CHAMBERS

Study THESAURUS

CHAMBERS

CHAMBERS
An imprint of Chambers Harrap Publishers Ltd
7 Hopetoun Crescent
Edinburgh, EH7 4AY

A CIP catalogue record for this book is available from the British Library.

ISBN 0-550-10045-8

Designed and typeset by Chambers Harrap Publishers Ltd, Edinburgh
Printed and bound in France

Contents

Contributors

Project Manager
Mary O'Neill

Study Supplement
Hazel Norris

Publishing Manager
Patrick White

Editorial Assistance
Ian Brookes
Paula McCulloch
Hazel Norris

Prepress
Paula McCulloch
David Reid

Preface

Chambers StudyThesaurus is specially designed for use by students aged 15 and older. It has been written taking into consideration the requirements of Key Stage 4 of the English and Welsh National Curriculum and beyond, but will also provide assistance for other students.

The thesaurus provides thousands of synonyms for words and phrases, giving the user many alternative ways to express themselves.This thesaurus also provides antonyms, that is, words and phrases which are opposite in meaning to the entry word, and these are clearly indicated by the symbol ⊠ . Illustrative examples guide the user to the group of synonyms they want. Labels show the register of words, so that each can be used appropriately. Notes are supplied at words that are often confused in their spelling or usage, such as *allude* and *elude*, *imply* and *infer*, helping the reader to use the right word with confidence.

Throughout the text there are hundreds of hyponym panels.These answer the question '*What kind of … are there?*' and list the names of, for example, **government systems** or **sciences**. Other panels contain useful lists of '*Terms used in…*', for example, the fields of **education** or **physics**; '*Parts of…*', for instance, an **engine** or a **plant**; and '*Colloquial ways of expressing…*', such as ideas connected with **happiness** or **money**.

Of particular interest to students is the Study Supplement, which aims to help the user get maximum benefit from the thesaurus. The section on Using Words Appropriately provides invaluable information on choosing the right vocabulary for the context, from formal and technical to slang, and on avoiding potential pitfalls. Other sections give sound advice on varying your word choices, for example in essays and job applications, so you can express your ideas creatively.The supplement demonstrates how *Chambers Study Thesaurus* can improve your use of language in academic assignments and the wider world.

Abbreviations

adj	adjective	*prep*	preposition
adv	adverb	*pron*	pronoun
Austral.	Australian English	®	trademark
colloq	colloquial	*Scot.*	Scottish English
conj	conjunction	*US*	American English
interj	interjection	*v*	verb
n	noun		

How to use the
Thesaurus

Headwords appear in bold type at the beginning of each entry.

Numbered sections show separate meanings of the word.

Technical words are labelled *technical*.

Parts of speech are given as abbreviations (*n* for *noun*, *v* for *verb*, etc) after the headword and treated in the same order within the entry.

Synonyms or alternative words are listed after the headword.

Notes on words easily confused are shown by the sign 📖.

Key synonyms (in small capitals) and examples are used in numbered sections to show different senses of the headword and help you find the meaning you want.

gorgeous *adj*
1 MAGNIFICENT, splendid, grand, glorious, superb, fine, impressive, rich, sumptuous, luxurious, brilliant, dazzling, resplendent, marvellous, wonderful, delightful, pleasing, lovely, enjoyable, good, showy, glamorous, *formal* opulent **2** ATTRACTIVE, beautiful, pretty, fine, sweet, glamorous, handsome, good-looking, lovely, *formal* pulchritudinous, *colloq.* sexy, stunning, ravishing
🔁 dull, plain

gory *adj*
bloody, bloodstained, blood-soaked, grisly, brutal, savage, violent, murderous, *formal* sanguinary

gospel *n*
1 LIFE OF CHRIST, teaching of christ, message of christ, good news, new testament **2** TEACHING, doctrine, creed, credo, certainty, truth, fact, *technical* kerygma, *formal* evangel, verity

gossamer *adj*
thin, light, delicate, flimsy, fine, cobwebby, insubstantial, sheer, shimmering, silky, airy, transparent, see-through, translucent, gauzy, *formal* diaphanous
🔁 heavy, opaque, thick

gossip *n, v*
▶ *n* **1** IDLE TALK, prattle, chitchat, tittle-tattle, rumour, hearsay, report, whisper, scandal, *colloq.* mudslinging, smear campaign **2** GOSSIP-MONGER, scandalmonger, whisperer, prattler, babbler, chatterbox, busybody, talebearer, tell-tale, tattler, blether, *colloq.* nosey parker
▶ *v* talk, chat, natter, chatter, blether, blather, gabble, prattle, babble, tattle, spread gossip, tell tales, whisper, rumour, spread/circulate a rumour, *colloq.* jabber, rabbit (on), gas, waffle, chinwag, jaw, chew the rag/fat

gouge *v*
chisel, cut, hack, incise, score, groove, scratch, claw, gash, slash, dig, scoop, hollow, extract

gourmand *n*
glutton, gormandizer, *formal* omnivore, *colloq.* gorger, guzzler, hog, pig
🔁 ascetic

📖 **gourmand** or **gourmet** ?
A *gourmand* is a glutton; a person who enjoys eating large quantities of food. A *gourmet* is a person who has an expert knowledge of, and a passion for, good food and wine.

gourmet *n*
gastronome, epicure, epicurean, connoisseur, bon vivant, *colloq.* foodie

govern *v*
1 RULE, reign, be in power, hold office, direct, manage, administer, be responsible for, superintend, supervise, oversee, preside, lead, head, be in charge of, command, order, control, influence, guide, conduct, steer, pilot **2** *govern your temper* dominate, master, control, regulate, curb, check, keep in check, hold/keep back, restrain, contain, quell, constrain, bridle, rein in, subdue, tame, discipline

governess *n*
teacher, guide, instructress, tutoress, tutress, mentor, companion, duenna, *old use* gouvernante

governing *adj*
ruling, controlling, regulatory, commanding, reigning, guiding, leading, supreme, uppermost, dominant, overriding, predominant, prevailing, transcendent, *formal* dominative

government *n*
1 *blame the government* administration, executive, ministry, Establishment, authorities, state, régime, congress, parliament, council, cabinet, leadership, *colloq.* powers that be **2** RULE, sovereignty, sway, direction, management, superintendence, supervision, surveillance, command, charge, authority, power, guidance, conduct, domination, dominion, control, regulation, restraint

Government systems include:
absolutism, autocracy, commonwealth, communism, democracy, despotism, dictatorship, empire, federation, hierocracy, junta, kingdom, monarchy, plutocracy, puppet government, republic, theocracy, triumvirate. *See also* PARLIAMENTS AND POLITICAL ASSEMBLIES.

Hyponym panels answer the question '*What kinds of ... are there?*'. Other types of panel are '*Technical terms*', eg terms used in **computing** and **music**; '*Parts of*', eg the **eye**, an **engine**; and '*Colloquial ways of expressing*', eg **anger**, **happiness**.

governor *n*
ruler, commissioner, administrator, executive, director, manager, leader, head, chief, president, viceroy, commander, superintendent, supervisor, commander, master, regulator, guide, warden, overseer, controller, *colloq.* boss

gown *n*
robe, dress, frock, dressing-gown, garment, habit, costume, *colloq.* garb

grab *v, n*
▶ *v* seize, snatch, take, pluck, snap up, catch/take/ lay hold of, grasp, clutch, grip, catch, capture, commandeer, usurp, annex, *formal* appropriate, *colloq.* nab, bag, collar, nail, swipe
▶ *n* grasp, grip, clutch, snatch, catch, capture
▷ **up for grabs** available, obtainable, at hand, *colloq.* for the asking, to be had

Register labels show the different and appropriate contexts in which synonyms can be used.

Phrases are highlighted separately.

grace *n, v*
▶ *n* **1** GRACEFULNESS, poise, beauty, attractiveness, loveliness, shapeliness, smoothness, elegance, ease, fluency, finesse, tastefulness, good taste, refinement, polish, breeding, cultivation, manners, etiquette, decorum, decency, consideration, courtesy, charm, *formal* propriety **2** KINDNESS, kindliness, compassion, consideration, goodness, virtue, generosity, charity, benevolence, goodwill, favour, forgiveness, indulgence, mercy, mercifulness, leniency, pardon, reprieve, quarter, *formal* beneficence, clemency **3** *say grace* blessing, benediction, thanksgiving, prayer
₣ **2** cruelty, harshness
▶ *v* favour, honour, dignify, distinguish, embellish, enhance, enrich, set off, trim, garnish, decorate, ornament, adorn
₣ spoil, detract from

The sign **₣** indicates antonyms – words that mean the opposite of the headword. Numbered sections within antonyms correspond to those of the synonyms.

graceful *adj*
easy, flowing, fluid, easy, smooth, supple, agile, deft, nimble, natural, slender, fine, tasteful, elegant, beautiful, attractive, appealing, charming, tasteful, cultured, refined, polished, cultivated, suave
₣ graceless, awkward, clumsy, ungainly

graft[1] *v, n*
▶ *v* *grafted onto a tree* engraft, implant, insert, transplant, join, splice, *formal* affix
▶ *n* implant, implantation, transplant, growth, splice, bud, sprout, shoot, scion

Words that have different origins but are spelt the same way have separate headwords highlighted by raised numbers, and the different meanings are explained by examples or key synonyms.

graft[2] *n*
1 EFFORT, hard work, toil, labour, *colloq.* sweat of your brow, slog **2** BRIBERY, corruption, dishonesty, extortion, *colloq.* con tricks, shady business, dirty tricks/ dealings, wheeling and dealing, sharp practices, rip-off, sting, *slang* scam

abandon *v, n*
▶ *v* **1** *abandon a baby* DESERT, leave (behind), maroon, strand, walk out on, *formal* forsake, *colloq.* run out on, jilt, ditch, chuck, dump, leave in the lurch, give the elbow to, break (it) off with, leave high and dry **2** *abandon the boat* vacate, evacuate, leave, depart from, withdraw from, go away from, bail out, escape, get out, break free from, break away, break loose, *colloq.* quit **3** *abandon an activity/your responsibilities* give up, stop (doing), let go, leave, abort, re-sign (from), surrender, waive, sacrifice, *formal* renounce, part with, desist, cease, discontinue, forego, forswear, relinquish, abdicate, yield, cede, *colloq.* drop, scrap, leave it at that, quit, jack in, pack in, kick the habit **4** *abandon yourself to despair* give way to, give yourself up to, yield to, be overcome by
Fa 1 support, maintain, stay (with), remain (with) **3** start, begin, continue
▶ *n* carelessness, recklessness, unrestraint, wildness, impetuosity, thoughtlessness
Fa restraint, caution, inhibition(s), moderation, care, carefulness

abandoned *adj*
1 *abandoned buildings* DESERTED, unoccupied, unused, empty, vacant, derelict, neglected, forlorn, desolate, *formal* forsaken **2** *abandoned young people* DISSOLUTE, wild, crazy, uninhibited, mad, wanton, wicked, debauched, immoral, corrupt, *formal* reprobate, profligate
Fa 1 (well-)kept, occupied **2** restrained, conscious, (self-)controlled

abandonment *n*
1 DESERTION, leaving (behind), neglect, marooning, stranding, *formal* forsaking, decampment, dereliction, *colloq.* running out on, jilting, ditching **2** *abandonment of an activity* giving-up, stopping, resignation (from), surrender, waiving, sacrifice, *formal* renunciation, relinquishment, cessation, discontinuation, discontinuance, abdication, cession, *colloq.* dropping, scrapping

abase *v*
humble, humiliate, *formal* debase, demean, mortify, belittle, malign, disparage
Fa elevate, honour, raise

abashed *adj*
ashamed, shamefaced, embarrassed, mortified, humiliated, humbled, affronted, confused, taken aback, bewildered, nonplussed, confounded, dumbfounded, *formal* perturbed, discomposed, disconcerted, discomfited, discountenanced, *colloq.* floored
Fa composed, at ease, *formal* audacious

abate *v*
1 *the storm abated* DECREASE, subside, reduce, sink, lessen, dwindle, die down, ease, moderate, taper off, fall off, wane, *formal* diminish, decline, attenuate, *colloq.* let up **2** *abate anger/pain* MODERATE, ease,

relieve, lessen, decrease, alleviate, soothe, mitigate, pacify, quell, subside, weaken, wane, slacken, slow, fade, *formal* remit, *colloq.* let up
Fa 1 increase, strengthen

abatement *n*
1 *the abatement of the storm*; *noise abatement* reduction, lessening, subsidence, dying-down, dwindling, easing, lowering, *formal* decline, diminution, attenuation **2** *abatement of anger* moderation, easing, relief, lessening, decrease, alleviation, mitigation, weakening, wane, slackening, *formal* remission, assuagement, palliation

abbey *n*
monastery, priory, friary, seminary, convent, nunnery, cloister, minster, cathedral

abbreviate *v*
shorten, cut (down), trim, clip, abridge, summarize, précis, abstract, digest, condense, compress, reduce, lessen, shrink, contract, *formal* truncate, curtail, constrict
Fa extend, lengthen, expand, amplify

abbreviation *n*
shortening, short form, shortened form, contraction, acronym, initialism, clipping, curtailment, abridgement, summary, synopsis, résumé, précis, abstract, digest, compression, reduction, *formal* truncated form, summarization, truncation
Fa long form, extension, expansion, amplification

abdicate *v*
1 *the king abdicated* resign, resign from the throne, stand down, give up, give up the throne, *formal* retire, relinquish/renounce the throne, *colloq.* quit **2** *abdicate responsibility* abandon, give up, reject, refuse to accept any longer, surrender, disown, *formal* renounce, relinquish, cede, yield, forego, abjure, abnegate, repudiate, *colloq.* shirk, quit, turn your back on, wash your hands of

abdication *n*
1 *the abdication of the king* resignation, retirement, standing-down, giving up of the throne, *formal* renunciation/relinquishment of the throne **2** *abdication of responsibilities* abandonment, rejection, refusal, surrender, giving-up, disowning, *formal* renunciation, relinquishment, abjuration, abnegation, repudiation

abdomen *n*
belly, stomach, midriff, *colloq.* guts, tummy, tum, paunch, pot belly, corporation

abdominal *adj*
coeliac, ventral, intestinal, visceral, ventricular, gastric, colic

abduct *v*
kidnap, seize, take (away) by force, carry off, make off with, snatch, shanghai, take as hostage, hold to ransom, spirit away, lay hold of, seduce, rape, *formal* appropriate, *colloq.* run away/off with

aberrant *adj*
deviant, deviating, divergent, different, irregular, anomalous, odd, peculiar, eccentric, rogue, defective, corrupt, *formal* incongruous, atypical, *colloq.* freakish, quirky
F3 regular, normal, typical

aberration *n*
1 *an aberration in behaviour* deviation, straying, wandering, divergence, instability, irregularity, abnormality, nonconformity, oversight, anomaly, oddity, peculiarity, eccentricity, lapse, delusion **2** *scientific aberrations* deviation, divergence, irregularity, abnormality, variation, anomaly, oddity, peculiarity, mistake
F3 1 conformity, regularity, normality

abet *v*
help, aid, assist, support, encourage, endorse, promote, sanction, spur, condone, *formal* succour, *colloq.* egg on
F3 prevent, hinder, discourage

abeyance *n*
▷ **in abeyance** no longer in use, cancelled temporarily, not in operation, disused, suspended, in (a state of) suspension, pending, *formal* dormant, *colloq.* hanging fire, on ice, shelved
F3 in use, in operation, continued

abhor *v*
hate, detest, loathe, recoil from, spurn, despise, have an aversion to, can't abide/bear, shudder at, shrink from, *formal* abominate, execrate, *colloq.* hate someone's guts, can't stand
F3 love, adore

abhorrence *n*
hate, hatred, aversion, loathing, horror, revulsion, disgust, distaste, contempt, *formal* abomination, repugnance, execration, detestation, animosity, enmity, malice, odium
F3 love, adoration

abhorrent *adj*
repugnant, detestable, loathsome, abominable, obnoxious, hated, hateful, horrible, horrid, offensive, repellent, repulsive, revolting, nauseating, disgusting, distasteful, *formal* execrable, heinous, odious
F3 delightful, attractive

abide *v*
1 *I can't abide that smell* BEAR, put up with, tolerate, accept, take, brook, endure, *colloq.* stand, stomach **2** *truths that abide* REMAIN, last, endure, continue, persist
▷ **abide by** obey, observe, follow, go along with, carry out, stand by, hold to, keep to, agree to, accept, respect, uphold, fulfil, *formal* comply with, adhere to, conform to, submit to, discharge, *colloq.* go by the book, stick to the rules, toe the line
F3 ignore, reject, *colloq.* flout

abiding *adj*
lasting, enduring, constant, continual, continuous, long-lasting, long-term, long-running, lifelong, persistent, unchanging, unchangeable, eternal, everlasting, immortal, unending, chronic, permanent, stable, firm, durable, *formal* immutable
F3 short-lived, short-term, *formal* ephemeral, transient

ability *n*
1 *the ability to teach* CAPABILITY, capacity, faculty, facility, power(s), resources, *formal* potentiality, potential, propensity **2** *someone of great ability* SKILL, competence, proficiency, qualification, talent, gift, calibre, endowment, expertise, forte, strength, dexterity, aptitude, deftness, adeptness, adroitness, prowess, motivation, *formal* competency, *colloq.* knack,

flair, touch, know-how, genius, the hang, what it takes, *savoir-faire*, savvy
F3 1 inability **2** incompetence, weakness

> **ability** or **capability** ?
>
> *Ability* is the more general term, referring to the possession of particular skills, knowledge, powers, etc or the simple fact of something being possible: *his ability to write a catchy tune; our ability to work together. Capability* may refer to the possession of an aptitude, especially one that derives from a person's character: *my mother's organizational capabilities.*

abject *adj*
1 *abject poverty* miserable, wretched, forlorn, hopeless, shameful, humiliating, pitiable, pathetic, outcast, degraded, *formal* execrable **2** *an abject coward* contemptible, worthless, base, low, mean, dishonourable, deplorable, despicable, vile, sordid, debased, degenerate, submissive, servile, grovelling, *formal* ignoble, ignominious
F3 2 proud, exalted

abjure *v*
renounce, abandon, disown, deny, reject, *formal* relinquish, retract, forswear, abdicate, abnegate, disavow, disclaim, renege on
F3 agree, assent, support

ablaze *adj*
1 BURNING, blazing, flaming, in flames, on fire, ignited, lighted, alight, incandescent, *formal* aflame, afire **2** *a house ablaze with lights* illuminated, luminous, glowing, aglow, radiant, flashing, gleaming, sparkling, brilliant, lit up, *formal* incandescent **3** *eyes ablaze with passion* impassioned, passionate, fervent, ardent, fiery, enthusiastic, excited, exhilarated, stimulated, aroused, angry, furious, fuming, raging, incensed, frenzied

able *adj*
capable, competent, fit, fitted, dexterous, adroit, deft, adept, proficient, qualified, practised, experienced, skilled, accomplished, clever, intelligent, expert, masterly, skilful, ingenious, talented, gifted, strong, powerful, effective, efficient, *colloq.* all there, on the ball, up to it, wised up, cut out for
F3 unable, incapable, incompetent, ineffective

able-bodied *adj*
fit, healthy, sound, in good health, strong, robust, hardy, tough, vigorous, powerful, hale, hearty, hale and hearty, fine, lusty, sturdy, rugged, strapping, stout, burly, stalwart, staunch
F3 disabled, handicapped, infirm, delicate

abnegation *n*
abstinence, self-denial, surrender, self-sacrifice, giving-up, temperance, *formal* renunciation, relinquishment, forbearance, abjuration, repudiation, eschewal

abnormal *adj*
odd, strange, peculiar, curious, queer, weird, eccentric, idiosyncratic, paranormal, unnatural, uncanny, extraordinary, exceptional, unusual, uncommon, unexpected, irregular, erratic, wayward, deviant, divergent, different, *formal* singular, anomalous, aberrant, atypical, outré, preternatural, *colloq.* oddball
F3 normal, regular, typical

abnormality *n*
oddity, peculiarity, eccentricity, strangeness, bizarreness, unnaturalness, unusualness, irregularity, exception, anomaly, deformity, flaw, malformation, dysfunction, deviation, divergence, difference, *formal* singularity, aberration, atypicality
F3 normality, regularity

abode *n*
home, dwelling, dwelling-place, lodgings, habitation, habitat, *formal* residence, domicile, *colloq.* pad

abolish *v*
cancel, end, stop, do away with, quash, repeal, revoke, annul, invalidate, rescind, suppress, destroy, eliminate, put an end to, exterminate, annihilate, obliterate, eradicate, overthrow, blot out, wipe out, get rid of, stamp out, subvert, overturn, *formal* terminate, discontinue, nullify, vitiate, abrogate, expunge, *colloq.* axe
🔛 create, introduce, establish, institute, retain, authorize, continue

abolition *n*
cancellation, ending, doing away with, repeal, suppression, destruction, elimination, annihilation, extinction, overthrow, blotting-out, quashing, withdrawal, *formal* termination, annulment, invalidation, nullification, voiding, rescindment, revocation, abrogation, rescission, obliteration, extermination, eradication, extirpation, dissolution, subversion, *colloq.* axe
🔛 creation, introduction, retention, authorization, continuation

abominable *adj*
loathsome, detestable, hateful, horrid, horrible, abhorrent, offensive, repulsive, repellent, disgusting, revolting, obnoxious, nauseating, foul, base, vile, atrocious, appalling, terrible, contemptible, despicable, wretched, cursed, damnable, *formal* execrable, odious, repugnant, heinous, reprehensible
🔛 delightful, pleasant, desirable

abominate *v*
abhor, hate, loathe, detest, despise, have an aversion to, condemn, *formal* execrate
🔛 love, adore

abomination *n*
1 *murder is an abomination* OUTRAGE, offence, disgrace, horror, atrocity, evil, curse, plague, torment, *formal* anathema **2** HATE, hatred, loathing, revulsion, disgust, distaste, aversion, hostility, *formal* abhorrence, execration, detestation, repugnance, odium
🔛 **2** adoration, delight

aboriginal *adj*
native, indigenous, original, earliest, first, primal, primeval, primitive, ancient, local, *formal* autochthonous

abort *v*
1 *abort a pregnancy* TERMINATE, miscarry, have a miscarriage **2** *abort a plan* end, bring/come to an end, stop, suspend, halt, call off, cut short, check, frustrate, thwart, fail, *formal* nullify, *colloq.* axe, pull the plug on
🔛 **2** continue, start, begin

abortion *n*
termination, miscarriage

abortive *adj*
failed, unsuccessful, fruitless, unproductive, barren, sterile, vain, idle, futile, useless, ineffective, *formal* unavailing, ineffectual
🔛 successful, fruitful

abound *v*
be plentiful, flourish, swell, increase, swarm, teem, crowd, be full, brim over, overflow, *formal* proliferate, thrive, superabound, exuberate, luxuriate

about *prep, adv*
▶ *prep* **1** *write about a subject* REGARDING, on, on the subject of, concerning, relating to, connected with, concerned with, as regards, referring to, with regard to, with respect to, with reference to, in the matter of, re, dealing with, *formal* apropos of **2** *somewhere about the house* close to, near, nearby, beside, adjacent to **3** *walk about the town* round, around, surrounding, throughout, all over, *formal* encircling, encompassing
▶ *adv* **1** *about twenty* around, more or less, approximately, roughly, in the region of, almost, nearly, approaching, nearing, *formal* circa **2** *run about* to and fro, here and there, from place to place, *old use* hither and thither
▷ **about to** going to, on the point of, on the verge of, all but, ready to, soon to, intending to, preparing to

about-turn *n*
about-face, volte-face, (complete) reversal, turnabout, *formal* enantiodromia, *colloq.* U-turn

above *prep, adv, adj*
▶ *prep* **1** *above the clouds* over, higher than, on top of, *formal* atop **2** *above the rank of sergeant* superior to, senior to, higher than, over **3** *temperatures above the average* in excess of, exceeding, beyond, *formal* surpassing **4** *above suspicion* beyond, not liable to, not open to, superior to
🔛 **1** below, under **2** below
▶ *adv* **1** *noise from above* overhead, high up, higher, *formal* aloft, on high **2** *as mentioned above* earlier, before, previously
🔛 **1** below, underneath **2** below
▶ *adj* above-mentioned, previous, earlier, preceding, *formal* above-stated, foregoing, prior, aforementioned, aforesaid

above-board *adj*
honest, legitimate, straight, true, open, frank, candid, straightforward, forthright, truthful, trustworthy, honourable, reputable, upright, *formal* guileless, veracious, *colloq.* on the level, fair and square, square
🔛 dishonest, underhand, shady

abrade *v*
rub, graze, scratch, scrape, scour, grate, grind, chafe, erode, wear away/down

abrasion *n*
graze, scratch, cut, scratching, scraping, scrape, scouring, grating, grinding, abrading, chafing, chafe, friction, rubbing, erosion, wearing away, wearing-down, *formal* excoriation

abrasive *adj*
1 *abrasive material* rough, scratching, scraping, grating, harsh, chafing, corrosive, *formal* erosive, frictional, attritional, erodent **2** *an abrasive person* harsh, brusque, caustic, sharp, biting, hurtful, nasty, unpleasant, irritating, annoying
🔛 **1** smooth **2** pleasant, kind

abreast *adv*
1 *walk abreast* side by side, level, beside/alongside each other, next to each other **2** *keep abreast of the news* acquainted, informed, knowledgeable, *au courant*, up to date, in touch, *au fait*, familiar, well up, *formal* conversant, *colloq.* in the picture, on the ball, with your finger on the pulse
🔛 **2** unaware, out of touch, unfamiliar

abridge *v*
shorten, cut (down), prune, curtail, abbreviate, contract, reduce, decrease, lessen, summarize, précis, abstract, digest, condense, compress, concentrate, *formal* synopsize, *colloq.* clip, lop
🔛 expand, amplify, *colloq.* pad out

abridgement *n*
1 *the abridgement of the story* SHORTENING, cutting, reduction, decrease, diminishing, concentration, contraction, restriction, *formal* diminution, truncation **2** *an abridgement of a report* SUMMARY, synopsis, résumé, short version, shortened version, outline, précis, abstract, digest, epitome, *formal* conspectus, abrégé
🔛 **1** expansion, *colloq.* padding (out)

abroad *adv*
1 *go abroad on business* OVERSEAS, in/to a foreign country, in/to foreign parts, out of the country, far and wide, widely **2** *news spread abroad* AT LARGE, widely, publicly, around, about, circulating, extensively, current
F4 **1** at home

abrogate *v*
abolish, cancel, end, stop, repeal, revoke, do away with, annul, invalidate, reverse, *formal* countermand, rescind, retract, dissolve, repudiate, disenact, *colloq.* axe, scrap
F4 establish, institute, introduce

abrupt *adj*
1 *come to an abrupt end* sudden, unexpected, unforeseen, unannounced, unceremonious, surprising, dramatic, quick, rapid, swift, hasty, hurried, instant, instantaneous, *formal* precipitate, *colloq.* snap **2** *an abrupt manner* BRUSQUE, curt, terse, brisk, gruff, rough, rude, offhand, impolite, blunt, direct, uncivil, *colloq.* short, snappy, snappish **3** *an abrupt slope* sheer, steep, sharp, *formal* precipitous, declivitous
F4 **1** gradual, slow, leisurely **2** friendly, expansive, ceremonious, polite

abscond *v*
run away, run off, make off, decamp, flee, fly, escape, disappear, vanish, bolt, *formal* take French leave, *colloq.* quit, scram, skedaddle, vamoose, clear out, make a quick getaway, beat it, run for it, do a runner, do a bunk, do a moonlight flit

absence *n*
1 *absence from school* non-attendance, truancy, non-appearance, absenteeism, non-existence **2** LACK, need, deficiency, scarcity, unavailability, default, omission, vacancy, *formal* want, dearth, privation, paucity, vacuity
F4 **1** presence, attendance, appearance **2** presence

absent *adj*
1 *absent from the meeting* MISSING, not present, not here, not there, not around, away, out, off, unavailable, gone, lacking, truant, *formal* in absentia, *colloq.* when someone's back is turned **2** INATTENTIVE, daydreaming, dreamy, faraway, elsewhere, absent-minded, blank, preoccupied, unaware, oblivious, unheeding, *formal* vacant, distracted
F4 **1** present, here, there **2** attentive, alert, aware

absent-minded *adj*
forgetful, scatterbrained, having a bad memory, absent, withdrawn, faraway, distracted, preoccupied, absorbed, engrossed, musing, dreaming, dreamy, wool-gathering, inattentive, unaware, oblivious, unconscious, heedless, unheeding, unthinking, impractical, abstracted, pensive, *formal* distrait(e), *colloq.* with a memory like a sieve, not all there, somewhere else, dead to the world, miles away, in a world of your own, scatty
F4 attentive

absolute *adj*
1 *in absolute confidence* utter, total, complete, entire, full, thorough, exhaustive, supreme, definitive, conclusive, final, definite, unquestionable, unambiguous, undivided, unlimited, categorical, decided, decisive, positive, sure, certain, genuine, pure, perfect, sheer, unmixed, unadulterated, unqualified, unconditional, unmitigated, unrestrained, unequivocal, unrestricted, downright, rank, out-and-out, outright, *formal* consummate, indubitable, peremptory **2** *absolute power/ruler* supreme, totalitarian, autocratic, tyrannical, despotic, dictatorial, sovereign, authoritarian, almighty, unlimited, unrestricted, plenary, *formal* omnipotent, autarchical

absolutely *adv*
utterly, totally, completely, entirely, fully, wholly, thoroughly, exhaustively, perfectly, supremely, unconditionally, finally, categorically, definitely, positively, in every way/respect, wholeheartedly, conclusively, unequivocally, unambiguously, unquestionably, decidedly, decisively, surely, certainly, infallibly, genuinely, truly, purely, exactly, precisely, *colloq.* dead

absolution *n*
forgiveness, pardon, deliverance, freedom, liberation, release, mercy, redemption, acquittal, amnesty, emancipation, *formal* exoneration, remission, vindication, discharge, exculpation, purgation, shrift

absolve *v*
excuse, clear, forgive, pardon, deliver, free, set free, liberate, release, loose, have mercy on, show mercy towards, emancipate, *formal* exonerate, vindicate, justify, acquit, discharge, exculpate, remit, *colloq.* let off

absorb *v*
1 *absorb liquid/heat* take in, draw in, soak up, drink in, suck up, assimilate, engulf, *formal* ingest, imbibe, consume, *colloq.* devour **2** *absorb facts* take in, digest, assimilate, understand, receive, hold, retain **3** *absorb your attention* ENGROSS, involve, fascinate, enthral, captivate, engage, hold, preoccupy, occupy, fill (up), monopolize, *colloq.* not be able to put down **4** *absorbed into a bigger company* incorporate, integrate, assimilate, *colloq.* swallow up
F4 **1** give out, *formal* exude

absorbed *adj*
engrossed, involved, fascinated, interested, enthralled, captivated, preoccupied, occupied, taken up with, riveted

absorbent *adj*
receptive, porous, permeable, pervious, soaking, blotting, retentive, *formal* absorptive, assimilative, sorbefacient, resorbent
F4 water-repellent, waterproof

absorbing *adj*
interesting, amusing, entertaining, enjoyable, diverting, engrossing, preoccupying, intriguing, fascinating, captivating, enthralling, spellbinding, gripping, riveting, compelling, compulsive, *colloq.* unputdownable
F4 boring, off-putting

absorption *n*
1 *the absorption of liquid/heat* taking-in, drawing-in, soaking-up, assimilation, *technical* osmosis, *formal* ingestion, consumption, *colloq.* devouring **2** *absorption of your attention* ENGROSSING, involvement, captivating, riveting, engagement, holding, preoccupation, occupation, attentiveness, concentration, intentness, monopoly

abstain *v*
1 *abstain from food* refuse, reject, resist, shun, avoid, keep from, give up, do/go without, stop, stop short of, hold back, keep from, *formal* refrain, decline, renounce, forbear, forego, desist, deny yourself, eschew, *colloq.* think twice before doing something **2** *abstain in an election* not vote, refuse to vote
F4 **1** indulge

abstemious *adj*
temperate, moderate, self-denying, self-disciplined, disciplined, sober, sparing, frugal, austere, ascetic, restrained, *formal* abstinent, self-abnegating
F4 intemperate, gluttonous, luxurious

abstention *n*
not voting, refusal to vote, declining to vote

abstinence *n*
1 *abstinence from sensual desires* abstaining, self-denial, non-indulgence, avoidance, refusal, giving-up,

going-without, restraint, self-restraint, self-control, self-discipline, *formal* abstemiousness, continence, forbearance, refraining, declension, renunciation, desistance, eschewal **2** *abstinence from alcohol* TEE-TOTALISM, temperance, moderation, frugality, asceticism, *formal* sobriety, nephalism
🗲 **1** indulgence, self-indulgence

abstract *adj, n, v*
▶ *adj* **1** *abstract nouns* non-concrete, conceptual, notional **2** *abstract reasoning* theoretical, conceptual, notional, intellectual, hypothetical, unpractical, unrealistic, general, generalized, indefinite, metaphysical, philosophical, academic, complex, deep, profound, subtle, *formal* abstruse, arcane, recondite **3** *abstract paintings* non-realistic, non-representational, contrived
🗲 **1, 2** concrete **2** real, actual, practical **3** representational, realistic, figurative
▶ *n* synopsis, outline, summary, recapitulation, résumé, précis, digest, abridgement, compression, *formal* epitome, conspectus
▶ *v* **1** *abstract a report* summarize, outline, précis, digest, condense, compress, abridge, abbreviate, shorten, cut (down) **2** *abstract coal from the ground* EXTRACT, remove, take away/out, withdraw, isolate, detach, separate, *formal* dissociate
🗲 **1** expand, lengthen **2** insert, put in

abstracted *adj*
preoccupied, absent-minded, distracted, forgetful, scatterbrained, absent, withdrawn, absorbed, engrossed, pensive, musing, dreaming, dreamy, bemused, wool-gathering, inattentive, unaware, oblivious, unconscious, heedless, unheeding, unthinking, impractical, *colloq.* scatty
🗲 attentive, alert, *colloq.* on the ball

abstraction *n*
1 IDEA, notion, concept, thought, conception, theory, hypothesis, theorem, formula, generalization, generality **2** INATTENTION, dream, dreaminess, absent-mindedness, preoccupation, remoteness, withdrawal, *formal* distraction, pensiveness, absorption, bemusedness **3** EXTRACTION, withdrawal, isolation, separation

abstruse *adj*
obscure, difficult to understand, deep, profound, complex, mysterious, cryptic, unfathomable, incomprehensible, perplexing, puzzling, *formal* arcane, esoteric, inscrutable, enigmatic, recondite
🗲 simple, obvious

absurd *adj*
ridiculous, ludicrous, preposterous, fantastic, illogical, paradoxical, unreasonable, irrational, nonsensical, meaningless, senseless, foolish, silly, stupid, idiotic, crazy, farcical, inane, comical, funny, humorous, harebrained, laughable, derisory, *formal* incongruous, implausible, untenable, risible, asinine, *colloq.* daft
🗲 reasonable, logical, rational, sensible

absurdity *n*
ridiculousness, ludicrousness, illogicality, unreasonableness, meaninglessness, senselessness, foolishness, folly, silliness, fatuousness, idiocy, stupidity, craziness, inanity, paradox, humour, farce, charade, travesty, joke, nonsense, rubbish, *formal* incongruity, irrationality, implausibility, *colloq.* daftness, twaddle, gibberish, drivel, claptrap, balderdash
🗲 reasonableness, logicality, rationality, (good) sense

abundance *n*
plenty, fullness, great supply, wealth, generosity, richness, riches, lavishness, overflow, land of milk and honey, glut, extravagance, excess, bonanza, fortune,

formal amplitude, bounty, plethora, copiousness, profusion, exuberance, luxuriance, munificence, plenitude, prodigality, opulence, affluence, *colloq.* bags, heaps, masses, piles, loads, stacks, lashings, oodles, lots, *US* scads
🗲 shortage, scarcity, *formal* dearth, paucity

abundant *adj*
plentiful, in plenty, full, filled, ample, copious, profuse, bountiful, exuberant, more than enough, well-supplied, ample, generous, rich, affluent, lavish, teeming, overflowing, galore, *formal* bounteous, luxuriant, opulent
🗲 scarce, sparse, scant, insufficient

abuse *n, v*
▶ *n* **1** *the abuse of drugs* misuse, exploitation, imposition, oppression, wrong, ill-treatment, maltreatment, *formal* misapplication **2** *child abuse* mistreatment, maltreatment, ill-treatment, cruelty, hurt, injury, molestation, damage, harm, beating, torture **3** *shout abuse* insult(s), swearing, swear-word, cursing, curse, offence, defamation, libel, slander, reproach, censure, scolding, *formal* affront, upbraiding, invective, castigation, malediction, vilification, vituperation, calumniation, calumny, contumely, denigration, derision, disparagement, tirade, diatribe, vitriol
🗲 **2** care, attention **3** compliment(s), praise
▶ *v* **1** *abuse authority* misuse, exploit, take advantage of, *formal* misapply **2** *abuse physically* ILL-TREAT, maltreat, hurt, injure, damage, harm, beat, hit, batter, oppress, exploit, wrong, torture, molest, rape, harass sexually **3** *abuse verbally* INSULT, swear at, curse, hurl abuse at, call names, be rude to, defame, libel, slander, pick on, bully, smear, scold, rail, victimize, *formal* malign, revile, upbraid, calumniate, castigate, denigrate, disparage, oppugn, *colloq.* slate, treat like dirt
🗲 **2** cherish, care for, look after **3** compliment, praise

---

🖉 **abuse** or **misuse** ?

Abuse refers to the use of something for the wrong purposes: *substance abuse*, eg glue-sniffing. *Misuse* refers to the use of substances or objects in an incorrect way: *Bacteria may acquire resistance to a particular antibiotic by its overuse or misuse.*

---

abusive *adj*
insulting, offensive, rude, scathing, hurtful, harmful, injurious, cruel, brutal, destructive, scathing, defamatory, libellous, slanderous, derogatory, disparaging, pejorative, maligning, reviling, reproachful, scolding, blasphemous, *formal* vilifying, censorious, upbraiding, railing, vituperative, castigating, calumniating, contumelious, denigrating, opprobrious
🗲 complimentary, polite

abut *v*
border, be next to, verge on, join, touch, impinge, *formal* adjoin, conjoin

abysmal *adj*
dismal, shocking, disgraceful, dreadful, appalling, awful, complete, utter

abyss *n*
fall into an abyss; *the abyss of war* gulf, chasm, crevasse, fissure, gorge, canyon, crater, pit, bottomless pit, depth(s), void, *formal* barathrum

academic *adj, n*
▶ *adj* **1** *academic qualifications* educational, instructional, scholastic, *formal* pedagogical **2** *she's very academic* SCHOLARLY, intellectual, educated, well-educated, learned, well-read, studious, bookish, literary, highbrow, serious, donnish, *formal* erudite, *colloq.* brainy, smart **3** *an academic, not practical,*

approach THEORETICAL, hypothetical, speculative, abstract, impractical, irrelevant, ivory-tower, *formal* conjectural, notional

🗲 **3** practical, relevant

▶ *n* teacher, professor, don, master, fellow, lecturer, tutor, educator, instructor, trainer, student, scholar, man/woman of letters, pedant, bookworm

accede *v*
1 *accede to a request* ACCEPT, bow to, agree to, admit, give in, back down, *formal* consent to, assent to, comply with, acquiesce, concur **2** *accede to the throne* come to, inherit, *formal* assume, attain, succeed (to)

accelerate *v*
1 *the car/driver accelerated* quicken, speed, speed up, drive faster, go faster, pick up/gather speed, gain momentum, *colloq.* open up, put your foot down, step on it/the gas/the juice, put on a spurt **2** *accelerate a process* speed up, hurry, step up, stimulate, facilitate, advance, further, promote, spur on, forward, *technical* festinate, *formal* hasten, expedite, precipitate

🗲 **1, 2** decelerate, slow down, delay

acceleration *n*
1 *the acceleration of a car* speeding-up, rate of increase, momentum **2** *acceleration of a process* speeding-up, stepping-up, stimulation, promotion, forwarding, *formal* advancement, furtherance, hastening, expedition

🗲 **1, 2** deceleration, slowing-down, delay

accent *n*
1 *speak with a strong Irish accent* PRONUNCIATION, articulation, brogue, tone, pitch, intonation, inflection, accentuation, stress, emphasis, intensity, force, rhythm, beat, pulse, *formal* enunciation, diction, modulation, cadence, pulsation, *colloq.* twang **2** *the accent is on ease of use* EMPHASIS, prominence, importance, priority, underlining, highlighting

accentuate *v*
accent, stress, emphasize, put the emphasis on, underline, underscore, highlight, give prominence to, heighten, intensify, strengthen, deepen, *colloq.* point up, drive the point home, make great play of, show up

🗲 weaken, *colloq.* play down

accept *v*
1 *accept a job/an offer* take, take up, receive, obtain, acquire, gain, secure, get, say yes to, not say no to, *formal* reply in the affirmative, *colloq.* jump at **2** *accept advice* take, welcome, *formal* embrace, *colloq.* take on board, take someone's point **3** *accept a decision* acknowledge, recognize, admit, allow, approve, agree to, take on, adopt, bow to, go along with, give in, back down, *formal* abide by, accede to, consent to, acquiesce in, concur with, comply with **4** *accept responsibility/blame* take on, undertake, bear, be responsible for, admit, acknowledge **5** *accept an explanation* believe (in), trust, be certain of, *colloq.* buy, swallow, fall for **6** *accept into the family* WELCOME, receive, receive warmly, integrate **7** *accept ill-treatment* TOLERATE, stand, bear, abide, face up to, take, endure, put up with, yield to, resign yourself to, be resigned to, come to terms with, let go of, *colloq.* stomach, swallow, make the best of

🗲 **1** refuse, turn down **2, 3, 4, 5, 6** reject

acceptable *adj*
1 *homework that is just acceptable* SATISFACTORY, tolerable, moderate, passable, adequate, reasonable, all right, unexceptionable, *colloq.* OK, so-so **2** *acceptable not to smoke* admissible, allowable, permissible, tolerable, agreeable, appropriate, desirable, *colloq.* the done thing **3** *a most acceptable present* welcome, delightful, pleasant, desirable, gratifying

🗲 **1** unacceptable, unsatisfactory **2** unacceptable

acceptance *n*
1 *acceptance of a job/an offer* taking (up), accepting, receipt, obtaining, getting, acquiring, gaining, securing **2** *acceptance of advice* taking, welcoming, *formal* embracing, *colloq.* taking on board, taking someone's point **3** *acceptance of the decision* acknowledgement, admission, recognition, approval, agreement, taking on, adoption, going along with, giving-in, backing-down, *formal* consent, assent, affirmation, accession, acquiescence, concurrence, endorsement, ratification, *colloq.* stamp of approval, OK **4** *acceptance of responsibility/blame* taking on, undertaking, assumption, admission, acknowledgement **5** *the idea gained acceptance* credence, belief, trust, faith **6** *acceptance into the family* welcome, receiving, recognition, integration **7** *acceptance of your situation* tolerance, bearing, facing up to, endurance, resignation, putting up with, *colloq.* making the best of

🗲 **1** refusal **2, 3, 4, 5, 6** rejection

accepted *adj*
recognized, established, authorized, approved, ratified, sanctioned, agreed, acknowledged, admitted, confirmed, acceptable, correct, appropriate, conventional, orthodox, traditional, customary, time-honoured, received, universal, regular, standard, normal, usual, common

🗲 unconventional, unorthodox, controversial

access *n*
1 *gain access to the building* means of approach/entry, entry, entering, entrance, gateway, door, way in, key, approach, passage, road, path, drive, driveway, course **2** *deny access to the prisoner* admission, admittance, right of entry, permission to enter/see, accessibility, *formal* entrée, ingress

🗲 **1** exit, outlet, *formal* egress

accessible *adj*
1 *accessible from the motorway* reachable, attainable, achievable, *colloq.* get-at-able **2** *financial help that is accessible to everyone* obtainable, available, on hand, ready, handy, convenient, near, nearby, *formal* procurable **3** *an accessible book/painting* UNDERSTANDABLE, intelligible, easy to understand, user-friendly

🗲 **1** inaccessible, remote, *colloq.* out of the way, off the beaten track **3** incomprehensible, unintelligible

accession *n*
1 *accession to the throne* inheritance, *formal* assumption, attaining, succession **2** *accessions to the library* addition, acquisition, increase, possession, purchase, gift

accessory *n, adj*
▶ *n* **1** *computer accessories* extra, supplement, addition, attachment, extension, component, fitting, *formal* appendage, adjunct **2** *accessories to match an outfit* decoration, adornment, ornament, frill, trimming, supplement, complement, gloves, hat, belt, shoes, handbag, jewellery, *formal* embellishment **3** *an accessory to a crime* ACCOMPLICE, partner, associate, colleague, confederate, assistant, helper, help, aid, *technical* accessory before the fact, accessory after the fact, particeps criminis, *formal* abettor, conniver

▶ *adj* additional, extra, supplementary, subsidiary, contributory, incidental, secondary, ancillary, auxiliary, subordinate, *formal* supplemental

accident *n*
1 *an accident with boiling water* mishap, casualty, calamity, disaster, tragedy, *formal* misfortune, mischance, misadventure, *colloq.* blow **2** *a car accident* collision, crash, fatality, *formal* contretemps, *colloq.* pile-up, smash-up, wreck, *slang* shunt, prang **3** *happen by accident* CHANCE, hazard, luck, good luck, fortune, good fortune, fate, coincidence, *formal*

fortuity, serendipity, contingency, happenstance, *colloq.* fluke

accidental *adj*
unintentional, unintended, inadvertent, unplanned, uncalculated, unpremeditated, unwitting, unexpected, unanticipated, unforeseen, unlooked-for, chance, uncertain, haphazard, random, casual, incidental, *formal* fortuitous, adventitious, serendipitous, aleatory, *colloq.* fluky
Ｆ intentional, deliberate, calculated, premeditated

accidentally *adv*
unintentionally, inadvertently, unexpectedly, by chance, by accident, by mistake, unwittingly, haphazardly, randomly, incidentally, *formal* fortuitously, bechance, adventitiously, serendipitously
Ｆ intentionally, deliberately

acclaim *v, n*
▶ *v* praise, commend, extol, exalt, honour, hail, salute, welcome, applaud, clap, cheer, celebrate, fanfare, toast, *formal* laud, eulogize, *colloq.* rave about, give rave reviews to, give a good press to
Ｆ condemn, criticize, *colloq.* give a bad press to
▶ *n* praise, commendation, homage, tribute, exaltation, honour, welcome, approval, bouquets, applause, ovation, clapping, cheers, cheering, shouting, celebration, *formal* acclamation, approbation, eulogy, extolment, laudation, plaudits
Ｆ criticism, disapproval, condemnation, *formal* vituperation, *colloq.* brickbats, bad press

acclamation *n*
praise, commendation, homage, tribute, exaltation, honour, welcome, approval, congratulations, applause, ovation, clapping, cheering, bravos, shouting, celebration, enthusiasm, *formal* approbation, eulogy, felicitations, paean, panegyric
Ｆ criticism, disapproval, condemnation

acclimatize *v*
adjust, adapt, accustom, get used to, find your way around, accommodate, familiarize, attune, conform, *formal* habituate, acculturate, inure, naturalize, *colloq.* find/get your bearings, find your feet

accolade *n*
award, honour, tribute, praise

accommodate *v*
1 *accommodate someone in a hotel* PUT UP, take in, house, shelter, provide shelter for, cater for, lodge, board, billet, *formal* domicile, *colloq.* put a roof over someone's head **2** *the hall accommodates 400* take, hold, have room/space for **3** *accommodate customers* help, be helpful to, oblige, assist, aid, serve, provide, supply, comply, conform, *colloq.* give/lend a (helping) hand to **4** *accommodate yourself to new developments* adapt, accustom, acclimatize, adjust, modify, fit, harmonize, reconcile, settle, compose

accommodating *adj*
obliging, indulgent, helpful, co-operative, agreeable, willing, kind, considerate, unselfish, sympathetic, friendly, hospitable, *formal* complaisant, pliable
Ｆ disobliging, selfish

accommodation *n*
1 *find accommodation* housing, shelter, board, quarter(s), lodging, *colloq.* a roof over someone's head **2** *reach an accommodation* agreement, compromise, negotiation(s), reconciliation, settlement, harmony, conformity

accompaniment *n*
1 *a musical accompaniment* support, background, backing, backup, *technical* obbligato, vamp **2** *wine as an accompaniment to food* complement, accessory, supplement, addition, *formal* concomitant, adjunct, coexistence

accompany *v*
1 *accompany someone on holiday* escort, attend, go (along) with, associate with, come (along) with, partner, chaperone, usher, conduct, follow, *formal* consort, convoy, squire, *colloq.* hang around with **2** *a book accompanied by a study guide* complement, supplement, belong to, go with, *formal* coexist, coincide **3** *accompany someone on the guitar* play with, provide backing/support for

accomplice *n*
assistant, helper, abettor, mate, henchman, conspirator, collaborator, ally, confederate, partner, associate, colleague, aide, participator, accessory, right-hand man, *colloq.* sidekick

accomplish *v*
achieve, attain, do, perform, carry out, manage, execute, fulfil, discharge, finish, complete, conclude, realize, bring about, bring off, engineer, produce, obtain, *formal* consummate, effect, effectuate, *colloq.* hack it, pull it off, deliver the goods, bring home the bacon

accomplished *adj*
skilled, professional, practised, proficient, gifted, talented, skilful, experienced, adroit, adept, expert, masterly, polished, cultivated, *formal* consummate
Ｆ unskilled, inexpert, incapable

accomplishment *n*
1 *the accomplishment of a task* achievement, attainment, doing, performance, carrying-out, execution, fulfilment, finishing, completion, management, conclusion, perfection, realization, fruition, production, *formal* discharge, consummation, effecting, futurition **2** *her great accomplishments* SKILL, talent, ability, capability, proficiency, gift, forte, art, *formal* aptitude, faculty **3** *no mean accomplishment* feat, achievement, deed, triumph, exploit, *colloq.* stroke

accord *v, n*
▶ *v* **1** *not accord with the truth* correspond, agree, harmonize, be in agreement/harmony, match, conform, suit, *formal* concur **2** *accord someone recognition* grant, give, tender, allow, endow, confer, *formal* bestow, vouchsafe
Ｆ **1** disagree **2** deny
▶ *n* agreement, assent, unanimity, unity, correspondence, conformity, harmony, sympathy, *formal* congruence, congruity, concurrence, accordance, concert
Ｆ conflict, discord, disharmony
▷ **of your own accord** voluntarily, of your own free will, freely, willingly, without being asked/forced
▷ **with one accord** unanimously, of one mind, in complete agreement

accordance *n*
▷ **in accordance with** in agreement with, consistent with, in keeping with, obedient to, in conformity with, in line with, in proportion to, in relation to, after, in the light of, in the manner of, *formal* commensurate with, in concert with, in consonance with

according *adj*
▷ **according to 1** *according to this book* as said/claimed/stated by, on the report of **2** *play according to the rules* in accordance with, in keeping with,

obedient to, in conformity with, in line with, consistent with, after, in the light of, in the manner of, after the manner of, as per **3** *be paid according to experience* in proportion to, in relation to, depending on, as per, *formal* commensurate with

accordingly *adv*
1 *he was dishonest and was distrusted accordingly* correspondingly, so, as a result, for that reason, consequently, in consequence, therefore, *formal* thus, hence, ergo **2** *act accordingly* appropriately, properly, suitably, consistently

accost *v*
approach, confront, waylay, stop, halt, detain, importune, solicit, attack, molest, *colloq.* buttonhole

account *n, v*
▶ *n* **1** *an account of what happened* story, tale, commentary, narrative, chronicle, history, memoir, record, statement, report, communiqué, write-up, version, narration, portrayal, sketch, description, presentation, explanation, detail(s) **2** *pay an account* BILL, statement, invoice, tab, charges **3** *the accounts of a business* ledger, books, register, inventory **4** *a matter of no account* importance, significance, consequence, *formal* distinction, esteem, import, regard
▷ **on account of** because of, owing to, the reason is
▷ **on no account** under no circumstances, certainly not
▶ *v* consider, assess, believe, count, hold, reckon, look upon, view as, value, *formal* adjudge, appraise, deem, esteem
▷ **account for 1** *account for the missing money* EXPLAIN, give reasons for, come up with an explanation, illuminate, clear up, rationalize, justify, answer for, say why, *formal* elucidate, vindicate **2** *exports account for half our income* make up, be responsible for, represent, supply, provide, give, *formal* constitute **3** *account for an enemy* defeat, destroy, kill

accountability *n*
responsibility, answerability, liability, amenability, reporting, obligation

accountable *adj*
responsible, answerable, liable, amenable, obliged, bound, charged with, chargeable, *formal* obligated

accoutrements *n*
paraphernalia, gear, equipment, decorations, fittings, fixtures, furnishings, appointments, kit, outfit, trimmings, adornments, *formal* appurtenances, caparison, *colloq.* bits and pieces, odds and ends

accredited *adj*
recognized, official, authorized, qualified, endorsed, appointed, approved, certified, licensed, commissioned, *formal* certificated, deputed

accrue *v*
accumulate, increase, mount (up), be added, build up, collect, amass, *formal* augment

accumulate *v*
gather, build up, assemble, collect, amass, accrue, grow, increase, multiply, pile up, hoard, stockpile, store, gain, acquire, *formal* aggregate, augment, cumulate, *colloq.* stash, snowball
☒ *formal* disseminate, diffuse

accumulation *n*
gathering, build-up, building-up, collection, growth, increase, multiplication, hoard, mass, pile, stockpile, store, stack, stock, reserve, conglomeration, gain, accrual, assembly, acquisition, *formal* aggregate, augmentation, cumulation
☒ *formal* dissemination

accuracy *n*
correctness, precision, exactness, authenticity, truth, truthfulness, closeness, faithfulness, carefulness,

meticulousness, *formal* veracity, fidelity, exactitude, scrupulosity, verity, veridicality
☒ inaccuracy

accurate *adj*
1 *an accurate report/translation* faithful, true, correct, exact, strict, literal, word-for-word, word-perfect, close, sound, truthful, valid, authentic, unerring, faultless, perfect, fair, *formal* veracious, letter-perfect, veridical **2** *accurate calculations* correct, precise, right, valid, rigorous, meticulous, *colloq.* spot on, bang on **3** *an accurate gun/throw* well-aimed, well-directed, precise
☒ **1, 2, 3** inaccurate **2** imprecise, inexact

accursed *adj*
damned, wretched, hateful, despicable, abominable, condemned, doomed, bewitched, *formal* execrable, anathematized, bedevilled
☒ blessed

accusation *n*
charge, allegation, denunciation, impeachment, recrimination, complaint, incrimination, blame, indictment, *formal* imputation, arraignment, inculpation, citation, crimination, gravamen, delation

accuse *v*
1 *accused of murder* make accusations, bring/press charges, prosecute, put on trial, allege, make allegations, denounce, impeach, confront, attribute, indict, incriminate, implicate, inform against, *formal* impugn, impute, arraign, cite, criminate, *colloq.* frame, book **2** *accuse someone of cheating* blame, hold responsible, *formal* censure, recriminate, *colloq.* point the finger at, throw the book at

accustom *v*
familiarize, adjust, adapt, accommodate, get used to, get familiar with, get acquainted with, conform, *formal* habituate, inure, attune

accustomed *adj*
1 *accustomed to the dark* used, in the habit of, given, acclimatized, acquainted, *formal* habituated, inured, wont, *colloq.* at home **2** *sitting in her accustomed chair* normal, usual, ordinary, familiar, everyday, conventional, routine, regular, customary, traditional, established, fixed, prevailing, general, *formal* habitual, wonted, consuetudinary
☒ **1** unaccustomed, unused

ace *n, adj*
▶ *n* champion, expert, genius, master, maestro, winner, virtuoso, *colloq.* dab hand, hotshot, whizz
▶ *adj* brilliant, excellent, first-class, superb, outstanding, great, perfect

acerbic *adj*
sharp, harsh, biting, stinging, abrasive, caustic, acrimonious, *formal* astringent, vitriolic, mordant, rancorous, trenchant
☒ mild, friendly, kind

ache *v, n*
▶ *v* **1** *my legs ache* HURT, be sore, pain, be painful, suffer, be in agony, agonize, throb, pound, twinge, smart, sting, *colloq.* kill **2** *aching to tell her* LONG, yearn, pine, hanker, desire, crave, hunger, thirst, itch
▶ *n* **1** *an ache in my neck* PAIN, hurt, soreness, suffering, anguish, agony, throb, throbbing, pounding, pang, twinge, smarting, stinging **2** *an ache for the past* longing, yearning, craving, itch, hankering

achieve *v*
accomplish, do, attain, reach, get, obtain, acquire, gain, earn, win, succeed, manage, do, perform, carry out, execute, fulfil, finish, complete, bring about, realize, produce, *formal* procure, consummate, effect, effectuate
☒ miss, fail

achievement *n*
1 *the achievement of our aims* accomplishment, attainment, performance, execution, fulfilment, completion, success, realization, fruition, *formal* procurement, consummation, acquirement, fruition 2 *great achievements* accomplishment, act, action, activity, deed, performance, exploit, feat, effort

achiever *n*
doer, performer, succeeder, *colloq.* high flyer, go-getter, success story

acid *n, adj*
▶ *n*

Types of acid include:
acetic, acrylic, amino, aqua fortis, aqua regia, ascorbic, benzoic, boric, carbolic, chloric, citric, DNA (deoxyribonucleic acid), fatty, folic, formic, hydrochloric, hydrocyanic, lactic, malic, nitric, nitrohydrochloric, nitrous, palmitic, pectic, phenol, phosphoric, prussic, RNA (ribonucleic acid), salicylic, spirits of salt, stearic, sulphuric, tannic, tartaric, uric. *See also* AMINO ACID.

▶ *adj* 1 *an acid taste* acidic, sour, bitter, tart, vinegary, sharp, pungent, acerbic, caustic, corrosive, *formal* acetic, acetous, acidulous 2 *an acid remark* bitter, unkind, critical, sarcastic, stinging, biting, cutting, incisive, harsh, morose, hurtful, *formal* acerbic, astringent, mordant, trenchant, vitriolic
🔁 1 alkaline 2 kind, complimentary

acknowledge *v*
1 *acknowledge a fact/an error* ADMIT, recognize, accept, agree to, declare, grant, allow, confess, own up to, concede, *formal* acquiesce, accede, affirm, avouch 2 *acknowledge him with a nod* greet, address, notice, recognize, *formal* salute, hail 3 *acknowledge a letter* answer, write back, reply to, respond to, react to, confirm 4 *acknowledge someone's help* thank, say thank you, express/show your appreciation, be grateful, express your thanks/gratitude, recognize
🔁 1 deny, disagree with 2 ignore

acknowledged *adj*
recognized, accepted, approved, accredited, declared, professed, confirmed, *formal* attested, avowed

acknowledgement *n*
1 *an acknowledgement of defeat* recognition, admission, confession, declaration, profession, acceptance 2 *a gesture of acknowledgement* greeting, notice, recognition, nod, smile, wave, *formal* salutation 3 *an acknowledgement of a letter* answer, reply, response, reaction, *formal* affirmation 4 *an acknowledgement of assistance* expression of gratitude/appreciation/thanks, gratefulness, tribute, credit

acme *n*
high point, height, peak, pinnacle, climax, culmination, crown, optimum, summit, *formal* apex, zenith, apogee
🔁 low point, *formal* nadir

acolyte *n*
follower, assistant, helper, attendant, adherent

acoustic *adj*
hearing, sound, *formal* auditory, aural, audile

acquaint *v*
familiarize, let know, accustom, tell, notify, advise, inform, make aware of, brief, enlighten, divulge, disclose, reveal, announce, *formal* make conversant, apprise

acquaintance *n*
1 *friends and acquaintances* associate, companion, colleague, friend, contact, *formal* confrère 2 *my acquaintance with them* FAMILIARITY, association, relationship, intimacy, social contact, fellowship, companionship 3 *some acquaintance with art* familiarity, awareness, knowledge, understanding, experience, *formal* cognizance

acquainted *adj*
1 *acquainted with him* FRIENDLY, on friendly terms, on good terms 2 *acquainted with that book* FAMILIAR, well-versed, knowledgeable, aware, abreast, *au fait*, *formal* conversant, cognizant, apprised, *colloq.* in the know
🔁 2 unfamiliar, unaware, ignorant

acquiesce *v*
consent, submit, agree, accept, allow, approve, defer, *formal* concur, accede, *colloq.* give in
🔁 disagree, object, resist

acquiescence *n*
consent, agreement, acceptance, approval, submission, yielding, deference, *formal* concurrence, compliance, assent
🔁 disagreement, resistance

acquiescent *adj*
consenting, agreeable, agreeing, accepting, approving, amenable, obedient, submissive, yielding, deferential, servile, *formal* acceding, concurrent, compliant, complaisant

acquire *v*
buy, purchase, obtain, get, come by, receive, collect, gather, amass, accumulate, net, gain, secure, earn, win, achieve, attain, realize, *formal* procure, appropriate, *colloq.* pick up, snap up, splash out on, *slang* bag, cop, collar
🔁 relinquish, forfeit, sell

acquisition *n*
1 *his latest acquisition* PURCHASE, buy, gain, possession, accession, takeover, property 2 *the acquisition of a skill* securing, gaining, obtaining, achievement, attainment, *formal* procurement, appropriation

acquisitive *adj*
greedy, covetous, grasping, *formal* avaricious, avid, predatory, rapacious, voracious

acquisitiveness *n*
greed, covetousness, graspingness, *formal* avarice, avidity, predatoriness, rapacity, voracity

acquit *v*
1 *acquitted of the crime* clear, reprieve, excuse, free, liberate, deliver, relieve, release, dismiss, discharge, settle, satisfy, repay, *formal* absolve, exonerate, exculpate, vindicate, *colloq.* let off, let off the hook 2 *acquit yourself well* perform, behave, act, do, conduct, *formal* comport, bear, *colloq.* make a good/bad job
🔁 1 convict, condemn

acquittal *n*
clearance, reprieve, excusing, freeing, liberation, deliverance, relief, release, dismissal, discharge, *formal* absolution, exoneration, exculpation, vindication, compurgation
🔁 conviction, condemnation

acrid *adj*
1 *an acrid smell* pungent, sharp, stinging, acid, sour, tart, harsh, burning, caustic, acerbic 2 *an acrid comment* caustic, biting, cutting, incisive, sarcastic, sardonic, bitter, acrimonious, harsh, nasty, malicious, venomous, *formal* acerbic, astringent, mordant, trenchant, virulent, vitriolic

acrimonious *adj*
bitter, biting, cutting, caustic, sharp, virulent, severe, spiteful, censorious, abusive, ill-tempered, waspish, venomous, *formal* acerbic, astringent, rancorous, trenchant, vitriolic, splenetic, irascible, petulant, *colloq.* crabbed
🔁 peaceable, kindly, *formal* irenic

acrimony *n*
bitterness, resentment, spite, ill-will, gall, ill temper, sarcasm, harshness, venom, *formal* causticity, rancour, petulance, irascibility, mordancy, trenchancy, vitriol, spleen, astringency, acerbity, asperity, acridity, virulence

acrobat *n*
gymnast, tumbler, balancer, somersaulter, contortionist, trapeze artist, rope-walker, rope-dancer, stuntman, stuntwoman, *formal* funambulist, aerialist, equilibrist

act *v*, *n*
▶ *v* **1** *act in a certain way*; *act fast* behave, be, move, do, take action, take steps, take measures, be active, be busy, go about, react, *formal* conduct yourself, acquit yourself, exert yourself, comport yourself **2** *the drug will act soon* TAKE EFFECT, have an effect, work, operate, function, *formal* be efficacious **3** *the gear acts as a brake* work, function, serve, operate, do, do the job of **4** *act upset* pretend, fake, put on, *formal* feign, affect, assume, simulate, dissemble, dissimulate, *colloq.* sham **5** *act in a play* perform, go on the stage, play, portray, represent, mime, characterize, enact, mimic, imitate, impersonate
▷ **act on 1** *act on orders* CARRY OUT, fulfil, comply with, conform to, obey, follow, heed, take **2** AFFECT, influence, alter, modify, change, transform
▷ **act up** not work, misbehave, behave badly, cause trouble, give bother, *colloq.* play up, mess about, muck around
▶ *n* **1** *acts of bravery* DEED, action, undertaking, enterprise, operation, manoeuvre, move, step, doing, execution, accomplishment, achievement, exploit, feat, stroke **2** *put on an act* pretence, make-believe, counterfeit, fake, *formal* feigning, dissimulation, dissemblance, affectation, *colloq.* sham, show, front **3** *an act of parliament* law, statute, ordinance, edict, decree, resolution, measure, ruling, bill **4** *a juggler's act* turn, item, routine, sketch, performance, *colloq.* skit, gig

acting *adj*, *n*
▶ *adj* temporary, provisional, interim, stopgap, supply, stand-by, stand-in, standing in for, in place of, covering, deputy, substitute, reserve, relief, pro tem, surrogate
▶ *n* theatre, drama, performing, performing arts, stagecraft, artistry, performance, play-acting, melodrama, dramatics, theatricals, histrionics, footlights, portrayal, characterization, impersonation, imitating

action *n*
1 *his prompt action* act, move, deed, exploit, step, measure, course of action, feat, accomplishment, achievement, performance, effort, endeavour, enterprise, undertaking, proceeding, process, activity **2** *put an idea into action* OPERATION, practice, effect, force, functioning, doing, performance, exercise, exertion, work, mechanism, movement, motion **3** *the action of a chemical on metal* EFFECT, operation, influence **4** *people of action* vitality, liveliness, spirit, energy, vigour, power, force, activity, *colloq.* get-up-and-go **5** *killed in action* warfare, battle, conflict, combat, fight, fray, engagement, encounter, skirmish, clash, *formal* affray **6** *a legal action* litigation, lawsuit, suit, case, prosecution

activate *v*
start, start working, set off, fire, switch/turn/put on, set in motion, mobilize, propel, move, stir, rouse, arouse, get going, set going, trigger (off), trip, stimulate, initiate, motivate, prompt, energize, excite, galvanize, *formal* actuate, animate, impel, bestir, *colloq.* push/press the button, throw the switch
🔁 deactivate, stop, arrest

active *adj*
1 *an active person* BUSY, occupied, industrious, diligent, hard-working, forceful, spirited, vital, vibrant, forward, hyperactive, manic, frenetic, *formal* indefatigable, astir, *colloq.* on the go **2** *active for his age* agile, nimble, spry, sprightly, light-footed, quick, alert, animated, lively, energetic, vigorous **3** *active members* devoted, engaged, involved, committed, contributing, militant, activist, enterprising, enthusiastic **4** *the system is active* in operation, functioning, working, running, in force
🔁 **1** passive **3** inactive

activity *n*
1 *the office is full of activity* business, liveliness, life, activeness, action, motion, movement, commotion, bustle, industry, labour, exertion, exercise, *colloq.* hurly-burly, a hive of activity/industry, comings and goings, toing and froing **2** *holiday activities* pursuit, hobby, pastime, interest, diversion, distraction, something to do, occupation, job, work, act, deed, project, scheme, task, venture, enterprise, endeavour, undertaking, *formal* avocation
🔁 **1** inactivity, passivity

actor, actress *n*
play actor, film actor, film star, movie star, comedian, tragedian, player, performer, stage performer, artist, dramatic artist, leading lady, leading man, understudy, extra, walk-on, impersonator, mime, mime artist, mummer, *formal* Thespian, Roscius, *colloq.* ham

actual *adj*
real, existent, substantial, tangible, material, physical, concrete, positive, definite, absolute, certain, unquestionable, indisputable, confirmed, verified, factual, truthful, true, genuine, legitimate, bona fide, authentic, realistic, *formal* de facto, *colloq.* real live
🔁 theoretical, apparent, imaginary

actuality *n*
reality, fact, substance, truth, *formal* factuality, historicity, corporeality, materiality, substantiality

actually *adv*
1 *Did you actually see him fall?* in fact, as a matter of fact, as it happens, in truth, in reality, really, truly, indeed, absolutely, *formal* de facto **2** *she took her degree eventually and actually got a first class* even, though it may seem strange, surprisingly, as it happens

actuate *v*
move, stir, stimulate, activate, motivate, instigate, prompt, rouse, arouse, kindle, start, start working, set off, set going, trigger (off), switch/turn on, set in motion

acumen *n*
astuteness, shrewdness, sharpness, keenness, quickness, penetration, insight, intuition, discrimination, discernment, judgement, perception, sense, wit, wisdom, intelligence, cleverness, ingenuity, *formal* judiciousness, percipience, perspicacity, perspicuity, sagacity, sapience, *colloq.* smartness, gumption

acute *adj*
1 *an acute shortage* SEVERE, intense, extreme, violent, critical, dangerous, serious, grave, urgent, crucial, vital, decisive, sharp, cutting, poignant, distressing **2** *an acute mind* SHARP, keen, incisive, penetrating, astute, shrewd, canny, judicious, discerning, clever, observant, perceptive, insightful,

sensitive, *formal* percipient, perspicacious, sapient, *colloq.* smart **3** *an acute illness* severe, serious, intense, dangerous, critical, grave

F3 1 mild, slight **3** mild, chronic, persistent

acutely *adv*
very, intensely, extremely, strongly, seriously, gravely, sharply, keenly

adage *n*
maxim, saying, axiom, proverb, byword, precept, saw, *formal* aphorism, apophthegm, paroemia

adamant *adj*
hard, resolute, determined, set, firm, insistent, rigid, stiff, inflexible, unbending, unrelenting, unyielding, stubborn, uncompromising, tough, fixed, immovable, unshakable, *formal* intransigent, obdurate

F3 hesitant, flexible, yielding

adapt *v*
1 *adapt to a new environment* ADJUST, acclimatize yourself, familiarize yourself, orientate yourself, accommodate yourself, get used/accustomed, *formal* habituate yourself **2** *adapt a building* ALTER, change, qualify, modify, adjust, convert, remodel, customize, fit, tailor, fashion, shape, harmonize, match, suit, conform, comply, prepare

adaptable *adj*
flexible, compliant, amenable, easy-going, versatile, plastic, malleable, alterable, changeable, variable, modifiable, adjustable, convertible, conformable

F3 inflexible, *formal* refractory

adaptation *n*
1 *adaptation to a different situation* ADJUSTMENT, acclimatization, familiarization, accommodation, getting used/accustomed, *formal* habituation **2** *adaptation of a novel for TV* ALTERATION, change, modification, shift, transformation, revision, variation, adjustment, conversion, remodelling, customization, fitting, refitting, fashioning, refashioning, reworking, shaping, reshaping, harmonization, matching, conformity, preparation

add *v*
1 *add an introduction to the book* put on, put in, include, increase, complete, improve, attach, supplement, combine, build on, *formal* adjoin, affix, append, annex, augment, *colloq.* throw in **2** *add numbers* count (up), total, work out/calculate the total, *colloq.* tot up **3** *'Thanks,' I added* tack on, continue, go on to say, carry on

F3 1 take away, reduce, decrease **2** subtract, take (away), deduct, remove

▷ **add up 1** *add up numbers* add, sum up, add together, total, tally, count (up), reckon, calculate, compute, *colloq.* tot up **2** *the total adds up to 100* amount, come to, include, spell, *formal* constitute **3** *it doesn't add up* be consistent, hang together, fit, be plausible, be reasonable, stand to reason, make sense, mean, signify, indicate, ring true

F3 1 subtract

added *adj*
additional, supplementary, extra, more, another, fresh, further, new, spare, *formal* adjunct

addendum *n*
appendix, addition, postscript, supplement, *formal* codicil, adjunct, appendage, augmentation, attachment, endorsement, allonge

addict *n*
1 *a drug addict* drug taker, drug user, *colloq.* junkie, user, dope-fiend, *slang* freak, head, coke-head, tripper, mainliner **2** *a chess addict* enthusiast, fan, devotee, follower, adherent, *colloq.* buff, fiend, freak

addicted *adj*
1 *addicted to drugs* dependent, drug-dependent, *colloq.* hooked, strung out **2** *addicted to TV* obsessed,

absorbed, devoted, dedicated, fond, inclined, *colloq.* hooked

addiction *n*
1 *alcohol addiction* dependence, craving, habit, *slang* monkey **2** *addiction to chocolate* craving, habit, obsession, compulsive behaviour, mania

addition *n*
1 *the index is a welcome addition* supplement, attachment, extra, increment, additive, rider, afterthought, postscript, annexe, addendum, appendix, accessory, *formal* adjunct, appendage, appurtenance **2** *the addition of a separate phone line* adding, extension, enlargement, increasing, increase, gain, *formal* annexation, accession, accretion **3** *addition of numbers* summing-up, totalling, counting, reckoning, inclusion, computation, *colloq.* totting-up

F3 2 removal, taking-away **3** subtraction, deduction

▷ **in addition** additionally, too, also, as well, besides, moreover, further, furthermore, over and above, not to mention, *colloq.* into the bargain

additional *adj*
added, extra, supplementary, spare, more, further, increased, other, new, fresh, another, *formal* adscititious, adventitious, supervenient, excrescent

additionally *adv*
in addition, too, also, as well, besides, moreover, further, furthermore, over and above, *colloq.* into the bargain, for good measure

additive *n*
supplement, addition, extra, preservative

addled *adj*
confused, befuddled, bewildered, flustered, mixed-up, muddled, perplexed

F3 clear

address *n, v*
▶ *n* **1** *write down an address and phone number* home, house, flat, apartment, lodging, directions, inscription, whereabouts, location, situation, place, poste restante, dwelling, *formal* (place of) residence, abode **2** SPEECH, talk, lecture, sermon, oration, discourse, monologue, soliloquy, dissertation, *formal* diatribe, philippic, apostrophe, disquisition **3** *forms of address* greeting, welcome, *formal* salutation, invocation

▶ *v* **1** *address an audience* lecture, speak to, talk to, give a talk/speech to, make/deliver a speech, *formal* sermonize, harangue, orate **2** *address a remark to someone* communicate, direct, convey, send, intend for, *formal* remit **3** *How should I address a duke?* call, speak/write to, designate

▷ **address (yourself) to** deal with, give your attention to, apply yourself to, devote yourself to, attend to, undertake, concentrate on, focus on, engage in, take care of

adduce *v*
cite, mention, allude to, refer to, put forward, point out, present, *formal* proffer, evidence

adept *adj, n*
▶ *adj* skilled, accomplished, expert, masterly, experienced, versed, practised, polished, proficient, competent, capable, good, clever, able, adroit, deft, nimble, *colloq.* ace, sharp, hot stuff, no flies on someone

F3 bungling, incompetent, inept

▶ *n* master, expert, genius, maestro, *colloq.* dab hand, hot stuff, nobody's fool, wizard

F3 bungler, incompetent

adequacy *n*
sufficiency, suitability, fitness, ability, competence, capability, serviceability, acceptability, satisfactoriness, reasonableness, passability, tolerability,

tolerableness, fairness, indifference, mediocrity, *formal* commensurateness, requisiteness
🔁 inadequacy, insufficiency

adequate *adj*
1 *adequate amounts of food* enough, sufficient, *formal* commensurate, requisite **2** *adequate work* acceptable, satisfactory, passable, reasonable, tolerable, unexceptional, indifferent, undistinguished, average, suitable, fit, able, competent, capable, serviceable, *colloq.* all right, OK, will do, could be better/worse, patchy, fair to middling, run of the mill, nothing (much) to write home about, not set the Thames on fire
🔁 **1** insufficient **2** inadequate

adhere *v*
1 STICK, stick together, glue, paste, cement, grip, fix, fasten, attach, join, link, combine, coalesce, cohere, hold, cling, *formal* cleave to, accrete **2** *adhere to the agreement* OBSERVE, follow, abide by, comply with, fulfil, obey, keep, heed, respect, stand by, *colloq.* stick **3** *adhere to an opinion* support, hold, defend, stand by, go along with, stick up for, *formal* espouse

adherent *n*
supporter, upholder, advocate, partisan, follower, disciple, satellite, henchman, devotee, admirer, fan, enthusiast, *formal* votary, aficionado, sectary, *colloq.* hanger-on, buff, freak, nut

adhesion *n*
adherence, adhesiveness, holding together, sticking together, bond, attachment, grip, cohesion

adhesive *adj, n*
▶ *adj* sticky, stick-on, tacky, self-adhesive, gummed, adhering, sticking, clinging, holding, attaching, cohesive, *formal* adherent, glutinous, mucilaginous, *colloq.* gummy, gluey
▶ *n* glue, gum, fixative, paste, cement, tape, sticky tape, Sellotape®, Elastoplast®, Band-aid®, Superglue®, Blue-tak®, *formal* mucilage

adieu *n*
goodbye, farewell, leave-taking, *au revoir, formal* valediction, valedictory, *colloq.* cheerio, cheers

adjacent *adj*
adjoining, touching, bordering, alongside, beside, next-door, neighbouring, next, closest, nearest, close, near, *formal* abutting, contiguous, juxtaposed, conterminant, conterminate, conterminous, proximate, vicinal
🔁 remote, distant

adjoin *v*
touch, meet, border, verge, neighbour, interconnect, link, connect, join, combine, unite, couple, attach, add, annex, *formal* abut, append, juxtapose

adjoining *adj*
adjacent, touching, bordering, near, neighbouring, next, next door, verging, interconnecting, linking, connecting, joining, combining, uniting, *formal* contiguous, impinging, abutting, proximate, juxtaposed, conjoining, vicinal

adjourn *v*
1 *adjourn a meeting* stop temporarily, interrupt, suspend, break off, delay, stay, defer, postpone, put off, pause, *formal* discontinue, prorogue **2** *adjourn to the lounge* withdraw, *formal* retire, repair
🔁 **1** assemble, convene

adjournment *n*
interruption, suspension, break, pause, interval, delay, stay, postponement, putting-off, *US* recess, intermission, *formal* discontinuation, deferment, deferral, dissolution, prorogation

adjudicate *v*
judge, arbitrate, umpire, referee, settle, determine, decide, pronounce, *formal* adjudge

adjust *v*
1 *adjust to new circumstances* become/grow accustomed, adapt, acclimatize yourself, become acclimatized, orientate yourself, accommodate yourself, reconcile yourself, harmonize, conform, *formal* habituate yourself, *colloq.* get used to **2** MODIFY, change, adapt, alter, convert, dispose, shape, remodel, fit, accommodate, suit, measure, amend, revise, make adjustments, rectify, regulate, balance, repair, reshape, refashion, temper, tune, fix, set, arrange, align, compose, settle, shape, square, *formal* coapt, *colloq.* fine-tune, tweak

adjustable *adj*
adaptable, modifiable, convertible, flexible, movable
🔁 fixed, immovable

adjustment *n*
1 *minor adjustments to the engine* MODIFICATION, change, adaptation, alteration, conversion, remodelling, shaping, fitting, accommodation, amendment, revision, rectification, regulation, tuning, fixing, setting, arranging, rearranging, arrangement, rearrangement, ordering, settlement **2** *adjustment to a new job* orientation, adaptation, acclimatization, accommodation, naturalization, reconciliation, harmonization, conforming, getting used to, *formal* habituation

ad-lib *v, adj, adv*
▶ *v* improvise, make up, invent, *formal* extemporize, *colloq.* speak off the cuff/off the top of your head
▶ *adj* impromptu, improvised, unprepared, without preparation, unpremeditated, unrehearsed, spontaneous, made-up, *formal* extempore, extemporaneous, extemporized, *colloq.* off-the-cuff, off the top of your head
🔁 prepared
▶ *adv* impromptu, spontaneously, impulsively, *formal* extempore, extemporaneously, *colloq.* off the cuff, off the top of your head

administer *v*
1 *administer a country/law/project* organize, direct, conduct, manage, run, control, regulate, superintend, supervise, oversee, govern, rule, lead, head, preside over, officiate **2** *administer a drug* GIVE, provide, supply, distribute, give out, measure out, mete out, execute, impose, apply, *formal* dispense, disburse, adhibit, *colloq.* dole out

administration *n*
1 *reduce the cost of administration* administering, management, running, paperwork, organization, direction, control, superintendence, supervision, overseeing, governing, ruling, leadership, execution, *colloq.* red tape **2** *a country's administration* government, governing body, regime, ministry, leadership, directorship, management, executive, term of office

administrative *adj*
management, managerial, governmental, legislative, authoritative, executive, organizational, regulatory, supervisory, *formal* directorial, gubernatorial

administrator *n*
manager, organizer, director, controller, superintendent, supervisor, overseer, governor, ruler, leader, president, chairman, chief executive, executive, managing director, head, chief, *formal* custodian, guardian, trustee, *colloq.* boss

admirable *adj*
praiseworthy, commendable, creditable, deserving, worthy, praiseworthy, respected, fine, excellent, superior, wonderful, exquisite, choice, rare, masterly, valuable, *formal* estimable, laudable, meritorious
🔁 contemptible, despicable, deplorable

admiration *n*
respect, (high) regard, reverence, worship, idolism, adoration, affection, adulation, approval, praise, acclaim, appreciation, kudos, pleasure, delight, wonder, astonishment, amazement, surprise, *formal* (high) esteem, approbation, veneration, laudation, fureur, *colloq.* yen
🖪 contempt, disrespect, scorn

admire *v*
1 *admire his honesty* respect, think highly of, have a high opinion of, look up to, like very much, revere, worship, idolize, adore, approve, praise, applaud, *formal* hold in high regard/esteem, esteem (highly), venerate, laud, prize, iconize, *colloq.* think the world of, hero-worship, put on a pedestal, take your hat off to 2 *admire a car* appreciate, value, like, approve of
🖪 1 despise, censure

admirer *n*
1 *a great admirer of classical music* follower, disciple, adherent, supporter, fan, enthusiast, devotee, worshipper, idolizer, idolater, *formal* aficionado, *colloq.* buff, fiend, freak 2 *a woman's admirers* suitor, boyfriend, girlfriend, sweetheart, lover, *formal* beau, wooer, gallant
🖪 1 critic, opponent

admissible *adj*
acceptable, allowable, permissible, allowed, permitted, lawful, legitimate, justifiable, tolerable, tolerated, passable, *formal* licit
🖪 inadmissible, illegitimate

admission *n*
1 *refuse admission* permission, entrance, access, right of access, *formal* ingress 2 *admission is £5* admission fee, entrance, entrance fee, entry charge 3 *an admission of guilt* CONFESSION, granting, acknowledgement, recognition, acceptance, allowance, concession, affirmation, declaration, profession, disclosure, divulgence, revelation, exposé, *formal* avowal, *mea culpa*, peccavi
🖪 1 exclusion, prohibition 3 denial, contradiction

> 🖉 **admission** or **admittance**?
> Each word means 'the act of entering' or 'permission to enter', but *admittance* is used in more formal styles: *Admission by ticket only*; *gain admittance to the palace of the President.*

admit *v*
1 *admit I was wrong* CONFESS, own up, grant, acknowledge, recognize, accept, allow, concede, agree, declare, profess, disclose, unburden yourself, divulge, reveal, *formal* affirm, *colloq.* blurt out, eat your words, come clean 2 *be admitted to the palace* LET IN, allow to enter, give access, give admission, accept, receive, take in, introduce, initiate, *formal* intromit
🖪 1 deny, hide 2 shut out, exclude, let out

admittance *n*
admitting, admission, letting in, (right of) access, entrance, (right of) entry, acceptance, reception, introduction, initiation, *formal* ingress
🖪 exclusion

admixture *n*
mixture, compound, combination, blend, amalgamation, mix, fusion, amalgam, alloy, *formal* commixture, intermixture, tincture

admonish *v*
scold, rebuke, reprimand, discipline, correct, reprove, warn, upbraid, chide, censure, exhort, counsel, *formal* berate, *colloq.* tell off

admonition *n*
rebuke, reprimand, reproof, scolding, correction, warning, censure, exhortation, counsel, *formal* berating, reprehension, *colloq.* telling-off

adolescence *n*
teens, teenage years, puberty, youth, minority, boyhood, girlhood, development, immaturity, youthfulness, boyishness, girlishness, *formal* pubescence, juvenescence, juvenility

adolescent *adj, n*
▶ *adj* 1 *an adolescent son* teenage, young, youthful, juvenile, boyish, girlish, growing, developing, *formal* pubescent, juvenescent 2 *adolescent behaviour* immature, puerile, childish
▶ *n* teenager, youth, young person, young adult, juvenile, minor

adopt *v*
1 *adopt children* take in, take as your own, foster 2 *adopt a policy* TAKE UP, take on, accept, assume, follow, choose, select, nominate, support, maintain, back, endorse, ratify, approve, *formal* appropriate, embrace, espouse
🖪 1 disown 2 reject

adoption *n*
1 *the adoption of children* taking as your own, taking-in, (long-term) fostering 2 *the adoption of a suggestion* taking-on, acceptance, taking-up, choice, selection, support, backing, endorsement, ratification, approval, *formal* appropriation, approbation, embracement, embracing, espousal

adorable *adj*
lovable, dear, darling, precious, appealing, sweet, winsome, charming, enchanting, captivating, winning, delightful, pleasing, attractive, wonderful, fetching, bewitching
🖪 hateful, abominable

adoration *n*
1 *adoration for someone* love, admiration, devotion, cherishing, doting on, (high) regard, *formal* esteem 2 *adoration of God* worship, praise, reverence, veneration, homage, idolization, exaltation, magnification, glorification
🖪 2 abhorrence, detestation

adore *v*
1 *adore your parents* love, cherish, be devoted to, dote on, hold dear, be fond of, admire, honour, revere, worship, *formal* esteem (highly), venerate, *colloq.* think the world of 2 *adore apricots* love, like very much, enjoy greatly, be fond of, enjoy, relish, be partial to, *colloq.* have a weakness for, not be able to resist
🖪 1, 2 hate, *formal* abhor

adorn *v*
decorate, deck, ornament, crown, trim, garnish, gild, enhance, embellish, enrich, grace, trim, *formal* festoon, bedeck, emblazon, furbish, gild, adonize, apparel, array, beautify, bedight, bedizen, begem, bejewel, bestick, impearl, miniate, *colloq.* doll up, tart up

adornment *n*
1 *bodily adornment* beautification, decorating, ornamentation, ornateness, enrichment, embellishment, *formal* bedizenment, garniture 2 *gold adornments* accessory, ornament, decoration, jewellery, frill, trappings, trimmings, garnish, flounce, frippery, *formal* falbala, fallal, fallalery, fandangle, figgery, furbelow, garnishry, gilding

adrift *adj*
1 *the boat had been cut adrift* at sea, drifting, off course, anchorless 2 *feel adrift and lonely* aimless, rootless, directionless, goalless, insecure, unsettled
🖪 1 anchored 2 stable

adroit *adj*
skilful, adept, able, clever, expert, masterful, proficient, deft, dexterous
Ea clumsy, inept, maladroit

adroitness *n*
skill, skilfulness, adeptness, ability, cleverness, expertise, mastery, facility, finesse, proficiency, competence, deftness, dexterity
Ea clumsiness, ineptitude

adulation *n*
flattery, idolization, personality cult, hero worship, praise, sycophancy, bootlicking, fawning, *formal* blandishment

adulatory *adj*
flattering, praising, bootlicking, fawning, servile, sycophantic, *formal* blandishing, fulsome, obsequious, unctuous
Ea unflattering

adult *adj*
1 *adult responsibilities* grown-up, of age, full-grown, fully-grown, developed, mature, ripe, ripened 2 *adult magazines* sexually explicit, pornographic, obscene
Ea 1 immature

adulterate *v*
contaminate, pollute, taint, corrupt, defile, debase, degrade, dilute, water down, weaken, devalue, deteriorate, make impure, *formal* attenuate, bastardize, vitiate
Ea purify, refine

adultery *n*
unfaithfulness, infidelity, affair, extramarital relations/relationship, extramarital sex, entanglement, flirtation, unchastity, *colloq.* cheating, a bit on the side, *slang* playing around, playing the field
Ea faithfulness, fidelity

advance *v, n*
▶ *v* 1 PROCEED, go forward, move on, move forward, come forward, surge forward, go ahead, progress, make progress, make headway, forge ahead, *colloq.* make great strides, come on in leaps and bounds 2 *advance the date of the wedding* bring forward, make earlier 3 ACCELERATE, speed (up), send forward, *formal* hasten, expedite 4 FURTHER, promote, upgrade, foster, support, assist, help, benefit, facilitate, increase, grow 5 *advance an idea* PRESENT, submit, put forward, suggest, allege, cite, bring forward, offer, provide, supply, furnish, *formal* proffer, adduce 6 *advance a sum of money* lend, loan, pay, pay beforehand, pay in advance, give
Ea 1 retreat 2 put back 3 *formal* retard 4 impede, hinder
▶ *n* 1 *recent advances in medicine* PROGRESS, forward movement, onward movement, moving forward, going forward, marching forward, headway, step, breakthrough, development, progression, growth, increase, improvement, *formal* advancement, furtherance, betterment, amelioration 2 *an advance of £500* deposit, down payment, prepayment, credit, loan, retainer
Ea 1 retreat, recession
▷ **in advance** beforehand, previously, early, earlier, sooner, ahead, in front, in the lead, in the forefront, *colloq.* up front
Ea later, behind

advanced *adj*
1 *an advanced design* up-to-date, leading, foremost, ahead, forward, precocious, progressive, forward-looking, hi-tech, state-of-the-art, avant-garde, ultramodern, ahead of the times, sophisticated, complex, higher, at the cutting/leading edge 2 *an advanced course of studies* high-level, complex
Ea 1 backward, retarded 2 elementary

advancement *n*
1 *advancement in a career* PROMOTION, furtherance, betterment, *formal* preferment 2 *the advancement of science* improvement, development, growth, rise, gain, advance, progress, headway
Ea 1 demotion 2 retardation

advances *n*
overtures, addresses, approach(es), attentions, moves, proposition

advantage *n*
1 *the advantages of electric light* asset, blessing, benefit, good, good point, plus, plus point, virtue, pro, boon, fruit, welfare, interest, service, help, aid, assistance, use, convenience, usefulness, utility, profit, gain, *formal* avail, *colloq.* beauty, pay-off 2 *an advantage over other candidates* edge, lead, upper hand, superiority, precedence, dominance, pre-eminence, sway, leverage, *colloq.* head start, everything going for you, the odds in your favour
Ea 1 disadvantage, drawback, hindrance

advantageous *adj*
beneficial, favourable, convenient, helpful, of assistance, of service, useful, worthwhile, valuable, profitable, gainful, remunerative, rewarding, *formal* opportune, propitious, furthersome
Ea disadvantageous, adverse, damaging

advent *n*
coming, appearance, approach, arrival, entrance, introduction, occurrence, onset, dawn, birth, beginning, *formal* accession, inception

adventure *n*
1 *exciting adventures* exploit, venture, undertaking, enterprise, risk, hazard, chance, speculation, experience, incident, occurrence 2 *a life of adventure* excitement, enterprise, risk, danger, peril, romance

adventurer *n*
opportunist, hero, heroine, traveller, venturer, voyager, wanderer

adventurous *adj*
1 *an adventurous person* daring, intrepid, bold, headstrong, audacious, impetuous, reckless, rash, risky, venturesome, enterprising, *colloq.* spunky, gutsy 2 *an adventurous life* exciting, enterprising, risky, dangerous, perilous, hazardous, romantic
Ea 1, 2 unadventurous 1 cautious, chary, prudent

adversary *n*
enemy, opponent, antagonist, assailant, attacker, competitor, contestant, foe, opposer, rival
Ea ally, supporter, friend

adverse *adj*
unfavourable, disadvantageous, hostile, antagonistic, opposing, opposite, counter, contrary, conflicting, counter-productive, negative, unfortunate, unlucky, detrimental, harmful, injurious, hurtful, unfriendly, uncongenial, *formal* inauspicious, inopportune, unpropitious, inexpedient, untoward
Ea advantageous, favourable

adversity *n*
misfortune, ill fortune, bad luck, ill luck, reverse, hardship, hard times, misery, wretchedness, affliction, suffering, distress, sorrow, woe, trouble, trial, calamity, disaster, catastrophe, *formal* tribulation, *colloq.* hell, living hell, *slang* the pits
Ea prosperity

advertise *v*
1 *advertise a product* publicize, promote, market, merchandise, sell, praise, tout, *colloq.* push, plug, hype 2 *advertise the time of a performance* announce, declare, proclaim, broadcast, publish, display, make known, make public, inform, notify, *formal* promulgate

advertisement *n*
commercial, publicity, promotion, marketing, jingle, display, blurb, announcement, notice, poster, bill, placard, leaflet, handbill, circular, handout, propaganda, trailer, *colloq.* advert, ad, plug, hype

advice *n*
1 *give someone advice* warning, caution, dos and don'ts, injunction, instruction, counsel, counselling, help, guidance, direction, suggestion, recommendation, opinion, view, tip, wisdom, word, constructive criticism, encouragement **2** *a remittance advice* notification, notice, memorandum, communication, information

advisability *n*
desirability, suitability, appropriateness, aptness, wisdom, judiciousness, prudence, soundness, *formal* expediency
☒ inadvisability, folly

advisable *adj*
suggested, recommended, sensible, wise, wisest, prudent, judicious, sound, profitable, beneficial, best, desirable, suitable, appropriate, apt, fitting, fit, proper, correct, *formal* politic
☒ inadvisable, foolish

advise *v*
1 COUNSEL, guide, give guidance, warn, forewarn, caution, instruct, teach, tutor, suggest, give/offer/make suggestions, recommend, give/offer/make recommendations, commend, urge, *formal* enjoin. **2** NOTIFY, inform, tell, acquaint, make known, report, give notice, *formal* apprise

adviser *n*
counsellor, consultant, authority, guide, teacher, tutor, instructor, coach, helper, aide, right-hand man/woman, therapist, mentor, guru, confidant(e), counsel, lawyer

advisory *adj*
advising, consultative, consulting, counselling, helping, recommending, *formal* consultatory

advocacy *n*
support, backing, adoption, campaigning, promotion, championing, defence, encouragement, patronage, proposal, recommendation, justification, upholding, propagation, *formal* espousal, advancement, promulgation

advocate *v, n*
▶ *v* defend, champion, campaign for, press for, argue for, plead for, justify, urge, encourage, advise, recommend, propose, promote, endorse, back (up), support, uphold, patronize, adopt, subscribe to, favour, believe in, sympathize with, lobby, *formal* espouse, countenance, *colloq.* be behind, be pro, throw your weight behind
☒ *formal* impugn, disparage, deprecate
▶ *n* **1** *an advocate of an idea* defender, supporter, upholder, champion, campaigner, pleader, vindicator, proponent, exponent, promoter, speaker, spokesperson **2** *the advocate in a court of law* lawyer, barrister, counsel, attorney
☒ **1** opponent, critic

aegis *n*
support, backing, auspices, guardianship, patronage, sponsorship, wing, advocacy, championship, favour

aeroplane *n*
See panel at AIRCRAFT.

affability *n*
friendliness, amiability, approachability, openness, geniality, good humour, good nature, mildness, benevolence, kindliness, graciousness, obligingness, courtesy, amicability, congeniality, cordiality,

warmth, sociability, pleasantness, *formal* benignity, conversableness
☒ unfriendliness, reserve, reticence, coolness

affable *adj*
friendly, amiable, approachable, open, expansive, genial, good-humoured, good-natured, mild, benevolent, kindly, gracious, obliging, courteous, amicable, congenial, cordial, warm, sociable, pleasant, agreeable
☒ unfriendly, reserved, reticent, cool

affair *n*
1 BUSINESS, transaction, operation, proceeding, undertaking, activity, project, responsibility, interest, concern, matter, question, issue, subject, topic, circumstance, happening, occurrence, incident, episode, event **2** *have an affair* relationship, liaison, intrigue, love affair, romance, amour, *colloq.* fling

affect *v*
1 *changes that affect the schedule* have an effect/influence on, concern, regard, involve, relate to, apply to, do to, bear upon, impinge upon, act on, change, transform, alter, modify, influence, sway, prevail over, impact **2** *deeply affected by the poverty* move, touch, impress, interest, stir, upset, disturb, trouble, overcome, *formal* perturb **3** *a disease affects the body* attack, strike, take hold of **4** *affect an attitude* adopt, put on, simulate, imitate, fake, counterfeit, sham, pretend, profess, *formal* feign, assume

---

> 📝 **affect** or **effect**?
>
> *Affect* is always a verb. Its most common meaning is 'to have an influence on; change the circumstances, etc of': *The accident affected his eyesight. Effect* is used as a noun or a verb: as a noun it means 'result or consequence': *recover from the effects of his illness.* As a verb it is used in formal styles to mean 'to cause or bring about': *effect a reconciliation with his parents.*

---

affectation *n*
airs, pretentiousness, mannerism, pose, act, show, appearance, façade, pretence, sham, false display, simulation, imitation, artificiality, insincerity, theatricism, airs and graces
☒ artlessness, ingenuousness

affected *adj*
put-on, simulated, artificial, fake, counterfeit, sham, contrived, studied, precious, mannered, pretentious, pompous, stiff, unnatural, insincere, twee, *formal* assumed, feigned, literose, minikin, *colloq.* la-di-da, phoney
☒ genuine, natural

affecting *adj*
moving, touching, impressive, piteous, pitiable, pitiful, poignant, pathetic, sad, stirring, troubling

affection *n*
fondness, attachment, devotion, love, tenderness, care, caring, warmth, feeling, kindness, friendliness, goodwill, favour, liking, partiality, inclination, passion, desire, *formal* amity, penchant, predilection, predisposition, proclivity, propensity
☒ dislike, antipathy

affectionate *adj*
fond, attached, devoted, doting, loving, tender, caring, warm, warm-hearted, kind, friendly, amiable, cordial
☒ cold, undemonstrative

affiliate *v*
join, associate, ally, amalgamate, unite, annex, combine, connect, incorporate, join, merge, syndicate, band together, *formal* confederate, conjoin

affiliation n
connection, relationship, link, tie, bond, alliance, union, amalgamation, association, coalition, combination, confederation, federation, incorporation, membership, joining, league, merger

affinity n
1 RAPPORT, attraction, compatibility, fondness, liking, good terms, bond, partiality, *formal* predisposition, propensity, *colloq.* chemistry **2** RESEMBLANCE, similarity, likeness, correspondence, analogy, comparability, *formal* similitude
Fd 1 hatred **2** dissimilarity

affirm v
confirm, corroborate, endorse, ratify, certify, witness, testify, swear, maintain, state, assert, declare, pronounce, *formal* asseverate, attest, aver, avouch, avow
Fd refute, deny

affirmation n
assertion, statement, declaration, attestation, certification, confirmation, corroboration, endorsement, ratification, oath, pronouncement, testimony, witness, *formal* affirmance, asseveration, averment, deposition, avouchment, avowal

affirmative adj
agreeing, concurring, approving, assenting, consenting, positive, confirming, corroborative, emphatic
Fd negative, dissenting

affix v
stick, glue, paste, pin on, tack, attach, add, annex, append, bind, connect, fasten, join, tag, *formal* adjoin, subjoin
Fd detach

afflict v
strike, visit, trouble, burden, oppress, distress, grieve, pain, hurt, wound, harm, try, harass, plague, torment, torture, *old use* smite, *formal* beset
Fd comfort, *formal* solace

> 🖉 **afflict** or **inflict**?
>
> *Afflict* means 'to cause pain or distress to': *Pre-fight nerves afflict almost everyone. Inflict* means 'to impose something unpleasant or unwanted': *They inflicted heavy casualties on the enemy.*

---

affliction n
distress, grief, sorrow, misery, depression, suffering, pain, torment, disease, illness, sickness, plague, curse, cross, ordeal, trial, trouble, hardship, adversity, misfortune, calamity, disaster, woe, wretchedness, *formal* tribulation
Fd comfort, blessing, *formal* consolation, solace

affluence n
wealthiness, wealth, riches, fortune, substance, property, prosperity, abundance, profusion, plenty, *colloq.* tidy sum, *slang* megabucks, *formal* opulence
Fd poverty

affluent adj
wealthy, rich, moneyed, well-off, prosperous, well-to-do, comfortable, *formal* opulent, *colloq.* well-heeled, flush, in the money, rolling in it, *slang* loaded
Fd poor, impoverished

afford v
1 *afford school fees* have enough for, pay for, be able to pay, spare, allow, manage, sustain, bear **2** *privileges afforded by the membership* provide, supply, furnish, give, grant, offer, impart, produce, yield, generate

affray n
brawl, brush, contest, disturbance, fight, quarrel, riot, row, feud, fracas, fray, mêlée, scuffle, set-to, skirmish, squabble, tussle, wrangle, *colloq.* fisticuffs, scrap, free-for-all

affront v, n
▶ v offend, insult, abuse, snub, slight, provoke, displease, irritate, annoy, anger, vex, incense, outrage, pique
Fd compliment, appease
▶ n offence, insult, slur, rudeness, discourtesy, disrespect, indignity, snub, slight, wrong, injury, abuse, provocation, vexation, outrage, *formal* aspersion, *colloq.* slap in the face, kick in the teeth
Fd compliment

afoot adj
about, around, circulating, current, going about, in the air, in the wind, brewing, *formal* abroad, *colloq.* in the pipeline

afraid adj
1 *afraid of spiders* FRIGHTENED, scared, alarmed, terrified, petrified, panic-stricken, fearful, timorous, daunted, intimidated, faint-hearted, cowardly, craven, reluctant, apprehensive, anxious, nervous, timid, distrustful, suspicious, *formal* tremulous, aghast **2** *I'm afraid she's badly hurt* sorry, concerned, regretful
Fd 1 unafraid, brave, bold, confident

afresh adv
anew, again, once again, once more, newly, over again

after prep
1 *life after death* following, subsequent to **2** *named after her mother* in honour of, given the same name as **3** *after the way I've been treated* because of, owing to, in consequence of, as a result of
Fd 1 before

aftermath n
after-effects, effects, results, outcome, consequences, end, repercussions, upshot, wake

afterwards adv
next, later (on), subsequently, after that, then

again adv
once more, once again, yet again, one more time, another time, over again, afresh, anew, encore
▷ **again and again** repeatedly, continually, constantly, over and over again, time and time again, time and again

against prep
1 *against the wall* adjacent to, close up to, touching, in contact with, on, *formal* abutting **2** *against corporal punishment* opposing, versus, opposed to, in opposition to, antagonistic to, hostile to, resisting, in defiance of, opposite to, facing, fronting, in the face of, confronting, in contrast to, *colloq.* anti
Fd 2 in favour of, for, *colloq.* pro

age n, v
▶ n **1** *the Ice Age* era, epoch, day, days, generation, date, time, period, duration, span, years, aeon **2** *the experience of age* old age, maturity, elderliness, seniority, dotage, senility, decline, advancing/declining years, *formal* senescence, decrepitude
Fd 2 youth, *colloq.* salad days
▶ v grow old/up, come of age, mature, ripen, mellow, season, decline, deteriorate, degenerate, wither
Fd obsolesce

aged adj
old, elderly, advanced (in years), ageing, geriatric, grey, hoary, patriarchal, superannuated, *formal* senescent, *colloq.* getting on, past it, over the hill, have seen better days, no spring chicken, not as young as you were, with one foot in the grave, ancient
Fd young, youthful

agency *n*
1 *a recruitment agency* bureau, office, department, organization, business, firm, company, work **2** MEANS, medium, instrumentality, power, force, influence, effect, intervention, action, activity, operation, mechanism, workings

agenda *n*
list, plan, programme, schedule, calendar, diary, timetable, to-do list, scheme of work, menu

agent *n*
1 *a travel agent* representative, broker, middleman, go-between, intermediary, negotiator, substitute, deputy, delegate, envoy, emissary, minister, proxy, trustee, assignee, mover, doer, performer, operator, operative, functionary, worker, factor, *colloq.* rep **2** *a secret agent* spy, double agent, *US* operative, *colloq.* mole **3** *water-purifying agents* instrument, vehicle, channel, means, agency, cause, force

agglomeration *n*
accumulation, build-up, collection, gathering, increase, store, aggregate, *formal* augmentation, aggregation

aggrandize *v*
make richer, make more powerful, advance, dignify, elevate, enhance, enlarge, ennoble, enrich, exaggerate, exalt, glamorize, glorify, inflate, amplify, magnify, promote, upgrade, widen
🖪 belittle, debase

aggravate *v*
1 *aggravate the problem* worsen, make worse, compound, inflame, increase, intensify, heighten, magnify, exaggerate, *formal* exacerbate, *colloq.* add fuel to the fire/flames, add insult to injury, rub salt in the wound **2** ANNOY, irritate, vex, irk, exasperate, incense, provoke, tease, pester, harass, *colloq.* get on someone's nerves, get up someone's nose, rub up the wrong way, needle
🖪 **1** improve, alleviate **2** soothe, appease, mollify

aggravation *n*
annoyance, exasperation, irritation, provocation, teasing, vexation, irksomeness, *colloq.* hassle, thorn in the flesh

aggregate *n*
total, sum, sum total, grand total, amount, total/ whole amount, whole, totality, entirety, generality, combination, collection, accumulation

aggression *n*
1 ANTAGONISM, provocation, offence, injury, attack, offensive, assault, onslaught, raid, incursion, strike, encroachment, infringement, invasion, intrusion **2** AGGRESSIVENESS, militancy, belligerence, combativeness, hostility, *formal* pugnacity, bellicosity
🖪 **1** peace, resistance **2** passivity, gentleness

aggressive *adj*
1 *an aggressive person* argumentative, quarrelsome, contentious, belligerent, hostile, offensive, provocative, intrusive, invasive, ruthless, brutal, savage, ferocious, destructive, *formal* pugnacious, *colloq.* cut-throat **2** *an aggressive sales rep* bold, assertive, go-ahead, forceful, vigorous, zealous, *colloq.* pushy, *slang* in-your-face
🖪 **1** peaceable, friendly, submissive, **2** unassertive, timid

aggressor *n*
invader, attacker, assailant, assaulter, intruder, offender, provoker
🖪 victim

aggrieved *adj*
bitter, resentful, pained, distressed, saddened, unhappy, upset, annoyed, wronged, offended, hurt, injured, insulted, maltreated, ill-used
🖪 pleased, happy

aghast *adj*
shocked, appalled, horrified, horror-struck, thunderstruck, stunned, stupefied, amazed, astonished, astounded, startled, confounded, dismayed

agile *adj*
1 *an agile person* active, lively, nimble, spry, sprightly, mobile, athletic, flexible, limber, lithe, fleet, quick, swift, brisk **2** *an agile mind* astute, sharp, acute, alert, quick-witted, clever
🖪 **1** clumsy, stiff **2** slow

agility *n*
1 *agility of movement* activeness, liveliness, nimbleness, mobility, flexibility, quickness, swiftness, briskness **2** *agility of thought* astuteness, sharpness, alertness, quick-wittedness
🖪 **1** clumsiness, stiffness **2** slowness

agitate *v*
1 *the news agitated them* worry, trouble, upset, alarm, disturb, unsettle, disquiet, discompose, fluster, ruffle, flurry, unnerve, confuse, distract, disconcert, *formal* perturb **2** *agitate for reform* campaign, argue, fight, rouse, arouse, stir up, excite, estimulate, incite, inflame, ferment, work up **3** *agitate the mixture* shake, rattle, rock, stir, beat, churn, toss, whisk
🖪 **1** calm, tranquillize

agitated *adj*
worried, troubled, upset, disturbed, anxious, unsettled, flustered, ruffled, distraught, unnerved, disconcerted, nervous, *colloq.* in a lather
🖪 calm, composed

agitator *n*
troublemaker, activist, subversive, rabble-rouser, revolutionary, *agent provocateur*, inciter, instigator, firebrand, fomenter, *colloq.* stirrer

agnostic *n*
unbeliever, sceptic, doubter, *colloq.* doubting Thomas

ago *adv*
from that time, gone, past, since, previously, earlier

agog *adj*
eager, excited, curious, enthralled, enthusiastic, impatient, in suspense, keen, avid, *colloq.* on the edge of your seat, on tenterhooks
🖪 incurious

agonize *v*
worry, labour, strain, strive, struggle, trouble, wrestle

agonizing *adj*
distressing, excruciating, harrowing, painful, tormenting, torturous, worrying, racking

agony *n*
anguish, torment, torture, pain, spasm, throes, suffering, affliction, tribulation, distress, hurt, woe, misery, wretchedness

agree *v*
1 *agree with someone* CONCUR, get on, settle, be of one mind, be of the same opinion, share the view, be at one, come to/reach an agreement, compromise, make concessions, *formal* accord, *colloq.* see eye to eye, go along with, go with, meet halfway **2** *agree to your request* CONSENT, allow, permit, accept, grant, admit, concede, yield, comply, say yes to, *formal* assent, accede, acquiesce in, *colloq.* give the go-ahead, give the thumbs-up, rubberstamp **3** *the reports do not agree* match, suit, fit, tally, correspond, conform
🖪 **1** disagree **2** refuse **3** disagree, differ, conflict

agreeable *adj*
1 *agreeable weather* pleasant, enjoyable, delightful, fine, nice, acceptable **2** *an agreeable person* pleasant, congenial, likable, nice, attractive, delightful, charming, friendly, good-natured, amicable,

sympathetic **3** *agreeable to a suggestion* willing, amenable, compliant
🔁 **1** disagreeable, nasty **2** unpleasant **3** unwilling, reluctant to accept

agreement *n*
1 *a trade agreement* settlement, covenant, treaty, pact, contract, deed, deal, bargain, arrangement, understanding, *formal* concordat, compact, indenture **2** *be in agreement* unanimity, union, harmony, sympathy, consensus, affinity, *formal* assent, complaisance **3** *the agreement of the reports* matching, fitting, tally, correspondence, consistency, conformity, compatibility, similarity, *formal* concurrence, accord, concord, consonance
🔁 **2** disagreement **3** inconsistency

agricultural *adj*
agronomic, agrarian, farming, farmed, cultivated, rural, pastoral, *formal* bucolic, geoponic, georgic, praedial

agriculture *n*
farming, husbandry, cultivation, tillage, *technical* agribusiness, agronomics, agronomy, agroscience, geoponics

aground *adj & adv*
ashore, beached, foundered, grounded, high and dry, marooned, stranded, stuck, wrecked, on the rocks
🔁 afloat

ahead *adv*
1 *glance ahead* forward, onward, leading, at the head, in front **2** *ahead on points* in the lead, winning, at an advantage, advanced, superior, to the fore, in the forefront **3** *plan ahead* in advance, before, earlier on

aid *v, n*
▶ *v* **1** *aid an invalid* help, assist, rally round, relieve, support, subsidize, sustain, second, serve, favour, co-operate with, *formal* succour, oblige, accommodate **2** *aid a process* promote, boost, encourage, facilitate, speed up, ease, *formal* expedite, hasten
🔁 **1** *colloq.* not lift a finger **2** hinder, impede, obstruct
▶ *n* **1** *aid for refugees* relief, benefit, assistance, subsidy, donation, gift, contribution, funding, grant, sponsorship, patronage, favour, encouragement, service, *formal* subvention **2** *turn to someone for aid* help, assistance, prop, support, backup, boost, *formal* succour, *colloq.* (helping) hand, a shot in the arm, a leg up
🔁 **2** hindrance, impediment, obstruction

aide *n*
adviser, assistant, right-hand person, right-hand man, supporter, adjutant, advocate, aide-de-camp, attaché, confidant, disciple, follower

ail *v*
afflict, trouble, upset, bother, distress, fail, irritate, pain, sicken, weaken, worry
🔁 comfort, flourish

ailing *adj*
unwell, ill, sick, poorly, suffering, languishing, sickly, diseased, invalid, infirm, unsound, unfit, frail, weak, feeble, failing, *formal* indisposed, debilitated, *colloq.* out of sorts, under the weather, off-colour
🔁 healthy, fit, thriving, flourishing

ailment *n*
illness, sickness, complaint, malady, disease, infection, disorder, affliction, infirmity, disability, weakness, *formal* indisposition

aim *v, n*
▶ *v* **1** POINT, direct, take aim, shoot at, level, train, sight, target, *colloq.* zero in on **2** *aim to achieve* plan, aspire, want, wish, seek, resolve, purpose, intend, propose, mean, design, strive, try, attempt, endeavour, set your sights on, *formal* resolve

▶ *n* purpose, motive, end, intention, object, objective, target, mark, goal, direction, course, plan, design, scheme, aspiration, mission, mission statement, ambition, hope, dream, desire, wish

aimless *adj*
pointless, purposeless, goalless, futile, unmotivated, irresolute, directionless, rambling, drifting, wandering, undirected, unguided, unsettled, stray, chance, random, haphazard, erratic, unpredictable, wayward
🔁 purposeful, positive, determined

air *n, v*
▶ *n* **1** *birds flying in the air* atmosphere, oxygen, sky, heavens, *formal* ether **2** *the air we breathe* breath, fresh air, puff, waft, draught, breeze, wind, blast, *formal* zephyr **3** APPEARANCE, look, aspect, aura, bearing, manner, character, effect, impression, feeling, carriage, *formal* ambience, demeanour
▶ *v* **1** *air a room* ventilate, aerate, freshen **2** *air an opinion* utter, voice, express, give vent to, make known, communicate, tell, declare, state, reveal, disclose, divulge, expose, make public, broadcast, publish, circulate, disseminate, publicize, *colloq.* speak your mind, have your say

aircraft *n*

Types of aircraft include:
aeroplane, plane, jet, jumbo, Concorde, airbus, helicopter, monoplane, two-seater, air-ambulance, freighter, sea-plane, glider, hang-glider, microlight, hot-air balloon; fighter, spitfire, bomber, *colloq.* kite, jump-jet, dive-bomber, *colloq.* chopper, spy plane, delta-wing, swing-wing, troop-carrier, airship, turbojet, VTOL (vertical take-off and landing), warplane, zeppelin.

airing *n*
1 *give clothes an airing* ventilation, aeration, freshening **2** *the airing of opinions* expression, making known, communication, declaration, statement, revelation, disclosure, divulgence, exposure, uttering, voicing, broadcast, publication, circulation, *formal* dissemination

airless *adj*
unventilated, badly/poorly ventilated, stuffy, musty, stale, suffocating, stifling, sultry, muggy, close, heavy, oppressive
🔁 airy, fresh

airs *n*
arrogance, artificiality, haughtiness, posing, pretensions, pretentiousness, superciliousness, *formal* affectation, affectedness, hauteur, pomposity, *colloq.* swank

airtight *adj*
closed, sealed, impenetrable, impermeable, tight-fitting

airy *adj*
1 *an airy room* roomy, spacious, open, draughty, well-ventilated, breezy, blowy, windy, gusty **2** CASUAL, cheerful, happy, light-hearted, high-spirited, lively, jaunty, nonchalant, offhand
🔁 **1** airless, stuffy, close, heavy, oppressive

aisle *n*
gangway, corridor, passage, passageway, alleyway, walkway, path, lane

alarm *n, v*
▶ *n* **1** FRIGHT, scare, fear, terror, panic, horror, shock, consternation, dismay, distress, anxiety, nervousness, apprehension, trepidation, uneasiness, *formal* perturbation **2** *a burglar alarm* danger signal,

alert, warning, distress signal, siren, bell, alarm-bell, *formal* tocsin
F3 1 calmness, composure
▶ *v* frighten, scare, startle, terrify, panic, make afraid, unnerve, daunt, dismay, distress, agitate, *formal* perturb, affright, *colloq.* put the wind up, rattle
F3 reassure, calm, soothe

alarming *adj*
frightening, scary, startling, terrifying, unnerving, daunting, ominous, worrying, threatening, dismaying, disturbing, distressing, shocking, dreadful, *formal* perturbing
F3 reassuring

alarmist *n*
scaremonger, pessimist, doomwatcher, *colloq.* doom and gloom merchant
F3 optimist

alcohol *n*
drink, liquor, spirits, strong drink, intoxicant, *colloq.* hard stuff, the bottle, Dutch courage, fire-water, *slang* booze

alcoholic *adj, n*
▶ *adj* intoxicating, inebriating, brewed, fermented, distilled, strong, hard, ardent, having a drink problem
▶ *n* drunk, drunkard, inebriate, drinker, hard drinker, heavy drinker, dipsomaniac, *colloq.* tippler, *slang* boozer, wino, lush, alkie, dipso, soak, toper

alcove *n*
niche, nook, recess, bay, corner, cubbyhole, compartment, cubicle, booth, carrel

alert *adj, v*
▶ *adj* attentive, awake, wide-awake, watchful, vigilant, on the lookout, sharp-eyed, observant, perceptive, sharp-witted, active, lively, spirited, quick, brisk, agile, nimble, ready, prepared, careful, heedful, circumspect, wary, *formal* on the qui vive, *colloq.* with your eyes open/peeled, on the ball, on your toes
F3 slow, listless, unprepared
▶ *v* warn, forewarn, notify, inform, tip off, signal, alarm

algae *n*

Types of algae and lichen include:
anabaena, badderlocks, bladderwrack, bull kelp, carrageen, Ceylon moss, chlorella, conferva, desmid, diatom, dinaflagellate, dulse, euglena, fucoid, fucus, gulfweed, Irish moss, kelp, laminaria, laver, lecanora, nostoc, nullipore, oak moss, oarweed, peacock's tail, redware, reindeer moss, rock tripe, rockweed, sargassum, sea lace, sea lettuce, sea tangle, seaware, sea wrack, Spanish moss, spirogyra, stonewort, wrack.

alias *n, adv*
▶ *n* pseudonym, false name, assumed name, *nom de guerre*, *nom de plume*, pen name, stage name, nickname, *formal* sobriquet, allonym, anonym
▶ *adv* also known as, also called, otherwise, otherwise known as, under the name of, formerly, *colloq.* aka

alibi *n*
defence, justification, story, explanation, excuse, cover-up, pretext, reason

alien *adj, n*
▶ *adj* 1 *an alien culture* foreign, exotic, extraterrestrial, extraneous, remote 2 *alien surroundings* strange, unfamiliar, outlandish, incongruous 3 *alien to her nature* opposed, contrary, conflicting, antagonistic, incompatible, *formal* repugnant, inimical

▶ *n* foreigner, immigrant, newcomer, stranger, outsider
F3 native, resident

alienate *v*
antagonize, estrange, set against, turn away, turn off, make hostile, separate, divorce, *formal* disaffect
F3 unite

alienation *n*
antagonization, estrangement, turning away, indifference, remoteness, rupture, separation, isolation, severance, divorce, disunion, diversion, *formal* disaffection
F3 endearment

alight¹ *adj*
1 *set the rubbish alight* lighted, lit, ignited, on fire, burning, blazing, ablaze, flaming, fiery 2 *eyes alight with excitement* lit up, illuminated, bright, radiant, shining, brilliant, lively, alive

alight² *v*
passengers alighting from buses descend, get down, get off, land, touch down, come down, come to rest, settle, light, perch, *formal* dismount, disembark, debark
F3 ascend, board, get on, get onto, rise

align *v*
1 *align yourself with a political party* ally, side, sympathize, associate, affiliate, join, co-operate, agree, join forces, combine, unite 2 *align two pieces of wood* arrange, straighten, range, line up, make parallel, even (up), adjust, regulate, regularize, order, co-ordinate

alignment *n*
1 *alignment with a political party* affiliation, association, alliance, co-operation, agreement, sympathy, siding 2 *alignment of the pieces* arrangement, straightening, line, lining up, order, ranging

alike *adj, adv*
▶ *adj* similar, resembling, comparable, akin, corresponding, equivalent, equal, the same, much the same, identical, indistinguishable, duplicate, parallel, even, uniform, *formal* analogous, cognate
F3 dissimilar, unlike, different
▶ *adv* similarly, in the same way, analogously, correspondingly, equally, in common

alive *adj*
1 *Are your parents alive still?* LIVING, having life, live, animate, breathing, existent, in existence, *formal* extant, *colloq.* (still) going strong, in the land of the living 2 *I like her because she is so alive* LIVELY, animated, spirited, awake, alert, active, brisk, energetic, full of life, vigorous, zestful, vivacious, vibrant, vital 3 *alive with tourists* full of, teeming with, abounding in, overflowing with, *colloq.* crawling with, swarming with 4 *alive to the danger* aware of, heedful of, alert to, sensitive to, *formal* cognizant of
F3 1 dead, extinct 2 lifeless, apathetic 4 unaware of, blind to, deaf to

all *adj, n, adv*
▶ *adj* 1 *all people are equal* each, every, each and every, every single, every one of, the whole of, every bit of, in its entirety, from start to finish 2 *run with all speed* complete, entire, full, total, utter, outright, perfect, greatest
F3 1 no, none
▶ *n* everything, everyone, everybody, sum, total, aggregate, total amount, whole amount, whole, entirety, utmost, comprehensiveness, universality, *colloq.* the lot
F3 nothing, none
▶ *adv* completely, entirely, wholly, fully, totally, utterly, altogether, wholesale

allay *v*
alleviate, relieve, soothe, ease, smooth, calm, tranquillize, compose, quiet, quell, pacify, mollify, soften, blunt, lessen, reduce, diminish, check, moderate
F3 exacerbate, intensify

allegation *n*
accusation, charge, claim, profession, assertion, affirmation, declaration, statement, testimony, plea, *formal* avowal, deposition, asseveration

allege *v*
assert, affirm, declare, state, maintain, insist, hold, put forward, contend, claim, profess, plead, *formal* attest

alleged *adj*
supposed, reputed, inferred, so-called, professed, declared, stated, claimed, described, designated, doubtful, dubious, suspect, *formal* ostensible, putative

allegiance *n*
loyalty, fidelity, faithfulness, constancy, duty, obligation, obedience, devotion, support, adherence, solidarity, friendship, *formal* fealty
F3 disloyalty, enmity

allegorical *adj*
figurative, representative, symbolic, metaphorical, symbolizing, typical, *formal* parabolic, emblematic, significative

allegory *n*
analogy, comparison, metaphor, symbol, parable, story, fable, myth, legend, tale, symbolism, *formal* emblem, apologue

allergic *adj*
1 *allergic to shellfish* sensitive, hypersensitive, susceptible, affected **2** *allergic to Mondays* averse, disinclined, opposed, hostile, antagonistic, *formal* dyspathetic

allergy *n*
1 *an allergy to dogs* sensitivity, hypersensitivity, susceptibility **2** *an allergy to work* opposition, hostility, antagonism, aversion, *formal* antipathy, disinclination, dyspathy

alleviate *v*
relieve, soothe, ease, mitigate, soften, cushion, dull, deaden, allay, abate, lessen, assuage, reduce, diminish, check, moderate, mollify, temper, subdue, *formal* palliate
F3 aggravate

alleviation *n*
relief, soothing, easing, mitigation, dulling, deadening, abatement, lessening, assuagement, reduction, moderation, mollification, *formal* palliation, diminution
F3 aggravation

alley *n*
alleyway, back street, lane, street, road, mall, passage, passageway, pathway, close, gate, walk

alliance *n*
partnership, confederation, federation, association, affiliation, coalition, league, bloc, cartel, conglomerate, consortium, syndicate, guild, union, marriage, agreement, compact, bond, pact, treaty, combination, connection
F3 separation, divorce, estrangement, enmity, hostility

allied *adj*
associated, connected, linked, bound, combined, in league, joined, joint, kindred, related, affiliated, amalgamated, coupled, unified, united, married, wed, *colloq.* hand in glove, in cahoots
F3 estranged

allocate *v*
assign, designate, budget, allow, earmark, set aside, allot, apportion, share out, distribute, dispense,

divide, parcel out, mete (out), ration, *formal* admeasure

allocation *n*
1 *the allocation of funds* apportionment, distribution, giving-out, allotment **2** *an allocation of tickets* share, measure, lot, portion, stint, ration, quota, budget, allowance, grant, *colloq.* cut, slice of the cake

allot *v*
divide, ration, apportion, share out, distribute, dispense, mete, allocate, assign, designate, budget, allow, grant, earmark, set aside, *formal* admeasure, *colloq.* dole out

allotment *n*
1 *dig an allotment* land, plot of land **2** *an allotment of funds* division, partition, allocation, apportionment, measure, percentage, lot, portion, share, stint, ration, quota, allowance, grant, *formal* apportionment

all-out *adj*
complete, full, total, undivided, comprehensive, exhaustive, thorough, intensive, thoroughgoing, wholesale, vigorous, powerful, full-scale, maximum, utmost, unlimited, unrestrained, unremitting, unstinted, resolute, determined, *colloq.* no-holds-barred
F3 perfunctory, half-hearted

allow *v*
1 PERMIT, let, enable, authorize, sanction, warrant, approve, say yes to, agree to, give leave, tolerate, put up with, endure, suffer, *formal* give your consent (to), consent (to), *colloq.* OK, okay, give the go-ahead, give the green light **2** ADMIT, confess, own, acknowledge, concede, grant, agree **3** *allow two hours for the journey* allot, allocate, assign, apportion, afford, give, provide, spare
F3 **1** forbid, prevent **2** deny
▷ **allow for** take into account, make provision for, make allowances for, provide for, foresee, plan for, arrange for, bear in mind, keep in mind, consider, include
F3 discount

allowable *adj*
permissible, acceptable, admissible, justifiable, all right, appropriate, approved, legal, legitimate, lawful, *formal* licit, sanctionable, *colloq.* legit
F3 unacceptable

allowance *n*
1 PAYMENT, remittance, pocket money, grant, income, maintenance, subsistence allowance, expenses, expense allowance, contribution, benefit, stipend, pension, annuity **2** REBATE, reduction, deduction, discount, concession, subsidy, weighting **3** ALLOCATION, lot, amount, portion, share, ration, quota
▷ **make allowances 1** TAKE INTO ACCOUNT, take into consideration, bear/keep in mind, consider **2** *make allowances for her inexperience* EXCUSE, pardon, forgive

alloy *n*
blend, compound, composite, amalgam, combination, mixture, fusion, coalescence, *formal* admixture, composite

all right *adj*, *adv*
▶ *adj* **1** SATISFACTORY, passable, unobjectionable, acceptable, reasonable, good enough, allowable, adequate, fair, average, *colloq.* OK **2** *Are you all right?* well, healthy, unhurt, uninjured, unharmed, unimpaired, whole, sound, safe, secure, *colloq.* right as rain
F3 **1** unacceptable, inadequate
▶ *adv* satisfactorily, well enough, passably, unobjectionably, acceptably, suitably, appropriately, adequately, reasonably, *colloq.* OK
F3 unsatisfactorily, unacceptably

allude *v*
mention, refer, remark, speak of, hint, imply, infer, insinuate, intimate, suggest, touch on/upon, *formal* adumbrate

 allude or **elude** ?
If you *allude* to something, you refer to it; if something *eludes* you, you cannot remember it or understand it.

allure *v, n*
▶ *v* lure, entice, seduce, lead on, tempt, coax, cajole, persuade, win over, disarm, charm, enchant, attract, interest, fascinate, captivate, entrance, beguile, *colloq.* give the come-on, work on
🖬 repel
▶ *n* lure, enticement, seduction, temptation, appeal, attraction, magnetism, fascination, glamour, captivation, charm, enchantment

alluring *adj*
attractive, fascinating, intriguing, interesting, captivating, winning, enchanting, engaging, enticing, arousing, beguiling, bewitching, fetching, seductive, sensuous, sexy, desirable, tempting, *colloq.* come-hither
🖬 repellent, unattractive

allusion *n*
mention, reference, citation, quotation, remark, observation, suggestion, hint, intimation, implication, insinuation

 allusion or **illusion** ?
An *allusion* to something is an indirect reference to it; an *illusion* is a false belief or appearance.

ally *n, v*
▶ *n* supporter, associate, consort, confederate, partner, colleague, co-worker, collaborator, helper, accomplice, accessory, friend, *colloq.* sidekick
🖬 enemy, antagonist
▶ *v* associate, collaborate, join forces, band together, team up, go into partnership, fraternize, confederate, affiliate, league, side, join, connect, link, marry, unite, unify, amalgamate, combine
🖬 estrange, separate

almanac *n*
yearbook, annual, calendar, register

almighty *adj*
1 *almighty God* all-powerful, supreme, absolute, great, invincible, *formal* omnipotent, plenipotent **2** ENORMOUS, severe, intense, overwhelming, overpowering, terrible, awful, desperate
🖬 **1** impotent, weak

almost *adv*
nearly, practically, virtually, just about, as good as, all but, well-nigh, more or less, to all intents and purposes, close to/on, not far from, approaching, nearing, not quite, about, approximately, *formal* quasi-, *colloq.* pretty much/well

alone *adj*
only, sole, single, unique, solitary, separate, detached, unconnected, isolated, cloistered, apart, by yourself, by itself, on your own, lonely, lonesome, deserted, abandoned, forsaken, forlorn, desolate, unaccompanied, unescorted, unattended, solo, single-handed, unaided, *formal* sequestered, *colloq.* on your tod
🖬 together, accompanied, escorted

aloof *adj*
distant, remote, offish, standoffish, haughty, supercilious, unapproachable, inaccessible, detached,

forbidding, cool, chilly, cold, unsympathetic, unresponsive, indifferent, uninterested, reserved, unforthcoming, unfriendly, unsociable, antisocial, formal
🖬 sociable, friendly, concerned

aloud *adv*
out loud, audibly, intelligibly, clearly, plainly, distinctly, loudly, resoundingly, sonorously, noisily, vociferously
🖬 silently

alphabet *n*

Alphabets and writing systems include:
Arabic, Byzantine, Chalcidian alphabet, cuneiform, Cyrillic, devanagari, estrangelo, finger-alphabet, futhark, Georgian, Glagol, Glossic, Greek, Gurmukhi, Hebrew, hieroglyphs, hiragana, ideograph, Initial Teaching Alphabet, (i.t.a.), International Phonetic Alphabet (IPA), kana, kanji, katakana, Kufic, linear A, linear B, logograph, nagari, naskhi, ogam, pictograph, romaji, Roman, runic, syllabary.

already *adv*
1 *I've read the book already* before now, beforehand, just now, previously, *formal* heretofore, hitherto **2** *he can already count* even now, even then, so soon (as this), so early, by now, by that time, by then, by this time

also *adv*
too, as well, and, plus, along with, including, as well as, additionally, in addition, besides, further, furthermore, moreover

alter *v*
change, vary, diversify, modify, qualify, shift, transpose, make different, adjust, adapt, convert, turn, transform, reform, reshape, remodel, recast, revise, amend, emend, *formal* metamorphose, transmute

alteration *n*
change, variation, variance, difference, diversification, shift, transposition, modification, adjustment, adaptation, conversion, transformation, transfiguration, reformation, reshaping, remodelling, revision, amendment, *formal* metamorphosis, transmutation, vicissitude

altercation *n*
argument, dispute, clash, disagreement, discord, dissension, fracas, quarrel, row, squabble, wrangle, *formal* logomachy

alternate *v, adj*
▶ *v* interchange, reciprocate, rotate, take turns, take it in turns, follow one another, replace each other, substitute, change, alter, vary, oscillate, fluctuate, intersperse, *colloq.* chop and change
▶ *adj* **1** *alternate weekends* alternating, every other, every second **2** *alternate bouts of depression and happiness* (repeated) one after the other, in turns, consecutive, interchanging, reciprocal, rotating

 alternate or **alternative** ?
Alternate refers to something happening or coming every second day, week, etc or in turns: *He visits them on alternate Tuesdays; alternate bursts of hot and cold water. Alternative* refers to the choice of two possibilities: *If that doesn't work, we'll have to think of an alternative plan.*

alternative *n, adj*
▶ *n* option, choice, selection, preference, other, recourse, substitute, back-up
▶ *adj* **1** *an alternative possibility* substitute, second,

another, other, different **2** *alternative medicine* unorthodox, unconventional, fringe, nontraditional
F3 2 conventional, traditional, orthodox, standard, regular

although *conj*
though, even though, despite/in spite of the fact that, while, even if, even supposing, granted that, *formal* albeit, whilst, howbeit, notwithstanding

altitude *n*
height, elevation, loftiness, tallness, stature, depth

altogether *adv*
1 *altogether more efficient* totally, completely, entirely, wholly, fully, utterly, absolutely, quite, perfectly, thoroughly **2** *the meal came to £40 altogether* in total, in all, all told, *in toto*, all in all

altruistic *adj*
selfless, unselfish, self-sacrificing, disinterested, public-spirited, philanthropic, charitable, humanitarian, benevolent, generous, considerate, humane
F3 selfish

always *adv*
1 *always be home by 6 o'clock* every time, all the time, consistently, invariably, without exception, habitually, unfailingly, regularly, perpetually, in perpetuum, evermore **2** *always criticizing others* again and again, continually, constantly, repeatedly, forever, endlessly, unceasingly, eternally
F3 1 never

amalgam *n*
mixture, blend, fusion, alloy, compound, coalescence, synthesis, combination, union, *formal* admixture, aggregate, commixture

amalgamate *v*
merge, blend, mingle, intermix, incorporate, alloy, integrate, compound, fuse, coalesce, synthesize, combine, unite, unify, ally, *formal* commingle, homogenize
F3 separate

amalgamation *n*
merger, blend, incorporation, integration, joining, compound, fusion, coalescence, synthesis, combination, unity, union, unification, alliance, *formal* admixture, commingling, homogenization
F3 separation

amass *v*
accumulate, accrue, assemble, collect, gather, heap (up), hoard, pile (up), store (up), gain, acquire, *formal* agglomerate, agglutinate, aggregate, foregather, garner

amateur *n*
non-professional, layman, lay person, dilettante, dabbler, enthusiast, fancier, *colloq.* ham, buff
F3 professional

amateurish *adj*
non-professional, lay, unpaid, unqualified, untrained, unskilful, inexpert, unprofessional, clumsy, crude, inept
F3 professional, expert, skilled

amaze *v*
surprise, startle, astonish, astound, stun, stupefy, daze, stagger, dumbfound, shock, dismay, disconcert, confound, bewilder, *colloq.* floor, flabbergast, bowl over, gobsmack, wow, blow your mind, knock for six, knock you down with a feather, strike dumb

amazement *n*
surprise, astonishment, shock, dismay, confusion, perplexity, bewilderment, admiration, wonder, marvel, *formal* stupefaction, wonderment

ambassador *n*
1 *a country's ambassador* envoy, diplomat, consul,

formal emissary, legate, plenipotentiary **2** *an ambassador of peace* representative, agent, deputy, delegate, minister

ambience *n*
atmosphere, air, aura, climate, milieu, mood, spirit, surroundings, environment, character, feel, feeling, flavour, impression, tenor, tone, *colloq.* vibes, vibrations

ambiguity *n*
double meaning, *double entendre*, ambivalence, polysemy, equivocality, equivocation, confusion, obscurity, unclearness, vagueness, woolliness, imprecision, indeterminateness, dubiousness, doubt, doubtfulness, uncertainty, enigma, puzzle, paradox, *formal* dubiety
F3 clarity

ambiguous *adj*
double-meaning, equivocal, multivocal, double-edged, two-edged, back-handed, cryptic, enigmatic, paradoxical, puzzling, confusing, obscure, unclear, vague, indefinite, imprecise, woolly, confused, dubious, doubtful, uncertain, inconclusive, indeterminate
F3 clear, definite

ambit *n*
scope, extent, range, compass, confines

ambition *n*
1 ASPIRATION, aim, goal, target, objective, intent, purpose, design, object, ideal, dream, hope, wish, desire, yearning, longing, hankering, craving, hunger **2** *a woman of ambition* enterprise, drive, push, thrust, striving, eagerness, commitment, initiative, zeal, *colloq.* get-up-and-go, what it takes
F3 2 apathy, diffidence

ambitious *adj*
1 ASPIRING, hopeful, desirous, intent, purposeful, bold, assertive, enterprising, driving, energetic, enthusiastic, eager, keen, striving, industrious, zealous, *colloq.* power-hungry, go-ahead, pushy, full of go, not backward in coming forward **2** FORMIDABLE, hard, difficult, arduous, strenuous, demanding, challenging, bold, exacting, impressive, grandiose, elaborate
F3 1 lazy, unassuming **2** modest, uninspiring

ambivalence *n*
contradiction, conflict, clash, opposition, inconsistency, confusion, fluctuation, wavering, hesitation, irresoluteness, uncertainty, doubt, inconclusiveness, *formal* vacillation
F3 certainty

ambivalent *adj*
contradictory, conflicting, clashing, warring, opposed, inconsistent, mixed, confused, fluctuating, wavering, hesitant, irresolute, undecided, unresolved, unsettled, uncertain, unsure, doubtful, debatable, inconclusive, *formal* vacillating
F3 unequivocal

amble *v*
walk, saunter, stroll, dawdle, wander, drift, meander, ramble, *formal* perambulate, promenade, *colloq.* mosey along, toddle
F3 stride, march

ambush *n, v*
▶ *n* waylaying, surprise attack, trap, snare, *formal* ambuscade
▶ *v* lie in wait, waylay, lay a trap for, surprise, trap, attack, ensnare, bushwhack, *formal* ambuscade, *colloq.* turn on, pounce on, jump

ameliorate *v*
alleviate, improve, better, amend, benefit, ease, elevate, enhance, mend, mitigate, promote, relieve
F3 exacerbate, worsen

amenable *adj*
accommodating, flexible, willing, open, agreeable, persuadable, compliant, submissive, responsive, susceptible, liable, responsible, *formal* tractable, acquiescent, complaisant
☒ unwilling, intractable

amend *v*
revise, correct, rectify, fix, repair, mend, remedy, redress, reform, change, alter, adjust, modify, qualify, enhance, improve, better, *formal* emend, emendate, ameliorate
☒ impair, worsen

📝 **amend** or **emend**?
If you *amend* a document, you alter or improve it; if you *emend* a text you correct errors in it.

---

amendment *n*
revision, correction, remedy, reform, change, alteration, adjustment, modification, improvement, qualification, enhancement, clarification, addition, attachment, adjunct, *formal* corrigendum, rectification, emendation, addendum
☒ impairment, deterioration

amends *n*
atonement, expiation, requital, satisfaction, recompense, compensation, indemnification, indemnity, reparation, redress, restoration, restitution

amenity *n*
facility, advantage, convenience, service, utility, resource

amiable *adj*
affable, friendly, approachable, genial, warm, cheerful, good-tempered, good-natured, kind, easy to get along/on with, obliging, charming, engaging, likable, pleasant, agreeable, congenial, companionable, sociable
☒ unfriendly, curt, hostile

📝 **amiable** or **amicable**?
Amiable is used to describe a person who is friendly, good-tempered and pleasant; *amicable* is used to describe relationships or agreements that are conducted in a friendly way without anger.

---

amicable *adj*
friendly, cordial, good-natured, civil, harmonious, civilized, peaceful
☒ hostile

amid *prep*
amidst, midst, in the midst of, in the thick of, among, amongst, in the middle of, surrounded by

amino acid *n*

Amino acids include:
alanine, arginine, asparagine, aspartic acid, cysteine, glutamic acid, glutamine, glycine, histidine, isoleucine, leucine, lysine, methionine, phenylalanine, proline, serine, threonine, trytophan, tyrosine, valine.

amiss *adj*
wrong, awry, defective, false, faulty, improper, out of order, inaccurate, inappropriate, incorrect, unsuitable, untoward, imperfect, out of kilter, *colloq.* wonky
☒ right, well

amity *n*
peace, peacefulness, understanding, accord, concord, cordiality, fellowship, fraternity, brotherliness, friendliness, friendship, goodwill, harmony, kindness, sympathy, *formal* comity
☒ discord, hostility

ammunition *n*
missiles, bullets, shells, rockets, projectiles, cartridges, slugs, grenades, bombs, shot, mine, gunpowder

amnesty *n*
pardon, forgiveness, absolution, mercy, lenience, indulgence, reprieve, remission, dispensation, immunity

amok *adv*
berserk, crazy, in a frenzy, frenzied, insanely, like a lunatic, madly, wildly, uncontrollably, violently

among *prep*
amongst, between, in the middle of, surrounded by, amid, amidst, midst, in the midst of, in the thick of, with, together with

amorous *adj*
passionate, loving, affectionate, tender, fond, erotic, impassioned, in love, lovesick, lustful, *formal* amatory, *colloq.* randy
☒ cold, indifferent

amorphous *adj*
formless, nebulous, shapeless, featureless, indeterminate, indistinct, irregular, undefined, unformed, unshapen, unstructured, vague, *formal* inchoate
☒ definite, distinctive, shapely

amount *n*
quantity, number, sum, total, sum total, whole, entirety, aggregate, lot, quota, supply, volume, mass, bulk, measure, magnitude, extent, expanse
▷ **amount to 1** *amount to a total* add up to, total, aggregate, come to, make, equal, run to, *colloq.* tot up, tot up to **2** *giving presents to potential customers amounts to bribery* mean, be tantamount to, be equivalent to, correspond to, come down to, boil down to

amphibian *n*

Amphibians include:
frog, bullfrog, tree frog, toad, horned toad, midwife toad, natterjack, newt, eft, salamander, conger eel, axolotl.

ample *adj*
1 *ample opportunity/space* (more than) enough, sufficient, considerable, substantial, plentiful, plenty, abundant, unrestricted, profuse, spacious, great, copious, *formal* commodious **2** *of ample proportions* large, big, extensive, expansive, broad, wide, full, generous, substantial, *formal* voluminous
☒ **1** insufficient, inadequate, meagre

amplify *v*
1 *amplify sound* MAKE LOUDER, increase, heighten, enhance, boost, intensify, strengthen, deepen, raise **2** *amplify a statement* enlarge on, expand, fill out, bulk out, add to, supplement, augment, increase, extend, lengthen, widen, broaden, develop, elaborate on, go into details, flesh out, *formal* expatiate on
☒ **1** reduce, decrease, soften

amplitude *n*
expanse, vastness, volume, bulk, capacity, extent, fullness, greatness, largeness, magnitude, mass, profusion, spaciousness, width, *formal* copiousness, plenitude, capaciousness

amputate *v*
cut off, remove, sever, dissever, separate, dock, lop, curtail, truncate

amulet *n*
charm, talisman, fetish, juju, lucky charm, *formal* braxas, pentacle, periapt, phylactery

amuse *v*
  1 *the joke amused them* make laugh, cheer (up), gladden, charm, delight, please, enthral, *colloq.* tickle, crease, crack, tickle your funny bone **2** *amuse yourselves while I'm away* OCCUPY, entertain, divert, regale, engross, absorb, interest, recreate, relax, *formal* disport
  ☞ **1** displease **2** bore

amusement *n*
  1 *a look of amusement at the joke* fun, enjoyment, pleasure, delight, merriment, mirth, hilarity, laughter, **2** *to the amusement of the onlookers* entertainment, diversion, distraction **3** PASTIME, game, sport, recreation, hobby, interest

amusing *adj*
  funny, humorous, hilarious, comical, laughable, ludicrous, droll, witty, facetious, jocular, jolly, waggish, enjoyable, pleasant, charming, delightful, entertaining, interesting
  ☞ dull, boring

anaemic *adj*
  bloodless, ashen, chalky, livid, pasty, pallid, sallow, whey-faced, pale, wan, colourless, insipid, weak, feeble, ineffectual, enervated, frail, infirm, sickly
  ☞ ruddy, sanguine, full-blooded

anaesthetic *n*
  painkiller, sedative, analgesic, anodyne, narcotic, opiate, palliative, soporific, epidural, stupefacient, stupefactive, premedication, local anaesthetic, general anaesthetic

anaesthetize *v*
  desensitize, numb, deaden, dull, drug, dope, stupefy

analogous *adj*
  comparable, similar, like, resembling, matching, kindred, parallel, corresponding, equivalent, relative, correlative, agreeing
  ☞ disparate

analogy *n*
  comparison, simile, metaphor, likeness, resemblance, similarity, parallel, correspondence, equivalence, relation, correlation, agreement, *formal* similitude, semblance

analyse *v*
  break down, separate, divide, take apart, dissect, reduce, resolve, sift, investigate, inquire, study, examine, scrutinize, review, interpret, test, judge, evaluate, estimate, consider, *formal* anatomize, assay

analysis *n*
  breakdown, separation, division, dissection, reduction, resolution, sifting, investigation, inquiry, study, examination, inspection, scrutiny, review, check, check-up, exposition, explication, explanation, interpretation, test, judgement, opinion, evaluation, estimation, reasoning, *formal* anatomization, assay

analytical *adj*
  analytic, detailed, in-depth, searching, critical, questioning, inquiring, inquisitive, investigative, dissecting, diagnostic, systematic, methodical, logical, rational, interpretative, explanatory, expository, studious

anarchic *adj*
  lawless, ungoverned, anarchistic, libertarian, nihilist, revolutionary, rebellious, mutinous, riotous, chaotic, disordered, confused, disorganized
  ☞ submissive, orderly

anarchist *n*
  revolutionary, rebel, insurgent, libertarian, nihilist, terrorist

anarchy *n*
  lawlessness, unrule, misrule, anarchism, revolution, rebellion, insurrection, mutiny, riot, pandemonium, chaos, disorder, confusion
  ☞ rule, control, order

anathema *n*
  aversion, abhorrence, abomination, object of loathing, *bête noire*, bugbear, bane, curse, proscription, taboo

anatomy *n*
  dissection, vivisection, zootomy, analysis, make-up, composition, constitution, construction, frame, framework, build, structure

ancestor *n*
  forebear, forefather, progenitor, predecessor, forerunner, precursor, antecedent, *formal* primogenitor
  ☞ descendant

ancestral *adj*
  familial, parental, genealogical, hereditary, genetic, *formal* lineal

ancestry *n*
  ancestors, forebears, forefathers, progenitors, parentage, family, family tree, lineage, line, descent, blood, race, stock, roots, pedigree, genealogy, extraction, derivation, origin, heritage, heredity

anchor *v*
  moor, berth, tie up, make fast, fasten, attach, affix, fix

Types of anchor include:
car, double fluked, drogue, grapnel, kedge, killick, mushroom, navy, sea, stocked, stockless, yachtsman.

ancient *adj*
  1 *ancient history* early, antediluvian, prehistoric, fossilized, primeval, primordial, immemorial old, aged, time-worn, age-old, antique, *formal* pristine, *colloq.* as old as the hills **2** OLD-FASHIONED, out-of-date, antiquated, archaic, outmoded, *passé*, obsolete, bygone, early, original, *formal* superannuated, atavistic
  ☞ **1** recent, contemporary **2** modern, up-to-date

ancillary *adj*
  auxiliary, supporting, helping, accessory, contributory, extra, secondary, subordinate, additional, subsidiary, supplementary, *formal* adjuvant, adminicular

and *conj*
  also, too, together (with), besides, as well (as), in addition (to), plus, including, furthermore, moreover, by the way, then, *colloq.* what's more

anecdote *n*
  story, tale, yarn, sketch, reminiscence

anew *adv*
  afresh, again, once again, once more

angel *n*
  1 *angel of God* divine messenger, heavenly messenger, heavenly being, principality, power **2** DARLING, treasure, saint, paragon, gem, ideal
  ☞ **1** devil, fiend

The nine orders of angels are:
seraph, cherub, throne, domination/dominion, virtue, power, principality, archangel, angel.

angelic *adj*
  cherubic, seraphic, celestial, heavenly, divine, holy, pious, saintly, pure, innocent, unworldly, virtuous, lovely, beautiful, adorable, *formal* beatific, ethereal, empyrean
  ☞ devilish, fiendish

anger *n, v*
▶ *n* annoyance, irritation, antagonism, displeasure, irritability, temper, pique, vexation, ire, rage, fury, wrath, exasperation, chagrin, outrage, indignation, gall, bitterness, rancour, resentment, fit of anger, paroxysm, *formal* choler, dudgeon, *US colloq.* conniption
🔁 forgiveness, forbearance
▶ *v* annoy, irritate, irk, vex, rile, make angry, needle, nettle, bother, ruffle, provoke, antagonize, offend, affront, gall, madden, enrage, incense, infuriate, exasperate, outrage, *colloq.* aggravate, wind up, miff, make your blood boil, *slang* nark
🔁 please, appease, calm

angle *n, v*
▶ *n* 1 CORNER, intersection, projection, nook, bend, flexure, hook, crook, elbow, knee, crotch, edge, point, gradient, inclination 2 ASPECT, outlook, facet, side, approach, direction, position, standpoint, viewpoint, point of view, slant, perspective
▶ *v* face, point, turn, direct, slant

angry *adj*
annoyed, cross, in a temper, irritated, displeased, irate, enraged, incensed, livid, seething, infuriated, furious, raging, passionate, heated, hot, exasperated, outraged, indignant, bitter, resentful, *colloq.* aggravated, uptight, mad, hopping mad, seeing red, in a lather, disgruntled, up in arms, hot under the collar, on the warpath, in a paddy
🔁 content, happy, calm

Colloquial ways of expressing becoming angry and losing your temper include:
blow up, blow a fuse, blow a gasket, blow your cool, blow your stack, blow your top, boil over, burst a blood vessel, do your nut, explode, flip your lid, fly into a rage, fly off the handle, go mad, go off the deep end, go up the wall, hit the ceiling, hit the roof, lose your cool, lose your patience, lose your rag, raise Cain, raise hell, see red, throw a tantrum, throw a wobbly, foam at the mouth, get all steamed up, *US* go ape, go ballistic, lose your marbles.

---

anguish *n*
agony, anxiety, desolation, distress, suffering, torment, torture, grief, heartache, heartbreak, misery, pain, pang, rack, sorrow, tribulation, woe, wretchedness, *formal* dole, dolour
🔁 happiness, solace

anguished *adj*
afflicted, tormented, stressed, distressed, harrowed, miserable, stricken, suffering, tortured, wretched, *formal* dolorous

angular *adj*
bony, thin, gaunt, gawky, lank, lanky, lean, rawboned, scrawny, skinny, spare

animal *n, adj*
▶ *n* 1 *wild animals* creature, mammal, beast 2 *that man is an animal* beast, brute, barbarian, savage, monster, *colloq.* swine, pig
▶ *adj* 1 *animal fats*, *formal* animalic, zoic 2 *animal instincts* bestial, brutish, inhuman, savage, wild, instinctive, bodily, physical, carnal, fleshly, sensual

---

Animals include:
cat, dog, hamster, gerbil, mouse, rat, rabbit, hare, fox, badger, beaver, mole, otter, weasel, ferret, ermine, mink, hedgehog, squirrel, horse, pig, cow, bull, goat, sheep; monkey, lemur, gibbon, ape, chimpanzee, orang-utan, baboon, gorilla; seal, sealion, dolphin, walrus, whale; lion, tiger,

---

cheetah, puma, panther, cougar, jaguar, ocelot, leopard; aardvark, armadillo, wolf, wolverine, hyena, mongoose, skunk, racoon, wombat, platypus, koala, polecat; deer, antelope, gazelle, eland, impala, reindeer, elk, caribou, moose; wallaby, kangaroo, bison, buffalo, gnu, camel, zebra, llama, panda, giant panda, grizzly bear, polar bear, giraffe, hippopotamus, rhinoceros, elephant. *See also* AMPHIBIAN; BIRD; BUTTERFLY; CAT; CATTLE; DOG; FISH; HORSE; INSECT; INVERTEBRATE; MAMMAL; MARSUPIAL; MOLLUSC; MONKEY; MOTH; REPTILE; RODENT. *See also* ANIMAL SOUNDS *at* SOUND[1]. *See also* COLLECTIVE NOUNS.

---

animate *adj, v*
▶ *adj* alive, living, live, breathing, conscious
🔁 inanimate
▶ *v* activate, enliven, arouse, instigate, invigorate, galvanize, goad, spur, impel, stimulate, incite, energize, excite, fire, kindle, move, quicken, reactivate, revive, rouse, spark, stir, urge, vitalize, encourage, inspire, *formal* embolden, vivify, inspirit, *colloq.* buck up
🔁 dull, inhibit

animated *adj*
lively, spirited, buoyant, vibrant, ebullient, vivacious, alive, vital, quick, brisk, vigorous, energetic, active, passionate, impassioned, vehement, ardent, fervent, glowing, radiant, excited, enthusiastic, eager, *colloq.* full of beans, bright and breezy
🔁 lethargic, sluggish, inert

animation *n*
liveliness, spirit, action, activity, ebullience, passion, elation, energy, enthusiasm, excitement, exhilaration, fervour, high spirits, life, radiance, sparkle, sprightliness, verve, vibrancy, vigour, vitality, zeal, zest, *colloq.* pep, zing
🔁 dullness, inertia

animosity *n*
ill feeling, ill-will, acrimony, bitterness, rancour, resentment, spite, malice, malignity, malevolence, hate, hatred, loathing, abhorrence, antagonism, hostility, enmity, feud, *formal* odium, animus
🔁 goodwill

annals *n*
archives, chronicles, records, registers, history, journals, memoirs, reports

annex *v*
1 ADD, append, affix, attach, adjoin, join, connect, unite, incorporate 2 SEIZE, appropriate, acquire, usurp, occupy, conquer, take over, *formal* arrogate

---

annex or **annexe** ?
Annex, stressed on the second syllable, is a verb meaning to add or acquire: *The USSR annexed Latvia in World War II*. The noun, stressed on the first syllable, may be spelt *annex* or *annexe*, but the form with -*e* is more common.

---

annexation *n*
seizure, appropriation, acquisition, usurping, occupation, conquest, takeover, *formal* arrogation

annexe *n*
wing, extension, attachment, addition, supplement, expansion

annihilate *v*
eliminate, eradicate, obliterate, erase, wipe out, murder, assassinate, exterminate, extinguish, raze,

destroy, abolish, conquer, defeat, rout, *formal* extirpate, *colloq.* liquidate, rub out, thrash, trounce, bring to their knees

annihilation *n*
elimination, eradication, obliteration, erasure, murder, assassination, extermination, extinction, destruction, abolition, defeat, *formal* extirpation, *colloq.* liquidation

anniversary *n*

Names of wedding anniversary include:
1st cotton, 2nd paper, 3rd leather, 4th flowers/fruit, 5th wood, 6th iron/sugar, 7th copper/wool, 8th bronze/pottery, 9th pottery/willow, 10th tin, 11th steel, 12th silk/linen, 13th lace, 14th ivory, 15th crystal, 20th china, 25th silver, 30th pearl, 35th coral, 40th ruby, 45th sapphire, 50th gold, 55th emerald, 60th diamond, 70th platinum.

annotate *v*
note, gloss, comment, explain, interpret, elucidate, *formal* marginalize, explicate

annotation *n*
note, footnote, gloss, comment, commentary, exegesis, explanation, elucidation, *formal* explication

announce *v*
declare, proclaim, report, state, make/issue a statement, reveal, disclose, divulge, make known, make public, notify, intimate, give out, publish, broadcast, advertise, publicize, blazon (abroad), *formal* promulgate, propound, preconize
F3 suppress

announcement *n*
1 *make an announcement* statement, declaration, proclamation, report, communiqué, dispatch, bulletin, message, information, notification, intimation, revelation, disclosure, divulgence, publication, broadcast, advertisement, publicity **2** *the announcement of the news* declaration, proclamation, reporting, revelation, disclosure, divulgence, making known/public, notification, intimation, giving-out, publication, publicizing

announcer *n*
broadcaster, newscaster, newsreader, commentator, compère, host, master of ceremonies, MC, presenter, anchorman, anchorwoman, town crier, herald, messenger

annoy *v*
irritate, rile, displease, anger, vex, irk, madden, exasperate, tease, provoke, ruffle, gall, trouble, nag, disturb, bother, pester, plague, harass, molest, *colloq.* aggravate, bug, hassle, rub up the wrong way, wind up, get on your nerves, get up your nose, get under your skin, get someone's goat, get on your wick, drive crazy/nuts, drive bananas, drive up the wall, drive round the bend/twist, get your back up, brass off, cheese off, make someone's hackles rise, give someone the hump, get your dander up, *US* tick/hack off
F3 please, gratify, comfort

annoyance *n*
1 NUISANCE, pest, disturbance, bother, trouble, bore, tease, provocation, irritant, *colloq.* bind, drag, headache, pain, pain in the neck, *slang* pain in the backside, *US* pain in the butt **2** *express your annoyance* irritation, displeasure, anger, vexation, exasperation, harassment, *colloq.* aggravation
F3 **2** pleasure

annoyed *adj*
irritated, cross, upset, displeased, angry, vexed,

piqued, exasperated, provoked, indignant, harassed, *colloq.* peeved, miffed, narked, bugged, hassled, driven crazy, driven nuts, cheesed off, got the hump, in a huff
F3 pleased

annoying *adj*
irritating, vexatious, irksome, troublesome, bothersome, tiresome, trying, maddening, exasperating, galling, offensive, teasing, provoking, disturbing, intrusive, unwelcome, harassing, *US* pesky, *colloq.* aggravating
F3 pleasing, welcome

annual *n, adj*
▶ *n* yearbook, almanac, calendar, register
▶ *adj* yearly

annul *v*
nullify, invalidate, void, rescind, abrogate, suspend, cancel, abolish, quash, repeal, revoke, countermand, negate, declare null and void, retract, recall, reverse
F3 enact, restore

annulment *n*
invalidation, voiding, rescindment, abrogation, suspension, cancellation, abolition, quashing, repeal, countermand, negation, nullification, recall, reverse, *formal* revocation, rescission
F3 enactment, restoration

anodyne *adj*
bland, inoffensive, neutral, deadening

anoint *v*
1 OIL, grease, lubricate, apply oil/lubrication, rub, smear, daub, *formal* embrocate **2** BLESS, consecrate, sanctify, dedicate, ordain

anomalous *adj*
abnormal, atypical, exceptional, irregular, inconsistent, incongruous, deviant, freakish, eccentric, peculiar, odd, unusual, singular, rare, *colloq.* freak
F3 normal, regular, ordinary

anomaly *n*
abnormality, exception, irregularity, inconsistency, incongruity, aberration, deviation, divergence, departure, freak, misfit, eccentricity, peculiarity, oddity, rarity

anonymous *adj*
unnamed, nameless, unsigned, unacknowledged, unspecified, unidentified, unknown, incognito, faceless, impersonal, nondescript, unexceptional, *formal* unattested, innominate
F3 named, signed, identifiable, distinctive

another *adj*
1 ADDITIONAL, further, extra, more, added, spare, second **2** DIFFERENT, other, some other, alternative, not the same, variant

answer *n, v*
▶ *n* **1** REPLY, acknowledgement, response, reaction, rejoinder, retort, riposte, retaliation, rebuttal, *formal* replication, *colloq.* comeback **2** SOLUTION, explanation, result, key, resolution, unravelling, *colloq.* quick fix
▶ *v* **1** REPLY, acknowledge, respond, write back, react, refute, retaliate, *colloq.* get/come back to **2** *answer a need* fulfil, fill, meet, satisfy, match up to **3** *answer (to) a description* fit, correspond to, correlate, conform, agree, suit, serve, pass
▷ **answer back** talk back, be cheeky to, retort, riposte, retaliate, retort, contradict, disagree, argue, dispute, rebut, *US colloq.* sass
▷ **answer for 1** *answer for her loyalty* vouch for, be responsible for, be liable for, speak for **2** *answer for the crimes* pay for, be punished for

answerable *adj*
liable, responsible, accountable, chargeable, blameworthy, to blame

antagonism n
hostility, opposition, enmity, rivalry, antipathy, ill feeling, ill-will, animosity, friction, discord, dissension, contention, conflict
F3 rapport, sympathy, agreement

antagonist n
opponent, adversary, enemy, foe, rival, competitor, contestant, contender
F3 ally, supporter

antagonistic adj
conflicting, opposed, adverse, at variance, incompatible, hostile, belligerent, contentious, unfriendly, ill-disposed, averse
F3 sympathetic, friendly

antagonize v
alienate, estrange, disaffect, repel, embitter, offend, insult, provoke, annoy, irritate, anger, incense, formal disaffect
F3 disarm

antecedent n
1 antecedents of the aeroplane precursor, forerunner, precedent 2 with Welsh antecedents ancestors, forebears, forefathers, extraction, genealogy

anthem n
hymn, song, chorale, psalm, song of praise, canticle, chant, formal paean

anthology n
selection, collection, compilation, compendium, digest, treasury, miscellany, omnibus edition, formal spicilege

anticipate v
1 FORESTALL, pre-empt, intercept, prevent, formal obviate, preclude, colloq. beat to it 2 EXPECT, foresee, predict, forecast, think likely, look for, await, look forward to, hope for, bank on, count on/upon, reckon on, prepare for, US figure on

anticipation n
1 in anticipation of the shortage expectation, preparation, prediction 2 eager anticipation excitement, expectancy, hope, colloq. bated breath

anticlimax n
comedown, let-down, disappointment, fiasco, formal bathos, colloq. non-event, damp squib, not all that it was cracked up to be

antics n
foolery, tomfoolery, silliness, buffoonery, clowning, horseplay, frolics, capers, skylarking, playfulness, mischief, tricks, monkey-tricks, pranks, stunts, doings

antidote n
1 an antidote to a sting cure, counter-agent, antitoxin, neutralizer, countermeasure, technical antivenin, mithridate, theriac 2 an antidote to depression remedy, cure, corrective

antipathy n
aversion, dislike, hate, hatred, loathing, abhorrence, distaste, disgust, repulsion, antagonism, animosity, ill-will, bad blood, enmity, hostility, opposition, incompatibility, formal animus, odium
F3 sympathy, affection, rapport

antiquated adj
obsolete, old-fashioned, outdated, outmoded, out-of-date, dated, bygone, anachronistic, ancient, antediluvian, archaic, démodé, fossilized, outworn, passé, colloq. on the way out, old hat
F3 forward-looking, modern

antique adj, n
▶ adj antiquarian, ancient, old, veteran, vintage, quaint, antiquated, old-fashioned, outdated, archaic, obsolete
▶ n antiquity, relic, bygone, period piece, heirloom,

curio, museum piece, curiosity, rarity, object of virtu

antiquity n
1 ancient times, time immemorial, distant past, olden days 2 of great antiquity age, old age, oldness, agedness
F3 1 modernity, novelty

antiseptic adj, n
▶ adj disinfectant, medicated, aseptic, germ-free, clean, pure, unpolluted, uncontaminated, sterile, sterilized, sanitized, sanitary, hygienic
▶ n disinfectant, germicide, bactericide, purifier, cleanser

antisocial adj
1 an antisocial person unfriendly, unsociable, uncommunicative, reserved, retiring, withdrawn, alienated, unapproachable 2 antisocial behaviour asocial, unacceptable, disruptive, disorderly, rebellious, lawless, belligerent, antagonistic, hostile, anarchic
F3 1 sociable, gregarious 2 acceptable

antithesis n
1 OPPOSITE, converse, reverse, opposite extreme 2 OPPOSITION, contrast, contradiction, reversal

anxiety n
worry, concern, care, distress, nervousness, apprehension, disquiet, dread, anguish, foreboding, misgiving, uneasiness, restlessness, fretfulness, impatience, suspense, tension, stress, strain, formal disquietude, worriment
F3 calm, composure, serenity

anxious adj
1 APPREHENSIVE, worried, concerned, nervous, afraid, fearful, uneasy, restless, fretful, impatient, in suspense, on tenterhooks, tense, taut, distressed, dismayed, disturbed, troubled, tormented, overwrought, tortured, formal solicitous, colloq. in a stew, having butterflies in your stomach/tummy, tearing your hair out 2 EAGER, keen, longing, enthusiastic, yearning, expectant
F3 1 calm, composed

apace adv
speedily, swiftly, double-quick, fast, hastily, quickly, rapidly, at full speed, at top speed, without delay

apart adv
1 stand apart from the others aside, to one side, away, afar, distant, aloof, excluded, isolated, cut off, separated, separate, distinct, piecemeal 2 live apart SEPARATELY, independently, separated, divorced, not together, not living together, individually, singly, alone, on your own, by yourself, privately 3 tear apart to pieces, to bits, into parts, in pieces, in bits, piecemeal
F3 2 connected 3 together
▷ **apart from** except (for), not counting, excepted, aside from, excluding, with the exception of, but for

apathetic adj
uninterested, uninvolved, indifferent, blasé, cool, unemotional, emotionless, impassive, unmoved, unconcerned, cold, unfeeling, numb, unresponsive, passive, listless, lethargic, unambitious, lukewarm, half-hearted
F3 enthusiastic, involved, concerned, feeling, responsive

apathy n
uninterestedness, indifference, coolness, impassivity, unconcern, lack of interest, lack of concern, lack of enthusiasm, coldness, insensibility, passivity, listlessness, lethargy, sluggishness, torpor, inertia, formal languor, acedia, accidie
F3 enthusiasm, interest, concern

ape v, n
▶ v copy, imitate, echo, mirror, parrot, mimic, take off, caricature, parody, mock, counterfeit, affect

▶ *n* monkey, chimpanzee, gibbon, gorilla, baboon, orang-utan

aperture *n*
gap, hole, opening, passage, perforation, breach, chink, cleft, crack, eye, fissure, rent, slit, slot, space, vent, mouth, *technical* orifice, foramen, *formal* interstice

apex *n*
top, high point, peak, pinnacle, point, summit, tip, climax, consummation, crest, crown, crowning point, culmination, height, *technical* acme, fastigium, apogee, vertex, zenith
🖪 nadir

aphorism *n*
maxim, adage, axiom, dictum, maxim, precept, proverb, saw, saying, witticism, *formal* apothegm, epigram, gnome

aphrodisiac *n, adj*
▶ *n* love potion, stimulant
▶ *adj* stimulant, erogenous, erotic, *formal* amative, amatory, erotogenous, venerous

aplomb *n*
poise, assurance, calmness, composure, confidence, coolness, balance, equanimity, sang-froid, savoir-faire, self-assurance, self-confidence, self-possession, audacity
🖪 discomposure

apocryphal *adj*
unauthenticated, unverified, unsubstantiated, unsupported, questionable, spurious, equivocal, doubtful, dubious, fabricated, concocted, fictitious, imaginary, legendary, mythical
🖪 authentic, true

apologetic *adj*
sorry, repentant, penitent, contrite, remorseful, conscience-stricken, regretful, rueful
🖪 unrepentant, impenitent, defiant

apologize *v*
say you are sorry, say sorry, regret, be apologetic, ask forgiveness, ask pardon, beg someone's pardon, acknowledge, confess, explain, justify, plead, *colloq.* swallow your pride, eat your words, eat humble pie

apology *n*
saying sorry, acknowledgement, confession, excuse, regrets, explanation, justification, vindication, defence, plea, *formal* palliation
🖪 defiance

apostasy *n*
defection, desertion, disloyalty, falseness, renunciation, treachery, unfaithfulness, heresy, *formal* perfidy, recreance, recreancy, renegation, recidivism
🖪 loyalty, orthodoxy

apostate *n*
renegade, defector, deserter, traitor, turncoat, heretic, *formal* recidivist, recreant, tergiversator
🖪 follower

apostle *n*
1 *Jesus Christ's apostles* disciple, messenger, evangelist, preacher, missionary, reformer, proselytizer 2 *apostles of a united Europe* advocate, champion, supporter, crusader, pioneer, proponent

appal *v*
horrify, shock, outrage, disgust, dismay, disconcert, daunt, intimidate, unnerve, alarm, scare, frighten, terrify
🖪 reassure, encourage

appalling *adj*
horrifying, horrific, harrowing, shocking, outrageous, atrocious, disgusting, awful, dreadful, frightful, terrible, dire, grim, hideous, ghastly, horrible, horrid, loathsome, daunting, intimidating, unnerving, alarming, frightening, terrifying, nightmarish
🖪 reassuring, encouraging

apparatus *n*
1 *gym apparatus* appliance, gadget, device, contraption, equipment, gear, tackle, outfit, tools, implements, utensils, materials, machine, machinery 2 *the apparatus of government* system, structure, network, set-up, mechanism, framework, means

apparel *n*
clothing, clothes, garments, dress, costume, garb, outfit, wardrobe

apparent *adj*
1 *his distrust was all too apparent* visible, evident, noticeable, perceptible, plain, clear, distinct, marked, unmistakable, conspicuous, be standing out, obvi-ous, manifest, patent, open, declared 2 *their apparent calmness* seeming, superficial, outward, visible, ostensible
🖪 1 hidden, obscure

apparently *adv*
seemingly, ostensibly, outwardly, on the face of it, to all appearances, superficially, on the surface, reputedly, plainly, clearly, obviously, manifestly, patently

apparition *n*
ghost, spectre, phantom, spirit, vision, manifestation, materialization, presence, *formal* chimera, visitant, *colloq.* spook

appeal *n, v*
▶ *n* 1 REQUEST, application, claim, approach, petition, suit, solicitation, plea, entreaty, supplication, prayer, invocation, *formal* imploration, adjuration, orison 2 ATTRACTION, allure, interest, fascination, enchantment, charm, attractiveness, winsomeness, beauty, charisma, magnetism 3 *an appeal in a law-court* retrial, reconsideration, review, re-evaluation, re-examination
▶ *v* 1 *appeal for help* ask (for), request, call, apply, claim, address, petition, solicit, plead, beg, beseech, implore, entreat, pray, invoke, call upon, *formal* supplicate, sue 2 ATTRACT, draw, allure, lure, tempt, entice, invite, interest, engage, fascinate, charm, please

appear *v*
1 ARRIVE, enter, turn up, attend, be present, materialize, develop, show (up), come into sight, come into view, come along, loom, rise, surface, arise, occur, crop up, come to light, come out, emerge, issue, be published 2 SEEM, look, give the impression of being, come across as, show signs of, take the guise of, turn out, *colloq.* pop up 3 *appear in a show* act, perform, play, take part, be a guest in, be on stage 4 *his book appeared in the shops* be published, come out, become available
🖪 1 disappear, vanish

appearance *n*
1 APPEARING, arrival, advent, coming, coming into view, rise, emergence, début, introduction, attendance, presence 2 LOOK, expression, face, aspect, air, bearing, manner, looks, figure, (outward) form, complexion, image, *formal* mien, visage, demeanour

---

Expressions used when talking about someone's appearance include:
a sight for sore eyes, as ugly as sin, beauty is in the eye of the beholder, beauty is only skin deep, cut a dash, done up like a dog's dinner, dressed up to the nines, easy on the eye, like something the cat brought in, like the wreck of the Hesperus, look like a million dollars, look like nothing on earth, look the part, look your best, mutton dressed as lamb, no oil painting, not a hair out of place, not much to look at, pretty as a picture.

---

3 *keep up an appearance* pretence, semblance, show,

front, guise, illusion, impression, outward impression, façade, image

F3 1 disappearance

appease *v*
placate, pacify, reconcile, satisfy, mitigate, make peace with, conciliate, propitiate

F3 aggravate

appellation *n*
epithet, name, title, designation, description, *formal* sobriquet

append *v*
add, affix, attach, fasten, join, tack on, *formal* adjoin, annex, conjoin, subjoin

appendage *n*
addendum, appendix, addition, supplement, adjunct, tailpiece

appendix *n*
addition, appendage, adjunct, addendum, supplement, epilogue, codicil, postscript, rider

appetite *n*
1 *a good appetite* hunger, stomach, relish, zest, taste 2 *appetite for sensation* hunger, taste, thirst, inclination, liking, desire, longing, propensity, yearning, craving, lust, eagerness, passion, zeal

appetizing *adj*
mouthwatering, tempting, inviting, appealing, palatable, tasty, delicious, succulent, piquant, savoury, *colloq.* scrumptious

F3 disgusting, distasteful

applaud *v*
1 *the audience applauded* clap, cheer, put your hands together for, give an ovation/a standing ovation to, give a round of applause, show your appreciation to, *colloq.* give a big hand to 2 *applaud the government's efforts* acclaim, compliment, congratulate, approve, commend, praise, *formal* laud, eulogize, extol

applause *n*
ovation, standing ovation, clapping, cheering, cheers, bravos, acclaim, acclamation, accolade, congratulation, approval, commendation, praise, *formal* encomium, *colloq.* a big hand

F3 criticism, censure

appliance *n*
machine, device, contrivance, contraption, gadget, tool, implement, instrument, apparatus, mechanism

applicable *adj*
relevant, apt, appropriate, fitting, suited, useful, suit-able, fit, proper, valid, legitimate, *formal* pertinent, apposite

F3 inapplicable, inappropriate

applicant *n*
candidate, interviewee, claimant, contestant, competitor, aspirant, suitor, petitioner, inquirer, *technical* postulant

application *n*
1 REQUEST, appeal, petition, suit, claim, inquiry, demand 2 RELEVANCE, function, purpose, use, value, bearing, significance, praxis, aptness, germaneness, *formal* pertinence 3 DILIGENCE, hard work, industry, effort, commitment, dedication, perseverance, keenness, attentiveness, *formal* assiduity, sedulousness

apply *v*
1 REQUEST, ask for, requisition, put in for, put in an application for, fill in a form for, order, write away/off for, appeal, petition, solicit, sue, claim, inquire 2 *apply yourself to a task* address, buckle down, settle down, commit, devote, dedicate, give, direct, concentrate, study, persevere, be industrious, work hard, make an effort, commit/devote yourself 3 USE, exercise, utilize, employ, bring into play, put into practice/operation, draw on, engage, harness, ply, wield,

administer, execute, implement, assign, direct, bring to bear, exert, practise, resort to 4 REFER, relate, be relevant, be significant, fit, suit, *formal* pertain, appertain 5 *apply ointment* put on, spread on, lay on, cover with, paint, anoint, smear, rub, treat with, *formal* adhibit

appoint *v*
1 NAME, nominate, be shortlisted, elect, install, choose, select, pick, engage, employ, take on, hire, recruit, commission, co-opt, delegate, assign, allot, designate, command, direct, charge, detail 2 DECIDE, determine, arrange, settle, fix, set, establish, ordain, decree, destine, designate, allot

F3 1 reject, dismiss, discharge

appointed *adj*
determined, decided, chosen, assigned, arranged, settled, fixed, set, established, ordained, decreed, destined, preordained, designated, allotted

appointment *n*
1 ARRANGEMENT, engagement, date, meeting, arrangement to meet, interview, consultation, rendezvous 2 JOB, position, situation, post, office, place 3 NAMING, nomination, election, choosing, choice, selection, commissioning, delegation

apportion *v*
assign, allocate, allot, distribute, divide, dispense, deal (out), hand out, grant, measure out, mete (out), ration (out), share (out), *formal* admeasure, *colloq.* dole out

apportionment *n*
allocation, allotment, distribution, division, dispensation, assignment, dealing, grant, ration(ing), share, *colloq.* handout

apposite *adj*
relevant, applicable, appropriate, apt, germane, suitable, suited, to the point, to the purpose, *formal* pertinent, apropos, befitting

F3 inapposite

appraisal *n*
evaluation, assessment, survey, inspection, review, examination, estimate, estimation, judgement, reckoning, opinion, appreciation, valuation, rating, *formal* assay, *colloq.* once-over

appraise *v*
evaluate, assess, survey, inspect, review, examine, estimate, sum up, judge, value, rate, *formal* assay, *colloq.* size up

---

appraise or apprise ?
If you *appraise* someone or something, you form an opinion about their quality, value, etc. If you are *apprised* of something, you are told about it.

---

appreciable *adj*
noticeable, significant, considerable, substantial, definite, perceptible, discernible, recognizable

F3 insignificant, imperceptible, negligible

appreciate *v*
1 ENJOY, relish, savour, prize, treasure, value, cherish, admire, respect, regard, esteem, like, welcome, take kindly to, think highly of 2 UNDERSTAND, comprehend, perceive, realize, recognize, grasp, be aware of, be conscious of, be sensitive to, acknowledge, sympathize with, know, see 3 *I appreciate your help* be grateful for, express your gratitude/appreciation, thank, be appreciative, be indebted to 4 *appreciate in value* grow, increase, rise, mount, go up, inflate, gain, strengthen, improve, enhance

F3 1 despise, hate 2 overlook, ignore 4 depreciate, go down

appreciation n
1 ENJOYMENT, relish, admiration, liking, respect, regard, esteem, valuing **2** send a present to show your appreciation gratitude, gratefulness, thankfulness, indebtedness, obligation **3** UNDERSTANDING, comprehension, perception, awareness, realization, recognition, grasp, acknowledgement, sympathy, sensitivity, responsiveness, valuation, assessment, estimation, judgement, knowledge, formal cognizance **4** REVIEW, critique, evaluation, analysis, assessment, commentary, notice, praise **5** GROWTH, increase, rise, inflation, gain, improvement, escalation, enhancement
F3 **1** ingratitude **5** depreciation

appreciative adj
1 GRATEFUL, thankful, obliged, indebted, pleased, formal beholden **2** ADMIRING, encouraging, enthusiastic, respectful, sensitive, responsive, perceptive, knowledgeable, conscious, mindful
F3 **1** ungrateful

apprehend v
1 CATCH, arrest, capture, detain, seize, colloq. bust, nick, collar, grab, nab, run in **2** UNDERSTAND, comprehend, grasp, believe, conceive, perceive, realize, recognize, see, colloq. twig

apprehension n
1 ANXIETY, dread, foreboding, misgiving, qualm, uneasiness, worry, concern, disquiet, nervousness, alarm, fear, trepidation, doubt, suspicion, mistrust, formal perturbation, colloq. butterflies (in your stomach), the willies **2** ARREST, capture, detention, seizure, taking **3** UNDERSTANDING, comprehension, grasp, belief, conception, perception, discernment, realization, recognition

apprehensive adj
nervous, anxious, worried, concerned, uneasy, doubtful, suspicious, mistrustful, distrustful, bothered, alarmed, afraid, fearful, colloq. on tenterhooks
F3 assured, confident

apprentice n
trainee, probationer, student, pupil, learner, novice, beginner, starter, recruit, newcomer, tyro, US colloq. rookie
F3 expert

apprise v
inform, notify, acquaint, advise, brief, communicate, enlighten, intimate, tell, warn, colloq. tip off

 apprise or **appraise** ? See panel at APPRAISE.

approach v, n
▶ v **1** GET CLOSER TO, come nearer/closer, advance towards, move towards, draw near, near, gain on, catch up, reach, meet, arrive **2** SPEAK TO, address, make conversation with, greet, accost **3** TACKLE, deal with, begin, commence, set about, embark on, undertake, introduce, mention, treat **4** APPLY TO, appeal to, sound out, contact, get in touch with, get on to, invite, make advances, make overtures, broach **5** a speed approaching 200 km/h REACH, come close to, come near to, compare with, approximate
▶ n **1** the approach of winter advance, coming, coming near/close, advent, arrival **2** ACCESS, road, av-enue, drive, driveway, way, passage, entrance, doorway, threshold **3** APPLICATION, appeal, overture(s), advances, invitation, proposition, proposal, request, plea **4** METHOD, manner, style, technique, procedure, means, modus operandi, strategy, system, tactics, course of action

approachable adj
1 FRIENDLY, easy to get on/along with, sociable, congenial, warm, affable, agreeable, open, informal **2** ACCESSIBLE, attainable, reachable, colloq. get-at-able
F3 **1** aloof, unapproachable **2** inaccessible, remote

appropriate adj, v
▶ adj suitable, applicable, relevant, to the point, well-chosen, apt, fitting, fit, befitting, germane, seemly, becoming, proper, right, correct, accepted, well-timed, timely, seasonable, opportune, formal pertinent, appurtenant, apropos, meet, felicitous, colloq. spot-on
F3 inappropriate, irrelevant, unsuitable
▶ v **1** SEIZE, take, take possession of, commandeer, requisition, confiscate, impound, assume, usurp, formal expropriate, arrogate **2** STEAL, pocket, filch, pilfer, embezzle, misappropriate, thieve, make off with, formal purloin, peculate, colloq. nick, pinch, swipe

approval n
1 ADMIRATION, esteem, regard, respect, good opinion, liking, appreciation, acceptance, favour, recommendation, praise, commendation, acclaim, acclamation, honour, applause, formal approbation **2** AGREEMENT, acceptance, assent, consent, permission, leave, sanction, authorization, licence, mandate, endorsement, blessing, certification, ratification, validation, confirmation, support, formal approbation, concurrence, imprimatur, colloq. go-ahead, green light, OK, rubber stamp, nod, wink, thumbs-up
F3 **1** disapproval, condemnation

approve v
1 ADMIRE, esteem, regard, like, think well/highly of, hold in high regard, be pleased with, appreciate, favour, recommend, praise, commend, acclaim, applaud **2** approve a proposal agree to, assent to, consent to, accede to, allow, permit, pass, sanction, authorize, mandate, bless, countenance, ratify, validate, endorse, support, uphold, second, back, accept, adopt, carry, confirm, formal concur, colloq. give the go-ahead to, give the green light to, OK, rubber-stamp, give the nod to, give the thumbs-up to, buy
F3 **1** disapprove, condemn **2** reject

approved adj
accepted, authorized, orthodox, official, recommended, sanctioned, correct, favoured, permissible, permitted, preferred, proper, recognized
F3 unauthorized, unorthodox

approximate adj, v
▶ adj estimated, guessed, rough, inexact, loose, close, near, like, similar, relative, colloq. ballpark
F3 exact
▶ v approach, come close to, border on, verge on, be tantamount to, resemble, be similar to

approximately adv
roughly, around, about, some, something like, odd, circa, more or less, loosely, round about, or thereabouts, approaching, close to, nearly, just about, not far off, in the region/neighbourhood/vicinity of, somewhere in the region of, in round numbers, rounded up/down, colloq. give or take
F3 exactly

approximation n
1 ESTIMATE, rough calculation, rough idea, guess, conjecture, colloq. guesstimate, ballpark figure **2** an approximation to a dress semblance, likeness, resemblance, correspondence

apropos adj, prep
▶ adj suitable, applicable, relevant, to the point, well-

chosen, apt, fitting, befitting, seemly, becoming, proper, right, correct, accepted, timely, seasonable, opportune, *formal* pertinent, felicitous
Fa inappropriate
▶ *prep* with reference to, with regard to, with respect to, in relation to, in respect of, on the subject of, in connection with, re, regarding, respecting

apt *adj*
1 RELEVANT, applicable, apposite, appropriate, fitting, acceptable, suitable, fit, germane, seemly, proper, correct, accurate, timely, seasonable, *colloq.* spot-on **2** *apt to do something* INCLINED, liable, prone, given, disposed, tending, likely, given, ready, subject
Fa 1 inapt, unsuitable

aptitude *n*
ability, natural ability, capability, capacity, faculty, gift, talent, flair, facility, skill, proficiency, cleverness, intelligence, quickness, bent, inclination, leaning, disposition, tendency
Fa inaptitude

aquatic *adj*
water, sea, river, marine, maritime, nautical, watery, fluid, liquid, *formal* fluvial

arable *adj*
cultivable, ploughable, tillable, fertile, productive, fruitful, *formal* fecund

arbiter *n*
1 ADJUDICATOR, judge, referee, umpire **2** *an arbiter of style* authority, expert, pundit, master, controller

arbitrary *adj*
1 RANDOM, chance, capricious, whimsical, inconsistent, discretionary, subjective, personal, instinctive, unreasoned, illogical, irrational, unreasonable **2** DESPOTIC, tyrannical, dictatorial, autocratic, absolute, imperious, magisterial, domineering, overbearing, high-handed, dogmatic
Fa 1 reasoned, rational, circumspect

arbitrate *v*
judge, adjudicate, pass judgement, sit in judgement, referee, umpire, mediate, settle, decide, determine

arbitration *n*
judgement, adjudication, intervention, mediation, negotiation, settlement, decision, determination, *formal* arbitrament

arbitrator *n*
judge, adjudicator, arbiter, referee, umpire, moderator, mediator, negotiator, intermediary, go-between

arc *n*
curve, curved line, bend, arch, bow, curvature, semicircle

arcade *n*
gallery, cloister, colonnade, covered way, mall, piazza, portico, precinct, shopping mall, shopping precinct, *technical* loggia, peristyle, stoa

arcane *adj*
secret, mysterious, concealed, obscure, hidden, abstruse, mystical, cryptic, enigmatic, esoteric, recondite, occult, profound

arch *n, v, adj*
▶ *n* **1** *the arches of a bridge* archway, bridge, span, dome, vault, concave **2** ARC, bend, curve, curvature, bow, semicircle
▶ *v* bend, curve, bow, arc, vault, camber
▶ *adj* mischievous, playful, mysterious, cunning, sly

archaeology *n*

Archaeological terms include :
agger, amphitheatre, amphora, artefact, barrow, beaker, blade, bogman, bowl, bracteate, burin, cairn, cartouche, cave art/rock art, cist, cromlech, cup, dolmen, earthwork, eolith, flake, flask, flint, handaxe, henge, hieroglyph, hill fort, hoard, hypocaust, incised decoration, jar, jug, kitchen-midden, kurgan, ley lines, loom weight, lynchet, megalith, microlith, mosaic, mound, mummy, neolith, obelisk, palmette, palstave, papyrus, potassium-argon dating, radiocarbon dating, rock shelter, sondage, spindle, stele, stone circle, tell, tumulus, urn, vallum, whorl.

archaic *adj*
antiquated, old-fashioned, outmoded, *passé*, outdated, out-of-date, obsolete, old, ancient, antique, quaint, bygone, primitive, medieval, antediluvian, *colloq.* old hat, out of the ark
Fa modern, recent

archetypal *adj*
model, standard, typical, representative, characteristic, original, classic, ideal, stock, *formal* exemplary

archetype *n*
pattern, model, standard, form, type, prototype, original, precursor, classic, paradigm, ideal, epitome, stereotype, *formal* exemplar

architect *n*
1 *the architect of the building* designer, planner, master builder, draughtsman **2** *the architect of modern economics* creator, author, inventor, engineer, maker, constructor, prime mover, originator, founder, instigator, shaper, *colloq.* mastermind

architecture *n*
1 *study architecture* designing, planning, building, construction, *technical* architectonics **2** *Victorian architecture* style, design, composition, structure, arrangement, make-up, framework

Architectural and building terms include :
alcove, annexe, architrave, baluster, barge-board, baroque, bas relief, capstone, classical, coping stone, Corinthian, corner-stone, cornice, coving, dado, dogtooth, dome, Doric, drawbridge, dry-stone, duplex, Early English, eaves, Edwardian, elevation, Elizabethan, façade, fascia, festoon, fillet, finial, flamboyant, Flemish bond, fletton, fluting, frieze, frontispiece, gargoyle, gatehouse, Georgian, Gothic, groin, groundplan, half-timbered, Ionic, jamb, lintel, mullion, Norman, pagoda, pantile, parapet, pinnacle, plinth, Queen-Anne, rafters, Regency, reveal, ridge, rococo, Romanesque, roof, rotunda, roughcast, sacristy, scroll, soffit, stucco, terrazzo, Tudor, Tuscan, wainscot, weathering. *See also* WALL.

archives *n*
records, annals, chronicles, memorials, papers, documents, deeds, ledgers, registers, memorabilia, roll

arctic *adj*
1 *the Arctic Ocean* polar, far north, *formal* boreal, hyperborean **2** *arctic weather* freezing, freezing cold, bitterly cold, frozen, glacial, subzero
Fa 1 Antarctic

ardent *adj*
fervent, fiery, warm, passionate, impassioned, fierce,

avid, vehement, intense, strong, spirited, enthusiastic, eager, keen, dedicated, devoted, zealous, hot, fervid

F3 apathetic, unenthusiastic

ardour *n*
fervour, passion, fire, heat, warmth, avidity, vehemence, intensity, spirit, enthusiasm, eagerness, animation, zest, keenness, dedication, devotion, zeal, lust, *formal* empressement

F3 apathy, coolness, indifference

arduous *adj*
hard, difficult, tough, rigorous, severe, harsh, formidable, strenuous, tiring, taxing, fatiguing, wearying, daunting, exhausting, backbreaking, punishing, gruelling, uphill, laborious, onerous, burdensome, heavy, *colloq.* be a slog, be murder

F3 easy

area *n*
1 *the Muslim areas of the city* locality, neighbourhood, quarter, environment, environs, patch, terrain, district, region, parish, zone, sector, department, precinct, province, enclave, catchment area, reserve area **2** *an area of land* expanse, width, breadth, stretch, part, portion, section, tract **3** *an area of activity/knowledge* FIELD, sphere, domain, world, realm, territory, department, province, branch, range, scope, compass, size, extent

arena *n*
1 STADIUM, field, ground, bowl, ring, area, amphitheatre, coliseum, hippodrome **2** *the political arena* sphere, scene, domain, world, realm, department, province, battlefield, battleground, area of conflict

arguable *adj*
debatable, open to question, questionable, disputable, contentious, uncertain, undecided, moot, *formal* controvertible

F3 incontrovertible, indisputable, certain

argue *v*
1 QUARREL, squabble, bicker, row, have a row, wrangle, haggle, remonstrate, take/join issue, fight, feud, fall out, disagree, dispute, *formal* altercate, *colloq.* be at each other's throats, be at loggerheads, have it out (with), have words, cross swords, have a bone to pick **2** REASON, assert, contend, hold, declare, maintain, claim, plead, *formal* expostulate **3** *argue the point* question, debate, discuss **4** *argued them out of leaving* persuade, talk out of, convince **5** BE EVIDENCE FOR, exhibit, display, show, manifest, demonstrate, indicate, denote, prove, suggest, imply

argument *n*
1 QUARREL, squabble, row, wrangle, controversy, debate, discussion, dispute, disagreement, clash, difference of opinion, heated exchange, conflict, fight, feud, rumpus, ruckus, *US* spat, *formal* altercation, *colloq.* tiff, barney, argy-bargy, running battle, shouting-match, slanging-match, set-to, dust-up, ding-dong, bust-up **2** REASONING, reason, logic, rationale, assertion, declaration, contention, claim, demonstration, evidence, argumentation, debate, defence, case, *formal* expostulation **3** *the argument of the book* synopsis, summary, theme, outline, plot, thesis

argumentative *adj*
quarrelsome, contentious, polemical, opinionated, belligerent, perverse, contrary, cantankerous, *formal* captious, disputatious, litigious, dissentious, *colloq.* stroppy

F3 complaisant

arid *adj*
1 *an arid landscape* dry, parched, waterless, moisture-

less, desiccated, torrid, dehydrated, baked, shrivelled up, barren, infertile, unproductive, desert, waste, *formal* torrefied **2** DULL, uninteresting, boring, monotonous, tedious, dry, sterile, dreary, drab, colourless, lifeless, spiritless, uninspired, vapid, jejune

F3 **1** fertile **2** lively, exciting

aright *adv*
rightly, accurately, exactly, properly, correctly, truly, fitly, suitably, aptly

arise *v*
1 OCCUR, emerge, issue, appear, come to light, come up, present itself, happen, begin, start, commence, come into being/existence, *colloq.* crop up **2** *points that arose from the report* result, be a result of, be caused by, ensue, follow, derive, stem, come, spring, proceed, flow **3** RISE, get up, stand up, get to your feet, rise up, go up, ascend, climb, mount, lift, soar, tower

aristocracy *n*
upper class, privileged class, gentry, nobility, noblemen, noblewomen, peerage, ruling class, gentility, high society, elite, *formal* patriciate, patricians, optimates, *haut monde*, *colloq.* top drawer, upper crust

F3 common people, lower classes, working class, proletariat, *colloq.* plebs, hoi polloi, riff-raff, proles

aristocrat *n*
noble, nobleman, noblewoman, peer, peeress, lord, lady, patrician, *formal* grandee, eupatrid, optimate, *colloq.* toff, nob

F3 commoner

aristocratic *adj*
upper-class, highborn, well-born, noble, patrician, blue-blooded, titled, lordly, courtly, elite, dignified, elegant, refined, thoroughbred, *colloq.* upper-crust

F3 plebeian, vulgar

arm¹ *n*
1 *with folded arms* limb, upper limb, appendage, *technical* brachium **2** *the air arm of the fighting forces* wing, section, division, detachment, department, branch, offshoot, extension, projection **3** *an arm of the sea* inlet, estuary, bay, channel, firth, passage, cove, creek

arm² *v*
arm someone with weapons/information provide, supply, issue, equip, rig, outfit, prime, prepare, forearm, rearm, gird, steel, brace, reinforce, strengthen, protect, *formal* array, furnish, fortify, accoutre

armada *n*
fleet, flotilla, navy, naval force, squadron

armaments *n*
weapons, arms, artillery, guns, cannon, munitions, ammunition, ordnance, weaponry

armistice *n*
ceasefire, truce, peace, peace treaty, agreement to end/cease/suspend hostilities

armour *n*
protective covering, panoply, mail, chain mail, ironcladding

Pieces of armour include:
beaver, besageur, brassard, breastplate, casque, chamfron, coudière, coutere, cubitière, cuirass, cuish, cuissard, cuissart, cuisse, épaulière, flanchard, gauntlet, genouillère, gorget, greave, habergeon, haubergeon, helmet, jambeau, knee piece, morion, neck guard, pallette, panache, pauldron, pavais, pavis, pavise, poitrel, poleyn, rear brace, rerebrace, sabaton, sabbaton, skull, solleret, suit of armour, taces, tasse, tasset, throat piece, vambrace, ventail, visor.

armoured *adj*
armour-plated, steel-plated, iron-clad, reinforced, protected, bullet-proof, bomb-proof

armoury *n*
arsenal, ordnance depot, ammunition dump, magazine, (arms) depot, repository, stock, stockpile, garderobe

arms *n*
1 WEAPONS, weaponry, firearms, guns, artillery, instruments of war, armaments, ordnance, munitions, ammunition **2** COAT-OF-ARMS, armorial bearings, insignia, heraldic device, escutcheon, shield, crest, heraldry, blazonry

army *n*
1 *a captain in the army* armed force, military, militia, land forces, soldiers, troops, infantry **2** *an army of workers* legions, cohorts, multitude, throng, host, horde, pack, mob, crowd, swarm

aroma *n*
smell, odour, scent, perfume, fragrance, bouquet, savour, *formal* fumet(te), redolence

aromatic *adj*
perfumed, fragrant, sweet-smelling, fresh, scented, balmy, savoury, spicy, pungent, *formal* redolent, odoriferous
F∃ acrid, foul-smelling

around *prep, adv*
▶ *prep* **1** SURROUNDING, round, encircling, encompassing, enclosing, on all sides of, on every side of, about, framed by, *formal* circumambient, circumjacent **2** *around a dozen* approximately, roughly, about, circa, more or less, close to, nearly
▶ *adv* **1** EVERYWHERE, all over, in all directions, on all sides, throughout, about, here and there, to and fro **2** CLOSE, close by, near, nearby, at hand

arouse *v*
1 *arouse suspicion* cause, instigate, induce, summon up, call forth, spark, kindle, inflame, whet, sharpen, quicken, animate, excite, prompt, provoke, stimulate, trigger, incur **2** *arouse someone to anger* provoke, incite, agitate, stir up, excite, evoke, rouse, startle, galvanize, goad, spur, whip up, get going **3** *arouse from sleep* wake up, waken, awaken **4** *arouse sexually* stimulate, excite, get going, *colloq.* turn on
F∃ 2 calm, lull, quieten

arraign *v*
accuse, call to account, charge, impeach, indict, prosecute, impugn, incriminate

arrange *v*
1 *arrange a meeting* decide, settle on, agree, plan, organize, set up, make (an appointment), *colloq.* fix (up), pencil in **2** ORGANIZE, co-ordinate, prepare, fix, plan, project, design, devise, contrive, determine, settle **3** ORDER, tidy, range, array, marshal, dispose, distribute, position, set out, lay out, align, line up, group, class, classify, categorize, sort (out), sift, grade, list, file, systematize, catalogue, codify, methodize, regulate, adjust **4** *arrange music* adapt, set, score, orchestrate, instrument, harmonize
F∃ 3 untidy, disorganize, muddle

arrangement *n*
1 *make arrangements* plan(s), preparation(s), detail(s), planning, preparing, groundwork **2** AGREEMENT, settlement, contract, terms, compromise, *modus vivendi* **3** ORDER, array, display, disposition, layout, line-up, positioning, grouping, classification, structure, system, method, set-up, organization, preparation, planning, plan, scheme, design, format, schedule **4** ADAPTATION, version, interpretation, setting, score, orchestration, instrumentation, harmonization

arrant *adj*
absolute, complete, utter, downright, extreme, out-and-out, outright, rank, thorough, thoroughgoing, brazen, flagrant, gross, blatant, unmitigated, incorrigible, infamous, notorious, barefaced, vile, *formal* egregious

array *n, v*
▶ *n* arrangement, display, show, exhibition, exposition, assortment, collection, muster, order, formation, line-up, parade, disposition, marshalling, *formal* assemblage
▶ *v* **1** ARRANGE, order, range, dispose, position, group, line up, align, draw up, marshal, assemble, muster, parade, display, show, exhibit **2** CLOTHE, dress, robe, deck, adorn, decorate, *formal* attire, accoutre, apparel, bedizen, habilitate

arrears *n*
debt(s), liabilities, outstanding payment/amount, sum of money owed, amount owed, liabilities, balance, deficit
▷ **in arrears** owing, outstanding, behind(hand), in debt, overdue, late

arrest *v, n*
▶ *v* **1** *arrest a criminal* capture, catch, seize, apprehend, detain, take into custody, *colloq.* bust, nick, collar, grab, nab, book, run in, pick up, do, nail **2** STOP, stem, check, restrain, inhibit, halt, interrupt, stall, delay, slow (down), retard, block, obstruct, impede, hinder, *colloq.* nip in the bud **3** *arrest your attention* capture, attract, catch, grip, engage, absorb, engross, rivet, fascinate, intrigue
▶ *n* capture, apprehension, detention, taking into custody, seizure
▷ **under arrest** in custody, helping police with their inquiries, in captivity

arresting *adj*
striking, amazing, surprising, stunning, extraordinary, impressive, remarkable, engaging, notable, noteworthy, conspicuous, noticeable, outstanding
F∃ inconspicuous, unremarkable

arrival *n*
1 *the arrival of the president/fresh supplies* appearance, entrance, entry, coming, approach, occurrence, emergence, *formal* advent **2** *welcome new arrivals* newcomer, incomer, visitor, guest, entrant, débutant(e), fresher, *US* freshman, *formal* visitant
F∃ 1 departure

arrive *v*
1 *arrive at the airport* come, reach, get to, get there, get here, be present, reach your destination, appear, put in an appearance, land, touch down, dock, pull in, come in, check in, clock in, materialize, enter, come on the scene, occur, happen, *colloq.* show (up), turn up, make it, drop in, blow in, roll up, surface **2** APPEAR, become available, come on the market, be produced **3** *arrive at a decision* reach, come to **4** *he thinks he's really arrived* succeed, *colloq.* make it, get to the top
F∃ 1 depart, leave

arrogance *n*
pride, conceit, boasting, haughtiness, vanity, superciliousness, disdain, scorn, contempt, superiority, egotism, condescension, lordiness, pomposity, high-handedness, imperiousness, self-importance, snobbishness, presumption, insolence, *formal* hauteur, hubris, contumely, *colloq.* nerve
F∃ humility, unassumingness, bashfulness

arrogant *adj*
proud, conceited, boastful, full of yourself, haughty, supercilious, disdainful, scornful, contemptuous, superior, egotistic, condescending, patronizing, imperious, lordly, overbearing, high-handed, self-important, snobbish, presumptuous, assuming, in-

arrogate

solent, *formal* hubristic, *colloq.* big-headed, stuck-up, high and mighty, uppity, toffee-nosed, hoity-toity

🔁 humble, unassuming, bashful

arrogate *v*
appropriate, seize, usurp, assume, presume, commandeer, misappropriate, possess yourself of

arrogation *n*
appropriation, assumption, commandeering

arrow *n*
1 *shoot with an arrow* shaft, bolt, dart, flight 2 *follow the arrows* marker, indicator, pointer

arsenal *n*
armoury, ordnance depot, ammunition dump, magazine, (arms) depot, repository, stock, stockpile, garderobe

arson *n*
fire-raising, incendiarism, pyromania

arsonist *n*
fire-raiser, fire-bug, incendiary, pyromaniac

art *n*
1 FINE ART, painting, sculpture, drawing, artwork, design, visual arts, craft, artistry, draughtsmanship, craftsmanship 2 *the art of public speaking* SKILL, knack, technique, craft, method, aptitude, facility, talent, flair, gift, dexterity, finesse, ingenuity, mastery, expertise, virtuosity, adroitness, profession, trade 3 ARTFULNESS, cunning, craftiness, slyness, guile, deceit, trickery, astuteness, shrewdness, wiliness

Schools of art include:
abstract, action painting, Aestheticism, Art Deco, Art Nouveau, Barbizon, Baroque, Bohemian, Byzantine, classical revival, classicism, Conceptual Art, Constructivism, Cubism, Dadaism, Etruscan art, Expressionism, Fauvism, Florentine, folk art, Futurism, Gothic, Hellenistic, Impressionism, junk art, Mannerism, medieval art, Minimal Art, Modernism, the Nabis, Naturalism, Neoclassicism, Neoexpressionism, Neoimpressionism, Neo-Plasticism, Op Art, plastic art, Pop Art, Postimpressionism, Post-Modernism, Purism, quattrocento, Realism, renaissance, Rococo, Romanesque, Romanticism, Suprematism, Surrealism, Symbolism, Venetian, Vorticism. *See also* PAINTING; PICTURE; SCULPTURE.

Arts and crafts include:
painting, oil painting, watercolour, fresco, portraiture; architecture, drawing, sketching, caricature, illustration; graphics, film, video; sculpture, modelling, woodcarving, woodcraft, marquetry, metalwork, enamelling, cloisonné, engraving, etching, pottery, ceramics, mosaic, jewellery, stained glass, photography, lithography, calligraphy, collage, origami, spinning, weaving, batik, silk-screen printing, needlework, tapestry, embroidery, patchwork, crochet, knitting. *See also* EMBROIDERY.

artefact *n*
thing, something, object, item, tool, piece of jewellery

artful *adj*
cunning, crafty, sly, foxy, wily, tricky, scheming, designing, deceitful, devious, subtle, sharp, shrewd, smart, clever, masterly, ingenious, resourceful, skilful, dexterous, *formal* vulpine

🔁 artless, naïve, ingenuous

article *n*
1 *articles in a magazine* feature, report, story, account, piece, item, review, commentary, write-up, composition, essay, paper, monograph, offprint 2 ITEM, thing, something, object, commodity, unit, artefact, part, constituent, piece, portion, *colloq.* thingummy, thingummyjig, thingummybob 3 *article 25 of the contract* paragraph, section, clause, point

articulate *adj, v*
▶ *adj* distinct, well-spoken, eloquent, clear, lucid, intelligible, comprehensible, understandable, coherent, fluent, vocal, expressive, meaningful

🔁 inarticulate, incoherent

▶ *v* say, utter, speak, talk, express, voice, vocalize, verbalize, state, pronounce, enunciate, breathe

articulated *adj*
coupled, linked, hinged, interlocked, joined, attached, connected, fastened, fitted together, joint

articulation *n*
saying, utterance, speaking, talking, expression, voicing, vocalization, verbalization, pronunciation, enunciation, diction, delivery

artifice *n*
1 TRICK, device, dodge, ruse, scheme, stratagem, strategy, subterfuge, tactic, wile, contrivance 2 DECEIT, trickery, artfulness, deception, fraud, guile, craft, craftiness, cunning, slyness, subtlety, chicanery, cleverness

artificial *adj*
1 *artificial flowers* SYNTHETIC, imitation, mock, plastic, man-made, manufactured, simulated, nonnatural, processed 2 *an artificial smile* false, fake, bogus, counterfeit, spurious, specious, sham, insincere, assumed, affected, mannered, studied, forced, contrived, made-up, feigned, pretended, simulated, *colloq.* phoney, pseudo, pseud

🔁 1 natural, real 2 genuine

artisan *n*
craftsman, craftswoman, artificer, journeyman, expert, skilled worker, mechanic, technician, operative

artist *n*

Types of artist include:
architect, graphic designer, designer, draughtsman, draughtswoman, illustrator, cartoonist, photographer, printer, engraver, goldsmith, silversmith, blacksmith, carpenter, potter, weaver, sculptor, painter; craftsman, craftswoman, master.

📖 **artist** or **artiste** ?
An *artist* is someone who paints pictures or is skilled in one of the fine arts. An *artiste*, or *artist*, is a performer in a theatre or circus or on television; *artiste* is now regarded as old-fashioned or affected.

artiste *n*
performer, entertainer, variety artist, vaudevillian, comic, comedian, comedienne, player, trouper, actor, actress, dancer, singer

artistic *adj*
1 *an artistic person* CREATIVE, sensitive, refined, cultured, gifted, cultivated, skilled, talented, imaginative 2 *an artistic design* aesthetic, ornamental, decorative, beautiful, attractive, exquisite, elegant, stylish, tasteful, graceful, harmonious

🔁 2 inelegant

artistry *n*
craftsmanship, workmanship, skill, craft, talent, flair,

ability, brilliance, genius, finesse, style, mastery, expertise, proficiency, accomplishment, deftness, touch, sensitivity, creativity

F3 ineptitude

artless *adj*
simple, natural, unpretentious, genuine, guileless, honest, ingenuous, sincere, straightforward, open, plain, pure, childlike, innocent, naïve, direct, frank, candid, true, trusting, unsophisticated, unwary, unworldly

F3 artful, cunning

as *conj & prep*
1 WHILE, when, whilst, at the same time (that/as), simultaneously **2** SUCH AS, for example, for instance, like **3** IN THE SAME MANNER THAT, in the same way that, like **4** BECAUSE, since, seeing that, considering that, inasmuch as, being, the reason is ..., through, on account of, as a result of, owing to

▷ **as for** with reference to, as regards, with regard to, on the subject of, in connection with, in relation to, with relation to, with respect to

▷ **as it were** so to speak, in a manner of speaking, in a way, in some way, so to say, as it might be

ascend *v*
rise, take off, lift off, go up, move up, gain height, slope upwards, climb, scale, mount, tower, float up, fly up, soar, arise

F3 descend, go down

ascendancy *n*
dominance, domination, authority, command, control, power, dominion, superiority, lordship, mastery, supremacy, edge, predominance, pre-eminence, influence, prevalence, sway, *formal* hegemony, *colloq.* upper hand

F3 decline, subordination

ascent *n*
1 ASCENDING, ascension, climb, climbing, scaling, escalation, rise, rising, mounting **2** SLOPE, gradient, incline, ramp, hill, elevation, *formal* acclivity **3** *their rapid ascent to power* rise, advance, progress, *formal* advancement

F3 1 descent

ascertain *v*
find out, learn, discover, get to know, determine, fix, establish, settle, locate, detect, identify, verify, confirm, make certain, *colloq.* suss out, pin down

ascetic *adj, n*
▶ *adj* self-denying, self-disciplined, austere, abstemious, abstinent, self-controlled, stern, strict, severe, rigorous, harsh, plain, puritanical, Spartan
▶ *n* hermit, recluse, solitary, anchorite, abstainer, celibate, monk, nun, puritan, fakir, dervish, yogi

ascribe *v*
attribute, credit, give credit to, put down, assign, charge, *formal* accredit, impute

ashamed *adj*
1 *ashamed of your behaviour* sorry, apologetic, remorseful, contrite, guilty, conscience-stricken, sheepish, embarrassed, blushing, red-faced, mortified, humiliated, discomfited, abashed, humbled, crestfallen, distressed, discomposed, confused, *colloq.* not able to look someone in the face, having your tail between your legs **2** *ashamed to admit his mistakes* reluctant, hesitant, unwilling, self-conscious, bashful, modest

F3 1 shameless, proud, defiant **2** proud

ashen *adj*
pallid, pale, pasty, wan, white, anaemic, blanched, bleached, colourless, ghastly, grey, leaden, livid

F3 ruddy

aside *adv, n*
▶ *adv* **1** *move aside* to one side, on one side, along-

side, apart, away, out of the way, separately, in isolation, alone, privately, secretly **2** *his money aside* apart, notwithstanding

▶ *n* digression, parenthesis, departure, soliloquy, monologue, stage whisper, whisper

asinine *adj*
silly, stupid, foolish, senseless, nonsensical, idiotic, moronic, imbecilic, absurd, half-witted, fatuous, inane, *colloq.* daft, potty, gormless

F3 intelligent, sensible

ask *v*
1 *ask a question* inquire, query, question, put a question to, pose, put forward, want to know the answer to, interrogate, propose, suggest, cross-examine, cross-question, poll, canvass, interview, press, *formal* posit, postulate, propound, *colloq.* grill, give a grilling to, pump, quiz, put on the spot **2** *ask for advice* REQUEST, appeal, petition, sue, plead, beg, entreat, implore, clamour, beseech, pray, supplicate, crave, demand, order, bid, require, seek, approach, solicit, invite, summon, requisition **3** *ask them to dinner* invite, have round/over, entertain,

askance *adv*
suspiciously, disapprovingly, contemptuously, scornfully, disdainfully, distrustfully, doubtfully, dubiously, mistrustfully, sceptically, indirectly, sideways, obliquely

askew *adv & adj*
crooked, lopsided, sideways, oblique, at an oblique angle, off-centre, out of line, asymmetric, crookedly, *colloq.* skew, skew-whiff

F3 straight, level

asleep *adj*
sleeping, napping, snoozing, fast asleep, sound asleep, resting, inactive, inert, unconscious, numb, dozing, *formal* dormant, reposing, *colloq.* flaked out, comatose, dead to the world, out like a light, having forty winks

aspect *n*
1 *many aspects of life* angle, direction, side, facet, feature, point, factor, dimension, position, standpoint, point of view, view, outlook, light **2** *take on a more promising aspect* appearance, look, air, manner, bearing, face, expression, countenance, **3** *a house with a northern aspect* direction, position, standpoint, point of view, view, outlook

asperity *n*
sharpness, acerbity, harshness, roughness, severity, acrimony, astringency, bitterness, churlishness, crabbedness, crossness, irascibility, irritability, peevishness, sourness, *formal* causticity

F3 mildness

aspersion *n*
▷ **cast aspersions on** make critical comments about, criticize, censure, defame, disparage, reproach, slander, *formal* denigrate, deprecate, vilify, *colloq.* throw/sling mud at, slur, smear

F3 commend, compliment

asphyxiate *v*
suffocate, choke, smother, stifle, strangle, strangulate, throttle

aspiration *n*
aim, intent, purpose, endeavour, object, objective, goal, ambition, hope, dream, ideal, wish, desire, yearning, longing, craving, hankering

aspire *v*
aim, intend, purpose, seek, pursue, hope, dream, wish, have as an ambition/aim/goal, desire, yearn, long, crave, hanker

aspiring *adj*
would-be, aspirant, striving, endeavouring, ambi-

tious, enterprising, budding, keen, eager, hopeful, optimistic, wishful, longing

ass *n*
1 *ride an ass* donkey, mule, burro, hinny, jackass, pony, *colloq.* moke **2** *call someone an ass* fool, idiot, imbecile, *colloq.* blockhead, nincompoop, ninny, nitwit, numskull, twerp, twit, dimwit, *slang* wally, dipstick, nerd

assail *v*
1 *assailed by the newspapers/foreign army* attack, criticize, lay into, set about, set upon, malign, maltreat, strike, invade, bombard, *colloq.* tear into **2** *assailed by doubts* beset, plague, worry, trouble, torment, bedevil, perplex

assailant *n*
attacker, invader, opponent, adversary, enemy, mugger, aggressor, assailer, assaulter, abuser, reviler

assassin *n*
murderer, killer, slayer, cut-throat, executioner, gunman, *colloq.* hatchet man, liquidator, contract man, hit-man

assassinate *v*
murder, kill, slay, dispatch, take someone's life, *colloq.* eliminate, liquidate, hit, bump off, do in

assault *n, v*
▶ *n* **1** ATTACK, offensive, onslaught, blitz, strike, raid, invasion, incursion, storm, storming, charge, act of aggression **2** *charged with assault* battery, violent act, grievous bodily harm, rape, abuse, molestation, *colloq.* GBH, mugging
▶ *v* attack, charge, invade, strike, hit, set upon, fall on, rape, molest, interfere with, abuse, bombard, *colloq.* go for, lay into, beat up, do over, mug

assemblage *n*
accumulation, collection, gathering, group, mass, multitude, rally, crowd, flock, throng

assemble *v*
1 GATHER, congregate, muster, summons, rally, convene, meet, join up, flock, group, collect, accumulate, amass, bring/come together, get together, round up, marshal, mobilize, mass **2** CONSTRUCT, build, put together, piece together, fit together, compose, make, connect, join, fabricate, manufacture, set up, collate
🔁 **1** scatter, disperse **2** dismantle

assembly *n*
1 GATHERING, rally, meeting, convention, conference, congress, council, group, body, body of people, company, congregation, flock, crowd, multitude, throng, collection, assemblage, *technical* agora, synod, gemot, gorsedd, indaba, kgotla, *formal* convocation, panegyry **2** CONSTRUCTION, building, fabrication, manufacture, putting together

assent *v, n*
▶ *v* agree, approve, accept, allow, consent, grant, permit, sanction, submit, subscribe, yield, *formal* accede, acquiesce, comply, concede, concur
🔁 disagree
▶ *n* agreement, approval, acceptance, capitulation, concession, consent, permission, sanction, submission, *formal* accord, acquiescence, compliance, concurrence, approbation

assert *v*
1 *assert a fact* DECLARE, state, pronounce, profess, affirm, confirm, attest, argue, swear, testify to **2** *assert your rights* maintain, insist on, establish, stress, protest, defend, vindicate, uphold, claim, stand up for, contend
🔁 **1** deny, refute
▷ **assert yourself** behave confidently, make your presence felt, make people sit up and take notice, make people sit up and listen

assertion *n*
affirmation, attestation, word, allegation, claim, contention, insistence, vindication, declaration, profession, statement, pronouncement, *formal* avowal, predication
🔁 denial

assertive *adj*
bold, confident, self-confident, self-assured, sure of yourself, positive, forward, insistent, emphatic, forceful, firm, decided, strong-willed, dogmatic, opinionated, presumptuous, assuming, overbearing, domineering, dominant, aggressive, *colloq.* pushy, not backward in coming forward
🔁 timid, diffident

assess *v*
1 *assess a situation* evaluate, gauge, estimate, appraise, review, judge, consider, weigh, size up, *colloq.* check out **2** *assess the value of something* compute, calculate, determine, estimate, fix, value, rate, tax, levy, impose, demand

assessment *n*
1 *the assessment of a situation* evaluation, estimation, appraisal, review, testing, judgement, consideration, opinion, *colloq.* recce **2** *a tax assessment* levy, computation, valuation, rate, toll, tariff, imposition, demand

asset *n*
1 *an asset to the school* strength, strong point, resource, virtue, benefit, advantage, blessing, boon, help, aid, liability, *colloq.* plus, plus point **2** *the assets of a company* estate, property, possessions, goods, holdings, securities, money, wealth, capital, funds, reserves, savings, valuables, resources, means

assiduous *adj*
industrious, diligent, hard-working, conscientious, constant, dedicated, devoted, attentive, persevering, persistent, steady, studious, unflagging, indefatigable, untiring, *formal* sedulous
🔁 negligent

assign *v*
1 ALLOCATE, apportion, grant, give, dispense, distribute, allot, consign, delegate, name, nominate, designate, appoint, choose, select, detail, commission, install, determine, set, fix, specify, stipulate **2** ATTRIBUTE, ascribe, put down, *formal* accredit, impute, *colloq.* chalk up to

assignation *n*
secret meeting, appointment, arrangement, date, engagement, rendezvous

assignment *n*
1 *written assignments* task, project, job, position, post, duty, responsibility, obligation, commission, errand, charge **2** *his assignment to the job* appointment, delegation, designation, nomination, selection, allocation, consignment, grant, distribution

assimilate *v*
1 *assimilate new ideas* ABSORB, take in, pick up, incorporate, learn **2** INTEGRATE, absorb, blend, mix, mingle, unite, accustom, adapt, adjust, acclimatize, accommodate
🔁 **1, 2** reject

assist *v*
1 *assist with someone's work/expenses* HELP, aid, give/lend a hand, abet, rally round, co-operate, collaborate, back (up), second, support, reinforce, sustain, relieve, *formal* succour, *colloq.* do your bit, give a leg up to **2** *assist in the operation of a task* facilitate, make easier, expedite, benefit, encourage, serve, enable, further, advance
🔁 **1** hinder **2** thwart

assistance *n*
help, aid, co-operation, collaboration, backing, support,

reinforcement, relief, benefit, service, boost, further-ance, *colloq.* a helping hand, a leg up, *formal* succour
🔁 hindrance, resistance

assistant *n*
1 DEPUTY, subordinate, right-hand man, auxiliary, an-cillary, backer, second, second-in-command, sup-porter, driving force 2 *a personal assistant* helper, aide, accomplice, accessory, abettor, collaborator, colleague, partner, ally, confederate, associate 3 *a shop assistant* salesperson, salesman, saleswoman, checkout person, *US* sales clerk

associate *v, n*
▶ *v* 1 CONNECT, link, think of together, couple, correl-ate, pair, identify, *colloq.* speak of in the same breath, go hand in hand 2 *associate with bad company* socialize, mingle, mix, keep company, fraternize, be involved, *formal* consort, *colloq.* hang around/out, hobnob, rub shoulders 3 AFFILIATE, confederate, ally, league, join, amalgamate, combine, unite, link, connect, relate, couple, attach, band together, syndicate, yoke
▶ *n* partner, ally, confederate, affiliate, collaborator, co-worker, mate, colleague, peer, compeer, fellow, comrade, companion, friend, assistant, helper, fol-lower, *colloq.* sidekick

association *n*
1 ORGANIZATION, corporation, company, partner-ship, league, alliance, coalition, confederation, con-federacy, federation, affiliation, consortium, cartel, syndicate, union, society, club, fraternity, fellowship, guild, clique, group, band, *formal* sodality 2 BOND, tie, connection, link, correlation, relation, relation-ship, involvement, intimacy, friendship, companion-ship, familiarity

assorted *adj*
miscellaneous, mixed, varied, different, differing, di-verse, sundry, motley, various, several, manifold, *formal* variegated, heterogeneous, multifarious

assortment *n*
miscellany, medley, potpourri, jumble, mix, mixture, variety, diversity, collection, selection, choice, ar-rangement, group(ing), lot, bunch, *technical* salma-gundi, olla-podrida

assuage *v*
1 *assuage grief/pain* relieve, ease, lessen, reduce, soften, allay, alleviate, calm, lighten, lower, lull, mitig-ate, moderate, soothe, mollify, pacify, palliate 2 *as-suage your thirst* alleviate, quench, satisfy, appease, *formal* slake
🔁 1 exacerbate, worsen

assume *v*
1 PRESUME, surmise, accept, take for granted, take as read, expect, understand, deduce, infer, guess, sup-pose, presuppose, think, believe, imagine, fancy, *for-mal* postulate, *colloq.* take it ..., take someone's word for it 2 AFFECT, take on, feign, counterfeit, simulate, put on, pretend 3 *assume great importance* take on, adopt, come to have 4 *assume command* undertake, adopt, enter upon, take upon yourself, embrace, seize, arrogate, commandeer, appropriate, usurp, pre-empt, take over

assumed *adj*
false, bogus, counterfeit, fake, sham, affected, feigned, simulated, pretended, made-up, fictitious, hypothetical, *formal* supposititious, putative, pseud-onymous, *colloq.* phoney
🔁 true, real, actual

assumption *n*
1 *make an assumption* presumption, surmise, infer-ence, supposition, presupposition, guess, conjecture, theory, hypothesis, premise, postulate, idea, notion, belief, expectation, fancy, *formal* postulation 2 *her*

assumption of power undertaking, adoption, taking upon yourself, embarkation, embrace, seizure, com-mandeering, takeover, *formal* arrogation, appropria-tion, usurpation, pre-emption

assurance *n*
1 GUARANTEE, pledge, promise, security, vow, de-claration, affirmation, assertion, word, undertaking, oath 2 CONFIDENCE, self-confidence, assuredness, self-assurance, aplomb, boldness, self-reliance, belief in yourself, audacity, courage, nerve, convic-tion, sureness, certainty
🔁 2 shyness, doubt, uncertainty

assure *v*
1 *assured me he would be safe* convince, persuade, encourage, hearten, reassure, soothe, comfort, 2 *success is assured* guarantee, warrant, pledge, prom-ise, seal, secure, ensure, confirm, affirm, vow, swear, certify, attest

assured *adj*
1 SURE, certain, indisputable, irrefutable, confirmed, promised, positive, definite, settled, fixed, ensured, guaranteed, secure, *colloq.* cut and dried 2 SELF-ASSURED, confident, self-confident, self-possessed, sure of yourself, bold, audacious, assertive
🔁 1 uncertain 2 shy, bashful

astonish *v*
surprise, startle, amaze, astound, stun, stupefy, daze, stagger, dumbfound, take aback, take your breath away, shock, confound, bewilder, *colloq.* floor, flab-bergast, wow

astonished *adj*
surprised, startled, amazed, astounded, stunned, dazed, staggered, dumbfounded, taken aback, shocked, confounded, bewildered, *colloq.* knocked for six, bowled over, flabbergasted

astonishing *adj*
surprising, startling, amazing, astounding, stunning, breathtaking, impressive, striking, startling, stagger-ing, shocking, bewildering, *colloq.* mind-boggling

astonishment *n*
surprise, amazement, shock, disbelief, dismay, con-sternation, confusion, bewilderment, wonder, *for-mal* stupefaction

astound *v*
surprise, startle, amaze, astonish, stun, take your breath away, stupefy, overwhelm, shock, bewilder, *colloq.* knock for six, bowl over

astounding *adj*
surprising, startling, amazing, astonishing, stunning, breathtaking, stupefying, overwhelming, staggering, shocking, bewildering

astray *adv*
adrift, off course, lost, missing, amiss, wrong, awry, off the mark, *colloq.* off the rails

astringent *adj*
1 *an astringent liquid* acerbic, acid, caustic, *tech-nical* styptic 2 *astringent criticism* caustic, biting, trenchant, scathing, hard, harsh, severe, stern, *formal* mordant
🔁 1, 2 bland

astronaut *n*
spaceman, spacewoman, space traveller, cosmonaut

astute *adj*
shrewd, prudent, sagacious, wise, canny, knowing, in-telligent, sharp, penetrating, keen, perceptive, dis-cerning, subtle, clever, crafty, cunning, sly, wily, *formal* perspicacious, sagacious
🔁 stupid, slow

asylum *n*
1 *seek political asylum* haven, sanctuary, refuge, shel-

ter, retreat, place of safety, *colloq.* port in a storm **2** *an asylum for the mentally ill* mental hospital, psychiatric hospital, institution, *colloq.* funny farm, loony bin, madhouse, nuthouse

asymmetrical *adj*
unsymmetrical, unbalanced, uneven, lopsided, crooked, awry, unequal, disproportionate, irregular, distorted, malformed
F₃ symmetrical

asymmetry *n*
imbalance, unevenness, crookedness, lopsidedness, inequality, disproportionateness, irregularity, distortion, malformation
F₃ symmetry

atheism *n*
unbelief, non-belief, disbelief, scepticism, irreligion, ungodliness, godlessness, impiety, infidelity, paganism, heathenism, freethinking, rationalism, *technical* nihilism

atheist *n*
unbeliever, non-believer, humanist, rationalist, disbeliever, sceptic, infidel, heretic, pagan, heathen, freethinker, *technical* nihilist, *formal* nullifidian

athlete *n*
sportsman, sportswoman, runner, gymnast, competitor, contestant, contender, player

athletic *adj*
1 *an athletic person* fit, energetic, vigorous, active, sporty, muscular, sinewy, brawny, strapping, robust, sturdy, strong, powerful, well-knit, well-proportioned, wiry **2** *athletic events* sports, gymnastic, games
F₃ 1 puny

athletics *n*
sports, games, matches, races, track events, field events, exercises, gymnastics, *technical* aerobics, callisthenics

atmosphere *n*
1 AIR, sky, aerospace, heavens, ether **2** AMBIENCE, environment, surroundings, setting, milieu, background, air, aura, feel, feeling, mood, climate, spirit, tone, tenor, character, quality, flavour

The different layers of the atmosphere are:
troposphere, stratosphere, mesosphere, thermosphere, ionosphere, exosphere.

atom *n*
molecule, particle, bit, morsel, crumb, fragment, grain, spot, speck, mite, shred, scrap, hint, trace, scintilla, jot, iota, whit

Subatomic particles include:
photon, electron, positron, neutrino, anti-neutrino, muon, pion, kaon, proton, anti-proton, neutron, anti-neutron, lambda particle, sigma particle, omega particle, psi particle.

atone *v*
make amends, pay for, remedy, indemnify, reconcile, repent, compensate, recompense, make up for, make right, make good, offset, redeem, redress, appease, propitiate, expiate

atonement *n*
amends, reparation, repayment, reimbursement, requital, restitution, restoration, satisfaction, compensation, indemnity, payment, penance, recompense, redress, appeasement, propitiation, expiation, *colloq.* eye for an eye

atrocious *adj*
atrocious behaviour/weather shocking, appalling,

abominable, dreadful, terrible, horrible, horrendous, hideous, ghastly, grievous, savage, vicious, monstrous, fiendish, wicked, brutal, cruel, ruthless, merciless, *formal* heinous, nefarious, flagitious
F₃ admirable, fine

atrocity *n*
outrage, abomination, enormity, horror, monstrosity, savagery, barbarity, brutality, cruelty, viciousness, evil, villainy, wickedness, violation, vileness, hideousness, atrociousness, *formal* heinousness, flagitiousness

atrophy *n, v*
▸ *n* withering, shrivelling, wasting (away), emaciation, decay, decline, degeneration, deterioration, diminution, *technical* marasmus, tabefaction
▸ *v* wither, shrivel, waste (away), emaciate, decay, decline, degenerate, deteriorate, diminish, dwindle, fade, shrink, *technical* tabefy

attach *v*
1 *attach a label* affix, stick, adhere, fasten, fix, secure, tie, bind, pin, nail, weld, join, unite, connect, link, couple, add, annex, make secure **2** *attach yourself to a group* join, affiliate with, associate with, combine with, ally, unite, *colloq.* latch on to **3** ASCRIBE, attribute, assign, put, place, associate, relate to, belong, *formal* impute **4** *a centre attached to the university* link, affiliate, associate, connect, assign, second
F₃ 1 detach, unfasten

attached *adj*
1 *very attached to her family* affectionate, fond, loving, tender, liking, friendly, devoted **2** *Is she attached?* married, engaged, spoken for, in a relationship, involved with someone, *colloq.* going steady
F₃ 1 unloving **2** single, unattached, on your own

attachment *n*
1 ACCESSORY, fitting, fixture, extension, extra, supplement, supplementary part, addition, adjunct, codicil, *formal* appendage, appurtenance, accoutrement **2** FONDNESS, affection, tenderness, love, liking, partiality, loyalty, devotion, friendship, affinity, attraction, bond, tie, link

attack *v, n*
▸ *v* **1** *attack a country/person* raid, strike, storm, rush, charge, assail, assault, besiege, set about, set upon, fall on, lay into, go for, pounce on, ambush, *colloq.* beat up, do over, mug, make a dead set at, jump, leave for dead, *slang* knock into the middle of next week, have your guts for garters, take to the cleaners **2** CRITICIZE, find fault with, censure, blame, denounce, revile, malign, abuse, reprove, rebuke, *formal* berate, impugn, revile, fulminate against, vilify, calumniate, decry, *colloq.* slate, slam, knock, pan, tear/pull to pieces, tear to shreds, pick holes in, have a go at, run down, bitch about, slag off **3** *the disease attacks the nerves* destroy, affect, infect **4** *attack a task* tackle, deal with, begin, start, get started on, commence, set about, embark on, undertake
F₃ 1 defend, protect
▸ *n* **1** OFFENSIVE, blitz, bombardment, invasion, incursion, foray, raid, strike, charge, storming, rush, onslaught, assault, sortie, push, sally, act of aggression, battery, *formal* irruption **2** *an attack on his reputation* criticism, censure, abuse, *formal* invective, impugnment, revilement, vilification, *colloq.* slating, slamming, knocking, flak **3** SEIZURE, fit, convulsion, bout, paroxysm, spasm, stroke, *formal* access

attacker *n*
assailant, aggressor, invader, raider, critic, detractor, reviler, abuser, persecutor, *colloq.* mugger
F₃ defender, supporter

attain v
accomplish, achieve, fulfil, complete, effect, realize, earn, reach, touch, arrive at, hit, grasp, find, get, acquire, obtain, procure, secure, gain, win, net

attainable adj
achievable, feasible, viable, manageable, obtainable, possible, potential, practicable, probable, reachable, realistic, within reach, at hand, accessible, imaginable, conceivable, colloq. doable
F₃ unattainable

attainment n
1 artistic attainments ACCOMPLISHMENT, achievement, feat, success, ability, capability, competence, proficiency, skill, art, talent, gift, aptitude, facility **2** the attainment of his ambitions fulfilment, completion, consummation, realization, accomplishment, mastery, formal procurement, acquirement

attempt v, n
▶ v try, have a try, endeavour, aspire, set out, seek, strive, undertake, tackle, venture, aim, experiment, see if you can do, try your hand, colloq. have a go/shot/crack/stab, give it a go/try/whirl, try your hand at, do your level best
▶ n try, endeavour, go, push, effort, struggle, bid, undertaking, venture, trial, experiment, colloq. shot, stab, bash, crack

attend v
1 attend a meeting be present, be here, be there, go/come along, appear, put in/make an appearance, go to, frequent, visit, colloq. turn up, show (up) **2** PAY ATTENTION, concentrate, listen, hear, heed, mind, mark, watch, note, notice, take note/notice, follow, observe **3** ESCORT, chaperone, accompany, usher, follow, guard **4** attend the sick look after, take care of, care for, nurse, tend, minister to, help, serve, wait upon
▷ **attend to** deal with, see to, take care of, look after, manage, handle, process, direct, control, oversee, supervise, follow up (on), heed

attendance n
presence, appearance, audience, house, crowd, gate, colloq. turnout, showing (up)

attendant n, adj
▶ n assistant, aide, helper, auxiliary, steward, waiter, servant, page, retainer, guide, marshal, usher, escort, companion, follower, guard, custodian
▶ adj accompanying, attached, associated, related, incidental, resultant, consequent, subsequent, formal concomitant

attention n
▶ **1** let your attention wander alertness, vigilance, concentration, heed, notice, observation, regard, mind, mindfulness, awareness, recognition, thought, focus of your thoughts, contemplation, consideration, preoccupation, formal advertence, advertency **2** attract great public attention notice, observation, regard, awareness, recognition, thought, contemplation, consideration, heed concern, colloq. limelight, high profile **3** receive medical attention care, treatment, therapy, help, service **4** flattered by his attentions respect, courtesy, politeness, compliments, gallantry
F₃ **1** inattention, disregard, daydreaming **2** inattention, disregard **3** carelessness
▷ **pay attention to** concentrate on, focus your mind/thoughts on, focus on, devote your attention to, take notice, listen/watch carefully

attentive adj
1 ALERT, awake, vigilant, aware, watchful, watching, observant, noticing, concentrating, heedful, mindful, careful, conscientious, on the qui vive, listening, formal advertent, colloq. all ears **2** CONSIDERATE, thoughtful, kind, obliging, accommodating, civil, polite, courteous, devoted, gracious, conscientious, chivalrous, gallant
F₃ **1** inattentive, heedless **2** inconsiderate

attest v
prove, confirm, corroborate, demonstrate, show, display, manifest, endorse, certify, affirm, assert, certify, declare, demonstrate, vouch for, bear witness to, verify, formal adjure, aver, asseverate, evince, evidence

attire n
dress, clothes, clothing, wear, garments, outfit, garb, costume, finery, formal habit, accoutrements, apparel, habiliments, colloq. gear, togs, rig-out

attired adj
clothed, dressed, arrayed, adorned, turned out, formal habilitated, colloq. decked out, rigged out

attitude n
1 OPINION, feeling, disposition, mood, aspect, manner, position, point of view, view, outlook, perspective, approach, way of thinking, mentality, mindset, world-view, Weltanschauung **2** POSTURE, bearing, pose, stance, stand, formal deportment, carriage

attract v
pull, draw, lure, allure, entice, seduce, tempt, invite, induce, incline, appeal to, bring in, pull in, magnetize, interest, engage, fascinate, enchant, charm, bewitch, captivate, excite
F₃ repel, disgust

attraction n
1 the attraction of an exotic lifestyle pull, draw, magnetism, lure, allure, bait, enticement, inducement, seduction, temptation, invitation, appeal, affinity, interest, fascination, enchantment, charm, captivation **2** tourist attractions sight, feature, building, activity, entertainment
F₃ **1** repulsion

attractive adj
1 an attractive person pretty, fair, fetching, handsome, good-looking, beautiful, gorgeous, striking, stunning, glamorous, elegant, lovely, pleasant, charismatic, picturesque, pleasing, cute, engaging, prepossessing, winsome, desirable, sexy, Scot. bonny **2** an attractive suggestion agreeable, appealing, winsome, winning, enticing, seductive, tempting, inviting, interesting, engaging, fascinating, charming, captivating, irresistible, magnetic

attribute v, n
▶ v ascribe, credit, assign, put down, blame, charge, refer, apply, formal accredit, impute
▶ n property, quality, virtue, point, aspect, facet, feature, trait, characteristic, idiosyncrasy, peculiarity, quirk, note, mark, side, streak, sign, indicator, symbol

attrition n
1 FRICTION, abrasion, rubbing, scraping, chafing, erosion, formal detrition **2** a war of attrition wearing away, wearing down, grinding, harassment, formal attenuation

attuned adj
acclimatized, assimilated, accustomed, familiarized, adapted, adjusted, regulated, co-ordinated, harmonized, set, tuned

atypical adj
uncharacteristic, unusual, exceptional, untypical, aberrant, abnormal, anomalous, deviant, divergent, eccentric, extraordinary, freakish
F₃ typical

auburn adj
reddish-brown, chestnut, tawny, russet, copper, rust, henna, Titian

audacious *adj*
adventurous, daring, enterprising, courageous, rash, reckless, risky, assuming, assured, unabashed, bold, brave, fearless, intrepid, dauntless, valiant, plucky, disrespectful, impertinent, forward, presumptuous, impudent, insolent, cheeky, pert, brazen, rude, shameless, *formal* venturesome
🔄 cautious, reserved, timid

audacity *n*
adventurousness, daring, enterprise, courage, rashness, recklessness, risk, boldness, bravery, fearlessness, intrepidity, dauntlessness, valour, pluck, disrespectfulness, impertinence, forwardness, presumption, impudence, insolence, cheek, pertness, brazenness, effrontery, defiance, rudeness, shamelessness
🔄 caution, reserve, timidity

audible *adj*
clear, distinct, recognizable, perceptible, discernible, detectable, appreciable, hearable, heard
🔄 inaudible, silent, unclear

audience *n*
1 *members of the audience* spectators, onlookers, house, auditorium, listeners, viewers, crowd, turnout, gathering, assembly, congregation, fans, devotees, regulars, following, public, ratings **2** MEETING, interview, hearing, consultation, reception, conference

audit *n, v*
▶ *n* examination, inspection, check, verification, investigation, scrutiny, analysis, review, statement, balancing
▶ *v* examine, inspect, check, verify, investigate, scrutinize, analyse, review, go over, go through, work through, balance

augment *v*
add to, amplify, boost, enlarge, build up, put on, expand, extend, grow, increase, make greater, magnify, multiply, raise, inflate, enhance, heighten, intensify, reinforce, strengthen, swell
🔄 decrease

augur *v*
herald, prophesy, foretell, predict, promise, be a sign of, signify, *formal* forebode, betoken, harbinger, bode, presage, portend

augury *n*
omen, herald, prophecy, prediction, foreboding, prognostication, forerunner, forewarning, harbinger, token, warning, portent, promise, sign, *formal* haruspication, prodrome

august *adj*
dignified, exalted, solemn, noble, impressive, imposing, glorious, grand, lofty, magnificent, majestic, stately, awe-inspiring

aura *n*
air, ambience, atmosphere, mood, quality, emanation, feel, feeling, hint, suggestion, vibrations, *formal* nimbus, *colloq.* vibes

auspices *n*
▷ **under the auspices of** under the aegis of, under the authority of, with the patronage/sponsorship of, with the backing/support/approval of, under the supervision/control/influence/guidance of, in the charge/care of

auspicious *adj*
favourable, encouraging, cheerful, bright, rosy, promising, hopeful, optimistic, fortunate, lucky, opportune, timely, happy, prosperous, *formal* propitious, felicitous
🔄 unfavourable, inauspicious, ominous

austere *adj*
1 STARK, bleak, plain, simple, basic, unadorned, unornamented, grim, forbidding, sombre **2** SEVERE, stern, strict, cold, formal, distant, rigid, rigorous, stringent, exacting, hard, harsh, spartan, grave, serious, solemn, sober, abstemious, unfeeling, unbending, inflexible, self-denying, restrained, economical, frugal, ascetic, self-disciplined, puritanical, chaste, *formal* self-abnegating
🔄 **1** ornate, elaborate **2** genial

austerity *n*
plainness, simplicity, severity, coldness, formality, hardness, harshness, solemnity, abstemiousness, abstinence, economy, asceticism, self-denial, self-discipline, inflexibility, puritanism
🔄 elaborateness, extravagance, materialism

authentic *adj*
1 *an authentic signature* genuine, real, actual, certain, bona fide, lawful, legal, legitimate, valid, *colloq.* the real thing, the genuine article, the real McCoy **2** *an authentic description* accurate, factual, true, true-to-life, correct, faithful, reliable, dependable, trustworthy, honest, credible, *colloq.* kosher
🔄 **1** false, fake, counterfeit, spurious **2** inaccurate, unfaithful

authenticate *v*
verify, validate, certify, endorse, confirm, ratify, corroborate, guarantee, warrant, vouch for, attest, authorize, prove, substantiate, *formal* accredit

authenticity *n*
genuineness, certainty, authoritativeness, validity, truth, veracity, truthfulness, honesty, accuracy, correctness, faithfulness, fidelity, reliability, dependability, credibility, trustworthiness, legality, legitimacy
🔄 spuriousness, invalidity

author *n*
1 WRITER, novelist, biographer, dramatist, playwright, poet, essayist, composer, contributor, screenwriter, librettist, lyricist, songwriter, reporter, journalist, pen, penman, penwoman **2** CREATOR, founder, originator, initiator, parent, prime mover, mover, inventor, designer, architect, planner, maker, producer

authoritarian *adj*
strict, disciplinarian, severe, harsh, rigid, tough, inflexible, unyielding, dogmatic, doctrinaire, absolute, autocratic, dictatorial, totalitarian, despotic, tyrannical, oppressive, domineering, imperious
🔄 liberal

---

authoritarian or **authoritative** ?

You describe a person or government as *authoritarian* if they try to control people instead of letting them have the freedom to make their own decisions. An *authoritative* account of something is one that is reliable; an *authoritative* person is one who inspires attention and obedience from others.

---

authoritative *adj*
1 *an authoritative person* self-confident, confident, self-assured, self-possessed, sure of yourself, bold, audacious, assertive, imposing, masterful **2** *an authoritative study* scholarly, learned, official, authorized, legitimate, valid, approved, sanctioned, accepted, definitive, decisive, authentic, factual, true, truthful, accurate, faithful, convincing, sound, reliable, dependable, trustworthy
🔄 **2** unofficial, unreliable

authority *n*
1 GOVERNMENT, administration, establishment, management, officialdom, state, council, bureaucracy, *colloq.* they, the powers that be **2** SOVEREIGNTY, supremacy, rule, sway, control, dominion,

influence, command, power, force, jurisdiction, *colloq.* clout, muscle **3** AUTHORIZATION, permission, sanction, permit, warrant, licence, credentials, right, power, prerogative, carte blanche **4** *an authority on antiques* expert, pundit, connoisseur, specialist, professional, master, scholar, sage, *colloq.* buff

authorization *n*
authority, permission, consent, sanction, approval, mandate, validation, ratification, confirmation, licence, entitlement, empowering, commission, warranty, permit, leave, credentials, *formal* accreditation, *colloq.* OK, okay, go-ahead, green light

authorize *v*
legalize, make legal, validate, ratify, confirm, license, entitle, empower, give authority to, enable, commission, warrant, permit, give permission, allow, let, consent to, sanction, approve, *formal* accredit, *colloq.* OK, okay, give the go-ahead, give the green light

autobiography *n*
memoirs, life story, story of your life, diary, journal

autocracy *n*
absolutism, totalitarianism, dictatorship, despotism, tyranny, authoritarianism, fascism
🔁 democracy

autocrat *n*
absolutist, totalitarian, dictator, despot, tyrant, authoritarian, fascist, *colloq.* (little) Hitler

autocratic *adj*
absolute, all-powerful, totalitarian, despotic, tyrannical, authoritarian, dictatorial, domineering, overbearing, imperious
🔁 democratic, liberal

autograph *n, v*
▶ *n* signature, name, initials, countersignature, inscription, endorsement, mark
▶ *v* sign, write your name, initial, countersign, endorse, put your mark

automatic *adj*
1 AUTOMATED, self-activating, mechanical, mechanized, programmed, self-regulating, computerized, push-button, robotic, self-propelling, unmanned **2** SPONTANEOUS, reflex, involuntary, mechanical, unwilled, unconscious, unthinking, natural, instinctive, routine, necessary, certain, inevitable, unavoidable, inescapable, uncontrollable, *colloq.* knee-jerk

autonomy *n*
self-government, self-rule, home rule, sovereignty, independence, self-determination, self-sufficiency, autarky, freedom, free will
🔁 subjection, compulsion

auxiliary *n, adj*
▶ *n* ancillary, subordinate, helper, partner, supporter, right-hand man, backer, second, second-in-command
▶ *adj* ancillary, assistant, subsidiary, accessory, secondary, supporting, supportive, helping, assisting, aiding, extra, supplementary, spare, reserve, backup, emergency, substitute

available *adj*
free, vacant, unoccupied, untaken, to hand, within reach, at hand, accessible, handy, convenient, on hand, at your disposal, disposable, ready, obtainable, usable, forthcoming, *formal* procurable, *colloq.* on tap, up your sleeve, up for grabs, yours for the asking/taking
🔁 unavailable, taken

avalanche *n*
landslide, landslip, cascade, torrent, deluge, flood, inundation, wave, barrage

avant-garde *adj*
innovative, innovatory, pioneering, experimental, un-

conventional, original, progressive, advanced, forward-looking, futuristic, enterprising, inventive, modern, contemporary, *colloq.* go-ahead, *slang* far-out, way-out
🔁 conservative

avarice *n*
covetousness, acquisitiveness, greed, greediness, meanness, miserliness, selfishness, materialism
🔁 generosity, liberality

avaricious *adj*
covetous, grasping, acquisitive, greedy, mercenary, mean, miserly, *formal* rapacious, pleonectic
🔁 generous, liberal

avenge *v*
take revenge for, take vengeance for, punish, requite, repay, pay back, retaliate, *colloq.* get even with, get back at, get your own back

average *n, adj*
▶ *n* mean, mid-point, median, norm, mode, standard, centre, rule, par, medium, mode, run
🔁 extreme, exception
▶ *adj* **1** *the average age* mean, medial, median, middle, intermediate, medium **2** *the average reader* ordinary, everyday, common, usual, normal, regular, standard, typical, routine, unexceptional **3** *an average performance* mediocre, moderate, satisfactory, fair, middling, fair to middling, indifferent, passable, tolerable, undistinguished, unexceptional, nothing special, *colloq.* run-of-the-mill, so-so, not up to much, nothing much to write home about, not much cop, no great shakes
🔁 **1** extreme **3** exceptional, remarkable

averse *adj*
reluctant, unwilling, loath, disinclined, ill-disposed, hostile, opposed, antagonistic, unfavourable, *formal* antipathetic
🔁 willing, keen, sympathetic

aversion *n*
dislike, hate, hatred, loathing, abomination, horror, phobia, reluctance, unwillingness, distaste, disgust, revulsion, repulsion, hostility, opposition, antagonism, *formal* detestation, abhorrence, repugnance, disinclination
🔁 liking, sympathy, desire

avert *v*
turn away, deflect, turn aside, parry, head off, fend off, ward off, stave off, forestall, frustrate, prevent, avoid, evade, stop, *formal* obviate, preclude

aviation *n*
aeronautics, flying, flight, aircraft industry

Aviation terms include :

aeronautics, aeroplane, aerospace, aileron, aircraft, airfield, air hostess, airline, air-miss, *US* airplane, airport, airship, airspace, air steward, airstrip, air-traffic control, airway, altitude, automatic pilot, biplane, black box, captain, *colloq.* chocks away, cockpit, console, control tower, crash-dive, crash-landing, dive, drag, fixed-wing, flap, flight, flight crew, flight deck, flight recorder, fly-by, fly-by-wire, fly-past, fuselage, *slang* George, glider, ground-control, ground-speed, hangar, helicopter, hop, hot-air balloon, jet, jet engine, jet propulsion, jetstream, joystick, jumbo jet, landing, landing-gear, landing-strip, lift-off, loop-the-loop, Mach number, maiden flight, mid-air collision, monoplane, night-flying, nose dive, overshoot, parachute, pilot, plane, pressurized cabin, *slang* prang, propeller, rotor blade, rudder, runway, solo flight, sonic boom, sound barrier, spoiler, supersonic, swing-wing, take-off, taxi, test flight, test pilot, thrust, touchdown, under-carriage, undershoot, vapour trail, vertical take-off and landing (VTOL), windsock, wingspan. *See also* AIRCRAFT.

avid *adj*
eager, earnest, keen, enthusiastic, fanatical, devoted, dedicated, zealous, ardent, fervent, intense, great, passionate, insatiable, ravenous, hungry, thirsty, greedy, grasping, covetous, *colloq.* crazy, mad
F3 indifferent

avoid *v*
evade, stay/keep away from, elude, sidestep, escape, run away from, get out of, bypass, get round, balk, prevent, avert, shun, abstain from, hold back from, shy away from, steer clear of, make a detour, keep your distance from, *formal* eschew, circumvent, refrain from, forbear, *colloq.* hedge, duck, dodge, shirk, wriggle/worm your way out of, give a miss, give a wide berth to

avoidable *adj*
escapable, preventable, *formal* avertible, eludible
F3 inevitable, inescapable

avowed *adj*
sworn, declared, professed, self-proclaimed, self-confessed, confessed, admitted, acknowledged, open, overt

await *v*
wait for, expect, hope for, look forward to, look for, be in store for, lie in wait

awake *adj, v*
▶ *adj* wakeful, wide awake, stirring, aroused, alert, vigilant, watchful, observant, attentive, conscious, aware, sensitive, alive, *colloq.* tossing and turning, not sleeping a wink
F3 asleep, sleeping
▶ *v* awaken, waken, wake, wake up, rouse, stir, arouse

awakening *n*
awaking, wakening, waking, rousing, arousal, stimulation, animating, enlivening, activation, revival, birth, *formal* vivification

award *n, v*
▶ *n* 1 *an award for bravery* prize, trophy, decoration, medal, certificate, presentation, commendation, citation, *slang* gong 2 *an award for compensation* endowment, gift, grant, allotment, allowance, dispensation, bestowal, conferral, adjudication, judgement, decision, order
▶ *v* give, present, distribute, dispense, bestow, confer, accord, endow, gift, grant, allot, allocate, assign, allow, determine, *formal* apportion, adjudge

aware *adj*
1 *aware of the problem* conscious, alive to, sensitive, appreciative, mindful, heedful, attentive, observant, sharp, alert, vigilant, *formal* sentient, sensible 2 *politically aware* familiar, conversant, acquainted, informed, enlightened, au courant, knowing, knowledgeable, shrewd, *formal* cognizant, apprised, *colloq.* clued up, in the know, on the ball
F3 1 unaware, oblivious, insensitive

awe *n*
wonder, reverence, respect, honour, admiration, amazement, astonishment, fear, terror, dread, apprehension, *formal* veneration, stupefaction
F3 contempt

awe-inspiring *adj*
wonderful, sublime, magnificent, stupendous, overwhelming, breathtaking, striking, spectacular, stupefying, stunning, astonishing, amazing, impressive, dazzling, imposing, majestic, solemn, exalted, sublime, moving, awesome, formidable, daunting, intimidating, fearsome, *formal* numinous
F3 contemptible, tame

awful *adj*
awful weather/injuries terrible, dreadful, fearful, frightful, ghastly, unpleasant, nasty, horrible, horrid, hideous, ugly, gruesome, dire, abysmal, unpleasant, atrocious, horrific, horrifying, shocking, appalling, alarming, disgusting, distressing, spine-chilling, *formal* heinous
F3 wonderful, excellent

awkward *adj*
1 CLUMSY, gauche, inept, inexpert, unskilful, bungling, ham-fisted, unco-ordinated, ungainly, graceless, ungraceful, ungainly, inelegant, cumbersome, unwieldy, lubberly, *formal* maladroit, *colloq.* all thumbs 2 *feeling awkward in their presence* uncomfortable, ill at ease, embarrassed, shy 3 *put me in an awkward position* difficult, tricky, embarrassing, uncomfortable, delicate, troublesome, perplexing, problematic, annoying, inconvenient, fiddly 4 OBSTINATE, stubborn, unco-operative, irritable, touchy, prickly, oversensitive, rude, unpleasant
F3 1 graceful, elegant, convenient, handy 2 comfortable, relaxed, at ease 3 straightforward, easy 4 amenable, pleasant

awry *adv & adj*
1 *clothing left awry* askew, asymmetrical, cock-eyed, crooked, misaligned, oblique, off-centre, skew-whiff, twisted, uneven, *colloq.* wonky 2 *plans gone awry* wrong, amiss
F3 1 straight, symmetrical

axe *n, v*
▶ *n* hatchet, chopper, cleaver, tomahawk, battle-axe
▷ **get the axe** be cancelled, *colloq.* get the boot, get the chop
▶ *v* 1 CUT DOWN, fell, hew, chop, cleave, split 2 CANCEL, terminate, discontinue, remove, withdraw, eliminate, get rid of, throw out, dismiss, discharge, *colloq.* cut, sack, fire

axiom *n*
principle, fundamental, truth, truism, precept, dictum, byword, maxim, adage, aphorism

axiomatic *adj*
manifest, assumed, certain, given, granted, self-evident, understood, unquestioned, presupposed, fundamental, accepted, proverbial, *formal* indubitable, aphoristic, apophthegmatic, gnomic

axis *n*
centre-line, vertical, horizontal, pivot, hinge

axle *n*
shaft, spindle, rod, pin, pivot

B

babble *v, n*
- ▶ *v* **1** CHATTER, gabble, jabber, gibber, cackle, prate, mutter, mumble, murmur, *colloq.* rabbit on, waffle **2** *the stream babbled* burble, gurgle
- ▶ *n* chatter, gabble, clamour, hubbub, babel, gibberish, burble, murmur

babe *n*
baby, child, infant, babe in arms

babel *n*
babble, hubbub, clamour, bedlam, hullabaloo, chaos, commotion, confusion, din, disorder, pandemonium, tumult, turmoil, uproar

baby *n, adj*
- ▶ *n* babe, infant, newborn baby, suckling, child, toddler, tiny tot, *Scot.* bairn, *technical* neonate, *slang* sprog
- ▶ *adj* miniature, small-scale, midget, small, little, tiny, minute, diminutive, dwarf, *Scot.* wee, *colloq.* mini

babyish *adj*
childish, juvenile, puerile, infantile, silly, foolish, baby, young, immature, naïve, *colloq.* soft, sissy
- 🔁 mature, precocious

back *n, v, adj, adv*
- ▶ *n* **1** *lie on your back* backbone, spine, *technical* dorsum, tergum **2** *the back of the house* rear, stern, end, rear end, tail, tail end, hind part, hindquarters, posterior, backside, reverse, reverse side, other side
- 🔁 front, face
- ▷ **behind your back** secretly, without your knowledge, deceitfully, slyly, furtively, covertly, sneakily, surreptitiously
- ▶ *v* **1** GO BACKWARDS, reverse, recede, backtrack, retreat, retire, withdraw, back away, recoil, *formal* regress **2** SUPPORT, sustain, assist, help, aid, abet, side with, champion, advocate, encourage, promote, boost, favour, confirm, bolster, sanction, countenance, endorse, second, countersign, sponsor, finance, subsidize, underwrite, *colloq.* throw your weight behind, get/be behind
- 🔁 **1** advance, approach **2** discourage, weaken
- ▷ **back away** retreat, withdraw, draw back, fall back, move back, give ground, recoil, step back, recede
- ▷ **back down** abandon, yield, submit, surrender, concede, give in, retreat, withdraw, back-pedal, backtrack, climb down
- ▷ **back out** abandon, give up, withdraw, resign, recant, go back on, cancel, *colloq.* pull out, get cold feet, chicken out
- ▷ **back up** support, confirm, corroborate, bear out, validate, substantiate, endorse, second, champion, reinforce, bolster, assist, aid
- ▶ *adj* **1** *the back door* rear, end, tail, posterior, hind, hindmost, reverse, other **2** *back copies* past, previous, earlier, former, outdated, elapsed, bygone, out of date, obsolete

- 🔁 **1** front
- ▶ *adv* backwards, to the rear, behind
- 🔁 forwards

backbiting *n*
criticism, slander, libel, defamation, abuse, disparagement, gossip, malice, scandalmongering, spite, spitefulness, *formal* aspersion, calumny, denigration, revilement, detraction, vilification, vituperation, *colloq.* bitchiness, cattiness, slagging off, mud-slinging
- 🔁 praise

backbone *n*
1 SPINE, spinal column, vertebrae, vertebral column. **2** *the backbone of an organization* mainstay, support, core, foundation, basis, nucleus **3** COURAGE, mettle, pluck, nerve, grit, determination, resolve, (strength of) character, firmness, tenacity, steadfastness, willpower, toughness, stamina, strength, power, *colloq.* bottle
- 🔁 **3** spinelessness, weakness

backbreaking *adj*
arduous, exhausting, gruelling, strenuous, hard, heavy, crushing, killing, laborious, punishing
- 🔁 easy

backer *n*
advocate, benefactor, promoter, second, seconder, sponsor, subscriber, supporter, underwriter, champion, patron, well-wisher

backfire *v*
1 *the engine backfired* explode, discharge, blow up, detonate **2** *the plans backfired* recoil, rebound, ricochet, boomerang, miscarry, fail, defeat itself, be self-defeating, be counterproductive, *colloq.* flop, come home to roost, score an own goal, blow up in your face

background *n*
1 SETTING, backdrop, backcloth, scene, surroundings, environment, milieu, context, framework, circumstances, influences, factors **2** HISTORY, record, credentials, experience, qualifications, grounding, preparation, education, upbringing, family, (family) circumstances, breeding, social standing, status, origins, culture, tradition

backhanded *adj*
ambiguous, double-edged, two-edged, indirect, oblique, dubious, equivocal, ironic, sarcastic, sardonic
- 🔁 sincere, wholehearted

backing *n*
support, accompaniment, aid, assistance, help, helpers, championing, advocacy, encouragement, moral support, commendation, favour, approval, sanction, promotion, endorsement, seconding, patronage, sponsorship, finance, funds, grant, subsidy

backlash *n*
reaction, response, repercussion, reprisal, retaliation, recoil, kickback, backfire, boomerang

backlog *n*
accumulation, stock, supply, resources, reserve, reserves, heap, excess, hoard, *colloq.* mountain

back-pedal *v*
take back, retract, change your mind, have second thoughts, abandon, yield, submit, surrender, concede, give in, submit, retreat, withdraw, backtrack, climb down, *formal* tergiversate, *colloq.* do a U-turn

backslide *v*
lapse, relapse, default, defect, turn away, turn your back, fall from grace, renege, desert, revert, go back, sin, slip, stray, go astray, *formal* apostatize, regress, tergiversate, *colloq.* leave the straight and narrow
₣ persevere

backslider *n*
apostate, defaulter, defector, deserter, renegade, reneger, turncoat, *formal* recidivist, recreant, tergiversator

backsliding *n*
lapse, relapse, apostasy, defection, desertion, defaulting, *formal* regression, tergiversation

backup *n*
support, help, assistance, aid, encouragement, confirmation, endorsement, reinforcement, additional equipment/resources

backward *adj*
1 *a backward step* rearward, reverse, to the back, retrograde, retrogressive, regressive 2 *a backward country/society* undeveloped, underdeveloped, unsophisticated 3 SHY, bashful, retiring, reluctant, unwilling, hesitant, hesitating, shrinking, timid, wavering 4 *a backward child* slow, immature, retarded, having learning difficulties, subnormal
₣ 1 forward 2 advanced, developed 3 precocious

backwards *adv*
rearwards, to the back, retrogressively, regressively

backwash *n*
1 *the backwash of a ship* wash, flow, swell, waves, wake, path 2 REPERCUSSIONS, aftermath, after-effect(s), result(s), consequence(s), reverberations

backwoods *n*
back of beyond, bush, outback, *colloq.* middle of nowhere, sticks

bacteria *n*
germs, viruses, microbes, micro-organisms, parasites, bacilli, *colloq.* bugs

bad *adj*
1 UNPLEASANT, disagreeable, nasty, dreadful, appalling, atrocious, undesirable, unfortunate, distressing, adverse, detrimental, harmful, damaging, hurtful, dangerous, injurious, unhealthy, unwholesome, destructive, ruinous, *formal* deleterious 2 EVIL, wicked, sinful, criminal, corrupt, dishonest, shameful, immoral, vile, offensive, degenerate, outrageous, deplorable, *formal* reprehensible, reprobate 3 *bad workmanship; bad at speaking French* poor, inferior, inadequate, weak, mediocre, substandard, imperfect, faulty, defective, deficient, unsatisfactory, unacceptable, second-rate, third-rate, useless, hopeless, incompetent, mismanaged, ineffective, *formal* ineffectual, *colloq.* awful, terrible, botched, lousy, pathetic, ropy, a load of rubbish, a load of garbage, *slang* poxy, crummy, naff, crappy, a load of crap 4 *feel bad today* unwell, sick, ill, poorly, indisposed, diseased, painful, in pain, aching, unhappy, despondent, gloomy, *colloq.* under the weather 5 ROTTEN, mouldy, decayed, spoilt, putrid, rancid, sour, off, tainted, contaminated, high, *formal* putrefactive, putrescent 6 *a bad child* naughty, mischievous, badly-behaved, ill-behaved, disobedient, unruly, wayward, *formal*

refractory, *colloq.* stroppy, bolshie 7 *have a bad cold* serious, grave, severe, intense, critical, acute, harsh 8 *a bad time to call* inconvenient, unfortunate, unfavourable, unsuitable, inappropriate, *formal* inauspicious
₣ 1 good, pleasant, mild 2 virtuous 3 skilled, skilful 4 well, happy 5 fresh 6 well-behaved, obedient 8 good, convenient, favourable, *formal* auspicious
▷ **not bad** quite good, all right, tolerable, passable, fair, average, adequate, reasonable, satisfactory, *colloq.* OK, so-so

badge *n*
1 *a school badge* identification, emblem, device, insignia, crest, shield, escutcheon, sign, mark, token, stamp, brand, trademark, logo, ensign 2 *a badge of power* sign, mark, token, symbol, indicator, indication

badger *v*
pester, plague, torment, harass, bait, bully, chivvy, goad, harry, hound, nag, *formal* importune, *colloq.* hassle

badinage *n*
banter, repartee, word-play, jocularity, teasing, waggery, chaff, drollery, give and take, humour, mockery, raillery, *formal* persiflage, *colloq.* ribbing

badly *adv*
1 *a badly directed play* poorly, inadequately, imperfectly, defectively, unsatisfactorily, unacceptably, uselessly, incompetently, wrongly, incorrectly, improperly, defectively, faultily, imperfectly, inadequately, unsatisfactorily, poorly, incompetently, negligently, carelessly, *formal* ineffectually, *colloq.* awfully, terribly, pathetically 2 *badly hurt* SERIOUSLY, acutely, bitterly, painfully, desperately, severely, critically, gravely, crucially 3 WICKEDLY, criminally, immorally, shamefully, dishonestly, sinfully, evilly, offensively, unfairly 4 UNFAVOURABLY, adversely, unfortunately, unsuccessfully, unhappily 5 *want something badly* very much, greatly, exceedingly, enormously, tremendously, desperately, intensely, extremely, deeply
₣ 2 slightly, mildly 3 well 4 favourably, fortunately

bad-tempered *adj*
irritable, cross, snappy, quick-tempered, grumpy, fractious, in a (bad) mood, narky, impatient, choleric, *formal* querulous, cantankerous, petulant, *colloq.* stroppy, in a huff, in a sulk, having got out of bed on the wrong side, having a short fuse, cross as a bear with a sore head, crotchety, crabbed, crabby, grouchy, shirty, ratty
₣ good-tempered, genial, equable

baffle *v*
puzzle, perplex, mystify, bemuse, bewilder, confuse, confound, dumbfound, daze, upset, disconcert, foil, thwart, frustrate, hinder, block, bar, check, defeat, *colloq.* bamboozle, flummox, stump, throw
₣ enlighten, help

baffling *adj*
puzzling, perplexing, mysterious, bewildering, confusing, stupefying, perplexing, disconcerting, surprising, amazing, astounding, bemusing, extraordinary, unfathomable
₣ enlightening, explanatory

bag *v, n*
▶ *v* 1 CATCH, capture, trap, land, kill, shoot 2 OBTAIN, acquire, get, gain, come by, corner, take, grab, appropriate, commandeer, reserve
▶ *n* container, receptacle

baggage *n*
luggage, suitcases, bags, belongings, things, equipment, gear, paraphernalia, effects, *formal* impedimenta, accoutrements

baggy *adj*
loose, loose-fitting, slack, roomy, ill-fitting, billowing,

bulging, ballooning, floppy, shapeless, sagging, droopy, oversize, extra large
🖪 tight, firm

bail n
security, surety, pledge, bond, guarantee, warranty, collateral
▷ **bail out 1** HELP, aid, assist, relieve, rescue, finance **2** (*also* **bale out**) withdraw, retreat, quit, back out, escape, get out, get clear

bait n, v
▶ n lure, incentive, inducement, bribe, temptation, snare, decoy, carrot, enticement, allurement, incitement, attraction
🖪 disincentive
▶ v tease, provoke, goad, irritate, annoy, hound, irk, harass, persecute, torment, badger, plague, harry, *colloq.* needle, hassle, give a hard time to

balance v, n
▶ v **1** STEADY, poise, stabilize, level, square, equalize, equate, match **2** *balance the cost against the benefits* equalize, equate, match, counterbalance, counteract, counterweigh, neutralize, offset, set, adjust, juggle, compensate for **3** COMPARE, consider, weigh, estimate, evaluate, appraise, review
🖪 **1** unbalance, overbalance
▶ n **1** EQUILIBRIUM, steadiness, stability, evenness, symmetry, equality, parity, equity, equivalence, correspondence, uniformity, *technical* stasis, *formal* equipoise **2** COMPOSURE, calmness, self-possession, poise, assurance, level-headedness, cool-headedness, equanimity, *formal* aplomb, sangfroid **3** REMAINDER, rest, residue, surplus, excess, difference
🖪 **1** imbalance, instability
▷ **on balance** in conclusion, all in all, taking everything into consideration

balanced adj
1 *a balanced report* objective, fair, impartial, unbiased, unprejudiced, equitable **2** *a balanced diet* well-rounded, healthy, complete **3** *a balanced person* calm, self-possessed, assured, level-headed, cool-headed, equitable, even-handed, sensible
🖪 **1** prejudiced, biased

balcony n
terrace, veranda, portico, loggia, gallery, upper circle, gods

bald adj
1 BALD-HEADED, hairless, smooth, uncovered, *technical* glabrous, glabrate, *formal* depilated, *colloq.* bald as a coot **2** BARE, naked, unadorned, plain, simple, severe, stark, barren, exposed, treeless, unsheltered, bleak **3** *a bald statement* forthright, direct, straight, blunt, outright, downright, straightforward, outspoken, simple, plain, unadorned
🖪 **1** hairy, hirsute **2** adorned

balderdash n
rubbish, nonsense, drivel, gibberish, trash, tripe, twaddle, *colloq.* bunk, bunkum, claptrap, piffle, bilge, poppycock, hot air, cobblers, rot, tommyrot

balding adj
receding, losing your hair, thin on top, bald

baldness n
bald-headedness, bareness, hair loss, hairlessness, starkness, *technical* calvities, calvousness, glabrousness, psilosis, *formal* alopecia
🖪 hirsuteness

bale n, v
▶ n bundle, truss, pack, package, parcel
▶ v ▷ **bale out** *see* BAIL OUT 2.

baleful adj
deadly, harmful, threatening, destructive, evil, hurtful, injurious, malevolent, malignant, menacing,

mournful, noxious, ominous, pernicious, ruinous, sinister, venomous
🖪 favourable

balk, baulk v
1 FLINCH, recoil, shrink, jib, boggle, hesitate, refuse, resist, dodge, evade, shirk, *formal* eschew **2** THWART, frustrate, foil, forestall, disconcert, baffle, hinder, obstruct, check, stall, bar, prevent, impede, defeat, counteract

ball¹ n
a golf ball sphere, globe, orb, globule, drop, conglomeration, projectile, pellet, pill, shot, bullet, *colloq.* slug
▷ **play ball** co-operate, collaborate, go along, play along, show willing, respond, reciprocate

ball² n
an invitation to a ball dance, dinner-dance, party, soirée, masquerade, carnival, assembly

ballad n
poem, song, folk-song, shanty, carol, ditty

ballet n
ballet-dancing, dancing, leg-business

Terms used in ballet include :

à pointe, arabesque, attitude, ballerina, prima ballerina, ballon, barre, battement, batterie, battu, bourrée, capriole, chassé, choreography, ciseaux, company, corps de ballet, coryphée, divertissement, écarté, élévation, entrechat, fish dive, five positions, fouetté, fouetté en tournant, glissade, jeté, grand jeté, leotard, pas de deux, pas de seul, pirouette, plié, pointes, sur les pointes, ports de bras, principal male dancer, régisseur, répétiteur, ballet shoe, point shoe, splits, stulchak, tutu.

balloon v
bag, belly, billow, blow up, bulge, dilate, enlarge, expand, inflate, puff out, swell, rocket, soar, *formal* distend

ballot n
poll, polling, vote, voting, election, referendum, plebiscite

ballyhoo n
fuss, hubbub, to-do, hullabaloo, clamour, commotion, excitement, disturbance, noise, racket, tumult, hue and cry, agitation, build-up, promotion, propaganda, publicity, advertising, hype

balm n
soothing balm for the skin/a troubled spirit cream, lotion, salve, sedative, unguent, balsam, bromide, calmative, curative, embrocation, emollient, lenitive, ointment, palliative, restorative, anodyne, comfort, consolation
🖪 irritant, vexation

balmy adj
warm, summery, gentle, mild, pleasant, soft, temperate, clement, soothing
🖪 inclement

bamboozle v
puzzle, perplex, mystify, bemuse, bewilder, confuse, confound, dumbfound, daze, upset, disconcert, trick, cheat, dupe, deceive, hoodwink, fool, swindle, *colloq.* con, gull

ban v, n
▶ v forbid, prohibit, disallow, bar, exclude, ostracize, outlaw, banish, suppress, veto, restrict, censor, disqualify, *formal* proscribe
🖪 allow, permit, authorize
▶ n prohibition, embargo, injunction, sanctions, veto, boycott, stoppage, restriction, suppression,

censorship, outlawry, bar, banishment, condemnation, denunciation, curse, taboo, *formal* interdiction, proscription

🔁 permission, dispensation

banal *adj*
trite, commonplace, ordinary, everyday, mundane, humdrum, boring, dull, unimaginative, nondescript, bland, hackneyed, clichéd, stock, stereotyped, stale, overused, threadbare, tired, unoriginal, inane, wearing thin, empty, vapid, *colloq.* corny

🔁 original, fresh, imaginative

banality *n*
triteness, ordinariness, dullness, unimaginativeness, staleness, tiredness, unoriginality, inaneness, emptiness, vapidity, fatuity, cliché, commonplace, bromide, platitude, prosaicism, triviality, truism

🔁 originality

band¹ *n*
a metal band
strip, belt, ribbon, tape, bandage, binding, tie, ligature, bond, strap, cord, chain, connection, link, shackle, manacle, fetter

band² *n, v*
▶ *n* **1** *bands of looters* TROOP, gang, crew, group, herd, flock, party, body, gathering, crowd, throng, horde, contingent, association, company, society, club, clique **2** *the band played on* group, music/musical group, pop group, orchestra, ensemble
▶ *v* group, gather, join, unite, join forces, close ranks, stand together, pull together, ally, collaborate, consolidate, amalgamate, merge, affiliate, federate, *colloq.* stick together

🔁 disband, disperse

bandage *n, v*
▶ *n* dressing, plaster, gauze, compress, ligature, tourniquet, swathe, swaddle
▶ *v* bind (up), dress, cover, swathe, swaddle

bandit *n*
robber, thief, brigand, marauder, plunderer, outlaw, highwayman, pirate, buccaneer, hijacker, cowboy, gunman, desperado, gangster, crook, criminal, racketeer

bandy¹ *v*
bandy words about exchange, swap, trade, barter, interchange, reciprocate, pass, toss, throw

bandy² *adj*
bandy-legged bow-legged, curved, bowed, bent, misshapen, crooked

bane *n*
ruin, adversity, destruction, scourge, affliction, torment, trial, trouble, vexation, woe, annoyance, *bête noire*, blight, burden, calamity, curse, disaster, distress, downfall, evil, irritation, misery, misfortune, nuisance, ordeal, plague, pest, pestilence

🔁 blessing

bang *n, v, adv*
▶ *n* **1** *a loud bang* explosion, detonation, pop, boom, clap, peal, clang, clash, thud, thump, slam, noise, shot, *formal* report **2** *a nasty bang on the head* BLOW, hit, knock, bump, crash, collision, crack, smack, punch, thump, stroke, bash, *colloq.* wallop, whack, sock
▶ *v* **1** STRIKE, hit, bump into, crash into, bash, knock, bump, rap, drum, hammer, pound, thump, stamp **2** EXPLODE, burst, detonate, boom, echo, resound, crash, slam, clatter, clang, peal, thunder
▶ *adv* straight, directly, headlong, right, exactly, precisely, absolutely, slap, smack, hard, noisily, suddenly, abruptly

banish *v*
1 *banish someone from their country* EXPEL, eject, evict, deport, transport, drive away, cast out, throw out, exile, outlaw, ban, bar, debar, exclude, shut out, ostracize, excommunicate, expatriate, repatriate, extradite, *formal* rusticate **2** *banish thoughts from your mind* dismiss, oust, dislodge, remove, get rid of, drive away, send away, shut out, discard, dispel, dislodge, eliminate, eradicate

🔁 **1** recall, welcome

banishment *n*
expulsion, eviction, deportation, expatriation, transportation, exile, exclusion, ostracism, excommunication, extradition, *formal* outlawry

🔁 return, recall, welcome

banisters *n*
railing, rail, handrail, balustrade

bank¹ *n, v*
▶ *n* **1** *a bank account* financial institution, high-street bank, clearing bank, merchant bank, savings bank, building society, finance company/house **2** *a blood bank* accumulation, fund, pool, reservoir, depository, repository, treasury, savings, reserve, store, stock, stockpile, hoard, cache
▶ *v* deposit, save (up), keep, store, accumulate, stockpile, lay by, put aside, *colloq.* save for a rainy day

🔁 spend

▷ **bank on** depend on, rely on, count on, bet on, trust, believe in, *colloq.* pin your hopes on

bank² *n, v*
▶ *n* **1** *the banks of a river* side, embankment, slope, tilt, edge, shore, margin **2** *a bank of ground* mound, earthwork, ridge, hillock, knoll, rampart, levee, parados, slope, rise, incline, heap, pile, mass
▶ *v* **1** SLOPE, incline, pitch, slant, tilt, tip **2** HEAP, pile, stack, mass, amass, accumulate, mound, drift

bank³ *n*
a bank of switches row, series, array, panel, bench, group, tier, rank, line, succession, sequence, train

banknote *n*
bill, note, paper money, treasury note, *US* greenback, *slang* flimsy

bankrupt *adj, v, n*
▶ *adj* **1** *the company went bankrupt* insolvent, in(to) liquidation, ruined, failed, folded, beggared, destitute, impoverished, spent, *formal* penurious, impecunious, *colloq.* bust, broke, hard up, gone to the wall, gone under, in the red, on the rocks, on your uppers **2** *bankrupt philosophies of life* deficient, lacking, wanting, deprived, exhausted, depleted

🔁 **1** solvent, wealthy, flourishing, prospering, rich, *colloq.* in the black
▶ *v* ruin, cripple
▶ *n* insolvent, debtor, pauper, beggar

bankruptcy *n*
insolvency, (financial) ruin, liquidation, disaster, exhaustion, failure, indebtedness, lack, *formal* penury, beggary, ruination

🔁 solvency, wealth

banner *n*
flag, standard, colours, ensign, pennant, streamer, placard, sign, banderol, burgee, fanion, pennon, labarum, gonfalon, vexillum

banquet *n*
feast, dinner, dinner party, meal, party, treat, spread, *formal* repast

banter *n, v*
▶ *n* joking, jesting, pleasantry, badinage, repartee, word play, chaff, chaffing, derision, mockery, ridicule, raillery, persiflage, *colloq.* kidding, ribbing
▶ *v* joke, jest, chaff, deride, mock, ridicule, make fun of, *colloq.* kid, rib, rag, pull someone's leg

baptism n
1 *the child's baptism* christening, immersion, sprinkling, affusion, aspersion, purification, naming, dedication 2 *a baptism of fire* beginning, initiation, introduction, début, launch, launching, inauguration

baptize v
christen, immerse, sprinkle, purify, cleanse, name, call, term, style, title, introduce, initiate, enrol, recruit

bar n, v, prep
▶ n 1 PUBLIC HOUSE, inn, tavern, saloon, taproom, lounge, lounge bar, grill, brasserie, counter, table, *colloq.* pub, hostelry, watering-hole, *slang* boozer 2 ROD, stick, shaft, pole, stake, stanchion, batten, crosspiece, rail, railing, paling, barricade 3 SLAB, cake, block, lump, chunk, wedge, ingot, nugget 4 OBSTACLE, impediment, hindrance, obstruction, barrier, stop, check, deterrent, drawback 5 *called to the Bar* barristers, lawyers, counsel, court, tribunal
▶ v 1 EXCLUDE, debar, ban, forbid, prohibit, prevent, hinder, obstruct, block, blockade, restrain, check, stop, disqualify, suspend, *formal* preclude 2 *bar the door* barricade, lock, bolt, latch, fasten, secure, padlock
▶ prep except, with the exception of, excepting, apart from, save, but for, excluding, omitting

barb n
1 *the barb on a fish hook* arrow, point, spike, needle, thorn, prickle, bristle, fluke 2 *critical barbs at leaders* gibe, insult, affront, sneer, rebuff, sarcasm, scorn, *colloq.* dig

barbarian n, adj
▶ n savage, brute, wild person, ruffian, hooligan, vandal, lout, oaf, boor, philistine, ignoramus, illiterate
▶ adj savage, brute, wild, rough, brutish, coarse, crude, uncivilized, uncouth, uncultivated, uncultured, unsophisticated, vulgar, loutish, hooligan, *formal* tramontane

barbaric adj
barbarous, primitive, wild, savage, fierce, ferocious, vicious, cruel, inhuman, brutal, brutish, bestial, murderous, ruthless, uncivilized, uncouth, vulgar, coarse, crude, rude
🔁 humane, civilized, gracious

barbarism n
wildness, savagery, fierceness, ferocity, viciousness, cruelty, inhumanness, brutality, brutishness, bestiality, murderousness, ruthlessness, uncivilizedness, corruption, enormity, uncouthness, vulgarity, coarseness, crudeness, rudeness

barbarity n
barbarousness, wildness, savagery, ferocity, viciousness, cruelty, inhumanity, brutality, ruthlessness, brutishness, atrocity, outrage, enormity
🔁 civilization, humanity, civility

barbarous adj
1 *barbarous behaviour* wild, savage, fierce, ferocious, vicious, cruel, inhuman, barbarian, barbaric, brutal, brutish, bestial, murderous, ruthless, heartless 2 *barbarous by modern standards* primitive, ignorant, uncivilized, unrefined, unsophisticated, uncultured, unlettered, vulgar, rough, rude, crude
🔁 2 civilized, cultured, educated

barbed adj
1 PRICKLY, spiny, thorny, spiked, pronged, hooked, jagged, toothed, pointed 2 *a barbed remark* cutting, caustic, acid, hurtful, unkind, nasty, snide, hostile, critical

bare adj
1 NAKED, nude, in the nude, unclothed, undressed, with nothing on, stripped, denuded, uncovered, exposed, *colloq.* in your birthday suit, in the raw 2 *bare*

shelves/rooms empty, vacant, unfurnished 3 *a bare tree/landscape* barren, denuded, exposed, bleak, desolate, unsheltered, treeless, unforested, unwooded, woodless, *formal* defoliated 4 *the bare facts/minimum* PLAIN, simple, unadorned, barren, bald, stark, basic, essential, straightforward, cold, hard, sheer, absolute, mere
🔁 1 clothed 2 full, decorated 3 wooded, sheltered, forested 4 detailed

barefaced adj
brazen, shameless, blatant, bold, brash, flagrant, glaring, arrant, impudent, insolent, unabashed, undisguised, unconcealed, audacious, naked, obvious, manifest, open, palpable, patent, transparent, bald

barefooted adj
barefoot, shoeless, unshod, *formal* discalced
🔁 shod

barely adv
hardly, scarcely, no sooner, only just, just, almost, *colloq.* be a near/close thing, by the skin of your teeth, by a whisker

bargain n, v
▶ n 1 DEAL, transaction, contract, treaty, pact, pledge, promise, covenant, agreement, understanding, arrangement, negotiation, *formal* concordat 2 DISCOUNT, reduction, special offer, good buy, value for money, *colloq.* snip, giveaway, steal
▷ **into the bargain** as well, besides, additionally
▶ v negotiate, haggle, beat down, deal, trade, traffic, barter, buy, sell, transact, settle, clinch
▷ **bargain for** expect, anticipate, plan for, be prepared for, include, reckon on, take into account, look for, foresee, imagine, contemplate, consider, figure on

bargaining n
negotiation, haggling, dealing(s), trade, trafficking, barter(ing), buying, selling, transaction, horse-trading, wheeling and dealing, wheeler-dealing

barge n, v
▶ n canal-boat, flatboat, narrow-boat, houseboat, lighter
▶ v push (in), push your way, force your way, shove, rush, bump, hit, collide, press, jostle, elbow, smash, plough
▷ **barge in** interrupt, butt in, burst in, break in, cut in, gatecrash, intrude, interfere

bark¹ v, n
▶ v 1 *the dog barked* yap, woof, yelp, snap, snarl, growl, bay, howl 2 *bark orders at someone* yell, shout, cry, bawl, thunder, snap, snarl
▶ n yap, woof, yelp, snap, snarl, growl, bay, howl

bark² n
the bark of a tree covering, casing, crust, husk, rind, peel, skin, hide, shell, *technical* cortex, integument

barmy adj
crazy, foolish, idiotic, insane, mad, odd, silly, stupid, *colloq.* daft, batty, dippy, dotty, loony, loopy, nuts, crackers, nutty, off your head/rocker/nutter, need your head examining, round the bend/twist, off your trolley, out to lunch
🔁 rational, sane, sensible, of sound mind

baroque adj
elaborate, ornate, rococo, florid, flamboyant, embellished, exuberant, vigorous, bold, convoluted, decorated, overdecorated, overwrought, extravagant, showy, fanciful, fantastic, whimsical, grotesque
🔁 plain, simple, unadorned, austere

barrack v
heckle, jeer, shout down, interrupt

barracks n
garrison, camp, encampment, fort, guardhouse, quarters, billet, lodging, accommodation, casern

barrage n
a barrage of fire/criticism bombardment, shelling, gunfire, cannonade, battery, volley, salvo, burst, broadside, assault, attack, onset, onslaught, deluge, torrent, flood, stream, storm, hail, rain, shower, mass, abundance, profusion

barrel n
cask, keg, tun, butt, water-butt, tierce, rundlet

barren adj
1 *barren land/activity* ARID, dry, desert, desolate, waste, uncultivable, empty, flat, dull, vapid, uninteresting, uninspiring, uninformative, uninstructive, unrewarding, unproductive, profitless, unfruitful, fruitless, pointless, useless, valueless, purposeless **2** INFERTILE, sterile, childless, unprolific, unbearing, *formal* infecund
🖪 **1** fertile, productive, fruitful, useful **2** fertile

barricade n, v
▶ n blockade, obstruction, obstacle, barrier, bar, fence, stockade, bulwark, rampart, palisade, protection, defence
▶ v block, obstruct, bar, close (up), shut (off), fortify, strengthen, defend, protect

barrier n
1 WALL, fence, railing, barricade, bar, gate, blockade, stockade, obstacle, roadblock, boom, rampart, fortification, ditch, frontier, boundary, bar, check **2** *a barrier to success* obstacle, hurdle, stumbling-block, impediment, obstruction, hindrance, handicap, limitation, restriction, drawback, check, restraint, difficulty

barring prep
except (for), except (in the event of), if, unless

barrister n
lawyer, advocate, attorney, counsel, QC

bartender n
barman, barmaid, barkeeper, publican

barter v, n
▶ v trade, exchange, bargain, swap, traffic, deal, haggle, negotiate, sell
▶ n trade, trading, exchange, bargaining, swapping, trafficking, dealing, haggling, negotiation

base¹ n, v
▶ n **1** *the base of the statue* BOTTOM, foot, pedestal, plinth, stand, stay, rest, support, prop, foundation, foundation stone, keystone, underneath, substructure, understructure, bed, groundwork, *technical* fundus **2** BASIS, foundation, fundamental, essential, component, principal, key, heart, core, essence, root, origin, source **3** HEADQUARTERS, centre, post, station, camp, settlement, depot, home, starting-point
▶ v **1** *research based on fact* found, establish, ground, build, construct, derive, have as a basis, depend, rest, hinge **2** *based in Edinburgh* locate, station, position, situate, site, install

base² adj
base behaviour abject, contemptible, despicable, wicked, corrupt, immoral, evil, vile, reprobate, vulgar, shameful, sordid, depraved, unprincipled, disgraceful, disreputable, wretched, worthless, ignominious, infamous, scandalous, low, lowly, low-minded, mean, miserable, pitiful, poor, valueless

baseless adj
groundless, unfounded, unsupported, unsubstantiated, unauthenticated, unconfirmed, unjustified, uncalled-for, gratuitous
🖪 justifiable, substantiated

basement n
cellar, crypt, vault

bash v, n
▶ v hit, strike, knock, punch, belt, smash, smack, slug, break, crash, *colloq.* wallop, whack, sock
▶ n **1** *have a bash at something* attempt, go, try, *colloq.* crack, whirl, shot, stab **2** *throw a bash* party, rave-up, *colloq.* thrash

bashful adj
shy, coy, demure, retiring, backward, reticent, reserved, unforthcoming, reluctant, hesitant, shrinking, nervous, timid, timorous, diffident, modest, self-effacing, inhibited, self-conscious, embarrassed, blushing, abashed, shamefaced, sheepish, faint-hearted
🖪 bold, confident, aggressive, assertive

bashfulness n
shyness, coyness, reticence, reserve, hesitancy, nervousness, timidity, diffidence, modesty, self-effacement, inhibition, self-consciousness, embarrassment, blushes, shamefacedness, sheepishness
🖪 boldness, confidence, assertiveness

basic adj
1 FUNDAMENTAL, elementary, primary, radical, root, underlying, key, central, inherent, intrinsic, essential, indispensable, vital, necessary, important, first, preparatory **2** *basic rate of pay* standard, minimum, lowest level, starting **3** *basic accommodation* primitive, elementary, plain, simple, staple, unadorned, spartan, stark, austere, crude, unsophisticated
🖪 **1** inessential, minor, peripheral **2** with commission, premium

basically adv
fundamentally, essentially, in essence, at bottom, at heart, inherently, radically, intrinsically, principally, primarily, substantially, mainly, in the main, when it comes down to it

basics n
fundamentals, essentials, rudiments, (first) principles, introduction, facts, necessaries, practicalities, realities, bedrock, rock bottom, core, *colloq.* brass tacks, nitty-gritty, nuts and bolts

basin n
1 *a pudding basin* bowl, dish, sink **2** *the basin of a river* bed, crater, cavity, hollow, depression, channel, dip

basis n
1 *research that forms the basis of the book* foundation, support, base, bottom, footing, ground(s), groundwork, cornerstone, bedrock, key, keynote, reason(s), rationale, fundamental(s), fundamental point, starting-point, premise, principle, first principles, main ingredient, alpha and omega, essential(s), essence, heart, core, thrust, *formal* quintessence, hypostasis **2** *on a particular basis* arrangement, procedure, method, system, principle, condition(s), terms, way, approach

bask v
1 *bask in the sun* sunbathe, lie, lounge, relax, laze, loll **2** *bask in someone's approval* revel, delight in, enjoy, take pleasure in, relish, savour, lap up, wallow, *formal* luxuriate

basket n
hamper, creel, pannier, punnet, bassinet, coop, skep, trug

bass adj
deep, deep-pitched, deep-toned, low, low-pitched, low-toned, grave, rich, resonant, sonorous

bastardize v
adulterate, pervert, defile, contaminate, corrupt,

debase, degrade, demean, depreciate, devalue, cheapen, distort

bastion *n*
stronghold, citadel, fortress, defence, bulwark, mainstay, support, prop, pillar, rock, protection, defence, *formal* redoubt

batch *n*
lot, consignment, parcel, pack, bunch, set, assortment, collection, assemblage, cluster, accumulation, mass, group, conglomeration, contingent, amount, quantity, aggregate, crowd

bath *n, v*
▶ *n* **1** *be in the bath* bathtub, tub, sauna, steam bath, Jacuzzi®, whirlpool, bath, slipper bath, Turkish bath, steam room, spa, hamman, thermae, *formal* balneary **2** *have/take a bath* wash, scrub, soak, shower, douche, tub, dip,
▶ *v* bathe, have/take a bath, wash, clean, soak, shower

bathe *v, n*
▶ *v* **1** *bathe in the sea* swim, bath, take a dip **2** *bathe a wound* wet, moisten, immerse, wash, cleanse, rinse, soak, steep, flood, cover, suffuse
▶ *n* swim, dip, paddle, wash, rinse, soak

bathos *n*
anticlimax, comedown, let-down

baton *n*
stick, rod, staff, truncheon

battalion *n*
1 *an infantry battalion* army, force, garrison, brigade, regiment, squadron, company, platoon, division, detachment, section, contingent, legion, troops, unit **2** *a battalion of people* horde, multitude, throng, host, mass, herd

batten *n, v*
▶ *n* strip, bar, board
▶ *v* barricade, board up, clamp down, fasten, fix, nail down, secure, tighten

batter *v*
1 *waves battering the pier* beat, pound, pummel, buffet, smash, dash, pelt, lash, damage, wear down, wear out, erode, mangle **2** *battering his wife* abuse, maltreat, ill-treat, hit, strike, knock about, club, bash, beat, assault, hurt, injure, bruise, disfigure, *colloq.* wallop, thrash, whack
▷ **batter down** break down, smash, demolish, destroy, ruin, wreck

battered *adj*
1 *a battered child* beaten, abused, ill-treated, injured, bruised **2** *a battered old shed* weather-beaten, dilapidated, tumbledown, ramshackle, shabby, crumbling, damaged, crushed

battery *n*
1 *a battery of tests/cameras* sequence, series, set, cycle, succession **2** *assault and battery* attack, beating, grievous bodily harm, force, striking, thrashing, violence, *colloq.* mugging **3** *the military battery* artillery, cannon, cannonry, emplacements, guns

battle *n, v*
▶ *n a battle against the enemy/cancer* war, warfare, hostilities, action, conflict, armed conflict, strife, combat, fight, engagement, final battle, Armageddon, encounter, attack, fray, skirmish, brawl, clash, struggle, free-for-all, contest, tournament, campaign, drive, race, competition, crusade, row, disagreement, confrontation, dispute, debate, controversy, *formal* altercation
▶ *v battle against the enemy/authorities* fight, combat, war, feud, contend, struggle, strive, campaign, crusade, agitate, clamour, contest, argue, quarrel, disagree, dispute

battle-axe *n*
dragon, disciplinarian, harridan, martinet, Tartar, termagant, virago

battle-cry *n*
war cry, war song, rallying cry/call, slogan, motto, watchword, catchword

battlefield *n*
battleground, field of battle, front, front line, war/combat zone, theatre of operations, arena

batty *adj*
crazy, foolish, idiotic, insane, mad, demented, odd, eccentric, peculiar, silly, stupid, *colloq.* daft, barmy, bats, bonkers, dippy, dotty, loony, loopy, nuts, crackers, nutty, off your head/rocker/nutter, need your head examining, round the bend/twist, out to lunch
🖭 rational, sane, sensible

bauble *n*
knick-knack, trinket, toy, plaything, trifle, ornament, bagatelle, bibelot, flamfew, gewgaw, gimcrack, kickshaw, tinsel

baulk *see* BALK.

bawd *n*
brothel-keeper, madam, panderess, pimp, procuress

bawdy *adj*
lewd, blue, pornographic, coarse, dirty, rude, vulgar, erotic, obscene, gross, improper, indecent, indecorous, indelicate, lecherous, lascivious, licentious, lustful, ribald, risqué, smutty, suggestive, *formal* libidinous, prurient, salacious
🖭 chaste, clean

bawl *v*
1 *the baby bawled* cry, weep, sob, blubber, wail, snivel, squall **2** *bawl loudly at someone* yell, shout, cry (out), bellow, howl, roar, call (out), scream, screech, *formal* vociferate, *colloq.* holler
▷ **bawl out** scold, rebuke, reprimand, yell at

bay¹ *n*
moor the ship in a bay gulf, bight, arm, sound, firth, inlet, indentation, cove, lagoon, estuary, loch

bay² *n*
a bay in the lounge recess, alcove, niche, nook, opening, compartment, cubicle, booth, stall, carrel

bay³ *v*
baying for blood howl, clamour, roar, bellow, bell, bawl, cry, bark, yelp, *colloq.* holler

bayonet *n, v*
▶ *n* knife, blade, pike, spear, dagger, poniard
▶ *v* stab, impale, knife, pierce, spear, stick

bazaar *n*
market, marketplace, mart, exchange, sale, fair, fête, bring-and-buy, souk

be *v*
1 EXIST, breathe, live, be alive, inhabit, be situated, be located, stand, lie, reside, dwell **2** STAY, remain, abide, last, endure, persist, continue, survive, stand, prevail, obtain **3** HAPPEN, occur, arise, come about, take place, come to pass, develop, transpire, *formal* befall **4** REPRESENT, constitute, make (up), form, amount to, add up to, account for

beach *n*
sand, sands, shingle, shore, strand, seashore, seaside, water's edge, coast, coastline, seaboard, *formal* littoral

beachcomber *n*
forager, loafer, loiterer, scavenger, scrounger, wayfarer

beacon *n*
signal, fire, watch fire, bonfire, light, beam, lighthouse, watchtower, flare, rocket, sign, warning light, danger signal, *formal* pharos

bead *n*
1 *a string of beads* ball, pearl, jewel, pellet globule, spheroid **2** *beads of sweat* drop, droplet, drip, blob, dot, bubble, *colloq.* glob

beak *n*
bill, mandibles, nib, neb, rostrum, nose, proboscis, snout

beaker *n*
glass, tumbler, jar, cup, mug, tankard

beam *n, v*
▸ *n* **1** *a beam of light* ray, shaft, gleam, stream, flash, flare, glint, glimmer, glow, bar **2** PLANK, board, timber, rafter, joist, girder, spar, boom, bar, support, stanchion, transom, lintel, cantilever, stringer, summer, lath, scantling
▸ *v* **1** *beam a TV signal* TRANSMIT, emit, broadcast, send, aim, direct, relay **2** *sunlight beaming through the window* shine, emit, radiate, glare, gleam, glitter, glow, glimmer, flash, sparkle, *formal* effulge **3** SMILE, grin

bean *n*

Varieties of bean and pulse include:
adzuki bean, alfalfa, beansprout, black-eyed pea, broad bean, butter bean, carob bean, chick pea, chilli bean, dal, dwarf runner bean, fava bean, French bean, garbanzo pea, green bean, haricot bean, kidney bean, legume, lentil, *US* lima bean, locust bean, mange tout, marrowfat pea, mung bean, *US* navy bean, okra, pea, *US* pinto bean, red kidney bean, runner bean, *US* scarlet runner, snap bean, soya bean, split pea, string bean, sugar bean, tonka bean, *US* wax bean.

bear *v*
1 CARRY, convey, transport, move, take, bring, fetch, *colloq.* hump, tote **2** SUPPORT, hold (up), shoulder, uphold, sustain **3** *bear children* give birth to, breed, propagate, beget, engender, produce, generate, develop, yield, bring forth, give up **4** TOLERATE, stand, put up with, endure, abide, suffer, like, permit, allow, admit, endorse, accept, take, live with, *colloq.* stomach **5** *bear signs of a struggle* carry, show, display, have **6** *bear the cost* pay, accept, support, shoulder **7** *bear someone malice* hold, have, maintain, entertain, harbour, cherish **8** *bear left at the junction* veer, turn, move, go, drive, diverge, deviate, bend, curve
▷ **bear in mind** keep in mind, remember, be mindful of, consider, note, take into account, make a mental note
▷ **bear out** confirm, endorse, support, back up, uphold, prove, demonstrate, corroborate, substantiate, validate, warrant, ratify, vindicate, justify, verify
▷ **bear up** persevere, cope, soldier on, carry on, suffer, endure, survive, withstand, *colloq.* grin and bear it, keep your pecker up
▷ **bear with** tolerate, put up with, endure, suffer, forbear, be patient with, make allowances for

bearable *adj*
tolerable, endurable, sufferable, supportable, sustainable, passable, acceptable, admissible, manageable
🔳 unbearable, intolerable

beard *n, v*
▸ *n* facial hair, stubble, bristle, beaver, goatee, imperial, vandyke, moustache, whiskers, five o'clock shadow, mutton chops, sideburns, sideboards, tuft
▸ *v* brave, challenge, confront, dare, defy, face, oppose, stand up against

bearded *adj*
unshaven, bristly, stubbly, whiskered, bewhiskered, tufted, hairy, hirsute, shaggy, bushy, *technical* pogoniate
🔳 beardless, clean-shaven, smooth

bearer *n*
1 *the bearer of bad news* conveyor, courier, messenger, runner **2** *the bearers of a coffin* carrier, conveyor, porter, transporter **3** *the bearer of a document* holder, possessor, beneficiary, consignee, payee

bearing *n*
1 *have no bearing on the matter* influence, relevance, significance, connection, relation, concern, reference, *formal* pertinence **2** MANNER, manner, air, aspect, attitude, behaviour, poise, carriage, gait, posture, stature, *formal* demeanour, comportment, deportment, mien **3** *find your bearings* orientation, position, situation, location, whereabouts, course, track, way, direction, aim

beast *n*
1 *birds and beasts* animal, creature, brute **2** *You selfish beast!* brute, monster, savage, barbarian, pig, swine, devil, ogre, fiend.

beastly *adj*
horrible, horrid, terrible, unpleasant, disagreeable, awful, nasty, rotten, foul, repulsive, rotten, brutal, cruel

beat *v, n, adj*
▸ *v* **1** HIT, flog, lash, whip, flay, cane, birch, strap, thrash, lay into, punch, strike, swipe, knock, bang, wham, club, bash, slap, smack, pound, hammer, batter, thump, drub, welt, thwack, buffet, pelt, bruise, box, cudgel, lambast, pummel, *old use* contuse, knubble, knout, vapulate, *colloq.* tan, wallop, whack, belt, clout, biff, fill in **2** *hear his heart beating* PULSATE, pulse, throb, thump, pound, race, palpitate, flutter, vibrate, quiver, tremble, shake, quake **3** *waves beating against the rocks* pound, strike, dash, batter **4** *beat a drum* hit, strike, bang **5** *a bird's wings beating* flap, flutter, shake, swing, quiver, vibrate **6** *beat the eggs* stir, mix, whisk, blend, combine **7** *beat metal* hammer, forge, knock, fashion, form, shape, stamp, *formal* malleate **8** DEFEAT, trounce, best, worst, conquer, overcome, overwhelm, overpower, subdue, rout, annihilate, outplay, outwit, outsmart, be more than a match for, have the edge on, drub, *formal* vanquish, subjugate, *colloq.* hammer, slaughter, clobber, lick, thrash, wipe the floor with **9** *beat the record* surpass, excel, exceed, outdo, outstrip, outrun, transcend
▷ **beat up** attack, assault, knock about, knock around, batter, *colloq.* do over, mug, rough up, knock someone's block off, beat the living daylights out of, knock into the middle of next week, batter
▸ *n* **1** *the beat of a drum* hit, stroke, strike, striking, bang, blow, knocking, pounding **2** PULSATION, pulse, stroke, throb, pounding, thump, palpitation, vibration, flutter **3** RHYTHM, time, tempo, metre, measure, rhyme, stress, accent, *formal* cadence **4** *a police officer's beat* round, rounds, territory, circuit, course, journey, way, path, route, walk
▸ *adj* exhausted, fatigued, tired, wearied, worn out, zonked, *colloq.* jiggered, *slang* zonked (out)

beaten *adj*
1 *beaten metal* HAMMERED, stamped, forged, wrought, worked, formed, shaped, fashioned **2** *beaten paths* trampled, trodden, well-trodden, well-worn, well-used **3** WHISKED, whipped, mixed, blended, frothy, foamy

beatific *adj*
blissful, blessed, divine, exalted, sublime, glorious, heavenly, joyful, ecstatic, rapturous, angelic, seraphic

beatify *v*
sanctify, bless, exalt, glorify, *formal* macarize

beating *n*
1 CORPORAL PUNISHMENT, hitting, whipping, flogging, caning, the cane/birch/strap, thrashing, lashing,

drubbing, punching, clubbing, slapping, smacking, battering, thumping, bruising, chastisement, *colloq.* tanning, whacking, walloping **2** DEFEAT, conquest, rout, ruin, downfall, overthrow, trouncing, overwhelming, overpowering, annihilation, outwitting, outsmarting, *formal* vanquishing, *colloq.* hammering, slaughter, clobbering, thrashing

beau *n*
admirer, suitor, sweetheart, boyfriend, lover, escort, fiancé, *colloq.* guy

beautician *n*
beauty specialist, cosmetician, hairdresser, friseur, *formal* visagiste

beautiful *adj*
attractive, fair, pretty, lovely, good-looking, handsome, gorgeous, radiant, ravishing, voluptuous, striking, stunning, pleasing, appealing, alluring, charming, pleasing, delightful, fine, graceful, exquisite, seemly, becoming, magnificent, *Scot.* bonny, *formal* comely, pulchritudinous, *colloq.* smashing, out of this world
 ugly, plain, hideous

beautify *v*
embellish, smarten (up), enhance, improve, grace, gild, garnish, decorate, ornament, deck, bedeck, adorn, array, glamorize, spruce up, *colloq.* titivate, tart up, doll up
 disfigure, spoil

beauty *n*
1 *the beauty of a woman/poem* attractiveness, prettiness, loveliness, (good) looks, handsomeness, gorgeousness, radiance, appeal, allure, charm, delight, grace, gracefulness, exquisiteness, seemliness, excellence, harmony, symmetry, *formal* pulchritude **2** *think her a real beauty* belle, charmer, siren, Venus, *femme fatale*, *colloq.* good-looker, smasher, corker, cracker, knockout, stunner, peach **3** *the beauties of the plan* attraction, advantage, benefit, good thing, plus point, good point, virtue, merit, glory, boon, blessing, bonus, dividend
 1 ugliness, repulsiveness **2** frump **3** disadvantage

beaver *v*
▷ **beaver away** work hard, work at, put a lot of effort in, persist, persevere, *colloq.* slog, plug away, slave away

becalmed *adj*
at a standstill, at a halt, idle, motionless, still, stranded, marooned, stuck

because *conj*
as, for, since, owing to, due to, on account of, as a result of, the reason is ..., through, thanks to, in view of the fact that, *formal* by reason of, by virtue of, forasmuch, *colloq.* seeing as

beckon *v*
1 *beckon to someone* summon, motion, gesture, signal, nod, wave, gesticulate **2** *fame beckons* call, invite, attract, pull, draw, lure, allure, entice, tempt, induce, persuade, coax

become *v*
1 *become old-fashioned* turn, grow (into), get, change into, be changed into, develop into, mature into, pass into, come to be, turn out to be, wax **2** SUIT, befit, flatter, look good on, enhance, grace, embellish, ornament, set off, harmonize

becoming *adj*
1 *a hat in a more becoming style* attractive, charming, flattering, graceful, elegant, tasteful, fetching, pretty, comely **2** *becoming behaviour* APPROPRIATE, suitable, fit, fitting, befitting, consistent, congruous, compatible
 1, 2 unbecoming

bed *n, v*
▷ *n* **1** *get out of bed* divan, couch, bunk, *slang* sack, hay, kip **2** LAYER, stratum, substratum, matrix, base, basis, bottom, floor, foundation, groundwork, watercourse, channel **3** *bed of flowers* garden, border, patch, area, space, strip, row, plot
▷ **go to bed with** sleep with, have sex with, have sexual intercourse with, make love to

Kinds of bed include:
berth, box bed, bunk bed, camp-bed, cot, cradle, crib, day bed, divan bed, double bed, foldaway bed, folding bed, four-poster, hammock, mattress, pallet, palliasse, Put-u-up®, put-you-up, single bed, sofa bed, trucklebed, trundlebed, twin bed, water-bed, Z-bed.

▷ *v* base, embed, establish, fix, found, ground, implant, inlay, insert, bury, plant, settle
▷ **bed down** sleep, go to bed, settle down, turn in, *slang* doss down, hit the hay/sack, kip down

bedclothes *n*
bedding, bed-linen, covers

bedeck *v*
beautify, decorate, deck, adorn, embellish, festoon, garnish, ornament, array, trick out, trim

bedevil *v*
afflict, torment, confound, frustrate, harass, irk, pester, plague, tease, annoy, besiege, torture, trouble, distress, vex, fret, worry, irritate

bedlam *n*
chaos, pandemonium, madhouse, commotion, confusion, furore, clamour, hubbub, hullabaloo, noise, tumult, turmoil, uproar, babel, anarchy
 calm

bedraggled *adj*
untidy, unkempt, dishevelled, disordered, scruffy, slovenly, messy, dirty, muddy, muddied, soiled, wet, soaked, soaking (wet), sodden, dripping, drenched
 neat, tidy, clean

bedridden *adj*
confined to bed, incapacitated, *colloq.* laid up, flat on your back

bedrock *n*
foundation, support, basis, base, bottom, footing, reason(s), rationale, fundamentals, basics, essentials, fundamental point, starting-point, premise, first principles, essence, heart

beef *v*
complain, criticize, grumble, moan, grouse, object, dispute, disagree, *colloq.* gripe
 approve
▷ **beef up** strengthen, consolidate, give new energy to, toughen, invigorate, build up, establish, reinforce, substantiate, flesh out
 weaken

beefy *adj*
brawny, muscular, bulky, burly, fat, fleshy, heavy, hefty, hulking, stalwart, stocky, robust, sturdy, *formal* corpulent
 slight

beer *n*
ale, bitter, stout, real ale, light ale, draught, bottled beer, lager, Pils, Pilsener, mild

beetle *v*
dash, hurry, nip, run, rush, scamper, scoot, scurry, tear, zip

beetling *adj*
overhanging, protruding, poking out, projecting, jutting, leaning over, sticking out, *formal* pendent

befall v

happen, take place, occur, arrive, chance, result, ensue, fall, follow, materialize, *formal* betide, supervene

befitting *adj*

appropriate, suitable, becoming, apt, correct, decent, fit, fitting, proper, right, seemly, *old use* meet

🔁 unbecoming

before *prep, adv*

▶ *prep* **1** *before breakfast* earlier than, previous to, prior to, not later than, sooner than, in preparation for, in anticipation of, on the eve of **2** *perform before the king* in front of, in the presence of, in the sight of **3** *all of his life before him* in front of, ahead of

▶ *adv* **1** *have been here before* earlier, formerly, previously, already **2** *go on before* ahead, in front, in advance

beforehand *adv*

in advance, preliminarily, already, before, previously, earlier, sooner

befriend v

help, aid, assist, succour, back, support, protect, defend, look after, stand by, uphold, sustain, comfort, encourage, welcome, favour, benefit, take under your wing, keep an eye on, make friends with, make a friend of, get to know, fall in with, stick up for, *formal* succour

🔁 neglect, oppose

befuddle v

confuse, muddle, baffle, bewilder, daze, disorient, puzzle, stupefy

beg v

1 *beg someone to do something* ask for, beseech, request, require, desire, crave, plead, appeal, turn to, entreat, implore, pray, supplicate, petition, solicit, importune **2** *beg for money* ask for money, cadge, *colloq.* bum, scrounge, sponge, *US* mooch (off)

beget v

1 CAUSE, bring about, create, breed, give rise to, occasion, result in, engender, *formal* effect **2** *beget a child* breed, father, generate, procreate, produce, propagate, sire, spawn

beggar *n, v*

▶ *n* mendicant, supplicant, pauper, down-and-out, tramp, vagrant, panhandler, *colloq.* cadger, scrounger, sponger, freeloader, bum; *US* moocher, *slang* bludger, *US* schnorrer

▶ *v* defy, baffle, challenge, exceed, surpass, transcend

beggarly *adj*

stingy, abject, meagre, mean, miserly, contemptible, despicable, inadequate, low, needy, niggardly, paltry, pathetic, pitiful, wretched

🔁 affluent, generous

begin v

start, commence, set about, embark on, set in motion, get going, launch into, do first, activate, actuate, set off, originate, initiate, arise, spring, emerge, appear, crop up, *colloq.* kick off, get cracking, set the ball rolling, take the plunge

🔁 end, stop, finish, cease, conclude

beginner *n*

novice, tiro, starter, learner, trainee, apprentice, student, probationer, initiate, freshman, fresher, recruit, raw recruit, cub, tenderfoot, fledgling, neophyte, *old use* abecedarian, *colloq.* greenhorn, rookie

🔁 veteran, old hand, expert

beginning *n*

start, commencement, onset, outset, first part, opening part, opening, preface, prelude, introduction,

initiation, establishment, inauguration, institution, launch, inception, starting-point, birth, dawn, origin, source, fountainhead, root, seed, conception, genesis, emergence, rise, fresh start, new beginnings, pastures new, *formal* inchoation, incipience, *colloq.* the word go, day one, square one, first base, kick-off, intro, new leaf

🔁 end, finish, conclusion

begrudge v

resent, grudge, mind, object to, envy, covet, be jealous of, stint

🔁 allow

beguile v

1 CHARM, enchant, bewitch, captivate, delight, attract, amuse, entertain, divert, distract, occupy, engross **2** DECEIVE, fool, hoodwink, dupe, trick, cheat, delude, mislead, seduce, cozen

beguiling *adj*

alluring, appealing, attractive, bewitching, captivating, charming, delightful, diverting, enchanting, entertaining, interesting, intriguing, enticing, seductive

🔁 offensive, repulsive

behalf *n*

▷ **on behalf of** for, representing, acting for, for the benefit/good of, for the sake of, in the name/authority of, for the good of, in the interests of, to the advantage/profit of

behave v

1 *behave aggressively* act, conduct yourself, be, acquit yourself, respond, react, perform, *formal* comport yourself **2** *tell the children to behave themselves* be good, be well behaved, act properly/politely, be on your best behaviour, mind your manners, stay out of trouble, *colloq.* act your age, keep your nose clean, not mess about/muck about, stop fooling around, mind your p's and q's, not put a foot wrong **3** *electrons behave like this* function, operate, work, act, perform, react

🔁 **2** misbehave, get into trouble, *colloq.* act up, be up to no good

behaviour *n*

1 *the child's behaviour* conduct, manner, manners, ways, habits, dealings, way of acting, response, reaction, attitudes, *formal* demeanour, comportment, deportment **2** *the behaviour of chemical elements* operation, performance, functioning, action, reaction

behead v

decapitate, execute, guillotine

behest *n*

▷ **at the behest of** with the authority of, at the bidding of, at the order/command of, at the request of, on the instruction(s) of, on the wishes of

behind *prep, adv, n*

▶ *prep* **1** *a shed behind the garage* at the back of, at the rear of, on the other side of, *US* in back of **2** *walk behind the others* after, following, at the back of, at the rear of, close on **3** *behind schedule* late, later than, running late, overdue, slow, slower than usual **4** *we are behind you in your decision* supporting, backing, endorsing, for, on the side of **5** *the reasons behind the change in policy* responsible for, explaining, accounting for, instigating, causing, initiating, giving rise to, at the bottom of

🔁 **1** in front of **2** ahead of

▶ *adv* **1** *with a garden behind* at the back/rear, in the rear **2** *with the stragglers following behind* after, following, at the back, next, subsequently **3** *be behind with work/payments* behindhand, late, overdue, in arrears, in debt

▶ *n* bottom, buttocks, backside, *colloq.* bum, posterior, *US* butt

behindhand *adv*
delayed, late, remiss, slow, tardy, backward, *formal* dilatory

behold *v, interj*
▶ *v* consider, contemplate, descry, discern, espy, look at, see, watch, note, observe, mark, perceive, regard, scan, gaze at, survey, view, witness
▶ *interj* look, mark, observe, see, watch, *voici, voila, ecce*, lo

beholden *adj*
indebted, obligated, obliged, under obligation, bound, grateful, owing, thankful

behove *v*
befit, be seemly, be proper, be to your advantage, benefit, profit, be advantageous, be necessary, be essential

beige *adj*
buff, fawn, mushroom, camel, sandy, khaki, coffee, oatmeal, tan, ecru, greige, neutral

being *n*
1 EXISTENCE, actuality, reality, life, animation, essence, substance, nature, soul, spirit, *technical* haecceity, esse **2** CREATURE, animal, beast, human being, human, man, woman, mortal, person, individual, thing, entity

belabour *v*
hit, attack, beat, flog, thrash, whip, belt, flay

belated *adj*
late, tardy, overdue, delayed, behindhand, unpunctual
𝔽 punctual, timely

belch *v, n*
▶ *v* **1** *the baby belched* burp, hiccup, bring up wind, *formal* eructate **2** *chimneys belching out smoke* emit, give out, give off, discharge, vent, eject, disgorge, spew
▶ *n* burp, hiccup, *formal* eructation

beleaguered *adj*
1 *a beleaguered person* harassed, pestered, badgered, bothered, worried, vexed, plagued, persecuted, beset **2** *a beleaguered city* BESIEGED, under siege, surrounded, blockaded

belie *v*
1 *the statistics belie the theory* disprove, contradict, deny, refute, negate, run counter to, *formal* gainsay, confute **2** *her looks belie her age* conceal, disguise, misrepresent, falsify, mislead, deceive

belief *n*
1 OPINION, persuasion, feeling, intuition, impression, notion, theory, view, viewpoint, point of view, conviction, judgement **2** CONFIDENCE, reliance, trust, faith, credit, assurance, certainty, sureness, presumption, expectation **3** IDEOLOGY, faith, creed, doctrine, teaching, dogma, theory, ism, tenet, principle
𝔽 **2** disbelief, doubt

believable *adj*
credible, imaginable, conceivable, acceptable, plausible, possible, likely, probable, authoritative, reliable, trustworthy, (well) within the bounds of possibility, not beyond the realms of possibility, with a ring of truth
𝔽 unbelievable, incredible, inconceivable, implausible, unconvincing

believe *v*
1 *I believe she's a professor* think, be of the opinion that, accept, suppose, gather, reckon, assume, consider, hold, maintain, understand, speculate, conjecture, guess, imagine, judge, *formal* deem, postulate,

opine **2** *believe him/that he is telling the truth* accept, trust, be convinced by, be persuaded by, be certain of, take someone's word for it, *colloq.* take on board, swallow, fall for, buy, wear, fall for/swallow hook line and sinker
𝔽 **2** disbelieve, doubt, question
▷ **believe in 1** *believe in God* be sure of the existence/reality of, be convinced of **2** *believe in hard work* approve of, favour, be in favour of, recommend, encourage, swear by, trust, be persuaded by, value highly, depend on, rely on, have confidence in, trust, accept the importance of, *formal* set great store by, *colloq.* rate

believer *n*
convert, proselyte, disciple, follower, adherent, devotee, zealot, supporter, upholder
𝔽 unbeliever, sceptic

belittle *v*
demean, minimize, play down, trivialize, dismiss, underrate, understate, undervalue, underestimate, lessen, diminish, detract from, decry, disparage, run down, deride, scorn, ridicule, *formal* deprecate
𝔽 exaggerate, praise

bellicose *adj*
aggressive, militant, argumentative, quarrelsome, contentious, combative, violent, bullying, antagonistic, warring, warlike, *formal* pugnacious
𝔽 peaceable

belligerence *n*
aggression, militancy, argumentativeness, provocation, quarrelsomeness, unfriendliness, contentiousness, combativeness, violence, bullying, antagonism, war, war-mongering, sabre-rattling, *formal* pugnacity
𝔽 complaisance

belligerent *adj*
aggressive, militant, argumentative, provocative, quarrelsome, contentious, combative, violent, bullying, antagonistic, warring, warlike, war-mongering, sabre-rattling, *formal* pugnacious, disputatious, truculent
𝔽 peaceable

bellow *v*
roar, yell, shout, bawl, cry, scream, shriek, howl, clamour, raise your voice, *colloq.* holler

belly *n*
stomach, abdomen, gut, guts, insides, intestines, paunch, pot-belly, beer belly, *technical* venter, *colloq.* tummy, corporation, *slang* bread basket.

belong *v*
1 *this book belongs to me* be owned by, be the possession of, be the property of, be under the ownership of, be yours **2** *belong to a rugby club* be a member of, be affiliated to, be connected with, be associated with, be in, be an adherent of **3** *this lid belongs to that pan* fit, go with, be part of, attach to, link up with, tie up with, be connected with, relate to **4** *Where do these toys belong?* have as its place/home, go, fit in, be sorted, be categorized, be classified, be included

belonging *n*
rapport, closeness, acceptance, affinity, association, attachment, compatibility, fellow-feeling, fellowship, kinship, link(s), loyalty, relationship
𝔽 antipathy

belongings *n*
possessions, property, chattels, goods, (personal) effects, paraphernalia, *formal* appurtenances, accoutrements, *colloq.* gear, stuff, things

beloved *adj, n*
▶ *adj* loved, much loved, adored, cherished, treasured, prized, precious, pet, favourite, dearest, dear, darling, admired, revered, worshipped

▶ *n* sweetheart, darling, dear, dearest, love, fiancé, fiancée, betrothed, boyfriend, girlfriend, special friend, partner, spouse, husband, wife, favourite, lover, pet, precious, sweet, *formal* inamorata, inamorato

below *adv, prep*
▶ *adv* **1** *the flat below* beneath, under, underneath, down, lower, lower down **2** *see below for details* later, at a later place, further on
Ⓕ₄ 1, 2 above
▶ *prep* **1** UNDER, underneath, beneath, lower than **2** INFERIOR TO, lower (in rank) than, lesser than, subordinate to, subject to
Ⓕ₄ 1, 2 above

belt *n, v*
▶ *n* **1** SASH, girdle, waistband, girth, strap, *formal* cummerbund, baldric, ceinture, cestus, cincture, cingulum **2** STRIP, area, region, district, zone, swathe, stretch, tract, extent, layer **3** THUMP, hit, punch, strike, swipe, knock, bang, bashing, slap, smack, pelt, bruise, box, *colloq.* tan, wallop, whack, clout
▶ *v* **1** HIT, strap, flog, lash, whip, flay, cane, birch, punch, strike, swipe, knock, bang, bash, slap, smack, thump, thwack, pelt, bruise, box, *colloq.* tan, wallop, whack, clout, biff **2** *belt along the road* dash, tear, fly, rush, career, zip, charge, speed
▷ **belt up** shut up, be quiet, *colloq.* pipe down, cut it out, *slang* put a sock in it, keep your trap shut, shut your mouth/face

bemoan *v*
lament, mourn, bewail, deplore, grieve for, regret, rue, sigh for, sorrow over, weep for
Ⓕ₄ gloat

bemuse *v*
confuse, bewilder, puzzle, perplex, daze, muddle, befuddle, stupefy
Ⓕ₄ enlighten, illuminate

bemused *adj*
bewildered, confused, puzzled, perplexed, disconcerted, dazed, overwhelmed, muddled, befuddled, stupefied, astounded, astonished
Ⓕ₄ clear-headed, clear, lucid

bench *n*
1 SEAT, form, settle, pew, ledge **2** *work at a bench* counter, table, stall, board, workbench, worktable **3** COURT, courtroom, tribunal, judiciary, judicature, judge, magistrate

benchmark *n*
criterion, example, level, model, norm, pattern, reference, reference-point, point of reference, guideline(s), standard, scale, touchstone, yardstick

bend *v, n*
▶ *v* **1** *bend down to pick up a pin* stoop, crouch, lean, incline, bow, kneel **2** *bend the wire* curve, make curved, turn, deflect, twist, contort, flex, shape, mould, arch, bow, loop, contort, buckle, warp, **3** *the road bends* curve, turn, deflect, veer, diverge, twist, wind, meander, zigzag, swerve, deviate, *formal* incurve **4** *bend to their will* mould, shape, persuade, influence, affect, sway, compel
Ⓕ₄ 2 straighten
▶ *n* curvature, curve, arc, bow, loop, hook, crook, elbow, angle, corner, hairpin bend, dog-leg, turn, twist, kink, zigzag, divergence, deflection, *technical* flexure, *formal* incurvation

beneath *adv, prep*
▶ *adv* below, under, underneath, lower, lower down
Ⓕ₄ above
▶ *prep* **1** UNDER, underneath, below, lower than **2** UNWORTHY OF, unbefitting, unbecoming
Ⓕ₄ 1 above

benediction *n*
blessing, prayer, thanksgiving, consecration, favour, grace, invocation, *formal* benison
Ⓕ₄ anathema, curse, *formal* execration

benefactor *n*
patron, sponsor, backer, supporter, promoter, donor, contributor, subscriber, provider, subsidizer, philanthropist, helper, friend, well-wisher, giver, *colloq.* angel
Ⓕ₄ opponent, persecutor

beneficent *adj*
altruistic, liberal, benevolent, benign, bountiful, charitable, compassionate, generous, helpful, kind, unselfish, *formal* munificent
Ⓕ₄ mean

beneficial *adj*
advantageous, favourable, useful, helpful, promising, profitable, serviceable, rewarding, valuable, improving, edifying, wholesome, salutary, *formal* propitious
Ⓕ₄ harmful, detrimental, useless

beneficiary *n*
payee, receiver, recipient, inheritor, legatee, heir, heiress, successor

benefit *n, v*
▶ *n* **1** *the benefits of exercise* advantage, good, good point, gain, profit, asset, blessing, boon, interest, favour, bonus, dividend, fringe benefit, perk, *colloq.* pay-off **2** *of benefit to children* good help, aid, assistance, service, use, avail, welfare **3** *child benefit; unemployment benefit* income, allowance, pension, sick pay, payment, social security, credit, support, Job Seekers Allowance (JSA), unemployment benefit, income support, *colloq.* dole, *US* welfare
Ⓕ₄ 1 disadvantage **2** harm, damage
▶ *v* help, aid, assist, serve, be of service to, avail, be of advantage to, do good to, profit, improve, enhance, better, further, advance, promote
Ⓕ₄ hinder, harm, undermine

benevolence *n*
philanthropy, humanitarianism, charitableness, generosity, liberality, magnanimity, altruism, humaneness, goodwill, kindness, kind-heartedness, friendliness, compassion, pity, mercy, grace, tolerance, care, considerateness, *formal* munificence
Ⓕ₄ meanness

benevolent *adj*
philanthropic, humanitarian, charitable, generous, liberal, magnanimous, altruistic, benign, humane, kind, kind-hearted, soft-hearted, friendly, kindly, well-disposed, compassionate, merciful, gracious, tolerant, caring, considerate, *formal* munificent
Ⓕ₄ mean, selfish, malevolent

benighted *adj*
ignorant, unenlightened, inexperienced, unknowing, uneducated, unschooled, uncultured, backward, illiterate, unlettered, unfortunate

benign *adj*
1 BENEVOLENT, charitable, good, gracious, gentle, kind, obliging, friendly, amiable, affable, genial, cordial, generous, liberal, sympathetic **2** *benign conditions/climate* FAVOURABLE, opportune, providential, beneficial, agreeable, temperate, mild, warm, refreshing, healthy, restorative, wholesome, *formal* auspicious, propitious, salubrious **3** *a benign tumour* curable, harmless, non-malignant, treatable
Ⓕ₄ 1 hostile **2** harmful, unpleasant **3** malignant, dangerous

bent *adj, n*
▶ *adj* **1** ANGLED, curved, bowed, arched, crooked, folded, doubled, twisted, hunched, stooped, warped, contorted **2** DISHONEST, illegal, criminal, corrupt, fraudulent, untrustworthy, *colloq.* crooked

■ 1 straight, upright 2 honest, trustworthy

▷ **bent on** determined to, resolved to, set on, fixed on, insistent on, intent on, inclined to, disposed to

▶ *n* tendency, inclination, disposition, leaning, preference, ability, capacity, faculty, aptitude, facility, gift, talent, fondness, knack, flair, forte, *formal* predisposition, predilecton, penchant, proclivity, propensity, *colloq.* cup of tea

bequeath *v*

1 *bequeathed in her will* leave, bestow, will, make over, give, endow, grant, consign, transfer, assign, entrust, commit 2 *social problems bequeathed by past generations* hand down, pass on, impart, transmit

bequest *n*

legacy, inheritance, heritage, trust, endowment, gift, donation, estate, settlement, *formal* devisal, bestowal, bequeathal

berate *v*

scold, chide, reprimand, rebuke, tell off, reproach, reprove, censure, chastise, chide, criticize, rail at, revile, upbraid, *formal* castigate, fulminate, vituperate, *colloq.* blast, slate, read the riot act to, jump down the throat of, dress down, tear a strip off, give a rocket to, give hell, *US* chew out

■ praise

bereaved *adj*

deprived, lost, dispossessed, divested, robbed, orphaned, widowed

bereavement *n*

loss, death, passing, passing-away, deprivation, dispossession, sadness, sorrow, grief

bereft *adj*

▷ **bereft of** deprived of, robbed of, stripped of, destitute of, devoid of, lacking, wanting, parted from, cut off from, minus

berserk *adj*

mad, crazy, demented, insane, deranged, frantic, frenzied, crazed, wild, raging, furious, violent, rabid, manic, maniacal, raving, hysterical, uncontrollable, *colloq.* out of your mind, off your head

■ sane, calm

berth *n, v*

▶ *n* 1 BED, bunk, hammock, billet 2 MOORING, anchorage, quay, wharf, dock, harbour, port

▶ *v* anchor, dock, drop/cast anchor, land, moor, tie up

■ weigh anchor, up anchor

beseech *v*

beg, call on, entreat, implore, ask, petition, plead, pray, solicit, appeal to, supplicate, crave, desire, *formal* adjure, importune, obsecrate, sue, exhort

beset *v*

assail, attack, harass, entangle, worry, pester, plague, torment, bedevil, hem in, surround, *colloq.* hassle

besetting *adj*

compulsive, habitual, persistent, dominant, inveterate, irresistible, uncontrollable, obsessive, prevalent, constant, recurring, troublesome, harassing

beside *prep*

next to, by, alongside, abreast of, adjacent, abutting, bordering, neighbouring, next door to, close to, near, overlooking

▷ **beside the point** irrelevant, immaterial, extraneous, inapplicable, incidental, inconsequential, pointless, unimportant, unrelated

▷ **beside yourself** berserk, insane, mad, crazy, crazed, delirious, demented, deranged, frantic, frenetic, frenzied, distraught, unbalanced, unhinged

besides *adv, prep*

▶ *adv* also, as well, too, in addition, additionally, further, furthermore, moreover, *colloq.* what's more

▶ *prep* apart from, other than, aside from, in addition to, over and above, as well as, excluding

besiege *v*

1 LAY SIEGE TO, blockade, surround, encircle, encompass, confine, beleaguer 2 *besieged by reporters* surround, encircle, encompass, confine, shut in, hem in 3 TROUBLE, worry, bother, importune, assail, beset, beleaguer, harass, pester, badger, nag, hound, plague

besmirch *v*

defame, defile, dishonour, slander, smear, soil, dirty, blacken, damage, stain, sully, tarnish

■ enhance

besotted *adj*

infatuated, doting, obsessed, smitten, hypnotized, spellbound, stupefied, bewitched, intoxicated

■ indifferent, disenchanted

bespeak *v*

demonstrate, indicate, reveal, show, signify, denote, display, exhibit, evidence, evince, attest, proclaim, suggest, imply

best *adj, adv, n, v*

▶ *adj* optimum, optimal, first, foremost, leading, top, ultimate, prime, record-breaking, unequalled, unsurpassed, unrivalled, unbeatable, matchless, peerless, incomparable, supreme, pre-eminent, of highest quality, greatest, highest, largest, finest, worthiest, excellent, outstanding, superlative, first-rate, first-class, ideal, perfect, *formal* nonpareil, *colloq.* ace, star, number one, (the) tops, second to none, the pick of the bunch, one in a million, a cut above the rest

■ worst

▶ *adv* greatly, extremely, exceptionally, excellently, outstandingly, superlatively, unsurpassedly, matchlessly, incomparably, supremely, most, to the greatest/highest degree

■ worst, least

▶ *n* 1 *students who are the best in their year* finest, cream, prime, elite, top, first, pick, choice, favourite, star, highlight, *colloq.* the pick of the bunch 2 *do your best* hardest, utmost, greatest effort, *colloq.* damnedest

■ 1 worst

▶ *v* defeat, trounce, worst, conquer, overcome, overwhelm, overpower, subdue, rout, annihilate, outplay, outwit, outsmart, be more than a match for, have the edge on, *formal* vanquish, *colloq.* hammer, slaughter, clobber, lick, thrash

bestial *adj*

cruel, savage, brutal, animal, barbaric, barbarous, beastly, inhuman, brutish, carnal, depraved, degraded, gross, sensual, sordid, vile, *formal* feral

■ civilized, humane

bestir *v*

arouse, exert, awaken, stimulate, energize, galvanize, incite, motivate, activate, actuate, animate

■ calm, lull, quell

bestow *v*

award, present, grant, confer, endow, bequeath, commit, entrust, impart, transmit, allot, apportion, accord, give, donate, lavish

■ withhold, deprive

bestride *v*

dominate, command, overshadow, bestraddle, sit astride, stand astride, straddle

bet *v, n*

▶ *v* 1 *bet money on a horse* wager, gamble, punt, speculate, risk, hazard, chance, venture, lay, stake, bid, pledge, back, put, place, *colloq.* play for money, have a flutter 2 *I bet she did it on purpose* be certain, be sure, be convinced, expect, not be surprised

▶ n 1 *place a bet* wager, gamble, speculation, risk, venture, stake, ante, bid, pledge, lottery, sweepstake, accumulator, *colloq.* flutter **2** *my bet is that he'll stay* opinion, feeling, intuition, impression, notion, theory, view, viewpoint, point of view, conviction, judgement **3** *your best bet* choice, option, course of action, alternative

bête noire *n*
bugbear, bane, abomination, anathema, aversion, curse, pet hate, pet aversion
F3 favourite

betide *v*
befall, chance, develop, ensue, happen, occur, overtake, *formal* supervene

betoken *v*
signal, indicate, signify, suggest, augur, bespeak, bode, forebode, portend, presage, declare, denote, evidence, represent, manifest, mark, prognosticate, promise

betray *v*
1 *betray a friend* inform on, double-cross, desert, abandon, forsake, turn traitor, be disloyal to, be unfaithful to, break faith with, deceive, delude, mislead, dupe, *colloq.* tell on, sell (out), sell down the river, stab in the back, squeal on, blow the whistle on, shop, walk out on, *slang* grass **2** DISCLOSE, give away, tell, divulge, expose, reveal, show, manifest, let slip, bring to light, unmask
F3 1 defend, protect, be loyal to **2** conceal, hide

betrayal *n*
treachery, treason, sell-out, disloyalty, unfaithfulness, double-dealing, double-crossing, duplicity, deception, trickery, duping, falseness, breaking faith, *formal* perfidy
F3 loyalty, faithfulness, protection

betrayer *n*
traitor, Judas, informer, double-crosser, deceiver, conspirator, renegade, apostate, *colloq.* whistle-blower, *slang* grass, supergrass
F3 protector, supporter

betrothal *n*
engagement, proposal of marriage, promise, vow(s), plighting of your troth, troth, *formal* espousal, fiançailles

betrothed *adj*
engaged, engaged to be married, contracted, promised, *formal* affianced, espoused

better *adj, v*
▶ adj 1 SUPERIOR, bigger, larger, longer, greater, worthier, of higher quality, finer, surpassing, preferable, more acceptable, more fitting, more advantageous, more valuable, *colloq.* a cut above **2** IMPROVING, progressing, on the mend, recovering, fitter, healthier, stronger, (fully) recovered, restored, cured, healed, well, *colloq.* on the mend
F3 1 inferior **2** worse
▶ v 1 IMPROVE, enhance, raise, make better, further, promote, forward, reform, mend, correct, rectify, enrich, *formal* ameliorate **2** SURPASS, top, beat, outdo, exceed, improve on, outstrip, overtake, cap, go one better than
F3 1 worsen, deteriorate

betterment *n*
improvement, furtherance, advancement, edification, enhancement, enrichment, *formal* amelioration, melioration
F3 deterioration, impairment

between *prep*
in the middle (of), among, halfway, mid, amid, amidst, amongst

bevel *n, v*
▶ n oblique, slant, slope, tilt, angle, bias, diagonal, mitre, basil, bezel, cant, chamfer
▶ v slant, slope, tilt, angle, mitre, bias, cant, chamfer

beverage *n*
drink, draught, liquor, liquid, refreshment, *formal* potation, potable

bevy *n*
gathering, group, band, company, assembly, collection, troupe, flock, gaggle, pack, bunch, crowd, throng

bewail *v*
grieve over, sorrow over, lament, bemoan, cry over, moan, mourn, regret, repent, rue, sigh over, deplore, keen
F3 gloat, glory, vaunt

beware *v*
watch out, look out, mind (out), be careful, be cautious, be wary, take heed, steer clear of, avoid, shun, guard against, be on your guard, be on the lookout for

bewilder *v*
confuse, muddle, mix up, disconcert, confound, baffle, puzzle, perplex, mystify, daze, stupefy, bemuse, disorient, *colloq.* bamboozle, stump

bewildered *adj*
confused, muddled, uncertain, disoriented, nonplussed, baffled, puzzled, perplexed, mystified, taken aback, bemused, surprised, speechless, stunned, *colloq.* bamboozled, (all) at sea
F3 unperturbed, collected

bewilderment *n*
perplexity, confusion, uncertainty, daze, disconcertion, disorientation, mystification, puzzlement, stupefaction, surprise, awe
F3 composure, confidence

bewitch *v*
charm, enchant, allure, beguile, spellbind, possess, enthral, captivate, enrapture, delight, obsess, fascinate, intrigue, tantalize, seduce, entrance, mesmerize, hypnotize, transfix
F3 disenchant, repel

beyond *prep* **1** *the fields beyond the house* on the far side of, on the other side of, further than, away from, remote from, apart from **2** *beyond the age of 16* after, past, later than, above, over, greater than, upwards of **3** *beyond me/my understanding* out of reach of, out of range of, further than the limitations of

bias *n, v*
▶ n 1 *racial bias* PREJUDICE, partiality, favouritism, one-sidedness, unfairness, bigotry, intolerance, stereotyping, distortion, bent, leaning, inclination, tendency, *formal* propensity, proclivity, predilection **2** *cut on the bias* diagonal, angle, slant, oblique, cross
F3 1 impartiality, fairness
▶ v prejudice, influence, sway, predispose, distort, jaundice, twist, angle, load, slant, warp, weight, *old use* earwig, *colloq.* load the dice

biased *adj*
prejudiced, one-sided, unfair, bigoted, blinkered, jaundiced, influenced, swayed, partial, predisposed, tendentious, subjective, partisan, slanted, angled, distorted, warped, twisted, loaded, weighted
F3 impartial, fair, objective

Bible *n*
1 *study the Christian Bible* Scriptures, holy Scriptures, Holy Bible, holy writ, Old Testament, New Testament, Apocrypha, writings, canon, revelation, Pentateuch, law, prophets, Gospels, epistles, letters, *colloq.* good book

The books of the Bible are:
the Old Testament: Genesis, Exodus, Leviticus, Numbers, Deuteronomy, Joshua, Judges, Ruth, 1 Samuel, 2 Samuel, 1 Kings, 2 Kings, 1 Chronicles, 2 Chronicles, Ezra, Nehemiah, Esther, Job, Psalms, Proverbs, Ecclesiastes, Song of Solomon (Song of Songs), Isaiah, Jeremiah, Lamentations, Ezekiel, Daniel, Hosea, Joel, Amos, Obadiah, Jonah, Micah, Nahum, Habakkuk, Zephaniah, Haggai, Zechariah, Malachi; *the New Testament*: Matthew, Mark, Luke, John, Acts of the Apostles, Romans, 1 Corinthians, 2 Corinthians, Galatians, Ephesians, Philippians, Colossians, 1 Thessalonians, 2 Thessalonians, 1 Timothy, 2 Timothy, Titus, Philemon, Hebrews, James, 1 Peter, 2 Peter, 1 John, 2 John, 3 John, Jude, Revelation; *the Apocrypha*: 1 Esdras, 2 Esdras, Tobit, Judith, Additions to Esther, Wisdom of Solomon, Ecclesiasticus, Baruch, Letter of Jeremiah, Prayer of Azariah, Song of the Three Young Men, History of Susanna, Bel and the Dragon, Prayer of Manasseh, 1 Maccabees, 2 Maccabees.

2 *the gardener's bible*; *the cyclist's bible* manual, handbook, authority, reference book, encyclopedia, dictionary, lexicon, guidebook, directory, companion, textbook, primer

bibliography *n*
book list, list of books, record, catalogue

bicker *v*
squabble, row, quarrel, wrangle, argue, spar, fight, clash, disagree, dispute, fall out, *formal* altercate, *colloq.* scrap
☲ agree, make up

bicycle *n*
cycle, two-wheeler, racer, mountain bike, all-terrain bike, tandem, unicycle, *colloq.* bike, push-bike

Parts of a bicycle include:
bell, brake, brake block, brake cable, brake caliper, brake lever, brake shoe, cable braking system, carrier, centre-pull brake cable, chain, chain guide, chain guard, chain link, chain stays, chain transmission, chain wheel, coaster brake, crank, crank lever, crankset, crossbar, derailleur gear, diamond frame, down tube, drum brake, dynamo, footrest, fork, frame, freewheel unit, gear, gear cable, gearwheel, handgrip, handlebars, handlebar stem, hub, hub gear, inner tube, kickstand, lamp, lamp bracket, mudguard, *US* fender, pannier, pedal, prop stand, pulley, pump, reflector, rim brake, rim tape, rod braking system, roller chain, saddle, saddle spring, seat pillar, seat stays, seat tube, side-pull brake cable, speedometer, spokes, spoke nipples, sprocket (wheel), stabilizer, steering head, steering tube, stirrup guide, toe clip, tool bag, tyre, *US* tire; tyre valve, Presta® valve, Schrader® valve, Woods® valve; wheel bearing, wheel lock, wheel nut, wheel rim, wheel spindle.

bid *v, n*
▶ *v* **1** *bid for a painting* offer, proffer, tender, submit, put forward, advance, propose **2** ASK, request, desire, instruct, direct, command, order, require, charge, call (for), demand, tell, summon, invite, solicit, *formal* enjoin **3** *bid them farewell* wish, greet, say, call, tell, wave
▶ *n* **1** OFFER, tender, sum, amount, price, advance, submission, proposal **2** ATTEMPT, effort, try, endeavour, venture, *colloq.* go

bidding *n*
request, desire, instruction, direction, command, order, charge, call, demand, summons, requirement, invitation, injunction, *formal* behest

big *adj*
1 *a big house* large, great, sizable, considerable, substantial, huge, enormous, immense, vast, massive, colossal, gigantic, giant, mammoth, extensive, spacious, cavernous, extra large, *formal* voluminous, *colloq.* whopping, jumbo, bumper, ginormous, humungous, *slang* mega **2** *a big person* large, burly, tall, huge, enormous, bulky, hulking, massive, beefy, brawny, muscular, fat, stout, obese, *formal* corpulent, *colloq.* hefty **3** *love your big brother* older, elder, grown-up, adult **4** *a big decision* important, significant, momentous, major, serious, weighty, salient, critical, radical, fundamental **5** *a big name in the fashion world* important, significant, well-known, famous, leading, main, principal, eminent, distinguished, prominent, influential, outstanding, noteworthy, valued **6** *that's big of you* generous, magnanimous, gracious, kind-hearted, benevolent, unselfish
☲ **1, 2** small, little **3** younger **4** insignificant **5** insignificant, unknown **6** mean, miserly, selfish

bigot *n*
sectarian, dogmatist, fanatic, zealot, chauvinist, racist, sexist, male chauvinist pig (MCP)
☲ liberal, humanitarian

bigoted *adj*
prejudiced, biased, intolerant, fanatical, illiberal, narrow-minded, narrow, blinkered, closed, dogmatic, opinionated, obstinate, jaundiced, influenced, swayed, partial, warped, twisted
☲ tolerant, liberal, broad-minded, enlightened

bigotry *n*
prejudice, discrimination, bias, injustice, unfairness, intolerance, partiality, narrow-mindedness, dogmatism, fanaticism, chauvinism, jingoism, sectarianism, racism, racialism, sexism
☲ tolerance

bigwig *n*
celebrity, dignitary, personage, somebody, VIP, notable, mogul, panjandrum, *colloq.* big gun, big noise, big shot, big cheese, heavyweight, nob
☲ nobody, nonentity

bile *n*
anger, bitterness, bad temper, short temper, ill-humour, irascibility, irritability, testiness, peevishness, rancour, choler, gall, spleen

bilge *n*
rubbish, nonsense, drivel, gibberish, trash, tripe, twaddle, *colloq.* claptrap, piffle, codswallop, poppycock, hot air, cobblers, rot, tommyrot

bilious *adj*
1 IRRITABLE, bad-tempered, short-tempered, ill-tempered, ill-humoured, choleric, cross, grumpy, crotchety, testy, grouchy, edgy, crabby, peevish **2** SICK, queasy, nauseated, sickly, *colloq.* out of sorts **3** *bilious colours* sickly, disgusting, nauseating, garish

bilk *v*
cheat, deceive, defraud, trick, swindle, *colloq.* con, do, do out of, diddle, bamboozle, *slang* fleece, sting

bill¹ *n, v*
▶ *n* **1** INVOICE, statement, account, charges, reckoning, tally, score, *US* check, *US, colloq.* tab **2** CIRCULAR, leaflet, handout, bulletin, handbill, broadsheet, advertisement, notice, announcement, poster, flyer, placard, playbill, programme, *colloq.* advert, ad **3** *parliamentary bill* proposal, measure, (piece of) legislation, statute, act
▶ *v* **1** *bill you at the end of the month* invoice, charge,

debit, list costs, send a statement, send an account/invoice **2** *be billed to appear in a show* advertise, announce, give notice, post

bill² *n*
a bird's bill
beak, mandible, neb, nib, rostrum

billet *n, v*
▶ *n* **1** ACCOMMODATION, quarters, living quarters, barracks, lodging, housing, berth **2** EMPLOYMENT, post, job, post, position, situation, office, occupation
▶ *v* accommodate, lodge, quarter, station

billow *v, n*
▶ *v* swell, expand, bulge, puff out, fill out, balloon, rise, heave, surge, roll, undulate
▶ *n* cloud, mass, surge, rush, wave, flood, breaker

billowy *adj*
billowing, swelling, surging, heaving, rippling, rolling, tossing, swirling, undulating, waving

bin *n*
container, receptacle, box, basket, chest

bind *v, n*
▶ *v* **1** FASTEN, tie, attach, fasten, secure, clamp, stick, lash, truss, rope, strap, fetter, tether, shackle, chain, bandage, cover, dress, wrap, tape **2** OBLIGE, force, compel, constrain, impel, require, necessitate, restrict, confine, restrain, hamper, yoke **3** *bound together by a common grief* UNITE, join, tie, unify, bond, stand together, pull together, close ranks
▶ *n* bore, difficulty, inconvenience, irritation, dilemma, embarrassment, hole, impasse, nuisance, predicament, quandary, *colloq.* drag, spot, tight spot

binding *adj, n*
▶ *adj* obligatory, compulsory, mandatory, necessary, requisite, permanent, conclusive, irrevocable, unalterable, indissoluble, unbreakable, strict, stringent, rigorous, tight, valid
▶ *n* cover, covering, wrapping, border, edging, trimming, tape, bandage

binge *n*
spree, bout, fling, orgy, jag, guzzle, *colloq.* do, beano, bender, blind
F∃ fast

biography *n*
life story, life, history, autobiography, memoirs, journals, diaries, letters, recollections, profile, curriculum vitae, cv, account, record, biopic, *formal* prosopography

biology *n*

Biological terms include :

bacteriology, biochemistry, biology, bionics, botany, cybernetics, cytology, Darwinism, neo-Darwinism, ecology, embryology, endocrinology, evolution, Haeckel's law, genetics, Mendelism, Lamarckism, marine biology, natural history, palaeontology, pathology, physiology, systematics, taxonomy, zoology; amino acid, anatomy, animal behaviour, animal kingdom, bacillus, bacteria, biologist, botanist, cell, chromosome, class, coccus, conservation, corpuscle, cultivar, cytoplasm, deoxyribonucleic acid (DNA), diffusion, ecosystem, ectoplasm, embryo, endoplasmic reticulum (ER), enzyme, evolution, excretion, extinction, flora and fauna, food chain, fossil, gene, genetic engineering, genetic fingerprinting, population genetics, germ, Golgi apparatus, hereditary factor, homeostasis, living world, meiosis, membrane, metabolism, microorganism, microbe, mitosis, molecule, mutation,

natural selection, nuclear membrane, nucleus, nutrition, order, organism, osmosis, parasitism, photosynthesis, pollution, protein, protoplasm, reproduction, respiration, reticulum, ribonucleic acid (RNA), ribosome, secretion, survival of the fittest, symbiosis, virus.

bird *n*

Birds include:
sparrow, thrush, starling, blackbird, bluetit, chaffinch, greenfinch, bullfinch, dunnock, robin, wagtail, swallow, tit, wren, martin, swift, crow, magpie, dove, pigeon, skylark, nightingale, linnet, warbler, jay, jackdaw, rook, raven, cuckoo, woodpecker, yellowhammer; duck, mallard, eider, teal, swan, goose, heron, stork, flamingo, pelican, kingfisher, moorhen, coot, lapwing, peewit, plover, curlew, snipe, avocet, seagull, guillemot, tern, petrel, crane, bittern, petrel, albatross, gannet, cormorant, auk, puffin, dipper; eagle, owl, hawk, sparrowhawk, falcon, kestrel, osprey, buzzard, vulture, condor; emu, ostrich, kiwi, peacock, penguin; chicken, grouse, partridge, pheasant, quail, turkey; canary, budgerigar, *colloq.* budgie, cockatiel, cockatoo, lovebird, parakeet, parrot, macaw, toucan, myna bird, mockingbird, kookaburra, bird of paradise.

birth *n*
1 CHILDBIRTH, labour, confinement, delivery, arrival, nativity, *formal* parturition, *colloq.* patter of tiny feet. **2** *of noble birth* ancestry, family, parentage, origin(s), descent, line, lineage, genealogy, derivation, pedigree, blood, stock, race, strain, house, extraction, background, breeding **3** BEGINNING, rise, emergence, arrival, appearance, origin(s), start, starting-point, commencement, source, dawn, derivation, fountainhead, root, seed, genesis, *formal* advent
F∃ 1 death **3** end, finish, conclusion

birthday *n*
anniversary, day of birth

birthmark *n*
blemish, discoloration, mole, patch, naevus, strawberry mark, port wine stain

birthplace *n*
place of origin, place of birth, native town, native country, fatherland, mother country, home, home town, root(s), provenance, source, fount, cradle

birthright *n*
privilege, prerogative, due, inheritance, legacy

biscuit *n*
cake, cookie, cracker, rusk, wafer, hardtack

bisect *v*
halve, cut in half, divide, divide into two, separate, split, intersect, cross, fork, *formal* bifurcate

bisexual *adj*
androgynous, hermaphrodite, *technical* gynandromorphic, gynandromorphous, monoclinous, epicene, *colloq.* bi
F∃ heterosexual, homosexual

bishop *n*
prelate, archbishop, primate, diocesan, metropolitan, patriarch, suffragan

bit *n*
fragment, part, segment, portion, piece, small piece, slice, crumb, grain, morsel, mouthful, drop, dash, chunk, lump, scrap, particle, atom, mite, whit, jot,

iota, tittle, shred, grain, flake, chip, sliver, speck, touch, hint, trace, scintilla, soupçon, vestige

▷ **a bit 1** *a bit boring* slightly, rather, a little, not much, not very **2** *wait a bit* a while, a moment, a short time, minute, few minutes, moment, few moments, *colloq.* jiffy, tick

▷ **bit by bit** gradually, little by little, in stages, step by step, slowly, piecemeal

🔁 all at once, wholesale

bitch *v*
complain, moan, grumble, criticize, find fault with, talk about behind their back, run down, malign, *formal* speak ill of, *colloq.* gripe, whinge, whine, slag off, bad-mouth

bitchy *adj*
catty, snide, nasty, mean, spiteful, malicious, vindictive, cutting, backbiting, venomous, cruel, vicious, *formal* rancorous

🔁 kind, loving

bite *v, n*
▶ *v* **1** CHEW, eat, munch, gnaw, nibble, peck, champ, crunch, crush, *formal* masticate **2** *the dog bit her hand* nip, snap, pierce, wound, tear, rend, sink/get your teeth into **3** SMART, sting, tingle **4** *the rise in costs was beginning to bite* GRIP, take effect, work, grip, hold, seize, pinch

▶ *n* **1** NIP, snap, wound, sting, smarting, pinch, prick, puncture, lesion **2** *have a bite to eat* snack, light meal, refreshment, mouthful, morsel, taste, piece, bit **3** PUNGENCY, piquancy, spiciness, *colloq.* kick, punch

biting *adj*
1 COLD, freezing, sharp, bitter, harsh, severe, penetrating, piercing, nipping, stinging **2** CUTTING, incisive, bitter, piercing, penetrating, raw, stinging, sharp, tart, caustic, scathing, cynical, hurtful, *formal* trenchant, mordant

🔁 **1** mild **2** bland

bitter *adj*
1 ACID, tart, sharp, sour, vinegary, unsweetened, pungent, tangy, *formal* acrid, astringent, acerbic **2** RESENTFUL, embittered, begrudging, indignant, aggrieved, angry, sour, morose, jaundiced, cynical, sullen, hostile, spiteful, vindictive, venomous, scathing, caustic, *formal* acrimonious, acerbic, rancorous, malevolent, vitriolic, vituperative, virulent, *colloq.* with a chip on your shoulder **3** INTENSE, severe, harsh, fierce, cruel, savage, merciless, painful, sad, unhappy, disappointing, tragic, distressing, harrowing, heartbreaking, heart-rending **4** *bitter winds* stinging, biting, sharp, freezing, freezing cold, arctic, icy, glacial, wintry, keen, raw, harsh, piercing, penetrating, *colloq.* parky

🔁 **1** sweet **2** contented **3** mild, happy **4** warm

bitterness *n*
1 ACIDITY, tartness, sharpness, sourness, vinegar, pungency, tanginess **2** RESENTMENT, embitterment, grudge, indignation, anger, sourness, moroseness, jaundice, cynicism, sullenness, hostility, spite, vindictiveness, venom, *formal* acrimony, acerbicity, rancour, malevolence, virulence **3** INTENSITY, severity, harshness, ferocity, cruelty, pain, painfulness, sadness, unhappiness, disappointment, tragedy, distress, heartbreaking, heart-rending **4** *the bitterness of the winter* sharpness, coldness, rawness, harshness, penetration, bite

bizarre *adj*
strange, odd, queer, curious, weird, peculiar, eccentric, outlandish, ludicrous, ridiculous, fantastic, comical, extravagant, grotesque, freakish, abnormal, deviant, unusual, uncommon, unconventional,

extraordinary, *colloq.* offbeat, oddball, wacky, *slang* way-out

🔁 normal, ordinary, standard

blab *v*
blurt out, tell, reveal, disclose, divulge, betray, let slip, let on, gossip, tattle, *colloq.* squeal, leak, let the cat out of the bag, spill the beans, give the game away

🔁 hide, hush up

black *adj, v, n*
▶ *adj* **1** JET-BLACK, coal-black, pitch-black, jet, ebony, raven, sable, inky, sooty, dusky, swarthy, *formal* nigrescent, *colloq.* black as coal **2** DARK, unlit, unilluminated, moonless, starless, overcast, dingy, dusky, dim, gloomy, overcast, sombre, funereal, pitch-black, *formal* crepuscular, tenebrous, fuliginous, subfusc, Cimmerian, Stygian **3** FILTHY, dirty, soiled, stained, grimy, sooty, grubby, muddy, unclean **4** *the future looks black* bleak, gloomy, sad, depressing, distressing, melancholy, dismal, hopeless, sombre, mournful, funereal, awful **5** *in a black mood* miserable, depressed, resentful, bitter, sullen, angry, threatening, menacing, *formal* lugubrious

🔁 **1** white **2** bright **3** clean **4** bright

▶ *v* **1** *black someone's eye* bruise, blacken, punch, hit, injure **2** *they blacked the imported goods* boycott, embargo, blacklist, ban, bar, taboo

▷ **black out 1** FAINT, pass out, lose consciousness, collapse, *colloq.* flake out **2** DARKEN, eclipse, cover up **3** CENSOR, conceal, suppress, withhold, censor, gag

▶ *n* ▷ **in the black** in credit, without debt, solvent, *colloq.* with your head above water

blackball *v*
vote against, ban, bar, blacklist, ostracize, shut out, drum out, throw out, exclude, expel, oust, reject, repudiate, snub, veto, *colloq.* give the cold shoulder to

blacken *v*
1 DARKEN, dirty, make dirty, soil, smudge, cloud **2** DEFAME, malign, slander, libel, revile, detract, smear, besmirch, sully, stain, tarnish, taint, defile, discredit, dishonour, *formal* impugn, calumniate, vilify, decry, *colloq.* run down

🔁 **2** praise, enhance

blackguard *n*
scoundrel, rascal, rogue, villain, devil, knave, miscreant, reprobate, wretch, *colloq.* bleeder, blighter, bounder, rotter, stinker, swine, scumbag

blacklist *v*
debar, disallow, exclude, ban, outlaw, bar, boycott, expel, ostracize, reject, shut out, repudiate, snub, taboo, veto, *formal* preclude, proscribe

🔁 accept, allow

blackmail *n, v*
▶ *n* extortion, intimidation, exaction, bribery, ransom, *formal* chantage, *colloq.* hush money
▶ *v* extort, exact, hold to ransom, threaten, force, compel, coerce, demand, *colloq.* bleed, milk, squeeze, lean on

blackmailer *n*
bloodsucker, extortioner, extortionist, vampire

blackout *n*
1 POWER FAILURE, power cut, electricity failure **2** FAINT, coma, unconsciousness, loss of consciousness, swoon, oblivion, *technical* syncope, *colloq.* flaking-out **3** *a news blackout* suppression, embargo, censorship, withholding, concealment, secrecy, *colloq.* cover-up

blade *n*
edge, cutting edge, knife, dagger, sword, scalpel, razor, vane

blame *v, n*
▶ *v* hold responsible, say something is someone's

fault, accuse, charge, tax, reprimand, chide, reprove, upbraid, reprehend, admonish, rebuke, reproach, censure, attribute liability, criticize, find fault with, find guilty, disapprove, condemn, scapegoat, *formal* berate, *colloq.* tear into, point the finger at
☒ exonerate, vindicate
▶ *n* censure, criticism, reprimand, reproof, reproach, recrimination, condemnation, accusation, charge, incrimination, guilt, fault, responsibility, accountability, liability, onus, *formal* culpability, berating, *slang* stick, rap

blameless *adj*
innocent, guiltless, clear, faultless, without fault, perfect, unblemished, stainless, virtuous, sinless, upright, above reproach, irreproachable, unblamable, unimpeachable
☒ guilty, blameworthy

blameworthy *adj*
at fault, guilty, discreditable, disreputable, shameful, unworthy, indefensible, inexcusable, reprehensible, reproachable, *formal* culpable, flagitious
☒ blameless

blanch *v*
1 *blanch at the sight* grow/become/turn pale, go/become/turn white, whiten, grow/become pallid 2 *blanch vegetables* boil, scald
☒ 1 colour, blush, redden

bland *adv*
1 *a bland person/statement* boring, monotonous, humdrum, tedious, dull, uninspiring, uninteresting, unexciting, nondescript, characterless, ordinary, mundane, inoffensive, flat, weak 2 TASTELESS, insipid, flavourless, weak, mild
☒ 1 exciting, lively, stimulating 2 tasty, piquant, rich

blandishments *n*
flattery, compliments, enticements, fawning, inducements, ingratiation, blarney, cajolery, coaxing, persuasiveness, sycophancy, wheedling, *formal* inveiglement, *colloq.* soft soap, sweet talk

blank *adj, n*
▶ *adj* 1 *a blank page* empty, unfilled, void, clear, bare, unmarked, unwritten, plain, clean, white 2 EXPRESSIONLESS, deadpan, poker-faced, impassive, emotionless, without feeling, lifeless, apathetic, uninterested, indifferent, glazed, empty, vacant, vacuous, inscrutable, uncomprehending
▶ *n* space, gap, break, void, emptiness, empty space, vacancy, vacuity, nothingness, vacuum

blanket *n, v, adj*
▶ *n* 1 *blankets on a bed* cover, covering, bedcover, coverlet, bedspread 2 *a blanket of snow* covering, coating, coat, layer, film, carpet, cloak, mantle, cover, sheet, film, envelope, overlay, wrapper, wrapping
▶ *v* cover, coat, overlay, eclipse, hide, conceal, mask, cloak, surround, muffle, deaden, obscure, suppress, cloud
▶ *adj* across-the-board, all-embracing, all-inclusive, comprehensive, inclusive, overall, global, total, sweeping, wide-ranging

blare *v*
trumpet, clamour, roar, blast (out), boom (out), resound, sound loudly, thunder, ring, peal, clang, hoot, toot, honk

blarney *n*
blandishments, cajolery, coaxing, flattery, persuasiveness, wheedling, *colloq.* soft soap, spiel, sweet talk

blasé *adj*
nonchalant, offhand, unimpressed, unmoved, unexcited, jaded, weary, bored, uninterested, uninspired, apathetic, indifferent, cool, lukewarm, unconcerned, *formal* phlegmatic
☒ excited, enthusiastic, responsive

blaspheme *v*
swear, curse, profane, utter profanities, utter oaths, desecrate, damn, revile, abuse, *formal* execrate, imprecate, anathematize, *colloq.* cuss

blasphemous *adj*
profane, impious, sacrilegious, godless, ungodly, irreligious, irreverent, *formal* imprecatory

blasphemy *n*
profanity, profaneness, curse, expletive, cursing, swearing, oaths, impiety, impiousness, ungodliness, irreverence, unholiness, sacrilege, desecration, violation, outrage, *formal* execration, imprecation

blast *n, v*
▶ *n* 1 EXPLOSION, detonation, bang, crash, clap, crack, volley, burst, outburst, discharge 2 *a blast of cold air* draught, gust, rush, gale, squall, storm, tempest 3 SOUND, blow, blare, blaring, roar, roaring, boom, booming, thunder, clamour, bellow, peal, hoot, toot, honk, wail, scream, shriek, clang
▶ *v* 1 EXPLODE, blow up, blow to pieces, burst, shatter, destroy, demolish, ruin, assail, attack 2 SOUND, blare (out), boom(out), roar, thunder, peal, bellow, hoot, toot, honk, wail, scream, shriek, clang 3 CRITICIZE, reprimand, rebuke, tell off, reprove, upbraid, *formal* berate
▷ **blast off** take off, lift off, be launched

blatant *adj*
flagrant, brazen, barefaced, arrant, open, overt, undisguised, ostentatious, glaring, conspicuous, manifest, patent, obtrusive, prominent, pronounced, obvious, sheer, outright, unmitigated, out and out

---

🖉 **blatant** or **flagrant** ?

Blatant means 'glaringly or shamelessly obvious': *a blatant lie/liar. Flagrant* implies a greater degree of condemnation and means 'scandalous, very obvious and wicked': *a flagrant misuse of his powers.*

---

blaze *n, v*
▶ *n* 1 FIRE, flames, inferno, bonfire, flare-up, explosion, blast, *formal* conflagration 2 *a blaze of colour* radiance, brilliance, beam, glare, flash, gleam, glitter, glow, light, burst, outburst
▶ *v* 1 *the fire was blazing* burn, flame, flare (up), ignite, catch fire, burst into flames 2 *blazing with light* shine, beam, glare, flash, flare, gleam, glitter, glow, light, burst, be radiant, be brilliant 3 *eyes blazing with anger* blow up, explode, erupt, burst, burn, fire, flash, rage, boil, seethe, *colloq.* see red

blazon *v*
proclaim, publicize, announce, make known, broadcast, celebrate, flourish, trumpet, flaunt, vaunt
☒ deprecate, hush up

bleach *v*
whiten, make white, blanch, decolour, decolorize, fade, pale, make pale, lighten, *technical* etiolate, peroxide

bleak *adj*
1 GLOOMY, sombre, leaden, grim, dreary, dismal, dark, drab, depressing, miserable, wretched, desperate, grim, joyless, cheerless, comfortless, hopeless, discouraging, disheartening, unpromising 2 *a bleak landscape* unsheltered, windy, windswept, exposed, open, barren, bare, empty, desolate, chilly, cold 3 COLD, chilly, raw, weather-beaten, dreary, dull
☒ 1 bright, cheerful 3 bright, fine, pleasant

bleary *adj*
bleary-eyed, blurred, blurry, cloudy, dim, tired, watery, rheumy

bleat *v*
1 *sheep bleating* baa, bray, cry, call, *US* blat 2 *bleating*

about price increases complain, grumble, moan, *colloq.* whine, whinge

bleed *v*
1 HAEMORRHAGE, lose blood, shed blood, gush, spurt, flow, run, exude, weep, ooze, seep, trickle, *technical* exsanguinate, phlebotomize, extravasate **2** DRAIN, suck dry, exhaust, squeeze, milk, sap, reduce, *formal* deplete **3** *bleed money* extort, extract, *colloq.* milk, squeeze

blemish *n, v*
▶ *n* **1** *a blemish on her skin* deformity, disfigurement, mark, speck, smudge, blotch, blot, stain, discoloration **2** *a blemish on his character* flaw, imperfection, defect, fault, stain, taint, disgrace, dishonour
▶ *v* tarnish, flaw, deface, disfigure, spoil, mar, damage, impair, spot, mark, blot, stain, sully, taint, compromise

blench *v*
falter, hesitate, recoil, flinch, shrink, shudder, cower, shy, start, wince, quail, quake, quiver

blend *v, n*
▶ *v* **1** MERGE, combine, mix, mingle, amalgamate, coalesce, compound, synthesize, fuse, unite, homogenize, alloy, interweave, intertwine, stir, beat, whisk, *formal* intermix, admix, commix, commingle **2** HARMONIZE, complement, fit, match, go (well) with, go together, suit, set off
🔁 **1** separate, divide
▶ *n* compound, composite, alloy, amalgam, amalgamation, merging, synthesis, fusion, combination, union, uniting, mix, mixture, cross between two things, concoction, *formal* admixture, commixture

bless *v*
1 ANOINT, sanctify, consecrate, hallow, dedicate, ordain **2** PRAISE, extol, magnify, glorify, exalt, thank, *formal* laud **3** *the priest blessed the congregation* ask God's favour for, as God's protection for
🔁 **1** curse **2** condemn

blessed *adj*
1 HOLY, sacred, hallowed, sanctified, revered, adored, divine **2** HAPPY, contented, glad, joyful, joyous, lucky, fortunate, prosperous **3** *blessed with a good memory* favoured, endowed, graced, provided
🔁 **1** cursed **2** unhappy, sad

blessing *n*
1 CONSECRATION, dedication, benediction, grace, thanksgiving, commendation, *technical* darshan, kiddush, *formal* invocation, benison **2** BENEFIT, advantage, favour, godsend, windfall, gift, gain, profit, help, service, bounty, good thing, good fortune **3** *give a proposal your blessing* approval, backing, support, agreement, authority, sanction, consent, permission, leave, *formal* approbation, concurrence
🔁 **2** curse, blight **3** condemnation

blight *n, v*
▶ *n* **1** *affected by planning blight* curse, misfortune, woe, trouble, calamity, bane, evil, scourge, affliction, decay, pollution, contamination, corruption **2** *potato blight* disease, fungus, mildew, rot, infestation, cancer, canker
🔁 **1** blessing, boon, benefaction, godsend, help, service, favour, bounty
▶ *v* spoil, mar, injure, undermine, ruin, wreck, crush, dash, shatter, destroy, damage, kill, annihilate, blast, wither, shrivel, frustrate, disappoint
🔁 bless

blind *adj, v, n*
▶ *adj* **1** SIGHTLESS, unsighted, unseeing, visionless, eyeless

---

> **Ways of describing sight impairment include**:
> amaurotic, astigmatic, having cataracts, colour-blind, far-sighted, glaucomatous, half-blind, hemeralopic, hypermetropic, long-sighted, myopic, near-sighted, night-blind, nyctalopic, partially-sighted, presbyopic, purblind, sand-blind, short-sighted, snow-blind, stone-blind, trachomatous, visually handicapped, visually impaired, *colloq.* blind as a bat.

2 *blind to their needs* UNAWARE, ignorant, oblivious, unconscious, unobservant, imperceptive, slow, inattentive, neglectful, indifferent, insensitive, thoughtless, inconsiderate **3** *love is blind* UNREASONING, uncritical, unthinking, irrational, injudicious, indiscriminate, heedless, mindless, impulsive, hasty, rash, impetuous, reckless, wild, mad, careless **4** CLOSED, obstructed, hidden, concealed, out of sight, obscured
🔁 **1** sighted **2** aware, sensitive **3** careful, cautious
▶ *v* **1** *blinded in the accident* make blind, cause to lose your vision, deprive of sight, deprive of vision, put the eyes out of, gouge the eyes out of **2** *blinded by the car's headlights* dazzle, block your vision, obscure your vision **3** *tolerance blinds you to faults* cause to lose reason/sense, deceive, mislead, trick, trap
▶ *n* **1** *a window blind* screen, cover, curtain, (window) shade, shutter, roller blind, Austrian blind, Venetian blind **2** *operate as a blind for illegal activities* cloak, mask, camouflage, masquerade, front, façade, distraction, smokescreen, cover, *colloq.* cover-up

blindly *adv*
1 *feel your way blindly* without vision, without sight, sightlessly, unseeingly **2** UNCRITICALLY, unthinkingly, irrationally, indiscriminately, mindlessly, senselessly, thoughtlessly, impulsively, rashly, impetuously, recklessly, wildly, madly, carelessly, incautiously
🔁 **2** critically, cautiously

blink *v*
1 *his eyes blinked* wink, *formal* nictate, nictitate **2** *the light blinked* flash, flicker, twinkle, shine, gleam, glimmer, glitter, sparkle, scintillate

bliss *n*
blissfulness, ecstasy, euphoria, rapture, joy, elation, happiness, gladness, blessedness, paradise, heaven, seventh heaven, utopia, nirvana
🔁 misery, hell, damnation

blissful *adj*
ecstatic, euphoric, elated, enraptured, idyllic, rapturous, delighted, enchanted, joyful, joyous, happy
🔁 miserable, wretched

blister *n*
sore, swelling, cyst, boil, abscess, ulcer, pustule, pimple, canker, carbuncle, *technical* bleb, bulla, furuncle, papilla, papula, pompholyx, vesicle, vesicula, wen

blistering *adj*
1 *blistering heat* hot, scorching, withering, intense, extreme **2** *blistering criticism* cruel, vicious, savage, fierce, caustic, scathing, sarcastic

blithe *adj*
casual, unthinking, thoughtless, careless, heedless, uncaring, unconcerned, carefree, untroubled, cheerful, cheery, light-hearted
🔁 morose, thoughtful, serious

blitz *n*
1 *the blitz during the war* bombardment, attack, offensive, raid, strike, campaign, onslaught, blitzkrieg **2** *have a blitz on the garden* effort, all-out effort, attack, exertion, attempt, endeavour, campaign

blizzard *n*
snowstorm, squall, storm, tempest

bloated *adj*
swollen, puffy, blown up, inflated, dilated, expanded, enlarged, full, stuffed, *formal* distended
F3 thin, shrunken, shrivelled

blob *n*
drop, droplet, globule, bead, pearl, bubble, dab, spot, splash, gob, lump, mass, ball, pellet, pill, *colloq.* glob

bloc *n*
alliance, group, league, coalition, federation, union, ring, syndicate, entente, axis, cabal, cartel, clique, faction

block *n, v*
▶ *n* **1** *a block of offices* building, development, structure **2** *a block of stone* piece, lump, mass, slab, chunk, hunk, square, cube, wedge, cake, brick, bar **3** *a block of seats/tickets* batch, cluster, quantity, series, section **4** OBSTACLE, barrier, bar, jam, blockage, stoppage, resistance, obstruction, impediment, hindrance, drawback, deterrent, stumbling-block, let, delay
▶ *v* *block a pipe/progress* choke, clog, plug, stop up, dam up, close, seal, bar, obstruct, be in the way, impede, hinder, stonewall, stop, check, arrest, halt, thwart, frustrate, scotch, deter, *colloq.* bung up

blockade *n, v*
▶ *n* barrier, barricade, siege, obstruction, restriction, obstacle, block, stoppage, closure, encirclement, *technical* investment
▶ *v* keep from, prevent, hinder, stop, check, obstruct, prevent entering/reaching, prevent using, besiege, encircle, surround

blockage *n*
obstruction, blocking, stoppage, occlusion, block, clot, jam, log-jam, congestion, hindrance, impediment, *formal* occlusion

blockhead *n* fool, idiot, imbecile, dunce, *colloq.* nincompoop, ninny, nitwit, numskull, twerp, twit, dimwit, *slang* wally, jerk, dipstick, nerd, dork, geek
F3 brain, genius

bloke *n*
man, boy, fellow, male, individual, character, *colloq.* chap, guy

blond, blonde *adj*
fair, flaxen, golden, fair-haired, golden-haired, light-coloured, tow-coloured, bleached

blood *n*
1 *lose blood* lifeblood, vital fluid, gore **2** *of aristocratic blood* extraction, birth, descent, lineage, family, kindred, relations, ancestry, descendants, kinship, relationship

bloodcurdling *adj*
horrifying, chilling, spine-chilling, hair-raising, terrifying, frightening, scary, dreadful, fearful, appalling, horrible, horrid, horrendous

bloodless *adj*
1 *a bloodless coup* peaceful, non-violent, strife-free, unwarlike **2** *her bloodless face* ASHEN, anaemic, colourless, pale, pallid, pasty, sallow, sickly, wan, chalky, cold, drained, feeble, insipid, languid, lifeless, listless, unfeeling, unemotional, passionless, spiritless, torpid
F3 **1** bloody, violent **2** bloody, ruddy, vigorous

bloodshed *n*
killing, murder, slaughter, slaying, massacre, bloodbath, butchery, carnage, pogrom, gore, bloodletting, decimation

bloodsucker *n*
blackmailer, extortioner, extortionist, *colloq.* leech, parasite, sponger

bloodthirsty *adj*
murderous, homicidal, warlike, savage, barbaric, barbarous, brutal, ferocious, vicious, cruel, inhuman, ruthless, *formal* sanguinary

bloody *adj*
bleeding, bloodstained, gory, murderous, bloodthirsty, savage, brutal, ferocious, fierce, cruel, *formal* sanguinary, sanguine, sanguineous, sanguinolent

bloom *n, v*
▶ *n* **1** BLOSSOM, flower, bud, *technical* efflorescence, florescence **2** PRIME, heyday, perfection, blush, flush, glow, rosiness, beauty, radiance, lustre, health, vigour, strength, freshness
▶ *v* **1** *the flowers were blooming* bud, sprout, blossom, flower, open **2** *the children are blooming* flourish, develop, mature, grow, blossom, prosper, thrive, glow
F3 **1** fade, wither

blooming *adj*
blossoming, healthy, flowering, rosy, ruddy, bonny, *technical* florescent
F3 ailing

blossom *n, v*
▶ *n* bloom, flower, bud, *technical* efflorescence, florescence
▶ *v* **1** *the trees were blossoming* bloom, flower, *formal* burgeon **2** *blossom into a beautiful young woman* develop, mature, bloom, flourish, thrive, prosper, succeed, *formal* burgeon
F3 **2** fade, wither

blot *n, v*
▶ *n* **1** *an ink blot* spot, stain, smudge, blotch, smear, mark, splodge, speck, blemish **2** *a blot on his reputation* blemish, flaw, fault, defect, imperfection, taint, stain, disgrace, tarnishing, black mark
▶ *v* **1** *blot a surface* spot, mark, stain, smudge, blur, dry (up), soak (up), absorb **2** *blotted his character* sully, taint, tarnish, spoil, mar, disfigure, disgrace
▷ **blot out** obliterate, cancel, delete, erase, darken, obscure, hide, conceal, screen, shadow, eclipse, *formal* efface, expunge

blotch *n*
patch, splodge, splotch, splash, smudge, blot, spot, mark, stain, blemish

blotchy *adj*
spotty, spotted, patchy, uneven, smeary, blemished, reddened, inflamed

blow¹ *v, n*
▶ *v* **1** *the wind was blowing* gust, blast, flurry **2** *blow leaves along the road* waft, fan, flutter, float, flow, stream, rush, whirl, whisk, sweep, fling, buffet, drive, blast **3** BREATHE, breathe out, pant, puff (out), *formal* exhale **4** *blow a horn* play, sound, pipe, trumpet, toot, blare, blast **5** *blow a lot of money* fritter away, misspend, spend freely, *formal* dissipate, *colloq.* spend like water, pour down the drain **6** *blow a chance/opportunity* waste, spoil, ruin, wreck, make a mess of, miss out on, *colloq.* miss the boat, *slang* screw up
▶ *n* puff, draught, flurry, gust, blast, wind, gale, squall, tempest
▷ **blow out** put out, smother, snuff out, *formal* extinguish
▷ **blow over** die down, subside, end, finish, cease, pass, vanish, disappear, be forgotten, fizzle out, peter out, *formal* dissipate
▷ **blow up** **1** EXPLODE, go off, go up, detonate, burst, blast, bomb **2** INFLATE, pump up, swell, fill (out), puff up, balloon, bloat, dilate, expand, enlarge, magnify, exaggerate, overstate, *formal* distend **3** LOSE YOUR TEMPER, become angry, get into a rage, take leave of your senses, *colloq.* blow your top, hit the roof, fly off

the handle, go mad, go ballistic, flip (your lid), *US, slang* go ape

blow² *n*

1 *a blow on the head* hit, concussion, box, cuff, clip, swipe, bash, slap, smack, buffet, bang, clap, knock, rap, stroke, thump, punch, hook, *colloq.* clout, whack, wallop, belt, *slang* biff, sock **2** MISFORTUNE, affliction, reverse, setback, comedown, disappointment, upset, jolt, shock, bombshell, calamity, catastrophe, disaster, *colloq.* shocker, bolt from the blue, rude awakening

blow-out *n*

1 PUNCTURE, flat tyre, burst tyre, *colloq.* flat **2** PARTY, celebration, feast, *colloq.* binge, bash, knees-up, rave, rave-up, beanfeast

blowy *adj*
breezy, windy, fresh, blustery, gusty, squally, stormy

blowzy *adj*
sloppy, slovenly, unkempt, untidy, bedraggled, dishevelled, ungroomed, tousled, messy, slipshod
◪ neat, smart

blubber *v*
cry, weep, blub, sob, snivel, sniffle, whimper

bludgeon *v, n*
▶ *v* **1** BEAT, strike, club, batter, hit, beat, cudgel, *colloq.* clobber, cosh **2** FORCE, coerce, compel, intimidate, bulldoze, badger, hector, harass, browbeat, bully, dragoon, pressurize, terrorize
▶ *n* club, baton, cosh, cudgel, truncheon

blue *adj*
1 AZURE, sky-blue, royal blue, sapphire, cobalt, ultramarine, navy blue, navy, indigo, aquamarine, turquoise, cyan, cerulean **2** DEPRESSED, low, dejected, downcast, dispirited, downhearted, despondent, gloomy, glum, dismal, sad, unhappy, miserable, melancholy, morose, *colloq.* fed up, down in the dumps **3** *a blue joke* obscene, offensive, indecent, improper, coarse, vulgar, lewd, dirty, pornographic, erotic, bawdy, smutty, risqué, *colloq.* adult, raunchy, steamy, near the bone, near the knuckle
◪ **2** cheerful, happy **3** decent, clean

blueprint *n*
design, outline, draft, sketch, pilot, guide, plan, scheme, strategy, project, programme, archetype, prototype, representation, model, pattern

blues *n*
depression, despondency, gloom, gloominess, moodiness, glumness, melancholy, miseries, dejection, doldrums, *colloq.* dumps
◪ euphoria

bluff¹ *v, n*
▶ *v* *was only bluffing* lie, pretend, feign, sham, fake, deceive, delude, mislead, hoodwink, blind, fool, *colloq.* bamboozle
▶ *n* lie, idle boast, bravado, humbug, pretence, show, sham, fake, fraud, trick, subterfuge, deceit, deception, feint, *formal* braggadocio

bluff² *adj, n*
▶ *adj* *a bluff man* blunt, candid, direct, downright, open, outspoken, plain-spoken, straightforward, frank, genial, good-natured, hearty, affable
◪ diplomatic, refined
▶ *n* cliff, crag, escarpment, peak, precipice, promontory, foreland, bank, brow, headland, height, ridge, scarp, escarp

blunder *n, v*
▶ *n* mistake, error, inaccuracy, misjudgement, slip, indiscretion, gaffe, *faux pas*, oversight, fault, *formal* solecism, *colloq.* howler, bloomer, clanger, boob, booboo, slip-up

▶ *v* make a mistake, stumble, flounder, bumble, err, miscalculate, misjudge, get wrong, go wrong, bungle, mismanage, *colloq.* botch, slip up, fluff, goof, *slang* screw up

blunt *adj, v*
▶ *adj* **1** UNSHARPENED, not sharp, dull, worn, pointless, edgeless, rounded, stubbed **2** FRANK, candid, direct, forthright, unceremonious, explicit, plainspoken, honest, straightforward, downright, outspoken, tactless, insensitive, rude, impolite, uncivil, brusque, curt, stark, abrupt, *colloq.* calling a spade a spade, speaking your mind, not beating about the bush, not mincing your words
◪ **1** sharp, pointed **2** subtle, tactful
▶ *v* dull, take the edge off, dampen, soften, deaden, numb, anaesthetize, alleviate, allay, abate, weaken, *formal* hebetate
◪ sharpen, intensify

blur *v, n*
▶ *v* **1** *the windscreen blurred* smear, smudge, spot, blotch, stain **2** *blurred memories/views* obscure, make vague/indistinct, mask, conceal, mist, fog, befog, cloud, becloud, veil, dim, dull, darken, soften
▶ *n* **1** *a blur on the picture* smear, smudge, spot, blotch, stain **2** *my memories are a blur* haze, mist, fog, cloudiness, fuzziness, indistinctness, obscurity, muddle, confusion, dimness

blurb *n*
advertisement, commendation, copy, puff, *colloq.* hype, spiel

blurred *adj*
out of focus, fuzzy, unclear, indistinct, vague, ill-defined, lacking definition, faint, hazy, misty, foggy, cloudy, clouded, bleary, dim, obscure, confused
◪ clear, distinct

blurt *v*
▷ **blurt out** exclaim, cry (out), call out, come out with, gush, spout, utter, tell, reveal, disclose, divulge, let out, leak, let slip, *formal* ejaculate, *colloq.* blab, let the cat out of the bag, give the game away, spill the beans
◪ bottle up, hush up

blush *v, n*
▶ *v* flush, redden, go red, turn red, colour, glow
◪ blanch
▶ *n* flush, reddening, rosiness, ruddiness, colour, glow

blushing *adj*
flushed, red, rosy, glowing, confused, embarrassed, ashamed, modest, *formal* erubescence
◪ pale, white, composed

bluster *v, n*
▶ *v* boast, brag, crow, swagger, strut, vaunt, show off, rant, roar, storm, bully, harangue, hector, *colloq.* talk big
▶ *n* boasting, crowing, bravado, bluff, swagger, domineering, *formal* braggadocio

blustery *adj*
windy, gusty, squally, stormy, tempestuous, violent, wild, boisterous
◪ calm

board *n, v*
▶ *n* **1** *a wooden board* sheet, panel, slab, plank, beam, timber, slat **2** COMMITTEE, council, panel, jury, commission, directorate, directors, trustees, governors, advisers, advisory group, working party, management, head office **3** MEALS, food, sustenance, provisions, rations, *formal* victuals, *slang* grub, nosh
▶ *v* get on, get in/into, embark, mount, enter, catch, *formal* embus, emplane, entrain

▷ **board up** close (up), cover (up), shut (up), seal

boast *v, n*

▶ *v* **1** *boasts about his qualifications* brag, crow, claim, exaggerate, overstate, bluster, trumpet, vaunt, strut, swagger, prate, show off, sing your own praises, *formal* gasconade, rodomontade, *colloq.* swank, talk big, loudmouth, blow your own trumpet, *US* blow your own horn **2** *boasts a new sauna* exhibit, possess, enjoy, pride yourself on

🔁 **1** *formal* belittle, deprecate

▶ *n* brag, crowing, blustering, self-praise, overstatement, claim, vaunt, pride, joy, gem, treasure, *formal* fanfaronade, gasconade, gasconism, rodomontade, jactation, *colloq.* hot air, swank

boastful *adj*
proud, conceited, vain, puffed up, bragging, crowing, cocky, swaggering, arrogant, self-flattering, egotistical, *formal* vainglorious, *colloq.* big-headed, swollen-headed, swanky

🔁 modest, self-effacing, humble

boat *n*

Types of boat or ship include:
canoe, dinghy, lifeboat, rowing-boat, kayak, coracle, skiff, punt, sampan, dhow, gondola, pedalo, catamaran, trimaran, yacht; cabin-cruiser, motor-boat, motor-launch, speedboat, trawler, barge, scow, narrow boat, houseboat, dredger, junk, smack, lugger; hovercraft, hydrofoil; clipper, cutter, ketch, packet, brig, schooner, square-rigger, galleon; ferry, paddle-steamer, tug, freighter, liner, container-ship, tanker; warship, battleship, destroyer, submarine, U-boat, frigate, aircraft-carrier, cruiser, dreadnought, corvette, minesweeper, man-of-war.

boatman *n*
ferryman, oarsman, oarswoman, rower, sailor, yachtsman, yachtswoman, waterman, bargee, gondolier, voyageur

bob *v*
1 *a raft bobbing up and down* bounce, float, move up and down shake, quiver, wobble, *formal* oscillate **2** *bobbed back into the house* leap, spring, jump, jerk, jolt, twitch, nod, bow, curtsy, hop, skip

▷ **bob up** appear, emerge, arrive, materialize, rise, surface, pop up, spring up, crop up, arise, *colloq.* show up

bode *v*
predict, foretell, prophesy, indicate, signify, intimate, herald, threaten, warn, *formal* augur, forebode, foreshadow, foreshow, forewarn, presage, betoken, portend, purport

bodily *adj, adv*

▶ *adj* physical, carnal, fleshly, real, actual, tangible, substantial, concrete, material, *formal* corporeal

🔁 spiritual

▶ *adv* altogether, en masse, collectively, as a whole, as one, completely, fully, wholly, entirely, totally, in toto

🔁 piecemeal

body *n*
1 *his whole body was aching* physique, build, form, frame, figure, anatomy, skeleton, trunk, torso **2** CORPSE, cadaver, carcase, dead body, *slang* stiff **3** *sit in the body of the church* main part, central part, largest part **4** ORGANIZATION, association, society, corporation, company, confederation, council, authority, bloc, cartel, syndicate, congress, collection, group, band, crowd, throng, multitude, mob, mass, phalanx **5** CONSISTENCY, density, solidity, firmness, bulk, mass, substance, essence, fullness, richness

bodyguard *n*
guard, protector, defender, guardian, *slang* minder

boffin *n*
scientist, engineer, designer, planner, inventor, mastermind, genius, brain, intellect, intellectual, thinker, *colloq.* egghead, wizard, backroom-boy

bog *n, v*

▶ *n* marsh, swamp, fen, mire, quagmire, quag, slough, morass, quicksands, marshland, swampland, wetlands

▶ *v* ▷ **bog down** encumber, hinder, overwhelm, deluge, sink, stick, slow down, slow up, delay, halt, hold up, set back, stall, *formal* impede, retard, mire

boggle *v*
astound, startle, amaze, surprise, overwhelm, stagger, alarm, confuse, *colloq.* bowl over, flabbergast

boggy *adj*
marshy, miry, swampy, muddy, oozy, morassy, quaggy, soft, spongy, waterlogged, fenny, *formal* paludal

🔁 arid

bogus *adj*
false, fake, counterfeit, forged, fraudulent, spurious, sham, make-believe, artificial, imitation, dummy, *colloq.* phoney, pseudo, pseud

🔁 genuine, true, real, valid

bohemian *adj, n*

▶ *adj* artistic, unconventional, unorthodox, nonconformist, alternative, original, avant-garde, eccentric, offbeat, bizarre, exotic, *colloq.* arty, oddball, off-the-wall, *slang* way-out

🔁 bourgeois, conventional, orthodox

▶ *n* beatnik, hippie, drop-out, nonconformist

🔁 conformist

boil¹ *v*
1 *boil water* SIMMER, stew, cook, heat, seethe, bring/come to the boil, brew, gurgle, bubble, fizz, effervesce, froth, foam, steam **2** *boil with anger* erupt, explode, rage, rave, storm, fume, *formal* fulminate, *colloq.* blow your top, fly into a rage, go off the deep end, hit the roof

▷ **boil down** amount, reduce, concentrate, distil, condense, digest, abstract, summarize, abridge

boil² *n*
a boil on the skin
pustule, abscess, gumboil, ulcer, tumour, pimple, carbuncle, blister, inflammation

boiling *adj*
1 *boiling water* turbulent, gurgling, bubbling, steaming, scalding **2** HOT, baking, roasting, scorching, sweltering, blistering, torrid, *US* broiling **3** ANGRY, indignant, incensed, infuriated, enraged, furious, fuming, flaming

boisterous *adj*
exuberant, rollicking, romping, bouncy, active, hyperactive, lively, spirited, turbulent, energetic, tumultuous, loud, noisy, clamorous, rowdy, rough, disorderly, riotous, wild, unrestrained, unruly, obstreperous, *colloq.* rumbustious

🔁 quiet, calm, restrained, docile

bold *adj*
1 BRAVE, dauntless, daring, audacious, fearless, undaunted, courageous, valiant, intrepid, heroic, gallant, intrepid, adventurous, venturesome, enterprising, plucky, spirited, confident, outgoing, *formal* valorous, *colloq.* bold as a lion **2** BRAZEN, brash, forward, shameless, unabashed, impudent, insolent, barefaced, *colloq.* cheeky, saucy, brassy, pert, bold as brass **3** EYE-CATCHING, striking, conspicuous, prom-inent, strong, pronounced, distinct, definite, bright, vivid, colourful, loud, flashy, showy, flamboyant

🔁 **1** cowardly, nervous, cautious, timid, shy **2** timid, modest, shy, diffident **3** faint, restrained

bolshie *adj*
awkward, obstinate, unhelpful, difficult, stubborn, unco-operative, irritable, touchy, prickly, oversensitive, rude, unpleasant, problem, *colloq*. stroppy, bloody-minded
E3 amenable, pleasant, co-operative, helpful

bolster *v, n*
▶ *v* boost, aid, assist, help, maintain, prop, reinforce, strengthen, supplement, support, brace, buoy up, buttress, firm up, shore up, stay, stiffen, revitalize, invigorate, *formal* augment
E3 undermine
▶ *n* pillow, support, cushion

bolt *n, v*
▶ *n* **1** *a bolt on a door* bar, rod, shaft, fastener, latch, catch, lock **2** *nuts and bolts* screw, pin, peg, rivet
▶ *v* **1** FASTEN, secure, bar, latch, lock, rivet, pin, screw **2** *bolt for the door* escape, flee, fly, run (away), run off, sprint, rush, dash, hurtle, *formal* abscond **3** *bolt your food down* gulp, wolf (down), gobble, gorge, guzzle, devour, cram, stuff

bomb *n, v*
▶ *n* atom bomb, nuclear bomb, hydrogen bomb, petrol bomb, neutron bomb, shell, bombshell, explosive, charge, grenade, mine, incendiary, fire-bomb, torpedo, depth charge, plastic bomb, time bomb, rocket, shell, missile, projectile, Molotov cocktail, stink bomb, car bomb, fire-bomb, letter bomb
▶ *v* bombard, shell, torpedo, attack, blow up, destroy

bombard *v*
1 *bombard the airport* attack, assail, pelt, pound, strafe, blast, bomb, shell, torpedo, stone, blitz, raid, besiege **2** *bombard with criticism* attack, hound, bother, harass, pester

bombardment *n*
1 *aerial bombardment* attack, assault, air raid, bombing, shelling, blitz, barrage, cannonade, fusillade, salvo, fire, flak **2** *bombardment of questions* attack, onslaught, besieging, hounding, bothering, harassing, pestering

bombastic *adj*
pompous, pretentious, grandiose, verbose, wordy, turgid, ostentatious, affected, high-flown, inflated, bloated, windy, *formal* grandiloquent, magniloquent, portentous, euphuistic, fustian
E3 reserved, restrained

bona fide *adj*
genuine, real, valid, true, actual, authentic, lawful, legal, legitimate, kosher, honest, *colloq*. the real McCoy
E3 bogus

bonanza *n*
windfall, sudden wealth, godsend, stroke of luck, blessing, boon

bond *n, v*
▶ *n* **1** *bonds of friendship* CONNECTION, relation, relationship, link, tie(s), binding, union, affiliation, attachment, rapport, affinity, chemistry, *formal* vinculum **2** CONTRACT, covenant, agreement, pledge, promise, pact, transaction, deal, treaty, word, obligation **3** FETTER, shackle, manacle, chain, cord, band, binding
▶ *v* connect, fasten, bind, unite, fuse, join, stick, attach, glue, gum, paste, weld, seal

bondage *n*
imprisonment, captivity, confinement, restraint, slavery, enslavement, serfdom, servitude, subservience, subjection, subjugation, yoke, *formal* incarceration, thraldom, vassalage
E3 freedom, independence

bone *n*

Human bones include:
clavicle, coccyx, collar-bone, femur, fibula, hip-bone, humerus, ilium, ischium, mandible, maxilla, metacarpal, metatarsal, patella, pelvic girdle, pelvis, pubis, radius, rib, scapula, shoulder-blade, skull, sternum, stirrup-bone, temporal, thigh-bone, tibia, ulna, vertebra.

bonny *adj*
attractive, lovely, beautiful, pretty, fine, fair, blooming, bouncing, cheerful, cheery, joyful, merry
E3 ugly

bonus *n*
1 *pay a bonus* commission, dividend, premium, prize, reward, honorarium, tip, gratuity, gift, fringe benefits, handout, *formal* lagniappe **2** *the good weather is a bonus* advantage, benefit, gain, extra, *formal* perquisite, *colloq*. plus, perk
E3 **2** disadvantage, disincentive

bony *adj*
thin, lean, angular, lanky, gawky, gangling, skinny, scrawny, scraggy, emaciated, skeletal, rawboned, gaunt, drawn
E3 fat, plump

book *n, v*
▶ *n* volume, tome, publication, work, booklet, tract

Types of book include:
hardback, paperback, bestseller; fiction, novel, story, thriller, detective, romantic novel, penny dreadful; children's book, primer, picture-book, annual; reference book, encyclopedia, dictionary, lexicon, thesaurus, concordance, anthology, compendium, omnibus, atlas, guidebook, gazetteer, directory, anthology, pocket companion, handbook, manual, cookbook, yearbook, almanac, catalogue; notebook, exercise book, textbook, scrapbook, album, sketchbook, diary, jotter, pad, ledger; libretto, manuscript, hymn-book, hymnal, prayer-book, psalter, missal, lectionary. *See also* LITERATURE.

▶ *v* **1** *book a ticket* arrange (in advance), reserve, make a reservation for, engage, charter, procure, order, organize, schedule, programme, *colloq*. bag **2** *booked for assault* charge, accuse (of), blame
E3 **1** cancel
▷ **book in** register, enrol, check in, record your arrival

bookbinding *n*

Terms used in bookbinding include :
adhesive binding, all edges gilt (aeg), backboard, backbone, back cornering, back lining, *US* binder's board, binder's brass, *US* binder's die, binding, blind blocking, blocking, boards, bolts, book block, buckram, case, casebound, casing-in, cloth-lined board, comb-binding, drawn-on, dust cover, embossing, endpaper, flyleaf, fore edge, front board, full bound, gather, half bound, hardback, head, headband, headcap, hinge, jacket, laminating, library binding, limp, lining, Linson®, loose-leaf, mechanical binding, millboard, morocco, notch binding, open-flat, paperback, pasteboard, perfect binding, quarter bound, raised band, ring binding, rounding and backing, saddle-stitch, sewing, shoulder, side-stitch, signature, smashing, soft-cover,

spine, spiral binding, square back, stab-stitch, *US* stamping, strawboard, tail, tailband, thermoplastic binding, thread sewing, unsewn binding, varnishing, whole bound, wire binding, wire stitching, wiro binding, yapp.

---

bookish *adj*
studious, well-read, academic, scholarly, cultured, erudite, highbrow, intellectual, learned, literary, scholastic, lettered, donnish, bluestocking, pedantic
F₃ lowbrow, unlettered

books *n*
accounts, ledgers, records, financial statement, balance sheet

boom *v, n*
▶ *v* **1** BANG, crash, roar, blare, thunder, roll, bellow, rumble, resound, reverberate, blast, explode **2** FLOURISH, thrive, prosper, succeed, develop, grow, do well, increase, gain, progress, expand, swell, surge, leap, escalate, intensify, strengthen, go from strength to strength, mushroom, explode
F₃ **2** fail, collapse, slump
▶ *n* **1** BANG, clap, crash, roar, thunder, rumble, reverberation, blast, blare, bellow, roll, explosion, burst, loud noise **2** INCREASE, growth, expansion, gain, upsurge, jump, surge, leap, spurt, boost, upturn, upswing, improvement, advance, progress, success, development, escalation, explosion
F₃ **2** failure, collapse, slump, recession, depression

boomerang *v*
rebound, bounce back, spring back, recoil, ricochet, backfire

boon *n*
blessing, advantage, benefit, bonus, help, godsend, windfall, favour, kindness, gift, present, grant, gratuity, *colloq.* plus
F₃ disadvantage, blight

boor *n*
oaf, lout, barbarian, philistine, vulgarian, rustic, yahoo, *colloq.* peasant, country bumpkin, clod, clodhopper, yokel

boorish *adj*
uncouth, oafish, loutish, ill-mannered, ill-bred, rude, coarse, rough, crude, vulgar, unrefined, uncivilized, gruff, impolite, rustic, uneducated, ignorant
F₃ polite, refined, cultured, genteel

boost *v, n*
▶ *v* **1** *boost confidence* bolster, lift, encourage, inspire, uplift, foster, support **2** *boost sales* increase, raise, put up, improve, enhance, develop, enlarge, expand, supplement, amplify, advance, help, aid, assist, maximize, promote, encourage, further, heighten, *formal* augment **3** *boost a product* advertise, promote, publicize, praise, *colloq.* plug, hype
F₃ **1** undermine **2** lower, deteriorate, hinder
▶ *n* **1** *a boost to morale* lift, uplift, fillip, encouragement, inspiration, stimulus, support, *colloq.* shot in the arm, ego-trip **2** *a boost to sales* increase, rise, improvement, enhancement, development, enlargement, expansion, increment, addition, supplement, amplification, advance, help, aid, assistance, furtherance, *formal* augmentation **3** *a boost for a product* advertisement, promotion, publicity, praise, *colloq.* plug, hype
F₃ **1** setback, blow **2** setback, deterioration

boot¹ *n, v*
▶ *n* gumboot, wellington, galosh, overshoe, walking-boot, climbing-boot, riding-boot, football boot, Doc Martens®, wader, bootee
▶ *v* kick, shove
▷ **boot out** dismiss, eject, expel, lay off, suspend,

shed, give notice, make redundant, *colloq.* kick out, fire, sack, give someone their cards, give the heave

boot² *v*
▷ **to boot** as well, in addition, *colloq.* into the bargain

booth *n*
cubicle, compartment, carrel, stall, stand, kiosk, hut, box

bootless *adj*
fruitless, futile, vain, ineffective, useless, pointless, profitless, sterile, unavailing, unsuccessful, worthless, unproductive, barren
F₃ profitable, useful

booty *n*
loot, plunder, pillage, spoil(s), haul, gains, takings, pickings, prize, profits, takings, winnings, *slang* swag

border *n, v*
▶ *n* **1** BOUNDARY, frontier, line, state line, marchlands, marches **2** *herbaceous borders* bed, edge, rim, brim, verge, margin, fringe, periphery, surround, perimeter, circumference, bound, bounds, confine, confines, limit, demarcation, borderline, brink, *technical* limb **3** HEM, frill, valance, skirt, trimming, frieze
▶ *v* **1** *Sweden borders Norway* lie/be next to, be adjacent to, join, touch, connect, *formal* adjoin, abut, impinge **2** *streets bordered with trees* edge, bound, skirt, flank, fringe, rim, surround, trim, hem, *formal* circumscribe
▷ **border on** verge on, be almost, be nearly, resemble, approximate to, approach

borderline *adj*
marginal, problematic, indefinite, doubtful, uncertain, indecisive, indeterminate, ambivalent, *colloq.* iffy
F₃ certain, definite, clear-cut

bore¹ *v, n*
▶ *v* *the speech bored them* tire, make tired, weary, wear out, fatigue, exhaust, pall on, be tedious to, jade, trouble, bother, worry, irritate, annoy, vex, irk, *colloq.* turn off, send to sleep, bore the pants off
F₃ interest, excite
▶ *n* nuisance, bother, *colloq.* bind, drag, turn-off, headache, pain, pain in the neck
F₃ pleasure, delight

bore² *v*
bore a hole drill, mine, pierce, perforate, penetrate, puncture, sink, dig (out), burrow, hollow (out), tap, tunnel, undermine, sap

bored *adj*
uninterested, unexcited, tired, wearied, exhausted, *formal* ennuied, ennuyé, *colloq.* bored to tears, bored stiff, bored out of your mind, cheesed off, fed up, turned off, sick and tired, in a rut, brassed off, browned off
F₃ interested, excited

boredom *n*
tedium, tediousness, monotony, humdrum, dullness, sameness, flatness, apathy, listlessness, weariness, world-weariness, frustration, *formal* ennui, malaise, acedia
F₃ interest, excitement

boring *adj*
tedious, dull, monotonous, routine, repetitious, uninteresting, unexciting, uneventful, dreary, humdrum, tiring, tiresome, unvaried, commonplace, trite, unimaginative, uninspired, dry, stale, flat, insipid, prosaic, long-winded, *old use* stultifying, jejune, *colloq.* samey, dull as ditchwater, soul-destroying, with the novelty worn off
F₃ interesting, exciting, stimulating, original

borrow *v*
1 *borrow a friend's car* have the use of, take/have on

loan, use temporarily, scrounge, cadge, take out a loan, rent, hire, charter, lease, *colloq.* sponge **2** *borrow words/ideas* adopt, take (over), draw, derive, obtain, use, acquire, *formal* appropriate
F3 1 lend

borrowing *n*
1 *borrowing of money* use, temporary use, loan, rental, hire, charter, leasing **2** *English borrowings in German* loan, loan-translation, loan-word, adoption, takeover, derivation, use, acquisition, *technical* calque
F3 1 lending

bosom *n, adj*
▶ *n* **1** BUST, breasts, chest, breast, *slang* boob **2** *in the bosom of the family* HEART, core, centre, midst, protection, shelter, sanctuary
▶ *adj* close, intimate, dear, devoted, loving, faithful, confidential

boss *n, v*
▶ *n* employer, master, owner, captain, head, chief, leader, supremo, administrator, executive, director, manager, superior, foreman, superintendent, overseer, governor, supervisor, *colloq.* gaffer
▶ *v* order around, order about, domineer, tyrannize, bully, bulldoze, browbeat, give orders to, dominate, *colloq.* push around, throw your weight about, lay down the law

bossy *adj*
authoritarian, autocratic, tyrannical, despotic, dictatorial, domineering, overbearing, oppressive, lordly, high-handed, dominating, imperious, insistent, assertive, demanding, exacting
F3 unassertive

botch *v, n*
▶ *v* bungle, mess (up), make a mess of, blunder, mar, mismanage, ruin, spoil, patch, *colloq.* foul up, fluff, muff, make a hash of, make a bad job of, goof, *slang* louse up, screw up
F3 accomplish, succeed
▶ *n* blunder, bungle, failure, muddle, mess, miscarriage, *colloq.* farce, shambles, fiasco, debacle, hash, *colloq.* pig's ear
F3 success

both *adj*
the two, each, the pair, the one and the other

bother *v, n*
▶ *v* **1** *not bother to reply* concern yourself, trouble, make the/an effort, think necessary **2** *the heat bothered us* concern, annoy, worry, upset, trouble dismay, alarm, distress, vex, *colloq.* bug **3** *don't bother her* disturb, inconvenience, put out, trouble, pester, plague, harass, nag, annoy, irritate, molest, *formal* incommode, *colloq.* hassle
▶ *n* **1** *not worth the bother* trouble, inconvenience, effort, problem, difficulty, fuss, exertion, pains, bustle, flurry, *colloq.* hassle **2** *office paperwork is a real bother* nuisance, annoyance, irritation, problem, difficulty, vexation, worry, strain, *colloq.* aggravation, pest, pain in the neck

bothersome *adj*
troublesome, annoying, irksome, irritating, infuriating, vexatious, vexing, inconvenient, distressing, exasperating, laborious, boring, tedious, tiresome, wearisome, *colloq.* aggravating

bottle *n, v*
▶ *n* container
▶ *v* ▷ **bottle up** hide, conceal, restrain, curb, keep back, hold back, keep in check, suppress, inhibit, restrict, shut in, enclose, contain, disguise
F3 unbosom, unburden

bottleneck *n*
hold-up, traffic jam, snarl-up, congestion, clogging,

blockage, obstruction, block, obstacle, restriction, constriction, narrowing

bottom *n, adj*
▶ *n* **1** UNDERSIDE, underneath, sole, base, foot, plinth, pedestal, support, foundation, substructure, underpinning, ground, nadir **2** *at the bottom of the sea* floor, bed, depths **3** *at the bottom of the garden* end, far end, furthest end, farthest end **4** *children at the bottom of the class* lowest level, least important position **5** *sitting on his bottom* rear, behind, buttocks, seat, rump, *colloq.* posterior, backside, bum, *US* butt, tail,
F3 1 top **2** surface **4** top
▶ *adj* lowest, lower, underside, undermost

bottomless *adj*
a bottomless pit/supply of funds deep, profound, fathomless, unfathomed, unplumbed, immeasurable, measureless, infinite, boundless, limitless, unlimited, inexhaustible
F3 shallow, limited

bough *n*
branch, limb

boulder *n*
rock, stone

boulevard *n*
avenue, mall, parade, promenade, drive, prospect, thoroughfare

bounce *v, n*
▶ *v* **1** *bounce a ball* rebound, spring back, bob, ricochet, recoil, throw **2** *children bouncing about* spring, jump, leap, bound
▷ **bounce back** recover, get better, get back to normal, improve
▶ *n* **1** SPRING, bound, springiness, elasticity, give, resilience, rebound, recoil **2** EBULLIENCE, exuberance, vitality, vivacity, energy, vigour, animation, dynamism, spiritedness, liveliness, *colloq.* go, get-up-and-go, zip

bouncing *adj*
healthy, lively, robust, strong, vigorous, thriving, blooming, bonny

bound¹ *adj*
1 *bound to go wrong* sure, certain, definite, fated, destined, doomed **2** LIABLE, committed, duty-bound, pledged, obliged, required, forced, compelled, constrained, beholden **3** FASTENED, secured, fixed, tied (up), chained, roped, fettered, tethered, held, attached, clamped, lashed, trussed, strapped, shackled, restricted, bandaged
▷ **bound up with** tied up with, connected with, linked with, related to, associated with, dependent on, *colloq.* (going) hand in hand with

bound² *adj*
be bound for Norway heading, headed, off (to), on your way to, travelling, going, coming, proceeding

bound³ *v, n*
▶ *v* *she bounded down the stairs* jump, leap, vault, hurdle, spring, bounce, bob, hop, skip, dance, frisk, gambol, frolic, caper, prance
▶ *n* jump, leap, vault, spring, bounce, bob, hop, skip, gambol, frolic, caper, dance, prance

bound *n, v*
▶ *n* **1** BORDER, line, limit, borderline, demarcation, confine(s), margin, verge, brink, edge, perimeter, circumference, extremity, termination **2** LIMITATION, limit, restriction, check, curb, restraint
▷ **out of bounds** forbidden, off-limits, disallowed, banned, barred, prohibited, taboo
▶ *v* **1** BORDER, outline, limit, enclose, edge, skirt, flank, fringe, surround **2** RESTRICT, regulate, control, moderate, restrain, contain, *formal* circumscribe

boundary *n*
border, frontier, barrier, line, borderline, demarcation, bounds, confines, limits, margin, fringe, verge, brink, edge, perimeter, extremity, termination, point of no return, Rubicon

bounded *adj*
enclosed, surrounded, bordered, edged, encircled, encompassed, limited, restrained, restricted, confined, walled in, hemmed in, controlled, defined, demarcated, *formal* circumscribed, delimited

bounder *n*
cad, cheat, blackguard, rogue, miscreant, cur, dastard, knave, *colloq.* blighter, rotter, pig, swine, rat, dirty dog

boundless *adj*
unbounded, limitless, unlimited, illimitable, unconfined, countless, incalculable, numberless, innumerable, untold, incalculable, vast, immense, measureless, immeasurable, infinite, endless, unending, never-ending, interminable, everlasting, inexhaustible, unflagging, indefatigable
◨ limited, restricted

bounds *n*
restrictions, confines, limits, borders, marches, demarcations, margins, fringes, boundaries, periphery, circumference, perimeter, edges, extremities, parameters, scope
▷ **out of bounds** off limits, prohibited, forbidden, not allowed

bountiful *adj*
abundant, plentiful, exuberant, profuse, ample, prolific, overflowing, ungrudging, unstinting, boundless, copious, generous, lavish, liberal, open-handed, princely, *formal* magnanimous, munificent, bounteous, plenteous, luxuriant
◨ meagre, mean, sparse

bounty *n*
1 REWARD, recompense, premium, bonus, gratuity, tip, gift, present, donation, grant, allowance 2 GENEROSITY, liberality, largesse, almsgiving, charity, philanthropy, kindness, *formal* munificence, beneficence

bouquet *n*
1 *a bouquet of flowers* bunch, posy, nosegay, spray, corsage, buttonhole, boutonnière, wreath, garland 2 AROMA, smell, odour, scent, perfume, fragrance, *formal* redolence, odoriferousness

bourgeois *adj*
middle-class, materialistic, money-orientated, conservative, traditional, conformist, conventional, hidebound, unadventurous, ordinary, dull, humdrum, banal, commonplace, trite, pedestrian, uninspired, unoriginal, uncreative, unimaginative, uncultured
◨ bohemian, unconventional, original

bout *n*
1 PERIOD, spell, time, stint, turn, term, stretch, run, course, session, spree, *colloq.* go 2 *a bout of illness* attack, fit, touch 3 FIGHT, battle, engagement, encounter, struggle, set-to, match, contest, competition, round, heat

bovine *adj*
1 *bovine animals* cattlelike, cowlike 2 *his bovine response* stupid, slow, dull, slow-witted, dim-witted, *colloq.* dense, dumb, thick, doltish
◨ 2 quick

bow¹ *v, n*
▶ *v* 1 *bow your head* incline, bend, nod, bob, curtsy, kowtow, salaam, stoop, curve, arch, crook, crouch, *formal* genuflect, make obeisance 2 YIELD, give in, give way to, consent, surrender, capitulate, submit, succumb, concede, accept, comply, defer, *formal* accede, acquiesce 3 SUBDUE, overpower, conquer,

crush, humble, humiliate, *formal* subjugate, vanquish
▷ **bow out** withdraw, pull out, desert, abandon, defect, back out, retire, resign, leave, stand down, step down, give up, *colloq.* chicken out, quit
▶ *n* inclination, bending, nod, bob, curtsy, arc, kowtow, salaam, salutation, acknowledgement, *formal* genuflexion, obeisance, prostration

bow² *n*
the bow of a ship front, beak, head, prow, stem, rostrum
◨ stern

bowdlerize *v*
censor, cut, edit, excise, expunge, expurgate, purge, clean up, purify, modify, blue-pencil

bowels *n*
1 INTESTINES, entrails, guts, colon, *technical* viscera, *colloq.* insides, innards 2 *in the bowels of the earth* DEPTHS, interior, inside, middle, centre, core, heart, belly, cavity

bower *n*
arbour, shelter, alcove, grotto, bay, recess, retreat, sanctuary

bowl¹ *n*
a washing-up bowl receptacle, container, vessel, dish, basin, sink

bowl² *v*
bowl a ball throw, hurl, fling, pitch, roll, spin, whirl, rotate, revolve
▷ **bowl over** 1 *bowled over by the news* overwhelm, affect deeply, impress greatly, surprise, amaze, astound, astonish, stagger, stun, dumbfound, *colloq.* flabbergast, floor 2 *bowl over a person* knock down, fell, topple, unbalance, push into

box¹ *n, v*
▶ *n* *boxes of books* container, receptacle, case, carton, packet, present, bijou, casket, pyxis, pyx, chest, coffret
▶ *v* package, pack, wrap, case, encase
▷ **box in** enclose, surround, block in, cordon off, hem in, shut in, fence in, corner, trap, confine, restrain, coop up, restrict, imprison, cage, contain, *formal* circumscribe

box² *v*
1 *learn to box* fight, spar, engage in fisticuffs 2 *box someone's ears* punch, hit, strike, slap, batter, thump, buffet, cuff, *colloq.* clout, wallop, whack, slug, *slang* sock

boxer *n*
fighter, prizefighter, sparring partner, *formal* pugilist

> **Weight divisions in professional boxing:**
> heavyweight, cruiserweight/junior-heavyweight, light-heavyweight, super-middleweight, middleweight, light-middleweight/junior-middleweight, welterweight, light-welterweight/junior-welterweight, lightweight, junior-lightweight/superfeatherweight, featherweight, super-bantamweight/junior-featherweight, bantamweight, super-flyweight/junior-bantamweight, flyweight, light-flyweight/junior-flyweight, mini-flyweight/straw-weight/minimum weight.

boxing *n*
prizefighting, fisticuffs, sparring, *formal* pugilism

boy *n*
son, lad, youngster, stripling, youth, junior, schoolboy, fellow, child, adolescent, teenager, young man, *colloq.* kid, nipper, whippersnapper, guttersnipe

boycott *v*
refuse, reject, embargo, black, ban, prohibit, disallow,

bar, exclude, blacklist, proscribe, outlaw, ostracize, ignore, avoid, spurn, *formal* eschew, *colloq.* cold-shoulder, send to Coventry
F≠ encourage, support, advocate, defend, champion, patronize

boyfriend *n*
young man, man, admirer, sweetheart, lover, suitor, fiancé, beau, partner, cohabitee, live-in lover, common-law spouse, *colloq.* fellow, bloke, date, toy-boy, steady, significant other

boyish *adj*
youthful, childlike, adolescent, childish, immature, innocent, juvenile, puerile, tomboy, unfeminine, unmaidenly, young, *colloq.* green

brace¹ *n, v*
▶ *n* fit braces to strengthen a wall support, stay, strap, prop, clamp, fastener, vice, beam, strut, reinforcement, truss, buttress, shoring, *formal* stanchion
▶ *v* strengthen, reinforce, bolster, buttress, prop (up), shore (up), support, hold up, steady, secure, tighten, fasten, tie, strap, bind, bandage, *formal* fortify

brace² *n*
a brace of pheasant pair, couple, twosome, duo

bracelet *n*
bangle, band, circlet

bracing *adj*
fresh, crisp, refreshing, reviving, strengthening, fortifying, tonic, rousing, stimulating, exhilarating, invigorating, enlivening, energizing, brisk, energetic, vigorous
F≠ weakening, draining, debilitating, *formal* enervating

brackish *adj*
bitter, briny, saline, salt, saltish, salty
F≠ fresh, clean, clear

brag *v*
bluster, boast, show off, swagger, vaunt, *formal* hyperbolize, *colloq.* blow your own trumpet, *US* blow your own horn, crow, talk big, lay it on thick/with a trowel
F≠ be modest, *formal* deprecate, *colloq.* run down

braggart *n*
boaster, bluffer, blusterer, show-off, boaster, braggadocio, fanfaron, gascon, rodomontader, swaggerer, swashbuckler, *colloq.* big mouth, windbag, loudmouth

bragging *n*
showing-off, bluster, boastfulness, boasting, bravado, exaggeration, *formal* vauntery, *colloq.* hot air
F≠ modesty, unobtrusiveness

braid *v*
plait, interweave, interlace, intertwine, weave, lace, twine, entwine, ravel, twist, wind
F≠ undo, unravel

brain *n*
1 *have a good brain* mind, head, intellect, intelligence, wit, reason, sense, common sense, shrewdness, understanding, *technical* encephalon, *formal* acumen, sagacity, sensorium, *colloq.* grey matter, brains, nous, savvy

---

Parts of the brain include:
brainstem, cerebellum, cerebral cortex (grey matter), cerebrum, corpus callosum, forebrain, frontal lobe, hindbrain, hypothalamus, medulla oblongata, mesencephalon, midbrain, occipital lobe, optic thalamus, parietal lobe, pineal body, pituitary gland, pons, spinal cord, temporal lobe, thalamus.

---

2 *the real brain in the family* mastermind, intellectual, scholar, expert, pundit, highbrow, genius, prodigy,

colloq. egghead, boffin, brainbox, cleverclogs
F≠ 2 simpleton, idiot

brainless *adj*
silly, stupid, crazy, daft, foolish, incompetent, half-witted, idiotic, inept, mindless, thoughtless, senseless
F≠ sensible, shrewd, wise

brainteaser *n*
riddle, puzzle, problem, conundrum, mind-bender, poser

brainwashing *n*
indoctrination, conditioning, pressurizing, grilling, re-education, intellectual suicide, mind-bending, persuasion, *formal* menticide

brainy *adj*
intellectual, intelligent, clever, gifted, smart, bright, brilliant, wise, *formal* sapient
F≠ dull, stupid

brake *n, v*
▶ *n* check, curb, rein, restraint, control, restriction, constraint, drag, *formal* retardment
▶ *v* slow, decelerate, reduce speed, retard, drag, slacken, moderate, check, halt, stop, pull up, *formal* retard
F≠ accelerate

branch *n*
1 *the branches of a tree* BOUGH, limb sprig, shoot, stem, offshoot, arm, wing, prong, *technical* ramus 2 *a different branch of the company* DEPARTMENT, office, local/regional office, part, section, division, subsidiary, subsection, subdivision, wing, discipline
▷ **branch off** divide, fork, diverge, separate, *formal* bifurcate, furcate
▷ **branch out** diversify, subdivide, vary, develop, expand, enlarge, extend, add to, broaden out, increase, multiply, proliferate, *formal* ramify

brand *n, v*
▶ *n* 1 *different brands of soap* MAKE, brand-name, tradename, trademark, logo, symbol, sign, emblem, label, stamp, hallmark 2 KIND, quality, class, kind, type, sort, line, variety, species 3 *identify cattle by their brand* MARK , tag, identification, identifying mark
▶ *v* 1 *branded as a troublemaker* mark, stamp, label, typecast, stigmatize, stain, taint, disgrace, discredit, denounce, censure, *formal* besmirch 2 *brand cattle* mark, stamp, burn (in), scar

brandish *v*
wave, flourish, shake, raise, swing, wield, flash, flaunt, exhibit, display, parade

brash *adj*
1 BRAZEN, forward, impertinent, impudent, insolent, rude, cocky, self-confident, assertive, assured, bold, audacious, *formal* temerarious, *colloq.* pushy 2 RECKLESS, rash, impetuous, impulsive, hasty, foolhardy, incautious, indiscreet, *formal* incautious, precipitate
F≠ 1 reserved, unassuming, modest, unobtrusive 2 cautious, wary, prudent

brass *n*
brazenness, impertinence, impudence, insolence, gall, rudeness, presumption, audacity, *formal* effrontery, temerity, *colloq.* cheek, nerve, chutzpah, brass neck, brass nerve
F≠ timidity, *formal* circumspection

brassy *adj*
1 *brassy music* NOISY, loud, blaring, dissonant, grating, hard, harsh, jangling, jarring, piercing, raucous, strident 2 *a brassy blonde* shameless, forward, brash, insolent, bold, loud, brazen, *colloq.* pushy, loudmouthed, saucy

brat *n*
kid, youngster, rascal, *colloq.* nipper, guttersnipe, jackanapes, puppy, whippersnapper

bravado *n*
swagger, boasting, bragging, bluster, talk, boast, showing-off, parade, show, pretence, *formal* vaunting, bombast, braggadocio, fanfaronade, rodomontade
🠲 modesty, restraint

brave *adj, v*
▶ *adj* courageous, plucky, unafraid, fearless, undaunted, unflinching, bold, daring, intrepid, stalwart, hardy, stoical, resolute, stout-hearted, lion-hearted, valiant, gallant, heroic, indomitable, *formal* dauntless, audacious, valorous, doughty, *colloq.* gutsy, spunky, gritty
🠲 cowardly, afraid, timid, craven, faint-hearted, *colloq.* yellow, spineless, wimpish, chicken
▶ *v* face, confront, defy, challenge, dare, stand up to, face up to, suffer, endure, bear, withstand, *colloq.* put up with, face the music, keep a stiff upper lip, put a bold/brave face on it, not turn a hair, keep your chin up
🠲 yield, capitulate, give in, *colloq.* get cold feet, chicken out

bravery *n*
courage, pluck, fearlessness, boldness, daring, stalwartness, hardiness, fortitude, resolution, tenacity, stout-heartedness, valour, gallantry, heroism, indomitability, mettle, spirit, dauntlessness, audacity, *formal* intrepidity, valiance, *colloq.* guts, grit, spunk
🠲 cowardice, fearfulness, faint-heartedness, timidity

> 📖 **bravery** or **bravado**?
> *Bravery* is courage: *soldiers decorated for bravery.*
> *Bravado* is a boastful act of bravery intended to impress or intimidate or a boastful pretence of bravery aimed at concealing cowardice: *She felt her defiant bravado disintegrate like shattered glass.*

brawl *n, v*
▶ *n* fight, scrap, scuffle, melee, free-for-all, fray, affray, broil, skirmish, fracas, rumpus, disorder, row, argument, quarrel, squabble, dispute, clash, fisticuffs, Donnybrook, *formal* altercation, *colloq.* punch-up, bust-up, dust-up, *US* ruckus
▶ *v* fight, scuffle, wrestle, tussle, argue, quarrel, squabble, wrangle, dispute, *formal* altercate, *colloq.* scrap, row

brawn *n*
strength, might, muscle, muscles, bulk, bulkiness, muscularity, power, robustness, sinews, *colloq.* beef, beefiness

brawny *adj*
muscular, sinewy, athletic, well-built, burly, hefty, solid, bulky, hulking, massive, strapping, strong, powerful, vigorous, sturdy, robust, hardy, stalwart, *colloq.* beefy, husky
🠲 slight, frail, skinny, weak, weedy

bray *v*
neigh, whinny, heehaw, blare, hoot, roar, screech, trumpet, bell, bellow

brazen *adj*
blatant, flagrant, brash, brassy, bold, forward, saucy, pert, barefaced, impudent, insolent, defiant, shameless, unashamed, unabashed, immodest, *formal* audacious, *colloq.* pushy, brassy
🠲 shy, shamefaced, modest, cautious
▷ **brazen it out** be unashamed, defy, be defiant, be impenitent, *colloq.* put a brave/bold face on it

breach *n, v*
▶ *n* 1 *a breach of the rules* breaking, violation, contravention, infringement, trespass, disobedience, offence, transgression, lapse, disruption, *formal* infraction 2 *a breach in international relations* quarrel, disagreement, dissension, difference, variance, schism, rift rupture, split, division, separation, parting, severance, alienation, dissociation, *formal* disaffection, estrangement 3 *a breach in the defences* break, crack, rift, rupture, fissure, cleft, crevice, opening, aperture, gap, space, hole, gulf, chasm
▶ *v* 1 *breach an agreement* violate, break, contravene, infringe 2 *breach the sea wall* rupture, break (open), open up, burst through, split

bread *n*
1 *bread and jam* crusts, roll, loaf, bap, plait, cob, sandwich, nan, chapati, paratha, pitta, matzo, croissant, baguette, brioche, bagel, French stick, pumpernickel 2 *our daily bread* food, provisions, diet, fare, nourishment, necessities, *formal* nutriment, sustenance, subsistence, victuals 3 *earn your daily bread* cash, money, funds

breadth *n*
1 *the breadth of the garden* WIDTH, broadness, wideness, latitude, thickness, size, magnitude, measure 2 *a great breadth of interests* RANGE, scale, reach, scope, compass, span, sweep, extent, expanse, spread, comprehensiveness, extensiveness, vastness, *formal* amplitude

break *v, n*
▶ *v* 1 *break a plate* fracture, crack, snap, split, sever, separate, divide, rend, smash, disintegrate, splinter, shiver, shatter, ruin, destroy, demolish 2 *break the law* violate, contravene, infringe, breach, disobey, flout, dishonour 3 *the televison has broken* stop working, fail, *formal* malfunction, *colloq.* go on the blink, pack up, conk out, go kaput, crash, cut out 4 *break for lunch* PAUSE, halt, stop, interrupt, suspend, rest, *formal* discontinue 5 *break a silence* INTERRUPT, suspend, interfere with, bring to an end, *formal* discontinue, *colloq.* cut off 6 *the news broke his spirit* overcome, subdue, tame, weaken, enfeeble, impair, undermine, demoralize 7 *the injury broke her skin* pierce, perforate, puncture, open (up) 8 *break the news* tell, inform, impart, divulge, disclose, reveal, announce 9 *break a record* EXCEED, beat, better, excel, surpass, outdo, outstrip 10 *the weather broke* change (for the better/worse), vary, improve, worsen 11 *break a code* CRACK, decipher, solve, work/figure out
🠲 1 mend, put together 2 keep, obey, observe, abide by 3 mend 4 start again 6 encourage, strengthen
▶ *n* 1 *a break in the defences/diplomatic relations* fracture, crack, split, rift, rupture, schism, separation, tear, gash, fissure, cleft, crevice, opening, gap, hole, breach, *formal* estrangement 2 *have a break for coffee* interval, intermission, interlude, interruption, stop, pause, halt, lull, respite, rest, *colloq.* let-up, breather, time-out 3 *away for a short break* time off, holiday, *US* vacation 4 *a lucky break* opportunity, chance, advantage, fortune, (stroke of) luck, opening
▷ **break away** separate, split (off), part company, detach, secede, leave, depart, quit, run away, escape, flee, fly, *colloq.* make a run for it
▷ **break down** 1 *the van broke down* fail, stop, stop working, give way, collapse, *colloq.* pack up, conk out, seize up 2 *negotiations broke down* fail, collapse, founder, *colloq.* fall through 3 *break down in tears* lose control, be overcome, collapse, *colloq.* go to pieces, crack up 4 *break down the figures* analyse, dissect, separate, itemize, detail
▷ **break in** 1 *break in with unhelpful remarks* INTERRUPT, butt in, cut in, interject, intervene, intrude, encroach, impinge, *formal* interpose 2 *break in and steal*

the money BURGLE, rob, raid, enter illegally **3** *break in a horse/pair of walking boots* train, condition, wear, accustom, get used to

▷ **break off 1** *break off a piece of ice* DETACH, separate, part, divide, disconnect, sever, *formal* dissever, *colloq.* snap off **2** *break off as the phone rang*; *break off a relationship* pause, interrupt, suspend, halt, stop, cease, end, finish, bring to an end, *formal* discontinue, terminate

▷ **break out 1** *war broke out in 1939* START, begin (suddenly), arise, emerge, happen, occur, erupt, *formal* commence, *colloq.* flare up, burst out **2** *break out of prison* ESCAPE, bolt, flee, formal abscond **3** *'Just a minute,' she broke out* exclaim, shout, *colloq.* burst out **4** *break out into a rash* erupt, come out in

▷ **break through** emerge, gain ground, leap forward, make headway, pass, penetrate, progress, succeed, overcome

▷ **break up 1** *break up a monopoly* dismantle, take apart, demolish, destroy, disintegrate, splinter, sever, divide, split (up), part, separate **2** *the couple broke up* separate, divorce, finish, *colloq.* split up **3** *the meeting broke up* disband, disperse, dissolve, adjourn, suspend, stop, finish, *formal* discontinue, terminate

▷ **break with** finish with, part with, reject, separate from, *formal* renounce, repudiate, *colloq.* drop, jilt, ditch

breakable *adj*
brittle, fragile, delicate, flimsy, insubstantial, frail, *formal* friable, frangible, *colloq.* jerry-built
🞂 unbreakable, durable, sturdy, long-lasting, shatterproof

breakaway *adj*
rebel, dissenting, renegade, heretical, *formal* apostate, schismatic, seceding, secessionist

breakdown *n*
1 *the breakdown of the talks/car* failure, collapse, disintegration, interruption, stoppage, *formal* malfunction **2** *a nervous breakdown* collapse, *colloq.* going to pieces, cracking-up **3** ANALYSIS, dissection, itemization, classification, categorization

breaker *n*
wave, roller, billow, white horses

break-in *n*
burglary, house-breaking, robbery, raid, invasion, intrusion, trespass, larceny

breakthrough *n*
discovery, find, finding, invention, innovation, advance, progress, headway, step, gain, leap, step/leap forward, quantum leap (forward), development, improvement, milestone

break-up *n*
divorce, separation, parting, split, rift, finish, dispersal, disintegration, crumbling, *formal* dissolution, termination, *colloq.* splitting-up

breakwater *n*
groyne, sea wall, mole, jetty, pier, quay, spur, wharf, dock, embankment

breast *n*
1 *beat your breasts in sorrow* bosom, bust, chest, front, heart, thorax **2** *a woman's breasts* bust, nipple, teat, cleavage, *technical* mamma, *slang* boob

breath *n*
1 *take deep breaths to relax* air, breathing, respiration, sigh, gasp, pant, gulp, *formal* flatus, inhalation, exhalation **2** *a breath of fresh air* breeze, puff, waft, gust, *formal* pneuma **3** *a breath of autumn in the air* aroma, smell, odour, whiff **4** *a breath of scandal* HINT, suggestion, suspicion, undertone, whisper, murmur

breathe *v*
1 *breathe deeply* sigh, gasp, pant, puff, snore, *formal* inhale, exhale, respire, expire **2** *not breathe a word to anyone* express, voice, murmur, whisper, tell, articulate, utter, impart **3** *breathe new life into a project* instil, imbue, infuse, inject, inspire, *formal* transfuse

breather *n*
break, rest, constitutional, pause, halt, recess, relaxation, rest, walk, *formal* respite, *colloq.* breathing-space

breathless *adj*
1 *breathless from climbing* short-winded, out of breath, panting, puffing, puffed (out), exhausted, winded, gasping, wheezing, choking **2** *breathless anticipation* expectant, impatient, in suspense, eager, agog, excited, feverish, anxious

breathtaking *adj*
awe-inspiring, impressive, magnificent, spectacular, overwhelming, amazing, astonishing, stunning, exciting, thrilling, stirring, moving

breed *v, n*
▸ *v* **1** *breed dogs* REPRODUCE, procreate, multiply, hatch, bear, give birth to, rear, raise, bring up, bring forth, *formal* propagate, pullulate **2** *breed suspicion* PRODUCE, create, originate, arouse, cause, occasion, give rise to, generate, make, foster, nurture, nourish, cultivate, develop, *formal* engender
▸ *n* **1** *breeds of cattle* SPECIES, strain, variety, family, stamp, stock, race, line, lineage, pedigree, hybrid, *formal* progeny **2** *the new breed of leader* kind, type, class

breeding *n*
1 *the breeding of cattle* REPRODUCTION, nurture, development, rearing, raising, upbringing, ancestry, lineage, stock, genetic engineering, *formal* procreation **2** *have breeding (good)* manners, politeness, gentility, refinement, culture, polish, education, training, *formal* civility, urbanity
🞂 **2** vulgarity, bad manners

breeding-ground *n*
nest, nursery, school, training ground, *colloq.* hotbed

breeze *n, v*
▸ *n* wind, gust, flurry, waft, puff, breath, draught, air
▸ *v* glide, sail, hurry, sweep, trip, wander, *colloq.* flit, sally

breezy *adj*
1 *a breezy day* WINDY, blowing, fresh, airy, gusty, blustery, squally **2** *a breezy manner* LIVELY, confident, animated, jaunty, buoyant, blithe, debonair, carefree, cheerful, casual, informal, light, bright, exhilarating, vivacious, *colloq.* easy-going
🞂 **1** still, calm, windless **2** staid, serious, quiet, sad

brevity *n*
1 *the brevity of the speech* briefness, shortness, conciseness, succinctness, pithiness, economy, crispness, incisiveness, abruptness, curtness, *formal* terseness, concision, laconism **2** *the brevity of life* briefness, shortness, *formal* impermanence, ephemerality, transience, transitoriness
🞂 **1** long-windedness, wordiness, *formal* verbosity, prolixity **2** permanence, *formal* longevity

brew *v, n*
▸ *v* **1** *brew tea* stew, boil, prepare, soak, steep, cook, *formal* infuse, seethe, ferment, prepare **2** *brew beer* ferment **3** *trouble/a storm is brewing* build up, gather, develop, plot, scheme, plan, project, devise, contrive, concoct, hatch, excite, foment
▸ *n* **1** *boil up a hot brew* drink, liquor, potion, *formal* beverage, infusion **2** *a powerful brew of sex and violence* mixture, blend, preparation, fermentation, distillation, *formal* concoction

bribe *n, v*
> *n* incentive, inducement, allurement, enticement, kickback, douceur, *colloq.* back-hander, refresher, sweetener, hush money, pay-off, slush fund, protection money, *US* payola, boodle
> *v* corrupt, reward, suborn, square, *colloq.* buy/pay off, grease, grease someone's palm, fix, take care of

bribery *n*
corruption, inducement, protection, *colloq.* palm-greasing, graft

bric-à-brac *n*
knick-knacks, ornaments, curios, antiques, trinkets, baubles, trumpery

brick *n*
1 *bricks and mortar* breeze block, adobe, firebrick, block, briquette, header, klinker, stretcher, rock, stone **2** *be a real brick for helping* mate, pal, real friend, chum, *US* buddy

bridal *adj*
wedding, nuptial, marriage, matrimonial, marital, conjugal, *formal* connubial

bride *n*
honeymooner, newly-wed, wife, spouse, marriage partner, war bride, GI bride

bridegroom *n*
honeymooner, newly-wed, husband, spouse, marriage partner, groom

bridge *n, v*
> *n* **1** *a bridge over the river* arch, span, causeway, link

Types of bridge include:
suspension bridge, arch bridge, cantilever bridge, flying bridge, flyover, overpass, footbridge, railway bridge, viaduct, aqueduct, humpback bridge, toll bridge, pontoon bridge, Bailey bridge, rope bridge, drawbridge, swing bridge.

2 *act as a bridge between the different factions* link, connection, bond, tie
> *v* span, cross, go over, reach across, fill, link, connect, couple, join, unite, bind, *formal* traverse

bridle *v, n*
> *v* **1** *bridle your temper* check, curb, restrain, control, govern, master, subdue, moderate, repress, contain **2** *bridle at someone's anger* bristle, become indignant, be offended by
> *n* check, halter, control, curb, restraint

brief *adj, n, v*
> *adj* **1** *a brief report/visit* short, terse, succinct, concise, pithy, crisp, compressed, condensed, abridged, thumbnail, *formal* aphoristic **2** *a brief manner* ABRUPT, sharp, short, brusque, blunt, curt, surly, *formal* laconic **3** *this brief life* short-lived, momentary, ephemeral, transient, fleeting, passing, transitory, temporary, limited, cursory, hasty, quick, swift, *formal* fugacious
> ⊠ **1** lengthy, long-winded, extensive, *formal* verbose, protracted
> *n* **1** *with a brief to reduce crime* RESPONSIBILITY, orders, instructions, directions, remit, mandate, directive, advice, briefing, data, information **2** *a brief of the day's events* outline, summary, précis, abstract, abridgement, digest **3** *a legal brief* dossier, case, defence, argument, evidence, data
> *v* instruct, direct, explain, guide, advise, prepare, prime, inform, *colloq.* fill in, gen up, give someone the run-down/low-down, put someone in the picture

briefing *n*
meeting, conference, preparation, priming, information, advice, guidance, directions, instructions, orders, *formal* intimation, *colloq.* filling-in, gen, run-down, low-down

briefly *adv*
1 *speak briefly* concisely, succinctly, cursorily, precisely, quickly, summarily, tersely, to the point **2** *briefly, the answer is no* in brief, in a word, in a few words, *colloq.* in a nutshell
> ⊠ **1** at length, fully

brigade *n*
group, band, body, company, unit, corps, crew, force, party, squad, team, troop, contingent

brigand *n*
bandit, robber, desperado, gangster, outlaw, marauder, plunderer, ruffian, highwayman, freebooter

bright *adj*
1 *bright lights/colours* BRILLIANT, luminous, illuminated, radiant, shining, beaming, flashing, gleaming, glistening, glittering, sparkling, twinkling, shimmering, glowing, glorious, splendid, dazzling, blinding, glaring, blazing, intense, vivid, *formal* resplendent, effulgent, refulgent, lustrous, incandescent **2** *look bright* HAPPY, cheerful, glad, joyful, merry, jolly, lively, *formal* vivacious **3** *the future looks bright* PROMISING, favourable, rosy, optimistic, hopeful, encouraging, *formal* propitious, auspicious **4** *bright students* CLEVER, smart, intelligent, quick-witted, quick, sharp, acute, keen, astute, perceptive, *colloq.* brainy, bright as a button **5** *a bright day* FINE, sunny, cloudless, unclouded, pleasant
> ⊠ **1** dull, drab, colourless, pale, dim, soft **2** sad, gloomy, depressed, *colloq.* down **3** depressing, gloomy, *formal* inauspicious **4** stupid, *colloq.* thick **5** dark, overcast, cloudy

brighten *v*
1 *brighten up a room* light up, illuminate, lighten, make bright **2** *brighten up the silver* polish, burnish, rub (up), shine, gleam, glow **3** *brighten at the prospect* CHEER UP, gladden, hearten, encourage, liven up, *formal* enliven, *colloq.* buck up, perk up, pep up
> ⊠ **1** darken, shadow **2** dull, tarnish

brilliance *n*
1 *brilliance at the piano* talent, virtuosity, genius, greatness, distinction, excellence, aptitude, cleverness, distinction **2** *the brilliance of the sun* RADIANCE, brightness, sparkle, dazzle, intensity, vividness, gloss, lustre, sheen, glamour, glory, magnificence, splendour, *formal* resplendence, effulgence, refulgence, fulgency, coruscation

brilliant *adj*
1 *a brilliant flautist* gifted, talented, accomplished, expert, skilful, masterly, exceptional, outstanding, superb, illustrious, famous, celebrated **2** *a brilliant light/show* sparkling, glittering, scintillating, dazzling, glaring, blazing, intense, vivid, bright, shining, glossy, showy, glorious, magnificent, splendid, *formal* resplendent, effulgent, refulgent, fulgent **3** *a brilliant mind* clever, bright, intelligent, quick, astute, *formal* erudite, *colloq.* brainy **4** *a brilliant performance* clever, skilful, masterly, remarkable, resourceful, enterprising **5** *What a brilliant game!* great, fantastic, superb, wonderful
> ⊠ **1** undistinguished, untalented **2** dull **3** stupid **4** ordinary, *colloq.* run-of-the-mill **5** awful, bad

brim *n, v*
> *n* rim, perimeter, circumference, lip, edge, margin, border, brink, verge, top, limit
> *v* be full with, be (packed) full with, be filled with, overflow with, be overflowing with

bring *v*
1 *bring a drink; bring you home later* take, carry, transport, fetch, deliver, escort, accompany, usher, guide, conduct, lead, convey, *formal* bear **2** *bring misery* cause, produce, result in, create, prompt, provoke, force, *formal* engender

▷ **bring about** cause, occasion, create, produce, generate, accomplish, achieve, fulfil, realize, manage, *formal* effect

▷ **bring down 1** *bring down the government* OVERTHROW, unseat, oust, defeat, destroy, *formal* vanquish, *colloq.* topple, knock down, shoot down **2** *bring down blood pressure/unemployment* REDUCE, lower, cause to fall/drop

▷ **bring forward** advance, put forward, make earlier

▟ postpone, put back

▷ **bring in 1** *bring in new laws* INTRODUCE, initiate, originate, pioneer, set up, usher in, *formal* inaugurate **2** *bring in £4,000* earn, net, gross, produce, fetch, return, yield, *formal* accrue, realize

▷ **bring off** succeed in, achieve, fulfil, perform, accomplish, win, *formal* execute, discharge, *colloq.* pull off

▷ **bring on 1** *bring on a headache* cause, lead to, give rise to, generate, inspire, prompt, provoke, *formal* occasion, induce, precipitate **2** *bring on the plant's growth* ADVANCE, accelerate, foster, nurture, improve, *formal* expedite

▷ **bring out 1** *bring out a point in a story* EMPHASIZE, stress, highlight, enhance, draw out, make someone aware of **2** *bring out a book* publish, print, issue, launch, introduce, produce

▷ **bring round 1** *bring round someone who is unconscious* REVIVE, resuscitate, bring to, rouse, awaken **2** *bring someone round to your way of thinking* PERSUADE, convince, win over, convert, coax, cajole

▷ **bring up 1** *bring up children* care for, raise, foster, nurture, educate, teach, train, form, *formal* rear **2** *bring up a matter for discussion* RAISE, introduce, broach, mention, submit, propose **3** *bring up food* vomit, regurgitate, *colloq.* throw up, puke

brink *n*
on the brink of the cliff edge/war verge, threshold, edge, margin, fringe, border, boundary, limit, extremity, lip, rim, brim, bank

brisk *adj*
1 *go for a brisk walk* energetic, vigorous, quick, snappy, lively, spirited, active, busy, bustling, agile, nimble, alert **2** *a brisk manner* lively, quick, businesslike, *colloq.* no-nonsense **3** *brisk business* busy, rapid, good **4** *brisk weather* invigorating, exhilarating, stimulating, bracing, refreshing, cold, fresh, crisp
▟ **1** unenergetic, slow **2** slow, lethargic **3** slow, sluggish

bristle *n, v*
▶ *n* **1** *shave off bristles* hair, whisker, stubble **2** *bristles on an animal's back* spine, prickle, barb, quill, thorn, awn
▶ *v* **1** *bristling with anger* seethe (with), draw oneself up, bridle at, be incensed at, *technical* horripilate **2** *bristling with police* teem with, swarm with, *formal* abound in, *colloq.* be thick with, hum with

bristly *adj*
hairy, whiskered, bearded, unshaven, stubbly, rough, spiny, prickly, spiky, thorny, *technical* hispid, barbellate, *formal* hirsute
▟ clean-shaven, smooth

brittle *adj*
1 BREAKABLE, easily broken, fragile, delicate, frail, hard, crisp, crumbly, crumbling, shattery, *formal* friable, frangible **2** *a brittle situation* unstable, fragile, delicate **3** *a brittle manner* tense, curt, irritable, nervous, *colloq.* nervy **4** *a brittle laugh* short hard, sharp, harsh, grating
▟ **1** durable, resilient, sturdy **2** stable, secure, constant

broach *v*
introduce, raise, mention, propose, suggest, hint at

broad *adj*
1 *broad avenues/valleys* WIDE, large, vast, roomy, spacious, ample, extensive, widespread, *formal* capacious, latitudinous **2** *a broad education* WIDE-RANGING, far-reaching, encyclopedic, extensive, all-embracing, inclusive, comprehensive, general, sweeping, universal, unlimited, *formal* catholic, eclectic, compendious **3** *the broad meaning of the term* general, vague, not detailed **4** *broad support* WIDESPREAD, extensive, general **5** *a broad hint* obvious, clear, plain, undisguised, unconcealed
▟ **1** narrow **2** limited, restricted **3** narrow, detailed, specific, precise **4** limited **5** veiled, disguised

📖 broad or **wide** ?
Broad refers to the extent across something and often has the connotation of spaciousness or ampleness, whereas *wide* refers to the distance separating, or the gap between, sides or edges: *a person's broad back*; *broad shoulders*; *wide sleeves*; *a wide doorway.*

broadcast *v, n*
▶ *v* **1** *broadcast TV programmes* TRANSMIT, air, show, beam, relay, televise, cable **2** *broadcast the decision widely* make known, report, announce, publicize, advertise, publish, circulate, spread, scatter, *formal* promulgate, disseminate
▶ *n* transmission, programme, show, access television, community broadcasting, simulcast, simultaneous transmission, television première, teletext, satellite programme

broaden *v*
the road broadens out; broaden the scope of the inquiry widen, spread, enlarge, expand, extend, stretch, increase, develop, open up, branch out, diversify, *formal* augment
▟ narrow, reduce, restrict

broad-minded *adj*
liberal, tolerant, permissive, forbearing, enlightened, free-thinking, progressive, indulgent, impartial, open-minded, receptive, unbiased, unprejudiced, dispassionate
▟ narrow-minded, intolerant, biased, prejudiced

broadside *n*
1 *fire a broadside at a ship* attack, assault, volley, battering, cannonade, blast, bombardment, counterblast **2** *verbal broadsides* criticism, denunciation, *formal* philippic, diatribe, fulmination, harangue, invective, *colloq.* brickbat, stick

brochure *n*
leaflet, booklet, pamphlet, prospectus, broadsheet, handbill, circular, handout, folder, flyer

broil *v*
grill, cook, fry, barbecue, roast

broiling *adj*
sweltering, boiling, baking, roasting, scorching, blistering

broke *adj*
penniless, bankrupt, ruined, poor, impoverished, poverty-stricken, destitute, *formal* insolvent, impecunious, penurious, indigent, *colloq.* bust, skint, stony-broke, strapped (for cash), cleaned out, on your uppers, on your beam ends, not having two pennies to rub together
▟ rich, affluent, solvent

broken *adj*
1 *a broken pipe* fractured, burst, ruptured, severed, separated, shattered, smashed, destroyed, demolished, *colloq.* broken to smithereens **2** *broken machinery* faulty, damaged, defective, out of order/

action, not working, gone wrong, *formal* malfunctioning, inoperative, *colloq.* bust, kaput, duff, on the blink, wonky **3** *broken sleep* disjointed, disconnected, fragmentary, interrupted, intermittent, spasmodic, erratic, *formal* discontinuous **4** *speak broken German* hesitating, stammering, halting, imperfect, disjointed **5** *a broken man* beaten, defeated, crushed, demoralized, weak, feeble, exhausted, tamed, subdued, oppressed, *formal* vanquished, *colloq.* down, knackered **F₃** **1** mended, intact, whole **2** mended, in order/action, working **3** continuous, uninterrupted **4** fluent

broken-down *adj*
1 *a broken-down machine* faulty, damaged, defective, out of order, *formal* inoperative, *colloq.* on the blink, bust, kaput, duff **2** *a broken-down old house* DILAPIDATED, in disrepair, decrepit, ruined, decayed, collapsed

broken-hearted *adj*
heartbroken, inconsolable, devastated, grief-stricken, desolate, despairing, miserable, wretched, mournful, sorrowful, sad, unhappy, dejected, despondent, crestfallen, disappointed, *formal* dolorous, forlorn, wretched, disconsolate, prostrated, *colloq.* down, down in the dumps

broker *n*
agent, middleman, dealer, factor, handler, intermediary, negotiator, stockbroker, jobber, stockjobber, *technical* arbitrageur

bromide *n*
platitude, banality, cliché, commonplace, stereotype, truism, *formal* anodyne

bronze *adj*
copper, copper-coloured, auburn, chestnut, reddish-brown, rust, rust-coloured, tan, Titian, suntanned, tanned, browned

brooch *n* badge, pin, clip, clasp, breastpin, tiepin

brood *v, n*
▶ *v* **1** *brood over lost opportunities* ponder, meditate, muse, mull over, go over, dwell on, worry about, sulk, agonize, *formal* rehearse, ruminate, *colloq.* fret, mope **2** *hens brood* incubate, sit, hatch
▶ *n* **1** *a brood of birds* clutch, chicks, hatch, litter, young, offspring, issue, progeny **2** *a brood of children* children, family

brook¹ *n*
a brook running by the cottage stream, rivulet, beck, burn, watercourse, channel, inlet, gill, runnel

brook² *v*
will brook no interference tolerate, allow, accept, allow, permit, bear, endure, stand, put up with, support, withstand, *formal* countenance, *colloq.* stomach

brothel *n*
bordello, bawdy-house, house of ill fame, house of ill repute, red light, bagnio

brother *n*
1 *brothers and sisters* sibling, blood-brother, relation, relative **2** *brothers in the struggle against injustice* comrade, friend, mate, partner, colleague, associate, fellow, companion, *colloq.* chum, mate, pal **3** *brothers in a monastery* monk, friar

brotherhood *n*
1 *feelings of brotherhood* fellowship, comradeship, friendship, friendliness cameraderie **2** *a brotherhood of monks* fraternity, association, society, league, confederation, confederacy, alliance, union, guild, fellowship, community, clique

brotherly *adj*
fraternal, loyal, affectionate, amicable, caring, sympathetic, friendly, kind, loving, benevolent, philanthropic **F₃** callous, unbrotherly

brow *n*
1 *sweat on your brow* forehead, temples **2** *the brow of the hill* summit, ridge, top, tip, peak, verge, brink, cliff

browbeat *v*
bully, coerce, force, intimidate, threaten, tyrannize, hound, dragoon, domineer, overbear, oppress, *colloq.* bulldoze
F₃ coax, flatter, *colloq.* sweet-talk

brown *adj, v*
▶ *adj* **1** *brown in colour* mahogany, chocolate, coffee, hazel, bay, chestnut, auburn, umber, sepia, ginger, beige, fawn, tan, tawny, russet, rust, rusty, brunette, dark, dusky **2** *brown from lying in the sun* sunburnt, tanned, bronze, bronzed, browned
▶ *v* cook, seal, fry, grill, toast

browned off *adj*
bored, fed up, discontented, discouraged, disheartened, weary, *colloq.* bored stiff, brassed off, cheesed off, disgruntled
F₃ fascinated, interested, intrigued

browse *v*
1 *browse through a book* survey, scan, leaf through, flick through, dip into, skim, *formal* peruse **2** *sheep browsing in the fields* GRAZE, pasture, feed, eat, nibble

bruise *v, n*
▶ *v* **1** *bruise your leg* discolour, blacken, mark, blemish, injure, wound **2** *bruise someone's feelings* hurt, injure, insult, offend, grieve, upset, crush **3** *bruise fruit* damage, mark, spoil, blemish, crush
▶ *n* discoloration, mark, blemish, injury, *technical* ecchymosis, *formal* contusion, *colloq.* black eye, shiner

brunt *n*
burden, thrust, (main) force, impact, impetus, pressure, (full) weight, shock, strain

brush¹ *n, v*
▶ *n* *sweep the room with a brush* broom, sweeper, besom, whisk
▶ *v* **1** *brush the room* clean, clean, sweep, flick, burnish, polish, shine **2** *brush against the table* touch, contact, graze, kiss, stroke, rub, scrape
▷ **brush aside** dismiss, ignore, flout, disregard, override, *formal* belittle, *colloq.* pooh-pooh
▷ **brush off** disregard, ignore, slight, snub, rebuff, dismiss, spurn, reject, repulse, disown, *formal* repudiate, *colloq.* cold-shoulder
▷ **brush up** **1** *brush up your Spanish* revise, relearn, improve, polish up, study, read up, *colloq.* swot, bone up on, cram **2** *go and brush up* refresh (yourself), freshen up, clean (yourself up), tidy (up)

brush² *n*
a ball lost in the brush bush, scrub, thicket, bushes, shrubs, brushwood, undergrowth, ground cover

brush³ *n*
a brush with the police confrontation, encounter, disagreement, argument, clash, conflict, fight, skirmish, tussle, fracas, *colloq.* dust-up, set-to, scrap

brush-off *n*
discouragement, dismissal, rebuff, refusal, rejection, repudiation, repulse, slight, snub, *formal* repudiation, *colloq.* cold shoulder, *US slang* kiss-off
F₃ encouragement

brusque *adj*
abrupt, sharp, short, terse, curt, gruff, surly, discourteous, impolite, uncivil, blunt, tactless, uncivil, undiplomatic
F₃ courteous, polite, tactful

brutal *adj*
1 *a brutal murder/attacker* savage, bloodthirsty, vicious, ferocious, cruel, inhumane, animal, inhuman,

beastly, brutish, remorseless, pitiless, merciless, ruthless, callous, *formal* bestial **2** *brutal frankness* harsh, insensitive, unfeeling, heartless, severe
☲ **1** kindly, humane, civilized **2** kind, gentle, sensitive

brutality *n*
savagery, bloodthirstiness, viciousness, ferocity, cruelty, inhumanity, violence, atrocity, ruthlessness, callousness, roughness, coarseness, barbarism, barbarity, brutishness, *formal* callosity
☲ gentleness, kindness

brute *n, adj*
▶ *n* animal, beast, swine, creature, monster, ogre, devil, fiend, savage, sadist, bully, lout, yahoo
▶ *adj* physical, senseless, unthinking, bodily, carnal, coarse, depraved, fleshly, gross, instinctive, mindless, sensual

brutish *adj*
brutal, uncivilized, barbarian, barbaric, barbarous, coarse, crass, crude, cruel, gross, loutish, savage, stupid, uncouth, vulgar, *formal* bestial, feral, ferine
☲ refined, civilized, polite

bubble *n, v*
▶ *n* **1** *soap bubbles* ball (of air), drop, droplet, bead, blister, fizz, foam, froth, head, lather, suds, effervescence, globule, spume, *formal* vesicle **2** *the bubble of all their dreams burst* delusion, fantasy, fraud, illusion, trifle, vanity
▶ *v* **1** SPARKLE, froth, foam, seethe, boil, burble, gurgle, effervesce, *colloq.* fizz **2** *bubble with enthusiasm* be filled, be excited, sparkle, be elated, *colloq.* bounce

bubbly *adj*
1 SPARKLING, carbonated, frothy, foaming, sudsy, effervescent, *colloq.* fizzy **2** LIVELY, happy, merry, elated, excited, exuberant, vivacious, alive and kicking, *formal* animated, ebullient, *colloq.* bouncy, full of beans
☲ **1** flat, still **2** lethargic

buccaneer *n*
pirate, corsair, filibuster, freebooter, privateer, sea-robber, sea-rover, sea-wolf

buck *v*
▷ **buck up 1** *buck someone up* cheer (up), encourage, improve, rally, stimulate, take heart, hearten, enliven, *formal* inspirit, *colloq.* perk up **2** *buck up or we'll be late!* hurry (up), *formal* hasten, *colloq.* get a move on, get your skates on, step on it
☲ **1** discourage **2** slow down

bucket *n*
pail, can, bail, scuttle, pitcher, vessel

buckle *n, v*
▶ *n* **1** *a buckle on a belt* clasp, clip, catch, fastener, hasp **2** *a buckle in metal* bulge, warp, distortion, twist, kink, *formal* contortion
▶ *v* **1** *buckle your belt* FASTEN, clasp, catch, hook, hitch, connect, close, secure **2** *the metal buckled* bend, warp, twist, distort, bulge, fold, wrinkle, crumple, collapse, *colloq.* cave in

bucolic *adj*
pastoral, rural, agrarian, agricultural, country, *formal* rustic, *colloq.* countrified
☲ industrial, urban

bud *n, v*
▶ *n* shoot, sprout, sprig, germ, embryo, *formal* knosp, plumule
▶ *v* shoot, sprout, develop, grow, *formal* burgeon, pullulate
☲ wither, waste away

budding *adj*
potential, promising, embryonic, developing, growing,

flowering, fledgling, *formal* incipient, nascent, burgeoning
☲ experienced, mature

budge *v*
1 *the door won't budge* move, stir, shift, remove, dislodge, push, roll, slide **2** *not budge from your position* change, bend, yield, give (way), give in, change your mind, not compromise, sway, influence, persuade, convince

budget *n, v*
▶ *n* finances, funds, resources, economics, means, allowance, allotment, quota, allocation, (financial) estimate, what you can afford
▶ *v* plan, estimate, allow, allot, allocate, set aside, ration, afford, *formal* apportion

buff¹ *adj, v*
▶ *adj buff-coloured envelopes* yellowish-brown, yellowish, straw, sandy, fawn, khaki, tan
▶ *v* polish, burnish, shine, smooth, rub, brush

buff² *n*
a computer buff expert, connoisseur, enthusiast, fan, admirer, devotee, addict, aficionado, *US* maven, *colloq.* freak, fiend

buffer *n*
shock-absorber, bumper, fender, pad, cushion, pillow, intermediary, screen, shield, bulwark

buffet¹ *n*
1 *a railway buffet* snackbar, counter, café, cafeteria **2** *a buffet supper* self-service, cold meal, smorgasbord, *colloq.* help yourself

buffet² *v, n*
▶ *v* *was buffeted by the storm* batter, hit, strike, knock, bang, bump, push, pound, pummel, beat, shove, thump, box, cuff, slap, *colloq.* clout
▶ *n* blow, knock, bang, bump, jar, jolt, push, thump, box, cuff, clout, slap, smack, shove, thump, box, cuff, slap, smack, *colloq.* clout

buffoon *n*
clown, comedian, comic, fool, harlequin, jester, joker, wag, droll

buffoonery *n*
clowning, jesting, pantomime, tomfoolery, waggishness, drollery, nonsense, silliness

bug *n, v*
▶ *n* **1** INSECT, flea, *colloq.* creepy-crawly **2** *a stomach bug* virus, bacterium, germ, microbe, micro-organism, infection, disease **3** *a bug in a computer program* fault, defect, flaw, blemish, imperfection, failing, error, *colloq.* gremlin **4** *bitten by the decorating bug* craze, fad, obsession **5** *put a bug in a room* hidden microphone, listening device, *colloq.* wire-tap, phone-tap
▶ *v* **1** *their attitude bugs me* ANNOY, irritate, vex, irk, bother, disturb, harass, *colloq.* needle, wind up **2** *bug an office* tap, listen in (on/to), *formal* eavesdrop (on), *colloq.* wire-tap, phone-tap

bugbear *n*
anathema, bane, bête noire, pet hate, dread, fiend, horror, nightmare

build *v, n*
▶ *v* **1** *build a new hotel* construct, put up, erect, raise, fabricate, make, form, constitute, assemble, put together, knock together, shape, fashion **2** *build a fairer society* develop, enlarge, extend, increase, escalate, intensify, *formal* augment
☲ **1** destroy, demolish, *colloq.* knock down **2** lessen
▶ *n* physique, figure, body, form, shape, size, frame, structure
▷ **build up 1** *build up a navy* ASSEMBLE, put together, piece together, extend, enlarge **2** *build up your strength* reinforce, extend, expand, develop, amplify,

increase, escalate, intensify, heighten, boost, improve, enhance, *formal* fortify **3** *build a person up as important* publicize, advertise, promote, *colloq.* plug, hype

building *n*
construction, development, fabrication, structure, erection, architecture, *formal* edifice, dwelling

Types of building include:
house, bungalow, cottage, block of flats, apartment, *US* condominium, cabin, farmhouse, villa, mansion, chateau, castle, palace; church, chapel, cathedral, abbey, monastery, temple, pagoda, mosque, synagogue; shop, store, garage, factory, warehouse, silo, office block, tower block, skyscraper, theatre, cinema, gymnasium, sports hall, restaurant, café, hotel, *colloq.* pub, public house, inn, school, college, museum, library, hospital, prison, power station, observatory; barracks, fort, fortress, monument, mausoleum; shed, barn, outhouse, stable, mill, lighthouse, pier, pavilion, boat-house, beach-hut, summerhouse, gazebo, dovecote, windmill. *See also* HOUSE; SHOP.

Types of building material include:
aluminium, ashlar, asphalt, bitumen, breeze block, brick, building block, cast iron, cement, chipboard, clay, concrete, reinforced concrete, fixings, flagstone, girder, glass, glass fibre, gravel, granite, grout, gypsum, hardboard, hard core, insulation, foam insulation, loose fill insulation, lagging, lintel, *US* lumber, marble, mortar, paving stone, pavior, plaster, plasterboard, plastic, plywood, sand, sandstone, shingle, slate, stainless steel, steel, steel beam, stone, tarmac, thatch, tile, floor tile, roof tile, timber, wattle and daub, wood.

build-up *n*
1 *a build-up of fat* enlargement, expansion, development, increase, gain, growth, accumulation, escalation, *formal* accretion **2** *build-up of nuclear weapons* ACCUMULATION, mass, load, heap, stack, drift, store, stockpile **3** *build-up to the competition* publicity, promotion, *colloq.* plug, hype
🔁 **1** reduction, decrease, contraction

built-in *adj*
1 *built-in wardrobes* FITTED, integral, in-built, included **2** *built-in safeguards* inherent, included, incorporated, implicit, in-built, inseparable, integral, intrinsic, essential, fundamental, necessary

bulb *n*

Plants grown from bulbs and corms include:
acidanthera, allium, amarylis, anemone, bluebell (endymion), chincherinchee, chionodoxa, crocosmia, crocus, autumn crocus (colchicum), cyclamen, daffodil, crown imperial (fritillaria), galtonia, garlic, gladioli, grape hyacinth (muscari), hyacinth, iris, ixia, jonquil, lily, montbretia, narcissus, nerine, ranunculus, scilla, snowdrop (galanthus), sparaxis, tulip, winter aconite.

bulbous *adj*
rounded, swollen, swelling, bulging, convex, bloated, *technical* pulvinate(d), *formal* distended

bulge *n, v*
▶ *n* **1** *a bulge on the wall* swelling, bump, lump, hump, *formal* projection, protuberance, distension **2** *a bulge*

in the production figures rise, increase, surge, upsurge, intensification
▶ *v* swell, hump, expand, enlarge, bulb, project, protrude, *formal* dilate, distend, *colloq.* puff out, sag

bulk *n*
1 *the vast bulk of the ship* size, magnitude, dimensions, extent, bigness, largeness, immensity, volume, mass, weight, substance, body, *formal* amplitude **2** *the bulk of the recruits* MAJORITY, most, nearly all, preponderance, *colloq.* lion's share

bulky *adj*
substantial, big, large, huge, enormous, immense, mammoth, massive, colossal, hulking, hefty, heavy, weighty, unmanageable, unwieldy, awkward, cumbersome, *formal* voluminous
🔁 insubstantial, small, handy

bulldoze *v*
1 *bulldoze buildings* clear, flatten, level, raze, *colloq.* knock down **2** *bulldoze someone into buying*; *bulldoze plans through a committee* FORCE, push (through), intimidate, browbeat, *formal* coerce, *colloq.* bully, steamroller

bullet *n*
shot, pellet, ball, missile, propellant, cartridge, cartouche, *formal* projectile, *colloq.* slug

bulletin *n*
1 *televison news bulletins* REPORT, newsflash, dispatch, communiqué, statement, announcement, notification, communication, message **2** *an office bulletin* news sheet, newspaper, newsletter, leaflet

bullish *adj*
optimistic, confident, hopeful, positive, cheerful, buoyant, *formal* sanguine, *colloq.* upbeat

bully *n, v*
▶ *n* persecutor, tormentor, browbeater, intimidator, bully-boy, ruffian, thug, bouncer, *colloq.* heavy, tough
▶ *v* persecute, torment, terrorize, bulldoze, coerce, browbeat, bullyrag, intimidate, cow, tyrannize, pick on, victimize, domineer, overbear, oppress, *colloq.* push around
🔁 coax, persuade, encourage

bulwark *n*
bastion, buttress, defence, guard, safeguard, security, support, mainstay, outwork, buffer, embankment, fortification, partition, rampart, *technical* redoubt

bumbling *adj*
bungling, awkward, inept, blundering, botching, clumsy, inefficient, incompetent, lumbering, muddled, stumbling, *formal* maladroit
🔁 competent, efficient

bump *v, n*
▶ *v* **1** *bump into the wall/against the table* hit, strike, knock, bang, crash, collide (with), *colloq.* slam, prang **2** *bump along a track* jolt, jerk, jar, jostle, rattle, shake, bounce
▶ *n* **1** *hear a bump* blow, hit, knock, bang, thump, thud, smash, crash, collision, impact, jolt, jar, shock **2** *a bump on your head* lump, swelling, bulge, injury, hump, *technical* papilla, knur, nodule, *formal* protrusion, protuberance, tumescence **3** *a bump on a road* lump, bulge, hump, protuberance, sleeping policeman
▷ **bump into** come across, meet (unexpectedly), meet by chance, encounter, *formal* chance upon, happen upon, light upon, *colloq.* run into
▷ **bump off** kill, murder, assassinate, remove, *colloq.* eliminate, liquidate, do in, rub out, blow away, top

bumper *adj*
plentiful, abundant, large, great, enormous, massive, excellent, exceptional
🔁 small, tiny

bumpkin n
country bumpkin, country yokel, boor, clodhopper, rustic, oaf, peasant, provincial, *colloq.* hillbilly, hick, hayseed

bumptious adj
self-important, pompous, officious, overbearing, pushy, assertive, over-confident, presumptuous, forward, full of yourself, impudent, arrogant, cocky, conceited, swaggering, boastful, full of yourself, egotistic, *colloq.* cocky, pushy
F₃ humble, modest, unassertive

bumpy adj
1 *a bumpy road* rough, lumpy, pot-holed, knobbly, knobby, uneven, irregular **2** *a bumpy ride* rough, uneven jerky, jolting, bouncy, choppy
F₃ 1 smooth, level **2** smooth, even, uncomfortable

bunch n, v
▶ n **1** *a bunch of grapes* bundle, sheaf, tuft, clump, cluster **2** *a bunch of keys/papers* batch, lot, wad, heap, pile, stack, mass, number, quantity, collection, assortment, *formal* agglomeration, fascicle, fascicule **3** *a bunch of flowers* BOUQUET, posy, spray, nosegay, corsage **4** *a bunch of people* gang, band, troop, crew, team, party, gathering, flock, swarm, crowd, mob, multitude
▶ v group, bundle, cluster, collect, gather, flock, herd, crowd, mass, pack, huddle, *formal* assemble, congregate
F₃ disperse, scatter, spread out

bundle n, v
▶ n **1** *a bundle of sticks* bunch, sheaf, roll, bale, truss, faggot, *formal* fascicle, fascicule **2** *carry bundles of clothes* pack, batch, parcel, package, packet, carton, box, bag, *formal* consignment **3** *a bundle of books/ paper* group, set, collection, assortment, quantity, mass, accumulation, pile, stack, heap
▶ v **1** *bundle papers together* pack, wrap, bale, truss, cluster, gather, parcel, bind, tie, fasten **2** *bundle someone into a van* rush, hurry, push roughly, shove

bungle v
mismanage, make a mess of, ruin, spoil, mar, fudge, blunder, *colloq.* foul up, mess up, louse up, bodge, botch, fluff, boob, muff, *slang* screw up

bungler n
incompetent, blunderer, *colloq.* botcher, butterfingers, duffer

bungling adj
awkward, clumsy, incompetent, inept, unskilful, *formal* maladroit, *colloq.* blundering, botching, cack-handed, ham-fisted, ham-handed

bunkum n
nonsense, rubbish, *colloq.* balderdash, baloney, bilge, bosh, bunk, garbage, cobblers, hooey, piffle, poppycock, rot, stuff and nonsense, tommyrot, trash, tripe, twaddle, *US* hogwash, horsefeathers, *slang* crap

buoy n
float, marker, signal, beacon, mooring
▷ **buoy up** support, sustain, raise, lift, boost, encourage, cheer (up), hearten
F₃ depress, discourage

buoyant adj
1 *a buoyant mood* light-hearted, carefree, bright, cheerful, optimistic, happy, joyful, lively, blithe, bullish, debonair, animated, vivacious, *colloq.* bouncy, peppy **2** *a buoyant raft* floatable, floating, afloat, light, weightless
F₃ 1 depressed, despairing **2** heavy

burble v
babble, gurgle, lap, murmur, purl

burden n, v
▶ n **1** *put down a heavy burden* cargo, load, weight, dead-weight, **2** *the burdens of office* OBLIGATION, responsibility, duty, onus, millstone, pressure, strain, stress, worry, anxiety, weight, care, trouble, trial, affliction, sorrow, *formal* encumbrance
▶ v *burdened with a heavy load/worldly cares* weigh down, handicap, bother, worry, tax, strain, overload, lie heavy/hard on, oppress, overwhelm, crush, *formal* encumber
F₃ unburden, relieve

burdensome adj
onerous, crushing, difficult, weighty, exacting, heavy, irksome, oppressive, taxing, troublesome, trying, wearisome
F₃ easy, light

bureau n
1 *the Federal Bureau of Investigation* office, service, agency, branch, department, division, counter **2** *sit at a bureau* desk, writing-desk

bureaucracy n
1 *a bureaucracy of thousands of civil servants* administration, government, ministry, civil service, the authorities, the system **2** *try to reduce bureaucracy* administration, rules and regulations, officialdom, officiousness, beadledom, *colloq.* red tape

bureaucrat n
officer, official, office-holder, administrator, civil servant, functionary, (government) minister, committee member, mandarin, apparatchik

bureaucratic adj
official, administrative, governmental, ministerial, complicated, procedural, inflexible

burglar n
housebreaker, robber, thief, pilferer, cat-burglar

burglary n
housebreaking, break-in, robbery, theft, stealing, pilferage, larceny, *colloq.* heist

burial n
burying, funeral, *formal* interment, entombment, obsequies, exequies, inhumation

burial place n
graveyard, cemetery, churchyard, God's acre, vault, crypt, catacomb, mausoleum, necropolis, tumulus

burlesque n, adj
▶ n caricature, mock, mockery, parody, ridicule, satire, travesty, *colloq.* take-off, send-up, spoof, mickey-taking
▶ adj comic, derisive, farcical, mocking, parodying, satirical, *formal* caricatural, hudibrastic
F₃ serious

burly adj
well-built, thickset, hulking, hefty, heavy, stocky, big, sturdy, brawny, beefy, muscular, athletic, strapping, strong, powerful
F₃ small, puny, thin, slim

burn v
1 *the fire's burning* be on/catch fire, be in flames, burst into flames, blaze, be/catch ablaze, go up in smoke, flame, flare (up), flash, glow, flicker, smoulder, smoke **2** *burn rubbish* ignite, light, set fire to, put a match to, kindle, incinerate, cremate, consume, corrode, burn down, destroy, go up in flames, gut, *formal* conflagrate, deflagrate **3** *burn your hand on the oven; burn a hole in a cardigan* SCALD, scorch, parch, shrivel, singe, char, toast, brand, sear, *formal* cauterize **4** *make your throat burn* smart, sting, bite, hurt, tingle **5** *burn with anger* FUME, simmer, seethe **6** *burn to be with someone* long, desire, yearn, itch, be eager

burning *adj*
　1 *a burning skyscraper* ablaze, aflame, afire, fiery, flaming, blazing, flashing, gleaming, glowing, smouldering, alight, lit, illuminated **2** *a burning forehead; a burning hot day* hot, scalding, scorching **3** *a burning sensation* searing, piercing, acute, smarting, stinging, prickling, tingling, biting, caustic, pungent, *formal* acrid **4** *burning desire* PASSIONATE, ardent, fervent, eager, earnest, intense, vehement, impassioned, frantic, frenzied, consuming, *formal* fervid **5** *a burning issue* URGENT, pressing, important, significant, crucial, essential, vital
　🔁 **2** cold **4** apathetic **5** unimportant

burnish *v*
　polish (up), brighten, buff, glaze, shine

burp *v*
　belch, bring up wind, *formal* eructate

burrow *n, v*
　▶ *n* warren, hole, earth, set, den, lair, retreat, shelter, tunnel
　▶ *v* **1** *burrow into the sand* TUNNEL, dig, delve, excavate, mine, undermine **2** *burrow for the keys* RUMMAGE, delve, search

burst *v, n*
　▶ *v* **1** *the tyre burst* puncture, rupture, tear, split, crack, break (open), fragment, shatter, shiver, disintegrate **2** *the dam burst* gush, spout, rush, erupt **3** *burst into a room* rush, run, hurry, race, dart, break in on, *colloq.* barge, push your way **4** *the bomb burst* explode, blow up
　▶ *n* **1** *have a burst on the motorway* puncture, *colloq.* blow-out **2** *a burst of gunfire; a sudden burst of activity* discharge, volley, gush, spurt, surge, rush, spate, torrent, outpouring, outburst, outbreak, fit, *formal* fusillade
　▷ **burst out 1** *burst out crying* begin, start, *formal* commence **2** *"That's what I've been trying to tell you,"* she burst out exclaim, cry (out), call out, utter, *colloq.* blurt out

bury *v*
　1 *bury the dead* lay to rest, shroud, *formal* inter, entomb, sepulchre, inhume, inearth, *colloq.* put six feet under **2** *bury your face in your hands; bury a memory* sink, submerge, plant, implant, embed, conceal, hide, cover, engulf, immerse, enclose, *formal* enshroud **3** *buried yourself in work* immerse, engross, occupy, engage, absorb
　🔁 **1** formal disinter, exhume **2** uncover, discover, expose

bush *n*
　1 *a rose bush* shrub, hedge, plant, thicket **2** *go camping in the bush* scrub, brush, scrubland, backwoods, brush, wilds
　▷ **not beat about the bush** speak plainly/openly, *colloq.* call a spade a spade

bushy *adj*
　shaggy, thick, bristling, bristly, fluffy, fuzzy, luxuriant, spreading, stiff, unruly, rough, wiry, *formal* dasyphyllous, dumose, dumous
　🔁 thin, neat, tidy, trim, well-kept

busily *adv*
　actively, diligently, assiduously, earnestly, energetically, hard, industriously, purposefully, briskly, speedily, strenuously

business *n*
　1 *do business* trade, commerce, industry, manufacturing, dealings, transactions, bargaining, trading, buying, selling, merchandising **2** *set up a new business* COMPANY, firm, industry, corporation, establishment, organization, concern, operation, franchise, enterprise, private enterprise, flagship, industry, venture, management buyout, consortium, syndicate, holding company, parent/subsidiary company, conglomerate, multinational **3** *a line of business* job, occupation, work, employment, trade, profession, line, calling, career, vocation, duty, task, responsibility, métier **4** *none of your business* affair, matter, issue, subject, topic, question, problem, point **5** *the business of the meeting* topic, subject, issue, question, matter

businesslike *adj*
　professional, efficient, thorough, systematic, methodical, organized, orderly, well-ordered, painstaking, practical, pragmatic, matter-of-fact, precise, correct, formal, impersonal
　🔁 inefficient, wasteful, disorganized, *colloq.* sloppy

businessman, businesswoman *n*
　executive, entrepreneur, industrialist, trader, merchant, tycoon, magnate, capitalist, financier, employer

busker *n*
　street-entertainer, street-musician

bust *n*
　1 *a bust of the President* sculpture, head, torso, statue **2** *a woman's bust* bosom, breasts, chest, breast, *slang* boobs

bustle *v, n*
　▶ *v* hurry, dash, rush, scamper, scurry, rush to and fro, scramble, fuss, *formal* hasten, bestir, *colloq.* tear, belt, to and fro
　▶ *n* activity, stir, commotion, tumult, agitation, excitement, fuss, scramble, flurry, hurry, hurly-burly, hustle and bustle, rush hour, the rush, *formal* haste, pother, ado, *colloq.* a hive of activity, comings and goings

bustling *adj*
　lively, active, energetic, busy, hectic, buzzing, rushing, crowded, eventful, full, humming, restless, stirring, swarming, teeming, *formal* astir, thronged
　🔁 quiet, sleepy, restful

busy *adj, v*
　▶ *adj* **1** *be busy at the moment* occupied, engaged, otherwise engaged, employed, unavailable, working, having a previous engagement/prior appointment, *colloq.* tied up, hard at it, busy as a bee **2** *a very busy day* active, lively, energetic, strenuous, tiring, full, crowded, swarming, vibrant, teeming, bustling, hectic, frantic, eventful **3** *busy preparing for the meeting* occupied, involved, engrossed, working **4** *a busy person* active, having a lot to do, energetic, lively, diligent, industrious, assiduous, restless, tireless, *formal* sedulous, *colloq.* on the go, having a lot on, having your hands full, fully stretched, rushed off your feet, under pressure, snowed under, up to your eyes in something
　🔁 **1** free, available **2** quiet, leisured, empty **3** unoccupied **4** lazy, idle, *colloq.* at a loose end
　▶ *v* occupy, involve, engage, employ, engross, absorb, immerse, interest, concern

busybody *n*
　meddler, interferer, intruder, pry, gossip, eavesdropper, snoop, snooper, troublemaker, scandalmonger, *formal* pantopragmatic, quidnunc, *colloq.* nosy parker

butcher *n, v*
　▶ *n* **1** *buy meat from the butcher's* meat counter, meat retailer, supermarket **2** *known as the Butcher* SLAUGHTERER, destroyer, killer, (mass) murderer, slayer
　▶ *v* slaughter, massacre, assassinate, destroy, exterminate, kill, liquidate, mutilate, slay, destroy

butchery *n*
　slaughter, massacre, (mass) murder, carnage, killing, mass destruction, blood-letting, bloodshed

butt¹ *n*
1 *the butt of a gun/tool* end, butt end, base, foot, shaft, stock, handle, haft **2** *the butt of a cigarette* stub, tip, tail end, *colloq.* fag-end, dog-end **3** *sit on your butt* bottom, buttocks, *colloq.* bum, posterior

butt² *n*
the butt of jokes target, mark, object, subject, victim, laughing-stock, dupe, scapegoat

butt³ *v*
butt someone with its horns hit, bump, knock, buffet, push, ram, thrust, shove, punch, jab, prod, poke
▷ **butt in** interrupt, cut in, intrude, meddle, interfere, *formal* interpose, interject, *colloq.* stick your nose in, put your oar in

butter *v*
▷ **butter up** flatter, praise, blarney, cajole, coax, pander to, wheedle, kowtow, *colloq.* suck up to, softsoap

butterfly *n*

Types of butterfly include:
red admiral, white admiral, apollo, cabbage white, chalkhill blue, common blue, brimstone, meadow brown, Camberwell beauty, clouded yellow, comma, large copper, small copper, fritillary, Duke of Burgundy fritillary, heath fritillary, gatekeeper, grayling, hairstreak, purple hairstreak, white letter hairstreak, hermit, monarch, orange-tip, painted lady, peacock, purple emperor, ringlet, grizzled skipper, swallowtail, tortoiseshell.

buttocks *n*
bottom, rump, hindquarters, rear, seat, breech, haunches, derrière, *technical* gluteus, nates, *colloq.* bum, behind, posterior; *US* butt

button *n*
1 *buttons on a shirt* fastener, fastening, catch, clasp **2** *press the button* knob, disc, switch

buttonhole *v*
accost, waylay, catch, take aside, detain, *formal* importune, *colloq.* grab, nab, corner

buttress *n, v*
▶ *n* support, prop, shore, stay, brace, pier, strut, mainstay, reinforcement, *formal* abutment, stanchion
▶ *v* support, prop up, shore up, hold up, back up, brace, underpin, strengthen, reinforce, bolster up, sustain
🖅 undermine, weaken

buxom *adj*
plump, ample, bosomy, busty, chesty, well-endowed, well-rounded, *formal* voluptuous, comely, *colloq.* busty
🖅 petite, slim, small

buy *v, n*
▶ *v* **1** *buy a car* pay for, acquire, obtain, get, go shopping, do the shopping, shop around, shop for, stock up on, invest in, speculate, *formal* purchase, procure, *colloq.* snap up, pick up, splash out on **2** *buy the tax man* bribe, buy off, suborn, *colloq.* fix, grease someone's palm
🖅 **1** sell
▶ *n* purchase, acquisition, bargain, deal

buyer *n*
purchaser, shopper, consumer, customer, client, patron, *formal* patron, vendee, emptor
🖅 seller, *formal* vendor

buzz *v, n*
▶ *v* **1** *bees buzzing round* hum, whirr, drone, murmur, *formal* bombilate, bombinate, susurrate **2** *buzz with excitement* hum, throb, pulse, bustle, race
▶ *n* **1** *the buzz of bees* hum, whirr, buzzing, drone, murmur, purr, *technical* tinnitus, *formal* bombilation, bombination, susurration, susurrus **2** *give someone a buzz* ring, (phone) call **3** *the latest buzz* rumour, gossip, scandal, latest, hearsay **4** *winning gives me a buzz* THRILL, excitement, stimulation, *colloq.* kick(s), high

by *prep, adv*
▶ *prep* **1** *a low table by the chair* near, next to, close to, beside, alongside **2** *enter by the window* along, over, through, via **3** *earn money by working hard* by means of, through the agency of, through, *formal* under the aegis of **4** *get home by noon* before, no later than, at **5** *by any standard* according to, in relation to
▶ *adv* near, close (by), handy, at hand, past, beyond, away, aside

bygone *adj*
past, ancient, departed, forgotten, former, previous, lost, olden, one-time, antiquated, *formal* erstwhile, forepast
🖅 modern, recent, future, forthcoming

bypass *v, n*
▶ *v* avoid, find a way round, sidestep, ignore, neglect, omit, *formal* circumvent, *colloq.* dodge, skirt
▶ *n* ring road, detour, diversion

by-product *n*
1 *cattle feed is a by-product of whisky* derivative, spin-off **2** *by-products of modern life* consequence, result, side effect, repercussion, after-effect, *colloq.* fallout

bystander *n*
spectator, onlooker, looker-on, watcher, observer, witness, eyewitness, passer-by, *colloq.* rubberneck
🖅 participant

byword *n*
1 *a byword for efficiency* SLOGAN, catchword, dictum, maxim, motto **2** PROVERB, saw, saying, precept, adage, aphorism, *formal* apophthegm

cab *n*
1 *hire a cab* taxi, taxicab, minicab, hackney carriage
2 *the cab in a lorry* compartment, driver's compartment, cabin, quarters

cabal *n*
clique, faction, party, plotters, coalition, league, set, coterie, conclave, junta, junto

cabaret *n*
entertainment, show, dancing, singing, comedy

cabin *n*
1 *a log cabin* HUT, shack, shanty, lodge, chalet, cottage, shed, shelter, *Scot.* bothy, refuge **2** BERTH, quarters, sleeping quarters, compartment, room, stateroom

cabinet *n*
1 *a medicine cabinet* cupboard, closet, dresser, case, store, chest, locker **2** *Cabinet ministers* government, ministers, leadership, senate, administration, executive

cable *n, v*
▶ *n* **1** *tie with cable* line, rope, cord, chain, guy, stay, hawser **2** *electric cable* wire, flex, lead **3** *send a message by cable* telegram, telegraph, Telemessage®, wire, fax, facsimile
▶ *v* send a telegram/telemessage/wire, send by telegraph, telegraph, wire, radio, fax

cache *n*
store, accumulation, collection, fund, hoard, reserve, stock, stockpile, storehouse, supply, garner, treasure-store, hidden treasure, *formal* repository, *colloq.* stash

cachet *n*
estimation, prestige, reputation, approval, favour, distinction, eminence, *formal* esteem, *colloq.* street cred

cackle *v*
laugh loudly, laugh unpleasantly, chortle, chuckle, crow, giggle, snigger, titter

cacophonous *adj*
raucous, strident, grating, harsh, discordant, dissonant, inharmonious, jarring, *formal* horrisonant
▣ harmonious, pleasant

cacophony *n*
raucousness, stridency, harshness, discord, dissonance, disharmony, jarring, caterwauling, *formal* horrisonance
▣ harmony

cad *n*
blackguard, scoundrel, rascal, rogue, villain, devil, knave, deceiver, miscreant, reprobate, wretch, *colloq.* bleeder, blighter, bounder, rotter, stinker, rat, swine, scumbag

cadaver *n*
dead body, body, corpse, remains, carcase, *slang* stiff

cadaverous *adj*
corpse-like, death-like, pale, ashen, wan, ghostly, gaunt, haggard, thin, emaciated, skeletal, *colloq.* like death warmed up

cadence *n*
intonation, lilt, modulation, inflection, accent, rhythm, beat, stress, tempo, measure, metre, pattern, swing, pulse, throb, rate

cadge *v*
scrounge, beg, *colloq.* sponge, bum

café *n*
coffee shop, tea shop, tea room, coffee bar, cybercafé, cafeteria, snackbar, bistro, wine bar, brasserie, restaurant, buffet

cafeteria *n*
self-service café, self-service restaurant, self-service canteen, café, canteen, restaurant, buffet

cage *n, v*
▶ *n* aviary, coop, hutch, enclosure, pen, pound, lock-up, corral
▶ *v* confine, imprison, impound, incarcerate, lock up, shut up, coop up

caged *adj*
encaged, cooped up, shut up, confined, restrained, fenced in, imprisoned, impounded, locked up, *formal* incarcerated
▣ released, let out, free

cagey *adj*
careful, chary, cautious, discreet, guarded, non-committal, secretive, shrewd, wary, wily, *formal* circumspect, *colloq.* playing your cards close to your chest
▣ frank, indiscreet, open

cajole *v*
coax, persuade, get round, wheedle, flatter, tempt, lure, seduce, entice, beguile, mislead, dupe, *formal* inveigle, *colloq.* sweet-talk, butter up, soft-soap
▣ bully, force, compel

cajolery *n*
coaxing, persuasion, wheedling, flattery, blarney, enticement, inducement(s), beguilement, misleading, duping, *formal* blandishments, inveigling, *colloq.* sweet talk, soft soap
▣ bullying, force, compulsion

cake *n, v*
▶ *n* **1** *tea and cakes* gateau, fancy, pastry, madeleine, bun, pie, tart, flan **2** LUMP, mass, bar, slab, block, cube, chunk, loaf
▶ *v* coat, cover, encrust, plaster, dry, harden, solidify, consolidate, coagulate, congeal, thicken

calamitous *adj*
disastrous, catastrophic, ruinous, devastating, deadly, fatal, cataclysmic, dire, ghastly, dreadful, wretched, tragic, woeful, grievous
▣ good, fortunate, happy

calamity *n*
disaster, catastrophe, mishap, misadventure, mischance, misfortune, adversity, scourge, reverse, trial,

tribulation, affliction, distress, tragedy, ruin, downfall, trouble
F3 blessing, godsend

calculate *v*
1 WORK OUT, compute, count, enumerate, reckon (up), figure, determine, make, derive, measure, weigh, rate, value, estimate, gauge **2** *a plan calculated to make him jealous* judge, consider, plan, intend, aim, design

calculated *adj*
considered, deliberate, intended, intentional, planned, purposeful, wilful, premeditated, *formal* purposed
F3 unintended, unplanned

calculating *adj*
crafty, cunning, sly, devious, scheming, designing, contriving, manipulative, sharp, shrewd, Machiavellian
F3 artless, naïve

calculation *n*
sum, computation, working-out, answer, result, reckoning, figuring, estimate, estimation, forecast, judgement, planning, deliberation

calibre *n*
1 DIAMETER, bore, gauge, size, measure **2** *candidates of the right calibre* talent, gifts, strength, worth, merit, quality, character, ability, capacity, faculty, excellence, competence, endowments, stature, distinction

call *v, n*
▶ *v* **1** NAME, christen, baptize, title, entitle, dub, style, term, label, brand, describe as, designate, rename, *formal* denominate **2** SHOUT, yell, exclaim, cry (out), scream, shriek, bellow, roar, bawl **3** TELEPHONE, phone (up), ring (up), contact, give someone a ring, *colloq.* buzz, give someone a buzz, give someone a tinkle **4** *call a doctor* ask to come in/round, ask for, send for, contact, order, *formal* summon **5** *call to collect the money* call in/round, drop in, pay a visit, stop by, come by, *colloq.* pop in **6** *call a meeting* invite, bid, assemble, *formal* convene, summon
▷ **call for 1** FETCH, collect, pick up, go for **2** DEMAND, require, need, make necessary, justify, involve, occasion, suggest, press for, push for, *formal* entail, necessitate, warrant
▷ **call off** cancel, drop, abandon, discontinue, break off, withdraw, *formal* rescind, revoke, *colloq.* scrub, shelve
▷ **call on 1** *call on a friend* pay someone a (short) visit, visit, look in on, go and see **2** *call on the government to resign* appeal, appeal to, ask, bid, demand, urge, request, plead, press for, *formal* request, summon, supplicate, entreat
▶ *n* **1** CRY, exclamation, shout, yell, scream, shriek **2** VISIT, ring, summons, invitation **3** *a telephone call* ring, *colloq.* buzz, tinkle, bell **4** *calls for his resignation* APPEAL, request, plea, order, command, claim, announcement, signal **5** *there's no call for it* demand, need, occasion, cause, excuse, justification, reason, grounds, right, run
▷ **on call** ready, on standby, standing by, on duty

calligraphy *n*
handwriting, script, penmanship, hand, text, words, copperplate, illumination, lettering, good hand, bold hand, *formal* chirography

calling *n*
mission, vocation, career, profession, occupation, job, trade, business, line, line of business/work, work, employment, field, province, pursuit, métier

callous *adj*
heartless, hard-hearted, cold, cold-hearted, cold-blooded, harsh, tough, indifferent, uncaring, unsym-

pathetic, unfeeling, insensitive, hardened, stony, stony-hearted, thick-skinned, *formal* obdurate, indurate, insensate
F3 kind, caring, sympathetic, sensitive

callow *adj*
inexperienced, immature, naïve, innocent, guileless, juvenile, puerile, raw, fledgling, uninitiated, unsophisticated, unfledged, untried, *formal* jejune, *colloq.* green
F3 experienced

calm *adj, v, n*
▶ *adj* **1** COMPOSED, self-possessed, self-controlled, collected, quiet, serene, cool, cool-headed, dispassionate, unemotional, impassive, unmoved, placid, sedate, poised, imperturbable, unexcitable, relaxed, unexcited, unruffled, unflustered, unperturbed, undisturbed, untroubled, unapprehensive, steady, *colloq.* laid back, unflappable **2** *calm waters/weather* smooth, still, waveless, windless, unclouded, mild, tranquil, serene, peaceful, quiet, undisturbed, restful
F3 1 excitable, worried, anxious, upset **2** rough, wild, windy, stormy
▶ *v* compose, soothe, relax, sedate, tranquillize, hush, lull, quieten, still, settle (down), allay, pacify, *formal* mollify, placate, appease, assuage, *colloq.* cool down, simmer down, keep your head, lighten up
F3 excite, worry, upset
▶ *n* calmness, stillness, tranquillity, restfulness, composure, contentment, serenity, peacefulness, peace, quiet, hush, impassiveness, impassivity, presence of mind, *formal* quietude, repose, placidity, equanimity, sang-froid, ataraxia, *colloq.* unflappability, cool
F3 storminess, restlessness, trouble, excitement

calumny *n*
slander, abuse, aspersion, backbiting, defamation, insult, libel, lying, misrepresentation, *formal* denigration, obloquy, revilement, derogation, detraction, disparagement, vilification, vituperation, *colloq.* slagging-off, smear

camaraderie *n*
brotherhood, brotherliness, companionship, comradeship, *esprit de corps*, fellowship, fraternization, good fellowship, sociability, closeness, affinity, intimacy, togetherness

camera *n*

Types of camera include:
automatic, bellows, binocular, box Brownie®, camcorder, camera obscura, cine, cinematographic, compact, daguerreotype, digital, disc, disposable, film, Instamatic®, large-format, miniature, subminiature, panoramic, plate, dry-plate, half-plate, quarter-plate, wet-plate, point-and-press, Polaroid®, press, reflex, folding reflex, single-lens reflex (SLR), twin-lens reflex (TLR), security, sliding box, sound, still, stereo, Super 8®, TV, video. *See also* PHOTOGRAPHIC.

Parts of a camera include:
accessory shoe, AF lenses, aperture, aperture setting control, autofocus (AF), autofocus sensor, automatic focusing system, battery chamber, blind, cable release, card door, card on/off key, card window, compact lens, compound lens, data panel/display, diaphragm, exposure meter, exposure mode button, film advance/transport, film gate, film holder, fisheye lens, flash contact, flash setting, focal plane shutter, focus control/setting, focusing hood, focusing ring, frame counter, function adjustment button, function selector key, iris diaphragm, leaf shutter, lens, lens

cap, lens release, light control, long-focus lens, magazine, medium focal-length lens, meter cell, mirror, mirror lens, mirror shutter, object lens, pentaprism, program card, program reset button, rangefinder window, reflex viewer, registration pin, release button, rewind handle/crank, shutter, shutter release, shutter speed control, shutter/film speed indicator, spool, spool knob, take-up reel/spool, telephoto lens, viewfinder eyepiece, viewfinder, viewing lens, wide-angle lens, zoom lens.

---

camouflage *n, v*
▶ *n* disguise, guise, masquerade, mask, cloak, screen, smokescreen, blind, front, cover, cover-up, protective colouring, concealment, deception, façade, dissimulation
▶ *v* disguise, mask, cloak, veil, screen, cover, cover up, conceal, hide, obscure
◆ uncover, reveal

camp[1] *n, v*
▶ *n* **1** *a Scout camp* campsite, camping-site, camping-ground, encampment, tents, bivouac **2** *the union camp* side, faction, group, party, section, set, crowd, caucus, clique
▶ *v* pitch tents, set up camp, sleep outdoors, *colloq.* rough it

camp[2] *adj*
camp behaviour affected, artificial, campy, exaggerated, mannered, ostentatious, posturing, theatrical, effeminate *colloq.* over the top

campaign *n, v*
▶ *n* *the election campaign; a bombing campaign* crusade, movement, promotion, drive, push, course of action, strategy, offensive, attack, battle, expedition, operation, war
▶ *v* crusade, promote, push, drive, advocate, work, fight, strive, struggle, battle, attack

camp-follower *n*
hanger-on, henchman, lackey, toady

can *n*
tin, container, receptacle, canister, jar, jerrycan, pail

canal *n*
1 *the Grand Union canal* waterway, watercourse, channel, zanja **2** *the alimentary canal* tube, channel, passage

cancel *v*
1 *cancel a concert* call off, abort, abandon, drop, postpone, *colloq.* scrap, scrub, shelve, axe **2** *cancel a reservation/debt* abolish, quash, stop, break off, repeal, delete, erase, obliterate, eliminate, dissolve, override, *formal* discontinue, countermand, rescind, revoke, annul, nullify, invalidate, retract, abrogate, vitiate
▷ **cancel out** offset, compensate, make up for, redeem, counterbalance, balance, neutralize, counteract, nullify

cancellation *n*
calling-off, abandoning, abandonment, abolition, dropping, stopping, deletion, elimination, neutralization, quashing, repeal, *formal* annulment, revocation, invalidation, nullifying, *colloq.* shelving, scrubbing

cancer *n*
1 TUMOUR, growth, malignancy, malignant growth, *technical* carcinoma **2** EVIL, blight, canker, pestilence, sickness, disease, plague, scourge, corruption, rot

candelabrum *n*
candlestick, menorah

candid *adj*
frank, open, truthful, honest, sincere, forthright, straightforward, ingenuous, guileless, simple, plain, plain-spoken, clear, unequivocal, blunt, outspoken
◆ guarded, evasive, devious

candidate *n*
1 *candidates for a job* applicant, aspirant, contender, contestant, competitor, seeker, runner, possibility, nominee **2** *candidates for an exam* entrant

candle *n*
taper, tallow-candle, cerge, wax-light

candour *n*
frankness, openness, truthfulness, honesty, plain-dealing, sincerity, forthrightness, straightforwardness, directness, brusqueness, ingenuousness, guilelessness, naïvety, artlessness, simplicity, plainness, unequivocalness, bluntness, outspokenness
◆ guardedness, evasiveness, deviousness

candy *n*
sweets, confectionery, chocolates, toffees

cane *n*
stick, staff, crook, rod, walking-stick, alpenstock, *formal* ferule

canker *n*
1 EVIL, blight, cancer, pestilence, sickness, disease, plague, scourge, bane, corrosion, corruption, rot **2** *canker in an animal's ear* sore, ulcer, boil, infection, lesion

cannabis *n*
marijuana, hemp, hashish, bhang, *colloq.* dope, ganja, grass, hash, pot, spliff, puff, tea, kef, *slang* blow, weed, skunk, punk, leaf, *US* locoweed

cannibal *n*
man-eater, people-eater, *technical* anthropophagite

cannibalism *n*
man-eating, people-eating, *technical* anthropophagy, endophagy, exophagy

cannon *n*
gun, mortar, field gun, howitzer, artillery, battery, ordnance, *colloq.* big gun

---

cannon or **canon** ?

A *cannon* is a large gun. A *canon* is a Christian priest who helps to run the work of a cathedral and also a general rule or belief: *the canons of literary taste*.

---

cannonade *n*
barrage, bombardment, shelling, volley, broadside, pounding, salvo

canny *adj*
shrewd, acute, sharp, astute, careful, cautious, prudent, clever, knowing, skilful, sly, subtle, wise, worldly-wise, artful, pawky, *formal* circumspect, perspicacious, judicious, sagacious, *colloq.* no flies on someone
◆ foolish, imprudent

canon *n*
1 *a cathedral canon* prebendary, clergyman, vicar, priest, minister, reverend **2** *the canons of literary taste* principle, rule, regulation, statute, criterion, standard, precept, dictate, yardstick

canonical *adj*
authorized, recognized, accepted, sanctioned, approved, authoritative, orthodox, regular

---

Names of canonical hours include:
matins, lauds, terce, sext, none, vespers, compline.

canopy *n*
awning, cover, covering, shade, shelter, sunshade, umbrella, tester, tilt, baldachin

cant *n*
1 *insincere cant* insincerity, hypocrisy, pretentiousness, sanctimoniousness **2** *underworld cant* argot, jargon, lingo, slang, vernacular

cantankerous *adj*
irritable, irascible, grumpy, grouchy, crusty, testy, bad-tempered, quick-tempered, ill-humoured, cross, peevish, difficult, perverse, contrary, quarrelsome, *colloq.* crabbed, crabby, crotchety
🔁 good-natured, pleasant, *colloq.* easy-going

canter *n & v*
amble, trot, jog, jogtrot, lope, gallop, run

canvass *v*
1 ELECTIONEER, agitate, campaign, solicit votes, ask for votes, seek votes, poll, drum up support **2** EXAMINE, inspect, find out, scrutinize, study, scan, investigate, explore, survey, examine, inquire into, analyse, sift, evaluate, poll, discuss, debate

canyon *n*
gorge, ravine, gully, valley, chasm, abyss

cap *n, v*
▶ *n* **1** HAT, bonnet, skullcap, beret, tam-o'-shanter, tammy, flat cap, school cap, peaked cap, baseball cap, balmoral, kalpak, forage-cap, glengarry, muffin-cap, kepi **2** LID, top, cover, stopper, plug, bung
▶ *v* **1** *cap someone's story* exceed, excel, surpass, transcend, better, beat, outdo, outstrip, outshine, eclipse **2** *mountains capped with snow* crown, top, cover, coat **3** *rate-cap a council* limit, restrict, curb, restrain, control

capability *n*
ability, capacity, faculty, power, potential, means, facility, competence, qualification, skill, skilfulness, accomplishment, proficiency, talent, aptitude, efficiency
🔁 inability, incompetence

 capability or **ability** ? *See panel at* ABILITY.

capable *adj*
1 *a capable person* able, competent, efficient, qualified, experienced, accomplished, skilful, adept, proficient, gifted, talented, masterly, clever, intelligent, smart, businesslike **2** *capable of winning* fitted, suited, apt to, liable to, disposed to, inclined to, tending to, having the inclination/tendency to, allowing, needing
🔁 **1** incompetent, useless **2** incapable

capacious *adj*
ample, big, vast, wide, broad, huge, large, roomy, sizable, spacious, comfortable, comprehensive, expansive, extensive, generous, liberal, substantial, *formal* commodious, voluminous
🔁 cramped, small

capacity *n*
1 CAPABILITY, ability, faculty, power, potential, competence, proficiency, efficiency, skill, gift, talent, genius, cleverness, intelligence, aptitude, resources, readiness **2** VOLUME, space, room, size, dimensions, proportions, magnitude, extent, largeness, compass, range, scope **3** *in her capacity as president* role, function, position, office, post, appointment, job

cape[1] *n*
wear a cape cloak, shawl, wrap, mantle, robe, poncho, pelisse, pelerine, coat

cape[2] *n*
the Cape of Good Hope headland, head, promontory, point, ness, neck, tongue, peninsula

caper *v, n*
▶ *v* cavort, frisk, frolic, gambol, bounce, bound, dance, hop, jump, leap, romp, skip, spring
▶ *n* antic, escapade, high jinks, jest, lark, mischief, prank, stunt, jape, affair, business, *US colloq.* dido

capital *n, adj*
▶ *n* **1** *need capital to expand the business* funds, finance, principal, money, cash, savings, investment(s), wealth, means, wherewithal, resources, assets, liquid assets, property, stock, reserves **2** *the capital of France* most important city, administrative centre, seat of government **3** *write in capitals* block letter, block capital, capital letter, upper-case letter, *formal* majuscule, uncial
▶ *adj* **1** PRINCIPAL, important, leading, primary, prime, main, major, cardinal, central, chief, first, foremost **2** *a capital offence* serious, punishable by death
🔁 **1** minor, unimportant **2** minor

capitalism *n*
private enterprise, free enterprise, private ownership, laissez-faire

capitalist *n*
banker, financier, investor, moneyman, tycoon, magnate, mogul, person of means, plutocrat, *colloq.* moneybags, money-spinner, *slang* fat cat

capitalize *v*
▷ **capitalize on** take advantage of, profit from, make the most of, exploit, *colloq.* cash in on

capitulate *v*
surrender, yield, give in, give up, relent, back down, submit, succumb, *colloq.* throw in the towel/sponge

capitulation *n*
surrender, yielding, giving-in, giving-up, relenting, backing-down, submission, succumbing

caprice *n*
whim, fad, fancy, impulse, whimsy, fantasy, notion, quirk, vagary, vapour, fickleness, fitfulness, inconstancy

capricious *adj*
changeable, inconstant, mercurial, erratic, fickle, uncertain, unpredictable, variable, wayward, fitful, fanciful, whimsical, freakish, impulsive, odd, queer, quirky
🔁 sensible, steady

capsize *v*
overturn, turn over, turn turtle, invert, keel over, tip over, roll over, upset

capsule *n*
1 *a capsule of medicine* pill, tablet, lozenge, receptacle, container **2** *a seed capsule* shell, sheath, pod **3** *a space capsule* craft, module, probe

captain *n*
officer, commander, master, skipper, pilot, head, chief, leader, *colloq.* boss

caption *n*
heading, note, title, legend, wording, inscription

captivate *v*
charm, enchant, bewitch, beguile, fascinate, delight, enthral, hypnotize, mesmerize, lure, allure, seduce, win, attract, enamour, infatuate, enrapture, dazzle
🔁 repel, disgust, appal

captivating *adj*
attractive, charming, fascinating, beautiful, enchanting, bewitching, beguiling, delightful, enthralling, alluring, seductive, winsome, dazzling
🔁 ugly, unattractive

captive *n, adj*
▶ *n* prisoner, hostage, slave, detainee, internee, convict, jailbird

▶ *adj* imprisoned, caged, confined, restricted, secure, locked up/away, shut up, interned, detained, held in custody, restrained, enchained, enslaved, ensnared, in bondage, *formal* incarcerated
F3 free, liberated

captivity *n*
custody, detention, imprisonment, internment, confinement, restraint, constraint, bondage, duress, slavery, *formal* incarceration, servitude
F3 freedom, liberation

capture *v, n*
▶ *v* **1** *capture a prisoner* catch, trap, entrap, hunt down, snare, ensnare, take, take possession of, seize, arrest, apprehend, imprison, recapture, pick up, secure, win, *colloq.* nab, collar, nick **2** *capture a mood* encapsulate, represent, record, embrace
▶ *n* catching, trapping, taking, taking captive, taking prisoner, seizure, arrest, imprisonment, *colloq.* nabbing, collaring, nicking

car *n*
automobile, motor car, motor vehicle, motor, vehicle

Types of car include:
saloon, hatchback, fastback, estate, sports car, cabriolet, convertible, limousine, *colloq.* limo, *colloq.* wheels, *colloq.* banger, Mini®, bubble-car, coupé, station wagon, shooting brake, veteran car, vintage car, jalopy, *colloq.* Beetle, four-wheel drive, Jeep®, buggy, Land Rover®, Range Rover®, panda car, patrol car, taxi, cab. *See also* MOTOR VEHICLE.

carafe *n*
bottle, decanter, flagon, flask, jug, pitcher

carbuncle *n*
boil, inflammation, pimple, sore, anthrax

carcase *n*
1 *the carcase of an animal* body, dead body, corpse, cadaver, remains **2** *the carcase of a building* shell, structure, framework, hulk, skeleton

card *n*
▷ **on the cards** likely, probable, possible, being a strong possibility, looking like, looking as if, *colloq.* the chances are

cardinal *adj*
chief, main, principal, fundamental, greatest, highest, important, key, leading, paramount, pre-eminent, primary, prime, central, essential, first, foremost, capital

care *n, v*
▶ *n* **1** *handle with care* CAREFULNESS, caution, forethought, watchfulness, pains, meticulousness, accuracy, *formal* prudence, vigilance, circumspection **2** *children need care* looking-after, regard, concern, attention, tending, minding, watching-over, heed, regard, consideration, interest, protection **3** *in their care* keeping, safekeeping, custody, guardianship, protection, ward, charge, responsibility, control, supervision, tutelage **4** *forget all your cares* WORRY, anxiety, stress, strain, pressure, responsibility, burden, concern, trouble, distress, affliction, fear, disquiet, *formal* tribulation, vexation, *colloq.* hang-up
F3 **1** carelessness **2** carelessness, thoughtlessness, inattention, neglect
▶ *v* worry, mind, bother, be concerned, be interested, *colloq.* give a damn
F3 neglect, ignore, be indifferent, *colloq.* not give a hoot/hang/hoot/damn/toss, not give a monkey's, not give a tinker's cuss/brass farthing
▷ **care for 1** LOOK AFTER, take care of, nurse, tend,

mind, watch over, protect, provide for, minister to, attend, maintain **2** *care for someone* BE FOND OF, feel affection for, love, be in love with, be keen on, be close to, enjoy, delight in, cherish **3** *Would you care for a cup of tea?* like, want, desire

career *n, v*
▶ *n* vocation, calling, life-work, occupation, pursuit, profession, trade, job, employment, métier, livelihood
▶ *v* rush, dash, tear, hurtle, race, run, gallop, speed, shoot, bolt

carefree *adj*
unworried, untroubled, unconcerned, blithe, breezy, happy-go-lucky, cheery, light-hearted, cheerful, happy, *formal* insouciant, nonchalant, *colloq.* easy-going, laid back
F3 worried, anxious, troubled, distressed, despondent

careful *adj*
1 CAUTIOUS, aware, wary, chary, vigilant, watchful, alert, attentive, mindful, heedful, discreet, tactful, guarded, *formal* prudent, circumspect, judicious, **2** METICULOUS, painstaking, conscientious, diligent, assiduous, scrupulous, fastidious, rigorous, thorough, detailed, showing great attention to detail, methodical, systematic, particular, accurate, precise, thoughtful, *formal* punctilious
F3 **1** careless, inattentive, thoughtless, reckless **2** careless

careless *adj*
1 UNTHINKING, thoughtless, inattentive, inconsiderate, uncaring, unconcerned, heedless, unmindful, forgetful, remiss, negligent, absent-minded, irresponsible, reckless, indiscreet, tactless, unguarded **2** *careless work* inaccurate, messy, untidy, disorganized, disorderly, neglectful, slack, lax, slipshod, slapdash, hasty, perfunctory, cursory, superficial, offhand, casual, *colloq.* sloppy **3** *careless charm* casual, carefree, unworried, untroubled, simple, artless, breezy, light-hearted, cheerful, happy-go-lucky, *formal* insouciant, nonchalant, *colloq.* easy-going, laid back
F3 **1** thoughtful, careful **2** careful, accurate, meticulous

caress *v, n*
▶ *v* stroke, pet, fondle, cuddle, hug, embrace, kiss, touch, rub, nuzzle, *colloq.* canoodle, grope
▶ *n* stroke, touch, pat, fondle, cuddle, hug, embrace, kiss, petting, *colloq.* slap and tickle

caretaker *n*
janitor, porter, watchman, keeper, custodian, curator, warden, superintendent, concierge, steward, ostiary, doorkeeper

careworn *adj*
tired, weary, worn, worn-out, exhausted, fatigued, gaunt, haggard
F3 lively, sprightly

cargo *n*
freight, load, pay-load, haul, lading, tonnage, shipment, consignment, contents, goods, merchandise, baggage

caricature *n, v*
▶ *n* cartoon, parody, lampoon, burlesque, satire, mimicry, imitation, representation, distortion, travesty, *colloq.* send-up, take-off
▶ *v* parody, mock, ridicule, satirize, mimic, distort, exaggerate, *colloq.* send up, take off

carnage *n*
bloodshed, bloodbath, butchery, slaughter, killing, murder, mass murder, massacre, genocide, ethnic cleansing, holocaust

carnal *adj*
sensual, sexual, erotic, fleshly, physical, human, natural, animal, bodily, impure, lascivious, lecherous,

lewd, licentious, lustful, *formal* corporeal, libidinous
🖬 chaste, pure, spiritual

carnival *n*
festival, fiesta, gala, jamboree, fête, fair, holiday, jubilee, celebration, merrymaking, revelry

carnivorous *adj*
meat-eating, *technical* creophagous, zoophagous

carol *n*
Christmas song, noel, song, hymn, strain, wassail, chorus

carouse *v*
make merry, revel, drink, drink freely, party, celebrate, quaff, roister, wassail, *formal* imbibe, *slang* booze

carousing *n*
celebrating, drinking, merrymaking, partying

carp *v*
complain, criticize, censure, reproach, find faults, nag, quibble, *formal* ultracrepidate, *colloq.* knock, nit-pick
🖬 praise, compliment

carpenter *n*
woodworker, joiner, cabinet-maker

carpet *n*
1 *fit a new carpet* floor-covering, covering, mat, rug, matting, Axminster, Aubusson, Wilton, Kidderminster, kali, kilim **2** *a carpet of leaves* layer, blanket, covering, bed

carriage *n*
1 COACH, wagon, cab, trap, hackney, hansom, gig, landau, car, vehicle **2** POSTURE, bearing, air, manner, attitude, stance, presence, guise, behaviour, conduct, *formal* deportment, demeanour, mien **3** CARRYING, conveyance, transport, transportation, delivery, freight, postage

carrier *n*
bearer, conveyor, delivery-person, roundsperson, messenger, porter, runner, transmitter, transporter, vehicle, vector

carry *v*
1 BRING, convey, transport, haul, move, transfer, relay, release, take, drive, fetch, shift, conduct, pipe, deliver, hand over, *colloq.* lug, cart, hump, tote **2** BEAR, shoulder, support, underpin, maintain, hold (up), uphold, sustain, suffer, stand, take someone's weight **3** *carry a disease* transmit, pass on, be infected with **4** *the proposal was carried* pass, vote for, vote in favour, accept, adopt, authorize, ratify, sanction **5** *drug-smuggling carries a risk* bear, involve, have (as a consequence), lead to, mean, *formal* entail **6** *the newspaper carried the story* cover, contain, display, show, present, communicate, print, release, broadcast, *formal* disseminate **7** *carry several brands* stock, sell, retail, have, have for sale
▷ **carry on 1** CONTINUE, proceed, last, endure, maintain, go on, keep on, keep up, persist, persevere, progress, return to, resume, restart **2** *carry on a business* operate, run, manage, conduct, administer **3** *children carrying on* misbehave, behave foolishly, *colloq.* mess around, play up **4** *carrying on with a colleague at work* have an affair, be involved
🖬 **1** stop, finish **3** behave (well)
▷ **carry out** do, perform, undertake, discharge, conduct, execute, implement, fulfil, accomplish, achieve, realize, bring off, put into effect/operation/practice, *formal* effect, *colloq.* deliver (the goods)

cart *n, v*
▶ *n* barrow, handcart, wheelbarrow, wagon, truck, dray
▶ *v* move, convey, transport, haul, bear, carry, transfer, shift, *colloq.* lug, hump, tote

carton *n*
box, packet, pack, case, container, package, parcel

cartoon *n*
1 *newspaper cartoons* sketch, drawing, picture, bubble, balloon, caricature, parody, lampoon, burlesque, *colloq.* send-up, take-off **2** *watch cartoons on TV* comic strip, animation, animated film

cartridge *n*
cassette, canister, cylinder, tube, container, case, capsule, shell, magazine, round, charge

carve *v*
1 *carve meat* cut (up), slice, chop, hack **2** *carve stone* sculpt, sculpture, shape, form, fashion, mould, hew, whittle, chisel, cut, chip **3** *carve a design* etch, engrave, incise, notch, indent
▷ **carve up** divide, share (out), separate, partition, parcel out, distribute, split (up)

carving *n*
bust, incision, sculpture, statue, statuette, *technical* dendroglyph, lithoglyph, petroglyph

cascade *n, v*
▶ *n* rush, gush, outpouring, flood, deluge, torrent, avalanche, cataract, waterfall, falls, fountain, chute, shower, trickle
▶ *v* rush, gush, surge, flood, overflow, spill, tumble, fall, descend, shower, pour, plunge, pitch

case¹ *n*
1 OCCURRENCE, circumstances, context, state, condition, position, situation, occasion, event, specimen, example, instance, illustration, point, *formal* contingency **2** LAWSUIT, suit, trial, proceedings, action, process, cause, argument, dispute **3** *a doctor's case* patient, invalid, victim, client

case² *n*
1 CONTAINER, receptacle, holder, trunk, crate, box, carton, casket, chest, cabinet, showcase, casing, cartridge, shell, capsule, sheath, cover, jacket, wrapper **2** SUITCASE, briefcase, vanity-case, bag, holdall, portmanteau, valise, overnight-bag, flight bag, hand-luggage, travel bag, attaché case, portfolio, trunk

cash *n, v*
▶ *n* **1** *pay by cash* money, hard money, ready money, banknotes, notes, coins, change, legal tender, currency, hard currency, bullion **2** *have no cash for a holiday* funds, resources, capital, wherewithal, *slang* bread, dough, dosh, readies, ready, lolly
▶ *v* exchange, realize, liquidate, turn into cash, encash

cashier¹ *n*
a bank cashier clerk, bank clerk, teller, treasurer, bursar, purser, banker, accountant, financial controller

cashier² *v*
be cashiered from the army discharge, dismiss, drum out, expel, break, discard, throw out, get rid of, *colloq.* sack, give someone the boot, unfrock

cask *n*
barrel, tun, keg, hogshead, firkin, vat, tub, butt

casket *n*
1 *keep jewels in a casket* box, case, chest, coffer, jewel-box, kist, pyxis **2** COFFIN, box, sarcophagus, *slang* pine overcoat, wooden overcoat

cast *v, n*
▶ *v* **1** THROW, hurl, lob, pitch, fling, toss, sling, heave, shy, launch, impel, drive, **2** *cast light* direct, project, shed, emit, give out, give off, radiate, diffuse, spread, scatter **3** *cast your eyes/a glance* look (at), glimpse, glance, see, view, catch sight **4** *cast doubt/suspicion* place, put, throw, put in jeopardy, *colloq.* put a question mark over **5** *cast your vote* vote, register, record,

mark with a cross **6** MOULD, shape, form, model, fashion, found

▷ **cast down** depress, discourage, dishearten, deject, sadden, crush, desolate

☒ cheer up, encourage

▶ *n* **1** COMPANY, troupe, actors, players, performers, entertainers, characters, dramatis personae **2** CASTING, mould, shape, form, model, covering

caste *n*
class, social class, social standing, order, group, position, rank, station, status, grade, lineage, background, degree, estate, stratum, race

castigate *v*
criticize, reprimand, chasten, chastise, rebuke, scold, discipline, punish, correct, censure, chide, reprove, upbraid, berate, *colloq.* dress down, haul over the coals, rap on the knuckles, tear a strip off

castle *n*
stronghold, fort, fortress, citadel, keep, tower, château, palace, mansion, stately home, country house

---

Parts of a castle include:
approach, bailey, barbican, bartizan, bastion, battlements, brattice, buttress, chapel, corbel, courtyard, crenel, crenellation, curtain wall, ditch, donjon, drawbridge, dungeon, embrasure, enclosure wall, fosse, gatehouse, inner wall, keep, lookout tower, merlon, moat, motte, mound, outer bailey, parapet, portcullis, postern, rampart, scarp, stockade, tower, turret, ward, watchtower.

---

castrate *v*
emasculate, geld, neuter, unman, unsex, *formal* evirate

casual *adj*
1 UNCONCERNED, nonchalant, blasé, lackadaisical, lukewarm, negligent, apathetic, indifferent, informal, offhand, relaxed, *formal* insouciant, *colloq.* couldn't-care-less, easy-going, laid back, happy-go-lucky, free-and-easy **2** *casual clothes* informal, comfortable, relaxed, leisure **3** *casual work* temporary, irregular, intermittent, occasional, part-time, short-term, provisional **4** *a casual meeting* chance, fortuitous, accidental, unintentional, unpremeditated, unexpected, unforeseen, irregular, random, occasional, incidental, superficial, cursory, *formal* serendipitous

☒ **1** worried, concerned **2** formal **3** permanent, regular, full-time **4** deliberate, planned

casualty *n*
injury, loss, death, fatality, victim, sufferer, injured, injured person, wounded, dead person, missing

casuistry *n*
chicanery, sophism, sophistry, speciousness, equivocation

cat *n*
tabby, kitten, mouser, tomcat, *colloq.* puss, pussy, pussy cat, mog, moggy, *old use* grimalkin

Breeds of cat include:
Abyssinian, American shorthair, Balinese, Birman, Bombay, British longhair, British shorthair, Burmese, Carthusian, chinchilla, Cornish rex, Cymric, Devon rex, domestic tabby, Egyptian Mau, Exotic shorthair, Foreign Blue, Foreign spotted shorthair, Foreign White, Havana, Himalayan, Japanese Bobtail, Korat, Maine Coon, Manx, Norwegian Forest, Persian, rag-doll, rex, Russian Blue, Scottish Fold, Siamese, silver tabby, Singapura, Somali, Tiffany, Tonkinese, Tortoiseshell, Turkish Angora, Turkish Van.

cataclysm *n*
disaster, calamity, catastrophe, debacle, devastation, upheaval, blow, collapse, convulsion

catacomb *n*
underground passages, underground rooms, underground tunnels, burial-vault, vault, tomb, crypt, *formal* ossuary

catalogue *n*, *v*
▶ *n* list, inventory, roll, register, roster, schedule, checklist, record, table, classification, index, directory, gazetteer, brochure, guide, prospectus, manifest, calendar, bulletin
▶ *v* list, compile/make a list, register, record, index, classify, alphabetize, file

catapult *v*
propel, hurl, fling, throw, pitch, toss, sling, hurtle, launch, shoot, fire

cataract *n*
waterfall, falls, rapids, force, cascade, downpour, torrent, deluge

catastrophe *n*
disaster, calamity, debacle, fiasco, failure, ruin, devastation, tragedy, blow, reverse, mischance, misfortune, adversity, trouble, upheaval, *formal* cataclysm, affliction

catastrophic *adj*
disastrous, tragic, fatal, calamitous, devastating, terrible, dreadful, awful, *formal* cataclysmic

catcall *n*
jeer, boo, gibe, hiss, whistle, barracking, *colloq.* raspberry

catch *v*, *n*
▶ *v* **1** *catch a ball* hold, grab, take, seize, grasp, snatch, grip, clutch **2** *catch an animal/a prisoner* capture, trap, entrap, hunt down, snare, ensnare, hook, net, seize, lay hold of, arrest, apprehend, corner, round up, recapture, *colloq.* nab, collar, nick **3** *catch what someone says* HEAR, make out, perceive, recognize, understand, follow, take in, fathom, grasp, comprehend, *colloq.* get the hang of, twig **4** *catch someone doing something wrong* SURPRISE, catch red-handed/in the act, expose, unmask, startle, find (out), discover, detect, discern **5** *catch a cold* get, develop, go down with, pick up, become infected with, become ill with, *formal* contract, succumb to **6** *catch someone's attention* attract, draw, grasp, hold

☒ **1** drop **2** release, free **3** miss

▷ **catch on 1** *the new style is catching on quickly* become popular, become fashionable, *colloq.* become all the rage **2** *catch on to what she said* understand, follow, take in, fathom, grasp, comprehend

▷ **catch up** draw level, gain on, overtake

▶ *n* **1** FASTENER, clip, hook, clasp, hasp, latch, lock, bolt, *Northern Eng.*, *Scot.* sneck **2** DISADVANTAGE, drawback, snag, hitch, obstacle, problem, difficulty, *colloq.* fly in the ointment

catching *adj*
infectious, contagious, communicable, transmittable, transmissible

catch phrase *n*
saying, slogan, motto, jingle, watchword, byword, catchword, formula, password

catchy *adj*
memorable, unforgettable, haunting, popular, melodic, tuneful, attractive, captivating, appealing

☒ dull, boring, instantly forgettable

catechize *v*
instruct, interrogate, question, cross-examine, examine, test, drill, *colloq.* grill, give the third degree

categorical *adj*
absolute, total, utter, unqualified, unreserved, unconditional, downright, positive, definite, emphatic, unequivocal, clear, conclusive, explicit, express, direct
F3 tentative, qualified, vague

categorize *v*
class, classify, group, sort, grade, rank, order, arrange, list, tabulate, stereotype, pigeonhole

category *n*
class, classification, group, grouping, kind, sort, type, variety, genre, section, division, department, chapter, head, heading, title, rubric, grade, rank, order, list, listing

cater *v*
1 *cater for people's needs/interests* provide, supply, furnish, serve, *formal* provision, victual **2** *cater to someone's desires* indulge, pander

caterwaul *v*
wail, scream, cry, screech, shriek, bawl, howl, miaow, squall, yowl

catharsis *n*
cleansing, purging, purification, purifying, release, *technical* abreaction, abstersion, epuration, lustration

cathartic *adj*
cleansing, purging, purifying, release, *technical* abreactive, abstersive, lustral

cathedral *n*
minster, dome, duomo

catholic *adj*
broad, broad-based, diverse, wide, wide-ranging, widespread, varied, universal, global, general, comprehensive, inclusive, all-inclusive, all-embracing, all-encompassing, liberal, tolerant, open-minded, broad-minded, *formal* eclectic
F3 narrow, limited, narrow-minded, bigoted

cattle *n*
cows, bulls, oxen, livestock, stock, beasts

Breeds of cattle include:
Aberdeen Angus, Africander, Alderney, Ankole, Ayrshire, Blonde d'Aquitaine, Brahman, Brown Swiss, cattabu, cattalo, Charolais, Chillingham, Devon, dexter, Durham, Friesian, Galloway, Guernsey, Hereford, Highland, Holstein, Jersey, Latvian, Limousin, Longhorn, Luing, Red Poll, Romagnola, Santa Gertrudis, Shetland, Shorthorn, Simmenthaler, Teeswater, Ukrainian, Welsh Black.

catty *adj*
bitchy, malicious, spiteful, venomous, vicious, mean, ill-natured, malevolent, back-biting, *formal* rancorous
F3 kind, pleasant

caucus *n*
assembly, meeting, session, convention, gathering, conclave, get-together, parley, set, clique

causative *adj*
causing, root, *technical* factitive, factive

cause *n, v*
▶ *n* **1** SOURCE, origin, beginning, root, basis, factor, spring, mainspring, originator, creator, producer, maker, author, mover, prime mover, agent, agency **2** REASON, motive, grounds, justification, explanation, basis, motivation, stimulus, incentive, inducement, impulse **3** *a worthy cause* object, purpose, end, aim, ideal, principle, belief, conviction, movement, undertaking, enterprise
F3 1 effect, result, consequence
▶ *v* begin, give rise to, be the cause of, be at the root

of, lead to, result in, occasion, bring about, make, make happen, produce, generate, originate, create, breed, precipitate, trigger (off), motivate, stimulate, provoke, incite, induce, prompt, force, compel, *formal* effect, render
F3 stop, prevent

caustic *adj*
1 *caustic chemicals* corrosive, acid, destructive, burning, stinging **2** *a caustic remark* biting, cutting, stinging, keen, pungent, bitter, sarcastic, scathing, virulent, severe, snide, *formal* acrimonious, astringent, mordant, trenchant
F3 1 soothing **2** mild, kind

cauterize *v*
burn, sterilize, disinfect, scorch, sear, singe, carbonize

caution *n, v*
▶ *n* **1** CARE, carefulness, watchfulness, alertness, mindfulness, heed, heedfulness, discretion, forethought, deliberation, wariness, *formal* prudence, vigilance, circumspection **2** WARNING, injunction, advice, counsel, *formal* admonition, caveat, *colloq.* tip-off
F3 1 carelessness, recklessness
▶ *v* warn, advise, counsel, urge, alert, deter, *formal* admonish, *colloq.* tip off

cautious *adj*
careful, watchful, alert, heedful, shrewd, discreet, tactful, chary, wary, guarded, tentative, unadventurous, *formal* prudent, circumspect, judicious, vigilant, *colloq.* cagey, softly-softly, gingerly
F3 reckless, rash, foolhardy

cavalcade *n*
procession, parade, march-past, troop, array, retinue, cortège, train

cavalier *n, adj*
▶ *n* **1** HORSEMAN, equestrian, horse soldier, cavalryman, knight, chevalier, Bashi-Bazouk, chasseur, Ironside, spahi **2** GENTLEMAN, gallant, escort, partner
▶ *adj* supercilious, patronizing, condescending, lordly, haughty, lofty, arrogant, swaggering, insolent, scornful, disdainful, curt, offhand, casual, free-and-easy

cavalry *n*
horsemen, equestrians, horse soldiers, cavalrymen, troopers, dragoons, hussars, lancers

cave *n, v*
▶ *n* cavern, grotto, hole, pothole, tunnel, dugout, underground chamber, hollow, cavity
▶ *v* ▷ **cave in** collapse, subside, give way, yield, fall (in), slip

caveat *n*
caution, warning, alarm, *formal* admonition

cavern *n*
cave, cavity, den, grotto, hollow, pothole, vault, tunnel, dugout, underground chamber

cavernous *adj*
hollow, concave, gaping, yawning, echoing, resonant, deep, unfathomable, bottomless, huge, immense, vast, spacious, dark, gloomy, sunken, depressed

cavil *v*
complain, carp, criticize, censure, reproach, find faults, nag, quibble, *colloq.* nit-pick
F3 praise, compliment

cavity *n*
hole, gap, dent, hollow, crater, pit, well, sinus, *technical* orifice, ventricle, aperture, lacuna

cavort *v*
caper, frolic, gambol, prance, skip, dance, frisk, sport, romp

cease *v*
stop, refrain, halt, call a halt, come/bring to a halt, break off, leave (off), finish, end, come/bring to an end, conclude, terminate, suspend, let up, abate, fail, die, *formal* discontinue, desist, *colloq.* fizzle out, peter out, pack in, quit
▄ begin, start, commence

ceaseless *adj*
endless, unending, never-ending, eternal, everlasting, continuous, non-stop, incessant, unceasing, interminable, constant, perpetual, continual, persistent, untiring, uninterrupted, unremitting
▄ occasional, irregular

cede *v*
surrender, give up, resign, abandon, yield, relinquish, convey, transfer, hand over, turn over, grant, deliver, allow, concede, *formal* abdicate, renounce

ceiling *n*
1 *a decorated ceiling* vault, plafond, roof, overhead, overhead covering, rafters, beams, awning, canopy **2** LIMIT, upper limit, maximum, most, cut-off point

celebrate *v*
1 *celebrate a birthday* commemorate, remember, observe, keep, mark, honour, do something in someone's honour, have/throw a party, rejoice, enjoy yourself, have fun, go out, toast, drink to, extol, revel, *colloq.* rave, binge, have a ball, live it up, whoop it up, go out on the town, go on the razzle, paint the town red, kill the fatted calf, put the flags out **2** *the priest celebrated Communion* bless, perform, solemnize

celebrated *adj*
famous, well-known, famed, renowned, illustrious, glorious, eminent, distinguished, great, notable, noted, prominent, outstanding, legendary, popular, acclaimed, exalted, revered, *colloq.* with your name in lights
▄ unknown, obscure, forgotten

celebration *n*
observance, merrymaking, jollification, revelry, festivity, *colloq.* rave, rave-up, binge, spree

celebrity *n*
star, personality, name, dignitary, famous person, superstar, legend, legend in their own lifetime, living legend, household name, *formal* personage, notable, luminary, worthy, *colloq.* VIP, big name, bigwig, big shot
▄ nobody, unknown, nonentity

celerity *n*
rapidity, fastness, quickness, speed, swiftness, velocity, dispatch, expedition, fleetness, haste, promptness
▄ slowness

celestial *adj*
heavenly, divine, godlike, spiritual, angelic, seraphic, elysian, empyrean, ethereal, paradisaic, eternal, immortal, sublime, supernatural, transcendental, astral, starry
▄ earthly, mundane

celibacy *n*
singleness, bachelorhood, spinsterhood, virginity, chastity, purity, self-denial, self-restraint, abstinence, continence, *formal* abnegation

celibate *adj*
chaste, pure, abstinent, virgin, single, bachelor, spinster

cell *n*
1 *a prison cell* prison, jail, dungeon, lock-up, room, cubicle, chamber, compartment, enclosure **2** *living cells* unit, organism, *technical* protoplasm, cytoplasm, protoplast, gamete, zygote, spore, nucleus, matrix **3** *a*

political cell faction, nucleus, group, party, unit, section, set, crowd, caucus, clique

cellar *n*
basement, crypt, vault, storeroom, wine cellar

cement *n, v*
▶ *n* plaster, mortar, concrete, screed, pointing, grouting, matrix, bonding, adhesive, glue, paste
▶ *v* stick, bond, weld, solder, join, cohere, unite, combine, bind, affix, attach, glue, gum

cemetery *n*
burial ground, burial place, burial site, graveyard, churchyard, graves, tombs, *formal* necropolis, charnel house, God's acre

censor *v, n*
▶ *v* cut, make cuts, ban, edit, delete, blue-pencil, bowdlerize, expurgate
▶ *n* inspector, examiner, editor, bowdlerizer, expurgator

✍ censor or **censure** ?

To *censor* books, films, etc is to examine them, deleting parts of them or forbidding publication: *His letters home were censored.* To *censure* someone is to criticize them severely: *The President was severely censured for abusing his powers.*

---

censorious *adj*
condemnatory, disapproving, disparaging, fault-finding, carping, cavilling, critical, hypercritical, severe, *formal* captious
▄ complimentary, approving

censure *v, n*
▶ *v* condemn, denounce, blame, criticize, disapprove of, reprehend, reprove, reproach, rebuke, reprimand, scold, *formal* castigate, admonish, remonstrate, upbraid, *colloq.* tell off, haul over the coals, come down heavy on, pull to pieces
▄ praise, compliment, approve
▶ *n* condemnation, blame, disapproval, criticism, denunciation, reprehension, reproof, reproach, rebuke, reprimand, scolding, *formal* admonition, admonishment, castigation, upbraiding, remonstrance, obloquy, vituperation, *colloq.* telling-off
▄ praise, compliments, approval

central *adj*
1 MIDDLE, mid, inner, interior, medial, median **2** PRINCIPAL, main, major, most important, chief, key, primary, fundamental, foremost, dominant, vital, crucial, significant, focal, pivotal, basic, essential, core, prime
▄ **1** peripheral **2** minor, secondary

centralize *v*
concentrate, converge, bring/gather together, incorporate, rationalize, focus, streamline, amalgamate, compact, condense, unify
▄ decentralize

centre *n, v*
▶ *n* middle, midpoint, heart, core, nucleus, kernel, pivot, hub, focus, focal point, crux, linchpin, arena, *colloq.* bull's-eye
▄ edge, periphery, outskirts
▶ *v* focus, concentrate, converge, gravitate, revolve, pivot, hinge

ceramics *n*
pottery, earthenware, ware, bisque, faience, ironstone, porcelain, raku. *See panel at* POTTERY.

cereal *n*
1 *cereal crops* barley, grain, corn, wheat, maize, millet, oats, rye, sorghum **2** *breakfast cereal* cornflakes, muesli, porridge, oatmeal.

ceremonial *adj, n*
► *adj* formal, official, stately, solemn, dignified, ritual, ritualistic
🔁 informal, casual
► *n* ceremony, formality, protocol, custom, solemnity, ritual, rite

> 📝 **ceremonial** or **ceremonious** ?
> *Ceremonial* means 'relating to or appropriate for a ceremony': *ceremonial dress; a ceremonial occasion.* *Ceremonious* means 'very formal or polite': *He ushered her through with a ceremonious bow.*

ceremonious *adj*
stately, dignified, grand, solemn, ritual, civil, official, polite, courteous, deferential, courtly, formal, stiff, starchy, exact, precise, scrupulous, *formal* punctilious, *colloq.* starchy
🔁 unceremonious, informal, relaxed

ceremony *n*
1 *wedding ceremony* service, rite, sacrament, ordinance, liturgy, commemoration, observance, festival, celebration, formality, function, custom, tradition, parade, anniversary, inauguration, dedication, induction, initiation, graduation, investiture, bar mitzvah, unveiling **2** ETIQUETTE, formality, protocol, form, niceties, ceremonial, ritual, pomp, pageantry, show, *formal* decorum, propriety

certain *adj*
1 *I'm certain he's telling the truth* SURE, positive, assured, confident, convinced, persuaded **2** *it's certain that she left yesterday* indisputable, unquestionable, undeniable, undoubted, evident, obvious, clear, plain, conclusive, absolute, convincing, true, *formal* indubitable, incontrovertible, irrefutable, *colloq.* no two ways about it, no ifs and buts, sure as eggs is eggs **3** *success is certain* INEVITABLE, unavoidable, inescapable, bound, bound to happen, meant to happen, destined, fated, doomed, *formal* inexorable, ineluctable, *colloq.* cut and dried, open-and-shut, home and dry, in the bag **4** *below a certain income* SPECIFIC, special, particular, individual, precise, express, fixed, established, settled, decided, definite, determined **5** *to a certain extent* some, partial
🔁 **1** uncertain, unsure, hesitant, doubtful **3** unlikely

certainly *adv*
surely, of course, naturally, obviously, clearly, plainly, definitely, for sure, undoubtedly, without a doubt, no doubt, undeniably, unquestionably, absolutely, by all means, doubtlessly, assuredly, positively

certainty *n*
1 *identify someone with certainty* sureness, positiveness, assurance, confidence, conviction, faith, trust, assuredness **2** *it's a certainty that she'll get the job* inevitability, foregone conclusion, truth, validity, fact, reality, *colloq.* sure thing, safe bet, dead cert

> **Expressions used to show one is certain or uncertain about something:**
> a dead cert, a safe bet, a sure thing, *US* as sure as God made little green apples, as sure as hell, beyond all doubt, beyond any shadow of a doubt, feel it in your bones/your water, for certain sure, I can guarantee it, I couldn't be more certain, I doubt it, I have my doubts, in two minds, *US* of two minds, not at all sure, sure as eggs are/is eggs.

🔁 **1** uncertainty, doubt, hesitation

certificate *n*
document, award, diploma, qualification, credentials,

testimonial, guarantee, endorsement, warrant, licence, authorization, pass, voucher

certify *v*
declare, assure, guarantee, endorse, confirm, pronounce, vouch, testify, witness, bear witness to, substantiate, verify, authenticate, validate, warrant, ratify, authorize, recognize, license, *formal* attest, aver, corroborate, accredit

certitude *n*
(full) assurance, assuredness, certainty, confidence, conviction, sureness, positiveness, *formal* plerophoria, plerophory
🔁 doubt

cessation *n*
halt, halting, ceasing, discontinuation, discontinuing, end, ending, remission, respite, rest, standstill, stay, stoppage, stopping, conclusion, suspension, termination, pause, recess, break, let-up, interruption, intermission, interval, *formal* abeyance, desistance, discontinuance, hiatus
🔁 beginning, start, commencement

chafe *v*
1 *chafe someone's skin* rub, grate, irritate, rasp, scrape, inflame, scratch, wear, *formal* abrade, excoriate **2** *chafing at the rules* anger, annoy, enrage, exasperate, incense, provoke, inflame, vex, *colloq.* peeve, get on someone's nerves, get on someone's wick

chaff *n*
husks, shells, pods, cases

chagrin *n, v*
► *n* annoyance, exasperation, indignation, disappointment, displeasure, irritation, vexation, disquiet, dissatisfaction, embarrassment, mortification, humiliation, shame, fretfulness, *formal* discomfiture, discomposure
🔁 delight, pleasure
► *v* annoy, exasperate, disappoint, displease, irritate, vex, irk, disquiet, dissatisfy, embarrass, humiliate, mortify, *colloq.* peeve

chain *n, v*
► *n* **1** FETTER, manacle, restraint, bond, shackle, trammel, link, coupling, union **2** *a hotel chain* group, company, firm **3** *a chain of islands* string, line, row, train, set, *formal* concatenation **4** *a chain of events* series, sequence, succession, progression
► *v* tether, fasten, secure, bind, tie, hitch, restrain, confine, fetter, shackle, manacle, handcuff, enslave
🔁 free, release, liberate

chair *n, v*
► *n* **1** *sit on a chair* armchair, recliner, swivel-chair, seat, stool, bench, form **2** *Sally is the new chair* chairperson, chairman, chairwoman, president, convener, organizer, director, master of ceremonies, MC, toastmaster, speaker
► *v* lead, act as chairperson/chairman/chairwoman, convene, direct, supervise, preside over

chalk *v*
▷ **chalk up** achieve, attain, gain, log, score, tally, register, record, accumulate, ascribe, attribute, charge, credit, put down

chalky *adj*
ashen, pale, pallid, white, wan, colourless, powdery, *formal* calcareous, cretaceous

challenge *v, n*
► *v* **1** DARE, defy, confront, brave, summon, invite, accost, provoke, *colloq.* throw down the gauntlet **2** *challenged his authority* QUESTION, dispute, query, protest, disagree with, object to, take exception to, call into question, *formal* demur **3** *challenged my ability* test, tax, try, stretch
► *n* **1** *the new job is a real challenge* test, trial, hurdle,

obstacle, problem, risk, hazard, opportunity **2** *take up the challenge to fight* dare, defiance, confrontation, provocation, call, summons, bidding **3** *a challenge to their powers* dispute, protest, opposition, defiance, disagreement, objection, calling into question, questioning, interrogation, stand, confrontation, ultimatum

challenging *adj*
exciting, exacting, demanding, testing, taxing, stretching
F3 undemanding

chamber *n*
1 HALL, assembly room, auditorium, meeting-place **2** ROOM, apartment, compartment, bedroom, boudoir **3** *the chambers of the heart* cavity, ventricle, compartment **4** *the upper chamber of parliament* assembly, legislature, parliament, council, house

champion *n, v*
▶ *n* **1** *the school chess champion* winner, victor, conqueror, title-holder, hero, ace, *colloq.* champ **2** *a champion of animal rights* guardian, protector, defender, vindicator, patron, backer, supporter, upholder, advocate, *colloq.* angel
▶ *v* defend, stand up for, back, support, protect, maintain, uphold, advocate, promote, *formal* espouse

chance *n, v, adj*
▶ *n* **1** *meet someone by chance* ACCIDENT, coincidence, luck, fortune, providence, fate, destiny, risk, gamble, speculation, *formal* fortuity, serendipity, *colloq.* fluke **2** *there's a chance that I'll be late* possibility, prospect, probability, likelihood, odds **3** *a second chance* opportunity, opening, occasion, time, *colloq.* break, golden opportunity, chance of a lifetime, your best shot
F3 **1** certainty
▶ *v* **1** RISK, hazard, take a chance, gamble, wager, stake, try, speculate, venture, *colloq.* chance your luck, push your luck, play a hunch, bet your boots/ life, bet your bottom dollar **2** HAPPEN, occur, come about, take place, arise, crop up, develop, result, follow
▷ **chance on/upon** meet, meet unexpectedly, find by chance, discover, come across, stumble on, *colloq.* run into, bump into
▶ *adj* fortuitous, casual, accidental, inadvertent, unintentional, unintended, unforeseen, unexpected, unanticipated, unlooked-for, random, arbitrary, haphazard, incidental, *formal* serendipitous, *colloq.* flukey
F3 deliberate, intentional, foreseen, certain

chancy *adj*
risky, speculative, tricky, uncertain, fraught, hazardous, dangerous, problematical, *colloq.* dicey, dodgy
F3 safe, secure

change *v, n*
▶ *v* **1** *water changes into ice; prices keep changing* make/become different, alter, vary, convert, turn, go, become, move, develop, modify, reorganize, reform, restructure, remodel, revise, renew, amend, adapt, customize, adjust, transform, evolve, transfer, move, shift, fluctuate, vacillate, be in a state of flux, *technical* mutate, transmutate, metamorphose, transfigure **2** *change one thing for another* substitute, replace, alternate, interchange, rotate, transpose, exchange, swap, trade, switch, barter, *colloq.* chop and change **3** *change buses* transfer, connect, make a connection
▶ *n* **1** *a change in the weather* difference, alteration, variation, conversion, modification, reorganization, shake-up, transition, trend, movement, diversion, novelty, innovation, variety, revolution, upheaval,

development, reform, restructuring, remodelling, reconstruction, revision, renewal, amendment, adaptation, customization, adjustment, transformation, evolution, transfer, move, shift, fluctuation, vacillation, state of flux, reversal, about-turn, about-face, volte-face, turnabout, ebb and flow, *technical* mutation, transmutation, metamorphosis, transfiguration, *formal* vicissitude, *colloq.* U-turn **2** *a change of government* exchange, transposition, interchange, substitution, substitute, replacement, alternation, rotation, swap, trade, switch, barter **3** *Have you got any change?* coins, cash, silver, coppers

changeable *adj*
variable, varying, fluctuating, fluid, kaleidoscopic, shifting, mobile, unsettled, unstable, uncertain, unpredictable, unreliable, erratic, irregular, inconstant, fickle, capricious, volatile, unstable, unsteady, wavering, vacillating, mercurial, labile, chameleonic, chameleon-like, Protean, *formal* mutable, vicissitudinous
F3 constant, settled, reliable

channel *n, v*
▶ *n* **1** *a channel for rainwater; irrigation channels* passage, duct, conduit, main, groove, furrow, trough, gutter, gully, canal, flume, watercourse, waterway, strait, neck, sound **2** *channels of communication* route, course, path, avenue, way, means, medium, approach, passage, agent, agency
▶ *v* direct, guide, conduct, convey, send, transmit, force, concentrate, focus

chant *n, v*
▶ *n* **1** *the football supporters' chants* shout, cry, slogan, warcry **2** *a religious chant* plainsong, psalm, song, melody, chorus, refrain, ditty, incantation, recitation, mantra
▶ *v* sing, chorus, recite, *formal* intone

chaos *n*
disorder, confusion, disorganization, anarchy, lawlessness, tumult, upheaval, disruption, pandemonium, uproar, riot, bedlam, madhouse, mess, *formal* tohu bohu, *colloq.* pig's breakfast, dog's dinner, shambles, *US slang* snafu
F3 order

chaotic *adj*
disordered, confused, disorganized, topsy-turvy, deranged, anarchic, lawless, orderless, riotous, tumultuous, unruly, uncontrolled, disrupted, *colloq.* shambolic, at sixes and sevens, all over the place/ shop, higgledy-piggledy, *US slang* snafu
F3 ordered, organized

chap *n*
fellow, man, boy, person, individual, character, sort, type, *colloq.* bloke, guy

chaperone, chaperon *n, v*
▶ *n* companion, escort, duenna
▶ *v* escort, accompany, attend, guard, protect, safeguard, shepherd, take care of, look after, mind, watch over

chapped *adj*
sore, chafed, cracked, raw

chapter *n*
1 *I read chapter 3* section, division, part, clause, portion, topic **2** *a new chapter in my life* EPISODE, period, phase, stage, time

char *v*
burn, cauterize, scorch, sear, singe, carbonize, brown

character *n*
1 *the cruel side of his character; the character of the countryside* nature, essential quality, essence, ethos, personality, disposition, temperament, temper, constitution, make-up, individuality, identity, peculiarity,

feature, attributes, characteristics, quality, property, type, stamp, calibre, reputation, psyche, status, position, trait, image, *formal* persona, *colloq.* what makes someone tick **2** *he has character; this house has character* strength, strength of purpose, determination, courage, honesty, integrity, uprightness, moral fibre, charm, appeal, attractiveness, attractive features, distinctive features, arresting qualities, specialness, style, interest **3** ECCENTRIC, eccentric person, original, oddity, *colloq.* oddball, case **4** *the characters in a play* individual, person, human being, role, part, sort, type, **5** LETTER, figure, symbol, sign, mark, type, device, logo, emblem, cipher, rune, hieroglyph, ideograph

characteristic *n, adj*
▶ *n* feature, trait, attribute, property, quality, essential quality, mark, hallmark, factor, peculiarity, idiosyncrasy, mannerism, symptom
▶ *adj* distinctive, distinguishing, individual, idiosyncratic, peculiar, specific, special, typical, representative, symbolic, symptomatic
☒ uncharacteristic, untypical

characterize *v*
1 *materialism that characterizes life* typify, mark, stamp, brand, identify, distinguish, indicate, specify, designate **2** DESCRIBE, represent, portray, present

charade *n*
farce, mockery, parody, pretence, fake, travesty, sham, pantomime

charge *v, n*
▶ *v* **1** *charge a high price* ask, ask for, ask someone to pay, demand, demand in payment, set/fix a price, levy, exact, debit, bill, put down to **2** ACCUSE, indict, impeach, incriminate, blame, *formal* arraign **3** ATTACK, assail, assault, storm, rush (forward), tear
▶ *n* **1** PRICE, cost, fee, rate, amount, expense, expenditure, outlay, payment, rent, rental, dues, toll, levy, tax **2** ACCUSATION, indictment, allegation, impeachment, blame, incrimination, *formal* arraignment, imputation **3** ATTACK, assault, onslaught, sortie, incursion, storming, rush, onrush **4** *in your charge* custody, keeping, care, safekeeping, guardianship, ward, protection, trust, responsibility, duty, burden, obligation
▷ **in charge of** responsible for, managing, leading, controlling, directing, supervising, overseeing, heading up, looking after, taking care of

charitable *adj*
philanthropic, humanitarian, benevolent, benign, kind, compassionate, sympathetic, understanding, considerate, generous, open-handed, liberal, tolerant, broad-minded, kindly, lenient, forgiving, indulgent, gracious, *formal* magnanimous, beneficent, bounteous, eleemosynary
☒ uncharitable, inconsiderate, unforgiving

charity *n*
1 fund, trust, foundation, caritas, voluntary organization **2** *live on charity* gift, donation, handout, aid, relief, contribution, funding, assistance, alms **3** GENEROSITY, goodwill, bountifulness, almsgiving, philanthropy, unselfishness, altruism, benevolence, benignness, kindness, goodness, humanity, compassion, considerateness, thoughtfulness, tenderheartedness, love, affection, tolerance, clemency, indulgence, *formal* beneficence
☒ **3** selfishness, malice

charlatan *n*
impostor, cheat, fake, fraud, confidence trickster, pretender, bogus caller/official, quack, sham, swindler, mountebank, *colloq.* phoney, con man

charm *n, v*
▶ *n* **1** ATTRACTION, allure, allurement, magnetism,

appeal, delightfulness, attractiveness, desirability, fascination, enchantment, captivation, *colloq.* what it takes **2** *lucky charm* trinket, ornament, talisman, mascot, amulet, fetish, idol, grisgris, juju, obi, periapt, porte-bonheur **3** *the magician's charm* spell, sorcery, magic, abracadabra
▶ *v* please, delight, enrapture, captivate, fascinate, beguile, enchant, bewitch, mesmerize, attract, draw, allure, intrigue, cajole, win, enamour, seduce
☒ repel, disgust

charming *adj*
pleasing, delightful, pleasant, lovely, captivating, enchanting, attractive, fetching, appealing, tasteful, sweet, cute, winsome, alluring, engaging, tempting, seductive, winning, irresistible, *formal* delectable
☒ ugly, unattractive, repulsive

chart *n, v*
▶ *n* **1** *a chart showing the patient's temperature* diagram, table, graph, map, plan, blueprint, bar chart, flow chart, pie chart, flow sheet, *technical* nomogram, nomograph **2** *number one in the charts* hit parade, top twenty, list, league
▶ *v* **1** *chart an area* map, map out, sketch, draw, draft, outline, delineate, mark, plot, place **2** MONITOR, document, record, keep a record of, put on record, note, register, observe, follow

charter *n, v*
▶ *n* right, privilege, prerogative, authority, authorization, permit, licence, franchise, concession, contract, covenant, indenture, deed, bond, warrant, sanction, document, *formal* accreditation
▶ *v* hire, rent, lease, commission, engage, employ, authorize, sanction, license

chary *adj*
careful, cautious, wary, guarded, heedful, uneasy, unwilling, reluctant, slow, suspicious, leery, *formal* prudent, circumspect
☒ heedless, unwary

chase *v, n*
▶ *v* pursue, follow, hunt, run after, give chase, track, trail, tail, shadow, hound, drive, expel, send away, rush, hurry, *colloq.* be hot on someone's heels
▶ *n* pursuit, trail, running after, hunt, hunting, coursing, rush

chasm *n*
1 *a chasm in the rocks* crack, rift, split, cleft, fissure, crevasse, canyon, gorge, ravine, gap, opening, gulf, abyss, void, hollow, cavity, crater, breach **2** *a chasm between two people* rift, split, gulf, gap, opening, gulf, breach, divorce, separation, estrangement, alienation, disagreement, quarrel

chassis *n*
framework, bodywork, frame, fuselage, skeleton, structure, substructure, undercarriage

chaste *adj*
1 *a chaste person* pure, virginal, unsullied, undefiled, immaculate, abstinent, continent, celibate, unmarried, single, virtuous, moral, innocent **2** *a chaste style* modest, decent, plain, simple, restrained, austere, unadorned, unembellished
☒ **1** promiscuous, immoral, corrupt **2** unrestrained, decorated

chasten *v*
humble, humiliate, tame, subdue, repress, curb, restrain, moderate, soften, discipline, punish, correct, reprove, *formal* chastise, castigate

chastise *v*
punish, discipline, reprimand, correct, reprove, admonish, scold, censure, beat, flog, whip, lash, scourge, smack, spank, strap, cane, *formal* castigate,

chastity *n*
purity, virginity, maidenhood, modesty, abstinence, temperateness, continence, celibacy, unmarried state, singleness, virtue, innocence, immaculateness
☒ promiscuity, immorality

chat *v, n*
▶ *v* talk, gossip, chatter, tittle-tattle, *formal* converse, *colloq.* natter, jabber, babble, rabbit (on), gas, waffle, prattle, chinwag, jaw, chew the rag/fat
▶ *n* talk, conversation, gossip, tête-à-tête, heart-to-heart, cosy chat, small talk, tittle-tattle, *colloq.* natter, confab, chinwag

chatter *v, n*
▶ *v* babble, chat, gossip, tattle, tittle-tattle, *colloq.* pass the time of day, natter, jabber, witter, babble, rabbit (on), gab, gas, waffle, prattle, chinwag, jaw, talk the hind legs off a donkey
▶ *n* talk, conversation, gossip, tête-à-tête, chit-chat, natter, jabber, witter, prattle, babble, tittle-tattle, jaw, *colloq.* natter, confab, chinwag

chatterbox *n*
chatterer, babbler, gossipper, gossip, conversationalist, jabberer, tittle-tattler, tattler, *colloq.* natterer, windbag, gasbag, gabber, big mouth, blabbermouth, loudmouth

chatty *adj*
1 *a chatty person* talkative, gossipy, conversational, garrulous, gushing, effusive, verbose, long-winded, glib, *formal* loquacious, *colloq.* gabby, mouthy **2** *a chatty letter* newsy, friendly, informal, colloquial, conversational, familiar
☒ **1** quiet, taciturn

chauvinism *n*
jingoism, nationalism, bias, prejudice, partisanship, flag-waving, sexism, male chauvinism

chauvinist *adj*
jingoist, nationalist, biased, prejudiced, flag-waving, sexist, male chauvinist

cheap *adj*
1 INEXPENSIVE, reasonable, dirt-cheap, low-price, low-cost, affordable, bargain, reduced, cut-price, knock-down, marked-down, discounted, slashed, rock-bottom, giveaway, budget, economy, sale, economical, no-frills, cheap-rate, reduced rate, concessional rate, on special offer, value for money, a good buy, *colloq.* a snip, a steal, going for a song, dirt-cheap, ten a penny, on a shoestring **2** SHODDY, cheap and nasty, tatty, tawdry, inferior, second-rate, worthless, vulgar, tasteless, common, poor, cheapjack, paltry, two-bit, *colloq.* cheapo, tacky **3** *cheap comments* mean, contemptible, despicable, low, vulgar, sordid
☒ **1** expensive, costly, dear **2** superior, good quality **3** noble, admirable

cheapen *v*
devalue, degrade, lower, demean, depreciate, belittle, disparage, discredit, downgrade, *formal* denigrate, derogate

cheat *v, n*
▶ *v* **1** *cheat someone* defraud, swindle, diddle, short-change, double-cross, mislead, deceive, dupe, fool, trick, hoodwink, gull, beguile, cozen, fiddle, fake, bluff, welsh, *colloq.* do, put one over on, rip off, con, sting, fleece, take for a ride, take to the cleaners, pull the wool over someone's eyes, two-time, bilk, fix, rig, bamboozle **2** *cheated out of their inheritance* prevent, deprive, deny, thwart, frustrate, check, *colloq.* do, have
▶ *n* cheater, dodger, crook, fraud, swindler, extortioner, double-crosser, impostor, charlatan, deceiver,

trickster, confidence trickster, rogue, cozener, *colloq.* con man, shark

check *v, n*
▶ *v* **1** EXAMINE, inspect, scrutinize, look at (closely), go through, scan, investigate, probe, inquire into, test, monitor, police, study, research, analyse, compare, cross-check, screen, take stock, make sure, confirm, verify, *formal* corroborate, substantiate, validate, *colloq.* give the once-over **2** *check an impulse* curb, bridle, restrain, control, limit, contain, rein in, repress, inhibit, damp, thwart, hinder, impede, obstruct, bar, delay, slow (down), stop, staunch, stem, arrest, halt, bring to a standstill, *formal* retard
▷ **check in** register, book in, enrol, record your arrival
▷ **check out 1** *check out of a hotel* leave, pay the bill, settle up **2** *check out the procedure* examine, investigate, test, study, look into, *colloq.* recce
▷ **check up** investigate, inspect, evaluate, assess, analyse, probe, inquire into, ascertain, make sure, confirm, verify
▶ *n* **1** EXAMINATION, inspection, scrutiny, check-up, investigation, inquiry, audit, test, research, monitoring, analysis, probe, confirmation, verification, *colloq.* once-over **2** BILL, invoice, statement, account, charges, reckoning, tally, *US* tab

check-up *n*
examination, inspection, scrutiny, investigation, inquiry, audit, test, research, monitoring, analysis, evaluation, appraisal, probe, confirmation, verification

cheek *n*
impertinence, impudence, insolence, disrespect, brazenness, audacity, gall, *formal* effrontery, temerity, *colloq.* nerve, sauce, gall, lip, mouth, brass neck, chutzpah

cheeky *adj*
impertinent, impudent, insolent, disrespectful, forward, brazen, pert, audacious, overfamiliar, *colloq.* fresh, saucy, lippy, *US* sassy
☒ respectful, polite

cheer *v, n*
▶ *v* **1** ACCLAIM, hail, clap, applaud, salute, welcome, celebrate, fanfare, shout, support, *colloq.* root for **2** COMFORT, console, brighten, gladden, warm, uplift, raise/lift the spirits of, elate, exhilarate, encourage, hearten, enliven, buoy up, *formal* solace, inspirit, *colloq.* buck up, perk up
☒ **1** boo, jeer **2** dishearten, discourage
▷ **cheer up** comfort, console, encourage, brighten, hearten, liven (up), take heart, rally, *colloq.* buck up, perk up
▶ *n* **1** *the cheers of the crowd* acclamation, hurrah, bravo, applause, clapping, ovation, *formal* plaudits **2** CHEERFULNESS, gladness, happiness, hopefulness, joyfulness, high spirits, light-heartedness, merriment, merrymaking, revelry
☒ criticism

cheerful *adj*
1 *a cheerful person* happy, glad, contented, joyful, joyous, blithe, carefree, light-hearted, cheery, good-humoured, sunny, optimistic, enthusiastic, hearty, genial, jovial, jolly, gay, merry, lively, animated, exuberant, bright, smiling, laughing, spirited, in good spirits, chirpy, breezy, jaunty, buoyant, sparkling **2** *painted in a cheerful yellow* attractive, pleasing, pleasant, agreeable, delightful, warm, sunny, bright, comforting, encouraging, heartening, inspiring, stirring
☒ **1** sad, dejected, depressed **2** depressing, disheartening

cheerio *interj*
goodbye, farewell, adieu, *au revoir*, *colloq.* cheers, so

long, bye, bye-bye, see you, see you later, ta-ta

cheerless adj
gloomy, dismal, dreary, dull, depressing, dejected, despondent, austere, barren, desolate, forlorn, grim, bleak, cold, sad, unhappy, sombre, sorrowful, comfortless, joyless, lonely, melancholy, miserable, mournful, dank, dark, dingy, disconsolate, drab, sullen, sunless, winterly, uninviting, formal dolorous
🔁 bright, cheerful

cheers interj
1 say cheers as a toast bottoms up, here's to you, your good health, here's looking to you, here's mud in your eye, here's to ..., to absent friends, down the hatch, happy landings, all the best, prosit, skol, slàinte **2** THANK YOU, thank you very much, bless you, much obliged, colloq. many thanks, thanks a lot, ta **3** GOODBYE, farewell, adieu, au revoir, colloq. so long, bye, bye-bye, see you, see you later, ta-ta

cheery adj
happy, glad, contented, joyful, carefree, light-hearted, cheerful, optimistic, enthusiastic, hearty, genial, jovial, jolly, gay, merry, lively, animated, exuberant, bright, smiling, laughing, spirited, in good spirits, chirpy, breezy, jaunty, buoyant, sparkling
🔁 downcast, sad

cheese n

Varieties of cheese include:
Amsterdam, Bel Paese, Bleu d'Auvergne, Blue Cheshire, Blue Vinny, Boursin, Brie, Caboc, Caerphilly, Camembert, Carré, Cheddar, Cheshire, Churnton, cottage cheese, cream cheese, Crowdie, curd cheese, Danish blue, Derby, Dolcelatte, Dorset Blue, Double Gloucester, Dunlop, Edam, Emmental, Emmentaler, ewe-cheese, Feta, fromage frais, Gloucester, Gorgonzola, Gouda, Gruyère, Huntsman, Jarlsberg, Killarney, Lancashire, Leicester, Limburg(er), Lymeswold, mascarpone, mouse-trap, mozzarella, Neufchâtel, Orkney, Parmesan, Petit Suisse, Pont-l'Évêque, Port Salut, processed cheese, quark, Red Leicester, Red Windsor, ricotta, Roquefort, sage Derby, Saint-Paulin, Stilton, stracchino, Vacherin, vegetarian cheese, Wensleydale.

chemical elements

The chemical elements (with their symbols) are:
actinium (Ac), aluminium (Al), americium (Am), antimony (Sb), argon (Ar), arsenic (As), astatine (At), barium (Ba), berkelium (Bk), beryllium (Be), bismuth (Bi), boron (B), bromine (Br), cadmium (Cd), caesium (Cs), calcium (Ca), californium (Cf), carbon (C), cerium (Ce), chlorine (Cl), chromium (Cr), cobalt (Co), copper (Cu), curium (Cm), dysprosium (Dy), einsteinium (Es), erbium (Er), europium (Eu), fermium (Fm), fluorine (F), francium (Fr), gadolinium (Gd), gallium (Ga), germanium (Ge), gold (Au), hafnium (Hf), hahnium (Ha), helium (He), holmium (Ho), hydrogen (H), indium (In), iodine (I), iridium (Ir), iron (Fe), krypton (Kr), lanthanum (La), lawrencium (Lr), lead (Pb), lithium (Li), lutetium (Lu), magnesium (Mg), manganese (Mn), mendelevium (Md), mercury (Hg), molybdenum (Mo), neodymium (Nd), neon (Ne), neptunium (Np), nickel (Ni), niobium (Nb), nitrogen (N), nobelium (No), osmium (Os), oxygen (O), palladium (Pd), phosphorus (P), platinum (Pt), plutonium (Pu), polonium (Po), potassium (K), praseodymium (Pr), promethium (Pm), protactinium (Pa), radium (Ra), radon (Rn), rhenium (Re), rhodium (Rh), rubidium (Rb), ruthenium (Ru), rutherfordium (Rf), samarium (Sm), scandium (Sc), selenium (Se), silicon (Si), silver (Ag), sodium (Na), strontium (Sr), sulphur (S), tantalum (Ta), technetium (Tc), tellurium (Te), terbium (Tb), thallium (Tl), thorium (Th), thulium (Tm), tin (Sn), titanium (Ti), tungsten (W), uranium (U), vanadium (V), xenon (Xe), ytterbium (Yb), yttrium (Y), zinc (Zn), zirconium (Zr).

chemistry n

Terms used in chemistry include :
analytical chemistry, biochemistry, inorganic chemistry, organic chemistry, physical chemistry; acid, alkali, analysis, atom, atomic number, atomic structure, subatomic particles, base, bond, buffer, catalysis, catalyst, chain reaction, chemical bond, chemical compound, chemical element, chemical equation, chemical reaction, chemist, chlorination, combustion, compound, corrosion, covalent bond, crystal, cycle, decomposition, diffusion, dissociation, distillation, electrochemical cell, electrode, electron, electrolysis, emulsion, fermentation, fixation, formula, free radical, gas, halogen, hydrolysis, immiscible, indicator, inert gas, ion, ionic bond, isomer, isotope, lipid, liquid, litmus paper, litmus test, mass, matter, metallic bond, mixture, mole, molecule, neutron, noble gas, nucleus, oxidation, periodic table, pH, polymer, proton, radioactivity, reaction, reduction, respiration, salt, solids, solution, solvent, substance, suspension, symbol, synthesis, valency, zwitterion. See also ACID; CHEMICAL ELEMENTS; GAS; MINERALS.

chequered adj
varied, mixed, diverse, with good and bad times/parts, with ups and downs, with sad and happy times/parts, with its fair share of rough and tumble

cherish v
1 cherish someone care for, look after, love, take (good) care of, hold dear, treasure, adore, support, foster, nurture, nourish, nurse, sustain **2** cherish a tradition/privilege foster, nurture, sustain, hold dear, value, prize, treasure **3** cherish hopes/memories harbour, shelter, entertain, hold dear, value, prize, treasure

cherub n
angel, seraph

cherubic adj
adorable, appealing, cute, sweet, innocent, lovable, lovely, heavenly, angelic, seraphic

chest n
1 a man with a hairy chest breast, technical sternum, thorax **2** a treasure chest trunk, crate, box, case, casket, coffer, strongbox

chew v
bite, gnaw, munch, champ, chomp, crunch, grind, formal masticate
▷ **chew over** consider, meditate on, mull over, ponder, weigh up, muse on, deliberate upon, formal ruminate on, colloq. put on your thinking cap

chic adj
elegant, fashionable, sophisticated, modish, smart,

stylish, dapper, à la mode, *colloq.* snazzy, trendy
F3 outmoded, unfashionable

chicanery *n*
trickery, deception, fraud, deceitfulness, dishonesty, deviousness, cheating, double-dealing, guile, hoodwinking, duplicity, artifice, intrigue, sharp practice, underhandedness, sophistry, subterfuge, wiles, *colloq.* dodge, jiggery-pokery,

chide *v*
scold, tell off, blame, criticize, censure, lecture, rebuke, reprehend, reprimand, reproach, reprove, *formal* admonish, berate, upbraid, objurgate
F3 praise

chief *adj, n*
► *adj* leading, foremost, uppermost, highest, supreme, grand, arch, head, premier, principal, main, key, central, prime, prevailing, predominant, dominant, pre-eminent, outstanding, vital, most important, essential, primary, major, controlling, directing, supervising
F3 minor, unimportant
► *n* ruler, chieftain, lord, overlord, master, supremo, head, principal, leader, commander, captain, governor, boss, director, manager, premier, prime minister, president, suzerain, chair, chairperson, chairman, chairwoman, chief executive, managing director, superintendent, superior, ringleader, *colloq.* boss, gaffer, top dog, big cheese, big noise, big gun

chiefly *adv*
mainly, mostly, for the most part, in the main, predominantly, principally, primarily, essentially, especially, generally, on the whole, usually

child *n*
youngster, young person, little one, young one, baby, infant, toddler, minor, juvenile, boy, little boy, girl, little girl, son, daughter, adolescent, teenager, youth, young adult, descendant, *formal* offspring, issue, progeny, *colloq.* tot, tiny tot, kid, nipper, brat, sprog

childbirth *n*
labour, delivery, confinement, child-bearing, lying-in, pregnancy, maternity, *technical* parturition, *formal* travail, accouchement, puerperal

childhood *n*
babyhood, infancy, boyhood, girlhood, schooldays, youth, adolescence, minority, immaturity

childish *adj*
babyish, boyish, girlish, infantile, puerile, juvenile, immature, irresponsible, silly, foolish, frivolous
F3 mature, sensible

📝 **childish** or **childlike** ?
You describe someone as *childish* if you think they are behaving in a silly immature way: *Stop being so childish! Childlike* is a neutral term: *childlike innocence.*

---

childlike *adj*
innocent, naïve, ingenuous, artless, guileless, credulous, trusting, trustful, simple, natural

chill *n, v, adj*
► *n* **1** *a wintry chill in the air* coolness, cold, coldness, rawness, bite, nip, crispness, iciness **2** *catch a chill* cold, fever, flu, influenza, virus **3** *a chill ran down my spine* shiver, fear, anxiety, apprehension, dread
F3 **1** warmth
► *v* **1** COOL, cool down, refrigerate, make/become cold(er), freeze, ice **2** FRIGHTEN, terrify, dismay, scare, dishearten, discourage, depress, dampen
F3 **1** warm, heat
▷ **chill out** calm down, relax, have a rest, *colloq.* take it easy
► *adj* cold, cool, raw, sharp, biting, icy, freezing,

wintry, chilly, frigid, depressing, bleak, *colloq.* nippy, parky
F3 warm, hot

chilly *adj*
1 *chilly weather* cold, fresh, brisk, crisp, cool, raw, sharp, biting, icy, freezing, frigid, wintry, *colloq.* nippy, parky **2** *a chilly response* cool, frigid, unsympathetic, unwelcoming, aloof, stony, distant, unresponsive, unfriendly, unenthusiastic, hostile
F3 **1** warm **2** friendly

chime *v*
sound, strike, toll, ring, peal, clang, ding, dong, jingle, tinkle, reverberate, boom, resound, *formal* tintinnabulate
▷ **chime in 1** *chime in when someone is talking* interrupt, *colloq.* chip in, butt in, cut in **2** *his analysis chimed in with mine* fit in, harmonize, correspond, blend, agree, be consistent, be similar

chimera *n*
illusion, fantasy, delusion, dream, fancy, idle fancy, figment of the imagination, hallucination, will-o'-the-wisp, spectre

chimney *n*
shaft, vent, flue, funnel, cleft, crevice, lum, femerall

china *n*
1 *a vase made of china* porcelain, ceramic, pottery, earthenware, terracotta **2** *serve the best china* crockery, plates, dishes, cups and saucers, tableware, dinner service

Chinese calendar *n*

The animals representing the years in which people are born:
rat, buffalo, tiger, rabbit (or hare), dragon, snake, horse, goat (or sheep), monkey, rooster, dog, pig.

---

chink *n*
crack, rift, cleft, fissure, crevice, cut, split, slit, slot, cavity, opening, aperture, gap, space

chip *n, v*
► *n* **1** *fish and chips* fried potato, (French) fry **2** NOTCH, nick, crack, scratch, dent, flaw **3** FRAGMENT, scrap, wafer, splinter, sliver, flake, shred, shard, shaving, paring **4** *gambling chips* counter, disc, token
► *v* chisel, whittle, nick, crack, fragment, break (off), crumble, notch, gash, snick, damage
▷ **chip in 1** CONTRIBUTE, make a donation, donate, club together, have a collection, pay, subscribe, *colloq.* have a whip-round **2** *chip in when someone is talking* interrupt, *formal* interpose, *colloq.* chime in, butt in, cut in

chirp *v & n*
chirrup, tweet, cheep, peep, trill, twitter, warble, sing, pipe, whistle

chirpy *adj*
cheerful, cheery, bright, happy, merry, gay, jaunty, blithe, *colloq.* perky
F3 downcast, sad

chit-chat *n*
chat, chatter, talk, conversation, gossip, idle gossip, tête-à-tête, heart-to-heart, cosy chat, small talk, tittle-tattle, *colloq.* natter, confab, chinwag

chivalrous *adj*
gentlemanly, polite, courteous, well-mannered, gallant, heroic, valiant, brave, courageous, bold, gracious, noble, honourable
F3 ungallant, cowardly

chivalry *n*
gentlemanliness, politeness, courtesy, graciousness, good manners, courtliness, gallantry, bravery, cour-

age, boldness, honour, truthfulness, integrity

chivvy *v*
badger, harass, annoy, hound, goad, nag, urge, pester, plague, pressure, hurry (up), prod, torment, *formal* importune, *colloq.* hassle

choice *n, adj*
▶ *n* **1** *a choice of several dishes; make a choice between two things* selection, variety, range, choosing, opting, picking, preference, decision, election, discrimination **2** *have no choice but to go* option, alternative, answer, solution
▶ *adj* select, best, superior, prime, plum, excellent, first-class, first-rate, fine, exquisite, exclusive, hand-picked, special, prize, valuable, precious
☲ inferior, poor

choke *v*
1 STRANGLE, throttle, asphyxiate, suffocate, stifle, smother, suppress, overpower, overwhelm **2** OB-STRUCT, constrict, congest, clog, block, dam (up), bar, close, stop, plug, *formal* occlude **3** COUGH, gag, retch
▷ **choke back** suppress, restrain, contain, control, check, curb, repress, inhibit, fight back

choleric *adj*
fiery, hot-tempered, angry, bad-tempered, ill-tempered, quick-tempered, testy, touchy, irascible, irritable, petulant, *colloq.* crabbed, crabby, crotchety
☲ calm, placid

choose *v*
1 *choose a new dress* pick (out), select, single out, take, go for, opt for, vote for, decide on, settle on, fix on, designate, adopt, take up, appoint, elect, predestine, *formal* espouse, *colloq.* plump for **2** *choose to do something* decide, prefer, wish, desire, make up your mind, want, favour, see fit

choosy *adj*
selective, discriminating, fussy, particular, finicky, fastidious, exacting, faddy, *colloq.* picky, pernickety
☲ undemanding

chop *v*
cut, hack, fell, hew, lop, saw, sever, truncate, slice, carve, cleave, divide, dissect, split, slash, axe
▷ **chop up** cut (up), cut into pieces, slice (up), divide, cube, dice, shred, mince, grind, grate

choppy *adj*
rough, turbulent, tempestuous, stormy, squally, blustery, ruffled, wavy, uneven, broken
☲ calm, still, peaceful

chore *n*
task, job, errand, routine, duty, burden, piece of work

chortle *v*
cackle, chuckle, guffaw, laugh, crow, snigger, snort

chorus *n*
1 REFRAIN, response, burden, strain, call, shout **2** CHOIR, choristers, singers, vocalists, ensemble, choral group

christen *v*
1 *christen a baby* baptize, name, give a name to, immerse, sprinkle **2** *christened it 'the emerald forest'* name, call, dub, title, style, term, designate **3** *christen the wine glasses* inaugurate, use for the first time, begin using

Christmas *n*
Xmas, Noel, Yule, Yuletide

chronic *adj*
1 *a chronic illness* PERSISTENT, deep-seated, recurring, incessant, constant, continual, long-lasting, long-standing, long-term, ingrained, deep-rooted **2** *a chronic worrier* inveterate, confirmed, habitual,

hardened **3** *the film was chronic* awful, terrible, dreadful, appalling, atrocious
☲ **1** temporary **3** excellent

chronicle *n, v*
▶ *n* account, record, register, annals, archives, diary, calendar, history, journal, narrative, story, saga, epic
▶ *v* recount, narrate, relate, report, tell, write down, set down, record, put on record, register, enter, list

chronicler *n*
historian, archivist, annalist, diarist, narrator, recorder, reporter, scribe, historiographer, chronographer, chronologer

chronological *adj*
consecutive, sequential, in sequence, progressive, ordered, in order, serial, historical

chubby *adj*
plump, fat, podgy, fleshy, flabby, stout, portly, round, full, tubby, paunchy, *formal* rotund
☲ slim, skinny

chuck *v*
1 THROW, cast, toss, fling, heave, hurl, jettison, pitch, shy, sling **2** *chuck a habit/your boyfriend* give up, abandon, reject, discard, get rid of, jilt, *formal* forsake, *colloq.* quit, dump, pack in, give the brush-off, give the elbow

chuckle *v*
laugh, laugh quietly, giggle, titter, snigger, chortle, snort, cackle, crow

chum *n*
friend, companion, comrade, *colloq.* mate, pal, crony, buddy
☲ enemy

chummy *adj*
friendly, affectionate, close, intimate, sociable, *colloq.* matey, pally, thick

chunk *n*
lump, hunk, mass, wedge, block, slab, piece, dollop, portion, *colloq.* wodge

church *n*
1 *go to church* place of worship, chapel, house of God, Lord's house, house of prayer, cathedral, minster, abbey, tabernacle, meeting-house, bethel, kirk, chantry, shrine **2** *the Methodist Church* denomination, tradition, grouping, sect, cult **3** CONGREGATION, assembly, fellowship, community, people of God, body of Christ, bride of Christ

---

Parts of a church or cathedral include:
aisle, almonry, altar, ambulatory, apse, arcade, arch, belfry, bell screen, bell tower, chancel, chapel, choir, clerestory, cloister, confessional, credence, crossing, crypt, fenestella, font, frontal, gallery, keystone, lectern, narthex, nave, parvis, pew, pinnacle, piscina, porch, portal, predella, presbytery, pulpit, reredos, ringing chamber, rood, rood screen, sacristy, sanctuary, sedile, shrine, slype, spire, squint, stall, steeple, stoup, tomb, tower, transept, triforium, vault, vestry.

---

churlish *adj*
bad-tempered, ill-tempered, harsh, impolite, morose, rough, brusque, rude, sullen, surly, uncivil, unmannerly, ill-mannered, ill-bred, discourteous, unneighbourly, unsociable, loutish, boorish, oafish, *colloq.* crabbed
🗲 polite, urbane

churn *v*
1 *my stomach is churning* heave, turn, vomit, be sick, retch, *colloq.* throw up, puke **2** *churn up mud* move about violently, agitate, beat, swirl, toss, writhe, convulse, boil, foam, froth, seethe
▷ **churn out** turn out, produce in great quantities, pump out, throw together, knock up

chute *n*
channel, incline, slide, slope, ramp, runway, shaft, funnel, gutter, trough

cigarette *n*
cigar, menthol, filter-tip, king-size, high-tar, low-tar, roll-up, roll-your-own, smoke, whiff, *colloq.* cig, ciggy, fag, fag end, dog end, gasper, joint, spliff, *slang* cancer-stick, coffin-nail

cinch *n*
colloq. child's play, doddle, piece of cake, snip, stroll, walkover, pushover, like falling off a log

cinders *n*
embers, ashes, clinker, charcoal, coke, slag

cinema *n*
1 FILMS, pictures, movies, *colloq.* or *old use* flicks, *colloq.* big screen, silver screen **2** PICTURE-HOUSE, film theatre, movie theatre, movies, entertainment centre, multiplex, picture-palace, *colloq.* fleapit

cipher *n*
1 CODE, secret system, coded message, cryptogram, cryptograph **2** NONENTITY, nobody, yes-man

circle *n, v*

Types of circle include:
annulus, ball, band, belt, circuit, circumference, coil, compass, cordon, coronet, crown, curl, cycle, disc, discus, eddy, ellipse, epicycle, girdle, globe, gyration, halo, hoop, lap, loop, orb, orbit, oval, perimeter, plate, revolution, ring, rotation, round, saucer, sphere, spiral, turn, tyre, vortex, wheel, whirlpool, whirlwind, wreath.

▶ *n circle of friends* group, band, company, crowd, set, clique, coterie, gang, club, society, assembly, fellowship, fraternity
▶ *v* **1** RING, loop, encircle, surround, belt, gird, encompass, enclose, envelop, hem in, hedge in, *formal* circumscribe, circumnavigate **2** ROTATE, revolve, move round, pivot, gyrate, circulate, whirl, turn, swivel, pivot, coil, wind

circuit *n*
1 *a racing circuit; run a circuit* race track, track, running-track, lap, orbit, revolution, course, route, round, beat, *formal* perambulation **2** *the circuit of the gardens* circumference, boundary, bounds, limit, range, compass, ambit **3** *a judge's circuit* tour, district, area, region

circuitous *adj*
roundabout, indirect, oblique, devious, tortuous, winding, meandering, rambling, *formal* periphrastic, labyrinthine
🗲 direct, straight

circular *adj, n*
▶ *adj* round, annular, ring-shaped, hoop-shaped, disc-shaped, spherical
▶ *n* handbill, leaflet, pamphlet, notice, announcement, advertisement, letter, flyer

circulate *v*
1 *circulate information* spread (around), diffuse, broadcast, transmit, publicize, publish, issue, give out, propagate, pass round, distribute, go/get around, *formal* disseminate, promulgate **2** GO ROUND, rotate, revolve, gyrate, whirl, swirl, flow

circulation *n*
1 BLOOD-FLOW, flow, motion, movement, rotation, circling **2** SPREAD, transmission, publication, readership, distribution, publicity, propagation, *formal* dissemination

circumference *n*
circuit, perimeter, rim, edge, girth, outline, boundary, border, bounds, limits, confines, extremity, margin, verge, fringe, periphery, circuit

circumlocution *n*
diffuseness, discursiveness, tautology, indirectness, euphemism, redundancy, roundaboutness, wordiness, *formal* convolution, periphrasis, pleonasm, verbosity, prolixity

circumlocutory *adj*
diffuse, discursive, tautological, indirect, euphemistic, redundant, roundabout, wordy, *formal* convoluted, periphrastic, pleonastic, verbose, prolix

circumscribe *v*
bound, limit, restrain, restrict, confine, curtail, trim, define, delimit, delineate, demarcate, surround, encircle, enclose, encompass, hem in, pen in

circumspect *adj*
careful, cautious, attentive, deliberate, discreet, guarded, observant, wary, canny, watchful, discriminating, wise, *formal* prudent, sagacious, judicious, vigilant, politic
🗲 unguarded, unwary, reckless

circumspection *n*
care, caution, deliberation, discretion, guardedness, canniness, chariness, wariness, *formal* prudence, vigilance
🗲 recklessness

circumstance *n*
1 *died in mysterious circumstances* condition, fact, factor, situation, position, state, state of affairs, background, environment, arrangement, detail, particular, item, thing, element, event, occurrence, happening, respect, lie of the land, how the land lies **2** *in impoverished circumstances* situation, means, resources, status, financial position, case, lifestyle, plight **3** *a victim of circumstance* fate, fortune, lot

circumstantial *adj*
conjectural, presumed, deduced, contingent, hearsay, incidental, indirect, provisional, inferential, *formal* evidential, presumptive

circumvent *v*
avoid, get round, get out of, get past, evade, bypass, sidestep, steer clear of, thwart, outwit

cistern *n*
tank, reservoir, sink, basin, vat

citadel *n*
fortress, stronghold, bastion, castle, keep, tower, fortification, acropolis

citation *n*
1 AWARD, commendation, honour **2** QUOTATION, quote, cutting, excerpt, illustration, mention, passage, reference, source

cite *v*
quote, mention, refer to, name, specify, allude to, exemplify, give an example, enumerate, advance, bring up, *formal* adduce, evidence

citizen *n*
city-dweller, townsman, townswoman, inhabitant,

denizen, resident, householder, voter, taxpayer, freeman, burgher, subject, urbanite, local, *formal* denizen, oppidan

city *n*
metropolis, town, urban district, conurbation, megalopolis, metropolitan area, inner city, city centre, downtown, concrete jungle, urban sprawl, precinct, ghetto, suburbia, megalopolis, municipality, *colloq.* big smoke

civic *adj*
city, metropolitan, urban, suburban, municipal, borough, local, public, communal, community

civil *adj*
1 *civil affairs* domestic, home, national, internal, interior, state, municipal, civic, public, communal, local, community, secular, civilian **2** POLITE, courteous, well-mannered, mannerly, well-bred, cultivated, courtly, refined, civilized, polished, urbane, affable, respectful, complaisant, obliging, accommodating
F3 **1** international, military, religious **2** uncivil, discourteous, rude

civility *n*
politeness, courteousness, courtesy, breeding, refinement, (good) manners, respect, urbanity, tact, graciousness, affability, pleasantness, amenity, *formal* comity
F3 discourtesy, rudeness, uncouthness

civilization *n*
1 *ancient civilizations* society, human society, culture, community, people **2** *modern western civilization* progress, advancement, development, education, enlightenment, cultivation, refinement, sophistication, urbanity
F3 **2** barbarity, primitiveness

civilize *v*
advance, enlighten, educate, instruct, cultivate, refine, polish, sophisticate, socialize, improve, perfect, tame, humanize

civilized *adj*
1 *a civilized society* advanced, developed, educated, enlightened, cultured, refined, sophisticated, cultivated, urbane, polite, sociable **2** *a polite, civilized manner* reasonable, sensible, polite, cultivated
F3 **1** uncivilized, barbarous, primitive **2** harsh, coarse, unreasonable, unsophisticated

clad *adj*
clothed, wearing, covered, dressed, *formal* attired, *colloq* rigged out

claim *v, n*
▶ *v* **1** MAINTAIN, allege, profess, state, affirm, assert, contend, hold, insist, pretend, profess, *formal* avow, aver, postulate, purport, assume **2** *claim a refund* ask, request, put in for, require, need, demand, exact, take, collect, lay claim to, have a right to, be entitled to, deserve, *formal* requisition **3** *claimed the lives of three people* take, cause, kill
▶ *n* **1** ALLEGATION, pretension, affirmation, assertion, contention, declaration, profession, insistence, *formal* avowal, averment **2** APPLICATION, petition, request, requirement, demand, call, right, privilege, entitlement

claimant *n*
applicant, candidate, petitioner, suppliant, supplicant, litigant, pretendant, pretender

clairvoyance *n*
psychic powers, ESP, extrasensory perception, telepathy, fortune-telling

clairvoyant *adj, n*
▶ *adj* psychic, prophetic, visionary, telepathic, extrasensory

▶ *n* psychic, fortune-teller, prophet, prophetess, visionary, seer, soothsayer, augur, oracle, diviner, telepath

clamber *v*
scramble, claw, climb, scrabble, shin, scale, mount, ascend, *US* shinny

clammy *adj*
damp, moist, sweaty, sweating, sticky, slimy, dank, muggy, heavy, close

clamorous *adj*
noisy, blaring, vociferous, deafening, lusty, riotous, tumultuous, uproarious, vehement, insistent
F3 quiet, silent

clamour *v, n*
▶ *v* demand, ask for noisily, call for, press for, claim, insist, urge
▶ *n* noise, uproar, commotion, shouting, din, racket, blare, agitation, hubbub, outcry, complaints, *formal* vociferation
F3 quietness, silence

clamp *n, v*
▶ *n* vice, grip, press, brace, clasp, bracket, fastener, immobilizer
▶ *v* fasten, secure, fix, clinch, clench, squeeze, press, grip, hold, brace, immobilize
▷ **clamp down on** control, limit, crack down on, come down hard on, restrict, confine, restrain, suppress, stop, put a stop to

clan *n*
1 *the Macleod clan* tribe, family, house, race, line, sept **2** GROUP, circle, society, brotherhood, fraternity, confraternity, sect, faction, band, set, clique, coterie

clandestine *adj*
secret, surreptitious, undercover, underhand, concealed, hidden, covert, fraudulent, sly, sneaky, stealthy, underground, closet, furtive, private, *colloq.* backroom, behind-door, cloak-and-dagger, under-the-counter
F3 open

clang *v & n*
clash, jangle, clank, clink, clunk, clatter, peal, bong, chime, resound, ring, toll

clanger *n*
mistake, error, blunder, inaccuracy, misjudgement, slip, indiscretion, gaffe, *faux pas*, oversight, fault, *formal* solecism, *colloq.* howler, bloomer, boob, booboo, slip-up

clank *v & n*
clang, clash, jangle, clink, clunk, clatter, resound, ring, toll

clannish *adj*
cliquey, cliquish, unfriendly, select, exclusive, insular, narrow, parochial, sectarian
F3 friendly, open

clap *v*
1 APPLAUD, acclaim, cheer, put your hands together for **2** SLAP, smack, strike, pat, bang, *colloq.* wallop, whack

claptrap *n*
rubbish, nonsense, drivel, gibberish, trash, tripe, twaddle, blarney, *colloq.* bunk, bunkum, claptrap, piffle, bilge, poppycock, hot air, cobblers, codswallop, rot, tommyrot

clarification *n*
explanation, simplification, interpretation, exposition, definition, gloss, illumination, *formal* elucidation
F3 *formal* obfuscation

clarify *v*
1 EXPLAIN, make clear, throw light on, simplify, resolve, spell out, clear up, make plain, define, illuminate,

gloss, *formal* elucidate **2** REFINE, purify, filter, clear
F3 1 obscure, confuse **2** cloud

clarity *n*
1 *clarity of thought* lucidity, simplicity, intelligibility, comprehensibility, plainness, explicitness, unambiguousness, obviousness **2** *clarity of the water/her diction* clearness, transparency, precision, sharpness, definition
F3 1 vagueness **2** obscurity, imprecision

clash *v, n*
▶ *v* **1** CRASH, bang, strike, clank, clang, jangle, clatter, rattle, jar **2** CONFLICT, disagree, quarrel, wrangle, grapple, fight, contend, feud, war **3** *two events clash* happen at the same time, coincide, *formal* co-occur **4** *the styles clash* not match, not go with, not go together, look unpleasant, be incompatible, be discordant, jar
F3 4 match, be compatible, harmonize, go well together
▶ *n* **1** CRASH, striking, bang, clank, clang, jangle, clatter, noise **2** *a clash with the police* confrontation, showdown, conflict, disagreement, fight, brush, collision, warring, fighting, feud, quarrel, wrangle

clasp *n, v*
▶ *n* **1** FASTENER, buckle, clip, pin, hasp, hook, fastening, catch **2** HOLD, grip, grasp, embrace, hug, cuddle
▶ *v* **1** HOLD, grip, grasp, clutch, embrace, enfold, hug, squeeze, press, cling to **2** FASTEN, connect, attach, grapple, hook, clip, pin

class *n, v*
▶ *n* **1** *a French class* lesson, period, lecture, seminar, tutorial, workshop, teach-in, course, year, form, grade, study group, set **2** *a social class* social order, social status, status, (social) standing, standing in society, social division, rank, level, (social) background, caste

Social classes/groups include:
aristocracy, nobility, gentry, landed gentry, gentlefolk, elite, *colloq.* nob, high society, *colloq.* top drawer, upper class, ruling class, jet set, middle class, lower class, working class, bourgeoisie, proletariat, hoi-polloi, commoner, serf, plebeian, *colloq.* pleb. *See also* NOBILITY.

3 CATEGORY, classification, group, set, section, division, department, sphere, grouping, order, league, rank, status, caste, quality, grade, type, genre, sort, kind, species, genus, style, *technical* phylum, *formal* denomination **4** *he has class* taste, style, stylishness, elegance, sophistication, distinction
▶ *v* categorize, classify, group, sort, rank, arrange, order, grade, rate, pigeonhole, designate, brand

classic *adj, n*
▶ *adj* **1** *a classic film* first-class, first-rate, outstanding, brilliant, ideal, best, finest, definitive, masterly, excellent, *formal* consummate **2** TYPICAL, prime, representative, characteristic, standard, regular, usual, true, *formal* paradigmatic, quintessential **3** *classic style* traditional, time-honoured, established, archetypal, model, exemplary, ageless, timeless, immortal, undying, lasting, enduring, abiding
F3 1 second-rate **2** unrepresentative
▶ *n* standard, model, prototype, exemplar, masterwork, masterpiece, established work, great, pièce de résistance

classical *adj*
1 *classical style/form* traditional, elegant, refined, excellent, plain, pure, restrained, well-proportioned, symmetrical, harmonious **2** *classical music* serious, traditional, concert, symphonic **3** *classical Greece* an-

cient Greek, Grecian, Hellenic, ancient Roman, Latin, Attic
F3 1 modern

classification *n*
categorization, sorting, classing, grading, grouping, arrangement, systematization, codification, tabulation, cataloguing, *technical* taxonomy

classify *v*
categorize, class, group, pigeonhole, sort, grade, rank, arrange, order, type, distribute, systematize, codify, tabulate, file, catalogue, *formal* dispose

classy *adj*
stylish, elegant, sophisticated, up-market, top-drawer, expensive, exclusive, exquisite, fine, grand, high-class, select, superior, gorgeous, *colloq.* posh, ritzy, swanky, swish
F3 dowdy, plain, unstylish

clatter *n & v*
bang, strike, clank, clunk, clang, jangle, crash, rattle, jar

clause *n*
article, item, part, section, subsection, paragraph, heading, chapter, passage, phrase, condition, proviso, provision, rider, specification, point, loophole

claw *n, v*
▶ *n* talon, nail, pincer, nipper, gripper, *technical* chela, unguis
▶ *v* scratch, scrabble, scrape, graze, tear, rip, lacerate, maul, mangle

clean *adj, adv*
▶ *adj* **1** WASHED, laundered, sterile, aseptic, antiseptic, hygienic, sanitary, sterilized, sterile, cleansed, laundered, decontaminated, purified, pure, unadulterated, fresh, unpolluted, uncontaminated, immaculate, spotless, unspotted, unstained, unsoiled, unsullied, perfect, speckless, spick and span, faultless, flawless, unblemished, *colloq.* clean as a new pin **2** *a clean life* innocent, guiltless, virtuous, pure, good, upright, moral, honest, honourable, righteous, reputable, upstanding, respectable, decent, chaste, *colloq.* squeaky-clean **3** *a clean sheet of paper* blank, new, fresh, unmarked, unused **4** *a clean game* fair, just, according to the rules, even-handed, proper, *colloq.* above board **5** *clean lines* simple, well-defined, clean-cut, smooth, regular, straight, neat, tidy
F3 1 dirty, polluted **2** dishonourable, indecent **4** dirty, rough **5** ragged
▶ *adv* completely, straight, directly, entirely, fully, totally, quite

Ways to clean include:
bath, bathe, bleach, brush, buff, cleanse, clear, comb, decontaminate, deodorize, disinfect, distil, dry-clean, dust, filter, floss, flush, freshen, freshen up, fumigate, groom, Hoover®, launder, mop, muck out, pasteurize, pick, polish, purge, purify, refine, rinse, rub, sandblast, sanitize, scour, scrape, scrub, shampoo, shine, shower, soak, soap, sponge, spring-clean, spruce, spruce up, steep, sterilize, swab, sweep, swill, tidy, vacuum, valet, wash, wipe.

cleaner *n*
char, charlady, charwoman, daily

cleanse *v*
1 *cleanse a wound* disinfect, sterilize, clean, bathe, wash, rinse, *formal* deterge **2** *cleansed from sin/ cleanse your soul* absolve, purify, purge, make free from, clear, *formal* lustrate
F3 1 dirty **2** defile

cleanser *n*
soap, soap powder, detergent, cleaner, solvent, scourer, scouring powder, purifier, disinfectant

clear *adj, v*
▶ *adj* **1** PLAIN, distinct, comprehensible, intelligible, coherent, lucid, explicit, precise, unambiguous, well-defined, apparent, evident, patent, obvious, manifest, conspicuous, unmistakable, unquestionable, explicit, sure, unequivocal, incontrovertible, beyond question, crystal-clear, beyond doubt, certain, positive, definite, convinced **2** *clear thinking* sharp, keen, perceptive, penetrating, quick, sensible, reasonable, logical **3** *clear water* transparent, limpid, crystalline, glassy, translucent, see-through, clean, unclouded, colourless, *formal* pellucid, diaphanous **4** *a clear day* cloudless, unclouded, fine, fair, bright, sunny, light, luminous, undimmed **5** UNOBSTRUCTED, unblocked, open, free, empty, unhindered, unimpeded **6** *a clear conscience* guiltless, innocent, blameless, in the clear, *formal* having no qualms, having/feeling no compunction **7** AUDIBLE, perceptible, pronounced, distinct, recognizable, *colloq.* clear as a bell
🖅 **1** unclear, vague, ambiguous, confusing, unsure **2** muddled **3** opaque, cloudy **4** dull, cloudy, rainy, misty **5** blocked **6** guilty **7** inaudible, indistinct, faint
▶ *v* **1** *clear the dishes/room* remove, take away, empty, unload, vacate, evacuate, move, shift, get rid of, rid, free, clean, fine, filter, tidy, wipe, erase, cleanse, refine, filter **2** UNBLOCK, unclog, unstop, decongest, free, rid, extricate, disentangle, loosen **3** *clear a fence* jump (over), vault, leap over, go over **4** ACQUIT, exonerate, absolve, pardon, vindicate, excuse, justify, free, liberate, release, let go, *formal* exculpate **5** *cleared for publication* permit, give permission, allow, authorize, approve, pass, sanction, *colloq.* give the green light, give the go-ahead **6** *clear £100* earn, take home, net, make a profit, make, gain, bring (in)
🖅 **1** dirty **2** block **4** condemn **5** prohibit
▷ **clear out 1** *been told to clear out* get out, leave, go away, depart, withdraw, *colloq.* beat it, clear off, push off, shove off, hop it, *slang* get lost **2** *clear out a cupboard* tidy (up), empty, sort (out), throw out
▷ **clear up 1** EXPLAIN, clarify, elucidate, unravel, solve, resolve, answer, straighten (out), sort out, iron out, *colloq.* crack **2** TIDY, order, sort, rearrange, put in order, straighten (up), remove **3** *the weather cleared up* clear, become fine, become sunny, stop raining, brighten(up), improve

clearance *n*
1 *clearance of old buildings* demolition, removal, taking-away, emptying, unloading, vacating, evacuation, clearing, moving, shifting, freeing, cleansing **2** AUTHORIZATION, sanction, endorsement, permission, consent, leave, *colloq.* OK, go-ahead, green light, say-so **3** SPACE, gap, room, headroom, margin, allowance

clear-cut *adj*
definite, explicit, well-defined, clear, precise, specific, straightforward, unambiguous, unequivocal, distinct, trenchant, plain, *colloq.* cut and dried
🖅 ambiguous, vague

clearing *n*
space, gap, opening, glade, dell

clearly *adv*
obviously, without doubt, undoubtedly, undeniably, evidently, incontestably, incontrovertibly, indisputably, unmistakably, manifestly, plainly, patently, distinctly, openly, markedly

cleave¹ *v*
cleave the tree in two split, divide, separate, sever, cut, slice, chop, crack, disunite, halve, hew, open, part, pierce, rend, *formal* dissever, sunder
🖅 join, unite

cleave² *v*
cleave to your marriage partner adhere, cling, cohere, hold, stick, remain, attach, unite

cleft *n*
fissure, opening, gap, fracture, breach, break, chasm, chink, crack, cranny, crevice, rent, split

clemency *n*
mercy, mercifulness, pity, compassion, forbearance, forgiveness, generosity, humanity, indulgence, kindness, sympathy, leniency, mildness, moderation, softheartedness, tenderness, *formal* magnanimity
🖅 harshness, ruthlessness

clench *v*
grip, hold, clasp, close (tightly), seal, fasten, shut, clutch, double, grasp, grit

clergy *n*
clergymen, churchmen, clerics, the church, the cloth, ministry, priesthood, holy orders

clergyman *n*
churchman, cleric, ecclesiastic, divine, man of God, man of the cloth, minister, priest, reverend, father, vicar, pastor, padre, parson, rector, canon, dean, deacon, deaconess, chaplain, curate, presbyter, rabbi, imam, muezzin, mullah

clerical *adj*
1 ADMINISTRATIVE, office, secretarial, white-collar, official, filing, typing, keyboarding, *colloq.* pen-pushing **2** ECCLESIASTICAL, pastoral, ministerial, priestly, episcopal, canonical, sacerdotal

Types of clerical vestment include:
alb, amice, biretta, cassock, chasuble, chimer, clerical collar, *colloq.* dog-collar, cope, cotta, cowl, dalmatic, ephod, frock, Geneva bands, Geneva gown, habit, hood, maniple, mantle, mitre, mozzetta, pallium, rochet, scapular, scarf, skullcap, soutane, stole, surplice, tallith, tippet, tunicle, wimple, yarmulka.

clerk *n*
account-keeper, record-keeper, assistant, official, administrative officer, administrator, notary, receptionist, secretary, typist, stenographer, shop-assistant, writer, copyist, protocolist, *colloq.* pen-pusher

clever *adj*
1 *a clever student* intelligent, bright, brilliant, smart, witty, gifted, talented, expert, knowledgeable, smart, apt, able, capable, quick, quick-witted, sharp, sharp-witted, keen, shrewd, knowing, perceptive, discerning, cunning, *formal* sapient, sagacious, *colloq.* brainy **2** *a clever plan* inventive, resourceful, sensible, rational, ingenious, shrewd
🖅 **1** foolish, stupid, senseless, ignorant **2** foolish

cliché *n*
platitude, hackneyed phrase/expression, commonplace, banality, truism, bromide, (old) chestnut, stereotype

click *v, n*
▶ *v* **1** *the machine clicked* clack, clink, snap, snick, snip, tick, beat **2** *it suddenly clicked* (begin to) understand, make sense, fall into place, *colloq.* twig, cotton on
▶ *n* beat, clack, clink, snap, snick, snip, tick

client *n*
customer, patron, regular, buyer, purchaser, shopper, consumer, user, patient, applicant

clientèle *n*
business, clients, customers, following, market,

patronage, patrons, regulars, trade, buyers, purchasers, shoppers, consumers, users

cliff *n*
precipice, overhang, bluff, face, rock-face, scar, scarp, escarpment, crag, tor, promontory

climactic *adj*
decisive, critical, crucial, exciting, paramount
F₃ trivial

climate *n*
1 *a cold climate* weather, weather conditions, temperature **2** *a hostile political climate* atmosphere, feeling, mood, temper, disposition, setting, milieu, environment, ambience, tendency, trend

climax *n*
culmination, height, high point, highlight, acme, zenith, peak, pinnacle, summit, apex, top, head, *formal* apogee
F₃ low point, *formal* nadir

climb *v*
1 *climb the stairs* go up, ascend, scale, shin up, clamber, mount, surmount **2** *climb into the car* move, shift, clamber, scramble **3** *unemployment is climbing* increase, go up, rise, soar, shoot up, top
▷ **climb down** retract, back down, admit that you are wrong, concede, retreat, *colloq.* eat your words

clinch *v*
settle, secure, seal, close, conclude, decide, determine, confirm, verify, *colloq.* land

cling *v*
1 *cling to a branch* clasp, clutch, grasp, grip, hold on to, stick, adhere, cleave, fasten, embrace, hug **2** *cling to old ideas* adhere, stick to, support, hold to, defend, stand by, be faithful to, stay true to

clinic *n*
medical centre, health centre, hospital, infirmary, doctor's, outpatients' department

clinical *adj*
1 *clinical trials of the drug* medical, hospital, patient **2** *a clinical design* simple, plain, austere, stark, basic, unadorned **3** *a clinical attitude* impersonal, analytic, business-like, cold, emotionless, unemotional, unfeeling, detached, disinterested, dispassionate, uninvolved, impassive, objective, scientific
F₃ 2 decorated, ornamented **3** warm, biased, subjective

clip *n, v*
▶ *n* **1** *a paper clip* fastener, staple, pin **2** *a clip from a newspaper* cutting, snippet, quotation, citation, passage, section, excerpt, extract **3** *a clip round the ear* punch, slap, cuff, box, *colloq.* clout, thump, wallop, whack
▶ *v* **1** *clipped the pen to her pocket* pin, staple, fasten, attach, fix, hold **2** *clip a bush* trim, snip, cut, cut short, prune, pare, shear, crop, dock, poll, pollard, truncate, curtail, shorten, abbreviate

clipping *n*
cutting, snippet, quotation, citation, passage, section, excerpt, extract, clip

clique *n*
circle, set, coterie, group, bunch, band, pack, gang, crowd, in-crowd, society, fraternity, faction, clan

cloak *n, v*
▶ *n* **1** *wear a cloak* cape, mantle, robe, wrap, shawl, cope, coat, cover **2** *a cloak of secrecy* coat, cover, shield, mask, front, screen, blind, veil, mantle, shroud, pretext
▶ *v* cover, veil, mask, screen, hide, conceal, obscure, shroud, disguise, shield, camouflage

clock *n, v*
▶ *n*

Types of clock or watch include:
alarm-clock, digital clock, analogue clock, mantel clock, bracket clock, carriage clock, quartz clock, cuckoo-clock, longcase clock, grandfather clock, grandmother clock, travelling clock, speaking clock, *colloq.* Tim; wrist-watch, fob-watch, repeating watch, chronograph, pendant watch, ring-watch, stop-watch; chronometer, sundial.

▶ *v* ▷ **clock up** reach, record, register, archive, attain, chalk up, notch up

clog *v*
block, choke, stop up, bung up, dam (up), congest, jam, obstruct, impede, hinder, hamper, encumber, burden, *formal* occlude
F₃ unblock, free

cloister *n*
walkway, pavement, corridor, aisle, arcade, portico, ambulatory

cloistered *adj*
sheltered, secluded, confined, restricted, enclosed, shielded, withdrawn, insulated, protected, isolated, *formal* reclusive, sequestered, cloistral, hermitic
F₃ open

close¹ *v, n*
▶ *v* **1** SHUT, shut up, fasten, secure, lock (up), bar, bolt, padlock **2** *close a road/bottle* obstruct, block, shut, clog, plug, cork, stop up, fill, seal, *formal* occlude **3** END, bring to an end, draw to an end, finish, complete, conclude, terminate, adjourn, wind up, round off, stop, *formal* cease, discontinue *the shop closes at 6 o'clock* shut, close for the night **5** *the factory closed in March* close down, close permanently, cease operating, cease operations, shut down, go bankrupt, fail, *colloq.* fold, go bust, go to the wall **6** *close a gap* join, unite, fuse, seal, narrow, lessen **7** *close a deal* settle, secure, seal, clinch, conclude, decide, determine, establish, confirm, verify
F₃ 1 open, separate **3** start, begin **4** open, open for business **6** widen
▷ **close in** come nearer, draw near, approach, surround, encircle
▶ *n* end, finish, completion, conclusion, culmination, ending, finale, dénouement, termination, adjournment, winding-up, stop, pause, *formal* cessation
F₃ start, beginning

close² *n*
live in a close courtyard, enclosure, quadrangle, square, place, court, row, terrace, lane, mews, cul-de-sac

close³ *adj*
1 NEAR, close by, nearby, at hand, not far, neighbouring, adjacent, adjoining, in the vicinity, in close proximity, impending, imminent, *colloq.* on your doorstep, in your own backyard, a stone's throw **2** INTIMATE, dear, familiar, attached, inseparable, devoted, loving, close-knit, tight, best, good, bosom **3** *a close resemblance* strong, near, similar, like, comparable, corresponding **4** *a close game* evenly matched, well-matched, hard-fought, *colloq.* neck and neck **5** OPPRESSIVE, heavy, stuffy, fuggy, muggy, humid, sultry, sweltering, airless, stifling, suffocating, unventilated, sticky **6** MISERLY, mean, stingy, niggardly, penny-pinching, *formal* parsimonious, *colloq.* tight **7** SECRETIVE, uncommunicative, unforthcoming, quiet, taciturn, reticent, private, secret, confidential **8** *a close*

translation exact, precise, accurate, strict, literal, faithful, true **9** *pay close attention* fixed, concentrated, thorough, rigorous, painstaking, detailed, methodical, careful, intense, keen, searching **10** DENSE, compact, condensed, solid, packed, crowded, cramped
⊠ 1 far, distant **2** cool, unfriendly, distant **5** fresh, airy, well-ventilated **6** generous **7** open **8** rough, loose

closet *n, adj*
▶ *n* cupboard, wardrobe, storage room
▶ *adj* secret, private, unrevealed, hidden, covert, furtive, underground, surreptitious, undercover
⊠ open, having come out

closure *n*
1 *the closure of the factory* closing-down, permanent closing, shutdown, failure, bankruptcy, *formal* cessation of operations, *colloq.* folding **2** *the closure of the road* obstruction, block, blocking, shutting, stopping-up

clot *n, v*
▶ *n* lump, mass, glob, clump, thrombus, thrombosis, clotting, obstruction, coagulation
▶ *v* coalesce, curdle, coagulate, congeal, thicken, solidify, set, gel

cloth *n*
1 FABRIC, material, stuff, textile, upholstery **2** RAG, face-cloth, flannel, dish-cloth, floorcloth, duster, towel

clothe *v*
dress, put on, robe, deck, outfit, fit out, rig, vest, drape, cover, *formal* attire, apparel, accoutre, habit, invest, bedizen, caparison
⊠ undress, strip, disrobe

clothes *n*
clothing, garments, wear, garb, outfit, dress, costume, wardrobe, vestments, *formal* attire, apparel, raiment, habiliments, vesture, *colloq.* gear, clobber, togs, get-up, hand-me-downs, cast-offs

Clothes include:
suit, trouser suit, dress suit, catsuit, jumpsuit, tracksuit, shell suit, wet suit; dress, frock, evening-dress, shirtwaister, caftan, kimono, sari; skirt, A-line skirt, mini skirt, dirndl, pencil-skirt, pinafore-skirt, divided-skirt, grass skirt, wrapover skirt, culottes, kilt, sarong; cardigan, jumper, jersey, sweater, polo-neck, turtle-neck, guernsey, pullover, twin-set, shirt, dress-shirt, sweat-shirt, tee-shirt, T-shirt, waistcoat, blouse, smock, tabard, tunic; uniform; trousers, jeans, Levis®, 501s®, denims, slacks, cords, flannels, drainpipes, bell-bottoms, dungarees, leggings, pedal-pushers, ski pants, breeches, plus-fours, jodhpurs, Bermuda shorts, hot pants, shorts; lingerie, bra, brassière, body stocking, camisole, liberty bodice, corset, girdle, garter, suspender belt, suspenders, shift, slip, petticoat, teddy, basque, briefs, pants, panties, French knickers, camiknickers, hosiery, pantihose, tights, stockings; underpants, boxer-shorts, Y-fronts, vest, string vest, singlet; swimsuit, bathing-costume, bikini, swimming costume, swimming trunks, leotard, salopettes; nightdress, *colloq.* nightie, pyjamas, bed-jacket, bedsocks, dressing-gown, housecoat, negligee; scarf, glove, mitten, muffler, earmuffs, leg-warmers, sock, tie, bow-tie, necktie, cravat, stole, shawl, belt, braces, cummerbund, veil, yashmak. *See also* CLERICAL; FOOTWEAR; HAT.

cloud *n, v*
▶ *n*

Types of cloud include:
cirrus, cirrostratus, cirrocumulus, altocumulus, altostratus, cumulus, stratocumulus, nimbostratus, fractostratus, fractocumulus, cumulonimbus, stratus.

▶ *v* mist, fog, blur, dull, dim, darken, shade, shadow, overshadow, eclipse, cover, veil, shroud, mantle, obscure, muddle, confuse, *formal* obfuscate
⊠ clear

cloudy *adj*
1 *a cloudy sky* overcast, dull, dark, murky, gloomy, sombre, grey, leaden, heavy, lowering, dim, sunless, hazy, misty, foggy **2** *a cloudy liquid* opaque, milky, muddy **3** *cloudy issues* indistinct, obscure, nebulous, hazy, misty, foggy, blurred, blurry, confused, muddled
⊠ 1 bright, sunny, cloudless **2** clear **3** clear, distinct, plain

clout *v, n*
▶ *v* punch, strike, smack, hit, slap, cuff, box, *colloq.* thump, wallop, whack, *slang* sock, slug
▶ *n* **1** *gave him a clout* punch, strike, smack, hit, slap, cuff, box, *colloq.* thump, wallop, whack, *slang* sock, slug **2** *political clout* influence, weight, authority, power, standing, prestige, *colloq.* pull, muscle

cloven *adj*
divided, split, bisected, cleft
⊠ solid

clown *n, v*
▶ *n* **1** *clowns at a circus* buffoon, comic, comedian, joker, jester, fool, harlequin, pierrot, zany **2** *some clown has parked in front of the gates* fool, idiot, blockhead, imbecile, *colloq.* nincompoop, ninny, nitwit, numskull, twerp, twit, dimwit, *slang* wally, jerk, dipstick, nerd, dork, geek
▶ *v* fool around, act foolishly, act/play the fool, jest, joke, *colloq.* mess around, muck about

cloying *adj*
disgusting, nauseating, sickening, sickly, excessive, choking, oversweet, fulsome
⊠ pleasing, pleasant

club *n, v*
▶ *n* **1** ASSOCIATION, society, organization, group, league, guild, order, union, auxiliary, fraternity, federation, company, brotherhood, set, circle, clique, social club **2** STICK, staff, bat, bludgeon, truncheon, cudgel, mace, *US* blackjack, *colloq.* cosh
▶ *v* hit, strike, beat (up), bash, clout, bludgeon, batter, pummel, *colloq.* clobber, clout, cosh

clue *n*
hint, tip, suggestion, idea, notion, lead, tip-off, pointer, sign, indication, evidence, trace, suspicion, inkling, intimation

clump *n, v*
▶ *n* cluster, bundle, bunch, tuft, thicket, mass, accumulation, collection, lot, group, *formal* agglomeration, agglutination
▶ *v* **1** *clump around* tramp, clomp, stamp, stomp, stumble, plod, trudge, lumber, thump, thud **2** *clump together* group, accumulate, amass, cluster, bunch, bundle

clumsy *adj*
1 *a clumsy person* awkward, unco-ordinated, bungling, ham-fisted, accident-prone, unhandy, heavy-handed, unskilful, inept, blundering, lumbering, gauche, ungainly, ungraceful, wooden, *formal* maladroit, *colloq.* gawky, all thumbs **2** *clumsy objects* awkward, unwieldy, ungainly, heavy, bulky, cumbersome, ill-made, shape-

less **3** *a clumsy attempt to comfort her* insensitive, rude, tactless, awkward, uncouth, rough, crude
F3 1 co-ordinated, skilful, careful, graceful, natural **2** elegant **3** sensitive, tactful

cluster *n, v*
▶ *n* bunch, clump, batch, group, knot, band, mass, crowd, gathering, huddle, collection, assembly, assortment, *technical* inflorescence, raceme, panicle, truss, *formal* assemblage, agglomeration
▶ *v* bunch, group (together), gather, collect, assemble, congregate, come together, flock

clustered *adj*
bunched, gathered, grouped, assembled, massed, *formal* glomerate

clutch *v, n*
▶ *v* hold, get/take hold of, clasp, grip, hang on to, grasp, cling to, clench, seize, snatch, grab, catch, grapple, embrace
▶ *n* **1** *in someone's clutches* control, grasp, grip, power, sway, dominion, possession, hands, keeping, custody, embrace, mercy, claws, jaws **2** *a clutch of eggs* set, setting, group, hatching, incubation

clutter *n, v*
▶ *n* litter, mess, jumble, untidiness, disorder, disarray, muddle, chaos, confusion
▶ *v* litter, encumber, fill (untidily), mess (up), make a mess, make untidy, cover, strew, scatter

coach *n, v*
▶ *n* **1** *travel by coach* express coach, bus, *US* Greyhound, *old use* charabanc, motor-bus, motor-coach **2** *a train of twelve coaches* carriage, car, wagon **3** *a football coach* trainer, instructor, tutor, teacher, educator, mentor **4** *a coach and horses* carriage, wagon, cab, trap, hackney, hansom, gig, landau, brougham
▶ *v* train, drill, instruct, teach, tutor, prime, cram, prepare

coagulate *v*
congeal, thicken, solidify, gel, melt, clot, curdle

coalesce *v*
amalgamate, join (together), blend, mix, unite, combine, consolidate, cohere, fuse, incorporate, integrate, merge, affiliate, *formal* commingle, commix

coalition *n*
alliance, merger, amalgamation, combination, integration, fusion, joining, league, bloc, compact, federation, confederation, confederacy, association, affiliation, union, *formal* conjunction, compact

coarse *adj*
1 ROUGH, unpolished, unfinished, uneven, lumpy, unpurified, unrefined, unprocessed, rugged, hairy, bristly, scaly, prickly **2** *coarse humour* bawdy, ribald, earthy, obscene, smutty, vulgar, crude, offensive, foul-mouthed, boorish, loutish, rude, impolite, ill-mannered, rough, gross, rank, indelicate, improper, indecent, immodest, *colloq.* blue, raunchy
F3 1 smooth, fine **2** refined, sophisticated, polite, clean

coarsen *v*
roughen, thicken, blunt, deaden, desensitize, dull, harden, *formal* indurate
F3 sensitize

coarseness *n*
bawdiness, ribaldry, obscenity, smut, smuttiness, vulgarity, crassitude, crudity, earthiness, indelicacy, offensiveness, indecency, immodesty
F3 delicacy, politeness, sophistication

coast *n, v*
▶ *n* coastline, seaboard, shore, seashore, beach, seaside, strand, foreshore, *formal* littoral
▶ *v* freewheel, glide, slide, sail, cruise, taxi, drift

coat *n, v*
▶ *n*

Types of coat include:
overcoat, greatcoat, redingote, car-coat, duffel coat, fleece, fur coat, Afghan, blanket, frock-coat, tail-coat, jacket, bomber jacket, dinner-jacket, donkey-jacket, hacking-jacket, reefer, pea-jacket, shooting-jacket, safari jacket, Eton jacket, matinee jacket, tuxedo, blazer, raincoat, trench-coat, mackintosh, *colloq.* mac, Burberry, parka, anorak, cagoul, windcheater, jerkin, blouson, cape, cloak, poncho.

1 FUR, hair, fleece, wool, pelt, hide, skin **2** LAYER, coating, covering, cover, overlay, film, blanket, sheet, mantle, glaze, varnish, finish, veneer, laminate, lamination, cladding, *technical* integument, pellicle
▶ *v* cover, paint, spread, layer, smear, daub, apply, put on/over, plaster, pave, cake, encrust

coating *n*
covering, layer, dusting, wash, coat, blanket, sheet, membrane, film, skin, finish, overlay, veneer, glaze, varnish, enamel, lamination, crust, *formal* patina

coax *v*
persuade, cajole, wheedle, get round, talk into, win over/round, flatter, beguile, allure, induce, entice, tempt, prevail upon, *formal* inveigle, *colloq.* sweet-talk, soft-soap

cobble *v*
▷ **cobble together** make/produce roughly, make/produce quickly, improvise, knock up, put together

cock *n, v*
▶ *n* rooster, capon, cockerel, chicken, chanticleer
▶ *v* lift, raise, point, slant, incline, tip

cock-eyed *adj*
1 CROOKED, lopsided, askew, asymmetrical, awry, skew-whiff **2** SENSELESS, absurd, crazy, ludicrous, nonsensical, preposterous, *colloq.* daft, barmy
F3 2 sensible, sober

cocky *adj*
arrogant, self-important, conceited, vain, swollen-headed, egotistical, swaggering, brash, cocksure, self-assured, self-confident, overconfident, bumptious, *formal* hubristic
F3 humble, modest, shy

cocoon *v*
protect, overprotect, isolate, preserve, defend, envelop, cushion, insulate, wrap, cover, cloister

coddle *v*
pamper, pet, spoil, protect, overprotect, mollycoddle, cosset, humour, indulge, baby

code *n*
1 ETHICS, rules, regulations, laws, principles, morals, morality, system, custom, convention, etiquette, manners, practice, conduct **2** *written in code* cipher, secret language, secret writing, secret message, cryptograph, cryptogram, Morse code **3** *a book's code number* numbers, letters, signs, symbols, bar code, postcode, postal code, zip code, dialling code, local code, national code, international code, machine code

coerce *v*
force, use force, drive, compel, constrain, pressurize, pressure, bully, intimidate, browbeat, bludgeon, dragoon, pressgang, *colloq.* bulldoze, strongarm, twist someone's arm, lean on

coercion *n*
force, duress, compulsion, constraint, pressure, bullying, intimidation, threats, direct action, browbeating, duress, strongarm tactics

coffer n
casket, case, box, chest, trunk, safe, strongbox, treasury, moneybox, repository

cogent adj
convincing, compelling, conclusive, potent, powerful, strong, forceful, forcible, influential, weighty, irresistible, persuasive, unanswerable, effective, urgent
▨ weak, ineffective, unsound

cogitate v
think deeply, consider, contemplate, deliberate, meditate, muse, ponder, reflect, mull over, formal ruminate, cerebrate

cognate adj
related, affiliated, associated, connected, kindred, akin, alike, allied, analogous, corresponding, similar, technical agnate, consanguine, congeneric
▨ unrelated, unconnected

cognition n
perception, awareness, consciousness, knowledge, apprehension, learning, discernment, insight, comprehension, understanding, thinking, intelligence, enlightenment, reason, reasoning, rationality

cognizance n
▷ **take cognizance of** acknowledge, regard, recognize, take notice of, become aware of, accept

cognizant adj
aware, conscious, conversant, familiar, informed, knowledgeable, acquainted, versed, witting
▨ unaware

cohabit v
live together, live together as man and wife, live with, sleep together, colloq. live in sin, slang shack up

cohere v
1 STICK, adhere, cling, fuse, unite, bind, combine, coalesce, consolidate **2** the argument does not cohere agree, square, correspond, harmonize, hold, hang together, make sense, add up
▨ separate

coherence n
agreement, harmony, consistency, correspondence, connection, sense, union, unity, formal congruity, consonance, concordance
▨ incoherence

coherent adj
articulate, intelligible, comprehensible, easy to understand, meaningful, lucid, clear, consistent, logical, reasoned, rational, sensible, orderly, systematic, organized, well-structured, well-planned
▨ incoherent, unintelligible, meaningless, disjointed, incomprehensible

cohesion n
union, unity, whole, agreement, harmony, consistency, correspondence, connection, sense

cohort n
1 Roman cohorts troop, division, legion, regiment, squadron, band, brigade, squad, body, column, company, contingent **2** COMPANION, partner, accomplice, assistant, supporter, associate, follower, myrmidon, colloq. mate, buddy, sidekick

coil v, n
▶ v wind, spiral, curl, loop, twist, writhe, snake, wreathe, twine, entwine, formal convolute
▶ n roll, curl, loop, ring, spiral, corkscrew, helix, twist, whorl, formal convolution, volution

coin n, v
▶ n piece, bit, money, cash, change, small change, loose change, silver, copper, formal specie

Types of coin include:
angel, bezant, colloq. bob, copper, crown, dandiprat, denarius, dime, doubloon, ducat, farthing, florin, groat, guilder, guinea, half-crown, half guinea, halfpenny, half sovereign, ha'penny, krugerrand, louis d'or, moidore, napoleon, nickel, noble, obol, penny, pound, colloq. quid, rap, real, sesterce, shilling, sixpence, solidus, sou, sovereign, spade guinea, stater, colloq. tanner, thaler, threepenny bit.

▶ v **1** coin a new word invent, make up, think up, conceive, dream up, devise, formulate, originate, create, fabricate, produce, neologize **2** coin money produce, mint, forge

coincide v
1 the two events coincided happen at the same time, happen together, clash, take place simultaneously, synchronize, formal concur **2** our opinions coincide be the same, agree, correspond, square, tally, accord, harmonize, be consistent with, match, formal concur

coincidence n
1 CHANCE, accident, luck, eventuality, formal fortuity, serendipity, colloq. fluke **2** COEXISTENCE, correspondence, happening at the same time, happening together, clash, clashing, taking place simultaneously, synchronization, formal concurrence, conjunction, correlation

coincidental adj
accidental, chance, casual, unintentional, unplanned, lucky, formal fortuitous, serendipitous, colloq. flukey
▨ deliberate, planned, arranged

coitus n
sexual intercourse, sex, union, copulation, coupling, love-making, marriage-bed, sleeping with someone, going to bed with someone, mating, formal coition

cold adj, n
▶ adj **1** UNHEATED, cool, chilled, ice-cold, chilly, chill, shivery, raw, biting, bitter, fresh, wintry, frigid, frosty, icy, rimy, glacial, arctic, Siberian, polar, freezing, frozen, numbed, keen, old use frore, formal gelid, brumal, brumous, colloq. nippy, parky **2** UNFEELING, unmoved, unsympathetic, unemotional, frigid, unfriendly, distant, remote, aloof, standoffish, reserved, clinical, undemonstrative, unresponsive, passionless, unexcitable, indifferent, lukewarm, stony, callous, insensitive, heartless, uncaring, antagonistic, hostile, formal phlegmatic
▨ **1** hot, warm **2** friendly, responsive, warm
▶ n coldness, chill, chilliness, coolness, frigidity, iciness, rawness, winter, frost, snow, ice
▨ warmth, heat

cold-blooded adj
cruel, inhuman, brutal, savage, barbaric, barbarous, merciless, ruthless, pitiless, callous, unfeeling, heartless
▨ compassionate, merciful

cold-hearted adj
unfeeling, unkind, uncaring, insensitive, unsympathetic, uncompassionate, callous, stony-hearted, cold, heartless, indifferent, detached, flinty, inhuman
▨ warm-hearted

collaborate v
1 WORK TOGETHER, co-operate, join, join forces, work jointly, work as partners, combine forces, team up, associate with, unite, participate **2** collaborate with the enemy conspire, collude, fraternize, betray, turn traitor

collaboration n
1 in collaboration with local industry association,

alliance, partnership, teamwork, co-operation, participation, union, combined/joint/collective effort **2** *collaboration with the enemy* conspiring, collusion, fraternizing

collaborator *n*
1 *collaborators in the research* co-worker, associate, partner, team-mate, colleague, assistant **2** *traitors and collaborators* conspirator, accomplice, traitor, turncoat, betrayer, colluder, fraternizer, quisling, renegade

collapse *v, n*
▶ *v* **1** *the bridge collapsed* fall down, fall in, fall to pieces, come apart, fall apart, sink, founder, disintegrate, crumble, subside, give way, cave in **2** *the business collapsed* fail, founder, break down, fall through, finish, disintegrate, come to an end, come to nothing, slump, *colloq.* fold, flop **3** *collapse with exhaustion* faint, pass out, lose consciousness, black out, keel over, swoon, crumple
▶ *n* **1** *the collapse of the roof* falling-down, falling-in, falling to pieces, coming apart, sinking, foundering, disintegration, subsidence, giving way, cave-in **2** *the collapse of the talks* failure, foundering, breakdown, falling-through, disintegration, downfall, ruin, debacle, *colloq.* flop **3** *his collapse in the street* fainting, passing-out, loss of consciousness, blackout, keeling-over, swoon

collar *n, v*
▶ *n* neckband, ring, dog-collar, gorget, ruff, bertha, rebato, ruche
▶ *v* stop, grab, capture, catch, seize, arrest, apprehend, *colloq.* nab, nick

collate *v*
gather, collect, sort, arrange, order, put in order, organize, compare, compose

collateral *n*
security, guarantee, pledge, surety, assurance, deposit, funds

colleague *n*
workmate, co-worker, team-mate, partner, collaborator, ally, associate, confederate, confrère, comrade, fellow worker, companion, aide, helper, assistant, auxiliary

collect *v*
1 *collect firewood* gather, accumulate, amass, heap, hoard, pile up, stockpile, *formal* aggregate **2** *a crowd collected* gather, form, come together, amass, mass, converge, congregate, assemble, convene, muster, rally **3** *collect them from the station* fetch, pick up, meet, get, call for, come for, go and get, go and take, go and bring **4** *collect for a charity* raise money, ask for money, ask people to give, solicit, acquire **5** *collect stamps* acquire, save, amass, have as a hobby, be interested in **6** *collect your thoughts* compose, gather (together), assemble, prepare
F3 **2** disperse, scatter **3** drop off

collected *adj*
composed, controlled, self-controlled, self-possessed, placid, serene, calm, unruffled, unshaken, unperturbed, imperturbable, poised, cool
F3 anxious, worried, agitated

collection *n*
1 *an art collection; the collection of information* group, cluster, accumulation, gathering, assembly, conglomeration, mass, heap, pile, hoard, stockpile, store, assortment, job-lot, *formal* assemblage **2** *a collection of poems* set, anthology, compilation, collected works **3** *a collection for charity* donation(s), gift(s), contribution(s), subscription, offering, offertory, *colloq.* whip-round

collective *adj, n*
▶ *adj* united, combined, concerted, co-operative, collaborative, joint, common, shared, corporate,

democratic, composite, aggregate, unanimous, cumulative
F3 individual
▶ *n* commune, co-operative, community, kibbutz, kolkhoz, moshav

collective nouns

Collective nouns (by animal) include:
shrewdness of *apes*, cete of *badgers*, sloth of *bears*, swarm of *bees*, obstinacy of *buffalos*, clowder of *cats*, drove of *cattle*, brood of *chickens*, bask of *crocodiles*, murder of *crows*, herd of *deer*, pack of *dogs*, school of *dolphins*, dole of *doves*, team of *ducks*, parade of *elephants*, busyness of *ferrets*, charm of *finches*, shoal of *fish*, skulk of *foxes*, army of *frogs*, gaggle/skein of *geese*, tribe of *goats*, husk of *hares*, cast of *hawks*, brood of *hens*, bloat of *hippopotami*, string of *horses*, pack of *hounds*, troop of *kangaroos*, kindle of *kittens*, exaltation of *larks*, leap of *leopards*, pride of *lions*, swarm of *locusts*, tittering of *magpies*, troop of *monkeys*, watch of *nightingales*, family of *otters*, parliament of *owls*, pandemonium of *parrots*, covey of *partridges*, muster of *peacocks*, muster of *penguins*, nye of *pheasants*, litter of *pigs*, school of *porpoises*, bury of *rabbits*, colony of *rats*, unkindness of *ravens*, crash of *rhinoceroses*, building of *rooks*, pod of *seals*, flock of *sheep*, murmuration of *starlings*, ambush of *tigers*, rafter of *turkeys*, turn of *turtles*, descent of *woodpeckers*, gam of *whales*, rout of *wolves*, zeal of *zebras*.

collector *n*

Names of collectors and enthusiasts include:
zoophile (*animals*), antiquary (*antiques*), tegestollogist (*beer mats*), campanologist (*bell-ringing*), ornithologist (*birds*), bibliophile (*books*), audiophile (*broadcast sound*), lepidopterist (*butterflies*), cartophilist (*cigarette cards*), numismatist (*coins/medals*), conservationist (*countryside*), environmentalist (*the environment*), xenophile (*foreigners*), gourmet (*good food*), gastronome (*good living*), discophile (*gramophone records*), chirographist (*handwriting*), hippophile (*horses*), entomologist (*insects*), phillumenist (*matches/matchboxes*), monarchist (*the monarchy*), deltiologist (*postcards*), arachnologist (*spiders/arachnids*), philatelist (*stamps*), arctophile (*teddy bears*), etymologist (*words*).

college *n*
educational institution, educational establishment, university, *formerly* polytechnic, *formerly* poly, institute, college of further education, technical college, adult education centre, academy, school, seminary

collide *v*
1 *the cars collided* crash (into), meet head on, smash (into), bump (into), run into, go into, plough into, hit, *colloq.* prang **2** *their opinions collided* CLASH, conflict, be in conflict, disagree, quarrel, wrangle, grapple, fight, contend, feud, war

collision *n*
1 *in collision with a lorry* CRASH, impact, bump, smash, accident, pile-up, wreck, disaster, *colloq.* prang **2** *a collision of interests* CLASH, conflict, confrontation, opposition, showdown, disagreement, fight, brush, warring, fighting, feud, quarrel, wrangle

colloquial *adj*
conversational, informal, familiar, everyday, vernacular, casual, idiomatic, chatty, popular, *formal* demotic
🖃 formal

collude *v*
conspire, plot, connive, collaborate, scheme, intrigue, *formal* machinate

collusion *n*
complicity, deceit, conspiracy, plot, connivance, collaboration, league, scheme, scheming, intrigue, artifice, *formal* machination, *colloq.* cahoots

colonist *n*
colonial, settler, immigrant, emigrant, pioneer

colonize *v*
settle, occupy, people, pioneer, found, populate, put down roots

colonnade *n*
arcade, cloisters, portico, covered walk, stoa, *formal* columniation, peristyle

colony *n*
1 *Britain's former colonies* settlement, outpost, dependency, dominion, protectorate, possession, satellite, satellite state, territory, province 2 *a colony of birds* group, association, community, settlement

colossal *adj*
huge, enormous, immense, vast, massive, great, gigantic, mammoth, monstrous, monumental, herculean, gargantuan, *formal* Brobdingnagian, *colloq.* whopping
🖃 tiny, minute

colour *n, v*
▶ *n* 1 HUE, shade, tinge, tone, tincture, tint, dye, paint, wash, pigment, pigmentation, colorant, coloration, complexion

The range of colours includes:
red, crimson, scarlet, vermilion, cherry, cerise, magenta, maroon, burgundy, ruby, orange, tangerine, apricot, coral, salmon, peach, amber, brown, chestnut, mahogany, bronze, auburn, rust, umber, copper, cinnamon, chocolate, tan, sepia, taupe, beige, fawn, yellow, lemon, canary, ochre, saffron, topaz, gold, chartreuse, green, eau de nil, emerald, jade, bottle, avocado, sage, khaki, turquoise, aquamarine, cobalt, blue, sapphire, gentian, indigo, anil, navy, violet, purple, mauve, plum, lavender, lilac, pink, rose, magnolia, cream, ecru, milky, white, grey, silver, charcoal, ebony, jet, black.

2 *the colour of her cheeks* rosiness, ruddiness, pinkness, glow 3 VIVIDNESS, liveliness, life, richness, brilliance, animation 4 *a nation's colours* flag, standard, banner, emblem, ensign, insignia, badge
▶ *v* 1 PAINT, crayon, dye, tint, stain, tinge, wash, highlight 2 BLUSH, flush, redden, go/turn red 3 *colour your judgement* affect, bias, prejudice, influence, sway, distort, slant, pervert, exaggerate, overstate, misrepresent, falsify, taint

colourful *adj*
1 MULTICOLOURED, kaleidoscopic, variegated, many-coloured, parti-coloured, vivid, bright, brilliant, rich, deep, intense, vibrant, gaudy, garish 2 *a colourful description* vivid, graphic, picturesque, animated, lively, stimulating, exciting, interesting, rich, vibrant
🖃 1 colourless, drab

colourless *adj*
1 TRANSPARENT, neutral, uncoloured, monochrome, in black and white, bleached, washed out, faded, pale, ashen, sickly, anaemic, wan 2 INSIPID, lacklustre, dull, dreary, drab, plain, characterless, unmemorable, boring, uninteresting, tame
🖃 1 colourful 2 bright, exciting

column *n*
1 PILLAR, post, shaft, upright, support, pier, obelisk, *technical* asta, caryatid, telamon, Atlas, pilaster 2 *a column of people* line, row, rank, file, procession, queue, string, parade, list 3 *a column in a newspaper* article, item, piece, feature, story

columnist *n*
journalist, reporter, reviewer, writer, correspondent, critic, editor

coma *n*
unconsciousness, hypnosis, insensibility, lethargy, oblivion, stupor, torpor, trance, drowsiness, *technical* catalepsy, sopor, *formal* somnolence

comatose *adj*
unconscious, out, out cold, in a coma, insensible, lethargic, drowsy, sleepy, sluggish, stupefied, stunned, dazed, torpid, *technical* cataleptic, soporose, *formal* somnolent
🖃 conscious

comb *v*
1 *comb your hair* groom, neaten, tidy, arrange, dress, untangle 2 SEARCH, hunt, scour, sweep, sift, screen, rake, rummage, ransack, go through, *colloq.* go over with a fine-tooth comb, turn upside down

combat *n, v*
▶ *n* war, warfare, hostilities, action, battle, fight, fighting, skirmish, struggle, conflict, clash, encounter, engagement, contest, bout, duel
▶ *v* fight, battle, do battle, war, wage war, take up arms, strive, struggle, contend, contest, oppose, resist, withstand, defy

combatant *n*
fighter, warrior, soldier, serviceman, servicewoman, enemy, opponent, adversary, antagonist, belligerent, contender

combative *adj*
aggressive, antagonistic, belligerent, argumentative, contentious, militant, quarrelsome, warlike, *formal* bellicose, pugnacious, truculent
🖃 pacific, peaceful

combination *n*
1 *in combination with other subjects* association, co-operation, conjunction, co-ordination, union, amalgamation, coalition, unification, alliance, federation, confederation, confederacy, combine, consortium, syndicate, merger, integration, synergy 2 BLEND, mix, mixture, composite, cross, amalgam, amalgamation, fusion, coalescence, collection, connection, group, synthesis, compound, solution

combine *v*
merge, amalgamate, bring together, put together, club together, unify, blend, stir, mix, mingle, integrate, incorporate, synthesize, compound, alloy, fuse, bond, bind, weld, join, join forces, connect, link, marry, unite, pool, ally, associate, team up, co-operate, *formal* admix, homogenize
🖃 divide, separate, detach

combustible *adj*
1 *combustible gas* explosive, flammable, incendiary, ignitable, inflammable 2 *a combustible temper* excitable, sensitive, explosive, stormy, tense, volatile, charged
🖃 incombustible, non-flammable, flameproof

combustion *n*
burning, igniting, ignition, firing

come v

1 *they came to me* advance, move towards, travel towards, move forward, approach, near, draw near **2** *come to the river/party* reach, attain, arrive, enter, get here, appear, put in an appearance, attend, materialize, *colloq.* turn up, show up, surface, burst in, barge in **3** *come to power* reach, attain, achieve, gain, secure, pass into **4** *the time for action has come* arrive, occur, take place, happen, come about, present itself, come to pass, transpire **5** *she comes from Belgium* originate, be, be a native of, be ... by birth, have as your home, hail, have as its source/origin **6** *his arrogance comes from his insecurity* result from, be caused by, follow, issue, develop, arise, stem, evolve **7** *it may come to war* pass into, become, turn, evolve into, develop into, enter, go as far as **8** *the idea came to me* think of, remember, strike, occur to, come to the mind of, dawn on

Ⓕ **1** go **2** depart, leave **3** fall from **8** forget

▷ **come about** happen, occur, come to pass, take place, result, arise, transpire, *formal* befall

▷ **come across** find (by chance), discover, meet by chance, stumble across, encounter, notice, *formal* chance upon, happen upon, *colloq.* run into, bump into

▷ **come along** progress, make progress, develop, get better, improve, show an improvement, make headway, advance, rally, mend, recover, recuperate

▷ **come apart** collapse, disintegrate, fall to bits/pieces, break (up), separate, split, tear, crumble

▷ **come between** separate, part, divide, split up, disunite, alienate, cause a rift between, *formal* estrange

▷ **come by** acquire, get, get hold of, obtain, secure, come into someone's possession, fall into someone's hands, *formal* procure

▷ **come clean** acknowledge, admit, confess, own up, reveal, tell all, *colloq.* make a clean breast of something, spill the beans

▷ **come down** decrease, fall, drop, reduce, descend, decline, deteriorate, worsen, degenerate

▷ **come down on** blame, criticize, rebuke, reprimand, find fault with, chide, reprove, upbraid, reprehend, admonish, *formal* berate, *colloq.* slate, tear into

▷ **come down to** mean, be tantamount to, be equivalent to, correspond to, amount to, boil down to

▷ **come down with** catch, fall ill with, get, develop, go down with, pick up, become infected with, become ill with, *formal* contract, succumb to

▷ **come forward** offer (yourself), offer your services, volunteer, step forward

▷ **come in** enter, appear, arrive, finish, receive, *colloq.* show up

Ⓕ go out

▷ **come in for** receive, get, suffer, endure, bear, undergo, experience, be subjected to

▷ **come into** inherit, be left, have bequeathed to you, acquire, receive

▷ **come off** succeed, be successful, be effective, go well, work (out), happen, occur, take place, end up

▷ **come on** begin, appear, advance, proceed, progress, make progress, develop, improve, show an improvement, get better, thrive, succeed, rally, mend, recover, recuperate

▷ **come out 1** *the magazine comes out monthly* be published, appear, be produced, become available, become known **2** *everything came out all right in the end* result, end (up), finish, conclude, terminate **3** *gay people coming out* come out of the closet, declare yourself to be, declare openly, admit, be outed by someone

▷ **come out with** say, state, affirm, declare, exclaim, disclose, divulge, exclaim, blurt out

▷ **come round 1** *come around from the anaesthetic* recover, recover/regain consciousness, wake, awake **2** YIELD, change your mind, agree, be converted to, be persuaded, be won over, relent, concede, allow, grant, accede

Ⓕ **1** pass out

▷ **come through** endure, withstand, survive, prevail, triumph, succeed, accomplish, achieve

▷ **come to 1** *come to after the operation* recover, recover/regain consciousness, wake, awake **2** *come to a total* add up to, total, aggregate, amount to, make, equal, run to

▷ **come up** rise, arise, happen, occur, present itself, crop up, turn up

▷ **come up to** reach, meet, match up to, measure up to, live up to, make the grade, compare with, approach, bear comparison with

▷ **come up with** suggest, put forward, propose, offer, present, think of, dream up, conceive, advance, produce, submit

comeback n

return, reappearance, resurgence, revival, recovery, rally

comedian n

comic, clown, humorist, funny man, funny woman, stand-up, entertainer, wit, joker, *colloq.* wag, gagster

comedown n

anticlimax, let-down, disappointment, deflation, blow, reverse, reversal, decline, descent, demotion, humiliation, degradation

comedy n

1 *comedy on TV* farce, entertainment, pantomime, burlesque, vaudeville, slapstick, satire, situation comedy, sitcom **2** *the comedy of the situation* humour, hilarity, funniness, drollery, clowning, wit, joking, jesting, facetiousness

Ⓕ **1** tragedy

comely adj

attractive, beautiful, pretty, lovely, good-looking, blooming, bonny, buxom, fair, graceful, pleasing, winsome, *formal* pulchritudinous

come-on n

encouragement, inducement, enticement, lure, allurement, temptation

come-uppance n

deserts, just deserts, what you deserve, dues, merit, punishment, rebuke, chastening, recompense, requital, retribution

comfort n, v

▶ n **1** EASE, relaxation, luxury, plenty, snugness, cosiness, well-being, satisfaction, contentment, enjoyment, freedom from pain, freedom from worry/unhappiness, freedom from difficulties, *formal* repose, opulence **2** CONSOLATION, compensation, cheer, reassurance, encouragement, condolence, alleviation, relief, help, aid, support, *formal* solace, succour

Ⓕ **1** discomfort **2** distress

▶ v ease, soothe, relieve, alleviate, assuage, console, cheer, gladden, reassure, hearten, encourage, help, support, sympathize, empathize, invigorate, strengthen, enliven, refresh, *formal* bring solace to, succour

comfortable adj

1 SNUG, cosy, relaxing, restful, easy, convenient, pleasant, agreeable, enjoyable, delightful, *colloq.* comfy **2** *comfortable clothes* well-fitting, loose-fitting, roomy **3** AFFLUENT, well-off, well-to-do, without financial problems, pleasant, prosperous, luxurious, *formal* opulent **4** *not feel comfortable talking about it* relaxed, at ease, unembarrassed, confident, happy, contented, safe

Ⓕ **1** uncomfortable, unpleasant **2** uncomfortable, tight **3** poor **4** uneasy, nervous, offended, awkward, embarrassed, threatened

comforting *adj*
soothing, reassuring, encouraging, heartening, heart-warming, helpful, cheering, consolatory, consoling, encouraging, *formal* inspiriting
🔁 worrying

comic *adj, n*
▶ *adj* funny, hilarious, side-splitting, comical, droll, humorous, witty, amusing, entertaining, diverting, joking, facetious, jocular, light, farcical, ridiculous, ludicrous, absurd, laughable, zany, *colloq.* priceless, rich
🔁 tragic, serious
▶ *n* comedian, clown, humorist, funny man, funny woman, stand-up, entertainer, wit, joker, buffoon, *colloq.* wag, gagster

comical *adj*
funny, hilarious, droll, humorous, witty, amusing, entertaining, diverting, laughable, farcical, absurd, ridiculous, ludicrous
🔁 sad, unamusing

coming *adj, n*
▶ *adj* 1 *in the coming months* next, forthcoming, upcoming, impending, imminent, due, approaching, advancing, near, nearing, future 2 *the coming man* aspiring, promising, rising, up-and-coming
▶ *n* advent, approach, arrival, nearing, birth, dawn, accession

command *v, n*
▶ *v* 1 ORDER, bid, give orders to, charge, enjoin, direct, instruct, require, demand, compel, *formal* adjure 2 LEAD, head, rule, reign, govern, control, have charge/command/control of, direct, dominate, manage, superintend, supervise, preside over 3 *command respect* be given, gain, receive, get, obtain, secure
▶ *n* 1 COMMANDMENT, decree, edict, precept, mandate, order, bidding, charge, injunction, dictate, directive, direction, instruction, requirement, *formal* behest 2 *be in command* power, authority, leadership, control, charge, domination, dominion, mastery, rule, sway, government, ascendancy, management, supervision, superintendence

commandeer *v*
seize, take possession of, confiscate, impound, hijack, usurp, *formal* appropriate, requisition, expropriate, arrogate, sequester, sequestrate

commander *n*
leader, head, chief, director, commander-in-chief, general, admiral, captain, commanding officer, officer, *colloq.* boss

commanding *adj*
1 *in a commanding lead* powerful, strong, superior, advantageous, dominant, dominating, controlling, directing 2 *a commanding personality* authoritative, forceful, powerful, assertive, confident, autocratic, *formal* peremptory 3 *the castle's commanding position* dominating, imposing, impressive, lofty

commemorate *v*
celebrate, solemnize, remember, mark, honour, pay tribute to, salute, immortalize, observe, keep, recognize, *formal* memorialize

commemoration *n*
celebration, observance, remembrance, memory, tribute, honour, honouring, ceremony, salute, recognition, dedication

commemorative *adj*
memorial, celebratory, remembering, marking, honouring, saluting, dedicatory, in memory of, in memoriam, in remembrance of, in honour of, as a tribute to, in recognition of

commence *v*
begin, make a beginning, start, make a start, embark on, originate, initiate, inaugurate, open, launch, go ahead
🔁 finish, end, *formal* cease

commend *v*
1 PRAISE, compliment, acclaim, extol, applaud, speak highly of, *formal* laud, eulogize 2 *commend this book* recommend, suggest, approve, propose, advocate, put in a good word for 3 COMMIT, entrust, trust, confide, consign, hand over, give, deliver, yield
🔁 1 criticize, censure

commendable *adj*
admirable, excellent, noble, praiseworthy, worthy, creditable, exemplary, deserving, estimable, *formal* laudable, meritorious
🔁 blameworthy, poor

commendation *n*
praise, acclaim, acclamation, accolade, applause, high/good opinion, good word, approval, credit, recognition, encouragement, recommendation, special mention, *formal* approbation, encomium, panegyric
🔁 blame, criticism

commensurate *adj*
proportionate, equivalent, corresponding, comparable, in proportion to, according to, corresponding to, consistent with, appropriate to, compatible with, acceptable, adequate, sufficient, due, fitting

comment *v, n*
▶ *v* remark, give an opinion, observe, note, mention, say, point out, explain, interpret, *formal* interpose, interject, elucidate, opine
▶ *n* opinion, statement, remark, observation, view, note, annotation, footnote, marginal note, explanation, illustration, exposition, commentary, criticism, *formal* elucidation

commentary *n*
1 *a commentary on a football match* narration, voice-over, analysis, description, report, account, review 2 *a Bible commentary* explanation, interpretation, analysis, notes, annotation, treatise, critique, *formal* elucidation, exegesis, exposition

commentator *n*
1 *a sports commentator* broadcaster, reporter, correspondent, sportscaster, newscaster, narrator, commenter 2 *a commentator on the text* annotator, interpreter, critic, *formal* expositor, exegete

commerce *n*
trade, business, industry, private enterprise, buying and selling, dealings, relations, dealing, traffic, trafficking, exchange, marketing, merchandising

commercial *adj, n*
▶ *adj* 1 *buildings for commercial use* trade, trading, business, industrial 2 *a commercial success* profitable, profit-making, sellable, saleable, popular, monetary, financial, entrepreneurial, profit-orientated, materialistic, mercenary, venal
▶ *n* advertisement, publicity, promotion, marketing, jingle, display, blurb, announcement, notice, poster, bill, placard, leaflet, handbill, circular, handout, propaganda, *colloq.* advert, ad, plug, hype

commiserate *v*
express/offer sympathy, send/offer condolences, sympathize, comfort, understand, console, show consideration

commiseration *n*
pity, sympathy, compassion, consolation, comfort, consideration, understanding, condolence, *formal* solace

commission *n, v*
▶ *n* 1 ASSIGNMENT, mission, errand, task, job, duty, function, appointment, employment, mandate, work,

piece of work, warrant, authority, charge, trust, responsibility **2** COMMITTEE, board, delegation, council, advisory group/body, deputation, representative **3** *commission on a sale* percentage, share, royalty, allowance, fee, brokerage, compensation, *colloq.* cut, rake-off

▶ *v* nominate, select, appoint, arrange, contract, engage, employ, assign, authorize, empower, delegate, depute, send, order, place/put in an order for, request, ask for, mandate

commit *v*
1 *commit a crime* do, carry out, get up to, indulge in, perform, execute, enact, *formal* effect, perpetrate **2** ENTRUST, trust, confide, commend, consign, deliver, hand over, give, assign, deposit **3** *commit yourself to do something* promise, pledge, bind, engage, decide, dedicate, bind, covenant, cross the Rubicon, *formal* obligate

commitment *n*
1 *show commitment* DEDICATION, involvement, adherence, devotion, allegiance, loyalty, hard work, effort **2** *too many commitments* DUTY, responsibility, undertaking, obligation, engagement, liability, tie **3** *make a commitment* UNDERTAKING, guarantee, assurance, promise, word, covenant, pledge, vow
F∃ **1** vacillation, wavering

committed *adj*
active, dedicated, devoted, loyal, involved, enthusiastic, zealous, fervent, red-hot, hardworking, diligent, industrious, studious, *colloq.* card-carrying, *formal* engagé
F∃ apathetic, uncommitted

commodious *adj*
roomy, spacious, large, ample, comfortable, expansive, extensive, *formal* capacious
F∃ cramped

commodity *n*
product, thing, article, item, goods, merchandise, output, produce, stock, wares

common *adj*
1 *a common name* frequent, familiar, customary, habitual, usual, daily, everyday, routine, regular, *colloq.* two a penny **2** *have a common belief* mutual, shared, joint, collective **3** *common land* communal, community, public **4** *common knowledge* widespread, prevalent, general, universal, conventional, accepted, popular, commonplace **5** *the common cold* ordinary, standard, average, plain, simple, workaday, run-of-the-mill, undistinguished, unexceptional **6** VULGAR, coarse, unrefined, crude, inferior, low, ill-bred, uncouth, loutish, plebeian, *colloq.* common as muck
F∃ **1** uncommon, unusual, rare, noteworthy **5** different, special **6** tasteful, refined

commonly *adv*
generally, normally, usually, typically, routinely, as a rule, for the most part
F∃ rarely

commonplace *adj*
ordinary, unexceptional, everyday, common, routine, humdrum, pedestrian, banal, trite, widespread, frequent, hackneyed, stock, stale, obvious, worn out, boring, uninteresting, threadbare, mundane
F∃ memorable, exceptional

common sense *n*
good sense, sense, sensibleness, level-headedness, sanity, soundness, reason, pragmatism, hardheadedness, realism, experience, discernment, wisdom, shrewdness, astuteness, judgement, native intelligence, practicality, *formal* prudence, judiciousness, *colloq.* gumption, nous, savvy
F∃ folly, stupidity

common-sense *adj*
commonsensical, matter-of-fact, sensible, level-headed, sane, sound, reasonable, practical, down-to-earth, pragmatic, hard-headed, realistic, experienced, wise, discerning, shrewd, astute, *formal* prudent, judicious
F∃ foolish, unreasonable, unrealistic

commonwealth *n*

Members of the Commonwealth are:
Antigua and Barbuda, Australia, the Bahamas, Bangladesh, Barbados, Belize, Botswana, Brunei, Canada, Cyprus, Dominica, the Gambia, Ghana, Grenada, Guyana, India, Jamaica, Kenya, Kiribati, Lesotho, Malawi, Malaysia, the Maldives, Malta, Mauritius, Namibia, Nauru, New Zealand, Nigeria, Pakistan, Papua New Guinea, St Christopher and Nevis, St Lucia, St Vincent and the Grenadines, Seychelles, Sierra Leone, Singapore, Solomon Islands, South Africa, Sri Lanka, Swaziland, Tanzania, Tonga, Trinidad and Tobago, Tuvalu, Uganda, United Kingdom, Vanuatu, Western Samoa, Zambia, Zimbabwe.

commotion *n*
agitation, hurly-burly, turmoil, tumult, excitement, ferment, fuss, bustle, ado, uproar, furore, racket, hubbub, rumpus, row, clamour, fracas, upheaval, disturbance, confusion, disorder, disquiet, riot, stir, *colloq.* ballyhoo, hullabaloo, to-do, brouhaha, bust-up

communal *adj*
public, community, shared, joint, collective, general, common
F∃ private, personal

commune *n, v*
▶ *n* collective, co-operative, kibbutz, community, fellowship, colony, settlement
▶ *v* converse, discourse, communicate, make contact, feel/get close to, feel/get in touch, relate spiritually

communicable *adj*
infectious, contagious, transmittable, transmissible, transferable, conveyable, catching, spreadable, *formal* infective

communicate *v*
1 ANNOUNCE, impart, inform, acquaint, intimate, notify, publish, broadcast, relay, spread, diffuse, pass on, transmit, convey, declare, proclaim, make known, report, reveal, disclose, divulge, unfold, express, *formal* disseminate **2** TALK, speak, converse, commune, correspond, write, phone, telephone, contact, get/be in touch, keep the lines open

communication *n*
information, intelligence, intimation, disclosure, contact, connection, transmission, *formal* dissemination

Forms of communication include:
media, mass media, broadcasting, radio, wireless, television, TV, cable TV, satellite, subscription TV, pay TV, pay-per-view, video, video-on-demand, teletext; telecommunications, data communication, information technology (IT); the Internet, the net, World Wide Web; newspaper, press, news, newsflash, magazine, journal, advertising, publicity, poster, leaflet, pamphlet, brochure, catalogue; post, dispatch, correspondence, letter, postcard, aerogram, e-mail, telegram, Telemessage®, cable, *colloq.* wire, chain letter, junk mail, mailshot;

conversation, word, message, dialogue, speech, gossip, *colloq.* grapevine; notice, bulletin, announcement, communiqué, circular, memo, note, report, statement, press release; telephone, intercom, answering machine, walkie-talkie, bleeper, tannoy, telex, teleprinter, facsimile, fax, computer, word processor, typewriter, dictaphone, megaphone, loud-hailer; radar, Morse code, semaphore, Braille, sign language. *See also* TELEPHONE.

communicative *adj*
talkative, voluble, expansive, informative, chatty, sociable, friendly, forthcoming, outgoing, extrovert, unreserved, free, open, frank, candid
F3 quiet, reserved, reticent, secretive

communion *n*
1 *communion with nature* sharing thoughts, sharing feelings, communing, closeness, sympathy, empathy, togetherness, unity, harmony, fellowship, participation, rapport, affinity, *formal* accord, concord, intercourse 2 *Holy Communion* Lord's Supper, Eucharist, Mass, Sacrament

communiqué *n*
announcement, bulletin, (official) communication, dispatch, message, report, statement, newsflash

communism *n*
collectivism, sovietism, revisionism, socialism, totalitarianism, Bolshevism, Leninism, Marxism, Stalinism, Trotskyism, Maoism,Titoism

community *n*
1 *the local community* district, locality, neighbourhood, population, people, populace, public, residents 2 *the Bangladeshi community* population, people, populace, public, residents, nation, state, section, group, colony, fellowship, brotherhood, fraternity 3 *a religious community* commune, kibbutz, society, association, fellowship, brotherhood, sisterhood, fraternity

commute *v*
1 *commute by train* travel to work, travel to and from, journey, shuttle 2 *commute the death sentence* REDUCE, decrease, shorten, curtail, lighten, soften, mitigate, remit, adjust, modify

commuter *n*
traveller, passenger, *colloq.* strap-hanger, suburbanite

compact¹ *adj, v*
▶ *adj a compact book* small, neat, short, brief, terse, succinct, concise, pithy, condensed, pocket, little, compressed, pressed together, close, dense, impenetrable, solid, firm
F3 large, rambling, diffuse
▶ *v* compress, press down, press together, condense, consolidate, pack down, cram, flatten, ram, squeeze, tamp

compact² *n*
the compact between the nations agreement, alliance, pact, treaty, arrangement, transaction, deal, settlement, bargain, understanding, bond, indenture, concordat, contract, covenant, entente

companion *n*
fellow, comrade, friend, intimate, confidant(e), ally, confederate, colleague, associate, partner, consort, escort, chaperon(e), attendant, aide, assistant, accomplice, follower, *colloq.* mate, pal, buddy, crony, sidekick

companionable *adj*
friendly, affable, sympathetic, familiar, genial, amiable, congenial, convivial, sociable, extrovert, out-going, approachable, gregarious, informal, neighbourly
F3 unfriendly

companionship *n*
fellowship, comradeship, camaraderie, *esprit de corps*, support, friendship, company, togetherness, conviviality, association, social intercourse, intimacy, sympathy, rapport

company *n*
1 *a manufacturing company* firm, business, business organization, concern, association, corporation, establishment, house, partnership, syndicate, cartel, trust, consortium, conglomerate, multinational, holding company, subsidiary, public limited company (PLC or plc), private limited company, limited company, limited liability company 2 TROUPE, group, band, ensemble, set, circle, crowd, throng, body, troop, crew, party, assembly, gathering, community, society, team 3 GUESTS, visitors, callers 4 *be glad of company* friendship, companionship, support, togetherness, fellowship, comradeship, conviviality, attendance, contact, presence

comparable *adj*
similar, like, alike, related, akin, corresponding, analogous, equivalent, tantamount, proportional, proportionate, commensurate, parallel, equal, *formal* cognate
F3 dissimilar, unlike, unequal

> **comparable** or **comparative** ?
> *Comparable* means 'of the same kind, to the same degree, etc': *cheaper than any comparable hotel.* *Comparative* means 'judged by comparing with something else': *After they had stopped playing so noisily there was a period of comparative silence.*

comparative *adj*
relative, by/in comparison

compare *v*
1 *compare the new edition with the old one* contrast, juxtapose, balance, weigh, measure, note the differences between, correlate 2 *compare her to an angel* liken, equate, link, correlate, regard as the same, show the similarities between, draw analogies with, draw a parallel between, *formal* analogize 3 *not compare with his predecessor* resemble, match, equal, parallel, bear comparison, be comparable to, be as good as, match, *colloq.* hold a candle to

comparison *n*
juxtaposition, analogy, parallel, correlation, relationship, likeness, resemblance, similarity, comparability, contrast, differences, differentiation, distinction

compartment *n*
section, division, subdivision, part, category, pigeonhole, cubbyhole, niche, alcove, bay, area, stall, booth, cubicle, locker, partition, carrel, cell, chamber, berth, carriage

compass *n*
limit(s), range, scope, stretch, space, extent, sphere, area, reach, field, realm(s), boundary, bounds, circle, circuit, circumference, enclosure, round, scale, zone

compassion *n*
kindness, gentleness, tenderness, tender-heartedness, fellow-feeling, humanity, mercy, pity, leniency, sympathy, commiseration, condolence, sorrow, benevolence, consideration, concern, care, understanding
F3 cruelty, indifference

compassionate *adj*
kind-hearted, kindly, tender-hearted, tender, gentle, caring, warm-hearted, benevolent, humanitarian, hu-

mane, merciful, clement, lenient, pitying, sympathetic, understanding, supportive
F̶ cruel, indifferent

compatible *adj*
harmonious, in harmony, consistent, matching, suitable, suited, reconcilable, adaptable, conformable, sympathetic, having rapport, like-minded, well-matched, well-suited, similar, *formal* congruous, congruent, accordant, consonant
F̶ incompatible, antagonistic, contradictory

compatriot *n*
fellow citizen, fellow national, countryman, fellow countryman, countrywoman, fellow countrywoman

compel *v*
force, make, constrain, oblige, necessitate, drive, urge, impel, insist on, coerce, pressure, pressurize, hustle, browbeat, bully, intimidate, press-gang, dragoon, *colloq.* bulldoze, strongarm, twist someone's arm, lean on, put the screws on

compelling *adj*
1 *a compelling story* fascinating, gripping, riveting, enthralling, spellbinding, absorbing, mesmeric, irresistible, compulsive, *colloq.* unputdownable **2** *compelling reasons* forceful, imperative, urgent, pressing, overriding, powerful, cogent, persuasive, convincing, weighty, conclusive, incontrovertible, irrefutable
F̶ **1** boring **2** weak, unconvincing

compendium *n*
companion, handbook, manual, digest, summary, synopsis, vade-mecum

compensate *v*
1 *compensate you for any loss* repay, refund, reimburse, indemnify, recompense, reward, remunerate **2** *compensate for doing wrong* make amends, make reparation, make good, make up for, restore, requite, atone, redeem, redress, satisfy **3** COUNTERACT, balance, counterbalance, cancel, neutralize, nullify, offset, *formal* countervail, counterpoise

compensation *n*
1 *pay compensation* recompense, reward, payment, remuneration, requital, repayment, refund, reimbursement, indemnification, indemnity, damages, reparation, return **2** *make compensation for wrongdoing* amends, redress, satisfaction, restoration, restitution, atonement, consolation, comfort

compère *n*
host, link person, presenter, master of ceremonies, MC, emcee, announcer, anchorman, anchorwoman

compete *v*
1 *compete against/with other firms* vie, contest, contend, fight, battle, struggle, strive, oppose, challenge, pit yourself, rival, jostle **2** *compete in a contest* contend, participate, enter, run, race, take part, go in for

competence *n*
ability, proficiency, capability, aptitude, capacity, skill, technique, experience, expertise, facility, fitness
F̶ incompetence

competent *adj*
1 *competent to deal with them* capable, able, adept, efficient, trained, qualified, well-qualified, skilled, skilful, accomplished, experienced, proficient, expert, masterly, equal **2** *competent work* satisfactory, acceptable, reasonable, passable, respectable, adequate, sufficient, fit, suitable, appropriate
F̶ **1** incompetent, incapable, unable, inefficient **2** excellent, outstanding

competition *n*
1 CONTEST, championship, tournament, cup, event, race, match, game, quiz, bout, meet **2** RIVALRY, opposition, challenge, contest, contention, conflict, struggle, strife, vying, competitiveness, combativeness **3** COMPETITORS, rivals, opponents, opposition, challengers, field

competitive *adj*
combative, contentious, antagonistic, aggressive, ambitious, keen, *colloq.* pushy, cut-throat, dog-eat-dog

competitiveness *n*
combativeness, contentiousness, antagonism, assertiveness, challenge, aggression, aggressiveness, rivalry, ambitious, ambitiousness, keenness, *formal* pugnacity, *colloq.* pushiness, rat race, survival of the fittest
F̶ backwardness, sluggishness

competitor *n*
contestant, contender, entrant, candidate, participant, challenger, player, opponent, adversary, antagonist, rival, emulator, competition, opposition

compilation *n*
composition, collection, accumulation, collation, anthology, selection, organization, arrangement, thesaurus, treasury, album, compendium, miscellany, omnibus, potpourri, corpus, opus, work, *formal* assemblage, amassment, collectanea, florilegium, chrestomathy

compile *v*
compose, put together, collect, gather, garner, cull, accumulate, amass, assemble, collate, marshal, organize, arrange

complacency *n*
smugness, self-satisfaction, gloating, triumph, pleasure, pride, self-righteousness, serenity, self-assurance, gratification, contentment, satisfaction
F̶ diffidence, discontent

complacent *adj*
smug, self-satisfied, gloating, triumphant, proud, self-righteous, unconcerned, serene, self-assured, pleased, gratified, contented, satisfied
F̶ diffident, concerned, discontented

✍ complacent or **complaisant**?

Complacent means 'smugly pleased with yourself or your own abilities': *One of the dangers of success is that you can become complacent. Complaisant* means 'being cheerfully willing to do what others want': *Franca's complaisant kindness was too much for him.*

---

complain *v*
1 *complain to the manager; always complaining* criticize, find fault, file/lodge a complaint, take something up with someone, kick up a fuss, object, protest, air your grievances, grumble, carp, fuss, lament, bemoan, bewail, moan, nag, whine, groan, growl, *formal* remonstrate, expostulate, repine, *colloq.* beef, belly-ache, grouse, gripe, bleat, whinge, have a bone to pick **2** *complain of an illness* suffer from, endure, be in pain, feel pain, hurt, ache

complainer *n*
grumbler, moaner, niggler, *colloq.* belly-acher, fusspot, grouser, nit-picker, whiner, whinger

complaint *n*
1 PROTEST, objection, grumble, moan, grievance, dissatisfaction, annoyance, fault-finding, criticism, carping, censure, accusation, charge, reproof, *colloq.* beefing, belly-aching, grouse, gripe, bleating, whingeing **2** *a chest complaint* ailment, illness, sickness, disease, disorder, trouble, upset, condition, *formal* indisposition, affliction, malady, malaise

complaisant *adj*
agreeable, amenable, amiable, accommodating, obli-

ging, solicitous, biddable, compliant, deferential, conciliatory, docile, obedient, conformable, *formal* tractable
F3 obstinate, perverse

 complaisant or **complacent**? *See panel at*
COMPLACENT.

complement *n, v*
▶ *n* **1** *wine as a complement to the dinner* companion, counterpart, addition, accessory, completion, *formal* consummation **2** *the ship's complement* allowance, quota, total, totality, aggregate, sum, capacity, entirety
▶ *v* go well with, go well together, combine well with, match, set off, contrast, round off, complete, crown

 complement, compliment or **supplement**?
One thing is a *complement* to another when it makes a pleasant contrast or makes the combination of the two things pleasantly balanced: *Yoghurt can be used as a complement to spicy dishes.* You pay someone a *compliment* when you praise them. A *supplement* is something added to something else that is already complete or to make up for a deficiency: *a magazine supplement; take vitamin supplements.*

complementary *adj*
finishing, completing, perfecting, reciprocal, interdependent, correlative, interrelated, corresponding, matching, twin, fellow, companion,
F3 contradictory, incompatible

 complementary, complimentary or **supplementary**?
Two things are *complementary* if they complement each other: *use complementary colours in all the furnishings.* You say something *complimentary* to someone as an expression of admiration or praise to them; a *complimentary* ticket is one given free of charge. You use *supplementary* to describe something that is added: *ask a supplementary question.*

complete *adj, v*
▶ *adj* **1** ENTIRE, integral, whole, full, unbroken, undivided, total, intact, plenary, unabbreviated, unabridged, unshortened, unedited, unexpurgated, detailed, comprehensive, exhaustive **2** FINISHED, ended, completed, concluded, over, done, accomplished, finalized, settled, achieved, *formal* terminated **3** UTTER, total, absolute, outright, downright, out-and-out, thorough, unqualified, unmitigated, unconditional, perfect
F3 **1** abridged **2** incomplete **3** partial
▶ *v* **1** *complete the work* finish, end, close, conclude, finalize, settle, perform, discharge, execute, fulfil, realize, accomplish, achieve, make up, crown, cap, round off, wind up, perfect, *formal* terminate, consummate, *colloq.* polish off, clinch **2** *complete a form* fill in, fill out, answer

completely *adv*
totally, utterly, wholly, fully, in full, absolutely, perfectly, quite, thoroughly, through and through, altogether, entirely, solidly, *colloq.* in every respect, lock stock and barrel, from first to last, root and branch, every inch, heart and soul, hook line and sinker

completion *n*
finish, end, close, conclusion, finalization, settlement, discharge, execution, fulfilment, realization, accomplishment, achievement, attainment, fruition, culmination, perfection, *formal* termination, consummation

complex *adj, n*
▶ *adj* complicated, intricate, elaborate, involved, difficult, circuitous, tortuous, devious, mixed, varied, diverse, multiple, composite, compound, ramified, *formal* convoluted, Byzantine
F3 simple, easy
▶ *n* **1** NETWORK, structure, system, scheme, composite, organization, establishment, institute, development, *formal* aggregation **2** FIXATION, obsession, preoccupation, phobia, disorder, neurosis, *colloq.* hang-up, thing

complexion *n*
1 SKIN, colour, colouring, tone, pigmentation **2** LOOK, appearance, aspect, attitude, guise, light, character, nature, cast, type, stamp, kind

complexity *n*
complication, intricacy, elaboration, involvement, circuitousness, tortuousness, deviousness, multifariousness, multiplicity, variety, diverseness, compositeness, entanglement, ramification, repercussion, *formal* convolution
F3 simplicity

compliance *n*
obedience, submissiveness, submission, agreement, assent, conformability, deference, passivity, yielding, *formal* acquiescence, complaisance, concurrence
F3 defiance, disobedience

compliant *adj*
obedient, submissive, subservient, pliable, accommodating, agreeable, biddable, conformable, deferential, passive, docile, yielding, indulgent, *formal* acquiescent, complaisant, tractable
F3 disobedient, intractable

complicate *v*
compound, elaborate, make difficult, involve, make involved, muddle, mix up, confuse, jumble, tangle, entangle
F3 simplify

complicated *adj*
complex, intricate, elaborate, involved, tortuous, difficult, puzzling, perplexing, problematic, cryptic, *formal* convoluted, *colloq.* fiddly
F3 simple, easy

complication *n*
difficulty, problem, drawback, snag, obstacle, problem, ramification, repercussion, complexity, intricacy, elaboration, convolution, tangle, web, confusion, mixture

complicity *n*
collusion, collaboration, connivance, involvement, agreement, approval, knowledge, *formal* concurrence, abetment
F3 ignorance, innocence

compliment *n, v*
▶ *n* **1** *pay someone a compliment* flattery, flattering remark, admiration, favour, approval, congratulations, tribute, honour, accolade, bouquet, commendation, praise, *formal* eulogy, homage, felicitation, encomium, laudation **2** *sends his compliments* greetings, regards, best wishes, congratulations, remembrances, respects, *formal* salutation, devoirs
F3 **1** insult, criticism
▶ *v* flatter, admire, commend, speak highly/well of, praise, extol, congratulate, applaud, salute, *formal* felicitate, laud, eulogize
F3 insult, condemn

 compliment, complement or **supplement**?
See panel at COMPLEMENT.

complimentary *adj*
1 FLATTERING, admiring, favourable, approving, appreciative, congratulatory, commendatory, *formal* eulogistic, panegyrical **2** *complimentary ticket* free, gratis, honorary, courtesy, *colloq.* on the house
F₃ 1 insulting, unflattering, critical

> **complimentary** or **complementary**? *See panel at* COMPLEMENTARY.

comply *v*
agree, consent, assent, yield, submit, defer, respect, observe, obey, abide by, conform, follow, perform, discharge, fulfil, satisfy, meet, oblige, accommodate, *formal* acquiesce, accord, accede
F₃ defy, disobey

component *n, adj*
▶ *n* part, constituent, constituent part, integral part, ingredient, element, factor, item, unit, piece, section, module, bit, spare part
▶ *adj* constituent, integral, essential, basic, intrinsic, inherent

comport *v*
acquit, conduct, carry, bear, act, behave, perform, *formal* demean, deport

compose *v*
1 *the board is composed of four directors* MAKE UP, constitute, form, comprise **2** CREATE, write, arrange, produce, make (up), think of/up, devise, form, fashion, build, construct, frame, invent, concoct, put together, assemble **3** CALM, calm down, soothe, quiet, collect, still, settle, steady, tranquillize, quell, assuage, pacify, control

composed *adj*
calm, calmed down, tranquil, quite, quietened down, serene, relaxed, unworried, unruffled, level-headed, cool, collected, cool and collected, self-possessed, controlled, self-controlled, confident, imperturbable, placid, sedate, at ease, *colloq.* unflappable, cool as a cucumber
F₃ agitated, worried, troubled

composer *n*
musician, arranger, songwriter, songsmith, tunesmith, author, writer, creator, maker, originator, producer, poet, bard

composite *adj, n*
▶ *adj* compound, conglomerate, complex, blended, combined, fused, mixed, patchwork, synthesized, *formal* heterogeneous, agglutinate
F₃ homogeneous, uniform
▶ *n* compound, conglomerate, blend, combination, alloy, amalgam, fusion, mixture, synthesis, pastiche, patchwork, *formal* agglutination

composition *n*
1 CONSTITUTION, make-up, combination, mixture, form, structure, configuration, layout, arrangement, organization, character, harmony, consonance, balance, symmetry, *formal* conformation **2** *a musical composition* creation, work, work of art, opus, piece, arrangement, adaptation, accompaniment, symphony, opera, study, exercise, poem, picture, painting, drawing, story, novel **3** MAKING, production, formation, creation, invention, arranging, devising, putting together, concoction, design, formulation, writing, compilation, proportion

compost *n*
fertilizer, humus, mulch, manure, peat, dressing

composure *n*
calm, tranquillity, serenity, ease, coolness, self-possession, self-control, level-headedness, confidence, assurance, self-assurance, poise, dignity,

imperturbability, placidity, equanimity, dispassion, impassivity, *formal* aplomb
F₃ agitation, nervousness, discomposure

compound¹ *n, adj, v*
▶ *n* *a chemical compound* blend, mixture, medley, hybrid, composite, amalgam, alloy, synthesis, fusion, composition, amalgamation, combination, conglomerate, *technical* admixture
▶ *adj* composite, blended, combined, fused, mixed, synthesized, multiple, complex, complicated, intricate, conglomerate
▶ *v* **1** COMBINE, put together, amalgamate, unite, fuse, coalesce, synthesize, alloy, blend, mix, mingle, intermingle **2** WORSEN, exacerbate, aggravate, make matters worse, complicate, intensify, heighten, magnify, add to, increase, *formal* augment, *colloq.* add insult to injury

compound² *n*
a prison compound enclosure, yard, pen, fold, pound, paddock, stockade, corral, court

comprehend *v*
1 UNDERSTAND, conceive, see, grasp, make sense of, fathom, penetrate, realize, appreciate, know, apprehend, perceive, discern, take in, assimilate, *colloq.* tumble to, twig **2** INCLUDE, comprise, take in, encompass, involve, contain, embrace, cover
F₃ 1 misunderstand

comprehensible *adj*
understandable, easy to understand, intelligible, graspable, discernible, conceivable, coherent, explicit, clear, lucid, plain, simple, accessible, straightforward
F₃ incomprehensible, obscure

comprehension *n*
understanding, conception, grasp, realization, appreciation, knowledge, apprehension, perception, discernment, judgement, sense, insight, intelligence, *colloq.* ken
F₃ incomprehension, unawareness

comprehensive *adj*
thorough, exhaustive, full, complete, encyclopedic, compendious, broad, wide, widespread, extensive, sweeping, general, blanket, inclusive, overall, all-inclusive, all-embracing, across-the-board
F₃ partial, incomplete, selective

compress *v*
1 *compress petrol and air* press, squeeze, crush, squash, flatten, jam, wedge, cram, tamp, stuff, compact, condense, constrict, consolidate, impact, pressurize, concentrate **2** *compress an article* abridge, condense, contract, telescope, shorten, abbreviate, reduce, summarize, synopsize, *old use* astrict, *formal* coarctate
F₃ 2 expand, diffuse

comprise *v*
1 *the flat comprises three rooms* consist of, be composed of, include, contain, take in, incorporate, embody, involve, encompass, cover, *formal* comprehend, embrace **2** *the countries that comprise Great Britain* make up, constitute, compose, form

compromise *v, n*
▶ *v* **1** NEGOTIATE, bargain, arbitrate, settle, agree, concede, make concessions, meet halfway, come to/reach an understanding, give and take, adapt, adjust **2** *compromise your principles* weaken, undermine, expose, endanger, imperil, jeopardize, risk, prejudice **3** DISHONOUR, discredit, shame, bring shame to, bring into disrepute, damage, embarrass, involve, implicate
▶ *n* settlement, agreement, concession, negotiation, mediation, understanding, bargain, deal, trade-off,

co-operation, accommodation, adjustment, give-and-take, balance
▢ disagreement, intransigence

compulsion n
1 *use compulsion to obtain something* force, coercion, duress, constraint, obligation, pressure, demand, insistence 2 *feel a compulsion to do something* urge, drive, impulse, desire, longing, need, necessity, temptation, obsession, preoccupation

compulsive adj
1 IRRESISTIBLE, overwhelming, overpowering, uncontrollable, obsessive, compelling, driving, besetting, urgent 2 *a compulsive gambler* obsessive, habitual, addicted, dependent, hardened, incorrigible, irredeemable, incurable, hopeless, *colloq.* pathological, hooked 3 *compulsive viewing* compelling, fascinating, gripping, riveting, enthralling, spellbinding, absorbing, mesmeric, irresistible

compulsory adj
obligatory, mandatory, imperative, forced, set, stipulated, binding, contractual, essential, necessary, required, requisite, *de rigueur*
▢ optional, voluntary, discretionary

compunction n
remorse, regret, repentance, penitence, shame, contrition, sorrow, qualm, misgiving, guilt, reluctance, hesitation, unease, uneasiness
▢ callousness, defiance

compute v
calculate, count (up), sum, tally, add up, total, enumerate, reckon, estimate, assess, evaluate, figure, measure, rate

computer n

Computer terms include :

mainframe, microcomputer, minicomputer, PC (personal computer), Applemac®; hardware, CPU (central processing unit), Pentium® processor, disk drive, joystick, keyboard, lap-top, light pen, microprocessor, modem, monitor, mouse, mouse mat, notebook computer, printer, bubblejet printer, daisywheel printer, dot-matrix printer, ink-jet printer, laser printer, screen, VDU (visual display unit); software, program, Windows®, WordPerfect®, Wordstar®, disk, magnetic disk, floppy disk, hard disk, optical disk, magnetic tape; programming language, BASIC, COBOL, FORTRAN; memory, backing storage, external memory, immediate access memory, internal memory, RAM (Random Access Memory), ROM (Read Only Memory), multimedia, CD-ROM (Compact Disc Read Only Memory); access, ASCII, backup, bit, boot, buffer, byte, kilobyte, megabyte, character, chip, silicon chip, printed circuit board, motherboard, computer game, computer graphics, computer literate, computer simulation, computer terminal, cursor, icon, graphical user interface (GUI), data, databank, database, default, desktop publishing (DTP), digitizer, directory, DOS (disk operating system), electronic mail, e-mail, the Internet, the net, World Wide Web, JANET®, format, function, grammar checker, graphics, hacking, hypertext, interface, macro, menu, MSDOS (Microsoft® disk operating system), network, peripheral, pixel, scrolling, spellchecker, spreadsheet, template, toggle, toolbar, user-friendly, user interface, video game, virtual reality (VR), virus, window, word-processing, work station, WYSIWYG (what you see is what you get).

comrade n
fellow, companion, friend, intimate, confidant(e), ally, confederate, colleague, associate, partner, consort, escort, chaperon(e), attendant, aide, assistant, accomplice, follower, *colloq.* mate, pal, buddy, crony, sidekick

con v, n
▶ v trick, cheat, hoax, dupe, deceive, mislead, hoodwink, double-cross, swindle, defraud, rook, *formal* inveigle, *colloq.* rip off, fleece, do, bamboozle
▶ n confidence trick, trick, bluff, deception, swindle, cheating, fraud, racket, *colloq.* fiddle, scam

concatenation n
sequence, series, course, progress, progression, succession, string, chain, connection, interlinking, interlocking, linking, nexus, thread, trail, procession, train

concave adj
hollow, hollowed, curved in, bending inwards, cupped, scooped, excavated, sunken, indented, depressed, *formal* incurvate, incurved
▢ convex

conceal v
1 *conceal a body* hide, obscure, disguise, camouflage, mask, screen, veil, cloak, shroud, cover, bury, submerge, keep hidden, keep out of sight, tuck away, *formal* secrete, *colloq.* stash 2 *conceal a secret* hide, keep dark, keep secret, keep quiet, suppress, *formal* - dissemble, *colloq.* cover up, hush up, sweep under the carpet, put the lid on, whitewash
▢ 1 uncover 2 reveal, disclose

concealed adj
hidden, covered, screened, unseen, covert, disguised, inconspicuous, latent, tucked away
▢ clear, plain

concealment n
1 *concealment of guns* hideaway, hideout, hiding, disguise, camouflage, mask, protection, screen, veil, shroud, cloak, cover, secrecy, shelter, *formal* secretion 2 *concealment of information* hiding, suppression, keeping dark, secrecy, *colloq.* cover-up, whitewash, smokescreen
▢ 1 uncovering 2 openness, revelation

concede v
1 ADMIT, confess, acknowledge, recognize, own (up), grant, allow, accept, *formal* accede 2 YIELD, give up, surrender, relinquish, forfeit, sacrifice, hand over, *formal* cede
▢ 1 deny

conceit n
conceitedness, pride, arrogance, vanity, haughtiness, immodesty, boastfulness, swagger, egotism, self-love, narcissism, self-importance, self-admiration, superciliousness, cockiness, self-satisfaction, complacency, *formal* vainglory
▢ modesty, diffidence

conceited adj
vain, proud, arrogant, haughty, boastful, swollen-headed, immodest, egotistical, narcissistic, self-important, full of yourself, puffed up, supercilious, self-satisfied, complacent, smug, *formal* vainglorious, *colloq.* cocky, big-headed, stuck-up, toffee-nosed, too big for your boots
▢ modest, self-effacing, diffident, humble

conceivable adj
imaginable, credible, believable, thinkable, tenable, possible, likely, probable
▢ inconceivable, unimaginable

conceive v
1 IMAGINE, envisage, visualize, see, picture, grasp, understand, perceive, apprehend, comprehend, realize, appreciate, believe, think, fancy, suppose

2 INVENT, design, devise, formulate, think of/up, come up with, create, originate, form, contrive, produce, develop **3** *conceive a baby* become pregnant, become fertilized, be fertile, become impregnated, become inseminated, reproduce, give birth to

concentrate *v, n*
▶ *v* **1** FOCUS, converge, centre, centralize, rivet, consolidate, cluster, crowd, congregate, gather, collect, accumulate, amass **2** APPLY YOURSELF, think, give your (undivided) attention, pay/devote attention, attend, put/keep your mind, consider, mind **3** CONDENSE, evaporate, boil down, reduce, compress, distil, thicken, intensify
☞ **1** disperse **3** dilute
▶ *n* essence, extract, distillation, juice, *technical* apozem, decoction, decocture, *formal* quintessence, elixir

concentrated *adj*
1 *concentrated liquid* condensed, evaporated, reduced, thickened, compressed, dense, rich, strong, undiluted **2** INTENSE, intensive, all-out, concerted, vigorous, hard, deep
☞ **1** diluted **2** half-hearted

concentration *n*
1 ATTENTION, deep/close thought, heed, absorption, application, mind, devotion, single-mindedness, engrossment, intensity **2** CONVERGENCE, centralization, focusing, cluster, crowd, grouping, collection, congregation, accumulation, consolidation, conglomeration, *formal* agglomeration **3** COMPRESSION, evaporation, boiling-down, distillation, reduction, consolidation, denseness, thickness
☞ **1** distraction **2** dispersal **3** dilution

concept *n*
idea, notion, plan, theory, hypothesis, thought, abstraction, conception, conceptualization, visualization, image, view, picture, impression

conception *n*
1 CONCEPT, idea, notion, thought, plan, theory, hypothesis, image, view, picture, impression **2** KNOWLEDGE, understanding, appreciation, perception, visualization, image, picture, impression, idea, inkling, clue **3** INVENTION, design, birth, beginning, origin, origination, outset, initiation, inauguration, formation, launching **4** *from conception to birth* impregnation, insemination, fertilization, pregnancy, reproduction, sexual intercourse, *formal* fecundation

concern *v, n*
▶ *v* **1** WORRY, distress, trouble, disturb, bother, upset, alarm, make worried, make anxious, prey on your mind, *formal* perturb **2** *concern yourself with their problems* give your attention to, involve, interest, busy, devote, affect, touch **3** BE ABOUT, relate to, refer to, regard, deal with, be connected with, have to do with, involve, apply to, bear on, *formal* appertain to, pertain to
▶ *n* **1** *a cause for concern* anxiety, worry, unease, disquiet, care, sorrow, distress, apprehension, disturbance, strain, pressure, anguish, *formal* perturbation **2** REGARD, consideration, attention, attentiveness, care, heed, thought **3** *it's not my concern* duty, responsibility, charge, job, task, field, business, affair, matter, problem, interest, involvement **4** COMPANY, firm, business, corporation, association, establishment, enterprise, organization, partnership, syndicate
☞ **1** joy **2** indifference

concerned *adj*
1 ANXIOUS, worried, uneasy, apprehensive, upset, unhappy, distressed, troubled, disturbed, bothered, *formal* perturbed **2** *concerned teachers* attentive, caring, considerate, kind, thoughtful, helpful, charitable,

unselfish, altruistic, gracious, sensitive **3** CONNECTED, related, implicated, interested, involved, affected
☞ **1** unconcerned, indifferent, apathetic **2** inconsiderate, thoughtless, selfish

concerning *prep*
about, regarding, with regard to, as regards, respecting, with respect to, with reference to, referring to, relating to, relevant to, in the matter of, on the subject of, re, *formal* apropos

concert *n*
1 *a musical concert* performance, entertainment, presentation, production, show, recital, appearance, engagement, rendering, rendition, gig, jam session, prom, soirée **2** *work in concert with others* agreement, harmony, unanimity, union, unison, *formal* accord, concord, concordance, consonance
☞ **2** disunity

concerted *adj*
combined, united, joint, collective, co-operative, shared, collaborative, co-ordinated, interactive, organized, concentrated, prearranged, planned
☞ separate, unco-ordinated, disorganized

concession *n*
1 YIELDING, giving-up, surrender, relinquishment, forfeit, sacrifice, handover, admission, acknowledgement, recognition, grant, allowance, compromise, adjustment, acceptance, *formal* ceding, *colloq.* sop **2** *tax concessions* reduction, decrease, cut, (special) right, (special) privilege, favour, grant, allowance, exception, *colloq.* bending of the rules

conciliate *v*
reconcile, pacify, placate, appease, restore harmony to, satisfy, soften, soothe, disarm, disembitter, mollify, propitiate
☞ antagonize

conciliation *n*
reconciliation, peacemaking, pacification, placation, appeasement, mollification, propitiation
☞ alienation, antagonization

conciliator *n*
reconciler, mediator, negotiator, peacemaker, intermediary, intercessor, dove
☞ troublemaker

conciliatory *adj*
reconciliatory, peacemaking, peaceable, appeasing, disarming, mollifying, pacific, assuaging, *formal* irenic, pacificatory, placatory, propitiative, propitiatory
☞ antagonistic

concise *adj*
short, brief, terse, succinct, pithy, crisp, compendious, compact, compressed, condensed, abridged, abbreviated, summary, to the point, *formal* synoptic, epigrammatic
☞ diffuse, wordy

conclave *n*
assembly, (secret) meeting, council, conference, session cabinet, cabal, *formal* confabulation, *colloq.* powwow, parley

conclude *v*
1 END, bring/come/draw to an end, close, finish, complete, culminate, *formal* consummate, cease, terminate, discontinue, *colloq.* wind up, polish off **2** INFER, deduce, come to the conclusion, assume, surmise, reason, gather, suppose, reckon, judge, decide, *formal* conjecture **3** SETTLE, resolve, close, decide, establish, determine, negotiate, accomplish, agree, arrange, work out, *formal* effect, *colloq.* wrap up, pull off, clinch
☞ **1** begin, start, commence

conclusion n
1 INFERENCE, deduction, assumption, opinion, conviction, judgement, verdict, decision, resolution, settlement, result, consequence, outcome, upshot, issue, answer, solution **2** END, close, finish, completion, culmination, finale, *formal* consummation, cessation, termination, discontinuance **3** SETTLING, resolution, decision, establishment, determination, negotiation, accomplishment, agreement, arrangement, working-out, *formal* effecting, *colloq.* pulling-off, clinching

conclusive adj
final, ultimate, definitive, decisive, clear, convincing, definite, undeniable, irrefutable, indisputable, incontrovertible, unarguable, unanswerable
🔁 inconclusive, questionable

concoct v
1 *concoct a meal* put together, mix, prepare, make, develop, blend, cook (up), brew, *colloq.* rustle up **2** *concoct a story* fabricate, invent, devise, contrive, formulate, plan, plot, hatch, *formal* decoct, *colloq.* cook up

concoction n
brew, potion, preparation, mixture, blend, combination, compound, creation

concomitant adj, n
▶ *adj* complementary, accompanying, associative, attendant, co-existent, coincidental, incidental, simultaneous, synchronous, concurrent, contributing, *formal* contemporaneous, conterminous, syndromic
🔁 accidental, unrelated
▶ *n* accompaniment, by-product, incidental, secondary, symptom, side effect, *formal* epiphenomenon

concord n
harmony, accord, agreement, friendship, entente, consensus, unanimity, unison, amicability, peace, compact, treaty, rapport, *formal* amity, consonance
🔁 discord

concourse n
1 *the station concourse* hall, entrance, foyer, lobby, lounge, piazza, plaza **2** *a concourse of people* gathering, multitude, crowd, swarm, throng, assembly, collection, meeting, crush, press

concrete adj
1 *concrete objects* real, actual, solid, physical, material, substantial, tangible, touchable, perceptible, visible **2** *concrete evidence* firm, definite, positive, specific, explicit, genuine, factual, solid
🔁 **2** abstract, vague

concubine n
mistress, kept woman, paramour, lover, courtesan

concupiscence n
appetite, desire, libido, lasciviousness, lechery, lewdness, lust, lustfulness, *formal* libidinousness, lubricity, *colloq.* randiness, horniness

concupiscent adj
lascivious, lecherous, lewd, lustful, *formal* libidinous, lubricious, *colloq.* randy, horny

concur v
agree, approve, comply, consent, co-operate, harmonize, be in harmony, *formal* accede, assent, accord, acquiesce
🔁 disagree

concurrence n
1 *concurrence on the decision* agreement, association, convergence, common ground, acceptance, approval, *formal* assent, acquiescence **2** *the concurrence of the two events* coincidence, coexistence, synchrony, *formal* contemporaneity, juxtaposition, simultaneity
🔁 **1** difference, disagreement

concurrent adj
simultaneous, synchronous, contemporaneous, coinciding, coincident, concomitant, coexisting, coexistent

condemn v
1 *condemn his actions* disapprove, criticize, reproach, blame, revile, deplore, denounce, *formal* reprehend, reprove, deprecate, berate, upbraid, castigate, disparage, censure, *colloq.* slam, slate **2** *condemn a prisoner* sentence, give/pass a sentence, punish, convict, judge, damn **3** *condemned to a life of poverty* doom, compel, coerce, force, consign, ordain **4** *condemn a building* declare unsafe, declare unfit, demolish, destroy, bar, ban
🔁 **1** praise, approve **2** acquit, pardon

condemnation n
disapproval, criticism, reproof, reproach, blame, denunciation, damnation, conviction, sentence, judgement, *formal* castigation, censure, deprecation, disparagement, *colloq.* thumbs-down
🔁 praise, approval

condemnatory adj
critical, disapproving, discouraging, incriminating, unfavourable, accusatory, accusing, damnatory, *formal* censorious, denunciatory, deprecatory, proscriptive, reprobative, reprobatory
🔁 approving, complimentary, indulgent, *formal* laudatory

condensation n
1 *condensation of liquid* distillation, liquefaction, precipitation, concentration, evaporation, reduction, boiling-down, consolidation, *technical* deliquescence **2** ABRIDGEMENT, précis, synopsis, digest, contraction, compression, curtailment

condense v
1 *condense a book* shorten, cut (down), curtail, abbreviate, abridge, précis, summarize, encapsulate, contract, compress, compact **2** DISTIL, precipitate, concentrate, evaporate, reduce, thicken, solidify, coagulate, compress, boil down, intensify, *technical* deliquesce
🔁 **1** expand **2** dilute

condensed adj
1 *a condensed book* shortened, cut (down), curtailed, abridged, abbreviated, summarized, abstracted, reduced, contracted, compact, concise **2** *condensed liquid* concentrated, evaporated, reduced, thickened, compressed, clotted, coagulated, dense, rich, strong, undiluted
🔁 **1** expanded **2** diluted

condescend v
1 *condescend to do something* deign, see fit, stoop, bend, lower yourself, demean yourself, humble yourself, descend **2** *condescend to people* patronize, talk down to, treat condescendingly, be snobbish to

condescending adj
patronizing, disdainful, supercilious, snooty, snobbish, haughty, lofty, superior, lordly, imperious, *colloq.* stuck-up, toffee-nosed
🔁 gracious, humble

condescension n
disdain, haughtiness, superciliousness, superiority, loftiness, snobbishness, lordliness, airs
🔁 humility

condition n, v
▶ *n* **1** STATE, circumstances, factor(s), case, position, situation, predicament, plight, quandary **2** *the conditions in which people work* surroundings, environment, milieu, setting, atmosphere, climate, background, context, circumstances, factors, way of life,

situation, state, set-up **3** REQUIREMENT, obligation, prerequisite, terms, stipulation, demand, necessity, essential, precondition, provision, proviso, qualification, limit, limitation, restriction, rule **4** *out of condition* fitness, health, state, state of health, shape, form, order, working order, fettle, kilter, *colloq.* nick **5** *a heart condition* disorder, defect, weakness, infirmity, problem, complaint, disease, illness, ailment, *formal* malady
▶ *v* **1** *a shampoo that conditions* tone, make healthy, restore, revive, treat, improve, groom **2** *conditioned by experience* influence, mould, educate, train, groom, equip, prepare, prime, accustom, familiarize, season, temper, adapt, adjust, tune, indoctrinate, brainwash

conditional *adj*
provisional, qualified, limited, restricted, tied, relative, subject, based, dependent, contingent
F3 unconditional, absolute

condolence *n*
sympathy, commiseration, compassion, pity, consolation, support
F3 congratulation

condom *n*
sheath, prophylactic, protective, female condom, Femidom®

condone *v*
forgive, pardon, excuse, overlook, ignore, disregard, tolerate, brook, let pass, allow, let someone off, make allowances for, *colloq.* turn a blind eye to, let something ride
F3 condemn, censure

conducive *adj*
leading, tending, contributing, contributory, productive, promoting, advantageous, beneficial, favourable, helpful, useful, instrumental, encouraging
F3 detrimental, adverse, unfavourable

conduct *v, n*
▶ *v* **1** CARRY OUT, perform, do, administer, manage, run, organize, direct, orchestrate, chair, control, be in charge of, handle, regulate **2** ACCOMPANY, show, take, bring, escort, usher, lead, guide, direct, pilot, steer **3** *conduct heat* convey, carry, bear, transmit **4** *conduct yourself* behave, acquit, act, *formal* comport
▶ *n* **1** *good conduct* behaviour, actions, ways, manners, bearing, practice, attitude, *formal* comportment, demeanour, deportment **2** ADMINISTRATION, management, direction, running, organization, operation, control, supervision, leadership, guidance

conduit *n*
channel, pipe, tunnel, passage, passageway, duct, tube, drain, gutter, culvert, ditch, flume, chute, watercourse, waterway, canal, main

confectionery *n*
sweets, chocolates, candy, toffees, rock, truffle, fudge, *Scot.* tablet, Turkish delight, bonbon

confederacy *n*
union, federation, alliance, coalition, confederation, league, partnership, *formal* compact

confederate *n, adj*
▶ *n* accomplice, ally, assistant, associate, colleague, friend, partner, supporter, collaborator, abettor, accessory, conspirator
▶ *adj* federate, federal, allied, associated, combined, united

confederation *n*
union, federation, alliance, association, coalition, amalgamation, confederacy, league, partnership, *formal* compact

confer *v*
1 DISCUSS, debate, deliberate, consult, talk, converse, exchange views **2** BESTOW, award, present, give (out), grant, accord, impart, lend

conference *n*
meeting, convention, congress, summit, symposium, forum, discussion, debate, consultation, dialogue, colloquium, seminar, *formal* convocation

confess *v*
admit, confide, own (up), accept blame, accept responsibility, grant, concede, acknowledge, recognize, affirm, assert, profess, declare, disclose, make known, divulge, expose, unbosom, unburden, *colloq.* come clean, make a clean breast of, get off your chest, come out with it, spill the beans, tell all
F3 deny, conceal

confession *n*
admission, acknowledgement, owning-up, affirmation, assertion, profession, declaration, disclosure, making known, divulgence, exposure, revelation, unbosoming, unburdening
F3 denial, concealment

confidant, confidante *n*
friend, close friend, bosom friend, intimate, companion, *colloq.* crony, pal, mate

confide *v*
confess, admit, tell a secret, reveal, disclose, divulge, whisper, breathe, tell, impart, intimate, unburden, unbosom, pour out your heart to, *colloq.* get off your chest
F3 hide, suppress, conceal

confidence *n*
1 *have confidence in someone* TRUST, faith, reliance, dependence, credence, belief, conviction, certainty **2** SELF-ASSURANCE, assurance, composure, calmness, self-possession, self-confidence, self-reliance, self-assurance, belief in yourself, poise, boldness, courage, *formal* aplomb **3** SECRET, confidential matter, private matter, intimacy
F3 **1** distrust **2** diffidence
▷ **in confidence** privately, in privacy, in private, confidentially, in secret, personally, between ourselves, *entre nous,* behind closed doors, within these four walls, *colloq.* between you and me, between you me and the gatepost/bedpost
F3 openly

confident *adj*
1 *confident that it will happen* sure, certain, positive, convinced, definite, unhesitating **2** *a confident person* assured, sure of yourself, composed, self-possessed, calm, cool, self-confident, self-reliant, self-assured, unselfconscious, bold, courageous, fearless, positive, optimistic, dauntless, unabashed, *colloq.* upbeat
F3 **1** doubtful **2** diffident, insecure

confidential *adj*
secret, top secret, classified, restricted, off-the-record, private, personal, intimate, sensitive

confidentially *adv*
privately, in privacy, in private, in confidence, in secret, personally, between ourselves, *entre nous,* behind closed doors, on the quiet, within these four walls, *formal* in camera, *colloq.* between you and me, between you me and the gatepost/bedpost
F3 openly

configuration *n*
arrangement, composition, figure, form, outline, shape, contour, cast, *formal* conformation, disposition

confine *v, n*
▶ *v* **1** *confine a disease; confine yourself to something* restrict, limit, keep within limits, bound, bind,

constrain, control, fix, regulate, *formal* circumscribe **2** *confine in prison* imprison, cage, enclose, shut (up), hold prisoner, hold captive, hold in custody, intern, impound, keep in, lock up/away, coop up, bind, shackle, trammel, restrain, repress, inhibit, *formal* incarcerate, immure
F3 1 derestrict **2** free
▶ *n* limit, limitation, restriction, scope, parameter, bound, boundary, frontier, border, circumference, perimeter, edge

confined *adj*
restricted, limited, narrow, constrained, controlled, enclosed, housebound, *formal* circumscribed
F3 free, unrestricted

confinement *n*
1 IMPRISONMENT, internment, custody, detention, captivity, house arrest, *formal* incarceration **2** CHILDBIRTH, birth, labour, delivery, *technical* parturition
F3 1 freedom, liberty

confirm *v*
1 PROVE, corroborate, substantiate, verify, check, validate, authenticate, give credence to, evidence, demonstrate, endorse, back, support **2** ESTABLISH, fix, settle, ratify, sanction, approve, authorize, warrant, endorse, *colloq.* clinch **3** *confirm that he will go* affirm, assert, assure, pledge, promise, guarantee, *formal* asseverate, aver **4** *confirmed me in my decision* strengthen, reinforce, harden, support, uphold, *formal* fortify
F3 1 refute, deny

confirmation *n*
affirmation, validation, authentication, corroboration, substantiation, verification, proof, evidence, testimony, ratification, sanction, approval, assent, acceptance, agreement, endorsement, backing, support, *formal* accreditation
F3 denial

confirmed *adj*
inveterate, entrenched, dyed-in-the-wool, rooted, fixed, set, established, long-established, habitual, long-standing, chronic, through and through, seasoned, hardened, incorrigible, incurable, *formal* inured

confiscate *v*
seize, remove, take away, take possession of, impound, commandeer, *formal* appropriate, expropriate, arrogate, sequester
F3 return, restore

confiscation *n*
seizure, removal, takeover, impounding, commandeering, *formal* appropriation, distrainment, distraint, escheat, expropriation, sequestration, forfeiture
F3 restoration

conflagration *n*
blaze, fire, inferno, holocaust, *formal* deflagration

conflict *n, v*
▶ *n* **1** DISAGREEMENT, quarrel, dissension, dispute, opposition, antagonism, hostility, friction, strife, unrest, confrontation, feud, discord, contention, ill-will, difference of opinion, variance, clash, row, *formal* antipathy, *colloq.* bust-up **2** BATTLE, war, warfare, combat, fight, contest, engagement, skirmish, fracas, brawl, quarrel, feud, encounter, row, clash, *colloq.* set-to, bust-up, scrap
F3 1 agreement, harmony, concord
▶ *v* differ, clash, collide, disagree, be at variance, be at loggerheads, be at odds, be inconsistent with, contradict, oppose, be in opposition, contest, fight, combat, battle, war, strive, struggle, contend
F3 agree, harmonize

confluence *n*
convergence, junction, meeting, meeting-point, concurrence, union, watersmeet, *formal* conflux

conform *v*
1 *conform to a law* obey, follow, comply, fall in with, observe, adapt, adjust, accommodate **2** *conform in your behaviour* follow, be conventional, be uniform, do the same thing, *colloq.* follow the crowd, go with the flow/stream, toe the line, jump on the bandwagon **3** *conform to a pattern* agree, accord, harmonize, match, correspond, tally, square
F3 1 disobey **2** rebel **3** differ, conflict

conformist *n*
conventionalist, traditionalist, *colloq.* yes-man, stick-in-the-mud, rubber-stamp
F3 bohemian, nonconformist

conformity *n*
1 *in conformity with the law* compliance, observance, obedience, allegiance, adaptation, adjustment, accommodation, affinity, agreement, harmony, correspondence, likeness, similarity, resemblance, *formal* consonance, congruity **2** *conformity in behaviour* conventionality, orthodoxy, traditionalism, uniformity
F3 1 disobedience **2** nonconformity, rebellion

confound *v*
1 CONFUSE, bewilder, baffle, perplex, mystify, puzzle, nonplus, surprise, startle, amaze, astonish, astound, dumbfound, stun, stupefy, *formal* discomfit, *colloq.* bamboozle, flabbergast, flummox **2** *confound their plans* thwart, frustrate, upset, beat, defeat, overwhelm, overthrow, destroy, demolish, ruin

confront *v*
1 *confront a problem* face, face up to, brave, tackle, address, deal with, cope with, contend with, reckon with, come to terms with, *colloq.* come to grips with, meet head on, face the music **2** *confront the enemy* face, face up to, meet, encounter, stand up to, challenge, oppose, brave, defy, resist, withstand, attack, assault, accost **3** *confront him with the facts* challenge, present, show

confrontation *n*
encounter, clash, conflict, collision, showdown, disagreement, fight, battle, quarrel, engagement, contest, *colloq.* set-to

confuse *v*
1 BEWILDER, baffle, perplex, mystify, confound, puzzle, bemuse, disorient, disconcert, fluster, discompose, upset, embarrass, mortify, *colloq.* throw, floor, tie in knots **2** MUDDLE, mix up, mistake, jumble, disarrange, disorder, tangle, entangle, involve, mingle **3** *to confuse matters further* complicate, make more difficult, compound, elaborate, make difficult, involve, make involved,
F3 1 enlighten, clarify **3** simplify

confused *adj*
1 BEWILDERED, baffled, perplexed, mystified, confounded, puzzled, bemused, nonplussed, disconcerted, flustered, disorientated, dazed, unbalanced, *colloq.* flummoxed, floored, not knowing whether you are coming or going, up a gumtree, in a flat spin, in a flap, all at sea, like a headless chicken **2** MUDDLED, jumbled, disarranged, disordered, untidy, disorderly, chaotic, disorganized, mixed-up, out of order, *colloq.* higgledy-piggledy, at sixes and sevens, have your wires crossed, *slang* have your knickers in a twist
F3 2 orderly

confusing *adj*
puzzling, baffling, bewildering, muddling, perplexing, unclear, difficult, ambiguous, complicated,

involved, contradictory, inconclusive, inconsistent, misleading, cryptic, tortuous
F3 clear, definite

confusion *n*
1 DISORDER, disarray, untidiness, mess, clutter, jumble, muddle, mix-up, disorganization, disarrangement, chaos, turmoil, commotion, upheaval, *colloq.* shambles **2** MISUNDERSTANDING, puzzlement, perplexity, mystification, bewilderment, bafflement, muddle
F3 **1** order **2** clarity

congeal *v*
clot, curdle, coalesce, coagulate, thicken, stiffen, harden, concentrate, fuse, solidify, set, cake, gel, freeze
F3 dissolve, melt, liquefy

congenial *adj*
agreeable, pleasant, pleasing, relaxing, delightful, favourable, friendly, companionable, genial, sympathetic, homely, compatible, complaisant, cosy, like-minded, suitable, well-suited
F3 disagreeable, unpleasant

congenital *adj*
1 *a congenital disease* hereditary, inborn, inbred, inherited, innate, inherent, constitutional, natural, *technical* connate **2** *a congenital liar* inveterate, entrenched, habitual, chronic, seasoned, hardened, incorrigible, incurable, complete, thorough, utter, *formal* inured

congested *adj*
1 *congested roads* blocked, clogged, jammed, packed, stuffed, crammed, full, crowded, overcrowded, overflowing, teeming **2** *a congested nose* blocked, clogged, choked
F3 **1, 2** clear

congestion *n*
1 *congestion on the roads* clogging, blockage, overcrowding, jam, traffic jam, snarl-up, gridlock, bottleneck **2** *nasal congestion* clogging, blockage, blocking, choking

conglomerate *n*
corporation, multinational, merger, cartel, trust, consortium, company, firm, business, business organization, concern, association, partnership, corporation, establishment

conglomeration *n*
mass, agglomeration, aggregation, accumulation, collection, assemblage, composite, medley, hotchpotch

congratulate *v*
praise, compliment, say well done to, wish well, wish happiness to, send/offer good wishes to, send/offer best wishes to, *formal* felicitate, *colloq.* take your hat off to, pat on the back
F3 commiserate

congratulations *n*
compliments, good wishes, best wishes, greetings, *formal* felicitations, *colloq.* pat on the back, bouquet(s)
F3 commiserations, condolences

congregate *v*
gather, assemble, collect, muster, rally, rendezvous, meet, convene, converge, flock, crowd, throng, form, mass, accumulate, cluster, clump
F3 disperse

congregation *n*
assembly, crowd, group, throng, mass, multitude, host, meeting, flock, parishioners, parish, laity, fellowship

congress *n*
assembly, conference, convention, council, legislature, meeting, gathering, forum, parliament, synod, diet, *formal* conclave, convocation

congruence *n*
correspondence, consistency, agreement, conformity, coincidence, harmony, compatibility, similarity, resemblance, identity, match, parallelism, *formal* concinnity, concurrence
F3 incongruity

conical *adj*
cone-shaped, pyramidal, pyramid-shaped, funnel-shaped, tapering, tapered, pointed, *formal* infundibular, infundibulate, turbinate

conjectural *adj*
hypothetical, assumed, surmised, tentative, theoretical, speculative, supposed, academic, suppositional, *formal* posited, postulated
F3 factual, real

conjecture *v, n*
▶ *v* speculate, theorize, hypothesize, guess, estimate, reckon, fancy, suppose, presuppose, surmise, assume, presume, infer, imagine, suspect
▶ *n* speculation, theory, hypothesis, fancy, notion, guesswork, guess, estimate, supposition, presupposition, surmise, suspicion, assumption, presumption, conclusion, inference, extrapolation, projection, *colloq.* guesstimate

conjugal *adj*
matrimonial, marital, nuptial, married, wedded, bridal, *formal* connubial, epithalamic, spousal, hymeneal

conjunction *n*
coincidence, co-occurrence, coexistence, combination, amalgamation, association, union, unification, *formal* concurrence, juxtaposition
▷ **in conjunction with** together with, with, along with, alongside, combined with, in partnership with, in collaboration with, in association with, in company with

conjure *v*
1 *conjuring at the children's party* do tricks, perform tricks, do magic, perform magic **2** *conjure handkerchiefs from a hat* summon, invoke, call up, evoke, make appear, rouse, raise, bewitch, charm, fascinate, compel
▷ **conjure up** evoke, create, produce, excite, awaken, recollect, recall, call/bring to mind

conjurer *n*
magician, illusionist, miracle-worker, sorcerer, wizard, *formal* prestidigitator, prestigiator, thaumaturge

conk *v*
▷ **conk out** break down, collapse, fail, *colloq.* pack up, go on the blink, go haywire

connect *v*
connect two objects; connected with the murder join, link, unite, couple, bridge, combine, fasten, secure, affix, tie, clamp, fuse, attach, relate (to), correlate, associate, bracket, identify, ally, *formal* concatenate
F3 disconnect, cut off, detach

connected *adj*
joined, linked, united, coupled, tied, combined, fastened, secured, related, akin, associated, affiliated, allied
F3 disconnected, unconnected

connection *n*
1 *a connection between pipes; a connection between smoking and cancer* junction, coupling, joint, fastening, attachment, clasp, bond, tie, link, association, alliance, relation, relationship, interrelation, contact, communication, parallel, correlation, analogy, correspondence, relevance, reference **2** *use your connections to get a job* friend, acquaintance, relation, relative, contact, sponsor, person of influence, person of importance
F3 **1** disconnection

connivance *n*
collusion, complicity, condoning, consent, abetment, abetting

connive *v*
1 *connive with someone to commit an offence* collude, conspire, intrigue, plot, scheme, *formal* complot, cabal, coact 2 *connive at wrongdoing* overlook, ignore, disregard, condone, tolerate, brook, let go, let pass, pass over, gloss over, allow, wink at, *colloq.* turn a blind eye to

conniving *adj*
scheming, colluding, conspiring, plotting, nasty, immoral, unscrupulous, corrupt

connoisseur *n*
authority, specialist, expert, judge, arbiter, pundit, specialist, devotee, aficionado, cognoscente, gourmet, gastronome, epicure, virtuoso, aesthete, *colloq.* buff

connotation *n*
implication, suggestion, intimation, hint, nuance, allusion, undertone, overtone, insinuation, colouring, association

connote *v*
imply, suggest, intimate, hint at, allude to, insinuate, signify, indicate, associate, *formal* import, purport, betoken

conquer *v*
1 *conquer an enemy/your fears* DEFEAT, beat, overthrow, overpower, rout, crush, subdue, quell, overrun, best, get the better of, worst, overcome, surmount, win, succeed, triumph over, prevail over, rise above, master, suppress, humble, *formal* vanquish, subjugate, *colloq.* trounce 2 SEIZE, take, annex, occupy, possess, take possession of, acquire, obtain, win, *formal* appropriate
F3 1 surrender, yield, give in

conqueror *n*
victor, winner, champion, hero, master, lord, *formal* vanquisher, subjugator, conquistador, *colloq.* champ

conquest *n*
1 *the conquest of the country* victory, triumph, win, success, defeat, beating, overthrow, overpowering, coup, rout, crushing, mastery, subjection, invasion, overrunning, possession, occupation, capture, seizing, annexation, acquisition, *formal* appropriation, subjugation, vanquishment, *colloq.* trouncing 2 *his latest conquest* captive, lover, catch, acquisition

conscience *n*
principles, standards, morals, ethics, sense of right, sense of right and wrong, moral sense, moral code, still small voice, voice within, scruples, qualms

conscience-stricken *adj*
ashamed, sorry, contrite, guilt-ridden, guilty, penitent, regretful, remorseful, repentant, disturbed, troubled, *formal* compunctious
F3 unashamed, unrepentant

conscientious *adj*
diligent, hard-working, scrupulous, painstaking, methodical, thorough, meticulous, punctilious, dedicated, assiduous, particular, careful, attentive, responsible, upright, honest, faithful, dutiful
F3 careless, irresponsible, unreliable

conscious *adj*
1 AWAKE, alive, responsive, sensible, rational, reasoning, alert, *formal* sentient 2 AWARE, self-conscious, heedful, mindful, alert, *formal* cognizant, percipient, sensible 3 *a conscious effort to be polite* deliberate, intentional, on purpose, calculated, premeditated, studied, knowing, wilful, voluntary, *formal* volitional

F3 1 unconscious 2 unaware 3 involuntary, unintentional

consciousness *n*
1 *enter his consciousness* awareness, mind, knowledge, intuition, perception, apprehension, realization, recognition, *formal* cognizance, sentience, sensibility 2 *lose consciousness* being awake, wakefulness, awareness, alertness
F3 2 unconsciousness

conscript *v, n*
▶ *v* recruit, enlist, draft, call up, take on, round up, muster
F3 volunteer
▶ *n* recruit, enlistee, draftee
F3 volunteer

consecrate *v*
sanctify, bless, anoint, hallow, make holy, dedicate, devote, vow, ordain, venerate, revere, exalt

consecutive *adj*
successive, sequential, serial, continuous, unbroken, uninterrupted, following, succeeding, running, one after the other, in turn, straight, *formal* seriate, *colloq.* on the trot, back to back
F3 discontinuous

consensus *n*
agreement, consent, harmony, majority view, unanimity, unity, *formal* concord, concurrence, consentience
F3 disagreement

consent *v, n*
▶ *v* agree, accept, approve, permit, allow, authorize, grant, admit, concede, yield, go along with, comply, *formal* concur, assent, accede, acquiesce, *colloq.* give the go-ahead, give the green light, give the thumbs-up
F3 refuse, decline, oppose
▶ *n* agreement, acceptance, approval, authorization, permission, clearance, sanction, concession, compliance, *formal* concurrence, assent, acquiescence, *colloq.* go-ahead, green light
F3 disagreement, refusal, opposition

consequence *n*
1 RESULT, outcome, issue, end, upshot, effect, side effect, eventuality, implication, repercussion, reverberation 2 *of no consequence* importance, significance, concern, value, weight, substance, note, eminence, prominence, distinction, *formal* import, moment
F3 1 cause 2 unimportance, insignificance

consequent *adj*
resultant, resulting, ensuing, subsequent, following, successive, sequential

consequently *adv*
as a result, therefore, with the result that, so that, accordingly, consequentially, necessarily, subsequently, then, *formal* inferentially, ergo, hence, thus

conservation *n*
keeping, safe-keeping, custody, saving, care, economy, husbandry, maintenance, upkeep, preservation, protection, safeguarding, ecology, environmentalism
F3 destruction

conservatism *n*
conservativeness, conventionalism, orthodoxy, traditionalism
F3 radicalism

conservative *adj, n*
▶ *adj* 1 *conservative politicians* Tory, right-wing, hidebound, die-hard, reactionary, establishmentarian 2 *conservative opinions/estimates* unprogressive, conventional, traditional, traditionalist, orthodox, inflexible, set in your ways, moderate, middle-of-the-road, careful, cautious, guarded, sober

⛝ 1 left-wing, radical **2** innovative
▶ *n* Tory, right-winger, die-hard, stick-in-the-mud, reactionary, traditionalist, moderate
⛝ left-winger, radical

conservatory *n*
1 *grow plants in the conservatory* greenhouse, glasshouse, hothouse **2** *study music at the conservatory* conservatoire, school, college, academy, institute, music school, drama college

conserve *v*
keep, keep back, keep in reserve, save, store up, hoard, maintain, preserve, protect, take care of, guard, safeguard
⛝ use, waste, squander

consider *v*
1 PONDER, deliberate, reflect, contemplate, meditate, muse, mull over, examine, study, weigh (up), respect, remember, note, make a mental note of, give thought to, bear/keep in mind, take into account/consideration, *formal* cogitate, ruminate, *colloq.* chew over, toy with **2** *consider it an honour* regard as, think, believe, judge, rate, count, hold, feel, *formal* deem

considerable *adj*
great, large, big, sizable, substantial, ample, plentiful, abundant, lavish, generous, marked, noticeable, perceptible, appreciable, reasonable, tolerable, respectable, important, significant, noteworthy, distinguished, influential, *colloq.* tidy
⛝ small, slight, insignificant, unremarkable

considerably *adv*
significantly, substantially, greatly, markedly, much, noticeably, remarkably, appreciably, abundantly
⛝ slightly

considerate *adj*
kind, thoughtful, caring, attentive, obliging, helpful, charitable, unselfish, concerned, selfless, altruistic, gracious, sympathetic, compassionate, generous, sensitive, tactful, discreet, solicitous
⛝ inconsiderate, thoughtless, selfish

consideration *n*
1 THOUGHT, deliberation, reflection, contemplation, meditation, examination, analysis, scrutiny, review, inspection, attention, notice, heed, regard, reckoning, account, *formal* cogitation, rumination **2** KINDNESS, thoughtfulness, care, attention, regard, respect, helpfulness, unselfishness, concern, selflessness, altruism, graciousness, sympathy, compassion, generosity, sensitivity, tact, discretion **3** *the cost is a major consideration* fact, circumstance, factor, issue, point
⛝ 1 disregard **2** thoughtlessness

considering *prep, adv*
▶ *prep* taking into account/consideration, bearing in mind, making allowances for, in view of, in the light of
▶ *adv* all things considered, all in all

consign *v*
entrust, assign, commend, commit, devote, hand over, give over, transfer, transmit, deliver, convey, ship, banish, relegate

consignment *n*
cargo, shipment, load, batch, delivery, goods

consist *v*
1 *a jury consists of twelve people* comprise, be composed of, be made up of, contain, include, incorporate, embody, be formed of, embrace, involve, amount to **2** *the poem's beauty consists in its simplicity* inhere, lie, reside, be contained in, have as its main feature

consistency *n*
1 *the consistency of the porridge* thickness, density,

firmness, cohesion, smoothness, *technical* viscosity **2** STEADINESS, regularity, evenness, uniformity, sameness, identity, constancy, steadfastness, stability, persistence, dependability, reliability, unchangeableness, lack of change **3** AGREEMENT, accordance, correspondence, compatibility, harmony, *formal* congruity, consonance
⛝ 3 inconsistency

consistent *adj*
1 STEADY, stable, regular, uniform, unchanging, undeviating, constant, same, persistent, unfailing, dependable **2** *not consistent with his colleague's version* agreeing, compatible, corresponding, coinciding, matching, harmonious, conforming, logical, *formal* accordant, consonant, congruous
⛝ 1 irregular, erratic **2** inconsistent

consolation *n*
comfort, cheer, encouragement, help, support, reassurance, aid, sympathy, commiseration, relief, ease, soothing, alleviation, *formal* solace, succour, assuagement
⛝ discouragement

console¹ *v*
console the bereaved comfort, cheer, hearten, help, encourage, support, reassure, sympathize with, commiserate with, relieve, soothe, calm, *formal* solace, succour
⛝ upset, agitate

console² *n*
an instrument console panel, control panel, board, dashboard, keyboard, instruments, controls, switches, knobs, dials, buttons, levers

consolidate *v*
1 *consolidate power/support* reinforce, strengthen, make strong(er), secure, make (more) secure, stabilize, make (more) stable, cement, *formal* fortify **2** *consolidate businesses* unite, join, combine, amalgamate, merge, unify, fuse

consolidation *n*
1 *consolidation of power* reinforcement, strengthening, securing, stabilization, cementing, *formal* fortification **2** *consolidation of businesses* uniting, joining, combination, amalgamation, merger, unification, affiliation, alliance, association, confederation, federation, fusion

consonance *n*
compatibility, agreement, consistency, conformity, correspondence, harmony, suitability, *formal* accordance, congruity, concord
⛝ dissonance

consonant *adj*
compatible, consistent, correspondent, conforming, harmonious, in harmony, agreeing, suitable, in accordance, according, *formal* accordant, congruous
⛝ dissonant

consort *n, v*
▶ *n* partner, companion, associate, escort, spouse, husband, wife
▶ *v* associate, spend time, keep company, fraternize, mingle, mix

consortium *n*
partnership, confederation, federation, association, affiliation, coalition, league, corporation, company, bloc, cartel, conglomerate, alliance, organization, syndicate, guild, union, marriage, agreement, compact, bond, pact, treaty, combination

conspicuous *adj*
apparent, visible, noticeable, easily seen/noticed, marked, clear, obvious, evident, recognizable, observable, discernible, perceptible, patent, manifest, prominent, striking, blatant, flagrant, glaring, osten-

tatious, showy, flashy, garish, *colloq.* standing out a mile
◱ inconspicuous, concealed, hidden

conspiracy *n*
plot, scheme, intrigue, stratagem, league, cabal, collusion, collaboration, connivance, treason, *formal* machination, *colloq.* fix, frame-up

conspirator *n*
conspirer, plotter, schemer, intriguer, colluder, collaborator, traitor

conspire *v*
1 *conspire to oust the president* plot, hatch a plot, scheme, intrigue, manoeuvre, connive, collude, collaborate, *formal* machinate **2** *events conspiring for their harm* combine, join, join forces, work/act together, connect, link, unite, ally, associate, co-operate

constancy *n*
1 STABILITY, steadiness, permanence, unchangeability, firmness, regularity, uniformity **2** LOYALTY, faithfulness, fidelity, devotion, steadfastness, dependability, trustworthiness, firmness, steadiness, persistence, resolution, perseverance, tenacity
◱ **1** change, irregularity **2** fickleness

constant *adj*
1 *a constant barrage of questions* CONTINUAL, unbroken, never-ending, non-stop, endless, interminable, incessant, eternal, everlasting, perpetual, persistent, chronic, continuous, unremitting, uninterrupted, without respite, relentless, unflagging, unwavering, *formal* ceaseless **2** *his temperature is constant* stable, steady, unchanging, unvarying, changeless, invariable, unalterable, permanent, firm, even, regular, uniform, *formal* immutable **3** *a constant friend* loyal, faithful, staunch, steadfast, dependable, trustworthy, true, devoted, firm, steady, persistent, resolute, persevering
◱ **1** fitful, occasional **2** variable, irregular **3** disloyal, fickle

constantly *adv*
always, continually, all the time, forever, permanently, continuously, endlessly, non-stop, everlastingly, incessantly, interminably, invariably, perpetually, relentlessly, ad nauseam, *formal* ceaselessly
◱ occasionally

constellation *n*

consternation *n*
alarm, dismay, anxiety, fear, distress, dread, horror, fright, shock, terror, panic, awe, bewilderment, *formal* disquietude, perturbation, trepidation
◱ composure

constituent *n, adj*
▶ *n* **1** *voting by constituents* elector, voter **2** *the constituents of the mixture* ingredient, element, factor, principle, component, component part, part, content, bit, section, unit
◱ **2** whole
▶ *adj* component, integral, essential, basic, intrinsic, inherent

constitute *v*
1 *six counties constitute the province* comprise, make up, form, compose **2** *his remarks constitute a challenge to the leadership* be, represent, mean, form, make, be equivalent to, amount to, add up to, be tantamount to, be regarded as **3** *constitute a committee* form, create, establish, set up, found, institute, appoint, authorize, commission, charter, empower

constitution *n*
1 *a country's constitution* laws, rules, statutes, basic principles, code, charter, codified law, bill of rights **2** *the constitution of the committee* COMPOSITION, make-up, structure, organization, formation, *formal* configuration **3** HEALTH, condition, physique, physical condition, make-up, disposition, temperament, character, nature

constitutional *adj, n*
▶ *adj* statutory, by law, according to the law, legal, legitimate, lawful, legislative, governmental, authorized, vested, codified, ratified
▶ *n* walk, stroll, saunter, amble, promenade, turn, airing

constrain *v*
1 *feel constrained to tell the whole truth* FORCE, compel, coerce, oblige, necessitate, drive, impel, pressurize, pressure, urge **2** *constrained by responsibilities* LIMIT, confine, constrict, restrain, check, curb, bind, restrict, hinder, hold back

constrained *adj*
uneasy, embarrassed, inhibited, reticent, reserved, guarded, stiff, forced, unnatural
◱ relaxed, free

constraint *n*
1 FORCE, duress, compulsion, coercion, pressure, necessity, obligation, demand, insistence **2** RESTRICTION, limitation, hindrance, restraint, check, curb, damper, impediment

constrict *v*
1 *constrict an air passage* squeeze, compress, pinch, cramp, narrow, make narrow, tighten, contract, shrink, choke, strangle, strangulate **2** *constricted by*

lower budgets limit, restrict, confine, constrain, check, curb, bind, hinder, impede, hold back, obstruct, hamper, inhibit
E **1** expand

constriction *n*
1 *feel a constriction in the chest* squeezing, narrowing, pressure, tightness, tightening, compression, cramp, blockage, *technical* stricture, stenosis, *formal* constringency **2** *constrictions in the budget* restriction, constraint, limitation, reduction, check, curb, hindrance, impediment
E **1** expansion

construct *v*
1 *construct a building* build, erect, raise, elevate, make, manufacture, fabricate, assemble, establish, put up, set up **2** *construct a theory* compose, form, put together, shape, fashion, fabricate, model, devise, design, engineer, create, found, establish, formulate
E **1** demolish, destroy

construction *n*
1 *houses under construction* building, erection, fabrication, assembly, elevation, making, manufacture, establishment **2** *the cathedral is a magnificent construction* structure, building, edifice, assembly, fabric, form, shape, framework, figure, model **3** *the construction put on his remarks* INTERPRETATION, meaning, inference, deduction, reading
E **1** demolition, destruction

constructive *adj*
practical, productive, positive, helpful, useful, valuable, beneficial, advantageous
E destructive, negative, unhelpful

construe *v*
interpret, explain, understand, see as, regard as, read, render, take to mean, deduce, infer, analyse, *formal* expound

consult *v*
1 *consult an expert* ask/seek advice, ask/seek information, ask someone's opinion, question, interrogate, turn to, *colloq.* pick someone's brains **2** *consult with business partners* confer, discuss, debate, deliberate **3** *consult a map* look up, refer to, turn to

consultant *n*
adviser, expert, authority, specialist

consultation *n*
discussion, deliberation, talk, dialogue, conference, meeting, hearing, interview, examination, appointment, forum, session

consultative *adj*
advisory, advising, consulting, counselling, helping, recommending, *formal* consultatory

consume *v*
1 EAT, eat up, drink (up), swallow, devour, gobble, take, *formal* ingest, *colloq.* tuck in, guzzle, scoff, polish off, touch **2** USE UP, absorb, spend, get through, go through, drain, exhaust, use, squander, waste, fritter away, *formal* deplete, dissipate, expend, utilize **3** DESTROY, demolish, annihilate, devastate, gut, ravage, lay waste **4** *consumed with jealousy* devour, dominate, absorb, engross, preoccupy, grip, obsess, monopolize, overwhelm, torment, *colloq.* eat up

consumer *n*
user, end-user, customer, buyer, purchaser, shopper, patron, client

consuming *adj*
dominating, compelling, absorbing, preoccupying, devouring, engrossing, gripping, obsessive, immoderate, monopolizing, overwhelming, tormenting

consummate *adj, v*
▶ *adj* absolute, complete, total, utter, perfect, supreme, superior, ultimate, superb, transcendent, unqualified, skilled, accomplished, gifted, practised, proficient, distinguished, matchless, polished
E imperfect
▶ *v* perfect, accomplish, fulfil, realize, complete, perform, achieve, crown, cap, end, finish, conclude, *formal* terminate, execute, effectuate

consummation *n*
perfection, accomplishment, fulfilment, realization, completion, performance, achievement, culmination, crowning, capping, end, finish, conclusion, *formal* termination, execution, actualization, effectuation

consumption *n*
1 EATING, drinking, swallowing, devouring, *formal* ingestion, *colloq.* tucking-in, guzzling, scoffing **2** USING-UP, absorption, spending, getting-through, going-through, draining, exhaustion, squandering, waste, *formal* depletion, expending, expenditure, utilization

contact *n, v*
▶ *n* **1** *in contact with an object* touching, touch, impact, meeting, junction, union, proximity, *formal* juxtaposition, contiguity **2** *in contact with old friends* touch, communication, connection, association **3** *use your contacts to get a job* friend, acquaintance, relation, relative, connection, sponsor, person of influence, person of importance, network of contacts
▶ *v* approach, get onto, apply to, reach, get hold of, get in touch with, get through to, communicate with, notify, write to, speak to, telephone, phone, ring, call, fax, e-mail

contagious *adj*
1 *a contagious disease* infectious, catching, communicable, transmissible, transmittable, spreading, epidemic, pandemic **2** *contagious laughter* infectious, compelling, irresistible, catching, spreading

contain *v*
1 INCLUDE, take in, comprise, incorporate, embody, involve, embrace, enclose, have inside, hold, carry, take, accommodate, seat **2** *contain your feelings* repress, suppress, stifle, restrain, control, keep under control, keep back, hold in, check, keep in check, curb, limit, stop, prevent from spreading
E **1** exclude

container *n*
receptacle, vessel, holder, *formal* repository

Types of container include:
bag, barrel, basin, basket, bath, beaker, bin, bottle, bowl, box, bucket, can, canister, carton, case, cask, casket, cauldron, chest, churn, cistern, crate, crock, cup, cylinder, dish, drum, dustbin, glass, hamper, jar, jug, keg, kettle, locker, mug, pack, packet, pail, pan, pannier, pitcher, pot, punnet, purse, sack, suitcase, tank, tea caddy, tea chest, teapot, tin, trough, trunk, tub, tube, tumbler, tureen, urn, vase, vat, waste bin, waste-paper basket, waterbutt, well.

contaminate *v*
infect, pollute, decay, adulterate, taint, soil, sully, defile, corrupt, harm, foul, spoil, make impure, deprave, debase, stain, tarnish, *formal* vitiate
E purify

contamination *n*
infection, pollution, decay, adulteration, taint, soiling, sullying, defilement, desecration, corruption, harm, foulness, rottenness, spoiling, filth, impurity, debasement, stain, tarnish, *formal* vitiation
E purification

contemplate *v*
1 *contemplate leaving; contemplate the meaning of life* CONSIDER, think about, deliberate, reflect on, ponder, meditate, muse, mull over, dwell, examine, study, weigh (up), turn over in your mind, have in mind/view, expect, foresee, envisage, plan, design, propose, intend, *formal* cogitate, ruminate **2** *contemplate the view* look at, regard, view, observe, scrutinize, survey, examine, inspect

contemplation *n*
1 *religious contemplation* CONSIDERATION, thought, deliberation, reflection, pondering, meditation, musing, mulling-over, dwell, examination, study, weighing (up), *formal* cogitation, rumination, cerebration **2** *contemplation of the view* gazing, regard, view, observation, scrutiny, survey, examination, inspection

contemplative *adj*
thoughtful, reflective, meditative, introspective, musing, pensive, rapt, intent, deep in thought, *formal* cerebral, ruminative
◪ impulsive, thoughtless

contemporary *adj*
1 MODERN, current, present, present-day, present-time, today's, topical, recent, latest, up-to-date, fashionable, up-to-the-minute, ultra-modern, avant-garde, futuristic, *colloq.* trendy, new-fangled, with it **2** CONTEMPORANEOUS, coexistent, synchronous, simultaneous, *formal* concurrent, coetaneous, coeval
◪ **1** out-of-date, old-fashioned

contempt *n*
scorn, disdain, condescension, derision, ridicule, mockery, disrespect, dishonour, disregard, neglect, dislike, loathing, hatred, *formal* detestation, contumely
◪ respect, admiration, regard

contemptible *adj*
despicable, shameful, low, mean, vile, base, detestable, lamentable, loathsome, abject, wretched, degenerate, unworthy, pitiful, paltry, worthless, *formal* ignominious
◪ admirable, honourable

contemptuous *adj*
scornful, disdainful, sneering, supercilious, condescending, arrogant, haughty, high and mighty, cynical, derisive, derisory, insulting, mocking, jeering, disrespectful, insolent, withering, *formal* contumelious
◪ respectful, polite, humble

contend *v*
1 *contend with a problem* deal, cope, grapple, face, face up to, brave, tackle, address, reckon, come to terms, *colloq.* come to grips, meet head on **2** MAINTAIN, state, hold, argue, allege, assert, declare, affirm, profess, claim, *formal* aver, asseverate **3** COMPETE, vie, contest, dispute, clash, wrestle, grapple, struggle, strive, tussle, oppose, challenge, fight, battle, combat, war

content¹ *n*
1 *the contents of the package* constituents, parts, elements, ingredients, components, component parts, load, items, what is contained, things inside **2** *the contents of the book* CHAPTER, division, section, subject, subject matter, topic, theme **3** SUBSTANCE, matter, material, essence, gist, meaning, significance, text, theme, subject matter, ideas, contents, load, burden **4** CAPACITY, volume, size, measure

content² *adj, n, v*
▶ *adj content with the arrangements* satisfied, fulfilled, contented, comfortable, unworried, untroubled, pleased, happy, glad, cheerful, willing, at ease
◪ dissatisfied, troubled

▶ *n* comfort, contentment, satisfaction, fulfilment, delight, pleasure, happiness, gladness, cheerfulness, peace, peacefulness, ease, serenity, gratification, *formal* equanimity
◪ discontent
▶ *v* satisfy, humour, indulge, gratify, please, be happy, be pleased, be glad, delight, appease, pacify, placate
◪ displease

contented *adj*
happy, glad, pleased, cheerful, comfortable, relaxed, content, satisfied, fulfilled, unworried, untroubled
◪ discontented, troubled, unhappy, annoyed

contention *n*
1 *it is my contention that ...* belief, opinion, persuasion, feeling, intuition, impression, notion, theory, view, viewpoint, point of view, thesis, conviction, claim, judgement, stand, position, assertion, argument **2** *a matter of contention* disagreement, argument, controversy, dispute, debate, discord, dissension, enmity, feuding, hostility, strife, struggle, rivalry, wrangling

contentious *adj*
1 *a contentious issue* controversial, polemical, disputed, doubtful, questionable, debatable, disputable **2** *a contentious person* argumentative, antagonistic, quarrelsome, hostile, perverse, querulous, bickering, captious, *formal* pugnacious
◪ **1** uncontroversial **2** co-operative, peaceable

contentment *n*
contentedness, happiness, gladness, cheerfulness, pleasure, gratification, comfort, ease, complacency, peace, peacefulness, serenity, equanimity, content, satisfaction, gratification, fulfilment
◪ unhappiness, discontent, dissatisfaction

contest *n, v*
▶ *n* competition, game, match, race, championship, tournament, event, encounter, fight, battle, combat, conflict, struggle, skirmish, dispute, vying, debate, controversy, *colloq.* set-to
▶ *v* **1** DISPUTE, debate, question, call into question, doubt, challenge, oppose, argue against, deny, refute, *technical* litigate **2** COMPETE, be in competition with, vie, contend, strive, struggle, fight, battle, try to beat, tussle
◪ **1** accept

contestant *n*
competitor, contender, player, participant, entrant, candidate, aspirant, rival, opponent, adversary

context *n*
background, setting, surroundings, framework, frame of reference, state of affairs, situation, general situation, position, circumstances, factors, conditions

contiguous *adj*
adjacent, adjoining, touching, beside, bordering, near, close, neighbouring, next, tangential, *technical* - vicinal, *formal* abutting, conjoining, conterminous, juxtaposed, juxtapositional

continent *n*
mainland, terra firma

The continents of the world are:
Africa, Antarctica, Asia, Australia, Europe, North America, South America.

contingency *n*
eventuality, possibility, accident, randomness, arbitrariness, chance, chance event, emergency, event, happening, incident, uncertainty, *formal* fortuity, juncture

contingent *n, adj*
▶ *n* body, company, deputation, delegation, mission, representatives, detachment, section, division, group, set, batch, quota, party, complement
▶ *adj* dependent, conditional, subject, based, relative

continual *adj*
constant, perpetual, incessant, interminable, eternal, everlasting, regular, frequent, recurrent, repeated, repetitive, persistent
🔃 occasional, intermittent, temporary

 continual or **continuous** ?
Continual means 'very frequent, happening again and again': *I've had continual interruptions all morning.*
Continuous means 'without a pause or break': *continuous rain.*

continually *adv*
constantly, perpetually, incessantly, interminably, forever, eternally, everlastingly, always, endlessly, nonstop, regularly, frequently, recurrently, repeatedly, persistently, habitually, all the time, *formal* ceaselessly
🔃 occasionally, intermittently

continuance *n*
continuation, duration, endurance, period, term, permanence, persistence, *formal* protraction

continuation *n*
1 *continuation after a pause* resumption, recommencement, starting again, renewal, maintenance, development, furtherance, addition, supplement, sequel **2** *the continuation of the road* prolongation, lengthening, extension, *formal* protraction
🔃 **1** *formal* cessation, termination

continue *v*
1 *continue doing something* go on, carry on, not stop, keep on (with), proceed, persist in, persevere in, progress, press on, *colloq.* stick at, soldier on **2** *the course continues next term* resume, recommence, renew, proceed (again), start again, begin again, take up again, carry on, go on, *colloq.* pick up the threads, pick up where you have left off **3** *if the storm continues* last, endure, remain, abide, survive, hold out, stay, rest, pursue, sustain, maintain, lengthen, prolong, extend, persist, keep on, project **4** *'I'm not sure,' she continued* start talking again, resume, go on **5** *continue on your way* keep going, keep travelling, keep walking, keep moving, keep on, carry on
🔃 **1, 2, 3, 4** stop

continuity *n*
flow, progression, succession, sequence, linkage, interrelationship, connection, cohesion, continuousness, uninterruptedness, unchangeableness
🔃 discontinuity

continuous *adj*
unbroken, uninterrupted, consecutive, non-stop, not stopping, without a break, endless, ceaseless, unending, never-ending, solid, unceasing, interminable, constant, unremitting, prolonged, extended, continued, lasting, *colloq.* with no let-up
🔃 discontinuous, broken, sporadic

 continuous or **continual** ? *See panel at* CONTINUAL.

contort *v*
twist, distort, warp, wrench, disfigure, deform, misshape, bend out of shape, gnarl, knot, writhe, squirm, wriggle, *formal* convolute

contortionist *n*
acrobat, gymnast, tumbler, balancer, somersaulter, trapeze artist, rope-walker, rope-dancer, stuntman, stuntwoman, *formal* funambulist, aerialist, equilibrist

contour *n*
outline, silhouette, shape, form, figure, curve, lines, relief, profile, character, aspect

contraband *n*
banned/black-market goods, smuggling, forbidden/illegal traffic, bootlegging, prohibited/unlawful goods, *formal* proscribed goods, *colloq.* hot goods

contraceptive *n*

Contraceptives and other forms of birth control include:
barrier contraceptive, barrier method, birth control pill, cervical cap, coil, coitus interruptus, combined pill, condom, contraceptive ring, contraceptive sponge, diaphragm, Dutch cap, female condom, Femidom®, injectable contraceptive, intrauterine device (IUD), loop, minipill, morning-after pill, oral contraceptive, pill, prophylactic, protective, rhythm method, sheath, spermicidal cream, spermicide, vaginal ring, withdrawal method.

contract *v, n*
▶ *v* **1** SHRINK, lessen, diminish, reduce, decrease, shorten, become shorter, become smaller, curtail, abbreviate, abridge, condense, compress, constrict, narrow, tighten, tense, draw in, shrivel, wrinkle **2** *contract pneumonia* catch, get, go/come down with, develop, pick up, become infected with, become ill with, *formal* succumb to **3** PLEDGE, promise, undertake, engage, agree, stipulate, arrange, agree terms, settle, negotiate, bargain
🔃 **1** expand, enlarge, lengthen
▶ *n* agreement, bond, commitment, engagement, covenant, treaty, convention, pact, transaction, deal, bargain, settlement, arrangement, understanding, *formal* compact, concordat

contraction *n*
1 *'Don't' is a contraction of 'do not'* abbreviation, shortening, shortened form, abridgement **2** *the contraction of muscles* constriction, compression, narrowing, tightening, tensing, drawing-in, shrivelling, shrinkage, lessening, reduction, curtailment, *technical* astringency
🔃 **2** expansion, growth

contradict *v*
1 *contradict someone* deny, challenge, oppose, dispute, rebut, counter, go against, *formal* disaffirm, confute, refute, impugn, gainsay **2** *one statement contradicts another* disagree, clash, conflict, contrast, go against, be at variance, be at odds, be in conflict, be inconsistent with, *formal* negate, *colloq.* fly in the face of
🔃 **1, 2** agree **2** confirm, *formal* corroborate

contradiction *n*
1 *the contradiction between theory and practice* clash, variance, odds, conflict, inconsistency, disagreement, paradox, *formal* incongruity, negation, antithesis **2** *contradiction of an earlier report* denial, challenge, opposition, dispute, rebuttal, counterargument, *formal* disaffirmance, disaffirmation, confutation, refutation
🔃 **1, 2** agreement

contradictory *adj*
contrary, opposite, opposing, paradoxical, conflicting, clashing, inconsistent, incompatible, antagonis-

tic, irreconcilable, opposed, *formal* discrepant, dissentient, repugnant, incongruous, antithetical
🖪 consistent

contraption *n*
contrivance, device, gadget, apparatus, rig, machine, mechanism, invention, *colloq.* thingumajig

contrary *adj, n*
▶ *adj* **1** OPPOSITE, counter, reverse, conflicting, clashing, inconsistent, incompatible, irreconcilable, antagonistic, opposed, opposing, adverse, hostile **2** PERVERSE, awkward, disobliging, difficult, wayward, obstinate, stubborn, headstrong, intractable, cantankerous, *formal* refractory, *colloq.* stroppy
🖪 **1** like **2** obliging
▶ *n* opposite, converse, reverse, *formal* antithesis
▷ **on the contrary** quite/just the reverse, quite/just the opposite

contrast *n, v*
▶ *n* difference, dissimilarity, divergence, distinction, differentiation, comparison, foil, opposite, opposition, relief, *formal* disparity, dissimilitude, antithesis
🖪 similarity, resemblance
▷ **in contrast to** as distinguished from, opposed to, in opposition to, rather than, as against
▶ *v* **1** *contrast two people* compare, differentiate, distinguish, discriminate **2** *her expression contrasted sharply with her dress* disagree, contradict, clash, conflict, differ, oppose, go against, be at variance, be at odds, be in conflict, be inconsistent with

contravene *v*
infringe, violate, break, breach, disobey, defy, flout, *formal* transgress
🖪 uphold, observe, obey

contretemps *n*
clash, brush, tiff, difficulty, accident, misadventure, misfortune, mishap, hitch, predicament

contribute *v*
1 *contribute money to charity* give, donate, give a donation, subscribe, grant, present, endow, provide, supply, furnish, *formal* bestow, *colloq.* chip in **2** *poor design contributed to the disaster* cause, play a part in, give rise to, lead to, result in, occasion, bring about, make, make happen, produce, generate, originate, create, promote, help, add to, be instrumental in, *formal* conduce **3** *contribute an article for a magazine* write, compose, create, compile, prepare, edit, supply, provide

contribution *n*
1 *a contribution of £1000* donation, subscription, gift, gratuity, handout, grant, present, endowment, offering, input, addition, *formal* bestowal **2** *a contribution to a magazine* article, story, feature, item, piece, column, report, review

contributor *n*
1 DONOR, subscriber, giver, patron, benefactor, sponsor, backer, supporter **2** WRITER, author, journalist, reporter, compiler, correspondent, reviewer, critic, columnist, freelance

contrite *adj*
sorry, regretful, remorseful, repentant, penitent, penitential, guilt-ridden, conscience-stricken, chastened, humble, ashamed

contrition *n*
remorse, sorrow, regret, shame, humiliation, penitence, repentance, sackcloth and ashes, self-reproach, *formal* compunction

contrivance *n*
1 INVENTION, device, contraption, gadget, implement, appliance, machine, mechanism, tool, apparatus, equipment, gear **2** STRATAGEM, ploy, trick, dodge, ruse, expedient, plan, design, project, scheme, plot, intrigue, *formal* machination, artifice

contrive *v*
1 *somehow contrived to blame me* manage, succeed, arrange, bring about, create, design, devise, find a way **2** *contrive a meeting between them* engineer, manoeuvre, orchestrate, stage-manage, plan, plot, scheme, fabricate, create, devise, invent, concoct, construct, *colloq.* set up, wangle

contrived *adj*
unnatural, artificial, false, forced, strained, laboured, mannered, elaborate, overdone, *colloq.* set-up
🖪 natural, genuine, spontaneous

control *n, v*
▶ *n* **1** POWER, charge, authority, command, mastery, dominance, sway, supremacy, government, rule, reign, direction, management, oversight, supervision, superintendence, discipline, guidance, influence, *formal* jurisdiction **2** RESTRAINT, self-restraint, self-control, self-discipline, constraint, check, curb, repression **3** *price controls* restriction, constraint, limitation, regulation, limit, reduction, brake, check, curb, hindrance, impediment **4** INSTRUMENT, dial, switch, button, knob, lever
▶ *v* **1** LEAD, be in charge of, have authority over, govern, rule, command, direct, manage, head, oversee, preside over, dominate, supervise, superintend, *colloq.* be the boss, be in the driving seat, be in the saddle, pull the strings, rule the roost, run the show, call the tune/shots, wear the trousers **2** *control a machine/the temperature* run, operate, work, make go, regulate, adjust, monitor, verify **3** *control wages* restrict, limit, regulate, constrain, reduce, check, curb, *colloq.* keep a tight rein on, put the brakes on **4** *control your temper* restrain, check, curb, subdue, repress, hold back, keep, contain

controversial *adj*
contentious, polemical, disputed, doubtful, questionable, debatable, disputable, at issue

controversy *n*
debate, discussion, war of words, difference of opinion, dispute, disagreement, argument, quarrel, squabble, wrangle, strife, contention, discord, friction, dissension, *formal* polemic, altercation
🖪 accord, agreement

contusion *n*
bruise, bump, discoloration, mark, blemish, injury, knock, lump, swelling, *technical* ecchymosis

conundrum *n*
puzzle, problem, enigma, poser, riddle, word game, anagram, brainteaser

convalescence *n*
recuperation, getting better, improvement, recovery, rehabilitation, restoration

convene *v*
1 *convene a meeting* call (together), rally, summon **2** *the court convened* assemble, meet, gather, collect, congregate, muster, *formal* convoke

convenience *n*
1 ACCESSIBILITY, availability, handiness, usefulness, use, ease of use, utility, serviceability, service, benefit, advantage, advantageousness, help, suitability, fitness, appropriateness, opportuneness, *formal* expediency, propitiousness, propinquity **2** *all modern conveniences* facility, amenity, appliance, device, labour-saving device, gadget, service, resource
🖪 **1** inconvenience

convenient *adj*
nearby, at hand, near/close at hand, within reach, within walking/driving distance, accessible, available, handy, useful, beneficial, helpful, labour-saving, adapted, fitted, suited, suitable, fit, fitting, appropriate, opportune, timely, well-timed, *formal* expedient, *col-*

loq. just/only round the corner, at your fingertips
🔄 inconvenient, awkward

convention *n*
1 CUSTOM, tradition, practice, usage, protocol, etiquette, formality, matter of form, code, *formal* propriety, punctilio **2** ASSEMBLY, congress, conference, meeting, gathering, council, delegates, representatives, synod, *formal* convocation, conclave **3** *the Geneva convention* agreement, bond, commitment, engagement, covenant, treaty, pact, transaction, deal, bargain, settlement, arrangement, understanding, *formal* compact, concordat

conventional *adj*
traditional, orthodox, formal, correct, proper, prevalent, prevailing, accepted, received, expected, unoriginal, conformist, conservative, ritual, routine, usual, customary, regular, standard, normal, ordinary, mainstream, straight, stereotyped, trite, hidebound, pedestrian, commonplace, common, *colloq.* common or garden, run-of-the-mill
🔄 unconventional, unusual, exotic, alternative

converge *v*
1 *crowds converged on the car* approach, move towards, gather, close in, form, mass, focus, concentrate **2** *the roads converge at the bridge* meet, join, combine, merge, coincide, unite, come together
🔄 **1** disperse **2** diverge

convergence *n*
concentration, approach, merging, combination, blending, meeting, coincidence, junction, intersection, union, *formal* confluence
🔄 divergence, separation

conversant *adj*
▷ **conversant with** familiar with, acquainted with, experienced in, informed about, knowledgeable about, practised in, proficient in, skilled in, versed in, *au fait* with, *formal* apprised of
🔄 ignorant of

conversation *n*
talk, chat, gossip, discussion, discourse, dialogue, exchange, communication, tête-à-tête, heart-to-heart, cosy chat, small talk, *formal* colloquy, *colloq.* chinwag, natter, confab

conversational *adj*
informal, chatty, colloquial, communicative, relaxed, casual

converse¹ *v*
converse with people talk, discuss, confer, communicate, chat, gossip, chatter, *formal* commune, discourse

converse² *n, adj*
▶ *n the converse is true* opposite, reverse, contrary, obverse, *formal* antithesis, *colloq.* other way round, other side of the coin
▶ *adj* opposite, opposing, reverse, counter, contrary, reversed, transposed, obverse, *formal* antithetical

conversion *n*
1 *a loft conversion* alteration, change, transformation, turning, adaptation, modification, remodelling, reshaping, reconstruction, reorganization, customization, adjustment, *technical* metamorphosis, transfiguration, mutation, transmutation **2** *conversion of pounds into francs* change, exchange, substitution, switch **3** *conversion to Judaism* persuasion, conviction, reformation, regeneration, rebirth, proselytization, preaching

convert *v, n*
▶ *v* **1** *convert the building* ALTER, change, turn, transform, make, adapt, customize, adjust, modify, go over to, transfer, switch, reform, restructure, remodel, reshape, refashion, restyle, revise, reorganize,

rebuild, reconstruct, *technical* metamorphose, transfigure, mutate, transmute **2** *convert inches into centimetres* change, exchange, substitute, turn into, switch from **3** WIN OVER, convince, persuade, cause to change beliefs/religion, reform, proselytize
▶ *n* disciple, believer, new person, changed person, proselyte, neophyte, adherent

convertible *adj*
adaptable, adjustable, exchangeable, modifiable, interchangeable, *formal* permutable

convex *adj*
rounded, curved out, bending outwards, bulging, swelling, protuberant, gibbous
🔄 concave, hollow

convey *v*
1 *convey feelings* COMMUNICATE, express, tell, relate, reveal, disclose, announce, make known, transmit, hand on, pass on, *formal* impart **2** TRANSPORT, carry, bear, bring, fetch, move, transport, drive, shift, send, forward, deliver, transfer, conduct, guide, channel, pipe

conveyance *n*
1 VEHICLE, car, bus, coach, bicycle, motorcycle, lorry, truck, van, wagon, carriage **2** *the conveyance of bicycles* transport, transportation, movement, transfer, transference **3** *the conveyance of property* transfer, transference, granting, transmission, consignment, delivery, bequeathal, ceding

convict *v, n*
▶ *v* condemn, find guilty, sentence, judge, imprison
▶ *n* criminal, law-breaker, felon, culprit, villain, offender, wrongdoer, prisoner, inmate, burglar, thief, robber, *colloq.* crook, jailbird, *slang* lag

conviction *n*
1 BELIEF, view, opinion, faith, creed, tenet, principle **2** *speak with conviction* assurance, confidence, fervour, earnestness, certainty, firmness, persuasion, *formal* certitude **3** *previous convictions* condemnation, pronouncement of guilt, sentence, judgement, imprisonment

convince *v*
assure, persuade, prove to, sway, talk into, win over, bring round, influence, prompt, *formal* prevail upon

convincing *adj*
persuasive, powerful, telling, impressive, credible, plausible, likely, probable, conclusive, compelling, forceful, incontrovertible, *formal* cogent
🔄 unconvincing, improbable

convivial *adj*
friendly, sociable, genial, cheerful, cordial, festive, hearty, jolly, jovial, lively, merry, fun-loving
🔄 taciturn

conviviality *n*
geniality, cheer, cordiality, sociability, gaiety, jollity, joviality, bonhomie, liveliness, mirth, festivity, merrymaking

convocation *n*
congress, convention, council, assembly, congregation, meeting, diet, synod, *formal* conclave, forgathering, assemblage

convoluted *adj*
convoluted carvings/ideas twisting, winding, meandering, tortuous, involved, complicated, complex
🔄 straight, straightforward

convolution *n*
1 *convolutions in the design* coil, twist, whorl, turn, spiral, helix, loop, coiling, winding, sinuousness, sinuosity, *technical* gyrus, *formal* curlicue **2** *convolutions in relationships* complexity, intricacy, complication, entanglement, involvement, tortuousness

convoy *n*
fleet, line, escort, guard, protection, attendance, train, group, company

convulse *v*
suffer a fit/seizure, shake uncontrollably/violently, jerk, seize, unsettle, disturb

convulsion *n*
1 FIT, seizure, attack, paroxysm, spasm, cramp, contraction, tic, tremor **2** *major political convulsions* ERUPTION, outburst, furore, disturbance, unrest, disorder, commotion, tumult, turmoil, agitation, turbulence, upheaval

convulsive *adj*
jerky, spasmodic, fitful, sporadic, uncontrolled, violent

cook *v*
prepare, heat, warm, put on, put together, improvise, undercook, underdo, overcook, overdo, burn, *colloq.* rustle up

Ways of cooking include:
bake, barbecue, boil, braise, broil, brown, casserole, coddle, curry, deep-fry, fricassee, fry, grill, microwave, oven-roast, parboil, poach, pot-roast, roast, sauté, scramble, simmer, spit-roast, steam, stew, stir-fry, toast.

Terms used in cookery include :
bake blind, bind, blend, bone, brown, caramelize, carve, chill, chop, cream, crumble, cure, defrost, deglaze, devil, drizzle, dust, fillet, flash fry, fold in, freeze, glaze, grate, grind, ice, joint, jug, knead, knock back, liquidize, marinate, mash, mince, mix, mull, peel, peppered, pickle, plate (up), potted, *colloq.* prep, preserve, prove, purée, reduce, re-heat, rest, rise, sear, sieve, sift, skim, smoke, souse, stir, strain, stuff, sweat, thicken, truss, whisk.
Terms used in French cookery include: à la crème, à la Grècque, au gratin, au poivre, Bolognese, brûlée, cacciatore, chasseur, cordon bleu, coulis, en cocotte, en croute, farci, frappé, galette, gougère, haute cuisine, Lyonnaise, mornay, Niçoise, nouvelle cuisine, Provençal, roux, sur le plat.
Terms used in Indian cookery include: akhni, aloo, balti, bargar, bhajee or bhaji, bhindi or bindi, bhoona or bhuna, dhal, dhansak, dopiaza, dum, gosht, kalia, karahi, kofta, korma, madras, masala, Moglai, paneer, tandoori, tikka, vindaloo.

▷ **cook up** concoct, prepare, brew, invent, make up, fabricate, contrive, devise, plan, plot, scheme, trump up, dream up

cool *adj, v, n*
▶ *adj* **1** CHILLY, fresh, breezy, nippy, cold, bracing, crisp, draughty **2** *a cool drink* cold, chilled, iced, ice-cold, refreshing **3** CALM, unruffled, unexcited, composed, self-possessed, level-headed, collected, unemotional, dispassionate, quiet, relaxed, impassive, unmoved, placid, sedate, poised, imperturbable, unexcitable, unflustered, unperturbed, undisturbed, untroubled, unapprehensive, *colloq.* laid back, unflappable, cool as a cucumber **4** *a cool reception* unfriendly, unwelcoming, cold, frigid, frosty, lukewarm, half-hearted, unenthusiastic, apathetic, uninterested, unresponsive, uncommunicative, undemonstrative, reserved, distant, aloof, standoffish **5** *look cool in that outfit* sophisticated, fashionable, elegant, smart, stylish, *colloq.* trendy, streetwise **6** *a*

really cool party great, wonderful, excellent, fantastic, marvellous
◪ **1** warm, hot **2** hot **3** excited, angry **4** friendly, welcoming
▶ *v* **1** CHILL, refrigerate, ice, freeze, make cold, make colder, get/turn cold, get/turn colder, air-condition, fan **2** MODERATE, lessen, temper, dampen, diminish, reduce, quiet, calm, allay, *formal* abate, assuage
◪ **1** warm, heat **2** excite
▶ *n* **1** *keep/lose your cool* composure, coolness, calmness, collectedness, poise, self-possession, self-discipline, self-control, control, temper **2** *the cool of the early morning* chill, freshness, breeze, nippiness, cold, crispness, draught, *technical* defervescence, defervescency

cooling *n, adj*
▶ *n* chilling, refrigeration, air-conditioning, ventilation, *technical* defervescence, defervescency
◪ heating, warming
▶ *adj* freezing, refrigerant, refrigerative, refrigeratory
◪ warming

coop *n, v*
▶ *n* cage, box, enclosure, pen, hutch, pound
▶ *v* ▷ **coop up** imprison, cage, enclose, shut (up), impound, keep in, lock up/away, pen, imprison, *formal* incarcerate, immure

co-operate *v*
collaborate, work together, pull together, band together, team up, help, assist, aid, contribute, participate, combine, unite, join forces, share, pool, conspire, *colloq.* play ball

co-operation *n*
helpfulness, help, helping hand, assistance, aid, contribution, participation, collaboration, teamwork, working together, unity, co-ordination, joint action, concerted action, give-and-take
◪ opposition, rivalry, competition

co-operative *adj*
1 COLLECTIVE, joint, shared, combined, united, concerted, co-ordinated, collaborative, working together **2** HELPFUL, helping, assisting, supportive, responsive, obliging, accommodating, willing, *formal* coactive, compliant
◪ **2** unco-operative, rebellious

co-ordinate *v*
organize, arrange, systematize, order, work together, co-operate, collaborate, tabulate, integrate, mesh, synchronize, harmonize, match, correlate, regulate, *colloq.* mix 'n'match

cope *v*
manage, carry on, survive, get by, get through, make do, succeed, take in your stride
▷ **cope with** deal with, encounter, contend with, struggle with, grapple with, wrestle with, handle, manage, treat, weather, endure
◪ *colloq.* not hack it

copious *adj*
abundant, plentiful, inexhaustible, overflowing, profuse, rich, lavish, bountiful, liberal, full, ample, generous, extensive, great, huge, *formal* plenteous, bounteous, luxuriant, *colloq.* bags of
◪ scarce, meagre

cop-out *n*
dodge, evasion, fraud, pretence, pretext, alibi, *colloq.* shirking, passing the buck

copse *n*
coppice, wood, thicket, grove, bush, brush

copulate *v*
mate, make love, have sex, have sexual intercourse, enjoy, gender, horse, line, *colloq.* go to bed with

copy *n, v*
▶ *n* **1** *copies of the letter* duplicate, facsimile, fax, carbon copy, photocopy, Photostat®, Xerox®, reproduction, print, tracing, transcript, transcription, replica, model, pattern, archetype, representation, image, likeness, counterfeit, forgery, fake, imitation, borrowing, plagiarism, crib **2** *buy a copy of the magazine* issue, sample, example, specimen
⊟ **1** original
▶ *v* duplicate, photocopy, Photostat®, Xerox®, reproduce, print, trace, transcribe, fax, scan, forge, counterfeit, pirate, simulate, imitate, impersonate, mimic, ape, parrot, repeat, echo, mirror, follow, emulate, borrow, plagiarize, crib, *formal* replicate

coquettish *adj*
flirtatious, amorous, dallying, flighty, flirty, inviting, teasing, *colloq.* come-hither, vampish

cord *n*
string, twine, rope, line, cable, flex, connection, link, bond, tie

cordial *adj*
friendly, amicable, affable, affectionate, agreeable, cheerful, genial, sociable, pleasant, heartfelt, warm, warm-hearted, welcoming, wholehearted, earnest, hearty, stimulating, invigorating
⊟ hostile, aloof, cool

cordiality *n*
friendliness, affability, affection, agreeableness, cheerfulness, geniality, sociability, heartiness, warmth, welcome, wholeheartedness, earnest, sincerity
⊟ coolness, hostility

cordon *n, v*
▶ *n* line, ring, barrier, chain, fence
▶ *v* ▷ **cordon off** close off, fence off, isolate, separate, encircle, enclose, surround

core *n*
kernel, nucleus, heart, centre, middle, nub, crux, essence, substance, gist, *formal* quintessence, *colloq.* nitty-gritty
⊟ surface, exterior

corn *n*
arable crop, cereal crop, cereal, wheat, barley, oats, rye, maize, grain

corner *n, v*
▶ *n* **1** *round the corner* angle, joint, crook, bend, curve, turning, fork, junction, intersection **2** NOOK, cranny, niche, recess, crevice, cavity, hole, hideout, hideaway, retreat **3** *in a tight corner* predicament, plight, situation, hardship, straits, *colloq.* tight spot, nowhere to turn, hole, pickle
▶ *v* **1** *corner an animal* force into a place, trap, hunt down, catch, cut off, block off, run to earth, confine **2** *corner the market* monopolize, control, dominate, have sole rights in, *colloq.* hog

corny *adj*
banal, commonplace, hackneyed, stale, overused, stereotyped, trite, clichéd, predictable, sentimental, dull, feeble, maudlin, mawkish, old-fashioned, platitudinous
⊟ new, original

corollary *n*
consequence, conclusion, result, upshot, deduction, induction, inference, *formal* illation

coronation *n*
enthronement, crowning, accession to the throne

coronet *n*
crown, diadem, tiara, circlet, wreath, garland

corporal *adj*
anatomical, bodily, fleshly, carnal, material, physical, tangible, corporeal, *formal* somatic
⊟ spiritual

corporate *adj*
combined, collective, concerted, joint, communal, merged, pooled, shared, united, allied, amalgamated, collaborative

corporation *n*
1 *a business corporation* firm, company, business, concern, association, organization, establishment, house, partnership, syndicate, cartel, trust, consortium, conglomerate, multinational, industry, holding company **2** *the Corporation of London* council, authority, authorities, governing body

corporeal *adj*
actual, material, physical, substantial, tangible, bodily, fleshly, human, mortal
⊟ spiritual

corps *n*
band, body, detachment, unit, squad, team, division, brigade, company, contingent, crew, regiment, squadron

corpse *n*
body, dead body, carcase, cadaver, skeleton, remains, mummy, zombie, *slang* stiff

corpulent *adj*
fat, fattish, large, obese, overweight, plump, stout, beefy, bulky, burly, fleshy, portly, pot-bellied, podgy, roly-poly, tubby, well-padded, *formal* rotund, adipose
⊟ thin

corpus *n*
collection, compilation, body, entirety, whole, *formal* aggregation

corral *n*
enclosure, fold, pound, stall, coop, sty, kraal

correct *adj, v*
▶ *adj* **1** *the correct answer* right, accurate, precise, exact, strict, true, truthful, actual, real, faithful, word-perfect, faultless, flawless, unerring, *colloq.* spot on, bang on **2** PROPER, acceptable, accepted, standard, regular, just, appropriate, suitable, fitting, conventional, *colloq.* OK
⊟ **1** incorrect, wrong, inaccurate
▶ *v* **1** *correct an error* rectify, put right, right, set right, put straight, remedy, cure, debug, redress, adjust, regulate, revise, improve, amend, *formal* emend, ameliorate, disabuse, *colloq.* put the record straight **2** PUNISH, discipline, reprimand, reprove, scold, rebuke, reform, *formal* admonish

correction *n*
1 *corrections to the text* rectification, remedying, adjustment, alteration, modification, amendment, improvement, *formal* emendation, amelioration **2** PUNISHMENT, discipline, reprimand, chastisement, reproof, scolding, rebuke, reformation, *formal* admonition

corrective *adj*
1 *corrective measures* remedial, curative, medicinal, palliative, restorative, therapeutic, *formal* emendatory **2** DISCIPLINARY, penal, punitive, reformatory, rehabilitative

correlate *v*
associate, compare, connect, show a connection/relationship, co-ordinate, correspond, agree, equate, interact, link, parallel, relate, link, tie in

correlation *n*
association, connection, relationship, correspondence, equivalence, interaction, interchange, interdependence, interrelationship, link, reciprocity

correspond *v*
1 MATCH, match up, fit (together), answer, conform, tally, square, agree, be in agreement, be consistent, coincide, harmonize, dovetail, complement, be simi-

lar, be equivalent, *formal* concur, correlate, accord, be analogous **2** COMMUNICATE, write, pen, exchange letters, keep in touch

correspondence *n*
1 COMMUNICATION, writing, letters, post, mail **2** CONFORMITY, agreement, coincidence, relation, analogy, comparison, comparability, similarity, resemblance, equivalence, harmony, match, *formal* concurrence, correlation, congruity, consonance
F3 2 divergence, incongruity

correspondent *n*
journalist, reporter, contributor, writer

corresponding *adj*
matching, complementary, reciprocal, interrelated, comparable, equivalent, similar, like, matching, parallel, identical, *formal* analogous

corridor *n*
aisle, passageway, passage, hallway, hall, lobby

corroborate *v*
confirm, prove, bear out, verify, support, back up, endorse, ratify, certify, substantiate, validate, authenticate, document, underpin, uphold, sustain, *formal* evidence
F3 contradict

corroborative *adj*
confirming, confirmatory, supporting, supportive, verifying, endorsing, substantiating, validating, *formal* confirmative, evidential, evidentiary, verificatory

corrode *v*
erode, wear away, eat away, consume, destroy, waste, rust, oxidize, tarnish, impair, deteriorate, rot, crumble, disintegrate, *formal* abrade

corrosive *adj*
corroding, acid, caustic, cutting, abrasive, wearing, consuming, destructive, wasting, *technical* erosive

corrugated *adj*
ridged, fluted, grooved, channelled, furrowed, wrinkled, folded, crinkled, rumpled, creased, *technical* striate

corrupt *adj, v*
▶ *adj* rotten, unscrupulous, unprincipled, unethical, immoral, evil, wicked, fraudulent, dishonest, untrustworthy, bribable, venal, depraved, degenerate, dissolute, tainted, contaminated, *colloq.* shady, bent, crooked
F3 ethical, virtuous, upright, honest, fair, trustworthy
▶ *v* contaminate, pollute, adulterate, taint, infect, mar, blight, defile, debase, debauch, pervert, deprave, warp, be a bad influence, lure, bribe, suborn, *formal* vitiate, *colloq.* lead astray, buy (off), grease someone's palm
F3 purify

corruption *n*
unscrupulousness, immorality, impurity, depravity, degeneration, degradation, perversion, debauchery, distortion, dishonesty, fraud, bribery, subornation, extortion, sharp practice, vice, wickedness, iniquity, evil, criminality, villainy, contamination, pollution, rottenness, *US* graft, *colloq.* wheeling and dealing, crookedness, shadiness
F3 honesty, virtue, fairness, trustworthiness

corset *n*
girdle, panty girdle, belt, bodice, corselet, foundation garment, roll-on, basque, stays

cortège *n*
procession, retinue, suite, train, column, entourage, cavalcade, parade

cosmetic *adj*
1 *a cosmetic substance* make-up, beauty, beautifying **2** *cosmetic changes* superficial, surface, external, shallow, peripheral, minor, slight, trivial
F3 2 basic, essential

cosmetics *n*

Types of cosmetics include:
blusher, cleanser, eyebrow pencil, eyelash dye, eyeliner, eye shadow, face cream, face mask, face pack, face powder, false eyelashes, foundation, greasepaint, kohl pencil, lip gloss, lip liner, lipstick, loose powder, maquillage, mascara, moisturizer, nail polish, nail varnish, pancake make-up, pressed powder, rouge, toner, *colloq.* war paint.

cosmic *adj*
1 *cosmic forces* worldwide, universal, in/from space, infinite, limitless, measureless **2** *changes of cosmic proportion* immense, vast, huge, grandiose, infinite, limitless, immeasurable, measureless

cosmonaut *n*
astronaut, spaceman, spacewoman, space traveller

cosmopolitan *adj*
1 *a very cosmopolitan city* international, universal, multiracial, multicultural **2** *a very cosmopolitan outlook* worldly, worldly-wise, well-travelled, broadminded, sophisticated, cultured, urbane
F3 2 insular, parochial

cosmos *n*
universe, creation, galaxy, system, worlds

cosset *v*
coddle, mollycoddle, baby, pamper, indulge, spoil, pet, fondle, cuddle, cherish

cost *n, v*
▶ *n* **1** EXPENSE, outlay, payment, expenditure, charge, price, selling price, asking price, rate, fee, quotation, amount, figure, value, valuation, worth, *formal* disbursement, *colloq.* damage **2** *cover costs* budget, expenses, expenditure, spending, outgoings, outlay, overheads **3** *the cost to her health* harm, injury, hurt, loss, suffering, deprivation, detriment, sacrifice, penalty, price
▶ *v* **1** *it costs £500* pay, charge, be priced at, ask for, sell for, retail at, buy for, be valued at, be worth, fetch, go for, come to, amount to, *colloq.* set back, knock back **2** *cost a job* price, estimate, cost out, quote, value, calculate, work out **3** *cost him his life* cause the loss/sacrifice of, cause harm/injury, deprive, harm, injure, hurt, be a high price to pay

costly *adj*
1 EXPENSIVE, dear, exorbitant, excessive, lavish, rich, splendid, valuable, precious, high-cost, high-priced, priceless, *colloq.* pricey, steep **2** HARMFUL, damaging, destructive, detrimental, disastrous, ruinous, catastrophic, loss-making, *formal* deleterious
F3 1 cheap, inexpensive

costume *n*
outfit, uniform, livery, ensemble, robes, vestments, dress, style of dress, fashion, clothes, clothing, garments, habit, fancy dress, *formal* apparel, attire, *colloq.* get-up

cosy *adj*
snug, comfortable, warm, sheltered, secure, safe, homely, congenial, intimate, *colloq.* comfy
F3 uncomfortable, cold

coterie *n*
set, circle, clique, group, club, association, community, faction, camp, caucus, cabal, gang

cottage *n*
lodge, chalet, bungalow, hut, cabin, shack

couch *n, v*
▶ *n* sofa, settee, chesterfield, chaise-longue, ottoman, divan, bed, day bed, sofa bed

▶ *v* express, frame, phrase, word, set, bear, support, utter, cradle

cough *v, n*
▶ *v* clear your throat, bark, hack, hawk, hem
▷ **cough up** pay up, pay, pay out, give, *colloq.* fork out, shell out, stump up
▶ *n* bark, hack, hawking, hem, clearing your throat, *technical* tussis, *colloq.* frog in your throat

council *n*
1 *the town council* local authority, cabinet, ministry, parliament, government, governing body, senate, administration **2** *the Arts Council* advisory body, advisory group, committee, panel, jury, commission, directorate, directors, trustees, governors, advisers, board, working party, management **3** *a ministerial council* congress, assembly, convention, conference, gathering, rally, meeting, group, body, body of people, company, congregation, flock, crowd, multitude, throng, *formal* convocation

---

🖉 **council** or **counsel**?
A *council* is 'a body of people who organize, control, advise or take decisions': *a county council. Counsel* is a rather formal word for 'advice': *give wise counsel.*

---

counsel *n, v*
▶ *n* **1** ADVICE, suggestion, recommendation, guidance, direction, information, consultation, deliberation, consideration, forethought, opinion, viewpoint, suggestion, *formal* exhortation, admonition **2** *counsel for the defence* lawyer, advocate, solicitor, attorney, barrister
▶ *v* advise, warn, caution, suggest, recommend, advocate, urge, exhort, guide, give guidance, direct, instruct, give your opinion, *formal* exhort, admonish

count *v, n*
▶ *v* **1** NUMBER, enumerate, list, include, reckon, calculate, compute, tell, check, add (up), total, score, tally, *colloq.* tot up **2** MATTER, be important, signify, qualify, carry weight, make a difference, make an impression, mean something, *colloq.* cut some ice, make waves **3** *count yourself lucky* consider, regard, judge, think, reckon, look upon, hold, *formal* esteem, deem **4** *if you count children* include, take account of, take into account, allow for
▷ **count on** depend on, rely on, bank on, lean on, reckon on, expect, believe, trust
▷ **count out** exclude, eliminate, ignore, leave out, omit, pass over, disregard, include out
☒ include, consider
▶ *n* numbering, enumeration, poll, reckoning, calculation, computation, sum, total, tally, whole, full amount, *colloq.* totting-up

countenance *n, v*
▶ *n* face, expression, appearance, features, look, *formal* mien, physiognomy, visage
▶ *v* tolerate, agree, allow, approve, brook, stand for, put up with, back, condone, endorse, endure, sanction

counter¹ *n*
1 *serve at the counter* worktop, surface, work surface, table, stand **2** *a counter in a game* disc, token, chip, piece, coin, marker

counter² *v, adv, adj*
▶ *v* *counter someone's argument* parry, resist, oppose, combat, dispute, offset, answer, respond, retaliate, retort, hit back at, return, meet
▶ *adv* against, in opposition, contrary to, conversely
▶ *adj* contrary, opposite, opposing, conflicting, contradictory, contrasting, opposed, against, adverse

counteract *v*
neutralize, counterbalance, offset, act against, oppose, resist, hinder, check, thwart, frustrate, foil, defeat, undo, annul, invalidate, *formal* negate, countervail
☒ support, assist

counterbalance *v*
balance, compensate for, make up for, equalize, neutralize, offset, undo, *formal* counterpoise, countervail

counterfeit *adj, n, v*
▶ *adj* fake, faked, false, forged, copied, pirate, fraudulent, bogus, sham, spurious, imitation, artificial, simulated, pretended, *formal* feigned, *colloq.* phoney, pseud, pseudo
☒ genuine, authentic, real
▶ *n* fake, forgery, copy, reproduction, imitation, fraud, sham
▶ *v* fake, forge, fabricate, copy, imitate, reproduce, pirate, impersonate, falsify, pretend, simulate, sham, *formal* feign

countermand *v*
cancel, reverse, annul, override, overturn, quash, repeal, *formal* abrogate, rescind, revoke

counterpart *n*
equivalent, opposite number, equal, complement, supplement, parallel, match, fellow, mate, twin, duplicate, copy, obverse

countless *adj*
innumerable, myriad, numberless, unnumbered, untold, incalculable, infinite, endless, without end, immeasurable, measureless, inexhaustible, limitless, boundless, *colloq.* umpteen
☒ finite, limited

countrified *adj*
rural, rustic, pastoral, provincial, idyllic, agricultural, agrarian, outback, *formal* bucolic, *colloq.* hick
☒ urban, *formal* oppidan

country *n, adj*
▶ *n* **1** STATE, nation, kingdom, realm, republic, power, community, principality, inhabitants, people, population, populace, residents, citizens, voters, electors **2** COUNTRYSIDE, green belt, farmland, moorland, rural area, outback, bush, *colloq.* provinces, backwater, backwoods, wilds, sticks, back of beyond, middle of nowhere **3** TERRAIN, land, territory, region, area, district, neighbourhood, locality
☒ **2** town, city
▶ *adj* rural, rustic, pastoral, landed, provincial, idyllic, agricultural, agrarian, *formal* bucolic
☒ urban

countryman, countrywoman *n*
1 *fellow countrywomen* compatriot, fellow citizen, fellow national **2** *local countrymen's skills* farmer, yokel, boor, clodhopper, rustic, peasant, provincial, backwoodsman, bushwhacker, *Scot.* hind, *colloq.* bumpkin, hillbilly, hick, hayseed

countryside *n*
landscape, scenery, country, green belt, farmland, moorland, rural area, outdoors

county *n*
shire, province, region, area, state, territory, district

coup *n*
1 *a military coup* coup d'état, overthrow, revolution, (military) takeover, uprising, palace revolution, putsch, rebellion, revolt **2** *a big coup for the company* feat, masterstroke, stroke, accomplishment, deed, exploit, stunt, action, manoeuvre, tour de force

coup de grâce *n*
death blow, *formal* quietus, *colloq.* clincher, kiss of death, come-uppance, kibosh, kill

coup d'état *n*
coup, overthrow, revolution, (military) takeover, uprising, palace revolution, putsch, rebellion, revolt

couple *n*, *v*
▶ *n* pair, husband and wife, newlyweds, partners, lovers, brace, twosome, duo, *colloq.* item
▶ *v* pair, match, marry, wed, unite, join, link, connect, combine, ally, associate, attach, fasten, hitch, clasp, bind, buckle, yoke, *formal* conjoin

coupon *n*
voucher, token, slip, check, stub, ticket, certificate, form

courage *n*
bravery, pluck, fearlessness, dauntlessness, heroism, gallantry, valour, boldness, audacity, intrepidity, daring, determination, resolution, spirit, mettle, backbone, *formal* fortitude, *colloq.* nerve, guts, bottle, spunk, grit
▣ cowardice, fear

courageous *adj*
brave, plucky, fearless, dauntless, indomitable, heroic, gallant, valiant, lion-hearted, stout-hearted, hardy, bold, audacious, daring, intrepid, adventurous, determined, resolute, *formal* valorous, *colloq.* gutsy, spunky
▣ cowardly, afraid

courier *n*
1 *the courier delivered the parcels* messenger, carrier, dispatch rider, runner, bearer, emissary, envoy, representative, herald, legate, nuncio, estafette, pursuivant **2** *a guided tour by the courier* guide, travel guide, tour guide, escort, company representative

course *n*, *v*
▶ *n* **1** CURRICULUM, syllabus, programme, schedule, classes, lessons, lectures, studies **2** FLOW, movement, advance, march, rise, progress, development, unfolding, furtherance, order, sequence, series, succession, progression **3** DURATION, time, period, lapse, term, spell, span, passing, passage **4** ROUTE, direction, way, passage, path, track, tack, road, lane, run, channel, trail, line, circuit, orbit, ambit, trajectory, flight path **5** *course of action* plan, schedule, programme, policy, procedure, system, process, manner, method, way, approach, tack, *formal* mode **6** *the last hole on the course* golf course, racecourse, racetrack, track, ground, circuit **7** *chicken for main course* dish, part, stage, remove, starters, hors d'oeuvres, appetizer, entrée, main course, dessert, sweet, pudding, entremets, *colloq.* afters **8** *a course of medical treatment* sequence, series, programme, schedule, regimen
▷ **in due course** in time, in due time, sooner or later, in the course of time, finally, eventually, to be sure
▷ **of course** naturally, certainly, surely, by all means, definitely, without a doubt, no doubt, undoubtedly, doubtlessly, needless to say, *formal* indubitably
▶ *v* **1** *tears coursing down her cheeks* flow, run, move, pour, gush, stream, surge, dash **2** *coursing hares* chase, hunt, pursue, run after, follow, track, race

court *n*, *v*
▶ *n* **1** LAWCOURT, bench, bar, judiciary, tribunal, trial, session, assizes

2 *tennis courts* playing area, game area, enclosure, track, ground, arena, ring, alley, green **3** COURTYARD, yard, quadrangle, square, patio, cloister, forecourt, enclosure, plaza, esplanade, *colloq.* quad **4** *at the king's court* palace, castle, royal residence **5** ENTOURAGE, attendants, household, retinue, suite, train, cortège
▶ *v* **1** *court a young lady* woo, pursue, chase, go out, go with, *colloq.* date, go steady **2** *court support/publicity* cultivate, try to win, solicit, flatter, pander to, attract, prompt, provoke, incite, seek, invite

courteous *adj*
polite, civil, respectful, well-mannered, well-bred, deferential, ladylike, gentlemanly, mannerly, gracious, obliging, considerate, kind, diplomatic, tactful, attentive, gallant, chivalrous, courtly, urbane, debonair, refined, polished
▣ discourteous, impolite, rude

courtesy *n*
politeness, civility, respect, (good) manners, (good) breeding, deference, graciousness, consideration, kindness, favour, generosity, tact, attention, gallantry, chivalry, refinement, urbanity
▣ discourtesy, rudeness

courtier *n*
noble, nobleman, lord, lady, lady-in-waiting, steward, page, attendant, cup-bearer, train-bearer, subject, liegeman, follower, flatterer, sycophant, toady

courtly *adj*
gracious, dignified, polite, refined, obliging, polished, elegant, stately, aristocratic, high-bred, lordly, ceremonious, gallant, chivalrous, civil, formal, decorous, flattering
▣ inelegant, provincial, rough

courtship *n*
wooing, pursuit, courting, chasing, going-out, dating, going steady, romance, affair

courtyard *n*
yard, quadrangle, area, enclosure, court, square, cloister, forecourt, plaza, patio, esplanade, atrium, *colloq.* quad

cove *n*
bay, bight, inlet, estuary, firth, fiord, creek

covenant *n*, *v*
▶ *n* arrangement, promise, contract, bond, commitment, deed, engagement, pact, pledge, treaty, trust, convention, stipulation, undertaking, *formal* indenture, compact, concordat
▶ *v* agree, contract, promise, stipulate, undertake, engage, pledge

cover *v*, *n*
▶ *v* **1** HIDE, put/place over, conceal, bury, obscure, shroud, veil, wreathe, screen, mask, disguise, camouflage **2** *covered with mud* be over, coat, spread, daub, plaster, cake, encase, wrap, envelop, blanket, swaddle, clothe, dress, overlay, *formal* attire, accoutre **3** SHELTER, put/place over, protect, shield, guard, safeguard, defend **4** *cover a topic* deal with, treat, consider, examine, investigate, give details of, review, survey, report, describe, encompass, embrace, incorporate, embody, involve, include, contain, comprise, take in **5** *cover 25 miles* travel (over), cross, go, go across, journey, do, *formal* traverse **6** *cover for a colleague* stand in for, deputize, relieve, replace, take over from, be a replacement/substitute for **7** *the estate*

covers some 500 acres extend over, stretch, continue, measure **8** *£50 to cover expenses* pay for, be enough for, recompense, make up for **9** *the insurance will cover it* protect, insure, provide for, *formal* indemnify

⊞ 1 uncover **2** strip **3** expose **4** exclude

▷ **cover up** conceal, hide, suppress, keep secret, keep dark, repress, gloss over; *formal* dissemble, *colloq.* whitewash, hush up

⊞ disclose, reveal

▸ *n* **1** SHELTER, refuge, protection, shield, guard, defence, concealment, hiding-place, sanctuary, refuge, disguise, camouflage **2** COVERING, coating, top, lid, cup, jacket, wrapper, binding, case, envelope, package, coat, layer, film, skin, carpet, mantle, clothing, dress, bedclothes, blankets, duvet, bedspread, canopy **3** *as a cover for illegal activity* cover-up, concealment, screen, smokescreen, veil, mask, front, façade, pretence, conspiracy, complicity, *colloq.* whitewash **4** *insurance cover* protection, insurance, compensation, assurance, *formal* indemnity, indemnification

coverage *n*
reporting, report(s), description, account, investigation, analysis, item, story, reportage

covering *n, adj*
▸ *n* layer, coat, coating, blanket, carpet, film, veneer, skin, crust, case, shell, casing, housing, wrapping, clothing, protection, shelter, mask, overlay, cover, top, shelter, roof, roofing
▸ *adj* accompanying, explanatory, descriptive, introductory

covert *adj*
hidden, secret, private, clandestine, concealed, disguised, veiled, sneaky, stealthy, sidelong, surreptitious, unsuspected, ulterior, underhand, *formal* dissembled, subreptitious, *colloq.* under the table

⊞ open

cover-up *n*
concealment, screen, smokescreen, front, façade, pretence, conspiracy, complicity, *colloq.* whitewash

covet *v*
desire, crave, long for, yearn for, hanker for, want, hunger/thirst for, lust after, envy, begrudge, *colloq.* fancy

covetous *adj*
yearning, craving, wanting, longing, hankering, hungering, thirsting, acquisitive, grasping, greedy, insatiable, jealous, envious, *formal* desirous, avaricious, rapacious

⊞ generous, temperate

covey *n*
cluster, flight, flock, group, bevy, nid, skein

cow *v*
intimidate, domineer, browbeat, bully, terrorize, frighten, scare, overawe, subdue, unnerve, daunt, dishearten, dismay, *colloq.* rattle

⊞ encourage

coward *n*
craven, faint-heart, poltroon, renegade, deserter, *old use* recreant, *colloq.* chicken, scaredy-cat, yellow-belly, sissy, cry-baby, wimp, *Austral.* sook

⊞ hero

cowardice *n*
cowardliness, faint-heartedness, timorousness, spinelessness, *formal* pusillanimity

⊞ courage, bravery, valour

cowardly *adj*
faint-hearted, craven, fearful, timorous, scared, unheroic, chicken-hearted, chicken-livered, spineless, weak, weak-kneed, soft, jittery, *formal* pusillanimous, *colloq.* chicken, gutless, wimpish, yellow-bellied, yellow, lily-livered

⊞ brave, courageous, bold, audacious, intrepid, daring, doughty, valiant

cowboy *n*
1 *cowboys to look after cattle* drover, cattleman, cowhand, herdsman, cattleherder, herder, stockman, rancher, ranchero, *US* bronco-buster, buckaroo, cowpoke, cowpuncher, gaucho, vaquero, waddy, wrangler **2** *a cowboy plumbing firm* bungler, incompetent, rascal, rogue, scoundrel

⊞ 2 professional

cower *v*
crouch, grovel, skulk, shrink, flinch, draw back, recoil, wince, cringe, quail, tremble, quake, shake, shiver

coy *adj*
modest, demure, prudish, prim, diffident, shy, bashful, timid, shrinking, backward, retiring, self-effacing, withdrawn, reserved, reticent, evasive, arch, flirtatious, coquettish, skittish, kittenish

⊞ bold, forward

crabbed, crabby *adj*
bad-tempered, cross, ill-tempered, irritable, morose, snappish, cantankerous, petulant, perverse, acrid, acrimonious, awkward, difficult, harsh, tough, sour, captious, churlish, fretful, snappy, surly, tart, testy, *formal* iracund, iracundulous, irascible, misanthropic, splenetic, *colloq.* crotchety, grouchy, prickly

⊞ calm, placid

crack *v, n, adj*
▸ *v* **1** SPLIT, burst, fracture, break, snap, shatter, splinter, split, fragment, chip **2** EXPLODE, go bang, bang, detonate, boom, burst, pop, crackle, snap, crash, bash, hit, clap, slap, bump, *colloq.* whack, wallop, clout **3** *crack under pressure* lose control, collapse, break down, go to pieces **4** *crack a code* decipher, work out, solve, unravel, figure out, find the answer to

▷ **crack down on** clamp down on, end, stop, put a stop to, crush, suppress, check, control, limit, restrict, confine, repress, act against

▷ **crack up** lose control, go to pieces, have a nervous breakdown, break down, collapse, go mad, go ballistic

▸ *n* **1** BREAK, fracture, flaw, chip, split, rift, breach, rupture, gap, crevice, fissure, cleft, cavity, chink, line, cranny **2** EXPLOSION, bang, boom, detonation, burst, pop, snap, crash, clap, blow, smack, slap, hit, bump, *formal* report, *colloq.* whack, clout **3** *have a crack at something* attempt, go, try, *colloq.* bash, shot, stab, whirl **4** JOKE, quip, witticism, one-liner, wisecrack, gibe, repartee, *colloq.* gag, dig

▸ *adj* first-class, first-rate, excellent, outstanding, brilliant, superior, choice, hand-picked, expert, *colloq.* top-notch

crackdown *n*
clampdown, crushing, end, check, stop, repression, suppression

cracked *adj*
1 *a cracked glass* broken, chipped, damaged, defective, flawed, imperfect, faulty, fissured, split, torn **2** *they're cracked* crazy, insane, deranged, crazed, foolish, idiotic, *colloq.* daft, barmy, batty, crackbrained, crackpot, loony, nuts, nutty, off your rocker, round the bend

⊞ 1 flawless, perfect **2** sane

crackers *adj*
cracked, crazy, mad, foolish, idiotic, *colloq.* daft, batty, crackbrained, crackpot, loony, nuts, nutty, round the bend

⊞ sane

crackle *v, n*
▸ *v* snap, crack, sizzle, rustle, *formal* crepitate, decrepitate

▶ *n* snap, crack, sizzle, rustle, *formal* crepitation, crepitus, decrepitation

crackpot *n*
idiot, fool, *colloq.* freak, loony, weirdo, oddball, nutter, *slang* dork

cradle *n, v*
▶ *n* **1** COT, carry-cot, travel-cot, crib, bassinet, bed **2** SOURCE, origin, spring, wellspring, fount, fountainhead, birthplace, starting-point, beginning
▶ *v* hold, support, rock, lull, nestle, nurse, shelter, nurture, tend

craft *n*
1 SKILL, expertise, mastery, talent, knack, flair, ability, skilfulness, expertness, aptitude, dexterity, cleverness, artistry, art, handicraft, handiwork, workmanship, technique **2** TRADE, business, calling, vocation, job, occupation, work, employment, line, pursuit **3** VESSEL, boat, ship, aircraft, spacecraft, spaceship, landing craft

craftsman, craftswoman *n*
artist, artisan, technician, expert, master, maker, skilled worker, wright, smith

craftsmanship *n*
artistry, workmanship, skill, technique, dexterity, expertise, mastery

crafty *adj*
sly, cunning, artful, wily, foxy, devious, subtle, scheming, calculating, conniving, designing, deceitful, fraudulent, sharp, shrewd, astute, canny, *formal* duplicitous, *colloq.* crooked
▄ artless, naïve, guileless

crag *n*
bluff, cliff, escarpment, scarp, ridge, peak, pinnacle, rock, tor

craggy *adj*
1 *a craggy cliff* precipitous, rocky, rough, rugged, cragged, stony, jagged, uneven **2** *a craggy face* rough, rugged, jagged, uneven
▄ **2** smooth

cram *v*
1 *cram sweets into your mouth* stuff, jam, ram, force, press, squeeze, crush, compress, pack, crowd, overcrowd, fill (up), overfill, glut, gorge, *formal* compact **2** *cram for an exam* revise, study hard, *colloq.* swot, mug up, bone up on, grind

cramp *n, v*
▶ *n* pain, ache, twinge, pang, contraction, convulsion, spasm, muscular contraction, crick, stitch, pins and needles, stiffness
▶ *v* hinder, hamper, obstruct, impede, inhibit, handicap, thwart, frustrate, check, restrict, limit, bridle, hamstring, arrest, constrain, restrain, confine, stymie, shackle, tie

cramped *adj*
narrow, tight, small, uncomfortable, restricted, confined, crowded, packed, squashed, squeezed, closed in, hemmed in, overcrowded, full, overfull, jampacked, congested, *colloq.* poky, no room to swing a cat
▄ spacious

crane *n*
derrick, hoist, tackle, winch, block and tackle, davit

crank *n*
eccentric, character, madman, idiot, *colloq.* freak, weirdo, oddball, nutter, crackpot, loony

cranky *adj*
1 ECCENTRIC, odd, peculiar, unconventional, strange, bizarre, freakish, idiosyncratic, *colloq.* wacky, dotty **2** BAD-TEMPERED, cross, ill-tempered, irritable, cantankerous, awkward, difficult, harsh, snappy, surly, tart, testy, *colloq.* crabby, crotchety, prickly
▄ **1** normal, sensible **2** calm, placid

cranny *n*
chink, cleft, crack, crevice, fissure, rent, gap, hole, nook, opening, cleavage, *formal* interstice

crash *n, v, adj*
▶ *n* **1** *a car crash* accident, collision, bump, pile-up, wreck, *colloq.* smash, smash-up, prang **2** BANG, clash, clatter, clang, clank, thud, thump, boom, explosion, thunder, smash, racket, din **3** *stock-market crash* collapse, failure, ruin, downfall, fall, bankruptcy, depression
▶ *v* **1** COLLIDE, hit, knock, bump, bang, run into, go into, drive into, smash into, plough into **2** BREAK, fracture, smash, batter, dash, shatter, splinter, shiver, fragment, disintegrate **3** FALL, topple, pitch, plunge, collapse, fail, fold (up), founder, go under, go into liquidation, *colloq.* go bust, go to the wall **4** *the computer crashed* cut out, break down, stop working, fail, *formal* malfunction, *colloq.* pack up, go on the blink
▶ *adj* intensive, rapid, accelerated, concentrated, telescoped, emergency, immediate, round-the-clock, urgent

crass *adj*
stupid, indelicate, insensitive, tactless, unrefined, unsophisticated, blundering, rude, crude, coarse, dense, oafish, unsubtle, witless, *formal* obtuse
▄ refined, sensitive

crate *n*
container, box, case, tea chest, packing-box, packing-case

crater *n*
hollow, depression, hole, dip, pit, cavity, chasm, abyss

crave *v*
hunger for, thirst for, long for, yearn for, pine for, sigh for, hanker after, pant for, lust after, desire, covet, want, dream of, wish, need, require, *colloq.* be dying for, fancy
▄ dislike

craven *adj*
cowardly, faint-hearted, fearful, timorous, scared, afraid, unheroic, chicken-hearted, chicken-livered, lily-livered, mean-spirited, spineless, weak, weak-kneed, soft, *old use* recreant, poltroon, *formal* pusillanimous, *colloq.* chicken, gutless, yellow
▄ brave, courageous, bold

craving *n*
appetite, hunger, thirst, longing, yearning, pining, sighing, hankering, panting, lust, desire, wish, need, urge
▄ dislike, distaste

crawl *v*
1 CREEP, go on all fours, move on your hands and knees, inch, edge, slither, wriggle, squirm, writhe, drag, move/advance slowly **2** GROVEL, cringe, toady, fawn, flatter, bow and scrape, curry favour, *colloq.* be all over, suck up, creep **3** *the city centre crawling with police* teem, swarm, seethe, bristle, be full of

craze *n*
fad, novelty, fashion, vogue, mode, trend, obsession, preoccupation, mania, frenzy, passion, infatuation, whim, enthusiasm, *colloq.* rage, the latest, thing

crazed *adj*
mad, insane, lunatic, unbalanced, deranged, demented, crazy, wild, berserk, unhinged, out of your mind, *colloq.* loony, nuts, off your rocker, round the bend, round the twist

crazy *adj*
1 MAD, insane, lunatic, unbalanced, disturbed,

deranged, demented, crazed, wild, berserk, unhinged, out of your mind, *colloq.* loony, loopy, bonkers, nuts, nutty, nutty as a fruitcake, doolally, off your rocker, out to lunch, needing your head examining, round the bend, round the twist, not all there, having lost your marbles, having several cards short of a full deck, with one sandwich short of a picnic **2** *What a crazy idea!* silly, foolish, idiotic, stupid, senseless, unwise, imprudent, nonsensical, absurd, odd, peculiar, ludicrous, ridiculous, preposterous, outrageous, impracticable, unrealistic, foolhardy, irresponsible, wild, *colloq.* daft, barmy, batty, potty, half-baked, hare-brained, crackbrained, crackpot **3** *crazy about golf* enthusiastic, fanatical, zealous, devoted, fond, keen, avid, ardent, passionate, infatuated, enamoured, smitten, mad, wild, *colloq.* daft, nuts
⊠ 1 sane **2** sensible **3** indifferent
▷ **go crazy** go mad, blow up, *colloq.* go ballistic, flip (your lid), lose your marbles, *US slang* go ape

creak *v*
squeak, groan, grate, scrape, rasp, scratch, grind, squeal, screech

creaky *adj*
squeaky, squeaking, groaning, grating, scraping, rasping, scratching, grinding, squealing, screeching, rusty, unoiled

cream *n, adj*
▶ *n* **1** PASTE, emulsion, oil, lotion, ointment, salve, cosmetic, *technical* emollient, liniment, unguent **2** BEST, pick, elite, flower, choice/select part, prime, pick of the bunch, *crème de la crème*
▶ *adj* yellowish-white, whitish-yellow, off-white, pale, pasty

creamy *adj*
1 CREAM-COLOURED, creamy, off-white, yellowish-white, whitish-yellow, pale, pasty **2** MILKY, buttery, oily, smooth, velvety, rich, thick

crease *v, n*
▶ *v* fold, pleat, wrinkle, pucker, crumple, rumple, crinkle, crimp, tuck, corrugate, groove, furrow, ridge
▷ **crease up** make laugh, amuse, *colloq.* make someone fall about, make someone split their sides, have rolling in the aisles
▶ *n* fold, line, pleat, tuck, wrinkle, pucker, ruck, crinkle, corrugation, furrow, ridge, groove

create *v*
invent, coin, formulate, compose, design, devise, concoct, hatch, originate, initiate, found, establish, set up, institute, cause, cause to happen, bring about, occasion, give rise to, produce, bring into being, bring into existence, generate, engender, make, form, shape, mould, develop, build, construct, erect, frame, fabricate, appoint, install, invest, inaugurate, ordain, lead to, result in
⊠ destroy

creation *n*
1 MAKING, formation, constitution, invention, concoction, origination, foundation, establishment, institution, production, generation, origin, conception, initiation, birth, development, construction, fabrication, *formal* procreation, genesis **2** *God's creation* world, universe, cosmos, nature, life, everything **3** INVENTION, innovation, brainchild, concept, product, achievement, work, work of art, handiwork, masterpiece, composition, design, *pièce de résistance, chef d'oeuvre*
⊠ 1 destruction

creative *adj*
artistic, inventive, original, imaginative, inspired, visionary, full of ideas, talented, gifted, clever, ingenious, resourceful, fertile, productive, intuitive
⊠ unimaginative

creativity *n*
artistry, inventiveness, originality, imagination, imaginativeness, inspiration, vision, talent, gift, cleverness, ingenuity, resourcefulness, fertility, productiveness
⊠ unimaginativeness

creator *n*
maker, inventor, designer, architect, author, originator, producer, initiator, builder, composer, founder, father, mother, prime mover, first cause, God

creature *n*
animal, beast, bird, fish, insect, organism, being, living thing, mortal, individual, person, human being, human, man, woman, body, soul, mortal

credence *n*
belief, confidence, trust, faith, dependence, reliance, support, credibility, credit
⊠ distrust

credentials *n*
diploma, certificate, reference, testimonial, recommendation, authorization, warrant, licence, permit, passport, identity card, proof of identity, papers, documents, deed, title, *formal* accreditation

credibility *n*
integrity, reliability, trustworthiness, plausibility, probability, likelihood, reasonableness
⊠ implausibility

credible *adj*
believable, imaginable, convincing, conceivable, thinkable, tenable, plausible, likely, probable, possible, reasonable, persuasive, sincere, honest, trustworthy, reliable, dependable, *colloq.* with a ring of truth
⊠ incredible, unbelievable, implausible, unreliable

---

credible, creditable or **credulous** ?

Credible means 'believable, even if untrue': *a credible theory*. *Creditable* means 'worthy of praise or respect': *a very creditable performance*. *Credulous* means 'too easily convinced; easily fooled': *Only the most credulous of voters would believe all the party's election promises.*

---

credit *n, v*
▶ *n* **1** *get the credit for his success* acknowledgement, recognition, thanks, approval, commendation, praise, acclaim, tribute, *formal* laudation **2** *your loyalty does you credit* glory, fame, prestige, distinction, honour, reputation, asset, boast, pride, esteem, estimation, *colloq.* feather in your cap, pride and joy **3** *give someone credit for their ability* belief, trust, faith, credence, confidence **4** *be in credit* money in your bank account, *colloq.* in the black
⊠ 1 blame, discredit, shame **4** overdraft, insolvency, *colloq.* in the red
▷ **on credit** on account, by instalments, by deferred payment, on hire purchase, *colloq.* on tick, on the slate, on the tab, on the never-never
▶ *v* **1** *credited with the invention* attribute, ascribe, put down, assign, charge, *formal* accredit, impute **2** *the reports are difficult to credit* believe, accept, subscribe to, trust, have faith, rely on, *colloq.* swallow, fall for, buy
⊠ 2 disbelieve

creditable *adj*
honourable, reputable, respectable, estimable, admirable, commendable, praiseworthy, good, excellent, exemplary, worthy, deserving, *formal* laudable, meritorious
⊠ shameful, blameworthy

creditor *n*
person/business you owe money to, lender, *formal* debtee, *colloq.* loan shark
F3 debtor

credulity *n*
naïvety, gullibility, credulousness, dupability, silliness, simplicity, stupidity, uncriticalness
F3 scepticism

credulous *adj*
naïve, gullible, wide-eyed, trusting, overtrusting, dupable, unsuspecting, uncritical
F3 sceptical, suspicious

 credulous, credible or **creditable** ? *See panel at* CREDIBLE.

creed *n*
belief, faith, persuasion, credo, catechism, doctrine, teaching, principles, tenets, articles, canon, dogma

creek *n*
inlet, estuary, cove, bay, bight, firth, fiord

creep *v, n*
► *v* crawl, inch, edge, tiptoe, steal, sneak, slink, move unnoticed, slither, worm, wriggle, squirm, grovel, writhe
► *n* **1** *You little creep!* sneak, fawner, sycophant, toady, *colloq.* yes-man, bootlicker **2** *gave me the creeps* fear, horror, revulsion, terror, alarm, unease, disquiet

creeper *n*
climber, climbing plant, trailer, trailing plant, plant, rambler, runner, trailing vine, liana

creepy *adj*
eerie, sinister, threatening, frightening, terrifying, hair-raising, bloodcurdling, spine-chilling, nightmarish, macabre, gruesome, horrible, horrifying, horrific, unpleasant, menacing, ominous, disturbing, weird, *colloq.* scary, spooky

crescent-shaped *adj*
bow-shaped, sickle-shaped, *formal* falcate, falcated, falciform, lunate, lunated, lunular

crest *n*
1 *the crest of the hill* ridge, crown, top, peak, summit, pinnacle, head, *formal* apex **2** TUFT, tassel, plume, comb, cockscomb, mane, aigrette, caruncle, panache **3** INSIGNIA, regalia, device, symbol, emblem, badge, coat of arms

crestfallen *adj*
disappointed, downhearted, dejected, sad, depressed, despondent, discouraged, disheartened, dispirited, downcast, *formal* disconsolate, *colloq.* cheesed off, in the doldrums, down in the dumps
F3 elated

crevasse *n*
abyss, chasm, cleft, crack, fissure, gap, bergschrund

crevice *n*
crack, fissure, split, rift, cleft, slit, chink, cranny, gap, hole, opening, break, *formal* interstice

crew *n*
team, party, squad, troop, corps, company, complement, force, gang, band, pack, group, unit, bunch, crowd, mob, set, lot

crib *n, v*
► *n* carry-cot, cot, travel-cot, bassinet, bed
► *v* copy, cheat, steal, pirate, plagiarize, *formal* purloin, *colloq.* lift, pinch

crick *n*
pain, spasm, stiffness, convulsion, cramp, twinge

crier *n*
announcer, proclaimer, messenger, bearer of tidings, herald, town crier

crime *n*
law-breaking, lawlessness, delinquency, illegal act, unlawful act, offence, felony, misdemeanour, misdeed, wrongdoing, misconduct, transgression, violation, sin, iniquity, vice, villainy, wickedness, atrocity, outrage, *formal* malfeasance

Crimes include:
theft, robbery, burglary, larceny, pilfering, mugging, poaching; assault, rape, grievous bodily harm, *colloq.* GBH, battery, manslaughter, homicide, murder, assassination; fraud, bribery, corruption, embezzlement, extortion, blackmail; arson, treason, terrorism, hijack, piracy, computer hacking, kidnapping, stalking, sabotage, vandalism, hooliganism, criminal damage, drug-smuggling, forgery, counterfeiting, perjury, joy-riding, drink-driving, drunk and disorderly.

criminal *n, adj*
► *n* law-breaker, felon, delinquent, offender, wrongdoer, miscreant, culprit, villain, convict, prisoner, gang, ring, (criminal) syndicate, underworld, *formal* malefactor
► *adj* **1** *a criminal offence* illegal, unlawful, illicit, lawless, law-breaking, wrong, indictable, dishonest, villainous, corrupt, wicked, evil, iniquitous, *formal* culpable, felonious, nefarious, *colloq.* crooked, bent **2** *a criminal waste* scandalous, deplorable, disgraceful, outrageous, infamous, disgusting, shameful, reprehensible, *colloq.* obscene
F3 **1** legal, lawful, honest, upright

crimp *v*
flute, pleat, fold, gather, furrow, ridge, corrugate, groove, wrinkle, pucker, crease, crumple, rumple, crinkle, tuck

cringe *v*
1 *the sight made me cringe* shrink, recoil, shy, start, flinch, draw back, wince, blench, quail, tremble, quiver, cower, crouch, bend, bow, stoop **2** GROVEL, toady, fawn, flatter, bow and scrape, curry favour, *colloq.* crawl, creep, be all over, suck up

crinkle *n, v*
► *n* fold, line, pleat, crease, tuck, ruffle, rumple, twist, wave, wrinkle, pucker, ruck, corrugation, furrow, ridge, groove
► *v* fold, pleat, crease, wrinkle, pucker, curl, twist, crumple, rumple, crimp, tuck, corrugate, groove, furrow, ridge

crinkly *adj*
fluted, pleated, folded, gathered, furrowed, ridged, corrugated, grooved, wrinkled, wrinkly, puckered, curly, frizzy, kinky, creased, crimped, crumpled, rumpled, crinkled, tucked
F3 smooth, straight

cripple *v*
crippled by the accident/the tax increase lame, paralyse, disable, handicap, injure, maim, mutilate, damage, impair, spoil, ruin, destroy, sabotage, weaken, hamstring, hamper, impede, spoil, *formal* incapacitate, debilitate, vitiate

crippled *adj*
lame, paralysed, disabled, handicapped, deformed, *formal* incapacitated

crisis *n*
emergency, extremity, catastrophe, disaster, calamity, critical situation, dilemma, quandary, predicament, difficulty, trouble, problem, *formal* exigency, *colloq.* crunch, mess, scrape, pickle, jam, fix, hole, hot water

crisp *adj*
1 *a crisp biscuit* crispy, crunchy, brittle, crumbly, breakable, firm, hard, *formal* friable **2** BRACING, invigorating, refreshing, fresh, brisk, chilly, cool **3** BRIEF, pithy, terse, short, succinct, clear, incisive, *colloq.* snappy
🗲 **1** soggy, limp, flabby **2** muggy **3** wordy, vague

criterion *n*
standard, norm, touchstone, benchmark, yardstick, measure, gauge, rule, scale, law, principle, model, canon, test, *formal* exemplar

critic *n*
1 *a music critic* reviewer, commentator, analyst, pundit, authority, expert, judge **2** *a critic of the government* judge, censor, censurer, carper, fault-finder, attacker, *colloq.* backbiter, carper, nit-picker, knocker

critical *adj*
1 *at the critical moment* crucial, vital, essential, important, all-important, momentous, major, deciding, decisive, historic, fateful, pivotal, urgent, serious, compelling, pressing, *formal* exigent, climacteric **2** *in a critical condition* dangerous, serious, grave, precarious, *formal* perilous **3** UNCOMPLIMENTARY, derogatory, disparaging, judgemental, disapproving, censorious, scathing, carping, fault-finding, captious, niggling, quibbling, hypercritical, venomous, vitriolic, *formal* vituperative, *colloq.* cavilling, nit-picking **4** ANALYTICAL, diagnostic, penetrating, probing, discerning, evaluative, explanatory, perceptive, *formal* expository
🗲 **1** unimportant **3** complimentary, appreciative

criticism *n*
1 CONDEMNATION, disapproval, disparagement, fault-finding, censure, reproof, blame, *formal* animadversion, *colloq.* brickbat, flak, slating, slamming, nit-picking, niggle, knocking, stick **2** REVIEW, critique, assessment, evaluation, appraisal, judgement, analysis, commentary, write-up, appreciation, explanation, interpretation, *formal* exposition, explication, *colloq.* bad press
🗲 **1** praise, commendation

criticize *v*
1 CONDEMN, disparage, carp, disapprove of, find fault with, denounce, attack, censure, blame, *formal* animadvert, excoriate, decry, denigrate, vituperate, *colloq.* nag, slate, slam, knock, snipe, run down, come down on, give someone some stick, go to town on, haul over the coals, pick holes in, pan, pull to pieces, tear to shreds, tear a strip off, nit-pick, do a hatchet job on, slag off, badmouth, rubbish, put the boot in **2** REVIEW, assess, evaluate, appraise, judge, analyse, explain, interpret
🗲 **1** praise, commend

critique *n*
review, essay, assessment, evaluation, appraisal, judgement, analysis, commentary, write-up, appreciation, explanation, interpretation, *formal* exposition, explication

croak *v*
rasp, squawk, caw, wheeze, speak harshly, gasp, grunt

crock *n*
jar, pot, vessel

crockery *n*
dishes, tableware, china, porcelain, earthenware, stoneware, pottery

croft *n*
farm, plot, smallholding, farmland

crony *n*
friend, companion, associate, colleague, accomplice, ally, comrade, follower, sidekick, *colloq.* mate, pal, chum, buddy

crook *n, v*
▶ *n* criminal, thief, robber, law-breaker, swindler, cheat, rogue, fraud, villain, *colloq.* shark, con man
▶ *v* bend, twist, tilt, slant, angle, hook, curve, flex, bow, distort, warp, deform

crooked *adj*
1 ASKEW, awry, lopsided, asymmetric, irregular, uneven, off-centre, tilted, slanting, bent, angled, hooked, curved, bowed, warped, distorted, misshapen, deformed, contorted, twisted, buckled, tortuous, sinuous, winding, zigzag, *formal* anfractuous, *colloq.* skew-whiff **2** CRIMINAL, illegal, unlawful, illicit, dishonest, deceitful, corrupt, fraudulent, shifty, underhand, treacherous, unscrupulous, unprincipled, unethical, *formal* nefarious, *colloq.* bent, shady
🗲 **1** straight **2** honest

croon *v*
sing, hum, warble, lilt, vocalize

crop *n, v*
▶ *n* **1** *grow crops* growth, yield, produce, fruits, harvest, vintage, gathering, reaping, gleaning **2** *this year's crop of graduates* batch, group, lot, set, collection
▶ *v* cut, snip, clip, shear, trim, pare, prune, mow, lop, shorten, reduce, curtail
▷ **crop up** arise, emerge, appear, arrive, occur, happen, come up, turn up, present itself, come to pass, take place

cross *n, v, adj*
▶ *n* **1** BURDEN, load, misfortune, trouble, adversity, worry, disaster, catastrophe, trial, grief, misery, pain, suffering, woe, *formal* affliction, tribulation **2** CROSSBREED, hybrid, mongrel, blend, mix, mixture, amalgam, combination

Types of cross include:
ankh, Avelian, botoné, Calvary, capital, cardinal, Celtic, Constantinian, Cornish, crosslet, crucifix, encolpion, fleury, fylfot, Geneva, Greek, Jerusalem, Latin, Lorraine, Maltese, moline, papal, patriarchal, potent, quadrate, rood, Russian, saltire, St Andrew's, St Anthony's, St George's, St Peter's, swastika, tau, Y-cross.

▶ *v* **1** *cross the river* go across, travel across, pass over, ford, bridge, span, *formal* traverse **2** INTERSECT, meet, join, converge, criss-cross, lace, interweave, intertwine **3** CROSSBREED, interbreed, mongrelize, hybridize, cross-fertilize, cross-pollinate, blend, mix **4** THWART, frustrate, foil, hinder, hamper, impede, obstruct, block, check, resist, oppose
▶ *adj* **1** IRRITABLE, annoyed, angry, vexed, bad-tempered, ill-tempered, grumpy, put out, irascible, short, snappy, snappish, surly, sullen, fractious, cantankerous, awkward, difficult, harsh, fretful, disagreeable, impatient, *formal* splenetic, *colloq.* peeved, shirty, crotchety, grouchy, crabby, prickly **2** TRANSVERSE, crosswise, oblique, diagonal, intersecting, opposite, reciprocal
🗲 **1** placid, pleasant

cross-examine *v*
interrogate, question, cross-question, quiz, examine, *colloq.* grill, pump, give someone the third degree

crossing *n*
1 *meet at the crossing* junction, intersection, crossroads **2** *a pedestrian crossing* pedestrian crossing, zebra crossing, pelican crossing, Toucan crossing, *US* crosswalk **3** *a sea crossing* journey, trip, passage, voyage

crosswise *adv*
diagonally, crossways, crisscross, across, over, sideways, transversely, aslant, obliquely, athwart, awry,

formal catercorner, catercornered

crotchety *adj*
grumpy, awkward, bad-tempered, cross, irritable, difficult, disagreeable, obstreperous, peevish, prickly, surly, testy, petulant, fractious, irascible, cantankerous, contrary, crusty, *formal* iracund, iracundulous, *colloq.* crabby, crabbed, grouchy
🔁 calm, placid, pleasant

crouch *v*
squat, kneel, stoop, bend, bow, hunch, duck, cower, cringe

crow *v*
bluster, boast, brag, show off, gloat, rejoice, triumph, exult, flourish, vaunt, *colloq.* blow your own trumpet, *US* blow your own horn

crowd *n, v*
▶ *n* **1** THRONG, multitude, army, host, mob, masses, populace, people, public, riff-raff, rabble, horde, swarm, flock, herd, drove, pack, press, crush, squash, assembly, collection, company **2** *all the college crowd* group, bunch, lot, set, circle, clique, fraternity **3** SPECTATORS, viewers, listeners, gate, attendance, audience, house, turnout
▶ *v* **1** *crowd around the pop star* cluster, gather, congregate, muster, converge, huddle, mass, mob, throng, swarm, flock, surge, stream **2** *crowd into a van* push, shove, elbow, jostle, thrust, press, squeeze, bundle, pile, pack, cram, jam, stuff, compress, congest, overflow

crowded *adj*
full, filled, packed, jammed, congested, crammed, cramped, crushed, overfull, overcrowded, overpopulated, busy, teeming, swarming, overflowing, *colloq.* full to bursting, jam-packed, packed like sardines, chock-a-block, thick on the ground
🔁 empty, deserted

crown *n, v*
▶ *n* **1** CORONET, diadem, tiara, circlet, wreath, garland **2** PRIZE, trophy, reward, honour, distinction, glory, kudos, garland, laurels **3** SOVEREIGN, monarch, king, queen, emperor, empress, ruler, sovereignty, monarchy, royalty, empire **4** TOP, tip, crest, summit, pinnacle, peak, climax, height, culmination, *formal* acme, apex
▶ *v* **1** *crown the king* enthrone, invest, induct, install, anoint, adorn, festoon, honour, dignify, reward **2** TOP, cap, complete, perfect, fulfil, finalize, round off, perfect, be the culmination of, *formal* consummate

crowning *adj, n*
▶ *adj* culminating, final, perfect, supreme, top, ultimate, unmatched, unsurpassed, paramount, sovereign, *formal* climactic, consummate
▶ *n* coronation, enthronement, installation, investiture, *formal* incoronation

crucial *adj*
urgent, pressing, vital, essential, key, pivotal, central, important, momentous, major, deciding, decisive, critical, trying, testing, compelling, pressing searching, historic, pivotal
🔁 unimportant, trivial

crucify *v*
1 *Christ was crucified* kill on the cross, execute, put to death on a cross **2** *crucified by the critics* criticize, mock, ridicule, persecute, torment, punish, torture, rack, *colloq.* slam, slate, tear to pieces

crude *adj*
1 RAW, unprocessed, unrefined, rough, coarse, unfinished, unpolished **2** *a crude cabin* rough, natural, primitive, makeshift, unfinished, undeveloped, simple, basic, rudimentary, *formal* rude **3** *a crude remark* vulgar, coarse, rude, indecent, obscene, uncouth, risqué,

offensive, gross, dirty, lewd, earthy, bawdy, smutty, *colloq.* raunchy, blue, hot, juicy
🔁 **1** refined, finished **3** polite, decent, tasteful

cruel *adj*
fierce, ferocious, vicious, savage, barbarous, barbaric, bloodthirsty, murderous, cold-blooded, sadistic, brutal, inhuman, inhumane, unkind, nasty, mean, evil, fiendish, spiteful, malicious, callous, heartless, unfeeling, merciless, pitiless, flinty, hard-hearted, stony-hearted, implacable, ruthless, remorseless, unrelenting, inexorable, grim, hellish, atrocious, bitter, severe, cutting, painful, excruciating, *formal* malevolent, vengeful, indurate
🔁 kind, compassionate, merciful

cruelty *n*
ferocity, viciousness, savagery, barbarity, bloodthirstiness, murderousness, violence, sadism, abuse, bullying, brutality, bestiality, inhumanity, spite, malice, venom, callousness, heartlessness, hard-heartedness, mercilessness, ruthlessness, tyranny, unkindness, meanness, harshness, severity
🔁 kindness, compassion, mercy

cruise *n, v*
▶ *n* holiday, voyage, sail, journey, trip
▶ *v* **1** *cruising round the Mediterranean* sail, travel, journey **2** *cruising along comfortably* sail, coast, drift, freewheel, glide, slide, taxi

crumb *n*
piece, scrap, morsel, bit, titbit, particle, grain, atom, flake, speck, iota, jot, mite, shred, sliver, snippet, soupçon

crumble *v*
1 *the plaster is crumbling* fragment, break up, come away, decompose, disintegrate, decay, degenerate, deteriorate, collapse, crush, pound, grind, powder, pulverize **2** *the organization began to crumble* collapse, fail, fall to pieces, fall apart, disintegrate, decay, degenerate, deteriorate, break down, rot

crumbly *adj*
brittle, powdery, short, *formal* friable, pulverulent

crummy *adj*
inferior, miserable, poor, rotten, shoddy, trashy, cheap, useless, weak, worthless, contemptible, second-rate, third-rate, *colloq.* grotty, pathetic, rubbishy, half-baked, *slang* crappy
🔁 excellent

crumple *v*
crush, wrinkle, pucker, crinkle, rumple, crease, fold, collapse, fall

crunch *v, n*
▶ *v* **1** *crunch a biscuit* munch, chomp, champ, chew, bite, grind, crush, *formal* masticate **2** *snow crunching* grind, crush, scrunch, smash
▶ *n* crisis, crux, critical situation, emergency, test, moment of truth, *colloq.* pinch

crusade *n, v*
▶ *n* **1** *the Crusades* holy war, jihad **2** *the crusade against nuclear power* campaign, drive, struggle, push, movement, cause, undertaking, expedition, strategy, offensive
▶ *v* campaign, promote, push, drive, advocate, work, fight, strive, struggle, battle, attack

crusader *n*
advocate, campaigner, champion, promoter, enthusiast, reformer, zealot, fighter, missionary

crush *v, n*
▶ *v* **1** SQUASH, compress, squeeze, mash, press, pulp, break (up), smash, mill, pound, pulverize, shatter, screw up, grind, crunch, crumble, crumple, crinkle, wrinkle, *formal* comminute, triturate **2** *the rebels were*

crushed conquer, demolish, devastate, overpower, overwhelm, overcome, quash, quell, suppress, subdue, put down, *formal* vanquish **3** *crushed by the criticism* upset, devastate, humiliate, shame, abash, *colloq.* put down
▸ *n* **1** *injured in the crush* crowd, pack, press, squash, jam **2** *a crush on the French teacher* infatuation, passion, obsession, love, liking, *colloq.* pash

crust *n*
surface, exterior, outside, covering, topping, coat, coating, layer, film, casing, mantle, skin, rind, shell, husk, scab, caking, *technical* incrustation, concretion

crusty *adj*
1 *crusty bread* crispy, crunchy, brittle, crumbly, breakable, firm, hard, well-done, baked, well-baked, *formal* friable **2** *a crusty old man* grumpy, awkward, bad-tempered, short-tempered, brusque, gruff, cross, irritable, difficult, disagreeable, obstreperous, peevish, prickly, surly, testy, touchy, petulant, fractious, irascible, cantankerous, contrary, *formal* splenetic, *colloq.* crabby, crabbed, grouchy
F4 **1** soft, soggy **2** calm, placid, pleasant

crux *n*
nub, heart, core, essence, centre, kernel, nucleus, *colloq.* the bottom line

cry *v, n*
▸ *v* **1** WEEP, sob, be in/shed tears, blubber, wail, howl, bawl, whimper, whine, snivel, *colloq.* burst into tears, cry your eyes out **2** SHOUT, call (out), exclaim, roar, bellow, yell, scream, howl, bawl, shriek, screech
▷ **cry off** cancel, withdraw, excuse yourself, back out, decide against, change your mind
▷ **cry out for** need, call for, demand, want, require, *formal* necessitate
▸ *n* **1** WEEP, weeping, sob, sobbing, tears, blubber, wail, howl, bawl, whimper, whine, snivel **2** SHOUT, call, plea, exclamation, roar, bellow, yell, scream, howl, bawl, shriek, screech

crypt *n*
tomb, vault, burial chamber, catacomb, mausoleum, undercroft

cryptic *adj*
enigmatic, ambiguous, equivocal, puzzling, perplexing, mysterious, strange, bizarre, secret, hidden, veiled, obscure, dark, occult, *formal* abstruse, esoteric
F4 straightforward, clear, obvious

crystallize *v*
1 *the substance crystallized* solidify, harden, materialize, form **2** *the idea crystallized* make/become clear, make/become definite, clarify, appear, emerge, form

cub *n*
1 *fox cubs* offspring, pup, puppy, whelp, baby **2** *a cub reporter* beginner, novice, tiro, starter, learner, trainee, apprentice, student, probationer, initiate, freshman, fresher, recruit, raw recruit, tenderfoot, fledgling, neophyte, youngster, youth, *colloq.* greenhorn, rookie

cubbyhole *n*
compartment, niche, pigeonhole, slot, recess, den, hideaway, hole, tiny room

cube *n*
dice, die, solid, block, cuboid, hexahedron

cuddle *v*
hug, embrace, clasp, hold, enfold, nurse, nestle, snuggle, pet, fondle, caress, *colloq.* snog, canoodle, neck, smooch

cuddly *adj*
cuddlesome, lovable, huggable, plump, soft, warm, cosy

cudgel *n, v*
▸ *n* club, stick, mace, bludgeon, bat, truncheon,

shillelagh, alpeen, bastinado, *colloq.* cosh
▸ *v* hit, strike, beat, club, bash, clout, thwack, pound, bludgeon, batter, *colloq.* clobber, cosh

cue *n*
signal, sign, nod, hint, suggestion, intimation, indication, reminder, prompt, incentive, stimulus

cuff *v*
hit, thump, box, clip, knock, buffet, slap, smack, strike, clout, beat, *colloq.* biff, clobber, belt, whack
▷ **off the cuff** impromptu, extempore, without preparation, ad lib, spontaneously, improvised, unprepared, unrehearsed, unscripted, *colloq.* off the top of your head, on the spur of the moment

cuisine *n*
cooking, cookery, *haute cuisine, cordon bleu, nouvelle cuisine*

cul-de-sac *n*
no through road, dead end, blind alley

cull *v*
1 *cull information* collect, gather, choose, pick (out), select, sift, glean, pluck, amass **2** *cull wild animals* kill, destroy, slaughter, thin (out)

culminate *v*
climax, come to a climax, end (up), terminate, close, conclude, finish, peak, *formal* consummate, *colloq.* wind up
F4 start, begin

culmination *n*
climax, height, high point, peak, pinnacle, summit, top, crown, perfection, finale, conclusion, completion, *formal* consummation, apex, acme, zenith
F4 start, beginning

culpable *adj*
to blame, wrong, in the wrong, at fault, responsible, guilty, liable, offending, answerable, blamable, blameworthy, censurable, reprehensible, sinful, *formal* peccant
F4 blameless, innocent

culprit *n*
guilty party, offender, wrongdoer, miscreant, lawbreaker, criminal, felon, delinquent, convict, villain

cult *n*
1 SECT, denomination, religion, faith, belief, affiliation, school, movement, party, faction **2** CRAZE, fad, fashion, vogue, obsession, trend, *colloq.* in-thing

cultivate *v*
1 FARM, till, work, plough, dig, prepare, grow, sow, plant, tend, raise, bring on, fertilize, produce, harvest **2** FOSTER, nurture, cherish, help, aid, assist, support, back, encourage, promote, further, forward, advance, enhance, work on, pursue, court, woo, develop, train, prepare, polish, refine, improve, enrich, enlighten
F4 **2** neglect

cultivated *adj*
refined, cultured, civilized, sophisticated, polished, genteel, urbane, advanced, enlightened, educated, well-read, well-informed, scholarly, highbrow, discerning, discriminating

cultural *adj*
1 *cultural events* artistic, aesthetic, liberal, civilizing, humanizing, enlightening, educational, educative, edifying, improving, broadening, developmental, enriching, elevating **2** *cultural heritage* communal, national, ethnic, folk, tribal, traditional, time-honoured, *technical* anthropological, *formal* societal

culture *n*
1 *popular culture* the arts, humanities, painting, philosophy, music, literature, history, learning **2** CIVILIZATION, society, lifestyle, way of life, customs, traditions, heritage, habits, behaviour, *formal* mores

3 *cell culture* growth, production, crop, tendering, nurturing

cultured *adj*
cultivated, civilized, advanced, enlightened, educated, well-educated, well-read, well-informed, learned, scholarly, highbrow, intellectual, erudite, artistic, well-bred, refined, polite, polished, sophisticated, genteel, tasteful, urbane, *colloq.* arty
🗲 uncultured, uneducated, ignorant

culvert *n*
channel, conduit, drain, duct, gutter, sewer, watercourse

cumbersome *adj*
1 *a cumbersome machine* awkward, inconvenient, bulky, unwieldy, unmanageable, burdensome, onerous, heavy, weighty, *formal* incommodious, cumbrous **2** *a cumbersome process* complicated, complex, involved, difficult, inefficient, badly organized, wasteful, slow
🗲 **1** convenient, manageable **2** simple, efficient

cumulative *adj*
increasing, growing, mounting, multiplying, enlarging, growing, collective, *colloq.* snowballing

cunning *adj, n*
▶ *adj* **1** *a cunning person* crafty, sly, artful, wily, tricky, devious, subtle, deceitful, guileful, manipulative, sharp, shrewd, astute, canny, knowing, deep, *colloq.* shifty, cunning as a fox **2** *a cunning plan* clever, imaginative, ingenious, skilful, inventive, resourceful, deft, dexterous, fiendish
🗲 **1** naïve, ingenuous, gullible
▶ *n* craftiness, slyness, artfulness, trickery, deviousness, subtlety, deceit, deceitfulness, guile, wiles, sharpness, shrewdness, astuteness, ingenuity, cleverness, imaginativeness, skill, inventiveness, resourcefulness, deftness, finesse, adroitness, fiendishness

cup *n*
1 *drink from a cup* mug, tankard, beaker, goblet, chalice **2** *win a cup* trophy, award, medal, prize, reward **3** *claret cup* punch, wine

cupboard *n*
cabinet, locker, closet, wardrobe, pantry, sideboard, tallboy, dresser, Welsh dresser, chest, chest of drawers

cupidity *n*
acquisitiveness, greed, greediness, avarice, graspingness, covetousness, eagerness, hunger, hankering, itching, longing, yearning, *formal* avidity, rapaciousness, rapacity, voracity

curative *adj*
healing, healthful, health-giving, therapeutic, tonic, medicinal, remedial, restorative, corrective, salutary, *technical* febrifugal, *formal* alleviative, vulnerary

curator *n*
keeper, attendant, conservator, custodian, caretaker, steward, warden, warder, guardian

curb *v, n*
▶ *v* restrain, constrain, restrict, contain, control, keep under control, check, keep in check, moderate, reduce, bridle, muzzle, hold back, suppress, subdue, repress, inhibit, hinder, impede, hamper, *formal* retard
🗲 encourage, foster
▶ *n* limitation, restriction, check, control, constraint, restraint, brake, rein, bridle, deterrent, damper, holding-back, suppression, repression, hindrance, hamper, impediment, *formal* retardant

curdle *v*
coagulate, congeal, clot, solidify, thicken, turn, sour, turn sour, ferment

cure *v, n*
▶ *v* **1** HEAL, remedy, correct, restore, treat, repair, fix, rectify, mend, relieve, ease, alleviate, remedy, help, make better, make well **2** PRESERVE, dry, smoke, salt, pickle, kipper
▶ *n* remedy, antidote, panacea, cure-all, solution, medicine, corrective, restorative, healing, treatment, therapy, alleviation, recovery, *technical* specific, *formal* elixir

curio *n*
antique, bygone, curiosity, knick-knack, trinket, bibelot, *objet d'art*, object of virtu, *objet de vertu*

curiosity *n*
1 INQUISITIVENESS, interest, questioning, querying, search, inquiry, prying, snooping, interference, *colloq.* nosiness **2** CURIO, *objet d'art*, antique, bygone, novelty, trinket, knick-knack **3** ODDITY, rarity, freak, phenomenon, spectacle, wonder, marvel, exotica

curious *adj*
1 INQUISITIVE, questioning, querying, searching, inquiring, interested, intrigued, fascinated, keen to know, wanting to learn, prying, meddling, snooping, meddlesome, interfering, *colloq.* nosy **2** *a curious sight* odd, queer, funny, strange, peculiar, bizarre, mysterious, puzzling, extraordinary, out of the ordinary, unusual, remarkable, rare, unique, novel, exotic, unconventional, weird, freakish, unorthodox, quaint
🗲 **1** uninterested, indifferent **2** ordinary, usual, normal

curl *v, n*
▶ *v* crimp, frizz, wave, crinkle, ripple, kink, bend, curve, meander, loop, turn, twist, wind, wreathe, twirl, twine, coil, spiral, snake, corkscrew, scroll
🗲 uncurl
▶ *n* wave, kink, swirl, twist, ring, ringlet, coil, curlicue, helix, spiral, whorl

curly *adj*
curled, crimped, permed, frizzy, fuzzy, wavy, kinky, curling, looping, turning, twisting, winding, wreathing, twirling, coiling, spiralled, spiralling, corkscrew
🗲 straight

currency *n*
1 MONEY, legal tender, coinage, coins, notes, cash, bills **2** ACCEPTANCE, publicity, popularity, vogue, circulation, prevalence, exposure, *formal* dissemination

current *adj, n*
▶ *adj* **1** *current events* present, ongoing, existing, contemporary, present-day, present-time, modern, fashionable, in fashion, up-to-date, up-to-the-minute, in vogue, popular, *formal* extant, *colloq.* trendy, in **2** *still current in the 1800s* (generally) accepted, widespread, prevalent, common, popular, general, prevailing, reigning, in circulation, *colloq.* going around
🗲 **1** obsolete, old-fashioned
▶ *n* draught, stream, mainstream, jet, flow, swirl, movement, drift, ebb, tide, course, progress, trend, direction, tendency, undercurrent, tenor, mood, feeling

curriculum *n*
syllabus, core curriculum, national curriculum, subjects, course of studies, discipline, course, course of study, module, educational programme, timetable

curse *v, n*
▶ *v* **1** SWEAR, use bad language, blaspheme, damn, condemn, denounce, blast, *formal* accurse, imprecate, anathematize, fulminate, *colloq.* cuss, put a jinx on **2** BLIGHT, plague, scourge, afflict, harm, ruin, trouble, beset, torment
🗲 **2** bless
▶ *n* **1** SWEAR-WORD, oath, expletive, blasphemy, obscenity, profanity, bad language, *formal* anathema,

imprecation, execration, *colloq.* four-letter word
2 JINX, spell, anathema, bane, evil, plague, scourge, affliction, trouble, torment, ordeal, calamity, misfortune, disaster, *formal* malediction, execration, tribulation
🔒 **2** blessing, advantage

cursed *adj*
damned, detestable, abominable, confounded, infernal, hateful, loathsome, odious, vile, fiendish, annoying, unpleasant, pernicious, infamous, *formal* execrable, *colloq.* blasted, blooming, flipping, dashed, dratted

cursory *adj*
brief, slight, summary, superficial, desultory, quick, rapid, fleeting, hasty, hurried, offhand, dismissive, passing, perfunctory, careless, casual, slapdash
🔒 painstaking, thorough

curt *adj*
abrupt, blunt, rude, sharp, brusque, gruff, laconic, offhand, short, short-spoken, tart, terse, snappish, unceremonious, uncivil, ungracious, brief, pithy, concise, succinct, summary
🔒 voluble

curtail *v*
reduce, limit, restrict, shorten, truncate, cut, cut down, cut short, cut back (on), trim, shrink, abridge, abbreviate, lessen, decrease, pare, pare down/back, prune, slim, guillotine
🔒 lengthen, extend, increase

curtailment *n*
reduction, limitation, restriction, shortening, truncation, cut, cutback, trimming, shrinkage, abridgement, abbreviation, contraction, lessening, decrease, paring, docking, pruning, slimming, guillotine, *formal* retrenchment
🔒 extension, lengthening, increase

curtain *n*
blind, screen, cover, shutter, net curtain, hanging, window hanging, backdrop, portière, drapery, tapestry, *US* drape

curtsy *v*
bob, bow, kowtow, salaam, *formal* genuflect

curvaceous *adj*
shapely, well-proportioned, well-rounded, well-stacked, buxom, comely, curvy, bosomy, voluptuous
🔒 skinny

curve *v, n*
▶ *v* bend, arch, arc, bow, bulge, swell, hook, crook, turn, wind, twist, round, swerve, loop, spiral, coil, *formal* incurve
▶ *n* bend, turn, bow, loop, arc, arch, circle, crescent, trajectory, helix, spiral, winding, meandering, camber, kink, curvature, flexure

curved *adj*
bent, arched, bowed, rounded, humped, bulging, swelling, convex, concave, bending, cupped, scooped, crooked, twisted, warped, sweeping, sinuous, tortuous, serpentine, *technical* arcuate, curviform
🔒 straight

cushion *n, v*
▶ *n* pillow, bolster, headrest, squab, beanbag, hassock, pad, padding, mat, buffer, shock absorber, *technical* pulvinus
▶ *v* soften, deaden, dampen, absorb, muffle, stifle, suppress, lessen, reduce, diminish, mitigate, protect, bolster, buttress, prop up, support

cushy *adj*
comfortable, easy, undemanding, *colloq.* jammy, soft, plum
🔒 demanding, tough

custodian *n*
caretaker, conservator, curator, guard, guardian, warden, warder, keeper, overseer, superintendent, watchdog, watchman, protector, castellan

custody *n*
1 KEEPING, possession, charge, care, safekeeping, protection, preservation, custodianship, trusteeship, guardianship, wardship, guidance, supervision, responsibility **2** DETENTION, confinement, imprisonment, captivity, arrest, *formal* incarceration

custom *n*
1 *national customs* tradition, usage, use, habit, routine, procedure, practice, policy, way, manner, style, form, fashion, way of behaving, convention, etiquette, ethos, formality, procedure, observance, ritual, rite, usage, institution **2** *take my custom elsewhere* business, trade, *formal* patronage

customarily *adv*
traditionally, conventionally, habitually, routinely, regularly, as a rule, usually, normally, ordinarily, commonly, generally, popularly, fashionably
🔒 unusually, occasionally, rarely

customary *adj*
traditional, conventional, accepted, established, set, habitual, routine, regular, usual, normal, ordinary, everyday, familiar, common, general, popular, fashionable, prevailing
🔒 unusual, rare

customer *n*
client, patron, regular, consumer, shopper, buyer, purchaser, clientèle, prospect, *colloq.* punter

customize *v*
adapt, convert, modify, tailor, alter, adjust, suit, fit, transform, *colloq.* fine-tune

cut *v, n*
▶ *v* **1** *cut the paper/your finger; cut a hole* slit, pierce, slice, sever, chop, hack, hew, carve, split, dock, lop, prune, excise **2** *cut meat* dissect, divide, carve, slice, chop (up), dice, mince, shred, grate, *formal* cleave **3** *cut hair/grass* shorten, trim, clip, crop, snip, shear, mow, shave, pare, prune, dock **4** *cut glass* engrave, incise, chisel, score **5** *cut someone's throat* stab, wound, nick, slash, lacerate **6** *cut costs* reduce, decrease, lower, diminish, curtail, curb, prune, *colloq.* slash, axe **7** *cut a story/broadcast* shorten, make shorter, curtail, abbreviate, abridge, condense, précis, summarize, edit, delete, omit, *formal* excise, expurgate **8** *cut someone dead* IGNORE, spurn, avoid, pretend not to see/notice, snub, slight, rebuff, insult, scorn, *colloq.* cut dead, cold-shoulder, look right through, send to Coventry, not give someone the time of day
▷ **cut across** transcend, surmount, go beyond, rise above, leave behind
▷ **cut back** check, crop, curb, curtail, decrease, economize, lessen, lop, lower, prune, reduce, trim, scale down, *formal* retrench, *colloq.* slash, downsize
▷ **cut down 1** *cut down a tree* fell, chop down, hew, saw, lop, level, raze **2** REDUCE, decrease, lower, lessen, diminish, curtail, curb, prune
▷ **cut in** interrupt, break in, butt in, intervene, intrude, *formal* interpose, interject, *colloq.* barge in
▷ **cut off 1** *cut off his head* remove, sever, detach, amputate, chop off, take off, break off, tear off **2** *feel cut off from friends* separate, isolate, keep apart, detach, seclude, sever, insulate, shelter **3** *cut off a supply* STOP, end, bring to an end, halt, suspend, disconnect, break off, block, obstruct, intercept, *formal* discontinue **4** *get cut off on the phone* disconnect, break off, unhook, separate, detach, intercept, interrupt
▷ **cut out 1** *cut out a coupon* extract, remove, separate, take out, tear out, *formal* excise **2** omit, cut, exclude, leave out, drop, delete, edit, *formal* excise **3** stop, refrain, *formal* cease, desist, discontinue,

colloq. quit, leave off, lay off, knock off, pack in **4** *the engine cut out* stop working, fail, break down, go wrong, *formal* malfunction, *colloq.* pack up, *slang* conk out
▷ **cut up** carve, slice (up), chop (up), dice, mince, dissect, dismember, divide, slash
▶ *n* **1** INCISION, wound, nick, gash, slit, slash, rip, laceration, notch, score **2** *go for a cut at the barber's* trim, clip, crop, shave **3** *spending cuts* reduction, decrease, lowering, cutback, saving, economy, lessening, *formal* retrenchment **4** *a cut of meat* section, slice, piece, bit, part **5** *a power cut* failure, fault, breakdown, breaking-down, cutting-out, *formal* malfunctioning **6** *a cut of the profits* SHARE, allocation, proportion, portion, quota, ration, *colloq.* slice, slice of the cake, whack **7** *the cut of a garment* shape, style, fashion, form, profile
▷ **cut and dried** clear, definite, certain, settled, fixed, organized, prearranged, automatic, *formal* predetermined, *colloq.* sewn up
▷ **cut out for** suitable, suited, right, appropriate, qualified, made, good

cutback *n*
cut, saving, economy, reduction, decrease, curtailment, lowering, lessening, *formal* retrenchment, *colloq.* slashing

cutlery *n*

Items of cutlery include:
knife, butter-knife, carving-knife, fish knife, steak knife, cheese knife, breadknife, vegetable knife, fork, fish fork, carving fork, spoon, dessert-spoon, tablespoon, teaspoon, soup-spoon, caddy spoon, salt spoon, apostle spoon, ladle, salad servers, fish slice, cake server, sugar tongs, chopsticks, canteen of cutlery.

cut-price *adj*
reduced, sale, discount, bargain, cheap, low-priced, cut-rate

cut-throat *adj*
ruthless, pitiless, relentless, fierce, highly/fiercely competitive, keen, keenly contested, cruel, brutal, *colloq.* dog-eat-dog

cutting *adj, n*
▶ *adj* *a cutting wind/comment* bitter, raw, chill, sharp, keen, pointed, incisive, penetrating, piercing, wounding, hurtful, stinging, biting, caustic, acid, scathing, sarcastic, snide, malicious, *formal* mordant, trenchant, *colloq.* bitchy
▶ *n* clipping, extract, excerpt, piece

cycle *n*
circle, round, rotation, oscillation, rhythm, biorhythm, body clock, revolution, rota, series, sequence, order, pattern, succession, phase, period, era, age, epoch, aeon

cyclone *n*
hurricane, monsoon, tempest, tropical storm, storm, tornado, typhoon, whirlwind

cylinder *n*
column, barrel, drum, reel, bobbin, spool, spindle

cynic *n*
sceptic, doubter, pessimist, killjoy, scoffer, *formal* misanthrope, *colloq.* knocker, spoilsport

cynical *adj*
sceptical, doubtful, doubting, distrustful, disillusioned, disenchanted, pessimistic, negative, critical, scornful, derisive, suspicious, contemptuous, sneering, surly, scoffing, mocking, sarcastic, sardonic, ironic

cynicism *n*
scepticism, doubt, disbelief, distrust, disillusionment, disenchantment, pessimism, scorn, suspicion, contempt, sneering, scoffing, mocking, sarcasm, irony, *formal* misanthropy

cyst *n*
growth, sac, vesicle, blister, wen, bladder, bleb, *technical* atheroma, utricle

D

dab *v, n*
▶ *v* pat, daub, swab, wipe, touch, press, tap
▶ *n* **1** BIT, drop, dash, speck, spot, trace, tinge, smear, smudge, fleck, *colloq.* dollop **2** TOUCH, pat, stroke, tap, press
▷ **dab hand** expert, pastmaster, wizard, ace, adept

dabble *v*
1 TRIFLE, play, tinker, toy, dally, potter **2** PADDLE, moisten, wet, dampen, sprinkle, dip, splash, splatter

dabbler *n*
amateur, lay person, dilettante, trifler, dallier, tinkerer
🔁 professional, expert

daft *adj*
1 FOOLISH, crazy, silly, stupid, absurd, ridiculous, ludicrous, preposterous, outrageous, nonsensical, senseless, unwise, imprudent, odd, peculiar, impracticable, unrealistic, foolhardy, irrational, irresponsible, wild, idiotic, fatuous, inane, *colloq.* dotty, dumb, barmy, batty, potty, half-baked, hare-brained, crackbrained, crackpot, wacky **2** INSANE, mad, lunatic, simple, crazy, unbalanced, disturbed, deranged, demented, crazed, wild, berserk, touched, unhinged, out of your mind, *colloq.* mental, loony, loopy, bonkers, nuts, nutty, nutty as a fruitcake, off your rocker, needing your head examining, round the bend, round the twist **3** INFATUATED, passionate, enamoured, smitten, mad, wild, enthusiastic, fanatical, zealous, devoted, fond, keen, avid, ardent, *colloq.* nuts, potty, sweet
🔁 **1** sensible **2** sane **3** indifferent

dagger *n*
bayonet, poniard, stiletto, knife, blade, skene, dirk, skene-dhu, kris, kukri, jambiya, misericord, yatagan

daily *adj, adv*
▶ *adj* **1** REGULAR, routine, everyday, customary, common, commonplace, ordinary, habitual **2** EVERYDAY, *formal* diurnal, quotidian, circadian
▶ *adv* every day, day after day, day by day

dainty *adj, n*
▶ *adj* **1** DELICATE, elegant, pretty, exquisite, petite, little, small, refined, fine, graceful, neat, trim, charming **2** *a dainty morsel* tasty, delectable, delightful, enjoyable, appetizing, palatable mouth-watering, luscious, succulent, juicy, savoury **3** FASTIDIOUS, fussy, particular, discriminating, finicky, scrupulous, *colloq.* choosy
🔁 **1** gross, clumsy **2** unpalatable
▶ *n* delicacy, fancy, titbit, sweetmeat, bonbon, bonne-bouche

dais *n*
platform, stage, rostrum, podium, stand

dale *n*
valley, vale, glen, dell, coomb, dingle, gill, glen, strath

dally *v*
1 DAWDLE, linger, loiter, delay, *formal* procrastinate, tarry **2** *dally with an idea* toy, play, flirt, trifle, frivol

🔁 **1** hasten, hurry

dam *n, v*
▶ *n* barrier, barrage, embankment, wall, blockage, barricade, obstruction, hindrance
▶ *v* block, confine, restrict, check, barricade, staunch, stem, obstruct

damage *v, n*
▶ *v* harm, injure, hurt, spoil, ruin, destroy, impair, mar, abuse, wreck, deface, vandalize, sabotage, desecrate, mutilate, weaken, tamper with, play/wreak havoc with, incapacitate, *formal* vitiate
🔁 mend, repair, fix
▶ *n* **1** *extensive damage after the fire* harm, injury, hurt, destruction, ruin, devastation, havoc, loss, abuse, suffering, mischief, mutilation, impairment, detriment, defacement, vandalism **2** *pay damages* compensation, fine, indemnity, reimbursement, reparation, restitution, satisfaction
🔁 **1** repair

damaging *adj*
harmful, hurtful, injurious, unfavourable, bad, detrimental, disadvantageous, pernicious, prejudicial, ruinous, *formal* deleterious
🔁 favourable, helpful

dame *n*
1 *Dame Edith Evans* lady, noblewoman, baroness, dowager, peeress, aristocrat **2** *US slang* WOMAN, female, broad

damn *v, n*
▶ *v* **1** CURSE, swear, blast, doom, blaspheme, use bad language, *formal* accurse, imprecate, execrate, maledict, anathematize, fulminate **2** CONDEMN, revile, denounce, criticize, censure, denunciate, *formal* berate, castigate, inveigh, excoriate, decry, denigrate, *colloq.* slam, slate, pan, knock, run down, come down on, pick holes in, pan, pull to pieces, tear to shreds
🔁 **1** bless **2** praise, commend
▶ *n* iota, jot, *slang* dash, hoot, toss, monkey's, brass farthing, two hoots, tinker's cuss

damnable *adj*
abominable, atrocious, horrible, despicable, detestable, iniquitous, cursed, infernal, offensive, wicked, *formal* execrable
🔁 admirable, praiseworthy

damnation *n*
condemnation, doom, denunciation, hell, perdition, excommunication, anathema, *formal* proscription

damned *adj*
1 *a damned soul* condemned, doomed, lost, cursed, accursed, reprobate, anathematized **2** *a damned disgrace* cursed, detestable, despicable, abominable, confounded, infernal, hateful, loathsome, odious, vile, fiendish, annoying, unpleasant, pernicious, *formal* execrable, *colloq.* blasted, blooming, flipping, darned, dashed, dratted
🔁 **1** blessed

damning *adj*
incriminating, condemning, implicating, *formal* accusatorial, condemnatory, damnatory, implicative, inculpatory

damp *adj, n, v*
▸ *adj* moist, wet, clammy, dank, humid, dewy, muggy, rainy, drizzly, misty, soggy, vaporous, rheumy
F3 dry, arid
▸ *n* dampness, moisture, clamminess, dankness, humidity, wet, wetness, dew, rain, drizzle, fog, mist
F3 dryness
▸ *v* ▷ **damp down** calm, dull, deaden, restrain, check, reduce, lessen, moderate, decrease, diminish

dampen *v*
1 MOISTEN, wet, spray, damp **2** DISCOURAGE, dishearten, damp down, deter, dash, dull, deaden, restrain, check, depress, dismay, reduce, lessen, moderate, decrease, diminish, put a damper on, muffle, inhibit, stifle, smother
F3 **1** dry **2** encourage

damper *n*
▷ **put a damper on** discourage, dishearten, damp down, deter, dash, dull, deaden, restrain, check, depress, dismay, reduce, lessen, moderate, decrease, diminish, muffle, inhibit, stifle, smother
F3 encourage

dampness *n*
damp, moisture, clamminess, dankness, humidity, wet, wetness, dew, rain, drizzle, fog, mist, vapour

damsel *n*
maiden, girl, lass, young woman, young lady

dance *v, n*
▸ *v* **1** *learn to dance* move to music, rock, spin, sway, twirl, pirouette, whirl, trip the light fantastic, *colloq.* hoof it, hop, jig, shake a leg **2** *dance for joy* skip, leap, jump, bounce, frisk, caper, frolic, gambol, juke, kantikoy, prance, skip, spin, stomp, sway, swing, tread a measure, whirl **3** *lights dancing on the water* leap, sway, flicker, twinkle, flash, shimmer, sparkle, waver, play, move lightly
▸ *n* ball, social, *colloq.* hop, knees-up, shindig

Dances include:
waltz, quickstep, foxtrot, tango, polka, one-step, military two-step, valeta, Lancers, rumba, samba, mambo, bossanova, beguine, fandango, flamenco, mazurka, bolero, paso doble, can-can; rock 'n' roll, jive, twist, stomp, bop, jitterbug, mashed potato; black bottom, Charleston, cha-cha, turkey-trot; Circassian circle, Paul Jones, jig, reel, quadrille, Highland fling, morris-dance, clog dance, hoedown, hokey-cokey, Lambeth Walk, conga, belly-dance; galliard, gavotte, minuet.

Types of dancing include:
ballet, tap, ballroom, old-time, disco, folk, country, Irish, Highland, Latin-American, flamenco, clog-dancing, line-dancing, morris dancing, limbo-dancing, break-dancing, robotics. *See also* BALLET.

Dance functions include:
disco, dance, social, tea dance, ceilidh, barn dance, ball, fancy dress ball, charity ball, hunt ball, *colloq.* hop, *colloq.* knees-up, *colloq.* shindig, *colloq.* rave, *US* prom.

dancer *n*
ballerina, ballet dancer, danseur, danseuse, coryphee, tap-dancer, belly-dancer

dandy *n, adj*
▸ *n* fop, coxcomb, beau, man about town, Adonis, beau, blade, dapperling, dude, exquisite, peacock, popinjay, swell, toff
▸ *adj* fine, capital, excellent, first-rate, great, splendid

danger *n*
1 *in danger of falling* insecurity, jeopardy, precariousness, liability, vulnerability, *formal* endangerment, imperilment **2** *the dangers of smoking* risk, threat, peril, hazard, menace, pitfall
F3 **1** safety, security **2** safety

dangerous *adj*
unsafe, insecure, risky, high-risk, fraught with danger, threatening, breakneck, hazardous, chancy, perilous, precarious, reckless, treacherous, vulnerable, defenceless, menacing, ominous, exposed, susceptible, alarming, critical, severe, serious, grave, daring, nasty, *formal* minacious, *colloq.* dicey, hairy
F3 safe, secure, harmless

dangle *v*
1 HANG, droop, swing, sway, flap, trail **2** TEMPT, entice, flaunt, flourish, lure, hold out, brandish, wave, tantalize

dank *adj*
damp, moist, wet, clammy, sticky, dewy, slimy, soggy
F3 dry

dapper *adj*
trim, well-dressed, well-turned-out, well-groomed, chic, dainty, neat, smart, spruce, stylish, nimble, active, brisk, spry, *colloq.* natty
F3 dishevelled, dowdy, scruffy, shabby, sloppy

dappled *adj*
speckled, mottled, spotted, stippled, dotted, flecked, freckled, variegated, bespeckled, piebald, pied, chequered

dare *v, n*
▸ *v* **1** RISK, venture, brave, be brave/bold enough, have the courage, hazard, adventure, endanger, stake, gamble **2** CHALLENGE, goad, provoke, taunt, *colloq.* throw down the gauntlet **3** DEFY, face, brave, confront, resist, flout, stand up to
▸ *n* challenge, venture, risk, provocation, taunt, goad, ultimatum, gauntlet

daredevil *n, adj*
▸ *n* adventurer, desperado, madcap, stuntman
F3 coward
▸ *adj* adventurous, daring, bold, fearless, dauntless, intrepid, brave, plucky, audacious, reckless, rash, impetuous, impulsive, valiant

daring *adj, n*
▸ *adj* bold, adventurous, intrepid, courageous, fearless, brave, plucky, audacious, valiant, dauntless, undaunted, reckless, wild, rash, impulsive, foolhardy
F3 cautious, timid, afraid
▸ *n* boldness, fearlessness, courage, bravery, adventurousness, audacity, intrepidity, valour, defiance, pluck, spirit, gall, prowess, wildness, rashness, foolhardiness, *colloq.* guts, nerve, grit
F3 caution, timidity, cowardice

dark *adj, n*
▸ *adj* **1** *a dark room/day* unlit, badly/poorly/dimly lit, overcast, black, dim, unilluminated, shady, shadowy, overcast, sunless, cloudy, misty, murky, foggy, dusky, gloomy, dingy, *formal* tenebrous **2** *dark hair/skin* black, brown, dark-haired, brunette, dark-skinned **3** *a dark manner* gloomy, grim, sad, cheerless, joyless, drab, dismal, bleak, forbidding, sombre, sinister, dejected, mournful, morose, ominous, menacing **4** *the dark days of war* unpleasant, awful, worrying, sad, gloomy, distressing, hopeless, frightening,

bleak, dismal, black **5** *dark secrets* hidden, mysterious, obscure, secret, unintelligible, puzzling, enigmatic, intricate, cryptic, *formal* abstruse, arcane, recondite, esoteric
🔁 **1** light, bright, clear **2** fair, light **3** bright, cheerful **4** happy, joyful **5** comprehensible
▶ *n* **1** DARKNESS, dimness, night, night-time, nightfall, evening, blackness, gloom, dusk, twilight, half-light, shadows, shade, shadiness, murkiness, sunlessness, cloudiness, mist, fog, *formal* tenebrity, tenebrosity **2** IGNORANCE, secrecy, privacy, concealment, obscurity, mystery
🔁 **1** light, brightness, daylight, lightness **2** enlightenment, openness

darken *v*
1 DIM, become/grow darker, obscure, blacken, cloud (over), fog, shadow, overshadow, shade, fade, eclipse, *old use* obnubilate **2** DEPRESS, sadden, deject, make gloomy, grow/become angry, look angry, frown
🔁 **1** lighten **2** brighten

darling *n, adj*
▶ *n* **1** *come here, darling* beloved, dear, dearest, favourite, sweetheart, love, pet, honey, angel, treasure **2** *the darling of the fashion world* FAVOURITE, pet, apple of your eye, *colloq.* blue-eyed boy, teacher's pet
▶ *adj* dear, dearest, beloved, adored, cherished, precious, treasured

darn *v*
mend, repair, stitch, sew (up)

dart *v, n*
▶ *v* **1** DASH, bound, sprint, flit, flash, fly, rush, run, race, spring, leap, tear, bolt, scurry, *colloq.* scoot **2** THROW, cast, hurl, fling, shoot, toss, sling, launch, project, propel, send
▶ *n* bolt, arrow, barb, feather, flight, shaft

dash *v, n*
▶ *v* **1** RUSH, fly, hurry, tear, dart, dive, race, sprint, run, speed, bolt, bound, hurtle, *colloq.* nip, pop **2** *waves dashing against rocks* smash, strike, lash, pound, beat, break, throw, crash, slam, hurl, fling **3** *dash your hopes* crush, smash, shatter, disappoint, discourage, dishearten, let down, depress, sadden, dampen, confound, blight, ruin, destroy, spoil, frustrate, thwart, devastate, ruin
▷ **dash off** scribble, jot down, scrawl
▶ *n* **1** DROP, pinch, grain, touch, flavour, soupçon, trace, suggestion, hint, tinge, bit, little, *colloq.* smidgen **2** SPRINT, dart, bolt, rush, spurt, race, run

dashing *adj*
1 LIVELY, vigorous, spirited, energetic, animated, gallant, daring, bold, plucky, exuberant **2** SMART, stylish, fashionable, elegant, debonair, showy, flamboyant, attractive
🔁 **1** lethargic **2** dowdy

dastardly *adj*
wicked, low, mean, base, contemptible, underhand, vile, cowardly, craven, despicable, faint-hearted, lily-livered, *formal* pusillanimous
🔁 heroic, noble

data *n*
information, documents, facts, input, statistics, figures, details, material, research, particulars

date *n, v*
▶ *n* **1** TIME, age, period, era, stage, epoch, day, week, month, year, decade, century, millennium **2** APPOINTMENT, engagement, meeting, rendezvous, *formal* assignation **3** FRIEND, boyfriend, girlfriend, partner, escort, *colloq.* steady
▷ **out of date** old-fashioned, unfashionable, outdated, obsolete, dated, outmoded, antiquated, archaic, *passé*
🔁 fashionable, modern
▷ **to date** so far, until now, until the present time, up to now, up to the present
▷ **up to date** fashionable, modern, current, contemporary, up to the minute, *colloq.* trendy
🔁 old-fashioned, dated
▶ *v* **1** *date back to the 18th century* originate, go back, come/exist from, belong to **2** *buy styles that won't date* become old-fashioned/obsolete, go out, go out of use, *formal* obsolesce **3** *date someone* go out with, take out, be together, go steady, court

dated *adj*
old-fashioned, obsolete, outdated, outmoded, out-of-date, *passé*, superseded, unfashionable, obsolescent, antiquated, archaic, *colloq.* old hat
🔁 fashionable, up-to-the-minute

daub *v, n*
▶ *v* smear, plaster, coat, paint, cover, smirch, smudge, spatter, splatter, stain, sully
▶ *n* smear, splash, splodge, splotch, spot, stain, blot, blotch

daughter *n*
girl, child, lass, lassie, offspring, descendant, inhabitant, disciple

daunt *v*
intimidate, unnerve, alarm, dismay, frighten, scare, disconcert, cow, overawe, take aback, discourage, dishearten, demoralize, disillusion, put off, dispirit, deter
🔁 encourage, hearten

dauntless *adj*
fearless, undaunted, resolute, brave, courageous, bold, intrepid, daring, plucky, valiant
🔁 discouraged, disheartened

dawdle *v*
delay, loiter, lag, go slowly, go at a snail's pace, hang about, linger, dally, take your time, take too long, trail, potter, *formal* tarry, *colloq.* dilly-dally
🔁 hurry

dawn *n, v*
▶ *n* **1** SUNRISE, daybreak, break of day, morning, daylight, first light, crack of dawn **2** BEGINNING, start, emergence, onset, origin, birth, arrival, rise, *formal* commencement, advent, inception, genesis
🔁 **1** dusk **2** end
▶ *v* **1** BREAK, brighten, lighten, become/grow light, gleam, glimmer **2** BEGIN, appear, emerge, open, develop, originate, be born, come into being, rise, *formal* commence
▷ **dawn on** realize, strike, occur to, sink in, come into your mind, *colloq.* hit, click

day *n*
1 DAYTIME, daylight **2** AGE, period, time, date, era, generation, epoch
🔁 **1** night
▷ **day after day** regularly, continually, endlessly, persistently, monotonously, perpetually, relentlessly
▷ **day by day** gradually, progressively, slowly but surely, steadily
▷ **have had its day** be no longer fashionable/popular, be no longer useful/successful, be out of date, *colloq.* be past it

daybreak *n*
sunrise, dawn, break of day, morning, daylight, first light, crack of dawn, cock-crow(ing), sun-up
🔁 sunset, sundown

daydream *n, v*
▶ *n* fantasy, imagining, reverie, castles in the air, pipe dream, vision, musing, wish, dream, inattention, figment
▶ *v* fantasize, imagine, muse, fancy, dream, be lost in space, not pay attention, let your thoughts wander, stare into space, *colloq.* switch off

daylight *n*
1 *during daylight hours* light, natural light, day, daytime, sunlight **2** SUNRISE, dawn, daybreak, break of day, morning, first light, crack of dawn
🔁 **1** night, dark

daze *v, n*
▶ *v* **1** STUN, stupefy, shock, numb, paralyse **2** DAZZLE, bewilder, blind, confuse, baffle, dumbfound, amaze, surprise, shock, stun, startle, perplex, astonish, astound, stagger, take aback, *colloq.* flabbergast
▶ *n* bewilderment, confusion, stupor, numbness, trance, shock, distraction

dazed *adj*
1 STUNNED, stupefied, shocked, numbed, paralysed, unconscious, *colloq.* out **2** DAZZLED, bewildered, confused, baffled, dumbfounded, speechless, amazed, surprised, shocked, stunned, startled, perplexed, astonished, astounded, staggered, taken aback, *colloq.* flabbergasted

dazzle *v, n*
▶ *v* **1** DAZE, blind, confuse, blur **2** SPARKLE, fascinate, impress, strike, overwhelm, awe, overawe, overpower, scintillate, bedazzle, amaze, astonish, bewitch, hypnotize, dumbfound, stupefy, *colloq.* bowl over, knock out, wow
▶ *n* sparkle, brilliance, brightness, magnificence, splendour, scintillation, glitter, gleam, glare, *colloq.* razzmatazz

dazzling *adj*
brilliant, splendid, impressive, stunning, awe-inspiring, breathtaking, spectacular, glaring, glittering, shining, sparkling, glorious, radiant, ravishing, scintillating, sensational, grand, superb

dead *adj, adv*
▶ *adj* **1** LIFELESS, inanimate, defunct, departed, perished, extinct, late, gone, no more, *formal* deceased, *colloq.* dead as a doornail **2** *dead leaves* inanimate, lifeless, inert, *formal* insentient, insensate, exanimate **3** *a dead language* obsolete, extinct, discontinued, no longer spoken **4** *that issue is dead* dated, out of date, passé, no longer of interest, *colloq.* old hat, dead as a dodo **5** *this town is dead* boring, dull, humdrum, tedious, uninteresting, unexciting, with nothing happening, quiet **6** *my fingers have gone dead* numb, unfeeling, not feeling anything, gone to sleep, paralysed **7** UNRESPONSIVE, apathetic, dull, indifferent, insensitive, numb, cold, emotionless, frigid, lukewarm, unsympathetic, torpid **8** *dead centre* EXACT, absolute, perfect, unqualified, utter, outright, complete, entire, total, downright, thorough **9** EXHAUSTED, tired, tired out, worn out, *colloq.* knackered, dead beat, ready to drop
🔁 **1** alive **3** living **7** lively **9** refreshed
▶ *adv* absolutely, completely, entirely, exactly, precisely, perfectly, very, quite, totally, thoroughly, utterly

deaden *v*
reduce, blunt, muffle, dull, lessen, quieten, suppress, weaken, numb, diminish, stifle, mitigate, alleviate, soothe, moderate, take the edge off, anaesthetize, desensitize, smother, check, abate, allay, assuage, subdue, dampen, hush, mute, paralyse
🔁 heighten

deadlock *n*
standstill, stalemate, checkmate, impasse, dead end, halt, stoppage

deadly *adj, adv*
▶ *adj* **1** *deadly poison* lethal, fatal, dangerous, venomous, toxic, destructive, pernicious, noxious, malignant, murderous, mortal **2** *deadly enemies* implacable, mortal, murderous, hated, grim, fierce, savage **3** *in deadly earnest* great, serious, marked, intense,

extreme **4** *a deadly lecture* dull, boring, uninteresting, unexciting, tedious, monotonous **5** *deadly aim* unerring, unfailing, precise, accurate, sure, effective, true
🔁 **1** harmless **4** exciting
▶ *adv* utterly, thoroughly, dreadfully, absolutely, completely, entirely, perfectly, quite, totally

deadpan *adj*
blank, empty, expressionless, unexpressive, impassive, inexpressive, inscrutable, poker-faced, straight-faced, dispassionate

deaf *adj*
1 HARD OF HEARING, stone-deaf, with impaired hearing, *colloq.* deaf as a post **2** UNCONCERNED, indifferent, impervious, unmoved, oblivious, heedless, unmindful
🔁 **2** aware, conscious

deafening *adj*
piercing, very loud, very noisy, ear-splitting, booming, resounding, thunderous, ringing, reverberating, roaring, overwhelming
🔁 quiet

deal *v, n*
▶ *v* **1** DISTRIBUTE, give out, share, dole out, divide, allot, dispense, assign, mete out, *formal* apportion, bestow **2** TRADE, do business, buy and sell, negotiate, traffic, export, bargain, handle, treat, operate, market, stock **3** *deal a blow* deliver, administer, direct, mete, inflict
▷ **deal with 1** *deal with a situation* attend to, concern, see to, manage, handle, tackle, cope with, get to grips with, take care of, look after, sort out, process **2** *her novel deals with the future* treat, consider, be about, concern, cover
▶ *n* **1** QUANTITY, lot, load, amount, extent, degree, portion, share **2** AGREEMENT, contract, understanding, pact, transaction, bargain, buy, arrangement **3** ROUND, hand, distribution

dealer *n*
trader, salesman, saleswoman, salesperson, merchant, retailer, wholesaler, marketer, merchandiser, vendor, trafficker, *colloq.* pusher, tout

dealings *n*
business, commerce, trade, operations, traffic, trafficking, transactions, negotiations, relations, *formal* intercourse, *colloq.* truck

dear *adj, n*
▶ *adj* **1** LOVED, beloved, treasured, valued, cherished, adored, favoured, precious, favourite, intimate, respected, close, darling, familiar, endearing, *formal* esteemed **2** EXPENSIVE, high-priced, costly, high-cost, overpriced, exorbitant, not cheap, *colloq.* pricey, steep
🔁 **1** disliked, hated **2** cheap
▶ *n* beloved, loved one, precious, darling, pet, sweetheart, honey, angel, treasure

dearly *adv*
1 *he loves her dearly* fondly, affectionately, with affection, lovingly, devotedly, adoringly, tenderly, intimately, with favour/respect **2** *I wish it dearly* greatly, extremely, very much, deeply, profoundly **3** *pay dearly for something* at a great cost, at a high price, with great loss

dearth *n*
scarcity, shortage, deficiency, insufficiency, inadequacy, lack, absence, scantiness, sparsity, need, poverty, famine, *formal* paucity, want
🔁 excess, abundance

death *n*
1 *people in danger of death* loss, departure, loss of life, fatality, passing, passing away, perishing, end, finish, the grave, *formal* expiration, decease, demise, quietus, *colloq.* last farewell, curtains **2** *the death of the*

welfare state ruin, destruction, end, finish, undoing, annihilation, downfall, extermination, dissolution, extinction, *formal* demise, obliteration, eradication, extirpation, termination, cessation
Fä 1 life, birth
▷ **put to death** execute, kill, hang, electrocute, shoot, guillotine, behead, exterminate, martyr

deathless *adj*
immortal, imperishable, eternal, everlasting, undying, never-ending, timeless, incorruptible, memorable, unforgettable

deathly *adj*
1 ASHEN, grim, haggard, pale, pallid, ghastly, wan, colourless, cadaverous **2** FATAL, deadly, mortal, intense, extreme, utmost

debacle *n*
fiasco, catastrophe, failure, collapse, defeat, devastation, disaster, downfall, havoc, cataclysm, overthrow, reversal, rout, turmoil, disintegration, ruin, ruination, stampede, farce

debar *v*
ban, bar, forbid, prohibit, eject, exclude, shut out, keep out, expel, stop, hamper, hinder, obstruct, prevent, segregate, restrain, deny, blackball, *formal* preclude, proscribe
Fä admit, allow

debase *v*
degrade, demean, devalue, disgrace, dishonour, discredit, shame, humble, humiliate, cheapen, lower, reduce, abase, defile, contaminate, pollute, corrupt, adulterate, alloy, dilute, taint, *formal* vitiate
Fä elevate, purify

debased *adj*
degraded, devalued, disgraced, dishonoured, discredited, shamed, humbled, humiliated, cheapened, abased, defiled, contaminated, impure, polluted, perverted, corrupt, debauched, fallen, low, degenerate, adulterated, tainted, base, sordid, vile
Fä elevated, pure

debasement *n*
degradation, devaluation, disgrace, dishonour, shame, humiliation, cheapening, depravation, abasement, defilement, contamination, pollution, perversion, corruption, degeneration, adulteration
Fä elevation, purification

debatable *adj*
questionable, arguable, uncertain, unsure, disputable, contestable, controversial, open to question, doubtful, contentious, undecided, unsettled, problematical, dubious, moot
Fä unquestionable, certain, incontrovertible

debate *n, v*
▶ *n* discussion, argument, controversy, deliberation, consideration, forum, contention, dispute, reflection, polemic, *formal* disputation, altercation
▶ *v* **1** DISPUTE, argue, reason, discuss, talk about/over, contend, contest, wrangle, *formal* altercate, *colloq.* kick around **2** CONSIDER, think over, deliberate, ponder, reflect, meditate on, mull over, weigh, *formal* cogitate

debauch *v*
corrupt, lead astray, deprave, over-indulge, pervert, pollute, subvert, ravish, ruin, seduce, violate
Fä cleanse, purge, purify

debauched *adj*
depraved, abandoned, immoral, corrupt, corrupted, debased, perverted, degenerate, degraded, intemperate, overindulgent, dissipated, dissolute, excessive, decadent, promiscuous, wanton, lewd, carousing, riotous, *formal* licentious
Fä decent, pure, virtuous

debauchery *n*
depravity, immorality, corruption, degeneracy, degradation, intemperance, overindulgence, rakishness, dissoluteness, excess, decadence, wantonness, lewdness, carousal, orgy, revel, lust, riot, *formal* dissipation, licentiousness, libertinism
Fä restraint, temperance

debilitate *v*
weaken, undermine, sap, incapacitate, wear out, exhaust, impair, cripple, *formal* enervate, enfeeble, devitalize
Fä strengthen, invigorate, energize

debilitating *adj*
weakening, undermining, incapacitating, wearing out, fatiguing, tiring, exhausting, impairing, crippling, *formal* enervating, enervative, enfeebling
Fä invigorating, strengthening

debility *n*
weakness, infirmity, tiredness, fatigue, exhaustion, faintness, feebleness, frailty, incapacity, infirmity, lack of energy/vitality
Fä strength, vigour, *technical* asthenia, atonicity, atony, *formal* decrepitude, enervation, enfeeblement, languor, malaise

debonair *adj*
suave, refined, urbane, well-bred, smooth, dashing, elegant, affable, breezy, buoyant, charming, courteous, cheerful, jaunty, light-hearted

debris *n*
remains, ruins, rubbish, waste, wreck, wreckage, litter, fragments, rubble, trash, pieces, bits, sweepings, drift, *formal* detritus

debt *n*
1 *£500 in debt* arrears, overdraft, money owing/due, due, liability, debit, duty, bill, hock, claim, score, *colloq.* the red, Queer Street **2** *in someone's debt for their kindness* indebtedness, obligation, commitment, liability
Fä 1 credit, asset

debtor *n*
borrower, bankrupt, insolvent, defaulter, mortgagor
Fä creditor

debunk *v*
expose, deflate, puncture, show up, ridicule, mock, explode, disprove, lampoon, *colloq.* cut down to size

début *n*
first appearance, first performance, first night, first recording, first time, introduction, launching, beginning, entrance, presentation, inauguration, première, coming-out, initiation

decadence *n*
corruption, debasement, debauchery, depravity, dissolution, immorality, degeneracy, degenerateness, degeneration, deterioration, self-indulgence, decay, decline, fall, perversion, *formal* dissipation, licentiousness, retrogression
Fä flourishing, rise

decadent *adj*
1 CORRUPT, debased, debauched, depraved, dissolute, dissipated, immoral, degenerate, degraded, self-indulgent, *formal* licentious **2** DECAYING, declining, degenerating, deteriorating, debased
Fä 1 moral

decamp *v*
make off, run away, take off, abscond, bolt, desert, escape, flee, flit, fly, *colloq.* scarper, skedaddle, vamoose, do a runner, do a bunk, do a moonlight flit, hightail it, absquatulate

decapitate *v*
behead, execute, guillotine, unhead

decay *v, n*
▸ *v* **1** ROT, go bad, decompose, spoil, fester, perish, rust, corrode, *formal* putrefy **2** DECLINE, deteriorate, disintegrate, corrode, crumble, waste away, degenerate, atrophy, wear away, weaken, dwindle, fail, shrivel, wither, sink
🖅 **2** flourish, grow
▸ *n* **1** ROT, going bad, decomposition, rotting, perishing, *formal* putrefaction, putrescence, putridity **2** DECLINE, deterioration, disintegration, degeneration, collapse, crumbling, decadence, weakening, wasting, failing, atrophy, withering, fading

decayed *adj*
rotten, bad, off, stale, sour, rank, addled, carious, decomposed, spoiled, mouldy, mildewed, perished, corroded, carrion, wasted, withered, *formal* putrefied, putrid

decease *n*
death, dying, demise, departure, passing, passing away, dissolution, *formal* expiration, demise

deceased *adj, n*
▸ *adj* dead, departed, former, late, lost, defunct, expired, gone, finished, extinct
▸ *n* dead, departed

deceit *n*
deception, pretence, cheating, misrepresentation, fraud, trickery, fraudulence, double-dealing, underhandedness, chicanery, fake, guile, sham, subterfuge, swindle, treachery, hypocrisy, artifice, ruse, cunning, slyness, craftiness, wiliness, stratagem, wile, imposition, feint, abuse, *formal* duplicity
🖅 honesty, openness, frankness

deceitful *adj*
dishonest, untruthful, lying, deceptive, deceiving, false, insincere, untrustworthy, double-dealing, fraudulent, treacherous, duplicitous, guileful, underhand, sneaky, counterfeit, crafty, sly, cunning, hypocritical, designing, illusory, knavish, *formal* mendacious, duplicitous, dissembling, perfidious, *colloq.* two-faced, tricky
🖅 honest, open

deceive *v*
mislead, delude, cheat (on), betray, fool, trick, hoax, bluff, dupe, swindle, outsmart, outwit, impose upon, lead on, misguide, outwit, hoodwink, beguile, set a trap for, entrap, ensnare, camouflage, abuse, seduce, gull, *formal* dissemble, *colloq.* con, kid, bamboozle, have on, take for a ride, string along, double-cross, two-time, pull someone's leg, pull a fast one on, pull the wool over someone's eyes, put up a smokescreen, lead up the garden path, put one over on

deceiver *n*
deluder, cheat, betrayer, fake, fraud, hypocrite, trickster, hoaxer, swindler, impostor, charlatan, abuser, seducer, mountebank, *formal* dissembler, inveigler, *colloq.* con man, diddler, crook, double-dealer

decelerate *v*
slow down, brake, put the brakes on, reduce speed

decency *n*
respectability, uprightness, integrity, civility, correctness, fitness, good taste, etiquette, courtesy, modesty, helpfulness, *old use* seemliness, *formal* propriety, decorum
🖅 impropriety, discourtesy

decent *adj*
1 *decent behaviour* RESPECTABLE, upright, worthy, proper, fitting, tasteful, chaste, virtuous, ethical, suitable, modest, appropriate, presentable, pure, fit, becoming, befitting, nice, *old use* seemly, *formal* decorous **2** *a decent person* KIND, obliging, courteous,

helpful, accommodating, generous, thoughtful, polite, gracious **3** ADEQUATE, acceptable, satisfactory, reasonable, sufficient, tolerable, competent, *colloq.* OK
🖅 **1** indecent **2** disobliging

decentralize *v*
devolve, regionalize, localize, delegate, deconcentrate, spread downwards/outwards
🖅 centralize

deception *n*
deceit, pretence, deceptiveness, insincerity, treachery, hypocrisy, cheating, misrepresentation, trickery, fraudulence, double-dealing, underhandedness, chicanery, trick, cheat, imposture, lie, hoax, fraud, bluff, ruse, snare, guile, sham, subterfuge, artifice, swindle, stratagem, illusion, wile, craftiness, cunning, *formal* dissembling, duplicity, *colloq.* con, put-up job, legpull, flim-flam
🖅 openness, honesty

deceptive *adj*
misleading, dishonest, false, fraudulent, cheating, cunning, sly, crooked, crafty, underhand, unreliable, illusive, fake, illusory, spurious, specious, mock, bogus, sham, ambiguous
🖅 genuine, artless, open, *formal* fallacious, dissembling, duplicitous

decide *v*
1 *decide to do something* MAKE UP YOUR MIND, come to/arrive at a decision, reach/make a decision, come to/reach a conclusion, determine, resolve **2** *decide an issue/a case* settle, resolve, determine, conclude, fix, establish, adjudicate, arbitrate, judge, rule, give a judgement/ruling **3** *decide on a new car* choose, pick, select, opt for, settle, *colloq.* go for, plump for

decided *adj*
1 DEFINITE, clear, certain, marked, obvious, undeniable, indisputable, unequivocal, absolute, clear-cut, pronounced, undisputed, unmistakable, unquestionable, positive, unambiguous, categorical, express, absolute, distinct, emphatic **2** RESOLUTE, decisive, determined, purposeful, firm, unhesitating, unswerving, unwavering, deliberate, forthright
🖅 **1** inconclusive **2** irresolute

decidedly *adv*
very, absolutely, certainly, downright, positively, quite, unquestionably, unequivocally, unmistakably, clearly, definitely, distinctly, obviously, decisively

decider *n*
clincher, *coup de grâce*, determiner, floorer

deciding *adj*
decisive, determining, conclusive, critical, crucial, significant, final, chief, influential, prime, principal, supreme, *colloq.* crunch
🖅 insignificant

decipher *v*
decode, unscramble, unravel, interpret, translate, make out, work out, understand, transliterate, *formal* construe, *colloq.* crack, figure out
🖅 encode

decision *n*
1 CONCLUSION, result, outcome, verdict, finding, settlement, resolution, judgement, arbitration, adjudication, ruling, decree, pronouncement, opinion **2** DETERMINATION, decisiveness, firmness, resolve, forcefulness, purpose, strong-mindedness

decisive *adj*
1 CONCLUSIVE, deciding, definite, definitive, determining, absolute, final, critical, crucial, influential, significant, momentous, prime, principal, fateful **2** *a decisive person* DETERMINED, resolute, decided, positive, firm, forceful, forthright, purposeful, strong, strong-minded, unwavering, unswerving

E 1 inconclusive, insignificant 2 indecisive

deck v
decorate, ornament, adorn, beautify, embellish, trim, garnish, garland, festoon, grace, enrich, prettify, trick out, *formal* array, bedeck, *colloq.* tart up, rig, tog

declaim v
speak boldly/dramatically, proclaim, hold forth, lecture, harangue, rant, sermonize, *formal* orate, perorate, *colloq.* spiel, spout

declamation n
speech, address, lecture, oration, sermon, harangue, tirade, rant, speechifying

declamatory adj
bold, dramatic, rhetorical, bombastic, discursive, grandiloquent, grandiose, high-flown, inflated, oratorical, overblown, pompous, stagy, theatrical, stilted, *formal* magniloquent, orotund, fustian

declaration n
1 ANNOUNCEMENT, notification, pronouncement, statement, proclamation, edict, decree, manifesto, broadcast, *formal* promulgation 2 AFFIRMATION, acknowledgement, assertion, statement, confession, testimony, confirmation, disclosure, profession, revelation, *formal* attestation, avowal, affidavit, averment

declare v
1 ANNOUNCE, proclaim, make known, pronounce, decree, publish, broadcast, *formal* promulgate 2 AFFIRM, assert, claim, profess, maintain, state, certify, pronounce, confess, confirm, disclose, make known, reveal, show, swear, testify, witness, validate, *formal* aver, avow, attest

decline v, n
▶ v 1 DIMINISH, become/get less, go/come down, decrease, dwindle, lessen, fade, fall, sink, subside, slide, drop, wane, weaken, wither, fade, ebb, flag, plummet, plunge, *formal* abate 2 REFUSE, turn down, say no to, reject, deny, repudiate, forego, avoid, balk, *colloq.* give the thumbs-down to 3 DECAY, deteriorate, worsen, degenerate, sink, rot, slip, fall off, lapse, *formal* regress 4 DESCEND, sink, slope, dip, slant
E 1 grow, increase 2 accept 3 improve 4 rise
▶ n 1 DETERIORATION, dwindling, lessening, decrease, reduction, decay, degeneration, weakening, worsening, failing, failure, downturn, dwindling, waning, fall, falling-off, recession, slump, *formal* diminution, abatement 2 DESCENT, dip, declination, hill, slope, incline, divergence, deviation, *formal* declivity
E 1 improvement 2 rise

decode v
decipher, interpret, unscramble, unravel, translate, make out, work out, understand, transliterate, uncipher, *formal* construe, *colloq.* crack, figure out
E encode

decomposable adj
biodegradable, degradable, destructible, decompoundable

decompose v
disintegrate, rot, decay, break down, break up, crumble, spoil, dissolve, separate, fester, *formal* putrefy

decomposition n
rot, going bad, decay, rotting, perishing, corruption, disintegration, dissolution, *formal* putrefaction, putrescence, putridity
E combination, unification

décor n
decoration, ornamentation, furnishings, colour scheme, scenery

decorate v
1 ORNAMENT, adorn, beautify, embellish, trim, garnish, deck, garland, festoon, grace, enrich, prettify, trick out, *formal* array, bedizen, bedaub, *colloq.* tart up 2 RENOVATE, paint, paper, wallpaper, colour, smarten, refurbish, *colloq.* do up 3 HONOUR, crown, cite, give a medal/honour to, give an award to, garland, bemedal

decoration n
1 ORNAMENT, adornment, ornamentation, trimming, embellishment, beautification, enhancement, décor, furnishings, mural, colour scheme, garnish, flourish, enrichment, elaboration, bunting, frill, scroll, trinket, bauble, knick-knack 2 AWARD, medal, order, badge, garland, crown, colours, ribbon, cross, laurel, wreath, star, emblem, insignia, honour, title

decorative adj
ornamental, fancy, adorning, beautifying, embellishing, non-functional, pretty, ornate, elaborate, enhancing, rococo
E plain

decorous adj
polite, refined, correct, courtly, decent, dignified, proper, well-behaved, appropriate, suitable, becoming, befitting, comely, *comme il faut*, fit, mannerly, modest, sedate, staid, *old use* seemly
E indecorous

decorum n
good manners, good form, etiquette, respectability, conformity, protocol, behaviour, decency, dignity, restraint, politeness, modesty, grace, breeding, *old use* seemliness, *formal* propriety, deportment
E bad manners, *formal* impropriety

decoy n, v
▶ n lure, trap, snare, pitfall, enticement, inducement, ensnarement, allurement, pretence, attraction, temptation, bait, diversion, dummy
▶ v bait, lure, entrap, entice, ensnare, allure, tempt, deceive, attract, seduce, lead, draw, *formal* inveigle

decrease v, n
▶ v lessen, make/become less, go/come down, lower, diminish, dwindle, decline, fall (off), reduce, subside, slide, plummet, plunge, cut back/down, contract, drop, ease, shrink, taper (off), wane, slim (down), let up, slacken, peter out, curtail, scale down, trim, *formal* abate
E increase
▶ n lessening, reduction, decline, lowering, drop, fall, falling-off, dwindling, loss, cutback, contraction, downturn, ebb, shrinkage, subsidence, step-down, *formal* diminution, abatement
E increase

decree n, v
▶ n order, command, law, ordinance, regulation, ruling, judgement, directive, rule, statute, act, enactment, edict, fiat, proclamation, mandate, manifesto, precept, *formal* interlocution, indiction, firman, rescript, psephism, irade, hatti-sherif
▶ v order, command, rule, lay down, dictate, direct, decide, determine, ordain, prescribe, proclaim, pronounce, enact, *formal* enjoin

decrepit adj
1 *a decrepit building* dilapidated, run-down, ramshackle, rickety, broken-down, battered, worn-out, old, in bad condition/shape, tumbledown, crumbling, falling apart/to bits, *colloq.* clapped-out 2 *a decrepit person* weak, aged, feeble, frail, worn-out, infirm, elderly, doddering, tottering, *formal* senescent

decrepitude n
ruin, dilapidation, decay, degeneration, deterioration, disability, debility, weakness, feebleness, infirmity, incapacity, dotage, old age, senility, *formal* senescence
E good repair, youth

decry *v*
criticize, condemn, disparage, carp, disapprove of, find fault with, denounce, attack, belittle, blame, depreciate, devalue, underrate, undervalue, *formal* censure, declaim against, animadvert, excoriate, derogate, inveigh against, denigrate, traduce, *colloq.* slate, knock, snipe, run down, come down on, pan, pull to pieces, tear to shreds, tear a strip off, nit-pick, do a hatchet job on
F3 praise, value

dedicate *v*
1 DEVOTE, commit, assign, give, give over to, pledge, present, offer, sacrifice, surrender **2** *dedicate a book* inscribe, address, name **3** CONSECRATE, bless, sanctify, set apart, hallow, make holy

dedicated *adj*
1 *a dedicated teacher* devoted, committed, enthusiastic, single-minded, wholehearted, single-hearted, zealous, given over to, purposeful, hard working, industrious, diligent **2** CUSTOMIZED, custom-built, bespoke
F3 1 uncommitted, apathetic

dedication *n*
1 COMMITMENT, devotion, single-mindedness, wholeheartedness, allegiance, attachment, adherence, faithfulness, loyalty, enthusiasm, zeal, self-sacrifice **2** INSCRIPTION, address **3** CONSECRATION, hallowing, blessing, sanctification, presentation
F3 1 apathy

deduce *v*
derive, infer, gather, conclude, come to the conclusion, reason, surmise, understand, draw, glean

deduct *v*
subtract, take away/off, remove, reduce by, decrease by, withdraw, *colloq.* knock off
F3 add

deduction *n*
1 INFERENCE, reasoning, finding, conclusion, corollary, surmising, assumption, presumption, result **2** SUBTRACTION, reduction, decrease, taking away/off, withdrawal, removal, discount, allowance, *formal* diminution, abatement
F3 2 addition, increase

deed *n*
1 ACTION, act, activity, achievement, performance, accomplishment, undertaking, exploit, feat, fact, truth, reality **2** DOCUMENT, contract, agreement, record, title, transaction, *formal* indenture

deem *v*
judge, believe, suppose, think, conceive, consider, estimate, hold, imagine, account, reckon, regard, *formal* adjudge, esteem

deep *adj, adv, n*
▶ *adj* **1** *a deep river/pit* PROFOUND, bottomless, unplumbed, fathomless, unfathomed, immeasurable, yawning, cavernous, immersed **2** *a deep sleep/crisis/ feeling* INTENSE, serious, earnest, extreme, profound, very great, severe, heart-felt, passionate, fervent, ardent, strong, vigorous, grave **3** *a deep person* PERCEPTIVE, discerning, profound, wise, learned, astute, clever, serious, intellectual, quiet, reserved, *formal* sagacious, perspicacious, *colloq.* deep as a well **4** LOW, low-pitched, bass, resonant, sonorous, resounding, booming, rich, strong, powerful **5** *a deep colour* STRONG, intense, rich, vivid, brilliant, warm, glowing, dark **6** OBSCURE, mysterious, difficult, *formal* abstruse, esoteric, recondite
F3 1 shallow, open **2** light **3** superficial, shallow, frivolous **4** high, high-pitched **5** light, pale **6** clear, plain, open
▶ *adv* far, a long way, a great distance
▶ *n* sea, high seas, ocean, main, *colloq.* briny

deepen *v*
1 INTENSIFY, grow, increase, strengthen, reinforce, heighten, extend, magnify, build up, deteriorate, worsen, get worse **2** EXCAVATE, hollow, dig out, scoop out

deeply *adv*
intensely, seriously, earnestly, extremely, completely, thoroughly, profoundly, very much, severely, passionately, fervently, ardently, movingly, strongly, vigorously, acutely, distressingly, feelingly, gravely, mournfully, sadly, to the quick, *colloq.* from the bottom of your heart
F3 slightly

deep-seated *adj*
ingrained, entrenched, deep-rooted, fixed, confirmed, deep, settled
F3 eradicable, temporary

deer *n*
buck, doe, hart, reindeer, roe, stag

deface *v*
damage, spoil, disfigure, blemish, impair, mutilate, mar, sully, tarnish, vandalize, deform, obliterate, injure, destroy
F3 repair

de facto *adv & adj*
actually, in effect, really; actual, existing, real
F3 de jure

defamation *n*
slander, libel, disparagement, slur, smear, smear campaign, innuendo, scandal, backbiting, *formal* vilification, aspersion, calumny, traducement, denigration, derogation, obloquy, opprobrium, malediction
F3 commendation, praise

defamatory *adj*
slanderous, libellous, disparaging, pejorative, insulting, injurious, derogatory, *formal* vilifying, denigrating, contumelious, calumnious, maledictory
F3 complimentary, appreciative

defame *v*
slander, libel, discredit, disgrace, dishonour, besmirch, disparage, libel, malign, blacken, smear, speak evil of, stigmatize, *old use* infame, *formal* cast aspersions, denigrate, asperse, calumniate, traduce, vilify, vituperate, *colloq.* run down, drag through the mud, sling/throw mud at
F3 compliment, praise

default *v, n*
▶ *v* fail, evade, defraud, neglect, dodge, swindle, backslide
▶ *n* failure, absence, neglect, negligence, non-payment, omission, deficiency, lapse, fault, lack, defect, *formal* want, dereliction

defaulter *n*
non-payer, offender, absentee, non-appearer

defeat *v, n*
▶ *v* **1** CONQUER, beat, overcome, overpower, get the better of, eclipse, excel, surpass, subdue, overthrow, worst, repel, overwhelm, rout, ruin, crush, quell, bring someone to their knees, reject, throw out, *formal* subjugate, vanquish, *colloq.* thrash, lick, hammer, thump, trounce, annihilate, smash, devastate, slaughter, make mincemeat (out) of, run rings round **2** FRUSTRATE, confound, balk, get the better of, disappoint, foil, thwart, baffle, puzzle, perplex, checkmate, block, obstruct
▶ *n* **1** CONQUEST, beating, overthrow, overcoming, rout, repulsion, ruin, crushing, rejection, debacle, *formal* subjugation, vanquishment, *colloq.* trouncing, thrashing **2** FRUSTRATION, failure, setback, reverse, breakdown, downfall, disappointment, thwarting, checkmate

defeatist *n, adj*
▶ *n* pessimist, quitter, yielder, doomwatcher, prophet of doom
▣ optimist
▶ *adj* pessimistic, resigned, fatalistic, despondent, helpless, hopeless, despairing, gloomy
▣ optimistic

defecate *v*
empty/move your bowels, evacuate, excrete, pass a motion, relieve yourself, void excrement, ease yourself, *formal* egest, *colloq.* poo, do number two, *slang* crap

defect *n, v*
▶ *n* imperfection, fault, flaw, deficiency, failing, mistake, error, inadequacy, blemish, taint, deformity, error, shortcoming, shortfall, weakness, frailty, lack, spot, weak spot, snag, absence, omission, *formal* want, *colloq.* bug
▶ *v* desert, abandon, break faith, change sides, rebel, revolt, turn traitor, *formal* renege, apostatize, tergiversate

defection *n*
desertion, abandonment, disloyalty, backsliding, rebellion, revolt, mutiny, betrayal, treason, *formal* renegation, apostasy, defalcation, dereliction, perfidy, tergiversation

defective *adj*
faulty, imperfect, out of order, flawed, deficient, broken, in disrepair, abnormal, *formal* malfunctioning, *colloq.* bust, duff, on the blink
▣ in order, working, *formal* operative

---

defective or **deficient** ?

Defective means 'having a fault or flaw': *The crash was caused by defective wiring in the signalling system.* *Deficient* means 'inadequate, lacking in what is needed': *a diet deficient in essential vitamins and minerals.*

---

defector *n*
deserter, traitor, turncoat, betrayer, rebel, Judas, quisling, mutineer, recreant, backslider, *formal* renegade, apostate, tergiversator, *colloq.* rat

defence *n*
1 PROTECTION, resistance, security, fortification, cover, safeguard, shelter, guard, shield, screen, deterrence, deterrent, barricade, bastion, keep, fortress, outpost, stronghold, garrison, immunity, bulwark, rampart, buttress **2** *a country's defences* military resources, armed forces, army, navy, air force, troops, soldiers, military, weapons, armaments **3** JUSTIFICATION, explanation, excuse, argument, plea, vindication, pleading, testimony, alibi, case, *formal* apologia, explication, extenuation, exoneration
▣ **1** attack, assault **3** accusation, attack

defenceless *adj*
unprotected, undefended, unarmed, unguarded, vulnerable, exposed, open to attack, weak, helpless, powerless, impotent
▣ protected, guarded

defend *v*
1 PROTECT, guard, safeguard, watch over, shelter, secure, preserve, shield, screen, cover, resist, withstand, oppose, keep from harm, contest, deter, barricade, garrison, buttress, *formal* fortify **2** SUPPORT, stand up for, stand by, back, uphold, endorse, vindicate, champion, bolster, argue for, speak up for, make a case for, explain, justify, plead, *formal* exonerate, *colloq.* stick up for
▣ **1** attack **2** accuse, attack

defendant *n*
accused, offender, prisoner, *technical* litigant, appellant, respondent

defender *n*
1 PROTECTOR, guard, bodyguard, keeper **2** SUPPORTER, guardian, advocate, vindicator, backer, endorser, upholder, preserver, champion, patron, sponsor, counsel, apologist
▣ **1** attacker **2** accuser

defensible *adj*
justifiable, tenable, arguable, permissible, plausible, valid, maintainable, safe, secure, unassailable, impregnable, pardonable, vindicable
▣ indefensible, insecure

defensive *adj*
1 PROTECTIVE, defending, safeguarding, protecting, wary, opposing, cautious, watchful **2** SELF-JUSTIFYING, apologetic, self-defensive

defer¹ *v*
defer a meeting delay, postpone, put off, adjourn, hold over, put back, shelve, suspend, waive, *formal* procrastinate, prorogue, protract, *colloq.* put on ice, put on the back burner, take a raincheck on
▣ bring forward

defer² *v*
defer to an expert opinion yield, give way, comply, submit, surrender, give in, capitulate, respect, bow, *formal* accede, acquiesce

deference *n*
1 RESPECT, regard, honour, reverence, courtesy, civility, politeness, attentiveness, consideration, thoughtfulness, *formal* esteem **2** SUBMISSION, submissiveness, obedience, yielding, *formal* compliance, acquiescence
▣ **1** contempt **2** resistance

deferential *adj*
respectful, reverent, reverential, courteous, civil, dutiful, polite, attentive, considerate, thoughtful, ingratiating, *formal* morigerous, regardful, complaisant, obeisant, obsequious
▣ arrogant, immodest

deferment *n*
delay, postponement, putting-off, adjournment, holding-over, shelving, suspension, stay, moratorium, waiving, *formal* procrastination, prorogation

defiance *n*
opposition, confrontation, resistance, challenge, disobedience, rebelliousness, contempt, insubordination, disregard, insolence, *formal* recalcitrance, truculence, contumacy
▣ compliance, acquiescence, submissiveness

defiant *adj*
challenging, resistant, antagonistic, aggressive, rebellious, insubordinate, disobedient, intransigent, bold, insolent, contemptuous, scornful, obstinate, unco-operative, militant, provocative, *formal* recalcitrant, refractory, truculent, contumacious
▣ compliant, acquiescent, submissive

deficiency *n*
1 SHORTAGE, lack, inadequacy, scarcity, insufficiency, dearth, want, scantiness, absence, deficit **2** IMPERFECTION, shortcoming, weakness, fault, defect, flaw, failing, frailty
▣ **1** excess, surfeit **2** perfection

deficient *adj*
inadequate, insufficient, scarce, short, lacking, meagre, scanty, skimpy, incomplete, unsatisfactory, inferior, weak, *formal* wanting, exiguous
▣ excessive

deficient or **defective**? *See panel at* DEFECTIVE.

deficit *n*
shortage, shortfall, deficiency, loss, arrears, lack, default
F3 excess

defile *v, n*
▶ *v* pollute, violate, contaminate, degrade, dishonour, desecrate, defame, debase, soil, dirty, infect, stain, spoil, sully, tarnish, taint, make impure/unclean, profane, treat sacrilegiously, corrupt, blacken, disgrace, *formal* denigrate, vitiate, inquinate
F3 clean, cleanse, purify
▶ *n* pass, gorge, valley, gully, passage, ravine

definable *adj*
ascertainable, definite, identifiable, describable, determinable, perceptible, definite, fixed, specific, exact, precise, *formal* explicable
F3 indefinable

define *v*
1 *define the boundaries* bound, limit, delimit, establish, demarcate, mark out, fix, *formal* circumscribe, delineate **2** *define the meaning* explain, characterize, describe, interpret, determine, designate, specify, spell out, detail, clarify, *formal* expound, elucidate

definite *adj*
1 CLEAR, clear-cut, exact, precise, specific, explicit, particular, firm, obvious, marked, noticeable **2** CERTAIN, settled, sure, positive, fixed, decided, determined, assured, guaranteed
F3 **1** vague **2** indefinite, provisional

 definite or **definitive**?
Definite means 'clear' or 'certain': *I'll give you a definite answer later. Definitive* means 'final, settling things once and for all': *a definitive study of Ben Jonson.*

definitely *adv*
positively, surely, unquestionably, without question, absolutely, certainly, categorically, undeniably, clearly, undoubtedly, doubtless, without doubt, no denying, unmistakably, plainly, obviously, indeed, easily, *formal* indubitably

definition *n*
1 EXPLANATION, meaning, significance, sense, description, interpretation, clarification, determination, *formal* exposition, elucidation **2** DISTINCTNESS, clarity, precision, clearness, focus, sharpness, visibility, contrast

definitive *adj*
decisive, conclusive, final, authoritative, standard, correct, ultimate, reliable, exhaustive, perfect, exact, absolute, complete, categorical
F3 interim

deflate *v*
1 FLATTEN, puncture, collapse, let down, exhaust, squash, empty, contract, void, shrink, squeeze **2** *deflate his opinion of himself* humiliate, debunk, dash, disappoint, dispirit, humble, mortify, chasten, disconcert, *colloq.* put down **3** DEPRECIATE, devalue, reduce, lessen, lower, diminish, decrease, depress
F3 **1** inflate **2** boost **3** inflate, increase

deflect *v*
deviate, diverge, turn (aside), swerve, veer, change course, sidetrack, drift, twist, avert, wind, glance off, bend, ricochet

deflection *n*
deviation, divergence, turning, turning aside, swerve, veer, changing course, sidetracking, drift, twisting,

glancing-off, bend, ricochet, *formal* aberration, refraction

deflower *v*
violate, assault, defile, rape, seduce, spoil, desecrate, force, harm, mar, molest, ruin, *formal* ravish, despoil

deform *v*
distort, contort, disfigure, deface, malform, misshape, warp, mar, pervert, ruin, spoil, damage, maim, mutilate, twist, buckle

deformation *n*
bend, curve, distortion, contortion, disfiguration, defacement, malformation, misshapenness, mutilation, twist, twisting, warp, buckle, *technical* diastrophism

deformed *adj*
distorted, misshapen, malformed, contorted, disfigured, crippled, crooked, gnarled, bent, twisted, warped, buckled, defaced, mangled, maimed, marred, ruined, mutilated, perverted, corrupted

deformity *n*
distortion, misshapenness, malformation, disfigurement, defacement, abnormality, irregularity, imperfection, misproportion, defect, ugliness, crookedness, vileness, grossness, monstrosity, corruption, perversion

defraud *v*
cheat, swindle, dupe, rob, trick, rook, deceive, delude, mislead, fool, hoodwink, outwit, embezzle, beguile, *formal* cozen, *colloq.* fiddle, fleece, sting, rip off, do, diddle, con

defray *v*
reimburse, refund, repay, recompense, discharge, meet, pay, settle
F3 incur

deft *adj*
adept, handy, dexterous, nimble, skilful, adroit, agile, expert, nifty, proficient, able, neat, clever
F3 clumsy, awkward

defunct *adj*
1 DEAD, deceased, departed, gone, expired, extinct **2** OBSOLETE, invalid, expired, *passé*, outmoded, bygone, *formal* inoperative
F3 **1** alive, live **2** functioning, *formal* operative

defy *v*
1 *defy the authorities* challenge, confront, resist, dare, brave, face, repel, spurn, beard, flout, slight, withstand, stand up to, disobey, rebel against, disrespect, disregard, ignore, scorn, despise, defeat, provoke, frustrate, thwart **2** *her writings defy categorization* elude, avoid, frustrate, baffle, foil
F3 **1** obey **2** permit, allow

degeneracy *n*
dissoluteness, debauchery, depravation, degradation, debasement, decadence, corruption, fallenness, immorality, vileness, wickedness, sinfulness, degeneration, perversion, deterioration, *formal* effeteness
F3 morality, uprightness

degenerate *adj, v*
▶ *adj* dissolute, debauched, depraved, degraded, debased, base, low, abandoned, decadent, corrupt, fallen, immoral, mean, ignoble, vile, wicked, sinful, degenerated, perverted, deteriorated, *formal* effete, profligate
F3 moral, upright
▶ *v* decline, deteriorate, sink, decay, rot, fail, slip, worsen, fall off, lapse, decrease, *formal* regress, *colloq.* go downhill, go to pot, go down the tube
F3 improve

degeneration *n*
decline, deterioration, debasement, decay, failure,

slip, worsening, falling-off, sinking, drop, slide, lapse, atrophy, decrease, *formal* regression
🗲 improvement

degradation *n*
1 ABASEMENT, humiliation, mortification, dishonour, disgrace, shame, ignominy, decadence, degeneracy, dissoluteness, debauchery, deprivation, debasement, corruption, fallenness, immorality, vileness, wickedness, sinfulness, degeneration, perversion 2 DETERIORATION, degeneration, decline, downgrading, demotion
🗲 1 enhancement 2 virtue

degrade *v*
1 DISHONOUR, disgrace, debase, abase, shame, humiliate, humble, discredit, mortify, demean, belittle, lower, devalue, weaken, impair, deteriorate, cheapen, adulterate, pervert, sully, defile, corrupt 2 DEMOTE, depose, downgrade, deprive, cashier, reduce/lower in rank, relegate, unseat, *colloq.* drum out, take down a peg or two
🗲 1 exalt 2 promote

degrading *adj*
humiliating, dishonourable, disgraceful, debasing, base, shameful, contemptible, discrediting, mortifying, demeaning, belittling, cheapening, ignoble, undignified, unworthy
🗲 enhancing

degree *n*
1 *to a great degree* EXTENT, measure, range, stage, step, level, amount, intensity, strength, standard 2 GRADE, class, rank, rung, order, position, standing, status, stage, level, limit, unit, point, mark

dehydrate *v*
dry, dry up, dry out, evaporate, lose water, drain, parch, *formal* desiccate, exsiccate, effloresce

deification *n*
exaltation, elevation, worship, glorification, idolization, extolling, immortalization, ennoblement, idealization, *formal* veneration, apotheosis, divinification, divinization

deify *v*
exalt, elevate, worship, glorify, idolize, extol, immortalize, ennoble, idealize, *formal* aggrandize, venerate

deign *v*
condescend, stoop, lower yourself, consent, demean yourself

deity *n*
god, goddess, divinity, divine being, supreme being, godhead, idol, demigod, spirit, power, eternal, immortal

dejected *adj*
downcast, despondent, depressed, downhearted, discouraged, disheartened, down, low, melancholy, sad, miserable, cast down, gloomy, glum, crestfallen, crushed, demoralized, dismal, wretched, doleful, morose, spiritless, dispirited, *formal* disconsolate, *colloq.* blue, down in the dumps
🗲 cheerful, high-spirited, happy

dejection *n*
despondency, depression, downheartedness, discouragement, low spirits, despair, melancholy, sadness, sorrow, unhappiness, misery, gloom, gloominess, wretchedness, dolefulness, moroseness, dispiritedness, *formal* disconsolateness, disconsolation, *colloq.* blues, dumps
🗲 happiness, high spirits

de jure *adv & adj*
legally, rightfully; legal, rightful
🗲 de facto

delay *v, n*
▶ *v* 1 OBSTRUCT, hinder, impede, hamper, hold up,

check, hold back, set back, stop, halt, detain, stonewall, filibuster, keep, restrain 2 POSTPONE, put off, defer, suspend, shelve, hold over, adjourn, stall, *formal* procrastinate, *colloq.* put on ice, put on the back burner 3 DAWDLE, hang on, linger, lag (behind), loiter, dither, hold back, *formal* tarry, *colloq.* dilly-dally
🗲 1 accelerate 2 bring forward 3 hurry, keep up
▶ *n* 1 OBSTRUCTION, hindrance, impediment, hold-up, check, setback, stay, stoppage, halt, interruption, lull, interval, wait 2 POSTPONEMENT, deferment, putting-off, adjournment, holding-over, shelving, suspension, stay, respite, moratorium, waiving, reprieve, *formal* procrastination, cunctation, mora 3 DAWDLING, lingering, loitering, stalling, *formal* tarrying, *colloq.* dilly-dallying
🗲 1 hastening, continuation 3 hurry

delectable *adj*
1 DELICIOUS, appetizing, palatable, tasty, dainty, luscious, mouth-watering, succulent, flavoursome, savoury, *colloq.* scrumptious, yummy 2 ATTRACTIVE, pleasant, delightful, adorable, charming, enchanting, engaging, exciting, pleasing, agreeable
🗲 1 unpalatable 2 unpleasant

delectation *n*
enjoyment, delight, happiness, pleasure, comfort, contentment, gratification, refreshment, relish, satisfaction, amusement, diversion, entertainment
🗲 distaste

delegate *n, v*
▶ *n* representative, agent, envoy, messenger, deputy, ambassador, spokesperson, spokesman, spokeswoman, legate, emissary, proxy, commissioner
▶ *v* authorize, appoint, depute, charge, commission, commit, give, pass on/over, assign, empower, entrust, devolve, consign, leave, designate, ordain, nominate, name, hand over

delegation *n*
1 DEPUTATION, representatives, commission, legation, mission, contingent, embassy 2 *delegation of responsibility* committal, transference, consignment, passing on/over, devolution, empowerment

delete *v*
erase, remove, cross out, cancel, rub out, strike (out), take out, obliterate, edit (out), cut (out), blot out, blue-pencil, *formal* excise, efface, expunge
🗲 add, insert

deleterious *adj*
destructive, detrimental, harmful, hurtful, injurious, bad, damaging, ruinous, pernicious, prejudicial, *formal* noxious
🗲 enhancing, helpful

deliberate *adj, v*
▶ *adj* 1 INTENTIONAL, planned, calculated, prearranged, premeditated, preplanned, preconceived, willed, conscious, designed, considered, advised 2 CAREFUL, unhurried, thoughtful, methodical, cautious, studied, prudent, slow, ponderous, steady, leisurely, measured, heedful, resolute, unhesitating, unwavering, *formal* circumspect
🗲 1 unintentional, accidental 2 hasty
▶ *v* consider, ponder, reflect, think (over), meditate, mull over, muse, debate, discuss, evaluate, weigh (up), consult, *formal* cogitate, ruminate, excogitate

deliberately *adv*
1 INTENTIONALLY, on purpose, consciously, pointedly, calculatingly, by design, in cold blood, knowingly, wittingly, wilfully, with malice aforethought 2 CAREFULLY, unhurriedly, thoughtfully, methodically, cautiously, prudently, slowly, ponderously, steadily, *formal* circumspectly

▣ **1** unintentionally, by accident, accidentally, by mistake **2** hastily

deliberation *n*
1 CONSIDERATION, reflection, thought, calculation, forethought, meditation, pondering, musing, mulling, brooding, study, evaluation, weighing-up, *formal* cogitation, rumination, excogitation **2** *secret deliberations* debate, discussion, consultation, conferring **3** CARE, carefulness, caution, thoughtfulness, unhurriedness, slowness, steadiness, prudence, *formal* circumspection

delicacy *n*
1 DAINTINESS, fineness, elegance, exquisiteness, lightness, fragility, precision **2** SENSITIVITY, tact, diplomacy, discretion, care, consideration, subtlety, finesse, discrimination, niceness **3** TITBIT, dainty, taste, treat, luxury, sweetmeat, savoury, relish, speciality
▣ **1** coarseness, roughness **2** tactlessness

delicate *adj*
1 FINE, dainty, exquisite, elegant, slight, graceful **2** FRAIL, sickly, weak, ailing, infirm, unwell, in poor health, faint, *formal* debilitated **3** *delicate china* fragile, breakable, easily damaged/broken, frail, flimsy, brittle, insubstantial **4** *a delicate situation* sensitive, tricky, difficult, problematic, critical, awkward, touchy, controversial **5** *needs delicate handling* tactful, sensitive, diplomatic, careful, considerate, discreet, *colloq.* softly-softly, kid-glove **6** SUBTLE, muted, pastel, pale, muted, subdued, soft, faint, mild, bland **7** *a delicate instrument* precision, sensitive, precise, exact, accurate
▣ **1** coarse **2** healthy, strong **3** strong **4** easy **6** strong, bold

delicious *adj*
1 TASTY, palatable, appetizing, mouth-watering, juicy, succulent, toothsome, savoury, good, choice, tempting, *formal* delectable, nectareous, ambrosial, *colloq.* morish, scrumptious, yummy **2** ENJOYABLE, pleasant, agreeable, delightful, charming, enchanting, captivating, pleasurable, pleasing, gratifying, entertaining, fascinating
▣ **1** unpalatable **2** unpleasant

delight *n, v*
▶ *n* happiness, joy, pleasure, contentment, enjoyment, gladness, glee, rapture, transport, bliss, euphoria, ecstasy, elation, gratification, jubilation, amusement, entertainment
▣ disgust, displeasure
▶ *v* **1** *the prospect of being parents delighted them* please, charm, gratify, cheer, gladden, excite, enchant, captivate, enrapture, tickle, thrill, ravish, amuse, entertain, *colloq.* bowl over, tickle pink **2** *delight in something* enjoy, relish, like, love, appreciate, revel in, take pleasure in, take pride in, glory in, boast of, wallow in, savour
▣ **1** disappoint, displease, dismay **2** dislike, hate

delighted *adj*
happy, pleased, glad, enchanted, captivated, enraptured, entranced, elated, euphoric, ecstatic, thrilled, excited, joyful, overjoyed, gleeful, jubilant, gratified, charmed, *formal* joyous, *colloq.* over the moon, tickled pink, happy as Larry/a sandboy, pleased as Punch
▣ disappointed, dismayed

delightful *adj*
charming, enchanting, captivating, enjoyable, pleasant, thrilling, exciting, agreeable, pleasurable, engaging, attractive, pleasing, gratifying, appealing, fascinating, amusing, diverting, entertaining, *formal* delectable, *colloq.* out of this world, great, magic, ace, divine, the tops

nasty, unpleasant, horrid, disagreeable, displeasing, distasteful

delimit *v*
bound, demarcate, determine, establish, fix, mark, define

delineate *v*
describe, define, depict, portray, set forth, outline, draw, sketch, trace, design, chart, render, represent, mark, bound, determine, establish, fix

delinquency *n*
crime, offence, misdeed, wrongdoing, misbehaviour, misconduct, law-breaking, misdemeanour, criminality, *formal* transgression

delinquent *n, adj*
▶ *n* offender, criminal, wrongdoer, law-breaker, hooligan, young offender, culprit, ruffian, vandal, *formal* miscreant
▶ *adj* criminal, offending, law-breaking, lawless, guilty, negligent, *formal* remiss, culpable
▣ blameless, careful

delirious *adj*
1 *delirious because of fever* demented, raving, incoherent, beside yourself, irrational, deranged, frenzied, light-headed, wild, mad, frantic, insane, crazy, unhinged, babbling, out of your mind **2** *delirious with excitement* ecstatic, euphoric, overjoyed, elated, jubilant, beside yourself, carried away, *colloq.* over the moon
▣ **1** sane

delirium *n*
1 *feverish delirium* derangement, raving, incoherence, irrationality, fever, frenzy, passion, wildness, madness, insanity, lunacy, craziness, hallucination, hysteria, *colloq.* jimjams **2** *the delirium of first love* ecstasy, euphoria, joy, elation, excitement, jubilation, wildness, passion
▣ **1** sanity

deliver *v*
1 *deliver a parcel* convey, bring, take, send, give, carry, supply, distribute, give out, *formal* dispatch **2** SURRENDER, hand over, relinquish, yield, transfer, grant, entrust, commit, *formal* cede **3** *deliver a speech* UTTER, make, speak, proclaim, declare, announce, pronounce, express, voice, give voice to, *formal* enunciate **4** ADMINISTER, deal, give, inflict, launch, direct, aim, strike **5** *deliver the promised benefits* FULFIL, provide, supply, do, carry out, implement **6** SET FREE, liberate, save, rescue, release, *formal* emancipate, ransom, redeem

deliverance *n*
rescue, liberation, salvation, freedom, release, escape, extrication, *formal* emancipation, ransom, redemption

delivery *n*
1 CONVEYANCE, supply, distribution, transport, transportation, carriage, consignment, transmission, transfer, shipment, *formal* dispatch **2** ARTICULATION, speech, utterance, intonation, elocution, *formal* enunciation **3** CHILDBIRTH, labour, confinement, *formal* parturition, travail

dell *n*
valley, vale, hollow, dean, dingle

delude *v*
deceive, mislead, beguile, dupe, fool, take in, lead on, trick, hoodwink, hoax, cheat, misguide, misinform, *colloq.* bamboozle, have on, take for a ride, double-cross, two-time, pull someone's leg, pull a fast one on, pull the wool over someone's eyes

deluge *n, v*
▶ *n a deluge of rain/letters* flood, inundation, down-

pour, overflowing, torrent, avalanche, spate, rush, wave
▶ *v* **deluged by rain/queries** flood, inundate, drench, drown, overwhelm, soak, swamp, engulf, submerge

delusion *n*
illusion, hallucination, fancy, misconception, misapprehension, false belief/impression, deception, misbelief, fallacy, misinformation, tricking

---

✒ **delusion** or **illusion** ?

A *delusion* is a false belief arising in your own mind, whereas an *illusion* is a false impression coming into your mind from the world outside it.

---

de luxe, deluxe *adj*
luxury, luxurious, select, choice, quality, expensive, costly, special, exclusive, grand, lavish, fine, elegant, palatial, rich, splendid, sumptuous, superior, *formal* opulent, *colloq.* plush

delve *v*
burrow, rummage, search, dig into, hunt in/through, poke, ransack, root, probe, examine, explore, investigate, go/look into, research

demagogue *n*
agitator, orator, firebrand, haranguer, rabble-rouser, tub-thumper

demand *v, n*
▶ *v* **1** ASK, request, tell, call for, insist on, urge, press for, hold out for, order, dictate, stipulate, solicit, claim, petition, exact, inquire, question, interrogate **2** REQUIRE, need, take, call for, involve, cry out for, *formal* necessitate
▶ *n* **1** REQUEST, question, claim, petition, plea, order, inquiry, desire, pressure, insistence, clamour, interrogation **2** NEED, necessity, call, requirement, want, *formal* exigency
▷ **in demand** popular, fashionable, asked for, requested, sought after, *colloq.* big, trendy

demanding *adj*
hard, difficult, challenging, exacting, taxing, tough, exhausting, wearing, back-breaking, insistent, nagging, harassing, pressing, testing, urgent, trying, *formal* exigent, *colloq.* a tall order
🖪 easy, undemanding, easy-going

demarcate *v*
determine, establish, fix, mark (out), delimit, define, bound

demarcation *n*
boundary, bound, differentiation, distinction, division, separation, enclosure, limit, line, margin, determination, establishment, fixing, marking off/out, delimitation, definition

demean *v*
lower, humble, degrade, belittle, deprecate, humiliate, debase, abase, descend, demote, stoop, condescend
🖪 exalt, enhance

demeanour *n*
manner, conduct, behaviour, air, *formal* bearing, deportment, mien, comportment

demented *adj*
made, insane, lunatic, unbalanced, disturbed, deranged, crazed, wild, berserk, unhinged, out of your mind, *colloq.* loony, loopy, bonkers, nuts, nutty, nutty as a fruitcake, off your rocker, needing your head examining, round the bend, round the twist
🖪 sane

demise *n*
1 DEATH, decease, end, passing, departure, *formal* termination, expiration, cessation **2** DOWNFALL, fall, collapse, failure, ruin

democracy *n*
self-government, commonwealth, autonomy, republic

democratic *adj*
self-governing, representative, egalitarian, autonomous, popular, populist, republican

demolish *v*
1 DESTROY, dismantle, knock down, pull down, flatten, bulldoze, raze, tear down, break up, pulverize, level **2** *demolish the opponents* beat, overcome, overpower, get the better of, conquer, excel, surpass, subdue, overthrow, repel, overwhelm, rout, ruin, crush, quell, bring someone to their knees, *formal* subjugate, vanquish, *colloq.* thrash, lick, hammer, annihilate, devastate, slaughter **3** *demolish an argument* destroy, ruin, wreck, overturn, undo
🖪 **1** build up, erect, construct

demolition *n*
1 DESTRUCTION, dismantling, knocking-down, pulling-down, flattening, razing, tearing-down, breaking-up, levelling, razing **2** *demolition of the opposing team* beating, overpowering, surpassing, overthrow, overwhelming, rout, *colloq.* thrashing, licking, hammering, annihilation, slaughter

demon *n*
1 DEVIL, fiend, evil spirit, fallen angel, imp, ghoul, daemon, cacodemon, afrit, rakshas, incubus, succubus **2** VILLAIN, devil, rogue, monster, fiend, beast, savage, brute **3** *a demon chess player* addict, fanatic, fiend, buff, wizard, *colloq.* ace, freak, dab hand

demonic *adj*
fiendish, devilish, diabolical, hellish, infernal, satanic, possessed, mad, maniacal, manic, crazed, frantic, frenetic, frenzied, furious

demonstrable *adj*
verifiable, provable, arguable, attestable, self-evident, obvious, evident, certain, clear, positive, *formal* evincible
🖪 unverifiable

demonstrate *v*
1 PROVE, determine, show, establish, verify, *formal* validate, substantiate **2** SHOW, display, exhibit, express, indicate, register, betray, *formal* manifest, testify to, bear witness to, evince, betoken, bespeak **3** EXPLAIN, illustrate, describe, show, teach, make clear, *formal* expound **4** PROTEST, march, parade, rally, picket, sit in

demonstration *n*
1 DISPLAY, expression, indication, exhibition, proof, confirmation, evidence, testimony, verification, *formal* manifestation, evincement, affirmation, substantiation, validation **2** EXPLANATION, illustration, description, presentation, test, trial, *formal* exposition, elucidation **3** PROTEST, march, rally, mass rally, picket, sit-in, parade, civil disobedience, *colloq.* demo

demonstrative *adj*
affectionate, expressive, extrovert, unreserved, effusive, gushing, expansive, emotional, open, loving, warm
🖪 reserved, introvert, cold, restrained

demoralize *v*
1 DISCOURAGE, dishearten, dispirit, undermine, depress, deject, cast down, crush, disconcert, make despondent, daunt, lower, undermine, weaken **2** CORRUPT, deprave, debase, pervert, contaminate, defile
🖪 **1** encourage, inspire confidence **2** improve

demote *v*
downgrade, reduce in rank, degrade, relegate, humble, cashier
🖪 promote, upgrade

demotic *adj*
popular, vernacular, colloquial, vulgar, *formal* enchorial, enchoric

demur *v, n*
▸ *v* disagree, dissent, object, take exception, refuse, protest, dispute, balk, cavil, scruple, doubt, express doubts, hesitate, be unwilling, refuse
▸ *n* disagreement, dissent, hesitation, objection, protest, misgiving, qualm, reservation, doubt, scruple, *formal* compunction, demurral

demure *adj*
modest, reserved, unassuming, reticent, coy, shy, timid, quiet, serious, retiring, prissy, grave, prudish, sober, strait-laced, prim, staid
✗ wanton, forward

den *n*
1 *a wolf's den* lair, hideout, hole, hollow 2 *a den of forgers* haunt, meeting-place, patch, pitch, *colloq.* dive, joint 3 *study in his den* retreat, study, hideaway, shelter, sanctuary

denial *n*
1 CONTRADICTION, opposition, disagreement, dissent, repudiation, disclaimer, dismissal, renunciation, *formal* negation, disavowal, disaffirmation, abjuration 2 REFUSAL, rebuff, rejection, dismissal, prohibition, veto 3 *denial of your parents* disowning, renunciation, repudiation, disavowal

denigrate *v*
run down, slander, belittle, abuse, assail, criticize, deprecate, *formal* disparage, revile, defame, malign, vilify, decry, besmirch, impugn, calumniate, vilipend, cast aspersions on, *colloq.* fling/sling/throw mud, pick holes in
✗ praise, acclaim

denizen *n*
citizen, dweller, inhabitant, occupant, resident, habitant, habitué

denomination *n*
1 RELIGION, persuasion, Church, sect, religious body/ group, belief, faith, creed, communion, cult, school, order, constituency 2 *the denomination of a banknote* value, face value, worth, unit, grade, class, kind, sort, designation

denote *v*
indicate, be a sign of, stand for, signify, represent, symbolize, mean, refer to, express, designate, typify, mark, show, imply, suggest, *formal* betoken

dénouement *n*
climax, culmination, conclusion, outcome, upshot, finale, resolution, clarification, unravelling, finish, last act, solution, close, *colloq.* pay-off

denounce *v*
condemn, censure, accuse, attack, criticize, inform against, betray, indict, *formal* deplore, revile, decry, castigate, impugn, vilify, arraign, declaim, fulminate, inculpate
✗ acclaim, praise

dense *adj*
1 *a dense crowd/forest* solid, packed, crammed, jammed together, close-packed, tightly packed, crowded, thick, compact, compressed, condensed, close, close-knit, heavy 2 *dense smoke* thick, opaque, impenetrable, concentrated 3 STUPID, crass, dull, slow, slow-witted, *formal* obtuse, *colloq.* thick, dim, dim-witted
✗ 1 thin, sparse 3 quick-witted, clever

density *n*
body, mass, bulk, closeness, compactness, consistency, denseness, solidity, solidness, thickness, tightness, impenetrability
✗ sparseness

dent *n, v*
▸ *n* hollow, depression, dip, concavity, indentation, crater, dimple, dint, pit
▸ *v* depress, gouge, push in, indent

denude *v*
strip, divest, expose, uncover, bare, deforest, defoliate
✗ cover, clothe

denunciation *n*
condemnation, denouncement, censure, accusation, incrimination, attack, criticism, *formal* invective, decrial, castigation, obloquy, fulmination
✗ acclaim, praise

deny *v*
1 *deny the allegations* contradict, oppose, disagree with, disprove, repudiate, rebut, *formal* refute, disaffirm, negate, nullify, abjure, gainsay 2 *deny him access to his children* REFUSE, turn down, forbid, prohibit, reject, withhold, dismiss, rebuff, veto, *formal* decline 3 *deny your parents* disown, disclaim, renounce, repudiate, turn your back on, *formal* disavow, recant
✗ 1 admit 2 allow

deodorant *n*
anti-perspirant, deodorizer, air-freshener, disinfectant, fumigant, fumigator

deodorize *v*
freshen, purify, refresh, sweeten, disinfect, fumigate, aerate, ventilate

depart *v*
1 GO, leave, withdraw, exit, make off, decamp, take your leave, absent yourself, set off, set out, start out, pull out, get going, remove, retreat, migrate, escape, disappear, retire, vanish, *colloq.* push along/off, make tracks, quit, scat, scoot, scram, take off, take to your heels, make yourself scarce, shove off, bunk off, clear off, split, scarper, skedaddle, vamoose, skive, do a runner, do a bunk, do a moonlight flit, hit the road/ trail, make a bolt/break for it, up sticks, hightail it, sling your hook 2 DEVIATE, digress, differ, diverge, fork, branch off, swerve, turn aside, veer, vary
✗ 1 arrive, return 2 keep to

departed *adj*
dead, gone, late, passed away, *formal* deceased, expired

department *n*
1 DIVISION, branch, subdivision, section, sector, wing, office, bureau, agency, organization, station, unit, branch, region, district 2 SPHERE, realm, province, domain, field, area, concern, responsibility, interest, function, speciality, line

departure *n*
1 EXIT, going, going away/off, leaving, leave-taking, removal, withdrawal, retirement, retreat, escape, exodus, setting-off, setting-out 2 DEVIATION, digression, divergence, variation, innovation, branching (out), forking, difference, change, shift, veering
✗ 1 arrival, return

depend *v*
1 *the cost depends on the quantity* HINGE ON, be dependent on, rest on, revolve around, be subject to, hang on, be decided by, be determined by, be based on, ride on, *formal* turn on, be contingent on 2 *depend on her for support* RELY ON, count on, calculate on, reckon on, build upon, trust in, have confidence in, lean on, need, not manage without, expect, *colloq.* bank on

dependable *adj*
reliable, trustworthy, steady, trusty, responsible, faithful, unfailing, sure, honest, conscientious, steadfast, certain, stable, *colloq.* tried and tested, a safe pair of hands
✗ unreliable, fickle

dependant *n*
child, minor, relative, charge, protégé, ward, client, hanger-on, henchman, minion, subordinate, parasite

dependence *n*
1 RELIANCE, confidence, faith, trust, need, expectation **2** ADDICTION, attachment, subservience, abuse, helplessness, subordination
F₃ **1** independence

dependency *n*
1 COLONY, province, protectorate **2** RELIANCE, helplessness, weakness, immaturity, support, subordination **3** ADDICTION, attachment, habit, subservience, abuse

dependent *adj*
1 RELIANT, helpless, weak, immature, subject, sustained, leaning, supported, subordinate, vulnerable **2** *the profit is dependent on the quantity bought* conditional, decided, determined, controlled, dictated, based, influenced, relative, subject, subordinate, *formal* contingent
F₃ **1, 2** independent

depict *v*
1 *depicted in a painting* portray, illustrate, sketch, outline, draw, picture, paint, trace, show, represent, describe **2** *novels depicting Victorian life* portray, describe, recount, characterize, detail, illustrate, outline, trace, show, represent, render, reproduce, record, *formal* delineate

depiction *n*
portrayal, description, characterization, detailing, drawing, illustration, image, likeness, picture, caricature, sketch, outline, representation, rendering, *formal* delineation

deplete *v*
empty, drain, exhaust, impoverish, bankrupt, weaken, evacuate, use up, consume, spend, expend, run down, reduce, lessen, decrease, diminish, eat into, erode, whittle away, *formal* attenuate
F₃ increase, *formal* augment

depletion *n*
exhaustion, impoverishment, weakening, evacuation, consumption, expenditure, reduction, lessening, decrease, deficiency, dwindling, lowering, shrinkage, *formal* attenuation, diminution
F₃ increase, supply, *formal* augmentation

deplorable *adj*
disgraceful, reprehensible, scandalous, outrageous, shameful, dishonourable, disreputable, blameworthy, abominable, despicable, lamentable, pitiable, grievous, regrettable, unfortunate, wretched, distressing, sad, miserable, heartbreaking, melancholy, disastrous, dire, appalling
F₃ excellent, commendable

deplore *v*
1 DISAPPROVE OF, condemn, criticize, reproach, blame, revile, denounce, *formal* reprehend, reprove, deprecate, berate, upbraid, castigate, disparage, censure, *colloq.* slam, slate **2** GRIEVE FOR, lament, mourn, regret, bemoan, bewail, pine, rue, weep, cry, shed tears
F₃ **1** extol

deploy *v*
arrange, position, station, spread out, scatter, use, utilize, distribute, *formal* dispose

depopulate *v*
empty, dispeople, unpeople

deport¹ *v*
deported from a country expel, banish, exile, extradite, repatriate, transport, oust, ostracize

deport² *v*
deport yourself well conduct, bear, behave, carry, hold, manage, act, *formal* acquit, comport

deportation *n*
expulsion, banishment, exile, extradition, repatriation, transportation, ousting, ostracism

deportment *n*
manner, air, appearance, aspect, bearing, behaviour, carriage, conduct, pose, posture, stance, etiquette, *formal* comportment, demeanour, mien

depose *v*
oust, overthrow, dismiss, remove, unseat, topple, disestablish, displace, demote, dethrone, discharge, downgrade, *colloq.* sack, fire

deposit *v, n*
▶ *v* **1** LAY, drop, plant, place, put (down), set (down), settle, park, sit, locate, *technical* precipitate, *colloq.* dump, bung **2** SAVE, store, hoard, bank, amass, consign, entrust, lodge, file, stow, put away, put by
▶ *n* **1** SECURITY, stake, down payment, pledge, retainer, instalment, part payment, money, *formal* earnest **2** SEDIMENT, accumulation, dregs, lees, silt, warp, *technical* alluvium, precipitate, precipitation, sublimate, *formal* deposition

deposition *n*
1 *the deposition of the ruler* ousting, dismissal, removal, unseating, toppling, displacement, dethronement **2** *the witness's deposition* affidavit, declaration, statement, testimony, evidence, information

depository *n*
storehouse, store, warehouse, bonded warehouse, depot, repository, arsenal

depot *n*
1 *military depot* storehouse, store, warehouse, depository, repository, cache, arsenal **2** *bus depot* station, garage, terminal, terminus

deprave *v*
corrupt, debauch, debase, degrade, pervert, subvert, infect, demoralize, lead astray, seduce, pollute, defile, contaminate
F₃ improve, reform

depraved *adj*
corrupt, debauched, degenerate, perverted, debased, reprobate, dissolute, immoral, obscene, base, shameless, wicked, sinful, vile, evil, iniquitous, criminal
F₃ moral, upright, *formal* licentious

depravity *n*
corruption, debauchery, degeneracy, perversion, debasement, reprobacy, dissoluteness, immorality, baseness, wickedness, sinfulness, vileness, evil, iniquity, vice, *formal* turpitude
F₃ uprightness

deprecate *v*
condemn, disapprove of, criticize, object to, protest at, reject, reproach, blame, revile, denounce, *formal* deplore, reprehend, reprove, deprecate, berate, upbraid, castigate, disparage, censure, *colloq.* slam, slate, knock
F₃ approve, commend

📖 **deprecate** or **depreciate** ?

Deprecate is a formal word meaning 'to disapprove of': *The government deprecated the soldiers' actions.*
Depreciate most commonly means 'to fall or cause to fall in value': *Property shares have depreciated rapidly.* A rarer meaning of *depreciate* is 'to speak of as having little value or importance': *to depreciate your achievements.*

deprecatory *adj*
disapproving, reproachful, dismissive, protesting, apologetic, regretful, *formal* censorious, condemnatory
◼ encouraging, *formal* commendatory

depreciate *v*
1 DEVALUE, deflate, downgrade, decrease/fall/go down in value, reduce, lower, drop, fall, lessen, decline, slump **2** BELITTLE, undervalue, underestimate, underrate, slight, run down, make light of, *formal* disparage, denigrate, revile, defame, malign
◼ **1** appreciate **2** overrate

depreciation *n*
1 DEVALUATION, deflation, depression, slump, fall, reduction in price/value, mark-down, cheapening **2** BELITTLEMENT, underestimation, *formal* disparagement, denigration

depredation *n*
desolation, destruction, devastation, laying waste, ravaging, marauding, pillage, looting, plunder, raiding, ransacking, harrying, robbery, theft, *formal* despoiling, denudation

depress *v*
1 DEJECT, sadden, make sad, dishearten, discourage, cast down, bring down, weigh down, oppress, upset, daunt, burden, overburden, *colloq.* get down, break someone's heart **2** WEAKEN, undermine, sap, tire, drain, exhaust, weary, impair, reduce, lessen, press, lower, level, *formal* enervate, debilitate **3** DEVALUE, bring down, reduce, lower, cut, depreciate, cheapen, *colloq.* slash
◼ **1** cheer **2** vitalize, *formal* fortify **3** increase, raise

depressant *n*
sedative, tranquillizer, downer, relaxant, calmant, calmative
◼ stimulant

depressed *adj*
1 DEJECTED, low-spirited, melancholy, dispirited, sad, unhappy, low, low in spirits, down, downcast, disheartened, miserable, moody, cast down, discouraged, gloomy, glum, downhearted, distressed, despondent, morose, crestfallen, pessimistic, *colloq.* fed up, blue, down in the dumps **2** POOR, disadvantaged, deprived, needy, run-down, destitute, poverty-stricken **3** SUNKEN, recessed, concave, hollow, indented, dented, pushed in
◼ **1** cheerful **2** thriving, affluent **3** convex, protuberant

depressing *adj*
dejecting, dismal, bleak, gloomy, saddening, cheerless, dreary, disheartening, unhappy, sad, melancholy, sombre, grey, black, daunting, discouraging, dispiriting, heartbreaking, distressing, hopeless, grave
◼ cheerful, happy, encouraging

depression *n*
1 DEJECTION, despair, despondency, melancholy, low spirits, unhappiness, sadness, gloom, gloominess, doldrums, glumness, downheartedness, pessimism, hopelessness, desolation, discouragement, *technical* melancholia, *colloq.* blues, dumps **2** RECESSION, slump, stagnation, crash, hard times, decline, inactivity, slowdown, standstill **3** INDENTATION, hollow, hole, dip, concavity, dent, dimple, valley, pit, sink, dint, bowl, cavity, basin, impression, dish, excavation
◼ **1** cheerfulness, happiness, euphoria **2** prosperity, boom **3** convexity, *formal* protuberance

deprivation *n*
1 *deprivation of sleep* denial, withdrawal, withholding, removal, lack, dispossession **2** *deprivation in inner cities* hardship, poverty, want, need, disadvantage, *formal* destitution, privation, penury

deprive *v*
take away, dispossess, strip, divest, rob, confiscate, bereave, deny, withhold, refuse, *formal* denude, expropriate
◼ endow, provide

deprived *adj*
poor, needy, in need, underprivileged, disadvantaged, impoverished, destitute, lacking, bereft
◼ prosperous

depth *n*
1 DEEPNESS, profoundness, extent, measure, drop, *formal* profundity **2** *depth of feeling* INTENSITY, strength, thoroughness, seriousness, severity, gravity, earnestness, passion, vigour, fervour **3** *a person of great depth* WISDOM, insight, discernment, perception, penetration, awareness, intuition, astuteness, cleverness, shrewdness, acumen, *formal* profundity **4** *the depths of their knowledge* extent, extensiveness, scope, amount, *formal* profundity **5** *depth of colour* intensity, strength, richness, vividness, brilliance, warmth, glow, darkness **6** *the depths of the sea* remotest area, bed, floor, bottom, abyss, deep, gulf, middle, midst
◼ **1** shallowness **6** surface
▷ **in depth** comprehensively, thoroughly, exhaustively, extensively, in detail
◼ superficially, broadly

deputation *n*
commission, delegation, embassy, mission, representatives, legation, committee

depute *v*
appoint, authorize, charge, commission, second, designate, nominate, empower, entrust, mandate, delegate, consign, hand over, *formal* accredit

deputize *v*
represent, stand in for, take over, substitute, replace, act for, understudy, take the place of, double, relieve, cover, *colloq.* sub for

deputy *n, adj*
▶ *n* representative, agent, delegate, proxy, substitute, stand-in, second-in-command, ambassador, envoy, commissioner, lieutenant, legate, surrogate, subordinate, assistant, locum, spokesperson, vice-president, vice-chairperson, vice-regent
▶ *adj* assistant, representative, substitute, stand-in, surrogate, subordinate, vice-, suffragan, coadjutor, depute

deranged *adj*
disordered, demented, crazy, mad, lunatic, insane, of unsound mind, *non compos mentis*, unbalanced, unhinged, unsettled, disturbed, irrational, confused, frantic, delirious, distraught, berserk, out of your mind, *colloq.* loony, loopy, bonkers, nuts, nutty, nutty as a fruitcake, off your rocker, needing your head examining, round the bend, round the twist, out to lunch
◼ sane, calm

derangement *n*
aberration, agitation, confusion, delirium, dementia, disorder, distraction, disturbance, frenzy, hallucination, mania, insanity, lunacy, madness
◼ order, sanity

derelict *adj, n*
▶ *adj* abandoned, neglected, deserted, forsaken, desolate, discarded, dilapidated, falling to pieces, ramshackle, tumbledown, run-down, ruined, in disrepair
▶ *n* tramp, vagrant, dosser, beggar, wretch, down-and-out, drifter, hobo, outcast, no-good, good-for-nothing, no-hoper, ne'er-do-well

dereliction *n*
1 DILAPIDATION, abandonment, neglect, desertion,

forsaking, desolation, ruin(s), disrepair **2** *dereliction of duty* abdication, abandonment, desertion, evasion, failure, faithlessness, forsaking, betrayal, neglect, negligence, relinquishment, remissness, renunciation, *formal* apostasy, renegation
F3 2 devotion, faithfulness, fulfilment

deride *v*
ridicule, mock, scoff, scorn, jeer, sneer, make fun of, satirize, gibe, insult, belittle, disdain, taunt, tease, rag, *formal* disparage, *colloq.* knock, pooh-pooh
F3 respect, praise

de rigueur *adj*
conventional, fitting, necessary, correct, decent, done, proper, required, right, *formal* decorous, *colloq.* the done thing

derision *n*
ridicule, mockery, scorn, contempt, scoffing, hissing, satire, sneering, taunting, disrespect, insult, teasing, ragging, disdain, *formal* disparagement
F3 respect, praise

derisive *adj*
mocking, scornful, contemptuous, scoffing, disrespectful, insulting, irreverent, jeering, disdainful, taunting
F3 respectful, flattering

📝 **derisive** or **derisory** ?
Derisive means 'mocking; showing derision': *derisive laughter. Derisory* means 'ridiculous; deserving mockery or derision': *The management offered a derisory pay increase.*

---

derisory *adj*
laughable, ludicrous, absurd, ridiculous, contemptible, insulting, outrageous, preposterous, tiny, paltry, *formal* risible

derivation *n*
source, origin, root, beginning, etymology, extraction, foundation, genealogy, ancestry, basis, descent, deduction, inference

derivative *adj, n*
▶ *adj* unoriginal, acquired, copied, borrowed, derived, imitative, obtained, second-hand, secondary, plagiarized, hackneyed, trite, *colloq.* cribbed, rehashed
F3 original, inventive, innovative
▶ *n* derivation, offshoot, by-product, development, branch, outgrowth, spin-off, product, descendant

derive *v*
1 *derive pleasure from something* GAIN, obtain, get, draw, extract, receive, acquire, borrow, *formal* procure **2** ORIGINATE, arise, spring, flow, have as the source, have its origin/roots in, descend, stem, issue, follow, develop, evolve, *formal* emanate, proceed

derogatory *adj*
insulting, pejorative, belittling, offensive, critical, disapproving, unfavourable, slighting, uncomplimentary, injurious, *formal* disparaging, depreciative, defamatory, vilifying, denigratory
F3 flattering, favourable, complimentary

descend *v*
1 GO DOWN, move down, drop, fall, plummet, plunge, tumble, swoop, sink, arrive, alight, dismount, dip, slope, incline, subside **2** CONDESCEND, deign, sink, stoop, lower yourself **3** DEGENERATE, deteriorate, decline, *colloq.* go downhill, go to the dogs **4** ORIGINATE, issue, spring, stem, *formal* proceed, emanate **5** *family descended on us* invade, arrive suddenly, swoop, take over
F3 1 ascent, rise

descendants *n*
offspring, children, issue, progeny, successors, lineage, line, scions, posterity, *formal* seed
F3 ancestors

descent *n*
1 FALL, going-down, drop, plunge, sinking, subsiding, dip, decline, incline, slope, slant, gradient, *formal* declivity **2** COMEDOWN, debasement, degradation, deterioration, decline, degeneracy, decadence **3** ANCESTRY, parentage, heredity, family tree, genealogy, lineage, line, stock, extraction, origin
F3 1 ascent, rise

describe *v*
1 *describe a situation* portray, depict, illustrate, characterize, specify, draw, define, detail, give details of, explain, express, tell, talk, write, narrate, outline, relate, recount, present, represent, report, *formal* delineate, elucidate **2** *describe someone as clever* call, portray, consider, think, style, label, designate, brand, hail **3** *skaters describing circles on the ice* mark out, draw, sketch, trace, outline, *formal* delineate

description *n*
1 PORTRAYAL, representation, characterization, account, depiction, sketch, portrait, presentation, report, statement, outline, explanation, narration, commentary, chronicle, profile, *formal* delineation, exposition, elucidation **2** SORT, type, kind, variety, specification, order, class, designation, category, breed, brand, make

descriptive *adj*
illustrative, explanatory, expressive, detailed, graphic, colourful, pictorial, striking, vivid, detailed, *formal* elucidatory

descry *v*
discern, catch sight of, mark, notice, observe, perceive, recognize, discover, distinguish, glimpse, see, spot, detect, *old use* espy

desecrate *v*
defile, violate, pervert, pollute, profane, contaminate, debase, dishallow, dishonour, insult, abuse, blaspheme, vandalize, violate

desecration *n*
defilement, violation, blasphemy, debasement, dishonouring, pollution, profanation, sacrilege, impiety, insult

desert¹ *n, adj*
▶ *n the Sahara desert* wasteland, wilderness, wilds, barrenness, void
▶ *adj* bare, barren, waste, wild, uninhabited, empty, uncultivated, dry, dried up, arid, parched, moistureless, infertile, unproductive, desolate, sterile, lonely, solitary

---
Deserts of the world, with locations, include:
Sahara, N Africa; Arabian, SW Asia; Gobi, Mongolia and NE China; Patagonian, Argentina; Great Basin, SW USA; Chihuahuan, Mexico; Great Sandy, NW Australia; Nubian, Sudan; Great Victoria, SW Australia; Thar, India/Pakistan; Sonoran, SW USA; Kara Kum, Turkmenistan; Kyzyl-Kum, Kazakhstan; Takla Makan, N China; Kalahari, SW Africa.

---

desert² *v*
1 *desert his family* abandon, leave, maroon, strand, give up, walk out on, *formal* renounce, forsake, relinquish, cast off, abscond, *colloq.* jilt, quit, run out on, leave in the lurch, leave high and dry, rat on **2** *the soldier deserted* decamp, defect, run away, fly, flee, go AWOL, *formal* abscond **3** *desert a political party* abandon, give up, turn your back on, deny, betray,

change sides, *formal* forsake, relinquish, renounce, recant, apostasize, tergiversate
☒ **1** stand by, support **3** support

desert³ *n*
1 DUE, right, reward, deserts, what you deserve, return, retribution, payment, recompense, remuneration, *colloq.* come-uppance **2** WORTH, merit, virtue

deserted *adj*
abandoned, empty, derelict, desolate, god-forsaken, neglected, underpopulated, stranded, isolated, bereft, left, vacant, betrayed, lonely, solitary, uninhabited, unoccupied, *formal* forsaken
☒ populous

deserter *n*
runaway, absconder, escapee, truant, renegade, defector, traitor, turncoat, fugitive, betrayer, backslider, delinquent, *formal* apostate, *colloq.* rat

desertion *n*
1 *desertion of his family* abandonment, leaving, give up, *formal* forsaking, relinquishment, absconding, casting-off, renunciation, *colloq.* jilting, quitting **2** *desertion from the armed forces* defection, decamping, running-away, flight, going AWOL, truancy, *formal* absconding, dereliction **3** *desertion of a political party* abandonment, giving-up, denial, betrayal, *formal* renunciation, forsaking, relinquishment, apostasy, renegation, tergiversation
☒ **3** support

deserve *v*
earn, be worthy of, merit, be entitled to, warrant, justify, have a right to, win, rate, incur

deserved *adj*
due, earned, merited, justifiable, justified, warranted, right, rightful, well-earned, suitable, proper, fitting, fair, just, appropriate, apt, legitimate, *formal* meet, apposite, condign
☒ gratuitous, undeserved

deserving *adj*
worthy, estimable, exemplary, praiseworthy, admirable, commendable, upright, righteous, virtuous, *formal* laudable, meritorious
☒ undeserving, unworthy

desiccated *adj*
dehydrated, drained, dried, dry, arid, dead, lifeless, parched, powdered, sterile, *formal* exsiccated

desiccation *n*
dehydration, dryness, aridity, parching, sterility, *formal* exsiccation, xeransis

design *v, n*
▶ *v* **1** DRAW, plan, sketch, draw up, draft, outline, plot, *formal* delineate **2** INVENT, originate, conceive, create, think up, develop, construct, fashion, form, model, fabricate, hatch, make **3** INTEND, plot, plan, devise, purpose, contrive, aim, scheme, shape, project, propose, tailor, mean, gear
▶ *n* **1** BLUEPRINT, draft, pattern, plan, prototype, sketch, drawing, outline, map, diagram, scheme, model, guide, *formal* delineation **2** MOTIF, style, pattern, logo, shape, form, figure, device, emblem, monogram, cipher, format, structure, organization, arrangement, composition, make-up, construction **3** AIM, intention, goal, purpose, plan, end, object, objective, scheme, plot, project, meaning, target, point, wish, desire, hope, dream, enterprise, undertaking
▷ **by design** intentionally, deliberately, on purpose, consciously, pointedly, calculatingly, knowingly, wittingly, wilfully

designate *v*
1 *designated as a listed building* call, name, title, entitle, term, dub, style, describe, christen **2** *designated*

to be chairman choose, appoint, nominate, select, elect, assign, specify, define, stipulate, earmark, set aside, show, denote, indicate

designation *n*
1 NAME, title, term, label, epithet, nickname, description, style, sobriquet, *formal* appellation, *colloq.* tag **2** INDICATION, specification, description, definition, denoting, marking, classification, category, stipulation **3** NOMINATION, appointment, selection, election

designer *n*
deviser, originator, maker, stylist, inventor, creator, contriver, producer, fashioner, planner, architect, author

designing *adj*
artful, crafty, scheming, conspiring, calculating, devious, intriguing, plotting, tricky, wily, sly, deceitful, cunning, guileful, underhand, sharp, shrewd
☒ artless, naïve

desirability *n*
1 *the desirability of qualifications* ADVANTAGE, profit, advisability, benefit, preference, usefulness, merit, worth, excellence, popularity **2** *the desirability of the woman* ATTRACTIVENESS, attraction, allure, seductiveness, *colloq.* sexiness
☒ **1** disadvantage, inadvisability, undesirability

desirable *adj*
1 *a desirable qualification* ADVANTAGEOUS, sought-after, profitable, worthwhile, advisable, appropriate, expedient, beneficial, preferable, sensible, eligible, good, pleasing, pleasant, agreeable, popular, in demand **2** *a desirable woman* ATTRACTIVE, alluring, seductive, fetching, tempting, tantalizing, *colloq.* sexy, *slang* beddable
☒ **1** undesirable **2** unattractive

desire *v, n*
▶ *v* **1** WANT, wish for, covet, long for, like, need, crave, hunger for, yearn for, set your heart on, fancy, hanker after, *colloq.* be dying for, have your eyes on, have designs on, give the world for **2** *desire a man* lust after, burn for, take to, *colloq.* fancy, be crazy about, have a crush on, take a shine to
▶ *n* **1** WANT, longing, wish, need, fancy, yearning, craving, hankering, lust, appetite, preference, aspiration, *formal* predilection, predisposition, proclivity, *colloq.* itch, yen **2** LUST, passion, sexual attraction, sexuality, sex drive, ardour, libido, sensuality, lasciviousness, *formal* concupiscence

desired *adj*
required, proper, accurate, appropriate, correct, exact, expected, fitting, necessary, particular, right
☒ undesired, unintentional

desirous *adj*
ready, willing, ambitious, aspiring, avid, burning, craving, itching, eager, enthusiastic, hopeful, hoping, keen, longing, anxious, wishing, yearning
☒ reluctant, unenthusiastic

desist *v*
stop, leave off, refrain, end, break off, give up, halt, abstain, suspend, pause, peter out, *formal* cease, discontinue, remit, forbear
☒ continue, resume

desk *n*
bureau, lectern, reading-desk, davenport, écritoire, secretaire, writing-table, ambo

desolate *adj, v*
▶ *adj* **1** DESERTED, uninhabited, unoccupied, abandoned, unfrequented, barren, bare, arid, bleak, gloomy, dismal, dreary, lonely, solitary, isolated, God-forsaken, forsaken, waste, depressing **2** FORLORN, bereft, depressed, dejected, forsaken, despondent,

distressed, melancholy, miserable, gloomy, unhappy, sad, disheartened, dismal, downcast, broken-hearted, heartbroken, wretched
Fa 1 populous **2** cheerful
▶ *v* devastate, upset, disconcert, overwhelm, take aback, confound, nonplus, get down, *formal* discomfit, *colloq.* shatter, floor

desolation *n*
1 DESTRUCTION, ruin, devastation, ravages, laying waste **2** BARRENNESS, bleakness, emptiness, forlornness, loneliness, isolation, solitude, remoteness, wildness **3** DEJECTION, despair, despondency, gloom, misery, sadness, melancholy, sorrow, unhappiness, broken-heartedness, anguish, depression, grief, distress, wretchedness

despair *v, n*
▶ *v* lose heart, lose hope, give up, give in, be despondent, be discouraged, collapse, surrender, *colloq.* hit rock bottom, throw in the towel
Fa hope
▶ *n* despondency, gloom, hopelessness, desperation, dejection, anguish, distress, inconsolability, inconsolableness, melancholy, misery, depression, pessimism, wretchedness
Fa cheerfulness, resilience

despairing *adj*
despondent, distraught, inconsolable, desolate, desperate, heartbroken, suicidal, grief-stricken, hopeless, depressed, discouraged, disheartened, dejected, miserable, anguished, wretched, sorrowful, pessimistic, dismayed, downcast, *formal* disconsolate
Fa cheerful, hopeful

desperado *n*
bandit, criminal, brigand, terrorist, gangster, gunman, outlaw, ruffian, thug, cut-throat, law-breaker, *colloq.* hoodlum, mugger

desperate *adj*
1 HOPELESS, inconsolable, wretched, despondent, abandoned, distraught, desolate, heartbroken, suicidal, grief-stricken, depressed, discouraged, disheartened, dejected, miserable, anguished, sorrowful, pessimistic, dismayed, downcast, *formal* disconsolate **2** RECKLESS, rash, impetuous, bold, audacious, daring, dangerous, do-or-die, foolhardy, risky, hazardous, hasty, wild, violent, frantic, frenzied, incautious, determined, *formal* precipitate **3** CRITICAL, dire, acute, crucial, serious, grave, severe, extreme, urgent, compelling, pressing, great, dangerous **4** *desperate to leave school* wanting very much, needing very much, crying out for, in great need, *colloq.* dying
Fa 1 hopeful **2** cautious

desperately *adv*
dangerously, critically, gravely, acutely, hopelessly, seriously, severely, badly, dangerously, urgently, greatly, extremely, dreadfully, fearfully, frightfully

desperation *n*
despair, despondency, anguish, hopelessness, gloom, misery, agony, distress, pain, wretchedness, sorrow, trouble, worry, anxiety, depression

despicable *adj*
contemptible, vile, worthless, detestable, disgusting, mean, degrading, wretched, disgraceful, disreputable, shameful, abominable, loathsome, reprobate, *formal* reprehensible
Fa admirable, noble

despise *v*
scorn, look down on, disdain, condemn, spurn, undervalue, slight, dislike, hate, detest, loathe, shun, mock, sneer, *formal* abhor, revile, deplore, deride, *colloq.* have a down on
Fa admire

despite *prep*
in spite of, regardless of, in the face of, undeterred by, against, defying, *formal* notwithstanding

despoil *v*
destroy, devastate, loot, maraud, pillage, plunder, ransack, ravage, deprive, dispossess, divest, rifle, rob, strip, vandalize, wreck, *formal* denude, depredate, spoliate
Fa adorn, enrich

despondency *n*
broken-heartedness, dejection, depression, despair, desperation, discouragement, dispiritedness, downheartedness, gloom, glumness, hopelessness, inconsolability, inconsolableness, melancholia, melancholy, distress, misery, sadness, sorrow, grief, wretchedness, *formal* disconsolateness, *colloq.* blues, heartache
Fa cheerfulness, hopefulness

despondent *adj*
depressed, dejected, disheartened, downcast, down, low, gloomy, glum, discouraged, distressed, miserable, melancholy, sad, sorrowful, doleful, despairing, heartbroken, inconsolable, mournful, wretched, *colloq.* down in the dumps, blue
Fa cheerful, heartened, hopeful

despot *n*
autocrat, tyrant, dictator, oppressor, absolute ruler, absolutist, boss

despotic *adj*
autocratic, tyrannical, imperious, oppressive, dictatorial, authoritarian, domineering, high-handed, absolute, overbearing, arbitrary, arrogant
Fa democratic, egalitarian, liberal, tolerant

despotism *n*
autocracy, totalitarianism, tyranny, dictatorship, absolutism, oppression, repression
Fa democracy, egalitarianism, liberalism, tolerance

dessert *n*
sweet, sweet dish, sweet course, pudding, *colloq.* afters, pud

destination *n*
1 GOAL, aim, objective, object, purpose, target, end, intention, aspiration, design, ambition **2** JOURNEY'S END, terminus, station, stop, final port of call, end of the line

destined *adj*
1 FATED, doomed, inevitable, certain, meant, unavoidable, inescapable, intended, designed, appointed, set apart, *formal* predetermined, ordained, foreordained **2** BOUND, directed, routed, en route, headed, heading, scheduled, assigned, booked

destiny *n*
fate, future, doom, fortune, luck, karma, kismet, *formal* lot, portion, predestination, predestiny

destitute *adj*
1 POOR, hard up, badly off, penniless, poverty-stricken, impoverished, distressed, bankrupt, *formal* impecunious, indigent, penurious, *colloq.* broke, stony-broke, down-and-out, on the breadline, cleaned out, strapped for cash, with your back to the wall, on your beam-ends, *slang* skint **2** LACKING, needy, wanting, innocent of, deprived, deficient, depleted, *formal* devoid of, bereft
Fa 1 prosperous, rich

destitution *n*
poverty, pennilessness, impoverishment, distress, bankruptcy, beggary, starvation, straits, *formal* impecuniousness, indigence, penury, pauperdom
Fa prosperity, wealth

destroy *v*
1 DEMOLISH, ruin, shatter, wreck, devastate, smash,

break, crush, subdue, overthrow, sabotage, undo, stamp out, dismantle, knock down, pull down, tear down, flatten, obliterate, thwart, undermine, waste, lay waste, gut, level, spoil, ravage, raze, ransack, torpedo, unshape, *formal* extirpate **2** KILL, annihilate, eliminate, extinguish, eradicate, dispatch, slaughter, put down, put to sleep, put out of its misery, *formal* slay, nullify, vitiate, *colloq.* decimate
F₃ 1 build up **2** create

destroyer *n*
wrecker, annihilator, demolisher, desolater, despoiler, ransacker, ravager, vandal, locust, kiss of death
F₃ creator

destruction *n*
1 RUIN, devastation, shattering, smashing, crushing, wreckage, demolition, knocking-down, pulling-down, tearing-down, vandalism, defeat, downfall, overthrow, ruination, desolation, obliteration, undoing, wastage, razing, levelling, dismantling, havoc, ravagement, *formal* depredation **2** ANNIHILATION, killing, extermination, eradication, elimination, extinction, slaughter, murder, massacre, end, liquidation, *formal* nullification
F₃ 2 creation

destructive *adj*
1 *destructive storms* devastating, damaging, catastrophic, disastrous, deadly, harmful, fatal, disruptive, lethal, ruinous, injurious, detrimental, hurtful, malignant, pernicious, mischievous, *formal* noxious, nullifying, deleterious, baneful, slaughterous **2** *destructive criticism* adverse, hostile, negative, discouraging, unfavourable, unfriendly, disparaging, contrary, derogatory, undermining, subversive, vicious, *formal* denigrating
F₃ 1 creative **2** constructive, favourable

desultory *adj*
random, erratic, aimless, disorderly, chaotic, haphazard, irregular, half-hearted, spasmodic, inconsistent, undirected, unco-ordinated, unsystematic, unmethodical, fitful, disconnected, rambling, loose, *formal* capricious
F₃ systematic, methodical

detach *v*
1 *detach the reply slip* separate, take/tear off, disconnect, unfasten, disjoin, cut off, disengage, remove, undo, uncouple, unhitch, sever, dissociate, isolate, loosen, free, unfix, unhitch, segregate, divide, disentangle **2** *detach yourself from something* separate, sever, split, cut off, dissociate, isolate, loosen, free, segregate, *formal* estrange
F₃ 1 attach **2** involve

detached *adj*
1 SEPARATE, disconnected, dissociated, severed, free, loose, divided, discrete **2** ALOOF, remote, dispassionate, impersonal, neutral, impartial, independent, indifferent, unconcerned, disinterested, cold, clinical, unemotional, objective
F₃ 1 connected **2** involved

detachment *n*
1 ALOOFNESS, remoteness, coolness, reserve, unconcern, indifference, impassivity, disinterestedness, neutrality, dispassionateness, lack of emotion, impartiality, objectivity, lack of bias, fairness **2** SEPARATION, disconnection, unfastening, uncoupling, disengagement, removal, withdrawal, undoing, severance, isolation, loosening, disentangling, *formal* disunion **3** SQUAD, unit, force, corps, brigade, patrol, task force
F₃ 1 concern, bias, prejudice

detail *n, v*
▶ *n* particular, item, factor, element, aspect, component, feature, point, fact, circumstance, respect, specific, specification, ingredient, attribute, count, respect, technicality, complication, intricacy, small print, complexity, minutiae, triviality, nicety, thoroughness, elaboration, meticulousness, refinement, *colloq.* ins and outs, nitty-gritty, nuts and bolts
▷ **in detail** point by point, carefully, thoroughly, comprehensively, exhaustively, fully, item by item, at length, in depth
▶ *v* **1** LIST, set out, enumerate, itemize, specify, catalogue, spell out, tabulate, describe, portray, depict, point out, recount, relate, *formal* delineate, rehearse **2** ASSIGN, appoint, choose, allocate, charge, delegate, commission

detailed *adj*
comprehensive, exhaustive, full, itemized, thorough, minute, in-depth, exact, precise, specific, particular, intricate, elaborate, complex, complicated, meticulous, descriptive, *formal* convoluted, *colloq.* blow-by-blow
F₃ cursory, general

detain *v*
1 DELAY, hold (up), make late, hold back, keep (back), hinder, impede, check, slow, stay, stop, *formal* retard, inhibit **2** CONFINE, arrest, intern, hold, restrain, keep, keep/hold in custody, lock up, put in prison, imprison, *formal* incarcerate
F₃ 2 release

detect *v*
1 NOTICE, ascertain, note, observe, perceive, make out, recognize, discern, distinguish, identify, sight, catch, spot, spy **2** UNCOVER, catch, discover, disclose, expose, find, turn up, track down, unearth, unmask, reveal, bring to light

detection *n*
1 NOTICING, ascertaining, note, observation, perception, recognition, discernment, distinguishing, identification, sighting, *US* operative **2** UNCOVERING, discovery, disclosure, exposé, exposure, tracking-down, smelling-out, sniffing-out, unearthing, unmasking, revelation

detective *n*
police officer, (private) investigator, plain-clothes officer, *colloq.* private eye, sleuth, sleuth-hound, gumshoe, shamus, dick, tail

detention *n*
1 DETAINMENT, custody, confinement, imprisonment, captivity, restraint, constraint, internment, quarantine, punishment, *formal* incarceration, **2** DELAY, hindrance, holding-back, slowing-up
F₃ 1 release

deter *v*
discourage, put off, talk out of, inhibit, frighten, intimidate, scare off, daunt, check, caution, warn, restrain, hinder, frighten, prevent, prohibit, stop, *formal* dissuade, disincline, *colloq.* turn off
F₃ encourage

detergent *n*
cleaner, cleanser, soap, washing powder, washing-up liquid, *technical* abstergent

deteriorate *v*
1 WORSEN, get worse, decline, degenerate, depreciate, drop, fail, fall off, lapse, slide, relapse, slip, wane, ebb, *formal* retrograde, retrogress, *colloq.* go downhill, go to pot, go down the tube, go/run to seed **2** DECAY, disintegrate, decompose, go bad, break up, fall apart, fall to pieces, weaken, fade
F₃ 1 improve, get better

deterioration *n*
worsening, decline, degeneration, drop, failure, falling-off, downturn, lapse, slide, relapse, slipping,

waning, ebb, atrophy, corrosion, debasement, degradation, disintegration, *formal* retrogression, exacerbation, pejoration
🔁 improvement

determinate *adj*
fixed, absolute, certain, clear-cut, distinct, explicit, express, conclusive, decided, decisive, defined, settled, specific, specified, definite, definitive, established, positive, precise, quantified
🔁 indeterminate

determination *n*
1 RESOLUTENESS, tenacity, firmness, willpower, perseverance, persistence, purpose, resolve, backbone, steadfastness, single-mindedness, will, insistence, conviction, dedication, push, drive, stamina, moral fibre, strength of character, firmness of purpose, *formal* fortitude, *colloq.* guts, grit, stay the course, hang on like grim death, hold your ground, dig your heels in **2** DECISION, judgement, settlement, conclusion, decree, verdict, opinion, *formal* resolution
🔁 **1** irresolution

> **Colloquial expressions showing determination include:**
> mean business, stick to your guns, go to great lengths, go all out, go to extremes, go the whole hog, go for it, move heaven and earth, stop at nothing, do your utmost, give your all, leave no stone unturned, pull out all the stops, put your heart and soul into, strain every nerve, be hell-bent, get stuck into.

determine *v*
1 AFFECT, influence, govern, control, condition, dictate, direct, guide, prompt, impel, regulate, ordain **2** DISCOVER, establish, find out, learn, ascertain, identify, check, detect, verify **3** DECIDE, settle, make up your mind, choose, conclude, agree on, establish, fix on, elect, finish, *formal* resolve, purpose, *colloq.* clinch

determined *adj*
resolute, firm, purposeful, strong-willed, single-minded, persevering, persistent, strong, strong-minded, steadfast, tenacious, dogged, insistent, intent, set, resolved, fixed, bent, dedicated, convinced, decided, unflinching, unwavering, uncompromising, stubborn, *colloq.* hell-bent, dead set, out
🔁 irresolute, wavering

deterrent *n*
hindrance, impediment, obstacle, repellent, check, bar, barrier, block, discouragement, disincentive, obstruction, curb, restraint, difficulty
🔁 incentive, encouragement

detest *v*
hate, loathe, dislike, recoil from, deplore, despise, *formal* abhor, abominate, execrate, *colloq.* can't stand
🔁 adore, love

detestable *adj*
hateful, loathsome, repellent, obnoxious, despicable, odious, contemptible, revolting, repulsive, repugnant, offensive, vile, disgusting, distasteful, heinous, shocking, sordid, *formal* abhorrent, abominable, execrable, accursed, reprehensible
🔁 adorable, admirable

detestation *n*
hate, hatred, loathing, dislike, digust, anathema, animosity, hostility, antipathy, aversion, repugnance, revulsion, *formal* abhorrence, abomination, execration, odium
🔁 adoration, approval, love

dethrone *v*
depose, oust, topple, unseat, unthrone, uncrown
🔁 crown, enthrone

detonate *v*
blow up, discharge, blast, explode, ignite, kindle, set off, let off, spark off, *formal* fulminate

detonation *n*
bang, blast, explosion, blow-up, boom, burst, discharge, igniting, ignition, *formal* fulmination, report

detour *n*
deviation, diversion, indirect route, circuitous route, roundabout route, scenic route, digression, byroad, byway, bypath, bypass

detract *v*
diminish, subtract from, take away from, spoil, mar, reduce, lessen, lower, devaluate, depreciate, belittle, *formal* disparage
🔁 add to, enhance, praise

detractor *n*
backbiter, belittler, defamer, slanderer, muck-raker, reviler, scandalmonger, enemy, *formal* denigrator, disparager, traducer, vilifier
🔁 flatterer, supporter, defender

detriment *n*
damage, harm, hurt, disadvantage, loss, ill, injury, impairment, disservice, wrong, evil, mischief, prejudice
🔁 advantage, benefit

detrimental *adj*
damaging, harmful, hurtful, adverse, disadvantageous, prejudicial, mischievous, pernicious, destructive, *formal* injurious, inimical
🔁 advantageous, favourable, beneficial

detritus *n*
remains, rubbish, debris, rubble, fragments, garbage, junk, litter, scum, waste, wreckage

devalue *v*
deflate, devaluate, lower, reduce, decrease, *formal* devalorize

devastate *v*
1 DESTROY, desolate, lay waste, demolish, spoil, despoil, wreck, ruin, ravage, waste, ransack, plunder, level, flatten, raze, pillage, sack **2** DISCONCERT, overwhelm, overcome, shock, take aback, confound, nonplus, discompose, traumatize, *formal* perturb, discomfit, *colloq.* shatter, floor

devastating *adj*
1 *devastating storms* destructive, disastrous, damaging, harmful, catastrophic **2** *a devastating argument* effective, incisive, overwhelming, shocking, stunning, *colloq.* shattering

devastation *n*
destruction, desolation, waste, havoc, ruin(s), damage, wreckage, ravages, demolition, annihilation, pillage, plunder, spoliation

develop *v*
1 ADVANCE, grow, evolve, expand, enlarge, progress, foster, nurture, flourish, mature, prosper, improve, branch out, spread **2** ELABORATE, amplify, enhance, unfold, work out, expand on, *formal* dilate on **3** ACQUIRE, begin, start, generate, create, invent, produce, originate, establish, set about/off, found, institute, *formal* contract, commence **4** RESULT, come about, grow, ensue, arise, follow, happen **5** *develop an illness* catch, get, go down with, pick up, become infected with, become ill with, *formal* contract, succumb to

development *n*
1 GROWTH, evolution, advance, blossoming, elaboration, furtherance, progress, progression, unfolding, expansion, enlargement, extension, spread, in-

crease, improvement, maturity, flourishing, prosperity, promotion, refinement, issue **2** OCCURRENCE, happening, event, incident, circumstance, change, outcome, situation, result, phenomenon **3** *property development* complex, centre, block, estate, land, area

deviant *adj, n*
▶ *adj* divergent, aberrant, anomalous, abnormal, irregular, variant, bizarre, eccentric, quirky, freakish, perverse, perverted, twisted, wayward, bent, *colloq.* kinky, oddball, with a screw loose, with bats in the belfry
◪ normal
▶ *n* freak, oddity, misfit, dropout, odd sort, pervert, *colloq.* oddball, kook, crank, weirdo, *slang* geek, goof
◪ straight

deviate *v*
diverge, veer, turn (aside), digress, swerve, deflect, change, vary, differ, depart, stray, yaw, wander, err, go astray, drift, part, *colloq.* go off the rails

deviation *n*
divergence, aberration, departure, abnormality, irregularity, difference, variance, variation, digression, eccentricity, anomaly, deflection, turning-aside, alteration, discrepancy, detour, fluctuation, inconsistency, change, drift, quirk, shift, freak, *formal* disparity
◪ conformity, regularity

device *n*
1 TOOL, implement, appliance, gadget, contrivance, contraption, apparatus, utensil, instrument, machine, mechanism, *colloq.* gizmo **2** SCHEME, ruse, strategy, stratagem, plan, plot, ploy, gambit, manoeuvre, wile, trick, artifice, stunt, manoeuvre, *formal* machination, *colloq.* dodge **3** EMBLEM, symbol, motif, logo, colophon, design, insignia, crest, badge, shield, seal, token, coat of arms

devil *n*
1 DEMON, Satan, fiend, evil spirit, arch-fiend, Lucifer, imp, Evil One, Prince of Darkness, Adversary, Beelzebub, Mephistopheles, *colloq.* Old Nick, Old Harry **2** BRUTE, rogue, monster, ogre, savage, beast, demon, terror, imp, rascal, wretch

devilish *adj*
diabolical, diabolic, fiendish, satanic, demonic, hellish, damnable, evil, infernal, wicked, vile, atrocious, dreadful, outrageous, shocking, disastrous, excruciating, accursed, *formal* execrable, nefarious

devil-may-care *adj*
careless, reckless, casual, cavalier, easy-going, flippant, frivolous, happy-go-lucky, heedless, nonchalant, unconcerned, unworried, swaggering, swashbuckling, *formal* insouciant

devious *adj*
1 UNDERHAND, deceitful, dishonest, double-dealing, unscrupulous, scheming, insidious, insincere, designing, calculating, crafty, cunning, evasive, wily, sly, artful, surreptitious, treacherous, misleading, *formal* disingenuous, *colloq.* tricky, slippery, crooked **2** INDIRECT, circuitous, rambling, roundabout, wandering, winding, deviating, tortuous, erratic
◪ **1** straightforward **2** direct

devise *v*
invent, contrive, plan, plot, design, conceive, come up with, work out, think up, dream up, put together, arrange, formulate, imagine, scheme, construct, originate, create, concoct, forge, fabricate, hatch, frame, project, shape, form, compose, create, *colloq.* cook up

devoid *adj*
lacking, wanting, without, free, bereft, destitute, deprived,

bare, barren, empty, vacant, void, *formal* deficient
◪ endowed

devolution *n*
decentralization, delegation of power, distribution, transference of power, dispersal
◪ centralization

devolve *v*
hand down, delegate, transfer, consign, convey, deliver, depute, entrust, commission, fall to, rest with

devote *v*
dedicate, consecrate, commit, give yourself, set apart, set aside, reserve, consign, apply, allocate, allot, sacrifice, enshrine, assign, appropriate, surrender, offer, give, put in, pledge

devoted *adj*
dedicated, ardent, committed, loyal, faithful, devout, loving, staunch, steadfast, true, constant, fond, unswerving, tireless, concerned, attentive, caring
◪ indifferent, disloyal

devotee *n*
enthusiast, fan, fanatic, addict, aficionado, follower, supporter, zealot, adherent, admirer, disciple, hound, *colloq.* buff, freak, merchant, fiend

devotion *n*
1 DEDICATION, commitment, consecration, ardour, loyalty, allegiance, adherence, trueness, staunchness, constancy, solidarity, zeal, support, love, passion, fervour, fondness, attachment, admiration, warmness, closeness, adoration, affection, faithfulness, reverence, steadfastness, regard, earnestness, *formal* fidelity **2** DEVOUTNESS, piety, godliness, faith, holiness, spirituality, sanctity **3** PRAYER, worship, observance
◪ **1** inconstancy **2** irreverence

devotional *adj*
devout, holy, pietistic, religious, reverential, sacred, solemn, spiritual, dutiful, pious

devour *v*
1 EAT, eat up, consume, finish off, guzzle, gulp, gorge, gobble, bolt, swallow, cram, gormandize, feast on, relish, revel in, *colloq.* wolf down, stuff, polish off, tuck into, scoff, put away, knock back **2** DESTROY, devastate, lay waste, consume, absorb, engulf, envelop, ravage, dispatch **3** *devour a book* be engrossed in, take in, drink in, appreciate, enjoy, relish, feast on

devout *adj*
1 PIOUS, godly, religious, reverent, prayerful, saintly, holy, orthodox, church-going, committed, practising **2** SINCERE, earnest, devoted, fervent, genuine, staunch, steadfast, ardent, passionate, serious, wholehearted, constant, faithful, intense, vehement, heartfelt, zealous, unswerving, deep, profound
◪ **1** irreligious **2** insincere

devoutly *adv*
1 *devoutly religious* piously, religiously, reverently, prayerfully **2** SINCERELY, deeply, earnestly, fervently, staunchly, steadfastly, ardently, passionately, wholeheartedly, faithfully, zealously

dewy *adj*
blooming, innocent, starry-eyed, youthful, *formal* roral, roric, rorid, roscid

dexterity *n*
deftness, adeptness, address, adroitness, agility, handiness, nimbleness, proficiency, mastery, readiness, skilfulness, ability, skill, expertise, aptitude, art, artistry, expertness, facility, knack, finesse, legerdemain, sleight, ingenuity, effortlessness
◪ clumsiness, awkwardness, ineptitude

dexterous *adj*
deft, adept, adroit, agile, able, nimble, proficient, skil-

ful, clever, expert, accomplished, nippy, handy, facile, nimble-fingered, neat-handed, *colloq.* nifty
🔁 clumsy, inept, awkward

diabolical *adj*
devilish, fiendish, demonic, hellish, damnable, evil, infernal, satanic, wicked, vile, sinful, dreadful, outrageous, shocking, appalling, disastrous, monstrous, excruciating, atrocious, nasty, *formal* execrable

diadem *n*
circlet, coronet, crown, tiara, headband, mitre, round

diagnose *v*
identify, determine, recognize, pinpoint, distinguish, analyse, explain, isolate, detect, interpret, investigate

diagnosis *n*
identification, verdict, explanation, conclusion, answer, interpretation, judgement, analysis, opinion, investigation, recognition, detection, examination, scrutiny

diagnostic *adj*
analytical, indicative, interpretative, interpretive, recognizable, symptomatic, demonstrative, distinguishing

diagonal *adj*
oblique, slanting, cross, crossing, crosswise, sloping, crooked, angled, cornerways

diagonally *adv*
obliquely, crossways, crosswise, at an angle, cornerwise, on the cross, on the slant, slantwise, aslant, on the bias

diagram *n*
plan, sketch, chart, bar chart, pie chart, flow chart, drawing, figure, representation, schema, illustration, outline, draft, graph, picture, exploded view, cutaway, layout, table, *formal* delineation

diagrammatic *adj*
diagrammatical, schematic, graphic, illustrative, representational, tabular
🔁 imaginative, impressionistic

dial *n, v*
► *n* circle, disc, face, clock, control
► *v* phone, telephone, ring, call (up), *colloq.* give a buzz/a bell

dialect *n*
idiom, language, regionalism, localism, patois, provincialism, vernacular, variety, argot, jargon, accent, speech, diction, *colloq.* lingo

dialectic *adj, n*
► *adj* dialectical, logical, rational, argumentative, analytical, rationalistic, logistic, polemical, inductive, deductive, *formal* disputatious
► *n* dialectics, logic, reasoning, rationale, analysis, debate, argumentation, contention, discussion, polemics, deduction, *formal* disputation, induction, ratiocination

dialogue *n*
1 CONVERSATION, communication, talk, chat, tête-à-tête, gossip, exchange, discussion, discourse, conference, *formal* interchange, converse, debate, colloquy, interlocution **2** LINES, script

diametrically *adv*
directly, completely, absolutely, utterly, *formal* antithetically

diaphanous *adj*
cobwebby, delicate, filmy, fine, gauzy, gossamer, gossamery, chiffony, light, see-through, sheer, thin, translucent, transparent, veily, *formal* pellucid
🔁 heavy, opaque, thick

diarrhoea *n*
looseness of the bowels, gippy tummy, holiday tummy, Montezuma's revenge, dysentery, *colloq.* the runs, the trots, Spanish tummy, Delhi belly
🔁 constipation

diary *n*
journal, day-book, logbook, chronicle, year-book, appointment book, engagement book, Filofax®

diatribe *n*
tirade, abuse, harangue, attack, onslaught, denunciation, criticism, insult, reviling, upbraiding, reproof, reprimand, rebuke, *formal* invective, vituperation, philippic, *colloq.* knocking, slating, slamming, running-down
🔁 praise, eulogy

dicey *adj*
risky, chancy, unpredictable, uncertain, tricky, problematic, dangerous, difficult, dubious, *colloq.* iffy, hairy, dodgy
🔁 certain

dicky *adj*
unsound, unsteady, weak, ailing, frail, infirm, shaky
🔁 healthy, robust

dictate *v, n*
► *v* **1** SAY, read, read aloud, read out, speak, utter, announce, pronounce, transmit **2** COMMAND, lay down, set down, impose, demand, insist, order, direct, decree, instruct, rule, *formal* prescribe, promulgate
► *n* command, decree, precept, principle, rule, direction, charge, injunction, edict, order, ruling, statute, requirement, law, bidding, mandate, ultimatum, word, *formal* ordinance, behest, promulgation

dictator *n*
despot, absolute ruler, autocrat, tyrant, oppressor, *formal* autarchist, *colloq.* supremo, Big Brother

dictatorial *adj*
tyrannical, despotic, totalitarian, all powerful, authoritarian, autocratic, oppressive, imperious, domineering, absolute, unlimited, unrestricted, repressive, overbearing, arbitrary, dogmatic, *formal* omnipotent, peremptory, autarchic, *colloq.* bossy
🔁 democratic, egalitarian, liberal

dictatorship *n*
tyranny, despotism, totalitarianism, authoritarianism, autocracy, absolute rule, fascism, police state, reign of terror, Hitlerism
🔁 democracy, egalitarianism

diction *n*
speech, articulation, language, elocution, intonation, pronunciation, inflection, fluency, delivery, expression, phrasing, *formal* enunciation

dictionary *n*
lexicon, glossary, thesaurus, vocabulary, wordbook, encyclopedia, concordance

dictum *n*
1 RULING, pronouncement, decree, dictate, edict, precept, command, order, *formal* fiat **2** SAYING, maxim, axiom, utterance, proverb, aphorism

didactic *adj*
instructive, educational, informative, prescriptive, pedantic, moralizing, moral, *formal* educative, pedagogic

die *v*
1 *he died in terrible pain* pass away, pass on, depart, depart this life, breathe your last, draw your last breath, lose your life, perish, *formal* expire, *colloq.* peg out, bite the dust, pop off, give up the ghost, have had it, meet your maker, push up daisies, go the way of all flesh, shuffle off this mortal coil, *slang* snuff it, cash in your chips, kick the bucket **2** DWINDLE, fade, pass, ebb, sink, wane, wilt, wither, decline, decay, decrease, finish, lapse, end, come to an end, disappear, vanish,

subside, dissolve, melt away, *colloq.* peter out **3** *the machine died* stop, break down, fail, lose power, *slang* conk out **4** LONG FOR, pine for, yearn, desire, be desperate, *colloq.* be crazy, be mad, be nuts, be wild, be raring

▷ **die away** fade, become weak, become faint, disappear

▷ **die down** decrease, subside, decline, quieten, stop

▷ **die out** become rarer/less common, disappear, vanish, *colloq.* peter out

F3 **1** live

die-hard *n*
reactionary, hardliner, ultra-conservative, rightist, fanatic, zealot, *formal* intransigent, *colloq.* blimp, old fogey, stick-in-the-mud

diet *n, v*
▶ *n* **1** FOOD, nutrition, rations, foodstuffs, fare, subsistence, *old use* provisions, *formal* sustenance, victuals, comestibles, viands **2** FAST, abstinence, regimen
▶ *v* lose weight, slim, fast, reduce, abstain, *colloq.* weight-watch

differ *v*
1 VARY, diverge, deviate, depart from, be a departure from, contradict, contrast, be unlike, be dissimilar **2** DISAGREE, argue, conflict, oppose, dispute, be at odds with, be at variance, clash, quarrel, fall out, debate, contend, not see eye to eye, *formal* dissent, altercate

F3 **1** conform **2** agree

difference *n*
1 DISSIMILARITY, unlikeness, discrepancy, divergence, diversity, variation, variance, variety, distinctness, distinction, deviation, differentiation, contrast, singularity, exception, *formal* dissimilitude, antithesis, incongruity, disparity **2** DISAGREEMENT, clash, dispute, conflict, argument, misunderstanding, quarrel, row, set-to, contention, *formal* controversy, disputation, altercation **3** REMAINDER, rest, balance, residue

F3 **1** conformity **2** agreement

different *adj*
1 DISSIMILAR, unlike, contrasting, divergent, inconsistent, deviating, at odds, at variance, clashing, opposed, *colloq.* a far cry, poles/worlds apart, different as chalk and cheese **2** VARIED, various, varying, separate, diverse, miscellaneous, assorted, many, numerous, several, sundry, other, another, *formal* disparate, discrete, *colloq.* mixed bag **3** UNUSUAL, unconventional, unique, distinct, distinctive, extraordinary, individual, original, special, strange, remarkable, odd, peculiar, rare, bizarre, anomalous, out of the ordinary

F3 **1** similar, identical **2** same **3** conventional, ordinary

differentiate *v*
distinguish, tell apart, discriminate, contrast, separate, mark off, individualize, particularize

differentiation *n*
distinction, distinguishing, discrimination, contrast, separation, demarcation, individualization, particularization, modification

F3 assimilation, association, confusion, connection

difficult *adj*
1 HARD, laborious, demanding, arduous, strenuous, tough, gruelling, tiring, wearisome, exhausting, back-breaking, uphill, formidable, exacting, burdensome, onerous **2** COMPLEX, complicated, intricate, hard, involved, obscure, dark, knotty, thorny, problematical, puzzling, perplexing, abstract, baffling, tricky, *formal* abstruse, intractable, recondite, arcane, esoteric **3** UNMANAGEABLE, awkward, perverse,

troublesome, trying, demanding, unco-operative, tiresome, stubborn, obstinate, *formal* intractable, recalcitrant, refractory

F3 **1** easy **2** straightforward, simple, intelligible **3** manageable, helpful

difficulty *n*
1 HARDSHIP, trouble, labour, strain, arduousness, strenuousness, painfulness, trial, struggle, awkwardness, *formal* tribulation, exigency **2** PROBLEM, predicament, complication, snag, dilemma, quandary, perplexity, embarrassment, plight, distress, hang-up, obstacle, hindrance, hurdle, impediment, objection, opposition, block, barrier, obstruction, pitfall, stumbling-block, cleft stick, *colloq.* fix, mess, jam, spot, hiccup, headache, hole, dire straits, pickle, tall order, hot/deep water, fly in the ointment, spanner in the works, catch-22, how-d'you-do, devil, tight spot, pretty pass, *slang* bitch

F3 **1** ease

▷ **in difficulties** having problems, in trouble, *colloq.* up against it, stumped, at the end of your tether, out of your depth, not knowing which way to turn, in the soup, in a fix/mess/jam/hole, in dire straits, in a scrape, in hot/deep water, in a tight spot, *slang* up the creek (without a paddle)

diffidence *n*
unassertiveness, modesty, shyness, timidity, self-consciousness, self-effacement, insecurity, reserve, bashfulness, humility, inhibition, meekness, self-distrust, self-doubt, hesitancy, reluctance, backwardness

F3 confidence

diffident *adj*
unassertive, modest, shy, timid, self-conscious, self-effacing, insecure, nervous, bashful, abashed, meek, reserved, withdrawn, tentative, shrinking, inhibited, hesitant, reluctant, unsure, shamefaced, sheepish

F3 assertive, confident

diffuse *v, adj*
▶ *v* spread, scatter, disperse, distribute, propagate, dispense, disseminate, permeate, circulate, *formal* dissipate, promulgate

F3 concentrate

▶ *adj* **1** *diffuse outbreaks of rain* scattered, unconcentrated, diffused, dispersed, disconnected **2** *a diffuse prose style* verbose, imprecise, wordy, rambling, long-winded, profuse, vague, discursive, *formal* prolix, loquacious, periphrastic, circumlocutory, *colloq.* waffling

F3 **1** concentrated **2** succinct

dig *v, n*
▶ *v* **1** EXCAVATE, penetrate, burrow, make a hole, mine, quarry, scoop, hollow, channel, tunnel, till, turn over, work, cultivate, harrow, plough, gouge, delve, pierce **2** POKE, prod, jab, punch **3** INVESTIGATE, probe, go into, research, search, delve

▷ **dig up** discover, unearth, uncover, root out, bring to light, disinter, expose, extricate, find, retrieve, track down, *formal* exhume

F3 bury, obscure

▶ *n* **1** *a dig in the ribs* poke, prod, jab, punch **2** GIBE, jeer, sneer, taunt, crack, insinuation, insult, wisecrack, compliment

digest *v, n*
▶ *v* **1** ABSORB, assimilate, incorporate, process, dissolve, break down, *formal* macerate **2** TAKE IN, absorb, understand, assimilate, grasp, study, consider, contemplate, meditate, mull over, ponder **3** SHORTEN, summarize, condense, compress, reduce, abridge, *formal* comprehend

▶ *n* summary, abridgement, abstract, précis, synopsis,

résumé, reduction, abbreviation, compression, compendium

digestion *n*
absorption, assimilation, breaking-down, transformation, *formal* ingestion, eupepsia

digestive system *n*

Parts of the human digestive system include:
alimentary canal, anus, bile, buccal cavity, colon, digestive enzymes, duodenum, gall bladder, gastric juices, ileum, intestine, large intestine, small intestine, jejenum, liver, mouth, oesophagus (gullet), pancreas, pancreatic juice, rectum, salivary glands, stomach.

---

dignified *adj*
stately, solemn, imposing, grand, majestic, noble, august, lordly, courtly, ceremonious, lofty, exalted, formal, distinguished, grave, impressive, reserved, honourable, *formal* decorous
F3 undignified, lowly

dignify *v*
honour, distinguish, grace, exalt, enhance, adorn, glorify, advance, elevate, ennoble, promote, raise, *formal* aggrandize, apotheosize
F3 degrade, demean

dignitary *n*
worthy, notable, high-up, personage, somebody, *formal* luminary, *colloq.* VIP, bigwig, big name, big gun, big shot, top brass

dignity *n*
stateliness, solemnity, nobleness, courtliness, self-possession, grandeur, loftiness, majesty, honour, eminence, importance, excellence, honourability, nobility, self-respect, self-esteem, self-importance, standing, poise, respectability, greatness, elevation, status, pride, *formal* propriety, decorum

digress *v*
diverge, deviate, stray, wander, go off at a tangent, go off the subject, drift, depart, ramble, turn aside, be sidetracked

digression *n*
divergence, deviation, straying, wandering, aside, departure, diversion, footnote, parenthesis, *formal* apostrophe, divagation, *obiter dictum*, excursus

dilapidated *adj*
ramshackle, shabby, broken-down, neglected, tumbledown, uncared-for, rickety, shaky, decrepit, crumbling, run-down, worn-out, ruined, in ruins, decayed, decaying, falling apart

dilapidation *n*
decay, ruin, disrepair, collapse, demolition, destruction, deterioration, disintegration, waste

dilate *v*
enlarge, expand, spread (out), broaden, widen, increase, extend, stretch, swell, bloat, inflate, *formal* distend
F3 contract, constrict, shorten

dilatory *adj*
delaying, slow, sluggish, lingering, dawdling, lazy, lackadaisical, slack, snail-like, time-wasting, postponing, stalling, *formal* procrastinating, tardy, tarrying
F3 prompt

dilemma *n*
quandary, conflict, predicament, problem, vicious circle, difficulty, puzzle, embarrassment, mess, perplexity, plight, *colloq.* catch-22, spot, no-win situation, tight corner

dilettante *n*
dabbler, amateur, trifler, potterer, *formal* aesthete, sciolist
F3 professional

diligence *n*
assiduity, assiduousness, industry, conscientiousness, attention, care, thoroughness, dedication, attentiveness, application, constancy, earnestness, intentness, laboriousness, perseverance, *formal* pertinacity, sedulousness
F3 laziness

diligent *adj*
assiduous, industrious, hard-working, conscientious, painstaking, busy, attentive, tireless, careful, thorough, dedicated, meticulous, persevering, persistent, studious, earnest, constant, *formal* sedulous
F3 negligent, lazy

dilly-dally *v*
dally, dawdle, delay, falter, hesitate, hover, linger, loiter, dither, potter, vacillate, waver, take your time, *formal* procrastinate, tarry, *colloq.* shilly-shally

dilute *v*
adulterate, water down, thin (out), make thinner, weaken, make weaker, diffuse, diminish, decrease, lessen, reduce, temper, moderate, tone down, *formal* attenuate, mitigate
F3 concentrate

dim *adj, v*
▶ *adj* **1** DARK, dull, dusky, cloudy, overcast, grey, shadowy, gloomy, leaden, sombre, dingy, unlit, lacklustre, feeble, *formal* crepuscular, tenebrous **2** INDISTINCT, blurred, hazy, ill-defined, obscure, misty, unclear, foggy, fuzzy, vague, faint, weak, feeble, pale, confused, imperfect, *formal* obfuscated **3** STUPID, dense, obtuse, slow-witted, doltish, *colloq.* thick, dumb, gormless, dim-witted **4** *dim prospects* unpromising, unfavourable, gloomy, discouraging, adverse, *formal* inauspicious
F3 **1** bright **2** distinct **3** bright, intelligent **4** hopeful, promising
▶ *v* darken, dull, obscure, cloud, blur, become blurred, fade, become faint, pale, tarnish, shade
F3 brighten, illuminate

dimension *n*
1 *the dimensions of the room* extent, measurement, measure, size, length, width, breadth, height, depth, area, proportions, scope, magnitude, largeness, volume, capacity, mass **2** *the dimensions of a problem* extent, size, scale, range, bulk, importance, magnitude, greatness **3** *add a new dimension to the matter* aspect, facet, side, factor, element, feature

diminish *v*
1 DECREASE, lessen, become/grow less, reduce, lower, contract, decline, dwindle, shrink, recede, taper off, wane, weaken, become/grow weaker, fade, sink, subside, deflate, ebb, slacken, die away, die out, cut, *formal* abate, retrench, *colloq.* peter out **2** BELITTLE, devalue, defame, *formal* disparage, deprecate, denigrate, derogate, vilify
F3 **1** increase, grow **2** exaggerate

diminution *n*
reduction, lessening, contraction, decline, ebb, decrease, cut, cutback, curtailment, deduction, decay, subsidence, weakening, shortening, shrinkage, *formal* abatement, retrenchment
F3 enlargement, increase, growth

diminutive *adj*
small-scale, tiny, little, undersized, small, miniature, minute, microscopic, infinitesimal, elfin, petite, midget, compact, Lilliputian, pocket(-sized), pygmy, dwarfish, *Scot.* wee, *formal* homuncular, *colloq.* mini,

teeny, teeny-weeny, dinky, pint-size(d)
🔁 big, large, oversized

dimple *n*
concavity, depression, dint, hollow, *technical* fovea, umbilicus

dimwit *n*
idiot, fool, blockhead, nitwit, dunce, dullard, dunderhead, ignoramus, *colloq.* bonehead, numskull, twit

din *n*
noise, loud noise, row, racket, clash, clatter, clamour, clangour, pandemonium, uproar, tumult, commotion, crash, hubbub, brouhaha, outcry, shout, shouting, yelling, babble, *colloq.* hullabaloo
🔁 quiet, calm

dine *v*
eat, have dinner, feast, sup, lunch, banquet, feed

dingy *adj*
dark, drab, grimy, murky, faded, dull, dim, shabby, soiled, discoloured, dirty, grimy, dreary, gloomy, dismal, cheerless, seedy, sombre, obscure, run-down, colourless, murky, dusky, worn
🔁 bright, clean

dinky *adj*
dainty, fine, small, petite, neat, trim, miniature, *colloq.* natty, mini

dinner *n*
meal, main meal, evening meal, supper, tea, banquet, feast, spread, *formal* repast, refection, *colloq.* blow-out

dinosaur *n*

> **Dinosaurs include:**
> Ornithischia, Saurischia; Allosaurus,
> Ankylosaurus, Apatosaurus, Barosaurus,
> Brachiosaurus, Brontosaurus, Camptosaurus,
> Coelophysis, Compsognathus, Corythosaurus,
> Deinonychus, Diplodocus, Heterodontosaurus,
> Iguanodon, Ophiacodon, Ornithomimus,
> Pachycephalosaurus, Parasaurolophus,
> Plateosaurus, Stegosaurus, Styracosaurus,
> Triceratops, Tyrannosaurus.

dint *n*
dent, indentation, impression, hollow, depression, blow, concavity, stroke
▷ **by dint of** by means of, by the agency of, through the medium of, with the assistance of, *formal* by virtue of

dip *v, n*
▶ *v* **1** PLUNGE, immerse, submerge, duck, dunk, lower, bathe, soak, douse, souse, sink **2** DESCEND, go down, decline, drop, fall, decrease, subside, slump, sink, lower **3** *the track dips* slope, descend, go down, decline, drop, fall, sink
▷ **dip into 1** *dip into a book* look at, leaf through, look through, run through, flick through, thumb through, skim, browse **2** *dip into your savings* spend, draw on, use
▶ *n* **1** HOLLOW, basin, decline, hole, drop, concavity, incline, descent, indentation, dent, depression, fall, slope, decrease, slump, lowering **2** BATHE, immersion, plunge, soaking, ducking, swim, drenching, dive, *formal* infusion **3** *an avocado dip* sauce, cream, dressing

diplomacy *n*
1 TACT, tactfulness, finesse, sensitivity, delicacy, discretion, savoir-faire, cleverness, subtlety, skill, craft, *formal* judiciousness, prudence **2** STATECRAFT, statesmanship, international relations, politics, negotiation, manoeuvring

diplomat *n*
go-between, mediator, negotiator, ambassador, envoy, emissary, legate, attaché, consul, plenipotentiary, *chargé d'affaires*, conciliator, peacemaker, arbitrator, moderator, politician, statesman

diplomatic *adj*
1 *diplomatic relations* consular, ambassadorial **2** TACTFUL, politic, discreet, subtle, sensitive, clever, skilful, *formal* judicious, prudent
🔁 tactless

dire *adj*
1 DISASTROUS, dreadful, terrible, frightful, awful, appalling, calamitous, catastrophic, horrible, atrocious, shocking, alarming, distressing **2** DESPERATE, urgent, grave, drastic, crucial, extreme, vital, pressing, ominous

direct *adj, v*
▶ *adj* **1** STRAIGHT, undeviating, unswerving, through, uninterrupted, non-stop, unbroken **2** STRAIGHTFORWARD, outspoken, blunt, bluff, frank, straight, forthright, plainspoken, unequivocal, sincere, candid, honest, explicit, unambiguous, *colloq.* up-front **3** IMMEDIATE, first-hand, face-to-face, personal
🔁 **1** indirect, circuitous **2** equivocal **3** indirect
▶ *v* **1** CONTROL, be in control of, manage, run, administer, be in charge of, organize, lead, govern, regulate, superintend, preside over, oversee, supervise, handle, mastermind, *colloq.* call the shots, be the boss of **2** INSTRUCT, command, order, give orders, issue instructions, charge, *formal* adjure **3** GUIDE, lead, conduct, point, show, steer, show/point the way, escort, usher **4** AIM, point, focus, turn, intend, mean, level

direction *n*
1 CONTROL, administration, management, government, running, handling, supervision, guidance, leadership, superintendency, overseeing, regulation **2** ROUTE, way, line, road, course, path, track, bearing, orientation **3** *change the direction of your career* course, trend, tendency, inclination, drift, tenor, current aim, orientation **4** *give someone directions* instructions, guidelines, orders, brief, briefing, guidance, recommendations, indication, plan, rules, regulations

directive *n*
command, instruction, order, regulation, ruling, imperative, dictate, decree, charge, bidding, mandate, injunction, ordinance, edict, notice, *formal* fiat

directly *adv*
1 IMMEDIATELY, instantly, at once, promptly, right away, speedily, forthwith, instantaneously, quickly, soon, presently, straightaway, without delay, as soon as possible, straight, right, exactly, *colloq.* pronto **2** FRANKLY, bluntly, candidly, honestly, straightforwardly, unequivocally, sincerely, clearly, plainly, explicitly, unambiguously

director *n*
manager, managing director, board of directors, head, boss, chief, controller, executive, chief executive, principal, governor, leader, president, superintendent, organizer, supervisor, overseer, administrator, producer, chairman, chairwoman, chairperson, chair, conductor, régisseur, *colloq.* top dog

dirge *n*
elegy, lament, funeral song, requiem, dead-march, coronach, threnody, monody

dirt *n*
1 EARTH, soil, clay, dust, mud, loam **2** FILTH, grime, soot, pollution, muck, mire, excrement, stain, smudge, sludge, slime, tarnish, *colloq.* gunge, yuck, grot, *slang* crud, gunk, grunge, crap **3** INDECENCY, impurity, obscenity, pornography, lewdness, sordidness, salaciousness, *colloq.* smut, sleaze

dirty *adj, v*
▶ *adj* **1** FILTHY, grimy, grubby, mucky, soiled, greasy, unclean, unwashed, unhygienic, foul, messy, muddy, dusty, sooty, polluted, slimy, squalid, dull, miry, scruffy, shabby, sullied, stained, defiled, tarnished, clouded, cloudy, dark, dull, *colloq.* grotty, yucky, flea-bitten, cruddy **2** INDECENT, improper, obscene, coarse, filthy, smutty, sordid, salacious, suggestive, risqué, vulgar, pornographic, contaminated, corrupt, lewd, bawdy, ribald, *colloq.* blue, raunchy, sleazy
◪ **1** clean **2** decent
▶ *v* pollute, soil, stain, foul, mess up, defile, contaminate, adulterate, smear, smirch, spoil, smudge, splash, sully, tarnish, muddy, blacken, *formal* besmirch, begrime
◪ clean, cleanse

disability *n*
handicap, disablement, disorder, inability, incapability, incapacity, infirmity, defect, unfitness, disqualification, illness, ailment, complaint, weakness, *formal* impairment, affliction, malady

disable *v*
1 *disable a person* cripple, lame, damage, handicap, hamstring, make unfit, disqualify, weaken, immobilize, invalidate, paralyse, prostrate, *formal* incapacitate, impair, debilitate, enfeeble **2** *disable a machine* immobilize, paralyse, stop, deactivate, put out of action, *formal* render inoperative

disabled *adj*
handicapped, infirm, unfit, crippled, lame, immobilized, maimed, weak, weakened, out of action, paralysed, bed-ridden, wrecked, *formal* incapacitated, impaired, indisposed, debilitated, enfeebled, *colloq.* physically challenged
◪ able, able-bodied

disadvantage *n*
1 DRAWBACK, snag, hindrance, liability, handicap, impediment, limitation, inconvenience, flaw, defect, nuisance, weakness, weak point, trouble, penalty, *colloq.* downside, minus, hang-up, spanner in the works, fly in the ointment, weak link in the chain, chink in your armour, Achilles heel **2** HARM, damage, detriment, hurt, injury, loss, prejudice, hardship, lack, disservice, *formal* privation
◪ **1** advantage, benefit, asset

disadvantaged *adj*
deprived, underprivileged, poor, poverty-stricken, handicapped, impoverished, struggling, in need, in distress, in want
◪ privileged

disadvantageous *adj*
unfavourable, harmful, detrimental, inopportune, prejudicial, adverse, unfortunate, unlucky, damaging, hurtful, injurious, inconvenient, ill-timed, inexpedient, *formal* hapless, deleterious
◪ advantageous, favourable, *formal* auspicious

disaffected *adj*
disloyal, hostile, alienated, antagonistic, rebellious, mutinous, dissatisfied, disgruntled, discontented, unfriendly, seditious, *formal* estranged
◪ loyal, friendly, satisfied

disaffection *n*
disloyalty, hostility, alienation, discontentment, resentment, ill-will, dissatisfaction, animosity, coolness, unfriendliness, antagonism, disharmony, discord, disagreement, aversion, dislike, *formal* estrangement
◪ loyalty, contentment

disagree *v*
1 *disagree with someone; the two sides disagree* conflict, contradict, diverge, differ, clash, agree to differ, not see eye to eye with, be at odds with, be at loggerheads with, quarrel, argue, bicker, wrangle, fight, squabble, contend, dispute, contest, take issue, beg to differ, *formal* dissent, *colloq.* fall out **2** *disagree with an idea* disapprove of, think wrong, oppose, object, contradict, take issue with, argue against, be against, *formal* dissent **3** *food disagreeing with you* upset, make unwell, cause illness
◪ **1** agree **2** approve, accept **3** agree

disagreeable *adj*
1 *disagreeable old man* bad-tempered, ill-humoured, impolite, difficult, unfriendly, ill-natured, awkward, unhelpful, peevish, rude, surly, churlish, irritable, nasty, disobliging, contrary, cross, brusque, *colloq.* grouchy **2** *a disagreeable taste* disgusting, unpleasant, offensive, repulsive, repellent, obnoxious, unsavoury, horrible, dreadful, abominable, objectionable, nasty, *formal* repugnant
◪ **1** amiable, pleasant **2** agreeable, pleasant

disagreement *n*
1 DISPUTE, argument, difference of opinion, friction, conflict, quarrel, row, clash, dissent, contention, strife, dissension, misunderstanding, squabble, wrangle, *formal* altercation, discord, disputation, *colloq.* falling-out, tiff

---

Ways of expressing disagreement include:
a bone of contention, a difference of opinion, agree to disagree, agree to differ, argue the toss, be at loggerheads with, be at odds with, beg to differ, I don't agree, not see eye to eye, not true!, on the contrary, put the opposite view/case, take issue with.

---

2 DIFFERENCE, variance, unlikeness, discrepancy, deviation, conformity, dissimilarity, incompatibility, inconsistency, divergence, diversity, *formal* disparity, incongruity, dissimilitude
◪ **1** agreement, harmony **2** similarity, conformity

disallow *v*
ban, cancel, forbid, prohibit, refuse, reject, debar, dismiss, embargo, disown, rebuff, repudiate, veto, say no to, exclude, *formal* abjure, disaffirm, disavow, disclaim, proscribe, interdict
◪ allow, permit

disappear *v*
1 VANISH, wane, recede, fade, evaporate, melt away, dissolve, ebb, go out of sight, pass from sight, get lost, go missing, dematerialize, *formal* evanesce, *colloq.* make tracks **2** GO, depart, withdraw, retire, exit, flee, fly, escape, hide, *colloq.* scarper, vamoose **3** END, perish, pass, die out, die away, become extinct, *formal* expire, cease
◪ **1** appear **3** emerge, start, begin

disappearance *n*
1 VANISHING, fading, passing from sight, evaporation, melting away, departure, withdrawal, exit, loss, going, passing, desertion, flight **2** END, passing, dying-out, expiry, extinction, *formal* evanescence
◪ **1** appearance, manifestation **2** start, beginning

disappoint *v*
let down, fail, dissatisfy, disillusion, dismay, discourage, depress, dispirit, disenchant, sadden, thwart, vex, baffle, frustrate, foil, dishearten, disgruntle, disconcert, hamper, hinder, deceive, defeat, delude, dash someone's hopes
◪ satisfy, please, delight

disappointed *adj*
let down, frustrated, thwarted, disenchanted, deflated, disillusioned, dissatisfied, upset, vexed,

discouraged, disgruntled, disheartened, distressed, downhearted, saddened, cast down, despondent, depressed, disenchanted, *colloq.* miffed
F3 pleased, satisfied

disappointing *adj*
unsatisfactory, inferior, inadequate, insufficient, unworthy, pathetic, sad, sorry, unhappy, discouraging, disconcerting, depressing, disagreeable, anticlimactic, *colloq.* not all it's cracked up to be, underwhelming
F3 encouraging, pleasant, satisfactory

disappointment *n*
1 FRUSTRATION, dissatisfaction, failure, disenchantment, disillusionment, displeasure, discouragement, discontent, distress, regret, chagrin, sadness, despondency, dispiritedness, *colloq.* cold comfort, bitter pill (to swallow) **2** FAILURE, let-down, anticlimax, setback, comedown, non-event, blow, misfortune, fiasco, disaster, calamity, *colloq.* washout, wipeout, damp squib, swiz, swizzle
F3 1 pleasure, satisfaction, delight **2** success

disapprobation *n*
blame, censure, condemnation, criticism, denunciation, disapproval, disfavour, dissatisfaction, dislike, displeasure, objection, exception, reproach, reproof, *formal* remonstration, disparagement
F3 approval, *formal* approbation

disapproval *n*
censure, condemnation, criticism, blame, displeasure, reproach, exception, objection, dissatisfaction, denunciation, dislike, rejection, veto, rebuke, reproof, *formal* remonstration, disparagement, *colloq.* disapprobation, the thumbs-down
F3 approval, *formal* approbation

disapprove *v*
censure, condemn, blame, take exception to, be against, object to, find unacceptable, deplore, denounce, disparage, dislike, reject, veto, spurn, look down on, think little of, hold in contempt, frown on, take a dim view of, take exception to, think badly of, have a low opinion of, not hold with, *formal* deprecate, discountenance, disallow, animadvert, *colloq.* look down your nose at, give the thumbs-down
F3 approve, agree, have a high opinion of

disapproving *adj*
censorious, condemnatory, critical, reproachful, derogatory, pejorative, *formal* deprecatory, disparaging, disapprobative, disapprobatory, improbative, improbatory

disarm *v*
1 DISABLE, unarm, demilitarize, demobilize, deactivate, disband, immobilize, lay down arms/weapons, make powerless, put out of action, *formal* render inoperative **2** APPEASE, conciliate, win over, mollify, placate, persuade, charm
F3 1 arm

disarmament *n*
demilitarization, demobilization, deactivation, laying-down of arms/weapons, arms control/limitation/reduction

disarming *adj*
charming, winning, persuasive, conciliatory, irresistible, likeable, mollifying

disarrange *v*
untidy, disorganize, disorder, confuse, disturb, jumble, mess, dislocate, shuffle, unsettle, derange
F3 arrange, tidy

disarray *n*
disorder, confusion, chaos, mess, muddle, disorganization, clutter, untidiness, dishevelment, unruliness,

unsettledness, jumble, clutter, indiscipline, tangle, upset, *colloq.* shambles
F3 order

disaster *n*
calamity, catastrophe, misfortune, reverse, reversal, adversity, tragedy, blow, accident, act of God, cataclysm, debacle, mishap, misadventure, setback, failure, fiasco, ruin, stroke, trouble, mischance, ruination, *colloq.* flop, wash out
F3 success, triumph

disastrous *adj*
calamitous, catastrophic, cataclysmic, devastating, ravaging, ruinous, tragic, unlucky, unfortunate, adverse, dreadful, dire, terrible, appalling, shocking, destructive, harmful, injurious, ill-fated, ill-starred, fatal, miserable
F3 successful, *formal* auspicious

disavowal *n*
repudiation, denial, contradiction, renunciation, rejection, dissent, *formal* disaffirmation, abjuration

disband *v*
disperse, break up, scatter, dismiss, demobilize, part company, separate, dissolve, go separate ways, *colloq.* demob
F3 assemble, gather, muster

disbelief *n*
unbelief, incredulity, doubt, scepticism, questioning, suspicion, distrust, mistrust, discredit, rejection, *formal* dubiety
F3 belief, conviction

Colloquial expressions of disbelief include:
a good one!; a likely story!; come, come!; come off it!; do me a favour!; don't give me that!; don't make me laugh!; don't tell me!; do you mean to say?; excuses, excuses!; fancy that!; get along (with you)!; get away (with you)!; go on!; go on with you!; good heavens!; good Lord!; goodness gracious me!; goodness me!; heavens above!; I ask you!; I bet!; I don't think; I'll eat my hat!; I've heard that one before!; if you believe that, you'd believe anything!; just fancy!; make me laugh!; my (giddy) aunt!; my foot!; my goodness!; my hat!; no kidding!; oh, yeah!; promises, promises!; pull the other one, it's got bells on!; says who?; says you!; sez who?; sez you!; stone me!; stone the crows!; strike a light!; strike me dead!; strike me pink!; stuff and nonsense!; tell it to the marines!; tell me another!; that's a tall story!; that's news to me!; that's rich!; the devil you do!; the hell you say!; what a load of cobblers!; you can't be serious!; you don't say!; you'll be lucky!; you must be joking!; you must be kidding!; you're kidding!; you're pulling my leg!; you what!

---

disbelieve *v*
discount, discredit, repudiate, reject, distrust, mistrust, suspect, question, doubt, be unconvinced, *colloq.* take something with a pinch of salt
F3 believe, trust, give credence to, accept

disbeliever *n*
doubter, agnostic, atheist, unbeliever, questioner, sceptic, scoffer, doubtingThomas, *formal* nullifidian
F3 believer

disburse *v*
pay out, spend, lay out, *formal* expend, *colloq.* fork out, shell out, cough up

disbursement *n*
payment, outlay, spending, expenditure, *formal* disbursal, disposal

disc *n*
1 CIRCLE, face, plate, ring, saucer, counter, discus
2 RECORD, album, LP, CD, vinyl, gramophone record
3 DISK, diskette, hard disk, floppy disk, compact disk, CD-ROM, microfloppy

discard *v*
reject, abandon, dispose of, get rid of, throw away, throw out, jettison, dispense with, cast aside, toss out, drop, scrap, shed, remove, relinquish, repudiate, *formal* forsake, *colloq.* ditch, dump, chuck away/out
🔁 retain, adopt

discern *v*
perceive, make out, observe, detect, recognize, see, ascertain, notice, determine, discover, distinguish, differentiate, judge, discriminate, *formal* descry

discernible *adj*
perceptible, noticeable, detectable, appreciable, distinct, distinguishable, observable, recognizable, visible, apparent, clear, obvious, plain, conspicuous, patent, discoverable, *formal* manifest
🔁 imperceptible

discerning *adj*
discriminating, perceptive, astute, clear-sighted, sensitive, shrewd, wise, ingenious, intelligent, clever, quick, sharp, subtle, penetrating, acute, piercing, critical, eagle-eyed, sound, *formal* sagacious, perspicacious, percipient, prudent, sapient

discernment *n*
judgement, discrimination, perception, perceptiveness, acuteness, clear-sightedness, shrewdness, wisdom, sharpness, ingenuity, insight, intelligence, cleverness, understanding, awareness, acumen, keenness, (good) taste, penetration, *formal* ascertainment, percipience, perspicacity, sagacity

discharge *v, n*
▶ *v* 1 LIBERATE, free, set free, let go, pardon, release, clear, absolve, acquit, relieve, dismiss, *formal* exonerate, exculpate 2 *discharge from employment* remove, dismiss, expel, get rid of, discard, oust, eject, *colloq.* sack, fire, turf out, boot out, give the boot to, give the elbow, axe 3 FULFIL, carry out, perform, do, fulfil, *formal* dispense 4 FIRE, shoot, let off, detonate, explode, set off 5 *discharge fumes* emit, let off/out, give off, release, exude, ooze, leak, disgorge, gush, *formal* excrete, disembogue 6 *discharge a debt* settle, pay, clear, honour, satisfy, meet
🔁 1 detain 2 appoint, hire 3 neglect
▶ *n* 1 LIBERATION, release, acquittal, clearance, absolution, *formal* exoneration, exculpation 2 *discharge from employment* dismissal, removal, expulsion, ousting, cashiering, *colloq.* sacking, the sack, firing, the boot, the elbow 3 EMISSION, secretion, ejection, flow, exuding, release, pus, *formal* excretion, suppuration 4 FULFILMENT, accomplishment, performance, doing, execution, achievement 5 *discharge of a debt* settling, payment, clearance, honouring
🔁 1 confinement, detention 2 hiring, appointment 3 absorption 4 neglect

disciple *n*
follower, convert, proselyte, adherent, believer, devotee, supporter, upholder, learner, pupil, student, votary

disciplinarian *n*
authoritarian, (hard) taskmaster, autocrat, stickler, despot, tyrant, martinet

discipline *n, v*
▶ *n* 1 TRAINING, exercise, drill, practice, routine, regimen 2 PUNISHMENT, correction, *formal* chastisement, castigation 3 STRICTNESS, control, self-control, restraint, self-restraint, regulation, orderliness

4 SUBJECT, area of study, field of study, course of study, branch, speciality
🔁 3 indiscipline
▶ *v* 1 TRAIN, instruct, drill, educate, exercise, break in, ground, *formal* inculcate, inure 2 CHECK, control, correct, restrain, govern, regulate, limit, restrict 3 PUNISH, chasten, rebuke, reprove, penalize, correct, reprimand, make an example of, teach someone a lesson, *formal* chastise, castigate

disclaim *v*
deny, disown, repudiate, abandon, renounce, reject, decline, refuse, *formal* abjure, disavow, *colloq.* wash your hands of
🔁 accept, confess

disclaimer *n*
denial, repudiation, renunciation, rejection, contradiction, *formal* abjuration, abnegation, disavowal, disaffirmation, disownment, retraction

disclose *v*
make known, reveal, tell, confess, let slip, blurt out, relate, publish, broadcast, communicate, make public, expose, reveal, show, exhibit, uncover, lay bare, unveil, bring to light, discover, *formal* divulge, impart, *colloq.* leak, blab, squeal, let the cat out of the bag, spill the beans
🔁 conceal, hide, keep secret, keep dark, dissemble, cover, mask, obscure

disclosure *n*
revelation, exposure, exposé, uncovering, publication, discovery, admission, confession, acknowledgement, announcement, publication, broadcast, declaration, bringing to light, laying bare, *formal* divulgence, *colloq.* leak

discoloration *n*
blemish, stain, spot, streak, mark, patch, blot, blotch, splotch, *technical* dyschroa, ecchymosis

discolour *v*
disfigure, fade, stain, soil, mark, mar, rust, streak, tarnish, tinge, weather

discomfit *v*
embarrass, disconcert, discompose, unsettle, demoralize, abash, confound, baffle, confuse, perplex, fluster, ruffle, frustrate, thwart, outwit, *formal* perturb, rattle, *colloq.* faze

discomfiture *n*
unease, embarrassment, confusion, abashment, discomposure, demoralization, frustration, disappointment, humiliation, chagrin

discomfort *n*
1 ACHE, pain, soreness, hurt, twinge, pang, *formal* malaise 2 UNEASE, embarrassment, trouble, distress, disquiet, hardship, vexation, irritation, annoyance, worry, apprehension, restlessness 3 INCONVENIENCE, difficulty, trouble, disadvantage, drawback, worry, nuisance, bother, irritation, annoyance
🔁 2 comfort, ease

discomposure *n*
unease, upset, agitation, restlessness, fluster, disturbance, anxiety, irritation, annoyance, *formal* disquietude, inquietude, perturbation
🔁 *formal* composure

disconcert *v*
unsettle, disturb, confuse, upset, unnerve, put off/out, shake, alarm, startle, take aback, throw off balance, surprise, fluster, ruffle, bewilder, nonplus, embarrass, baffle, perplex, dismay, *formal* perturb, *colloq.* faze, rattle, put someone's nose out of joint, *US slang* discombobulate

disconcerting *adj*
disturbing, confusing, upsetting, unnerving, daunt-

ing, alarming, bewildering, distracting, embarrassing, awkward, baffling, perplexing, dismaying, bothersome, *formal* perturbing, *colloq.* off-putting

disconnect *v*
cut off, disengage, uncouple, sever, separate, detach, unplug, undo, unhook, unhitch, part, divide, split
F3 attach, connect, join, unite

disconnected *adj*
confused, incoherent, garbled, rambling, wandering, unco-ordinated, unintelligible, loose, rambling, irrational, disjointed, illogical, jumbled, mixed-up, abrupt, staccato
F3 coherent, connected

disconsolate *adj*
desolate, dejected, dispirited, sad, melancholy, depressed, unhappy, wretched, miserable, despondent, gloomy, downcast, forlorn, inconsolable, low, low-spirited, down, crushed, heavy-hearted, hopeless, heartbroken, wretched, grief-stricken, *colloq.* down in the dumps
F3 cheerful, joyful

discontent *n*
uneasiness, dissatisfaction, disquiet, disaffection, restlessness, fretfulness, unrest, impatience, vexation, regret, displeasure, misery, unhappiness, wretchedness
F3 content, satisfaction, happiness

discontented *adj*
dissatisfied, disgruntled, unhappy, restless, impatient, disaffected, miserable, wretched, exasperated, displeased, complaining, *colloq.* fed up, browned off, cheesed off
F3 contented, satisfied, happy

discontinue *v*
stop, come to a stop, end, come to an end, finish, break off, refrain, do away with, halt, drop, suspend, abolish, abandon, cancel, interrupt, *formal* cease, terminate, *colloq.* quit, scrap
F3 begin, continue, produce

discontinuity *n*
disjointedness, disconnectedness, incoherence, interruption, breach, disconnection, disruption, disunion, rupture
F3 continuity, coherence

discontinuous *adj*
intermittent, broken, disconnected, fitful, interrupted, irregular, spasmodic, periodic, punctuated
F3 continuous

discord *n*
1 CONFLICT, disagreement, dissension, clashing, disunity, incompatibility, difference, difference of opinion, dispute, contention, friction, division, opposition, strife, split, wrangling, argument, row, dissent, *formal* discordance **2** DISCORD OF SOUNDS, disharmony, jangle, jangling, jarring, harshness, *formal* dissonance, cacophony
F3 1 concord, agreement **2** harmony

discordant *adj*
1 DISAGREEING, conflicting, at odds, at variance, opposing, clashing, hostile, contradictory, differing, dissenting, incompatible, inconsistent, *formal* incongruous **2** DISSONANT, grating, jangling, jarring, harsh, strident, sharp, flat, *technical* atonal, *formal* cacophonous
F3 1 agreeing **2** harmonious

discount *n, v*
▶ *n* reduction, rebate, allowance, cut price, cut, concession, deduction, mark-down
▶ *v* **1** DISREGARD, ignore, overlook, disbelieve, pass over, gloss over **2** REDUCE, deduct, mark down, take off, *colloq.* knock off, slash
F3 1 pay attention to **2** increase

discourage *v*
1 DISHEARTEN, dampen, dispirit, depress, demoralize, dismay, unnerve, put off, daunt, deject, disappoint, cast down, put a damper on **2** DETER, dissuade, hinder, put off, restrain, prevent, hold back, talk out of, advise against
F3 1 encourage, hearten **2** encourage, persuade

discouraged *adj*
disheartened, let-down, deflated, dispirited, depressed, demoralized, dejected, dismayed, downcast, glum, pessimistic, daunted, dashed, crestfallen
F3 encouraged, heartened

discouragement *n*
1 DOWNHEARTEDNESS, despondency, pessimism, dismay, depression, dejection, despair, disappointment, hopelessness, gloom **2** DETERRENT, damper, setback, impediment, obstacle, curb, barrier, disincentive, opposition, hindrance, restraint, rebuff
F3 1 encouragement **2** incentive

discouraging *adj*
disheartening, dispiriting, depressing, disappointing, demoralizing, off-putting, unfavourable, dampening, daunting, *formal* dehortatory, dissuasive, dissuasory, inauspicious, unpropitious
F3 encouraging, heartening

discourse *n, v*
▶ *n* **1** CONVERSATION, dialogue, chat, communication, talk, discussion, *formal* converse, colloquy, confabulation **2** SPEECH, address, lecture, sermon, essay, treatise, dissertation, homily, *formal* oration, disquisition
▶ *v* converse, talk, speak, discuss, debate, confer, lecture, preach

discourteous *adj*
rude, bad-mannered, ill-mannered, impolite, boorish, uncouth, disrespectful, unpleasant, offensive, ill-bred, uncivil, unmannerly, ungracious, unceremonious, impertinent, impudent, insolent, offhand, curt, brusque, abrupt, short, gruff
F3 courteous, polite

discourtesy *n*
rudeness, bad manners, impoliteness, disrespectfulness, ill-breeding, unmannerliness, ungraciousness, incivility, impertinence, insolence, curtness, brusqueness, rebuff, slight, snub, insult, affront, *formal* indecorousness, indecorum
F3 courtesy, politeness

discover *v*
1 FIND OUT ABOUT, determine, realize, notice, recognize, perceive, see, spot, discern, establish, learn, detect, come to know, fathom (out), *formal* ascertain, *colloq.* twig, suss out, get wise to, rumble, get onto, get wind of **2** FIND, come across, uncover, unearth, dig up, disclose, reveal, stumble across/on, turn up, come to light, ferret out, light on, locate **3** ORIGINATE, invent, pioneer, devise, create, work out, compose
F3 1 conceal, cover (up) **2** miss

discoverer *n*
explorer, finder, founder, pioneer, initiator, inventor, originator, author, deviser, creator

discovery *n*
1 FINDING, determination, realization, recognition, discernment, learning, disclosure, detection, revelation, location **2** BREAKTHROUGH, find, finding(s), origination, introduction, innovation, research, invention, devising, exploration, pioneering

discredit *v, n*
▶ *v* **1** *discredit someone* dishonour, degrade, defame, damage, disgrace, bring into disrepute, give someone a bad name, belittle, slander, slur, smear, tarnish, reproach, reflect (badly) on, put in a bad light, *formal* disparage, vilify, cast aspersions on **2** *discredit a*

theory DISBELIEVE, distrust, doubt, question, mistrust, challenge, invalidate, deny, discard, reject, explode, debunk, shake your faith in, *formal* refute
🔁 **1** honour **2** believe
▶ *n* dishonour, disrepute, censure, disgrace, blame, shame, reproach, slur, stigma, smear, scandal, infamy, humiliation, *formal* aspersion, opprobrium, ignominy

discreditable *adj*
improper, dishonourable, disreputable, disgraceful, scandalous, blameworthy, shameful, infamous, degrading, *formal* reprehensible
🔁 creditable

discreet *adj*
tactful, careful, diplomatic, cautious, delicate, reserved, guarded, wary, sensible, wise, considerate, *formal* politic, prudent, judicious, circumspect
🔁 tactless, indiscreet

---

 discreet or **discrete**?

Discreet means 'prudent, cautious, not saying or doing anything that might cause trouble': *My secretary won't ask awkward questions; she's very discreet. Discrete* means 'separate, not attached to others': *a suspension of discrete particles in a liquid.*

---

discrepancy *n*
inconsistency, difference, variance, variation, dissimilarity, deviation, divergence, disagreement, conflict, contradiction, inequality, *formal* disparity, discordance, incongruity

discrete *adj*
separate, distinct, detached, disconnected, unattached, individual, discontinuous, disjoined, *formal* disjunct

discretion *n*
1 TACT, diplomacy, caution, wisdom, discernment, judgement, good sense, care, carefulness, reserve, consideration, wariness, guardedness, *formal* judiciousness, prudence, circumspection, volition, predilection **2** CHOICE, freedom, preference, will, wish, desire, inclination
🔁 **1** indiscretion

discretionary *adj*
optional, voluntary, elective, open
🔁 fixed, mandatory, compulsory, automatic

discriminate *v*
1 DISTINGUISH, differentiate, discern, tell apart, tell/recognize the differences, draw/make a distinction, segregate, separate **2** BE PREJUDICED, be biased, victimize, treat differently, be intolerant
🔁 **1** confuse, confound **2** favour

discriminating *adj*
discerning, fastidious, selective, critical, perceptive, particular, tasteful, keen, astute, shrewd, sensitive, cultivated

discrimination *n*
1 BIAS, prejudice, intolerance, unfairness, bigotry, favouritism, narrow-mindedness, inequity, segregation, racism, sexism, male chauvinism, ageism, homophobia **2** DISCERNMENT, judgement, acumen, perception, acuteness, insight, shrewdness, astuteness, penetration, subtlety, keenness, sensitivity, refinement, taste, *formal* perspicacity

discriminatory *adj*
biased, prejudiced, favouring, inequitable, prejudicial, unfair, unjust, discriminative, partial, partisan, preferential, loaded, weighted, one-sided
🔁 fair, impartial, unbiased

discursive *adj*
rambling, digressing, wandering, wordy, long-winded, meandering, wide-ranging, circuitous, diffuse, verbose, *formal* prolix
🔁 terse

discuss *v*
debate, talk about/over, confer, argue, consider, go into, weigh up, deliberate, converse, consult, exchange views on, examine, study, review, analyse, *old use* parley, *formal* discourse, confabulate, *colloq.* kick around, put your heads together

discussion *n*
debate, conference, argument, conversation, talk, talks, dialogue, exchange, consultation, forum, negotiations, deliberation, consideration, analysis, review, examination, study, scrutiny, seminar, symposium, *old use* parley, *formal* discourse, colloquium, *colloq.* powwow

disdain *n, v*
▶ *n* scorn, contempt, arrogance, haughtiness, derision, sneering, dislike, snobbishness, *formal* disparagement, deprecation, contumely
🔁 admiration, respect
▶ *v* scorn, look down on, despise, slight, disregard, snub, ignore, reject, spurn, rebuff, turn down, belittle, sneer at, undervalue, *formal* contemn, deride, disavow, *colloq.* pooh-pooh, cold shoulder
🔁 admire, respect

disdainful *adj*
scornful, contemptuous, derisive, haughty, aloof, arrogant, supercilious, sneering, slighting, pompous, superior, proud, insolent, *formal* disparaging
🔁 respectful

disease *n*
illness, sickness, ill-health, infirmity, complaint, disorder, ailment, indisposition, condition, disability, infection, contagion, epidemic, *formal* malady, affliction, *colloq.* bug, virus
🔁 health

Diseases and disorders include:
Addison's disease, AIDS, alopecia, Alzheimer's disease, anaemia, angina, anorexia nervosa, anthrax, arthritis, asbestosis, asthma, athlete's foot, autism, Bell's palsy, beriberi, Black Death, botulism, Bright's disease, bronchitis, brucellosis, bubonic plague, bulimia, cancer, cerebral palsy, chickenpox, cholera, cirrhosis, coeliac disease, common cold, consumption, croup, cystic fibrosis, diabetes, diphtheria, dropsy, dysentery, eclampsia, emphysema, encephalitis, endometriosis, enteritis, farmer's lung, *colloq.* flu, foot-and-mouth disease, gangrene, German measles, gingivitis, glandular fever, glaucoma, gonorrhoea, haemophilia, hepatitis, herpes, Hodgkin's disease, Huntington's chorea, hydrophobia, impetigo, influenza, Lassa fever, Legionnaire's Disease, leprosy, leukaemia, lockjaw, malaria, mastoiditis, measles, meningitis, motor neurone disease, multiple sclerosis (MS), mumps, muscular dystrophy, myalgic encephalomyelitis (ME), nephritis, osteomyelitis, osteoporosis, Paget's disease, Parkinson's disease, peritonitis, pneumonia, poliomyelitis, psittacosis, psoriasis, pyorrhoea, rabies, rheumatic fever, rheumatoid arthritis, rickets, ringworm, rubella, scabies, scarlet fever, schistosomiasis, schizophrenia, scurvy, septicaemia, shingles, silicosis, smallpox, syphilis, tapeworm, tetanus, thrombosis, thrush, tinnitus, tuberculosis (TB), typhoid, typhus, vertigo, whooping cough, yellow fever.

diseased *adj*
sick, ill, unhealthy, unwell, infirm, ailing, unsound, contaminated, infected, blighted
🖪 healthy, well

disembark *v*
land, arrive, dismount, leave, get off, step off, *formal* alight, debark, detrain, deplane
🖪 embark

disembodied *adj*
bodiless, ghostly, phantom, spiritual, immaterial, intangible, *formal* incorporeal, discarnate, spectral

disembowel *v*
disbowel, draw, embowel, gut, gralloch, paunch, *formal* eviscerate, exenterate

disenchanted *adj*
disillusioned, disappointed, let down, discouraged, jaundiced, cynical, soured, blasé, indifferent, *colloq.* fed up

disenchantment *n*
disillusionment, disillusion, disappointment, cynicism, revulsion

disengage *v*
disconnect, disunite, detach, loosen, free, extricate, undo, unfasten, untie, uncouple, unhitch, unhook, release, liberate, separate, loosen, disentangle, withdraw
🖪 connect, engage, unite

disengaged *adj*
detached, liberated, loose, released, free(d), disentangled, separate(d), unattached, unconnected, unhitched
🖪 connected, joined, united

disentangle *v*
1 LOOSE, release, free, extricate, disconnect, untangle, unwind, unfasten, disengage, detach, unravel, unsnarl, untwist, undo, unknot, separate, unfold, straighten **2** RESOLVE, clarify, simplify, distinguish, separate, distance
🖪 **1** entangle

disfavour *n*
1 *fall into disfavour* unpopularity, discredit, disrepute, *formal* ignominy, opprobrium **2** *look with disfavour at someone* dislike, disapproval, displeasure, distaste, dissatisfaction, disregard, low opinion, *formal* disapprobation, disesteem
🖪 **1, 2** favour

disfigure *v*
deface, blemish, mutilate, maim, scar, mar, deform, distort, damage, injure, ruin, spoil, flaw, make ugly
🖪 adorn, embellish

disfigurement *n*
blemish, defacement, defect, deformity, mutilation, scar, spot, blotch, stain, disgrace, impairment, injury, distortion, uglification
🖪 adornment

disgorge *v*
discharge, empty, eject, expel, vomit, spew, spout, belch, regurgitate, relinquish, renounce, surrender, *formal* effuse, *colloq.* throw up

disgrace *n, v*
▶ *n* shame, disrepute, disrespect, dishonour, disfavour, humiliation, loss of face, defamation, degradation, infamy, discredit, scandal, reproach, blot, slur, smear, stain, stigma, black mark, *formal* ignominy, debasement, disapprobation, opprobrium, obloquy, *colloq.* skeleton in the cupboard
🖪 honour, esteem
▶ *v* shame, bring shame on, put to shame, dishonour, abase, defame, humiliate, cause to lose face, put someone's nose out of joint, blot someone's copybook, disfavour, degrade, debase, belittle, discredit, reproach, blame, slur, sully, taint, stain, stigmatize, *formal* disparage, denigrate, *colloq.* drag through the mud
🖪 honour, respect

disgraced *adj*
discredited, shamed, dishonoured, humiliated, degraded, branded, stigmatized, *colloq.* in the doghouse
🖪 honoured, respected

disgraceful *adj*
shameful, dishonourable, disreputable, scandalous, outrageous, despicable, contemptible, blameworthy, shocking, unworthy, dreadful, terrible, awful, appalling, *formal* ignominious, culpable, reprehensible
🖪 honourable, respectable

disgruntled *adj*
discontented, dissatisfied, displeased, annoyed, exasperated, grumpy, irritated, peeved, peevish, resentful, sulky, sullen, testy, vexed, put out, petulant, *formal* malcontent, *colloq.* fed up, hacked off, cheesed off, browned off, brassed off
🖪 pleased, satisfied

disguise *n, v*
▶ *n* concealment, camouflage, cloak, cover, costume, mask, front, façade, masquerade, deception, misrepresentation, false picture, pretence, travesty, screen, veil, shroud
▶ *v* **1** CONCEAL, cover, cover up, be under cover, camouflage, mask, hide, dress up, impersonate, cloak, screen, veil, shroud, suppress, repress, *colloq.* put on a brave face **2** FALSIFY, deceive, pretend, misrepresent, gloss over, fake, fudge, *formal* dissemble, feign, *colloq.* cook the books, whitewash, put up a smokescreen
🖪 **1** reveal, expose

disguised *adj*
camouflaged, cloaked, veiled, hidden, made up, masked, incognito, undercover, unrecognizable, fake, false, *formal* covert, feigned

disgust *v, n*
▶ *v* offend, displease, nauseate, revolt, sicken, repel, outrage, put off, make your gorge rise, *colloq.* turn off, turn your stomach
🖪 delight, please
▶ *n* revulsion, repulsion, distaste, aversion, nausea, loathing, hatred, disapproval, displeasure, *formal* repugnance, abhorrence, detestation

disgusted *adj*
repelled, repulsed, revolted, sickened, offended, appalled, outraged, put off, *colloq.* up in arms
🖪 attracted, delighted

disgusting *adj*
repellent, repulsive, revolting, offensive, sickening, nauseating, nauseous, off-putting, odious, foul, unappetizing, unpalatable, distasteful, unpleasant, bad, vile, obscene, abominable, detestable, disgraceful, appalling, objectionable, nasty, shocking, outrageous, *formal* repugnant, rebarbative, *colloq.* yucky, gross
🖪 delightful, pleasant, acceptable

dish *n, v*
▶ *n* plate, bowl, platter, food, fare, recipe, speciality, delicacy, course
▶ *v* ▷ **dish out** distribute, give out, share out, hand out, hand round, pass round, dole out, allocate, mete out, inflict
▷ **dish up** serve, present, ladle, spoon, scoop, dispense, offer, present

disharmony *n*
conflict, clash, discord, friction, incompatibility, *formal* disaccord, discordance, dissonance
🖪 harmony

dishearten v
discourage, dispirit, dampen, cast down, depress, make depressed, dismay, dash, disappoint, deject, weigh down, daunt, crush, deter, put a damper on
⊞ encourage, hearten

disheartened adj
discouraged, dispirited, downcast, depressed, disappointed, dismayed, downhearted, dejected, daunted, crestfallen, crushed
⊞ encouraged, heartened

dishevelled adj
tousled, unkempt, uncombed, untidy, bedraggled, messy, in a mess, ruffled, rumpled, slovenly, disordered, formal disarranged
⊞ neat, tidy

dishonest adj
untruthful, fraudulent, deceitful, false, lying, deceptive, double-dealing, cheating, treacherous, untrustworthy, unscrupulous, unprincipled, swindling, corrupt, disreputable, dishonourable, crafty, cunning, sly, devious, irregular, formal perfidious, mendacious, duplicitous, colloq. crooked, shady, bent, shifty, fishy, iffy
⊞ honest, trustworthy, scrupulous

dishonesty n
deceit, falsehood, falsity, fraudulence, fraud, criminality, insincerity, untruthfulness, treachery, cheating, double-dealing, corruption, unscrupulousness, trickery, chicanery, sharp practice, irregularity, formal duplicity, improbity, perfidy, colloq. crookedness, shadiness, dirty trick

---

Expressions used when talking about dishonesty or dishonest behaviour:
a bad apple, a bad egg, a fast talker, a pack of lies, a slippery customer, a snake in the grass, a tall story, a tissue of lies, be economical with the truth, be up to no good, catch someone red-handed, catch someone with their hand in the till, cook the books, daylight robbery, duck and dive, fall off the back of a lorry, feed someone a line, funny business, Austr get a five-finger discount [= shoplift something], have light fingers, have the shirt off someone's back, lie through/in your teeth, lift anything that isn't nailed down, on the fiddle, on the sly, pull a fast one, pull the wool over someone's eyes, put one over on someone, rob someone blind, US sell someone a bill of goods, sell someone a pup, sharp practice, smell fishy, spin a yarn, take someone for a ride, under false pretences, under the counter, under the table.

⊞ honesty, truthfulness

dishonour v, n
▶ v 1 dishonour the family's name disgrace, shame, humiliate, debase, defile, degrade, defame, discredit, stain, sully, abuse, insult, offend, affront, demean, debauch 2 dishonour an agreement/a cheque refuse, reject, turn down
⊞ 1 honour 2 honour, accept
▶ n disgrace, abasement, humiliation, shame, degradation, disrepute, infamy, indignity, reproach, slight, slur, scandal, stigma, insult, offence, outrage, abuse, discourtesy, formal discredit, ignominy, disfavour, aspersion, debasement, opprobrium
⊞ honour

dishonourable adj
disreputable, unprincipled, unscrupulous, untrustworthy, unethical, unworthy, corrupt, discreditable, treacherous, scandalous, shameful, shameless, disgraceful, contemptible, despicable, infamous,

ignoble, formal ignominious, perfidious, colloq. shady
⊞ honourable

disillusion v
disenchant, disappoint, formal disabuse

disillusioned adj
disenchanted, undeceived, disappointed, let down, formal disabused

disincentive n
deterrent, barrier, constraint, damper, determent, discouragement, dissuasion, hindrance, impediment, obstacle, repellent, restriction, turn-off
⊞ encouragement, incentive

disinclination n
reluctance, unwillingness, hesitation, dislike, loathness, objection, opposition, resistance, alienation, averseness, aversion, formal antipathy, repugnance
⊞ inclination, enthusiasm

disinclined adj
reluctant, unwilling, resistant, indisposed, unenthusiastic, loath, opposed, hesitant, formal averse
⊞ inclined, willing, enthusiastic

disinfect v
sterilize, fumigate, sanitize, decontaminate, cleanse, purify, purge, clean
⊞ contaminate, infect

disinfectant n
antiseptic, sterilizer, sanitizer, fumigant, decontaminant, bactericide, germicide

disingenuous adj
insincere, deceitful, dishonest, devious, designing, guileful, wily, sly, crafty, artful, cunning, two-faced, shifty, insidious, uncandid
⊞ artless, frank, ingenuous, naïve, formal duplicitous, feigned

disinherit v
cut off, renounce, reject, abandon, dispossess, impoverish, repudiate, cut someone out of your will, colloq. cut off without a penny, turn your back on

disintegrate v
break up, decompose, fall apart, break apart, crumble, rot, decay, moulder, separate, shatter, smash, splinter, fall to pieces

disinterest n
disinterestedness, impartiality, neutrality, detachment, unbiasedness, dispassionateness, fairness

disinterested adj
unbiased, neutral, impartial, objective, unprejudiced, dispassionate, detached, uninvolved, open-minded, fair, equitable, just, even-handed, unselfish
⊞ biased, prejudiced, concerned

🖉 disinterested or uninterested ?
Disinterested means 'not biased, not influenced by private feelings or selfish motives': I think we need the opinions of a few disinterested observers. Uninterested means 'not interested, not showing any interest': uninterested in politics.

---

disjointed adj
1 INCOHERENT, aimless, directionless, confused, disordered, loose, unconnected, bitty, wandering, rambling, spasmodic 2 DISCONNECTED, dislocated, divided, separated, disunited, displaced, broken, fitful, split, disarticulated
⊞ 1 coherent

dislike n, v
▶ n aversion, hatred, hostility, distaste, disapproval, displeasure, resentment, animosity, antagonism, enmity, detestation, disgust, loathing, formal repug-

nance, disinclination, disapprobation, disesteem, antipathy, animus
F3 liking, *formal* predilection
▶ *v* hate, detest, object to, loathe, abominate, disapprove, regard with distaste, shun, despise, scorn, *formal* abhor, execrate, disfavour, disrelish, *colloq.* not stand the sight of, not be someone's cup of tea, be sick to the back teeth of, be no love lost between
F3 like, favour

dislocate *v*
1 *dislocate a bone* disjoint, put out of joint/place, displace, misplace, twist, strain, sprain, pull, disengage, put out, disorder, shift, disconnect, disunite, *technical* luxate, *colloq.* do in **2** *dislocate plans* DISRUPT, disturb, disorganize, confuse, throw into confusion

dislocation *n*
disruption, disturbance, disarray, disorder, disorganization
F3 order

dislodge *v*
displace, eject, remove, oust, extricate, force out, shift, move, uproot

disloyal *adj*
treacherous, faithless, false, traitorous, deceitful, double-dealing, two-faced, unfaithful, untrue, unpatriotic, *formal* apostate, perfidious
F3 loyal, faithful, trustworthy, constant

disloyalty *n*
treachery, unfaithfulness, falseness, falsity, breach of trust, betrayal, treason, double-dealing, deceit, infidelity, adultery, *formal* apostasy, inconstancy, perfidiousness, perfidy, sedition
F3 loyalty, faithfulness

dismal *adj*
dreary, gloomy, depressing, bleak, cheerless, dull, dark, dingy, drab, low-spirited, melancholy, desolate, sad, cheerless, sombre, forlorn, despondent, miserable, sorrowful, hopeless, discouraging, *formal* lugubrious, *colloq.* long-faced
F3 cheerful, bright

dismantle *v*
demolish, take apart, disassemble, strip (down), pull apart, separate, take to pieces
F3 assemble, put together

dismay *n, v*
▶ *n* alarm, distress, agitation, dread, fear, fright, horror, terror, discouragement, disappointment, *formal* consternation, apprehension, trepidation
F3 boldness, encouragement
▶ *v* alarm, daunt, frighten, unnerve, unsettle, upset, scare, put off, dispirit, cast down, distress, disconcert, disturb, shock, take aback, dishearten, discourage, disillusion, depress, horrify, worry, bother, concern, disappoint, *formal* perturb
F3 encourage, hearten

dismember *v*
disjoint, amputate, dissect, dislocate, mutilate, sever, divide, separate, break up
F3 assemble, join, unify

dismiss *v*
1 *the class was dismissed* discharge, free, let go, release, send away, remove, dissolve, drop, discord, banish **2** *dismiss employees* make redundant, give notice, suspend, give someone their papers, lay off, discharge, relegate, expel, remove, cashier, *colloq.* send packing, boot out, sack, fire, give someone their cards, give someone the sack/push/boot/elbow, show someone the door **3** *dismiss it from your mind* discount, disregard, banish, reject, repudiate, set aside, put away, put out of your mind, shelve, spurn, pour cold water on

F3 **1** retain, gather **2** appoint, hire **3** accept, think about

dismissal *n*
notice, redundancy, laying-off, discharge, removal, expulsion, marching-orders, *colloq.* papers, sacking, firing, sack, push, boot, elbow
F3 appointment, hiring

dismissive *adj*
contemptuous, disdainful, scornful, sneering, offhand, *formal* dismissory
F3 concerned, interested

dismount *v*
descend, get down, *formal* alight, disembark, light, unmount
F3 mount

disobedience *n*
unruliness, waywardness, defiance, rebellion, wilfulness, contrariness, indiscipline, mutiny, revolt, *formal* contumacity, contumacy, infraction, insubordination, recalcitrance
F3 obedience

disobedient *adj*
unruly, wayward, defiant, rebellious, wilful, contrary, disorderly, obstreperous, naughty, mischievous, *formal* contumacious, froward, insubordinate, intractable, refractory, recalcitrant, recusant
F3 obedient

disobey *v*
infringe, go against someone's wishes, overstep, step out of line, flout, disregard, defy, ignore, resist, rebel, *formal* contravene, violate, transgress
F3 obey, comply with

disobliging *adj*
unhelpful, unwilling, unco-operative, unaccommodating, awkward, disagreeable, discourteous, rude, uncivil, bloody-minded
F3 obliging, helpful

disorder *n*
1 CONFUSION, chaos, muddle, disarray, mess, untidiness, clutter, disorganization, disorderliness, jumble, *colloq.* shambles **2** DISTURBANCE, unrest, tumult, riot, breach of the peace, confusion, disruption, commotion, uproar, fracas, brawl, fight, rumpus, rout, clamour, quarrel, brouhaha, mêlée **3** ILLNESS, complaint, disease, sickness, disability, ailment, condition, *formal* affliction, malady
F3 **1** neatness, order **2** law and order, peace

disordered *adj*
1 UNTIDY, messy, confused, muddled, disorganized, jumbled, cluttered, upside-down **2** DISTURBED, deranged, confused, troubled, upset, maladjusted, unbalanced
F3 **1** organized, tidy

disorderly *adj*
1 DISORGANIZED, confused, chaotic, messy, irregular, untidy, jumbled, cluttered, in disarray, *colloq.* at sixes and sevens **2** UNRULY, undisciplined, unmanageable, uncontrollable, obstreperous, rowdy, rough, boisterous, tumultuous, turbulent, rebellious, wild, lawless, disobedient, *formal* refractory
F3 **1** neat, tidy **2** well-behaved

disorganization *n*
disarray, chaos, confusion, disorder, disruption, untidiness, muddle, *colloq.* shambles
F3 order, tidiness

disorganize *v*
disorder, disrupt, disturb, disarrange, muddle, upset, confuse, discompose, jumble, play havoc with, unsettle, break up, mess up, mix up, destroy
F3 organize

disorganized *adj*
1 CONFUSED, disordered, haphazard, jumbled, muddled, chaotic, unsorted, unsystematized, topsy-turvy, *colloq.* shambolic 2 UNMETHODICAL, unorganized, unstructured, unsystematic, careless, muddled, *colloq.* untogether
🔁 1 organized, tidy 2 organized, methodical

disorientate *v*
confuse, disorient, mislead, perplex, puzzle, upset, muddle, *colloq.* faze

disorientated *adj*
disoriented, confused, bewildered, mixed up, muddled, perplexed, puzzled, unsettled, unbalanced, lost, adrift, astray, at sea, upset

disown *v*
repudiate, renounce, disclaim, deny, cast off, disallow, reject, turn your back on, abandon, *formal* forsake, disavow, abnegate
🔁 accept, acknowledge

disparage *v*
belittle, criticize, defame, slander, decry, degrade, detract from, disdain, discredit, dishonour, malign, ridicule, scorn, run down, minimize, dismiss, underestimate, underrate, undervalue, *formal* denigrate, deprecate, deride, vilify, traduce, vilipend, derogate, calumniate, cast aspersions on
🔁 praise

disparagement *n*
belittlement, condemnation, criticism, slander, contempt, denunciation, discredit, disdain, ridicule, scorn, debasement, degradation, detraction, underestimation, *formal* derision, deprecation, aspersion, derogation, decrial, decrying, contumely, vilification
🔁 praise

disparaging *adj*
derisive, derogatory, mocking, scornful, critical, insulting, dismissive, *formal* deprecatory, *colloq.* snide
🔁 flattering, praising

disparate *adj*
contrasting, different, dissimilar, unequal, unlike, contrary, diverse, distinct, *formal* discrepant
🔁 equal, similar

disparity *n*
difference, contrast, discrepancy, gap, gulf, dissimilarity, distinction, imbalance, inequality, unevenness, unlikeness, disproportion, bias, unfairness, *formal* dissimilitude, incongruity, inequity
🔁 equality, similarity, parity

dispassionate *adj*
detached, objective, impartial, neutral, disinterested, unbiased, unprejudiced, equitable, impersonal, fair, cool, calm, calm and collected, composed, unemotional, unexcited, self-possessed, self-controlled
🔁 biased, emotional, involved

dispatch, despatch *v, n*
▶ *v* 1 SEND, mail, post, express, transmit, forward, consign, expedite, convey, remit, accelerate 2 DISPOSE OF, finish, perform, discharge, conclude, settle, perform 3 KILL, murder, execute, put to death, assassinate, slaughter, *colloq.* bump off, knock off, do in
🔁 1 receive
▶ *n* 1 COMMUNICATION, message, report, bulletin, communiqué, news, letter, article, account, item, piece 2 PROMPTNESS, speed, expedition, celerity, haste, rapidity, swiftness, *formal* alacrity, promptitude
🔁 2 slowness

dispel *v*
banish, drive away, chase away, get rid of, rid, dismiss, disperse, allay, eliminate, expel, rout, scatter, melt away, *formal* dissipate, disseminate

dispensable *adj*
unnecessary, disposable, expendable, inessential, non-essential, replaceable, superfluous, needless, gratuitous, useless
🔁 indispensable, essential

dispensation *n*
1 PERMISSION, exemption, exception, release, remission, relief, reprieve, immunity, licence 2 ISSUE, distribution, allocation, allotment, apportionment, handing out, sharing out, *formal* endowment, bestowal 3 AUTHORITY, order, system, organization, arrangement, plan, scheme, direction, administration, discharge, application, *formal* economy

dispense *v*
1 DISTRIBUTE, give out, deal out, hand out, dole out, divide out, mete out, bestow, *formal* confer 2 ADMINISTER, carry out, apply, implement, enforce, discharge, execute, operate, *formal* effectuate
▷ **dispense with** dispose of, get rid of, abolish, do away with, do without, not need, discard, omit, disregard, give up, cancel, forgo, ignore, waive, renounce, relinquish, *formal* rescind, revoke

disperse *v*
scatter, dispel, spread, distribute, diffuse, dissolve, break up, melt away, thin out, dismiss, disband, separate, go their separate ways, *formal* dissipate, disseminate
🔁 gather

dispersion *n*
spreading, scattering, distribution, circulation, dispersal, diffusion, broadcast, *technical* diaspora, *formal* dissemination, dissipation

dispirit *v*
dishearten, discourage, deject, depress, dash, dampen, damp, sadden, put a damper on, deter
🔁 encourage, hearten

dispirited *adj*
disheartened, discouraged, dejected, depressed, despondent, sad, downcast, cast down, crestfallen, gloomy, glum, morose, low, *colloq.* fed up, cheesed off, down, down in the dumps, brassed off, browned off
🔁 encouraged

displace *v*
1 DISLODGE, move, shift, misplace, disturb, dislocate, relocate 2 DEPOSE, oust, remove, force out, dislodge, replace, dismiss, discharge, supplant, eject, expel, evict, succeed, supersede, *colloq.* turf out, boot out

displacement *n*
disarrangement, dislodging, dislocation, shifting, moving, disturbance, misplacement, *technical* ectopia, ectopy, heterotaxis, heterotopia
🔁 order, arrangement

display *v, n*
▶ *v* 1 EXHIBIT, present, demonstrate, show, put on show, unveil, advertise, promote, publicize 2 BETRAY, disclose, reveal, show, expose, *formal* evince, manifest 3 SHOW OFF, flourish, parade, flaunt, boast, blazon
🔁 1 conceal 2 disguise
▶ *n* show, exhibition, exhibit, demonstration, presentation, parade, spectacle, pageant, array, revelation, evidence, disclosure, *formal* manifestation, evincement

displease *v*
offend, annoy, irritate, anger, upset, dissatisfy, infuriate, offend, provoke, exasperate, incense, irk, vex, disturb, *formal* perturb, discompose, *colloq.* put out, aggravate, bug
🔁 please, satisfy

displeased *adj*
annoyed, angry, exasperated, furious, infuriated, irritated, offended, upset, disgruntled, peeved, piqued, *colloq.* aggravated, put out
☒ pleased

displeasure *n*
offence, annoyance, disapproval, irritation, resentment, discontentment, disfavour, dissatisfaction, distaste, disgust, anger, exasperation, indignation, chagrin, ire, pique, wrath, *formal* disapprobation, perturbation
☒ pleasure

disport *v*
divert, amuse, entertain, cheer, delight, play, revel, romp, frisk, frolic, cavort, gambol, sport

disposable *adj*
disposable plastic cups throwaway, expendable, nonreturnable, biodegradable

disposal *n*
1 ARRANGEMENT, grouping, order 2 CONTROL, direction, command 3 REMOVAL, riddance, throwing-away, clearance, discarding, jettisoning, scrapping
▷ **at someone's disposal** available, obtainable, at/to hand, ready, *colloq.* on tap

dispose *v*
1 *dispose of a problem* DEAL WITH, decide, settle, determine, finish, attend to, see to, handle, tackle, look after, take care of, sort out 2 *dispose of old books* GET RID OF, discard, throw away/out, shed, scrap, destroy, jettison, clear out, *colloq.* dump, get shot of, chuck out 3 *dispose troops* arrange, align, group, place, position, put, situate, order, organize, line up 4 *dispose of a person* kill, murder, destroy, do away with, put to death, *colloq.* do in, bump off
☒ 2 keep

disposed *adj*
liable, inclined, prone, likely, apt, minded, subject, ready, prepared, willing, eager, *formal* predisposed
☒ *formal* disinclined

disposition *n*
1 *a friendly disposition; a disposition to obey* character, nature, temperament, inclination, make-up, bent, leaning, constitution, habit, mood, temper, spirit, humour, tendency, proneness, *formal* predisposition, propensity, predilection, proclivity, *colloq.* what makes someone tick 2 *the disposition of troops* arrangement, alignment, placing, positioning, order, line-up, pattern, grouping, sequence, system 3 *the disposition of property* distribution, giving-over, allocation, disposal, transfer, conveyance

dispossess *v*
deprive, take away, divest, strip, rob, eject, evict, expel, oust, dislodge
☒ give, provide

disproportion *n*
inequality, unevenness, imbalance, lopsidedness, discrepancy, inadequacy, insufficiency, *formal* asymmetry, disparity, incommensurateness
☒ balance, equality

disproportionate *adj*
unequal, uneven, unbalanced, excessive, unreasonable, out of proportion, *formal* incommensurate
☒ balanced, *formal* commensurate

disprove *v*
rebut, discredit, invalidate, contradict, prove false, deny, expose, give the lie to, *formal* refute, negate, controvert, confute, *colloq.* debunk
☒ confirm, prove

disputable *adj*
arguable, debatable, questionable, controversial, doubtful, dubious, uncertain, moot, *formal* litigious
☒ indisputable, unquestionable

disputation *n*
debate, argument, argumentation, controversy, dispute, deliberation, polemics, *technical* quodlibet, *formal* dissension

disputatious *adj*
argumentative, contentious, polemical, quarrelsome, cantankerous, captious, *formal* litigious, pugnacious

dispute *v, n*
▶ *v* argue, debate, question, call into question, contend, challenge, contest, discuss, doubt, contest, contradict, deny, quarrel, clash, wrangle, bicker, squabble
☒ agree
▶ *n* argument, debate, disagreement, controversy, conflict, contention, quarrel, row, wrangle, feud, strife, squabble, *formal* altercation
☒ agreement, settlement

disqualified *adj*
eliminated, ineligible, struck off, *formal* debarred, precluded, disentitled
☒ accepted, eligible, qualified

disqualify *v*
1 *disqualified from the competition* rule out, declare ineligible, eliminate, prohibit, suspend, strike off, *formal* preclude, disentitle, debar 2 INCAPACITATE, disable, invalidate, immobilize, handicap, *formal* impair, debilitate
☒ 1 qualify, accept

disquiet *n, v*
▶ *n* anxiety, worry, concern, uneasiness, nervousness, restlessness, alarm, distress, agitation, fretfulness, fear, foreboding, anguish, dread, disturbance, upset, trouble, *formal* disquietude, inquietude, perturbation
☒ calm, reassurance
▶ *v* worry, make anxious, unsettle, make uneasy, unnerve, distress, agitate, annoy, bother, trouble, upset, concern, disturb, fret, shake, ruffle, harass, pester, plague, vex, *formal* discompose, incommode, perturb, *colloq.* hassle
☒ calm, reassure

disquisition *n*
explanation, dissertation, paper, essay, thesis, treatise, monograph, sermon, *formal* discourse, exposition

disregard *v, n*
▶ *v* 1 IGNORE, overlook, discount, neglect, take no notice of, pass over, gloss over, disobey, flout, make light of, set aside, brush aside, *colloq.* turn a blind eye to, laugh off 2 SLIGHT, snub, shun, insult, despise, disdain, *formal* disparage, denigrate, *colloq.* cold shoulder
☒ 1 heed, pay attention to, listen to 2 respect
▶ *n* neglect, negligence, carelessness, inattention, oversight, indifference, disrespect, contempt, disdain, *formal* denigration, *colloq.* brush-off
☒ attention, heed, notice

disrepair *n*
dilapidation, deterioration, decay, collapse, ruin, rack and ruin, shabbiness
☒ good repair

disreputable *adj*
1 DISGRACEFUL, discreditable, dubious, suspicious, dishonourable, unprincipled, unrespectable, notorious, infamous, scandalous, outrageous, shameful, unworthy, base, contemptible, corrupt, low, mean, shocking, *formal* ignominious, opprobrious, *colloq.* shady, shifty, dodgy 2 SCRUFFY, shabby, seedy, unkempt, slovenly, untidy, dishevelled
☒ 1 honourable, respectable 2 smart

disrepute n
disgrace, dishonour, shame, disfavour, discredit, disreputation, infamy, *formal* disesteem, ignominy, obloquy
▆ honour, *formal* esteem

disrespect n
impoliteness, disregard, discourtesy, incivility, irreverence, rudeness, dishonour, contempt, scorn, insolence, impertinence, impudence, cheek, *formal* misesteem
▆ respect, politeness, civility, consideration

disrespectful adj
rude, discourteous, inconsiderate, impertinent, impolite, impudent, insolent, uncivil, unmannerly, cheeky, insulting, irreverent, contemptuous, *US colloq.* sassy
▆ polite, respectful, civil, considerate

disrobe v
undress, unclothe, take off, bare, uncover, strip, remove, shed, denude, *formal* divest, disapparel
▆ cover, dress

disrupt v
disturb, disorganize, confuse, cause confusion in, interfere with, interrupt, butt in, break up, unsettle, intrude, upset, throw into disorder/disarray, disarrange, hamper, impede, sabotage, *colloq.* throw a spanner in the works, put a spoke in someone's wheel

disruption n
disorder, confusion, disorganization, turmoil, disarray, disorderliness, disturbance, interference, interruption, stoppage, upheaval, upset

disruptive adj
troublesome, unruly, undisciplined, obstreperous, disorderly, boisterous, noisy, turbulent, distracting, disturbing, unsettling, upsetting
▆ well-behaved, manageable

dissatisfaction n
discontent, displeasure, dislike, discomfort, disappointment, disapproval, frustration, restlessness, anger, annoyance, irritation, exasperation, unhappiness, regret, resentment, vexation, chagrin, *formal* disapprobation
▆ satisfaction

dissatisfied adj
discontented, displeased, disgruntled, disappointed, disillusioned, disenchanted, frustrated, angry, annoyed, irritated, exasperated, unfulfilled, unhappy, unsatisfied, *colloq.* fed up, cheesed off, brassed off, browned off
▆ fulfilled, satisfied

dissatisfy v
displease, disappoint, discontent, disgruntle, anger, annoy, irritate, exasperate, frustrate, put out, vex, give cause for complaint

dissect v
1 DISMEMBER, cut up, vivisect, *formal* anatomize **2** ANALYSE, break down, investigate, scrutinize, examine, inspect, study, probe, explore, pore over

dissection n
1 dismemberment, cutting up, vivisection, *technical* autopsy, necropsy **2** analysis, breakdown, investigation, scrutiny, examination, inspection, study, probe, exploration

dissemble v
feign, pretend, hide, conceal, disguise, simulate, camouflage, cloak, mask, counterfeit, fake, falsify, sham, play possum, *formal* affect, dissimulate, *colloq.* cover up
▆ admit

dissembler n
pretender, deceiver, hypocrite, impostor, trickster, charlatan, fake, feigner, fraud, whited sepulchre, *formal* dissimulator, *colloq.* con man

disseminate v
circulate, distribute, spread, broadcast, scatter, sow, diffuse, disperse, publish, publicize, propagate, proclaim, *formal* promulgate

dissemination n
circulation, distribution, spread, broadcasting, publishing, publication, diffusion, dispersion, propagation, *formal* promulgation

dissension n
disagreement, discord, dissent, dispute, contention, argument, conflict, strife, friction, quarrel, variance, difference of opinion
▆ agreement

dissent v, n
▸ v disagree, differ, protest, object, dispute, refuse, quibble
▆ assent
▸ n disagreement, difference, dissension, discord, friction, dispute, difference of opinion, controversy, resistance, opposition, objection, protest
▆ agreement, conformity

dissenter n
dissident, objector, protestant, protester, demonstrator, nonconformist, disputant, rebel, recusant, heretic, revolutionary, sectary, schismatic

dissentient adj
disagreeing, dissenting, dissident, opposing, protesting, conflicting, differing, rebellious, heretical, revolutionary, recusant
▆ arguing

dissertation n
thesis, treatise, critique, essay, monograph, paper, *technical* prolegomena, propaedeutic, *formal* discourse, disquisition, exposition

disservice n
disfavour, injury, wrong, bad turn, harm, hurt, unkindness, injustice, sharp practice, *colloq.* dirty trick, con trick, kick in the teeth
▆ favour

dissidence n
disagreement, discordance, dispute, dissent, feud, recusancy, rupture, schism, variance
▆ agreement, peace

dissident adj, n
▸ adj disagreeing, differing, discordant, nonconformist, opposing, protesting, conflicting, rebellious, heretical, revolutionary, *formal* dissenting, heterodox
▆ acquiescent, orthodox
▸ n dissenter, protester, objector, nonconformist, rebel, agitator, revolutionary, heretic, schismatic, recusant
▆ assenter

dissimilar adj
unlike, different, divergent, deviating, unrelated, contrasting, incompatible, mismatched, distinct, diverse, varying, various, *formal* disparate, heterogeneous
▆ similar, like, alike

dissimilarity n
unlikeness, difference, discrepancy, divergence, distinction, unrelatedness, contrast, incomparability, diversity, variety, incompatibility, *formal* disparity, dissimilitude, heterogeneity
▆ compatibility, similarity

dissimulate v
feign, pretend, hide, lie, fake, conceal, mask, cloak, disguise, camouflage, *formal* dissemble, affect, *colloq.* cover up

dissipate v

1 *he dissipated his inheritance* spend, waste, exhaust, squander, use up, expend, consume, lavish, drain, deplete, fritter away, burn up, run/get through **2** *the clouds dissipated* disperse, drive away, scatter, break up, vanish, disappear, dispel, diffuse, evaporate, dissolve, melt away

F3 **1** accumulate **2** appear, gather

dissipated *adj*

dissolute, debauched, abandoned, self-indulgent, rakish, wasted, corrupt, wild, depraved, degenerate, *formal* intemperate, profligate, licentious

F3 conserved, virtuous, upright

dissipation *n*

1 *the dissipation of all fears* dispersal, diffusion, evaporation, disappearance, squandering, expenditure, consumption, depletion **2** DEBAUCHERY, extravagance, licence, immorality, abandonment, self-indulgence, excess, prodigality, corruption, depravity, *formal* intemperance, licentiousness

F3 **1** conservation **2** virtue

dissociate v

1 *dissociate one thing from another* separate, detach, break off/up, disunite, disassociate, disengage, disconnect, cut off, sever, disband, set apart, divorce, disrupt, isolate, segregate **2** *dissociate yourself from something* distance, disconnect, cut off, withdraw, separate, *formal* secede, *colloq.* quit

F3 associate, join

dissociation *n*

separation, detachment, break, division, divorce, disconnection, disengagement, dissevering, distancing, segregation, isolation, setting apart, cutting-off, severance, severing, split, *formal* disunion

F3 association, union

dissolute *adj*

dissipated, debauched, degenerate, depraved, wanton, self-indulgent, abandoned, corrupt, immoral, lewd, rakish, unrestrained, wild, *formal* intemperate, profligate, licentious

F3 restrained, virtuous

dissolution *n*

1 *the dissolution of an organization/a marriage* ending, break-up, conclusion, suspension, divorce, annulment, *formal* termination, discontinuation **2** *the dissolution of the monarchy* break-up, destruction, overthrow **3** *dissolution of family life* break-up, disintegration, collapse, decomposition, separation, division, disposal, evaporation, disappearance

dissolve v

1 *sugar dissolves in water* liquefy, melt, go into solution, *technical* deliquesce, solvate **2** *the marriage/partnership dissolved* end, bring to an end, finish, break up, disintegrate, wind up, dismiss, disband, separate, disperse, *formal* terminate, discontinue **3** *my fears gradually dissolved* disappear, vanish, evaporate, disperse, dwindle, melt away, crumble, *formal* dissipate, evanesce **4** *dissolve into tears* collapse, be overcome with, lose control, break, burst, begin, start

dissonance *n*

discord, clash, disagreement, dissension, difference, incompatibility, inconsistency, variance, disharmony, discordance, discrepancy, harshness, jangle, stridency, grating, jarring, cacophony, *formal* disparity, incongruity

F3 harmony, agreement

dissonant *adj*

discordant, clashing, jarring, disagreeing, jangling, grating, differing, harsh, incompatible, irregular, inconsistent, irreconcilable, raucous, strident, cacophonous, unmusical, tuneless, unmelodious, *formal* anomalous, incongruous

F3 compatible, harmonious

dissuade v

deter, discourage, put off, stop, discourage, persuade not to, talk out of, disincline

F3 persuade

dissuasion *n*

discouragement, deterrence, deterring, caution, *formal* expostulation, remonstrance, remonstration

F3 persuasion

distance *n, v*

▶ *n* **1** SPACE, interval, gap, separation, extent, stretch, range, reach, span, length, width, breadth, depth, height **2** REMOTENESS, farness, inaccessibility **3** ALOOFNESS, reserve, coolness, coldness, remoteness, formality, unfriendliness, stiffness

F3 **1** closeness **2** accessibility **3** approachability, closeness, warmth

▶ *v* separate, cut off, dissociate, remove, withdraw, break, *formal* secede

distant *adj*

1 FAR, faraway, far-flung, far-off, out-of-the-way, remote, outlying, isolated, abroad, dispersed, *colloq.* back of beyond **2** *a distant relative* not close, slight, remote **3** ALOOF, cool, reserved, formal, cold, unfriendly, restrained, detached, stiff, unapproachable, uncommunicative, unresponsive, antisocial, withdrawn, *colloq.* stand-offish

F3 **1** close, nearby **2** close **3** approachable, warm

distaste *n*

dislike, aversion, disgust, revulsion, horror, loathing, disfavour, displeasure, *formal* repugnance, abhorrence, antipathy

F3 liking

distasteful *adj*

disagreeable, offensive, displeasing, unpleasant, disgusting, revolting, objectionable, repellent, repulsive, obnoxious, undesirable, uninviting, unsavoury, detestable, loathsome, abhorrent, *formal* repugnant

F3 pleasing

distend v

bloat, swell, dilate, enlarge, expand, fill out, inflate, bulge, balloon, puff, stretch, widen, *technical* intumesce

F3 deflate

distended *adj*

bloated, swollen, dilated, enlarged, expanded, inflated, puffed-out, puffy, stretched, astrut, *technical* emphysematous, tumescent, varicose

F3 deflated

distension *n*

swelling, bloating, enlargement, expansion, extension, spread, dilation, *technical* emphysema, intumescence, tumescence

distil v

vaporize, evaporate, condense, extract, press out, draw out, derive, express, drip, trickle, leak, flow, purify, refine, *technical* rectify, sublimate

distillation *n*

extract, extraction, evaporation, condensation, essence, spirit

distinct *adj*

1 CLEAR, plain, evident, obvious, clear-cut, apparent, marked, defined, well-defined, sharp, definite, noticeable, recognizable, unambiguous, unmistakable, *formal* manifest **2** SEPARATE, different, detached, individual, dissimilar, unconnected, unassociated, *formal* discrete, disparate

F3 **1** indistinct, vague

distinct or **distinctive** ?

Distinct means 'definite', 'clearly or easily seen, heard, smelt, etc': *a distinct smell of alcohol; a distinct Scottishness in her pronunciation. Distinctive* means 'characteristic', 'distinguishing one person or thing from others': *She has a very distinctive walk; the distinctive call of a barn owl.*

distinction *n*
1 DIFFERENTIATION, discrimination, discernment, separation, difference, dissimilarity, division, contrast, *formal* contradistinction, dissimilitude **2** EXCELLENCE, renown, fame, celebrity, prominence, eminence, importance, significance, reputation, greatness, honour, prestige, repute, superiority, worth, merit, credit, quality, *formal* consequence **3** CHARACTERISTIC, peculiarity, individuality, feature, quality, mark
F₃ 2 unimportance, obscurity

distinctive *adj*
characteristic, distinguishing, individual, peculiar, different, typical, unique, particular, special, original, noteworthy, extraordinary, idiosyncratic, *formal* singular
F₃ ordinary, common

distinctly *adv*
clearly, plainly, obviously, evidently, definitely, markedly, noticeably, unmistakably, unambiguously, *formal* manifestly

distinguish *v*
1 DIFFERENTIATE, tell apart, set apart, discriminate, determine, tell the difference between, single out, mark off, characterize, particularize, typify, mark, stamp, categorize, characterize, classify **2** DISCERN, perceive, identify, ascertain, make out, recognize, see, detect, notice, pick out, discriminate, *formal* descry **3** *distinguish yourself academically* excel, do well, acquit yourself well, bring fame to, bring honour to, bring acclaim to, glorify, dignify

distinguishable *adj*
recognizable, discernible, clear, plain, plainly seen, evident, noticeable, conspicuous, obvious, perceptible, appreciable, observable, *formal* manifest
F₃ indistinguishable

distinguished *adj*
famous, eminent, celebrated, well-known, acclaimed, illustrious, prominent, notable, noted, renowned, famed, honoured, acclaimed, outstanding, striking, marked, extraordinary, noble, aristocratic, refined, conspicuous, *formal* esteemed
F₃ insignificant, obscure, unimpressive

distinguishing *adj*
differentiating, different, distinctive, individual, individualistic, marked, peculiar, typical, characteristic, unique, discriminative, discriminatory, *formal* singular, diacritical

distort *v*
1 DEFORM, contort, bend, misshape, disfigure, twist, warp, buckle **2** FALSIFY, misrepresent, pervert, slant, twist, bias, colour, garble, tamper with, *colloq.* cook the books

distorted *adj*
1 DEFORMED, bent, misshapen, out of shape, disfigured, twisted, warped, awry, skew, skewed, wry **2** FALSE, biased, perverted, misrepresented
F₃ 1 straight **2** accurate

distortion *n*
1 DEFORMITY, twist, bend, buckle, contortion, crookedness, skew, slant, warp **2** MISREPRESENTATION, falsification, perversion, bias, twisting, colouring, garbling

distract *v*
1 DIVERT, sidetrack, deflect, draw away, turn aside/away, put off **2** AMUSE, occupy, divert, entertain, engross **3** CONFUSE, disconcert, bewilder, confound, disturb, perplex, puzzle, fluster, discompose

distracted *adj*
1 DISTRAUGHT, agitated, anxious, overwrought, upset, distressed, grief-stricken, beside yourself, worked up, frantic, hysterical, raving, mad, wild, crazy **2** *their attention was distracted* abstracted, wandering, absent-minded, preoccupied, inattentive, dreaming, *colloq.* miles away, not with it
F₃ 1 calm, untroubled **2** attentive

distracting *adj*
disturbing, disconcerting, confusing, bewildering, annoying, irritating, *formal* perturbing, *colloq.* off-putting

distraction *n*
1 DISTURBANCE, interruption, diversion, interference, confusion, *formal* derangement **2** DIVERSION, amusement, entertainment, game, sport, hobby, pastime, recreation, divertissement
▷ **drive someone to distraction** upset, annoy, anger, madden, exasperate, *colloq.* drive crazy, get someone's blood up, make someone's blood boil

distraught *adj*
agitated, anxious, overwrought, upset, distressed, distracted, beside yourself, worked up, frantic, hysterical, raving, mad, wild, crazy, *colloq.* in a state, het up
F₃ calm, untroubled

distress *n, v*
▶ *n* **1** ANGUISH, grief, misery, sorrow, heartache, suffering, discomfort, torment, wretchedness, sadness, worry, anxiety, unease, desolation, pain, agony, torture, *formal* woe, tribulation, affliction, perturbation **2** ADVERSITY, hardship, poverty, need, destitution, calamity, misfortune, trouble, difficulties, trial, *formal* privation, indigence, penury
F₃ 1 content **2** comfort, ease
▶ *v* upset, cause suffering to, grieve, disturb, trouble, sadden, make miserable, worry, make anxious, pain, vex, torment, harass, harrow, hurt, agonize, break someone's heart, *formal* afflict, perturb, *colloq.* cut up
F₃ comfort

distribute *v*
1 DISPENSE, allocate, give out, hand out, pass round, dole out, dish out, share, deal (out), divide, measure out, mete out, allot, issue, *formal* apportion **2** DELIVER, supply, hand out, spread, issue, circulate, pass round **3** SCATTER, diffuse, disperse, *formal* disseminate
F₃ 2 collect

distribution *n*
1 DELIVERY, supply, transport, transportation, dealing, handling, conveyance **2** ALLOCATION, giving-out, handing-out, division, sharing, *formal* apportionment **3** CIRCULATION, spreading, scattering, dispersal, *formal* dissemination **4** ARRANGEMENT, grouping, classification, organization, placement, position
F₃ 1 collection

district *n*
region, area, quarter, neighbourhood, locality, sector, precinct, zone, block, parish, place, locale, community, vicinity, ward, constituency, domain, territory

distrust *v, n*
▶ *v* mistrust, doubt, have doubts about, disbelieve, suspect, be suspicious of, question, be sceptical about, discredit
F₃ trust

▶ *n* mistrust, doubt, doubtfulness, disbelief, suspicion, misgiving, wariness, scepticism, question, questioning, qualm, chariness, discredit
F₃ trust, confidence, faith

distrustful *adj*
mistrustful, distrusting, doubtful, doubting, dubious, disbelieving, suspicious, wary, sceptical, untrustful, untrusting, chary, uneasy, cynical
F₃ trustful, unsuspecting

disturb *v*
1 DISRUPT, interrupt, put off, distract, bother, butt in on, break someone's train of thought, pester **2** AGITATE, trouble, unsettle, upset, distress, worry, make anxious, fluster, annoy, bother, concern, disconcert, dismay, discompose, stir, *formal* discomfit, perturb **3** DISARRANGE, disorder, confuse, upset, disorganize, muddle, unsettle, throw into confusion
F₃ **2** reassure **3** order

disturbance *n*
1 DISRUPTION, agitation, interference, interruption, distraction, intrusion, upheaval, upset, confusion, disorder, muddle, annoyance, bother, trouble, hindrance **2** DISORDER, uproar, commotion, tumult, turmoil, fracas, fray, brawl, riot, row, rumpus, hullabaloo, racket **3** *emotional disturbance* illness, sickness, disorder, complaint, neurosis
F₃ **1** peace **2** order

disturbed *adj*
1 *disturbed by the news* anxious, apprehensive, bothered, concerned, troubled, worried, upset, confused, discomposed, uneasy, flustered **2** *emotionally disturbed* maladjusted, neurotic, unbalanced, psychotic, mentally ill, paranoid, upset, *colloq.* screwed-up, hung-up
F₃ **1** calm

disturbing *adj*
alarming, distressing, troubling, unsettling, upsetting, worrying, disconcerting, bewildering, confusing, dismaying, disquieting, discouraging, agitating, frightening, startling, threatening, *formal* disturbant, disturbative, perturbing
F₃ reassuring, comforting

disunited *adj*
divided, split, separated, disrupted, alienated, *formal* estranged
F₃ unify

disunity *n*
disagreement, conflict, discord, division, dissension, dissent, rupture, schism, split, strife, alienation, breach, *formal* estrangement, discordance
F₃ unity

disuse *n*
neglect, abandonment, decay, *formal* desuetude, discontinuance
F₃ use

disused *adj*
unused, neglected, abandoned, decayed, *formal* discontinued
F₃ used

ditch *n, v*
▶ *n* trench, dyke, channel, canal, gully, gutter, furrow, moat, drain, level, watercourse
▶ *v* abandon, get rid of, throw away/out, discard, dispose of, drop, jettison, scrap, *colloq.* dump, chuck

dither *v, n*
▶ *v* hesitate, waver, vacillate, hang back, delay, take your time, *colloq.* be in two minds, shilly-shally, dilly-dally
▶ *n* panic, indecision, bother, flutter, fluster, *colloq.* flap, pother, stew, tizzy
F₃ decision

divan *n*
couch, settee, sofa, chaise-longue, day bed, lounge, lounger, ottoman, chesterfield

dive *v, n*
▶ *v* **1** *dive into water* plunge, jump, plummet, dip, submerge, leap, nose-dive, fall, drop, swoop, descend, go down/under, pitch **2** *dive for cover* move quickly, leap, dash, rush, hurry, fly, tear, bolt
▶ *n* **1** PLUNGE, lunge, header, jump, leap, plummet, nose-dive, swoop, dash, spring, fall, drop **2** *make a dive for the door* leap, dash, rush, dart **3** BAR, club, pub, saloon, nightclub, *colloq.* dump, joint, hole

diverge *v*
1 DIVIDE, branch (off), fork, part, separate, spread (out), split, subdivide, radiate, *formal* bifurcate **2** DIFFER, vary, disagree, dissent, conflict, clash, contradict, be at variance **3** DEVIATE, digress, stray, wander, depart, drift, *formal* divagate
F₃ **1** converge **2** agree

divergence *n*
difference, disagreement, variation, clash, conflict, deviation, separation, parting, deflection, departure, digression, branching-out, *formal* disparity
F₃ agreement

divergent *adj*
different, differing, disagreeing, conflicting, dissimilar, variant, varying, separate, diverging, diverse, deviating, tangential
F₃ similar

divers *adj*
varying, varied, various, different, many, numerous, several, some, miscellaneous, sundry, *formal* manifold, multifarious

diverse *adj*
various, varied, varying, sundry, all means of, different, differing, assorted, mixed, unlike, dissimilar, contrasting, miscellaneous, separate, several, distinct, *formal* discrete, heterogeneous
F₃ similar, identical

diversify *v*
vary, change, expand, extend, branch out, bring variety to, spread out, modify, alter, mix, assort, *formal* variegate

diversion *n*
1 DEVIATION, detour, alternative route, redirection, rerouteing, switching **2** AMUSEMENT, entertainment, distraction, hobby, pastime, recreation, relaxation, play, game, sport, fun, divertissement **3** ALTERATION, change, redirection, deviation

diversionary *adj*
distracting, deflecting, divertive

diversity *n*
variety, dissimilarity, difference, diversification, variance, assortment, miscellany, range, mixture, medley, *formal* variegation, dissimilitude, pluralism, heterogeneity
F₃ similarity, likeness

divert *v*
1 DEFLECT, redirect, reroute, switch, sidetrack, avert, distract, deflect, draw/turn away **2** AMUSE, entertain, occupy, distract, delight, occupy, interest, absorb, engross, intrigue

diverting *adj*
enjoyable, entertaining, amusing, fun, pleasant, pleasurable, funny, humorous, witty
F₃ irritating

divest *v*
divest of power/clothes deprive, strip, remove, dispossess, undress, unclothe, disrobe, *old use* doff, *formal* denude, despoil
F₃ clothe

divide *v*
1 SPLIT, separate, sever, part, cut (up), break up/down, detach, bisect, disconnect, segregate, diverge, branch, fork **2** DISTRIBUTE, share, allocate, deal out, allot, dispense, hand out, dole out, measure out, *formal* apportion **3** DISUNITE, separate, alienate, split (up), break up, come between, set someone against another, *formal* estrange **4** CLASSIFY, group, sort, grade, arrange, order, rank, categorize, segregate
F3 1 join **2** collect **3** unite
▷ **divide up** share (out), allocate, allot, dole out, measure out, parcel out, *formal* apportion

dividend *n*
1 *shareholders' dividends* share, bonus, portion, surplus, gain, *colloq.* cut, divvy, whack **2** BENEFIT, bonus, extra, gain, plus

divination *n*
clairvoyance, divining, foretelling, prophecy, prediction, fortune-telling, dukkeripen, second sight, soothsaying, augury, necromancy, presage, *Scot.* taghairm, *formal* hariolation, prognostication, rhabdomancy

divine *adj, n, v*
▶ *adj* **1** GODLIKE, godly, superhuman, supernatural, mystical, celestial, heavenly, angelic, seraphic, saintly, spiritual **2** HOLY, sacred, sanctified, consecrated, spiritual, transcendent, exalted, glorious, religious, supreme **3** DELIGHTFUL, beautiful, charming, lovely, wonderful, excellent, glorious, heavenly
F3 1 human **2** mundane
▶ *n* churchman, churchwoman, clergyman, clergywoman, minister, priest, pastor, parson, reverend, cleric, ecclesiastic, prelate
▶ *v* guess, deduce, suppose, infer, surmise, suspect, understand, foretell, apprehend, perceive, *formal* conjecture, intuit, prognosticate

diviner *n*
astrologer, augur, oracle, prophet, seer, soothsayer, haruspex, sibyl, water-finder, dowser

divinity *n*
1 *worship a divinity; claims to divinity* god, goddess, deity, divineness, godliness, holiness, sanctity, godhead, spirit **2** THEOLOGY, religious studies, religious education, religious knowledge, religion

division *n*
1 SEPARATION, dividing, detaching, parting, cutting (up), disunion, severance **2** BREACH, rupture, split, schism, rift, disunion, disagreement, feud, discord, conflict, alienation, difference of opinion, *formal* estrangement **3** DISTRIBUTION, sharing (out), allotment, allocation, *formal* apportionment **4** SECTION, group, sector, segment, part, department, category, class, compartment, branch, arm **5** BOUNDARY, divide, dividing-line, frontier, border, partition, demarcation line
F3 1 union **2** unity **3** collection **4** whole

divisive *adj*
alienating, damaging, injurious, disruptive, troublesome, troublemaking, inharmonious, *formal* discordant, estranging
F3 harmonious, unifying

divorce *n, v*
▶ *n* dissolution, annulment, break-up, split-up, split, rupture, separation, breach, division, partition, disunion, severance
▶ *v* separate, part, annul, break up, split up, sever, dissolve, divide, detach, dissociate, disconnect, disunite, isolate, *colloq.* bust up
F3 marry, unite

divulge *v*
reveal, disclose, make known, tell, communicate,

broadcast, publish, proclaim, confess, declare, let slip, betray, expose, uncover, *formal* impart, promulgate, *colloq.* leak, break the news, let the cat out of the bag, spill the beans, blow the gaff, put your cards on the table

dizzy *adj*
1 GIDDY, faint, light-headed, wobbly, shaky, reeling, off-balance, weak at the knees, with your head swimming, *formal* vertiginous, *colloq.* woozy **2** CONFUSED, bewildered, dazed, muddled **3** *a dizzy blonde* silly, irresponsible, foolish, feather-brained, scatterbrained, *US colloq.* ditsy

do *v, n*
▶ *v* **1** PERFORM, carry out, execute, accomplish, achieve, fulfil, implement, complete, discharge, undertake, work, put on, present, end, finish, put into practice, *formal* conclude, effectuate **2** BEHAVE, act, conduct yourself, *formal* comport yourself **3** *do the tea* prepare, get ready, fix, organize, arrange, deal with, look after, take care of, manage, be in charge of, be responsible for, produce, make, create, cause, proceed **4** *Will this do?* be enough, be adequate, be sufficient, be satisfactory, fit the bill, satisfy, serve, *formal* suffice **5** *What do you do?* have a job, work as, be employed as, earn a living as **6** *do something about a problem* try to solve, deal with, work out, find the answer to, sort out, figure out, tackle, *formal* resolve, *colloq.* crack, get to the bottom of **7** *do French at school* study, learn, master, read, work at/on, take, major in **8** *do deliveries for you* provide, supply, furnish, offer **9** *do 150 kph* travel at, go at, reach, achieve **10** *do well/badly; How are you doing?* get on, get along, come on, come along, fare, progress, develop, manage, make a good/bad job of **11** CHEAT, defraud, swindle, trick, deceive, dupe, hoodwink, *colloq.* con, rip off, have, fleece, take for a ride
▷ **do away with 1** GET RID OF, discard, dispose of, abolish, remove, eliminate, *formal* discontinue, nullify, annul **2** KILL, murder, slaughter, slay, exterminate, assassinate, *colloq.* do in, knock off, bump off
▷ **do down** criticze, condemn, blame, censure, find fault with
▷ **do in** kill, murder, slaughter, slay, exterminate, assassinate, *colloq.* knock off, bump off
▷ **do out of** prevent from having, deprive of, cheat out of, trick out of, swindle out of, *colloq.* con out of, diddle out of, fleece
▷ **do up 1** FASTEN, tie, lace, button, zip up, pack **2** RENOVATE, redecorate, decorate, restore, modernize, repair, recondition
▷ **do without** go without, manage without, give up, dispense with, deny yourself, refrain, *formal* forgo, abstain from, relinquish
▶ *n* function, affair, event, gathering, party, celebration, soirée, occasion, *colloq.* bash, knees-up, rave-up
▷ **dos and don'ts** rules, regulations, code, instructions, standards, customs, etiquette

docile *adj*
tractable, co-operative, manageable, submissive, obedient, amenable, controllable, controlled, obliging, yielding, *formal* compliant
F3 truculent, unco-operative

docility *n*
amenability, tractability, manageability, submissiveness, obedience, biddableness, meekness, pliability, pliancy, *formal* complaisance, compliance, ductility
F3 truculence, unco-operativeness

dock[1] *n, v*
▶ *n* *the ship is in dock* harbour, wharf, quay, boatyard, pier, waterfront, jetty, marina
▶ *v* anchor, moor, drop anchor, land, berth, put in, tie up

dock² *v*
1 *dock an animal's tail* crop, clip, cut, shorten, curtail, truncate **2** *dock someone's pay* deduct, reduce, lessen, withhold, decrease, subtract, remove, diminish

docket *n, v*
▶ *n* certificate, ticket, label, receipt, tab, tag, bill, chit, chitty, counterfoil, tally, documentation, paperwork
▶ *v* label, mark, tab, tag, ticket, register, catalogue, file, index

doctor *n, v*
▶ *n* physician, medical officer, consultant, clinician, *colloq.* medic

Types of medical doctor include:
general practitioner, GP, family doctor, family practitioner, locum, hospital doctor, houseman, intern, resident, registrar, consultant, medical officer (MO), *colloq.* doc, *colloq.* bones, *colloq.* quack, dentist, veterinary surgeon, *colloq.* vet. *See also* MEDICAL SPECIALISTS.

▶ *v* **1** ALTER, tamper with, interfere with, falsify, misrepresent, pervert, adulterate, change, disguise, dilute **2** CONTAMINATE, drug, weaken, lace, add drugs/poison to, adulterate, *colloq.* spike **3** STERILIZE, castrate, spay, neuter

doctrinaire *adj*
dogmatic, inflexible, rigid, insistent, opinionated, pedantic, biased, fanatical
🖅 flexible

doctrine *n*
dogma, creed, belief, tenet, principle, teaching, precept, conviction, opinion, canon, credo

document *n, v*
▶ *n* paper, certificate, deed, record, proof, evidence, report, form, charter, *technical* affidavit, *formal* instrument
▶ *v* **1** RECORD, put on record, keep on record, report, chronicle, list, detail, register, cite, chart **2** SUPPORT, back up, prove, verify, give weight to, *formal* corroborate, substantiate, validate

documentary *adj*
recorded, chronicled, detailed, charted, written

doddering *adj*
decrepit, weak, aged, feeble, frail, infirm, elderly, tottering

doddery *adj*
unsteady, shaky, weak, faltering, doddering, tottery, feeble, infirm, aged
🖅 hale, youthful

dodge *v, n*
▶ *v* avoid, elude, evade, swerve, jump away, bypass, get out of, get round, side-step, shirk, shun, shift, steer clear of, fend off, veer, *colloq.* duck
▶ *n* trick, ruse, ploy, wile, scheme, stratagem, manoeuvre, device, contrivance, subterfuge, deception, sharp practice, *formal* machination

dodger *n*
evader, avoider, shirker, trickster, slacker, layabout, dreamer, *colloq.* lead-swinger, skiver, slyboots, lazybones

dodgy *adj*
chancy, dangerous, delicate, dubious, disreputable, difficult, problematical, risky, ticklish, tricky, uncertain, suspect, unreliable, unsafe, *colloq.* dicey, dicky, shifty
🖅 easy, safe

doer *n*
achiever, activist, organizer, worker, accomplisher,

executor, bustler, dynamo, *colloq.* go-getter, live wire, power-house
🖅 thinker, contemplatist

doff *v*
take off, discard, remove, shed, throw off, lift, raise, tip, touch
🖅 don

dog *n, v*
▶ *n* **1** *cats and dogs* hound, cur, mongrel, canine, puppy, pup, bitch, *colloq.* mutt, pooch **2** VILLAIN, scoundrel, rascal, rogue, wretch

Breeds of dog include:
Afghan hound, alsatian, basset-hound, beagle, Border collie, borzoi, bulldog, bull-mastiff, bullterrier, cairn terrier, chihuahua, chow, cocker spaniel, collie, corgi, dachshund, Dalmatian, Doberman pinscher, foxhound, fox-terrier, German Shepherd, golden retriever, Great Dane, greyhound, husky, Irish wolfhound, Jack Russell, King Charles spaniel, Labrador, lhasa apso, lurcher, Maltese, Old English sheepdog, Pekingese, pit bull terrier, pointer, poodle, pug, Rottweiler, saluki, sausage-dog, schnauzer, Scottie, Scottish terrier, Sealyham, setter, sheltie, shih tzu, springer spaniel, St Bernard, terrier, West Highland terrier, Westie, whippet, wolf-hound, Yorkshire terrier.

▶ *v* pursue, follow, trail, track, tail, hound, shadow, plague, harry, haunt, trouble, worry

dogged *adj*
determined, resolute, persistent, persevering, intent, tenacious, firm, steadfast, staunch, single-minded, tireless, indefatigable, steady, unshakable, stubborn, obstinate, relentless, unyielding, unflagging, unfaltering, *formal* indomitable, obdurate, pertinacious
🖅 irresolute, apathetic

doggedness *n*
determination, resolution, persistence, perseverance, tenaciousness, tenacity, firmness, steadfastness, steadiness, single-mindedness, stubbornness, obstinacy, relentlessness, endurance, *formal* indomitability, pertinacity

dogma *n*
doctrine, creed, belief, precept, principle, code (of belief), article (of faith), credo, tenet, conviction, teaching, opinion, maxim

dogmatic *adj*
opinionated, assertive, authoritative, canonical, positive, doctrinaire, domineering, dictatorial, doctrinal, categorical, emphatic, overbearing, arbitrary, insistent, arrogant, imperious, intolerant, authoritarian, ex cathedra, unquestionable, unchallengeable, pontifical

dogmatism *n*
opinionatedness, assertiveness, imperiousness, dictatorialness, bigotry, presumption, arbitrariness, positiveness, *formal* peremptoriness

dogsbody *n*
gofer, drudge, slave, lackey, doormat, galley-slave, menial, factotum, maid-of-all-work, man-of-all-work, *colloq.* skivvy

doings *n*
activities, actions, acts, exploits, feats, achievements, enterprises, deeds, events, goings-on, happenings, dealings, affairs, concerns, adventures, handiwork, proceedings, transactions

doldrums *n*
depression, dejection, downheartedness, gloom, list-

lessness, low-spiritedness, apathy, boredom, tedium, dullness, inertia, stagnation, sluggishness, torpor, *formal* ennui, lassitude, malaise, acedia, *colloq.* blues, dumps

dole *n, v*
▶ *n* benefit, Job Seekers Allowance (JSA), unemployment benefit, social security, allowance, payment, income, credit, support
▶ *v* ▷ **dole out** distribute, allocate, give out, hand out, dish out, allot, mete out, share (out), divide (up), deal (out), issue, ration, dispense, administer, assign, *formal* apportion

doleful *adj*
cheerless, depressing, distressing, dismal, dreary, forlorn, gloomy, melancholy, miserable, wretched, sad, sorrowful, mournful, sombre, rueful, painful, pathetic, pitiful, woeful, *formal* dolorous, lugubrious, woebegone, disconsolate, *colloq.* blue, down in the dumps
🗲 cheerful

doll *n*
figure, puppet, marionette, plaything, toy, figurine, moppet, dolly, Barbie®, Sindy®
▷ **doll up** dress up, preen, primp, deck out, trick out, titivate, *colloq.* tart up

dollop *n*
lump, blob, clump, bunch, ball, glob, gob, gobbet, helping, portion, serving

dolorous *adj*
anguished, distressing, melancholy, miserable, wretched, sad, sorrowful, doleful, grievous, harrowing, heart-rending, painful, mournful, rueful, sombre, woeful, *formal* lugubrious, woebegone
🗲 happy

dolour *n*
anguish, distress, grief, misery, sadness, sorrow, heartache, heartbreak, mourning, suffering, lamentation

dolt *n*
fool, idiot, imbecile, simpleton, *colloq.* ass, blockhead, nincompoop, ninny, nitwit, numskull, twerp, dope, chump, clot, nutcase, twit, dimwit, *slang* wally, dipstick, nerd

domain *n*
1 DOMINION, kingdom, realm, territory, region, empire, estate, lands, province 2 FIELD, area, speciality, concern, section, department, region, province, realm, sphere, world, discipline, jurisdiction

dome *n*
cupola, vault, rotunda, mound, hemisphere

domestic *adj, n*
▶ *adj* 1 HOME, family, household, home-loving, stay-at-home, homely, domesticated, house-trained, tame, pet, private, personal, *formal* domiciliary 2 INTERNAL, indigenous, native, home
🗲 2 foreign, international, export
▶ *n* servant, maid, charwoman, char, daily help, domestic help, hired help, daily, au pair, housekeeper, major-domo

domestic appliance *n*

Types of domestic appliance include:
washing machine, washer, washer/drier, tumble-drier, clothes airer, iron, steam iron, steam press, trouser press; dishwasher, vacuum cleaner, upright cleaner, cylinder cleaner, wet-and-dry cleaner, Hoover®, floor polisher, carpet sweeper, carpet shampooer; oven, Aga®, barbecue, cooker, Dutch oven, electric cooker, fan oven, gas stove, kitchen range, microwave oven, stove, hob, hotplate, grill,

electric grill, griddle, rotisserie, spit, waffle iron, deep fryer, slow cooker, sandwich maker, toaster; food processor, mixer, blender, liquidizer, ice-cream maker, juicer, juice extractor, food slicer, electric knife, knife sharpener, kettle, tea/coffee maker, percolator, coffee mill, electric tin opener, timer, water filter; refrigerator, *colloq.* fridge, icebox, fridge/freezer, freezer, deep-freeze; hostess-trolley, humidifier, ionizer, fire extinguisher.

domesticate *v*
tame, house-train, break, break in, train, accustom, familiarize, acclimatize, naturalize, assimilate, *formal* habituate

domesticated *adj*
tame, tamed, pet, house-trained, broken (in), domestic, home-loving, homely, house-proud, housewifely, naturalized
🗲 feral, wild

domesticity *n*
homemaking, housecraft, homecraft, housekeeping, home economics, domestic science, domestication

domicile *n, v*
▶ *n* home, house, residence, lodging(s), residency, mansion, quarters, settlement, *formal* abode, dwelling, habitation
▶ *v* make your home, settle, establish, take up residence, put down roots

dominance *n*
supremacy, authority, power, command, control, pre-eminence, rule, domination, sway, leadership, mastery, government, *formal* ascendancy, hegemony, paramountcy

dominant *adj*
1 AUTHORITATIVE, controlling, governing, ruling, powerful, all-powerful, strong, assertive, influential 2 PRINCIPAL, main, outstanding, chief, major, key, important, most important, predominant, primary, paramount, prime, prominent, leading, pre-eminent, supreme, prevailing, prevalent, commanding
🗲 1 submissive 2 subordinate

dominate *v*
1 CONTROL, domineer, govern, preside, rule, direct, command, monopolize, predominate, master, lead, overrule, prevail, overbear, intimidate, tyrannize, *formal* have ascendancy over, *colloq.* have the upper/whip hand over, have under your thumb, have over a barrel, throw your weight around 2 OVERSHADOW, eclipse, dwarf, overlook, tower over

domination *n*
command, control, authority, influence, power, leadership, rule, sway, mastery, supremacy, superiority, despotism, dictatorship, oppression, subjection, subordination, suppression, repression, tyranny, pre-eminence, predominance, *formal* ascendancy

domineering *adj*
overbearing, authoritarian, imperious, autocratic, dictatorial, despotic, masterful, high-handed, iron-handed, forceful, coercive, oppressive, tyrannical, arrogant, haughty, aggressive, *formal* peremptory, *colloq.* bossy, pushy
🗲 meek, servile

dominion *n*
1 POWER, authority, domination, command, control, rule, direction, sway, jurisdiction, government, lordship, mastery, supremacy, sovereignty, *formal* ascendancy 2 DOMAIN, country, territory, province, colony, realm, kingdom, empire

don *v, n*
▸ *v* put on, get into, dress in, slip into, clothe yourself in
🔁 doff
▸ *n* lecturer, teacher, tutor, academic, scholar, professor

donate *v*
give, give away, contribute, present, make a gift, make a donation, pledge, bequeath, subscribe, *formal* bestow, confer, *colloq.* cough up, fork out, chip in, club together, shell out
🔁 receive

donation *n*
gift, present, offering, grant, gratuity, largess(e), contribution, presentation, subscription, alms, charity, bequest, *formal* benefaction

done *adj, interj*
▸ *adj* **1** FINISHED, over, accomplished, complete, completed, ended, settled, realized, fulfilled, executed, *formal* concluded, terminated, consummated **2** CONVENTIONAL, acceptable, proper, right, correct, suitable, appropriate, fitting, *old use* seemly, *formal* decorous **3** COOKED, well-done, ready, prepared, finished, baked, boiled, browned, fried, roasted, stewed
▷ **done for** ruined, destroyed, finished, lost, wrecked, undone, doomed, beaten, broken, dashed, defeated, foiled, *formal* vanquished, *colloq.* for the high jump
▷ **done in** exhausted, tired out, weary, fatigued, *colloq.* all in, bushed, dead, dead beat, dog-tired, fagged out, knackered, pooped, zonked, on your last legs, bushed, flaked out, shattered, worn to a frazzle
▷ **done with** finished with, over with, no longer involved/associated with, *colloq.* over and done with
▸ *interj* settled, agreed, accepted, arranged, decided, right, absolutely, *colloq.* OK

Don Juan *n*
ladies' man, lady-killer, womanizer, lover, Casanova, philander(er), romeo, gigolo

donkey *n*
ass, mule, burro, hinny, jackass, jenny, *colloq.* moke

donnish *adj*
academic, serious, intellectual, bookish, erudite, learned, pedantic, scholarly, scholastic, formalistic, pedagogic

donor *n*
giver, donator, benefactor, backer, supporter, contributor, philanthropist, provider, *colloq.* fairy godmother, angel
🔁 beneficiary

doom *n, v*
▸ *n* **1** FATE, fortune, destiny, portion, lot **2** DESTRUCTION, catastrophe, downfall, disaster, ruin, ruination, death, death-knell, rack and ruin **3** CONDEMNATION, judgement, sentence, verdict, pronouncement
▸ *v* condemn, damn, consign, judge, sentence, decree, pronounce, destine, fate, *formal* predestine

doomed *adj*
condemned, damned, fated, ill-fated, star-crossed, ill-omened, cursed, destined, ruined, hopeless, unlucky, luckless, ill-starred, bedevilled

door *n*
1 *the door of the house* opening, entrance, entry, exit, doorway, portal, hatch **2** OPPORTUNITY, open door, entrance, opening, way in, access, route, way, gateway, road

doorkeeper *n*
commissionaire, doorman, gatekeeper, usher, janitor, porter, concierge, ostiary

dope *n, v*
▸ *n* **1** NARCOTIC, drugs, marijuana, cannabis, opiate, hallucinogen, barbiturate, amphetamine, crack, acid,

LSD, *colloq.* grass, weed, hash, pot, speed, coke, *slang* ecstasy, E **2** FOOL, dolt, idiot, dunce, simpleton, *colloq.* half-wit, dimwit, clot, blockhead, nincompoop, ninny, nitwit, twerp, twit **3** INFORMATION, facts, inside information, details, specifics, particulars, *colloq.* low-down, info, gen
▸ *v* drug, sedate, anaesthetize, stupefy, medicate, narcotize, inject, knock out, doctor, *colloq.* spike

dopey *adj*
1 SLEEPY, dozy, groggy, drowsy, nodding, lethargic, *formal* somnolent, torpid **2** STUPID, foolish, silly, daft, dozy, simple
🔁 **1** awake, alert **2** clever, bright

dormant *adj*
1 INACTIVE, asleep, sleeping, inert, resting, slumbering, sluggish, hibernating, latent, fallow, *technical* comatose, *formal* torpid, quiescent **2** LATENT, unrealized, potential, undeveloped, undisclosed
🔁 **1** active, awake **2** realized, developed

dose *n, v*
▸ *n* measure, dosage, amount, portion, quantity, draught, potion, prescription, shot
▸ *v* medicate, administer, prescribe, dispense, treat

dot *n, v*
▸ *n* point, spot, speck, mark, fleck, dab, circle, pinpoint, atom, particle, decimal point, full stop, iota, jot
▷ **on the dot** punctually, promptly, precisely, exactly on time, sharp
▸ *v* spot, speckle, mark, scatter, pepper, sprinkle, stud, dab, stipple, punctuate

dotage *n*
old age, senility, second childhood, infirmity, weakness, feebleness, imbecility, *formal* decrepitude

dote *v*
▷ **dote on** adore, idolize, worship, treasure, admire, love, hold dear, indulge, pamper, spoil

doting *adj*
adoring, devoted, fond, loving, affectionate, tender, soft, indulgent

dotty *adj*
crazy, eccentric, feeble-minded, peculiar, touched, weird, *colloq.* daft, barmy, batty, loony, potty
🔁 sensible

double *adj, v, n*
▸ *adj* **1** *double doors; a double yellow line* dual, twofold, twice, duplicate, twin, paired, doubled, two-ply, coupled, *formal* bifarious, binal, binate **2** AMBIGUOUS, double-meaning, double-edged, two-edged, ambivalent, equivocal, paradoxical
🔁 single, half
▸ *v* **1** *double your income* duplicate, enlarge, increase twofold, repeat, multiply by two, fold, magnify **2** *double as someone/something* have a second job/purpose, have a dual/second role **3** *double for someone* substitute, stand in, understudy, be an understudy
▷ **double back** return, reverse, backtrack, circle, dodge, evade, loop, go back the way you came, retrace your steps
▸ *n* twin, duplicate, copy, clone, replica, *doppelgänger*, lookalike, match, image, facsimile, counterpart, impersonator, *colloq.* spitting image, ringer
▷ **at the double** immediately, at once, without delay, right away, straight away, quickly, at full speed

double-cross *v*
cheat, swindle, defraud, trick, hoodwink, betray, mislead, *colloq.* con, two-time, pull a fast one on, take for a ride

double-dealing *n*
cheating, swindling, betrayal, treachery, defrauding,

tricking, hoodwinking, misleading, two-facedness, two-timing, *formal* dissembling, duplicity, perfidy, mendacity, *colloq.* two-timing, crookedness

double entendre *n*
double meaning, innuendo, suggestiveness, ambiguity, play on words, wordplay, pun

doubly *adv*
twice, twofold, again, especially, extra, *formal* bis

doubt *n, v*
▶ *n* 1 DISTRUST, suspicion, mistrust, scepticism, reservation, misgiving, qualm, mixed feeling, incredulity, apprehension, hesitation, uneasiness 2 UNCERTAINTY, difficulty, confusion, ambiguity, problem, indecision, hesitation, perplexity, dilemma, quandary
F3 1 trust, confidence, faith 2 certainty, belief
▷ **in doubt** uncertain, undecided, unresolved, unreliable, ambiguous, in question, open to question, questionable, open to debate, debatable, *colloq.* up in the air
▷ **no doubt** doubtless, without doubt, undoubtedly, definitely, unquestionably, certainly, surely, of course, no denying, probably, most likely, presumably
▶ *v* 1 DISTRUST, mistrust, query, question, suspect, be suspicious, have misgivings/qualms about, fear, *formal* disbelieve, *colloq.* take with a pinch of salt 2 BE UNCERTAIN, be dubious, hesitate, vacillate, waver, be undecided, *formal* demur
F3 1 believe, trust, have confidence in 2 be certain, decide

doubter *n*
questioner, sceptic, disbeliever, unbeliever, agnostic, doubting Thomas, cynic, scoffer
F3 believer

doubtful *adj*
1 *it is doubtful that he will win* unlikely, improbable, uncertain, in doubt, open to question, debatable, *colloq.* touch and go 2 *doubtful about his future* uncertain, unsure, undecided, suspicious, distrustful, uneasy, apprehensive, having reservations/misgivings, irresolute, wavering, hesitant, vacillating, tentative, sceptical, *colloq.* in two minds 3 *writing of doubtful origin* dubious, questionable, suspect, unclear, inconclusive, ambiguous, vague, obscure, debatable, *colloq.* fishy, shady, iffy
F3 1 certain 2 certain, decided, confident 3 definite, settled, trustworthy

doubtless *adv*
certainly, without doubt, undoubtedly, unquestionably, indisputably, no doubt, clearly, surely, of course, truly, precisely, probably, presumably, most likely, seemingly, supposedly

dour *adj*
1 GLOOMY, dismal, forbidding, grim, morose, unfriendly, unsmiling, dreary, austere, sour, sullen, churlish, gruff 2 HARD, harsh, inflexible, unyielding, rigid, severe, stern, rigorous, strict, obstinate
F3 1 cheerful, bright 2 easy-going

douse, dowse *v*
1 SOAK, pour water over, saturate, flood, deluge, steep, submerge, immerse, immerge, wet, dip, souse, duck, drench, dunk, plunge, splash 2 EXTINGUISH, put out, blow out, smother, quench, snuff

dovetail *v*
fit together, correspond, match, coincide, conform, agree, tally, harmonize, join, interlock, link, *formal* accord

dowdy *adj*
unfashionable, ill-dressed, frumpish, drab, shabby, frowsy, dingy, old-fashioned, slovenly, *colloq.* tatty, tacky
F3 fashionable, smart

down[1] *prep, adv, adj, v*
▶ *prep & adv*
down the road to a lower level/position, to the ground, to the floor, to the bottom
F3 up
▷ **down with** get rid of, away with
▶ *adj* 1 SAD, depressed, unhappy, melancholy, miserable, downhearted, dejected, downcast, dispirited, wretched, low, *colloq.* blue, down in the dumps 2 *the computer is down* out of order, out of action, not working, crashed, *formal* inoperative, *colloq.* bust, *slang* conked out
F3 1 happy 2 operational
▶ *v* 1 KNOCK DOWN, fell, floor, bring down, prostrate, throw, topple 2 SWALLOW, consume, drink, gulp, *colloq.* swig, put away, knock back, toss off, swill

down[2] *n*
quilts made of down soft feathers, fine hair, wool, pile, shag, nap, fluff, floss, fuzz, floccus, flue, bloom, *technical* pappus

down-and-out *adj, n*
▶ *adj* derelict, destitute, impoverished, on your uppers, penniless, ruined
▶ *n* tramp, vagrant, vagabond, *US* hobo, *colloq.* loser, *slang* dosser

down-at-heel *adj*
shabby, poor, ill-dressed, frayed, tattered, ragged, drab, frowsy, dowdy, dingy, run-down, slovenly, *colloq.* tatty, tacky, seedy

downbeat *adj*
1 RELAXED, calm, low, downcast, informal, casual, nonchalant, unhurried, unworried, *formal* insouciant, *colloq.* laid back 2 GLOOMY, pessimistic, fearing the worst, negative, depressed, low, downcast, despondent, cheerless, cynical
F3 1 upbeat 2 happy

downcast *adj*
dejected, depressed, despondent, sad, unhappy, wretched, miserable, down, low, disheartened, downhearted, dispirited, discouraged, disappointed, crestfallen, daunted, dismayed, glum, gloomy, *formal* disconsolate, *colloq.* blue, fed up
F3 cheerful, happy, elated

downfall *n*
fall, ruin, failure, collapse, destruction, disgrace, debasement, degradation, debacle, undoing, overthrow
F3 rise

downgrade *v*
1 DEGRADE, demote, lower, humble, reduce/lower in rank, relegate, depose, deflate, *formal* disparage, denigrate, *colloq.* take down a peg or two, take the wind out of someone's sails 2 BELITTLE, decry, minimize, defame, make light of, *colloq.* run down, do down, sell short
F3 1 upgrade, improve 2 praise

downhearted *adj*
depressed, dejected, despondent, sad, downcast, disappointed, discouraged, disheartened, dispirited, low-spirited, daunted, unhappy, gloomy, glum, dismayed, disappointed, *formal* disconsolate
F3 cheerful, enthusiastic

downpour *n*
cloudburst, deluge, rainstorm, flood, inundation, torrent

downright *adv, adj*
▶ *adv* absolutely, plainly, utterly, clearly, completely, totally, thoroughly, categorically
▶ *adj* outright, complete, total, out-and-out, absolute, plain, utter, clear, sheer, thorough, wholesale, categorical, unqualified, unequivocal

down-to-earth *adj*
commonsense, commonsensical, hard-headed, mat-

ter-of-fact, mundane, no-nonsense, plain-spoken, practical, realistic, sane, sensible, unsentimental, idealistic

F3 fantastic, impractical

down-trodden *adj*
oppressed, subservient, exploited, trampled on, weighed-down, burdened, overwhelmed, abused, tyrannized, bullied, victimized, helpless, powerless, *formal* subjugated

downward *adj*
descending, declining, going/moving down, downhill, sliding, slipping

F3 upward

dowry *n*
marriage settlement, marriage portion, inheritance, legacy, portion, provision, share, wedding-dower, dot, dower, endowment, faculty, gift, talent

doze *v, n*
▶ *v* sleep, nap, catnap, take a nap, drift off, go off, nod off, drop off, *colloq.* snooze, kip, *slang* zizz
▶ *n* nap, catnap, siesta, *colloq.* snooze, forty winks, kip, shut-eye, *slang* zizz

drab *adj*
dull, dingy, dreary, dismal, gloomy, flat, grey, colourless, lacklustre, cheerless, lifeless, sombre, shabby, featureless, tedious, boring

F3 bright, cheerful

draft *n, v*
▶ *n* **1** OUTLINE, sketch, rough sketch, plan, abstract, rough, preliminary version, drawing, blueprint, *formal* delineation, protocol **2** *a bank draft* bill of exchange, cheque, money order, letter of credit, postal order
▶ *v* draw (up), outline, sketch, plan, design, formulate, compose, *formal* delineate

drag *v, n*
▶ *v* **1** DRAW, pull, haul, lug, tug, trail, tow, yank **2** GO SLOWLY, creep, crawl, lag, become boring/tedious, wear on, go on and on, go on for ever
▷ **drag out** spin out, prolong, draw out, extend, hang on, lengthen, persist, *formal* protract
▷ **drag up** rake up, remind, bring up, raise, mention, introduce, revive
▶ *n* bore, annoyance, nuisance, bother, pest, trouble, *colloq.* pain, pain in the neck, bind, headache

dragoon *v*
coerce, compel, constrain, drive, force, harass, impel, intimidate, browbeat, bully, *colloq.* strongarm

drain *v, n*
▶ *v* **1** EMPTY, remove, evacuate, draw off, pump off, extract, withdraw, strain, dry, milk, bleed, tap, *formal* void **2** *waste draining into the stream* trickle, flow out, seep out, leak, ooze, *formal* discharge, exude, effuse **3** EXHAUST, consume, sap, use up, drink up, swallow, strain, tax, *formal* deplete

F3 **1** fill

▶ *n* **1** CHANNEL, conduit, culvert, duct, outlet, trench, ditch, pipe, gutter, sewer **2** *a drain on resources* exhaustion, consumption, sap, strain, tax, *formal* depletion

drama *n*
1 PLAY, acting, theatre, show, piece, spectacle, stagecraft, scene, comedy, melodrama, tragedy, dramatics, dramaturgy **2** EXCITEMENT, thrill, sensation, crisis, dilemma, tension, turmoil, histrionics

dramatic *adj*
1 *a dramatic change* striking, sudden, marked, significant, abrupt, noticeable, distinct **2** EXCITING, striking, stirring, thrilling, tense, spectacular, vivid, graphic, sensational, expressive, effective, impressive, unexpected **3** HISTRIONIC, theatrical, exaggerated, melodramatic,

flamboyant, artificial **4** *dramatic art* theatrical, stage, Thespian

dramatist *n*
playwright, scriptwriter, play-writer, screen writer, comedian, dramaturge, dramaturgist, tragedian

dramatize *v*
1 STAGE, put on, adapt, present as a play/film, arrange for **2** EXAGGERATE, play-act, act, overdo, overstate, *colloq.* ham (up), lay it on thick, blow up out of all proportion, make a big thing of

drape *v*
hang, cover, wrap, envelop, overlay, shroud, cloak, veil, arrange, decorate, adorn, fold, drop, droop, suspend

drapery *n*
cloth, covering(s), curtain(s), hanging(s), blind(s), arras, backdrop, tapestry, valance

drastic *adj*
extreme, radical, strong, forceful, severe, harsh, rigorous, far-reaching, desperate, dire, Draconian

F3 moderate, cautious

draught *n*
1 PUFF, current, flow, movement, *formal* influx **2** DRINK, quantity, cup, potion **3** PULLING, dragging, drawing, traction

draw *v, n*
▶ *v* **1** *draw a picture* sketch, portray, trace, pencil, paint, represent, map out, depict, design, chart, scribble, doodle, *formal* delineate **2** *the procession drew nearer* MOVE, go, proceed, progress, travel, come, approach, advance **3** PULL, drag, haul, tow, tug, lug, trail **4** *draw a knife; draw water from a well* take out, pull out, bring out, produce, extract, remove, withdraw **5** *draw a breath* breathe in, *formal* inhale, respire, inspire **6** *draw money from a bank* take, get, receive, obtain, *formal* procure **7** *draw attention to something* ATTRACT, allure, lure, entice, bring in, influence, persuade, elicit, prompt **8** *draw a conclusion* conclude, deduce, infer, gather, come to, reason **9** *draw lots* pick, choose, select, decide on, go for, *colloq.* plump for **10** TIE, be equal, be even, *colloq.* be all square

F3 **3** push **7** repel

▷ **draw back** recoil, wince, flinch, shrink, start back, withdraw, retract, retreat
▷ **draw on** make use of, use, put to use, exploit, apply, employ, quarry, rely on, have recourse to, *formal* utilize
▷ **draw out 1** *the train drew out of the station* pull out, move out, set out, depart, leave, start **2** EXTEND, prolong, lengthen, spin out, elongate, stretch, *formal* protract **3** *draw someone out* encourage to talk, induce to talk/speak, put at ease, make feel less nervous

F3 **2** shorten

▷ **draw up 1** DRAFT, compose, formulate, prepare, frame, write out, put in writing **2** PULL UP, stop, halt, run in
▶ *n* **1** ATTRACTION, enticement, lure, allure, appeal, bait, interest, magnetism **2** TIE, stalemate, dead heat

drawback *n*
disadvantage, snag, hitch, obstacle, hurdle, barrier, impediment, hindrance, difficulty, problem, flaw, fault, catch, stumbling-block, nuisance, trouble, defect, weak spot, handicap, deficiency, liability, limitation, imperfection, damper, discouragement, *colloq.* fly in the ointment

F3 advantage, benefit

drawing *n*
sketch, picture, outline, representation, portrayal, illustration, cartoon, graphic, portrait, composition,

depiction, diagram, study, *formal* delineation

drawl *v*
speak slowly, draw out your vowels, drone, haw-haw, protract, twang

drawn *adj*
tired, fatigued, worn, haggard, gaunt, pinched, strained, stressed, taut, tense, fraught, harassed, sapped, washed out, *colloq.* hassled

dread *v, n, adj*
▶ *v* fear, shrink from, quail, cringe at, flinch, shy, shudder, tremble, be afraid of, be scared of, be terrified by, be frightened (to death) by, be anxious/worried about, *colloq.* get cold feet about
☒ look forward to
▶ *n* fear, apprehension, misgiving, dismay, alarm, horror, terror, fright, fit of terror, blind panic, cold sweat, hair standing on end, disquiet, worry, qualm, *formal* trepidation, perturbation, *colloq.* (blue) funk
☒ confidence, security
▶ *adj* dreaded, feared, frightening, frightful, terrifying, terrible, dreadful, awful, awe-inspiring, alarming, ghastly, grisly, gruesome, horrible, dire

dreadful *adj*
awful, terrible, frightful, horrible, appalling, dire, shocking, outrageous, frightening, terrifying, alarming, ghastly, horrendous, horrific, grim, tragic, grievous, hideous, unpleasant, nasty, *formal* heinous
☒ wonderful, comforting

dream *n, v, adj*
▶ *n* 1 VISION, illusion, reverie, trance, fantasy, daydream, nightmare, hallucination, delusion, imagination, phantasmagoria 2 ASPIRATION, ambition, wish, hope, desire, yearning, ideal, goal, design, aim, plan, speculation, expectation, castles in the air 3 DAYDREAM, fantasy, reverie, pipe dream, inattention 4 *their new house is a dream* ideal, beauty, perfection, joy, marvel
▶ *v* 1 *dream during sleep* imagine, envisage, fantasize, fancy, hallucinate 2 DAYDREAM, fantasize, imagine, muse, fancy, be lost in space, not pay attention, let your thoughts wander, stare into space, *colloq.* switch off 3 *dream of becoming a doctor* want very much, long, desire, yearn, crave
▷ **dream up** invent, devise, conceive, think up, conjure up, imagine, concoct, hatch, create, fabricate, spin, contrive
▷ **not dream of** not think, not imagine, not consider, not conceive
▶ *adj* perfect, ideal, model, supreme, superb, excellent, wonderful

dreamer *n*
idealist, visionary, fantasist, romancer, daydreamer, star-gazer, theorizer, romantic, Utopian, Don Quixote, Walter Mitty
☒ realist, pragmatist

dreamlike *adj*
surreal, illusory, unreal, trance-like, hallucinatory, insubstantial, unsubstantial, visionary, chimerical, phantom, phantasmagoric, phantasmagorical, *formal* ethereal

dreamy *adj*
1 FANTASTIC, unreal, imaginary, shadowy, unclear, indistinct, vague, misty, hazy, faint, ethereal, dim 2 IMPRACTICAL, fanciful, daydreaming, fantasizing, romantic, idealistic, visionary, faraway, absent, musing, pensive, thoughtful, absent-minded, preoccupied, abstracted, *colloq.* with your head in the clouds 3 *dreamy music* relaxing, soothing, lulling, calming, gentle, soft, romantic
☒ 1 real, clear 2 practical, down-to-earth

dreary *adj*
gloomy, depressing, drab, dismal, bleak, sombre, cheerless, sad, mournful, overcast, dark, boring, tedious,

uninteresting, uneventful, dull, humdrum, routine, monotonous, unvaried, wearisome, commonplace, colourless, lifeless, featureless, run-of-the-mill
☒ cheerful, interesting

dredge *v*
▷ **dredge up** dig up, discover, uncover, unearth, raise, drag up, draw up, fish up, rake up, scoop up

dregs *n*
1 SEDIMENT, deposit, residue, lees, grounds, scourings, scum, dross, trash, waste, *technical* precipitate, sublimate, *formal* residuum, detritus 2 OUTCASTS, rabble, riff-raff, scum, down-and-outs, tramps, vagrants, *slang* dossers

drench *v*
soak, soak to the skin, saturate, steep, wet, douse, souse, immerse, inundate, duck, flood, swamp, imbue, drown, permeate

dress *n, v*
▶ *n* 1 FROCK, gown, robe 2 CLOTHES, clothing, garment(s), outfit, costume, ensemble, garb, *formal* attire, apparel, habiliment, *colloq.* get-up, gear, togs
▶ *v* 1 CLOTHE, put on, get into, slip into, garb, rig, robe, wear, don, decorate, deck, garnish, trim, adorn, turn out, fit (out), drape, *formal* attire, array, accoutre, *colloq.* throw on 2 *dress your hair* ARRANGE, adjust, dispose, prepare, groom, straighten, tidy, comb, do, primp, preen 3 BANDAGE, bind up, put a plaster on, clean, cover, tend, treat, swathe 4 *dress meat* clean, prepare, get ready
☒ 1 strip, undress
▷ **dress down** rebuke, reprimand, reprove, scold, chide, *formal* berate, castigate, upbraid, *colloq.* carpet, haul over the coals, tear off a strip, tell off, give someone an earful
▷ **dress up** beautify, improve, adorn, decorate, ornament, embellish, deck, gild, disguise, *colloq.* doll up, tart up, tog up

dressing *n*
1 *a salad dressing* sauce, condiment, relish, salad dressing, French dressing, Thousand Island dressing 2 BANDAGE, plaster, Elastoplast®, gauze, lint, compress, poultice, tourniquet, pad, spica, ligature

dressmaker *n*
tailor, tailoress, couturier, modiste, needlewoman, seamstress, sewing woman, midinette

dressy *adj*
elegant, formal, smart, stylish, elaborate, ornate, *colloq.* classy, natty, ritzy, swish
☒ dowdy, scruffy

dribble *v, n*
▶ *v* 1 TRICKLE, drip, leak, run, seep, drop, ooze, *formal* exude 2 DROOL, slaver, slobber, drivel
▶ *n* drip, trickle, droplet, leak, seepage, sprinkling

dried *adj*
arid, dehydrated, desiccated, drained, parched, wilted, withered, wizened, shrivelled, mummified

drift *v, n*
▶ *v* 1 WANDER, waft, stray, float, freewheel, coast, go with the stream, be carried along, roam, rove 2 GATHER, accumulate, pile up, bank, drive, amass
▶ *n* 1 ACCUMULATION, mound, pile, bank, mass, heap 2 TREND, tendency, course, direction, flow, movement, current, variation, digression, rush, sweep 3 MEANING, intention, implication, gist, vein, tenor, thrust, course, direction, trend, tendency, significance, essence, core, substance, aim, point, design, scope, *formal* import, purport

drifter *n*
wanderer, traveller, nomad, vagrant, itinerant, rover, tramp, vagabond, rolling stone, swagman, beachcomber, *US* hobo

drill *n, v*
> ► *n* **1** BORER, awl, bit, gimlet **2** INSTRUCTION, training, practice, coaching, grounding, exercise, repetition, tuition, preparation, discipline, indoctrination, procedure, routine, *formal* inculcation
> ► *v* **1** TEACH, train, instruct, coach, practise, school, rehearse, exercise, discipline, ground, put someone through their paces, *formal* inculcate **2** BORE, pierce, make a hole in, penetrate, puncture, perforate, prick, punch

drink *v, n*
> ► *v* **1** IMBIBE, swallow, have, sip, drain, down, gulp, sup, quaff, absorb, guzzle, swill, *formal* partake of, *colloq.* swig, knock back **2** GET DRUNK, have one too many, have (a drop) too much, indulge, carouse, revel, be a hard drinker, be a heavy drinker, have a drink problem, *colloq.* tipple, tank up, have one over the eight, drink like a fish, hit the bottle, knock back a few, polish off, *slang* booze, lush **3** *drink someone's health* drink to, toast, propose a toast to, salute, wish someone success
> ► *n* **1** BEVERAGE, liquid, brew, infusion, soft drink, cold drink, hot drink, thirst-quencher, refreshment, draught, sip, swallow, gulp, *colloq.* swig

Types of non-alcoholic drink include:
Assam tea, Indian tea, Earl Grey, China tea, lapsang souchong, green tea, herbal tea, fruit tea, camomile tea, peppermint tea, rosehip tea, lemon tea, tisane, julep, mint-julep; coffee, café au lait, café filtre, café noir, cappuccino, espresso, Irish coffee, Turkish coffee; cocoa, hot chocolate, Horlicks®, Ovaltine®; milk, milk shake, float; fizzy drink, *colloq.* pop, cherryade, Coca Cola®, *colloq.* Coke®, cream soda, ginger beer, lemonade, limeade, Pepsi®, root beer, sarsaparilla, cordial, squash, barley water, Ribena®, fruit juice, mixer, bitter lemon, Canada Dry®, ginger ale, soda water, tonic water, mineral water, Perrier®, seltzer, Vichy water, Lucozade®, Wincarnis®, beef tea.

2 ALCOHOL, strong drink, spirits, liquor, tot, *colloq.* tipple, the bottle, stiffener, hard stuff, *slang* booze

Alcoholic drinks include:
ale, beer, cider, lager, shandy, stout, Guinness®; alcopop; aquavit, Armagnac, bourbon, brandy, Calvados, Cognac, gin, gin-and-tonic, G&T, pink gin, sloe gin, rum, grog, rye, vodka, whisky, Scotch and soda, hot toddy; wine, red wine, vin rouge, vin rosé, white wine, vin blanc, champagne, *colloq.* bubbly, hock, mead, perry, *colloq.* vino, *colloq.* plonk, absinthe, advocaat, Benedictine, Chartreuse, black velvet, bloody Mary, Buck's fizz, Campari, cherry brandy, cocktail, Cointreau®, crème de menthe, daiquiri, eggnog, ginger wine, kirsch, Marsala, Martini®, ouzo, Pernod®, pina colada, port, punch, retsina, sake, sangria, schnapps, sherry, snowball, tequila, Tom Collins, vermouth. *See also* WINE.

drinkable *adj*
clean, safe, fit to drink, potable

drinker *n*
hard/serious drinker, heavy drinker, drunk, drunkard, inebriate, dipsomaniac, imbiber, *colloq.* tippler, *slang* boozer, wino, lush, alkie, dipso, soak, hophead, toper, sot
▪ abstainer, teetotaller

drip *v, n*
> ► *v* drop, dribble, trickle, leak, ooze, plop, drizzle, splash, sprinkle, weep, filter, percolate
> ► *n* **1** DROP, trickle, dribble, leak, splash, plop, bead, tear **2** WEAKLING, bore, *colloq.* wimp, softy, wet, ninny, nerd, dork

drive *v, n*
> ► *v* **1** STEER, ride, travel (by car), go/come (by car), motor, be behind/at the wheel, be at the controls **2** TRANSPORT, take, convey, carry, move, send, run, chauffeur, give someone a lift, take someone somewhere **3** PROPEL, impel, direct, control, manage, operate, run, handle, hurl, press, thrust **4** FORCE, compel, impel, coerce, constrain, press, move, push, urge, spur, prod, herd, round up, dragoon, goad, guide, oblige, leave someone with no choice/option **5** MOTIVATE, force, compel, pressure, pressurize, impel, lead, prompt, actuate, incite, provoke, persuade, move, spur **6** STRIKE, hammer, knock, thump, dash, dig, sink, ram, thrust, plunge **7** OVERBURDEN, overwork, tax, overtax, work too hard, overdo it, burden, *colloq.* kill yourself
> ▷ **drive at** imply, allude to, intimate, mean, suggest, hint, have in mind, intend, refer to, signify, insinuate, indicate, aim at, *colloq.* get at
> ► *n* **1** EXCURSION, outing, journey, ride, run, trip, jaunt, *colloq.* spin, turn **2** AVENUE, driveway, road, roadway **3** ENERGY, enterprise, ambition, initiative, vigour, verve, motivation, determination, will, resolve, spirit, effort, action, *formal* tenacity, *colloq.* get-up-and-go, pizazz, zip, *slang* vim **4** CAMPAIGN, crusade, appeal, effort, action, fight, struggle, battle, *colloq.* push **5** POWER, thrust, surge, pressure, propulsion, transmission, propeller shaft **6** URGE, instinct, impulse, pressure, need, desire

drivel *n*
nonsense, rubbish, gibberish, gobbledygook, garbage, *old use* balderdash, *colloq.* bunkum, mumbo-jumbo, waffle, rot, poppycock, tripe, hogwash, claptrap, twaddle, *slang* crap

driver *n*
motorist, motorcyclist, rider, chauffeur, cabbie, trucker

driving *adj*
compelling, forceful, vigorous, dynamic, energetic, forthright, heavy, violent, sweeping

drizzle *n, v*
> ► *n* mist, mizzle, (light) rain, spray, shower
> ► *v* spit, spray, sprinkle, rain, spot, shower, mizzle

droll *adj*
bizarre, odd, queer, eccentric, peculiar, comical, amusing, humorous, ridiculous, laughable, ludicrous, funny, clownish, zany, farcical, waggish, whimsical, witty, comic, diverting, entertaining, jocular, *formal* risible

drone *v, n*
> ► *v* **1** HUM, buzz, purr, thrum, vibrate, whirr, drawl, chant, bombilate, bombinate **2** *the lecturer droned on and on* go on and on, speak interminably, talk monotonously, intone
> ► *n* **1** HUM, buzz, purr, thrum, vibration, whirr, whirring, murmuring, chant **2** LAZY PERSON, idler, loafer, slacker, dreamer, layabout, parasite, leech, hanger-on, *colloq.* lazybones, sponger, scrounger

drool *v*
1 DRIBBLE, slobber, slaver, salivate, drivel, water at the mouth **2** *drool over the new baby* dote, enthuse, gloat, gush, slobber over

droop *v*
1 HANG DOWN, dangle, sag, bend, wilt, stoop, bow, fall down, sink, drop, slump **2** LANGUISH, decline,

drop *v, n*
▶ *v* **1** FALL, sink, decline, plunge, plummet, tumble, dive, descend, droop **2** LOWER, let fall, let go **3** DRIP, trickle, leak, dribble, plop **4** LOWER, decrease, lessen, weaken, diminish, decline, dwindle, slacken off, plummet, plunge, sink **5** ABANDON, give up, desert, reject, jilt, disown, walk out on, *formal* forsake, relinquish, repudiate, renounce, *colloq.* chuck, ditch, run out on, throw over **6** END, stop, finish, leave out, miss out, omit, exclude, *formal* cease, dispense with, discontinue, terminate, forgo, relinquish, repudiate, renounce, *colloq.* quit **7** DISMISS, discharge, make redundant, *colloq.* sack, fire, turf out, boot out
F3 **1** rise
▷ **drop back** fall behind, lag (behind), fall back, *formal* retreat
▷ **drop in** call (round), call by, come over, come round, visit, come by, *colloq.* pop in
▷ **drop off 1** FALL ASLEEP, drift off, go off, catnap, *colloq.* nod off, doze, snooze, have forty winks **2** DECLINE, fall off, plummet, decrease, dwindle, lessen, diminish, slacken off, plummet, plunge, sink **3** DELIVER, set down, deposit, unload, hand in
F3 **1** wake up **2** increase
▷ **drop out** withdraw, leave, give up, abandon, *formal* renounce, forsake, *colloq.* back out, cry off, quit
▷ **drop out of** back out of, withdraw from, leave, opt out, pull out, abandon, *formal* renounce, renege, *colloq.* cry off from, quit
▶ *n* **1** DROPLET, bead, tear, drip, bubble, blob, globule, trickle, *formal* goutte, globulet, spheroid, gutta **2** LITTLE, mouthful, sprinkle, bit, pinch, sip, nip, tot, trace, dab, splash, *US* tad, *formal* modicum, *colloq.* dash, spot, smidgen **3** DESCENT, fall, precipice, cliff, slope, chasm, abyss, plunge, *formal* declivity **4** DECLINE, falling-off, fall-off, lowering, downturn, decrease, reduction, cutback, slump, plunge, depreciation, devaluation, deterioration

dropout *n*
non-conformist, rebel, Bohemian, dissenter, hippie, loner, deviant, *formal* dissentient, malcontent, renegade

droppings *n*
excrement, dung, manure, ordure, spraint, *technical* excreta, stools, *formal* egesta, faeces

dross *n*
rubbish, remains, refuse, trash, waste, scum, debris, dregs, impurity, lees, slag, *technical* scoria

drought *n*
dryness, aridity, parchedness, dehydration, shortage, want, *formal* desiccation

drove *n*
herd, horde, gathering, crowd, multitude, swarm, throng, flock, pack, host, company, mob, press, crush

drown *v*
1 SUBMERGE, immerse, inundate, go under, flood, sink, deluge, engulf, drench **2** OVERWHELM, overpower, overcome, swamp, wipe out, extinguish

drowsiness *n*
sleepiness, tiredness, weariness, lethargy, sluggishness, *formal* oscitancy, somnolence, torpor, *colloq.* dopiness, doziness, grogginess

drowsy *adj*
sleepy, tired, weary, lethargic, nodding, dreamy, dozy, yawning, half-asleep, hardly able to keep your eyes open, *formal* somnolent, torpid, *colloq.* dopey
F3 alert, awake

drubbing *n*
defeat, beating, flogging, pounding, pummelling, trouncing, walloping, whipping, hammering, *colloq.* clobbering, licking, thrashing

drudge *n, v*
▶ *n* toiler, menial, hack, labourer, toiler, servant, slave, factotum, worker, galley-slave, lackey, *colloq.* dogsbody, skivvy
▶ *v* plod, toil, work, slave, labour, *colloq.* plug away, grind, beaver, slog away, keep your nose to the grindstone, work your fingers to the bone
F3 idle, laze

drudgery *n*
labour, menial work, hack-work, slavery, sweat, sweated labour, toil, skivvying, chore, *colloq.* donkeywork, slog, grind

drug *n, v*
▶ *n* medication, medicine, remedy, potion, cure

Types of drug include:
anaesthetic, analgesic, antibiotic, antidepressant, antihistamine, barbiturate, narcotic, opiate, hallucinogenic, sedative, steroid, stimulant, tranquillizer; chloroform, aspirin, codeine, paracetamol, morphine, penicillin, diazepam, Valium®, Prozac®, cortisone, insulin, digitalis, laudanum, quinine, progesterone, oestrogen, cannabis, marijuana, smack, LSD, acid, ecstasy, *slang* E, heroin, opium, cocaine, crack, *colloq.* dope, amphetamine, downer, *slang* speed. *See also* MEDICINE.

▶ *v* medicate, sedate, tranquillize, anaesthetize, make unconscious, dose, stupefy, deaden, numb, *colloq.* dope, knock out

drug addict *n*
colloq. junkie, user, dope-fiend, *slang* freak, head, coke-head, tripper, mainliner

drugged *adj*
stupefied, *technical* comatose, *colloq.* knocked out, high, spaced out, turned on, doped, zonked, on a trip, stoned

drum *v*
beat, pulsate, tap, throb, thrum, tattoo, reverberate, rap, knock
▷ **drum into** din into, drive home, hammer, harp on, instil, reiterate, inculcate
▷ **drum out** expel, discharge, dismiss, *colloq.* throw out
▷ **drum up** obtain, round up, collect, gather, summon, solicit, canvass, petition, attract, get

drunk *adj, n*
▶ *adj* under the influence, drunken, *formal* inebriated, intoxicated, crapulent, *colloq.* merry, tight, tipsy, tiddly, well-oiled, blotto, drunk as a lord/newt, blind drunk, roaring drunk, the worse for drink, soused, squiffy, happy, legless, plastered, sozzled, pickled, bibulous, woozy, one over the eight, under the table, bevvied, having had a few, *slang* stoned, tanked up, loaded, lit up, canned, paralytic, sloshed, smashed, stewed, bombed, wasted, wrecked
F3 sober, temperate, abstinent, teetotal
▶ *n* drunkard, alcoholic, inebriate, drinker, hard drinker, heavy drinker, dipsomaniac, *colloq.* tippler, *slang* boozer, wino, lush, alkie, dipso, soak, hophead, toper, sot

drunkard *n*
drunk, alcoholic, inebriated, drinker, hard drinker, heavy drinker, dipsomaniac, *colloq.* tippler, *slang* boozer, wino, lush, alkie, dipso, soak, hophead, toper, sot

drunken adj
 1 DRUNK, formal inebriate, intoxicated, crapulent, colloq. merry, tight, tipsy, tiddly, happy, slang boozy, stoned, loaded, lit up, sloshed, bombed 2 a drunken party debauched, dissipated, riotous, intemperate, bacchanalian, formal crapulent
 ⊟ 1 sober

drunkenness n
 intemperance, alcoholism, hard/serious drinking, debauchery, dipsomania, formal inebriation, inebriety, insobriety, intoxication, crapulence, colloq. bibulousness, tipsiness
 ⊟ sobriety

dry adj, v
 ▶ adj 1 ARID, parched, scorched, thirsty, dehydrated, barren, unwatered, rainless, moistureless, torrid, shrivelled, withered, wilted, technical xeric, formal desiccated, colloq. dry as a bone 2 BORING, dull, dreary, tedious, monotonous, uninteresting, wearisome, flat, colloq. dry as dust 3 dry humour witty, ironic, subtle, cynical, droll, deadpan, sarcastic, cutting, low-key, laconic
 ⊟ 1 wet, damp 2 interesting, imaginative
 ▶ v dehydrate, parch, scorch, drain, shrivel, wither, wilt, formal desiccate
 ⊟ soak, wet
 ▷ **dry up** 1 FAIL, stop being productive, come to an end, disappear, stop, fade, die out 2 STOP TALKING, forget your lines, shut up, someone's mind goes blank

dryness n
 aridity, aridness, drought, barrenness, dehydration, thirst, thirstiness
 ⊟ wetness

dual adj
 double, twofold, duplicate, duplex, binary, combined, paired, coupled, twin, two-piece, matched

dub v
 name, call, entitle, confer, designate, label, nickname, style, tag, term, christen, formal bestow

dubiety n
 doubt, doubtfulness, indecision, uncertainty, misgiving, scepticism, suspicion, mistrust, qualm, hesitation, formal incertitude
 ⊟ certainty

dubious adj
 1 DOUBTFUL, uncertain, undecided, unsure, wavering, vacillating, unsettled, suspicious, sceptical, hesitant, irresolute 2 QUESTIONABLE, debatable, unreliable, untrustworthy, ambiguous, suspect, suspicious, obscure, colloq. fishy, shady, iffy, shifty
 ⊟ 1 certain 2 trustworthy

duck v
 1 CROUCH, stoop, bob, bend, bow down, drop, squat 2 AVOID, evade, shirk, shun, sidestep, steer clear of, elude, colloq. dodge, wriggle out of, worm your way out of 3 DIP, immerse, plunge, dunk, dive, submerge, douse, souse, wet, lower

duct n
 pipe, tube, channel, conduit, passage, vessel, canal, funnel

ductile adj
 amenable, biddable, flexible, plastic, malleable, manageable, pliable, pliant, tractable, manipulable, yielding, formal compliant
 ⊟ intractable, formal refractory

dud n, adj
 ▶ n failure, flop, colloq. washout
 ▶ adj broken, failed, valueless, worthless, formal inoperative, nugatory, colloq. bust, duff, kaput
 ⊟ working

due adj, adv, n
 ▶ adj 1 OWED, owing, payable, unpaid, outstanding, in arrears 2 RIGHTFUL, right, fitting, appropriate, proper, merited, deserved, justified, suitable, correct 3 ADEQUATE, enough, sufficient, ample, plenty of, formal requisite 4 EXPECTED, scheduled, anticipated, long-awaited, required
 ⊟ 1 paid 3 inadequate
 ▷ **due to** owing to, as a result of, caused by, because of
 ▶ adv exactly, direct(ly), precisely, straight, colloq. dead
 ▶ n 1 give him his due rights, (just) deserts, merits, prerogative, privilege, birthright, colloq. comeuppance 2 pay dues charge(s), contribution, fee, membership fee, levy, subscription

duel n
 affair of honour, combat, contest, fight, clash, struggle, battle, competition, rivalry, engagement, encounter

duffer n
 bungler, blunderer, fool, idiot, ignoramus, oaf, colloq. bonehead, clod, clot, dolt, dimwit

dulcet adj
 sweet, sweet-sounding, gentle, pleasant, melodious, harmonious, mellow, soothing, soft, agreeable, formal mellifluous

dull adj, v
 ▶ adj 1 BORING, uninteresting, unexciting, flat, dreary, monotonous, stereotyped, tedious, tiresome, wearisome, stultifying, uneventful, humdrum, unimaginative, pedestrian, dismal, lifeless, plain, bland, insipid, heavy, ponderous, colloq. dull as ditchwater 2 DARK, sombre, gloomy, drab, dreary, murky, indistinct, grey, dark, cloudy, lacklustre, matt, opaque, dim, overcast 3 UNINTELLIGENT, dense, dim, stupid, slow, colloq. dimwitted, thick, dumb, bird-brained, slow on the uptake 4 dull weather overcast, grey, cloudy, dim, dark, leaden, dreary, sombre, gloomy 5 feel dull sluggish, slow, inactive, inert, idle, heavy, lethargic, formal torpid 6 a dull pain weak, faint, mild, troublesome, uncomfortable, distressing 7 a dull sound/thud muted, indistinct, weak, feeble, muffled 8 BLUNT, unsharpened, edgeless
 ⊟ 1 interesting, exciting, lively 2 bright 3 intelligent, clever 4 fine, sunny 5 lively, energetic 6 sharp, intense, acute 7 sharp 8 sharp
 ▶ v 1 BLUNT, alleviate, moderate, lessen, reduce, decrease, diminish, relieve, soften, allay, assuage, tone down, formal mitigate 2 DEADEN, numb, paralyse, stupefy, drug, tranquillize 3 DISCOURAGE, dampen, subdue, sadden, dishearten, depress, deject 4 DIM, obscure, darken, fade, wash out

dullard n
 idiot, imbecile, ignoramus, moron, oaf, simpleton, dunce, colloq. blockhead, bonehead, chump, clod, clot, dimwit, dolt, dope, dunderhead, nitwit, numskull
 ⊟ brain

dullness n
 dreariness, emptiness, flatness, dryness, plainness, monotony, slowness, tedium, sluggishness, formal torpor, vacuity, vapidity
 ⊟ excitement, interest, sharpness, brightness, clarity

duly adv
 accordingly, appropriately, correctly, fitly, fittingly, properly, rightfully, suitably, sure enough, deservedly, formal befittingly, decorously

dumb adj
 1 deaf and dumb silent, mute, soundless, speechless,

tongue-tied, inarticulate, without speech, at a loss for words, lost for words, *colloq.* mum, *slang* shtoom **2** STUPID, unintelligent, foolish, dense, *colloq.* dim-witted, thick, brainless, gormless

dumbfounded *adj*
astonished, amazed, astounded, overwhelmed, speechless, taken aback, startled, stunned, over-come, confounded, lost for words, staggered, con-fused, baffled, bewildered, dumb, nonplussed, paralysed, *colloq.* thrown, flabbergasted, bowled over, floored, gobsmacked, knocked for six

dummy *n, adj*
▶ *n* **1** COPY, duplicate, imitation, counterfeit, substi-tute, representation, reproduction, sample **2** MODEL, lay-figure, mannequin, figure, form **3** TEAT, pacifier **4** IDIOT, imbecile, fool, oaf, *colloq.* blockhead, chump, clot, dimwit, numskull, nitwit
▶ *adj* **1** ARTIFICIAL, fake, imitation, false, bogus, mock, sham, *colloq.* phoney **2** *a dummy run* SIMU-LATED, practice, trial

dump *v, n*
▶ *v* **1** DEPOSIT, put down, place, drop, offload, throw down, let fall, fling down, unload, empty out, tip out, discharge, pour out, park, *colloq.* plonk, bung **2** GET RID OF, discard, scrap, throw away, throw out, dispose of, ditch, tip, jettison, *col-loq.* chuck away **3** *he dumped his girlfriend* leave, abandon, walk out on, *formal* forsake, *colloq.* ditch, chuck
▶ *n* **1** RUBBISH TIP, junkyard, rubbish heap, tip, scrapyard **2** HOVEL, slum, shack, shanty, mess, *colloq.* hole, joint, tip, pigsty
▷ **down in the dumps** sad, depressed, unhappy, mel-ancholy, miserable, downhearted, dejected, down-cast, dispirited, low, *colloq.* blue

dumpy *adj*
short, plump, stout, chubby, chunky, podgy, pudgy, squab, squat, stubby, tubby
☒ tall

dun *adj*
greyish-brown, dull, dingy, mud-coloured, mouse-coloured

dunce *n*
fool, idiot, imbecile, *colloq.* blockhead, bonehead, nincompoop, ninny, nitwit, numskull, twerp, twit, dimwit, *slang* wally, dipstick, nerd
☒ brain, intellectual

dung *n*
excrement, animal waste, droppings, manure, ordure, spraint, *formal* faeces

dungeon *n*
cell, prison, jail, gaol, cage, lock-up, keep, oubliette, vault

dupe *v, n*
▶ *v* deceive, delude, fool, trick, outwit, cheat, hoax, swindle, take in, hoodwink, defraud, *colloq.* con, rip off, bamboozle
▶ *n* victim, fool, gull, pawn, puppet, instrument, sim-pleton, *colloq.* sucker, mug, push-over, fall guy, stooge

duplicate *v, adj, n*
▶ *v* copy, reproduce, repeat, do again, photocopy, Xerox®, fax, facsimile, double, clone, echo, *formal* replicate
▶ *adj* identical, matching, twin, twofold, correspond-ing, paired, matched
▶ *n* copy, replica, reproduction, model, photocopy, Xerox®, carbon (copy), match, mate, facsimile, fax, double, twin, clone, imitation, forgery, *colloq.* look-alike, (dead) ringer, spitting image

duplication *n*
repetition, copy(ing), photocopy(ing), reproduction, doubling, clone, cloning, *formal* dittography, gemina-tion, replication

duplicity *n*
deceit, deception, dishonesty, falsehood, fraud, guile, hypocrisy, double-dealing, treachery, betrayal, artifice, chicanery, *formal* dissimulation, mendacity, perfidy

durability *n*
permanence, imperishability, persistence, stability, strength, endurance, constancy, lastingness
☒ fragility, impermanence, weakness, *formal* dur-ableness, longevity

durable *adj*
lasting, enduring, long-lasting, abiding, hard-wear-ing, heavy-duty, reinforced, strong, solid, sturdy, tough, robust, unchanging, unfading, substantial, sound, reliable, dependable, stable, resistant, persis-tent, persisting, constant, permanent, firm, fixed, fast
☒ changeable, perishable, weak, fragile

duration *n*
time, time span, time scale, extent, continuation, con-tinuance, perpetuation, prolongation, fullness, length, length of time, period, span, spell, stretch
☒ shortening

duress *n*
constraint, coercion, compulsion, pressure, restraint, threat, force, enforcement, exaction, *colloq.* arm-twisting

during *conj*
at/in the time of, for the time of, in, throughout, in the course of, all the while

dusk *n*
twilight, sunset, nightfall, evening, sundown, gloam-ing, darkness, dark, gloom, shadows, shade
☒ dawn, brightness

dusky *adj*
shadowy, dark, dim, gloomy, murky, cloudy, foggy, misty, hazy, twilit, *formal* crepuscular, tenebrous, fuli-ginous, subfusc
☒ bright

dust *n, v*
▶ *n* powder, particles, dirt, earth, soil, ground, clay, grit, grime, soot, smut
▶ *v* **1** CLEAN, wipe, brush, mop, burnish, polish, spray **2** SPRINKLE, powder, scatter, cover, spread, fleck, speckle

dust-up *n*
conflict, disagreement, quarrel, argument, distur-bance, encounter, fight, fracas, brawl, brush, commo-tion, scuffle, skirmish, tussle, *colloq.* argy-bargy, punch-up, scrap, set-to

dusty *adj*
1 DIRTY, grubby, grimy, filthy, dust-covered, sooty **2** POWDERY, granular, crumbly, chalky, sandy, *formal* friable
☒ **1** clean **2** solid, hard

dutiful *adj*
obedient, respectful, conscientious, devoted, filial, reverential, deferential, submissive, thoughtful, con-siderate, *formal* compliant

duty *n*
1 OBLIGATION, responsibility, burden, onus, assign-ment, calling, charge, part, role, task, job, chore, busi-ness, function, work, office, service, commission, mission, requirement **2** OBEDIENCE, respect, loyalty, allegiance, faithfulness, *formal* fidelity **3** TAX, toll, tar-iff, levy, customs, excise, dues
▷ **off duty** not working, on holiday, off, off work, free, resting, inactive
▷ **on duty** at work, working, on call, engaged, busy, occupied, active, *colloq.* tied up

dwarf *n, adj, v*
▶ *n* **1** PERSON OF RESTRICTED GROWTH, midget, pygmy, TomThumb, Lilliputian **2** GNOME, goblin
▶ *adj* miniature, small, tiny, pocket, diminutive, petite, Lilliputian, baby, pygmy, stunted, undersized, *colloq.* mini
🔁 large
▶ *v* **1** STUNT, retard, check, arrest, *formal* atrophy **2** OVERSHADOW, tower over, dominate, *colloq.* stand head and shoulders above

dwell *v*
live, inhabit, stay, settle, populate, people, lodge, rest, *formal* reside, abide, be domiciled, *colloq.* hang out
▷ **dwell on** brood on, think about, meditate on, turn over in your mind, reflect on, mull over, harp on, linger over, elaborate, emphasize, *formal* expatiate, ruminate on
🔁 pass over

dweller *n*
inhabitant, occupant, occupier, resident, *formal* denizen

dwelling *n*
home, house, establishment, residence, quarters, dwelling-house, lodge, lodging, cottage, hut, shanty, tent, *formal* abode, domicile, habitation

dwindle *v*
diminish, decrease, decline, become/grow less, lessen, subside, ebb, fade, weaken, taper off, tail off, shrink, fall, wane, waste away, die out, wither, shrivel, vanish, disappear, *colloq.* peter out
🔁 increase, grow

dye *n, v*
▶ *n* colour, colouring, agent, stain, wash, pigment, tint, shade, hue, tinge
▶ *v* colour, tint, stain, shade, pigment, tinge, imbue

dyed-in-the-wool *adj*
entrenched, inveterate, deep-rooted, die-hard, established, long-standing, settled, fixed, hard-core, hardened, inflexible, unchangeable, uncompromising, unshakable, through and through, thorough, confirmed, complete, card-carrying
🔁 superficial

dying *adj*
passing, final, going, mortal, close/near to death, not long for this world, at death's door, on your deathbed, perishing, failing, fading, vanishing, ebbing, *formal* moribund, *colloq.* with one foot in the grave, on your last legs
🔁 reviving

dynamic *adj*
forceful, powerful, active, strong, energetic, full of energy, vigorous, high-powered, driving, effective, self-starting, spirited, vital, lively, active, potent, *colloq.* go-ahead, magnetic, go-getting
🔁 inactive, apathetic

dynamism *n*
energy, forcefulness, drive, initiative, liveliness, vigour, enterprise, *colloq.* get-up-and-go, go, pep, pizzazz, push, vim, zap, zip
🔁 apathy, inactivity, slowness

dynasty *n*
house, line, succession, dominion, regime, government, authority, rule, jurisdiction, empire, sovereignty

dyspeptic *adj*
bad-tempered, crabbed, crabby, crotchety, gloomy, grouchy, peevish, short-tempered, snappish, testy, touchy

E

each *adj, pron, adv*
- *adj* every, every single, every individual
- *pron* each one, each in their own way, each and every one
- *adv* apiece, individually, per capita, per head, per person, respectively, separately, singly

eager *adj*
1 ENTHUSIASTIC, keen, fervent, intent, earnest, wholehearted, zealous, impatient, avid, ardent, diligent **2** LONGING, yearning, anxious, keen, intent, wishing, greedy, thirsty, hungry
🔁 **1** unenthusiastic, indifferent, reluctant

eagerly *adv*
keenly, enthusiastically, fervently, intently, earnestly, wholeheartedly, impatiently, ardently, avidly, zealously, greedily
🔁 apathetically, listlessly

eagerness *n*
keenness, enthusiasm, fervency, fervour, intentness, earnestness, wholeheartedness, impatience, ardour, avidity, impetuosity, zeal, longing, yearning, greediness, hunger, thirst, *formal* fervidity
🔁 apathy, disinterest

ear *n*
1 ATTENTION, heed, notice, regard, attentiveness **2** *an ear for language* perception, sensitivity, discrimination, appreciation, hearing, skill, ability, taste
▷ **play it by ear** ad-lib, extemporize, improvise, *colloq.* take things as they come, think on your feet

---

Parts of the ear include:

anvil (incus), auditory canal, auditory nerve, auricle, cochlea, concha, eardrum, Eustachian tube, hammer (malleus), helix, labyrinth, lobe, oval window, pinna, round window, semicircular canal, stirrup (stapes), tragus, tympanum, vestibular nerve, vestibule.

---

early *adj, adv*
- *adj* **1** *early symptoms/stages* forward, advanced, premature, untimely, undeveloped, precocious, first, initial, opening **2** *early theatre* primitive, ancient, *technical* autochthonous, *formal* primeval, primordial
- *adv* **1** *early in the day* in the (early) morning, at dawn, at daybreak **2** AHEAD OF TIME, ahead of schedule, in good time, beforehand, before the usual/arranged/expected time, with time to spare, in advance, too soon, prematurely
🔁 **1** late

earmark *v*
set aside, put aside, designate, allocate, keep back, reserve, label, mark out, tag

earn *v*
1 *earn a good salary* receive, be/get paid, obtain, make, get, draw, clear, gain, realize, gross, net, collect, pocket, take home, reap, *colloq.* bring in, pull in

2 *earn your reputation* deserve, merit, be owed, be someone's by right, warrant, win, rate, obtain, secure, attain, achieve
🔁 **1** spend, lose

earnest¹ *adj*
1 SERIOUS, sincere, solemn, grave, heartfelt, intense, dedicated, committed, thoughtful, zealous, *formal* assiduous **2** RESOLUTE, devoted, ardent, conscientious, intent, keen, fervent, firm, fixed, eager, enthusiastic, steady
🔁 **1** frivolous, flippant **2** apathetic
▷ **in earnest 1** SERIOUSLY, resolutely, ardently, conscientiously, intently, steadily, wholeheartedly, passionately **2** SINCERE, genuine, serious, not joking
🔁 **2** in jest, as a joke

earnest² *n*
the earnest of heavenly gifts deposit, down payment, guarantee, pledge, token, security, assurance

earnestly *adv*
seriously, sincerely, intently, resolutely, firmly, keenly, eagerly, fervently, warmly, zealously
🔁 flippantly, listlessly

earnestness *n*
seriousness, sincerity, gravity, purposefulness, resolution, intentness, determination, ardour, devotion, eagerness, enthusiasm, fervency, fervour, zeal, keenness, passion, vehemence, warmth
🔁 apathy, flippancy

earnings *n*
pay, income, salary, wages, profits, take home pay, net pay, gross pay, gain, proceeds, reward, receipts, return, revenue, fee, remuneration, honorarium, stipend, *formal* emolument
🔁 expenditure, outgoings

earth *n*
1 WORLD, planet, globe, sphere, orb **2** LAND, ground, soil, turf, clay, loam, sod, humus, dirt

earthenware *n*
pottery, ceramics, crockery, stoneware, pots

earthly *adj*
1 *our earthly life* material, physical, human, worldly, mortal, mundane, fleshly, secular, sensual, materialistic, profane, temporal, *formal* terrestrial, tellurian, telluric **2** *no earthly explanation* possible, likely, imaginable, conceivable, slightest, feasible
🔁 **1** spiritual, heavenly

earthquake *n*
earth-tremor, tremor, quake, seism, shake, upheaval, aftershock

earthy *adj*
crude, coarse, rude, vulgar, bawdy, rough, ribald, robust, down-to-earth, natural, unsophisticated, uninhibited, *formal* indecorous, *colloq.* raunchy, blue
🔁 refined, modest, inhibited

ease *n, v*

▸ *n* **1** FACILITY, effortlessness, skilfulness, deftness, adroitness, dexterity, naturalness, cleverness **2** COMFORT, contentment, enjoyment, peace, affluence, prosperity, wealth, leisure, relaxation, rest, quiet, happiness, lap of luxury, *formal* repose, opulence, *colloq.* bed of roses, easy street, life of Riley
🖃 **1** difficulty **2** discomfort

▷ **at ease** relaxed, natural, composed, calm, secure, at home, comfortable

▸ *v* **1** *ease the pain* alleviate, moderate, grow/become less, lessen, reduce, diminish, lighten, relieve, relent, allay, assuage, relax, comfort, calm, soothe, facilitate, smooth, quieten, salve, *formal* mitigate, abate, ameliorate, palliate **2** *ease it into position* inch, steer, edge, slide, manoeuvre, guide
🖃 **1** aggravate, intensify, worsen

▷ **ease off** decrease, become less, die away, die down, diminish, moderate, relent, slacken, subside, wane, *formal* abate
🖃 increase

easily *adv*

1 EFFORTLESSLY, comfortably, readily, simply, fluently, straightforwardly **2** *easily the best* BY FAR, undoubtedly, indisputably, definitely, certainly, doubtlessly, clearly, far and away, undeniably, simply, surely, probably, well
🖃 **1** laboriously

easy *adj*

1 SIMPLE, effortless, uncomplicated, undemanding, straightforward, foolproof, manageable, painless, natural, *colloq.* cushy, a cinch, a doddle, a piece of cake, a pushover, easy as ABC, child's play, like falling off a log **2** RELAXED, carefree, easy-going, comfortable, informal, calm, natural, leisurely, casual, unforced, *colloq.* laid-back
🖃 **1** difficult, hard, demanding, exacting **2** tense, uneasy

easy-going *adj*

relaxed, tolerant, lenient, amenable, undemanding, carefree, nonchalant, calm, even-tempered, serene, placid, *formal* insouciant, imperturbable, *colloq.* laid-back, happy-go-lucky
🖃 strict, intolerant, critical

eat *v*

1 CONSUME, feed, swallow, devour, chew, munch, have a snack, breakfast, lunch, dine, gulp down, bolt down, gobble, *formal* ingest, partake of, *colloq.* scoff, put away, wolf down, tuck into, polish off, graze **2** CORRODE, erode, wear away, decay, rot, crumble, dissolve, undermine

eatable *adj*

edible, palatable, good, wholesome, digestible, *formal* comestible
🖃 inedible, unpalatable

📗 **eatable** or **edible** ?

If something is *edible,* it is by nature safe or good to eat, whereas if it is *eatable,* it is in a condition that makes it possible to eat it (whether or not it is safe to do so). Poisonous mushrooms are *eatable* but they are not *edible,* while a bag of flour is perfectly *edible* but would scarcely be *eatable.*

---

eavesdrop *v*

listen in, spy, overhear, monitor, *colloq.* snoop, tap, bug

eavesdropper *n*

listener, monitor, spy, *colloq.* snoop, snooper

ebb *v, n*

▸ *v* **1** *the tide ebbed* fall, fall back, flow back, go out,

recede, *formal* retrocede **2** *his confidence ebbed away* decline, decrease, diminish, drop, dwindle, flag, weaken, deteriorate, decay, degenerate, fade away, shrink, sink, slacken, subside, recede, lessen, wane, *formal* abate, *colloq.* peter out
🖃 **1** rise **2** increase, rise

▸ *n* **1** *at ebb tide* low tide, low water, ebb tide, fall, going out, flowing-back, retreat **2** *her health is at a low ebb* decline, decrease, drop, decay, lagging, lessening, deterioration, degeneration, slackening, weakening, subsidence, wane, waning, dwindling
🖃 **1** rise, flow **2** increase

ebony *adj*

black, dark, jet, jet-black, jetty, sable, sooty

ebullience *n*

exhilaration, effusiveness, enthusiasm, excitement, exuberance, brightness, buoyancy, elation, vivacity, high spirits, breeziness, zest, *colloq.* chirpiness
🖃 apathy, dullness, lifelessness

ebullient *adj*

exhilarated, effusive, enthusiastic, excited, exuberant, bright, buoyant, elated, gushing, vivacious, effervescent, breezy, irrepressible, zestful, *colloq.* chirpy
🖃 apathetic, dull, lifeless

eccentric *adj, n*

▸ *adj* odd, peculiar, abnormal, unconventional, strange, quirky, weird, queer, outlandish, idiosyncratic, bizarre, freakish, erratic, singular, *formal* aberrant, *colloq.* way-out, wacky, dotty, off-beat, nutty, loony, loopy, *US* kooky
🖃 conventional, orthodox, normal

▸ *n* nonconformist, oddity, *colloq.* oddball, crank, freak, character, case, nut, nutter, weirdo, crackpot, *US* kook, odd fish, square peg in a round hole, fish out of water, *slang* geek

eccentricity *n*

unconventionality, strangeness, peculiarity, nonconformity, abnormality, oddity, bizarreness, weirdness, idiosyncrasy, singularity, quirk, freakishness, anomaly, *formal* aberration, capriciousness
🖃 conventionality, ordinariness

ecclesiastic *n*

churchman, churchwoman, cleric, clergyman, clergywoman, man/woman of God, man/woman of the cloth, minister, priest, reverend, father, vicar, pastor, padre, parson, rector, canon, dean, deacon, deaconess, chaplain, curate, presbyter

ecclesiastical *adj*

church, churchly, religious, clerical, priestly, holy, divine, spiritual, pastoral, *formal* sacerdotal
🖃 secular, temporal

echelon *n*

level, rank, grade, rung, tier, degree, position, place, status

echo *n, v*

▸ *n* **1** REVERBERATION, ringing, resounding, reiteration, repetition, reflection **2** IMITATION, copy, reproduction, reflection, mirror image, image, parallel, repeat, clone, duplicate **3** REMINDER, memory, remembrance, allusion, hint, trace, *formal* evocation

▸ *v* **1** REVERBERATE, resound, repeat, reflect, reiterate, ring **2** IMITATE, copy, reproduce, mirror, reflect, resemble, mimic, repeat, parallel, parrot

éclat *n*

effect, glory, brilliance, lustre, ostentation, show, distinction, display, success, splendour, acclaim, renown, acclamation, applause, approval, fame, celebrity, *formal* plaudits
🖃 disapproval, dullness

eclectic *adj*

diverse, wide-ranging, many-sided, catholic, broad,

comprehensive, diversified, general, all-embracing, liberal, varied, selective, *formal* heterogeneous, multifarious
F3 narrow, one-sided, exclusive

eclipse *v, n*
► *v* **1** BLOT OUT, obscure, cloud, cover, conceal, veil, shroud, darken, dim, cast a shadow over **2** OUTDO, overshadow, outshine, surpass, exceed, transcend, excel, dwarf, put into the shade, leave someone standing, *colloq.* run rings around
► *n* **1** OVERSHADOWING, blotting-out, darkening, concealing, covering, veiling, shading, dimming, *formal* obscuration **2** DECLINE, failure, fall, loss, ebb, weakening

economic *adj*
1 COMMERCIAL, business, industrial, trade **2** FINANCIAL, budgetary, fiscal, monetary **3** PROFITABLE, profit-making, money-making, productive, cost-effective, viable, remunerative

---

 economic or **economical**?

Economic means 'relating to economics or the economy of a country': *economic history; the country's economic future*. It also means 'giving an adequate profit or fair return', as in *We must charge an economic rent/price. Economical* means 'thrifty','not wasteful, expensive, or extravagant': *This car is very economical on petrol; the economical use of limited supplies.*

---

economical *adj*
1 THRIFTY, careful, saving, sparing, frugal, scrimping, skimping, *formal* prudent, parsimonious **2** CHEAP, inexpensive, low-priced, low-cost, low-budget, reasonable, cost-effective, budget, modest, efficient
F3 **1** wasteful **2** expensive, uneconomical

economize *v*
save, cut back, budget, cut expenditure, use less, buy cheaply, keep down costs, live on the cheap, cut costs, be economical, scrimp and save, *formal* retrench, *colloq.* tighten your belt, cut corners, cut your coat according to your cloth
F3 waste, squander

economy *n*
1 *the country's economy* system of wealth, financial state, financial resources, financial system, financial organization, business resources **2** THRIFT, saving, restraint, carefulness, care, frugality, parsimony, providence, husbandry, scrimping, skimping, *formal* prudence
F3 **2** extravagance

ecstasy *n*
delight, rapture, bliss, elation, joy, jubilation, euphoria, frenzy, exultation, fervour, transports of delight, pleasure
F3 misery, torment

ecstatic *adj*
elated, blissful, joyful, jubilant, rapturous, enraptured, overjoyed, euphoric, delirious, frenzied, fervent, *formal* rhapsodic, *colloq.* jumping for joy, on cloud nine, in seventh heaven, over the moon, tickled pink, high as a kite
F3 downcast

eddy *n, v*
► *n* whirlpool, swirl, swirling, vortex, twist, maelstrom
► *v* swirl, whirl

edge *n, v*
► *n* **1** BORDER, rim, boundary, frontier, limit, brim, threshold, brink, fringe, margin, outline, outer limit, side, verge, line, extremity, perimeter, periphery, lip

2 ADVANTAGE, superiority, force, dominance, *formal* ascendancy, *colloq.* upper hand, whip hand **3** SHARPNESS, acuteness, keenness, incisiveness, severity, zest, bite, sting, *formal* pungency, acerbity, causticity, trenchancy
▷ **on edge** nervous, tense, anxious, apprehensive, ill at ease, keyed-up, touchy, edgy, irritable, *colloq.* uptight, nervy
F3 calm, at ease
► *v* creep, crawl, inch, ease, steal, sidle, elbow, worm, pick your way

edgy *adj*
on edge, nervous, tense, anxious, ill at ease, keyed-up, touchy, irritable, *colloq.* uptight, nervy
F3 calm, at ease

edible *adj*
eatable, fit to eat, palatable, digestible, wholesome, good, harmless, *formal* comestible
F3 inedible

---

edible or **eatable**? *See panel at* EATABLE.

---

edict *n*
command, order, proclamation, law, decree, regulation, pronouncement, rule, ruling, act, mandate, statute, fiat, injunction, manifesto, pronunciamento, ukase

edification *n*
instruction, improvement, enlightenment, guidance, education, teaching, coaching, upbuilding, elevation, uplifting

edifice *n*
building, construction, structure, erection

edify *v*
instruct, build up, improve, enlighten, inform, guide, educate, tutor, nurture, teach, school, coach, elevate, uplift

edit *v*
1 *edit a text* correct, revise, rewrite, rephrase, reorder, rearrange, adapt, modify, check, compile, select, polish, annotate, blue pencil, *formal* emend, redact **2** *edit a newspaper* be in charge of, direct, head (up), be responsible for

edition *n*
copy, volume, impression, printing, publication, issue, version, number

educable *adj*
instructible, teachable, trainable
F3 ineducable

educate *v*
teach, train, instruct, tutor, coach, school, inform, cultivate, edify, enlighten, drill, improve, prepare, prime, discipline, indoctrinate, develop, *formal* inculcate

educated *adj*
learned, taught, schooled, literate, trained, knowledgeable, enlightened, informed, instructed, lettered, well-read, cultured, civilized, cultivated, wise, tutored, refined, well-bred, *formal* erudite, sagacious, *colloq.* brainy, all there, clever-clever
F3 uneducated, uncultured

education *n*
teaching, training, schooling, tuition, tutoring, coaching, guidance, instruction, informing, drilling, cultivation, culture, letters, scholarship, improvement, enlightenment, edification, knowledge, nurture, preparation, fostering, upbringing, development, indoctrination, *formal* inculcation

educational *adj*
academic, learning, teaching, cultural, edifying, enlightening, educative, improving, informative, in-

structive, *formal* didactic, scholastic, pedagogic, pedagogical
Ⅎ uninformative

Educational establishments include:
kindergarten, nursery school, infant school, primary school, middle school, combined school, comprehensive school, secondary school, secondary modern, upper school, high school, grammar school, grant-maintained school, foundation school, preparatory school, public school, private school, boarding-school, college, sixth-form college, college of further education, city technical college, CTC, technical college, university, adult-education centre, academy, seminary, finishing school, business school, secretarial college, Sunday school, convent school, summer-school.

Educational terms include :
adult education, assisted places scheme, A-level, AS-level, (international) baccalaureate, board of governors, break time, bursar, campus, catchment area, certificate, classroom, coeducation, common entrance, course, course of studies, curriculum, degree, diploma, discipline, double-first, educational programme, eleven-plus, enrolment, examination, exercise book, final exam, finals, further education, GCSE (General Certificate of Secondary Education), governor, graduation, half-term, head boy, head girl, head teacher, higher education, Higher Grade, homework, intake, invigilator, lecture, literacy, matriculation, matron, mixed-ability teaching, modular course, module, national curriculum, newly qualified teacher, NVQ (national vocational qualification), numeracy, O-level, opting out, parent governor, PTA (parent teacher association), playground, playtime, prefect, primary education, proctor, professor, pupil, quadrangle, qualification, refresher course, register, report, scholarship, school term, secondary education, special education, Standard Grade, statemented, streaming, student, student grant, student loan, study, subject, syllabus, teacher, teacher training, test paper, textbook, thesis, timetable, truancy, university entrance, work experience.

educative *adj*
instructive, improving, informative, edifying, educational, enlightening, *formal* catechetic, catechismal, catechistic(al), didactic
Ⅎ uninformative

educator *n*
instructor, teacher, tutor, schoolteacher, schoolmaster, schoolmistress, educationalist, lecturer, professor, academic, trainer, coach, *formal* pedagogue

eerie *adj*
weird, strange, unnatural, unearthly, mysterious, uncanny, ghostly, frightening, scaring, scary, bloodcurdling, *colloq.* spooky, creepy, spine-chilling

efface *v*
remove, destroy, delete, rub out, wipe out, cancel, eliminate, eradicate, obliterate, erase, blank out, blot out, cross out, *formal* excise, expunge, extirpate

effect *n, v*
► *n* **1** OUTCOME, result, conclusion, consequence,

upshot, fruit, impact, aftermath, issue **2** POWER, force, impact, impression, strength, influence, *formal* efficacy **3** MEANING, significance, sense, drift, tenor, *formal* import, purport **4** *personal effects* belongings, possessions, property, goods, movables, paraphernalia, baggage, luggage, things, trappings, *formal* chattels, accoutrements, *colloq.* gear, things, stuff
▷ **in effect** in fact, actually, in actual fact, really, in reality, in truth, to all intents and purposes, in practice, for all practical purposes, essentially, effectively, virtually
▷ **take effect** be effective, become operative, come into force, come into operation, be implemented, become valid, begin, work, produce results, function
► *v* cause, execute, bring about, carry out, create, achieve, accomplish, perform, produce, make, initiate, give rise to, fulfil, complete, *formal* generate, effectuate

 effect or **affect** ? *See panel at* AFFECT.

effective *adj*
1 EFFICIENT, productive, adequate, capable, useful, successful, *formal* efficacious **2** OPERATIVE, in force, functioning, valid, current, active **3** STRIKING, impressive, forceful, powerful, exciting, attractive, persuasive, convincing, potent, telling, *formal* cogent **4** ACTUAL, practical, virtual, essential
Ⅎ **1** ineffective, powerless **4** theoretical

effective or **effectual** ?
Effective has a number of meanings: 'producing, or likely to produce, the intended result': *Aspirin is effective against many types of pain*; 'impressive', 'powerful': *He's a very effective speaker*; 'in operation, in force': *The new regulations become effective at midnight*; 'in reality, even if not in theory': *Although not the king, he was the effective ruler of the country for twenty years. Effectual* puts more emphasis on the actual achievement of the desired result than *effective* does. If the police take *effective* measures to combat the rising crime rate, these measures have the desired effect, or are expected to, whereas if the police take *effectual measures,* there is no doubt that these measures are succeeding in reducing the crime rate.

effectiveness *n*
success, strength, force, influence, use, power, ability, capability, efficiency, validity, vigour, weight, *formal* cogency, efficacy, potency, *colloq.* clout
Ⅎ ineffectiveness, uselessness

effectual *adj*
1 *an effectual plan* successful, effective, useful, capable, influential, serviceable, operative, sound, powerful, productive, forcible **2** *effectual contracts* binding, authoritative, lawful, legal, valid
Ⅎ **1** ineffective, useless

effeminate *adj*
unmanly, womanly, womanish, feminine, delicate, *colloq.* sissy, wimpish
Ⅎ manly

effervesce *v*
1 *mineral water effervescing* sparkle, bubble, fizz, boil, foam, froth, ferment **2** *effervescing with conversation* be lively, be vivacious, be animated, be exhilarated, *formal* ebullient

effervescence *n*
1 SPARKLE, bubbles, bubbling, fizz, foam, foaming, froth, frothing, ferment, fermentation **2** LIVELINESS, vivacity, vitality, animation, buoyancy, enthusiasm,

high spirits, excitedness, excitement, exhilaration, exuberance, *formal* ebullience, *colloq.* vim, zing, zip

effervescent *adj*
1 BUBBLY, bubbling, sparkling, fizzy, fizzing, frothy, carbonated, foaming, fermenting **2** LIVELY, vivacious, animated, buoyant, exhilarated, enthusiastic, exuberant, sparkling, excited, vital, *formal* ebullient
Fl 1 flat **2** dull

effete *adj*
weak, feeble, enfeebled, exhausted, drained, fruitless, unfruitful, unproductive, played out, spent, sterile, tired out, worn out, spoiled, used up, unprolific, wasted, decayed, barren, corrupt, debased, decrepit, degenerate, decadent, *formal* debilitated, enervated, ineffectual, infecund
Fl vigorous

efficacious *adj*
effective, productive, capable, useful, successful, competent, powerful, potent, strong, adequate, sufficient, active, effectual, operative
Fl ineffective, useless

efficacy *n*
effectiveness, effect, usefulness, use, success, power, energy, force, influence, potency, strength, capability, ability, competence, virtue
Fl ineffectiveness, uselessness

efficiency *n*
effectiveness, competence, proficiency, skill, expertise, skilfulness, capability, ability, productivity, organization
Fl inefficiency, incompetence

efficient *adj*
effective, competent, proficient, skilful, capable, able, productive, organized, well-organized, well-ordered, streamlined, rationalized, businesslike, workmanlike, powerful, well-run, well-conducted, expert
Fl inefficient, incompetent

effigy *n*
figure, statue, carving, representation, likeness, picture, portrait, image, icon, idol, dummy, guy

effluent *n*
waste, discharge, sewage, emission, outflow, pollutant, pollution, *formal* effluence, effluvium, efflux, emanation, exhalation

effort *n*
1 EXERTION, strain, application, struggle, sweat, trouble, energy, hard work, power, force, stress, toil, striving, pains, labour, muscle power, *formal* travail, *colloq.* elbow grease, sweat of your brow, beef, muscles

---

Expressions about effort include:
be at pains, beaver away, blood, sweat and tears, break the back of something, bust a gut, can't be bothered, do your bit, do your utmost, fight tooth and nail, go all out, go out of your way, go the extra mile, go to a lot of trouble, go to great lengths, go to the trouble of, have your nose to the grindstone, huff and puff, knock your pan in, make a point of doing something, make the effort, pull out all the stops, pull your finger out, pull your socks up, pull your weight, put your back into something, put your shoulder to the wheel, stay the course, sweat blood over something, take a bit of doing, take the trouble to, use a bit of elbow grease, use a sledgehammer to crack a nut, work your guts out.

---

2 ATTEMPT, try, endeavour, *colloq.* go, shot, stab, crack, bash, whirl **3** ACHIEVEMENT, accomplishment, feat, attainment, exploit, production, creation, deed, product, result, work, opus

effortless *adj*
easy, simple, undemanding, facile, painless, uncomplicated, unexacting, straightforward, smooth
Fl difficult, complicated, exacting, demanding

effrontery *n*
audacity, impertinence, insolence, impudence, temerity, boldness, brazenness, cheekiness, gall, nerve, presumption, disrespect, arrogance, brashness, *colloq.* cheek, nerve, face, brass, lip, chutzpah
Fl respect, timidity

effulgent *adj*
brilliant, radiant, shining, glowing, splendid, glorious, *formal* resplendent, refulgent, incandescent

effusion *n*
outpouring, outburst, outflow, gush, discharge, emission, stream, shedding, *formal* effluence, efflux, voidance

effusive *adj*
fulsome, gushing, unrestrained, unreserved, expansive, demonstrative, profuse, overflowing, enthusiastic, exuberant, extravagant, lavish, talkative, voluble, lyrical, *formal* ebullient, rhapsodic, *colloq.* gabby, gassy, over the top, OTT, all mouth, big-mouthed
Fl reserved, restrained

egg *v*
▷ **egg on** encourage, incite, push, urge, drive, excite, stimulate, spur, prompt, coax, talk into, goad, prod, prick, *formal* exhort
Fl discourage

egghead *n*
boffin, brain, intellect, intellectual, academic, scholar, thinker, bookworm, genius, Einstein, *colloq.* know-all, know-it-all

ego *n*
self, (sense of) identity, self-esteem, self-importance, self-confidence, self-image, self-worth

egoism *n*
self-interest, self-centredness, self-importance, self-absorption, self-love, self-regard, self-seeking, selfishness, narcissism, egocentricity, egomania, egotism, amour-propre
Fl altruism

egoist *n*
self-seeker, narcissist, egotist, egomaniac

egoistic *adj*
self-absorbed, self-important, self-involved, self-centred, self-pleasing, self-seeking, narcissistic, egocentric, egoistical, egotistic, egotistical, egomaniacal
Fl altruistic

egotism *n*
egoism, egomania, self-centredness, no thought for others, self-importance, egocentricity, selfishness, superiority, conceitedness, self-regard, self-love, self-conceit, narcissism, self-admiration, pride, boastfulness, vanity, snobbery, *formal* braggadocio, *colloq.* bigheadedness, swank, blowing your own trumpet, *US* blowing your own horn
Fl humility

egotist *n*
boaster, bluffer, show-off, self-admirer, braggart, egoist, egomaniac, swaggerer, braggadocio, *colloq.* bighead, big mouth, smart alec, clever clogs, clever dick

egotistic *adj*
egoistic, egocentric, self-centred, self-important, selfish, self-admiring, narcissistic, conceited, superior, vain, proud, boasting, bragging, *colloq.* swollen-headed, bigheaded
Fl humble

egregious *adj*
grievous, outrageous, scandalous, shocking, gross, rank, infamous, notorious, insufferable, intolerable, monstrous, flagrant, glaring, arrant, heinous
🖅 slight

egress *n*
exit, way out, outlet, vent, issue, exodus, emergence, leaving, departure, escape

ejaculate *v*
1 DISCHARGE, eject, spurt, emit, release, expel, *colloq.* come 2 EXCLAIM, call (out), blurt (out), cry (out), shout (out), yell, utter, scream

ejaculation *n*
1 *ejaculation of semen* discharge, ejection, emission, spurt, release, expulsion, orgasm, climax, *colloq.* coming 2 EXCLAMATION, call, cry, scream, shout, yell, utterance

eject *v*
1 EMIT, expel, discharge, release, spout, spew, disgorge, evacuate, vomit, *formal* exude, excrete 2 OUST, evict, get rid of, throw out, drive out, turn out, expel, remove, banish, deport, dismiss, discharge, exile, kick out, *colloq.* fire, sack, boot out, turf out, chuck out, give someone their cards, show someone the door 3 BAIL OUT, propel, thrust out, throw out, get out

ejection *n*
eviction, expulsion, removal, banishment, dismissal, discharge, exile, deportation, ousting, *colloq.* firing, sacking, the boot, the sack

eke *v*
▷ **eke out** 1 *eke out supplies* make something stretch, stretch, spin out, fill out, husband, economize on, be economical with, add to, increase, supplement, *colloq.* go easy with 2 *eke out a living* scrimp and save, scrape, scratch, get by, survive, *colloq.* live from hand to mouth, feel the pinch

elaborate *adj, v*
▶ *adj* 1 *elaborate plans* detailed, complicated, complex, careful, thorough, exact, extensive, painstaking, precise, perfected, minute, laboured, studied 2 *elaborate designs* intricate, complex, complicated, involved, ornamental, ornate, fancy, decorated, extravagant, ostentatious, showy, fussy, rococo
🖅 2 simple, plain
▶ *v* amplify, develop, enlarge on, expand on, flesh out, polish, improve, refine, enhance, devise, explain, *formal* expatiate
🖅 précis, simplify

élan *n*
panache, liveliness, flair, flourish, style, spirit, verve, vigour, vivacity, animation, confidence, zest, dash, esprit, *colloq.* brio, oomph, pizzazz
🖅 apathy, lifelessness

elapse *v*
pass, lapse, go by, go on, slip away, slip by

elastic *adj*
1 PLIABLE, flexible, stretchable, stretchy, supple, resilient, yielding, springy, rubbery, pliant, plastic, bouncy, buoyant 2 ADAPTABLE, accommodating, flexible, tolerant, adjustable, fluid, *formal* compliant, *colloq.* easy
🖅 1 rigid 2 inflexible

elasticity *n*
1 PLIABILITY, flexibility, resilience, stretch, stretchiness, springiness, suppleness, plasticity, bounce, buoyancy, *colloq.* give 2 ADAPTABILITY, flexibility, tolerance, adjustability
🖅 1 rigidity 2 inflexibility

elated *adj*
exhilarated, excited, delighted, euphoric, ecstatic, rapturous, exultant, jubilant, overjoyed, joyful, blissful, *formal* joyous, rhapsodic, *colloq.* over the moon, on cloud nine
🖅 despondent, downcast

elation *n*
exhilaration, delight, transports of delight, euphoria, ecstasy, rapture, bliss, exultation, glee, high spirits, joy, joyfulness, jubilation, *formal* joyousness
🖅 depression, despondency

elbow *v*
jostle, nudge, push, bump, knock, crowd, shoulder, *colloq.* shove, barge

elbow-room *n*
space, room, breathing-space, play, scope, leeway, freedom, latitude, Lebensraum

elder *adj*
older, senior, first-born, ancient
🖅 younger

elderly *adj, n*
▶ *adj* aging, aged, old, grey-haired, hoary, senile, *formal* senescent, *colloq.* not as young as you were, not getting any younger, over the hill, long in the tooth, past it, not long for this world
🖅 young, youthful
▶ *n* old people, older generation, older adults, senior citizens, retired people, pensioners, old-age pensioners, OAPs, *colloq.* oldies, wrinklies, has-beens, *slang* fossils

eldest *adj*
first, first-born, oldest
🖅 youngest

elect *v, adj*
▶ *v* choose, pick, opt for, select, vote for, cast a vote, go to the polls, decide on, prefer, adopt, designate, appoint, determine, *colloq.* plump for
▶ *adj the elect; the president-elect* choice, elite, chosen, designated, designate, picked, prospective, selected, to be, preferred, hand-picked

election *n*
choice, selection, vote, voting, ballot, poll, hustings, referendum, appointment, determination, decision, preference, choosing, picking

elector *n*
voter, selector, constituent, electorate

electric *adj*
1 *an electric light* electric-powered, mains-operated, battery-operated, rechargeable, cordless, powered, live 2 *the atmosphere was electric* electrifying, exciting, stimulating, thrilling, startling, charged, dynamic, stirring, tense, rousing
🖅 2 unexciting, flat

electrical components

Types of electrical components and devices include:
adaptor, ammeter, armature, battery, bayonet fitting, cable, ceiling rose, circuit breaker, conduit, continuity tester, copper conductor, dimmer switch, dry-cell battery, earthed plug, electrical screwdriver, electricity meter, extension lead, fluorescent tube, fuse, fusebox, fuse carrier, high voltage tester, insulating tape, lampholder, light bulb, multimeter, neon lamp, socket, test lamp, three-core cable, three-pin plug, transducer, transformer, two-pin plug, universal test meter, voltage doubler, wire strippers.

electricity n

Electricity and electronic terms include :

alternating current (AC), alternator, amp, ampere, amplifier, analogue signal, anode, band-pass filter, battery, bioelectricity, capacitance, capacitor, cathode, cathode-ray tube, cell, commutator, condenser, conductivity, coulomb, digital signal, diode, direct current (DC), Dolby (system), dynamo, eddy current, electrode, electrolyte, electromagnet, electron tube, farad, Faraday cage, Foucault current, frequency modulation, galvanic, galvanometer, generator, grid system, henry, impedance, induced current, inductance, integrated circuit, isoelectric, isoelectronic, logic gate, loudspeaker, microchip, mutual induction, ohm, optoelectronics, oscillator, oscilloscope, piezoelectricity, polarity, power station, reactance, resistance, resistor, rheostat, semiconductor, siemens, silicon chip, solenoid, solid state circuit, static electricity, step-down transformer, superconductivity, switch, thermionics, thermistor, thyristor, transformer, transistor, triode, truth table, turboalternator, tweeter, valve, volt, voltage amplifier, voltaic, watt, Wheatstone bridge, woofer.

electrify v
thrill, excite, shock, charge, invigorate, animate, stimulate, stir, rouse, fire, jolt, galvanize, amaze, astonish, astound, stagger
🖪 bore

elegance n
style, chic, fashionableness, sophistication, smartness, refinement, polish, beauty, dignity, distinction, grace, gracefulness, discernment, taste, gentility, politeness, tastefulness, poise, exquisiteness, grandeur, luxury, sumptuousness, *formal* propriety
🖪 inelegance

elegant adj
stylish, chic, fashionable, modish, smart, refined, pol-ished, cultivated, genteel, charming, sophisticated, smooth, tasteful, lovely, fine, exquisite, beautiful, cultured, graceful, handsome, delicate, neat, artistic
🖪 inelegant, unrefined, unfashionable

elegiac adj
lamenting, funereal, mournful, doleful, melancholic, sad, plaintive, valedictory, keening, *formal* threnetic, threnetical, threnodial, threnodic
🖪 happy

elegy n
dirge, lament, requiem, funeral poem, funeral song, plaint, *formal* threnody, threnode

element n
1 *the elements of our discussion* factor, component, constituent, ingredient, member, part, piece, fragment, feature, strand **2** *the elements of a subject* BASICS, foundations, fundamentals, principles, rudiments, essentials **3** *an element of truth* small amount, grain, trace, touch, hint, suspicion, soupçon **4** *the criminal element in society* individual(s), group, faction, set, party, clique **5** *exposed to the elements* weather, wind and rain, storms, climate, atmospheric conditions, atmospheric forces
🖪 **1** whole

elemental adj
basic, fundamental, natural, rudimentary, primitive, radical, immense, powerful, forceful, uncontrolled

elementary adj
basic, fundamental, rudimentary, principal, primary, clear, easy, introductory, straightforward, uncomplicated, simple
🖪 advanced, complicated

elephantine adj
large, vast, immense, huge, enormous, massive, bulky, hulking, heavy, weighty, awkward, clumsy, lumbering

elevate v
1 LIFT, raise, hoist, uplift, heighten, intensify, magnify, exalt, *colloq.* hike up **2** PROMOTE, advance, exalt, aggrandize, refine, ennoble, upgrade, *colloq.* move up the ladder, put on a pedestal, kick upstairs **3** UPLIFT, rouse, boost, buoy up, brighten, cheer, gladden, give a lift to
🖪 **1** lower **2** downgrade **3** depress

elevated adj
1 IMPORTANT, great, lofty, exalted, grand, noble, dignified **2** *elevated thoughts* advanced, lofty, exalted, grand, noble, dignified, moral, *formal* sublime **3** *elevated ground* raised, lifted (up), rising, high, hoisted, uplifted

elevation n
1 RISE, promotion, advancement, preferment, upgrading, aggrandizement, *colloq.* step up the ladder, leg-up, go-getting **2** EXALTATION, loftiness, grandeur, eminence, nobility, dignity, *formal* sublimity **3** HEIGHT, altitude, tallness, hill, rise, mound, mount
🖪 **1** demotion **3** dip

elf n
fairy, sprite, imp, goblin, hobgoblin, gnome, brownie, leprechaun, troll, banshee, puck

elfin adj
small, petite, delicate, charming, elfish, elflike, frolicsome, sprightly, playful, impish, mischievous, puckish

elicit v
evoke, draw out, bring out, derive, extract, obtain, exact, extort, cause, wrest, *formal* call forth, educe, *colloq.* worm out

eligible adj
qualified, fit, fitting, appropriate, suitable, acceptable, worthy, proper, desirable
🖪 ineligible

eliminate v
1 GET RID OF, remove, cut out, take out, exclude, delete, dispense with, put an end/a stop to, rub out, omit, reject, disregard, dispose of, drop, do away with, eradicate, expel, extinguish, stamp out **2** DEFEAT, conquer, beat, overwhelm, *colloq.* knock out, thrash, lick, hammer, annihilate **3** KILL, murder, do away with, exterminate, *colloq.* wipe out, liquidate, rub out, bump off, do in
🖪 **1** include, accept

elite n, adj
▶ n best, pick, cream, elect, aristocracy, upper classes, nobility, gentry, crème de la crème, establishment, high society, *colloq.* pick of the bunch, jet set
▶ adj choice, best, exclusive, selected, first-class, aristocratic, noble, upper-class

elixir n
cure-all, panacea, remedy, solution, mixture, concentrate, essence, extract, pith, potion, principle, quintessence, syrup, tincture, nostrum

elliptical adj
1 OVAL, egg-shaped, oviform, ovoid(al) **2** OBLIQUE, cryptic, obscure, ambiguous, incomprehensible, unfathomable, concise, concentrated, condensed, laconic, terse, *formal* abstruse, recondite
🖪 **2** clear, direct

elocution *n*
delivery, articulation, diction, pronunciation, voice production, rhetoric, speech, utterance, phrasing, *formal* enunciation, oratory

elongate *v*
lengthen, extend, draw out, prolong, make longer, stretch, *formal* protract

elongated *adj*
lengthened, extended, prolonged, protracted, stretched, long

elope *v*
run off, run away, decamp, bolt, make off, abscond, flee, escape, slip away, steal away, leave, disappear, *colloq.* do a bunk

eloquence *n*
expressiveness, fluency, flow of words, expression, persuasiveness, articulateness, diction, facility, forcefulness, oratory, rhetoric, *formal* facundity, *colloq.* gift of the gab, blarney, gassiness
🖬 inarticulateness

eloquent *adj*
articulate, fluent, well-expressed, well-spoken, glib, expressive, vocal, voluble, persuasive, moving, forceful, graceful, plausible, stirring, effective, vivid
🖬 inarticulate, tongue-tied

elsewhere *adv*
somewhere else, in/to another place, not here, absent, removed, abroad
🖬 here, present

elucidate *v*
explain, clarify, make clear, clear up, interpret, spell out, simplify, state simply, illustrate, illuminate, unfold, throw/shed light on, fill in, exemplify, give an example, *formal* explicate, expound
🖬 confuse

elucidation *n*
explanation, clarification, comment, commentary, illumination, illustration, interpretation, footnote, gloss, annotation, marginalia, *formal* explication, exposition

elude *v*
1 AVOID, escape, evade, shirk, shake off, flee, get away from, give someone the slip, throw someone off the scent, *formal* circumvent, *colloq.* dodge, duck, slip through someone's fingers 2 PUZZLE, frustrate, baffle, confound, thwart, stump, foil

elusive *adj*
1 INDEFINABLE, difficult to describe, intangible, unanalysable, subtle, puzzling, baffling, deceptive, misleading, transient, transitory 2 EVASIVE, difficult to find, hard to catch, slippery, tricky, *colloq.* shifty, dodgy

emaciated *adj*
thin, gaunt, lean, haggard, drawn, wasted, anorexic, scrawny, skinny, skeletal, pinched, meagre, *formal* attenuated, cadaverous, *colloq.* thin as a rake, all skin and bone
🖬 plump, well-fed

emaciation *n*
thinness, gauntness, leanness, haggardness, scrawniness, *formal* atrophy
🖬 plumpness

emanate *v*
1 RADIATE, send out, emit, give out, give off, discharge, *formal* exhale 2 ORIGINATE, proceed, arise, derive, issue, spring, stem, flow, come, emerge

emanation *n*
discharge, emission, flow, effluent, effluence, radiation, *formal* effluvium, efflux, effluxion, effusion

emancipate *v*
free, liberate, release, set free, enfranchise, deliver, discharge, loose, set loose, unchain, untie, un-shackle, unfetter, unyoke, *formal* manumit
🖬 enslave

emancipation *n*
liberation, freedom, setting free, release, deliverance, liberty, discharge, enfranchisement, unbinding, un-fettering, unchaining, *formal* manumission
🖬 enslavement

emasculate *v*
1 CASTRATE, geld, neuter, spay 2 WEAKEN, impoverish, cripple, debilitate, soften, *formal* enervate
🖬 2 boost, vitalize

embalm *v*
preserve, mummify, store, lay out, enshrine, cherish, consecrate, conserve, treasure

embankment *n*
causeway, dam, rampart, levee, earthwork

embargo *n, v*
▶ *n* restriction, ban, prohibition, restraint, bar, barrier, impediment, check, hindrance, obstruction, blockage, stoppage, seizure, *formal* proscription, interdiction
▶ *v* restrict, ban, bar, prohibit, restrain, block, check, impede, obstruct, seize, stop, *formal* interdict, proscribe
🖬 allow

embark *v*
board (ship), go aboard, take ship
🖬 disembark
▷ **embark on** begin, start, commence, set about, launch into, undertake, venture into, enter (on), initiate, engage
🖬 complete, finish

embarrass *v*
make awkward/ashamed, disconcert, mortify, show up, discompose, fluster, humiliate, shame, distress, upset, confuse, *formal* discomfit, discountenance

embarrassed *adj*
awkward, uncomfortable, self-conscious, upset, confused, distressed, disconcerted, ashamed, shamed, guilty, shown up, humiliated, mortified, abashed, *formal* discomfited, *colloq.* sheepish
🖬 unembarrassed

embarrassing *adj*
awkward, uncomfortable, disconcerting, distressing, upsetting, sensitive, mortifying, humiliating, shameful, shaming, tricky, compromising, painful, *formal* discomfiting, indelicate, discountenancing, *colloq.* touchy

embarrassment *n*
1 DISCOMPOSURE, self-consciousness, mortification, humiliation, shame, guilt, awkwardness, confusion, distress, bashfulness, *formal* chagrin, discomfiture 2 DIFFICULTY, constraint, predicament, distress, dilemma, mess, plight, *colloq.* fix, scrape, pickle 3 *an embarrassment of riches* abundance, surplus, excess, superabundance, *formal* profusion

embassy *n*
consulate, legation, ministry, delegation, deputation, mission

embed *v*
implant, plant, fix, insert, root, set, sink, hammer, drive

embellish *v*
adorn, ornament, decorate, deck, dress up, beautify, gild, garnish, trim, festoon, elaborate, embroider, enrich, exaggerate, enhance, varnish, grace, *formal* bedeck, bespangle
🖬 simplify, *formal* denude

embellishment *n*
adornment, ornament, ornamentation, decoration, elaboration, garnish, trimming, gilding, enrichment,

enhancement, embroidery, exaggeration

embers n
ashes, cinders, charcoal, residue

embezzle v
steal, swindle, pilfer, rob, *formal* appropriate, misappropriate, purloin, defalcate, peculate, *colloq.* filch, pinch, nab, nick, rip off, have your fingers/hand in the till

embezzlement n
pilfering, fraud, stealing, theft, *formal* appropriation, misappropriation, defalcation, *colloq.* filching, nabbing, nicking

embezzler n
cheat, fraud, thief, robber, *formal* defalcator, peculator, *colloq.* crook, diddler, con man

embittered adj
bitter, resentful, disaffected, sour, disillusioned, disenchanted, angry, exasperated, piqued, rankled

emblazon v
1 DECORATE, adorn, ornament, blazon, embellish, depict, colour, illuminate, paint 2 PROCLAIM, publicize, publish, extol, praise, glorify, trumpet, *formal* laud

emblem n
symbol, sign, token, representation, logo, insignia, device, crest, mark, badge, figure, image

emblematic adj
representative, representing, symbolic, symbolical, figurative, emblematical

embodiment n
incarnation, personification, exemplification, expression, epitome, example, type, model, incorporation, realization, representation, concentration, *formal* manifestation

embody v
1 PERSONIFY, exemplify, represent, stand for, typify, symbolize, incorporate, express, *formal* manifest 2 INCLUDE, contain, integrate, incorporate, assimilate, collect, combine, bring together, take in

embolden v
encourage, inspire, make brave/bold, give courage to, invigorate, reassure, rouse, stimulate, stir, strengthen, vitalize, animate, fire, cheer, hearten, inflame, nerve
🔁 dishearten

embrace v, n
▶ v 1 HUG, clasp, cuddle, hold, grasp, put/throw your arms around, take into your arms, squeeze, *colloq.* neck, canoodle, smooch 2 INCLUDE, encompass, incorporate, contain, cover, involve, take in, span, *formal* comprise 3 ACCEPT, take up, welcome, receive eagerly, receive wholeheartedly, *formal* espouse, *colloq.* take on board
▶ n hug, cuddle, hold, clasp, squeeze, *colloq.* clinch, necking, slap and tickle, smooch

embrocation n
cream, lotion, ointment, salve, *formal* epithem

embroider v
1 DECORATE, sew, stitch 2 EMBELLISH, enrich, exaggerate, colour, enhance, elaborate, dress up, garnish

embroidery n
fancywork, needlework, sewing, tapestry, tatting, needlepoint

embroil v
involve, implicate, entangle, enmesh, mix up, catch up in, draw into, incriminate

embryo n
1 UNBORN CHILD, foetus 2 *the embryo of the plan* nucleus, germ, beginning, root, rudiments, basics

embryonic adj
undeveloped, rudimentary, immature, beginning, unformed, early, germinal, elementary, primary, *formal* incipient, inchoate
🔁 developed

emend v
correct, rectify, edit, revise, rewrite, polish, refine, improve, alter, amend, *formal* redact

 emend or **amend** ? *See panel at* AMEND.

emendation n
correction, editing, revision, rewriting, refinement, improvement, alteration, amendment, *formal* corrigendum, rectification, redaction

emerge v
1 *emerge from the office* come out, come forth, come into view, emanate, issue, proceed, arise, rise, surface, appear, develop, turn up, materialize 2 *the facts emerged* become known, come out, come to light, appear, transpire, turn out, *colloq.* crop up
🔁 1 disappear

emergence n
appearance, rise, coming, dawn, development, arrival, springing-up, unfolding, disclosure, issue, *formal* advent
🔁 disappearance

emergency n, adj
▶ n crisis, danger, accident, catastrophe, disaster, calamity, difficulty, predicament, plight, pinch, strait, dilemma, quandary, *formal* exigency, *colloq.* scrape, mess, pickle, fix, hot water
▶ adj alternative, back-up, reserve, spare, substitute, extra, fall-back

emergent adj
budding, coming (out), developing, emerging, embryonic, rising, independent
🔁 declining, disappearing

emetic adj, n
▶ adj emetical, vomitive, vomitory
▶ n vomit, vomitory, vomitive

emigrate v
migrate, move abroad, relocate, move, depart, leave your home/native country, resettle

emigration n
moving abroad, migration, removal, departure, exodus, journey, relocation, expatriation

eminence n
distinction, fame, pre-eminence, prominence, renown, reputation, illustriousness, greatness, importance, esteem, celebrity, notability, note, prestige, dignity, rank

eminent adj
distinguished, famous, prominent, illustrious, outstanding, notable, pre-eminent, prestigious, celebrated, renowned, noteworthy, conspicuous, esteemed, important, well-known, elevated, respected, great, high-ranking, grand, superior
🔁 unknown, obscure, unimportant

eminently adv
highly, well, very, greatly, exceedingly, exceptionally, extremely, outstandingly, prominently, remarkably, notably, signally, strikingly, conspicuously, surpassingly, par excellence

emissary *n*
ambassador, agent, envoy, messenger, delegate, herald, courier, representative, scout, deputy, intermediary, go-between, spy

emission *n*
discharge, issue, ejection, emanation, giving-out, giving-off, diffusion, transmission, exhalation, radiation, release, production, exudation, vent

emit *v*
discharge, issue, eject, emanate, exude, pour out, give out, throw out, give off, send out, send forth, diffuse, radiate, release, shed, vent, ooze, leak, produce, let out, express, *formal* excrete
🔁 absorb

emollient *adj, n*
▶ *adj* 1 SOOTHING, assuaging, mollifying, softening, *formal* assuasive, balsamic, demulcent, lenitive, mitigative 2 CONCILIATORY, placatory, appeasing, calming, *formal* propitiatory
▶ *n* cream, lotion, moisturizer, oil, ointment, balm, poultice, salve, *formal* lenitive, liniment, unguent

emolument *n*
pay, salary, wages, payment, remuneration, return, reward, allowance, benefit, earnings, fee, gain, profit(s), hire, honorarium, stipend, compensation, recompense

emotion *n*
feeling, passion, sensation, sense, sentiment, ardour, fervour, warmth, reaction, vehemence, excitement, joy, happiness, ecstasy, sadness, sorrow, grief, fear, despair, dread, hate, anger

emotional *adj*
1 FEELING, passionate, sensitive, responsive, loving, ardent, tender, warm, roused, demonstrative, excitable, enthusiastic, fervent, impassioned, moved, sentimental, zealous, hot-blooded, heated, tempestuous, overcharged, temperamental, fiery 2 EMOTIVE, moving, poignant, thrilling, touching, stirring, heartwarming, soul-stirring, exciting, sentimental, pathetic, *colloq.* tear-jerking, soppy, schmaltzy
🔁 1 unemotional, cold, detached, calm

emotionless *adj*
cold, cold-blooded, cool, distant, undemonstrative, unemotional, unfeeling, impassive, detached, clinical, indifferent, remote, blank, toneless, frigid, glacial, *formal* imperturbable, phlegmatic
🔁 emotional

emotive *adj*
controversial, delicate, inflammatory, sensitive, awkward, touchy

empathize *v*
share, identify with, feel for, comfort, support, understand, be sensitive towards, *colloq.* put yourself in someone's shoes

emperor *n*
ruler, sovereign, imperator, kaiser, mikado, shogun, tsar

emphasis *n*
1 IMPORTANCE, stress, weight, significance, priority, underscoring, accent, accentuation, force, power, prominence, pre-eminence, attention, intensity, strength, urgency, positiveness, insistence, mark, moment 2 *the emphasis is on the second syllable* stress, accent, weight, force

emphasize *v*
1 *emphasize the differences* stress, accentuate, underline, highlight, call attention to, accent, feature, dwell on, weight, point up, spotlight, play up, insist on, press home, intensify, heighten, strengthen, punctuate, bring to the fore, *colloq.* drive the point home 2 *em-phasize a syllable* put stress on, accent, stress, accentuate
🔁 1 play down, understate

emphatic *adj*
forceful, positive, insistent, certain, definite, decided, unequivocal, absolute, categorical, earnest, marked, pronounced, significant, unmistakable, distinctive, strong, striking, vigorous, distinct, energetic, forcible, important, impressive, momentous, powerful, punctuated, telling, vivid, direct
🔁 tentative, hesitant, understated

empire *n*
1 DOMAIN, dominion, kingdom, realm, province, commonwealth, territory 2 SUPREMACY, sovereignty, rule, authority, dominion, command, government, jurisdiction, control, power, sway

empirical *adj*
practical, pragmatic, experimental, observed, *formal* experiential
🔁 theoretical, conjectural, speculative

employ *v*
1 ENGAGE, hire, appoint, take on, recruit, sign up, enlist, commission, put on the payroll, retain, fill, occupy, take up, apprentice 2 USE, utilize, make use of, put to use, apply, draw on, exploit, bring to bear, bring into play, ply, exercise, exert

employed *adj*
working, in work, in employment, with a job, earning, hired, occupied, engaged, active, preoccupied, busy
🔁 unemployed, jobless

employee *n*
worker, working man, working woman, working person, blue-collar worker, white-collar worker, office worker, member of staff, job-holder, hand, wage-earner, assistant, labourer, operative, artisan, craftsman, tradesman

employer *n*
proprietor, owner, manager, head, management, director, executive, company, firm, business, establishment, organization, *colloq.* boss, skipper, gaffer

employment *n*
1 JOB, work, occupation, situation, business, calling, profession, vocation, trade, service, métier, pursuit, craft, *colloq.* line 2 ENLISTMENT, employ, engagement, hire, hiring, taking-on, recruitment, apprenticeship, signing-up
🔁 1 unemployment

emporium *n*
shop, store, establishment, bazaar, market, market-place, mart, fair

empower *v*
1 AUTHORIZE, warrant, enable, license, certify, sanction, permit, entitle, commission, delegate, qualify, *formal* accredit 2 EQUIP, enable, give power/means to

emptiness *n*
1 VACUUM, vacantness, void, voidness, hollowness, hunger, bareness, barrenness, desolation, *formal* hiatus 2 FUTILITY, meaninglessness, uselessness, worthlessness, aimlessness, purposelessness, senselessness, ineffectiveness, insubstantiality, unreality
🔁 1 fullness

empty *adj, v*
▶ *adj* 1 VACANT, with nothing in it, containing nothing, void, unoccupied, free, available, uninhabited, unfilled, deserted, barren, bare, hollow, desolate, blank, clear 2 *an empty gesture* FUTILE, aimless, meaningless, senseless, trivial, vain, idle, worthless, useless, fruitless, unreal, insubstantial, ineffective, insincere, *formal* ineffectual 3 *an empty period of*

life aimless, meaningless, senseless, purposeless, futile, vain, hollow, worthless, useless **4** VACUOUS, inane, expressionless, blank, vacant, deadpan
F₃ 1 full **2** meaningful **3** interesting, eventful
▶ *v* drain, exhaust, discharge, issue, clear, turn out, evacuate, vacate, leave, go out, pour out, flow out, use up, unload, void, gut
F₃ fill

empty-headed *adj*
inane, silly, stupid, foolish, frivolous, *colloq.* scatter-brained, scatty, feather-brained, daft, dopey, batty, dotty
F₃ intelligent

emulate *v*
match, copy, mimic, follow, imitate, model yourself on, echo, compete with, contend with, rival, vie with, *colloq.* take a leaf out of someone's book

emulation *n*
copying, mimicry, following, imitation, echoing, matching, challenge, competition, contention, contest, rivalry, strife

enable *v*
1 AUTHORIZE, equip, qualify, entitle, empower, sanction, warrant, allow, permit, prepare, equip, fit, license, commission, endue, *formal* accredit, validate **2** FACILITATE, make possible, make easier, allow, permit, help, further, clear/pave the way for
F₃ prevent, inhibit, forbid

enact *v*
1 DECREE, ordain, order, authorize, command, legislate, rule, sanction, ratify, pass, make law, establish **2** ACT OUT, perform, play, portray, represent, depict, appear as
F₃ 1 repeal, rescind

enactment *n*
1 PASSING, authorization, approval, sanction, ratification, legislation, rule, bill, act, statute, law, order, decree, edict, command, commandment, ordinance, regulation **2** PERFORMANCE, play, playing, performing, acting, portrayal, representation, staging
F₃ 1 repeal

enamoured *adj*
charmed, infatuated, in love with, enchanted, captivated, entranced, bewitched, enthralled, smitten, keen, wild, mad, taken, fascinated, fond

encampment *n*
camp, camping-ground, campsite, base, bivouac, quarters, tents

encapsulate *v*
sum up, summarize, typify, exemplify, epitomize, capture, include, contain, take in, represent, condense, digest, abridge, compress, précis

enchant *v*
1 CAPTIVATE, charm, fascinate, enrapture, enamour, attract, allure, appeal, delight, thrill **2** ENTRANCE, enthral, bewitch, beguile, spellbind, hypnotize, mesmerize
F₃ 1 repel

enchanter *n*
conjurer, magician, magus, mesmerist, necromancer, reim-kennar, sorcerer, spellbinder, warlock, witch, wizard

enchanting *adj*
charming, delightful, attractive, fascinating, appealing, lovely, pleasant, wonderful, alluring, bewitching, captivating, endearing, entrancing, irresistible, mesmerizing, ravishing, winsome
F₃ boring, repellent

enchantment *n*
1 DELIGHT, fascination, charm, appeal, attractive-

ness, allure, allurement, glamour, bliss, rapture, ecstasy **2** SPELL, magic, witchcraft, wizardry, hypnotism, sorcery, incantation, charm, mesmerism, *formal* conjuration, necromancy
F₃ 1 disenchantment

enchantress *n*
1 SORCERESS, magician, spellbinder, witch, conjurer, Circe, lamia, *formal* necromancer **2** SEDUCTRESS, charmer, siren, vamp, femme fatale

encircle *v*
surround, encompass, compass, ring, circle, orbit, girdle, enclose, enfold, envelop, crowd, close in, hem in, *formal* circumscribe, gird

enclose *v*
1 SURROUND, encircle, encompass, ring, circle, fence, hedge, hem in, bound, encase, embrace, envelop, confine, frame, cage, cocoon, hold, shut in, close in, wrap, pen, cover, corral, *formal* circumscribe **2** INCLUDE, insert, contain, put in, send with, *formal* comprehend

enclosure *n*
1 *herded into the enclosure* pen, pound, compound, paddock, fold, stockade, sty, run, arena, area, corral, kraal, court, yard, ring, fencing, close, cloister **2** INSERTION, inclusion, addition

encompass *v*
1 ENCIRCLE, circle, ring, surround, envelop, close in, shut in, hem in, confine, enclose, hold, *formal* gird, circumscribe **2** INCLUDE, cover, embrace, contain, take in, admit, incorporate, involve, embody, span, *formal* comprise, comprehend

encore *n*
repeat, repetition, additional/extra performance

encounter *v, n*
▶ *v* **1** *encounter difficulties* confront, face, be faced with, experience, be/come up against, deal with, cope with **2** MEET, come across, run across, stumble across, *formal* happen on, chance upon, *colloq.* run into, bump into **3** FIGHT, clash with, combat, engage, grapple with, struggle, strive, contend, tussle, do battle with, come into conflict with, *colloq.* cross swords with
▶ *n* **1** MEETING, contact, rendezvous, brush, confrontation **2** CLASH, fight, combat, conflict, struggle, contest, battle, dispute, engagement, action, skirmish, run-in, collision, *colloq.* set-to

encourage *v*
1 HEARTEN, stimulate, motivate, spur, reassure, rally, give moral support to, be supportive to, animate, stir, inspire, incite, buoy up, cheer, urge, rouse, comfort, embolden, console, *formal* exhort **2** *encourage someone to do something* persuade, influence, sway, win over, convince, prompt, talk into, *formal* exhort, *colloq.* egg on **3** PROMOTE, advance, aid, boost, forward, further, foster, back, support, help, assist, advocate, favour, strengthen
F₃ 1 discourage, depress **2** discourage, dissuade **3** discourage

encouragement *n*
1 REASSURANCE, inspiration, motivation, cheer, incitement, urging, persuasion, stimulation, consolation, *formal* exhortation, succour, *colloq.* pep talk **2** PROMOTION, help, aid, assistance, boost, incentive, support, backing, stimulus, furtherance, *colloq.* shot in the arm
F₃ 1 discouragement, disapproval

encouraging *adj*
heartening, promising, hopeful, reassuring, stimulating, inspiring, uplifting, cheering, comforting, bright, rosy, cheerful, satisfactory, *formal* auspicious
F₃ discouraging

encroach *v*
intrude, invade, impinge, trespass, infringe, usurp, overstep, overrun, infiltrate, make inroads, *colloq.* muscle in on, tread on someone's toes

encroachment *n*
intrusion, invasion, trespassing, infringement, overstepping, infiltration, *formal* incursion

encumber *v*
1 BURDEN, overload, weigh down, saddle, strain, stress, oppress, handicap, hamper, hinder, impede, restrain, slow down, obstruct, constrain, inconvenience, prevent, check, cramp, *formal* retard **2** BLOCK, congest, jam, pack, stuff, cram

encumbrance *n*
burden, load, weight, cross, millstone, albatross, difficulty, restraint, constraint, handicap, impediment, obstruction, obstacle, inconvenience, strain, stress, hindrance, liability, obligation, responsibility, *formal* cumbrance

encyclopedic *adj*
complete, exhaustive, comprehensive, thorough, wide-ranging, vast, all-inclusive, broad, all-embracing, all-encompassing, universal, compendious
🗲 incomplete, narrow

end *n, v*
▶ *n* **1** FINISH, conclusion, close, ending, completion, culmination, epilogue, finale, dénouement, *formal* termination, cessation **2** EXTREMITY, boundary, border, edge, limit, margin, tip **3** REMAINDER, tip, butt, left-over, remnant, stub, scrap, vestige, fragment, left-overs **4** AIM, object, objective, purpose, intention, goal, target, point, reason, motive, design, *formal* intent **5** RESULT, outcome, consequence, issue, upshot **6** DEATH, destruction, extermination, downfall, doom, ruin, extinction, dissolution, *formal* demise **7** PART, aspect, side, area, field, section, department, branch
🗲 **1** beginning, start **6** birth
▷ **the end** intolerable, unbearable, unendurable, too much, enough, beyond endurance, insufferable, the worst, *colloq.* the limit, the last straw, the final blow
▶ *v* **1** FINISH, come/bring to an end, close, stop, be over, expire, complete, round off, culminate, break off, die out, fade away, run out, *formal* cease, conclude, terminate, discontinue, *colloq.* wind up **2** DESTROY, annihilate, exterminate, extinguish, ruin, abolish, dissolve
🗲 **1** begin, start, *formal* commence

endanger *v*
hazard, risk, put at risk, jeopardize, put in jeopardy, expose, threaten, put in danger, compromise, *formal* imperil
🗲 protect

endearing *adj*
lovable, charming, appealing, attractive, winsome, engaging, delightful, sweet, adorable, captivating, enchanting

endearment *n*
love, affection, fondness, attachment, diminutive, pet-name, sweet nothing, *formal* hypocorism

endeavour *v, n*
▶ *v* attempt, try, strive, struggle, aim, aspire, undertake, venture, try your hand at, labour, take pains, do your best, *formal* seek
▶ *n* attempt, effort, try, undertaking, enterprise, aim, venture, striving, *colloq.* go, shot, stab, bash, crack

ending *n*
end, close, finish, completion, conclusion, culmination, climax, resolution, dénouement, finale, epilogue, *formal* termination, consummation, cessation
🗲 beginning, start

endless *adj*
1 INFINITE, without end, unending, boundless, limitless, unlimited, measureless **2** EVERLASTING, perpetual, constant, continual, continuous, undying, eternal, interminable, boring, monotonous, *formal* ceaseless **3** UNBROKEN, continuous, constant, uninterrupted, entire, whole
🗲 **1** finite, limited **2** temporary

endorse *v*
1 APPROVE, sanction, authorize, support, back, be/get behind, favour, ratify, confirm, vouch for, advocate, uphold, warrant, recommend, subscribe to, sustain, adopt, *formal* affirm, *colloq.* throw your weight behind **2** SIGN, countersign

endorsement *n*
1 APPROVAL, sanction, authorization, support, backing, ratification, confirmation, advocacy, warrant, recommendation, commendation, seal of approval, testimonial, *formal* affirmation, *colloq.* OK **2** SIGNATURE, countersignature

endow *v*
1 LEAVE, will, give, donate, grant, boast, present, award, finance, fund, support, make over, furnish, provide, supply, *formal* bestow, bequeath, confer **2** HAVE, possess, give, provide, present, enjoy, boast, be endued with, be blessed with

endowment *n*
1 LEGACY, award, grant, fund, finance, gift, present, provision, settlement, donation, dowry, income, revenue, *formal* bequest, bestowal, benefaction **2** TALENT, attribute, faculty, gift, aptitude, capability, ability, quality, flair, power, capacity, genius, qualification, attribute

endurable *adj*
bearable, tolerable, supportable, manageable, withstandable, sustainable, sufferable
🗲 intolerable, unbearable

endurance *n*
patience, staying power, stamina, resignation, stoicism, sufferance, tenacity, perseverance, resolution, stability, durability, backbone, persistence, strength, toleration, *formal* fortitude, *colloq.* guts, spunk, bottle, stickability

endure *v*
1 *endure hardship* bear, stand, put up with, tolerate, abide, weather, brave, cope with, face, go through, encounter, meet, experience, submit to, suffer, sustain, swallow, undergo, withstand, take, stick, allow, permit, support, *colloq.* stomach **2** *a peace that will endure for ever* last, remain, live, survive, stay, persist, continue, hold, prevail, *formal* abide

enduring *adj*
lasting, long-lasting, durable, permanent, perpetual, abiding, remaining, continuing, long-standing, stable, steady, firm, steadfast, persistent, persisting, chronic, prevailing, surviving, unfaltering, unwavering, eternal, immortal, imperishable
🗲 changeable, fleeting, brief, ephemeral, momentary, passing

enemy *n*
adversary, opponent, rival, antagonist, the opposition, competitor, the competition, opposer, other side, *formal* foe
🗲 friend, ally

energetic *adj*
lively, vigorous, active, animated, dynamic, spirited, tireless, boisterous, zestful, brisk, strong, forceful, potent, powerful, strenuous, high-powered, indefatigable, *colloq.* bursting with energy, full of beans, go-getting, zippy, punchy
🗲 lethargic, sluggish, inactive, idle

energize *v*
stimulate, arouse, stir, motivate, enliven, invigorate, liven, quicken, animate, vitalize, vivify, activate, electrify, galvanize, *colloq.* pep up
🖪 daunt

energy *n*
liveliness, vigour, activity, animation, drive, dynamism, enthusiasm, life, spirit, verve, vivacity, vitality, sparkle, effervescence, zest, zeal, ardour, fire, efficiency, force, forcefulness, effectiveness, strength, power, potency, intensity, exertion, stamina, *formal* might, *colloq.* get-up-and-go, zip, push, brio, pizzazz
🖪 lethargy, inertia, weakness

enervated *adj*
tired, weak, exhausted, feeble, fatigued, worn out, weakened, incapacitated, paralysed, undermined, unmanned, unnerved, sapped, devitalized, limp, spent, *formal* debilitated, effete, enfeebled, *colloq.* done in, run-down, washed-out
🖪 active, energetic

enfeeble *v*
weaken, exhaust, fatigue, reduce, diminish, wear out, sap, geld, undermine, unhinge, unnerve, deplete, devitalize, *formal* debilitate, enervate
🖪 strengthen

enfold *v*
1 ENCLOSE, envelop, shroud, swathe, encircle, encompass, fold, enwrap, wrap (up) 2 EMBRACE, clasp, hug, hold

enforce *v*
1 IMPOSE, administer, implement, carry out, apply, execute, discharge, fulfil 2 COMPEL, insist on, oblige, urge, constrain, require, necessitate, force, pressure, pressurize, coerce, prosecute, reinforce

enforced *adj*
compulsory, binding, necessary, required, unavoidable, imposed, involuntary, forced, obliged, compelled, constrained, dictated, ordained, prescribed

enforcement *n*
imposition, administration, implementation, application, execution, discharge, fulfilment, insistence, coercion, obligation, compulsion, constraint, pressure, prosecution, requirement, *formal* coaction

enfranchise *v*
give the right to vote to, give the vote to, free, liberate, release, *formal* emancipate, manumit, give suffrage to
🖪 disenfranchise

enfranchisement *n*
giving the right to vote, voting rights, freedom, freeing, liberating, liberation, release, *formal* emancipation, manumission, suffrage
🖪 disenfranchisement

engage *v*
1 PARTICIPATE, take part, embark on, take up, practise, do, enter into, undertake, join in, involve, become involved in/with 2 ATTRACT, allure, draw, win, gain, captivate, charm, catch 3 OCCUPY, engross, absorb, employ, fill, hold, preoccupy, busy, tie up, grip 4 EMPLOY, hire, appoint, take on, sign up/on, enlist, enrol, commission, recruit, contract, put on the payroll 5 INTERLOCK, mesh, enmesh, interconnect, join, fit together, interact, attach 6 FIGHT, battle with, attack, take on, encounter, assail, clash with, combat, join in battle with, wage war with
🖪 2 repel 4 dismiss, discharge 5 disengage

engaged *adj*
1 *engaged in his work* occupied, busy, engrossed, immersed, absorbed, preoccupied, involved, active, employed, *colloq.* tied up 2 *engaged to be married* promised, pledged, committed, *formal* betrothed, affianced, plighted, espoused, *colloq.* spoken for 3 *the*

phone is engaged busy, unavailable, in use, taken, *colloq.* tied up

engagement *n*
1 APPOINTMENT, meeting, interview, date, arrangement, commitment, assignation, fixture, rendezvous 2 PROMISE, pledge, commitment, obligation, agreement, contract, bond, assurance, vow, *formal* betrothal, troth 3 FIGHT, battle, combat, conflict, attack, clash, war, assault, strife, struggle, offensive, action, encounter, confrontation, contest

engaging *adj*
charming, attractive, appealing, captivating, pleasing, delightful, winsome, winning, lovable, adorable, sweet, likable, pleasant, fetching, fascinating, enchanting, agreeable
🖪 repulsive, repellent

engender *v*
cause, produce, occasion, bring about, give rise to, instigate, lead to, incite, induce, create, inspire, generate, arouse, excite, encourage, nurture, kindle, breed, propagate, provoke, *old use* beget, *formal* effect

engine *n*
motor, machine, machinery, mechanism, appliance, contraption, apparatus, device, instrument, tool, implement, locomotive, generator, dynamo

Types of engine include:
diesel, donkey, fuel-injection, internal-combustion, jet, petrol, steam, turbine, turbojet, turboprop, V-engine.

Parts of an automotive engine and its ancillaries include:
air filter, alternator, camshaft, camshaft cover, carburettor, choke, connecting rod, *colloq.* con-rod, cooling fan, crankshaft, crankshaft pulley, cylinder block, cylinder head, drive belt, exhaust manifold, exhaust valve, fan belt, flywheel, fuel and ignition ECU (electronic control unit), fuel injector, gasket, ignition coil, ignition distributor, inlet manifold, inlet valve, oil filter, oil pump, oil seal, petrol pump, piston, piston ring, power-steering pump, push-rod, radiator, rocker arm, rocker cover, rotor arm, spark plug, starter motor, sump, tappet, thermostat, timing belt, timing pulley, turbocharger.

---

engineer *n, v*
▶ *n* 1 MECHANIC, technician, operator, driver, engine driver 2 DESIGNER, originator, planner, builder, inventor, deviser, mastermind, architect, civil engineer, electrical engineer, mechanical engineer, chemical engineer, sound engineer
▶ *v* plan, contrive, devise, manoeuvre, cause, manipulate, control, direct, bring about, mastermind, originate, arrange, orchestrate, plot, scheme, stage-manage, manage, create, rig, *formal* effect

engrave *v*
1 INSCRIBE, cut, carve, chisel, etch, mark, print, imprint, impress, incise, chase 2 *engraved on her mind* imprint, impress, fix, stamp, lodge, set, embed, engrain, brand

engraving *n*
print, impression, imprint, inscription, carving, etching, cutting, cut, woodcut, plate, block, cutting, chiselling, mark, *technical* dry-point, intaglio

engross *v*
absorb, occupy, engage, interest, grip, hold, preoccupy, rivet, fascinate, captivate, enthral, arrest, involve, intrigue

engrossed *adj*
absorbed, occupied, taken up, preoccupied, gripped, engaged, caught up, enthralled, fascinated, captivated, immersed, intent, intrigued, rapt, riveted, mesmerized, wrapped, lost, fixated
🔁 bored, disinterested

engrossing *adj*
absorbing, fascinating, enthralling, captivating, intriguing, gripping, interesting, compelling, riveting, suspenseful, *colloq.* unputdownable
🔁 boring

engulf *v*
overwhelm, swamp, flood, deluge, drown, inundate, plunge, immerse, submerge, overrun, overtake, swallow up, devour, consume, bury, absorb, engross, envelop

enhance *v*
heighten, intensify, increase, improve, upgrade, elevate, add to, enrich, magnify, swell, exalt, raise, lift, boost, strengthen, emphasize, stress, reinforce, embellish, *formal* augment
🔁 reduce, minimize

enhancement *n*
heightening, increase, improvement, elevation, enrichment, magnification, intensification, boost, emphasis, stress, reinforcement, *formal* augmentation

enigma *n*
mystery, riddle, puzzle, paradox, conundrum, problem, dilemma, quandary, brain-teaser, *colloq.* poser

enigmatic *adj*
mysterious, mystifying, puzzling, cryptic, obscure, strange, baffling, perplexing, paradoxical, incomprehensible, inexplicable, unfathomable, *formal* arcane, esoteric, recondite
🔁 simple, straightforward

enjoin *v*
1 ORDER, command, demand, urge, direct, instruct, decree, ordain, advise, require, charge **2** PROHIBIT, forbid, ban, bar, *formal* disallow, interdict, proscribe

enjoy *v*
1 *enjoy dancing* take pleasure in, delight in, appreciate, like, relish, revel in, love, be fond of, rejoice in, savour, *colloq.* fancy **2** *enjoy a benefit* have, possess, be blessed with, be endowed with, be favoured with
🔁 **1** dislike, hate
▷ **enjoy yourself** have a good time, have fun, make merry, *colloq.* have a whale of a time, live it up, let your hair down, paint the town red

enjoyable *adj*
pleasant, agreeable, delightful, pleasing, entertaining, amusing, fun, pleasurable, delicious, fine, lovely, good, nice, satisfying, *formal* gratifying, delectable
🔁 disagreeable

enjoyment *n*
1 PLEASURE, delight, amusement, entertainment, relish, joy, fun, gladness, happiness, diversion, recreation, indulgence, zest, satisfaction, *formal* gratification, delectation

---

Expressions of enjoyment include:
a night on the town, bask in, carpe diem, enjoy it while you can, enter into the spirit of things, get into the swing of things, have a ball, have a field day, have a great time, have a whale of a time, have the time of your life, hit the spot, in raptures about something, it's yummy!, kick off your shoes, lap it up, let your hair down, live for the day, live it up, make a night of it, make merry, make the most of it, mmm!, paint the town red, rave it up, seize the day, sow your wild oats, take pleasure in, the life of Riley.

---

2 POSSESSION, use, advantage, benefit, privilege, favour, blessing
🔁 **1** displeasure

enlarge *v*
1 *enlarge the garden; glands enlarging* make/become larger, make/become bigger, increase, expand, extend, magnify, add to, supplement, inflate, swell, stretch, multiply, develop, amplify, widen, broaden, lengthen, heighten, *technical* distend, dilate, intumesce, *formal* augment, elongate **2** *enlarge a photograph* make bigger, blow up **3** *enlarge on something* expand on, go into details, elaborate on, *formal* expatiate on, dilate on
🔁 **1** diminish, shrink

enlargement *n*
1 *enlargement of the building/a gland* increase, expansion, extension, magnification, inflation, swelling, stretching, multiplication, development, amplification, *technical* distension, dilation, intumescence, oedema, *formal* augmentation **2** *a photographic enlargement* blow up, magnification
🔁 **2** contraction, decrease, reduction

enlighten *v*
instruct, edify, cultivate, educate, inform, illuminate, teach, tutor, counsel, apprise, advise, make aware
🔁 confuse

enlightened *adj*
informed, aware, knowledgeable, educated, civilized, cultivated, refined, cultured, sophisticated, conversant, wise, learned, intellectual, reasonable, liberal, broad-minded, open-minded, literate, *formal* erudite
🔁 ignorant, confused

enlightenment *n*
awareness, knowledge, teaching, understanding, education, instruction, wisdom, information, insight, comprehension, civilization, cultivation, refinement, learning, literacy, edification, sophistication, broad-mindedness, open-mindedness, *formal* erudition, sapience
🔁 confusion, ignorance

enlist *v*
enlist in the army; enlist someone's help engage, enrol, register, sign up, recruit, conscript, hire, take on, employ, volunteer, join (up), gather, muster, secure, obtain, enter, *formal* procure

enliven *v*
excite, exhilarate, brighten, cheer (up), gladden, hearten, invigorate, rouse, wake up, liven (up), stimulate, revitalize, inspire, animate, buoy up, fire, kindle, quicken, spark, *formal* vivify, *colloq.* pep up, perk up, give a lift to
🔁 subdue

en masse *adv*
all at once, all together, as a group, as a whole, as one, ensemble, in a body, together, en bloc, wholesale

enmity *n*
animosity, hostility, antagonism, discord, strife, feud, antipathy, bitterness, hate, hatred, aversion, ill-will, bad blood, rancour, malice, venom, *formal* acrimony, malevolence
🔁 friendship, reconciliation

ennoble *v*
dignify, uplift, elevate, raise, exalt, enhance, glorify, honour, magnify, *formal* aggrandize, nobilitate

ennui *n*
boredom, tiredness, dissatisfaction, tedium, lassitude, listlessness, languor, *formal* accidie, acedia, *colloq.* the doldrums

enormity *n*
atrocity, outrage, iniquity, horror, evil, crime, abom-

ination, violation, monstrosity, outrageousness, wickedness, vileness, depravity, evilness, atrociousness, viciousness

---

 enormity or **enormousness**?

Of these two nouns, only *enormousness* should be used when referring to size: *the enormousness of his ambitions*. *Enormity* means 'great wickedness, seriousness (of a crime, etc)': *the enormity of his assault on the little girl*.

---

enormous *adj*
huge, immense, vast, gigantic, massive, colossal, large-scale, gross, gargantuan, astronomic, monstrous, mammoth, considerable, tremendous, stupendous, prodigious, *colloq.* jumbo, great big, whopping
F⃫ small, tiny

enormously *adv*
extremely, to a vast/huge/immense extent, hugely, exceptionally, extraordinarily, exceedingly, massively, tremendously, immensely

enormousness *n*
hugeness, immenseness, vastness, massiveness, largeness, greatness, magnitude, expanse, extensiveness

enough *adj, n, adv*
▶ *adj* sufficient, adequate, ample, plenty, abundant
F⃫ insufficient, inadequate
▶ *n* sufficiency, adequacy, plenty, abundance, ample supply, *formal* amplitude
▶ *adv* sufficiently, adequately, reasonably, tolerably, passably, moderately, fairly, satisfactorily, amply

en passant *adv*
in passing, by the way, while on the subject, incidentally, cursorily

enquire, enquirer, enquiring, enquiry *see* INQUIRE, INQUIRER, INQUIRING, INQUIRY.

enrage *v*
incense, infuriate, anger, make angry, annoy, madden, provoke, incite, inflame, agitate, exasperate, irritate, rile, irk, vex, *colloq.* needle, bug, wind up, drive someone up the wall, drive someone round the bend, make someone's blood boil, make someone's hackles rise, put/get someone's back up, push too far
F⃫ calm, placate

enraged *adj*
incensed, infuriated, angry, angered, furious, livid, raging, storming, inflamed, annoyed, irritated, irate, exasperated, fuming, *colloq.* aggravated, mad, wild
F⃫ calm

enrapture *v*
enchant, fascinate, charm, thrill, delight, captivate, bewitch, beguile, enthral, entrance, spellbind, transport, ravish

enrich *v*
1 ENDOW, enhance, improve, refine, develop, cultivate, add to, supplement, *formal* augment, aggrandize, ameliorate **2** ADORN, ornament, beautify, embellish, decorate, garnish, grace, gild
F⃫ 1 impoverish

enrol *v*
1 REGISTER, enlist, sign on, sign up, join up, recruit, go in for, enter, put your name down, engage, admit **2** RECORD, list, note, enter, put down, *formal* inscribe

enrolment *n*
registration, recruitment, enlistment, enlisting, signing on/up, joining up, admission, acceptance

en route *adv*
in transit, on the move, on the way, on the road

ensconce *v*
install, settle, establish, entrench, nestle, put, place, lodge, protect, shelter, shield, screen, locate

ensemble *n*
1 WHOLE, total, entirety, sum, set, group, collection, accumulation, *formal* aggregate, *colloq.* whole caboodle, whole (bang) shoot **2** OUTFIT, costume, suit, co-ordinates, *colloq.* get-up, rig-out **3** GROUP, band, company, troupe, circle, chorus, cast

enshrine *v*
preserve, protect, guard, shield, treasure, cherish, immortalize, consecrate, dedicate, exalt, hallow, revere, sanctify, idolize, embalm, *formal* apotheosize

enshroud *v*
cloak, cloud, shroud, veil, pall, wrap, conceal, hide, cover, enclose, enfold, envelop, enwrap, obscure

ensign *n*
banner, standard, flag, colours, pennant, jack, badge, crest, shield, coat of arms

enslave *v*
subject, dominate, bind, enchain, yoke, trap, *formal* subjugate
F⃫ free, emancipate

enslavement *n*
slavery, subjection, servitude, bondage, captivity, oppression, repression, serfdom, vassalage, *formal* dulosis, enthralment, subjugation, thraldom
F⃫ emancipation

ensnare *v*
trap, catch, capture, net, snare, embroil, enmesh, entangle, entrap

ensue *v*
follow, issue, proceed, succeed, result, arise, happen, occur, transpire, turn out, flow, derive, stem, come next, *formal* befall
F⃫ precede

ensure *v*
1 MAKE CERTAIN, make sure, guarantee, warrant, secure, certify, *formal* effect **2** PROTECT, make safe, guard, safeguard, secure

entail *v*
involve, necessitate, occasion, need, require, call for, demand, cause, produce, bring about, give rise to, lead to, result in

entangle *v*
1 *entangled in the net* tangle, twist, knot, ravel, intertwine, enmesh, ensnare, snare, mix up **2** EMBROIL, involve, implicate, complicate, confuse, jumble, muddle
F⃫ 1, 2 disentangle

entanglement *n*
1 TANGLE, knot, mesh, tie, trap, jumble, ensnarement, entrapment, snare **2** INVOLVEMENT, complication, embarrassment, confusion, muddle, snarl-up, difficulty, mess, mix-up, predicament, liaison, affair
F⃫ 1, 2 disentanglement

entente *n*
agreement, arrangement, friendship, deal, pact, treaty, understanding, entente cordiale, *formal* compact

enter *v*
1 COME IN TO, go in (to), get in (to), arrive, cross the threshold, burst in, sneak in, break in, worm your way in, insert, introduce, board, infiltrate, penetrate, occupy, *colloq.* pop in **2** JOIN, become a member of, enlist, set about, sign up, put your name down for, take up, participate, take part, go in for, undertake, embark upon, enrol, start, begin, engage in, *formal* commence **3** RECORD, log, note, list, register, put down, take down, set down, inscribe, lodge, put on record, submit, input
F⃫ 1 depart **3** delete

enterprise *n*
1 UNDERTAKING, venture, project, plan, effort, operation, campaign, programme, endeavour, task, scheme 2 INITIATIVE, resourcefulness, drive, adventurousness, courage, boldness, ambition, energy, enthusiasm, strong feeling, spirit, vitality, *colloq.* get-up-and-go, push, oomph 3 BUSINESS, company, firm, establishment, operation, concern, industry
F∃ 2 apathy

enterprising *adj*
venturesome, adventurous, bold, daring, imaginative, resourceful, entrepreneurial, self-reliant, enthusiastic, energetic, keen, eager, zealous, ambitious, aspiring, spirited, vigorous, active, *colloq.* go-ahead, pushy
F∃ unenterprising, lethargic

entertain *v*
1 AMUSE, divert, please, delight, cheer, interest, occupy, engage, engross, charm, captivate 2 RECEIVE, have guests, ask over/round, have round, invite over/round, accommodate, play host to, provide hospitality, put up, treat, host, regale 3 HARBOUR, contemplate, consider, think about, imagine, conceive, foster, nurture, cherish, *formal* countenance
F∃ 2 bore 3 reject

entertainer *n*

Entertainers include:
acrobat, actor, actress, artiste, busker, chat-show host, clown, comedian, comic, conjurer, contortionist, dancer, disc jockey, *colloq.* DJ, escapologist, fire-eater, game-show host, hypnotist, ice-skater, impressionist, jester, juggler, magician, mime artist, mimic, mind-reader, minstrel, musician, performer, player, presenter, prima ballerina, singer, song-and-dance act, stand-up comic, striptease-artist, *colloq.* stripper, trapeze-artist, tight-rope walker, unicyclist, ventriloquist. *See also* MUSICIAN; SINGER.

entertaining *adj*
amusing, diverting, fun, recreational, enjoyable, delightful, interesting, pleasant, pleasing, pleasurable, humorous, funny, comical, witty
F∃ boring

entertainment *n*
1 AMUSEMENT, diversion, recreation, enjoyment, play, hobby, pastime, fun, sport, leisure, activity, distraction, pleasure 2 SHOW, spectacle, performance, play, presentation, extravaganza

Forms of entertainment include:
cinema, cartoon show, video, radio, television, theatre, pantomime; dance, disco, discothèque, concert, recital, musical, opera, variety show, music hall, revue, karaoke, cabaret, night-club, casino; magic-show, puppet show, Punch-and-Judy show, circus, gymkhana, waxworks, laser-light show, zoo, rodeo, carnival, pageant, fête, festival, firework party, barbecue, show business, *colloq.* show biz. *See also* THEATRICAL.

enthral *v*
captivate, entrance, enchant, fascinate, charm, beguile, bewitch, thrill, enrapture, delight, intrigue, spellbind, hypnotize, mesmerize, engross, grip, rivet, absorb
F∃ bore

enthralling *adj*
captivating, entrancing, enchanting, fascinating, intriguing, beguiling, charming, thrilling, riveting, gripping, compulsive, compelling, spellbinding, hypnotizing, mesmerizing, mesmeric
F∃ boring

enthuse *v*
praise, rave, wax lyrical, gush, drool, excite, inspire, motivate, fire, bubble over, effervesce

enthusiasm *n*
1 ZEAL, ardour, fervour, passion, keenness, eagerness, vehemence, warmth, zest, frenzy, fire, excitement, earnestness, relish, spirit, wholeheartedness, commitment, devotion 2 INTEREST, hobby, pastime, passion, craze, mania, rage, *colloq.* thing
F∃ 1 apathy

enthusiast *n*
devotee, zealot, admirer, fan, supporter, follower, fanatic, aficionado, lover, *colloq.* buff, freak, fiend

enthusiastic *adj*
keen, ardent, eager, fervent, vehement, passionate, warm, wholehearted, zealous, vigorous, spirited, earnest, devoted, avid, committed, excited, fanatical, exuberant, *formal* ebullient, *colloq.* crazy, mad, wild, daft, nuts, potty
F∃ unenthusiastic, apathetic

entice *v*
tempt, lure, attract, seduce, lead on, draw, coax, persuade, induce, beguile, cajole, *formal* inveigle, *colloq.* sweet-talk

enticement *n*
inducement, lure, attraction, seduction, bait, persuasion, coaxing, temptation, decoy, allurement, beguilement, cajolery, *formal* blandishments, inveiglement, *colloq.* come-on, sweet-talk

entire *adj*
complete, whole, total, full, absolute, intact, sound, perfect
F∃ incomplete, partial

entirely *adv*
completely, wholly, totally, fully, utterly, unreservedly, absolutely, in toto, thoroughly, altogether, perfectly, only, solely, exclusively, in every respect, in every way, every inch
F∃ partially

entirety *n*
totality, fullness, completeness, wholeness, whole

entitle *v*
1 AUTHORIZE, give someone the right, qualify, empower, enable, make eligible, allow, permit, license, warrant, sanction, *formal* accredit 2 NAME, call, term, title, give the title, know as, style, christen, dub, label, designate

entity *n*
being, existence, thing, body, creature, individual, organism, substance, object

entombment *n*
burial, interment, *formal* inhumation, sepulture

entourage *n*
retinue, attendants, company, companions, followers, following, escort, staff, suite, court, train, retainers, associates, cortège, coterie

entrails *n*
intestines, offal, viscera, bowels, internal organs, vital organs, giblets, umbles, *colloq.* guts, innards, insides

entrance[1] *n*
1 OPENING, way in, entry, access, door, doorway, gate, gateway, approach, threshold, drive, driveway, passageway, lobby, porch, hall, vestibule, foyer, anteroom 2 ARRIVAL, appearance, debut, initiation, introduction, start 3 ACCESS, admission, admittance, entry, right of entry, entrée, *formal* ingress
F∃ 1 exit 2 departure

entrance² *v*
entranced by her beauty charm, enchant, enrapture, captivate, enthral, bewitch, beguile, spellbind, fascinate, charm, delight, ravish, transport, hypnotize, mesmerize
F3 repel

entrant *n*
1 NOVICE, beginner, starter, newcomer, new arrival, initiate, convert, probationer, apprentice, fresher, freshman, learner, student, pupil, trainee **2** COMPETITOR, candidate, contestant, contender, entry, applicant, participant, player, rival, opponent

entrap *v*
1 CATCH, trap, capture, snare, ensnare, entangle, enmesh, embroil, ambush, net **2** TRICK, deceive, delude, entice, seduce, implicate, beguile, allure, lure, *formal* inveigle

entreat *v*
beg, implore, plead with, crave, pray, ask, petition, solicit, request, appeal to, *formal* beseech, supplicate, invoke, importune

entreaty *n*
appeal, plea, prayer, petition, suit, cry, solicitation, request, *formal* supplication, invocation

entrench *v*
establish, fix, embed, dig in, ensconce, install, lodge, root, ingrain, settle, seat, plant, anchor, set, stop a gap, take up position
F3 dislodge

entrenched *adj*
deep-rooted, deep-seated, rooted, well-established, firm, fixed, implanted, ingrained, inbred, set, inflexible, diehard, unshakable, dyed-in-the-wool, indelible, ineradicable, *formal* intransigent, *colloq.* stick-in-the-mud

entrepreneur *n*
business executive, businessman, businesswoman, financier, industrialist, middleman, promoter, agent, dealer, broker, contractor, magnate, tycoon, speculator, money-maker, manager, impresario

entrepreneurial *adj*
business, commercial, industrial, trade, contractual, managerial, financial, monetary, economic, budgetary, professional

entrust *v*
trust, commit, make someone responsible for, put in charge, confide, consign, authorize, charge, assign, turn over, hand over, commend, depute, invest, delegate, deliver

entry *n*
1 ENTRANCE, appearance, admittance, admission, access, entrée, introduction **2** RECORD, item, minute, note, memorandum, description, statement, account, listing **3** ENTRANT, competitor, contestant, candidate, applicant, participant, player, rival, opponent **4** OPENING, entrance, door, doorway, access, threshold, way in, passage, gate, gateway, approach, lobby, porch, hall, vestibule, foyer, anteroom
F3 **4** exit

entwine *v*
wind, twist, intertwine, interlace, interlink, interweave, intwine, braid, knit, plait, twine, weave, wreathe, knot, ravel, entangle, embroil
F3 unravel

enumerate *v*
list, name, itemize, cite, detail, specify, count, number, relate, recount, spell out, tell, mention, calculate, quote, recite, reckon

enunciate *v*
1 ARTICULATE, pronounce, vocalize, voice, express, say, speak, utter, sound **2** STATE, declare, express, utter, proclaim, announce, put forward, *formal* affirm, propound, promulgate

envelop *v*
wrap, enfold, enwrap, encase, cover, swathe, shroud, engulf, enclose, encircle, encompass, surround, cloak, veil, blanket, conceal, obscure, hide

envelope *n*
wrapper, wrapping, cover, case, casing, sheath, covering, shell, skin, holder, jacket, coating

enviable *adj*
desirable, privileged, favoured, blessed, fortunate, lucky, desirable, advantageous, sought-after, excellent, fine
F3 unenviable

envious *adj*
covetous, jealous, resentful, green (with envy), dissatisfied, grudging, begrudging, jaundiced, *colloq.* green-eyed

environment *n*
surroundings, conditions, climate, circumstances, milieu, atmosphere, habitat, situation, element, medium, background, ambience, scene, setting, locale, context, mood, influences, territory, domain, *colloq.* the lie of the land, which way the wind is blowing

environmentalist *n*
conservationist, ecologist, preservationist, Friend of the Earth, *colloq.* ecofreak, econut, green

environs *n*
neighbourhood, surroundings, surrounding area, vicinity, outskirts, suburbs, district, locality, precincts, purlieus, *formal* circumjacencies, vicinage

envisage *v*
visualize, imagine, picture, see coming, envision, conceive of, preconceive, predict, anticipate, foresee, image, see, think of, contemplate

envoy *n*
agent, representative, ambassador, diplomat, messenger, legate, consul, attaché, emissary, minister, delegate, deputy, courier, mediator, intermediary, go-between

envy *n, v*
▶ *n* covetousness, jealousy, resentfulness, resentment, dissatisfaction, grudge, ill-will, malice, spite
▶ *v* covet, resent, begrudge, grudge, crave

ephemeral *adj*
transient, short-lived, fleeting, brief, momentary, passing, short, temporary, transitory, impermanent, flitting, *formal* evanescent, fugacious, fungous
F3 enduring, lasting, perpetual

epic *adj, n*
▶ *adj* heroic, grand, majestic, elevated, exalted, lofty, imposing, impressive, vast, ambitious, long, large, large-scale, great, colossal, huge, *formal* grandiloquent, sublime
F3 ordinary
▶ *n* long story/poem, narrative, history, legend, saga, myth

epicure *n*
gourmet, connoisseur, *bon vivant, bon viveur,* gastronome, epicurean, gourmand, glutton, hedonist, sensualist, Sybarite, voluptuary

epicurean *adj*
gourmet, gastronomic, gormandizing, sensual, voluptuous, luxurious, self-indulgent, gluttonous, luscious, lush, unrestrained, hedonistic, Sybaritic, libertine

epidemic *adj, n*
▶ *adj* widespread, prevalent, extensive, rife, rampant, sweeping, wide-ranging, pervasive, prevailing, endemic, *formal* pandemic

▶ *n* plague, outbreak, scourge, spread, rash, spate, upsurge, growth, increase, rise, wave

epigram *n*
witticism, quip, *bon mot*, saying, proverb, maxim, aphorism, gnome, *technical* apophthegm

epigrammatic *adj*
concise, succinct, brief, short, terse, laconic, pithy, aphoristic, incisive, piquant, pointed, sharp, pungent, witty, ironic

epilogue *n*
afterword, postscript, PS, appendix, coda, conclusion, swan song
F3 foreword, prologue, preface

episode *n*
1 INCIDENT, event, occurrence, happening, occasion, circumstance, experience, adventure, affair, matter, business **2** INSTALMENT, part, chapter, passage, section, scene

episodic *adj*
periodic, intermittent, irregular, occasional, spasmodic, sporadic, disconnected, disjointed, digressive, anecdotal, *formal* picaresque

epistle *n*
letter, communication, message, missive, correspondence, bulletin, note, line, encyclical

epitaph *n*
commemoration, inscription, rest in peace, RIP, obituary, funeral oration, *technical* lapidary expression

epithet *n*
description, descriptive adjective, descriptive phrase/expression, designation, name, nickname, tag, title, sobriquet, *formal* appellation, denomination

epitome *n*
1 PERSONIFICATION, embodiment, representation, model, example, archetype, type, prototype, essence, *formal* quintessence, exemplar **2** SUMMARY, abstract, abridgement, digest, synopsis, outline, précis, résumé

epitomize *v*
1 PERSONIFY, embody, represent, exemplify, encapsulate, illustrate, typify, symbolize, sum up, *formal* incarnate **2** ABRIDGE, shorten, summarize, abbreviate, abstract, précis, reduce, compress, condense, contract, curtail, cut
F3 **2** elaborate, expand

epoch *n*
age, era, period, time, date

equable *adj*
1 *an equable person* even-tempered, placid, calm, cool and collected, serene, unexcitable, tranquil, composed, level-headed, easy-going, *formal* imperturbable, *colloq.* unflappable, unfazed, laid-back **2** *an equable climate* uniform, even, consistent, constant, regular, moderate, temperate, unchanging, unvarying, steady, stable, smooth
F3 **1** excitable **2** variable, extreme

📖 **equable** or **equitable** ?
Equable means 'even-tempered': *That child would infuriate the most equable parent*; 'not extreme and without great variation': *an equable climate*. *Equitable* means 'fair, just': *a more equitable distribution of profits*.

---

equal *adj, n, v*
▶ *adj* **1** IDENTICAL, the same, alike, like, equivalent, corresponding, commensurate, comparable **2** EVEN, uniform, regular, constant, level, unchanging, symmetrical, unvarying, balanced, well balanced, matched, evenly matched, on an equal footing, *colloq.* fifty-fifty, neck and neck **3** IMPARTIAL, fair, just, unbiased, neutral, non-partisan **4** *equal to a task* COMPETENT, able, adequate, sufficient, fit, strong, capable, suitable, suited
F3 **1** different **2** unequal **3** biased **4** unsuitable
▶ *n* peer, counterpart, equivalent, coequal, match, parallel, twin, fellow, mate, compeer
▶ *v* **1** *equal a number* match, correspond to, be the same as, add up to, amount to, balance, parallel, square with, tally with, coincide with, equalize, equate with, make, total **2** *equal someone's score* match, rival, emulate, be level with, be on a par with, measure up to, come up to

equality *n*
1 UNIFORMITY, evenness, equivalence, correspondence, comparability, parallelism, balance, parity, par, symmetry, proportion, identity, sameness, likeness, similarity **2** IMPARTIALITY, fairness, justice, neutrality, partisanship, equal rights, equal opportunities, egalitarianism
F3 **2** inequality

equalize *v*
level, even up, make even, even out, match, equal, equate, draw level, keep pace, balance, redress the balance, square, standardize, regularize, compensate, smooth

equanimity *n*
composure, calm, tranquillity, serenity, ease, coolness, self-possession, self-control, level-headedness, confidence, assurance, self-assurance, poise, dignity, placidity, impassivity, *formal* imperturbability, aplomb, sangfroid, *colloq.* unflappability
F3 alarm, anxiety, discomposure

equate *v*
1 *equate wealth with happiness* compare with, liken to, match with, identify with, connect with, link with, pair with, juxtapose with, regard as the same, bracket together **2** *costs equate to a quarter of the income* correspond to, correspond with, balance, parallel, equalize, be equal, offset, square with, agree with, tally with

equation *n*
equality, correspondence, equivalence, balancing, agreement, parallel, pairing, comparison, match, matching, likeness, identity, similarity, *formal* juxtaposition

equestrian *n, adj*
▶ *n* horseman, horsewoman, rider, courier, cavalryman, knight, cavalier, hussar, trooper, cowboy, cowgirl, rancher, herder, jockey
▶ *adj* mounted, riding, horse-riding, *formal* equine

equilibrium *n*
1 BALANCE, poise, symmetry, evenness, stability, steadiness, *technical* stasis, *formal* equipoise, counterpoise **2** EQUANIMITY, self-possession, composure, calmness, coolness, serenity, tranquillity, self-control, level-headedness, confidence, assurance, self-assurance, poise, dignity, *formal* imperturbability, aplomb, sangfroid, *colloq.* unflappability
F3 **1** imbalance, instability **2** anxiety

equip *v*
provide, fit out, supply, furnish, prepare, arm, issue, fit up, kit out, stock, endow, rig, dress, deck out, *formal* array, accoutre

equipment *n*
apparatus, gear, supplies, tackle, kit, tools, material, furnishings, luggage, baggage, outfit, paraphernalia, stuff, things, accessories, furniture, *formal* accoutrements, *colloq.* rig-out

equipoise *n*
equilibrium, balance, evenness, stability, steadiness, symmetry, poise, ballast, counterbalance, counterweight, *formal* counterpoise, equibalance, equiponderance
🎦 imbalance

equitable *adj*
even-handed, fair, proper, reasonable, right, rightful, due, fair-and-square, square, honest, ethical, impartial, just, unbiased, unprejudiced, legitimate, disinterested, dispassionate, objective
🎦 inequitable, unfair

> **equitable** or **equable** ? *See panel at* EQUABLE.

equity *n*
even-handedness, equitableness, fairness, fair play, fair-mindedness, reasonableness, righteousness, uprightness, honesty, integrity, justice, justness, objectivity, impartiality, disinterestedness, *formal* rectitude
🎦 inequity

equivalence *n*
identity, correspondence, agreement, likeness, equality, interchangeability, comparability, similarity, substitutability, correlation, parallel, conformity, sameness, *formal* parity
🎦 unlikeness, dissimilarity

equivalent *adj, n*
▶ *adj* equal, same, similar, identical, substitutable, corresponding, alike, like, comparable, interchangeable, even, twin, *technical* homologous, *formal* tantamount, commensurate
🎦 unlike, different
▶ *n* counterpart, opposite number, equal, parallel, match, fellow, double, twin, peer, alternative, correspondent, *technical* homologue, *formal* correlative

equivocal *adj*
ambiguous, uncertain, ambivalent, obscure, vague, indefinite, evasive, oblique, misleading, dubious, questionable, suspicious, confusing, indefinite
🎦 unequivocal, clear, definite

equivocate *v*
prevaricate, evade, dodge, fence, hedge, mislead, change your mind, *formal* tergiversate, vacillate, *colloq.* shilly-shally, pussyfoot, waffle, chop and change, change your tune, beat about the bush, hedge your bets, run with the hare and hunt with the hounds

equivocation *n*
prevarication, evasion, dodging the issue, hedging, double talk, quibbling, shifting, shuffling, *formal* tergiversation, *colloq.* waffle, weasel words, pussyfooting
🎦 directness

era *n*
age, epoch, period, date, day, days, time, times, generation, aeon, season, cycle, stage, century

eradicate *v*
eliminate, annihilate, get rid of, remove, root out, uproot, suppress, destroy, exterminate, extinguish, weed out, stamp out, wipe out, crack down on, abolish, erase, obliterate, *formal* efface, expunge, extirpate

eradication *n*
elimination, annihilation, removal, riddance, obliteration, abolition, suppression, destruction, extermination, extinction, *formal* effacement, extirpation, deracination, expunction

erasable *adj*
removable, washable, eradicable, *formal* effaceable
🎦 permanent, ineradicable

erase *v*
obliterate, rub out, delete, blot out, wipe out, cancel, get rid of, remove, eradicate, put out of your mind, *formal* expunge, efface, excise

erasure *n*
obliteration, deletion, elimination, eradication, removal, cancellation, cleansing, *formal* erasement, effacement, expunction

erect *v, adj*
▶ *v* **1** BUILD, construct, put up, put together, establish, set up, elevate, assemble, raise, rear, lift, mount, pitch, create **2** *erect an organization* found, form, institute, initiate, put up, create, organize, establish
▶ *adj* **1** UPRIGHT, straight, vertical, upstanding, standing, raised **2** RIGID, hard, firm, stiff

erection *n*
1 BUILDING, construction, edifice, structure, assembly, establishment, manufacture, fabrication, creation, elevation, raising, *colloq.* pile **2** RIGIDITY, stiffness, *technical* tumescence

ergo *adv*
therefore, consequently, accordingly, for this reason, in consequence, so, then, this being the case, *formal* hence, thus

erode *v*
wear away, eat away, eat into, wear down, corrode, consume, grind down, destroy, disintegrate, deteriorate, fragment, deplete, spoil, undermine, *formal* abrade, excoriate

erosion *n*
wear, wearing away, corrosion, disintegration, deterioration, destruction, undermining, *formal* abrasion, attrition, denudation, excoriation

erotic *adj*
aphrodisiac, seductive, sensual, titillating, pornographic, lascivious, stimulating, suggestive, erogenous, sexually arousing, amorous, venereal, carnal, lustful, voluptuous, *formal* amatory, *colloq.* sexy, adult, blue, raunchy, steamy, dirty

err *v*
1 MAKE A MISTAKE, be wrong, be incorrect, miscalculate, mistake, misjudge, make a slip, blunder, misunderstand, misconstrue, *colloq.* slip up, boob, make a booboo, bark up the wrong tree, get hold of the wrong end of the stick, put your foot in it, be wide of the mark, *slang* louse up **2** DO WRONG, sin, misbehave, go astray, trespass, lapse, offend, deviate, fall from grace, *formal* transgress

errand *n*
task, job, duty, chore, commission, charge, mission, undertaking, assignment, message

errant *adj*
1 WAYWARD, wrong, erring, stray, straying, deviant, offending, criminal, lawless, disobedient, sinful, sinning, loose, *formal* aberrant, peccant **2** ROAMING, rambling, roving, itinerant, journeying, wandering, nomadic, *formal* peripatetic

erratic *adj*
changeable, variable, fitful, fluctuating, inconsistent, intermittent, sporadic, irregular, unsteady, unstable, shifting, varying, inconstant, unpredictable, volatile, unsettled, unreliable, abnormal, eccentric, wandering, meandering, *formal* aberrant, capricious, desultory
🎦 steady, consistent, stable

erring *adj*
wayward, wrong, errant, stray, straying, deviant, offending, criminal, lawless, disobedient, guilty, sinful, sinning, loose, *formal* peccant

erroneous *adj*
incorrect, wrong, mistaken, false, untrue, spurious, specious, inaccurate, inexact, invalid, illogical, unfounded, faulty, flawed, misguided, misplaced, *formal* fallacious
F3 correct, right

error *n*
mistake, inaccuracy, slip, blunder, gaffe, *faux pas*, lapse, slip of the tongue, mix-up, miscalculation, misunderstanding, misinterpretation, misjudgement, misconception, misapprehension, misprint, literal, spelling mistake, oversight, omission, fallacy, flaw, fault, wrong, *formal* solecism, aberration, *colloq.* slip-up, howler, boob

ersatz *adj*
fake, substitute, imitation, artificial, synthetic, man-made, simulated, counterfeit, sham, bogus, *colloq.* phoney

erstwhile *adj*
one-time, former, sometime, ex, late, old, once, past, previous, bygone

erudite *adj*
learned, scholarly, well-educated, knowledgeable, lettered, educated, well-read, literate, academic, cultured, intellectual, wise, highbrow, profound, *colloq.* brainy
F3 illiterate, ignorant

erudition *n*
learning, scholarship, education, knowledge, facts, knowledgeableness, learnedness, scholarliness, wisdom, culture, letters, *formal* profundity, reconditeness

erupt *v*
break out, explode, belch, pour forth, discharge, burst, gush, spew, spout, eject, vent, expel, emit, flare up, vomit, break, *formal* eruct, eructate

eruption *n*
1 OUTBURST, discharge, ejection, emission, venting, explosion, flare-up **2** RASH, outbreak, inflammation

escalate *v*
increase, intensify, grow, accelerate, rise, step up, heighten, raise, spiral, magnify, mushroom, enlarge, expand, extend, develop, mount, ascend, climb, soar, amplify, *colloq.* rocket, go through the roof, hit the roof
F3 decrease, diminish

escalator *n*
lift, elevator, moving staircase, moving walkway, travolator

escapable *adj*
avoidable, evadable, avertible, eludible
F3 inevitable

escapade *n*
adventure, exploit, fling, prank, frolic, caper, romp, spree, antic, stunt, trick, *colloq.* lark, skylarking

escape *v, n*
▶ *v* **1** GET AWAY, break free, run away, make your escape, make your getaway, bolt, abscond, flee, fly, decamp, break loose, break out, flit, slip away, shake off, slip, *colloq.* scoot, scram, scat, scarper, do a runner/bunk, do a moonlight flit, make a bolt/break for it, take to your heels, run for your life, slip through someone's fingers **2** AVOID, evade, elude, skip, shun, steer clear of, sidestep, *formal* circumvent, *colloq.* dodge, duck **3** LEAK, seep, flow, drain, spurt, gush, issue, discharge, ooze, trickle, pour out/forth, pass **4** *his name escapes me* forget, not place, not be remembered/recalled, not know, *colloq.* be on the tip of your tongue, not be able to put your finger on
▶ *n* **1** GETAWAY, flight, bolt, flit, breakout, absconding,

decampment, jailbreak, *colloq.* bunk **2** AVOIDANCE, evasion, *formal* circumvention, *colloq.* dodging, ducking **3** LEAK, seepage, leakage, outflow, gush, drain, discharge, issue, emission, spurt, outpour, emanation, *formal* efflux **4** ESCAPISM, diversion, distraction, dreaming, fantasy, fantasizing, wishful thinking, recreation, relaxation, pastime, safety-valve

escapee *n*
absconder, jailbreaker, defector, deserter, fugitive, runaway, truant, refugee

escapism *n*
diversion, distraction, dreaming, fantasy, fantasizing, wishful thinking, recreation, relaxation, pastime, safety-valve
F3 realism

escapist *n*
dreamer, daydreamer, fantasizer, wishful thinker, non-realist, *colloq.* ostrich
F3 realist

eschew *v*
avoid, give up, refrain from, abandon, keep clear of, repudiate, shun, spurn, disdain, *formal* abjure, abstain from, forgo, forswear, renounce
F3 embrace

escort *n, v*
▶ *n* **1** COMPANION, chaperon(e), partner, attendant, aide, squire, guide, bodyguard, protector, defender, beau, *colloq.* date **2** ENTOURAGE, company, retinue, suite, train, guard, convoy, cortège, attendants
▶ *v* accompany, partner, chaperon(e), bring, come (along) with, take, take out, attend on, guide, lead, usher, conduct, guard, protect, defend, shepherd, walk

esoteric *adj*
obscure, cryptic, inscrutable, mysterious, mystic, mystical, occult, hidden, secret, confidential, private, inside, *formal* recondite, abstruse, arcane
F3 well-known, familiar

especial *adj*
particular, special, marked, specific, striking, pre-eminent, notable, noteworthy, exceptional, outstanding, express, unique, exclusive, extraordinary, peculiar, singular, signal, uncommon, unusual, remarkable

especially *adv*
1 PARTICULARLY, specially, markedly, notably, exceptionally, outstandingly, expressly, supremely, uniquely, exclusively, unusually, extraordinarily, uncommonly, remarkably, strikingly, very **2** CHIEFLY, mainly, principally, primarily, pre-eminently, above all, most of all

espionage *n*
counter-intelligence, infiltration, intelligence, investigation, probing, reconnaissance, spying, surveillance, intercepting, industrial espionage, undercover operations/work, fifth column, *colloq.* snooping, bugging, wiretapping

espousal *n*
adoption, embracing, support, advocacy, backing, promotion, choice, defence, championing, championship, maintenance

espouse *v*
take up, adopt, embrace, support, advocate, back, choose, stand up for, defend, champion, patronize, maintain, opt for

espy *v*
notice, see, catch sight of, glimpse, observe, detect, discern, perceive, make out, sight, spot, spy, discover, distinguish, behold

essay *n, v*
▶ *n* composition, dissertation, paper, article, assign-

ment, thesis, piece, commentary, critique, treatise, review, leader, tract, *formal* discourse, disquisition
▶ *v* try, attempt, endeavour, test, go for, take on, strain, strive, struggle, tackle, undertake, *colloq.* have a bash, have a crack, have a go, have a stab

essence *n*
1 NATURE, character, essential character, being, substance, reality, actuality, soul, spirit, core, centre, heart, meaning, point, quality, significance, life, entity, crux, kernel, marrow, pith, characteristics, attributes, principle, *formal* quintessence **2** CONCENTRATE, extract, concentration, distillation, spirits, *formal* distillate
▷ **in essence** basically, fundamentally, essentially, substantially, to all intents and purposes
▷ **of the essence** crucial, indispensable, necessary, vital, requisite, required, needed, important

essential *adj, n*
▶ *adj* **1** FUNDAMENTAL, basic, intrinsic, inherent, innate, underlying, principal, main, key, central, characteristic, definitive, typical, constituent **2** CRUCIAL, indispensable, necessary, vital, requisite, required, needed, important
F3 **1** incidental **2** dispensable, inessential
▶ *n* necessity, prerequisite, requisite, requirement, basic, fundamental, necessary, principle, gist, main point(s), key point(s), *formal* sine qua non, *colloq.* must

establish *v*
1 SET UP, found, start, form, institute, bring into being, open, create, begin, organize, inaugurate, introduce, install, plant, settle, secure, lodge, base **2** PROVE, demonstrate, show, authenticate, ratify, verify, certify, confirm, attest, *formal* substantiate, validate, corroborate, affirm
F3 **1** uproot **2** refute

established *adj*
respected, experienced, traditional, conventional, secure, settled, entrenched, ensconced, fixed, steadfast, proved, proven, tried and tested
F3 impermanent, unreliable

establishment *n*
1 FORMATION, setting up, founding, forming, creation, foundation, installation, institution, organization, inauguration, *formal* inception **2** BUSINESS, company, firm, institute, organization, concern, institution, corporation, enterprise, shop, store **3** RULING CLASS, the system, the authorities, the powers that be

estate *n*
1 POSSESSIONS, effects, assets, belongings, holdings, property, goods, lands, landholding, real estate, manor **2** AREA, development, centre, land, region, tract **3** STATUS, standing, situation, position, class, place, condition, state, rank

estate agent *n*
property agent, *US* realtor, real-estate agent

esteem *n, v*
▶ *n* respect, regard, good opinion, appreciation, estimation, judgement, admiration, honour, consideration, reverence, credit, reckoning, count, account, love, *formal* veneration, approbation
▶ *v* respect, admire, honour, regard highly, revere, reverence, value, cherish, reckon, rate, regard, think, view, consider, treasure, count, judge, hold, believe, account, *formal* adjudge, deem, venerate

esteemed *adj*
admired, respected, well-respected, well-thought-of, worthy, highly-regarded, honoured, revered, treasured, valued, honourable, admirable, reputable, respectable, distinguished, excellent, prized, *formal* venerated

estimable *adj*
esteemed, respected, worthy, creditable, admirable, commendable, distinguished, reputable, respectable, honourable, excellent, good, notable, noteworthy, praiseworthy, valuable, valued, *formal* laudable, meritorious
F3 despicable, insignificant

estimate *v, n*
▶ *v* assess, reckon, evaluate, calculate roughly, work out approximately, gauge, guess, value, *formal* conjecture
▶ *n* **1** ROUGH CALCULATION, approximate cost/price/value/quantity, quotation, reckoning, valuation, judgement, (rough) guess, approximation, assessment, estimation, evaluation, computation, *colloq.* guesstimate, ballpark figure **2** JUDGEMENT, consideration, opinion, belief, view, thinking, conclusion, evaluation, assessment, reckoning

estimation *n*
1 JUDGEMENT, opinion, belief, consideration, estimate, view, (way of) thinking, feeling, evaluation, assessment, reckoning, conception, calculation, computation, conclusion **2** RESPECT, regard, appreciation, esteem, credit **3** ROUGH CALCULATION, approximate cost/price/value/quantity, valuation, (rough) guess, assessment, estimate, evaluation

estrange *v*
alienate, disaffect, antagonize, disunite, divide, divorce, split up, break up, separate, sever, drive apart, part, set at variance, set against, withhold, withdraw, *colloq.* drive a wedge between, put a barrier between
F3 attract, bind, unite

estranged *adj*
divided, separate, separated, divorced, alienated, disaffected, antagonized
F3 reconciled, united

estrangement *n*
alienation, disaffection, antagonization, disunity, division, dissociation, parting, separation, severance, split, breach, break-up, hostility, unfriendliness, antipathy, withdrawal, withholding

estuary *n*
inlet, mouth, firth, fjord, creek, cove, bay, arm, sea-loch

et cetera *adv*
and so on, and so forth, and the like, and the rest, &c, and suchlike, et al, *colloq.* and what have you, and/or whatever

etch *v*
cut, carve, engrave, burn, furrow, dig, groove, impress, imprint, incise, ingrain, inscribe, bite, corrode, stamp

etching *n*
carving, cut, engraving, inscription, impression, imprint, print, sketch

eternal *adj*
1 *eternal bliss* unending, endless, ceaseless, everlasting, never-ending, infinite, limitless, immortal, deathless, undying, imperishable, indestructible **2** *eternal truths* unchanging, timeless, enduring, lasting, perennial, abiding **3** *eternal quarrelling* constant, continuous, perpetual, persistent, incessant, interminable, endless, never-ending, non-stop, relentless, remorseless, *formal* unremitting
F3 **1** ephemeral, temporary **2** changeable

eternally *adv*
1 EVERLASTINGLY, endlessly, ceaselessly, indestructibly, for ever **2** INTERMINABLY, constantly, lastingly, always, for ever, perpetually, incessantly
F3 briefly, temporarily

eternity n

1 EVERLASTINGNESS, endlessness, everlasting, imperishability, infinity, timelessness, perpetuity, immutability, after-life, hereafter, immortality, deathlessness, everlasting life, heaven, paradise, next world, world to come, world without end **2** AGE, ages, long time, ages and ages, *colloq.* donkey's years

ethereal *adj*

1 DELICATE, immaterial, dainty, exquisite, fine, light, gossamer, subtle, tenuous, insubstantial, intangible, airy-fairy, impalpable, *formal* diaphanous **2** HEAVENLY, spiritual, celestial, refined, rarefied, unearthly, unworldly, elemental, *formal* empyreal, empyrean
 2 earthly, solid

ethical *adj*

moral, principled, just, right, proper, virtuous, honourable, fair, upright, decent, above reproach, righteous, honest, good, correct, high-minded, commendable, fitting, noble, *formal* decorous
 unethical

ethics n

moral values, values, morality, morals, principles, moral principles, standards, moral standards, code, moral code, moral philosophy, rules, beliefs, conscience, equity, principles of behaviour, principles of right and wrong, *formal* propriety

ethnic *adj*

racial, native, indigenous, traditional, tribal, folk, cultural, national, aboriginal, *formal* autochthonous

ethos n

attitude, beliefs, standards, manners, ethics, morality, code, principles, spirit, tenor, flavour, rationale, character, disposition

etiquette n

code, code of behaviour, formalities, standards, correctness, conventions, customs, code of practice, code of conduct, rules, manners, good manners, form, good form, politeness, courtesy, ceremony, decency, unwritten law, *formal* protocol, civility, decorum, propriety

etymology n

word history, word origins, word-lore, linguistics, origin, derivation, source, philology, semantics, lexicology

eulogize *v*

praise, acclaim, sing/sound the praises of, wax lyrical, applaud, approve, celebrate, exalt, extol, glorify, honour, magnify, commend, compliment, congratulate, *formal* laud, panegyrize, *colloq.* rave about, hype, plug
 condemn

eulogy n

praise, tribute, acclaim, acclamation, accolade, commendation, exaltation, glorification, compliment, applause, plaudit, *formal* encomium, laud, laudation, laudatory, paean, panegyric
 condemnation

euphemism n

evasion, polite term, indirect expression, substitution, softening, genteelism, politeness, understatement
 dysphemism

euphemistic *adj*

polite, neutral, vague, indirect, evasive, soft-toned, genteel, understated

euphonious *adj*

harmonious, melodious, melodic, musical, silvery, soft, sweet, dulcet, mellow, sweet-sounding, sweet-toned, tuneful, clear, *formal* canorous, consonant,

dulcifluous, dulciloquent, euphonic, mellifluous, symphonious
 cacophonous

euphoria n

elation, ecstasy, bliss, rapture, high spirits, buoyancy, well-being, exhilaration, exultation, joy, intoxication, jubilation, transport, glee, exaltation, enthusiasm, cheerfulness, *colloq.* high
 depression, despondency

euphoric *adj*

elated, ecstatic, blissful, rapturous, exhilarated, enraptured, enthusiastic, buoyant, intoxicated, exultant, exulted, joyful, gleeful, happy, cheerful, jubilant, *formal* joyous, *colloq.* high
 depressed, despondent

euthanasia n

mercy killing, release, happy/merciful release, quietus

evacuate *v*

1 LEAVE, go away from, depart, withdraw, remove, move out of, retreat, retire from, abandon, desert, vacate, decamp, relinquish, *formal* forsake, *colloq.* quit, clear (out), pull out of **2** EMPTY, make empty, eject, void, clear, expel, discharge, eliminate, purge, *formal* defecate, excrete

evacuation n

1 DEPARTURE, leaving, withdrawal, retreat, exodus, flight, removal, desertion, abandonment, clearance, relinquishment, retirement, vacating, *formal* forsaking, *colloq.* quitting **2** EMPTYING, expulsion, ejection, discharge, elimination, purging, urination, *formal* defecation

evade *v*

1 *evade your duties* elude, avoid, escape, shirk, steer clear of, shun, sidestep, get round, balk, fend off, *formal* circumvent, *colloq.* dodge, duck, skive, chicken out, cop out **2** *evade a question* prevaricate, equivocate, fence, fudge, avoid, parry, quibble, *colloq.* hedge, dodge, duck, beat about the bush
 1 confront, face

evaluate *v*

value, assess, estimate, reckon, calculate, gauge, measure, judge, determine, rate, size up, weigh, compute, rank, *formal* appraise

evaluation n

valuation, assessment, estimation, estimate, judgement, reckoning, calculation, opinion, determination, computation, *formal* appraisal

evanescent *adj*

ephemeral, fading, fleeting, brief, short-lived, transient, transitory, impermanent, momentary, temporary, unstable, disappearing, vanishing, passing, evaporating, insubstantial, perishable
 permanent

evangelical *adj*

1 *evangelical Christianity* biblical, Bible-believing, scriptural, orthodox, fundamentalist, missionary, crusading, *colloq.* Bible-bashing, Bible-thumping, Bible-punching **2** ENTHUSIASTIC, zealous, campaigning, crusading, evangelistic, missionary, propagandizing, propagandist, proselytizing

evangelist n

preacher, missionary, missioner, revivalist, crusader, campaigner

evangelize *v*

preach, campaign, spread the word, crusade, convert, proselytize, baptize, gospelize, missionarize, missionize, propagandize

evaporate *v*

1 DISAPPEAR, dematerialize, vanish, melt (away), dissolve, disperse, dispel, fade, *formal* dissipate, evanesce **2** VAPORIZE, dry, dehydrate, exhale, *formal* desiccate

evaporation *n*
vaporization, drying, dehydration, condensation, distillation, dematerialization, dissolution, fading, melting, vanishing, *formal* desiccation

evasion *n*
1 AVOIDANCE, equivocation, prevarication, escape, shirking, trickery, subterfuge, fencing, steering clear of, shunning, *formal* circumvention, tergiversation, *colloq.* hedging, ducking **2** *evasions rather than straight answers* excuse, quibble, deception, deceit, trickery, fudging, prevarication, equivocation, *colloq.* ducking, hedging, dodge, dodging
⊠ **1** frankness, directness

evasive *adj*
equivocating, indirect, vague, prevaricating, devious, unforthcoming, misleading, deceitful, deceptive, fudging, quibbling, oblique, secretive, tricky, cunning, *colloq.* shifty, slippery, cagey, waffling
⊠ direct, frank

eve *n*
day before, time before, period before, verge, brink, edge, threshold

even *adj, adv, v*
▶ *adj* **1** LEVEL, flat, smooth, horizontal, flush, parallel, uniform, true, plane **2** STEADY, unvarying, unchanging, stable, constant, regular, uniform, consistent, unwavering **3** EQUAL, balanced, matching, same, similar, like, alike, evenly matched, on an equal footing, symmetrical, level, side by side, *colloq.* fifty-fifty, neck and neck **4** EVEN-TEMPERED, calm, placid, serene, tranquil, composed, cool, equable, unruffled, unexcitable, *formal* unperturbable, *colloq.* unflappable **5** EVEN-HANDED, balanced, equitable, fair, impartial, just, neutral, non-partisan
⊠ **1** uneven **3** unequal
▶ *adv* **1** *even worse* all the more, still, yet, more, to a greater extent/degree **2** *even a child could do that* surprisingly, unexpectedly, unusually, oddly, as well, also, too, still more, likewise **3** *sad, even depressed* more exactly, more precisely, indeed **4** *not even write his own name* hardly, scarcely, at all, so much as
▷ **even so** however, but, all the same, despite that, in spite of that, however that may be, nevertheless, nonetheless, still, yet, *formal* notwithstanding that
▶ *v* smooth, flatten, level, plane, match, regularize, balance, equalize, make equal, make uniform, align, square, stabilize, steady, straighten, *colloq.* strike a balance

even-handed *adj*
fair, just, impartial, balanced, disinterested, dispassionate, equitable, neutral, unbiased, unprejudiced, reasonable, non-discriminatory, square, fair and square, without fear or favour
⊠ inequitable, discriminatory

evening *n*
nightfall, dusk, close of day, eve, eventide, twilight, sunset, sundown

event *n*
1 HAPPENING, occurrence, incident, occasion, affair, circumstance, episode, experience, matter, case, adventure, business, fact, possibility, milestone, *formal* eventuality **2** GAME, match, fixture, competition, contest, round, race, tournament, engagement, meeting, item **3** CONSEQUENCE, result, outcome, conclusion, end, aftermath, upshot, effect, issue, *formal* termination

even-tempered *adj*
calm, level-headed, equable, placid, stable, tranquil, serene, composed, cool, cool and collected, steady,

peaceful, peaceable, *formal* imperturbable, *colloq.* unflappable, unfazed, laid-back
⊠ excitable, erratic

eventful *adj*
busy, exciting, lively, active, full, interesting, remarkable, important, significant, memorable, momentous, historic, crucial, critical, notable, noteworthy, unforgettable, *colloq.* action-packed
⊠ dull, ordinary

eventual *adj*
final, ultimate, last, resulting, closing, concluding, ensuing, future, later, subsequent, prospective, projected, planned, impending

eventuality *n*
possibility, probability, likelihood, chance, contingency, event, happening, circumstance, case, outcome, crisis, emergency, mishap, *formal* happenstance

eventually *adv*
finally, ultimately, at last, in the end, at length, subsequently, after all, sooner or later, in the long run, in the fullness of time, *colloq.* at the end of the day, when all is said and done, in the final analysis

ever *adv*
1 ALWAYS, evermore, for ever, perpetually, permanently, constantly, at all times, continually, incessantly, endlessly, eternally, until the end of time, till doomsday, till your dying day, *colloq.* till the cows come home, till hell freezes over **2** AT ANY TIME, in any case, in any circumstances, at all, on any account, on any occasion
⊠ **1** never
▷ **ever so** very, very much, really, extremely

everlasting *adj*
1 ETERNAL, undying, never-ending, endless, immortal, infinite, imperishable, constant, permanent, perpetual, indestructible, timeless **2** *everlasting noise* constant, continuous, perpetual, persistent, incessant, interminable, endless, never-ending, non-stop, relentless, remorseless, *formal* unremitting
⊠ temporary, transient

evermore *adv*
always, for ever, eternally, ever, ever after, for ever and a day, for ever and ever, unceasingly, to the end of time, till doomsday, *formal* henceforth, hereafter, in perpetuum

every *adj*
1 EACH, every single, every individual **2** *make every effort* all possible, as much as possible **3** *have every confidence* all, complete, total, full, entire

everybody *n*
everyone, one and all, each one, each person, every person, all and sundry, the whole world

everyday *adj*
ordinary, common, commonplace, day-to-day, familiar, run-of-the-mill, regular, standard, basic, plain, routine, usual, workaday, normal, average, customary, stock, accustomed, conventional, daily, habitual, monotonous, unimaginative, frequent, simple, informal, *colloq.* common-or-garden
⊠ unusual, exceptional, special

everyone *n*
everybody, one and all, each one, each person, every person, all and sundry, the whole world, *colloq.* all the world and his wife, every Tom, Dick and Harry, every man Jack, Uncle Tom Cobleigh and all

everything *n*
all, all things, each thing, the lot, the whole lot, the entirety, the sum, the total, lock, stock and barrel, *formal* the aggregate, *colloq.* the whole caboodle, the

whole kit and caboodle, the whole shooting-match, the whole shebang, the whole bag of tricks, the works, everything but the kitchen sink

everywhere adv
all around, in/to all places, in/to each place, the world over, all over, throughout, far and near, near and far, far and wide, high and low, ubiquitous, colloq. left, right and centre, here there and everywhere, US every place

evict v
expel, eject, dispossess, put out, turn out, throw out, force out, force to leave, remove, cast out, oust, dislodge, formal expropriate, colloq. turf out, kick out, chuck out, show someone the door, throw out on the streets, turn out of house and home

eviction n
expulsion, ejection, dispossession, removal, clearance, dislodgement, formal defenestration, expropriation, colloq. the bum's rush, the boot, the push, the elbow

evidence n, v
▶ n **1** PROOF, verification, confirmation, grounds, support, documentation, data, formal affirmation, substantiation, corroboration **2** TESTIMONY, declaration, technical affidavit, formal attestation **3** INDICATION, suggestion, sign, trace, mark, hint, demonstration, token, symptom, formal manifestation
▷ **in evidence** clear, obvious, apparent, plain, patent, visible, conspicuous, noticeable, clear-cut, unmistakable
▶ v show, indicate, reveal, demonstrate, display, exhibit, prove, witness, signify, confirm, establish, betray, formal affirm, attest, denote, evince, manifest

evident adj
clear, obvious, apparent, plain, patent, visible, conspicuous, noticeable, clear-cut, unmistakable, perceptible, distinct, discernible, tangible, undoubted, incontestable, indisputable, incontrovertible, formal manifest

evidently adv
1 CLEARLY, apparently, plainly, patently, obviously, undoubtedly, doubtless(ly), indisputably, formal manifestly **2** SEEMINGLY, apparently, outwardly, as it would seem/appear, so it seems/appears, to all appearances, formal ostensibly

evil adj, n
▶ adj **1** WICKED, wrong, sinful, bad, immoral, vicious, vile, cruel, base, corrupt, malicious, malignant, devilish, demonic, diabolic, depraved, mischievous, sinister, black, formal malevolent, iniquitous, reprehensible, nefarious, heinous **2** HARMFUL, pernicious, destructive, injurious, deadly, detrimental, hurtful, bad, poisonous, formal deleterious **3** DISASTROUS, ruinous, calamitous, catastrophic, adverse, dire, unfortunate, unlucky, formal inauspicious, unpropitious **4** OFFENSIVE, noxious, foul, stinking, formal noisome
🔁 **1** good **3** fortunate
▶ n **1** WICKEDNESS, wrongdoing, wrong, immorality, misconduct, badness, sin, sinfulness, vice, viciousness, vileness, depravity, baseness, corruption, devilishness, mischief, formal iniquity, malignity, heinousness **2** ADVERSITY, calamity, disaster, misfortune, suffering, sorrow, ruin, catastrophe, blow, curse, distress, hurt, harm, ill, pain, injury, misery, woe, formal affliction

evildoer n
wrongdoer, bad person, criminal, delinquent, offender, miscreant, reprobate, sinner, scoundrel, rogue, villain

evince v
show, reveal, indicate, display, exhibit, express, sig-

nify, demonstrate, confess, declare, betray, establish, formal attest, bespeak, betoken, evidence, manifest
🔁 conceal, suppress

eviscerate v
disembowel, gut, draw, gralloch, formal exenterate

evocation n
summoning-up, calling, elicitation, invocation, inducing, arousal, stirring, stimulation, suggestion, activation, excitation, kindling, recall, echo

evocative adj
suggestive, expressive, indicative, reminiscent, vivid, graphic, memorable, formal redolent

evoke v
summon (up), call, elicit, invoke, induce, arouse, stir, raise, kindle, stimulate, bring about, cause, call forth, call up, conjure up, awaken, provoke, excite, recall, bring back memories of, make someone think of
🔁 suppress

evolution n
development, growth, progression, progress, expansion, increase, ripening, derivation, descent, unrolling, unfolding, unravelling, working-out, opening-out

evolve v
develop, grow, increase, mature, progress, unravel, unroll, unfold, work out, open out, expand, enlarge, emerge, descend, derive, result, elaborate

exacerbate v
aggravate, worsen, make worse, make things/matters worse, compound the problem, heighten, increase, provoke, sharpen, intensify, exaggerate, inflame, exasperate, deepen, embitter, enrage, infuriate, irritate, vex, colloq. add fuel to the fire/flames, fan the flames, add insult to injury, rub salt in the wound
🔁 soothe

exact adj, v
▶ adj **1** PRECISE, accurate, correct, faithful, literal, flawless, faultless, right, true, definite, explicit, detailed, specific, strict, unerring, close, just, factual, identical, express, word-perfect, formal veracious, colloq. blow-by-blow, on the nail, spot on, bang on, on the button **2** CAREFUL, scrupulous, particular, rigorous, precise, methodical, meticulous, orderly, exacting, painstaking, thorough, formal punctilious
🔁 **1** inexact, imprecise **2** careless
▶ v extort, extract, claim, insist on, wrest, wring, compel, demand, command, call for, force, impose, require, squeeze, colloq. milk, bleed

exacting adj
demanding, challenging, difficult, hard, laborious, arduous, onerous, stringent, tiring, rigorous, taxing, tough, harsh, firm, painstaking, severe, strict, stern, unsparing, unyielding
🔁 easy

exactitude n
accuracy, precision, exactness, correctness, faultlessness, carefulness, care, meticulousness, orderliness, rigorousness, rigour, scrupulousness, thoroughness, conscientiousness, painstakingness, perfectionism, strictness, detail
🔁 inaccuracy, carelessness, imprecision

exactly adv, interj
▶ adv **1** PRECISELY, accurately, literally, faithfully, correctly, specifically, rigorously, scrupulously, verbatim, carefully, faultlessly, without error, unerringly, strictly, religiously, to the letter, particularly, methodically, explicitly, expressly, formal veraciously, colloq. dead **2** ABSOLUTELY, definitely, precisely, indeed, certainly, truly, quite, just, unequivocally, colloq. bang on, spot on, on the dot, on the button, on the nail, to a T, smash, plumb
🔁 **1** inaccurately, roughly, vaguely

▶ *interj* precisely, quite, of course, just so, indeed, absolutely, agreed, certainly, right, true

exactness *n*
accuracy, precision, exactitude, correctness, faultlessness, carefulness, care, meticulousness, orderliness, rigorousness, rigour, scrupulousness, thoroughness, strictness
◨ inaccuracy, carelessness, imprecision

exaggerate *v*
overstate, overdo, magnify, overemphasize, emphasize, stress, make too much of, dramatize, overdramatize, embellish, embroider, colour, stretch the truth, enlarge, amplify, enhance, oversell, overplay, *formal* aggrandize, *colloq.* lay/pile it on, lay/pile it on thick, lay/pile it on with a trowel, make a mountain out of a molehill, blow something up out of all proportion, shoot a line, make a drama out of a crisis
◨ understate, play down

exaggerated *adj*
overstated, overdone, overestimated, overcharged, excessive, extravagant, pretentious, embellished, amplified, bombastic, inflated, overblown, caricatured, burlesqued, exalted, *technical* euphuistic, *formal* hyperbolic, *colloq.* tall
◨ understated, played down

exaggeration *n*
overstatement, overemphasis, emphasis, magnification, overestimation, excess, extravagance, embellishment, enlargement, pretentiousness, amplification, burlesque, caricature, parody, *formal* hyperbole
◨ meiosis, understatement

exalt *v*
1 PRAISE, extol, glorify, magnify, acclaim, applaud, bless, honour, adore, revere, worship, reverence, eulogize, *formal* laud, venerate 2 DELIGHT, elate, overjoy, transport, promote, raise, prefer, elevate, upgrade, enliven, excite, exhilarate, *formal* aggrandize

exaltation *n*
1 ELATION, ecstasy, rapture, bliss, joy, jubilation, excitement, exhilaration, high spirits 2 PRAISE, glorification, acclaim, honour, glory, reverence, worship, adoration, eulogy, *formal* veneration

exalted *adj*
1 LOFTY, high, elevated, grand, regal, lordly, eminent, stately, noble, idealistic, virtuous, moral 2 ELATED, ecstatic, blissful, joyful, happy, jubilant, rapturous, in high spirits, *colloq.* in seventh heaven

exam *n*
test, examination, exercises, questions, multiple-choice questions, practical, quiz, paper, viva, oral, final

examination *n*
1 INSPECTION, inquiry, scrutiny, study, survey, search, analysis, assessment, exploration, investigation, probe, observation, research, review, scan, perusal, check, check-up, audit, critique, post-mortem, *formal* appraisal, *colloq.* once-over 2 TEST, exam, quiz, questioning, cross-examination, cross-questioning, trial, inquisition, interrogation, viva, oral

examine *v*
1 INSPECT, investigate, scrutinize, study, look at, look into, observe, survey, analyse, explore, inquire, consider, probe, research, review, scan, check (out), check over, ponder, pore over, sift, vet, weigh up, assess, audit, peruse, *technical* assay, *formal* appraise, *slang* case 2 TEST, quiz, question, cross-examine, cross-question, interrogate, *formal* catechize, *colloq.* grill, pump, give the third degree to, give someone a roasting, go to town on, put the screws on

examinee *n*
entrant, candidate, competitor, contestant, applicant, interviewee

examiner *n*
adjudicator, assessor, tester, inspector, interviewer, judge, marker, questioner, reviewer, reader, analyst, censor, critic, auditor, arbiter, scrutineer, scrutinizer, *technical* assayer, *formal* examinant, interlocutor, scrutator

example *n*
1 SAMPLE, specimen, prototype, *formal* exemplar, archetype 2 INSTANCE, case, case in point, illustration, exemplification, representation, typical case, epitome 3 MODEL, role model, guide, pattern, ideal, standard, criterion, type, *formal* precedent, paradigm 4 LESSON, warning, caution, punishment, *formal* admonition
▷ **for example** eg, for instance, as an example/instance, say, to illustrate, by way of illustration, to give as an illustration

exasperate *v*
infuriate, annoy, anger, incense, irritate, madden, provoke, enrage, irk, rile, rankle, rouse, goad, vex, gall, *colloq.* get on someone's nerves, get to, needle, bug, wind up, drive up the wall, make someone's blood boil, put someone's back up
◨ appease, pacify

exasperated *adj*
infuriated, annoyed, angry, indignant, angered, incensed, irritated, maddened, provoked, riled, vexed, piqued, irked, galled, goaded, *colloq.* aggravated, at the end of your tether, bugged, fed up, needled, nettled, peeved
◨ calm, satisfied

exasperating *adj*
infuriating, annoying, bothersome, maddening, provoking, troublesome, disagreeable, irksome, irritating, vexing, galling, pernicious, vexatious, *colloq.* aggravating

excavate *v*
dig (out), dig up, hollow, burrow, tunnel, delve, unearth, mine, quarry, disinter, cut, gouge, scoop, reveal, uncover, *formal* exhume

excavation *n*
hole, hollow, pit, quarry, mine, colliery, dugout, dig, diggings, burrow, cavity, crater, trench, trough, shaft, ditch, cutting

exceed *v*
surpass, go beyond, be greater/larger than, be more than, outnumber, outdo, outstrip, beat, better, be superior to, pass, overtake, top, outshine, eclipse, outreach, outrun, outweigh, transcend, cap, overdo, overstep, go over

exceedingly *adv*
very, very much, extremely, greatly, highly, unusually, exceptionally, especially, enormously, excessively, hugely, immensely, vastly, inordinately, unprecedentedly, superlatively, surpassingly, amazingly, astonishingly, extraordinarily

excel *v*
1 BE EXCELLENT, succeed, shine, stand out, be outstanding, be skilful, be pre-eminent, predominate 2 SURPASS, outdo, beat, be superior to, outclass, outperform, outrank, outrival, eclipse, better, be better than

excellence *n*
superiority, pre-eminence, distinction, merit, supremacy, quality, worth, value, fineness, skill, eminence, goodness, greatness, virtue, perfection, purity, transcendence

excellent *adj*
wonderful, brilliant, marvellous, fantastic, superior, first-class, first-rate, high-quality, very good, prime, superlative, unequalled, unparalleled, matchless, exceptional, outstanding, surpassing, remarkable, distinguished, great, eminent, flawless, faultless, perfect, good, exemplary, select, superb, admirable, commendable, splendid, pre-eminent, praiseworthy, noteworthy, notable, noted, fine, worthy, inspired, *formal* sterling, *colloq.* top-notch, smashing, terrific, neat, ace, brill, out of this world, second to none, *slang* mega, cool, wicked, stonking, radical, crucial, way-out, groovy
F3 inferior, second-rate

except *prep, v*
▶ *prep* excepting, but, but for, apart from, other than, with the exception of, aside from, save, omitting, not counting, leaving out, excluding, except for, besides, bar, barring, minus, less
▶ *v* leave out, omit, bar, exclude, reject, rule out, pass over

exception *n*
oddity, deviation, departure, abnormality, irregularity, peculiarity, inconsistency, rarity, special case, freak, quirk, *formal* anomaly
▷ **with the exception of** excepting, but, apart from, other than, save, omitting, not counting, leaving out, excluding, except for, besides, bar, barring, minus, less

exceptionable *adj*
objectionable, unpleasant, disagreeable, offensive, unacceptable, disgusting, deplorable, abhorrent, *formal* repugnant
F3 acceptable, agreeable

exceptional *adj*
1 OUTSTANDING, remarkable, marvellous, excellent, extraordinary, brilliant, phenomenal, notable, noteworthy, superior, unequalled, *formal* prodigious **2** ABNORMAL, unusual, strange, odd, irregular, extraordinary, out of the ordinary, peculiar, special, rare, atypical, uncommon, *formal* anomalous, aberrant, singular
F3 1 mediocre **2** normal

exceptionally *adv*
1 EXTREMELY, extraordinarily, notably, outstandingly, especially, amazingly, remarkably, wonderfully **2** UNUSUALLY, uncommonly, irregularly, abnormally, rarely

excerpt *n*
extract, passage, portion, section, selection, quote, quotation, part, piece, cutting, clip, clipping, citation, scrap, fragment, *technical* pericope

excess *n, adj*
▶ *n* **1** SURFEIT, too much, more than enough, overabundance, oversupply, glut, superabundance, surplus, backlog, overflow, overkill, remainder, residue, leftovers, *formal* plethora, superfluity, *colloq.* bellyful **2** OVERINDULGENCE, dissoluteness, immoderateness, immoderation, extravagance, unrestraint, debauchery, *formal* dissipation, intemperance, prodigality
F3 1 deficiency **2** restraint
▶ *adj* extra, surplus, too much, spare, redundant, remaining, residual, left-over, additional, superfluous, *formal* supernumerary
F3 inadequate

excessive *adj*
immoderate, inordinate, extreme, too much, undue, uncalled-for, disproportionate, overdone, unnecessary, unneeded, needless, unwarranted, superfluous, superabundant, unreasonable, lavish, exorbitant, extravagant, *colloq.* steep, over the top, OTT
F3 insufficient

excessively *adv*
immoderately, inordinately, extremely, too much, to a fault, unduly, unreasonably, overly, overmuch, disproportionately, unnecessarily, needlessly, superfluously, exorbitantly, exaggeratedly, extravagantly, intemperately
F3 insufficiently, inadequately

exchange *v, n*
▶ *v* barter, change, trade, swap, switch, replace, interchange, convert, commute, transpose, substitute, stand in for, reciprocate, bargain, bandy
▶ *n* **1** INTERCHANGE, swap, switch, replacement, substitution, *formal* reciprocity, *colloq.* give and take **2** TRADE, commerce, dealing, market, traffic, barter, bargain, trade-off **3** CONVERSATION, discussion, chat, argument

excise¹ *n*
excise *duty* duty, tax, VAT, customs, levy, surcharge, tariff, toll, *formal* impost

excise² *v*
excise *sensitive material* cut, cut out, remove, extract, destroy, eradicate, erase, delete, exterminate, *formal* expunge, expurgate, extirpate, rescind

excision *n*
removal, deletion, eradication, destruction, expunction, *formal* expurgation, extermination, extirpation

excitable *adj*
temperamental, volatile, passionate, emotional, highly-strung, fiery, hot-headed, hasty, nervous, hot-tempered, irascible, quick-tempered, sensitive, susceptible, *formal* choleric, mercurial, *colloq.* edgy
F3 calm, stable

excite *v*
1 *excite a feeling* stir up, thrill, impress, touch, move, agitate, disturb, upset, arouse, rouse, animate, awaken, evoke, engender, inspire, kindle, fire, inflame, ignite, *colloq.* turn on **2** *excite an action* provoke, motivate, stimulate, bring about, instigate, incite, induce, galvanize, generate, sway **3** *excite sexually* arouse, stimulate, awaken, titillate, *colloq.* turn on
F3 1 calm

excited *adj*
aroused, roused, stimulated, stirred, exhilarated, thrilled, elated, in high spirits, enthusiastic, eager, moved, beside yourself, animated, worked up, wrought-up, overwrought, agitated, restless, frantic, frenzied, wild, *colloq.* high, on the edge of your seat, on tenterhooks, thrilled to bits, turned on, uptight, hyper, fired up
F3 calm, apathetic

excitement *n*
1 *the excitement of winning* thrill, passion, adventure, emotion, pleasure, animation, elation, enthusiasm, restlessness, ferment, fever, eagerness, stimulation, agitation, discomposure, exhilaration, *formal* perturbation, *colloq.* kick(s) **2** UNREST, ado, action, activity, commotion, stir, fuss, tumult, flurry, furore
F3 1 apathy **2** calm

exciting *adj*
stimulating, stirring, intoxicating, exhilarating, thrilling, dramatic, rousing, moving, enthralling, electrifying, striking, breathtaking, sensational, provocative, inspiring, interesting, *colloq.* nail-biting, cliffhanging, action-packed, sexy
F3 dull, unexciting

exclaim *v*
cry (out), declare, come out with, blurt (out), call, yell, shout, roar, shriek, bellow, proclaim, utter, *formal* vociferate, ejaculate

exclamation *n*
cry, call, yell, shout, expletive, interjection, outcry,

utterance, roar, shriek, bellow, *formal* ejaculation

exclude *v*
1 BAN, bar, prohibit, refuse, disallow, veto, forbid, blacklist, *formal* interdict **2** OMIT, leave out, miss out, delete, keep out, refuse, reject, ignore, shut out, rule out, ostracize, eliminate, *formal* preclude, *colloq.* drop, skip **3** EXPEL, eject, evict, throw out, remove, excommunicate, *colloq.* boot out, turf out, kick out
F3 **1** admit **2** include, consider

exclusion *n*
1 OMISSION, rejection, elimination, ruling out, refusal, repudiation, *formal* preclusion **2** BAN, bar, prohibition, embargo, veto, boycott, *formal* interdict, proscription **3** EJECTION, expulsion, eviction, removal, boycott, exception
F3 **1** inclusion **2** allowance **3** admittance

exclusive *adj*
1 SOLE, single, individual, unique, only, undivided, unshared, complete, whole, total, peculiar **2** RESTRICTED, limited, closed, private, narrow, restrictive, choice, select, discriminative, cliquey, chic, elegant, fashionable, up-market, upper crust, snobbish, *colloq.* classy, posh, snazzy, ritzy, plush, swish
▷ **exclusive of** except, except for, with the exception of, excepting, excluding, not including, not counting, omitting, leaving out, ruling out, barring, debarring
F3 inclusive of

excommunicate *v*
ban, banish, eject, denounce, exclude, expel, remove, bar, blacklist, debar, outlaw, repudiate, disfellowship, unchurch, *formal* anathematize, proscribe, execrate

excoriate *v*
condemn, carp, disapprove of, find fault with, denounce, attack, censure, blame, *formal* animadvert, disparage, decry, denigrate, vituperate, *colloq.* nag, slate, slam, knock, snipe, run down, come down on, give someone some stick, nit-pick

excrement *n*
waste matter, excretion, dung, ordure, droppings, *technical* egesta, frass, scats, guano, *formal* faeces, stool, *slang* crap, poop

excrescence *n*
1 GROWTH, swelling, bump, lump, knob, appendage, outgrowth, projection, prominence, tumour, wart, boil, cancer, *formal* intumescence, protuberance **2** MONSTROSITY, blot, disfigurement, eyesore

excrete *v*
void, pass, eject, discharge, expel, evacuate, exude, secrete, *formal* defecate, urinate, *slang* crap

excretion *n*
discharge, excrement, droppings, dung, evacuation, ordure, perspiration, *formal* defecation, excreta, urination, faeces, stool, *slang* crap

excruciating *adj*
agonizing, painful, severe, tormenting, unbearable, insufferable, acute, intolerable, intense, sharp, piercing, extreme, atrocious, racking, harrowing, savage, burning, bitter

exculpate *v*
clear, discharge, excuse, free, justify, let off, pardon, release, vindicate, forgive, deliver, absolve, acquit, *formal* exonerate
F3 blame, condemn

excursion *n*
1 OUTING, trip, day trip, jaunt, expedition, journey, tour, airing, breather, ride, drive, walk, ramble, *colloq.* junket **2** DIGRESSION, departure, straying, wandering, detour, diversion

excusable *adj*
understandable, minor, slight, allowable, permiss-

ible, defensible, explainable, forgivable, pardonable, justifiable
F3 blameworthy

excuse *v, n*
▶ *v* **1** FORGIVE, pardon, overlook, absolve, acquit, tolerate, make allowances for, ignore, indulge, *formal* exonerate, exculpate **2** RELEASE, free, discharge, liberate, let off, relieve, spare, exempt **3** CONDONE, explain, justify, vindicate, defend, apologize for, *formal* mitigate
F3 **1** criticize **2** punish
▶ *n* justification, explanation, grounds, defence, plea, alibi, reason, vindication, apology, pretext, pretence, evasion, shift, substitute, *formal* exoneration, mitigation, mitigating circumstances, *colloq.* cop-out, front, cover-up

execrable *adj*
deplorable, abhorrent, abominable, disgusting, foul, appalling, atrocious, despicable, detestable, offensive, shocking, repulsive, revolting, horrible, loathsome, vile, nauseous, obnoxious, odious, damnable, accursed, hateful, *formal* heinous
F3 admirable, estimable

execrate *v*
deplore, hate, abhor, loathe, abominate, condemn, denounce, denunciate, despise, detest, revile, curse, damn, imprecate, *formal* excoriate, fulminate, inveigh against, vilify, anathematize, *colloq.* blast
F3 commend, praise

execute *v*
1 PUT TO DEATH, kill, hang, electrocute, shoot, guillotine, behead, crucify, *formal* decapitate, *colloq.* liquidate **2** CARRY OUT, perform, do, accomplish, achieve, fulfil, complete, bring off, discharge, put into effect, put into practice, enact, deliver, enforce, finish, implement, administer, engineer, realize, dispatch, validate, serve, render, stage, *formal* effect, consummate, expedite

execution *n*
1 DEATH PENALTY, death sentence, capital punishment, putting to death, killing

Means of execution include:
beheading, burning, crucifixion, decapitation, electrocution, firing squad, garrotting, gassing, guillotining, hanging, lethal injection, lynching, shooting, stoning, *colloq.* stringing up.

2 ACCOMPLISHMENT, operation, performance, completion, achievement, administration, effect, enactment, implementation, realization, fulfilment, discharge, dispatch, enforcement, *formal* consummation, effecting **3** STYLE, technique, rendition, rendering, delivery, performance, staging, manner, mode, presentation

executioner *n*
hangman, firing squad, headsman, axeman, killer, murderer, exterminator, assassin, slayer, *colloq.* hit man, liquidator

executive *n, adj*
▶ *n* **1** ADMINISTRATOR, manager, organizer, leader, controller, director, governor, official **2** ADMINISTRATION, management, government, leadership, hierarchy, *colloq.* top brass, big guns, big shots
▶ *adj* administrative, managerial, controlling, supervisory, regulating, decision-making, governing, law-making, organizing, directing, directorial, organizational, leading, guiding

exegesis *n*
explanation, interpretation, clarification, opening-up, *formal* exposition, expounding, explication

exemplar *n*
example, standard, model, pattern, type, ideal, proto-type, paragon, copy, criterion, yardstick, epitome, il-lustration, instance, specimen, *formal* archetype, embodiment, exemplification, paradigm

exemplary *adj*
1 MODEL, ideal, perfect, admirable, excellent, fault-less, flawless, correct, good, commendable, praise-worthy, worthy, honourable, *formal* laudable, es-timable, meritorious **2** CAUTIONARY, warning, *formal* admonitory
F3 1 imperfect, unworthy

exemplify *v*
illustrate, be an example of, demonstrate, show, in-stance, cite, represent, typify, characterize, embody, personify, epitomize, exhibit, depict, display, *formal* manifest

exempt *v, adj*
▶ *v* excuse, release, relieve, let off, free, grant immu-nity to, absolve, discharge, dismiss, liberate, spare, exclude, waive, make an exception, *formal* exonerate
▶ *adj* excused, not liable, not subject, immune, re-leased, spared, absolved, discharged, excluded, free, liberated, dismissed, clear
F3 liable

exemption *n*
exception, exclusion, immunity, privilege, indul-gence, release, freedom, indemnity, discharge, *formal* absolution, dispensation, exoneration
F3 liability

exercise *v, n*
▶ *v* **1** USE, utilize, employ, make use of, apply, exert, practise, implement, bring to bear, bring into play, wield, try, discharge, exploit **2** TRAIN, do exercises, drill, practise, keep fit, exert yourself, *colloq.* work out **3** WORRY, disturb, trouble, upset, burden, dis-tress, vex, annoy, agitate, afflict, preoccupy, *formal* perturb
▶ *n* **1** TRAINING, drill, movement, practice, effort, ex-ertion, activity, keep-fit, aerobics, sports, gymnastics, PE, physical education, PT, physical training, warm-up, jogging, running, isometrics, eurhythmics, cal-listhenics, labour, *colloq.* physical jerks, workout **2** USE, utilization, employment, application, imple-mentation, practice, operation, discharge, assign-ment, fulfilment, accomplishment, exertion **3** TASK, lesson, work, discipline, problem, piece of work

exert *v*
use, utilize, employ, apply, exercise, bring to bear, bring into play, wield, spend, expend
▷ **exert yourself** strive, struggle, try hard, strain, make every effort, take pains, do your best/utmost, toil, labour, work, endeavour, apply yourself, give your all, *colloq.* sweat, go all out, pull out all the stops

exertion *n*
1 EFFORT, industry, labour, toil, work, exercise, strug-gle, diligence, assiduousness, perseverance, pains, endeavour, attempt, strain, stress, trial, *formal* travail **2** USE, utilization, employment, application, exercise, operation, action
F3 1 idleness, rest

exhale *v*
breathe (out), give off, blow, discharge, emit, expel, issue, respire, steam, evaporate, *formal* emanate, ex-pire
F3 inhale

exhaust *v, n*
▶ *v* **1** TIRE (OUT), weary, fatigue, tax, sap, drain, strain, weaken, overwork, overtax, wear out, *formal* enervate, *colloq.* do in, fag out, knock out, whack, take it out of, nearly/almost kill **2** CONSUME, empty,

drain, sap, spend, expend, waste, squander, impover-ish, use up, finish, dry, bankrupt, *formal* deplete, dis-sipate
F3 1 refresh **2** renew
▶ *n* emission, exhalation, discharge, fumes, smoke, steam, vapour, *formal* emanation

exhausted *adj*
1 TIRED OUT, dead tired, worn out, fatigued, weak, washed-out, drained, jaded, *formal* enfeebled, ener-vated, *colloq.* dead beat, all in, done (in), whacked, fagged out, knackered, bushed, burnt out, dog-tired, ready to drop, zonked **2** EMPTY, finished, consumed, spent, used up, drained, dry, worn out, void, *formal* de-pleted
F3 1 vigorous **2** fresh

exhausting *adj*
tiring, strenuous, taxing, wearing, gruelling, arduous, hard, laborious, backbreaking, draining, severe, test-ing, punishing, formidable, *formal* debilitating, ener-vating
F3 refreshing, invigorating

exhaustion *n*
fatigue, tiredness, weariness, weakness, feebleness, lethargy, jet-lag, *formal* debility, enervation
F3 freshness, liveliness

exhaustive *adj*
comprehensive, all-embracing, all-inclusive, far-reaching, complete, total, extensive, encyclopedic, full-scale, thorough, full, in-depth, intensive, de-tailed, definitive, all-out, sweeping
F3 incomplete, restricted

exhibit *v, n*
▶ *v* display, put on display, show, present, demon-strate, expose, unveil, parade, reveal, express, make clear, make plain, reveal, disclose, indicate, air, flaunt, offer, set out, set forth, *formal* manifest, array
F3 conceal, hide
▶ *n* display, exhibition, show, showing, demonstra-tion, illustration, model, presentation

exhibition *n*
display, show, demonstration, exhibit, presentation, spectacle, showing, fair, performance, airing, repre-sentation, showcase, indication, expression, revela-tion, disclosure, *formal* manifestation, exposition, *colloq.* expo

exhibitionist *n*
show-off, extrovert, poseur, poser, self-advertiser

exhilarate *v*
thrill, excite, make excited, elate, make happy, cheer up, delight, gladden, animate, enliven, invigorate, vi-talize, revitalize, raise/lift the spirits of, stimulate, brighten, lift, *colloq.* perk up
F3 bore, discourage

exhilarating *adj*
thrilling, exciting, delightful, cheerful, gladdening, cheering, enlivening, stimulating, revitalizing, invig-orating, heady, breathtaking, *colloq.* mind-blowing
F3 boring, discouraging

exhilaration *n*
excitement, thrill, happiness, cheerfulness, gladness, delight, elation, joy, joyfulness, exaltation, glee, high spirits, liveliness, vivacity, zeal, enthusiasm, anima-tion, ardour, invigoration, revitalization, stimulation, gusto, dash, gaiety, mirth, hilarity, *formal* élan
F3 boredom, discouragement

exhort *v*
urge, persuade, encourage, implore, goad, incite, in-flame, inspire, instigate, spur, warn, bid, call upon, press, advise, counsel, caution, prompt, *formal* ad-monish, beseech, enjoin, entreat

exhortation *n*
urging, persuasion, encouragement, goading, incitement, advice, caution, warning, counsel, bidding, lecture, sermon, *formal* admonition, beseeching, enjoinder, entreaty, paraenesis, protreptic

exhume *v*
disinter, dig up, disentomb, excavate, unbury, unearth, resurrect, *formal* disinhume
⬛ bury

exigency *n*
1 DEMAND, requirement, need, necessity **2** EMERGENCY, urgency, crisis, criticalness, difficulty, distress, imperativeness, pressure, plight, quandary, predicament, stress

exigent *adj*
urgent, demanding, insistent, necessary, pressing, stringent, exacting, critical, crucial

exiguous *adj*
meagre, insufficient, scant, scanty, negligible, sparse, slight, slim, bare

exile *n, v*
▶ *n* **1** BANISHMENT, deportation, expatriation, expulsion, uprooting, ostracism, separating, separation, transportation **2** EXPATRIATE, refugee, émigré, expat, deportee, displaced person, outcast, outlaw, pariah
▶ *v* banish, expel, deport, extradite, expatriate, repatriate, drive out, cast out, uproot, separate, ostracize, oust, excommunicate, eject, outlaw, ban, bar

exist *v*
1 BE, live, have life, abide, continue, endure, have being, have existence, breathe, have breath **2** SUBSIST, survive, live, eke out a living, eke out an existence **3** BE PRESENT, occur, happen, be available, remain, last, continue, prevail

existence *n*
1 BEING, life, living, reality, actuality, fact, continuance, continuation, endurance, survival, breath, subsistence **2** WAY OF LIFE, way of living, life, lifestyle, *formal* mode of living **3** ENTITY, creature, being, thing **4** CREATION, the world
⬛ **1** death, non-existence

existent *adj*
existing, actual, real, current, present, living, alive, enduring, remaining, surviving, standing, abiding, prevailing, *formal* obtaining, extant, *colloq.* around
⬛ non-existent

exit *n, v*
▶ *n* **1** DEPARTURE, going, leaving, retreat, withdrawal, leave-taking, retirement, farewell, exodus, flight **2** DOOR, way out, doorway, gate, vent, outlet, *formal* egress
⬛ **1** entrance, arrival **2** entrance
▶ *v* depart, leave, go, retire, withdraw, take your leave, retreat, issue
⬛ arrive, enter

exodus *n*
departure, evacuation, mass departure, mass evacuation, flight, fleeing, escape, leaving, migration, retirement, long march, retreat, withdrawal, exit, hegira

exonerate *v*
1 ABSOLVE, acquit, clear, excuse, vindicate, justify, pardon, declare innocent, discharge, *formal* exculpate **2** EXEMPT, excuse, spare, let off, free, liberate, discharge, release, relieve
⬛ **1** incriminate

exoneration *n*
1 ACQUITTAL, clearing, excusing, vindication, justification, pardon, discharge, amnesty, absolution, dismissal, *formal* exculpation **2** EXEMPTION, excusing,

discharge, liberation, freeing, release, relief, immunity, indemnity
⬛ **1** incrimination

exorbitant *adj*
excessive, unreasonable, unwarranted, undue, inordinate, immoderate, extravagant, extortionate, enormous, preposterous, monstrous, *colloq.* daylight robbery, a rip-off
⬛ reasonable, moderate, fair

exorcism *n*
casting out, deliverance, freeing, expulsion, purification, *old use* exsufflation, *formal* adjuration

exorcize *v*
cast out, drive out, free, expel, purify, *old use* exsufflate, *formal* adjure

exotic *adj*
1 FOREIGN, alien, imported, introduced, tropical, external, non-native **2** UNUSUAL, striking, different, remarkable, unfamiliar, extraordinary, bizarre, curious, strange, impressive, fascinating, colourful, glamorous, peculiar, outlandish, extravagant, outrageous, sensational
⬛ **1** native **2** ordinary, common

expand *v*
increase, grow, become/make larger/bigger, extend, enlarge, develop, amplify, spread, stretch, swell, widen, lengthen, thicken, intensify, escalate, magnify, multiply, inflate, amplify, broaden, blow up, open out, fill out, fatten, puff out, unfold, unfurl, pad, branch out, diversify, *formal* distend, dilate, intumesce
⬛ contract
▷ **expand on** enlarge on, elaborate on, embroider, go into details, *formal* expatiate on, dilate on

expanse *n*
extent, space, area, breadth, range, stretch, region, sweep, field, plain, tract, vastness, extensiveness

expansion *n*
growth, increase, extension, development, amplification, spread, expanse, swelling, enlargement, lengthening, thickening, broadening, magnification, multiplication, inflation, unfolding, unfurling, diversification, *formal* augmentation, diffusion, dilation, distension, dilatation
⬛ contraction

expansive *adj*
1 EXTENSIVE, broad, comprehensive, wide, wide-ranging, widespread, all-embracing, thorough **2** FRIENDLY, genial, outgoing, open, affable, sociable, talkative, warm, communicative, effusive, uninhibited, *formal* loquacious **3** EXPANDING, growing, increasing, enlarging, developing, diversifying, magnifying, multiplying
⬛ **1** restricted, narrow **2** reserved, cold **3** contracting

expatiate *v*
expand, enlarge, amplify, elaborate, embellish, develop, expound, dwell on, *formal* dilate

expatriate *n, v, adj*
▶ *n* emigrant, émigré, exile, refugee, displaced person, ex-pat, outcast
▶ *v* banish, exile, deport, extradite, drive out, uproot, expel, oust, repatriate, ostracize, *formal* proscribe
▶ *adj* banished, exiled, deported, expelled, uprooted, emigrant, émigré

expect *v*
1 *expect you're right* suppose, assume, believe, think, presume, imagine, reckon, trust, *formal* surmise, conjecture, *colloq.* guess **2** *expect the money soon* anticipate, await, look forward to, hope for, look for, watch for, bank on, bargain for, envisage, predict, forecast, contemplate, project, foresee **3** *expect you to com-*

ply require, want, wish, insist on, demand, call for, look for, hope for, rely on, count on

expectancy *n*
anticipation, eagerness, expectation, hope, suspense, waiting, curiosity, *formal* conjecture

expectant *adj*
1 AWAITING, anticipating, looking forward, hopeful, in suspense, ready, apprehensive, anxious, watchful, eager, on tenterhooks, with bated breath, curious 2 PREGNANT, going to have a baby, *technical* gravid, *formal* with child, enceinte, *colloq.* expecting, in the family way, in the club, *slang* preggers, with a bun in the oven

expectantly *adv*
in anticipation, eagerly, expectingly, hopefully, in suspense, apprehensively, optimistically

expectation *n*
hope, belief, anticipation, assumption, presumption, surmise, supposition, calculation, forecast, projection, prediction, eagerness, requirement, demand, insistence, promise, want, wish, reliance, trust, prospect, confidence, assurance, suspense, optimism, possibility, probability, outlook, *formal* conjecture

expecting *adj*
pregnant, going to have a baby, expectant, *technical* gravid, *formal* with child, enceinte, *colloq.* in the family way, in the club

expedience *n*
convenience, suitability, appropriateness, fitness, aptness, advantageousness, effectiveness, desirability, helpfulness, properness, profitableness, usefulness, practicality, pragmatism, advisability, benefit, advantage, profitability, expediency, utility, utilitarianism, *formal* judiciousness, propriety, prudence

expedient *adj, n*
▶ *adj* convenient, suitable, appropriate, fitting, opportune, politic, in your own interest, profitable, useful, beneficial, advantageous, advisable, sensible, practical, pragmatic, tactical, *formal* prudent
◰ inexpedient
▶ *n* stratagem, scheme, means, method, tactic, ploy, manoeuvre, plan, trick, shift, contrivance, device, stopgap, *colloq.* dodge

expedite *v*
speed up, accelerate, step up, quicken, hasten, hurry, further, facilitate, assist, promote, press, dispatch, discharge, hurry through, *formal* precipitate
◰ delay

expedition *n*
1 JOURNEY, excursion, trip, voyage, tour, outing, exploration, trek, safari, hike, sail, ramble, raid, quest, pilgrimage, adventure, undertaking, enterprise, project, campaign, mission, crusade 2 TEAM, group, party, crew, company 3 PROMPTNESS, speed, swiftness, haste, *formal* alacrity, celerity

expeditious *adj*
quick, efficient, rapid, speedy, swift, fast, hasty, immediate, instant, diligent, prompt, active, alert, brisk, ready, *colloq.* meteoric
◰ slow

expel *v*
1 DRIVE OUT, eject, evict, banish, throw out, cast out, ban, bar, oust, dismiss, reject, exile, outlaw, expatriate, *formal* proscribe, *colloq.* boot out, chuck out, kick out 2 DISCHARGE, eject, belch, evacuate, void, cast out, spew out
◰ 1 welcome

expend *v*
1 SPEND, pay, buy, afford, overspend, waste, fritter, squander, *formal* purchase, disburse, procure, *colloq.*

fork out, lay out, shell out, blow, splash out 2 CONSUME, use (up), get through, go through, exhaust, empty, drain, sap, employ, utilize, *formal* dissipate, deplete
◰ 1 save 2 conserve

expendable *adj*
dispensable, disposable, replaceable, unimportant, unnecessary, inessential, non-essential
◰ indispensable, necessary

expenditure *n*
1 *huge amounts of public expenditure* spending, expense, expenses, costs, outlay, outgoings, payment, output, waste, squandering, *formal* disbursement 2 *the expenditure of effort* use, application, consumption, draining, sapping, employment, utilization, *formal* dissipation
◰ income

expense *n*
1 *underestimate the expense of moving house* spending, expenditure, outlay, payment, paying-out, loss, cost, price, charge, fee, rate, *formal* disbursement 2 *expenses will be reimbursed* costs, outgoings, incidentals, outlay, overheads, incidental expenses, out-of-pocket expenses, miscellaneous expenses, spending 3 *at the expense of his life* cost, sacrifice, loss, harm, disadvantage, detriment

expensive *adj*
dear, high-priced, costly, costing a lot, exorbitant, extortionate, overpriced, extravagant, lavish, *colloq.* steep, pricey, sky-high, costing an arm and a leg, costing the earth, costing a bomb, daylight robbery
◰ cheap, inexpensive

experience *n, v*
▶ *n* 1 KNOWLEDGE, familiarity, contact, skill, involvement, exposure, participation, practice, training, understanding, learning, observation, *colloq.* know-how 2 INCIDENT, event, episode, happening, encounter, occurrence, circumstance, adventure, affair, case, ordeal
◰ 1 inexperience
▶ *v* undergo, go through, live through, suffer, feel, endure, encounter, face, meet, know, try, perceive, sustain, become familiar with, participate in

experienced *adj*
1 PRACTISED, knowledgeable, familiar, capable, competent, proficient, adept, well-versed, expert, accomplished, qualified, skilful, skilled, tried, trained, professional, *au fait*, *au courant* 2 MATURE, seasoned, wise, veteran, sophisticated, worldly wise, *colloq.* around, streetwise
◰ 1 inexperienced, unskilled 2 inexperienced, unsophisticated

experiment *n, v*
▶ *n* trial, test, testing, investigation, experimentation, research, inquiry, demonstration, examination, observation, analysis, trial run, venture, try-out, trial and error, attempt, procedure, proof, pilot study, piloting, dummy run, dry run
▶ *v* try (out), test, investigate, examine, research, sample, verify, observe, explore, carry out tests, conduct an experiment

experimental *adj*
trial, test, exploratory, tentative, provisional, investigative, observational, speculative, pilot, preliminary, trial-and-error, at the trial/exploratory stage, *formal* empirical, peirastic

expert *n, adj*
▶ *n* specialist, connoisseur, authority, pundit, master, past master, old master, professional, maestro, virtuoso, *colloq.* pro, dab hand, old hand, ace, buff, egghead, wise guy, *US* mavin, *US* maven
▶ *adj* proficient, adept, skilled, skilful, knowledgeable, experienced, able, practised, professional, ac-

complished, masterly, excellent, brilliant, specialist, qualified, virtuoso, dexterous, *colloq.* top-notch, up on, well up on, crack, ace
F3 amateurish, novice

expertise *n*
expertness, proficiency, ability, skill, skilfulness, deftness, knowledge, professionalism, mastery, command, dexterity, facility, cleverness, virtuosity, *savoir-faire*, *colloq.* know-how, knack
F3 inexperience, inexpertness

expiate *v*
atone for, make amends for, purge, do penance for, make up for, pay for, redress

expiation *n*
atonement, redemption, ransom, reparation, redress, penance, amends, recompense, shrift

expire *v*
1 END, come to an end, cease, finish, stop, close, run out, be no longer valid, lapse, *formal* terminate, conclude, discontinue **2** DIE, depart, perish, pass away, pass on, depart this life, breathe your last, lose your life, *formal* decease, *colloq.* peg out, bite the dust, pop off, give up the ghost, have had it, meet your maker, *slang* snuff it, cash in your chips, kick the bucket
F3 1 begin, be valid **2** live, be born

expiry *n*
end, finish, close, expiration, lapse, *formal* cessation, conclusion, termination, discontinuation
F3 beginning, continuation

explain *v*
1 INTERPRET, clarify, describe, define, make clear, throw/shed light on, simplify, resolve, solve, spell out, translate, elaborate, unfold, unravel, untangle, decipher, decode, illustrate, demonstrate, disclose, teach, set out, *formal* elucidate, expound, delineate, explicate **2** JUSTIFY, excuse, account for, rationalize, vindicate, defend, give a reason for, explain away, lie behind
F3 1 obscure, confound

explanation *n*
1 INTERPRETATION, clarification, definition, illustration, demonstration, account, description, note, comment, commentary, gloss, footnote, annotation, unfolding, deciphering, decoding, *formal* elucidation, exegesis, expounding, delineation, explication **2** JUSTIFICATION, excuse, reason, account, motive, meaning, answer, warrant, rationalization, vindication, defence, alibi, *formal* apologia

explanatory *adj*
descriptive, demonstrative, illustrative, justifying, *formal* interpretative, interpretive, explicative, expository, exegetical, elucidatory

expletive *n*
swear-word, oath, curse, blasphemy, obscenity, profanity, bad language, *formal* anathema, imprecation, execration, *colloq.* four-letter word

explicable *adj*
explainable, accountable, definable, determinable, intelligible, justifiable, resolvable, understandable, solvable, *formal* interpretable, exponible

explicate *v*
explain, interpret, clarify, describe, define, make clear, illustrate, demonstrate, spell out, set forth, unfold, unravel, untangle, work out, *formal* elucidate, expound
F3 confuse, obscure

explicit *adj*
1 CLEAR, distinct, clearly expressed, exact, categorical, absolute, direct, certain, positive, precise, speci-

fic, unequivocal, unambiguous, express, definite, declared, detailed, stated, straightforward **2** OPEN, direct, frank, candid, outspoken, straightforward, forthright, unreserved, unrestrained, uninhibited, plain, plain-spoken
F3 1 implicit, unspoken, vague **2** reserved, restrained

explode *v*
1 BLOW UP, burst, go off, go up, set off, detonate, discharge, blast, *formal* erupt, *colloq.* go bang **2** *explode with rage* blow up, erupt, flare up, burst out, *colloq.* blow a fuse, blow your cool, blow your top, boil over, burst a blood vessel, do your nut, fly into a rage, fly off the handle, go off the deep end, go up the wall, hit the ceiling, hit the roof, lose your cool, lose your rag, see red **3** DISCREDIT, disprove, give the lie to, debunk, invalidate, rebut, repudiate, *formal* refute **4** GROW RAPIDLY, increase suddenly, escalate, accelerate, boom, leap, surge, mushroom, rocket
F3 3 prove, confirm

exploit *n, v*
▶ *n* deed, feat, adventure, achievement, accomplishment, attainment, activity, action, act, stunt
▶ *v* **1** USE, apply, employ, draw on, put to good use, utilize, capitalize on, use to good advantage, profit by, turn to account, take advantage of, make capital out of, tap, *colloq.* cash in on, milk **2** MISUSE, abuse, take advantage of, take liberties, profiteer, oppress, ill-treat, impose on, manipulate, *colloq.* rip off, fleece, milk, bleed, take for a ride, put something across someone, pull a fast one on, walk all over, play off against

exploration *n*
1 INVESTIGATION, examination, inquiry, research, scrutiny, study, inspection, observation, analysis, probe **2** EXPEDITION, survey, reconnaissance, search, trip, tour, voyage, travel, safari

exploratory *adj*
investigative, fact-finding, experimental, pilot, probing, searching, analytic, tentative, trial

explore *v*
1 INVESTIGATE, examine, look into, study, inspect, research, scrutinize, probe, analyse, consider, survey, inquire into, review **2** TRAVEL, tour, search, reconnoitre, prospect, scout, survey, *formal* traverse, *colloq.* see the world, do

explorer *n*
traveller, discoverer, navigator, tourer, prospector, scout, surveyor, reconnoitrer

explosion *n*
1 DETONATION, blast, burst, outburst, discharge, eruption, bang, boom, outbreak, clap, crack, thunder, rumble, roll, fit, *formal* report **2** *population explosion* boom, surge, leap, sudden increase, dramatic growth **3** *explosion of anger* outburst, eruption, fit, flare-up, rage, tantrum, paroxysm

explosive *n, adj*
▶ *n* dynamite, gelignite, gunpowder, jelly, nitroglycerine, TNT, cordite, Semtex®
▶ *adj* **1** *an explosive device* charged, hazardous, dangerous, unstable, volatile, *formal* perilous **2** *an explosive situation* tense, sensitive, fraught, charged, critical, nerve-racking, unstable, volatile **3** FIERY, angry, unstable, volatile, overwrought, worked-up, violent, stormy, unrestrained, wild, raging, sensitive, touchy **4** *explosive growth* sudden, dramatic, rapid, unexpected, mushrooming, rocketing, burgeoning, abrupt, *colloq.* meteoric
F3 1, 2 stable, calm **3** composed

exponent *n*
1 ADVOCATE, promoter, supporter, upholder, defender, backer, adherent, spokesman, spokeswoman,

spokesperson, champion, *formal* proponent **2** PRAC-TITIONER, adept, expert, master, specialist, player, performer

export *v, n*
▶ *v* trade, deal with, sell abroad/overseas, traffic in, transport
▶ *n* exported product/commodity/goods, transfer, trade, foreign trade, international trade

expose *v*
1 REVEAL, show, exhibit, display, disclose, uncover, bring to light, bring out into the open, make known, present, detect, divulge, betray, unveil, unmask, unearth, lay bare, denounce, *formal* manifest, *colloq.* blow the whistle, take the lid off **2** ENDANGER, jeopardize, imperil, risk, hazard, put at risk, put in jeopardy, make vulnerable **3** *expose the public to art* familiarize with, bring into contact with, acquaint with, introduce to, lay open to, subject to
🔁 **1** conceal, cover up **2** protect

exposé *n*
disclosure, divulgence, exposure, revelation, uncovering, account, article

exposed *adj*
bare, open, in the open, revealed, laid bare, unprotected, without protection, open to the elements, vulnerable, exhibited, on display, on view, on show, shown, susceptible
🔁 covered, sheltered

exposition *n*
1 EXPLANATION, description, analysis, unfolding, clarification, illumination, commentary, interpretation, account, illustration, critique, presentation, paper, study, thesis, monograph, *formal* discourse, elucidation, exegesis, explication **2** EXHIBITION, show, fair, display, demonstration, *colloq.* expo

expository *adj*
explanatory, descriptive, illustrative, interpretative, *technical* exegetic, hermeneutic, *formal* declaratory, elucidative, explicatory, interpretive

expostulate *v*
protest, argue, plead, reason, dissuade, *formal* remonstrate

exposure *n*
1 REVELATION, uncovering, disclosure, exposé, showing, unmasking, unveiling, display, airing, exhibition, presentation, publicity, discovery, detection, divulgence, denunciation, *formal* manifestation **2** FAMILIARITY, experience, knowledge, contact, acquaintance, awareness **3** JEOPARDY, danger, hazard, risk, vulnerability, susceptibility **4** PUBLICITY, public attention, advertising, promotion, *colloq.* plug, hype

expound *v*
explain, analyse, dissect, unfold, unravel, untangle, clarify, illuminate, describe, illustrate, interpret, comment on, set forth, set out, spell out, preach, sermonize, *formal* elucidate, explicate

express *v, adj*
▶ *v* **1** ARTICULATE, verbalize, put into words, utter, voice, give voice to, say, speak, state, communicate, put/get over, pronounce, word, tell, announce, report, assert, declare, put across, formulate, point out, intimate, testify, convey, vent, ventilate, air, *formal* enunciate **2** SHOW, demonstrate, exhibit, disclose, divulge, reveal, indicate, denote, depict, embody, couch, *formal* manifest **3** SYMBOLIZE, stand for, represent, signify, designate
▶ *adj* **1** SPECIFIC, explicit, exact, definite, clear, categorical, precise, distinct, well-defined, clear-cut, certain, plain, particular, stated, unambiguous, unequivocal, special, sole, *formal* manifest **2** FAST,

speedy, rapid, quick, swift, high-speed, brisk, nonstop, *formal* expeditious
🔁 **1** vague

expression *n*
1 LOOK, air, aspect, appearance, scowl, grimace, gesture, *formal* countenance, mien **2** REPRESENTATION, demonstration, indication, exhibition, communication, illustration, embodiment, show, sign, symbol, style, *formal* manifestation **3** UTTERANCE, verbalization, voicing, communication, articulation, statement, assertion, proclamation, announcement, declaration, pronouncement, speech, wording, intimation **4** PHRASE, word, wording, term, turn of phrase, saying, set phrase, phrasing, idiom, language **5** TONE, intonation, delivery, style, idiom, diction, enunciation, modulation, phrasing, *formal* locution **6** FEELING, emotion, passion, depth, force, power, vigour, vividness, intensity, imagination, artistry, creativity

expressionless *adj*
dull, blank, deadpan, impassive, emotionless, straightfaced, inscrutable, empty, vacuous, glassy, *colloq.* poker-faced
🔁 expressive

expressive *adj*
1 ELOQUENT, articulate, meaningful, forceful, telling, revealing, informative, communicative, demonstrative, emphatic, moving, evocative, poignant, lively, striking, animated, suggestive, significant, thoughtful, vivid, sympathetic **2** INDICATIVE, showing, demonstrating, revealing, suggesting

expressly *adv*
specifically, explicitly, exactly, definitely, clearly, categorically, absolutely, precisely, distinctly, plainly, particularly, unambiguously, unequivocally, specially, solely, especially, decidedly, intentionally, on purpose, purposely, pointedly, *formal* manifestly

expropriate *v*
take, take away, seize, commandeer, confiscate, impound, usurp, assume, dispossess, annex, unhouse, *technical* disseise, *formal* appropriate, arrogate, requisition, sequester

expulsion *n*
1 EJECTION, eviction, exile, banishment, removal, discharge, exclusion, dismissal, throwing out, rejection, *colloq.* sacking, the sack, the boot **2** DISCHARGE, ejection, belching, evacuation, voiding, excretion

expunge *v*
erase, remove, wipe out, cancel, obliterate, eradicate, destroy, exterminate, extinguish, raze, get rid of, abolish, annihilate, annul, blot out, delete, cross out, rub out, *formal* efface, extirpate

expurgate *v*
censor, cut, emend, clean up, blue-pencil, bowdlerize, purge, purify, sanitize

exquisite *adj*
1 BEAUTIFUL, attractive, dainty, delicate, fine, charming, elegant, delightful, lovely, pretty, pleasing, fragile **2** PERFECT, flawless, fine, excellent, choice, precious, rare, outstanding **3** REFINED, discriminating, meticulous, sensitive, discerning, cultivated, cultured, impeccable **4** INTENSE, keen, sharp, acute, piercing, poignant
🔁 **1** ugly **2** flawed **3** unrefined

extant *adj*
surviving, remaining, existent, existing, in existence, alive, living, subsistent, subsisting
🔁 extinct, non-existent, dead

extempore *adv, adj*
▶ *adv* impromptu, ad lib, on the spur of the moment, spontaneously, *colloq.* off the cuff, off the top of your head

▶ *adj* impromptu, improvised, ad-lib, unscripted, spontaneous, unplanned, unrehearsed, unprepared, extemporaneous, *colloq.* off-the-cuff
F3 planned

extemporize *v*
ad-lib, improvise, play it by ear, think on your feet, make up

extend *v*
1 SPREAD, stretch, reach, continue, carry on, run, last, come (up/down) to, go as far as, go down/up to **2** ENLARGE, increase, expand, develop, amplify, intensify, step up, lengthen, widen, broaden, draw out, stretch, prolong, spin out, drag out, unwind, *formal* elongate, protract, augment **3** OFFER, give, grant, hold out, reach out, impart, present, *formal* bestow, confer, proffer
F3 **2** contract, shorten **3** withhold

extended *adj*
lengthy, long, lengthened, increased, enlarged, expanded, developed, amplified

extension *n*
1 ENLARGEMENT, increase, stretching, broadening, widening, lengthening, expansion, development, enhancement, continuation, prolongation, *formal* elongation, protraction **2** ADDITION, supplement, appendix, annexe, wing, add-on, adjunct, *formal* addendum **3** DELAY, postponement, more/additional time

extensive *adj*
1 BROAD, comprehensive, far-reaching, large-scale, thorough, wide, wide-ranging, widespread, universal, complete, extended, all-inclusive, unlimited, boundless, general, pervasive, prevalent **2** LARGE, huge, roomy, spacious, vast, long, lengthy, wide, substantial, fair-sized, sizeable, *formal* capacious, commodious, voluminous
F3 **1** restricted, narrow **2** small

extent *n*
1 DIMENSION(S), amount, magnitude, expanse, size, area, bulk, degree, level, breadth, quantity, spread, coverage, stretch, volume, width, measure, length, duration, term, time **2** LIMIT, bounds, lengths, range, reach, scope, compass, stretch, sphere, play, sweep

extenuate *v*
diminish, excuse, lessen, minimize, modify, qualify, soften, *formal* mitigate

extenuating *adj*
moderating, qualifying, justifying, palliative, diminishing, excusing, lessening, minimizing, modifying, softening, *formal* exculpatory, extenuative, extenuatory, mitigating

exterior *n, adj*
▶ *n* outside, surface, outer surface, covering, coating, face, façade, shell, skin, finish, externals, external surface, appearance
F3 inside, interior
▶ *adj* outer, outside, outermost, surface, external, superficial, surrounding, outward, peripheral, extrinsic
F3 inside, interior

exterminate *v*
annihilate, kill, eradicate, destroy, eliminate, massacre, slaughter, abolish, wipe out, *formal* extirpate

extermination *n*
annihilation, killing, eradication, elimination, destruction, massacre, genocide, *formal* extirpation

external *adj*
1 OUTER, surface, outside, exterior, superficial, outward, outermost, apparent, visible, extraneous, peripheral, extrinsic **2** *external students* extramural,

independent, visiting, non-resident, outside
F3 **1** internal **2** resident

extinct *adj*
1 DEFUNCT, dead, died out, non-existent, gone, obsolete, ended, exterminated, terminated, vanished, lost, wiped out, abolished **2** EXTINGUISHED, quenched, inactive, out, burnt out **3** OBSOLETE, invalid, expired, *passé*, outmoded, bygone, antiquated, *formal* terminated
F3 **1** living, existing, existent **2** active, erupting

extinction *n*
annihilation, extermination, death, dying-out, vanishing, eradication, obliteration, destruction, abolition, excision, *formal* termination

extinguish *v*
1 PUT OUT, blow out, snuff out, stifle, smother, choke, douse, quench, dampen down, stub out **2** ANNIHILATE, exterminate, eliminate, destroy, kill, eradicate, erase, abolish, remove, end, suppress, *formal* expunge, extirpate

extirpate *v*
destroy, annihilate, eliminate, wipe out, eradicate, cut out, remove, root out, uproot, abolish, exterminate, extinguish, erase, *formal* deracinate, expunge

extol *v*
praise, acclaim, exalt, magnify, glorify, sing the praises of, applaud, celebrate, commend, *formal* laud, eulogize, rhapsodize
F3 blame, *formal* denigrate

extort *v*
extract, wring, exact, coerce, force, get out of, wrest, blackmail, squeeze, bully, *colloq.* milk, bleed

extortion *n*
force, coercion, blackmail, oppression, demand, exaction, racketeering, *colloq.* milking

extortionate *adj*
exorbitant, excessive, outrageous, grasping, exacting, immoderate, unreasonable, inordinate, preposterous, oppressive, severe, hard, harsh, *formal* rapacious

extra *adj, n, adv*
▶ *adj* **1** ADDITIONAL, added, auxiliary, supplementary, new, another, more, further, ancillary, fresh, other, subsidiary **2** EXCESS, excessive, spare, superfluous, surplus, unused, unneeded, unnecessary, left-over, reserve, redundant, *formal* supernumerary
F3 **1** integral **2** essential
▶ *n* **1** ADDITION, supplement, extension, accessory, appendage, bonus, complement, additive, adjunct, attachment, *formal* addendum **2** *employ extras in the film* bit player, supernumerary, spear-carrier, walk-on part, minor role
▶ *adv* **1** ESPECIALLY, exceptionally, extraordinarily, particularly, unusually, remarkably, uncommonly, extremely **2** IN ADDITION, also, as well, together with, along with, besides, too, additionally, and so on, not to mention, not forgetting, let alone, above and beyond, *colloq.* into the bargain

extract *v, n*
▶ *v* **1** REMOVE, take out, draw out, cut out, get out, pull out, exact, uproot, prize, pluck, wrench, withdraw, *formal* deracinate **2** DERIVE, draw, distil, obtain, get, gather, glean, wrest, wring, elicit, worm **3** CHOOSE, select, cull, abstract, copy, cite, quote, reproduce
F3 **1** insert
▶ *n* **1** DISTILLATION, essence, concentrate, spirits, decoction, juice, *formal* distillate **2** EXCERPT, passage, selection, clip, clipping, cutting, quotation, abstract, citation

extraction *n*
1 REMOVAL, taking out, uprooting, drawing, pulling, withdrawal, separation, obtaining, derivation 2 ORIGIN, descent, ancestry, birth, blood, lineage, derivation, family, stock, parentage, pedigree, race
⊟ 1 insertion

extradite *v*
send back, send home, deport, repatriate, banish, expel, exile

extradition *n*
sending back, deportation, banishment, expulsion, exile

extraneous *adj*
superfluous, supplementary, redundant, irrelevant, immaterial, inapplicable, inappropriate, inessential, inapt, incidental, tangential, needless, unnecessary, unneeded, non-essential, unessential, unrelated, unconnected, extra, additional, peripheral, exterior, external, extrinsic, alien, strange, foreign, *formal* inapposite
⊟ integral, essential

extraordinary *adj*
remarkable, unusual, exceptional, notable, noteworthy, outstanding, unique, special, unexpected, strange, peculiar, odd, bizarre, curious, unconventional, rare, uncommon, surprising, amazing, astounding, wonderful, unprecedented, marvellous, fantastic, significant, particular, *formal* singular, *colloq.* out of this world
⊟ commonplace, ordinary

extravagance *n*
1 OVERSPENDING, squandering, waste, wastefulness, thriftlessness, recklessness, *formal* profligacy, prodigality, improvidence, imprudence 2 EXCESS, exaggeration, immoderation, recklessness, profusion, outrageousness, folly, wildness, pretentiousness, lavishness
⊟ 1 thrift 2 moderation, restraint

extravagant *adj*
1 WASTEFUL, spendthrift, squandering, thriftless, reckless, *formal* prodigal, profligate, improvident, imprudent 2 IMMODERATE, exaggerated, excessive, flamboyant, preposterous, outrageous, ostentatious, pretentious, lavish, ornate, fanciful, fantastic, wild, unrestrained, *colloq.* flashy, over the top, OTT 3 OVERPRICED, exorbitant, expensive, excessive, extortionate, costly, dear, *colloq.* steep
⊟ 1 thrifty 2 moderate, restrained 3 reasonable

extravaganza *n*
spectacular, pageant, display, show, spectacle

extreme *adj, n*
▶ *adj* 1 INTENSE, great, immoderate, inordinate, utmost, uttermost, out-and-out, maximum, acute, downright, extraordinary, exceptional, greatest, highest, supreme, ultimate, unreasonable, remarkable 2 FARTHEST, far-off, faraway, distant, endmost, outermost, outlying, remotest, most remote, uttermost, final, last, terminal, ultimate, endmost 3 RADICAL, zealous, extremist, fanatical, hardline, immoderate, excessive, unreasonable 4 DRASTIC, dire, uncompromising, unrelenting, unyielding, stern, strict, rigid, severe, harsh, stringent, Draconian
⊟ 1 mild 3 moderate
▶ *n* extremity, limit, maximum, ultimate, utmost, excess, top, mark, line, pinnacle, peak, height, end, climax, depth, edge, pole, *formal* termination, acme, apex, zenith
▷ **in the extreme** exceedingly, excessively, very, exceptionally, extraordinarily, intensely, remarkably, utterly, greatly, highly, immoderately, uncommonly, inordinately

extremely *adv*
exceedingly, excessively, very, really, exceptionally, extraordinarily, intensely, thoroughly, remarkably, utterly, greatly, highly, unusually, unreasonably, immoderately, uncommonly, inordinately, acutely, severely, decidedly, *colloq.* awfully, terribly, dreadfully, frightfully, terrifically

extremism *n*
fanaticism, radicalism, zeal, excessiveness, unreasonableness, terrorism, *formal* zealotry
⊟ moderation

extremist *n*
fanatic, hardliner, fundamentalist, militant, radical, zealot, diehard, ultra, terrorist
⊟ moderate

extremity *n*
1 EXTREME, limit, boundary, brink, verge, periphery, bound, border, frontier, height, tip, top, edge, excess, end, termination, peak, pinnacle, margin, terminal, terminus, ultimate, pole, maximum, minimum, depth, *formal* apex, acme, zenith, apogee 2 *extremities of the body* limb, arm, hand, finger, foot, leg, toe 3 CRISIS, danger, emergency, plight, hardship, adversity, misfortune, trouble, *formal* indigence, exigency

extricate *v*
disentangle, extract, clear, disengage, detach, let loose, free, deliver, liberate, release, rescue, relieve, remove, get out, withdraw
⊟ involve

extrinsic *adj*
external, extraneous, exterior, outside, alien, exotic, foreign, imported
⊟ intrinsic

extrovert *n*
mixer, socializer, mingler, outgoing person, sociable person, conversationalist, joiner, life and soul of the party

extroverted *adj*
outgoing, friendly, sociable, amicable, amiable, exuberant, hearty, demonstrative
⊟ introverted

extrude *v*
force out, squeeze out, press out, mould

exuberance *n*
1 LIVELINESS, vitality, high spirits, zest, effervescence, enthusiasm, eagerness, excitement, animation, elation, buoyancy, exhilaration, effusiveness, cheerfulness, fulsomeness, life, vigour, energy, *formal* ebullience, vivacity, *colloq.* pizzazz 2 ABUNDANCE, copiousness, lushness, richness, superabundance, lavishness, luxuriance, rankness, exaggeration, excessiveness, *formal* plenitude, prodigality, profusion
⊟ 1 apathy, lifelessness 2 scantiness

exuberant *adj*
1 LIVELY, vivacious, spirited, zestful, high-spirited, effervescent, enthusiastic, sparkling, excited, animated, elated, buoyant, exhilarated, effusive, cheerful, full of life, vigorous, energetic, unrestrained, fulsome, irrepressible, exaggerated, *formal* ebullient 2 PLENTIFUL, lavish, overflowing, luxurious, lush, rich, profuse, abundant, thriving, rank, *formal* plenteous
⊟ 1 apathetic 2 scarce

exude *v*
1 *exude confidence* radiate, ooze, display, show, emanate, emit, exhibit, *formal* manifest 2 DISCHARGE, issue, flow out, bleed, excrete, leak, secrete, seep, perspire, sweat, trickle, weep, well

exult *v*
rejoice, revel, delight, be joyful, be delighted, glory,

celebrate, relish, crow, gloat, triumph, *colloq.* be over the moon

exultant *adj*
delighted, rejoicing, revelling, elated, exulting, gleeful, joyful, overjoyed, jubilant, transporting, enraptured, triumphant, *formal* joyous, *colloq.* cock-a-hoop, over the moon
F3 depressed

exultation *n*
rejoicing, joy, delight, elation, glee, revelling, glory, glorying, joyfulness, jubilation, merriness, transport, triumph, celebration, crowing, gloating, *formal* joyousness, paean, eulogy
F3 depression

eye *n, v*
▶ *n* **1** APPRECIATION, discrimination, discernment, perception, awareness, recognition, judgement, sensitivity, taste **2** VISION, sight, eyesight, power of seeing, faculty of sight, observation **3** VIEWPOINT, opinion, view, point of view, judgement, mind, estimation, belief **4** WATCH, observation, lookout, view, notice, watchfulness, vigilance, surveillance
▷ **keep an eye on** watch closely, mind, attend to, take responsibility for, look after, take care of, monitor, keep tabs on
▷ **see eye to eye** agree, be of one mind, be at one, reach an agreement, *colloq.* go along with, go with, speak the same language, be on the same wavelength
▷ **set eyes on** see, notice, observe, come across, come upon, lay eyes on, clap eyes on, meet, encounter, *formal* behold
▷ **up to your eyes** busy, occupied, involved, engrossed, overwhelmed, inundated, *colloq.* snowed

under, fully stretched, overstretched, having your hands full, tied up
F3 free, idle

Parts of the eye include:
anterior chamber, aqueous humour, blind spot, choroid, ciliary body, cone, conjunctiva, cornea, eyelash, fovea, iris, lacrimal duct, lens, lower eyelid, ocular muscle, optic nerve, papilla, posterior chamber, pupil, retina, rod, sclera, suspension ligament, upper eyelid, vitreous humour.

▶ *v* look at, watch, regard, observe, stare at, gaze at, glance at, view, scrutinize, scan, examine, peruse, study, survey, inspect, contemplate, look up and down, assess

eye-catching *adj*
striking, arresting, attractive, spectacular, captivating, beautiful, stunning, gorgeous, imposing, impressive, showy, conspicuous, noticeable, prominent
F3 plain, unattractive

eyesight *n*
vision, sight, perception, observation, power of seeing, faculty of sight, view

eyesore *n*
ugliness, blemish, scar, monstrosity, blot, blot on the landscape, disfigurement, defacement, horror, blight, disgrace, atrocity, mess, carbuncle

eyewitness *n*
witness, observer, spectator, looker-on, onlooker, bystander, viewer, passer-by, watcher

F

fable *n*
allegory, parable, story, tale, moral tale, yarn, myth, legend, epic, saga, fiction, fabrication, invention, lie, untruth, falsehood, yarn, *colloq.* tall story, old wives' tale, *formal* apologue

fabled *adj*
legendary, renowned, famous, famed, remarkable
🏳 unknown

fabric *n*
1 CLOTH, material, textile, stuff, web, texture **2** STRUCTURE, framework, construction, make-up, constitution, organization, infrastructure, foundations

Fabrics include:
alpaca, angora, astrakhan, barathea, bouclé, cashmere, chenille, duffel, felt, flannel, fleece, Harris tweed®, mohair, paisley, serge, sheepskin, Shetland wool, tweed, vicuña, wool, worsted; brocade, buckram, calico, cambric, candlewick, canvas, chambray, cheesecloth, chino, chintz, cord, corduroy, cotton, crepe, denim, drill, jean, flannelette, gaberdine, gingham, jersey, lawn, linen, lisle, madras, moleskin, muslin, needlecord, piqué, poplin, sateen, seersucker, terry towelling, ticking, Viyella®, webbing, winceyette; grosgrain, damask, Brussels lace, chiffon, georgette, gossamer, voile, organza, organdie, tulle, net, crepe de Chine, silk, taffeta, shantung, velvet, velour; polycotton, polyester, rayon, nylon, Crimplene®, Terylene®, Lurex®, lamé; hessian, horsehair, chamois, kid, leather, leather-cloth, sharkskin, suede.

fabricate *v*
1 FAKE, falsify, forge, counterfeit, invent, make up, trump up, concoct, hatch, *colloq.* cook up **2** MANUFACTURE, make, construct, assemble, build, erect, put together, produce, form, shape, fashion, create, frame, devise
🏳 **2** demolish, destroy

fabrication *n*
1 FAKE, falsehood, forgery, invention, concoction, fable, fiction, figment, story, myth, untruth, *colloq.* cock-and-bull story, fairy story **2** MANUFACTURE, assembly, building, construction, erection, production, *formal* assemblage
🏳 **1** truth

fabulous *adj*
1 WONDERFUL, marvellous, fantastic, remarkable, great, superb, breathtaking, spectacular, phenomenal, amazing, astounding, astonishing, unbelievable, incredible, inconceivable, unimaginable, *colloq.* out of this world, top-notch, great, super, cool, magic, radical, *slang* way-out **2** *a fabulous beast* mythical, le-

gendary, fabled, fantastic, fictitious, fictional, invented, made-up, imaginary, unreal
🏳 **2** real

façade *n*
1 FRONT, exterior, frontage, face **2** SHOW, semblance, appearance, cover, cloak, veil, guise, mask, disguise, pretence, veneer

face *n, v*
▶ *n* **1** *she has a lovely face* features, façade, *formal* countenance, visage, physiognomy, *colloq.* mug, kisser, phiz, pan, clock, dial, *slang* puss **2** EXPRESSION, look, appearance, air, aspect, *formal* mien, demeanour **3** *pull a face* grimace, frown, scowl, pout **4** EXTERIOR, outside, surface, cover, front, frontage, façade, aspect, side **5** *changing the face of the city* appearance, nature, look(s), aspect, form **6** *save/lose face* reputation, prestige, name, standing, respect, honour, admiration
▷ **face to face** opposite, facing, eye to eye, confronting, in confrontation, *colloq.* eyeball to eyeball
▷ **fly in the face of** contradict, oppose, disagree, clash, conflict, contrast, go against, be at variance, be at odds, be in conflict, be inconsistent with
▷ **on the face of it** apparently, seemingly, ostensibly, outwardly, to all appearances, superficially, on the surface, reputedly, plainly, clearly, obviously, manifestly, patently
▷ **pull a face** frown, grimace, lour, pout, scowl, sulk, glower, knit your brows
▶ *v* **1** BE OPPOSITE, give on to, front, overlook, look onto **2** CONFRONT, face up to, deal with, come up against, cope with, tackle, brave, defy, oppose, brave, resist, withstand, have to reckon with, encounter, meet, experience **3** COVER, line, coat, dress, clad, overlay, smooth, polish, veneer
▷ **face up to** accept, come to terms with, resign yourself to, acknowledge, recognize, cope with, deal with, confront, meet head-on, stand up to

facelift *n*
1 COSMETIC SURGERY, plastic surgery, *technical* rhytidectomy **2** REDECORATION, renovation, restoration

facet *n*
surface, plane, slant, side, face, aspect, element, angle, point, feature, characteristic, factor

facetious *adj*
flippant, frivolous, playful, jocular, jocose, jesting, joking, tongue-in-cheek, light-hearted, funny, amusing, humorous, comic, comical, droll, witty
🏳 serious

facile *adj*
shallow, superficial, easy, simple, simplistic, uncomplicated, ready, quick, hasty, glib, fluent, smooth, slick, plausible
🏳 complicated, profound

facilitate *v*
ease, help, assist, encourage, further, smooth,

smooth the way, promote, advance, forward, accelerate, speed up, *formal* expedite

facility *n*
1 *a facility for learning languages* effortlessness, ease, readiness, quickness, fluency, eloquence, articulateness, smoothness, proficiency, skill, skilfulness, talent, gift, knack, ability, dexterity 2 *sports facilities* amenity, service, utility, convenience, resource, prerequisite, appliance, equipment, means, opportunity, advantage, aid, *colloq.* mod con

facing *n*
coating, covering, lining, cladding, dressing, reinforcement, façade, overlay, surface, trimming, veneer, false front, *technical* revetment

facsimile *n*
copy, imitation, reproduction, repro, replica, carbon copy, carbon, duplicate, image, fax, photocopy, Photostat®, Xerox®, mimeograph, transcript, print

fact *n*
1 *facts and figures* information, datum, detail, particular, specific, point, item, feature, factor, circumstance, component, element, event, incident, occurrence, happening, act, deed, fait accompli, *colloq.* gen, info, low-down, score, ins and outs 2 REALITY, actuality, factuality, certainty, truth
🔁 2 fiction
▷ **in fact** actually, in actual fact, in point of fact, as a matter of fact, in practice, in reality, really, indeed, truly, in truth

faction *n*
1 SPLINTER GROUP, ginger group, minority, division, section, contingent, party, band, side, group, camp, set, sector, ring, caucus, clique, coterie, cabal, junta, lobby, pressure group 2 DISAGREEMENT, conflict, argument, friction, quarrels, discord, disharmony, division, trouble, contention, infighting, strife

factious *adj*
conflicting, clashing, divisive, partisan, sectarian, quarrelsome, discordant, quarrelling, at odds, at loggerheads, warring, troublemaking, turbulent, tumultuous, dissident, rival, contentious, mutinous, seditious, insurrectionary, rebellious, *formal* disputatious, refractory
🔁 calm, co-operative

factor *n*
cause, influence, circumstance, contingency, consideration, element, ingredient, component, constituent, part, point, aspect, facet, fact, item, detail, characteristic, feature, *formal* determinant

factory *n*
works, plant, mill, shop floor, assembly line, workshop, foundry, manufactory

factotum *n*
do-all, handyman, jack-of-all-trades, maid-of-all-work, Man (or Girl) Friday, odd-jobman

factual *adj*
true, historical, actual, real, genuine, authentic, true-to-life, correct, accurate, truthful, precise, exact, literal, faithful, close, strict, detailed, realistic, unbiased, unprejudiced, objective
🔁 false, fictitious, imaginary, fictional

faculties *n*
wits, senses, intelligence, reason, powers, capabilities

faculty *n*
1 ABILITY, capability, capacity, power, facility, proficiency, knack, flair, gift, talent, skill, aptitude, bent 2 *Faculty of Medicine* department, organization, division, section

fad *n*
craze, mania, (passing) fashion, mode, vogue, trend,

enthusiasm, whim, fancy, *formal* affectation, *colloq.* rage

faddy *adj*
fussy, particular, fastidious, finicky, hard-to-please, exact, *colloq.* pernickety, choosy, picky, nit-picking

fade *v*
1 DISCOLOUR, lose colour, bleach, blanch, blench, pale, become paler, tone down, whiten, dim, dull, wash out, *technical* etiolate, *colloq.* go as white as a sheet 2 DECLINE, fall, diminish, dwindle, ebb (away), wane, fail, waste away, disappear, vanish, recede, melt (away), dissolve, pale, flag, weaken, become weaker, droop, wilt, wither, shrivel, perish, die (away), *formal* evanesce, *colloq.* peter out, fizzle out
🔁 brighten

faeces *n*
waste matter, body waste, excrement, droppings, dung, ordure, manure, *technical* excreta, stools, *slang* poo, crap

fag *n*
1 CIGARETTE, filter-tip, king-size, high-tar, low-tar, roll-up, roll-your-own, smoke, whiff, *colloq.* cig, ciggy, fag end, dog end, gasper, joint, *slang* cancer-stick, coffin-nail 2 NUISANCE, inconvenience, irritation, bind, bore, bother, chore, pest, *colloq.* drag

fagged *adj*
exhausted, fatigued, weary, worn out, jaded, wasted, *colloq.* all in, beat, knackered, on your last legs, *slang* zonked
🔁 refreshed

fail *v*
1 GO WRONG, be unsuccessful, break down, collapse, miscarry, abort, fall through, founder, get nowhere, *colloq.* flop, fold, flunk, not come off, not make it, not come up to scratch, fall flat, come undone, not come up with the goods, fizzle out, score an own goal 2 *fail to pay the bill* omit, neglect, forget, not do something 3 LET DOWN, disappoint, leave, desert, neglect, abandon, *formal* forsake 4 *the engine failed* break down, go wrong, stop, not work, cut out, not start, *formal* malfunction, *colloq.* pack up, crash, go kaput, *slang* conk out 5 *the business failed* collapse, founder, go bankrupt, go bust, go under, become insolvent, sink, *colloq.* fold, flop, crash, go bust, go broke, go to the wall, go into the red 6 *his health failed* weaken, fade, wane, ebb, sink, collapse, flag, decline, dwindle, diminish, decay, deteriorate, droop
🔁 1 succeed 4 work 5 prosper
▷ **without fail** without exception, unfailingly, constantly, regularly, dependably, conscientiously, reliably, faithfully, predictably, punctually, religiously, *colloq.* like clockwork
🔁 unpredictably, unreliably

failing *n, prep*
▶ *n* weakness, foible, fault, defect, imperfection, flaw, blemish, drawback, deficiency, shortcoming, failure, lapse, error, weak spot
🔁 strength, advantage
▶ *prep* in the absence of, lacking, without, in default of, wanting

failure *n*
1 *our efforts ended in failure* lack of success, defeat, collapse, breakdown, downfall, miscarriage, abortion, frustration, coming to nothing, *colloq.* flop, washout, let-down, mess 2 *the plan was a failure* disappointment, misfortune, disaster, calamity, miss, fiasco, *colloq.* flop, washout, shambles, slip-up, no go, wipeout 3 *his failure to return home* omission, neglect, negligence, disregard, oversight, forgetfulness, default, *formal* dereliction 4 *feel that you are a failure* loser, born loser, misfit, reject, victim, *colloq.* drop-

out, non-starter, washout, write-off, no-hoper, also-ran, flop, has-been, dead loss, waste of space **5** *the failure of the machine* breakdown, cutting-out, shut-down, stopping, stalling, *formal* malfunctioning, *colloq.* crash, packing-up, *slang* conking-out **6** *the failure of the business* collapse, bankruptcy, ruin, insolvency, foundering, *colloq.* crash, folding, flop, going under, going to the wall **7** *the failure of his health* weakening, fading, decline, sinking, flagging, waning, ebbing, collapse, breakdown, deterioration

---

Expressions used when talking about failing or failure include:
a dead duck, a lost cause, a miss is as good as a mile, be pipped at the post, bite the dust, blow it, blow your chances, *US* bomb, come a cropper, come to grief, come to nothing, come unstuck, cut your losses, die a death, *US* die a natural death, draw a blank, *US* drop the ball, fall at the first hurdle, fall down on the job, fight a losing battle, fluff it, give something up as a bad job, *US* go belly-up, go bust, go down like a lead balloon, go down the tubes, go phut, go to the wall, go under, have had your chips, if all else fails, make a mess/muck/pig's ear of something, not come up to scratch/the mark, on the rocks, the beginning of the end, the nail in someone's coffin, whistle in the wind.

F3 **1, 2** success **3** observance **4** success **6** prosperity

faint *adj, v, n*
▶ *adj* **1** SLIGHT, weak, feeble, soft, low, hushed, muffled, subdued, muted, faded, bleached, mild, light, pale, dull, dim, hazy, indistinct, unclear, obscure, blurred, vague **2** *I feel faint* dizzy, giddy, unsteady, light-headed, weak, feeble, exhausted, *colloq.* woozy **3** *a faint smile* slight, feeble, weak, unenthusiastic, half-hearted
F3 **1** strong, clear
▶ *v* black out, lose consciousness, pass out, collapse, drop, *colloq.* flake out, keel over
▶ *n* blackout, loss of consciousness, collapse, unconsciousness, *technical* syncope

faint-hearted *adj*
timid, timorous, weak, lily-livered, spiritless, diffident, half-hearted, irresolute, *colloq.* yellow
F3 courageous, confident

faintly *adv*
slightly, vaguely, a little, a bit, weakly, feebly, softly

fair¹ *adj*
1 JUST, equitable, square, even-handed, dispassionate, impartial, objective, disinterested, unbiased, unprejudiced, detached, right, proper, above board, lawful, legitimate, honest, trustworthy, upright, honourable, *colloq.* on the level, straight up, legit, kosher, going/done/played by the book **2** *a fair number; a fair chance of success* reasonable, moderate, respectable, satisfactory, modest, decent, sporting **3** FAIR-HAIRED, fair-headed, blond(e), yellow, light, light-haired **4** *fair skin* pale, cream, light **5** ADEQUATE, sufficient, middling, not bad, all right, satisfactory, acceptable, tolerable, reasonable, passable, mediocre, *colloq.* OK, so-so **6** *fair weather* fine, dry, sunny, bright, clear, cloudless, unclouded
F3 **1** unfair **3** dark **5** excellent, poor **6** inclement, cloudy

fair² *n*
a trade fair exhibition, show, exposition, trade fair, market, craft fair, bazaar, exchange, fete, festival, carnival, gala, *colloq.* expo

fairly *adv*
1 QUITE, rather, somewhat, reasonably, tolerably, moderately, adequately, pretty **2** POSITIVELY, absolutely, impartially, really, fully, veritably **3** JUSTLY, equitably, honestly, objectively, unbiasedly, properly, legally, lawfully
F3 **3** unfairly

fairness *n*
justice, equitableness, equity, even-handedness, unbiasedness, impartiality, legitimacy, rightfulness, rightness, uprightness, disinterestedness, decency, legitimateness
F3 unfairness

fairy *n*
elf, fay, pixie, imp, brownie, leprechaun, sprite, Robin Goodfellow, Puck, hob, hobgoblin, nymph, rusalka, peri, fée

fairy tale *n*
1 FAIRY STORY, folk-tale, myth, romance, fiction, fantasy **2** LIE, untruth, invention, fabrication, *colloq.* cock-and-bull story, tall story

faith *n*
1 BELIEF, trust, reliance, dependence, conviction, confidence, assurance, *formal* credit, credence **2** RELIGION, denomination, persuasion, church, belief, creed, teaching, doctrine, dogma, sect **3** FAITHFULNESS, fidelity, loyalty, obedience, commitment, devotion, dedication, honour, sincerity, honesty, truthfulness
F3 **1** mistrust **3** unfaithfulness, treachery

faithful *adj, n*
▶ *adj* **1** LOYAL, devoted, committed, dedicated, staunch, steadfast, constant, trusty, trustworthy, reliable, dependable, unwavering, unflagging, unswerving, obedient, true **2** *a faithful description* accurate, precise, exact, strict, close, true, truthful
F3 **1** disloyal, treacherous **2** inaccurate, vague
▶ *n* adherents, followers, supporters, believers, congregation, communicants, brethren

faithfulness *n*
1 LOYALTY, fidelity, devotion, dedication, commitment, allegiance, steadfastness, constancy, trustworthiness, reliability, dependability, staunchness **2** ACCURACY, closeness, exactness, strictness, scrupulousness
F3 **1** disloyalty, treachery **2** inaccuracy

faithless *adj*
1 DISLOYAL, unfaithful, inconstant, fickle, false, false-hearted, unreliable, untrue, untrustworthy, untruthful, traitorous, treacherous, adulterous, *formal* perfidious **2** UNBELIEVING, doubting, disbelieving, *formal* nullifidian
F3 believing, faithful

faithlessness *n*
unfaithfulness, disloyalty, deceit, infidelity, fickleness, inconstancy, treachery, betrayal, adultery, apostasy, *formal* perfidy
F3 belief, faithfulness

fake *adj, v, n*
▶ *adj* forged, counterfeit, false, spurious, pseudo, bogus, fraudulent, assumed, sham, artificial, simulated, mock, imitation, reproduction, *formal* affected, *colloq.* phoney, pseud, pretend
F3 genuine
▶ *v* forge, fabricate, counterfeit, copy, pirate, imitate, simulate, feign, sham, pretend, put on, assume, *formal* affect
▶ *n* forgery, copy, reproduction, replica, imitation, mountebank, simulation, sham, counterfeit, hoax, fraud, impostor, charlatan, *colloq.* phoney, quack

fall *v, n*
▶ *v* **1** TUMBLE, stumble, trip, fall down, slip, topple,

keel over, collapse, slump, crash, slide, pitch (forward) **2** DESCEND, go down, come down, drop, slope, incline, slant, slide, sink, dive, plunge, plummet, nose-dive, pitch **3** DECREASE, lessen, decline, go down, diminish, dwindle, fall off, subside, recede, slump, plummet, plunge, dive, nose-dive **4** *fall asleep* pass (into), become, grow (into), turn, come to be **5** *fall in battle* be killed, die, perish, lose your life, *formal* be slain **6** *the town fell in the battle* lose control, be defeated, be conquered, be taken, surrender, yield, capitulate, give in, pass into enemy hands, *formal* be vanquished **7** *my birthday falls on a Tuesday this year* - happen, occur, take place, come about

F3 **2** rise **3** increase

▷ **fall apart** break, break into pieces, fall to bits/pieces, come/go to pieces, go to bits, break up, come away, shatter, disintegrate, collapse, dissolve, crack up, crumble, decompose, decay, rot

▷ **fall back** retreat, withdraw, recoil, draw back, pull back, disengage, depart

▷ **fall back on** resort to, make use of, have recourse to, use, employ, turn to, look to, call on, call into play

▷ **fall behind** lag (behind), trail, drop back, not keep up

F3 keep up, make progress, keep pace

▷ **fall for 1** FALL IN LOVE WITH, be attached to, become infatuated with, desire, take to, *colloq.* fancy, be crazy about, have a crush on, fall head over heels in love with **2** ACCEPT, be taken in by, be fooled by, be deceived by, *colloq.* swallow, buy

▷ **fall in** cave in, come down, collapse, crash, give way, subside, sink

▷ **fall in with** agree with, go along with, accept, comply with, co-operate with, support, *formal* assent to

▷ **fall off** decrease, lessen, drop (off), slump, decline, deteriorate, worsen, slow, slacken

▷ **fall on** attack, descend on, set upon, lay into, pounce on, snatch, assail, assault

▷ **fall out** quarrel, argue, squabble, bicker, fight, clash, disagree, differ

F3 agree

▷ **fall through** come to nothing, go wrong, fail, miscarry, abort, founder, collapse, come to grief

F3 come off, succeed

▷ **fall to** apply yourself, begin, get stuck in, set about, set to, start, *formal* commence

▶ *n* **1** TUMBLE, stumble, trip, topple, keeling-over, collapse, slip, slide, crash **2** DROP, fall-off, decrease, decline, cut, reduction, lessening, dwindling, slump, crash, plunge, plummeting, nose-dive **3** DEFEAT, capture, conquest, overthrow, loss of control, downfall, collapse, ruin, failure, destruction, surrender, capitulation, yielding, giving-in, resignation, *formal* demise

fallacious *adj*
false, wrong, untrue, incorrect, mistaken, deceptive, erroneous, inaccurate, inexact, illogical, misleading, spurious, delusive, delusory, illusory, fictitious, *formal* casuistical, sophistic, sophistical

F3 correct, true

fallacy *n*
misconception, misapprehension, miscalculation, delusion, mistake, mistaken belief, error, flaw, inconsistency, falsehood, false idea, illusion, myth, *formal* casuistry, sophism, sophistry

F3 truth

fallen *adj*
1 *fallen in battle* killed, died, dead, lost, perished, slaughtered, *formal* slain **2** *fallen women* immoral, loose, promiscuous, degenerate, shamed, disgraced

F3 **2** chaste

fallible *adj*
imperfect, errant, erring, frail, weak, flawed, human, mortal, ignorant, uncertain

F3 infallible

fallow *adj*
uncultivated, unploughed, unplanted, unsown, undeveloped, unused, idle, inactive, unproductive, dormant, resting, barren

false *adj*
1 WRONG, incorrect, mistaken, untrue, erroneous, inaccurate, inexact, misleading, faulty, invalid, illusory, *formal* fallacious **2** ARTIFICIAL, synthetic, imitation, simulated, mock, fake, counterfeit, fraudulent, forged, fabricated, invented, feigned, pretended, sham, bogus, assumed, fictitious, *colloq.* phoney, pretend, trumped-up **3** *false friends* disloyal, unfaithful, faithless, lying, unreliable, deceitful, dishonest, insincere, untrustworthy, hypocritical, two-faced, double-dealing, treacherous, traitorous, *formal* duplicitous, perfidious

F3 **1** true, right **2** real, genuine **3** faithful, reliable, genuine

falsehood *n*
untruth, lie, fib, story, fairy story, fiction, fabrication, invention, untruthfulness, deceit, deception, dishonesty, insincerity, hypocrisy, two-facedness, double dealing, treachery, *technical* perjury, *formal* duplicity, perfidy, *colloq.* tall story

F3 truth, truthfulness

falsification *n*
alteration, tampering, distortion, perversion, misrepresentation, change, adulteration, deceit, forgery, *formal* dissimulation

falsify *v*
alter, tamper with, doctor, distort, adulterate, twist, pervert, misrepresent, misstate, forge, counterfeit, fake, rig, fiddle, manipulate, massage, *colloq.* cook

falter *v*
1 TOTTER, stumble, be unsteady, be shaky **2** *falter while talking* stammer, stutter, stumble, *colloq.* fluff your lines **3** HESITATE, waver, vacillate, delay, flinch, quail, shake, tremble, flag, fail, *colloq.* shilly-shally, dilly-dally, be in two minds, sit on the fence, drag your feet, take your time

faltering *adj*
uncertain, hesitant, unsteady, weak, tentative, irresolute, stammering, stumbling, timid, broken, failing, flagging

F3 firm, strong

fame *n*
renown, celebrity, stardom, prominence, distinction, eminence, notability, note, illustriousness, glory, honour, greatness, importance, reputation, name, *formal* esteem

famed *adj*
renowned, well-known, widely-known, famous, recognized, noted, celebrated, acclaimed, *formal* esteemed

F3 unknown

familiar *adj*
1 EVERYDAY, usual, routine, repeated, conventional, household, common, commonplace, ordinary, accustomed, customary, frequent, habitual, run-of-the-mill, well-known, known, recognizable, unmistakable **2** INTIMATE, close, near, dear, confidential, friendly, informal, free, free-and-easy, easy, relaxed, casual, comfortable, sociable, open, natural, unceremonious, unreserved, *colloq.* pally, chummy **3** *familiar with the procedure* aware, acquainted, abreast, knowledgeable, versed, conversant, well up, *au fait*, *au courant* **4** FORWARD, over-familiar, over-friendly, pre-

sumptuous, impertinent, bold, disrespectful, *colloq.* pushy, smarmy

F3 1 unfamiliar, strange **2** formal, reserved **3** unfamiliar, ignorant

familiarity *n*
1 INTIMACY, liberty, closeness, nearness, friendliness, ease, sociability, openness, naturalness, informality, casualness, unceremoniousness, *colloq.* palliness, chumminess **2** AWARENESS, acquaintance, experience, skill, knowledge, understanding, comprehension, grasp, mastery **3** FORWARDNESS, overfamiliarity, over-friendliness, presumption, liberty, liberties, impertinence, boldness, disrespect, impudence, intrusiveness, *colloq.* pushiness

familiarize *v*
accustom, acclimatize, make familiar, make aware, make acquainted, teach, school, train, coach, instruct, indoctrinate, prime, brief, *formal* habituate

family *n*
1 RELATIVES, relations, household, nuclear family, extended family, one-parent family, single-parent family, next of kin, kin, kindred, kinsmen, people, parents, your own flesh and blood, you and yours, ancestors, forebears, children, offspring, issue, progeny, descendants, scions, stirps, *colloq.* folk, little ones, kids, patter of tiny feet **2** CLAN, tribe, race, dynasty, house, pedigree, ancestry, parentage, descent, line, lineage, extraction, blood, stock, strain, birth **3** CLASS, group, species, genus, type, class, kind, classification, *technical* stirps
▷ **family tree** ancestry, pedigree, genealogy, line, lineage, extraction, background

Members of a family include:
ancestor, forebear, forefather, descendant, offspring, heir; husband, wife, spouse, parent, father, dad, *colloq.* daddy, *colloq.* old man, mother, *colloq.* mum, *colloq.* mummy, *US colloq.* mom, grandparent, grandfather, grandmother, granny, *colloq.* nanny, grandchild, son, daughter, brother, half-brother, sister, half-sister, sibling, uncle, aunt, nephew, niece, cousin, godfather, godmother, godchild, stepfather, stepdad, stepmother, stepmum, foster-parent, foster-child.

famine *n*
starvation, hunger, malnutrition, lack, deprivation, scarcity, shortage of food, dearth, lack, death, *formal* destitution, want
F3 plenty

famished *adj*
starved, starving, famishing, ravenous, hungry, undernourished, voracious
F3 sated

famous *adj*
well-known, famed, renowned, celebrated, acclaimed, world-famous, noted, great, distinguished, illustrious, eminent, honoured, respected, glorious, legendary, remarkable, notable, popular, prominent, signal, venerable, having (made) a name for yourself, someone's name is on everyone's lips, notorious, infamous, *formal* esteemed
F3 unheard-of, unknown, obscure

fan¹ *n*
football fans enthusiast, admirer, supporter, backer, follower, adherent, devotee, addict, lover, aficionado, *colloq.* buff, fiend, freak, nut

fan² *v, n*
▶ *v* **1** COOL, ventilate, air, air-condition, air-cool, blow, freshen, refresh **2** INCREASE, provoke, intensify,

stimulate, incite, instigate, rouse, arouse, excite, agitate, ignite, kindle, stir up, work up, whip up
▷ **fan out** spread out, move out, open out, unfold, unfurl
▶ *n* extractor fan, ventilator, air-conditioner, blower, cooler, air cooler, propeller, vane

fanatic *n*
zealot, devotee, enthusiast, addict, maniac, visionary, radical, bigot, extremist, militant, activist, fundamentalist, *colloq.* fiend, freak

fanatical *adj*
overenthusiastic, extreme, passionate, zealous, fervent, burning, mad, wild, frenzied, rabid, obsessive, fundamentalist, activist, militant, immoderate, extremist, radical, single-minded, bigoted, dogmatic, narrowminded
F3 moderate, unenthusiastic

fanaticism *n*
extremism, monomania, single-mindedness, fundamentalism, activism, militancy, obsessiveness, madness, wildness, frenzy, infatuation, bigotry, narrowmindedness, zeal, fervour, dogmatism, enthusiasm, dedication
F3 moderation

fanciful *adj*
1 IMAGINARY, mythical, flighty, fabulous, fantastic, legendary, visionary, romantic, unrealistic, unreal, make-believe, illusory, fairy-tale, airy-fairy, vaporous, whimsical, wild **2** ELABORATE, ornate, decorated, extravagant, wild, creative, imaginative, fantastic, curious
F3 1 real, ordinary, realistic **2** simple, plain

fancy *v, n, adj*
▶ *v* **1** LIKE, want, feel like, wish, prefer, favour, desire, take a liking to, take to, go for, have in mind, not mind, not say no to, long for, yearn for **2** BE ATTRACTED TO, find attractive, desire, take to, go for, have a soft spot for, think the world of, be interested in, lust after, *colloq.* have a crush on, have eyes for, be mad about, want, *slang* have the hots for **3** THINK, conceive, imagine, dream of, picture, believe, suppose, reckon, guess, *formal* conjecture, surmise
F3 1 dislike
▶ *n* **1** DESIRE, whim, caprice, raving, urge, want, wish, liking, fondness, longing, yearning, inclination, preference, *formal* penchant, predilection, *colloq.* itch, yen **2** NOTION, thought, idea, opinion, impression, imagination, creativity, dream, fantasy, vision, illusion, delusion
F3 1 dislike, aversion **2** fact, reality
▶ *adj* elaborate, ornate, decorated, adorned, ornamented, embellished, rococo, baroque, elegant, extravagant, ostentatious, showy, lavish, fantastic, fanciful, far-fetched
F3 plain, ordinary, simple

fanfare *n*
flourish, trumpet call, trump, fanfarade

fang *n*
tooth, prong, tusk, tang, venom-tooth

fantasize *v*
imagine, daydream, dream, hallucinate, invent, romance, *colloq.* build castles in the air, live in a dream

fantastic *adj*
1 WONDERFUL, marvellous, sensational, superb, excellent, first-rate, tremendous, impressive, terrific, great, brilliant, incredible, unbelievable, amazing, overwhelming, enormous, extreme, *colloq.* top notch, super, cool, magic, ace, radical, brill, out of this world, *US* neat **2** STRANGE, weird, odd, eccentric, bizarre, exotic, outlandish, extravagant, wild, absurd, fanciful, fabulous, imaginary, illusory, unreal, imaginative, visionary, romantic
F3 1 ordinary **2** real

fantasy n

dream, daydream, reverie, pipe-dream, nightmare, vision, hallucination, illusion, mirage, apparition, figment of the imagination, invention, fancy, flight of fancy, myth, speculation, delusion, misconception, creativity, imagination, originality, unreality, moonshine, *colloq.* cloud-cuckoo-land, pie in the sky

F3 reality

far adv, adj

▶ *adv* a long way, a good way, great distance, some distance, nowhere near, much, very much, greatly, considerably, extremely, markedly, decidedly, incomparably, immeasurably, *colloq.* miles

F3 near, close

▷ **far and wide** extensively, far and near, widely, everywhere, in/from all places, all about, broadly, worldwide

▷ **far out** extreme, strange, exotic, radical, bizarre, weird, outlandish, *colloq.* way out

F3 orthodox, conventional

▷ **go far** be successful, achieve success, get on, *colloq.* get on in the world, make your mark, make a name for yourself, go places

▷ **so far** up to now, up to this point, up to the present moment, till now, to date, *formal* thus far, hitherto

▶ *adj* distant, far-off, faraway, far-flung, remote, inaccessible, secluded, out-of-the-way, Godforsaken, removed, far-removed, further, opposite, other, *US colloq.* in the boondocks/boonies

F3 nearby, close, accessible

faraway adj

1 DISTANT, remote, outlying, far-flung, far-off, far **2** DREAMY, absent-minded, absent, abstracted, preoccupied, lost

F3 1 nearby **2** alert

farce n

1 COMEDY, slapstick, buffoonery, satire, parody, burlesque **2** TRAVESTY, sham, parody, joke, mockery, ridiculousness, absurdity, nonsense, *colloq.* shambles

farcical adj

ridiculous, absurd, ludicrous, preposterous, nonsensical, stupid, laughable, comic, silly, derisory, diverting

F3 sensible

fare n, v

▶ *n* **1** *pay your fare* charge, cost, price, fee, ticket, passage **2** FOOD, eatables, nourishment, nutriment, rations, meals, diet, menu, board, table, *formal* sustenance, victuals, viands, *colloq.* nosh, eats

▶ *v* be, do, get along, get on, go, go on, happen, make out, manage, proceed, progress, prosper, succeed, turn out

far-fetched adj

implausible, unrealistic, improbable, unlikely, dubious, incredible, unbelievable, unconvincing, fantastic, fanciful, preposterous, crazy

F3 plausible

farm n, v

▶ *n* ranch, farmstead, grange, croft, homestead, station, co-operative, land, farmland, holding, acreage, acres

▶ *v* cultivate, till, plough, work the land, plant, operate

▷ **farm out** subcontract, pass/give to others, delegate, contract out

farmer n

agriculturist, crofter, smallholder, husbandman, rancher, crofter, grazier, yeoman, *technical* agronomist

farming n

agriculture, cultivation, husbandry, tilling, crofting, *technical* agribusiness, agronomy, agroscience, geoponics

farrago n

hotchpotch, jumble, medley, miscellany, mixture, mélange, pot-pourri, hash, mishmash, gallimaufry, salmagundi, *colloq.* dog's breakfast

far-reaching adj

broad, extensive, widespread, sweeping, important, wide-ranging, wide, comprehensive, global, thorough, significant, momentous

F3 limited, restricted, insignificant

far-sighted adj

wise, forward-looking, far-seeing, shrewd, discerning, cautious, acute, canny, provident, *formal* circumspect, judicious, politic, prescient, prudent

F3 imprudent, unwise

farther adj, adv

▶ *adj* further, more distant, remoter, more extreme

▶ *adv* to a greater distance, to a more distant/remote/onward/advanced point

farthest adj

furthest, most distant, remotest, most extreme

fascinate v

absorb, engross, intrigue, delight, charm, allure, lure, draw, attract, entice, captivate, enchant, beguile, spellbind, enthral, enrapture, rivet, transfix, hypnotize, mesmerize

F3 bore, repel

fascinated adj

absorbed, engrossed, curious, intrigued, delighted, charmed, enticed, spellbound, enthralled, entranced, captivated, bewitched, beguiled, hypnotized, mesmerized, infatuated, smitten, *colloq.* hooked

F3 bored, uninterested

fascinating adj

intriguing, gripping, exciting, interesting, engaging, engrossing, irresistible, compelling, alluring, bewitching, captivating, enchanting, riveting, enticing, seductive, tempting, charming, absorbing, stimulating, delightful, mesmerizing

F3 boring, uninteresting

fascination n

interest, attraction, delight, appeal, lure, allure, compulsion, magnetism, pull, draw, charm, captivation, enchantment, spell, sorcery, magic

F3 boredom, repulsion

fascism n

autocracy, dictatorship, absolutism, authoritarianism, totalitarianism, Hitlerism

fascist adj, n

▶ *adj* autocratic, absolutist, authoritarian, totalitarian, Hitlerist, Hitlerite

▶ *n* autocrat, absolutist, authoritarian, totalitarian, Blackshirt, Hitlerite, Hitlerist

fashion n, v

▶ *n* **1** MANNER, way, method, mode, approach, style, system, shape, form, make, design, pattern, line, cut, look, appearance, type, sort, kind **2** VOGUE, trend, mode, style, fad, craze, custom, tendency, practice, convention, *colloq.* rage, latest **3** COUTURE, clothes, clothes industry, haute couture, fashion business, high fashion, designer label, *colloq.* rag trade

▷ **after a fashion** not very well, to some extent, in a manner of speaking

▶ *v* create, form, shape, mould, model, design, fit, tailor, alter, adjust, adapt, suit

fashionable adj

chic, smart, elegant, stylish, designer, modish, à la mode, in vogue, in, popular, prevailing, current, latest, up-to-the-minute, up-to-date, contemporary, modern, *colloq.* trendy, all the rage, natty, glitzy, ritzy,

snazzy, swanky, funky, hip, with it, swinging, in thing, cool, dressed to the nines
🔁 unfashionable

fast¹ *adj, adv*
▶ *adj* **1** QUICK, swift, rapid, brisk, accelerated, speedy, express, high-speed, hasty, hurried, flying, *colloq.* nippy **2** FASTENED, shut, closed, secure, fixed, immovable, immobile, firm, tight
🔁 **1** slow, unhurried **2** loose
▶ *adv* **1** QUICKLY, swiftly, rapidly, speedily, hastily, hurriedly, in a hurry, apace, presto, *colloq.* like a flash, like a shot, as fast as your legs will carry you, before you can say Jack Robinson, at a rate of knots, hell for leather, like greased lightning, like mad/crazy, like the wind, like lightning, like a bat out of hell, like the clappers, lickety-spit **2** FIRMLY, securely, tightly, immovably, fixedly, resolutely, doggedly, stubbornly **3** *fast asleep* sound, deeply, fully
🔁 **1** slowly, gradually

fast² *v, n*
▶ *v fast for religious reasons* go hungry, diet, slim, deny yourself, starve, refrain, *formal* abstain
▶ *n* fasting, diet, starvation, abstinence
🔁 gluttony, self-indulgence

fasten *v*
1 FIX, affix, attach, clamp, grip, anchor, rivet, nail, pin, clip, tack, seal, close, latch, shut, lock, bolt, secure, tie, tether, hitch, bind, chain, link, interlock, connect, join, unite, do up, button, zip up, lace, buckle **2** *fasten your attention* focus, direct, concentrate, fix, rivet, point aim
🔁 **1** unfasten, untie, undo

fastidious *adj*
fussy, particular, finicky, hard-to-please, faddy, discriminating, hypercritical, meticulous, precise, punctilious, overnice, squeamish, difficult, dainty, *colloq.* choosy, pernickety, picky
🔁 undemanding

fat *adj, n*
▶ *adj* **1** PLUMP, overweight, obese, tubby, dumpy, stout, portly, round, paunchy, well-endowed, pot-bellied, large, heavy, solid, chubby, podgy, fleshy, buxom, sonsy, *formal* rotund, corpulent, steatopygous, *colloq.* beefy, flabby, gross, fat as a pig **2** FATTY, oily, pinguid, greasy, *formal* oleaginous, adipose, sebaceous **3** *a fat book* thick, wide, broad, big, heavy, solid, substantial **4** *fat profits* large, handsome, considerable, generous, sizeable
🔁 **1** thin, slim **2** low-fat **3** narrow, slim, thin **4** slim, meagre, miserable, poor
▶ *n* **1** FATNESS, obesity, plumpness, stoutness, solidness, bulk, chubbiness, overweight, paunch, pot (belly), blubber, *formal* corpulence, *colloq.* flab **2** *fats such as cream* butter, margarine, cream, cheese, lard, suet, animal fat, vegetable fat, polyunsaturated fat, tallow, blubber

fatal *adj*
deadly, lethal, mortal, killing, incurable, malignant, terminal, final, destructive, calamitous, catastrophic, disastrous
🔁 harmless

📖 **fatal** or **fateful** ?
Fatal means 'causing death or disaster': *a fatal accident*; *She made the fatal mistake of telling him what she really thought.* *Fateful* means 'of great importance, having important consequences, etc', as in: *At last the fateful day arrived, the day she was to be married.*

---

fatalism *n*
resignation, stoicism, acceptance, passivity, endurance, *formal* predestination, preordination, foreordination

fatality *n*
death, mortality, loss, casualty, dead, deadliness, lethality, disaster, catastrophe

fate *n*
destiny, providence, God's will, kismet, karma, chance, future, luck, fortune, horoscope, stars, lot, doom, end, issue, outcome, ruin, disaster, destruction, catastrophe, defeat, death

fated *adj*
doomed, destined, predestined, preordained, fore-ordained, unavoidable, inevitable, inescapable, certain, sure, *formal* ineluctable
🔁 avoidable

fateful *adj*
crucial, critical, decisive, important, momentous, significant, pivotal
🔁 unimportant

📖 **fateful** or **fatal** ? *See panel at* FATAL.

---

father *n, v*
▶ *n* **1** PARENT, patriarch, ancestor, *formal* begetter, procreator, progenitor, sire, paterfamilias, pater, *colloq.* dad, daddy, pop, pa, papa, old man **2** ANCESTOR, patriarch, elder, forefather, forebear, predecessor, progenitor **3** FOUNDER, creator, originator, inventor, initiator, maker, architect, author, patron, leader, prime mover **4** PRIEST, padre, pastor, parson, clergyman, abbé, curé
▶ *v* produce, engender, give life to, *formal* procreate

fatherland *n*
native land, home, homeland, land of your birth, mother-country, motherland, old country

fatherly *adj*
paternal, kind, kindly, affectionate, protective, supportive, benevolent, benign, tender, forbearing, indulgent, patriarchal, *formal* avuncular
🔁 cold, harsh, unkind

fathom *v*
1 MEASURE, gauge, plumb, sound, probe, estimate **2** UNDERSTAND, comprehend, grasp, see, perceive, work out, search out, interpret, penetrate, get to the bottom of

fatigue *n, v*
▶ *n* tiredness, weariness, exhaustion, lethargy, listlessness, lassitude, weakness, *formal* debility, enervation
🔁 energy
▶ *v* tire, wear out, weary, exhaust, drain, sap, tax, weaken, overwork, *formal* debilitate, enervate, *colloq.* take it out of
🔁 invigorate, refresh

fatigued *adj*
exhausted, jaded, jiggered, overtired, tired, tired out, wasted, weary, *colloq.* all in, beat, bushed, dead-beat, fagged (out), knackered, whacked, zonked, done in
🔁 refreshed

fatness *n*
plumpness, overweight, obesity, bulk, bulkiness, heaviness, largeness, tubbiness, stoutness, portliness, podginess, grossness, *formal* corpulence, rotundity, *colloq.* flab

fatten *v*
feed, feed up, nourish, nurture, build up, overfeed, cram, stuff, bloat, swell, fill out, spread, expand, widen, broaden, thicken, pinguefy

fatty *adj*
fat, greasy, oily, creamy, buttery, fleshy, waxy, pinguid, *formal* oleaginous, oleic, adipose, sebaceous, lipoid, unctuous

fatuous *adj*
idiotic, foolish, silly, stupid, ludicrous, ridiculous, absurd, daft, inane, mindless, vacuous, moronic, puerile, brainless, lunatic, dense, asinine, weak-minded, witless
🖅 sensible

fault *n, v*
▸ *n* **1** DEFECT, flaw, blemish, imperfection, deficiency, shortcoming, weak point, weakness, failing, foible, negligence, omission, oversight, *colloq.* bug, glitch, hitch **2** ERROR, mistake, blunder, slip, lapse, indiscretion, peccadillo, foible, misdeed, offence, wrong, wrongdoing, sin, *formal* misdemeanour, *colloq.* slip-up, boob, booboo **3** *it's your fault* responsibility, accountability, liability, answerability, blameworthiness, *formal* culpability
▷ **at fault** (in the) wrong, blameworthy, to blame, responsible, accountable, guilty, *formal* culpable
▷ **to a fault** excessively, extremely, too much, inordinately, unduly, unnecessarily, disproportionately, in the extreme, to extremes, immoderately, out of all proportion, *colloq.* over the top
▸ *v* find fault with, criticize, censure, blame, call to account, *formal* impugn, *colloq.* pick holes in, knock, slate, slam, pull to pieces
🖅 praise, approve

fault-finding *n, adj*
▸ *n* criticism, grumbling, complaining, carping, quibbling, cavilling, nagging, niggling, hypercriticism, *formal* ultracrepidation, *colloq.* finger-pointing, hairsplitting, nit-picking
🖅 praise
▸ *adj* critical, grumbling, nagging, captious, carping, cavilling, censorious, hypercritical, *formal* querulous, ultracrepidarian, *colloq.* nit-picking
🖅 complimentary

faultless *adj*
perfect, flawless, unblemished, spotless, immaculate, impeccable, unsullied, pure, blameless, exemplary, model, correct, accurate
🖅 faulty, imperfect, flawed

faulty *adj*
1 NOT WORKING, defective, imperfect, damaged, out of order, out of action, broken, *formal* malfunctioning, inoperative, *colloq.* on the blink, bust, kaput, duff **2** FLAWED, defective, inaccurate, incorrect, wrong, erroneous, illogical, invalid, weak, *formal* fallacious, casuistic
🖅 **1** working **2** sound

faux pas *n*
blunder, gaffe, indiscretion, mistake, *formal* impropriety, solecism, *colloq.* boob, booboo, clanger, goof, slip-up, howler

favour *n, v*
▸ *n* **1** APPROVAL, support, backing, sympathy, kindness, friendliness, goodwill, patronage, assistance, aid, favouritism, preference, partiality, *formal* esteem, approbation **2** *he did me a favour* kindness, service, good turn, good deed, courtesy, benefit
🖅 **1** disapproval
▷ **in favour of** for, all for, pro, supporting, on the side of, backing, behind
🖅 against
▸ *v* **1** PREFER, choose, select, opt for, like, pick, approve, support, back, recommend, endorse, advocate, champion, sanction, take kindly to, *colloq.* go for, plump for **2** HELP, assist, aid, benefit, promote, encourage, pamper, spoil, indulge, *formal* succour
🖅 **1** dislike **2** mistreat

favourable *adj*
1 *a favourable reaction* positive, sympathetic, agreeable, well-disposed, approving, complimentary, enthusiastic, friendly, amicable, kind, understanding, encouraging, reassuring, heartening **2** *a favourable impression* positive, good, agreeable, pleasing, effective, promising **3** *favourable conditions* good, advantageous, beneficial, promising, fair, encouraging, convenient, suitable, appropriate, opportune, *formal* auspicious, propitious
🖅 **1** negative **2** negative **3** unhelpful

favourably *adv*
well, positively, sympathetically, agreeably, approvingly, enthusiastically, helpfully, advantageously, fortunately, conveniently, opportunely, profitably, *formal* auspiciously, propitiously
🖅 unfavourably

favoured *adj*
preferred, chosen, selected, recommended, favourite, privileged, advantaged, blessed, elite, *formal* predilected

favourite *adj, n*
▸ *adj* preferred, favoured, pet, best-loved, most-liked, dearest, beloved, treasured, chosen, special, *formal* esteemed
🖅 hated
▸ *n* preference, choice, first choice, number one, pick, pet, beloved, darling, idol, *colloq.* blue-eyed boy, teacher's pet, the apple of your eye
🖅 *bête noire*, pet hate

favouritism *n*
nepotism, preferential treatment, preference, partiality, prejudice, inequality, inequity, one-sidedness, partisanship, bias, unfairness, injustice
🖅 impartiality, equality

fawn¹ *adj*
a fawn coat beige, buff, yellowish-brown, sandy, sand-coloured, khaki

fawn² *v*
fawning over someone famous flatter, grovel, bow and scrape, court, curry favour, dance attendance, kowtow, pay court, ingratiate yourself, toady, *colloq.* bootlick, crawl, creep, cringe, smarm, lick someone's boots, suck up to, butter up, soft-soap

fawning *adj*
obsequious, servile, sycophantic, deferential, flattering, grovelling, ingratiating, bowing and scraping, abject, toadying, toadyish, *formal* unctuous, *colloq.* bootlicking, crawling, cringing,
🖅 cold, proud

fear *n, v*
▸ *n* **1** TERROR, dread, alarm, fright, panic, fearfulness, agitation, apprehension, foreboding, dismay, distress, trembling, shaking, quivering, phobia, aversion, terror, horror, nightmare, *bête noire*, *formal* trepidation, consternation **2** ANXIETY, worry, concern, unease, uneasiness, qualms, misgivings, disquiet, suspicion, doubt, *formal* solicitude **3** AWE, reverence, respect, wonder, honour, fear, fear of God, terror, dread, *formal* veneration **4** *no fear of being misunderstood* chance, risk, likelihood, possibility, probability, prospect, expectation, scope

---

Expressions used when talking about fear or being frightened include:
a chill/shiver runs down your spine, be a bundle of nerves, bottle out, frightened of your own shadow, get cold feet, get the wind up, give someone a start, give someone the shivers, give someone the willies, give you the collywobbles, have butterflies, have the heebie-jeebies, have your heart in your mouth, heart-stopping, in fear of your life, lose your bottle, lose your nerve, make someone's blood run cold,

make someone's hair stand on end, naked fear, pluck up your courage, put the fear of God into someone, rooted to the spot, scare the living daylights out of, scared out of your wits, shake like a jelly/leaf, the fright of your life, turn to jelly.

F 1 courage, bravery, confidence **3** contempt
▸ *v* BE AFRAID OF, be scared of, dread, shudder at, shrink from, tremble, lose your nerve, take fright at, have a horror of, have a phobia about, panic, *colloq.* have your heart in your mouth, your heart melts, your stomach turns, get the wind up, be in a cold sweat, freak out, lose your bottle **2** WORRY, be anxious about, be uneasy about, be concerned about, have misgivings/qualms about, tremble for **3** *fear God* stand in awe of, revere, hold in reverence, reverence, wonder at, *formal* venerate **4** *I fear I can't help you* be afraid, suspect, expect, foresee, anticipate

fearful *adj*
1 FRIGHTENED, afraid, scared, alarmed, in dread, nervous, anxious, tense, uneasy, apprehensive, agitated, trembling, shaking, quivering, petrified, hesitant, nervy, panicky, faint-hearted, timid, *colloq.* spineless, yellow **2** TERRIBLE, dreadful, awful, frightful, atrocious, shocking, dire, harrowing, distressing, appalling, horrific, monstrous, gruesome, hideous, ghastly, horrible, grim, *formal* fearsome
F 1 brave, courageous, fearless **2** wonderful, delightful

fearfully *adv*
1 APPREHENSIVELY, anxiously, nervously, hesitantly, timidly, in fear and trembling **2** *fearfully insecure* extremely, highly, intensely, unusually, exceedingly, *colloq.* awfully, terribly, frightfully, dreadfully

fearless *adj*
bold, brave, confident, courageous, daring, intrepid, valiant, heroic, gallant, plucky, dauntless, unafraid, unapprehensive, unabashed, undaunted, unflinching, lion-hearted, unblenching, unblinking, *formal* doughty, indomitable, valorous, *colloq.* game, gutsy, spunky, gritty
F afraid, timid

fearsome *adj*
formidable, awe-inspiring, awesome, awful, daunting, frightening, frightful, hair-raising, horrendous, horrible, horrific, horrifying, menacing, terrible, unnerving, alarming, appalling, dismaying
F delightful

feasibility *n*
practicability, achievability, workability, reasonableness, possibility, viability, expedience

feasible *adj*
practicable, practical, workable, doable, achievable, attainable, realizable, accomplishable, viable, expedient, reasonable, possible, likely, realistic
F impossible

feast *n, v*
▸ *n* **1** BANQUET, dinner, spread, junket, *formal* repast, *colloq.* blow-out, binge, beano, slap-up meal **2** *a feast for the eyes* wealth, abundance, cornucopia, *formal* profusion **3** FESTIVAL, holiday, gala, fête, celebration, saint's day, feast day, religious festival, holy day, revels, festivities
▸ *v* gorge, eat your fill, wine and dine, indulge in, treat, entertain, regale, *formal* partake of

feat *n*
exploit, deed, act, action, accomplishment, achievement, attainment, performance

feather *n*
plume, quill, down, tuft, crest, *technical* penna, plumule, plumula, aigrette, egret, pinion

feathery *adj*
1 *feathery birds* feathered, featherlike, fleecy, fluffy, wispy, downy, *technical* pennaceous, penniform, plumate, plumed, plumose, plumous, plumy **2** *feathery clouds* soft, light, delicate, fluffy, wispy

feature *n, v*
▸ *n* **1** ASPECT, facet, point, factor, attribute, quality, property, side, trait, characteristic, peculiarity, mark, hallmark, speciality, highlight, attraction, focal point **2** *a person's facial features* face, looks, *formal* countenance, lineaments, physiognomy, visage, *colloq.* mug, phiz, kisser, pan, clock, dial **3** *a magazine feature* column, article, report, story, piece, item, comment
▸ *v* **1** EMPHASIZE, highlight, spotlight, play up, accentuate, promote, show, present **2** APPEAR, figure, participate, act, perform, star

febrile *adj*
feverish, delirious, fevered, flushed, sweating, fiery, hot, inflamed, burning, *formal* pyretic, *colloq.* having a temperature

feckless *adj*
incompetent, weak, feeble, useless, worthless, aimless, futile, hopeless, irresponsible, *formal* ineffectual
F efficient, sensible

fecund *adj*
fertile, productive, fruitful, prolific, teeming, *formal* feracious, fructiferous, fructuous
F infertile

fecundity *n*
fertility, productiveness, fruitfulness, *formal* feracity, fructiferousness
F infertility

fed up *adj*
depressed, bored, discontented, annoyed, dismal, dissatisfied, gloomy, glum, tired, weary, have had enough, *colloq.* blue, brassed off, browned off, cheesed off, down, sick and tired, hacked off, have had it up to here, at the end of your tether
F contented

federal *adj*
confederated, amalgamated, allied, integrated, unified, united, in league, combined, associated

federate *v*
confederate, amalgamate, integrate, join together, league, syndicate, unify, unite, combine, associate
F disunite, separate

federation *n*
confederation, confederacy, alliance, league, amalgamation, association, coalition, combination, syndicate, union, copartnership, federacy

fee *n*
charge, terms, bill, account, pay, remuneration, payment, cost, price, retainer, subscription, reward, recompense, hire, rent, retainer, honorarium, toll, *formal* emolument

feeble *adj*
1 WEAK, faint, exhausted, frail, slight, delicate, puny, sickly, infirm, ailing, failing, powerless, helpless, decrepit, *formal* effete, debilitated, enervated **2** *a feeble excuse* inadequate, lame, poor, weak, futile, thin, flimsy, unconvincing, tame, ineffective, unsuccessful, *formal* ineffectual **3** *a feeble person* ineffective, weak, incompetent, indecisive, *formal* ineffectual, *colloq.* wimpish, wet
F 1 strong, powerful

feeble-minded *adj*
slow-witted, half-witted, stupid, moronic, simple, weak-minded, retarded, deficient, idiotic, imbecilic,

colloq. dim-witted, dumb, slow on the uptake, soft in the head, two bricks short of a load
🔁 bright, intelligent

feed *v, n*
▶ *v* **1** *feed the baby* give food to, nurture, nourish, cater for, provide for, suckle, eat, dine (on), consume, take in, *formal* partake of **2** *animals feeding* graze, pasture, browse, crop, *formal* ruminate **3** *feed your sense of self-worth* strengthen, gratify, fuel, foster, nurture, encourage **4** *feed data into a computer* put, insert, give, introduce, provide, supply, slide, slip
▶ *n* food, fodder, forage, pasture, silage, provender

feel *v, n*
▶ *v* **1** EXPERIENCE, be, go through, live through, undergo, suffer, bear, endure, be overcome by, give way to, harbour, nurse, know, enjoy **2** TOUCH, finger, handle, manipulate, hold, contact, stroke, massage, rub, caress, fondle, paw, maul, poke, fumble, grope, clutch, grasp **3** *feel soft* seem, appear, look **4** THINK, believe, consider, reckon, judge, hold, *formal* deem **5** SENSE, perceive, notice, observe, know, understand, realize, be aware of, feel in your bones
▷ **feel for** pity, sympathize (with), empathize with, commiserate (with), be sorry for, be moved by, grieve for, weep for, pity
▷ **feel like** want, desire, wish, fancy
▶ *n* **1** *the feel of the material* texture, surface, finish, touch, consistency **2** *have a feel for computer-programming* touch, knack, ability, skill, aptitude, gift, talent, faculty, flair, bent **3** *the feel of a place* atmosphere, impression, feeling, quality, mood, air, aura, ambience, *colloq.* vibes

feeler *n*
1 ANTENNA, horn, tentacle, sense-organ, *technical* palp, palpus **2** *put out feelers* advance, approach, overture(s), probe, trial balloon, ballon d'essai

feeling *n*
1 EMOTION, passion, intensity, warmth, compassion, love, sympathy, understanding, pity, concern, affection, fondness, ardour, sentiment, sentimentality, susceptibility, sensibility, sensitivity, appreciation, fervour, intensity, *formal* sentience **2** SENSE, perception, sensation, instinct, intuition, hunch, theory, suspicion, inkling, impression, idea, thought, notion, opinion, view, point of view, way of thinking **3** *hurt someone's feelings* emotions, passions, self-esteem, sensitivities, susceptibilities, ego, *formal* affections **4** AIR, aura, atmosphere, mood, quality, feel, impression, *colloq.* vibes

feign *v*
simulate, assume, fabricate, fake, forge, imitate, pretend, put on, put it on, sham, make a show of, invent, counterfeit, act, *formal* affect, dissemble, dissimulate

feint *n*
play, pretence, ruse, artifice, distraction, expedient, gambit, manoeuvre, stratagem, subterfuge, blind, bluff, deception, mock-assault, wile, *colloq.* dodge

felicitous *adj*
1 APPOSITE, appropriate, apt, fitting, suitable, well-chosen, opportune, timely, well-timed, well-turned, fortunate, *formal* apropos **2** DELIGHTFUL, happy, inspired, fortunate, *formal* propitious
🔁 inappropriate

felicity *n*
1 BLISS, joy, delight, ecstasy, happiness, *formal* delectation **2** APPROPRIATENESS, applicability, aptness, eloquence, suitability, suitableness, *formal* propriety
🔁 **1** sadness **2** inappropriateness

feline *adj*
catlike, graceful, sleek, slinky, smooth, stealthy, seductive, sensual, sinuous, leonine

fell *v*
cut down, hew, knock down, strike down, floor, level, clear, flatten, raze, raze to the ground, demolish, overthrow

fellow *n, adj*
▶ *n* **1** MAN, male, boy, individual, person, character, *colloq.* chap, bloke, guy, lad **2** PEER, compeer, equal, partner, associate, colleague, co-worker, confrère, contemporary, compatriot, companion, comrade, friend, counterpart, match, mate, twin, double, *colloq.* crony, pal, chum, buddy
▶ *adj* co-, associate, associated, related, like, similar

fellow feeling *n*
commiseration, compassion, sympathy, understanding, empathy

fellowship *n*
1 COMPANIONSHIP, camaraderie, comradeship, communion, familiarity, friendship, amiability, affability, intimacy, *colloq.* chumminess, matiness, palliness **2** ASSOCIATION, league, guild, society, club, union, affiliation, fraternity, brotherhood, sisterhood, order

female *adj*
feminine, she-, girlish, womanly, ladylike
🔁 male

Female terms include:
girl, lass, maiden, woman, lady, daughter, sister, girlfriend, fiancée, bride, wife, mother, aunt, niece, grandmother, matriarch, godmother, widow, dowager, dame, madam, mistress, virgin, spinster, old-maid, crone; cow, heifer, bitch, duck, doe, ewe, hen, mare, filly, nanny-goat, sow, tigress, vixen.

feminine *adj*
1 FEMALE, womanly, ladylike, pretty, graceful, gentle, tender, delicate **2** EFFEMINATE, unmanly, womanish, girlish, weak, *colloq.* sissy
🔁 **1** masculine **2** manly

femininity *n*
feminineness, womanhood, womanishness, womanliness, girlishness, effeminacy, prettiness, gracefulness, gentleness, tenderness, delicacy, *colloq.* sissiness
🔁 masculinity

feminism *n*
women's movement, women's lib(eration), female emancipation, women's rights

femme fatale *n*
charmer, seductress, enchantress, temptress, siren, vamp

fen *n*
bog, marsh, morass, moss, quag, quagmire, slough, swamp

fence *n, v*
▶ *n* barrier, railing, rail, paling, wall, hedge, windbreak, guard, defence, barricade, stockade, enclosure, rampart, palisade
▶ *v* **1** SURROUND, encircle, bound, hedge, wall, enclose, shut in, pen, coop, confine, restrict, separate, protect, secure, guard, defend, *formal* fortify, circumscribe **2** PARRY, evade, hedge, equivocate, quibble, stonewall, prevaricate, *formal* vacillate, tergiversate, *colloq.* dodge, pussyfoot, shilly-shally, beat about the bush
▷ **sit on the fence** be irresolute, be uncommitted, be

undecided, be unsure, be uncertain, vacillate, dither, *colloq.* shilly-shally

fencing *n*

Fencing terms include :

appel, attack, balestra, barrage, coquille, disengage, en garde, épée, feint, flèche, foible, foil, forte, hit, lunge, on guard, parry, counter-parry, pink, piste, plastron, remise, reprise, riposte, counter-riposte, sabre, tac-au-tac, thrust, touch, touché, volt.

fend *v*
1 *fend for yourself* look after, take care of, support, maintain, sustain, provide **2** *fend off an attack* ward off, beat off, parry, deflect, divert, avert, resist, repel, repulse, hold at bay, keep off, stave off, shut out, turn aside

feral *adj*
wild, ferocious, fierce, savage, vicious, brutal, brutish, bestial, undomesticated, unbroken, untamed
🖃 tame, domesticated

ferment *v, n*
▶ *v* **1** BUBBLE, effervesce, froth, foam, boil, seethe, smoulder, fester, work, brew, rise **2** ROUSE, arouse, stir up, excite, work up, agitate, foment, incite, provoke, inflame, cause, heat
▶ *n* unrest, agitation, turbulence, stir, excitement, turmoil, disruption, commotion, confusion, fuss, tumult, hubbub, stew, uproar, furore, brouhaha, frenzy, fever
🖃 calm

ferocious *adj*
1 VICIOUS, savage, fierce, wild, untamed, barbarous, barbaric, brutal, inhuman, cruel, sadistic, murderous, bloodthirsty, violent, merciless, pitiless, bitter, ruthless, *formal* feral **2** INTENSE, wild, vigorous, strong, extreme, severe, deep
🖃 **1** tame **2** gentle, mild

ferocity *n*
savagery, fierceness, violence, bloodthirstiness, ruthlessness, cruelty, inhumanity, brutality, viciousness, sadism, barbarity, wildness, intensity, severity, extremity
🖃 gentleness, mildness

ferret *v*
search, rummage, hunt, go through, scour, forage, rifle
▷ **ferret out** discover, search out, find, hunt down, track down, trace, elicit, extract, unearth, dig up, nose out, root out, worm out, run to earth, *colloq.* suss out

ferry *n, v*
▶ *n* ferry-boat, car ferry, ship, boat, vessel, packet, packet boat, shuttle
▶ *v* transport, ship, convey, carry, take, shuttle, taxi, drive, run, move, shift, ply

fertile *adj*
1 *fertile soil* fruitful, productive, rich, abundant, *formal* fecund, luxuriant **2** *a fertile imagination* creative, resourceful, inventive, prolific, productive, imaginative, inspired, visionary **3** *fertile animals* generative, prolific, able to have children, potent, reproductive, virile, *formal* fecund
🖃 **1** unfruitful, unproductive **2** barren **3** sterile, infertile, barren

fertility *n*
1 FRUITFULNESS, productiveness, abundance, richness, *formal* luxuriance, fecundity **2** *fertility tests* generativeness, prolificness, potency, reproductiveness, virility
🖃 **1** aridity **2** barrenness, sterility

fertilization *n*
impregnation, implantation, insemination, pollination, propagation, *formal* fecundation, procreation

fertilize *v*
1 IMPREGNATE, inseminate, pollinate, make pregnant, make fruitful, *formal* procreate, fecundate, fructify **2** *fertilize land* enrich, feed, dress, compost, manure, dung, mulch, top-dress

fertilizer *n*
dressing, compost, manure, dung, top-dressing, plant food, mulch, bone meal, humus

fervent *adj*
ardent, earnest, eager, sincere, enthusiastic, wholehearted, excited, energetic, vigorous, fiery, spirited, intense, vehement, passionate, full-blooded, zealous, devout, impassioned, heartfelt, emotional, warm
🖃 cool, indifferent, apathetic

fervour *n*
ardour, eagerness, earnestness, sincerity, enthusiasm, excitement, animation, energy, vigour, spirit, verve, intensity, wholeheartedness, fire, vehemence, passion, emotion, zeal, warmth
🖃 apathy, indifference

fester *v*
1 *the wound was festering* infect, ulcerate, gather, suppurate, discharge, *technical* maturate **2** *the food was festering* rot, decay, go bad, decompose, perish, *formal* putrefy **3** *hatred was festering* rankle, irk, chafe, anger, annoy, gall, rankle, smoulder

festival *n*
celebration, commemoration, anniversary, jubilee, holiday, feast, gala, gala day, fair, fête, carnival, fiesta, party, merrymaking, entertainment, festivities

festive *adj*
celebratory, holiday, gala, carnival, festal, happy, joyful, merry, hearty, cheerful, cheery, light-hearted, jolly, jovial, cordial, jubilant, convivial, *formal* joyous
🖃 gloomy, sombre, sober

festivity *n*
celebration, jubilation, feasting, banqueting, fun, enjoyment, pleasure, entertainment, festival, party, fun and games, carousal, junketing, sport, amusement, cheerfulness, cheeriness, merriment, merrymaking, revelry, revel, jollity, joviality, conviviality

festoon *v, n*
▶ *v* adorn, deck, garland, wreathe, drape, hang, swathe, decorate, ornament, garnish, *formal* bedeck, array
▶ *n* garland, wreath, swathe, chaplet, swag

fetch *v*
1 *fetch a bucket* get, go and get, collect, bring, carry, transport, deliver, escort, convey, conduct **2** SELL FOR, go for, bring in, yield, realize, make, earn

fetching *adj*
attractive, pretty, sweet, cute, charming, enchanting, fascinating, captivating, alluring, winsome
🖃 repellent

fête *n, v*
▶ *n* fair, bazaar, sale of work, garden party, gala, carnival, festival
▶ *v* entertain, treat, regale, welcome, honour, lionize

fetid *adj*
stinking, disgusting, foul, filthy, sickly, nauseating, smelly, odorous, offensive, rancid, rank, reeking, *formal* malodorous, noisome, noxious, mephitic
🖃 fragrant

fetish *n*
1 FIXATION, obsession, mania, *idée fixe, colloq.* thing **2** CHARM, amulet, talisman, idol, image, cult object, ju-ju, totem

fetter *v*
hamper, restrain, hinder, obstruct, restrict, impede, constrain, bind, chain, confine, encumber, curb, shackle, tie (up), hamstring, manacle, truss, entrammel
F⃞ free

fetters *n*
1 CONSTRAINTS, obstructions, restraints, restrictions, hindrances, checks, curbs, inhibitions, captivity, bondage **2** CHAINS, bonds, bracelets, handcuffs, irons, shackles, manacles

feud *n, v*
▶ *n* vendetta, quarrel, row, argument, disagreement, dispute, bickering, conflict, strife, discord, animosity, ill will, bitterness, enmity, hostility, antagonism, rivalry, bad blood
F⃞ agreement, peace
▶ *v* quarrel, argue, row, squabble, bicker, clash, contend, dispute, duel, fight, brawl, war, wrangle, be at odds, *formal* altercate
F⃞ agree

fever *n*
1 FEVERISHNESS, (high) temperature, delirium, ague, *technical* pyrexia **2** EXCITEMENT, agitation, turmoil, unrest, restlessness, heat, passion, ecstasy, frenzy, ferment

feverish *adj*
1 DELIRIOUS, with a temperature, hot, burning, flushed, red **2** EXCITED, impatient, agitated, restless, nervous, overwrought, worked up, passionate, frenzied, frantic, hectic, rushed, hasty, hurried, flustered, troubled, bothered, *colloq.* hot and bothered, in a kerfuffle, in a tizzy, in a tizz, in a dither
F⃞ **1** cool **2** calm

few *adj, pron*
▶ *adj* scarce, rare, uncommon, sporadic, infrequent, sparse, thin, scant, scanty, meagre, negligible, inconsiderable, inadequate, insufficient, in short supply, *colloq.* thin on the ground
F⃞ many
▶ *pron* not many, hardly any, scarcely any, one or two, a couple, a small number of, scattering, sprinkling, handful, some, a minority
F⃞ many

fiancé, fiancée *n*
betrothed, intended, husband-to-be, bridegroom-to-be, future/prospective husband, wife-to-be, bride-to-be, future/prospective wife

fiasco *n*
failure, catastrophe, calamity, collapse, debacle, disaster, ruin, rout, mess, *colloq.* cropper, damp squib, flop, washout
F⃞ success

fiat *n*
order, command, directive, edict, decree, injunction, mandate, sanction, warrant, authorization, ordinance, permission, dictate, precept, dictum, proclamation, diktat, *colloq.* OK

fib *n, v*
▶ *n* lie, untruth, white lie, falsehood, story, tale, yarn, concoction, fantasy, fiction, invention, misrepresentation, evasion, prevarication, *colloq.* whopper
▶ *v* evade, fabricate, falsify, fantasize, invent, lie, prevaricate, sidestep, *formal* dissemble

fibre *n*
1 FILAMENT, strand, thread, tendril, fibril, nerve, sinew, pile, texture, material, cloth, substance, stuff **2** *moral fibre* character, nature, make-up, disposition, temperament, calibre, backbone, strength, stamina, toughness, courage, resolution, determination, resoluteness, willpower, strength of character, firmness (of purpose)

fickle *adj*
inconstant, disloyal, unfaithful, faithless, treacherous, unreliable, unpredictable, variable, changeable, irresolute, vacillating, volatile, unstable, unsteady, inconstant, flighty, *formal* capricious, mercurial, labile
F⃞ constant, steady, stable

fickleness *n*
inconstancy, disloyalty, unfaithfulness, faithlessness, treachery, unreliability, unpredictability, changeability, changeableness, volatility, unsteadiness, instability, fitfulness, flightiness, *formal* capriciousness
F⃞ constancy

fiction *n*
1 *read fiction* novels, fantasy, romance, story, tale, yarn, fable, parable, legend, myth, story-telling **2** PRETENCE, lie, falsehood, untruth, fabrication, invention, concoction, *colloq.* fib, tall story, cock-and-bull story
F⃞ **1** non-fiction **2** fact, truth

fictional *adj*
literary, invented, made-up, imaginary, make-believe, legendary, mythical, mythological, fabulous, non-existent, unreal
F⃞ factual, real

fictitious *adj*
false, untrue, invented, made-up, fabricated, fake, apocryphal, imaginary, non-existent, bogus, counterfeit, sham, spurious, assumed, supposed, concocted, improvised
F⃞ true, genuine

fiddle *v, n*
▶ *v* **1** *fiddling with her necklace* play, tinker, toy, trifle, tamper, mess around, fool around, meddle, interfere, fidget, fuss **2** CHEAT, swindle, juggle, manoeuvre, racketeer, *colloq.* cook the books, diddle, graft
▶ *n* swindle, fraud, racket, sharp practice, *colloq.* con, rip-off, graft, fix

fiddling *adj*
trifling, petty, trivial, insignificant, negligible, paltry
F⃞ important, significant

fidelity *n*
1 FAITHFULNESS, loyalty, allegiance, devotion, devotedness, constancy, reliability, dependability, trustworthiness **2** ACCURACY, exactness, precision, closeness, adherence, strictness, faithfulness, authenticity
F⃞ **1** disloyalty, unfaithfulness, infidelity, inconstancy, treachery **2** inaccuracy

fidget *v*
squirm, wriggle, writhe, toss and turn, shuffle, twitch, jerk, jump, jiggle, twiddle, fret, fuss, bustle, fiddle, mess about, play around, tinker, toy, trifle, tamper

fidgety *adj*
restless, impatient, uneasy, nervous, agitated, excited, jumpy, twitchy, on edge, *formal* restive, *colloq.* jittery, uptight, afraid of your shadow, like a cat on hot bricks
F⃞ still

field *n, v*
▶ *n* **1** GRASSLAND, meadow, pasture, paddock, playing-field, ground, pitch, green, lawn **2** RANGE, scope, bounds, limits, confines, territory, area, province, domain, sphere, environment, department, discipline, speciality, line, forte, regime, scene **3** PARTICIPANTS, entrants, contestants, competitors, contenders, runners, candidates, applicants, opponents, opposition, competition, possibles
▶ *v* **1** CATCH, retrieve, stop, pick up, return **2** ANSWER, cope with, deal with, handle, parry, deflect

fiend n
1 EVIL SPIRIT, demon, devil, monster, savage, beast, brute, ogre 2 *a health fiend* enthusiast, fanatic, fan, addict, devotee, aficionado, *colloq.* freak, nut, buff

fiendish adj
1 *a fiendish person/plot* devilish, diabolical, infernal, wicked, malevolent, cunning, cruel, inhuman, savage, brutal, aggressive, vicious, ferocious, ruthless, bloodthirsty, barbaric, monstrous, unspeakable 2 *a fiendish problem/plan* difficult, intricate, involved, complex, complicated, obscure, horrendous, challenging, cunning, clever, imaginative, ingenious, resourceful

fierce adj
1 FEROCIOUS, vicious, savage, cruel, brutal, wild, merciless, ruthless, aggressive, dangerous, bloodthirsty, murderous, frightening, menacing, threatening, stern, grim, terrible, relentless 2 INTENSE, strong, powerful, passionate, wild, raging, violent, furious, tempestuous, severe, grave, keen, cut-throat, hot, uncontrolled, relentless
🔁 1 gentle, kind 2 calm

fiercely adv
ferociously, viciously, savagely, cruelly, brutally, wildly, mercilessly, murderously, ruthlessly, aggressively, dangerously, menacingly, threateningly, sternly, terribly, intensely, implacably, fanatically, bitterly, strongly, powerfully, passionately, relentlessly, violently, furiously, tempestuously, severely, keenly, *colloq.* tooth and nail
🔁 gently, kindly

fiery adj
1 BURNING, afire, flaming, aflame, blazing, ablaze, red-hot, glowing, aglow, flushed, hot, torrid, sultry 2 PASSIONATE, inflamed, ardent, fervent, impatient, excitable, impetuous, impulsive, hot-headed, fierce, violent, heated 3 SPICY, spiced, seasoned, hot, pungent, piquant, sharp
🔁 1 cold 2 impassive

fight v, n
▶ v 1 WRESTLE, box, fence, joust, brawl, punch, hit, set about, take on, scuffle, tussle, skirmish, combat, battle, do battle, war, wage war, make war, be at war, clash, cross swords, engage, attack, grapple, struggle, contend, come to blows, *colloq.* scrap, lay into, weigh into 2 QUARREL, argue, have a row, dispute, squabble, bicker, wrangle, feud, be at odds, *formal* altercate, *colloq.* fall out, be at each other's throats 3 OPPOSE, contest, campaign against, champion, work for, resist, withstand, defy, hold out against, stand up to, dispute, object to, take issue with, strive
▷ **fight back 1** RETALIATE, defend yourself, resist, put up a fight, counter-attack, hold out against, retort, reply 2 *fight back tears* hold back, force back, restrain, curb, control, repress, contain, suppress, check, *colloq.* bottle up
▷ **fight off** hold off, keep/hold at bay, ward off, stave off, resist, repel, rebuff, beat off, rout, put to flight
▶ n 1 BOUT, contest, duel, combat, action, battle, war, warfare, bloodshed, hostilities, attack, brawl, scuffle, tussle, struggle, brush, skirmish, exchange, clash, engagement, encounter, confrontation, conflict, fray, row, disturbance, free-for-all, fracas, rout, ruckus, ruction, riot, mêlée, ruffle, shindy, Donnybrook, *colloq.* aggro, bovver, scrap, set-to, punch-up, pasting, bashing 2 QUARREL, row, disagreement, difference of opinion, argument, dispute, *colloq.* dust-up, *formal* dissension, discord, altercation 3 *the fight for freedom* campaign, crusade, movement, drive, struggle, battle 4 *lose all his fight* determination, willpower, tenacity, firmness, resoluteness, drive, spirit, aggression, will to live

fighter n
combatant, contestant, contender, rival, opponent, adversary, antagonist, attacker, disputant, boxer, wrestler, prizefighter, sparring partner, soldier, trouper, mercenary, warrior, man-at-arms, swordsman, gladiator, *formal* pugilist

figment n
▷ **a figment of your imagination** invention, fabrication, falsehood, fancy, fiction, illusion, delusion, improvisation, fable, deception, concoction

figurative adj
metaphorical, symbolic, emblematic, representative, allegorical, parabolic, descriptive, pictorial, naturalistic
🔁 literal

figure n, v
▶ n 1 NUMBER, numeral, digit, integer, sum, amount, total 2 *good at figures* arithmetics, mental arithmetic, calculations, mathematics, maths, statistics 3 SHAPE, form, outline, silhouette 4 BODY, frame, build, physique, torso 5 *public figure* dignitary, celebrity, leader, personality, character, person, personage, notable, worthy 6 DIAGRAM, illustration, picture, drawing, sketch, image, representation, symbol, sign, emblem, design, pattern
▷ **figure of speech** figure, image, imagery, rhetorical device, turn of phrase. *See panel at* RHETORICAL.
▶ v 1 RECKON, guess, estimate, judge, think, believe, consider, conclude 2 FEATURE, appear, crop up, be mentioned in, be included in
▷ **figure out** work out, calculate, make, compute, reckon, count, estimate, puzzle out, resolve, fathom, reason, understand, see, make out, decipher, *colloq.* twig, tumble to, latch onto, get the picture

figurehead n
1 *the president is merely a figurehead* front man, name, mouthpiece, dummy, puppet, image, man of straw, nominal head, titular head, token 2 *a figurehead on a ship's prow* figure, bust, carving

filament n
fibre, strand, thread, hair, whisker, wire, tendril, string, cord, cable, pile

filch v
steal, take, pilfer, thieve, rob, embezzle, palm, crib, *formal* misappropriate, peculate, purloin, *colloq.* lift, nick, pinch, rip off, knock off, snaffle, snitch, swipe

file¹ n, v
▶ n 1 FOLDER, dossier, papers, portfolio, binder, case, box, record, document, data, information, particulars, details 2 LINE, queue, column, row, procession, cortège, train, string, stream, trail
▶ v 1 *file papers* record, register, note, enter, process, store, classify, categorize, pigeonhole, organize, catalogue, put in place 2 *file a complaint/file for divorce* make, put in, submit, apply, ask 3 *file out of the building* walk in line, trail, process, stream, march, parade, troop

file² v
file a rough surface rub (down), sand, abrade, scour, scrape, grate, rasp, hone, whet, shave, plane, smooth, polish, shape

filial adj
dutiful, loyal, respectful, devoted, affectionate, loving, fond, daughterly
🔁 disloyal, unfilial

filibuster n, v
▶ n delay, impediment, obstruction, postponement, hindrance, *formal* procrastination, speechifying, peroration
▶ v delay, obstruct, impede, put off, prevent, hinder, *formal* procrastinate, speechify, perorate
🔁 expedite

filigree *n*
fretwork, lacework, lattice, latticework, interlace, lace, scrollwork, tracery, wirework

fill *v, n*
▶ *v* **1** *fill a bucket with water* MAKE FULL, stock, supply, furnish, satisfy, provide, pack, crowd, occupy, cram, stuff, congest, block, clog, plug, bung, cork, stop (up), close, seal, *formal* replenish **2** PERVADE, imbue, permeate, soak, impregnate, saturate, charge, spread throughout, riddle, *formal* suffuse **3** *fill a post* take up, hold, occupy, fulfil, complete, perform
Ⅎ **1** empty, drain
▷ **fill in 1** *fill in a form* complete, fill out, answer **2** STAND IN, deputize, understudy, substitute, replace, represent, act for **3** INFORM, brief, advise, acquaint, bring up to date
▷ **fill out 1** *fill out a form* complete, fill in, answer **2** *the child filled out* become/grow fatter, put on/gain weight, become plumper/chubbier
▶ *n* enough, abundance, ample, plenty, sufficiency, sufficient, all you want, more than enough, all you can take

filling *n, adj*
▶ *n* contents, inside, stuffing, padding, wadding, filler, substance
▶ *adj* satisfying, nutritious, rich, square, solid, stodgy, substantial, heavy, large, big, generous, ample
Ⅎ insubstantial

fillip *n*
boost, incentive, stimulus, inducement, encouragement, motivation, goad, impetus, spur, prod, push, *colloq.* shove
Ⅎ damper

film *n, v*
▶ *n* **1** MOTION PICTURE, picture, video, cassette, videocassette, cartridge, reel, spool, feature film, short, documentary, screenplay, footage, *colloq.* movie, flick

Kinds of film include:
action, adult, adventure, animated, avant-garde, biopic, B-movie, black comedy, blockbuster, *colloq.* blue, buddy, burlesque, Carry-on, cartoon, chapter-play, Charlie Chaplin, cinéma-vérité, classic, cliff-hanger, comedy, comedy thriller, comic-book hero, cowboy and Indian, crime, cult, detective, disaster, Disney, documentary, Ealing comedy, epic, erotic, escapist, ethnographic, expressionist, family, fantasy, farce, film à clef, film noir, flashback, gangster, gay-lesbian, historical romance, Hitchcock, Hollywood, horror, James Bond, kitchen sink, love story, low-budget, medieval, melodrama, multiple-story, murder, murder mystery, musical remake, newsreel, new wave, nouvelle vague, passion, period epic, police, police thriller, political, pornographic, psychological thriller, realist, re-make, rites of passage, robbery, romantic, romantic tragedy, satirical, science-fiction, screenplay, serial, sexual fantasy, short, silent, social comedy, social problem, space-age, space exploration, Spielberg, spy, surrealist, *colloq.* tear-jerker, thriller, thrillomedy, tragedy, tragicomedy, travelogue, underground, Victorian adaptation, *colloq.* vogue, war, war hero, western, whodunnit.

2 LAYER, covering, cover, dusting, coat, coating, glaze, skin, membrane, tissue, sheet, veil, blanket, screen, cloud, mist, haze, veil

▶ *v* photograph, shoot, record on film, televise, video, videotape
▷ **film over** cloud over, mist over, glaze, become blurred, blur, dull

filmy *adj*
cobwebby, delicate, fragile, fine, gauzy, gossamer, gossamery, light, chiffony, see-through, sheer, shimmering, thin, translucent, transparent, insubstantial, flimsy, floaty, *formal* diaphanous
Ⅎ opaque

filter *v, n*
▶ *v* strain, sieve, sift, riddle, screen, refine, purify, clarify, percolate, ooze, seep, leak, trickle, dribble, drain, leach, *formal* filtrate
▶ *n* strainer, sieve, sifter, colander, mesh, netting, gauze, riddle, membrane

filth *n*
1 DIRT, grime, muck, dung, manure, excrement, sewage, refuse, rubbish, garbage, trash, slime, sludge, effluent, pollution, contamination, corruption, defilement, impurity, uncleanness, foulness, sordidness, squalor, *formal* faeces, putrefaction, putrescence, *colloq.* gunge, yuck, grot, *slang* crud, gunk, grunge, crap **2** OBSCENITY, pornography, indecency, vulgarity, coarseness, dirty books, *colloq.* smut, sleaze, porn, hard porn, blue films, sexploitation, raunchiness
Ⅎ **1** cleanness, cleanliness, purity

filthy *adj*
1 DIRTY, soiled, unwashed, grimy, grubby, black, mucky, muddy, slimy, sooty, unclean, contaminated, polluted, decaying, rotten, impure, foul, gross, sordid, squalid, vile, low, mean, base, nasty, contemptible, despicable, *formal* faecal, putrid, putrefying, *colloq.* yucky, *slang* crappy **2** OBSCENE, dirty, foul, pornographic, smutty, bawdy, suggestive, indecent, explicit, offensive, foul-mouthed, vulgar, coarse, lewd, corrupt, depraved, *colloq.* blue, adult **3** DESPICABLE, contemptible, worthless, wretched, nasty, vile, low
Ⅎ **1** clean, pure **2** decent

final *adj*
1 LAST, latest, closing, concluding, finishing, end, ultimate, terminal, dying, last-minute, eventual, *formal* terminating **2** CONCLUSIVE, definitive, decisive, definite, settled, incontrovertible, indisputable, irrevocable, irrefutable, *formal* determinate
Ⅎ **1** first, initial

finale *n*
climax, dénouement, culmination, crowning glory, end, ending, conclusion, close, final act, curtain, epilogue

finality *n*
conclusiveness, conviction, decidedness, decisiveness, definiteness, certitude, firmness, resolution, inevitability, inevitableness, unavoidability, incontrovertibility, irreversibility, irrevocability, *formal* ultimacy

finalize *v*
conclude, finish, complete, round off, work out, resolve, settle, agree, decide, close, *colloq.* clinch, sew up, wrap up, put the icing on the cake, put the finishing touches to

finally *adv*
lastly, in conclusion, to conclude, ultimately, eventually, at last, at length, in the end, conclusively, once and for all, for ever, for good, permanently, irreversibly, irrevocably, decisively, definitely, *colloq.* when all is said and done

finance *n, v*
▶ *n* **1** *corporate finance* economics, money management, accounting, banking, investment, stock market, business, commerce, trade, money, funding, sponsorship, subsidy **2** *the company's finances*

accounts, affairs, budget, bank account, income, revenue, liquidity, resources, funding, assets, means, capital, wealth, money, cash, funds, wherewithal, savings
▶ *v* pay for, fund, sponsor, back, support, underwrite, guarantee, subsidize, capitalize, float, set up

Terms used in accounting and finance include :
above the line, accounting period, accounts rendered, accounts payable, accounts receivable, accrual basis, allowable expense, annual accounts, annual report, appreciation, APR [= Annual Percentage Rate], asset-stripping, audit, authorized capital, bad debt, balance sheet, below the line, benefit in kind, bookkeeping, break-even point, budgetary control, capital expenditure, capital gain, capitalization, cash flow, circulating capital, collateral, compound interest, consolidated accounts, cost accounting, cost-benefit analysis, creative accounting, credit control, creditor, current assets, current liabilities, debit, debt/equity ratio, debtor, deferred credit, deferred expenditure, deferred liability, deficit, depreciating asset, depreciation, direct costs, disinvestment, dividend, double-entry bookkeeping, earnings per share, equity, fiduciary loan, fictitious assets, financial year, first cost, fiscal year, fixed assets, fixed capital, fixed costs, fixtures and fittings, floating capital, frozen assets, funds flow statement, gearing, going concern, gross margin, gross profit, gross receipts, grossing up, historic cost, income, intangible assets, interim accounts, ledger, liability, liquid assets, liquidation, liquidity, loan capital, loss, net assets, net profit, nominal capital, overheads, outgoings, payroll, petty cash, poison pill, profit and loss account, rate of return, realization of assets, refinance, replacement cost, reserves, return on capital, revenue expenditure, ring fencing (funds), running costs, secured loan, simple interest, statutory income, statutory returns, takeover, hostile takeover, tangible assets, tax loss, taxable profits, total costs, trading account, trial balance, turnover, unit costs, variable costs, wasting asset, watering, white knight, windfall profit, write off.

financial *adj*
monetary, money, economic, fiscal, budgetary, commercial, entrepreneurial, *formal* pecuniary

financier *n*
financialist, banker, stockbroker, money-maker, investor, speculator

find *v, n*
▶ *v* 1 DISCOVER, locate, track down, trace, retrieve, recover, regain, get back, unearth, uncover, dig out, turn up, expose, reveal, bring to light, come across, come by, stumble across/on, meet, encounter, detect, recognize, notice, observe, perceive, realize, learn, *formal* happen upon, chance upon 2 ATTAIN, achieve, win, reach, gain, earn, acquire, obtain, get, *formal* procure 3 *find it difficult* consider, think, judge, rate, gauge, declare, *formal* deem
☒ 1 lose
▷ **find out** 1 LEARN, ascertain, establish, identify, pinpoint, discover, detect, note, observe, perceive, see, gather, realize, *colloq.* get wind of, suss out 2 UNMASK, expose, show up, uncover, reveal, disclose, get at, detect, bring to light, lay bare, catch, *colloq.* suss out, tumble to, *slang* rumble
▶ *n* acquisition, asset, catch, coup, discovery, boon,

godsend, bargain, good buy

finding *n*
1 FIND, discovery, breakthrough, innovation 2 DECISION, conclusion, judgement, verdict, order, pronouncement, decree, recommendation, award

fine¹ *adj*
1 EXCELLENT, outstanding, exceptional, first-class, great, superior, exquisite, splendid, magnificent, admirable, brilliant, beautiful, handsome, attractive, lovely, nice, good, select, choice 2 HEALTHY, in good health, well, fit, strong, flourishing, vigorous 3 SATISFACTORY, acceptable, all right, agreeable, good, *colloq.* OK 4 *fine weather* bright, sunny, clear, cloudless, dry, fair, clement, temperate 5 THIN, slender, slim, slight, sheer, gauzy, powdery, flimsy, light, fragile, delicate, dainty, narrow 6 POWDERY, ground, crushed, fine-grained, gossamer 7 EXPENSIVE, elegant, smart, fashionable, stylish 8 *a fine distinction* EXACT, precise, accurate, nice, critical, *colloq.* hair-splitting
☒ 1 mediocre 4 cloudy, dull, inclement, stormy 5 thick, coarse

fine² *n, v*
▶ *n a speeding fine* penalty, punishment, forfeit, forfeiture, damages, *formal* amercement, mulct
▶ *v* penalize, punish, *formal* amerce, mulct, *colloq.* sting

finery *n*
decorations, frippery, best clothes, Sunday best, jewellery, ornaments, showiness, splendour, gaudery, trappings, *formal* bedizenment, *colloq.* glad rags, best bib and tucker

finesse *n, v*
▶ *n* skill, flair, expertise, deftness, adeptness, adroitness, cleverness, delicacy, diplomacy, tact, discretion, subtlety, *savoir-faire*, elegance, gracefulness, polish, neatness, refinement, sophistication, quickness, *colloq.* know-how
▶ *v* bluff, evade, manipulate, manoeuvre, trick

finger *v*
touch, handle, manipulate, feel, stroke, caress, fondle, paw, fiddle with, toy with, play about with, meddle with
▷ **put your finger on** pinpoint, indicate, isolate, pin down, hit upon, identify, discover, find out, remember, place, locate, recall, *colloq.* hit the nail on the head

finicky *adj*
1 PARTICULAR, finickety, fussy, fastidious, meticulous, scrupulous, critical, hypercritical, selective, discriminating, faddy, *colloq.* pernickety, choosy, nit-picking, picky 2 FIDDLY, intricate, tricky, difficult, delicate
☒ 1 easy-going 2 easy

finish *v, n*
▶ *v* 1 END, bring/come to an end, stop, be over, complete, accomplish, attain, achieve, fulfil, carry out, discharge, deal with, do, close, settle, round off, culminate, perfect, *formal* conclude, terminate, cease, discontinue, *colloq.* wind up, polish off, pack in, wrap up, sew up, be done with, get shot of, be through, call it a day 2 USE UP, use, consume, devour, eat, drink, exhaust, drain, empty, run out of, *formal* deplete, expend 3 DESTROY, ruin, exterminate, get rid of, annihilate, defeat, overcome, overwhelm, overpower, conquer, rout, overthrow, crush, bring down, get the better of, *colloq.* wipe out
☒ 1 begin, start, *formal* commence
▶ *n* 1 END, completion, conclusion, close, ending, finale, culmination, accomplishment, achievement, perfection, fulfilment, discharge, ruin, destruction,

formal termination, cessation, *colloq.* winding-up, wind-up, curtains **2** SURFACE, appearance, texture, grain, polish, shine, gloss, glaze, coating, veneer, lacquer, lustre, smoothness

F₄ 1 beginning, start, *formal* commencement

finished *adj*
1 COMPLETED, complete, concluded, dealt with, over, at an end, *colloq.* over and done with, through, wrapped up, sewn up **2** USELESS, defeated, ruined, doomed, drained, exhausted, empty, spent, undone, unwanted, unpopular, *colloq.* done for, played out, zonked **3** *a finished performance* accomplished, proficient, professional, expert, polished, impeccable, faultless, flawless, perfect, masterly, consummate, refined, sophisticated, urbane, virtuoso

F₄ 1 unfinished, incomplete **2** useful, productive **3** incompetent, *colloq.* hopeless

finite *adj*
limited, restricted, bounded, demarcated, terminable, definable, fixed, measurable, calculable, countable, numbered

F₄ infinite

fire *n, v*
▶ *n* **1** FLAMES, blaze, bonfire, inferno, burning, combustion, holocaust, *formal* conflagration **2** GUNFIRE, attack, bombing, shelling, sniping, bombardment, barrage, cannonade, fusillade, salvo, fire, flak **3** HEATER, radiator, convector, fan **4** PASSION, feeling, ardour, excitement, eagerness, enthusiasm, spirit, energy, liveliness, life, vigour, animation, vivacity, verve, fervour, intensity, heat, radiance, inventiveness, creativity, sparkle
▶ *v* **1** IGNITE, light, put a match to, kindle, set fire to, set on fire, set alight, set ablaze **2** *fire a missile* shoot, launch, set off, let off, detonate, discharge, explode, trigger, hurl **3** DISMISS, discharge, eject, get rid of, *colloq.* sack, axe, boot out, show someone the door, give someone their cards, give someone the sack/ push/boot/elbow **4** EXCITE, whet, enliven, galvanize, electrify, stir (up), arouse, rouse, motivate, stimulate, inspire, animate, inflame, incite, spark off, trigger off
▷ **on fire 1** IN FLAMES, burning, alight, ignited, flaming, aflame, blazing, ablaze, fiery **2** ENTHUSIASTIC, passionate, excited, eager, ardent, energetic, creative, inventive, sparkling, inspired

firearm *n*
gun, weapon, automatic, handgun, pistol, revolver, rifle, shotgun, musket

fireworks *n*
1 PYROTECHNICS, explosions, illuminations, feux d'artifice **2** UPROAR, trouble, outburst, frenzy, fit, rage, rows, storm, temper, sparks, hysterics

firm¹ *adj*
1 *firm ground* dense, compressed, compact, close-grained, concentrated, set, solid, solidified, substantive, hard, hardened, unyielding, stiff, rigid, inflexible, inelastic **2** FIXED, embedded, established, fast, tight, secure, fastened, anchored, riveted, immovable, tight, motionless, unshakable, stationary, steady, stable, set, sturdy, strong **3** *a firm decision* definite, settled, fixed, decided, established, unchangeable, unalterable **4** ADAMANT, unshakable, resolute, resolved, decided, determined, dogged, unwavering, unfaltering, unswerving, unflinching, strict, hard, inflexible, stubborn, obstinate, constant, steadfast, staunch, tenacious, *formal* obdurate **5** *firm friends* close, dependable, true, sure, committed, unchanging, constant, long-standing, long-lasting, steady, stable, steadfast, staunch

F₄ 1 soft, flabby **2** unsteady **3** changeable **4** hesitant

firm² *n*
a firm of accountants company, corporation, business, enterprise, concern, house, establishment, institution, organization, association, partnership, syndicate, conglomerate

firmly *adv*
securely, tightly, steadily, stably, sturdily, strongly, robustly, unshakably, unwaveringly, strictly, immovably, unalterably, unchangeably, unflinchingly, resolutely, inflexibly, decisively, definitely, determinedly, doggedly, enduringly, staunchly, steadfastly

F₄ hesitantly, uncertainly, unsoundly

firmness *n*
1 STIFFNESS, hardness, rigidity, solidity, density, compactness, inflexibility, inelasticity, tautness, tension, fixity, immovability, tightness **2** STRENGTH, strength of will, determination, resolution, resolve, dependability, reliability, staunchness, steadfastness, steadiness, willpower, constancy, conviction, changelessness, stability, strictness, resistance, sureness, doggedness, *formal* indomitability, obduracy

F₄ 1 softness **2** uncertainty

first *adj, adv, n*
▶ *adj* **1** INITIAL, opening, introductory, preliminary, beginning, inaugural, elementary, primary, basic, fundamental **2** ORIGINAL, earliest, earlier, prior, primitive, oldest, eldest, senior, *formal* primeval, primordial **3** CHIEF, main, key, cardinal, principal, head, leading, foremost, ruling, sovereign, highest, greatest, uppermost, paramount, best, prime, supreme, predominant, pre-eminent

F₄ 1 last, final
▶ *adv* initially, to begin with, at first, first of all, in the first place, to start with, first and foremost, at the outset, beforehand, before anything else, originally, in preference, rather, sooner
▶ *n* beginning, start, opening, introduction, outset, origin(s), original, prototype, unveiling, première, *formal* commencement, inception, *colloq.* the word go, square one

first-born *adj*
elder, eldest, older, oldest, senior, *formal* aîné(e), primogenital, primogenitary, primogenitive

firsthand *adj & adv*
direct(ly), immediate(ly), personal(ly), in service, on the job, *colloq.* straight from the horse's mouth, hands-on

F₄ indirect(ly)

first name *n*
forename, Christian name, given name, baptismal name

first-rate *adj*
first-class, second-to-none, matchless, peerless, top, top-flight, leading, supreme, superior, prime, excellent, outstanding, superlative, premier, exceptional, splendid, superb, fine, admirable, *colloq.* super, top-notch, A1, ace, crack, out of this world, *slang* way-out, cool, radical, mega

F₄ inferior

fiscal *adj*
financial, monetary, money, economic, budgetary, treasury, capital, *formal* pecuniary

fish *n, v*
▶ *n*

Types of fish include:
bloater, brisling, cod, coley, Dover sole, haddock, hake, halibut, herring, jellied eel, kipper, mackerel, pilchard, plaice, rainbow trout, salmon, sardine, sole, sprat, trout, tuna, turbot, whitebait; bass, Bombay duck, bream, brill, carp, catfish,

chub, conger eel, cuttlefish, dab, dace, dogfish, dory, eel, goldfish, guppy, marlin, minnow, monkfish, mullet, octopus, perch, pike, piranha, roach, shark, skate, snapper, squid, stickleback, stingray, sturgeon, swordfish, tench, whiting; clam, cockle, crab, crayfish, *US* crawfish, kingprawn, lobster, mussel, oyster, prawn, scallop, shrimp, whelk. *See also* SHARK.

▶ *v* **1** GO FISHING, angle, trawl **2** *fished in her bag for a pen* delve, hunt, search, grope
▷ **fish out** produce, take out, extract, find, retrieve, haul out, pull out, come up with, dredge up

fisherman *n*
angler, fisher, rodfisher, rodman, rodsman, rodster, *formal* piscator, piscatorian

fishing *n*
angling, trawling

fishy *adj*
1 *a fishy taste* fish-like, *formal* piscatorial, piscatory, piscine **2** ODD, suspicious, questionable, shady, suspect, doubtful, dubious, implausible, improbable, funny, irregular, queer
☑ honest, legitimate

fission *n*
splitting, breaking, division, rupture, parting, rending, schism, severance, scission, cleavage

fissure *n*
crack, opening, cleft, fracture, breach, break, cranny, crevasse, crevice, rent, rift, rupture, chasm, hole, gap, gash, slit, split, chink, fault, *technical* grike, foramen, sulcus, *formal* cleavage, interstice, scissure

fist *n*
palm, hand, *colloq.* paw, *slang* mitt

fit¹ *adj, v*
▶ *adj* **1** HEALTHY, well, in good health, able-bodied, in good form, in good shape, in shape, in good condition, in trim, sound, sturdy, strong, hardy, robust, vigorous, flourishing, hale and hearty **2** SUITABLE, appropriate, apt, fitting, correct, right, proper, due, convenient, ready, prepared, able, capable, competent, qualified, equipped, trained, eligible, worthy, *formal* decorous, pertinent
☑ **1** unfit **2** unsuitable, unworthy
▶ *v* **1** *Do the shoes fit you?* get into, be the right size for, be the right shape for, be a good fit, *colloq.* fit like a glove **2** MATCH, correspond, conform, follow, agree, tally, suit, be suitable, harmonize, go, be right, be consistent, belong, dovetail, interlock, connect, join, put together, meet, accommodate, *formal* concur, be consonant **3** *fit a washing-machine* install, insert, put in, arrange, position, place, put in position/place, attach, arrange, fix **4** ALTER, modify, change, adjust, adapt, regulate, tailor, shape, fashion, accommodate **5** EQUIP, qualify, train, make suitable, prepare, make ready, prime, condition, arm, coach, groom, tailor
▷ **fit in** match, correspond, conform, agree, square, belong, slot, squeeze, *formal* accord, concur
▷ **fit out** equip, rig out, kit out, outfit, provide, supply, furnish, prepare, arm, *formal* accoutre

fit² *n*
1 SEIZURE, convulsion, spasm, paroxysm, attack, *technical* ictus **2** OUTBREAK, bout, spell, burst, surge, outburst, eruption, explosion, tantrum
▷ **in fits and starts** sporadically, fitfully, intermittently, occasionally, irregularly, unevenly, brokenly, erratically, off and on
☑ regularly, steadily

fitful *adj*
sporadic, intermittent, occasional, spasmodic, erratic, irregular, disconnected, haphazard, uneven, broken, disturbed
☑ steady, regular

fitness *n*
1 SUITABILITY, qualifications, readiness, preparedness, eligibility, appropriateness, aptness, competence, adequacy, applicability, condition, *formal* pertinence **2** HEALTH, healthiness, strength, vigour, condition, shape, trim, good health, robustness, haleness
☑ **1** unsuitability **2** unfitness

fitted *adj*
1 *fitted wardrobe* built-in, permanent, fixed **2** EQUIPPED, rigged out, provided, furnished, appointed, prepared, armed, tailored **3** SUITED, right, suitable, fit, qualified, cut out

fitting *adj, n*
▶ *adj* apt, appropriate, suitable, fit, correct, right, proper, desirable, deserved, *formal* decorous
☑ unsuitable, improper
▶ *n* **1** *light fittings* attachment, accessory, connection, part, component, piece, unit, fitment, fixture, unit **2** *the price includes fittings* equipment, furnishings, furniture, fixtures, installations, fitments, accessories, extras, *formal* accoutrements, appointments

fix *v, n*
▶ *v* **1** FASTEN, secure, tie, bind, attach, join, connect, link, couple, anchor, clamp, pin, nail, screw, rivet, stick, glue, cement, set, harden, solidify, stiffen, stabilize, plant, root, implant, embed, establish, install, station, locate, situate, position **2** *fix a date* arrange, set, specify, define, agree on, decide, determine, name, settle, resolve, finalize, arrive at, sort **3** MEND, repair, patch up, correct, rectify, adjust, restore, remedy, see to, put right **4** *fix your eyes/attention* direct, aim, focus, concentrate, turn, level **5** *fix your hair* arrange, tidy, groom, adjust, dress, prepare, put in order, order, do, straighten, comb **6** *fix a race* rig, falsify, fake, manoeuvre, tamper with, manipulate **7** *fix some food for you* prepare, make, get ready, put together, cook
☑ **1** move, shift **3** damage **5** untidy
▷ **fix up** arrange, organize, settle, agree on, plan, lay on, provide, supply, furnish, equip, settle, sort out, produce, bring about
▶ *n* **1** DILEMMA, quandary, predicament, plight, difficulty, corner, mess, muddle, *colloq.* hole, (tight) spot, bind, pickle, scrape, jam, the soup **2** INJECTION, dose, shot, hit, *colloq.* score, slug, bang

fixation *n*
preoccupation, obsession, mania, fetish, infatuation, compulsion, complex, *idée fixe*, phobia, *colloq.* thing, hang-up

fixed *adj*
decided, settled, established, constant, definite, arranged, planned, set, firm, rigid, inflexible, entrenched, immobile, steady, secure, fast, rooted, permanent, *colloq.* cast/set in stone
☑ variable, varying, flexible, mobile

fixity *n*
permanence, persistence, constancy, stability, steadiness, fixedness, *formal* immutability

fixture *n*
1 *fixtures and fittings* equipment, furnishings, furniture, installations **2** *a sports fixture* event, match, game, competition, contest, race, round, meeting

fizz *v*
effervesce, sparkle, bubble, froth, foam, fizzle, hiss

fizzle *v*
▷ **fizzle out** collapse, come to nothing, die away, die

down, fall through, fail, come to grief, stop, subside, disappear, evaporate, taper off, *formal* dissipate, *colloq.* fold, peter out, flop

fizzy *adj*
effervescent, sparkling, aerated, carbonated, gassy, bubbly, bubbling, frothy, foaming

flabbergasted *adj*
amazed, confounded, astonished, astounded, staggered, dumbfounded, speechless, stunned, dazed, nonplussed, overcome, overwhelmed, *colloq.* bowled over

flabby *adj*
fleshy, soft, yielding, flaccid, limp, floppy, drooping, hanging, sagging, slack, loose, lax, weak, feeble, fat, overweight, plump
🖃 firm, strong, lean, toned

flaccid *adj*
limp, drooping, flabby, floppy, lax, loose, sagging, slack, soft, toneless, weak, nerveless, relaxed, clammy
🖃 firm, hard

flag¹ *n, v*
  ▶ *n* fly the *Japanese flag*

> **Types of flag include:**
> banderol, banner, bunting, burgee, colours, cornet, ensign, gonfalon, jack, oriflamme, pennant, pilot flag, signal flag, standard, streamer, swallow tail, vexillum.

  ▶ *v* **1** SIGNAL, wave, salute, motion, hail, wave down, signal to stop **2** MARK, indicate, label, tag, note

flag² *v*
spirits were beginning to flag lessen, diminish, decline, fall (off), subside, wane, ebb, sink, slump, dwindle, peter out, taper off, fade, fail, weaken, slow, falter, tire, grow tired, weary, wilt, droop, hang down, sag, flop, faint, die, *formal* abate
🖃 revive

flagellation *n*
beating, whipping, flogging, lashing, scourging, thrashing, flaying, whaling, *formal* castigation, chastisement, vapulation

flagging *adj*
lessening, diminishing, declining, subsiding, sinking, dwindling, ebbing, waning, decreasing, fading, failing, weakening, slowing, faltering, sagging, tiring, drooping, wilting, *formal* abating
🖃 returning, reviving

flagon *n*
bottle, decanter, carafe, jug, pitcher, flask, ewer, vessel

flagrant *adj*
scandalous, outrageous, glaring, disgraceful, dreadful, shameless, blatant, ostentatious, open, atrocious, enormous, heinous, infamous, notorious, bold, brazen, audacious, barefaced, conspicuous, unashamed, undisguised, overt, rank, gross, arrant, *formal* egregious
🖃 covert, secret

 flagrant or **blatant** ? *See panel at* BLATANT.

flail *v*
wave uncontrollably, swing wildly, thresh, thrash, batter, beat, whip, strike

flair *n*
skill, ability, natural ability, aptitude, faculty, gift, talent, bent, facility, knack, mastery, genius, feel, taste, discernment, acumen, style, elegance, stylishness, panache

🖃 inability, ineptitude

flak *n*
criticism, blame, censure, complaints, disapproval, fault-finding, hostility, opposition, abuse, condemnation, *formal* animadversions, aspersions, disapprobation, disparagement, invective, *colloq.* bad press, brickbats, stick

flake *n, v*
  ▶ *n* scale, peeling, paring, shaving, scurf, sliver, wafer, chip, splinter, bit, particle, fragment, *technical* desquamation, exfoliation, furfur
  ▶ *v* scale, peel, chip, splinter, blister, *technical* desquamate, exfoliate
  ▷ **flake out** collapse, pass out, faint, keel over, drop, fall asleep, relax completely

flaky *adj*
dry, scaly, scurfy, laminar, layered, *technical* desquamative, desquamatory, exfoliative, furfuraceous, scabrous

flamboyance *n*
showiness, ostentation, colour, brilliance, glamour, extravagance, style, dash, élan, panache, theatricality, *colloq.* pizzazz
🖃 diffidence, restraint

flamboyant *adj*
showy, ostentatious, flashy, gaudy, bright, colourful, brilliant, exciting, dazzling, striking, dashing, extravagant, rich, glamorous, elaborate, ornate, florid, theatrical
🖃 modest, restrained

flame *v, n*
  ▶ *v* burn, catch fire, flare, blaze, burst into flames, glare, flash, beam, shine, glow, sparkle, gleam, radiate
  ▶ *n* **1** FIRE, blaze, light, brightness, gleam, glow, heat, warmth, *formal* conflagration **2** PASSION, ardour, fervour, warmth, fervency, excitement, enthusiasm, eagerness, keenness, zeal, intensity, radiance, fire **3** *an old flame* lover, partner, boyfriend, girlfriend, sweetheart

flaming *adj*
1 *a flaming torch* burning, alight, aflame, blazing, on fire, in flames, fiery, brilliant, scintillating, red-hot, glowing, raging, smouldering **2** *a flaming red* intense, vivid, bright, brilliant, blazing **3** *a flaming temper* furious, angry, enraged, raging, infuriated, incensed, mad, violent

flammable *adj*
inflammable, ignitable, combustible
🖃 non-flammable, incombustible, flameproof, fire-resistant, flame-resistant

flank *n, v*
  ▶ *n* the *animal's/enemy's flank* side, edge, quarter, wing, loin, haunch, hip, thigh
  ▶ *v* edge, fringe, skirt, line, border, bound, confine, wall, screen

flannel *n*
nonsense, rubbish, flattery, blarney, *colloq.* waffle, rot, sweet talk, soft soap

flap *v, n*
  ▶ *v* flutter, vibrate, wave, agitate, shake, wag, waggle, swing, sway, swish, thrash, thresh, beat, move up and down, move from side to side
  ▶ *n* **1** FOLD, fly, lapel, overhang, overlap, covering, tab, lug, tag, tail, skirt, apron, aileron, lappet **2** FLUTTER, fluttering, wave, shake, wag, waggle, swing, sway, swish **3** PANIC, fuss, commotion, fluster, agitation, flutter, dither, *colloq.* state, tizzy, stew

flare *v, n*
  ▶ *v* **1** FLAME, burn, blaze, glare, glow, gleam, glitter, sparkle, flash, flicker, burst, explode, erupt **2** BROADEN,

widen, flare out, spread out, splay

▷ **flare up** erupt, break out, blaze, burst out, lose your temper, lose control, *colloq.* explode, blow up, boil over, lose your cool

▶ *n* **1** FLAME, blaze, glare, flash, flicker, burst, glimmer, gleam, dazzle **2** SIGNAL, distress signal, warning signal, beacon, light, rocket, beam **3** BROADENING, widening, spread, splay

flash *v, n, adj*

▶ *v* **1** BEAM, shine, light up, flare, blaze, glare, gleam, glimmer, glisten, glint, flicker, twinkle, sparkle, glitter, shimmer, scintillate, dance, *formal* coruscate, fulgurate **2** *the train flashed past* streak, fly, shoot, speed, dart, race, dash, tear, zoom, rush, bolt, career, bound **3** *flashed her engagement ring* flourish, brandish, flaunt, show off, display

▶ *n* **1** *flash of lightning* beam, ray, shaft, spark, blaze, flare, burst, streak, glare, glimmer, glitter, gleam, glint, flicker, twinkle, sparkle, shimmer **2** *a flash of inspiration* burst, outburst, outbreak, sudden appearance, show, display, exhibition

▷ **in a flash** in an instant, in a moment, in a split second, in a twinkling, in the twinkling of an eye, in no time (at all), in less than no time, in a trice, *colloq.* pronto, in a jiffy, in two shakes of a lamb's tail, before you can say Jack Robinson

▶ *adj* showy, ostentatious, smart, fashionable, expensive, glamorous, gaudy, kitsch, pretentious

flashy *adj*

showy, ostentatious, flamboyant, glamorous, bold, loud, garish, gaudy, jazzy, flash, pretentious, tawdry, cheap, vulgar, tasteless, kitsch, showing poor taste, *colloq.* tacky, glitzy

🖃 plain, tasteful

flask *n*

bottle, carafe, flagon, decanter, matrass, flacket, lekythos

flat *n, adj, adv*

▶ *n* apartment, penthouse, maisonette, tenement, flatlet, rooms, suite, bed-sit(ter), *colloq.* pad

▶ *adj* **1** LEVEL, plane, even, smooth, uniform, unbroken, levelled, horizontal, outstretched, prostrate, prone, recumbent, reclining, low, spread-eagled, *technical* homaloidal, *formal* supine, *colloq.* flat as a pancake **2** SHALLOW, not deep, not thick, not tall **3** *a flat tyre* punctured, burst, deflated, collapsed, ruptured, *colloq.* blown-out **4** DULL, boring, monotonous, tedious, uninteresting, unexciting, stale, lifeless, dead, spiritless, lacklustre, vapid, insipid, bland, weak, watery, empty, pointless **5** *a flat refusal* absolute, utter, total, unequivocal, categorical, pos-itive, unconditional, unqualified, outright, out and out, downright, point-blank, direct, straight, explicit, plain, final, definite, complete **6** *feel flat* depressed, low, discouraged, dejected, downcast, miserable, inactive, sluggish, slack, slow, *colloq.* down **7** *charge a flat price* set, fixed, standard, definite, stock, firm, rigid, planned, arranged

🖃 **1** bumpy, vertical, upright **2** deep, thick, tall **4** exciting, full **5** equivocal **6** happy, cheerful, lively **7** variable, negotiable

▶ *adv* directly, outright, categorically, absolutely, straight, point-blank, completely, totally, utterly, entirely, exactly, plainly, precisely

▷ **flat out** at top speed, at full speed, all out, for all you are worth

flatly *adv*

categorically, point-blank, positively, absolutely, completely, uncompromisingly, unconditionally, unhesitatingly, *formal* peremptorily

flatness *n*

1 EVENNESS, levelness, smoothness, horizontality, uniformity **2** DULLNESS, monotony, tedium, boredom, staleness, emptiness, tastelessness, insipidity, vapidity, *formal* languor

flatten *v*

1 SMOOTH, iron, press, roll, crush, squash, compress, plane, level, make flat, make even, even out **2** KNOCK DOWN, knock to the ground, prostrate, floor, fell, demolish, raze, tear down, overwhelm, subdue

flatter *v*

1 PRAISE, compliment, adulate, fawn, sing the praises of, wheedle, toady, kowtow, humour, play up to, court, curry favour with, *formal* sycophantize, eulogize, inveigle, *colloq.* sweet-talk, butter up, creep, suck up to, make up to, soft-soap, play up to **2** *that dress flatters you* show off, make someone look attractive, look good on, become, suit, enhance, embellish, grace, show to advantage, befit

🖃 **1** criticize

flatterer *n*

adulator, fawner, groveller, lackey, toady, bootlicker, lickspittle, *formal* encomiast, sycophant, eulogizer, *colloq.* back-scratcher, creeper, crawler

🖃 critic, opponent

flattering *adj*

complimentary, kind, favourable, enhancing, gratifying, becoming, adulatory, ingratiating, fawning, fulsome, effusive, servile, smooth-spoken, smoothtongued, honeyed, honey-tongued, sugared, sugary, *formal* laudatory, obsequious, sycophantic, unctuous

🖃 candid, uncompromising, unflattering

flattery *n*

adulation, praise, blarney, fulsomeness, compliments, cajolery, fawning, toadyism, ingratiation, servility, *formal* eulogy, sycophancy, blandishments, laudation, *colloq.* sweet talk, soft soap, flannel

🖃 criticism

flatulence *n*

wind, windiness, gas, gassiness, *formal* eructation, flatus, borborygmus, ventosity, *colloq.* farting

flatulent *adj*

windy, gassy, *formal* ventose

flaunt *v*

show off, display, parade, flourish, brandish, exhibit, boast, air, sport, vaunt, wield, dangle, flash

---

📝 **flaunt** or **flout** ?

To *flaunt* something is 'to show it off or display it ostentatiously': *She was flaunting her new fur coat in front of her colleagues.* Flout means 'to treat with contempt, to refuse to obey or comply with': *He constantly flouts authority/the law.*

---

flavour *n, v*

▶ *n* **1** TASTE, tang, smack, savour, relish, piquancy, zest, aroma, odour, *colloq.* zing **2** QUALITY, property, character, style, aspect, feeling, feel, atmosphere, tone, spirit, essence, nature, soul **3** HINT, suggestion, touch, tinge, tone

▶ *v* season, spice, ginger up, infuse, imbue, lace

flavouring *n*

seasoning, flavour, zest, tang, relish, piquancy, essence, extract, additive, *colloq.* zing

flaw *n*

defect, imperfection, fault, weakness, weak spot, foible, shortcoming, failing, fallacy, lapse, slip, error, mistake, blemish, spot, mark, speck, crack, crevice, fissure, cleft, rent, split, tear, rift, chip, break, fracture

flawed *adj*
imperfect, defective, faulty, blemished, marked, damaged, spoilt, marred, cracked, chipped, broken, unsound, fallacious, erroneous
☒ flawless, perfect

flawless *adj*
perfect, faultless, unblemished, spotless, immaculate, impeccable, stainless, sound, intact, whole, unbroken, undamaged, unimpaired
☒ flawed, imperfect, blemished

flay *v*
skin, skin alive, upbraid, revile, scourge, flog, *formal* excoriate, castigate, execrate, lambast, *colloq.* pull to pieces, tear a strip off

fleck *v, n*
▶ *v* dot, spot, mark, speckle, dapple, mottle, stipple, freckle, streak, sprinkle, dust, spatter
▶ *n* dot, point, spot, mark, speck, speckle, freckle, streak

fledgling *n*
beginner, newcomer, novice, apprentice, learner, recruit, trainee, tiro, neophyte, novitiate, tenderfoot, *colloq.* greenhorn, rookie

flee *v*
run away, bolt, fly, take flight, take off, make off, cut and run, escape, get away, rush, decamp, abscond, leave, depart, withdraw, retreat, vanish, disappear, make yourself scarce, *colloq.* clear off, take to your heels, scarper, scoot, scram, vamoose
☒ stay

fleece *n, v*
▶ *n* down, coat, wool
▶ *v* swindle, rob, steal, cheat, defraud, overcharge, plunder, mulct, bilk, *colloq.* bleed, con, diddle, rip off, squeeze, sting, fiddle, gull, have someone on, string along, take for a ride, take to the cleaners, pull a fast one

fleecy *adj*
downy, woolly, soft, velvety, shaggy, nappy, fluffy, hairy, *formal* floccose, flocculate, lanuginose, pilose, eriophorous
☒ bald, smooth

fleet *n, adj*
▶ *n* flotilla, armada, navy, task force, naval force, squadron
▶ *adj* swift, fast, quick, rapid, nimble, flying, speedy, light-footed, winged, mercurial, meteoric, *formal* expeditious
☒ slow

fleeting *adj*
short, brief, flying, short-lived, short, quick, sudden, rushed, momentary, ephemeral, transient, transitory, passing, temporary, *formal* evanescent, fugacious, *colloq.* here today and gone tomorrow
☒ lasting, permanent

flesh *n, v*
▶ *n* **1** *an animal's flesh* body, tissue, fat, muscle, brawn, skin, meat, pulp **2** SUBSTANCE, matter, physicality, pith, stuff, solidity, significance, weight **3** *pleasures of the flesh* human nature, physical nature, sinful nature, carnal nature, carnality, physicality, corporeality, sensuality
▷ **flesh and blood** family, relative, relations, kin, *colloq.* folks
▷ **in the flesh** in person, in real life, in actual life, before your own eyes
▶ *v* ▷ **flesh out** add/give details, elaborate, make complete, make more substantial

fleshly *adj*
wordly, earthy, physical, earthly, corporal, corporeal, bodily, human, animal, sensual, sexual, bestial, carnal, lustful, erotic, material, brutish
☒ spiritual

fleshy *adj*
fat, ample, beefy, chubby, chunky, brawny, hefty, meaty, obese, plump, podgy, portly, tubby, stout, paunchy, overweight, well-padded, *formal* corpulent, rotund, *colloq.* flabby
☒ thin, slim

flex *n, v*
▶ *n* cable, wire, lead, cord
▶ *v* bend, bow, curve, angle, crook, ply, double up, stretch, tighten, contract
☒ straighten, extend

flexibility *n*
1 BENDABILITY, pliability, pliancy, elasticity, resilience, spring, springiness, suppleness, give, flexion, *formal* tensility **2** ADAPTABILITY, agreeability, adjustability, amenability, *formal* complaisance
☒ **1, 2** inflexibility

flexible *adj*
1 BENDABLE, pliable, pliant, plastic, malleable, mouldable, elastic, stretchy, springy, yielding, supple, lithe, limber, double-jointed, agile, mobile, *colloq.* bendy **2** ADAPTABLE, adjustable, changeable, amenable, accommodating, variable, open, open-ended, yielding, manageable
☒ **1** inflexible, rigid **2** fixed, inflexible, rigid

flick *v, n*
▶ *v* hit, strike, rap, tap, touch, dab, flip, swish, snap, click, jerk, whip, lash
▷ **flick through** flip through, browse through, thumb through, leaf through, glance at, glance over, skip, skim, scan
▶ *n* rap, tap, touch, dab, flip, jerk, click, snap, swish

flicker *v, n*
▶ *v* flash, blink, wink, twinkle, sparkle, glimmer, glitter, flare, glint, shimmer, gutter, flutter, vibrate, bat, quiver, waver
▶ *n* flash, gleam, glint, twinkle, glimmer, glitter, spark, sparkle, trace, drop, iota, atom, indication

flight[1] *n*
a seagull in flight **1** FLYING, aviation, aeronautics, air transport, air travel **2** JOURNEY, trip, voyage, shuttle, globe-trotting **3** *a flight of steps* staircase, set, stairway, stairs, steps

flight[2] *n*
his flight from the police fleeing, escape, running away/off, getaway, breakaway, rush, absconding, exit, departure, exodus, retreat, withdrawal
▷ **take flight** run away, bolt, fly, take off, make off, cut and run, escape, get away, rush, decamp, abscond, leave, depart, withdraw, retreat, vanish, disappear

flighty *adj*
inconstant, scatterbrained, impetuous, impulsive, changeable, irresponsible, silly, skittish, thoughtless, fickle, frivolous, light-headed, rattle-brained, rattle-headed, unstable, unsteady, volatile, unbalanced, wild, mercurial, *formal* capricious, *colloq.* bird-brained, hare-brained
☒ steady, responsible, sensible

flimsy *adj*
1 *flimsy clothing/structures* thin, fine, light, slight, insubstantial, ethereal, lightweight, fragile, delicate, filmy, sheer, shaky, rickety, ramshackle, jerry-built, makeshift **2** *flimsy excuse* weak, feeble, meagre, inadequate, shallow, superficial, trivial, poor, thin, trifling, unconvincing, implausible
☒ **1** sturdy, strong **2** convincing, plausible

flinch *v*
wince, start, cringe, cower, crouch, quail, tremble,

shake, quake, shudder, shiver, shrink, blench, recoil, draw back, pull back, balk, shy away, avoid, shirk, withdraw, retreat, flee, *colloq.* duck, dodge

fling *v, n*
▶ *v* throw, hurl, pitch, lob, toss, cast, sling, catapult, launch, propel, send, send flying, let fly, heave, jerk, *colloq.* chuck
▶ *n* **1** THROW, hurl, pitch, lob, toss, cast, shot, heave **2** SPREE, venture, indulgence, gamble, binge, whirl, go, trial, try, turn, attempt, *colloq.* crack

flip *v, n*
▶ *v* flick, spin, twirl, twist, turn, toss, throw, cast, pitch, jerk, flap, click, snap
▷ **flip through** flick through, browse through, thumb through, leaf through, glance at, glance over, skip, skim, scan
▶ *n* flick, spin, twirl, twist, turn, toss, jerk, flap, click, snap

flippancy *n*
facetiousness, light-heartedness, frivolity, superficiality, shallowness, thoughtlessness, disrespect, disrespectfulness, glibness, pertness, impertinence, irreverence, levity, *formal* persiflage, *colloq.* cheek, cheekiness, sauciness
F3 earnestness, seriousness

flippant *adj*
facetious, light-hearted, frivolous, superficial, shallow, thoughtless, offhand, glib, pert, impudent, impertinent, rude, disrespectful, irreverent, irresponsible, *formal* insouciant, *colloq.* saucy, cheeky
F3 serious, respectful

flirt *v, n*
▶ *v* chat up, make eyes at, ogle, eye up, make a pass at, make up to, lead on, philander, dally
▷ **flirt with** consider, entertain, toy with, play with, trifle with, dabble in, try
▶ *n* tease, vamp, trifler, heart-breaker, philanderer, wanton, hussy, coquet(te), gillet, *slang* chippy

flirtation *n*
affair, chatting up, dalliance, dallying, philandering, coquetry, intrigue, teasing, toying, trifling, sport, *formal* amour

flirtatious *adj*
provocative, coquettish, flirty, loose, promiscuous, teasing, sportive, amorous, wanton, *colloq.* comehither, come-on

flit *v*
dart, speed, dash, rush, flash, fly, wing, flutter, flitter, whisk, skim, slip, pass, bob, dance

float *v*
1 GLIDE, stay afloat, sail, swim, bob, be buoyant, slide, drift, waft, hover, wander, hang, suspend **2** LAUNCH, initiate, set up, establish, promote, get going, get off the ground, be in at the beginning of, get the show on the road **3** *float an idea with you* suggest, recommend, put forward, submit, present, propose
F3 1 sink

floating *adj*
1 AFLOAT, buoyant, unsinkable, sailing, swimming, bobbing, drifting, wafting, hovering **2** VARIABLE, fluctuating, movable, migratory, transitory, wandering, unsettled, unattached, free, uncommitted
F3 1 sinking, submerged **2** fixed, settled

flock *v, n*
▶ *v* herd, swarm, troop, converge, mass, bunch, cluster, huddle, mill, crowd, throng, group, assemble, come together, gather, collect, congregate
▶ *n* herd, pack, crowd, throng, drove, fold, host, multitude, mass, bunch, cluster, group, gathering, collection, assembly, congregation

flog *v*
1 BEAT, whip, lash, scourge, birch, cane, strap, flay, drub, thrash, belt, chastise, punish, horsewhip, *formal* flagellate, *colloq.* whack, wallop **2** SELL, deal in, handle, trade, peddle, hawk, offer for sale, put up for sale

flogging *n*
beating, whipping, lashing, scourging, birching, caning, flaying, strapping, belting, thrashing, hiding, horsewhipping, *formal* flagellation, *colloq.* whacking, walloping

flood *v, n*
▶ *v* **1** DELUGE, inundate, soak, drench, saturate, fill, overflow, surge, swell, brim over, immerse, submerge, engulf, swamp, overwhelm, drown, smother **2** FLOW, pour, stream, rush, surge, gush, saturate
▶ *n* **1** DELUGE, inundation, downpour, torrent, flash flood, flow, tide, stream, rush, spate, outpouring, overflow **2** EXCESS, torrent, abundance, glut, *formal* profusion, superfluity, plethora
F3 1 drought, trickle **2** trickle, dearth, lack

floor *n, v*
▶ *n* **1** FLOORING, ground, base, basis **2** *on the third floor* storey, level, stage, landing, deck, tier
▶ *v* **1** BAFFLE, defeat, overwhelm, beat, frustrate, confound, perplex, nonplus, dumbfound, puzzle, bewilder, disconcert, throw, *formal* discomfit, *colloq.* stump **2** KNOCK DOWN, strike down, fell, level, prostrate

flop *v, n*
▶ *v* **1** COLLAPSE, slump, tumble, droop, hang, dangle, sag, drop, fall, topple **2** FAIL, be unsuccessful, collapse, misfire, fall flat, founder, sink, *colloq.* fold, pack up, crash, go bust, go broke, go to the wall, go into the red, *US* bomb
▶ *n* failure, fiasco, debacle, disaster, *colloq.* washout, non-starter, shambles, slip-up, no-hoper, alsoran, has-been

floppy *adj*
droopy, hanging, dangling, sagging, limp, loose, baggy, soft, flabby
F3 firm

flora *n*
botany, plant life, plants, vegetable kingdom, vegetation, herbage, plantage

florid *adj*
1 FLOWERY, ornate, elaborate, fussy, overelaborate, extravagant, embellished, verbose, pompous, bombastic, baroque, rococo, flamboyant, *technical* melismatic, *formal* grandiloquent **2** *a florid complexion* ruddy, red, red-faced, reddish, blushing, flushed, purple, *formal* rubicund
F3 1 plain, simple **2** pale

flotsam *n*
jetsam, wreckage, floating wreckage, debris, rubbish, junk, oddments, odds and ends, *formal* detritus

flounce¹ *v*
bounce, spring, stamp, storm, toss, jerk, twist, throw, fling, bob

flounce² *n*
frill, fringe, ruffle, trimming, valance, falbala

flounder *v*
wallow, thresh about, flail about, struggle, grope, fumble, blunder, stagger, stumble, falter, dither, be confused, be in difficulties, go under, be out of your depth, not know which way to turn

flourish *v, n*
▶ *v* **1** THRIVE, grow, wax, increase, flower, blossom, bloom, bear fruit, be strong, develop, progress, get on, do well, prosper, succeed, boom, *formal* burgeon **2** BRANDISH, wave, shake, twirl, swing, swish, wag, display, wield, flaunt, show off, parade, exhibit, vaunt

1 decline, languish, fail
▶ *n* **1** DISPLAY, parade, show, gesture, wave, sweep, fanfare, ornament, decoration, panache, élan, *colloq.* pizzazz **2** *a flourish on the lettering* swirl, curlicue, serif, twist

flourishing *adj*
thriving, blooming, blossoming, prosperous, successful, booming

flout *v*
defy, disobey, break, disregard, spurn, treat with contempt, show contempt for, disdain, reject, scorn, jeer at, scoff at, sneer at, mock, laugh at, ridicule, *formal* violate
1 obey, respect, regard

flow *v, n*
▶ *v* **1** CIRCULATE, move, run, proceed, ooze, seep, trickle, ripple, bubble, well, spout, spew, spurt, squirt, gush, jet, leak, drip, spill, pour, cascade, rush, stream, teem, flood, overflow, surge, sweep, drift, slip, slide, babble, gurgle, glide, roll, swirl, whirl **2** ORIGINATE, derive, arise, spring, emerge, issue, result, stem, proceed, *formal* emanate
▶ *n* course, flux, tide, current, drift, outpouring, stream, deluge, cascade, spurt, gush, flood, spate, abundance, plenty, *formal* effusion, plethora

flower *n, v*
▶ *n* **1** BLOOM, blossom, bud, floret, floweret, *technical* efflorescence, florescence, inflorescence **2** BEST, cream, pick, finest, choice, select, elite, crème de la crème

---

Parts of a flower include:
anther, calyx, capitulum, carpel, corolla, corymb, dichasium, filament, gynoecium, monochasium, nectary, ovary, ovule, panicle, pedicel, petal, pistil, raceme, receptacle, sepal, spadix, spike, stalk, stamen, stigma, style, thalamus, torus, umbel.

Flowers include:
African violet, alyssum, anemone, aster, aubrietia, azalea, begonia, bluebell, busy lizzie (impatiens), calendula, candytuft, carnation, chrysanthemum, cornflower, cowslip, crocus, cyclamen, daffodil, dahlia, daisy, delphinium, forget-me-not, foxglove (digitalis), freesia, fuchsia, gardenia, geranium, gladioli, hollyhock, hyacinth, iris (flag), lily, lily-of-the-valley, lobelia, lupin, marigold, narcissus, nasturtium, nemesia, nicotiana, night-scented stock, orchid, pansy, petunia, pink (dianthus), phlox, poinsettia, polyanthus, poppy, primrose, primula, rose, salvia, snapdragon (antirrhinum), snowdrop, stock, sunflower, sweet pea, sweet william, tulip, verbena, viola, violet, wallflower, zinnia. *See also* BULB; PLANT; SHRUB; WILD FLOWER.

▶ *v* bud, bloom, blossom, open, sprout, come out, develop, grow, mature, prosper, thrive, flourish, succeed, *formal* burgeon

flowery *adj*
florid, ornate, elaborate, fancy, baroque, rhetorical, high-flown, verbose, pompous, bombastic, *technical* euphuistic, *formal* grandiloquent
1 plain, simple

flowing *adj*
1 *flowing rivers/traffic* moving, oozing, seeping, bubbling, welling, gushing, pouring, rushing, cascading, streaming, surging, sweeping, overflowing **2** FLUENT, effortless, easy, smooth, continuous, uninterrupted,

unbroken **3** *flowing hair* hanging, hanging loose, hanging freely, falling, rolling

fluctuate *v*
vary, change, alter, shift, rise and fall, seesaw, go up and down, ebb and flow, alternate, swing, sway, undulate, vacillate, waver, hesitate, *formal* oscillate, *colloq.* chop and change
1 be steady

fluctuation *n*
variation, change, shift, swing, alternation, variability, instability, unsteadiness, wavering, irresolution, inconstancy, ambivalence, fickleness, *formal* oscillation, capriciousness, vacillation

flue *n*
shaft, pipe, duct, vent, channel, passage, chimney

fluency *n*
ease, eloquence, smoothness, articulateness, assurance, command, control, facility, readiness, glibness, slickness, *formal* facundity, volubility
1 incoherence

fluent *adj*
flowing, smooth, easy, effortless, fluid, natural, graceful, elegant, articulate, eloquent, silver-tongued, slick, glib, ready, *formal* voluble, mellifluous
1 broken, inarticulate, tongue-tied

fluff *n, v*
▶ *n* down, nap, pile, fuzz, floss, lint, dust
▶ *v* botch, do badly, make a bad job of, mismanage, bungle, mess up, make a mess of, muck up, muddle, fumble, muff, spoil, *colloq.* blot your copybook, boob, put your foot in it, foul up, mess up, blow, *slang* screw up
1 bring off

fluffy *adj*
furry, fuzzy, downy, feathery, fleecy, woolly, hairy, shaggy, velvety, silky, soft

fluid *n, adj*
▶ *n* liquid, solution, liquor, juice, gas, vapour
▶ *adj* **1** LIQUID, liquefied, aqueous, watery, flowing, running, runny, melted, molten **2** *a fluid situation* variable, changeable, unstable, inconstant, shifting, mobile, adjustable, adaptable, flexible, open, unsettled, fluctuating, unsteady, unstable, *formal* protean **3** *fluid movements* flowing, smooth, effortless, easy, graceful, elegant, natural
1 solid **2** inflexible, fixed

fluke *n*
stroke, stroke of luck, lucky break, accident, quirk, blessing, windfall, break, chance, coincidence, *formal* fortuity, serendipity, *colloq.* freak

fluky *adj*
accidental, lucky, chance, fortunate, coincidental, uncertain, incalculable, *formal* fortuitous, serendipitous, *colloq.* freakish

flummox *v*
confuse, confound, baffle, bewilder, mystify, perplex, puzzle, nonplus, fox, stump, defeat, stymie, *colloq.* bamboozle

flummoxed *adj*
baffled, confounded, bewildered, confused, perplexed, puzzled, mystified, nonplussed, stumped, foxed, stymied, at a loss, at sea

flunkey *n*
lackey, assistant, menial, minion, slave, manservant, valet, underling, drudge, footman, hanger-on, cringer, toady, bootlicker, yes-man

flurry *n, v*
▶ *n* **1** BURST, outbreak, spell, shower, bout, spurt, gust, blast, squall **2** BUSTLE, hurry, hubbub, fluster, fuss, commotion, tumult, whirl, disturbance, agitation, excitement, stir, *formal* perturbation, *colloq.* to-do, flap

▶ *v* fluster, hurry, hustle, agitate, bewilder, bother, bustle, flutter, fuss, unsettle, upset, confuse, ruffle, disconcert, disturb, *formal* discountenance, perturb, *colloq.* hassle, rattle

flush¹ *v, n, adj*
▶ *v* **1** BLUSH, go/turn red, redden, crimson, colour, burn, glow, flame, *formal* suffuse **2** CLEANSE, wash, rinse, hose, swab, clear, empty, eject, evacuate, expel
▶ *n* bloom, freshness, vigour, glow, blush, colour, redness, rosiness, ruddiness
▶ *adj* **1** ABUNDANT, lavish, generous, full, overflowing, rich, wealthy, moneyed, prosperous, well-off, well-heeled, well-to-do **2** LEVEL, even, smooth, flat, plane, square, true

flush² *v*
flush the enemy out of the forest force out, drive out, run to earth, discover, uncover, expel, eject, start, rouse, disturb

flushed *adj*
1 RED, rosy, ruddy, blushing, burning, crimson, scarlet, aflame, ablaze, glowing, aglow, hot, embarrassed, *formal* rubicund **2** ELATED, thrilled, enthused, excited, exhilarated, exultant, animated, aroused, inspired, intoxicated, sanguine
🖬 **1** pale

fluster *v, n*
▶ *v* bother, upset, embarrass, disturb, agitate, ruffle, discompose, confuse, confound, unsettle, unnerve, make nervous, disconcert, put off, distract, *formal* perturb, *colloq.* rattle, faze
🖬 calm
▶ *n* flurry, bustle, commotion, disturbance, confusion, agitation, upset, turmoil, agitation, panic, embarrassment, *formal* perturbation, *colloq.* state, flap, dither, tizzy, tizz
🖬 calm

fluted *adj*
grooved, furrowed, channelled, corrugated, ribbed, ridged

flutter *v, n*
▶ *v* flap, wave, beat, bat, flicker, vibrate, palpitate, agitate, shake, tremble, quiver, shiver, ruffle, flitter, ripple, twitch, pulsate, toss, waver, fluctuate, dance, hover
▶ *n* **1** FLAPPING, wave, beat, flicker, vibration, palpitation, tremble, tremor, quiver, shiver, shudder, twitch, ripple, ruffle **2** BET, gamble, wager, speculation, risk

flux *n*
fluctuation, instability, unrest, change, alteration, modification, fluidity, flow, movement, motion, transition, development, mutation
🖬 stability, rest

fly¹ *v*
1 TAKE OFF, rise, ascend, mount, soar, glide, float, hover, flit, flutter, wing **2** *fly an aeroplane* control, operate, pilot, guide, manoeuvre, steer **3** *fly a flag* show, wave, display, exhibit, present, reveal **4** RACE, sprint, dash, tear, rush, go/pass quickly, slip by, hurry, speed, zoom, shoot, bolt, dart, career, jet, *formal* hasten
▷ **fly at** attack, go for, fall upon, hit, strike, lay into, charge, lash out at, let someone have it, let fly, *colloq.* bite someone's head off, jump down someone's throat

fly² *adj*
he's a fly fellow alert, artful, sharp, shrewd, astute, canny, careful, cunning, *formal* prudent, sagacious, *colloq.* nobody's fool, on the ball, smart

fly-by-night *adj*
cowboy, discreditable, disreputable, questionable, shady, unreliable, untrustworthy, undependable, irresponsible, dubious, ephemeral, short-lived, *colloq.*

here today gone tomorrow
🖬 reliable

flying *adj*
1 *flying insects* gliding, floating, hovering, flapping, fluttering, airborne, winged, winging, wind-borne, soaring, mobile **2** *a flying visit* BRIEF, hurried, fleeting, rapid, fast, hasty, rushed, speedy

foam *n, v*
▶ *n* froth, lather, suds, head, bubbles, fizz, spume, effervescence
▶ *v* froth, lather, bubble, effervesce, fizz, boil, seethe, spume

foamy *adj*
frothy, lathery, bubbly, foaming, spumy, sudsy, *formal* spumescent

fob *v*
▷ **fob off** foist, pass off, get rid of, dump, unload, inflict, impose, deceive, put off, *colloq.* palm off

focus *n, v*
▶ *n* focal point, target, centre, heart, core, nucleus, kernel, crux, hub, axis, linchpin, pivot, hinge
▷ **in focus** clear, sharp, distinct, well-defined
▷ **out of focus** blurred, ill-defined, indistinct, hazy, fuzzy, blurry, muzzy
▶ *v* concentrate, aim, direct, turn, fix, spotlight, pinpoint, home in, zoom in, converge, meet, join, centre, bring into focus, *colloq.* zero in

fodder *n*
feed, food, foodstuff, forage, nourishment, rations, silage, provender, lucerne, browsing, proviant, pabulum

foe *n*
enemy, adversary, antagonist, opponent, combatant, rival, ill-wisher
🖬 friend

foetus *n*
unborn child, embryo

fog *n, v*
▶ *n* **1** MIST, haze, mistiness, haziness, cloud, gloom, murkiness, smog, pea-souper **2** PERPLEXITY, puzzlement, confusion, bewilderment, bafflement, disorientation, daze, trance, stupor, vagueness, obscurity, blur, haze
▶ *v* mist, steam up, cloud, dull, dim, darken, obscure, blur, confuse, muddle, bewilder, baffle, perplex, *formal* obfuscate

foggy *adj*
misty, hazy, smoggy, cloudy, clouded, overcast, murky, dark, grey, shadowy, gloomy, dim, indistinct, vague, obscure, unclear
🖬 clear

foible *n*
quirk, weakness, weak point, idiosyncrasy, imperfection, eccentricity, oddity, failing, fault, defect, oddness, peculiarity, shortcoming, strangeness, habit

foil¹ *v*
foil someone's plans defeat, outwit, frustrate, thwart, prevent, baffle, counter, nullify, stop, check, baulk, obstruct, block, elude, hinder, hamper, *formal* circumvent, *colloq.* scuttle, scupper
🖬 abet

foil² *n*
a foil to her dark hair contrast, complement, balance, setting, background, relief, *formal* antithesis

foist *v*
force, impose, introduce, thrust, unload, pass off, get rid of, fob off, wish on, *colloq.* palm off

fold¹ *v, n*
▶ *v* **1** BEND, ply, double, overlap, tuck, pleat, crease, gather, turn under, turn down, crumple, crimp, crinkle

2 ENFOLD, embrace, hug, clasp, squeeze, envelop, wrap (up), enclose, entwine, intertwine **3** *the business folded* fail, shut down, close, collapse, crash, go out of business, *colloq.* flop, pack up, go to the wall, go bust
► *n* bend, turn, layer, ply, overlap, tuck, pleat, gather, crease, knife-edge, line, wrinkle, crinkle, pucker, furrow, corrugation

fold² *n*
1 ENCLOSURE, pen, pound, compound, paddock, stockade, court, yard, ring, kraal **2** CONGREGATION, church, assembly, flock, gathering, parishioners, fellowship

folder *n*
file, binder, folio, portfolio, envelope, holder, wallet, pocket

foliage *n*
leaves, greenery, leafage, vegetation, foliation, *technical* frondescence, foliature, vernation, *formal* verdure

folk *n, adj*
► *n* **1** PEOPLE, society, nation, public, population, race, tribe, clan, ethnic group **2** RELATIONS, family, parents, relatives, kin, kindred
► *adj* ethnic, national, traditional, popular, native, indigenous, tribal, ancestral

folklore *n*
fables, folktales, legends, myths, mythology, lore, stories, tales, customs, beliefs, tradition, superstitions

follow *v*
1 *night follows day* come after, succeed, come next, replace, supersede, supplant, take the place of, step into the shoes of **2** CHASE, pursue, go after, run after, hunt, track, trail, shadow, tail, stalk, dog, give chase, hound, catch, be at someone's heels **3** ACCOMPANY, go (along) with, escort, attend, trail, go behind, walk behind, tread behind, tag along **4** RESULT, ensue, develop, emanate, arise, issue, spring, flow, proceed **5** OBEY, adhere to, heed, mind, observe, note, accept, yield to, conform to, carry out, practise, *formal* comply with **6** GRASP, understand, comprehend, fathom, take in, appreciate, *colloq.* twig, latch onto **7** KEEP UP WITH, support, be interested in, be devoted to, be a fan of, be a supporter of, keep up to date with
1 precede **3** abandon, desert **5** disobey
▷ **follow through** continue, pursue, see through, finish, complete, conclude, fulfil, implement, bring to completion
▷ **follow up** investigate, check out, look into, research, continue, pursue, reinforce, consolidate

follower *n*
backer, supporter, admirer, enthusiast, fan, devotee, disciple, apostle, pupil, imitator, emulator, adherent, hanger-on, believer, convert, attendant, retainer, helper, companion, escort, *colloq.* sidekick, freak, buff

following *adj, n*
► *adj* subsequent, next, succeeding, successive, resulting, ensuing, consequent, later
previous
► *n* followers, suite, retinue, entourage, circle, fans, admirers, adherents, supporters, support, body of support, backing, backers, patrons, patronage, clientèle, audience, public, coterie

folly *n*
1 FOOLISHNESS, stupidity, senselessness, rashness, recklessness, irresponsibility, indiscretion, craziness, inanity, madness, lunacy, insanity, idiocy, imbecility, silliness, ludicrousness, ridiculousness, absurdity, nonsense, illogicality, *formal* imprudence, fatuousness **2** MONUMENT, tower, whim, belvedere, gazebo
1 wisdom, prudence, sanity

foment *v*
incite, instigate, excite, stir up, agitate, arouse, rouse,

encourage, kindle, promote, prompt, provoke, raise, activate, stimulate, spur, quicken, goad, whip up, work up, foster, brew
quell

fond *adj*
1 *fond of someone/something* liking, partial to, attached to, keen on, having a soft spot for, addicted to, *formal* enamoured of, *colloq.* hooked on **2** AFFECTIONATE, warm, tender, caring, loving, adoring, devoted, doting, indulgent, amorous **3** *fond expectations* foolish, naïve, deluded, credulous, absurd, impractical, over-optimistic, vain

fondle *v*
caress, stroke, pat, pet, hug, cuddle, *colloq.* touch up

fondness *n*
affection, devotion, kindness, tenderness, love, liking, fancy, attachment, enthusiasm, inclination, leaning, partiality, preference, weakness, soft spot, taste, susceptibility, *formal* penchant, predilection
aversion, hate

food *n*
1 FOODSTUFFS, comestibles, provisions, meals, stores, rations, refreshments, sustenance, nourishment, nutrition, nutriment, subsistence, feed, fodder, diet, fare, dish, speciality, delicacy, cooking, cuisine, menu, board, table, *formal* viands, victuals, *colloq.* eatables, eats, tuck, *slang* grub, nosh, chow, scoff **2** *food for thought* mental stimulation, something to be seriously considered, something to think about

Kinds of food include:
soup, broth, minestrone, bouillabaisse, borsch, cockaleekie, consommé, gazpacho, goulash, vichyssoise; chips, French fries, ratatouille, sauerkraut, bubble-and-squeak, nut cutlet, cauliflower cheese, chilladas, hummus, macaroni cheese; pasta, cannelloni, fettuccine, ravioli, spaghetti bolognese, tortellini, lasagne; fish and chips, fishcake, fish-finger, fisherman's pie, kedgeree, gefilte fish, kipper, pickled herring, scampi, calamari, prawn cocktail, caviar; meat, casserole, cassoulet, hotpot, shepherd's pie, cottage pie, chilli con carne, biriyani, chop suey, moussaka, paella, samosa, pizza, ragout, risotto, tandoori, vindaloo, Wiener schnitzel, smorgasbord, stroganoff, Scotch woodcock, Welsh rarebit, faggot, haggis, sausage, frankfurter, hot dog, fritter, hamburger, McDonald's®, Big Mac®, Wimpy®, bacon, egg, omelette, quiche, tofu, Quorn®, Yorkshire pudding, toad-in-the-hole; ice cream, charlotte russe, egg custard, fruit salad, fruit cocktail, gateau, millefeuilles, pavlova, profiterole, Sachertorte, soufflé, summer pudding, Bakewell tart, trifle, yogurt, sundae, syllabub, queen of puddings, Christmas pudding, tapioca, rice pudding, roly-poly pudding, spotted dick, zabaglione; doughnut, Chelsea bun, Eccles cake, éclair, flapjack, fruitcake, Danish pastry, Genoa cake, Battenburg cake, Madeira cake, lardy cake, hot-cross-bun, ginger nut, gingerbread, ginger snap, macaroon, digestive, digestive biscuit, oatcake, Garibaldi biscuit; bread, French bread, French toast, pumpernickel, cottage loaf, croissant; baguette, brioche, bagel, gravy, fondue, salad cream, mayonnaise, French dressing; sauces: tartare, Worcestershire, bechamel, white, barbecue, tomato ketchup, hollandaise, Tabasco®, apple, mint, cranberry, horseradish, pesto. *See also* CHEESE; FISH; FRUIT; MEAT; NUT; PASTA; PASTRY; SUGAR; SWEET; VEGETABLE.

fool *n, v*
▶ *n* blockhead, fat-head, dunce, dimwit, simpleton, halfwit, idiot, cretin, imbecile, ignoramus, moron, dupe, stooge, butt, laughing-stock, clown, comic, buffoon, jester, *colloq.* nincompoop, ass, chump, ninny, clot, dope, twit, nitwit, nit, sucker, mug, twerp, birdbrain, *slang* wally, jerk, dumbo, pillock, prat, dork, geek, plonker, git
▷ **play the fool** fool around, fool about, mess about, mess around, clown around, monkey around, *colloq.* act the fool
▶ *v* 1 DECEIVE, take in, delude, mislead, beguile, make a fool of, dupe, gull, hoodwink, put one over on, trick, hoax, cheat, swindle, bluff, tease, joke, jest, play tricks, pretend, feign, sham, *colloq.* con, diddle, string along, have on, kid, bamboozle, make believe 2 *fooling about* lark about, play about, monkey about, monkey around, *colloq.* horse around, mess about, mess around

foolery *n*
silliness, folly, fooling, nonsense, tomfoolery, antics, buffoonery, drollery, waggery, zanyism, capers, carry-on, clowning, farce, childishness, horseplay, larks, high jinks, mischief, practical jokes, pranks, monkey tricks, shenanigans

foolhardy *adj*
rash, reckless, ill-advised, irresponsible, incautious, impulsive, bold, daring, daredevil, *formal* imprudent, temerarious
☒ cautious, *formal* prudent

foolish *adj*
stupid, senseless, silly, absurd, ridiculous, ludicrous, nonsensical, unwise, ill-advised, ill-considered, short-sighted, half-baked, crazy, mad, insane, idiotic, moronic, hare-brained, half-witted, simple-minded, simple, ignorant, unintelligent, inept, inane, point-less, unreasonable, *formal* fatuous, risible, injudicious, *colloq.* daft, crack-brained, gormless, dumb, dotty, potty, batty, barmy, nutty, not in your right mind, out of your mind, with a screw missing, needing to have your head examined
☒ wise, *formal* prudent, judicious

foolishly *adv*
stupidly, senselessly, absurdly, ridiculously, unwisely, ill-advisedly, idiotically, incautiously, indiscreetly, mistakenly, ineptly, short-sightedly, *formal* fatuously, imprudently, injudiciously
☒ wisely

foolishness *n*
stupidity, silliness, senselessness, absurdity, irresponsibility, weakness, craziness, madness, lunacy, nonsense, rubbish, folly, foolery, inanity, ineptitude, indiscretion, *formal* imprudence, incaution, unreason, unwisdom, *colloq.* bunkum, claptrap, baloney, daftness, hogwash, rot, piffle, poppycock, bunk, bunkum, claptrap, bilge, cobblers, *slang* crap

> **Expressions used when talking about being or appearing foolish include:**
> a fool and his money are easily parted, a fool's errand, a fool to himself/herself, act/play the fool, act the (giddy) goat, be daft as a brush, don't be a fool!, don't be daft/silly!, fall on your face, fools rush in where angels fear to tread, have egg on your face, live in a fool's paradise, look a Charley, make a fool of yourself, More fool you!, The more fool you!, play somebody for a fool.

☒ wisdom, *formal* prudence

foolproof *adj*
idiot-proof, infallible, unfailing, safe, fail-safe, sure, certain, dependable, trustworthy, guaranteed, *colloq.* sure-fire
☒ unreliable

foot *n*
1 *an animal's feet* paw, hoof, pad, trotter, leg, toe, sole, heel, *technical* pes 2 *at the foot of the hill* bottom, end, far end, limit, extremity, border, foundation
☒ 2 head, top, summit

footing *n*
1 BASIS, base, foundation, ground, relations, relation-ship, terms, conditions, state, standing, status, grade, rank, position 2 FOOTHOLD, balance, support, position, grip

footling *adj*
paltry, trifling, minor, trivial, insignificant, petty, irrelevant, *colloq.* piffling

footnotes *n*
annotation, note, marginal note, gloss, commentary, marginalia, *formal* scholia

footprint *n*
footmark, track, trail, trace, step, tread, *formal* vestige

footstep *n*
footmark, track, step, tread, footfall, plod, tramp, trudge

footwear *n*

> **Types of footwear include:**
> shoe, court-shoe, brogue, casual, *colloq.* lace-up, *colloq.* slip-on, slingback, sandal, espadrille, stiletto heel, platform heel, moccasin, Doc Martens®, slipper, mule, pantofle, *colloq.* flip-flop, boot, walking-boot, climbing-boot, riding-boot, overshoe, football boot, wader, bootee, wellington boot, *colloq.* welly, galosh, gumboot, football boot, rugby boot, tennis shoe, plimsoll, pump, sneaker, trainer, ballet shoe, clog, sabot, snow-shoe, *slang* beetle-crushers, *slang* brothel-creepers.

forage *n, v*
▶ *n* fodder, pasturage, feed, food, foodstuffs, provender
▶ *v* rummage, search, seek, cast about, scour, scratch, hunt, scavenge, ransack, plunder, assault, ravage, loot, raid, invade

foray *n*
raid, offensive, attack, assault, ravage, sortie, sally, swoop, invasion, inroad, incursion, reconnaissance

forbear *v*
refrain, avoid, decline, hesitate, hold, hold back, keep from, stop, withhold, stay, restrain yourself, omit, pause, *formal* abstain, desist, cease, eschew

forbearance *n*
self-control, patience, moderation, endurance, leniency, mildness, restraint, temperance, tolerance, toleration, avoidance, clemency, long-suffering, resignation, refraining, sufferance, *formal* abstinence
☒ intolerance

forbearing *adj*
long-suffering, patient, moderate, lenient, self-controlled, restrained, tolerant, merciful, mild, easy, forgiving, indulgent, clement
☒ intolerant, merciless

forbid *v*
prohibit, disallow, not allow, not let, ban, veto, refuse, deny, outlaw, debar, blacklist, exclude, rule out, prevent, block, hinder, inhibit, *formal* proscribe, interdict, preclude

🖪 allow, permit, let, approve

forbidden *adj*
prohibited, banned, excluded, taboo, vetoed, debarred, illicit, outlawed, out of bounds, *formal* proscribed

forbidding *adj*
stern, formidable, awesome, severe, harsh, grim, unfriendly, daunting, off-putting, uninviting, menacing, threatening, ominous, sinister, foreboding, frightening
🖪 approachable, friendly, congenial

force *v, n*
▶ *v* **1** COMPEL, make, oblige, urge, coerce, constrain, press, pressure, pressurize, put pressure on, pressgang, bulldoze, bully, railroad, drive, propel, impel, push, thrust, impose, inflict, *formal* necessitate, *colloq.* lean on, put the screws on, twist someone's arm, breathe down someone's neck **2** PRISE, force open, crack, blast, wrench, wrest, extort, exact, wring, extract
▶ *n* **1** COMPULSION, impulse, necessity, influence, coercion, constraint, pressure, duress, enforcement, violence, aggression, *colloq.* arm-twisting, strongarm tactics, the screws, the third degree **2** POWER, might, strength, intensity, effort, energy, vigour, exertion, stamina, muscle, momentum, impetus, drive, dynamo, dynamism, vitality, passion, vehement, determination, stress, emphasis, influence, power, significance, persuasiveness, effectiveness **3** MEANING, sense, substance, significance, gist, essence, thrust **4** ARMY, troop, body, corps, regiment, squad, platoon, squadron, battalion, division, unit, detachment, patrol
🖪 **2** weakness
▷ **in force 1** IN OPERATION, functioning, valid, binding, working, effective, current, on the statute book, *formal* operative **2** IN STRENGTH, in crowds, in large/great numbers, in flocks, in droves

forced *adj*
1 UNNATURAL, stiff, wooden, stilted, laboured, strained, false, artificial, contrived, feigned, insincere, overdone, *formal* affected **2** COMPULSORY, obligatory, involuntary, enforced, compelled, *formal* mandatory
🖪 **1** spontaneous, natural, sincere

forceful *adj*
strong, mighty, powerful, potent, effective, compelling, convincing, impressive, persuasive, telling, valid, weighty, urgent, emphatic, vehement, forcible, dynamic, assertive, energetic, vigorous, *formal* cogent
🖪 weak, feeble

forcible *adj*
1 VIOLENT, aggressive, coercive, forced, by/using force **2** POWERFUL, strong, compelling, compulsory, effective, impressive, telling, weighty, cogent, energetic, forceful, vehement, mighty, potent
🖪 **1, 2** feeble, weak

forcibly *adv*
violently, by force, using force, against your will, compulsorily, obligatorily, under compulsion, under duress, vigorously, vehemently, emphatically, willy-nilly

ford *n*
causeway, crossing, drift

forebear *n*
ancestor, forefather, father, predecessor, forerunner, antecedent, *formal* progenitor, primogenitor
🖪 descendant

foreboding *n*
misgiving, anxiety, worry, apprehension, apprehensiveness, suspicion, dread, fear, omen, sign, token, premonition, warning, prediction, intuition, feeling,

sixth sense, *formal* presentiment, prognostication

forecast *v, n*
▶ *v* predict, prophesy, foretell, foresee, forewarn, anticipate, expect, tip off, estimate, calculate, *formal* conjecture, prognosticate, portend, divine, augur
▶ *n* prediction, prophecy, expectation, forewarning, outlook, projection, guess, tip, speculation, *formal* prognosis, conjecture, prognostication, augury, *colloq.* guesstimate

forefather *n*
ancestor, forebear, father, predecessor, forerunner, antecedent, *formal* progenitor, primogenitor
🖪 descendant

forefront *n*
front, front line, firing line, van, vanguard, spearhead, lead, fore, leading/foremost position, avant-garde
🖪 rear

forego *v*
give up, yield, surrender, sacrifice, forfeit, waive, abandon, resign, pass up, do without, go without, refrain from, *formal* relinquish, renounce, abstain from, eschew, abjure

foregoing *adj*
preceding, above, previous, earlier, former, prior, *formal* antecedent, precedent, aforementioned
🖪 following

foregone *adj*
foreseen, fixed, inevitable, anticipated, predictable, cut-and-dried, open-and-shut, *formal* predetermined, preordained
🖪 unpredictable

foreground *n*
fore, forefront, front, prominence, leading/foremost position, centre, limelight
🖪 background

forehead *n*
brow, temples, front, *technical* metope

foreign *adj*
alien, immigrant, imported, international, external, outside, overseas, exotic, ethnic, migrant, faraway, distant, remote, strange, unfamiliar, outlandish, peculiar, odd, unknown, uncharacteristic, unconnected, extraneous, borrowed, *formal* incongruous, inapposite
🖪 native, indigenous

foreigner *n*
alien, immigrant, incomer, stranger, outsider, newcomer, visitor
🖪 native

foreknowledge *n*
foresight, premonition, forewarning, clairvoyance, second sight, *technical* precognition, prescience, *formal* prevision, prognostication

foreman *n*
supervisor, superintendent, manager, leader, overseer, steward, ganger, overman, charge hand, *colloq.* boss, gaffer, *US* honcho

foremost *adj*
first, leading, most important, front, chief, main, principal, primary, first, top, cardinal, paramount, central, highest, advanced, uppermost, supreme, premier, pre-eminent

foreordained *adj*
fated, destined, appointed, preordained, prearranged, foredoomed, *formal* predestined, predetermined

forerunner *n*
precursor, predecessor, ancestor, antecedent, forefather, harbinger, herald, envoy, sign, token
🖪 successor, follower

foresee v
envisage, anticipate, expect, forecast, predict, prophesy, foretell, foreknow, forebode, *formal* prognosticate, divine

foreshadow v
predict, prophesy, signal, indicate, signify, mean, suggest, promise, *formal* bode, prefigure, presage, augur, portend

foresight n
anticipation, planning, forward planning, forethought, far-sightedness, vision, caution, discernment, discrimination, care, readiness, preparedness, provision, precaution, *formal* prudence, circumspection, perspicacity, judiciousness
🔁 improvidence

forest n
wood, woodland, woods, trees, greenwood, monte, plantation, urman

forestall v
pre-empt, anticipate, stop, avert, head off, ward off, stave off, parry, balk, frustrate, thwart, obstruct, hinder, prevent, impede, intercept, get ahead of, *formal* preclude, obviate

forestry n
forestation, woodcraft, woodmanship, forest management, *technical* afforestation, arboriculture, dendrology, silviculture

foretaste n
forewarning, foretoken, preview, trailer, sample, appetizer, specimen, example, whiff, indication, warning, premonition

foretell v
prophesy, forecast, predict, foresee, signify, foreshadow, indicate, forewarn, *formal* prognosticate, augur, presage, divine

forethought n
preparation, planning, forward planning, provision, precaution, anticipation, foresight, far-sightedness, caution, discernment, *formal* circumspection, prudence, perspicacity, judiciousness
🔁 improvidence, carelessness

forever adv
1 ETERNALLY, always, ever, evermore, for all time, permanently, till the end of time, *colloq.* till kingdom come, till the cows come home, for good, until hell freezes over **2** CONTINUALLY, constantly, always, persistently, incessantly, perpetually, endlessly, *formal* interminably, *colloq.* all the time

forewarn v
alert, advise, caution, tip off, give advance warning to, *formal* apprise, admonish, dissuade, previse

foreword n
preface, introduction, preliminary matter, prelims, frontmatter, prologue, *formal* prolegomenon
🔁 appendix, postscript, epilogue

forfeit v, n
▶ v lose, give up, hand over, surrender, sacrifice, forego, abandon, *formal* relinquish, renounce
▶ n penalty, loss, surrender, confiscation, fine, damages, relinquishment, *technical* sequestration, amercement

forfeiture n
giving up, surrender, confiscation, loss, relinquishment, sacrifice, foregoing, *technical* escheat, attainder, sequestration, *formal* déchéance

forge¹ v
1 MAKE, mould, cast, shape, form, fashion, found, beat out, hammer out, beat into shape, work, create, construct, invent, frame, devise, put together **2** *forge a document* fake, counterfeit, falsify, copy, imitate, simulate, feign

forge²
▷ **forge ahead** *building is forging ahead* progress, make progress, move steadily, advance, go/move forward, make headway, push forward

forger n
counterfeiter, contriver, faker, falsifier, framer, coiner, fabricator

forgery n
fake, counterfeit, copy, replica, reproduction, imitation, sham, fraud, faking, falsification, counterfeiting, *colloq.* dud, phoney
🔁 original

forget v
omit, fail, fail to remember, have no recollection of, neglect, let slip, overlook, disregard, ignore, lose sight of, dismiss, think no more of, unlearn, not place, slip your mind, put out of your mind, put behind you, put aside, *colloq.* go in one ear and out the other, have a memory like a sieve
🔁 remember, recall, recollect
▷ **forget yourself** misbehave, behave badly, be guilty of misconduct

forgetful adj
absent-minded, scatterbrained, preoccupied, distracted, abstracted, dreamy, inattentive, oblivious, negligent, neglectful, remiss, lax, careless, heedless, unheeding, *formal* pensive, *colloq.* with a memory like a sieve, not all there
🔁 attentive, mindful, heedful

forgetfulness n
absent-mindedness, inattention, obliviousness, oblivion, dreaminess, heedlessness, carelessness, wool-gathering, abstraction, amnesia, lapse, laxness, *formal* oblivisence
🔁 attentiveness, heedfulness

forgivable adj
excusable, pardonable, minor, petty, slight, trifling, innocent, venial
🔁 unforgivable

forgive v
pardon, absolve, excuse, acquit, remit, let off, let it go, clear, spare, overlook, condone, forgive and forget, let bygones be bygones, *formal* exonerate, exculpate, *colloq.* shake hands, shake on it, think no more of, bury the hatchet
🔁 punish, censure

forgiveness n
pardon, absolution, acquittal, remission, amnesty, mercy, clemency, leniency, *formal* exoneration
🔁 punishment, censure, blame

forgiving adj
merciful, clement, lenient, tolerant, forbearing, indulgent, kind, humane, compassionate, soft-hearted, mild, *formal* magnanimous
🔁 merciless, censorious, harsh

forgo see FOREGO.

forgotten adj
unremembered, unrecalled, blotted out, disregarded, ignored, neglected, obliterated, overlooked, omitted, out of mind, past recollection, past recall, gone, left behind, buried, bygone, past, lost, irrecoverable, irretrievable, unretrieved
🔁 remembered

fork v, n
▶ v split, divide, part, separate, diverge, branch (off), go separate ways, *formal* bifurcate, divaricate
▷ **fork out** pay (up), give, *colloq.* cough up, shell out, stump up
▶ n branching, divergence, separation, split, division,

junction, intersection, *formal* bifurcation, divarication, furcation

forked *adj*
branched, branching, divided, split, separated, Y-shaped, pronged, *formal* tined, bifurcate, divaricated, forficate, furcate, furcal, furcular

forlorn *adj*
deserted, abandoned, forsaken, forgotten, neglected, bereft, friendless, lonely, lost, homeless, uncared-for, destitute, desolate, desperate, despairing, hopeless, cheerless, unhappy, miserable, sad, wretched, helpless, pathetic, pitiable, *formal* disconsolate
🖬 cheerful

form *n, v*
▶ *n* **1** APPEARANCE, shape, mould, cast, cut, guise, outline, silhouette, figure, build, construction, frame, framework, structure, format, formation, model, pattern, design, arrangement, planning, order, organization, system, *formal* configuration, disposition, manifestation **2** *a form of punishment* type, kind, sort, order, species, genus, variety, genre, style, manner, nature, character, description **3** CLASS, year, grade, stream **4** *on top form* health, fitness, shape, trim, fettle, condition, spirits **5** ETIQUETTE, protocol, custom, convention, ritual, behaviour, polite behaviour, manners, *colloq.* the done thing **6** QUESTIONNAIRE, document, application (form), paper, sheet
▶ *v* **1** SHAPE, mould, model, fashion, forge, make, manufacture, produce, create, found, establish, build, construct, assemble, put together, set up, devise, arrange, organize, order, line up, develop, acquire **2** COMPRISE, constitute, make (up), compose, serve as, be a part of **3** APPEAR, take shape, materialize, crystallize, come into existence, show up, grow, develop, become visible

formal *adj*
1 OFFICIAL, ceremonial, ritual, stately, solemn, conventional, customary, traditional, established, orthodox, correct, prescribed, approved, proper, fixed, set, standard, regular, ordered, organized, methodical **2** PRIM, starchy, stiff, strait-laced, strict, rigid, inflexible, unbending, precise, exact, punctilious, ceremonious, stilted, remote, reserved, aloof **3** *a formal garden* symmetrical, ordered, controlled, regular, conventional
🖬 **2** informal, casual

formality *n*
custom, convention, ceremony, ceremoniousness, ritual, procedure, rule, custom, form, matter of form, bureaucracy, red tape, protocol, etiquette, form, correctness, politeness, *formal* decorum, propriety, punctilio
🖬 informality

format *n*
appearance, form, order, presentation, design, layout, pattern, plan, shape, structure, style, arrangement, make-up, look, type, construction, dimensions, *formal* configuration

formation *n*
1 STRUCTURE, construction, composition, constitution, format, order, organization, arrangement, layout, make-up, grouping, pattern, design, figure, *formal* configuration, disposition, phalanx **2** CREATION, generation, production, construction, building, making, shaping, manufacture, appearance, development, starting, founding, institution, establishment, inauguration

formative *adj*
determining, controlling, influential, dominant, shaping, growing, guiding, moulding, developmental, impressionable, teachable, malleable, mouldable,

pliant, susceptible, sensitive, *formal* determinative
🖬 destructive

former *adj*
past, ex-, one-time, sometime, late, departed, old, old-time, ancient, bygone, historical, earlier, prior, previous, preceding, long ago, long-gone, first, first-mentioned, antecedent, foregoing, above, *formal* erstwhile, quondam, of yore
🖬 current, present, future, following

formerly *adv*
once, in the past, previously, historically, earlier, at an earlier time, before, at one time, once, *formal* heretofore, hitherto, erst, erstwhile
🖬 currently, now, later

formidable *adj*
daunting, redoubtable, challenging, intimidating, threatening, menacing, frightening, terrifying, horrifying, alarming, terrific, frightful, horrific, fearful, great, huge, colossal, mammoth, tremendous, impressive, powerful, awesome, dreadful, overwhelming, staggering, *formal* prodigious, *colloq.* scary, mind-blowing, spooky

formless *adj*
amorphous, shapeless, confused, chaotic, disorganized, indefinite, indeterminate, incoherent, nebulous, vague, unshaped, unformed, *formal* inchoate, indigest
🖬 definite, orderly

formula *n*
recipe, prescription, proposal, blueprint, code, fixed/set expression, wording, rubric, rule, principle, form, precept, procedure, technique, convention, method, way

formulate *v*
devise, create, compose, prepare, conceive, think up, invent, originate, found, form, give form to, work out, plan, design, map out, draw up, frame, define, express, articulate, state, set down, put down, specify, detail, itemize, develop, evolve

fornication *n*
sexual intercourse, sex, sexual relations, making love, love-making, going to bed/sleeping with someone, *formal* coitus, copulation

forsake *v*
desert, abandon, throw over, discard, jettison, cast off, reject, repudiate, set aside, disown, leave, give up, surrender, *formal* relinquish, renounce, forego, *colloq.* jilt, quit, ditch, leave in the lurch, have done with, turn your back on

forsaken *adj*
abandoned, deserted, neglected, God-forsaken, remote, isolated, desolate, forlorn, lonely, marooned, solitary, derelict, dreary, destitute, cast off, discarded, disowned, rejected, shunned, outcast, ignored, friendless, *colloq.* jilted, left in the lurch

forswear *v*
abandon, give up, repudiate, drop, disown, disclaim, reject, deny, do without, renege, lie, perjure yourself, *formal* forsake, forego, renounce, recant, disavow, abjure, retract, *colloq.* cut out, pack in, jack in
🖬 revert to

fort *n*
fortress, castle, tower, watchtower, citadel, keep, stronghold, fortification, turret, battlements, parapet, garrison, station, camp, donjon, redoubt

forte *n*
strong point, strength, skill, speciality, gift, talent, aptitude, bent, métier
🖬 weak point, inadequacy

forth *adv*
out, away, off, outside, onwards, forwards, into

existence, into view

forthcoming *adj*
1 *their forthcoming wedding* impending, imminent, approaching, coming, future, prospective, projected, expected **2** AVAILABLE, accessible, obtainable, ready, at your disposal, *colloq.* on tap, up for grabs, yours for the asking/taking **3** COMMUNICATIVE, talkative, chatty, conversational, sociable, informative, expansive, open, frank, direct, *formal* loquacious, voluble
F3 3 reticent, reserved

forthright *adj*
direct, straightforward, blunt, frank, candid, plain, plain-spoken, open, honest, bold, outspoken
F3 devious, secretive

forthwith *adv*
immediately, at once, directly, instantly, straightaway, right away, without delay, quickly, *colloq.* pronto

fortification *n*
defence, strengthening, reinforcement, protection, castle, citadel, fort, fortress, keep, stronghold, earthwork, rampart, bulwark, bastion, battlements, parapet, barricade, palisade, buttressing, embattlement, entrenchment, munition, outwork, redoubt, stockade

fortify *v*
1 STRENGTHEN, reinforce, brace, shore up, buttress, garrison, defend, guard, protect, secure, cover, embattle **2** INVIGORATE, sustain, support, boost, revive, energize, brace, encourage, hearten, cheer, reassure, strengthen, buoy up
F3 1 weaken

fortitude *n*
courage, bravery, valour, pluck, nerve, resolution, determination, tenacity, perseverance, patience, firmness, strength of mind, backbone, mettle, willpower, hardihood, endurance, stoicism, *formal* forbearance, *colloq.* grit, spine
F3 cowardice, fear

fortress *n*
stronghold, castle, citadel, fortification, fastness, tower, keep, garrison, battlements

fortuitous *adj*
accidental, chance, random, arbitrary, casual, haphazard, incidental, unforeseen, unexpected, unplanned, unintentional, lucky, fortunate, providential, *colloq.* fluky
F3 intentional, planned, anticipated

fortunate *adj*
lucky, providential, happy, prosperous, flourishing, successful, well-off, timely, well-timed, opportune, convenient, advantageous, favourable, encouraging, promising, profitable, blessed, favoured, *formal* felicitous, propitious, auspicious, providential
F3 unlucky, unfortunate, unhappy

fortunately *adv*
luckily, happily, conveniently, encouragingly, *formal* providentially
F3 unfortunately

fortune *n*
1 WEALTH, riches, treasure, income, means, substance, assets, estate, property, possessions, affluence, prosperity, success, *formal* opulence, *colloq.* mint, pile, packet, bundle, bomb, *slang* megabucks, big bucks **2** LUCK, chance, coincidence, accident, providence, fate, destiny, doom, lot, portion, cup, life, history, future, *formal* serendipity **3** *the fortunes of the company* experience, circumstances, position, condition, situation, state of affairs

fortune-teller *n*
prophet, prophetess, visionary, soothsayer, seer, au-

gur, diviner, oracle, sibyl, psychic, telepath

forum *n*
meeting, meeting-place, arena, rostrum, stage, assembly, conference, discussion, debate, symposium

forward *adj, adv, v*
▶ *adj* **1** FIRST, head, front, fore, foremost, leading, advance, onward, advancing, progressing, progressive, prospective, future, forward-looking, enterprising, *formal* frontal, *colloq.* go-ahead **2** CONFIDENT, over-confident, assertive, over-assertive, bold, audacious, brazen, brash, barefaced, impudent, impertinent, familiar, overfamiliar, presumptuous, presuming, aggressive, thrusting, *colloq.* cheeky, fresh, cocky, pushy **3** EARLY, advance, precocious, premature, advanced, well-advanced, well-developed
F3 1 backward, retrograde **2** shy, modest **3** late, retarded
▶ *adv* forwards, ahead, on, onward, onwards, out, forth, into view, into the open
▶ *v* advance, promote, further, foster, encourage, support, back, favour, help, assist, aid, facilitate, accelerate, speed (up), step up, hurry, hasten, dispatch, send (on), pass on, post, mail, transport, deliver, ship, *formal* expedite
F3 impede, obstruct, hinder, slow

forward-looking *adj*
far-sighted, enterprising, progressive, reforming, modern, innovative, dynamic, enlightened, avant-garde, liberal, *colloq.* go-getting, goey, go-ahead
F3 conservative, retrograde

forwardness *n*
confidence, over-confidence, boldness, audacity, brashness, brazenness, pertness, presumption, presumptuousness, impertinence, impudence, aggressiveness, *colloq.* cheek, cheekiness, pushiness
F3 reserve, retiring

forwards *adv*
forward, ahead, on, onwards, out, forth

fossil *n*
remains, remnant, petrified remains/impression, ammonite, relic, reliquiae, *technical* graptolite, coprolite, trilobite

fossilized *adj*
1 HARDENED, petrified, ossified, stony **2** OUT OF DATE, archaic, obsolete, old-fashioned, *passé*, outmoded, prehistoric, antediluvian, anachronistic, antiquated, extinct, dead
F3 2 up-to-date

foster *v*
raise, rear, bring up, nurse, care for, take care of, look after, nourish, feed, sustain, help, assist, aid, back, support, uphold, promote, advance, encourage, stimulate, further, boost, cultivate, nurture, hold, cherish, entertain, harbour
F3 neglect, discourage

foul *adj, v*
▶ *adj* **1** DISGUSTING, offensive, repulsive, revolting, dirty, soiled, filthy, unclean, tainted, infected, impure, defiled, polluted, contaminated, rank, fetid, stinking, smelly, foul-smelling, putrid, decayed, rotting, rotten, sickening, nauseating, abominable, loathsome, odious, squalid, *formal* fetid, putrescent, putrefactive **2** *foul language* obscene, lewd, smutty, dirty, filthy, indecent, coarse, off-colour, ribald, lewd, indelicate, vulgar, gross, low, blasphemous, profane, offensive, abusive, *colloq.* blue **3** NASTY, disagreeable, wicked, vicious, vile, base, mean, low, loathsome, despicable, offensive, revolting, repulsive, disgusting, abhorrent, detestable, horrible, disgraceful, shameful, contemptible, *formal* iniquitous, heinous, execrable, nefarious **4** *foul weather* bad, nasty, unpleasant, disagreeable,

rainy, wet, stormy, squally, blustery, rough, dirty, wild
Fa 1 clean **2** clean **4** fine
▷ **foul play** criminal violence, crime, unfair/dishonest behaviour, breach of the rules, deception, dirty work, double-dealing, *colloq.* funny business, sharp practice
Fa fair play, justice
▶ *v* **1** DIRTY, soil, stain, sully, muddy, blacken, defile, taint, pollute, contaminate **2** ENTANGLE, catch, snarl, twist, ensnare, tangle **3** BLOCK, obstruct, clog, choke, jam, foul up
Fa 1 clean **2** disentangle **3** clear

foul-mouthed *adj*
coarse, obscene, offensive, profane, abusive, blasphemous, *formal* foul-spoken

found *v*
1 START, originate, create, bring into being, organize, initiate, institute, inaugurate, set up, constitute, develop, establish, endow **2** BASE, ground, bottom, root, rest, set, ground, settle, fix, plant, locate, position, raise, build, erect, construct

foundation *n*
1 BASE, foot, bottom, ground, bedrock, substance, basis, footing, underpinning, understructure, substructure, substratum **2** BASIS, support, base, groundwork, bedrock, key, keynote, reason(s), rationale, fundamental(s), fundamental point, starting-point, premise, principle, first principles, main ingredient, alpha and omega, essential(s), essence, heart, core, thrust, *formal* quintessence, hypostasis **3** SETTING-UP, establishment, founding, institution, inauguration, initiation, creation, constitution, endowment, organization, groundwork

founder¹ *n*
the founder of the university originator, initiator, father, mother, benefactor, creator, author, architect, designer, inventor, prime mover, maker, builder, constructor, organizer, institutor, establisher, developer, discoverer

founder² *v*
the ship/plan foundered sink, go down, go to the bottom, submerge, capsize, subside, collapse, break down, fall, come to grief, fail, misfire, miscarry, abort, fall through, come to nothing, go wrong
Fa succeed

foundling *n*
stray, orphan, waif, outcast, urchin, enfant trouvé

fountain *n*
1 SPRAY, jet, spout, spring, spurt, fount, well, wellspring, source, reservoir, waterworks **2** SOURCE, origin, fount, rise, well, cause, birth, beginning, mainspring, fountainhead, wellhead, *formal* commencement, inception

four-square *adv*
firmly, squarely, resolutely, solidly, frankly, honestly

fowl *n*
bird, duck, chicken, cock, hen, bantam, goose, turkey, pheasant, wildfowl, poultry

foxy *adj*
crafty, canny, devious, cunning, artful, astute, sharp, shrewd, sly, tricky, wily, fly, knowing, guileful
Fa naïve, open

foyer *n*
entrance hall, hall, reception, lobby, vestibule, antechamber, anteroom

fracas *n*
brawl, disturbance, fight, free-for-all, quarrel, riot, trouble, uproar, row, rumpus, scuffle, barney, affray, ruckus, ruction, rout, ruffle, shindy, melee, *formal* Donnybrook, *colloq.* aggro

fraction *n*
proportion, amount, ratio, subdivision, part, bit

fractious *adj*
awkward, quarrelsome, cross, irritable, touchy, bad-tempered, petulant, testy, unruly, captious, fretful, peevish, *formal* choleric, querulous, recalcitrant, refractory, *colloq.* crabby, crotchety, grouchy, grumpy
Fa complaisant, placid

fracture *n, v*
▶ *n* break, breakage, crack, fissure, cleft, rupture, split, splitting, rift, rent, schism, breach, gap, opening, aperture, slit
▶ *v* break, crack, rupture, split, splinter, chip
Fa join

fragile *adj*
1 BRITTLE, breakable, frail, delicate, flimsy, dainty, fine, slight, insubstantial, unstable, *formal* frangible **2** *feel fragile after an illness* weak, feeble, infirm
Fa 1 robust, tough, durable, sturdy **2** strong

fragility *n*
brittleness, breakableness, delicacy, frailty, weakness, feebleness, infirmity, *formal* frangibility
Fa durability, robustness, strength

fragment *n, v*
▶ *n* piece, bit, part, portion, fraction, particle, crumb, morsel, scrap, remainder, remains, remnant, shred, snip, snippet, chip, splinter, shiver, sliver, chink, shard
▶ *v* break, shatter, splinter, shiver, crumble, disintegrate, come to pieces, come apart, break up, divide, split (up), disunite, smash to pieces/smithereens
Fa hold together, join

fragmentary *adj*
bitty, piecemeal, scrappy, broken, disjointed, disconnected, separate, scattered, sketchy, partial, incomplete, uneven, discontinuous, incoherent
Fa whole, complete

fragrance *n*
perfume, scent, smell, sweet smell, odour, aroma, bouquet, balm, attar, otto, *formal* redolence

fragrant *adj*
perfumed, scented, sweet-smelling, sweet, balmy, aromatic, odorous, *formal* redolent, odoriferous
Fa unscented

frail *adj*
delicate, brittle, breakable, easily broken, fragile, flimsy, insubstantial, slight, puny, weak, feeble, infirm, unwell, unsound, vulnerable, susceptible, *formal* frangible
Fa robust, tough, strong

frailty *n*
weakness, weak point, foible, failing, deficiency, shortcoming, fault, defect, flaw, blemish, imperfection, infirmity, fallibility, susceptibility, vulnerability, brittleness, fragility, delicacy
Fa strength, robustness, toughness

frame *n, v*
▶ *n* **1** STRUCTURE, fabric, framework, skeleton, carcase, shell, casing, chassis, substructure, foundation, construction, support, bodywork, body, build, form, physique, figure, size, shape **2** MOUNT, mounting, setting, surround, border, edge
▷ **frame of mind** state (of mind), mood, condition, humour, temper, disposition, spirit, outlook, attitude
▶ *v* **1** COMPOSE, formulate, conceive, establish, create, devise, contrive, concoct, plan, map out, plot, sketch, draw up, draft, shape, form, model, fashion, mould, forge, assemble, put together, build, set up, erect, construct, fabricate, make, manufacture, *colloq.* cook up **2** SURROUND, enclose, box in, case, encase, mount **3** *I've been framed* trap, incriminate, plant, *colloq.* set up, fit up, pin on, cook up a charge

frame-up *n*
fabrication, trap, *colloq.* fit-up, fix, put-up job, trumped-up charge

framework *n*
structure, fabric, bare bones, skeleton, shell, frame, casing, outline, plan, foundation, groundwork, substructure, trestle, trestlework, lattice, rack, scheme, constraints, parameters

franchise *n*
concession, licence, charter, warrant, authorization, permission, privilege, right, prerogative, liberty, freedom, immunity, exemption, *formal* consent, suffrage, enfranchisement

frank *adj, v*
▸ *adj* honest, truthful, sincere, genuine, candid, blunt, open, free, plain, plain-spoken, direct, forthright, straight, straightforward, downright, outspoken, explicit, bluff, *colloq.* straight from the shoulder, up-front
⊟ insincere, evasive
▸ *v* stamp, mark, postmark, cancel

frankly *adv*
to be frank, to be honest, to be blunt, in truth, honestly, candidly, bluntly, truthfully, openly, freely, plainly, directly, straight, explicitly
⊟ insincerely, evasively

frankness *n*
bluntness, candour, forthrightness, plain speaking, openness, directness, sincerity, outspokenness, truthfulness, *formal* ingenuousness
⊟ reserve

frantic *adj*
agitated, overwrought, fraught, desperate, beside yourself, furious, raging, mad, wild, raving, frenzied, berserk, frenetic, distressed, distracted, distraught, out of control, panic-stricken, hectic, *colloq.* at your wits' end
⊟ calm, composed

fraternity *n*
comradeship, brotherhood, kinship, camaraderie, companionship, set, society, association, circle, club, company, guild, order, league, union, fellowship, clan

fraternize *v*
mix, mingle, socialize, associate, keep company, go around, affiliate, unite, sympathize, *formal* consort, *colloq.* hang about, hobnob, pal up with, gang up with, rub shoulders
⊟ shun, ignore

fraud *n*
1 DECEIT, deception, guile, fraudulence, cheating, swindling, double-dealing, sharp practice, embezzlement, fake, counterfeit, forgery, sham, hoax, trick, trickery, racket, *formal* duplicity, chicanery, *colloq.* con, rip-off, riddle, scam, fix, diddle, swiz **2** CHARLATAN, impostor, pretender, sham, fake, bluffer, hoaxer, cheat, swindler, embezzler, double-dealer, trickster, quack, mountebank, *colloq.* phoney, con man

fraudulent *adj*
dishonest, criminal, deceitful, deceptive, false, bogus, sham, counterfeit, swindling, cheating, double-dealing, unscrupulous, exploitative, shameless, *formal* duplicitous, *colloq.* crooked, shady, phoney
⊟ honest, genuine

fraught *adj*
1 FULL, filled, charged, abounding, accompanied, attended, bristling, *formal* laden, replete **2** ANXIOUS, tense, agitated, worried, under stress, distressed, distraught, overwrought, *colloq.* uptight, stressed out
⊟ calm, untroublesome

fray *v, n*
▸ *v* **1** *the rope is fraying* become ragged, become threadbare, wear, unravel, wear thin **2** *tempers were fraying* irritate, vex, strain, stress, tax, overtax, make tense, make nervous, push too far, put on edge
▸ *n* brawl, scuffle, free-for-all, set-to, clash, conflict, fight, combat, battle, quarrel, row, rumpus, disturbance, riot, excitement, challenge, *colloq.* dust-up

frayed *adj*
ragged, tattered, worn, threadbare, unravelled, thin, worn thin

freak *n, adj*
▸ *n* **1** MONSTER, mutant, mutation, freak of nature, monstrosity, deformity, irregularity, *formal* malformation **2** ANOMALY, abnormality, aberration, oddity, curiosity, quirk, whim, vagary, twist, turn, *formal* caprice, *colloq.* oddball, weirdo **3** ENTHUSIAST, fanatic, addict, devotee, fan, aficionado, *colloq.* buff, fiend, nut
▸ *adj* abnormal, atypical, unusual, exceptional, odd, queer, bizarre, erratic, unpredictable, unexpected, surprise, chance, *formal* aberrant, capricious, fortuitous, *colloq.* fluky
⊟ normal, common

freakish *adj*
unusual, odd, abnormal, strange, unconventional, unpredictable, weird, outlandish, freaky, whimsical, fanciful, fantastic, grotesque, monstrous, malformed, arbitrary, fitful, changeable, erratic, *formal* aberrant, capricious
⊟ ordinary, normal

free *adj, v, adv*
▸ *adj* **1** *free tickets* gratis, without charge, free of charge, for nothing, at no cost, at no extra cost, complimentary, *colloq.* on the house, *slang* buckshee **2** *free to move* AT LIBERTY, at large, loose, on the loose, unattached, unrestrained, unconfined, out, *colloq.* free as a bird **3** *a free country* LIBERATED, emancipated, sovereign, independent, democratic, self-governing, self-ruling, autonomous **4** *free of dirt* lacking, without, unaffected by, immune to, exempt from, safe from, clear of, *formal* devoid of **5** *free time; a free seat* spare, available, idle, unemployed, unoccupied, with time on your hands, untaken, vacant, empty **6** CLEAR, unobstructed, unimpeded, open, unblocked, unhampered **7** GENEROUS, liberal, open-handed, lavish, charitable, giving, hospitable, unstinting, *formal* munificent **8** *with his free hand* unattached, unfastened, loose, unsecured **9** *a free translation* loose, rough, general, broad, vague, inexact, imprecise **10** *his free manner; free movement* easy, relaxed, easy-going, smooth, natural, uninhibited, casual, spontaneous, fluid, *colloq.* doing your own thing, doing as you please
⊟ **2** imprisoned, bound, tied, fettered, confined, restricted **4** liable to, affected by **5** busy, occupied, at work, reserved, engaged, *colloq.* tied up **6** blocked, obstructed **7** mean, stingy **8** attached **9** literal, rigorous, exact, precise **10** inhibited, formal, tense
▷ **free and easy** casual, informal, easy-going, relaxed, happy-go-lucky, carefree, spontaneous, tolerant, *colloq.* laid-back
⊟ inhibited, formal
▷ **free hand** authority, freedom, latitude, liberty, carte blanche, permission, power, scope, discretion
▸ *v* *free a prisoner; free someone trapped; free someone from debt* release, let go, let out, loose, turn loose, set loose, set free, untie, unbind, unchain, unleash, liberate, emancipate, rescue, deliver, save, ransom, disentangle, disengage, extricate, clear, make available, rid, relieve, unburden, exempt, excuse, except, absolve, acquit

▣ imprison, confine

▸ *adv* **1** FOR NOTHING, for free, without charge, gratis, freely, for love **2** GENEROUSLY, liberally, lavishly, extravagantly, abundantly, copiously
▣ **2** meanly

free will *n*
freedom, liberty, independence, self-determination, self-sufficiency, spontaneity, *technical* autarky, *formal* volition, autonomy

freedom *n*
1 LIBERTY, emancipation, deliverance, release, exemption, immunity, impunity **2** INDEPENDENCE, autonomy, self-government, sovereignty, democracy, emancipation, home rule **3** RANGE, scope, play, leeway, margin, latitude, licence, privilege, right, power, prerogative, free rein, free hand, opportunity, informality, flexibility
▣ **1** captivity, confinement **3** restriction

freely *adv*
1 READILY, willingly, voluntarily, of your own volition, of your own free will, spontaneously, easily **2** *give freely* generously, liberally, lavishly, extravagantly, amply, abundantly **3** *speak freely* frankly, candidly, bluntly, unreservedly, openly, plainly
▣ **2** grudgingly **3** evasively, cautiously

freethinker *n*
rationalist, sceptic, agnostic, doubter, deist, unbeliever, infidel

freeze *v, n*
▸ *v* **1** ICE OVER, ice up, congeal, solidify, set, harden, stiffen, *technical* glaciate **2** DEEP-FREEZE, ice, refrigerate, chill, cool **3** GET COLD, shiver, quiver, catch a chill, turn blue with cold, your teeth be chattering **4** STOP, suspend, fix, immobilize, halt, stand still, stop dead in your tracks, hold **5** FIX, hold, suspend, peg
▸ *n* **1** FROST, freeze-up **2** STOPPAGE, halt, standstill, shutdown, suspension, interruption, postponement, stay, embargo, moratorium

freezing *adj*
icy, frosty, glacial, arctic, polar, Siberian, wintry, raw, bitter, bitterly cold, biting, cutting, piercing, penetrating, numbing, stinging, numb, cold, chilly
▣ hot, warm

freight *n*
cargo, load, lading, payload, contents, goods, merchandise, consignment, shipment, transportation, conveyance, carriage, haulage, freightage, portage

frenetic *adj*
frantic, wild, frenzied, hectic, overwrought, demented, distraught, excited, unbalanced, mad, insane, berserk, hysterical, maniacal, obsessive, hyperactive
▣ calm, placid

frenzied *adj*
frantic, frenetic, hectic, feverish, desperate, furious, overwrought, distraught, distracted, crazed, wild, uncontrolled, mad, berserk, amok, raving, demented, hysterical, panic-stricken, out of control, uncontrolled, beside yourself, obsessive, at your wits' end
▣ calm, composed

frenzy *n*
1 TURMOIL, agitation, wildness, distraction, madness, lunacy, insanity, mania, hysteria, delirium, fever **2** BURST, fit, bout, spasm, paroxysm, convulsion, seizure, outburst, transport, passion, rage, fury
▣ **1** calm, composure

frequency *n*
frequentness, incidence, prevalence, recurrence, repetition, commonness, oftenness, constancy, *formal* periodicity
▣ infrequency

frequent *adj, v*
▸ *adj* common, commonplace, happening often, normal, everyday, familiar, usual, customary, habitual, prevailing, prevalent, predominant, numerous, countless, incessant, constant, continual, persistent, repeated, recurring, regular
▣ infrequent
▸ *v* visit, go to frequently, go to regularly, patronize, attend, haunt, associate with, *colloq.* hang out at, hang about with, hang out with

frequenter *n*
regular, regular visitor, customer, client, patron, haunter, habitué

frequently *adv*
often, commonly, many times, much, many a time, over and over, repeatedly, persistently, continually, habitually, customarily, oftentimes, *colloq.* nine times out of ten, more times than you've had hot dinners
▣ infrequently, seldom

fresh *adj*
1 ADDITIONAL, supplementary, extra, more, further, other **2** NEW, novel, innovative, original, different, brand-new, unconventional, revolutionary, modern, up-to-date, recent, latest, exciting, unusual, *colloq.* new-fangled **3** REFRESHING, bracing, invigorating, brisk, crisp, keen, cool, chilly, fair, bright, clean, clear, pure, unfaded, unpolluted **4** *fresh fruit* RAW, natural, unprocessed, crude, unpreserved, uncured, undried **5** REFRESHED, revived, restored, renewed, rested, invigorated, stimulated, energetic, vigorous, lively, vibrant, alert, vital, bouncing, *colloq.* raring to go, ready for more, yourself again, a new person, fresh as a daisy **6** *a fresh complexion* HEALTHY, glowing, bright, clear, blooming, fair, pink, rosy **7** PERT, disrespectful, impudent, insolent, bold, brazen, forward, familiar, overfamiliar, presumptuous, *colloq.* saucy, cheeky, cocky
▣ **2** old, hackneyed **3** stale **4** preserved, tinned, processed **5** tired

freshen *v*
1 AIR, ventilate, purify, clean, clear, deodorize **2** REFRESH, restore, revitalize, revive, reinvigorate, liven (up), enliven, stimulate, rouse, *colloq.* tart up
▣ **2** tire
▷ **freshen up** tidy yourself up, wash yourself, get washed, spruce yourself up, get spruced up

freshman *n*
first-year, fresher, underclassman

freshness *n*
brightness, cleanness, clearness, newness, originality, novelty, bloom, shine, glow, sparkle, vigour, wholesomeness
▣ staleness, tiredness

fret *v*
1 WORRY, be anxious, be upset, agonize, anguish, be distressed, brood, pine, mope, brood, make a fuss **2** VEX, irritate, nettle, bother, trouble, anger, annoy, exasperate, infuriate, rile, torment

fretful *adj*
worried, anxious, unhappy, upset, distressed, disturbed, uneasy, fearful, tense, restless, troubled, *colloq.* edgy, uptight
▣ calm

friable *adj*
brittle, crumbly, crisp, powdery, *formal* pulverizable
▣ solid

friar *n*
monk, religioner, mendicant, religious, prior, abbot, brother

friction *n*
1 DISAGREEMENT, dispute, disharmony, clashing,

conflict, strife, quarrelling, arguing, antagonism, hostility, opposition, rivalry, animosity, bad/ill feeling, bad blood, resentment, *formal* dissension, discord, disputation **2** RUBBING, chafing, irritation, scraping, grating, rasping, erosion, gnawing, wearing away, resistance, traction, *formal* abrasion, abrading, attrition, excoriation

friend *n*
1 COMPANION, good friend, close friend, best friend, intimate, confidant(e), bosom friend, soul mate, comrade, ally, partner, associate, familiar, playmate, penfriend, acquaintance, well-wisher, *colloq.* mate, pal, chum, buddy, crony **2** SUPPORTER, backer, patron, well-wisher, sponsor, benefactor, subscriber
🖅 **1** enemy **2** opponent

friendless *adj*
alone, companionless, unpopular, unloved, unbefriended, solitary, shunned, ostracized, lonely, isolated, forlorn, abandoned, lonesome, lonely-heart, deserted, forsaken, unattached, unbeloved, by yourself, with no one to turn to, *colloq.* cold shouldered

friendliness *n*
affability, amiability, companionability, congeniality, conviviality, approachability, kindness, kindliness, warmth, neighbourliness, sociability, geniality, *Gemütlichkeit, colloq.* matiness
🖅 coldness, unsociableness

friendly *adj*
1 AMIABLE, affable, genial, convivial, cordial, kind, kindly, warm, neighbourly, helpful, sympathetic, fond, affectionate, familiar, intimate, inseparable, close, companionable, sociable, outgoing, approachable, receptive, hospitable, comradely, amicable, peaceable, well-disposed, favourable, agreeable, good-natured, sympathetic, *colloq.* maty, pally, chummy, thick, tight **2** *a friendly atmosphere* convivial, congenial, cordial, welcoming, warm, close, amicable, familiar
🖅 **1** hostile, unsociable, unfriendly **2** cold

friendship *n*
companionship, closeness, intimacy, familiarity, amiability, affinity, rapport, attachment, affection, fondness, warmth, love, harmony, concord, understanding, goodwill, friendliness, kindliness, friendly relationship, alliance, fellowship, comradeship, *formal* amity
🖅 enmity, animosity

fright *n*
shock, scare, alarm, dismay, dread, apprehension, fear, fearfulness, terror, horror, panic, disquiet, *formal* trepidation, consternation, perturbation, *colloq.* blind panic, cold sweat, hair standing on end, blood running cold, knocking knees, shivers, jitters, creeps, willies, heebie-jeebies, funk, blue funk, bombshell, bolt from the blue

frighten *v*
alarm, daunt, unnerve, unman, dismay, intimidate, terrorize, scare, startle, scare stiff, give someone a fright, terrify, petrify, horrify, appal, shock, panic, *colloq.* rattle, scare out of your wits, make your blood run cold, scare the living daylights out of, make your hair stand on end, make someone jump out of their skin, put the frighteners on, put the wind up, give someone the heebie-jeebies
🖅 reassure, calm

frightened *adj*
afraid, dismayed, scared, terrified, unnerved, terrorized, terror-stricken, alarmed, cowed, frozen, petrified, scared stiff, startled, trembly, quivery, panicky, panic-stricken, *colloq.* scared out of your wits, scared to death, having kittens, in a blue funk, shaking like a

leaf, with your heart in your mouth
🖅 calm, courageous

frightening *adj*
alarming, daunting, formidable, grim, fearsome, forbidding, terrifying, hair-raising, creepy, blood-curdling, spine-chilling, petrifying, traumatic, *colloq.* scary, hairy, spooky

frightful *adj*
unpleasant, disagreeable, awful, nasty, dreadful, fearful, terrible, alarming, appalling, shocking, harrowing, unspeakable, dire, grim, ghastly, hideous, horrible, horrid, grisly, macabre, gruesome, revolting, repulsive, abhorrent, odious, loathsome, unbearable
🖅 pleasant, agreeable

frigid *adj*
1 FROZEN, bitter, freezing, icy, frosty, glacial, arctic, cold, chill, chilly, wintry, polar, Siberian **2** UNFEELING, unresponsive, passionless, unloving, cool, chilly, icy, distant, formal, aloof, passive, lifeless
🖅 **1** hot **2** responsible, enthusiastic, approachable

frigidity *n*
unresponsiveness, unapproachability, frostiness, iciness, impassivity, lifelessness, passivity, stiffness, cold-heartedness, coldness, aloofness, chill, chilliness
🖅 responsiveness, warmth

frill *n*
1 *a blouse with frills* flounce, gathering, ruff, ruffle, trimming, tuck, valance, fold, fringe, furbelow, ruche, ruching, purfle, orphrey **2** *the basic model without the frills* trimmings, addition, extra, ornamentation, decoration, embellishment, fanciness, accessory, ostentation, superfluity, finery, frilliness, fandangle, frippery

frilly *adj*
ruffled, crimped, gathered, frilled, trimmed, lacy, fancy, ornate
🖅 plain

fringe *n, adj, v*
▶ *n* **1** MARGIN, periphery, outskirts, edge, perimeter, limit, rim, border, verge, borderline **2** BORDER, edging, trimming, tassel, frill, valance
▶ *adj* unconventional, unorthodox, unofficial, alternative, avant-garde, experimental
🖅 conventional, mainstream
▶ *v* border, edge, trim, skirt, surround, enclose

fringed *adj*
bordered, edged, fringy, trimmed, tasselled, tassely, *technical* fimbriated

frippery *n*
finery, adornments, decorations, ornaments, ostentation, pretentiousness, showiness, gaudiness, fanciness, flashiness, frilliness, fussiness, tawdriness, triviality, baubles, fandangles, trinkets, knick-knacks, gewgaws, trifles, trivia, frills, froth, nonsense, glad rags, foppery, *formal* meretriciousness
🖅 plainness, simplicity

frisk *v*
1 JUMP, leap, skip, hop, bounce, prance, caper, dance, gambol, frolic, romp, cavort, play, sport, trip **2** BODY-SEARCH, search, inspect, check, *US* shake down

frisky *adj*
lively, active, spirited, high-spirited, in high spirits, exuberant, dashing, frolicsome, playful, romping, rollicking, bouncy, *colloq.* high, alive and kicking, full of beans, hyper
🖅 quiet, subdued

fritter *v*
waste, squander, go through, get through, idle, mis-

use, misspend, overspend, *formal* dissipate, *colloq.* spend like water, *slang* blow

frivolity *n*
fun, gaiety, flippancy, facetiousness, jest, lightheartedness, levity, triviality, superficiality, inanity, silliness, folly, foolishness, pettiness, nonsense, senselessness
F3 seriousness

frivolous *adj*
trifling, trivial, unimportant, petty, shallow, superficial, inane, light, merry, zany, flippant, jocular, lighthearted, juvenile, puerile, flighty, facetious, foolish, silly, idle, vain, pointless, senseless, futile
F3 serious, sensible

frizzy *adj*
curled, curly, crimped, crisp, frizzed, wiry, corrugated
F3 straight

frolic *v, n*
► *v* gambol, caper, romp, play, lark around, rollick, make merry, frisk, prance, cavort, dance, leap, skip, hop, bounce, sport
► *n* fun, fun and games, amusement, sport, game, gaiety, jollity, merriment, mirth, revel, romp, prank, lark, caper, spree, high jinks, antics, escapade, *colloq.* razzle, razzle-dazzle

frolicsome *adj*
playful, frisky, lively, merry, gay, sprightly, sportive, rollicking, coltish, skittish
F3 quiet, serious, solemn

front *n, adj, v*
► *n* **1** *the front of the building* face, aspect, frontage, façade, outside, exterior, facing, cover, obverse, top, head, lead, vanguard, forefront, front line, firing line, foreground, forepart, bow **2** PRETENCE, show, air, appearance, look, expression, manner, exterior, façade, cover, mask, disguise, pretext, cover-up, blind, *formal* countenance
F3 **1** back, rear
► *adj* leading, foremost, head, first, fore
F3 back, rear, last
▷ **in front** leading, ahead, first, in advance, to the fore, before, preceding
F3 behind
► *v* face, confront, look over, look out on, meet, oppose, overlook

frontier *n*
border, boundary, borderline, limit, edge, perimeter, confines, marches, bounds, verge

frost *n*
freeze, freeze-up, Jack Frost, hoar-frost, rime, coldness

frosty *adj*
1 ICY, frozen, freezing, frigid, wintry, cold, bitterly cold, chilly, rimy, glacial, frigid, arctic, Siberian, polar, *colloq.* nippy, parky **2** UNFRIENDLY, unwelcoming, cool, cold, icy, aloof, standoffish, stiff, discouraging, hostile
F3 **1** warm, hot **2** warm, friendly responsive, welcoming, enthusiastic

froth *n, v*
► *n* bubbles, effervescence, fizz, foam, lather, suds, head, scum, spume
► *v* foam, lather, ferment, fizz, effervesce, bubble, spume

frothy *adj*
1 BUBBLING, bubbly, foaming, foamy, yeasty, sudsy, *formal* spumescent, spumous, spumy, *colloq.* fizzy **2** INSUBSTANTIAL, empty, trivial, frivolous, trifling, slight, vain
F3 **1** flat **2** substantial, significant

frown *v, n*
► *v* scowl, glower, lour, glare, grimace, pout, *colloq.* give someone a dirty look, look daggers at
▷ **frown on** disapprove of, object to, dislike, discourage, take a dim view of, not take kindly to, think badly of, have a low opinion of, raise your eyebrows
F3 approve of, go along with
► *n* scowl, glower, glare, grimace, raised eyebrow, *colloq.* dirty look

frowsy *adj*
untidy, dishevelled, unwashed, unkempt, ungroomed, dirty, messy, frumpish, frumpy, slatternly, sloppy, slovenly
F3 well-groomed

frozen *adj*
iced, chilled, icy, frosty, icebound, ice-covered, arctic, ice-cold, bitterly cold, raw, polar, Siberian, frigid, freezing, numb, hard, frosted, solidified, stiff, frozen-stiff, rigid, fixed
F3 warm

frugal *adj*
thrifty, penny-wise, niggardly, penny-pinching, stingy, miserly, careful, provident, saving, economical, sparing, meagre, paltry, scanty, inadequate, *formal* parsimonious, prudent, *colloq.* scrimping and saving
F3 wasteful, generous

fruit *n*
1 CROP, harvest, produce, fruitage

> **Varieties of fruit include:**
> apple, Bramley, Cox's Orange Pippin, Golden Delicious, Granny Smith, crab apple; pear, William, Conference; orange, Jaffa, mandarin, mineola, clementine, satsuma, tangerine, Seville; apricot, peach, plum, nectarine, cherry, sloe, damson, greengage, grape, gooseberry, *colloq.* goosegog, rhubarb, tomato; banana, pineapple, olive, lemon, lime, ugli fruit, star fruit, lychee, passion fruit, date, fig, grapefruit, kiwi fruit, mango, avocado; melon, honeydew, cantaloupe, watermelon; strawberry, raspberry, blackberry, bilberry, loganberry, elderberry, blueberry, boysenberry, cranberry; redcurrant, blackcurrant.

2 BENEFIT, consequence, advantage, effect, outcome, reward, return, result, yield, product, profit

fruitful *adj*
1 FERTILE, rich, teeming, plentiful, abundant, prolific, productive, fruit-bearing, *formal* fecund, feracious **2** REWARDING, profitable, advantageous, beneficial, effective, worthwhile, well-spent, useful, successful, productive, *formal* effectual, efficacious
F3 **1** barren **2** fruitless

fruitfulness *n*
productiveness, profitability, fertility, usefulness, *formal* fecundity, feracity
F3 fruitlessness

fruition *n*
realization, fulfilment, attainment, achievement, completion, maturity, ripeness, perfection, success, enjoyment, *formal* consummation

fruitless *adj*
unsuccessful, abortive, useless, futile, pointless, vain, idle, hopeless, worthless, unproductive, barren, sterile, *formal* ineffectual
F3 fruitful, successful, profitable, productive

fruity *adj*
1 *a fruity voice* rich, mellow, resonant, full **2** INDECENT, bawdy, indelicate, juicy, suggestive, saucy,

risqué, titillating, vulgar, salacious, spicy, sexy, smutty, racy, *colloq.* blue
F∃ **2** decent

frumpy *adj*
dowdy, dreary, drab, badly-dressed, dingy, ill-dressed, dated, out of date
F∃ chic, well-groomed

frustrate *v*
1 DISAPPOINT, discourage, dishearten, dissatisfy, embitter, depress, anger, annoy, irritate, *formal* circumvent, *colloq.* stymie **2** THWART, foil, balk, baffle, block, check, stop, defeat, hinder, obstruct, hamper, impede, forestall, counter, nullify, neutralize, inhibit, *colloq.* spike, nobble
F∃ **1** encourage **2** further, promote

frustrated *adj*
disappointed, discontented, discouraged, dissatisfied, disheartened, embittered, resentful, angry, annoyed, thwarted, blighted, repressed
F∃ fulfilled, satisfied

frustration *n*
1 DISAPPOINTMENT, discouragement, dissatisfaction, resentment, annoyance, anger, vexation, irritation **2** THWARTING, foiling, balking, blocking, defeat, curbing, failure, non-fulfilment, obstruction, contravention, *formal* circumvention
F∃ **1** fulfilment **2** furthering, promoting

fuddled *adj*
hazy, confused, muddled, stupefied, muzzy, bemused, drunk, groggy, woozy, inebriated, intoxicated, sozzled, tipsy
F∃ clear, sober

fuddy-duddy *n, adj*
▶ *n* conservative, museum piece, fossil, *colloq.* old fogey, stick-in-the-mud, square, back number, stuffed shirt
▶ *adj* old-fashioned, old-fogeyish, stick-in-the-mud, stuffy, carping, censorious, prim
F∃ up-to-date

fudge *v*
avoid, dodge, equivocate, evade, hedge, stall, shuffle, misrepresent, fake, falsify, *colloq.* cook, fiddle, fix

fuel *n, v*
▶ *n* **1** COMBUSTIBLE, propellant, motive power **2** PROVOCATION, incitement, encouragement, ammunition, goading, incentive, stimulus, material
▶ *v* incite, inflame, fire, encourage, fan, feed, nourish, sustain, stoke up
F∃ discourage, damp down

fug *n*
stuffiness, staleness, reek, stink, frowstiness, fustiness, *formal* fetidness
F∃ airiness

fuggy *adj*
stuffy, airless, close, stale, suffocating, unventilated, foul, fetid, frowsty, fusty, *formal* noisome, noxious
F∃ airy

fugitive *n, adj*
▶ *n* escapee, runaway, deserter, refugee
▶ *adj* **1** RUNAWAY, refugee **2** FLEETING, transient, transitory, passing, short, short-lived, momentary, brief, flying, temporary, ephemeral, elusive, *formal* evanescent, fugacious
F∃ **2** permanent

fulfil *v*
complete, finish, perfect, realize, achieve, accomplish, perform, execute, discharge, implement, carry out, comply with, observe, keep, obey, conform to, satisfy, fill, meet, answer, *formal* conclude, consummate, effect
F∃ fail, break

fulfilled *adj*
satisfied, gratified, pleased, happy, content
F∃ dissatisfied, discontented, unhappy

fulfilment *n*
completion, perfection, realization, achievement, accomplishment, success, performance, execution, discharge, implementation, observance, satisfaction, *formal* consummation
F∃ failure

full *adj, adv, n*
▶ *adj* **1** FILLED, loaded, laden, packed, crowded, crammed, stuffed, overflowing, bulging, well-stocked, flush, jammed, filled to capacity, full to the brim, *colloq.* chock-a-block, packed out, bursting at the seams, packed like sardines **2** ENTIRE, whole, intact, total, complete, unabridged, unexpurgated **3** THOROUGH, comprehensive, exhaustive, all-inclusive, broad, vast, extensive, detailed, ample, filled, generous, abundant, plentiful, copious, profuse, sufficient **4** *feel full* satisfied, gorged, sated, stuffed, *formal* satiated, replete, *colloq.* bursting **5** *a full sound* rich, resonant, loud, deep, clear, strong, distinct, fruity **6** *at full speed* maximum, top, highest, greatest, utmost **7** *lead a full life* busy, active, lively, eventful, tiring, hectic, frantic **8** *a full figure* plump, chubby, stout, fat, overweight, large, round, shapely, buxom, obese, *formal* corpulent, rotund **9** *a full skirt* wide, baggy, loose-fitting, *formal* voluminous
F∃ **1** empty **2** partial, incomplete **3** superficial **4** hungry **6** minimum **7** unoccupied, empty
▶ *adv* directly, squarely, straight, right, exactly, *colloq.* bang, smack
▶ *n* ▷ **in full** fully, completely, wholly, in detail, with all the details, in its entirety, in total, uncut, with nothing missed out
▷ **to the full** to the greatest possible extent, to the utmost, fully, completely, entirely, thoroughly, utterly

full-blooded *adj*
committed, dedicated, devoted, enthusiastic, whole-hearted, thorough, vigorous, hearty
F∃ half-hearted

full-grown *adj*
adult, grown-up, fully-grown, of age, mature, ripe, developed, fully-developed, fully-fledged, full-blown, full-scale
F∃ young, undeveloped

fullness *n*
1 THOROUGHNESS, comprehensiveness, vastness, extensiveness, abundance, plenty, profusion, ampleness, completeness, totality, richness, resonance, strength, loudness, wholeness, variety **2** SATISFACTION, glut, fill, satedness, *formal* satiation, satiety, repletion **3** BREADTH, wideth, largeness, shapeliness, plumpness, curvaceousness **4** SWELLING, enlargement, inflammation, growth, *technical* tumescence, *formal* dilation
F∃ **1** incompleteness **2** emptiness
▷ **in the fullness of time** eventually, in due course, finally, ultimately, in the end, *colloq.* when all is said and done, in the final analysis

full-scale *adj*
exhaustive, extensive, complete, sweeping, thorough, thoroughgoing, wide-ranging, comprehensive, all-out, in-depth, all-encompassing, intensive, major
F∃ partial

fully *adv*
completely, totally, utterly, wholly, entirely, in all respects, thoroughly, altogether, quite, positively, without reserve, unreservedly, perfectly, satisfactorily, sufficiently
F∃ partly

fully-fledged *adj*
professional, qualified, trained, senior, graduate,

mature, proficient, experienced, fully-developed, full-blown
🔄 inexperienced

fulminate v
criticize, condemn, curse, denounce, protest, rage, rail, fume, thunder, *formal* animadvert, inveigh, vituperate, declaim, decry
🔄 praise

fulmination n
condemnation, criticism, denunciation, thundering, tirade, detonation, *formal* diatribe, invective, obloquy, philippic, decrial
🔄 praise

fulsome adj
extravagant, excessive, immoderate, overdone, gross, inordinate, insincere, adulatory, effusive, fawning, ingratiating, sycophantic, unctuous, sickening, nauseating, cloying, nauseous, offensive, saccharine, *colloq.* smarmy, slimy, buttery, over the top
🔄 sincere

fumble v
grope, feel, scrabble, blunder, bungle, botch, mishandle, mismanage, flounder, spoil

fume v
1 SMOKE, smoulder, boil, steam 2 RAGE, be furious, storm, rant, rave, seethe, boil, be livid, *colloq.* rant and rave, blow your cool, burst a blood vessel, hit the roof

fumes n
exhaust, smoke, gas, vapour, haze, fog, smog, pollution, stink, smell, stench, reek, *formal* exhalation

fumigate v
deodorize, disinfect, sterilize, purify, cleanse, sanitize

fuming adj
angry, enraged, furious, livid, incensed, raging, seething, boiling, *colloq.* steamed up
🔄 calm

fun n, adj
▶ n enjoyment, pleasure, amusement, entertainment, relaxation, diversion, distraction, recreation, play, sport, game, foolery, tomfoolery, buffoonery, horseplay, skylarking, romp, merrymaking, celebration, laughter, laughs, mirth, cheerfulness, gladness, jollity, jocularity, hilarity, joy, joking, jesting
▷ **for fun** for a laugh, for enjoyment, for no particular reason, *colloq.* for kicks, for the hell of it
▷ **in fun** as a joke, jokingly, for a laugh, to tease, in jest, mischievously, teasingly, tongue in cheek
▷ **make fun of** ridicule, mock, jeer at, scoff at, sneer at, tease, taunt, humiliate, poke fun at, *formal* deride, *colloq.* rib, send up, pull someone's leg, take the mickey
▶ adj entertaining, amusing, diverting, recreational, delightful, pleasurable, enjoyable, lively, witty

function n, v
▶ n 1 ROLE, part, office, duty, charge, responsibility, concern, capacity, job, post, chore, task, occupation, situation, employment, business, activity, purpose, mission, use 2 RECEPTION, party, gathering, affair, dinner, luncheon, *colloq.* do
▶ v work, be in working order, operate, run, go, serve, act, perform, behave, play the part of, have the job of
🔄 break down, *formal* malfunction, *slang* conk out

functional adj
working, operational, operative, running, working, practical, useful, utilitarian, utility, plain, hardwearing, serviceable
🔄 useless, decorative

functionary n
bureaucrat, employee, officer, official, office-bearer, office-holder, dignitary

fund n, v
▶ n 1 *contribute to the restoration fund* pool, kitty, reserve, treasury, grant, endowment, foundation, investment 2 *raise funds for the repairs* money, finance, backing, capital, resources, savings, wealth, cash, means, assets 3 *a fund of funny stories* reserve, repository, storehouse, store, stock, collection, accumulation, hoard, cache, stack, mine, well, source, supply, reservoir
▶ v finance, provide finance for, capitalize, endow, subsidize, pay for, underwrite, sponsor, back, support, promote, float

fundamental adj
basic, primary, first, elementary, underlying, integral, central, principal, cardinal, prime, main, chief, key, essential, indispensable, vital, necessary, crucial, important, initial, original, profound, *formal* rudimentary, basal, elemental

fundamentally adv
basically, essentially, in essence, at bottom, at heart, deep down, inherently, intrinsically, primarily

fundamentals n
basics, essentials, first principles, laws, rules, rudiments, facts, necessaries, practicalities, *colloq.* brass tacks, nitty-gritty, nuts and bolts

funeral n
burial, cremation, wake, *formal* interment, entombment, inhumation, exequies, obsequies

funereal adj
solemn, serious, grave, mournful, sad, sombre, depressing, dismal, dreary, gloomy, lamenting, woeful, sepulchral, dark, deathlike, *formal* exequial, funebral, funebrial, lugubrious
🔄 happy, lively

funk v
balk at, flinch from, recoil from, blench, duck out of, shirk from, *colloq.* chicken out of, cop out, dodge

funnel v
channel, direct, convey, move, transfer, pass, go, pour, siphon, filter

funny adj
1 HUMOROUS, amusing, entertaining, diverting, comic, comical, hilarious, witty, facetious, droll, farcical, laughable, ridiculous, absurd, silly, hysterical, side-splitting, riotous, uproarious, riotous, rich, *formal* risible, *colloq.* killing, corny, rum, a scream, a hoot 2 ODD, strange, peculiar, curious, queer, weird, bizarre, unusual, remarkable, puzzling, perplexing, mysterious, suspicious, dubious, *colloq.* shady, oddball, way-out, off-beat, wacky
🔄 1 serious, solemn, sad 2 normal, ordinary, usual

fur n
coat, hair, hide, down, fleece, pelt, fell, skin, wool, pelage

furious adj
1 ANGRY, livid, indignant, irate, enraged, infuriated, incensed, inflamed, raging, fuming, boiling, seething, frenzied, purple with rage, *colloq.* mad, hopping mad, sizzling, up in arms, in a stew, in a paddy, in a lather, in a huff, gone off the deep end, hot under the collar, foaming at the mouth 2 VIOLENT, wild, fierce, intense, vigorous, frantic, boisterous, stormy, tempestuous, vehement
🔄 1 calm, pleased 2 restrained

furnish v
equip, fit out, decorate, rig, appoint, stock, provide, supply, afford, grant, give, offer, present, endue, appoint, *formal* bestow
🔄 divest

furniture n
equipment, appliances, furnishings, fittings, appoint-

ments, fitments, household goods, movables, possessions, effects, things

Types of furniture include:
table, dining-table, gateleg table, refectory table, lowboy, side-table, coffee-table, card table; chair, easy chair, armchair, rocking-chair, recliner, dining-chair, carver, kitchen chair, stool, swivel-chair, high-chair, suite, settee, sofa, couch, studio couch, chesterfield, pouffe, footstool, bean-bag; bed, four-poster, chaise-longue, daybed, bed-settee, divan, camp-bed, bunk, water-bed, cot, cradle; desk, bureau, secretaire, bookcase, cupboard, cabinet, china cabinet, Welsh dresser, sideboard, buffet, dumb-waiter, fireplace, overmantel, fender, firescreen, hallstand, umbrella-stand, mirror, magazine rack; wardrobe, armoire, dressing-table, vanity unit, washstand, chest-of-drawers, tallboy, chiffonier, commode, ottoman, chest, coffer, blanket box.

furore *n*
uproar, disturbance, outcry, commotion, fuss, frenzy, fury, hullabaloo, outburst, rage, stir, to-do, tumult, storm, excitement, *colloq.* flap
F3 calm

furrow *n, v*
▶ *n* **1** GROOVE, channel, trench, hollow, trough, rut, track, *technical* sulcus **2** WRINKLE, line, crease, crinkle, crow's foot
▶ *v* crease, wrinkle, draw together, knit, seam, flute, channel, corrugate, gouge, plough, groove

further *adj, v, adv*
▶ *adj* **1** MORE, additional, supplementary, extra, fresh, new, other **2** FARTHER, more distant, remoter, more extreme
F3 **2** nearer
▶ *v* advance, forward, promote, champion, encourage, contribute to, foster, help, aid, assist, ease, facilitate, speed (up), hasten, accelerate, *formal* expedite, *colloq.* push
F3 stop, frustrate
▶ *adv* moreover, furthermore, besides, in addition, additionally, also, as well, too, *colloq.* what's more

furtherance *n*
advancement, promotion, advancing, backing, boosting, encouragement, help, carrying-out, facilitation, championship, promoting, advocacy, pursuit, *formal* preferment

furthermore *adv*
moreover, in addition, further, besides, also, too, as well, additionally, *colloq.* what's more

furthest *adj*
farthest, furthermost, remotest, outermost, outmost, extreme, ultimate, utmost, uttermost
F3 nearest

furtive *adj*
surreptitious, sly, stealthy, secretive, underhand, hidden, cloaked, veiled, covert, secret, sneaky, *formal* clandestine
F3 open

fury *n*
anger, rage, wrath, ire, frenzy, madness, passion, vehemence, fierceness, ferocity, violence, wildness, intensity, severity, force, turbulence, power
F3 calm, peacefulness

fuse *v*
combine, integrate, unite, join, amalgamate, blend, coalesce, meld, melt, solder, weld, smelt, merge, synthesize, intermix, *formal* agglutinate, commingle, intermingle

fusillade *n*
barrage, volley, discharge, burst, fire, hail, outburst, salvo, broadside

fusion *n*
melting, smelting, welding, union, synthesis, blending, coalescence, amalgamation, integration, merger, federation

fuss *n, v*
▶ *n* bother, trouble, palaver, furore, squabble, row, commotion, stir, fluster, confusion, upset, worry, agitation, excitement, bustle, flurry, hurry, *colloq.* hassle, to-do, hoo-ha, flap, carry-on, kerfuffle, bally-hoo, tizzy, a song and dance, storm in a teacup
F3 calm
▶ *v* complain, grumble, fret, worry, panic, take pains, bother, bustle, fidget, *colloq.* flap, stir, make a song and dance, be in a tizzy

fussiness *n*
choosiness, finicality, finicalness, pernicketiness, perfectionism, meticulousness, niceness, niggling, particularity, busyness
F3 unfastidiousness

fusspot *n*
worrier, perfectionist, hyper-critic, stickler, fidget, *colloq.* nit-picker, old woman

fussy *adj*
1 PARTICULAR, fastidious, scrupulous, finicky, finical, difficult, hard to please, discriminating, faddy, demanding, quibbling, pettifogging, pedantic, selective, *colloq.* pernickety, choosy, picky, nit-picking **2** FANCY, elaborate, ornate, overdecorated, cluttered, busy, baroque, rococo
F3 **1** casual, uncritical **2** plain, simple

fusty *adj*
1 OLD-FASHIONED, antiquated, archaic, outdated, out-of-date, *passé, colloq.* old-fogeyish **2** STALE, damp, dank, airless, stuffy, unventilated, fuggy, ill-smelling, musty, mouldy, mouldering, frowsty, rank, *formal* malodorous
F3 **1** up-to-date **2** airy

futile *adj*
pointless, useless, worthless, vain, in vain, idle, wasted, fruitless, profitless, unavailing, to no avail, unsuccessful, abortive, unprofitable, unproductive, ineffective, barren, empty, hollow, forlorn, *formal* ineffectual
F3 fruitful, profitable

futility *n*
pointlessness, uselessness, fruitlessness, worthlessness, ineffectiveness, waste, unproductiveness, vanity, emptiness, hollowness, barrenness, aimlessness
F3 use, purpose, success

future *n, adj*
▶ *n* hereafter, tomorrow, time to come, coming times, outlook, prospects, expectations
F3 past
▶ *adj* prospective, next, designate, to be, to come, forthcoming, in the offing, imminent, impending, coming, approaching, expected, planned, unborn, later, subsequent, eventual, fated, destined
F3 past

fuzz *n*
down, floss, fluff, fug, hair, lint, nap, pile, fibre, flock

fuzzy *adj*
1 FRIZZY, fluffy, furry, woolly, fleecy, downy, linty, velvety, napped **2** BLURRED, unfocused, ill-defined, indefinite, unclear, indistinct, vague, faint, hazy, foggy, shadowy, woolly, muffled, distorted, fuddled, confused, *colloq.* muzzy
F3 **2** clear, distinct, focused

gab *v, n*
▶ *v* chatter, talk, drivel, gossip, jaw, prattle, tattle, babble, blabber, jabber, blather, blether, buzz, *colloq.* yak
▶ *n* chat, chatter, chitchat, conversation, prattle, prattling, gossip, blab, blarney, blethering, small talk, tittle-tattle, tongue-wagging, *formal* loquacity, *colloq.* yackety-yak, yak

gabble *v, n*
▶ *v* babble, chatter, jabber, prattle, spout, splutter, cackle, sputter, gaggle, gibber, rattle, blab, blabber, blether
▶ *n* babble, chatter, blabber, cackling, prattle, twaddle, blethering, waffle, nonsense, drivel, gibberish

gad *v*
▷ **gad about** gallivant, run around, travel, roam, wander, range, rove, flit about, ramble, stray, traipse, dot about

gadabout *n*
gallivanter, rambler, rover, runabout, wanderer, pleasure-seeker, *Scot.* stravaiger

gadget *n*
tool, implement, appliance, device, instrument, apparatus, mechanism, contrivance, invention, contraption, thing, novelty, gimmick, *colloq.* thingummy, gismo, widget, whatsit, whatnot

gaffe *n*
blunder, mistake, slip, indiscretion, *faux pas*, gaucherie, *formal* solecism, *colloq.* bloomer, boob, booboo, brick, clanger, goof, howler

gaffer *n*
foreman, manager, overseer, superintendent, supervisor, overman, ganger, *colloq.* boss

gag¹ *v*
1 SILENCE, muffle, muzzle, quiet, stifle, smother, block, plug, clog, put a gag on, throttle, suppress, restrain, curb, check, still **2** RETCH, choke, heave, nearly vomit

gag² *n*
a comedian telling gags joke, jest, quip, wisecrack, one-liner, pun, witticism, *colloq.* crack, funny

gaiety *n*
happiness, glee, cheerfulness, joy, pleasure, delight, *joie de vivre*, jollity, merriment, mirth, gladness, blitheness, hilarity, fun, merrymaking, revelry, festivity, celebration, frolics, joviality, good humour, high spirits, light-heartedness, liveliness, exuberance, buoyancy, brightness, brilliance, sparkle, glitter, colour, colourfulness, show, showiness, *formal* vivacity
☒ sadness, drabness

gaily *adv*
happily, joyfully, merrily, cheerfully, blithely, light-heartedly, brightly, brilliantly, colourfully, flamboyantly
☒ sadly, dully

gain *v, n*
▶ *v* **1** EARN, make, produce, realize, gross, net, clear, profit, yield, bring in, reap, harvest, gather, win, achieve, capture, secure, get, obtain, acquire, *formal* procure **2** REACH, arrive at, come to, get to, attain, achieve, realize **3** *gain speed* increase, pick up, gather, collect, add, advance, progress, improve
☒ **1** lose **3** lose
▷ **gain on** close with, close in on, narrow the gap, approach, get nearer/closer to, catch up, level with, overtake, outdistance
☒ leave behind
▷ **gain time** delay, stall, temporize, *formal* procrastinate, *colloq.* drag your feet, dilly-dally
▶ *n* earnings, proceeds, income, revenue, winnings, pickings, takings, profit, return, reward, yield, interest, dividend, growth, addition, increase, increment, rise, advance, progress, headway, improvement, advantage, benefit, attainment, achievement, acquisition, *formal* emolument, advancement, augmentation, accretion
☒ loss

gainful *adj*
profitable, beneficial, advantageous, fruitful, lucrative, remunerative, moneymaking, paying, productive, rewarding, financially rewarding, useful, worthwhile, *formal* fructuous
☒ useless

gainsay *v*
deny, contradict, disagree with, dispute, oppose, challenge, *formal* contravene, controvert, disaffirm
☒ agree

gait *n*
walk, pace, step, stride, tread, bearing, carriage, manner

gala *n*
festivity, celebration, party, festival, carnival, jubilee, jamboree, fête, fair, pageant, procession

galaxy *n*
1 STARS, star system, solar system, the Milky Way, constellation, cluster, nebula **2** ARRAY, host, collection, gathering, group, assembly, mass

gale *n*
1 WIND, squall, storm, hurricane, tornado, typhoon, cyclone **2** BURST, outburst, outbreak, fit, eruption, explosion, blast

gall¹ *n*
1 *had the gall to ask for more money* IMPERTINENCE, impudence, brazenness, insolence, presumption, presumptuousness, *formal* effrontery, *colloq.* nerve, neck, cheek, chutzpah, sauciness, brass, brass neck **2** BITTERNESS, rancour, sourness, spite, animosity, hostility, enmity, antipathy, malice, venom, virulence, *formal* acrimony, animus, malevolence
☒ **1** modesty, reserve **2** friendliness

gall² *v*
it galls me to have to ask his permission annoy, irritate,

irk, exasperate, vex, bother, get to, nettle, peeve, pester, provoke, plague, rile, rankle, ruffle, harass, nag, *colloq.* aggravate
F3 please

gallant *adj*
chivalrous, gentlemanly, courteous, polite, gracious, attentive, thoughtful, considerate, courtly, noble, honourable, dashing, manly, heroic, valiant, brave, courageous, fearless, dauntless, intrepid, audacious, bold, daring, plucky
F3 ungentlemanly, cowardly

gallantry *n*
chivalry, gentlemanliness, courtesy, courteousness, politeness, graciousness, attentiveness, thoughtfulness, consideration, courtliness, nobility, honour, manliness, heroism, valour, bravery, courage, courageousness, spirit, fearlessness, dauntlessness, boldness, intrepidity, audacity, pluck, daring, *formal* valiance
F3 cowardice, ungentlemanliness

gallery *n*
art gallery, exhibition area, museum, arcade, passage, walk, balcony, circle, spectators, *colloq.* gods

galling *adj*
annoying, irritating, irksome, exasperating, humiliating, infuriating, vexing, provoking, nettling, plaguing, rankling, vexatious, bitter, embittering, bothersome, harassing, *colloq.* aggravating
F3 pleasing

gallivant *v*
gad about, run around, travel, roam, wander, ramble, range, rove, stray, traipse, flit about, dot about, *Scot.* stravaig

gallop *v*
bolt, canter, run, sprint, race, career, fly, dash, tear, speed, zoom, scurry, shoot, dart, rush, hurry, *formal* hasten
F3 amble

gallows *n*
scaffold, gibbet, the rope

galore *adj*
in abundance, lots of, plenty, in numbers, to spare, everywhere, *formal* in profusion, *colloq.* heaps of, tons of, stacks of, millions of
F3 scarce

galvanize *v*
electrify, shock, jolt, prod, spur, urge, provoke, stimulate, stir, startle, move, arouse, rouse, awaken, excite, fire, inspire, enliven, animate, invigorate, vitalize, energize

gambit *n*
device, manoeuvre, move, ploy, tactic(s), ruse, play, stratagem, trick, wile, artifice, *formal* machination

gamble *v, n*
▶ *v* bet, wager, try your luck, put money on, back, punt, play, play for money, play the horses, game, stake, chance, chance it, take a chance, risk, take a risk, hazard, venture, *colloq.* have a flutter
▶ *n* bet, wager, punt, lottery, chance, risk, hazard, venture, speculation, pot luck, *colloq.* flutter, leap in the dark, toss-up

gambler *n*
better, punter, risk-taker, tipster, bookmaker, turf accountant, desperado, daredevil

gambol *v*
caper, frolic, frisk, cavort, dance, skip, leap, romp, jump, bound, spring, hop, bounce, prance

game¹ *n*
1 RECREATION, play, sport, pastime, diversion, distraction, entertainment, amusement, merriment, fun, frolic, romp, joke, jest, prank, trick

Types of indoor game include:
board game; backgammon, *US* checkers, chess, Cluedo®, draughts, halma, ludo, mah-jongg, Monopoly®, nine men's morris, Scrabble®, snakes and ladders, Trivial Pursuit®; card game, baccarat, beggar-my-neighbour, bezique, blackjack, brag, bridge, canasta, chemin de fer, *colloq.* crib, cribbage, faro, gin rummy, rummy, happy families, *colloq.* nap, napoleon, newmarket, old maid, patience, Pelmanism, picquet, poker, draw poker, stud poker, pontoon, vingt-et-un, snap, solitaire, twenty-one, whist, partner whist, solo whist; bagatelle, pinball, billiards, snooker, pool, bowling, ten-pin bowling, bowls, darts, dice, craps, dominoes, roulette, shove ha'penny, table tennis, ping pong.

Types of children's games include:
battleships, blind man's buff, charades, Chinese whispers, consequences, fivestones, forfeits, hangman, hide-and-seek, I-spy, jacks, jackstraws, musical chairs, noughts and crosses, pass the parcel, piggy-in-the-middle, pin the tail on the donkey, postman's knock, sardines, Simon says, spillikins, spin the bottle, tiddlywinks.

2 COMPETITION, contest, match, round, tournament, event, meeting, meet, bout, round **3** GAME BIRDS, animals, wild animals, meat, flesh, wild fowl, prey, quarry, bag, spoils **4** ACTIVITY, business, enterprise, profession, occupation, line, trade **5** SCHEME, trick, intention, ploy, plot, strategy, device, stratagem, tactic(s), ruse

game² *adj*
1 *game for anything* willing, inclined, interested, ready, prepared, eager, enthusiastic, *formal* desirous
2 BOLD, daring, intrepid, brave, courageous, fearless, resolute, spirited, unflinching, gallant, plucky, valiant, lion-hearted
F3 **1** unwilling **2** cowardly, afraid, fearful

gamekeeper *n*
keeper, warden, *old use* venerer

gamut *n*
scale, series, range, sweep, scope, compass, spectrum, sequence, field, area, variety

gang *n*
group, band, ring, pack, herd, mob, crowd, gathering, horde, circle, clique, coterie, set, lot, club, team, crew, squad, shift, party, troupe, company

gangling *adj*
lanky, gawky, gangly, skinny, spindly, bony, angular, raw-boned, loose-jointed, awkward, tall, ungainly, rangy, gauche

gangster *n*
mobster, desperado, hoodlum, ruffian, rough, tough, thug, terrorist, racketeer, bandit, brigand, robber, criminal, *colloq.* crook, *slang* heavy

gaol *see* JAIL.

gaoler *see* JAILER.

gap *n*
1 SPACE, blank, void, hole, cavity, aperture, opening, crack, chink, crevice, cleft, cranny, breach, rift, fracture, rent, divide, gulf, divergence, difference, *formal* orifice, lacuna, vacuity, discontinuity, disparity **2** INTERRUPTION, break, recess, pause, lull, interlude, intermission, interval, hiatus

gape *v*
1 STARE, gaze, wonder, goggle, *colloq.* gawp, gawk,

US slang rubberneck **2** OPEN, yawn, part, split, crack

gaping *adj*
open, yawning, broad, wide, vast, cavernous
F3 tiny

garage *n*
lock-up, car port, petrol station, service station

garb *n, v*
▶ *n* **1** CLOTHES, clothing, garment, costume, dress, outfit, wear, robes, uniform, vestments, habiliment, *formal* apparel, array, attire, raiment, *colloq.* gear, get-up, rig-out, togs **2** APPEARANCE, guise, aspect, look, form, fashion, style
▶ *v* clothe, cover, dress, robe, *formal* apparel, array, attire, habilitate, *colloq.* rig out

garbage *n*
1 WASTE, rubbish, refuse, remains, leftovers, scourings, scraps, slops, swill, filth, muck, debris, dross, junk, litter, bits and pieces, odds and ends, sweepings, *formal* detritus, *Scot.* trash **2** NONSENSE, rubbish, gibberish, trash, tripe, twaddle, *colloq.* bunk, bunkum, claptrap, piffle, bilge, poppycock, hot air, cobblers, rot, tommyrot

garble *v*
confuse, muddle, jumble, scramble, mix up, twist, distort, corrupt, pervert, warp, slant, doctor, misrepresent, misinterpret, falsify, tamper with, mutilate
F3 decipher

garden *n*
yard, backyard, plot, park

gargantuan *adj*
colossal, huge, enormous, giant, gigantic, massive, immense, vast, tremendous, towering, mammoth, large, big, monumental, titanic, monstrous, elephantine, *formal* leviathan, prodigious, Brobdingnagian
F3 small, tiny, minute

garish *adj*
gaudy, lurid, loud, glaring, flashy, showy, flaunting, tawdry, vulgar, tasteless, cheap, glittering, tinselly, raffish, *formal* meretricious, *colloq.* glitzy, flash
F3 quiet, tasteful

garland *n, v*
▶ *n* wreath, festoon, decoration, flowers, laurels, honours, crown, coronet, coronal, headband, lei, bays, chaplet, stemma
▶ *v* wreathe, festoon, decorate, deck, adorn, crown

garments *n*
clothes, clothing, wear, outfit, dress, costume, uniform, *formal* attire, apparel, *colloq.* gear, togs, get-up, garb

garner *v*
gather, collect, accumulate, amass, assemble, heap, pile up, stack up, hoard, lay up, put by, reserve, save, stockpile, cull, store, stow away, deposit, treasure, husband
F3 dissipate

garnish *v, n*
▶ *v* decorate, adorn, ornament, trim, deck (out), festoon, embellish, enhance, grace, set off, beautify, *colloq.* jazz up
F3 divest
▶ *n* decoration, ornament, ornamentation, adornment, trimming, embellishment, enhancement, relish

garrison *n, v*
▶ *n* **1** ARMED FORCE, detachment, troops, unit, command **2** FORT, fortress, fortification, stronghold, station, post, base, barracks, camp, encampment, casern, zareba
▶ *v* **1** PROTECT, defend, guard **2** OCCUPY, position, place, mount, station, assign, furnish, man, post

garrulous *adj*
talkative, chatty, windy, long-winded, verbose, wordy, gabby, gassy, glib, yabbering, gossiping, gushing, chattering, babbling, effusive, prattling, prating, mouthy, *formal* loquacious, prolix, voluble
F3 taciturn, terse

gas *n*

Types of gas include:
acetylene, ammonia, black damp, butane, carbon dioxide, carbon monoxide, chloroform, choke damp, CS gas, cyanogen, ether, ethylene, fire damp, helium, hydrogen sulphide, krypton, laughing gas, marsh gas, methane, mustard gas, natural gas, neon, nerve gas, niton, nitrous oxide, ozone, propane, radon, tear gas, town gas, xenon.

gash *v, n*
▶ *v* cut, wound, slash, slit, incise, lacerate, tear, rend, split, score, gouge, nick
▶ *n* cut, wound, slash, slit, incision, laceration, tear, rent, split, score, gouge, nick

gasp *v, n*
▶ *v* pant, puff, blow, breathe, catch your breath, wheeze, heave, choke, gulp
▶ *n* pant, puff, blow, breath, choke, gulp, exclamation

gastric *adj*
stomach, intestinal, abdominal, coeliac, stomachic, enteric

gate *n*
barrier, door, doorway, gateway, opening, entrance, exit, access, passage, *formal* portal

gather *v*
1 CONGREGATE, convene, muster, rally, round up, assemble, summon, marshal, collect, come/bring together, meet, group, crowd, cluster, attract, draw, pull in, amass, mass, accumulate, converge, hoard, stockpile, heap, pile up, hoard up, build, rake in, garner, *colloq.* stash away **2** INFER, deduce, conclude, surmise, assume, understand, learn, hear, believe **3** *gather flowers* pick, pluck, cull, select, reap, harvest, crop, glean, collect, garner **4** *gather speed* gain, increase, grow, pick up, build up, add, advance, progress, improve, develop **5** FOLD, pleat, tuck, pucker, ruffle, shirr
F3 **1** scatter, dissipate

gathering *n*
assembly, convention, meeting, round-up, rally, get-together, jamboree, party, group, band, company, congregation, mass, crowd, flock, throng, mob, horde, turnout, *formal* convocation, conclave, assemblage

gauche *adj*
awkward, clumsy, shy, ungainly, inelegant, ungraceful, unpolished, gawky, graceless, uncultured, unsophisticated, ignorant, ill-bred, ill-mannered, insensitive, inept, farouche, tactless, *formal* maladroit
F3 graceful, elegant, urbane

gaudy *adj*
bright, too bright, brilliant, colourful, multicoloured, glaring, garish, loud, shrieking, harsh, stark, flashy, showy, kitsch, flaunting, ostentatious, tinselly, tawdry, vulgar, tasteless, raffish, *formal* meretricious, *colloq.* glitzy, flash, snazzy
F3 drab, plain, simple

gauge *v, n*
▶ *v* estimate, guess, judge, assess, evaluate, value,

rate, reckon, figure, calculate, compute, count, measure, weigh, determine, check, *formal* apprise, ascertain, *colloq.* guesstimate
▶ *n* **1** STANDARD, basic, guide, norm, criterion, benchmark, yardstick, touchstone, rule, guideline, indicator, measure, meter, test, sample, example, model, pattern, *formal* exemplar **2** SIZE, magnitude, measure, capacity, bore, calibre, thickness, width, span, extent, area, scope, height, depth, degree

gaunt *adj*
1 HAGGARD, hollow-eyed, angular, bony, thin, lean, lank, skinny, skin and bones, scraggy, scrawny, spindly, skeletal, emaciated, wasted, *formal* cadaverous **2** BLEAK, stark, bare, barren, desolate, forlorn, dismal, dreary, forbidding, grim, harsh
F3 **1** plump

gauzy *adj*
filmy, flimsy, delicate, sheer, thin, transparent, light, see-through, gossamer, insubstantial, unsubstantial, *formal* diaphanous
F3 heavy, thick

gawk *v*
gape, goggle, stare, gaze, look, look vacantly, ogle, *colloq.* rubberneck, gawp

gawky *adj*
awkward, clumsy, gauche, inept, loutish, oafish, ungainly, gangling, lanky, unco-ordinated, graceless, lumbering, *formal* maladroit
F3 graceful

gay *adj, n*
▶ *adj* **1** HOMOSEXUAL, lesbian, bisexual **2** HAPPY, joyful, jolly, merry, cheerful, bright, blithe, sunny, carefree, debonair, fun-loving, pleasure-seeking, vivacious, lively, animated, exuberant, sprightly, playful, light-hearted, in good/high spirits **3** *gay colours* vivid, rich, bright, brilliant, sparkling, festive, colourful, gaudy, garish, flashy, showy, flamboyant
F3 **1** heterosexual, *slang* straight **2** sad, gloomy
▶ *n* homosexual, lesbian
F3 heterosexual, *colloq.* straight

gaze *v, n*
▶ *v* stare, stare fixedly/intently, contemplate, regard, watch, view, look, gape, wonder, goggle, eye, *colloq.* gawk
▶ *n* stare, look, fixed look, gape

gazebo *n*
belvedere, summerhouse, shelter, pavilion, hut, arbour, bower

gazette *n*
newspaper, journal, magazine, news-sheet, periodical, paper, organ, dispatch, notice

gear *n, v*
▶ *n* **1** EQUIPMENT, kit, outfit, tackle, apparatus, tools, implements, instruments, appliances, accessories, supplies, utensils, contrivances, *formal* accoutrements, *colloq.* stuff, things **2** GEARWHEEL, cogwheel, tooth-wheel, toothed wheel, ratchet, cog, gearing, mechanism, machinery, works, *formal* engrenage **3** BELONGINGS, possessions, personal possessions, things, baggage, luggage, paraphernalia, kit, *formal* effects, *colloq.* stuff **4** CLOTHES, clothing, garments, dress, *formal* attire, apparel, *colloq.* garb, togs, get-up
▶ *v* adapt, fit, design, tailor, devise, prepare, organize

gel, jell *v*
set, congeal, coagulate, crystallize, harden, thicken, solidify, materialize, come together, finalize, form, take shape

gelatinous *adj*
jelly-like, jellied, congealed, rubbery, glutinous,

gummy, gluey, sticky, viscous, viscid, *formal* mucilaginous, *colloq.* gooey

geld *v*
emasculate, castrate, neuter, unman, unsex

gem *n*
1 GEMSTONE, precious stone, stone, jewel **2** TREASURE, prize, masterpiece, *pièce de résistance*, crème de la crème, *colloq.* pride and joy

Gems and gemstones include:
diamond, white sapphire, zircon, cubic zirconia, marcasite, rhinestone, pearl, moonstone, onyx, opal, mother-of-pearl, amber, citrine, fire opal, topaz, agate, tiger's eye, jasper, morganite, ruby, garnet, rose quartz, beryl, cornelian, coral, amethyst, sapphire, turquoise, lapis lazuli, emerald, aquamarine, bloodstone, jade, peridot, tourmaline, jet.

gen *n, v*
▶ *n* information, facts, details, data, knowledge, background, *colloq.* info, low-down, dope
▶ *v* ▷ **gen up on** find out about, be well-informed about, research, read up on, study, *colloq.* swot up on, bone up on, brush up on

genealogy *n*
family tree, family history, pedigree, lineage, ancestry, descent, derivation, extraction, family, dynasty, line, birth, parentage, breeding

general *adj*
1 *a general statement* broad, sweeping, blanket, all-inclusive, comprehensive, universal, global, total, across-the-board, widespread, wide-ranging, prevailing, prevalent, extensive, overall, accepted, popular, panoramic **2** VAGUE, broad, ill-defined, indefinite, imprecise, inexact, approximate, loose, rough, unspecific **3** USUAL, regular, normal, typical, ordinary, standard, everyday, customary, conventional, common, habitual, public **4** *a general store* mixed, varied, assorted, diverse, miscellaneous, *formal* heterogeneous, variegated
F3 **1** particular, limited **2** specific, detailed, precise **3** rare

generality *n*
1 GENERALIZATION, sweeping statement, general statement, impreciseness, indefiniteness, inexactness, looseness, approximateness, vagueness **2** COMMONNESS, extensiveness, popularity, prevalence, universality, comprehensiveness, breadth, catholicity, ecumenicity, miscellaneity
F3 **1** detail, exactness, particular **2** uncommonness

generally *adv*
usually, normally, in general, ordinarily, commonly, habitually, customarily, as a rule, by and large, for the most part, on the whole, mostly, in most cases, predominantly, mainly, chiefly, broadly, largely, at large, universally

generate *v*
produce, engender, whip up, arouse, cause, bring about, bring into being, give rise to, create, originate, initiate, occasion, make, form, breed, propagate
F3 prevent

generation *n*
1 AGE GROUP, age, days, era, epoch, period, time **2** PRODUCTION, creation, origination, formation, engendering, reproduction, propagation, breeding, *formal* genesis, procreation

generic *adj*
1 GENERAL, common, comprehensive, inclusive, universal, sweeping, wide, all-inclusive, blanket, all-

encompassing, collective **2** *generic drugs* unbranded, non-trademarked, non-registered, non-proprietary
🗄 **1** particular **2** branded, trademarked, registered, proprietary

generosity *n*
liberality, open-handedness, bounty, charity, magnanimity, philanthropy, kindness, big-heartedness, benevolence, goodness, lavishness, unselfishness, selflessness, *formal* munificence
🗄 meanness, selfishness

generous *adj*
1 LIBERAL, free, bountiful, open-handed, free-handed, unstinting, unsparing, lavish **2** MAGNANIMOUS, charitable, philanthropic, public-spirited, unselfish, selfless, altruistic, kind, big-hearted, benevolent, good, high-minded, noble, lofty, *formal* beneficent, munificent, *colloq.* big **3** AMPLE, lavish, full, substantial, plentiful, abundant, rich, copious, overflowing
🗄 **1** mean, miserly **2** selfish **3** meagre

genesis *n*
origin, beginning, birth, outset, root, source, start, foundation, founding, generation, initiation, engendering, formation, propagation, creation, dawn, *formal* commencement, inception
🗄 end, finish

genial *adj*
affable, amiable, friendly, amicable, convivial, cordial, kindly, kind, sociable, warm-hearted, warm, hearty, jovial, jolly, cheerful, happy, good-natured, good-humoured, agreeable, pleasant, *colloq.* easygoing
🗄 cold, unfriendly

geniality *n*
affability, amiability, friendliness, conviviality, congenialness, cordiality, kindliness, kindness, warmheartedness, warmth, joviality, jollity, cheerfulness, happiness, gladness, cheeriness, good nature, agreeableness, pleasantness
🗄 coldness, unfriendliness

genie *n*
spirit, fairy, demon, jinni, jinnee, jann

genitals *n*
sexual organs, reproductive organs, private parts, vulva, clitoris, labia majora/minora, vagina, womb, uterus, penis, scrotum, testicles, *technical* pudenda, pudendum, *formal* genitalia, *colloq.* privates, willy

genius *n*
1 VIRTUOSO, maestro, prodigy, master, past master, expert, adept, intellectual, mastermind, brain, intellect, sage, *colloq.* egghead, brains, boffin **2** INTELLIGENCE, brightness, brilliance, cleverness, fine mind, intellect, wisdom, ability, aptitude, gift, talent, flair, knack, bent, inclination, capacity, faculty, *formal* propensity, *colloq.* brains, nous, grey matter, little grey cells

genocide *n*
extermination, massacre, slaughter, ethnocide, ethnic cleansing

genre *n*
type, form, style, class, fashion, brand, group, kind, sort, variety, category, character, school, strain, *technical* genus

genteel *adj*
respectable, refined, cultivated, polished, elegant, polite, stylish, fashionable, cultured, aristocratic, formal, civil, gentlemanly, graceful, mannerly, well-mannered, well-bred, courteous, courtly, ladylike, urbane
🗄 crude, rough, unpolished, vulgar

gentility *n*
1 NOBILITY, aristocracy, high birth, gentle birth, good family, upper class, nobles, rank, breeding, elite, gentry, blue blood **2** COURTESY, respectability, formality, elegance, politeness, etiquette, civility, courtliness, manners, mannerliness, refinement, culture, urbanity, *formal* decorum, propriety
🗄 crudeness, discourteousness, roughness

gentle *adj*
1 KIND, kindly, amiable, tender, tender-hearted, soft-hearted, compassionate, sympathetic, lenient, humane, merciful, charitable, benign, mild, placid, calm, tranquil, serene, soft **2** *a gentle slope* gradual, slow, easy, smooth, moderate, slight, light, imperceptible **3** SOOTHING, peaceful, serene, quiet, soft, smooth **4** *gentle winds* mild, light, moderate, calm, pleasant, balmy
🗄 **1** unkind, rough, harsh, wild **2** steep, severe **4** strong, violent

gentlemanly *adj*
courteous, polite, refined, polished, urbane, well-bred, well-mannered, cultivated, civilized, civil, honourable, mannerly, gentlemanlike, noble, gallant, genteel, reputable, suave, obliging
🗄 impolite, rough

gentry *n*
nobility, nobles, upper class, aristocracy, elite, gentility

genuine *adj*
1 REAL, actual, natural, pure, original, authentic, factual, veritable, true, sound, bona fide, legitimate, legal, lawful, unadulterated, pukka, *colloq.* real McCoy **2** HONEST, sincere, frank, candid, earnest, with integrity, truthful, open, natural
🗄 **1** artificial, false, fake, counterfeit **2** insincere, deceitful

genus *n*
species, race, breed, genre, order, sort, set, type, division, subdivision, kind, group, category, class, *technical* taxon

geological timescale *n*

A scale into which the Earth's geological history can be subdivided:
Cenozoic: Quaternary (2 million years ago to present: Holocene, Pleistocene), Tertiary (65 million years ago to 2 million years ago: Pliocene, Miocene, Oligocene, Eocene, Palaeocene); *Mesozoic:* Cretaceous (140 million years ago to 65 million years ago), Jurassic (210 million yeas ago to 140 million years ago), Triassic (250 million years ago to 210 million years ago); *Palaeozoic:* Permian (290 million years ago to 250 million years ago), Carboniferous (360 million years ago to 290 million years ago: Pennsylvanian, Mississippian), Devonian (410 million yeas ago to 360 million years ago), Silurian (440 million years ago to 410 million years ago), Ordovician (505 million years ago to 440 million years ago), Cambrian (580 million years ago to 505 million years ago); *Precambrian* (before 580 million years ago).

germ *n*
1 MICRO-ORGANISM, microbe, bacterium, bacillus, virus, *colloq.* bug **2** BEGINNING, start, origin, source, fountain, cause, spark, rudiment, nucleus, root, seed, embryo, bud, sprout, *formal* commencement, inception

germane *adj*
relevant, appropriate, suitable, apt, applicable, fitting,

material, proper, related, connected, akin, allied, *formal* pertinent, apposite, apropos

🔁 irrelevant

germinal *adj*
generative, developing, embryonic, seminal, preliminary, rudimentary, undeveloped

germinate *v*
bud, sprout, shoot, develop, originate, grow, swell, spring up, take root, *formal* burgeon

gestation *n*
development, incubation, pregnancy, conception, evolution, ripening, planning, drafting, *formal* maturation

gesticulate *v*
wave, signal, gesture, motion, indicate, sign, make a sign

gesticulation *n*
wave, signal, gesture, motion, movement, indication, sign, *formal* chironomy

gesture *n, v*
► *n* movement, motion, indication, sign, signal, wave, gesticulation, act, action
► *v* indicate, sign, motion, beckon, point, signal, wave, gesticulate

get *v*
1 OBTAIN, acquire, come by, receive, be given, earn, gain, buy, bring in, clear, make, win, secure, achieve, realize, *formal* procure, purchase **2** *it's getting dark* become, turn, go, grow, come to be **3** *get him to help* persuade, coax, induce, talk into, urge, influence, sway, win over, convince, *formal* prevail upon **4** MOVE, go, come, reach, arrive **5** FETCH, collect, pick up, bring, take, catch, capture, seize, grab **6** *get a disease* catch, pick up, develop, come down with, become infected with, be afflicted by, *formal* contract **7** *get to see the exhibition* succeed, manage, have the opportunity, organize, arrange **8** *get breakfast* prepare, get ready, cook, put together, *US* fix, *colloq.* rustle up **9** *get a joke* understand, see, follow, grasp, fathom, *formal* comprehend, *colloq.* twig, get the hang of, get the point **10** *get a thief/an animal* catch, capture, trap, hunt down, snare, lay hold of, arrest, hit, kill, *colloq.* nab, collar, nick **11** *his snoring really gets me* annoy, irritate, infuriate, exasperate, vex, provoke, bother, *colloq.* bug, get on someone's nerves, rub someone up the wrong way, drive crazy

🔁 **1** lose **4** leave

▷ **get about** move about, move around, go/travel (widely)

▷ **get across** communicate, transmit, convey, impart, put across, put over, get over, bring home to

▷ **get ahead** advance, progress, get on, thrive, flourish, prosper, do well, succeed, make good, make it, *colloq.* go places, get there, get somewhere, go great guns, make the big time, make your mark, go up in the world

🔁 fall behind, fail

▷ **get along 1** COPE, manage, get by, survive, fare, progress, develop **2** AGREE, be on friendly terms, harmonize, get on, be on the same wavelength, *colloq.* hit it off

▷ **get at 1** REACH, attain, find, discover, obtain **2** BRIBE, suborn, corrupt, influence **3** MEAN, intend, imply, insinuate, hint, suggest **4** CRITICIZE, find fault with, pick on, attack, make fun of, *colloq.* knock, slate, slam, pick holes in

▷ **get away** escape, get out, break out, break away, break free, run away, flee, depart, leave

▷ **get back 1** RETURN, go/come back, go/come home **2** RECOVER, regain, recoup, repossess, retrieve **3** PAY BACK, retaliate, get even with, take vengeance on, avenge yourself on

▷ **get by** cope, get along, manage, survive, exist, fare, *formal* subsist, *colloq.* make ends meet, scrape through, hang on, keep your head above water, keep the wolf from the door, weather the storm, see it through

▷ **get down 1** DEPRESS, sadden, dishearten, dispirit **2** DESCEND, dismount, disembark, alight, get off

🔁 **1** encourage **2** board

▷ **get even** pay back, reciprocate, repay, requite, revenge yourself, *colloq.* get your own back, settle a score

▷ **get in** enter, penetrate, infiltrate, arrive, come, land, embark

▷ **get off 1** *get off a train* alight, leave, get out (of), dismount, climb off, descend, *formal* disembark **2** REMOVE, detach, separate, shed, get down

🔁 **1** get on **2** put on

▷ **get on 1** BOARD, climb on, get in, get into, embark, mount, ascend **2** COPE, manage, fare, get along, make out, prosper, succeed, be on friendly terms with, *colloq.* hit it off with **3** CONTINUE, proceed, press on, advance, progress

🔁 **1** get off

▷ **get out 1** ESCAPE, flee, break out, extricate yourself, free yourself, leave, depart, withdraw, vacate, evacuate, clear out, *colloq.* quit, clear off **2** *she got out a pen* take out, produce **3** *the news got out* become public, become known, come out, leak out, be leaked, spread, circulate

▷ **get out of** avoid, escape, evade, shirk, *colloq.* dodge, skive

▷ **get over 1** RECOVER FROM, shake off, recuperate from, pull through, get well/better, respond to treatment, be restored, survive **2** SURMOUNT, overcome, master, get round, defeat, deal with, complete **3** COMMUNICATE, get across, convey, put over, impart, explain

▷ **get ready** prepare, arrange, fix up, ready, rehearse, set out

▷ **get rid of** do away with, dispense with, dispose of, throw away, rid yourself of, shake off, remove, unload, dump, eject, eliminate, expel, jettison, *colloq.* get shot of

🔁 accumulate, acquire

▷ **get round 1** BYPASS, evade, avoid, *formal* circumvent **2** PERSUADE, win over, talk round, coax, induce, sway, *formal* prevail upon

▷ **get there** advance, arrive, prosper, succeed, make good, *colloq.* go places, make it

▷ **get together** meet, assemble, collect, gather, congregate, rally, join, unite, collaborate, organize

▷ **get up** stand (up), arise, rise, ascend, climb, mount, scale

getaway *n*
escape, breakout, flight, start, absconding, decampment, break

get-together *n*
party, reception, meeting, reunion, function, gathering, rally, assembly, social, soirée, *colloq.* do

get-up *n*
set, outfit, clothes, clothing, garments, *colloq.* rigout, gear, togs

ghastly *adj*
1 AWFUL, dreadful, frightful, frightening, terrifying, terrible, grim, gruesome, hideous, horrible, horrid, horrendous, loathsome, nasty, repellent, shocking, appalling **2** *look/feel ghastly* ill, sick, unwell, poorly, rotten, dreadful, awful, terrible, *colloq.* lousy, ropy, off colour, under the weather **3** *a ghastly mistake* serious, bad, grave, critical, dangerous, awful, terrible, dreadful, frightful, shocking, appalling, unrepeatable

🔁 **1** delightful, attractive **2** well, healthy

ghost *n*
1 SPECTRE, phantom, apparition, visitant, spirit, wraith, soul, shade, shadow, presence, *colloq.* spook
2 TRACE, suggestion, hint, shadow, impression, semblance

ghostly *adj*
eerie, creepy, weird, supernatural, unearthly, ghostlike, spectral, wraith-like, phantom, illusory, shadowy, *colloq.* spooky

ghoulish *adj*
grisly, gruesome, macabre, morbid, unhealthy, unwholesome, revolting, sick

giant *n, adj*
▶ *n* monster, titan, colossus, Goliath, Hercules, behemoth, ogre, Cyclops
▶ *adj* gigantic, colossal, titanic, mammoth, king-size, huge, enormous, massive, immense, vast, monumental, prodigious, gargantuan, cyclopean, Brobdingnagian, large, *colloq.* jumbo, great big, whopping

gibber *v*
babble, blab, blabber, blather, gabble, jabber, prattle, chatter, cackle, cant

gibberish *n*
nonsense, rubbish, drivel, jargon, twaddle, balderdash, prattle, yammer, *colloq.* gobbledygook, mumbo-jumbo, poppycock, tommyrot, cobblers, bunkum
🔁 sense

gibe, jibe *n, v*
▶ *n* jeer, sneer, mockery, ridicule, teasing, taunt, derision, scoff, poke, quip, *colloq.* dig, crack
▶ *v* jeer, sneer, mock, ridicule, taunt, tease, scoff, make fun of, *formal* deride

giddiness *n*
1 DIZZINESS, faintness, light-headedness, wooziness, wobbliness, nausea, vertigo **2** EXCITEMENT, dizziness, frenzy, exhilaration, thrill, animation

giddy *adj*
1 DIZZY, faint, light-headed, unsteady, reeling, *formal* vertiginous, *colloq.* woozy **2** EXCITED, wild, dizzy, exhilarated, stirred, stimulated, thrilled, elated, frenzied, *colloq.* high

gift *n, v*
▶ *n* **1** PRESENT, offering, donation, contribution, bounty, largesse, gratuity, tip, bonus, inheritance, legacy, bequest, endowment, *colloq.* freebie **2** TALENT, genius, flair, skill, aptitude, aptness, bent, knack, facility, endowment, proficiency, power, faculty, attribute, ability, capability, capacity, turn
▶ *v* present, offer, contribute, donate, *formal* bestow, confer

gifted *adj*
talented, endowed, adept, skilful, expert, masterly, skilled, accomplished, able, capable, proficient, clever, intelligent, bright, brilliant, sharp, *colloq.* smart

gigantic *adj*
huge, enormous, immense, vast, giant, massive, colossal, king-size, monumental, titanic, mammoth, gargantuan, Brobdingnagian, *colloq.* jumbo, great big, whopping
🔁 tiny, Lilliputian

giggle *v & n*
titter, snigger, chuckle, chortle, laugh, snicker

gild *v*
enhance, ornament, deck, enrich, adorn, grace, beautify, embellish, embroider, festoon, garnish, brighten, dress up, paint, coat, trim, *formal* array, bedeck

gilded *adj*
gilt, gold, golden, gold-plated, gold-layered

gimcrack *adj*
cheap, shoddy, tawdry, trashy, rubbishy, trumpery, *colloq.* tacky
🔁 solid, well-made

gimmick *n*
attraction, publicity, novelty, ploy, stratagem, ruse, scheme, trick, stunt, dodge, device, contrivance, gadget

gingerly *adv*
tentatively, hesitantly, warily, watchfully, cautiously, with caution, carefully, charily, attentively, delicately, *formal* judiciously, prudently
🔁 boldly, carelessly

gird *v*
1 PREPARE, ready, get ready, brace, steel, *formal* fortify **2** FASTEN, belt, bind, girdle, hem in, pen, surround, encircle, enclose, ring, encompass, enfold

girdle *n, v*
▶ *n* belt, sash, band, waistband, corset, *formal* cummerbund, ceinture, cestus, cincture, cingulum
▶ *v* surround, encircle, circle, enclose, encompass, go round, gird, bind, bound, hem, ring

girl *n*
lass, young woman, young lady, schoolgirl, girlfriend, sweetheart, maiden, daughter, child, teenager, adolescent, au pair, *colloq.* kid, nipper

girlfriend *n*
young lady, girl, lass, partner, date, sweetheart, lover, fiancée, mistress, old flame, cohabitee, live-in lover, common-law spouse, *colloq.* date, steady, significant other

girlish *adj*
youthful, childlike, adolescent, childish, immature, innocent, unmasculine

girth *n*
circumference, perimeter, measure, size, bulk, strap, band

gist *n*
pith, essence, marrow, substance, matter, meaning, significance, sense, idea, drift, direction, point, crux, nucleus, nub, core, keynote, *formal* import, quintessence

give *v*
1 PRESENT, award, let someone have, slip, offer, lend, donate, contribute, provide, supply, distribute, administer, furnish, grant, endow, gift, make over, hand over, turn over, deliver, entrust, bequeath, leave, will, commit, devote, *formal* confer, bestow, accord, proffer **2** *give news* communicate, transmit, transfer, convey, tell, utter, announce, declare, pronounce, publish, set forth, *formal* impart **3** CONCEDE, allow, admit, yield, give way, give up, surrender, *formal* cede **4** *give trouble* cause, occasion, make, create, produce, do, perform **5** *give an impression* show, indicate, display, present, exhibit, reveal, set forth, *formal* manifest **6** *give attention to something* concentrate, direct, aim, focus, turn **7** *give someone a fright* cause to experience/undergo, make, do, perform, occasion, create, give rise to **8** *give something a value* allow, offer, estimate, grant **9** SINK, yield, bend, buckle, give way, break (down), collapse, fall, fall apart **10** *give a party* organize, arrange, put on, be responsible for, take charge of, lay on, *colloq.* throw **11** *be given to understand something* lead, make, cause, move, dispose, incline, prompt, induce
🔁 **1** take, withhold **5** withstand
▷ **give away** betray, inform on, expose, uncover, divulge, disclose, reveal, leak, let out, let slip, concede
🔁 keep
▷ **give in** surrender, capitulate, submit, yield, give way, concede, admit/concede defeat, give up, suc-

cumb, *colloq.* quit, throw in the towel/sponge, chuck it in, pack it in, jack in, call it a day, show the white flag
F3 hold out
▷ **give off** emit, discharge, release, give out, send out, throw out, pour out, exhale, vent, exude, produce
▷ **give on to** lead to, open on to, overlook
▷ **give out 1** DISTRIBUTE, disperse, hand out, pass around, share out, dole out, mete out, allot, deal, *colloq.* dish out **2** ANNOUNCE, declare, broadcast, publish, make known, circulate, disseminate, communicate, transmit, impart, notify, advertise **3** STOP WORKING, break down, *colloq.* pack up, *slang* conk out **4** RUN OUT, come to an end, be (all) mixed up, be exhausted, *formal* be depleted
▷ **give up 1** STOP, resign, abandon, renounce, waive, leave off, sacrifice, *formal* cease, relinquish, discontinue, forswear, *colloq.* quit, cut out **2** SURRENDER, capitulate, give in, concede, concede defeat, *colloq.* quit, throw in the towel, turn in
F3 1 start **2** hold out

give-and-take *n*
adaptability, compromise, negotiation, flexibility, goodwill, willingness, compliance

given *adj, prep*
▶ *adj* **1** *a given number* specified, particular, definite, specific, individual, distinct **2** INCLINED, disposed, likely, liable, prone
▶ *prep* considering, taking into account/consideration, bearing in mind, making allowances for, in view of, in the light of, assuming

giver *n*
benefactor, patron, sponsor, backer, supporter, promoter, donor, contributor, subscriber, provider, subsidizer, philanthropist, helper, friend, well-wisher, *colloq.* angel, fairy godmother
F3 opponent, persecutor

glacial *adj*
1 FREEZING, frozen, biting, bitter, chill, chilly, cold, frosty, raw, wintry, stiff, frigid, icy, piercing, polar, arctic, Siberian, *formal* brumous, gelid **2** UNFRIENDLY, antagonistic, cold, icy, hostile, *formal* inimical
F3 1, 2 warm

glad *adj*
1 PLEASED, delighted, gratified, contented, satisfied, happy, joyful, overjoyed, thrilled, elated, merry, cheerful, cheery, gleeful, welcome, bright, *colloq.* over the moon, chuffed, tickled pink **2** WILLING, eager, keen, ready, prepared, inclined, happy, pleased, *formal* disposed
F3 1 sad, unhappy **2** unwilling, reluctant

gladden *v*
brighten, cheer, encourage, delight, please, hearten, gratify, rejoice, elate, enliven, exhilarate, raise the spirits of, *colloq.* buck up
F3 sadden

gladly *adv*
happily, cheerfully, freely, willingly, readily, with good grace, with pleasure, *old use* fain
F3 sadly, unwillingly, reluctantly

gladness *n*
happiness, joy, cheerfulness, delight, pleasure, brightness, high spirits, jollity, glee, hilarity, mirth, gaiety, *formal* felicity, joyousness
F3 sadness

glamorous *adj*
smart, elegant, well-dressed, attractive, beautiful, lovely, gorgeous, enchanting, captivating, alluring, charming, appealing, fascinating, exciting, thrilling, dazzling, glittering, glossy, colourful, *colloq.* glitzy, flashy, ritzy
F3 plain, drab, boring

glamour *n*
attraction, attractiveness, allure, appeal, fascination, excitement, thrill, captivation, enchantment, charm, magic, beauty, elegance, glitter, prestige

glance *v, n*
▶ *v* peep, peek, glimpse, catch a glimpse of, view, look, look quickly/briefly at, scan, skim, leaf, flip, flick, thumb, dip, browse
▷ **glance off** bounce off, rebound, ricochet, spring back
▶ *n* peep, peek, glimpse, look, quick/brief look, *colloq.* butcher's, dekko, gander

gland *n*

Types of gland include:
adrenal, apocrine, cortex, eccrine, endocrine, exocrine, holocrine, lachrymal, lymph, lymph node, mammary, medulla, merocrine, ovary, pancreas, parathyroid, parotid, pineal, pituitary, prostate, sebaceous, testicle, thymus, thyroid.

glare *v, n*
▶ *v* **1** GLOWER, look, frown, scowl, stare, *colloq.* look daggers, give someone a dirty look **2** DAZZLE, blaze, flame, flare, shine, beam, reflect
▶ *n* **1** *his fiery glare* frown, scowl, stare, look, *colloq.* dirty look, black look **2** BRIGHTNESS, brilliance, glow, blaze, flame, flare, dazzle, spotlight

glaring *adj*
blatant, flagrant, open, conspicuous, patent, obvious, overt, outrageous, gross, lurid, *formal* manifest
F3 hidden, concealed, minor

glass *n*
1 BEAKER, tumbler, goblet **2** CRYSTAL, glassware, vitrics **3** SPECTACLES, lens, contact lenses, lorgnette, eyeglasses, opera-glasses, pince-nez, monocle, *colloq.* specs. *See also* SPECTACLES.

glassy *adj*
1 GLASSLIKE, smooth, polished, slippery, icy, shiny, glossy, transparent, clear, crystal clear, mirrorlike **2** *a glassy stare* expressionless, blank, empty, vacant, dazed, unmoving, fixed, deadpan, glazed, vacuous, cold, lifeless, dull

glaze *v, n*
▶ *v* coat, cover, enamel, gloss, varnish, lacquer, polish, burnish
▶ *n* coat, coating, finish, enamel, varnish, lacquer, polish, shine, lustre, gloss

gleam *n, v*
▶ *n* glint, flash, beam, ray, shaft, flare, flicker, glimmer, shimmer, sparkle, glitter, gloss, glow, lustre, brightness
▶ *v* glint, flash, glance, flare, shine, radiate, beam, glisten, glimmer, glitter, sparkle, scintillate, shimmer, glow

glean *v*
gather, collect, find out, learn, pick (up), select, accumulate, amass, harvest, garner, reap, cull

glee *n*
delight, cheerfulness, pleasure, fun, joy, joyfulness, merriment, mirth, gladness, liveliness, exhilaration, exuberance, exultation, elation, hilarity, jocularity, jollity, joviality, gaiety, gratification, triumph, verve, *formal* joyousness

gleeful *adj*
delighted, cheerful, pleased, happy, beside yourself, joyful, overjoyed, elated, exuberant, exultant, merry, mirthful, jubilant, jovial, gratified, triumphant, *formal* joyous, *colloq.* over the moon, cock-a-hoop
F3 sad

glib *adj*

fluent, easy, facile, quick, ready, talkative, plausible, insincere, smooth, slick, suave, smooth-tongued, smooth-talking, silver-tongued, *formal* loquacious, voluble, *colloq.* with the gift of the gab, gabby, gassy
🔁 tongue-tied, implausible

glide *v*

slide, move smoothly/effortlessly, slip, skate, skim, fly, float, drift, sail, coast, roll, run, flow, pass

glimmer *v, n*

▶ *v* glow, shimmer, glisten, glitter, sparkle, twinkle, wink, blink, flash, flicker, gleam, shine
▶ *n* **1** GLOW, shimmer, shine, sparkle, twinkle, flicker, glint, gleam, ray, flash **2** TRACE, hint, suggestion, inkling, grain, flicker, ray

glimpse *n, v*

▶ *n* peep, peek, squint, glance, look, quick/brief look, sight, sighting, view
▶ *v* spy, espy, spot, catch sight of, sight, view

glint *v, n*

▶ *v* flash, gleam, shine, reflect, glitter, sparkle, glisten, twinkle, glimmer, shimmer, scintillate
▶ *n* flash, gleam, shine, reflection, glitter, sparkle, glistening, twinkle, glimmer, shimmer

glisten *v*

shine, gleam, glint, glitter, flash, sparkle, twinkle, flicker, glimmer, shimmer, *formal* coruscate

glitter *v, n*

▶ *v* sparkle, spangle, scintillate, twinkle, shimmer, glimmer, flicker, glisten, glint, gleam, flash, shine, dazzle, *formal* coruscate
▶ *n* **1** SPARKLE, scintillation, twinkle, shimmer, glimmer, flicker, glint, gleam, flash, shine, lustre, sheen, brightness, radiance, brilliance, splendour, *formal* coruscation **2** SHOWINESS, glamour, tinsel, flashiness, *colloq.* glitz, razzle-dazzle, razzmatazz

gloat *v*

triumph, glory, exult, rejoice, revel in, delight in, relish, crow, boast, vaunt, *colloq.* rub it in

global *adj*

1 WORLDWIDE, universal, international **2** GENERAL, all-encompassing, total, thorough, exhaustive, comprehensive, all-inclusive, encylopedic, wide-ranging
🔁 **1** parochial **2** limited

globe *n*

world, earth, planet, sphere, ball, orb, round

globular *adj*

ball-shaped, round, globate, spherical, *formal* orbicular, spheroid

globule *n*

bead, ball, bubble, drop, droplet, globulet, pearl, pellet, particle, *technical* vesicle, vesicula

gloom *n*

1 DARK, darkness, blackness, shade, shadow, dusk, twilight, dimness, obscurity, cloud, cloudiness, dullness, murkiness **2** DEPRESSION, low spirits, despondency, dejection, sadness, unhappiness, glumness, melancholy, grief, sorrow, woe, misery, hopelessness, pessimism, desolation, despair, *colloq.* the blues
🔁 **1** brightness **2** cheerfulness, happiness

gloomy *adj*

1 DARK, sombre, shadowy, dim, obscure, overcast, dull, dreary, dismal, dingy, unlit, *formal* tenebrous, crepuscular **2** DEPRESSED, down, low, despondent, dejected, downcast, dispirited, downhearted, sad, miserable, glum, morose, dreary, drear, pessimistic, cheerless, melancholy, sorrowful, dismal, depressing, desolate, in low spirits, *formal* disconsolate, *colloq.* down in the dumps
🔁 **1** bright **2** happy, cheerful

glorify *v*

1 *glorify God* praise, worship, exalt, adore, honour, thank, bless, magnify, revere, extol, sanctify, *formal* laud, venerate **2** *glorify violence/war* celebrate, praise, magnify, hail, lionize, idolize, elevate, enshrine, immortalize, romanticize, panegyrize, *formal* eulogize
🔁 **1** denounce, *formal* vilify

glorious *adj*

1 ILLUSTRIOUS, eminent, distinguished, famous, renowned, honoured, noted, great, noble, celebrated, famed, splendid, magnificent, grand, majestic, supreme, excellent, victorious, triumphant **2** MARVELLOUS, splendid, beautiful, gorgeous, superb, perfect, excellent, wonderful, delightful, dazzling, heavenly, *colloq.* super, terrific, great **3** *glorious weather* FINE, bright, radiant, shining, brilliant
🔁 **1** unknown

glory *n, v*

▶ *n* **1** FAME, renown, celebrity, illustriousness, greatness, eminence, distinction, honour, recognition, acclaim, prestige, accolade, kudos, triumph **2** PRAISE, homage, tribute, worship, veneration, adoration, exaltation, blessing, thanksgiving, gratitude **3** BRIGHTNESS, radiance, brilliance, beauty, splendour, resplendence, magnificence, pomp, grandeur, majesty, dignity, impressiveness
▶ *v* revel, delight, exult, pride yourself, rejoice, triumph, relish, boast, crow, gloat

gloss[1] *n, v*

▶ *n* **1** SHEEN, polish, varnish, lustre, shine, brightness, gleam, shimmer, sparkle, brilliance **2** SHOW, appearance, semblance, surface, front, façade, veneer, camouflage, mask, disguise, veil, window-dressing
▶ *v* ▷ **gloss over** conceal, hide, veil, draw a veil over, mask, disguise, camouflage, cover up, whitewash, explain away, evade, avoid, ignore, smooth over, deal with quickly

gloss[2] *n, v*

▶ *n glosses to the text* annotation, note, footnote, explanation, interpretation, translation, definition, comment, commentary, *formal* elucidation, explication, scholion
▶ *v* annotate, add glosses to, define, explain, interpret, construe, translate, comment, *formal* elucidate

glossy *adj*

shiny, sheeny, lustrous, sleek, silky, smooth, glassy, polished, burnished, glazed, gleaming, enamelled, bright, shining, shimmering, sparkling, brilliant
🔁 matt

glove *n*

mitten, mitt, gauntlet, gage, mousquetaire glove, oven glove

glow *n, v*

▶ *n* **1** LIGHT, gleam, glimmer, radiance, brightness, vividness, richness, brilliance, splendour, *technical* phosphorescence, *formal* luminosity, incandescence **2** ARDOUR, fervour, intensity, warmth, passion, enthusiasm, excitement, happiness, satisfaction **3** FLUSH, blush, rosiness, redness, reddening, pinkness, burning
▶ *v* **1** SHINE, radiate, gleam, glimmer, burn, smoulder **2** *their faces glowed* flush, blush, colour, redden, grow/look pink

glower *v, n*

▶ *v* glare, frown, scowl, stare, frown, *colloq.* look daggers, give someone a dirty look
▶ *n* glare, frown, scowl, stare, look, *colloq.* black look, dirty look

glowing *adj*

1 BRIGHT, luminous, vivid, vibrant, rich, warm,

flushed, red, ruddy, flaming, smouldering, *technical* phosphorescent, *formal* incandescent **2** *a glowing review* complimentary, enthusiastic, favourable, ecstatic, rhapsodic, *formal* laudatory, eulogistic, panegyrical, *colloq.* rave

F3 **1** dull, colourless **2** restrained

glue *n, v*

▶ *n* adhesive, gum, paste, size, cement, fixative, mortar

▶ *v* stick, affix, gum, paste, seal, bond, cement, fix, *formal* agglutinate

gluey *adj*

adhesive, gummy, sticky, viscid, viscous, *formal* glutinous

glum *adj*

gloomy, unhappy, forlorn, sad, miserable, depressed, despondent, moody, dejected, morose, pessimistic, doleful, crestfallen, sour, sulky, sullen, surly, grumpy, gruff, ill-humoured, churlish, crabbed, *colloq.* down, low, down in the dumps

F3 ecstatic, happy

glut *n, v*

▶ *n* surplus, excess, superfluity, surfeit, overabundance, superabundance, saturation, overflow

F3 scarcity, lack

▶ *v* saturate, oversupply, overload, inundate, flood, deluge, overfeed, sate, satiate, stuff, gorge, fill, cram, choke, clog

glutinous *adj*

adhesive, sticky, cohesive, gluey, gummy, mucous, viscous, *formal* mucilaginous, viscid

glutton *n*

gourmand, gormandizer, gobbler, *colloq.* guzzler, greedy guts, gorger, pig

F3 ascetic

gluttonous *adj*

greedy, gluttonish, voracious, ravenous, insatiable, gormandizing, *formal* edacious, esurient, omnivorous, rapacious, *colloq.* gutsy, hoggish, piggish

F3 abstemious, ascetic

gluttony *n*

gourmandise, gourmandism, greed, greediness, voracity, insatiability, *formal* edacity, esurience, *colloq.* piggishness

F3 abstinence, asceticism

gnarled *adj*

gnarly, knotted, knotty, bumpy, lumpy, twisted, contorted, distorted, rough, wrinkled, rugged, weatherbeaten, leathery

gnash *v*

grind, grate, grit, scrape

gnaw *v*

1 BITE, nibble, munch, chew, crunch, eat, devour, consume, erode, wear, *formal* masticate **2** WORRY, nag, niggle, fret, trouble, plague, prey, torment, harass, harry, haunt

go *v, n*

▶ *v* **1** MOVE, pass, advance, progress, proceed, make for, head, drive, travel, journey, walk, start, begin, go away, depart, leave, take your leave, set off, set out, retreat, withdraw, disappear, vanish, melt away, *formal* repair, *colloq.* quit, scat, scoot, scram, make tracks **2** OPERATE, function, work, run, act, perform, be in working order **3** EXTEND, spread, stretch, reach, lead, span, continue, unfold **4** *time goes quickly* pass, elapse, lapse, proceed, roll on, go by, slip away, tick away **5** *go mad* become, turn, get, grow, come to be, be changed into **6** *the machine goes 'beep'* emit, sound, make a sound, give off, send out, release **7** *the books go here* belong, have as its usual place, fit

in, be found, be located, be situated **8** *the interview went well* turn out, work out, progress, proceed, manage, fare, occur, result, end up, *formal* eventuate, *colloq.* pan out **9** *Where does all the money go?* be used up, be spent, be finished, be exhausted, be consumed **10** *100 jobs will go* get rid of, be discarded, be thrown away, be dismissed, be made redundant, *colloq.* be axed, be sacked, be fired, be given their cards, be shown the door **11** *most of the income goes on rent* be spent on, be given to, be allotted to, be assigned to, be awarded to

F3 **1** stop **2** break down, fail

▷ **go about** approach, begin, set about, address, tackle, attend to, undertake, do, engage in, perform

▷ **go ahead** begin, proceed, carry on, continue, advance, progress, make progress, move

▷ **go along with** accept, agree with, obey, follow, support, abide by, *formal* comply with, concur with

▷ **go around** circulate, be spread around, be passed round, be talked about, go about

▷ **go at** set about, tackle, attack, blame, criticize, argue

▷ **go away** depart, leave, abscond, withdraw, retreat, disappear, vanish, *colloq.* get knotted, sling your hook

---

Colloquial expressions telling someone to go away include:

away!, away with you!, be off!, beat it!, buzz off!, clear off!, clear out!, do me a favour!, get lost!, get out of here!, get out!, get the hell out of here!, go and jump in the lake!, go fly a kite!, hop it!, never darken my door again!, off with you!, off you go!, on your way!, out of my sight!, push off!, run along!, scarper!, scat!, scram!, shove off!, skeddadle!, take a running jump!, vamoose!

▷ **go back** return, revert, backslide, retreat

▷ **go back on** renege on, default on, deny, break your promise

▷ **go by 1** PASS, elapse, lapse, flow **2** *go by the rules* observe, follow, obey, heed, *formal* comply with

▷ **go down 1** DESCEND, sink, be submerged, set, fall (down), drop, decrease, be reduced, decline, deteriorate, degenerate, fail, founder, go under, collapse, *colloq.* fold **2** LOSE, be beaten, be defeated, suffer defeat, fail, *colloq.* come a cropper **3** *the joke went down badly* be received, have as a response, be reacted to, be met with, sustain

▷ **go down with** become ill with, catch, get, develop, pick up, become infected with, fall ill with, *formal* contract, succumb to

▷ **go far** be successful, achieve success, get on, *colloq.* get on in the world, make your mark, make a name for yourself, go places, get ahead

▷ **go for 1** CHOOSE, select, prefer, favour, aim for, like, admire, enjoy **2** ATTACK, assail, assault, rush at, set about, lunge at

▷ **go in for** enter, take part in, participate in, engage in, go into, take up, embrace, adopt, undertake, practise, pursue, follow, *formal* espouse

▷ **go into** discuss, consider, review, examine, study, research, look into, scrutinize, investigate, inquire into, check out, probe, delve into, analyse, dissect

▷ **go off 1** DEPART, leave, set out, abscond, vanish, disappear, *colloq.* quit **2** EXPLODE, blow up, blast, burst, detonate, be fired, be discharged, *colloq.* go bang **3** *the milk has gone off* deteriorate, turn, sour, go bad, rot, go stale

▷ **go on 1** CONTINUE, carry on, proceed, persist, stay, endure, last, remain **2** CHATTER, ramble on, *colloq.* rabbit, witter, natter, gab, gas, talk the hind legs off a donkey **3** HAPPEN, occur, take place

▷ **go out 1** EXIT, depart, leave, withdraw **2** *go out with a boy* go with, court, see each other, *colloq.* date, go steady

▷ **go over** examine, peruse, study, revise, scan, read, look over, inspect, discuss, think about, check, review, repeat, rehearse, list

▷ **go through 1** SUFFER, undergo, experience, bear, tolerate, endure, withstand, stand, be subjected to **2** INVESTIGATE, check, examine, look through, search, hunt, explore **3** USE UP, consume, exhaust, spend, squander, get through

▷ **go together** match, harmonize, fit, suit, blend, co-ordinate, complement, *formal* accord

▷ **go under 1** CLOSE DOWN, collapse, default, die, fail, go out of business, founder, go bankrupt, *colloq.* fold, flop, go to the wall, go bust **2** SINK, go down, founder, submerge, succumb, drown

▷ **go with 1** MATCH, harmonize, co-ordinate, blend, complement, suit, fit, correspond **2** ACCOMPANY, escort, take, usher

☒ **1** clash

▷ **go without** abstain, deny yourself, forgo, do without, manage without, lack, want

▶ *n* **1** *have a go* attempt, try, bid, turn, endeavour, effort, *colloq.* shot, bash, stab, whirl **2** ENERGY, vitality, life, force, spirit, dynamism, vigour, animation, *colloq.* get-up-and-go, push, pizzazz

goad *v*
prod, prick, spur, impel, push, drive, jolt, provoke, incite, induce, instigate, arouse, stimulate, inspire, motivate, pressurize, prompt, urge, nag, hound, harass, taunt, annoy, irritate, vex

go-ahead *n, adj*
▶ *n* permission, authorization, clearance, sanction, approval, assent, consent, warranty, agreement, confirmation, *colloq.* green light, OK, thumbs-up
☒ ban, veto, embargo
▶ *adj* enterprising, pioneering, progressive, ambitious, forward, forward-looking, opportunist, up-and-coming, dynamic, vigorous, energetic, aggressive, *colloq.* go-getting, pushy
☒ unenterprising, sluggish

goal *n*
target, mark, objective, aim, intention, object, purpose, end, design, ambition, ideal, aspiration

gobble *v*
bolt, guzzle, gorge, cram, stuff, devour, consume, swallow, gulp, *colloq.* put away, wolf, scoff

gobbledygook *n*
jargon, journalese, computerese, psychobabble, buzz words, nonsense, rubbish, drivel, twaddle, balderdash, prattle

go-between *n*
intermediary, mediator, liaison, contact, middleman, broker, dealer, agent, factor, messenger, medium

goblin *n*
imp, brownie, fiend, hobgoblin, gnome, elf, sprite, spirit, gremlin, nixie, red-cap, bogey, kelpie, kobold, demon

God *n*
Deity, Supreme Being, Divine Being, Godhead, prime mover, Creator, Maker, Providence, Lord, King, Almighty, Holy One, Jehovah, Yahweh, Father, Allah, Brahma, Zeus, Judge, Saviour, Eternal, Everlasting

god, goddess *n*
deity, divine being, divinity, spirit, power, icon, idol, graven image

God-forsaken *adj*
remote, isolated, lonely, bleak, desolate, abandoned, deserted, forlorn, dismal, dreary, gloomy, miserable, wretched, depressing

godless *adj*
ungodly, atheistic, heathen, pagan, irreligious, agnostic, faithless, unholy, unrighteous, impious, sacrilegious, profane, irreverent, bad, evil, sinful, wicked, *formal* nullifidian
☒ godly, pious

godlike *adj*
divine, celestial, heavenly, exalted, saintly, holy, sacred, perfect, sublime, transcendent, superhuman, *formal* deiform, theomorphic

godly *adj*
religious, holy, pious, devout, God-fearing, believing, righteous, good, moral, virtuous, saintly, pure, innocent
☒ godless, impious

godsend *n*
blessing, boon, stroke of luck, bonanza, windfall, benediction, miracle
☒ blow, setback

goggle *v*
stare, gaze, wonder, *colloq.* gawp, gawk

going-over *n*
1 EXAMINATION, inspection, investigation, study, survey, analysis, check, check-up, review, scrutiny **2** BEATING, attack, criticism, reprimand, scolding, rebuke, pasting, chiding, thrashing, whipping, row, *formal* castigation, chastisement, *colloq.* dressing-down, trouncing

goings-on *n*
events, activities, occurrences, happenings, affair, scenes, business, misbehaviour, mischief, *colloq.* funny business

gold *n*
bullion, nugget, bar, ingot, precious metal

golden *adj*
1 GOLD, gilded, gilt, gold-coloured, yellow, blond(e), fair, flaxen, bright, shining, gleaming, brilliant, dazzling, lustrous, *formal* resplendent **2** PROSPEROUS, successful, glorious, excellent, treasured, precious, happy, joyful, delightful, rosy, favourable, promising, flourishing, bright, rewarding, *formal* auspicious, propitious

golf club *n*

Types of golf club include:
driver, brassie, spoon, wood, iron, driving iron, midiron, midmashie, mashie iron, mashie, spade mashie, mashie niblick, pitching niblick, niblick, putter, pitching wedge, sand wedge.

gone *adj*
departed, absent, away, astray, defunct, disappeared, vanished, lost, missing, finished, done, over, elapsed, past, used, spent, dead, extinct, *colloq.* over and done with

goo *n*
matter, ooze, slime, stickiness, slush, sludge, mud, scum, mire, muck, grease, grime, *colloq.* gunge, yuck, grot, *slang* crud, gunk, grunge

good *adj, n, interj*
▶ *adj* **1** *have a good day; do good work* enjoyable, cheerful, pleasing, pleasurable, satisfying, commendable, excellent, first-class, first-rate, superior, fine, wonderful, marvellous, fantastic, terrific, superb, exceptional, acceptable, satisfactory, pleasant, agreeable, nice, adequate, passable, reasonable, tolerable, desirable, *colloq.* great, super **2** *good at her job* competent, proficient, skilled, expert, accomplished, professional, skilful, clever, talented, gifted, fit, brilliant, able, capable, dependable, reliable, effi-

cient, adept, dexterous **3** KIND, considerate, gracious, friendly, sympathetic, benevolent, charitable, altruistic, philanthropic, kind-hearted, well-disposed **4** VIRTUOUS, exemplary, moral, upright, honest, trustworthy, worthy, honourable, noble, admirable, righteous, ethical, *colloq.* salt of the earth **5** ADVANTAGEOUS, beneficial, favourable, helpful, useful, worthwhile, profitable, convenient, appropriate, suitable, fitting, lucky, fortunate, *formal* auspicious, propitious **6** WELL-BEHAVED, obedient, well-mannered, polite, respectful, under control, *formal* compliant, *colloq.* good as gold **7** *in good health* fine, healthy, strong, vigorous, sound, hale and hearty, *colloq.* in the pink, the picture of health, fit as a fiddle **8** *a good reason* sound, sensible, valid, right, genuine **9** *be good friends* close, dear, intimate, best, loving, bosom **10** THOROUGH, complete, whole, substantial, considerable, sizeable, large

🖅 **1** bad, poor **2** incompetent **3** unkind, inconsiderate **4** wicked, immoral **5** inconvenient, useless **6** disobedient, naughty **7** poor **8** bad

▷ **make good 1** PUT RIGHT, make amends for, make recompense for, compensate for, make restitution for **2** SUCCEED, get ahead, go far, progress, be successful, get on in the world **3** *make good a threat/ promise* fulfil, carry out, do, live up to, put into action, *formal* effect

▶ *n* **1** VIRTUE, morality, goodness, integrity, honesty, honour, uprightness, righteousness, right, ethics, morals, *formal* rectitude **2** USE, purpose, avail, advantage, profit, gain, worth, merit, usefulness, service **3** *for your own good* benefit, welfare, well-being, interest, sake, behalf, convenience

▷ **for good** for ever, always, ever, evermore, for all time, permanently, till the end of time, eternally, *colloq.* till kingdom come, till the cows come home

▶ *interj* fine, perfect, all right, very well, right, agreed, indeed, just so, *colloq.* OK

goodbye *interj, n*
▶ *interj* farewell, adieu, *au revoir, auf Wiedersehen, ciao, colloq.* cheerio, bye, bye-bye, cheers, see you (later), see you around, be seeing you, all the best, mind how you go, take care, have a nice day, ta-ta, so long
▶ *n* farewell, adieu, *au revoir*, leave-taking, parting, swan song, *formal* valediction

---

Some ways of saying goodbye and expressions used when leaving include:

adios, bye, bye bye, cheerio, chow, good afternoon, good day, goodbye, goodnight, have a nice day, see you later, see you later, alligator, in a while, crocodile, see you when I see you, seeya, ta ta, ta ta for now, take your leave, ttfn, until later.

---

good-for-nothing *adj, n*
▶ *adj* lazy, useless, worthless, idle, irresponsible, reprobate, no-good, *formal* profligate, indolent, feckless
🖅 conscientious, successful
▶ *n* layabout, ne'er-do-well, reprobate, idler, waster, wastrel, *formal* profligate, *colloq.* black sheep, lazybones, loafer, *slang* bum
🖅 achiever, success, winner

good-humoured *adj*
cheerful, happy, jovial, genial, affable, amiable, friendly, congenial, pleasant, good-tempered, approachable
🖅 ill-humoured

good-looking *adj*
attractive, handsome, beautiful, fair, pretty, lovely, personable, presentable, *old use* comely
🖅 ugly, plain

goodly *adj*
substantial, sizeable, considerable, ample, large, good, significant, sufficient, *colloq.* tidy
🖅 inadequate

good-natured *adj*
kind, kindly, kind-hearted, sympathetic, benevolent, generous, helpful, neighbourly, gentle, good-tempered, warm-hearted, approachable, friendly, tolerant, patient
🖅 ill-natured

goodness *n*
virtue, uprightness, integrity, righteousness, honesty, kindness, compassion, graciousness, mercy, goodwill, excellence, benefit, benevolence, unselfishness, generosity, altruism, friendliness, helpfulness, wholesomeness, *formal* rectitude, probity, beneficence
🖅 badness, wickedness, selfishness

goods *n*
1 PROPERTY, chattels, effects, possessions, belongings, paraphernalia, things, *colloq.* gear, stuff, *formal* accoutrements, appurtenances **2** MERCHANDISE, wares, commodities, products, things, lines, stock, freight

goodwill *n*
benevolence, kindness, compassion, generosity, favour, friendliness, friendship, zeal, *formal* amity
🖅 ill-will

goody-goody *adj*
self-righteous, sanctimonious, pious, priggish, *formal* unctuous, ultra-virtuous

gooey *adj*
1 STICKY, soft, gluey, glutinous, viscous, tacky, thick, syrupy, *formal* mucilaginous, viscid, *colloq.* gungy **2** SENTIMENTAL, slushy, sloppy, syrupy, nauseating, maudlin, mawkish

gore *v, n*
▶ *v* pierce, penetrate, stab, spear, stick, impale, wound
▶ *n* blood, bloodiness, bloodshed, slaughter, butchery, carnage, *technical* cruor, grume

gorge *n, v*
▶ *n* canyon, ravine, gully, defile, chasm, abyss, crevice, cleft, fissure, rift, gap, pass
▶ *v* feed, guzzle, gobble, devour, bolt, gulp, swallow, cram, stuff, fill, sate, surfeit, glut, overeat, *colloq.* wolf
🖅 fast

gorgeous *adj*
1 MAGNIFICENT, splendid, grand, glorious, superb, fine, impressive, rich, sumptuous, luxurious, brilliant, dazzling, resplendent, marvellous, wonderful, delightful, pleasing, lovely, enjoyable, good, showy, glamorous, *formal* opulent **2** ATTRACTIVE, beautiful, pretty, fine, sweet, glamorous, handsome, good-looking, lovely, *formal* pulchritudinous, *colloq.* sexy, stunning, ravishing
🖅 dull, plain

gory *adj*
bloody, bloodstained, blood-soaked, grisly, brutal, savage, violent, murderous, *formal* sanguinary

gospel *n*
1 LIFE OF CHRIST, teaching of Christ, message of Christ, good news, New Testament **2** TEACHING, doctrine, creed, credo, certainty, truth, fact, *technical* kerygma, *formal* evangel, verity

gossamer *adj*
thin, light, delicate, flimsy, fine, cobwebby, insubstantial, sheer, shimmering, silky, airy, transparent, see-through, translucent, gauzy, *formal* diaphanous
🖅 heavy, opaque, thick

gossip *n, v*
▶ *n* **1** IDLE TALK, prattle, chitchat, tittle-tattle, rumour, hearsay, report, whisper, scandal, *colloq.* mudslinging, smear campaign **2** GOSSIP-MONGER, scandalmonger, whisperer, prattler, babbler, chatterbox, busybody, talebearer, tell-tale, tattler, blether, *colloq.* nosey parker
▶ *v* talk, chat, natter, chatter, blether, blather, gabble, prattle, babble, tattle, spread gossip, tell tales, whisper, rumour, spread/circulate a rumour, *colloq.* jabber, rabbit (on), gas, waffle, chinwag, jaw, chew the rag/fat

gouge *v*
chisel, cut, hack, incise, score, groove, scratch, claw, gash, slash, dig, scoop, hollow, extract

gourmand *n*
glutton, gormandizer, *formal* omnivore, *colloq.* gorger, guzzler, hog, pig
F∃ ascetic

📝 **gourmand** or **gourmet** ?

A *gourmand* is a glutton; a person who enjoys eating large quantities of food. A *gourmet* is a person who has an expert knowledge of, and a passion for, good food and wine.

gourmet *n*
gastronome, epicure, epicurean, connoisseur, bon vivant, *colloq.* foodie

govern *v*
1 RULE, reign, be in power, hold office, direct, manage, administer, be responsible for, superintend, supervise, oversee, preside, lead, head, be in charge of, command, order, control, influence, guide, conduct, steer, pilot **2** *govern your temper* dominate, master, control, regulate, curb, check, keep in check, hold/keep back, restrain, contain, quell, constrain, bridle, rein in, subdue, tame, discipline

governess *n*
teacher, guide, instructress, tutoress, tutress, mentor, companion, duenna, *old use* gouvernante

governing *adj*
ruling, controlling, regulatory, commanding, reigning, guiding, leading, supreme, uppermost, dominant, overriding, predominant, prevailing, transcendent, *formal* dominative

government *n*
1 *blame the government* administration, executive, ministry, Establishment, authorities, state, régime, congress, parliament, council, cabinet, leadership, *colloq.* powers that be **2** RULE, sovereignty, sway, direction, management, superintendence, supervision, surveillance, command, charge, authority, power, guidance, conduct, domination, dominion, control, regulation, restraint

Government systems include:
absolutism, autocracy, commonwealth, communism, democracy, despotism, dictatorship, empire, federation, hierocracy, junta, kingdom, monarchy, plutocracy, puppet government, republic, theocracy, triumvirate. *See also* PARLIAMENTS AND POLITICAL ASSEMBLIES.

governor *n*
ruler, commissioner, administrator, executive, director, manager, leader, head, chief, president, viceroy, commander, superintendent, supervisor, commander, master, regulator, guide, warden, overseer, controller, *colloq.* boss

gown *n*
robe, dress, frock, dressing-gown, garment, habit, costume, *colloq.* garb

grab *v, n*
▶ *v* seize, snatch, take, pluck, snap up, catch/take/lay hold of, grasp, clutch, grip, catch, capture, commandeer, usurp, annex, *formal* appropriate, *colloq.* nab, bag, collar, nail, swipe
▶ *n* grasp, grip, clutch, snatch, catch, capture
▷ **up for grabs** available, obtainable, at hand, *colloq.* for the asking, to be had

grace *n, v*
▶ *n* **1** GRACEFULNESS, poise, beauty, attractiveness, loveliness, shapeliness, smoothness, elegance, ease, fluency, finesse, tastefulness, good taste, refinement, polish, breeding, cultivation, manners, etiquette, decorum, decency, consideration, courtesy, charm, *formal* propriety **2** KINDNESS, kindliness, compassion, consideration, goodness, virtue, generosity, charity, benevolence, goodwill, favour, forgiveness, indulgence, mercy, mercifulness, leniency, pardon, reprieve, quarter, *formal* beneficence, clemency **3** *say grace* blessing, benediction, thanksgiving, prayer
F∃ **2** cruelty, harshness
▶ *v* favour, honour, dignify, distinguish, embellish, enhance, enrich, set off, trim, garnish, decorate, ornament, adorn
F∃ spoil, detract from

graceful *adj*
easy, flowing, fluid, easy, smooth, supple, agile, deft, nimble, natural, slender, fine, tasteful, elegant, beautiful, attractive, appealing, charming, tasteful, cultured, refined, polished, cultivated, suave
F∃ graceless, awkward, clumsy, ungainly

graceless *adj*
clumsy, awkward, unattractive, forced, gauche, gawky, ungainly, ungraceful, inelegant, rough, rude, vulgar, coarse, crude, uncouth, unsophisticated, impolite, improper, unmannerly, ill-mannered, barbarous, shameless, *formal* indecorous
F∃ graceful, refined

gracious *adj*
1 POLITE, courteous, well-mannered, refined, considerate, sweet, obliging, accommodating, kind, compassionate, kind-hearted, kindly, friendly, pleasant, benevolent, generous, magnanimous, charitable, hospitable, forgiving, indulgent, lenient, mild, clement, merciful, *formal* beneficent **2** ELEGANT, luxurious, comfortable, tasteful, sumptuous
F∃ **1** ungracious

gradation *n*
change, progression, degree, grading, sorting, ordering, progress, succession, arrangement, sequence, series, stage, step, level, mark, shading, rank, *formal* array

grade *n, v*
▶ *n* rank, status, standing, station, place, position, level, stage, degree, step, rating, rung, notch, mark, brand, quality, standard, condition, size, order, group, type, class, category, classification, *formal* echelon
▷ **make the grade** succeed, pass, come/win through, reach the expected standard
▶ *v* sort, arrange, categorize, order, group, class, rate, size, rank, range, classify, evaluate, assess, value, mark, brand, label, pigeonhole, type

gradient *n*
slope, incline, hill, bank, rise, grade, *formal* acclivity, declivity

gradual *adj*
slow, leisurely, unhurried, easy, gentle, moderate,

regular, even, measured, steady, continuous, progressive, step-by-step
🖪 sudden, steep, precipitate

gradually *adv*
little by little, bit by bit, imperceptibly, inch by inch, step by step, successively, continuously, progressively, by degrees, piecemeal, slowly, gently, cautiously, gingerly, moderately, regularly, evenly, steadily

graduate *v, n*
▶ *v* **1** *graduate from medical school* pass, qualify, complete studies **2** CALIBRATE, mark off, measure out, proportion, grade, arrange, range, order, rank, sort, group, classify, categorize **3** PROGRESS, move up, move forward, advance, be promoted, make headway, go/forge ahead
▶ *n* qualified/skilled person, expert, specialist, consultant, professional, bachelor, doctor, master, fellow, member, graduand, alumna, alumnus, valedictorian, *colloq.* whizz kid

graft¹ *v, n*
▶ *v grafted onto a tree* engraft, implant, insert, transplant, join, splice, *formal* affix
▶ *n* implant, implantation, transplant, growth, splice, bud, sprout, shoot, scion

graft² *n*
1 EFFORT, hard work, toil, labour, *colloq.* sweat of your brow, slog **2** BRIBERY, corruption, dishonesty, extortion, *colloq.* con tricks, shady business, dirty tricks/dealings, wheeling and dealing, sharp practices, rip-off, sting, *slang* scam

grain *n*
1 BIT, piece, fragment, scrap, morsel, crumb, granule, particle, molecule, atom, jot, iota, mite, speck, modicum, trace, hint, suggestion, soupçon, scintilla **2** SEED, kernel, corn, cereals, wheat, rye, barley, oats, maize **3** TEXTURE, fabric, fibre, weave, pattern, marking, surface, nap

grand *adj*
1 MAJESTIC, regal, stately, palatial, splendid, magnificent, glorious, superb, sublime, exalting, fine, excellent, outstanding, first-rate, impressive, imposing, striking, monumental, large, luxurious, lavish, sumptuous, noble, lordly, lofty, pompous, pretentious, grandiose, showy, ostentatious, ambitious, *formal* opulent **2** SUPREME, pre-eminent, leading, head, chief, main, principal, arch, highest, senior, great, illustrious **3** *have a grand day out* excellent, wonderful, splendid, marvellous, fantastic, superb, enjoyable, delightful, outstanding, first-rate, *colloq.* great, super, terrific, smashing, *slang* mega, cool, wicked **4** *a grand total* complete, final, comprehensive, inclusive, all-inclusive, in full
🖪 **1** humble, plain, simple, common, poor

grandeur *n*
majesty, stateliness, pomp, state, dignity, splendour, magnificence, impressiveness, luxuriousness, lavishness, nobility, greatness, illustriousness, importance, fame, renown, eminence, prominence, *formal* opulence
🖪 humbleness, lowliness, simplicity

grandfather *n*
grandpa, grand(d)ad, grand(d)addy

grandiloquent *adj*
exaggerated, pretentious, high-flown, high-sounding, inflated, pompous, bombastic, flowery, rhetorical, fustian, euphuistic, swollen, turgid, *formal* grandiloquous, magniloquent, orotund
🖪 plain, restrained, simple

grandiose *adj*
pompous, pretentious, high-flown, high-sounding, lofty, ambitious, extravagant, ostentatious, showy,

flamboyant, grand, majestic, splendid, striking, stately, magnificent, impressive, imposing, monumental, *colloq.* over-the-top
🖪 unpretentious

grandmother *n*
grandma, granny, gran, nan

grant *v, n*
▶ *v* **1** GIVE, donate, present, award, impart, transmit, dispense, assign, allot, allocate, provide, supply, contribute, *formal* confer, bestow, apportion, furnish **2** ADMIT, acknowledge, concede, allow, permit, accept, agree to, *formal* consent to, accede to, vouchsafe
🖪 **1** withhold **2** deny
▶ *n* allowance, subsidy, concession, award, bursary, scholarship, gift, donation, endowment, bequest, annuity, pension, honorarium, contribution

granular *adj*
grainy, granulated, gritty, sandy, lumpy, rough, crumbly, friable

granule *n*
piece, particle, grain, scrap, crumb, bead, speck, fragment, iota, jot, atom, molecule, pellet, seed

graph *n*
diagram, chart, table, grid, plot, curve, bar graph, bar chart, pie chart, scatter diagram, *technical* nomogram, nomograph

graphic *adj*
1 VIVID, descriptive, expressive, striking, telling, lively, realistic, explicit, effective, clear, lucid, specific, detailed, well-defined, blow-by-blow, *formal* cogent **2** VISUAL, pictorial, diagrammatic, drawn, illustrative, representational, *formal* delineative
🖪 **1** vague, impressionistic

grapple *v*
1 GRASP, seize, snatch, grab, grip, clutch, clasp, hold, lay hold of, wrestle, tussle, struggle, contend, battle, fight, combat, clash, engage, close **2** *grapple with a problem* face, confront, encounter, tackle, address, deal with, cope with, get to grips with
🖪 **1** release **2** avoid, evade

grasp *v, n*
▶ *v* **1** HOLD, clasp, clutch, grip, grapple, seize, snatch, grab, catch, lay hold of, clench **2** *grasp a concept* understand, comprehend, follow, see, perceive, master, realize, take in, catch on, latch onto, *formal* apprehend, *colloq.* get
▶ *n* **1** GRIP, clasp, hold, embrace, clutches, possession, control, power, command, rule, dominion, mastery **2** UNDERSTANDING, comprehension, apprehension, mastery, familiarity, knowledge, awareness, perception

grasping *adj*
greedy, acquisitive, covetous, mercenary, mean, selfish, miserly, close-fisted, tight-fisted, stingy, niggardly, *formal* avaricious, rapacious, parsimonious
🖪 generous

grass *n*
turf, lawn, green, grassland, common, field, meadow, pasture, downs, prairie, pampas, savanna, steppe, veld, veldt, *old use* lea, mead, sward

grate *v*
1 GRIND, shred, mince, pulverize, rub, rasp, scrape, scratch, *formal* triturate **2** JAR, set your teeth on edge, annoy, irritate, vex, irk, exasperate, gall, rankle, *colloq.* aggravate, peeve, get on someone's nerves, get under your skin, get someone's goat

grateful *adj*
thankful, appreciative, indebted, obliged, obligated, *formal* beholden
🖪 ungrateful

gratification *n*
pleasure, satisfaction, contentment, delight, elation, enjoyment, joy, thrill, relish, indulgence, glee, *colloq.* kicks
🔁 frustration, disappointment

gratify *v*
1 PLEASE, cheer, charm, gladden, delight, thrill, make happy 2 SATISFY, fulfil, indulge, pander to, humour, favour, pamper, spoil, cosset, placate
🔁 1 frustrate 2 thwart

grating[1] *adj*
a grating noise harsh, rasping, scraping, grinding, scratching, squeaky, screeching, strident, discordant, raucous, jarring, annoying, irritating, galling, unpleasant, disagreeable, offensive, exasperating, irksome
🔁 harmonious, pleasing

grating[2] *n*
a grating over a window grate, grille, grid, lattice, trellis, frame, *technical* graticule

gratis *adv*
free, without charge, free of charge, for nothing, at no cost, complimentary, *colloq.* on the house, *slang* buckshee

gratitude *n*
gratefulness, thankfulness, thanks, appreciation, acknowledgement, recognition, indebtedness, obligation
🔁 ingratitude, ungratefulness

gratuitous *adj*
1 VIOLENT, wanton, unnecessary, needless, superfluous, unwarranted, unjustified, groundless, unfounded, undeserved, unprovoked, uncalled-for, unasked-for, unmerited, unsolicited, without reason 2 VOLUNTARY, free, free of charge, gratis, for nothing, complimentary, unrewarded, unpaid
🔁 1 justified, provoked

gratuity *n*
tip, bonus, gift, present, donation, reward, recompense, bounty, boon, largesse, baksheesh, pourboire, *formal* perquisite, *colloq.* perk

grave[1] *n*
1 *buried in a grave* burial place, tomb, vault, crypt, last resting-place, sepulchre, mausoleum, pit, burial mound, burial site, barrow, tumulus, cairn 2 DEATH, loss of life, loss, departure, fatality, passing, passing away, *formal* expiration, decease, demise, *colloq.* last farewell, curtains

grave[2] *adj*
1 SOLEMN, dignified, sober, sedate, serious, earnest, sombre, severe, thoughtful, pensive, grim, gloomy, long-faced, quiet, reserved, subdued, restrained, staid 2 *a grave mistake* important, significant, weighty, momentous, serious, critical, vital, crucial, urgent, pressing, acute, severe, menacing, threatening, dangerous, hazardous, *formal* exigent, perilous
🔁 1 cheerful, smiling 2 trivial, light, slight

gravel *n*
shingle, grit, pebbles, stones, chesil, hogging, *old use* grail

gravelly *adj*
1 GRAINY, granular, pebbly, shingly, gritty, *old use* glareous, *formal* sabulose, sabulous 2 *a gravelly voice* harsh, rough, thick, hoarse, guttural, throaty, grating, gruff
🔁 2 clear, fine

gravestone *n*
tombstone, headstone, stone, memorial

graveyard *n*
cemetery, burial ground, burial place, burial site, churchyard, *formal* necropolis, charnel house, God's acre

gravitate *v*
fall, descend, drop, head for, move, precipitate, sink, incline, lean, tend, drift, be attached to, be drawn to, settle

gravity *n*
1 IMPORTANCE, significance, seriousness, weightiness, momentousness, consequence, urgency, acuteness, severity, danger, hazard, *formal* exigency, peril 2 SOLEMNITY, dignity, seriousness, earnestness, severity, thoughtfulness, sombreness, grimness, gloominess, reserve, restraint, *formal* sobriety 3 GRAVITATION, attraction, pull, weight, heaviness
🔁 1 triviality 2 levity

graze[1] *v*
the cattle are grazing crop, feed, fodder, pasture, browse, *formal* ruminate

graze[2] *v, n*
▶ *v* 1 SCRATCH, scrape, skin, bruise, rub, chafe, *formal* abrade 2 BRUSH, skim, touch, kiss, shave, glance off
▶ *n* scratch, scrape, abrasion

grease *n*
oil, lubrication, fat, lard, dripping, tallow

greasy *adj*
oily, fatty, lardy, buttery, smeary, slimy, slippery, smooth, waxy, *formal* oleaginous, oleic, adipose, sebaceous, unctuous

great *adj*
1 LARGE, big, huge, enormous, massive, colossal, gigantic, mammoth, immense, vast, extensive, boundless, spacious, impressive, *colloq.* great big, whopping, jumbo, ginormous, *slang* mega 2 *with great care* considerable, pronounced, substantial, sizeable, extreme, excessive, inordinate 3 FAMOUS, renowned, celebrated, famed, illustrious, eminent, distinguished, prominent, noteworthy, notable, noted, remarkable, outstanding, *formal* august 4 FINE, grand, glorious, impressive, imposing, magnificent, splendid 5 IMPORTANT, significant, serious, major, crucial, critical, principal, primary, main, chief, leading, essential, momentous, vital, paramount, salient 6 EXCELLENT, first-rate, superb, wonderful, marvellous, admirable, splendid, tremendous, fantastic, fabulous, *colloq.* super, terrific, smashing, ace, top-notch, *slang* cool, mega, wicked 7 EXPERT, proficient, adept, skilled, skilful, knowledgeable, experienced, able, practised, professional, accomplished, masterly, excellent, brilliant, specialist, qualified, virtuoso, dexterous, *colloq.* top-notch, up on, well up on, crack, ace
🔁 1 small, limited 2 slight 3 unknown 5 unimportant, insignificant 7 amateurish, novice

greatly *adv*
much, considerably, enormously, highly, extremely, immensely, vastly, noticeably, significantly, remarkably, impressively, notably, substantially, markedly, mightily, tremendously, hugely, powerfully, exceedingly, abundantly

greatness *n*
fame, renown, illustriousness, eminence, heroism, distinction, note, significance, importance, weight, momentousness, seriousness, power, magnitude, intensity, excellence, glory, genius, grandeur
🔁 insignificance, pettiness, smallness

greed *n*
1 HUNGER, ravenousness, gluttony, gourmandism, insatiability, *formal* voracity, edacity, esurience, *colloq.* piggishness, hoggishness, bingeing, stuffing yourself 2 ACQUISITIVENESS, covetousness, desire, craving, longing, eagerness, impatience, selfishness, *formal* avarice, rapacity, cupidity
🔁 1 abstemiousness, self-restraint

greedy *adj*
1 HUNGRY, starving, ravenous, gluttonous, gormandizing, insatiable, *formal* voracious, edacious, esurient, omnivorous, *colloq.* hoggish, piggish, bingeing **2** ACQUISITIVE, covetous, desirous, craving, grabbing, eager, impatient, grasping, selfish, *formal* avaricious, rapacious, cupidinous, *colloq.* on the make, grabby
F3 **1** abstemious

green *adj, n*
▶ *adj* **1** GRASSY, leafy, unripe, lush, unseasoned, tender, raw, fresh, budding, blooming, flourishing, healthy, vigorous, *formal* verdant, glaucous, viridescent, virescent, verdurous **2** ECOLOGICAL, environmental, conservationist, eco-friendly, environmentally aware, environmentally friendly **3** IMMATURE, naïve, simple, unsophisticated, ignorant, unqualified, inexperienced, untrained, inexpert, unversed, raw, new, recent, young, *colloq.* wet behind the ears **4** *green with envy* envious, covetous, jealous, grudging, resentful
F3 **3** mature, experienced, qualified, expert
▶ *n* common, lawn, grass, turf, field, grassland, meadow, pasture

greenery *n*
foliage, vegetation, greenness, *formal* verdure, verdancy, viridity, viridescence, virescence

greenhorn *n*
novice, apprentice, beginner, learner, initiate, recruit, neophyte, tenderfoot, tiro, newcomer, fledgling, *colloq.* rookie
F3 veteran, *colloq.* old hand

greenhouse *n*
glasshouse, hothouse, conservatory, pavilion, vinery, orangery

greet *v*
salute, acknowledge, hail, address, say hello to, shake hands with, kiss, wave to, nod to, accost, meet, receive, welcome
F3 ignore

greeting *n*
salutation, acknowledgement, wave, hallo, nod, handshake, the time of day, seasonal greeting, address, reception, welcome

greetings *n*
regards, kind/warm regards, respects, compliments, best wishes, good wishes, congratulations, respects, love, salutations

gregarious *adj*
sociable, outgoing, extrovert, friendly, affable, social, companionable, convivial, cordial, warm, hospitable
F3 unsociable

grey *adj*
1 *a grey colour* neutral, colourless, pale, pallid, ashen, wan, leaden **2** *a grey morning* dull, cloudy, overcast, dim, dark, dismal, dreary, bleak, cheerless, foggy, misty, murky **3** GLOOMY, dismal, cheerless, depressing, dreary, bleak, dull, uninteresting, colourless **4** *a grey area* unclear, uncertain, doubtful, ambiguous, debatable, open to question

grid *n*
grating, frame, grille, grill, gridiron, lattice, trellis, *technical* graticule

grief *n*
sorrow, sadness, unhappiness, depression, dejection, desolation, despondency, despair, distress, misery, woe, heartbreak, mourning, bereavement, heartache, anguish, agony, pain, suffering, trouble, regret, remorse, *formal* affliction, lamentation, tribulation
F3 happiness, delight

grief-stricken *adj*
sorrowful, sad, unhappy, sorrowing, grieving, mourning, depressed, dejected, desolate, despondent, distressed, despairing, broken, broken-hearted, heartbroken, inconsolable, overcome, overwhelmed, devastated, crushed, anguished, troubled, wretched, *formal* disconsolate, woebegone, afflicted
F3 overjoyed, delighted

grievance *n*
complaint, resentment, objection, protest, charge, wrong, injustice, unfairness, offence, injury, damage, trouble, hardship, trial, *formal* affliction, tribulation, *colloq.* moan, grumble, grouse, gripe, bone to pick

grieve *v*
1 SORROW, lament, mourn, wail, cry, weep, sob, mope, brood, pine away, ache, suffer **2** SADDEN, upset, dismay, distress, afflict, pain, hurt, wound, crush, horrify, offend, shock, break someone's heart
F3 **1** rejoice **2** please, gladden

grievous *adj*
1 SEVERE, grave, tragic, appalling, distressing, dreadful, atrocious, burdensome, calamitous, devastating, damaging, shameful, harmful, outrageous, overwhelming, shocking, deplorable, intolerable, unbearable, monstrous, flagrant, glaring, *formal* sorrowful **2** WOUNDING, injurious, hurtful, painful, damaging, sore, *formal* afflicting

grim *adj*
1 STERN, severe, harsh, dour, forbidding, formidable, fierce, menacing, threatening, surly, sullen, morose, gloomy, depressing, unattractive **2** UNPLEASANT, horrible, horrid, horrendous, dire, ghastly, gruesome, grisly, sinister, dreadful, awful, frightening, fearsome, terrible, shocking, appalling, harrowing, unspeakable **3** RESOLUTE, determined, dogged, tenacious, persistent, stubborn, inexorable, unyielding, unshakable, *formal* obdurate
F3 **1** attractive **2** pleasant

grimace *n, v*
▶ *n* frown, scowl, pout, smirk, sneer, face
▶ *v* pull a face, make a face, frown, scowl, pout, smirk, mouth, sneer

grime *n*
dirt, muck, filth, soot, dust, mud, *colloq.* gunge, yuck, grot, *slang* crud, grunge

grimy *adj*
dirty, mucky, grubby, soiled, stained, filthy, sooty, smutty, dusty, muddy, smudgy, *formal* besmirched
F3 clean

grind *v, n*
▶ *v* **1** CRUSH, pound, pulverize, crumble, powder, mill, granulate, grate, scrape, gnash, *formal* kibble, levigate, comminute, triturate **2** SHARPEN, whet, smooth, polish, sand, file, rub, abrade **3** GRATE, scrape, rub, rasp
▷ **grind down** wear down, oppress, crush, trouble, persecute, plague, torment, harass, harry, hound, tyrannize, *formal* afflict
▶ *n* drudgery, chore, toil, labour, round, routine, exertion, task, slavery, sweat

grip *n, v*
▶ *n* **1** HOLD, grasp, clasp, clutch, embrace, clench, hug **2** CONTROL, power, command, influence, mastery, domination, clutches **3** BAG, case, hold-all, kitbag, shoulder-bag, valise, suitcase, overnight bag, travelling bag
▷ **come/get to grips with** deal with, tackle, cope with, take care of, look after, encounter, confront, face up to, take on, grasp
▶ *v* **1** HOLD, grasp, clasp, get/catch/grab hold of, clutch, clench, latch onto, cling, seize, grab, catch

2 FASCINATE, thrill, enthral, spellbind, mesmerize, hypnotize, entrance, rivet, engross, absorb, involve, engage, compel

gripe *v, n*
▶ *v* complain, grumble, protest, moan, nag, groan, *colloq.* beef, bellyache, carp, grouch, grouse, whine, whinge, bitch, have a bone to pick
▶ *n* complaint, groan, grumble, moan, objection, protest, grievance, *colloq.* beef, grouch, grouse, griping, bitch

gripping *adj*
fascinating, thrilling, enthralling, compelling, compulsive, exciting, suspenseful, spellbinding, entrancing, riveting, engrossing, absorbing, *colloq.* unputdownable

grisly *adj*
gruesome, gory, grim, macabre, horrid, horrible, horrifying, ghastly, awful, frightful, terrible, dreadful, repulsive, revolting, disgusting, hideous, macabre, loathsome, abhorrent, abominable, appalling, shocking
🖃 delightful

grit *n, v*
▶ *n* **1** GRAVEL, pebbles, shingle, sand, dust **2** DETERMINATION, courage, bravery, strength, resolve, resolution, hardness, toughness, mettle, endurance, perseverance, doggedness, steadfastness, tenacity, *colloq.* backbone, guts
▶ *v* clench, gnash, grate, rasp, scrape, grind

gritty *adj*
1 GRAINY, dusty, gravelly, sandy, shingly, pebbly, powdery, granular, rough, abrasive, *formal* sabulous, sabulose **2** DETERMINED, courageous, brave, resolute, hardy, tough, mettlesome, dogged, tenacious, steadfast, spirited, plucky, *colloq.* spunky
🖃 **1** fine, smooth **2** cowardly, *colloq.* spineless

grizzle *v*
cry, whimper, whine, whinge, sniffle, snivel, snuffle, fret, moan, complain, grumble

grizzled *adj*
grey, grey-haired, grey-headed, greying, hoary, hoar, pepper-and-salt, *technical* griseous, *formal* canescent

groan *n, v*
▶ *n* **1** MOAN, sigh, cry, whine, whimper, wail, lament **2** COMPLAINT, grumble, objection, protest, outcry, grievance, moan, *colloq.* beef, grouch, grouse, griping
▶ *v* **1** MOAN, sigh, cry, whine, whimper, wail, lament **2** COMPLAIN, grumble, object, protest, *colloq.* whine, whinge, beef, bellyache, grouse

grocer *n*
dealer, storekeeper, supplier, supermarket, greengrocer, *formal* purveyor, victualler

groggy *adj*
weak, dopey, unsteady, wobbly, shaky, staggering, stunned, dazed, confused, befuddled, bewildered, stupefied, punch-drunk, dizzy, faint, reeling, *colloq.* muzzy, woozy
🖃 healthy, strong, lucid

groom *v, n*
▶ *v* **1** SMARTEN, neaten, tidy (up), spruce up, prepare, put in order, arrange, adjust, fix, do, smooth **2** CLEAN, brush, curry, preen, dress **3** *groomed for her new post* prepare, make ready, train, school, teach, educate, instruct, tutor, drill, coach, prime
▶ *n* **1** BRIDEGROOM, honeymooner, newly-wed, husband, spouse, marriage partner **2** STABLEBOY, stableman, stable lad/lass, stable hand

groove *n*
furrow, rut, track, slot, channel, canal, chamfer,

gutter, trough, ditch, trench, hollow, gouge, indentation, cut, score, ridge, *technical* rabbet, rebate, sulcus

grooved *adj*
channelled, fluted, furrowed, rutted, scored, chamfered, *technical* rabbeted, scrobiculate, *formal* sulcal, sulcate, exarate
🖃 ridged

grope *v*
1 FUMBLE, feel, scrabble, flounder, pick **2** SEARCH, hunt, scrabble, fish, probe, cast about

gross *adj, v*
▶ *adj* **1** *gross misconduct* serious, grievous, blatant, flagrant, glaring, obvious, plain, sheer, utter, outright, shameful, shocking, outrageous, *formal* manifest, egregious **2** OBSCENE, lewd, improper, dirty, filthy, risqué, pornographic, indecent, offensive, rude, coarse, crude, vulgar, ribald, bawdy, smutty, earthy, improper, tasteless, *colloq.* blue **3** FAT, obese, overweight, big, large, huge, colossal, immense, massive, hulking, bulky, heavy, *formal* corpulent **4** TASTELESS, vulgar, unpleasant, uncultured, unsophisticated, unrefined, insensitive, coarse, boorish **5** *gross earnings* inclusive, all-inclusive, total, entire, complete, comprehensive, whole, before deductions, before tax, *formal* aggregate
🖃 **2** polite **3** slight **4** tasteful **5** net
▶ *v* earn, make, take, bring in, accumulate, total, *formal* aggregate, *colloq.* rake in

grotesque *adj*
bizarre, odd, weird, strange, peculiar, unnatural, freakish, monstrous, hideous, ugly, unsightly, misshapen, deformed, malformed, distorted, twisted, fantastic, fanciful, whimsical, extravagant, ridiculous, ludicrous, absurd, outlandish, surreal, macabre
🖃 normal, graceful

grotto *n*
cave, cavern, chamber, catacomb, underground chamber, subterranean (chamber)

grouch *n*
1 COMPLAINER, grumbler, moaner, fault-finder, murmurer, mutterer, grouser, *formal* malcontent, *colloq.* belly-acher, crosspatch, whiner, whinger, **2** COMPLAINT, grievance, grumble, objection, moan, *colloq.* gripe, grouse, whinge

grouchy *adj*
bad-tempered, irritable, cross, dissatisfied, discontented, grumpy, sulky, surly, complaining, grumbling, testy, ill-tempered, irascible, captious, churlish, peevish, petulant, *formal* cantankerous, querulous, truculent, *colloq.* crotchety
🖃 contented

ground *n, v*
▶ *n* **1** EARTH, soil, clay, loam, dirt, dust, dry land, terra firma, land, terrain, bottom, foundation, surface **2** *a football ground* field, pitch, stadium, arena, park **3** *the palace grounds* estate, property, territory, domain, gardens, park, campus, surroundings, fields, acres, land, terrain, holding, plot **4** *no grounds for such harsh treatment* base, foundation, justification, excuse, vindication, reason, motive, inducement, cause, occasion, call, score, account, argument, principle, basis **5** *coffee grounds* dregs, sediment, deposit, residue, lees, scourings, *technical* precipitate
▶ *v* **1** BASE, found, establish, set, fix, settle **2** PREPARE, introduce, initiate, familiarize with, acquaint with, inform, instruct, teach, educate, train, drill, coach, tutor

groundless *adj*
baseless, unfounded, unsubstantiated, unsupported, empty, imaginary, false, illusory, unjustified, unwar-

ranted, unprovoked, uncalled-for, without reason
F3 well-founded, reasonable, justified

groundwork *n*
basis, base, essentials, foundation, fundamentals, preparation, preliminaries, research, homework, cornerstone, footing, spadework, underpinnings

group *n, v*
▶ *n* band, gang, pack, team, crew, troop, squad, detachment, unit, party, faction, set, circle, clique, coterie, contingent, club, society, association, guild, league, organization, company, gathering, congregation, body, assembly, crowd, flock, collection, bunch, clump, cluster, knot, batch, lot, combination, element, bracket, formation, grouping, class, category, classification, genus, species, family, school, *formal* conglomeration
▶ *v* GATHER, collect, assemble, congregate, mass, cluster, clump, bunch, huddle **2** *group them according to size* sort, range, arrange, marshal, line up, organize, order, rank, grade, class, classify, categorize, band, bracket, link, associate

grouse *v, n*
▶ *v* complain, grumble, moan, find fault, *colloq.* beef, bellyache, carp, grouch, gripe, whine, whinge, bitch
F3 acquiesce
▶ *n* complaint, groan, grumble, moan, objection, protest, grievance, *colloq.* bellyache, gripe, grouch, whine, whinge

grove *n*
wood, woodland, thicket, spinney, coppice, copse, plantation, covert, arbour, avenue

grovel *v*
1 INGRATIATE YOURSELF, crawl, creep, toady, flatter, fawn, cringe, cower, kowtow, defer, demean yourself, *colloq.* butter someone up, suck up, bow and scrape, lick someone's boots, kiss up to **2** CRAWL, creep, kneel, crouch, stoop, lie low, prostrate yourself, lie down, bow down, cower, fall on your knees

grow *v*
1 BECOME LARGER, become taller/bigger, increase in size/height, extend, develop, expand, enlarge, lengthen, elongate, widen, broaden, thicken, deepen, swell, fill out **2** GERMINATE, shoot, sprout, spring, bud, flower, mature, develop, *formal* burgeon **3** INCREASE, rise, expand, enlarge, swell, spread, extend, stretch, develop, multiply, escalate, mushroom, wax, *formal* proliferate **4** *grow cold* become, get, go, turn, come to be, change, develop **5** PROGRESS, thrive, flourish, prosper, succeed, improve, advance, make headway **6** ORIGINATE, arise, issue, stem, spring **7** CULTIVATE, farm, produce, propagate, breed, raise, sow, plant, harvest
F3 1 shrink **3** decrease **5** fail

growl *v*
snarl, snap, yap, bark, howl, yelp, rumble, roar

grown-up *adj, n*
▶ *adj* adult, mature, of age, full-grown, fully-grown, fully-developed, fully-fledged
F3 young, immature
▶ *n* adult, man, woman
F3 child

growth *n*
1 INCREASE, rise, extension, enlargement, expansion, spread, multiplication, magnification, amplification, deepening, development, evolution, progress, advance, improvement, success, headway, prosperity, *formal* proliferation, augmentation, aggrandizement **2** GERMINATION, shooting, sprouting, springing, budding, flowering, development, *formal* maturation, burgeoning **3** TUMOUR, lump, swelling,

protuberance, outgrowth, *technical* intumescence, excrescence
F3 1 decrease, decline, failure

grub *v, n*
▶ *v* dig, burrow, delve, excavate, probe, root, rummage, forage, ferret, hunt, search, scour, unearth, uncover, explore
▶ *n* **1** LARVA, maggot, worm, pupa, caterpillar, chrysalis **2** FOOD, provision, meals, refreshment(s), sustenance, nutrition, *colloq.* eats, tuck, *slang* nosh

grubby *adj*
dirty, soiled, unwashed, mucky, grimy, filthy, squalid, seedy, messy, scruffy, shabby
F3 clean

grudge *n, v*
▶ *n* resentment, bitterness, envy, jealousy, pique, spite, malice, enmity, antagonism, hate, hatred, venom, dislike, animosity, antipathy, aversion, ill-will, hard feelings, grievance, *formal* malevolence, rancour, animus
F3 favour
▶ *v* begrudge, resent, envy, covet, be jealous of, dislike, take exception to, object to, mind

grudging *adj*
reluctant, unwilling, hesitant, half-hearted, unenthusiastic, resentful, envious, jealous

gruelling *adj*
hard, difficult, taxing, demanding, tiring, exhausting, laborious, arduous, strenuous, trying, backbreaking, draining, crushing, grinding, harsh, severe, tough, punishing
F3 easy

gruesome *adj*
horrible, disgusting, repellent, repugnant, repulsive, revolting, sickening, hideous, grisly, macabre, grim, ghastly, awful, terrible, horrific, horrid, frightful, dreadful, appalling, shocking, monstrous, abhorrent, abominable, loathsome
F3 pleasant

gruff *adj*
1 CURT, brusque, abrupt, blunt, rude, surly, sour, sullen, grumpy, bad-tempered, churlish, testy, tetchy, impolite, unfriendly, discourteous, *colloq.* crotchety, crabbed **2** *a gruff voice* rough, harsh, rasping, guttural, throaty, husky, hoarse, croaking, thick
F3 1 friendly, courteous, polite

grumble *v, n*
▶ *v* **1** COMPLAIN, moan, object, protest, bleat, find fault, *colloq.* bellyache, beef, grouch, gripe, whine, whinge, carp **2** RUMBLE, murmur, gurgle, growl
▶ *n* **1** COMPLAINT, moan, grievance, objection, protest, *colloq.* beef, gripe, grouch, grouse, whinge, bleat, bitch **2** RUMBLE, murmur, muttering, gurgle, growl, roar

grumpy *adj*
bad-tempered, ill-tempered, churlish, cross, irritable, surly, sullen, sulky, tetchy, snappy, petulant, discontented, *formal* cantankerous, *colloq.* crotchety, crabbed, grouchy, ratty, in a huff, in a sulk, having got out of bed on the wrong side
F3 contented

guarantee *n, v*
▶ *n* warranty, insurance, assurance, promise, word of honour, pledge, oath, bond, covenant, contract, security, collateral, surety, endorsement, testimonial, *formal* earnest
▶ *v* assure, give an assurance, promise, pledge, swear, vouch for, answer for, warrant, certify, underwrite, provide security/collateral/surety for, endorse, support, back, sponsor, secure, protect, insure, ensure, make sure, make certain

guarantor *n*
underwriter, guarantee, sponsor, supporter, backer, surety, warrantor, referee, voucher, bondsman, bailsman, covenantor, *colloq.* angel

guard *v, n*
▶ *v* protect, safeguard, save, preserve, shield, secure, screen, shelter, cover, defend, patrol, police, escort, supervise, oversee, watch, keep watch, be alert, look out, take care, mind, beware
▶ *n* **1** PROTECTOR, defender, custodian, warder, escort, bodyguard, keeper, conductor, watch, scout, watchman, lookout, sentry, sentinel, picket, patrol, security, guardian, *slang* minder **2** PROTECTION, safeguard, defence, wall, barrier, fence, screen, shield, bumper, fender, buffer, pad, cushion
▷ **off your guard** careless, unprepared, unaware(s), unready, unwary, inattentive, napping, unsuspecting, surprised, with your defences down, *colloq.* red-handed, with your pants down
▷ **on your guard** alert, watchful, vigilant, cautious, careful, ready, prepared, attentive, on the lookout, wary, wide awake, on the alert, *formal* circumspect

guarded *adj*
cautious, wary, chary, careful, watchful, discreet, noncommittal, reluctant, reticent, reserved, restrained, secretive, *formal* circumspect, *colloq.* cagey
F3 communicative, frank

guardian *n*
trustee, curator, custodian, steward, caretaker, keeper, warden, protector, preserver, defender, champion, guard, warder, escort, attendant

guardianship *n*
trust, care, guidance, trusteeship, curatorship, custodianship, custody, tutelage, stewardship, patronage, attendance, guard, hands, keeping, wardenship, wardship, preservation, protection, safekeeping, defence, *formal* aegis

guerrilla *n*
freedomfighter, terrorist, irregular, resistance fighter, partisan, sniper, guerrillero, franc-tireur, haiduck, bushwhacker, maquisard

guess *v, n*
▶ *v* speculate, make a guess, predict, estimate, reckon, hypothesize, work out, put something at, suppose, assume, think, believe, judge, consider, imagine, fancy, feel, suspect, *formal* conjecture, surmise, postulate, *colloq.* guesstimate
▶ *n* prediction, estimate, speculation, assumption, belief, judgement, reckoning, fancy, idea, notion, theory, hypothesis, guesswork, opinion, feeling, suspicion, intuition, hunch, *formal* conjecture, supposition, surmise, *colloq.* guesstimate, ballpark figure, shot in the dark

guesswork *n*
speculation, estimation, reckoning, prediction, assumption, intuition, theory, hypothesis, *formal* conjecture, supposition, surmise, *colloq.* guesstimate

guest *n*
visitor, caller, boarder, lodger, resident, patron, regular, *formal* visitant

guesthouse *n*
boarding-house, hostel, hostelry, inn, hotel, pension, rooming-house, *formal* xenodochium

guidance *n*
leadership, direction, management, rule, charge, control, teaching, instruction, advice, counsel, counselling, help, assistance, information, instructions, directions, guidelines, indication(s), pointer(s), hint(s), tip(s), recommendation(s), suggestion(s)

guide *v, n*
▶ *v* **1** LEAD, conduct, direct, navigate, point, steer, pilot, manoeuvre, usher, escort, show, show the way, accompany, attend, *colloq.* hold someone's hand **2** CONTROL, govern, manage, direct, be in charge of, rule, preside over, oversee, supervise, superintend, command **3** ADVISE, counsel, give directions/recommendations to, influence, educate, teach, instruct, train
▶ *n* **1** MANUAL, handbook, guidebook, catalogue, directory, key, ABC **2** LEADER, courier, navigator, pilot, helmsman, steersman, conductor, director, ranger, usher, escort, chaperon(e), attendant, companion **3** ADVISER, counsellor, mentor, guru, teacher, instructor, tutor **4** GUIDELINE, example, model, pattern, norm, gauge, standard, criterion, measure, benchmark, yardstick, tombstone, indication, pointer, signpost, sign, signal, key, marker, mark, beacon, *formal* exemplar, archetype

guideline *n*
instruction, recommendation, suggestion, direction, advice, information, indication, rule, regulation, standard, criterion, measure, benchmark, yardstick, touchstone, framework, parameter, constraint, procedure, principle, terms

guild *n*
organization, association, alliance, federation, society, club, union, fellowship, league, order, company, chapel, brotherhood, lodge, fraternity, sorority, corporation, incorporation

guile *n*
deceit, deception, cunning, treachery, double-dealing, fraud, trickery, trickiness, wiliness, cleverness, slyness, craft, craftiness, deviousness, artfulness, artifice, ruse, gamesmanship, knavery, *formal* duplicity
F3 artlessness, guilelessness

guileless *adj*
artless, direct, straight, straightforward, genuine, honest, frank, sincere, trusting, truthful, innocent, naïve, candid, natural, open, simple, transparent, unreserved, unsophisticated, unworldly, *formal* ingenuous
F3 artful, cunning

guilt *n*
1 *he confessed his guilt* responsibility, blame, blameworthiness, disgrace, dishonour, wrong, wrongdoing, criminality, misconduct, unlawfulness, *formal* culpability **2** *a feeling of guilt* guilty conscience, conscience, disgrace, dishonour, shame, self-condemnation, self-reproach, self-accusation, regret, remorse, contrition, repentance, penitence, *formal* compunction
F3 **1** innocence, righteousness **2** shamelessness

guiltless *adj*
blameless, innocent, clear, clean, pure, irreproachable, above reproach, sinless, spotless, faultless, stainless, immaculate, impeccable, unblamable, unimpeachable, undefiled, unspotted, unsullied, untainted, untarnished, *formal* inculpable
F3 guilty, tainted

guilty *adj*
1 *guilty of a crime* responsible, blamable, blameworthy, to blame, at fault, offending, wrong, illegal, unlawful, illicit, sinful, wicked, delinquent, criminal, convicted, evil, *formal* culpable **2** CONSCIENCE-STRICKEN, ashamed, guilt-ridden, bad, with a bad conscience, shamefaced, sheepish, sorry, regretful, remorseful, contrite, penitent, repentant, *formal* compunctious
F3 **1** innocent, guiltless, blameless **2** shameless

guise *n*
appearance, form, shape, features, likeness, manner, disguise, mask, pretence, show, façade, front, behaviour, custom, air, aspect, face, semblance, *formal* demeanour

gulf *n*
1 BAY, bight, cove, inlet, basin **2** GAP, opening, separation, division, rift, split, breach, cleft, fissure, crevice, chasm, gorge, hole, ravine, abyss, void, hollow, canyon

gullet *n*
throat, craw, crop, maw, *technical* oesophagus

gullibility *n*
credulity, innocence, simplicity, naïvety, trustfulness, foolishness
Ⓕ astuteness

gullible *adj*
credulous, suggestible, impressionable, trusting, trustful, ingenuous, unsuspecting, easily deceived, foolish, naïve, green, inexperienced, unsophisticated, innocent, *colloq.* wet behind the ears
Ⓕ astute

gully *n*
channel, ravine, gorge, valley, canyon, watercourse, gutter, ditch

gulp *v, n*
▶ *v* swallow, swig, swill, quaff, bolt, gobble, guzzle, devour, stuff, *colloq.* knock back, wolf, tuck into
Ⓕ sip, nibble
▶ *n* swallow, swig, draught, mouthful

gum *n, v*
▶ *n* adhesive, glue, paste, cement, fixative, resin
▶ *v* stick, glue, paste, fix, cement, seal, clog, *formal* affix
▷ **gum up** obstruct, hinder, impede, choke, clog

gummy *adj*
sticky, adhesive, gluey, gooey, tacky, viscous, *formal* viscid

gumption *n*
common sense, initiative, resourcefulness, cleverness, astuteness, nous, enterprise, shrewdness, wit, discernment, acumen, ability, acuteness, *formal* sagacity, *colloq.* savvy
Ⓕ foolishness

gun *n*
firearm, handgun, pistol, revolver, automatic repeater, Colt®, Winchester®, rifle, shotgun, machine-gun, airgun, carbine, bazooka, howitzer, flintlock, blunderbuss, musket, cannon, mortar, machine-gun, fusil, *colloq.* shooter, shooting iron

gunman *n*
assassin, terrorist, thug, killer, murderer, bandit, gangster, sniper, shootist, bravo, desperado, gunslinger, *colloq.* hatchet man, hit man, *US colloq.* mobster

gurgle *v, n*
▶ *v* **1** BABBLE, bubble, burble, murmur, ripple, lap, splash, plash, crow **2** BURBLE, crow, babble
▶ *n* **1** BABBLE, bubbling, murmur, ripple **2** BURBLE, crow, babble

guru *n*
expert, authority, instructor, master, teacher, tutor, leader, mentor, luminary, guiding light, pundit, maharishi, Svengali, swami, sage

gush *v, n*
▶ *v* **1** FLOW, run, pour, stream, surge, cascade, flood, rush, burst, spurt, spout, jet, well, issue **2** ENTHUSE, effervesce, bubble over, effuse, chatter, babble, fuss, jabber, blather, drivel, *colloq.* go on

▶ *n* flow, outflow, stream, surge, torrent, cascade, flood, tide, rush, burst, outburst, spurt, spout, outpouring, spate, jet

gushing *adj*
effusive, over-enthusiastic, excessive, cloying, emotional, saccharine, sentimental, sickly, fulsome, gushy, mawkish
Ⓕ restrained, sincere

gust *n, v*
▶ *n* blast, burst, rush, flurry, blow, puff, breeze, wind, gale, storm, squall, surge, outburst, outbreak, fit, eruption
▶ *v* blast, blow, puff, squall, bluster, breeze, rush, surge, burst out, erupt

gusto *n*
zest, relish, appreciation, enjoyment, pleasure, delight, enthusiasm, exhilaration, exuberance, energy, fervour, élan, verve, zeal
Ⓕ distaste, apathy

gusty *adj*
stormy, blowy, squally, windy, blustering, blustery, breezy, tempestuous
Ⓕ calm

gut *n, v, adj*
▶ *n* **1** INTESTINES, bowels, viscera, entrails, vital organs, insides, belly, stomach, *colloq.* innards **2** *have the guts to own up* courage, bravery, pluck, boldness, audacity, tenacity, nerve, mettle, *formal* fortitude, *colloq.* grit, backbone, bottle, spunk
▶ *v* **1** *gut fish* disembowel, draw, clean (out), *formal* eviscerate, exenterate **2** STRIP, clear, empty, rifle, ransack, plunder, loot, sack, rob, destroy, devastate, ravage, clear out
▶ *adj* instinctive, intuitive, emotional, unthinking, basic, deep-seated, heartfelt, innate, involuntary, natural, spontaneous, strong

gutless *adj*
weak, cowardly, feeble, irresolute, timid, fainthearted, craven, abject, *colloq.* chicken, chicken-hearted, chicken-livered, lily-livered, spineless
Ⓕ courageous

gutsy *adj*
bold, brave, courageous, determined, resolute, plucky, indomitable, mettlesome, passionate, spirited, staunch, gallant, game
Ⓕ quiet, timid

gutter *n*
drain, sluice, sewer, ditch, trench, trough, channel, duct, conduit, culvert, passage, pipe, tube

guttural *adj*
rasping, throaty, croaking, hoarse, harsh, gruff, rough, grating, gravelly, husky, deep, low, thick
Ⓕ dulcet

guy *n*
fellow, man, boy, youth, lad, person, individual, character, *colloq.* bloke, chap

guzzle *v*
bolt, devour, gobble, gormandize, stuff, cram, gulp, swallow, swill, quaff, swig, *colloq.* wolf, scoff, polish off, put away, tuck into, knock back

gyrate *v*
turn, revolve, rotate, twirl, pirouette, spin, whirl, wheel, swirl, swivel, circle, spiral

gyration *n*
turn, revolution, rotation, twirl, pirouette, spin, spinning, whirl, whirling, swirl, swivel, wheeling, circle, spiral, *formal* convolution

H

habit *n*

1 CUSTOM, usage, practice, routine, rule, procedure, matter of course, second nature, way(s), manner, mannerism, mode, policy, wont, inclination, tendency, leaning, bent, mannerism, quirk, *formal* propensity, proclivity **2** ADDICTION, dependence, fixation, obsession, weakness **3** GARMENT, costume, dress, clothing, outfit, uniform, robe, vestment, *colloq.* get-up, gear, togs

habitable *adj*
fit to live in, suitable to live in, good enough to live in, inhabitable

habitat *n*
home, domain, element, environment, surroundings, dwelling, locality, territory, terrain, *formal* abode

habitation *n*

1 OCCUPANCY, occupation, quarters, residence, tenancy, housing, lodging, inhabitance, inhabitancy, inhabitation **2** HOME, house, cottage, accommodation, flat, apartment, hut, quarters, living quarters, lodging, mansion, *formal* abode, domicile, dwelling, dwelling-place, residence, residency, *colloq.* digs, pad, joint, roof over your head

habitual *adj*

1 CUSTOMARY, traditional, accustomed, routine, usual, ordinary, common, natural, normal, set, standard, regular, recurrent, fixed, established, familiar, *formal* wonted **2** *habitual drinker* confirmed, inveterate, chronic, hardened, addicted, dependent, constant, persistent, obsessive
🖃 **1** occasional, infrequent

habituate *v*
acclimatize, accustom, make used to, adapt, familiarize, make familiar with, break in, condition, train, school, discipline, tame, harden, inure, season

habitué *n*
regular, regular customer, frequenter, patron, denizen

hack¹ *v*
hacked them to death cut, chop, hew, fell, saw, clear, notch, gash, slash, lacerate, mutilate, mangle

hack² *n*
write as a hack scribbler, writer, journalist, drudge, slave

hackle *n*
▷ **make someone's hackles rise** anger, annoy, irritate, irk, vex, rile, make angry, needle, nettle, bother, ruffle, provoke, antagonize, offend, affront, gall, madden, enrage, incense, infuriate, exasperate, outrage, *colloq.* aggravate, miff, make your blood boil, bug, hassle, rub up the wrong way, get someone's blood up, get on someone's nerves

hackneyed *adj*
stale, overworked, overused, tired, worn-out, time-worn, threadbare, wearing thin, unoriginal, cliché-ridden, clichéed, stereotyped, stock, banal, trite,

commonplace, common, pedestrian, uninspired, unimaginative, *formal* platitudinous, *colloq.* corny, run-of-the-mill, yawn-making
🖃 original, new, fresh

hag *n*
crone, witch, shrew, gorgon, termagant, vixen, virago, harridan, fury, harpy, *colloq.* battle-axe

haggard *adj*
drawn, gaunt, careworn, thin, wasted, drained, shrunken, pinched, hollow-cheeked, pale, pallid, wan, ghastly
🖃 hale

haggle *v*
bargain, negotiate, barter, beat down, chaffer, higgle, wrangle, squabble, bicker, quarrel, dispute, *US* dicker

hail¹ *v*

1 GREET, address, acknowledge, salute, say hello to, nod to, wave to **2** SIGNAL TO, flag down, wave to, call out to **3** ACCLAIM, applaud, honour, welcome, praise, cheer, exalt, *formal* laud **4** *hail from Malawi* come, originate, have your home/roots in, be born in

hail² *n, v*
▶ *n a hail of arrows* barrage, bombardment, volley, torrent, shower, rain, storm
▶ *v* pelt, bombard, shower, rain, batter, attack, assail

hair *n*
locks, tresses, shock, mop, mane, fleece, wool, coat, fur, pelt, hide
▷ **let your hair down** relax, let yourself go, throw off your inhibitions, *colloq.* hang loose, loosen up, *slang* let it all hang out, chill out
▷ **not turn a hair** calm, remain composed, *colloq.* see it coming, not bat an eyelid, keep your cool, stay cool
▷ **split hairs** find fault, quibble, cavil, argue over unimportant details, *colloq.* nit-pick

hairdo *n*
hairstyle, coiffure, cut, haircut, style, set

hairdresser *n*
hairstylist, stylist, barber, coiffeur, coiffeuse

hairless *adj*
bald, bald-headed, shorn, tonsured, shaven, clean-shaven, beardless
🖃 hairy, hirsute

hair-raising *adj*
frightening, scary, terrifying, horrifying, shocking, bloodcurdling, spine-chilling, petrifying, eerie, alarming, startling, thrilling, exciting, *colloq.* creepy

hair's-breadth *n*
fraction, hair, inch, jot, *colloq.* whisker
🖃 mile

hairstyle *n*
style, coiffure, cut, haircut, set, *colloq.* hairdo

hairy *adj*
hirsute, bearded, shaggy, bushy, fuzzy, furry, woolly,

fleecy, unshaven, *formal* pilose, crinose, crinigerous, crinite
🔳 bald, clean-shaven

halcyon *adj*
peaceful, happy, flourishing, prosperous, carefree, calm, balmy, mild, gentle, golden, pacific, placid, quiet, serene, still, tranquil, undisturbed
🔳 stormy

hale *adj*
healthy, fit, well, youthful, strong, sound, vigorous, robust, flourishing, athletic, hearty, able-bodied, blooming, *colloq.* in the pink, in fine fettle, full of vim, fit as a fiddle
🔳 ill

half *n, adj, adv*
▶ *n* fifty per cent, equal part/share, bisection, hemisphere, semicircle, section, segment, portion, share, fraction
▶ *adj* semi-, halved, divided, divided in two, bisected, hemispherical, fractional, part, partial, incomplete, moderate, limited, slight
🔳 whole
▶ *adv* partly, partially, incompletely, inadequately, insufficiently, moderately, slightly, barely
🔳 completely
▷ **by half** very, considerably, excessively, too
▷ **by halves** incompletely, imperfectly, inadequately, insufficiently
🔳 thoroughly
▷ **not half 1** *not half as clever* not at all, not nearly **2** *not half get into trouble* very, very much, really, indeed

half-baked *adj*
impractical, stupid, ill-conceived, unplanned, undeveloped, unrealistic, unworkable, ill-judged, shortsighted, silly, crazy, foolish, senseless, *colloq.* harebrained, crackpot
🔳 sensible, thought out

half-hearted *adj*
lukewarm, cool, weak, feeble, passive, apathetic, lacklustre, listless, uninterested, unenthusiastic, indifferent, unconcerned, neutral
🔳 whole-hearted, enthusiastic

halfway *adv, adj*
▶ *adv* midway, in/to the middle, centrally
▶ *adj* middle, central, equidistant, mid, midway, intermediate, mean, median
▷ **meet someone halfway** compromise, negotiate, make concessions, come to/reach an understanding, give and take, steer a middle course, find a happy medium, make a deal, *colloq.* go fifty-fifty with, split the difference

halfwit *n*
fool, blockhead, fat-head, dunce, dimwit, simpleton, idiot, cretin, imbecile, ignoramus, moron, dupe, stooge, butt, laughing-stock, clown, comic, buffoon, jester, *colloq.* nincompoop, ass, chump, ninny, clot, dope, twit, nitwit, nit, sucker, mug, twerp, birdbrain, *slang* wally, dumbo, pillock, prat, dork, geek, plonker
🔳 brain

half-witted *adj*
simple-minded, feeble-minded, silly, foolish, idiotic, stupid, crazy, dull, moronic, simple, *colloq.* dim-witted, crack-brained, crackpot, dumb, dotty, potty, batty, barmy, nutty, two bricks short of a load
🔳 clever

hall *n*
1 HALLWAY, corridor, passage, passageway, entrance-hall, foyer, vestibule, lobby **2** CONCERT-HALL, auditorium, chamber, assembly room, conference hall

hallmark *n*
1 *a hallmark on gold* official mark/stamp, mark/stamp

of authenticity **2** *the hallmark of her music* typical quality, distinctive feature, stamp, mark, trademark, brand-name, sign, indication, indicator, symbol, emblem, device, badge

hallowed *adj*
honoured, revered, sacred, sacrosanct, blessed, sanctified, consecrated, holy, dedicated, established, inviolable, age-old

hallucinate *v*
dream, imagine, imagine things, see things, see visions, daydream, fantasize, *slang* freak out, trip

hallucination *n*
illusion, mirage, vision, apparition, dream, daydream, fantasy, figment, figment of the imagination, delusion, delirium, phantasmagoria, *colloq.* freak-out, trip

halo *n*
circle of light, crown, ring, corona, glory, nimbus, radiance, aura, aureole, aureola, gloria, gloriole, halation

halt *v, n*
▶ *v* stop, come/bring to a stop, draw up, pull up, pause, wait, rest, break off, finish, bring/draw to a close, end, put an end to, check, stem, curb, obstruct, block, arrest, crush, hold back, impede, *formal* discontinue, cease, desist, terminate, *colloq.* quit, call it a day
🔳 start, continue
▶ *n* stop, stoppage, arrest, interruption, break, interval, pause, rest, respite, breathing-space, standstill, end, close, deadlock, stalemate, *formal* termination, cessation, discontinuance, discontinuation, desistance
🔳 start, continuation

halting *adj*
hesitant, stuttering, stammering, faltering, stumbling, fumbling for words, uncertain, broken, imperfect, laboured, awkward, unsteady
🔳 fluent, certain

halve *v*
bisect, cut in half, split in two, divide, divide equally, split, sever, share, cut down, reduce, lessen, *formal* dichotomize

halved *adj*
divided, split, cut, shared, bisected, *formal* dimidiate

ham-fisted *adj*
clumsy, awkward, unco-ordinated, bungling, accident-prone, unhandy, heavy-handed, unskilful, inept, blundering, lumbering, gauche, *colloq.* all thumbs

hammer *v, n*
▶ *v* **1** HIT, strike, beat, drum, bang, bash, slap, pound, batter, knock, drive, shape, form, make, mould, fashion **2** CRITICIZE, condemn, attack, blame, censure, *formal* decry, denigrate, *colloq.* slate, slam, knock, run down, tear a strip off **3** *hammer the opposition* BEAT, trounce, defeat, overcome, overwhelm, rout, annihilate, outplay, *colloq.* clobber, slaughter, lick, thrash **4** *hammer an idea into someone* FORCE, drum, din, drive home, instil, reiterate **5** *hammer away at his essay* PERSEVERE, pound, persist, keep on, labour, plug, grind, drudge, slog
▷ **hammer out** settle, sort out, negotiate, thrash out, achieve eventually, produce, bring about, work out, carry through, accomplish, complete, finish, resolve
▶ *n* mallet, gavel, beetle

hamper *v, n*
▶ *v* hinder, impede, obstruct, slow down, hold up, stop, inhibit, frustrate, thwart, baulk, prevent, handicap, hamstring, shackle, cramp, restrict, curb, restrain, block, check, bridle, encumber, fetter, foil, *formal* retard, *colloq.* stymie
🔳 aid, facilitate
▶ *n* basket, box, container, creel, pannier

hamstring *v*
hinder, impede, hold up, stop, frustrate, baulk, thwart, cramp, restrict, restrain, block, check, encumber, foil, cripple, disable, handicap, incapacitate, paralyse, *colloq.* stymie

hand *n, v*
▸ *n* 1 FIST, palm, *technical* manus, *colloq.* paw, *slang* mitt, fin 2 *give me a hand* HELP, helping hand, aid, assistance, support, participation, part, influence, *formal* succour 3 *in someone's hands* RESPONSIBILITY, care, custody, possession, charge, authority, command, control, power, management, supervision, clutches 4 *give someone a hand* APPLAUSE, clapping, handclap, cheering, acclaim, ovation 5 INDICATOR, pointer, needle, arrow, marker 6 HANDWRITING, writing, script, penmanship, calligraphy, *colloq.* fist 7 WORKER, employee, operative, workman, labourer, farm-hand, hireling
▷ **at hand** near, close, to hand, handy, accessible, available, at someone's disposal, ready, imminent, about to happen
▷ **by hand** manually, using your hands
▷ **from hand to mouth** precariously, dangerously, insecurely, uncertainly, in poverty, from day to day, *colloq.* on the breadline
▷ **hand in glove** very closely, in close collaboration/co-operation, in close association
▷ **hand in hand 1** HOLDING HANDS, with hands joined/clasped/held 2 CLOSELY RELATED, closely together, in close association
▷ **in hand 1** BEING DEALT WITH, under way, considered, attended to, under control 2 SPARE, in reserve, put by, ready, available
▷ **to hand** near, close, at hand, handy, accessible, available, at someone's disposal, ready, imminent, about to happen
▷ **try your hand** attempt, try, seek, strive, see if you can do, *colloq.* have a go, have a shot/crack/stab
▷ **win hands down** win easily/effortlessly, win without effort
▸ *v* give, pass, offer, submit, present, yield, deliver, hand over, transmit, conduct, convey
▷ **hand down** bequeath, will, pass on, pass down, transfer, give, grant, leave
▷ **hand out** distribute, deal out, pass out, give out, share out, mete out, *formal* dispense, disseminate, *colloq.* dish out
▷ **hand over** yield, relinquish, surrender, turn over, deliver, consign, release, give, donate, present, pass, transfer
🔁 keep, retain

handbill *n*
circular, leaflet, pamphlet, flyer, notice, announcement, advertisement, letter

handbook *n*
manual, instruction book, book of directions, ABC, guide, guidebook, companion, prospectus

handcuff *v*
fetter, shackle, manacle, fasten, secure, tie

handcuffs *n*
manacles, fetters, cuffs, shackles, wristlets, *colloq.* darbies

handful *n*
1 SMALL NUMBER, few, little, small amount, sprinkling, scattering, smattering 2 NUISANCE, bother, pest, *colloq.* pain in the neck, thorn in the flesh, pain
🔁 1 a lot, many

handicap *n, v*
▸ *n* obstacle, obstruction, check, block, barrier, impediment, stumbling-block, hindrance, encumbrance, constraint, drawback, disadvantage, restriction, limitation, penalty, disability, impairment, abnormality, defect, shortcoming
🔁 assistance, advantage
▸ *v* impede, hinder, disadvantage, put at a disadvantage, hold back, hamper, impair, obstruct, block, check, bridle, curb, burden, encumber, restrict, limit, disable, *formal* retard
🔁 help, assist

handicraft *n*
craft, art, craftwork, craftsmanship, skill, handwork, handiwork, workmanship

handiwork *n*
work, doing, responsibility, achievement, action, product, result, design, invention, creation, production, skill, workmanship, craftsmanship, artisanship, handicraft, craft, art, craftwork

handle *n, v*
▸ *n* grip, handgrip, knob, stock, shaft, hilt, haft
▸ *v* 1 TOUCH, finger, feel, fondle, pick up, hold, grasp, grip, *colloq.* paw 2 *handle a situation* tackle, treat, deal with, manage, cope with, control, supervise, be in charge of, take care of 3 *handle a car* operate, control, drive, steer, work 4 TRADE IN, do business in, deal in, market, stock, traffic, operate

handling *n*
management, conduct, approach, operation, running, treatment, direction, administration, discussion, transaction, manipulation

handout *n*
1 CHARITY, alms, gifts, dole, largesse, share, issue, free sample, *colloq.* freebie 2 LEAFLET, circular, bulletin, statement, press release, brochure, pamphlet, literature

hand-picked *adj*
choice, select, selected, chosen, elect, elite, picked, screened, recherché

handsome *adj*
1 GOOD-LOOKING, attractive, fair, personable, elegant, fine, dignified, stately, *colloq.* gorgeous, dishy, hunky 2 GENEROUS, liberal, large, considerable, ample, lavish, plentiful, abundant, bountiful, sizeable, magnanimous, unsparing, unstinting
🔁 1 ugly, unattractive 2 mean

handsomely *adv*
generously, lavishly, plentifully, richly, amply, abundantly, bountifully, liberally, magnanimously, unsparingly, unstintingly, *formal* munificently
🔁 stingily

handwriting *n*
writing, script, hand, penmanship, calligraphy, autograph, *colloq.* fist, scrawl, scribble

handy *adj*
1 CONVENIENT, practical, useful, helpful, functional, practicable 2 AVAILABLE, to hand, ready, at hand, near, nearby, accessible, within reach, *colloq.* at your fingertips 3 SKILFUL, proficient, expert, skilled, clever, practical, dexterous, adroit, adept, nimble
🔁 2 inconvenient 3 clumsy

handyman *n*
DIYer, odd-jobman, odd-jobber, Jack-of-all-trades, factotum

hang *v*
1 SUSPEND, be suspended, hang down, put up, dangle, swing, drape, drop, flop, droop, sag, trail, lean, bend 2 FASTEN, attach, fix, stick, glue, paste, cement, *formal* affix, append 3 *hang in the air* float, drift, hover, flit, flutter, linger, remain, cling 4 *the prisoners were hanged* execute, lynch, put to death, send to the gallows/scaffold/gibbet, kill, *colloq.* string up
▷ **get the hang** understand, grasp, comprehend,

fathom, get the knack of, *colloq.* twig
▷ **hang about** hang around, linger, loiter, dawdle, waste time, associate with, keep company with, frequent, haunt
▷ **hang back** hold back, be reluctant, hesitate, shy away, shrink back, recoil, stay behind, *formal* demur
▷ **hang fire** hold back, hang back, delay, hold on, stall, stick, stop, wait, *formal* procrastinate, vacillate
🖪 press on
▷ **hang on 1** WAIT, hold on, remain, hold out, endure, continue, carry on, persevere, persist **2** GRIP, grasp, cling, clutch, hold fast **3** DEPEND ON, hinge on, turn on, rest on, be conditional on, be determined by, *formal* be contingent on
🖪 **1** give up
▷ **hang over** impend, loom, menace, threaten, approach

hangdog *adj*
abject, browbeaten, defeated, guilty, shamefaced, cowed, cringing, downcast, miserable, wretched, sneaking, furtive
🖪 bold

hanger-on *n*
follower, minion, henchman, lackey, toady, sycophant, parasite, freeloader, dependant, *colloq.* sponger

hanging *adj, n*
▶ *adj* suspended, dangling, swinging, draping, drooping, flopping, floppy, flapping, loose, unattached, unsupported, *formal* pendent, pendulous, pensile
▶ *n* drape, drapery, drop, frontal, drop-scene, dossal, dossel

hang-out *n*
haunt, den, meeting-place, home, patch, local, *colloq.* dive, joint, watering-hole

hangover *n*
after-effects, katzenjammer, morning after, the morning after the night before, *formal* crapulence

hang-up *n*
inhibition, difficulty, problem, obsession, preoccupation, fixation, phobia, *idée fixe*, block, mental block, *colloq.* thing

hank *n*
skein, coil, loop, length, roll, piece, twist, *Scot.* fank

hanker *v*
▷ **hanker after/for** crave, hunger for, thirst for, want, wish for, desire, covet, yearn for, long for, pine for, itch for, set your heart on, *colloq.* be dying for

hankering *n*
craving, hunger, thirst, wish, desire, yearning, longing, pining, itch, urge

hanky-panky *n*
mischief, trickery, tricks, deception, dishonesty, jiggery-pokery, nonsense, cheating, chicanery, subterfuge, devilry, *formal* machinations, *colloq.* funny business, monkey business, shenanigans
🖪 openness

haphazard *adj*
random, chance, casual, arbitrary, hit-or-miss, indiscriminate, irregular, aimless, orderless, unsystematic, disorganized, disorderly, careless, slapdash, slipshod, unmethodical, unplanned
🖪 methodical, orderly

hapless *adj*
unlucky, unhappy, unfortunate, wretched, miserable, ill-fated, ill-starred, cursed, luckless, jinxed, star-crossed
🖪 lucky

happen *v*
1 OCCUR, take place, fall, arise, crop up, develop, present itself, turn up, go on, come about, come true, result, ensue, follow, turn out, appear, come into being,

formal transpire, supervene, eventuate, *colloq.* materialize **2** *happen to do something* have the good/bad luck to, have the good/bad fortune to **3** *happen on something* find, discover, hit on, light on, stumble on, come across, chance on

happening *n*
occurrence, phenomenon, event, incident, episode, occasion, adventure, experience, accident, chance, proceedings, circumstance, case, affair, thing, action, scene, business, *formal* eventuality

happily *adv*
1 GLADLY, joyfully, merrily, cheerfully, gleefully, heartily, delightedly, contentedly, agreeably, enthusiastically, willingly, *formal* joyously **2** FORTUNATELY, luckily, providentially, by chance, fittingly, *formal* auspiciously, opportunely, propitiously
🖪 **1, 2** unhappily

happiness *n*
joy, joyfulness, gladness, cheerfulness, cheeriness, contentment, pleasure, delight, enjoyment, gaiety, glee, merriment, merriness, light-heartedness, exuberance, high spirits, good spirits, elation, bliss, ecstasy, euphoria, *formal* blitheness, felicity

---

Ways of expressing happiness include:
couldn't be happier, floating on air, full of the joys of spring, happy as a sandboy, I'm/he's a happy chappie, in high spirits, in seventh heaven, joy unbounded, jump for joy, make someone's day, on cloud nine, on top of the world, over the moon, thrilled to bits, tickled pink, walking on air, weigh-hey!

🖪 unhappiness, sadness

happy *adj*
1 JOYFUL, jolly, merry, cheerful, glad, pleased, delighted, thrilled, elated, ecstatic, rapturous, overjoyed, exuberant, gleeful, euphoric, satisfied, gratified, in good/high spirits, in a good mood, content, contented, gay, carefree, light-hearted, jovial, radiant, smiling, untroubled, unconcerned, unworried, *formal* joyous, blithe, *colloq.* cock-a-hoop, on top of the world, happy as Larry/a sandboy, over the moon, on cloud nine, in seventh heaven, walking/floating on air, tickled pink **2** *a happy coincidence* lucky, fortunate, favourable, advantageous, convenient, helpful, beneficial, appropriate, apt, fitting, proper, opportune, *formal* felicitous, auspicious, propitious, apposite
🖪 **1** unhappy, sad, discontented **2** unfortunate, inappropriate

happy-go-lucky *adj*
easy-going, carefree, casual, nonchalant, cheerful, devil-may-care, light-hearted, unconcerned, untroubled, unworried, reckless, irresponsible, heedless, improvident, *formal* blithe, insouciant
🖪 anxious, wary

harangue *n, v*
▶ *n* diatribe, tirade, lecture, speech, address, *formal* peroration, exhortation
▶ *v* lecture, preach, hold forth, spout, address, *formal* declaim

harass *v*
pester, badger, harry, plague, torment, hound, dragoon, persecute, exasperate, vex, annoy, nag, provoke, antagonize, irritate, fret, bother, disturb, trouble, worry, stress, tire, wear out, exhaust, fatigue, *colloq.* hassle, have it in for, put the wind up, put the frighteners on, drive round the bend/twist

harassed *adj*
distraught, pressurized, pressured, stressed, under pressure, under stress, strained, distressed, troubled,

worried, careworn, hounded, pestered, plagued, tormented, harried, vexed, *colloq.* hassled, stressed out, uptight
☒ carefree

harassment *n*
annoyance, nuisance, pestering, trouble, molest, molestation, persecution, pressuring, torment, bother, distress, aggravation, badgering, bedevilment, irritation, vexation, *colloq.* hassle
☒ assistance

harbinger *n*
herald, forerunner, precursor, messenger, omen, portent, warning, sign, indication, *avant-courier, formal* foretoken

harbour *n, v*
▶ *n* port, dock, quay, wharf, marina, mooring, anchorage, haven, shelter, refuge
▶ *v* **1** HIDE, conceal, protect, shield, shelter, house, take in **2** *harbour a feeling* hold, retain, cling to, entertain, maintain, foster, nurse, nurture, cherish, believe, imagine

hard *adj, adv*
▶ *adj* **1** SOLID, firm, unyielding, tough, strong, dense, condensed, compressed, compact, compacted, impenetrable, resistant, stiff, rigid, inflexible, unpliable, *colloq.* hard as stone/iron/rock **2** *a hard question/ problem* COMPLICATED, difficult, complex, involved, intricate, knotty, baffling, puzzling, perplexing, bewildering **3** *building a wall is hard work* STRENUOUS, difficult, arduous, onerous, laborious, tough, tiring, toilsome, exhausting, backbreaking, heavy, exacting, rigorous **4** HARSH, severe, strict, callous, unfeeling, unsympathetic, cruel, cold-hearted, hardhearted, stern, tyrannical, oppressive, pitiless, merciless, ruthless, implacable, unsparing, unyielding, unrelenting, distressing, painful, unpleasant, *formal* obdurate, *colloq.* hard as flint, standing no nonsense, ruling with a rod of iron **5** *hard times* tough, unpleasant, difficult, harsh, grim, severe, painful, distressing, uncomfortable, disagreeable, austere **6** *a hard worker* hard-working, industrious, diligent, assiduous, conscientious, zealous, enthusiastic, keen, busy, energetic, *formal* sedulous **7** *a hard push* forceful, powerful, strong, intense, heavy, sharp, violent **8** *a hard winter* cold, severe, harsh, raw, bitter, freezing **9** *hard evidence* true, indisputable, undeniable, unquestionable, definite, actual, certain, real, verified **10** *hard drugs* addictive, harmful, habit-forming, narcotic, heavy, strong,potent
☒ **1** soft, yielding **2** easy, simple **4** kind, pleasant, compassionate, gentle **5** easy, comfortable **6** lazy, idle **8** mild **9** uncertain
▶ *adv* **1** FORCEFULLY, powerfully, energetically, intensely, strongly, heavily, sharply, violently, vigorously, *formal* with all your might **2** *work hard* diligently, industriously, assiduously, conscientiously, energetically, intensely, busily, enthusiastically, eagerly, keenly **3** *look/think hard* carefully, attentively, closely, intently, sharply, keenly **4** *a hard-won victory* with difficulty, arduously, strenuously, laboriously, after a struggle, vigorously **5** *snowing hard* intensely, severely, strongly, heavily, steadily
☒ **3** carelessly **4** effortlessly **5** lightly
▷ **hard and fast** binding, fixed, definite, immutable, incontrovertible, inflexible, invariable, rigid, set, strict, stringent, unalterable, unchangeable, unchanging, uncompromising
☒ flexible
▷ **hard up** penniless, impoverished, in the red, bankrupt, short, lacking, *formal* impecunious, *colloq.* broke, bust, stony broke, skint, cleaned out, strapped (for cash), on your uppers, on your

beam ends, not having two pennies to rub together
☒ rich

hard-bitten *adj*
callous, case-hardened, cynical, down-to-earth, hard-boiled, hard-headed, hard-nosed, toughened, inured, matter-of-fact, practical, realistic, ruthless, shrewd, tough, unsentimental
☒ callow

hard-boiled *adj*
tough, cynical, hard-headed, down-to-earth, unsentimental

hard-core *adj*
steadfast, dedicated, blatant, obstinate, rigid, staunch, explicit, extreme, intransigent, dyed-in-the-wool, diehard
☒ moderate

harden *v*
solidify, set, freeze, congeal, bake, cake, stiffen, petrify, strengthen, reinforce, buttress, brace, steel, gird, nerve, toughen, temper, deaden, season, accustom, train, inure, *technical* anneal, vulcanize, *formal* fortify, habituate, indurate
☒ soften, weaken

hardened *adj*
incorrigible, inveterate, irredeemable, seasoned, set, shameless, toughened, inured, reprobate, habitual, accustomed, habituated, chronic, unfeeling, callous, *formal* obdurate
☒ soft, callow

hard-headed *adj*
shrewd, astute, businesslike, sharp, level-headed, clear-thinking, cool-headed, sensible, realistic, rational, pragmatic, practical, hard-bitten, hard-boiled, tough, unsentimental, down-to-earth, *colloq.* hard-nosed
☒ unrealistic, sentimental, idealistic, impractical

hard-hearted *adj*
callous, unfeeling, uncaring, unconcerned, unkind, cold, hard, stony, stony-hearted, heartless, unsympathetic, cruel, inhuman, pitiless, merciless
☒ kind, merciful, compassionate, concerned

hard-hitting *adj*
condemnatory, critical, unsparing, boldly, directly, frankly, straight, vigorous, forceful, tough, uncompromising, *colloq.* no-holds-barred, pulling no punches
☒ mild

hardiness *n*
robustness, toughness, resilience, resolution, boldness, courage, valour, ruggedness, sturdiness, intrepidity, *formal* fortitude
☒ timidity

hardline *adj*
strict, tough, extreme, immoderate, inflexible, militant, uncompromising, unyielding, undeviating, *formal* intransigent
☒ moderate, flexible

hardly *adv*
barely, scarcely, just, only just, not quite, not at all, almost not, by no means

hardness *n*
toughness, severity, harshness, sternness, firmness, rigidity, difficulty, laboriousness, insensitivity, pitilessness, inhumanity, coldness
☒ ease, mildness, softness

hard-pressed *adj*
hard-pushed, hard put, harassed, harried, pushed, under pressure, overburdened, overtaxed, *colloq.* up against it, in a corner, with your back to the wall
☒ untroubled

hardship n
misfortune, adversity, trouble, difficulty, affliction, pain, distress, suffering, burdens, trial, want, need, austerity, poverty, destitution, deprivation, misery, *formal* tribulation, privation
$\blacksquare$ ease, comfort, prosperity

hard-wearing adj
durable, lasting, well-made, made/built to last, strong, tough, sturdy, stout, rugged, resilient, heavy-duty, infrangible
$\blacksquare$ delicate

hard-working adj
industrious, diligent, assiduous, conscientious, enthusiastic, keen, zealous, busy, energetic, *formal* sedulous, *colloq.* with your nose to the grindstone, with your shoulder to the wheel
$\blacksquare$ idle, lazy

hardy adj
1 STRONG, tough, sturdy, durable, heavy-duty, robust, vigorous, fit, sound, healthy 2 BRAVE, courageous, plucky, fearless, undaunted, bold, daring, intrepid, stalwart, stoical, stout, stout-hearted, heroic, indomitable
$\blacksquare$ weak, unhealthy

hare-brained adj
foolish, stupid, silly, wild, daft, ill-conceived, careless, rash, reckless, inane, giddy, dizzy, *colloq.* half-baked, crackpot, scatty, scatterbrained, airheaded, birdbrained
$\blacksquare$ sensible

hark v
listen, hear, give ear, mark, note, notice, pay attention, pay heed, *old use* hearken
$\triangleright$ **hark back** remember, recall, recollect, go back, turn back, revert, *formal* regress

harlequin n & adj
fool, jester, clown, comic, buffoon, zany, jester, joker

harm n, v
$\blacktriangleright$ n damage, loss, injury, hurt, pain, detriment, ill, misfortune, adversity, suffering, ruin, destruction, loss, wrong, abuse, impairment, disservice
$\blacksquare$ benefit, service
$\blacktriangleright$ v damage, impair, work against, blemish, spoil, mar, ruin, hurt, destroy, injure, wound, ill-treat, maltreat, abuse, molest, misuse, be detrimental to
$\blacksquare$ benefit, improve

harmful adj
damaging, detrimental, bad, pernicious, unhealthy, unwholesome, injurious, wounding, dangerous, hazardous, poisonous, toxic, destructive, *formal* noxious, deleterious
$\blacksquare$ harmless

harmless adj
safe, innocuous, non-toxic, benign, inoffensive, unobjectionable, unexceptionable, gentle, mild, blameless, innocent, friendly
$\blacksquare$ harmful, dangerous, destructive

harmonious adj
1 MELODIOUS, tuneful, musical, sweet-sounding, harmonizing, rhythmic, symphonious, euphonious, pleasant, mellow, *formal* mellifluous 2 MATCHING, co-ordinated, balanced, compatible, *formal* congruous, concordant 3 *a harmonious relationship* agreeable, cordial, amiable, amicable, friendly, sympathetic, like-minded, peaceful, peaceable, compatible
$\blacksquare$ 1 discordant

harmonize v
match, co-ordinate, balance, mix, blend, fit in, suit, tone, correspond, go together, get on with, agree, reconcile, coincide, accommodate, adapt, arrange, compose, *formal* be congruous, be congruent, accord
$\blacksquare$ clash, conflict

harmony n
1 TUNEFULNESS, tune, melody, melodiousness, euphony, *formal* mellifluousness 2 *live in harmony* AGREEMENT, unison, unanimity, oneness, unity, compatibility, like-mindedness, peace, goodwill, rapport, sympathy, understanding, amicability, friendliness, co-operation, *formal* accord, concord, amity, assent, concurrence 3 CO-ORDINATION, balance, blending, symmetry, correspondence, conformity, *formal* concord, consonance
$\blacksquare$ 1 discord 2 conflict

harness n, v
$\blacktriangleright$ n tackle, gear, equipment, reins, straps, tack, *formal* accoutrements

Parts of a horse's harness include:
backband, bellyband, bit, *US* blinders, blinkers, breeching, bridle, collar, crupper, girth, hackamore, halter, hames, *US* headstall, martingale, noseband, reins, saddle, saddlepad, stirrup, *US* throatlatch/throatlash, traces.

$\blacktriangleright$ v control, channel, use, utilize, exploit, make use of, employ, mobilize, apply
$\triangleright$ **in harness 1** CO-OPERATING, in co-operation, collaborating, together 2 *back in harness* at work, working, busy, active, employed

harp v
$\triangleright$ **harp on** keep talking about, dwell on, labour, press, reiterate, renew, repeat, nag, *colloq.* go on and on about

harpoon n
arrow, barb, dart, spear, trident, grains

harridan n
virago, vixen, witch, dragon, harpy, nag, scold, shrew, tartar, fury, gorgon, termagant, Xanthippe, hell-cat, *colloq.* battle-axe

harried adj
worried, anxious, agitated, troubled, bothered, distressed, harassed, hard-pressed, pressured, pressurized, plagued, tormented, ravaged, beset, *colloq.* hassled
$\blacksquare$ untroubled

harrowing adj
distressing, upsetting, heart-rending, disturbing, alarming, daunting, tormenting, frightening, terrifying, nerve-racking, traumatic, agonizing, excruciating, *formal* perturbing
$\blacksquare$ encouraging, heartening

harry v
badger, pester, nag, chivvy, harass, oppress, plague, torment, persecute, annoy, vex, worry, trouble, bother, disturb, molest, *colloq.* hassle

harsh adj
1 SEVERE, austere, barren, stark, bitter, bleak, grim, comfortless, desolate, wild, inhospitable, Spartan 2 CRUEL, strict, abrasive, severe, stern, grim, savage, brutal, unsympathetic, unfeeling, hard, inhuman, pitiless, ruthless, merciless, Draconian, *formal* acerbic 3 *a harsh sound* RASPING, rough, coarse, croaking, guttural, hoarse, gruff, grinding, grating, jarring, jangling, discordant, strident, ear-piercing, raucous, sharp, shrill, unpleasant, dissonant, metallic 4 BRIGHT, dazzling, glaring, showy, flashy, gaudy, lurid, garish, bold
$\blacksquare$ 1 mild, comfortable, lenient 2 compassionate, feeling 3 harmonious, soft, gentle 4 gentle

harshness n
bitterness, coarseness, roughness, severity, ill-temper, rigour, starkness, sternness, strictness, hardness,

sourness, abrasiveness, brutality, *formal* acerbity, acrimony, asperity
☐ mildness, softness, gentleness

harum-scarum *adj*
reckless, hasty, rash, impetuous, irresponsible, ill-considered, wild, careless, haphazard, erratic, *formal* imprudent, precipitate, *colloq.* hare-brained, scatterbrained, scatty
☐ sensible

harvest *n, v*
▶ *n* **1** HARVEST-TIME, ingathering, reaping, harvesting, collection, store, supply, stock, accumulation, hoard **2** CROP, yield, return, produce, product, fruits, result, consequence, effect, returns
▶ *v* reap, mow, pick, glean, pluck, garner, gather (in), collect, accumulate, amass, hoard, gain, obtain, acquire, secure

hash *n*
1 MESS, botch, muddle, bungle, mix-up, jumble, confusion, mismanagement, hotchpotch, mishmash **2** GOULASH, stew, hotpot, lobscouse, lob's course

hashish *n*
hash, hemp, marijuana, bhang, cannabis, *colloq.* dope, ganja, grass, pot

hassle *n, v*
▶ *n* bother, inconvenience, nuisance, difficulty, trouble, problem, struggle, argument, disagreement, quarrel, squabble, trial, upset, fight, dispute, bickering, wrangle, *formal* altercation, *colloq.* aggro
☐ agreement, peace
▶ *v* bother, pester, trouble, annoy, badger, harass, hound, harry, chivvy, *colloq.* bug
☐ assist, calm

haste *n*
hurry, rush, hustle, bustle, speed, velocity, rapidity, swiftness, quickness, briskness, fastness, urgency, rashness, recklessness, carelessness, foolhardiness, impulsiveness, impetuosity, *formal* alacrity, celerity, expeditiousness
☐ slowness

hasten *v*
hurry (up), be quick, go fast/quickly, rush, run, sprint, dash, tear, race, fly, bolt, accelerate, speed (up), quicken, dispatch, urge, assist, help, aid, boost, press, advance, forward, step up, push forward, *old use* make haste, *formal* expedite, precipitate, *colloq.* get a move on, step on it/the gas, hotfoot it, put your foot down
☐ dawdle, delay

hastily *adv*
1 RASHLY, recklessly, hurriedly, impetuously, heedlessly, impulsively, *formal* precipitately **2** FAST, quickly, rapidly, speedily, promptly, straightaway, apace, *colloq.* double-quick, chop-chop
☐ **1** carefully, deliberately **2** slowly

hasty *adj*
1 *a hasty decision* hurried, rushed, rash, reckless, heedless, thoughtless, careless, impetuous, impulsive, impatient, headlong, hotheaded, *formal* precipitate **2** FAST, quick, rapid, swift, speedy, rushed, hurried, brisk, prompt, short, brief, cursory, fleeting, transitory, perfunctory, *formal* expeditious
☐ **1** careful, deliberate **2** slow

hat *n*

Hats include:
trilby, bowler, fedora, top-hat, Homburg, *US* derby, pork-pie hat, flat cap, beret, bonnet, tam-o'-shanter, tammy, deerstalker, hunting-cap, stovepipe hat, stetson, ten-gallon hat, boater, sunhat, panama, straw hat, picture-hat, pill-box, cloche, *US* beanie, poke-bonnet, mob-cap, turban, fez, sombrero, sou'wester, glengarry, bearskin, busby, peaked cap, sailor-hat, baseball cap, balaclava, hood, snood, toque, helmet, mortarboard, skullcap, yarmulka, mitre, biretta.

hatch *v*
1 INCUBATE, brood, sit on, breed **2** CONCOCT, formulate, originate, think up, dream up, invent, conceive, devise, contrive, plot, scheme, design, plan, project

hatchet *n*
axe, chopper, cleaver, tomahawk, battle-axe, mattock, pickaxe, machete

hate *v, n*
▶ *v* **1** DISLIKE, despise, detest, loathe, not stand, recoil from, have an aversion to, feel revulsion at, *formal* abhor, abominate, execrate, *colloq.* hate someone's guts **2** *I hate to disturb you* regret, apologize, be sorry, be reluctant, be unwilling, be loath
☐ **1** like, love
▶ *n* hatred, aversion, dislike, loathing, animosity, ill-will, grudge, bitterness, resentment, antagonism, hostility, enmity, *formal* abhorrence, abomination, rancour
☐ liking, love

hateful *adj*
horrid, horrible, loathsome, detestable, abominable, offensive, disgusting, obnoxious, odious, revolting, repulsive, nasty, unpleasant, disagreeable, despicable, vile, contemptible, foul, evil, heinous, *formal* abhorrent, execrable, repellent, repugnant
☐ pleasing

hatred *n*
hate, aversion, dislike, loathing, disgust, revulsion, animosity, ill-will, grudge, bitterness, resentment, antagonism, hostility, enmity, *formal* detestation, repugnance, abhorrence, abomination, execration, rancour, antipathy, animus
☐ liking, love

haughtiness *n*
arrogance, pride, conceit, contempt, contemptuousness, disdain, aloofness, loftiness, snobbishness, superciliousness, airs, hauteur, insolence, pomposity, *colloq.* snootiness
☐ friendliness, humility

haughty *adj*
arrogant, proud, conceited, vain, swollen-headed, lofty, imperious, high and mighty, supercilious, cavalier, contemptuous, disdainful, scornful, superior, self-important, egotistical, overbearing, condescending, patronizing, snobbish, *colloq.* snooty, stuck-up, high and mighty, on your high horse
☐ humble, modest

haul *v, n*
▶ *v* pull, heave, tug, draw, tow, drag, trail, move, transport, convey, ship, convoy, carry, cart, lug, push, *colloq.* hump
▶ *n* loot, booty, plunder, spoils, takings, gain, yield, find, *slang* swag

haunches *n*
thighs, hips, buttocks, nates, huckles, hucks, hunkers

haunt *v, n*
▶ *v* **1** *a ghost haunts the house* walk, visit, appear often in, materialize, spook, possess, curse, *colloq.* show up **2** FREQUENT, patronize, visit (regularly), *colloq.* hang about/around in **3** *memories haunted her* plague, torment, trouble, disturb, worry, burden, recur, prey on, beset, harry, oppress, obsess, possess
▶ *n* resort, stamping-ground, den, local, meeting-place, rendezvous, favourite spot, *colloq.* hang-out

haunted *adj*
1 POSSESSED, cursed, eerie, ghostly, jinxed, hag-

ridden, *colloq.* spooky **2** TROUBLED, worried, plagued, tormented, obsessed, preoccupied

haunting *adj*
memorable, unforgettable, persistent, recurrent, evocative, nostalgic, atmospheric, poignant
▰ unmemorable

have *v*
1 OWN, possess, get, obtain, gain, be given, acquire, secure, take, receive, accept, keep, hold, use, *formal* procure **2** FEEL, experience, enjoy, suffer, undergo, submit to, be subjected to, endure, tolerate, put up with, go through, find, meet, encounter **3** CONTAIN, include, take in, embody, incorporate, consist of, *formal* comprise, embrace, comprehend **4** *have a party* hold, arrange, organize, take part in, participate in **5** *have to go now* must, be forced, be compelled, be obliged, be required, ought, should **6** *have someone do something* cause, make, arrange, get, oblige, require, persuade, talk into, ask, tell, request, order, command, bid, force, compel, coerce, *formal* enjoin, prevail upon **7** *have pity on someone* show, demonstrate, display, exhibit, express, feel, *formal* manifest **8** *have food/drink* eat, swallow, consume, take, drink, devour, down, gulp, guzzle, *formal* partake of, *colloq.* put away, tuck into, knock back **9** *have a baby* give birth to, bear, bring into the world, be delivered of **10** *I won't have such behaviour* tolerate, put up with, take, accept, allow, permit, stand, abide, brook **11** *you've been had* deceive, dupe, fool, trick, cheat, swindle, take in, *colloq.* con, diddle
▰ **1** lack
▷ **have done with** finish with, give up, stop, be through with, *formal* cease, desist, *colloq.* throw over, wash your hands of
▷ **have had it** be in trouble, have no hope, be defeated, be exhausted, be lost, have no chance of success, *colloq.* bite the dust, come to a sticky end
▷ **have on 1** WEAR, be dressed in, be clothed in **2** *What have you got on this week?* have an engagement, have an appointment, have arranged, have planned **3** TEASE, trick, play a joke on, *colloq.* kid, rag, pull someone's leg

haven *n*
harbour, port, dock, bay, anchorage, shelter, refuge, sanctuary, asylum, retreat, oasis

haversack *n*
backpack, rucksack, knapsack, kitbag

havoc *n*
chaos, confusion, disorder, disruption, mayhem, damage, destruction, ruin, ruination, wreck, wreckage, rack and ruin, devastation, waste, ravaging, desolation, *formal* despoliation, *colloq.* shambles

hawk¹ *n*
hawks and other birds of prey buzzard, kite, harrier, sparrowhawk, falcon, haggard, goshawk, tercel

hawk² *v*
hawking goods at people's houses sell, offer for sale, peddle, market, offer, cry, tout, vend, bark

hawker *n*
pedlar, vendor, door-to-door salesman, crier, huckster, colporteur, barrow-boy, chapman, costermonger, coster

haywire *adj*
wrong, out of control, crazy, mad, wild, chaotic, confused, disordered, disorganized, tangled, topsy-turvy

hazard *n, v*
▶ *n* risk, danger, jeopardy, menace, threat, deathtrap, pitfall, accident, chance, luck, *formal* peril
▰ safety
▶ *v* **1** RISK, endanger, jeopardize, expose to danger, put at risk, put in jeopardy **2** CHANCE, gamble, stake,

venture, suggest, put forward, submit, offer, speculate

hazardous *adj*
risky, dangerous, unsafe, precarious, menacing, threatening, insecure, chancy, uncertain, unpredictable, difficult, tricky, *formal* perilous, *colloq.* hairy
▰ safe, secure

haze *n*
1 MIST, fog, smog, cloud, steam, vapour, film, mistiness, fogginess, cloudiness, smokiness, dimness, obscurity **2** BLUR, confusion, muddle, bewilderment, uncertainty, indistinctness, vagueness

hazy *adj*
misty, foggy, smoky, clouded, cloudy, overcast, milky, fuzzy, blurred, muzzy, ill-defined, veiled, obscure, dim, faint, unclear, indistinct, vague, indefinite, uncertain
▰ clear, bright, definite

head *n, adj, v*
▶ *n* **1** SKULL, cranium, *technical* caput, *colloq.* noddle, nut, conk, bonce **2** MIND, brain, mentality, mental abilities, intellect, intelligence, wit(s), sense, understanding, wisdom, thought, reasoning, common sense, *colloq.* brains, loaf, noddle, little grey cells, grey matter, upper storey **3** TOP, peak, summit, crown, crest, tip, apex, vertex, height, climax **4** FRONT, fore, forefront, vanguard, van, lead **5** LEADER, chief, captain, commander, director, manager, managing director, superintendent, supervisor, principal, head teacher, headmaster, headmistress, ruler, controller, administrator, president, governor, chair, chairman, chairwoman, chairperson, *colloq.* boss **6** COMMAND, control(s), leadership, directorship, management, supervision, charge **7** *come to a head* CRISIS, critical point, climax, emergency, catastrophe, calamity, dilemma, *colloq.* crunch **8** *the head of a river* source, origin, fount, spring, rise, wellspring, wellhead **9** *no head on the beer* froth, foam, bubbles, fizz, suds, lather
▰ **1** foot, tail **3** base, foot **4** back **5** subordinate
▷ **go to your head 1** MAKE DRUNK, intoxicate, inebriate, make dizzy, befuddle, *colloq.* make woozy **2** *success has gone to his head* make arrogant, make conceited, make proud, make someone full of themselves, *colloq.* puff up
▷ **head over heels** completely, utterly, uncontrollably, wholeheartedly, recklessly, thoroughly, intensely, wildly
▷ **keep your head** keep calm, stay calm and collected, keep control of yourself, keep/maintain your composure, *colloq.* keep your cool
▷ **lose your head** panic, lose control of yourself, lose your composure, *colloq.* lose your cool, flap, go round like a headless chicken
▶ *adj* leading, front, foremost, first, chief, main, prime, principal, top, topmost, highest, supreme, premier, dominant, pre-eminent
▶ *v* **1** *head the queue* be at the front of, be first in, go first, lead **2** LEAD, rule, govern, command, direct, be in charge of, be in control of, manage, run, superintend, oversee, supervise, administer, control, guide, steer
▷ **head for** make for, go/move/travel towards, direct towards, go in the direction of, aim for, point to, turn for, steer for
▷ **head off** forestall, intercept, intervene, deflect, divert, turn aside, cut off, fend off, ward off, avert, prevent, stop, *formal* interpose
▷ **head up** lead, direct, manage, be in charge of, take charge of, be responsible for

headache *n*
1 *suffer from headaches* migraine, neuralgia, *technical* cephalalgia, hemicrania **2** BOTHER, nuisance, trouble,

inconvenience, problem, worry, pest, vexation, bane, *colloq.* hassle

heading *n*
title, name, headline, rubric, caption, section, division, classification, subject, category, class, head

headland *n*
promontory, cape, head, point, ness, foreland

headlong *adj, adv*
▶ *adj* hasty, impetuous, impulsive, rash, reckless, careless, impetuous, impulsive, dangerous, breakneck, head-first, *formal* precipitate
▶ *adv* head first, hurriedly, hastily, prematurely, rashly, recklessly, carelessly, heedlessly, impetuously, impulsively, thoughtlessly, without thinking, wildly, *formal* precipitately

headman *n*
chief, leader, captain, ruler, muqaddam, sachem

head-on *adj*
a head-on crash/confrontation direct, full-frontal, straight-on, straight, *colloq.* eyeball-to-eyeball

headquarters *n*
HQ, base (camp), head office, main office, centre of operations, nerve centre

headstrong *adj*
stubborn, obstinate, intractable, wayward, pigheaded, wilful, self-willed, not listening to reason, perverse, contrary, unruly, ungovernable, *formal* obdurate, refractory, recalcitrant, intransigent
F∃ tractable, docile

headway *n*
advance, progress, ground, way, improvement, development

heady *adj*
intoxicating, strong, stimulating, overpowering, exhilarating, invigorating, thrilling, exciting, ecstatic, euphoric, rousing

heal *v*
cure, make better, make well, remedy, mend, restore, improve, treat, soothe, comfort, salve, settle, reconcile, make good, patch up, put/set right, *formal* assuage, palliate

health *n*
fitness, constitution, form, shape, trim, fettle, condition, tone, state, healthiness, good condition, wellbeing, welfare, good shape, soundness, robustness, strength, vigour
F∃ illness, infirmity

healthy *adj*
1 WELL, fit, good, fine, in condition, in good shape, in fine fettle, sound, sturdy, robust, strong, vigorous, hale and hearty, blooming, flourishing, thriving, able-bodied, *colloq.* hardy, fit as a fiddle, right as rain, in the pink, a picture of health **2** *healthy food* wholesome, nutritious, nourishing, bracing, good, beneficial, invigorating, healthful **3** *healthy fresh air* bracing, invigorating, refreshing, stimulating, *formal* salubrious **4** *a healthy economy* successful, strong, sound, robust, vigorous **5** *a healthy respect for authority* wise, sensible, sound, *formal* prudent, judicious
F∃ **1** ill, sick, infirm **2** *colloq.* junk **3** ailing

heap *n, v*
▶ *n* **1** MOUND, pile, stack, mountain, lot, mass, bundle, accumulation, collection, hoard, stockpile, supply, store, *formal* assemblage, agglomeration **2** A LOT, great deal, plenty, abundance, quantities, lots, mass, lashings, *colloq.* load(s), stack(s), tons, oodles, pot(s), millions, scores
▶ *v* **1** PILE, stack, mound, bank, build, amass, accumulate, collect, gather, assemble, hoard, stockpile, store (up), load, burden **2** *heap criticism/praise*

on someone shower, lavish, *formal* confer, bestow

hear *v*
1 LISTEN, catch, pick up, make out, perceive, be in touch with, overhear, eavesdrop, heed, pay attention, take in, *colloq.* latch onto **2** LEARN, find out, discover, pick up, understand, gather, be informed, be told, *formal* ascertain **3** JUDGE, pass judgement, try, examine, investigate, consider, inquire, adjudicate

hearing *n*
1 EARSHOT, sound, range, hearing distance, reach, ear, perception **2** TRIAL, inquiry, investigation, examination, review, judgement, inquest, inquisition, adjudication, audition, interview, audience

hearsay *n*
rumour, word of mouth, talk, common talk, common knowledge, gossip, tittle-tattle, report, *colloq.* buzz

heart *n*
1 SOUL, mind, character, disposition, nature, temperament **2** FEELING, emotion, sentiment, love, affection, passion, tenderness, kindness, compassion, concern, sympathy, pity, responsiveness, warmth **3** *lose heart* courage, bravery, boldness, heroism, fearlessness, intrepidity, pluck, stout-heartedness, spirit, resolution, determination, enthusiasm, eagerness, keenness, *formal* fortitude, *colloq.* guts **4** CENTRE, middle, core, substance, kernel, nucleus, nub, crux, essence, essential part, pith, marrow, *formal* quintessence
F∃ 3 cowardice **4** periphery

Parts of the heart include:

aortic valve, ascending aorta, bicuspid valve, carotid artery, descending thoracic aorta, inferior vena cava, left atrium, left pulmonary artery, left pulmonary veins, left ventricle, mitral valve, myocardium, papillary muscle, pulmonary valve, right atrium, right pulmonary artery, right pulmonary veins, right ventricle, superior vena cava, tricuspid valve, ventricular septum.

▷ **at heart** basically, really, fundamentally, essentially, in essence, at bottom
▷ **by heart** by rote, parrot-fashion, pat, off pat, word for word, verbatim
▷ **change of heart** change of mind, rethink, second thoughts
▷ **from the bottom of your heart** deeply, sincerely, earnestly, profoundly, devoutly
▷ **heart and soul** eagerly, enthusiastically, completely, unreservedly, wholeheartedly, devotedly, gladly, heartily, absolutely, entirely
▷ **set your heart on** wish for, long for, desire, yearn, crave
▷ **take heart** be encouraged, brighten up, cheer up, rally, revive, *colloq.* buck up, perk up
▷ **take to heart** be affected by, be moved by, be upset by, be disturbed by

heartache *n*
sorrow, anxiety, worry, grief, despair, anguish, agony, heartbreak, pain, suffering, despondency, dejection, bitterness, distress, remorse, torment, torture, *formal* affliction

heartbreak *n*
distress, sadness, suffering, sorrow, dejection, despair, pain, grief, misery, agony, anguish, desolation
F∃ elation, joy, relief

heartbreaking *adj*
distressing, sad, tragic, harsh, harrowing, heart-rending, pitiful, agonizing, painful, excruciating, grievous, bitter, cruel, disappointing, poignant
F∃ heartwarming, heartening

heartbroken *adj*
broken-hearted, desolate, sad, miserable, sorrowful, in low spirits, dejected, despondent, downcast, suffering, crestfallen, disappointed, disheartened, dispirited, grieved, desolate, crushed, anguished
F3 delighted, elated

hearten *v*
comfort, console, reassure, cheer (up), encourage, boost, inspire, invigorate, stimulate, energize, revitalize, animate, rouse, raise the spirits of, *colloq.* buck up, pep up
F3 dishearten, depress, dismay

heartfelt *adj*
deep, profound, sincere, honest, genuine, unfeigned, devout, earnest, ardent, fervent, wholehearted, warm, compassionate
F3 insincere, false

heartily *adv*
1 ENTHUSIASTICALLY, eagerly, earnestly, deeply, profoundly, warmly, gladly, cordially, feelingly, sincerely, resolutely, unfeignedly, zealously, vigorously, genuinely 2 ABSOLUTELY, completely, very, totally, thoroughly

heartless *adj*
unfeeling, uncaring, cold, hard, hard-hearted, cold-hearted, cold-blooded, callous, unkind, cruel, inhuman, harsh, brutal, ruthless, pitiless, merciless, unsympathetic, unmoved, inconsiderate
F3 kind, considerate, sympathetic, merciful

heart-rending *adj*
harrowing, heartbreaking, agonizing, pitiful, piteous, pathetic, tragic, sad, distressing, moving, affecting, poignant

heartsick *adj*
sad, heavy-hearted, despondent, dejected, disappointed, depressed, downcast, melancholy, glum

heart-throb *n*
pin-up, star, idol, *colloq.* dreamboat

heart-to-heart *n*
cosy chat, private conversation, tête-à-tête, friendly talk, honest talk, personal conversation

heartwarming *adj*
cheering, heartening, encouraging, uplifting, gladdening, touching, moving, affecting, pleasing, gratifying, rewarding, satisfying
F3 heartbreaking

hearty *adj*
1 ENTHUSIASTIC, eager, wholehearted, unreserved, heartfelt, sincere, genuine, unfeigned, warm, affable, friendly, cordial, jovial, cheerful, ebullient, effusive, exuberant 2 *a hearty breakfast* large, sizeable, substantial, filling, solid, nourishing, nutritious, ample, abundant, generous 3 STRONG, energetic, vigorous, boisterous, robust, healthy, sound, hardy, stalwart
F3 1 inhibited, reserved, cold, half-hearted 3 weak, feeble

heat *n, v*
▶ *n* 1 HOTNESS, warmth, sultriness, torridness, swelter, closeness, heaviness, high temperature, fever, feverishness, *technical* calefaction 2 ARDOUR, fervour, fervency, fieriness, passion, warmth, intensity, vehemence, fury, anger, excitement, impetuosity, earnestness, eagerness, enthusiasm, zeal
F3 1 cold(ness) 2 coolness
▶ *v* 1 WARM, boil, toast, cook, microwave, bake, roast, reheat, warm up, *technical* calefy 2 INFLAME, excite, animate, stir, rouse, arouse, stimulate, enrage, annoy, flush, glow
F3 1 cool (down), chill

heated *adj*
angry, furious, raging, passionate, impassioned, fiery, stormy, tempestuous, bitter, fierce, intense, vehement, violent, frenzied, enraged, inflamed, excited, animated, stirred, fired, roused, stimulated, *colloq.* worked-up
F3 calm

heathen *n, adj*
▶ *n* pagan, unbeliever, infidel, philistine, nations, idolater, idolatress, barbarian, savage, *formal* nullifidian
F3 believer
▶ *adj* pagan, unbelieving, infidel, philistine, uncivilized, unenlightened, idolatrous, godless, irreligious, savage, barbaric, *formal* nullifidian
F3 godly, believing

heave *v*
1 PULL, haul, drag, tug, raise, lift, hitch, hoist, lever, rise, surge 2 THROW, fling, hurl, cast, toss, send, pitch, let fly, *colloq.* chuck, sling 3 RETCH, vomit, be sick, spew, gag, *colloq.* throw up 4 *heave a sigh* give, utter, express, let out, breathe

heaven *n*
1 PARADISE, home of God, bliss, next world, hereafter, life to come, afterlife, utopia, Elysium, elysian fields, happy hunting-ground, Zion, nirvana, Valhalla, Swarga, *formal* abode of God, *colloq.* up there 2 SKY, firmament, skies, the blue, ether 3 ECSTASY, rapture, bliss, happiness, complete happiness, joy, delight, transports of delight, *colloq.* seventh heaven
F3 1 hell

heavenly *adj*
1 CELESTIAL, unearthly, supernatural, extraterrestrial, cosmic, other-worldly, spiritual, divine, godlike, angelic, seraphic, cherubic, immortal, holy, sublime, blessed, beatific, *formal* empyreal, empyrean 2 BLISSFUL, wonderful, glorious, marvellous, rapturous, beautiful, lovely, exquisite, perfect, enchanting, delightful, enjoyable, *colloq.* out of this world, divine
F3 1 infernal, mundane 2 hellish

heavily *adv*
1 PONDEROUSLY, slowly, clumsily, awkwardly, laboriously, painfully, hard, sluggishly, weightily, woodenly 2 COMPACTLY, closely, densely, solidly, thick, thickly 3 COMPLETELY, utterly, decisively, thoroughly, roundly, soundly 4 EXCESSIVELY, to excess, too much, abundantly, copiously
F3 1 lightly 2 loosely

heaviness *n*
1 WEIGHT, weightiness, ponderousness, heftiness, bulk, density, solidity, thickness 2 *a heaviness in the air* dejection, depression, despondency, melancholy, sadness, seriousness, oppression, oppressiveness, burdensomeness, onerousness, drowsiness, sleepiness, sluggishness, deadness, gloom, gloominess, *formal* languor, lassitude, somnolence
F3 2 lightness, liveliness

heavy *adj*
1 WEIGHTY, hefty, ponderous, burdensome, cumbersome, awkward, massive, substantial, large, bulky, hulking, solid, dense, thick, *colloq.* weighing a ton, heavy as lead 2 *heavy work* hard, difficult, tough, arduous, laborious, strenuous, troublesome, demanding, taxing, exacting, harsh, severe 3 SERIOUS, intense, grave, sombre, deep, profound, dull, tedious, dry, uninteresting 4 *heavy fighting; a heavy shower* severe, intense, extreme, excessive, considerable, strong, great, immoderate, inordinate 5 *a heavy blow on the head* forceful, hard, powerful, strong, intense, sharp, violent 6 *heavy responsibilities* burdensome,

onerous, unbearable, intolerable, crushing, difficult, weighty, exacting, irksome, oppressive, taxing, troublesome, trying, wearisome **7** *with a heavy heart* sad, miserable, despondent, depressed, discouraged, downcast, gloomy, crushed **8** *a heavy meal* filling, substantial, solid, big, large, stodgy, indigestible, starchy **9** *tables heavy with food* laden, loaded, full, burdened, weighed down, encumbered, groaning **10** *the weather is heavy* sultry, humid, muggy, close, steamy, sticky **11** *a heavy sky* dark, cloudy, overcast, dull, grey, gloomy, leaden
F3 **1** light **2** easy **3** light **4** light **5** gentle **6** light **8** light **10** cool, fresh **11** bright

heavy-handed *adj*
clumsy, awkward, blundering, bungling, unsubtle, tactless, insensitive, thoughtless, inept, oppressive, forceful, severe, harsh, stern, overbearing, domineering, autocratic, despotic, *formal* maladroit, *colloq.* ham-fisted, cack-handed, all fingers and thumbs, like a bull in a china shop
F3 skilful

heavy-hearted *adj*
sorrowful, sad, depressed, discouraged, disappointed, disheartened, downcast, downhearted, despondent, gloomy, miserable, morose, mournful, melancholy, glum, forlorn, crushed, heartsick
F3 light-hearted

heckle *v*
barrack, shout down, interrupt, disrupt, jeer, taunt, pester, gibe, catcall, bait

hectic *adj*
busy, frantic, frenetic, chaotic, fast, feverish, excited, bustling, heated, furious, frenzied, tumultuous, turbulent, wild
F3 leisurely

hector *v*
bully, intimidate, badger, chivvy, harass, menace, threaten, nag, provoke, worry, browbeat, bluster, bullyrag, huff, *colloq.* bulldoze

hedge *n, v*
▶ *n* **1** FENCE, hedgerow, screen, windbreak, barrier, protection, dyke, boundary **2** SAFEGUARD, protection, shield, cover, guard
▶ *v* **1** SURROUND, enclose, encircle, edge, hem in, confine, restrict, limit, guard, shield, protect, safeguard, cover, insure, *formal* fortify **2** STALL, equivocate, dodge, sidestep, evade, quibble, prevaricate, *formal* temporize, *colloq.* duck, dodge

hedonism *n*
gratification, luxuriousness, self-indulgence, sensualism, sensuality, voluptuousness, pleasure-seeking, Epicureanism, epicurism, *dolce vita*, sybaritism
F3 asceticism

hedonist *n*
pleasure-seeker, sensualist, voluptuary, epicure, epicurean, *bon vivant, bon viveur*, sybarite
F3 ascetic

hedonistic *adj*
luxurious, pleasure-seeking, self-indulgent, voluptuous, epicurean, sybaritic
F3 ascetic, austere

heed *v, n*
▶ *v* listen, pay attention, mind, mark, attend to, take note/notice, take into account, take into consideration, bear in mind, consider, note, regard, observe, follow, obey
F3 ignore, disregard
▶ *n* attention, regard, note, notice, consideration, mind, thought, watchfulness, care, caution, heedfulness, respect, ear, *formal* animadversion
F3 inattention, indifference, unconcern

heedful *adj*
attentive, watchful, mindful, observant, careful, cautious, vigilant, chary, wary, *formal* circumspect, prudent, regardful
F3 heedless, unthinking

heedless *adj*
oblivious, unthinking, careless, negligent, rash, reckless, foolhardy, inattentive, unobservant, unwary, thoughtless, regardless, unconcerned, unmindful, *formal* precipitate
F3 heedful, mindful, attentive, watchful, vigilant

hefty *adj*
1 LARGE, big, huge, strapping, burly, hulking, beefy, muscular, brawny, strong, powerful, vigorous, robust, massive, stout **2** *a hefty blow* FORCEFUL, hard, heavy, weighty, powerful, vigorous, solid, substantial, massive, immense, colossal, bulky, awkward, unwieldy **3** *a hefty sum of money* SUBSTANTIAL, considerable, generous, ample, sizeable
F3 **1** small, slight **2** weak **3** small

height *n*
1 HIGHNESS, altitude, elevation, tallness, loftiness, stature **2** TOP, summit, peak, pinnacle, mountain top, hill top, apex, crest, crown, culmination, climax, perfection, extremity, maximum, limit, ultimate, uttermost, ceiling, *technical* vertex, zenith, apogee
F3 **1** depth

heighten *v*
raise, elevate, lift, increase, add to, build up, magnify, intensify, strengthen, sharpen, improve, boost, amplify, enhance, exalt, *formal* augment
F3 lower, decrease, diminish

heinous *adj*
evil, monstrous, atrocious, abominable, detestable, loathsome, contemptible, despicable, iniquitous, outrageous, shocking, flagrant, vicious, wicked, awful, hideous, villainous, revolting, hateful, odious, infamous, unspeakable, grave, *formal* abhorrent, execrable, facinorous, nefarious

heir, heiress *n*
beneficiary, co-heir, inheritor, inheritress, inheritrix, successor, scion, *technical* parcener, legatee

helix *n*
spiral, twist, coil, curl, whorl, loop, wreathe, screw, corkscrew, *technical* curlicue, volute

hell *n*
1 *heaven and hell* underworld, inferno, infernal regions, lower regions, nether world, abyss, fire, bottomless pit, Hades, Acheron, Gehenna, Tophet, Abaddon, Tartarus, Malebolge, *formal* perdition, abode of the devil, *colloq.* down there, blazes **2** TORTURE, suffering, anguish, agony, torment, ordeal, nightmare, misery, wretchedness, *formal* tribulation
F3 **1** heaven
▷ **give someone hell** trouble, annoy, torment, pester, vex, harass, punish, scold, beat, flog
▷ **hell for leather** very fast, hurriedly, quickly, rapidly, swiftly, recklessly, rashly, wildly, post-haste, *formal* precipitately
▷ **raise hell** object noisily, protest loudly, be very angry, be furious, *colloq.* hit the roof

hell-bent *adj*
determined, bent, intent, fixed, resolved, set, settled, tenacious, dogged, inflexible, unhesitating, unwavering, *formal* intransigent, obdurate

hellish *adj, adv*
▶ *adj* infernal, devilish, satanic, diabolical, demonic, fiendish, accursed, damnable, monstrous, savage, barbaric, wicked, cruel, abominable, atrocious,

dreadful, nasty, disagreeable, unpleasant, *formal* nefarious, execrable
🖪 heavenly
▶ *adv* dreadfully, awfully, extremely, unpleasantly

helm *n*
tiller, rudder, wheel
▷ **at the helm** in control, in command, in charge, leading, directing, in the driving seat, holding the reins, in the saddle

help *v, n*
▶ *v* **1** AID, assist, be of assistance, lend a hand, do something for, do someone a good turn, serve, be of use, guide, collaborate, co-operate, back, stand by, rally round, support, back, encourage, oblige, contribute to, promote, nurse, give a boost to, *colloq.* do your bit **2** IMPROVE, relieve, soothe, assuage, cure, heal, remedy, ease, facilitate, further, *formal* ameliorate, alleviate, mitigate **3** *can't help laughing* be able to stop, control, prevent yourself, *formal* be able to refrain/abstain
🖪 **1** hinder **2** worsen
▶ *n* **1** AID, assistance, helping hand, collaboration, co-operation, encouragement, boost, backup, support, backing, advice, guidance, service, charity, relief, use, utility, avail, benefit, advantage, *formal* succour, *colloq.* shot in the arm, tower of strength **2** REMEDY, relief, cure, healing, improvement, restorative, moderator, balm, salve, *formal* alleviation, amelioration, mitigation, *colloq.* oil on troubled waters
🖪 **1** hindrance

helper *n*
assistant, deputy, auxiliary, subsidiary, attendant, aide, adjutant, right-hand man/woman, PA, mate, helpmate, partner, associate, colleague, collaborator, accomplice, worker, co-worker, subordinate, ally, supporter, second, second-in-command, employee, man/girl Friday, maid, servant

helpful *adj*
1 USEFUL, of use, practical, of service, constructive, worthwhile, valuable, beneficial, profitable, advantageous **2** *a helpful person* CO-OPERATIVE, obliging, accommodating, neighbourly, friendly, caring, considerate, kind, benevolent, charitable, sympathetic, supportive
🖪 **1** useless, futile **2** unfriendly, cruel

helping *n*
serving, portion, share, ration, amount, plateful, bowlful, spoonful, piece, *colloq.* dollop

helpless *adj*
weak, feeble, powerless, dependent, vulnerable, exposed, unprotected, defenceless, abandoned, friendless, destitute, forlorn, desolate, incapable, incompetent, infirm, disabled, impotent, paralysed, *formal* debilitated, *colloq.* helpless as a newborn babe
🖪 strong, independent, competent

helpmate *n*
partner, support, assistant, associate, companion, consort, helper, helpmeet, better half, other half, spouse, husband, wife

helter-skelter *adv, adj*
▶ *adv* carelessly, confusedly, recklessly, wildly, hastily, hurriedly, pell-mell, rashly, impulsively, headlong
▶ *adj* confused, disordered, disorganized, jumbled, muddled, random, unsystematic, hit-or-miss, haphazard, topsy-turvy, higgledy-piggledy

hem *n, v*
▶ *n* edge, edging, border, margin, fringe, trim, trimming, frill, valance, flounce, *technical* fimbria
▶ *v* fringe, edge, trim, bind, border, skirt, fold, *technical* fimbriate

▷ **hem in** surround, enclose, box in, close in, shut in, confine, restrict, limit, hedge in, pen in, trap, constrain

hence *adv*
therefore, thus, for this reason, accordingly, consequently, *formal* ergo

henceforth *adv*
from now on, from this time on, in the future, henceforward, hereafter, hereinafter, hence

henchman *n*
aide, associate, subordinate, supporter, attendant, follower, right-hand man/woman, minion, bodyguard, lackey, underling, *colloq.* heavy, hit man, hatchet man, crony, minder, sidekick

henpecked *adj*
dominated, subjugated, browbeaten, bullied, intimidated, criticized, harassed, pestered, badgered, tormented, meek, timid, *colloq.* under someone's thumb, tied to someone's apron strings, like a puppet on a string
🖪 dominant

herald *n, v*
▶ *n* messenger, courier, announcer, crier, forerunner, precursor, usher, omen, token, signal, sign, indication, *formal* harbinger, portent, augury
▶ *v* **1** ANNOUNCE, proclaim, broadcast, advertise, publicize, make known, make public, trumpet, *formal* promulgate **2** PRECEDE, usher in, show, indicate, promise, foreshadow, *formal* harbinger, augur, portend, presage, *colloq.* pave the way

heraldry *n*

Heraldic terms include :

shield, crest, coat of arms, arms, badge, hatchment, emblazonry, emblem, ensign, insignia, regalia, mantling, helmet, supporters, field, charge, compartment, motto, dexter, centre, sinister, annulet, fleur-de-lis, martlet, mullet, rampant, passant, sejant, caboched, statant, displayed, couchant, dormant, urinant, volant, chevron, pile, pall, saltire, quarter, orle, bordure, gyronny, lozenge, impale, escutcheon, antelope, camelopard, cockatrice, eagle, griffin, lion, phoenix, unicorn, wivern, addorsed, bezant, blazon, canton, cinquefoil, quatrefoil, roundel, semé, tierced, undee, urdé.

herbs and spices

Herbs and spices include:
angelica, anise, basil, bay, bergamot, borage, camomile, catmint, chervil, chives, comfrey, cumin, dill, fennel, garlic, hyssop, lavender, lemon balm, lovage, marjoram, mint, oregano, parsley, rosemary, sage, savory, sorrel, tarragon, thyme; allspice, caper, caraway seeds, cardamon, cayenne pepper, chilli, cinnamon, cloves, coriander, curry, ginger, mace, mustard, nutmeg, paprika, pepper, saffron, sesame, turmeric, vanilla.

herculean *adj*
arduous, laborious, onerous, toilsome, demanding, strong, tough, exacting, difficult, enormous, powerful, exhausting, strenuous, tremendous, colossal, large, gigantic, massive, great, huge, mammoth, formidable, daunting, gruelling, heavy, hard

herd *n, v*
▶ *n* drove, flock, swarm, pack, collection, press, crush, mass, horde, throng, multitude, crowd, mob, host, the masses, rabble, *colloq.* riff-raff, plebs, proles

▶ *v* **1** FLOCK, congregate, gather, collect, get together, assemble, rally, huddle, muster **2** LEAD, guide, shepherd, round up, urge, drive, goad, force

herdsman *n*
shepherd, cowherd, cowman, drover, stockman, grazier, wrangler, *US* vaquero

here *adv*
1 *come here* in/to/at this place, present, around, in **2** *I must finish here* at this point, at this time, now, at this stage
🖃 **1** there, away, absent, missing **2** then

hereafter *adv, n*
▶ *adv* from now on, from this time forward/onwards, hence, henceforth, henceforward, in the future, later, eventually
▶ *n* afterlife, heaven, paradise, life after death, life to come, next world, elysian fields, happy hunting-ground

here and there *adv*
in different places, hither and thither, to and fro, sporadically, *colloq.* from pillar to post

hereditary *adj*
1 *a hereditary title* inherited, bequeathed, handed down, family, ancestral, left, willed, transferred **2** *hereditary diseases* inborn, inbred, innate, inherent, inherited, natural, congenital, genetic, transmissible

heresy *n*
heterodoxy, unorthodoxy, nonconformity, free-thinking, apostasy, dissidence, dissent, unbelief, atheism, agnosticism, scepticism, schism, error, sectarianism, separatism, revisionism, blasphemy
🖃 orthodoxy

heretic *n*
free-thinker, nonconformist, apostate, dissident, dissenter, unbeliever, atheist, agnostic, sceptic, revisionist, separatist, schismatic, sectarian, renegade
🖃 conformist

heretical *adj*
heterodox, unorthodox, free-thinking, dissident, dissenting, revisionist, separatist, sectarian, renegade, unbelieving, atheistic, agnostic, sceptical, revisionist, rationalistic, schismatic, impious, irreverent, iconoclastic, blasphemous
🖃 orthodox, conventional, conformist

heritage *n*
1 INHERITANCE, legacy, bequest, endowment, lot, portion, share, estate, birthright, due **2** HISTORY, past, tradition, culture, cultural traditions, background, ancestry, descent, lineage, family, extraction, dynasty

hermetic *adj*
airtight, sealed, watertight, shut, hermetical

hermit *n*
recluse, solitary, loner, monk, ascetic, anchorite, anchoress, ancress, eremite, stylite, pillarist, pillar-saint

hermitage *n*
retreat, refuge, haven, sanctuary, cloister, shelter, asylum, hideaway, hideout, hiding place

hero *n*
1 *the hero of a play* protagonist, leading male role/part, leading actor, male lead, lead **2** *heroes in battle* conqueror, victor, champion, man/person of courage, cavalier, lion, celebrity, *colloq.* goody **3** IDOL, star, superstar, pin-up, ideal, paragon, celebrity, god, *colloq.* heart-throb
🖃 **1** villain

heroic *adj*
brave, courageous, fearless, dauntless, undaunted, lion-hearted, stout-hearted, valiant, bold, daring, intrepid, adventurous, gallant, chivalrous, noble, determined, selfless, *formal* valorous, doughty
🖃 cowardly, timid

heroine *n*
1 *the heroine of a play* protagonist, leading female role/part, leading actress/lady, female lead, lead, diva, prima donna, prima ballerina **2** *heroines in battle* conqueror, victor, champion, woman/person of courage, cavalier, lion, celebrity, *colloq.* goody **3** IDOL, star, superstar, pin-up, ideal, paragon, celebrity, goddess
🖃 **1** villain

heroism *n*
bravery, courage, valour, fearlessness, dauntlessness, boldness, daring, intrepidity, gallantry, chivalry, prowess, selflessness, determination, stout-heartedness, lion-heartedness, *formal* fortitude, doughtiness
🖃 cowardice, timidity, *formal* pusillanimity

hero-worship *n*
admiration, idolization, adoration, worship, exaltation, glorification, adulation, idealization, deification, *formal* veneration, *colloq.* putting on a pedestal

hesitancy *n*
reluctance, misgiving, qualm, scruples, unwillingness, doubt, doubtfulness, reservation, uncertainty, indecision, wavering, *formal* disinclination, demur, irresolution
🖃 willingness, certainty

hesitant *adj*
hesitating, reluctant, unwilling, half-hearted, uncertain, unsure, doubtful, sceptical, dubious, indecisive, irresolute, vacillating, delaying, stalling, wavering, tentative, wary, shy, timid, halting, stammering, stuttering, *formal* disinclined, demurring
🖃 decisive, resolute, confident, fluent

hesitate *v*
1 PAUSE, delay, wait, think twice, hold back, hang back, falter, stumble, halt, stammer, stutter **2** BE RELUCTANT, be unwilling, shrink from, scruple, boggle, vacillate, waver, stall, be uncertain, dither, *formal* demur, be disinclined, *colloq.* shilly-shally, dilly-dally
🖃 **2** decide

hesitation *n*
pause, delay, holding-back, hanging-back, waiting, reluctance, unwillingness, hesitance, scruple(s), qualm(s), misgivings, doubt, doubtfulness, scepticism, second thoughts, vacillation, wavering, uncertainty, unsureness, indecision, stalling, faltering, stumbling, stammering, stuttering, *formal* irresolution, disinclination, demur, cunctation, *colloq.* dilly-dallying, shilly-shallying
🖃 eagerness, assurance

heterodox *adj*
unorthodox, unsound, dissident, dissenting, free-thinking, heretical, schismatic, iconoclastic, revisionist
🖃 orthodox

heterogeneous *adj*
diverse, varied, miscellaneous, assorted, different, mixed, motley, diversified, divergent, catholic, opposed, unlike, unrelated, dissimilar, contrary, contrasted, discrepant, *technical* polymorphic, *formal* multiform, disparate, incongruous
🖃 homogeneous

heterosexual *adj & n*
colloq. straight, *slang* hetero
🖃 homosexual, gay

hew *v*
1 CHOP cut, fell, saw, axe, lop, hack, sever, prune, trim, split **2** FORM, carve, sculpt, sculpture, chip, whittle, chisel, hammer, fashion, model, shape, make

heyday n
peak, pinnacle, prime, flush, bloom, flowering, culmination, golden age, boom time

hiatus n
break, gap, breach, opening, rift, space, void, chasm, blank, discontinuity, pause, rest, lull, interruption, interval, lapse, suspension, *formal* aperture, discontinuance, lacuna

hidden adj
1 *a hidden door* CONCEALED, covered, shrouded, veiled, masked, disguised, camouflaged, unseen, secret, out of sight 2 OBSCURE, dark, occult, secret, covert, close, cryptic, indistinct, mysterious, abstruse, mystical, latent, ulterior, *formal* arcane, recondite, *colloq.* under wraps
🗲 1 showing, apparent, revealed, visible, on view 2 obvious, clear, distinct

hide¹ v
1 CONCEAL, cover, cloak, shroud, veil, draw a veil over, put out of sight, screen, mask, disguise, camouflage, obscure, shadow, eclipse, darken, cloud, obstruct, bury, store, stow, secrete, withhold, keep dark, suppress, *formal* dissemble, *colloq.* stash away, bottle up, keep under your hat, sweep under the carpet, keep under wraps 2 TAKE COVER, shelter, conceal yourself, lie low, go to ground, go into hiding, keep out of sight, cover your tracks, lurk, *colloq.* hole up, disappear into thin air, keep a low profile, lie doggo, lay a false scent
🗲 1 reveal, show, display

hide² n
the hide of an animal skin, pelt, fell, fur, coat, fleece, leather

hideaway n
retreat, hiding place, hideout, refuge, sanctuary, shelter, cloister, hermitage, haven, nest, den, lair, hole

hidebound adj
set, rigid, fixed, entrenched, narrow, narrow-minded, intolerant, strait-laced, conventional, bigoted, ultra-conservative, uncompromising, reactionary, *formal* intractable
🗲 liberal, progressive

hideous adj
ugly, repulsive, repellent, grotesque, monstrous, unsightly, horrid, ghastly, awful, dreadful, frightful, terrible, grim, gruesome, macabre, abominable, terrifying, shocking, outrageous, appalling, horrifying, disgusting, revolting, horrible, horrendous
🗲 beautiful, attractive

hideout n
retreat, hiding place, hideaway, refuge, sanctuary, shelter, cloister, hermitage, haven, nest, den, lair, hole

hiding¹ n
go into hiding concealment, cover, veiling, screening, disguise, shroud, veil, mask, camouflage

hiding² n
give someone a good hiding beating, flogging, whipping, caning, spanking, thrashing, drubbing, battering, *colloq.* walloping, tanning, whacking, belting, licking

hiding place n
hideaway, hideout, lair, den, hole, hide, nest, cache, cover, shelter, refuge, haven, sanctuary, retreat, cloister

hierarchy n
pecking order, ranking, grading, scale, series, ladder, echelons, strata, system, structure

higgledy-piggledy adv, adj
▶ *adv* any old how, anyhow, indiscriminately, untidily, confusedly, haphazardly, pell-mell, topsy-turvy
▶ *adj* confused, disorderly, disorganized, jumbled, untidy, muddled, haphazard, indiscriminate, topsy-turvy

high adj, n
▶ *adj* 1 TALL, lofty, elevated, soaring, towering 2 GREAT, strong, powerful, forceful, vigorous, violent, intense, extreme 3 IMPORTANT, influential, powerful, eminent, distinguished, notable, prominent, chief, top, principal, leading, senior, high-ranking, elevated, exalted 4 *a higher form of life* advanced, complex, elaborate, progressive, ultra-modern, hi-tech 5 *a high standard* good, excellent, fine, outstanding, great, perfect, exemplary, commendable, noteworthy, first-class, first-rate, superior, superlative, surpassing, unequalled, unparalleled, select, choice, quality, de luxe, gilt-edged, tiptop, top-class, blue-chip, *colloq.* classy 6 *have a high opinion of someone* favourable, good, positive, well-disposed, approving, complimentary, admiring, agreeable, appreciative 7 *high moral principles* noble, moral, ethical, lofty, virtuous, upright, admirable, honourable, worthy 8 *a high price* expensive, dear, costly, exorbitant, excessive, inflated, extortionate, *colloq.* steep 9 HIGH-PITCHED, soprano, treble, falsetto, sharp, shrill, tinny, piping, piercing, penetrating, acute 10 *high on drugs* intoxicated, inebriated, hallucinating, *colloq.* turned on, having your mind blown, doped, on a trip, stoned, freaked out, spaced out, wasted, zonked, *US* wired, *slang* bombed, loaded, blitzed, blasted, out of it 11 *meat going high* bad, off, rotting, smelling, decayed, putrid, rancid
🗲 1 low, short 2 low, slight 3 unimportant, lowly 4 low 5 low, poor, inferior 6 low, poor, bad 7 low 8 cheap 9 deep, low
▷ **high and dry** abandoned, marooned, stranded, helpless, bereft, destitute, *colloq.* ditched, dumped
▷ **high and mighty** arrogant, conceited, haughty, overbearing, self-important, snobbish, superior, proud, egotistic, condescending, patronizing, disdainful, cavalier, imperious, overweening, *colloq.* stuck-up, swanky
▶ *n* 1 *feeling on a high* intoxication, inebriation, hallucination, *colloq.* trip, turn-on, freak-out 2 RECORD, height, summit, peak, top, *formal* zenith
🗲 1, 2 low

high-born adj
noble, aristocratic, blue-blooded, thoroughbred, well-born, patrician
🗲 low-born

highbrow n, adj
▶ *n* intellectual, scholar, genius, mastermind, academic, *colloq.* egghead, brains, brainbox, know-all, clever clogs, boffin
▶ *adj* intellectual, sophisticated, cultured, cultivated, academic, scholarly, bookish, deep, profound, serious, classical, *colloq.* brainy
🗲 lowbrow

high-class adj
upper-class, top-class, top-flight, high-quality, quality, de luxe, luxurious, élite, elegant, superior, excellent, first-rate, choice, select, exclusive, *colloq.* posh, classy, super
🗲 ordinary, mediocre

highfalutin, highfaluting adj
pretentious, pompous, supercilious, bombastic, grandiose, high-flown, high-sounding, lofty, *formal* affected, magniloquent, *colloq.* la-di-da, swanky

high-flown adj
florid, extravagant, exaggerated, elaborate, flamboyant, ornate, ostentatious, pretentious, grandiose, high-sounding, pompous, bombastic, turgid, artificial, stilted, affected, lofty, highfalutin, supercilious, *formal* grandiloquent, *colloq.* la-di-da

high-handed adj
overbearing, domineering, arrogant, haughty, imperious,

dictatorial, autocratic, despotic, tyrannical, oppressive, arbitrary, *formal* peremptory, *colloq.* bossy

highland *n*
mountain, hill, upland, elevation, rise, mound, mount, height, ridge, plateau

highlight *n*, *v*
▶ *n* high point, high spot, most interesting/exciting part, most significant feature, focus, peak, climax, best, cream
▶ *v* underline, emphasize, put emphasis on, stress, accentuate, accent, play up, point up, spotlight, illuminate, show up, set off, focus on, feature, call attention to

highly *adv*
1 VERY, very much, greatly, considerably, decidedly, extremely, certainly, immensely, vastly, hugely, tremendously, exceptionally, extraordinarily **2** *think highly of someone* favourably, approvingly, enthusiastically, warmly, well, appreciatively

highly-strung *adj*
sensitive, neurotic, nervous, easily upset, nervy, jumpy, edgy, on edge, temperamental, excitable, restless, overwrought, tense, stressed, *colloq.* wound up, uptight
F⁊ calm

high-minded *adj*
lofty, noble, pure, moral, ethical, principled, idealistic, elevated, virtuous, upright, righteous, honourable, fair, good, worthy
F⁊ immoral, unscrupulous

high-pitched *adj*
soprano, treble, falsetto, sharp, shrill, tinny, piping, piercing, penetrating, acute
F⁊ deep, low

high-powered *adj*
powerful, forceful, driving, aggressive, insistent, dynamic, ambitious, enterprising, assertive, energetic, vigorous, *colloq.* go-ahead, pushy

high-priced *adj*
expensive, dear, costly, exorbitant, excessive, extortionate, high, pricey, unreasonable, *colloq.* steep, stiff
F⁊ cheap

high-sounding *adj*
grandiose, flamboyant, ostentatious, overblown, pompous, florid, artificial, bombastic, extravagant, high-flown, ponderous, pretentious, stilted, strained, *formal* affected, grandiloquent, magniloquent, orotund

high-spirited *adj*
boisterous, bouncy, exuberant, effervescent, frolicsome, ebullient, sparkling, animated, vigorous, vibrant, vivacious, lively, active, dynamic, energetic, spirited, dashing, bold, daring
F⁊ quiet, sedate, placid, *colloq.* full of beans

high spirits *n*
boisterousness, exhilaration, exuberance, ebullience, animation, energy, spirit, boldness, liveliness, sparkle, good cheer, vivacity, capers, hilarity, buoyancy, *joie de vivre*, *colloq.* bounce

highwayman *n*
bandit, robber, land-pirate, rank-rider, knight of the road, footpad

hijack *v*
commandeer, skyjack, seize, take over, *formal* expropriate

hike *v*, *n*
▶ *v* **1** RAMBLE, walk, trek, wander, march, tramp, trudge, plod **2** RAISE, increase, put up, lift, pull up, *colloq.* jack up, push up **3** *hike up your clothing* pull, tug, jerk, hoist, jack, hitch, raise, lift, *colloq.* yank

▶ *n* ramble, walk, trek, wander, tramp, trudge, march

hilarious *adj*
funny, amusing, comical, humorous, side-splitting, farcical, laughable, riotous, uproarious, noisy, boisterous, rollicking, merry, entertaining, jolly, jovial, *formal* risible, *colloq.* hysterical, killing, a scream
F⁊ serious, grave

hilarity *n*
mirth, laughter, fun, amusement, comedy, levity, frivolity, merriment, jollity, conviviality, high spirits, boisterousness, exuberance, exhilaration
F⁊ seriousness, gravity

hill *n*
1 HILLOCK, knoll, mound, hummock, prominence, eminence, elevation, rise, rising ground, hilltop, foothill, down, fell, tor, mountain, mount, height, *US* mesa **2** *a steep hill* slope, incline, gradient, ramp, rise, ascent, drop, descent, declivity, *formal* acclivity

hillock *n*
mound, hummock, knoll, dune, barrow, knap, knob, monticle, monticulus, tump, *Scot.* knowe

hilt *n*
handle, grip, handgrip, shaft, haft, heft, helve
▷ **to the hilt** completely, fully, as fully as possible, wholly, entirely, utterly, to the full, to the end, to the maximum extent, in every respect, *colloq.* all the way, from first to last, from beginning to end

hind *adj*
rear, back, hinder, tail, after, posterior, caudal
F⁊ fore

hinder *v*
hamper, obstruct, block, impede, encumber, handicap, hamstring, hold up, delay, slow down, hold back, check, curb, halt, stop, forestall, arrest, prevent, foil, frustrate, thwart, balk, oppose, inhibit, interfere with, interrupt, *formal* retard, *colloq.* stymie, put a spoke in someone's wheel
F⁊ help, aid, assist

hindmost *adj*
last, farthest behind, furthest back, rearmost, tail, endmost, furthest, final, remotest, trailing, ultimate, concluding, terminal
F⁊ foremost

hindrance *n*
obstruction, impediment, handicap, encumbrance, obstacle, stumbling-block, block, barrier, bar, check, curb, restraint, restriction, thwarting, interference, interruption, stoppage, hold-up, delay, limitation, difficulty, drag, snag, hitch, drawback, disadvantage, inconvenience, deterrent, foil
F⁊ help, aid, assistance

hinge *v*
centre, turn, revolve, pivot, hang, depend, rest, *formal* be contingent

hint *n*, *v*
▶ *n* **1** TIP, advice, suggestion, help, clue, inkling, suspicion, tip-off, cue, reminder, indication, sign, pointer, mention, allusion, intimation, whisper, insinuation, implication, innuendo, *colloq.* wrinkle **2** *a hint of garlic* touch, trace, tinge, taste, dash, soupçon, sprinkling, speck, whiff, suspicion, suggestion, nuance
▶ *v* suggest, prompt, indicate, signal, imply, insinuate, intimate, allude, mention, *colloq.* tip off, tip someone the wink

hinterland *n*
interior, hinderland, back-country, backveld, back-blocks

hip *n*
haunch, loin, pelvis, hindquarters, posterior, buttocks, rump, croup, huck, huckle

hippie *n*
beatnik, flower child, rebel, loner, bohemian, deviant, *colloq.* dropout

hire *v, n*
▶ *v* **1** RENT, let, lease, charter, commission, book, reserve **2** EMPLOY, take on, sign up, sign on, engage, appoint, enlist, retain
▣ **2** dismiss, *colloq.* fire
▶ *n* rental, rent, lease, fee, charge, pay, cost, price, salary, wage

hire-purchase *n*
instalment plan, easy terms, *colloq.* never-never

hirsute *adj*
hairy, bearded, unshaven, bristly, bewhiskered, shaggy, *technical* hispid, *formal* crinal, crinate, crinigerous, crinose, crinite
▣ bald, hairless

hiss *v, n*
▶ *v* **1** WHISTLE, shrill, whizz, sizzle, *formal* sibilate **2** JEER, mock, scoff at, scorn, ridicule, taunt, boo, hoot, shout down, catcall, *formal* deride, *colloq.* blow raspberries
▶ *n* **1** WHISTLE, hissing, buzz, *formal* sibilance, sibilation **2** JEER, mockery, scoffing, scorn, taunting, contempt, hoot, boo, catcall, *formal* derision, *colloq.* raspberry

historian *n*
chronicler, archivist, annalist, diarist, narrator, recorder, historiographer, chronologer

historic *adj*
famous, famed, renowned, celebrated, momentous, important, significant, epoch-making, notable, memorable, remarkable, outstanding, extraordinary, *formal* consequential, *colloq.* red-letter
▣ unimportant, insignificant, unknown

---

historic or **historical**?

Historic means 'famous or important in history': *a historic battle. Historical* means 'of or about history': *books on military and historical topics*; or 'having actually happened or lived, in contrast to existing only in legend or fiction': *Is Macbeth a historical person?*

---

historical *adj*
1 *of historical interest* past, old, former, prior, ancient, bygone, *formal* of yore **2** REAL, actual, authentic, factual, documented, recorded, chronicled, confirmed, verified, verifiable, *formal* attested
▣ **2** legendary, fictional

history *n*
1 PAST, bygone/olden days, former times, days of old, the (good) old days, antiquity, yesterday, *formal* yesteryear, days of yore **2** CHRONICLE, record(s), annals, archives, chronology, account, study, report(s), narrative, story, tale, saga, biography, life, autobiography, memoirs **3** BACKGROUND, experience, record, credentials, qualifications, education, family, circumstances

histrionic *adj*
dramatic, exaggerated, theatrical, melodramatic, insincere, sensational, unnatural, forced, artificial, bogus, ham, *formal* affected

histrionics *n*
overacting, theatricality, dramatics, performance, artificiality, insincerity, unnaturalness, sensationalism, staginess, tantrums, scene, *formal* affectation, *colloq.* ranting and raving

hit *v, n*
▶ *v* **1** STRIKE, knock, tap, smack, slap, thrash, bash, bat, thump, punch, beat, pound, batter, buffet, cuff, box, thrash, *colloq.* whack, belt, wallop, clout, biff, sock, clobber, zap **2** BUMP, collide with, bang, crash into, smash into, run into, meet head-on, plough into, damage, harm **3** AFFECT, have an effect on, upset, disturb, trouble, overwhelm, move, touch, *formal* perturb, *colloq.* knock for six **4** *the thought hit me* come to mind, come to, strike, be remembered, be thought of, occur to, dawn on
▷ **hit back** retaliate, reciprocate, counter-attack, strike back, criticize in return
▷ **hit it off** get along with, get on (well) with, be/become friendly with, become friends, warm to, grow to like, relate well to each other, get on good terms with, *colloq.* become thick as thieves
▷ **hit on** realize, arrive at, guess, think of, chance on, stumble on, light on, uncover, discover, invent
▷ **hit out** lash out, assail, attack, rail, strike out, denounce, condemn, criticize, *formal* denounce, inveigh, vilify
▶ *n* **1** STROKE, shot, blow, knock, tap, slap, smack, buffet, thrashing, beating, punch, cuff, box, bash, bump, collision, impact, crash, smash, *colloq.* clout, whack, belt, wallop, clobbering, biff, sock **2** SUCCESS, triumph, *colloq.* winner
▣ **2** failure

hitch *v, n*
▶ *v* **1** FASTEN, attach, tie, harness, tether, bind, yoke, couple, connect, join, unite **2** PULL, heave, tug, jerk, hoist, *colloq.* yank, hike (up)
▣ **1** unhitch, unfasten
▶ *n* snag, delay, hold-up, trouble, problem, difficulty, mishap, setback, hiccup, drawback, catch, impediment, hindrance, obstacle, block, check, barrier, obstruction

hitherto *adv*
until now, up to now, till now, so far, previously, beforehand, thus far, *formal* heretofore

hit-or-miss *adj*
disorganized, haphazard, indiscriminate, undirected, unplanned, careless, offhand, casual, aimless, random, trial-and-error, perfunctory, lackadaisical, apathetic, cursory, uneven
▣ directed, planned, organized

hoard *n, v*
▶ *n* collection, accumulation, mass, heap, pile, fund, reservoir, supply, reserve, store, stockpile, cache, treasure-trove, *formal* aggregation, conglomeration, *colloq.* stash
▶ *v* collect, gather, amass, accumulate, heap (up), stack up, buy up, save, set aside, put by, put away, lay in, lay up, store, stock up, stockpile, pile up, keep, treasure, *colloq.* stash away
▣ use, spend, squander

---

 hoard or **horde**?

A *hoard* is a store or hidden stock of something: *He had a hoard of chocolate bars under the bed.* A *horde* is a crowd or large number of people, etc: *Hordes of tourists come here every year.*

---

hoarder *n*
collector, saver, gatherer, miser, niggard, magpie, squirrel

hoarse *adj*
husky, croaky, croaking, throaty, guttural, gravelly, gruff, growling, rough, harsh, rasping, raspy, grating, raucous, discordant
▣ clear, smooth

hoary *adj*
1 WHITE-HAIRED, white, grey, grey-haired, silvery, grizzled, venerable, old, aged, ancient, antique,

antiquated, *formal* canescent, senescent **2** *that hoary old joke* old, familiar, ancient, archaic, *colloq.* old-hat

hoax *n, v*

▶ *n* trick, prank, practical joke, put-on, joke, jest, ruse, fake, fraud, deception, bluff, humbug, cheat, swindle, *colloq.* leg-pull, con, put-up job, frame-up, fast one, scam, spoof

▶ *v* trick, deceive, play a practical joke on, take in, fool, dupe, gull, delude, swindle, cheat, hoodwink, bluff, *colloq.* con, bamboozle, have on, pull someone's leg, take for a ride, lead up the garden path, pull the wool over someone's eyes, pull a fast one on, double-cross, two-time

hoaxer *n*
joker, practical joker, prankster, trickster, hoodwinker, mystifier, humbug, *colloq.* bamboozler, spoofer

hobble *v*
limp, walk with a limp, stumble, falter, stagger, totter, reel, dodder, shuffle, walk awkwardly, walk lamely

hobby *n*
pastime, interest, diversion, recreation, relaxation, pursuit, leisure activity/pursuit, sideline, game, sport, entertainment, amusement, divertissement

hobgoblin *n*
goblin, imp, elf, dwarf, gnome, spectre, spirit, evil spirit, sprite, apparition, bugbear, bogey, bogeyman, bugaboo

hobnob *v*
associate, fraternize, keep company, mingle, mix, go around, socialize, *formal* consort, *colloq.* hang about, pal around

hocus-pocus *n*
trickery, swindle, deception, delusion, chicanery, gibberish, humbug, imposture, nonsense, mumbo-jumbo, rigmarole, sleight of hand, legerdemain, trompe-l'oeil, artifice, cant, jargon, gobbledygook, abracadabra, cheat, hoax, deceit, conjuring, *formal* prestidigitation

hog *n, v*

▶ *n* pig, boar, wild boar, porker, grunter, swine

▶ *v* monopolize, control, dominate, corner, take over, keep to yourself

hogwash *n*
rubbish, nonsense, drivel, gibberish, trash, tripe, twaddle, *colloq.* bunk, bunkum, claptrap, piffle, bilge, poppycock, hot air, cobblers, eyewash, hooey, tosh, balderdash, rot, tommyrot

hoi polloi *n*
the common people, the ordinary people, the masses, the proletariat, the third estate, *formal* the populace, *colloq.* riff-raff, the plebs, the peasants, the rabble, the herd, the great unwashed, the proles

☲ aristocracy, élite, nobility

hoist *v, n*

▶ *v* lift, elevate, raise, erect, jack up, winch up, heave, rear, uplift

▶ *n* jack, winch, crane, tackle, pulley, capstan, lift, elevator

hoity-toity *adj*
arrogant, proud, overweening, conceited, haughty, scornful, snobbish, supercilious, lofty, disdainful, pompous, *colloq.* stuck-up, high and mighty, toffee-nosed, snooty, uppity

hold *v, n*

▶ *v* **1** GRIP, have in your hand(s), grasp, clutch, clasp, seize, cling to, embrace, enfold, hug, have, own, possess, keep, retain **2** *hold a meeting* run, organize, conduct, carry on, continue, call, summon, convene,

assemble, preside over **3** *hold someone's attention* keep, engage, occupy, maintain, catch, arrest, absorb, engross, fascinate, enthral, captivate, rivet, fill, monopolize **4** CONSIDER, regard, judge, reckon, suppose, view, treat, think, believe, maintain, assume, presume, *formal* esteem, deem **5** BEAR, support, hold up, keep up, sustain, carry, take, buttress, prop up, brace **6** IMPRISON, detain, confine, impound, hold in custody, lock up, stop, arrest, check, curb, restrain, *formal* incarcerate **7** CLING, stick, adhere, stay, remain **8** *the memories that they held dear* cherish, treasure, value, prize, hold dear **9** *the bus holds 53 passengers* contain, accommodate, take, have a capacity of, *formal* compromise **10** *hold office as prime minister* occupy, fill, take up, continue, fulfil, have, hold down **11** *the fine weather will hold* continue, carry on, last, remain, stay, keep up **12** *the invitation/theory still holds* stay, apply, remain, remain valid/true, be in force/operation, hold up

☲ **1** drop **5** collapse, fall, break **6** release, free, liberate

▷ **hold back 1** CONTROL, keep back, curb, check, bar, restrain, impede, stop, delay, prevent, obstruct, suppress, stifle, retain, withhold, repress, contain, inhibit, *formal* retard **2** HESITATE, delay, shrink, refuse, *formal* desist, refrain, forbear

☲ **1** release, disclose

▷ **hold down 1** *hold down a job* keep, have, occupy, continue in **2** *hold someone down* keep down, oppress, dominate, tyrannize, suppress

▷ **hold forth** speak, talk, lecture, discourse, preach, harangue, *formal* orate, declaim, *colloq.* spout

▷ **hold off 1** FEND OFF, fight off, ward off, stave off, keep off, keep at bay, repel, rebuff **2** DELAY, postpone, put off, defer, avoid, wait

▷ **hold on 1** GRASP, grip, clutch, clasp, seize, cling to **2** CONTINUE, endure, remain, persevere, carry on, keep going, survive, *colloq.* hang on

▷ **hold out 1** OFFER, give, present, extend, *formal* proffer **2** LAST, last out, continue, carry on, persist, endure, persevere, stand fast, stand firm, resist, withstand, *colloq.* hang on

☲ **2** give in, yield

▷ **hold over** defer, postpone, put off, delay, adjourn, suspend, shelve

▷ **hold up 1** SUPPORT, bear, carry, hold, sustain, brace, shore up, prop up, lift, raise **2** DELAY, detain, slow, hinder, impede, obstruct, set/put back, *formal* retard **3** ROB, steal from, burgle, knock over, break into, *US* burglarize, *colloq.* mug, stick up, knock off, nobble

▷ **hold water** bear scrutiny/examination, convince, be convincing, make sense, ring true, work, stand up, pass the test, *colloq.* wash

▷ **hold with** agree with, go along with, approve of, support, subscribe to, accept, *formal* countenance

▷ **hold your own** resist, withstand, survive, stand fast, stand firm, stand your ground, *colloq.* keep your head above water

☲ be defeated, lose ground

▶ *n* **1** GRIP, grasp, clasp, embrace, hug **2** INFLUENCE, power, sway, mastery, dominance, dominion, authority, control, grip, leverage, *colloq.* clout

▷ **get hold of 1** OBTAIN, get, acquire, get your hands on **2** CONTACT, reach, speak to, communicate with, get through to

▷ **put on hold** delay, postpone, put off, hold off, defer, *colloq.* put on the back burner

holder *n*
1 *holders of tickets* bearer, owner, possessor, proprietor, keeper, purchaser, custodian, occupant, incumbent **2** CONTAINER, receptacle, case, housing, casing, cover, sheath, rest, stand

holdings *n*
investments, shares, stocks, securities, bonds, assets, resources, land, real estate, possessions, property, estate, tenure

hold-up *n*
1 DELAY, wait, hitch, setback, snag, difficulty, problem, trouble, obstruction, stoppage, (traffic) jam, bottleneck **2** ROBBERY, burglary, theft, break-in, raid, *colloq.* mugging, *slang* heist, stick-up, stick-up job

hole *n, v*
▶ *n* **1** *dig a hole* dent, dimple, depression, excavation, crater, mine, shaft, pothole, scoop, hollow, cavity, pit, chasm, cave, cavern, chamber, pocket, recess **2** *a hole in the roof* aperture, opening, space, break, gap, pore, puncture, perforation, eyelet, tear, split, crack, fissure, breach, rift, vent, notch, slit, gash, rent, outlet, shaft, slot, *formal* orifice **3** *an animal's hole* burrow, nest, lair, den, covert, set **4** *a hole in a theory* flaw, fault, mistake, error, defect, loophole, inconsistency, discrepancy, weakness **5** HOVEL, slum, shack, *colloq.* dump, tip, pigsty **6** *in a hole* predicament, difficulty, quandary, snag, plight, *colloq.* fix, mess, jam, spot, pickle, hot/deep water, pretty pass
▷ **pick holes in** criticize, find fault with, *colloq.* run down, pull to pieces, nit-pick
▶ *v* puncture, perforate, pierce, breach, break, crack, stab, spike, slit, gash, rent
▷ **hole up** hide, conceal yourself, take cover, lie low, go to ground, go into hiding

hole-and-corner *adj*
secretive, secret, underhand, clandestine, covert, furtive, stealthy, surreptitious, *colloq.* back-door, backstairs, hush-hush, sneaky, under-the-counter
🖪 open, public

holiday *n*
1 *go on holiday* vacation, trip, recess, leave, leave of absence, time off, day off, break, rest, half-term, furlough **2** *a national holiday* public holiday, bank holiday, legal holiday, feast day, festival, celebration, anniversary, saint's day, holy day

holier-than-thou *adj*
self-righteous, sanctimonious, self-satisfied, complacent, self-approving, smug, priggish, pietistic, pious, religiose, *formal* unctuous, *colloq.* goody-goody
🖪 humble, modest, meek

holiness *n*
sacredness, sanctity, spirituality, divinity, piety, devoutness, godliness, consecration, dedication, saintliness, blessedness, religiousness, goodness, virtuousness, righteousness, purity, perfection, sinlessness
🖪 impiety

holler *n & v*
yell, shout, bawl, bellow, roar, call, cheer, shriek, clamour, cry, howl, yelp, yowl, whoop

hollow *adj, n, v*
▶ *adj* **1** CONCAVE, indented, depressed, caved-in, sunken, deep-set, deep, cavernous, empty, vacant, void, unfilled, *formal* incurvate **2** FALSE, artificial, deceptive, insincere, hypocritical, pretended, deceitful, sham, meaningless, empty, vain, futile, fruitless, useless, pointless, profitless, worthless, valueless, unavailing, of no avail, Pyrrhic **3** *a hollow sound* dull, flat, low, muffled, deep, rumbling, echoing, reverberant
🖪 **1** solid **2** real
▷ **beat someone hollow** defeat soundly/convincingly, rout, overwhelm, crash, *colloq.* thrash, lick, hammer, trounce, annihilate, devastate, slaughter
▶ *n* **1** HOLE, pit, well, cavity, crater, excavation,

cavern, cave, depression, basin, bowl, cup, dimple, dent, dip, niche, recess, nook, cranny, indentation, groove, channel, trough, *formal* concavity **2** VALLEY, gorge, ravine, dell, glen, dale, cirque
▶ *v* dig, excavate, burrow, tunnel, scoop, gouge, channel, groove, furrow, pit, dent, indent

holocaust *n*
conflagration, flames, inferno, destruction, devastation, annihilation, extermination, extinction, massacre, carnage, mass murder, genocide, ethnic cleansing, sacrifice, slaughter, pogrom, hecatomb, *formal* immolation

holy *adj*
1 *holy ground* sacred, hallowed, consecrated, sanctified, sacrosanct, dedicated, blessed, venerated, revered, religious, spiritual, divine **2** PIOUS, religious, devout, godly, God-fearing, pietistic, saintly, virtuous, good, righteous, moral, faithful, pure, perfect, sinless
🖪 **1** unsanctified **2** impious, irreligious

homage *n*
recognition, acknowledgement, tribute, honour, praise, adulation, admiration, regard, respect, deference, reverence, adoration, awe, worship, devotion, *formal* esteem, veneration

home *n, adj, v*
▶ *n* **1** *invite someone to your home* HOUSE, flat, apartment, bungalow, cottage, address, *formal* residence, abode, domicile, dwelling, dwelling-place, habitation, *colloq.* pad, digs, semi, roof over your head, somewhere to live **2** BIRTHPLACE, roots, home town, native town, homeland, native country, country of origin, mother country, motherland, fatherland **3** INSTITUTION, residential home, nursing home, retirement home, old people's home, sheltered housing, children's home, Dr Barnardo's home, refuge, hostel, centre, retreat, asylum, safe place **4** *the home of jazz* PLACE OF ORIGIN, birthplace, source, fount, cradle, habitat, natural environment, element
▷ **at home 1** COMFORTABLE, relaxed, at ease **2** FAMILIAR, knowledgeable, experienced, skilled, conversant, competent, *colloq.* well up
▷ **bring home** make someone understand, make someone aware, impress, emphasize, instil, inculcate
▷ **nothing to write home about** not interesting, not exciting, dull, drab, boring, ordinary, mediocre, inferior, predictable, *colloq.* not enough to set the Thames on fire, no great shakes, nothing earthshattering
▶ *adj* domestic, household, family, internal, local, national, native, inland, interior
🖪 foreign, international, overseas
▶ *v* ▷ **home in on** pinpoint, aim, direct, focus, concentrate, zero in on, zoom in on

homeland *n*
native land, country of origin, native country, fatherland, motherland, mother country

homeless *adj, n*
▶ *adj* itinerant, travelling, nomadic, wandering, vagrant, rootless, unsettled, displaced, dispossessed, evicted, exiled, outcast, abandoned, forsaken, destitute, *formal* of no fixed abode, *colloq.* down-and-out, *slang* dossing
▶ *n* travellers, vagabonds, vagrants, tramps, squatters, *formal* derelicts, *colloq.* down-and-outs, *slang* dossers

homely *adj*
1 *a homely room* HOMELIKE, homey, comfortable, cosy, snug, relaxed, informal, friendly, welcoming, cheerful, hospitable, intimate, familiar **2** SIMPLE, plain, everyday, ordinary, domestic, natural, modest, unassuming, unpretentious, unsophisticated, folksy, homespun **3** *a homely person* PLAIN, unattractive, unlovely, ugly, unprepossessing, *colloq.* not much to look at

⊠ **1** grand, formal **2** sophisticated **3** attractive, lovely, good-looking

homespun *adj*
plain, simple, uncomplicated, unpolished, unrefined, unsophisticated, rough, rude, crude, rustic, homely, home-made, inelegant, amateurish, coarse, artless, folksy
⊠ sophisticated

homicidal *adj*
deadly, lethal, murderous, violent, bloodthirsty, mortal, death-dealing, maniacal, *formal* sanguinary

homicide *n*
murder, manslaughter, assassination, killing, bloodshed, slaughter, slaying, massacre, butchery, foul play

homily *n*
sermon, lecture, talk, speech, address, harangue, preaching, *formal* discourse, postil, oration, *colloq.* spiel

homogeneity *n*
uniformity, consistency, identicalness, similarity, sameness, resemblance, likeness, oneness, correspondence, agreement, analogousness, comparability, *formal* consonancy, similitude
⊠ difference, disagreement

homogeneous *adj*
uniform, consistent, unvarying, unvaried, identical, similar, alike, (all) the same, of the same kind, all of a piece, akin, kindred, analogous, corresponding, comparable, harmonious, compatible, *formal* cognate, correlative
⊠ heterogeneous, different

homogenize *v*
blend, merge, combine, amalgamate, coalesce, fuse, unite

homologous *adj*
related, matching, similar, parallel, comparable,analogous, equivalent, like, correspondent, corresponding
⊠ different, dissimilar

homosexual *n, adj*
▶ *n* gay, lesbian, bisexual
⊠ heterosexual, *colloq.* straight
See also LESBIAN; GAY.
▶ *adj* gay, lesbian

hone *v*
sharpen, whet, point, edge, grind, file, polish, develop, acuminate

honest *adj*
1 LAW-ABIDING, virtuous, upright, upstanding, ethical, moral, principled, high-minded, right-minded, scrupulous, honourable, dependable, reputable, respectable, reliable, trustworthy, incorruptible, true, genuine, real **2** TRUTHFUL, sincere, frank, candid, blunt, outspoken, direct, straight, outright, forthright, straightforward, plain, simple, open, plain-speaking, *colloq.* up front **3** FAIR, just, impartial, objective, equitable, above-board, legitimate, legal, lawful, *colloq.* on the level, fair and square, honest as the day is long, straight as a die
⊠ **1** dishonourable **2** dishonest **3** unjust

honestly *adv*
1 REALLY, truly, truthfully, sincerely, frankly, to be honest, directly, outright, plainly, openly, *colloq.* straight up, not to put too fine a point on it **2** LEGITIMATELY, legally, lawfully, morally, ethically, fairly, justly, objectively, honourably, in good faith, *colloq.* on the level
⊠ **2** dishonestly, dishonourably

honesty *n*
1 VIRTUE, uprightness, honour, integrity, morality, morals, ethics, principles, righteousness, incorrupt-

ibility, scrupulousness, trustworthiness, genuineness, veracity, *formal* probity, rectitude **2** TRUTHFULNESS, sincerity, frankness, candour, bluntness, outspokenness, forthrightness, straightforwardness, plain-speaking, explicitness, openness **3** FAIRNESS, legitimacy, legality, equity, justness, objectivity, impartiality, balance, even-handedness
⊠ **2** dishonesty **3** bias, prejudice, partiality

honorarium *n*
fee, pay, salary, remuneration, recompense, reward, *formal* emolument

honorary *adj*
unpaid, unofficial, titular, nominal, in name only, honorific, ex officio, formal
⊠ paid

honour *n, v*
▶ *n* **1** REPUTATION, good name, repute, renown, fame, glory, distinction, regard, respect, credit, dignity, self-respect, pride, integrity, uprightness, honesty, morals, ethics, principles, virtue, goodness, morality, decency, righteousness, trustworthiness, truthfulness, *formal* esteem, rectitude, probity **2** AWARD, accolade, decoration, prize, reward, trophy, crown, title, distinction, laurel, commendation, acknowledgement, compliment, recognition, tribute, favour, privilege **3** PRAISE, acclaim, acclamation, applause, homage, admiration, reverence, worship, adoration
⊠ **1** dishonour, disgrace
▶ *v* **1** PRAISE, acclaim, applaud, commend, have a high regard for, compliment, exalt, glorify, pay homage to, pay tribute to, acknowledge, recognize, decorate, crown, celebrate, commemorate, remember, admire, respect, revere, worship, prize, value, *formal* esteem, venerate **2** *honour a promise* KEEP, observe, respect, fulfil, carry out, discharge, execute, perform, be true to **3** *honour a cheque/bill* PAY, accept, clear
⊠ **1** dishonour, disgrace

honourable *adj*
great, eminent, distinguished, renowned, famous, notable, noted, illustrious, respected, worthy, prestigious, trusty, reputable, respectable, admirable, virtuous, upright, upstanding, straight, honest, trustworthy, truthful, true, sincere, dependable, reliable, noble, high-minded, principled, high-principled, moral, ethical, fair, just, right, righteous, good, decent
⊠ dishonourable, unworthy, dishonest

hood *n*
cowl, scarf, capuche, capeline, domino

hoodlum *n*
1 HOOLIGAN, ruffian, rowdy, vandal, mobster, thug, tough, lout, brute, *colloq.* mugger, *slang* bovver boy, yob **2** CRIMINAL, law-breaker, felon, offender, gangster, armed robber, gunman, *US colloq.* mobster, hood

hoodwink *v*
deceive, dupe, fool, take in, delude, mislead, outwit, hoax, trick, cheat, rook, gull, defraud, swindle, get the better of, *colloq.* bamboozle, have on, con, take for a ride, pull a fast one on, pull the wool over someone's eyes

hoof *n*
foot, trotter, cloven hoof, cloot, *technical* ungula

hoofed *adj*
cloven-footed, cloven-hoofed, *technical* ungulate, unguligrade

hook *n, v*
▶ *n* **1** *a hook on a door/dress* CATCH, peg, barb, fastener, clasp, hasp, clip **2** SICKLE, scythe **3** BEND, curve, crook, angle, loop, elbow, bow, arc **4** BLOW,

hit, stroke, box, thump, punch, cuff, clip, knock, rap, *colloq.* clout, wallop

▷ **off the hook** cleared, acquitted, in the clear, *formal* exonerated, vindicated, *colloq.* scot free

▶ *v* **1** BEND, crook, curve, curl **2** CATCH, capture, bag, grab, trap, entrap, snare, ensnare, enmesh, entangle **3** FASTEN, clasp, hitch, fix, secure

hooked *adj*
1 CURVED, bent, curled, beaked, barbed, beaky, aquiline, sickle-shaped, *formal* falcate, hamate, hamose, hamous, hamular, hamulate, uncate, unciform, uncinate **2** ADDICTED, dependent, devoted, obsessed, enamoured

hooligan *n*
ruffian, rowdy, hoodlum, mobster, thug, tough, rough, lout, vandal, delinquent, *colloq.* mugger, *slang* bovver boy, yob

hoop *n*
ring, circle, round, loop, wheel, band, girdle, circlet

hoot *v, n*
▶ *v* **1** *an owl hooting* call, cry, whoop, screech, tu-whit tu-whoo, *formal* ululate **2** *the car hooted* toot, beep, whistle **3** *the audience hooted* shout, shriek, whoop, howl, sneer, ridicule, taunt, mock, jeer, boo, hiss, howl down
▶ *n* **1** *the hoot of an owl* call, cry, whoop, screech, tu-whit tu-whoo **2** *the hoot of a car* toot, beep, whistle **3** *the hoots of the audience* shout, shriek, whoop, howl, sneer, ridicule, taunt, mock, jeer, boo, hiss

hop *v, n*
▶ *v* **1** JUMP, leap, spring, bound, vault, skip, dance, prance, frisk, limp, hobble **2** *hop over to Paris* pop, nip, fly quickly
▶ *n* **1** JUMP, leap, spring, bound, vault, bounce, step, skip, dance **2** *a quick hop by plane* (quick) flight, trip, journey, excursion, jaunt **3** DANCE, disco, social, party, *colloq.* knees-up, rave, shindig

hope *n, v*
▶ *n* hopefulness, optimism, ambition, aspiration, wish, desire, longing, yearning, craving, dream, expectation, anticipation, prospect, promise, belief, confidence, assurance, conviction, assumption, faith
F3 pessimism, despair
▶ *v* aspire, wish, desire, long, yearn, crave, dream, expect, be hopeful, await, look forward to, anticipate, be ambitious, contemplate, foresee, believe, trust, have confidence, rely, reckon on, assume, *colloq.* keep your fingers crossed, pin your hopes on, hope against hope
F3 despair

hopeful *adj*
1 OPTIMISTIC, confident, assured, expectant, sanguine, cheerful, buoyant, aspiring, aspirant, positive, *colloq.* bullish **2** *a hopeful sign* promising, encouraging, heartening, gladdening, reassuring, optimistic, pleasant, favourable, positive, rosy, bright, cheerful, *formal* propitious, auspicious
F3 **1** pessimistic, despairing **2** discouraging

hopefully *adv*
1 *hopefully the weather will improve* I hope, if all goes well, with luck, all being well, probably, conceivably, it is to be hoped that **2** EXPECTANTLY, with hope, with anticipation, confidently, eagerly, optimistically, expectedly, *formal* sanguinely, *colloq.* bullishly

hopeless *adj*
1 PESSIMISTIC, defeatist, negative, despairing, desperate, gloomy, demoralized, downhearted, dejected, downcast, despondent, forlorn, wretched **2** UNATTAINABLE, unachievable, impracticable, impossible, vain, grave, foolish, futile, useless, pointless, worthless, poor, helpless, lost, irreversible, irremediable,

beyond remedy, irreparable, beyond repair, incurable **3** *hopeless at speaking French* useless, incompetent, bad, weak, *colloq.* lousy, pathetic, awful
F3 **1** hopeful, optimistic **2** curable **3** skilled, expert

horde *n*
band, gang, pack, troop, crew, herd, drove, flock, swarm, crowd, mob, throng, mass, multitude, host, army

 horde or **hoard** ? *See panel at* HOARD.

horizon *n*
1 SKYLINE, vista, prospect, range, range of vision **2** *widen your horizons* scope, perspective, compass, outlook, perception

horizontal *adj*
level, flat, plane, smooth, levelled, on its side, *formal* supine

horny *adj*
1 *a horny shell* hard, corny, callous, *technical* ceratoid, *formal* corneous **2** LUSTFUL, ardent, sexy, lascivious, lecherous, ruttish, *formal* concupiscent, libidinous, *colloq.* randy
F3 **2** cold, frigid

horrendous *adj*
horrific, shocking, appalling, horrifying, terrifying, frightening, terrible, dreadful, frightful

horrible *adj*
1 *horrible scenes of murder* horrific, shocking, appalling, horrifying, terrifying, frightening, harrowing, bloodcurdling, hair-raising, terrible, dreadful, frightful, repulsive, revolting, abominable, grim, hideous, gruesome, ghastly, awful, *colloq.* scary **2** *that fish smells horrible* unpleasant, disagreeable, nasty, unkind, obnoxious, horrid, disgusting, revolting, loathsome, repulsive, detestable, abominable, offensive, ghastly, awful, terrible, dreadful, frightful
F3 **1** attractive **2** pleasant, agreeable, lovely

horrid *adj*
1 HORRIFIC, shocking, appalling, horrifying, terrifying, frightening, harrowing, bloodcurdling, hair-raising, terrible, dreadful, frightful, repulsive, revolting, abominable, grim, hideous, gruesome, ghastly, awful **2** UNKIND, mean, nasty, awful, cruel, dreadful, obnoxious, hateful, *colloq.* beastly
F3 **1, 2** lovely, pleasant

horrific *adj*
horrifying, shocking, appalling, awful, terrible, frightful, dreadful, ghastly, gruesome, terrifying, frightening, harrowing, bloodcurdling, *colloq.* scary

horrify *v*
shock, appal, offend, outrage, scandalize, disgust, repel, revolt, sicken, nauseate, dismay, alarm, startle, scare, panic, frighten, terrify, terrorize, intimidate, *colloq.* make your blood run cold, make your hair stand on end, put the wind up, put the frighteners on, scare out of your wits, scare the living daylights out of, scare to death
F3 please, delight

horror *n*
1 *recoil in horror* shock, outrage, disgust, distaste, revulsion, repugnance, abhorrence, loathing, abomination, hate, dismay, alarm, fright, fear, terror, panic, dread, apprehension, *formal* consternation, trepidation, detestation **2** GHASTLINESS, awfulness, frightfulness, hideousness, unpleasantness
F3 **1** approval, delight

horror-struck *adj*
appalled, shocked, frightened, horrified, terrified, horror-stricken, aghast, stunned, petrified
F3 delighted, pleased

horse n

steed, mount, stallion, nag, mustang, mare, colt, filly, bay, sorrel, roan, hack, bronc(h)o, charger, cob, dobbin, hackney, centaur

The points of a horse are:

back, breast, cannon, chestnut, crest of the neck, croup/crupper/rump, ear, elbow, eye, face, fetlock, forearm, forefoot, forehead, forelock, gaskin, haunch, head, hind leg, hip, hock, hoof, knee, loins, lower jaw, lower/under lip, mane, mouth, neck, nose, nostril, pastern, root/dock of the tail, shoulder, spur vein, stifle (joint), tail, throat, upper lip, withers.

Breeds of horse include:

Akhal-Teké, Alter-Réal, American Quarter Horse, American Saddle Horse, American Trotter, Andalusian, Anglo-Arab, Anglo-Norman, Appaloosa, Arab, Ardennias, Auxois, Barb, Bavarian Warmblood, Boulonnais, Brabançon, Breton, British Warmblood, Brumby, Budyonny, Calabrese, Charollais Halfbred, Cleveland Bay, Clydesdale, Comtois, Criollo, Danubian, Døle Gudbrandsdal, Døle Trotter, Don, Dutch Draught, East Bulgarian, East Friesian, Einsiedler, Finnish, Frederiksborg, Freiberger, French Saddle Horse, French Trotter, Friesian, Furioso, Gelderland, German Trotter, Groningen, Hanoverian, Hispano, Holstein, Iomud, Irish Draught, Irish Hunter, Italian Heavy Draught, Jutland, Kabardin, Karabair, Karabakh, Kladruber, Knabstrup, Kustanair, Latvian Harness Horse, Limousin Halfbred, Lipizzaner, Lithuanian Heavy Draught, Lokai, Lusitano, Mangalarga, Maremmana, Masuren, Mecklenburg, Metis Trotter, Morgan, Muraköz, Murgese, Mustang, New Kirgiz, Nonius, North Swedish, Oldenburg, Orlov Trotter, Palomino, Paso Fino, Percheron, Peruvian Stepping Horse, Pinto, Pinzgauer Noriker, Plateau Persian, Poitevin, Rhineland Heavy Draught, Russian Heavy Draught, Salerno, Sardinian, Shagya Arab, Shire, Suffolk Punch, Swedish Halfbred, Tchenaran, Tennessee Walking Horse, Tersky, Thoroughbred, Toric, Trait du Nord, Trakehner, Vladimir Heavy Draught, Waler, Welsh Cob, Württemberg.

Breeds of pony include:

Connemara, Dales, Dartmoor, Exmoor, Falabella, Fell, Hackney, Highland, New Forest, Przewalski's Horse, Shetland, Welsh Mountain Pony, Welsh Pony.

horseman, horsewoman n

equestrian, rider, jockey, cavalryman, horse soldier, hussar, dragoon, knight

horseplay n

clowning, buffoonery, foolery, fooling, fooling around, tomfoolery, skylarking, pranks, capers, antics, high jinks, practical jokes, fun and games, rough-and-tumble, colloq. monkey business

hortatory adj

encouraging, edifying, heartening, inspiriting, instructive, practical, stimulating, homiletic, formal didactic, exhortative, exhortatory, hortative, preceptive, colloq. pep

horticulture n

gardening, cultivation, formal arboriculture, floriculture

hosanna n

praise, worship, alleluia, save us, formal laudation

hose n

pipe, tube, tubing, channel, conduit, duct

hosiery n

socks, stockings, tights, leggings, leg-coverings, hose

hospitable adj

friendly, sociable, welcoming, neighbourly, receptive, cordial, amicable, congenial, convivial, genial, warm, helpful, kind, kind-hearted, gracious, generous, open-handed, liberal, bountiful

🗲 inhospitable, unfriendly, hostile

hospital n

medical centre, health centre, clinic, infirmary, institute, sanatorium, hospice

hospitality n

friendliness, sociability, welcome, neighbourliness, accommodation, entertainment, congeniality, conviviality, warmth, cheer, generosity, kindness, liberality, helpfulness, open-handedness

🗲 unfriendliness, hostility

host¹ n, v

▶ n 1 COMPÈRE, master of ceremonies, MC, presenter, announcer, anchorman, anchorwoman, linkman, media personality, colloq. emcee 2 PUBLICAN, innkeeper, landlord, landlady, proprietor, proprietress
▶ v present, introduce, give, compère

host² n

a host of letters multitude, myriad, array, army, horde, crowd, throng, mass, swarm, pack, troop, herd, mob, crush, band

hostage n

prisoner, captive, pawn, surety, security, pledge

hostel n

youth hostel, bed and breakfast, boarding-house, guesthouse, hotel, inn, motel, pension, formal residence, slang dosshouse

hostile adj

1 BELLIGERENT, warlike, ill-disposed, unsympathetic, unfriendly, inhospitable, inimical, antagonistic, opposed, formal bellicose, malevolent 2 ADVERSE, unfavourable, contrary, opposite, formal inauspicious

🗲 1 receptive, friendly, welcoming 2 favourable

hostilities n

war, warfare, battle, fighting, conflict, strife, action, bloodshed

hostility n

opposition, aggression, belligerence, militancy, enmity, antagonism, animosity, unfriendliness, cruelty, ill-will, malice, resentment, hate, hatred, dislike, aversion, formal estrangement, abhorrence, bellicosity, malevolence

🗲 friendliness, friendship

hot adj

1 WARM, heated, fiery, burning, scalding, scorching, blistering, red hot, roasting, baking, boiling, piping, steaming, sizzling, sweltering, parching, searing, sultry, torrid, tropical 2 SPICY, peppery, piquant, sharp, pungent, strong, fiery 3 FEVERISH, delirious, burning, flushed, red, with a temperature 4 his hot temper fiery, furious, angry, indignant, raging, boiling, seething, fuming, livid, violent, heated, inflamed, incensed, enraged 5 hot competition fierce, intense, strong, furious, keen, cut-throat 6 not very hot on the idea keen, enthusiastic, eager, warm, earnest, zealous, diligent, devoted 7 hot news recent, new, fresh, latest, up-to-date, exciting 8 hot goods illegally obtained/imported, contraband, stolen, pilfered, ill-gotten

🗲 1 cold, cool, chilly 2 mild, bland 4 calm 7 old, stale

▷ **hot air** nonsense, empty talk, emptiness, mere words, blather, blether, bluster, bombast, vapour, foam, froth, *formal* verbiage, *colloq.* balderdash, bosh, bunk, bunkum, claptrap, gas, cobblers, piffle, bilge
🖪 wisdom

hotbed *n*
breeding-ground, den, hive, nest, seedbed, cradle, nursery, school, forcing-house

hot-blooded *adj*
temperamental, excitable, spirited, wild, rash, impulsive, impetuous, high-spirited, heated, fervent, fiery, bold, eager, ardent, passionate, lustful, sensual, lusty, *formal* perfervid, precipitate
🖪 cool, dispassionate

hotchpotch *n*
mishmash, medley, miscellany, collection, mix, mixture, melange, jumble, confusion, mess, *US* hodgepodge

hotel *n*
boarding-house, guesthouse, pension, motel, inn, public house, tavern, hostel, hostelry, *colloq.* pub

hotfoot *adv*
speedily, at top speed, quickly, rapidly, swiftly, without delay, hurriedly, in haste, hastily, posthaste, helter-skelter, pell-mell
🖪 slowly, *formal* dilatorily

hothead *n*
tearaway, terror, madcap, madman, daredevil, desperado, hotspur

hotheaded *adj*
headstrong, impetuous, impulsive, hasty, rash, foolhardy, reckless, wild, fiery, excitable, volatile, explosive, volcanic, hot-tempered, quick-tempered, short-tempered, irascible
🖪 cool, calm

hothouse *n*
greenhouse, glasshouse, conservatory, orangery, vinery

hot-tempered *adj*
fiery, choleric, explosive, quick-tempered, short-tempered, violent, volcanic, testy, hasty, irascible, irritable, petulant
🖪 calm, cool, *formal* imperturbable

hound *v*
chase, pursue, follow, hunt (down), track, stalk, trail, drive, force, goad, prod, urge, chivvy, nag, pester, disturb, bully, badger, harry, harass, provoke, persecute

house *n, v*
▶ *n* **1** BUILDING, home, *formal* dwelling, residence, domicile, habitation **2** HOUSEHOLD, family, family circle, home, ménage **3** *a publishing/design house* firm, company, establishment, business, enterprise, corporation, organization **4** ASSEMBLY, body, chamber, legislature, parliament, congress **5** *a full house at the theatre* audience, auditorium, gathering, assembly, turnout, spectators, onlookers, listeners, viewers **6** DYNASTY, family, clan, tribe, line, lineage, ancestry, blood, strain, race, kindred
▷ **on the house** free, free of charge, without charge/cost, for nothing, at no (extra) cost

Types of house include:
semi-detached, *colloq.* semi, detached, terraced, town house, council house, cottage, thatched cottage, *colloq.* prefab, pied-à-terre, bungalow, chalet bungalow; flat, bedsit, apartment, studio, maisonnette, penthouse, granny flat, *US* duplex, *US* condominium, manor, hall, lodge, grange, villa, mansion, rectory, vicarage, parsonage, manse, croft, farmhouse, homestead, ranchhouse, chalet, log cabin, shack, shanty, hut, igloo, hacienda.

▶ *v* **1** LODGE, quarter, billet, board, accommodate, put up, take in, have room/space for, shelter, harbour **2** HOLD, contain, protect, cover, guard, shelter, sheathe, place, keep, store

household *n, adj*
▶ *n* family, family circle, house, home, ménage, establishment, set-up
▶ *adj* domestic, home, family, ordinary, plain, everyday, common, familiar, well-known, established

householder *n*
resident, tenant, occupier, occupant, owner, landlady, freeholder, leaseholder, proprietor, landlord, home-owner, head of the household

housekeeping *n*
home economics, domestic science, household management, running a home, domestic work/matters, homemaking, housewifery

houseman *n*
1 DOCTOR, house-physician, house-surgeon, intern(e), resident **2** MANSERVANT, servant, butler, valet, retainer, gentleman's gentleman

house-trained *adj*
domesticated, tame, tamed, well-mannered, house-broken
🖪 unsocial

housing *n*
1 ACCOMMODATION, houses, homes, shelter, *formal* dwellings, habitation **2** CASING, case, container, holder, covering, guard, cover, sheath, jacket, protection

hovel *n*
shack, shanty, cabin, hut, shed, *colloq.* dump, hole

hover *v*
1 HANG, poise, float, drift, fly, flutter, flap **2** *he hovered by the door* pause, linger, hang about, hesitate, waver, fluctuate, alternate, seesaw, *formal* vacillate, oscillate

however *adv*
nevertheless, nonetheless, still, yet, even so, regardless, though, anyhow, just the same, *formal* notwithstanding

howl *n & v*
wail, cry, shriek, scream, bawl, shout, yell, roar, bellow, bay, yelp, yowl, hoot, moan, groan

howler *n*
error, mistake, blunder, gaffe, malapropism, *formal* solecism, *colloq.* bloomer, clanger, boob

hub *n*
centre, middle, focus, focal point, axis, pivot, linch-pin, nerve centre, core, heart

hubbub *n*
noise, racket, din, clamour, commotion, disturbance, riot, uproar, hullabaloo, rumpus, confusion, disorder, tumult, hurly-burly, chaos, pandemonium
🖪 peace, quiet

huckster *n*
hawker, dealer, salesperson, barker, tinker, vendor, haggler, packman, pedlar, pitcher

huddle *v, n*
▶ *v* cluster, gravitate, converge, meet, gather, congregate, crowd, flock, cram, pack, herd, throng, press, squeeze, cuddle, snuggle, nestle, curl up, crouch, hunch
🖪 disperse
▶ *n* **1** CLUSTER, clump, knot, mass, crowd, heap, muddle, jumble **2** MEETING, conclave, conference, discussion, consultation, *colloq.* powwow

hue *n*
colour, shade, tint, dye, tinge, nuance, tone, complexion, aspect, light

hue and cry *n*
furore, fuss, hullabaloo, outcry, rumpus, uproar, brouhaha, clamour, ado, chase, *colloq.* ruction, to-do

huff *n*
pique, sulks, mood, bad mood, anger, rage, passion

huffy *adj*
cross, angry, resentful, snappy, disgruntled, grumpy, irritable, offended, sulky, surly, testy, touchy, moping, morose, moody, crusty, short, peevish, petulant, waspish, *formal* querulous, *colloq.* crabbed, crotchety, miffed, shirty
F3 cheery, happy

hug *v, n*
▶ *v* embrace, cuddle, squeeze, enfold, hold, hold close, press, clasp, clutch, grip, cling to, stay close to, follow closely, enclose
▶ *n* embrace, cuddle, squeeze, clasp, hold, clinch

huge *adj*
immense, vast, enormous, massive, colossal, titanic, giant, gigantic, mammoth, monumental, tremendous, stupendous, great big, large, extensive, monstrous, Herculean, gargantuan, bulky, heavy, unwieldy, *formal* prodigious, *colloq.* jumbo
F3 tiny, minute

hulk *n*
1 WRECK, shipwreck, remains, derelict, frame, hull, shell 2 LOUT, lump, lubber, oaf, *colloq.* clod

hulking *adj*
massive, heavy, weighty, unwieldy, cumbersome, bulky, awkward, clumsy, lumbering, ungainly
F3 small, delicate

hull¹ *n*
the hull of a ship body, frame, framework, skeleton, structure, casing, covering

hull² *n, v*
▶ *n the hull of a fruit* husk, pod, capsule, legume, skin, rind, peel, shell, *US* shuck, *technical* epicarp
▶ *v* husk, pare, peel, shell, strip, skin, trim, *US* shuck

hullabaloo *n*
fuss, palaver, outcry, furore, hue and cry, noise, din, racket, brouhaha, uproar, pandemonium, rumpus, disturbance, commotion, hubbub, turmoil, tumult, *colloq.* to-do, ruction
F3 calm, peace

hum *v, n*
▶ *v* 1 BUZZ, whirr, purr, drone, thrum, croon, sing 2 MURMUR, mumble 3 *humming with activity* throb, pulse, vibrate, buzz
▶ *n* buzz, buzzing, whirr, whirring, purring, thrum, drone, murmur, mumble, throb, throbbing, pulsation, vibration

human *adj, n*
▶ *adj* 1 MORTAL, physical, fleshly, fallible, flesh and blood, weak, susceptible, vulnerable, reasonable, rational, *formal* anthropoid 2 KIND, considerate, understanding, humane, compassionate, sympathetic
F3 2 inhuman
▶ *n* human being, mortal, man, woman, child, person, individual, body, soul, *technical* homo sapiens

humane *adj*
kind, compassionate, sympathetic, understanding, kind-hearted, good-natured, considerate, gentle, tender, loving, mild, lenient, merciful, forgiving, forbearing, kindly, generous, benevolent, charitable, humanitarian, good, benign
F3 inhumane, cruel

humanitarian *adj, n*
▶ *adj* benevolent, charitable, philanthropic, public-spirited, welfare, compassionate, humane, kind, sym-

pathetic, understanding, considerate, generous, altruistic, unselfish
F3 selfish, self-seeking
▶ *n* philanthropist, benefactor, good Samaritan, do-gooder, altruist
F3 egoist, self-seeker

humanitarianism *n*
benevolence, charitableness, charity, goodwill, philanthropy, humanism, compassionateness, generosity, loving-kindness, *formal* beneficence
F3 egoism, self-seeking

humanity *n*
1 HUMAN RACE, humankind, mankind, womankind, mortals, mortality, people, man, *technical* homo sapiens 2 HUMANENESS, kindness, compassion, fellow-feeling, brotherly love, understanding, tenderness, sympathy, gentleness, thoughtfulness, benevolence, tolerance, generosity, goodwill, kind-heartedness, goodness, pity, mercy
F3 2 inhumanity, cruelty

humanize *v*
improve, better, polish, refine, domesticate, tame, civilize, cultivate, educate, enlighten, edify

humble *adj, v*
▶ *adj* 1 MEEK, submissive, unassertive, modest, unassuming, self-effacing, polite, respectful, deferential, servile, subservient, sycophantic, obsequious, prideless 2 LOWLY, low, mean, insignificant, unimportant, common, commonplace, ordinary, poor, inferior, low-ranking, plain, simple, modest, unassuming, unpretentious, unostentatious, undistinguished, unrefined
F3 1 proud, assertive 2 important, pretentious
▶ *v* bring down, lower, bring low, abase, demean, sink, discredit, belittle, disgrace, shame, put to shame, humiliate, mortify, chasten, crush, deflate, subdue, *formal* disparage, *colloq.* put someone in their place, bring/take someone down a peg or two
F3 exalt

humbly *adv*
modestly, unassumingly, meekly, respectfully, simply, submissively, unpretentiously, deferentially, diffidently, docilely, obsequiously, subserviently, servilely, *colloq.* sheepishly, cap in hand
F3 confidently, defiantly

humbug *n*
1 DECEPTION, pretence, sham, fraud, swindle, trick, hoax, deceit, trickery, cheating, *colloq.* con 2 NONSENSE, rubbish, bluff, cant, hypocrisy, *colloq.* bunkum, claptrap, eyewash, balderdash, poppycock, cobblers, rot, *slang* baloney 3 CHARLATAN, fraud, cheat, bluffer, actor, swindler, impostor, fake, sham, trickster, rogue, *colloq.* con man, swank, poser

humdrum *adj*
boring, tedious, monotonous, routine, dull, repetitious, tiresome, dreary, uninteresting, uneventful, unvaried, ordinary, mundane, everyday, commonplace, run-of-the-mill, banal
F3 varied, lively, unusual, exceptional

humid *adj*
damp, moist, dank, wet, clammy, sticky, close, heavy, oppressive, muggy, sultry, steamy
F3 dry

humidity *n*
humidness, damp, dampness, moisture, moistness, dankness, wetness, stickiness, closeness, heaviness, clamminess, mugginess, sultriness, steaminess, sogginess, vaporousness, dew, mist, *formal* vaporosity
F3 dryness

humiliate *v*
mortify, embarrass, confound, crush, break, deflate,

chasten, shame, put to shame, bring shame on, disgrace, abash, discredit, degrade, demean, humble, bring low, abase, *formal* discomfit, *colloq.* put down, put someone in their place, make someone lose face, bring/take someone down a peg or two, cut someone down to size, take the wind out of someone's sails
F3 dignify, exalt

humiliating *adj*
humbling, mortifying, shaming, crushing, chastening, deflating, degrading, embarrassing, disgraceful, ignominious, inglorious, disgracing, snubbing, *formal* discomfiting, humiliant, humiliative, humiliatory
F3 gratifying, triumphant

humiliation *n*
mortification, embarrassment, shame, disgrace, chastening, crushing, confounding, dishonour, discredit, indignity, ignominy, abasement, humbling, degradation, deflation, snub, rebuff, affront, *formal* discomfiture, *colloq.* put-down, loss of face, humble pie
F3 gratification, triumph

humility *n*
modesty, unassertiveness, unassumingness, self-effacement, diffidence, meekness, submissiveness, deference, self-abasement, servility, humbleness, lowliness, unpretentiousness
F3 pride, arrogance, assertiveness

hummock *n*
hillock, hump, knoll, mound, barrow, elevation, prominence

humorist *n*
wit, satirist, caricaturist, cartoonist, comedian, comic, joker, wag, jester, clown

humorous *adj*
funny, amusing, comic, entertaining, witty, satirical, facetious, playful, waggish, droll, whimsical, comical, farcical, ludicrous, absurd, ridiculous, laughable, hilarious, side-splitting, *formal* jocular, risible, *colloq.* zany
F3 serious, humourless

humour *n, v*
▶ *n* 1 WIT, wittiness, gags, drollery, jokes, jesting, badinage, repartee, facetiousness, absurdity, ridiculousness, hilarity, satire, comedy, farce, fun, amusement, *formal* jocularity, *colloq.* wisecracks 2 *in a bad humour* mood, temper, frame/state of mind, spirits, disposition, temperament
▶ *v* go along with, comply with, accommodate, satisfy, gratify, indulge, pamper, spoil, cosset, favour, permit, please, mollify, flatter, pander to, tolerate, *formal* acquiesce in

humourless *adj*
boring, tedious, dull, dry, solemn, serious, grave, sombre, glum, morose, unsmiling, unlaughing, grim, long-faced
F3 humorous, witty

hump *n, v*
▶ *n* 1 HUNCH, lump, knob, bump, projection, protuberance, outgrowth, bulge, swelling, mound, mass, prominence, protrusion, *formal* excrescence, intumescence 2 *get/give the hump* unhappiness, annoyance, irritation, vexation, exasperation, sadness, depression, gloom, *formal* aggravation
▶ *v* 1 ARCH, curve, crook 2 CARRY, lug, lift, heave, hoist, shoulder

hump-backed *adj*
crookbacked, hunchbacked, hunched, crooked, stooped, humped, deformed, misshapen, gibbous, *technical* kyphotic
F3 straight, upright

humped *adj*
arched, bent, curved, crooked, hunched, gibbous
F3 flat, straight

hunch *n, v*
▶ *n* premonition, intuition, suspicion, feeling, impression, idea, inkling, guess, sixth sense, *formal* presentiment
▶ *v* hump, bend, curve, arch, stoop, crouch, squat, huddle, draw in, curl up

hunger *n, v*
▶ *n* 1 HUNGRINESS, emptiness, starvation, malnutrition, famine, famishment, appetite, ravenousness, greed, greediness, *formal* voracity, esurience, esuriency 2 *hunger for power* desire, craving, longing, yearning, pining, hankering, want, need, yen, itch, thirst, appetite
▶ *v* starve, want, wish, desire, need, crave, have a craving for, hanker, long, have a longing for, yearn, pine, ache, itch, thirst

hungry *adj*
1 STARVING, underfed, undernourished, malnourished, empty, hollow, famished, ravenous, greedy, insatiable, *formal* voracious, *colloq.* peckish, could eat a horse 2 *hungry for knowledge* desirous, craving, longing, aching, yearning, pining, hankering, itching, thirsty, eager, avid, needing, covetous
F3 1 satisfied, full

hunk *n*
chunk, lump, piece, block, slab, wedge, mass, dollop, clod, gobbet

hunt *v, n*
▶ *v* 1 CHASE, pursue, follow, shadow, hound, dog, stalk, track, trail 2 SEEK, look for, search, try to find, scour, rummage, fish, ferret, forage, investigate
▶ *n* chase, pursuit, search, stalking, tracking, scouring, rummaging, quest, investigation

hunter *n*
huntsman, chaser, chasseur, woodman, woodsman, jäger, montero, venator, venerer

hurdle *n*
jump, fence, wall, hedge, railing, bar, barrier, barricade, obstacle, obstruction, stumbling-block, hindrance, impediment, handicap, problem, snag, difficulty, complication

hurl *v*
throw, toss, fling, sling, pitch, cast, heave, catapult, project, propel, fire, launch, send, let fly, *colloq.* chuck

hurly-burly *n*
bustle, hustle, commotion, confusion, trouble, disorder, disruption, unrest, pandemonium, uproar, chaos, furore, upheaval, tumult, turbulence, turmoil, frenzy, distraction, agitation, hubbub, brouhaha, bedlam, *colloq.* hassle

hurricane *n*
gale, tornado, typhoon, cyclone, whirlwind, squall, storm, tempest

hurried *adj*
rushed, hectic, hasty, speedy, fast, quick, breakneck, swift, rapid, passing, fleeting, transient, transitory, brief, short, cursory, superficial, offhand, perfunctory, shallow, careless, slapdash, *formal* precipitate, *colloq.* rush job
F3 leisurely, unhurried

hurry *v, n*
▶ *v* rush, dash, run, fly, hasten, make haste, press on, quicken, speed (up), accelerate, hustle, push, *formal* expedite, *colloq.* get a move on, run like hell, show your heels, get cracking, cut and run, put your foot down, step on it, go all out, pull your finger out, shake a leg
F3 slow down, delay
▶ *n* rush, haste, quickness, swiftness, fastness, rapidity, speed, urgency, hustle, bustle, flurry, commotion, hubbub, confusion, *formal* expedition, celerity
F3 leisureliness, calm

hurt *v, n, adj*
▶ *v* **1** *my leg hurts* ACHE, be painful, be sore, pain, throb, sting, smart, burn, tingle **2** INJURE, wound, maltreat, ill-treat, bruise, cut, scratch, lacerate, damage, burn, torture, maim, impair, disable, *formal* debilitate **3** DAMAGE, impair, harm, mar, spoil, blemish, blight **4** UPSET, sadden, cause sadness, grieve, distress, wound, offend, annoy, *formal* afflict
▶ *n* pain, soreness, aching, throbbing, burning, tingling, smarting, discomfort, suffering, injury, wound, cut, bruise, scratch, damage, harm, distress, sadness, upset, sorrow, grief, misery, *formal* affliction
▶ *adj* **1** INJURED, wounded, bruised, grazed, cut, scarred, lacerated, maimed, painful, sore, aching, throbbing, burning, tingling, smarting **2** UPSET, sad, saddened, sorrowful, grief-stricken, miserable, in anguish, distressed, aggrieved, annoyed, offended, affronted

hurtful *adj*
1 UPSETTING, wounding, vicious, cruel, mean, unkind, nasty, malicious, spiteful, catty, derogatory, offensive, distressing, scathing, cutting, *formal* injurious, malefactory **2** HARMFUL, damaging, pernicious, destructive, ruinous, *formal* injurious, deleterious
🖬 **1** helpful, kind, innocuous **2** advantageous

hurtle *v*
dash, tear, race, fly, shoot, speed, rush, career, charge, plunge, dive, crash, rattle

husband *n, v*
▶ *n* spouse, partner, mate, groom, married man, *colloq.* hubby, better half, other half
▶ *v* conserve, economize, eke out, use sparingly, use carefully, preserve, reserve, put aside, put by, budget, save, save up, store, ration, hoard
🖬 squander, waste

husbandry *n*
1 FARMING, agriculture, cultivation, tillage, land management, farm management, conservation, *technical* agribusiness, agronomics, agronomy **2** MANAGEMENT, saving, thrift, thriftiness, frugality, economy, good housekeeping
🖬 **2** wastefulness, squandering

hush *v, n, interj*
▶ *v* quieten, silence, shush, still, settle, compose, calm, soothe, mollify, subdue, *colloq.* pipe down, shut up, cut the cackle, dry up
🖬 disturb, rouse
▷ **hush up** keep dark, keep secret, suppress, conceal, cover up, stifle, smother, gag
🖬 publicize
▶ *n* quietness, quiet, silence, peace, peacefulness, stillness, calm, calmness, tranquillity, serenity, *formal* repose
🖬 noise, clamour
▶ *interj* quiet, hold your tongue, shut up, not another word

hush-hush *adj*
secret, confidential, classified, restricted, top-secret, *colloq.* under wraps
🖬 open, public

husk *n*
covering, case, shell, pod, capsule, legume, hull, rind, peel, skin, bran, chaff, *US* shuck, *technical* epicarp, integument

husky *adj*
1 HOARSE, croaky, croaking, low, deep, throaty, guttural, gruff, gravelly, rasping, rough, thick, coarse, harsh **2** BRAWNY, muscular, burly, hefty, strong, strapping, well-built, broad-shouldered, stalwart, rugged, powerful, *colloq.* beefy

hustle *v, n*
▶ *v* rush, hurry, dash, fly, bustle, hasten, force, pressurize, push, shove, thrust, bundle, elbow, nudge, jostle, crowd
▶ *n* bustle, activity, stir, commotion, tumult, agitation, fuss, hurry, rush, hurly-burly

hut *n*
cabin, shack, shanty, booth, shed, lean-to, shelter, den

hybrid *n, adj*
▶ *n* cross, crossbreed, half-breed, half-blood, mongrel, composite, combination, mixture, amalgam, compound, *formal* conglomeration
▶ *adj* crossbred, mongrel, composite, combined, mixed, heterogeneous, compound
🖬 pure-bred

hybridize *v*
crossbreed, cross, interbreed, bastardize, reproduce together, cross-polinate

hygiene *n*
sanitariness, sanitation, sterility, disinfection, cleanliness, purity, wholesomeness
🖬 insanitariness

hygienic *adj*
sanitary, sterile, sterilized, aseptic, germ-free, disinfected, clean, pure, healthy, wholesome, *formal* salubrious
🖬 unhygienic, insanitary, contaminated, polluted

hymn *n*
song of praise, song, chorus, spiritual, psalm, anthem, carol, chant, cantata, canticle, motet, doxology, antiphon, introit, choral(e), offertory, paean, paraphrase, plainsong

hype *n, v*
▶ *n* publicity, advertisement, advertising, promotion, puffing, ballyhoo, build-up, racket, fuss, *colloq.* plugging, razzmatazz
▶ *v* promote, publicize, advertise, build up, *colloq.* plug

hyperbole *n*
overstatement, exaggeration, excess, magnification, extravagance, overkill
🖬 understatement, *technical* meiosis

hypercritical *adj*
fault-finding, over-particular, pedantic, finicky, fussy, quibbling, hair-splitting, niggling, captious, carping, strict, cavilling, censorious, *formal* ultracrepidarian, *colloq.* nit-picking, pernickety, choosy, picky
🖬 tolerant, uncritical

hypnotic *adj*
mesmerizing, soporific, sleep-inducing, sedative, numbing, spellbinding, fascinating, compelling, irresistible, magnetic, *formal* somniferous, stupefactive

hypnotism *n*
hypnosis, mesmerism, suggestion, auto-suggestion

hypnotize *v*
mesmerize, put into a state of unconsciousness, put to sleep, spellbind, bewitch, enchant, entrance, fascinate, captivate, beguile, magnetize

hypochondria *n*
neurosis, hypochondrianism, hypochondriasis, *formal* valetudinarianism

hypochondriac *n, adj*
▶ *n* hypochondriast, *formal* valetudinarian
▶ *adj* hypochondriacal, neurotic, *formal* valetudinarian

hypocrisy *n*
insincerity, double-talk, double-dealing, falsity, two-facedness, dishonesty, deceit, deceitfulness, deception, pretence, pretended goodness, lip service, cant, pharisaism, *formal* dissembling, duplicity, *colloq.* phoneyness
🖬 sincerity

hypocrite *n*
deceiver, fraud, impostor, pretender, mountebank, Pharisee, canter, charlatan, whited sepulchre, Holy Willie, *formal* dissembler, *colloq.* phoney, pseud, pseudo

hypocritical *adj*
insincere, two-faced, self-righteous, sanctimonious, double-dealing, false, specious, hollow, deceptive, fraudulent, spurious, deceitful, dishonest, lying, pharisaical, Pecksniffian, *formal* dissembling, perfidious, duplicitous, *colloq.* phoney
F3 sincere, genuine, truthful

hypothesis *n*
theory, thesis, theorem, axiom, proposition, supposition, presumption, assumption, speculation, *formal* premise, postulate, conjecture

hypothetical *adj*
theoretical, imaginary, imagined, supposed, assumed, presumed, proposed, speculative, *formal* conjectural
F3 real, actual

hysteria *n*
agitation, frenzy, panic, hysterics, neurosis, mania, delirium, madness, *colloq.* (screaming) habdabs
F3 calm, composure, control

hysterical *adj*
1 FRANTIC, frenzied, berserk, out of control, uncontrollable, mad, raving, crazed, beside yourself, delirious, demented, overwrought, neurotic, in a panic
2 HILARIOUS, extremely funny, uproarious, side-splitting, *colloq.* priceless, rich
F3 1 calm, composed, self-possessed

hysterics *n*
agitation, frenzy, panic, hysteria, neurosis, mania, delirium, madness, *colloq.* (screaming) habdabs

I

ice *n, v*
> ► *n* **1** FROZEN WATER, frost, rime, icicle, glacier **2** ICI-NESS, frostiness, coldness, chill, coolness, unresponsiveness, distance
> ▷ **put on ice** shelve, delay, postpone, put off, defer, *formal* hold/leave in abeyance, *colloq.* put on the back burner
> ► *v* freeze (over), refrigerate, chill, cool, frost, glaze, harden

ice-cold *adj*
frozen, iced, chilled, icy, frosty, icebound, arctic, bitterly cold, raw, polar, glacial, Siberian, frigid, freezing, numb, hard, frosted, solidified, stiff, frozen-stiff, chilled to the bone, rigid, fixed, *technical* algid, *formal* gelid
☒ warm, hot

icon *n*
idol, portrait, image, likeness, figure, representation, symbol, portrait, portrayal

iconoclast *n*
critic, denouncer, dissenter, denunciator, dissident, radical, sceptic, rebel, opponent, questioner, heretic, unbeliever, image-breaker
☒ devotee, believer

iconclastic *adj*
critical, dissident, irreverent, innovative, questioning, radical, rebellious, sceptical, subversive, heretical, impious, *formal* denunciatory, dissentient
☒ uncritical, unquestioning, trustful

icy *adj*
1 ICE-COLD, glacial, freezing, frozen, frosty, raw, bitter, biting, cold, chill, chilly, frigid, arctic, polar, Siberian, *formal* gelid **2** *icy roads* frosty, slippery, glassy, frozen, icebound, frostbound, rimy, slippy **3** HOSTILE, cold, stony, cool, frigid, frosty, indifferent, unfriendly, aloof, stiff, reserved, restrained, distant, formal
☒ **1** hot **3** friendly, warm, welcoming, responsive

idea *n*
1 THOUGHT, concept, notion, theory, hypothesis, guess, belief, opinion, feeling, view, viewpoint, judgement, conception, conceptualization, vision, image, impression, perception, interpretation, understanding, inkling, suspicion, fancy, clue, *formal* conjecture, abstraction **2** *a good idea* brainwave, suggestion, proposal, proposition, recommendation, plan, scheme, design **3** AIM, intention, purpose, reason, point, end, goal, target, object, objective

ideal *n, adj*
► *n* **1** PERFECTION, epitome, paragon, example, model, pattern, prototype, type, image, criterion, standard, yardstick, benchmark, *formal* acme, exemplar, archetype, nonpareil **2** PRINCIPLE, morals, ethics, moral standards/values, ethical standards/values
► *adj* **1** PERFECT, dream, utopian, best, optimum, optimal, supreme, highest, complete, absolute, model,

formal archetypal, quintessential, consummate **2** UN-REAL, imaginary, conceptual, philosophical, theoretical, hypothetical, abstract, unattainable, impractical, visionary, romantic, fanciful, idealistic, utopian

idealism *n*
impracticality, perfectionism, romanticism, utopianism
☒ pragmatism, realism

idealist *n*
perfectionist, visionary, dreamer, optimist, romantic, romanticist
☒ realist, pragmatist

idealistic *adj*
perfectionist, utopian, visionary, romantic, quixotic, starry-eyed, optimistic, unrealistic, impractical, impracticable
☒ realistic, pragmatic, practical

idealization *n*
romanticization, romanticizing, glamorization, glorification, worship, exaltation, idolization, ennoblement, *formal* apotheosis

idealize *v*
utopianize, romanticize, glamorize, glorify, exalt, worship, idolize
☒ caricature

ideally *adv*
perfectly, in a perfect world, in an ideal world, at best, in theory, theoretically, hypothetically

idée fixe *n*
fixation, obsession, complex, hang-up, leitmotiv, fixed idea, *formal* monomania

identical *adj*
same, self-same, one and the same, indistinguishable, interchangeable, twin, duplicate, like, alike, similar, corresponding, matching, equal, equivalent, *colloq.* as like as two peas in a pod
☒ different

identifiable *adj*
recognizable, discernible, noticeable, known, perceptible, detectable, distinguishable, unmistakable, *formal* ascertainable
☒ unidentifiable, indefinable, unfamiliar, unknown

identification *n*
1 RECOGNITION, detection, spotting, pointing-out, diagnosis, naming, labelling, classification **2** EMPATHY, association, involvement, connection, rapport, relationship, sympathy, fellow feeling **3** IDENTITY CARD, documents, ID, papers, credentials, badge

identify *v*
1 RECOGNIZE, know, pick out, single out, point out, distinguish, perceive, make out, discern, discover, find out, establish, notice, detect, diagnose, name, label, tag, specify, pinpoint, spot, place, catalogue, classify, *formal* ascertain **2** ASSOCIATE, connect, relate, involve, place, think of together, couple **3** *identify*

with other sufferers empathize with, relate to, associate with, respond to, sympathize with, feel for

identity *n*
1 INDIVIDUALITY, particularity, distinctiveness, uniqueness, self, selfhood, personhood, name, ego, personality, character, existence, *formal* singularity **2** SAMENESS, likeness, selfsameness, closeness, similarity, resemblance, indistinguishability, interchangeability, correspondence, equality, equivalence

ideologist *n*
thinker, theorist, visionary, philosopher, teacher, doctrinaire, ideologue

ideology *n*
philosophy, world-view, ideas, principles, teaching, theory, tenets, doctrine(s), convictions, belief(s), opinion(s), faith, dogma, thesis, *formal* creed, credo

idiocy *n*
folly, stupidity, silliness, senselessness, lunacy, craziness, absurdity, foolhardiness, insanity, inanity, *formal* fatuousness, *colloq.* daftness
🔁 wisdom, sanity

idiom *n*
phrase, expression, colloquialism, language, turn of phrase, phraseology, style, usage, jargon, speech, talk, vernacular, *formal* locution

idiomatic *adj*
colloquial, everyday, vernacular, native, grammatical, correct, dialectal, dialectical, idiolectal
🔁 unidiomatic

idiosyncrasy *n*
peculiarity, individuality, speciality, oddity, eccentricity, freak, quirk, habit, mannerism, trait, feature, characteristic, quality, *formal* singularity

idiosyncratic *adj*
personal, individual, characteristic, distinctive, peculiar, odd, eccentric, quirky, *formal* singular
🔁 general, common

idiot *n*
fool, imbecile, fat-head, dunce, dimwit, simpleton, halfwit, cretin, clown, ignoramus, *colloq.* thickhead, numskull, nincompoop, ass, chump, ninny, clot, dope, twit, nitwit, nit, sucker, mug, twerp, birdbrain, *slang* jerk, nerd, wally, dumbo, pillock, prat, dork, geek, plonker

idiotic *adj*
foolish, stupid, senseless, silly, absurd, ridiculous, ludicrous, nonsensical, unwise, ill-advised, ill-considered, short-sighted, half-baked, crazy, mad, insane, idiotic, moronic, hare-brained, half-witted, simple-minded, simple, ignorant, unintelligent, inept, inane, pointless, unreasonable, *formal* fatuous, risible, injudicious, *colloq.* thick-headed, daft, crackbrained, dumb, dotty, potty, batty, barmy, nutty
🔁 sensible, sane

idle *adj, v*
▶ *adj* **1** INACTIVE, not working, inoperative, unused, dormant, dead, mothballed, unoccupied, unemployed, jobless, redundant, *colloq.* on the dole **2** LAZY, work-shy, lethargic, sluggish, lackadaisical, do-nothing, loafish, *formal* indolent, slothful **3** *idle threats* empty, futile, vain, pointless, useless, worthless, pointless, fruitless, unsuccessful, ineffective, unproductive, *formal* ineffectual **4** *idle gossip* casual, trivial, petty, foolish, shallow, unimportant, insignificant
🔁 **1** active, hardworking **2** busy **4** important, deep
▶ *v* **1** DO NOTHING, laze, lounge, while, take it easy, sit back, relax, kill time, while away, potter, loiter, dawdle, dally, fritter, waste, loaf, slack, shirk, *colloq.* skive, horse around, *slang* bum around **2** *the engine*

is idling tick over, be operational, be ready to work/run, move
🔁 **1** work, be busy

idleness *n*
laziness, lazing, sluggishness, torpor, inaction, inactivity, inertia, vegetating, shiftlessness, leisure, loafing, pottering, ease, unemployment, *formal* indolence, sloth, slothfulness, *colloq.* skiving
🔁 activity, employment, occupation

idler *n*
loafer, dawdler, slacker, lounger, malingerer, shirker, good-for-nothing, laggard, sluggard, waster, wastrel, layabout, do-nothing, drone, clock-watcher, *formal* sloth, *colloq.* dodger, lazybones, skiver

idol *n*
1 HERO, heroine, favourite, darling, star, superstar, pet, beloved, *colloq.* blue-eyed boy, pin-up **2** *worship idols* effigy, icon, image, graven image, likeness, god, deity, fetish, mammet

idolater *n*
admirer, worshipper, adorer, devotee, idolatress, idol-worshipper, idolist, iconolater, votary

idolatrous *adj*
adoring, worshipping, glorifying, lionizing, adulatory, idolizing, idol-worshipping, reverential, uncritical, pagan, heretical

idolatry *n*
worshipping, admiration, reverence, adoration, adulation, deification, exaltation, glorification, hero-worship, idolizing, idolism, iconolatry, icon worship, paganism, heathenism, fetishism
🔁 vilification

idolize *v*
hero-worship, lionize, exalt, glorify, worship, deify, revere, admire, adore, adulate, reverence, love, dote on, *formal* venerate, *colloq.* put on a pedestal
🔁 despise

idyllic *adj*
perfect, idealized, heavenly, blissful, delightful, wonderful, charming, picturesque, pastoral, rustic, unspoiled, peaceful, romantic, happy
🔁 unpleasant, spoiled, noisy

if *conj*
in the event of, in case of, on condition that, as/so long as, provided, providing, assuming (that), supposing (that)

iffy *adj*
uncertain, doubtful, dubious, undecided, unsettled, *colloq.* dodgy

ignite *v*
set fire to, set alight, light, catch fire, flare up, burn, burst into flames, conflagrate, fire, inflame, kindle, touch off, put a match to, spark off
🔁 quench

ignoble *adj*
low, mean, petty, base, vulgar, wretched, contemptible, despicable, shameful, vile, infamous, disgraceful, dishonourable, *formal* heinous
🔁 noble, worthy, honourable

ignominious *adj*
humiliating, mortifying, degrading, undignified, shameful, dishonourable, discreditable, sorry, disreputable, disgraceful, despicable, infamous, abject, base, despicable, contemptible, scandalous, embarrassing
🔁 triumphant, honourable, glorious

ignominy *n*
humiliation, mortification, degradation, shame, dishonour, discredit, disgrace, disrepute, reproach, scandal, contempt, indignity, infamy, stigma, *formal* obloquy, odium, opprobrium
🔁 credit, honour, dignity

ignoramus *n*
dunce, dimwit, halfwit, imbecile, simpleton, fool, illiterate, know-nothing, blockhead, dullard, *colloq.* numskull, bonehead, ass, duffer, dolt
🖪 scholar, intellectual, highbrow

ignorance *n*
unintelligence, illiteracy, unawareness, unconsciousness, oblivion, unfamiliarity, inexperience, innocence, naïvety, stupidity, *colloq.* greenness, thickness
🖪 knowledge, wisdom, education, intelligence

ignorant *adj*
uneducated, illiterate, innumerate, backward, unread, untaught, untrained, inexperienced, unschooled, unlearned, stupid, uninitiated, unenlightened, uninformed, ill-informed, unwitting, unaware, unfamiliar, unacquainted, unconscious, oblivious, blind, innocent, naïve, *formal* nescient, *colloq.* clueless, dense, thick, thick as two short planks, dumb, in the dark, not all there, a brick short of a load
🖪 educated, knowledgeable, learned, clever, wise, *formal* conversant

ignore *v*
disregard, take no notice of, not take any notice of, overlook, take for granted, pay no attention to, be oblivious to, pass over, neglect, omit, brush aside, shrug off, reject, snub, spurn, slight, cut (dead), *colloq.* close/shut your eyes to, turn a blind eye to, look the other way, turn a deaf ear to, not listen to, cold-shoulder, turn your back on, keep in the dark, bury your head in the sand, run away from
🖪 notice, observe, pay attention to

ilk *n*
kind, sort, type, make, style, variety, brand, breed, class, stamp, character, description

ill *adj, n, adv*
▶ *adj* **1** SICK, poorly, unwell, laid up, ailing, off-colour, seedy, queasy, diseased, unhealthy, infirm, frail, weak, feeble, bedridden, *formal* afflicted, indisposed, valetudinarian, *colloq.* in a bad way, dicky, out of sorts, under the weather, run down, rough, groggy, like death warmed up **2** *an ill omen* bad, evil, damaging, harmful, unpleasant, injurious, destructive, ruinous, detrimental, adverse, unfavourable, unpromising, sinister, ominous, threatening, unlucky, unfortunate, difficult, harsh, severe, *formal* inauspicious, unpropitious, infelicitous, deleterious **3** *ill feelings* unkind, unfriendly, antagonistic, hostile, resentful, belligerent
🖪 **1** well, healthy **2** good, favourable, fortunate **3** kind, friendly
▷ **ill at ease** uncomfortable, awkward, fidgety, hesitant, embarrassed, self-conscious, strange, unsure, nervous, on edge, restless, tense, unrelaxed, unsettled, uneasy, worried, anxious, disquieted, disturbed, *colloq.* edgy, like a cat on hot bricks, on tenterhooks
🖪 at ease
▶ *n* trouble, problem, trial(s), pain, misfortune, suffering, disaster, unpleasantness, harm, evil, hurt, cruelty, destruction, injury, sorrow, *formal* tribulation, affliction
🖪 good, benefit
▶ *adv* **1** BADLY, unfavourably, unkindly, disapprovingly, adversely, unfortunately, unsuccessfully, unluckily, wrongfully, *formal* inauspiciously **2** SCARCELY, hardly, barely, by no means, insufficiently, inadequately, poorly, scantily, amiss
🖪 **1** well

ill-advised *adj*
unwise, foolish, ill-considered, thoughtless, careless, hasty, rash, reckless, short-sighted, misguided,

inappropriate, *formal* imprudent, injudicious
🖪 wise, sensible, well-advised, cautious, *formal* politic, circumspect

ill-assorted *adj*
incompatible, inharmonious, discordant, unsuited, mismatched, uncongenial, misallied, *formal* incongruous
🖪 harmonious, well-matched

ill-bred *adj*
bad-mannered, ill-mannered, discourteous, impolite, rude, loutish, boorish, coarse, crude, vulgar, crass, uncouth, indelicate, uncivil, uncivilized, *formal* unseemly
🖪 well-bred, polite, gentlemanly, ladylike

ill-considered *adj*
ill-advised, ill-judged, careless, foolish, hasty, heedless, rash, unwise, overhasty, *formal* improvident, imprudent, injudicious, precipitate
🖪 sensible, wise

ill-defined *adj*
indistinct, unclear, vague, nebulous, imprecise, indefinite, blurred, fuzzy, hazy, woolly, blurry, dim, shadowy
🖪 clear

ill-disposed *adj*
unfriendly, unsympathetic, hostile, antagonistic, opposed, unco-operative, unwelcoming, against, *formal* averse, inimical, *colloq.* anti
🖪 well-disposed

illegal *adj*
unlawful, illicit, criminal, wrong, forbidden, prohibited, illegitimate, fraudulent, banned, outlawed, barred, unauthorized, under-the-counter, black-market, unconstitutional, wrongful, *formal* felonious, proscribed, interdicted
🖪 legal, lawful, permitted, allowed

illegality *n*
wrong, wrongfulness, wrongness, crime, criminality, illegitimacy, illicitness, lawlessness, unconstitutionality, unlawfulness, *technical* felony
🖪 legality

illegible *adj*
unreadable, indecipherable, hard to read, scrawled, obscure, faint, indistinct, unintelligible, hieroglyphic
🖪 legible, clear

illegitimate *adj*
1 *an illegitimate child* natural, love, fatherless, misbegotten, adulterine, unfathered, *formal* born out of wedlock, *colloq.* born on the wrong side of the blanket **2** ILLEGAL, unlawful, illicit, lawless, unauthorized, unwarranted, unlicensed, improper **3** ILLOGICAL, incorrect, inadmissible, spurious, invalid, unsound, wrongly inferred
🖪 **1** legitimate **2** legal **3** well-reasoned

ill-fated *adj*
doomed, ill-starred, ill-omened, blighted, unfortunate, unlucky, luckless, unhappy, *formal* hapless
🖪 lucky

ill-favoured *adj*
hideous, plain, repulsive, ugly, unattractive, unlovely, unprepossessing, unsightly, *US* homely
🖪 beautiful, attractive

ill-feeling *n*
ill-will, bad blood, bitterness, grudge, hard feelings, resentment, sourness, spite, malice, hostility, enmity, animosity, antagonism, dissatisfaction, frustration, offence, anger, indignation, wrath, disgruntlement, dudgeon, *formal* animus, odium, rancour
🖪 friendship, goodwill

ill-founded *adj*
baseless, groundless, without foundation, unjustified, unsupported, unconfirmed
▣ substantiated, verified

ill-humoured *adj*
bad-tempered, cross, impatient, irascible, quick-tempered, irritable, sharp, snappy, snappish, disagreeable, grumpy, sulky, sullen, huffy, moody, morose, peevish, tart, testy, waspish, *formal* acrimonious, cantankerous, petulant, *colloq.* crabbed, crabby, crotchety, grouchy
▣ amiable

illiberal *adj*
mean, narrow-minded, intolerant, petty, prejudiced, reactionary, small-minded, bigoted, hidebound, ungenerous, uncharitable, stingy, miserly, niggardly, close-fisted, tight, *formal* parsimonious, *colloq.* tight-fisted
▣ broad-minded, liberal

illicit *adj*
illegal, unlawful, criminal, wrong, illegitimate, improper, forbidden, prohibited, banned, barred, unauthorized, unlicensed, black-market, contraband, ill-gotten, under-the-counter, furtive, clandestine, secretive, surreptitious, stealthy
▣ legal, permissible

illiterate *adj*
ignorant, uneducated, unschooled, unlearned, untaught, unlettered, untutored, uncultured, *technical* analphabetic, *formal* benighted
▣ literate

ill-judged *adj*
ill-advised, ill-considered, short-sighted, unwise, foolish, foolhardy, misguided, hasty, overhasty, rash, reckless, incautious, indiscreet, wrong-headed, *formal* impolitic, imprudent, injudicious, *colloq.* daft
▣ sensible

ill-mannered *adj*
rude, impolite, badly-behaved, insolent, discourteous, ill-bred, ill-behaved, unmannerly, uncivil, loutish, uncouth, boorish, churlish, coarse, crude, insensitive
▣ polite, well-mannered

ill-natured *adj*
spiteful, vindictive, nasty, perverse, mean, surly, sulky, sullen, unfriendly, unkind, unpleasant, vicious, bad-tempered, cross, disagreeable, malicious, malignant, churlish, *formal* malevolent, petulant, *colloq.* crabbed
▣ good-natured

illness *n*
disease, disorder, complaint, condition, ailment, sickness, ill/poor health, indisposition, infirmity, disability, attack, bout, touch, *formal* malady, affliction
See panel at DISEASE.

illogical *adj*
irrational, unreasonable, unscientific, untenable, invalid, unsound, faulty, specious, spurious, inconsistent, fallible, senseless, meaningless, absurd, incorrect, wrong, *formal* fallacious, sophistical, casuistic
▣ logical, rational, reasonable

illogicality *n*
irrationality, unreasonableness, unreason, unsoundness, absurdity, senselessness, speciousness, fallacy, inconsistency, invalidity, *formal* fallaciousness
▣ logicality

ill-starred *adj*
doomed, ill-fated, unfortunate, unhappy, unlucky, star-crossed, blighted, *formal* inauspicious, hapless
▣ fortunate

ill-tempered *adj*
bad-tempered, cross, ill-natured, ill-humoured, impatient, irritable, irascible, spiteful, vicious, curt, grumpy, testy, tetchy, touchy, choleric, sharp
▣ good-tempered

ill-timed *adj*
inopportune, inconvenient, inappropriate, unseasonable, untimely, wrong-timed, unwelcome, unfortunate, awkward, tactless, inept, crass
▣ well-timed

ill-treat *v*
mistreat, abuse, maltreat, injure, harm, damage, neglect, mishandle, misuse, wrong, oppress

ill-treatment *n*
abuse, mistreatment, maltreatment, damage, harm, injury, ill-use, manhandling, mishandling, misuse, neglect
▣ care

illuminate *v*
1 LIGHT, light up, shine on, throw light on, floodlight, brighten, *formal* illumine 2 CLARIFY, clear up, elucidate, illustrate, explain, edify, instruct, enlighten 3 DECORATE, ornament, adorn, embellish, illustrate
▣ 1 darken 2 mystify

illuminating *adj*
informative, instructive, helpful, edifying, enlightening, revealing, *formal* explanatory, revelatory
▣ unhelpful

illumination *n*
1 LIGHT, lights, lighting, beam, ray, irradiation, brightness, radiance 2 ENLIGHTENMENT, awareness, insight, understanding, instruction, perception, learning, education, revelation 3 DECORATION, ornamentation, adornment, embellishment, illustration
▣ 1 darkness

illusion *n*
apparition, mirage, spectre, phantom, will-o'-the-wisp, hallucination, figment of the imagination, fantasy, fancy, delusion, misapprehension, misconception, misjudgement, error, false impression, deception, *formal* chimera, fallacy
▣ reality, truth

 illusion or **allusion** ? *See panel at* ALLUSION.

 illusion or **delusion** ? *See panel at* DELUSION.

illusory *adj*
illusive, illusionary, deceptive, misleading, apparent, seeming, deluding, delusive, unreal, delusory, fancied, imagined, specious, unsubstantial, sham, false, untrue, mistaken, erroneous, *formal* chimerical, fallacious
▣ real, actual

illustrate *v*
1 DEMONSTRATE, exemplify, instance, explain, interpret, clarify, draw, sketch, depict, picture, show, exhibit, *formal* elucidate 2 ILLUMINATE, decorate, ornament, adorn, embellish, *formal* miniate

illustrated *adj*
decorated, embellished, illuminated, pictorial, *formal* miniated

illustration *n*
1 PICTURE, plate, half-tone, photograph, drawing, sketch, figure, diagram, chart, artwork, design, representation, decoration, ornamentation, adornment, embellishment 2 EXAMPLE, specimen, instance, case, sample, analogy, demonstration, exemplification, explanation, interpretation, clarification, *formal* exemplar, elucidation

illustrative *adj*
explanatory, descriptive, representative, typical, exemplifying, sample, specimen, diagrammatic, graphic, pictorial, interpretative, *formal* explicatory, expository, delineative, illustrational, illustratory

illustrious *adj*
great, noble, eminent, distinguished, celebrated, acclaimed, honoured, famous, famed, renowned, well-known, noted, prominent, outstanding, pre-eminent, remarkable, notable, brilliant, excellent, splendid, magnificent, glorious, exalted, *formal* esteemed
🖃 ignoble, inglorious

ill-will *n*
hostility, antagonism, bad blood, enmity, unfriendliness, malevolence, malice, spite, animosity, ill-feeling, resentment, hard feelings, bad blood, grudge, dislike, aversion, hatred, antipathy, anger, indignation, wrath, *formal* animus, rancour, odium
🖃 goodwill, friendship

image *n*
1 IDEA, notion, concept, conception, thought, fancy, impression, perception, vision **2** REPRESENTATION, likeness, resemblance, picture, portrait, icon, graven image, effigy, figure, figurine, statue, statuette, bust, idol, replica, doll **3** REPRODUCTION, reflection, photograph, picture, copy, facsimile **4** *the image of his father* likeness, representation, double, twin, duplicate, copy, clone, replica, *doppelgänger*, lookalike, match, *colloq.* spitting image, (dead) ringer **5** *images in a poem* figure of speech, figurative expression, turn of phrase, rhetorical device, imagery, simile, metaphor

imaginable *adj*
conceivable, thinkable, believable, credible, supposable, feasible, plausible, likely, possible, probable
🖃 unimaginable, inconceivable

imaginary *adj*
imagined, fanciful, fancied, illusory, hallucinatory, visionary, pretend, make-believe, dreamy, shadowy, ghostly, spectral, insubstantial, unreal, non-existent, fictional, fantastic, fabulous, legendary, mythological, mythical, made-up, invented, fictitious, assumed, supposed, hypothetical, notional, *formal* chimerical
🖃 real

imagination *n*
1 CREATIVITY, imaginativeness, inventiveness, fancifulness, originality, inspiration, insight, ingenuity, resourcefulness, enterprise, wit, vision **2** *see them in my imagination* mind's eye, fancy, illusion, vision, dream, conceptualization, *formal* chimera
🖃 **1** unimaginativeness **2** reality

imaginative *adj*
creative, inventive, innovative, full of ideas, original, inspired, visionary, ingenious, clever, resourceful, enterprising, fanciful, whimsical, fantastic, vivid
🖃 unimaginative

imagine *v*
1 PICTURE, form a picture of, visualize, see, see in your mind's eye, envisage, conceive, fancy, fantasize, daydream, dream, pretend, make believe, conjure up, dream up, think up, invent, devise, create, scheme, plan, project **2** *I imagine so* think, believe, judge, suppose, guess, reckon, assume, presume, gather, fancy, *formal* conjecture, deem, surmise, *colloq.* take it

imbalance *n*
unevenness, inequality, disproportion, unfairness, partiality, bias, *formal* disparity, inequity
🖃 balance, parity

imbecile *n, adj*
▶ *n* idiot, halfwit, simpleton, moron, cretin, fool, blockhead, bungler, dunce, dimwit, *colloq.* ass, clot, twit, nitwit

▶ *adj* stupid, silly, foolish, idiotic, inane, ludicrous, absurd, crazy, moronic, witless, asinine, *formal* fatuous, *colloq.* doltish, thick, daft, dotty, dopey, barmy
🖃 intelligent, sensible

imbecility *n*
foolishness, idiocy, inanity, stupidity, incompetence, cretinism, asininity, childishness, *technical* amentia, *formal* fatuity
🖃 intelligence, sense

imbibe *v*
1 DRINK, consume, swallow, gulp, sip, *formal* ingest, *colloq.* knock back, quaff, swig **2** ABSORB, take in, assimilate, drink in, receive, soak up, acquire, gain, gather, *colloq.* lap up

imbroglio *n*
entanglement, tangle, involvement, confusion, difficulty, dilemma, muddle, mess, quandary, embroilment, *colloq.* scrape

imbue *v*
permeate, impregnate, pervade, suffuse, fill, saturate, inject, ingrain, inspire, charge, steep, inculcate, instil, tinge, tint

imitate *v*
1 COPY, take as a model, follow, follow suit, do likewise, ape, mimic, impersonate, do an impression of, caricature, parody, mock, parrot, repeat, echo, mirror, *formal* emulate, *colloq.* take a leaf out of someone's book **2** REPRODUCE, duplicate, simulate, copy, fake, counterfeit, forge, *formal* replicate

imitation *n, adj*
▶ *n* **1** MIMICRY, impersonation, aping, apery, impression, caricature, parody, mocking, mockery, travesty, *colloq.* take-off, send-up, spoof **2** COPY, duplicate, reproduction, replica, simulation, counterfeit, fake, forgery, sham, likeness, resemblance, reflection, dummy, *formal* emulation
▶ *adj* artificial, synthetic, man-made, ersatz, fake, mock, reproduction, simulated, sham, dummy, *colloq.* phoney, pseudo
🖃 genuine

imitative *adj*
copying, mimicking, parrot-like, unoriginal, derivative, plagiarized, second-hand, simulated, mock, *formal* emulating, mimetic, *colloq.* me-too
🖃 original

imitator *n*
mimic, impersonator, impressionist, parrot, ape, echo, parodist, plagiarist, copier, copyist, follower, epigone, *formal* emulator, *colloq.* copycat

immaculate *adj*
perfect, unblemished, flawless, faultless, impeccable, spotless, unsoiled, clean, spick and span, pure, unsullied, undefiled, incorrupt, untainted, stainless, blameless, guiltless, sinless, innocent, *colloq.* squeaky clean
🖃 blemished, stained, contaminated

immaterial *adj*
irrelevant, insignificant, unimportant, minor, trivial, petty, trifling, inconsequential, of no account
🖃 relevant, important

immature *adj*
young, under-age, adolescent, juvenile, childish, puerile, infantile, babyish, raw, crude, callow, inexperienced, naïve, unripe, undeveloped, unmellowed, incomplete, unready, unprepared, *formal* ingenuous, *colloq.* wet behind the ears, innocent as a newborn babe, green
🖃 mature, fully-developed, grown-up

immaturity n
youth, adolescence, juvenility, childishness, puerility, babyishness, rawness, crudeness, crudity, callowness, inexperience, immatureness, unpreparedness, imperfection, unripeness, greenness
E3 maturity, mellowness

immeasurable adj
vast, immense, infinite, limitless, unlimited, illimitable, boundless, fathomless, unfathomable, unbounded, endless, never-ending, interminable, bottomless, inexhaustible, incalculable, inestimable
E3 limited

immediacy n
urgency, importance, criticalness, instancy, spontaneity, instantaneity, promptness, swiftness, simultaneity, directness, imminence
E3 remoteness, distance

immediate adj
1 INSTANT, instantaneous, direct, sudden, without delay, prompt, swift, speedy 2 URGENT, pressing, important, vital, crucial, critical, current, present, existing, pressing, colloq. top-priority, high-priority 3 NEAREST, closest, next, adjacent, next-door, near, close, recent, formal adjoining, abutting 4 the immediate cause of death direct, primary, basic, fundamental, chief, main, principal
E3 1 delayed 3 distant 4 indirect

immediately adv
now, straight away, right away, right now, at once, instantly, instantaneously, directly, speedily, quickly, forthwith, without delay, no sooner ... than, as soon as, promptly, unhesitatingly, without hesitation, without question, this minute/instant, colloq. pronto, yesterday, before you know it, before you can say Jack Robinson, in two shakes of a lamb's tail, like a shot
E3 eventually, never

immemorial adj
age-old, timeless, ancient, archaic, long-standing, fixed, time-honoured, hoary, traditional, ancestral, formal of yore
E3 recent

immense adj
vast, great, extremely large, huge, enormous, massive, giant, gigantic, colossal, extensive, cosmic, tremendous, monumental, mammoth, herculean, elephantine, titanic, Brobdingnagian, colloq. whopping, bumper, jumbo, ginormous, humungous, mega
E3 tiny, minute

immensely adv
enormously, greatly, extremely, extraordinarily, massively

immensity n
magnitude, bulk, expanse, vastness, greatness, hugeness, enormousness, massiveness, giganticness, extensiveness
E3 minuteness

immerse v
1 PLUNGE, submerge, submerse, sink, duck, dip, dunk, douse, souse, saturate, drench, soak, bathe, baptize 2 ENGROSS, preoccupy, occupy, absorb, bury, wrap up in, engage, involve, engulf

immersed adj
absorbed, engrossed, involved, occupied, preoccupied, consumed, buried, busy, deep, taken up, wrapped up in, rapt, sunk

immersion n
1 SUBMERSION, plunging, sinking, ducking, dip, dipping, dunking, dousing, saturation, drenching, soaking, baptism, bathe 2 PREOCCUPATION, absorption, engrossing, engagement, involvement, concentration

immigrant n
incomer, settler, migrant, newcomer, new arrival, alien
E3 native

immigrate v
come in, move in, migrate, settle, resettle, remove
E3 emigrate

imminence n
approach, nearness, closeness, immediacy, instancy, menace, threat, formal propinquity
E3 remoteness

imminent adj
impending, forthcoming, in the offing, approaching, fast approaching, coming, on the way, near, close, looming, menacing, threatening, brewing, in the air, at hand, about to happen, almost upon you, on the horizon, colloq. round the corner
E3 remote, far-off

immobile adj
motionless, stationary, unmoving, immobilized, at rest, still, stock-still, static, immovable, rooted, fixed, frozen, rigid, stiff, riveted
E3 mobile, moving

immobility n
motionlessness, immovability, steadiness, stillness, firmness, fixedness, fixity, stability, inertness, disability
E3 mobility

immobilize v
stop, halt, inactivate, freeze, transfix, paralyse, disable, cripple, put out of action/operation
E3 mobilize

immoderate adj
excessive, unreasonable, unjustified, unwarranted, undue, exaggerated, fulsome, enormous, exorbitant, lavish, extravagant, extreme, wanton, inordinate, uncalled-for, uncontrolled, unrestrained, outrageous, unlimited, unrestricted, unbridled, uncurbed, intemperate, self-indulgent, formal unconscionable, profligate, hubristic, distemperate, egregious, colloq. over the top, OTT, steep
E3 moderate

immoderately adv
excessively, exorbitantly, extravagantly, extremely, inordinately, exaggeratedly, unduly, unjustifiably, unrestrainedly, without measure, unreasonably, wantonly
E3 moderately

immoderation n
excess, excessiveness, exorbitance, extravagance, lavishness, immoderateness, intemperance, overindulgence, unreason, unrestraint, formal prodigality, dissipation
E3 moderation

immodest adj
indecent, revealing, shameless, forward, bold, boastful, impudent, brazen, improper, immoral, obscene, lewd, coarse, risqué, formal indecorous, colloq. cheeky, fresh, cocky, saucy
E3 modest

immodesty n
audacity, boldness, forwardness, gall, impudence, shamelessness, temerity, bawdiness, coarseness, impurity, lewdness, obscenity, indelicacy, formal indecorousness, indecorum, colloq. brass
E3 modesty

immoral adj
unethical, wrong, bad, sinful, evil, wicked, unscrupulous, unprincipled, dishonest, vile, corrupt, depraved, base, degenerate, debauched, reprobate, dissolute,

loose, lewd, indecent, pornographic, obscene, licentious, impure, *formal* iniquitous, nefarious, *colloq.* blue, raunchy, juicy
F3 moral, right, good

immorality *n*
wrong, wrongdoing, badness, sin, sinfulness, evil, wickedness, dishonesty, vileness, corruption, vice, depravity, dissoluteness, debauchery, impurity, lewdness, indecency, pornography, obscenity, licentiousness, *formal* iniquity, profligacy, turpitude
F3 morality

immortal *adj, n*
► *adj* **1** UNDYING, deathless, imperishable, indestructible, unfading, eternal, everlasting, perpetual, endless, ceaseless, lasting, enduring, abiding, constant, perennial, timeless, ageless, *formal* sempiternal **2** *recall those immortal words* memorable, unforgettable, well-known, celebrated, famous, honoured, distinguished
F3 mortal
► *n* deity, god, goddess, divinity, great, hero, genius, Olympian

immortality *n*
1 ETERNAL LIFE, everlasting life, eternity, endlessness, deathlessness, incorruptibility, imperishability, indestructibility, timelessness, perpetuity **2** FAME, glorification, gloriousness, glory, greatness, renown, celebrity, honour, distinction
F3 **1** mortality

immortalize *v*
celebrate, commemorate, memorialize, perpetuate, glorify, enshrine, eternalize, *formal* laud

immovable *adj*
1 FIXED, rooted, immobile, stuck, fast, secure, stable, moored, riveted, anchored, jammed, constant, firm, set **2** STEADFAST, determined, resolute, adamant, unshakable, stubborn, obstinate, uncompromising, unyielding, set, firm, constant, inflexible, dogged, unwavering, unswerving, *formal* intransigent
F3 **1** movable **2** flexible

immune *adj*
invulnerable, unsusceptible, resistant, proof, protected, safe, exempt, free, clear, secure, spared, excused, released, relieved, absolved
F3 susceptible, liable, subject, affected

immune system *n*

The immune system's components and responses include:
antibody, antigen [= antibody generator], commensals, complement system, cytotoxic cells, histamine, immunoglobins, interferon, leucocyte, lymphocyte, B-lymphocytes, T-cells, T-lymphocytes, killer T-cells, helper T-cells, memory T-cells, lysosome, lysozyme, phagocyte, plasma cells, receptor (binding) site; acquired immunity, artificially acquired immunity (immunization), naturally acquired immunity, passive immunity, cell-mediated immunity, cellular response, humoral immunity/response, adaptive immune system, innate immune system, non-specific immune response, specific immune response, autoimmune response, primary response, secondary response, inflammatory response, immunosurveillance, allergy, phagocyte action (adherence/ingestion/digestion), phagocytosis, sneeze reflex, tissue rejection.

---

immunity *n*
resistance, protection, immunization, vaccination, inoculation, safety, exemption, indemnity, exception,

impunity, freedom, liberty, release, licence, franchise, privilege, right, permission, *formal* exoneration
F3 susceptibility

immunization *n*
vaccination, inoculation, injection, protection, jab

immunize *v*
vaccinate, inoculate, inject, protect, safeguard, shield

immure *v*
enclose, confine, wall in, shut up, cage, imprison, incarcerate, jail, cloister, enwall
F3 free

immutability *n*
changelessness, immutableness, invariability, unalterableness, unchangeableness, permanence, constancy, durability, fixedness, stability
F3 mutability

immutable *adj*
changeless, inflexible, invariable, unalterable, unchangeable, perpetual, permanent, abiding, constant, enduring, fixed, lasting, stable, steadfast, sacrosanct
F3 mutable, changeable

imp *n*
1 SPRITE, demon, devil, goblin, hobgoblin, gnome, puck **2** MISCHIEVOUS CHILD, rascal, rogue, scamp, brat, minx, troublemaker, mischief-maker, trickster, prankster, flibbertigibbet, gamin, urchin

impact *n, v*
► *n* **1** *the impact of the reforms* effect, consequences, results, repercussions, impression, power, influence, significance, meaning **2** COLLISION, crash, smash, bang, bump, blow, knock, whack, contact, clash, jolt, force, shock, brunt
► *v* **1** COLLIDE, crash, hit, clash, crush, fix, strike, press together **2** AFFECT, have an effect on, influence, apply to, impinge

impair *v*
damage, harm, injure, hinder, mar, spoil, cripple, disable, worsen, deteriorate, undermine, weaken, reduce, decrease, lessen, diminish, blunt, *formal* debilitate, enervate, vitiate, enfeeble
F3 improve, enhance

impaired *adj*
defective, faulty, flawed, poor, weak, disabled, imperfect, damaged, spoilt, unsound, *formal* vitiated
F3 enhanced

impairment *n*
disability, disablement, injury, weakness, damage, deterioration, reduction, harm, hurt, fault, flaw, ruin, *formal* dysfunction, vitiation
F3 enhancement

impale *v*
pierce, puncture, perforate, run through, spear, lance, spike, skewer, spit, stick, stab, prick, transfix, disembowel

impalpable *adj*
imperceptible, inapprehensible, insubstantial, unsubstantial, elusive, indistinct, intangible, shadowy, tenuous, thin, fine, delicate, airy, *formal* incorporeal
F3 palpable

impart *v*
1 CONVEY, tell, relate, communicate, make known, transmit, disclose, divulge, reveal, report, pass on **2** GIVE, grant, offer, contribute, lend, assign, *formal* confer, bestow, accord
F3 **1, 2** withhold

impartial *adj*
objective, dispassionate, detached, disinterested, neutral, non-partisan, unbiased, unprejudiced, open-minded, fair, fair-minded, just, equitable, even-handed, equal
F3 biased, prejudiced

impartiality n
neutrality, non-partisanship, objectivity, unbiasedness, fairness, justice, even-handedness, open-mindedness, detachment, disinterest, disinterestedness, dispassion, equality, equity
🔁 bias, prejudice, favouritism, discrimination

impassable adj
blocked, closed, obstructed, unnavigable, unpassable, pathless, trackless, impenetrable, insurmountable, insuperable, unassailable, invincible
🔁 passable

impasse n
deadlock, stalemate, checkmate, dead end, cul-de-sac, blind alley, halt, standstill

impassioned adj
fervent, ardent, passionate, intense, inspired, stirring, spirited, rousing, emotional, enthusiastic, eager, excited, fervid, vigorous, forceful, violent, furious, fiery, vehement, animated, glowing, inflamed, blazing, heated
🔁 apathetic, mild

impassive adj
expressionless, emotionless, calm, composed, unruffled, unconcerned, apathetic, cool, unfeeling, unemotional, unmoved, unruffled, unexcitable, stoical, indifferent, dispassionate, formal imperturbable, phlegmatic, colloq. unflappable, laid back
🔁 responsive, moved

impatience n
eagerness, keenness, excitability, restlessness, agitation, anxiety, nervousness, edginess, uneasiness, irritability, intolerance, shortness, brusqueness, abruptness, curtness, tenseness, haste, rashness, impetuosity
🔁 patience

impatient adj
eager, keen, excitable, restless, fidgety, fretful, agitated, anxious, nervous, edgy, irritable, jittery, snappy, testy, hot-tempered, quick-tempered, angry, intolerant, brusque, abrupt, short, curt, tense, impetuous, hasty, headlong, formal restive, querulous, precipitate, colloq. champing at the bit, straining/panting at the leash
🔁 patient

impeach v
accuse, charge, denounce, criticize, revile, attack, censure, blame, technical indict, arraign, formal impugn, disparage

impeachment n
accusation, charge, technical arraignment, indictment, formal disparagement

impeccable adj
perfect, faultless, precise, exact, correct, exemplary, flawless, unblemished, stainless, immaculate, pure, upright, irreproachable, blameless, innocent
🔁 faulty, flawed, corrupt

impecunious adj
poor, poverty-stricken, insolvent, destitute, impoverished, penniless, needy, formal indigent, penurious, colloq. broke, stony-broke, skint, cleaned out
🔁 rich

impede v
hinder, hamper, obstruct, block, handicap, clog, slow (down), hold up, hold back, delay, check, curb, restrain, thwart, disrupt, stop, bar, formal retard
🔁 aid, promote, further

impediment n
1 HINDRANCE, obstacle, obstruction, barrier, bar, block, setback, stumbling-block, snag, difficulty, handicap, burden, encumbrance, check, curb, restraint, restriction 2 a speech impediment DEFECT, handicap, stutter, stammer
🔁 1 aid

impedimenta n
baggage, luggage, equipment, gear, belongings, formal effects, accoutrements, colloq. things, stuff

impel v
urge, force, oblige, compel, constrain, drive, propel, get going, push, press, pressure, pressurize, spur, prod, goad, prompt, incite, stimulate, excite, instigate, motivate, inspire, move
🔁 deter, dissuade

impending adj
imminent, forthcoming, in the offing, approaching, coming, close, near, at hand, on the way, looming, menacing, threatening, brewing, in the air, about to happen, on the horizon
🔁 remote, far-off

impenetrable adj
1 impenetrable jungle impassable, solid, thick, dense, overgrown 2 UNINTELLIGIBLE, incomprehensible, unfathomable, indiscernible, puzzling, baffling, mysterious, cryptic, enigmatic, obscure, dark, inscrutable, formal abstruse, recondite
🔁 2 accessible, understandable

impenitence n
impenitency, stubbornness, hard-heartedness, defiance, incorrigibility, formal obduracy
🔁 penitence

impenitent adj
unrepentant, unremorseful, uncontrite, unashamed, defiant, hardened, incorrigible, remorseless, un-abashed, unreformed, unregenerate, formal obdurate
🔁 penitent, contrite

imperative adj
vital, essential, crucial, pressing, urgent, compulsory, critical, necessary, obligatory, indispensable
🔁 optional, unimportant

imperceptible adj
inappreciable, indiscernible, unapparent, indistinguishable, undetectable, inaudible, unapparent, faint, slight, muffled, negligible, impalpable, infinitesimal, microscopic, minute, tiny, minuscule, small, fine, subtle, gradual, unclear, obscure, vague, indistinct, indefinite
🔁 perceptible, noticeable, clear

imperceptibly adv
inappreciably, indiscernibly, unnoticeably, unobtrusively, unseen, slowly, subtly, gradually, bit by bit, little by little, formal insensibly
🔁 perceptibly

imperfect adj
faulty, flawed, defective, damaged, broken, blemished, impaired, chipped, deficient, inadequate, insufficient, incomplete
🔁 perfect, whole

imperfection n
fault, flaw, defect, blemish, deformity, crack, dent, break, tear, cut, scratch, blot, blotch, stain, taint, spot, deficiency, impairment, shortcoming, foible, weakness, failing, inadequacy, insufficiency
🔁 perfection

imperial adj
sovereign, supreme, absolute, royal, regal, monarchical, kingly, queenly, majestic, grand, magnificent, glorious, splendid, great, noble, lofty, stately

imperial or **imperious**?

Imperial means 'of an empire or emperor': *the imperial crown. Imperious* means 'proud and overbearing', 'behaving as if expecting to be, or in the habit of being, obeyed': *She disliked his imperious manner.*

imperialism *n*
empire-building, colonialism, expansionism, acquisitiveness, adventurism

imperil *v*
endanger, put in danger, jeopardize, put in jeopardy, risk, expose to risk, hazard, take a chance, expose, compromise, threaten

imperious *adj*
overbearing, domineering, autocratic, despotic, tyrannical, dictatorial, high-handed, lordly, masterful, commanding, assertive, arrogant, haughty, *formal* peremptory, overweening
 F3 humble

imperishable *adj*
enduring, permanent, incorruptible, indestructible, inextinguishable, undying, unfading, unforgettable, abiding, perpetual, perennial, eternal, everlasting, immortal, deathless
 F3 perishable

impermanent *adj*
transient, temporary, passing, short-lived, momentary, transitory, inconstant, brief, elusive, fleeting, flying, unfixed, unsettled, unstable, mortal, perishable, fugitive, *formal* ephemeral, evanescent, fugacious, *colloq.* fly-by-night
 F3 permanent

impermeable *adj*
impervious, impenetrable, impassable, sealed, hermetic, non-porous, damp-proof, waterproof, proof, water-resistant, resistant, water-repellent
 F3 permeable, porous

impersonal *adj*
1 COLD, cool, frigid, formal, official, aloof, remote, distant, clinical, stiff, stuffy, businesslike, detached, unemotional, unfeeling **2** OBJECTIVE, neutral, dispassionate, detached, unbiased, unprejudiced, nonpartisan
 F3 1 friendly, informal **2** biased

impersonate *v*
imitate, mimic, parody, caricature, mock, ape, masquerade as, pose as, pass off as, act, portray, *colloq.* take off

impersonation *n*
imitation, impression, mimicry, parody, caricature, aping, apery, burlesque, *colloq.* take-off

impertinence *n*
rudeness, impoliteness, disrespect, discourtesy, insolence, impudence, effrontery, audacity, boldness, brazenness, forwardness, presumption, shamelessness, *colloq.* cheek, brass, brass neck, nerve, sauce, lip, gall, face, mouth
 F3 politeness, respect, civility

impertinent *adj*
rude, impolite, ill-mannered, unmannerly, discourteous, disrespectful, insolent, impudent, pert, bold, audacious, brash, brazen, forward, presumptuous, shameless, *colloq.* cheeky, saucy, fresh, *US* sassy
 F3 polite, respectful

imperturbability *n*
calmness, composure, coolness, complacency, self-possession, tranquillity, *formal* equanimity
 F3 jitteriness, touchiness

imperturbable *adj*
unexcitable, calm, tranquil, composed, collected, even-tempered, self-possessed, cool, impassive, unmoved, unruffled, untroubled, complacent, *colloq.* unflappable, calm and collected
 F3 excitable, ruffled

impervious *adj*
1 IMPERMEABLE, waterproof, damp-proof, proof, non-porous, watertight, hermetic, closed, sealed, resistant, impenetrable **2** *impervious to criticism* immune, invulnerable, untouched, unaffected, unmoved, closed, resistant
 F3 1 porous, pervious **2** responsive, vulnerable

impetuosity *n*
impetuousness, impulsiveness, rashness, haste, hastiness, spontaneity, foolhardiness, recklessness, thoughtlessness, impatience, dash, élan, vehemence, *formal* precipitateness
 F3 caution, wariness, *formal* circumspection

impetuous *adj*
impulsive, spontaneous, unplanned, unthinking, unpremeditated, spur-of-the-moment, hasty, impatient, headlong, uncontrolled, brash, foolhardy, rash, reckless, thoughtless, unthinking, ill-conceived, unreasoned, *formal* precipitate
 F3 cautious, wary, *formal* circumspect

impetuously *adv*
rashly, impulsively, unthinkingly, recklessly, spontaneously, passionately, vehemently, *formal* precipitately
 F3 cautiously

impetus *n*
stimulus, incentive, motivation, influence, encouragement, inspiration, actuation, impulse, momentum, force, energy, power, drive, urging, boost, push, goad, spur

impiety *n*
irreverence, irreligion, profaneness, profanity, sinfulness, ungodliness, unholiness, unrighteousness, wickedness, godlessness, blasphemy, sacrilege, sacrilegiousness, *formal* iniquity, hubris
 F3 piety, reverence

impinge *v*
encroach, infringe, affect, influence, hit, touch (on), intrude, trespass, invade

impious *adj*
irreverent, irreligious, profane, sinful, ungodly, godless, unholy, unrighteous, wicked, blasphemous, sacrilegious, *formal* iniquitous, hubristic
 F3 pious, reverent

impish *adj*
mischievous, naughty, roguish, rascally, sportive, devilish, elfin, gamin, tricksome, frolicsome, tricksy, pranksome, waggish

implacability *n*
implacableness, inexorability, relentlessness, remorselessness, mercilessness, pitilessness, ruthlessness, unforgivingness, vengefulness, irreconcilability, inflexibility, *formal* intransigence, intractability, rancorousness
 F3 placability

implacable *adj*
inexorable, relentless, unrelenting, remorseless, merciless, pitiless, unappeasable, irreconcilable, vengeful, cruel, heartless, unforgiving, ruthless, inflexible, adamant, uncompromising, unyielding, *formal* intransigent, intractable, rancorous
 F3 compassionate, forgiving

implant *v*
1 *implant ideas in someone's mind* sow, plant, fix, root, instil, inculcate, introduce **2** *implant a new heart/new*

skin tissue insert, place, put, engraft, graft, transplant **3** EMBED, fix, sow, plant, place, root

implausible *adj*
improbable, unlikely, hard to believe, unbelievable, inconceivable, incredible, far-fetched, dubious, doubtful, questionable, suspect, unconvincing, weak, flimsy, thin, transparent
F⁊ plausible, likely, reasonable

implement *n, v*
▶ *n* tool, instrument, utensil, gadget, device, apparatus, appliance, contrivance
▶ *v* ›enforce, bring about, carry out, perform, do, fulfil, complete, accomplish, realize, put into effect, put into action/operation, *formal* discharge, execute, effect

implementation *n*
carrying out, performance, performing, fulfilling, fulfilment, accomplishment, completion, operation, action, enforcement, realization, *formal* discharge, effecting, execution

implicate *v*
involve, embroil, entangle, incriminate, compromise, include, concern, connect, associate, be a part of, be (a) party to, *formal* inculpate
F⁊ absolve, *formal* exonerate

implicated *adj*
involved, embroiled, entangled, incriminated, compromised, included, concerned, connected, associated, responsible, party to, suspected, *formal* inculpated
F⁊ exonerated

implication *n*
1 INFERENCE, deduction, insinuation, suggestion, meaning, significance, overtone, undertone, ramification, repercussion, effect, consequence, conclusion **2** INVOLVEMENT, entanglement, embroilment, incrimination, connection, association, *formal* inculpation

implicit *adj*
1 IMPLIED, inferred, deducible, insinuated, suggested, hinted, indirect, unsaid, unspoken, unexpressed, unstated, tacit, understood, inherent, hidden, latent **2** *implicit belief* unquestioning, unhesitating, utter, total, full, entire, complete, absolute, perfect, sheer, positive, unqualified, unreserved, unconditional, steadfast, wholehearted
F⁊ **1** explicit **2** half-hearted

implicitly *adv*
absolutely, totally, utterly, completely, unconditionally, unhesitatingly, unquestioningly, unreservedly, steadfastly, wholeheartedly, firmly
F⁊ explicitly

implied *adj*
implicit, tacit, indirect, insinuated, suggested, hinted, assumed, understood, unspoken, unexpressed, unstated, undeclared, inherent
F⁊ stated

implore *v*
beg, entreat, ask, appeal, request, press, crave, plead, pray, *formal* importune, solicit, supplicate, beseech

imply *v*
suggest, insinuate, hint, intimate, infer, say indirectly, give someone to understand/believe, mean, signify, point to, indicate, signal, involve, require, entail, state, *formal* denote

 imply or **infer** ?
Imply means 'to suggest or hint at (something) without actually stating it': *Are you implying that I'm a liar? Infer* means 'to form an opinion by reasoning from what you know': *I inferred from your silence that you were angry.*

impolite *adj*
rude, discourteous, bad-mannered, unmannerly, ill-mannered, ill-bred, uncivil, unrefined, ungentlemanly, unladylike, indecorous, ungracious, inconsiderate, disrespectful, impertinent, insolent, rough, loutish, boorish, coarse, crude, vulgar, abrupt,*colloq.* cheeky
F⁊ polite, courteous

impoliteness *n*
rudeness, discourtesy, bad manners, unmannerliness, disrespect, insolence, impertinence, incivility, inconsiderateness, boorishness, churlishness, crassness, indelicacy, roughness, coarseness, abruptness, gaucherie
F⁊ politeness, courtesy

impolitic *adj*
unwise, ill-advised, inexpedient, ill-judged, misguided, ill-considered, short-sighted, undiplomatic, indiscreet, rash, foolish, *formal* injudicious, imprudent, maladroit, *colloq.* daft
F⁊ wise, *formal* politic, prudent

import *n, v*
▶ *n* **1** *exports and imports* imported product/commodity/goods, foreign product/commodity/goods, foreign trade **2** IMPORTANCE, consequence, significance, weight, substance **3** CONTENT, sense, substance, nub, meaning, implication, intention, thrust, message, drift, essence, gist, *formal* purport
▶ *v* betoken, bring in, imply, indicate, introduce, mean, purport, signify

importance *n*
1 MOMENTOUSNESS, significance, urgency, criticalness, graveness, substance, matter, concern, interest, usefulness, value, worth, weight, *formal* consequence **2** *people of importance in society* influence, power, mark, prominence, eminence, distinction, noteworthiness, prestige, status, standing, *formal* esteem
F⁊ **1, 2** unimportance, insignificance

important *adj*
1 MOMENTOUS, noteworthy, significant, meaningful, relevant, material, salient, urgent, critical, paramount, crucial, vital, essential, key, central, primary, principal, major, main, chief, priority, substantial, valuable, valued, weighty, serious, grave, far-reaching, pivotal, historic, fateful, *formal* seminal **2** *the most important person in the school* LEADING, foremost, high-level, high-ranking, influential, chief, main, powerful, pre-eminent, prestigious, prominent, outstanding, eminent, notable, distinguished, valued, noted, *formal* esteemed
F⁊ **1** unimportant, insignificant, trivial **2** powerless

importunate *adj*
insistent, persistent, troublesome, impatient, tenacious, dogged, pressing, urgent, *formal* pertinacious

importune *v*
pester, badger, harass, hound, cajole, plague, appeal, request, press, urge, plead with, solicit, beset, *formal* supplicate

importunity *n*
insistence, persistence, pressing, pestering, harassing, hounding, urgency, urging, solicitation, harassment, cajolery, entreaties

impose *v*
1 ENFORCE, exact, levy, apply, charge, set, fix, put (on), place (on), lay (on), introduce, institute, establish, decree, inflict, burden, encumber, saddle, force, thrust, foist **2** FOIST, force yourself, thrust yourself, intrude, butt in, break in, encroach, trespass, obtrude, presume, exploit, put upon, abuse, mislead, take liberties, take advantage of

imposing *adj*
impressive, striking, grand, stately, majestic, splendid, dignified, lofty, august
F3 unimposing, modest

imposition *n*
1 ENFORCEMENT, introduction, infliction, exaction, levying, application, setting, fixing, establishment, decree, institution **2** CHARGE, tax, tariff, toll, burden, constraint, load, encumbrance, duty, task, punishment **3** INTRUSION, encroachment, trespassing

impossibility *n*
hopelessness, impracticability, unattainableness, unobtainableness, unacceptability, untenability, unviability, inability, inconceivability, preposterousness, absurdity, ludicrousness, ridiculousness
F3 possibility

impossible *adj*
hopeless, impracticable, unworkable, unattainable, unachievable, unobtainable, insoluble, unreasonable, unacceptable, beyond you, inconceivable, unimaginable, unthinkable, out of the question, preposterous, incredible, unbelievable, absurd, ludicrous, ridiculous, outlandish, intolerable, unbearable, *colloq.* out, not by any stretch of the imagination, and pigs might fly
F3 possible

impostor *n*
fraud, fake, quack, charlatan, sham, mountebank, impersonator, pretender, deceiver, deluder, hoodwinker, swindler, cheat, trickster, defrauder, rogue, *colloq.* phoney, con man

imposture *n*
deception, fraud, impersonation, quackery, swindle, trick, counterfeit, cheat, hoax, artifice, *colloq.* con, con trick

impotence *n*
powerlessness, helplessness, uselessness, inability, inadequacy, incapacity, incompetence, ineffectiveness, weakness, feebleness, frailty, disability, infirmity, paralysis, *formal* enervation, inefficacy, impuissance
F3 strength

impotent *adj*
powerless, helpless, useless, worthless, futile, unable, incapable, ineffective, incompetent, inadequate, weak, feeble, frail, worn out, exhausted, infirm, disabled, incapacitated, paralysed, crippled, *formal* debilitated, enervated, impuissant
F3 potent, strong

impound *v*
1 CONFISCATE, seize, remove, take away, take possession of, commandeer, *formal* appropriate, expropriate **2** CONFINE, shut up, cage, keep in, lock up, coop up, hem in, *formal* incarcerate, immure

impoverish *v*
bankrupt, break, ruin, beggar, weaken, reduce, deplete, exhaust, drain, diminish, denude, *formal* pauperize
F3 enrich

impoverished *adj*
1 POOR, needy, poverty-stricken, destitute, down-and-out, bankrupt, penniless, ruined, *formal* impecunious, penurious, indigent, *colloq.* bust, skint, stony-broke, cleaned out, on your uppers, on your beam ends, not having two pennies to rub together **2** WEAKENED, drained, exhausted, desolate, empty, waste, dead, barren, bare
F3 **1** rich

impracticability *n*
unworkability, infeasibility, unsuitableness, unviability, uselessness, impossibility, futility, hopelessness
F3 practicability

impracticable *adj*
unworkable, unfeasible, unattainable, unachievable, impossible, out of the question, unviable, useless, unserviceable, inoperable
F3 practicable, feasible

> **impracticable** or **impractical** ?
> *Impracticable* means 'that cannot be carried out or put into practice': *The whole project has become completely impracticable.* When referring to suggestions, plans, etc, *impractical* means 'possible to carry out but not sensible or convenient': *In a modern economy barter is totally impractical*; 'not able to do or make things in a sensible and efficient way': *He was impractical and dreamy, with a head full of foolish notions.*

impractical *adj*
unrealistic, idealistic, romantic, starry-eyed, visionary, theoretical abstract, academic, ivory-tower, impracticable, unworkable, impossible, awkward, inconvenient, unserviceable
F3 practical, realistic, sensible

impracticality *n*
idealism, romanticism, unworkability, unworkableness, impossibility, hopelessness, infeasibility
F3 practicality

imprecation *n*
curse, blasphemy, denunciation, abuse, anathema, *formal* execration, malediction, profanity, vituperation, vilification

imprecise *adj*
inexact, inaccurate, approximate, estimated, rough, loose, indefinite, vague, woolly, blurred, hazy, ill-defined, sloppy, inexplicit, ambiguous, equivocal
F3 precise, exact

impregnable *adj*
impenetrable, unconquerable, invincible, unbeatable, unassailable, indestructible, inviolable, fortified, strong, solid, secure, safe, invulnerable, unquestionable, irrefutable
F3 vulnerable

impregnate *v*
1 SOAK, steep, saturate, drench, fill, permeate, pervade, suffuse, imbue, infuse, penetrate **2** INSEMINATE, fertilize, make pregnant, *formal* fecundate

impregnation *n*
fertilization, fertilizing, insemination, saturation, imbuing, *formal* fructification, fructifying, fecundation

impresario *n*
manager, organizer, director, producer, promoter, exhibitor

impress *v*
1 *I'm not impressed* strike, move, touch, sway, affect, influence, stir, inspire, rouse, excite, *colloq.* grab **2** STAMP, imprint, print, engrave, mark, indent, instil, inculcate, fix deeply, emphasize, stress, highlight, underline, bring home

impressed *adj*
moved, excited, affected, struck, influenced, marked, taken, touched, stamped, stirred, overawed, *colloq.* grabbed, turned on, knocked out
F3 unimpressed

impression *n*
1 FEELING, awareness, consciousness, sense, sensation, illusion, idea, notion, opinion, belief, thought, conviction, suspicion, fancy, hunch, memory, recollection, *colloq.* funny feeling, gut feeling, vibes **2** *make a good impression* effect, impact, influence, power, control, sway **3** STAMP, mark, print, dent, indentation, imprint, pressure, outline **4** IMPERSONATION,

imitation, parody, mimicry, caricature, burlesque, *colloq.* take-off, send-up

impressionability *n*
naïvety, gullibility, susceptibility, vulnerability, sensitivity, receptiveness, receptivity, suggestibility, greenness, *formal* ingenuousness

impressionable *adj*
naïve, gullible, persuadable, susceptible, vulnerable, sensitive, pliable, mouldable, responsive, open, receptive, *formal* ingenuous

impressive *adj*
striking, imposing, grand, breathtaking, spectacular, powerful, effective, dazzling, awe-inspiring, awesome, stirring, inspiring, exciting, rousing, moving, affecting, touching
▸ unimpressive, uninspiring

imprint *n, v*
▸ *n* print, mark, stamp, impression, indentation, sign, logo, emblem, badge, colophon
▸ *v* stamp, print, mark, brand, impress, fix, establish, engrave, emboss, etch

imprison *v*
put in prison, send to prison, jail, intern, detain, lock up, cage, pen, confine, shut in, *formal* incarcerate, immure, *colloq.* send down, put away, bang up
▸ release, free

imprisoned *adj*
jailed, locked up, behind bars, confined, caged, captive, *formal* incarcerated, immured, *colloq.* inside, put away, sent down, doing time, doing bird, doing porridge
▸ free

imprisonment *n*
internment, detention, custody, captivity, confinement, *formal* incarceration
▸ freedom, liberty

improbability *n*
uncertainty, doubt, doubtfulness, dubiousness, unlikelihood, unlikeliness, far-fetchedness, preposterousness, ridiculousness, implausibility, *formal* dubiety
▸ probability

improbable *adj*
uncertain, questionable, doubtful, unlikely, dubious, implausible, unconvincing, far-fetched, preposterous, ridiculous, unbelievable, incredible
▸ probable, likely, convincing

impromptu *adj, adv*
▸ *adj* improvised, extempore, ad-lib, off the cuff, unscripted, unrehearsed, unprepared, spontaneous
▸ rehearsed
▸ *adv* without preparation, extempore, ad lib, spontaneously, *colloq.* on the spur of the moment, off the top of your head, off the cuff

improper *adj*
1 INDECENT, rude, vulgar, shocking, risqué, indelicate, *formal* unseemly, indecorous, unbecoming **2** WRONG, incorrect, irregular, false, erroneous, unlawful **3** UNSUITABLE, inappropriate, unfitting, inopportune, inadequate, out of place, *formal* incongruous
▸ **1** decent **2** correct, lawful **3** suitable, appropriate

impropriety *n*
mistake, lapse, slip, blunder, *faux pas*, gaffe, bad taste, vulgarity, gaucherie, immodesty, indecency, unsuitability, *formal* incongruity, indecorousness, indecorum, solecism, unseemliness
▸ *formal* propriety

improve *v*
better, make better, ameliorate, enhance, enrich, perfect, polish, touch up, mend, rectify, put right, set right, correct, amend, revise, reform, help, upgrade, modernize, streamline, revamp, increase, rise, pick up, develop, look up, advance, grow, progress, make headway, get better, recover, convalesce, recuperate, rally, rehabilitate, gain strength, *colloq.* be on the up and up, get your act together, turn over a new leaf, mend your ways, perk up, look up, give a facelift to, do up, fix up
▸ worsen, deteriorate, decline

improvement *n*
betterment, enhancement, rectification, rectifying, correction, amendment, revision, reform, reformation, rehabilitation, upgrading, modernizing, increase, rise, upswing, gain, development, advance, growth, progress, headway, furtherance, recovery, rally, upswing, *formal* amelioration
▸ deterioration, decline, worsening

improvident *adj*
thriftless, unthrifty, spendthrift, extravagant, shiftless, uneconomical, wasteful, careless, reckless, heedless, inattentive, thoughtless, negligent, unprepared, underprepared, Micawberish, *formal* imprudent, prodigal, profligate
▸ thrifty, economical

improvisation *n*
ad-lib, ad-libbing, extemporizing, impromptu, invention, spontaneity, makeshift, expedient, vamp, *formal* autoschediasm

improvise *v*
1 CONTRIVE, devise, concoct, invent, put together quickly, make do, *colloq.* throw together, cobble together, knock up, rig up, run up **2** EXTEMPORIZE, ad-lib, compose/perform without preparation, vamp, *colloq.* say whatever comes into your head/mind, speak off the cuff, speak off the top of your head, play by ear, have a brainwave

improvised *adj*
extempore, ad-lib, spontaneous, extemporaneous, extemporized, makeshift, off-the-cuff, unrehearsed, unprepared, unscripted
▸ rehearsed

imprudent *adj*
unwise, ill-advised, ill-considered, ill-judged, foolish, foolhardy, short-sighted, rash, reckless, hasty, irresponsible, unthinking, careless, heedless, thoughtless, indiscreet, *formal* impolitic, injudicious, improvident
▸ wise, cautious, wary, *formal* prudent

impudence *n*
impertinence, boldness, brazenness, pertness, insolence, rudeness, presumption, *formal* effrontery, *colloq.* cheek, nerve, sauciness, lip, face, mouth, brass neck
▸ politeness

impudent *adj*
impertinent, bold, forward, shameless, immodest, cocky, brazen, insolent, rude, impolite, disrespectful, presumptuous, audacious, pert, *colloq.* cheeky, saucy, fresh
▸ polite

impugn *v*
challenge, attack, assail, question, call in question, criticize, oppose, resist, dispute, *formal* berate, censure, revile, vilify, vituperate, traduce, vilipend
▸ praise, compliment

impulse *n*
1 URGE, wish, desire, inclination, whim, notion, caprice, instinct, feeling, passion, drive **2** IMPETUS, momentum, force, pressure, drive, thrust, propulsion, impulsion, surge, push, incitement, incentive, inducement, stimulation, stimulus, motive, motivation

impulsive *adj*
impetuous, rash, reckless, foolhardy, thoughtless, un-thinking, impatient, madcap, headstrong, hasty, quick, sudden, ill-judged, ill-considered, spontaneous, automatic, instinctive, emotional, passionate, intuitive, *formal* precipitate
Ⓕ cautious, premeditated

impulsiveness *n*
impetuosity, impetuousness, rashness, recklessness, foolhardiness, thoughtlessness, impatience, haste, hastiness, quickness, suddenness, spontaneity, instinct, emotion, passion, intuitiveness, *formal* precipitateness, precipitation
Ⓕ caution

impunity *n*
exemption, freedom, immunity, liberty, licence, dispensation, permission, security, amnesty, excusal
Ⓕ liability

impure *adj*
1 UNREFINED, adulterated, alloyed, mixed, blended, combined, diluted, contaminated, polluted, tainted, infected, corrupt, defiled, debased, sullied, unclean, dirty, foul, filthy **2** OBSCENE, indecent, dirty, crude, coarse, vulgar, offensive, immoral, shameless, improper, promiscuous, depraved, unchaste, sexy, immodest, lustful, lewd, lecherous, licentious, risqué, suggestive, pornographic, erotic, smutty, bawdy, ribald
Ⓕ 1 pure **2** chaste, decent

impurity *n*
1 *impurities in the petrol* adulteration, mixture, blend, dilution, contamination, pollution, taint, infection, corruption, debasement, dirtiness, contaminant, pollutant, dirt, filth, grime, foulness, dross, foreign body, mark, spot **2** OBSCENITY, indecency, crudity, coarseness, vulgarity, offensiveness, immorality, shamelessness, impropriety, promiscuity, unchastity, looseness, immodesty, lustfulness, lewdness, licentiousness, pornography, eroticism, smut
Ⓕ 2 purity

impute *v*
ascribe, assign, attribute, put down to, charge, credit, refer, *formal* accredit

in *adj*
fashionable, in vogue, popular, current, smart, stylish, modish, *colloq.* all the rage, trendy, cool

inability *n*
incapability, incapacity, powerlessness, impotence, inadequacy, incompetence, ineffectiveness, weakness, ineptitude, handicap, disability, uselessness
Ⓕ ability

inaccessible *adj*
isolated, remote, out of the way, god-forsaken, unfrequented, unapproachable, unreachable, out of reach, beyond reach, unattainable, impenetrable, unavailable, *colloq.* unget-at-able
Ⓕ accessible

inaccuracy *n*
mistake, error, miscalculation, slip, blunder, gaffe, fault, defect, imprecision, inexactness, unreliability, erroneousness, mistakenness, *formal* corrigendum, erratum, fallaciousness, *colloq.* boo-boo, slip-up, howler
Ⓕ accuracy, precision

inaccurate *adj*
incorrect, wrong, erroneous, mistaken, false, faulty, flawed, imperfect, defective, imprecise, inexact, out, loose, unreliable, unfaithful, untrue, unsound, *formal* fallacious
Ⓕ accurate, correct, true, right, sound

inaccurately *adv*
incorrectly, wrongly, erroneously, falsely, imperfectly,

defectively, imprecisely, inexactly, unreliably, unfaithfully, loosely, wildly, carelessly, clumsily
Ⓕ accurately, correctly

inaction *n*
inactivity, immobility, motionlessness, inertia, rest, idleness, passivity, slowness, lifelessness, sluggishness, lethargy, stagnation, *formal* torpor
Ⓕ action

inactivate *v*
disable, immobilize, paralyse, stop, cripple, mothball, stabilize, *colloq.* knock the bottom out of, scupper
Ⓕ activate

inactive *adj*
immobile, motionless, stationary, inert, idle, unused, unemployed, dormant, passive, sedentary, lazy, slow, lifeless, lethargic, sluggish, vegetating, stagnant, sleepy, *formal* inoperative, indolent, torpid, quiescent
Ⓕ active, working, busy, working, functioning, in use

inactivity *n*
immobility, inaction, inertia, inertness, idleness, unemployment, dormancy, passivity, laziness, sluggishness, lifelessness, lethargy, sloth, vegetation, stagnation, hibernation, languor, dullness, heaviness, *technical* stasis, *formal* indolence, lassitude, quiescence, dilatoriness, torpor, abeyance
Ⓕ activeness

inadequacy *n*
1 INSUFFICIENCY, lack, shortage, deficit, dearth, deficiency, scarcity, scantiness, meagreness, *formal* want, paucity **2** DEFECTIVENESS, ineffectiveness, inability, incapability, incompetence, ineffectiveness, *formal* inefficacy **3** *the inadequacies of the system* fault, defect, imperfection, weakness, foible, failing, shortcoming, flaw
Ⓕ 1 adequacy **3** strong point

inadequate *adj*
1 INSUFFICIENT, short, wanting, deficient, too little/few, scanty, scant, scarce, skimpy, sparse, meagre, niggardly **2** INCOMPETENT, bad, incapable, inexpert, unproficient, careless, not good enough, unequal, unqualified, ineffective, faulty, defective, imperfect, unsatisfactory, unfit, substandard, disappointing, *formal* ineffectual, inefficacious, *colloq.* not up to scratch
Ⓕ 1 adequate, enough **2** satisfactory

inadequately *adv*
insufficiently, poorly, meagrely, scantily, sketchily, skimpily, sparsely, thinly, imperfectly, badly, carelessly
Ⓕ adequately

inadmissible *adj*
unacceptable, irrelevant, immaterial, inappropriate, disallowed, prohibited, improper, *formal* precluded, inapposite
Ⓕ admissible

inadvertent *adj*
accidental, chance, unintentional, unintended, unplanned, unpremeditated, uncalculated, careless, negligent, thoughtless, unwitting, unconscious, involuntary
Ⓕ deliberate, conscious, careful

inadvertently *adv*
accidentally, by accident, by mistake, by chance, unintentionally, unthinkingly, unwittingly, unconsciously, involuntarily, carelessly, heedlessly, negligently, mistakenly, remissly, thoughtlessly
Ⓕ deliberately

inadvisable *adj*
unwise, foolish, silly, ill-advised, ill-judged, inexpedient, ill-considered, misguided, indiscreet, *formal* imprudent, injudicious
Ⓕ advisable, wise

inalienable *adj*
inherent, inviolable, unassailable, non-negotiable, non-transferable, untransferable, unremovable, permanent, sacrosanct, absolute
F3 impermanent

inane *adj*
senseless, foolish, stupid, unintelligent, silly, idiotic, absurd, ridiculous, ludicrous, frivolous, trifling, puerile, mindless, nonsensical, vapid, empty, vacuous, vain, worthless, futile, *formal* fatuous
F3 sensible

inanimate *adj*
lifeless, dead, defunct, extinct, unconscious, inactive, lazy, inert, dormant, immobile, stagnant, spiritless, dull, apathetic, lethargic, wooden, *technical* insentient, insensate, *formal* torpid
F3 animate, living, alive

inanity *n*
senselessness, folly, foolishness, stupidity, silliness, absurdity, ridiculousness, ludicrousness, frivolity, puerility, imbecility, vapidity, vacuity, asininity, emptiness, *formal* fatuity, *colloq.* daftness, waffle
F3 sense

inapplicable *adj*
irrelevant, immaterial, inapt, inappropriate, unsuitable, unsuited, unrelated, unconnected, *formal* inapposite, inconsequent
F3 applicable, *formal* germane, pertinent

inapposite *adj*
unsuitable, inappropriate, irrelevant, immaterial, unsuitable, out of place

inappropriate *adj*
unsuitable, inapt, ill-suited, ill-fitted, irrelevant, out of place, untimely, ill-timed, inopportune, tactless, improper, unbecoming, unfitting, tasteless, *formal* inapposite, incongruous, unseemly, indecorous
F3 appropriate, suitable

inapt *adj*
inappropriate, unsuitable, unsuited, ill-suited, ill-fitted, irrelevant, out of place, ill-timed, inopportune, unfortunate, *formal* inapposite, infelicitous
F3 apt

inarticulacy *n*
inarticulateness, incoherence, unintelligibility, incomprehensibility, mumbling, indistinctness, hesitancy, stumbling, stammering, stuttering, speechlessness, tongue-tiedness
F3 articulacy

inarticulate *adj*
incoherent, unintelligible, incomprehensible, unclear, indistinct, mumbled, blurred, muffled, hesitant, hesitating, stumbling, stammering, stuttering, trembling, shaking, quavery, faltering, disjointed, halting, tongue-tied, speechless, voiceless, dumb, mute, soundless
F3 articulate

inattention *n*
carelessness, negligence, disregard, heedlessness, thoughtlessness, unmindfulness, inattentiveness, absent-mindedness, forgetfulness, daydreaming, dreaminess, preoccupation, distraction

inattentive *adj*
distracted, dreamy, daydreaming, preoccupied, absent-minded, wool-gathering, unmindful, heedless, regardless, disregarding, careless, thoughtless, negligent, forgetful, remiss, *formal* distrait, *colloq.* miles away, in a world of your own, somewhere else
F3 attentive

inaudible *adj*
silent, noiseless, imperceptible, faint, indistinct,

muffled, stifled, muted, soft, dull, low, mumbled, muttered, murmured, whispered
F3 audible, loud

inaugural *adj*
opening, introductory, first, initial, launching, original, maiden, *formal* exordial

inaugurate *v*
1 *inaugurate a scheme* institute, originate, begin, start, set up, open, launch, introduce, usher in, initiate, set in motion, put into operation, get going, *formal* commence, *colloq.* set/start the ball rolling **2** *inaugurate the president* induct, invest, install, ordain, instate, enthrone **3** *inaugurate a new building* dedicate, consecrate, open officially, commission

inauguration *n*
1 INSTITUTION, setting up, starting, opening, launch, launching, initiation, *formal* commencement **2** INDUCTION, ordination, investiture, consecration, enthronement, installation, installing

inauspicious *adj*
unfavourable, bad, unlucky, unfortunate, unpromising, untimely, ill-fated, ill-starred, discouraging, threatening, ominous, black, *formal* infelicitous, unpropitious
F3 promising, *formal* auspicious

inborn *adj*
innate, inherent, natural, native, congenital, inbred, hereditary, inherited, in the family, ingrained, instinctive, intuitive, *formal* connate
F3 learned

inbred *adj*
innate, inherent, natural, native, ingrained, constitutional, *formal* connate, ingenerate
F3 learned

incalculable *adj*
countless, innumerable, numberless, without number, untold, inestimable, immeasurable, measureless, limitless, boundless, unlimited, endless, infinite, immense, vast, enormous
F3 limited, restricted

incandescent *adj*
glowing, aglow, shining, dazzling, gleaming, brilliant, bright, white-hot

incantation *n*
chant, charm, spell, abracadabra, formula, magic formula, invocation, mantra, mantram, rune, hex, *formal* conjuration

incapable *adj*
unable, powerless, impotent, helpless, useless, weak, feeble, unfit, unsuited, unqualified, unfitted, incompetent, inept, inadequate, ineffective, *formal* ineffectual, *colloq.* not up to scratch, not hacking it, out of your league
F3 capable, experienced

incapacitate *v*
disable, cripple, paralyse, immobilize, disqualify, put out of action, lay up, *formal* debilitate, *colloq.* scupper

incapacitated *adj*
disabled, crippled, paralysed, immobilized, disqualified, out of action, unfit, unwell, hamstrung, prostrate, drunk, *formal* indisposed, *colloq.* laid up, scuppered, tipsy
F3 operative

incapacity *n*
incapability, inability, disability, unfitness, disqualification, powerlessness, impotence, ineffectiveness, ineptitude, weakness, feebleness, inadequacy, incompetence, incompetency, uselessness, *formal* ineffectuality
F3 capability

incarcerate v
imprison, put in prison, jail, gaol, put in jail, lock up, intern, confine, impound, commit, detain, put away, restrain, restrict, cage, encage, coop up, wall in, *formal* immure, *colloq.* send down
☒ free, release

incarceration n
imprisonment, internment, jail, custody, detention, confinement, bondage, captivity, restraint, restriction
☒ freedom, liberation

incarnate adj
human, in human form, embodied, made flesh, in the flesh, fleshly, personified, typified, *formal* corporeal

incarnation n
human form, appearance in the flesh, personification, embodiment, manifestation, impersonation

incautious adj
careless, ill-judged, ill-advised, ill-considered, unthinking, thoughtless, inconsiderate, inattentive, unwary, unwatchful, unobservant, foolish, foolhardy, rash, reckless, hasty, impulsive, *formal* imprudent, injudicious, uncircumspect, precipitate
☒ cautious, careful, vigilant

incendiary adj, n
▶ adj **1** *an incendiary bomb* fire-raising, flammable, combustible, pyromaniac **2** INCITING, inflammatory, provocative, stirring, seditious, subversive, dissentious, rabble-rousing, *formal* proceleusmatic
☒ **2** calming
▶ n **1** AGITATOR, insurgent, revolutionary, rabble-rouser, demagogue, firebrand **2** FIRE-RAISER, pyromaniac, arsonist, firebug, pétroleur, pétroleuse **3** FIRE-BOMB, bomb, explosive, charge, grenade, mine, petrol bomb

incense[1] n
smell the incense perfume, scent, aroma, balm, bouquet, fragrance, joss-stick

incense[2] v
incense his teacher anger, enrage, infuriate, madden, exasperate, inflame, agitate, irritate, irk, vex, nettle, rile, provoke, excite, *colloq.* aggravate, hassle, get someone's blood up, make someone's blood boil, get under someone's skin, drive up the wall, get someone's dander up
☒ calm

incensed adj
enraged, angry, fuming, furious, exasperated, mad, maddened, steamed up, indignant, infuriated, irate, ireful, wrathful, *formal* furibund, *colloq.* in a paddy, on the warpath, up in arms
☒ calm

incentive n
bait, lure, enticement, reward, encouragement, inducement, incitement, reason, motive, impetus, spur, stimulus, goad, lure, bait, stimulant, motivation, *colloq.* carrot, sweetener
☒ disincentive, discouragement, deterrent

inception n
inauguration, initiation, opening, installation, beginning, start, birth, origin, dawn, outset, rise, *formal* commencement, *colloq.* kick-off
☒ end

incessant adj
ceaseless, unceasing, endless, never-ending, unending, continual, persistent, constant, perpetual, eternal, everlasting, continuous, unbroken, uninterrupted, recurrent, unremitting, non-stop, *formal* interminable
☒ intermittent, sporadic, periodic, temporary

incidence n
frequency, commonness, prevalence, extent, range, amount, degree, rate, occurrence

incident n
1 EVENT, occurrence, happening, episode, adventure, experience, proceeding, affair, matter, occasion, instance, circumstance **2** CONFRONTATION, clash, conflict, fight, skirmish, commotion, disturbance, scene, row, fracas, brush, upset, mishap

incidental adj
accidental, chance, by chance, random, minor, nonessential, petty, trivial, small, secondary, subordinate, background, subsidiary, ancillary, peripheral, supplementary, accompanying, attendant, related, contributory, *formal* fortuitous, concomitant
☒ important, essential

incidentally adv
1 BY THE WAY, in passing, secondarily, parenthetically, *en passant*, apropos, *colloq.* by the by **2** ACCIDENTALLY, by accident, coincidentally, unexpectedly, by chance, casually, digressively, *formal* fortuitously

incinerate v
burn, cremate, reduce to ashes, carbonize

incipient adj
beginning, originating, starting, inaugural, developing, rudimentary, embryonic, newborn, impending, *formal* commencing, inceptive, inchoate, nascent
☒ developed

incise v
cut, cut into, carve, chisel, engrave, sculpt, sculpture, etch, gash, slit, slash, nick, notch

incision n
cut, opening, slit, gash, notch, slash, nick

incisive adj
cutting, keen, sharp, acute, piercing, penetrating, biting, stinging, pungent, caustic, acid, astute, perceptive, shrewd, sarcastic, *formal* trenchant, mordant, perspicacious

incisiveness n
keenness, sharpness, acuteness, penetration, astuteness, acidity, pungency, sarcasm, tartness, *formal* perspicacity, astucity, trenchancy

incite v
prompt, instigate, rouse, arouse, inflame, foment, stir up, whip up, work up, agitate, excite, animate, provoke, stimulate, spur, goad, prod, induce, impel, drive, urge, encourage, *colloq.* egg on
☒ restrain

incitement n
prompting, instigation, rousing, agitation, provocation, spur, goad, prod, impetus, stimulus, stimulation, animation, urging, drive, motivation, encouragement, inducement, incentive
☒ discouragement

inciting adj
incendiary, rabble-rousing, inflammatory, provocative, stirring, seditious, subversive, *formal* proceleusmatic
☒ calming

incivility n
impoliteness, discourtesy, discourteousness, rudeness, disrespect, unmannerliness, bad manners, ill-breeding, inurbanity, boorishness, coarseness, roughness, vulgarity
☒ civility

inclemency n
harshness, bitterness, rawness, severity, storminess, tempestuousness, roughness, foulness
☒ clemency

inclement *adj*
intemperate, harsh, bitter, harsh, raw, severe, stormy, tempestuous, rough, foul, nasty, blustery, squally
F₃ fine, clement

inclination *n*
1 LIKING, fondness, affection, attraction, affinity, taste, preference, partiality, bias, tendency, trend, disposition, leaning, *formal* propensity, proclivity, predisposition, predilection, penchant **2** *an inclination of 45 degrees* angle, slope, gradient, incline, ascent, steepness, bank, ramp, lift, pitch, slant, tilt, bend, bow, nod, *formal* acclivity, declivity
F₃ **1** disinclination, dislike

incline *v, n*
▶ *v* **1** DISPOSE, influence, persuade, affect, sway, bend, bias, prejudice, tend **2** LEAN, slope, slant, bank, tilt, tip, bend, curve, list, bow, nod, stoop, list, veer, deviate, swing
▶ *n* slope, gradient, ramp, hill, rise, ascent, dip, descent, *formal* acclivity, declivity

inclined *adj*
liable, likely, tending, given, apt, disposed, of a mind, willing, *formal* predisposed, wont

include *v*
comprise, incorporate, embody, contain, enclose, hold, encompass, cover, take in, span, admit, insert, introduce, add, enter, put in, allow for, take into account, involve, let in on, *formal* comprehend, embrace, subsume, *colloq.* rope in, throw in
F₃ exclude, omit, eliminate

including *prep*
counting, inclusive of, with, together with, included
F₃ excluding

inclusion *n*
incorporation, involvement, embodiment, encompassing, addition, insertion, *formal* comprehension
F₃ exclusion

inclusive *adj*
comprehensive, full, all-in, all-inclusive, across-the-board, all-embracing, general, catch-all, overall, sweeping, *colloq.* blanket
F₃ exclusive, narrow

incognito *adj*
in disguise, disguised, masked, veiled, camouflaged, unmarked, unidentified, unrecognizable, unidentifiable, keeping your identity secret, unknown, under an assumed/a false name, nameless
F₃ undisguised

incognizant *adj*
unaware, unconscious, unacquainted, uninformed, unenlightened, ignorant, unknowing, unobservant, inattentive
F₃ aware, *formal* apprised

incoherence *n*
unintelligibility, incomprehensibility, inarticulateness, stammer, stutter, mumble, mutter, brokenness, garbledness, muddle, mix-up, jumble, confusion, wildness, disconnectedness, disjointedness, illogicality, inconsistency
F₃ coherence

incoherent *adj*
unintelligible, incomprehensible, inarticulate, wandering, rambling, stammering, stuttering, mumbled, muttered, unconnected, disconnected, broken, garbled, scrambled, confused, muddled, mixed-up, jumbled, disjointed, disordered, illogical, inconsistent, unclear
F₃ coherent, intelligible

incombustible *adj*
fireproof, flameproof, fire-resistant, flame-resistant, flame-retardant, non-flammable, non-inflammable, unburnable
F₃ combustible

income *n*
revenue, returns, proceeds, gains, profits, interest, takings, receipts, earnings, pay, salary, wages, means, remuneration
F₃ expenditure, expenses

incoming *adj*
arriving, entering, approaching, coming, homeward, returning, ensuing, succeeding, next, new
F₃ outgoing

incommensurate *adj*
disproportionate, insufficient, inadequate, unequal, excessive, extravagant, extreme, *formal* inequitable, inordinate
F₃ appropriate

incommunicable *adj*
indescribable, inexpressible, unspeakable, unutterable, unimpartable, *formal* ineffable
F₃ expressible, communicable

incomparable *adj*
matchless, unmatched, beyond compare, unequalled, without equal, unparalleled, without parallel, unrivalled, unsurpassed, peerless, inimitable, nonpareil, paramount, supreme, superlative, superb, brilliant
F₃ ordinary, run-of-the-mill, poor

incomparably *adv*
by far, far and away, beyond compare, immeasurably, infinitely, easily, supremely, superbly, superlatively, eminently, brilliantly
F₃ poorly, slightly

incompatibility *n*
irreconcilability, contradiction, clash, conflict, variance, inconsistency, difference, disagreement, discrepancy, antagonism, mismatch, uncongeniality, *formal* disparateness, disparity, incongruity
F₃ compatibility

incompatible *adj*
irreconcilable, contradictory, conflicting, at odds, at variance, inconsistent, clashing, antagonistic, disagreeing, discordant, ill-matched, mismatched, unsuited, uncongenial, wrong, poles apart, worlds apart, *formal* incongruous, disparate, *colloq.* like a fish out of water, like a square peg in a round hole, like chalk and cheese
F₃ compatible, complementary, going well together

incompetence *n*
incapability, inability, unfitness, unsuitability, stupidity, uselessness, ineptitude, ineptness, ineffectiveness, inefficiency, inadequacy, insufficiency, bungling, *formal* ineffectuality, ineffectualness
F₃ competence

incompetent *adj*
incapable, unable, unfit, unqualified, unsuitable, inefficient, inexpert, amateurish, unskilful, bungling, awkward, clumsy, fumbling, stupid, useless, botched, ineffective, inadequate, insufficient, deficient
F₃ competent, able

incomplete *adj*
deficient, lacking, short, unfinished, unaccomplished, undeveloped, abridged, shortened, partial, part, fragmentary, broken, scrappy, piecemeal, imperfect, defective, *formal* wanting
F₃ complete, accomplished, exhaustive, total

incomprehensible *adj*
unintelligible, unreadable, impenetrable, unfathomable, complex, complicated, involved, above your head, puzzling, perplexing, baffling, deep, profound,

enigmatic, mysterious, inscrutable, obscure, opaque, *formal* abstruse, recondite
⧉ comprehensible, intelligible

inconceivable *adj*
unthinkable, unimaginable, staggering, unheard-of, impossible, unbelievable, incredible, implausible, ridiculous, ludicrous, absurd, outrageous, shocking, *colloq.* mind-boggling
⧉ conceivable, imaginable, not on

inconclusive *adj*
unsettled, undecided, indefinite, open, open to question, uncertain, indecisive, ambiguous, vague, unconvincing, unsatisfying, *formal* indeterminate, *colloq.* up in the air, left hanging
⧉ conclusive, *colloq.* open-and-shut

incongruity *n*
inappropriateness, unsuitability, inconsistency, incompatibility, conflict, clash, irreconcilability, contradiction, discrepancy, inharmoniousness, inaptness, *formal* disparity, dissociability, dissociableness
⧉ consistency, harmoniousness

incongruous *adj*
inappropriate, unsuitable, out of place, out of keeping, inconsistent, conflicting, clashing, jarring, incompatible, irreconcilable, contradictory, contrary, at odds, odd, absurd, strange
⧉ consistent, compatible

inconsequential *adj*
minor, trivial, trifling, petty, unimportant, insignificant, negligible, immaterial, inappreciable
⧉ important, significant

inconsiderable *adj*
small, slight, negligible, trivial, petty, trifling, minor, unimportant, insignificant, negligible
⧉ considerable, large

inconsiderate *adj*
unkind, uncaring, unconcerned, uncharitable, selfish, self-centred, egotistic, intolerant, insensitive, tactless, rude, thoughtless, unthinking, careless, heedless, undiscerning
⧉ considerate, thoughtful, gracious, kind

inconsiderateness *n*
unkindness, unconcern, self-centredness, selfishness, intolerance, insensitivity, tactlessness, rudeness, thoughtlessness, carelessness
⧉ considerateness, thoughtfulness, kindness

inconsistency *n*
1 CONFLICT, variance, odds, contradiction, irreconcilability, incompatibility, discrepancy, disagreement, divergence, paradox, *formal* contrariety, disparity, incongruity **2** CHANGEABLENESS, unpredictability, instability, unsteadiness, unreliability, fickleness, inconstancy
⧉ **1, 2** consistency **2** constancy

inconsistent *adj*
1 CONFLICTING, at variance, at odds, out of place/ keeping, in opposition, incompatible, contradictory, contrary, differing, discordant, irreconcilable, *formal* incongruous **2** CHANGEABLE, variable, irregular, erratic, unpredictable, varying, unstable, unsteady, inconstant, fickle, capricious, mercurial
⧉ **1, 2** consistent **2** constant

inconsolable *adj*
heartbroken, brokenhearted, devastated, desolate, despairing, wretched, miserable, grief-stricken, *formal* disconsolate

inconspicuous *adj*
unobtrusive, plain, ordinary, indistinct, unremarkable, undistinguished, discreet, low-key, hidden,

concealed, camouflaged, modest, unassuming, quiet, retiring, insignificant, in the background
⧉ conspicuous, noticeable, obtrusive

inconstant *adj*
changeable, variable, varying, changeful, erratic, mutable, unsteady, fluctuating, inconsistent, unsettled, unstable, volatile, wavering, uncertain, undependable, unreliable, unfaithful, irresolute, capricious, mercurial, wayward, fickle, *formal* vacillating
⧉ constant

incontestable *adj*
incontrovertible, indisputable, undeniable, unquestionable, certain, obvious, clear, evident, self-evident, sure, *formal* indubitable, irrefutable
⧉ uncertain

incontinent *adj*
uncontrollable, uncontrolled, ungovernable, ungoverned, unrestrained, unbridled, unchecked, loose, promiscuous, unchaste, dissipated, dissolute, debauched, lewd, licentious, lascivious, lecherous, lustful, wanton
⧉ continent

incontrovertible *adj*
indisputable, unquestionable, beyond question, beyond doubt, undeniable, beyond doubt, certain, clear, self-evident, *formal* irrefutable, indubitable
⧉ questionable, uncertain

inconvenience *n, v*
▸ *n* awkwardness, difficulty, problem, unsuitability, inappropriateness, annoyance, worry, vexation, nuisance, hindrance, drawback, bother, trouble, fuss, upset, nuisance, disturbance, disruption, disadvantage, burden, *colloq.* drag, pain, bore, bind, headache, turn-off
⧉ convenience
▸ *v* bother, disturb, disrupt, put out, trouble, upset, irk, annoy, worry, fuss, burden, impose upon, *formal* discommode
⧉ convenience

inconvenient *adj*
awkward, ill-timed, untimely, inopportune, unseasonable, unsuitable, inappropriate, inexpedient, difficult, embarrassing, annoying, troublesome, bothersome, unwieldy, unmanageable, cumbersome
⧉ convenient, suitable, handy

incorporate *v*
include, embody, contain, take in, absorb, assimilate, integrate, combine, amalgamate, unite, unify, merge, blend, mix, fuse, coalesce, consolidate, *formal* subsume, embrace
⧉ separate

incorporation *n*
inclusion, absorption, embodiment, assimilation, integration, combination, amalgamation, unification, unifying, blend, fusion, coalescence, association, company, merger, society, federation, *formal* subsuming
⧉ separation, splitting off

incorporeal *adj*
bodiless, unfleshy, spiritual, unreal, illusory, intangible, ethereal, spectral, phantasmal, phantasmic, ghostly
⧉ real, fleshy

incorrect *adj*
wrong, not right, mistaken, erroneous, inaccurate, imprecise, inexact, false, untrue, faulty, ungrammatical, improper, illegitimate, inappropriate, unsuitable, *formal* fallacious, *colloq.* (way) off beam
⧉ correct, accurate

incorrectness *n*
wrongness, mistakenness, erroneousness, error, in-

accuracy, imprecision, inexactitude, falseness, faultiness, impreciseness, inexactness, speciousness, unsoundness, unsuitability, *formal* fallacy
🖪 correctness, accuracy

incorrigible *adj*
irredeemable, incurable, inveterate, hardened, hopeless, beyond, hope, beyond redemption, dyed-in-the-wool
🖪 redeemable

incorruptibility *n*
honesty, honour, integrity, uprightness, virtue, morality, trustworthiness, justness, nobility, *formal* probity
🖪 corruptibility

incorruptible *adj*
honest, straight, upright, virtuous, moral, ethical, honourable, high-principled, trustworthy, unbribable, just
🖪 corruptible, dishonest

increase *v, n*
▶ *v* **1** *the number of tourists has increased* become greater, go up, be on the increase, climb, rise, mount, soar, improve, advance, progress, grow, develop, build up, intensify, strengthen, heighten, extend, expand, spread, swell, multiply, proliferate, escalate, mushroom, snowball, rocket, skyrocket, spiral, *colloq.* go through the roof **2** *increase the public's awareness* raise, boost, add to, improve, enhance, advance, further, step up, intensify, strengthen, heighten, develop, build up, accumulate, enlarge, magnify, broaden, widen, deepen, extend, prolong, expand, spread, breed, propagate, scale up, *formal* augment, *colloq.* hike up, bump up, bring to a head, bring to the boil
🖪 **1** decline, fall **1, 2** decrease, reduce
▶ *n* rise, growth, surge, upsurge, upturn, gain, boost, addition, increment, advance, step-up, build-up, intensification, heightening, development, enlargement, extension, expansion, spread, proliferation, escalation, mushrooming, snowballing, rocketing, *formal* augmentation, *colloq.* hike
🖪 decrease, reduction, decline

increasingly *adv*
more and more, all the more, more so, to an increasing degree/extent, progressively, cumulatively

incredible *adj*
1 *give some incredible excuse* unbelievable, improbable, implausible, far-fetched, preposterous, absurd, impossible, inconceivable, beyond/past belief, unthinkable, unimaginable **2** *walk an incredible distance* extraordinary, amazing, surprising, astonishing, astounding, fantastic, remarkable, exceptional, marvellous, wonderful, great
🖪 **1** credible, believable

📝 **incredible** or **incredulous** ?

Incredible means 'unbelievable'; *incredulous* means 'not believing, showing disbelief'. If you are told an *incredible* story, you may be *incredulous*.

---

incredulity *n*
unbelief, disbelief, scepticism, cynicism, suspicion, doubt, distrust, mistrust
🖪 credulity

incredulous *adj*
unbelieving, disbelieving, unconvinced, sceptical, cynical, suspicious, doubting, distrusting, distrustful, suspicious, dubious, doubtful, uncertain
🖪 credulous

increment *n*
increase, gain, addition, step-up, advancement,

extension, supplement, growth, enlargement, expansion, *formal* accretion, accrual, accrument, addendum, augmentation
🖪 decrease

incriminate *v*
implicate, involve, accuse, charge, impeach, blame, put the blame on, *technical* indict, arraign, *formal* inculpate, *colloq.* point the finger at
🖪 exonerate

inculcate *v*
instil, drum into, hammer into, din into, drill into, implant, fix, imprint, engrain, impress, infuse, teach, indoctrinate

inculpate *v*
blame, put the blame on, censure, accuse, charge, impeach, incriminate, involve, implicate, recriminate, *technical* indict, arraign
🖪 exonerate

incumbent *adj, n*
▶ *adj* binding, necessary, obligatory, compulsory, prescribed, up to, *formal* mandatory
▶ *n* office-holder, office-bearer, official, officer, functionary, member

incur *v*
sustain, suffer, provoke, arouse, bring upon yourself, lay yourself open to, expose yourself to, experience, arouse, meet with, run up, gain, earn

incurable *adj*
1 *an incurable disease* TERMINAL, fatal, untreatable, unhealable, inoperable, hopeless **2** INCORRIGIBLE, inveterate, hardened, hopeless, beyond hope, beyond redemption, dyed-in-the-wool
🖪 **1** curable

incursion *n*
raid, attack, assault, invasion, onslaught, foray, sortie, sally, infiltration, inroads, penetration, *formal* irruption

indebted *adj*
obliged, grateful, thankful, appreciative, *formal* beholden

indecency *n*
immodesty, impurity, obscenity, pornography, lewdness, licentiousness, vulgarity, coarseness, crudity, foulness, grossness, offensiveness, *formal* indecorum
🖪 decency, modesty

indecent *adj*
1 IMPURE, immodest, improper, indelicate, suggestive, offensive, obscene, pornographic, lewd, immoral, corrupt, perverted, depraved, degenerate, licentious, vulgar, coarse, crude, dirty, filthy, smutty, foul, gross, bawdy, ribald, risqué, outrageous, shocking **2** *indecent haste* improper, unbecoming, unsuitable, inappropriate, *formal* unseemly, indecorous
🖪 **1** decent, modest

indecipherable *adj*
indistinguishable, unreadable, illegible, unintelligible, indistinct, unclear, tiny, crabbed, cramped
🖪 readable

indecision *n*
indecisiveness, irresolution, wavering, fluctuation, hesitation, hesitancy, ambivalence, uncertainty, tentativeness, doubt, *formal* vacillation, *colloq.* shilly-shallying
🖪 decisiveness, resolution

indecisive *adj*
1 UNDECIDED, irresolute, undetermined, fluctuating, wavering, ambivalent, hesitating, hesitant, faltering, tentative, uncertain, unsure, indefinite, doubtful, *formal* vacillating, *colloq.* in two minds, weak-willed,

pussyfooting, shilly-shallying, wishy-washy, blowing hot and cold, chopping and changing, sitting on the fence **2** INCONCLUSIVE, indefinite, unclear, open, undecided, unsettled, *formal* indeterminate, *colloq.* up in the air, hanging in the balance
🔁 **1, 2** decisive **2** *colloq.* open-and-shut

indecorous *adj*
undignified, improper, immodest, indecent, rough, impolite, rude, vulgar, in bad taste, tasteless, uncouth, unsuitable, inappropriate, coarse, crude, uncivil, unmannerly, ungentlemanly, unladylike, ill-mannered, ill-bred, boorish, churlish, *formal* unseemly, untoward
🔁 decorous

indecorum *n*
immodesty, indecency, roughness, rudeness, impoliteness, uncivility, tastelessness, bad taste, coarseness, crudity, vulgarity, *formal* impropriety, unseemliness

indeed *adv*
really, actually, in fact, in truth, certainly, absolutely, positively, truly, undeniably, undoubtedly, without doubt, doubtlessly, for sure, to be sure, *formal* nay

indefatigable *adj*
untiring, tireless, untireable, unflagging, unfailing, unwearied, unwearying, unwearieable, unresting, relentless, unremitting, dogged, inexhaustible, diligent, patient, persevering, indomitable, undying
🔁 flagging, slothful

indefensible *adj*
1 UNJUSTIFIABLE, inexcusable, unforgivable, unpardonable, insupportable, untenable, wrong, faulty, flawed, specious **2** *an indefensible place* vulnerable, exposed, defenceless, unshielded, unarmed, disarmed, unprotected, unguarded, ill-equipped, *formal* unfortified
🔁 **1, 2** defensible **1** excusable **2** protected, guarded

indefinable *adj*
indescribable, inexpressible, indistinct, unrealized, nameless, obscure, unclear, vague, subtle, dim, hazy, impalpable
🔁 definable

indefinite *adj*
unknown, uncertain, unsettled, unresolved, inconclusive, undecided, undetermined, unfixed, undefined, unspecified, unlimited, ill-defined, vague, indistinct, unclear, blurred, confused, hazy, fuzzy, obscure, ambivalent, equivocal, ambiguous, doubtful, imprecise, inexact, loose, general, nondescript, *formal* indeterminate, *colloq.* the jury is still out on
🔁 definite, limited, clear

indefinitely *adv*
for ever, eternally, endlessly, without limit, continually, ad infinitum

indelible *adj*
lasting, enduring, permanent, fast, unfading, ineffaceable, ineradicable, ingrained, imperishable, indestructible
🔁 erasable

indelicacy *n*
immodesty, indecency, obscenity, rudeness, vulgarity, offensiveness, suggestiveness, tastelessness, bad taste, coarseness, crudity, grossness, smuttiness, *formal* impropriety
🔁 delicacy

indelicate *adj*
rude, embarrassing, suggestive, immodest, improper, indecent, offensive, tasteless, in bad taste, unbecoming, vulgar, coarse, crude, gross, low, obscene, risqué, *formal* indecorous, unseemly, untoward, *colloq.* blue, off-colour
🔁 delicate

indemnify *v*
protect, secure, underwrite, guarantee, insure, endorse, exempt, free, reimburse, compensate, repair, repay, requite, satisfy, pay, remunerate

indemnity *n*
compensation, reimbursement, remuneration, repayment, restitution, requital, redress, reparation, insurance, assurance, guarantee, security, protection, safeguard, immunity, exemption, amnesty

indent *v*
1 CUT, mark, nick, notch, dent, dint, pink, serrate, scallop **2** ORDER, ask for, request, demand, *formal* requisition

indentation *n*
notch, nick, cut, serration, dent, groove, furrow, depression, dip, hollow, pit, dimple

indenture *n*
contract, agreement, certificate, deed, bond, covenant, commitment, deal, settlement

independence *n*
autonomy, self-government, self-determination, self-rule, home rule, sovereignty, freedom, liberty, individualism, separation, self-sufficiency, self-reliance, *technical* autarky
🔁 dependence

independent *adj*
1 AUTONOMOUS, self-governing, self-determining, self-ruling, self-legislating, sovereign, absolute, non-aligned, neutral, impartial, unbiased, *technical* autarkic, *formal* autarchic **2** FREE, free-thinking, liberated, unconstrained, unrestrained, freelance, individualistic, individualist, unconventional, self-sufficient, self-supporting, self-reliant, unaided, *colloq.* standing on your own two feet, doing your own thing, with a mind of your own, going your own way, doing something off your own bat, paddling your own canoe **3** SEPARATE, self-contained, individual, unconnected, unattached, unrelated, free-standing, distinct
🔁 **1** dependent

independently *adv*
alone, by yourself, on your own, individually, separately, solo, unaided, autonomously, *colloq.* under your own steam, on your tod
🔁 together

indescribable *adj*
inexpressible, indefinable, unutterable, unspeakable, incredible, extraordinary, exceptional, amazing, *formal* ineffable
🔁 describable

indestructible *adj*
unbreakable, durable, tough, strong, lasting, enduring, abiding, permanent, eternal, everlasting, immortal, endless, undecaying, inextinguishable, imperishable, *formal* infrangible
🔁 breakable, mortal

indeterminate *adj*
indefinite, unspecified, unstated, undefined, unknown, unfixed, imprecise, inexact, unclear, vague, hazy, ill-defined, open-ended, undecided, undetermined, unpredictable, uncertain, ambiguous, equivocal, ambivalent
🔁 known, specified, fixed

index *n*
1 *an index of names* table, key, list, catalogue, directory, guide **2** INDICATOR, pointer, needle, hand, sign, token, mark, indication, hint, clue, symptom

indicate *v*
1 *shrugging shoulders indicates a lack of care* show, reveal, display, mark, signify, mean, express, tell, make known, display, suggest, imply, represent, be sympto-

matic of, *formal* manifest, evince, denote **2** *indicate the way to someone* point out, show, point to, designate, specify **3** *the gauge indicates temperature* show, register, record, read

indicated *adj*
needed, required, suggested, desirable, necessary, called-for, advisable, recommended

indication *n*
sign, mark, evidence, symptom, signal, record, register, warning, omen, intimation, suggestion, hint, clue, note, explanation, *formal* manifestation, augury, portent

indicative *adj*
symptomatic, suggestive, demonstrative, characteristic, typical, significant, symbolic, *formal* denotative, exhibitive, indicatory, indicant

indicator *n*
pointer, needle, marker, hand, index, sign, symbol, token, signal, display, dial, gauge, meter, index, guide, mark, signpost, *US* turn signal

indict *v*
charge, accuse, impeach, summon, summons, prosecute, put on trial, incriminate, *technical* arraign, *formal* inculpate
F3 absolve, *formal* exonerate

indictment *n*
charge, accusation, impeachment, allegation, recrimination, summons, prosecution, incrimination, *technical* arraignment, *formal* inculpation
F3 exoneration

indifference *n*
apathy, unconcern, lack of concern, lack of interest, lack of feeling, coldness, coolness, inattention, disregard, heedlessness, negligence, impassivity, nonchalance, neutrality, disinterestedness
F3 interest, concern

indifferent *adj*
1 UNINTERESTED, unenthusiastic, unexcited, apathetic, unconcerned, unmoved, unresponsive, unfeeling, unemotional, uncaring, unsympathetic, blasé, callous, cold, cool, distant, aloof, detached, dispassionate, uninvolved, impassive, neutral, nonchalant, disinterested, careless, heedless, *colloq.* easy, all the same to you **2** MEDIOCRE, average, middling, passable, moderate, fair, adequate, undistinguished, ordinary, medium, bad, not good, *colloq.* OK, so-so, could be better/worse, run of the mill
F3 1 interested, caring **2** excellent

indigence *n*
poverty, distress, destitution, deprivation, necessity, need, want, *formal* penury, privation
F3 affluence

indigenous *adj*
native, aboriginal, original, local, home-grown, *formal* autochthonous
F3 foreign

indigent *adj*
poverty-stricken, impoverished, poor, destitute, needy, penniless, in dire straits, in want, in need, *formal* penurious, impecunious, necessitous, *colloq.* down and out, bust, skint, broke, stony-broke, cleaned out, on your uppers, on your beam ends, not having two pennies to rub together
F3 affluent

indigestion *n*
dyspepsia, dyspepsy, heartburn, cardialgia, acidity, pyrosis, water-brash

indignant *adj*
annoyed, angry, irate, heated, fuming, livid, furious, incensed, infuriated, enraged, exasperated, outraged, riled, disgruntled, wrathful, *colloq.* mad, up in arms, peeved, miffed, narked, got the hump, in a huff
F3 pleased, delighted

indignation *n*
annoyance, anger, ire, wrath, rage, fury, exasperation, outrage, pique, scorn, contempt
F3 pleasure, delight

indignity *n*
humiliation, abuse, insult, slight, snub, affront, contempt, mistreatment, offence, disgrace, outrage, reproach, dishonour, disrespect, incivility, injury, *formal* contumely, obloquy, opprobrium, *colloq.* slap in the face, kick in the teeth, cold shoulder, putdown
F3 honour

indirect *adj*
1 ROUNDABOUT, circuitous, divergent, devious, oblique, wandering, rambling, curving, winding, meandering, zigzag, tortuous, discursive, *formal* periphrastic, circumlocutory **2** *an indirect effect* secondary, incidental, unintended, subordinate, subsidiary, ancillary
F3 1 direct **2** primary

indirectly *adv*
roundaboutly, obliquely, second-hand, deviously, in a roundabout way, hintingly, *formal* periphrastically, circumlocutorily
F3 directly

indiscernible *adj*
imperceptible, minuscule, minute, microscopic, tiny, undiscernible, undetectable, unapparent, indistinct, unclear, indistinct, obscure, indistinguishable, invisible, hidden, impalpable
F3 clear, apparent

indiscreet *adj*
tactless, undiplomatic, insensitive, unwise, ill-advised, ill-judged, ill-considered, foolish, foolhardy, rash, reckless, hasty, careless, heedless, unthinking, unwary, immodest, indelicate, shameless, *formal* impolitic, injudicious, imprudent
F3 discreet, cautious

indiscretion *n*
mistake, error, slip, *faux pas*, gaffe, blunder, lapse, tactlessness, rashness, recklessness, foolishness, folly, carelessness, immodesty, indelicacy, shamelessness, *formal* imprudence, *colloq.* boob, slip-up
F3 caution, diplomacy, etiquette

indiscriminate *adj*
general, sweeping, wholesale, random, haphazard, hit or miss, hit and miss, aimless, careless, confused, chaotic, unsystematic, unmethodical, unselective, undifferentiating, undiscriminating, mixed, varied, diverse, motley, miscellaneous
F3 selective, specific, precise

indiscriminately *adv*
generally, wholesale, haphazardly, randomly, unselectively, aimlessly, carelessly, unsystematically, unmethodically, without fear or favour, in the mass
F3 deliberately, selectively

indispensable *adj*
vital, essential, absolutely, essential, basic, fundamental, important, key, crucial, imperative, required, requisite, needed, necessary, needful
F3 dispensable, unnecessary

indisposed *adj*
1 ILL, sick, unwell, poorly, ailing, confined to bed, laid up, *formal* incapacitated, *colloq.* groggy, under the weather, out of sorts, like death warmed up **2** RELUCTANT, unwilling, not willing, not of a mind (to), disinclined, averse, loath
F3 1 well **2** inclined

indisposition *n*
1 ILLNESS, ailment, disease, complaint, disorder, sickness, ill health, bad health, *formal* malady **2** RELUCTANCE, unwillingness, hesitancy, disinclination, aversion, dislike, distaste
F∃ 1 health 2 inclination

indisputable *adj*
incontrovertible, unquestionable, undeniable, incontestable, absolute, undisputed, definite, positive, certain, sure, beyond question, *formal* indubitable, irrefutable
F∃ doubtful, uncertain

indissoluble *adj*
indestructible, permanent, inseparable, imperishable, incorruptible, enduring, lasting, eternal, fixed, inviolable, abiding, binding, solid, unbreakable, *formal* sempiternal
F∃ impermanent, short-lived

indistinct *adj*
unclear, ill-defined, out of focus, blurred, fuzzy, misty, hazy, shadowy, obscure, dim, pale, faded, faint, low, muted, muffled, muttered, confused, unintelligible, indistinguishable, indecipherable, vague, woolly, ambiguous, indefinite, undefined
F∃ distinct, clear, in focus

indistinguishable *adj*
identical, interchangeable, same, twin, alike, hard to make out the difference, cloned, tantamount, *colloq.* like as two peas in a pod
F∃ distinguishable, unalike, different, dissimilar

individual *n, adj*
▶ *n* person, being, human being, creature, party, body, soul, mortal, type, sort, character, fellow
▶ *adj* distinctive, characteristic, typical, idiosyncratic, peculiar, unique, exclusive, original, special, personal, own, lone, solitary, isolated, proper, respective, several, separate, distinct, specific, personalized, particular, single, sole, private, *formal* singular
F∃ collective, shared, general

individualism *n*
independence, originality, self-direction, freethinking, self-interest, self-reliance, freethought, eccentricity, egocentricity, egoism, anarchism, libertarianism
F∃ conventionality

individualist *n*
independent, freethinker, free spirit, egoist, egocentric, nonconformist, original, bohemian, eccentric, maverick, loner, lone wolf, libertarian, anarchist
F∃ conventionalist

individualistic *adj*
independent, individual, non-conformist, unorthodox, eccentric, bohemian, original, self-reliant, unconventional, egocentric, egoistic, idiosyncratic, special, typical, unique, particular, libertarian, anarchistic
F∃ conventional

individuality *n*
character, personality, distinctiveness, peculiarity, uniqueness, originality, separateness, distinction, *formal* singularity
F∃ sameness

individually *adv*
separately, singly, one by one, independently, particularly, *formal* severally
F∃ together

indivisible *adj*
inseparable, undividable, indissoluble, impartible, *formal* indiscerptible
F∃ divisible

indoctrinate *v*
brainwash, propagandize, teach, instruct, school, ground, train, drill, impress, inculcate, instil

indoctrination *n*
brainwashing, instruction, schooling, training, teaching, grounding, inculcation, drilling, instilling, *formal* catechesis, catechetics

indolence *n*
idleness, laziness, inactivity, inertia, inertness, lethargy, heaviness, listlessness, do-nothingism, apathy, slacking, sloth, sluggishness, *formal* languidness, languor, torpidity, torpidness, torpitude, torpor, *colloq.* shirking
F∃ activeness, enthusiasm, industriousness

indolent *adj*
idle, lazy, inactive, inert, lethargic, listless, shiftless, do-nothing, apathetic, slack, slow, sluggish, slothful, sluggard, lackadaisical, lumpish, *formal* fainéant, languid, torpid
F∃ active, enthusiastic, industrious

indomitable *adj*
invincible, unconquerable, unbeatable, undefeatable, impregnable, unassailable, brave, courageous, fearless, valiant, bold, intrepid, stalwart, lionhearted, resolute, staunch, firm, intransigent, determined, steadfast, undaunted, unflinching, unyielding
F∃ compliant, timid, submissive

indubitable *adj*
indisputable, beyond dispute, unanswerable, undeniable, beyond doubt, undoubted, undoubtable, unquestionable, unarguable, incontestable, incontrovertible, sure, absolute, certain, obvious, evident, *formal* irrefutable, irrebuttable, irrefragable
F∃ arguable

induce *v*
1 CAUSE, bring about, occasion, give rise to, lead to, set in motion, incite, instigate, originate, prompt, provoke, produce, generate, *formal* effect **2** COAX, prevail upon, encourage, press, persuade, talk into, move, influence, draw, tempt, inspire, motivate, urge, actuate, impel
F∃ 2 discourage, deter

inducement *n*
lure, bait, attraction, enticement, encouragement, incentive, impetus, incitement, influence, reward, spur, goad, stimulus, motive, reason, *colloq.* carrot, sweetener
F∃ disincentive

induct *v*
inaugurate, initiate, install, invest, ordain, introduce, consecrate, enthrone, swear in

induction *n*
1 INAUGURATION, initiation, installation, institution, investiture, ordination, introduction, enthronement, consecration **2** INFERENCE, conclusion, deduction, generalization

indulge *v*
1 GRATIFY, satisfy, humour, pander to, go along with, give in to, yield to, give way to, cater to, favour, pet, cosset, mollycoddle, pamper, spoil, treat, regale **2** *indulge in something* give way to, give free rein to, give yourself up to, revel in, wallow in, luxuriate in

indulgence *n*
1 EXTRAVAGANCE, luxury, treat, excess, gratification, satisfaction, fulfilment, immoderation, intemperance, dissipation, dissoluteness **2** FAVOUR, tolerance, generosity, lenience, pardon, remission
F∃ 1 restraint

indulgent *adj*
tolerant, lenient, permissive, generous, forgiving,

merciful, compassionate, sympathetic, humane, liberal, kind, fond, tender, understanding, patient, pampering, humouring, spoiling, cosseting, mollycoddling, *formal* forbearing, *colloq.* easy-going
⊟ strict, harsh

industrial *adj*
manufacturing, commercial, business, trade

industrialist *n*
manufacturer, producer, magnate, tycoon, baron, captain of industry, capitalist, financier

industrious *adj*
busy, productive, hard-working, hard, diligent, assiduous, conscientious, laborious, steady, dedicated, studious, zealous, active, energetic, tireless, indefatigable, persistent, persevering, determined, dogged, vigorous, *formal* sedulous, *colloq.* busy as a bee, on the go, slogging your guts out
⊟ lazy, idle

industriously *adv*
diligently, conscientiously, assiduously, steadily, hard, perseveringly, doggedly, sedulously, *colloq.* with your nose to the grindstone
⊟ lazily

industry *n*
1 *the steel industry* business, trade, commerce, manufacturing, production, service, enterprise, line, field
2 INDUSTRIOUSNESS, diligence, conscientiousness, assiduousness, assiduity, application, intentness, concentration, effort, labour, laboriousness, toil, persistence, hard work, zeal, energy, vigour, activity, perseverance, steadiness, determination, productiveness, tirelessness, *formal* sedulity, sedulousness, *colloq.* stickability

inebriated *adj*
under the influence, drunk, drunken, *formal* intoxicated, crapulant, *colloq.* merry, tight, tipsy, tiddly, well-oiled, blotto, drunk as a lord/newt, blind drunk, roaring drunk, the worse for drink, soused, squiffy, happy, legless, plastered, sozzled, pickled, bibulous, woozy, one over the eight, under the table, bevvied, have had a few, *slang* stoned, tanked up, loaded, lit up, canned, paralytic, sloshed, smashed, stewed, bombed, wasted, wrecked
⊟ sober, temperate, abstinent, teetotal

inedible *adj*
uneatable, unpalatable, stale, indigestible, not fit to eat, unconsumable, rotten, off, bad, rancid, harmful, noxious, poisonous, deadly
⊟ edible, wholesome

ineducable *adj*
unteachable, incorrigible, indocile
⊟ educable

ineffable *adj*
indescribable, inexpressible, unspeakable, unutterable, beyond words, incommunicable, unimpartible
⊟ describable

ineffective *adj*
1 *an ineffective attempt* useless, worthless, vain, idle, futile, unavailing, to no avail, abortive, profitless, fruitless, unproductive, unsuccessful, *formal* ineffectual 2 POWERLESS, impotent, inadequate, weak, feeble, inept, idle, lame, incompetent
⊟ 1, 2 effective

ineffectual *adj*
1 *ineffectual methods* useless, vain, futile, worthless, fruitless, unproductive, unavailing, abortive, *formal* inefficacious 2 *an ineffectual person* weak, feeble, powerless, inadequate, incompetent, impotent, inept, lame
⊟ 1, 2 effectual

inefficacy *n*
ineffectiveness, unproductiveness, uselessness, futility, inadequacy, *formal* ineffectuality, ineffectualness
⊟ efficacy

inefficiency *n*
waste, wastefulness, disorganization, carelessness, negligence, slackness, laxity, ineptitude, sloppiness, incompetence, muddle
⊟ efficiency

inefficient *adj*
uneconomic, wasteful, money-wasting, incompetent, time-wasting, ineffective, inexpert, unworkmanlike, slipshod, sloppy, slack, lax, inept, careless, disorganized, unorganized, negligent
⊟ efficient

inelegant *adj*
graceless, ungraceful, clumsy, awkward, gauche, ungainly, laboured, ugly, unrefined, ill-bred, crude, vulgar, unpolished, rough, unsophisticated, uncultured, uncultivated, unfinished, uncouth
⊟ elegant

ineligible *adj*
disqualified, ruled out, unacceptable, undesirable, unworthy, unsuitable, unfit, unfitted, unqualified, unequipped, *technical* incompetent
⊟ eligible

inept *adj*
awkward, clumsy, bungling, heavy-handed, incompetent, incapable, inadequate, unskilful, inexpert, unsuccessful, foolish, stupid, useless, appalling, *formal* maladroit, *colloq.* pathetic, cack-handed, lousy, ham-fisted
⊟ competent, skilful

ineptitude *n*
ineptness, awkwardness, clumsiness, bungling, unhandiness, gaucheness, gaucherie, incompetence, incapability, unskilfulness, inexpertness, stupidity, unfitness, uselessness, crassness, *formal* fatuity, incapacity
⊟ aptitude, skill

inequality *n*
unequalness, imbalance, difference, discrepancy, contrast, variation, diversity, dissimilarity, nonconformity, unevenness, roughness, irregularity, disproportion, bias, prejudice, discrimination, *formal* disparity
⊟ equality, balance

inequitable *adj*
unfair, unjust, unequal, wrongful, one-sided, biased, prejudiced, discriminatory, bigoted, intolerant, partisan, partial, preferential
⊟ equitable

inequity *n*
unfairness, unjustness, injustice, maltreatment, mistreatment, abuse, inequality, wrongfulness, onesidedness, prejudice, bias, discrimination, partiality
⊟ equity

inert *adj*
1 IMMOBILE, motionless, unmoving, still, stock-still, inactive, static, stationary, inanimate, lifeless, dead, passive, cold, unresponsive, *formal* comatose 2 SLUGGISH, lethargic, lazy, inactive, slack, listless, dull, apathetic, idle, dormant, stagnant, torpid, sleepy, *formal* indolent
⊟ 1 moving 2 lively, animated

inertia *n*
immobility, motionlessness, stillness, stagnation, inactivity, inaction, passivity, unresponsiveness, apathy, idleness, laziness, sloth, slothfulness, lethargy, listlessness, *formal* indolence, languor, torpor
⊟ activity, liveliness

inescapable *adj*
inevitable, unavoidable, destined, fated, certain, sure, assured, irrevocable, unalterable, inexorable, *formal* ineluctable
F3 escapable, preventable

inessential *adj, n*
▶ *adj* unnecessary, irrelevant, superfluous, surplus, redundant, non-essential, needless, unasked-for, uncalled-for, unimportant, secondary, spare, accidental, unessential, dispensable, expendable, extraneous, optional, extrinsic
F3 essential, necessary
▶ *n* non-essential, extra, extravagance, luxury, superfluity, accessory, trimming, appendage
F3 essential

inestimable *adj*
incalculable, measureless, infinite, immeasurable, invaluable, precious, priceless, unlimited, uncountable, unfathomable, incomputable, immense, vast, untold, *formal* prodigious, *colloq.* mind-boggling, worth a fortune
F3 insignificant

inevitable *adj*
unavoidable, inescapable, necessary, definite, certain, sure, decreed, ordained, destined, fated, automatic, assured, fixed, settled, unalterable, irrevocable, inexorable, unpreventable, *formal* predestined, ineluctable
F3 avoidable, uncertain, alterable

inevitably *adv*
unavoidably, inescapably, irrevocably, inexorably, necessarily, definitely, certainly, surely, automatically, assuredly
F3 avoidably

inexact *adj*
imprecise, approximate, inaccurate, incorrect, erroneous, indefinite, indistinct, fuzzy, loose, woolly, lax, muddled, *formal* indeterminate, fallacious
F3 exact, accurate

inexactitude *n*
inexactness, impreciseness, imprecision, inaccuracy, incorrectness, indefiniteness, approximation, miscalculation, woolliness, looseness, mistake, blunder, error
F3 exactitude, accuracy

inexcusable *adj*
indefensible, unforgivable, unpardonable, unjustifiable, intolerable, unacceptable, outrageous, shameful, blameworthy, *formal* reprehensible
F3 excusable, justifiable

inexhaustible *adj*
1 *an inexhaustible supply* UNLIMITED, limitless, boundless, unbounded, unrestricted, measureless, infinite, endless, never-ending, abundant, *formal* illimitable **2** INDEFATIGABLE, tireless, untiring, unflagging, unfailing, unwearied, unwearying, weariless
F3 **1** limited

inexorable *adj*
relentless, unrelenting, remorseless, unalterable, inevitable, unpreventable, unavertable, irresistible, irrevocable, inescapable, immovable, unyielding, unceasing, incessant, unstoppable, unfaltering, ordained, destined, fated, definite, certain, sure, *formal* ineluctable
F3 avoidable, preventable

inexorably *adv*
relentlessly, remorselessly, inescapably, irresistibly, inevitably, irrevocably, definitely, certainly, surely, resistlessly, implacably, pitilessly, mercilessly, *formal* ineluctably

inexpedient *adj*
unwise, unsuitable, inappropriate, disadvantageous, misguided, detrimental, unadvisable, unfavourable, indiscreet, foolish, senseless, wrong, ill-advised, inadvisable, ill-chosen, ill-judged, inconvenient, impractical, undesirable, undiplomatic, *formal* impolitic, imprudent, injudicious
F3 expedient

inexpensive *adj*
cheap, low-priced, low-price, reasonable, modest, bargain, budget, low-cost, cut-rate, economical, reduced, discounted
F3 expensive, dear

inexperience *n*
inexpertness, ignorance, unfamiliarity, strangeness, newness, freshness, rawness, immaturity, naïveness, innocence
F3 experience

inexperienced *adj*
inexpert, untrained, unqualified, untutored, new to the job, unskilled, amateur, probationary, apprentice, unacquainted, uninformed, ignorant, unfamiliar, unaccustomed, unseasoned, new, fresh, raw, callow, young, immature, naïve, unsophisticated, innocent, *colloq.* green, wet behind the ears, out of your depth, wide-eyed
F3 experienced, mature

inexpert *adj*
unskilled, unskilful, untaught, untrained, unpractised, unworkmanlike, unprofessional, untutored, unqualified, amateur, amateurish, awkward, clumsy, unhandy, incompetent, inept, bungling, blundering, *formal* maladroit, *colloq.* cack-handed, ham, ham-fisted
F3 expert

inexplicable *adj*
incomprehensible, unexplainable, unintelligible, unaccountable, strange, mystifying, puzzling, perplexing, baffling, bewildering, mysterious, insoluble, enigmatic, weird, unfathomable, incredible, unbelievable, miraculous, *formal* abstruse
F3 explicable

inexplicably *adv*
incomprehensibly, unexplainably, incredibly, unaccountably, strangely, mysteriously, mystifyingly, bafflingly, puzzlingly, miraculously
F3 explicably

inexpressible *adj*
indescribable, undescribable, unspeakable, unutterable, incommunicable, indefinable, nameless, unsayable, untellable, *formal* ineffable

inexpressive *adj*
unexpressive, expressionless, deadpan, poker-faced, inscrutable, blank, vacant, empty, lifeless, dead, cold, emotionless, impassive
F3 expressive

inextinguishable *adj*
unquenchable, indestructible, imperishable, irrepressible, unconquerable, unquellable, unsuppressible, deathless, enduring, lasting, eternal, everlasting, undying, immortal
F3 impermanent, perishable

inextricable *adj*
inseparable, indissoluble, indivisible, indistinguishable, intricate, irretrievable, irreversible

inextricably *adv*
inseparably, indissolubly, indivisibly, indistinguishably, intricately, irresolubly, irretrievably, irreversibly

infallibility *n*
accuracy, unerringness, faultlessness, inerrancy, per-

fection, dependability, reliability, safety, supremacy, sureness, trustworthiness, impeccability, irreproachability, *formal* irrefutability, omniscience
🖅 fallibility

infallible *adj*
accurate, unerring, unfailing, foolproof, fail-safe, certain, sure, reliable, dependable, trustworthy, sound, perfect, flawless, faultless, impeccable, *colloq.* surefire
🖅 fallible

infamous *adj*
notorious, ill-famed, disreputable, disgraceful, discreditable, dishonourable, shameful, shocking, outrageous, abominable, detestable, scandalous, evil, bad, base, vile, wicked, hateful, *formal* iniquitous, ignominious, egregious, nefarious
🖅 illustrious, glorious

infamy *n*
notoriety, disrepute, disgrace, discredit, shame, dishonour, discredit, wickedness, evil, baseness, vileness, depravity, villainy, *formal* ignominy, turpitude
🖅 glory

infancy *n*
1 BABYHOOD, childhood, youth **2** BEGINNING, start, outset, birth, dawn, cradle, genesis, emergence, rise, origin(s), early stages, *formal* commencement, inception
🖅 **1** adulthood

infant *n, adj*
▶ *n* baby, toddler, child, little one, *Scot.* bairn, *formal* babe, babe in arms, *colloq.* tot
🖅 adult
▶ *adj* newborn, baby, young, youthful, juvenile, immature, beginning, growing, developing, dawning, emergent, rudimentary, early, initial, new, *formal* nascent
🖅 adult, mature

infantile *adj*
babyish, childish, puerile, juvenile, young, youthful, adolescent, immature
🖅 adult, mature

infatuated *adj*
besotted, obsessed, enamoured, in love, spellbound, bewitched, mesmerized, captivated, fascinated, enraptured, ravished, carried away, *formal* entêté(e), *colloq.* crazy, mad, daft, nuts, sweet, wild, sold, far gone, having a thing, smitten, head over heels in love
🖅 indifferent, disenchanted

infatuation *n*
besottedness, obsession, craze, fixation, mania, passion, love, fondness, fascination, *colloq.* crush, thing, pash, shine
🖅 indifference, disenchantment

infect *v*
contaminate, pollute, defile, taint, blight, mar, spoil, ulcerate, poison, corrupt, pervert, spread to, pass on, influence, affect, excite, stimulate, animate, move, touch, inspire

infection *n*
illness, disease, complaint, condition, virus, bacteria, germ, epidemic, contagion, pestilence, contamination, pollution, defilement, taint, tainting, spoiling, fouling, blight, poison, corruption, influence, *technical* sepsis, *colloq.* bug

infectious *adj*
1 *an infectious disease* contagious, communicable, transmissible, transmittable, infective, catching, spreading, epidemic, virulent, deadly, toxic, contaminating, polluting, defiling, corrupting, *technical* septic, *formal* noxious **2** *infectious laughter* contagious, compelling, irresistible, catching, spreading

infelicitous *adj*
1 INAPPROPRIATE, unfitting, unsuitable, unfortunate, inopportune, untimely, disadvantageous, *formal* incongruous **2** UNHAPPY, unfortunate, sad, miserable, sorrowful, unlucky, despairing, wretched
🖅 **1** appropriate, apt **2** happy

infer *v*
deduce, derive, extrapolate, conclude, come to a conclusion, reason, assume, presume, surmise, gather, understand, allude, *formal* conjecture, *colloq.* figure out

 infer or **imply**? *See panel at* IMPLY.

inference *n*
deduction, conclusion, consequence, assumption, presumption, construction, interpretation, reasoning, reading, *formal* extrapolation, corollary, conjecture, surmise

inferior *adj, n*
▶ *adj* **1** LOWER, lesser, minor, secondary, junior, subordinate, ancillary, subsidiary, second-class, low, lowly, humble, menial, subservient, *colloq.* not in the same league **2** *inferior work* substandard, second-rate, low-quality, mediocre, bad, poor, awful, unsatisfactory, imperfect, defective, incompetent, slipshod, shoddy, cheap, *colloq.* crummy, ropy, *slang* naff
🖅 **1** superior **2** excellent
▶ *n* subordinate, junior, underling, minion, vassal, menial
🖅 superior

inferiority *n*
1 SUBORDINATION, subservience, humbleness, lowliness, subservience, meanness, insignificance **2** MEDIOCRITY, imperfection, inadequacy, faultiness, defectiveness, low/poor/bad quality, unsatisfactoriness, slovenliness, shoddiness, incompetence
🖅 **1** superiority **2** excellence, perfection

infernal *adj*
1 HELLISH, satanic, devilish, diabolical, demonic, fiendish, accursed, damned, Hadean **2** WICKED, evil, vile, atrocious, *formal* execrable, malevolent **3** *What an infernal mess!* damned, wretched, cursed, confounded, fiendish, *colloq.* blasted, flipping, blooming, darned, dashed
🖅 **1** heavenly

infertile *adj*
barren, sterile, childless, unproductive, unfruitful, non-productive, arid, parched, dried-up, *formal* effete, unfructuous, infecund
🖅 fertile, fruitful, productive, prolific

infertility *n*
barrenness, sterility, unfruitfulness, unproductiveness, aridity, aridness, *formal* effeteness, infecundity
🖅 fertility

infest *v*
swarm, teem, crawl, bristle, throng, flood, overrun, overspread, spread through, plague, take over, beset, invade, infiltrate, penetrate, permeate, pervade, ravage

infested *adj*
swarming, teeming, crawling, bristling, beset, alive, pervaded, plagued, ravaged, ridden, overrun, overspread, infiltrated, permeated, vermined

infidel *n*
pagan, heathen, disbeliever, unbeliever, heretic, sceptic, atheist, freethinker, irreligionist, *formal* nullifidian
🖅 believer

infidelity *n*
1 ADULTERY, unfaithfulness, cheating, falseness, af-

fair, relationship, liaison, intrigue, romance, armour **2** DISLOYALTY, faithlessness, treachery, betrayal, *formal* duplicity, perfidy, *colloq.* fooling around, playing around
F3 1 fidelity **2** faithfulness

infiltrate *v*
penetrate, enter, creep into, insinuate, intrude, invade, slip, pervade, permeate, filter, percolate, seep, soak

infiltration *n*
penetration, entr(y)ism, insinuation, intrusion, pervasion, invasion, permeation, percolation, *formal* interpenetration

infiltrator *n*
penetrator, insinuator, intruder, spy, subversive, subverter, seditionary, entr(y)ist

infinite *adj*
limitless, unlimited, boundless, unbounded, endless, never-ending, interminable, inexhaustible, bottomless, fathomless, innumerable, numberless, without number, uncountable, countless, untold, incalculable, inestimable, immeasurable, unfathomable, vast, extensive, immense, enormous, huge, absolute, total, *formal* indeterminable
F3 finite, limited

> ### ⚠ **infinite** or **infinitesimal**?
> *Infinite* means 'without limits', or, loosely, 'extremely large or great': *If we follow that course of action, the dangers are infinite*; *infinitesimal* means 'infinitely small'or, loosely, 'extremely small': *Personally, I consider the dangers infinitesimal.*

infinitesimal *adj*
tiny, minute, microscopic, minuscule, inconsiderable, insignificant, trifling, negligible, inappreciable, imperceptible, *Scot.* wee, *colloq.* teeny
F3 great, large, enormous

infinity *n*
eternity, perpetuity, limitlessness, boundlessness, endlessness, inexhaustibility, countlessness, immeasurableness, extensiveness, vastness, immensity, enormousness
F3 finiteness, limitation

infirm *adj*
weak, feeble, frail, ailing, ill, unwell, poorly, sickly, decrepit, failing, faltering, unsteady, shaky, wobbly, doddery, old, lame, disabled, *formal* debilitated
F3 healthy, strong

infirmity *n*
weakness, feebleness, frailty, ailment, illness, ill health, disease, complaint, sickness, sickliness, disorder, failing, decrepitude, vulnerability, instability, dodderiness, *formal* debility, malady
F3 health, strength

inflame *v*
anger, enrage, infuriate, incense, exasperate, madden, rile, provoke, stimulate, work up, stir, excite, rouse, arouse, agitate, stir (up), whip up, foment, impassion, kindle, ignite, fire, heat, fan, fuel, increase, intensify, worsen, make worse, aggravate, *formal* exacerbate
F3 cool, quench

inflamed *adj*
sore, swollen, septic, infected, festered, poisoned, red, hot, heated, fevered, angry, feverish, flushed, reddened, glowing

inflammable *adj*
flammable, combustible, burnable, ignitable, ignitible
F3 non-flammable, incombustible, flameproof, fire-resistant, flame-resistant

inflammation *n*
soreness, painfulness, tenderness, swelling, abscess, festering, infection, redness, heat, hotness, rash, sore, irritation, eruption, *technical* empyema, erythema, sepsis, septicity

inflammatory *adj*
1 PROVOCATIVE, incendiary, explosive, fiery, rabble-rousing, rabid, riotous, seditious, insurgent, intemperate, inciting, incitative, inflaming, instigative, anarchic, demagogic **2** SORE, painful, tender, swollen, allergic, festering, septic, infected
F3 1 calming, pacific

inflate *v*
1 *inflate a life-jacket* blow up, pump up, bloat, expand, dilate, enlarge, aerate, swell, puff out, *formal* distend **2** *inflated prices* increase, raise, boost, step up, escalate, amplify, extend, intensify, *formal* augment, *colloq.* hike up, push up **3** *inflate the importance of something* exaggerate, overstate, overrate, overestimate, boost, magnify, *formal* aggrandize
F3 1 deflate **2** decrease, lower **3** understate, play down

inflated *adj*
1 BLOWN UP, swollen, puffed out, dilated, bloated, ballooned, *formal* distended, tumefied, tumid **2** INCREASED, raised, escalated, extended, intensified **3** EXAGGERATED, overblown, ostentatious, pompous, bombastic, *formal* grandiloquent, magniloquent, euphuistic
F3 deflated

inflation *n*
expansion, increase, rise, escalation, hyperinflation
F3 deflation

inflection *n*
change of tone/intonation, pitch, modulation, stress, emphasis, rhythm

inflexibility *n*
rigidity, hardness, stiffness, fixity, immovability, immutability, immutableness, inelasticity, obstinacy, stubbornness, stringency, unsuppleness, *formal* intractability, intransigence, obduracy
F3 flexibility

inflexible *adj*
an inflexible mass; *inflexible rules/people* rigid, stiff, hard, solid, set, fixed, unelastic, unsupple, fast, immovable, immutable, unchangeable, unvarying, uniform, standard, standardized, firm, rigorous, taut, strict, stringent, unbending, unbendable, unyielding, adamant, resolute, relentless, pitiless, merciless, implacable, intolerant, uncompromising, unaccommodating, stubborn, obstinate, steely, entrenched, dyed-in-the-wool, *formal* intransigent, obdurate, intractable
F3 flexible, yielding, adaptable

inflict *v*
impose, enforce, perpetrate, wreak, administer, apply, deliver, deal (out), mete out, lay, burden, exact, levy

> ### ⚠ **inflict** or **afflict**? *See panel at* AFFLICT.

infliction *n*
imposition, enforcement, perpetration, wreaking, administration, application, delivery, affliction, exaction, burden, punishment, trouble, worry, penalty, *formal* retribution, castigation, chastisement

influence *n*, *v*
▶ *n* power, sway, rule, authority, domination, dominance, supremacy, mastery, rule, hold, control, direction, guidance, bias, prejudice, pull, pressure, effect, impact, weight, importance, prestige, standing, mark, toll, *colloq.* clout, pull, whip hand, drag

▶ *v* dominate, control, manipulate, direct, guide, determine, manoeuvre, change, alter, modify, transform, affect, have an effect on, impress, move, mould, shape, stir, arouse, rouse, sway, persuade, impact on, induce, incite, instigate, prompt, impel, motivate, dispose, incline, colour, condition,. bias, prejudice, *colloq.* have clout, carry weight, pull strings, pull wires, have under your thumb, hold over a barrel, twist someone's arm, wheel and deal

influential *adj*
dominant, controlling, leading, authoritative, charismatic, persuasive, meaningful, convincing, compelling, inspiring, moving, powerful, potent, effective, telling, strong, far-reaching, prestigious, weighty, momentous, important, significant, instrumental, guiding
🖅 ineffective, unimportant

influx *n*
inflow, inrush, invasion, arrival, intrusion, stream, flow, inflow, rush, flood, inundation, *formal* ingress, incursion

inform *v*
1 TELL, advise, notify, communicate, announce, relate, impart, leak, tip off, acquaint, brief, instruct, enlighten, illuminate, *colloq.* fill in, put in the picture, clue up, put wise, wise up, keep posted, *formal* apprise **2** *inform on your friends* betray, incriminate, denounce, blab, *colloq.* tell on, shop, squeal, rat, blow the whistle on, sell down the river, split, snitch, *slang* grass **3** CHARACTERIZE, typify, mark, stamp, brand, identify, distinguish, permeate

informal *adj*
unofficial, unceremonious, casual, everyday, relaxed, easy, easygoing, free, natural, simple, unpretentious, familiar, colloquial, vernacular
🖅 formal, solemn, serious, official

informality *n*
unceremoniousness, casualness, congeniality, ease, freedom, familiarity, naturalness, relaxation, simplicity, unpretentiousness, approachability, homeliness, cosiness
🖅 formality, ceremony

informally *adj*
unofficially, unceremoniously, casually, easily, familiarly, simply, colloquially, freely, confidentially, privately, on the quiet
🖅 formally

information *n*
facts, details, particulars, data, input, intelligence, news, report, bulletin, communiqué, propaganda, message, word, advice, counsel, notice, briefing, instruction, knowledge, enlightenment, file, record, dossier, database, databank, clues, evidence, *formal* tidings, *colloq.* gen, info, low-down, dope, *slang* bumf

informative *adj*
educational, instructive, edifying, enlightening, illuminating, revealing, forthcoming, communicative, chatty, gossipy, newsy, helpful, useful, constructive
🖅 uninformative

informed *adj*
1 *we'll keep you informed* familiar, conversant, acquainted, enlightened, briefed, primed, posted, up to date, abreast, *au fait, colloq.* in the know **2** *an informed opinion* well-informed, authoritative, expert, versed, well-versed, well-read, well-briefed, erudite, learned, knowledgeable, well-researched
🖅 **1** ignorant, unaware

informer *n*
informant, betrayer, traitor, Judas, tell-tale, sneak, spy, *colloq.* mole, rat, finger, squealer, whistle-blower, snitch, *slang* grass, supergrass, stool pigeon, nark

infraction *n*
breaking, breach, violation, infringement, contravention, encroachment, *formal* transgression
🖅 observance, compliance

infrequent *adj*
exceptional, intermittent, occasional, rare, scanty, sparse, spasmodic, sporadic, uncommon, unusual, *colloq.* few and far between, like gold dust
🖅 frequent

infringe *v*
1 BREAK, violate, contravene, overstep, disobey, defy, flout, ignore, *formal* transgress **2** INTRUDE, encroach, impinge, trespass, invade

infringement *n*
1 *infringement of the rules* breach, breaking, disobedience, violation, defiance, contravention, evasion, noncompliance, non-observance, *formal* infraction, transgression **2** INTRUSION, encroachment, trespass, invasion

infuriate *v*
anger, vex, enrage, incense, exasperate, madden, inflame, provoke, rouse, annoy, irritate, rile, antagonize, *colloq.* bug, get, make someone's blood boil, rub up the wrong way, get on someone's nerves, get under someone's skin
🖅 calm, pacify

infuriated *adj*
angry, exasperated, enraged, agitated, provoked, roused, vexed, furious, incensed, irate, irritated, violent, wild, heated, beside yourself, *colloq.* flaming, maddened, peeved, miffed, narked
🖅 calm, gratified, pleased

infuriating *adj*
annoying, exasperating, irritating, unbearable, intolerable, frustrating, galling, provoking, thwarting, *formal* vexatious, *colloq.* pesky, maddening, aggravating, *US* pesky
🖅 agreeable, pleasing

infuse *v*
fill, breathe into, imbue, impart to, introduce, implant, inculcate, inspire, instil, inject, steep, soak, saturate, brew, draw

infusion *n*
implantation, inculcation, infusing, instillation, steeping, soaking, brew

ingenious *adj*
clever, shrewd, astute, adept, adroit, cunning, crafty, wily, sly, sharp, smart, skilful, masterly, bright, brilliant, imaginative, creative, inventive, resourceful, talented, gifted, original, innovative
🖅 unimaginative

✎ ingenious or **ingenuous** ?

Ingenious means 'clever, skilful' or 'cleverly made or thought out': *an ingenious plan. Ingenuous* means 'frank, trusting, not cunning or deceitful': *It was rather ingenuous of you to believe a compulsive liar like him.*

---

ingenuity *n*
ingeniousness, cleverness, shrewdness, astuteness, sharpness, skill, skilfulness, creativeness, adroitness, cunning, slyness, innovativeness, invention, inventiveness, deftness, originality, resourcefulness, genius, gift, faculty, flair, knack
🖅 clumsiness, dullness

ingenuous *adj*
artless, guileless, innocent, honest, sincere, genuine, frank, candid, open, direct, forthright, plain, simple, unsophisticated, naïve, trusting, trustful, *formal* undissembling
🖅 cunning, deceitful, artful, sly

ingenuousness *n*
artlessness, guilelessness, innocence, genuineness, honesty, openness, naïvety, trustfulness, candour, frankness, forthrightness, directness, unsophisticatedness, unreserve
🖪 deceit, cunning, slyness, artfulness, subterfuge

inglorious *adj*
shameful, disgraceful, discreditable, dishonourable, disreputable, humiliating, blameworthy, ignoble, infamous, mortifying, unsuccessful, unhonoured, unheroic, unknown, obscure, unsung, *formal* ignominious
🖪 glorious

ingrain *v*
fix, root, entrench, engrain, embed, build in, impress, imprint, imbue, implant, infix, instil, dye

ingrained *adj*
fixed, implanted, rooted, deep-rooted, deep-seated, entrenched, embedded, immovable, ineradicable, permanent, inbuilt, built-in, inborn, inbred, inherent

ingratiate *v*
curry favour, flatter, creep, crawl, grovel, fawn, get in with, toady, play up to, *colloq.* suck up to, lick someone's boots, bow and scrape, get on the right side of, get into someone's good books

ingratiating *adj*
flattering, obsequious, servile, crawling, fawning, toadying, unctuous, smooth-tongued, suave, time-serving, *formal* sycophantic, *colloq.* bootlicking

ingratitude *n*
ungratefulness, thanklessness, unappreciativeness, unthankfulness, ungraciousness
🖪 gratitude, thankfulness, appreciation

ingredient *n*
constituent, element, factor, unit, component, item, feature, part

ingress *n*
access, means of approach/entry, entrance, entry, admission, admittance, right of entry, permission to enter

inhabit *v*
live in, occupy, possess, colonize, settle, make your home in, people, populate, stay in, *formal* dwell in, reside in

inhabitant *n*
resident, citizen, native, settler, occupier, occupant, inmate, tenant, lodger, *formal* dweller, habitant

inhabited *adj*
lived-in, occupied, peopled, populated, settled, possessed, colonized, held, developed, tenanted, overrun
🖪 uninhabited

inhalation *n*
breathing, breath, inhaling, inspiration, suction, *technical* respiration, spiration

inhale *v*
breathe in, draw in, draw, suck in, inspire, whiff, *technical* respire, *formal* inbreathe

inharmonious *adj*
1 UNMELODIOUS, unharmonious, tuneless, grating, harsh, strident, clashing, jangling, jarring, discordant, raucous, cacophonous, untuneful, unmusical, atonal **2** INCOMPATIBLE, conflicting, contradictory, clashing, irreconcilable, unfriendly, unsympathetic, quarrelsome, perverse, *formal* dissonant, antipathetic, inconsonant, *colloq.* stroppy
🖪 **1, 2** harmonious

inherent *adj*
inborn, inbred, innate, inherited, hereditary, in the blood, native, natural, inbuilt, built-in, intrinsic, ingrained, essential, fundamental, basic

inherit *v*
succeed to, assume, take over, come into, be left, receive, be bequeathed, *formal* accede to

inheritance *n*
legacy, bequest, heritage, endowment, birthright, heredity, descent, succession, *formal* accession

inheritor *n*
heir, heiress, inheritress, inheritrix, successor, beneficiary, recipient, reversionary, *technical* devisee, legatee, legatary, *formal* heritor, heritress, heritrix

inhibit *v*
discourage, repress, hold back, suppress, curb, rein in, check, bridle, restrain, constrain, hinder, impede, obstruct, restrict, interfere with, frustrate, thwart, hamper, balk, prevent, stop, stanch, stem, slow down
🖪 encourage, assist

inhibited *adj*
repressed, self-conscious, shy, embarrassed, reticent, withdrawn, introverted, self-restrained, reserved, guarded, subdued, restrained, constrained, frustrated, *colloq.* uptight
🖪 uninhibited, open, relaxed

inhibition *n*
1 *lose all our inhibitions* repression, shyness, self-consciousness, reticence, reserve, *colloq.* hang-up **2** RESTRAINT, curb, check, hindrance, impediment, obstruction, restriction, interference, hampering, frustration, thwarting, bar
🖪 **1** openness **2** freedom

inhospitable *adj*
1 *an inhospitable place* uninhabitable, forbidding, bare, barren, bleak, desolate, empty, lonely, uncongenial, unfavourable, hostile, *formal* inimical **2** *an inhospitable person* unwelcoming, unfriendly, unreceptive, unsociable, antisocial, ungenerous, unkind, unneighbourly, uncivil, cold, cool, aloof, xenophobic
🖪 favourable, hospitable

inhuman *adj*
1 BARBARIC, barbarous, animal, bestial, vicious, savage, sadistic, cold-blooded, brutal, cruel, merciless, ruthless, diabolical, fiendish **2** NON-HUMAN, strange, odd, animal
🖪 **1, 2** human

✒ **inhuman** or **inhumane**?

When referring to cruel conditions, treatment, behaviour, etc, *inhuman* is stronger than *inhumane*. *Inhumane* means 'unkind, cruel, showing lack of compassion', whereas *inhuman* means 'showing such cruelty and lack of compassion to a degree almost unbelievable in a human being'.

---

inhumane *adj*
unkind, insensitive, inconsiderate, callous, unfeeling, uncaring, unsympathetic, heartless, cold-hearted, hard-hearted, pitiless, cruel, harsh
🖪 humane, kind, compassionate

inhumanity *n*
atrocity, barbarism, barbarity, savageness, brutality, brutishness, cruelty, cold-bloodedness, viciousness, pitilessness, ruthlessness, sadism, callousness, unkindness, cold-heartedness, hard-heartedness, heartlessness
🖪 humanity

inimical *adj*
hostile, adverse, antagonistic, destructive, opposed, harmful, injurious, hurtful, pernicious, intolerant, unfavourable, unfriendly, unwelcoming, inhospitable, ill-disposed, disaffected, antipathetic, contrary, *formal* noxious, repugnant
🖪 favourable, friendly, sympathetic

inimitable *adj*
unique, incomparable, matchless, unmatched, unparalleled, unrivalled, unsurpassable, unsurpassed, unequalled, peerless, consummate, sublime, superlative, supreme, distinctive, exceptional, nonpareil, unexampled

iniquitous *adj*
evil, wicked, unrighteous, immoral, unjust, sinful, accursed, atrocious, base, vicious, awful, dreadful, criminal, abominable, infamous, reprobate, *formal* nefarious, reprehensible, heinous, flagitious
☒ virtuous

iniquity *n*
wickedness, injustice, offence, misdeed, wrong, wrongdoing, evil, evil-doing, sin, sinfulness, enormity, baseness, vice, viciousness, infamy, abomination, crime, lawlessness, unrighteousness, ungodliness, *formal* heinousness, transgression
☒ virtue

initial *adj, v*
▶ *adj* first, beginning, opening, starting, introductory, inaugural, original, primary, prime, early, basic, elementary, foundational, formative, *formal* commencing, inceptive, inchoate, incipient
☒ final, last
▶ *v* write your initials on, sign, endorse, countersign

initially *adv*
at first, at the beginning, at the start, to begin with, to start with, originally, first, firstly, first of all
☒ finally, in the end

initiate *v, n*
▶ *v* **1** BEGIN, start, originate, pioneer, institute, set up, introduce, launch, open, inaugurate, instigate, activate, trigger, prompt, stimulate, cause, *formal* commence, *colloq.* kick off, set the ball rolling, set the wheels in motion, get off the ground, get under way, set in motion, get things moving **2** TEACH, instruct, train, drill, crash, tutor, inculcate, instil **3** *initiated into the organization* accept, admit, let in, introduce, receive, welcome, enrol, sign up, induct, install, invest, ordain
▶ *n* member, recruit, entrant, learner, newcomer, novice, beginner, convert, catechumen, novitiate, neophyte, probationer, proselyte, tenderfoot, tiro, authority, expert, connoisseur, sage, *colloq.* greenhorn, rookie

initiation *n*
1 BEGINNING, start, origination, setting-up, launching, opening, inauguration, *formal* inception **2** ADMISSION, reception, entrance, entry, debut, introduction, admittance, enrolment, enlistment, induction, investiture, installation, ordination, inauguration, baptism, rite of passage

initiative *n*
1 ENTERPRISE, resourcefulness, inventiveness, originality, innovativeness, creativity, energy, drive, dynamism, ambition, *colloq.* get-up-and-go, go, push **2** SUGGESTION, recommendation, action, lead, first move, opening move, first step

inject *v*
1 *inject drugs* inoculate, immunize, vaccinate, syringe, *colloq.* jab, *slang* shoot (up), mainline **2** INTRODUCE, insert, add, bring (in), infuse, instil

injection *n*
1 INOCULATION, immunization, vaccination, dose, *colloq.* jab, shot, *slang* fix **2** INTRODUCTION, insertion, addition, infusion, instilling

injudicious *adj*
ill-advised, ill-judged, inexpedient, ill-timed, unwise, inadvisable, incautious, inconsiderate, foolish, stupid, hasty, rash, misguided, unthinking, indiscreet, wrong-headed, *formal* impolitic, imprudent
☒ wise, cautious, *formal* judicious, prudent

injunction *n*
command, order, directive, ruling, mandate, direction, instruction, precept, dictum, dictate, *formal* admonition

injure *v*
1 HURT, harm, damage, impair, spoil, mar, ruin, disfigure, deface, blemish, blight, weaken, undermine, mutilate, mangle, deform, wound, cut, break, fracture, maim, disable, cripple, lame **2** OFFEND, ill-treat, maltreat, abuse, wrong, upset, put out

injured *adj*
1 HURT, harmed, damaged, wounded, lame, disabled, crippled, weakened **2** OFFENDED, ill-treated, maltreated, misused, pained, put out, wronged, upset, unhappy, aggrieved, maligned, abused, defamed, insulted, grieved, displeased, disgruntled, cut to the quick

injurious *adj*
damaging, detrimental, harmful, hurtful, disadvantageous, destructive, prejudicial, unconducive, pernicious, adverse, corrupting, baneful, ruinous, unhealthy, unjust, bad, wrongful, insulting, libellous, slanderous, *formal* calumnious, deleterious, iniquitous, noxious
☒ beneficial, favourable

injury *n*
1 WOUND, cut, bruise, sore, lesion, fracture, gash, abrasion, laceration, trauma, hurt, mischief, ill, harm, damage, impairment, ruin, disfigurement, mutilation, *technical* contusion, *formal* affliction **2** WRONG, ill-treatment, abuse, insult, grievance, offence, injustice

injustice *n*
unfairness, unjustness, wrong, injury, abuse, offence, ill-treatment, inequality, discrimination, oppression, bias, prejudice, one-sidedness, partisanship, partiality, favouritism, *formal* disparity, iniquity, inequity
☒ justice, fairness

inkling *n*
suspicion, idea, notion, glimmering, clue, hint, intimation, insinuation, innuendo, suggestion, allusion, indication, sign, pointer, *colloq.* faintest, foggiest, whisper

inky *adj*
black, jet-black, coal-black, pitch-black, jet, sooty, dark-blue

inlaid *adj*
set, inset, enamelled, mosaic, tiled, lined, studded, enchased, damascened, *formal* tessellated, empaestic

inland *adj*
interior, inner, internal, central, domestic, up-country

inlay *n*
setting, inset, enamel, mosaic, tiling, lining, studding, damascene, *formal* tessellation, emblema

inlet *n*
bay, cove, bight, creek, fiord, firth, opening, entrance, passage, sound

inmate *n*
patient, prisoner, convict, detainee, case, client

inn *n*
public house, tavern, hostelry, hotel, bar, *colloq.* pub, local

innards *n*
1 *the innards of an animal* insides, guts, internal organs, interior, intestines, entrails, entera, organs, umbles, viscera, vitals **2** *the innards of a machine* works, mechanism, inner workings

innate *adj*
inborn, inbred, congenital, inherited, hereditary, inherent, intrinsic, native, indigenous, natural, instinctive, intuitive, *formal* connate
☒ acquired, learnt

inner *adj*
internal, interior, inside, inward, innermost, central, middle, concealed, obscure, hidden, secret, private, personal, intimate, restricted, mental, psychological, spiritual, emotional, *formal* esoteric
🔁 outer, outward, revealed

innermost *adj*
deepest, deep, central, inmost, intimate, personal, dearest, private, secret, confidential, closest, essential, hidden, buried, basic, *formal* esoteric

innkeeper *n*
landlord, landlady, hotel-keeper, hotelier, publican, host, hostess, mine host, bar-keeper, restaurateur, innholder, padrone

innocence *n*
1 GUILTLESSNESS, blamelessness, irreproachability, unimpeachability, honesty, integrity, virtue, righteousness, sinlessness, faultlessness, impeccability, immaculateness, stainlessness, spotlessness, purity, chastity, virginity, incorruptibility, *formal* inculpability **2** ARTLESSNESS, guilelessness, ingenuousness, naïveness, naïvety, inexperience, ignorance, naturalness, simplicity, openness, frankness, unsophistication, unworldliness, childlikeness, credulity, gullibility, trustfulness **3** HARMLESSNESS, innocuousness, inoffensiveness, safety, playfulness
🔁 **1** guilt **2** experience **3** harmfulness

innocent *adj, n*
▶ *adj* **1** *innocent of the crime* guiltless, blameless, clear, irreproachable, above suspicion, unblameworthy, unimpeachable, honest, upright, virtuous, righteous, sinless, faultless, impeccable, stainless, spotless, immaculate, unsullied, unblemished, untainted, uncontaminated, pure, chaste, virginal, uncorrupted, incorrupt, *formal* inculpable **2** ARTLESS, guileless, ingenuous, naïve, inexperienced, fresh, natural, simple, open, frank, unsophisticated, unworldly, childlike, angelic, credulous, gullible, trusting, trustful, *colloq.* green, wet behind the ears, innocent as a newborn babe **3** HARMLESS, inoffensive, innocuous, safe, playful, unsuspicious
🔁 **1** guilty, to blame **2** experienced, sophisticated **3** harmful, offensive
▶ *n* beginner, infant, novice, child, tenderfoot, babe, babe in arms, neophyte, ingénue, greenhorn
🔁 connoisseur, expert

innocently *adv*
naïvely, artlessly, blamelessly, harmlessly, innocuously, inoffensively, unoffendingly, trustfully, trustingly, simply, ingenuously, credulously, unsuspiciously, *colloq.* like a lamb to the slaughter

innocuous *adj*
harmless, safe, inoffensive, unobjectionable, innocent, playful, mild, bland, unobtrusive
🔁 harmful

innovation *n*
new product, new method, newness, novelty, neologism, introduction, modernization, progress, reform, change, alteration, variation, departure

innovative *adj*
new, fresh, original, creative, imaginative, inventive, resourceful, enterprising, go-ahead, progressive, reforming, bold, daring, adventurous
🔁 conservative, unimaginative

innuendo *n*
insinuation, slur, whisper, hint, intimation, suggestion, implication, allusion, overtone, *formal* aspersion

innumerable *adj*
countless, uncountable, numerous, numberless, unnumbered, untold, incalculable, infinite, many, *colloq.* umpteen

inoculate *v*
immunize, vaccinate, inject, protect, safeguard, *colloq.* give a jab/shot to

inoculation *n*
vaccination, immunization, protection, injection, *colloq.* shot, jab

inoffensive *adj*
harmless, innocuous, safe, innocent, unobjectionable, peaceable, mild, bland, unobtrusive, unassertive, quiet, retiring
🔁 offensive, harmful, provocative

inoperable *adj*
incurable, untreatable, unhealable, unremovable, irremovable, terminal, fatal, deadly, hopeless, *formal* intractable
🔁 operable

inoperative *adj*
not working, not operative, out of order, out of action, out of service, out of commission, defective, broken, broken-down, non-functioning, unserviceable, unused, unworkable, useless, invalid, idle, ineffective, inadequate, inefficient, futile, worthless, *formal* ineffectual, inefficacious, nugatory, *colloq.* kaput
🔁 working, operative

inopportune *adj*
untimely, inconvenient, unsuitable, inappropriate, tactless, ill-timed, ill-chosen, mistimed, wrong-timed, unfortunate, unseasonable, clumsy, *formal* inauspicious, infelicitous, unpropitious, infelicitous
🔁 opportune

inordinate *adj*
excessive, immoderate, extreme, exorbitant, unwarranted, unrestricted, unrestrained, undue, unreasonable, outrageous, preposterous, disproportionate, great
🔁 moderate, reasonable

input *v, n*
▶ *v* feed in, insert, key in, code, capture, process, store
▶ *n* information, data, facts, figures, statistics, material, details, particulars, resources
🔁 output

inquest *n*
inquiry, investigation, examination, hearing, postmortem, inspection

inquietude *n*
uneasiness, restlessness, worry, anxiety, nervousness, agitation, unease, apprehension, discomposure, disquiet, jumpiness, *formal* disquietude, perturbation, solicitude
🔁 composure

inquire, enquire *v*
ask, question, quiz, query, investigate, look into, research, study, probe, examine, inspect, scrutinize, scan, search, explore, interrogate, *colloq.* snoop

inquirer, enquirer *n*
questioner, student, seeker, researcher, searcher, explorer, interrogator, investigator

inquiring, enquiring *adj*
inquisitive, interested, questioning, searching, curious, analytical, eager, investigative, investigatory, interrogatory, outward-looking, probing, prying, wondering, doubtful, sceptical, *formal* zetetic, *colloq.* nosy
🔁 incurious, unquestioning

inquiry, enquiry *n*
question, query, investigation, inquest, hearing, inquisition, interrogation, examination, inspection, scrutiny, study, survey, poll, search, probe, exploration, sounding, survey, reconnaissance

inquisition *n*
interrogation, cross-examination, cross-questioning, examination, investigation, questioning, quizzing, inquiry, inquest, *colloq.* grilling, third degree, witch hunt

inquisitive *adj*
curious, inquiring, questioning, probing, searching, scrutinizing, prying, peeping, peering, snooping, spying, nosy, interfering, meddlesome, intrusive, *colloq.* snoopy

inroad *n*
advance, progress, encroachment, foray, impingement, incursion, intrusion, trespassing, invasion, irruption, onslaught, attack, assault, offensive, charge, raid, sally, sortie, trespass

insane *adj*
1 MAD, crazy, mentally ill, lunatic, demented, deranged, unhinged, disturbed, out of your mind, *non compos mentis, colloq.* mental, crazy, loony, loopy, bonkers, nuts, nutty, nutty as a fruitcake, soft in the head, off your rocker, not all there, off your trolley, crackers, barmy, needing your head examining, round the bend, round the twist **2** FOOLISH, stupid, senseless, mad, crazy, impractical, idiotic, nonsensical, absurd, ridiculous, *colloq.* daft, potty, barmy
🖅 **1** sane **2** sensible

insanitary *adj*
unhygienic, unsanitary, unclean, impure, unhealthy, unsanitized, dirty, dirtied, contaminated, polluted, infected, disease-ridden, filthy, foul, infested, *formal* unhealthful, noisome, noxious, insalubrious, feculent
🖅 sanitary, clean

insanity *n*
1 *suffer from insanity* madness, craziness, lunacy, mental illness, neurosis, mania, dementia, delirium, frenzy, derangement, *technical* psychosis **2** FOLLY, madness, craziness, lunacy, foolishness, stupidity, senselessness, absurdity, ridiculousness, irresponsibility, *colloq.* daftness
🖅 **1** sanity **2** sensibleness

insatiable *adj*
voracious, unquenchable, unsatisfiable, unappeasable, ravenous, hungry, greedy, gluttonous, craving, avid, immoderate, inordinate, *formal* rapacious

inscribe *v*
1 ENGRAVE, etch, carve, cut, incise, imprint, impress, stamp, brand, mark, print **2** WRITE, sign, enrol, enlist, register, record, address, autograph, dedicate

inscription *n*
engraving, etching, epitaph, caption, legend, lettering, words, writing, signature, autograph, message, dedication

inscrutable *adj*
incomprehensible, unfathomable, impenetrable, deep, unintelligible, inexplicable, unexplainable, unreadable, baffling, puzzling, mysterious, enigmatic, cryptic, hidden, *formal* arcane
🖅 comprehensible, expressive

insect *n*

Insects include:
fly, gnat, midge, mosquito, tsetse-fly, locust, dragonfly, cranefly, *colloq.* daddy longlegs, horsefly, mayfly, butterfly, moth, bee, bumblebee, wasp, hornet, aphid, blackfly, greenfly, whitefly, froghopper, ladybird, water boatman, lacewing; beetle, cockroach, *US* roach, earwig, stick insect, grasshopper, cricket, cicada, flea, louse, nit, leatherjacket, termite, glowworm, woodworm, weevil, woodlouse.

Arachnids include:
spider, black widow, tarantula, scorpion, mite, tick.

Parts of an insect:
abdomen, antenna, cercus, compound eye, forewing, head, hindwing, legs, mandible, mouthpart, ocellus, ovipositor, segment, spiracle, thorax.

insecure *adj*
1 ANXIOUS, worried, nervous, uncertain, unsure, lacking confidence, afraid, apprehensive, fearful, hesitant, doubtful **2** UNSAFE, dangerous, hazardous, perilous, precarious, unsteady, unstable, shaky, loose, weak, frail, flimsy, unprotected, unguarded, defenceless, exposed, vulnerable, open to attack
🖅 **1** confident, self-assured **2** secure, safe, protected

insecurity *n*
1 ANXIETY, worry, nervousness, uncertainty, unsureness, apprehension, fear, uneasiness, lack of confidence **2** UNSAFETY, unsafeness, danger, hazard, peril, precariousness, unsteadiness, shakiness, instability, weakness, frailness, flimsiness, defencelessness, vulnerability
🖅 **1** confidence **2** safety, security

insensible *adj*
1 UNCONSCIOUS, anaesthetized, numb, senseless, unresponsive, *formal* insentient, comatose, *colloq.* out, zonked, knocked out, out for the count, dead to the world **2** UNAWARE, unconscious, oblivious, unmindful, ignorant, blind, deaf **3** CALLOUS, insensitive, unfeeling, emotionless, detached, untouched, unmoved, unaffected, cold, hard, aloof, distant **4** IMPERCEPTIBLE, indiscernible, indistinguishable, undetectable, unapparent, faint, slight
🖅 **1** conscious **2** aware, knowing **3** sensitive

insensitive *adj*
hardened, tough, resistant, impenetrable, impervious, immune, unsusceptible, thick-skinned, unfeeling, impassive, oblivious, indifferent, unaffected, unresponsive, unmoved, untouched, unsympathetic, uncaring, unconcerned, callous, heartless, thoughtless, tactless, crass, *technical* hypalgesic
🖅 sensitive, responsive, affected

insensitivity *n*
hardness, toughness, resistance, impenetrability, imperviousness, immunity, unresponsiveness, hardheadedness, unconcern, bluntness, callousness, indifference, tactlessness, crassness, obtuseness, *technical* hypalgesia, hypalgia
🖅 sensitivity, responsiveness

inseparable *adj*
indivisible, indissoluble, undividable, inextricable, close, intimate, bosom, constant, devoted
🖅 separable

insert *v, n*
▶ *v* put, place, press, put in, enclose, stick in, push in, thrust in, slide in, slip in, introduce, enter, implant, embed, engraft, infix, inlay, set, inset, let in, interleave, interject, *formal* interpose, interpolate, intercalate
▶ *n* insertion, enclosure, inset, notice, advertisement, circular, supplement, addition, inlay

insertion *n*
addition, entry, inclusion, insert, inset, introduction, implant, supplement, intrusion, *formal* intercalation, interpolation, intromission

inside *n, adv, adj*
▶ *n* interior, content, contents, middle, centre, heart, core, *colloq.* guts, belly
🖅 outside

▸ *adv* within, indoors, internally, inwardly, secretly, privately

▣ outside

▸ *adj* **1** INTERIOR, internal, inner, implicit, inherent, intrinsic, innermost, inward **2** SECRET, classified, confidential, internal, private, restricted, reserved

insider *n*
member, participant, staff member, co-worker, *colloq.* one of us, one of the in-crowd

insides *n*
internal organs, entrails, guts, intestines, bowels, organs, viscera, belly, stomach, abdomen, *colloq.* innards

insidious *adj*
subtle, sly, crafty, cunning, wily, artful, deceptive, deceitful, dishonest, devious, stealthy, surreptitious, furtive, sneaking, sneaky, tricky, treacherous, insincere, Machiavellian, *formal* duplicitous, perfidious

▣ direct, straightforward

insight *n*
awareness, knowledge, comprehension, understanding, realization, grasp, apprehension, perception, intuition, sensitivity, discernment, judgement, acumen, penetration, sharpness, shrewdness, observation, vision, wisdom, intelligence, *formal* perspicacity

insightful *adj*
perceptive, astute, sharp, shrewd, observant, penetrating, understanding, acute, discerning, intelligent, knowledgeable, wise, *formal* perspicacious, prudent, sagacious, percipient

▣ superficial

insignia *n*
emblem, badge, regalia, crest, sign(s), ensign, medallion, ribbon, decoration, mark, hallmark(s), symbol, trademark, brand

insignificance *n*
unimportance, irrelevance, meaninglessness, immateriality, inconsequence, inconsequentiality, negligibility, smallness, pettiness, paltriness, tininess, insubstantiality, triviality, meanness, worthlessness, *formal* nugatoriness

▣ significance

insignificant *adj*
unimportant, irrelevant, meaningless, immaterial, inconsequential, minor, trivial, trifling, petty, paltry, meagre, scanty, slight, small, tiny, insubstantial, inconsiderable, negligible, non-essential, peripheral, not worth mentioning, *formal* nugatory, *colloq.* piddling, cutting no ice, no great shakes, small-time

▣ significant, important

insincere *adj*
hypocritical, two-faced, double-dealing, lying, untruthful, dishonest, deceitful, underhand, devious, unfaithful, faithless, disloyal, untrue, treacherous, false, feigned, pretended, hollow, *formal* mendacious, disingenuous, dissembling, duplicitous, perfidious, *colloq.* phoney

▣ sincere, genuine

insincerity *n*
hypocrisy, untruthfulness, dishonesty, deceitfulness, deviousness, pretence, hollowness, falseness, falsity, faithlessness, artificiality, cant, evasiveness, *formal* disingenuousness, dissembling, dissimulation, duplicity, mendacity, perfidy, *colloq.* phoniness, humbug, lip service

▣ sincerity

insinuate *v*
imply, suggest, allude, hint, mention, intimate, indicate, *colloq.* get at, whisper

▷ **insinuate yourself** curry favour, get in with, ingratiate, sidle, work, worm, wriggle

insinuation *n*
suggestion, implication, allusion, hint, intimation, introduction, slant, slur, innuendo, *formal* aspersion

insipid *adj*
tasteless, flavourless, unsavoury, unappetizing, watery, weak, thin, bland, anaemic, colourless, drab, dull, monotonous, boring, tedious, wearisome, uninteresting, tame, flat, lifeless, inanimate, spiritless, vapid, characterless, trite, banal, unimaginative, dry, *colloq.* wishy-washy

▣ tasty, spicy, piquant, appetizing

insist *v*
demand, require, urge, entreat, stress, emphasize, repeat, reiterate, dwell on, harp on, assert, declare, state firmly, ask for firmly, maintain, claim, contend, hold, vow, swear, persist, stand firm, stand your ground, refuse to accept an alternative, *formal* aver, *colloq.* put your foot down, not take no for an answer

insistence *n*
demand, requirement, entreaty, urging, stress, emphasis, repetition, reiteration, maintenance, assertion, declaration, claim, contention, persistence, determination, resolution, firmness, *formal* exhortation

insistent *adj*
demanding, importunate, emphatic, resolute, determined, emphatic, adamant, forceful, pressing, urgent, dogged, tenacious, persistent, persevering, constant, repeated, relentless, unrelenting, unremitting, unyielding, inexorable, incessant, *formal* importunate, exigent

insobriety *n*
drunkenness, hard drinking, intemperance, inebriation, inebriety, intoxication, *formal* crapulence, *colloq.* tipsiness

▣ sobriety

insolence *n*
rudeness, abuse, insults, impudence, impertinence, arrogance, audacity, boldness, forwardness, pertness, presumption, presumptuousness, disrespect, contemptuousness, defiance, insubordination, offensiveness, incivility, *formal* hubris, effrontery, contumely, *colloq.* cheek, cheekiness, sauce, sauciness, gall, nerve, lip, mouth, chutzpah

▣ politeness, respect

insolent *adj*
rude, abusive, insulting, disrespectful, ill-mannered, impertinent, impudent, bold, audacious, brazen, brash, forward, presumptuous, arrogant, defiant, contemptuous, insubordinate, *colloq.* cheeky, saucy, fresh

▣ polite, respectful

insoluble *adj*
unsolvable, unexplainable, inexplicable, incomprehensible, unfathomable, impenetrable, inscrutable, enigmatic, indecipherable, complex, intricate, involved, obscure, mysterious, mystifying, puzzling, perplexing, baffling

▣ explicable

insolvency *n*
bankruptcy, default, failure, liquidation, ruin, indebtedness, destitution, impoverishment, pennilessness, *formal* impecuniosity

▣ solvency

insolvent *adj*
bankrupt, failed, in debt, liquidated, ruined, penniless, impoverished, destitute, *formal* impecunious, *colloq.* bust, broke, skint, strapped (for cash), on your beam ends, gone to the wall, gone under, in the red, on the rocks, in queer street

▣ solvent

insomnia *n*
sleeplessness, restlessness, wakefulness, *formal* insomnolence
⚠ sleep

insouciance *n*
nonchalance, unconcern, carefreeness, heedlessness, indifference, light-heartedness, flippancy, airiness, breeziness, jauntiness, ease
⚠ anxiety, care

insouciant *adj*
nonchalant, unconcerned, untroubled, unworried, indifferent, heedless, carefree, casual, easy-going, free and easy, flippant, happy-go-lucky, airy, breezy, buoyant, jaunty, light-hearted
⚠ anxious, careworn

inspect *v*
check, vet, look over, go over, pore over, examine, search, investigate, appraise, assess, audit, scrutinize, study, scan, survey, view, superintend, supervise, oversee, visit, reconnoitre, see over, tour

inspection *n*
check, check-up, examination, scrutiny, scan, study, survey, review, search, investigation, vetting, analysis, appraisal, assessment, audit, supervision, visit, tour, *colloq.* once-over, look-over, recce, dekko

inspector *n*
supervisor, superintendent, overseer, surveyor, controller, appraiser, assessor, auditor, scrutineer, scanner, checker, tester, examiner, investigator, reviewer, critic, visitor

inspiration *n*
1 CREATIVITY, originality, imagination, genius, inventiveness, muse, influence, encouragement, stimulation, incitement, stirring, arousing, motivation, spur, goad, stimulus, fillip 2 IDEA, bright idea, stroke of genius, brainwave, insight, illumination, revelation, enlightenment, awakening

inspire *v*
encourage, hearten, influence, impress, animate, breathe, enliven, quicken, energize, galvanize, fire, kindle, inflame, stir, arouse, rouse, trigger, instigate, produce, bring about, spark off, touch off, prompt, spur, goad, motivate, provoke, stimulate, excite, exhilarate, thrill, enthral, enthuse, imbue, infuse

inspired *adj*
brilliant, impressive, superlative, wonderful, outstanding, exciting, dazzling, memorable, thrilling, enthralling, marvellous, exceptional, splendid, remarkable
⚠ dull, uninspired

inspiring *adj*
encouraging, heartening, uplifting, invigorating, stirring, rousing, interesting, enthusiastic, invigorating, stimulating, exciting, exhilarating, thrilling, enthralling, moving, affecting, memorable, impressive
⚠ uninspiring, dull

inspirit *v*
encourage, inspire, move, stimulate, nerve, hearten, invigorate, quicken, refresh, reinvigorate, enliven, exhilarate, fire, galvanize, incite, animate, rouse, cheer, gladden, embolden

instability *n*
unsteadiness, shakiness, vacillation, wavering, oscillation, irresolution, uncertainty, impermanence, transience, unpredictability, changeableness, variability, fluctuation, volatility, capriciousness, flightiness, fitfulness, fickleness, inconstancy, unreliability, insecurity, precariousness, unsafeness, unsoundness, flimsiness, frailty
⚠ stability

install *v*
1 *install a new phone system* fix, fit, lay, put (in), insert, place, position, locate, lodge, site, situate, station, plant, settle, establish, set up, introduce 2 *install her as president* institute, inaugurate, invest, induct, ordain, consecrate, instate

installation *n*
1 FITTING, insertion, positioning, location, placing, siting 2 EQUIPMENT, machinery, plant, system 3 *her installation as president* inauguration, investiture, instatement, induction, consecration, ordination 4 *a military installation* base, station, post, centre, site, settlement, establishment, headquarters

instalment *n*
1 *pay in instalments* payment, part payment, repayment, portion, hire purchase 2 EPISODE, chapter, part, section, division, portion, segment

instance *n, v*
▶ *n* 1 *several instances of bullying* case, example, illustration, exemplification, case in point, citation, occurrence, occasion, sample 2 *at his instance* request, urging, incitement, demand, initiative, insistence, entreaty, instigation, pressure, prompting, solicitation, *formal* behest, exhortation, importunity
▶ *v* mention, quote, refer to, specify, give, name, cite, point to, exemplify, *formal* adduce

instant *n, adj*
▶ *n* flash, twinkling, trice, moment, split second, second, minute, time, occasion, juncture, *colloq.* tick, jiffy, twinkling of an eye, two shakes of a lamb's tail
▶ *adj* 1 INSTANTANEOUS, immediate, on-the-spot, direct, prompt, urgent, unhesitating, quick, fast, rapid, swift 2 *instant food* quickly prepared, easily prepared, ready mixed, convenience
⚠ 1 slow

instantaneous *adj*
immediate, instant, direct, prompt, rapid, unhesitating, sudden, on-the-spot
⚠ eventual

instantaneously *adv*
at once, directly, forthwith, immediately, right away, instantly, on the spot, promptly, speedily, quickly, rapidly, straight away, there and then, unhesitatingly, without hesitation, without delay, *colloq.* pronto, before you can say Jack Robinson, in two shakes of a lamb's tail
⚠ eventually

instantly *adv*
immediately, instantaneously, at once, right away, straight away, there and then, forthwith, now, on the spot, without delay, directly, *colloq.* pronto
⚠ eventually

instead *adv*
alternatively, preferably, rather, else, by/in contrast, as an alternative, substitute, replacement
▷ **instead of** as opposed to, in contrast to, in place of, in lieu of, on behalf of, in preference to, in favour of, as an alternative to, rather than

instigate *v*
initiate, set on, start, begin, cause, bring about, induce, press, generate, inspire, move, influence, persuade, encourage, urge, spur, prod, goad, prompt, provoke, stimulate, kindle, incite, stir up, whip up, foment, rouse, excite, *colloq.* egg on

instigation *n*
initiation, incitement, initiative, encouragement, prompting, urging, inducement, insistence, incentive, bidding, *formal* behest

instigator *n*
leader, motivator, prime mover, provoker, ringleader, spur, goad, incendiary, inciter, mischief-maker,

troublemaker, *agent provocateur*, agitator, fomenter, firebrand

instil *v*
infuse, imbue, insinuate, introduce, inject, implant, inculcate, impress, teach, drill, *colloq.* din into

instinct *n*
1 NATURAL RESPONSE, inbred response, intuition, sixth sense, impulse, urge, drive, feeling, hunch, tendency, *formal* predisposition, *colloq.* gut feeling/reaction **2** FLAIR, knack, gift, talent, bent, feel, faculty, ability, aptitude

instinctive *adj*
natural, native, inborn, innate, inherent, intuitive, impulsive, involuntary, unintentional, automatic, mechanical, reflex, spontaneous, immediate, unlearned, untaught, unthinking, unpremeditated, visceral, *colloq.* gut
◼ conscious, voluntary, deliberate

instinctively *adv*
intuitively, naturally, spontaneously, unthinkingly, without thinking, automatically, involuntarily, mechanically
◼ consciously, deliberately, voluntarily

institute *v, n*
▶ *v* **1** START, originate, initiate, introduce, enact, begin, create, establish, develop, set up, organize, found, inaugurate, open, launch, *formal* commence **2** APPOINT, install, invest, induct, ordain, initiate
◼ **1** cancel, abolish, *formal* discontinue
▶ *n* **1** *an institute for advanced research* school, college, academy, conservatory, seminary, foundation, institution, organization **2** LAW, principle, rule, custom, regulation, decree

institution *n*
1 ORGANIZATION, association, society, guild, league, club, concern, corporation, foundation, establishment, institute, hospital, home, centre **2** CUSTOM, tradition, usage, practice, ritual, convention, rule, law, system **3** INITIATION, starting, introduction, enactment, creation, establishment, setting-up, formation, creation, founding, foundation, installation, *formal* commencement, inception

institutional *adj*
established, organized, establishment, accepted, customary, conventional, formal, methodical, orderly, systematic, orthodox, regimented, set, routine, uniform, ritualistic, bureaucratic, clinical, impersonal, cold, unwelcoming, dreary, dull, drab, forbidding, monotonous, cheerless
◼ individualistic, unconventional

instruct *v*
1 TEACH, educate, tutor, coach, train, drill, ground, school, discipline, prime, prepare **2** ORDER, command, direct, demand, require, charge, mandate, tell, inform, notify, make known, advise, counsel, guide, enlighten, *formal* enjoin, bid

instruction *n*
1 *give someone instructions* order, direction, recommendation, advice, guidance, information, charge, command, requirement, injunction, mandate, directive, ruling, briefing **2** EDUCATION, schooling, lesson(s), classes, tuition, tutoring, tutelage, teaching, training, coaching, drilling, grounding, preparation, priming, guidance, enlightenment **3** *read the instructions carefully* directions, orders, recommendations, rules, brief, information, advice, key, legend, guidance, guidelines, book of words, handbook, manual

instructive *adj*
informative, educational, educative, doctrinal, uplift-

ing, edifying, enlightening, illuminating, helpful, useful
◼ unenlightening

instructor *n*
teacher, lecturer, educator, master, mistress, tutor, coach, trainer, demonstrator, exponent, adviser, mentor, guide, pedagogue, counsellor, guru

instrument *n*
1 TOOL, implement, utensil, appliance, gadget, contraption, device, contrivance, apparatus, mechanism, *colloq.* gismo **2** GAUGE, meter, measure, indicator, rule, guideline, yardstick **3** AGENT, agency, vehicle, organ, medium, factor, channel, way, means. *See also panel at* MUSICAL INSTRUMENTS.

instrumental *adj*
active, involved, contributory, conducive, influential, important, significant, useful, helpful, auxiliary, subsidiary
◼ obstructive, unhelpful

insubordinate *adj*
disobedient, rebellious, defiant, ungovernable, unruly, disorderly, undisciplined, rude, riotous, seditious, insurgent, mutinous, turbulent, impertinent, impudent, *formal* contumacious, recalcitrant, refractory
◼ docile, obedient, compliant

insubordination *n*
disobedience, defiance, rebellion, insurrection, mutinousness, mutiny, revolt, riotousness, sedition, rudeness, ungovernability, indiscipline, impertinence, impudence, *formal* recalcitrance
◼ docility, obedience, compliance

insubstantial *adj*
1 FLIMSY, frail, feeble, weak, tenuous, poor, slight, thin **2** UNREAL, false, illusory, fanciful, imaginary, idle, vaporous, immaterial, incorporeal, moonshine, *formal* chimerical, ephemeral
◼ **1** solid, strong **2** real

insufferable *adj*
intolerable, unbearable, unendurable, detestable, loathsome, revolting, dreadful, shocking, outrageous, impossible, too much to bear, more than you can bear
◼ pleasant, tolerable

insufficiency *n*
inadequacy, shortage, deficiency, lack, scarcity, dearth, need, poverty, short supply, *formal* want
◼ sufficiency, excess

insufficient *adj*
inadequate, not enough, short, deficient, lacking, wanting, meagre, sparse, scanty, scant, scarce, in short supply
◼ sufficient, enough, excessive

insular *adj*
parochial, provincial, cut off, detached, isolated, remote, withdrawn, separate, solitary, insulated, inward-looking, blinkered, closed, narrow-minded, narrow, limited, restricted, petty, bigoted, biased, prejudiced, xenophobic, *colloq.* parish-pump
◼ open-minded

insularity *n*
isolation, detachment, narrow-mindedness, solitariness, pettiness, parochiality, parochialness, bigotry, bias, prejudice, xenophobia
◼ open-mindedness, openness

insulate *v*
cushion, pad, lag, cocoon, protect, wrap, cover, shield, shelter, isolate, separate, cut off, exclude, detach, segregate, encase, envelop, *formal* sequester

insulation *n*
cushioning, padding, lagging, cladding, cocooning,

protection, wrapping, cover, covering, stuffing, shield, shelter, isolation, separation, exclusion, detachment, segregation

insult *v, n*
▶ *v* abuse, call names, taunt, ridicule, bait, rebuff, libel, slander, malign, slight, slur, snub, injure, hurt, wound, offend, outrage, mortify, *formal* affront, disparage, revile, impugn, calumniate, traduce, *colloq.* kick in the teeth, slap in the face, give the cold shoulder
🖅 compliment, praise
▶ *n* abuse, rudeness, insolence, gibe, taunt, defamation, libel, slander, slight, slur, barb, snub, indignity, offence, outrage, *formal* affront, aspersions, disparagement, revilement, *colloq.* put-down, backhanded compliment, cold shoulder
🖅 compliment, praise

insulting *adj*
offensive, abusive, rude, hurtful, injurious, contemptuous, degrading, slighting, outrageous, insolent, scurrilous, libellous, slanderous, *formal* affronting, disparaging, reviling
🖅 complimentary, respectful

insuperable *adj*
insurmountable, formidable, overwhelming, invincible, unconquerable, unassailable, impassable
🖅 surmountable

insupportable *adj*
intolerable, unbearable, unendurable, insufferable, dreadful, loathsome, hateful, detestable, unacceptable, untenable, unjustifiable, indefensible
🖅 bearable

insuppressible *adj*
irrepressible, lively, unstoppable, uncontrollable, ungovernable, unruly, unsubduable, obstreperous, incorrigible, energetic, *colloq.* go-getting
🖅 suppressible

insurance *n*
cover, protection, assurance, safeguard, security, surety, provision, assurance, indemnity, guarantee, indemnification, warranty, policy, premium

insure *v*
cover, protect, assure, underwrite, indemnify, guarantee, warrant

insurer *n*
assurer, underwriter, protector, indemnifier, guarantor, warrantor

insurgent *n, adj*
▶ *n* rebel, revolter, revolutionary, rioter, insurrectionist, seditionist, mutineer, partisan, revolutionist, resister
▶ *adj* rebellious, revolting, revolutionary, mutinous, riotous, seditious, disobedient, insubordinate, insurrectionary, partisan

insurmountable *adj*
insuperable, unconquerable, invincible, unassailable, overwhelming, hopeless, impossible
🖅 surmountable

insurrection *n*
rising, uprising, insurgence, riot, rebellion, mutiny, revolt, revolution, sedition, coup, *coup d'état*, putsch

intact *adj*
unbroken, (all) in one piece, whole, complete, integral, entire, perfect, faultless, flawless, sound, undamaged, unharmed, unhurt, uninjured, unscathed
🖅 broken, incomplete, damaged

intangible *adj*
insubstantial, imponderable, elusive, fleeting, airy, unclear, shadowy, vague, subtle, obscure, indefinite, undefinable, indescribable, abstract, unreal, invisible, immeasurable
🖅 tangible, real

integral *adj*
1 *an integral part* intrinsic, constituent, component, inherent, elemental, basic, fundamental, necessary, essential, indispensable, *formal* requisite **2** COMPLETE, entire, full, whole, total, undivided, intact
🖅 **1** extra, additional, unnecessary

integrate *v*
assimilate, merge, join, unite, combine, amalgamate, consolidate, incorporate, coalesce, fuse, knit, mesh, mix, intermix, mingle, blend, homogenize, harmonize, desegregate
🖅 divide, separate, segregate

integrated *adj*
mixed, desegregated, assimilated, merged, joined, unified, unseparated, united, combined, amalgamated, consolidated, incorporated, coalesced, fused, meshed, mingled, blended, harmonized, harmonious, cohesive, connected, interrelated, *colloq.* part and parcel
🖅 unintegrated, segregated

integration *n*
assimilation, merger, unity, unification, combination, amalgamation, consolidation, incorporation, fusion, blend, harmony, mix, desegregation
🖅 separation, segregation

integrity *n*
1 HONESTY, uprightness, incorruptibility, purity, morality, principle, sincerity, honour, decency, virtue, goodness, fairness, righteousness, truthfulness, *formal* probity, rectitude **2** COMPLETENESS, wholeness, unity, entirety, totality, coherence, cohesion, unification
🖅 **1** dishonesty **2** incompleteness

intellect *n*
1 *a person of considerable intellect* mind, brain(s), brainpower, brilliance, intelligence, genius, reason, thought, understanding, comprehension, sense, wisdom, judgement **2** THINKER, academic, highbrow, mastermind, genius, intellectual, *colloq.* egghead
🖅 **1** stupidity

intellectual *adj, n*
▶ *adj* academic, scholarly, intelligent, studious, learned, thoughtful, mental, logical, highbrow, bookish, cultural, well-educated, well-read, *formal* cerebral, erudite
🖅 low-brow
▶ *n* thinker, academic, highbrow, mastermind, genius, intellect, *colloq.* egghead
🖅 low-brow

intelligence *n*
1 INTELLECT, reason, wit(s), brainpower, cleverness, brightness, brilliance, aptitude, quickness, alertness, sharpness, acumen, discernment, perception, thought, understanding, comprehension, *colloq.* brain(s), grey matter, little grey cells, nous **2** INFORMATION, facts, data, knowledge, findings, notification, news, report, notice, account, rumour, warning, advice, *colloq.* low-down, tip-off, gen, dope **3** SURVEILLANCE, spying, espionage, observation
🖅 **1** stupidity, foolishness

intelligent *adj*
clever, bright, smart, brilliant, quick, alert, quickwitted, sharp, acute, discerning, perceptive, knowing, knowledgeable, well-informed, thinking, educated, rational, sensible, *formal* perspicacious, sagacious, *colloq.* brainy, quick on the uptake, no flies on someone, knowing a thing or two, knowing how many beans make five, using your loaf, all there
🖅 unintelligent, stupid, foolish

intelligentsia *n*
academics, intellectuals, cognoscenti, literati, highbrows, illuminati, *colloq.* brains, eggheads

intelligibility *n*
comprehensibility, comprehensibleness, clearness, clarity, plainness, lucidity, lucidness, explicitness, distinctness, legibility, precision, simplicity
 unintelligibility

intelligible *adj*
comprehensible, understandable, clear, plain, lucid, distinct, open, explicit, legible, decipherable, fathomable, penetrable
 unintelligible

intemperance *n*
excess, immoderation, self-indulgence, overindulgence, unrestraint, extravagance, drunkenness, intoxication, insobriety, licence, *formal* crapulence, inebriation
 temperance

intemperate *adj*
extreme, immoderate, inordinate, unrestrained, unbridled, uncontrolled, uncontrollable, irrestrainable, ungovernable, severe, violent, wild, tempestuous, passionate, excessive, unreasonable, extravagant, self-indulgent, drunken, intoxicated, dissolute, incontinent, prodigal, licentious, profligate, *formal* inebriated, *colloq.* over the top
 temperate

intend *v*
aim, have a mind, have in mind, contemplate, mean, be going, be looking, propose, choose, plan, project, scheme, devise, plot, design, expect, purpose, determine, be determined, destine, mark out, earmark, set apart, *formal* resolve

intended *adj, n*
► *adj* designated, destined, deliberate, intentional, planned, proposed, designate, future, prospective, betrothed
 accidental
► *n* fiancé, fiancée, husband-to-be, wife-to-be, betrothed

intense *adj*
1 EXTREME, great, deep, profound, strong, powerful, vigorous, potent, forceful, fierce, harsh, severe, acute, sharp, keen, enthusiastic, zealous, eager, earnest, ardent, fervent, excited, passionate, impassioned, vehement, consuming, burning, energetic, violent, intensive, concentrated, heightened, *formal* fervid 2 *an intense person* serious, thoughtful, impassioned, emotional, tense, nervous, heavy
 1 moderate, mild, weak 2 easy-going

📖 **intense** or **intensive** ?

Intense means 'very great': *the intense heat from the furnace*; *intense bitterness*. *Intensive* means 'concentrated, thorough, taking great care': *an intense search*; *the intensive care ward of a hospital*.

---

intensely *adv*
extremely, deeply, very, strongly, greatly, profoundly, fiercely, ardently, fervently, passionately, *colloq.* with a vengeance
 mildly

intensification *n*
increase, stepping-up, strengthening, reinforcement, magnification, escalation, heightening, building-up, build-up, boost, aggravation, acceleration, worsening, deepening, concentration, emphasis, enhancement, *formal* augmentation, exacerbescence
 lessening

intensify *v*
increase, step up, build up, escalate, heighten, maximize, fire, boost, fuel, fan, aggravate, worsen, add to,

broaden, widen, strengthen, reinforce, magnify, sharpen, whet, quicken, deepen, concentrate, emphasize, enhance, *formal* augment, exacerbate, *colloq.* hot up, bump up, hike up, add fuel to the flames, bring to a head
 reduce, weaken

intensity *n*
greatness, extremity, intenseness, depth, profundity, strength, power, vigour, potency, force, fierceness, severity, acuteness, keenness, eagerness, earnestness, ardour, enthusiasm, zeal, fanaticism, fervency, fervour, fire, emotion, passion, concentration, energy, vehemence, strain, tension

intensive *adj*
concentrated, thorough, exhaustive, comprehensive, detailed, in-depth, thoroughgoing, all-out, intense
 superficial

📖 **intensive** or **intense** ? *See panel at* INTENSE.

---

intent *adj, n*
► *adj* 1 *intent on doing something* determined, resolved, set, bent, eager, keen, committed, firm 2 *an intent look* attentive, alert, concentrating, fixed, close, hard, keen, absorbed, occupied, wrapped up, focused, engrossed, preoccupied, steady, rapt, enrapt, searching, watchful
 2 absent-minded, distracted
► *n* intention, purpose, meaning, objective, plan, aim, goal, target, point, idea, view, design, object, end
▷ **to all intents and purposes** almost, nearly, practically, virtually, more or less, just about, as good as, pretty much, pretty well

intention *n*
aim, purpose, object, end, point, target, goal, objective, idea, plan, design, view, intent, meaning, ambition, wish, aspiration

intentional *adj*
designed, wilful, conscious, planned, purposeful, deliberate, prearranged, premeditated, preconceived, considered, calculated, studied, intended, weighed-up, meant, on purpose
 unintentional, accidental

intentionally *adv*
deliberately, on purpose, wilfully, by design, designedly, meaningly, with malice aforethought
 accidentally

intently *adv*
attentively, watchfully, carefully, closely, steadily, searchingly, staringly, fixedly, hard, keenly
 absent-mindedly

inter *v*
bury, lay to rest, entomb, inearth, sepulchre, inhume, *formal* inurn
 exhume

interbreed *v*
cross, crossbreed, cross-fertilize, mongrelize, hybridize, reproduce together, *formal* miscegenate

interbreeding *n*
cross-breeding, crossing, hybridization, *formal* miscegenation

intercede *v*
mediate, arbitrate, intervene, plead, speak, petition, negotiate, *formal* entreat, beseech, interpose

intercept *v*
head off, ambush, interrupt, deflect, cut off, stop, arrest, catch, commandeer, take, seize, check, block, impede, obstruct, delay, frustrate, thwart

intercession *n*
mediation, arbitration, negotiation, intervention,

plea, pleading, advocacy, agency, solicitation, prayer, good offices, *formal* beseeching, entreaty, supplication, interposition

interchange *n, v*
▶ *n* **1** EXCHANGE, trading, barter, swap, alternation, reciprocation, interplay, crossfire, *colloq.* give-and-take **2** INTERSECTION, junction, crossroad(s), crossing
▶ *v* exchange, swap, switch, alternate, reciprocate, replace, substitute, trade, barter, bandy, transpose, reverse

interchangeable *adj*
reciprocal, exchangeable, transposable, equivalent, corresponding, comparable, similar, identical, the same, synonymous, standard
F∃ different

intercourse *n*
1 *sexual intercourse* sex, sexual relations, intimacy, intimate relations, love-making, copulation, carnal knowledge, the sex act, *colloq.* sleeping with someone, nookie, going to bed with someone, *formal* coition, coitus **2** ASSOCIATION, communication, communion, contact, connection, dealings, conversation, converse, correspondence, commerce, trade, intercommunication, congress, traffic

interdict *v, n*
▶ *v* ban, bar, debar, forbid, prohibit, prevent, embargo, rule out, veto, outlaw, *formal* disallow, preclude, proscribe
F∃ allow
▶ *n* ban, injunction, prohibition, bar, embargo, taboo, veto, *formal* disallowance, interdiction, proscription, preclusion
F∃ permission

interest *n, v*
▶ *n* **1** *have an interest in dance* curiosity, inquisitiveness, concern, care, attention, attentiveness, notice, regard, heed, charm, allure, appeal, attraction, fascination, involvement, engagement **2** IMPORTANCE, significance, consequence, moment, consideration, magnitude, relevance, prominence, weight, value, note, urgency, priority, seriousness, gravity **3** *leisure interests* activity, pursuit, pastime, hobby, diversion, recreation, amusement **4** ADVANTAGE, good, benefit, profit, gain **5** *business interests* share, stake, concern, business, claim, involvement, participation, portion, investment, stock, equity **6** *earn interest* dividend, return, profit, gain, receipts, revenue, proceeds, credits, bonus, premium, percentage
F∃ **1** boredom **2** meaninglessness **4** loss
▷ **in the interests of** for the sake of, on behalf of, to the advantage of, for the benefit of
▶ *v* concern, involve, touch, move, attract, appeal to, divert, amuse, occupy, engage, rivet, absorb, engross, fascinate, intrigue, captivate, grip
F∃ bore

interested *adj*
1 ATTENTIVE, curious, absorbed, engrossed, fascinated, intent, captivated, gripped, enthralled, riveted, intrigued, enthusiastic, keen, attracted, *colloq.* having the ... bug **2** CONCERNED, involved, affected, implicated
F∃ **1** uninterested, indifferent, apathetic **2** disinterested, unaffected

interesting *adj*
attractive, appealing, entertaining, engaging, absorbing, engrossing, exciting, fascinating, captivating, intriguing, compelling, compulsive, gripping, riveting, stimulating, thought-provoking, amusing, curious, unusual, *colloq.* unputdownable
F∃ uninteresting, boring, monotonous, tedious

interfere *v*
1 INTRUDE, pry, interrupt, intervene, meddle, tamper, *colloq.* poke/stick your nose in, stick/put your oar in, put in your two pennyworth, muscle in on, butt in, *US* put in your two cents' worth **2** HINDER, hamper, obstruct, block, check, impede, handicap, cramp, inhibit, trammel, balk, thwart, conflict, clash, *colloq.* get in the way of **3** MOLEST, abuse, assault, sexually assault, attack, rape
F∃ **1** *colloq.* mind your own business **2** assist

interference *n*
1 INTRUSION, prying, interruption, intervention, meddling, meddlesomeness **2** OBSTRUCTION, hindrance, hampering, blocking, checking, impediment, handicap, inhibiting, trammel(s), thwarting, opposition, conflict, clashing
F∃ **2** assistance

interim *adj, n*
▶ *adj* temporary, provisional, stopgap, makeshift, improvised, stand-in, acting, caretaker, *colloq.* pro tem
▶ *n* meantime, meanwhile, interval, interregnum

interior *adj, n*
▶ *adj* **1** INTERNAL, inside, inner, innermost, central, inward, intrinsic **2** *interior thoughts* inner, mental, personal, private, intimate, spiritual, emotional, psychological, secret, hidden, involuntary, spontaneous, impulsive, intuitive, instinctive, innate **3** HOME, domestic, central, local, inland, up-country, remote
F∃ **1** exterior, external **3** external, coastal
▶ *n* inside, inside part, centre, middle, core, heart, nucleus, depths
F∃ exterior, outside

interject *v*
cry, shout, call, utter, introduce, interrupt, exclaim, *formal* ejaculate, interpose, interpolate

interjection *n*
exclamation, cry, shout, call, utterance, interruption, *formal* ejaculation, interpolation

interlace *v*
entwine, braid, twine, knit, plait, cross, enlace, interweave, interlock, intertwine, intermix, intersperse, interwreathe, *formal* reticulate

interlink *v*
link, link together, interconnect, lock together, interlock, mesh, knit, intergrow, intertwine, interweave, clasp together
F∃ separate, divide

interlock *v*
lock together, interconnect, link, link together, mesh, clasp together, intertwine, *formal* interdigitate

interloper *n*
intruder, uninvited guest, trespasser, encroacher, invader, *colloq.* gate-crasher

interlude *n*
interval, intermission, break, breathing-space, pause, rest, recess, stop, stoppage, respite, wait, delay, halt, spell, *formal* hiatus, *colloq.* breather, let-up

intermediary *n*
mediator, go-between, negotiator, arbitrator, middleman, broker, agent

intermediate *adj*
midway, halfway, in-between, middle, mid, median, medial, mean, intermediary, intervening, transitional
F∃ extreme

interment *n*
burial, burying, funeral, *formal* inhumation, exequies, obsequies, obsequy, sepulture
F∃ exhumation

interminable *adj*
endless, never-ending, perpetual, limitless, boundless, unlimited, without end, everlasting, eternal, long, long-winded, long-drawn-out, dragging, wearisome, tedious, boring, dull, monotonous, *formal* ceaseless, prolix, loquacious
Ⅎ limited, brief

intermingle *v*
mix, mix together, merge, blend, amalgamate, combine, fuse, interlace, interweave, mix up, *formal* commingle, commix, intermix
Ⅎ separate

intermission *n*
interval, interlude, break, recess, rest, respite, breathing-space, pause, lull, remission, suspension, interruption, halt, stop, stoppage, *formal* cessation, *colloq.* breather, let-up

intermittent *adj*
occasional, periodic, sporadic, spasmodic, fitful, erratic, irregular, cyclic, broken, off and on, *formal* discontinuous
Ⅎ continuous, constant

intern *v*
confine, detain, hold, hold in custody, jail, imprison
Ⅎ free, release

internal *adj*
1 INSIDE, inner, interior, inward **2** HOME, domestic, in-house, local **3** *internal processes of the mind* subjective, intimate, private, personal, spiritual, mental, emotional, psychological
Ⅎ **1** external

international *adj*
global, worldwide, intercontinental, cosmopolitan, universal, general
Ⅎ national, local, parochial

internecine *adj*
fierce, violent, bloody, deadly, mortal, fatal, destructive, ruinous, murderous, exterminating, family, civil, internal

Internet *n*

Internet terms include :

ad click, address, ADSL (Asynchronous Digital Subscriber Line), alias, anonymous FTP, applet, attachment, backbone, backbone cabling, bandwidth, banner, BBS (Bulletin Board System), bookmark, bounced mail, bps (bits per second), broadband, browser, cable-free connection, chat, chatroom, connect time, cookie, country code, cybercafé, cyberspace, dialer, dial up connection, dedicated line, digital signing, DNS (Domain Name Server/System), domain name, dotcom, download, e-commerce, email *or* e-mail, emoticon, encryption, e-tailing, extranet, firewall, flame, FTP (File Transfer Protocol), gateway, heavy site, helper application, hit, home page, host, host name, HTML (HyperText Markup Language), HTTP *or* http (Hypertext Transfer Protocol), hyperlink, hypertext, IMAP (Internet Message Access Protocol), intelligent agent, Internet access provider (IAP), Internet Protocol (IP), Internet Relay Chat (IRC), Internet service provider (ISP), intranet, ISDN (Integrated Services Digital Network), Java, JPEG (Joint Photographics Experts Group), junk mail, kill file, latency, link, mailbox, mailing list, mail server, Microsoft Internet Explorer®, MIME (Multipurpose Internet Mail Extensions), modem, moderated mailing lists/newsgroup, Netscape Navigator®, newsgroup, newsreader, NNTP (Network News Transfer Protocol), node, offline, online, online service, packet, plain text, plug-in, POP (Point of Presence), POP3 (Post Office Protocol), portal, postmaster, PPP (Point to Point Protocol), private commercial community, protocol, protocol name, search engine, server, set-top box, signature file, smiley, snail mail, spam, surf, TCP/IP (Transmission Control Protocol/Internet Protocol), timeout, upload, URL (Uniform *or* Universal Resource Locator), Usenet, user name, viral email, WAN (wide area network), WAP (Wireless Application Protocol), Web cam, web page, website, World Wide Web (WWW *or* www).

interplay *n*
exchange, interchange, interaction, reciprocation, alternation, transposition, *colloq.* give-and-take

interpolate *v*
insert, add, put in, introduce, *formal* interpose, interject, intercalate

interpolation *n*
insert, insertion, addition, introduction, aside, *formal* intercalation, interjection

interpose *v*
insert, introduce, interject, add, put in, thrust in, interrupt, intrude, interfere, come between, put/place between, intervene, step in, mediate, arbitrate, intercede, *formal* interpolate, *colloq.* barge in, butt in, muscle in, poke your nose in, put your oar in

interpret *v*
explain, clarify, make clear, throw/shed light on, define, paraphrase, translate, render, decode, decipher, solve, make sense of, understand, read, take, *formal* expound, elucidate, construe, explicate, *colloq.* read between the lines

interpretation *n*
explanation, clarification, analysis, translation, rendering, version, paraphrase, performance, reading, understanding, sense, meaning, opinion, decoding, deciphering, *technical* anagogy, *formal* expounding, exposition, elucidation, exegesis, explication, construe

interpretative *adj*
explanatory, clarificatory, interpretive, *technical* hermeneutic, *formal* exegetic, explicatory, expository

interpreter *n*
translator, linguist, commentator, annotator, *technical* hermeneutist, *formal* elucidator, exegete, exponent, expositor

interrogate *v*
question, quiz, examine, cross-examine, debrief, cross-question, *colloq.* grill, give a going-over, give the third degree, pump, give a roasting

interrogation *n*
questioning, quizzing, cross-questioning, examination, cross-examination, inquisition, inquiry, inquest, *colloq.* grilling, going-over, third degree, pumping

interrogative *adj*
questioning, quizzical, curious, inquisitive, probing, inquiring, interrogatory, *formal* inquisitional, inquisitorial, catechetical, erotetic

interrupt *v*
1 *interrupt a conversation* cut in, intrude, break in, disturb, punctuate, cut in, cut short, cut off, heckle, barrack, *colloq.* barge in, butt in, chip in, put your oar in
2 *interrupt an event* disturb, disrupt, hold up, stop, halt, end, suspend, delay, postpone, cancel, cut off, disconnect, break, punctuate **3** *interrupt a view* obstruct, block, cut off, disturb, interfere with

interruption n

1 *work without interruption* intrusion, interference, disturbance, cutting-in, disruption, suspension, breaking-off, delay, disconnection, *formal* discontinuance, cessation, *colloq.* barging-in, butting-in **2** *no interruptions are allowed* question, remark, interjection, obstruction, impediment, obstacle, hitch, *formal* interpolation **3** PAUSE, break, halt, stop, interval, intermission, recess, *colloq.* breather, let-up

intersect v

cross, criss-cross, cut across, bisect, divide, meet, converge, overlap

intersection n

junction, interchange, crossroads, crossing, meeting

intersperse v

scatter, distribute, spread, dispense, pepper, sprinkle, dot, intermix, diversify, *formal* interpose, interlard

intertwine v

entwine, interweave, interlace, interlink, link together, connect, interwind, twirl, twist, twine, coil, cross, weave, blend, mix

interval n

1 BREAK, interlude, intermission, rest, pause, space, lull, gap, delay, wait, interim, period, time, recess, meantime, meanwhile, *colloq.* breathing-space, breather **2** SPACE, gap, opening, distance, period, spell, time, season

intervene v

1 STEP IN, mediate, arbitrate, intercede, negotiate, involve yourself in, interfere, interrupt, intrude **2** OCCUR, happen, pass, arise, come to pass, *formal* elapse, befall

intervening adj

between, *formal* interposing, intervenient, interjacent, mediate

intervention n

involvement, stepping-in, mediation, arbitration, negotiation, agency, intercession, interference, interruption, intrusion

interview n, v

▶ n discussion, audience, consultation, talk, dialogue, meeting, conference, press conference, evaluation, appraisal, assessment, oral examination, viva
▶ v question, interrogate, examine, talk to, sound out, cross-examine, cross-question, evaluate, assess, vet

interviewer n

examiner, questioner, investigator, reporter, correspondent, evaluator, appraiser, assessor, interrogator, inquisitor, *formal* interlocutor, interrogant

interweave v

intertwine, entwine, interlace, interlink, interwind, interlock, twist, twine, coil, knit, cross, criss-cross, weave, intertangle, intertwist, interwork, interwreathe, braid, splice, blend, link together, interconnect, intermingle, connect, mix, *formal* reticulate

intestinal adj

internal, abdominal, gastric, duodenal, visceral, *technical* coeliac, ileac, enteric, *formal* stomachic

intestines n

bowels, guts, entrails, insides, colon, offal, viscera, vitals, *colloq.* innards

intimacy n

1 CLOSENESS, close relationship, friendship, familiarity, confidence, confidentiality, privacy, warmth, affection, love, understanding **2** SEXUAL INTERCOURSE, sexual relations, intimate relations, lovemaking, copulation, carnal knowledge, sleeping with someone, going to bed with someone, *formal* coition, coitus

☲ distance

intimate¹ adj, n

▶ adj **1** *an intimate friend; an intimate atmosphere* close, near, dear, bosom, cherished, friendly, informal, familiar, cosy, warm, affectionate, *colloq.* thick, matey, pally, chummy, tight **2** *an intimate conversation* confidential, secret, private, personal, internal, innermost **3** *intimate knowledge of art* deep, profound, in-depth, penetrating, detailed, exhaustive, thorough

☲ **1** unfriendly, cold, distant **3** superficial

▶ n friend, close friend, best friend, bosom friend, confidant(e), associate, *colloq.* mate, pal, chum, buddy, crony

☲ stranger

intimate² v

initmated that he'd be willing to help hint, insinuate, imply, suggest, indicate, signal, communicate, impart, tell, state, declare, announce, make known, let it be known

intimately adv

1 CLOSELY, affectionately, personally, tenderly, warmly, familiarly **2** CONFIDENTIALLY, confidingly, privately **3** DEEPLY, fully, in detail, exhaustively, thoroughly, inside out

☲ **1** coldly, distantly **3** superficially

intimation n

hint, inkling, insinuation, implication, suggestion, indication, announcement, communication, signal, declaration, notice, statement, reference, warning, reminder, allusion

intimidate v

daunt, cow, overawe, domineer, appal, dismay, alarm, scare, frighten, terrify, subdue, threaten, extort, blackmail, menace, tyrannize, terrorize, bully, browbeat, bulldoze, coerce, compel, pressure, pressurize, warn off, *colloq.* get at, lean on, twist someone's arm, put the screws on, put the frighteners on, turn the heat on

intimidation n

frightening, terrifying, menaces, threats, threatening, threatening behaviour, terrorization, terrorizing, domineering, tyrannization, bullying, browbeating, coercion, compulsion, pressure, fear, terror, *colloq.* arm-twisting, screws, frighteners, big stick

☲ persuasion

intolerable adj

unbearable, unendurable, insupportable, unacceptable, insufferable, loathsome, detestable, impossible, more than you can bear, *colloq.* too bad, awful, dreadful, the limit, the end, the last straw, the straw that broke the camel's back

☲ tolerable

intolerance n

impatience, prejudice, discrimination, narrowness, narrow-mindedness, small-mindedness, insularity, bigotry, opinionativeness, dogmatism, fanaticism, extremism, illiberality, uncharitableness, chauvinism, jingoism, racialism, racism, sexism, ageism, xenophobia, anti-Semitism

☲ tolerance

intolerant adj

impatient, prejudiced, biased, discriminating, partisan, one-sided, bigoted, narrow, narrow-minded, small-minded, provincial, parochial, insular, opinionated, dogmatic, fanatical, extremist, illiberal, uncharitable, chauvinistic, jingoistic, racist, racialist, sexist, ageist, xenophobic, anti-Semitic

☲ tolerant

intonation n

modulation, tone, accentuation, emphasis, stress, inflection, pitch, timbre, lilt, cadence

intone v
chant, croon, intonate, monotone, enunciate, pronounce, recite, sing, say, speak, voice, utter, *formal* declaim

intoxicate n
1 MAKE DRUNK, befuddle, fuddle, stupefy, *formal* inebriate **2** EXCITE, elate, exhilarate, stimulate, thrill, animate, enthuse, inspire, inflame

intoxicated adj
1 DRUNK, drunken, under the influence, *formal* inebriated, crapulent, *colloq.* merry, tight, tipsy, tiddly, well-oiled, blotto, drunk as a lord/newt, blind drunk, roaring drunk, the worse for drink, soused, squiffy, happy, legless, plastered, sozzled, pickled, bibulous, woozy, one over the eight, under the table, bevvied, have had a few, *slang* stoned, tanked up, loaded, lit up, canned, paralytic, sloshed, smashed, stewed, bombed **2** EXCITED, elated, exhilarated, thrilled, moved, stirred, stimulated, enthusiastic, worked up, in high spirits, *colloq.* carried away
🖪 **1** sober

intoxicating adj
1 *intoxicating liquor* alcoholic, strong, stimulant, *formal* inebriant, *colloq.* going to your head **2** EXCITING, stimulating, heady, exhilarating, thrilling, stirring, dramatic, rousing, moving, enthralling, inspiring
🖪 **1** sobering

intoxication n
1 DRUNKENNESS, intemperance, alcoholism, hard/serious drinking, debauchery, dipsomania, *technical* methysis, *formal* inebriation, inebriety, insobriety, intoxication, crapulence, *colloq.* bibulousness, tipsiness **2** EXCITEMENT, elation, exhilaration, thrill, pleasure, animation, enthusiasm, stimulation, euphoria, rapture
🖪 **1** sobriety

intractability n
unmanageableness, uncontrollableness, ungovernability, unco-operativeness, unamenability, waywardness, stubbornness, obstinacy, perverseness, perversity, awkwardness, pig-headedness, indiscipline, incorrigibility, cantankerousness, contrariness, *formal* obduracy
🖪 amenability

intractable adj
unmanageable, uncontrollable, unyielding, unbending, unco-operative, undisciplined, ungovernable, unamenable, wild, unruly, obstinate, perverse, self-willed, wilful, wayward, pig-headed, stubborn, disobedient, awkward, difficult, fractious, headstrong, cantankerous, contrary, *formal* intransigent, obdurate, refractory
🖪 amenable

intransigent adj
stubborn, obstinate, uncompromising, unamenable, unbending, unpersuadable, unyielding, unbudgeable, unrelenting, relentless, inexorable, immovable, irreconcilable, implacable, hardline, determined, rigid, tenacious, tough, *formal* intractable, obdurate, *colloq.* uppity
🖪 amenable, flexible

intrepid adj
bold, daring, brave, courageous, plucky, valiant, audacious, lion-hearted, fearless, dauntless, undaunted, undismayed, unflinching, stout-hearted, spirited, stalwart, gallant, heroic, *formal* doughty, valorous, *colloq.* gutsy, spunky, gritty
🖪 cowardly, timid, afraid

intrepidness n
boldness, bravery, daring, intrepidity, audacity, val-

our, courage, heroism, dauntlessness, fearlessness, gallantry, lion-heartedness, stout-heartedness, undauntedness, pluck, prowess, spirit, nerve, *formal* doughtiness, fortitude, *colloq.* guts
🖪 cowardice, timidity

intricacy n
complexity, complexness, complexedness, complication, intricateness, elaborateness, entanglement, sophistication, involvement, knottiness, obscurity, enigma, involution, *formal* convolution(s)
🖪 simplicity, straightforwardness

intricate adj
complex, complicated, elaborate, sophisticated, involved, tortuous, tangled, entangled, ravelled, knotty, twisty, perplexing, baffling, puzzling, difficult, enigmatic, fancy, ornate, rococo, *formal* convoluted
🖪 simple, plain, straightforward

intrigue n, v
▶ n **1** PLOT, scheme, conspiracy, conniving, manoeuvre, stratagem, artifice, ruse, wile, trickery, cabal, double-dealing, *formal* collusion, machination, *colloq.* sharp practice, dodge **2** ROMANCE, liaison, affair, love affair, amour, intimacy
▶ v **1** FASCINATE, arouse your curiosity, rivet, tantalize, attract, pull, draw, charm, captivate, absorb, interest, puzzle **2** PLOT, scheme, conspire, connive, manoeuvre, *formal* machinate
🖪 **1** bore

intriguer n
plotter, schemer, conspirator, collaborator, conniver, Machiavellian, intrigant(e), *formal* machinator, *colloq.* wangler, wheeler-dealer, wire-puller

intriguing adj
fascinating, appealing, charming, absorbing, riveting, compelling, captivating, diverting, exciting, interesting, beguiling, attractive, tantalizing, titillating, puzzling
🖪 boring, uninteresting, dull

intrinsic adj
basic, central, essential, fundamental, natural, underlying, built-in, in-built, inborn, inbred, interior, inherent, inward, native, indigenous, congenital, constitutional, elemental, genuine
🖪 extrinsic

introduce v
1 INSTITUTE, begin, start, establish, found, originate, organize, develop, inaugurate, launch, usher in, open, bring in, initiate, put/set in motion, *formal* commence **2** PUT FORWARD, advance, submit, offer, propose, suggest **3** PRESENT, announce, acquaint, familiarize **4** PREFACE, precede, begin, start, lead in, lead into, *formal* commence
🖪 **1** end, conclude **2** remove, take away **4** conclude, end, finish

introduction n
1 INSTITUTION, beginning, start, establishment, origination, organization, development, inauguration, launch, presentation, debut, initiation, *formal* commencement **2** FOREWORD, preface, preamble, prologue, preliminaries, front matter, overture, prelude, lead-in, opening, *formal* prolegomenon, exordium, proem, *colloq.* intro **3** PRESENTATION, announcement, familiarization, acquainting **4** BASICS, fundamentals, essentials, rudiments, first principles
🖪 **1** removal, withdrawal **2** appendix, conclusion

introductory adj
preliminary, preparatory, opening, inaugural, first, beginning, starting, initial, early, elementary, basic, fundamental, essential, rudimentary, *formal* prefatory, initiatory, precursory, exordial, isagogic

introspection *n*
self-examination, contemplation, pensiveness, brooding, thoughtfulness, self-analysis, self-centredness, self-observation, soul-searching, heart-searching, introversion, *colloq.* navel-gazing, navel-contemplation

introspective *adj*
inward-looking, contemplative, meditative, pensive, thoughtful, brooding, musing, introverted, subjective, self-centred, self-absorbed, self-examining, self-analysing, self-observing, reserved, withdrawn
F3 outward-looking

introverted *adj*
introspective, inward-looking, self-centred, self-absorbed, self-examining, introspective, withdrawn, shy, reserved, quiet
F3 extroverted

intrude *v*
interrupt, meddle, interfere, violate, invade, infringe, encroach, trespass, *formal* interject, obtrude, interlope, *colloq.* gatecrash, barge in, chip in, butt in
F3 withdraw, stand back

intruder *n*
trespasser, prowler, burglar, raider, housebreaker, robber, pilferer, thief, unwelcome guest, invader, infiltrator, *formal* interloper, *colloq.* gatecrasher

intrusion *n*
interruption, interference, meddling, violation, infringement, encroachment, trespass, invasion, *formal* incursion, obtrusion, *colloq.* gatecrashing
F3 withdrawal

intrusive *adj*
disturbing, interfering, irritating, annoying, troublesome, invasive, obtrusive, interrupting, trespassing, meddlesome, uncalled-for, unwanted, unwelcome, uninvited, forward, impertinent, officious, presumptuous, *formal* importunate, *colloq.* nosy, pushy, snooping, go-getting
F3 unintrusive, welcome

intuition *n*
instinct, sixth sense, perception, discernment, insight, hunch, feeling, extrasensory perception, *formal* presentiment, *colloq.* gut feeling, feeling in your bones
F3 reasoning

intuitive *adj*
instinctive, intuitional, spontaneous, involuntary, automatic, innate, inborn, unlearned, untaught
F3 reasoned

inundate *v*
flood, deluge, swamp, engulf, submerge, soak, immerse, drown, saturate, bury, overwhelm, overburden, overrun, overflow

inundation *n*
flood, deluge, swamp, overflow, torrent, spate, tidal wave, excess, surplus, glut
F3 trickle

inure *v*
accustom, familiarize, acclimatize, harden, temper, strengthen, desensitize, toughen, train, *formal* habituate

invade *v*
1 *invade a country* enter (by force), penetrate, infiltrate, burst in, descend on, attack, assault, raid, seize, storm, maraud, plunder, pillage, occupy, take over, march into, overrun, swarm over, infest, pervade **2** *invade someone's privacy* intrude, encroach, infringe, violate, trespass, interrupt, *formal* obtrude
F3 withdraw, evacuate

invader *n*
aggressor, attacker, assailant, raider, plunderer, marauder, pillager, intruder, trespasser, infringer

invalid[1] *n, adj*
▶ *n* visit *an invalid in hospital* patient, sufferer, convalescent, *formal* valetudinarian
▶ *adj* sick, ill, unwell, poorly, ailing, sickly, weak, feeble, frail, infirm, disabled, bedridden, *formal* debilitated, valetudinarian
F3 healthy

invalid[2] *adj*
1 FALSE, unsound, ill-founded, unfounded, baseless, groundless, unjustified, unsubstantiated, untenable, unacceptable, unwarranted, illogical, irrational, unscientific, wrong, incorrect, weak, mistaken, erroneous, *formal* fallacious **2** ILLEGAL, null, void, null and void, worthless, abolished, cancelled, quashed, overturned, *formal* inoperative, revoked, rescinded, nullified
F3 1 valid, sound **2** legal, binding

invalidate *v*
annul, cancel, quash, void, veto, discredit, negate, undo, overrule, overthrow, undermine, weaken, *formal* abrogate, nullify, rescind, vitiate, revoke, terminate
F3 validate

invalidity *n*
incorrectness, falsity, irrationality, unsoundness, sophism, speciousness, illogicality, inconsistency, voidness, *formal* fallaciousness, fallacy

invaluable *adj*
priceless, inestimable, incalculable, indispensable, precious, valuable, costly, useful
F3 worthless, cheap

invariable *adj*
fixed, set, unvarying, unchanging, unchangeable, unalterable, changeless, permanent, constant, steady, consistent, stable, unwavering, uniform, rigid, inflexible, habitual, regular, *formal* immutable, invariant
F3 variable, changeable

invariably *adv*
always, without exception, without fail, unfailingly, consistently, regularly, repeatedly, constantly, habitually, inevitably
F3 never

invasion *n*
1 *an invasion of a country* attack, offensive, onslaught, raid, foray, breach, occupation, storming, penetration, infiltration, *formal* incursion **2** *invasion of privacy* interference, interruption, intrusion, encroachment, infringement, violation
F3 1 withdrawal, evacuation

invective *n*
abuse, denunciation, reproach, scolding, reprimand, rebuke, tirade, diatribe, recrimination, sarcasm, tongue-lashing, *formal* censure, revilement, fulmination, berating, castigation, obloquy, philippic, vilification, vituperation, contumely
F3 praise

inveigh *v*
criticize, blame, condemn, upbraid, denounce, scold, rail, recriminate, reproach, sound off, tongue-lash, *formal* censure, fulminate, castigate, berate, lambast, expostulate, vituperate
F3 praise

inveigle *v*
cajole, persuade, beguile, coax, allure, lure, seduce, entrap, ensnare, entice, wile, decoy, manipulate, manoeuvre, lead on, wheedle, *colloq.* bamboozle, con, sweet-talk

invent *v*
1 CONCEIVE, think up, design, discover, create, originate, innovate, be the brainchild of, pioneer, formulate, frame, devise, contrive, improvise, coin, come up with, hit upon, dream up, fabricate **2** *invent an ex-*

cuse make up, concoct, cook up, trump up, imagine, dream up

invention *n*

1 *her latest invention* design, creation, brainchild, innovation, discovery, development, construction, device, machine, system, contrivance, gadget **2** *the invention of the steam engine* design, creation, discovery, development, innovation, contriving **3** LIE, falsehood, falsification, untruth, deceit, fabrication, concoction, fake, forgery, fiction, fantasy, myth, figment, *colloq.* tall story, fib **4** INVENTIVENESS, imagination, creativity, innovation, originality, ingenuity, resourcefulness, skill, artistry, talent, gift, inspiration, genius
F3 **3** truth

inventive *adj*
imaginative, creative, innovative, original, ingenious, resourceful, fertile, skilful, inspired, artistic, talented, gifted, clever

inventor *n*
designer, discoverer, creator, originator, innovator, deviser, author, architect, developer, maker, producer, framer, scientist, engineer, father, mother

inventory *n*
list, listing, checklist, record, register, catalogue, tally, file, account, description, schedule, roll, roster, equipment, supply, stock

inverse *adj, n*
▶ *adj* inverted, upside down, transposed, reversed, opposite, other, contrary, counter, reverse, converse, obverse
F3 converse
▶ *n* opposite, contrary, reverse, converse, obverse, *colloq.* the other side of the coin

inversion *n*
opposite, reversal, reverse, converse, transposal, transposition, contrary, *technical* hysteron-proteron, *formal* antithesis, contrariety, contraposition

invert *v*
upturn, turn upside down, turn back to front, turn inside out, turn around, overturn, capsize, turn turtle, upset, transpose, reverse
F3 right

invertebrate *n*

Invertebrates include:
sponges: calcareous, glass, horny; *jellyfish, corals and sea anemones:* Portuguese man-of-war, box jellyfish, sea wasp, dead-men's fingers, sea pansy, sea gooseberry, Venus's girdle; *echinoderms:* sea lily, feather star, starfish, crown-of-thorns, brittle star, sea urchin, sand dollar, sea cucumber; *worms:* annelid worm, arrow worm, blood fluke, bristle worm, earthworm, eelworm, flatworm, fluke, hookworm, leech, liver fluke, lugworm, peanut worm, pinworm, ragworm, ribbonworm, roundworm, sea mouse, tapeworm, threadworm; *crustaceans:* acorn barnacle, barnacle, brine shrimp, crayfish, daphnia, fairy shrimp, fiddler crab, fish louse, goose barnacle, hermit crab, krill, lobster, mantis shrimp, mussel shrimp, pill bug, prawn, sand hopper, seed shrimp, spider crab, spiny lobster, tadpole shrimp, water flea, whale louse, woodlouse; centipede, millipede, velvet worm. *See also* BUTTERFLY; INSECT; MOLLUSC; MOTH.

invest *v*
1 SPEND, lay out, put in, sink, subsidize, fund **2** *invest time/energy in something* spend, put in, devote, dedicate, give, contribute **3** PROVIDE, supply, give, endow,

grant, entrust, vest, empower, authorize, sanction, *formal* confer, bestow **4** *invest a person in authority* induct, install, inaugurate, ordain

investigate *v*
inquire into, look into, consider, examine, study, inspect, scrutinize, analyse, research, go into, delve into, probe, explore, search, sift, *colloq.* check out, suss out, give the once-over, see how the land lies, see which way the wind is blowing

investigation *n*
inquiry, inquest, hearing, consideration, examination, study, research, survey, review, inspection, scrutiny, analysis, probe, exploration, search, sifting, fact-finding mission/visit

investigative *adj*
fact-finding, investigating, inspecting, research, researching, analytical, exploratory, *formal* heuristic, zetetic

investigator *n*
examiner, researcher, inquirer, reviewer, inspector, searcher, scrutineer, scrutinizer, analyst, analyser, explorer, prober, questioner, detective, private detective, *colloq.* sleuth, private eye

investiture *n*
installation, induction, inauguration, investing, investment, ordination, coronation, enthronement, admission, instatement

investment *n*
asset, speculation, venture, stake, risk, contribution, outlay, expenditure, capital, cash, savings, wealth, resources, money, funds, finance, principal, property, stock, reserve, transaction

inveterate *adj*
chronic, habitual, hardened, diehard, dyed-in-the-wool, entrenched, confirmed, established, hard-core, obstinate, incorrigible, incurable, irreformable, inured, addicted, long-standing
F3 impermanent

invidious *adj*
awkward, difficult, undesirable, unpleasant, objectionable, hateful, obnoxious, offensive, slighting, odious, discriminating, discriminatory, *formal* repugnant
F3 desirable, pleasant

invigorate *v*
vitalize, energize, animate, enliven, liven up, quicken, strengthen, brace, motivate, stimulate, inspire, exhilarate, excite, rouse, refresh, freshen, revitalize, rejuvenate, *formal* fortify, *colloq.* perk up, pep up, buck up, soup up, give a new lease of life to
F3 tire, weary, dishearten

invigorating *adj*
energizing, stimulating, refreshing, animating, exhilarating, fresh, bracing, uplifting, rejuvenating, vivifying, restorative, tonic, healthful, generous, *formal* inspiriting, salubrious
F3 tiring, disheartening, wearying

invincible *adj*
unbeatable, unconquerable, insuperable, unsurmountable, undefeatable, unassailable, impregnable, impenetrable, invulnerable, indestructible, unyielding, unshakable, *formal* indomitable
F3 beatable, surmountable

inviolability *n*
inalienability, inviolableness, inviolacy, invulnerability, sacrosanctness, sanctity, sacredness, holiness
F3 violability

inviolable *adj*
inalienable, unalterable, untouchable, sacred, sacrosanct, holy, hallowed, *formal* intemerate
F3 violable, alienable

inviolate *adj*
entire, intact, complete, whole, undisturbed, unbroken, unhurt, undamaged, unharmed, uninjured, untouched, unpolluted, unprofaned, undefiled, unstained, unsullied, unspoiled, stainless, pure, sacred, virgin, *formal* intemerate
☒ sullied

invisible *adj*
unseen, out of sight, hidden, concealed, disguised, unnoticed, unobserved, inconspicuous, indiscernible, imperceptible, imperceivable, undetectable, indistinguishable, infinitesimal, microscopic, imaginary, non-existent
☒ visible

invitation *n*
request, call, summons, bidding, petition, appeal, temptation, enticement, allurement, lure, bait, draw, attraction, encouragement, inducement, provocation, incitement, challenge, welcome, overture, *formal* solicitation, *colloq.* come-on

invite *v*
1 ASK, have round/over, entertain, call, summon, bid, petition, appeal, welcome, encourage, bring on, provoke, ask for, seek, look for, *formal* request, solicit, request the pleasure of someone's company **2** ATTRACT, lead, draw, tempt, entice, allure

inviting *adj*
welcoming, appealing, attractive, tempting, seductive, enticing, alluring, pleasing, pleasant, agreeable, delightful, captivating, fascinating, enchanting, entrancing, intriguing, beguiling, bewitching, tantalizing, engaging, winning, irresistible
☒ uninviting, unappealing, unattractive, disagreeable, unpleasant, *colloq.* off-putting

invocation *n*
appeal, petition, prayer, *formal* request, supplication, solicitation, beseeching, entreaty, conjuration, imploration, epiclesis

invoice *n*
account bill, statement of account, charges, reckoning

invoke *v*
1 *invoke God for help* call upon, appeal to, petition, implore, beg, pray, *formal* request, supplicate, beseech, entreat, solicit, imprecate, conjure **2** *invoke a law* turn to, resort to, have recourse to, make use of

involuntary *adj*
1 SPONTANEOUS, unconscious, automatic, mechanical, reflex, instinctive, conditioned, impulsive, unthinking, blind, uncontrolled, unintentional, forced **2** FORCED, compelled, coerced, reluctant, unwilling, against your wishes
☒ **1** deliberate, intentional

involve *v*
1 REQUIRE, mean, assume, presuppose, imply, entail, include, incorporate, encompass, cover, take in, affect, concern, *formal* necessitate, denote, embrace, comprehend **2** IMPLICATE, incriminate, draw in, let yourself in for, mix up, embroil, associate, connect, cause to take part, *formal* inculpate **3** ENGAGE, interest, occupy, absorb, engross, preoccupy, hold, grip, rivet
☒ **1** exclude

involved *adj*
1 CONCERNED, associated, taking part, implicated, incriminated, mixed up, caught up, participating, *formal* inculpated, *colloq.* in on **2** *an involved explanation* complicated, complex, intricate, difficult, elaborate, tangled, jumbled, knotty, tortuous, confusing, confused, *formal* convoluted
☒ **1** uninvolved **2** simple

involvement *n*
concern, interest, responsibility, association, connection, participation, contribution, share, part, implication, entanglement, attachment

invulnerability *n*
safety, security, strength, unassailability, impenetrability, invincibility, impregnability, inviolability, insusceptibility
☒ vulnerability

invulnerable *adj*
safe, secure, unassailable, impenetrable, invincible, indestructible
☒ vulnerable

inward *adj*
incoming, entering, inside, interior, internal, inner, innermost, inmost, hidden, personal, private, intimate, secret, confidential
☒ outward, external

inwardly *adv*
inside, to yourself, within, at heart, in your heart of hearts, deep down, deep inside you, privately, secretly
☒ externally, outwardly

iota *n*
scrap, bit, mite, jot, whit, speck, trace, hint, grain, morsel, fraction, particle, atom, *colloq.* tad

irascibility *n*
snappishness, bad temper, cantankerousness, irritability, irritation, petulance, impatience, ill-temper, crossness, shortness, testiness, touchiness, fieriness, *colloq.* crabbiness, edginess
☒ placidness

irascible *adj*
quick-tempered, short-tempered, bad-tempered, ill-natured, ill-tempered, hot-tempered, cantankerous, petulant, irritable, testy, touchy, choleric, cross, hasty, *formal* querulous, iracund, iracundulous, *colloq.* crabbed, crabby, narky, prickly
☒ placid

irate *adj*
annoyed, irritated, indignant, up in arms, angry, enraged, furious, infuriated, incensed, worked up, fuming, raging, ranting, livid, exasperated, vexed, *colloq.* mad
☒ calm, composed

ire *n*
anger, wrath, exasperation, annoyance, fury, rage, indignation, passion, displeasure, choler
☒ calmness

iridescent *adj*
shimmering, sparkling, multicoloured, prismatic, rainbow, rainbow-coloured, rainbow-like, dazzling, glittering, shot, pearly, polychromatic, *formal* opalescent, variegated

irk *v*
annoy, anger, exasperate, incense, infuriate, irritate, provoke, put out, ruffle, get, get to, vex, weary, nettle, distress, gall, disgust, rile, *colloq.* aggravate, bug, miff, peeve, hassle, rub up the wrong way, make someone's blood boil
☒ please

irksome *adj*
annoying, irritating, infuriating, exasperating, vexing, vexatious, wearisome, bothersome, burdensome, disagreeable, tiresome, troublesome, trying, tedious, boring, *colloq.* aggravating
☒ pleasing

iron *adj, v*
▶ *adj* rigid, inflexible, adamant, determined, hard, steely, tough, strong, firm
☒ pliable, weak
▶ *v* press, smooth, flatten

▷ **iron out** resolve, settle, sort out, straighten out, clear up, put right, reconcile, harmonize, deal with, get rid of, eradicate, eliminate

ironic *adj*
ironical, sarcastic, sardonic, scornful, contemptuous, derisive, sneering, scoffing, ridiculing, ridiculous, mocking, satirical, wry, paradoxical, *colloq.* rich

irons *n*
chains, bonds, fetters, shackles, trammels, manacles

irony *n*
sarcasm, mockery, ridicule, scorn, satire, paradox, contrariness, *formal* incongruity

irradiate *v*
brighten, enlighten, light up, lighten, illume, illuminate, illumine, expose, radiate, shine on

irrational *adj*
unreasonable, unsound, illogical, inconsistent, invalid, groundless, implausible, arbitrary, ridiculous, absurd, crazy, wild, foolish, silly, senseless, nonsensical, unwise
F rational, reasonable

irrationality *n*
unreasonableness, unreason, unsoundness, illogicality, groundlessness, absurdity, ridiculousness, senselessness, preposterousness, madness, lunacy, insanity
F rationality

irreconcilable *adj*
incompatible, opposed, contrary, opposite, at odds, conflicting, clashing, contradictory, inconsistent, uncompromising, hardline, inflexible, implacable, inexorable, *formal* incongruous, intransigent
F reconcilable

irrecoverable *adj*
irretrievable, lost, unrecoverable, unsavable, irredeemable, irreclaimable, irremediable, irreparable, unsalvageable
F recoverable

irrefutable *adj*
undeniable, incontrovertible, indisputable, incontestable, unquestionable, beyond doubt/question, indubitable, unanswerable, certain, sure, definite, positive, decisive

irregular *adj*
1 ROUGH, bumpy, lumpy, uneven, pitted, crooked, ragged, jagged, crooked, asymmetric, lopsided **2** VARIABLE, fluctuating, wavering, unsteady, uneven, shaky, erratic, fitful, intermittent, sporadic, spasmodic, occasional, random, haphazard, disorganized, fragmentary, disorderly, unmethodical, unsystematic, inconsistent **3** ABNORMAL, unconventional, unorthodox, unofficial, improper, unusual, exceptional, anomalous, out of order, aberrant, extraordinary, freak, odd, strange, peculiar **4** DISHONEST, lawless, deceitful, fraudulent, false, cheating, unprincipled, immoderate, indecent, improper
F **1** smooth, level, uniform **2** regular **3** conventional **4** honest

irregularity *n*
1 ROUGHNESS, bumpiness, unevenness, raggedness, jaggedness, crookedness, asymmetry, lopsidedness, lumpiness **2** VARIABILITY, fluctuation, wavering, fitfulness, intermittence, spasm, occasionalness, randomness, haphazardness, disorderliness, unpunctuality, inconsistency, unsteadiness, uncertainty, inconstancy, disorganization, patchiness **3** ABNORMALITY, unconventionality, unorthodoxy, anomaly, deviation, breach, aberration, oddity, peculiarity, eccentricity, freak, *formal* singularity **4** DISHONESTY, lawlessness, deceit, fraudulence, fraud, cheating, malpractice

F **1** smoothness, levelness **2** regularity **3** conventionality

irregularly *adv*
occasionally, now and again, off and on, unevenly, spasmodically, haphazardly, intermittently, jerkily, unmethodically, anyhow, disconnectedly, eccentrically, erratically, fitfully, *colloq.* by/in fits and starts
F regularly

irrelevance *n*
inappropriateness, inaptness, unimportance, unrelatedness, inconsequence, irrelevancy, *formal* inappositeness, *colloq.* red herring
F relevance, bearing

irrelevant *adj*
immaterial, beside/off the point, inapplicable, inappropriate, inapt, unimportant, out of place, having no bearing, unrelated, unconnected, inconsequent, peripheral, tangential, *formal* inapposite, *colloq.* neither here nor there, not coming into it, making no difference, not matter
F relevant

irreligious *adj*
atheistic, unbelieving, ungodly, unreligious, godless, undevout, unholy, unrighteous, agnostic, sceptical, heathenish, pagan, heathen, heretical, sacrilegious, iconoclastic, impious, irreverent, blasphemous, freethinking, profane, rationalistic, sinful, wicked, *formal* nullifidian
F pious, religious

irremediable *adj*
irreparable, irretrievable, irrecoverable, irreversible, remediless, irredeemable, incurable, inoperable, incorrigible, terminal, unmedicinable, deadly, fatal, final, hopeless, mortal
F remediable

irremovable *adj*
durable, immovable, indestructible, ineradicable, ingrained, inoperable, fast, fixed, set, stuck, permanent, persistent, rooted, obstinate, *formal* obdurate
F removable

irreparable *adj*
irreversible, irreclaimable, irrecoverable, irremediable, irretrievable, incurable, unrepairable
F recoverable, remediable

irreplaceable *adj*
indispensable, essential, vital, unique, priceless, precious, peerless, matchless, unmatched, special
F replaceable

irrepressible *adj*
ebullient, bubbly, uninhibited, buoyant, effervescent, animated, vivacious, resilient, boisterous, uncontrollable, unrestrainable, ungovernable, unstoppable, insuppressible, uncontainable

irreproachable *adj*
irreprehensible, blameless, unblamable, innocent, beyond reproach, unimpeachable, faultless, guiltless, flawless, impeccable, perfect, unblemished, immaculate, stainless, spotless, sinless, pure
F blameworthy, *formal* culpable

irresistible *adj*
1 *irresistible desire* overwhelming, overpowering, forceful, unavoidable, inevitable, inescapable, inexorable, unpreventable, uncontrollable, irrepressible, potent, compelling, imperative, pressing, urgent **2** *irresistible beauty* tempting, enticing, alluring, captivating, tantalizing, seductive, ravishing, enchanting, charming, fascinating
F **1** resistible, avoidable **2** unattractive, repulsive

irresolute *adj*
indecisive, hesitating, hesitant, unsure, uncertain,

doubtful, dubious, ambivalent, wavering, fluctuating, shifting, dithering, variable, weak, faint-hearted, fickle, undecided, unsettled, undetermined, unstable, unsteady, half-hearted, tentative, *formal* vacillating, *colloq.* shilly-shallying, pussyfooting, in two minds, (sitting) on the fence
F3 resolute, decisive

irrespective *adj*
▷ **irrespective of** regardless of, disregarding, no matter, without considering, ignoring, not affecting, however, whatever, whichever, whoever, never mind, *formal* notwithstanding

irresponsible *adj*
unreliable, untrustworthy, careless, negligent, thoughtless, unwise, heedless, ill-considered, rash, reckless, wild, carefree, flighty, erratic, scatterbrained, light-hearted, immature, *formal* injudicious
F3 responsible, dependable, cautious

irretrievable *adj*
irreparable, irrecoverable, irreversible, irredeemable, irremediable, unrecoverable, unrecallable, lost, hopeless, unsalvageable, damned, *formal* irrevocable
F3 recoverable, reversible

irreverence *n*
1 IMPIETY, godlessness, ungodliness, irreligion, heresy, profanity, sacrilege, blasphemy **2** DISRESPECT, disrespectfulness, discourtesy, rudeness, impoliteness, insolence, impudence, impertinence, mockery, flippancy, levity, cheekiness, *colloq.* sauce, cheek
F3 **1, 2** reverence

irreverent *adj*
1 IMPIOUS, godless, ungodly, irreligious, heretical, profane, sacrilegious, blasphemous **2** DISRESPECTFUL, discourteous, rude, impolite, impudent, impertinent, insolent, mocking, flippant, *colloq.* cheeky, saucy
F3 **1** reverent **2** respectful, deferential

irreversible *adj*
irrevocable, unalterable, final, permanent, lasting, irreparable, irremediable, irretrievable, incurable, unrectifiable, hopeless
F3 reversible, remediable, curable

irrevocable *adj*
unalterable, unchangeable, changeless, invariable, final, fixed, settled, irreversible, irretrievable, *formal* immutable, predetermined
F3 alterable, flexible, reversible

irrigate *v*
water, flood, inundate, wet, soak, moisten, dampen, spray, sprinkle

irritability *n*
crossness, bad temper, ill-temper, impatience, grumpiness, prickliness, touchiness, fretfulness, edge, edginess, hypersensitivity, testiness, tetchiness, irascibility, peevishness, petulance, fractiousness
F3 cheerfulness, complacence, good humour, bonhomie

irritable *adj*
cross, bad-tempered, ill-tempered, quick-tempered, grumpy, crusty, cantankerous, testy, short-tempered, snappish, snappy, short, impatient, touchy, edgy, thin-skinned, hypersensitive, prickly, peevish, fretful, fractious, irascible, *colloq.* crotchety, crabby, ratty, stroppy, shirty
F3 good-tempered, cheerful

irritant *n*
annoyance, nuisance, trouble, bother, menace, provocation, vexation, goad, *colloq.* pain, thorn in the flesh
F3 pleasure, sweetness

irritate *v*
1 ANNOY, bother, harass, rouse, provoke, rile, irk, vex, goad, nettle, anger, enrage, infuriate, incense, exasperate, put out, grate, jar, *colloq.* aggravate, bug, get, get on your nerves, get your blood up, rub up the wrong way, get your back up, get under your skin, drive crazy/nuts, drive round the bend/up the wall, peeve **2** INFLAME, chafe, rub, fret, hurt, tickle, itch
F3 **1** please, gratify

irritated *adj*
annoyed, bothered, angry, cross, exasperated, irked, irritable, nettled, vexed, ruffled, roused, riled, edgy, impatient, uptight, harassed, flustered, discomposed, displeased, piqued, *formal* exacerbated, *colloq.* peeved, put out, ratty, narked, miffed, in a huff
F3 composed, gratified, pleased

irritating *adj*
1 ANNOYING, infuriating, maddening, troublesome, bothersome, irksome, tiresome, grating, worrisome, vexatious, vexing, disturbing, upsetting, nagging, displeasing, galling, provoking, thorny, trying, *colloq.* aggravating, pesky **2** ABRASIVE, rubbing, chafing, sore, ticklish, itchy
F3 **1** pleasant, pleasing

irritation *n*
1 *express your irritation* displeasure, dissatisfaction, annoyance, aggravation, provocation, anger, vexation, pique, indignation, fury, exasperation, irritability, crossness, testiness, snappiness, impatience **2** NUISANCE, annoyance, disturbance, bother, trouble, pest, *colloq.* pain, pain in the neck, thorn in the flesh, drag, bind
F3 pleasure, satisfaction, delight

island *n*
isle, islet, atoll, archipelago, eyot, holm, cay, key, skerry

The world's largest islands include:
Australia, Greenland, New Guinea, Borneo, Madagascar, Sumatra, Baffin (Canada), Honshu (Japan), Great Britain, Victoria (Canada).

isolate *v*
set apart, seclude, keep apart, segregate, quarantine, insulate, abstract, cut off, strand, maroon, detach, remove, disconnect, separate, divorce, alienate, shut out/away, ostracize, exclude, *formal* sequester, *colloq.* cold-shoulder, send to Coventry
F3 assimilate, incorporate, integrate

isolated *adj*
1 REMOTE, out-of-the-way, outlying, God-forsaken, deserted, unfrequented, secluded, detached, cut off, lonely, solitary, alone, separated, segregated, apart, single, *colloq.* off the beaten track **2** *an isolated occurrence* unique, special, exceptional, atypical, untypical, solitary, single, unusual, uncommon, freak, abnormal, anomalous, unrelated
F3 **1** populous **2** typical, common

isolation *n*
quarantine, solitude, solitariness, loneliness, aloneness, remoteness, seclusion, retirement, withdrawal, exile, segregation, insulation, separation, separateness, detachment, disconnection, dissociation, alienation, abstraction, *formal* sequestration
F3 contact

issue *n, v*
▶ *n* **1** MATTER, affair, concern, problem, point, subject, topic, question, debate, argument, dispute, controversy **2** PUBLICATION, release, distribution, supply, supplying, delivery, circulation, broadcast, announcement, *formal* promulgation, dissemination

3 *last week's issue* copy, number, instalment, edition, impression, version, printing **4** RESULT, consequence, upshot, outcome, conclusion, effect, finale, *colloq.* pay-off **5** OFFSPRING, descendants, children, family, progeny, heirs, successors, seed, young, *formal* scions **6** OUTFLOW, discharge, rush, jet, spurt, gush, *formal* effusion, effluence

▷ **at issue** being discussed, under discussion, in question, being debated

▷ **take issue** disagree, argue, challenge, quarrel, fight, dispute, contest, protest, be at odds with, object, take exception, call into question

▶ *v* **1** PUBLISH, put out, release, distribute, supply, deliver, give out, deal out, circulate, broadcast, announce, proclaim, *formal* promulgate, disseminate **2** ORIGINATE, stem, result, spring, rise, emerge, burst forth, gush, flow, proceed, emanate, arise **3** COME OUT, emit, produce, discharge, emanate, emerge, burst forth, gush, flow, exude, ooze, seep

itch *v, n*

▶ *v* **1** TICKLE, irritate, tingle, prickle, crawl **2** *be itching to do something* die, long, burn, pine, crave, hanker, yearn, ache

▶ *n* **1** ITCHINESS, tickle, irritation, prickling, tingling

2 EAGERNESS, keenness, desire, ache, hunger, thirst, longing, yearning, hankering, craving, burning

itching *adj*

dying, longing, burning, hankering, aching, eager, greedy, impatient, inquisitive, avid, raring

item *n*

1 OBJECT, article, thing, piece, component, ingredient, element, factor, point, detail, particular, aspect, feature, consideration, matter, circumstance **2** *an item in the local paper* article, piece, feature, report, story, account, notice, entry, paragraph, bulletin

itemize *v*

list, record, specify, detail, document, instance, particularize, count, mention, overname, number, enumerate, tabulate, make an inventory

itinerant *adj*

travelling, peripatetic, roving, roaming, wandering, journeying, wayfaring, drifting, rambling, nomadic, migratory, vagrant, rootless, unsettled, vagabond

🡢 stationary, settled

itinerary *n*

route, course, journey, tour, circuit, plan, arrangements, programme, schedule, timetable

J

jab *v, n*
- ▶ *v* poke, prod, dig, nudge, stab, push, elbow, lunge, punch, box, tap, thrust
- ▶ *n* poke, prod, dig, nudge, stab, push, punch, box, tap, shot, injection

jabber *v*
chatter, gab, gabble, prattle, rabbit, ramble, tattle, babble, blather, blether, jaw, prate, rattle, mumble, witter, yap

jack *v*
▷ **jack up 1** LIFT, raise, hoist, elevate **2** *jack up prices* increase, inflate, put up, push up, hike (up)

jacket *n*
CASING, cover, covering, wrapping, wrap, wrapper, case, sheath, shell, skin, envelope, folder. *See panel at* COAT.

jackpot *n*
prize, first prize, winnings, kitty, pool, pot, reward, award, bonanza, stakes, *colloq.* big time

jaded *adj*
fatigued, exhausted, dulled, played-out, tired, tired out, weary, wearied, worn out, spent, bored, unenthusiastic, *colloq.* fagged, done in, bushed, fed up, cheesed off
🖪 fresh, refreshed

jag *n*
barb, point, projection, protrusion, snag, notch, spur, tooth, *technical* denticle, dentil

jagged *adj*
uneven, irregular, notched, indented, rough, serrated, saw-edged, toothed, ragged, pointed, ridged, craggy, snagged, snaggy, barbed, spiked, nicked, broken, *technical* denticulate
🖪 even, smooth

jail, gaol *n, v*
- ▶ *n* prison, jailhouse, custody, lock-up, penitentiary, detention centre, guardhouse, *colloq.* inside, nick, *slang* clink, cooler, slammer, quod, jug, can, choky
- ▶ *v* imprison, lock up, put away, send down, send to prison, confine, detain, intern, impound, immure, *formal* incarcerate

jailer, gaoler *n*
prison officer, warden, warder, guard, keeper, captor, *slang* screw

jam¹ *n*
bread and jam conserve, preserve, jelly, spread, marmalade, confiture

jam² *v, n*
- ▶ *v* **1** CRAM, pack, wedge, squash, squeeze, press, crush, crowd, congest, ram, stuff, insert, confine, force, thrust, push, press **2** BLOCK, clog, obstruct, close (off), stall, stick
- ▶ *n* **1** CRUSH, crowd, press, congestion, pack, herd, swarm, mob, throng, horde, multitude **2** *a traffic jam* bottleneck, congestion, gridlock, hold-up, obstruc-

tion **3** PREDICAMENT, trouble, quandary, plight, straits, *colloq.* fix, hole, (tight) spot, bind, pickle, scrape, the soup

jamboree *n*
celebration, party, rally, festivity, festival, carnival, jubilee, junket, fête, frolic, revelry, spree, carouse, merriment, field day, gathering, get-together, convention, *colloq.* shindig

jangle *v, n*
- ▶ *v* **1** CLANK, clash, jar, clang, clatter, clink, jingle, chime, rattle, vibrate **2** *jangle someone's nerves* upset, irritate, disturb, bother, trouble, make anxious
- ▶ *n* clang, clash, rattle, clatter, jar, jarring, cacophony, clink, din, discord, racket, reverberation, clangour, stridor, *formal* dissonance
🖪 euphony

janitor *n*
caretaker, doorkeeper, doorman, custodian, concierge, porter, *technical* ostiary

jar¹ *n*
a jam jar pot, container, vessel, receptacle, crock, pitcher, urn, vase, flask, flagon, carafe, jug, mug

jar² *v*
1 JOLT, agitate, rattle, shake, jerk, vibrate **2** GRATE, upset, disturb, trouble, jangle, irritate, annoy, offend, irk, *colloq.* nettle **3** CLASH, be in conflict, be at odds, be at variance, quarrel, disagree, bicker

jargon *n*
1 SPECIALIST LANGUAGE, journalese, computerese, computerspeak, legalese, psychobabble, buzz words, parlance, slang, cant, argot, vernacular, idiom, usage **2** NONSENSE, gibberish, *colloq.* gobbledegook, mumbo-jumbo

jarring *adj*
discordant, jangling, harsh, grating, irritating, cacophonous, rasping, strident, upsetting, disturbing, troubling, jolting

jaundiced *adj*
1 BITTER, cynical, pessimistic, sceptical, distrustful, disbelieving, biased, prejudiced, bigoted, envious, jealous, hostile, jaded, suspicious, resentful, unenthusiastic, misanthropic **2** DISTORTED, biased, prejudiced, bigoted, preconceived

jaunt *n*
trip, outing, excursion, holiday, tour, ride, drive, spin, ramble, stroll

jaunty *adj*
sprightly, lively, perky, breezy, energetic, bouncy, buoyant, high-spirited, self-confident, carefree, airy, cheeky, debonair, dapper, smart, trim, showy, flashy, spruce, stylish
🖪 depressed, dowdy

jaw *n, v*
- ▶ *n* **1** *the lower jaw* mandible, mouth, muzzle, *technical* maxilla, *colloq.* chops, trap **2** TALK, gossip, chat,

conversation, discussion, *colloq.* chinwag, natter, confab **3** *the jaws of death* clutches, grasp, control, power, claws, threshold
▶ *v* chat, chatter, gossip, talk, gabble, *colloq.* natter, rabbit (on), jabber, babble

jazz *n, v*
▶ *n*

Kinds of jazz include:
acid jazz, Afro-Cuban, avant-garde, bebop, blues, boogie-woogie, bop, cool, Dixieland, free-form, fusion, hot jazz, jive, mainstream, modern, New Orleans, post-bop, ragtime, soul jazz, spiel, swing, third stream, West Coast.

▶ *v* ▷ **jazz up** liven up, enliven, smarten up, brighten up

jazzy *adj*
lively, smart, spirited, stylish, bold, wild, fancy, gaudy, vivacious, zestful, *colloq.* flashy, snazzy, swinging
Ⓕ conservative, square

jealous *adj*
1 ENVIOUS, covetous, desirous, grudging, begrudging, resentful, *colloq.* green, green-eyed **2** SUSPICIOUS, wary, doubting, distrustful, anxious, possessive, insecure **3** PROTECTIVE, watchful, mindful, careful, vigilant, wary
Ⓕ **1** contented, satisfied

jealousy *n*
1 ENVY, covetousness, grudge, grudgingness, resentment, bitterness, spite, ill-will, *colloq.* green-eyed monster **2** SUSPICION, distrust, mistrust, doubt, possessiveness, insecurity **3** PROTECTIVENESS, watchfulness, mindfulness, carefulness, vigilance, wariness

jeer *v, n*
▶ *v* mock, scoff, taunt, gibe, ridicule, sneer, make fun of, scorn, chaff, barrack, tease, twit, heckle, shout down, hiss, boo, banter, *formal* deride, *colloq.* knock, *US* razz
▶ *n* mockery, ridicule, banter, taunt, gibe, sneer, scoff, teasing, abuse, catcall, hiss, boo, hoot, *formal* derision, *colloq.* dig

jejune *adj*
1 UNSOPHISTICATED, simple, naïve, immature, childish, juvenile, puerile, silly, callow **2** DULL, uninteresting, unoriginal, arid, trite, banal, senseless, barren, empty, colourless, vapid, insipid, prosaic, wishy-washy, dry, spiritless
Ⓕ **1** mature **2** meaningful

jell *see* GEL.

jeopardize *v*
endanger, expose to danger, risk, put at risk, put in jeopardy, hazard, venture, gamble, chance, take a chance, threaten, menace, expose, stake, *formal* imperil
Ⓕ protect, safeguard

jeopardy *n*
danger, risk, hazard, endangerment, venture, vulnerability, precariousness, menace, threat, insecurity, exposure, liability, *formal* peril
Ⓕ safety, security

jerk *v, n*
▶ *v* jolt, tug, twitch, jog, yank, wrench, pull, jiggle, lurch, pluck, thrust, shrug, throw, bounce
▶ *n* **1** JOLT, tug, twitch, jar, jog, yank, wrench, pull, pluck, lurch, throw, thrust, shrug **2** IDIOT, fool, *colloq.* clot, dope, twerp, twit, *slang* nerd, wally, pillock, prat, geek

jerky *adj*
fitful, twitchy, spasmodic, jumpy, jolting, lurching,

convulsive, disconnected, bumpy, bouncy, shaky, shaking, rough, unco-ordinated, uncontrolled, incoherent
Ⓕ smooth

jerry-built *adj*
insubstantial, ramshackle, thrown together, quickly built, built on the cheap, rickety, unstable, cheap, shoddy, defective, faulty, flimsy, unsubstantial, slipshod, cheapjack
Ⓕ firm, stable, substantial

jersey *n*
sweater, jumper, pullover, sweatshirt, top, woolly

jest *n, v*
▶ *n* joke, quip, witticism, banter, fooling, prank, practical joke, trick, hoax, *colloq.* wisecrack, crack, gag, kidding, leg-pull
▷ **in jest** in fun, as a joke, jokingly, to tease, mischievously
▶ *v* joke, tell jokes, quip, fool, tease, mock, jeer, *colloq.* kid

jester *n*
clown, fool, comic, buffoon, comedian, humorist, joker, wag, zany, wit, prankster, quipster, juggler, joculator, patch, pantaloon, harlequin, merryman, mummer, motley, merry-andrew, droll

jet¹ *n, v*
▶ *n* *a jet of water* gush, spurt, spout, spray, spring, sprinkler, sprayer, fountain, flow, stream, rush, squirt
▶ *v* **1** GUSH, spurt, spray, spring, flow, stream, rush, squirt **2** FLY, zoom, rush, shoot, career

jet² *adj*
jet black black, pitch-black, ebony, sable, raven, sooty, inky

jetsam *see* FLOTSAM.

jettison *v*
discard, scrap, throw away, get rid of, abandon, offload, unload, eject, expel, heave, *colloq.* ditch, dump, chuck
Ⓕ load, take on

jetty *n*
breakwater, pier, dock, harbour, groyne, mole, quay, wharf

jewel *n*
1 GEM, precious stone, gemstone, ornament, *colloq.* rock, sparkler **2** TREASURE, gem, find, prize, masterpiece, showpiece, rarity, paragon, pearl, jewellery, pride and joy, crème de la crème, *pièce de résistance*

jewellery *n*
jewels, gems, ornaments, trinkets, regalia, treasure, bijoux, bijouterie, finery, gemmery, gauds

Types of jewellery include:
bangle, bracelet, charm bracelet, anklet, cufflink, tiepin, hatpin, brooch, cameo, earring, stud, nose-ring, ring, signet-ring, solitaire ring, necklace, rivière, necklet, choker, pendant, locket, chain, beads, amulet, torque, tiara, coronet, diadem.

Jewish calendar

The Jewish calendar and its Gregorian equivalents:
Tishri (September-October), Hesshvan (October-November), Kislev (November-December), Tevet (December-January), Shevat (January-February), Adar (February-March), Adar Sheni (leap years only), Nisan (March-April), Iyar (April-May), Sivan (May-June), Tammuz (June-July), Av (July-August), Elul (August-September).

Jezebel *n*
seductress, temptress, *femme fatale*, hussy, scarlet woman, Delilah, wanton

jib *v*
balk, shrink, recoil, back off, stall, refuse, retreat, stop short

jibe *see* GIBE.

jiffy *n*
instant, moment, second, sec, split second, flash, twinkling, twinkling of an eye, minute, tick, two ticks, trice, no time, *colloq.* two shakes of a lamb's tail
⊞ age

jig *v*
jerk, prance, caper, hop, jump, leap, twitch, skip, bounce, bob, wiggle, shake, wobble

jigger *v*
wreck, destroy, break, ruin, spoil, undermine, *formal* vitiate, *colloq.* botch up, kibosh, louse up, make a pig's ear of, scupper

jiggery-pokery *n*
deceit, trickery, dishonesty, fraud, deception, mischief, subterfuge, chicanery, funny business, hanky-panky, skulduggery, shenanigans, *colloq.* monkey business, hocus-pocus
⊞ straightforwardness, honesty

jiggle *v*
jerk, jump, bounce, twitch, fidget, shift, shake, agitate, jig, jog, joggle, waggle, wiggle, wobble

jilt *v*
abandon, reject, desert, discard, brush off, leave, drop, spurn, betray, cast aside, *colloq.* ditch, chuck, pack in

jingle *v, n*
▶ *v* clink, tinkle, ring, ding, chime, chink, jangle, clatter, rattle, *formal* tintinnabulate
▶ *n* **1** CLINK, tinkle, ringing, chime, ding, clang, rattle, jangle, clangour, *formal* tintinnabulation **2** RHYME, verse, song, carol, tune, ditty, doggerel, melody, poem, chant, chorus, refrain

jingoism *n*
chauvinism, flag-waving, patriotism, nationalism, imperialism, warmongering, insularity

jinx *n, v*
▶ *n* spell, curse, bad luck, evil eye, hex, voodoo, hoodoo, black magic, charm, plague, *formal* malediction, affliction, *colloq.* gremlin
▶ *v* curse, bewitch, bedevil, cast a spell on, doom, plague

jitters *n*
nerves, nervousness, tenseness, anxiety, fidgets, agitation, trembling, uneasiness, *colloq.* heebie-jeebies, habdabs, the creeps, the shakes, the shivers, the willies, jimjams

jittery *adj*
nervous, anxious, agitated, uneasy, flustered, quivering, shaky, shivery, trembling, jumpy, fidgety, quaking, panicky, *formal* perturbed, *colloq.* edgy, nervy
⊞ calm, composed, confident

job *n*
1 *she has a good job* work, employment, occupation, position, post, pursuit, situation, profession, line of work/business, career, calling, vocation, trade, métier, capacity, business, (means of) livelihood **2** *it's a difficult job* task, piece of work, chore, duty, responsibility, charge, commission, assignment, mission, activity, affair, concern, assignment, business, proceeding, project, enterprise, office, capacity, pursuit, role, undertaking, venture, province, part, place, share, errand, function, contribution, stint, consignment, charge

▷ **have a job doing something** find something difficult, find it a problem, have a hard time doing something, find something (to be) troublesome

jobless *adj*
unemployed, out of work, without work, workless, laid off, on the dole, inactive, idle, redundant
⊞ employed

jockey *n, v*
▶ *n* equestrian, horseman, horsewoman, rider
▶ *v* manipulate, manoeuvre, engineer, negotiate, wheedle, cajole, coax, induce, ease, edge, manage, *formal* inveigle

jocose *adj*
humorous, playful, funny, jesting, mischievous, pleasant, teasing, comical, droll, facetious, witty, sportive, waggish, jovial, joyous, merry, mirthful, *formal* lepid
⊞ morose

jocular *adj*
joking, jesting, funny, humorous, jovial, amusing, hilarious, comical, comic, entertaining, facetious, droll, whimsical, teasing, playful, witty, waggish, roguish, *formal* jocose
⊞ serious

jocularity *n*
jesting, funniness, humour, joviality, amusement, entertainment, laughter, hilarity, merriment, gaiety, jolliness, comicality, drollery, wit, whimsicality, waggishness, pleasantry, facetiousness, playfulness, sportiveness, sport, roguishness, fooling, teasing, *formal* jocosity, jocoseness, desipience

jog *v, n*
▶ *v* **1** JOLT, jar, bump, jostle, jerk, joggle, nudge, poke, shake, prod, bounce, push, rock, elbow **2** PROMPT, remind, stir, arouse, activate, stimulate **3** RUN, trot, canter
▶ *n* **1** JOLT, bump, jerk, nudge, shove, push, poke, prod, shake **2** RUN, trot, canter

joie de vivre *n*
cheerfulness, enjoyment, buoyancy, joyfulness, joy, enthusiasm, merriment, mirth, pleasure, relish, zest, gaiety, gusto, *formal* blitheness, ebullience, *colloq.* bounce, get-up-and-go
⊞ depression

join *v*
1 UNITE, connect, combine, attach, link, amalgamate, ally, unify, fasten, merge, converge, marry, couple, yoke, tie, splice, knit, weld, fuse, bind, cement, glue, add, adhere, annex, *formal* conjoin **2** BORDER (ON), verge on, touch, meet, coincide, march with, *formal* abut, adjoin, conjoin **3** ASSOCIATE, affiliate, become a member of, accompany, cooperate, collaborate, ally, enlist, enrol, enter, sign up, team up with
⊞ **1** divide, separate **3** leave
▷ **join in** take part in, participate, partake, cooperate, pitch in, lend a hand, help, contribute, chip in, *colloq.* muck in
▷ **join up** enlist, sign up, enrol, enter

joint *n, adj, v*
▶ *n* **1** JUNCTION, connection, union, coupling, juncture, join, intersection, hinge, knot, articulation, seam, *formal* nexus **2** CLUB, dive, bar, nightclub, pub, haunt, place **3** CIGARETTE, *colloq.* reefer, spliff, stick, roach
▶ *adj* combined, common, communal, joined, shared, united, collective, amalgamated, mutual, co-operative, co-ordinated, consolidated, concerted
▶ *v* **1** JOIN, connect, couple, unite, fasten, fit, articulate **2** CUT UP, carve, divide, sever, dismember, dissect

joke *n, v*
▶ *n* **1** JEST, quip, witticism, funny story, pun, hoot,

whimsy, yarn, banter, repartee, *colloq.* crack, gag, wisecrack, one-liner **2** TRICK, jape, lark, prank, practical joke, hoax, spoof, fun, play, sport
▸ *v* jest, tell jokes, quip, clown, fool (around), pun, tease, banter, mock, laugh, frolic, gambol, *colloq.* kid, wisecrack, pull someone's leg, have someone on, kid on, take for a ride, pull a fast one on

joker *n*
comedian, comic, wit, humorist, jester, trickster, quipster, prankster, hoaxer, practical joker, wag, clown, buffoon, kidder, droll, character, sport, *colloq.* wisecracker, card

jolly *adj, adv*
▸ *adj* **1** *a jolly person* jovial, merry, glad, cheerful, cheery, playful, hearty, happy, exuberant, lively, gay, joyful, gleeful, mirthful **2** ENJOYABLE, happy, delightful, pleasurable, convivial, festive
🔛 **1** sad, unhappy
▸ *adv* extremely, very, exceptionally, intensely, greatly, highly, certainly

jolt *v, n*
▸ *v* **1** JAR, jerk, jog, bump, jounce, jostle, push, knock, bounce, lurch, shake, shove, push, bang, nudge **2** UPSET, startle, shock, shake (up), surprise, stun, amaze, astound, astonish, discompose, disconcert, disturb, *formal* perturb
▸ *n* **1** JAR, jerk, jog, bump, blow, bang, knock, push, shove, hit, impact, lurch, shake, start **2** SHOCK, surprise, reversal, setback, start, upset, blow, fright of your life, *colloq.* bombshell, thunderbolt, bolt from the blue, turn-up for the book

jostle *v*
1 PUSH, shove, jog, bump, elbow, hustle, jolt, crowd, shoulder, joggle, shake, squeeze, throng, bang, collide **2** COMPETE, vie, contend, fight, battle, struggle

jot *n, v*
▸ *n* iota, glimmer, trace, fraction, scrap, atom, gleam, grain, hint, speck, trifle, whit, bit, particle, mite, morsel, scintilla, tittle, ace, detail, *colloq.* smidgen
▸ *v* ▷ **jot down** write down, take down, note (down), put down, list, record, scribble, register, enter

journal *n*
1 MAGAZINE, periodical, newspaper, paper, publication, review, weekly, monthly **2** DIARY, gazette, daybook, log, record, account, register, chronicle

journalism *n*
reporting, writing, news, news coverage, reportage, feature-writing, press, Fleet Street, fourth estate, copy-writing, correspondence, media, broadcasting, radio, television

journalist *n*
reporter, news-writer, correspondent, editor, columnist, feature-writer, commentator, broadcaster, contributor, reviewer, editor, subeditor, newshound, paparazzo, freelance, stringer, *colloq.* hack, sub, journo, scribe

journey *n, v*
▸ *n* voyage, trip, travel(s), expedition, passage, trek, tour, ramble, roving, outing, excursion, jaunt, wanderings, cruise, ride, crossing, flight, drive, safari, progress, globetrotting, *formal* odyssey, peregrination
▸ *v* travel, voyage, go, cruise, sail, trek, hike, tour, roam, rove, proceed, wander, tramp, ramble, range, fly, gallivant, *formal* peregrinate

journeyer *n*
tourist, traveller, tripper, voyager, wanderer, wayfarer, rambler, pilgrim, trekker, *formal* peregrinator

joust *v, n*
▸ *v* fight, spar, vie, compete, contest, quarrel, skirmish, wrangle

▸ *n* fight, encounter, contest, tournament, trial, engagement, skirmish, tilt, tourney

jovial *adj*
jolly, happy, cheerful, glad, cheery, merry, affable, animated, cordial, genial, lively, buoyant, mirthful, gleeful, gay, in good spirits, sociable
🔛 gloomy, sad, depressed

joviality *n*
jollity, happiness, cheerfulness, cheeriness, gladness, merriment, mirth, glee, ebullience, fun, gaiety, affability, buoyancy, hilarity
🔛 moroseness, sadness

joy *n*
1 HAPPINESS, gladness, delight, pleasure, bliss, ecstasy, elation, joyfulness, enjoyment, exultation, rejoicing, gratification, rapture, glee, *formal* felicity, *colloq.* seventh heaven, cloud nine **2** *the joys of childhood* treasure, delight, pleasure, thrill, treat, prize, gem **3** *get no joy from the inquiry desk* satisfaction, achievement, success, successful/positive result, victory, accomplishment
🔛 **1** despair, grief

joyful *adj*
happy, pleased, delighted, glad, elated, ecstatic, overjoyed, euphoric, thrilled, gratified, triumphant, gleeful, merry, cheerful, jubilant, *colloq.* tickled pink, over the moon, on top of the world, on cloud nine, in seventh heaven
🔛 sorrowful, mournful

joyless *adj*
miserable, discouraging, depressing, sad, unhappy, sombre, downcast, dreary, forlorn, gloomy, glum, grim, despondent, dejected, cheerless, bleak, dismal, dispirited, doleful, dour
🔛 joyful

joyous *adj*
happy, joyful, cheerful, glad, gleeful, merry, jubilant, rapturous, ecstatic, festal, festive, gladsome
🔛 sad

jubilant *adj*
joyful, rejoicing, overjoyed, delighted, elated, triumphant, exuberant, exultant, excited, ecstatic, euphoric, thrilled, rhapsodic, *colloq.* tickled pink, over the moon, on top of the world, on cloud nine, in seventh heaven

jubilation *n*
euphoria, ecstasy, elation, triumph, excitement, exultation, jollification, joy, celebration, festivity, jamboree, jubilee
🔛 depression, lamentation

jubilee *n*
celebration, commemoration, anniversary, festival, festivity, holiday, gala, fête, carnival, feast day

Judas *n*
traitor, betrayer, deceiver, renegade, quisling, turncoat, *formal* tergiversator

judge *n, v*
▸ *n* **1** JUSTICE, Law Lord, magistrate, sheriff, recorder, coroner, judiciary, procurator fiscal, district attorney, seneschal, arbiter, adjudicator, arbitrator, mediator, ombudsman, moderator, referee, umpire, assessor, *slang* beak, his/her nibs **2** CONNOISSEUR, authority, expert, evaluator, assessor, critic, reviewer
▸ *v* **1** ADJUDICATE, arbitrate, try, sit in judgement, deliver/pronounce a verdict, referee, umpire, decree, mediate, examine, sentence, pass sentence, give a sentence, review, rule, find, *formal* adjudge **2** ASCERTAIN, determine, decide, assess, appraise, evaluate, estimate, value, weigh (up), gauge, review, examine, distinguish, discern, reckon, believe, think, form an opinion, consider, conclude, rate **3** CONDEMN, criticize, doom, convict, damn

judgement *n*
1 VERDICT, sentence, ruling, adjudication, decree, conclusion, decision, arbitration, finding, result, mediation, order, opinion **2** DISCERNMENT, discrimination, understanding, wisdom, common sense, good sense, sense, intelligence, taste, shrewdness, perception, penetration, acumen, enlightenment, *formal* prudence, judiciousness, sagacity, perspicacity **3** OPINION, assessment, evaluation, appraisal, estimate, view, belief, diagnosis, conviction **4** CONVICTION, damnation, punishment, doom, fate, misfortune, *formal* retribution

judicial *adj*
legal, judiciary, magistral, forensic, official, discriminating, critical, impartial

---

📖 **judicial** or **judicious**?
Judicial is a formal word meaning 'relating to judges and lawcourts'. *Judicious* means 'showing wisdom and good sense': *a judicious choice of words.*

---

judicious *adj*
wise, careful, cautious, astute, discerning, informed, discriminating, shrewd, thoughtful, reasonable, sensible, clever, intelligent, smart, sound, well-judged, well-advised, considered, common-sense, *formal* prudent, sagacious, circumspect
🔁 injudicious

jug *n*
pitcher, carafe, crock, ewer, flagon, urn, jar, decanter, vessel, Toby jug, container, receptacle

juggle *v*
alter, change, manipulate, falsify, tamper with, fake, rearrange, balance, equalize, adjust, massage, rig, disguise, *colloq.* doctor, cook

juice *n*
liquid, fluid, extract, essence, sap, secretion, nectar, liquor, serum

juicy *adj*
1 SUCCULENT, moist, wet, lush, watery, flowing **2** INTERESTING, colourful, vivid, thrilling, exciting, sensational, racy, risqué, suggestive, scandalous, lurid, spicy
🔁 **1** dry

jumble *v, n*
▶ *v* disarrange, confuse, disorganize, mix (up), muddle, shuffle, tangle
🔁 order
▶ *n* disorder, disarray, confusion, mess, chaos, mix-up, mixture, muddle, clutter, mixture, hotch-potch, miscellany, medley, potpourri, *colloq.* mishmash, shambles

jumbled *adj*
muddled, confused, chaotic, disorganized, disordered, disarrayed, mixed-up, tangled, unsorted, untidy, shuffled, tumbled, miscellaneous
🔁 orderly, tidy

jumbo *adj*
gigantic, colossal, giant, extra-large, mammoth, huge, enormous, immense, vast, *colloq.* whopping

jump *v, n*
▶ *v* **1** LEAP, spring, bound, vault, clear, go over/across, hurdle, bounce, skip, hop, caper, cavort, frisk, romp, sport, prance, frolic, gambol **2** START, flinch, jerk, recoil, shake, quiver, twitch, jump out of your skin, wince, quail **3** OMIT, leave out, miss, skip, pass over, cut out, bypass, disregard, overlook, ignore, avoid, digress **4** RISE, increase, go up, gain, appreciate, ascend, escalate, mount, advance, surge, spiral **5** POUNCE ON, attack, assault, spring on, swoop on, set upon, *colloq.* mug, beat up, do over

▷ **jump at** accept, agree to, fall for, leap at, grab, seize, pounce on, snatch, swallow
▷ **jump on** criticize, blame, reprimand, rebuke, reprove, scold, chide, fly at, tick off, reproach, upbraid, *formal* berate, castigate, censure, revile
▶ *n* **1** LEAP, spring, bound, vault, hop, skip, bounce, prance, frisk, frolic, pounce **2** START, flinch, jerk, jolt, jar, lurch, shock, spasm, quiver, shiver, shake, quiver, twitch **3** BREAK, gap, space, interruption, lapse, omission, interval, breach, switch, *formal* hiatus, lacuna **4** RISE, increase, escalation, boost, advance, increment, upsurge, elevation, upturn, mounting, *colloq.* hike **5** HURDLE, fence, gate, hedge, barricade, barrier, obstacle, rail

jumper *n*
sweater, jersey, pullover, sweatshirt, woolly

jumpy *adj*
1 NERVOUS, anxious, agitated, apprehensive, uneasy, jittery, tense, panicky, fidgety, shaky, on edge, *formal* restive, *colloq.* edgy, twitchy **2** FITFUL, twitchy, spasmodic, jerky, jolting, lurching, convulsive, disconnected, bumpy, bouncy, shaky, shaking, rough, unco-ordinated, uncontrolled, incoherent
🔁 **1** calm, composed

junction *n*
1 *a road junction* intersection, crossing, crossroads, interchange, meeting-point, confluence **2** JOINT, join, joining, connection, bond, seam, juncture, union, intersection, link, linking, coupling, welding

---

📖 **junction** or **juncture**?
A *junction* is a point or place where things meet: *a road junction*; *a junction box for wires*. A *juncture* is a point in time: *at this/that juncture.*

---

juncture *n*
point, period, stage, time, occasion, minute, moment, crisis, emergency, crux, predicament

jungle *n*
1 *tigers in the dense jungle* tropical forest, rainforest, equatorial rainforest, bush, growth **2** *a jungle of building regulations* mass, heap, tangle, confusion, disorder, disarray, chaos, snarl, clutter, hotch-potch, mishmash, miscellany, medley, maze, labyrinth, web

junior *adj, n*
▶ *adj* younger, minor, lesser, lower, subordinate, secondary, subsidiary, inferior
🔁 senior
▶ *n* minor, subordinate, inferior, subsidiary, minion, servant

junk *n, v*
▶ *n* rubbish, refuse, trash, debris, garbage, waste, scrap, litter, clutter, oddments, bric-à-brac, rummage, leftovers, leavings, dregs, wreckage
▶ *v* throw out, get rid of, ditch, jettison, discard, dispose of, *colloq.* dump, chuck

junta *n*
faction, clique, gang, group, ring, set, party, cartel, coterie, council, league, conclave, confederacy, cabal, camarilla

jurisdiction *n*
1 *under the council's jurisdiction* power, authority, control, influence, dominion, province, sovereignty, administration, leadership, mastery, command, domination, rule, right, sway, *formal* prerogative **2** AREA, field, orbit, bounds, scope, range, reach, sphere, zone

jury *n*
jurors, panel, jurymen, jurywomen

just *adj, adv*
▶ *adj* **1** *a just ruler* fair, equitable, impartial, unbiased, unprejudiced, fair-minded, even-handed, neutral, objective, disinterested, righteous, upright, virtuous, moral, ethical, truthful, sincere, honourable, good, honest, irreproachable, upstanding, principled **2** *a just punishment* deserved, merited, earned, fitting, well-deserved, appropriate, suitable, apt, due, justified, valid, sound, well-grounded, well-founded, proper, reasonable, rightful, lawful, legitimate, legal
F3 1 unjust **2** undeserved
▶ *adv* **1** *he's just left* a short time ago, a moment ago, recently, lately **2** *that's just like him* exactly, precisely, perfectly, completely, absolutely, quite, *colloq.* bang on, spot on, to a T **3** *she's just a child* only, merely, simply, purely, nothing but, barely, hardly, scarcely
▷ **just about** practically, almost, virtually, nearly, as good as, all but, well-nigh, more or less, to all intents and purposes

justice *n*
1 FAIRNESS, equity, fair play, impartiality, objectivity, neutrality, equitableness, fair-mindedness, even-handedness, justness, legitimacy, honesty, honour, uprightness, integrity, right, rightfulness, rightness, righteousness, morals, ethics, justifiableness, lawfulness, validity, soundness, reasonableness, *formal* rectitude, propriety **2** LEGALITY, law, penalty, punishment, recompense, amends, redress, reparation, satisfaction, compensation **3** JUDGE, Justice of the Peace, JP, magistrate, sheriff
F3 1 injustice, unfairness, bias

justifiable *adj*
defensible, excusable, warranted, reasonable, within reason, sustainable, supportable, justified, lawful, legal, legitimate, acceptable, explainable, forgivable, pardonable, understandable, plausible, valid, well-founded, sound, sensible, right, proper, fit, tenable, *formal* explicable

F3 unjustifiable

justification *n*
defence, plea, mitigation, apology, explanation, excuse, vindication, verification, confirmation, warrant, rationalization, reason, grounds, basis

justify *v*
vindicate, warrant, defend, acquit, absolve, clear, excuse, forgive, explain, pardon, validate, uphold, show to be right/reasonable, sustain, support, stand up for, maintain, establish, prove, rationalize, verify, confirm, bear out, deserve, *formal* exculpate, exonerate, substantiate

justly *adv*
properly, justifiably, duly, equitably, even-handedly, rightfully, rightly, with reason, fairly, honestly, impartially, lawfully, legitimately, conscientiously, objectively, equally
F3 unjustly

jut (out) *v*
project, protrude, stick out, overhang, extend, beetle, extrude
F3 recede

juvenile *n, adj*
▶ *n* child, youth, minor, young person, youngster, adolescent, teenager, boy, girl, infant, *colloq.* kid
▶ *adj* young, youthful, minor, junior, immature, inexperienced, childish, puerile, infantile, adolescent, babyish, unsophisticated, callow, *colloq.* green, wet behind the ears
F3 mature

juxtapose *v*
put/place together, place side by side, put next to each other

juxtaposition *n*
proximity, nearness, closeness, contact, vicinity, immediacy, *formal* contiguity

K

kaleidoscopic *adj*
1 MANY-COLOURED, multicoloured, variegated, many-splendoured, motley, *technical* poikilitic, *formal* polychromatic, polychrome **2** EVER-CHANGING, changeable, fluctuating, manifold, fluid, *formal* multifarious
F3 1 dull, monochrome, monotonous

kaput *adj*
broken, finished, ruined, wrecked, smashed, undone, defunct, destroyed, extinct, *colloq.* conked out

karate *n*

keel *v*
▷ **keel over 1** OVERTURN, capsize, turn upside down, turn turtle, founder, collapse, upset **2** FAINT, pass out, lose consciousness, black out, fall, drop, stagger, topple over

keen *adj, v*
▶ *adj* **1** EAGER, avid, fervent, enthusiastic, earnest, devoted, diligent, industrious, conscientious, assiduous, intent, impatient **2** ASTUTE, sharp, shrewd, clever, perceptive, wise, discerning, discriminating, quick, quick-witted, sharp-witted, penetrating, deep, sensitive, *formal* perspicacious **3** SHARP, piercing, penetrating, incisive, acute, pointed, intense, pungent, acid, biting, *formal* trenchant, mordant **4** *keen competition* fierce, intense, strong, wild, ruthless, cut-throat, *colloq.* dog-eat-dog **5** *keen on something/ someone* fond of, devoted to, liking, attached to, loving, caring, *colloq.* having a soft spot for
F3 1 apathetic **2** superficial **3** dull
▶ *v* wail, grieve, mourn, lament, sob, howl, cry, sorrow

keenness *n*
1 ENTHUSIASM, eagerness, diligence, earnestness, industriousness, industry, sedulity **2** ASTUTENESS, sharpness, shrewdness, cleverness, discernment, penetration, sensitivity, wisdom, incisiveness, *formal* sagacity, sapience, trenchancy
F3 1 apathy **2** bluntness, dullness

keep *v, n*
▶ *v* **1** RETAIN, hold, preserve, hold on to, hang on to, not part with, save, store (up), stock, deal in, carry, possess, keep possession of, amass, hoard, accumulate, collect, stack, conserve, deposit, heap, pile (up), place, maintain, furnish, sustain **2** CARRY ON, keep at/on, continue, persevere, persist, remain, stay, maintain **3** LOOK AFTER, tend, care for, keep in good order, have charge of, have custody of, maintain, provide for, subsidize, support, sustain, be responsible for, foster, superintend, mind, protect, shelter, guard, defend, watch (over), shield, safeguard, feed, nurture, manage **4** DETAIN, delay, check, hinder, hold (up), hold back, impede, obstruct, prevent, block, curb, interfere with, restrain, limit, inhibit, deter, hamper, keep back, control, constrain, arrest, withhold, confine, *formal* retard **5** OBSERVE, comply with, respect, obey, fulfil, adhere to, abide by, carry out, recognize, keep up, keep faith with, commemorate, celebrate, hold, maintain, perform, perpetuate, mark, honour, solemnize, *formal* effectuate
▷ **keep at** persevere, stick at, be steadfast, continue, carry on, complete, endure, finish, last, maintain, remain, stay, persist, plug away at, toil, grind, drudge, labour, beaver away at, *colloq.* slog at
F3 abandon, neglect
▷ **keep back 1** RESTRAIN, check, constrain, curb, impede, limit, prohibit, stop, control, delay, *formal* retard **2** HOLD BACK, restrict, suppress, withhold, conceal, censor, hide, hush up, stifle, reserve, keep secret, retain
▷ **keep from** prevent, resist, stop, halt, *formal* forbear, desist
▷ **keep in 1** REPRESS, keep back, inhibit, bottle up, conceal, stifle, suppress, hide, control, restrain, quell, stop up **2** CONFINE, detain, shut in, coop up
F3 1 declare **2** release
▷ **keep off** avoid, stay away from, stay off, keep away, avoid going near, not go near, keep at a distance from, steer clear of, keep at arm's length, *colloq.* give a wide berth to
▷ **keep on** continue, carry on, endure, persevere, persist, keep at it, last, remain, stay, stay the course, hold on, retain, maintain, *colloq.* soldier on, stick at it
▷ **keep on at** go on at, nag, pester, plague, pursue, badger, chivvy, harass, harry, *formal* importune
▷ **keep secret** hide, conceal, keep back, keep dark, suppress, *formal* dissemble, *colloq.* keep under your hat, keep under wraps, your lips be sealed
▷ **keep to** observe, comply with, respect, obey, fulfil, adhere to, stick to
▷ **keep track of** follow, grasp, keep up with, monitor, oversee, plot, record, trace, track, understand, watch
▷ **keep up** maintain, continue, persevere, go along with, support, sustain, preserve, keep pace, equal, contend, compete, vie, rival, match, emulate
F3 fall behind
▶ *n* **1** SUBSISTENCE, board, board and lodgings, livelihood, living, maintenance, support, upkeep, means, food, nourishment, sustenance, nurture **2** FORT, fortress, tower, castle, citadel, stronghold, dungeon, donjon
▷ **for keeps** for ever, always, for all time, *colloq.* for good

keeper *n*
guard, custodian, curator, caretaker, attendant, guard-

ian, overseer, steward, warder, jailer, gaoler, warden, supervisor, bodyguard, escort, inspector, defender, governor, superintendent, administrator, surveyor, *formal* conservator, *colloq.* minder

keeping *n*
1 CUSTODY, guardianship, supervision, care, charge, safe-keeping, retention, protection, maintenance, surveillance, trust, tutelage, ward, cure, patronage, *formal* auspices, aegis **2** *in keeping with the architecture* agreement, harmony, conformity, correspondence, consistency, balance, proportion, *formal* accord, congruity

keepsake *n*
memento, souvenir, remembrance, relic, reminder, token, pledge, emblem

keg *n*
barrel, butt, cask, drum, tun, vat, firkin, hogshead

ken *n*
knowledge, understanding, perception, awareness, appreciation, comprehension, realization, field, grasp, notice, range, reach, scope, acquaintance, compass, *formal* cognizance

kernel *n*
core, crux, grain, seed, stone, nut, nucleus, centre, heart, nub, essence, germ, marrow, substance, gist, *formal* quintessence, *colloq.* nitty-gritty, nuts and bolts, innards

key *n, adj*
 ▶ *n* **1** CLUE, cue, indicator, pointer, explanation, guide, gloss, sign, answer, solution, interpretation, means, secret, *formal* explication **2** GUIDE, glossary, translation, legend, code, table, index **3** *in a low key* pitch, tone, style, mood
 ▶ *adj* important, essential, vital, crucial, necessary, principal, decisive, central, chief, main, major, leading, basic, fundamental

keynote *n*
core, centre, heart, substance, theme, gist, pith, marrow, essence, emphasis, accent, stress

keystone *n*
cornerstone, core, crux, base, basis, foundation, ground, linchpin, principle, root, mainspring, source, spring, motive

kick *v, n*
 ▶ *v* **1** BOOT, hit, strike, knee, jolt **2** GIVE UP, quit, stop, leave off, abandon, desist from, break
 ▷ **kick against** resist, rebel, oppose, spurn, defy, withstand, protest, hold out against
 ▷ **kick around** discuss, talk about, play with, toy with
 ▷ **kick off** begin, start, open, get under way, open the proceedings, introduce, inaugurate, initiate, *formal* commence, *colloq.* set/start the ball rolling
 ▷ **kick out** eject, evict, expel, oust, remove, discharge, dismiss, get rid of, throw out, reject, *colloq.* chuck out, sack, boot out, show someone the door, give the sack/push/boot/elbow to
 ▶ *n* **1** BLOW, recoil, jolt, striking **2** STIMULATION, thrill, excitement, fun, pleasure, *colloq.* buzz, lift, lark, high **3** *a drink with a kick* power, strength, potency, effect, stimulus, *colloq.* punch, pep, bite, zing, zip

kick-off *n*
beginning, start, outset, opening, introduction, *formal* commencement, inception, *colloq.* word go

kid¹ *n*
she has three kids child, young one, little one, toddler, youngster, young person, youth, juvenile, infant, girl, boy, adolescent, teenager, lad, *colloq.* nipper, tot

kid² *v*
I was only kidding; don't kid yourself tease, joke, hoax, fool, pretend, trick, delude, dupe, jest, hoodwink,

deceive, humbug, gull, *colloq.* have on, pull someone's leg, con, bamboozle

kidnap *v*
abduct, capture, seize, hold to ransom, snatch, hijack, take/hold as hostage, steal

kill *v, n*
 ▶ *v* **1** SLAUGHTER, murder, take someone's life, slay, put to death, exterminate, assassinate, stab to death, do to death, finish off, massacre, execute, destroy, put down, put to sleep, do away with, butcher, annihilate, hang, execute, guillotine, behead, shoot, electrocute, send to the electric chair, *formal* smite, decapitate, *colloq.* do in, bump off, eliminate, dispatch, liquidate, knock off, rub out, wipe out, decimate, polish off, take out, waste, blow away, zap **2** *kill a project* end, destroy, put an end to, ruin, abolish, devastate, eradicate **3** *my feet are killing me* hurt, ache, cause pain, be painful, be sore, suffer, throb, pound, twinge, sting, smart **4** *don't kill yourself with all this work* strain, exhaust, tire out, weary, fatigue, sap, drain **5** *kill time* pass, spend, occupy, fill, use (up), while away **6** *kill pain/noise* STIFLE, deaden, dull, smother, quash, quell, suppress, muffle
 ▶ *n* death, shoot-out, death-blow, end, finish, climax, conclusion, *coup de grâce*, dénouement, dispatch, mop-up

killer *n*
murderer, assassin, executioner, destroyer, slayer, slaughterer, exterminator, cut-throat, gunman, homicide, *colloq.* butcher, hatchet man, hit-man, liquidator

killing *n, adj*
 ▶ *n* **1** SLAUGHTER, murder, massacre, butchery, genocide, homicide, assassination, execution, slaying, manslaughter, extermination, carnage, bloodshed, elimination, destruction, fatality, *formal* patricide, matricide, infanticide, fratricide, sororicide, uxoricide, *colloq.* liquidation **2** GAIN, fortune, windfall, booty, profit, lucky break, coup, success, stroke of luck, hit, big hit, *colloq.* clean-up, bonanza
 ▶ *adj* **1** FUNNY, hilarious, comical, amusing, uproarious, ludicrous, absurd, rib-tickling, *colloq.* side-splitting, a scream **2** EXHAUSTING, hard, taxing, arduous, tiring, fatiguing, wearing, draining, *formal* debilitating, enervating

killjoy *n*
spoilsport, moaner, complainer, dampener, damper, misery, cynic, pessimist, sceptic, grouch, whiner, prophet of doom, Weary Willie, *colloq.* wet blanket
 ☒ enthusiast, optimist, sport

kin *n*
relatives, relations, family, people, flesh and blood, cousins, blood, lineage, extraction, clan, stock, tribe, *formal* consanguinity

kind *n, adj*
 ▶ *n* sort, type, class, category, set, variety, character, genus, genre, style, brand, family, breed, race, nature, persuasion, description, species, strain, stamp, temperament, character, manner
 ▶ *adj* benevolent, kind-hearted, kindly, good-hearted, good-natured, helpful, obliging, humane, generous, magnanimous, big-hearted, compassionate, merciful, forbearing, pitying, charitable, benign, philanthropic, altruistic, humanitarian, amiable, friendly, amicable, congenial, soft-hearted, thoughtful, warm, warm-hearted, genial, considerate, courteous, sympathetic, patient, cordial, tender-hearted, loving, affectionate, understanding, lenient, mild, gentle, humane, indulgent, tolerant, unselfish, selfless, neighbourly, tactful, giving, nice, good, gracious, *formal* bounteous
 ☒ cruel, inconsiderate, unhelpful

▷ **in kind** in like manner, in return, in exchange, similarly, tit for tat

kind-hearted *adj*
kind, warm, warm-hearted, sympathetic, tender-hearted, kindly, generous, considerate, compassionate, amicable, good-hearted, good-natured, obliging, gracious, benign, big-hearted, helpful, philanthropic, altruistic, humanitarian, humane
🆘 ill-natured

kindle *v*
1 IGNITE, light, set alight, set on fire, set fire to **2** INFLAME, fire, stir, thrill, stimulate, rouse, arouse, awaken, excite, fan, incite, induce, provoke

kindliness *n*
kindness, benevolence, compassion, friendliness, sympathy, warmth, generosity, charity, amiability, *formal* beneficence, benignity, loving-kindness
🆘 cruelty, meanness, unkindness

kindly *adj*
benevolent, kind, kind-hearted, compassionate, charitable, good, good-natured, helpful, considerate, thoughtful, warm, generous, magnanimous, big-hearted, cordial, favourable, giving, indulgent, pleasant, nice, agreeable, sympathetic, understanding, tender, gentle, mild, humane, patient, friendly, amicable, cordial, polite
🆘 cruel, uncharitable

kindness *n*
1 BENEVOLENCE, kindliness, charity, magnanimity, compassion, fellow feeling, generosity, hospitality, humanity, humaneness, courtesy, friendliness, pleasantness, good will, philanthropy, altruism, humanitarianism, niceness, goodness, grace, patience, indulgence, tolerance, leniency, understanding, sympathy, considerateness, consideration, warmth, warm-heartedness, love, affection, helpfulness, thoughtfulness, gentleness, mildness, *formal* loving-kindness **2** FAVOUR, good turn, assistance, help, aid, service
🆘 **1** cruelty, inhumanity **2** disservice

kindred *n, adj*
▶ *n* relatives, relations, flesh and blood, family, people, folk, connections, clan, relationship, kinsfolk, lineage, *formal* consanguinity
▶ *adj* similar, common, related, matching, like, corresponding, affiliated, connected, allied, akin, *formal* cognate

king *n*
1 MONARCH, ruler, sovereign, majesty, emperor, chief, chieftain, prince, lord, supremo **2** *the king of football* supremo, kingpin, star, chief, leader, master, *colloq.* leading light, top dog, big cheese/shot/noise, the greatest

kingdom *n*
monarchy, sovereignty, reign, realm, empire, dominion, commonwealth, nation, principality, state, country, domain, dynasty, province, sphere, territory, land, grouping, division

kingly *adj*
sovereign, majestic, royal, regal, imperial, imperious, lordly, noble, stately, supreme, splendid, glorious, grand, imposing, grandiose, dignified, *formal* august, monarchical, sublime

kink *n, v*
▶ *n* **1** CURL, twist, twirl, bend, dent, indentation, knot, loop, crimp, coil, tangle, entanglement, crinkle, wrinkle **2** QUIRK, eccentricity, idiosyncrasy, whim, foible, deviation, perversion, fetish, *formal* caprice
▶ *v* bend, curl, twist, curve, coil, tangle, crimp, wrinkle

kinky *adj*
1 STRANGE, odd, unconventional, freakish, eccentric, outlandish, queer, quirky, idiosyncratic, peculiar, perverted, deviant, unnatural, warped, weird, bizarre, whimsical, degenerate, depraved, licentious, *formal* capricious **2** CURLED, coiled, twisted, crumpled, tangled, curly, wavy, wrinkled, crimped, frizzy

kinsfolk *n*
relatives, relations, family, clan, cousins, connections

kinship *n*
1 KIN, family, blood, relation, relationship, ties, lineage, ancestry, *formal* consanguinity **2** AFFINITY, similarity, association, alliance, connection, correspondence, equivalence, relationship, tie, community, likeness, kindred, conformity

kiosk *n*
booth, stall, stand, news-stand, bookstall, cabin, box, counter

kismet *n*
destiny, fate, doom, fortune, lot, portion, providence, karma, *formal* predestiny

kiss *v, n*
▶ *v* **1** CARESS, *formal* osculate, *colloq.* peck, give someone a peck, smooch, neck, canoodle, bill and coo, *slang* snog **2** TOUCH, touch gently/lightly, graze, glance off, brush, lick, scrape, fan
▶ *n formal* osculation, *colloq.* peck, smack, smacker, *slang* snog

kit *n, v*
▶ *n* **1** EQUIPMENT, gear, apparatus, supplies, tackle, provisions, outfit, implements, set, tools, trappings, rig, instruments, paraphernalia, utensils, effects, luggage, baggage, *formal* accoutrements, appurtenances, *colloq.* things, stuff **2** *football kit* tackle, clothing, outfit, rig, colours, *colloq.* rig-out, gear, strip, togs, get-up, clobber
▶ *v* ▷ **kit out** equip, fit out, outfit, supply, provide, fix up, furnish, prepare, arm, deck out, dress, rig out

kitchen utensils

Kitchen utensils include:
baster, blender, bottle opener, breadbin, breadboard, butter curler, butter dish, can-opener, cheese board, cheese slicer, chopping-board, colander, corer, corkscrew, cruet set, dough hook, egg separator, egg slicer, egg-timer, fish slice, flour dredger, food processor, fork, garlic press, grater, herb mill, ice-cream scoop, icing syringe, jelly mould, kitchen scales, knife block, lemon squeezer, liquidizer, mandolin, measuring jug, meat thermometer, mincer, mixing bowl, nutcracker, nutmeg grater, pasta maker, pastry board, pastry brush, pastry cutter, peeler, pepper mill, pie funnel, potato masher, pudding basin, punch bowl, rolling-pin, salad spinner, scissors, sharpening steel, shears, sieve, sifter, skewer, spatula, spice rack, stoner, storage jar, tea caddy, tea infuser, tea strainer, toast rack, tongs, tureen, vegetable brush, whisk, wine cooler, wine rack, yoghurt maker, zester; *types of knife*: boning knife, bread knife, butter-knife, carving knife, cheese knife, cleaver, cocktail knife, cook's knife, fish knife, grapefruit knife, Kitchen Devils®, palette knife, paring knife, steak knife, table knife, vegetable knife; *types of spoon*: dessert spoon, draining spoon, ladle, measuring spoon, serving spoon, skimmer, straining spoon, tablespoon, teaspoon, wooden spoon.

Types of cooking utensil include:
baking sheet, bun tin, cake tin, flan tin, loaf tin, muffin tin, pie plate, quiche dish; bain-marie, brochette, casserole, cocotte, deep-fat fryer, egg coddler, egg poacher, fish kettle, fondue set, frying-pan, grill pan, milk pan, preserving pan, pressure cooker, ramekin, roasting pan, saucepan, skillet, slow cooker, soufflé dish, steamer, stockpot, terrine, vegetable steamer, wok.

kittenish *adj*
playful, sportive, frolicsome, frisky, cute, coquettish, flirtatious
🔁 staid

knack *n*
flair, faculty, facility, bent, skill, competence, proficiency, talent, genius, gift, trick, ability, capability, adroitness, expertise, skilfulness, aptitude, forte, capacity, handiness, dexterity, quickness, turn, *formal* propensity, *colloq.* hang

knapsack *n*
bag, pack, haversack, rucksack, backpack, duffel bag, flight bag, hold-all, kitbag, shoulder-bag

knave *n*
rogue, scoundrel, villain, swindler, rascal, cheat, reprobate, scamp, scallywag, swine

knavery *n*
knavishness, mischief, roguery, trickery, villainy, devilry, corruption, deceit, deception, dishonesty, double-dealing, fraud, chicanery, imposture, *formal* duplicity, *colloq.* hanky-panky, monkey business

knavish *adj*
roguish, mischievous, rascally, fiendish, wicked, contemptible, corrupt, fraudulent, deceitful, deceptive, dishonest, dishonourable, unprincipled, unscrupulous, reprobate, scoundrelly, villainous, devilish
🔁 honest, honourable, scrupulous

knead *v*
manipulate, press, massage, work, ply, squeeze, shape, rub, form, mould, knuckle, *formal* malax, malaxate

kneel *v*
fall to your knees, bow (down), get down on your knees, stoop, bend, curtsy, revere, defer to, kowtow, *formal* genuflect, make obeisance

knell *n*
toll, ringing, ring, chime, peal, sound, end

knickers *n*
pants, panties, briefs, underwear, lingerie, bikini briefs, camiknickers, knickerbockers, Directoire knickers, bloomers, *colloq.* drawers, smalls

knick-knack *n*
trinket, trifle, bauble, gewgaw, gimcrack, bagatelle, ornament, bric-à-brac, plaything

knife *n, v*
▶ *n* blade, cutter, scalpel, carver, dagger, dirk, skenedhu, penknife, pocket knife, switchblade, jackknife, machete, flick knife, craft knife, Stanley knife®, Kitchen Devils®
▶ *v* cut, rip, slash, stab, pierce, wound, lacerate, bayonet

knight *n*
cavalier, horseman, equestrian, cavalryman, man-at-arms, soldier, warrior, chevalier, gallant, freelance, champion, knight-errant, banneret, kempery-man, kemper

knightly *adj*
chivalrous, bold, courageous, valiant, dauntless, gallant, heroic, noble, honourable, intrepid, soldierly, courtly, gracious, *formal* valorous
🔁 cowardly, ignoble, ungallant

knit *v*
1 JOIN, unite, secure, bind, ally, connect, tie, fasten, link, draw together, mend, interlace, intertwine 2 KNOT, loop, crochet, purl, weave 3 WRINKLE, furrow, crease, gather

knob *n*
1 HANDLE, door-handle, switch 2 LUMP, ball, boss, protrusion, bump, projection, protuberance, nub, *technical* umbo, capitulum 3 KNOT, knurl, gnarl, swell, knub, swelling, tumour, tuber, *technical* tubercle

knock *v, n*
▶ *v* 1 *knock on the door* TAP, hit, strike, rap, thump, pound, slap, smack 2 *knock someone down* hit, strike, smack, slap, punch, box, cuff, clip, swipe, bang, batter, *colloq.* clout, wallop, whack, belt 3 *knocked her head against the wall* bang, bump, hit, strike, collide, bash, pound, thump, stamp, dash, crash, jolt 4 CRITICIZE, condemn, find fault with, attack, *formal* disparage, deprecate, censure, *colloq.* slate, slam, pan, run down, pick holes in, pull/tear to pieces
🔁 4 boost, praise
▷ **knock about 1** WANDER, travel, roam, rove, saunter, traipse, ramble, gad, gallivant, range 2 ASSOCIATE, go around, *formal* consort, *colloq.* hang around 3 BEAT UP, batter, abuse, mistreat, hurt, hit, strike, punch, bash, damage, maltreat, injure, wound, manhandle, bruise, buffet
▷ **knock down 1** DEMOLISH, destroy, fell, pull down, floor, level, wreck, raze, pound, batter, clout, smash, wallop 2 RUN OVER, hit, knock over, run down 3 *knocked down prices* reduce, lower, decrease
▷ **knock off 1** FINISH, finish/stop work, stop, clock off, clock out, *formal* cease, terminate, *colloq.* pack (it) in 2 STEAL, rob, pilfer, filch, *colloq.* pinch, nick, lift, rip off, snaffle, snitch, swipe 3 DEDUCT, take away 4 KILL, murder, slay, assassinate, get rid of, do away with, *colloq.* bump off, do in, *slang* - waste
▷ **knock out 1** *knock someone out* make unconscious, floor, strike down, fell, level, prostrate; *colloq.* KO 2 *knocked out of a competition* defeat, eliminate, beat, overcome, get the better of, overwhelm, rout, crush, *colloq.* thrash, hammer, run rings round 3 STUN, astound, impress, amaze, surprise, startle, astonish, shock, overwhelm, take your breath away, *colloq.* bowl over, knock for six
🔁 1 bring round
▷ **knock up** build quickly, jerry-build, make quickly, put together hurriedly, improvise
🔁 demolish
▶ *n* 1 *a knock at the door* tap, rap, hit, pounding, banging, hammering 2 BLOW, bump, bang, box, rap, thump, cuff, clip, pounding, hammering, slap, smack, *colloq.* clip, whack, belt, clout, wallop 3 MISFORTUNE, blow, setback, failure, rejection, reversal, rebuff, defeat, bad experience/luck

knockout *n*
success, triumph, sensation, attraction, coup, hit, winner, *colloq.* smash, smash-hit, stunner
🔁 flop, loser

knoll *n*
hill, hillock, mound, barrow, elevation, hummock, koppie, *Scot.* knowe

knot *v, n*
▶ *v* tie, secure, bind, loop, tether, leash, lash, entangle, tangle, knit, entwine, ravel, weave
▶ *n* 1 TIE, bond, joint, fastening, loop, splice, twist, ligature

Types of knot include:
bend, Blackwall hitch, blood knot, bow, bowline, running bowline, carrick bend, clove hitch, common whipping, double-overhang, Englishman's tie (or knot), figure of eight, fisherman's bend, fisherman's knot, flat knot, granny knot, half hitch, highwayman's hitch, hitch, Hunter's bend, loop knot, overhand knot or thumb knot, reef knot or square knot, rolling hitch, round turn and two half hitches, seizing, sheepshank, sheet bend or common bend or swab hitch, slipknot, spade-end knot, surgeon's knot, tie, timber hitch, Turk's head, turle knot, wall knot, weaver's knot, Windsor knot.

2 BUNCH, cluster, clump, group, circle, ring, band, gathering, crowd **3** *a knot on a tree* knob, lump, gnarl, knurl, swelling, knub

knotty *adj*
1 COMPLICATED, complex, intricate, difficult, hard, perplexing, thorny, tricky, troublesome, puzzling, baffling, mystifying, problematical, Byzantine, *formal* anfractuous **2** GNARLED, knobby, knotted, rugged, rough, bumpy, nodose, nodous, nodular

know *v*
1 *know French* understand, comprehend, apprehend, perceive, sense, notice, be aware, be conscious of, fathom, be well-versed in, be conversant with, experience, realize, see, undergo, go through, *formal* be cognizant of, *colloq.* be clued up, have at your fingertips, know like the back of your hand, know what's what, have something taped **2** *I know George* be acquainted with, be familiar with, be friends with, associate with, be on good terms with, recognize, know by sight, identify **3** *know a good wine* distinguish, discriminate, discern, differentiate, identify, make out, tell (apart)

know-all *n*
know-it-all, wiseacre, *colloq.* clever clogs, clever dick, wise guy, smart alec, smartypants

know-how *n*
expertise, knowledge, experience, proficiency, competence, gumption, *savoir-faire*, ability, capability, skill, ingenuity, dexterity, aptitude, adroitness, adeptness, talent, faculty, bent, flair, knack, *colloq.* savvy

knowing *adj*
meaningful, expressive, perceptive, shrewd, significant, discerning, conscious, cunning, astute, aware

knowingly *adj*
intentionally, willingly, on purpose, purposely, consciously, studiedly, wilfully, wittingly, deliberately, designedly, by design, calculatedly

knowledge *n*
1 LEARNING, scholarship, education, schooling, letters, instruction, wisdom, tuition, enlightenment, information, data, facts, *formal* erudition, *colloq.* know-how **2** ACQUAINTANCE, familiarity, awareness, intimacy, consciousness, *formal* cognizance **3** UNDERSTANDING, comprehension, apprehension, recognition, judgement, discernment, wisdom, intelligence, ability, grasp, skill, expertise, proficiency, conversance, *formal* cognition, *colloq.* know-how
F3 1 ignorance **2** unawareness

knowledgeable *adj*
1 EDUCATED, scholarly, learned, informed, well-informed, well-read, lettered, intelligent, enlightened, *formal* erudite, *colloq.* a mine of information **2** AWARE, acquainted, conscious, familiar, *au fait*, conversant, experienced, expert, well-versed, *colloq.* in the know
F3 1 ignorant

known *adj*
acknowledged, recognized, well-known, noted, obvious, patent, plain, admitted, revealed, familiar, avowed, commonplace, published, proclaimed, confessed, celebrated, famous

knuckle *v*
▷ **knuckle down** buckle down, start to work hard, begin to study
▷ **knuckle under** submit, yield, give way, give in, succumb, surrender, capitulate, defer, buckle under, *formal* accede, acquiesce, *colloq.* throw in the towel, raise the white flag

kowtow *v*
defer, cringe, fawn, grovel, pander, curry favour, pay court, flatter, kneel, *colloq.* suck up, toady, bow and scrape

kudos *n*
fame, glory, applause, praise, honour, laurels, prestige, renown, repute, reputation, distinction, acclaim, plaudits, *formal* esteem, regard, laudation

L

label *n, v*
▶ *n* **1** TAG, ticket, docket, tab, mark, marker, sticker, trademark **2** DESCRIPTION, categorization, identification, characterization, classification, designation, tag, badge, brand, name, title, nickname, epithet **3** TRADEMARK, brand, brand name, proprietary name
▶ *v* **1** TAG, mark, stamp, attach a label to, mark, stamp, ticket **2** DESCRIBE, brand, classify, categorize, classify, characterize, identify, class, designate, define, term, call, dub, name

laboratory apparatus

> **Laboratory apparatus includes:** autoclave, beaker, bell jar, boiling tube, Buchner funnel, Bunsen burner, burette, centrifuge, clamp, condenser, conical flask, crucible, cylinder, desiccator, distillation apparatus, dropper, evaporating dish, filter flask, filter paper, flask, fume cupboard, funnel, glove box, Kipp's apparatus, Liebig condenser, measuring cylinder, microscope, mortar, pestle, Petri dish, pipette, retort, separating funnel, slide, spatula, stand, still, stirrer, stop clock, test tube, test tube rack, thermometer, top-pan balance, tripod, trough, U-tube, volumetric flask, Woulfe bottle.

laborious *adj*
1 HARD, arduous, difficult, strenuous, tough, backbreaking, wearisome, wearying, tiresome, tiring, fatiguing, uphill, onerous, tedious, heavy, toilsome **2** HARD-WORKING, industrious, painstaking, indefatigable, diligent, careful, assiduous
☒ **1** easy, effortless **2** lazy

labour *n, v*
▶ *n* **1** WORK, task, job, employment, chore, toil, effort, hard work, exertion, drudgery, industriousness, diligence, *colloq.* grind, slog, sweat **2** WORKERS, employees, workforce, labourers, workmen, hands **3** CHILDBIRTH, birth, delivery, labour pains, pangs, throes, contractions, *technical* parturition
☒ **1** ease, leisure **2** management
▶ *v* **1** WORK, toil, work hard, drudge, slave, strive, exert yourself, endeavour, struggle, plod, *formal* travail, *colloq.* grind, sweat, kill yourself **2** OVERDO, overemphasize, dwell on, elaborate, overstress, put too much emphasis on, strain **3** *labour hard to get results* struggle, strive, endeavour, work hard, *colloq.* do your best, give your all, go all out **4** *labour under a mistaken belief* suffer, be misled, be deceived, be blinded **5** TOSS, pitch, roll, pitch, turn
☒ **1** laze, idle, lounge

laboured *adj*
awkward, unnatural, forced, difficult, complicated, heavy, overdone, overwrought, stiff, stilted, strained, ponderous, studied, contrived, *formal* affected
☒ easy, natural

labourer *n*
manual worker, blue-collar worker, unskilled worker, navvy, hand, worker, workman, drudge, menial, hireling

labyrinth *n*
maze, winding, warren, complexity, intricacy, complication, network, puzzle, riddle, enigma, tangle, entanglement, jungle, confusion

labyrinthine *adj*
complex, intricate, complicated, perplexing, puzzling, involved, knotty, tangled, tortuous, winding, mazelike, confused, mazy, Byzantine, *formal* convoluted
☒ simple, straightforward

lace *n, v*
▶ *n* **1** NETTING, mesh-work, open work, tatting, crochet, filigree **2** STRING, cord, twine, thong, tie, shoelace, bootlace, lacing
▶ *v* **1** TIE, do up, fasten, secure, thread, close, bind, attach, string, twine, intertwine, interweave **2** ADD TO, mix in, flavour, blend, strengthen, *formal* fortify, *colloq.* spike

lacerate *v*
tear, rip, rend, cut (open), gash, slash, wound, claw, mangle, maim, injure, mutilate, torture, torment, harrow, hurt, distress, *formal* afflict

laceration *n*
tear, cut, gash, rip, rent, slash, wound, injury, mutilation, maim

lachrymose *adj*
tearful, crying, weeping, weepy, mournful, sad, melancholy, sobbing, teary, woeful, *formal* dolorous, lugubrious
☒ happy, laughing

lack *n, v*
▶ *n* need, scarcity, shortage, insufficiency, dearth, deficiency, absence, scantiness, vacancy, void, deprivation, destitution, emptiness, *formal* want, paucity, privation
☒ abundance, profusion
▶ *v* need, have need of, not have, not have enough of, miss, be deficient in, require, *formal* want, *colloq.* be clean/fresh out of

lackadaisical *adj*
apathetic, lazy, lethargic, inert, limp, spiritless, listless, indifferent, idle, dreamy, dull, lukewarm, half-hearted, abstracted, *formal* enervated, indolent, languorous, languid
☒ active, dynamic, energetic, vigorous

lackey *n*
1 FAWNER, sycophant, toady, flatterer, hanger-on, parasite, minion, pawn, instrument, tool, *colloq.* yesman, doormat **2** ATTENDANT, steward, servant, manservant, footman, menial, valet

lacking *adj*
needing, without, short of, missing, minus, inad-

equate, deficient, defective, flawed, *formal* wanting

lacklustre *adj*
drab, dull, flat, boring, tedious, dry, leaden, lifeless, spiritless, uninteresting, unimaginative, uninspired, commonplace, dim, insipid, vapid, *colloq.* run-of-the-mill
F∃ brilliant, inspired, lively, bright

laconic *adj*
terse, succinct, pithy, concise, incisive, crisp, taciturn, short, curt, brief, economical, blunt, abrupt, to the point
F∃ verbose, wordy

lacuna *n*
gap, omission, space, void, break, blank, cavity, *formal* hiatus

lad *n*
1 BOY, youth, youngster, juvenile, schoolboy, son, *colloq.* kid **2** CHAP, fellow, *colloq.* guy, bloke

laden *adj*
loaded, charged, weighed down, burdened, oppressed, packed, stuffed, weighted, full, chock-full, fraught, encumbered, hampered, taxed, jammed
F∃ empty

la-di-da *adj*
pretentious, posh, conceited, snobbish, snooty, mannered, over-refined, foppish, *formal* affected, *colloq.* highfalutin, put-on, stuck-up, toffee-nosed

ladle *v*
shovel, spoon, lade, dish, scoop, bail, dip
▷ **ladle out** hand out, distribute, disburse, dish out, dole out

lady *n*
woman, young woman, female, matron, noblewoman, dame, damsel, gentlewoman

ladylike *adj*
refined, well-bred, well-mannered, polite, courteous, proper, respectable, polished, modest, cultured, elegant, courtly, queenly, genteel, matronly, *formal* decorous

lag *v*
dawdle, loiter, hang back, linger, fall behind, straggle, trail, bring up the rear, saunter, delay, shuffle, idle, dally, *formal* tarry, *colloq.* shilly-shally, lounge, drag your feet, kick your heels
F∃ hurry, lead, keep up

laggard *n*
dawdler, loiterer, lingerer, straggler, sluggard, idler, saunterer, snail, loafer, *colloq.* slowcoach, lounger
F∃ dynamo, live wire, *colloq.* go-getter

lagoon *n*
pool, pond, shallows, lake, marsh, bog, fen, swamp, *US* bayou

laid up *adj*
housebound, bedridden, ill, sick, incapacitated, disabled, hors de combat, immobilized, injured, out of action, on the sick list

laid-back *adj*
relaxed, at ease, casual, leisurely, easy-going, unhurried, untroubled, unworried, calm, cool, passionless, free and easy, *formal* imperturbable, *colloq.* unflappable
F∃ tense, *colloq.* uptight

lair *n*

Lairs and homes of creatures include:
sett (*badger*); den (*bear*); lodge (*beaver*); hive (*bee*); nest (*bird*); byre (*cow*); eyrie (*eagle*); coop (*fowl*); earth (*fox*); form (*hare*); den (*lion*); fortress (*mole*); hole, nest (*mouse*); holt (*otter*); sty (*pig*); dovecote (*pigeon*); burrow, warren (*rabbit*); pen, fold (*sheep*); shell (*snail*); drey (*squirrel*); nest, vespiary (*wasp*).

laissez-faire *adj*
permissive, non-interfering, non-interventionist, free-enterprise, free-market, free-trade, *colloq.* live and let live

lake *n*
pond, pool, lagoon, reservoir, dam, basin, mere, tarn, *Scot.* loch, *US* bayou

lam *v*
beat, batter, hit, knock, pound, thump, strike, thrash, leather, pelt, pummel, *colloq.* clout, wallop, whack

lambaste *v*
1 CRITICIZE, reprimand, rebuke, scold, upbraid, *formal* berate, castigate, censure, reprove, *colloq.* roast **2** BEAT, whip, flog, thrash, strike, drub, thump, batter, flay, leather, *colloq.* clout, wallop, whack, tan

lame *adj*
1 DISABLED, handicapped, crippled, hurt, injured, maimed, limping, hobbling, halting, *formal* incapacitated, *colloq.* gammy, poorly **2** WEAK, feeble, flimsy, inadequate, unsatisfactory, defective, poor, thin, unconvincing
F∃ 1 able-bodied **2** convincing

lament *v, n*
▶ *v* mourn, bewail, grieve, sorrow, cry, weep, sob, wail, keen, complain, groan, moan, deplore, regret, *formal* bemoan, ululate
F∃ rejoice, celebrate
▶ *n* lamentation, dirge, elegy, keen, requiem, complaint, moan, groan, wail, grieving, crying, weeping, sobbing, tears, howl, *formal* threnody

lamentable *adj*
1 DEPLORABLE, regrettable, mournful, distressing, sorrowful, tragic, unfortunate, terrible, wretched, grievous, woeful **2** MEAGRE, low, inadequate, insufficient, mean, unsatisfactory, pitiful, miserable, niggardly, poor, disappointing, *colloq.* measly, lousy, grotty

lamentation *n*
dirge, elegy, lament, wailing, mourning, weeping, moan, sobbing, sorrow, grief, grieving, keen, keening, jeremiad, *formal* ululation, deploration, threnody, plaint
F∃ celebration, rejoicing

laminate *v*
cover, layer, plate, stratify, veneer, coat, face, flake, separate, split, *technical* foliate, *formal* exfoliate

lamp *n*
light, lantern, bulb, light bulb. *See panel at* LIGHT.

lampoon *n, v*
▶ *n* satire, skit, caricature, parody, spoof, burlesque, travesty, pasquinade, *colloq.* send-up, take-off
▶ *v* satirize, caricature, parody, spoof, make fun of, ridicule, mock, burlesque, pasquinade, *colloq.* send up, take off

lampooner *n*
satirist, caricaturist, parodist, pasquinader, pasquilant, pasquiler

lance *v, n*
▶ *v* pierce, slit, cut (open), puncture, prick, incise
▶ *n* spear, javelin, pike, harpoon, bayonet, lancet

land *n, v*
▶ *n* **1** EARTH, ground, soil, loam, terrain, dry land, terra firma **2** PROPERTY, grounds, real estate, country, countryside, fields, rural area, open space, farmland, agricultural land, tract, acres, acreage,

manor **3** COUNTRY, nation, region, area, district, territory, province, domain, realm, state, fatherland, motherland, native country
▶ *v* **1** ALIGHT, disembark, dismount, dock, berth, unload, touch down, come/bring in to land, bring/take down, go ashore, come to rest **2** ARRIVE, deposit, reach, get, find yourself, drop, settle, turn up, *colloq.* wind up, end up **3** OBTAIN, secure, gain, get, acquire, net, capture, achieve, win, *formal* procure **4** *land you with another bill* saddle, weigh down, burden, oppress, trouble, tax, encumber **5** *land a blow on the ear* hit, deal, give, catch, deliver, administer, direct, inflict, *colloq.* fetch

landlady, landlord *n*
publican, innkeeper, hotelier, hotel-keeper, owner, proprietor, host, mine host, restaurateur, freeholder, tenant

landmark *n*
feature, monument, signpost, turning-point, crisis, watershed, milestone, milepost, boundary, beacon, cairn

landscape *n*
scene, scenery, view, panorama, outlook, vista, prospect, perspective, countryside, aspect

landslide *n, adj*
▶ *n* landslip, earthfall, rockfall, avalanche
▶ *adj* overwhelming, decisive, emphatic, runaway

lane *n*
way, track, passage(way), alley(way), footpath, footway, path(way), towpath, byroad, byway, driveway, avenue, channel

language *n*
1 SPEECH, vocabulary, terminology, communication, speaking, uttering, verbalizing, vocalizing, *formal* parlance **2** TALK, conversation, utterance, *formal* discourse, converse **3** WORDING, style, phraseology, phrasing, expression, utterance, rhetoric, diction

Language terms include :

brogue, dialect, idiom, patois, regionalism, localism, dialect, tongue, pidgin, creole, vernacular, argot, cant, jargon, doublespeak, gobbledygook, buzz word, colloquialism, journalese, *colloq.* lingo, patter, slang, cockney rhyming slang; etymology, lexicography, lingua franca, linguistics, phonetics, semantics, syntax, usage, grammar, orthography, socio-linguistics.

languages

Languages of the world include:
Aborigine, Afghan, Afrikaans, Arabic, Balinese, Bantu, Basque, Bengali, Burmese, Belorussian, Catalan, Celtic, Chinese, Cornish, Croat, Czech, Danish, Dutch, English, Eskimo, Esperanto, Estonian, Ethiopian, Farsi, Finnish, Flemish, French, Gaelic, German, Greek, Haitian, Hawaiian, Hebrew, Hindi, Hindustani, Hottentot, Hungarian, Icelandic, Indonesian, Irish, Iranian, Iraqi, Italian, Japanese, Kurdish, Lapp, Latin, Latvian, Lithuanian, Magyar, Malay, Maltese, Mandarin, Manx, Maori, Mexican, Norwegian, Persian, Polish, Portuguese, Punjabi, Romany, Romanian, Russian, Sanskrit, Scottish, Serbian, Siamese, Sinhalese, Slavonic, Slovak, Slovenian, Somali, Spanish, Swahili, Swedish, Swiss, Tamil, Thai, Tibetan, Turkish, Ukrainian, Urdu, Vietnamese, Volapük, Welsh, Yiddish, Zulu.

languid *adj*
listless, sluggish, lethargic, slow, inactive, lazy, feeble, heavy, uninterested, unenthusiastic, spiritless, indifferent, inert, lackadaisical, drooping, dull, weak, faint, weary, pining, limp, sickly, *formal* debilitated, enervated, languorous, torpid
F3 alert, lively, vivacious

languish *v*
1 WILT, droop, fade, fail, flag, wither, waste away, rot, deteriorate, weaken, sink, faint, decline, mope, waste, grieve, sorrow, sigh, brood, sicken **2** PINE, yearn, want, long, desire, hanker, hunger, sigh
F3 **1** flourish

languor *n*
lethargy, listlessness, laziness, faintness, fatigue, weariness, silence, inertia, drowsiness, dreaminess, sleepiness, feebleness, weakness, frailty, calm, lull, relaxation, oppressiveness, heaviness, ennui, sloth, stillness, *formal* debility, enervation, indolence, lassitude, torpor, indolence
F3 alacrity, gusto

lank *adj*
1 *lank hair* limp, straggling, scraggy, drooping, lifeless, lustreless **2** *lank young people* tall, thin, long, emaciated, skinny, gaunt, lanky, lean, slender, slim, scrawny, rawboned
F3 burly

lanky *adj*
gaunt, gangling, scrawny, tall, thin, lean, slender, slim, scraggy, weedy
F3 short, squat

lap[1] *n, v*
▶ *n* **1** CIRCUIT, round, orbit, ambit, tour, loop, course, circle, compass, distance **2** *a lap on a journey* stage, section, leg
▶ *v* wrap, fold, wind, envelop, enfold, swathe, encase, surround, cover, swaddle, overlap

lap[2] *v*
animals lapping milk drink, sip, sup, lick
▷ **lap up** accept eagerly, take in enthusiastically, listen in, absorb

lapse *n, v*
▶ *n* **1** ERROR, slip, mistake, negligence, omission, oversight, fault, failing, indiscretion, backsliding, relapse, *formal* aberration, dereliction **2** FALL, descent, decline, drop, downturn, deterioration, worsening, degeneration, backslide, slipping **3** BREAK, gap, interval, lull, interruption, intermission, pause, *formal* hiatus
▶ *v* **1** DECLINE, fall, sink, drop, deteriorate, slide, slip, sink, drift, fail, worsen, degenerate, backslide, *colloq.* go downhill, go to pot, go to the dogs, go to rack and ruin, go down the tube(s) **2** EXPIRE, run out, end, stop, become void/invalid, *formal* terminate, cease **3** PASS, elapse, go by, go on, slip away, slip by
F3 **2** continue

lapsed *adj*
ended, expired, run out, finished, out of date, outdated, invalid, obsolete, unrenewed, *formal* discontinued
F3 renewed, continued

larceny *n*
stealing, theft, burglary, robbery, pilfering, piracy, *formal* misappropriation, purloining, expropriation, *slang* heist

larder *n*
pantry, storeroom, storage room, scullery

large *adj*
1 BIG, huge, immense, massive, vast, sizable, great, giant, gigantic, bulky, heavy, ample, enormous, colossal, king-sized, broad, considerable, monumental,

prodigious, stupendous, mammoth, substantial, high, tall, *formal* commodious, voluminous, *colloq.* jumbo, whopping, bumper, ginormous, dirty great, humungous **2** FULL, extensive, generous, liberal, ample, roomy, plentiful, spacious, grand, far-reaching, sweeping, broad, comprehensive, exhaustive, grandiose
 1 small, tiny
▷ **at large 1** GENERALLY, in general, by and large, on the whole, chiefly, mainly **2** FREE, at liberty, on the loose, on the run, independent, unconfined
▷ **by and large** on the whole, generally, mostly, generally speaking, as a rule, for the most part, all things considered

largely *adv*
mainly, in the main, principally, chiefly, generally, primarily, predominantly, mostly, for the most part, considerably, by and large, to a large extent, widely, extensively, greatly

large-scale *adj*
extensive, far-reaching, broad, nationwide, countrywide, wide, wide-ranging, expansive, wholesale, global, vast, sweeping, epic
 minor

largesse *n*
generosity, kindness, liberality, philanthropy, benefaction, open-handedness, bounty, donation, gift, present, aid, grant, handout, endowment, bequest, charity, allowance, alms, *formal* munificence
 meanness

lark *n, v*
▶ *n* **1** ESCAPADE, antic, fling, prank, romp, revel, mischief, fooling, horseplay, frolic, caper, cavorting, play, game, *colloq.* skylark **2** *this writing lark* activity, task, job, chore
▶ *v* play, play tricks, have fun, fool around/about, mess about, cavort, frolic, caper, romp, sport, rollick, gambol, *colloq.* skylark

lascivious *adj*
lecherous, lewd, licentious, lustful, ribald, sensual, obscene, pornographic, crude, vulgar, coarse, bawdy, wanton, dirty, indecent, offensive, suggestive, salacious, scurrilous, unchaste, *formal* libidinous, prurient, *colloq.* blue, horny, randy, smutty

lash *n, v*
▶ *n* blow, whip, stroke, swipe, hit
▶ *v* **1** WHIP, flog, beat, hit, thrash, strike, scourge, flail, batter, *colloq.* wallop, whack **2** ATTACK, criticize, lay into, scold, reprove, rebuke, *formal* censure, fulminate, berate, *colloq.* bawl out, tear a strip off, tear to shreds **3** TIE, bind, fasten, secure, make fast, join, affix, rope, tether, strap **4** *waves lashing the shore* strike, smash, dash, break, beat, pound, buffet **5** *an animal lashing its tail* flick, swish, whip, switch, wag
▷ **lash out** *at someone* hit out at, attack strongly, speak out against, criticize fiercely, have a go at **2** *lash out on new clothes* spend a lot of money, spend extravagantly, *colloq.* splash out on, spend a fortune on, spend money like water

lass *n*
girl, young woman, schoolgirl, lassie, miss

lassitude *n*
sluggishness, tiredness, weariness, lethargy, listlessness, drowsiness, apathy, dullness, exhaustion, fatigue, heaviness, inertia, *formal* enervation, languor, torpor
 energy, vigour

last¹ *adj, adv, n*
▶ *adj* **1** *last Sunday* most recent, latest, previous **2** FINAL, ultimate, closing, latest, rearmost, hindmost, terminal, furthest, concluding, finishing, end-

ing, remotest, utmost, extreme **3** *the last person to expect help from* least likely, least suitable, most unlikely, most unsuitable
 1 next **2** first, initial **3** first, most likely
▷ **last word 1** final decision, final say, final statement, conclusive/definite comment, ultimatum **2** latest, best, pick, cream, ultimate, vogue, rage, perfection, crème de la crème, *dernier cri*, *ne plus ultra*, *formal* quintessence
▶ *adv* finally, ultimately, behind, after, at the end, at the back/rear
 first, firstly
▶ *n* finish, close, end, ending, conclusion, completion
▷ **at last** eventually, finally, in the end, in conclusion, ultimately, in due course, at length

last² *v*
it lasts six hours continue, go on, take, endure, remain, persist, carry on, keep (on), survive, hold out, hold on, exist, wear, stay, hold on, stand up, *formal* abide, subsist
 cease, stop, fade

last-ditch *adj*
final, desperate, frenzied, wild, last-chance, straining, struggling, frantic, heroic, *colloq.* all-out, eleventh-hour, last-gasp

lasting *adj*
enduring, unchanging, unceasing, unending, abiding, surviving, continuing, persisting, permanent, durable, perpetual, external, everlasting, undying, never-ending, lifelong, long-lived, long-standing, long-term, *formal* interminable, ceaseless
 brief, fleeting, short-lived

lastly *adv*
finally, ultimately, in conclusion, in the end, to sum up
 firstly

latch *n, v*
▶ *n* fastening, catch, bar, bolt, lock, hook, hasp
▶ *v* fasten, bar, bolt, lock, hook, catch, make secure
▷ **latch on to 1** ATTACH YOURSELF TO, not want to leave, follow **2** UNDERSTAND, comprehend, grasp, learn, realize, *formal* apprehend, *colloq.* twig

late *adj, adv*
▶ *adj* **1** OVERDUE, behind, behindhand, behind schedule, behind time, slow, unpunctual, delayed, last-minute, *formal* tardy **2** FORMER, previous, departed, dead, deceased, past, preceding, old, defunct **3** RECENT, up-to-date, current, fresh, new, up-to-the-minute, latest
 1 early, punctual
▶ *adv* unpunctually, behindhand, behind schedule, behind time, in arrears, slowly, belatedly, formerly, recently, *formal* dilatorily, tardily
 early, punctually
▷ **of late** recently, lately, not long ago, newly, latterly

lately *adv*
recently, of late, not long ago, newly, latterly

lateness *n*
belatedness, delay, unpunctuality, *formal* dilatoriness, retardation, tardiness
 earliness

latent *adj*
potential, possible, dormant, inactive, undeveloped, unrealized, lurking, unexpressed, unseen, unrevealed, secret, concealed, hidden, invisible, underlying, veiled, passive, *formal* quiescent
 active, conspicuous, apparent

later *adv, adj*
▶ *adv* next, afterwards, subsequently, after, successively, in the (near) future, at a future time/date, at a

later time, later on, in due course, in a while, some other time
F⃝ earlier
▶ *adj* next, subsequent, following, succeeding

lateral *adj*
sideways, side, oblique, indirect, slanting, sideward, edgeways, marginal, flanking

latest *adj*
modern, newest, most recent, ultimate, up-to-date, current, now, fashionable, *colloq.* in, with it, up-to-the-minute
F⃝ earliest

lather *n, v*
▶ *n* **1** FOAM, suds, soapsuds, froth, bubbles, soap, shampoo **2** AGITATION, fluster, anxiety, fuss, dither, flutter, fever, *colloq.* state, flap, tizzy, sweat, stew
▶ *v* foam, froth, rub, soap, shampoo, whip up

latitude *n*
freedom, liberty, unrestrictedness, laxity, indulgence, carte blanche, licence, leeway, scope, range, room, space, play, clearance, breadth, width, spread, sweep, reach, span, field, extent

latter *adj*
last-mentioned, last, later, closing, final, end, concluding, ensuing, succeeding, successive, second
F⃝ former

latter-day *adj*
modern, contemporary, current, present-day

latterly *adv*
lately, recently, most recently, of late, *formal* hitherto
F⃝ formerly

lattice *n*
lattice-work, openwork, fretwork, mesh, web, grate, grating, network, espalier, grid, grille, tracery, trellis, *formal* reticulation

laud *v*
praise, admire, approve, magnify, acclaim, applaud, celebrate, glorify, extol, honour, hail
F⃝ blame, condemn, curse, damn

laudable *adj*
praiseworthy, commendable, estimable, of note, excellent, exemplary, worthy, admirable, creditable, sterling, *formal* meritorious
F⃝ damnable, execrable

laudation *n*
praise, acclaim, acclamation, reverence, adulation, blessing, accolade, celebrity, commendation, devotion, extolment, glorification, glory, kudos, homage, tribute, *formal* encomium, encomion, eulogy, panegyric, paean, veneration
F⃝ condemnation, criticism

laudatory *adj*
complimentary, commendatory, adulatory, acclamatory, approving, celebratory, glorifying, *formal* approbatory, encomiastic(al), eulogistic, panegyrical
F⃝ damning

laugh *v, n*
▶ *v* chuckle, burst out laughing, dissolve into laughter, roar/shriek with laughter, cackle, giggle, guffaw, snigger, titter, chortle, hoot, roar, peal, *colloq.* split your sides, fall about, crease up, break up, be rolling in the aisles, be in stitches, laugh like a drain
▷ **laugh at** mock, ridicule, make jokes about, jeer, make/poke fun of, scoff at, scorn, taunt, make a fool of, *formal* deride
▷ **laugh off** dismiss, disregard, ignore, brush aside, belittle, shrug off, make little of, minimize
▶ *n* **1** *have a good laugh* giggle, chuckle, snigger, titter, guffaw, chortle, lark, roar, peal, *colloq.* scream, hoot **2** JOKE, jest, prank, hoax, trick, sport, fun, play

laughable *adj*
1 FUNNY, amusing, comical, comic, humorous, hilarious, uproarious, droll, farcical, diverting, entertaining, *colloq.* side-splitting **2** RIDICULOUS, absurd, ludicrous, preposterous, nonsensical, derisory, derisive
F⃝ **1** serious

laughing-stock *n*
figure of fun, butt, dupe, victim, target, fair game, stooge, Aunt Sally

laughter *n*
laughing, giggling, chuckling, chortling, guffawing, sniggering, tittering, hilarity, amusement, merriment, mirth, happiness, cheerfulness, glee, convulsions

launch *v*
1 PROPEL, dispatch, discharge, fire, send off, project, float, set afloat, set in motion, throw, fire **2** BEGIN, start, embark on, set up, establish, found, open, initiate, inaugurate, institute, introduce, organize, instigate, *formal* commence, *colloq.* set in motion, set the ball rolling

laundry *n*
1 WASHING, (dirty) clothes, wash **2** LAUNDERETTE, dry cleaner's, *US* Laundromat®

lavatory *n*
toilet, WC, bathroom, cloakroom, washroom, Ladies' room, water closet, public convenience, urinal, latrine, privy, powder room, *US* rest room, comfort station, *colloq.* loo, the ladies, the gents, bog, *slang* kazi, *US slang* john

lavish *adj, v*
▶ *adj* **1** ABUNDANT, copious, lush, luxuriant, plentiful, profuse, unlimited, prolific, splendid, grand, gorgeous, rich **2** GENEROUS, liberal, open-handed, free, bountiful, extravagant, wasteful, thriftless, prodigal, wasteful, profligate, immoderate, excessive, wild, intemperate, unsparing, unstinting
F⃝ **1** scant **2** frugal, thrifty, mean
▶ *v* spend, expend, heap, pour, shower, deluge, squander, waste, dissipate, *formal* bestow

law *n*
1 RULE, act, legislation, decree, edict, order, directive, statute, regulation, command, commandment, pronouncement, ordinance, charter, code, constitution, enactment **2** PRINCIPLE, axiom, maxim, criterion, standard, precept, rule, formula, tenet, code, direction, instruction, canon, guideline **3** JURISPRUDENCE, legislation, lawsuit, litigation

law-abiding *adj*
obedient, upright, orderly, lawful, complying, honest, honourable, decent, virtuous, good, righteous, upstanding, dutiful
F⃝ lawless

law-breaker *n*
offender, wrongdoer, criminal, felon, miscreant, culprit, delinquent, convict, outlaw, sinner, transgressor, trespasser, *formal* infractor, *colloq.* crook

lawful *adj*
legal, legitimate, permissible, legalized, constitutional, authorized, recognized, allowable, sanctioned, warranted, valid, just, proper, rightful, *formal* licit
F⃝ illegal, unlawful, illicit

lawless *adj*
disorderly, rebellious, anarchic(al), unruly, ungoverned, riotous, mutinous, insurgent, insurrectionary, rebellious, revolutionary, seditious, unrestrained, chaotic, illegal, wrongdoing, law-breaking, criminal, wild, reckless
F⃝ law-abiding

lawlessness *n*
anarchy, disorder, chaos, insurgency, insurrection, rebellion, revolution, sedition, mob-rule, piracy, racketeering, *formal* ochlocracy, *colloq.* mobocracy, rent-a-mob
F3 order

lawsuit *n*
litigation, suit, action, legal action, proceedings, legal proceedings, case, prosecution, dispute, process, trial, argument, contest, cause, *technical* indictment

lawyer *n*
solicitor, barrister, advocate, attorney, counsel, QC, legal adviser, legal representative, legal practitioner, *colloq.* brief

lax *adj*
1 CASUAL, careless, heedless, easy-going, slack, lenient, indulgent, permissive, tolerant, negligent, neglectful, remiss, slipshod, sloppy, inattentive 2 IMPRECISE, inexact, indefinite, loose, inaccurate, vague, general, broad
F3 1 strict, careful 2 exact, rigorous, specific

laxative *n*
loosener, purgative, evacuant, purge, salts, senna, ipecacuanha, *technical* aperient, cathartic, eccoprotic

laxity *n*
1 CARELESSNESS, neglect, heedlessness, indulgence, negligence, slovenliness, slackness, sloppiness, tolerance, permissiveness, softness, leniency, freedom, indifference, nonchalance, latitude, latitudinarianism, laissez-faire 2 IMPRECISION, inexactness, indefiniteness, looseness
F3 1 severity, strictness 2 exactness

lay¹ *v*
1 PUT, place, deposit, set down, settle, lodge, plant, set, establish, leave, *formal* posit 2 ARRANGE, position, set out, locate, work out, devise, make, prepare, plan, design, present, submit, offer, put forward, *formal* dispose 3 ATTRIBUTE, ascribe, assign, charge, impute, allot 4 *lay a burden on someone* impose, put, burden, inflict, apply, thrust, encumber, saddle, oppress, weigh down 5 *lay a bet* place, bet, wager, gamble, risk, chance, hazard 6 *lay eggs* produce, bear, deposit, give birth to, breed, engender, *technical* oviposit
▷ **lay aside** 1 PUT ASIDE, save, keep, store 2 REJECT, set aside, put out of your mind, abandon, discard, dismiss, shelve, postpone, put off, cast aside
▷ **lay bare** disclose, divulge, explain, expose, reveal, show, uncover, unveil, exhibit
▷ **lay down** 1 SURRENDER, yield, give up, give, discard, drop, *formal* relinquish 2 STIPULATE, assert, postulate, affirm, state, establish, formulate, prescribe, ordain
▷ **lay down the law** dictate, crack down, emphasize, dogmatize, *formal* pontificate, *colloq.* read the riot act, rule the roost
▷ **lay hands on** 1 ATTACK, assault, beat up, lay into, seize, set on, grab, clasp, clutch, get, lay hold of, grip 2 FIND, get hold of, locate, bring to light, acquire, discover, grasp, unearth 3 BLESS, consecrate, ordain, confirm
▷ **lay in** store (up), stock up, amass, accumulate, hoard, stockpile, gather, collect, build up, glean, squirrel away, salt away
▷ **lay into** attack, assail, pitch into, set about, tear into, let fly at, hit out at, have a go at, lash out at
▷ **lay it on** exaggerate, overdo it, flatter, overpraise, *colloq.* butter up, soft-soap, sweet-talk
▷ **lay off** 1 DISMISS, discharge, make redundant, pay off, let go, *colloq.* sack 2 GIVE UP, drop, stop, leave off, leave alone, let up, refrain, *formal* cease, desist, discontinue, *colloq.* quit

▷ **lay on** provide, supply, cater, furnish, give, set up, organize
▷ **lay out** 1 DISPLAY, set out, put out, spread out, exhibit, arrange, plan, design 2 KNOCK OUT, fell, floor, flatten, demolish 3 SPEND, pay, give, contribute, invest, *formal* disburse, *colloq.* shell out, fork out
▷ **lay up** store up, hoard, accumulate, amass, keep, save, put away
▷ **lay waste** desolate, ravage, destroy, devastate, raze, ruin, sack, spoil, pillage, rape, vandalize, *formal* depredate, despoil

---

🖊 lay or lie ?
Lay means 'to place in a flat, prone or horizontal position.' It is a transitive verb, ie it requires an object: *If you lay the pen down there, it will roll off the table.* *Lie* means 'to be or move into a flat, prone or horizontal position.' It is an intransitive verb, ie, it does not have an object. The past tense is *lay*: *She went into the bedroom and lay on the bed.*

---

lay² *adj*
1 LAIC, secular 2 AMATEUR, non-professional, non-specialist
F3 1 clergy, ordained 2 expert, professional

lay³ *n*
heavenly lays song, poem, ballad, lyric, madrigal, ode

layabout *n*
good-for-nothing, ne'er-do-well, waster, idler, laggard, lounger, *colloq.* loafer, shirker, skiver, lazy-bones, lounge-lizard

layer *n*
1 COVER, coating, coat, covering, film, blanket, mantle, sheet, lamina 2 STRATUM, seam, vein, band, deposit, thickness, tier, bed, plate, row, ply

layman, laywoman or **layperson** *n*
1 LAYPERSON, parishioner 2 AMATEUR, outsider, non-professional
F3 1 clergyman 2 expert, professional

lay-off *n*
redundancy, discharge, dismissal, unemployment, *colloq.* sack, sacking, papers, firing, push, boot, elbow

layout *n*
arrangement, design, outline, plan, format, sketch, draft, map, geography

laze *v*
idle, lounge, sit around, lie around, loll, relax, *colloq.* loaf, bum around, not pull your weight
F3 work

laziness *n*
idleness, sloth, slothfulness, inactivity, slowness, sluggishness, lethargy, slackness, *formal* dilatoriness, fainéance, indolence, tardiness, langour
F3 industriousness

lazy *adj*
idle, slothful, slack, work-shy, inactive, inert, slow, slow-moving, good-for-nothing, lethargic, sluggish, *formal* indolent, torpid, languid, languorous, tardy, fainéant, *colloq.* bone idle
F3 industrious, hard-working

lazy-bones *n*
idler, slouch, laggard, sluggard, good-for-nothing, layabout, ne'er-do-well, *colloq.* loafer, lounger, shirker, skiver

leach *v*
drain, extract, filter, strain, seep, filtrate, percolate, *technical* osmose, *formal* lixiviate

lead¹ *v, n, adj*
▶ *v* 1 GUIDE, conduct, escort, steer, pilot, usher

2 RULE, govern, head, be at the head of, be in charge of, preside over, direct, supervise, command, manage, regulate, *colloq.* call the shots **3** CAUSE, result in, produce, bring about, bring on, contribute to, call forth, tend towards, provoke **4** INFLUENCE, persuade, incline, sway, prompt, induce, move, dispose **5** SURPASS, outdo, excel, outstrip, outrun, outdistance, exceed, eclipse, transcend, be in lead, be in front, come first **6** PASS, spend, live, have, undergo, experience

▱ **1** follow

▷ **lead off** begin, commence, open, get going, start (off), inaugurate, initiate, *colloq.* kick off, start the ball rolling

▷ **lead on** entice, lure, seduce, tempt, draw on, beguile, persuade, string along, deceive, trick, mislead, dupe

▷ **lead up to** prepare (the way) for, approach, introduce, make overtures, pave/open the way

▷ **lead the way** go in front, go first, show, show the way, guide

▸ *n* **1** PRIORITY, precedence, first place, advance position, start, van, vanguard, forefront, advantage, supremacy, pre-eminence, edge, interval, gap, margin **2** LEADERSHIP, guidance, direction, example, model, pattern **3** CLUE, hint, indication, indicator, guide, pointer, tip, suggestion, *colloq.* tip-off **4** TITLE ROLE, starring part, principal, principal part, leading role

▸ *adj* leading, first, principal, chief, main, foremost, head, premier, primary, prime, star, top

lead² *n*
1 BULLETS, shot, ammunition, pellets, balls, slugs **2** WEIGHT, heavy weight, plumb, sinker

leaden *adj*
1 GREY, overcast, cloudy, gloomy, dingy, dismal, dreary, ashen, greyish, oppressive, sombre **2** DULL, heavy, burdensome, onerous, laboured, lifeless, lacklustre, listless, spiritless, sluggish, humdrum, inert, stilted, *formal* languid **3** CUMBERSOME, wooden, stiff, heavy, laboured, plodding, lead

leader *n*
1 HEAD, chief, figurehead, director, ruler, principal, manager, governor, superintendent, overseer, supervisor, commander, captain, superior, chieftain, ringleader, guide, conductor, skipper, mover and shaker, *colloq.* boss **2** GUIDE, courier, escort, usher **3** PIONEER, innovator, developer, expert, authority, leading light, guiding light, discoverer, inventor, founder, architect, trailblazer, pathfinder, groundbreaker, front-runner

▱ **1** follower

leadership *n*
direction, control, command, management, authority, rule, guidance, supervision, superintendency, domination, pre-eminence, premiership, captaincy, administration, sway, directorship, governorship, headship

leading *adj*
main, principal, chief, primary, first, front, supreme, outstanding, foremost, dominant, ruling, directing, guiding, superior, greatest, highest, governing, paramount, top-rank, pre-eminent, number one

▱ subordinate

leaf *n, v*
▸ *n the leaves of a tree* **1** BLADE, bract, frond, pad, calyx, needle, sepal, leaflet, *technical* cotyledon, foliole

---

Leaf parts include:
auxiliary bud, blade, chloroplasts, epidermis, leaf axil, leaf cells, margin, midrib, petiole, sheath, stipule, stomata, tip, vein.

Leaf shapes include:
abruptly pinnate, acerose, ciliate, cordate, crenate, dentate, digitate, doubly dentate, elliptic, entire, falcate, hastate, lanceolate, linear, lobed, lyrate, obovate, orbicular, ovate, palmate, peltate, pinnate, pinnatifid, reniform, runcinate, sagittate, spathulate, subulate, ternate, trifoliate.

---

2 PAGE, sheet, folio
▸ *v* thumb (through), browse, flip, glance, skim

leaflet *n*
pamphlet, booklet, brochure, circular, handout, bill, handbill, flyer, tract

leafy *adj*
green, leafed, leaved, wooded, woody, shady, shaded, bosky, frondescent, frondose, *technical* dasyphyllous, foliose, *formal* verdant

league *n, v*
▸ *n* **1** ASSOCIATION, confederation, alliance, union, federation, confederacy, coalition, affiliation, group, combination, band, syndicate, conglomerate, corporation, guild, consortium, cartel, combine, partnership, co-operative, fellowship, compact **2** CATEGORY, class, level, group

▷ **in league** allied, in co-operation, co-operating, linked, in partnership, in alliance, in collusion, in tandem, collaborating, conspiring, *colloq.* hand in glove, in cahoots

▱ at odds

▸ *v* amalgamate, associate, band together, co-operate, collaborate, combine, confederate, conspire, join forces, unite, link, ally, consort

leak *n, v*
▸ *n* **1** CRACK, hole, opening, puncture, crevice, chink, fissure, break, cut **2** LEAKAGE, leaking, seeping, seepage, drip, oozing, discharge, escape, percolation **3** DISCLOSURE, divulgence, revelation, exposure, exposé, uncovering, bringing to light

▸ *v* **1** SEEP, drip, ooze, escape, spill, trickle, percolate, exude, discharge **2** DISCLOSE, reveal, let slip, make known, make public, tell, relate, give away, pass on, *formal* divulge, impart, *colloq.* blab, squeal, let on, let the cat out of the bag, spill the beans

leaky *adj*
leaking, holey, perforated, punctured, split, cracked, porous, permeable

lean¹ *v*
1 SLANT, slope, incline, bend, tilt, list, bank, be at an angle **2** RECLINE, prop, rest, *formal* repose **3** INCLINE, favour, prefer, tend, have an inclination/preference for, *formal* have a propensity for

▷ **lean on** **1** RELY ON, depend on, trust in, have confidence in, not manage without, *colloq.* bank on **2** FORCE, force, persuade, pressurize, put pressure on

lean² *adj*
1 THIN, skinny, bony, gaunt, lank, angular, slim, slender, scraggy, scrawny, emaciated, *colloq.* all skin and bones **2** SCANTY, inadequate, insufficient, bare, barren, unproductive, unfruitful, sparse, scanty, poor, arid

▱ **1** fat, flabby

leaning *n*
tendency, inclination, preference, partiality, liking, fondness, attraction, bent, bias, disposition, aptitude, *formal* propensity, proclivity, penchant, predilection

leap *v, n*
▸ *v* **1** JUMP (OVER), bound, spring, vault, clear, skip, hop, dance, bounce, caper, gambol, romp, frisk, frolic, cavort **2** SOAR, surge, mount, increase, rocket, skyrocket, escalate, rise

▱ **2** drop, fall

▷ **leap at** jump at, accept eagerly, agree to, fall for, grab, seize, pounce on, snatch, swallow
▶ *n* **1** JUMP, bound, spring, vault, hop, skip, caper, *technical* entrechat **2** INCREASE, upsurge, upswing, surge, rise, soaring, escalation
▷ **by/in leaps and bounds** rapidly, swiftly, quickly

learn *v*
1 GRASP, comprehend, understand, master, acquire, train, study, pick up, take in, digest, gather, assimilate, absorb, discern, familiarize yourself in, gain knowledge of, acquire skill in, *colloq.* get the hang of **2** MEMORIZE, learn by heart, commit to memory, have off pat, remember **3** DISCOVER, find out, ascertain, understand, hear, detect, determine, hear, see, gather, realize, become aware of, become informed about, *colloq.* get wind of

learned *adj*
scholarly, erudite, well-informed, well-read, well-educated, knowledgeable, cultured, academic, lettered, literary, studious, literate, widely read, intellectual, versed, pedantic
☒ uneducated, illiterate

learner *n*
novice, beginner, student, trainee, pupil, scholar, apprentice, tiro, neophyte, *colloq.* rookie, greenhorn

learning *n*
scholarship, erudition, education, schooling, knowledge, information, letters, study, wisdom, tuition, culture, edification, intellect, research, pedantry

lease *v, n*
▶ *v* let, loan, rent, hire, sublet, charter
▶ *n* agreement, contract, chapter

leash *n*
lead, tether, rein, hold, cord, check, control, curb, restraint, discipline

least *adj*
smallest, lowest, minimum, fewest, slightest, poorest
☒ most

leathery *adj*
hard, hardened, durable, rough, rugged, tough, wrinkled, wizened, leathern, *technical* coriaceous, corious

leave¹ *v*
1 DEPART, go, go away, set out, take your leave, pull out, decamp, exit, move, retire, withdraw, retreat, emigrate, disappear, *colloq.* push off, push along, quit, scoot, take off, make tracks, do a bunk, up sticks, hook it **2** ABANDON, desert, forsake, give up, drop, pull out, surrender, *formal* relinquish, renounce, desist, cease, *colloq.* run out on, ditch, jilt, chuck, damp, turn your back on, leave high and dry **3** ASSIGN, commit, entrust, allot, consign, make over, hand over, deliver, transmit **4** *leave property in your will* will, hand down, leave behind, endow, give over, *technical* devise, *formal* bequeath
☒ **1** arrive **3** receive
▷ **leave off** stop, refrain, lay off, break off, end, halt, *formal* cease, discontinue, desist, abstain, terminate, *colloq.* quit, give over, knock off
▷ **leave out** omit, exclude, overlook, ignore, except, disregard, pass over, count out, cut (out), eliminate, neglect, reject, cast aside, bar
☒ include

leave² *n*
1 PERMISSION, authorization, consent, allowance, sanction, warrant, concession, indulgence, liberty, freedom, *formal* dispensation, *colloq.* say-so, OK, green light **2** HOLIDAY, time off, day off, break, leave of absence, vacation, sabbatical, furlough, sick leave, compassionate leave
☒ **1** refusal, rejection

leaven *v*
1 RAISE, cause to rise, puff up, ferment, expand, swell, work **2** INSPIRE, stimulate, lighten, quicken, pervade, permeate, imbue, suffuse

leavings *n*
remains, remainder, residue, remnants, leftovers, dregs, detritus, dross, fragments, bits, pieces, oddments, sweepings, scraps, refuse, rubbish, debris, waste, spoil

lecher *n*
womanizer, adulterer, seducer, sensualist, debauchee, libertine, profligate, libidinist, rake, roué, fornicator, wanton, Casanova, Don Juan, *colloq.* dirty old man, flasher, goat, wolf

lecherous *adj*
lewd, womanizing, carnal, promiscuous, lustful, lascivious, degenerate, debauched, dissolute, dissipated, unchaste, wanton, salacious, libidinous, *formal* concupiscent, licentious, prurient, *colloq.* randy, raunchy, horny

lechery *n*
lewdness, womanizing, carnality, libertinism, debauchery, rakishness, lust, lustfulness, libidinousness, licentiousness, salaciousness, sensuality, wantonness, lasciviousness, *formal* concupiscence, prurience, *colloq.* randiness, raunchiness

lecture *n, v*
▶ *n* **1** ADDRESS, lesson, speech, talk, instruction, sermon, *formal* discourse, disquisition, homily **2** REPRIMAND, rebuke, reproof, scolding, harangue, censure, upbraiding, chiding, reproach, *formal* berating, *colloq.* telling-off, talking-to, dressing-down, rocket
▶ *v* **1** TALK, give a talk, teach, hold forth, speak, make a speech, expound, address, instruct, give lessons in **2** REPRIMAND, reprove, rebuke, scold, admonish, harangue, chide, censure, *formal* berate, *colloq.* tell off, haul over the coals, tear/pull to pieces, pick holes in

lecturer *n*
teacher, tutor, talker, speech-maker, speechifier, orator, expounder, speaker, reader, instructor, academic, pedagogue, sermonizer, preacher, haranguer, *formal* declaimer

ledge *n*
shelf, sill, mantel, mantelpiece, mantelshelf, ridge, projection, overhang, step

lee *n*
shelter, refuge, protection, cover, sanctuary

leech *n*
hanger-on, parasite, sycophant, toady, bloodsucker, freeloader, extortioner, usurer, *colloq.* sponger, scrounger

leer *v, n*
▶ *v* eye, ogle, look lecherously at, stare, wink, squint, gloat, goggle, grin, smirk, sneer
▶ *n* ogle, lecherous look, stare, wink, squint, grin, smirk, sneer

leery *adj*
wary, careful, cautious, guarded, uncertain, unsure, chary, suspicious, on your guard, distrustful, doubting, dubious, sceptical

lees *n*
deposit, dregs, grounds, residue, sediment, refuse, settlings, draff, *formal* precipitate

leeway *n*
space, room, latitude, elbow-room, play, scope, slack, margin, flexibility

left *adj*
1 LEFT-HAND, port, *formal* sinistral **2** LEFT-WING,

socialist, radical, progressive, revolutionary, liberal, communist, *colloq.* red
🇫 1 right **2** right-wing

left-handed *adj*
ambiguous, dubious, equivocal, awkward, clumsy, gauche, insincere, hypocritical, unlucky, *formal* sinistral

left-over *n & adj*
remaining, settled, excess, surplus, unused, uneaten

leftovers *n*
leavings, remainder, remains, remnants, residue, surplus, scraps, sweepings, refuse, dregs, excess

leg *n, v*
▶ *n* **1** LIMB, member, shank, *technical* crus, *colloq.* pin, stump, peg **2** SUPPORT, prop, upright, brace, underpinning **3** STAGE, part, bit, section, portion, stretch, segment, lap
▷ **not have a leg to stand on** be unjustified, be unproved, lack support, lack an excuse
▷ **on its last legs** weak, failing, fading fast, ailing, nearing collapse, about to fail/collapse, near to death, *colloq.* at death's door
▷ **pull someone's leg** tease, trick, joke, play a joke on, make fun of, fool, deceive, *colloq.* kid, rib, have on, wind up, lead up the garden path, pull a fast one on
▶ *v* ▷ **leg it** run, hurry, walk, go by foot, *colloq.* hoof it

legacy *n*
bequest, endowment, gift, heritage, heritance, inheritance, birthright, estate, heirloom, *formal* bequeathal, patrimony

legal *adj*
1 LAWFUL, legitimate, within the law, permissible, permitted, sanctioned, allowed, authorized, licensed, allowable, legalized, constitutional, valid, warranted, above-board, right, sound, proper, rightful, acceptable, admissible, *formal* licit **2** JUDICIAL, forensic **3** JUDICIARY, statutory, constitutional
🇫 1 illegal

legal terms

Legal terms include :

criminal law: acquittal, age of consent, alibi, arrest, bail, caution, charge, confession, contempt of court, dock, fine, guilty, indictment, innocent, malice aforethought, pardon, parole, plead guilty, plead not guilty, prisoner, probation, remand, reprieve, sentence; *marriage and divorce*: adultery, alimony, annulment, bigamy, decree absolute, decree nisi, divorce, maintenance, settlement; *people*: accessory, accomplice, accused, advocate, Attorney General, barrister, *colloq.* brief, clerk of the court, client, commissioner for oaths, convict, coroner, criminal, defendant, Director of Public Prosecutions (DPP), executor, felon, judge, jury, justice of the peace (JP), juvenile, Law Lord, lawyer, Lord Advocate, Lord Chancellor, Lord Chief Justice, liquidator, magistrate, notary public, offender, plaintiff, procurator fiscal, receiver, Queen's Counsel (QC), sheriff, solicitor, witness, young offender; *property or ownership*: asset, conveyance, copyright, deed, easement, endowment, estate, exchange of contracts, fee simple, foreclosure, freehold, inheritance, intestacy, lease, leasehold, legacy, local search, mortgage, patent, tenancy, title, trademark, will; *miscellaneous*: act of God, Act of Parliament, adjournment, affidavit, agreement, allegation, amnesty, appeal, arbitration, bar, bench, Bill of Rights, brief, by-law, charter, civil law, claim,

codicil, common law, constitution, contract, covenant, courtcase, court martial, cross-examine, custody, damages, defence, demand, equity, eviction, evidence, extradition, grant, hearing, hung jury, indemnity, injunction, inquest, inquiry, judgment, judiciary, lawsuit, legal aid, liability, mandate, misadventure, miscarriage of justice, oath, party, penalty, power of attorney, precedent, probate, proceedings, proof, proxy, public inquiry, repeal, sanction, settlement, statute, subpoena, sue, summons, testimony, trial, tribunal, verdict, waiver, ward of court, warrant, will, writ. *See also* COURT; CRIME.

legality *n*
lawfulness, legitimacy, validity, rightness, rightfulness, soundness, admissibleness, permissibility, constitutionality
🇫 illegality

legalize *v*
legitimize, license, permit, sanction, allow, decriminalize, authorize, warrant, validate, approve, ratify, accept, admit

legate *n*
representative, ambassador, delegate, deputy, emissary, envoy, agent, commissioner, messenger, nuncio

legatee *n*
beneficiary, recipient, inheritor, heir, co-heir(ess), devisee, inheritrix

legation *n*
mission, commission, consulate, embassy, ministry, deputation, delegation, representation

legend *n*
1 MYTH, story, traditional story, tale, folk-tale, fable, fiction, romance, narrative, saga **2** INSCRIPTION, caption, motto, key, cipher, explanation

legendary *adj*
1 MYTHICAL, fabulous, fabled, story-book, fictitious, fictional, fanciful, traditional **2** FAMOUS, celebrated, renowned, well-known, illustrious, glorious, acclaimed, honoured, remembered, popular, immortal

legerdemain *n*
trickery, sleight of hand, deception, cunning, craftiness, chicanery, artifice, artfulness, subterfuge, contrivance, manipulation, manoeuvring, feint, *formal* prestidigitation, thaumaturgics, sophistry, *colloq.* hocus-pocus

legible *adj*
readable, easy to read, intelligible, decipherable, clear, distinct, neat, plain
🇫 illegible

legion *n, adj*
▶ *n* **1** *Roman legions* army, battalion, brigade, company, division, regiment, unit, cohort, troop, force **2** *legions of foreign tourists* host, number, multitude, myriad, swarm, throng, drove, mass, horde
▶ *adj* countless, numerous, myriad, numberless, innumerable, illimitable, multitudinous

legislate *v*
enact, ordain, decree, order, authorize, codify, establish, formulate, *formal* constitutionalize, prescribe

legislation *n*
1 LAW, statute, regulation, bill, act, charter, enactment, ordinance, code, authorization, ruling, rules, measure **2** LAW-MAKING, enactment, codification, formulation, *formal* prescription

legislative *adj*
law-making, law-giving, judicial, parliamentary, congressional, senatorial, *technical* jurisdictive

legislator *n*
law-maker, law-giver, member of parliament, parliamentarian, politician, representative, congressman, congresswoman, senator

legislature *n*
assembly, chamber, house, parliament, congress, senate

legitimate *adj*
1 LEGAL, lawful, authorized, warranted, sanctioned, statutory, rightful, proper, correct, real, genuine, acknowledged, *formal* licit 2 REASONABLE, sensible, rational, logical, admissible, plausible, acceptable, justifiable, justified, warranted, well-founded, sound, fair, valid, true, credible
F₃ 1 illegal 2 invalid

legitimize *v*
sanction, authorize, permit, allow, warrant, license, validate, charter, entitle, legalize, decriminalize, *formal* legitimate

leisure *n*
relaxation, rest, spare time, free time, time off, ease, freedom, liberty, recreation, retirement, holiday, vacation, break, time out
F₃ work
▷ **at your leisure** when you want to, at your convenience, unhurriedly, in your own time, in your spare time, when you get round to it

leisurely *adj*
unhurried, slow, relaxed, comfortable, easy, easygoing, unhasty, tranquil, restful, gentle, carefree, lazy, slow, loose, *colloq.* laid-back
F₃ rushed, hectic

lend *v*
1 LOAN, advance, allow to have, allow to use, let someone use 2 *lend your support to something* give, grant, provide, supply, contribute, donate, add, *formal* bestow, furnish, confer, impart
F₃ 1 borrow
▷ **lend an ear** listen, pay attention, take notice, heed, give ear, *formal* hearken
▷ **lend a hand** help, help out, assist, aid, give a helping hand, *colloq.* do your bit, pitch in
▷ **lend itself to** be suitable for, be appropriate for, be easily/readily used for

length *n*
1 EXTENT, distance, measure, reach, span 2 DURATION, period, term, stretch, space, span 3 PIECE, portion, section, segment
▷ **at length** 1 THOROUGHLY, in great detail, comprehensively, exhaustively 2 EVENTUALLY, finally, in due course, at last
▷ **go to any lengths** be very determined, try very hard, do anything, go to extremes

lengthen *v*
stretch, extend, draw out, grow longer, prolong, protract, spin out, eke (out), pad out, increase, expand, continue, *formal* elongate
F₃ reduce, shorten

lengthwise *adv*
lengthways, endways, endwise, endlong, horizontally, vertically

lengthy *adj*
long, prolonged, extended, lengthened, overlong, long-drawn-out, long-winded, rambling, diffuse, wordy, verbose, drawn-out, interminable, tedious, *formal* protracted, prolix
F₃ brief, concise

leniency *n*
lenience, tolerance, forbearance, permissiveness, indulgence, mercy, forgiveness, soft-heartedness, softness, kindness, mildness, tenderness, gentleness, compassion, humaneness, generosity, magnanimity, moderation, *formal* clemency
F₃ severity

lenient *adj*
tolerant, forbearing, sparing, indulgent, liberal, merciful, forgiving, soft-hearted, kind, mild, tender, gentle, compassionate, humane, generous, magnanimous, moderate
F₃ strict, severe

lenitive *adj*
alleviating, calming, easing, palliative, relieving, soothing, assuaging, appeasing, mollifying, *formal* mitigating
F₃ irritant

lens *n*
See panel at SPECTACLES.

leper *n*
outcast, social outcast, undesirable, untouchable, pariah, lazar

lesbian *n, adj*
▶ *n* gay, homosexual, sapphist, tribade
▶ *adj* gay, homosexual, Sapphic, tribadic

lesion *n*
injury, wound, abrasion, sore, scratch, scrape, bruise, cut, gash, laceration, impairment, hurt, trauma, *technical* contusion

less *n, adv*
▶ *n* fewer, smaller amount, not as/so much, not as/so many
F₃ more
▶ *adv* to a lesser degree/extent, to a smaller extent, not as/so much
F₃ more

lessen *v*
decrease, go/come down, reduce, diminish, decline, plunge, plummet, curtail, lower, ease (off), contract, die down, let up, dwindle, lighten, slow down, weaken, shrink, abridge, de-escalate, erode, minimize, narrow, moderate, subside, ebb, wane, slack, slacken, flag, fail, dull, deaden, relieve, impair, *formal* abate, *colloq.* nosedive, peter out
F₃ grow, increase

lessening *n*
decrease, reduction, decline, curtailment, easing, contraction, dwindling, weakening, shrinkage, de-escalation, erosion, minimization, moderation, ebbing, waning, slackening, flagging, failure, deadening, let-up, *formal* abatement, diminution, *colloq.* petering out
F₃ increase

lesser *adj*
lower, secondary, inferior, smaller, subordinate, slighter, minor
F₃ greater

lesson *n*
1 CLASS, period, instruction, lecture, seminar, sermon, tutorial, teaching, coaching, course 2 ASSIGNMENT, exercise, homework, schoolwork, practice, task, drill 3 EXAMPLE, model, warning, deterrent, moral

let¹ *v*
1 PERMIT, allow, give permission, authorize, agree to, sanction, grant, enable, tolerate, *formal* give leave, consent to, assent to, *colloq.* OK, give the OK, give the go-ahead, give the green light to, give the nod, say the magic word 2 *let something happen* allow, cause, enable, make 3 LEASE, hire, rent, let out
F₃ 1 prohibit, forbid
▷ **let alone** not to mention, not forgetting, never mind, apart from, also, as well as

▷ **let down** fail, disappoint, disillusion, dissatisfy, disenchant, fall short, abandon, betray, desert, *colloq.* leave in the lurch
🔁 satisfy
▷ **let go** release, set free, stop holding, free, liberate, unhand, *formal* manumit
🔁 catch, imprison
▷ **let in** admit, allow to enter, accept, receive, take in, include, incorporate, greet, welcome
🔁 prohibit, bar, forbid
▷ **let off 1** EXCUSE, absolve, pardon, exempt, discharge, reprieve, forgive, acquit, spare, ignore, liberate, release, *formal* exonerate **2** DISCHARGE, detonate, fire, explode, emit, give off, release
🔁 **1** punish
▷ **let on** disclose, reveal, let slip, make known, make public, tell, relate, give away, pass on, *formal* divulge, impart, *colloq.* blab, squeal, let the cat out of the bag, spill the beans
▷ **let out 1** FREE, release, let go, discharge, *colloq.* leak **2** REVEAL, disclose, make known, utter, betray, let slip, *colloq.* blab, squeal, let the cat out of the bag, spill the beans
🔁 **1** keep in
▷ **let up** subside, ease (off), lessen, moderate, slacken, diminish, decrease, moderate, stop, end, halt, die down, *formal* abate, cease
🔁 continue

let² *n*
without let or hindrance check, constraint, impediment, hindrance, obstacle, obstruction, prohibition, restriction, restraint, interference
🔁 assistance

let-down *n*
disappointment, anticlimax, disillusionment, setback, betrayal, desertion, *colloq.* washout

lethal *adj*
fatal, deadly, deathly, mortal, dangerous, poisonous, toxic, murderous, ruinous, disastrous, destructive, devastating, *formal* noxious
🔁 harmless, safe

lethargic *adj*
listless, sluggish, dull, lifeless, inert, slow, lazy, inactive, idle, slothful, apathetic, drowsy, heavy, sleepy, weary, *formal* debilitated, enervated, hebetant, languid, somnolent, torpid
🔁 lively

lethargy *n*
listlessness, sluggishness, dullness, lifelessness, inertia, slowness, laziness, idleness, sloth, apathy, inactivity, inaction, indifference, sleepiness, drowsiness, weariness, stupor, *formal* lassitude, torpor, languor, somnolence
🔁 liveliness

letter *n*
1 NOTE, message, line, correspondence, dispatch, communication, chit, acknowledgement, reply, circular, *formal* missive, epistle **2** CHARACTER, symbol, sign, *technical* grapheme **3** *a woman of letters* literature, books, culture, education, learning, humanities, writing, scholarship, academia, belles-lettres, *formal* erudition
▷ **to the letter** exactly, strictly, strictly speaking, word for word, literally, religiously, punctiliously, in every detail, by the book

lettered *adj*
learned, scholarly, educated, informed, knowledgeable, academic, well-educated, well-read, widely read, cultivated, cultured, literary, literate, studied, versed, accomplished, *formal* erudite, *colloq.* highbrow
🔁 ignorant

let-up *n*
break, interval, lessening, pause, recess, remission, slackening, respite, lull, *formal* abatement, cessation, *colloq.* breather
🔁 continuation

level *adj, n, v*
▶ *adj* **1** FLAT, smooth, even, flush, plane, uniform, horizontal, aligned, plane **2** EQUAL, balanced, aligned, even, on a par, neck and neck, matching, uniform, level pegging **3** STEADY, stable, constant, unchanging, regular, uniform **4** CALM, unemotional, steady, composed, self-possessed, *colloq.* unflappable
🔁 **1** uneven **2** unequal **3** unsteady **4** emotional
▶ *n* **1** HEIGHT, elevation, altitude, highness **2** POSITION, point, rank, status, class, degree, grade, mark, standard, standing, station, plane, layer, stratum, storey, stage, zone, *formal* echelon **3** MEASURE, degree, extent, quantity, size, magnitude, amount, volume
▷ **on the level** honest, open, candid, fair, straight, *colloq.* fair and square, straight-up, upfront, above board
▶ *v* **1** DEMOLISH, destroy, devastate, flatten, knock down, raze, raze to the ground, pull down, bulldoze, tear down, lay waste **2** EVEN OUT, flush, plane, smooth, equalize, even up, stabilize, make level, make flat **3** DIRECT, point, aim, train, focus, concentrate, zero in on **4** *level with someone* admit, open up, confess, divulge, tell, tell all, speak plainly, be frank, keep nothing back, *formal* avow, *colloq.* come clean, put your cards on the table, be upfront, give it to someone straight, tell it like it is, bring out in the open

level-headed *adj*
calm, balanced, even-tempered, sensible, steady, reasonable, rational, composed, cool, cool-headed, sane, self-possessed, dependable, *formal* circumspect, prudent, imperturbable, *colloq.* unflappable

lever *n, v*
▶ *n* **1** HANDLE, bar, pull, switch, joystick **2** CROWBAR, bar, jemmy, handspike
▶ *v* force, prise, pry, raise, lift, hoist, dislodge, jemmy, shift, move, heave

leverage *n*
force, strength, power, advantage, authority, influence, rank, weight, *formal* ascendancy, purchase, *colloq.* clout, pull

leviathan *n*
giant, mammoth, hulk, colossus, monster, sea monster, behemoth, whale, Titan

levitate *v*
float, glide, waft, drift, fly, hover, suspend, hang

levity *n*
light-heartedness, light-mindedness, frivolity, carefreeness, facetiousness, flippancy, irreverence, hilarity, triviality, silliness, fun
🔁 seriousness

levy *v, n*
▶ *v* tax, impose, exact, demand, charge, raise, gather, collect
▶ *n* tax, toll, subscription, contribution, duty, customs, excise, duties, due, fee, tariff, collection, assessment, tithe, *technical* impost

lewd *adj*
obscene, smutty, indecent, suggestive, bawdy, pornographic, salacious, licentious, lascivious, impure, vulgar, unchaste, lustful, lecherous, carnal, promiscuous, degenerate, debauched, dissolute, *formal* concupiscent, *colloq.* blue, raunchy, randy
🔁 decent, chaste

lewdness *n*
obscenity, smut, smuttiness, indecency, bawdiness,

pornography, salaciousness, licentiousness, lasciviousness, impurity, unchastity, lustfulness, lechery, vulgarity, wantonness, carnality, crudity, debauchery, depravity, *formal* concupiscence, *colloq.* randiness
🔁 chasteness, politeness

lexicon *n*
dictionary, glossary, vocabulary, wordbook, word-list, phrase book, encyclopedia

liability *n*
1 ACCOUNTABILITY, duty, obligation, responsibility, answerability, blameworthiness, *formal* culpability **2** DEBIT, arrears, obligation, dues, indebtedness **3** DRAWBACK, disadvantage, inconvenience, hindrance, impediment, burden, onus, nuisance, encumbrance, *colloq.* drag, millstone around your neck
🔁 **1** unaccountability **2** asset **3** advantage

liable *adj*
1 INCLINED, likely, apt, disposed, prone, tending, susceptible, vulnerable, exposed, subject, open, *formal* predisposed **2** RESPONSIBLE, answerable, accountable, amenable, changeable, to blame, at fault
🔁 **1** unlikely **2** unaccountable

liaise *v*
contact, communicate, intercommunicate, work together, co-operate, collaborate, exchange information, relate to, network, interface

liaison *n*
1 CONTACT, connection, communication, interchange, go-between, link, co-operation, collaboration, working together, exchange of information **2** LOVE AFFAIR, affair, relationship, romance, intrigue, amour, flirtation, entanglement

liar *n*
falsifier, perjurer, deceiver, prevaricator, false witness, *colloq.* fibber

libation *n*
drink offering, sacrifice, *formal* oblation

libel *n, v*
▶ *n* defamation, false report, untrue statement, slur, smear, slander, denigration, *formal* disparagement, vilification, aspersion, calumny, *colloq.* muck-raking, mudslinging
▶ *v* defame, slander, malign, abuse, denigrate, *formal* cast aspersions on, vilify, revile, disparage, calumniate, traduce, *colloq.* slur, smear, drag someone's name through the mud, throw mud at, *US* badmouth

> ✏️ **libel** or **slander**?
> In English law, *libel* is an untrue defamatory statement made in a permanent form such as print, writing or pictures or broadcast on radio or television, whereas *slander* is one made by means of the spoken word (not broadcast) or gesture. In Scots law, both are *slander*.

libellous *adj*
defamatory, abusive, slanderous, derogatory, maligning, injurious, scurrilous, false, untrue, denigratory, *formal* vilifying, disparaging, calumniatory, traducing

liberal *adj*
1 BROAD-MINDED, open-minded, enlightened, tolerant, lenient, unprejudiced, unbiased, impartial, broad-based, wide-ranging, catholic, libertarian **2** PROGRESSIVE, reformist, forward-looking, advanced, radical, moderate **3** GENEROUS, ample, bountiful, lavish, plentiful, abundant, copious, profuse, handsome, open-handed, magnanimous, big-hearted, unsparing, munificent, philanthropic, altruistic
🔁 **1** narrow-minded **2** conservative **3** mean, miserly

liberalism *n*
progressivism, radicalism, free-thinking, humanitarianism, libertarianism, latitudinarianism
🔁 conservatism, narrow-mindedness

liberality *n*
1 GENEROSITY, benevolence, free-handedness, large-heartedness, kindness, magnanimity, open-handedness, largesse, charity, bounty, philanthropy, altruism, *formal* beneficence, munificence **2** BROAD-MINDEDNESS, liberalism, impartiality, open-mindedness, permissiveness, breadth, tolerance, toleration, progressivism, catholicity, libertarianism
🔁 **1** meanness **2** illiberality

liberate *v*
free, emancipate, release, let loose, set loose, let go, let out, set free, deliver, unchain, unfetter, uncage, unshackle, discharge, rescue, ransom, *formal* redeem, manumit
🔁 imprison, enslave, restrict

liberation *n*
freedom, freeing, liberating, liberty, emancipation, release, deliverance, loosing, unchaining, uncaging, unfettering, unshackling, unpenning, ransoming, enfranchisement, *formal* manumission, redemption
🔁 enslavement, imprisonment, restriction

liberator *n*
rescuer, deliverer, freer, saviour, ransomer, redeemer, emancipator, *formal* manumitter
🔁 enslaver, jailer

libertine *n, adj*
▶ *n* debauchee, reprobate, seducer, sensualist, womanizer, rake, profligate, lecher, voluptary, loose-liver, roué, Don Juan, Casanova
▶ *adj* debauched, degenerate, debauched, womanizing, lecherous, reprobate, dissolute, promiscuous, lustful, salacious, *formal* licentious

liberty *n*
1 FREEDOM, emancipation, deliverance, release, liberation, independence, autonomy, self-government, self-rule, self-determination, sovereignty, *formal* manumission **2** LICENCE, permission, sanction, right, privilege, prerogative, entitlement, authorization, dispensation, franchise **3** FAMILIARITY, disrespect, overfamiliarity, presumption, impertinence, impudence, insolence, *formal* impropriety
🔁 **1** imprisonment **3** respect, politeness
▷ **at liberty** free, allowed, permitted, entitled, unconstrained, unrestricted, unhindered, without restraint, not confined

libidinous *adj*
lustful, debauched, impure, promiscuous, loose, lascivious, lecherous, carnal, lewd, salacious, unchaste, sensual, wanton, wicked, *formal* concupiscent, cupidinous, prurient, ruttish, *colloq.* randy, horny
🔁 modest, temperate

libido *n*
sexual desire, sex drive, sexual appetite, sexual urge, erotic desire, passion, ardour, lust, eroticism, *colloq.* randiness, the hots

libretto *n*
words, text, lines, lyrics, script, book

licence *n*
1 PERMIT, warrant, certificate, charter, document, pass, authority, grant, imprimatur **2** PERMISSION, warranty, authorization, authority, sanction, certification, right, entitlement, prerogative, privilege, dispensation, carte blanche, freedom, liberty, approval, exemption, independence, *formal* leave, consent, accreditation **3** ABANDON, dissipation, excess, immoderation, indulgence, self-indulgence, intem-

perance, lawlessness, unruliness, anarchy, disorder, debauchery, decadence, dissoluteness, licentiousness, immorality, impropriety, irresponsibility
F₃ 2 prohibition, restriction **3** decorum, moderation, restraint, control

license *v*
permit, give permission, allow, authorize, certify, warrant, entitle, empower, sanction, commission, franchise, *formal* accredit, consent
F₃ ban, prohibit

licentious *adj*
debauched, dissolute, dissipated, depraved, decadent, profligate, lascivious, immoral, abandoned, lewd, lecherous, promiscuous, libertine, impure, lax, lustful, disorderly, wanton, unchaste
F₃ modest, chaste

licentiousness *n*
debauchery, dissoluteness, immorality, abandon, lewdness, lechery, promiscuity, libertinism, impurity, lust, lustfulness, salaciousness, salacity, wantonness, dissipation, *formal* cupidinousness, prurience
F₃ modesty, temperance

lick *v, n*
▶ *v* **1** *lick the chocolate* tongue, wet, moisten, lap, taste, wash, keep, stretch, reach, stand, continue, *formal* flick, ripple **3** DEFEAT, beat, conquer, *formal* vanquish, *colloq.* thrash, hammer, trounce
▷ **lick your lips** enjoy, savour, drool over, relish, anticipate
▶ *n* bit, dab, little, speck, spot, touch, taste, stroke, sample, brush, smidgeon, hint

licking *n*
thrashing, whipping, flogging, hiding, smacking, spanking, tanning, beating, defeat, drubbing

lid *n*
top, cover, covering, cap, stopper

lie¹ *n, v*
▶ *n tell lies*
falsehood, untruth, perjury, falsification, fabrication, invention, fiction, half-truth, deceit, falsity, white lie, prevarication, *colloq.* fib, whopper, porky, pork pie, tall story, made-up story, cock-and-bull story, *slang* - crap
F₃ truth
▷ **give the lie to** disprove, rebut, contradict, invalidate, prove false
▶ *v* perjure, misrepresent, tell a lie, fabricate, falsify, invent, make up a story, equivocate, prevaricate, *formal* forswear yourself, dissemble, dissimulate, *colloq.* fib, lie through your teeth

lie² *v*
1 BE, exist, be located, be found, belong, extend, remain, stay, keep, stretch, reach, stand, continue, *formal* dwell **2** *lie down for a rest* rest, recline, stretch out, sprawl out, lounge, couch, laze, *formal* repose
▷ **lie in wait for** ambush, waylay, lay a trap for, trap, attack, surprise, *formal* ambuscade
▷ **lie low** go into hiding, hide, hide away, hide out, conceal yourself, go to earth, take cover, lurk, skulk, *colloq.* hole up, lie doggo, keep a low profile

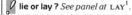 **lie or lay** ? *See panel at* LAY¹.

lieutenant *n*
assistant, second-in-command, deputy, subordinate, right-hand man/woman

life *n*
1 BEING, existence, animation, breath, viability, aliveness, entity, soul **2** LIVING THINGS, human life, animal life, plant, fauna, flora, fauna and flora **3** *the loss*

of many lives person, individual, human being, man, woman, child **4** DURATION, lifetime, existence, life expectancy, course, span, lifespan, career **5** *the machine has a limited life* duration, continuance, span, lifespan, time, course, period of usefulness, time of being active, lifetime **6** *see life* (wide) experience, varied activities, travelling, meeting people **7** LIFE STORY, biography, autobiography, diary, diaries, memoirs, journal **8** LIVELINESS, vigour, vitality, vivacity, animation, high spirits, exuberance, enthusiasm, excitement, verve, zest, energy, élan, spirit, sparkle, effervescence, activity, cheerfulness, *colloq.* oomph, pizzazz
F₃ 1 death
▷ **come to life** become active, become interesting, become lively, become exciting, come alive, wake up
▷ **give your life** sacrifice yourself for, give up/sacrifice your life, offer up/surrender your life, die for, dedicate yourself to, devote yourself to

life-and-death *adj*
important, all-important, crucial, vital, serious, critical

lifeblood *n*
essential part/factor, life-force, spirit, soul, core, centre, heart, inspiration

lifeless *adj*
1 DEAD, deceased, defunct, cold, unconscious, gone, inanimate, insensible, stiff **2** LETHARGIC, listless, sluggish, lacklustre, dull, apathetic, passive, insipid, uninspired, uninspiring, colourless, slow, flat, wooden, stiff **3** BARREN, bare, empty, desolate, stark, uninhabited, arid, sterile, unproductive, empty
F₃ 1 alive, exciting **2** lively

lifelike *adj*
realistic, true-to-life, real, true, vivid, natural, authentic, faithful, exact, graphic
F₃ unrealistic, unnatural

lifelong *adj*
lifetime, for all your life, long-lasting, long-standing, persistent, lasting, enduring, abiding, permanent, constant
F₃ impermanent, temporary

lifestyle *n*
way of life, life, way of living, manner of living, living conditions, position, situation

lifetime *n*
duration, existence, life, lifespan, span, period, time, course, day(s), career

lift *v, n*
▶ *v* **1** *she lifted the chair* raise, pick up, elevate, hoist, uplift, upraise, hold up, hold high **2** *he lifted their spirits* uplift, exalt, buoy up, boost, raise, elevate **3** *the ban has been lifted* cancel, end, stop, relax, remove, withdraw, annul, *formal* revoke, rescind, terminate **4** *lift people out of the war zone* fly, transport, move, transfer, airlift, convey, shift **5** *the fog lifted* clear, disperse, vanish, disappear, scatter, dissolve, thin out **6** DIG UP, dig out of the ground, pull up, pick, root out, unearth **7** *lift someone else's material* copy, plagiarize, steal, borrow, *colloq.* crib
F₃ 1 drop **2** lower **3** start **5** come down **6** plant, sow
▶ *n* **1** ELEVATOR, escalator, hoist, paternoster **2** *give you a life home* drive, hitch, ride, run, transport **3** BOOST, fillip, encouragement, pick-me-up, uplift, spur, reassurance, *colloq.* shot in the arm
F₃ 3 discouragement

ligature *n*
band, binding, bond, link, tie, connection, cord, rope, string, thong, strap, bandage, tourniquet, ligament

light¹ *n, v, adj*
▶ *n* **1** ILLUMINATION, brightness, brilliance, radi-

ance, glow, ray, beam, shaft, shine, glare, gleam, glint, lustre, flash, blaze, *formal* luminescence, effulgence, lambency **2** LAMP, lantern, lighter, match, torch, candle, taper, bulb, beacon, *technical* luminosity, incandescence, *US* flashlight **3** DAY, daybreak, daylight, daytime, dawn, sunrise, first light, crack of dawn, cockcrow **4** ENLIGHTENMENT, illumination, explanation, understanding, comprehension, insight, knowledge, *formal* elucidation **5** *presented in a different light* aspect, way, approach, manner, style, angle, side, dimension, point of view
F3 **1** darkness **3** night

Sources of light include:
natural light: aurora borealis, daylight, lightning, moonlight, starlight, sunlight; infrared, ultraviolet; *electric light:* Belisha beacon, break light, chandelier, courtesy light, fairy light, flashgun, floodlight, fluorescent light, fog lamp, footlight, halogen light, headlamp, headlight, indicator light, laser, light bulb, light buoy, lighthouse, navigation light, neon light, night light, pedestrian light, range light, runway light, searchlight, sidelight, spotlight, standard lamp, streetlight, strip light, strobe light, sun-lamp, tail-light, torch, traffic light; *fire light:* bonfire, candle, candlelight, fire, firework, flare, flame, spark, taper, gaslight, hurricane lamp, lighter, match, oil lamp, pilot light.

▶ *v* **1** IGNITE, fire, set alight, set fire to, set burning, kindle **2** ILLUMINATE, light up, lighten, floodlight, brighten, animate, cheer (up), make cheerful, switch on, turn on, put on, *formal* irradiate
F3 **1** extinguish **2** darken
▶ *adj* **1** ILLUMINATED, bright, brilliant, luminous, glowing, shining, well-lit, sunny **2** PALE, pastel, fair, blond, blonde, bleached, faded, whitish, faint
F3 **1** dark **2** black
▷ **bring to light** make known, notice, reveal, expose, discover, uncover
▷ **come to light** become obvious, be made known, be noticed, be discovered, be uncovered, be exposed
▷ **in the light of** considering, taking into consideration, taking into account, because of, in view of, bearing/keeping in mind, being mindful of, remembering
▷ **shed/throw/cast light on** clarify, make clear, explain, make plain, illuminate, *formal* elucidate

light² *adj*
1 WEIGHTLESS, insubstantial, lightweight, delicate, fine, airy, buoyant, flimsy, thin, feathery, floaty, slight **2** *light rain; light winds* slight, mild, gentle, weak, faint **3** *light machinery* small, portable, easily moved, easy to carry around **4** *light work* easy, effortless, moderate, undemanding, unexacting, untaxing **5** *a light punishment* mild, lenient, slight **6** *light movements* graceful, quick, nimble, agile **7** TRIVIAL, inconsiderable, trifling, superficial, unimportant, inconsequential, worthless, petty **8** CHEERFUL, cheery, carefree, light-hearted, lively, happy, merry, gay, *formal* blithe **9** ENTERTAINING, diverting, amusing, funny, humorous, frivolous, light-hearted, witty, pleasing **10** *light food* easy to digest, digestible, modest, delicately flavoured **11** *light soil* easily dug, porous, loose, crumbly
F3 **1** heavy, weighty, thick **2, 3, 4** heavy **5** severe, harsh **7** important, serious **8** solemn **9** serious **10** heavy, rich **11** solid, dense

light³ *v*
▷ **light on/upon** *eyes lighting upon an object* find, come across, discover, notice, hit on, spot, stumble on, *formal* chance on, encounter, happen upon

lighten¹ *v*
the sky lightened illuminate, illumine, make lighter, brighten, make brighter, light up, shine, glow
F3 darken

lighten² *v*
1 EASE, lessen, make lighter, unload, lift, relieve, reduce, calm, *formal* mitigate, alleviate, allay, assuage **2** BRIGHTEN, cheer (up), encourage, hearten, uplift, lift, gladden, restore, revive, elate, buoy up, inspire, *formal* inspirit, *colloq.* park up
F3 **1** burden **2** depress

light-fingered *adj*
dishonest, pilfering, stealing, thieving, thievish, shoplifting, crafty, furtive, shifty, sly, *colloq.* crooked, filching
F3 honest

light-footed *adj*
agile, active, nimble, sprightly, spry, swift, lithe, graceful
F3 clumsy, slow

light-headed *adj*
1 FAINT, giddy, dizzy, unsteady, airy, delirious, *formal* vertiginous, *colloq.* woozy **2** FLIGHTY, foolish, frivolous, silly, superficial, shallow, empty-headed, flippant, vacuous, trifling, *colloq.* scatter-brained, feather-brained
F3 **2** level-headed, solemn

light-hearted *adj*
cheerful, joyful, jolly, happy, happy-go-lucky, bright, in good spirits, in high spirits, carefree, untroubled, merry, sunny, glad, elated, gay, jovial, playful, frolicsome, amusing, entertaining, *formal* blithe, *colloq.* chirpy, bouncy, high
F3 sad, unhappy, serious

lighthouse *n*
beacon, tower, danger/warning signal, fanal, pharos

lightly *adv*
1 SLIGHTLY, gently, faintly, delicately, softly, thinly, sparingly, sparsely, slightingly **2** EASILY, effortlessly, readily, airily, breezily, gaily, facilely, gingerly **3** FRIVOLOUSLY, flippantly, carelessly, heedlessly, thoughtlessly **4** LENIENTLY, mildly, easily
F3 **1** heavily **3** soberly

lightness *n*
1 *lightness of the clothes* weightlessness, slightness, airiness, buoyancy, crumbliness, porosity, porousness, sandiness, delicacy, delicateness, flimsiness, thinness **2** *lightness of movement* grace, gracefulness, agility, gentleness, litheness, nimbleness, mildness **3** *lightness of spirit* cheerfulness, cheeriness, light-heartedness, liveliness, gaiety, animation, *formal* blitheness **4** FICKLENESS, triviality, frivolity, levity
F3 **1** heaviness, solidity **2** clumsiness **3** heaviness **4** sadness, severity, sobriety

lightning *n*
1 *thunder and lightning* forked lightning, sheet lightning, ball lightning, summer lightning, lightning strike, thunderbolt, thunderclap, clap of thunder, thunderdart, thunderstorm, electric storm **2** *he works like lightning* speedily, quickly, rapidly, hastily, immediately, *colloq.* wildfire, a rocket

lightweight *adj*
1 LIGHT, insubstantial, delicate, flimsy, thin, feathery, weightless **2** UNIMPORTANT, insignificant, inconsequential, trivial, worthless, negligible, trifling, petty, slight, paltry, *formal* nugatory
F3 **1** heavy **2** important, major, heavyweight

like¹ *adj, n, prep*
▶ *adj like minds* similar, resembling, alike, same, much the same, having an affinity, identical, equi-

valent, akin, comparable, corresponding, related, relating, parallel, allied, approximating, of a kind, *formal* analogous

🗲 unlike, dissimilar

▶ *n* equal, match, counterpart, equivalent, opposite number, fellow, mate, twin, parallel, peer

▶ *prep* in the same way/manner as, along/on the lines of, similar to

like² *v*

1 ENJOY, delight in, find enjoyable/interesting, find pleasant, take pleasure in, take to, appeal to, care for, admire, appreciate, be fond of, find attractive, be keen on, love, adore, hold dear, cherish, prize, relish, revel in, approve, welcome, take (kindly) to, be to someone's liking, *formal* esteem, *colloq.* have a soft spot for, dig **2** PREFER, choose, select, decide on, feel inclined, desire, want, wish, would rather, would sooner, would more willingly/readily, *colloq.* go for, fancy, go a bundle on, take a shine to

🗲 **1** dislike **2** reject

likeable *adj*

lovable, pleasing, appealing, nice, agreeable, charming, engaging, winsome, winning, pleasant, genial, amiable, congenial, attractive, sympathetic

🗲 unpleasant, disagreeable

likelihood *n*

likeliness, probability, possibility, chance, prospect, liability

🗲 improbability, unlikeliness

likely *adj, adv*

▶ *adj* PROBABLE, possible, anticipated, expected, to be expected, liable, prone, tending, inclined, predictable, inclined, foreseeable, *colloq.* odds-on, on the cards, in the wind **2** CREDIBLE, believable, plausible, feasible, reasonable, acceptable **3** PROMISING, appropriate, acceptable, proper, fitting, fit, right, promising, hopeful, pleasing

🗲 **1** unlikely **3** unsuitable

▶ *adv* probably, presumably, in all probability, no doubt, doubtlessly, *colloq.* (as) like as not

like-minded *adj*

agreeing, in agreement, of one mind, of the same mind, unanimous, in harmony, in rapport, compatible, harmonious, *formal* in accord

🗲 disagreeing

liken *v*

compare, equate, match, parallel, link, relate, juxtapose, associate, set beside, *formal* correlate, analogize

likeness *n*

1 SIMILARITY, resemblance, comparison, affinity, correspondence, parallelism, *formal* similitude, analogy **2** REPRESENTATION, image, copy, reproduction, replica, facsimile, statue, bust, sculpture, effigy, drawing, painting, picture, sketch, portrait, study, photograph, icon, counterpart **3** SEMBLANCE, guise, appearance, form, shape

🗲 **1** dissimilarity, unlikeness

likewise *adv*

1 SIMILARLY, in the same way, by the same token, in like manner **2** ALSO, moreover, furthermore, in addition, further, besides, too

liking *n*

fondness, love, affection, preference, partiality, affinity, taste, attraction, appreciation, proneness, inclination, tendency, bias, leaning, bent, desire, weakness, fancy, *formal* predilection, penchant, propensity, proclivity, *colloq.* soft spot, thing

🗲 dislike, aversion, hatred

lilt *n*

rise and fall, rhythm, sway, swing, song, measure, beat, cadence, air

lily-white *adj*

faultless, pure, spotless, virtuous, virgin, blameless, chaste, incorrupt, innocent, irreproachable, uncorrupt, uncorrupted, unsullied, untainted, untarnished, milk-white

🗲 corrupt

limb *n*

1 *stretch your limbs* arm, leg, member, appendage, extremity **2** BRANCH, projection, offshoot, wing, fork, extension, section, part, spur, bough

▷ **out on a limb** exposed, isolated, in a weak position, vulnerable, in a risky/precarious situation

limber *v, adj*

▶ *v* ▷ **limber up** loosen up, warm up, work out, exercise, prepare

▶ *adj* flexible, supple, pliant, plastic, elastic, agile, graceful, lithe, loose-jointed, loose-limbed, pliable, lissom

🗲 stiff

limbo *n*

▷ **in limbo** in a state of uncertainty, awaiting action, left hanging, left in the air, *formal* in abeyance, *colloq.* up in the air, on the back burner

limelight *n*

fame, celebrity, spotlight, stardom, recognition, renown, attention, notice, eminence, notability, prominence, publicity, public eye

limit *n, v*

▶ *n* **1** EXTREMITY, ultimate, utmost, extreme, maximum, terminus, greatest extent, greatest amount, lid, ceiling, maximum, cut-off point, saturation point, deadline **2** BOUNDARY, confines, parameters, bound(s), brim, border, frontier, edge, brink, threshold, verge, end, perimeter, rim, compass, demarcation, termination **3** CHECK, curb, restraint, restriction, constraint, limitation

▷ **the limit** enough, intolerable, too much, the end, the worst, *colloq.* the final blow, the last straw

▶ *v* restrict, check, curb, restrain, constrain, hold in check, confine, demarcate, delimit, control, bound, hem in, ration, reduce, specify, hinder, impede, *formal* circumscribe

limitation *n*

1 CHECK, restriction, curb, control, constraint, restraint, delimitation, demarcation, block, hindrance, impediment **2** INADEQUACY, shortcoming, incapability, inability, weakness, weak point, defect, disadvantage, drawback, snag, condition, qualification, reservation

🗲 **1** extension **2** advantage, strong point

limited *adj*

restricted, constrained, controlled, confined, checked, defined, finite, qualified, fixed, minimal, small, basic, narrow, inadequate, insufficient, scanty, incomplete, imperfect, *formal* circumscribed

🗲 limitless, boundless

limitless *adj*

unlimited, unbounded, boundless, illimited, undefined, immeasurable, measureless, incalculable, infinite, countless, endless, never-ending, unending, interminable, inexhaustible, untold, vast, unspecified

🗲 limited

limp¹ *v, n*

▶ *v limp down the road* hobble, falter, stumble, hop, shuffle, shamble, stagger, totter, walk with a limp, walk unevenly

▶ *n* hobble, lameness, hitch, shuffle, uneven walk, *technical* claudication

limp² *adj*

1 FLABBY, drooping, flaccid, floppy, loose, slack, relaxed, lax, soft, flexible, pliable, limber **2** TIRED, weary, exhausted, fatigued, spent, weak, frail, feeble, worn out, lethargic, *formal* debilitated, enervated

F3 1 stiff, firm **2** vigorous, energetic

limpid *adj*
1 CLEAR, crystal-clear, transparent, translucent, pure, glassy, bright, still, unruffled, untroubled, *formal* pellucid **2** INTELLIGIBLE, comprehensible, clear, flowing, coherent, lucid

F3 1 muddy, ripply, *formal* turbid **2** unintelligible

line¹ *n, v*
▶ *n* **1** STROKE, band, bar, stripe, mark, strip, rule, dash, slash, strand, streak, seam, belt, underline, score, underscore, scratch **2** ROW, rank, queue, file, column, sequence, series, procession, parade, chain, string, trail, tier, bank **3** LIMIT, boundary, border, borderline, edge, perimeter, periphery, frontier, demarcation, margin **4** STRING, rope, cord, cable, thread, strand, filament, wire, twine **5** PROFILE, contour, outline, silhouette, figure, shape, appearance, pattern, style, formation, *formal* configuration, delineation **6** CREASE, wrinkle, furrow, groove, crow's feet, corrugation **7** COURSE, path, direction, track, route, channel, way, trajectory, axis **8** APPROACH, avenue, course (of action), belief, ideology, attitude, policy, system, position, practice, procedure, method, way, scheme, *modus operandi* **9** OCCUPATION, business, trade, profession, vocation, work, job, line of business/work, career, activity, interest, employment, department, calling, field, province, forte, area, activity, pursuit, specialization, specialty, specialism, speciality **10** *chat-up line* spiel, patter, talk, sales talk, pitch **11** *drop you a line* note, letter, card, postcard, message, word, report, memo, memorandum, information **12** WORDS, part, text, script, book, libretto **13** *a shipping line* company, business, firm, transport business **14** *enemy lines* defences, position, front, front line, firing-line, battleground, battlefield, battle zone **15** *a line of products* brand, make, type, kind, sort, variety, type **16** ANCESTRY, family, descent, extraction, parentage, heritage, lineage, strain, pedigree, stock, race, breed

▷ **draw the line** refuse, say not to, exclude, limit, reject, rule out, stop short of, stand firm, *colloq.* put your foot down

▷ **in line 1** IN A ROW, in a queue, in a column, in series **2** *bring the two systems in line with each other* in agreement, in step, in harmony, *formal* in accord **3** *in line for promotion* due, likely, being considered, in the running, *colloq.* on the cards

▷ **lay/put on the line** risk, put in jeopardy, jeopardize, endanger, imperil

▷ **toe the line** conform, keep/follow the rules, be conventional

▶ *v* **1** BORDER, skirt, verge, edge, bound, fringe, rim **2** CREASE, score, furrow, mark, draw, hatch, inscribe, rule

▷ **line up 1** ALIGN, range, straighten, marshal, order, group, regiment, queue up, stand in line, wait in line, form ranks, fall in, assemble, *formal* array **2** ORGANIZE, arrange, prepare, produce, secure, obtain, *formal* procure, *colloq.* lay on

line² *v*
line a box with paper encase, panel, cover, fill, inlay, pad, back, face, stuff, reinforce

lineage *n*
ancestry, descent, extraction, genealogy, family, line, pedigree, race, stock, birth, breed, house, heredity, ancestors, forebears, descendants, offspring, succession

lineaments *n*
features, face, lines, outline(s), appearance, aspect,

profile, traits, *formal* countenance, visage, physiognomy, configuration

lined *adj*
1 RULED, feint **2** WRINKLED, furrowed, creased, wizened, worn

F3 1 unlined, blank **2** smooth

linen *n*
bed linen, sheets, pillowcases, tablecloths, table linen, napkins, tea towels, white goods, *formal* napery

line-up *n*
array, arrangement, queue, row, line, selection, cast, team, bill, list

linger *v*
1 LOITER, delay, dally, wait, remain, stay, hang on, hang around, lag, dawdle, idle, stop, take your time, *formal* tarry, procrastinate, *colloq.* dilly-dally **2** CONTINUE, endure, hold out, last, persist, survive, remain

F3 1 leave, rush

lingerie *n*
underclothes, underwear, underclothing, undergarments, panties, knickers, camiknickers, camisole, slip, half-slip, teddy, body stocking, panty girdle, brassiere, bra, suspender belt, unmentionables, inexpressibles, *colloq.* frillies, undies, smalls

lingering *adj*
persistent, remaining, slow, dragging, long-drawn-out, prolonged, *formal* protracted

F3 quick

lingo *n*
language, tongue, patois, speech, talk, jargon, idiom, vernacular, terminology, vocabulary, parlance, dialect, argot, cant, patter

liniment *n*
cream, lotion, salve, ointment, embrocation, emollient, balm, balsam, wash, *formal* unguent

lining *n*
inlay, interfacing, facing, padding, backing, encasement, stiffening, panelling, reinforcement

link *n, v*
▶ *n* **1** CONNECTION, bond, tie, association, joint, relationship, tie-up, union, knot, liaison, attachment, communication, partnership **2** RING, loop, bond, tie, knot, joint **3** PART, piece, element, member, constituent, component, division
▶ *v* connect, join, attach, couple, tie, fasten, unite, bind, amalgamate, merge, associate, ally, bracket, identify, relate, yoke, attach, hook up, join forces, team up

F3 separate, unfasten

▷ **link up** connect, join (up), ally, amalgamate, meet up, join forces, merge, team up, unify, hook up, dock

F3 separate

link-up *n*
connection, alliance, amalgamation, association, relationship, partnership, merger, tie-in, union

F3 separation

lion-hearted *adj*
bold, brave, courageous, heroic, daring, gallant, intrepid, stout-hearted, valiant, fearless, dauntless, resolute, stalwart, dreadless, *formal* valorous

F3 cowardly

lionize *v*
glorify, hero-worship, treat as a hero, honour, idolize, magnify, fête, exalt, celebrate, praise, sing the praises of, acclaim, adulate, *formal* aggrandize, eulogize, *colloq.* put on a pedestal

F3 vilify

lip *n*
1 EDGE, brim, border, brink, rim, margin, verge

2 IMPERTINENCE, impudence, insolence, rudeness, effrontery, backchat, *colloq.* cheek, sauce
🔁 politeness

liquefaction *n*
dissolution, dissolving, fusion, liquefying, melting, thawing, *formal* deliquescence
🔁 solidification

liquefy *v*
dissolve, fuse, liquidize, melt, smelt, run, thaw, flux, fluidize, *formal* liquesce, deliquesce
🔁 solidify

liquid *n, adj*
▶ *n* liquor, fluid, juice, drink, sap, solution, lotion
▶ *adj* **1** FLUID, flowing, liquefied, watery, wet, running, runny, sloppy, thin, melted, molten, thawed, clear, *formal* aqueous, hydrous **2** SMOOTH, flowing, steady, even, regular, unbroken, uninterrupted, mellow, melodious
🔁 **1** solid, gas

liquidate *v*
1 PAY (OFF), close down, dissolve, break up, clear, discharge, wind up, sell (off), disband, cash in, convert to cash **2** ANNIHILATE, terminate, do away with, put an end to, dissolve, kill, murder, massacre, assassinate, destroy, dispatch, abolish, eliminate, exterminate, remove, finish off, *colloq.* rub out, wipe out

liquidize *v*
process, blend, crush, purée, mix, synthesize

liquor *n*
1 ALCOHOL, intoxicant, strong drink, spirits, drink, *colloq.* hard stuff, hoo(t)ch, plonk, vino, juice, Dutch courage, grog, sauce, firewater, *slang* booze **2** LIQUID, juice, gravy, essence, extract, stock, broth, infusion

lissom *adj*
graceful, supple, pliable, flexible, pliant, light, nimble, agile, limber, lithe, lithesome, loose-jointed, loose-limbed, willowy
🔁 stiff, awkward

list¹ *n ,v*
▶ *n a shopping list* catalogue, roll, inventory, register, enumeration, schedule, programme, agenda, index, (list of) contents, listing, record, file, directory, table, tabulation, tally, series, syllabus, calendar, recipe, roster, rota, checklist, invoice
▶ *v* enumerate, register, itemize, classify, catalogue, alphabetize, index, tabulate, record, programme, file, schedule, enrol, enter, note, bill, book, set down, write down, compile

list² *v*
the ship is listing lean (over), incline, tilt, slope, slant, heel (over), tip, cant

listen *v*
attend, pay attention, hear, heed, hang on (someone's) words, prick up your ears, take notice, mind, lend an ear, give ear
▷ **listen in** eavesdrop, overhear, tap, wiretap, monitor, pin back your ears, prick up your ears, *colloq.* bug

listless *adj*
sluggish, lethargic, spiritless, languishing, lackadaisical, limp, lifeless, dull, passive, inert, inactive, impassive, indifferent, uninterested, vacant, apathetic, depressed, bored, heavy, *formal* languid, torpid, enervated, indolent
🔁 energetic, enthusiastic

listlessness *n*
lethargy, sluggishness, spiritlessness, lifelessness, sloth, inattention, indifference, ennui, apathy, *formal* enervation, indolence, languidness, languor, torpidity, torpor, supineness
🔁 liveliness

litany *n*
1 PRAYER, petition, supplication, devotion, *formal* invocation **2** CATALOGUE, account, enumeration, list, repetition, recital, recitation

literacy *n*
ability to read, ability to write, proficiency, education, culture, cultivation, intelligence, knowledge, learning, scholarship, learnedness, articulacy, articulateness, *formal* erudition
🔁 illiteracy

literal *adj*
1 VERBATIM, word-for-word, strict, close, actual, precise, faithful, exact, accurate, factual, true, genuine, undistorted, unexaggerated, unembellished, unvarnished **2** PROSAIC, unimaginative, uninspired, colourless, matter-of-fact, down-to-earth, humdrum, boring, dull, tedious
🔁 **1** imprecise, loose, deviating **2** imaginative

literally *adv*
1 *many people in Africa are literally starving* actually, really, truly, certainly **2** *translate literally* exactly, faithfully, to the letter, strictly, precisely, closely, plainly, word for word, verbatim
🔁 **2** imprecisely, loosely

literary *adj*
1 EDUCATED, well-read, bookish, learned, scholarly, lettered, literate, widely-read, cultured, cultivated, refined, *formal* erudite **2** *literary phrases* formal, poetic, old-fashioned
🔁 **1** ignorant, illiterate **2** everyday, colloquial, informal

literate *adj*
able to read, able to write, proficient, educated, well-educated, cultured, intelligent, learned, intellectual, knowledgeable

literature *n*
1 WRITINGS, printed works, published works, letters, paper(s) **2** INFORMATION, facts, data, leaflet(s), pamphlet(s), circular(s), brochure(s), hand-out(s), printed matter, advertising material, *colloq.* bumf

Types of literature include:
allegory, anti-novel, autobiography, *formal* belles-lettres, biography, classic novel, criticism, drama, epic, epistle, essay, fiction, Gothic novel, lampoon, libretto, magnum opus, non-fiction, novel, novella, parody, pastiche, *colloq.* penny dreadful, picaresque novel, poetry, polemic, postil, prose, roman novel, saga, satire, thesis, tragedy, treatise, triad, trilogy, verse. *See also* POEM; STORY.

lithe *adj*
agile, supple, flexible, pliable, pliant, lissom, limber, lithesome, double-jointed, loose-jointed, loose-limbed
🔁 stiff

litigant *n*
contender, contestant, disputant, claimant, complainant, litigator, plaintiff, party

litigation *n*
lawsuit, action, dispute, suit, case, legal case, prosecution, process, contention

litigious *adj*
argumentative, quarrelsome, contentious, disputatious, disputable, belligerent
🔁 easy-going

litter *n, v*
▶ *n* **1** RUBBISH, debris, refuse, odds and ends, waste, mess, disorder, clutter, confusion, disarray, untidiness, muck, jumble, fragments, shreds, *US* trash, garbage, *formal* detritus, *colloq.* junk, shambles, grot

2 OFFSPRING, young, brood, family, *formal* progeny, issue

▶ *v* strew, scatter, mess up, make a mess of, disorder, clutter, make untidy

F3 tidy

little *adj, adv, n*

▶ *adj* **1** SMALL, short, tiny, minute, diminutive, miniature, infinitesimal, mini, microscopic, petite, baby, midget, dwarf, Lilliputian, slender, slight, younger, *colloq.* wee, teeny, pint-size(d) **2** SHORT-LIVED, brief, short, fleeting, passing, momentary, transient, transitory, *formal* ephemeral **3** INSUFFICIENT, sparse, scant, meagre, paltry, skimpy, *formal* exiguous **4** INSIGNIFICANT, unimportant, inconsiderable, negligible, trivial, petty, minor, paltry, nominal, trifling, *formal* nugatory, *colloq.* peanuts **5** *a nice little house* pleasant, attractive, nice, sweet, cute

F3 **1** big **2** long, lengthy **3** ample **4** considerable, serious

▶ *adv* barely, hardly, scarcely, slightly, rarely, seldom, infrequently, not much, next to nothing, a drop in the ocean

F3 frequently

▷ **little by little** gradually, bit by bit, progressively, slowly, step by step, by degrees, imperceptibly, piecemeal

F3 all at one go, quickly

▶ *n* bit, dash, pinch, small amount, spot, trace, drop, dab, speck, touch, taste, soupçon, smattering, particle, hint, fragment, modicum, trifle, trickle

F3 lot

liturgical *adj*

ceremonial, ritual, solemn, sacramental, formal, eucharistic, *formal* sacerdotal, hieratic

F3 secular

liturgy *n*

service, office, form, formula, rite, usage, worship, ceremony, ritual, observance, sacrament, ordinance, celebration

live¹ *v*

1 BE, be alive, have life, exist, breathe, draw breath **2** LAST, endure, continue, remain, persist, stay, survive, support yourself, earn your living, *formal* abide **3** *live in Leeds* have your home, be settled, inhabit, lodge, stay, squat, *formal* reside, abide, dwell, *colloq.* hang out **4** PASS, spend, lead, behave, *formal* comport, conduct **5** *live while you're young* enjoy life, enjoy life to the full, see life, make the most of your life

F3 **1** die **2** cease

▷ **live it up** revel, celebrate, go on a spree, *colloq.* have a ball, make merry, make whoopee, paint the town red

▷ **live on** live on fruit and vegetables, feed, live off, depend for nourishment, rely on, exist, *formal* subsist

live² *adj*

1 ALIVE, living, having life, existent, breathing, animate **2** LIVELY, vital, active, energetic, dynamic, alert, vigorous **3** BURNING, glowing, blazing, flaming, hot, ignited, alight **4** *a live TV programme* not prerecorded, not recorded, with an audience **5** *live cables* connected, charged, electrically charged, active **6** *a live bomb* unexploded, explosive, unstable, volatile **7** *a live issue* RELEVANT, current, topical, controversial, active, important, vital, lively, urgent, pressing, *formal* pertinent

F3 **1** dead **2** apathetic **4** prerecorded **5** disconnected, disconnected **6** defused **7** irrelevant

▷ **live wire** self-starter, *colloq.* life and soul of the party, ball of fire, dynamo, go-getter, eager beaver, whizz kid

F3 wet blanket

liveable *adj*

1 INHABITABLE, habitable **2** BEARABLE, tolerable,

supportable, comfortable, endurable, acceptable, adequate, satisfactory, worthwhile

F3 **1** uninhabitable **2** unbearable

▷ **liveable with** companionable, sociable, *gemütlich*, compatible, congenial, harmonious, passable, tolerable, bearable

F3 impossible, unbearable

livelihood *n*

occupation, employment, job, work, profession, trade, living, means, means of support, income, source of income, maintenance, work, support, subsistence, sustenance, upkeep

liveliness *n*

animation, energy, quickness, spirit, vitality, vivacity, dynamism, activity, boisterousness, briskness, smartness, sprightliness, *colloq.* brio, oomph

F3 apathy, inactivity

livelong *adj*

complete, entire, full, whole, enduring, long, protracted

F3 partial

lively *adj*

1 ANIMATED, alert, active, energetic, alive, high-spirited, spirited, enthusiastic, dynamic, vivacious, vigorous, sprightly, spry, agile, nimble, quick, keen **2** CHEERFUL, blithe, merry, frisky, perky, playful, jaunty, breezy, frolicsome, buoyant, *colloq.* chirpy, bouncy **3** *a lively discussion* animated, enthusiastic, heated, interesting, exciting, stimulating **4** BUSY, bustling, quick, brisk, rapid, crowded, eventful, exciting, buzzing, teeming, swarming, hectic **5** VIVID, bright, strong, colourful, graphic, striking, exciting, imaginative, stimulating, stirring, invigorating, racy, refreshing, sparkling

F3 **1** moribund, apathetic **3** dull **4** inactive, dull

liven *v*

enliven, vitalize, put life into, rouse, invigorate, animate, energize, brighten, stir (up), spice (up), *colloq.* buck up, pep up, perk up, hot up

F3 dishearten

liverish *adj*

irritable, snappy, testy, tetchy, crusty, grumpy, disagreeable, ill-humoured, quick-tempered, irascible, peevish, splenetic, *colloq.* crabbed, crabby, crotchety

F3 calm, easy-going

livery *n*

uniform, costume, regalia, dress, clothes, clothing, garments, vestments, suit, garb, habit, *formal* apparel, attire, habiliments, *colloq.* get-up, gear, clobber, togs

livid *adj*

1 ANGRY, furious, infuriated, irate, outraged, enraged, raging, seething, fuming, indignant, incensed, exasperated, *colloq.* mad **2** LEADEN, black-and-blue, bruised, discoloured, greyish, purple, purplish **3** PALE, deathly pale, pallid, ashen, blanched, white, bloodless, wan, waxy, ghastly, pasty

F3 **1** calm

living *adj, n*

▶ *adj* **1** ALIVE, breathing, existing, live, animate **2** CURRENT, surviving, continuing, active, operative, strong, vigorous, active, lively, vital, animated, *formal* extant, *colloq.* going strong **3** *a living likeness* close, exact, identical, precise, true, genuine

F3 **1** dead **2** dead, sluggish **3** inexact

▶ *n* **1** BEING, life, animation, existence **2** LIVELIHOOD, maintenance, support, means of support, income, source of income, subsistence, sustenance, work, job, occupation, profession, trade, way of life, lifestyle, *technical* benefice

living-room *n*

lounge, sitting-room, drawing-room, parlour, front room, salon, common room

load *n, v*
► *n* **1** CARGO, consignment, shipment, goods, lading, freight, contents, burden, charge **2** BURDEN, onus, responsibility, duty, obligation, encumbrance, weight, pressure, charge, trouble, worry, strain, oppression, millstone, albatross, *formal* tribulation **3** *loads of money* a lot, lots, heaps, dozens, scores, hundreds, thousands, a million, millions, hordes, tons
► *v* **1** PACK, pile, heap, freight, fill (up), stack, lade, charge **2** BURDEN, weigh down, encumber, overburden, oppress, overwhelm, worry, trouble, weight, strain, tax, saddle with

loaded *adj*
1 BURDENED, charged, laden, full, filled, weighted, packed, piled, heaped, stacked, *colloq.* snowed under **2** WEIGHTED, biased, to your disadvantage **3** RICH, wealthy, well-off, affluent, *colloq.* well-heeled, flush, in the money, rolling in it **4** DRUNK, under the influence, drunken, *formal* inebriated, intoxicated, crapulant, *colloq.* merry, tight, tipsy, tiddly, well-oiled, blotto, drunk as a lord/newt, blind drunk, roaring drunk, the worse for drink, soused, squiffy, happy, legless, plastered, sozzled, pickled, bibulous, woozy, one over the eight, under the table, bevvied, have had a few, *slang* stoned, tanked up, lit up, canned, paralytic, sloshed, smashed, stewed, bombed

loaf¹ *n*
1 *a loaf of bread* block, slab, brick, mass, lump, cube, cake **2** *use your loaf* common sense, sense, head, noddle, *colloq.* brains, gumption, nous,

loaf² *v*
loafing about/around stand about, idle, laze, loiter, *colloq.* take it easy, hang around, lounge around, mooch
🖪 toil

loafer *n*
idler, shirker, sluggard, wastrel, lounger, ne'er-do-well, *colloq.* layabout, skiver, lazybones

loan *n, v*
► *n* advance, credit, mortgage, allowance, lending
► *v* lend, advance, credit, allow

loath *adj*
reluctant, unwilling, resisting, disinclined, opposed, grudging, hesitant, indisposed, against, *formal* averse
🖪 willing

loathe *v*
hate, detest, despise, dislike, not stand, recoil from, have an aversion to, feel revulsion at, *formal* abominate, abhor, execrate
🖪 adore, love

loathing *n*
hatred, hate, detestation, repugnance, revulsion, repulsion, dislike, disgust, aversion, odium, ill-will, horror, *formal* abhorrence, abomination, antipathy, execration
🖪 affection, love

loathsome *adj*
detestable, odious, repulsive, hateful, repugnant, repellent, offensive, horrible, disgusting, odious, nauseating, vile, revolting, nasty, obnoxious, despicable, contemptible, disagreeable, *formal* abhorrent, abominable, execrable

lob *v*
throw, toss, hurl, pitch, fling, heave, launch, lift, shy, loft, *colloq.* chuck

lobby *v, n*
► *v* campaign for, press for, demand, persuade, call for, urge, influence, solicit, pressure, promote, *colloq.* push for
► *n* **1** VESTIBULE, foyer, porch, anteroom, hall, hall-

way, waiting-room, entrance hall, entrance, corridor, passage, passageway **2** PRESSURE GROUP, campaign, ginger group, lobbyists

local *adj, n*
► *adj* regional, provincial, community, district, neighbourhood, municipal, city, urban, town, village, parish, parochial, vernacular, small-town, limited, narrow, restricted, parish(-pump)
🖪 national
► *n* **1** INHABITANT, citizen, resident, native **2** PUB, bar, inn, public house, tavern, *colloq.* hostelry, watering-hole, *slang* boozer

locale *n*
place, position, scene, setting, site, spot, venue, area, locality, location, neighbourhood, environment, zone, *formal* locus

locality *n*
neighbourhood, vicinity, district, area, locale, environment, region, position, place, site, spot, scene, setting, surrounding area

localize *v*
1 IDENTIFY, specify, zero in on, narrow down, pinpoint, ascribe, assign **2** RESTRAIN, limit, restrict, confine, contain, concentrate, delimit, delimitate, *formal* circumscribe

locate *v*
1 FIND, discover, uncover, unearth, come across, track down, detect, pinpoint, identify, *colloq.* run to earth, lay your hands on, hit upon **2** SITUATE, settle, fix, establish, place, position, put, set, site, station, seat, build

location *n*
position, situation, place, whereabouts, venue, site, locale, bearings, spot, point, setting, scene, *formal* locus

lock¹ *n, v*
► *n* *fit locks to windows* fastening, bolt, clasp, catch, padlock, mortise lock, combination lock, spring lock, Chubb® lock, Yale® lock

Parts of a lock include:
barrel, bolt, cylinder, cylinder hole, dead bolt, escutcheon, face plate, hasp, key, key card, keyhole, keyway, knob, latch, latch bolt, latch follower, latch lever, mortise bolt, pin, push button, rose, sash, sash bolt, spindle, spindle hole, spring, strike plate, staple.

► *v* **1** FASTEN, secure, bolt, latch, bar, seal, shut, padlock **2** JOIN, unite, engage, link, mesh, entangle, entwine, clench, interlock, jam **3** CLASP, hug, embrace, grasp, encircle, enclose, clutch, grapple
🖪 unlock
▷ **lock out** shut out, refuse admittance/entrance to, keep out, exclude, bar, debar
▷ **lock up** imprison, jail, confine, shut in, shut up, put behind bars, put under lock and key, secure, cage, pen, detain, wall in, close up, *formal* incarcerate
🖪 free

lock² *n*
locks of hair strand, tress, tuft, plait, ringlet, curl

locker *n*
cupboard, container, cabinet, compartment

lock-up *n*
1 JAIL, gaol, prison, penitentiary, cell, *slang* can, clink, cooler, jug, quod **2** GARAGE, lock-up, storeroom, depository, warehouse

locomotion *n*
movement, motion, moving, progress, progression,

travel, travelling, headway, action, walking, *formal* ambulation, perambulation

locution *n*
1 STYLE, diction, articulation, accent, intonation, inflection **2** WORDING, term, phrase, phrasing, cliché, turn of phrase, expression, idiom, collocation

lodge *n, v*
▶ *n* **1** HUT, cabin, cottage, chalet, gatehouse, house, hunting-lodge **2** BRANCH, chapter, section, group, club, society, association, meeting-place **3** HAUNT, retreat, shelter, nest, lair, den
▶ *v* **1** ACCOMMODATE, quarter, board, billet, shelter, harbour, *colloq.* put up **2** LIVE, stay, have your home, be settled, room, *formal* reside, dwell, sojourn **3** FIX, imbed, implant, get stuck, get caught **4** DEPOSIT, place, put, submit, register, bank **5** *lodge a complaint* register, make, submit, record, file

lodger *n*
boarder, paying guest, resident, tenant, guest

lodgings *n*
accommodation, quarters, billet, board, boarding-house, rooms, place, *formal* dwelling, abode, residence, *colloq.* digs, pad, a roof over your head

lofty *adj*
1 *lofty ideals* noble, grand, exalted, distinguished, illustrious, majestic, sublime, stately, imposing, dignified, imperial, renowned, *formal* esteemed **2** HIGH, tall, sky-high, elevated, raised, towering, soaring **3** ARROGANT, proud, haughty, condescending, disdainful, patronizing, supercilious, superior, lordly, snooty, *colloq.* high and mighty, toffee-nosed
F⃞ **2** low **3** humble, lowly, modest

log *n, v*
▶ *n* **1** TIMBER, trunk, block, chunk, piece **2** RECORD, diary, journal, logbook, daybook, account, tally, register, chart
▶ *v* record, register, write up, note, set down, book, chart, tally, file

loggerheads *n*
▷ *at loggerheads* disagreeing, in conflict, at odds, in opposition, quarrelling, *colloq.* at daggers drawn, at each other's throats, like cat and dog

logic *n*
reasoning, reason, sense, judgement, deduction, rationale, coherence, argument, argumentation, *technical* dialectics, *formal* ratiocination

logical *adj*
reasonable, rational, reasoned, well-reasoned, well-founded, well-thought-out, coherent, consistent, relevant, valid, sound, well-founded, clear, sensible, wise, intelligent, thinking, deducible, methodical, well-organized, *formal* cogent, judicious
F⃞ illogical, irrational

logistics *n*
organization, co-ordination, management, masterminding, orchestration, strategy, tactics, planning, plans, direction, engineering

logo *n*
symbol, sign, trademark, representation, insignia, emblem, device, mark, badge, figure, image

loiter *v*
dawdle, hang about/around, idle, waste time, take your time, linger, dally, delay, mooch, lag, saunter, *formal* tarry, *colloq.* dilly-dally, loaf, lounge

loll *v*
1 RELAX, slouch, slump, sprawl, *formal* recline, *colloq.* loaf, lounge **2** HANG, flop, droop, drop, dangle, flap, sag

lone *adj*
1 BY YOURSELF, single, sole, alone, one, only, isol-ated, solitary, separate, unmarried, divorced **2** *a lone parent* by yourself, on your own, single, unmarried, unattached, divorced, separated, without a partner **3** ISOLATED, uninhabited, remote, out-of-the-way, unfrequented, secluded, abandoned, deserted, forsaken, desolate, barren
F⃞ **1** accompanied

loneliness *n*
aloneness, isolation, lonesomeness, solitariness, solitude, seclusion, desolation

lonely *adj*
1 ALONE, friendless, lone, lonesome, solitary, abandoned, forsaken, companionless, reclusive, unaccompanied, destitute, rejected, outcast, sad, unhappy, miserable, wretched **2** ISOLATED, uninhabited, remote, out-of-the-way, unfrequented, secluded, abandoned, deserted, forsaken, desolate, barren, God-forsaken, *colloq.* off the beaten track
F⃞ **1** popular **2** crowded, populous

loner *n*
individualist, recluse, solitary, hermit, *formal* solitudinarian, *colloq.* lone wolf

lonesome *adj*
1 ALONE, lonely, friendless, lone, lonesome, solitary, abandoned, forsaken, companionless, reclusive, unaccompanied, destitute, rejected, outcast, sad, unhappy, miserable, wretched **2** ISOLATED, lonely, uninhabited, remote, out-of-the-way, unfrequented, secluded, abandoned, deserted, forsaken, desolate, barren

long *adj, v*
▶ *adj* lengthy, extensive, extended, expanded, elongated, prolonged, stretched (out), spread out, sustained, expansive, far-reaching, long-drawn-out, overlong, spun out, marathon, interminable, slow, *formal* protracted, verbose, tardy
F⃞ short, brief, fleeting, abbreviated
▷ *before long* soon, shortly, in a short time, in a moment, in a minute or two, in the near future
▶ *v* yearn, crave, want, wish, desire, hope, dream, hanker, pine, thirst, hunger, lust, covet, itch, *colloq.* yen for

long-drawn-out *adj*
lengthy, long-winded, spun out, overlong, prolonged, interminable, tedious, marathon, overextended, long-drawn, *formal* protracted, prolix, *colloq.* dragging on
F⃞ brief, curtailed

longing *n, adj*
▶ *n* craving, desire, yearning, hunger, hungering, hankering, pining, thirst, wish, wanting, dream, hope, urge, coveting, itch, aspiration, ambition, *colloq.* yen
▶ *adj* wishful, eager, craving, pining, yearning, wistful, languishing, hungry, anxious, avid, ardent, *formal* desirous

long-lasting *adj*
permanent, imperishable, enduring, unchanging, unfading, continuing, abiding, chronic, lingering, long-standing, prolonged, *formal* protracted
F⃞ short-lived, ephemeral, transient

long-lived *adj*
enduring, lasting, durable, long-lasting, long-standing, *technical* macrobian, macrobiotic, *formal* longevous
F⃞ brief, short-lived, *formal* ephemeral

long-standing *adj*
established, long-established, well-established, long-lived, long-lasting, enduring, abiding, traditional, time-honoured

long-suffering *adj*
uncomplaining, forbearing, forgiving, tolerant, indulgent, easy-going, patient, stoical, resigned
F⃞ complaining

long-winded *adj*
lengthy, overlong, prolonged, long-drawn-out, diffuse, verbose, wordy, garrulous, discursive, repetitious, rambling, tedious, *formal* prolix, protracted, voluble
F3 brief, terse

long-windedness *n*
lengthiness, verbosity, wordiness, diffuseness, discursiveness, repetitiousness, tediousness, garrulity, *formal* volubility, prolixity, longueur, macrology
F3 brevity, curtness

look *v, n*
▶ *v* **1** WATCH, see, take a look, observe, view, survey, regard, gaze, eye, study, stare, examine, inspect, focus, check, take in, consider, scrutinize, glance, contemplate, scan, peep, gape, *colloq.* gawp, run your eyes over, give the once-over, give a going-over, get a load of, get an eyeful of, take a squint at, take a dekko at, take a gander at, take a butcher's at, take a shufti at, *US* eyeball **2** SEEM, appear, give the appearance of, show, exhibit, display **3** *the house looks onto the fields* face, front, front on, give on (to), overlook, be opposite, look onto
▷ **look after** take care of, mind, care for, attend to, take charge of, maintain, tend, keep an eye on, watch over, nurse, protect, supervise, guard, babysit, sit, childmind
F3 neglect, disregard, ignore
▷ **look back** remember, recall, think back, reminisce, reflect on the past
▷ **look down on** despise, scorn, sneer at, hold in contempt, disdain, spurn, think of as inferior/unimportant, patronize, talk down to, act/speak condescendingly, *formal* disparage, *colloq.* look down your nose at, turn your nose up at
F3 esteem, approve
▷ **look for** try to find, search for, seek, quest, hunt for, hunt out, forage for
▷ **look forward to** anticipate, await, expect, hope for, long for, envisage, envision, count on, wait for, look for
▷ **look into** investigate, probe, research, study, go into, search into, examine, inquire about, ask about, explore, inspect, scrutinize, look over, plumb, fathom, dig, delve, *colloq.* check out
▷ **look like** resemble, take after, be similar (in appearance) to, have the appearance of, remind you of
▷ **look on/upon** consider, regard, think, judge, count, hold, *formal* deem
▷ **look out** pay attention, watch out, beware, be careful, be alert, be on your guard, guard yourself, keep your eyes open/peeled/skinned, be on the qui vive, keep an eye out, *colloq.* look/mind where you're going
▷ **look over** inspect, examine, check, cast an/your eye over, look through, go through, scan, read through, view, monitor, *colloq.* check out, give a once-over
▷ **look to** expect, hope for, reckon on, rely on, turn to, count on, anticipate, think about, await
▷ **look up 1** SEARCH FOR, research, seek, consult, hunt for, find, track down **2** VISIT, call on, drop in on, look in on, pay a visit to, stop by, drop by **3** IMPROVE, get better, pick up, progress, make progress, develop, advance, make headway, come on/along, *formal* ameliorate, *colloq.* perk up
▷ **look up to** admire, respect, regard highly, revere, honour, have a high opinion of, think highly of, *formal* esteem
▶ *n* **1** VIEW, survey, inspection, examination, study, contemplation, observation, sight, review, glance, glimpse, stare, gaze, gape, peek, peep, *colloq.* once-over, squint, eyeful, dekko, gander, butcher's, shufti

2 APPEARANCE, aspect, manner, air, effect, impression, semblance, expression, face, guise, features, façade, complexion, *formal* countenance, mien, bearing

look-alike *n*
double, replica, twin, image, living image, exact likeness, clone, *doppelgänger*, *colloq.* spitting image, spit, (dead) ringer

lookout *n*
1 GUARD, sentry, watch, watch-tower, watchman, sentinel, tower, post, observation post **2** CONCERN, responsibility, worry, affair, business, problem, *colloq.* pigeon
▷ **keep a lookout** remain alert, watch, keep guard, be vigilant, be on the qui vive

loom *v*
the ship loomed out of the mist; her exams are looming appear, emerge, take shape, become visible, menace, threaten, impend, be imminent, hang over, dominate, tower, overhang, rise, soar, mount, overshadow, over-top

loop *n, v*
▶ *n* hoop, ring, circle, noose, coil, eyelet, loophole, spiral, curve, curl, oval, kink, twist, whorl, twirl, turn, bend, *formal* convolution
▶ *v* coil, encircle, surround, roll, bend, circle, curve round, turn, curl, twist, spiral, wind, connect, join, tie, knot, fasten, fold, braid

loophole *n*
let-out, escape, omission, escape, clause, evasion, excuse, pretext, plea, pretence, mistake

loose *adj, v*
▶ *adj* **1** FREE, unfastened, untied, at large, unconfined, released, undone, untethered, uncoupled, unlocked, let go, escaped, off, movable, unattached, insecure, wobbly, unsteady **2** SLACK, lax, baggy, hanging, loose-fitting, sagging, flowing, shapeless, unbound, untied **3** IMPRECISE, vague, inexact, ill-defined, indefinite, inaccurate, indistinct, general, broad, rambling **4** *loose morals* promiscuous, dissolute, lax, unchaste, fast, debauched, disreputable, immoral, corrupt, wanton, degenerate, abandoned
F3 **1** firm, fixed, secure **2** tight **3** precise, specific, literal **4** chaste
▷ **at a loose end** with nothing to do, bored, out of action, idle, off duty, *colloq.* fed up, twiddling your thumbs, with time to kill
▶ *v* **1** RELEASE, set free, free, let go, liberate, loosen, unbind, unclasp, unfasten, untie, disconnect, disengage, detach, unleash, unhook, uncouple, undo, unlock, unmoor, unpen **2** RELAX, slacken, ease, moderate, lessen, loosen, weaken, diminish, reduce
F3 **1** bind, fasten, fix, secure **2** tighten

loosen *v*
1 EASE, relax, loose, slacken, moderate, weaken, diminish, undo, unbind, untie, unfasten **2** FREE, set free, release, let go, set loose, let out, deliver
F3 **1** tighten
▷ **loosen up 1** RELAX, unwind, let up, go easy, lessen, ease up, *colloq.* hang loose, cool it, chill out **2** LIMBER UP, warm up, work out, exercise, prepare

loot *n, v*
▶ *n* spoils, booty, plunder, stolen money, stolen goods, pickings, riches, haul, prize, *colloq.* swag
▶ *v* steal, plunder, pillage, rob, steal (from), burgle, sack, rifle, raid, maraud, ransack, ravage, *formal* despoil

lop *v*
chop, cut (off), dock, prune, sever, trim, clip, crop, hack, shorten, curtail, detach, remove, take off, reduce, truncate

lope *v*
run, lollop, bound, spring, stride, canter, gallop

lop-sided *adj*
asymmetrical, unbalanced, askew, off balance, uneven, unequal, crooked, squint, tilting, one-sided
☒ balanced, symmetrical

loquacious *adj*
talkative, chatty, chattering, babbling, blathering, gossipy, wordy, garrulous, *formal* voluble, multiloquent, multiloquous, *colloq.* gabby, gassy
☒ succinct, taciturn, terse, reserved

loquacity *n*
talkativeness, chattiness, garrulity, effusiveness, *formal* volubility, multiloquence, multiloquy, *colloq.* gassiness
☒ succinctness, taciturnity, terseness

lord *n*
1 PEER, noble, nobleman, earl, duke, count, viscount, baron, aristocrat 2 MASTER, ruler, superior, overlord, leader, chief, captain, commander, governor, king, prince, sovereign, monarch, emperor 3 *God, the Lord* God, Creator, Maker, King, Almighty, Holy One, Jehovah, Yahweh, Father, Eternal, Christ, Jesus Christ, the Word, Redeemer, Saviour, Son of God, Son of Man
▷ **lord it over** domineer, tyrannize, be overbearing, order around, queen it over, oppress, repress, pull rank, swagger, *formal* put on airs, *colloq.* act big, boss around

lordly *adj*
1 NOBLE, dignified, aristocratic, magnificent, splendid, majestic, grand, grandiose, stately, imperial, impressive, lofty 2 PROUD, arrogant, disdainful, haughty, imperious, condescending, patronizing, supercilious, dictatorial, high-handed, domineering, overbearing, over-confident, *formal* peremptory, hubristic, *colloq.* big-headed, stuck-up, high and mighty, uppity, toffee-nosed, hoity-toity, too big for your boots
☒ 1 lowly 2 humble

lore *n*
knowledge, wisdom, learning, scholarship, traditions, folklore, teaching, beliefs, legends, stories, sayings, superstitions, *formal* erudition

lorry *n*
truck, trailer, articulated lorry, pantechnicon, removal van, vehicle, wagon, juggernaut, pick-up, float

lose *v*
1 MISLAY, misplace, forget, miss, not find, forfeit, drop 2 FAIL, fall short, suffer defeat, be defeated, be beaten, be conquered, go down, be unsuccessful, *colloq.* come to grief, throw in the towel 3 ELUDE, evade, throw off, shake off, leave behind, outrun 4 BE DEPRIVED OF, no longer have, stop having, be taken away, be bereaved of, be dispossessed of, *formal* be divested of 5 *lose an opportunity* not take advantage of, fail to grasp, neglect, miss, disregard, ignore, waste, squander, fritter 6 *lose your way* wander from, stray from, depart from, go astray, get lost, lose your bearings 7 WASTE, squander, spend, consume, use up, exhaust, expend, spend, drain, *formal* dissipate, deplete
☒ 1 find, keep, gain 2 win 3 win 5 grasp, take advantage of 6 find 7 make
▷ **lose yourself in something** be absorbed in, be preoccupied in, be occupied in, be taken up with, be engrossed in, be fascinated by, be enthralled by, be captivated by, be riveted by
▷ **lose out** suffer, miss out, be unsuccessful, be at a disadvantage, be disadvantaged

loser *n*
failure, runner-up, the defeated, *colloq.* also-ran, flop, no-

hoper, washout, non-starter, write-off, has-been, dead loss
☒ winner

loss *n*
1 MISLAYING, misplacement, missing, forfeiture, forgetting, dropping 2 DEPRIVATION, disappearance, bereavement, dispossession, disadvantage, harm, hurt, impairment, undoing, waste, *formal* privation 3 *losses in war* casualties, fatalities, death toll, dead, missing, wounded 4 *the business made a loss* deficit, debt, deficiency
☒ 1 finding 2 gain 4 profit
▷ **at a loss** puzzled, perplexed, bewildered, mystified, not knowing what to do/say

lost *adj*
1 MISLAID, missing, vanished, disappeared, misplaced, astray, strayed, disoriented, disorientated, off course 2 CONFUSED, disoriented, bewildered, puzzled, baffled, perplexed, nonplussed, at a loss 3 WASTED, squandered, ruined, destroyed, wrecked, demolished, neglected, missed, frittered away, unrecoverable 4 *a lost civilization* past, dead, defunct, extinct, bygone, long-forgotten, vanished, untraceable 5 *lost souls* damned, fallen, condemned, doomed, cursed, irredeemable 6 *lost in thought* absorbed, preoccupied, occupied, taken up with, engrossed, fascinated, enthralled, captivated, riveted, spellbound, absent-minded, dreamy
☒ 1 found

lot *n*
1 *lots of food*; *a lot of people* large amount, great number, many, a quantity, a good/great deal, *colloq.* oodles, tons, loads, masses, heaps, piles, stacks, dozens, hundreds, thousands, millions, miles 2 COLLECTION, batch, bundle, assortment, quantity, group, set, consignment, crowd, gathering, *colloq.* bunch 3 SHARE, portion, allowance, ration, quota, percentage, part, piece, parcel, *colloq.* cut 4 *content with your lot in life* destiny, fate, fortune, circumstances, situation 5 PLOT, allotment, parcel, piece of land, piece of ground
▷ **a lot** much, to a great extent/degree, often, frequently, for a long time
▷ **throw in your lot with** join forces, align yourself with, team up with, combine with, pitch in, take part in, *colloq.* muck in

lotion *n*
ointment, balm, balsam, cream, salve, emollient, embrocation, liniment

lottery *n*
1 DRAW, raffle, sweepstake, bingo, tombola, gambling game 2 SPECULATION, venture, risk, gamble, chance, hazard, luck

loud *adj*
1 NOISY, deafening, rowdy, booming, resounding, resonant, reverberating, roaring, ear-piercing, ear-splitting, piercing, penetrating, thundering, blaring, clamorous, insistent, emphatic, vehement, vociferous, strident, shrill, raucous, rowdy, aggressive, brazen, loud-mouthed, full-mouthed, *formal* stentorian 2 GARISH, gaudy, glaring, flashy, flamboyant, brash, showy, bold, obtrusive, ostentatious, tasteless, vulgar, *colloq.* flash
☒ 1 quiet, soft 2 subdued

loudly *adv*
noisily, strongly, deafeningly, resoundingly, clamorously, vehemently, shrilly, vigorously, uproariously, vociferously, lustily, stridently, *technical* fortissimo, *formal* streperously, strepitantly
☒ quietly, softly

loudmouth *n*
boaster, braggart, brag, blusterer, braggadocio,

swaggerer, *colloq.* windbag, gasbag, big mouth

loud-mouthed *adj*
noisy, aggressive, bold, brazen, boasting, blustering, bragging, coarse, vulgar

lounge *v, n*
▶ *v* relax, loll (about), idle, laze, waste time, kill time, lie about/around, sprawl, recline, lie back, slump, *formal* repose, *colloq.* take it easy
▶ *n* sitting-room, living-room, drawing-room, day-room, parlour

lour, lower *v*
1 DARKEN, blacken, cloud over, threaten, menace, loom, impend, be brewing **2** SCOWL, frown, glare, glower, *colloq.* give a dirty look, look daggers

louring, lowering *adj*
menacing, threatening, forbidding, ominous, grim, impending, foreboding, gloomy, cloudy, overcast, dark, darkening, grey, black, heavy

lousy *adj*
1 BAD, rotten, poor, second-rate, no good, inferior, contemptible, miserable, low, *colloq.* awful, terrible, mingy, *slang* crap **2** ILL, unwell, sick, poorly, off-colour, seedy, queasy, *colloq.* awful, out of sorts, under the weather
🖅 **1** excellent, superb **2** well

lout *n*
oaf, boor, dolt, barbarian, yahoo, gawk, lubber, *colloq.* clod, clodhopper, hick, hobbledehoy, slob, yob, yobbo, bumpkin

loutish *adj*
uncouth, oafish, boorish, doltish, ill-mannered, ill-bred, gawky, rude, coarse, rough, crude, vulgar, churlish, unmannerly, unrefined, uncivilized, gruff, impolite, rustic, uneducated, ignorant, bungling, *colloq.* clodhopping
🖅 polite, refined, cultured, genteel

lovable *adj*
adorable, endearing, winsome, appealing, captivating, enchanting, bewitching, dear, charming, engaging, attractive, fetching, sweet, lovely, pleasing, delightful, likeable, cute
🖅 detestable, hateful

love *v, n*
▶ *v* **1** *he loves his wife* be fond of, like very much, adore, cherish, dote on, treasure, hold dear, be attracted to, feel affection for, be devoted to, care for, prize, desire, long for, be infatuated with, idolize, worship, think the world of, mean the world to someone, *colloq.* be mad on, be sweet on, be daft/nuts on, be sold on, have a crush on, *slang* have the hots for **2** *I love macaroons* take pleasure in, enjoy, delight in, like very much, appreciate, desire, fancy, have a liking for, be partial to, savour, relish
🖅 detest, hate
▶ *n* **1** FONDNESS, affection, adoration, attachment, care, regard, concern, liking, amorousness, ardour, intimacy, desire, devotion, adulation, passion, rapture, tenderness, warmth, inclination, infatuation, lust, delight, enjoyment, weakness, taste, friendship, brotherhood, sympathy, kindness, *colloq.* soft spot **2** *a love of power* pleasure, enjoyment, delight, liking, appreciation, weakness, partiality, relish, *colloq.* soft spot **3** *come here, my love* darling, beloved, dear, dear one, dearest, favourite, sweetheart, honey, angel, pet, treasure
🖅 **1** hate, hatred, dislike **2** detestation, loathing
▷ **fall in love with** fall for, become infatuated with, burn with passion, take to, lose your heart to, *colloq.* fall head over heels in love, have a thing for, fancy, be crazy about, have a crush on, take a shine to, have it bad

▷ **in love with** attracted to, smitten, sweet/soft on, besotted, charmed, doting, enamoured, infatuated, *colloq.* mad/crazy/wild about, have a crush on, hooked, nuts about, stuck on, head over heels, swept off one's feet

▷ **love affair** affair, romance, liaison, relationship, love, intrigue, passion, amour, involvement, attachment, entanglement, courtship, flirtation, *affaire de coeur*, dalliance, *colloq.* fling

▷ **make love** have sex with, *colloq.* sleep with, sleep together, go to bed with

loveless *adj*
cold, cold-hearted, hard, icy, insensitive, unresponsive, unloved, unloving, passionless, unfeeling, unfriendly, unappreciated, friendless, disliked, frigid, forsaken, unvalued, heartless, uncherished
🖅 passionate

lovelorn *adj*
infatuated, desiring, longing, pining, yearning, languishing, lovesick, unrequited in love

lovely *adj*
1 ATTRACTIVE, beautiful, charming, delightful, attractive, enchanting, pleasing, pleasant, good-looking, pretty, handsome, fair, adorable, sweet, winning, exquisite **2** MARVELLOUS, wonderful, enjoyable, pleasing, delightful, agreeable
🖅 **1** ugly, hideous

love-making *n*
sexual intercourse, intercourse, sex, sexual relations, sexual union, copulation, intimacy, foreplay, mating, *formal* carnal knowledge, coition, coitus, congress, *colloq.* sleeping with someone, going to bed with someone

lover *n*
1 BELOVED, loved one, admirer, boyfriend, man friend, girlfriend, woman friend, sweetheart, partner, live-in partner, suitor, mistress, lady love, fiancé(e), other man, other woman, significant other, *colloq.* flame, bit on the side, date, fella, toy boy, heart-throb **2** ENTHUSIAST, devotee, admirer, fan, supporter, follower, fanatic, *colloq.* buff, freak, fiend

lovesick *adj*
infatuated, desiring, longing, pining, yearning, languishing, lovelorn, unrequited in love

loving *adj*
amorous, affectionate, devoted, doting, fond, adoring, ardent, passionate, warm, warm-hearted, kind, tender, caring, friendly, sympathetic

low[1] *adj, n*
▶ *adj* **1** SHORT, small, squat, stunted, little, shallow **2** INADEQUATE, insufficient, deficient, poor, sparse, meagre, paltry, trifling, scant, scanty, little, insignificant, reduced **3** *low land* close to the ground, sea-level, ground-level, depressed, deep, sunken, flat **4** LOWLY, humble, low-born, obscure, poor, plebeian, plain, simple, common, modest, ordinary, inferior, junior, low-ranking, peasant, meek, mild, mean, submissive, subordinate, unimportant **5** *have a low opinion of someone* poor, unfavourable, bad, negative, adverse, hostile, opposing, antagonistic **6** *low notes* DEEP, low-pitched, bass, resonant, sonorous, rich **7** *low achiever* unintelligent, foolish, slow, dull, mediocre, inadequate, deficient, below standard **8** UNHAPPY, depressed, downcast, gloomy, low-spirited, miserable, despondent, sad, downhearted, disheartened, glum, *formal* disconsolate, *colloq.* down, down in the dumps, blue, fed up, cheesed off **9** BASE, coarse, vulgar, bad, evil, wicked, mean, contemptible, nasty, despicable, dishonourable, depraved, immoral, obscene, indecent, smutty, *formal* heinous **10** CHEAP, inexpensive, reasonable,

moderate, modest, reduced, slashed, sale, rock-bottom **11** SUBDUED, muted, soft, quiet, quietened, gentle, hushed, muffled, whispered
F3 1 high **2** high **3** high **4** high, important **5** high, good **6** high **8** cheerful **9** honourable **10** high, exorbitant **11** loud, noisy
▸ *n* all-time low, lowest point, bottom, low point, low-watermark
F3 high, *formal* nadir

low² *v*
cattle lowing bellow, moo

low-born *adj*
humble, poor, mean-born, plebeian, unexalted, lowly, low-ranking, peasant, obscure
F3 high-born, noble

lowbrow *adj*
ignorant, uncultivated, uncultured, unrefined, uneducated, unlearned, unscholarly, unlettered, crude, rude
F3 highbrow, intellectual

low-down *n*
information, news, facts, data, inside story, intelligence, *colloq.* dope, gen, info

lower¹ *adj, v*
▸ *adj* **1** *the lower jaw* UNDER, bottom, undermost, nether **2** INFERIOR, lesser, subordinate, secondary, minor, second-class, low-level, lowly, junior
F3 1 upper **2** higher
▸ *v* **1** DROP, depress, sink, descend, let down, let fall, take down **2** REDUCE, decrease, cut, lessen, diminish, curtail, slash, bring down, cheapen, *formal* abate **3** *lower your eyes* look down, move downwards, set down, bring low **4** *lower your voice* speak (more) quietly, quieten, hush **5** *not lower yourself by doing something* debase, belittle, degrade, demean, disgrace, dishonour, abase, *formal* disparage
F3 1 raise **2** increase **3** raise

lower² *see* LOUR.

lowering *see* LOURING.

low-grade *adj*
bad, inferior, poor, poor-quality, substandard, below standard, second-class, second-rate, third-rate, cheapjack, *colloq.* not up to scratch
F3 good, quality

low-key *adj*
muted, quiet, restrained, subdued, understated, easygoing, relaxed, subtle, slight, soft
F3 showy, impressive

lowly *adj*
humble, low-born, obscure, poor, plebeian, plain, simple, common, modest, ordinary, inferior, junior, low-ranking, peasant, meek, mild, mean, submissive, subordinate, unimportant
F3 lofty, noble, pretentious

low-pitched *adj*
deep, low, bass, resonant, sonorous, rich
F3 high, high-pitched

low-spirited *adj*
depressed, gloomy, heavy-hearted, low, down-hearted, despondent, dejected, discouraged, sad, unhappy, miserable, moody, glum, *colloq.* down, fed up, cheesed off, down in the dumps
F3 high-spirited, cheerful

loyal *adj*
true, faithful, steadfast, staunch, devoted, constant, firm, unchanging, trustworthy, truehearted, trusty, reliable, dependable, dedicated, committed, sincere, patriotic
F3 disloyal, treacherous

loyalty *n*
allegiance, faithfulness, fidelity, devotion, dedication,

commitment, staunchness, steadfastness, constancy, trustworthiness, reliability, dependability, sincerity, patriotism
F3 disloyalty, treachery

lozenge *n*
pastille, gumdrop, tablet, cough-drop, jujube, *technical* troche, trochiscus, trochisk

lubber *n*
oaf, boor, dolt, barbarian, yahoo, gawk, lout, *colloq.* clod, clodhopper, hick, hobbledehoy, slob, yob, yobbo, bumpkin

lubberly *adj*
clumsy, awkward, blundering, gawky, ungainly, heavy-handed, bungling, churlish, loutish, oafish, uncouth, doltish, lumbering, clownish, lumpish, coarse, dense, crude, *colloq.* clodhopping

lubricant *n*
oil, grease, lubrication, fat, lard

lubricate *v*
oil, grease, smear, wax, polish, make smooth, lard

lucid *adj*
1 *lucid writing* CLEAR, comprehensible, plain, explicit, distinct, intelligible, obvious, evident **2** CLEAR-HEADED, sane, rational, reasonable, intelligible, sensible, sober, sound, of sound mind, compos mentis **3** SHINING, bright, brilliant, beaming, transparent, translucent, gleaming, radiant, glassy, luminous, resplendent, crystalline, pure, *formal* diaphanous, effulgent, limpid, pellucid
F3 1 unclear **2** unintelligible **3** dark, murky

luck *n*
1 CHANCE, fortune, accident, fate, the stars, hazard, destiny, *formal* fortuity, predestination, *colloq.* fluke **2** GOOD FORTUNE, good luck, success, prosperity, godsend, *colloq.* break
F3 1 design **2** misfortune
▷ **in luck** fortunate, happy, favoured, successful, advantaged, timely, opportune, *formal* auspicious, *colloq.* jammy
▷ **out of luck** unlucky, unfortunate, luckless, hapless, unsuccessful, disadvantaged, *formal* inauspicious, *colloq.* down on your luck

luckily *adv*
as luck would have it, by good luck, by chance, by accident, fortunately, happily, providentially, *formal* fortuitously
F3 unfortunately

luckless *adj*
unlucky, unfortunate, hopeless, ill-fated, ill-starred, jinxed, cursed, doomed, hapless, star-crossed, miserable, unhappy, unsuccessful, disastrous, calamitous, catastrophic, *formal* unpropitious
F3 lucky, fortunate

lucky *adj*
fortunate, in luck, promising, favoured, charmed, successful, prosperous, timely, opportune, expedient, providential, *formal* auspicious, fortuitous, propitious, *colloq.* jammy
F3 unlucky

lucrative *adj*
profitable, well-paid, remunerative, profit-making, money-making, high-paying, gainful, productive, financially rewarding, advantageous, worthwhile
F3 unprofitable

lucre *n*
money, cash, riches, wealth, profit(s), gain(s), proceeds, winnings, pay, income, remuneration, spoils, mammon, *slang* dough, dosh, bread

ludicrous *adj*
absurd, ridiculous, preposterous, nonsensical, laugh-

lug
able, farcical, silly, comical, comic, humorous, amusing, hilarious, funny, droll, outlandish, zany, odd, eccentric, *formal* risible, *colloq.* crazy
🖅 serious

lug *v*
pull, drag, haul, carry, bear, tow, tote, heave, tug, hump

luggage *n*
baggage, belongings, paraphernalia, *formal* impedimenta, *colloq.* gear, things, stuff

> **Types of luggage include:**
> case, suitcase, vanity-case, bag, holdall, portmanteau, valise, overnight-bag, kit-bag, flight bag, hand-luggage, travel bag, Gladstone bag, grip, rucksack, knapsack, haversack, backpack, briefcase, attaché case, portfolio, satchel, basket, hamper, trunk, chest, box.

lugubrious *adj*
melancholy, morose, gloomy, glum, sad, woeful, woebegone, sorrowful, sombre, serious, dismal, doleful, dreary, mournful, funereal, sepulchral
🖅 cheerful, jovial, merry

lukewarm *adj*
1 *lukewarm water* tepid, slightly warm, warmish, cool 2 HALF-HEARTED, cool, apathetic, tepid, indifferent, unenthusiastic, uninterested, unresponsive, unconcerned, impassive, Laodicean

lull *n, v*
▶ *n* calm, calmness, peace, quiet, tranquillity, stillness, let-up, pause, hush, silence
🖅 agitation
▶ *v* soothe, subdue, calm, silence, hush, pacify, quieten down, quiet, quell, still, allay, ease, compose, *formal* assuage
🖅 agitate

lullaby *n*
cradle song, *berceuse*

lumber¹ *n, v*
▶ *n* 1 *store away lumber* clutter, jumble, rubbish, refuse, bits and pieces, odds and ends, junk, trash 2 TIMBER, wood
▶ *v* burden, encumber, saddle, land, load, hamper, impose, charge

lumber² *v*
lumber round the house clump, shamble, plod, shuffle, stump, stamp, trundle, trudge, stumble

lumbering *adj*
awkward, clumsy, heavy-footed, ungainly, unwieldy, heavy, blundering, bumbling, lumpish, ponderous, hulking, massive, elephantine, bovine, *colloq.* like a bull in a china shop
🖅 agile, nimble

luminary *n*
expert, authority, leader, leading light, celebrity, VIP, dignitary, worthy, notable, personage, star, superstar, *colloq.* big name, bigwig

luminescent *adj*
glowing, bright, luminous, fluorescent, radiant, shining, *formal* effulgent, luciferous, phosphorescent

luminous *adj*
glowing, illuminated, lit, lighted, radiant, shining, dazzling, fluorescent, brilliant, lustrous, bright, *formal* luminescent, effulgent

lump¹ *n, v*
▶ *n* 1 MASS, cluster, clump, clod, ball, dab, wad, cluster, bunch, piece, chunk, cake, hunk, nugget, wedge 2 SWELLING, growth, bulge, bump, protuberance,
bruise, protrusion, tumour, carbuncle, *formal* tumescence
▶ *v* collect, mass, gather, put together, cluster, combine, pool, blend, fuse, coalesce, group, consolidate, unite, mix together, conglomerate

lump² *v*
like it or lump it put up with, bear (with), endure, tolerate, stand, suffer, swallow, take, brook, *Scot.* thole, *colloq.* stomach

lumpish *adj*
awkward, heavy, clumsy, ungainly, hulking, gawky, bungling, lumbering, lethargic, elephantine, stupid, dull-witted, oafish, boorish, doltish, obtuse, stolid

lumpy *adj*
clotted, curdled, bunched, bumpy, cloggy, knobbly, grainy, granular, *formal* nodous, nodose
🖅 even, smooth

lunacy *n*
madness, insanity, aberration, derangement, dementia, dementedness, mania, idiocy, imbecility, folly, foolishness, absurdity, nonsense, stupidity, preposterousness, outrageousness, irresponsibility, silliness, inanity, ridiculousness, illogicality, irrationality, senselessness, *formal* imprudence, *colloq.* craziness
🖅 sanity

lunatic *n, adj*
▶ *n* psychotic, psychopath, madman, madwoman, insane person, imbecile, maniac, manic-depressive, neurotic, *colloq.* loony, nutcase, nutter, fruitcake, psycho, headcase, oddball, *slang* dipstick
▶ *adj* mad, insane, deranged, psychotic, unbalanced, disturbed, demented, irrational, foolish, idiotic, absurd, stupid, illogical, nonsensical, senseless, silly, inane, *colloq.* crazy, bonkers, loony, loopy, nuts, nutty, daft, barmy, potty, hare-brained, crackpot, off your rocker, round the bend/twist
🖅 sane

lunch *n*
midday meal, luncheon, light lunch, ploughman's lunch, packed lunch, brunch, Sunday lunch, dinner

lunge *v, n*
▶ *v* thrust, jab, stab, pounce, plunge, pitch into, charge, dart, dash, dive, poke, strike (at), fall upon, grab (at), hit (at), leap, spring, bound
▶ *n* thrust, stab, pounce, charge, jab, poke, pass, cut, spring, plunge, leap, bound

lurch *v*
roll, rock, pitch, sway, swerve, veer, stagger, totter, stumble, reel, list

lure *v, n*
▶ *v* tempt, entice, draw, attract, allure, induce, decoy, seduce, ensnare, beguile, lead on, *formal* inveigle
▶ *n* temptation, enticement, attraction, draw, allurement, bait, decoy, inducement, seduction, *colloq.* carrot

lurid *adj*
1 SENSATIONAL, shocking, startling, explicit, graphic, exaggerated, melodramatic 2 MACABRE, gruesome, gory, ghastly, grisly, horrific, revolting 3 BRIGHTLY COLOURED, garish, glaring, loud, showy, vivid, brilliant, dazzling, intense
🖅 1 restrained 3 pale

lurk *v*
skulk, prowl, slink, lie in wait, crouch, lie low, hide, conceal yourself, snoop, sneak

luscious *adj*
1 *luscious food* delicious, juicy, succulent, appetizing, mouth-watering, sweet, tasty, savoury, *formal* delectable, *colloq.* scrumptious, yummy, morish 2 *a luscious blonde* attractive, beautiful, voluptuous, desirable,

gorgeous, sensuous, stunning, ravishing, sexy, *colloq.* smashing

lush *adj, n*
▸ *adj* **1** FLOURISHING, luxuriant, abundant, prolific, teeming, dense, overgrown, green, profuse, *formal* verdant **2** SUMPTUOUS, opulent, ornate, plush, rich, luxurious, grand, lavish, extravagant, palatial
▸ *n* drunk, drunkard, alcoholic, inebriated, drinker, hard drinker, heavy drinker, dipsomaniac, *colloq.* tippler, *slang* boozer, wino, alkie, dipso, soak, toper, sot

lust *n*
1 SENSUALITY, sexual desire, libido, sexual drive, lechery, licentiousness, lewdness, lasciviousness, *formal* concupiscence, prurience, *colloq.* randiness, raunchiness, horniness, the hots **2** CRAVING, desire, appetite, longing, passion, greed, greediness, covetousness, hunger, yearning, avidity, *formal* cupidity
▷ **lust after** desire, crave, yearn for, want, need, hunger for, thirst for, covet, long for

lustful *adj*
sensual, passionate, licentious, lewd, lascivious, lecherous, carnal, unchaste, wanton, craving, hankering, salacious, *formal* concupiscent, libidinous, prurient, cupidinous, *colloq.* horny, randy, raunchy

lustily *adv*
loudly, hard, robustly, strongly, vigorously, forcefully, powerfully, stoutly, with all your might, *formal* with might and main
🖬 weakly, feebly

lustiness *n*
power, robustness, sturdiness, vigour, health, healthiness, strength, energy, haleness, hardiness, toughness, stoutness, virility

lustre *n*
1 SHINE, gloss, sheen, gleam, glow, brilliance, brightness, radiance, sparkle, shimmer, resplendence, burnish, glitter, glint, *formal* refulgence, lambency **2** GLORY, honour, prestige, renown, distinction, fame, illustriousness, merit, credit

lustrous *adj*
bright, shiny, shining, glossy, glowing, dazzling, gleaming, glistening, glittering, shimmering, sparkling, twinkling, burnished, luminous, radiant, *formal* lambent
🖬 dull, lacklustre, matt

lusty *adj*
robust, strong, sturdy, vigorous, tough, hale, hearty, hale and hearty, healthy, blooming, energetic, lively, strapping, rugged, forceful, powerful, virile, *colloq.* gutsy
🖬 weak, feeble

luxuriance *n*
abundance, copiousness, lushness, denseness, rankness, fertility, lavishness, profusion, sumptuousness, richness, excess, exuberance, *formal* fecundity

luxuriant *adj*
1 ABUNDANT, prolific, lush, superabundant, sumptu-

ous, profuse, plentiful, plenteous, overflowing, ample, lavish, teeming, thriving, rich, riotous, rank, copious, dense, productive, fertile, *formal* fecund **2** ELABORATE, extravagant, fancy, ornate, flamboyant, flowery, opulent, excessive, rococo, baroque, *formal* florid
🖬 barren, infertile

📖 **luxuriant or luxurious** ?

Luxuriant means 'abundant, prolific, growing vigorously': *the luxuriant growth of the jungle plants.*
Luxurious means 'relating to luxury and riches, expensive': *a luxurious house.*

---

luxuriate *v*
delight, enjoy, revel, relish, savour, thrive, bask, abound, wallow, relax in, indulge, prosper, flourish, grow, bloom, burgeon, *colloq.* live in the lap of luxury, live off the fat of the land, live the life of Riley, live in clover, live on easy street, have a ball

luxurious *adj*
sumptuous, opulent, lavish, de luxe, magnificent, splendid, rich, expensive, costly, affluent, self-indulgent, pampered, comfortable, grand, well-appointed, *colloq.* plush, posh, cushy, glitzy, swanky
🖬 austere, spartan

luxury *n*
1 SUMPTUOUSNESS, opulence, hedonism, splendour, affluence, richness, expensiveness, costliness, magnificence, grandness, grandeur, pleasure, indulgence, self-indulgence, gratification, comfort, *colloq.* lap of luxury *life's little luxuries* EXTRAVAGANCE, satisfaction, extra, treat
🖬 **1** austerity **2** essential

lying *adj, n*
▸ *adj* deceitful, dishonest, false, untruthful, double-dealing, *formal* mendacious, dissembling, dissimulating, *colloq.* two-faced, crooked
🖬 honest, truthful
▸ *n* dishonesty, untruthfulness, deceit, falsity, perjury, falsification, fabrication, invention, double-dealing, *formal* duplicity, *colloq.* fibbing, white lies, crookedness
🖬 honesty, truthfulness

lynch *v*
hang, hang by the neck, execute, put to death, kill, *colloq.* string up

lyric *adj*
emotional, passionate, personal, subjective, direct, strong, poetic, musical

lyrical *adj*
1 POETIC, musical, romantic **2** ENTHUSIASTIC, emotional, rapturous, rhapsodic, ecstatic, effusive, passionate, carried away, expressive, impassioned, inspired

lyrics *n*
text, words, book, libretto

M

macabre *adj*
gruesome, chilling, grisly, grim, horrible, gory, horrific, frightful, frightening, terrifying, shocking, dreadful, morbid, ghostly, eerie, hideous, ghastly

mace *n*
rod, stick staff, club, cudgel

macerate *v*
soak, steep, soften, liquefy, mash, blend, pulp

Machiavellian *adj*
devious, crafty, designing, scheming, shrewd, sly, cunning, wily, artful, astute, calculating, deceitful, double-dealing, guileful, underhand, opportunist, foxy, intriguing, unscrupulous, *formal* perfidious

machination *n*
scheme, intrigue, plot, design, manoeuvre, conspiracy, tactic, wile, ruse, ploy, stratagem, trick, device, dodge, cabal, *formal* artifice, *colloq.* shenanigans

machine *n*
1 INSTRUMENT, device, contrivance, tool, contraption, mechanism, engine, motor, apparatus, appliance, gadget, hardware **2** AGENCY, organization, structure, instrument, tool, organ, vehicle, influence, catalyst, system, workings **3** AUTOMATON, robot, mechanical person, tool, mechanism, zombie, android

machine-gun *n*
See panel at WEAPONS.

machinery *n*
1 INSTRUMENTS, mechanism, tools, apparatus, equipment, tackle, gear, gadgetry

> **Types of heavy machinery include:**
> all-terrain fork lift, bulldozer, caterpillar tractor, combine harvester, concrete mixer, concrete pump, crane, crawler crane, crawler tractor, digger, dragline excavator, dredger, dumper, dump truck, dustcart, excavator, fertilizer spreader, fire appliance, fork-lift truck, gantry crane, grader, grapple, gritter, hydraulic bale loader, hydraulic shovel, JCB®, muck spreader, pick-up loader, pile-driver, platform hoist, riding mower, road roller, road-sweeping lorry, Rotovator®, silage harvester, snowplough, straw baler, threshing machine, tower crane, tracklayer, tractor, tractor-scraper, truck crane, wheel loader.

2 ORGANIZATION, channel(s), structure, system, procedure, workings, agency

machinist *n*
worker, operator, operative, factory hand, mechanic

machismo *n*
masculinity, maleness, manliness, virility, toughness, strength

macrocosm *n*
universe, solar system, cosmos, creation, world, planet, society, civilization, community, culture, humanity, totality, (single) entity, system
🖪 microcosm

mad *adj*
1 INSANE, lunatic, unbalanced, psychotic, deranged, maniacal, demented, out of your mind, out of your senses, of unsound mind, unhinged, crazed, unstable, *non compos mentis*, frenzied, manic **2** ANGRY, furious, enraged, raging, infuriated, incensed, irate, blazing, fuming, livid, hopping mad, seeing red, hot under the collar **3** IRRATIONAL, illogical, unreasonable, absurd, ludicrous, preposterous, foolish, foolhardy, idiotic, insane, stupid, silly, nonsensical, wild, *colloq.* crazy, daft, barmy, potty, hare-brained, crackbrained, crackpot **4** FANATICAL, enthusiastic, infatuated, ardent, zealous, devoted, fond, keen, avid, passionate, wild, *colloq.* crazy, daft, nuts **5** UNCONTROLLED, wild, frantic, furious, reckless, violent, energetic, intense, rapid, hasty, hurried, unrestrained, frenzied, abandoned, excited
🖪 **1** sane **2** calm **3** sensible **4** apathetic **5** controlled
▷ **like mad** energetically, quickly, furiously, wildly, frantically, hurriedly, enthusiastically, fanatically, zealously avidly

madcap *adj, n*
▶ *adj* foolhardy, rash, reckless, impulsive, silly, thoughtless, wild, lively, flighty, heedless, ill-advised, hotheaded, crazy, *formal* imprudent, *colloq.* bird-brained, hare-brained
▶ *n* adventurer, tearaway, hothead, daredevil, firebrand, fury, desperado, *colloq.* crackpot

madden *v*
anger, enrage, infuriate, incense, annoy, upset, agitate, exasperate, provoke, annoy, irritate, inflame, irk, vex, *colloq.* aggravate, bug, hassle, rub up the wrong way, get someone's blood up, make your blood boil, get on your nerves, get up your nose, get under your skin, get someone's goat, get on your wick, drive crazy/nuts, drive up the wall, drive round the bend/twist, get your back up, get your dander up
🖪 calm, pacify

maddening *adj*
infuriating, exasperating, annoying, troublesome, irritating, vexatious, galling, upsetting, disturbing

made-up *adj*
1 INVENTED, make-believe, unreal, untrue, false, fictional, imaginary, specious, fabricated, fairy-tale, mythical, *colloq.* trumped-up **2** WEARING MAKE-UP, painted, powdered, done up
🖪 **1** real, factual, true

madhouse *n*
1 BEDLAM, chaos, disarray, disorder, uproar, turmoil, pandemonium, Babel **2** MENTAL HOSPITAL, lunatic asylum, asylum, mental institution, psychiatric hospital, *colloq.* funny farm, loony bin, nut-house

madly *adv*
1 *he rolled his eyes madly* insanely, dementedly, hysterically, frenziedly, deliriously, wildly, distractedly, *colloq.* crazily **2** *madly cleaning up* wildly, excitedly, frantically, furiously, recklessly, violently, energetically, intensely, rapidly, hastily, fast, hurriedly **3** *madly in love* intensely, wildly, fervently, devotedly, devotedly **4** EXTREMELY, wildly, exceedingly, exceptionally, utterly, unreasonably

madman, madwoman *n*
lunatic, psychotic, psychopath, maniac, imbecile, *colloq.* loony, nutter, nut, crackpot, crank, headcase, nutcase, fruitcake, screwball, oddball, basket case, *US* hook, *slang* psycho

madness *n*
1 INSANITY, lunacy, dementia, psychosis, mental instability, mania, derangement, distraction, delusion, *colloq.* craziness

---

Some colloquial expressions used when talking about madness:

crazy, nuts, nutty, nutty as a fruitcake, barmy, bonkers, batty, crackers, dippy, daffy, bananas, loony, loopy, off the wall, needing your head examined, having bats in the belfry, barking (mad), Dagenham [= two stops up from Barking], doolally, have a few tiles missing, have a screw loose, have lost your marbles, lose your mind, mad as a hatter, mad as a March hare, not playing with a full deck, off your chump, off your head, off your rocker, off your trolley, out of your mind, out to lunch, round the bend, round the twist, running on three wheels, stir-crazy.

---

2 FURY, rage, raving, frenzy, hysteria, anger, agitation, exasperation, wrath, ire **3** FOLLY, craziness, irrationality, unreasonableness, insanity, stupidity, silliness, inanity, absurdity, nonsense, foolishness, foolhardiness, preposterousness, wildness, *colloq.* daftness **4** KEENNESS, enthusiuasm, ardour, craze, abandon, zeal, wildness, unrestraint, uproar, riot, passion, excitement, fanaticism, infatuation, intoxication
F3 **1** sanity **2** calmness **3** reasonableness

maelstrom *n*
confusion, disorder, turmoil, mess, pandemonium, tumult, uproar, bedlam, chaos, vortex, whirlpool, Charybdis

maestro *n*
expert, master, genius, prodigy, virtuoso, *colloq.* wizard, ace

magazine *n*
1 JOURNAL, periodical, publication, paper, weekly, monthly, quarterly, supplement, colour supplement **2** ARSENAL, storehouse, ammunition dump, depot, ordnance

magic *n, adj*
▶ *n* **1** SORCERY, enchantment, supernatural, occult, occultism, black magic, black art, witchcraft, wizardry, wonder-working, voodoo, hoodoo, magical powers, spell, curse, *formal* necromancy, thaumaturgy **2** CONJURING, illusion, sleight of hand, deception, trickery, legerdemain, *formal* prestidigitation **3** CHARM, fascination, glamour, enticement, allure, allurement, enchantment, magnetism, pull
▶ *adj* **1** SUPERNATURAL, occult, mysterious, demonic **2** CHARMING, enchanting, bewitching, fascinating, spellbinding, entrancing, captivating, irresistible, magnetic **3** WONDERFUL, excellent, great, tremendous, marvellous, *colloq.* terrific, smashing, brill, ace, *slang* mega, cool, wicked

magician *n*
1 SORCERER, miracle-worker, enchanter, wizard, witch, warlock, spellbinder, spellworker, wonderworker, *formal* necromancer, thaumaturge **2** CONJURER, illusionist, juggler **3** GENIUS, maestro, expert, master, virtuoso, *colloq.* wizard, ace

magisterial *adj*
authoritative, commanding, masterful, assertive, authoritarian, domineering, imperious, high-handed, dictatorial, lordly, overbearing, arrogant, despotic, *formal* peremptory, *colloq.* bossy

magistrate *n*
judge, justice, justice of the peace, JP, stipendiary, bailiff, tribune, aedile, *colloq.* beak

magnanimity *n*
generosity, liberality, open-handedness, benevolence, selflessness, unselfishness, charity, charitableness, big-heartedness, bountifulness, kindness, high-mindedness, nobility, philanthropy, altruism, mercy, forgiveness, largesse, *formal* beneficence, munificence
F3 meanness, vindictiveness

magnanimous *adj*
generous, liberal, open-handed, benevolent, selfless, charitable, big-hearted, bountiful, kind, kindly, noble, philanthropic, altruistic, unselfish, ungrudging, merciful, forgiving, *formal* beneficent, munificent
F3 mean

magnate *n*
tycoon, captain of industry, industrialist, mogul, entrepreneur, financier, plutocrat, baron, executive, personage, notable, leader, *colloq.* fat cat, moneybags, bigwig, big shot, big noise, big timer

magnet *n*
draw, bait, lure, allurement, charm, enticement, appeal, attraction, centre of attraction, focus, focal point, lodestone, solenoid
F3 repellent

magnetic *adj*
attractive, alluring, fascinating, appealing, enthralling, charming, engaging, mesmerizing, hypnotic, seductive, tempting, tantalizing, irresistible, entrancing, bewitching, enchanting, captivating, gripping, absorbing, charismatic
F3 repellent, repulsive

magnetism *n*
attraction, allure, fascination, enchantment, captivation, charm, temptation, seductiveness, lure, appeal, drawing power, draw, pull, hypnotism, mesmerism, charisma, grip, magic, power, spell

magnification *n*
1 ENLARGEMENT, amplification, increase, expansion, intensification, enhancement, inflation, heightening, deepening, dilation, build-up, boost, extolment, lionization, *formal* aggrandizement, augmentation **2** EXAGGERATION, dramatization, overemphasis, overstatement, overdoing, embellishment, embroidery
F3 **1** diminution, reduction

magnificence *n*
splendour, grandeur, impressiveness, glory, gorgeousness, brilliance, excellence, majesty, sumptuousness, nobility, luxuriousness, luxury, lavishness, pomp, stateliness, *formal* resplendence, opulence, sublimity
F3 modesty, plainness, simplicity

magnificent *adj*
splendid, grand, imposing, grandiose, impressive, striking, elegant, glorious, gorgeous, brilliant, dazzling, excellent, marvellous, wonderful, majestic, superb, sumptuous, noble, exalted, elegant, fine, lavish,

luxurious, rich, royal, stately, *formal* resplendent, opulent, august, sublime
F₃ modest, humble, poor

magnify *v*
1 ENLARGE, enlarge, amplify, increase, expand, intensify, enhance, boost, enhance, extend, greaten, heighten, broaden, deepen, dilate, build up **2** EXAGGERATE, dramatize, overemphasize, overplay, overstate, overdo, embellish, embroider, *colloq.* blow up, blow up out of all proportion, make a mountain out of a molehill
F₃ **1** reduce, diminish **2** belittle, play down

magniloquence *n*
pomposity, pretentiousness, bombast, loftiness, rhetoric, euphuism, turgidity, fustian, *formal* grandiloquence, orotundity
F₃ simplicity, straightforwardness

magniloquent *adj*
pompous, high-sounding, lofty, overblown, elevated, exalted, bombastic, fustian, high-flown, pretentious, rhetorical, declamatory, euphuistic, sonorous, turgid, stilted, *formal* grandiloquent, orotund
F₃ simple, straightforward

magnitude *n*
1 SIZE, extent, measure, amount, expanse, dimensions, mass, proportions, quantity, weight, volume, capacity, bulk, largeness, greatness, space, strength, amplitude **2** IMPORTANCE, consequence, significance, weight, greatness, eminence, fame, distinction, moment, note, intensity

magnum opus *n*
masterpiece, masterwork, chef d'oeuvre, *pièce de résistance*

maid *n*
servant, domestic, waitress, kitchenmaid, chambermaid, housemaid, girl, au pair, maidservant, servingmaid, lady's maid, handmaiden, soubrette, abigail, maid-of-all-work, *colloq.* skivvy

maiden *n, adj*
▶ *n* girl, young girl, young lady, young woman, virgin, lass, lassie, miss, nymph, *formal* damsel
▶ *adj* **1** *a maiden voyage* FIRST, inaugural, new, introductory, initial, initiatory **2** CHASTE, decent, demure, gentle, girlish, female, modest, proper, pure, reserved, undefiled, unsullied, unbroached, vestal, virgin, unmarried, unwed, virginal, virtuous, *formal* decorous
F₃ **2** defiled, deflowered, unchaste

maidenly *adj*
becoming, chaste, decent, demure, gentle, girlish, female, modest, proper, pure, reserved, undefiled, unsullied, unbroached, vestal, virgin, unmarried, unwed, virginal, virtuous, *formal* decorous
F₃ immodest

mail¹ *n, v*
▶ *n* **1** *deliver the mail* post, letters, correspondence, communications, packages, parcels, packets, delivery, registered mail, recorded mail, special delivery, direct mail, airmail, surface mail, international mail, electronic mail, e-mail, *colloq.* junk mail, snail mail **2** POSTAL SERVICE, postal system, post, Post Office
▶ *v* post, send, dispatch, forward

mail² *n*
chain mail armour, chain mail, iron-cladding, panoply, protective covering

maim *v*
mutilate, disfigure, wound, incapacitate, injure, disable, hurt, impair, mar, cripple, lame, put out of action

main *adj, n*
▶ *adj* principal, chief, leading, first, foremost, major,

key, predominant, dominant, pre-eminent, primary, most important, prime, premier, supreme, paramount, central, head, cardinal, outstanding, essential, critical, crucial, necessary, vital, fundamental, pivotal
F₃ minor, unimportant, insignificant
▶ *n* pipe, duct, conduit, channel, cable, line
▷ **in the main** chiefly, mostly, on the whole, for the most part, generally, in general, especially, as a rule, by and large, commonly, usually, largely

mainly *adv*
primarily, principally, chiefly, first and foremost, in the main, mostly, on the whole, for the most part, generally, in general, especially, as a rule, by and large, commonly, usually, above all, largely, overall

mainspring *n*
motive, motivation, cause, reason, driving force, impulse, incentive, inspiration, origin, prime mover, generator, source, fountainhead, wellspring

mainstay *n*
support, buttress, bulwark, linchpin, prop, pillar, anchor, backbone, foundation, basis, base

mainstream *adj*
normal, average, central, general, typical, regular, standard, conventional, established, orthodox, received, accepted, mainline
F₃ heterodox, peripheral, marginal

maintain *v*
1 CARRY ON, continue, keep (up), keep going, sustain, preserve, perpetuate, conserve, retain **2** CARE FOR, conserve, look after, keep (up), take care of, preserve, keep in good condition/repair **3** PROVIDE FOR, keep, support, finance, supply, feed, sustain, nourish, nurture **4** ASSERT, claim, profess, contend, declare, announce, hold, state, insist, believe, stand by, fight for, support, *formal* affirm, avow, aver, asseverate
F₃ **2** neglect **4** deny

maintenance *n*
1 CONTINUATION, continuance, carrying-on, preservation, conservation, perpetuation **2** CARE, conservation, preservation, support, repairs, protection, upkeep, running **3** KEEP, subsistence, feeding, sustenance, nourishment, nurture, living, livelihood, financing, support, upkeep, allowance, alimony, aliment
F₃ **2** neglect

majestic *adj*
magnificent, grand, glorious, dignified, distinguished, noble, royal, queenly, kingly, princely, lordly, stately, splendid, imperial, marvellous, impressive, elevated, exalted, awesome, imposing, regal, superb, lofty, monumental, pompous, *formal* resplendent, sublime, august
F₃ lowly, unimpressive, unimposing

majesty *n*
grandeur, grandness, glory, dignity, magnificence, beauty, awesomeness, nobility, nobleness, royalty, regality, splendour, stateliness, pomp, exaltedness, impressiveness, loftiness, *formal* resplendence, sublimity

major *adj*
greater, chief, main, larger, bigger, higher, leading, outstanding, notable, supreme, prime, paramount, uppermost, significant, crucial, important, serious, key, keynote, great, senior, older, superior, pre-eminent, vital, weighty
F₃ minor, unimportant, trivial

majority *n*
1 BULK, mass, preponderance, (the) many, most, greater/larger part, more than half, nearly all, *colloq.* lion's share **2** ADULTHOOD, maturity, manhood, wo-

manhood, legal age, age of consent, years of discretion

 1 minority

make *v, n*

▶ *v* **1** CREATE, manufacture, mass-produce, fabricate, construct, assemble, build, erect, produce, turn out, put together, put up, originate, compose, form, shape, fashion, mould, model **2** CAUSE, bring about, produce, accomplish, occasion, create, give rise to, engender, generate, render, perform, *formal* effect **3** CARRY OUT, accomplish, achieve, do, perform, undertake, discharge, *formal* effect, execute, *colloq.* deliver (the goods), get down to, wrap up **4** COERCE, force, urge, oblige, constrain, compel, impel, prevail upon, pressure, pressurize, press, drive, require, dragoon, *colloq.* bulldoze, strongarm, put the screws on **5** APPOINT, vote in, elect, select, designate, nominate, name, ordain, install, create, vote **6** COMPOSE, create, write, arrange, prepare, produce, devise, think up, form, formulate, frame, construct, draw up **7** EARN, gain, net, gross, obtain, acquire, get, bring in, secure, win, take home, clear, *formal* realize **8** CONSTITUTE, compose, comprise, add up to, amount to, come to, total **9** SCORE, gain, chalk up, *colloq.* notch up **10** PREPARE, get ready, put together, cook, *US colloq.* fix **11** CALCULATE, work out, compute, reckon (up), estimate **12** SERVE AS, have the qualifications for, become, act as, play the role/part of, achieve

 1 dismantle **7** spend, lose

▷ **make away with 1** STEAL, run off with, walk off with, snatch, seize, carry off, kidnap; *colloq.* pinch, lift, nick, nab, swipe **2** KILL, do away with, murder, slaughter, assassinate, *colloq.* do in, knock off, bump off

▷ **make believe** pretend, play, play-act, imagine, dream, enact, fantasize, act, *formal* feign, *colloq.* make castles in the air

▷ **make do** cope, manage, survive, get along, get by, improvise, make out, muddle through, *colloq.* scrape by, make the best of a bad job, keep your head above water

▷ **make for 1** HEAD FOR, aim for, go towards, move towards **2** PRODUCE, lead to, promote, contribute to, facilitate, favour, forward, further, be conducive to

▷ **make it** succeed, be successful, get on, come through, arrive, pull through, reach, survive, prosper

 fail

▷ **make off** run off, run away, depart, bolt, leave, fly, *colloq.* cut and run, beat a hasty retreat, clear off, make a getaway, take to your heels, skedaddle, scarper, beat it

▷ **make off with** run off with, carry off, steal, swipe, walk off with, pilfer, kidnap, abduct, *formal* appropriate, purloin, *colloq.* filch, knock off, nab, nick, pinch

▷ **make out 1** DISCERN, manage to see/hear, perceive, decipher, distinguish, recognize, see, detect, discover **2** UNDERSTAND, work out, grasp, comprehend, follow, fathom **3** DRAW UP, complete, fill in, write out **4** MAINTAIN, imply, claim, assert, declare, describe, demonstrate, prove, establish, *formal* affirm, aver **5** MANAGE, get on, get along, get by, cope, progress, succeed, *formal* fare **6** WRITE OUT, fill in/out, complete

▷ **make over** transfer, sign over, convey, assign, bequeath, leave

▷ **make up 1** CREATE, invent, devise, fabricate, construct, originate, formulate, frame, dream up, compose, think up, concoct, hatch **2** COMPLETE, fill, supply, provide, meet, supplement, round off **3** COMPRISE, constitute, compose, form **4** BE RECONCILED, make peace, settle differences, become friends again, shake hands, repent, *colloq.* bury the hatchet, forgive

and forget, call it quits **5** PUT MAKE-UP ON, powder, rouge, perfume, paint, *colloq.* put on your face, doll up, tart up

▷ **make up for** compensate for, make amends for, make recompense for, offset, redress, *formal* atone for

▷ **make up to** curry favour with, toady to, court, fawn on, butter up, make overtures to, *colloq.* chat up

▷ **make up your mind** decide, choose, determine, resolve, settle

 waver

▷ **make way** allow to pass, make room/space for, stand back for, not stand in the way of, allow to succeed

▶ *n* brand, sort, type, style, variety, manufacture, model, mark, kind, form, structure

make-believe *n, adj*

▶ *n* pretence, imagination, fantasy, unreality, fabrication, play-acting, role-play, dream, dreaming, daydreaming, masquerade, charade

 reality

▶ *adj* imaginary, imagined, made-up, imitated, pretended, fantasy, fantasized, dream, simulated, unreal, mock, sham, *formal* feigned, *colloq.* pretend

 real

maker *n*

creator, manufacturer, constructor, builder, producer, director, architect, author, fabricator

makeshift *adj*

temporary, improvised, rough and ready, thrown together, cobbled together, provisional, substitute, stopgap, stand-by, expedient, make-do

 permanent

make-up *n*

1 COSMETICS, paint, powder, greasepaint, maquillage, *colloq.* war paint. *See panel at* COSMETICS. **2** CONSTITUTION, nature, composition, character, construction, form, format, formation, arrangement, organization, style, structure, assembly, *formal* configuration **3** PERSONALITY, temperament, temper, nature, character, disposition, style

making *n*

1 PRODUCTION, producing, creation, creating, manufacture, assembly, building, composition, construction, fabrication, modelling, moulding, forging **2** POTENTIAL, qualities, potentiality, promise, capability, capacity, possibilities, beginnings, materials, ingredients **3** EARNINGS, income, profits, proceeds, revenue, returns, takings

 1 dismantling

▷ **in the making** budding, potential, promising, coming, developing, emergent, up and coming, *formal* nascent, burgeoning, incipient

maladjusted *adj*

disturbed, unstable, confused, alienated, disordered, neurotic, *formal* estranged, *colloq.* dotty, round the bend, screwed-up, *slang* schizo, psycho, gaga

 well-adjusted, *colloq.* together

maladministration *n*

inefficiency, incompetence, mismanagement, mishandling, misrule, blundering, bungling, misgovernment, misconduct, corruption, dishonesty, malpractice, stupidity, *technical* malfeasance, misfeasance, *formal* malversation

maladroit *adj*

clumsy, awkward, bungling, unskilful, unhandy, gauche, graceless, inelegant, inept, inexpert, tactless, insensitive, thoughtless, inconsiderate, undiplomatic, ill-timed, *formal* untoward, *colloq.* cack-handed, ham-fisted

 1 skilful **2** adroit, tactful

malady *n*
illness, disease, sickness, complaint, infirmity, ailment, disorder, breakdown, *formal* affliction, malaise, indisposition

malaise *n*
uneasiness, unease, discontent, depression, discomfort, disquiet, weariness, anxiety, anguish, doldrums, *angst*, illness, disease, sickness, weakness, *formal* lassitude, melancholy, indisposition, enervation
☒ happiness, well-being

malapropism *n*
wrong word, misuse, misapplication, solecism, error, slip of the tongue

malapropos *adj, adv*
▶ *adj* inappropriate, unsuitable, untimely, ill-timed, inopportune, misapplied, inapt, uncalled-for, tactless, *formal* inapposite, unseemly
☒ appropriate, tactful
▶ *adv* inappropriately, unsuitably, inaptly, unseasonably, tactlessly, inopportunely, *formal* inappositely
☒ appropriately, tactfully

malcontent *n, adj*
▶ *n* grumbler, complainer, moaner, rebel, agitator, mischief-maker, troublemaker, *colloq.* belly-acher, grouch, grouser, nit-picker, whinger
▶ *adj* dissatisfied, unhappy, unsatisfied, discontented, disgruntled, ill-disposed, disaffected, morose, rebellious, fault-finding, resentful, *formal* restive, dissentious, *colloq.* belly-aching
☒ contented

male *adj*
masculine, manly, virile, boyish, he-, manlike
☒ female

> Male terms include:
> boy, lad, youth, man, gentleman, *colloq.* gent, bachelor, *colloq.* fellow, *colloq.* chap, *colloq.* bloke, *colloq.* guy, son, brother, boyfriend, beau, *colloq.* toy boy, fiancé, bridegroom, husband, father, uncle, nephew, grandfather, patriarch, godfather, widower; bull, dog, buck, tup, cock, cockerel, stallion, billy-goat, boar, dog fox, stag, ram, tom cat, drake, gander.

malediction *n*
curse, cursing, denunciation, anathema, anathematization, damnation, damning, *formal* execration, imprecation, malison
☒ blessing, praise

malefactor *n*
law-breaker, criminal, offender, felon, convict, outlaw, delinquent, wrongdoer, evildoer, culprit, villain, *technical* misfeasor, *formal* miscreant, transgressor, *colloq.* crook

malevolence *n*
malice, malignancy, malignity, maliciousness, spite, spitefulness, vindictiveness, vengefulness, ill-will, hostility, unfriendliness, hate, hatred, bitterness, venom, viciousness, fierceness, balefulness, cruelty, *formal* rancour
☒ benevolence

malevolent *adj*
malicious, malign, spiteful, vindictive, vengeful, ill-natured, hostile, unfriendly, bitter, resentful, vicious, fierce, cruel, venomous, pernicious, evil-minded, *formal* rancorous, baleful, maleficent
☒ benevolent, kind

malformation *n*
deformity, misshapenness, disfigurement, irregularity, distortion, warp

malformed *adj*
deformed, misshapen, irregular, disfigured, distorted, twisted, warped, crooked, bent
☒ perfect

malfunction *v, n*
▶ *v* break down, go wrong, fail, stop working, *colloq.* go kaput, pack up, *slang* conk out
▶ *n* fault, defect, failure, breakdown, flaw, impairment, glitch

malice *n*
maliciousness, enmity, hostility, animosity, ill-will, hatred, hate, bad blood, spite, vindictiveness, venom, spleen, bitterness, resentment, *formal* malevolence, animus, rancour, *colloq.* bone to pick, bloody-mindedness, bitchiness
☒ love

malicious *adj*
ill-natured, hostile, malign, spiteful, venomous, vicious, vengeful, evil, evil-minded, pernicious, bitter, resentful, *formal* malevolent, baleful, rancorous
☒ friendly, kind

malign *v, adj*
▶ *v* defame, slander, libel, abuse, harm, injure, insult, *formal* disparage, calumniate, vilify, traduce, *colloq.* run down, smear, slur, badmouth, stab in the back, kick in the teeth, drag through the mud
☒ praise
▶ *adj* harmful, malignant, bad, evil, hurtful, injurious, destructive, hostile, *formal* malevolent
☒ benign, kind

malignant *adj*
1 EVIL, hostile, malicious, spiteful, vicious, venomous, spiteful, destructive, harmful, hurtful, pernicious, *formal* malevolent, rancorous 2 FATAL, deadly, lethal, incurable, dangerous, life-threatening, cancerous, uncontrollable, virulent
☒ 1 kind 2 benign

malignity *n*
malice, maliciousness, harmfulness, hate, hurtfulness, ill-will, hatred, bad blood, bitterness, deadliness, perniciousness, gall, destructiveness, hostility, wickedness, vengefulness, vindictiveness, spite, venom, viciousness, animosity, *formal* animus, balefulness, malevolence, rancour
☒ harmlessness, kindness

malinger *v*
pretend, pretend to be ill, slack, *colloq.* dodge, loaf, shirk, skive, put it on, swing the lead
☒ work

malingerer *n*
slacker, *colloq.* dodger, loafer, shirker, skiver, lead-swinger
☒ worker

mall *n*
shopping centre, shopping precinct, galleria, plaza

malleable *adj*
1 SUPPLE, plastic, pliable, pliant, flexible, soft, workable, *formal* ductile 2 IMPRESSIONABLE, manageable, receptive, flexible, susceptible, persuadable, pliant, pliable, adaptable, biddable, governable, *formal* compliant, tractile, tractable
☒ 1 rigid 2 *formal* intractable

malnutrition *n*
starvation, undernourishment, underfeeding, hunger, unhealthy diet, anorexia (nervosa), *formal* inanition
☒ nourishment

malodorous *adj*
foul-smelling, evil-smelling, fetid, nauseating, niffy, offensive, putrid, rank, reeking, smelly, stinking,

formal noisomemephitic, miasmal, miasmatic, miasmatous, miasmic, miasmous,
🖃 sweet-smelling

malpractice *n*
misconduct, unethical behaviour, unprofessional conduct, mismanagement, negligence, carelessness, impropriety, wrongdoing, offence, abuse, misdeed, *formal* dereliction of duty

maltreat *v*
mistreat, ill-treat, treat badly, misuse, abuse, injure, harm, damage, hurt, bully, hound, victimize, torture
🖃 care for

maltreatment *n*
mistreatment, ill-treatment, ill-usage, ill-use, abuse, misuse, injury, harm, damage, hurt, bullying, victimization, torture
🖃 care

mammal *n*

Mammals include:
aardvark, African black rhinoceros, African elephant, anteater, antelope, armadillo, baboon, Bactrian camel, badger, bat, bear, beaver, bushbaby, cat, chimpanzee, chipmunk, cow, deer, dog, dolphin, duck-billed platypus, dugong, echidna, flying lemur, fox, gerbil, gibbon, giraffe, goat, gorilla, guinea pig, hamster, hare, hedgehog, hippopotamus, horse, human being, hyena, Indian elephant, kangaroo, koala, lemming, leopard, lion, manatee, marmoset, marmot, marsupial mouse, mole, mouse, opossum, orang utan, otter, pig, porcupine, porpoise, rabbit, raccoon, rat, sea cow, sea lion, seal, sheep, shrew, sloth, squirrel, tamarin, tapir, tiger, vole, wallaby, walrus, weasel, whale, wolf, zebra. *See also* CAT; CATTLE; DOG; HORSE; MARSUPIAL; MONKEY; RODENT.

mammoth *adj*
enormous, huge, vast, colossal, gigantic, giant, massive, immense, stupendous, monumental, mighty, prodigious, gargantuan, herculean, leviathan, Brobdingnagian, *colloq.* whopping, jumbo, bumper, ginormous
🖃 tiny, minute

man *n, v*
▸ *n* **1** MALE, gentleman, *colloq.* guy, chap, bloke, boy, lad, fellow **2** HUMAN BEING, person, individual, adult, human, mortal **3** HUMANITY, human race, human beings, humankind, mankind, people, *Homo sapiens*, mortals **4** MANSERVANT, servant, worker, workman, labourer, employee, helper, hand, soldier, valet, houseman, houseboy, page, attendant, factotum, man-of-all-work, jack-of-all-trades, odd-jobman **5** PARTNER, husband, lover, boyfriend, spouse, *colloq.* fellow, bloke, guy, toy boy
▷ **to a man** without exception, unanimously, as one, with one voice, one and all, bar none
▸ *v* staff, crew, take charge of, be in charge of, work, operate, occupy

manacle *v*
handcuff, shackle, restrain, fetter, chain, put in chains, bind, curb, check, hamper, inhibit
🖃 free, unshackle

manacles *n*
handcuffs, chains, fetters, cuffs, shackles, wristlets, irons, bonds, *colloq.* bracelets, darbies

manage *v*
1 ADMINISTER, direct, run, organize, command, govern, be in charge of, be responsible for, head (up), be

head of, lead, guide, preside over, rule, superintend, supervise, control, oversee, conduct **2** ACCOMPLISH, succeed, achieve, bring about, bring off, engineer, *formal* effect **3** CONTROL, influence, deal with, master, handle, operate, manipulate, work, guide, use, wield **4** COPE, deal with, survive, get by, get along, get on, make do, *formal* fare, *colloq.* make out
🖃 **1** mismanage **2** fail

manageable *adj*
1 *a manageable amount of work* reasonable, doable, feasible, attainable, practicable, acceptable, viable, tolerable **2** CONTROLLABLE, governable, amenable, accommodating, yielding, submissive, docile, pliant, pliable, flexible, *formal* tractable
🖃 **1, 2** unmanageable

management *n*
1 ADMINISTRATION, direction, control, government, command, leadership, organization, running, ruling, overseeing, superintendence, supervision, charge, care, handling, conduct **2** MANAGERS, directors, directorate, executive, executives, governors, board, owners, employers, proprietors, supervisors, *colloq.* bosses
🖃 **1** mismanagement **2** workers

manager *n*
director, executive, employer, president, chairman, chief executive, managing director, administrator, controller, superintendent, supervisor, commissioner, overseer, governor, organizer, head, chief, head of department, comptroller, *colloq.* boss, gaffer, guv, *US* honcho

mandate *n*
order, command, decree, edict, injunction, dictate, charge, directive, direction, ordinance, ruling, law, statute, bidding, warrant, authorization, authority, instruction, commission, sanction

mandatory *adj*
obligatory, compulsory, binding, required, necessary, essential, imperative, *formal* requisite
🖃 optional

manful *adj*
brave, manly, gallant, courageous, heroic, intrepid, bold, lion-hearted, determined, resolute, stalwart, stout, stout-hearted, valiant, strong, powerful, indomitable, hardy, daring, unflinching, vigorous, noble, noble-minded
🖃 half-hearted, timid

manfully *adv*
bravely, courageously, valiantly, heroically, intrepidly, boldly, gallantly, pluckily, determinedly, hard, vigorously, strongly, powerfully, unflinchingly, desperately, resolutely, stalwartly, stoutly, steadfastly, nobly
🖃 half-heartedly, timidly

manger *n*
trough, feeding trough, feeder, crib

mangle *v*
1 MUTILATE, disfigure, mar, maim, butcher, destroy, deform, wreck, twist, maul, distort, crush, cut, hack, tear, lacerate, rend **2** SPOIL, butcher, ruin, bungle, *colloq.* botch, mess up, make a mess of, *slang* screw up

mangy *adj*
seedy, shabby, scruffy, scabby, shoddy, moth-eaten, worn, filthy, dirty, mean, *colloq.* tatty

manhandle *v*
1 *the porters manhandled the baggage* haul, heave, pull, push, shove, tug, *colloq.* hump **2** *the police manhandled the demonstrators* maul, mistreat, maltreat, misuse, abuse, handle roughly, push, shove, *colloq.* knock about, rough up

manhood *n*
1 ADULTHOOD, maturity 2 MASCULINITY, virility, manliness, manfulness, maleness, *colloq.* machismo

mania *n*
1 MADNESS, insanity, lunacy, dementia, psychosis, derangement, disorder, aberration, frenzy, wildness, raving, hysteria, *colloq.* craziness

Manias (by name of disorder) include:
dipsomania (*alcohol*), bibliomania (*books*), ailuromania (*cats*), demomania (*crowds*), thanatomania (*death*), cynomania (*dogs*), narcomania (*drugs*), pyromania (*fire-raising*), anthomania (*flowers*), hippomania (*horses*), mythomania (*lying and exaggerating*), egomania (*yourself*), ablutomania (*personal cleanliness*), hedonomania (*pleasure*), megalomania (*power*), theomania (*religion*), monomania (*single idea or thing*), kleptomania (*stealing*), tomomania (*surgery*), logomania (*talking*), ergomania (*work*). *See also* PHOBIA.

2 PASSION, craze, rage, obsession, compulsion, fetish, preoccupation, enthusiasm, infatuation, fixation, craving, urge, desire, fascination, *colloq.* fad

maniac *n*
1 LUNATIC, madman, madwoman, psychotic, psychopath, deranged person, *colloq.* loony, nutter, nut, nutcase, fruitcake, crackpot, crank, headcase, *US* hook, *slang* screwball, oddball, psycho 2 ENTHUSIAST, fan, fanatic, *colloq.* fiend, freak

manifest *adj, v*
▶ *adj* obvious, evident, clear, apparent, plain, open, patent, distinct, noticeable, conspicuous, perceptible, glaring, blatant, unmistakable, visible, unconcealed, transparent
☒ unclear
▶ *v* show, exhibit, display, demonstrate, reveal, set forth, present, express, declare, indicate, expose, make clear/plain, prove, illustrate, establish, *formal* evince
☒ conceal, hide

manifestation *n*
display, exhibition, demonstration, show, presentation, declaration, revelation, exposure, disclosure, appearance, expression, illustration, exemplification, evidence, sign, indication, token, mark, *formal* exposition

manifesto *n*
statement, declaration, announcement, proclamation, publication, policies, platform

manifold *adj*
many, several, numerous, varied, various, diverse, multiple, kaleidoscopic, abundant, copious, *formal* multifarious, multitudinous

manipulate *v*
1 MANOEUVRE, influence, control, exploit, work, engineer, guide, direct, steer, use/turn to your advantage, negotiate, capitalize on, *colloq.* wangle, cash in on, pull strings, have in the palm of your hand, twist round your little finger, have over a barrel, wheel and deal, frame, fit up 2 FALSIFY, rig, juggle with, massage, tamper with, distort, alter, *colloq.* doctor, cook, fiddle 3 HANDLE, control, wield, operate, work, knead, use, utilize, employ, process, ply

manipulator *n*
1 EXPLOITER, puller of strings, puppet master, puppeteer, controller, manoeuvrer, influencer, schemer, engineer, director, negotiator, *colloq.* wheeler-dealer, smoothy, smart guy 2 HANDLER, operator, user, worker, controller, wielder

mankind *n*
human race, humanity, human beings, humankind, man, *Homo sapiens*, people, mortals

manliness *n*
masculinity, maleness, virility, manfulness, bravery, boldness, courage, valour, fearlessness, heroism, intrepidity, resolution, stout-heartedness, stalwartness, hardihood, independence, manhood, strength, vigour, mettle, firmness, *formal* fortitude, *colloq.* machismo
☒ timidity, unmanliness

manly *adj*
masculine, male, virile, manful, brave, courageous, bold, intrepid, fearless, heroic, determined, strong, powerful, firm, tough, rugged, vigorous, sturdy, robust, *colloq.* macho

man-made *adj*
synthetic, manufactured, simulated, imitation, artificial, *colloq.* ersatz
☒ natural

manner *n*
1 WAY, method, means, fashion, style, variety, procedure, technique, approach, practice, process, routine, form, *formal* mode 2 BEHAVIOUR, conduct, appearance, look, character, attitude, posture, stance, *formal* bearing, demeanour, air, mien, aspect, deportment 3 *good manners* behaviour, conduct, way of behaving, etiquette, politeness, courtesy, protocol, good form, formalities, social graces, *formal* decorum, propriety, demeanour, bearing, *colloq.* p's and q's, the done thing

mannered *adj*
artificial, posed, pretentious, stilted, precious, *formal* affected, euphuistic, *colloq.* pseudo, put-on
☒ natural

mannerism *n*
idiosyncrasy, peculiarity, characteristic, quirk, trait, feature, foible, habit

mannerly *adj*
polite, courteous, refined, well-behaved, well-bred, well-mannered, gentlemanly, ladylike, respectful, civil, civilized, deferential, gracious, formal, genteel, polished, *formal* decorous
☒ unmannerly

mannish *adj*
masculine, unfeminine, unladylike, unwomanly, tomboyish, viraginian, viraginous, viragoish, Amazonian, *formal* virilescent, *colloq.* butch, laddish
☒ womanish

mannishness *n*
masculinity, unfemininity, unladylikeness, unwomanliness, virilism, *formal* virilescence, *colloq.* butchness
☒ womanishness

manoeuvre *v, n*
▶ *v* 1 MOVE, manipulate, handle, guide, pilot, steer, navigate, negotiate, jockey, direct, drive, exercise 2 CONTRIVE, engineer, plot, scheme, intrigue, manipulate, manage, plan, devise, negotiate, *colloq.* wangle, pull strings, jockey for position
▶ *n* 1 EXERCISE, move, movement, operation, deployment, action 2 MANIPULATION, skilful plan, ploy, plot, ruse, stratagem, device, gambit, tactic, trick, scheme, subterfuge, *formal* machination, artifice, *colloq.* dodge, wangle

manor *n*
house, country house, seat, hall, villa, barony, château, Schloss, Hof

manse *n*
vicarage, rectory, parsonage, deanery, glebe-house

manservant *n*
  butler, gentleman's gentleman, valet, retainer

mansion *n*
  home, hall, house, manor, manor-house, castle, château, Schloss, villa, seat, *formal* abode, dwelling, habitation, residence

manslaughter *n*
  killing, slaughter, murder, massacre, butchery, genocide, homicide, assassination, execution, slaying, extermination, carnage, bloodshed, elimination, destruction, fatality, *formal* patricide, matricide, infanticide, fratricide, sororicide, uxoricide, *colloq.* liquidation

mantle *n, v*
  ▶ *n* 1 CLOAK, cape, hood, shawl, veil, wrap, shroud, screen 2 COVER, covering, veil, shroud, blanket, layer, cloak, mask, cloud, envelope
  ▶ *v* cover, cloak, veil, mask, wrap, blanket, shroud, cloud, envelop, hide, disguise, conceal

manual *n, adj*
  ▶ *n* handbook, guide, guidebook, instruction book, instructions, ABC, companion, bible, prospectus, vade-mecum, directions, *colloq.* book of words
  ▶ *adj* hand-operated, by hand, (done) with your hands, physical, human
  ◪ mental, automatic

manufacture *v, n*
  ▶ *v* 1 MAKE, produce, construct, build, fabricate, create, assemble, mass-produce, put together, turn out, fashion, process, forge, model, form 2 INVENT, make up, devise, construct, frame, concoct, fabricate, think up, dream up
  ▶ *n* production, making, construction, building, fabrication, mass-production, assembly, processing, creation, formation, fashioning, modelling, forming

manufacturer *n*
  maker, producer, industrialist, constructor, factory-owner, builder, creator

manure *n*
  fertilizer, compost, muck, dung, animal excrement, droppings, guana, ordure, *formal* animal faeces

manuscript *n*
  document, text, paper, parchment, scroll, vellum

many *adj, n*
  ▶ *adj* a lot of, a large number of, several, numerous, innumerable, countless, various, multiple, copious, varied, sundry, diverse, *formal* manifold, multitudinous, *colloq.* lots of, umpteen, scores, hundreds, thousands, millions, billions, zillions, masses, piles, heaps, stacks, oodles, scads, wads, tons
  ◪ few
  ▶ *n* a lot, a large number of people/things, a mass, a multitude, plenty, *colloq.* lots of, umpteen, scores, hundreds, thousands, millions, billions, zillions, masses, piles, heaps, stacks, oodles, scads, wads, tons

map *n, v*
  ▶ *n* chart, plan, town plan, street plan, street guide, road-map, atlas, gazetteer, graph, plot
  ▶ *v* chart, plot, plan, mark, sketch, *formal* delineate
  ▷ **map out** sketch, draw (up), draft, outline, work out

mar *v*
  spoil, impair, harm, hurt, damage, blemish, deface, deform, disfigure, mutilate, injure, maim, scar, detract from, mangle, ruin, wreck, taint, tarnish, contaminate, stain
  ◪ enhance

maraud *v*
  plunder, raid, ravage, ransack, loot, pillage, harry, forage, foray, sack, *formal* despoil, spoliate, depredate

marauder *n*
  bandit, brigand, robber, raider, plunderer, looter, pillager, pirate, buccaneer, freebooter, outlaw, highwayman, ravager, predator, rustler, rover

march *v, n*
  ▶ *v* walk, file, parade, pace, step, tread, stride, tramp, hike, stalk, strut, swagger, forward, advance, progress, make headway
  ▶ *n* 1 STEP, pace, stride, walk, gait 2 WALK, route-march, trek, hike, tramp, *colloq.* footslog 3 PROCESSION, parade, demonstration, *colloq.* demo 4 ADVANCE, development, progress, evolution, passage, headway, evolution

margin *n*
  1 BORDER, edge, boundary, bound, periphery, perimeter, frontier, demarcation line, rim, brim, brink, limit(s), confine(s), verge, side, skirt 2 ALLOWANCE, play, leeway, latitude, scope, room, room for manoeuvre, difference, differential, space, surplus, extra

marginal *adj*
  borderline, doubtful, peripheral, on the edge, negligible, minute, minimal, insignificant, minor, slight, tiny, low, small
  ◪ central, core, mainstream

marijuana *n*
  cannabis, hemp, hashish, bhang, *colloq.* dope, ganja, grass, hash, pot, spliff, puff, tea, kef, *slang* blow, weed, skunk, punk, leaf, *US* locoweed

marina *n*
  dock, harbour, mooring, port, yacht station

marinade *v*
  steep, soak, immerse, marinate, souse, saturate, imbue, permeate, infuse

marine *adj*
  sea, maritime, naval, nautical, seafaring, seagoing, ocean-going, oceanic, saltwater, seawater, aquatic, *formal* pelagic, thalassian, thalassic

mariner *n*
  sailor, seaman, seafarer, deckhand, navigator, *colloq.* tar, Jack Tar, matlo, matlow, matelot, sea dog, salt, limey

marital *adj*
  conjugal, matrimonial, married, marriage, wedding, wedded, *formal* nuptial, connubial

maritime *adj*
  marine, nautical, naval, seafaring, sea, seaside, seagoing, oceanic, coastal, *formal* littoral, pelagic

mark *n, v*
  ▶ *n* 1 SPOT, stain, blemish, patch, pimple, freckle, birthmark, blot, blotch, smudge, smear, dent, impression, trace, fingerprint(s), track(s), imprint, speck, notch, chip, cut, scar, scratch, bruise, score, line, nick, *formal* stigma, *colloq.* zit 2 SIGN, indication, character, symbol, stamp, token, characteristic, feature, quality, attribute, symptom, clue, proof, hint, evidence, impression, print 3 SCORE, grade, percentage, tick, assessment, evaluation, letter, number, symbol, emblem, brand, stamp, seal, badge, device, logo, trademark, motto, monogram 4 *inflation reaching the 5% mark* point, level, stage, norm, standard, criterion, gauge, scale, measure, yardstick 5 TARGET, goal, aim, objective, object, purpose, end, intention, bull's-eye
  ▷ **make one's mark** succeed, be successful, prosper, get on, *colloq.* make it, hit/make the big time
  ▷ **wide of the mark** incorrect, inaccurate, imprecise, irrelevant, beside the point, off target
  ▶ *v* 1 STAIN, blemish, blot, smudge, discolour, dent, scar, scratch, bruise, dent, chip, cut, score, nick 2 BRAND, label, stamp, tag, flag, characterize, identify, distinguish 3 EVALUATE, assess, correct, grade,

formal appraise **4** WRITE DOWN, note (down), indicate, name, label, specify, designate, jot down **5** CHARACTERIZE, identify, stamp, brand, typify, distinguish **6** *mark an event/occasion* observe, remember, celebrate, commemorate, keep, honour, recognize **7** *mark my words* listen, mind, note, spot, mind, observe, regard, see, notice, take note of, discern, pay attention to, bear in mind, take to heart, *formal* heed, take heed of

▷ **mark down** reduce, lower, decrease, cut, *colloq.* slash

🔁 mark up

▷ **mark out 1** *mark out a football pitch* draw lines, demarcate, show the boundaries of, fix, delimit **2** DISTINGUISH, differentiate, tell apart, set apart, discriminate, single out, tell the difference between

▷ **mark up** increase, raise, put up, *colloq.* hike up, jack up

marked *adj*
1 SPOTTED, spotty, stained, blemished, blotched, blotchy, scarred, pimply, freckled, bruised, scarred, scratched **2** NOTICEABLE, obvious, conspicuous, prominent, signal, evident, clear, pronounced, distinct, noted, decided, emphatic, considerable, remarkable, apparent, glaring, striking, blatant, unmistakable **3** SUSPECTED, watched, doomed, condemned

🔁 **1** unnoticeable, slight

markedly *adj*
noticeably, obviously, conspicuously, prominently, signally, evidently, clearly, distinctly, decidedly, emphatically, considerably, remarkably, glaringly, strikingly, blatantly, unmistakably

market *n, v*
▶ *n* **1** *buy goods at the market* mart, market-place, shopping centre, mall, bazaar, fair, exchange, outlet, *formal* agora **2** *no market for these goods* demand, call, requirement, need, occasion, want, desire **3** BUSINESS, trade, trading, buying, selling, industry, dealings
▶ *v* sell, retail, hawk, peddle, offer for sale

🔁 buy

▷ **on the market** for sale, on sale, up for sale, available

marketable *adj*
in demand, sought after, wanted, saleable, sellable, merchantable, *formal* vendible

🔁 unsaleable

marketing *n*

Terms used in marketing include :

above-the-line advertising, account executive (AE), ACORN [= A Classification of Residential Neighbourhoods], adopter, after-sales service, AIDA [= attention, interest, desire, action], aided or prompted recall, area sampling, articles of ostentation, ASA [= Advertising Standards Authority], attitude research, audience research, below-the-line advertising, blanket coverage, blind advertisement, BOGO(F)F [= buy one get one (for) free], brand awareness, brand image, brand leader, brand loyalty, buyers' market, buying motives, call rate, campaign, cannibalism, canvass, captive audience, captive market, classified advertising, cluster sampling, cold call, commando salesman, commercial, comparative advertising, competitive market, concentrated marketing, concept testing, consumer panel, consumer research, consumer sovereignty, co-operative advertising, corner a market, corporate identity, corporate image, coverage, credibility gap, customer orientation, customer profile, DAGMAR [= Defining Advertising Goals for Measured Advertising Results], dealer brand, demarketing, early adopter, elasticity of demand, face-to-face selling, family brand, family life cycle, field selling, filter question, flash pack, FMCGs [= fast moving consumer goods], focus group survey, four p's [= product, price, promotion and place], free gift/ sample, frequency, Gallup poll, gap analysis, generic, geographical concentration, Giffen good, gimmick, give-away, group discussion; growth-share matrix, cash cow, dog, star, problem children or wildcats; halo effect, hard sell, harvesting strategy, heavy user, heterogeneous products, hierarchy of effects, hierarchy of needs, high-involvement products, high-pressure selling, hit rate, horizontal marketing, homogeneous products, house-to-house, impulse buying, incentive marketing, industrial advertising, inertia selling, institutional advertising, international marketing, island display, jingle, journey planning, key prospects, launch, leading question, loss leader, low-involvement products, low-pressure selling, loyalty card, macro marketing, mailshot, market demand, market leader, market orientation, market penetration, market potential, market profile, market research, market segmentation, market share, marketing audit, marketing board, marketing concept, marketing intelligence, marketing mix, matched sample, media buyer, media independent, media planner, media research, merchandising, micro marketing, missionary selling, mock-up, motivation research, multi-brand strategy, necessity good, Nielsen index, normal good, observation, opportunity to see, opinion leaders, outdoor advertising, own label, paired comparisons, party selling, perceptual map, perfect competition, personal selling, personality promotion, piggy-back promotion, predatory pricing, product differentiation/orientation/positioning, promotion, psychographic measurement, pyramid selling, random sampling, recognition, reference group, response rate, retail audit, rolling launch, sales aid, sales campaign, sales drive, saturation point, shout, skimming pricing, slogan, social marketing, socio-economic groups, solus position, static market, subliminal advertising, tachistoscope, target audience, Target Group Index, telephone selling, test marketing, unaided recall, undifferentiated marketing, unprompted response, up-market, USP [= unique selling proposition], vertical marketing, viral marketing, visualizer.

marksman, markswoman *n*
crack shot, dead shot, sharpshooter, sniper, bersagliere

maroon *v*
abandon, strand, cast away, forsake, desert, put ashore, strand, leave (behind), isolate, turn your back on, *colloq.* leave in the lurch, leave high and dry

marriage *n*
1 *the marriage ceremony* union, married relationship, married state, wedding, *formal* matrimony, nuptials, spousage **2** UNION, alliance, partnership, merger, coupling, fusion, amalgamation, unification, combi-

nation, link, connection, association, confederation, affiliation
F3 1 divorce **2** separation

married *adj*
marital, wedded, united, wed, joined, husbandly, wifely, wived, yoked, *formal* conjugal, connubial, matrimonial, nuptial, spousal, *colloq.* hitched, spliced
F3 divorced, single

marrow *n*
essence, heart, nub, kernel, core, nucleus, centre, pith, soul, spirit, substance, quick, stuff, gist, *formal* quintessence, *colloq.* nitty-gritty, nuts and bolts

marry *v*
1 WED, get married, become husband and wife, intermarry, elope, *formal* join in matrimony, become espoused, *colloq.* tie the knot, get hitched, get spliced, take the plunge, lead to the altar, make an honest woman of **2** UNITE, ally, join (together), merge, combine, amalgamate, couple, affiliate, match, link, connect, associate, weld, fuse, knit
F3 1 divorce **2** separate

marsh *n*
marshland, bog, swamp, fen, morass, mire, quagmire, slough, *US* bayou

marshal *v*
1 ARRANGE, dispose, order, line up, align, array, rank, organize, put in order, assemble, gather (together), muster, group, collect, draw up, deploy **2** GUIDE, lead, take, escort, conduct, usher, shepherd

marshy *adj*
boggy, fenny, fennish, swampy, quaggy, waterlogged, wet, muddy, squelchy, miry, slumpy, spongy, *formal* paludal, paludinal, paludine, paludinous
F3 solid, firm, dry

marsupial *n*

Marsupials include:
bandicoot, cuscus, kangaroo, rat kangaroo, tree kangaroo, wallaroo, koala, marsupial anteater, marsupial mouse, marsupial mole, marsupial rat, opossum, pademelon, phalanger, Tasmanian Devil, Tasmanian wolf, wallaby, rock wallaby, wombat.

martial *adj*
warlike, military, army, soldierly, militant, heroic, brave, belligerent, combative, aggressive, *formal* pugnacious, bellicose

martinet *n*
disciplinarian, stickler, tyrant, taskmaster, taskmistress, formalist, *colloq.* slave-driver

martyr *v*
put to death, make a martyr of, crucify, stone, persecute, torture, torment, burn at the stake, throw to the lions, put on the rack, *colloq.* give the works, give the third degree

martyrdom *n*
death, suffering, torture, torment, persecution, excruciation, ordeal, agony, anguish, witness

marvel *v, n*
▶ *v* wonder, gape, gaze, stare, goggle, not expect, be amazed at, stand in amazement, *colloq.* gawp, be flabbergasted, not believe your eyes, not know what to say
▶ *n* wonder, miracle, surprise, something amazing/incredible, phenomenon, prodigy, spectacle, sensation, genius, *colloq.* eye-opener, quite something

marvellous *adj*
1 WONDERFUL, excellent, splendid, superb, great, magnificent, terrific, super, fantastic, *colloq.* ace,

brill, magic, *slang* awesome, wicked, bad, cool, mega **2** EXTRAORDINARY, amazing, surprising, astonishing, astounding, sensational, spectacular, miraculous, remarkable, awesome, unbelievable, incredible, stupendous, glorious
F3 1 terrible, awful **2** ordinary, run-of-the-mill

masculine *adj*
1 MALE, manlike, manly, mannish, virile, *colloq.* macho, butch **2** VIGOROUS, strong, strapping, robust, powerful, muscular, rugged, red-blooded, bold, brave, gallant, fearless, heroic, determined, confident, resolute, stout-hearted
F3 1 feminine

masculinity *n*
manliness, maleness, virility, manfulness, bravery, boldness, courage, valour, fearlessness, heroism, intrepidity, resolution, stout-heartedness, stalwartness, hardihood, independence, manhood, strength, vigour, strength, mettle, firmness, *formal* fortitude, *colloq.* machismo
F3 femininity

mash *v, n*
▶ *v* crush, pulp, beat, pound, purée, pulverize, pummel, grind, smash, squash
▶ *n* mush, pulp, crush, purée, squash, pap, paste

mask *n, v*
▶ *n* disguise, camouflage, façade, front, concealment, cover-up, cover, guise, pretence, semblance, cloak, veil, blind, screen, show, veneer, visor, goggles
▶ *v* disguise, camouflage, cover (up), conceal, cloak, veil, hide, obscure, screen, shield
F3 expose, uncover

masquerade *n, v*
▶ *n* **1** MASQUE, masked ball, costume ball, fancy-dress party **2** DISGUISE, counterfeit, cover-up, cover, deception, front, pose, pretence, guise, cloak
▶ *v* disguise, impersonate, pose, pass yourself off, mask, play, pretend, profess, *formal* dissimulate

mass¹ *n, adj, v*
▶ *n* **1** HEAP, pile, load, accumulation, collection, combination, entirety, whole, total, totality, sum, lot, group, batch, bunch, *formal* aggregate, conglomeration, assemblage **2** QUANTITY, abundance, multitude, throng, troop, crowd, band, horde, mob, *colloq.* loads, heaps, bags, piles, lots, tons, scores, oodles **3** MAJORITY, body, bulk, greater part, most, preponderance **4** SIZE, dimension, magnitude, immensity, bulk, capacity **5** LUMP, piece, chunk, block, hunk, *colloq.* wodge **6** *the masses* crowd, herd, mob, lower classes, working class(es), common people, proletariat, rabble, hoi polloi, the rank and file, *colloq.* plebs, riff-raff
▶ *adj* widespread, large-scale, extensive, comprehensive, general, universal, indiscriminate, popular, across-the-board, sweeping, wholesale, blanket, *formal* pandemic
F3 limited, small-scale
▶ *v* collect, gather, assemble, congregate, amass, accumulate, draw together, come/bring together, crowd, rally, cluster, muster, swarm, throng
F3 separate

mass² *n*
go to mass Eucharist, Communion, Holy Communion, Lord's Supper, Lord's Table

massacre *n, v*
▶ *n* slaughter, murder, homicide, extermination, carnage, butchery, wholesale slaughter, indiscriminate killing, holocaust, bloodbath, annihilation, killing, genocide, ethnic cleansing, pogrom, liquidation, decimation
▶ *v* slaughter, butcher, murder, mow down, exterminate,

annihilate, kill (off), slay, decimate, liquidate, *colloq.* wipe out

massage *n, v*
▶ *n* manipulation, kneading, rub, rubbing, rubdown, pummelling, reflexology, aromatherapy, acupressure, shiatsu, Jacuzzi®, osteopathy, physiotherapy, Reichian therapy
▶ *v* manipulate, knead, rub (down), pummel

massive *adj*
huge, immense, enormous, vast, colossal, mammoth, gigantic, big, bulky, monumental, solid, hulking, hefty, weighty, substantial, heavy, large, large-scale, great, extensive, mighty, *colloq.* whopping, jumbo, ginormous
◪ tiny, small

mast *n*
pole, shaft, rod, bar, spar, boom, yard, heel, post, staff, stick, upright, support, transmitter, pylon, aerial, flagpole, flagstaff

master *n, adj, v*
▶ *n* 1 RULER, chief, governor, head, lord, captain, employer, commander, controller, director, manager, superintendent, overseer, principal, overlord, owner, *colloq.* boss, gaffer, skipper, guv, *US* honcho 2 EXPERT, genius, professional, pundit, virtuoso, past master, grand master, maestro, adept, *colloq.* dab hand, ace, pro, buff, egghead, wise guy, *US* mavin, maven 3 TEACHER, tutor, mentor, instructor, schoolteacher, schoolmaster, schoolmistress, guide, guru, *formal* pedagogue, preceptor
◪ 1 servant, underling 2 amateur 3 learner, pupil
▶ *adj* 1 CHIEF, principal, main, leading, foremost, most important, prime, predominant, controlling, great, grand 2 EXPERT, masterly, skilled, skilful, experienced, proficient, practised, adept, dexterous
◪ 1 subordinate 2 inept
▶ *v* 1 CONQUER, defeat, subdue, triumph over, overcome, overpower, quell, suppress, rule, control, govern, tame, bridle, check, curb, *formal* subjugate, vanquish 2 LEARN, grasp, acquire, manage, *colloq.* get the hang of

masterful *adj*
arrogant, authoritative, domineering, overbearing, overweening, controlling, commanding, highhanded, despotic, dictatorial, autocratic, tyrannical, powerful, dominating, imperious, *formal* peremptory, *colloq.* bossy, pushy
◪ humble, downtrodden, *colloq.* hen-pecked

ℓ **masterful** or **masterly** ?

Masterful means 'showing power, authority or determination': *The directors show a masterful approach to their employees.* *Masterly* means 'showing the skill of a master': *a masterly display of swordsmanship.*

---

masterly *adj*
expert, professional, accomplished, polished, skilled, skilful, dexterous, adept, adroit, first-rate, excellent, superb, superior, supreme, *formal* consummate, *colloq.* ace, crack, top-notch
◪ inept, clumsy

mastermind *v, n*
▶ *v* devise, think up, contrive, engineer, direct, organize, manage, originate, plan, conceive, design, dream up, frame, hatch, forge, inspire, be behind
▶ *n* organizer, initiator, manager, planner, creator, director, originator, authority, genius, intellect, engineer, architect, prime mover, virtuoso, *colloq.* brains, brainbox, bright spark

masterpiece *n*
masterwork, *pièce de résistance*, *chef d'oeuvre*, magnum opus, work of art, creation, jewel

mastery *n*
1 PROFICIENCY, skill, ability, capability, command, expertise, virtuosity, knowledge, understanding, comprehension, know-how, dexterity, familiarity, grasp, *formal* prowess 2 CONTROL, command, domination, supremacy, superiority, victory, triumph, dominion, authority, sovereignty, rule, direction, *formal* ascendancy, *colloq.* upper hand
◪ 1 incompetence 2 subjugation

masticate *v*
champ, chew, munch, chomp, crunch, eat, ruminate, knead, *formal* manducate

masturbation *n*
self-gratification, self-stimulation, autoeroticism, onanism, self-abuse, tribadism, tribady, frottage

mat *n, v*
▶ *n* 1 CARPET, doormat, felt, rug, underfelt, underlay, drugget, table mat, place mat, coaster 2 TANGLE, knot, twist, cluster, mass
▶ *v* entangle, knot, snarl, ravel, interweave, interlace, intertwine, intertwist, ensnare, entrap, enmesh

match¹ *n, v*
▶ *n* 1 CONTEST, competition, bout, game, test, trial, event, meet, tournament 2 EQUAL, equivalent, peer, counterpart, fellow, mate, rival, competitor, one of a pair, copy, double, companion, complement, replica, lookalike, twin, duplicate, *colloq.* dead ringer 3 MARRIAGE, alliance, union, combination, partnership, affiliation, pairing, merger, coupling
▶ *v* 1 EQUAL, compare, measure up to, rival, parallel, compete, oppose, contend, vie, keep up with, pit against 2 FIT, go with, agree, suit, correspond, harmonize, tally, co-ordinate, blend, complement, adapt, go together, relate, tone with, accompany, connect, *formal* accord 3 JOIN, marry, unite, mate, link, couple, combine, ally, pair (up), yoke, team, *colloq.* hitch up
◪ 2 clash, conflict 3 separate, divorce

match² *n*
light the fire with matches light, safety match, spill, taper, fuse, vesta

matching *adj*
corresponding, comparable, complementing, equivalent, parallel, like, identical, co-ordinating, blending, harmonizing, complementary, similar, duplicate, same, twin, paired, double, coupled, *formal* analogous
◪ clashing, conflicting

matchless *adj*
unequalled, without equal, peerless, incomparable, beyond compare, unmatched, unparalleled, unsurpassed, unexcelled, unrivalled, inimitable, perfect, unique
◪ ordinary

mate *n, v*
▶ *n* 1 FRIEND, companion, comrade, colleague, partner, fellow worker, coworker, workmate, associate, *formal* compeer, *colloq.* chum, crony, buddy, pal 2 PARTNER, husband, wife, spouse, boyfriend, girlfriend, companion, *colloq.* better half, other half, hubbie, missis, missus 3 ASSISTANT, helper, subordinate, apprentice, accomplice, partner 4 MATCH, fellow, twin, equivalent, counterpart
▶ *v* 1 COUPLE, pair, breed, copulate 2 JOIN, match, marry, wed

material *n, adj*
▶ *n* 1 STUFF, substance, body, matter, medium 2 FABRIC, textile, cloth, stuff 3 INFORMATION, facts, facts and figures, numbers, data, details, particulars,

ideas, evidence, constituents, work, notes, *colloq.* low-down, gen, info
► *adj* **1** PHYSICAL, bodily, concrete, tangible, palpable, substantial, earthly, worldly, *formal* corporeal **2** RELEVANT, significant, important, momentous, consequential, meaningful, essential, vital, key, indispensable, serious, weighty, *formal* pertinent, germane, apposite
F₃ **1** spiritual, abstract **2** irrelevant

materialistic *adj*
mercenary, money-grabbing, mammonist, mammonistic
F₃ spiritual

materialize *v*
appear, arise, become visible, show/reveal yourself, take shape, turn up, happen, occur, take place, come into being
F₃ disappear

materially *adv*
significantly, essentially, fundamentally, substantially, basically, considerably, seriously, gravely, greatly, much
F₃ insignificantly

maternal *adj*
motherly, motherlike, nurturing, nourishing, loving, caring, kind, protective, vigilant, doting
F₃ paternal

mathematics *n*

Mathematical terms include :

acute angle, addition, algebra, algorithm, analysis, angle, apex, approximate, arc, area, argument, arithmetic, arithmetic progression, asymmetrical, average, axis, axis of symmetry, bar chart, bar graph, base, bearing, binary, binomial, breadth, calculus, capacity, cardinal number, Cartesian coordinates, chance, chord, circumference, coefficient, combination, commutative operation, complement, complementary angle, complex number, concave, concentric circles, congruent, conjugate angles, constant, continuous distribution, converse, convex, coordinate, correlation, cosine, covariance, cross section, cube, cube root, curve, decimal, degree, denominator, depth, derivative, determinant, diagonal, diameter, differentiation, directed number, distribution, dividend, division, divisor, edge, equal, equation, equidistant, even number, exponent, exponential, face, factor, factorial, Fibonacci sequence, formula, fraction, function, geometric progression, geometry, gradient, graph, greater than, group, harmonic progression, height, helix, histogram, horizontal, hyperbola, hypotenuse, identity, infinity, integer, integration, irrational number, latitude, length, less than, linear, line, locus, logarithm, longitude, magic square, matrix, maximum, mean, measure, median, minimum, minus, mirror image, mirror symmetry, Möbius strip, mode, modulus, multiple, multiplication, natural logarithm, natural number, negative number, number, numerator, oblique, obtuse angle, odd number, operation, ordinal number, origin, parabola, parallel lines, parallel planes, parameter, percentage, percentile, perimeter, permutation, perpendicular, pi, pie chart, place value, plane figure, plus, point, positive number, prime number, probability, product, proportion, protractor, Pythagoras's theorem, quadrant, quadratic equation, quadrilateral, quartile,

quotient, radian, radius, random sample, ratio, rational number, real numbers, reciprocal, recurring decimal, reflection, reflex angle, regression, remainder, right-angle, right-angled triangle, root, rotation, rotational symmetry, sample, scalar segment, secant, sector, set, side, simultaneous equation, sine, speed, spiral, square, square root, standard deviation, statistics, straight line, subset, subtractor, supplementary angles, symmetry, tangent, three-dimensional, total, transcendental number, triangulation, trigonometry, unit, universal set, variable, variance, vector, velocity, Venn diagram, vertex, vertical, volume, whole number, width, zero. *See also* SHAPE.

mating *n*
breeding, copulating, sexual intercourse, copulation, coupling, fusing, uniting, pairing, jointing, matching, twinning, *formal* coition

matrimonial *adj*
marital, marriage, wedding, married, wedded, spousal, *formal* nuptial, conjugal

matrimony *n*
marriage, married relationship/state, union, *formal* espousals, nuptials, spousage

matted *adj*
knotted, tangled, entangled, tangly, tousled, dishevelled, uncombed
F₃ tidy, untangled

matter *n, v*
► *n* **1** SUBJECT, issue, topic, question, affair, business, case, point, concern, event, occurrence, happening, situation, proceeding, circumstance, episode, incident, thing **2** IMPORTANCE, significance, consequence, momentousness, interest, value, note, weight, *formal* import **3** *What's the matter?* TROUBLE, problem, difficulty, distress, upset, worry, bother, nuisance, inconvenience, shortcoming, weakness **4** SUBSTANCE, stuff, material, medium, physical elements, body, content **5** DISCHARGE, pus, secretion, *formal* purulence, suppuration
► *v* count, be important, be of importance, be relevant, have influence, carry weight, make a difference, mean something, *colloq.* make a stir, make waves, cut a lot of ice
▷ **as a matter of fact** in fact, actually, as it happens, really, truly, in actual fact
▷ **no matter** never mind, it does not matter, it is unimportant

matter-of-fact *adj*
unemotional, prosaic, down-to-earth, emotionless, unsentimental, straightforward, sober, pedestrian, unimaginative, lifeless, dry, dull, flat, *colloq.* deadpan
F₃ emotional

mature *adj, v*
► *adj* **1** ADULT, grown-up, grown, full-grown, of age, sensible, responsible, balanced, experienced, wise, fully fledged, complete, finished, finalized, perfect, perfected, well-developed, well-thought-out **2** RIPE, ripened, seasoned, mellow, ready
F₃ **1** childish **2** immature
► *v* grow up, become adult, become sensible, come of age, develop, be fully developed, become ripe, become mellow, mellow, ripen, perfect, age, bloom, evolve, fall due

maturity *n*
1 ADULTHOOD, full growth, majority, coming of age, womanhood, manhood, wisdom, experience,

responsibility, sensibleness **2** RIPENESS, readiness, mellowness, perfection

F∃ **1** childishness **2** immaturity

maudlin *adj*
sentimental, mawkish, emotional, tearful, half-drunk, drunk, fuddled, tipsy, *formal* lachrymose, *colloq.* gushy, schmaltzy, mushy, sickly, slushy, soppy, weepy

F∃ pleasant

maul *v*
attack, abuse, ill-treat, mutilate, mangle, manhandle, maltreat, assault, molest, paw, beat (up), claw, lacerate, thrash, *colloq.* batter, wallop, belt, do over, mug, knock about, rough up, knock someone's block off

maunder *v*
mutter, ramble, babble, blather, chatter, gabble, *colloq.* prattle, witter, natter, jabber, waffle, rabbit (on)

mausoleum *n*
tomb, crypt, vault, burial chamber, catacomb, sepulchre, undercroft

maverick *n*
outsider, rebel, agitator, nonconformist, individualist, *colloq.* fish out of water

maw *n*
mouth, jaws, throat, stomach, gullet, gulf, abyss, chasm

mawkish *adj*
sentimental, maudlin, emotional, offensive, nauseous, nauseating, feeble, flat, disgusting, foul, loathsome, *colloq.* soppy, gushy, schmaltzy, mushy, sickly, slushy

F∃ matter-of-fact, pleasant

maxim *n*
saying, proverb, adage, axiom, aphorism, saw, epigram, motto, byword, precept, rule, *formal* gnome

maximum *adj, n*
▶ *adj* greatest, highest, largest, biggest, most, utmost, supreme, top, topmost

F∃ minimum

▶ *n* most, top (point), utmost, uttermost, upper limit, peak, pinnacle, summit, height, ceiling, extremity, *formal* zenith, apogee, acme

F∃ minimum

maybe *adv*
perhaps, possibly, conceivably, for all you know, *formal* perchance, peradventure

F∃ definitely

mayhem *n*
chaos, disorder, confusion, disorganization, tumult, disruption, uproar, riot, bedlam, madhouse, mess, anarchy, lawlessness

maze *n*
labyrinth, network, tangle, jungle, web, mesh, complex, confusion, puzzle, intricacy

meadow *n*
field, grassland, grass, pasture, pastureland, paddock, green

meagre *adj*
1 SCANTY, sparse, inadequate, insufficient, deficient, skimpy, paltry, negligible, small, poor, slight, stingy, niggardly, *formal* exiguous, *colloq.* measly **2** THIN, puny, insubstantial, bony, emaciated, scraggy, gaunt, scrawny, slight

F∃ **1** ample **2** fat

meagreness *n*
scantiness, sparseness, inadequacy, insufficiency, deficiency, smallness, slightness, stinginess, puniness, *colloq.* measliness

mealy-mouthed *adj*
hestitant, indirect, mincing, over-squeamish, over-

delicate, reticent, plausible, equivocal, flattering, smooth-tongued, euphemistic, prim, glib

mean¹ *v*
1 SIGNIFY, represent, stand for, symbolize, show, designate, convey, express, suggest, indicate, imply, intimate, *formal* denote, betoken, purport, connote **2** INTEND, aim, propose, design, purpose, plan, aspire, wish, wont, have in mind, think of **3** CAUSE, give rise to, lead to, bring about, produce, involve, entail, result in, *formal* effect **4** *it was meant to happen* destine, fate, design, intend, appoint, *formal* ordain

mean² *adj*
1 MISERLY, niggardly, selfish, grasping, tight-fisted, close-fisted, *formal* parsimonious, *colloq.* tight, stingy, penny-pinching, mingy **2** UNKIND, unpleasant, nasty, bad-tempered, cruel, disagreeable, unfriendly, cross, spiteful, *colloq.* crotchety, crabby, grouchy **3** LOWLY, base, poor, humble, ordinary, common, obscure, wretched, shabby, dirty, miserable, dismal, squalid

F∃ **1** generous **2** kind **3** noble, splendid

mean³ *adj, n*
▶ *adj the mean score* average, intermediate, middle, medium, middling, halfway, median, normal

F∃ extreme

▶ *n* average, middle, mid-point, norm, median, mode, compromise, middle course, middle way, medium, happy medium, golden mean

F∃ extreme

meander *v*
1 WIND, zigzag, turn, twist, snake, bend, curve **2** WANDER, stray, amble, ramble, stroll, roam, rove, ease, shuffle, inch, *colloq.* laze, mosey, mooch

meandering *adj*
wandering, winding, twisting, turning, rambling, tortuous, circuitous, snaking, serpentine, sinuous, indirect, roundabout, meandrous, *formal* convoluted

F∃ straight, direct

meaning *n*
1 SIGNIFICANCE, sense, implication, message, expression, gist, drift, substance, essence, thrust, trend, definition, explanation, interpretation, *formal* import, signification, connotation, explication, elucidation **2** AIM, intention, purpose, plan, goal, object, objective, aspiration, wish, idea **3** VALUE, worth, point, significance, purpose

meaningful *adj*
1 IMPORTANT, significant, relevant, valid, useful, worthwhile, material, purposeful, serious **2** EXPRESSIVE, speaking, suggestive, eloquent, pregnant, warning, pointed

F∃ **1** unimportant, worthless

meaningless *adj*
1 SENSELESS, pointless, purposeless, useless, insignificant, incomprehensible, unintelligible, aimless, motiveless, irrational, futile, insubstantial, trifling, trivial **2** EMPTY, hollow, vacuous, vain, worthless, nonsensical, absurd

F∃ **1** important, meaningful **2** worthwhile

meanness *n*
mean-spiritedness, miserliness, narrow-mindedness, niggardliness, tight-fistedness, close-fistedness, closehandedness, illiberality, *formal* parsimony, penuriousness, *colloq.* stinginess

F∃ generosity, kindness

means *n*
1 METHOD, way, manner, medium, course, agency, process, instrument, avenue, channel, vehicle, *formal* mode **2** RESOURCES, funds, money, income, wealth, capital, riches, substance, wherewithal, fortune, affluence, assets, property

▷ **by all means** of course, naturally, certainly, surely, with pleasure
▷ **by means of** using, with, through, via, with the help of, with the aid of, as a result of, *formal* by dint of
▷ **by no means** certainly not, not at all, never, *colloq.* no way

meantime, meanwhile *adv*
at the same time, for the time being, for now, for the moment, in the meantime, in the meanwhile, in the interim, in the interval, concurrently, simultaneously

measly *adj*
mean, miserable, paltry, meagre, pitiful, scanty, skimpy, petty, poor, puny, trivial, ungenerous, miserly, niggardly, beggarly, contemptible, *colloq.* stingy, piddling, pathetic, mingy
🖬 generous

measurable *adj*
perceptible, significant, quantifiable, noticeable, appreciable, determinable, assessable, computable, gaugeable, fathomable, material, quantitative, *formal* mensurable
🖬 measureless

measure *n, v*
▶ *n* **1** SIZE, quantity, magnitude, amount, degree, extent, range, scope, proportion(s), dimension(s), area, expanse, capacity, height, depth, length, width, weight, volume, mass, bulk **2** RULE, gauge, ruler, scale, level, standard, system, unit(s), criterion, norm, touchstone, yardstick, benchmark, test, meter **3** STEP, course, action, act, deed, expedient, procedure, proceeding, means, method, act, bill, statute, resolution **4** PORTION, ration, share, piece, part, allocation, quota, division, lot, allotment, *colloq.* rakeoff, cut
▷ **beyond measure** beyond belief, immensely, infinitely, endlessly, incalculably, inestimably
▷ **for good measure** as well, besides, in addition, furthermore, over and above, as a bonus
▶ *v* quantify, evaluate, assess, weigh, value, gauge, judge, sound, fathom, read, record, meter, time, determine, calculate, estimate, size (up), rate, plumb, survey, compute, measure out, measure off, *formal* appraise
▷ **measure off** mark out, measure (out), determine, fix, lay down, limit, pace out, delimit, demarcate, *formal* circumscribe
▷ **measure out** share out, divide, distribute, proportion, dispense, deal out, dole out, allot, apportion, hand out, mete out, parcel out, pour out, issue, assign
▷ **measure up** do, come up to standard, make the grade, pass muster, fit/fill the bill, *formal* suffice, *colloq.* come up to scratch, shape up
▷ **measure up to** equal, meet, live up to, come up to, match, match up to, compare with, touch, rival, make the grade

measured *adj*
deliberate, planned, reasoned, slow, unhurried, steady, regular, studied, well-thought-out, calculated, careful, considered, premeditated, precise

measureless *adj*
endless, immeasurable, inestimable, incalculable, innumerable, limitless, unbounded, infinite, boundless, bottomless, immense, vast
🖬 measurable

measurement *n*
1 DIMENSION, size, extent, amount, proportion(s), amplitude, unit, magnitude, area, range, expanse, capacity, height, depth, length, width, weight, volume, mass, bulk, quantity

SI (Système International d'Unités) base units include:
ampere, candela, kelvin, kilogram, metre, mole,
second; *SI derivatives and other measurements include:* acre, angstrom, atmosphere, bar, barrel, becquerel, bushel, cable, calorie, centimetre, century, chain, coulomb, cubic centimetre, cubic foot, cubic inch, cubic metre, cubic yard, day, decade, decibel, degree, dyne, erg, farad, fathom, fluid ounce, fresnel, foot, foot-pound, furlong, gallon, gill, gram, hand, hectare, hertz, horsepower, hour, hundredweight, inch, joule, kilometre, knot, league, litre, lumen, micrometre, mile, millennium, millibar, millilitre, minute, month, nautical mile, newton, ohm, ounce, pascal, peak, pint, pound, pound per square inch, radian, rod, siemens, span, square centimetre, square foot, square inch, square kilometre, square metre, square mile, square yard, steradian, stone, therm, ton, tonne, volt, watt, week, yard, year.

2 ASSESSMENT, evaluation, estimation, computation, calculation, calibration, quantification, sizing, weighing, reading, gauging, judgement, appraisal, appreciation, survey

meat *n*
1 FLESH

Kinds of meat include:
beef, pork, lamb, mutton, ham, bacon, gammon, chicken, turkey, goose, duck, rabbit, hare, venison, pheasant, grouse, partridge, pigeon, quail; offal, liver, heart, tongue, kidney, brains, brawn, pig's knuckle, trotters, oxtail, sweetbread, tripe; steak, minced beef, sausage, rissole, faggot, beefburger, hamburger, black pudding, paté.

Cuts of meat include:
shoulder, collar, hand, loin, hock, leg, chop, shin, knuckle, rib, spare-rib, breast, brisket, chine, cutlet, fillet, rump, scrag, silverside, topside, sirloin, flank, escalope, neck, saddle.

2 FOOD, rations, provisions, nourishment, sustenance, subsistence, fare, comestibles, *formal* viands, victuals, *colloq.* eats, eatables, tuck, *slang* grub, nosh **3** ESSENCE, substance, fundamentals, heart, kernel, marrow, core, crux, nub, nucleus, pith, point, gist

meaty *adj*
1 FLESHY, hearty, solid, heavy, brawny, beefy, burly, muscular, strapping, sturdy, *colloq.* hunky **2** SUBSTANTIAL, interesting, significant, meaningful, profound, rich, pithy

mechanic *n*
engineer, repairman, operative, operator, technician, machinist, mechanician, artificer

mechanical *adj*
1 *a mechanical device* automatic, automated, machine-powered, power-driven, electric **2** AUTOMATIC, involuntary, instinctive, routine, machinelike, habitual, impersonal, emotionless, unemotional, unconscious, cold, matter-of-fact, unfeeling, perfunctory, lifeless, dead, dull
🖬 **2** conscious

mechanism *n*
1 MACHINE, machinery, engine, appliance, instrument, tool, contraption, motor, works, workings, action, movement, system, gadget, device, apparatus, contrivance, gears, components, *colloq.* guts **2** MEANS, method, agency, process, procedure, system, technique, medium, channel, structure, workings, operation, functioning, performance

medal *n*
award, medallion, prize, trophy, decoration, honour, reward, *slang* gong

meddle *v*
interfere, intervene, pry, intrude, butt in, tamper, *colloq.* poke/stick your nose in, stick/put your oar in, snoop

meddlesome *adj*
interfering, meddling, prying, intrusive, intruding, mischievous, *colloq.* nosy

mediate *v*
arbitrate, conciliate, intervene, referee, umpire, intercede, moderate, reconcile, act as mediator/intermediary/peacemaker, negotiate, resolve, settle, step in, *formal* interpose

mediation *n*
arbitration, reconciliation, negotiation, conciliation, intercession, peacemaking, good offices, intervention, *formal* interposition

mediator *n*
arbitrator, referee, umpire, intermediary, negotiator, go-between, interceder, judge, arbiter, reconciler, middleman, intervener, moderator, intercessor, conciliator, peacemaker, Ombudsman

medical equipment

Medical and surgical equipment include:
aspirator, audiometer, aural speculum, auriscope, autoclave, body scanner, bronchoscope, cannula, catheter, CAT scanner, clamp, CT (computed tomography) scanner, curette, defibrillator, disposable enema pack, ear syringe, ECG (electrocardiograph), electroencephalograph, endoscope, first aid kit, forceps, haemodialysis unit, hypodermic needle, hypodermic syringe, incubator, inhaler, instrument table, iron lung, isolator tent, kidney dish, laparoscope, laryngoscope, microscope, MRI (magnetic resonance imaging) scanner, nebulizer, obstetrical forceps, oesophagoscope, operating table, ophthalmoscope, oxygen cylinder, oxygen mask, rectoscope, respirator, resuscitator, retractor, rhinoscope, scales, scalpel, sliding-weight scales, specimen glass, speculum, sphygmomanometer, sterile donor-pack, sterilizer, stethoscope, stomach pump, surgical mask, surgical suture materials, swabs, syringe, thermometer, tracheostomy tube, traction apparatus, tweezers, ultrasound, urethroscope, vaginal speculum, X-ray unit.

medical specialists

Medical specialists include:
anaesthetist, bacteriologist, cardiologist, chiropodist, chiropractor, dentist, dermatologist, dietician, doctor, embryologist, endocrinologist, forensic pathologist, gastroenterologist, geriatrician, gerontologist, gynaecologist, haematologist, homoeopath, immunologist, microbiologist, neurologist, obstetrician, oncologist, ophthalmologist, optician (or optometrist), orthodontist, orthopaedist, orthoptist, paediatrician, pathologist, pharmacist, pharmacologist, physiotherapist, psychiatrist, psychologist, rheumatologist, toxicologist. *See also* DOCTOR; NURSE.

medical terms

Medical terms include :
abortion, allergy, amputation, analgesic, antibiotics, antiseptic, bandage, barium meal, biopsy, blood bank, blood count, blood donor, blood group, blood pressure, blood test, caesarean, cardiopulmonary resuscitation (CPR), case history, casualty, cauterization, cervical smear, check-up, childbirth, circulation, circumcision, clinic, complication, compress, consultant, consultation, contraception, convulsion, cure, diagnosis, dialysis, dislocate, dissection, doctor, donor, dressings, enema, examination, gene, health screening, home visit, hormone replacement therapy (HRT), hospice, hospital, immunization, implantation, incubation, infection, inflammation, injection, injury, inoculation, intensive care, labour, miscarriage, mouth-to-mouth, nurse, ointment, operation, paraplegia, post-mortem, pregnancy, prescription, prognosis, prosthesis, psychosomatic, quarantine, radiotherapy, recovery, rehabilitation, relapse, remission, respiration, resuscitation, scan, side effect, sling, smear test, specimen, splint, sterilization, steroid, surgery, suture, symptom, syndrome, therapy, tourniquet, tranquillizer, transfusion, transplant, trauma, treatment, tumour, ultrasound scanning, vaccination, vaccine, virus, X-ray. *See also* THERAPY.

medicinal *adj*
therapeutic, healing, remedial, health-giving, curative, restorative, medical

medicine *n*
medication, drug, cure, remedy, medicament, prescription, pharmaceutical, panacea, *technical* analeptic

Types of medicine include:
tablet, capsule, pill, painkiller, lozenge, pastille, gargle, linctus, tonic, laxative, suppository, antacid, ointment, arnica, eye drops, ear drops, nasal spray, inhaler, Ventolin®, antibiotic, penicillin, emetic, gripe-water, paregoric. *See also* DRUG.

Forms of alternative medicine include:
acupuncture, aromatherapy, chiropractic, herbal remedies, homeopathy, naturopathy, osteopathy, reflexology.

medieval *adj*
1 *medieval history* of the Middle Ages, of the Dark Ages, historic, old, archaic **2** OLD-FASHIONED, obsolete, primitive, antiquated, archaic, antique, antediluvian, old-world, outmoded, unenlightened

mediocre *adj*
ordinary, average, middling, medium, indifferent, unexceptional, undistinguished, commonplace, pedestrian, insignificant, second-rate, passable, adequate, inferior, uninspired, tolerable, *colloq.* so-so, run-of-the-mill, fair to middling, not up to much, not all that it is cracked up to be, nothing much to write home about, no great shakes, not much cop
Fa exceptional, extraordinary, distinctive

mediocrity *n*
1 ORDINARINESS, unimportance, averageness, unexceptionableness, adequacy, passableness, insignificance, poorness, inferiority, indifference **2**

NONENTITY, nobody, nothing, *colloq.* non-starter, no-hoper, dead loss

🖅 **1** distinction, exceptionableness

meditate *v*
reflect, ponder, ruminate, contemplate, muse, brood, think (over), consider, deliberate, mull over, study, concentrate, speculate, scheme, plan, devise, design, intend, have in mind, *formal* cogitate, *colloq.* put on your thinking cap

meditation *n*
contemplation, reflection, pondering, musing, thought, ruminating, rumination, deliberation, brooding, mulling over, speculation, study, reverie, concentration, brown study, *formal* cerebration, cogitation, excogitation

meditative *adj*
contemplative, deliberative, reflective, thoughtful, studious, museful, pensive, ruminant, ruminative, *formal* cogitative

medium *adj, n*
▶ *adj* average, middle, median, mean, medial, intermediate, middling, midway, midpoint, standard, fair
▶ *n* **1** AVERAGE, middle, median, mean, mode, intermediate point, midpoint, middle ground, norm, compromise, centre, happy medium, golden mean **2** MEANS, means of expression, way of expressing, agency, channel, vehicle, instrument, way, form, substance, material, stuff, avenue, organ, *formal* instrumentality, mode **3** ENVIRONMENT, element, setting, surroundings, atmosphere, conditions, habitat, circumstances, influences, ambience, milieu **4** PSYCHIC, spiritualist, spiritist, clairvoyant, necromancer

medley *n*
assortment, mixture, mix, miscellany, variety, melange, potpourri, hotchpotch, hodge-podge, confusion, farrago, salmagundi, smorgasbord, collection, pastiche, patchwork, gallimaufry, jumble, *formal* conglomeration, *colloq.* mixed bag, mishmash, omniumgatherum

meek *adj*
modest, long-suffering, forbearing, humble, docile, patient, unassuming, quiet, lowly, mild, unpretentious, resigned, gentle, peaceful, tame, timid, submissive, yielding, deferential, weak, spiritless, *formal* compliant, *colloq.* spineless

🖅 arrogant, assertive, rebellious

meekness *n*
modesty, long-suffering, forbearance, humility, docility, patience, unpretentiousness, lowliness, mildness, gentleness, humbleness, peacefulness, submission, submissiveness, deference, tameness, softness, self-abasement, self-disparagement, self-effacement, timidity, spiritlessness, resignation, weakness, *formal* acquiescence, compliance, *colloq.* spinelessness

🖅 arrogance, assertiveness

meet *v*
1 ENCOUNTER, come across, run across, run into, make contact with, join up with, chance on, *formal* happen upon, *colloq.* bump into **2** GATHER, get together, collect, come together, muster, assemble, congregate, rally, rendezvous, *formal* convene, convoke, forgather **3** FULFIL, satisfy, match, answer, come up to, measure up to, equal, comply with, discharge, perform, execute **4** EXPERIENCE, encounter, face, come across, go through, undergo, bear, endure, suffer **5** *meet a challenge* deal with, manage, handle, tackle, look after, cope with, get to grips with **6** *meet the cost* - pay (for), settle, discharge, honour **7** JOIN, converge, come together, connect, link (up), cross, intersect, touch, unite, *formal* abut, adjoin

🖅 **4** scatter, disperse **7** diverge, separate

meeting *n*
1 ENCOUNTER, confrontation, rendezvous, appointment, date, engagement, contact, assignation, introduction, *formal* tryst **2** ASSEMBLY, gathering, session **3** CONVERGENCE, confluence, junction, intersection, union, venue, (point of) contact, interface, watersmeet, *formal* concourse, abutment, conjunction

megalomania *n*
overestimation, self-importance, exaggerated sense of power, delusions of grandeur, *folie de grandeur*, conceitedness

melancholy *adj, n*
▶ *adj* depressed, dejected, downcast, downhearted, downcast, gloomy, glum, low, low-spirited, heavy-hearted, sad, unhappy, despondent, dispirited, miserable, mournful, dismal, sorrowful, moody, *formal* disconsolate, lugubrious, woeful, woebegone, *colloq.* down, blue, down in the dumps, in the doldrums

🖅 cheerful, elated, joyful

▶ *n* depression, dejection, gloom, despondency, low spirits, sadness, unhappiness, sorrow, misery, pessimism, *colloq.* blues, doldrums, dumps

🖅 cheerfulness, elation, joy

melange *n*
assortment, mixture, mix, miscellany, variety, potpourri, hotchpotch, hodge-podge, confusion, farrago, salmagundi, smorgasbord, collection, pastiche, patchwork, gallimaufry, jumble, *formal* conglomeration, *colloq.* mixed bag, mishmash, omniumgatherum

melee *n*
1 BRAWL, rumpus, scuffle, set-to, fight, tussle, ruckus, ruction, broil, affray, fracas, fray, free-for-all, scrum, *Scot.* stramash **2** MUDDLE, confusion, chaos, disorganization, disorder, mess, mix-up, jumble, clutter, tangle

mellifluous *adj*
smooth, sweet-sounding, sweet, soothing, soft, tuneful, harmonious, dulcet, mellow, honeyed, silvery, *formal* canorous, euphonious

🖅 discordant, grating, harsh

mellow *adj, v*
▶ *adj* **1** MATURE, ripe, juicy, soft, tender, sweet, full-flavoured, luscious, mild **2** GENIAL, cordial, affable, pleasant, relaxed, easy-going, good-natured, amiable, amicable, placid, gentle, serene, tranquil, cheerful, happy, jolly, jovial, kind, kind-hearted **3** SMOOTH, melodious, tuneful, harmonious, smooth, rich, rounded, full, soft, sweet, dulcet, *formal* euphonious

🖅 **1** unripe **2** cold **3** harsh

▶ *v* mature, ripen, improve, sweeten, soften, temper, make/become less extreme, season, perfect

melodious *adj*
tuneful, musical, melodic, harmonious, dulcet, sweet, sweet-sounding, silvery, *formal* euphonious

🖅 discordant, grating, harsh

melodramatic *adj*
histrionic, theatrical, overdramatic, exaggerated, extravagant, overemotional, sensational, overdone, stagy, *colloq.* hammy

melody *n*
1 TUNE, music, song, refrain, harmony, rhythm, theme, air, strain **2** TUNEFULNESS, musicality, musicalness, harmony, harmoniousness, sweetness, *formal* euphony

melt *v*
1 LIQUEFY, dissolve, thaw, defrost, unfreeze, fuse, *formal* deliquesce **2** *melt someone's heart* soften, move, affect, touch, make/become tender, moderate, calm

🖅 **1** freeze, solidify **2** harden

▷ **melt away** disappear, vanish, fade (away), evaporate,

dissolve, disperse, *formal* evanesce, *colloq.* disappear into thin air

member *n*
1 *members of a club* adherent, associate, subscriber, representative, comrade, fellow **2** PART, limb, arm, leg, appendage, extremity, organ, element

membership *n*
1 *membership of a club* affiliation, adherence, allegiance, participation, enrolment, fellowship **2** MEMBERS, associates, body, adherents, subscribers, representatives, comrades, fellows, fellowship

membrane *n*
sheet, film, skin, tissue, layer, veil, partition, diaphragm, *technical* integument, septum, velum, hymen

memento *n*
souvenir, keepsake, remembrance, reminder, token, memorial, trophy, record, vestige, relic

memoir *n*
account, biography, essay, journal, life, monograph, narrative, chronicle, record, register, report

memoirs *n*
reminiscences, recollections, memories, autobiography, life story, diary, diaries, chronicles, annals, journals, records, confessions, experiences

memorable *adj*
unforgettable, remarkable, significant, impressive, striking, notable, noteworthy, historic, extraordinary, important, consequential, distinguished, distinctive, special, outstanding, momentous, unique
☒ forgettable, trivial, unimportant

memorandum *n*
message, note, reminder, *colloq.* memo, memory-jogger

memorial *n, adj*
▶ *n* remembrance, monument, statue, stone, plaque, shrine, cenotaph, mausoleum, record, souvenir, memento
▶ *adj* commemorative, celebratory, monumental

memorize *v*
learn, learn by heart, learn by rote, commit to memory, remember
☒ forget

memory *n*
1 RECALL, powers of recall, retention, recollection, remembrance, reminiscence **2** COMMEMORATION, remembrance, tribute, honour, observance, recognition
☒ **1** forgetfulness

menace *n, v*
▶ *n* **1** THREAT, intimidation, terrorism, ominousness, threatening behaviour, terrorizing, tyrannization, bullying, browbeating, coercion, pressure, warning, *colloq.* screws, frighteners, big stick **2** DANGER, peril, hazard, jeopardy, risk, threat **3** NUISANCE, annoyance, pest, bother, troublemaker, *colloq.* pain, thorn in your side/flesh
▶ *v* threaten, frighten, alarm, daunt, dismay, appal, intimidate, scare, terrorize, terrify, browbeat, coerce, press, pressure, pressurize, bully, loom, lour

menacing *adj*
threatening, intimidating, intimidatory, warning, ominous, alarming, frightening, dangerous, looming, sinister, grim, louring, Damoclean, *formal* impending, portentous, minacious, minatory

mend *v*
1 REPAIR, fix, renovate, restore, renew, refit, patch (up), put back together, cobble, darn, stick, sew, cure, heal, make whole **2** RECOVER, get better, improve, recuperate **3** REMEDY, correct, rectify, reform, revise,

amend, improve, put right, put in order, *formal* ameliorate, emend
☒ **1** break **2** deteriorate **3** destroy
▷ **on the mend** convalescing, convalescent, recovering, improving, recuperating, reviving, healing

mendacious *adj*
untruthful, untrue, false, fictitious, insincere, deceitful, deceptive, dishonest, lying, perjured, fraudulent, *formal* fallacious, perfidious, duplicitous
☒ honest, truthful, *formal* veracious

mendacity *n*
untruthfulness, untruth, lie, lying, misrepresentation, distortion, falsehood, falsification, insincerity, deceit, deceitfulness, dishonesty, fraudulence, perjury, *formal* inveracity, duplicity, perfidy
☒ honesty, truthfulness, *formal* veracity

mendicant *adj, n*
▶ *adj* begging, scrounging, *formal* petitionary, supplicant, *colloq.* cadging
▶ *n* beggar, supplicant, pauper, down-and-out, tramp, vagabond, vagrant, beachcomber, *US* hobo, *colloq.* bum, cadger, scrounger, *US* moocher

menial *adj, n*
▶ *adj* low, lowly, humble, base, dull, humdrum, routine, boring, degrading, demeaning, ignominious, unskilled, subservient, servile, slavish
▶ *n* servant, domestic, labourer, minion, attendant, drudge, slave, underling, *colloq.* skivvy, dogsbody

menstruation *n*
period, menstrual cycle, monthly flow, courses, flow, menses, menorrhoea, *technical* catamenia, *colloq.* monthlies, the usual, the curse

mensuration *n*
measurement, measuring, calibration, computation, estimation, calculation, assessment, evaluation, survey, surveying, valuation, *technical* metage

mental *adj*
1 INTELLECTUAL, abstract, unconscious, conceptual, theoretical, rational, *formal* cognitive, cerebral **2** MAD, insane, lunatic, crazy, deranged, psychotic, disturbed, *colloq.* (mentally) unbalanced, loony, nuts, barmy, bonkers, off your head, off your trolley, having a screw loose
☒ **1** physical **2** sane

mentality *n*
1 FRAME OF MIND, mind, way of thinking, (mental) attitude, make-up, character, disposition, personality, psychology, outlook, mindset **2** INTELLECT, intelligence, understanding, mind, comprehension, faculty, rationality, *colloq.* brains, little grey cells, grey matter

mentally *adv*
intellectually, in the mind, inwardly, psychologically, rationally, temperamentally, subjectively, emotionally

mention *v, n*
▶ *v* **1** SPEAK OF, refer to, say, name, acknowledge, report, make known, impart, introduce, declare, communicate, divulge, disclose, broach, cite, reveal, state, quote **2** TOUCH ON, allude to, cite, refer to, speak about briefly, bring up, hint at, intimate, point out
▷ **don't mention it** not at all, don't worry, forget it, it was nothing, it's a pleasure, think nothing of it
▷ **not to mention** not including, to say nothing of, besides, as well as, let alone, not forgetting
▶ *n* reference, allusion, citation, observation, recognition, remark, statement, acknowledgement, announcement, notification, tribute, indication

mentioned *adj*
quoted, reported, stated, cited, *formal* abovementioned, forementioned, forenamed, fore-quoted, foresaid, aforesaid, fore-cited

mentor n
teacher, tutor, adviser, counsellor, guru, swami, guide, coach, instructor, pedagogue, therapist

menu n
bill of fare, tariff, list, card, *carte du jour*

mercantile adj
trade, trading, commercial, merchantable, marketable, saleable

mercenary adj, n
▶ adj **1** GREEDY, covetous, grasping, acquisitive, money-orientated, materialistic, mammonistic, sordid, *formal* avaricious, *colloq.* money-grubbing, on the make **2** HIRED, paid, venal
▶ n soldier of fortune, hired soldier, freelance, free companion, hireling, condottiere, galloglass, landsknecht, lansquenet, *colloq.* merc

merchandise n, v
▶ n goods, commodities, stock, produce, products, wares, cargo, freight, shipment, *formal* vendibles
▶ v **1** TRADE, deal in, market, retail, sell, buy and sell, carry, distribute, supply, traffic in, peddle, *formal* vend **2** ADVERTISE, publicize, promote, market, sell, *colloq.* push, plug, hype

merchant n
trader, dealer, broker, trafficker, wholesaler, distributor, retailer, seller, salesperson, salesman, saleswoman, sales executive, shopkeeper, vendor

merciful adj
compassionate, forgiving, forbearing, humane, lenient, sparing, tender-hearted, soft-hearted, pitying, gracious, humanitarian, kind, liberal, tolerant, sympathetic, generous, mild
Ⓕ hard-hearted, merciless

merciless adj
pitiless, relentless, unmerciful, ruthless, barbarous, hard-hearted, hard, heartless, implacable, inexorable, intolerant, inhumane, unforgiving, remorseless, unpitying, unsympathetic, unfeeling, unsparing, severe, rigid, stern, cruel, callous, harsh, inhuman
Ⓕ compassionate, merciful

mercurial adj
volatile, temperamental, unpredictable, unstable, variable, changeable, inconstant, erratic, fickle, impetuous, impulsive, irrepressible, flighty, lighthearted, lively, spirited, sprightly, active, mobile, *formal* capricious
Ⓕ saturnine

mercy n
1 COMPASSION, grace, forgiveness, forbearance, leniency, pity, humaneness, humanitarianism, kindness, tender-heartedness, tenderness, mildness, sympathy, generosity, *formal* clemency **2** BLESSING, godsend, boon, favour, good luck, stroke of good luck, relief
Ⓕ **1** cruelty, harshness
▷ **at the mercy of** in the control of, in the power of, in someone's clutches, defenceless against, unarmed against, exposed to, vulnerable to, unprotected against, at the whim of

mere adj
sheer, plain, simple, pure and simple, no more than, bare, utter, pure, absolute, complete, stark, unadulterated, common, paltry, petty

merely adv
simply, just, only, purely, nothing but, barely, hardly, scarcely

merge v
join, unite, combine, come/bring together, join forces, team up, converge, amalgamate, blend, coalesce,

mix, intermix, mingle, melt into, run into, fuse, meet, meld, be swallowed up in, be assimilated in, become lost in, be engulfed, incorporate, consolidate

merger n
amalgamation, union, fusion, combination, coalition, alliance, consolidation, confederation, incorporation, convergence, blend, assimilation

merit n, v
▶ n worth, excellence, value, quality, high quality, good, goodness, virtue, worthiness, asset, credit, advantage, strong point, talent, justification, reward, recompense, due, deserts, claim, *colloq.* plus
Ⓕ fault, drawback, *colloq.* minus
▶ v deserve, be worthy of, be worth, earn, justify, have a right to, be entitled to, warrant

merited adj
deserved, earned, justified, entitled, fitting, appropriate, warranted, worthy, due, just, rightful, *formal* condign
Ⓕ inappropriate, unjustified

meritorious adj
commendable, deserving, right, righteous, virtuous, excellent, good, honourable, praiseworthy, worthy, estimable, admirable, creditable, exemplary, *formal* laudable
Ⓕ unworthy

merriment n
fun, jollity, hilarity, laughter, conviviality, high spirits, joyfulness, cheerfulness, gaiety, festivity, amusement, revelry, frolic, liveliness, joviality, buoyance, carefreeness, *formal* mirthfulness, mirth, jocundity, blitheness
Ⓕ gloom, seriousness

merry adj
1 JOLLY, light-hearted, jovial, joyful, happy, high-spirited, in good spirits, convivial, festive, cheerful, cheery, amusing, carefree, glad, *formal* mirthful, blithe **2** TIPSY, slightly drunk, happy, tiddly, *colloq.* squiffy
Ⓕ **1** gloomy, melancholy **2** sober
▷ **make merry** have fun, enjoy yourself, celebrate, have a party, sing, dance, drink, carouse

merry-go-round n
roundabout, carousel, joy-wheel, whirligig

merrymaking n
merriment, celebration, fun, gaiety, jollification, rejoicings, conviviality, festivity, party, carousal, carousing, revel, revelry

mesh n, v
▶ n net, network, netting, lattice, latticework, tracery, trellis, web, tangle, entanglement, snare, trap
▶ v engage, interlock, dovetail, fit together (closely), connect, harmonize, match, co-ordinate, combine, go/come together

mesmerize v
transfix, hypnotize, magnetize, spellbind, hold spellbound, captivate, enthral, fascinate, grip, entrance, stupefy, benumb

mess n
1 CHAOS, untidiness, disorder, disarray, confusion, muddle, jumble, clutter, litter, turmoil, disorganization, mix-up, dirt, dirtiness, filth, filthiness, squalor, *colloq.* shambles, hole, dump, tip, dog's breakfast, pig's breakfast, dog's dinner **2** DIFFICULTY, trouble, predicament, plight, dilemma, quandary, *colloq.* fix, (tight) spot, jam, pickle, hiccup, hole, stew, hot/deep water, pretty pass **3** BOTCH, bungle, muddle, failure, *colloq.* farce, shambles, hash
Ⓕ order, tidiness
▷ **mess about/around** mess around, fool around, play, play around, play about, potter about, fiddle

around, *colloq.* muck about, faff about/around

▷ **mess about/around with** interfere with, treat badly, upset, bother, trouble, inconvenience, meddle with, play (about/around) with, fool about/around with, tamper with

▷ **mess up 1** DISARRANGE, jumble, untidy, clutter up, throw into disorder, disrupt, confuse, muddle, tangle, dishevel, dirty, foul **2** BOTCH, bungle, spoil, ruin, make a mess of, *colloq.* muck up, bodge, botch, fluff, muff, foul up, make a hash of, *slang* louse up, screw up

F3 **1** order, tidy

message *n*
1 COMMUNICATION, bulletin, dispatch, communiqué, report, news, piece of information, word, errand, task, letter, memorandum, note, notice, fax, cable, *formal* missive, tidings, epistle, *colloq.* memo **2** MEANING, idea, sense, significance, point, theme, implication, gist, drift, essence, thrust, moral, *formal* purport

▷ **get the message** understand, take in, follow, see, grasp, *formal* comprehend, *colloq.* get it, get the point, get the idea, get the hang, catch the drift, catch on, latch onto, cotton on, tumble to

messenger *n*
courier, envoy, go-between, herald, runner, errand-boy, errand-girl, carrier, bearer, harbinger, agent, ambassador, Hermes, *formal* emissary

messy *adj*
untidy, unkempt, dishevelled, disordered, disorganized, in disarray, chaotic, sloppy, slovenly, confused, muddled, dirty, grubby, filthy, muddled, cluttered, littered, *colloq.* shambolic, slobbish

F3 neat, ordered, tidy

metallic *adj*
1 *metallic elements* copper, iron, tin, lead, nickel, steel, gold, silver, shiny, polished, gleaming **2** *metallic sounds* harsh, grating, jarring, unpleasant, rough, dissonant, jangling

metamorphose *v*
change, alter, transform, remake, remodel, reshape, convert, modify, translate, *technical* mutate, transubstantiate, *formal* transmute, transfigure, *colloq.* transmogrify

metamorphosis *n*
change, alteration, rebirth, regeneration, transfiguration, conversion, modification, change-over, *technical* mutation, *formal* transformation, transmutation, *colloq.* transmogrification

metaphor *n*
figure of speech, allegory, analogy, symbol, emblem, emblematic, visual, picture, image, representation, *formal* trope

metaphorical *adj*
figurative, allegorical, symbolic, analogical, emblematic, visual, representational

F3 literal

metaphysical *adj*
philosophical, theoretical, abstract, unreal, essential, fundamental, basic, subjective, spiritual, supernatural, transcendental, unsubstantial, insubstantial, general, immaterial, speculative, intellectual, ideal, high-flown, intangible, deep, profound, universal, eternal, *formal* abstruse, esoteric, impalpable, incorporeal, recondite

mete *v*
▷ **mete out** allot, apportion, deal out, dole out, hand out, measure out, share out, ration out, portion, distribute, dispense, divide out, assign, administer

meteor *n*
meteorite, meteoroid, bolide, comet, shooting star, fireball, aerolite, aerolith

meteoric *adj*
rapid, speedy, swift, quick, fast, breakneck, accelerated, sudden, lightning, overnight, instantaneous, momentary, brief, transient, spectacular, brilliant, dazzling, flashing

meteorologist *n*
weather forecaster, climatologist, weatherman, weathergirl, weatherlady, met man, met officer, weather prophet

method *n*
1 WAY, approach, means, course, manner, fashion, form, process, procedure, system, practice, route, technique, style, plan, arrangement, scheme, rule, programme, *modus operandi, formal* mode **2** ORGANIZATION, order, structure, system, pattern, arrangement, form, design, plan, planning, regularity, orderliness, routine

methodical *adj*
systematic, structured, organized, ordered, orderly, well-ordered, logical, tidy, regular, planned, efficient, disciplined, businesslike, deliberate, neat, scrupulous, precise, meticulous, painstaking

F3 chaotic, irregular, confused

meticulous *adj*
precise, scrupulous, careful, conscientious, rigorous, exact, punctilious, fussy, particular, detailed, accurate, thorough, fastidious, painstaking, strict

F3 careless, slapdash

métier *n*
calling, vocation, line, line of business, business, occupation, profession, sphere, field, forte, trade, pursuit, speciality, specialty, craft

metropolis *n*
capital, city, main city, large city, municipality, megalopolis, industrial/cultural centre, conurbation, *colloq.* concrete jungle, big smoke

mettle *n*
1 CHARACTER, temperament, disposition, nature, calibre, personality, personal qualities, make-up **2** SPIRIT, courage, bravery, vigour, nerve, boldness, daring, intrepidity, indomitability, fearlessness, pluck, nerve, resolve, determination, endurance, valour, gallantry, fortitude, *colloq.* guts, backbone, spunk

mew *v*
miaow, meow, mewl, caterwaul, whine

mewl *v*
whine, whimper, whinge, cry, blubber, grizzle, snivel

miasma *n*
odour, smell, stench, stink, pollution, reek, *formal* fetor, effluvium, mephitis

miasmal *adj*
foul, noxious, putrid, reeking, smelly, stinking, polluted, unwholesome, *formal* fetid, malodorous, noisome, mephitic, miasm(at)ic, miasm(at)ous

microbe *n*
micro-organism, bacterium, bacillus, germ, virus, pathogen, *colloq.* bug

microscopic *adj*
minute, tiny, extremely small, minuscule, infinitesimal, indiscernible, imperceptible, negligible

F3 huge, enormous

midday *n*
noon, twelve, twelve o'clock, twelve noon, lunchtime, *formal* noonday, noontide

middle *adj, n*
▸ *adj* central, mid, midway, halfway, mean, medium, medial, median, equidistant, intermediate, inner, inside, intervening
▸ *n* centre, halfway point, midpoint, mean, median, heart, core, midst, inside, *colloq.* bull's eye

extreme, end, edge, beginning, border
▷ **in the middle of** busy with, during, engaged in, in the process of, occupied with, surrounded by, while, in the midst of, among

middle-class adj
conventional, suburban, professional, white-colour, gentrified, bourgeois

middleman n
intermediary, go-between, negotiator, entrepreneur, distributor, retailer, broker, fixer

middling adj
mediocre, medium, ordinary, moderate, average, fair, unexceptional, unremarkable, run-of-the-mill, indifferent, modest, adequate, passable, tolerable, *colloq.* so-so, OK

midget n, adj
▶ n person of restricted growth, pygmy, dwarf, Lilliputian, Tom Thumb, gnome, manikin, homunculus
🔁 giant
▶ adj tiny, small, minute, diminutive, dwarf, miniature, little, baby, pocket, pocket-sized, toy, pygmy, Lilliputian, *colloq.* teeny, itsy-bitsy, teeny-weeny
🔁 giant

midst n
middle, centre, midpoint, heart, core, bosom, nucleus, hub, depths, thick, interior
▷ **in the midst** during, in the middle of, among, surrounded by, in the thick of

midway adv
halfway, in the middle, at the midpoint, in the centre, equidistant between, betwixt and between

mien n
appearance, look, manner, aspect, expression, air, complexion, presence, semblance, aura, *formal* bearing, carriage, countenance, demeanour, deportment

miffed adj
annoyed, irritated, displeased, aggrieved, nettled, hurt, offended, put out, resentful, upset, vexed, irked, disgruntled, chagrined, piqued, *colloq.* in a huff, narked, peeved
🔁 delighted, pleased, *colloq.* chuffed

might n
power, strength, force, forcefulness, energy, powerfulness, ability, capability, capacity, sway, vigour, stamina, heftiness, muscularity, potency, valour, prowess, *formal* efficacy, puissance, *colloq.* clout, muscle

mightily adv
exceedingly, very, very much, much, extremely, greatly, highly, hugely, decidedly, intensely, powerfully, strongly, vigorously, energetically, forcefully, lustily, manfully, strenuously

mighty adj
1 STRONG, powerful, potent, forceful, vigorous, hefty, robust, tough, stalwart, stout, strapping, muscular, dominant, influential, doughty, grand, hardy, indomitable, lusty, manful 2 LARGE, enormous, colossal, huge, immense, vast, massive, gigantic, great, tremendous, towering, titanic, stupendous, monumental, bulky, prodigious
🔁 1 frail, weak 2 small

migrant n, adj
▶ n traveller, wanderer, itinerant, emigrant, immigrant, rover, nomad, transient, globetrotter, drifter, Gypsy, tinker, vagrant
▶ adj travelling, wandering, peripatetic, itinerant, immigrant, roving, nomadic, shifting, transient, globetrotting, drifting, Gypsy, migratory, vagrant

migrate v
move, resettle, relocate, wander, roam, rove, journey, emigrate, travel, voyage, hike, trek, drift

migration n
movement, travel, journey, voyage, wandering, roving, emigration, shift, trek, *technical* diaspora, *formal* transhumance

migratory adj
travelling, wandering, peripatetic, itinerant, immigrant, roving, nomadic, shifting, transient, globetrotting, drifting, Gypsy, migrant, vagrant

mild adj
1 *mild manners* gentle, calm, peaceable, placid, tender, tender-hearted, sensitive, soft, soft-hearted, good-natured, kind, sympathetic, warm, warm-hearted, meek, easy-going, amiable, lenient, humane, compassionate, merciful, forbearing 2 *mild weather* calm, temperate, warm, balmy, clement, fair, moderate, pleasant 3 *mild food* bland, mellow, smooth, subtle, soothing, tasteless, insipid
🔁 1 harsh, aggressive, fierce 2 cold, stormy 3 strong, sharp, spicy

mildewy adj
rotten, fusty, musty, *formal* fetid, mucedinous, mucid

mildness n
1 GENTLENESS, calmness, placidity, tenderness, softness, docility, kindness, sympathy, warmth, meekness, indulgence, leniency, lenity, compassion, mercy, forbearance, tranquillity, passivity 2 TEMPERATENESS, calmness, warmth, clemency, moderation 3 BLANDNESS, mellowness, smoothness, tastelessness, insipidness
🔁 1 harshness, aggressiveness, violence 2 storminess 3 sharpness

milieu n
environment, location, scene, setting, surroundings, background, locale, medium, arena, element, sphere

militant adj, n
▶ adj aggressive, belligerent, vigorous, fighting, combative, embattled, warring, assertive, activist, *formal* pugnacious
🔁 pacifist, peaceful
▶ n activist, combatant, fighter, struggler, soldier, warrior, aggressor, belligerent, partisan

military adj, n
▶ adj martial, armed, army, soldierly, warlike, service, disciplined
▶ n army, armed forces, soldiers, forces, services, militia, air force, navy

---

Military terms include :

about turn, absent without leave (AWOL), action stations, action, adjutant, aide-de-camp (ADC), air cover, air-drop, Airborne Warning and Control System (AWACS), allies, ambush, arm, armed forces, armistice, army, arsenal, artillery, assault course, atomic warfare, attack, attention, barracks, base, battle fatigue, battle, beachhead, billet, bivouac, blockade, bomb, bombardment, brevet, bridgehead, briefing, brigade, bugle call, call up, camouflage, camp, campaign, canteen, carpet-bombing, cease-fire, charge, citation, colours, combat, command, commission, company, conquest, conscript, conscription, corps, counter-attack, court-martial, crossfire, debriefing, decamp, decoration, defeat, defence, demilitarize, *colloq.* demob, demotion, depot, desertion, detachment, detail, disarmament, discharge, dispatches, division, draft, drill, duty, encampment, enemy, enlist, ensign, epaulette, evacuation, excursion, expedition, fall out, fatigues, firing line, first post, flank, fleet, flight, flotilla, foe, foray, forced march, friendly fire, front line, fusillade, garrison, guard, incursion, infantry, insignia, inspection, installation, insubordination, intelligence, invasion, kitbag, landing, last post, latrine, leave, left wheel, liaison, lines, logistics, manoeuvres, march, marching orders, march past, married quarters, martinet, minefield, mission, mobilize, munitions, muster, mutiny, national service, navy, Navy, Army and Air Force Institutes (NAAFI), nuclear warfare, observation post, offensive, operational command, operational fleet, operations, orders, ordnance, outpost, padre, parade, parade ground, parley, parole, patrol, pincer movement, platoon, posting, prisoner of war (POW), quartermaster, quarters, quick march, radar, range, rank, ration, rearguard, *colloq.* recce, recruit, regiment, reinforcements, requisition, retreat, reveille, rifle range, roll-call, rout, route march, salute, sentry, shell, shell-shock, signal, skirmish, slow march, sniper, sortie, squad, squadron, *slang* square-bashing, standard, stores, strategy, supplies, surrender, tactics, tank, target, task-force, tattoo, the front, training, trench, trench warfare, troop, truce, unit, vanguard, victory, wing. *See also* ARMED SERVICES; RANK[1]; SAILOR; SOLDIER.

militate *v*
▷ **militate against** oppose, discourage, counter, counteract, go/count against, act/tell against, weigh against, be detrimental to, be harmful to, be disadvantageous to, damage, hurt, prejudice, be a decisive factor against, contend, resist
▷ **militate for** help, promote, speak for, back, further, advance, aid

militia *n*
reserve, reservists, Territorial Army, yeomanry, National Guard, minutemen

milk *v*
1 DRAIN, bleed, tap, extract, draw (off), exploit, use, express, press, pump, siphon, squeeze, wring **2** EXPLOIT, use, squeeze, wring, pump, take advantage of, oppress, impose on, manipulate, *colloq.* bleed, rip off

milksop *n*
coward, weakling, namby-pamby, sissy, *colloq.* wimp, mummy's boy

milky *adj*
white, milk-white, chalky, opaque, clouded, cloudy

mill *n, v*
▶ *n* **1** FACTORY, plant, processing plant, works, workshop, shop, foundry **2** GRINDER, crusher, quern, roller
▶ *v* grind, pulverize, powder, pound, crush, crunch, roll, press, grate, *formal* comminute
▷ **mill around** move about, crowd around, throng, swarm, stream, press around

millstone *n*
burden, load, encumbrance, weight, obligation, duty, onus, trouble, affliction, grindstone, quernstone, *colloq.* cross to bear

mime *n, v*
▶ *n* dumb show, pantomime, gesture, mimicry, mummery, charade
▶ *v* gesture, signal, indicate, act out, represent, simulate, impersonate, mimic, imitate

mimic *v, n*
▶ *v* imitate, parody, caricature, copy, ape, parrot, impersonate, echo, mirror, resemble, simulate, look like, *formal* emulate, *colloq.* take off, send up

▶ *n* imitator, impersonator, impressionist, mimicker, caricaturist, parrot, copy, copyist, *colloq.* copycat

mimicry *n*
imitation, imitating, impersonation, copying, parody, impression, caricature, aping, burlesque, *colloq.* take-off

mince *v*
1 CHOP, cut, cut into very small pieces, hash, dice, grind, crumble **2** *not mince your words* suppress, diminish, play down, tone down, speak indirectly, hold back, moderate, weaken, soften, spare **3** WALK AFFECTEDLY, attitudinize, pose, strike a pose, posture, simper, walk in an effeminate/a dainty way

mincing *adj*
dainty, effeminate, nice, precious, foppish, pretentious, minikin, niminy-piminy, coxcombic(al), *formal* affected, *colloq.* la-di-da, sissy

mind *n, v*
▶ *n* **1** INTELLIGENCE, intellect, reason, powers of reasoning, judgement, sense, understanding, comprehension, wits, mentality, thinking, thoughts, subconscious, head, genius, concentration, application, attention, spirit, psyche, *technical* psyche, *formal* ratiocination, *colloq.* brains, brainbox, grey matter, little grey cells **2** MEMORY, remembrance, recollection, recall, retention **3** OPINION, view, viewpoint, point of view, way of thinking, belief, attitude, judgement, outlook, feeling, sentiment **4** INCLINATION, disposition, tendency, will, wish, intention, desire, fancy, urge, notion **5** THINKER, intellect, intellectual, genius, mastermind, scholar, expert, *colloq.* egghead, brain, brainbox
▷ **be in two minds** be uncertain, hesitate, be hesitant, be unsure, be undecided, waver, vacillate, dither, *colloq.* shilly-shally, dilly-dally
▷ **bear/keep in mind** consider, remember, note, take note of, make a mental note of, take into account/consideration, give thought to
▷ **cross your mind** think of, remember, occur to, come to, strike, hit
▷ **make up your mind** decide, come to/arrive at a decision, reach/make a decision, choose, determine, settle, resolve
▷ **mind's eye** imagination, mind, head, contemplation, memory, recollection, remembrance
▶ *v* **1** OBJECT (TO), take offence (at), be offended by, be bothered by, be annoyed by, care about, resent, disapprove, dislike **2** *mind the traffic* WATCH, be careful, heed, pay attention, pay heed to, regard, note, obey, respect, listen to, concentrate on, comply with, follow, mark, observe, watch **3** MAKE SURE, ensure, make certain, take care, remember, not forget, note **4** LOOK AFTER, take care of, watch over, guard, have charge of, attend to, *colloq.* keep an eye on
▷ **mind out** be careful, take care, look out, watch out, watch, pay attention, beware, be on your guard, keep your eyes open
▷ **never mind 1** TAKE NO NOTICE OF, not bother about, don't worry, forget it **2** LET ALONE, not to mention, not forgetting, apart from, also, as well as, too

mindful *adj*
aware, conscious, alive (to), alert, attentive, paying attention to, careful, watchful, wary, chary, heedful
🖪 heedless, inattentive, *formal* cognizant, sensible

mindless *adj*
1 THOUGHTLESS, senseless, illogical, irrational, stupid, foolish, witless, dull, unintelligent, gratuitous, negligent, *colloq.* dumb, dopey, thick, bird-brained **2** MECHANICAL, automatic, tedious, routine, involuntary, instinctive
🖪 **1** thoughtful, intelligent

mine *n, v*
▶ *n* **1** PIT, colliery, coalfield, excavation, quarry, well, vein, lode, seam, shaft, trench, deposit

Parts of a coalmine include:

air lock; bord-and-pillar, long-wall, long-wall face, retreat long-wall; bunker, cage, cage-winding system, capping, charging conveyor, coal seam, coal-bearing rock; coal-cutter, jib coal-cutter, plough coal-cutter, scraper chain, pan, shearer loader; fan drift, fault line, gallery, goaf/gob/waste, overburden; pit prop, hydraulic pit prop, powered support; pithead frame, pithead gear; shaft, main shaft, staple shaft, lateral; skip winding system, spoil, sump/sink, tunnelling machine, ventilation shaft, winding engine.

2 SUPPLY, source, stock, store, storehouse, reserve, reservoir, quarry, fund, repository, hoard, treasury, wealth **3** LAND MINE, explosive, depth charge, bomb
▶ *v* excavate, dig for, dig up, delve, quarry, extract, unearth, tunnel, remove, undermine

miner *n*
coalminer, collier, pitman

minerals *n*

Minerals include:

alabaster, albite, anhydrite, asbestos, aventurine, azurite, bentonite, blacklead, bloodstone, blue john, borax, cairngorm, calamine, calcite, calcspar, cassiterite, chalcedony, chlorite, chrysoberyl, cinnabar, corundum, dolomite, emery, feldspar, fluorite, fluorspar, fool's gold, French chalk, galena, graphite, gypsum, haematite, halite, haüyne, hornblende, hyacinth, idocrase, jacinth, jargoon, jet, kandite, kaolinite, lapis lazuli, lazurite, magnetite, malachite, meerschaum, mica, microcline, montmorillonite, olivine, orthoclase, peridot, plumbago, pyrites, quartz, rock salt, rutile, saltpetre, sanidine, silica, smithsonite, sodalite, spar, sphalerite, spinel, talc, uralite, uranite, vesuvianite, wurtzite, zircon.

mingle *v*
1 MIX, intermingle, intermix, combine, blend, merge, unite, alloy, fuse, amalgamate, coalesce, join, compound **2** ASSOCIATE, socialize, circulate, *formal* commingle, *colloq.* hobnob, rub shoulders

miniature *adj*
tiny, small, small-scale, scaled-down, minute, reduced, diminutive, midget, toy, dwarf, baby, pocket-sized, little, *Scot.* wee, *colloq.* pint-size(d), mini
F3 giant

minimal *adj*
least, smallest, minimum, slightest, littlest, negligible, minute, token, nominal

minimize *v*
1 REDUCE, decrease, diminish, cut, curtail, shrink, *colloq.* slash **2** BELITTLE, make light of, make little of, deprecate, discount, play down, underestimate, underrate, trivialize, laugh off, *formal* disparage, decry, *colloq.* soft-pedal
F3 **1** maximize **2** emphasize, play up

minimum *n, adj*
▶ *n* least, lowest, lowest point, lowest number, smallest quantity, slightest, bottom, *formal* nadir
F3 maximum
▶ *adj* minimal, least, lowest, slightest, smallest, littlest, tiniest
F3 maximum

minion *n*
1 ATTENDANT, follower, underling, lackey, flunkey, hireling, servant, menial, drudge **2** DEPENDANT, hanger-on, favourite, darling, sycophant, fawner, parasite, leech, *colloq.* yes-man, bootlicker

minister *n, v*
▶ *n* **1** OFFICIAL, office-holder, politician, dignitary, diplomat, ambassador, delegate, legate, envoy, emissary, representative, consul, cabinet minister, agent, aide, administrator, executive, department secretary **2** CLERGYMAN, churchman, cleric, parson, priest, dean, pastor, vicar, rector, verger, curate, deacon, elder, chaplain, preacher, divine, padre, *formal* ecclesiastic
▶ *v* attend, serve, tend, take care of, look after, administer, wait on, cater to, accommodate, nurse

ministration *n*
help, aid, assistance, care, service, relief, supervision, backing, support, favour, patronage, *formal* succour

ministry *n*
1 GOVERNMENT, cabinet, department, office, bureau, administration **2** THE CHURCH, holy orders, the priesthood

minor *adj*
lesser, secondary, small, smaller, inferior, subordinate, subsidiary, junior, younger, unimportant, insignificant, inconsiderable, unknown, little known, negligible, petty, trivial, trifling, second-class, unclassified, slight, light
F3 major, significant, important

minstrel *n*
singer, musician, troubadour, bard, rhymer, joculator, jongleur

mint *v, adj, n*
▶ *v* **1** COIN, stamp, strike, cast, forge, punch, make, manufacture, produce, construct, devise, fashion **2** INVENT, make up, coin, fabricate, forge, falsify, fake, trump up, concoct, hatch
▶ *adj* perfect, brand-new, new, as new, fresh, immaculate, undamaged, unblemished, unused, excellent, first-class
▶ *n* fortune, wealth, riches, *colloq.* pile, packet, bomb, bundle, heap, stack, million

minuscule *adj*
tiny, fine, little, very small, minute, miniature, microscopic, infinitesimal, diminutive, Lilliputian, *colloq.* teeny, teeny-weeny, itsy-bitsy
F3 gigantic, huge

minute¹ *n*
1 *ten minutes* moment, second, instant, short (length of) time, flash, *colloq.* jiffy, tick **2** *the minute something happens* the moment, immediately, the instant, the point, directly, no sooner, as soon as
▷ **in a minute** soon, very soon, shortly, in a moment, in a flash, before long, in the near future, *colloq.* pronto, in a jiffy/tick, in two shakes of a lamb's tail, before you can say Jack Robinson
▷ **up to the minute** latest, most modern, newest, most recent, fashionable, *colloq.* with it, in, all the rage

minute² *adj*
1 TINY, very small, infinitesimal, minuscule, microscopic, diminutive, miniature, inconsiderable, insignificant, infinitesimal, negligible, slight, trifling, trivial, Lilliputian **2** DETAILED, precise, accurate, exact, meticulous, painstaking, close, strict, critical, exhaustive, punctilious
F3 **1** gigantic, huge **2** cursory, superficial

minutely *adv*
closely, in detail, meticulously, painstakingly, scrupu-

lously, systematically, precisely, exactly, exhaustively, critically, *colloq.* with a fine-tooth comb

minutes *n*
proceedings, record(s), notes, memorandum, transcript, transactions, details, tapes

minutiae *n*
details, fine details, finer points, intricacies, complexities, particulars, niceties, subtleties, trifles, trivialities, *colloq.* small print

miracle *n*
wonder, marvel, prodigy, phenomenon

miraculous *adj*
1 WONDERFUL, marvellous, phenomenal, extraordinary, remarkable, incredible, amazing, astounding, astonishing, unbelievable **2** SUPERNATURAL, inexplicable, unaccountable, phenomenal, extraordinary, remarkable, unbelievable, superhuman
◻ natural, normal

mirage *n*
illusion, optical illusion, hallucination, fantasy, phantasm, phantasmagoria

mire *n, v*
▶ *n* **1** QUAGMIRE, quag, marsh, marshland, morass, bog, fen, swamp, slough, *Scot.* glaur **2** MUCK, mud, dirt, slime, ooze **3** DIFFICULTIES, trouble, mess, *colloq.* spot, jam, pickle, fix, hole, stew
▶ *v* sink, bog down, overwhelm, deluge

mirror *n, v*
▶ *n* **1** GLASS, looking-glass, reflector **2** REFLECTION, likeness, exact likeness, image, double, twin, copy, clone, *colloq.* dead ringer, spitting image
▶ *v* reflect, echo, imitate, copy, follow, represent, show, depict, mimic, parrot, ape, *formal* emulate

mirth *n*
merriment, hilarity, gaiety, fun, laughter, enjoyment, pleasure, jollity, jocularity, amusement, frolics, revelry, glee, cheerfulness, light-heartedness, high spirits, buoyancy, *formal* blitheness
◻ gloom, melancholy

mirthful *adj*
merry, hilarious, laughing, laughable, uproarious, pleasurable, jolly, jovial, amusing, funny, amused, happy, gay, cheerful, cheery, glad, gladsome, light-hearted, light-spirited, vivacious, buoyant, playful, sportive, frolicsome, festive, *formal* blithe, jocund
◻ gloomy, glum, melancholy, mirthless

miry *adj*
marshy, swampy, boggy, fenny, muddy, mucky, dirty, oozy, slimy, *Scot.* glaury

misadventure *n*
bad luck, hard luck, accident, ill fortune, ill luck, misfortune, mischance, calamity, catastrophe, tragedy, mishap, disaster, failure, debacle, cataclysm, reverse, setback

misanthropic *adj*
antisocial, unfriendly, surly, unsociable, unsympathetic, malevolent, egoistic, inhumane
◻ philanthropic

misanthropy *n*
antisociality, unsociableness, malevolence, egoism, inhumanity
◻ philanthropy

misapply *v*
misuse, use unwisely/unsuitably, pervert, misappropriate, misemploy, abuse, exploit

misapprehend *v*
misunderstand, misinterpret, miscomprehend, misconceive, misconstrue, mistake, misread, get the wrong idea, get a false impression, *colloq.* get hold of the wrong end of the stick
◻ apprehend

misapprehension *n*
misunderstanding, misconception, misinterpretation, misreading, error, mistake, wrong idea, false impression, fallacy, delusion

misappropriate *v*
steal, embezzle, pocket, thieve, pilfer, rob, swindle, misspend, misuse, misapply, abuse, pervert, *formal* peculate, defalcate, *colloq.* filch, pinch, nab, nick, have your fingers/hand in the till

misappropriation *n*
embezzlement, stealing, theft, pilfering, robbing, pocketing, misapplication, misuse, *formal* defalcation, peculation

misbegotten *adj*
1 DISHONEST, disreputable, stolen, unlawful, illicit, ill-gotten, shady, *formal* purloined **2** ILL-CONCEIVED, ill-advised, poorly thought-out, abortive, *colloq.* hare-brained **3** ILLEGITIMATE, natural, born out of wedlock

misbehave *v*
behave unacceptably/badly, be naughty, be rude, mess about, fool about/around, be beyond the pale, get up to mischief, offend, disobey, lapse, trespass, *formal* transgress, *colloq.* muck about, play up, act up, carry on

misbehaviour *n*
unacceptable/bad behaviour, misconduct, bad manners, disobedience, naughtiness, mischief, insubordination, *formal* misdemeanour, impropriety, *colloq.* mucking about, carryings-on

misbelief *n*
wrong belief, delusion, illusion, error, mistake, misapprehension, misunderstanding, misconception, fallacy, heresy, unorthodoxy, heterodoxy

miscalculate *v*
misjudge, get wrong, go wrong, make a mistake, slip up, blunder, err, miscount, overestimate, underestimate, *colloq.* boob

miscarriage *n*
1 *have a miscarriage* spontaneous abortion **2** FAILURE, breakdown, abortion, aborting, mishap, mismanagement, error, perversion, ruination, disappointment
◻ **2** success, fulfilment

miscarry *v*
1 *she miscarried* abort, lose the baby, have a spontaneous abortion **2** FAIL, abort, come to nothing, fall through, go wrong, go amiss, misfire, founder, come to grief, *colloq.* flop, fold, not come off, come a cropper, bite the dust
◻ **2** succeed

miscellaneous *adj*
mixed, varied, various, assorted, diverse, diversified, sundry, motley, jumbled, indiscriminate, *formal* heterogeneous, multifarious, variegated

miscellany *n*
assortment, mixture, mix, variety, collection, anthology, medley, potpourri, hotch-potch, jumble, diversity, pastiche, patchwork, gallimaufry, farrago, salmangundi, smorgasbord, *formal* conglomeration, *colloq.* mixed bag, mishmash, omnium-gatherum

mischance *n*
accident, misfortune, bad break, ill-chance, ill-fortune, ill-luck, misadventure, disaster, tragedy, calamity, mishap, blow, contretemps, *formal* infelicity

mischief *n*
1 TROUBLE, harm, hurt, evil, damage, injury, disruption **2** MISBEHAVIOUR, bad behaviour, naughtiness, impishness, roguishness, devilment, pranks, tricks, escapade, wrongdoing, *colloq.* monkey business, shenanigans, carry-on, hanky-panky, jiggery-pokery,

funny business **3** IMP, monkey, rascal, rogue, stirrer, scallywag, scamp, nuisance, pest, tyke, villain, devil

mischievous *adj*
1 MALICIOUS, evil, spiteful, vicious, wicked, malignant, pernicious, destructive, harmful, hurtful, injurious, detrimental **2** NAUGHTY, badly-behaved, bad, disobedient, misbehaving, impish, rascally, roguish, playful, teasing, frolicsome, troublesome
F₃ 1 kind **2** well-behaved, good

misconceive *v*
misunderstand, misapprehend, misinterpret, misread, misjudge, misconstrue, mistake, *colloq.* get hold of the wrong end of the stick

misconception *n*
misapprehension, misunderstanding, misreading, misinterpretation, error, mistake, fallacy, delusion, wrong idea, false impression, *colloq.* the wrong end of the stick

misconduct *n*
misbehaviour, bad/unacceptable behaviour, malpractice, unethical/unprofessional behaviour, mismanagement, wrongdoing, *formal* impropriety, misdemeanour

misconstrue *v*
misinterpret, misjudge, misread, misunderstand, misconceive, misapprehend, mistranslate, misreckon, mistake, take the wrong way, *colloq.* get hold of the wrong end of the stick

miscreant *n*
wrongdoer, criminal, evildoer, sinner, rogue, rascal, scoundrel, scamp, scallywag, villain, vagabond, wretch, reprobate, profligate, mischief-maker, knave, dastard, troublemaker, *formal* malefactor
F₃ worthy

misdeed *n*
wrong, wrongdoing, crime, felony, offence, peccadillo, delinquency, error, fault, misconduct, villainy, sin, trespass, *formal* misdemeanour, transgression

misdemeanour *n*
wrongdoing, wrong, misdeed, offence, infringement, lapse, fault, error, indiscretion, misbehaviour, misconduct, trespass, peccadillo, *formal* malfeasance, transgression

miser *n*
niggard, skinflint, cheeseparer, Scrooge, *colloq.* penny-pincher, cheapskate, meanie, tightwad, money-grubber
F₃ spendthrift

miserable *adj*
1 UNHAPPY, sad, sorrowful, dejected, despondent, depressed, downcast, downhearted, heartbroken, low-spirited, wretched, distressed, crushed, desolate, forlorn, gloomy, glum, *formal* disconsolate, melancholic, *colloq.* down, down in the dumps, blue **2** *miserable weather* CHEERLESS, depressing, dreary, gloomy, dismal, disagreeable, unpleasant, forlorn, joyless **3** *miserable living conditions* impoverished, shabby, squalid, poor, wretched **4** CONTEMPTIBLE, despicable, ignominious, detestable, vile, base, mean, disgraceful, deplorable, low, shameful **5** MEAGRE, paltry, niggardly, scanty, poor, worthless, pathetic, pitiful, *colloq.* measly **6** GRUMPY, bad-tempered, ill-tempered, irritable, surly, sullen, *colloq.* grouchy, crotchety
F₃ 1 cheerful, happy **2** pleasant **3** happy **5** generous

miserliness *n*
meanness, niggardliness, tightness, tight-fistedness, close-fistedness, frugality, parsimony, penny-pinching, cheeseparing, covetousness, avarice, *formal* penuriousness, *colloq.* minginess, stinginess
F₃ generosity, lavishness, *formal* prodigality

miserly *adj*
mean, niggardly, tight, tight-fisted, close-fisted, sparing, parsimonious, cheeseparing, beggarly, *formal* penurious, *colloq.* stingy, penny-pinching, mingy, money-grubbing
F₃ generous, spendthrift

misery *n*
1 UNHAPPINESS, sadness, suffering, sorrow, distress, depression, discomfort, despair, anguish, agony, gloom, grief, wretchedness, adversity, misfortune, *formal* woe, melancholy, affliction **2** DEPRIVATION, hardship, poverty, want, oppression, destitution, *formal* privation, penury, indigence **3** SPOILSPORT, pessimist, killjoy, moaner, complainer, prophet of doom, Jeremiah, *colloq.* wet blanket, grouch, whiner, whinger, sourpuss
F₃ 1 contentment **2** comfort

misfire *v*
miscarry, go wrong, go amiss, go awry, abort, fail, fall through, founder, fizzle out, come to grief, *colloq.* flop, not come off, come a cropper, bite the dust
F₃ succeed

misfit *n*
individualist, nonconformist, eccentric, maverick, dropout, loner, lone wolf, *colloq.* oddball, weirdo, freak, odd one out, fish out of water, square peg in a round hole
F₃ conformist

misfortune *n*
bad luck, mischance, mishap, ill-luck, hard luck, misadventure, setback, reverse, failure, calamity, catastrophe, disaster, blow, accident, tragedy, trouble, adversity, evil, sorrow, hardship, trial, *formal* tribulation, affliction, woe
F₃ luck, success

misgiving *n*
doubt, uncertainty, unease, hesitation, qualm, reservation, apprehension, scruple, suspicion, distrust, second thoughts, niggle, anxiety, worry, fear
F₃ confidence

misguided *adj*
misled, misconceived, ill-considered, ill-advised, ill-judged, imprudent, rash, misdirected, misinformed, misplaced, deluded, foolish, erroneous, wrong, mistaken, *formal* fallacious, injudicious
F₃ sensible, wise

mishandle *v*
mismanage, make a mess of, bungle, misjudge, mess up, *colloq.* botch, make a hash of, make a pig's ear of, muff, *slang* screw up
F₃ cope, manage

mishap *n*
misfortune, ill-fortune, stroke of bad luck, misadventure, accident, reverse, setback, calamity, catastrophe, disaster, adversity, blow, incident, trouble, trial, *formal* tribulation

mishmash *n*
hotchpotch, hodge-podge, jumble, medley, potpourri, pastiche, mess, muddle, salad, hash, farrago, gallimaufry, salmagundi, olla-podrida, olio, *formal* conglomeration

misinform *v*
mislead, misdirect, misguide, deceive, bluff, hoodwink, *colloq.* lead up the garden path, take for a ride, give a bum steer

misinformation *n*
disinformation, misleading, misdirection, nonsense, bluff, lies, baloney, *colloq.* bum steer, dope, eyewash, guff, hype

misinterpret *v*
misconstrue, misread, misunderstand, mistake, mis-

judge, misconceive, misapprehend, distort, garble, take the wrong way, *colloq.* get hold of the wrong end of the stick

misjudge *v*
miscalculate, mistake, misinterpret, misconstrue, misunderstand, overestimate, underestimate, have a wrong opinion about

mislay *v*
lose, misplace, miss, forget where you have put, lose sight of, lose track of, be unable to find, misfile

mislead *v*
misinform, misdirect, misguide, misrepresent, deceive, fool into, delude, lead astray, fool, hoodwink, *colloq.* send on a wild-goose chase, lead up the garden path, take for a ride, pull a fast one on, pull the wool over someone's eyes

misleading *adj*
deceptive, deceiving, confusing, unreliable, equivocal, ambiguous, biased, loaded, evasive, delusive, illusory, *formal* fallacious, *colloq.* tricky
🔝 unequivocal, authoritative, informative

mismanage *v*
mishandle, botch, bungle, make a mess of, mess up, misrule, misspend, misjudge, foul up, mar, waste, *colloq.* botch, make a hash of, make a pig's ear of, muff, *slang* screw up

mismatched *adj*
clashing, discordant, ill-assorted, incompatible, unmatching, misallied, mismated, unsuited, unreconcilable, irregular, *formal* incongruous, disparate, antipathetic
🔝 compatible, matching

misogynist *n*
woman-hater, anti-feminist, male chauvinist, male supremacist, sexist, misogamist, *colloq.* male chauvinist pig (MCP)
🔝 feminist

misplace *v*
lose, mislay, miss, misapply, misassign, misfile, forget where you have put, lose sight of, lose track of, be unable to find

misprint *n*
mistake, error, literal, printing error, typographical error, *formal* corrigendum, erratum, *colloq.* typo

misquote *v*
misrepresent, misreport, muddle, misstate, twist, distort, pervert, falsify, garble, misremember

misrepresent *v*
distort, falsify, slant, pervert, twist, garble, misquote, exaggerate, minimize, misconstrue, misinterpret, misreport, misstate, give a false/wrong account of

misrule *n*
disorder, disorganization, maladministration, misgovernment, mismanagement, chaos, confusion, indiscipline, lawlessness, anarchy, riot, tumult, turmoil, turbulence, unreason

miss[1] *v, n*
▶ *v* 1 *miss a target* FAIL, lose, let slip, let go, omit, fail, fail to hit/get/catch, miscarry, overlook, pass over, slip, leave out, mistake, trip, misunderstand, err, *colloq.* blow, muff 2 *miss a meeting* be absent from, be away from, fail to attend, not take part in, not go to, not go to see, not see, not be part of, be too late for 3 *miss an opportunity* let go, let slip, fail to seize, not take advantage of, neglect, disregard, overlook 4 NOT NOTICE, not spot, fail to notice, fail to notice the absence of, overlook, disregard 5 AVOID, escape, evade, dodge, forego, skip, bypass, sidestep, *formal* circumvent 6 PINE FOR, long for, yearn for, regret, feel

the loss of, grieve for, mourn, sorrow for, ache for, want, wish, need, lament
🔝 1 hit, get, catch 2 take part in 3 seize 4 notice, spot
▷ **miss out** bypass, dispense with, disregard, ignore, jump, leave out, omit, pass over, skip
▶ *n* failure, error, blunder, mistake, omission, oversight, fault, slip, fiasco, *colloq.* flop

miss[2] *n*
Miss Bancroft girl, schoolgirl, young lady, young woman, teenager, Ms, mademoiselle, damsel, lass, maid, maiden

missal *n*
breviary, formulary, mass-book, office-book, prayer-book, servicebook, euchologion, Triodion

misshapen *adj*
deformed, distorted, twisted, malformed, warped, contorted, crooked, crippled, bent, misproportioned, grotesque, ugly, monstrous
🔝 regular, shapely

missile *n*
projectile, shot, guided missile, ballistic missile, arrow, shaft, dart, rocket, bomb, shell, flying bomb, grenade, torpedo, weapon

missing *adj*
absent, lost, lacking, gone, mislaid, unaccounted-for, wanting, disappeared, astray, gone astray, strayed, misplaced, nowhere to be found
🔝 found, present

mission *n*
1 TASK, undertaking, assignment, operation, campaign, crusade, business, errand, work, duty, chore 2 CALLING, duty, purpose, vocation, *raison d'être*, aim, goal, quest, pursuit, charge, office, job, work 3 COMMISSION, ministry, delegation, deputation, task-force, legation, embassy

missionary *n*
evangelist, campaigner, preacher, converter, proselytizer, apostle, minister, crusader, propagandist, champion, promoter, emissary, envoy, ambassador

missive *n*
communication, dispatch, letter, line, message, report, note, bulletin, communiqué, memorandum, *formal* epistle, *colloq.* memo

misspent *adj*
wasted, frittered away, squandered, thrown away, idle, idled away, misused, profitless, misapplied, dissipated, unprofitable, *formal* prodigal
🔝 profitable

misstate *v*
misreport, misrepresent, misquote, misrelate, pervert, twist, distort, falsify, garble, misremember

mist *n, v*
▶ *n* haze, fog, vapour, smog, cloud, condensation, film, spray, drizzle, mizzle, dew, steam, veil, dimness
▶ *v* ▷ **mist over/up** cloud over, become cloudy, become hazy, fog (up), dim, blur, become blurred, steam up, obscure, veil, glaze
🔝 clear

mistake *n, v*
▶ *n* error, inaccuracy, slip, oversight, aberration, lapse, slip of the tongue, blunder, gaffe, fault, *faux pas*, indiscretion, misjudgement, miscalculation, misunderstanding, misapprehension, misprint, misspelling, misreading, mispronunciation, *formal* solecism, erratum, corrigendum, *colloq.* bloomer, howler, clanger, slip-up, muff, fluff, goof, botch-up, boob, booboo, a bad move, blooper
▶ *v* 1 MISUNDERSTAND, misapprehend, misconstrue, misjudge, misread, miscalculate, get wrong, slip up, blunder, err, *colloq.* muff, boob, goof (it), put

your foot in it, get your wires crossed **2** *mistake a person for another* confuse, mix up, confound, muddle (up)

mistaken *adj*
wrong, incorrect, in error, erroneous, inaccurate, inexact, untrue, unfounded, inappropriate, ill-judged, inauthentic, false, deceived, deluded, misguided, misinformed, misled, faulty, at fault, *formal* fallacious, *colloq.* having got hold of the wrong end of the stick, get the wrong idea, wide of the mark
Fa correct, right

mistakenly *adv*
wrongly, by mistake, erroneously, incorrectly, falsely, inaccurately, inappropriately, misguidedly, unfairly, unjustly, *formal* fallaciously
Fa appropriately, correctly, fairly, justly

mistimed *adj*
inconvenient, unfortunate, untimely, ill-timed, inopportune, unseasonable, unsynchronized, tactless, *formal* infelicitous, malapropos
Fa opportune

mistreat *v*
abuse, misuse, ill-treat, ill-use, maltreat, treat badly, mishandle, harm, hurt, bully, batter, injure, molest, maul, *colloq.* knock about, beat up, walk (all) over
Fa cosset, pamper

mistreatment *n*
maltreatment, abuse, ill-treatment, ill-use, harm, hurt, battering, injury, molestation, bullying, cruelty, unkindness, manhandling, mauling, mishandling, misuse, ill-usage, brutalization
Fa cosseting, pampering

mistress *n*
1 LOVER, live-in lover, partner, girlfriend, kept woman, concubine, courtesan, paramour, woman, ladylove, inamorata, hetaera, *colloq.* bit on the side **2** TEACHER, schoolteacher, governess, tutor

mistrust *n, v*
▸ *n* distrust, doubt, suspicion, wariness, misgiving, reservations, qualm, hesitancy, chariness, caution, uncertainty, scepticism, apprehension
Fa trust
▸ *v* distrust, doubt, have doubts about, have no faith in, suspect, be suspicious of, be wary of, beware, have reservations, have misgivings, fear
Fa trust

mistrustful *adj*
distrustful, doubtful, dubious, hesitant, sceptical, suspicious, uncertain, wary, cautious, apprehensive, fearful, shy, chary, cynical, *colloq.* leery
Fa trustful

misty *adj*
hazy, foggy, cloudy, blurred, fuzzy, murky, smoky, unclear, dim, indistinct, obscure, opaque, vague, nebulous, veiled
Fa clear, distinct

misunderstand *v*
misapprehend, misconstrue, misinterpret, misread, misjudge, mistake, get wrong, get the wrong idea, get a false impression, miss the point, mishear, *colloq.* get hold of the wrong end of the stick, not make head or tail of, get your wires crossed
Fa understand

misunderstanding *n*
1 MISTAKE, error, misapprehension, misconception, misjudgement, misinterpretation, wrong idea, false impression, misreading, mix-up, *colloq.* the wrong end of the stick, crossed wires **2** DISAGREEMENT, argument, dispute, conflict, clash, difference, difference of opinion, breach, quarrel, rift, row, squabble, *formal* discord, *colloq.* falling-out, tiff
Fa **1** understanding **2** agreement

misunderstood *adj*
misappreciated, misconstrued, misjudged, misread, misrepresented, mistaken, unappreciated, unrecognized, misheard, misinterpreted, ill-judged

misuse *n, v*
▸ *n* mistreatment, maltreatment, mishandling, injury, abuse, wrong use, harm, ill-treatment, misapplication, misemployment, misappropriation, waste, squandering, perversion, corruption, exploitation
▸ *v* abuse, misapply, misemploy, ill-use, ill-treat, treat badly, harm, mistreat, wrong, distort, injure, hurt, corrupt, pervert, waste, squander, misappropriate, exploit, dissipate

> **misuse** or **abuse** ? *See panel at* ABUSE.

mite *n*
bit, trace, spark, whit, touch, atom, morsel, scrap, grain, jot, iota, modicum, ounce, *colloq.* smidgen, tad

mitigate *v*
moderate, temper, alleviate, reduce, lessen, calm, pacify, soften, soothe, still, subdue, tone down, weaken, placate, quiet, decrease, diminish, dull, check, ease, mollify, lighten, modify, blunt, *formal* abate, allay, appease, assuage, extenuate, palliate, remit, lenify
Fa increase, exacerbate, aggravate

mitigating *adj*
extenuating, justifying, vindicating, tempering, modifying, qualifying, vindicatory, *formal* palliative

mitigation *n*
moderation, lessening, tempering, reduction, relief, easement, alleviation, decrease, diminution, qualification, mollification, *formal* abatement, allaying, appeasement, assuagement, extenuation, palliation, remission
Fa increase, exacerbation, aggravation

mix *v, n*
▸ *v* **1** COMBINE, blend, mingle, put together, intermingle, intermix, amalgamate, compound, homogenize, synthesize, merge, join, unite, coalesce, fuse, alloy, incorporate, stir, whisk, mash, emulsify, infiltrate, introduce, fold in, *formal* interpolate **2** ASSOCIATE, consort, fraternize, socialize, meet others, mingle, join, *colloq.* hobnob **3** BE COMPATIBLE, harmonize, get along/on, agree, complement, go well with, suit, *colloq.* be on the same wavelength
Fa **1** divide, separate
▷ **mix in** add in, blend, merge, introduce, incorporate, infiltrate, *formal* interpolate
Fa extract, isolate
▷ **mix up** confuse, bewilder, muddle (up), mistake, perplex, puzzle, confound, mix, jumble, get jumbled up, complicate, garble, involve, implicate, disturb, upset, snarl up
▸ *n* mixture, blend, amalgam, amalgamation, assortment, combination, union, compound, merger, coalition, alloy, fusion, synthesis, medley, composite, *formal* conglomerate, *colloq.* mishmash

mixed *adj*
1 *mixed race* combined, hybrid, mingled, crossbred, mongrel, interbred, blended, composite, compound, incorporated, united, alloyed, amalgamated, fused **2** *mixed biscuits* assorted, varied, miscellaneous, diverse, diversified, motley **3** *mixed feelings* ambivalent, equivocal, conflicting, contradicting, uncertain, unsure
▷ **mixed up 1** *a mixed-up person* maladjusted, disturbed, disordered, disoriented, distracted, distraught, confused, bewildered, muddled, perplexed, puzzled, upset, chaotic, complicated, désorienté, *slang* screwed up **2** *mixed up in a crime* INVOLVED,

embroiled, incriminated, caught up, entangled, implicated, *formal* inculpated, *colloq.* in on

mixer *n*
1 *a food mixer* blender, food processor, liquidizer, beater, whisk **2** EXTROVERT, joiner, socializer, everybody's friend, *colloq.* life and soul of the party, social butterfly **3** INTERFERER, busybody, disrupter, meddler, mischief-maker, subversive, troublemaker, *colloq.* stirrer
F₃ 2 introvert, loner, recluse **3** peacemaker

mixing *n*
1 AMALGAMATION, combination, synthesis, intermingling, coalescence, blending, union, fusion, hybridization, interbreeding, interflow, *formal* minglement **2** ASSOCIATION, fraternization, socializing, mingling
F₃ 1 separation

mixture *n*
mix, blend, combination, amalgamation, amalgam, compound, composite, coalescence, alloy, brew, synthesis, union, fusion, concoction, cross, hybrid, assortment, variety, miscellany, medley, melange, farrago, smorgasbord, pastiche, patchwork, potpourri, jumble, hotchpotch, *formal* conglomeration, *colloq.* mixed bag, mishmash

mix-up *n*
mess, mistake, misunderstanding, muddle, nonsense, chaos, confusion, jumble, disorder, complication, snarl-up, tangle, *colloq.* foul-up, *US* snafu

moan *n, v*
► *n* **1** GROAN, lament, lamentation, sob, wail, howl, whimper, whine **2** COMPLAINT, grumble, grievance, groan, dissatisfaction, annoyance, fault-finding, criticism, carping, censure, accusation, charge, representation, *colloq.* beefing, beef, belly-aching, grouse, gripe, bleating, whingeing, whinge
► *v* **1** GROAN, wail, sob, weep, howl, whimper, mourn, lament, sigh, grieve **2** COMPLAIN, grumble, whine, carp, *colloq.* whinge, gripe, grouse, bleat, belly-ache, beef, kick up a fuss
F₃ 1 rejoice

mob *n, v*
► *n* **1** CROWD, mass, throng, multitude, horde, rabble, host, swarm, gathering, group, collection, body, flock, herd, drove, brood, pack, press, set, tribe, troop, company, crew, gang, *formal* assemblage **2** POPULACE, rabble, masses, hoi polloi, great unwashed, *canaille*, *colloq.* plebs, riff-raff
► *v* crowd, crowd round, surround, swarm round, gather round, jostle, overrun, set upon, fall upon, besiege, descend on, throng, pack, fill, pester, attack, charge

mobile *adj*
1 MOVING, movable, able to move, portable, transportable, travelling, roaming, roving, itinerant, wandering, migrant, *formal* peripatetic, motile, locomotive, ambulatory **2** FLEXIBLE, adjustable, adaptable, supple, agile, active, energetic, nimble **3** CHANGING, changeable, ever-changing, expressive, lively
F₃ 1 immobile

mobility *n*
movability, movableness, portability, flexibility, motion, expressiveness, vivacity, agility, animation, suppleness, *formal* locomobility, locomotion, locomotivity, motility, motivity
F₃ immobility, inflexibility, rigidity

mobilize *v*
assemble, marshal, rally, conscript, muster, call up, enlist, call into action, activate, cause to take action, galvanize, organize, prepare, get ready, make ready, ready, summon, animate

mob rule *n*
lynch law, ochlocracy, Reign of Terror, *colloq.* mobocracy

mock *v, adj*
► *v* **1** RIDICULE, jeer, make fun of, poke fun at, laugh at, scoff, sneer, taunt, gibe, scorn, insult, tease, chaff, *formal* disparage, deride, *colloq.* kid, rib, rag, knock, take the mickey out of **2** IMITATE, simulate, mimic, ape, caricature, parody, burlesque, lampoon, satirize, *formal* emulate, *colloq.* send up, take off
► *adj* imitation, counterfeit, artificial, sham, simulated, synthetic, substitute, ersatz, false, fake, forged, fraudulent, bogus, pseudo, spurious, feigned, faked, pretended, dummy, *colloq.* phoney, pretend
F₃ genuine

mocker *n*
jeerer, ridiculer, scoffer, scorner, sneerer, satirist, tease, tormentor, flouter, lampooner, lampoonist, critic, detractor, pasquinader, *formal* derider, reviler, vilifier, iconoclast
F₃ flatterer, supporter

mockery *n*
1 RIDICULE, jeering, scoffing, scorn, sneer, sneering, taunting, teasing, contempt, disdain, disrespect, sarcasm, *formal* derision, disparagement, contumely, *colloq.* kidding, ribbing, ragging, mickey-taking **2** PARODY, satire, sham, travesty, caricature, farce, burlesque, lampoon, apology, *formal* emulation, *colloq.* send-up, take-off, spoof

mocking *adj*
scornful, derisive, derisory, contemptuous, sarcastic, satirical, taunting, scoffing, sardonic, sneering, insulting, irreverent, impudent, disrespectful, disdainful, cynical, *colloq.* snide

mode *n*
1 WAY, style, manner, approach, condition, method, form, plan, practice, procedure, process, technique, system, convention **2** FASHION, style, custom, trend, vogue, fad, look, *colloq.* craze, latest thing, rage, *dernier cri*

model *n, adj, v*
► *n* **1** COPY, replica, representation, facsimile, image, imitation, mock-up, dummy **2** EXAMPLE, pattern, design, standard, ideal, epitome, paragon, perfect example, embodiment, mould, original, type, prototype, sample, template, version, *formal* exemplar, archetype, paradigm **3** DESIGN, style, form, sort, kind, variety, type, version, mark, *formal* mode **4** MANNEQUIN, fashion model, artist's model, photographer's model, dummy, sitter, subject, poser
► *adj* exemplary, perfect, typical, ideal, *formal* archetypal, prototypical
► *v* **1** MAKE, form, fashion, mould, sculpt, carve, cast, shape, work, create, design, plan, base **2** DISPLAY, wear, sport, pose, show off

moderate *adj, v, n*
► *adj* **1** MEDIOCRE, medium, modest, ordinary, fair, fairish, indifferent, average, middling, adequate, tolerable, passable, middle-of-the-road, *colloq.* so-so, fair to middling, not up to much, no great shakes, not much cop, nothing much to write home about **2** REASONABLE, restrained, fair, just, modest, sensible, calm, steady, sober, controlled, temperate, cool, mild, well-regulated
F₃ 1 exceptional, extreme **2** immoderate, excessive
► *v* control, regulate, decrease, lessen, slacken, soften, restrain, tone down, play down, diminish, ease, curb, calm, check, keep in check, keep under control, modulate, repress, subdue, soft-pedal, tame, subside, pacify, dwindle, *formal* attenuate, mitigate, allay, alleviate, abate, appease, assuage, palliate

▶ *n* nonextremist, centrist, liberal, neutral person, don't know
☒ extremist, hardliner

moderately *adv*
reasonably, somewhat, quite, rather, fairly, slightly, passably, within reason, to some extent, to a certain degree
☒ extremely

moderation *n*
1 RESTRAINT, self-control, self-restraint, caution, control, composure, sobriety, abstemiousness, temperance, temperateness, reasonableness 2 DECREASE, reduction, lessening, regulation, curbing, subsidence, *formal* attenuation, mitigation, alleviation, abatement
☒ 1 indulgence, self-indulgence
▷ **in moderation** within limits, within bounds, within reason, moderately, with self-control
☒ to excess

modern *adj*
current, contemporary, up-to-date, existing, new, fresh, latest, late, novel, present, present-day, recent, up-to-the-minute, advanced, avant-garde, progressive, modernistic, innovative, inventive, state-of-the-art, go-ahead, forward-looking, futuristic, fashionable, in fashion, stylish, in vogue, in style, voguish, modish, *colloq.* newfangled, in, trendy, with it, spanking new, faddish, all the rage, the latest, hot off the press, hip, cool
☒ old-fashioned, old, out-of-date, antiquated, traditional

modernity *n*
innovation, innovativeness, newness, novelty, originality, contemporaneity, fashionableness, freshness, recentness
☒ antiquatedness, antiquity

modernize *v*
renovate, refurbish, rejuvenate, regenerate, streamline, revamp, renew, make modern, update, bring up-to-date, improve, do up, redesign, reform, remake, remodel, refresh, transform, modify, progress, *colloq.* do over, do up, fix up, move with the times, get with it
☒ regress

modest *adj*
1 UNASSUMING, humble, self-effacing, quiet, self-deprecating, reserved, retiring, unpretentious, discreet, bashful, shy, self-conscious, coy, timid 2 MODERATE, ordinary, unexceptional, fair, satisfactory, reasonable, tolerable, passable, adequate, limited, small 3 *a modest house* unassuming, unpretentious, simple, plain, inexpensive 4 *modest behaviour* proper, discreet, decent, chaste, virtuous, demure, *formal* decorous
☒ 1 immodest, conceited, arrogant 2 exceptional, excessive 3 pretentious, expensive, extravagant

modesty *n*
1 HUMILITY, humbleness, self-effacement, self-deprecation, reticence, reserve, quietness, shyness, bashfulness, coyness, self-consciousness, timidity 2 *modesty of behaviour* decency, propriety, demureness, chasteness, *formal* decorum 3 UNPRETENTIOUSNESS, simplicity, plainness, inexpensiveness
☒ 1 immodesty, vanity, conceit 3 extravagance

modicum *n*
little, bit, small amount, little bit, particle, molecule, fragment, grain, scrap, shred, speck, touch, degree, trace, tinge, atom, crumb, dash, drop, pinch, ounce, hint, suggestion, inch, iota, mite, *colloq.* tad

modification *n*
adaptation, adjustment, alteration, change, revision, variation, improvement, transformation, mutation, refinement, reformation, reorganization, remoulding, reworking, recasting, limitation, moderation, qualification, restriction, tempering, *formal* modulation

modify *v*
1 CHANGE, alter, redesign, revise, vary, adapt, adjust, transform, reform, convert, improve, reorganize, reshape, remould, rework, recast 2 MODERATE, reduce, lessen, decrease, diminish, temper, tone down, limit, soften, dull, qualify, *formal* abate, mitigate

modish *adj*
fashionable, stylish, smart, vogue, voguish, contemporary, current, modern, modernistic, avant-garde, chic, now, *à la mode*, *colloq.* all the rage, hip, in, jazzy, latest, mod, trendy, up-to-the-minute, with it
☒ dowdy, old-fashioned

modulate *v*
modify, adjust, balance, alter, soften, temper, moderate, lower, regulate, change, vary, harmonize, inflect, tune

modulation *n*
modification, adjustment, balance, alteration, softening, lowering, moderation, regulation, change, variation, harmonization, tuning, tone, shift, inflection, inflexion, intonation, accent, shade

modus operandi *n*
method, way, operation, plan, practice, procedure, process, manner, technique, system, rule, rule of thumb, *formal* praxis

mogul *n*
magnate, tycoon, baron, potentate, notable, personage, supremo, *colloq.* big cheese, big gun, big noise, big pot, big shot, big wheel, bigwig, Mr Big, top dog, VIP
☒ nobody

moist *adj*
damp, clammy, dank, humid, wet, wettish, dewy, rainy, dewy, muggy, marshy, drizzly, drizzling, watery, soggy, dripping
☒ dry, arid

moisten *v*
moisturize, dampen, damp, wet, make wet, soak, water, humidify, humify, lick, irrigate
☒ dry

moisture *n*
water, liquid, wetness, wet, wateriness, damp, dampness, dankness, humidity, vapour, rain, drizzle, dew, mugginess, condensation, soaking, steam, spray, perspiration, sweat
☒ dryness

mole¹ *n*
a mole on the skin spot, blemish, blotch, speckle, freckle

mole² *n*
a mole in the organization agent, infiltrator, secret agent, spy, double agent

mole³ *n*
a mole stretching out to sea barrier, breakwater, pier, causeway, dyke, groyne, jetty, embankment

molest *v*
1 ANNOY, disturb, bother, harass, irritate, agitate, vex, exasperate, persecute, pester, nag, chivvy, harry, plague, tease, torment, hound, upset, fluster, worry, trouble, provoke, badger, *colloq.* aggravate, needle, hassle, bug 2 ATTACK, accost, assail, hurt, ill-treat, maltreat, mistreat, abuse, interfere with, (sexually) assault, rape, harm, injure, *formal* ravish

mollify *v*
placate, appease, calm, pacify, compose, conciliate, cushion, ease, relax, relieve, lessen, moderate, tem-

per, modify, quell, soften, soothe, lull, quiet, blunt, sweeten, mellow, *formal* abate, allay, mitigate, assuage, propitiate

F3 aggravate, anger

mollusc *n*

> **Molluscs include:**
> abalone, conch, cowrie, cuttlefish, clam, cockle, limpet, mussel, nautilus, nudibranch, octopus, oyster, periwinkle, scallop, sea slug, slug, freshwater snail, land snail, marine snail, squid, tusk shell, whelk.

mollycoddle *v*
pamper, coddle, indulge, spoil, overprotect, pander to, cosset, spoon-feed, mother, pet, baby, ruin

F3 ill-treat, neglect

moment *n*
1 *stop for a moment* second, instant, (very) short time, less than no time, point in time, minute, split second, sec, flash, twinkling of an eye, trice, *colloq.* mo, jiffy, tick, two ticks, two shakes of a lamb's tail **2** *the moment something happens* the minute, immediately, the instant, the point, directly, no sooner …, as soon as **3** IMPORTANCE, significance, substance, note, interest, value, worth, concern, consequence, gravity, seriousness, weight, weightiness, *formal* import

F3 3 insignificance

momentarily *adv*
briefly, for a moment, for a short time, for a second, for an instant, fleetingly, temporarily

momentary *adj*
brief, short, short-lived, temporary, transient, transitory, fleeting, hasty, quick, passing, spasmodic, *formal* ephemeral, evanescent

F3 lasting, permanent

momentous *adj*
significant, important, of importance, of consequence, of significance, critical, crucial, decisive, weighty, grave, serious, vital, consequential, fateful, historic, pivotal, earth-shaking, earth-shattering, world-shattering, epoch-making, eventful, major

F3 insignificant, unimportant, trivial

momentum *n*
impetus, force, energy, impulse, drive, power, driving-power, thrust, propulsion, speed, velocity, impact, incentive, stimulus, urge, strength, push

monarch *n*
sovereign, crowned head, ruler, king, queen, emperor, empress, prince, princess, tsar, potentate

monarchy *n*
1 KINGDOM, empire, principality, realm, sovereign state, domain, dominion **2** ROYALISM, sovereignty, kingship, autocracy, absolutism, despotism, tyranny, *formal* monocracy

monastery *n*
friary, priory, nunnery, convent, abbey, cloister, charterhouse, religious community, *formal* coenobium

monastic *adj*
reclusive, withdrawn, secluded, cloistered, canonical, austere, ascetic, celibate, meditative, contemplative, *formal* sequestered, eremitic, anchoritic, coenobitic

F3 secular, worldly

monasticism *n*
asceticism, austerity, recluseness, reclusion, seclusion, monkhood, *formal* monachism, eremitism, coenobitism

monetary *adj*
financial, money, fiscal, budgetary, economic, capital, cash, *formal* pecuniary

money *n*
currency, cash, legal tender, banknotes, coin, funds, finances, assets, means, savings, resources, capital, riches, wealth, prosperity, affluence, *colloq.* the necessary, readies, *slang* megabucks, dough, dosh, bread, lolly, spondulicks, brass, loot, gravy, *US* greens, rhino, shekels, moolah, gelt.

> **Expressions used when talking about money include:**
> be on the take, bring home the bacon, cash cow, cash in hand, *US* cash on the barrel(head), coin it, cost a bomb, cost a packet, cost an arm and a leg, cost the earth, divvy up, easy money, feather your own nest, get-rich-quick, great oaks out of little acorns grow, have money to burn, I'm not made of money, in pocket, in the money, make a bomb, make a bundle, make a fast buck, make a few bob, make a fortune/a bundle/a killing, make your pile, making money hand over fist, money for jam/old rope, money is no object, money talks, not cost a bean, not cost a penny, *Austr* not have a brass razoo, not have two halfpennies to rub together, on easy street, on your uppers, out of pocket, pay over the odds, pay through the nose for something, pay your way, poor as a church mouse, quids in, rich as Croesus, rolling in it, scratching, see the colour of someone's money, spend money like it's going out of fashion, spend money like water, spondulicks, stoney broke, throw good money after bad, throw money around, throw money at something, what's the damage?, where there's muck there's brass.

▷ **in the money** rich, wealthy, affluent, prosperous, well-off, well-to-do, *colloq.* rolling in it, well-heeled, flush, *slang* loaded

F3 poor

money-box *n*
cash box, chest, safe, coffer, piggy-bank

moneyed *adj*
wealthy, rich, affluent, comfortable, well-off, prosperous, well-to-do, *formal* opulent, *colloq.* flush, well-heeled, rolling in it, *slang* loaded

F3 poor, impoverished

money-grubbing *adj*
acquisitive, grasping, miserly, mercenary, mammonish, mammonistic, *formal* quaestuary

money-making *adj*
profitable, profit-making, lucrative, commercial, remunerative, paying, successful

mongrel *n, adj*
▶ *n* cross, crossbreed, hybrid, half-breed, mixed breed, cur
▶ *adj* crossbred, hybrid, half-bred, mixed, of mixed breed, ill-defined

F3 pure-bred, pedigree

monitor *v, n*
▶ *v* check, watch, keep track of, keep under surveillance, keep an eye on, keep track of, follow, track, supervise, oversee, observe, note, survey, trace, scan, record, plot, detect
▶ *n* **1** SCREEN, display, VDU, recorder, scanner, detector, security camera, CCTV **2** SUPERVISOR, watchdog, observer, overseer, invigilator, adviser, prefect, head boy, head girl

monk *n*
brother, religious, friar, frater, prior, abbot, hermit,

monastic, mendicant, contemplative, cloisterer, coenobite, beguin, conventual, religieux, religionary, religioner, anchorite, gyrovague

monkey *n, v*
▶ *n* **1** PRIMATE, simian

Monkeys include:
ape, baboon, capuchin, colobus monkey, drill and mandrill, guenon, guereza, howler monkey, langur, leaf monkey, macaque, mangabey, marmoset, night monkey (or douroucouli), proboscis monkey, rhesus monkey, saki, spider monkey, squirrel money, tamarin, titi, toque, uakari (or cacajou), woolly monkey.

2 SCAMP, imp, urchin, brat, rogue, rascal, mischiefmaker, *colloq.* scallywag
▷ **monkey business** mischief, tomfoolery, trickery, chicanery, clowning, pranks, dishonesty, skulduggery, legerdemain, sleight-of-hand, foolery, *colloq.* carry-on, hanky-panky, jiggery-pokery, monkey tricks, shenanigans, funny business
🖪 honesty
▶ *v* play, fool, tinker, tamper, trifle, fiddle, fidget, interfere, meddle, mess, potter

monochrome *adj*
black-and-white, monotone, sepia, monochromatic, monotonous, *formal* monochroic, unicolor, unicolorate, unicolorous, unicolour, unicoloured
🖪 kaleidoscopic, multicoloured

monocle *n*
eyeglass, glass

monogamous *adj*
having only one marriage partner, *formal* monandrous, monogamic, monogynous
🖪 bigamous, polygamous

monogamy *n*
state of having only one marriage partner, practice/custom of having only one marriage partner, *formal* monandry, monogyny
🖪 bigamy, polygamy

monolingual *adj*
speaking one language only, using/involving one language only, expressed in one language only, *formal* monoglot, unilingual
🖪 polyglot

monolith *n*
megalith, standing stone, shaft, menhir, sarsen

monolithic *adj*
massive, vast, colossal, gigantic, huge, monumental, giant, immovable, immobile, rigid, solid, unmoving, unchanging, inflexible, faceless, undifferentiated, fossilized, hidebound, intractable, unvaried

monologue *n*
speech, soliloquy, lecture, sermon, address, oration, homily, *colloq.* spiel
🖪 conversation, dialogue, discussion

monomania *n*
obsession, fixation, ruling passion, fanaticism, *idée fixe*, mania, neurosis, fetish, *colloq.* bee in one's bonnet, hobby-horse, thing

monopolize *v*
dominate, take over, keep to yourself, have (all) to yourself, corner, control, not share with others, have exclusive/sole rights, engross, occupy, preoccupy, take up, tie up, *formal* appropriate, *colloq.* hog
🖪 share

monopoly *n*
domination, control, corner, exclusive right(s), sole right(s), *technical* monopsony, *formal* ascendancy

monotonous *adj*
boring, dull, tedious, uninteresting, unexciting, tiresome, wearisome, unchanging, uneventful, unvarying, unvaried, all the same, uniform, toneless, flat, colourless, repetitive, repetitious, routine, mechanical, plodding, humdrum, soul-destroying, *colloq.* run-of-the-mill, samey, deadly, ho-hum
🖪 lively, varied, colourful

monotony *n*
tedium, dullness, boredom, sameness, tiresomeness, uneventfulness, flatness, wearisomeness, uniformity, routine, routineness, repetitiveness, repetition
🖪 liveliness, colour, variety, excitement, interest

monster *n, adj*
▶ *n* **1** *sea monsters* frightening creature, imaginary creature, mythical creature, Frankenstein, dragon, Medusa, Gorgon, Minotaur, Sphinx, hippocampus, kraken, wivern, windigo **2** BEAST, fiend, brute, barbarian, savage, villain, Frankenstein, giant, ogre, ogress, devil, troll **3** FREAK, freak of nature, monstrosity, mutant, malformation, miscreation, *formal* teratism **4** MAMMOTH, jumbo, giant, colossus, leviathan, behemoth, cyclops, Brobdingnagian
▶ *adj* huge, gigantic, giant, colossal, enormous, immense, massive, monstrous, jumbo, mammoth, vast, tremendous, *colloq.* whopping, ginormous, mega
🖪 tiny, minute

monstrosity *n*
1 EYESORE, blot on the landscape, atrocity, abnormality, enormity, freak, monster, mutant, miscreation, obscenity, *technical* teras **2** DREADFULNESS, frightfulness, hideousness, loathsomeness, horror, hellishness, evil, *formal* heinousness

monstrous *adj*
1 WICKED, evil, vicious, savage, cruel, criminal, outrageous, scandalous, shocking, disgraceful, abominable, atrocious, abhorrent, dreadful, frightful, horrible, horrifying, grisly, terrible, vile, foul, nasty, inhuman, *formal* heinous **2** UNNATURAL, inhuman, freakish, abnormal, grotesque, hideous, gruesome, deformed, malformed, misshapen, *technical* teratoid **3** HUGE, enormous, colossal, gigantic, vast, immense, tremendous, massive, mammoth

monument *n*
memorial, cenotaph, headstone, gravestone, tombstone, shrine, mausoleum, cairn, barrow, cross, marker, obelisk, pillar, column, statue, relic, remembrance, commemoration, witness, testament, reminder, record, memento, evidence, token

monumental *adj*
1 IMPRESSIVE, imposing, striking, awe-inspiring, awesome, overwhelming, significant, important, epoch-making, historic, magnificent, remarkable, majestic, memorable, unforgettable, notable, outstanding, abiding, permanent, enduring, immortal, lasting, classic **2** HUGE, immense, enormous, colossal, vast, tremendous, extraordinary, massive, great, exceptional **3** COMMEMORATIVE, celebratory, memorial
🖪 **1** insignificant, unimportant

mood *n*
1 DISPOSITION, frame of mind, state of mind, temper, humour, vein, spirit, tenor, whim **2** BAD TEMPER, bad mood, sulk, the sulks, pique, melancholy, low spirits, depression, doldrums, *colloq.* blues, dumps **3** ATMOSPHERE, feeling, feel, spirit, tenor, tone, climate, ambience
▷ **in the mood for** wanting to do/have, feeling like, willing to, eager to, keen on/to, inclined to, in the right frame of mind to, *formal* disposed to

moody *adj*
changeable, temperamental, unpredictable, volatile,

unstable, irritable, short-tempered, bad-tempered, crotchety, testy, touchy, morose, angry, broody, irritable, irascible, cantankerous, petulant, mopy, sulky, sullen, gloomy, melancholy, miserable, downcast, in a huff, in a (bad) mood, doleful, glum, impulsive, fickle, flighty, *formal* capricious, *colloq.* crabby, crusty
F3 equable, cheerful

moon *n, v*
▶ *n* ▷ **once in a blue moon** very rarely, seldom, not often, hardly ever
▷ **over the moon** ecstatic, elated, blissful, joyful, jubilant, rapturous, enraptured, overjoyed, euphoric, delirious, frenzied, fervent, *formal* rhapsodic, *colloq.* jumping for joy, on cloud nine, in seventh heaven, tickled pink, high as a kite
▶ *v* idle, loaf, languish, pine, mope, brood, daydream, dream, fantasize, *colloq.* mooch

moonlike *adj*
lunar, moon-shaped, crescent, crescentic, moony, *technical* lunate, *formal* lunular, meniscoid, selenic

moonshine *n*
1 NONSENSE, rubbish, fantasy, stuff, *colloq.* hot air, guff, hogwash, baloney, blather, blether, bosh, bunk, bunkum, claptrap, eyewash, tommyrot, tosh, tripe, twaddle, piffle, rot, *slang* crap **2** SPIRITS, liquor, bootleg, hoo(t)ch, pot(h)een
F3 1 sense

moor¹ *v*
to moor a boat fasten, secure, tie up, drop anchor, anchor, berth, dock, make fast, fix, fix firmly, hitch, lash, bind
F3 loose

moor² *n*
the Yorkshire moors moorland, heath, fell, upland

moot *v, adj*
▶ *v* put forward, propose, suggest, submit, advance, bring up, broach, introduce, pose, discuss, argue, debate, *formal* propound
▶ *adj* controversial, problematic, difficult, questionable, vexed, unsettled, unresolved, unresolvable, undecided, undetermined, disputed, disputable, arguable, doubtful, insoluble, knotty, open, open to debate, debatable, crucial, contestable, academic

mop *n, v*
▶ *n* **1** *a floor mop* sponge, wiper, swab, squeegee **2** *a mop of hair* head of hair, shock, mane, tangle, thatch, mat, mass
▶ *v* swab, sponge, wipe, clean, wash, absorb, soak
▷ **mop up 1** WIPE UP, wash, absorb, soak up, sponge, swab, clean up, tidy up **2** FINISH OFF, deal with, wipe up, dispose of, account for, round up, neutralize, eliminate, secure, take care of

mope *v, n*
▶ *v* brood, fret, sulk, pine, languish, droop, despair, grieve
▷ **mope about** idle, wander, moon, languish, *colloq.* mooch, lounge, loll
▶ *n* melancholic, misery, depressive, pessimist, killjoy, melancholiac, moaner, introvert, *colloq.* grouch, grump, moper

moral *adj, n*
▶ *adj* **1** ETHICAL, virtuous, good, right, principled, honourable, decent, upright, upstanding, straight, righteous, high-minded, honest, incorruptible, proper, blameless, chaste, clean-living, pure, just, noble **2** *give moral support* encouraging, emotional, psychological
F3 1 immoral
▶ *n* lesson, message, significance, teaching, point, dictum, meaning, maxim, adage, precept, saying, proverb, aphorism, epigram

morale *n*
confidence, spirit(s), *esprit de corps*, self-esteem, self-confidence, state of mind, heart, mood, optimism, hopefulness

morality *n*
ethics, morals, moral values, ideals, principles, principles of behaviour, principles of right and wrong, standards, virtue, righteousness, decency, purity, chastity, goodness, honesty, integrity, justice, uprightness, conduct, manners, *formal* rectitude, propriety
F3 immorality

moralize *v*
preach, lecture, pontificate, edify, sermonize, *formal* discourse, ethicize

morals *n*
morality, moral values, moral code, ethics, principles, principles of behaviour, principles of right and wrong, standards, ideals, integrity, scruples, behaviour, conduct, habits, manners

morass *n*
1 QUAGMIRE, bog, moss, marsh, marshland, swamp, slough, mire, fen, quag, quicksand **2** CONFUSION, clutter, chaos, mess, jam, jumble, muddle, mix-up, tangle, *colloq.* can of worms

moratorium *n*
delay, postponement, halt, freeze, suspension, stay, standstill, stoppage, respite, ban, embargo
F3 *colloq.* go-ahead, green light

morbid *adj*
1 GHOULISH, obsessed with death, ghastly, gruesome, grisly, macabre, hideous, horrible, horrid, dreadful, grim **2** GLOOMY, pessimistic, melancholy, dejected, morose, sombre, *formal* lugubrious **3** SICK, ailing, diseased, unhealthy, unwholesome, *formal* insalubrious

mordant *adj*
biting, acid, caustic, bitter, astringent, critical, scathing, sharp, harsh, incisive, waspish, stinging, wounding, vicious, venomous, cutting, sarcastic, pungent, edged, *formal* acerbic, acrimonious, trenchant
F3 gentle, mild, sparing

more *adj, adv, pron*
▶ *adj* further, extra, additional, added, new, fresh, increased, other, another, supplementary, repeated, alternative, spare
F3 less
▶ *adv* further, longer, again, besides, moreover, better
F3 less
▶ *pron* greater number/quantity, additional people/things, extra

moreover *adv*
furthermore, further, besides, in addition, as well, also, additionally, what is more

morgue *n*
mortuary, funeral parlour, deadhouse, charnel house

moribund *adj*
1 DYING, failing, fading, expiring, declining, wasting away, senile, in extremis, *technical* comatose, *colloq.* on your last legs, on the way out, with one foot in the grave, not long for this world **2** WEAK, feeble, lifeless, declining, wasting away, waning, ebbing, stagnating, stagnant, obsolescent, doomed, dwindling, collapsing, crumbling
F3 1 alive, lively, *formal* nascent **2** flourishing

morning *n*
before noon, a.m., dawn, sunrise, daybreak, break of day, daylight

moron *n*
fool, blockhead, fat-head, dolt, dunce, dimwit, simpleton, halfwit, idiot, cretin, imbecile, ignoramus,

dupe, stooge, butt, laughing-stock, clown, comic, buffoon, jester, *colloq.* nincompoop, ass, chump, ninny, clot, dope, twit, nitwit, nit, sucker, mug, twerp, birdbrain, *slang* wally, jerk, dumbo, pillock, prat, dork, geek, plonker *US* schmuck

moronic *adj*
foolish, stupid, senseless, silly, absurd, ridiculous, ludicrous, nonsensical, unwise, ill-advised, ill-considered, shortsighted, half-baked, crazy, mad, insane, idiotic, hare-brained, half-witted, simple-minded, simple, ignorant, unintelligent, inept, inane, pointless, unreasonable, *colloq.* daft, crack-brained, gormless, dumb, dotty, potty, batty, barmy, nutty, not in your right mind, out of your mind, with a screw missing, needing to have your head examined

morose *adj*
ill-tempered, bad-tempered, moody, sombre, sullen, sulky, surly, gloomy, grim, gruff, sour, taciturn, glum, saturnine, depressed, mournful, melancholic, pessimistic, *formal* lugubrious, *colloq.* grouchy, crabby
■ cheerful, communicative

morsel *n*
bit, scrap, piece, fragment, crumb, bite, mouthful, nibble, taste, soupçon, titbit, slice, segment, fraction, modicum, grain, atom, part, particle

mortal *adj, n*
▶ *adj* **1** WORLDLY, earthly, bodily, fleshly, human, perishable, transient, temporal, *formal* corporeal, ephemeral **2** FATAL, lethal, deadly, killing, murderous **3** EXTREME, great, severe, intense, grave, awful, dire, terrible, unbearable **4** *mortal enemies* implacable, relentless, unrelenting, deadly, cruel, bitter, vengeful
■ **1** immortal
▶ *n* human being, human, individual, person, man, woman, being, body, creature, earthling
■ immortal, god

mortality *n*
1 HUMANITY, death, impermanence, worldliness, earthliness, perishability, transience, *formal* ephemerality **2** FATALITY, death, death rate, killing, slaughter, carnage, casualty, loss of life
■ **1** immortality

mortgage *n*
loan, pledge, security, bond, debenture, *Scot.* wadset, *formal* lien

mortification *n*
1 EMBARRASSMENT, humiliation, confounding, shame, disgrace, dishonour, loss of face, abasement, annoyance, chastening, vexation, *formal* chagrin, discomfiture, ignominy **2** DISCIPLINE, punishment, asceticism, control, self-control, denial, self-denial, conquering, *formal* subjugation

mortified *adj*
humiliated, horrified, shamed, ashamed, disgraced, dishonoured, humbled, embarrassed, crushed, confounded, defeated

mortify *v*
1 HUMILIATE, horrify, shame, put to shame, embarrass, offend, disgrace, dishonour, chastise, chasten, abash, confound, humble, bring low, crush, deflate, affront, annoy, disappoint, *formal* discomfit, chagrin, *colloq.* take down a peg or two **2** DISCIPLINE, restrain, suppress, deny, die, control, conquer, subdue

mortifying *adj*
embarrassing, humbling, humiliating, salutary, shaming, ignominious, overwhelming, crushing, chastening, punishing, thwarting, *formal* discomfiting

mortuary *n*
morgue, funeral parlour, deadhouse, charnel house

most *n*
bulk, mass, majority, overwhelming majority, preponderance, greatest/largest part, almost all, nearly all, *colloq.* lion's share

mostly *adv*
mainly, on the whole, principally, especially, chiefly, generally, in general, usually, largely, predominantly, overall, for the most part, in the main, as a rule, above all

moth *n*

Types of moth include:
brown-tail, buff-tip, burnet, six-spot, carpet, cinnabar, clothes, emperor, garden tiger, gypsy, death's head hawkmoth, privet hawkmoth, Kentish glory, lackey, lappet, leopard, lobster, magpie, oak hook-tip, pale tussock, peach blossom, peppered, puss, red underwing, silkworm, silver-Y, swallowtail, turnip, wax, winter.

moth-eaten *adj*
old, worn, worn-out, old-fashioned, obsolete, outdated, outworn, ragged, tattered, threadbare, dated, ancient, antiquated, archaic, decrepit, dilapidated, decayed, musty, shabby, stale, mouldy, mangy, moribund, seedy
■ fresh, new

mother *n, v*
▶ *n* **1** PARENT, dam, matriarch, ancestor, matron, *formal* procreator, progenitress, materfamilias, mater, *colloq.* mum, mummy, ma, mam, mumsy, mamma, old woman, *US* mom, mommy **2** ORIGIN, source, spring, fount, foundation, base, cause, derivation, roots, wellspring
▶ *v* **1** BEAR, produce, bring forth, nurture, raise, rear, tend, nurse, care for, take care of, look after, cherish **2** PAMPER, spoil, baby, indulge, overprotect, fuss over

motherly *adj*
maternal, caring, comforting, affectionate, kind, loving, protective, warm, tender, gentle, fond
■ neglectful, uncaring

motif *n*
theme, idea, topic, concept, pattern, design, figure, form, logo, shape, device, emblem, ornament, decoration

motion *n, v*
▶ *n* **1** MOVEMENT, action, mobility, moving, activity, locomotion, travelling, travel, transit, going, changing place(s), passage, passing, progress, change, flow, inclination, *formal* motility **2** GESTURE, gesticulation, movement, act, action, indication, signal, sign, wave, nod **3** PROPOSAL, suggestion, recommendation, proposition, plan, scheme, project, manifesto, presentation, bid, offer
▷ **in motion** under way, moving, on the move, going, on the go, travelling, in progress, functioning, running, operational
■ stationary, at rest
▶ *v* signal, gesture, gesticulate, sign, wave, nod, beckon, direct, usher

motionless *adj*
unmoving, still, stationary, static, immobile, unmovable, at a standstill, stock-still, fixed, halted, at rest, resting, standing, paralysed, inanimate, inert, lifeless, frozen, transfixed, rigid, stagnant
■ active, moving

motivate *v*
prompt, incite, impel, spur, provoke, stimulate, drive, lead, stir, urge, goad, push, propel, persuade, move, inspire, encourage, cause, trigger, actuate, activate, induce, kindle, draw, excite, arouse, bring, initiate
■ deter, discourage, prevent, inhibit

motivation *n*
reason, incitement, inducement, prompting, spur, stimulus, provocation, drive, push, hunger, desire, wish, urge, impulse, incentive, ambition, inspiration, instigation, momentum, motive, persuasion, interest
F discouragement, prevention

motive *n*
ground(s), cause, reason, basis, purpose, motivation, occasion, object, intention, influence, rationale, thinking, incentive, impulse, stimulus, inspiration, incitement, inducement, urge, goad, spur, encouragement, inspiration, design, desire, attraction, lure, consideration, persuasion
F deterrent, disincentive

motley *adj*
1 ASSORTED, varied, mixed, miscellaneous, diverse, diversified, multifarious, *formal* heterogeneous 2 MULTICOLOURED, variegated, particoloured, colourful, many-hued, pied, piebald, tabby, dappled, brindled, mottled, spotted, striped, streaked
F 1 uniform, homogeneous 2 monochrome

motor vehicle
See CAR.

Parts of a motor vehicle include:
ABS (anti-lock braking system), accelerator, airbag, air brake, air-conditioner, air inlet, antidazzle mirror, antiglare switch, anti-roll bar, antitheft device, ashtray, axle, *US* backup light, battery, bench seat, bezel, bodywork, bonnet, boot, brake drum, brake light, brake pad, brake shoe, bumper, car radio, car phone, catalytic converter, central locking, centre console, chassis, child-safety seat, cigarette-lighter, clock, clutch, courtesy light, crankcase, cruise control, dashboard, differential gear, dimmer, disc brake, door, door-lock, drive shaft, drum brake, electric window, emergency light, engine, exhaust pipe, *US* fender, filler cap, flasher switch, fog lamp, folding seat, four-wheel drive, fuel gauge, *US* gas tank, gear, gearbox, gear-lever (or gear-stick), glove compartment, grill, handbrake, hazard warning light, headlight, headrest, heated rear window, heater, *US* hood, horn, hub-cap, hydraulic brake, hydraulic suspension, ignition, ignition key, indicator, instrument panel, jack, jump lead, kingpin, *US* license plate, *US* lift gate, monocoque, number plate, oil gauge, overrider, parcel shelf, parking-light, petrol tank, pneumatic tyre, power brake, prop shaft, quarterlight, rack and pinion, radial-ply tyre, rear light, rear-view mirror, reclining seat, reflector, *colloq.* rev counter, reversing light, roof rack, screen-washer bottle, seat belt, shaft, shock absorber, sidelight, side-impact bar, side mirror, silencer, sill, solenoid, spare tyre, speedometer, spoiler, steering-column, steering-wheel, *US* stick shift, stoplight, sunroof, sun visor, suspension, temperature gauge, towbar, track rod, transmission, *US* trunk, tyre, vent, wheel, wheel arch, windscreen, windscreen-washer, windscreen-wiper, *US* windshield, wing, wing mirror. *See also* ENGINE.

---

mottled *adj*
speckled, dappled, blotchy, blotched, flecked, piebald, stippled, streaked, marbled, splotchy, tabby, spotted, freckled, brinded, brindled, brindle, variegated, *technical* poikilitic
F monochrome, uniform

motto *n*
saying, slogan, maxim, watchword, cry, catchword, byword, precept, proverb, aphorism, saw, axiom, adage, formula, rule, golden rule, dictum, truism, *formal* epigram, gnome

mould¹ *n, v*
▶ *n* 1 CAST, form, shape, die, template, pattern, matrix, frame, framework, blister pack 2 SHAPE, form, format, pattern, structure, style, type, build, construction, formation, cast, cut, figure, design, kind, model, sort, stamp, arrangement, brand, frame, character, nature, quality, calibre, line, outline, make, *formal* configuration
▶ *v* 1 FORGE, cast, shape, stamp, make, form, fashion, create, design, construct, sculpt, carve, model, work, frame 2 INFLUENCE, affect, form, shape, direct, control

mould² *n*
a smell of mould mildew, must, fungus, mouldiness, mustiness, blight, rot

moulder *v*
decay, decompose, perish, rot, waste, corrupt, crumble, disintegrate, turn to dust, humify

mouldy *adj*
mildewed, blighted, musty, decaying, corrupt, rotten, fusty, putrid, bad, spoiled, stale
F fresh, wholesome

mound *n*
1 HILL, hillock, hummock, rise, knoll, bank, dune, elevation, ridge, embankment, earthwork, tump, tumulus, barrow 2 HEAP, pile, stack, accumulation, collection, supply, store, hoard, abundance, mountain, lot, stack, bundle, stockpile

mount *v, n*
▶ *v* 1 PRODUCE, put on, set up, prepare, stage, exhibit, display, launch, arrange, organize, install 2 INCREASE, grow, build (up), accumulate, pile up, multiply, rise, intensify, escalate, soar, swell, accrue 3 CLIMB (UP), ascend, get up, go up, get on, clamber up, scale, climb on (to), jump on(to), get astride
F 2 decrease, descend 3 descend, dismount, go down
▶ *n* 1 HORSE, steed 2 SUPPORT, mounting, backing, base, fixture, stand, frame

mountain *n*
1 HEIGHT, elevation, mount, peak, pinnacle, hill, fell, mound, alp, tor, massif 2 HEAP, pile, mound, stack, mass, abundance, accumulation, lot, stack, backlog

mountaineering *n*

Mountaineering and climbing terms include :
abseiling, abseil station, adze, *US* adz, Alpinism, arête, ascender, ascent, avalanche; axe, *US* ax, ice axe, hammer axe; base camp; belay, belayer, non-belayer, self-belaying; bivouac; bolting, debolting; bouldering, cam, carabiner *or* karabiner, chalk bag, chalk cliff climbing, chimney, chock, chockstone,

cleft, climbing wall, col, cornice, corrie, crag, crampon, crevasse, descender, descent, Dülfer seat, étrier, fissure, glacier, gully; harness, climbing harness, sit harness; hand hold, helmet, helmet lamp, hut, ice climbing, ice ridge, ice screw, ice slope, ice step, Munro; nut, wallnut; overhang, pick, piolet, pitch; piton, abseil piton, corkscrew piton, drive-in ice piton, ice piton, ringed piton; prusik knot, prusik loop, rapelling, ridge, rock, rock face, rock spike, rock wall; rope, dynamic rope, kernmantel rope, standing rope, on the rope, unrope; saddle, scree, sérac, Sherpa, shunt; sling, abseil sling, rope sling, sling seat, wrist sling; solo ascent, snow bridge, snow cornice, snow gaiters, snow goggles, spike, sport climbing, spur; stack, sea stack; summit, top out, trad route, traverse, tying in.

mountainous adj
1 CRAGGY, rocky, hilly, high, highland, upland, alpine, soaring, lofty, towering, steep 2 HUGE, towering, enormous, immense, vast, colossal, massive, gigantic
🖅 1 flat 2 tiny

mountebank n
charlatan, swindler, cheat, fake, fraud, impostor, pretender, rogue, trickster, colloq. con man, phoney, pseud, quack

mourn v
grieve, lament, sorrow, bemoan, bewail, miss, regret, deplore, weep, wail, keen
🖅 rejoice

mourner n
griever, bereaved, sorrower, mute, keener

mournful adj
sorrowful, sad, unhappy, desolate, doleful, grief-stricken, heavy-hearted, heartbroken, broken-hearted, cast-down, downcast, miserable, tragic, melancholy, funereal, sombre, depressed, dejected, gloomy, dismal, formal woeful, lugubrious, disconsolate, elegiac
🖅 happy, joyful, cheerful

mourning n
grief, grieving, bereavement, lamentation, sadness, sorrow, sorrowing, desolation, weeping, wailing, keening
🖅 rejoicing

moustache n
whiskers, mustachio, handlebar moustache, toothbrush moustache, walrus, colloq. face fungus

mousy adj
1 BROWNISH, greyish, colourless, drab, dull, plain, uninteresting, diffident 2 SHY, quiet, timid, withdrawn, unassertive, unforthcoming, self-effacing, formal timorous
🖅 2 assertive, bright, extrovert, irrepressible

mouth n, v
▶ n 1 LIPS, jaws, embouchure, colloq. chops, kisser, slang trap, gob, traphole, cakehole

---

Parts of the mouth include:
cleft palate, gum, hard palate, hare lip, inferior dental arch, isthmus of fauces, labial commissure, lower lip, palatoglossal arch, palato-pharyngeal arch, soft palate, superior dental arch, tongue, tonsil, upper lip, uvula. See also TOOTH.

---

2 OPENING, aperture, cavity, vent, entrance, door, doorway, gateway, hatch, portal, inlet, estuary, outlet, delta, technical stoma, formal orifice 3 BOASTING, bragging, bragging, blustering, babble, empty/idle talk, colloq. hot air, gas 4 CHEEK, impudence, impertinence, insolence, disrespect, rudeness, backchat, formal effrontery, colloq. nerve, sauce, gall, lip, brass neck
▶ v enunciate, articulate, utter, say, pronounce, whisper, form

mouthful n
sample, morsel, spoonful, swallow, taste, bite, nibble, bit, gulp, sip, titbit, drop, forkful, slug, sup, bonne-bouche

mouthpiece n
spokesperson, spokesman, spokeswoman, representative, agent, delegate, propagandist, journal, periodical, publication, organ

movable adj
mobile, portable, transportable, changeable, alterable, adjustable, flexible, transferable, formal portative
🖅 fixed, immovable

movables n
belongings, possessions, goods, furniture, property, formal chattels, effects, impedimenta, plenishings, colloq. gear, stuff, things

move v, n
▶ v 1 GO, advance, travel, walk, shift, stir, change, pass, act, take action, proceed, progress, make strides, colloq. budge 2 TRANSPORT, carry, bring, take, fetch, relocate, transfer, shift, switch, shunt, swing, formal transpose 3 DEPART, go away, leave, transfer, decamp, migrate, remove, move house, move away, relocate 4 PROMPT, stimulate, incline, urge, impel, drive, cause, lead, propel, actuate, motivate, incite, excite, rouse, arouse, push, persuade, induce, inspire, influence, provoke 5 AFFECT, touch, agitate, stir, impress, excite, disturb, upset, agitate 6 PROPOSE, put forward, request, suggest, advocate, recommend
▶ n 1 MOVEMENT, motion, manoeuvre, gesture, gesticulation, activity 2 REMOVAL, relocation, migration, transfer, repositioning, change of address 3 MEASURE, step out, act, manoeuvre, action, activity, action, device, stratagem, tack
▷ **get a move on** hurry up, speed up, make haste, colloq. get cracking, shake a leg, put your food down
▷ **on the move** moving, travelling, journeying, progressing, advancing, moving forward, active, on the go, astir, under way

movement n
1 REPOSITIONING, move, moving, gesture, gesticulation, relocation, activity, act, action, agitation, stirring, shifting, transfer, transportation, passage 2 CHANGE, development, variation, advance, improvement, breakthrough, evolution, passage, current, drift, flow, current, fall, rise, swing, shift, progress, progression, trend, tendency 3 CAMPAIGN, crusade, drive, group, organization, party, coalition, faction, wing 4 MECHANISM, works, workings, system, action, colloq. guts 5 a movement in a symphony section, part, division, piece, bit, portion, passage

movie n
film, motion picture, picture, feature film, video, silent, talkie, flick

moving adj
1 MOBILE, active, dynamic, in motion, astir, manoeuvrable, technical kinetic, formal motile 2 TOUCH-ING, affecting, poignant, impressive, emotive, arousing, stirring, emotional, inspiring, inspirational, exciting, thrilling, persuasive, stimulating, disturbing, upsetting, worrying, pathetic 3 the moving force/spirit driving, motivating, leading,

influential, dynamic, stimulating, inspiring, urging
F3 1 immobile, fixed 2 unemotional

mow *v*
cut, trim, crop, clip, shear, scythe
▷ **mow down** butcher, slaughter, massacre, shoot down, decimate, cut down, cut to pieces

much *adv, adj, n*
▶ *adv* greatly, to a great extent, a great deal, considerably, a lot, frequently, often
▶ *adj* copious, plentiful, ample, considerable, a lot, abundant, great, substantial, a great number of, extensive, widespread, *colloq.* lots
▶ *n* plenty, a great deal, a lot, *colloq.* lots, loads, heaps, lashings
F3 little

muck *n*
1 DIRT, mire, filth, mud, slime, grime, scum, sludge, *colloq.* gunge, yuck, *slang* grunge, crud 2 EXCREMENT, dung, manure, ordure, sewage, *technical* guano, *formal* faeces
▷ **muck about/around** 1 FOOL AROUND, play around, play about, *colloq.* mess about/around, lark about/around 2 INCONVENIENCE, upset, bother, trouble, *colloq.* lead a merry dance, lead up the garden path, send on a wild goose chase, make life hell for 3 INTERFERE, tamper, meddle, untidy, disorder, disarrange, dishevel, mess up
▷ **muck up** ruin, wreck, spoil, mess up, make a mess of, botch, bungle, *slang* screw up, louse up

mucky *adj*
begrimed, bespattered, dirty, filthy, grimy, messy, miry, mud-caked, muddy, oozy, slimy, soiled, sticky
F3 clean

mucous *adj*
gelatinous, glutinous, gummy, viscous, viscid, slimy, snotty, *formal* mucilaginous

mud *n*
clay, mire, ooze, dirt, soil, sludge, silt

muddle *n, v*
▶ *n* chaos, confusion, disorganization, disorder, disarray, mess, mix-up, jumble, clutter, tangle
▶ *v* 1 DISORGANIZE, disorder, throw into disorder, mix up, mess up, jumble (up), scramble, tangle 2 CONFUSE, bewilder, bemuse, perplex, daze, puzzle, confound, befuddle
▷ **muddle through** get by, get along, cope, make

muddled *adj*
confused, chaotic, disorganized, disordered, jumbled, mixed-up, tangled, scrambled, disarrayed, messy, loose, higgledy-piggledy, disorient(at)ed, perplexed, bewildered, unclear, vague, woolly, befuddled, stupefied, dazed, incoherent, *colloq.* at sea

muddy *adj, v*
▶ *adj* 1 DIRTY, filthy, foul, miry, mucky, grimy, grubby, slimy, slushy, oozy, marshy, boggy, swampy, quaggy, grimy 2 CLOUDY, indistinct, obscure, opaque, murky, turbid, hazy, smoky, blurred, fuzzy, dull, dingy
F3 1 clean 2 clear
▶ *v* 1 DIRTY, soil, smear, smirch, cloud, begrime, bespatter, bedash, bedaub 2 CONFUSE, cloud, make unclear, mix up, jumble (up), disorganize, scramble, tangle
F3 1 clean 2 clarify

muff *v*
botch, bungle, mess up, mismanage, miss, spoil, mishit, *colloq.* fluff

muffle *v*
1 WRAP, wrap up, envelop, cloak, swathe, swaddle, cover (up) 2 DEADEN, dull, quieten, soften, mute, hush, silence, stifle, dampen, muzzle, suppress, smother, gag
F3 2 amplify

mug[1] *n*
drink *coffee from a mug* cup, beaker, pot, tankard

mug[2] *v*
mugged on his way home set upon, attack, assault, waylay, steal from, rob, beat up, bash, jump (on), knock about, *colloq.* do over, rough up, batter, knock someone's block off, knock into the middle of next week

mug[3] *n*
like a mug, I agreed fool, simpleton, gull, *colloq.* sucker, chump, muggins, soft touch

mug *n*
his ugly mug face, features, *formal* countenance, visage, *colloq.* kisser, mush, clock, phiz
▷ **mug up** bone up, con, cram, get up, study, swot

muggy *adj*
humid, sticky, stuffy, sultry, close, clammy, oppressive, airless, sweltering, moist, damp
F3 dry

mulish *adj*
obstinate, stubborn, defiant, difficult, headstrong, inflexible, self-willed, stiff-necked, unreasonable, wilful, perverse, rigid, wrong-headed, *formal* intractable, intransigent, recalcitrant, refractory, *colloq.* pig-headed

mull *v*
▷ **mull over** reflect on, ponder, contemplate, think over, think about, consider, weigh up, muse on, chew over, meditate, study, examine, deliberate, *formal* ruminate

multicoloured *adj*
variegated, particoloured, colourful, motley, pied, piebald, dappled, brindled, spotted, striped

multifarious *adj*
diverse, diversified, different, miscellaneous, varied, sundry, variegated, numerous, many, multiple, multitudinous, legion, *formal* manifold, multiform

multiple *adj*
many, numerous, various, several, sundry, collective, *formal* manifold

multiplicity *n*
abundance, array, number, numerousness, profusion, variety, diversity, mass, host, lot, myriad, *formal* manifoldness, *colloq.* heaps, loads, lots, oodles, piles, scores, stacks, tons

multiply *v*
increase, proliferate, expand, grow, spread, reproduce, propagate, breed, accumulate, intensify, extend, build up, boost, *formal* augment
F3 decrease, lessen

multitude *n*
1 CROWD, throng, horde, swarm, mob, mass, herd, congregation, assembly, host, lot, legion, *colloq.* lots 2 PUBLIC, people, populace, crowd, mob, common people, rabble, hoi polloi, herd, common herd, *colloq.* plebs, riff-raff
F3 1 few, scattering

multitudinous *adj*
numerous, many, profuse, swarming, copious, considerable, abundant, abounding, teeming, innumerable, countless, great, infinite, legion, myriad, *formal* manifold, *colloq.* umpteen

mum *adj*
quiet, mute, dumb, silent, reticent, secretive, tight-lipped, close-lipped, close-mouthed, uncommunicative, unforthcoming

mumble *v*
murmur, rumble, talk to yourself, talk under your breath, stutter, splutter, speak unclearly, speak softly, speak in a low voice, slur

mumbo-jumbo *n*
nonsense, claptrap, gibberish, incantation, jargon, magic, superstition, spell, chant, cant, charm, ritual, rite, mummery, rigmarole, abracadabra, *formal* conjuration, *colloq.* double talk, gobbledygook, hocus-pocus, humbug

munch *v*
eat, chew, crunch, champ, chomp, *formal* masticate

mundane *adj*
1 ORDINARY, banal, hackneyed, boring, stale, trite, everyday, common, commonplace, usual, normal, typical, regular, customary, prosaic, humdrum, workaday, routine **2** WORLDLY, secular, earthly, terrestrial, fleshly, temporal
 1 extraordinary **2** spiritual

municipal *adj*
civic, city, civil, town, metropolitan, urban, borough, community, public

municipality *n*
city, town, township, borough, department, district, precinct, council, local government, burgh, département

munificence *n*
generosity, generousness, liberality, magnanimousness, open-handedness, bounty, benevolence, philanthropy, charitableness, altruism, hospitality, *formal* largesse, beneficence, bounteousness
 meanness

munificent *adj*
generous, open-handed, big-hearted, bountiful, free-handed, magnanimous, lavish, liberal, hospitable, benevolent, philanthropical, charitable, altruistic, rich, unstinting, princely, *formal* beneficent, bounteous
 mean

murder *n, v*
▶ *n* **1** KILLING, homicide, manslaughter, slaying, slaughter, assassination, execution, massacre, butchery, bloodshed, foul play, *formal* patricide, matricide, infanticide, fratricide, sororicide, uxoricide, *colloq.* liquidation **2** *driving in town is murder* hell, torment, torture, agony, ordeal, nightmare, misery, wretchedness, suffering, anguish
▶ *v* **1** KILL, slaughter, slay, put to death, assassinate, butcher, massacre, *colloq.* do in, bump off, eliminate, liquidate, knock off, rub out, wipe out, take out, waste, blow away **2** RUIN, spoil, destroy, botch, mess up, wreck, make a mess of **3** DEFEAT EASILY, beat, overwhelm, rout, annihilate, outplay, outwit, outsmart, trounce, *colloq.* slaughter, hammer, clobber, lick, thrash, wipe the floor with

murderer *n*
killer, homicide, slayer, slaughterer, assassin, butcher, cut-throat

murderous *adj*
1 HOMICIDAL, brutal, barbarous, bloodthirsty, bloody, cut-throat, killing, lethal, fatal, mortal, cruel, savage, ferocious, deadly **2** DIFFICULT, exhausting, strenuous, arduous, punishing, unpleasant, dangerous, *colloq.* killing

murky *adj*
1 DARK, dismal, gloomy, dreary, cheerless, dull, overcast, misty, foggy, dim, cloudy, obscure, veiled, grey **2** *murky water* dirty, dark, dingy, cloudy, turbid **3** MYSTERIOUS, shady, dark, secret, suspicious, questionable
 1 bright, clear, fine **2** clear

murmur *n, v*
▶ *n* **1** MUMBLE, muttering, whisper, undertone, humming, rumble, drone, grumble **2** GRUMBLE, complaint, moan, grievance, protest, objection,

dissatisfaction, annoyance, fault-finding, criticism, carping, censure, *colloq.* grouse, gripe, beefing, belly-aching, whingeing
▶ *v* **1** MUTTER, mumble, whisper, intone, buzz, drone, hum, rustle, rumble, purr, purl, burble, babble **2** COMPLAIN, criticize, find fault, object, protest, grumble, carp, fuss, whine, *colloq.* beef, belly-ache, grouse, gripe, whinge

murmuring *adj, n*
▶ *adj* mumbling, murmurous, muttering, rumbling, whispering, buzzing, droning, purring
▶ *n* drone, mumble, mumbling, muttering, rumble, rumbling, whisper(ing), buzz(ing), purr(ing), *formal* murmuration, susurrus

muscle *n, v*
▶ *n* **1** *strong muscles* sinew, tendon, ligament **2** FORCE, brawn, beef, power, forcefulness, strength, stamina, potency, sturdiness, weight, *colloq.* clout, *formal* might
▶ *v* ▷ **muscle in** butt in, push in, shove, strongarm, impose yourself, force your way in, elbow your way in, jostle

muscular *adj*
brawny, sinewy, fibrous, athletic, powerfully built, strapping, hefty, burly, powerful, husky, robust, stalwart, rugged, sturdy, vigorous, strong, potent, *colloq.* beefy
 puny, flabby, weak

muse *v*
ponder, think, think over, meditate, mull over, weigh, contemplate, consider, brood, reflect, review, chew, dream, deliberate, speculate, *formal* cogitate, ruminate

mush *n*
1 PASTE, pulp, pap, dough, corn, slush, swill, mash, cream, purée **2** SENTIMENTALITY, mawkishness, *colloq.* schmaltz

mushroom *v*
proliferate, shoot up, grow, increase, expand, flourish, boom, spread, spring up, sprout, luxuriate, *formal* burgeon

mushy *adj*
1 PULPY, pappy, pulpous, squashy, squelchy, squidgy, soft, doughy, wet **2** SENTIMENTAL, sloppy, slushy, maudlin, mawkish, saccharine, sugary, syrupy, weepy, *colloq.* schmaltzy

music *n*

Types of music include:
acid house, ballet, ballroom, bluegrass, blues, boogie-woogie, chamber, choral, classical, country-and-western, dance, disco, Dixieland, doo-wop, electronic, folk, folk rock, *colloq.* funk, garage, gospel, grunge, hard rock, heavy metal, hip-hop, honky-tonk, house, incidental, instrumental, jazz, jazz-funk, jazz-pop, jazz-rock, jive, karaoke, operatic, orchestral, pop, punk rock, ragtime, rap, reggae, rhythm and blues (R B), rock and roll, rock, sacred, ska, skiffle, soft rock, soul, swing, *slang* thrash metal. *See also* JAZZ.

musical *adj*
tuneful, melodious, melodic, harmonious, mellow, dulcet, sweet-sounding, lyrical, *formal* euphonious, mellifluous
 discordant, unmusical

musical instruments

Musical instruments include:
balalaika, banjo, cello, double-bass, guitar, harp,

hurdy-gurdy, lute, lyre, mandolin, sitar, spinet, ukulele, viola, violin, *colloq.* fiddle, zither; accordion, concertina, *colloq.* squeeze-box, clavichord, harmonium, harpsichord, keyboard, melodeon, organ, Wurlitzer®, piano, grand piano, Pianola®, player-piano, synthesizer, virginals; bagpipes, bassoon, bugle, clarinet, cor anglais, cornet, didgeridoo, euphonium, fife, flugelhorn, flute, French horn, harmonica, horn, kazoo, mouth-organ, oboe, Pan-pipes, piccolo, recorder, saxophone, sousaphone, trombone, trumpet, tuba; castanets, cymbal, glockenspiel, maracas, marimba, tambourine, triangle, tubular bells, xylophone; bass-drum, bongo, kettle-drum, snare-drum, tenor-drum, timpani, tom-tom.

musical terms

Musical terms include :

accelerando, acciaccatura, accidental, accompaniment, acoustic, adagio, ad lib, a due, affettuoso, agitato, al fine, al segno, alla breve, alla cappella, allargando, allegretto, allegro, al segno, alto, amoroso, andante, animato, appoggiatura, arco, arpeggio, arrangement, a tempo, attacca, bar, bar line, double bar line, baritone, bass, beat, bis, breve, buffo, cadence, cantabile, cantilena, chord, chromatic, clef, alto clef, bass clef, tenor clef, treble clef, coda, col canto, con brio, concert, con fuoco, con moto, consonance, contralto, counterpoint, crescendo, crotchet, cross-fingering, cue, da capo, decrescendo, demisemiquaver, descant, diatonic, diminuendo, dissonance, dolce, doloroso, dominant, dotted note, dotted rest, downbeat, drone, duplet, triplet, quadruplet, quintuplet, sextuplet, encore, ensemble, expression, finale, fine, fingerboard, flat, double flat, forte, fortissimo, fret, glissando, grave, harmonics, harmony, hemidemisemiquaver, hold, imitation, improvisation, interval, augmented interval, diminished interval, second interval, third interval, fourth interval, fifth interval, sixth interval, seventh interval, major interval, minor interval, perfect interval, intonation, key, key signature, langsam, larghetto, largo, leading note, ledger line, legato, lento, lyric, maestoso, major, manual, marcato, mediant, medley, melody, metre, mezza voce, mezzo forte, microtone, middle C, minim, minor, moderato, mode, modulation, molto, mordent, movement, mute, natural, non troppo, note, obbligato, octave, orchestra, orchestration, ostinato, part, pause, pedal point, pentatonic, perdendo, phrase, pianissimo, piano, piece, pitch, pizzicato, presto, quarter tone, quaver, rallentando, recital, refrain, resolution, rest, rhythm, rinforzando, ritenuto, root, scale, score, semibreve, semiquaver, semitone, semplice, sempre, senza, sequence, shake, sharp, double sharp, slur, smorzando, solo, soprano, sostenuto, sotto voce, spiritoso, staccato, staff, stave, subdominant, subito, submediant, sul ponticello, supertonic, swell, syncopation, tablature, tacet, tanto, tempo, tenor, tenuto, theme, tie, timbre, time signature, compound time, simple time, two-two time, three-four time, four-four time, six-eight time, tone, tonic sol-fa, transposition, treble, tremolo, triad, trill, double trill, tune, tuning, turn, tutti, upbeat, unison, vibrato, vigoroso, virtuoso, vivace.

musician *n*

Musicians include:

instrumentalist, accompanist, performer, player, composer, bard, virtuoso; bugler, busker, cellist, clarinettist, drummer, flautist, fiddler, guitarist, harpist, oboist, organist, pianist, piper, soloist, trombonist, trumpeter, violinist; singer, vocalist, balladeer, diva, prima donna; conductor, maestro; band, orchestra, group, backing group, ensemble, chamber orchestra, choir, duo, duet, trio, quartet, quintet, sextet, octet, nonet.

musing *n*
thinking, meditation, introspection, dreaming, daydreaming, wool-gathering, abstraction, absent-mindedness, contemplation, reflection, reverie, brown study, *formal* cerebration, cogitation, ponderment, rumination

muss *v*
ruffle, make untidy, dishevel, tousle, disarrange, make a mess of

must *n*
necessity, prerequisite, obligation, requirement, stipulation, essential, fundamental, imperative, duty, basic, provision, sine qua non, *formal* requisite

muster *v, n*
▶ *v* assemble, convene, gather (together), call together, mobilize, round up, marshal, bring/come together, congregate, collect, group, meet, rally, mass, throng, call up, summon (up), enrol, *formal* convoke
▶ *n* gathering, assembly, collection, congregation, convention, mass, mobilization, rally, round-up, meeting, parade, review, march past, throng, concourse, *formal* assemblage, convocation
▷ **pass muster** be acceptable, be accepted, come up to standard, measure up, fit/fill the bill, make the grade, *colloq.* come up to scratch, shape up

musty *adj*
mouldy, mildewy, mildewed, stale, stuffy, fusty, damp, dank, airless, decayed, decaying, smelly

mutability *n*
changeableness, interchangeability, alterability, variability, permutability, variation

mutable *adj*
changing, interchangeable, changeable, adaptable, alterable, vacillating, variable, volatile, wavering, inconsistent, uncertain, undependable, unreliable, unsettled, inconstant, fickle, flexible, irresolute, unstable, unsteady, permutable
🔁 constant, invariable, permanent

mutation *n*
change, alteration, variation, modification, adaptation, transformation, deviation, anomaly, evolution, *formal* metamorphosis, *colloq.* transmogrification

mute *adj, v*
▶ *adj* silent, dumb, voiceless, uncommunicative, taciturn, wordless, speechless, unspoken, noiseless, unexpressed, unpronounced, *technical* aphasic, *colloq.* mum
🔁 vocal, talkative
▶ *v* tone down, subdue, muffle, lower, moderate, dampen, deaden, dull, smother, quieten, stifle, suppress, soften, silence, *colloq.* soft-pedal
🔁 intensify

muted *adj*
quiet, soft, softened, low-key, subtle, discreet, subdued, restrained, faint, dull, muffled, suppressed, dampened, stifled

mutilate *v*
1 MAIM, injure, dismember, disable, disfigure, lame, cripple, mangle, lacerate, cut to pieces, cut up, butcher, hack (up) **2** SPOIL, mar, damage, impair, ruin, distort, mangle, cut, censor, *formal* bowdlerize, *colloq.* hack, butcher

mutilation *n*
amputation, maiming, disfigurement, dismembering, damage, *formal* detruncation

mutinous *adj*
rebellious, insurgent, insubordinate, disobedient, disorderly, uncontrollable, ungovernable, seditious, revolutionary, riotous, anarchistic, subversive, unruly, *formal* refractory, contumacious, *colloq.* bolshie
☒ obedient, compliant

mutiny *n, v*
▶ *n* rebellion, insurrection, revolt, revolution, rising, uprising, insurgence, insubordination, disobedience, defiance, resistance, riot, strike, protest
▶ *v* rebel, revolt, rise up, resist, protest, disobey, defy, strike

mutt *n*
1 MONGREL, dog, cur, hound, bitch, *colloq.* pooch **2** FOOL, idiot, imbecile, ignoramus, moron, dolt, *colloq.* dunderhead, thickhead

mutter *v*
1 MUMBLE, murmur, talk to yourself, talk under your breath, stutter, splutter, rumble **2** COMPLAIN, grumble, criticize, find fault, object, protest, carp, fuss, whine, *colloq.* grouse, beef, belly-ache, gripe, whinge

mutual *adj*
reciprocal, shared, common, joint, collective, interchangeable, interchanged, exchanged, complementary

muzzle *v*
restrain, inhibit, check, stifle, suppress, gag, fetter, mute, silence, censor, choke

muzzy *adj*
1 GROGGY, tipsy, confused, dazed, befuddled, addled, muddled, bewildered **2** FUZZY, blurred, unfocused, unclear, indistinct, faint, hazy
☒ **2** clear

myopic *adj*
1 *myopic vision* short-sighted, near-sighted, purblind, half-blind **2** *myopic attitudes* short-sighted, unwise, ill-considered, thoughtless, narrow, narrow-minded, localized, parochial, short-term, *formal* imprudent, uncircumspect
☒ **2** far-sighted

myriad *adj, n*
▶ *adj* countless, innumerable, limitless, immeasurable, incalculable, untold, boundless, *formal* multitudinous
▶ *n* multitude, throng, horde, army, flood, host, swarm, sea, *colloq.* scores, thousands, millions, zillions, mountain

mysterious *adj*
1 ENIGMATIC, cryptic, mystifying, inexplicable, incomprehensible, puzzling, perplexing, obscure, strange, unfathomable, unsearchable, inscrutable, mystical, baffling, curious, hidden, insoluble, *formal*

abstruse, arcane, recondite **2** SECRET, as if by magic, weird, secretive, veiled, dark, furtive, obscure, strange, mystical, baffling, curious, hidden, surreptitious, reticent
☒ **1** straightforward, comprehensible

mystery *n*
1 ENIGMA, puzzle, secret, riddle, problem, conundrum, question, question mark **2** OBSCURITY, mystique, secrecy, ambiguity, curiosity, strangeness, weirdness, incomprehensibility, inexplicability, inscrutability, unfathomability, furtiveness, surreptitiousness, reticence

mystical *adj*
occult, arcane, mystic, esoteric, spiritual, supernatural, paranormal, other-worldly, transcendental, metaphysical, hidden, mysterious, obscure, incomprehensible, inexplicable, unfathomable, strange, weird, baffling, *formal* preternatural, abstruse, arcane, recondite
☒ rational, logical

mystify *v*
puzzle, bewilder, baffle, perplex, confound, confuse, *colloq.* bamboozle

mystique *n*
mystery, secrecy, fascination, glamour, magic, spell, charm, appeal, charisma, awe

myth *n*
1 LEGEND, fable, fairy tale, fairy story, allegory, parable, saga, story, tale, folk tale, bestiary **2** FICTION, fancy, fallacy, delusion, fantasy, invention, fabrication, lie, untruth, pretence, *colloq.* fib, tall story

mythical *adj*
1 MYTHOLOGICAL, legendary, fabled, fairytale, fictitious, *formal* chimerical, fabulous, fantastic **2** FICTITIOUS, imaginary, made-up, invented, non-existent, unreal, untrue, fantasy, fabricated, pretended, fanciful, *colloq.* make-believe, pretend, put-on, phoney
☒ **1** historical **2** actual, real, true

mythological *adj*
legendary, mythical, traditional, mythic, fabled, fairytale, fictitious, *formal* fabulous, folkloric

---

Mythological creatures and spirits include: abominable snowman (or yeti), afrit, basilisk, bunyip, Cecrops, centaur, Cerberus, Chimera, cockatrice, Cyclops, dragon, dryad, Echidna, elf, Erinyes (or Furies), Fafnir, fairy, faun, Frankenstein's monster, genie, Geryon, Gigantes, gnome, goblin, golem, Gorgon, griffin, Harpies, hippocampus, hippogriff, hobgoblin, imp, kelpie, kraken, lamia, leprechaun, Lilith, lindworm, Loch Ness monster, Medusa, mermaid, merman, Minotaur, naiad, nereid, nymph, ogre, ogress, orc, oread, Pegasus, phoenix, pixie, roc, salamander, sasquatch, satyr, sea serpent, Siren, Sphinx, sylph, troll, Typhoeus, unicorn, werewolf, windigo, wivern.

---

mythology *n*
legend, myths, lore, tradition(s), stories, folklore, folk tales, tales

N

nab *v*
catch, arrest, capture, grab, seize, snatch, *formal* apprehend, *colloq.* collar, nail, nick, nobble

nabob *n*
celebrity, magnate, personage, tycoon, VIP, millionaire, multimillionaire, billionaire, financier, *formal* luminary, *colloq.* bigwig

nadir *n*
low point, lowest point, minimum, zero, bottom, depths, all-time low, low-watermark, *colloq.* rock bottom
🖪 zenith, peak, *formal* acme, apex

nag¹ *v*
1 SCOLD, pester, badger, plague, torment, harass, harry, vex, upbraid, pick on, keep on at, moan, complain, *formal* berate, *colloq.* henpeck, hassle, grouse **2** NIGGLE, tease, worry, bother, trouble, annoy, irritate,
colloq. bug, aggravate, get someone's back up

nag² *n*
ride a nag horse, hack, jade, keffel, rip, Rosinante, *colloq.* plug

nagging *adj*
1 *a nagging pain* continuous, critical, distressing, upsetting, worrying, irritating, niggling, painful, aching, persistent **2** SCOLDING, shrewish, critical, tormenting, moaning, *colloq.* nit-picking

nail *v, n*
▶ *v* **1** FASTEN, attach, secure, pin, tack, fix, join, hammer **2** CATCH, arrest, capture, grab, seize, trap, snatch, corner, pin down, *formal* apprehend, *colloq.* collar, nick, nab, nobble **3** EXPOSE, detect, identify, reveal, uncover, unearth, unmask
▶ *n* **1** FASTENER, pin, tack, rivet, brad, sprig, clout, sparable, spike, skewer, screw **2** FINGERNAIL, toenail, nipper, pincer, claw, talon

naïve *adj*
unsophisticated, ingenuous, innocent, unaffected, artless, guileless, simple, unrealistic, natural, frank, childlike, inexperienced, immature, open, candid, trusting, born yesterday, unsuspecting, unsuspicious, unaffected, unworldly, gullible, unpretentious, credulous, wide-eyed, *formal* jejune, *colloq.* green, wet behind the ears
🖪 experienced, sophisticated

naïvety *n*
ingenuousness, innocence, inexperience, immaturity, naturalness, artlessness, guilelessness, childlikeness, simplicity, openness, frankness, candidness, gullibility, credulity
🖪 experience, sophistication

naked *adj*
1 NUDE, bare, with nothing on, undressed, unclothed, uncovered, exposed, stripped, stark-naked, disrobed, denuded, *colloq.* in the altogether, starkers, in your birthday suit, in the raw, in the buff, not a stitch on, naked as the day you were born **2** OPEN, unadorned, undisguised, unqualified, unvarnished, plain, stark, bald, simple, evident, overt, patent, blatant, flagrant, glaring, exposed **3** DEFENCELESS, exposed, unprotected, unguarded, uncovered, weak, vulnerable, helpless, powerless **4** *a naked landscape* denuded, stripped, grassless, treeless, exposed, barren, bare, stark
🖪 **1** clothed, covered **2** concealed, veiled

nakedness *n*
1 NUDITY, bareness, undress, starkness, *colloq.* the altogether, the buff **2** PLAINNESS, openness, simplicity, baldness, barrenness, bareness, starkness

namby-pamby *adj*
sentimental, feeble, spineless, weak, weedy, wet, wishy-washy, mawkish, vapid, maudlin, insipid, colourless, anaemic, pretty-pretty, prim, prissy

name *n, v*
▶ *n* **1** TITLE, designation, label, tag, style, term, epithet, nickname, *formal* appellation, denomination, cognomen, *colloq.* handle, monicker

Kinds of name include:
full name, first name, given name, Christian name, baptismal name, second name, middle name; surname, family name, last name; maiden name; nickname, sobriquet, agnomen, pet name, term of endearment, diminutive; false name, pseudonym, alias, stage-name, nom-de-plume, assumed name, pen-name; proper name; place name; brand name, trademark; code name.

2 REPUTATION, character, repute, renown, eminence, prominence, fame, honour, prestige, distinction, note, standing, popularity, celebrity, *formal* esteem **3** STAR, expert, authority, leading light, celebrity, dignitary, VIP, luminary, hero, *colloq.* big noise, big name, bigwig, a somebody
▶ *v* **1** CALL, christen, baptize, give name to, term, title, entitle, dub, label, tag, style, identify, *formal* denominate **2** DESIGNATE, nominate, mention, cite, choose, pick, select, specify, classify, commission, appoint

named *adj*
called, known as, by the name of, labelled, termed, titled, entitled, dubbed, styled, baptized, christened, identified, designated, mentioned, chosen, picked, selected, singled out, specified, classified, commissioned, cited, nominated, appointed, dit, *formal* denominated
🖪 nameless

nameless *adj*
1 UNNAMED, anonymous, unidentified, untitled, unlabelled, unspecified, undesignated, unknown, obscure, *formal* innominate **2** INEXPRESSIBLE, inde-

scribable, unutterable, unspeakable, unmentionable, unheard-of

🖪 **1** named

namely *adv*
that is, ie, specifically, viz, that is to say, in other words, *formal* to wit

nap¹ *n, v*
▶ *n* have a nap rest, lie-down, doze, sleep, light sleep, siesta, catnap, *colloq.* snooze, forty winks, kip
▶ *v* doze, sleep, sleep lightly, nod (off), drop off, catnap, lie down, rest, *colloq.* snooze, kip, have forty winks, get some shut-eye

nap² *n*
the nap of the carpet down, pile, weave, shag, surface, texture, fibre, grain, fuzz, downiness

nappy *n*
diaper, napkin, towel, serviette

narcissism *n*
self-love, egotism, egomania, egocentricity, self-centredness, self-regard, self-conceit, conceit, vanity

narcissistic *adj*
self-loving, egotistic, egomaniacal, egocentric, self-centred, conceited, vain

narcotic *n, adj*
▶ *n* drug, opiate, sedative, tranquillizer, sleeping pill, painkiller, analgesic, anodyne, anaesthetic, palliative, soporific, *slang* upper, downer
▶ *adj* soporific, sleep-inducing, hypnotic, sedative, analgesic, anaesthetic, tranquillizing, opiate, pain-killing, numbing, dulling, pain-dulling, calming, stupefying, *formal* somnolent, stupefacient

narked *adj*
annoyed, bothered, irritated, piqued, irked, exasperated, provoked, riled, vexed, galled, *colloq.* bugged, miffed, nettled, peeved

narrate *v*
tell, read, report, describe, portray, unfold, recite, state, explain, set out, detail, chronicle, *formal* relate, recount, rehearse, set forth

narration *n*
account, story, tale, description, explanation, telling, report, statement, history, chronicle, detail, sketch, portrayal, reading, recital, story-telling, voice-over, *formal* rehearsal, recountal

narrative *n*
story, tale, chronicle, account, history, report, description, sketch, portrayal, reading, detail, statement

narrator *n*
storyteller, chronicler, reporter, raconteur, anecdotist, commentator, writer, author, describer, relater, annalist, *formal* recounter

narrow *adj, v*
▶ *adj* **1** TIGHT, confined, constricted, cramped, small, slim, slender, thin, fine, spare, tapering, close, *formal* attenuated **2** LIMITED, restricted, cramped, squeezed, tight, close, meagre, scant, *formal* circumscribed, incommodious, exiguous **3** NARROW-MINDED, biased, bigoted, prejudiced, dogmatic, intolerant, illiberal, reactionary, hidebound, strait-laced, dyed-in-the-wool, close-minded, set, rigid, conservative, small-minded, insular, petty **4** *in the narrow sense of the word* strict, literal, exact, precise, true, original

🖪 **1** wide **2** broad **3** broad-minded, tolerant **4** broad
▶ *v* constrict, limit, tighten, confine, restrict, cramp, reduce, diminish, taper, simplify, *formal* attenuate, circumscribe

🖪 broaden, widen, increase

narrowing *n*
compression, constriction, curtailment, contraction, reduction, tapering, thinning, emaciation, constipation, *technical* stenosis, *formal* attenuation

🖪 broadening, widening

narrowly *adv*
1 BARELY, scarcely, just, only just, *colloq.* by a hair's breadth, by a whisker **2** CAREFULLY, closely, strictly, scrutinizingly, precisely, exactly, painstakingly

narrow-minded *adj*
illiberal, biased, bigoted, prejudiced, reactionary, hidebound, strait-laced, dyed in the wool, opinionated, diehard, small-minded, close-minded, set, rigid, inflexible, entrenched, conservative, ultra-conservative, blimpish, intolerant, insular, provincial, parochial, twisted, warped, jaundiced, petty, petty-minded, exclusive, unreasonable

🖪 broad-minded, liberal, tolerant

narrowness *n*
1 THINNESS, tightness, slenderness, limitation, restrictedness, nearness, constriction, closeness, meagreness, *formal* attenuation **2** NARROW-MINDEDNESS, insularity, parochialism, exclusiveness, bias, bigotry, prejudice, intolerance, pettiness, small-mindedness, rigidity, conservatism

🖪 **1** breadth, width **2** broad-mindedness, tolerance

narrows *n*
straits, sound, channel, passage, waterway

nascent *adj*
budding, developing, growing, rising, young, embryonic, beginning, evolving, advancing, *formal* burgeoning, incipient, naissant

🖪 dying

nastiness *n*
1 UNPLEASANTNESS, repulsiveness, horribleness, disagreeableness, offensiveness, filth, dirtiness, defilement, filthiness, foulness, impurity, pollution, squalor, uncleanliness, unsavouriness **2** OBSCENITY, indecency, filth, pornography, *colloq.* porn, smuttiness **3** MALICE, spitefulness, spite, viciousness, meanness, *formal* malevolence

nasty *adj*
1 UNPLEASANT, awful, repulsive, hateful, loathsome, objectionable, disagreeable, offensive, distasteful, disgusting, obnoxious, revolting, sickening, horrible, dirty, filthy, squalid, foul, vile, odious, polluted, rank, *formal* repellent, repugnant, noisome, malodorous, *colloq.* grotty, yucky **2** OBSCENE, offensive, indecent, dirty, filthy, pornographic, ribald, *colloq.* blue, smutty **3** MALICIOUS, mean, spiteful, vicious, cruel, unkind, bad-tempered, disagreeable, unpleasant, *formal* malevolent **4** SERIOUS, grave, critical, dangerous, worrying, alarming, disquieting, unpleasant, difficult, tricky **5** *nasty weather* stormy, wet, rainy, foggy, foul, disagreeable, unpleasant, vile, filthy, awful

🖪 **1** agreeable, nice, pleasant, decent, palatable **3** benevolent, kind **5** fine

nation *n*
country, people, race, tribe, state, kingdom, land, realm, republic, population, community, society

national *adj, n*
▶ *adj* countrywide, civil, civic, domestic, nationwide, state, internal, domestic, native, general, governmental, federal, public, widespread, comprehensive, social
▶ *n* citizen, native, subject, inhabitant, resident

nationalism *n*
patriotism, allegiance, loyalty, chauvinism, xenophobia, jingoism

nationalistic *adj*
patriotic, loyal, chauvinistic, jingoistic, xenophobic, *formal* ethnocentrist

nationality n
race, nation, ethnic group, birth, tribe, clan

nationwide adj
national, countrywide, general, overall, extensive, widespread, comprehensive, state, coast-to-coast

native adj, n
▶ adj **1** INDIGENOUS, local, domestic, vernacular, home, home-grown, aboriginal, mother, original, formal autochthonous **2** INHERENT, inborn, innate, inbred, ingrained, hereditary, inherited, congenital, instinctive, intuitive, natural, built-in, intrinsic, formal natal, connate
▶ n inhabitant, resident, national, citizen, dweller, aborigine, formal autochthon
F₃ foreigner, outsider, stranger, alien

nativity n
birth, childbirth, delivery, formal parturition

natter v, n
▶ v chat, chatter, gossip, talk, confabulate, colloq. blather, blether, confab, gab, gabble, jabber, jaw, prattle, rabbit (on), chinwag, witter
▶ n chat, conversation, talk, gossip, prattle, chit-chat, colloq. blather, blether, chinwag, confab, gab, gabble, jaw

natty adj
smart, neat, dapper, chic, elegant, well-dressed, fashionable, spruce, stylish, trim, colloq. ritzy, snazzy, swanky

natural adj
1 ORDINARY, normal, common, regular, standard, everyday, routine, run-of-the-mill, usual, typical **2** INNATE, inborn, inbred, ingrained, built-in, normal, instinctive, intuitive, inherent, inherited, congenital, native, indigenous, formal connate **3** natural fibres genuine, pure, authentic, additive-free, chemical-free, organic, raw, virgin, unrefined, unprocessed, unmixed, plain, real, whole **4** SINCERE, unaffected, genuine, artless, ingenuous, guileless, simple, unpretentious, unsophisticated, frank, open, candid, spontaneous
F₃ **1** unnatural **2** acquired **3** artificial, man-made, synthetic **4** affected, disingenuous, contrived

naturalist n
life scientist, plant scientist, botanist, biologist, zoologist, ecologist, evolutionist, Darwinist, creationist

naturalistic adj
natural, realistic, true-to-life, representational, lifelike, graphic, real-life, photographic, factual
F₃ idealistic, unrealistic

naturalize v
introduce, adopt, incorporate, familiarize, acclimatize, accept, assimilate, accustom, adapt, enfranchise, domesticate, formal acclimate, acculturate, endenizen, habituate

naturally adv
1 OF COURSE, obviously, as a matter of course, simply, logically, typically, certainly, absolutely, as you would expect, colloq. natch **2** NORMALLY, genuinely, sincerely, instinctively, spontaneously, artlessly, ingenuously, candidly, frankly

naturalness n
sincerity, genuineness, artlessness, ingenuousness, simpleness, simplicity, plainness, pureness, purity, wholeness, candidness, frankness, openness, realism, unpretentiousness, unaffectedness, spontaneousness, spontaneity, informality

nature n
1 ESSENCE, quality, character, essential quality/character, identity, features, disposition, attributes, personality, stamp, make-up, characteristic(s), complexion, constitution, temperament, mood, outlook, humour, temper, colloq. chemistry **2** KIND, sort, type, description, category, variety, style, species, class, category **3** UNIVERSE, world, creation, cosmos, earth, mother earth/nature, environment **4** COUNTRYSIDE, country, landscape, scenery, natural history

naught n
nothing, nothingness, zero, nought, nil, colloq. zilch

naughty adj
1 BAD, badly behaved, misbehaving, mischievous, disobedient, wayward, defiant, undisciplined, unruly, exasperating, playful, roguish, perverse, incorrigible, formal refractory **2** INDECENT, obscene, bawdy, risqué, vulgar, off-colour, coarse, ribald, lewd, smutty, colloq. blue
F₃ **1** good, well-behaved **2** decent

nausea n
1 VOMITING, sickness, retching, gagging, queasiness, biliousness, morning sickness, travel sickness, motion sickness, seasickness, carsickness, airsickness, colloq. throwing up, puking **2** DISGUST, revulsion, loathing, aversion, distaste, hatred, formal repugnance, abhorrence, detestation

nauseate v
sicken, make sick, disgust, revolt, repel, offend, make your gorge rise, colloq. turn off, turn your stomach, US gross out

nauseating adj
sickening, disgusting, repulsive, offensive, distasteful, repellent, odious, loathsome, nauseous, revolting, formal abhorrent, detestable, repugnant

nauseous adj
queasy, nauseated, sick, ill, travel sick, seasick, carsick, airsick, colloq. under the weather, about to throw up

nautical adj
naval, maritime, seagoing, sailing, oceanic, boating, yachting

Nautical terms include :

afloat, aft, air-sea rescue, amidships, ballast, beam, bear away, beat, bow-wave, breeches buoy, broach, capsize, cargo, cast off, chandler, circumnavigate, coastguard, compass bearing, convoy, course, cruise, current, Davy Jones's locker, dead reckoning, deadweight, disembark, dock, dockyard, dry dock, ebb tide, embark, ferry, fleet, float, flotilla, flotsam, foghorn, fore, foreshore, go about, gybe, harbour, harbour-bar, harbour dues, harbour-master, haven, head to wind, heave to, heavy swell, heel, helm, high tide, inflatable life-raft, jetsam, jetty, knot, launch, lay a course, lay up, lee, lee shore, leeward, life buoy, life-jacket, life-rocket, list, low tide, make fast, marina, marine, maroon, mayday, moor, mooring, mutiny, navigation, neap tide, on board, pitch and toss, plane, put in, put to sea, quay, reach, reef, refit, ride out, riptide, roll, row, run, run aground, run before the wind, salvage, seafaring, sea lane, sea legs, seamanship, seasick, seaworthy, set sail, sheet in, shipping, shipping lane, ship's company, ship water, shipwreck, shipyard, shore leave, sink, slip anchor, slipway, stevedore, stowaway, tack, tide, trim, voyage, wake, wash, watch, wave, weather, weigh anchor, wharf, wreck. See also SAIL.

naval adj
marine, maritime, nautical, sea, seagoing, seafaring

navel *n*
umbilicus, centre, middle, hub, *formal* omphalos, *colloq.* belly-button, tummy-button

navigable *adj*
passable, crossable, negotiable, open, clear, unblocked, unobstructed, surmountable, *formal* traversable

navigate *v*
steer, drive, direct, pilot, guide, handle, manoeuvre, negotiate, cruise, sail, voyage, journey, cross, helm, plot, plan, *colloq.* skipper

navigation *n*
sailing, steering, piloting, pilotage, directing, direction, guiding, guidance, cruising, voyaging, seamanship, helmsmanship, manoeuvring

Navigational aids include:
astro-navigation, bell buoy, channel-marker buoy, chart, chronometer, conical buoy, Decca® navigator system, depth gauge, dividers, echo-sounder, flux-gate compass, Global Positioning System (GPS), gyrocompass, lighthouse, lightship, log, loran (long-range radio navigation), magnetic compass, marker buoy, nautical table, parallel ruler, pilot, radar, sectored leading-light, sextant, VHF radio.

navigator *n*
pilot, seaman, helmsman, mariner

navvy *n*
labourer, common labourer, worker, manual worker, workman, digger, ganger

navy *n*
fleet, ships, flotilla, armada, warships

nay *adv*
indeed, really, actually, in fact, in truth, certainly, absolutely, to be sure

near¹ *adj*
1 NEARBY, close, close by, within reach, within range, at hand, accessible, convenient, bordering, adjacent, alongside, local, neighbouring, surrounding, *formal* adjoining, contiguous, *colloq.* a stone's throw from **2** IMMINENT, close, impending, forthcoming, coming, looming, immediate, approaching, in the offing, *formal* proximate **3** DEAR, familiar, close, related, closely related, intimate, akin **4** SIMILAR, close, like, alike, comparable, corresponding
1 far, far off, far-away **2** distant **3** remote
▷ **near thing** near miss, narrow escape, nasty moment, close call, *colloq.* close shave

near² *adv, prep, v*
▶ *adv* nearby, close, close by, not far away, at close quarters, alongside, within reach, at hand, within close range, *colloq.* a stone's throw away
▶ *prep* nearby, close to, next to, bordering on, adjacent to, alongside, in the neighbourhood of, within reach of, *formal* adjoining, contiguous to
▶ *v* approach, get closer to, come nearer/closer, advance towards, come/move towards, draw near to, close in on, cling to
withdraw, keep your distance

nearby *adj, adv*
▶ *adj* near, close, neighbouring, adjoining, adjacent, accessible, convenient, handy, within reach
faraway
▶ *adv* near, within reach, at close quarters, close at hand, not far away, a short distance away, in the vicinity, *colloq.* on your doorstep, in your own backyard

nearly *adv*
almost, practically, virtually, as good as, closely, close

to, approximately, more or less, all but, just about, roughly, well-nigh
completely, totally

nearness *n*
1 CLOSENESS, vicinity, handiness, accessibility, availability, immediacy, imminence, *formal* proximity, contiguity, propinquity **2** INTIMACY, dearness, familiarity, closeness, chumminess

near-sighted *adj*
short-sighted, myopic, half-blind, purblind

neat *adj*
1 TIDY, orderly, ordered, well-ordered, organized, well-organized, straight, smart, spruce, dapper, trim, clean, shipshape, *colloq.* natty, spick-and-span, in apple-pie order, shipshape and Bristol fashion **2** DEFT, clever, adroit, nimble, skilful, practised, dexterous, expert, *colloq.* nifty **3** COMPACT, handy, dainty, convenient, efficient, well-designed, well-made, user-friendly **4** *a neat solution* clever, convenient, nice, simple, apt, sensible, ingenious, elegant **5** GREAT, excellent, wonderful, marvellous, superb, admirable, tremendous, fantastic, fabulous, *colloq.* super, terrific, smashing, *slang* cool, mega, wicked **6** UNDILUTED, unmixed, unadulterated, straight, pure
1 untidy, scruffy, shabby, slovenly **2** clumsy **6** diluted

neaten *v*
tidy (up), straighten, smarten (up), spruce up, clean (up), arrange, trim, edge, round off, groom, put to rights

neatly *adv*
1 TIDILY, smartly, stylishly, sprucely, methodically, systematically, efficiently **2** CLEVERLY, conveniently, handily, aptly, nicely, daintily, elegantly **3** DEFTLY, skilfully, adeptly, adroitly, agilely, nimbly, dexterously, effortlessly, expertly, precisely, accurately, gracefully
1 untidily **2** inelegantly **3** unskilfully, inexpertly

neatness *n*
1 TIDINESS, smartness, trimness, spruceness, stylishness, style, orderliness, straightness, methodicalness **2** CLEVERNESS, aptness, efficiency, handiness, elegance, daintiness, niceness, nicety **3** SKILFULNESS, skill, adeptness, deftness, adroitness, agility, dexterity, gracefulness, grace, nimbleness, expertness, preciseness, precision, accuracy
1 untidiness, disorderliness **2** inelegance

nebulous *adj*
vague, hazy, imprecise, indefinite, indistinct, cloudy, misty, shadowy, obscure, uncertain, unclear, dim, ambiguous, confused, fuzzy, abstract, shapeless, unformed, *formal* amorphous, indeterminate
clear

necessarily *adv*
inevitably, incontrovertibly, certainly, compulsorily, by definition, inescapably, of necessity, inexorably, of course, naturally, consequently, automatically, therefore, thus, accordingly, axiomatically, willy-nilly, *nolens volens, formal* ineluctably, perforce

necessary *adj*
needed, required, essential, compulsory, indispensable, vital, crucial, de rigueur, obligatory, needful, unavoidable, sure, inevitable, inescapable, inexorable, certain, *old use* needful, *formal* mandatory, imperative, requisite, ineluctable
unnecessary, inessential, unimportant

necessitate *v*
require, involve, entail, make necessary, need, take, call for, demand, oblige, exact, force, constrain, compel

necessity *n*
1 REQUIREMENT, obligation, prerequisite, essential,

fundamental, indispensable, need, want, compulsion, demand, *formal* exigency, requisite, desideratum, sine qua non, *colloq.* must **2** INDISPENSABILITY, inevitability, certainty, inescapability, inexorability, obligation, needfulness **3** POVERTY, destitution, hardship, want, need, deprivation, *formal* penury, privation, indigence

F◸ **1, 3** luxury

neck *n, v*
▶ *n* nape, scruff, scrag, halse, *technical* cervix
▶ *v* kiss, caress, *colloq.* smooch, canoodle, *slang* snog

necklace *n*
chain, string, band, pearls, beads, jewels, choker, locket, pendant, lavallière, negligee, torque, torc, gorget, carcanet, rivière

necromancer *n*
magician, conjurer, diviner, sorcerer, sorceress, witch, wizard, warlock, spiritist, spiritualist, *formal* thaumaturge, thaumaturgist

necromancy *n*
divination, enchantment, wonder-working, magic, magical powers, black magic, black art, sorcery, witchcraft, witchery, spiritism, spiritualism, wizardry, demonology, voodoo, hoodoo, *formal* conjuration, thaumaturgy

necropolis *n*
cemetery, graveyard, burial ground, burial place, burial site, churchyard, *formal* charnel house, God's acre

need *v, n*
▶ *v* miss, lack, want, require, demand, call for, have need of, be necessary to have, have occasion for, have to, must, be compelled/obliged to, desire, crave, pine for, yearn for, be desperate for, cry out for, be dependent on, depend on, be reliant on, rely on, *formal* necessitate
▶ *n* **1** *a need for caution* call, demand, obligation, want, wish, justification, requirement, *formal* exigency **2** *the country's needs* essential, necessity, prerequisite, *formal* requisite, desideratum **3** *a need for equipment* want, lack, insufficiency, inadequacy, neediness, demand, shortage
▷ **in need** poor, impoverished, penniless, disadvantaged, deprived, poverty-stricken, underprivileged, *formal* destitute, penurious, indigent, impecunious, *colloq.* on the breadline, hard up, unable to keep the wolf from the door

needed *adj*
called for, desired, required, wanted, lacking, compulsory, necessary, obligatory, essential, *formal* requisite

F◸ unnecessary, unneeded

needful *adj*
required, needed, necessary, essential, indispensable, vital, stipulated, needy, *formal* requisite

F◸ excess, needless, superfluous

needle *n, v*
▶ *n* **1** *needle and thread* knitting needle, pin, nib, bodkin, hypodermic needle, stylus **2** POINTER, indicator, arrow, marker, hand **3** THORN, prickle, spike, splinter, barb, spine, quill, briar, bristle, bramble, *formal* spicule
▶ *v* annoy, irritate, harass, pester, goad, spur, provoke, ruffle, prick, rile, bait, prod, nag, irk, taunt, torment, sting, *colloq.* aggravate, nettle, niggle, wind up, cheese off

needless *adj*
unnecessary, gratuitous, uncalled-for, unwanted, undesired, redundant, dispensable, superfluous, expendable, useless, pointless, purposeless, luxury

F◸ necessary, essential, indispensable

needlework *n*
embroidery, fancywork, stitching, sewing, crocheting, tapestry, tatting, needlepoint

needy *adj*
poor, impoverished, in need, penniless, disadvantaged, deprived, poverty-stricken, underprivileged, *formal* destitute, penurious, indigent, impecunious, *colloq.* on the breadline, hard up, unable to keep the wolf from the door

F◸ affluent, wealthy, well-off

ne'er-do-well *n*
good-for-nothing, idler, layabout, wastrel, waster, *colloq.* black sheep, loafer, shirker, skiver

nefarious *adj*
wicked, detestable, dreadful, evil, foul, loathsome, vile, vicious, shameful, outrageous, horrendous, terrible, odious, monstrous, villainous, abominable, atrocious, base, sinful, unholy, criminal, depraved, infamous, horrible, satanic, infernal, *formal* execrable, heinous, iniquitous, opprobrious

F◸ exemplary

negate *v*
1 CANCEL, annul, invalidate, undo, neutralize, quash, reverse, wipe out, void, repeal, *formal* nullify, countermand, abrogate, retract, revoke, rescind **2** DENY, contradict, oppose, disprove, repudiate, renounce, reject, discredit, *formal* refute, gainsay, *colloq.* explode, squash

F◸ **2** affirm

negation *n*
1 CANCELLATION, repeal, neutralization, veto, *formal* disavowal, nullification, abrogation, countermanding **2** DENIAL, contradiction, rejection, renunciation, disclaimer **3** OPPOSITE, reverse, contrary, *formal* inverse, antithesis, converse

F◸ **2** affirmation

negative *adj, n*
▶ *adj* **1** CONTRADICTORY, contrary, denying, refusing, opposing, opposed, invalidating, neutralizing, annulling, *formal* nullifying, dissenting, gainsaying **2** UNCO-OPERATIVE, cynical, pessimistic, defeatist, gloomy, unenthusiastic, uninterested, unwilling, unhelpful, critical, weak, spineless

F◸ **1** affirmative, positive **2** constructive, positive
▶ *n* contradiction, denial, opposite, refusal, rejection, *formal* dissension

neglect *v, n*
▶ *v* **1** DISREGARD, ignore, overlook, leave alone, leave out, abandon, pass by, rebuff, scorn, disdain, slight, spurn, *formal* forsake **2** FORGET, fail (in), omit, overlook, let slide, shirk, skimp, be lax about

F◸ **1** cherish, appreciate **2** remember, pay attention to, attend to
▶ *n* negligence, disregard, carelessness, failure, inattention, disrepair, indifference, slackness, laxity, forgetfulness, ignoring, rebuff, scorn, disdain, slight, spurning, oversight, slight, disrespect, *formal* remissness, default, dereliction of duty, heedlessness

F◸ care, attention, concern

neglected *adj*
uncared-for, disregarded, abandoned, derelict, overgrown, uncultivated, unmaintained, untended, untilled, unweeded, unhusbanded, underestimated, undervalued, unappreciated

F◸ cherished, treasured

neglectful *adj*
uncaring, careless, inattentive, disregardful, forgetful, thoughtless, unmindful, indifferent, lax, negligent, oblivious, *formal* heedless, remiss, *colloq.* sloppy

F◸ attentive, careful

negligence *n*
inattentiveness, inattention, carelessness, laxity, neglect, slackness, thoughtlessness, forgetfulness, indifference, omission, oversight, disregard, shortcoming, failure, *formal* default, remissness, dereliction of duty, heedlessness, *colloq.* sloppiness
🔁 attentiveness, care, regard

negligent *adj*
neglectful, inattentive, thoughtless, casual, lax, cursory, careless, indifferent, offhand, nonchalant, slack, uncaring, unmindful, forgetful, *formal* remiss, heedless, dilatory, *colloq.* sloppy
🔁 attentive, careful, scrupulous

negligible *adj*
unimportant, insignificant, small, imperceptible, inappreciable, trifling, trivial, petty, paltry, minor, minute, tiny, not worth bothering about
🔁 significant

negotiable *adj*
1 DEBATABLE, arguable, questionable, contestable, open to discussion/question, undecided, unsettled **2** NAVIGABLE, passable, crossable, open, clear, unblocked, unobstructed, surmountable, *formal* traversable
🔁 **1** non-negotiable, fixed, definite

negotiate *v*
1 *negotiate an agreement* deal, mediate, arbitrate, intervene, intercede, debate, haggle, bargain, arrange, agree, come to an agreement, hammer out, thrash out, pull off, transact, work out, manage, complete, settle, fulfil, consult, contract, talk, discuss, reach a compromise, *formal* confer, resolve, execute, conclude, *colloq.* parley, wheel and deal **2** GET ROUND, cross, clear, surmount, pass (over/through), *formal* traverse

negotiation *n*
mediation, arbitration, debate, conference, discussion, diplomacy, bargaining, haggling, parleying, transaction, reaching an agreement, thrashing-out, hammering-out, pulling-off, talks, *colloq.* parley, wheeling and dealing

negotiator *n*
arbitrator, go-between, mediator, intermediary, bargainer, haggler, moderator, intercessor, adjudicator, broker, ambassador, diplomat, *colloq.* parleyer, wheeler-dealer

neigh *v*
whinny, hinny, bray, nicker

neighbourhood *n*
district, locality, vicinity, community, locale, quarter, part, precinct, environs, confines, surroundings, area, region, *formal* proximity, purlieus
▷ **in the neighbourhood of** near, close to, about, roughly, almost, approximately, nearby, next to

neighbouring *adj*
adjacent, bordering, near, nearby, nearest, near at hand, close at hand, local, connecting, next, surrounding, *formal* adjoining, abutting, contiguous
🔁 distant, remote, far away

neighbourly *adj*
sociable, friendly, amiable, kind, generous, helpful, genial, warm, cordial, easy to get on/along with, affable, hospitable, obliging, considerate, companionable

nemesis *n*
retribution, vengeance, punishment, just punishment, destruction, ruin, downfall, destiny, fate

neologism *n*
new word, new expression, new phrase, innovation, coinage, novelty, vogue word

neophyte *n*
beginner, learner, novice, newcomer, apprentice, probationer, trainee, recruit, raw recruit, new member, tiro, rookie, *formal* noviciate, novitiate, *colloq.* greenhorn

nepotism *n*
favouritism, bias, partiality, preferential treatment, keeping it in the family, looking after your own, *colloq.* jobs for the boys, old-boy network, old-school tie

nerve *n, v*
▶ *n* **1** COURAGE, bravery, mettle, pluck, spirit, vigour, intrepidity, valour, daring, fearlessness, cool-headedness, hardihood, firmness, resolution, steadfastness, will, determination, endurance, force, *formal* fortitude, *colloq.* guts, spunk, grit, bottle **2** AUDACITY, impudence, effrontery, brazenness, gall, boldness, impertinence, insolence, presumption, temerity, *colloq.* cheek, chutzpah, face, neck, brass neck, sauce, mouth, lip
🔁 **1** weakness **2** timidity
▶ *v* steel, strengthen, invigorate, encourage, bolster, brace, hearten, embolden, *formal* fortify
🔁 unnerve

nerveless *adj*
feeble, weak, flabby, inert, slack, nervous, spineless, timid, unnerved, afraid, cowardly, *formal* debilitated, enervated
🔁 bold, brave, strong

nerve-racking *adj*
harrowing, distressing, trying, stressful, tense, maddening, worrying, anxious, disquieting, difficult, frightening, *colloq.* nail-biting

nerves *n*
nervousness, tension, nervous tension, stress, anxiety, worry, strain, fretfulness, apprehensiveness, *colloq.* jitters, butterflies, butterflies in your stomach, collywobbles, willies, heebie-jeebies

nervous *adj*
highly-strung, excitable, anxious, agitated, on edge, edgy, tense, strained, fidgety, apprehensive, neurotic, shaky, uneasy, worried, flustered, disquieted, fretful, quaking, on tenterhooks, fearful, timid, timorous, *formal* perturbed, *colloq.* nervy, twitchy, het up, keyed up, wound up, jumpy, jittery, uptight, with butterflies in your stomach, on pins and needles, shaking like a leaf/jelly, with your heart in your mouth, in a sweat, in a stew, in a tizzy, *slang* screwed-up
🔁 calm, relaxed

nervous breakdown *n*
mental breakdown, nervous disorder, neurosis, crisis, depression, clinical depression, melancholia, *colloq.* cracking-up

nervousness *n*
anxiety, tension, strain, stress, edginess, worry, uneasiness, disquiet, apprehensiveness, agitation, restlessness, fluster, excitability, timidity, timorousness, tremulousness, *formal* perturbation, *colloq.* habdabs, heebie-jeebies, touchiness, willies
🔁 calmness, coolness

nervy *adj*
highly-strung, excitable, anxious, agitated, on edge, edgy, tense, strained, fidgety, apprehensive, neurotic, shaky, uneasy, worried, flustered, fearful, *colloq.* twitchy, het up, keyed up, wound up, jumpy, jittery, uptight, with butterflies in your stomach, on pins and needles, shaking like a leaf/jelly, with your heart in your mouth
🔁 calm, relaxed

nescient *adj*
ignorant, uneducated, illiterate, innumerate, backward, unread, untaught, untrained, inexperienced,

unschooled, unlearned, stupid, uninitiated, unenlightened, uninformed, ill-informed, unwitting, unaware, unfamiliar, unacquainted, *colloq.* clueless, dense, thick, thick as two short planks
Fa educated, knowledgeable, learned, clever, *formal* conversant

nest *n*
1 *a bird's nest* breeding-ground, den, roost, perch, eyrie, lair, cote, dovecote, vespiary, nesting-box, *US* bird-house **2** RETREAT, refuge, resort, shelter, haunt, haven, hideaway, hideout, hiding place, den, mew

nest egg *n*
fund(s), reserve(s), savings, store, cache, deposit, bottom drawer, *colloq.* money saved for a rainy day

nestle *v*
snuggle (up), huddle (together), cuddle (up), nuzzle, curl up

nestling *n*
fledgling, chick, suckling, weanling, baby

net¹ *n, v*
▶ *n a fishing net* mesh, meshwork, web, webbing, network, netting, open work, tracery, lattice, latticework, filigree, lace, fishnet, drag, dragnet, drift, driftnet, drop-net, seine, seine net, snare, trap, *formal* reticulum
▶ *v* catch, trap, capture, take captive, bag, ensnare, snare, enmesh, entangle, *colloq.* nab, collar, nick

net² *adj, v*
▶ *adj* **1** *a net salary* nett, clear, after tax, after deductions, take-home, final, lowest **2** OVERALL, general, broad, total, inclusive, final, ultimate
Fa **1** gross
▶ *v* bring in, clear, earn, take, take home, raise, get, make, receive, gain, pocket, obtain, accumulate, *formal* realize, *colloq.* pull in, rake in

nether *adj*
1 LOWER, under, lower-level, bottom, below, beneath, underground, *formal* basal, inferior **2** INFERNAL, hellish, underworld, Plutonian, Stygian

nettle *v*
annoy, chafe, discountenance, exasperate, fret, goad, harass, incense, irritate, needle, pique, provoke, ruffle, sting, tease, torment, vex, *colloq.* bug, hassle, aggravate, get on someone's nerves, rub up the wrong way, get someone's blood/back up, drive round the bend/twist

nettled *adj*
annoyed, offended, irritated, angry, aggrieved, incensed, exasperated, cross, harassed, provoked, piqued, riled, ruffled, stung, vexed, galled, goaded, huffy, irritable, *colloq.* miffed, needled, peeved, narked

network *n*
1 NET, maze, mesh, labyrinth, circuitry, grill, meshwork, web, webbing, network, netting, open work, tracery, lattice, latticework, filigree, lace, *formal* convolution **2** SYSTEM, organization, arrangement, structure, interconnections, complex, grid, matrix, channels, tracks, *formal* nexus, *colloq.* grapevine, bush telegraph, Old-Boy network, old-school tie

neurosis *n*
(mental) disorder, psychological disorder, affliction, abnormality, disturbance, instability, maladjustment, derangement, deviation, fixation, obsession, phobia

neurotic *adj*
paranoid, irrational, disturbed, maladjusted, deranged, anxious, nervous, overwrought, hysterical, unstable, unhealthy, deviant, abnormal, compulsive, obsessive, phobic

neuter *v*
castrate, emasculate, doctor, geld, spay, dress, caponize, sterilize, *colloq.* fix

neutral *adj*
1 IMPARTIAL, uncommitted, unbiased, unprejudiced, non-aligned, disinterested, undecided, non-partisan, non-committal, objective, detached, indifferent, dispassionate, uninvolved, even-handed, open-minded **2** DULL, bland, inoffensive, unexceptionable, unremarkable, unassertive, ordinary, uninteresting, nondescript, colourless, insipid, drab, expressionless, indistinct, anodyne **3** *a neutral colour* pale, pastel, indefinite, indistinct, grey, fawn, beige
Fa **1** biased, prejudiced, partisan **2** remarkable, exciting **3** colourful

neutrality *n*
unbiasedness, impartiality, impartialness, detachment, disinterest, disinterestedness, non-alignment, non-intervention, non-involvement

neutralize *v*
counteract, counterbalance, offset, balance, compensate for, make up for, negate, cancel (out), invalidate, annul, undo, frustrate, incapacitate, *formal* nullify

never *adv*
at no time, not ever, not for a moment, under no circumstances, not at all, on no account, *colloq.* not on your life, not on your nellie, when pigs fly, no way, not in a month of Sundays, not in a million years
Fa always

never-ending *adj*
everlasting, eternal, non-stop, endless, unending, without end, perpetual, unceasing, uninterrupted, continuous, unbroken, unremitting, interminable, incessant, unbroken, permanent, persistent, constant, unchanging, relentless, infinite, boundless, limitless
Fa fleeting, transitory

nevertheless *adv*
nonetheless, still, anyway, even so, yet, however, by any means, in any case/event, by some means, anyhow, but, regardless, for all that, all/just the same, at the same time, *formal* notwithstanding

new *adj*
1 MODERN, contemporary, current, latest, recent, state-of-the-art, present-day, up-to-date, up-to-the-minute, topical, modish, ultra-modern, futuristic, advanced, avant-garde, *colloq.* trendy, newfangled, way out **2** NOVEL, original, fresh, different, creative, resourceful, imaginative, innovative, pioneering, revolutionary, ground-breaking, experimental, ingenious, unfamiliar, strange, unconventional, unusual, brand-new, mint, unknown, unused, newly discovered, virgin, newborn **3** CHANGED, altered, modernized, improved, renewed, refreshed, reinvigorated, restored, remodelled, redesigned, *colloq.* born-again **4** ADDED, additional, another, further, extra, more, supplementary **5** *new to the work* unfamiliar, unacquainted, unknown, inexperienced, unversed, unaccustomed, ignorant, a stranger, alien
Fa **1** out-of-date, old-fashioned, outdated **2** usual, ordinary, just another **3** old **5** familiar

newcomer *n*
1 IMMIGRANT, alien, foreigner, incomer, colonist, settler, (new) arrival, outsider, intruder, stranger **2** NOVICE, beginner, learner, pupil, trainee, recruit, probationer, apprentice, *formal* neophyte, *colloq.* greenhorn, rookie

newfangled *adj*
modern, new, recent, state-of-the-art, contemporary, ultra-modern, futuristic, fashionable, modernistic, novel, gimmicky, *colloq.* trendy
Fa old-fashioned

newly *adv*
recently, lately, latterly, just, freshly, of late, afresh, anew

newness *n*
freshness, innovation, novelty, originality, oddity, uniqueness, unusualness, strangeness, unfamiliarity, *formal* recency
⚋ oldness, ordinariness

news *n*
report, account, information, data, facts, intelligence, dispatch, message, communication, announcement, press release, communiqué, bulletin, news item, newsflash, newscast, gossip, hearsay, rumour, statement, story, word, latest, developments, scandal, revelation, exposé, disclosure, advice, *formal* tidings, *colloq.* lowdown, gen, info, dope

newspaper *n*
daily, paper, publication, broadsheet, tabloid, sheet, journal, periodical, magazine, weekly, press, gazette, organ, *colloq.* rag

newsworthy *adj*
reportable, hitting/making the headlines, important, significant, interesting, remarkable, stimulating, notable, noteworthy, arresting, unusual

next *adj, adv*
▶ *adj* 1 ADJACENT, neighbouring, bordering, along, alongside, beside, nearest, closest, *formal* adjoining, contiguous, tangential 2 FOLLOWING, succeeding, successive, ensuing, later, *formal* subsequent
⚋ 2 previous, preceding
▶ *adv* afterwards, later, then, *formal* subsequently, thereafter

nibble *n, v*
▶ *n* bite, peck, gnaw, munch, morsel, taste, titbit, bit, crumb, snack, piece
▶ *v* bite, eat, peck, pick at, munch, gnaw, *colloq.* snack, *slang* nosh

nice *adj*
1 *have a nice time* pleasant, agreeable, enjoyable, lovely, good, delightful, satisfying, acceptable, pleasurable, fine, appealing, amusing, entertaining, welcome, *formal* delectable 2 *he seems a nice man* pleasant, agreeable, delightful, charming, likeable, attractive, good, good-natured, good-humoured, kind, kindly, friendly, genial, sweet, amiable, sympathetic, understanding, endearing, well-mannered, polite, respectable, civil, courteous 3 SUBTLE, delicate, fine, minute, fastidious, refined, particular, discriminating, scrupulous, meticulous, precise, exact, accurate, careful, strict, close
⚋ 1 unpleasant, horrible 2 nasty, disagreeable, unpleasant 3 careless

nicely *adv*
satisfactorily, well, agreeably, delightfully, pleasurably, pleasantly, pleasingly, respectably, properly
⚋ unpleasantly, disagreeably, nastily

niceness *n*
pleasantness, kindness, agreeableness, friendliness, delightfulness, likeableness, attractiveness, charm, amiability, politeness, respectability
⚋ unpleasantness, disagreeableness, nastiness

nicety *n*
1 SUBTLETY, refinement, delicacy, distinction, nuance, fine point 2 PRECISION, accuracy, meticulousness, exactness, scrupulousness, minuteness, finesse

niche *n*
1 POSITION, place, vocation, calling, métier, slot, specialized/specialist area 2 RECESS, alcove, hollow, nook, cranny, cubbyhole, corner, opening

nick *n, v*
▶ *n* 1 NOTCH, indentation, chip, cut, groove, dent, scar, scratch, mark 2 PRISON, jail, jailhouse, police station, *colloq.* inside, *slang* clink, cooler, slammer, jug 3 *in good nick* condition, shape, form, state, health, fettle
▶ *v* 1 NOTCH, cut, dent, indent, chip, score, scratch, scar, mark, damage, snick 2 STEAL, pilfer, take, pocket, *colloq.* knock off, pinch, swipe, lag, snitch 3 ARREST, catch, capture, pick up, *formal* apprehend, *colloq.* nab, collar, run in, *slang* bust

nickname *n*
pet name, familiar name, sobriquet, epithet, diminutive

nifty *adj*
slick, neat, clever, pleasing, enjoyable, excellent, quick, skilful, deft, chic, smart, stylish, spruce, sharp, adroit, agile, nippy, apt

niggardliness *n*
1 MEANNESS, miserliness, closeness, grudgingness, ungenerousness, *formal* parsimony, *colloq.* stinginess, tight-fistedness, cheese-paring 2 MEAGRENESS, paltriness, smallness, scantiness, skimpiness, inadequacy, insufficiency
⚋ 1 generosity 2 bountifulness

niggardly *adj*
1 MEAN, miserly, close, ungenerous, ungiving, sparing, grudging, hard-fisted, *formal* parsimonious, *colloq.* stingy, tight-fisted, cheese-paring 2 MEAGRE, small, miserable, scanty, skimpy, paltry, inadequate, insufficient, *colloq.* measly
⚋ 1 generous 2 bountiful

niggle *v*
1 BOTHER, worry, trouble, annoy, irritate, upset, *colloq.* bug 2 NAG, criticize, keep on at, pick on, complain, moan, carp, quibble, *colloq.* nit-pick, hassle, henpeck

night *n*
night-time, darkness, hours of darkness, dark, dead of night
⚋ day, daytime

nightclub *n*
club, disco, discotheque, cabaret, nightspot, *colloq.* niterie, nitery

nightfall *n*
sunset, dusk, twilight, dark, evening, sundown, *formal* gloaming, crepuscule
⚋ dawn, sunrise

nightmare *n*
1 BAD DREAM, hallucination, *formal* incubus 2 ORDEAL, horror, torment, torture, trial, calamity, agony, anguish, awful experience

nightmarish *adj*
terrifying, alarming, dreadful, frightening, harrowing, horrible, horrific, agonizing, disturbing, scaring, unreal, *colloq.* creepy

nihilism *n*
rejection, repudiation, negation, denial, pessimism, scepticism, nothingness, oblivion, emptiness, nonexistence, lawlessness, anarchy, terrorism, disorder, agnosticism, atheism, cynicism, disbelief, negativism, *formal* abnegation, nullity, renunciation

nihilist *n*
pessimist, revolutionary, extremist, agitator, anarchist, terrorist, negationist, negativist, agnostic, atheist, disbeliever, cynic, sceptic, antinomian

nil *n*
nothing, zero, none, nought, naught, love, *colloq.* duck, zilch

nimble *adj*
1 AGILE, active, lively, sprightly, spry, smart, graceful,

lithe, quick, quick-moving, brisk, deft, light-footed, prompt, ready, swift, *colloq.* nippy **2** ALERT, quick-witted, quick, quick-thinking, clever, smart, sharp-witted, sharp-eyed
F3 1 clumsy, slow **2** slow

nimbleness *n*
agility, adroitness, dexterity, grace, lightness, deftness, finesse, sprightliness, spryness, smartness, skill, alertness, *formal* alacrity, *colloq.* niftiness, nippiness

nimbly *adv*
smartly, agilely, fast, sharply, snappily, speedily, swiftly, spryly, quickly, readily, promptly, actively, proficiently, dexterously, deftly, briskly, easily, alertly, quick-wittedly
F3 awkwardly, clumsily

nincompoop *n*
fool, idiot, dunce, dimwit, simpleton, ignoramus, dolt, *colloq.* blockhead, nitwit, numskull, chump, clot, twit, twerp, *slang* nerd, plonker, wally

nip¹ *v*
1 BITE, pinch, squeeze, snip, clip, dock, lop, tweak, catch, grip, nibble **2** DASH, go, hurry, rush, fly, tear, run, *colloq.* pop
▷ **nip in the bud** halt, arrest, stop, stem, check, block, frustrate, obstruct, impede

nip² *n*
a nip of brandy dram, draught, shot, swallow, mouthful, drop, sip, taste, portion

nipple *n*
teat, udder, breast, pap, papilla, dug, *technical* mamilla

nippy *adj*
1 CHILLY, cold, biting, sharp, raw, nipping, piercing, stinging **2** FAST, quick, speedy, nimble, brisk, active, agile, sprightly, spry
F3 1 warm **2** slow

nirvana *n*
enlightenment, paradise, tranquillity, bliss, joy, peace, ecstasy, exaltation, serenity

nit-picking *adj*
quibbling, carping, finicky, fussy, hair-splitting, hypercritical, pedantic, captious, cavilling

nitty-gritty *n*
basics, essentials, fundamentals, main points, key points, *colloq.* bottom line, nuts and bolts, brass tacks

nitwit *n*
fool, idiot, dimwit, simpleton, *colloq.* dummy, nincompoop, ninny, numskull, nit, twit

no *adv*
not at all, not really, of course not, absolutely not, most certainly not, no thanks, under no circumstances, *colloq.* no way, nope, not on your life, over my dead body

nob *n*
VIP, aristocrat, personage, *colloq.* big shot, bigwig, fat cat, toff

nobble *v*
1 BRIBE, buy (off), influence, warn off, threaten, intimidate **2** DOPE, drug, interfere with, disable, incapacitate, hamstring, *colloq.* get at **3** CATCH, arrest, grab, seize, *colloq.* nab, collar, nick **4** STEAL, grab, take, pilfer, pinch, *colloq.* nick, knock off, snitch, swipe **5** THWART, frustrate, foil, check, defeat, hinder

nobility *n*
1 NOBLENESS, dignity, grandeur, grandness, illustriousness, stateliness, majesty, magnificence, splendour, impressiveness, eminence, excellence, superiority, uprightness, integrity, honour, virtue, worthiness, generosity, magnanimity **2** ARISTOCRACY, peerage, peers, nobles, gentry, élite, lords, high society, *colloq.* nobs, toffs

F3 1 baseness **2** proletariat

Titles of the nobility include:
aristocrat, baron, baroness, baronet, count, countess, dame, dowager, duchess, duke, earl, governor, grand duke, knight, lady, laird, liege, liege lord, life peer, lord, marchioness, marquess, marquis, noble, nobleman, noblewoman, peer, peeress, ruler, seigneur, squire, thane, viscount, viscountess.

noble *n, adj*
▶ *n* aristocrat, peer, lord, lady, nobleman, noblewoman
F3 commoner
▶ *adj* **1** ARISTOCRATIC, high-born, titled, landed, high-ranking, patrician, *colloq.* blue-blooded, born with a silver spoon in your mouth **2** MAGNIFICENT, magnanimous, splendid, stately, generous, dignified, distinguished, fine, eminent, grand, great, exalted, lofty, honoured, honourable, venerated, imposing, impressive, majestic **3** VIRTUOUS, unselfish, honourable, worthy, excellent, elevated, fine, gentle, generous, self-sacrificing, magnanimous
F3 1 low-born **3** ignoble, base, contemptible

nobody *pron n*
▶ *pron* no one, nothing
F3 somebody
▶ *n* nonentity, menial, cipher, mediocrity, *colloq.* lightweight
F3 somebody

nod *v, n*
▶ *v* **1** GESTURE, indicate, sign, signal, salute, acknowledge, incline, dip, bow **2** AGREE, approve, support, accept, say yes to, *formal* assent **3** SLEEP, fall asleep, doze (off), drowse, nap, *formal* slumber, *colloq.* drop off
▶ *n* gesture, indication, sign, signal, salute, greeting, beck, acknowledgement

node *n*
swelling, protuberance, lump, knob, knot, growth, bud, bump, nodule, carbuncle

noise *n, v*
▶ *n* sound, din, racket, row, clamour, clash, clatter, commotion, outcry, hubbub, uproar, cry, blare, talk, pandemonium, tumult, babble
F3 quiet, silence
▶ *v* report, rumour, publicize, announce, circulate

noiseless *adj*
silent, inaudible, soundless, quiet, mute, still, hushed
F3 loud, noisy

noisome *adj*
disgusting, offensive, repulsive, disagreeable, obnoxious, nauseating, harmful, hurtful, injurious, pernicious, bad, unhealthy, unwholesome, smelly, stinking, foul, putrid, reeking, poisonous, *formal* deleterious, fetid, malodorous, mephitic, noxious, pestiferous, pestilential
F3 balmy, pleasant, wholesome

noisy *adj*
booming, roaring, thundering, loud, deafening, blasting, blaring, ear-splitting, clamorous, piercing, vocal, tumultuous, rowdy, rumbustious, boisterous, obstreperous, clamorous, turbulent, *formal* vociferous, *colloq.* so loud you can't hear yourself think
F3 quiet, silent, peaceful

nomad *n*
traveller, wanderer, itinerant, transient, rambler, roamer, rover, migrant, vagabond, vagrant

nomadic *adj*
travelling, itinerant, wandering, roaming, migrant,

migratory, drifting, roving, roaming, Gypsy, unsettled, vagrant, *formal* peregrinating, peripatetic

nom-de-plume *n*
pseudonym, pen-name, assumed name, alias

nomenclature *n*
naming, classification, vocabulary, terminology, phraseology, *technical* taxonomy, *formal* codification, locution

nominal *adj*
1 TITULAR, in name only, supposed, professed, ostensible, so-called, theoretical, formal, self-styled, puppet, symbolic, *formal* purported **2** TOKEN, minimal, trifling, trivial, insignificant, small, symbolic
F3 1 actual, genuine, real

nominate *v*
1 PROPOSE, designate, submit, suggest, recommend, present, *colloq.* put up **2** APPOINT, choose, select, name, elect, assign, commission, elevate, term

nomination *n*
1 PROPOSAL, submission, suggestion, recommendation **2** APPOINTMENT, choice, selection, designation, election

nominee *n*
candidate, entrant, contestant, appointee, runner, assignee

non-aligned *adj*
neutral, independent, impartial, non-partisan, uncommitted, undecided, uninvolved

nonchalance *n*
calm, cool, composure, indifference, detachment, unconcern, self-possession, *formal* equanimity, imperturbability, insouciance, sang-froid, aplomb, pococurant(e)ism
F3 anxiousness, worriedness

nonchalant *adj*
unconcerned, detached, dispassionate, offhand, blasé, indifferent, casual, cool, calm, collected, apathetic, careless, *formal* insouciant, imperturbable, *colloq.* laid-back, cool and collected, cool as a cucumber
F3 concerned, careful

non-committal *adj*
guarded, unrevealing, cautious, wary, reserved, ambiguous, discreet, equivocal, evasive, careful, neutral, indefinite, tactful, diplomatic, tentative, vague, *formal* circumspect, prudent, politic, *colloq.* sitting on the fence, playing your cards close to your chest

non compos mentis *adj*
of unsound mind, insane, mentally ill, deranged, unbalanced, unhinged, crazy
F3 sane, stable

nonconformist *n, adj*
▶ *n* dissenter, rebel, individualist, dissident, radical, protester, heretic, iconoclast, eccentric, maverick, seceder, secessionist, *formal* dissentient, *colloq.* fish out of water, square peg in a round hole
F3 conformist
▶ *adj* rebel, dissident, unco-operative, radical, heretical, eccentric, individualist, *formal* dissentient

nonconformity *n*
unconventionality, originality, eccentricity, dissent, deviation, heterodoxy, heresy, secession
F3 conformity, conventionality

nondescript *adj*
featureless, indeterminate, undistinctive, undistinguished, indistinguishable, unexceptional, ordinary, outrage, commonplace, plain, dull, vague, bland, anaemic, insipid, uninspiring, uninteresting, unattractive, unremarkable, unclassified, *colloq.* run of

the mill, common or garden
F3 distinctive, remarkable

none *pron*
no one, not any, not one, not even one, not a single one, nothing, nobody, not a soul, nil, zero

nonentity *n*
nobody, nothing, menial, cipher, mediocrity, *colloq.* lightweight
F3 somebody

non-essential *adj*
unnecessary, unimportant, superfluous, redundant, unneeded, inessential, peripheral, dispensable, excessive, extraneous, expendable, supplementary
F3 essential, necessary

nonetheless *adv*
nevertheless, still, anyway, even so, yet, however, anyhow, but, regardless, *formal* notwithstanding

non-existence *n*
unreality, fancy, illusion, illusiveness, insubstantiality, unbeing, *formal* chimera
F3 existence, reality

non-existent *adj*
missing, unreal, null, legendary, mythical, fictitious, fictional, fancied, fanciful, hallucinatory, illusory, hypothetical, imaginary, imagined, fantasy, immaterial, insubstantial, *formal* chimerical, incorporeal, suppositional
F3 actual, existing, real

non-flammable *adj*
not flammable, fire-proof, fire-resistant, flame-resistant, incombustible, uninflammable
F3 flammable, inflammable

non-intervention *n*
non-involvement, non-participation, non-alignment, non-interference, laissez-faire, inaction, inertia, passivity, apathy, *colloq.* hands-off policy

nonpareil *adj*
unparalleled, incomparable, beyond compare, without equal, unequalled, matchless, unrivalled, unique, inimitable

non-partisan *adj*
unbiased, unprejudiced, impartial, independent, neutral, objective, even-handed, detached, dispassionate
F3 partisan, biased, prejudiced

nonplus *v*
puzzle, perplex, take aback, baffle, bewilder, confound, confuse, dumbfound, stun, stump, astonish, astound, dismay, embarrass, disconcert, mystify, *formal* discomfit, discountenance, *colloq.* flabbergast, flummox, faze

nonplussed *adj*
disconcerted, confounded, taken aback, at a loss, stunned, bewildered, astonished, astounded, dumbfounded, perplexed, puzzled, baffled, dismayed, embarrassed, *colloq.* stumped, flabbergasted, flummoxed, fazed, floored, out of your depth

nonsense *n*
rubbish, trash, drivel, balderdash, gibberish, gobbledygook, senselessness, stupidity, silliness, foolishness, folly, blather, twaddle, ridiculousness, *colloq.* stuff and nonsense, double Dutch, mumbo-jumbo, bunk, bunkum, claptrap, cobblers, poppycock, piffle, waffle, flannel, rot, tripe, tosh, bosh, tommy-rot, codswallop, baloney, humbug, hooey, bilge, bull, *slang* crap
F3 sense, wisdom

nonsensical *adj*
ridiculous, meaningless, senseless, foolish, stupid, inane, irrational, silly, incomprehensible, unintelligible, ludicrous, preposterous, absurd, fatuous, *colloq.*

crazy, crackpot, potty, nutty, dotty, barmy, harebrained, wacky
F3 reasonable, sensible, logical

non-stop *adj, adv*
▶ *adj* never-ending, uninterrupted, continuous, unceasing, ceaseless, incessant, constant, endless, interminable, persistent, relentless, unending, unbroken, without interruption, unfaltering, round-the-clock, ongoing
F3 intermittent, occasional
▶ *adv* uninterruptedly, continuously, constantly, incessantly, unceasingly, ceaselessly, endlessly, interminably, unendingly, unbrokenly, round-the-clock, unfalteringly, steadily, relentlessly, unrelentingly, unremittingly
F3 intermittently, occasionally

non-violent *adj*
peaceable, peaceful, pacifist, passive, irenic, dovish
F3 violent

nook *n*
1 RECESS, alcove, corner, cranny, niche, cubbyhole
2 SHELTER, retreat, hideout, hideaway, den, refuge, cavity, opening

noon *n*
midday, twelve o'clock, twelve noon, lunchtime

norm *n*
average, mean, standard, rule, usual rule, pattern, type, criterion, gauge, model, yardstick, benchmark, touchstone, measure, scale, reference

normal *adj*
usual, standard, general, commonplace, common, ordinary, conventional, popular, average, regular, routine, everyday, accepted, typical, mainstream, natural, habitual, accustomed, well-adjusted, straight, rational, reasonable, *colloq.* run-of-the-mill
F3 abnormal, irregular, peculiar, deviant

normality *n*
usualness, commonness, ordinariness, regularity, routine, conventionality, balance, adjustment, averageness, typicality, naturalness, reason, reasonableness, rationality
F3 abnormality, irregularity, peculiarity

normally *adv*
ordinarily, usually, as usual, as a rule, generally, typically, commonly, conventionally, characteristically, naturally, regularly, routinely
F3 abnormally, exceptionally

northern *adj*
north, northerly, polar, Arctic, *old use* septentrional, *formal* boreal, hyperborean
F3 southern

nose *n, v*
▶ *n* **1** *the animal's nose* bill, neb, *formal* proboscis, *colloq.* beak, boko, hooter, schnozzle, snitch, snout, snoot, *slang* conk **2** *a nose for a good story* sense, flair, feel, perception, instinct
▶ *v* nudge, inch, edge, ease, push
▷ **nose around** poke around, search, pry, *colloq.* snoop, rubberneck, poke your nose in
▷ **nose out** discover, detect, find out, uncover, reveal, inquire, *colloq.* sniff out

nosedive *v, n*
▶ *v* plummet, dive, drop, plunge, decline, get worse, go down, submerge, swoop
▶ *n* plummet, dive, drop, plunge, swoop, header, purler

nosegay *n*
bouquet, posy, spray, bunch

nosh *n*
food, foodstuffs, comestibles, provisions, meals, stores, rations, refreshments, sustenance, nourishment, nutrition, nutriment, subsistence, feed, fodder, diet, fare, dish, speciality, delicacy, cooking, cuisine, menu, board, table, *formal* viands, victuals, *colloq.* eatables, eats, tuck, *slang* grub

nostalgia *n*
yearning, longing, wistfulness, regretfulness, regret(s), remembrance, recollection(s), reminiscence(s), homesickness, pining

nostalgic *adj*
yearning, longing, pining, wistful, emotional, regretful, sentimental, homesick, reminiscent

nostrum *n*
medicine, pill, drug, potion, cure, remedy, elixir, panacea, cure-all, cure for all ills, universal cure/remedy

nosy *adj*
inquisitive, meddlesome, prying, interfering, curious, eavesdropping, probing, *colloq.* snooping

notability *n*
1 NOTEWORTHINESS, impressiveness, importance, significance, distinction, fame, eminence, renown, *formal* esteem **2** CELEBRITY, dignitary, magnate, worthy, luminary, *formal* notable, personage, *colloq.* somebody, VIP, bigwig, big shot, big noise, heavyweight, top brass, someone
F3 nonentity

notable *adj, n*
▶ *adj* noteworthy, remarkable, noticeable, particular, striking, extraordinary, impressive, outstanding, special, important, significant, marked, unusual, uncommon, celebrated, distinguished, famous, great, illustrious, eminent, pre-eminent, well-known, momentous, notorious, memorable, renowned, unforgettable, rare
F3 ordinary, commonplace, usual
▶ *n* celebrity, notability, VIP, personage, somebody, dignitary, luminary, star, worthy
F3 nobody, nonentity

notably *adv*
markedly, noticeably, particularly, significantly, remarkably, strikingly, signally, conspicuously, distinctly, especially, impressively, outstandingly, extraordinarily, eminently, uncommonly

notation *n*
symbols, characters, code, cipher, signs, alphabet, system, script, hieroglyphics, noting, record, shorthand

notch *n, v*
▶ *n* **1** CUT, nick, indentation, incision, dent, score, groove, gouge, cleft, gash, scratch, mark, snip **2** DEGREE, grade, step, level, stage
▶ *v* cut, nick, score, dent, gouge, groove, indent, mark, gash, scratch
▷ **notch up** achieve, gain, attain, make, score, record, register, *colloq.* chalk up

notched *adj*
jagged, jaggy, pinked, serrate(d), serrulate(d), eroded, *formal* crenellate(d), emarginate, erose

note *n, v*
▶ *n* **1** MESSAGE, letter, communication, memorandum, reminder, line, jotting, account, record, comment, *formal* epistle, missive, *colloq.* memo **2** ANNOTATION, comment, commentary, explanation, gloss, footnote, remark, *formal* explication, marginalia **3** INDICATION, signal, element, tone, inflection, token, mark, symbol **4** EMINENCE, distinction, consequence, fame, renown, greatness, illustriousness, reputation, pre-eminence, prestige **5** HEED, attention, attentiveness, care, mindfulness, regard, notice, observation, consideration

▸ *v* **1** NOTICE, observe, perceive, heed, detect, mark, remark, mention, allude to, refer to, touch on, see, witness **2** RECORD, register, log, write down, enter, put in writing, put down, jot down

noted *adj*
famous, well-known, renowned, notable, celebrated, eminent, pre-eminent, prominent, great, of note, acclaimed, illustrious, distinguished, respected, recognized
⇄ obscure, unknown

notes *n*
jottings, record, impressions, report, commentary, sketch, impressions, outline, synopsis, transcript, minutes, draft

noteworthy *adj*
remarkable, significant, important, notable, memorable, striking, exceptional, impressive, extraordinary, unusual, outstanding, marked
⇄ commonplace, unexceptional, ordinary

nothing *n*
1 NOUGHT, zero, not a thing, naught, nothingness, *colloq.* zilch, sweet Fanny Adams **2** NON-EXISTENCE, emptiness, void, oblivion, *formal* nullity, *colloq.* lightweight **3** NOBODY, nonentity, menial, cipher, mediocrity
⇄ **1, 2, 3** something
▷ **for nothing 1** FREE, gratis, without charge, free of charge, at no cost, *colloq.* on the house **2** IN VAIN, unsuccessfully, futilely, needlessly, with no result, to no avail

nothingness *n*
non-existence, oblivion, vacuum, void, emptiness, *formal* nihilism, nihility, nullity
⇄ life, existence

notice *v, n*
▸ *v* note, remark, perceive, observe, mind, see, discern, distinguish, make out, mark, detect, spot, become aware of, take note of, pay attention to, *formal* heed, take heed of, behold, espy
⇄ ignore, overlook, miss
▸ *n* **1** ANNOUNCEMENT, notification, information, declaration, communication, intimation, intelligence, news, warning, instruction, advice, order, *formal* apprisal **2** ADVERTISEMENT, poster, sign, bill, handbill, bulletin, leaflet, pamphlet, circular, information sheet **3** REVIEW, comment, criticism, critique, write-up, *colloq.* crit **4** ATTENTION, observation, awareness, note, regard, thought, interest, watchfulness, consideration, *formal* heed, cognizance

noticeable *adj*
perceptible, observable, appreciable, unmistakable, conspicuous, visible, discernible, evident, clear, distinct, significant, striking, plain, patent, obvious, detectable, distinguishable, measurable, *formal* manifest
⇄ inconspicuous, unnoticeable

notification *n*
announcement, information, notice, declaration, advice, warning, telling, informing, intelligence, message, publication, statement, communication, divulgence, disclosure

notify *v*
inform, tell, make known, advise, announce, declare, communicate, broadcast, warn, acquaint, caution, alert, publish, disclose, reveal, divulge, *formal* apprise

notion *n*
1 IDEA, thought, concept, conception, belief, impression, view, opinion, conviction, theory, hypothesis, assumption, understanding, apprehension, *formal* conceptualization **2** INCLINATION, desire, wish, whim, fancy, caprice

notional *adj*
theoretical, abstract, imaginary, hypothetical, illusory, conceptual, speculative, fanciful, fancied, unfounded, unreal, visionary, thematic, classificatory, *formal* ideational
⇄ real

notoriety *n*
infamy, disrepute, dishonour, disgrace, scandal, *formal* ignominy, obloquy, opprobrium

notorious *adj*
infamous, disreputable, scandalous, dishonourable, ill-famed, of ill repute, disgraceful, flagrant, blatant, glaring, well-known, *formal* ignominious, egregious, opprobrious

notoriously *adv*
infamously, disreputably, scandalously, dishonourably, disgracefully, flagrantly, blatantly, glaringly, overtly, notably, obviously, openly, particularly, patently, arrantly, spectacularly, *formal* egregiously, opprobriously, ignominiously

notwithstanding *adv prep*
nevertheless, nonetheless, although, though, even so, however, yet, despite, in spite of, regardless of

nought *n*
zero, nil, naught, nothing, nothingness, *colloq.* zilch

nourish *v*
1 NURTURE, feed, foster, care for, provide for, take care of, sustain, support, attend to, tend, nurse, bring up, rear, maintain, have, cherish **2** STRENGTHEN, encourage, promote, cultivate, stimulate, foster, further, forward, advance, boost, help, aid, assist

nourishing *adj*
nutritious, wholesome, healthful, health-giving, good, beneficial, substantial, strengthening, invigorating, *technical* alimentative, *formal* nutritive

nourishment *n*
nutrition, food, sustenance, diet, nutriment, subsistence, *colloq.* eats, tuck, *slang* grub, nosh

novel *adj, n*
▸ *adj* new, original, fresh, innovative, unfamiliar, unique, rare, unusual, uncommon, different, creative, imaginative, resourceful, ingenious, inventive, unconventional, unorthodox, modern, unprecedented, pioneering, ground-breaking, strange
⇄ hackneyed, familiar, ordinary
▸ *n* fiction, story, tale, narrative, romance, book

novelty *n*
1 NEWNESS, originality, freshness, innovation, unfamiliarity, unusualness, uniqueness, rareness, difference, creativity, imaginativeness, unconventionality, strangeness **2** GIMMICK, gadget, trifle, memento, knick-knack, curiosity, souvenir, trinket, bauble, gimcrack

novice *n*
beginner, tiro, learner, student, pupil, trainee, probationer, recruit, raw recruit, apprentice, amateur, newcomer, *formal* neophyte, noviciate, *colloq.* greenhorn, rookie
⇄ expert

noviciate *n*
apprenticeship, trainee period, training, initiation, trial period

now *adv*
1 AT PRESENT, right now, just now, at the moment, for the time being, at the present time, at the moment, at this moment in time, at this time, currently, nowadays, today, these days, *US* presently **2** IMMEDIATELY, at once, directly, instantly, straight away, right away, promptly, without delay, next
▷ **now and then** at times, sometimes, from time to

time, now and again, occasionally, on and off, on occasion, once in a while, periodically, infrequently, intermittently, spasmodically, sporadically, *formal* desultorily

nowadays *adv*
at present, today, at the present time, at the moment, at this moment in time, at this time, currently, these days, in this day and age, *US* presently

noxious *adj*
harmful, poisonous, pernicious, toxic, injurious, unhealthy, deadly, destructive, ruinous, damaging, detrimental, malignant, foul, disgusting, threatening, menacing, *formal* noisome, deleterious
🖅 innocuous, wholesome

nuance *n*
subtlety, suggestion, shade, shading, hint, suspicion, gradation, (fine) distinction, overtone, refinement, touch, trace, tinge, degree, nicety

nub *n*
centre, heart, core, nucleus, kernel, crux, gist, pith, marrow, meat, pivot, focus, point, essence

nubile *adj*
mature, adult, marriageable, attractive, desirable, voluptuous, *colloq.* sexy

nucleus *n*
centre, heart, nub, core, kernel, basis, marrow, meat, pivot, focus, crux

nude *adj*
naked, bare, with nothing on, undressed, unclothed, stripped, stark-naked, uncovered, exposed, *colloq.* starkers, in your birthday suit, in the altogether, in the raw, in the buff, not a stitch on, naked as the day you were born
🖅 clothed, dressed

nudge *v n*
poke, prod, jab, shove, dig, jog, prompt, push, elbow, bump

nudity *n*
nakedness, bareness, undress, state of undress, nudism, dishabille, déshabillé, *colloq.* the altogether

nugatory *adj*
worthless, futile, useless, vain, valueless, unavailing, null and void, invalid, inoperative, insignificant, inconsequential, trifling, trivial, inadequate, *formal* ineffectual
🖅 important, significant

nugget *n*
lump, mass, piece, chunk, clump, hunk, wad, wodge

nuisance *n*
annoyance, inconvenience, bother, irritation, irritant, vexation, pest, bore, difficulty, problem, trial, trouble, weight, burden, plague, inconvenience, drawback, *formal* affliction, tribulation, *colloq.* pain, drag, thorn in your side/flesh

null *adj*
void, invalid, invalidated, annulled, revoked, cancelled, useless, vain, worthless, powerless, inoperative, *formal* ineffectual, nullified, abrogated
🖅 valid

nullify *v*
annul, revoke, cancel, invalidate, declare null and void, abolish, rescind, quash, repeal, void, set aside, bring to an end, reverse, offset, counteract, *formal* abrogate, negate, countermand, renounce, discontinue
🖅 validate

nullity *n*
non-existence, voidness, characterlessness, immateriality, invalidity, powerlessness, uselessness, worthlessness, *formal* incorporeality, ineffectualness
🖅 validity

numb *adj, v*
▶ *adj* benumbed, insensible, unfeeling, deadened, dead, insensitive, without feeling, drugged, anaesthetized, stunned, dazed, frozen, paralysed, immobilized, in shock, *formal* insensible, insensate
🖅 sensitive
▶ *v* deaden, benumb, anaesthetize, drug, freeze, immobilize, paralyse, dull, daze, stupefy, stun
🖅 sensitize

number *n, v*
▶ *n* **1** FIGURE, numeral, digit, integer, unit, character, cipher, fraction, decimal, statistics, data **2** TOTAL, sum, aggregate, tally, score, count, sum, collection, amount, quantity, several, many, company, crowd, group, multitude, throng, horde **3** COPY, issue, edition, impression, imprint, volume, printing
▶ *v* **1** COUNT, calculate, enumerate, reckon, total, add (up to), compute, estimate, include **2** *your days are numbered* limit, restrict, restrain, delimit, specify

numberless *adj*
innumerable, countless, endless, uncounted, many, unnumbered, unsummed, infinite, untold, myriad, immeasurable, *formal* multitudinous

numbness *n*
deadness, paralysis, anaesthetization, unfeelingness, dullness, insensitivity, stupefaction, stupor, torpor, *formal* insensateness, insensibility
🖅 sensitivity

numeral *n*
number, figure, digit, integer, unit, character, cipher

numerous *adj*
many, innumerable, countless, endless, abundant, several, quite a few, legion, plentiful, copious, profuse, various, sundry, *formal* manifold, multitudinous, *colloq.* a good few
🖅 few, scarce, rare

numerousness *n*
plentifulness, abundance, copiousness, countlessness, plurality, profusion, *formal* manifoldness, multiplicity, multitudinousness, multeity
🖅 scantiness, scarcity

numskull *n*
fool, dimwit, dunce, simpleton, *colloq.* clot, dummy, fat head, thickhead, twit, nit, nitwit, twerp, birdbrain

nun *n*
sister, abbess, prioress, vowess, mother superior, anchoress, ancress, canoness, vestal

nuncio *n*
representative, envoy, ambassador, legate

nunnery *n*
convent, priory, cloister, abbey

nuptial *adj*
wedding, wedded, marital, bridal, *formal* matrimonial, conjugal, connubial, hymeneal, epithalamial, epithalamic

nuptials *n*
wedding celebrations, wedding, marriage, bridal, *formal* matrimony, spousals, espousal

nurse *v*
1 TEND, care for, look after, treat, attend to, take care of **2** BREAST-FEED, feed, suckle, wet-nurse, nurture, nourish **3** PRESERVE, sustain, support, nourish, cherish, harbour, entertain, encourage, keep, foster, boost, promote, advance, further, nurture, help, aid, assist

Nurses include:
charge nurse, children's nurse, dental nurse, district nurse, healthcare assistant, health visitor, home nurse, Iain Rennie nurse, locality manager,

Macmillan nurse, matron, midwife, nanny, night nurse, night sister, nursemaid, nursery nurse, nurse tutor, occupational health nurse, psychiatric nurse, Registered General Nurse (RGN), school nurse, sister, staff nurse, State Enrolled Nurse (SEN), State Registered Nurse (SRN), theatre sister, ward sister, wet nurse.

nurture *n, v*
▶ *n* **1** FOOD, nourishment, nutrition, sustenance, diet, subsistence, *colloq.* eats, tuck, *slang* grub, nosh **2** REARING, upbringing, training, care, cultivation, stimulation, encouragement, fostering, promotion, help, aid, assistance, furtherance, advance, boosting, development, education, tending, feeding, schooling, discipline
▶ *v* **1** FEED, nourish, nurse, tend, care for, foster, support, sustain **2** BRING UP, rear, cultivate, develop, stimulate, promote, foster, help, aid, assist, further, advance, boost, educate, instruct, train, school, coach, tutor, discipline

nut *n*
1 *a bag of mixed nuts* kernel, pip, seed, stone

Varieties of nut include:
almond, beech nut, brazil nut, cashew, chestnut, cobnut, coconut, filbert, hazelnut, macadamia, monkey nut, peanut, pecan, pistachio, walnut.

2 MANIAC, insane person, lunatic, psychopath, madman, madwoman, *colloq.* loony, nutcase, nutter, fruitcake, basket-case, *slang* psycho, headcase, oddball **3** ENTHUSIAST, fan, fanatic, follower, supporter, de-

votee, zealot, admirer, aficionado, *colloq.* buff, freak, fiend

nutriment *n*
food, nourishment, nutrition, sustenance, diet, subsistence, *colloq.* eats, tuck, *slang* grub, nosh

nutrition *n*
food, nourishment, sustenance, diet, nutriment, subsistence, *colloq.* eats, tuck, *slang* grub, nosh

nutritious *adj*
nourishing, nutritive, wholesome, healthful, healthgiving, good, beneficial, strengthening, substantial, invigorating
🔁 bad, unwholesome

nuts *adj*
1 MAD, crazy, insane, lunatic, unbalanced, disturbed, deranged, demented, crazed, wild, berserk, unhinged, out of your mind, *colloq.* loony, loopy, bonkers, nutty, nutty as a fruitcake, off your rocker, out to lunch, doolally, round the bend, round the twist **2** *nuts about computers* crazy, enthusiastic, fanatical, zealous, devoted, fond, keen, avid, ardent, passionate, infatuated, enamoured, smitten, mad, wild, *colloq.* daft
🔁 **1** sane **2** indifferent

nuts and bolts *n*
basics, essentials, fundamentals, details, components, bits and pieces, practicalities, *colloq.* nitty-gritty

nuzzle *v*
snuggle, cuddle, pet, nestle, fondle, nudge, burrow

nymph *n*
sprite, sylph, dryad, hamadryad, naiad, oread, undine, girl, damsel, lass, maid, maiden

oaf *n*
lout, boor, dolt, yahoo, barbarian, gawk, lubber, *colloq.* clod, hick, hobbledehoy, slob, yobbo, bumpkin

oafish *adj*
boorish, churlish, doltish, lumpish, lubberly, stolid, swinish, uncouth, unmannerly, bungling, rough, coarse, gross, ill-bred, ill-mannered, gawky, lumpen, *colloq.* clodhopping

oasis *n*
1 SPRING, watering-hole **2** REFUGE, haven, island, sanctuary, retreat, hideaway, hideout, *formal* sanctum

oath *n*
1 VOW, pledge, promise, bond, word, assurance, word of honour, *formal* affirmation, avowal, attestation **2** CURSE, swear-word, four-letter word, obscenity, bad language, blasphemy, *formal* imprecation, profanity, expletive, malediction

obdurate *adj*
obstinate, stubborn, inflexible, hard-hearted, implacable, iron, stiff-necked, stony, unfeeling, immovable, unyielding, unbending, unrelenting, persistent, dogged, headstrong, strong-minded, self-willed, steadfast, firm, determined, adamant, wilful, *formal* intractable, intransigent, *colloq.* pig-headed, bloody-minded
🔁 submissive, tender

obedience *n*
submissiveness, submission, respect, reverence, amenableness, amenability, malleability, allegiance, conformability, accordance, agreement, deference, duty, dutifulness, passivity, subservience, observance, docility, *formal* compliance, acquiescence, tractability
🔁 disobedience, rebellion

obedient *adj*
submissive, docile, yielding, conforming, pliable, malleable, amenable, dutiful, biddable, law-abiding, deferential, respectful, well-trained, disciplined, subservient, observant, *formal* compliant, acquiescent, tractable, obsequious
🔁 disobedient, rebellious, wilful

obeisance *n*
respect, reverence, submission, deference, homage, bow, curtsy, kowtow, salaam, salute, *formal* genuflection, salutation, veneration

obelisk *n*
pillar, column, monument, memorial, needle

obese *adj*
fat, overweight, tubby, stout, big, large, portly, fleshy, round, well-endowed, paunchy, ponderous, plump, podgy, chubby, roly-poly, heavy, bulky, outsize, Falstaffian, *formal* corpulent, rotund, *colloq.* gross, flabby
🔁 skinny, slender, thin

obesity *n*
fatness, overweight, stoutness, plumpness, portliness, chubbiness, podginess, tubbiness, bulk, *formal* corpulence, rotundity, *colloq.* grossness, flabbiness
🔁 thinness, slenderness, skinniness

obey *v*
1 *obey an order* follow, observe, abide by, adhere to, conform, heed, keep (to), mind, respond, submit, surrender, yield, be ruled by, bow to, take orders from, do as you are told, defer (to), respect, give way, *formal* comply, consent to, acquiesce in, *colloq.* stick to the rules, go by the book, toe the line **2** CARRY OUT, discharge, execute, act upon, fulfil, perform
🔁 **1** disobey

obfuscate *v*
obscure, cover, blur, confuse, muddle, complicate, conceal, cloud, hide, disguise, mask, overshadow, shadow, shade, cloak, veil, shroud

object¹ *n*
1 THING, article, item, entity, body, something, device, gadget, phenomenon **2** AIM, objective, purpose, goal, target, intention, point, idea, motive, end, reason, ambition, design, *formal* intent **3** TARGET, focus, recipient, butt, victim

object² *v*
object to something protest, oppose, take exception, disapprove, refuse, complain, rebut, repudiate, withstand, resist, argue, challenge, beg to differ, take issue, take a stand against, *formal* demur, expostulate, remonstrate
🔁 agree, approve, *formal* acquiesce, accede, assent

objection *n*
protest, dissent, disapproval, opposition, complaint, dissatisfaction, argument, challenge, grievance, scruple, *formal* demur, expostulation, remonstration
🔁 agreement, approval, assent

objectionable *adj*
unacceptable, unpleasant, offensive, obnoxious, disagreeable, hateful, detestable, deplorable, despicable, contemptible, intolerable, loathsome, revolting, repulsive, nauseating, sickening, *formal* repugnant, abhorrent, repellent, reprehensible
🔁 acceptable, pleasant, delightful

objective *adj, n*
▶ *adj* **1** IMPARTIAL, unbiased, detached, unprejudiced, open-minded, equitable, dispassionate, even-handed, neutral, disinterested, uninvolved, just, fair **2** *objective information* factual, real, true, actual, authentic, genuine
🔁 **1** subjective
▶ *n* object, aim, goal, end, purpose, ambition, mark, target, intention, point, idea, design, *formal* intent

objectively *adv*
impartially, equitably, dispassionately, disinterestedly, even-handedly, neutrally, justly, fairly, with an open mind

objectivity *n*
impartiality, detachment, disinterest, disinterestedness, equitableness, even-handedness, justness, justice, fairness, open-mindedness, open mind
F3 subjectivity, bias, prejudice

obligate *v*
compel, constrain, coerce, require, make, necessitate, force, impel, pressurize, pressure, press, bind

obligation *n*
duty, responsibility, onus, charge, task, function, assignment, job, commitment, liability, accountability, requirement, agreement, bond, deed, covenant, contract, debt, indebtedness, burden, trust, compulsion, demand, command, pressure, duress

obligatory *adj*
compulsory, statutory, required, binding, essential, necessary, unavoidable, enforced, *formal* mandatory, imperative, requisite
F3 optional

oblige *v*
1 COMPEL, constrain, coerce, require, make, necessitate, force, impel, pressurize, pressure, press, bind, obligate, leave/be given no option 2 HELP, assist, accommodate, do someone a favour, serve, do someone a service, put yourself out for, gratify, please

obliged *adj*
under an obligation, indebted, in debt (to), grateful, thankful, gratified, appreciative, bound, forced, compelled, constrained, duty-bound, honour-bound, required, obligated, under compulsion, *formal* beholden

obliging *adj*
accommodating, co-operative, helpful, considerate, willing, generous, pleasant, agreeable, friendly, kind, good-natured, polite, courteous, civil, indulgent, *formal* complaisant
F3 unhelpful

oblique *adj, n*
▶ *adj* 1 SLANTING, sloping, inclined, angled, tilted 2 INDIRECT, roundabout, circuitous, divergent, devious, rambling, winding, meandering, zigzag, tortuous, discursive, *formal* periphrastic, circumlocutory
▶ *n* diagonal, slant, slash, stroke, *formal* virgule

obliquely *adv*
1 DIAGONALLY, at an angle, aslant, aslope, askance, askant, slantwise 2 INDIRECTLY, in a roundabout way, circuitously, evasively, not in so many words

obliterate *v*
eradicate, destroy, eliminate, annihilate, strike out, delete, blot out, wipe out, rub out, erase, *formal* efface, expunge, extirpate

obliteration *n*
eradication, destruction, elimination, annihilation, blotting out, deletion, erasure, *formal* effacement, expunction, extirpation

oblivion *n*
1 UNCONSCIOUSNESS, blankness, darkness, stupor, void, limbo 2 OBSCURITY, nothingness, disuse, nonexistence 3 UNAWARENESS, unconsciousness, inattentiveness, unmindfulness, absent-mindedness, carelessness, blindness, deafness, ignorance
F3 3 awareness

oblivious *adj*
unaware, unconscious, inattentive, unmindful, preoccupied, absent-minded, careless, forgetful, heedless, unheeding, blind, deaf, ignorant, negligent, unconcerned, *formal* insensible
F3 aware, conscious

obloquy *n*
disgrace, dishonour, discredit, disfavour, shame, reproach, humiliation, criticism, attack, abuse, blame, censure, defamation, slander, detraction, bad press, *formal* animadversion, aspersion, calumny, contumely, ignominy, invective, odium, opprobrium, stigma, vilification

obnoxious *adj*
unpleasant, disagreeable, disgusting, offensive, objectionable, unacceptable, loathsome, nasty, horrid, horrible, odious, vile, repulsive, revolting, sickening, nauseating, hateful, detestable, contemptible, deplorable, intolerable, *formal* repugnant, abhorrent, repellent
F3 pleasant

obscene *adj*
1 INDECENT, rude, improper, immoral, immodest, shameless, unchaste, impure, coarse, vulgar, filthy, dirty, foul, gross, vile, bawdy, lewd, licentious, pornographic, scurrilous, suggestive, sexy, risqué, smutty, off-colour, disgusting, foul, *formal* carnal, lubricious, prurient, *colloq.* near the knuckle/bone, blue, raunchy, fruity, sleazy 2 SHOCKING, shameless, offensive, objectionable, outrageous, disgraceful, immoral, scandalous
F3 1 decent, wholesome

obscenity *n*
1 INDECENCY, immodesty, immorality, impurity, impropriety, unchasteness, lewdness, licentiousness, bawdiness, suggestiveness, eroticism, pornography, dirtiness, filthiness, foulness, coarseness, grossness, indelicacy, vulgarity, shamelessness, salaciousness, lasciviousness, *formal* carnality, prurience, lubricity, *colloq.* raunchiness, sleaze 2 ATROCITY, evil, outrage, offence, wickedness, vileness, *formal* heinousness 3 SWEAR-WORD, four-letter word, curse, bad language, *formal* profanity, expletive, imprecation, malediction

obscure *adj, v*
▶ *adj* 1 UNKNOWN, unimportant, insignificant, little-known, unheard-of, remote, out-of-the-way, God-forsaken, undistinguished, nameless, unsung, unrecognized, inconspicuous, humble, minor, *colloq.* off the beaten track 2 INCOMPREHENSIBLE, unclear, complex, involved, enigmatic, cryptic, opaque, mysterious, unexplained, inexplicable, unfathomable, impenetrable, deep, hidden, concealed, confusing, puzzling, perplexing, *formal* recondite, esoteric, arcane, abstruse 3 INDISTINCT, unclear, indefinite, uncertain, doubtful, shadowy, blurred, cloudy, faint, hazy, fuzzy, dim, misty, shady, vague, murky, dark, gloomy, dusky
F3 1 famous, renowned 2 intelligible, straightforward 3 clear, definite
▶ *v* conceal, cloud, hide, cover, blur, confuse, muddle, complicate, disguise, mask, overshadow, shadow, shade, cloak, veil, shroud, darken, dim, eclipse, screen, block out, *formal* obfuscate
F3 clarify, illuminate

obscurity *n*
1 UNIMPORTANCE, insignificance, lowliness, namelessness, inconspicuousness, lack of fame/recognition, inconspicuousness 2 INCOMPREHENSIBILITY, impenetrability, unclearness, complexity, intricacy, ambiguity, mystery, confusion, mysticism, *formal* abstruseness, reconditeness
F3 1 fame 2 intelligibility, clarity, lucidity

obsequious *adj*
servile, ingratiating, grovelling, fawning, menial, sycophantic, cringing, toadying, deferential, flattering, unctuous, oily, submissive, subservient, slavish, abject, *colloq.* smarmy, bootlicking, creepy

observable *adj*
noticeable, perceptible, discernible, appreciable, de-

tectable, recognizable, measurable, significant, visible, apparent, clear, obvious, evident, open, patent, perceivable

observance *n*
1 ADHERENCE, performance, execution, obedience, keeping, following, fulfilment, honouring, notice, attention, *formal* compliance, heeding, discharge **2** RITUAL, custom, ceremony, rite, practice, tradition, formality, service, celebration, festival

observant *adj*
1 ATTENTIVE, alert, vigilant, on guard, watchful, mindful, perceptive, sharp, sharp-eyed, hawk-eyed, eagle-eyed, wide-awake, on the lookout, *formal* heedful, *colloq.* with your eyes skinned/peeled, with eyes like a hawk **2** DUTIFUL, committed, devoted, obedient, practising, orthodox
☒ 1 unobservant

observation *n*
1 ATTENTION, notice, noticing, seeing, viewing, examination, inspection, scrutiny, monitoring, study, review, watching, consideration, discernment, perception **2** REMARK, comment, utterance, thought, statement, pronouncement, declaration, reflection, opinion, finding, result, description, note, information, data, *formal* annotation

observe *v*
1 WATCH, see, view, spot, study, notice, note, contemplate, inspect, examine, monitor, keep an eye on, discern, perceive, detect, catch sight of, keep watch on, keep under surveillance, *formal* behold, espy, *colloq.* keep tabs on, miss nothing, keep an eye on, keep your eyes skinned/peeled, watch like a hawk **2** REMARK, comment, say, mention, utter, state, declare **3** *observe the law* ABIDE BY, honour, keep, follow, obey, adhere to, fulfil, celebrate, mark, commemorate, remember, recognize, perform, conform to, respect, execute, *formal* comply with, discharge
☒ 1 miss **3** break, violate

observer *n*
watcher, spectator, viewer, witness, reporter, looker-on, onlooker, sightseer, eyewitness, commentator, bystander, *formal* beholder

obsess *v*
preoccupy, dominate, rule, control, monopolize, haunt, hound, torment, bedevil, grip, have a grip/hold on, plague, prey on, possess, engross, consume, be uppermost in your mind

obsessed *adj*
preoccupied, dominated, gripped, in the grip of, immersed in, haunted, hounded, plagued, infatuated, bedevilled, beset, *colloq.* hung up on
☒ detached, indifferent, unconcerned

obsession *n*
preoccupation, fixation, *idée fixe*, ruling passion, compulsion, fetish, infatuation, mania, complex, phobia, enthusiasm, fascination, *colloq.* hang-up, thing, one-track mind

obsessive *adj*
consuming, compulsive, gripping, fixed, haunting, tormenting, maddening

obsolescent *adj*
out of date, old-fashioned, outdated, dated, dying out, disappearing, declining, fading, waning, ageing, redundant, on the way out, past its prime, on the decline, on the wane, *formal* moribund

obsolete *adj*
outmoded, disused, in disuse, discarded, out of date, old-fashioned, out of fashion, *passé*, dated, outworn, old, ancient, antiquated, antique, superannuated, dead, extinct, bygone, behind the times, on the way out, past its prime, *formal* discontinued, *colloq.* past

its sell-by date, old hat, on the shelf, out of the ark, antediluvian
☒ modern, current, up-to-date, in use

obstacle *n*
barrier, bar, obstruction, blockade, barricade, impediment, hurdle, hindrance, check, snag, stumbling-block, blockage, drawback, handicap, difficulty, hitch, catch, stoppage, stop, curb, interference, interruption, deterrent, *colloq.* hiccup, no-no, fly in the ointment, spanner in the works
☒ advantage, help

obstinacy *n*
stubbornness, inflexibility, hard-heartedness, persistence, perseverance, resoluteness, tenacity, wilfulness, wrong-headedness, perversity, firmness, doggedness, relentlessness, mulishness, *formal* frowardness, intransigence, obduracy, pertinacity, *colloq.* pig-headedness
☒ co-operativeness, flexibility, submissiveness

obstinate *adj*
stubborn, inflexible, hard-hearted, immovable, unyielding, unbending, unrelenting, persistent, dogged, headstrong, strong-minded, self-willed, steadfast, firm, persevering, determined, adamant, wilful, *formal* intractable, intransigent, refractory, recalcitrant, *colloq.* pig-headed, bloody-minded, obstinate as a mule
☒ flexible, tractable

obstreperous *adj*
disorderly, unruly, tumultuous, unmanageable, undisciplined, wild, uncontrolled, out of hand, noisy, loud, boisterous, clamorous, raucous, riotous, rip-roaring, tempestuous, rowdy, rough, turbulent, uproarious, vociferous, *formal* refractory, restive, intractable, *colloq.* stroppy, bolshie, bloody-minded
☒ calm, disciplined, quiet

obstruct *v*
block, impede, hinder, prevent, check, frustrate, hamper, clog, choke, bar, barricade, stop, halt, bridle, stall, restrict, limit, thwart, encumber, hamstring, inhibit, hold up, brake, curb, arrest, slow down, delay, interrupt, interfere with, shut off, cut off, obscure, *formal* retard, arrest
☒ assist, further

obstruction *n*
barrier, blockage, bar, barricade, hindrance, impediment, obstacle, stumbling-block, check, stop, stoppage, restriction, embargo, sanction, difficulty, deterrent
☒ help

obstructive *adj*
hindering, delaying, blocking, stalling, unhelpful, unco-operative, awkward, difficult, restrictive, inhibiting, interrupting
☒ co-operative, helpful

obtain *v*
1 ACQUIRE, get, gain, gain possession of, come by, attain, secure, seize, earn, achieve, *formal* procure, *colloq.* get your hands on **2** PREVAIL, exist, hold, be in force, be the case, be effective, be in use, hold sway, stand, reign, rule, be prevalent

obtainable *adj*
available, at hand, ready, to be had, accessible, achievable, attainable, realizable, on call, *formal* procurable, *colloq.* on tap
☒ unobtainable, unavailable

obtrusive *adj*
1 PROMINENT, protruding, projecting, noticeable, obvious, conspicuous, blatant, flagrant, bold, forward **2** INTRUSIVE, interfering, forward, prying, meddling, *colloq.* nosy, pushy
☒ 1 unobtrusive

obtuse *adj*
slow, slow-witted, stupid, unintelligent, dull, dense, crass, stolid, dull-witted, thick-skinned, *colloq.* thick, dumb, dim, dim-witted
🄵 bright, sharp

obviate *v*
avert, prevent, divert, forestall, remove, counter, counteract, anticipate, *formal* preclude

obvious *adj*
evident, self-evident, manifest, patent, clear, crystal-clear, plain, visible, distinct, transparent, undeniable, unmistakable, conspicuous, glaring, apparent, open, unconcealed, visible, noticeable, detectable, perceptible, pronounced, recognizable, self-explanatory, straightforward, clear-cut, prominent, *colloq.* as plain as a pikestaff, as clear as daylight, staring you in the face, sticking out a mile, right under your nose, shouting from the rooftops
🄵 unclear, indistinct, obscure

obviously *adv*
plainly, clearly, evidently, noticeably, patently, undeniably, unmistakably, without doubt, undoubtedly, certainly, distinctly, of course, *formal* manifestly

occasion *n, v*
▶ **1** EVENT, occurrence, incident, episode, experience, situation, circumstance, happening, affair, time, instance, point, chance, case, opportunity, juncture **2** REASON, cause, excuse, justification, call, ground(s) **3** CELEBRATION, function, affair, party, *colloq.* do, get-together
▶ *v* cause, bring about, bring on, make, produce, create, give rise to, generate, induce, lead to, provoke, prompt, evoke, elicit, influence, inspire, persuade, originate, engender, *formal* effect

occasional *adj*
periodic, intermittent, irregular, sporadic, infrequent, uncommon, incidental, odd, rare, casual
🄵 frequent, regular, constant

occasionally *adv*
sometimes, on occasion, from time to time, at times, at intervals, now and then, now and again, irregularly, periodically, every so often, once in a while, off and on, on and off, infrequently, intermittently, sporadically
🄵 frequently, often, always

occult *adj, n*
▶ *adj* mystical, supernatural, magical, magic, mysterious, concealed, obscure, secret, hidden, veiled, *formal* esoteric, arcane, recondite, abstruse, transcendental, preternatural
▶ *n* the supernatural, black arts, mysticism, supernaturalism

Terms associated with the occult include :

amulet, astral projection, astrologer, astrology, bewitch, black cat, black magic, black mass, cabbala, charm, chiromancer, chiromancy, clairvoyance, clairvoyant, conjure, coven, crystal ball, curse, déjà vu, divination, diviner, divining-rod, dream, ectoplasm, evil eye, evil spirit, exorcism, exorcist, extrasensory perception (ESP), familiar, fetish, fortune-teller, garlic, Hallowe'en, hallucination, hoodoo, horoscope, horseshoe, hydromancer, hydromancy, illusion, incantation, jinx, juju, magic, magician, mascot, medium, necromancer, necromancy, obi, omen, oneiromancer, oneiromancy, Ouija board®, palmist, palmistry, paranormal, pentagram, planchette, poltergeist, possession, prediction, premonition, psychic, rabbit's foot, relic, rune, satanic, Satanism, Satanist, séance, second sight, shaman, shamrock, sixth sense, sorcerer, sorcery, spell, spirit, spiritualism, spiritualist, supernatural, superstition, talisman, tarot card, tarot reading, telepathist, telepathy, totem, trance, vision, voodoo, Walpurgis Night, warlock, white magic, witch, witchcraft, witch doctor, witch's broomstick, witch's sabbath.

occupancy *n*
tenancy, residence, tenure, term, occupation, owner-occupancy, ownership, possession, holding, use, *formal* domiciliation, habitation, inhabitancy

occupant *n*
occupier, owner-occupier, holder, inhabitant, resident, householder, tenant, user, renter, leaseholder, lessee, squatter, inmate, incumbent

occupation *n*
1 JOB, profession, work, career, vocation, employment, employ, trade, post, calling, business, field, line, province, pursuit, craft, walk of life, activity, métier **2** INVASION, seizure, conquest, control, possession, capture, overthrow, foreign rule, foreign domination, takeover, *formal* subjugation **3** OCCUPANCY, possession, holding, tenancy, tenure, residence, use, *formal* habitation

occupational *adj*
job-related, professional, vocational, career, work, employment, trade, business

occupied *adj*
1 UNAVAILABLE, in use, taken, busy, full, tenanted **2** ABSORBED, engrossed, taken up, employed, engaged, preoccupied, immersed, busy, working, tied up, *colloq.* hard at it
🄵 **1** unoccupied, vacant

occupy *v*
1 INHABIT, live in, possess, reside in, stay in, make your home in, settle, people, tenant, take possession of, own, *formal* dwell in **2** ABSORB, take up, engross, employ, engage, hold, involve, preoccupy, immerse, amuse, entertain, busy, interest, divert **3** INVADE, seize, capture, overrun, take over, take possession of **4** FILL, take up, use (up), hold, have

occur *v*
1 HAPPEN, come about, take place, chance, come to pass, turn out, materialize, develop, crop up, turn up, result, *formal* transpire, befall, eventuate **2** EXIST, be present, be found, have its being, arise, appear, *formal* obtain, manifest itself **3** *the idea occurred to me* come to you, dawn on, strike, hit, suggest itself, come to mind, cross your mind, enter your head, present itself, spring to mind, sink in

occurrence *n*
1 INCIDENT, event, happening, affair, proceedings, circumstance, episode, instance, case, development, action **2** INCIDENCE, existence, appearance, arising, springing-up, development, *formal* manifestation

ocean *n*
main, profound, sea, the deep, *colloq.* briny, the drink

The world's oceans and largest seas include:
Pacific Ocean, Atlantic Ocean, Indian Ocean, Arctic Ocean, Antarctic (Southern) Ocean, South China Sea, Caribbean Sea, Mediterranean Sea, Bering Sea, Gulf of Mexico, Sea of Okhotsk.

odd *adj*
1 UNUSUAL, strange, uncommon, peculiar, funny, ab-

normal, exceptional, curious, atypical, abnormal, different, queer, bizarre, eccentric, deviant, singular, idiosyncratic, remarkable, unconventional, uncanny, weird, irregular, wild, extraordinary, outlandish, rare, *colloq.* out of the ordinary, freaky, kinky, wacky, oddball, rum, zany, barmy, crackers, off the wall, *slang* far-out, way-out **2** OCCASIONAL, incidental, haphazard, irregular, periodic, seasonal, random, casual, part-time, temporary, *formal* fortuitous **3** UNMATCHED, unpaired, single, spare, surplus, superfluous, left-over, remaining, sundry, various, miscellaneous
Fa 1 normal, usual **2** regular
▷ **odd one out** nonconformist, eccentric, odd man out, odd woman out, *colloq.* freak, oddball, weirdo, odd bod, fish out of water, square peg in a round hole

oddity *n*
1 ABNORMALITY, strangeness, peculiarity, queerness, rarity, eccentricity, idiosyncrasy, phenomenon, twist, quirk **2** CURIOSITY, anomaly, rarity, phenomenon, character, misfit, *colloq.* freak

oddment *n*
bit, scrap, piece, leftover, fragment, offcut, end, remnant, shred, snippet, patch

odds *n*
1 LIKELIHOOD, probability, chances **2** ADVANTAGE, edge, lead, superiority, supremacy, *formal* ascendancy
▷ **at odds** disagreeing, in disagreement, in conflict, differing, clashing, quarrelling, arguing, at loggerheads
▷ **odds and ends** litter, bits and pieces, bits, oddments, junk, remnants, rubbish, scraps, cuttings, snippets, tat, debris, flotsam and jetsam, leavings, *colloq.* odds and sods, this and that

odious *adj*
offensive, loathsome, unpleasant, disagreeable, obnoxious, disgusting, hateful, objectionable, repulsive, revolting, foul, detestable, horrible, horrid, vile, contemptible, despicable, *formal* repugnant, execrable, abhorrent, abominable, heinous
Fa pleasant

odium *n*
dislike, hatred, disapproval, disrepute, dishonour, shame, disgrace, disfavour, discredit, censure, condemnation, contempt, *formal* abhorrence, detestation, disapprobation, animosity, antipathy, obloquy, opprobrium, infamy, reprobation, execration

odorous *adj*
scented, sweet-smelling, balmy, aromatic, fragrant, perfumed, pungent, *formal* odoriferous, redolent
Fa odourless

odour *n*
smell, scent, aroma, fragrance, bouquet, perfume, stench, *formal* redolence, *colloq.* stink, pong, niff, whiff

odyssey *n*
journey, voyage, trek, travels, wandering, adventure, *formal* peregrination

off *adj, adv*
▶ *adj* **1** ROTTEN, bad, sour, turned, high, spoilt, rancid, mouldy, decomposed **2** CANCELLED, postponed, called off, abandoned, dropped, *colloq.* shelved, scrapped **3** AWAY, absent, gone, unavailable, unobtainable **4** SUBSTANDARD, below par, disappointing, unsatisfactory, slack, wrong, incorrect
▶ *adv* **1** AWAY, elsewhere, out, at a distance, apart, aside **2** ILL, out of sorts, unwell, sick, off form, poorly, *formal* indisposed, *colloq.* under the weather

offbeat *adj*
unorthodox, weird, unconventional, untraditional,

abnormal, strange, unusual, bizarre, out of the ordinary, *colloq.* oddball, freaky, kooky, wacky, *slang* far-out, way-out

off-colour *adj*
1 ILL, out of sorts, unwell, sick, off form, poorly, *formal* indisposed, *colloq.* under the weather, run down **2** RUDE, indecent, improper, immoral, coarse, vulgar, impure, filthy, dirty, pornographic, suggestive, sexy, risqué, smutty

off-duty *adj*
off, off work, not at work, on holiday, free, at leisure
Fa on duty

offence *n*
1 *a criminal offence* infringement, crime, trespass, wrong, wrongdoing, illegal act, breach of the law, sin, *formal* misdemeanour, transgression, violation, misdeed, infraction **2** AFFRONT, insult, injury, hurt, outrage, snub, slight, indignity, atrocity, ire **3** RESENTMENT, indignation, anger, annoyance, exasperation, disapproval, pique, umbrage, outrage, hurt, hard feelings, *formal* antipathy
▷ **take offence** resent, be indignant, be angry, be annoyed, be exasperated, be hurt, be offended, be insulted, be upset, be/feel put out, take exception, take personally, take umbrage, *colloq.* be miffed, get huffy, get one's nose out of joint

offend *v*
1 HURT, insult, injure, affront, wrong, wound, displease, snub, upset, annoy, anger, outrage, exasperate, incense, provoke, *colloq.* miff, needle, put someone's back up, rub someone up the wrong way, put someone's nose out of joint, raise someone's hackles **2** DISGUST, repel, sicken, revolt, nauseate, put off **3** BREAK THE LAW, do wrong, sin, err, go astray, *formal* transgress, violate
Fa 1 please

offended *adj*
upset, hurt, resentful, disgruntled, affronted, displeased, angered, annoyed, exasperated, incensed, outraged, wounded, smarting, stung, piqued, pained, disgusted, *colloq.* huffy, in a huff, miffed, put out, touchy
Fa pleased, happy

offender *n*
wrongdoer, culprit, criminal, miscreant, guilty party, law-breaker, delinquent, *formal* malefactor, transgressor

offensive *adj, n*
▶ *adj* **1** DISAGREEABLE, unpleasant, objectionable, displeasing, disgusting, odious, obnoxious, revolting, loathsome, vile, sickening, nauseating, nasty, foul, detestable, abominable, *formal* repellent, repugnant, abhorrent **2** INSOLENT, abusive, rude, insulting, affronting, upsetting, hurtful, wounding, annoying, exasperating, impolite, disrespectful, discourteous, impertinent
Fa 1 pleasant **2** polite
▶ *n* attack, assault, onslaught, invasion, raid, drive, thrust, push, sortie, charge, *formal* incursion

offer *v, n*
▶ *v* **1** PRESENT, make available, advance, extend, put forward, submit, suggest, propose, recommend, hold out, *formal* propound, proffer **2** PROVIDE, give, supply, sell, put on the market, *formal* afford **3** *offer £100* propose, bid, put in a bid, tender **4** VOLUNTEER, come forward, make yourself available, be at someone's service, *colloq.* show willing **5** *offer prayers/a sacrifice* offer up, sacrifice, dedicate, present, worship, give, consecrate, celebrate **6** *offer resistance* show, express, give, present, try, attempt
▶ *n* proposal, bid, submission, tender, suggestion,

proposition, overture, approach, attempt, presentation

offering *n*
1 GIFT, present, donation, handout, contribution, subscription **2** SACRIFICE, dedication, consecration, tithe, celebration, *formal* oblation

offhand *adj, adv*
▶ *adj* casual, unconcerned, uninterested, indifferent, unceremonious, discourteous, rude, brusque, abrupt, curt, terse, perfunctory, cursory, informal, cavalier, careless, blasé, *colloq.* take-it-or-leave-it, happy-go-lucky, free-and-easy, laid-back, couldn't-care-less
▶ *adv* impromptu, immediately, ad lib, without thinking about it, without checking, *formal* extempore, *colloq.* off the cuff, off the top of one's head
F̄ calculated, planned

office *n*
1 RESPONSIBILITY, duty, obligation, charge, commission, occupation, tenure, situation, post, position, employment, function, work, appointment, business, role, place, service **2** WORKPLACE, workroom, place of business, base, bureau **3** *through the offices of someone* support, advocacy, help, aid, favour, recommendation, word, back-up, backing, patronage, mediation, intervention, referral, *formal* auspices, aegis, intercession

officer *n*
official, office-holder, office-bearer, public servant, functionary, dignitary, bureaucrat, committee member, administrator, representative, executive, board member, agent, appointee, envoy, messenger, deputy

official *adj, n*
▶ *adj* **1** AUTHORIZED, authoritative, legal, lawful, legitimate, formal, accepted, recognized, licensed, certified, validated, endorsed, sanctioned, approved, authenticated, authentic, bona fide, proper, *formal* accredited, *colloq.* kosher **2** *official activities* formal, ceremonial, stately, dignified, solemn, ritual
F̄ **1** unofficial
▶ *n* office-bearer, office-holder, officer, functionary

official or officious ?

Official means 'done by someone in authority; relating to authority': *We think she has won, but we're still waiting for the official result of the race. Officious* means 'too eager to meddle, offering unwanted advice or assistance' or, more often, 'holding too rigidly to rules and regulations': *An officious little man told us that we would have to move our bicycles.*

officiate *v*
preside, superintend, conduct, chair, take the chair, manage, oversee, run, be in charge, take charge

officious *adj*
obtrusive, domineering, dictatorial, intrusive, interfering, prying, meddlesome, meddling, inquisitive, over-zealous, self-important, forward, opinionated, bustling, *formal* importunate, *colloq.* bossy, pushy

officious or official ? *See panel at* OFFICIAL.

offing *n*
▷ **in the offing** imminent, near, coming/happening soon, coming up, (close) at hand, just round the corner, in sight, on the way, on the horizon, *colloq.* on the cards
F̄ far off

offish *adj*
standoffish, aloof, cool, haughty, unsociable, *colloq.* stuck-up
F̄ friendly, sociable

off-key *adj*
out of tune, discordant, unsuitable, inappropriate, out of keeping, inharmonious, jarring, *formal* dissonant
F̄ in tune

offload *v*
unburden, unload, jettison, drop, deposit, get rid of, shift, discharge, *formal* disburden, *colloq.* dump, chuck

off-putting *adj*
intimidating, daunting, frightening, disconcerting, discouraging, disheartening, dispiriting, formidable, unnerving, unsettling, demoralizing, disturbing, upsetting, *formal* discomfiting

offset *v*
counterbalance, compensate for, cancel out, counteract, make up for, balance (out), neutralize, *formal* counterpoise, countervail

offshoot *n*
1 BRANCH, outgrowth, limb, arm **2** SPIN-OFF, by-product, product, result, consequence, outcome, development, branch, appendage

offspring *n*
child, children, young, young one(s), family, brood, heirs, successors, descendants, *formal* issue, progeny, fruit of your loins, *colloq.* kid(s), nipper(s)
F̄ parent(s)

often *adv*
frequently, repeatedly, regularly, generally, again and again, over and over again, time after time, time and (time) again, day in day out, week in week out, month in month out, many times, many a time, much
F̄ rarely, seldom, never

ogle *v*
eye, eye up, leer, make eyes at, look, stare

ogre *n*
1 GIANT, monster, devil, demon, troll, fiend, bogey, bogeyman **2** *his father is a bit of an ogre* monster, beast, brute, villain, savage, barbarian, fiend

oil *v, n*
▶ *v* lubricate, grease, make smooth, anoint
▶ *n* lubricant, grease, ointment, lotion, liniment, cream, balm, salve, *formal* unguent

oil rig *n*

Parts of an offshore oil rig include:
drilling platform, production platform, jack-up rig, semi-submersible; accommodation module, control room, derrick, drill, rotary drill, emergency flare stack, helicopter deck, hoisting equipment, lifeboats, main deck, materials store, pedestal crane, pig trap, pipe, drilling pipes, pipe rack, power station, production oil and gas separator, test oil and gas separator, pumping station, seawater desalination plant, substructure, valve, whipstock, workshop.

oily *adj*
1 GREASY, fatty, buttery, *formal* oleaginous **2** UNCTUOUS, smooth, smooth-talking, obsequious, ingratiating, glib, suave, urbane, flattering, servile, subservient, *colloq.* smarmy

ointment *n*
salve, balm, cream, gel, lotion, liniment, *technical* emollient, *formal* embrocation

OK *adj, n, v, interj*
▶ *adj* acceptable, all right, fine, permitted, in order, fair, satisfactory, reasonable, tolerable, passable, good, adequate, convenient, correct, accurate, *colloq.* not bad, so-so, up to par, up to scratch
▶ *n* authorization, approval, endorsement, permis-

sion, agreement, sanction, *formal* consent, approbation, *colloq.* go-ahead, green light, thumbs-up
▶ *v* approve, authorize, pass, rubber-stamp, agree to, say yes to, *formal* consent to, *colloq.* give the go-ahead to, give the green light to, give the thumbs-up to
▶ *interj* all right, fine, very well, very good, agreed, right, yes

old *adj*
1 AGED, ageing, elderly, advanced in years, mature, sensible, wise, past your prime, grey, senile, *formal* senescent, *colloq.* getting on, past it, no spring chicken, not as young as you were, not getting any younger, over the hill, (a bit) long in the tooth, not long for this world, gaga **2** ANCIENT, age-old, bygone, antique, classic, vintage, veteran, original, primitive, early, earlier, earliest, antiquated, primeval, prehistoric, primordial, primal, *formal* pristine **3** LONG-STANDING, long-established, long-lived, enduring, lasting, time-honoured, traditional, age-old, *colloq.* old as the hills **4** OBSOLETE, old-fashioned, unfashionable, out of date, behind the times, outdated, *passé*, archaic, *colloq.* on the way out, past it, past its sell-by date, Dickensian, out of the ark, antediluvian **5** WORN OUT, cast-off, torn, shabby, decayed, decaying, decrepit, broken down, crumbling, ramshackle, tumbledown, *colloq.* having seen better days **6** FORMER, previous, earlier, one-time, sometime, ex-, *formal* erstwhile, quondam
F₃ 1 young **2** new **4** modern, contemporary, state-of-the-art, up-to-date, fashionable, new **5** new **6** current
▷ **old age** age, agedness, oldness, elderliness, advancing years, declining years, second childhood, senility, dotage, twilight of your life, *formal* senescence
F₃ youth

old-fashioned *adj*
outmoded, out of date, outdated, dated, old, unfashionable, out of fashion, obsolete, past, bygone, ancient, old-time, dead, moth-eaten, written off, behind the times, antiquated, archaic, *passé*, obsolescent, *colloq.* antediluvian, out of the ark, fuddy-duddy, old hat, past it, square, past its sell-by date, on the way out
F₃ modern, up-to-date

old-time *adj*
old fashioned, outmoded, out of date, outdated, dated, old, unfashionable, out of fashion, obsolete, past, bygone, behind the times, antiquated, archaic, *passé*

old-world *adj*
old-fashioned, quaint, traditional, picturesque, antiquated, past, archaic, bygone

omen *n*
sign, warning, token, premonition, foreboding, indication, forecast, prediction, harbinger, *formal* portent, augury, auspice, presentiment, prodrome, prodromus

ominous *adj*
menacing, foreboding, sinister, fateful, unpromising, unlucky, unfavourable, threatening, sinister, *formal* portentous, inauspicious, unpropitious, minatory
F₃ favourable, *formal* auspicious

omission *n*
exclusion, gap, exception, leaving-out, erasure, oversight, failure, lack, neglect, negligence, disregard, default, avoidance, *formal* lacuna, expunction, dereliction
F₃ inclusion

omit *v*
leave out, exclude, miss (out), pass over, except, overlook, drop, skip, eliminate, forget, neglect, leave un-

done, fail, fail to mention, disregard, edit out, erase, delete, cross out, rub out, *formal* expunge
F₃ include, mention

omnibus *adj, n*
▶ *adj* comprehensive, inclusive, wide-ranging, all-embracing, compendious, encyclopedic
F₃ selective
▶ *n* anthology, collection, compilation, compendium, encyclopedia

omnipotence *n*
absolute/total power, complete authority, all-powerfulness, almightiness, divine right, invincibility, mastery, sovereignty, supremacy, *formal* plenipotence
F₃ impotence

omnipotent *adj*
all-powerful, almighty, invincible, supreme, *formal* plenipotent
F₃ impotent

omnipresent *adj*
universal, all-present, present everywhere, pervasive, all-pervasive, limitless, infinite, ubiquitous, *formal* ubiquity

omniscient *adj*
all-knowing, all-seeing, all-wise, *formal* pansophic

omnivorous *adj*
all-devouring, eating anything, gluttonous, indiscriminate, undiscriminating

on *adv*
▷ **on and off** now and then, occasionally, on occasion, off and on, periodically, sometimes, from time to time, now and again, every so often, irregularly, at intervals, intermittently, spasmodically, sporadically, fitfully, *formal* discontinuously

once¹ *adv*
formerly, previously, in the past, at one time, on one occasion, at one point, one time, long ago, in times past, in times gone by, once upon a time, in the old days
▷ **at once 1** IMMEDIATELY, instantly, directly, right away, straight away, without delay, now, right now, promptly, *formal* forthwith, *colloq.* pronto, before you know it, before you can say Jack Robinson, in two shakes of a lamb's tail, like a shot, yesterday **2** SIMULTANEOUSLY, together, at the same time, at the same moment
▷ **once and for all** permanently, decisively, definitively, conclusively, positively, finally, for good, for the last time
▷ **once in a while** now and again, now and then, at times, sometimes, from time to time, occasionally, on and off, on occasion, periodically, infrequently, intermittently, sporadically

once² *conj*
after, immediately after, as soon as, when

oncoming *adj*
approaching, advancing, upcoming, looming, nearing, onrushing, gathering

one *adj*
1 SINGLE, solitary, lone, individual, only, sole, ace **2** UNITED, joined, fused, bound, married, wedded, harmonious, like-minded, whole, entire, complete, equal, identical, alike

oneness *n*
singleness, unity, completeness, wholeness, identity, individuality, identicalness, sameness, consistency

onerous *adj*
oppressive, burdensome, demanding, tiring, wearying, laborious, arduous, strenuous, back-breaking, crushing, hard, taxing, difficult, troublesome, exact-

ing, fatiguing, exhausting, heavy, weighty, *formal* exigent

oneself *pron*
▷ **by oneself 1** ALONE, by yourself, on your own, lonely, lonesome, deserted, isolated, abandoned, forsaken, forlorn, desolate, unaccompanied, unescorted, unattended, solo **2** ON YOUR OWN, independently, unaided, unassisted, without help, without assistance, singly, single-handed, unaccompanied

one-sided *adj*
1 UNBALANCED, unequal, uneven, lopsided **2** UNFAIR, unjust, prejudiced, biased, bigoted, partial, partisan, narrow-minded, discriminatory, inequitable **3** UNILATERAL, independent, one-way, separate, separated, disconnected
🖅 **1** balanced **2** impartial **3** bilateral, multilateral

one-time *adj*
former, previous, ex-, late, sometime, *formal* erstwhile, quondam

ongoing *adj*
1 CONTINUING, continuous, unending, unbroken, uninterrupted, non-stop, constant, incessant **2** DEVELOPING, evolving, progressing, advancing, growing, in progress, current, unfinished, unfolding

onlooker *n*
bystander, observer, spectator, looker-on, eyewitness, witness, sightseer, watcher, viewer, *colloq.* rubberneck, gawper

only *adv, adj*
▶ *adv* just, at most, merely, simply, purely, barely, not more than, no more than, nothing but, exclusively, solely
▶ *adj* sole, single, one and only, solitary, lone, unique, exclusive, individual

onrush *n*
surge, rush, push, stream, flood, flow, charge, cascade, career, onset, onslaught, stampede

onset *n*
1 BEGINNING, start, outset, outbreak, *formal* commencement, inception, *colloq.* kick-off **2** ASSAULT, attack, onslaught, onrush, charge
🖅 **1** end, finish

onslaught *n*
attack, assault, offensive, charge, onrush, storming, raid, drive, push, thrust, foray, bombardment, blitz

onus *n*
burden, responsibility, weight, load, obligation, duty, charge, encumbrance, liability, task, *colloq.* millstone, albatross

onwards *adv*
forward(s), on, ahead, in front, beyond, *formal* forth
🖅 backward(s)

oodles *n*
lots, masses, abundance, *colloq.* bags, heaps, lashings, loads, tons
🖅 scarcity

oomph *n*
vitality, sparkle, vigour, energy, vivacity, enthusiasm, exuberance, animation, *colloq.* bounce, get-up-and-go, pep, pizzazz, zing, sexiness

ooze *v, n*
▶ *v* seep, exude, leak, percolate, escape, dribble, drip, trickle, drop, discharge, bleed, secrete, emit, flow, overflow with, pour forth, filter, drain, *formal* filtrate, excrete
▶ *n* sludge, silt, slime, muck, mire, mud, sediment, deposit, *formal* alluvium

oozy *adj*
sludgy, muddy, slimy, mucky, miry, dripping, dewy, moist, weeping, sweaty, sloppy, *formal* uliginous

opacity *n*
1 CLOUDINESS, opaqueness, dullness, unclearness, impermeability, milkiness, murkiness, filminess, density **2** OBSCURITY, impenetrability, incomprehensibility, unintelligibility, *formal* obfuscation
🖅 **1** transparency **2** clarity

opalescent *adj*
shimmering, sparkling, multicoloured, rainbow, rainbow-coloured, rainbow-like, prismatic, dazzling, glittering, shot, pearly, polychromatic, *formal* iridescent, variegated

opaque *adj*
1 CLOUDY, clouded, murky, unclear, dull, dim, hazy, misty, muddied, muddy, dingy, blurred, dense, thick, turbid **2** OBSCURE, unclear, impenetrable, unfathomable, incomprehensible, unintelligible, enigmatic, cryptic, difficult, confusing, baffling, puzzling, *formal* abstruse, recondite, esoteric, *colloq.* as clear as mud
🖅 **1** transparent **2** clear, obvious

open *adj, v*
▶ *adj* **1** UNCLOSED, ajar, gaping, wide open, uncovered, unfastened, unbolted, unlocked, unsealed, unbarred, unlatched, yawning, lidless, topless, coverless **2** UNRESTRICTED, free, unobstructed, unblocked, passable, navigable, unenclosed, unfenced, clear, accessible, exposed, unprotected, unsheltered, vacant, wide, obtainable, available, unoccupied **3** OVERT, obvious, plain, clear, visible, patent, evident, noticeable, apparent, flagrant, blatant, conspicuous, unhidden, unconcealed, undisguised, *formal* manifest **4** UNDECIDED, unresolved, unsettled, debatable, arguable, problematic, moot **5** FRANK, candid, honest, guileless, natural, simple, ingenuous, unreserved, forthright, blunt, direct **6** LOOSELY WOVEN, airy, holey, openwork, porous, honeycombed, cellular, spongelike **7** *an open secret* widely known, well known, public, general, accessible, unrestricted **8** *open to misinterpretation* liable, vulnerable, susceptible, receptive, exposed, disposed, accessible
🖅 **1** shut, closed **2** restricted **3** hidden, concealed **4** decided, resolved **5** reserved **6** close **7** private, closed
▶ *v* **1** UNFASTEN, undo, unlock, unlatch, uncover, unseal, untie, unbolt, unblock, uncork, crack, broach, break open, burst open, slide open, push open, force open, prise open, clear, expose **2** EXPLAIN, divulge, expose, disclose, bare, lay bare, pour out **3** EXTEND, spread (out), unroll, unfold, unfurl, flower, come apart, separate, split **4** BEGIN, start, commence, inaugurate, initiate, set in motion, launch, *colloq.* set the ball rolling, kick off, get cracking, take the plunge
🖅 **1** close, shut **2** hide **4** end, finish
▷ **open onto** give onto, overlook, lead to, command a view of, face

open-air *adj*
outdoor, out-of-doors, outside, afield, alfresco
🖅 indoor

open-and-shut *adj*
straightforward, obvious, simple, clear, easily decided, easily solved

open-handed *adj*
generous, free, liberal, large-hearted, lavish, bountiful, unstinting, *formal* bounteous, eleemosynary, munificent
🖅 tight-fisted

opening *n, adj*
▶ *n* **1** APERTURE, breach, gap, space, break, chink, crack, fissure, cleft, crevice, chasm, hole, cave, slot, split, inlet, outlet, vent, rupture, *formal* orifice, interstice **2** START, onset, beginning, outset, inauguration, birth, dawn, launch, *formal* inception, *colloq.* the word

go, square one, kick-off, first base **3** OPPORTUNITY, chance, occasion, place, vacancy, job, position, *colloq.* break

F2 2 close, end

▶ *adj* first, beginning, starting, introductory, initial, early, primary, *formal* commencing, inaugural

F2 closing

openly *adv*
overtly, frankly, candidly, directly, forthrightly, bluntly, honestly, blatantly, flagrantly, plainly, unashamedly, brazenly, unreservedly, glaringly, in public, in full view, immodestly, shamelessly, *colloq.* with no holds barred

F2 secretly, slyly

open-minded *adj*
unprejudiced, unbiased, broad-minded, broad, impartial, tolerant, liberal, receptive, reasonable, objective, free, catholic, dispassionate, enlightened, *formal* latitudinarian

F2 bigoted, intolerant, prejudiced, narrow-minded

open-mouthed *adj*
amazed, astounded, spellbound, dumbfounded, shocked, clamorous, thunderstruck, expectant, *colloq.* flabbergasted

operate *v*
1 *it operates on batteries* function, act, perform, run, work, go **2** *she can operate that machine* control, handle, manage, work, run, be in charge of, use, utilize, employ, manoeuvre

operation *n*
1 FUNCTIONING, action, running, motion, movement, performance, working **2** INFLUENCE, manipulation, handling, control, working, running, management, use, using, utilization **3** UNDERTAKING, enterprise, affair, procedure, proceeding, process, exercise, activity, business, deal, job, task, transaction, effort **4** CAMPAIGN, action, task, manoeuvre, exercise, attack, assault, charge, raid

▷ **in operation** operational, in force, functioning, active, effective, efficient, in action, working, workable, viable, serviceable, functional, valid

operational *adj*
working, in working order, in use, usable, functioning, functional, in action, going, viable, workable, ready, prepared, in service

F2 out of order

operative *adj, n*
▶ *adj* **1** OPERATIONAL, in operation, in force, functioning, active, effective, efficient, in action, working, workable, viable, serviceable, functional, valid **2** KEY, crucial, important, relevant, significant, vital

F2 1 inoperative, out of service

▶ *n* **1** WORKER, workman, employee, labourer, hand, mechanic, machinist, operator, artisan **2** DETECTIVE, private detective, (private) investigator, *colloq.* vate eye, sleuth, gumshoe, shamus, dick **3** SECRET AGENT, agent, spy, double agent, *colloq.* mole

operator *n*
1 OPERATIVE, worker, mechanic, machinist, technician, mover, driver, practitioner **2** TRADER, contractor, dealer, manager, director, administrator, handler **3** MANIPULATOR, machinator, punter, manoeuvrer, shyster, speculator, *colloq.* wheeler-dealer

opiate *n*
drug, narcotic, sedative, pacifier, anodyne, tranquillizer, soporific, stupefacient, depressant, bromide, *formal* nepenthe, *colloq.* downer

opine *v*
think, believe, suppose, suggest, guess, say, volunteer, presume, declare, judge, conceive, conclude, suspect, venture, *formal* conjecture, surmise

opinion *n*
belief, judgement, view, point of view, viewpoint, thought, idea, perception, stance, standpoint, theory, impression, feeling(s), sentiment, assumption, assessment, conception, mind, notion, way of thinking, thought(s), school of thought, conviction, persuasion, attitude, *formal* estimation

opinionated *adj*
dogmatic, doctrinaire, dictatorial, arrogant, inflexible, obstinate, stubborn, pigheaded, uncompromising, with preconceived ideas, single-minded, adamant, prejudiced, biased, bigoted, self-important, pompous, cocksure, pontifical

F2 open-minded

opponent *n*
adversary, enemy, antagonist, foe, competitor, contestant, challenger, opposer, opposition, rival, contender, objector, dissident, *formal* dissentient

F2 ally, friend, supporter

opportune *adj*
suitable, proper, convenient, appropriate, advantageous, apt, fit, seasonable, timely, well-timed, favourable, providential, fitting, fortunate, good, lucky, happy, *formal* auspicious, felicitous, pertinent, propitious

F2 unsuitable, *formal* inopportune

opportunism *n*
exploitation, expediency, pragmatism, realism, taking advantage, unscrupulousness, Machiavellianism, *colloq.* making hay while the sun shines

opportunity *n*
chance, opening, occasion, possibility, hour, moment, *colloq.* break, look-in

oppose *v*
1 RESIST, withstand, counter, attack, combat, contest, challenge, contradict, disapprove of, argue against, disagree with, stand up to, take a stand against, be against, take issue with, confront, defy, face, fight, hinder, obstruct, bar, check, prevent, thwart, *colloq.* fly in the face of **2** COMPARE, contrast, match, offset, balance, counterbalance, set against, play off, *formal* juxtapose

F2 1 defend, support

opposed *adj*
in opposition, against, hostile, conflicting, disagreeing, opposing, opposite, antagonistic, clashing, contrary, incompatible, *formal* averse, inimical, *colloq.* anti

F2 in favour

opposing *adj*
opposite, contrary, differing, at odds, at variance, rival, clashing, conflicting, irreconcilable, incompatible, opposed, contentious, enemy, hostile, antagonistic, fighting, contending, warring, combatant, *formal* antipathetic, disputatious, oppugnant

opposite *adj, n*
▶ *adj* **1** FACING, face to face, fronting, corresponding **2** OPPOSED, antagonistic, conflicting, contrary, hostile, contradictory, clashing, irreconcilable, unlike, reverse, inconsistent, different, contrasted, differing, at odds, at variance, *formal* adverse, antithetical, dissident, *colloq.* poles apart

F2 2 same

▶ *n* reverse, converse, contrary, contradiction, inverse, *formal* antithesis, *colloq.* flip side, the other side of the coin, the other side of the fence

F2 same

opposition *n*
1 ANTAGONISM, hostility, resistance, confrontation, obstructiveness, unfriendliness, dislike, disapproval **2** OPPONENT, adversary, enemy, antagonist,

rival, foe, opposing side, other side, competition
⊟ 1 co-operation, support **2** ally, supporter

oppress *v*
1 OVERWHELM, subjugate, suppress, subdue, over-power, crush, trample, tyrannize, repress, enslave, quell, quash, persecute, maltreat, abuse, *colloq.* bring someone to their knees, treat like dirt, use as a door-mat, walk all over **2** BURDEN, afflict, lie heavy on, weigh down, crush, harass, depress, sadden, dis-courage, dishearten, deject, dispirit, torment, vex, *formal* desolate

oppressed *adj*
tyrannized, burdened, downtrodden, enslaved, sub-ject, crushed, repressed, harassed, abused, mal-treated, misused, persecuted, troubled, disad-vantaged, underprivileged, *formal* subjugated
⊟ free

oppression *n*
tyranny, overwhelming, overpowering, subjection, re-pression, despotism, suppression, injustice, cruelty, brutality, ruthlessness, abuse, persecution, maltreat-ment, harshness, hardship, *formal* subjugation

oppressive *adj*
1 TYRANNICAL, despotic, overbearing, overwhelm-ing, repressive, iron-fisted, domineering, crushing, harsh, unjust, inhuman, cruel, brutal, ruthless, piti-less, merciless, burdensome, onerous, intolerable, Draconian **2** AIRLESS, stuffy, close, stifling, suffocat-ing, sultry, muggy, heavy
⊟ 1 just, gentle **2** airy

oppressor *n*
tyrant, bully, (hard) taskmaster, slave-driver, despot, dictator, persecutor, tormentor, torturer, intimidator, autocrat, *formal* subjugator

opprobrious *adj*
contemptuous, insulting, offensive, scandalous, abu-sive, damaging, defamatory, derogatory, insolent, scurrilous, vitriolic, venomous, *formal* calumniatory, calumnious, contumelious, invective, vituperative

opprobrium *n*
censure, disgrace, dishonour, reproach, disrepute, disfavour, discredit, degradation, debasement, shame, infamy, scurrility, stigma, *formal* calumny, contumely, ignominy, obloquy, odium, *colloq.* slur

opt *v*
choose, pick, decide (on), elect, prefer, select, settle on, single out, *colloq.* go for, plump for

optimistic *adj*
confident, assured, sanguine, hopeful, positive, cheerful, buoyant, bright, idealistic, expectant, bull-ish, pollyann(a)ish, Panglossian, Panglossic, *colloq.* upbeat, happy-go-lucky, looking on the bright side/ through rose-coloured spectacles
⊟ pessimistic

optimum *adj*
best, ideal, model, perfect, optimal, flawless, supreme, highest, superlative, top, choice, most favourable, utopian
⊟ worst

option *n*
choice, alternative, preference, possibility, selection

optional *adj*
voluntary, discretionary, elective, free, unforced
⊟ compulsory, required, *formal* mandatory

opulence *n*
1 RICHES, fortune, wealth, prosperity, affluence, *colloq.* easy street **2** SUMPTUOUSNESS, lavishness, richness, luxury, plenty **3** ABUNDANCE, fullness, co-piousness, profusion, superabundance, luxuriance, cornucopia
⊟ 1 poverty, *formal* penury

opulent *adj*
1 RICH, wealthy, prosperous, affluent, well-to-do, well-off, moneyed, *colloq.* well-heeled, rolling in it **2** SUMPTUOUS, lavish, luxurious, *colloq.* plush, posh **3** ABUNDANT, copious, prolific, plentiful, profuse, superabundant, luxuriant
⊟ 1 poor, *formal* penurious

opus *n*
work, piece, production, composition, creation, oeuvre, brainchild

oracle *n*
1 SEER, prophet, sage, soothsayer, wizard, sibyl, high priest, augur **2** AUTHORITY, adviser, mentor, ex-pert, specialist, *colloq.* guru, mastermind, pundit **3** PROPHECY, vision, divination, prediction, revelation, answer, augury, *formal* prognostication

oracular *adj*
prophetic, wise, significant, positive, authoritative, dogmatic, dictatorial, grave, predictive, obscure, mysterious, cryptic, Delphic, venerable, ominous, portentous, ambiguous, equivocal, two-edged, *for-mal* arcane, abstruse, auspicious, haruspical, pres-cient, sage

oral *adj*
verbal, spoken, said, uttered, unwritten, vocal
⊟ written

orate *v*
speak, talk, hold forth, sermonize, pontificate, dis-course, harangue, speechify, *formal* declaim

oration *n*
address, speech, lecture, sermon, discourse, ha-rangue, homily, *formal* declamation, *colloq.* spiel

orator *n*
public speaker, speaker, lecturer, rhetorician, dema-gogue, declaimer, spellbinder, phrasemonger, *colloq.* spieler

oratorical *adj*
rhetorical, eloquent, sonorous, high-flown, elocu-tionary, silver-tongued, smooth-tongued, Ciceronian, Demosthenic, *formal* bombastic, declamatory, gran-diloquent, magniloquent

oratory *n*
rhetoric, eloquence, public speaking, speech, speechifying, speech-making, diction, elocution, declamation, *formal* grandiloquence

orb *n*
ball, sphere, globe, circle, ring, mound, round, globule, spherule

orbit *n, v*
▶ *n* **1** CIRCUIT, cycle, circle, course, path, trajectory, track, revolution, rotation, *formal* circumgyration **2** RANGE, scope, reach, domain, influence, sphere of influence, sweep, ambit, compass
▶ *v* revolve, circle, encircle, circumnavigate

orchestrate *v*
arrange, co-ordinate, organize, stage-manage, put to-gether, prepare, present, mastermind, fix, integrate, score, compose

ordain *v*
1 CONSECRATE, invest, appoint, call, elect, anoint, frock **2** DECREE, order, require, instruct, rule, set, lay down, fix, dictate, pronounce, will, fate, destine, *for-mal* foreordain, predestine, predetermine, prescribe

ordeal *n*
trial, test, trouble(s), suffering, anguish, distress, ag-ony, pain, torment, persecution, torture, nightmare, *formal* tribulation(s), affliction

order *n, v*
▶ *n* **1** COMMAND, directive, decree, injunction, sum-mons, writ, warrant, instruction, direction, edict, dic-

tate, ordinance, stipulation, mandate, regulation, rule, precept, law **2** REQUISITION, request, requirement, booking, commission, reservation, application, demand, call, notification **3** ARRANGEMENT, organization, grouping, sequence, cycle, categorization, classification, codification, method, form, pattern, plan, system, rota, regularity, uniformity, symmetry, array, layout, line-up, set-up, structure, *formal* disposition **4** ORDERLINESS, neatness, tidiness, method, system **5** PEACE, quiet, calm, tranquillity, harmony, law and order, lawfulness, discipline **6** ASSOCIATION, society, club, community, fellowship, fraternity, brotherhood, sisterhood, sorority, lodge, guild, league, company, organization, denomination, sect, union, secret society **7** CLASS, kind, sort, type, group, variety, species, genus, rank, position, level, grade, degree, station, hierarchy, family, caste, *colloq.* pecking order

3 disorder **4** confusion, chaos **5** anarchy

▷ **in order 1** WORKING, functioning, operative, mended **2** ORDERED, orderly, organized, tidy, neat, shipshape, arranged, well-organized, systematic, regular, methodical, categorized, classified, in sequence, in alphabetical order **3** ACCEPTABLE, proper, correct, right, lawful, allowed, permitted, suitable, appropriate, fitting, all right, done, *colloq.* OK

▷ **in order to** with the purpose of, with the intention of, intending to, to, with a view to, so that, with the result that

▷ **out of order 1** BROKEN, broken down, not working, not functioning, inoperative, out of commission, *colloq.* gone phut, haywire, on the blink, *slang* conked out **2** DISORDERED, disorganized, untidy, messy, confused, muddled, out of sequence **3** UNSEEMLY, improper, un-called-for, incorrect, wrong, irregular, unacceptable, inappropriate, unsuitable, unlawful

▶ *v* **1** COMMAND, instruct, direct, bid, decree, rule, legislate, require, authorize, *formal* prescribe, enjoin **2** REQUEST, reserve, book, apply for, call for, send away for, write off for, *formal* requisition **3** ARRANGE, organize, systematize, dispose, classify, group, marshal, tidy up, sort out, lay out, manage, control, regulate, catalogue, codify

▷ **order around** order about, domineer, dominate, tyrannize, bully, bulldoze, browbeat, boss around, *colloq.* push around, throw your weight about, lay down the law

orderly *adj*
1 ORDERED, systematic, neat, tidy, regular, methodical, efficient, businesslike, in order, well-organized, well-regulated, trim, *colloq.* in apple-pie order **2** WELL-BEHAVED, controlled, disciplined, restrained, law-abiding, ruly

1 chaotic **2** disorderly

ordinance *n*
1 REGULATION, law, rule, ruling, command, decree, dictum, directive, injunction, canon, statute, edict, enactment, fiat **2** SACRAMENT, ceremony, order, practice, observance, rite, ritual, institution

ordinarily *adv*
as a rule, usually, commonly, normally, in general, generally, familiarly, customarily, habitually, conventionally

ordinary *adj*
normal, usual, customary, common, commonplace, regular, routine, standard, mainstream, average, everyday, workaday, quotidian, unexceptional, unremarkable, fair, typical, plain, familiar, habitual, simple, conventional, modest, mediocre, indifferent, uninteresting, dull, mundane, banal, bland, nondescript, pedestrian, prosaic, undistinguished, un-

pretentious, unmemorable, *colloq.* run-of-the-mill, common-or-garden

extraordinary, unusual

▷ **out of the ordinary** unusual, exceptional, remarkable, memorable, noteworthy, extraordinary, different, unique, rare, outstanding, surprising, unexpected

ordnance *n*
munitions, weapons, military supplies, arms, artillery, cannon, guns, *colloq.* big guns

organ *n*
1 DEVICE, instrument, implement, tool, element, constituent, part, component, process, structure, unit, member **2** MEDIUM, agency, forum, vehicle, voice, mouthpiece, publication, newspaper, paper, magazine, periodical, journal

organic *adj*
1 *organic matter* biological, living, animate, natural, *technical* biotic **2** *organic vegetables* natural, not artificial, non-chemical, pesticide-free, additive-free **3** *an organic whole* structured, organized, ordered, harmonious

organism *n*
1 LIVING THING, being, creature, entity, body, structure, cell, animal, plant, bacterium **2** SYSTEM, structure, entity, whole, unity, set-up

organization *n*
1 ASSOCIATION, institution, institute, society, company, firm, corporation, concern, operation, federation, group, body, union, league, club, confederation, consortium, conglomeration, syndicate, authority, council, outfit **2** ARRANGEMENT, management, running, co-ordination, administration, development, establishment **3** SYSTEM, classification, methodology, order, formation, grouping, method, plan, structure, unity, whole, set-up, pattern, composition, design, *formal* configuration

organize *v*
1 ARRANGE, co-ordinate, structure, manage, run, see to, administer, be in charge of, be responsible for, order, standardize, group, marshal, dispose, put in order, sort out, classify, systematize, tabulate, catalogue **2** ESTABLISH, found, set up, create, originate, start, begin, institute, prepare, develop, form, mould, frame, construct, assemble, put together, shape

1 disorganize

organized *adj*
arranged, neat, tidy, orderly, planned, ordered, well-ordered, structured, systematic, efficient, regular, methodical, businesslike, in order, well-organized, well-regulated

disorganized

orgy *n*
1 PARTY, wild party, debauch, carousal, revelry, revel(s), bout, bacchanalia, *colloq.* binge, splurge **2** INDULGENCE, excess, spree, frenzy, *colloq.* binge, splurge

orient *v*
accustom, accommodate, familiarize, acclimatize, adapt, adjust, orientate, align, get your bearings, *formal* habituate

orientation *n*
1 SITUATION, bearings, location, direction, position, alignment, placement, attitude, inclination **2** INDUCTION, initiation, training, guiding, leading, acclimatization, familiarization, adaptation, adjustment, getting your bearings, settling-in

orifice *n*
opening, hole, gap, space, breach, break, inlet, pore, rent, slit, slot, vent, mouth, cleft, crack, rift, crevice, fissure, perforation, *formal* aperture

origin *n*
1 SOURCE, spring, fount, foundation, basis, base, cause, derivation, root(s), fountain, fountainhead, well-spring, etymology, *formal* provenance **2** BEGINNING, start, inauguration, foundation, launch, birth, dawn, dawning, creation, conception, emergence, *formal* commencement, inception, genesis **3** ANCESTRY, descent, extraction, heritage, family, lineage, parentage, pedigree, birth, paternity, stock
F₃ **2** end, termination

original *adj, n*
▶ *adj* **1** FIRST, early, earliest, initial, primary, archetypal, rudimentary, embryonic, starting, opening, commencing, first-hand, primitive, primeval, primal, primordial, *formal* autochthonous **2** CREATIVE, innovative, new, novel, fresh, imaginative, ingenious, inventive, resourceful, unconventional, unorthodox, unusual, unique, pioneering, ground-breaking **3** GENUINE, real, authentic, true
F₃ **1** latest **2** hackneyed, unoriginal **3** copied
▶ *n* prototype, master, paradigm, model, pattern, archetype, standard, type
F₃ copy

originality *n*
inventiveness, creativeness, creativity, imaginativeness, imagination, freshness, boldness, cleverness, creative spirit, daring, innovativeness, innovation, ingenuity, individuality, resourcefulness, newness, novelty, unconventionality, unorthodoxy, singularity, eccentricity

originally *adv*
initially, at first, at the start, at the outset, in the beginning, first, to begin with, in origin, by derivation, by birth

originate *v*
1 RISE, arise, spring, stem, issue, flow, emanate, proceed, derive, result, come, evolve, emerge, be born **2** CREATE, invent, inaugurate, introduce, give birth to, develop, discover, establish, begin, start, set up, set in motion, launch, pioneer, conceive, form, produce, generate, be the father/mother of, *formal* commence
F₃ **1** end, terminate

originator *n*
architect, author, creator, designer, father, mother, founder, generator, developer, establisher, innovator, discoverer, inventor, initiator, pioneer, prime mover, *colloq.* the brains

ornament *n, v*
▶ *n* **1** ADORNMENT, decoration, embellishment, garnish, trimming, accessory, frill, pattern **2** TRINKET, decoration, bauble, jewel, accessory, gewgaw, furbelow, fallal
▶ *v* decorate, adorn, embellish, garnish, trim, beautify, brighten, dress up, deck, gild

ornamental *adj*
decorative, embellishing, adorning, embroidering, attractive, showy, fancy

ornamentation *n*
decoration, adornment, embellishment, embroidery, ornateness, elaboration, garniture, frills, fallalery

ornate *adj*
elaborate, ornamented, fancy, decorated, embellished, showy, ostentatious, baroque, rococo, florid, flowery, flamboyant, fussy, busy, grandiose, sumptuous, *colloq.* flash
F₃ plain

orotund *adj*
1 *orotund voices* full, loud, ground, powerful, strong, deep, rich, sonorous, booming, resonating **2** *orotund speaking* dignified, imposing, ornate, pompous, strained, pretentious, *formal* magniloquent

orthodox *adj*
1 CONFORMIST, conventional, accepted, correct, official, traditional, usual, regular, well-established, established, received, customary, conservative, recognized, authoritative **2** *orthodox religious views* sound, conservative, correct, true, faithful, devout, traditional, strict
F₃ **1** nonconformist, unorthodox

orthodoxy *n*
1 CONVENTIONALITY, conformity, conformism, correctness, properness, authoritativeness, received wisdom **2** TRADITIONALISM, soundness, conservatism, devoutness, devotion, trueness, faithfulness, inflexibility, strictness

oscillate *v*
fluctuate, vary, waver, sway, swing, vacillate, move backwards and forwards, move to and fro, vibrate, wigwag, go from one extreme to the other, *colloq.* seesaw, yo-yo

oscillation *n*
fluctuation, wavering, variation, vacillation, swinging, swing, instability, *colloq.* shilly-shallying, seesawing

ossify *v*
fossilize, harden, solidify, make/become fixed, make/become hard, *formal* indurate, petrify, rigidify

ostensible *adj*
alleged, apparent, presumed, seeming, supposed, so-called, professed, claimed, outward, pretended, superficial, specious, *formal* feigned, purported
F₃ real, genuine

ostensibly *adv*
allegedly, apparently, professedly, supposedly, seemingly, reputedly, outwardly, superficially, *formal* purportedly

ostentation *n*
showiness, showing off, flamboyance, pretension, pretentiousness, show, flaunting, vaunting, pomp, exhibitionism, boasting, display, flourish, pageantry, parade, trappings, window-dressing, *formal* affectation, *colloq.* flashiness, swank, tinsel
F₃ unpretentiousness

ostentatious *adj*
showy, pretentious, vulgar, loud, obtrusive, flaunting, demonstrative, garish, gaudy, flamboyant, conspicuous, extravagant, *formal* affected, *colloq.* flashy, flash, kitsch, glitzy, over the top, OTT
F₃ restrained, modest

ostracism *n*
exclusion, isolation, rejection, barring, avoidance, banishment, boycott, exile, expulsion, excommunication, *formal* disfellowship, proscription, *colloq.* cold shoulder
F₃ acceptance, reinstatement, welcome

ostracize *v*
exclude, banish, exile, expel, excommunicate, reject, segregate, isolate, send to Coventry, shun, snub, boycott, bar, outlaw, avoid, *colloq.* cold-shoulder, cut
F₃ accept, welcome

other *adj*
1 DIFFERENT, dissimilar, unlike, variant, separate, distinct, contrasting, *formal* disparate **2** MORE, further, extra, additional, supplementary, spare, alternative

otherwise *adv*
1 UNLESS, if not, or, or else, failing that **2** DIFFERENTLY, in a different way, along different lines, in other respects

otherworldly *adj*
dreamy, absent-minded, ethereal, preoccupied, rapt, bemused, fey
F₃ worldly, mundane, solid, substantial

ounce *n*
particle, scrap, speck, spot, trace, iota, jot, shred, whit, atom, crumb, drop, grain, modicum, morsel

oust *v*
expel, eject, depose, displace, turn out, throw out, overthrow, evict, drive out, thrust out, force out, put out, get rid of, dismiss, unseat, dislodge, dispossess, disinherit, replace, topple, *colloq.* sack, fire, boot out, show the door to, give someone the boot/elbow
⊟ install, settle

out *adj*
1 AWAY, absent, elsewhere, not at home, gone, outside, abroad **2** UNCONSCIOUS, knocked out, out cold, *technical* comatose, *formal* insensible, *colloq.* KO'd **3** *the book is out* published, available, obtainable, ready, in print **4** REVEALED, exposed, known, disclosed, divulged, public, evident, in the open, *formal* manifest **5** FORBIDDEN, unacceptable, impossible, excluded, inadmissible, unwelcome, undesirable, inappropriate, unsuitable, *formal* disallowed **6** OUT OF DATE, unfashionable, old-fashioned, dated, *passé*, antiquated, *démodé*, *colloq.* old hat **7** EXTINGUISHED, finished, expired, dead, not burning, doused, not shining, used up **8** *the flowers are out* in bloom, in full bloom, blooming, blossoming, in flower **9** *out to make money* determined, bent, insistent, intent, set
⊟ **1** in, here, at home **2** conscious **3** out of print **4** hidden, concealed **5** allowed **6** up-to-date, *colloq.* in

out-and-out *adj*
absolute, thorough, total, complete, utter, outright, perfect, downright, inveterate, thoroughgoing, unmitigated, unqualified, uncompromising, *formal* arrant, consummate, *colloq.* dyed-in-the-wool

outbreak *n*
eruption, outburst, explosion, flare-up, upsurge, sudden start, flash, rash, burst, epidemic, *formal* recrudescence

outburst *n*
outbreak, eruption, explosion, flare-up, outpouring, burst, fit, gush, surge, storm, spasm, seizure, gale, attack, fit of temper, paroxysm

outcast *n*
castaway, exile, pariah, outsider, untouchable, leper, refugee, evacuee, reject, *persona non grata*

outclass *v*
surpass, outshine, beat, excel over, be much better than, outrival, transcend, top, eclipse, outdo, outdistance, outrank, outstrip, overshadow, leave standing, put in the shade

outcome *n*
result, consequence, upshot, conclusion, effect, after-effect, product, issue, sequel, end result

outcry *n*
protest, complaint, protestation, objection, dissent, indignation, uproar, cry, exclamation, clamour, row, fuss, commotion, noise, tumult, hue and cry, outburst, *colloq.* hullabaloo, racket

outdated *adj*
out of date, old-fashioned, out of fashion, dated, unfashionable, outmoded, behind the times, obsolete, obsolescent, superseded, antediluvian, antiquated, antique, archaic, *passé*, *démodé*, *colloq.* old hat, square, old-fogeyish
⊟ fashionable, modern

outdistance *v*
outstrip, outpace, outrun, pass, overtake, pull ahead of, shake off, overhaul, surpass, leave behind, leave standing

outdo *v*
surpass, exceed, beat, excel, outstrip, outshine, get

the better of, have the advantage over, come first, overcome, defeat, outclass, outdistance, eclipse, transcend, *colloq.* cap, gain the upper/whip hand over, stand/be head and shoulders above, run rings/circles round

outdoors *adv*
out, outside, in the open air, out-of-doors, alfresco, en plein air
⊟ indoors

outer *adj*
1 EXTERNAL, exterior, outside, outermost, outward, surface, superficial, peripheral **2** OUTLYING, distant, remote, further, fringe, peripheral, far-away
⊟ **1** internal **2** inner

outface *v*
brave, confront, defy, outstare, stare down, brazen out, beard
⊟ capitulate, *formal* succumb

outfit *n, v*
▶ *n* **1** CLOTHES, dress, suit, costume, ensemble, *colloq.* get-up, togs, garb, gear **2** EQUIPMENT, kit, tools, apparatus, rig, trappings, paraphernalia, *colloq.* gear **3** ORGANIZATION, firm, business, company, corporation, group, team, unit, set, set-up, clique, coterie, crew, gang, squad
▶ *v* fit out, furnish, provide, supply, equip, stock, turn out, fit up, kit out, appoint, provision, *formal* accoutre, apparel, attire

outfitter *n*
tailor, clothier, costumer, costumier, dressmaker, sartor, modiste, haberdasher, couturier, couturière

outflow *n*
discharge, rush, spout, gush, jet, emergence, effusion, emanation, outrush, outpouring, drainage, ebb, outfall, *formal* debouchment, disemboguement, effluence, effluent, effluvium, efflux, effluxion
⊟ inflow

outflowing *adj*
discharging, gushing, leaking, rushing, spurting, effluent, emanant, *formal* debouching

outgoing *adj*
1 SOCIABLE, friendly, unreserved, affable, amiable, warm, affectionate, approachable, expansive, open, talkative, extrovert, gregarious, cordial, genial, easy-going, communicative, demonstrative, sympathetic **2** DEPARTING, retiring, leaving, former, last, past, ex-
⊟ **1** reserved **2** incoming

outgoings *n*
costs, expenditure, outlay, overheads, spending, expenses, *formal* disbursal, disbursement
⊟ income

outgrowth *n*
1 CONSEQUENCE, effect, product, offshoot, by-product, spin-off, emanation **2** SWELLING, shoot, sprout, *formal* protuberance, excrescence

outing *n*
excursion, expedition, jaunt, pleasure trip, tour, mystery tour, spin, picnic, *colloq.* trip

outlandish *adj*
unconventional, unfamiliar, unheard-of, unknown, bizarre, strange, odd, unusual, peculiar, weird, eccentric, alien, exotic, curious, quaint, barbarous, grotesque, foreign, extraordinary, preposterous, unreasonable, *colloq.* freaky, oddball, wacky, *slang* way-out, far-out
⊟ familiar, ordinary

outlandishness *n*
bizarreness, oddness, unusualness, strangeness,

weirdness, queerness, eccentricity, exoticness, quaintness, grotesqueness
🖪 commonplaceness, familiarity

outlast *v*
survive, come through, outlive, outstay, ride, weather

outlaw *n, v*
► *n* fugitive, bandit, brigand, robber, desperado, highwayman, criminal, marauder, pirate, outcast, exile
► *v* ban, disallow, forbid, prohibit, exclude, embargo, bar, debar, banish, excommunicate, condemn, *formal* proscribe, interdict
🖪 allow, legalize

outlay *n*
expenditure, expenses, outgoings, payment, charge, cost, price, spending, *formal* disbursement
🖪 income

outlet *n*
1 RETAILER, retail outlet, shop, store, market, supplier **2** EXIT, way out, vent, duct, escape, outfall, opening, release, valve, safety valve, channel, culvert, conduit, *formal* egress **3** *an outlet for your feelings* channel, means of release, means of expression, safety valve
🖪 **2** entry, inlet

outline *n, v*
► *n* **1** SUMMARY, sketch, synopsis, précis, résumé, main points, rough idea, bare facts, bare bones, thumbnail sketch, abstract **2** PROFILE, sketch, tracing, form, shape, design, layout, plan, contour, silhouette, *formal* configuration, delineation, lineament
► *v* sketch (out), summarize, draft, trace, rough out, give a rough idea of, *formal* delineate

outlive *v*
survive, outlast, come through, live through, weather
🖪 predecease

outlook *n*
1 VIEW, viewpoint, point of view, attitude, perspective, frame of mind, interpretation, angle, slant, standpoint, opinion **2** EXPECTATIONS, future, forecast, prospect, prognosis **3** *a house with a pleasant outlook* view, prospect, aspect, panorama

outlying *adj*
distant, remote, isolated, far-off, far-away, far-flung, outer, out-of-the-way, inaccessible, provincial, *colloq.* off the beaten track
🖪 inner

outmanoeuvre *v*
outdo, outthink, outwit, outsmart, outfox, beat, outflank, outgeneral, get the better of, *formal* circumvent

outmoded *adj*
out of date, old-fashioned, out of fashion, dated, unfashionable, behind the times, obsolete, obsolescent, superseded, antediluvian, antiquated, archaic, *passé*, *démodé*, *colloq.* old hat, square, old-fogeyish
🖪 modern, new, fashionable, fresh

out of date *adj*
old-fashioned, outdated, outmoded, out of fashion, dated, unfashionable, behind the times, obsolete, obsolescent, superseded, antediluvian, antiquated, archaic, *passé*, *démodé*, *colloq.* old hat, square, old-fogeyish
🖪 modern, new, fashionable, fresh

out-of-the-way *adj*
remote, isolated, far-flung, far-off, far-away, distant, outlying, outer, inaccessible, lonely, little-known, obscure, unfrequented, peripheral, *colloq.* off the beaten track

out of work *adj*
unemployed, redundant, out of a job, jobless, idle, laid off, workless, *colloq.* on the dole
🖪 employed, occupied, busy

outpace *v*
outstrip, outrun, outdistance, outdo, beat, pass, overtake, surpass, overhaul

outpouring *n*
flood, deluge, torrent, stream, spate, spurt, flow, outflow, flux, cascade, effusion, emanation, *formal* debouchment, disemboguement, effluence, efflux

output *n*
production, productivity, product, manufacture, achievement, performance, accomplishment, gain, yield, fruits, harvest, return

outrage *n, v*
► *n* **1** ANGER, fury, rage, indignation, shock, affront, horror, wrath **2** ATROCITY, offence, injury, enormity, barbarism, brutality, crime, violation, evil, scandal, horror, affront
► *v* **1** APPAL, anger, infuriate, affront, incense, enrage, madden, disgust, injure, offend, shock, horrify, scandalize **2** ASSAULT, violate, abuse, desecrate, defile, ravish, ravage

outrageous *adj*
1 ATROCIOUS, abominable, shocking, scandalous, offensive, disgraceful, dreadful, terrible, monstrous, unspeakable, horrible, ghastly, gruesome, vile, foul, unacceptable, intolerable, unbearable, insufferable, *formal* heinous **2** EXCESSIVE, exorbitant, immoderate, unreasonable, extortionate, scandalous, obscene, inordinate, preposterous
🖪 **2** acceptable, reasonable

outré *adj*
unconventional, unusual, strange, odd, extraordinary, eccentric, weird, bizarre, shocking, outrageous, *colloq.* oddball, freaky, *slang* way-out, far-out

outrider *n*
advance guard, escort, attendant, guard, bodyguard, vanguard, herald, precursor

outright *adj, adv*
► *adj* **1** TOTAL, utter, absolute, complete, downright, out-and-out, unqualified, unconditional, unmitigated, perfect, pure, thorough, direct **2** CLEAR, definite, categorical, unequivocal, unmistakable, undeniable, straightforward
🖪 ambiguous, indefinite
► *adv* **1** TOTALLY, absolutely, completely, wholly, entirely, categorically, utterly, thoroughly, openly, without restraint, straightforwardly, positively, directly, explicitly **2** *killed outright* instantaneously, at once, there and then, instantly, immediately, straight away

outrun *v*
outstrip, outpace, outdistance, overtake, outdo, shake off, pass, overhaul, surpass, exceed, excel, beat, lose, leave behind

outset *n*
start, beginning, opening, inauguration, *formal* inception, commencement, *colloq.* kick-off
🖪 end, conclusion

outshine *v*
outclass, outstrip, outdo, overshadow, transcend, eclipse, surpass, beat, best, upstage, excel, dwarf, outrank, top, put in the shade, put to shame

outside *adj, n*
► *adj* **1** EXTERNAL, exterior, outer, surface, superficial, outward, extraneous, outdoor, outermost, extreme **2** *an outside chance* remote, marginal, distant, small, faint, slight, slim, slender, vague, negligible, improbable, unlikely
🖪 **1** inside **2** likely, real, substantial
► *n* exterior, façade, front, surface, outer surface, face, appearance, cover
🖪 inside

outsider *n*
stranger, intruder, alien, non-member, non-resident, foreigner, newcomer, visitor, emigrant, émigré, immigrant, outlander, intruder, interloper, misfit, gatecrasher, *colloq.* odd one out

outskirts *n*
suburbs, suburbia, vicinity, neighbourhood, environs, periphery, fringes, borders, boundary, limit, frontier, edge, margin, perimeter
🖪 centre

outsmart *v*
outwit, outperform, outmanoeuvre, best, outthink, beat, get the better of, deceive, trick, dupe, outfox, *colloq.* kid, con, have on, take for a ride, pull a fast one on

outspoken *adj*
candid, frank, forthright, free, unreserved, unequivocal, unceremonious, plain-spoken, plain, direct, straightforward, explicit, blunt, brusque, rude
🖪 diplomatic, reserved

outspread *adj*
spread out, outstretched, open, opened, wide, wide open, unfolded, unfurled, stretched, extended, fanned out, flared, expanded

outstanding *adj*
1 EXCELLENT, distinguished, eminent, pre-eminent, famous, famed, well-known, renowned, celebrated, exceptional, superior, remarkable, prominent, superb, great, notable, impressive, striking, superlative, important, noteworthy, memorable, special, extraordinary, arresting 2 OWING, unpaid, due, unsettled, unresolved, uncollected, pending, payable, remaining, unfinished, ongoing, left-over
🖪 1 ordinary, unexceptional 2 paid, settled

outstandingly *adv*
exceptionally, remarkably, greatly, notably, extremely, especially, extraordinarily, impressively, strikingly, amazingly

outstrip *v*
surpass, exceed, better, outdo, beat, top, transcend, outshine, pass, gain on, leave behind, leave standing, outrun, outdistance, overtake, eclipse

outward *adj*
external, exterior, outer, outside, outermost, surface, superficial, visible, apparent, perceptible, noticeable, discernible, observable, evident, supposed, professed, public, obvious, ostensible
🖪 inner, private

outwardly *adv*
apparently, externally, to all appearances, visibly, superficially, supposedly, seemingly, on the surface, on the outside, at first sight, as far as you can see, on the face of it

outweigh *v*
exceed, surpass, be greater than, be more than, be superior to, override, prevail over, overcome, take precedence over, cancel out, make up for, compensate for, predominate, *formal* preponderate

outwit *v*
outsmart, outthink, outmanoeuvre, get the better of, be cleverer than, trick, better, beat, dupe, cheat, deceive, defraud, swindle, *colloq.* kid, con, have on, take for a ride, pull a fast one on

outworn *adj*
outdated, out of date, outmoded, ancient, antiquated, archaic, stale, discredited, defunct, old-fashioned, behind the times, hackneyed, rejected, obsolete, obsolescent, disused, rejected, exhausted, abandoned, *colloq.* old hat, moth-eaten, past its sell-by date
🖪 fresh, new

oval *adj*
egg-shaped, elliptical, ovoid, ovate, ellipsoidal, *technical* obovate, oviform, *formal* vulviform

ovation *n*
applause, acclaim, acclamation, praise(s), tribute, clapping, handclapping, cheering, cheers, accolade, bravos, *formal* plaudits, laudation, *colloq.* bouquet
🖪 abuse, catcalls

over *adj, adv, prep*
▶ *adj* finished, ended, at an end, done with, past, gone, no more, completed, closed, in the past, settled, up, forgotten, accomplished, *formal* concluded, terminated, *colloq.* over and done with, ancient history
▶ *adv* 1 ABOVE, beyond, overhead, on high, *formal* aloft 2 EXTRA, remaining, surplus, superfluous, left, left over, unclaimed, unused, unwanted, in excess, in addition
▷ **over and over (again)** again and again, repeatedly, frequently, often, continually, endlessly, time and (time) again, ad infinitum, ad nauseam
▶ *prep* 1 ABOVE, on, on top of, upon, in charge of, in command of, higher than, superior to 2 EXCEEDING, more than, in excess of
▷ **over and above** in addition to, on top of, together with, plus, along with, as well as, besides, added to, let alone, not to mention

overabundance *n*
surplus, surfeit, excess, glut, oversupply, *embarras de choix, embarras de richesse, formal* superfluity, superabundance, profusion, plethora, *colloq.* too much of a good thing
🖪 lack, dearth

overact *v*
overplay, exaggerate, overdo, *colloq.* ham, lay/pile it on, lay/pile it on thick, lay/pile it on with a trowel
🖪 underact, underplay

overall *adj, adv*
▶ *adj* total, all-inclusive, all-embracing, comprehensive, inclusive, complete, sweeping, general, universal, global, broad, all-over, *colloq.* blanket, umbrella
🖪 narrow, specific
▶ *adv* in general, on the whole, by and large, broadly, generally speaking

overawe *v*
intimidate, daunt, dismay, disconcert, abash, frighten, scare, terrify, petrify, alarm, awe, unnerve, browbeat, cow
🖪 reassure, comfort

overbalance *v*
lose your balance, fall over, tip over, topple over, trip, slip, tumble, upset, somersault, lose your footing, capsize, keel over, overturn, turn turtle

overbearing *adj*
imperious, domineering, arrogant, officious, dictatorial, despotic, lordly, tyrannical, high-handed, haughty, proud, cavalier, autocratic, dogmatic, oppressive, presumptuous, contemptuous, disdainful, *colloq.* bossy, la-di-da, snobby, snooty, snotty, stuck-up, toffee-nosed, too big for your boots
🖪 meek, unassertive

overblown *adj*
overstated, overdone, overestimated, overcharged, excessive, extravagant, pretentious, embellished, amplified, bombastic, inflated, caricatured, burlesqued, exalted, self-important, *colloq.* over the top, OTT

overcast *adj*
cloudy, clouded (over), grey, dull, dark, darkened, sombre, gloomy, dreary, dismal, sunless, hazy, misty, foggy, leaden, louring
🖪 bright, clear

overcharge v
surcharge, short-change, cheat, extort, swindle, *colloq.* rip off, sting, do, diddle, fleece, rook
⊟ undercharge

overcome v, adj
▶ v conquer, defeat, beat, surmount, prevail, triumph over, get the better of, be victorious over, rise above, master, overpower, overwhelm, overthrow, subdue, trounce, best, worst, rout, outplay, outwit, outsmart, be more than a match for, have the edge on, *formal* vanquish, subjugate, *colloq.* hammer, slaughter, clobber, lick, thrash, wipe the floor with
▶ adj overwhelmed, overpowered, moved, broken, speechless, *colloq.* lost for words, bowled over, swept off your feet, *formal* affected

over-confident adj
arrogant, brash, cocksure, self-assured, blustering, swaggering, presumptuous, overweening, foolhardy, rash, incautious, over-optimistic, sanguine, *formal* hubristic, temerarious, *colloq.* cocky, uppity, uppish
⊟ cautious, diffident

overcritical adj
overparticular, fault-finding, hypercritical, hard to please, pedantic, purist, captious, carping, cavilling, over-nice, Zoilean, *formal* ultra-crepidarian, *colloq.* nit-picking, pernickety, hair-splitting
⊟ easy-going, tolerant, uncritical

overcrowded adj
congested, packed (out), crammed full, chock-full, overpopulated, overloaded, swarming, teeming, overrun, full to overflowing, *colloq.* jam-packed, packed like sardines
⊟ deserted, empty

overdo v
exaggerate, go too far, carry to excess, overindulge, overstate, overact, overplay, *colloq.* ham it, go overboard, camp it up, lay/pile it on, lay/pile it on thick, lay/pile it on with a trowel, stretch a point
▷ **overdo it** overwork, work too hard, do too much, overstretch yourself, strain yourself, overreach yourself, overexert yourself, *colloq.* sweat blood, burn yourself out, bite off more than you can chew, run yourself into the ground, burn the candle at both ends, work your fingers to the bone, crack up

overdone adj
1 OVERCOOKED, burnt, spoiled, dried up, overbaked, charred, *colloq.* burnt to a cinder, burnt to a frazzle
2 EXAGGERATED, overstated, overelaborate, undue, unnecessary, overplayed, excessive, immoderate, fulsome, effusive, gushing, inordinate, histrionic, *colloq.* over the top
⊟ 1 underdone, raw 2 underplayed, understated

overdraft n
overdrawn account, debt, arrears, liabilities, borrowings, unpaid amounts, deficit, insufficient funds

overdue adj
late, behindhand, behind schedule, delayed, owing, unpaid, due, unsettled, pending, payable, unpunctual, slow, *formal* tardy, belated
⊟ early

overeat v
gorge, overindulge, guzzle, eat too much, go on a binge, stuff yourself, gormandize, *colloq.* binge, make a pig of yourself, pig out, have eyes bigger than your stomach
⊟ abstain, starve

overeating n
guzzling, overindulgence, gluttony, bulimia, hyperphagia, gourmandise, gourmandism, gormandism, *colloq.* bingeing
⊟ abstemiousness, abstention

overemphasize v
exaggerate, overstress, lay/put too much emphasis on, attach too much importance to, make too much of, labour, belabour, overdramatize, *colloq.* make a mountain out of a molehill, blow up out of all proportion
⊟ minimize, play down, underplay, understate, belittle

overexert v
▷ **overexert yourself** overdo it, overstrain yourself, overtax yourself, overtire yourself, overwork, strain yourself, wear yourself out, drive yourself too hard, work too hard, run yourself into the ground, fatigue, work yourself to death, push yourself too hard, *colloq.* burn the candle at both ends, knock yourself out
⊟ idle, laze

overflow v, n
▶ v spill (over), overrun, run over, pour over, well over, flow over, brim over, bubble over, surge, discharge, flood, cover, inundate, deluge, shower, submerge, soak, swamp, teem
▶ n overspill, spill, inundation, flood, spillage, overabundance, surplus

overflowing adj
crowded, filled, full, swarming, teeming, thronged, bountiful, abounding, superabundant, brimful, plentiful, copious, profuse, rife, *formal* inundant, plenteous
⊟ lacking, scarce

overgrowth n
escalation, overabundance, overdevelopment, superabundance, *technical* hypertrophy
⊟ decline, failure, shrinkage, wasting

overhang v
jut (out), project, bulge (out), protrude, stick out, stand out, extend, beetle

overhanging adj
projecting, protruding, jutting (out), bulging (out), sticking out, standing out, beetling, *formal* pensile

overhaul v, n
▶ v 1 RENOVATE, repair, service, recondition, revamp, mend, examine, inspect, investigate, check, check over/up, survey, go over, re-examine, fix
2 OVERTAKE, pull ahead of, outpace, outstrip, outdistance, gain on, pass, get ahead of
▶ n reconditioning, repair, renovation, check, checkup, service, examination, inspection, *colloq.* going-over

overhead adv, adj
▶ adv above, up above, on high, upwards
⊟ below, underfoot
▶ adj elevated, aerial, overhanging, raised

overheads n
running costs, outgoings, operating costs, regular costs, expenses, expenditure, burden, oncost, *formal* disbursement
⊟ income, profit

overheated adj
angry, agitated, inflamed, fiery, flaming, overwrought, passionate, roused, impassioned, excited, overexcited
⊟ calm, cool, impassive, dispassionate

overindulge v
1 GORGE, gormandize, gluttonize, guzzle, debauch, eat/drink too much, satiate, sate, *colloq.* binge, pig out, make a pig of yourself, *slang* booze 2 PAMPER, mollycoddle, spoil, cosset, pander, pet, *colloq.* spoon-feed
⊟ 1 abstain

overindulgence *n*
excess, immoderation, overeating, intemperance, surfeit, debauch, *colloq.* binge
🇫 abstemiousness, abstention

overjoyed *adj*
delighted, elated, euphoric, ecstatic, in raptures, joyful, enraptured, rapturous, thrilled, jubilant, in transports of delight, *colloq.* over the moon, tickled pink, on cloud nine, in seventh heaven, on top of the world, like a child with a new toy, pleased as Punch, high as a kite
🇫 sad, disappointed

overlap *v*
coincide, cover, overlay, overlie, flap over, *technical* imbricate, shingle

overlay *v*
cover, wrap, envelop, blanket, inlay, decorate, ornament, adorn, veneer, varnish, laminate

overload *v*
burden, overburden, oppress, strain, tax, overtax, weigh down, overcharge, encumber, saddle, lumber

overlook *v*
1 FRONT ONTO, face, look onto, open onto, look over, command/have a view of 2 MISS, disregard, ignore, omit, neglect, pass over, leave, forget, take no notice of, let pass, let ride, slight 3 EXCUSE, forgive, pardon, condone, wink at, turn a blind eye to
🇫 2 notice, observe 3 penalize, condemn

overlooked *adj*
unhonoured, unvalued, unregarded, unnoted, unremarked, unprized, unconsidered, unheeded
🇫 appreciated, prized, sought-after, valued

overly *adv*
too, over, unduly, excessively, exceedingly, immoderately, unreasonably, inordinately
🇫 inadequately, insufficiently

overnice *adj*
overfastidious, over-meticulous, overparticular, overprecise, oversensitive, overscrupulous, oversubtle, finical, *colloq.* nit-picking, pernickety
🇫 casual, uncritical

overplay *v*
exaggerate, overstate, overdo, magnify, overemphasize, emphasize, stress, make too much of, dramatize, overdramatize, embellish, embroider, colour, stretch the truth, enlarge, amplify, enhance, oversell, *formal* aggrandize, *colloq.* lay/pile it on, lay/pile it on thick, lay/pile it on with a trowel, make a mountain out of a molehill, blow something up out of all proportion, shoot a line
🇫 understate, play down

overpopulated *adj*
overcrowded, congested, packed (out), crammed full, chock-full, overloaded, swarming, teeming, overrun, full to overflowing, *colloq.* jam-packed, packed like sardines
🇫 deserted, empty

overpower *v*
1 OVERWHELM, overcome, conquer, defeat, beat, trounce, rout, subdue, overthrow, quash, quell, crush, immobilize, master, gain mastery over, gain the upper hand over, *formal* vanquish, subjugate 2 *overpowered by a feeling* move, affect deeply/strongly, touch, confuse, perplex, daze, stagger, dumbfound, leave speechless, take aback, *colloq.* bowl over, floor, flabbergast, knock for six

overpowering *adj*
overwhelming, powerful, strong, forceful, irresistible, undeniable, irrefutable, uncontrollable, compelling, extreme, oppressive, suffocating, stifling, unbearable, nauseating, sickening

overrate *v*
overestimate, overvalue, overpraise, magnify, overprize, make too much of, attach too much importance to, *colloq.* blow up
🇫 underrate

overreach *v*
▷ **overreach yourself** overstretch yourself, try to do too much, overdo it, go too far, strain yourself, *colloq.* bite off more than you can chew, spread yourself too thinly, burn yourself out

override *v*
1 OUTWEIGH, be more important than, exceed, surpass, be greater than, be superior to, prevail over, overcome 2 OVERRULE, cancel, annul, set aside, supersede, quash, reverse, disregard, ignore, trample over, *formal* abrogate, countermand, nullify, rescind, vanquish, *colloq.* ride roughshod over

overriding *adj*
most important, most significant, principal, first, major, predominant, primary, prime, supreme, compelling, dominant, essential, final, ultimate, overruling, prior, prevailing, ruling, paramount, pivotal, cardinal, determining, number one
🇫 insignificant, unimportant

overrule *v*
overturn, override, countermand, revoke, set aside, disallow, reject, reverse, invalidate, cancel, annul, vote down, *formal* abrogate, rescind, nullify

overrun *v*
1 INVADE, occupy, besiege, attack, storm, infest, overwhelm, inundate, permeate, penetrate, spread over, swamp, swarm over, surge over, ravage, overgrow, *colloq.* run riot, spread like wildfire 2 EXCEED, go over, overshoot, overstep, overreach

overseas *adj, adv*
▶ *adj* foreign, international, external, exotic, faraway, distant, remote
🇫 domestic, home
▶ *adv* abroad, in/to a foreign country, out of the country, in/to foreign parts, in/to foreign climes, far and wide, widely

overseer *n*
supervisor, chief, foreman, forewoman, manager, manageress, superintendent, *colloq.* boss, gaffer

overshadow *v*
1 OBSCURE, cloud, darken, dim, mar, spoil, blight, veil, take the edge off, put a damper on 2 OUTSHINE, eclipse, excel, surpass, be superior to, dominate, dwarf, put in the shade, rise above, tower above

oversight *n*
1 LAPSE, omission, fault, error, mistake, blunder, carelessness, neglect, *formal* dereliction, *colloq.* slipup, howler, boob 2 SUPERVISION, responsibility, care, charge, control, custody, superintendence, handling, keeping, administration, management, surveillance, direction

overstate *v*
exaggerate, overdo, magnify, overemphasize, emphasize, stress, make too much of, dramatize, overdramatize, embellish, embroider, colour, stretch the truth, enlarge, amplify, enhance, oversell, *formal* aggrandize, *colloq.* lay/pile it on, lay/pile it on thick, lay/pile it on with a trowel, make a mountain out of a molehill, blow something up out of all proportion, shoot a line
🇫 understate, play down

overstatement *n*
exaggeration, overemphasis, emphasis, magnification, overestimation, excess, extravagance, embellishment, enlargement, pretentiousness, amplification, burlesque, caricature, parody, *formal* hyperbole
🇫 meiosis, understatement

overt *adj*
open, plain, evident, patent, observable, obvious, noticeable, visible, conspicuous, apparent, public, professed, unconcealed, undisguised, *formal* manifest
🔁 covert, secret

overtake *v*
1 PASS, go past, drive/run past, catch up with, outdistance, leave behind, outstrip, draw level with, pull ahead of, overhaul **2** COME UPON, happen to, happen suddenly/unexpectedly to, take by surprise, catch unawares, strike, overwhelm, engulf, *formal* befall

overthrow *v, n*
▶ *v* **1** DEPOSE, oust, bring down, topple, unseat, displace, dethrone, conquer, beat, defeat, crush, overcome, overpower, overwhelm, quash, quell, trounce, best, worst, subdue, master, abolish, upset, *formal* vanquish **2** OVERTURN, upset, upturn, tip over, topple, overbalance, keel over, knock over, spill, turn over, invert
🔁 **1** install, protect, reinstate, restore
▶ *n* ousting, unseating, defeat, deposition, dethronement, fall, rout, undoing, suppression, downfall, end, humiliation, destruction, ruin, *formal* vanquishing

overtone *n*
suggestion, intimation, nuance, hint, undercurrent, insinuation, innuendo, connotation, hidden meaning, indirect reference, association, feeling, implication, sense, flavour

overture *n*
1 APPROACH, advance(s), offer, invitation, proposal, proposition, suggestion, signal, move(s), motion **2** PRELUDE, opening, introduction, opening move, (opening) gambit

overturn *v*
1 CAPSIZE, upset, upturn, tip over, topple, overbalance, keel over, knock over, spill, turn over, invert, skittle **2** OVERRULE, repeal, override, reverse, cancel, annul, abolish, destroy, quash, set aside, veto, *formal* abrogate, nullify, rescind, revoke **3** OVERTHROW, depose, oust, bring down, topple, unseat, displace, dethrone, conquer, beat, defeat, crush, overcome, overpower, overwhelm, *formal* vanquish

overused *adj*
overworked, hackneyed, trite, stereotyped, worn, tired, unoriginal, stale, played out, commonplace, bromidic, clichéd, threadbare, *formal* platitudinous
🔁 fresh, original, new

overweening *adj*
arrogant, conceited, haughty, proud, self-confident, supercilious, vain, presumptuous, overblown, highhanded, cocksure, excessive, immoderate, inflated, extravagant, swollen, opinionated, lordly, egotistical, cavalier, pompous, insolent, *colloq.* cocky, *formal* hubristic, vainglorious
🔁 unassuming, modest, diffident

overweight *adj*
fat, plump, stout, massive, huge, chunky, obese, ample, hefty, bulky, outsize, podgy, portly, pot-bellied, fleshy, heavy, tubby, chubby, buxom, *formal* corpulent, *colloq.* flabby, gross, well-padded, well-upholstered
🔁 underweight, thin, skinny, emaciated

overwhelm *v*
1 OVERCOME, overpower, overthrow, destroy, defeat, beat, trounce, worst, best, subdue, quash, quell, prevail, get the better of, be victorious over, outplay, outwit, outsmart, be more than a match for, have the edge on, crush, rout, devastate, *formal* vanquish, subju-

gate, *colloq.* hammer, slaughter, clobber, lick, thrash, wipe the floor with **2** OVERRUN, deluge, inundate, bury, submerge, overburden, swamp, engulf, *colloq.* snow under **3** CONFUSE, stagger, move, affect deeply/strongly, daze, touch, *colloq.* bowl over, floor, knock for six

overwhelming *adj*
1 OVERPOWERING, powerful, strong, forceful, irresistible, undeniable, irrefutable, uncontrollable, compelling, extreme, oppressive, suffocating, stifling, unbearable, nauseating, sickening **2** *an overwhelming majority* great, large, vast, immense, huge
🔁 **1** resistible **2** insignificant, negligible

overwork *v*
overstrain, overload, exploit, exhaust, overuse, overtax, strain, wear out, oppress, burden, weary, work too hard, overdo it, do too much, overstretch yourself, strain yourself, overreach yourself, overexert yourself, *colloq.* sweat blood, burn yourself out, bite off more than you can chew, run yourself into the ground, burn the candle at both ends, work your fingers to the bone, crack up

overworked *adj*
1 *overworked employees* overstrained, exhausted, worn out, overtaxed, *colloq.* stressed out **2** *an overworked expression* hackneyed, trite, stereotyped, worn, tired, unoriginal, stale, played out, commonplace, bromidic, clichéd, threadbare, *formal* platitudinous
🔁 fresh, original, new

overwrought *adj*
tense, distraught, agitated, keyed up, on edge, edgy, worked up, wound up, nervous, highly-strung, frantic, overcharged, overexcited, excited, beside yourself, *colloq.* uptight, nervy
🔁 calm

owe *v*
be in debt to, be overdrawn, get into debt, run up debts, be indebted to, be in arrears to, be under an obligation to, *colloq.* be in the red, be up to your ears in debt

owing *adj*
unpaid, due, owed, in arrears, outstanding, payable, unsettled, overdue
▷ **owing to** because of, as a result of, on account of, thanks to

own *adj, v*
▶ *adj* personal, individual, private, particular, idiosyncratic
▷ **on your own** alone, isolated, by yourself, singly, unaccompanied, unaided, unassisted, independently, *colloq.* off your own bat, on your tod
▶ *v* possess, have, have got, have as your belongings/property, have in your possession, have (all) to yourself, monopolize, hold, retain, keep, enjoy, use, occupy
▷ **own up** admit, confess, tell the truth, acknowledge, *colloq.* come clean, make a clean breast of it

owner *n*
possessor, holder, keeper, householder, home-owner, landlord, landlady, proprietor, proprietress, master, mistress, freeholder

ownership *n*
possession, proprietary rights, right of possession, proprietorship, rights, freehold, dominion, *technical* title

ox *n*
bull, bullock, steer, buffalo, bison, yak

P

pace *n, v*
▶ *n* **1** STEP, stride, walk, gait, tread **2** SPEED, movement, motion, progress, rate, rate of progress, velocity, quickness, rapidity, swiftness, tempo, measure, *formal* celerity
▶ *v* step, stride, walk, walk up and down, march, tramp, pound, patrol, mark out, measure

pacific *adj*
peaceable, peaceful, peace-loving, mild, peacemaking, pacifist, irenic, appeasing, friendly, gentle, equable, placid, still, unruffled, quiet, serene, tranquil, smooth, calm, conciliatory, nonbelligerent, non-violent, diplomatic, dovelike, dovish, *formal* complaisant, pacificatory, placatory, propitiatory, halcyon
☒ belligerent, aggressive, contentious, *formal* pugnacious

pacifism *n*
non-violence, pacificism, passive resistance, satyagraha

pacifist *n*
peacemaker, pacificist, peace-lover, conscientious objector, peace-monger, dove, *colloq.* conchy
☒ warmonger, hawk

pacify *v*
appease, conciliate, placate, mollify, calm, calm down, compose, soothe, assuage, allay, defuse, moderate, soften, lull, still, quiet, quieten, silence, quell, crush, put down, tame, subdue, *formal* propitiate
☒ anger

pack *n, v*
▶ *n* **1** PACKET, box, carton, container, parcel, package, bundle, truss, bale, burden, load **2** BAG, backpack, rucksack, haversack, knapsack, kitbag **3** GROUP, company, set, troop, crew, herd, flock, drove, band, bunch, crowd, gang, mob
▶ *v* **1** WRAP, wrap up, tie up, parcel, package, bundle, put in, cover, crate, stow, store **2** FILL, load, charge, cram, stuff, crowd, throng, mob, jam, press, squeeze, ram, wedge, compact, compress
▷ **pack in 1** CRAM IN, fill, load, charge, stuff, crowd, throng, mob, jam, press, squeeze, ram, wedge **2** STOP, end, give up, leave, resign, *colloq.* throw in, jack in, chuck
▷ **pack off** send, dismiss, dispatch, bundle off
▷ **pack up 1** TIDY UP, tidy away, clear up, put things away **2** STOP, finish, end, give up, *colloq.* throw in, jack in, wrap up, call it a day **3** BREAK DOWN, stop working, fail, *formal* malfunction, *colloq.* seize up, *slang* conk out

package *n, v*
▶ *n* **1** PARCEL, pack, packet, box, container, carton, bale, consignment **2** WHOLE, unit, group, set, entity, package deal
▶ *v* parcel (up), wrap (up), pack (up), gift-wrap, box, batch

packaging *n*
container, box, packet, packing, wrapping(s), wrapper(s), presentation

packed *adj*
filled, full, crammed, jammed, crowded, congested, brimful, overflowing, overloaded, *colloq.* jam-packed, chock-a-block, packed like sardines
☒ empty, deserted

packet *n*
1 PACK, carton, box, bag, package, parcel, case, container, wrapper, wrapping, packing, padded bag, padded envelope, Jiffy bag® **2** *cost a packet* a lot, lots, fortune, small fortune, king's ransom, *colloq.* mint, pile, pots, pretty penny, a bob or two, bomb, bundle, tidy sum

pact *n*
treaty, convention, covenant, bond, alliance, cartel, contract, deal, bargain, settlement, agreement, arrangement, entente, understanding, *formal* compact, concordat
☒ disagreement, quarrel

pad[1] *n, v*
▶ *n* **1** CUSHION, pillow, bolster, wad, wadding, buffer, padding, stuffing, protection **2** WRITING-PAD, notepad, jotter, notebook, block, *colloq.* memo pad **3** *an animal's pad* FOOT, paw, sole, print, footprint **4** HOME, place, room, rooms, quarters, penthouse, flat, apartment, *colloq.* hang-out
▶ *v* fill, stuff, wad, pack, wrap, line, cushion, protect
▷ **pad out** expand, inflate, fill out, amplify, elaborate, increase, flesh out, lengthen, stretch, spin out, *formal* augment, protract

pad[2] *v*
to pad softly walk, move, step, run, tread, trudge, tramp, tiptoe, lope

padding *n*
1 FILLING, stuffing, wadding, packing, cushioning, lining, protection **2** VERBOSITY, verboseness, wordiness, bombast, hot air, *formal* verbiage, prolixity, *colloq.* waffle

paddle[1] *n, v*
▶ *n the paddles of a canoe* oar, scull, sweep
▶ *v* row, oar, scull, propel, pull, punt, steer

paddle[2] *v*
children paddling in the water wade, splash, slop, dabble, plunge

paddock *n*
enclosure, field, pen, fold, yard, pound, compound, stockade, corral

paddy *n*
rage, tiff, temper, tantrum, fit of temper, fury, passion, taking, bate, *colloq.* pet

padlock *n*
lock, mortise lock, spring lock, fastening, bolt, clasp, catch

padre *n*
chaplain, minister, priest, pastor, vicar, cleric, curate, reverend, father, parson, rector, deacon, deaconess, clergyman, churchman

paean *n*
eulogy, song of praise, ode to joy, hymn, doxology, anthem, psalm, ovation, *formal* dithyramb, encomium, panegyric
🔁 denunciation, satire

pagan *n, adj*
▶ *n* heathen, atheist, unbeliever, nonbeliever, infidel, idolater, *formal* nullifidian
🔁 believer
▶ *adj* heathen, irreligious, atheistic, godless, infidel, idolatrous, pantheistic, *formal* nullifidian

page¹ *n*
1 *write on a new page* leaf, sheet, folio, side, recto, verso **2** *start a new page of your life* episode, incident, event, period, stage, chapter, phase, era, epoch

page² *n, v*
▶ *n a page at a wedding* pageboy, attendant, servant, messenger, bell-boy, footman, *US* bell-hop
▶ *v* call, ask for, send for, summon, bid, announce

pageant *n*
procession, parade, show, display, tableau, scene, play, representation, cavalcade, spectacle, extravaganza

pageantry *n*
pomp, ceremony, grandeur, magnificence, splendour, glamour, glitter, flourish, spectacle, parade, display, show, showiness, extravagance, theatricality, drama, melodrama

pail *n*
bucket, can, tub, bail, scuttle, pitcher, vessel, churn, piggin

pain *n, v*
▶ *n* **1** HURT, ache, throb, cramp, stitch, spasm, twinge, pang, stab, sting, smart, smarting, soreness, irritation, aching, throbbing, tenderness, discomfort, distress, suffering, trouble, anguish, agony, torment, torture, *formal* affliction **2** ANGUISH, grief, sorrow, agony, anxiety, desolation, distress, suffering, torment, torture, heartache, heartbreak, brokenheartedness, misery, pang, rack, woe, wretchedness, *formal* tribulation **3** NUISANCE, bother, pest, annoyance, vexation, burden, *colloq.* bore, drag, headache, pain in the neck/backside
▶ *v* **1** HURT, ache, be sore, sting, smart, irritate, be tender **2** AFFLICT, torment, torture, agonize, distress, worry, trouble, upset, make miserable, make anxious, sadden, grieve
🔁 **2** please, delight, gratify

pained *adj*
hurt, injured, wounded, stung, offended, aggrieved, reproachful, distressed, upset, worried, unhappy, sad, saddened, grieved, piqued, vexed
🔁 pleased, gratified

painful *adj*
1 SORE, tender, hurting, irritating, inflamed, aching, throbbing, smarting, stabbing, agonizing, excruciating **2** *a painful experience* unpleasant, disagreeable, distressing, upsetting, saddening, wretched, miserable, agonizing, disturbing, harrowing, traumatic, *formal* disquieting **3** EMBARRASSING, awkward, uncomfortable, disconcerting, distressing, upsetting, sensitive, mortifying, humiliating, shameful, shaming, *formal* discomfiting, *colloq.* touchy **4** HARD, difficult, tough, trying, exacting, laborious, tedious, arduous, rigorous, strenuous
🔁 **1** painless, soothing **2** pleasant, agreeable **4** easy, simple

painfully *adv*
distressingly, dreadfully, terribly, excessively, clearly, markedly, alarmingly, pitiably, pitifully, sadly, unfortunately, wretchedly, agonizingly, excruciatingly, woefully, deplorably

painkiller *n*
analgesic, anodyne, anaesthetic, palliative, sedative, drug, remedy, lenitive

painless *adj*
pain-free, trouble-free, effortless, easy, simple, undemanding, *colloq.* cushy, a piece of cake, child's play, like falling off a log, plain sailing
🔁 painful, difficult

pains *n*
trouble, bother, effort, labour, care, diligence, assiduousness
▷ **be at pains** be anxious, be concerned, make every effort, try hard, take care, bother, go to great lengths

painstaking *adj*
careful, meticulous, scrupulous, thorough, conscientious, attentive, diligent, assiduous, industrious, hardworking, dedicated, devoted, persevering, searching, *formal* punctilious, sedulous
🔁 careless, negligent

paint *n, v*
▶ *n* colour, colouring, pigment, colorant, vinyl, wash, dye, tint, stain
▶ *v* **1** COLOUR, dye, tint, stain, lacquer, varnish, glaze, apply, daub, wash, whitewash, coat, plaster, smear, cover, spray, respray, decorate, redecorate **2** PORTRAY, depict, tell, describe, narrate, draw, sketch, picture, evoke, represent, *formal* recount, delineate
▷ **paint the town red** celebrate, have/throw a party, rejoice, enjoy yourself, have fun, go out, *colloq.* rave, binge, have a ball, live it up, whoop it up, go out on the town, go on the razzle, kill the fatted calf, put the flags out

painter *n*
artist, colourist, oil painter, watercolourist, miniaturist, dauber, limner, depicter, *formal* delineator

painting *n*
oil painting, oil, watercolour, picture, portrait, landscape, portrayal, representation, likeness, still life, miniature, illustration, fresco, mural, *formal* delineation

Painting terms include :
abstract, alla prima, aquarelle, aquatint, art gallery, bleeding, bloom; brush, filbert brush, flat brush, round brush, sable brush; brush strokes, canvas, canvas board, capriccio, cartoon, charcoal, chiaroscuro, collage, composition, craquelure, diptych, drawing, easel, encaustic, facture, *fête champêtre, fête galante*, figurative, foreshortening, fresco, frieze, frottage, gallery, genre painting, gesso, gouache, grisaille, grotesque, hard edge, icon, illustration, impasto, landscape, mahlstick, miniature, monochrome, montage, mural, oil painting, paint, palette, palette knife, pastels, pastoral, paysage, pencil sketch, pentimento, perspective, picture, pieta, pigment, pochade box, pointillism, portrait, primer, scumble, seascape, secco, sfumato, sgraffito, silhouette, sketch, skyscape, still life, stipple, tempera, thinners, tint, tondo, tone, triptych, trompe l'oeil, turpentine, underpainting, vignette, wash, watercolour. *See also* ART; PICTURE.

pair *n, v*
▶ *n* couple, brace, two, twosome, duo, twins, two of a kind, set

► *v* match (up), twin, team (up), mate, marry, wed, unite, splice, join (up), couple, link (up), bracket, put together, arrange in pairs
F3 separate, part

paired *adj*
coupled, joined, linked, matched, double, twinned, in twos, yoked, mated, associated, bracketed
F3 single

pal *n*
friend, comrade, companion, partner, confidant(e), intimate, soul mate, *colloq.* buddy, chum, crony, mate, sidekick
F3 enemy, opponent

palace *n*
castle, château, mansion, stately home, basilica, dome

palatable *adj*
1 TASTY, appetizing, eatable, edible, flavoursome, flavorous, succulent, mouth-watering, savoury, *formal* delectable, *colloq.* yummy, morish, scrumptious, scrummy, done to a turn 2 ACCEPTABLE, satisfactory, pleasant, pleasing, nice, agreeable, enjoyable, attractive
F3 1 unpalatable 2 unacceptable, unpleasant, disagreeable

palate *n*
taste, sense of taste, appreciation, liking, relish, gout, enjoyment, enthusiasm, appetite, stomach, heart

palatial *adj*
grand, magnificent, splendid, majestic, regal, stately, grandiose, imposing, luxurious, de luxe, sumptuous, opulent, spacious, *colloq.* plush, posh, ritzy

palaver *n*
fuss, bother, fuss about nothing, rigmarole, procedure, carry-on, activity, business, bustle, commotion, fluster, *colloq.* song and dance, to-do, flap

pale[1] *adj, v*
► *adj* 1 PALLID, livid, ashen, ashy, white, whitish, colourless, chalky, pasty, pasty-faced, waxen, waxy, wan, peaky, sallow, anaemic, drained, *colloq.* washed-out 2 *pale blue* light, pastel, faded, bleached, colourless, insipid, vapid, weak, muted, feeble, thin, faint, dim, restrained, low-key, *formal* etiolated, *colloq.* washed-out
F3 1 ruddy 2 dark, strong, intense
► *v* 1 WHITEN, blanch, bleach, fade, dim, grow white, grow pale 2 *pale into insignificance* fade, dim, lessen, diminish, melt, dwindle
F3 1 colour, blush

pale[2] *n*
▷ **beyond the pale** *such behaviour is beyond the pale* unacceptable, intolerable, unreasonable, improper, unsuitable, inappropriate, inadmissible, *formal* unseemly

palisade *n*
fence, paling, defence, enclosure, barricade, bulwark, fortification, stockade

pall[1] *n*
a pall over a coffin; *a pall of smoke* shroud, veil, mantle, cloak, cloud, shadow, gloom, damper
▷ **cast a pall over** spoil, mar, upset, impair, harm, ruin, destroy, wreck

pall[2] *v*
interest began to pall wear off, tire, weary, become tired, become bored, lose its attraction, jade, sate, satiate, cloy, sicken

palliate *v*
ease, diminish, moderate, mollify, relieve, soften, soothe, temper, lessen, lighten, allay, alleviate, excuse, minimize, mitigate, cover, conceal, cloak,

formal abate, assuage, extenuate, lenify

palliative *adj, n*
► *adj* sedative, soothing, mollifying, alleviative, calming, lenitive, calmative, anodyne, *technical* demulcent, paregoric, *formal* mitigative, mitigatory, assuasive
F3 irritant
► *n* analgesic, anodyne, painkiller, sedative, tranquillizer, calmative, lenitive, *technical* demulcent, paregoric

pallid *adj*
1 PALE, pasty, whitish, sallow, colourless, pasty-faced, ashen, ashy, bloodless, anaemic, wan, waxen, waxy, whey-faced, *formal* etiolated, *Scot.* peelie-wally, formal etiolated 2 UNEXCITING, weak, dull, boring, uninteresting, bland, uninspired, tame, sterile, tired, lifeless, insipid, spiritless, vapid
F3 1 vigorous, ruddy, high-complexioned 2 lively, exciting

pallor *n*
paleness, whiteness, pallidness, wanness, sallowness, bloodlessness, chalkiness, *formal* etiolation
F3 ruddiness

pally *adj*
friendly, close, affectionate, familiar, intimate, *colloq.* chummy, thick
F3 unfriendly

palm *n, v*
► *n* hand, *colloq.* paw, *slang* mitt
► *v* take, grab, snatch, appropriate
▷ **palm off** foist, impose, fob off, thrust, offload, unload, pass off, get rid of

palmist *n*
fortune-teller, clairvoyant, palm reader

palmistry *n*
fortune-telling, clairvoyancy, palm reading, chirognomy, chiromancy

palmy *adj*
carefree, thriving, prosperous, flourishing, successful, fortunate, happy, glorious, triumphant, joyous, luxurious, golden, *formal* halcyon

palpable *adj*
1 SOLID, substantial, material, concrete, real, touchable, tangible 2 OBVIOUS, visible, apparent, clear, plain, evident, patent, conspicuous, glaring, blatant, unmistakable, *formal* manifest
F3 1 intangible 2 impalpable, imperceptible, elusive

palpitate *v*
flutter, quiver, tremble, shiver, vibrate, quake, shake, beat, pulse, pulsate, pound, thump, thud, throb

paltry *adj*
meagre, derisory, contemptible, mean, low, miserable, wretched, poor, sorry, small, slight, trifling, inconsiderable, negligible, trivial, minor, contemptible, petty, unimportant, insignificant, puny, worthless, *colloq.* measly, piddling
F3 substantial, significant, valuable

pamper *v*
spoil, cosset, coddle, mollycoddle, humour, gratify, indulge, overindulge, pander, pet, fondle, *colloq.* spoonfeed, wait on someone hand and foot
F3 neglect, ill-treat

pampered *adj*
spoilt, cosseted, coddled, mollycoddled, indulged, overfed, high-fed, petted
F3 abused, neglected

pamphlet *n*
leaflet, brochure, booklet, folder, circular, handout, notice

pan[1] *n, v*
► *n* pots and pans saucepan, frying-pan, fryer, pot,

skillet, casserole, wok, container, vessel, pancheon
► *v* criticize, censure, flay, find fault with, hammer, *colloq.* knock, pull to pieces, roast, rubbish, slam, slate
Ⅎ praise
▷ **pan out** work out, turn out, result, happen, yield, culminate, come to an end, be exhausted, *formal* eventuate

pan² *v*
pan the camera sweep, scan, move, turn, follow, track, swing, circle, *formal* traverse

panacea *n*
cure-all, universal remedy, elixir, nostrum, *formal* catholicon, diacatholicon, panpharmacon

panache *n*
flourish, flamboyance, ostentation, style, flair, élan, dash, spirit, enthusiasm, zest, brio, energy, vigour, verve

pancake *n*
crêpe, waffle, wafer, blini, griddle-cake, tortilla, *Scot.* bannock, *US* battercake, flapjack

pandemic *adj*
widespread, extensive, general, common, prevalent, far-reaching, rife, pervasive, universal, global

pandemonium *n*
chaos, disorder, confusion, commotion, rumpus, turmoil, turbulence, tumult, uproar, din, bedlam, hubbub, hullabaloo, hue and cry, *colloq.* to-do
Ⅎ order, calm, peace

pander *v*
▷ **pander to** humour, indulge, pamper, please, gratify, satisfy, fulfil, provide, cater to

panegyric *n, adj*
► *n* eulogy, praise, tribute, commendation, homage, accolade, citation, *formal* paean, encomium, eulogium
Ⅎ censure, criticism
► *adj* eulogistic, favourable, flattering, glowing, praiseful, praising, complimentary, commendatory, *formal* encomiastic, laudatory, panegyrical
Ⅎ censorious, critical, damning

panel *n*
1 *a wooden panel* board, sheet, slab, plank, beam, timber, cartouche **2** *a panel of judges* board, committee, council, jury, team, commission, directorate, trustees, advisory group **3** *a control panel* board, console, dashboard, instrument panel, instruments, controls, switches, knobs, dials, buttons, levers

panelling *n*
panel-work, wainscot, wainscot(t)ing, dado

pang *n*
pain, ache, twinge, stab, sting, prick, stitch, gripe, spasm, throe, misgiving, scruple, qualm, agony, anguish, uneasiness, discomfort, distress

panic *n, v*
► *n* agitation, alarm, dismay, fright, fear, horror, terror, frenzy, hysteria, *formal* consternation, disquiet, trepidation, perturbation, *colloq.* flap
Ⅎ calmness, confidence
► *v* lose your nerve, lose your head, overreact, unnerve, *colloq.* flap, go to pieces, lose your cool, have kittens, get the jitters, get the shakes, get the willies, feel your hair stand on end, run round like a headless chicken
Ⅎ relax

panic-stricken *adj*
alarmed, frightened, horrified, terrified, terror-stricken, petrified, scared, scared stiff, aghast, in a cold sweat, panicky, frantic, frenzied, hysterical, *formal* perturbed, *colloq.* in a tizzy

Ⅎ relaxed, confident

panoply *n*
array, range, equipment, show, regalia, insignia, armour, dress, raiment, trappings, *formal* attire, *colloq.* garb, gear, get-up, turn-out

panorama *n*
view, wide/broad view, bird's eye view, vista, prospect, scenery, landscape, scene, spectacle, perspective, overview, survey

panoramic *adj*
scenic, wide, broad, sweeping, extensive, far-reaching, wide-ranging, widespread, overall, comprehensive, general, universal
Ⅎ narrow, restricted, limited

pant *v, n*
► *v* **1** PUFF, blow, gasp, wheeze, breathe, sigh, heave, throb, palpitate, *colloq.* huff and puff **2** LONG, pine, desire, want, yearn, covet, crave, hanker, sigh, ache, thirst, *colloq.* yen
► *n* gasp, puff, huff, throb, wheeze

panting *adj*
1 PUFFED OUT, breathless, out of breath, gasping, short-winded, winded, puffing, puffed **2** ANXIOUS, eager, impatient, longing, craving, hankering

pantomime *n*
show, charade, farce, commedia dell'arte, harlequinade, masque, *colloq.* panto

pants *n*
1 UNDERPANTS, drawers, panties, briefs, knickers, camiknickers, teddy, panty girdle, Y-fronts, boxer shorts, trunks, shorts, *colloq.* undies, smalls, frillies **2** TROUSERS, slacks, jeans

pap *n*
1 MUSH, pulp, purée, soft food, semi-liquid food, *colloq.* goo **2** RUBBISH, drivel, trash, nonsense, gibberish, *colloq.* rot, claptrap, *slang* crap

paper *n, v*
► *n* **1** NEWSPAPER, daily, broadsheet, tabloid, magazine, periodical, weekly, journal, organ, *colloq.* rag **2** DOCUMENT, credential, authorization, identification, identity card, ID, certificate, record, deed, paperwork, *colloq.* red tape **3** *a paper on alternative medicine* essay, composition, dissertation, thesis, treatise, article, study, report, work, examination, analysis, *formal* monograph
▷ **on paper 1** IN WRITING, written down, officially, on the record, recorded, in black and white **2** IN THEORY, hypothetically, ideally, theoretically, seemingly, in your mind's eye

Types of paper include:
art paper, bank, blotting paper, bond, carbon paper, cartridge paper, crêpe paper, graph paper, greaseproof paper, manila, notepaper, parchment, rice paper, silver paper, sugar paper, tissue paper, toilet paper, tracing paper, vellum, wallpaper, wrapping paper, writing-paper; card, cardboard, pasteboard; A4, foolscap, quarto, atlas, crown.

► *v* ▷ **paper over** hide, conceal, cover up, obscure, put out of sight, disguise, camouflage

papery *adj*
thin, paper-thin, light, lightweight, delicate, insubstantial, flimsy, fragile, frail, translucent

par *n*
level, standard, norm, usual, correspondence, similarity, equivalence, equal footing, equality, balance, equilibrium, accordance, average, mean, *technical* median, *formal* parity
▷ **below par 1** UNSATISFACTORY, inadequate, infer-

ior, below average, not up to par, *colloq.* not up to scratch **2** UNWELL, under par, tired, out of sorts, *colloq.* under the weather
▷ **on a par with** equal to, equivalent to, as good as, the same standard as
▷ **par for the course** typical, normal, standard, usual, predictable, only to be expected

parable *n*
fable, allegory, lesson, moral tale, story, story with a moral

parade *n, v*
▶ *n* **1** PROCESSION, cavalcade, motorcade, march, column, file, train, progression, review, ceremony **2** SPECTACLE, pageant, show, display, demonstration, exhibition, *formal* array
▶ *v* **1** MARCH, process, file past **2** SHOW, display, exhibit, show off, vaunt, flaunt, brandish

paradigm *n*
pattern, model, example, original, ideal, framework, prototype, *formal* archetype, exemplar

paradise *n*
1 HEAVEN, home of God, bliss, next world, hereafter, life to come, afterlife, utopia, Elysium, elysian fields, happy hunting ground, Shangri-la, Eden, Garden of Eden **2** ECSTASY, rapture, bliss, happiness, complete happiness, joy, delight, transports of Delight, *formal* felicity, *colloq.* seventh heaven
⊟ 1 hell, Hades

paradox *n*
contradiction, inconsistency, absurdity, oddity, mystery, enigma, riddle, puzzle, *formal* incongruity, anomaly

paradoxical *adj*
self-contradictory, contradictory, conflicting, inconsistent, absurd, illogical, improbable, impossible, mysterious, enigmatic, puzzling, baffling, *formal* incongruous, anomalous

paragon *n*
ideal, epitome, model, pattern, crème de la crème, masterpiece, prototype, standard, criterion, *formal* exemplar, quintessence, archetype, nonpareil, *colloq.* the bee's knees

paragraph *n*
passage, section, part, portion, segment, subsection, subdivision, article, piece, clause, item

parallel *adj, n, v*
▶ *adj* **1** ALIGNED, equidistant, alongside, coextensive, collateral **2** SIMILAR, like, matching, resembling, equivalent, comparable, uniform, corresponding, *formal* analogous, homologous
⊟ 2 divergent, different
▶ *n* **1** MATCH, equal, twin, duplicate, equivalent, counterpart, *formal* analogue **2** SIMILARITY, resemblance, likeness, correspondence, equivalence, analogy, comparison, *formal* correlation
▶ *v* match, echo, be similar to, resemble, be like, be equivalent, equal, conform, agree, correspond, compare, liken, *formal* be analogous, correlate
⊟ diverge, differ

paralyse *v*
1 *paralysed his leg* cripple, lame, disable, incapacitate, immobilize, anaesthetize, numb, dull, deaden, freeze, shock, terrify, transfix, *formal* debilitate **2** *paralyse the transport system* bring to a standstill, immobilize, cripple, halt, stop, disable

paralysed *adj*
paralytic, paraplegic, quadriplegic, crippled, lame, disabled, incapacitated, immobilized, numb
⊟ able-bodied

paralysis *n*
1 *paralysis in the legs* paraplegia, quadriplegia, palsy,

numbness, deadness, immobility, powerlessness, *technical* paresis, *formal* debilitation **2** *paralysis of the transport system* standstill, halt, stoppage, shutdown, breakdown, immobility

paralytic *adj*
1 CRIPPLED, disabled, paralysed, incapacitated, lame, immobilized, immobile, numb, palsied, quadriplegic, monoplegic, hemiplegic **2** DRUNK, inebriated, intoxicated, *colloq.* legless, plastered, pie-eyed, *slang* stoned, sloshed, smashed, stewed
⊟ 2 (stone-cold) sober

parameter *n*
variable, guideline, indication, criterion, specification, factor, limiting factor, limitation, restriction, framework, limit, boundary

paramount *adj*
supreme, highest, topmost, predominant, pre-eminent, prime, principal, main, chief, outstanding, cardinal, primary, first, foremost, first and foremost, most important, of greatest importance
⊟ lowest, last

paramour *n*
lover, beloved, beau, courtesan, mistress, woman, kept woman, inamorato, inamorata, concubine, hetaera, *colloq.* fancy man, fancy woman, bit on the side

paranoia *n*
obsession, delusions, psychosis, megalomania, monomania, persecution complex

paranoid *adj*
suspicious, distrustful, bewildered, confused, afraid, fearful, fazed

parapet *n*
1 WALL, railing, fence, rail, paling, barrier **2** EMBANKMENT, defence, guard, battlement, bulwark, fortification, rampart, barbican, bastion

paraphernalia *n*
equipment, gear, tackle, apparatus, tools, implements, materials, accessories, trappings, belongings, possessions, stuff, things, baggage, *formal* effects, accoutrements, *colloq.* bits and pieces, odds and ends

paraphrase *v, n*
▶ *v* reword, rephrase, restate, put in other words, express differently, interpret, render, translate, gloss, *colloq.* rehash
▶ *n* rewording, rephrasing, restatement, different expression, other form of words, version, interpretation, rendering, translation, gloss

parasite *n*
1 LEECH, bloodsucker, *technical* endophyte, entozoon, endozoon, epiphyte, epizoon, epizoan **2** *parasites in society* hanger-on, passenger, leech, drone, bloodsucker, *colloq.* sponger, scrounger, cadger, freeloader, bum, moocher

parasitic *adj*
1 *parasitic animals* parasitical, biogenous, leechlike, *technical* epizoan, epizoic **2** *a parasitic person* bloodsucking, freeloading, *colloq.* cadging, scrounging, sponging

parcel *n, v*
▶ *n* **1** PACKAGE, packet, pack, box, carton, bundle **2** *a parcel of land* plot, patch, area, piece, portion, lot, allotment, tract **3** GROUP, company, troop, herd, flock, band, crowd, gang, mob **4** LOT, deal, transaction, package, pack, collection
▶ *v* package, pack (up), wrap (up), gift-wrap, bundle (up), tie up
▷ **parcel out** divide (out), carve up, apportion, allocate, allot, share out, distribute, hand out, dispense,

dole out, deal out, mete out

parch *v*
dry (up), dehydrate, bake, burn, scorch, sear, blister, wither, shrivel, *formal* desiccate

parched *adj*
1 ARID, waterless, dry, dried up, dehydrated, baked, burnt, seared, blistered, scorched, withered, shrivelled, *formal* desiccated, sear, sere, *colloq.* dry as a bone **2** THIRSTY, dry, dehydrated, *colloq.* gasping

parchment *n*
scroll, vellum, document, certificate, charter, diploma, palimpsest

pardon *v, n*
▶ *v* forgive, condone, overlook, excuse, absolve, let off, reprieve, free, liberate, release, *formal* vindicate, acquit, remit, exonerate, exculpate, *colloq.* let off the hook
⊟ punish, discipline
▶ *n* forgiveness, mercy, clemency, indulgence, forbearance, lenience, amnesty, excuse, absolution, reprieve, release, discharge, *formal* acquittal, condonation, exoneration, exculpation
⊟ punishment, condemnation

pardonable *adj*
forgivable, excusable, justifiable, warrantable, understandable, allowable, permissible, slight, minor, venial, condonable
⊟ inexcusable

pare *v*
peel, skin, shear, clip, trim, crop, cut, dock, lop, prune, cut back, whittle, reduce, decrease

parent *n, v*
▶ *n* **1** *a single parent* father, mother, biological/birth parent, single parent, guardian, foster parent, custodial parent, dam, sire, *old use* begetter, *formal* progenitor, procreator **2** SOURCE, origin, root, cause, creator, originator, author, architect, prototype, forerunner
▶ *v* be the father/mother of, bring into the world, create, look after, take care of, nurture, bring up, raise, foster, educate, teach, train, *old use* beget, *formal* rear, procreate

parentage *n*
family, birth, origin, source, stock, extraction, filiation, affiliation, ancestry, lineage, derivation, descent, line, race, pedigree, paternity, *formal* stirps

parenthetical *adj*
in parenthesis, incidental, qualifying, explanatory, bracketed, inserted, extraneous, *formal* elucidative, interposed, intervening
⊟ basic, original

pariah *n*
outcast, outlaw, exile, castaway, leper, undesirable, unperson, untouchable, Ishmael, *colloq.* black sheep

paring *n*
peel, peeling, skin, shaving, shred, clipping, trimming, fragment, cutting, flake, rind, slice, sliver, snippet, flaught

parish *n*
1 DISTRICT, community, village, town **2** PARISHIONERS, church, churchgoers, congregation, flock, fold

parity *n*
equality, equivalence, parallelism, consistency, conformity, analogy, agreement, correspondence, similarity, resemblance, likeness, sameness, uniformity, unity, semblance, affinity, par, *formal* congruence, congruity, consonance, similitude

park *n, v*
▶ *n* grounds, woodland, grassland

Types of park include:
amusement park, arboretum, botanical garden, car park, estate, game reserve, industrial park, municipal park, national park, park-and-ride, parking lot, parkland, play area, playground, pleasance, pleasure garden, pleasure ground, recreation ground, reserve, sanctuary, theme park, wildlife park.

▶ *v* put, position, place, deposit, set, leave, stop, *colloq.* plonk

parlance *n*
phraseology, language, talk, speech, tongue, idiom, jargon, diction, argot, cant, *colloq.* lingo

parley *n, v*
▶ *n* talk(s), negotiation, meeting, conference, council, deliberation, discussion, get together, dialogue, tête-à-tête, *formal* colloquy, *colloq.* confab, powwow
▶ *v* talk, speak, discuss, negotiate, consult, deliberate, *formal* confer, *colloq.* powwow

parliament *n*
legislature, senate, congress, house, lower house, upper house, assembly, convocation, council, diet

parliamentary *adj*
governmental, senatorial, congressional, legislative, law-making, law-giving, elected, democratic, popular, representative, official, republican, *formal* legislatorial

parliaments and political assemblies

Names of parliaments and political assemblies include:
House of Representatives, Senate (*Australia*); Nationalrat, Bundesrat (*Austria*); Narodno Sobraniye (*Bulgaria*); House of Commons, Senate (*Canada*); National People's Congress (*China*); Folketing (*Denmark*); People's Assembly (*Egypt*); Eduskunta (*Finland*); National Assembly, Senate (*France*); Bundesrat, Bundestag, Landtag (*Germany*); Althing (*Iceland*); Lok Sabha, Rajya Sabha (*India*); Majlis (*Iran*); Dáil, Seanad (*Ireland*); Knesset (*Israel*); Camera dei Deputati, Senato (*Italy*); Diet (*Japan*); Staten-Generaal (*Netherlands*); House of Representatives (*New Zealand*); Storting (*Norway*); Sejm (*Poland*); Cortes (*Portugal*); Congress of People's Deputies, Supreme Soviet (*Russia*); House of Assembly (*South Africa*); Cortes (*Spain*); Riksdag (*Sweden*); Nationalrat, Ständerat, Bundesrat (*Switzerland*); Porte (*Turkey*); House of Commons, House of Lords (*UK*); House of Representatives, Senate (*US*); National Assembly (*Vietnam*).

---

parochial *adj*
insular, provincial, parish-pump, small-town, petty, small-minded, narrow-minded, narrow, inward-looking, blinkered, limited, restricted, confined, *colloq.* hick
⊟ national, international

parochialism *n*
insularity, provincialism, small-mindedness, pettiness, narrow-mindedness, narrowness

parody *n, v*
▶ *n* caricature, lampoon, burlesque, satire, pasquinade, skit, mimicry, imitation, travesty, distortion, corruption, misrepresentation, perversion, *colloq.* send-up, spoof, take-off
▶ *v* caricature, lampoon, burlesque, satirize, mimic, imitate, ape, *colloq.* send up, spoof, take off

paroxysm n
fit, seizure, spasm, convulsion, attack, eruption, flare-up, outbreak, outburst, explosion

parrot v, n
▶ v repeat, copy, imitate, mimic, echo, rehearse, reiterate, ape
▶ n mimic, repeater, imitator, copy-cat, phraser, ape

parrot-fashion adv
by rote, mechanically, mindlessly, unthinkingly, automatically

parry v
ward off, fend off, repel, repulse, rebuff, field, deflect, stave off, block, avert, turn aside, avoid, evade, keep/hold at bay, sidestep, steer clear of, shun, formal circumvent, colloq. duck, dodge

parsimonious adj
mean, niggardly, miserly, tight-fisted, stinting, sparing, scrimpy, saving, close, cheese-paring, close-fisted, close-handed, frugal, grasping, formal penurious, colloq. mingy, penny-pinching, stingy, tight
F3 generous, liberal, open-handed

parsimony n
meanness, miserliness, frugality, niggardliness, tight-fistedness, colloq. minginess, penny-pinching, stinginess, tightness
F3 generosity, liberality

parson n
vicar, rector, priest, minister, pastor, preacher, clergyman, reverend, cleric, churchman

part n, v, adj
▶ n 1 COMPONENT, constituent, module, element, factor, ingredient, side, dimension, aspect, facet, piece, bit, particle, fragment, slice, scrap, segment, fraction, proportion, percentage, portion, extract, excerpt, share, section, division, department, branch, sector, wing 2 ROLE, character, duty, job, work, charge, task, responsibility, chore, office, function, capacity, involvement, participation 3 SECTION, chapter, volume, book, passage, scene, episode, instalment 4 AREA, district, sector, region, neighbourhood, territory, quarter 5 a person of many parts skill, gift, talent, ability, capability, attribute, accomplishment, faculty, endowment, expertise, genius, intellect, intelligence, calibre
F3 1 whole, totality
▷ **for the most part** by and large, on the whole, generally, usually, mostly, mainly, in the main, chiefly, largely, commonly
▷ **in part** to some degree, partly, somewhat, to some extent, to a certain extent, to a certain degree, up to a point, slightly
▷ **take part in** join in, be involved in, participate in, share in, engage in, help with, assist in, play a part in, play a role in, contribute to, formal partake
▶ v 1 SEPARATE, detach, disconnect, sever, split, tear, break, break up, take apart, dismantle, come apart, split up, divide, formal disjoin, cleave 2 PART COMPANY WITH, split up from, separate from, divorce from, get divorced from, leave, withdraw from, go away from, go your separate ways, depart from, take your leave, say goodbye, get going, colloq. push along/off, split, scarper, clear off, take off, hit the road/trail, make tracks 3 DISPERSE, separate, diverge, disband, scatter, split up, break up
F3 1, 2 join
▷ **part with** relinquish, let go of, give up, yield, surrender, renounce, forego, abandon, discard, jettison
F3 hold onto
▶ adj partial, half, not complete, limited, restricted, imperfect, fragmentary, unfinished

partake v
take part, share, participate, be involved, engage, enter
▷ **partake of 1** partake of food consume, eat, drink 2 partake of the divine nature receive, share, have, show, demonstrate, take, suggest, evoke, formal evince, manifest

partial adj
1 a partial victory incomplete, in part, part, limited, restricted, imperfect, fragmentary, unfinished 2 BIASED, prejudiced, partisan, one-sided, discriminatory, preferential, unfair, unjust, inequitable, coloured, affected, formal predisposed
F3 1 complete, total 2 impartial, disinterested, unbiased, fair
▷ **partial to** fond of, liking, loving, keen on, taken with, with a weakness for, formal with a penchant for, colloq. crazy about, mad about, with a soft spot for

partiality n
1 BIAS, prejudice, discrimination, unfairness, injustice, inequity, inequitableness, partisanship 2 LIKING, fondness, love, inclination, preference, formal predilection, predisposition, proclivity

partially adv
incompletely, not fully, fractionally, somewhat, in part, partly

participant n
entrant, competitor, contestant, contributor, participator, member, party, co-operator, helper, associate, partner, worker, sharer, shareholder

participate v
take part, join in, contribute, engage, be involved, be associated, enter, share, play a part, play a role, co-operate, help, assist, formal partake

participation n
involvement, sharing, partnership, co-operation, contribution, assistance, association, formal partaking

particle n
bit, piece, fragment, scrap, trace, touch, shred, sliver, speck, morsel, mite, crumb, iota, whit, jot, tittle, atom, molecule, grain, drop, colloq. smidgen, tad

parti-coloured adj
motley, variegated, piebald, formal polychromatic, polychromic, versicoloured
F3 monochromatic, plain

particular adj, n
▶ adj 1 on that particular day specific, precise, exact, distinct, certain, individual, special, peculiar 2 EXCEPTIONAL, remarkable, notable, marked, outstanding, thorough, unusual, uncommon, peculiar, notable, noteworthy, formal especial 3 FUSSY, discriminating, finicky, fastidious, selective, meticulous, painstaking, exacting, colloq. choosy, pernickety, picky 4 EXACT, detailed, thorough, precise, faithful, accurate
F3 1 general
▶ n detail, specific, point, feature, item, fact, circumstance
▷ **in particular** particularly, especially, specifically, exactly, precisely, to be specific, in detail

particularity n
feature, trait, detail, instance, fact, item, circumstance, characteristic, idiosyncrasy, individuality, point, property, distinctiveness, uniqueness, peculiarity, quirk, singularity

particularize v
detail, specify, itemize, stipulate, individualize, enumerate, formal individuate

particularly adv
especially, exceptionally, remarkably, notably, mark-

edly, extraordinarily, unusually, uncommonly, surprisingly, in particular, specifically, explicitly, distinctly, expressly

parting *n, adj*
▶ *n* **1** DEPARTURE, going, leaving, leave-taking, farewell, goodbye, adieu, *formal* valediction **2** DIVERGENCE, separation, divorce, division, partition, rift, split, rupture, breaking, breaking-up
🔁 **1** meeting **2** convergence
▶ *adj* departing, leaving, farewell, goodbye, last, dying, final, closing, concluding, *formal* valedictory
🔁 first, arriving, opening

partisan *n, adj*
▶ *n* **1** SUPPORTER, devotee, adherent, follower, party man, disciple, backer, upholder, champion, fan, votary, stalwart **2** GUERRILLA, irregular, freedom fighter, resistance fighter
▶ *adj* biased, prejudiced, unfair, unjust, inequitable, partial, predisposed, discriminatory, one-sided, factional, sectarian
🔁 impartial

partisanship *n*
bias, prejudice, partiality, partyism, sectarianism, factionalism
🔁 impartiality

partition *n, v*
▶ *n* **1** DIVIDER, barrier, wall, dividing wall, panel, screen, room-divider, dividing screen, separator, *technical* membrane, diaphragm **2** DIVISION, break-up, splitting, separation, segregation, parting, severance, subdivision
▶ *v* **1** SEPARATE, separate off, divide, subdivide, bar, wall off, fence off, screen (off) **2** SHARE, divide (up), split up, break up, segregate, sever, parcel out

partly *adv*
somewhat, to some extent, to some degree, a little, to a certain extent, to a certain degree, up to a point, slightly, fractionally, in some measure, moderately, relatively, in part, partially, incompletely, half
🔁 completely, totally, fully, wholly

partner *n*
1 ASSOCIATE, ally, confederate, colleague, co-worker, team-mate, collaborator, co-operator, accomplice, helper, mate, companion, comrade, consort, spouse, husband, wife, *colloq.* sidekick, oppo **2** *bring your partner to the party* spouse, husband, wife, boyfriend, girlfriend, friend, companion, consort, *colloq.* other half

partnership *n*
1 *the partnership between teachers and parents* association, alliance, co-operation, collaboration, participation, sharing, confederation, affiliation, combination, union, fellowship, fraternity, brotherhood **2** *a business partnership* company, firm, corporation, syndicate, co-operative, association, society, conglomerate

party *n*
1 CELEBRATION, festivity, social, get-together, gathering, reunion, function, reception, at-home **2** *a search party* team, squad, crew, gang, band, group, body, company, unit, contingent, detachment **3** *a political party* faction, side, league, cabal, alliance, association, affiliation, grouping, camp, combination **4** PERSON, individual, litigant, plaintiff, defendant

parvenu *n*
upstart, pretender, climber, arriviste, *nouveau riche*, new rich, vulgarian

pass¹ *v, n*
▶ *v* **1** GO, move, proceed, travel, progress, flow, run, drive, make your way **2** OVERTAKE, go past, drive/run past, outdistance, outstrip, beat, lose, lap, leave

behind, draw level with, pull ahead of, overhaul **3** GO THROUGH, go across, go over, get across, get over, run, move, traverse **4** *pass the salt* hand, give, reach, let someone have, transfer, transmit **5** *time passes quickly* go by, go past, elapse, proceed, advance, slip by, slip away, drag **6** *pass time wisely* spend, fill, occupy, employ, use up, take up, devote, while away **7** EXCEED, surpass, go beyond, go over, outdo, outstrip **8** *pass an exam* succeed, be successful in, get through, qualify, graduate, pass with flying colours, sail/breeze through, scrape through **9** *the examiner passed him* declare successful, approve, accept, declare satisfactory **10** *pass a new law* enact, ratify, validate, adopt, authorize, sanction, approve, vote for, agree to, accept **11** *pass from one state to another* CHANGE, go, move, turn, become, develop, transfer, evolve **12** HAPPEN, take place, occur, come about, *formal* transpire, befall **13** *the estate passed to her daughter* be left, be willed, be bequeathed, be inherited, be made over, be given, be handed down, be endowed, be granted, be consigned, transfer **14** *pass the ball* throw, kick, move, swing, lunge **15** *pass urine* discharge, expel, emit, let out, release, *formal* excrete
🔁 **2** fall behind **7** fail to reach **8** fail **9** fail
▷ **pass as/for** appear to be, be taken for, be mistaken for, be regarded as
▷ **pass away** die, pass on, *formal* expire, decease, *colloq.* give up the ghost, peg out, pop off, kick the bucket
▷ **pass off 1** HAPPEN, occur, take place, go off **2** *the effects passed off quickly* wear off, fade away, die down, disappear, vanish **3** FEIGN, counterfeit, fake, palm off
▷ **pass out 1** FAINT, lose consciousness, black out, collapse, drop *colloq.* flake out, keel over **2** GIVE OUT, hand out, distribute, deal out, allocate, allot, share out, dole out
▷ **pass over** disregard, ignore, overlook, miss, omit, leave, neglect, forget, take no notice of, not take into consideration, turn a blind eye to, turn a deaf ear to
▷ **pass up** not take advantage of, ignore, miss, refuse, neglect, reject, let slip
▶ *n* **1** THROW, kick, move, lunge, swing **2** PERMIT, passport, visa, identification, ticket, licence, authorization, warrant, permission **3** *make a pass at someone* advances, approach, overture, suggestion, proposition, play

pass² *n*
a pass through the mountains col, defile, gorge, ravine, canyon, gap, passage

passable *adj*
1 SATISFACTORY, acceptable, allowable, tolerable, average, ordinary, unexceptional, moderate, fair, adequate, all right, mediocre, *colloq.* OK, run-of-the-mill, so-so, nothing to write home about, not much cop, no great shakes **2** CLEAR, unobstructed, unblocked, open, navigable, traversable
🔁 **1** unacceptable, excellent **2** obstructed, blocked, impassable

passably *adv*
fairly, rather, somewhat, tolerably, relatively, reasonably, moderately, after a fashion

passage *n*
1 PASSAGEWAY, aisle, corridor, hall, hallway, lobby, vestibule, doorway, opening, entrance, exit **2** THOROUGHFARE, way, route, road, avenue, path, track, lane, alley **3** CHANNEL, duct, conduit, main, groove, furrow, trough, gutter, gully, canal, flume, watercourse, waterway, strait, neck, sound **4** MOVEMENT, flow, running, course **5** TRANSITION, progress, advance, change, transfer, turning, development, *technical* mutation, metamorphosis **6** *the passage of a*

bill acceptance, approval, adoption, authorization, validation, sanction, enactment, ratification **7** *grant passage through a country* access, admission, permission to travel through, safe conduct **8** EXTRACT, excerpt, quotation, text, paragraph, section, piece, clause, verse, *formal* citation **9** JOURNEY, voyage, trip, crossing, tour, trek

passageway *n*
passage, corridor, hall, hallway, lobby, entrance, exit, aisle, lane, path, way, track, alley

passé *adj*
outdated, old-fashioned, out of date, dated, obsolete, outmoded, unfashionable, outworn, *démodé*, antiquated, past its best, *colloq.* old hat, out
F₃ fashionable, in

passenger *n*
1 TRAVELLER, voyager, commuter, rider, fare, farepayer, hitchhiker **2** *get rid of passengers who don't work* hanger-on, drone, *colloq.* freeloader, sponger, bum

passer-by *n*
bystander, witness, looker-on, onlooker, observer, spectator, eyewitness, *colloq.* rubberneck, gawper

passing *adj, n*
▶ *adj* **1** SHORT-LIVED, temporary, momentary, transitional, fleeting, brief, short, *formal* ephemeral, transient **2** CASUAL, incidental, cursory, hasty, quick, slight, superficial, shallow
F₃ 1 lasting, permanent
▶ *n* death, departure, passing away, perishing, end, finish, loss, *formal* decease, demise, expiration, quietus, termination
▷ **in passing** incidentally, by the way, parenthetically, *en passant*, *colloq.* by the by(e)

passion *n*
1 FEELING, emotion, ardour, zeal, fervour, warmth, heat, spirit, intensity, fire, vehemence **2** OUTBURST, explosion, anger, indignation, wrath, rage, fit, temper, fury, tantrum **3** LOVE, desire, sexual desire, ardour, lust, adoration, infatuation, fondness, affection, craving **4** ENTHUSIASM, obsession, mania, craze, fascination, eagerness, keenness, avidity, zest, fanaticism, zeal
F₃ 1 coolness, indifference

passionate *adj*
1 ARDENT, fervent, eager, keen, avid, enthusiastic, fanatical, zealous, warm, hot, fiery, inflamed, aroused, excited, impassioned, intense, strong, fierce, vehement, violent, stormy, tempestuous, wild, frenzied **2** EMOTIONAL, excitable, hot-headed, intense, impetuous, impulsive, frenzied, quick-tempered, irritable **3** LOVING, affectionate, ardent, aroused, lustful, erotic, sexy, sensual, sultry, *colloq.* turned on, randy
F₃ 1 phlegmatic, *colloq.* laid back **3** frigid

passionless *adj*
emotionless, unfeeling, unemotional, unloving, impassive, calm, cold, cold-hearted, frigid, callous, frosty, icy, cold-blooded, apathetic, restrained, unresponsive, uncaring, indifferent, insensible, uninvolved, detached, dispassionate, impartial, neutral, withdrawn
F₃ passionate, caring, sensitive, sympathetic

passive *adj*
1 DOCILE, receptive, unassertive, yielding, submissive, unresisting, non-violent, patient, resigned, compliant, long-suffering **2** UNEMOTIONAL, apathetic, lifeless, emotionless, unmoved, indifferent, detached, distant, uninvolved, unenterprising, non-participating, remote, aloof, dispassionate, inert, inactive
F₃ 1 involved, lively, active **2** responsive

passport *n*
1 *show your passport at the border* travel documents, papers, identity card, ID, visa, permit, pass, authorization, laissez-passer **2** *the passport to success* key, entry, door, doorway, avenue, path, way, route, admission, means of access

password *n*
watchword, signal, key, word, open sesame, parole, shibboleth, countersign

past *adj, n*
▶ *adj* **1** OVER, ended, finished, completed, done, over and done with **2** FORMER, previous, preceding, foregoing, foregone, late, sometime, last, latter, recent, *formal* erstwhile **3** ANCIENT, bygone, olden, early, gone, gone by, elapsed, long ago, no more, extinct, defunct, forgotten
F₃ 2 future, next
▶ *n* **1** *in the past* history, former times, olden days, olden times, days gone by, bygone times/days, good old days, antiquity, *formal* days of yore **2** LIFE, background, experience, record, track record
F₃ 1 future

pasta *n*

Forms and shapes of pasta include:
agnolotti, anelli, angel's hair, bombolotti, bucatini, cannelloni, capelletti, casarecci, conchiglie, crescioni, ditali, elbow macaroni, farfalline, fedelini, fettuccine, fiochetti, fusilli, gnocchi, lasagne, lasagne verde, linguini, lumache, macaroni, mafalde, manicotti, maruzze, mezzani, noodle, noodle farfel, penne, pennine, ravioli, rigatoni, ruoti, spaghetti, spaghetti bolognese, stelline, tagliatelle, tortellini, trofie, vermicelli, ziti.

paste *n, v*
▶ *n* **1** ADHESIVE, glue, gum, mastic, putty, cement **2** *fish paste* pap, pulp, mush, blend, purée, spread, mixture
▶ *v* stick, glue, gum, cement, fix, fasten

pastel *adj, n*
▶ *adj* soft, soft-hued, light, light-coloured, pale, delicate, subtle, discreet, muted, low-key, subdued, faint
▶ *n* **1** CHALK, crayon, pastille **2** DRAWING, sketch, vignette

pastiche *n*
assortment, mixture, mix, miscellany, variety, melange, potpourri, hotchpotch, hodgepodge, confusion, farrago, salmagundi, smorgasbord, mish, collection, medley, patchwork, gallimaufry, jumble, *formal* conglomeration, *colloq.* mixed bag, mishmash, omnium-gatherum

pastille *n*
lozenge, pastel, sweet, tablet, cough sweet, cough drop, confection, jujube, troche

pastime *n*
hobby, activity, leisure activity, game, sport, recreation, play, fun, amusement, entertainment, diversion, distraction, relaxation
F₃ work, employment

past master *n*
expert, proficient, virtuoso, adept, artist, *colloq.* ace, old hand, dab hand, wizard
F₃ incompetent

pastor *n*
minister, clergyman, priest, rector, vicar, parson, cleric, churchman, canon, prebendary, divine, ecclesiastic

pastoral *adj*
1 RURAL, country, rustic, agricultural, agrarian, simple, idyllic, *formal* bucolic 2 ECCLESIASTICAL, clerical, priestly, ministerial
☐ 1 urban

pastry *n*

> **Types of pastry include:**
> American crust, biscuit-crumb, cheese pastry, choux, Danish, filo, flaky, flan pastry, hot-water crust, one-stage pastry, pâte savarin, pâte brisée, pâte frolle, pâte sablée, pâte sucrée, plain pastry, pork-pie pastry, puff, rich shortcrust, rough-puff, short, shortcrust, suetcrust, sweet pastry.

pasture *n*
grass, grassland, meadow, field, paddock, pasturage, grazing, grazing land

pasty *adj*
sallow, pale, pallid, wan, anaemic, pasty-faced, sickly, unhealthy
☐ ruddy, healthy

pat *v, n, adj, adv*
▶ *v* tap, dab, slap, clap, touch, stroke, caress, fondle, pet
▷ **pat someone on the back** congratulate, praise, compliment, say well done to, *colloq.* take your hat off to
▶ *n* tap, dab, slap, touch, stroke, caress
▶ *adj* glib, fluent, smooth, slick, ready, easy, facile, simplistic
▶ *adv* precisely, exactly, perfectly, flawlessly, faultlessly, fluently
☐ imprecisely, inaccurately, wrongly

patch *n, v*
▶ *n* 1 *a patch of land* bed, plot, lot, parcel, tract, area, piece, spot 2 COVER, material, cloth, covering, shield, protection 3 *go through a bad patch* phase, period, stretch, time, term, spell
▶ *v* mend, repair, sew, stitch, fix, cover, reinforce

patchwork *n*
medley, jumble, mixture, farrago, gallimaufry, hash, hotchpotch, pastiche, *colloq.* mishmash

patchy *adj*
uneven, irregular, inconsistent, varying, variable, random, fitful, erratic, sketchy, bitty, spotty, blotchy
☐ even, uniform, regular, consistent

patent *adj, n*
▶ *adj* obvious, evident, conspicuous, clear, plain, transparent, apparent, visible, unmistakable, palpable, unequivocal, open, overt, blatant, flagrant, glaring, *formal* manifest
☐ hidden, opaque
▶ *n* privilege, right, certificate, licence, invention, copyright, registered trademark

paternal *adj*
fatherly, fatherlike, protective, benevolent, concerned, vigilant

path *n*
1 FOOTPATH, pathway, bridleway, trail, towpath, track, walk 2 ROUTE, course, direction, approach, way, circuit, passage, road, avenue, lane

pathetic *adj*
1 PITIABLE, poor, sorry, lamentable, miserable, wretched, sad, dismal, distressing, moving, affecting, touching, pitiful, poignant, plaintive, heart-rending, heartbreaking, woeful 2 CONTEMPTIBLE, derisory, deplorable, miserable, useless, worthless, inadequate, unsatisfactory, meagre, poor, sorry, feeble, woeful
☐ 1 cheerful 2 admirable, excellent, valuable

pathological *adj*
compulsive, habitual, inveterate, obsessive, confirmed, chronic, hardened, addicted, dependent, persistent

pathos *n*
poignancy, misery, sadness, pitiableness, pitifulness, plaintiveness, inadequacy

patience *n*
calmness, composure, self-control, equanimity, even-temperedness, restraint, tolerance, forbearance, endurance, fortitude, long-suffering, submission, resignation, stoicism, tranquillity, serenity, inexcitability, persistence, perseverance, diligence, doggedness, tenacity, *formal* imperturbability, *colloq.* unflappability, cool, stickability
☐ impatience, intolerance, exasperation

patient *adj, n*
▶ *adj* calm, composed, serene, self-possessed, self-controlled, restrained, even-tempered, mild, lenient, indulgent, understanding, forgiving, tolerant, accommodating, forbearing, long-suffering, uncomplaining, submissive, resigned, philosophical, stoical, persistent, persevering, *formal* imperturbable, *colloq.* patient as Job, unflappable, cool, hanging in there
☐ impatient, restless, intolerant, exasperated
▶ *n* invalid, sufferer, case, client

patois *n*
dialect, vernacular, local parlance, local speech, argot, cant, lingo, lingua franca, patter, slang, jargon

patriarch *n*
elder, father, grandfather, paterfamilias, greybeard, founder, sire, *colloq.* grand old man

patrician *n, adj*
▶ *n* aristocrat, noble, nobleman, gentleman, grandee, peer
☐ commoner, plebeian
▶ *adj* aristocratic, noble, lordly, high-class, highborn, gentle, thoroughbred, well-born, *colloq.* blue-blooded
☐ common, humble

patrimony *n*
inheritance, legacy, bequest, heritage, estate, property, possessions, birthright, revenue, share, portion

patriot *n*
nationalist, loyalist, chauvinist, flag-waver, jingoist, jingo

patriotic *adj*
nationalistic, nationalist, chauvinistic, jingoistic, loyal, loyalist, flag-waving

patriotism *n*
chauvinism, flag-waving, jingoism, loyalty, nationalism

patrol *v, n*
▶ *v* police, guard, keep guard on, protect, defend, keep watch on/over, monitor, go the rounds, make/do the/your rounds, be on the beat, tour, inspect
▶ *n* 1 GUARD, patrolman, patrolwoman, sentry, sentinel, police officer, security guard, night-watchman, watchman 2 *on patrol* watch, guard, vigil, surveillance, policing, patrolling, protection, defence, round, beat

patron *n*
1 BENEFACTOR, philanthropist, sponsor, backer, supporter, friend, promoter, sympathizer, advocate, upholder, champion, defender, protector, guardian, guardian angel, helper, *colloq.* angel, fairy godmother 2 CUSTOMER, client, frequenter, shopper, buyer, purchaser, subscriber, *colloq.* regular

Occupations with a patron saint include:
Accountants (Matthew), Actors (Genesius; Vitus),
Advertisers (Bernardino of Siena), Architects
(Thomas, Apostle), Artists (Luke; Angelico),
Astronauts (Joseph of Cupertino), Astronomers
(Dominic), Athletes (Sebastian), Authors (Francis
de Sales), Aviators (Our Lady of Loreto), Bakers
(Honoratus), Bankers (Bernardino (Feltre)),
Barbers (Cosmas and Damian), Blacksmiths
(Eligius), Bookkeepers (Matthew), Book trade
(John of God), Brewers (Amand; Wenceslaus),
Builders (Barbara; Thomas, Apostle), Butchers
(Luke), Carpenters (Joseph), Chemists (Cosmas
and Damian), Comedians (Vitus), Cooks
(Lawrence; Martha), Dancers (Vitus), Dentists
(Apollonia), Doctors (Cosmas and Damian; Luke),
Editors (Francis de Sales), Farmers (Isidore),
Firemen (Florian), Fishermen (Andrew; Peter),
Florists (Dorothy; Thérèse of Lisieux), Gardeners
(Adam; Fiacre), Glassworkers (Luke; Lucy),
Gravediggers (Joseph of Arimathea), Grocers
(Michael), Hotelkeepers (Amand; Julian the
Hospitaler), Housewives (Martha), Jewellers
(Eligius), Journalists (Francis de Sales), Labourers
(James; John Bosco), Lawyers (Ivo; Thomas More),
Librarians (Jerome; Catherine of Alexandria),
Merchants (Francis of Assisi), Messengers
(Gabriel), Metalworkers (Eligius), Midwives
(Raymond Nonnatus), Miners (Anne; Barbara),
Motorists (Christopher), Musicians (Cecilia;
Gregory the Great), Nurses (Camillus de Lellis;
John of God), Philosophers (Thomas Aquinas;
Catherine of Alexandria), Poets (Cecilia; David),
Police (Michael), Postal workers (Gabriel), Priests
(Jean-Baptiste Vianney), Printers (John of God),
Prisoners (Leonard), Radio workers (Gabriel),
Sailors (Christopher; Erasmus; Francis of Paola),
Scholars (Thomas Aquinas), Scientists (Albert the
Great), Sculptors (Luke; Louis), Secretaries
(Genesius), Servants (Martha; Zita), Shoemakers
(Crispin; Crispinian), Singers (Cecilia; Gregory),
Soldiers (George; Joan of Arc; Martin of Tours;
Sebastian), Students (Thomas Aquinas),
Surgeons (Luke; Cosmas and Damian),
Tailors (Homobonus), Tax collectors (Matthew),
Taxi drivers (Fiacre), Teachers (Gregory the
Great; John Baptist de la Salle), Theologians
(Augustine; Alphonsus Liguori; Thomas Aquinas),
Television workers (Gabriel), Undertakers
(Dismas; Joseph of Arimathea), Waiters (Martha),
Writers (Lucy)

patronage *n*
1 SPONSORSHIP, funding, backing, support, promotion, financial help/aid/assistance, encouragement
2 CUSTOM, business, trade, commerce, buying, purchasing, shopping, subscription

patronize *v*
1 LOOK DOWN ON, talk down to, despise, scorn, act/
speak condescendingly to, *formal* disparage, *colloq.*
look down your nose at, turn your nose up at **2** SPONSOR, fund, finance, back, support, maintain, protect,
help, assist, aid, promote, champion, foster, encourage **3** FREQUENT, shop at, buy from, deal with,
colloq. be a regular at

patronizing *adj*
condescending, stooping, overbearing, high-handed,
haughty, lofty, superior, snobbish, supercilious, scornful, contemptuous, disdainful, *colloq.* snooty, toffee-

nosed, stuck-up, high-and-mighty, on your high horse
◼ humble, lowly

patter¹ *v, n*
▶ *v rain pattering on the window* tap, pat, pitter-patter, drum, pound, beat, pelt, trip, scuttle, scurry
▶ *n* pattering, tapping, pitter-patter, beating

patter² *n*
a salesman's patter chatter, gabble, jabber, line, pitch,
jargon, monologue, *colloq.* spiel, lingo, yak

pattern *n, v*
▶ *n* **1** SYSTEM, method, order, plan, arrangement
2 DECORATION, ornamentation, ornament, figure,
motif, device, design, style, markings **3** MODEL, template, stencil, guide, plan, design, instruction, original, prototype, blueprint, standard, norm, ideal,
example **4** *a book of fabric patterns* sample, swatch
▶ *v* model, style, order, form, follow, imitate, match,
stencil, emulate, copy, decorate, design, shape,
mould, trim

patterned *adj*
decorated, ornamented, figured, printed, watered,
moiré
◼ plain

paucity *n*
lack, shortage, insufficiency, scarcity, scantiness,
poverty, rarity, fewness, sparseness, sparsity, want,
dearth, deficiency, smallness, slightness, slenderness, meagreness, paltriness, *formal* exiguousness
◼ abundance

paunch *n*
fat stomach, abdomen, belly, pot-belly, beer belly,
colloq. corporation

paunchy *adj*
pot-bellied, fat, podgy, pudgy, portly, tubby, *technical*
adipose, *formal* corpulent, rotund

pauper *n*
insolvent, down-and-out, have-not, bankrupt, beggar, mendicant, church-mouse, *formal* indigent

pause *v, n*
▶ *v* halt, stop, break off, interrupt, adjourn, take a
break, rest, wait, delay, hold back, hesitate, *formal*
cease, discontinue, desist, *colloq.* let up, take a
breather, take a rest, take five
▶ *n* halt, stoppage, interruption, break, rest, lull, stay,
respite, gap, interval, interlude, intermission, wait,
delay, hesitation, *formal* cessation, *colloq.* breather,
breathing space, let-up, time out

pave *v*
flag, tile, floor, surface, cover, asphalt, tar, macadamize, tarmac, concrete
▷ **pave the way for** get/make ready for, prepare for,
lead up to, introduce, take steps/measures, clear the
ground, lay the groundwork for, do the spadework for

pavement *n*
footpath, footway, path, way, floor, bed, causeway, *US*
sidewalk

paw *n, v*
▶ *n* foot, pad, forefoot, hand
▶ *v* maul, touch, stroke, manhandle, mishandle, molest, *colloq.* touch up

pawn¹ *n*
mere pawns in the power struggle dupe, puppet, tool,
instrument, toy, plaything, *colloq.* cat's-paw, stooge

pawn² *v*
pawn your watch deposit, pledge, stake, mortgage,
formal impignorate, *colloq.* hock, pop, lay in lavender

pawnbroker *n*
pawnshop, lender, money-lender, usurer, gombeenman, *mont-de-piété*, *monte di pietà*, *colloq.* pop-shop,
slang uncle

pay *v, n*
▶ *v* **1** *pay money to someone* spend, pay out, meet the cost of, lay out, outlay, hand over, recompense, invest, reimburse, repay, refund, settle, settle up, discharge, reward, *formal* remunerate, remit, expend, disburse, indemnify, *colloq.* dip (your hand) into your pocket, foot the bill, pick up the tab, fork out, shell out, cough up, stump up **2** BENEFIT, profit, pay off, bring in, produce, yield, return, be beneficial to, be advantageous to, be worthwhile to, *colloq.* rake in **3** ATONE, make amends, compensate, avenge yourself on, pay back, answer, suffer
▷ **pay back 1** REPAY, refund, return, reimburse, recompense, settle, pay off, give back, square **2** RETALIATE, get your own back, take revenge, avenge yourself on, get even with, punish, repay, reciprocate, counter-attack
▷ **pay for** answer for, atone, be punished for, compensate, make amends, suffer, pay a penalty for, pay the price for, count the cost (of), cost dearly, *colloq.* face the music, get your deserts
▷ **pay off 1** DISCHARGE, settle, square, clear, meet, honour, repay, pay in full **2** DISMISS, discharge, make redundant, lay off, *colloq.* fire, sack **3** *the preparations paid off* succeed, be successful, work, get results **4** BRIBE, buy off, take care of, *colloq.* fix, grease, grease someone's palm
▷ **pay out** spend, hand over, part with, lay out, *formal* disburse, remit, *colloq.* fork out, shell out
▶ *n* wages, salary, earnings, income, commission, fee, stipend, honorarium, payment, reward, recompense, compensation, reimbursement, *formal* remuneration, emoluments

payable *adj*
owed, owing, unpaid, to be paid, outstanding, in arrears, due, mature

payment *n*
settlement, discharge, clearance, premium, outlay, advance, deposit, instalment, amount, contribution, donation, allowance, reward, pay, fee, hire, fare, toll, *formal* remittance, remuneration

pay-off *n*
1 RESULT, outcome, benefit, advantage, reward, settlement, consequence, upshot, *colloq.* crunch, moment of truth, punchline **2** BRIBE, inducement, allurement, enticement, *colloq.* back-hander, sweetener, hush money, slush fund, protection money

peace *n*
1 CALM, quiet, quietness, peacefulness, hush, silence, still, stillness, rest, restfulness, relaxation, tranquillity, calmness, serenity, composure, contentment, placidity, *formal* repose **2** ARMISTICE, truce, ceasefire, peace treaty, non-violence, non-aggression, conciliation, harmony, friendship, amicableness, goodwill, agreement, treaty, *formal* concord, amity, accord
☒ **1** noise, disturbance **2** war, disagreement, discord

peaceable *adj*
pacific, peace-loving, unwarlike, non-violent, non-aggressive, conciliatory, friendly, cordial, even-tempered, good-natured, irenic, amicable, harmonious, inoffensive, gentle, placid, mild, *colloq.* easy-going
☒ aggressive, quarrelsome, belligerent

peaceful *adj*
quiet, still, restful, relaxing, tranquil, serene, calm, placid, sleepy, unruffled, undisturbed, untroubled, friendly, harmonious, amicable, peaceable, pacific, gentle, *formal* reposeful, in repose
☒ noisy, disturbed, troubled, violent

peacemaker *n*
appeaser, conciliator, mediator, arbitrator, intercessor, peace-monger, pacifier, pacifist

peacemaking *adj*
appeasing, conciliatory, pacific, irenic(al), mediating, mediative, mediatorial, mediatory

peak *n, v*
▶ *n* top, summit, pinnacle, crest, crown, height, high point, elevation, mountain, mount, hill, summit, maximum, climax, culmination, apex, tip, point, *formal* apogee, zenith
☒ trough, *formal* nadir
▶ *v* climax, culminate, come to a head

peaky *adj*
pale, pallid, wan, ill, sick, unwell, off-colour, sickly, poorly, *colloq.* under the weather, washed-out
☒ healthy, *colloq.* in the pink

peal *n, v*
▶ *n* chime, carillon, toll, knell, ring, clang, ringing, reverberation, resounding, rumble, boom, roar, crash, clap, *formal* tintinnabulation
▶ *v* chime, toll, ring (out), clang, resonate, reverberate, resound, rumble, boom, roll, roar, crash

peasant *n*
rustic, provincial, country person, yokel, bumpkin, oaf, boor, lout, churl, *colloq.* country bumpkin

pebble *n*
stone, agate, chip, gallet

peccadillo *n*
error, fault, indiscretion, lapse, slip, minor offence, misdeed, misdemeanour, delinquency, *formal* infraction, *colloq.* boob, slip-up

peck *v*
nip, jab, tap, rap, hit, strike, bite, prick, kiss

peculiar *adj*
1 *a peculiar sound* strange, odd, curious, funny, queer, weird, bizarre, quaint, extraordinary, unusual, abnormal, exceptional, unconventional, offbeat, droll, eccentric, outlandish, freakish, grotesque, exotic, *slang* way-out **2** CHARACTERISTIC, distinctive, distinguishing, specific, particular, special, distinct, remarkable, individual, individualistic, personal, idiosyncratic, unique, singular **3** *feel peculiar* unwell, ill, sick, poorly, out of sorts, dizzy, *colloq.* under the weather
☒ **1** ordinary, normal **2** general
▷ **peculiar to** unique to, characteristic of, typical of, representative of

peculiarity *n*
oddity, bizarreness, weirdness, abnormality, exception, eccentricity, quirk, foible, mannerism, feature, trait, mark, hallmark, quality, attribute, property, characteristic, distinctiveness, particularity, idiosyncrasy

pecuniary *adj*
monetary, financial, fiscal, commercial, *formal* nummary, nummulary

pedagogic *adj*
educational, teaching, instructional, tuitional, academic, scholastic, didactic

pedagogue *n*
teacher, instructor, educator, master, mistress, educationalist, educationist, schoolmaster, schoolmistress, don, pedant, dogmatist, preceptor, dominie

pedagogy *n*
teaching, instruction, training, tuition, tutelage, didactics, pedagogics

pedant *n*
purist, formalist, literalist, perfectionist, precisionist, precisian, dogmatist, quibbler, casuist, doctrinaire, academic, intellectual, pettifogger, Dryasdust, scholastic, *colloq.* hair-splitter, nit-picker, egghead, highbrow

pedantic *adj*
stilted, fussy, purist, perfectionist, literalist, formalist, particular, precise, exact, meticulous, punctilious, scrupulous, quibbling, finical, pompous, pretentious, academic, intellectual, bookish, stuffy, erudite, *colloq.* hair-splitting, nit-picking
🔄 imprecise, informal, casual

pedantry *n*
punctiliousness, exactness, meticulousness, cavilling, finicality, quibbling, pomposity, pretentiousness, academicness, intellectualism, bookishness, stuffiness, pedagogism, pedagoguishness, pedantism, *colloq.* hair-splitting, nit-picking

peddle *v*
sell, vend, hawk, tout, push, trade, traffic, market, offer/present for sale, *colloq.* flog

pedestal *n*
plinth, pillar, column, stand, support, mounting, foot, base, foundation, platform, podium
▷ **put on a pedestal** idolize, hero-worship, exalt, revere, admire, adulate

pedestrian *n, adj*
▶ *n* walker, foot-traveller, hiker
▶ *adj* dull, boring, flat, uninspired, unexciting, unimaginative, banal, mundane, commonplace, humdrum, ordinary, mediocre, indifferent, prosaic, stodgy, plodding, turgid, *colloq.* run-of-the-mill, not up to much, no great shakes, nothing much to write home about
🔄 exciting, imaginative

pedigree *n, adj*
▶ *n* genealogy, family tree, lineage, ancestry, descent, line, line of descent, family, parentage, derivation, extraction, race, breed, stock, strain, blood, *formal* stirps
▶ *adj* pure-bred, full-blooded, thoroughbred, aristocratic

pedlar *n*
seller, hawker, huckster, vendor, walker, street-trader, colporteur, chapman, gutter-man, gutter-merchant, boxwallah, cheap-jack, *Scot.* yagger

peek *v, n*
▶ *v* peep, glance, peer, spy, look, *colloq.* have a gander, have a look-see
▶ *n* peep, glance, glimpse, look, blink, *colloq.* dekko, look-see, shufti, *slang* gander

peel *v, n*
▶ *v* pare, skin, strip, scale, flake (off), take off, remove, *formal* decorticate, desquamate
▶ *n* skin, rind, zest, peeling, *technical* epicarp, exocarp, integument
▷ **keep your eyes peeled** watch closely, observe, monitor, keep a lookout for, be alert, keep your eyes skinned

peep[1] *v, n*
▶ *v* peep through the keyhole look, peek, glimpse, spy, squint, peer, emerge, issue, appear
▶ *n* look, peek, glimpse, glance, squint, *colloq.* dekko, look-see, shufti, *slang* gander

peep[2] *v, n*
▶ *v* birds peeping chirp, cheep, chirrup, pipe, tweet, chatter, twitter, warble, squeak
▶ *n* chirp, cheep, chirrup, pipe, tweet, chatter, twitter, warble, squeak, cry, utterance, sound, noise, word

peephole *n*
spyhole, keyhole, pinhole, hole, opening, aperture, slit, chink, slink, crack, fissure, cleft, crevice, Judas-hole, Judas-window, *formal* interstice

peer[1] *v*
peer through the window look, gaze, scan, scrutinize, examine, inspect, spy, snoop, peep, squint

peer[2] *n*
1 ARISTOCRAT, noble, nobleman, lord, duke, marquess, marquis, earl, count, viscount, baron, patrician **2** EQUAL, counterpart, equivalent, like, match, fellow, confrère, compeer

peerage *n*
aristocracy, nobility, lords and ladies, *colloq.* upper crust, top drawer

peeress *n*
aristocrat, noble, noblewoman, lady, dame, duchess, marchioness, countess, viscountess, baroness

peerless *adj*
matchless, without equal, unequalled, unexcelled, unmatched, incomparable, beyond compare, unparalleled, unrivalled, unsurpassed, unbeatable, unique, supreme, excellent, paramount, outstanding, superlative, *formal* nonpareil, *colloq.* second to none

peeve *v*
annoy, exasperate, irritate, vex, irk, gall, *colloq.* rub someone up the wrong way, get someone's blood up, get on someone's nerves, get under someone's skin, drive up the wall

peeved *adj*
annoyed, irritated, exasperated, put out, upset, vexed, irked, galled, riled, sore, piqued, nettled, *colloq.* miffed, narked, having the hump, in a huff

peevish *adj*
petulant, querulous, fractious, fretful, touchy, complaining, irritable, cross, grumpy, ill-tempered, in a bad mood, cantankerous, crusty, snappy, short-tempered, moody, testy, tetchy, churlish, surly, sullen, sulky, *colloq.* ratty, crotchety, crabbed, touchy
🔄 good-tempered

peevishness *n*
ill-temper, irritability, perversity, petulance, querulousness, testiness, pique, pet, captiousness, acrimony, *formal* protervity

peg *n, v*
▶ *n* pin, nail, screw, spike, brad, dowel, hook, knob, marker, post, stake
▷ **take/bring down a peg or two** humiliate, bring/cut down to size, put someone in their place, take the wind out of someone's sails
▶ *v* **1** FASTEN, secure, fix, attach, join, mark **2** peg prices control, stabilize, limit, freeze, fix, set
▷ **peg away** apply yourself, work away, persevere, persist, plug away, beaver away, plod along, *colloq.* hang in, keep at it, stick at it

pejorative *adj*
derogatory, disparaging, belittling, slighting, unflattering, uncomplimentary, unpleasant, bad, negative, *formal* deprecatory
🔄 complimentary

pellet *n*
ball, shot, bullet, pill, drop, capsule, lozenge, *colloq.* slug

pell-mell *adv*
hurriedly, hastily, feverishly, precipitously, posthaste, recklessly, rashly, heedlessly, impetuously, at full tilt, *colloq.* helter-skelter, hurry-scurry

pellucid *adj*
clear, limpid, transparent, translucent, pure, glassy, bright

pelt[1] *v*
1 THROW, hurl, bombard, shower, attack, assail, batter, beat, hit, strike **2** POUR, teem, *colloq.* bucket (down), rain cats and dogs **3** RUSH, hurry, charge, tear, race, dash, run, speed, sprint, career, *colloq.* belt, zip

pelt² *n*
a *beaver pelt* skin, coat, fur, fleece, hide, fell

pen¹ *n, v*
▶ *n write with a pen* fountain pen, ballpoint, ballpoint pen, Biro®, felt-tip pen, felt-tip
▶ *v* write (down), compose, draft, scribble, jot down

pen² *n, v*
▶ *n a sheep pen* enclosure, fold, pound, compound, stall, sty, coop, cage, hutch, mew, corral
▶ *v* enclose, fence, hedge, hem in, confine, cage, coop, shut (up)

penal *adj*
punitive, disciplinary, corrective, retaliatory, retributive, vindictive

penalize *v*
punish, discipline, correct, fine, disadvantage, handicap, *formal* castigate, chastise
🖅 reward

penal servitude *n*
hard labour, stretch, time, *colloq.* bird, lag, porridge

penalty *n*
1 PUNISHMENT, retribution, sentence, fine, forfeit, chastisement, *formal* mulct, castigation **2** DISADVANTAGE, handicap, drawback, snag, weak point, *colloq.* downside, minus
🖅 **1** reward **2** advantage, benefit

penance *n*
atonement, reparation, punishment, penalty, self-punishment, self-abasement, mortification

penchant *n*
fondness, liking, tendency, taste, preference, affinity, bent, inclination, leaning, bias, partiality, weakness, soft spot, proneness, *formal* disposition, predilection, predisposition, proclivity, propensity
🖅 dislike

pendant *n*
medallion, locket, necklace

pendent *adj*
hanging, suspended, dangling, drooping, swinging, *formal* pendulous, pensile, nutant

pending *adj, prep*
▶ *adj* imminent, impending, in the offing, forthcoming, coming, approaching, nearing, near, undecided, unsettled, awaiting settlement, uncertain, *colloq.* in the balance, up in the air
🖅 finished, settled
▶ *prep* until, till, to, before, so long as, while, whilst, throughout

pendulous *adj*
sagging, hanging, suspended, dangling, drooping, droopy, swaying, swinging, *formal* pendent

penetrable *adj*
clear, open, passable, permeable, pervious, porous, fathomable, understandable, intelligible, accessible, comprehensible, explicable
🖅 impenetrable

penetrate *v*
1 PIERCE, stab, prick, perforate, puncture, spike, probe, sink, bore **2** GET INTO, enter, infiltrate, make your way, permeate, fill, seep, saturate, pervade, suffuse, imbue **3** GRASP, understand, fathom, comprehend, make out, work out, see, register, sink in, *colloq.* crack, cotton on, twig, get to the bottom of

penetrating *adj*
1 PIERCING, stinging, biting, incisive, sharp **2** *a penetrating sound* loud, clear, strident, shrill, piercing, carrying **3** *a penetrating mind* keen, acute, shrewd, discerning, discriminating, wise, perceptive, observant, profound, deep, searching, probing
🖅 **1** blunt

penetration *n*
1 PIERCING, puncturing, perforation, stabbing, pricking, incision **2** ENTRANCE, entry, inroad, infiltration, permeation, pervasion, invasion, *formal* interpenetration **3** DISCERNMENT, perception, insight, acumen, astuteness, sharpness, keenness, acuteness, shrewdness, wit, *formal* perspicacity

peninsula *n*
cape, point, mull, tongue, chersonese, doab, promontary, headland

penis *n*
male organ of copulation, *formal* phallus, membrum virile, *colloq.* willy

penitence *n*
repentance, contrition, sorrow, shame, remorse, regret, self-reproach, *formal* compunction, ruefulness

penitent *adj*
repentant, contrite, sorry, sorrowful, apologetic, remorseful, ashamed, regretful, conscience-stricken, shamefaced, humble, *formal* rueful
🖅 unrepentant, hard-hearted, callous

pen-name *n*
assumed name, pseudonym, stage-name, nom-de-plume, false name, *formal* allonym

pennant *n*
flag, banner, ensign, standard, streamer, colours, banderol, gonfalon, jack

penniless *adj*
poor, poverty-stricken, impoverished, destitute, bankrupt, ruined, bust, *formal* indigent, *colloq.* broke, stony-broke, down and out, on the breadline, cleaned out, strapped for cash, on your beam-ends, *slang* skint
🖅 rich, wealthy, affluent

penny-pincher *n*
miser, niggard, skinflint, cheeseparer, Scrooge, *colloq.* meanie, cheapskate, money-grubber

penny-pinching *adj*
miserly, mean, close, tight-fisted, niggardly, scrimping, cheese-paring, ungenerous, frugal, *formal* parsimonious, *colloq.* mingy, stingy
🖅 generous, open-handed

pension *n*
old-age pension, retirement pension, state pension, personal pension, company pension, index-linked pension, annuity, superannuation, support, welfare, social assistance, income, allowance, benefit

pensioner *n*
retired person, old-age pensioner, senior citizen

pensive *adj*
thoughtful, reflective, contemplative, meditative, thinking, pondering, musing, ruminative, absorbed, preoccupied, absent-minded, dreamy, wistful, solemn, serious, sober, *formal* cogitative
🖅 carefree

pent-up *adj*
repressed, inhibited, restrained, bridled, curbed, suppressed, stifled, held in, *colloq.* bottled-up

penurious *adj*
1 POOR, impoverished, destitute, poverty-stricken, beggarly, penniless, hard up, in straitened circumstances, inadequate, *formal* impecunious, indigent, parsimonious, *colloq.* tight, cheese-paring, bust, flat broke, stingy **2** MISERLY, mean, niggardly, close, close-fisted, grudging, ungenerous, *colloq.* tight-fisted
🖅 **1** wealthy, generous

penury *n*
poverty, destitution, pauperism, impoverishment, insolvency, straitened circumstances, straits, defi-

ciency, need, want, dearth, beggary, *formal* indigence, mendicity
🖃 prosperity

people *n, v*
▶ *n* 1 PERSONS, individuals, humans, human beings, the human race, mankind, humankind, humanity, mortals, folk(s) 2 CITIZENS, ordinary citizens, public, general public, populace, rank and file, population, men women and children, inhabitants, community, society, electorate, masses, mob, rabble, *colloq.* the plebs, riff-raff 3 NATION, race, tribe, clan 4 *his people are from Wales* parents, relations, relatives, folks, family, kith and kin
▶ *v* populate, inhabit, occupy, settle, colonize

pep *n*
energy, vigour, verve, spirit, sparkle, vitality, life, liveliness, exuberance, effervescence, high spirits, *formal* ebullience, *colloq.* get-up-and-go, pizzazz
▷ **pep up** invigorate, vitalize, liven up, quicken, stimulate, animate, excite, exhilarate, inspire, energize
🖃 tone down

pepper *v*
1 BOMBARD, attack, assail, pelt, blitz 2 SPRINKLE, shower, scatter, spatter, bespatter, strew, dot

peppery *adj*
1 SPICY, hot, pungent, seasoned, piquant 2 QUICK-TEMPERED, hot-tempered, irritable, irascible, choleric, testy, fiery, grumpy, snappish, *colloq.* touchy 3 INCISIVE, sharp, sarcastic, biting, stinging, astringent, caustic, waspish, *formal* trenchant

perceive *v*
1 SEE, discern, make out, detect, discover, spot, catch sight of, glimpse, notice, observe, view, remark, note, distinguish, recognize, *formal* espy, behold 2 SENSE, feel, apprehend, learn, realize, appreciate, be aware of, discern, recognize, see, know, grasp, understand, gather, deduce, conclude, comprehend, *formal* be cognizant of, *colloq.* get wind of

perceptible *adj*
perceivable, discernible, detectable, appreciable, distinguishable, observable, noticeable, obvious, evident, conspicuous, clear, plain, distinct, patent, apparent, tangible, visible, *formal* manifest
🖃 imperceptible, inconspicuous

perception *n*
1 VIEW, interpretation, understanding, sense, feeling, impression, idea, conception, knowledge, apprehension 2 DISCERNMENT, awareness, consciousness, observation, recognition, insight, understanding, grasp, discrimination, sensitivity, responsiveness, *formal* cognizance

perceptive *adj*
discerning, observant, sensitive, responsive, aware, alert, quick, quick-witted, keen, sharp, sharp-eyed, astute, penetrating, discriminating, shrewd, understanding, *formal* perspicacious
🖃 unobservant

perch *v*
land, alight, settle, sit, roost, balance, rest

perchance *adv*
perhaps, maybe, possibly, conceivably, feasibly

percipience *n*
perception, discernment, astuteness, awareness, insight, intuition, understanding, sensitivity, penetration, judgement, alertness, acuteness, *formal* perspicacity, sagacity

percipient *adj*
perceptive, observant, discerning, discriminating, sharp, aware, alive, astute, alert, penetrating, quick-

witted, knowing, intelligent, wide-awake, *formal* judicious, perspicacious
🖃 unaware, obtuse

percolate *v*
filter, strain, seep, ooze, leach, leak, drip, drain, sift, sieve, penetrate, pass through, spread (slowly) through, trickle through, permeate, pervade

perdition *n*
damnation, hell, everlasting punishment, condemnation, hellfire, destruction, doom, downfall, ruin, ruination, annihilation

peregrination *n*
travel, travelling, voyage, wandering, roaming, roving, journey, tour, expedition, exploration, trek, trekking, trip, excursion, globe-trotting, wayfaring, odyssey

peremptory *adj*
imperious, commanding, dictatorial, autocratic, tyrannical, lordly, authoritative, assertive, high-handed, overbearing, domineering, dogmatic, absolute, irrefutable, abrupt, curt, summary, arbitrary, *colloq.* bossy

perennial *adj*
lasting, enduring, abiding, everlasting, eternal, immortal, undying, imperishable, unceasing, endless, unending, incessant, never-ending, constant, continual, unchanging, uninterrupted, unfailing, perpetual, persistent, unfailing, permanent, *formal* ceaseless

perfect *adj, v*
▶ *adj* 1 FAULTLESS, impeccable, flawless, immaculate, sinless, unmarred, unblemished, spotless, blameless, pure, superb, wonderful, excellent, matchless, peerless, incomparable, superlative 2 IDEAL, model, textbook, exemplary, ultimate, expert, accomplished, finished, completed, experienced, skilful, *formal* consummate, *colloq.* just the job 3 EXACT, precise, accurate, right, correct, true, faithful 4 *perfect strangers* utter, absolute, sheer, complete, entire, total, thorough, downright, out-and-out
🖃 1 imperfect, flawed, blemished 2 inexperienced, unskilled 3 inaccurate, wrong
▶ *v* fulfil, complete, finish, better, improve, polish, refine, elaborate, *formal* consummate
🖃 spoil, mar

perfection *n*
1 EXCELLENCE, faultlessness, flawlessness, superiority, immaculateness, impeccability 2 IMPROVEMENT, betterment, polishing, refinement, completion, realization, *formal* consummation 3 IDEAL, model, paragon, crown, pinnacle, peak of perfection, ultimate, *ne plus ultra*, acme, *colloq.* one in a million
🖃 3 imperfection, flaw

perfectionist *n*
idealist, purist, pedant, formalist, stickler, precisionist

perfectly *adv*
1 UTTERLY, absolutely, quite, thoroughly, completely, entirely, wholly, totally, fully, altogether 2 FAULTLESSLY, flawlessly, immaculately, without blemish, impeccably, ideally, wonderfully, superbly, exactly, correctly, to perfection
🖃 1 partially 2 imperfectly, badly

perfidious *adj*
treacherous, untrustworthy, deceitful, dishonest, disloyal, double-dealing, double-faced, false, traitorous, two-faced, unfaithful, faithless, corrupt, Machiavellian, treasonous, Punic, *formal* duplicitous
🖃 faithful, honest, loyal

perfidy *n*
treachery, betrayal, deceit, falsity, faithlessness, infi-

delity, disloyalty, double-dealing, traitorousness, treason, *formal* duplicity, perfidiousness
🖪 faithfulness, honesty, loyalty

perforate *v*
hole, make holes in, punch, drill, bore, pierce, prick,
puncture, spike, stab, gore, burst, rupture, tear, split,
penetrate

perforated *adj*
pierced, holed, bored, drilled, punctured, punched,
porous, *technical* ethmoid, fenestrate(d), fenestrial,
foraminous

perforation *n*
hole, bore, prick, puncture, dotted line, *technical*
fenestration, foramen

perforce *adv*
unavoidably, inevitably, necessarily, of necessity,
willy-nilly

perform *v*
1 DO, carry out, discharge, fulfil, satisfy, complete,
achieve, accomplish, conduct, bring off, pull off, bring
about, *formal* execute, effect **2** *perform a play* stage,
put on, present, enact, represent, act, do, play, appear
as **3** FUNCTION, work, operate, go, run, behave, produce

performance *n*
1 SHOW, appearance, presentation, production, interpretation, representation, portrayal, acting **2** AC-
TION, deed, doing, carrying out, implementation,
discharge, fulfilment, conducting, completion,
achievement, accomplishment, *formal* execution, effecting **3** FUNCTIONING, operation, running, going,
behaviour, conduct

performer *n*
1 *circus performer* actor, actress, player, musician,
singer, dancer, comic, comedian, clown, artiste, entertainer, trouper, Thespian. *See panels at* ENTER-
TAINER; MUSICIAN; SINGERS. **2** ACHIEVER, doer,
operator, author, *formal* executor

perfume *n*
scent, fragrance, smell, odour, aroma, bouquet,
sweetness, balm, essence, cologne, eau-de-cologne,
eau-de-toilette, toilet water, incense, *formal* redolence

perfunctory *adj*
quick, careless, superficial, cursory, negligent, offhand, slipshod, slovenly, inattentive, hurried, heedless, automatic, mechanical, routine, stereotyped,
indifferent, brief, wooden
🖪 careful, enthusiastic

perhaps *adv*
maybe, possibly, conceivably, feasibly, *formal* perchance

peril *n*
danger, hazard, risk, jeopardy, uncertainty, insecurity,
threat, menace
🖪 safety, security

perilous *adj*
dangerous, unsafe, hazardous, risky, chancy, precarious, insecure, unsure, vulnerable, fraught with danger, exposed, menacing, threatening, dire
🖪 safe, secure

perimeter *n*
circumference, edge, border, boundary, frontier, lim-
it(s), outer limits, bounds, confines, fringe, margin,
periphery
🖪 middle, centre, heart

period *n*
1 TIME, season, stretch, duration, space, span, spell,
stint, shift, term, while, turn, session, interval, cycle
2 STAGE, phase, era, epoch, age, eon, generation,
date, years **3** CLASS, lesson, lecture, seminar, tutorial,

instruction **4** *a woman's monthly period* menstruation, menstrual flow, monthlies, *formal* menses,
colloq. the curse **5** *a period at the end of the sentence*
full stop, full point, point **6** *you may not go, period* full
stop, stop, end, finish, conclusion

periodic *adj*
occasional, infrequent, sporadic, intermittent, once
in a while, recurrent, recurring, repeated, regular,
periodical, seasonal, cyclical, cyclic

periodical *n*
magazine, journal, publication, weekly, monthly,
quarterly, review, organ

peripatetic *adj*
travelling, itinerant, journeying, mobile, roaming,
roving, migrant, migratory, nomadic, wandering, vagabond, vagrant, *formal* ambulant, ambulatory
🖪 fixed

peripheral *adj*
1 MINOR, secondary, lesser, incidental, unimportant,
irrelevant, subsidiary, ancillary, unnecessary, marginal, borderline, surface, superficial, *colloq.* beside the
point, neither here nor there **2** OUTLYING, outer, outermost, surrounding
🖪 **1** major, crucial **2** central

periphery *n*
edge, boundary, border, circumference, fringe, perimeter, brim, brink, rim, skirt, outskirts, outer regions,
margin, verge, hem, circuit, ambit
🖪 centre, nub, middle

periphrastic *adj*
roundabout, indirect, circuitous, wandering, oblique,
discursive, tortuous, rambling, long-drawn-out, *formal* circumlocutory

perish *v*
1 DIE, pass away, lose your life, depart, breathe your
last, *formal* expire, *colloq.* peg out, bite the dust, pop
off, have had it, kick the bucket **2** COLLAPSE, disintegrate, crumble, fail, fall, come to an end, disappear,
vanish, die away, rot, decay, decompose, go off

perishable *adj*
destructible, biodegradable, decomposable, short-
lived
🖪 imperishable, durable

perjure *v*
▷ **perjure yourself** lie, commit perjury, bear false wit-
ness/testimony, make false statements, give false evidence, *formal* forswear yourself

perjury *n*
false evidence, false testimony, false witness, false
swearing, false oath, false statement, falsification,
formal forswearing, mendacity

perk *n*
fringe benefit, benefit, bonus, advantage, dividend,
gratuity, tip, extra, baksheesh, *formal* perquisite,
colloq. plus, freebie, golden handshake
▷ **perk up** brighten (up), cheer up, take heart, revive,
rally, liven up, make/become lively, recover, improve,
look up, *colloq.* buck up, pep up

perky *adj*
lively, jaunty, spirited, vivacious, sprightly, cheerful,
cheery, gay, bright, animated, bouncy, buoyant, bubbly, effervescent, peppy, sunny, *formal* ebullient
🖪 cheerless, dull, gloomy

permanence *n*
fixedness, stability, imperishability, indestructibility,
perpetuity, constancy, endurance, steadfastness, persistence, durability
🖪 impermanence, transience

permanent *adj*
1 LASTING, enduring, durable, imperishable, inde-

structible, unfading, eternal, everlasting, lifelong, perpetual, constant, steadfast, immutable, invariable, unchangeable, indelible, perennial, long-lasting **2** FIXED, stable, unchanging, constant, established
F3 1 temporary, fleeting, *formal* ephemeral

permanently *adv*
always, continually, constantly, ceaselessly, endlessly, eternally, perpetually, in perpetuity, incessantly, unceasingly, unremittingly, unendingly, once and for all, indelibly, everlastingly, ever more, for ever, for ever and ever, for all time, *colloq.* for keeps, till doomsday, till kingdom come, till the cows come home, till hell freezes over
F3 temporarily

permeable *adj*
porous, absorbent, absorptive, penetrable, passable, spongy
F3 impermeable, watertight

permeate *v*
pass through, soak through, filter through, seep through, spread through, penetrate, infiltrate, percolate, pervade, imbue, saturate, impregnate, fill, diffuse

permissible *adj*
permitted, allowable, allowed, admissible, all right, tolerable, acceptable, proper, authorized, sanctioned, lawful, legal, legitimate, *colloq.* OK, kosher
F3 prohibited, banned, forbidden

permission *n*
consent, assent, agreement, approval, allowance, clearance, go-ahead, authorization, sanction, leave, warrant, permit, licence, dispensation, freedom, liberty, *formal* approbation, *colloq.* green light, thumbs up
F3 prohibition

permissive *adj*
liberal, broad-minded, tolerant, forbearing, lenient, indulgent, overindulgent, lax, free, *formal* latitudinarian, *colloq.* easy-going
F3 strict, rigid, narrow-minded

permit *v, n*
▶ *v* allow, let, consent, agree, admit, grant, authorize, enable, empower, sanction, warrant, license, *colloq.* give the go-ahead to, give the green light to, give the thumbs up to, give the nod to
F3 prohibit, forbid
▶ *n* pass, passport, visa, licence, warrant, authorization, sanction, permission
F3 prohibition

permutation *n*
alteration, change, shift, transformation, variation, *formal* transposition, configuration, transmutation, commutation

pernicious *adj*
harmful, damaging, dangerous, destructive, ruinous, detrimental, bad, hurtful, injurious, offensive, malicious, poisonous, venomous, pestilent, toxic, wicked, evil, malignant, fatal, deadly, unhealthy, unwholesome, *formal* deleterious, maleficent, malevolent, noisome, noxious
F3 innocuous

pernickety *adj*
fussy, particular, over-particular, over-precise, carping, nice, punctilious, fastidious, fiddly, finical, finicky, exacting, detailed, careful, painstaking, fine, tricky, *colloq.* choosy, picky, hair-splitting, nit-picking

peroration *n*
1 SUMMING-UP, summary, conclusion, closing remarks, reiteration, recapitulation, *colloq.* recapping **2** SPEECH, lecture, talk, address, *formal* oration, diatribe, declamation

perpendicular *adj*
vertical, upright, erect, straight, at right angles, sheer, steep, abrupt, precipitous, plumb
F3 horizontal

perpetrate *v*
commit, carry out, execute, do, be responsible for, be to blame for, perform, inflict, wreak, *formal* effect, effectuate

perpetual *adj*
eternal, everlasting, infinite, endless, unending, never-ending, interminable, ceaseless, unceasing, incessant, continuous, unbroken, uninterrupted, unremitting, constant, persistent, continual, repeated, recurrent, perennial, permanent, lasting, enduring, abiding, persisting, unchanging, unfailing, undying, unvarying, intermittent
F3 temporary, *formal* ephemeral, transient

perpetually *adv*
eternally, endlessly, interminably, ceaselessly, unceasingly, incessantly, unremittingly, constantly, persistently, continually, permanently

perpetuate *v*
continue, keep up, maintain, sustain, preserve, keep alive, keep going, immortalize, commemorate, eternalize, memorialize

perpetuity *n*
▷ **in perpetuity** for ever, for ever and ever, for all time, always, endlessly, eternally, perpetually, ever more

perplex *v*
puzzle, baffle, mystify, stump, confuse, confound, muddle, bewilder, dumbfound, *colloq.* bamboozle, nonplus

perplexed *adj*
puzzled, baffled, bewildered, mystified, stumped, confused, muddled, confounded, disconcerted, fuddled, worried, at a loss, *colloq.* bamboozled, nonplussed

perplexing *adj*
puzzling, baffling, bewildering, confusing, mystifying, amazing, complex, complicated, intricate, inexplicable, hard, strange, weird, paradoxical, difficult, taxing, involved, knotty, thorny, enigmatic, mysterious, *formal* labyrinthine
F3 easy, simple

perplexity *n*
1 PUZZLEMENT, bafflement, bewilderment, confusion, incomprehension, mystification, nonplus **2** COMPLEXITY, complication, difficulty, intricacy, involvement, dilemma, enigma, mystery, puzzle, paradox, obscurity, labyrinth, *formal* obfuscation

perquisite *n*
perk, fringe benefit, benefit, bonus, advantage, dividend, gratuity, tip, extra, baksheesh, plus, *colloq.* freebie

persecute *v*
1 ILL-TREAT, abuse, mistreat, maltreat, oppress, tyrannize, victimize, martyr, distress, afflict, torment, torture, crucify **2** HARASS, hound, pursue, hunt, bother, worry, annoy, pester, badger, molest, *colloq.* hassle
F3 1 pamper, spoil

persecution *n*
ill-treatment, mistreatment, abuse, maltreatment, discrimination, oppression, harassment, molestation, suppression, tyranny, victimization, punishment, torture, martyrdom, crucifixion, *formal* subjugation

perseverance *n*
persistence, determination, resolution, resolve, doggedness, tenacity, diligence, application, assiduity, dedication, commitment, purpose, purposefulness,

constancy, steadfastness, stamina, endurance, indefatigability, *formal* pertinacity, intransigence, *colloq.* stickability, *US* stick-to-it-iveness

persevere *v*
continue, carry on, go on, keep going, struggle on, soldier on, persist, remain, be persistent, be determined, be resolute, stand firm, stand fast, hold on, hang on, *colloq.* stick at it, plug away, hang in there, go the whole distance, stick to your guns, leave no stone unturned, mean business
F₃ give up, stop, *formal* discontinue

persist *v*
1 CONTINUE, carry on, go on, keep on, keep going, soldier on, keep at it, persevere, stand firm, stand fast, hold on, hang on, be persistent, be determined, be resolute, insist, *colloq.* stick at it, plug away **2** REMAIN, keep on, hold, linger, last, endure, continue, *formal* abide
F₃ 1 stop, give up, *formal* desist

persistence *n*
perseverance, determination, endurance, doggedness, diligence, assiduousness, assiduity, constancy, resolution, tenacity, steadfastness, tirelessness, stamina, indefatigableness, *formal* pertinacity, sedulity, *colloq.* grit, stickability, *US* stick-to-it-iveness

persistent *adj*
1 INCESSANT, endless, never-ending, interminable, continuous, unceasing, ceaseless, lasting, unrelenting, relentless, unremitting, constant, steady, continual, repeated, perpetual, lasting, enduring **2** *persistent effort* persevering, determined, resolute, purposeful, diligent, assiduous, dogged, tenacious, stubborn, obstinate, steadfast, zealous, tireless, unflagging, indefatigable, *formal* intractable, obdurate, pertinacious, *colloq. US* stick-to-it-ive

person *n*
individual, human being, human, being, man, woman, mortal, body, soul, character, type, someone, somebody
▷ **in person** personally, face to face, bodily, *colloq.* in the flesh, as large as life

persona *n*
image, face, public face, role, part, character, personality, front, façade, mask

personable *adj*
pleasant, pleasing, likeable, presentable, nice, agreeable, amiable, affable, attractive, good-looking, handsome, charming, warm, winning, outgoing
F₃ unpleasant, disagreeable, unattractive

personage *n*
celebrity, name, notable, worthy, public figure, personality, luminary, dignitary, headliner, *colloq.* VIP, big shot, somebody, big noise, bigwig

personal *adj*
1 *give you my personal attention* individual, special, particular, exclusive, in person **2** *your personal style* individual, idiosyncratic, peculiar, characteristic, distinctive, unique, own, subjective **3** PRIVATE, confidential, intimate, secret **4** *personal remarks* offensive, insulting, critical, rude, abusive, hurtful, wounding, disrespectful, upsetting
F₃ 2 general, universal **3** public, official

personality *n*
1 CHARACTER, nature, disposition, temperament, temper, individuality, psyche, traits, make-up, charm, charisma, magnetism **2** CELEBRITY, notable, personage, public figure, dignitary, worthy, star, *colloq.* VIP

personally *adv*
1 INDIVIDUALLY, in person, specially, particularly, exclusively, solely, alone, independently, subjectively,

idiosyncratically, distinctively, characteristically, uniquely, privately, confidentially **2** *take something personally* directed against you, as personal criticism, as hurtful comments, insultingly, offensively

personification *n*
essence, embodiment, incarnation, likeness, image, representation, recreation, portrayal, semblance, *formal* delineation, manifestation, quintessence

personify *v*
embody, epitomize, typify, exemplify, symbolize, represent, mirror, be the incarnation of

personnel *n*
staff, workforce, workers, employees, crew, human resources, labour force, manpower, people, members, *colloq.* liveware

perspective *n*
1 VIEW, point of view, viewpoint, aspect, angle, slant, attitude, frame of mind, vantage point, standpoint, vista, scene, prospect, outlook **2** *get things into perspective* proportion, relation, equilibrium

perspicacious *adj*
discerning, observant, sensitive, responsive, aware, alert, quick, quick-witted, keen, sharp, sharp-eyed, astute, penetrating, discriminating, shrewd, understanding, *formal* sagacious, percipient, judicious
F₃ unobservant, obtuse

perspicacity *n*
discernment, astuteness, perceptiveness, discrimination, insight, acuteness, cleverness, sharpness, keenness, acumen, shrewdness, penetration, wit, *formal* percipience, perspicaciousness, perspicuity, sagaciousness, sagacity, *colloq.* brains

perspicuity *n*
clarity, clearness, plainness, precision, lucidity, straightforwardness, distinctness, explicitness, intelligibility, comprehensibility, comprehensibleness, penetrability, transparency, *formal* limpidity, limpidness

perspicuous *adj*
clear, crystal-clear, unambiguous, plain, obvious, self-evident, transparent, understandable, lucid, straightforward, apparent, explicit, distinct, intelligible, comprehensible, *formal* limpid, manifest

perspiration *n*
sweat, secretion, moisture, wetness, *technical* sudor, diaphoresis, hidrosis, *formal* exudation

perspire *v*
sweat, secrete, swelter, drip, *technical* sudate, *formal* exude

persuadable *adj*
amenable, agreeable, flexible, persuasible, malleable, pliable, receptive, susceptive, impressionable, *formal* acquiescent, compliant
F₃ firm, inflexible, stubborn

persuade *v*
coax, prevail upon, cajole, wheedle, talk into, induce, bring round, win over, convince, satisfy, convert, lobby, sway, influence, tempt, lure, lead on, incite, prompt, urge, coerce, *formal* inveigle, *colloq.* lean on, sweet-talk, soft-soap, swing it, pull strings, twist someone's arm, put the screws on
F₃ dissuade, deter, discourage, talk out of, put off

persuasion *n*
1 COAXING, prevailing, cajolery, wheedling, talking into, winning over, inducement, enticement, pull, power, influence, sway, conviction, conversion, incitement, prompting, urging, coercion, *colloq.* clout, sweet-talking, arm-twisting **2** OPINION, school (of thought), party, faction, side, camp, affiliation, philosophy, conviction, faith, belief, view, point of view, viewpoint, denomination, sect

persuasive *adj*
convincing, plausible, sound, valid, influential, forceful, weighty, effective, slick, telling, potent, compelling, moving, touching, *formal* cogent, effectual, *colloq.* pushy, smooth-talking
F3 unconvincing

pert *adj*
impudent, cheeky, presumptuous, impertinent, insolent, bold, brash, gay, forward, fresh, flippant, lively, spirited, brisk, daring, sprightly, jaunty, tossy, *colloq.* perky, saucy, cocky
F3 coy, shy

pertain *v*
relate, apply, be appropriate, be part of, be relevant, bear on, have a bearing on, befit, belong, come under, concern, refer, regard, *formal* appertain

pertinacious *adj*
persistent, persevering, determined, dogged, purposeful, tenacious, relentless, resolute, uncompromising, unyielding, wilful, headstrong, inflexible, obstinate, stubborn, self-willed, strong-willed, perverse, mulish, *formal* intractable, obdurate

pertinent *adj*
relevant, suitable, appropriate, fitting, apt, apposite, to the point, material, applicable, *formal* germane, apropos, *ad rem*
F3 inappropriate, unsuitable, irrelevant

pertness *n*
impudence, cheek, cheekiness, impertinence, insolence, presumption, rudeness, effrontery, forwardness, freshness, boldness, brashness, audacity, brazenness, *colloq.* sauciness, brass, cockiness, face, chutzpah

perturb *v*
worry, alarm, disturb, bother, trouble, upset, make anxious, disconcert, unsettle, discompose, disquiet, ruffle, fluster, confuse, agitate, vex
F3 reassure, compose

perturbed *adj*
worried, anxious, alarmed, upset, fearful, shaken, troubled, nervous, restless, disturbed, unsettled, discomposed, disconcerted, flustered, agitated, uncomfortable, uneasy, harassed, flurried
F3 calm, composed

perusal *n*
read, look, scrutiny, study, examination, inspection, check, browse, glance, skim, run-through

peruse *v*
study, pore over, read, scan, scrutinize, examine, inspect, check, browse, look through, run through, leaf through, glance through, skim

pervade *v*
affect, penetrate, permeate, percolate, charge, fill, pass through, spread through, be disseminated through, imbue, infuse, suffuse, diffuse, infiltrate, saturate, impregnate

pervasive *adj*
prevalent, common, extensive, widespread, general, universal, inescapable, rife, diffuse, ubiquitous, *formal* omnipresent, immanent

perverse *adj*
contrary, wayward, wrong-headed, wilful, headstrong, stubborn, obstinate, unyielding, disobedient, awkward, unruly, difficult, rebellious, troublesome, uncontrollable, unmanageable, ill-tempered, cantankerous, unreasonable, senseless, incorrect, improper, deviant, *formal* intransigent, obdurate, refractory, intractable, *colloq.* stroppy, bolshie, bloody-minded, nit-picking, pig-headed
F3 obliging, co-operative, reasonable

perversion *n*
1 CORRUPTION, depravity, debauchery, immorality, vice, wickedness, deviance, abnormality, irregularity, *colloq.* kinkiness **2** TWISTING, distortion, misrepresentation, travesty, misinterpretation, deviation, misuse, misapplication, falsification, *formal* aberration

perversity *n*
contrariness, waywardness, wrong-headedness, wilfulness, stubbornness, obstinacy, disobedience, awkwardness, unruliness, rebelliousness, troublesomeness, uncontrollability, unreasonableness, senselessness, contradictoriness, frowardness, gee, *formal* contumacy, intransigence, obduracy, refractoriness

pervert *v, n*
▶ *v* **1** *pervert the truth* twist, warp, distort, misrepresent, falsify, garble, misinterpret, misdirect, turn aside, deflect, avert **2** CORRUPT, lead astray, deprave, debauch, debase, degrade, warp, abuse, misuse, misapply, *formal* vitiate
▶ *n* deviate, deviant, debauchee, degenerate, *colloq.* weirdo, oddball

perverted *adj*
corrupt, depraved, debauched, debased, immoral, evil, wicked, corrupted, deviant, unnatural, abnormal, unhealthy, twisted, warped, distorted, *formal* vitiated, *colloq.* kinky
F3 natural, normal

pessimism *n*
defeatism, fatalism, hopelessness, cynicism, depression, dejection, despair, gloom, gloominess, glumness, despondency, doomwatch, melancholy, negative thinking, distrust, Weltschmerz, *colloq.* looking on the black side
F3 optimism, hopefulness

pessimist *n*
defeatist, fatalist, alarmist, doubter, cynic, melancholic, worrier, prophet of doom, gloom-monger, doomster, doomwatcher, doubting Thomas, *colloq.* dismal Jimmy, gloom and doom merchant, killjoy, wet blanket, no-hoper
F3 optimist, hopeful

pessimistic *adj*
negative, cynical, fatalistic, defeatist, resigned, distrustful, suspicious, doubting, hopeless, alarmist, discouraging, depressing, off-putting, despairing, despondent, dejected, downhearted, glum, morose, melancholy, depressed, dismal, gloomy, bleak, *colloq.* looking on the black side
F3 optimistic

pest *n*
nuisance, bother, annoyance, irritation, irritant, vexation, trial, curse, scourge, bane, blight, bug, *colloq.* pain, pain in the neck, thorn in the flesh

pester *v*
nag, badger, hound, harass, plague, torment, provoke, worry, irk, fret, bother, disturb, annoy, irritate, pick on, *colloq.* hassle, get at, get on someone's nerves, drive round the bend, drive up the wall

pestilence *n*
plague, epidemic, disease, sickness, infection, contagion, infestation, cholera, *formal* pandemic

pestilent *adj*
1 HARMFUL, destructive, ruinous, diseased, disease-ridden, plague-ridden, poisonous, contaminated, contagious, infectious, infected, communicable, catching, corrupting, detrimental, pernicious, *formal* deleterious **2** INFURIATING, troublesome, annoying, bothersome, irritating, tiresome, vexing, irksome

pestilential *adj*
infuriating, troublesome, annoying, bothersome, irri-

tating, tiresome, vexing, irksome, pernicious

pet¹ *n, adj, v*
▶ *n* teacher's *pet* favourite, darling, idol, treasure, jewel, *colloq.* teacher's pet, apple of your eye, blue-eyed boy/girl
▶ *adj* favourite, favoured, preferred, dear, dearest, cherished, prized, preferred, chosen, special, particular, personal
▶ *v* stroke, caress, fondle, cuddle, embrace, kiss, *colloq.* neck, canoodle, smooch, *slang* snog

pet² *n*
in a pet bad mood, bad temper, temper, sulk(s), tantrum, *colloq.* paddy, hump, huff, stew, grumps, the pits

peter *v*
▷ **peter out** dwindle, taper off, fade, wane, evaporate, ebb, diminish, fail, cease, stop, die away, come to an end, come to nothing, *colloq.* fizzle out

petite *adj*
dainty, small, slight, little, delicate, bijou, dinky
🔁 big, large

petition *n, v*
▶ *n* appeal, round robin, protest, application, request, solicitation, plea, entreaty, prayer, supplication, *formal* invocation
▶ *v* appeal, call upon, ask, crave, solicit, bid, urge, press, implore, beg, plead, entreat, beseech, pray, request, *formal* supplicate, adjure, sue

pet name *n*
diminutive, endearment, term of endearment, nickname, *formal* hypocorisma

petrified *adj*
terrified, terror-stricken, aghast, horrified, horror-stricken, appalled, scared stiff, stunned, dumbfounded, shocked, speechless, stupefied, transfixed, numb, benumbed, dazed, frozen

petrify *v*
1 TERRIFY, horrify, frighten, alarm, panic, appal, paralyse, numb, stupefy, stun, dumbfound 2 TURN TO STONE, ossify, fossilize

pettifogging *adj*
mean, petty, quibbling, paltry, captious, niggling, over-refined, subtle, sophistical, cavilling, casuistic, equivocating, *colloq.* hair-splitting, nit-picking

pettish *adj*
peevish, sulky, irritable, petulant, thin-skinned, tetchy, grumpy, bad-tempered, ill-humoured, fractious, cross, fretful, querulous, snappish, waspish, *formal* splenetic, *colloq.* huffy, touchy

petty *adj*
1 MINOR, unimportant, insignificant, inconsequential, inessential, trivial, secondary, lesser, small, little, slight, trifling, paltry, inconsiderable, negligible, *colloq.* measly, grotty, piffling, piddling, no great shakes 2 SMALL-MINDED, narrow-minded, mean, ungenerous, grudging, spiteful
🔁 1 important, significant 2 generous

petulance *n*
bad temper, irritability, ill-temper, ill-humour, sulkiness, sullenness, waspishness, peevishness, pique, *formal* procacity, querulousness, spleen, *colloq.* crabbedness, crabbiness

petulant *adj*
fretful, peevish, cross, irritable, snappish, bad-tempered, ill-humoured, complaining, impatient, moody, sullen, sulky, sour, ungracious, *formal* querulous, *colloq.* crotchety, crabby, crabbed, touchy, ratty, browned off, in a paddy, in a stew

phantom *n*
ghost, spectre, spirit, apparition, wraith, vision, hallu-

cination, illusion, figment, *formal* revenant, *colloq.* spook

pharisaical *adj*
sanctimonious, self-righteous, holier-than-thou, formal, hypocritical, insincere, pietistic, preachy, moralizing, *colloq.* goody-goody

Pharisee *n*
hypocrite, fraud, pietist, whited sepulchre, *formal* dissembler, dissimulator, *colloq.* phoney, humbug

phase *n, v*
▶ *n* stage, step, time, juncture, period, spell, season, chapter, position, part, point, aspect, form, shape, state, condition
▶ *v* ▷ **phase in** introduce, ease in, bring in, start, start using, initiate
▷ **phase out** wind down, run down, ease off, taper off, wind up, eliminate, dispose of, get rid of, remove, withdraw, close, stop, stop using, *formal* terminate

phenomenal *adj*
marvellous, sensational, stupendous, amazing, astounding, astonishing, breath-taking, remarkable, extraordinary, exceptional, unprecedented, unparalleled, unique, singular, unheard of, unusual, unbelievable, incredible, wonderful, fantastic, *colloq.* mind-blowing, mind-boggling, too good to be true

phenomenon *n*
1 OCCURRENCE, happening, event, incident, episode, circumstance, fact, experience, appearance, sight 2 WONDER, marvel, miracle, prodigy, rarity, curiosity, spectacle, sensation

philander *v*
womanize, flirt, dally, play/fool around, have an affair, *colloq.* sleep around

philanderer *n*
womanizer, ladies' man, flirt, dallier, libertine, playboy, Casanova, Don Juan, *colloq.* lady-killer, stud, wolf

philanthropic *adj*
humanitarian, public-spirited, altruistic, unselfish, selfless, benevolent, kind, kind-hearted, humane, charitable, alms-giving, generous, liberal, open-handed, *formal* munificent, bounteous, bountiful
🔁 misanthropic

philanthropist *n*
humanitarian, benefactor, patron, sponsor, giver, donor, helper, backer, contributor, alms-giver, altruist
🔁 misanthrope

philanthropy *n*
humanitarianism, public-spiritedness, altruism, unselfishness, selflessness, social concern/awareness, social conscience, benevolence, kind-heartedness, charity, alms-giving, giving, patronage, sponsorship, help, backing, generosity, liberality, open-handedness, *formal* beneficence, munificence, bounteousness, bountifulness
🔁 misanthropy

philippic *n*
diatribe, tirade, abuse, harangue, attack, onslaught, denunciation, criticism, insult, reviling, upbraiding, reproof, reprimand, rebuke, *formal* invective, vituperation

philistine *n, adj*
▶ *n* lowbrow, ignoramus, barbarian, bourgeois, vulgarian, yahoo, *colloq.* boor, lout
▶ *adj* uncultivated, uncultured, uneducated, unrefined, unread, unlettered, ignorant, lowbrow, tasteless, boorish, bourgeois, crass

philosopher *n*
philosophizer, thinker, theorist, theorizer, analyser, scho-

lar, expert, guru, metaphysicist, sage, logician, *technical* epistemologist, dialectician, *formal* deipnosophist

philosophical *adj*
1 *a philosophical discussion* metaphysical, abstract, theoretical, analytical, rational, logical, erudite, learned, wise, thoughtful, pensive, reflective, contemplative, meditative **2** RESIGNED, patient, stoic, stoical, self-possessed, dispassionate, unruffled, calm, composed, collected, cool, rational, logical, realistic, *formal* phlegmatic, imperturbable

philosophy *n*
1 *study philosophy* reason, thought, thinking, wisdom, knowledge **2** IDEOLOGY, world-view, doctrine, beliefs, convictions, tenets, values, principles, attitude, viewpoint, point of view, view

Philosophical terms include :

absolutism, aesthetics, agnosticism, altruism, antinomianism, a posteriori, a priori, ascetism, atheism, atomism, behaviourism, deduction, deism, deontology, determinism, dialectical materialism, dogmatism, dualism, egoism, empiricism, entailment, Epicureanism, epistemology, ethics, existentialism, fatalism, hedonism, historicism, humanism, idealism, identity, induction, instrumentalism, interactionism, intuition, jurisprudence, libertarianism, logic, logical positivism, materialism, metaphysics, monism, naturalism, nihilism, nominalism, objectivism, ontology, pantheism, phenomenalism, phenomenology, positivism, pragmatism, prescriptivism, rationalism, realism, reductionism, relativism, scepticism, scholasticism, sensationalism, sense data, solipsism, stoicism, structuralism, subjectivism, substance, syllogism, teleology, theism, transcendentalism, utilitarianism.

phlegmatic *adj*
placid, stolid, impassive, calm, tranquil, cool, unemotional, unconcerned, indifferent, matter-of-fact, stoical, dispassionate, *formal* imperturbable, *colloq.* cool and collected
🢒 emotional, passionate, nervous

phobia *n*
fear, irrational fear, terror, dread, anxiety, neurosis, obsession, aversion, dislike, hatred, horror, loathing, revulsion, repulsion, *formal* antipathy, detestation, *colloq.* hang-up, thing
🢒 love, liking

Phobias (by name of fear) include:
zoophobia (*animals*), apiphobia (*bees*), ailurophobia (*cats*), necrophobia (*corpses*), scotophobia (*darkness*), cynophobia (*dogs*), claustrophobia (*enclosed places*), panphobia (*everything*), pyrophobia (*fire*), xenophobia (*foreigners*), phasmophobia (*ghosts*), acrophobia (*high places*), hippophobia (*horses*), entomophobia (*insects*), astraphobia (*lightning*), autophobia (*loneliness*), agoraphobia (*open spaces*), toxiphobia (*poison*), herpetophobia (*reptiles*), ophiophobia (*snakes*), tachophobia (*speed*), arachnophobia (*spiders*), triskaidekaphobia (*thirteen*), brontophobia (*thunder*), hydrophobia (*water*).

phone *n, v*
🢒 *n* **1** TELEPHONE, receiver, handset, mobile phone,

car phone, *colloq.* blower **2** *give me a quick phone* ring, call, phone call, *colloq.* buzz, tinkle, bell
🢒 *v* telephone, ring (up), call (up), dial, contact, get in touch, give someone a call, make a call, *colloq.* give a buzz, give a tinkle, give a bell

phonetic alphabet *n*

Communications code words for the letters of the alphabet are:
Alpha, Bravo, Charlie, Delta, Echo, Foxtrot, Golf, Hotel, India, Juliet, Kilo, Lima, Mike, November, Oscar, Papa, Quebec, Romeo, Sierra, Tango, Uniform, Victor, Whisky, X-ray, Yankee, Zulu.

phoney *adj, n*
🢒 *adj* fake, counterfeit, forged, fraudulent, bogus, trick, false, mock, spurious, assumed, feigned, simulated, affected, put-on, contrived, sham, imitation, ersatz, *colloq.* pseudo
🢒 real, genuine
🢒 *n* impostor, pretender, fraud, sham, fake, faker, forgery, counterfeit, mountebank, *colloq.* humbug, pseud, quack

phosphorescent *adj*
glowing, bright, luminescent, luminous, radiant, *technical* noctilucent, noctilucous, *formal* refulgent

photocopy *v, n*
🢒 *v* copy, duplicate, photostat, xerox, print, run off
🢒 *n* copy, duplicate, facsimile, Photostat®, Xerox®

photograph *n, v*
🢒 *n* photo, snap, snapshot, print, shot, still, slide, transparency, videotape, picture, image, likeness, *colloq.* mug shot
🢒 *v* snap, take, take a picture of, take a photograph of, take a snapshot of, film, shoot, video, record, capture on film/videotape

photographic *adj*
1 *photographic equipment* filmic, graphic, cinematic, pictorial **2** *photographic memory* accurate, exact, detailed, faithful, precise, realistic, retentive, vivid, minute, visual, lifelike, natural, naturalistic, representational

Photographic equipment includes:
camera, boom arm, flash umbrella, stand, tripod; developer bath, developing tank, dry mounting press, easel, enlarger, enlarger timer, film-drying cabinet, fixing bath, focus magnifier, light-box, negative carrier, print washer, contact printer, print-drying rack, paper drier, safelight, stop bath, Vertoscope®, viewer; slide viewer, slide projector, film projector, screen.

Photographic accessories include:
air-shutter release, battery, cable release, camera bag, eye-cup, eyepiece magnifier, film, cartridge film, cassette film, disc film, film pack, filter, colour filter, heat filter, polarizing filter, skylight filter, flashbulb, flashcube, flashgun, flash unit, hot shoe, lens, afocal lens, auxiliary lens, close-up lens, fisheye lens, macro lens, supplementary lens, telephoto lens, teleconverter, wide-angle lens, zoom lens, lens cap, lens hood, lens shield, light meter, exposure meter, spot meter, diffuser, barn doors, honeycomb diffuser, parabolic reflector, snoot, slide mount, viewfinder, right-angle finder; camcorder battery discharger/charger/tester, cassette adaptor, remote control, tele-cine converter, video editor, video light, video mixer. *See also* CAMERA.

phrase *n, v*
▶ *n* construction, clause, idiom, expression, group of words, saying, utterance, remark, comment, language, phraseology, usage, way/style of speaking
▶ *v* word, formulate, frame, couch, present, put, express, say, utter, pronounce

phraseology *n*
terminology, phrase, phrasing, wording, expression, idiom, language, parlance, speech, writing, style, syntax, diction, argot, cant, patois

physical *adj*
1 BODILY, corporeal, fleshy, fleshly, carnal, incarnate, mortal, earthly, unspiritual, *formal* somatic **2** MATERIAL, concrete, solid, substantial, tangible, palpable, visible, real, actual
F3 1 mental, spiritual **2** abstract, theoretical

physician *n*
doctor, medical practitioner, general practitioner, GP, houseman, intern, registrar, consultant, specialist, healer, *colloq.* medic, doc, quack, medico

physics *n*

Terms used in physics include :

absolute zero, acceleration, acoustics, alpha particles, analogue signal, applied physics, Archimedes principle, area, atom, beta particles, Big Bang theory, boiling point, bubble-chamber, capillary action, centre of gravity, centre of mass, centrifugal force, chain reaction, charge, charged particle, circuit, circuit-breaker, couple, critical mass, cryogenics, density, diffraction, digital, dynamics, efficiency, elasticity, electric current, electric discharge, electricity, electrodynamics, electromagnetic spectrum, electromagnetic waves, electron, energy, engine, entropy, equation, equilibrium, evaporation, field, flash point, force, formula, freezing point, frequency, friction, fundamental constant, gamma ray, gas, gate, grand united theory (GUT), gravity, half-life, heat, heavy water, hydraulics, hydrodynamics, hydrostatics, incandescence, indeterminacy principle, inertia, infrared, interference, ion, Kelvin effect, kinetic energy, kinetic theory, laser (light amplification by stimulated emission of radiation), latent heat, law, laws of motion, laws of reflection, laws of refraction, laws of thermodynamics, lens, lever, light, light emission, light intensity, light source, liquid, longitudinal wave, luminescence, Mach number, magnetic field, magnetism, mass, mechanics, microwaves, mirror, Mohs scale, molecule, moment, momentum, motion, neutron, nuclear, nuclear fission, nuclear fusion, nuclear physics, nucleus, optical centre, optics, oscillation, parallel motion, particle, periodic law, perpetual motion, phonon, photon, photosensitivity, polarity, potential energy, power, pressure, principle, process, proton, quantum chromodynamics (QCD), quantum electrodynamics (QED), quantum mechanics, quantum theory, quark, radiation, radioactive element, radioactivity, radioisotope, radio wave, ratio, reflection, refraction, relativity, resistance, resonance, rule, semiconductor, sensitivity, separation, SI unit, sound, sound wave, specific gravity, specific heat capacity, spectroscopy, spectrum, speed, states of matter, statics, substance, superstring theory, supersymmetry, surface tension, temperature, tension, theory, theory of

relativity, thermodynamics, Thomson effect, transverse wave, ultrasound, ultraviolet, uncertainty principle, velocity, visible spectrum, viscosity, volume, wave, wave property, weight, white heat, work, X-ray.
See also ATOM; ELECTRICITY.

physiognomy *n*
face, features, look, *old use* visnomy, *formal* countenance, visage, *colloq.* clock, dial, mug, phiz, phizog, kisser

physique *n*
body, figure, shape, form, build, frame, structure, constitution, make-up

pick *v, n*
▶ *v* **1** SELECT, choose, go for, opt for, decide on, settle on, fix on, single out, prefer, favour, make up your mind, *colloq.* plump for **2** GATHER, collect, pluck, pull, harvest, cull, take in **3** *pick a lock/safe* open, crack, break open, prise open, force open **4** *pick a quarrel* cause, start, begin, provoke, produce, lead to, prompt, give rise to
▷ **pick at** nibble, peck, play with, toy with, eat small amounts of
▷ **pick off 1** SHOOT, hit, kill, remove, strike, fire at, take out **2** REMOVE, detach, take away, pull off
▷ **pick on** bully, torment, persecute, criticize, blame, find fault with, nag, bait, *colloq.* get at, needle
▷ **pick out** discern, make out, spot, notice, perceive, recognize, distinguish, tell apart, discriminate, separate, single out, hand-pick, choose, select
▷ **pick up 1** LIFT, raise, hoist, take up **2** *I'll pick you up at eight* call for, fetch, collect, give a lift/ride **3** LEARN, master, grasp, acquire, get to know, gather **4** IMPROVE, get better, rally, recover, make progress, make headway, *colloq.* perk up **5** ARREST, take into custody, apprehend, *colloq.* nick, nab, collar, run in, take in **6** RESUME, begin again, start again, continue, go on, carry on **7** OBTAIN, acquire, gain, learn, hear, find, discover, come across, buy, purchase, *formal* chance upon **8** *pick up an infection* catch, contract, get, become ill with, become infected with, go down with **9** *pick up a radio signal* receive, detect, get, hear
▶ *n* **1** CHOICE, selection, option, decision, preference, favour **2** BEST, cream, choicest, prize, flower, elite, elect, crème de la crème

picket *n, v*
▶ *n* **1** PICKETER, protester, objector, rebel, dissident, demonstrator, striker **2** GUARD, sentry, watch, patrol, lookout, outpost **3** STAKE, post, spike, upright, pike, stanchion, pale, paling
▶ *v* protest, demonstrate, boycott, blockade, go on a picket line, enclose, surround

pickings *n*
proceeds, profits, returns, rewards, earnings, yield, take, spoils, booty, loot, plunder, *slang* gravy

pickle *n, v*
▶ *n* **1** *cheese and pickle* chutney, relish, vinegar, sauce, flavouring, seasoning, condiment **2** MESS, difficulty, dilemma, predicament, crisis, quandary, straits, *formal* exigency, *colloq.* bind, fix, hot water, jam, pinch, scrape, spot, tight spot
▶ *v* preserve, conserve, souse, marinade, steep, cure, salt

pick-me-up *n*
tonic, boost, refreshment, restorative, fillip, stimulant, stimulus, cordial, *technical* roborant, *colloq.* shot in the arm

pick-pocket *n*
thief, snatcher, pick-purse, *old use* file, *colloq.* dip, diver, wire

picnic n

1 *a picnic lunch* outing, excursion, outdoor meal, *fête champêtre*, wayzgoose **2** *minding young children is no picnic*, *colloq.* child's play, cinch, doddle, piece of cake, pushover, walkover

pictorial adj

graphic, diagrammatic, schematic, representational, vivid, striking, expressive, illustrated, picturesque, scenic, in pictures, in photographs

picture n, v

▸ *n* **1** DESCRIPTION, portrayal, depiction, account, report, story, narrative, tale, semblance, impression, *formal* delineation, similitude

Kinds of picture include:
abstract, cameo, canvas, caricature, cartoon, collage, design, doodle, drawing, effigy, engraving, etching, fresco, graffiti, graphics, icon, identikit, illustration, image, kakemono, landscape, likeness, miniature, montage, mosaic, *colloq.* mug shot, mural, negative, oil-painting, old master, painting, passport photo, Photofit®, photograph, photogravure, pin-up, plate, portrait, print, representation, reproduction, self-portrait, silhouette, sketch, slide, *colloq.* snap, snapshot, still, still life, study, tableau, tapestry, tracing, transfer, transparency, triptych, trompe l'oeil, vignette, watercolour.

2 *the picture of health* embodiment, personification, epitome, essence, *formal* archetype, exemplar, quintessence **3** FILM, motion picture, *old use colloq.* flick **4** *go to the pictures* cinema, movies, picture-house, film theatre, entertainment centre, multiplex, picture-palace, *old use colloq.* flicks
▷ **get the picture** understand, grasp, take in, follow, see, *formal* comprehend, *colloq.* get the message, get it, get the idea, get the point, cotton on, tumble to
▷ **put someone in the picture** inform, tell, notify, communicate, explain, update, *colloq.* fill in, clue up, keep posted
▸ *v* **1** IMAGINE, envisage, envision, conceive, visualize, call to mind, see, see in your mind's eye **2** DEPICT, describe, represent, reproduce, show, portray, draw, sketch, paint, photograph, illustrate, appear, *formal* delineate

picturesque adj

1 ATTRACTIVE, beautiful, pretty, lovely, delightful, charming, pleasant, pleasing, quaint, idyllic, scenic **2** DESCRIPTIVE, graphic, vivid, colourful, striking, impressive
F3 **1** unattractive **2** dull, boring

piddling adj

paltry, meagre, derisory, contemptible, mean, low, miserable, wretched, poor, sorry, small, slight, trifling, inconsiderate, negligible, trivial, minor, contemptible, petty, unimportant, insignificant, puny, worthless, *colloq.* measly, piffling
F3 substantial, significant, valuable

pie n

pastry, tart
▷ **pie in the sky** daydream, dream, delusion, fantasy, reverie, romance, mirage, notion, *colloq.* jam tomorrow, hot air, castle in Spain, castle in the air

piebald adj

black and white, dappled, flecked, mottled, pied, spotted, speckled, variegated, brindle(d), skewbald

piece n, v

▸ *n* **1** FRAGMENT, bit, scrap, crumb, morsel, flake, speck, fleck, titbit, mouthful, bite, lump, chunk, wedge, hunk, dollop, block, slab, bar, slice, sliver, snippet, chip, splinter, shred, offcut, length, sample, component, constituent, element; part, segment, section, unit, division, fraction, share, allocation, allotment, percentage, quota, portion, quantity, *US* tidbit, *colloq.* smithereen, cut **2** ARTICLE, item, study, work, opus, story, review, composition, report, illustration, creation, specimen, example, instance
▷ **all in one piece** intact, unbroken, whole, complete, integral, entire, undamaged, unharmed, unhurt, uninjured
F3 broken, incomplete, damaged
▷ **go to pieces** lose control, break down, be overcome, collapse, *colloq.* crack up
▷ **in pieces** in bits, broken, damaged, disintegrated, ruined, shattered, smashed, *colloq.* kaput, in smithereens
▸ *v* ▷ **piece together** assemble, join, put together, unite, attach, compose, fit, mend, fix, repair, patch, restore

pièce de résistance n

masterpiece, masterwork, prize, showpiece, magnum opus, *chef-d'oeuvre*, jewel

piecemeal adv, adj

▸ *adv* little by little, intermittently, parcel-wise, partially, at intervals, slowly, bit by bit, by degrees, fitfully, *colloq.* in dribs and drabs
F3 completely, entirely, wholly
▸ *adj* fragmentary, intermittent, interrupted, partial, unsystematic, scattered, patchy, sporadic, *formal* discrete
F3 complete, entire, whole, wholesale

pied adj

flecked, irregular, motley, mottled, multicoloured, parti-coloured, piebald, dappled, brindle(d), spotted, streaked, skewbald, varicoloured, variegated

pier n

1 JETTY, breakwater, landing-stage, dock, quay, wharf **2** SUPPORT, upright, pile, pillar, post, column

pierce v

1 PENETRATE, enter, pass through, stick into, puncture, drill, bore, probe, perforate, punch, prick, stab, lance, bayonet, run through, spear, skewer, spike, impale, transfix **2** *pierce someone's spirit* stab, sting, pain, hurt, move, prick, cut to the quick **3** *pierce the darkness* burst through, penetrate, fill, enter, light up

pierced adj

perforated, impaled, punctured, stung, *formal* pertusate, pertuse(d)

piercing adj

1 *a piercing cry* shrill, high-pitched, loud, ear-splitting, ear-piercing, penetrating, sharp, keen **2** PENETRATING, probing, searching, discerning, perceptive, shrewd, alert, astute, sharp, sharp-witted **3** COLD, bitter, raw, biting, numbing, keen, fierce, severe, wintry, frosty, freezing, Arctic **4** PAINFUL, agonizing, excruciating, extreme, severe, intense, stabbing, lacerating, shooting

piety n

piousness, devoutness, godliness, saintliness, holiness, sanctity, spirituality, religiousness, religion, faith, devotion, reverence, respect, deference
F3 impiety, irreligion

piffle n

nonsense, rubbish, trash, tripe, drivel, balderdash, rot, tarradiddle, *colloq.* bunk, bunkum, codswallop, guff, hooey, poppycock, tommy-rot, tosh, twaddle

pig n, v

▸ *n* **1** SWINE, hog, sow, boar, grunter, piglet, *colloq.* piggy **2** ANIMAL, beast, brute, boor **3** GLUTTON, gormandizer, gourmand, *colloq.* greedy guts, guzzler

▶ *v* gorge, guzzle, stuff, *colloq.* wolf

pigeonhole *n, v*
▶ *n* **1** COMPARTMENT, niche, slot, cubbyhole, cubicle, locker, box, place, section **2** CATEGORY, class, classification, compartment
▶ *v* **1** LABEL, compartmentalize, categorize, classify, sort, file, tag, slot, catalogue, alphabetize **2** SHELVE, defer, postpone, put off, *colloq.* put on the back burner

pig-headed *adj*
stubborn, obstinate, perverse, self-willed, stiff-necked, inflexible, contrary, mulish, stupid, unyielding, wilful, wrong-headed, headstrong, bull-headed, *old use* froward, *formal* intractable, intransigent
➡ flexible, tractable

pigment *n*
colour, hue, tint, dye, stain, paint, colouring, tincture, colourant

pile[1] *n, v*
▶ *n* **1** STACK, heap, bundle, mound, mountain, mass, accumulation, collection, assortment, hoard, stockpile, store, *formal* assemblage **2** LARGE QUANTITY, a great deal, a lot, quantities, *colloq.* loads, lots, lashings, stacks, heaps, oodles, millions, thousands, hundreds, tons **3** *make a pile* fortune, wealth, riches, *colloq.* mint, packet, bundle, bomb, *slang* megabucks, big bucks **4** *a pile in the country* large building, imposing/impressive building, edifice
▶ *v* **1** STACK, heap, mass, amass, accumulate, build up, gather, assemble, collect, hoard, stockpile, store, load **2** PACK, jam, crush, squeeze, crowd, flock, flood, stream, rush, charge
▷ **pile it on** exaggerate, overstate, overdo, magnify, overemphasize, emphasize, stress, make too much of, overplay, dramatize, overdramatize, *colloq.* lay it on, lay/pile it on thick, lay/pile it on with a trowel, make a mountain out of a molehill, blow something up out of all proportion
➡ understate, play down
▷ **pile up** mount up, increase, grow, accumulate, multiply, escalate, soar

pile[2] *n*
houses built on piles post, piling, column, upright, support, bar, beam, foundation

pile[3] *n*
the pile of a carpet nap, shag, plush, fur, hair, fluff, fuzz, down, wool, (soft) surface, texture

pile-up *n*
crash, accident, collision, bump, wreck, *colloq.* smash, smash-up, prang

pilfer *v*
steal, filch, shoplift, rob, thieve, *formal* purloin, peculate, *colloq.* pinch, nick, knock off, lift, snaffle, swipe, nobble, have sticky fingers, snitch

pilgrim *n*
crusader, traveller, wanderer, wayfarer, worshipper, devotee, palmer, hadji

pilgrimage *n*
crusade, mission, expedition, journey, trip, tour, hadj

pill *n*
tablet, capsule, lozenge, pellet, ball, bolus

pillage *v, n*
▶ *v* plunder, raid, sack, vandalize, maraud, loot, spoil, ransack, ravage, raze, freeboot, rifle, rob, strip, *formal* depredate, despoil, spoliate
▶ *n* plunder, sack, devastation, marauding, harrying, seizure, spoils, robbery, loot, booty, *formal* depredation, rapine, spoliation

pillar *n*
1 COLUMN, shaft, pole, post, mast, pier, upright, pile, support, prop, stanchion, *technical* cippus **2** *a pillar of society* mainstay, bastion, support, rock, tower of strength

pillory *v*
ridicule, mock, pour scorn on, laugh at, denounce, lash, hold up to shame, show up, brand, cast a slur on, stigmatize

pillow *n*
cushion, bolster, rest, headrest, bed

pilot *n, v, adj*
▶ *n* **1** FLYER, aviator, airman, airwoman, captain, commander, first officer, flight engineer, crew, aircrew **2** NAVIGATOR, steersman, helmsman, coxswain, captain, leader, director, guide
▶ *v* fly, drive, steer, direct, control, handle, manoeuvre, manage, operate, run, conduct, lead, guide, navigate
▶ *adj* experimental, trial, test, model

pimp *n*
pander, panderer, procurer, go-between, fancy man, fleshmonger, solicitor, *slang* hustler, mack

pimple *n*
spot, blackhead, boil, swelling, papula, papule, pustule, *colloq.* zit

pin *v, n*
▶ *v* **1** TACK, nail, fix, stick, affix, attach, join, staple, clip, fasten, secure **2** HOLD DOWN, hold fast, restrain, constrain, press, immobilize **3** *pin the blame on someone* attach, put, place, lay, attribute, ascribe, *formal* impute
▷ **pin down 1** PINPOINT, identify, define, determine, specify, *colloq.* nail down, put your finger on **2** FORCE, make, compel, press, pressurize, hold down, hold fast, restrain, constrain, *colloq.* nail down
▶ *n* tack, nail, screw, spike, rivet, bolt, peg, dowel, fastener, clip, staple, brooch

pincers *n*
forceps, tweezers, forfex

pinch *v, n*
▶ *v* **1** SQUEEZE, compress, crush, press, tweak, nip, hurt, confine, cramp, grip, grasp **2** STEAL, pilfer, filch, snatch, *formal* appropriate, purloin, peculate, *colloq.* nick, walk off with, knock off, lift **3** ECONOMIZE, save, cut back, budget, keep costs down, live on the cheap, scrimp and save, *colloq.* tighten your belt, cut your coat according to your cloth, scrape a living **4** ARREST, capture, catch, seize, detain, *colloq.* bust, nick, collar, nab, book, run in, pick up, nail
▶ *n* **1** SQUEEZE, tweak, nip **2** DASH, soupçon, trace, taste, bit, touch, speck, jot, mite, *colloq.* smidgen, tad **3** EMERGENCY, crisis, predicament, difficulty, hardship, pressure, stress
▷ **at a pinch** if necessary, if absolutely necessary, in an emergency, with great difficulty

pinched *adj*
pale, thin, drawn, haggard, gaunt, peaky, careworn, worn, narrowed, straightened, starved
➡ healthy, chubby

pine *v*
1 YEARN, long, ache, sigh, wish, desire, crave, hanker, hunger, thirst **2** *pine away from grief* grieve, mourn, fret, weaken, fade, languish, waste away

pinion *v*
pin down, tie, fasten, confine, bind, chain, fetter, manacle, shackle, hobble, immobilize, truss

pink[1] *adj, n*
▶ *adj* *pink flowers* reddish, flushed, rose, rosy, salmon, roseate
▶ *n* perfection, height, peak, extreme, best, flower, summit, top, tiptop, *formal* acme
▷ **in the pink** fit, healthy, well, very well, in good

pink² *v*

to pink cloth cut, notch, serrate, perforate, score, incise, prick, punch, scallop, *formal* crenellate

pinnacle *n*

1 PEAK, summit, top, cap, crown, crest, apex, vertex, height, eminence, culmination, *formal* acme, zenith, apogee **2** SPIRE, steeple, turret, pyramid, cone, obelisk, needle

pinpoint *v*

identify, spot, distinguish, locate, place, home in on, pin down, discover, determine, specify, define, *colloq.* zero in on, nail down, put your finger on

pint-size *adj*

pint-sized, little, small, pocket, pocket-sized, tiny, diminutive, miniature, dwarf, midget, *Scot.* wee

F3 1 giant, huge, enormous

pioneer *n, v*

▶ *n* **1** SETTLER, colonist, frontiersman, frontierswoman, explorer **2** *a pioneer in science* developer, pathfinder, trail-blazer, ground-breaker, leader, innovator, inventor, discoverer, founder, founding father

▶ *v* invent, discover, originate, create, initiate, instigate, begin, start, launch, institute, introduce, found, establish, set up, develop, open up, prepare the way for, lead the way, spearhead, break new ground, blaze a trail, make the first move, *colloq.* set/start the ball rolling, pave the way

pious *adj*

1 DEVOUT, godly, saintly, holy, spiritual, religious, reverent, sanctified, faithful, dedicated, devoted, good, virtuous, righteous, moral **2** SANCTIMONIOUS, self-righteous, unctuous, hypocritical, insincere, *colloq.* holier-than-thou, goody-goody, pi

F3 1 impious, irreligious, irreverent

pipe *n, v*

▶ *n* **1** TUBE, hose, piping, tubing, pipeline, line, main, flue, duct, conduit, drainpipe, channel, passage, cylinder, conveyor, overflow **2** *pipe and tobacco* clay, claypipe, hookah, hubble-bubble, kalian, water pipe, brier, dudeen, meerschaum, narghile, calumet, peace-pipe

▶ *v* **1** CHANNEL, funnel, siphon, carry, bring, take, convey, conduct, duct, transmit, supply, deliver **2** WHISTLE, chirp, tweet, cheep, chirrup, peep, twitter, sing, warble, trill, shrill, play, sound

▷ **pipe down** be quiet, stop talking, *colloq.* shut up

pipe dream *n*

daydream, dream, delusion, fantasy, reverie, romance, mirage, notion, *formal* chimera, vagary, *colloq.* castle in Spain, castle in the air, pie in the sky

pipeline *n*

passage, pipe, tube, line, conduit, channel, duct, conveyor

▷ **in the pipeline** in preparation, planned, already started, under way

pipsqueak *n*

nobody, nonentity, nothing, *colloq.* upstart, squirt, twerp, whippersnapper, creep, hobbledehoy

F3 somebody

piquancy *n*

1 SPICINESS, pungency, tang, pepperiness, spice, relish, flavour, sharpness, ginger, bite **2** LIVELINESS, excitement, interest, vigour, vitality, spirit, zest, colour, raciness, punch, *colloq.* edge, kick, pep, pizzazz, zip

piquant *adj*

1 *piquant sauce* spicy, tangy, savoury, salty, peppery, seasoned, highly seasoned, pungent, zesty, sharp, bit-

ing, tart, stinging **2** LIVELY, spirited, stimulating, provocative, interesting, sparkling, intriguing, fascinating, sharp, racy, colourful, *colloq.* juicy

F3 1 bland, insipid **2** dull, banal

pique *n, v*

▶ *n* annoyance, anger, irritation, gall, vexation, displeasure, offence, resentment, grudge, umbrage, *colloq.* huff

▶ *v* **1** AROUSE, stimulate, excite, goad, rouse, provoke, stir, spur, whet, kindle, galvanize **2** ANNOY, anger, irritate, affront, displease, gall, irk, get, put out, rile, incense, offend, mortify, vex, wound, sting, *formal* miff, nettle, peeve

piqued *adj*

annoyed, irritated, vexed, riled, angry, displeased, offended, put out, resentful, *colloq.* miffed, peeved

piracy *n*

buccaneering, freebooting, bootlegging, robbery, stealing, theft, hijacking, infringement, plagiarism, *formal* rapine

pirate *n, v*

▶ *n* **1** BUCCANEER, brigand, freebooter, filibuster, corsair, marauder, raider, rover, picaroon, sea robber, sea rover, sea wolf, sea rat, water rat, marque **2** INFRINGER, plagiarist, plagiarizer

▶ *v* copy, reproduce illegally, steal, pinch, plagiarize, poach, *formal* appropriate, *colloq.* borrow, crib, lift, nick

pirouette *n, v*

▶ *n* gyration, spin, turn, twirl, whirl, pivot

▶ *v* gyrate, spin, turn, twirl, whirl, pivot

pistol *n*

gun, handgun, revolver, sidearm, six-shooter, Luger®, dag, *US* derringer, *colloq.* gat, iron, piece, rod

pit *n, v*

▶ *n* **1** *dig a pit* hole, cavity, crater, pothole, gulf, chasm, abyss, mine, coalmine, quarry, diggings, trench, ditch, excavations, workings **2** HOLLOW, depression, dent, indentation, pockmark

▶ *v* pockmark, blemish, scar, mark, dent, notch, depress, indent, dimple, pothole

▷ **pit against** compete, match, oppose, set against

pitch¹ *v, n*

▶ *v* **1** THROW, fling, toss, cast, lob, bowl, hurl, heave, sling, fire, launch, aim, direct, *colloq.* chuck **2** PLUNGE, dive, plummet, drop, fall, fall headlong, topple, tumble **3** *pitch camp* erect, put up, set up, place, station, settle, plant, fix **4** MOVE UP AND DOWN, lurch, sway, roll, reel, keel, list, flounder, wallow

▷ **pitch in** join in, co-operate, be involved, participate, help, lend a hand, *colloq.* muck in, do your bit

▶ *n* **1** *cricket pitch* ground, field, sports field, playing-field, park, arena, stadium **2** SOUND, tone, timbre, tonality, modulation, frequency, level **3** GRADIENT, incline, slope, slant, tilt, angle, degree, inclination, steepness, cant **4** *reach a high pitch* level, degree, extent, height, point, position, intensity, grade, mark **5** THROW, fling, toss, lob, hurl, *colloq.* chuck **6** TALK, patter, line, gabble, chatter, jargon, *colloq.* spiel, yak

pitch² *n*

to coat a surface with pitch tar, bitumen, asphalt

pitch-black *adj*

pitch-dark, black, dark, jet-black, inky, coal-black, unilluminated, unlit

pitcher *n*

jug, ewer, jar, vessel, crock, bottle, can, container, urn

piteous *adj*

poignant, moving, touching, distressing, heartbreaking, heart-rending, plaintive, mournful, sad, sorrowful, woeful, wretched, pitiful, pitiable, pathetic

 piteous, pitiable or **pitiful** ?

Pitiful means 'very sad, arousing or deserving pity': *She was a pitiful sight*; and also 'arousing or deserving contempt, very bad, very poor': *a pitiful attempt at catching the ball. Pitiable* means the same as *pitiful* but is less common: *He was in a pitiable condition; That was a pitiable attempt you made. Piteous* is a rather formal word meaning 'arousing or deserving pity': *She gave a piteous cry.*

pitfall *n*
danger, peril, hazard, trap, snare, stumbling-block, catch, snag, drawback, difficulty

pith *n*
gist, essence, essential part, salient point, point, crux, nub, heart, core, meat, kernel, marrow, importance, significance, moment, weight, value, consequence, substance, forcefulness, vigour, matter, *formal* import, quintessence

pithy *adj*
succinct, concise, compact, terse, short, brief, condensed, summary, pointed, expressive, meaningful, forceful, incisive, telling, *formal* trenchant, cogent
 wordy, verbose

pitiable *adj*
contemptible, distressed, distressful, distressing, doleful, grievous, lamentable, miserable, mournful, piteous, poor, sad, sorry, woeful, woesome, wretched, *colloq.* pathetic

 pitiable, piteous or **pitiful** ? *See panel at* PITEOUS.

pitiful *adj*
1 PITEOUS, doleful, mournful, distressing, heartbreaking, heart-rending, affecting, moving, pathetic, pitiable, sad, miserable, wretched, poor, sorry **2** CONTEMPTIBLE, meagre, despicable, low, base, mean, poor, vile, shabby, miserable, deplorable, lamentable, woeful, inadequate, hopeless, insignificant, paltry, worthless, *colloq.* pathetic

 pitiful, piteous or **pitiable** ? *See panel at* PITEOUS.

pitiless *adj*
merciless, cold-hearted, unsympathetic, unfeeling, uncaring, heartless, hard-hearted, callous, cruel, inhuman, inhumane, brutal, cold-blooded, ruthless, relentless, unremitting, inexorable, harsh, severe
 merciful, compassionate, kind, gentle

pittance *n*
modicum, crumb, drop (in the ocean), trifle, *colloq.* chickenfeed, *slang* peanuts

pitted *adj*
dented, holey, potholed, pockmarked, blemished, scarred, marked, notched, depressed, indented, rough

pity *n, v*
▶ *n* **1** SYMPATHY, commiseration, regret, sorrow, sadness, distress, understanding, fellow-feeling, feeling, emotion, condolence, compassion, kindness, tenderness, mercy, forgiveness, grace, *formal* forbearance **2** *What a pity!* shame, disappointment, misfortune, unfortunate thing, bad luck, *colloq.* crying shame
 1 cruelty, anger, scorn
▶ *v* feel sorry for, feel for, sympathize with, be sympathetic towards, empathize with, show understanding towards, feel/have compassion for, commiserate

with, grieve for, weep for
▷ **take pity on** feel sorry for, feel for, sympathize with, be sympathetic towards, empathize with, show understanding towards, feel/have compassion for, commiserate with, show mercy, have mercy on, pardon, spare

pivot *n, v*
▶ *n the wheel turns on a pivot; the pivot of her life* axis, hinge, axle, spindle, fulcrum, kingpin, linchpin, swivel, hub, central point, focal point, focus, centre, heart
▶ *v* **1** SWIVEL, turn, spin, revolve, rotate, swing **2** DEPEND, rely, revolve, hinge, hang, lie, *formal* turn, be contingent

pivotal *adj*
vital, important, focal, central, critical, crucial, decisive, determining, climactic, axial

pixie *n*
elf, brownie, goblin, leprechaun, fairy, sprite

placard *n*
poster, bill, notice, sticker, sign, advertisement, *colloq.* ad, advert

placate *v*
appease, pacify, conciliate, win over, mollify, calm (down), assuage, soothe, lull, quiet, *formal* propitiate
 anger, enrage, incense, infuriate

placatory *adj*
appeasing, calming, soothing, mollifying, conciliatory, peacemaking, *formal* pacificatory, propitiatory, propitiative

place *n, v*
▶ *n* **1** SITE, locale, venue, location, scene, setting, situation, spot, point, position, part, whereabouts, seat, space, room **2** *a place name* city, town, village, hamlet, locality, neighbourhood, whereabouts, district, area, region, state, country **3** BUILDING, establishment, hotel, restaurant, institution, property, accommodation, house, flat, apartment, home, *formal* dwelling, residence, abode, domicile, *colloq.* pad, digs **4** JOB, position, appointment, situation, role, part, niche, status, standing, grade, rank, footing **5** *not your place to comment* role, function, task, duty, responsibility, right, concern, business
▷ **in place** arranged, in order, in the correct position, set up, working
▷ **in place of** instead of, in lieu of, as a replacement for, as an alternative to, in exchange for, as a substitute for, taking the place of
▷ **out of place** inappropriate, unsuitable, unfitting, improper, tactless, unbecoming, *formal* unseemly, inapposite
▷ **put someone in their place** humble, humiliate, shame, crush, deflate, bring low, bring/take someone down a peg or two, take the wind out of someone's sail
▷ **take place** happen, occur, come about, be held, come off, fall, *formal* transpire, come to pass, befall, betide
▷ **take the place of** replace, substitute for, supersede, stand in for, act for
▶ *v* **1** PUT, put down, set, set down, plant, fix, position, locate, situate, station, rest, settle, install, establish, lay, lay down, stand, deposit, lodge, leave **2** ARRANGE, put, class, sort, classify, categorize, group, rank, grade **3** *I can't quite place her* recognize, know, remember, identify, establish, pinpoint, categorize **4** *place graduates in companies* find a job for, find employment for, find accommodation for, allocate, assign

placement *n*
locating, location, installation, ordering, arrangement, deployment, appointment, positioning, rank-

ing, stationing, distribution, classification, job, assignment, disposition, engagement, employment, *formal* emplacement

placid *adj*
1 *a placid person* calm, composed, unmoved, undisturbed, unruffled, untroubled, unexcitable, cool, self-possessed, level-headed, imperturbable, mild, gentle, equable, serene, unemotional, even-tempered, peaceable, tranquil, *colloq.* easy-going, unflappable **2** *live in placid surroundings* tranquil, still, quiet, calm, peaceful, restful, *formal* pacific
F₃ 1 excitable, agitated, disturbed

plagiarism *n*
infringement, copying, reproduction, counterfeiting, piracy, theft, *formal* appropriation, *colloq.* borrowing, cribbing, lifting

plagiarist *n*
copier, robber, thief, pirate, imitator

plagiarize *v*
copy, reproduce, imitate, counterfeit, pirate, infringe copyright, poach, steal, lift, borrow, *formal* appropriate, *colloq.* crib, lift, nick

plague *n, v*
▶ *n* **1** PESTILENCE, epidemic, disease, sickness, infection, contagion, infestation, cholera, bubonic plague, pneumonic plague, Black Death, *formal* pandemic **2** *a plague of rats* infestation, influx, swarm, invasion, huge number, epidemic **3** NUISANCE, annoyance, curse, scourge, trial, affliction, torment, calamity, *colloq.* thorn in the flesh, pain in the neck
▶ *v* annoy, vex, bother, disturb, trouble, distress, upset, irritate, worry, cause problems for, pester, harass, hound, dog, hamper, hinder, haunt, bedevil, afflict, torment, torture, persecute, *colloq.* bug, hassle, aggravate, cause headaches to

plain *adj, adv, n*
▶ *adj* **1** *plain cookery* ordinary, basic, simple, unpretentious, unsophisticated, modest, unadorned, unelaborate, restrained, stark, austere, Spartan **2** *plain fabric* undecorated, unadorned, unembellished, unpatterned, unvariegated, uncoloured, self-coloured, restrained, muted **3** OBVIOUS, evident, patent, clear, understandable, apparent, noticeable, perceptible, discernible, visible, overt, unmistakable, transparent, *formal* manifest, *colloq.* plain as a pikestaff **4** UNATTRACTIVE, ordinary, ugly, unprepossessing, unlovely, *US* homely **5** *plain language* clear, intelligible, understandable, lucid, unambiguous, uncomplicated, simple, direct, straightforward, accessible **6** FRANK, candid, blunt, outspoken, direct, forthright, straightforward, unambiguous, plain-spoken, open, honest, sincere, truthful, simple, unassuming
F₃ 1 fancy, elaborate **2** patterned **3** unclear, obscure **4** attractive, beautiful, good-looking **5** complicated, obscure **6** devious, deceitful
▶ *adv* completely, utterly, totally, thoroughly, undeniably, simply, quite
▶ *n* grassland, prairie, steppe, lowland, pampas, flat, flatland, plateau, tableland, savannah, tundra

plain-spoken *adj*
candid, frank, open, honest, blunt, outspoken, straightforward, direct, truthful, unequivocal, outright, explicit, forthright, downright

plaintive *adj*
doleful, mournful, melancholy, wretched, woeful, wistful, sad, unhappy, sorrowful, grief-stricken, heart-broken, piteous, pitiful, heart-rending, high-pitched, *formal* disconsolate

plan *n, v*
▶ *n* **1** IDEA, suggestion, intention, aim, arrangement, proposal, proposition, project, scheme, plot, system,

method, means, way, policy, procedure, strategy, formula, programme, schedule, scenario **2** BLUEPRINT, layout, diagram, chart, map, drawing, scale drawing, sketch, representation, illustration, design, *formal* delineation
▶ *v* **1** PLOT, scheme, design, invent, think of, devise, contrive, develop, formulate, frame, shape, draft, outline, sketch, map out, work out, prepare, organize, arrange, schedule, programme, mastermind **2** AIM, intend, want, wish, propose, purpose, mean, seek, contemplate, envisage, foresee, *formal* resolve

plane¹ *n, adj*
▶ *n* **1** FLAT SURFACE, level surface, flat, level **2** LEVEL, stage, position, class, condition, degree, rank, footing, rung, stratum, echelon
▶ *adj* level, smooth, uniform, regular, plain, flat, flush, even, horizontal, *technical* homaloidal, *formal* planar

plane² *n, v*
▶ *n* *travel by plane* aeroplane, aircraft, jet, jumbo jet, jumbo, airliner, glider, bomber, fighter, seaplane, swing-wing, VTOL, *US* airplane. *See also panel at* AIRCRAFT.
▶ *v* skim, skate, fly, glide, sail, volplane, wing

planet *n*

Planets within the Earth's solar system (nearest the sun shown first) are:
Mercury, Venus, Earth, Mars, Jupiter, Saturn, Uranus, Neptune, Pluto.

plant *n, v*
▶ *n* **1** *garden plants* flower, shrub, herb, bush, vegetable

Plants include:
annual, biennial, perennial, herbaceous plant, evergreen, succulent, cultivar, hybrid, house plant, pot plant; flower, herb, shrub, bush, tree, vegetable, grass, vine, weed, cereal, wild flower, air-plant, water-plant, cactus, fern, moss, algae, lichen, fungus; bulb, corm, seedling, sapling, bush, climber. *See also* ALGAE AND LICHEN; BULB; FLOWER; GRASS; LEAF; POISONOUS; SHRUB; WILD FLOWER.

Parts of a plant include:
bark, cambium, cork cambium, cellulose, conducting tissue, cotyledon, monocotyledon, dicotyledon, flower, fruit, leaf, meristem, phellogen, phloem, root, lateral root, root cap, root hair, rootlet, seed, seed leaf, stem, tap root, vascular bundle, vascular tissue, xylem.

2 FACTORY, works, foundry, mill, shop, yard, workshop, machinery, apparatus, equipment, gear
▶ *v* **1** SOW, seed, scatter, implant, put into the ground, bury, transplant **2** INSERT, put, place, set, position, situate, fix, lodge, imbed, root, settle, found, establish **3** HIDE, put secretly, conceal, bury, disguise, put out of sight, *formal* secrete

plaque *n*
plate, slab, tablet, panel, sign, plaquette, brass, shield, medal, medallion, badge, brooch, *technical* cartouche

plaster *n, v*
▶ *n* **1** *apply plaster to walls* stucco, mortar, plasterwork, gypsum, plaster of Paris, plasterboard **2** *put a plaster on a wound* sticking-plaster, patch, dressing, adhesive dressing, bandage, Band-aid®, Elastoplast®

▶ *v* daub, bedaub, smear, coat, cover, cover thickly, overlay, spread

plastic *adj*
1 *plastic toys* soft, pliable, flexible, supple, malleable, mouldable, ductile, shapeable **2** EASILY INFLU-ENCED, receptive, malleable, pliable, pliant, impressionable, manageable, mouldable, *formal* compliant, tractable **3** ARTIFICIAL, unnatural, false, synthetic, man-made, *colloq.* phoney
F₃ **1** rigid, inflexible **2** inflexible, *formal* intractable **3** natural

Types of plastic include:
Bakelite®, Biopol®, celluloid®, epoxy
resin, Perspex®, phenolic resin, plexiglass,
polyester, polyethylene, polymethyl
methacrylate, polynorbornene,
polypropylene, polystyrene, polythene,
polyurethane, PTFE (polytetrafluoroethylene),
PVC (polyvinyl chloride), uPVC, silicone,
Teflon®, transpolyisoprene, urea formaldehyde,
vinyl.

plasticity *n*
flexibility, softness, suppleness, pliancy, pliableness, pliability, malleability, *formal* tractability
F₃ inflexibility, rigidity

plate *n, v*
▶ *n* **1** DISH, platter, salver, helping, serving, portion, ashet **2** SHEET, slab, pane, panel, sign, plaque, tablet, *formal* lamina **3** ILLUSTRATION, photograph, picture, print, lithograph
▶ *v* coat, cover, overlay, veneer, laminate, electroplate, anodize, galvanize, platinize, gild, silver, tin

plateau *n*
1 *a grassy plateau* plane, highland, tableland, table, upland, mesa **2** STABILITY, level, grade, stage

platform *n*
1 STAGE, podium, dais, rostrum, stand, *colloq.* soapbox **2** POLICY, party line, principles, tenets, manifesto, programme, objectives, aims, ideas, intentions, strategy

platitude *n*
banality, commonplace, truism, cliché, bromide, inanity, stereotype, hackneyed statement, trite expression, overworked phrase, *colloq.* chestnut

platitudinous *adj*
banal, commonplace, truistic, trite, clichéd, hackneyed, overworked, stale, stereotyped, set, stock, inane, tired, dull, flat, well-worn, vapid, *colloq.* corny

platonic *adj*
non-physical, spiritual, non-romantic, non-sexual, intellectual, ideal, idealistic, transcendent, *formal* incorporeal
F₃ sexual

platoon *n*
company, group, patrol, battery, team, squad, squadron, outfit

platter *n*
plate, dish, salver, tray, charger, trencher

plaudits *n*
commendation, approval, praise, acclaim, acclamation, applause, congratulations, hurrahs, accolade, ovation, standing ovation, clapping, *formal* approbation, *colloq.* hand, bouquet, pat on the back, rave review, good press
F₃ criticism

plausible *adj*
credible, believable, reasonable, logical, likely, possible, probable, imaginable, conceivable, convincing,

persuasive, smooth-talking, glib, *formal* cogent
F₃ implausible, unlikely, improbable

play *v, n*
▶ *v* **1** AMUSE YOURSELF, have fun, enjoy yourself, play games, occupy yourself, divert yourself, revel, sport, romp, frolic, caper, gambol, frisk, cavort **2** PAR-TICIPATE, take part, join in, be involved in, do, compete **3** *France played Italy* oppose, compete against, vie with, rival, challenge, take on **4** ACT, perform, play the part of, portray, represent, impersonate **5** *light playing on the water* dance, move lightly, flicker, twinkle, flash
F₃ **1** work
▷ **play around with 1** FIDDLE WITH, toy with, fidget with, meddle with, tamper with, interfere with **2** DALLY WITH, mess around with, flirt with, fool with, trifle with, womanize with, philander with
▷ **play at** pretend (to be), put on an act, make out, *formal* affect, *colloq.* go through the motions
▷ **play down** minimize, make light of, gloss over, underplay, downplay, understate, undervalue, underestimate
F₃ exaggerate, emphasize, play up
▷ **play on** exploit, take advantage of, turn to account, profit by, trade on, capitalize on
▷ **play out** continue, go on, carry on, unfold, be revealed, act, enact
▷ **play up 1** EXAGGERATE, highlight, spotlight, accentuate, emphasize, stress, underline, point up, call attention to **2** MISBEHAVE, be mischievous, be naughty, give trouble, be difficult to control, trouble, bother, annoy, hurt **3** MALFUNCTION, not work, go wrong, *colloq.* go/be on the blink
F₃ **1** play down, underplay **3** work properly
▷ **play up to** flatter, ingratiate yourself, suck up to, curry favour with, blandish, fawn, toady, *colloq.* bootlick, butter up, soft-soap
▶ *n* **1** FUN, amusement, enjoyment, entertainment, diversion, leisure, recreation, sport, game, hobby, pastime, merrymaking **2** DRAMA, tragedy, comedy, farce, show, melodrama, plot, performance **3** MOVE-MENT, action, flexibility, freedom of movement, slack, looseness, leeway, latitude, freedom, liberty, free rein, margin, scope, range, licence, room, space, *colloq.* give **4** ACTION, operation, exercise, interaction, interplay, transaction **5** JEST, fun, joking, teasing, laugh, *colloq.* kicks
F₃ **1** work

playboy *n*
philanderer, womanizer, ladies' man, lady-killer, rake, libertine, roué, debauchee, *colloq.* man about town, socialite

player *n*
1 CONTESTANT, competitor, participant, sportsman, sportswoman **2** PERFORMER, entertainer, artiste, actor, actress, artist, comedian, trouper, player, musician, instrumentalist, accompanist

playful *adj*
1 *as playful as a kitten* frisky, sportive, frolicsome, lively, fun-loving, spirited, mischievous, roguish, impish, puckish, kittenish **2** *a playful remark* humorous, tongue-in-cheek, jesting, joking, facetious, waggish, teasing
F₃ **2** serious

playground *n*
park, playing-field, play area, adventure playground, amusement park, pleasure ground, recreation ground

playmate *n*
friend, companion, comrade, neighbour, playfellow, *colloq.* buddy, chum, pal

plaything *n*
toy, trifle, amusement, game, puppet, trinket, pastime, bauble, gewgaw, gimcrack

playwright *n*
dramatist, writer, scriptwriter, screen writer, dramaturge, dramaturgist, tragedian

plea *n*
1 APPEAL, petition, request, entreaty, supplication, prayer, *formal* invocation, imploration **2** DEFENCE, justification, excuse, explanation, claim, pretext, *formal* vindication

plead *v*
1 BEG, implore, entreat, appeal, petition, ask, request, *formal* beseech, solicit, make supplication **2** *plead ignorance* assert, state, argue, maintain, claim, allege, put forward, *formal* adduce

pleasant *adj*
1 *a pleasant chat* ENJOYABLE, agreeable, nice, fine, lovely, delightful, charming, amusing, pleasing, gratifying, satisfying, acceptable, welcome, entertaining, refreshing **2** *a pleasant person* FRIENDLY, amiable, affable, likeable, cheerful, congenial, good-humoured, charming, nice, lovely, winsome
🔁 **1, 2** unpleasant, nasty **2** unfriendly

pleasantry *n*
1 *exchange pleasantries about the weather* friendly remark, polite comment, casual remark **2** JOKE, jest, banter, badinage, quip, sally, witticism, *bon mot*

please *v*
1 DELIGHT, make happy, give pleasure to, charm, attract, appeal to, captivate, entertain, amuse, divert, cheer (up), gladden, humour, indulge, gratify, satisfy, fulfil, content, suit **2** WANT, will, wish, desire, like, prefer, choose, think fit, see fit
🔁 **1** displease, annoy, anger, sadden

pleased *adj*
contented, satisfied, gratified, glad, happy, cheerful, delighted, thrilled, euphoric, elated, *colloq.* chuffed, over the moon, tickled pink
🔁 displeased, annoyed

pleasing *adj*
gratifying, satisfying, acceptable, good, pleasant, pleasurable, agreeable, nice, fine, delightful, enjoyable, amusing, entertaining, charming, attractive, engaging, winning
🔁 unpleasant, disagreeable

pleasurable *adj*
enjoyable, delightful, fun, good, lovely, nice, pleasant, gratifying, welcome, entertaining, amusing, diverting, agreeable, congenial, *colloq.* groovy
🔁 bad, disagreeable

pleasure *n*
1 HAPPINESS, contentment, joy, delight, gladness, enjoyment, satisfaction, gratification, *formal* solace **2** *the pleasure of playing a sport* joy, delight, enjoyment, thrill, glory, treasure, prize, gem **3** *combine business with pleasure* recreation, amusement, entertainment, leisure, fun **4** PREFERENCE, wish, will, desire, choice, inclination
🔁 **1** sorrow, pain, trouble, displeasure **2** disappointment, sadness

pleat *v*
tuck, fold, crease, flute, crimp, gather, pucker

plebeian *adj, n*
▶ *adj* **1** LOWER-CLASS, working-class, proletarian, low-born, peasant, mean **2** COMMON, uncultured, unrefined, uncultivated, coarse, base, ignoble, low, *colloq.* non-U
🔁 **1** aristocratic, noble, patrician **2** refined, sophisticated

▶ *n* common person, commoner, person in the street, proletarian, worker, peasant, *colloq.* pleb, prole
🔁 aristocrat, noble, patrician

plebiscite *n*
vote, referendum, ballot, poll, straw poll

pledge *n, v*
▶ *n* **1** PROMISE, vow, word of honour, word, oath, bond, covenant, guarantee, warrant, commitment, assurance, undertaking **2** DEPOSIT, security, surety, bail, guarantee, pawn, *formal* collateral
▶ *v* **1** PROMISE, vow, give your word, swear, take an oath, commit, contract, engage, undertake, give an undertaking, vouch, guarantee, secure **2** GUARANTEE, mortgage, *formal* put up as collateral

plenary *adj*
full, complete, entire, open, absolute, unrestricted, whole, general, integral, unconditional, unlimited, unqualified, thorough, sweeping

plenipotentiary *n*
ambassador, envoy, minister, dignitary, emissary, legate, nuncio

plenitude *n*
abundance, plenty, plentifulness, profusion, fullness, completeness, copiousness, bounty, excess, wealth, cornucopia, entireness, *formal* amplitude, plenteousness, plethora, repletion
🔁 scarcity

plenteous *adj*
abundant, plentiful, bountiful, copious, fruitful, lavish, abounding, ample, generous, liberal, productive, fertile, profuse, prolific, overflowing, inexhaustible, infinite, *formal* bounteous, luxuriant, *colloq.* bumper
🔁 scarce, paltry

plentiful *adj*
ample, abundant, profuse, copious, overflowing, lavish, generous, liberal, bountiful, fruitful, productive, inexhaustible, infinite, *formal* bounteous, *colloq.* bumper
🔁 scarce, scanty, rare

plenty *n*
1 ABUNDANCE, profusion, copiousness, enough, fullness, sufficiency, quantity, mass, volume, fund, mine, store, *formal* plethora, plenteousness **2** AFFLUENCE, wealth, wealthiness, riches, fortune, substance, prosperity
🔁 **1** scarcity, lack, want **2** need
▷ **plenty of** many, large amount, large number, enough, more than enough, more than is needed, *colloq.* lots, loads, masses, heaps, piles, stacks

plethora *n*
surfeit, surplus, excess, glut, overabundance, profusion, overfullness, superabundance, *formal* superfluity

pliability *n*
1 BENDABILITY, elasticity, flexibility, plasticity, ductility **2** ADAPTABILITY, amenability, susceptibility, malleability, suggestibility, impressionableness, docility, *formal* compliance, tractableness
🔁 **1, 2** inflexibility, rigidity

pliable *adj*
1 *pliable pieces of wood* pliant, flexible, bendable, supple, lithe, malleable, elastic, plastic, *colloq.* bendy **2** *a pliable person* yielding, adaptable, flexible, accommodating, manageable, docile, biddable, persuadable, responsive, receptive, impressionable, susceptible, *formal* tractable, compliant
🔁 **1** rigid, inflexible **2** headstrong

pliant *adj*
1 *pliant pieces of wood* pliable, flexible, bendable, supple, lithe, malleable, elastic, plastic, *colloq.* bendy **2** *a pliant person* yielding, adaptable, flexible, accom-

modating, manageable, docile, biddable, persuadable, responsive, receptive, impressionable, susceptible, *formal* tractable, compliant
F∃ 1 rigid, inflexible **2** headstrong

plight¹ *n*
the plight of starving children predicament, quandary, dilemma, extremity, trouble, difficulty, difficult/distressing situation, straits, dire straits, state, condition, situation, circumstances, case, *colloq.* jam, hole, tight spot, scrape, pickle

plight² *v*
plight your troth promise, pledge, vow, swear, contract, covenant, engage, guarantee, propose, vouch

plod *v*
1 TRUDGE, tramp, stump, clump, stomp, lumber, walk heavily, plough through **2** DRUDGE, labour, toil, grind, slog, persevere, peg away, plug away, soldier on

plodder *n*
drudge, dullard, toiler, slogger, mug, sap
F∃ high-flier

plot *n, v*
▶ *n* **1** CONSPIRACY, intrigue, scheme, plan, ruse, stratagem, cabal, *formal* machination **2** STORY, narrative, action, subject, theme, storyline, thread, outline, scenario **3** *plot of land* patch, tract, area, allotment, lot, parcel
▶ *v* **1** CONSPIRE, intrigue, collude, connive, scheme, hatch, lay, devise, contrive, plan, project, design, draft, concoct, frame, *formal* machinate, *colloq.* cook up **2** CHART, map (out), mark, locate, draw, sketch, calculate

plotter *n*
conspirator, intriguer, schemer, planner, *formal* machinator

plough *v*
cultivate, dig, till, work, ridge, spade, break, turn up, furrow
▷ **plough into** crash into, drive into, smash into, run/go into, hit, collide, bump into
▷ **plough through** plod through, move through laboriously, trudge through, wade through

ploy *n*
manoeuvre, stratagem, tactic, move, device, contrivance, scheme, game, trick, artifice, dodge, wile, ruse, subterfuge

pluck *v, n*
▶ *v* **1** PULL, draw, tug, snatch, pull (off), remove, extract, pick, collect, gather, take in, harvest, *colloq.* yank **2** *pluck a guitar* pick, twang, strum, finger
▶ *n* courage, bravery, daring, boldness, spirit, intrepidity, audacity, fearlessness, mettle, backbone, resolution, determination, *formal* fortitude, valour, *colloq.* nerve, guts, grit
F∃ cowardice

plucky *adj*
brave, courageous, bold, daring, audacious, fearless, intrepid, heroic, valiant, spirited, determined, *colloq.* gutsy, spunky, gritty
F∃ cowardly, weak, feeble

plug *n, v*
▶ *n* **1** STOPPER, bung, cork, seal, spigot **2** ADVERTISEMENT, publicity, commercial, promotion, blurb, mention, puff, good word, *colloq.* hype, ad, push **3** *a plug of tobacco* chew, wad, twist, cake
▶ *v* **1** STOP (UP), bung, cork, block, choke, close, seal, fill, pack, stuff, *colloq.* hype, push **2** ADVERTISE, publicize, promote, market, tout, mention, *colloq.* - push
▷ **plug away** keep trying, preserve, plod on, slog away, peg away, soldier on

plum *adj*
first-class, best, choice, prize, especially valued, excellent, *colloq.* cushy

plumb *adv, v*
▶ *adv* **1** VERTICALLY, perpendicularly, sheer, straight up, straight down, up and down **2** PRECISELY, right, exactly, dead, *colloq.* slap, bang, spot on
▶ *v* sound (out), fathom, measure, gauge, penetrate, delve into, probe, search (out), examine, investigate, explore
▷ **plumb the depths of** experience the worst extremes of, hit the lowest point/level, reach rock bottom

plume *n*
feather, crest, pinion, quill, tuft, aigrette, *technical* pappus
▷ **plume yourself on** congratulate yourself, boast about, pride yourself, preen yourself, exult in, *colloq.* pat yourself on the back

plummet *v*
plunge, dive, nosedive, descend, drop, fall, drop/fall rapidly, decrease quickly, tumble, hurtle
F∃ soar

plump¹ *adj*
a plump person fat, obese, dumpy, tubby, stout, round, well-rounded, portly, chubby, podgy, fleshy, full, ample, buxom, *formal* rotund, corpulent, *colloq.* well-upholstered, beefy, flabby, gross
F∃ thin, skinny

plump² *v*
plump the sacks on the floor put down, set down, deposit, drop, flop, sink, slump, collapse, descend, fall, *colloq.* dump
▷ **plump for** choose, select, prefer, opt for, back, side with, support, favour

plumpness *n*
fatness, fleshiness, chubbiness, stoutness, portliness, tubbiness, podginess, pudginess, *formal* corpulence, obesity, rotundity
F∃ thinness, skinniness

plunder *v, n*
▶ *v* loot, pillage, ravage, lay waste, devastate, sack, raid, ransack, maraud, rifle, steal, rob, strip, fleece, *formal* despoil, depredate
▶ *n* loot, pillage, booty, spoils, pickings, ill-gotten gains, prize, *slang* swag

plunge *v, n*
▶ *v* **1** DIVE, jump, nosedive, swoop, dive-bomb, plummet, descend, go down, sink, drop, fall, drop/fall rapidly, decrease quickly, throw, pitch, tumble, hurtle, career, charge, dash, rush, tear **2** THRUST, push, drive, stick, stab, shove, ram, jab **3** IMMERSE, submerge, dip, sink
▶ *n* dive, nosedive, jump, swoop, descent, drop, fall, tumble, charge, rush, hurtle, immersion, submersion

plurality *n*
diversity, variety, number, numerousness, profusion, mass, bulk, majority, most, *formal* multiplicity, multitudinousness, preponderance, *colloq.* galaxy

plus *n, prep*
▶ *n* advantage, benefit, bonus, good point, asset, credit, gain, extra, surplus, *colloq.* perk
F∃ disadvantage, drawback, *colloq.* minus
▶ *prep* and, with, together with, as well as, in addition to, over and above, *colloq.* not to mention
F∃ minus

plush *adj*
luxurious, luxury, lavish, de luxe, palatial, stylish, affluent, sumptuous, costly, rich, *formal* opulent, *colloq.* ritzy, glitzy, posh, swanky

plutocrat *n*
rich man, capitalist, millionaire, tycoon, magnate, billionaire, multimillionaire, Dives, Croesus, *colloq.* fat cat, moneybags

ply¹ *v*
1 KEEP SUPPLYING, provide, supply, furnish, feed, lavish, assail, beset, bombard, harass, importune **2** TRAVEL, go, ferry, make regular journeys between/along **3** *ply a trade* practise, carry on, follow, pursue, exercise, work at **4** *ply a tool* use, employ, utilize, wield, handle, manipulate

ply² *n*
three-ply wool thickness, strand, leaf, layer, sheet, fold

poach *v*
1 STEAL, pilfer, copy, take, *formal* appropriate, *colloq.* lift, borrow, nick **2** TRESPASS, encroach, infringe, intrude, catch/hunt illegally

pocket *n, adj, v*
▶ *n* **1** *a pocket on the back of the seat* pouch, bag, envelope, receptacle, compartment, hollow, cavity **2** *the fees are a drain on my pocket* resources, funds, means, money, finances, budget, assets, capital, wherewithal **3** *pocket of resistance/unemployment* patch, small area, isolated area, small group
▶ *adj* small, little, concise, abridged, potted, compact, portable, miniature, *colloq.* mini, pint-size
▶ *v* take, gain, win unfairly, help yourself to, pilfer, filch, steal, *formal* appropriate, purloin, *colloq.* lift, nick, pinch

pockmark *n*
blemish, pock, pit, scar, pockpit

pod *n*
shell, husk, case, hull, *technical* legume

podgy *adj*
fat, chubby, paunchy, plump, fleshy, roly-poly, squat, chunky, dumpy, stout, tubby, stubby, stumpy, *formal* corpulent, rotund
F₃ thin, skinny

podium *n*
dais, platform, stage, stand, rostrum

poem *n*

> **Types of poem include:**
> ballad, bucolic, clerihew, couplet, ditty, eclogue, elegy, epic, epigram, epithalamium, epode, epopee, georgic, haiku, idyll, lay, limerick, lipogram, lyric, madrigal, monody, nursery rhyme, ode, palinode, pastoral, prothalamion, rhyme, rondeau, roundelay, song, sonnet, tanka, triolet, verse, verselet, versicle. *See also* SONG.

poet *n*
versifier, verse-maker, rhymer, rhymester, rhymist, lyricist, idyllist, sonneteer, balladeer, elegist, bard, minstrel, poetaster, poeticule

poetic *adj*
poetical, lyrical, moving, artistic, graceful, flowing, expressive, sensitive, beautiful, creative, imaginative, metrical, rhythmical, rhyming, prosaic, figurative, symbolic

poetry *n*
verse, lyrics, rhyme, rhyming, versing, poems, poesy, free verse, versification, vers libre, pennill, iambics, muse, Parnassus

pogrom *n*
slaughter, murder, homicide, extermination, carnage, butchery, wholesale slaughter, indiscriminate killing, holocaust, bloodbath, annihilation, killing, genocide, ethnic cleansing, liquidation, decimation

poignancy *n*
pathos, feeling, sentiment, emotion, evocativeness, intensity, keenness, painfulness, piquancy, tenderness, piteousness, sharpness, pungency, sadness, pain, distress, tragedy, misery, wretchedness, bitterness

poignant *adj*
moving, touching, affecting, emotional, tender, distressing, tragic, upsetting, heartbreaking, heart-rending, heartfelt, piteous, pathetic, sorrowful, sad, tearful, painful, agonizing, miserable, wretched

point *n, v*
▶ *n* **1** *the main points of the argument* issue, matter, subject, topic, question, item **2** FEATURE, attribute, quality, aspect, characteristic, trait, property, facet, detail, particular, item, subject, topic **3** *What's the point?* use, sense, purpose, motive, reason, object, objective, intention, aim, end, goal **4** ESSENCE, main point, crux, core, central point, heart, heart of the matter, pith, gist, nub, meat, marrow, thrust, meaning, significance, importance, theme, vein, tenor, drift, burden, keynote **5** PLACE, position, situation, location, locality, area, site, spot **6** MOMENT, instant, juncture, stage, time, period, position **7** DOT, spot, mark, speck, full stop, stop, full point, period, decimal point **8** *the point of a needle* sharp end, end, extremity, tip, top, taper, spike, tine, nib **9** HEADLAND, head, foreland, promontory, cape, ness **10** MARK, score, goals, runs, hits, total
▷ **beside the point** irrelevant, immaterial, unrelated, unconnected, out of place, *colloq.* neither here nor there
▷ **in point of fact** actually, in fact, as a matter of fact, in reality, really
▷ **on the point of** on the verge of, about to, going to, ready to, preparing to
▷ **point of view 1** OPINION, view, belief, judgement, attitude, feeling, sentiment, position, standpoint, viewpoint **2** PERSPECTIVE, outlook, approach, angle, slant, aspect
▷ **to the point** relevant, related, connected, germane, applicable, appropriate, *formal* apposite, pertinent
▷ **up to a point** partly, somewhat, to some extent/degree, slightly
▶ *v* **1** *point a gun* aim, direct, train, level **2** INDICATE, signal, gesture at/towards, show, signify, designate, suggest, *formal* denote, evidence
▷ **point out** show, indicate, draw/call attention to, point to, reveal, identify, specify, mention, bring up, allude to, remind
▷ **point up** emphasize, stress, underline, highlight, call attention to

point-blank *adv, adj*
▶ *adv* outright, directly, forthrightly, straightforwardly, straight, plainly, explicitly, openly, bluntly, frankly, candidly, rudely, abruptly, unequivocally
▶ *adj* **1** OUTRIGHT, direct, forthright, straightforward, plain, explicit, open, unreserved, blunt, frank, candid **2** AT CLOSE RANGE, closely, close to, near, touching

pointed *adj*
1 SHARP, keen, edged, tapering, barbed, *technical* acicular, cuspidate(d), *formal* aculeate(d), fastigiate, lanceolate(d), mucronate(d) **2** *a pointed comment* cutting, incisive, biting, forceful, penetrating, telling, striking, clear, obvious, *formal* trenchant

pointer *n*
1 ARROW, indicator, needle, hand **2** TIP, recommendation, suggestion, sign, hint, guide, guideline, clue, indication, indicator, advice, piece of advice, warning, caution **3** STICK, rod, cane, pole

pointless *adj*
useless, futile, vain, fruitless, unproductive, unprof-

itable, worthless, senseless, valueless, absurd, ridiculous, nonsensical, foolish, inane, meaningless, insignificant, a waste of time/effort, aimless, to no avail, unavailing, *colloq.* a mug's game
F3 useful, profitable, meaningful

poise *n, v*
► *n* calmness, composure, self-control, presence of mind, self-possession, assurance, self-assurance, dignity, elegance, grace, serenity, balance, equilibrium, *formal* equanimity, aplomb, *colloq.* cool, coolness
► *v* balance, position, steady, hover, hang, suspend, support

poised *adj*
1 DIGNIFIED, graceful, calm, composed, collected, self-possessed, self-controlled, self-confident, assured, serene, suave, urbane, *colloq.* cool, cool calm and collected, unruffled, unflappable **2** *poised for action* prepared, ready, set, all set, waiting, expectant

poison *n, v*
► *n* **1** *poison such as arsenic* toxin, venom **2** *a poison spreading through society* bane, blight, cancer, malignancy, contagion, pollution, contamination, corruption, canker
► *v* kill by poison, infect, contaminate, pollute, taint, adulterate, corrupt, deprave, defile, pervert, warp, spoil, blight

poisonous *adj*
1 TOXIC, venomous, lethal, deadly, fatal, mortal **2** HARMFUL, noxious, pernicious, malicious, vicious, spiteful, virulent, malignant, contaminating, corrupting, cancerous, cankerous

Poisonous plants include:
aconite, amanita, anemone, banewort, belladonna, black nightshade, castor oil plant, common nightshade, cowbane, cuckoo pint, deadly nightshade, digitalis, dwale, foxglove, giant hockweed, helmet flower, hemlock, hemlock water dropwort, jimson-weed, laburnum, lantana, lords-and-ladies, meadow saffron, monkshood, naked boys, naked lady, oleander, poison ivy, stinkweed, stramonium, thorn apple, wake-robin, wild arum, windflower, wolfsbane.

poke *v, n*
► *v* prod, stab, jab, stick, thrust, push, shove, nudge, elbow, dig, butt, hit, punch
▷ **poke around** grope around, search for, look (all over) for, rummage around, rake through
▷ **poke fun at** ridicule, mock, jeer, make fun of, tease, parody, *colloq.* rag, rib, send up, spoof, take the mickey
▷ **poke out** stick out, jut out, protrude, project, overhang, extend, beetle, extrude
▷ **poke your nose into** meddle in, interfere in, tamper with, pry in, *colloq.* put/stick your oar in, butt in
► *n* prod, jab, thrust, shove, nudge, dig, butt, punch

poky *adj*
confined, cramped, small, tight, tiny, narrow, crowded, *formal* incommodious
F3 spacious, roomy

polar *adj*
1 COLD, freezing, frozen, icy, glacial, arctic, Siberian **2** OPPOSITE, completely/utterly different, diametrically opposed, conflicting, ambivalent, contradictory, *formal* antithetical, dichotomous

polarity *n*
opposition, oppositeness, contradiction, ambivalence, contrariety, duality, paradox, *formal* antithesis, dichotomy

pole[1] *n*
a telegraph pole bar, rod, stick, shaft, spar, upright, pillar, support, post, stake, mast, staff

pole[2] *n*
views that represent opposite poles extremity, extreme, limit
▷ **poles apart** completely different, incompatible, irreconcilable, worlds apart, *colloq.* like chalk and cheese

polemic *n, adj*
► *n* argument, controversy, debate, dispute
► *adj* argumentative, contentious, controversial, polemical, *formal* disputatious, eristic(al)

polemicist *n*
debater, controversialist, arguer, contender, disputer, disputant, polemist, *formal* logomachist

polemics *n*
debate, dispute, argument, controversy, contention, argumentation, *formal* disputation, logomachy

police *n, v*
► *n* police force, constabulary, *colloq.* the Law, the Force, cops, *slang* the (old) Bill, the fuzz, rozzers, pigs
► *v* **1** PATROL, guard, protect, defend, keep watch, keep the peace **2** CHECK, control, keep under control, regulate, monitor, watch, observe, supervise, oversee

police officer *n*
officer, policeman, policewoman, constable, PC, *colloq.* the Law, cop, copper, bobby, rozzer, boy in blue, the (old) Bill, *slang* pig, nark, the fuzz, flatfoot, bluebottle, bull

policy *n*
1 CODE OF PRACTICE, rules, guidelines, procedure, method, system, practice, custom, protocol **2** COURSE OF ACTION, line, course, plan, programme, scheme, schedule, stance, position, approach

polish *v, n*
► *v* **1** SHINE, brighten, smooth, rub (up), buff, burnish, furbish, clean, wax **2** IMPROVE, enhance, brush up, touch up, finish, perfect, refine, cultivate
F3 **1** tarnish, dull
▷ **polish off 1** EAT UP, consume, devour, put away, bolt, gobble, finish, complete, dispose of, down, stuff, *colloq.* wolf **2** MURDER, kill, eliminate, *colloq.* bump off, liquidate, rub out
► *n* **1** *a tin of polish* wax, varnish **2** SHINE, gloss, sheen, lustre, brightness, brilliance, sparkle, smoothness, finish, glaze, veneer, burnish **3** REFINEMENT, cultivation, class, breeding, sophistication, finesse, style, elegance, grace, poise
F3 **2** dullness **3** clumsiness

polished *adj*
1 SHINING, shiny, waxed, burnished, glossy, lustrous, gleaming, smooth, glassy, slippery **2** FAULTLESS, flawless, impeccable, perfect, outstanding, superlative, remarkable, excellent, masterly, expert, professional, skilful, accomplished, proficient, adept, perfected, *formal* consummate **3** REFINED, cultivated, genteel, well-bred, well-mannered, polite, sophisticated, civilized, urbane, suave, elegant, graceful
F3 **1** tarnished **2** inexpert **3** gauche

polite *adj*
1 COURTEOUS, well-mannered, respectful, civil, well-bred, well-behaved, deferential, refined, cultured, gentlemanly, ladylike, gallant, chivalrous, gracious, obliging, thoughtful, considerate, tactful, diplomatic **2** *in polite society* refined, cultured, genteel, well-bred, well-mannered, polite, sophisticated, civilized, urbane, suave, elegant
F3 **1** impolite, rude, discourteous

politeness *n*
courtesy, manners, good manners, deference, cordi-

ality, gentility, mannerliness, polish, refinement, elegance, courtliness, culture, thoughtfulness, cultivation, civility, considerateness, graciousness, grace, gentlemanliness, respect, respectfulness, diplomacy, tact, discretion, attention, *formal* complaisance
F3 impoliteness, rudeness, discourtesy

politic *adj*
wise, prudent, shrewd, sensible, tactful, diplomatic, advisable, advantageous, opportune, expedient, *formal* judicious, sagacious, sage
F3 impolitic

 politic or **political** ?

Politic is a rather formal word meaning 'wise, sensible': *He considered it politic to leave before there was any further trouble. Political* means 'relating to politics': *the political system of the USA*; *party political broadcasts.*

political *adj*
governmental, parliamentary, constitutional, ministerial, administrative, executive, bureaucratic, civil, public, judicial, party political

 political or **politic** ? *See panel at* POLITIC.

political ideology *n*

Political ideologies include:
absolutism, anarchism, authoritarianism, Bolshevism, Christian democracy, collectivism, communism, conservatism, democracy, egalitarianism, fascism, federalism, holism, imperialism, individualism, liberalism, Maoism, Marxism, nationalism, Nazism, neocolonialism, neo-fascism, neo-nazism, pluralism, republicanism, social democracy, socialism, syndicalism, Thatcherism, theocracy, totalitarianism, Trotskyism, unilateralism, Whiggism.

politics *n*
1 *go into politics* public affairs, civics, affairs of state, statecraft, government, national government, regional government, local government, diplomacy, statesmanship, political science, party politics, political views/beliefs **2** *office politics* power struggle, power game, power politics, manipulation, manoeuvring, *formal* machination(s), *colloq.* wheeler-dealing

Terms used in politics include :
alliance, apartheid, ballot, bill, blockade, cabinet, campaign, civil service, coalition, constitution, council, *coup d'état*, détente, election, electoral register, ethnic cleansing, general election, glasnost, go to the country, government, green paper, Hansard, judiciary, left wing, lobby, local government, majority, mandate, manifesto, nationalization, parliament, party, party line, perestroika, prime minister's question time, privatization, propaganda, proportional representation, rainbow coalition, referendum, right wing, sanction, shadow cabinet, sovereignty, state, summit, summit conference, term of office, trade union, veto, vote, welfare state, threeline whip, whip, white paper.

Political parties include:
Alliance, Communist, Conservative and Unionist, Co-operative, Democratic, Democratic Left, Democratic Unionist, Fianna Fáil, Fine Gael, Green, Labour, Liberal, Liberal Democratic, Militant Labour, National Front, Parliamentary, Parliamentary Labour, Plaid Cymru, Progressive Democrats, Republican, Scottish Conservative and Unionist, Scottish Liberal Democratic, Scottish National, Sinn Féin, Social and Liberal Democratic, Social Democratic and Labour, Ulster Democratic Unionist, Ulster Popular Unionist, Ulster Unionist, Welsh Liberal Democratic. *See also* GOVERNMENT SYSTEMS; PARLIAMENTS AND ASSEMBLIES; POLITICAL IDEOLOGY.

poll *n, v*
▶ *n* ballot, ballot-box, vote, voting, plebiscite, referendum, straw poll, straw vote, head count, show of hands, sampling, canvass, opinion poll, market research, Gallup poll, survey, returns, census, count, tally
▶ *v* **1** WIN, net, get, receive, return, gain, obtain **2** BALLOT, survey, canvass, sample, question, interview, solicit, electioneer, campaign **3** CLIP, cut, trim, shear, pollard, dod, dishorn

pollute *v*
contaminate, infect, poison, taint, adulterate, debase, corrupt, dirty, make dirty, foul, befoul, soil, defile, deprave, warp, sully, stain, tarnish, blacken, mar, spoil, *formal* vitiate

pollution *n*
impurity, contamination, infection, taint, adulteration, corruption, dirtiness, filthiness, foulness, fouling, defilement, debasement, depravity, sullying, staining, tarnishing, blackening, *colloq.* muckiness
F3 purification, purity, cleanness

polychromatic *adj*
multicoloured, many-coloured, kaleidoscopic, manyhued, mottled, motley, rainbow, variegated, varicoloured, polychrome, parti-coloured, *technical* poikilitic
F3 monochromatic, monochrome, black and white

polyglot *adj, n*
▶ *adj* multilingual, cosmopolitan, international, multiracial, *formal* polyglottal, polyglottic
F3 monoglot
▶ *n* linguist, multilinguist

polymath *n*
all-rounder, oracle, mine of information, *formal* pansophist, polyhistor, *colloq.* know-all, walking encyclopedia
F3 ignoramus

pomp *n*
ceremony, ceremonial, ritual, solemnity, formality, ceremoniousness, state, grandeur, splendour, magnificence, pageantry, show, display, parade, spectacle, ostentation, flourish, brilliance, glory, majesty, *colloq.* glitter
F3 austerity, simplicity

pomposity *n*
1 VANITY, arrogance, self-importance, pride, haughtiness, presumption, pretension, pretentiousness, imperiousness, superciliousness, condescension, airs, *formal* affectation **2** BOMBAST, turgidity, rhetoric, stuffiness, preachiness, *formal* euphuism, fustian, grandiloquence, magniloquence
F3 **1** modesty **2** simplicity, economy

pompous *adj*
1 SELF-IMPORTANT, arrogant, proud, haughty, conceited, vain, presumptuous, grandiose, supercilious, patronizing, condescending, overbearing, imperious, magisterial, pretentious, ostentatious, *formal* af-

fected, *colloq.* snooty **2** *pompous language* elaborate, grand, bombastic, high-flown, overblown, windy, stilted, flowery, ostentatious, turgid, stuffy, *formal* euphuistic, magniloquent, *colloq.* preachy, la-di-da
F₃ 1 unassuming, modest, unaffected **2** simple

pond *n*
pool, puddle, lake, mere, tarn, waterhole, watering-hole

ponder *v*
deliberate, give thought to, reflect, reason, think, contemplate, meditate, consider, brood, examine, analyse, study, ruminate over, weigh, muse, puzzle over, mull over, *formal* cerebrate, cogitate, excogitate, ratiocinate

ponderous *adj*
1 *ponderous writing* dull, serious, dreary, tedious, stilted, long-winded, plodding, verbose, laborious, pedantic, pedestrian, stodgy, stolid, humourless, laboured, lifeless, *formal* prolix **2** CLUMSY, unwieldy, awkward, cumbersome, graceless, heavy, bulky, weighty, heavy-handed, heavy-footed, huge, massive, hefty, slow-moving, lumbering, elephantine
F₃ 1 light, simple **2** delicate

ponderousness *n*
seriousness, tedium, heaviness, laboriousness, stodginess, stolidity, weightiness, humourlessness, gravitas
F₃ delicacy, lightness, subtlety

pontifical *adj*
1 PAPAL, apostolic, ecclesiastical, prelatic **2** SELF-IMPORTANT, pompous, overbearing, condescending, imperious, pretentious, magisterial, dogmatic, didactic, portentous, sermonizing, *colloq.* preachy
F₃ 2 reticent, unassuming

pontificate *v*
preach, hold forth, lecture, expound, pronounce, sermonize, sound off, harangue, dogmatize, moralize, *formal* declaim, perorate, *colloq.* lay down the law

pony *n*
See panel at HORSE.

pooh-pooh *v*
dismiss, scorn, make little of, belittle, brush aside, ridicule, disdain, disregard, slight, sneer, sniff at, scoff, spurn, reject, play down, minimize, *formal* deride, disparage, *colloq.* turn up your nose at
F₃ exaggerate, magnify

pool¹ *n*
a pool of water puddle, pond, lake, mere, tarn, waterhole, watering-hole, paddling-pool, swimming-pool, swimming-bath(s)

pool² *n, v*
▶ *n* **1** FUND, reserve, supply, accumulation, bank, kitty, purse, pot, jackpot, ante **2** SYNDICATE, cartel, ring, combine, consortium, collective, group, team
▶ *v* share, merge, combine, amalgamate, contribute, *colloq.* chip in, muck in

poor *adj*
1 IMPOVERISHED, poverty-stricken, badly off, in need, hard up, bankrupt, penniless, without means, without the wherewithal, destitute, deprived, underprivileged, disadvantaged, reduced, humble, lowly, mean, miserable, wretched, distressed, straitened, needy, *formal* penurious, impecunious, exiguous, indigent, *colloq.* broke, stony-broke, skint, on your uppers, on your beam-ends, not having two pennies to rub together, not having a penny to your name, on the breadline, poor as a church mouse **2** BAD, substandard, unsatisfactory, inferior, mediocre, below standard, below par, low, low-quality, low-grade, second-rate, third-rate, shoddy, imperfect, defective, faulty, jerry, weak, feeble, sorry, worthless, fruitless, unpro-

ductive, barren, *colloq.* pathetic, rubbish, ropy, rotten, measly, crummy, *slang* naff **3** LACKING, deficient, inadequate, insufficient, scanty, skimpy, meagre, sparse, paltry, depleted, exhausted **4** UN-FORTUNATE, unlucky, luckless, ill-fated, ill-starred, unhappy, miserable, wretched, sorry, sad, spiritless, pathetic, pitiable, pitiful, *formal* hapless
F₃ 1 rich, wealthy, affluent **2** good, superior, impressive **3** sufficient, ample **4** fortunate, lucky

poorly *adj, adv*
▶ *adj* ill, sick, unwell, indisposed, ailing, sickly, off colour, below par, seedy, groggy, *colloq.* out of sorts, under the weather, rotten
F₃ well, healthy
▶ *adv* badly, inadequately, unsatisfactorily, unsuccessfully, faultily, incompetently, inexpertly, insufficiently, inferiorly, rottenly, shabbily, shoddily, meanly, feebly
F₃ well

pop *v, n*
▶ *v* **1** BURST, explode, go off, bang, crack, snap **2** RUSH, dash, hurry, go quickly, leave quickly, go for a short time, *colloq.* nip **3** PUT, push, insert, slide, slip, thrust, drop, shove
▷ **pop off** die, pass away, pass on, *colloq.* peg out, have had it, *slang* snuff it, kick the bucket
▷ **pop up** appear, occur, materialize, crop up, turn up, show up, come along
▶ *n* **1** BANG, crack, snap, burst, explosion, boom, *formal* report **2** FIZZY DRINK, fizzy lemonade, cola, soda

pope *n*
pontiff, sovereign pontiff, Bishop of Rome, Holy Father, Vicar of Christ, His Holiness

popinjay *n*
dandy, fop, beau, coxcomb, peacock, swell, dude, *colloq.* toff
F₃ he-man, macho

poppycock *n*
nonsense, rubbish, trash, garbage, drivel, balderdash, gibberish, gobbledygook, stupidity, silliness, foolishness, folly, blather, twaddle, havers, *colloq.* stuff and nonsense, bunk, rot, claptrap, cobblers, piffle, waffle, flannel, rot, tripe, tosh, bosh, tommy-rot, codswallop, baloney, humbug, hooey, bilge, bull, *slang* crap
F₃ sense

populace *n*
inhabitants, natives, residents, citizens, occupants, community, society, people, folk, general public, crowd, masses, proletariat, public, mob, multitude(s), common herd, canaille, hoi polloi, *colloq.* plebs, punters, rabble, rank and file
F₃ aristocracy, élite, nobility

popular *adj*
1 WELL-LIKED, favourite, liked, favoured, in favour, admired, wanted, desired, approved, in demand, sought-after, fashionable, modish, *colloq.* trendy, in, hip, cool, big, all the rage **2** FAMOUS, well-known, celebrated, renowned, acclaimed, noted, idolized **3** PREVAILING, current, accepted, usual, customary, conventional, standard, stock, common, prevalent, widespread, universal, general, generally recognized, household **4** *a popular history of science* general, non-specialist, non-technical, understandable, accessible, simple, simplified, ordinary, mass-market
F₃ 1 unpopular, disliked, out of favour **2** unheard-of, obscure, unknown **3** rare, unusual **4** specialist, technical, expert, professional

popularity *n*
approval, acceptance, recognition, reputation, favour, vogue, kudos, mass appeal, regard, fame,

renown, currency, repute, acclaim, adoration, adulation, glory, worship, idolization, lionization, *formal* approbation, esteem
F3 unpopularity

popularize *v*
spread, propagate, familiarize, universalize, democratize, generalize, give currency to, simplify, make understandable, make accessible

popularly *adv*
commonly, widely, universally, generally, usually, customarily, ordinarily, regularly, conventionally, traditionally

populate *v*
people, occupy, settle, colonize, inhabit, live in, overrun, *formal* dwell

population *n*
inhabitants, natives, residents, citizens, occupants, community, society, people, folk, *formal* populace

populous *adj*
crowded, packed, swarming, teeming, crawling, densely populated, overpopulated, overpeopled
F3 deserted, empty

porcelain *n*

Types of porcelain include:
biscuit, bisque, blue and white, bone china, Canton, Capodimonte, chinoiserie, Compagnie des Indes, copper red, eggshell, faience, famille-rose, famille-verte, First Period Worcester, hard paste, Imari, Kakiemon, Kraak, nankeen, Parian, salt-glazed, soapstone paste, soft paste, Yingqing.

Famous makes of porcelain include:
Arita, Belleek, Bow, Bristol, Caughley, Chantilly, Chelsea, Coalport, Copeland, Derby, Dresden, Limoges, Meissen, Ming, Minton, Nanking, Rockingham, Royal Doulton, Royal Worcester, Satsuma, Sèvres, Vienna, Wedgwood, Worcester.

porch *n*
vestibule, hall, hallway, entrance-hall, lobby, foyer

pore¹ *v*
▷ **pore over** *pore over a book* study, study intensely, examine, examine closely, scrutinize, go over, read, scan, contemplate, ponder, dwell on, brood, *formal* peruse

pore² *n*
sweating from every pore hole, opening, perforation, aperture, outlet, vent, *technical* foramen, *formal* orifice

pornographic *adj*
obscene, indecent, dirty, filthy, blue, risqué, off-colour, bawdy, coarse, gross, lewd, salacious, erotic, titillating, *formal* prurient, *colloq.* porn

pornography *n*
indecency, obscenity, filth, dirt, smut, erotica, grossness, bawdiness, facetiae, *colloq.* porn, porno, sexploitation, girlie magazines

porous *adj*
permeable, pervious, penetrable, absorbent, spongy, spongelike, honeycombed, cellular, holey, open, airy, *technical* foraminous, foveate
F3 impermeable, impervious

port *n*
seaport, harbour, jetty, dock, anchorage, harbourage, haven, roads, roadstead, hithe

portable *adj*
movable, transportable, compact, lightweight, manageable, conveyable, handy, convenient
F3 fixed, immovable

portend *v*
indicate, point to, be a sign of, be an indication of, warn of, announce, forecast, predict, foretell, promise, signify, threaten, herald, *formal* augur, bode, forebode, foreshadow, forewarn, harbinger, bespeak, betoken, foretoken, prognosticate, adumbrate, presage

portent *n*
sign, indication, warning, threat, omen, precursor, forecast, foreboding, forerunner, prefiguration, premonition, *formal* augury, signification, prognostication, foreshadowing, forewarning, prognostic, presage, presentiment, prodrome, harbinger

portentous *adj*
1 FOREBODING, ominous, sinister, fateful, menacing, threatening, momentous **2** REMARKABLE, significant, important, amazing, astounding, extraordinary, awe-inspiring, earth-shaking, epoch-making, miraculous, crucial **3** POMPOUS, ponderous, solemn, weighty, self-important, pontifical
F3 **2** insignificant, unimportant, unimpressive

porter¹ *n*
a porter at a hotel bearer, carrier, baggage-attendant, baggage-handler, baggage-carrier

porter² *n*
a porter at a college doorman, commissionaire, doorkeeper, gatekeeper, door attendant, janitor, caretaker, concierge

portion *n, v*
▶ *n* **1** SHARE, allocation, tranche, allotment, parcel, quantity, allowance, ration, quota, measure, part, section, division, fraction, percentage, bit, fragment, morsel, piece, segment, slice, wedge, serving, helping, *colloq.* cut, whack, rake-off **2** DESTINY, fate, lot, kismet, fortune, luck, chance
▶ *v* distribute, divide, deal, share out, allocate, allot, apportion, assign, slice up, parcel, partition, *colloq.* carve up, dole out

portliness *n*
ampleness, stoutness, roundness, plumpness, fatness, paunchiness, obesity, heaviness, fullness, dumpiness, tubbiness, chubbiness, fleshiness, *formal* corpulence, rotundity, *colloq.* beefiness

portly *adj*
stout, round, fat, plump, obese, overweight, stocky, ample, heavy, large, *formal* corpulent, rotund
F3 slim, thin, slight

portrait *n*
picture, painting, drawing, sketch, caricature, miniature, icon, photograph, likeness, image, representation, vignette, profile, study, thumbnail sketch, characterization, description, depiction, portrayal, story, account

portray *v*
1 DRAW, sketch, paint, illustrate, picture, represent **2** DESCRIBE, depict, picture, represent, characterize, illustrate, evoke **3** PLAY, act, play/act the part of, perform, impersonate, characterize, personify

portrayal *n*
representation, characterization, depiction, description, picture, painting, drawing, sketch, study, evocation, presentation, acting, performance, interpretation, rendering, *formal* delineation

pose *v, n*
▶ *v* **1** MODEL, sit, position, arrange **2** PRETEND, feign, act, put on an act, put on airs, masquerade, pass yourself off, impersonate, attitudinize, *formal* affect **3** *pose a question* put forward, ask, submit, suggest, pro-

pose, put, set, advance, *formal* posit, postulate, propound **4** *pose a problem/threat* create, present, cause, produce, give rise to, lead to, result in
▸ *n* **1** POSITION, stance, air, posture, attitude, *formal* bearing, carriage, deportment **2** PRETENCE, sham, façade, front, masquerade, airs, role, act, *formal* affectation

poser¹ *n*
he's a poser poseur, poseuse, posturer, attitudinizer, exhibitionist, show-off, play-actor, charlatan, sham, impostor, *colloq.* pseud, phoney

poser² *n*
this is a poser puzzle, riddle, conundrum, brainteaser, mystery, enigma, problem, dilemma, vexed question

poseur *n*
poser, poseuse, posturer, attitudinizer, exhibitionist, show-off, play-actor, charlatan, sham, impostor, *colloq.* pseud, phoney

posh *adj*
smart, stylish, fancy, fashionable, elegant, high-class, upper-class, grand, luxurious, lavish, sumptuous, luxury, de luxe, rich, up-market, exclusive, select, *formal* opulent, *colloq.* la-di-da, swanky, classy, swish, plush
🖩 inferior, cheap

posit *v*
put forward, pose, advance, state, submit, assert, assume, presume, *formal* postulate, predicate, propound

position *n, v*
▸ *n* **1** PLACE, situation, location, site, spot, scene, setting, area, locality, whereabouts, point **2** POSTURE, stance, pose, attitude, arrangement, disposition, *formal* bearing **3** JOB, post, occupation, employment, situation, appointment, office, duty, function, role, capacity **4** RANK, grade, level, place, status, standing, ranking, influence, prestige **5** SITUATION, state, condition, state of affairs, circumstances, case, factor(s), background, plight, predicament **6** OPINION, point of view, belief, view, outlook, viewpoint, attitude, stance, standpoint, stand
▸ *v* put, place, set, settle, fix, stand, arrange, dispose, lay out, deploy, station, locate, situate, site, install, establish, *formal* array

positive *adj*
1 SURE, certain, convinced, confident, assured **2** OPTIMISTIC, hopeful, confident, encouraged, cheerful, promising, encouraging, *colloq.* upbeat **3** *positive criticism* helpful, constructive, practical, useful, productive **4** DEFINITE, decisive, conclusive, real, actual, concrete, clear, clear-cut, unmistakable, explicit, precise, unequivocal, express, direct, firm, emphatic, categorical, undeniable, indisputable, incontestable, incontrovertible, *formal* irrefutable **5** ABSOLUTE, utter, sheer, complete, rank, perfect, unmitigated, outright, out-and-out, thorough, veritable, *formal* consummate
🖩 **1** uncertain **2, 3** negative **4** indefinite, vague

positively *adv*
absolutely, definitely, categorically, firmly, finally, decisively, emphatically, expressly, conclusively, certainly, assuredly, surely, unmistakably, unquestionably, incontestably, incontrovertibly, indisputably, unequivocally, undeniably, uncompromisingly

possess *v*
1 OWN, have, hold, be in possession of, acquire, gain, get, enjoy, be endowed with, be gifted with **2** SEIZE, take, obtain, acquire, take over, take possession of, get, occupy **3** INFLUENCE, control, dominate, bewitch, haunt, enchant, infatuate, obsess

possessed *adj*
dominated, controlled, mesmerized, enchanted, berserk, bedevilled, bewitched, haunted, cursed, hagridden, frenzied, demented, crazed, maddened, raving, consumed, infatuated, obsessed, besotted

possession *n*
OWNERSHIP, title, tenure, occupation, holding, tenancy, custody, proprietorship, control, hold, grip

possessions *n*
lose your possessions belongings, property, baggage, luggage, paraphernalia, effects, goods, chattels, goods and chattels, movables, assets, estate, wealth, riches, *formal* accoutrements, *colloq.* things, stuff, gear, (all your) worldly wealth

possessive *adj*
selfish, clinging, overprotective, domineering, dominating, controlling, jealous, covetous, acquisitive, grasping, greedy
🖩 unselfish, sharing

possibility *n*
1 LIKELIHOOD, probability, odds, chance, risk, danger, hazard, hope, prospect, potentiality, conceivability, practicability, feasibility, attainability **2** *a place with possibilities* promise, potential, prospects, advantages, capabilities, expectations, talent, *formal* potentiality **3** OPTION, alternative, choice, preference, recourse
🖩 **1** impossibility, impracticability **2** disadvantages, liabilities

possible *adj*
likely, probable, promising, potential, imaginable, conceivable, practicable, feasible, that can be done, viable, tenable, credible, workable, achievable, attainable, doable, accomplishable, realizable, *colloq.* on the cards, odds-on
🖩 impossible, unthinkable, impracticable, unattainable

possibly *adv*
perhaps, maybe, conceivably, by any means, at all, by any chance, *formal* peradventure, *colloq.* hopefully

post¹ *n, v*
▸ *n* *a fence post* pole, stake, picket, pale, pillar, column, shaft, standard, support, prop, baluster, banister, palisade, upright, newel, stanchion, strut, leg
▸ *v* **1** DISPLAY, stick up, pin (up), put up, attach, affix **2** ANNOUNCE, advertise, publicize, make known, circulate, report, publish, broadcast

post² *n, v*
▸ *n* *a teaching post* office, job, employment, position, situation, place, vacancy, appointment, assignment, station, beat
▸ *v* station, locate, situate, position, place, put, appoint, assign, second, transfer, move, send

post³ *n, v*
▸ *n* **1** *deliver the post* MAIL, letters, correspondence, communications, packages, parcels, packets, delivery, registered mail, recorded mail, special delivery, direct mail, airmail, surface mail, international mail, electronic mail, e-mail, *colloq.* junk mail, snail mail **2** POSTAL SERVICE, postal system, mail, Post Office
▸ *v* mail, send, dispatch, transmit, forward
▷ **keep someone posted** inform, keep up to date, give the latest information, *colloq.* fill in, keep in the picture

poster *n*
notice, bill, sign, placard, sticker, advertisement, bulletin, announcement, *colloq.* ad, advert

posterior *adj, n*
▸ *adj* rear, rearward, behind, back, hind, hinder, after, ensuing, following, subsequent, succeeding, later, latter, *technical* dorsal, posticous

Ξ anterior, front, previous
▶ *n* bottom, rear, behind, buttocks, rump, seat, haunches, hinder end, hindquarters, *colloq.* backside, bum, *US* butt, tail

posterity *n*
descendants, successors, future generations, succeeding generations, heirs, offspring, seed, children, *formal* progeny, issue

posthaste *adv*
quickly, speedily, straight away, immediately, at once, directly, promptly, hastily, swiftly, with all speed, *colloq.* double-quick, full tilt, pronto
Ξ eventually, gradually, slowly

postman, postwoman *n*
delivery officer, letter-carrier, mail-carrier, mail handler, postal worker, *US* mailman, *colloq.* postie

post-mortem *n*
autopsy, dissection, necropsy, analysis, examination, review

postpone *v*
put off, defer, put back, do later, hold over, delay, adjourn, suspend, reschedule, shelve, pigeonhole, freeze, *formal* prorogue, procrastinate, *colloq.* put on ice, put on the back burner, take a raincheck on
Ξ advance, forward, bring forward

postponed *adj*
put off, adjourned, deferred, shelved, suspended, pigeonholed, frozen, *formal* in abeyance, *colloq.* on ice, on the back burner
Ξ advanced

postponement *n*
adjournment, put-off, deferment, delay, deferral, moratorium, freeze, suspension, stay, respite, *formal* prorogation

postscript *n*
addition, supplement, afterthought, addendum, appendix, afterword, epilogue, *technical* codicil, *colloq.* PS
Ξ introduction, prologue

postulate *v*
theorize, suppose, assume, presume, presuppose, propose, advance, lay down, stipulate, *formal* hypothesize, posit

posture *n, v*
▶ *n* 1 POSITION, stance, pose, attitude, disposition, *formal* bearing, carriage, deportment 2 ATTITUDE, opinion, point of view, belief, view, outlook, viewpoint, stance, standpoint, stand
▶ *v* pose, put on airs, show off, strike attitudes, attitudinize, strut, *formal* affect

posy *n*
bouquet, spray, buttonhole, nosegay, corsage

pot *n*
1 RECEPTACLE, vessel, teapot, coffee pot, urn, jar, vase, bowl, basin, pan, cauldron, crucible 2 KITTY, purse, fund, reserve

pot-bellied *adj*
bloated, corpulent, distended, fat, gor-bellied, obese, overweight, paunchy, portly, tubby

pot-belly *n*
belly, beer belly, paunch, gut, pot, *colloq.* corporation, spare tyre

potency *n*
power, strength, force, influence, potential, vigour, control, authority, effectiveness, persuasiveness, energy, sway, capacity, *formal* cogency, efficaciousness, efficacy, might, puissance, *colloq.* headiness, kick, muscle, punch
Ξ weakness, impotence

potent *adj*
effective, powerful, mighty, strong, intoxicating, pungent, impressive, convincing, persuasive, eloquent, compelling, forceful, dynamic, energetic, vigorous, authoritative, commanding, dominant, influential, overpowering, *formal* cogent, efficacious, puissant
Ξ impotent, weak

potentate *n*
ruler, monarch, sovereign, autocrat, head of state, king, queen, despot, dictator, tyrant, emperor, empress, prince, chief, chieftain, mogul, leader, dynast, overlord

potential *adj, n*
▶ *adj* possible, likely, probable, prospective, future, aspiring, would-be, promising, budding, developing, embryonic, inherent, undeveloped, dormant, latent, hidden, concealed, unrealized
▶ *n* possibility, ability, capability, capacity, aptitude, gift, flair, talent, promise, powers, resources

potentiality *n*
likelihood, possibilities, potential, promise, prospect, virtuality, ability, capability, aptitude, capacity

potion *n*
mixture, concoction, brew, beverage, drink, draught, dose, medicine, tonic, elixir, philtre, potation

potpourri *n*
medley, mixture, assortment, jumble, hotchpotch, miscellany, collection, melange, confusion, smorgasbord, pastiche, patchwork, gallimaufry, *colloq.* mishmash

potter *v*
dawdle, amble, loiter, *colloq.* mess about, toddle, dilly-dally
▷ **potter about** tinker about/around, fiddle about/around, fool about/around, play about/around, *colloq.* mess about/around, muck about/around

pottery *n*
ceramics, crockery, china

Terms used in pottery include :

armorial, art pottery, basalt, blanc-de-chine, bronzing, celadon, ceramic, china clay, cloisonné, crackleware, crazing, creamware, delft, earthenware, enamel, faience, fairing, figure, firing, flambé, flatback, glaze, grotesque, ground, ironstone, jasper, kiln, lustre, maiolica, majolica, maker's mark, mandarin palette, model, monogram, overglaze, porcelain, sagger, scratch blue, sgraffito, slip, slipcast, spongeware, Staffordshire, stoneware, terracotta, tin-glazed earthenware, transfer printing, underglaze, Willow pattern. *See also* PORCELAIN.

potty *adj*
crazy, foolish, eccentric, demented, silly, touched, soft, *colloq.* daft, nuts, nutty, bananas, barmy, bonkers, crackers, dippy, dotty

pouch *n*
bag, purse, pocket, container, receptacle, sack, wallet, sporran, poke, *technical* marsupium, sac, *formal* reticule

pounce *v, n*
▶ *v* fall on, dive on, swoop, drop, descend, attack, strike, ambush, spring, jump, leap, bound, lunge, snatch, grab, take by surprise, catch/take unawares, catch off guard
▶ *n* attack, assault, bound, dive, grab, jump, leap, swoop, lunge, spring

pound¹ *n*
it cost 100 pounds pound coin, pound sterling, *colloq.* quid, *slang* nicker, smacker, smackeroo, oncer, sov

pound² *n*
keep animals in a pound enclosure, compound, corral, yard, pen, fold

pound³ *v*
1 STRIKE, thump, beat, drum, pelt, hammer, batter, bang, bash, smash, pummel **2** PULVERIZE, powder, grind, mash, bray, pestle, crush, beat, smash, granulate, *formal* levigate, comminute, triturate **3** *his heart was pounding* throb, pulsate, palpitate, thump, thud **4** *pound the streets* tread, tramp, walk, pace, trudge, plod, stomp

pour *v*
1 *pour a drink* make flow, serve, pour out, decant, tip, spill, sprinkle **2** SPILL, issue, come out, discharge, flow, emit, leak, ooze, stream, run, rush, spout, spew, jet, spurt, gush, course, cascade, flood, crowd, throng, swarm, *formal* disgorge, disembogue **3** RAIN, team down, pelt down, *colloq.* rain cats and dogs, bucket down, come down in buckets/stair rods/torrents

pout *v, n*
▶ *v* scowl, glower, lour, grimace, pull a face, sulk, mope
🔁 grin, smile
▶ *n* scowl, glower, grimace, long face, moue
🔁 grin, smile

poverty *n*
poorness, impoverishment, insolvency, bankruptcy, pennilessness, destitution, deprivation, distress, hardship, need, necessity, want, lack, deficiency, shortage, inadequacy, insufficiency, depletion, scarcity, meagreness, paucity, dearth, *formal* penury, impecuniosity, indigence, privation
🔁 wealth, richness, affluence, plenty

poverty-stricken *adj*
poor, penniless, impoverished, needy, destitute, distressed, bankrupt, beggared, *formal* impecunious, obolary, indigent, penurious, *colloq.* broke, skint, stony, stony-broke, strapped, on your beam-ends, on your uppers
🔁 rich, affluent

powder *n, v*
▶ *n* dust, grains, pounce, bran, talc, *formal* triturate, pulvil, pulville, pulvil(l)io
▶ *v* **1** PULVERIZE, powder, grind, mash, bray, pestle, crush, beat, smash, granulate, *formal* levigate, comminute, triturate **2** SPRINKLE, scatter, cover, dust, strew

powdery *adj*
dusty, sandy, grainy, granular, granulated, powdered, pulverized, ground, fine, loose, dry, floury, crumbly, chalky, *formal* friable, pulverulent, levigate

power *n*
1 COMMAND, authority, sovereignty, rule, dominion, domination, control, say, influence, mastery, supremacy, sway, *formal* ascendancy, *colloq.* clout, pull, muscle, teeth, clutches **2** RIGHT, authority, privilege, prerogative, authorization, licence, warrant **3** POWERFULNESS, strength, intensity, energy, force, forcefulness, effectiveness, vigour, potency, *formal* might, *colloq.* juice **4** ABILITY, capability, capacity, potential, faculty, competence, *formal* potentiality
🔁 **1** subjection **3** weakness, impotence **4** inability

powerful *adj*
1 INFLUENTIAL, dominant, prevailing, leading, high-powered, authoritative, commanding, potent, effective, energetic, forceful, telling, impressive, convincing, persuasive, compelling, winning, overwhelming, all-powerful **2** STRONG, mighty, robust, tough, muscular, brawny, strapping, burly, hardy
🔁 **1** powerless, ineffective, impotent **2** weak

powerfully *adv*
strongly, vigorously, hard, forcefully, forcibly, potently, convincingly, persuasively, impressively, tellingly, *formal* cogently, mightily, with might and main

powerless *adj*
helpless, unfit, unable, impotent, incapable, ineffective, weak, having a say, feeble, frail, infirm, incapacitated, disabled, paralysed, vulnerable, defenceless, unarmed, *formal* debilitated, ineffectual
🔁 powerful, influential, able, potent

practicability *n*
possibility, feasibility, practicality, viability, workability, workableness, handiness, operability, use, usefulness, value, utility
🔁 impracticability

practicable *adj*
possible, feasible, performable, achievable, doable, attainable, viable, workable, practical, realistic
🔁 impracticable

---

 practicable or **practical** ?

Practicable means 'able to be done, used, carried out, etc': *a practicable plan*. *Practical,* when applied to things, suggestions, etc also means 'able to be done, used, or carried out' but has the further connotation of 'efficient, sensible, useful': *Both these suggested courses of action are practicable, but John's is certainly the more practical of the two; High heels aren't very practical for hill-walking.* Applied to people, *practical* means 'able to do, make, or deal with things well or efficiently': *He's not a very practical person: he has lots of ideas for redesigning the bathroom but he doesn't have a clue how to put up a shelf.*

---

practical *adj*
1 *put knowledge to practical use* applied, hands on, real, actual **2** *a practical person* down-to-earth, matter-of-fact, sensible, realistic, pragmatic, hard-headed, businesslike, efficient, experienced, trained, qualified, skilled, accomplished, proficient, *colloq.* hard-nosed, having both feet on the ground **3** *practical ideas* realistic, workable, feasible, sensible, commonsense, applied, workaday, practicable **4** *wear practical shoes* sensible, strong, suitable, utilitarian, functional, working, everyday, ordinary, serviceable, useful, handy **5** *a practical walkover* virtual, effective, essential
🔁 **1** theoretical **2** impractical, unskilled **3, 4** impractical

---

🔁 **practical** or **practicable** ? *See panel at* PRACTICABLE.

---

practicality *n*
sense, common sense, realism, basics, experience, practicability, pragmatism, practicalness, serviceability, soundness, usefulness, utility, workability, feasibility, practice, *colloq.* nitty-gritty, nuts and bolts

practically *adv*
1 ALMOST, nearly, well-nigh, virtually, all but, just about, in principle, in effect, essentially, fundamentally, to all intents and purposes, *colloq.* pretty much, pretty well **2** REALISTICALLY, sensibly, reasonably, rationally, pragmatically, matter-of-factly

practice *n*
1 CUSTOM, tradition, convention, usage, habit, routine, way, method, system, procedure, policy, *formal* wont **2** REHEARSAL, run-through, dry run, dummy run, try-out, training, drill, exercise, work-out, study, preparation, warm-up, experience **3** *in practice* effect, reality, actuality, action, operation, performance,

use, exercise, application **4** *the practice of medicine* business, work, profession, career, occupation, employment, job, following, pursuit
F3 **3** theory, principle

practise *v*
1 DO, perform, implement, carry out, apply, put into practice, observe, follow, pursue, engage in, undertake, *formal* execute **2** REHEARSE, run through, go through, go over, repeat, drill, exercise, train, study, work on, work at, prepare, perfect, refine, polish

practised *adj*
experienced, seasoned, veteran, trained, qualified, accomplished, skilled, skilful, versed, knowing, knowledgeable, able, adept, proficient, expert, masterly, finished, *formal* consummate
F3 unpractised, inexperienced, inexpert

pragmatic *adj*
practical, realistic, sensible, matter-of-fact, businesslike, efficient, utilitarian, hard-headed, unsentimental, *colloq.* hard-nosed
F3 unrealistic, idealistic, romantic

pragmatism *n*
practicality, realism, utilitarianism, hard-headedness, humanism, practicalism, opportunism, unidealism
F3 idealism, romanticism

pragmatist *n*
realist, utilitarian, opportunist, practicalist
F3 idealist, romantic

praise *v, n*
▸ *v* commend, congratulate, express approval of, speak highly of, speak well of, admire, compliment, flatter, sing the praises of, wax lyrical, extol, promote, applaud, cheer, acclaim, hail, recognize, acknowledge, pay tribute to, honour, glorify, magnify, exalt, worship, adore, bless, *formal* eulogize, laud, *colloq.* rave over
F3 criticize, revile

Expressions used when praising someone:
can't praise him/her/them highly enough, clever boy/girl!, congratulations!, you deserve a medal, encore!, *Irish* fair play to you, give that person a coconut, good for you!, *US* good job!, good show!, good work!, *US* nice job!, nice one!, sing someone's praises, ten out of ten, *US* way to go!, well done!, you beauty!

▸ *n* approval, admiration, commendation, congratulation, compliment, flattery, adulation, applause, plaudits, ovation, cheering, acclaim, recognition, testimonial, tribute, accolade, homage, honour, glory, worship, adoration, devotion, thanks, thanksgiving, hallelujah, *formal* approbation, eulogy, encomium, laudation, panegyric, *colloq.* bouquets, puff
F3 criticism, revilement

praiseworthy *adj*
commendable, fine, excellent, admirable, exemplary, worthy, deserving, honourable, reputable, estimable, sterling, *formal* laudable
F3 blameworthy, dishonourable, ignoble

praising *adj*
approving, complimentary, congratulatory, favourable, flattering, commendatory, adulatory, recommendatory, promotional, worshipful, *formal* approbatory, eulogistic, encomiastic, laudative, laudatory, panegyric, plauditory
F3 condemnatory, critical

prance *v*
1 LEAP, jump, spring, skip, dance, frisk, frolic, gam-

bol, cavort, caper, bound, romp, vault **2** SHOW OFF, strut, swagger, stalk, parade, curvet, *colloq.* swank

prank *n*
trick, practical joke, joke, stunt, caper, frolic, lark, antic, escapade

prattle *v, n*
▸ *v* chat, chatter, witter, gabble, rattle, twitter, twaddle, twattle, patter, drivel, gossip, blather, blether, *colloq.* babble, jabber
▸ *n* chat, chatter, gossip, talk, jaw, gab, tattle, blather, blether, nonsense, prating, gibberish, foolishness, drivel, *colloq.* hot air, bubble

prattler *n*
chatterer, talker, gossip, blether, gabbler, tatler, tattler, magpie, *colloq.* babbler, blabbermouth, chatterbox, loudmouth, windbag
F3 clam

pray *v*
1 *pray to God* invoke, call on, commune with, talk to, speak to, say a prayer, be at prayer, say your prayers, praise, worship, adore, confess, thank **2** ENTREAT, implore, plead, beg, petition, ask, request, crave, solicit, *formal* supplicate, beseech

prayer *n*
1 *prayer to God* collect, litany, devotion, doxology, communion, invocation, fellowship, intercession, praise, worship, the Lord's Prayer, Our Father, Paternoster, Kyrie eleison, Hail Mary, Ave Maria, Agnus Dei, Magnificat, Benedictus, Nunc Dimittis, Sursum Corda, Gloria, Om, mantra **2** ENTREATY, plea, appeal, petition, request, *formal* supplication

prayer-book *n*
ordinal, service-book, missal, breviary, mahzor, euchologion, euchology, formulary, Triodion

preach *v*
address, lecture, teach, proclaim, harangue, pontificate, sermonize, evangelize, give a sermon, spread the gospel, moralize, exhort, advise, admonish, urge, advocate

preacher *n*
minister, clergyman, parson, evangelist, televangelist, missionary, revivalist, sermonizer, moralizer, pulpite(e)r, ranter, homilist, pontificater

preaching *n*
teaching, instruction, doctrine, precepts, message, homiletics, homilies, dogma, gospel, sermons, sermonizing, evangelism, pontificating, *technical* evangel, kerygma, *formal* exhortation

preachy *adj*
moralizing, pontificating, sermonizing, religiose, pietistic, pharisaic, pontifical, sanctimonious, self-righteous, dogmatic, didactic, edifying, homiletic, *formal* exhortatory, hortatory, *colloq.* holier-than-thou

preamble *n*
introduction, lead-in, preliminaries, preparation, prelude, foreword, preface, prologue, overture, *formal* exordium, proem, prolegomenon
F3 postscript, epilogue

precarious *adj*
unsafe, dangerous, treacherous, risky, hazardous, chancy, uncertain, unsure, unsettled, dubious, doubtful, unpredictable, unreliable, undependable, unsteady, unstable, shaky, wobbly, insecure, vulnerable, *colloq.* chancy, dicey, dodgy, hairy, iffy, dicky
F3 safe, certain, stable, secure

precaution *n*
safeguard, security, preventive/preventative measure, protection, insurance, providence, forethought,

care, caution, attentiveness, foresight, farsightedness, anticipation, preparation, provision, *formal* prudence, circumspection

precautionary *adj*
safety, protective, preventive, preventative, provident, cautious, far-sighted, preparatory, preliminary, *formal* prudent, judicious

precede *v*
come before, lead, come first, go before, go ahead of, take precedence, introduce, herald, usher in, head, preface, *formal* antecede, antedate, prevene
F3 follow, succeed

precedence *n*
priority, preference, pride of place, superiority, supremacy, eminence, pre-eminence, lead, first place, seniority, rank, *formal* ascendancy
▷ **take precedence over** take priority over, come before, be more important than

precedent *n*
example, instance, case, parallel, pattern, model, standard, criterion, yardstick, *formal* paradigm, exemplar

preceding *adj*
above, earlier, former, past, previous, prior, precedent, foregoing, antecedent, *formal* aforementioned, aforesaid, supra, precursive, anterior
F3 following, later

precept *n*
principle, axiom, command, commandment, charge, direction, directive, ordinance, regulation, guideline, order, injunction, institute, law, instruction, decree, dictum, mandate, rule, statute, convention, canon, maxim, motto, saying, sentence, rubric

precinct *n*
1 ZONE, area, district, quarter, sector, division, section, shopping centre, mall, galleria **2** BOUNDARY, limit, bound, confine, enclosure, close, court, neighbourhood, surrounds, locality, vicinity, environs, milieu, purlieus

preciosity *n*
artificiality, pretentiousness, floweriness, over-refinement, affectation, tweeness, chichi

precious *adj*
1 VALUED, treasured, prized, cherished, beloved, dear, dearest, darling, favourite, loved, revered, adored, idolized **2** VALUABLE, expensive, costly, high-priced, dear, priceless, inestimable, rare, choice, fine **3** AFFECTED, overrefined, simulated, contrived, artificial, mannered, pretentious, flowery, twee, chichi

precipice *n*
cliff, cliff face, bluff, brink, steep, escarpment, crag, drop, height, escarp, scarp, krantz

precipitate *v, adj*
▶ *v* **1** HASTEN, hurry, speed (up), accelerate, quicken, expedite, advance, further, bring about, bring on, induce, trigger, cause, occasion **2** THROW, plunge, hurl, heave, thrust, fling
▶ *adj* sudden, unexpected, abrupt, quick, swift, speedy, rapid, brief, hasty, hurried, headlong, breakneck, frantic, violent, impatient, hot-headed, impetuous, impulsive, rash, reckless, heedless, indiscreet
F3 cautious, careful

---

precipitate or **precipitous** ?

Precipitate means 'hasty or too hasty': *precipitate decision. Precipitous* means 'very steep, like a precipice': *The path through the mountains is narrow and precipitous.*

---

precipitation *n*

Types of precipitation include:
dew, downpour, drizzle, fog, hail, mist, rain, rainfall, rainstorm, shower, sleet, snow, snowfall, snowflake.

precipitous *adj*
steep, sheer, perpendicular, vertical, abrupt, sharp, high, sudden
F3 gradual

---

precipitous or **precipitate** ? *See panel at* PRECIPITATE

---

précis *n, v*
▶ *n* summary, abridgement, contraction, abbreviation, condensation, synopsis, abstract, digest, epitome, outline, résumé, sketch, compendium, rundown, table, *formal* conspectus, encapsulation
▶ *v* summarize, shorten, sum up, outline, abstract, abridge, condense, synopsize, digest, abbreviate, encapsulate, epitomize, contract, compress
F3 amplify, expand

precise *adj*
exact, accurate, right, punctilious, correct, factual, faithful, authentic, literal, word-for-word, actual, express, definite, explicit, unequivocal, unambiguous, clear-cut, distinct, detailed, blow-by-blow, minute, nice, particular, specific, fixed, rigid, strict, careful, scrupulous, punctilious, meticulous, conscientious, rigorous, fastidious
F3 imprecise, inexact, ambiguous, careless

precisely *adv*
exactly, absolutely, just so, accurately, on the dot, dead on, correctly, literally, verbatim, word for word, strictly, minutely, clearly, distinctly, *US* on the button, *colloq.* dead on, bang on, spot on, plumb, slap, smack, to a T

precision *n*
exactness, exactitude, accuracy, correctness, faithfulness, explicitness, distinctness, detail, particularity, rigour, care, reliability, meticulousness, scrupulousness, punctiliousness, conscientiousness, neatness, fastidiousness
F3 imprecision, inaccuracy

preclude *v*
prevent, exclude, eliminate, rule out, hinder, inhibit, prohibit, restrain, stop, avoid, check, debar, forestall, *formal* obviate
F3 incur, involve

precocious *adj*
forward, ahead, far ahead, advanced, early, premature, mature, developed, gifted, talented, clever, bright, brilliant, smart, quick, fast
F3 backward, slow, stupid

preconceive *v*
presuppose, presume, assume, anticipate, project, imagine, conceive, envisage, expect, visualize, picture

preconception *n*
presupposition, presumption, assumption, notion, anticipation, expectation, prejudgement, bias, prejudice, *formal* conjecture, predisposition

precondition *n*
condition, stipulation, requirement, prerequisite, essential, necessity, *formal* sine qua non, *colloq.* must

precursor *n*
forerunner, antecedent, sign, indication, prelude, herald, harbinger, messenger, usher, pioneer, trail-

blazer, curtain-raiser, ancestor, forebear, *formal* progenitor
F3 follower, successor

precursory *adj*
preceding, warning, introductory, antecedent, preliminary, preparatory, previous, prior, prefatory, anterior, *formal* preambulatory, precursive, preludial, prelusive, prevenient, prodromal
F3 following, resulting, subsequent

predatory *adj*
hunting, preying, voracious, carnivorous, greedy, acquisitive, avaricious, covetous, despoiling, thieving, ravaging, plundering, marauding, pillaging, wolfish, lupine, vulturine, vulturous, *formal* predacious, predative, rapacious, raptatorial, raptorial

predecessor *n*
ancestor, forefather, forebear, antecedent, forerunner, precursor, *formal* progenitor
F3 successor, descendant

predestination *n*
destiny, fate, lot, doom, foreordination, *formal* predetermination

predestine *v*
intend, mean, destine, fate, foreordain, preordain, pre-elect, doom, foredoom, *formal* predestinate, predetermine

predetermined *adj*
1 PREDESTINED, destined, fated, doomed, ordained, foreordained 2 PREARRANGED, arranged, agreed, fixed, set, settled

predicament *n*
situation, plight, trouble, mess, fix, quandary, dilemma, impasse, crisis, emergency, *colloq.* spot, tight spot, scrape, pickle, jam, hiccup, hole, stew, hot/deep water, can of worms, kettle of fish

predicate *v*
1 ASSERT, affirm, state, declare, proclaim, contend, *formal* aver, avouch, avow, posit, postulate, premise 2 BE DEPENDENT, rest, base, build, found, establish, maintain, ground

predict *v*
forecast, foretell, prophesy, foresee, project, *formal* prognosticate, vaticinate, augur, portend, presage, divine, auspicate, *colloq.* second-guess

predictable *adj*
foreseeable, expected, anticipated, likely, probable, imaginable, foreseen, foregone, certain, sure, reliable, dependable, *colloq.* on the cards, odds-on
F3 unpredictable, unforeseeable, uncertain

prediction *n*
prophecy, forecast, prognosis, fortune-telling, soothsaying, *formal* augury, divination, prognostication, auspication

predictive *adj*
prophetic, foretelling, diagnostic, *formal* augural, divinatory, prognostic

predilection *n*
fondness, preference, inclination, leaning, liking, affection, love, partiality, tendency, bent, bias, enthusiasm, fancy, taste, affinity, soft spot, weakness, *formal* penchant, predisposition, proclivity, propensity
F3 dislike, disinclination, *formal* antipathy

predispose *v*
dispose, incline, prompt, induce, make, make liable, sway, move, influence, persuade, affect, bias, prejudice

predisposed *adj*
inclined, liable, prepared, ready, susceptible, willing, disposed, well-disposed, minded, not unwilling, subject, agreeable, amenable, favourable, prone, biased, prejudiced
F3 unwilling, reluctant, loath

predisposition *n*
likelihood, inclination, leaning, tendency, preference, disposition, bent, proneness, willingness, liability, susceptibility, vulnerability, bias, prejudice, *formal* penchant, potentiality, predilection, proclivity, propensity

predominance *n*
dominance, dominion, power, control, leadership, mastery, prevalence, superiority, supremacy, influence, sway, weight, hold, numbers, *formal* hegemony, ascendancy, paramountcy, preponderance, prepotence, prepotency, prepollence, prepollency, *colloq.* edge, upper hand
F3 ineffectiveness, weakness

predominant *adj*
dominant, prevailing, chief, main, principal, primary, capital, paramount, supreme, sovereign, ruling, controlling, in control, leading, powerful, potent, prime, important, most important, influential, forceful, strong, most noticeable, most obvious, *formal* preponderant, ascendant, in the ascendancy
F3 minor, lesser, weak

predominate *v*
prevail, dominate, outnumber, outweigh, override, overrule, overshadow, transcend, tell, reign, rule, *formal* obtain, preponderate

pre-eminence *n*
supremacy, distinction, excellence, fame, prestige, renown, repute, predominance, prominence, superiority, incomparability, peerlessness, matchlessness, paramountcy, transcendence

pre-eminent *adj*
supreme, unsurpassed, unrivalled, unequalled, unmatched, matchless, incomparable, inimitable, chief, first, most important, foremost, leading, eminent, distinguished, renowned, famous, prominent, outstanding, exceptional, excellent, superlative, transcendent, superior
F3 inferior, unknown

pre-eminently *adv*
especially, notably, particularly, exceptionally, eminently, signally, superlatively, singularly, strikingly, surpassingly, par excellence, exclusively, supremely, emphatically, conspicuously, incomparably, inimitably, matchlessly, peerlessly

pre-empt *v*
prevent, forestall, anticipate, assume, acquire, secure, seize, usurp, *formal* appropriate, arrogate

preen *v*
1 CLEAN, smooth, groom, plume, trim, spruce up, dress up, trick out, doll up, slick, prettify, adorn, beautify, deck, primp, prink, *formal* array, *colloq.* do up, tart up 2 CONGRATULATE, pride, exult, bask, plume, gloat, pique, *colloq.* pat yourself on the back

preface *n, v*
▶ *n* foreword, introduction, preamble, prologue, prelude, frontmatter, preliminaries, *formal* proem, prolegomenon, exordium, *colloq.* prelims
F3 epilogue, postscript
▶ *v* precede, prefix, lead up to, introduce, launch, open, begin, start
F3 end, finish, complete

prefatory *adj*
introductory, opening, preparatory, preliminary, explanatory, antecedent, *formal* exordial, preambulatory, precursory, prefatorial, preludial, prelusive, prelusory, proemial, prolegomenal
F3 closing, final

prefect n
monitor, administrator, supervisor, praeposter, prepositor, praefect

prefer v
1 *I prefer tea to coffee* favour, like better, would rather, would sooner, be partial to, want, wish, desire, choose, select, pick (out), opt (for), go for, single out, advocate, recommend, back, support, elect, adopt, *colloq.* plump for, fancy 2 PROMOTE, favour, advance, move up, raise, elevate, exalt, honour, *formal* aggrandize 3 *prefer charges* bring, file, lodge, press, present, place
 1 reject 2 demote

preferable adj
better, superior, nicer, preferred, favoured, more desired, chosen, desirable, advantageous, advisable, recommended
 inferior, undesirable

preferably adv
rather, much rather, sooner, much sooner, from choice, for choice, by/for preference, first

preference n
1 FAVOURITE, first choice, choice, pick, selection, option, wish, desire, *colloq.* cup of tea 2 LIKING, fancy, inclination, bent, leaning, bias, discrimination, predilection, partiality, favouritism, priority, precedence, preferential treatment

preferential adj
better, superior, favoured, privileged, special, favourable, advantageous, partial, partisan, biased
 equal

preferment n
promotion, advancement, furtherance, improvement, rise, step up, betterment, dignity, elevation, exaltation, upgrading, *formal* aggrandizement
 demotion

preferred adj
favoured, selected, approved, choice, chosen, desired, recommended, authorized, sanctioned, *formal* predilect
 rejected, undesirable

pregnancy n
child-bearing, conception, fertilization, impregnation, gestation, *technical* parturition, *formal* gravidity, *colloq.* family way

pregnant adj
1 *a pregnant woman* expectant, expecting, *technical* parturient, *formal* with child, enceinte, *colloq.* in the family way, in the club, *slang* preggers, with a bun in the oven 2 *a pregnant pause* meaningful, significant, eloquent, rich, expressive, suggestive, telling, pointed, charged, loaded, heavy, full, filled, fraught, *formal* replete
 2 jejune

prehistoric adj
primitive, primeval, primordial, earliest, early, ancient, archaic, antiquated, old, obsolete, out of date, outmoded, *colloq.* antediluvian, out of the ark, before the flood
 modern

prejudge v
judge prematurely, anticipate, presume, assume, presuppose, forejudge, *formal* predetermine, prejudicate

prejudice n, v
 n 1 BIAS, partiality, partisanship, discrimination, preference, one-sidedness, unfairness, injustice, intolerance, narrow-mindedness, bigotry, chauvinism, racism, sexism, misogyny, ageism, xenophobia, misanthropy, anti-Semitism 2 HARM, damage, impairment, hurt, injury, detriment, disadvantage, loss, ruin

 1 fairness, tolerance 2 benefit, advantage
 v 1 BIAS, incline, sway, influence, condition, colour, jaundice, slant, distort, load, weight, *formal* predispose 2 HARM, damage, impair, be detrimental to, be disadvantageous to, hinder, undermine, hurt, injure, mar, spoil, ruin, wreck
 2 benefit, help, advance

prejudiced adj
biased, partial, subjective, partisan, one-sided, discriminatory, unfair, unjust, loaded, weighted, intolerant, narrow-minded, bigoted, blinkered, chauvinist, chauvinistic, xenophobic, anti-Semitic, racist, sexist, ageist, jaundiced, distorted, warped, influenced, conditioned, insular, parochial, *formal* predisposed
 impartial, fair, tolerant

prejudicial adj
harmful, damaging, hurtful, injurious, detrimental, disadvantageous, counter-productive, unfavourable, inimical, *formal* deleterious, noxious
 beneficial, advantageous

preliminary adj, n
 adj preparatory, prior, advance, exploratory, experimental, trial, test, pilot, early, earliest, first, initial, beginning, primary, qualifying, inaugural, introductory, opening, prefatory, *formal* precursory, exordial
 final, closing
 n preparation, groundwork, foundations, basics, rudiments, formalities, introduction, preface, foreword, prelude, preamble, opening, beginning, start, *formal* proem, exordium, prolegomenon, prodrome

prelude n
overture, introduction, preface, foreword, preamble, prologue, opening, opener, preliminary, preparation, beginning, start, forerunner, herald, harbinger, precursor, curtain-raiser, *formal* proem, exordium, prolegomenon, prodrome, commencement
 finale, epilogue

premature adj
early, soon, too early, too soon, immature, green, unripe, embryonic, half-formed, incomplete, undeveloped, abortive, hasty, ill-considered, rash, impetuous, impulsive, precipitate, untimely, inopportune, ill-timed, *colloq.* jumping the gun
 late, *formal* tardy

premeditated adj
planned, intended, intentional, deliberate, wilful, conscious, cold-blooded, calculated, considered, contrived, preplanned, prearranged, predetermined
 unpremeditated, spontaneous

premeditation n
planning, prearrangement, purpose, intention, deliberation, deliberateness, determination, forethought, design, scheming, plotting, *technical* malice aforethought, *formal* predetermination
 impulse, spontaneity

premier n, adj
 n head of government, prime minister, chief minister, first minister, chancellor, secretary of state
 adj principal, leading, highest, top, head, foremost, chief, primary, prime, main, supreme, paramount, pre-eminent, first, cardinal, earliest, original, initial

première n
first performance, first showing, opening, opening night, first night, début

premise n, v
 n proposition, statement, assertion, postulate, thesis, argument, basis, supposition, hypothesis, assumption, *formal* presupposition, postulate
 v lay down, state, assert, assume, stipulate, take as

true, presuppose, *formal* hypothesize, posit, postulate, predicate

premises *n*
building, property, establishment, office, grounds, estate, site, place

premium *n*
1 *pay an insurance premium* regular payment, instalment **2** *pay a premium rate* extra sum/charge, surcharge, overcharging, *colloq.* an arm and a leg, daylight robbery
▷ **at a premium** scarce, rare, hard to come by, in short supply, in great demand, few and far between, *colloq.* like gold dust
▷ **put a premium on** value greatly, treasure, appreciate, favour, hold dear, attach great/special importance to, regard highly, set great store by

premonition *n*
feeling, intuition, sixth sense, hunch, idea, suspicion, sneaking suspicion, foreboding, misgiving, fear, apprehension, anxiety, worry, warning, omen, sign, *formal* presentiment, presage, portent, *colloq.* feeling in your bones, funny feeling, gut feeling

preoccupation *n*
1 OBSESSION, fixation, concern, interest, enthusiasm, hobby-horse, *colloq.* hang-up, thing, bee in your bonnet, one-track mind **2** DISTRACTION, absent-mindedness, daydreaming, reverie, abstraction, heedlessness, obliviousness, oblivion, inattentiveness, absorption, engrossment

preoccupied *adj*
1 OBSESSED, intent, immersed, engrossed, absorbed, engaged, taken up, wrapped up, involved, pensive, deep in thought **2** DISTRACTED, abstracted, absent-minded, daydreaming, absorbed, faraway, heedless, oblivious, *formal* distrait

preoccupy *v*
occupy, absorb, engage, take up, involve, obsess, occupy the attention of

preordain *v*
destine, prearrange, foreordain, doom, fate, *formal* predestine, predetermine

preparation *n*
1 *preparations for the wedding; in preparation for the event* planning, plan, arrangement, organization, development, basics, rudiments, preliminaries, readiness, provision, supply, equipping, assembly, composition, construction, production, homework, foundation, groundwork, spadework **2** TRAINING, coaching, study, revision, practice **3** MIXTURE, compound, composition, concoction, potion, medicine, lotion, application, cosmetic

preparatory *adj*
preliminary, introductory, opening, initial, primary, basic, fundamental, rudimentary, elementary, *formal* precursory, prefatory
▷ **preparatory to** before, in advance of, in anticipation of, in expectation of, previous to, prior to, as a preparation for

prepare *v*
1 GET READY, make ready, make preparations for, set up, plan, organize, arrange, adjust, provide, supply, equip, fit out, rig out, prime, put together, construct, assemble, concoct, contrive, devise, draft, fashion, draw up, compose, pave the way, do your homework for, lay the foundations for, lay the groundwork for, do the spadework for, take the necessary steps for, set the scene for, *colloq.* gear up, psych up, tee up **2** TRAIN, exercise, coach, study, practise, prime, warm up, get into shape, make ready **3** *prepare a meal* make, produce, concoct, put together, throw together, get ready, *US* fix

▷ **prepare yourself** brace yourself, steel yourself, gird yourself, *formal* fortify yourself, gird up your loins

prepared *adj*
ready, willing, disposed, waiting, set, fit, inclined, arranged, planned, organized, in order, fixed, *formal* predisposed
🔁 unprepared, unready

preparedness *n*
readiness, preparation, order, fitness, alertness, anticipation, expectancy
🔁 unreadiness

preponderance *n*
dominance, supremacy, greater number, superiority, majority, bulk, mass, extensiveness, prevalence, predominance, domination, dominion, power, force, sway, weight, *formal* ascendancy, *colloq.* lion's share

preponderant *adj*
greater, larger, superior, predominant, prevailing, overriding, overruling, controlling, foremost, important, significant

preponderate *v*
dominate, predominate, prevail, outnumber, override, overrule, rule, tell, weigh with, turn the balance, turn the scales

prepossessing *adj*
attractive, charming, good-looking, winning, winsome, appealing, beautiful, likeable, lovable, amiable, delightful, fair, handsome, pleasing, striking, captivating, bewitching, enchanting, engaging, inviting, alluring, magnetic, fascinating, fetching, taking
🔁 unattractive, unprepossessing

preposterous *adj*
incredible, unbelievable, absurd, ridiculous, ludicrous, foolish, farcical, crazy, nonsensical, irrational, unreasonable, senseless, monstrous, shocking, outrageous, asinine, intolerable, unthinkable, incredible, impossible
🔁 sensible, reasonable, acceptable

prerequisite *n, adj*
▶ *n* condition, proviso, qualification, requirement, imperative, necessity, essential, *formal* precondition, requisite, sine qua non, *colloq.* must
🔁 extra
▶ *adj* indispensable, necessary, obligatory, required, needed, needful, essential, basic, fundamental, vital, imperative, *formal* mandatory, requisite
🔁 unnecessary, superfluous

prerogative *n*
privilege, right, authority, advantage, choice, sanction, exemption, immunity, liberty, due, claim, licence, carte blanche, birthright, *technical* droit

presage *v, n*
▶ *v* indicate, point to, be a sign of, be an indication of, warn of, announce, forecast, predict, foretell, promise, signify, threaten, herald, foretoken, *formal* augur, portend, bode, forebode, foreshadow, forewarn, harbinger, bespeak, betoken, adumbrate, prognosticate
▶ *n* sign, indication, warning, threat, omen, precursor, forecast, foreboding, forerunner, prefiguration, premonition, *formal* augury, portent, signification, prognostication, foreshadowing, forewarning, prognostic, presentiment, harbinger

prescience *n*
foreknowledge, foresight, far-sightedness, second sight, prophecy, clairvoyance, propheticness, *formal* precognition, prevision

prescient *adj*
foreknowing, far-sighted, far-seeing, prophetic, foresighted, perceptive, discerning, clairvoyant, divina-

tory, divining, psychic, *formal* previsional

🖩 imperceptive

prescribe *v*

1 *prescribe medicine* advise, act, specify, stipulate 2 *prescribe a duty* ordain, decree, dictate, rule, command, order, require, direct, specify, stipulate, lay down, set, appoint, impose, fix, define, limit

---

 prescribe or **proscribe** ?

To *prescribe* is to advise or order: *The doctor prescribed a course of antibiotics*; *The law prescribes severe penalties for such offences*. To *proscribe* is to ban, outlaw or forbid: *This book was formerly proscribed by the church*; *Such actions are proscribed by law*.

---

prescribed *adj*

laid down, specified, stipulated, set, ordained, assigned, decreed, *formal* formulary

prescription *n*

1 INSTRUCTION, direction, formula, recipe, advice, recommendation, guideline(s) 2 MEDICINE, drug, preparation, mixture, remedy, treatment

prescriptive *adj*

dictatorial, legislating, prescribing, didactic, dogmatic, rigid, authoritarian, customary, *formal* preceptive

presence *n*

1 ATTENDANCE, company, companionship, occupancy, residence, existence, being 2 AURA, air, appearance, dignity, poise, self-confidence, self-assurance, attraction, personality, charisma, appeal, magnetism, *formal* demeanour, bearing, carriage 3 NEARNESS, closeness, proximity, neighbourhood, vicinity, *formal* propinquity 4 SPIRIT, ghost, phantom, spectre, apparition, visitant, shadow

🖩 1 absence 3 remoteness, distance

▷ **presence of mind** calmness, self-possession, composure, coolness, self-assurance, self-command, level-headedness, alertness, poise, *formal* aplomb, imperturbability, sang-froid, *colloq.* cool, unflappability

🖩 agitation, confusion

present¹ *adj, n*

▶ *adj* 1 ATTENDING, here, there, near, nearby, at hand, close at hand, to hand, available, ready, existing 2 *at the present time* current, contemporary, present-day, immediate, instant, existent, existing

🖩 1 absent 2 past, out of date

▷ **the present day** today, now, nowadays, at this time, currently

▶ *n* ▷ **at present** at the moment, now, at this time, today, currently

▷ **for the present** for the time being, for the moment, for now, in the meantime, pro tem

present² *v*

1 AWARD, grant, give, donate, hand over, entrust, extend, hold out, *formal* confer, bestow 2 OFFER, tender, submit, *formal* proffer 3 SHOW, display, put on display, exhibit, demonstrate, organize, mount, stage, perform, put on, introduce, host, make known 4 *present a television show* introduce, compère, host, announce 5 *the story presents her sympathetically* DESCRIBE, depict, represent, portray, characterize, picture, *formal* delineate

▷ **present oneself** 1 *present yourself somewhere* appear, arrive, attend, show up, turn up, *colloq.* pop up 2 *an idea presents itself* occur, arise, crop up, emerge, materialize, come to light, happen

present³ *n*

Christmas presents gift, offering, donation, contribu-

tion, handout, award, grant, endowment, bounty, largesse, gratuity, tip, favour, *formal* benefaction, *colloq.* prezzie, freebie, perk, sweetener

presentable *adj*

neat, tidy, clean, smart, smartly dressed, spruce, respectable, decent, proper, suitable, acceptable, satisfactory, tolerable

🖩 unpresentable, untidy, shabby

presentation *n*

1 APPEARANCE, arrangement, organization, structure, system, layout, form, format 2 AWARD, presenting, granting, donating, investiture, *formal* conferral, bestowal 3 TALK, address, lecture, speech, seminar, *formal* disquisition 4 SHOW, performance, production, staging, showing, mounting, representation, rendition, display, exhibition, demonstration, introduction, making known, launch

present-day *adj*

current, present, existing, living, contemporary, modern, up to date, fashionable

🖩 past, future

presenter *n*

host, announcer, compère, anchorman, anchorwoman, frontman, master of ceremonies, MC, *colloq.* emcee

presentiment *n*

premonition, intuition, apprehension, fear, feeling, misgiving, hunch, anticipation, foreboding, expectation, forecast, forethought, *formal* forebodement, presage, *colloq.* bad vibes

presently *adv*

1 SOON, shortly, in a short time, in a short while, in a minute, before long, by and by 2 CURRENTLY, at present, now, at the moment, at the present time, these days, at this moment in time

preservation *n*

protection, defence, maintenance, keeping, guarding, safeguarding, safekeeping, safety, security, conservation, storage, upkeep, support, retention, upholding, continuation, perpetuation

🖩 destruction, ruin

preserve *v, n*

▶ *v* 1 PROTECT, safeguard, guard, defend, shield, shelter, care for, look after, take care of, maintain, uphold, secure, sustain, continue, perpetuate, keep, retain, conserve, save, store 2 *preserve food* bottle, tin, can, pickle, salt, cure, dry, smoke

🖩 1 destroy, ruin

▶ *n* 1 *home made preserves* conserve, jam, marmalade, jelly, pickle 2 DOMAIN, realm, sphere, area, field, speciality 3 RESERVATION, sanctuary, reserve, game reserve, safari park

preside *v*

chair, be in the chair, be the chairman/chairwoman/chairperson of, officiate, conduct, direct, manage, administer, control, run, head, lead, govern, rule, be responsible for, be in charge of, *colloq.* head up, call the shots

president *n*

head of state, ruler, leader, controller, governor, head, director, manager, principal, chief, *colloq.* boss

press *v, n*

▶ *v* 1 CRUSH, squash, squeeze, mash, pinch, knead, compress, stuff, jam, cram, crowd, push (down), depress, surge, swarm, throng, trample 2 *press clothes* iron, smooth (out), flatten, roll 3 HUG, embrace, clasp, enfold, grasp, squeeze, caress, cuddle, crush 4 URGE, plead, petition, campaign, demand, call for, insist on, exhort, entreat, implore, push for, push forward, compel, constrain, force, coerce, pres-

sure, pressurize, put pressure on, harass, besiege, afflict, vex, worry, trouble, *formal* supplicate
▷ **press on** press ahead, continue, carry on, go on, go ahead, proceed
▶ *n* **1** CROWD, throng, multitude, mob, horde, troop, swarm, pack, crush, flock, push **2** JOURNALISTS, reporters, correspondents, photographers, paparazzi, newspapermen, newspaperwomen, pressmen, presswomen, the media, news media, newspapers, papers, Fleet Street, journalism, fourth estate, *colloq.* hacks **3** PRINTING PRESS, printing-machine, rotary press **4** *get a good/bad press* coverage, treatment, articles, reviews, praise, criticism

pressed *adj*
1 FORCED, pressured, pressurized, coerced, bullied, browbeaten, constrained, hurried, pushed, rushed, harassed **2** *be pressed for time* short of, having little, not having enough, lacking, deficient in
🔁 **1** unhurried **2** well-off

pressing *adj*
urgent, needing to be dealt with immediately, high-priority, burning, crucial, demanding, vital, essential, imperative, serious, important, critical, key, *formal* exigent
🔁 unimportant, trivial

pressure *n*
1 FORCE, power, load, burden, weight, heaviness, compression, crushing, squeezing, stress, strain **2** COMPULSION, force, constraints, coercion, duress, bullying, harassment **3** STRESS, tension, difficulty, problem, demand, adversity, burden, trouble, constraint, obligation, *colloq.* hassle, aggro

pressurize *v*
force, compel, constrain, oblige, drive, bulldoze, dragoon, coerce, press, pressure, put pressure on, browbeat, bully, *colloq.* lean on, put the screws on

prestige *n*
status, reputation, standing, stature, eminence, distinction, regard, importance, authority, influence, fame, renown, kudos, credit, honour, *formal* esteem
🔁 humbleness, unimportance

prestigious *adj*
respected, reputable, important, influential, distinguished, high-ranking, great, eminent, prominent, illustrious, renowned, celebrated, famous, well-known, exalted, imposing, impressive, up-market, *formal* esteemed, *colloq.* blue-chip
🔁 humble, modest

presumably *adv*
most likely, very likely, in all likelihood, in all probability, as like as not, doubtless, doubtlessly, no doubt, probably, apparently, seemingly

presume *v*
1 ASSUME, take it, think, believe, imagine, suppose, surmise, infer, presuppose, deduce, take for granted, *formal* hypothesize **2** *presume to criticize* dare, make so bold, have the audacity, take the liberty, go so far, venture, undertake
▷ **presume on** count on, rely on, depend on, bank on, trust, take (unfair) advantage of, exploit

presumption *n*
1 ASSUMPTION, belief, opinion, surmise, deduction, inference, guess, likelihood, probability, *formal* hypothesis, presupposition, supposition, conjecture **2** PRESUMPTUOUSNESS, boldness, arrogance, effrontery, temerity, audacity, impertinence, impudence, insolence, forwardness, assurance, *colloq.* cheek, nerve
🔁 **2** humility

presumptive *adj*
expected, assumed, believed, designate, prospective, likely, possible, probable, reasonable, supposed, un-

derstood, believable, conceivable, credible, inferred, plausible, *formal* hypothetical
🔁 known, unlikely

presumptuous *adj*
bold, audacious, impertinent, impudent, insolent, over-familiar, forward, arrogant, over-confident, conceited, cocksure, *colloq.* pushy, cheeky, cocky, big-headed, too big for your boots
🔁 humble, modest

presuppose *v*
assume, presume, suppose, accept, consider, imply, take for granted, *formal* posit, postulate, premise

presupposition *n*
assumption, presumption, belief, supposition, theory, preconception, *formal* hypothesis, premise, premiss

pretence *n*
show, display, appearance, cover, front, charade, façade, veneer, cloak, veil, mask, masquerade, guise, sham, feigning, faking, false show, semblance, hypocrisy, simulation, deception, trickery, wile, ruse, excuse, pretext, bluff, falsehood, deceit, lie, fabrication, invention, acting, play-acting, make-believe, posturing, posing, showiness, ostentation, pretentiousness, *formal* affectation, dissimulation, dissembling
🔁 honesty, openness

pretend *v*
1 *pretend to be asleep* put on, assume, feign, sham, counterfeit, fake, fabricate, simulate, bluff, impersonate, pass yourself off, act, play-act, put on an act, mime, go through the motions, *formal* affect, dissemble, *colloq.* keep up appearances **2** CLAIM, allege, profess, *formal* purport **3** IMAGINE, make believe, suppose

pretended *adj*
artificial, put-on, alleged, ostensible, professed, supposed, spurious, bogus, fake, false, feigned, sham, fictitious, counterfeit, so-called, imaginary, specious, *formal* affected, avowed, purported, supposititious, *colloq.* phoney, pretend, pseudo
🔁 real

pretender *n*
claimant, aspirant, claimer, candidate

pretension *n*
1 PRETENTIOUSNESS, pomposity, self-importance, airs, conceit, vanity, snobbishness, hypocrisy, pretence, show, showiness, floweriness, ostentation, *formal* affectation, magniloquence **2** CLAIM, profession, demand, aspiration, ambition, *formal* purporting
🔁 **1** modesty, humility, simplicity

pretentious *adj*
pompous, self-important, conceited, immodest, snobbish, twee, mannered, flaunting, showy, ostentatious, extravagant, flamboyant, elaborate, bombastic, exaggerated, high-sounding, artificial, inflated, grandiose, ambitious, overambitious, *colloq.* over the top, OTT, *formal* affected, magniloquent, vainglorious
🔁 modest, humble, simple, straightforward

pretentiousness *n*
ostentation, posing, pretension, show, theatricality, floweriness, floridness, flamboyance, attitudinizing, *formal* posturing, *colloq.* pseudery
🔁 humbleness, modesty, simplicity, straightforwardness

preternatural *adj*
extraordinary, unusual, exceptional, abnormal

pretext *n*
excuse, alleged/ostensible reason, ploy, ruse, cover, cloak, mask, veil, guise, sham, semblance, appear-

ance, pretence, show, *colloq.* red herring

prettify *v*
decorate, smarten up, ornament, adorn, beautify, bedeck, deck, deck out, embellish, gild, garnish, trick out, trim, *colloq.* do up, doll up, tart up
🗲 mar, uglify

pretty *adj, adv*
▶ *adj* attractive, good-looking, beautiful, fair, lovely, delightful, nice, cute, pleasant, pleasing, engaging, personable, prepossessing, winsome, appealing, charming, handsome, dainty, graceful, elegant, fine, delicate, *Scot.* bonny
🗲 plain, unattractive, ugly
▶ *adv* fairly, somewhat, rather, quite, reasonably, moderately, tolerably

prevail *v*
1 WIN, triumph, be victorious, succeed, overcome, overrule, conquer, reign, rule, gain mastery, *formal* gain ascendancy, *colloq.* carry the day **2** PREDOMINATE, abound, hold sway, occur, be common, be customary, be present, be normal, be accepted, be current, *formal* preponderate, obtain
🗲 **1** lose
▷ **prevail upon** persuade, talk into, prompt, induce, incline, sway, influence, convince, urge, win over, bring round, pressure, pressurize, *colloq.* sweet-talk, lean on, soft-soap, pull strings, twist someone's arm

prevailing *adj*
predominant, preponderant, main, principal, chief, supreme, dominant, controlling, powerful, compelling, influential, reigning, ruling, current, fashionable, in fashion, in style, in vogue, popular, mainstream, accepted, established, set, usual, most usual, customary, general, common, most common, prevalent, widespread, *formal* prepotent, ascendant
🗲 minor, subordinate

prevalence *n*
commonness, currency, frequency, pervasiveness, acceptance, popularity, predominance, universality, regularity, rule, hold, mastery, sway, profusion, *formal* ascendancy, omnipresence, preponderance, primacy, ubiquity
🗲 uncommonness

prevalent *adj*
widespread, extensive, rampant, rife, pervasive, frequent, general, customary, usual, universal, established, accepted, set, ubiquitous, common, everyday, popular, current, prevailing, dominant
🗲 uncommon, rare

prevaricate *v*
equivocate, quibble, evade, shift, shuffle, lie, deceive, *formal* cavil, tergiversate, *colloq.* hedge, dodge, shilly-shally, waffle, pussy-foot, beat about the bush, sit on the fence

---

📝 **prevaricate** or **procrastinate**?
To *prevaricate* is 'to talk evasively in order to avoid telling the truth, coming to the point, or answering a question': *When faced with difficult questions, politicians usually prevaricate.* To *procrastinate* is 'to put off until later things that should be done immediately'.

---

prevarication *n*
evasion, equivocation, pretence, quibbling, lie, falsehood, untruth, falsification, fibbing, fib(s), half-truth, misrepresentation, deception, deceit, *formal* cavilling, tergiversation

prevaricator *n*
evader, equivocator, quibbler, liar, hypocrite, deceiver, *formal* casuist, caviller, dissembler, sophist,

colloq. dodger, fibber

prevent *v*
stop, avert, avoid, keep from, halt, arrest, hold back, inhibit, head off, ward off, fend off, stave off, intercept, forestall, anticipate, frustrate, thwart, restrain, hinder, hamper, impede, obstruct, block, check, hold in check, foil, balk, deter, bar, *formal* preclude, obviate
🗲 cause, help, foster, encourage, allow

prevention *n*
avoidance, halting, arresting, heading off, warding off, fending off, staving off, frustration, check, hindrance, impediment, obstruction, obstacle, bar, elimination, precaution, safeguard, deterrence, hampering, foiling, balking, *technical* prophylaxis, *formal* preclusion, obviation
🗲 cause, help

preventive *adj, n*
▶ *adj* preventative, anticipatory, pre-emptive, inhibitory, obstructive, precautionary, protective, counteractive, deterrent, *technical* prophylactic
🗲 causative, fostering
▶ *n* prevention, protection, precautionary measure, protective, impediment, hindrance, deterrent, block, obstruction, obstacle, safeguard, remedy, shield, neutralizer, *technical* prophylactic
🗲 cause, encouragement, incitement

previous *adj*
preceding, foregoing, earlier, prior, past, former, ex-, one-time, sometime, antecedent, *formal* erstwhile, quondam
🗲 following, subsequent, later

previously *adv*
formerly, once, earlier, until now, before, beforehand, at one time, in the past, *formal* heretofore, hitherto, erst, erstwhile
🗲 later

prey *n, v*
▶ *n* quarry, game, kill, victim, target, *colloq.* mug, fall guy
▶ *v* **prey on 1** HUNT, kill, seize, catch, devour, eat, feed on, live off, exploit, take advantage of, *colloq.* con, fleece, bleed **2** *prey on one's mind* haunt, trouble, distress, worry, burden, weigh down, hang over, oppress, plague, torment

price *n, v*
▶ *n* **1** *the price of the car* value, worth, cost, expense(s), outlay, expenditure, fee, charge, levy, toll, rate, bill, assessment, valuation, estimate, quotation, figure, amount, sum, payment, reward **2** *publicity is the price of fame* penalty, forfeit, sacrifice, consequences, result
▷ **at a price** expensive, at a high price, at a high cost
▷ **at any price** at any cost, whatever it takes, whatever the cost, no matter what it costs
▶ *v* value, rate, cost, evaluate, assess, estimate, set/fix the price at, *formal* appraise, valorize

priceless *adj*
1 INVALUABLE, inestimable, incalculable, expensive, costly, dear, precious, valuable, prized, treasured, cherished, irreplaceable, incomparable, rare, *colloq.* worth its weight in gold **2** FUNNY, amusing, comic, hilarious, riotous, side-splitting, *colloq.* killing, rich, a scream
🗲 **1** cheap, run-of-the-mill

pricey *adj*
costly, dear, excessive, exorbitant, expensive, extortionate, high-priced, *colloq.* steep, over the odds, costing an arm and a leg
🗲 cheap

prick *v, n*
▶ *v* **1** PIERCE, puncture, perforate, punch, jab, jag, nick, slit, gash, wound, spike, bore, stab, sting, bite,

prickle, itch, tingle, smart **2** *prick your conscience* trouble, distress, worry, torment, plague, harass, harry, gnaw at, prey on
▶ *n* puncture, perforation, pinhole, hole, stab, jab, jag, nick, wound, pang, twinge, sting, pain, smarting, tingle, bite

prickle *n, v*
▶ *n* **1** THORN, spine, barb, spur, point, spike, needle, prong, tine, *formal* acantha **2** *feel a prickle of fear* sensation, sting, stinging, itching, smarting, twinge, pang, tingle, *technical* paraesthesia, *formal* formication, *colloq.* pins and needles
▶ *v* tingle, itch, smart, sting, prick, nip

prickly *adj*
1 THORNY, brambly, spiny, barbed, spiky, spiked, pronged, bristly, rough, scratchy **2** IRRITABLE, edgy, touchy, grumpy, short-tempered, bad-tempered, *colloq.* stroppy, ratty, crabby, crotchety, grouchy **3** *a prickly subject* complicated, difficult, hard, thorny, problematical, tough, troublesome, tricky
🖬 **1** smooth **2** relaxed, *colloq.* easy-going

pride *n, v*
▶ *n* **1** SATISFACTION, gratification, sense of achievement, pleasure, delight, joy **2** DIGNITY, self-respect, self-esteem, self-image, self-worth, ego, honour **3** CONCEIT, vanity, egotism, big-headedness, boastfulness, smugness, disdain, arrogance, self-importance, self-conceit, presumption, haughtiness, superciliousness, snobbery, pretentiousness
🖬 **1** shame **3** humility, modesty
▶ *v* ▷ **pride yourself on** take satisfaction in, congratulate yourself, flatter yourself, take pride in, revel in, glory in, exult in, vaunt, crow about, boast about, brag about, *colloq.* pat yourself on the back for
🖬 belittle, humble

priest *n*
minister, vicar, parson, pastor, padre, father, man/woman of God, man/woman of the cloth, clergyman, clergywoman, churchman, churchwoman, deacon, deaconess

priestess *n*
clergywoman, canoness, deaconess, nun, prioress, sister, abbess, religious, vestal, beguine, mambo

priestly *adj*
clerical, ecclesiastical, canonical, pastoral, priestlike, sacerdotal, Aaronic(al), *formal* hieratic

prig *n*
prude, puritan, killjoy, precisian, old maid, Mrs Grundy, *colloq.* goody-goody, holy Joe, holy Willie

priggish *adj*
smug, self-righteous, sanctimonious, puritanical, prim, prudish, narrow-minded, starchy, stuffy, strait-laced, *colloq.* goody-goody, holier-than-thou
🖬 broad-minded

prim *adj*
prudish, strait-laced, formal, demure, proper, priggish, prissy, fussy, particular, stuffy, starchy, puritanical, precise, fastidious, school-marmish, old-maidish, *colloq.* fuddy-duddy
🖬 relaxed, *colloq.* easy-going

primacy *n*
supremacy, dominance, paramountcy, pre-eminence, sovereignty, superiority, command, seniority, dominion, leadership, *formal* ascendancy
🖬 inferiority

primal *adj*
original, basic, earliest, fundamental, primitive, first, primary, initial, major, greatest, highest, main, central, chief, paramount, principal, prime, *formal* primeval, primordial
🖬 later, minor

primarily *adv*
chiefly, principally, mainly, mostly, basically, first, firstly, fundamentally, especially, particularly, predominantly, essentially, in essence, in the main, in the first place

primary *adj*
1 CHIEF, principal, main, dominant, leading, foremost, supreme, prime, predominant, cardinal, capital, paramount, greatest, highest, ultimate **2** FIRST, basic, fundamental, essential, radical, rudimentary, elementary, simple, earliest, original, initial, introductory, beginning, opening, *formal* elemental, primeval, primordial
🖬 **1** secondary, subsidiary, minor

prime¹ *adj, n*
▶ *adj* **1** BEST, choice, select, quality, first-class, first-rate, excellent, top, top-grade, supreme, highest, pre-eminent **2** CHIEF, principal, main, leading, foremost, supreme, predominant **3** CLASSIC, typical, standard, characteristic, *formal* paradigmatic, quintessential
🖬 second-rate, secondary
▶ *n* height, peak, pinnacle, zenith, heyday, flower, blossom, bloom, culmination, best part, maturity, perfection, *formal* acme

prime² *v*
1 PREPARE, equip, get ready, coach, train **2** BRIEF, inform, notify, fill, fill in, *colloq.* clue up, gen up

primer *n*
introduction, manual, textbook, *formal* prodrome, prodromus

primeval *adj*
earliest, first, original, early, old, ancient, prehistoric, primitive, instinctive, *formal* primordial, autochthonal
🖬 modern

primitive *adj*
1 CRUDE, rough, unsophisticated, uncivilized, simple, natural, uncultured, undeveloped, barbarian, wild, savage **2** EARLY, elementary, rudimentary, primary, first, original, earliest, ancient, *formal* primeval, primordial
🖬 **1** advanced, sophisticated, civilized

primordial *adj*
earliest, first, original, early, old, ancient, prehistoric, primitive, instinctive, *formal* primeval, autochthonal
🖬 modern

primp *v*
groom, smarten, tidy, dress up, spruce up, beautify, preen, *colloq.* titivate, doll up, tart up, put on your best bib and tucker, put on your glad rags

prince *n*
lord, ruler, monarch, potentate, sovereign

princely *adj*
1 SOVEREIGN, imperial, royal, regal, majestic, stately, grand, imposing, magnificent, splendid, noble **2** *princely sum* handsome, generous, liberal, lavish, sumptuous, magnificent, magnanimous, *formal* bounteous

principal *adj, n*
▶ *adj* main, chief, key, major, essential, cardinal, primary, first, foremost, leading, controlling, dominant, in charge, prime, paramount, pre-eminent, most important, supreme, highest, arch
🖬 minor, subsidiary, lesser, least
▶ *n* **1** HEAD, head teacher, headmaster, headmistress, rector, chief, leader, director, manager, superintendent, controller, ruler, *colloq.* boss **2** MONEY, capital, capital sum, capital funds, assets

---

📝 **principal** or **principle**?

As an adjective, *principal* means 'most important':
Shipbuilding and coal-mining were two of Britain's

principal industries. As a noun, *principal* means 'the head of a school, college or university'. *Principle* can only be used as a noun. It means 'a general rule' or 'the theory underlying a method or way of working': *the principles of economic theory.*

principally *adv*
mainly, mostly, chiefly, primarily, predominantly, above all, particularly, especially, in the main, for the most part, first and foremost

principle *n*
1 RULE, formula, law, canon, axiom, dictum, precept, maxim, truth, tenet, doctrine, creed, dogma, code, theory, idea, standard, criterion, proposition, basis, fundamental, essential, *formal* postulate **2** *a man of principle* honour, integrity, uprightness, virtue, decency, morality, morals, ethics, standards, scruples, conscience, *formal* rectitude
▷ **in principle** theoretically, in theory, ideally, in essence, *en principe*

 principle or **principal** ? *See panel at* PRINCIPAL.

principled *adj*
upright, virtuous, moral, ethical, high-minded, honourable, conscientious, decent, righteous, just, right-minded, scrupulous
🔁 unprincipled

print *v, n*
▶ *v* mark, stamp, imprint, impress, engrave, etch, copy, reproduce, run off, publish, issue, *colloq.* put to bed
▶ *n* **1** LETTERS, characters, lettering, type, typescript, typeface, fount **2** MARK, impression, fingerprint, footprint **3** COPY, reproduction, replica, design, picture, engraving, lithograph, photograph, photo, snapshot, *colloq.* snap
▷ **in print** published, available, obtainable, in circulation
🔁 out of print

Printing methods include:
bubble-jet printing, collotype, colour-process printing, copper engraving, die-stamping, duplicating, electrostatic printing, engraving, etching, flexography, gravure, ink-jet printing, intaglio, laser printing, letterpress, lino blocking, litho, lithography, offset lithography, offset printing, photoengraving, rotary press, screen printing, silk-screen printing, stencilling, thermography, twin-etching, xerography.

Printing terms include :
anodized plate, author's proof, back margin, backing-up, bad break, base alignment, batter, bi-directional printing, black printer, blanket-to-blanket press, bold face, bromide, camera-ready copy, carding, caret, cast-off, catchword, centre, character set, chase, cliché, cold composition, collograph, colour control bar, colour separation, column inch/centimetre, compose, composing room, composition size, compositor, condensed, copy, cylinder press, dampers, dot-etching, dot gain, drum printer, electrotype, em, en, end even, expanded type, feathering, finishing, first proof, flat-bed press, flong, font, forme, galley, gutter, hard hyphen, hot-metal typesetting, image printing, imposition, impression, indent, initial caps, inking roller, Intertype®, italic,

justification, keep standing, kern, kiss impression, large print, leaders, leading, letterset, line printer, Linotype®, literal, logotype, lower-case, machine composition, machine proof, mackle, makeready, manuscript, margin, matrix, misprint, moiré, Monophoto®, Monotype®, mottling, newsprint, non-image area, non-impact printing, offprint, orphan, overprint, Ozalid®, perfecting, phototypesetting, planographic, printing press, progressive proofs, proof, quoin, ragged right/left, registration, relief printing, reprint, roman, run-around, running head, running text, sans serif, see-through, signature, small capitals, soft hyphen, specimen page, spoilage, stereotype, stet, strike-on, strip in, take in, take over, text, thermal printer, tint, trim marks, type, typeface, type scale, typescript, typesetting, type spec, typo, *US* typographer, upper-case, web-fed, web offset, widow, woodcut, wood engraving, zinco.

prior *adj*
earlier, preceding, foregoing, previous, former
🔁 later
▷ **prior to** before, preceding, earlier than, until
🔁 after, following

priority *n*
1 *a top priority* most important thing, most urgent matter, matter of highest/greatest importance, main thing, supreme matter, first concern, primary issue, essential, requirement, pole position, *colloq.* top of the tree **2** PRECEDENCE, right of way, seniority, rank, superiority, pre-eminence, supremacy, paramountcy, the lead, first/highest place
🔁 **2** inferiority

priory *n*
monastery, abbey, cloister, friary, convent, nunnery, religious house, béguinage

prise *v*
lever, force, jemmy, pry, raise, lift, hoist, dislodge, shift, move, winkle

prison *n*
jail, penitentiary, cell, lock-up, cage, dungeon, imprisonment, confinement, detention, custody, *colloq.* nick, inside, *slang* clink, cooler, slammer, jug, can, choky, quod

prisoner *n*
captive, hostage, convict, prisoner of war, POW, inmate, internee, detainee, recidivist, *colloq.* jailbird, con, lifer, (old) lag, yardbird

prissy *adj*
prim, squeamish, prudish, strait-laced, formal, demure, proper, priggish, fussy, particular, stuffy, starchy, puritanical, precise, fastidious, schoolmarmish, old-maidish, *colloq.* finicky, po-faced

pristine *adj*
1 IMMACULATE, undefiled, uncorrupted, untouched, virgin, unspoiled, unsullied **2** ORIGINAL, earliest, first, initial, former, primary, primitive, primal, *formal* primeval, primordial, primigenial
🔁 **1** spoiled **2** developed, later

privacy *n*
secrecy, confidentiality, independence, solitude, quietness, isolation, seclusion, privateness, concealment, retirement, retreat, *formal* sequestration
🔁 publicness, interruption, interference

private *adj, n*
▶ *adj* **1** *private discussions* CONFIDENTIAL, classified, secret, privileged, unofficial, off the record,

colloq. hush-hush **2** *your private life/feelings* personal, confidential, intimate, innermost, secret, individual **3** *a private bathroom* exclusive, particular, own, special, individual, personal **4** *a private person* quiet, reserved, withdrawn, independent, solitary, retiring, separate, self-contained **5** *a private place* secluded, isolated, hidden, concealed, secret, remote, undisturbed, quiet, out-of-the-way, *formal* sequestered **6** *private industries* independent, commercial, free-enterprise, privatized, non-governmental, denationalized, self-governing, self-determining
▰ **1** official, public **5** public **6** public, state-controlled, state-run, nationalized
▷ **private detective** private eye, private investigator, pinkerton, shamus
▷ **private parts** genitals, sexual organs, reproductive organs, vagina, womb, penis, *technical* pudenda, *formal* genitalia, *colloq.* privates
▶ *n* enlisted man, private soldier, Tommy, squaddy, swad, swaddy, *colloq.* Tommy Atkins
▷ **in private** privately, in confidence, confidentially, secretly, in secret, behind closed doors, in camera, *sub rosa*
▰ publicly, openly

privateer *n*
buccaneer, pirate, brigand, filibuster, freebooter, corsair, marque, sea robber, sea wolf

privation *n*
hardship, destitution, deprivation, affliction, neediness, poverty, suffering, lack, need, austerity, loss, misery, distress, *formal* indigence, penury, want
▰ affluence, wealth

privilege *n*
advantage, benefit, concession, birthright, title, due, right, prerogative, entitlement, honour, freedom, liberty, franchise, licence, sanction, dispensation, authority, immunity, exemption
▰ disadvantage

privileged *adj*
1 FAVOURED, advantaged, special, indulgent, sanctioned, authorized, immune, excepted, exempt, elite, honoured, ruling, powerful **2** CONFIDENTIAL, private, classified, secret, unofficial, off the record
▰ **1** disadvantaged, under-privileged **2** public

privy *n*
toilet, lavatory, water closet, WC, public convenience, washroom, cloakroom, latrine, powder room, bathroom, *colloq.* bog, loo
▷ **privy to** aware of, cognizant of, informed about, wise to, *formal* apprised of, *colloq.* in on, in the know about
▰ unaware of

prize *n, adj, v*
▶ *n* **1** REWARD, trophy, medal, award, winnings, jackpot, purse, premium, stake(s), honour, accolade, laurels, pennant **2** AIM, goal, gain, hope, desire, honour **3** BOOTY, loot, spoils, plunder, pickings, capture, pillage, trophy
▶ *adj* best, top, first-rate, excellent, outstanding, champion, winning, prize-winning, award-winning, *colloq.* top-notch, terrific, smashing, out of this world
▰ second-rate
▶ *v* treasure, value, appreciate, revere, cherish, love, hold dear, think highly of, hold in high regard, set great store by, *formal* esteem
▰ despise, undervalue

prize-winner *n*
winner, champion, cup-winner, medallist, prizeman, prizewoman, dux, *colloq.* champ

probability *n*
likelihood, likeliness, odds, chance(s), expectation, prospect, possibility
▰ improbability

probable *adj*
likely, expected, to be expected, anticipated, credible, believable, plausible, feasible, foreseeable, predictable, possible, apparent, seeming, *colloq.* odds-on, on the cards, a fair bet
▰ improbable, unlikely

probably *adv*
in all likelihood, in all probability, likely, it looks like, the chances are, most likely, as likely as not, doubtless, presumably, possibly, perhaps, maybe, *colloq.* (as) like as not, a fair bet
▰ improbably

probation *n*
trial period, experimental period, trial, test, test period, apprenticeship, supervision

probe *v, n*
▶ *v* **1** INVESTIGATE, scrutinize, examine, study, inquire, analyse, research, go into, look into, search, sift, test **2** PROD, poke, pierce, penetrate, sound, plumb, check, explore, examine
▶ *n* **1** INQUIRY, inquest, investigation, exploration, examination, test, scrutiny, scrutinization, study, analysis, research **2** BORE, drill

probity *n*
uprightness, righteousness, integrity, honour, honourableness, virtue, morality, worth, honesty, goodness, equity, fairness, justice, truthfulness, trustworthiness, sincerity, *formal* fidelity, rectitude
▰ *formal* improbity

problem *n, adj*
▶ *n* **1** TROUBLE, worry, predicament, quandary, plight, dilemma, difficulty, complication, snag, *colloq.* hassle, hole, pickle, fix, mess, tight spot, dire straits, no-win situation, catch-22 **2** QUESTION, issue, matter, poser, puzzle, brain-teaser, conundrum, riddle, enigma
▶ *adj* difficult, unmanageable, uncontrollable, unruly, troublesome, disobedient, delinquent, *formal* recalcitrant, intransigent
▰ well-behaved, manageable

problematic *adj*
1 DIFFICULT, fraught with difficulties, troublesome, awkward, hard, puzzling, perplexing, intricate, involved, tricky, thorny, problematical, enigmatic, moot, *colloq.* a can of worms, a minefield **2** UNCERTAIN, questionable, debatable, doubtful, dubious
▰ **1** easy, straightforward **2** certain

procedure *n*
routine, process, method, methodology, system, technique, custom, practice, means, measure, policy, formula, way, course, course of action, scheme, strategy, plan of action, move, step, action, conduct, operation, *modus operandi*, performance

proceed *v*
1 *permission to proceed* advance, go ahead, move on, go on, go forward, progress, continue, carry on, press on, make your way **2** START, begin, make a start, take steps, get under way, set in motion **3** ORIGINATE, derive, flow, start, stem, spring, arise, issue, emanate, result, ensue, follow, come
▰ **1** stop, retreat

proceedings *n*
1 MATTERS, affairs, business, dealings, transactions, report, account, minutes, records, archives, annals **2** EVENTS, activities, happenings, deeds, doings, moves, steps, measures, action, course of action, operations, procedures, manoeuvres **3** *legal proceedings* lawsuit, case, trial, action, process, litigation

proceeds *n*
revenue, income, returns, receipts, takings, earnings, gain, profit(s), yield, produce
🖪 expenditure, outlay

process *n, v*
▶ *n* **1** PROCEDURE, operation, practice, action, method, system, technique, means, manner, way, stage, step, *formal* mode **2** COURSE, progression, advance, progress, development, change(s), evolution, formation, growth, movement, action, proceeding
▷ **in the process of** in the course of, in the middle of, being, in the making, in preparation
▶ *v* deal with, handle, treat, prepare, refine, transform, convert, change, alter

procession *n*
march, parade, cavalcade, motorcade, cortège, file, column, train, succession, stream, series, sequence, course, run

proclaim *v*
announce, declare, pronounce, give out, publish, advertise, circulate, broadcast, make known, notify, profess, testify, blazon, trumpet, show, indicate, *formal* affirm, promulgate

proclamation *n*
announcement, declaration, pronouncement, publication, circulation, advertisement, notice, notification, broadcast, manifesto, order, rule, command, decree, edict, *formal* affirmation, promulgation

proclivity *n*
tendency, leaning, inclination, weakness, disposition, bent, bias, liability, proneness, liableness, *formal* penchant, predilection, predisposition, propensity
🖪 disinclination

procrastinate *v*
defer, put off, postpone, delay, stall, play for time, dally, drag your feet, prolong, protract, *formal* retard, temporize, *colloq.* dilly-dally
🖪 advance, proceed

 procrastinate or **prevaricate** ? *See panel at* PREVARICATE.

procrastination *n*
delaying, deferral, stalling, delaying tactics, *formal* temporizing, dilatoriness, vacillation, *colloq.* dilly-dallying, humming and hawing

procreate *v*
reproduce, produce, father, mother, breed, conceive, generate, propagate, multiply, engender, sire, spawn, *old use* beget

procure *v*
1 ACQUIRE, buy, purchase, get, obtain, find, come by, pick up, lay hands on, earn, gain, win, secure, get hold of, *formal* appropriate, requisition **2** *procure a prostitute* pimp, pander, solicit, importune, *colloq.* hook, hustle
🖪 **1** lose

procurer *n*
procuress, pimp, pander, panderer, bawd, madam

prod *v, n*
▶ *v* **1** POKE, jab, dig, elbow, nudge, push, butt, thrust, *colloq.* shove **2** URGE, goad, spur, prompt, stimulate, motivate, stir, move, encourage, incite, *colloq.* egg on
▶ *n* **1** POKE, jab, dig, elbow, nudge, push, *colloq.* shove **2** PROMPT, prompting, reminder, stimulus, spur, goad, motivation, encouragement

prodigal *adj, n*
▶ *adj* wasteful, extravagant, squandering, excessive, improvident, intemperate, unsparing, unthrifty, wanton, reckless, spendthrift, immoderate, lavish, profuse, sumptuous, exuberant, bountiful, copious, *formal* bounteous, luxuriant, profligate
🖪 modest, thrifty, parsimonious
▶ *n* squanderer, waster, spendthrift, spendall, wastrel, *formal* profligate, *colloq.* big spender

prodigality *n*
wastefulness, extravagance, recklessness, squandering, waste, wantonness, unthriftiness, immoderation, intemperance, dissipation, excess, abandon, exuberance, richness, profusion, lavishness, sumptuousness, plenty, abundance, *formal* luxuriance, plenteousness, profligacy, bounteousness, amplitude, copiousness
🖪 modesty, thrift, parsimony

prodigious *adj*
1 ENORMOUS, gigantic, huge, massive, vast, immense, colossal, giant, mammoth, immeasurable **2** EXTRAORDINARY, marvellous, startling, amazing, astounding, staggering, fabulous, fantastic, flabbergasting, striking, impressive, miraculous, wonderful, monumental, inordinate, spectacular, remarkable, stupendous, tremendous, phenomenal, unusual, exceptional, abnormal
🖪 **1** small **2** commonplace, unremarkable

prodigy *n*
genius, virtuoso, child genius, wonder child, gifted child, mastermind, wonder, marvel, miracle, phenomenon, sensation, freak, curiosity, rarity, *colloq.* whizz kid

produce *v, n*
▶ *v* **1** CAUSE, occasion, give rise to, provoke, bring about, result in, create, evoke, originate, invent, develop, prepare, make, manufacture, fashion, fabricate, build, construct, put together, assemble, compose, generate, yield, bear, breed, grow, deliver, *formal* effect **2** ADVANCE, put forward, present, offer, give, supply, provide, furnish, bring out, bring forward, bring forth, show, exhibit, demonstrate, come up with, *formal* proffer **3** *produce a play* direct, stage, present, perform, manage, organize, arrange, mount, put on
▶ *n* crop, harvest, yield, output, product(s), food, foodstuffs, fruit, vegetables, dairy products, eggs

producer *n*
director, presenter, impresario, manager, régisseur, manufacturer, maker, farmer, grower

product *n*
1 COMMODITY, merchandise, goods, wares, end-product, artefact, work, article, item, creation, invention, production, output, yield, produce, fruit, return **2** RESULT, consequence, effect, outcome, issue, upshot, fruit, offshoot, spin-off, by-product, legacy
🖪 **2** cause

production *n*
1 MAKING, manufacture, manufacturing, producing, building, fabrication, construction, assembly, creation, origination, preparation, formation, composition, development **2** OUTPUT, yield, harvest, fruit(s), return(s), productivity, manufacture, achievement, performance **3** *an amateur production* staging, mounting, performance, presentation, direction, management, organization **4** SHOW, play, drama, concert, musical, opera, film, revue, presentation, performance
🖪 **1** consumption

productive *adj*
fruitful, profitable, rewarding, valuable, beneficial, worthwhile, useful, constructive, gainful, creative, inventive, fertile, prolific, rich, high-yielding, teeming, busy, energetic, vigorous, efficient, effective, *formal*

fecund, fructiferous
🔁 unproductive, fruitless, useless

productivity *n*
productiveness, yield, output, production, capacity, work rate, efficiency

profane *adj, v*
▶ *adj* 1 SACRILEGIOUS, irreligious, blasphemous, idolatrous, godless, ungodly, irreverent, disrespectful, abusive, crude, vulgar, coarse, foul, filthy, unclean 2 SECULAR, temporal, lay, worldly, unconsecrated, unhallowed, unsanctified, unholy, impious
🔁 1 sacred 2 religious, respectful
▶ *v* desecrate, pollute, contaminate, defile, debase, pervert, abuse, misuse, misemploy
🔁 revere, honour

profanity *n*
1 SACRILEGE, irreverence, profaneness, impiety, blasphemy, abuse, *formal* execration, imprecation, malediction 2 OBSCENITY, swear-word, swearing, expletive, curse, cursing, *colloq.* four-letter word
🔁 1 politeness, reverence

profess *v*
1 CLAIM, maintain, allege, lay claim to, make out, pretend, *formal* dissemble 2 DECLARE, admit, confess, acknowledge, own, confirm, certify, announce, proclaim, state, assert, affirm, *formal* aver, avow

professed *adj*
1 SELF-ACKNOWLEDGED, self-confessed, self-styled, so-called, *soi-disant*, confirmed, declared, certified, acknowledged, proclaimed, *formal* avowed 2 PRETENDED, supposed, ostensible, alleged, would-be, *formal* purported

profession *n*
1 CAREER, job, occupation, employment, business, line (of work), walk of life, craft, trade, vocation, calling, métier, craft, office, appointment, post, position, situation 2 ADMISSION, confession, acknowledgement, declaration, announcement, statement, testimony, assertion, affirmation, claim, *formal* averment, avowal

professional *adj, n*
▶ *adj* qualified, licensed, trained, experienced, practised, skilful, skilled, educated, expert, masterly, adept, proficient, competent, businesslike, efficient
🔁 amateur, unprofessional
▶ *n* expert, authority, specialist, master, past master, virtuoso, *colloq.* pro, dab hand, wizard, ace
🔁 amateur

proffer *v*
offer, tender, advance, extend, hold out, hand, suggest, present, propose, submit, volunteer, *formal* propound

proficiency *n*
skill, skilfulness, expertise, experience, mastery, talent, knack, dexterity, finesse, aptitude, accomplishment, capability, ability, competence, aptness, adeptness
🔁 incompetence

proficient *adj*
able, capable, skilled, qualified, trained, experienced, accomplished, expert, masterly, gifted, talented, clever, skilful, competent, efficient, effective, apt, adept
🔁 unskilled, incompetent

profile *n*
1 SIDE VIEW, outline, contour, silhouette, shape, form, line(s), figure, sketch, drawing, diagram, chart, graph 2 BIOGRAPHY, curriculum vitae, CV, thumbnail sketch, vignette, portrait, sketch, study, analysis, examination, survey, review

profit *n, v*
▶ *n* 1 *the company's profits* revenue, return, yield, proceeds, receipts, takings, earnings, winnings, dividend, interest, bonus, gain, surplus, excess, bottom line, *colloq.* fast buck, gravy, killing, rake-off 2 ADVANTAGE, benefit, gain, use, avail, value, worth
🔁 1, 2 loss
▶ *v* gain, make money, pay, serve, avail, benefit, *colloq.* line your pockets
🔁 lose
▷ **profit by/from** exploit, take advantage of, use, utilize, turn to advantage, put to good use, gain a benefit from, gain an advantage from, capitalize on, reap the benefit of, *colloq.* cash in on, milk

profitable *adj*
cost-effective, economic, commercial, money-making, lucrative, remunerative, paying, rewarding, successful, fruitful, productive, advantageous, beneficial, useful, valuable, worthwhile, *formal* gainful, *colloq.* in the black
🔁 unprofitable, loss-making, non-profit-making

profiteer *n, v*
▶ *n* racketeer, exploiter, extortioner, extortionist
▶ *v* exploit, extort, racketeer, overcharge, *colloq.* fleece, make a fast buck, make a quick killing

profiteering *n*
exploitation, extortion, racketeering, Rachmanism

profitless *adj*
useless, worthless, fruitless, futile, vain, pointless, thankless, ineffective, idle, unavailing, unproductive, unprofitable, unremunerative, gainless, *formal* ineffectual
🔁 profitable

profligacy *n*
1 WASTE, wastefulness, extravagance, excess, unrestraint, lavishness, unthriftiness, recklessness, squandering, improvidence, prodigality 2 IMMORALITY, promiscuity, corruption, debauchery, degeneracy, depravity, libertinism, licentiousness, wantonness, dissipation, dissoluteness
🔁 morality, parsimony, thrift, uprightness

profligate *adj, n*
▶ *adj* 1 WASTEFUL, extravagant, squandering, immoderate, excessive, improvident, reckless, spendthrift, prodigal 2 IMMORAL, corrupt, dissolute, unprincipled, wicked, loose, dissipated, depraved, degenerate, debauched, iniquitous, promiscuous, licentious, wanton, libertine
🔁 1 thrifty, *formal* parsimonious 2 upright, moral
▶ *n* 1 WASTER, wastrel, squanderer, spendthrift, prodigal 2 REPROBATE, debauchee, libertine, degenerate, rake, roué

profound *adj*
1 DEEP, great, intense, extreme, heartfelt, sincere, marked, thorough, thoroughgoing, far-reaching, radical, extensive, exhaustive 2 *a profound remark* serious, weighty, deep, penetrating, discerning, thoughtful, philosophical, wise, learned, impenetrable, *formal* sagacious, erudite, esoteric, abstruse
🔁 1 shallow, slight, mild 2 shallow

profoundly *adv*
deeply, intensely, extremely, seriously, acutely, greatly, heartily, thoroughly, keenly, sincerely
🔁 slightly

profundity *n*
depth, profoundness, extremity, intensity, severity, strength, seriousness, penetration, learning, insight, intelligence, wisdom, perceptiveness, acumen, *formal* abstruseness, erudition, perspicuity, perspicacity, sagacity
🔁 shallowness

profuse *adj*
ample, abundant, plentiful, copious, generous, liberal, lavish, rich, excessive, immoderate, extravagant, fulsome, unstinting, overabundant, superabundant, overflowing, *formal* luxuriant, inordinate, *colloq.* over the top
 inadequate, sparse

profusion *n*
abundance, copiousness, plenty, wealth, multitude, glut, riot, excess, surplus, superfluity, superabundance, extravagance, *formal* plethora, plenitude, *colloq.* loads, lots, heaps, tons
 inadequacy, scarcity

progenitor *n*
1 ANCESTOR, forebear, forefather, father, mother, parent, *old use* begetter, *formal* procreator, primogenitor **2** ORIGINATOR, forerunner, founder, instigator, precursor, predecessor, antecedent, source

progeny *n*
offspring, children, young, descendants, family, issue, lineage, race, breed, seed, stock, quiverful, *formal* posterity, scions

prognosis *n*
diagnosis, expectation, forecast, prediction, outlook, projection, assessment, evaluation, prospect, speculation, surmise, *formal* prognostication

prognosticate *v*
forecast, foreshadow, foretell, predict, prophesy, herald, indicate, soothsay, divine, *formal* augur, betoken, harbinger, portend, presage

prognostication *n*
prediction, projection, forecast, expectation, speculation, surmise, horoscope, prophecy, *formal* prognosis

programme *n, v*
▶ *n* **1** SCHEDULE, timetable, agenda, calendar, order of events, listing, list, line-up, plan, plan of action, scheme, project, syllabus, prospectus, curriculum **2** *radio programme* broadcast, transmission, show, performance, production, presentation, episode, simulcast
▶ *v* arrange, plan, schedule, work out, formulate, itemize, lay on, line up, design, list, map out, book, prearrange

progress *n, v*
▶ *n* movement, progression, passage, going, journey, way, advance, headway, step(s) forward, breakthrough, development, evolution, growth, increase, improvement, upgrading, betterment, promotion, *formal* advancement
 recession, deterioration, decline
▷ **in progress** under way, proceeding, going on, happening, occurring, continuing, in preparation, not finished, not completed, *colloq.* in the pipeline, on the stocks
▶ *v* proceed, advance, go forward, move forward, forge ahead, make progress, make headway, make your way, make strides, continue, go on, come on, develop, grow, mature, blossom, flourish, improve, better, recover, prosper, increase, *colloq.* be getting there, shape up
 deteriorate, decline

progression *n*
cycle, chain, string, succession, series, sequence, stream, train, order, course, advance, headway, passage, progress, development, forward movement, *formal* advancement

progressive *adj*
1 MODERN, avant-garde, advanced, forward-looking, forward-thinking, enlightened, liberal, radical, revolutionary, reformist, innovative, dynamic, enter-prising, go-ahead, up-and-coming **2** ADVANCING, continuing, developing, growing, increasing, escalating, intensifying, accelerating
 1 conservative **2** regressive

prohibit *v*
forbid, ban, bar, veto, outlaw, rule out, prevent, exclude, stop, hinder, hamper, impede, obstruct, restrict, *formal* proscribe, preclude, interdict
 permit, allow, authorize

prohibited *adj*
forbidden, banned, barred, taboo, vetoed, embargoed, verboten, *formal* disallowed, interdicted, proscribed
 permitted, allowed

prohibition *n*
forbidding, forbiddance, ban, bar, constraint, veto, restriction, obstruction, exclusion, prevention, negation, embargo, injunction, *formal* disallowance, forbiddal, interdict, interdiction, proscription
 permission

prohibitionist *n*
teetotaller, abolitionist, dry, pussyfoot

prohibitive *adj*
forbidding, preposterous, excessive, exorbitant, extortionate, impossible, restrictive, restraining, suppressive, repressive, prohibiting, prohibitory, *formal* proscriptive, *colloq.* sky-high, steep
 encouraging, reasonable

project *n, v*
▶ *n* scheme, campaign, plan, venture, programme, design, proposal, assignment, contract, task, job, work, occupation, activity, enterprise, undertaking, idea, conception
▶ *v* **1** PREDICT, forecast, plan, propose, extrapolate, estimate, reckon, calculate, gauge, expect, design, map out, *formal* predetermine **2** THROW, fling, hurl, cast, launch, propel, discharge **3** PROTRUDE, stick out, stand out, extend, bulge, jut out, overhang, *formal* obtrude

projectile *n*
missile, rocket, shell, shot, grenade, bullet, ball, mortar-bomb

projecting *adj*
overhanging, protruding, protrusive, beetling, *formal* exsertile, extrusive, extrusory, protrudent

projection *n*
1 PREDICTION, forecast, expectation, extrapolation, estimate, estimation, reckoning, calculation, computation, plan, design **2** PROTUBERANCE, bulge, jutting, overhang, ledge, sill, shelf, ridge

proletariat *n*
working class, common people, masses, mob, lower classes, rabble, herd, hoi polloi, canaille, commoners, commonalty, *colloq.* great unwashed, plebs, proles, riff-raff

proliferate *v*
multiply, reproduce, grow quickly, breed, increase, build up, intensify, extend, escalate, mushroom, snowball, rocket, spread, expand, flourish, thrive, *formal* burgeon
 dwindle

proliferation *n*
multiplication, increase, intensification, escalation, expansion, spread, extension, build-up, concentration, duplication, mushrooming, snowballing, rocketing
 decrease

prolific *adj*
productive, fruitful, fertile, profuse, copious, abundant, rank, *formal* fecund, luxuriant
 unproductive

prolix *adj*
long-winded, verbose, lengthy, prolonged, prosy, discursive, digressive, long, diffuse, rambling, tedious, tiresome, wordy, *technical* pleonastic, *formal* protracted
F3 succinct

prolixity *n*
long-windedness, verboseness, verbiage, wordiness, prosiness, rambling, discursiveness, diffuseness, wandering, verbosity, boringness, tediousness, *technical* pleonasm
F3 succinctness

prologue *n*
introduction, foreword, preface, preamble, preliminary, prelude, *formal* exordium, proem, prolegomena, prooemion, prooemium

prolong *v*
lengthen, extend, elongate, stretch (out), protract, draw out, spin out, drag out, delay, continue, perpetuate, *formal* protract
F3 shorten

promenade *n, v*
▶ *n* **1** SEAFRONT, walkway, front, parade, esplanade, prom, boulevard, terrace **2** WALK, stroll, breather, airing, saunter, turn, walkabout, *formal* constitutional
▶ *v* walk, stroll, saunter, strut, swagger, sally forth, parade, *formal* perambulate, *colloq.* mosey

prominence *n*
1 FAME, celebrity, renown, eminence, pre-eminence, illustriousness, distinction, greatness, note, importance, conspicuousness, reputation, name, standing, stature, rank, prestige, weight, top billing **2** BULGE, protuberance, swelling, jutting, protruding, bump, hump, lump, mound, rise, elevation, projection, process, headland, promontory, pinnacle, crest, height, cliff, crag
F3 **1** unimportance, insignificance

prominent *adj*
1 NOTICEABLE, conspicuous, obvious, unmistakable, striking, eye-catching **2** BULGING, protuberant, projecting, jutting (out), standing out, sticking out, protruding, obtrusive, protrusive **3** *a prominent writer* famous, well-known, celebrated, renowned, noted, notable, eminent, pre-eminent, distinguished, respected, illustrious, leading, foremost, chief, main, important, popular, outstanding, top, acclaimed
F3 **1** inconspicuous **3** unknown, unimportant, insignificant

promiscuity *n*
looseness, laxity, permissiveness, wantonness, immorality, dissoluteness, dissipation, licentiousness, debauchery, depravity, *formal* profligacy, proterivity
F3 chastity, morality

promiscuous *adj*
loose, immoral, licentious, dissolute, debauched, dissipated, abandoned, wanton, fast, of easy virtue, casual, random, haphazard, indiscriminate, *formal* profligate
F3 chaste, moral

promise *v, n*
▶ *v* **1** vow, pledge, swear, take an oath, contract, give an undertaking, undertake, give your word, vouch, warrant, guarantee, assure, give an assurance **2** *clouds that promise rain* indicate, suggest, hint at, signify, denote, be a sign of, *formal* augur, presage, betoken
▷ **promised land** paradise, Zion, land of milk and honey, Shangri-la
▶ *n* **1** vow, pledge, oath, word, word of honour, bond, guarantee, assurance, contract, undertaking, engagement, commitment, *formal* compact, covenant **2** POTENTIAL, ability, capability, aptitude, talent, flair

3 *a promise of autumn sunshine* sign, hint, suggestion, indication, evidence

promising *adj*
favourable, rosy, bright, encouraging, optimistic, hopeful, talented, able, gifted, budding, *formal* auspicious, propitious, *colloq.* up-and-coming
F3 unpromising, inauspicious, discouraging

promontory *n*
cliff, headland, head, foreland, bluff, precipice, point, projection, prominence, ridge, spur, cape, naze, ness, peninsula

promote *v*
1 UPGRADE, advance, move up, raise, elevate, exalt, honour, *formal* aggrandize, prefer **2** ENCOURAGE, recommend, advocate, champion, endorse, sponsor, support, back, help, aid, assist, advance, foster, nurture, further, forward, boost, stimulate, urge, contribute to, *formal* espouse **3** ADVERTISE, publicize, popularize, market, sell, push, *colloq.* plug, hype, puff up
F3 **1** demote, relegate **2** discourage, hinder, *formal* disparage

promotion *n*
1 ADVANCEMENT, upgrading, rise, elevation, exaltation, move up, *formal* preferment, aggrandizement **2** ENCOURAGEMENT, support, recommendation, advocacy, urging, fostering, contribution, backing, furtherance, development, boosting, *formal* espousal **3** ADVERTISING, publicity, campaign, propaganda, marketing, *colloq.* plugging, hype, pushing
F3 **1** demotion **2** discouragement, obstruction, *formal* disparagement

prompt *adj, adv, v, n*
▶ *adj* punctual, on time, immediate, instantaneous, instant, direct, quick, swift, rapid, speedy, unhesitating, willing, ready, alert, eager, responsive, timely, early, *formal* expeditious
F3 slow, hesitant, late
▶ *adv* promptly, punctually, exactly, on time, on the dot, to the minute, sharp, *colloq.* dead on, bang on, spot on
▶ *v* cause, give rise to, result in, lead, occasion, produce, make, instigate, call forth, elicit, provoke, induce, incite, urge, encourage, inspire, move, stimulate, motivate, spur, impel, prod, remind, *formal* expedite
F3 deter, dissuade
▶ *n* reminder, cue, refresher, encouragement, hint, help, jolt, prod, spur, stimulus

prompting *n*
encouragement, reminder, reminding, advice, assistance, hint, influence, jogging, prodding, pushing, suggestion, urging, persuasion, incitement, pressing, pressure, *formal* admonition, protreptic
F3 dissuasion

promptly *adv*
1 IMMEDIATELY, instantly, directly, unhesitatingly, quickly, speedily, swiftly, *formal* forthwith, *colloq.* pronto **2** PUNCTUALLY, on time, on target, exactly, on the dot, to the minute, sharp, as soon as possible, posthaste, *colloq.* bang on, spot on, dead on, pronto, ASAP, pdq, pretty damn quick

promptness *n*
punctuality, quickness, readiness, speed, swiftness, willingness, briskness, dispatch, eagerness, alertness, haste, *formal* alacrity, expedition, promptitude
F3 *formal* tardiness

promulgate *v*
announce, proclaim, declare, decree, promote, circulate, notify, communicate, publish, spread, publicize, broadcast, advertise, issue, *formal* disseminate

promulgation n
announcement, communication, declaration, proclamation, publication, publicizing, issuance, promulgating, *formal* dissemination

prone adj
1 LIKELY, given, inclined, disposed, bent, apt, liable, subject, susceptible, vulnerable, *formal* predisposed **2** *she lay prone* face down, prostrate, flat, horizontal, full-length, stretched, *formal* recumbent, procumbent
F3 1 unlikely, immune **2** upright, supine

proneness n
inclination, leaning, tendency, susceptibility, aptness, bent, bias, disposition, liability, weakness, *formal* penchant, proclivity, propensity
F3 dislike

prong n
point, spike, projection, spur, tine, tip, fork, grain

pronounce v
1 SAY, utter, speak, express, voice, vocalize, sound, enunciate, articulate, stress **2** DECLARE, announce, proclaim, decree, judge, affirm, assert

pronounceable adj
speakable, utterable, sayable, vocable, articulable, enunciable, expressible
F3 unpronounceable

pronounced adj
clear, distinct, definite, positive, decided, marked, noticeable, conspicuous, evident, obvious, striking, unmistakable, strong, broad, thick
F3 faint, vague

pronouncement n
declaration, statement, announcement, judgement, notification, proclamation, assertion, decree, edict, manifesto, dictum, *formal* pronunciamento, *ipse dixit*, promulgation

pronunciation n
speech, diction, elocution, enunciation, articulation, saying, uttering, voicing, vocalization, delivery, accent, stress, inflection, intonation, modulation

proof n, adj
▶ n evidence, documentation, demonstration, verification, confirmation, corroboration, certification, validation, substantiation, authentication, *formal* attestation
▶ adj impenetrable, impervious, proofed, repellent, resistant, strong, tight, treated, fireproof, weatherproof, waterproof, rainproof, leakproof, windproof, bombproof, bulletproof, childproof, foolproof, tamperproof, soundproof
F3 permeable, untreated

prop v, n
▶ v **1** SUPPORT, sustain, uphold, hold up, maintain, shore (up), stay, brace, buttress, bolster (up), underpin, set, underwrite **2** *propped against the wall* lean, rest, stand, balance, steady
▶ n **1** *a clothes prop* support, stick, post, column, shaft, stay, mainstay, strut, buttress, upright, bolster, brace, truss, stanchion **2** *drink is the prop in his life* mainstay, support, pillar, column, supporter, anchor

propaganda n
advertising, publicity, promotion, information, indoctrination, brainwashing, disinformation, *colloq.* hype

propagandist n
promoter, advocate, canvasser, publicist, pamphleteer, evangelist, proselytizer, indoctrinator, *formal* proponent, *colloq.* plugger

propagate v
1 SPREAD, transmit, broadcast, communicate, distribute, proclaim, diffuse, circulate, publish, publicize, promote, *formal* disseminate, promulgate **2** IN-

CREASE, multiply, proliferate, grow, generate, produce, breed, spawn, reproduce, *formal* procreate

propagation n
1 COMMUNICATION, spread, spreading, transmission, promotion, distribution, circulation, diffusion, *formal* dissemination, promulgation **2** INCREASE, generation, breeding, multiplication, proliferation, spawning, reproduction, *old use* procreation

propel v
move, drive, impel, force, thrust, push (forward), launch, shoot, send, *colloq.* shove
F3 stop

propensity n
tendency, liability, susceptibility, inclination, leaning, disposition, aptness, proneness, bent, bias, readiness, foible, weakness, *formal* penchant, predisposition, proclivity
F3 disinclination

proper adj
1 RIGHT, correct, accurate, exact, precise, true, genuine, real, actual **2** ACCEPTED, correct, suitable, appropriate, fitting, acceptable, conventional, orthodox, established, decent, respectable, polite, refined, genteel, strict, gentlemanly, ladylike, prim, prudish, formal
F3 1 wrong, incorrect **2** improper, indecent

property n
1 ESTATE, land, real estate, acres, premises, buildings, house(s), wealth, riches, resources, means, capital, assets, holding(s), belongings, possessions, goods, chattels, paraphernalia, *formal* effects, *colloq.* gear **2** FEATURE, trait, quality, attribute, characteristic, idiosyncrasy, quirk, peculiarity, mark

prophecy n
prediction, forecast, prognosis, second sight, fortune-telling, divination, soothsaying, *formal* augury, prognostication

prophesy v
predict, foresee, augur, foretell, forewarn, forecast, *formal* prognosticate, augur

prophet n
seer, soothsayer, foreteller, forecaster, oracle, clairvoyant, fortune-teller, *formal* prognosticator
▷ **prophet of doom** pessimist, doomwatcher, Jeremiah, Cassandra, *colloq.* doom merchant, doomster

prophetic adj
forecasting, predictive, prognostic, foreshadowing, oracular, fey, *formal* sibylline, presaging, prescient, augural, divinatory, fatidical, mantic, vatic, vaticidal
F3 unprophetic

prophylactic adj
preventive, preventative, anticipatory, pre-emptive, inhibitory, obstructive, precautionary, protective, counteractive, deterrent
F3 causative, fostering

propinquity n
nearness, closeness, connection, tie, vicinity, neighbourhood, proximity, adjacency, relation, relationship, blood, kinship, affiliation, affinity, *formal* consanguinity, contiguity, kindredness, kindredship
F3 remoteness

propitiate v
reconcile, pacify, placate, satisfy, appease, conciliate, mollify, soothe
F3 anger, provoke

propitiation n
reconciliation, peacemaking, appeasement, conciliation, mollification, pacification, placation, pacifying
F3 angering, provocation

propitiatory *adj*
reconciliatory, peacemaking, soothing, pacifying, pacificatory, appeasing, conciliatory, mollifying, assuaging, *formal* placative, placatory, propitiative
☒ provocative

propitious *adj*
favourable, fortunate, advantageous, happy, friendly, gracious, opportune, timely, promising, prosperous, encouraging, reassuring, well-disposed, bright, lucky, kindly, rosy, benign, beneficial, benevolent, *formal* auspicious
☒ inauspicious

proponent *n*
advocate, supporter, backer, proposer, subscriber, apologist, partisan, defender, enthusiast, exponent, upholder, vindicator, champion, friend, patron, *formal* propounder
☒ opponent, enemy

proportion *n*
1 PERCENTAGE, fraction, part, segment, portion, measure, division, share, quota, amount, *colloq.* cut, split, whack, slice of the cake, piece of the action **2** RATIO, relationship, correspondence, symmetry, balance, distribution, quotient **3** *a task/building of huge proportions* dimensions, measurements, size, magnitude, extent, volume, capacity, bulk, mass, height, length, depth, breadth, width, scale
☒ 2 disproportion, imbalance

proportional *adj*
proportionate, relative, equivalent, commensurate, consistent, corresponding, analogous, comparable, equitable, even
☒ disproportionate

proportionally *adv*
proportionately, relatively, correspondingly, comparably, commensurately, evenly, pro rata
☒ disproportionately

proposal *n*
plan, scheme, project, design, programme, manifesto, presentation, proposition, suggestion, recommendation, motion, bid, offer, tender, terms

propose *v*
1 SUGGEST, recommend, move, advance, put forward, introduce, bring up, advocate, table, submit, present, offer, tender, *formal* proffer, propound **2** INTEND, mean, aim, purpose, plan, design, have in mind **3** NOMINATE, put up, name, recommend, suggest **4** *propose marriage* ask to marry, ask for someone's hand in marriage, *colloq.* pop the question, go down on bended knee
☒ 1 withdraw

proposition *n, v*
▶ *n* **1** PROPOSAL, suggestion, theory, plan, project, programme, recommendation, scheme, manifesto, motion, tender, *formal* theorem **2** TASK, activity, undertaking, venture **3** *a sexual proposition* advance, overture, approach, indecent proposal/suggestion, pass
▶ *v* accost, solicit, make sexual advances/overtures to, make an indecent proposal to, make a pass at

propound *v*
put forward, suggest, propose, advance, set forth, advocate, contend, lay down, present, submit, *formal* move, postulate
☒ oppose

proprietor, proprietress *n*
landlord, landlady, title-holder, freeholder, leaseholder, landowner, owner, possessor, deed holder

propriety *n*
1 MODESTY, decorum, decency, civility, etiquette, protocol, delicacy, respectability, refinement, rightness, correctness, manners, good manners, politeness, courtesy, breeding, appropriateness, aptness, becomingness, suitableness, fitness, gentlemanliness, ladylikeness, *formal* punctilio, rectitude **2** *observe proprieties* civility, standard, etiquette, convention, decency, nicety, *colloq.* the done thing, p's and q's
☒ 1, 2 impropriety

propulsion *n*
drive, driving force, power, pressure, push, thrust, motive force, momentum, impetus, impulse, impulsion

prosaic *adj*
mundane, ordinary, routine, dull, stale, boring, commonplace, humdrum, matter-of-fact, unimaginative, uninspired, uninspiring, monotonous, bland, tame, trite, banal, vacuous, vapid, pedestrian, workaday, flat, dry, hackneyed, everyday
☒ imaginative, interesting

proscribe *v*
forbid, prohibit, ban, outlaw, bar, banish, condemn, embargo, reject, exclude, boycott, censure, damn, doom, black, blackball, denounce, deport, expel, exile, excommunicate, expatriate, ostracize, *formal* interdict, disallow
☒ allow, permit

 proscribe or **prescribe** ? *See panel at* PRESCRIBE.

proscription *n*
prohibition, ban, bar, barring, embargo, outlawry, censure, condemnation, damning, denunciation, ostracism, rejection, banishment, boycott, deportation, expulsion, ejection, eviction, exclusion, exile, excommunication, expatriation, *formal* interdict
☒ admission, allowing

prosecute *v*
accuse, sue, charge, bring charges, bring an action against, prefer charges, take to court, litigate, summon, put on trial, try, *formal* arraign, indict
☒ defend

proselytize *v*
convert, evangelize, make converts, persuade, win over, propagandize, spread the gospel, bring into the fold, bring to God

prosody *n*

Forms of prosody include:
abstract verse, Alcaic verse, alexandrine, alliteration, amphibrach, amphimacer, Anacreontic verse, anacrusis, analysed rhyme, anapaest, antibacchius, antispast, Archilochian verse, asclepiad, assonance, asynartete, ballade, blank verse, bouts rimés, broken rhyme, caesura, canto, catalexis, choliamb, choree, choriamb, cinquain, couplet, dactyl, decastich, dipody, dispondee, distich, ditrochee, dizain, dochmius, elision, enjambment, envoy, epitrite, epode, eye rhyme, false quantity, feminine caesura, feminine ending, feminine rhyme, foot, free verse, galliambic, glyconic, heptameter, heptapody, heroic couplet, hexameter, hexastich, hypermetrical, iamb, ictus, Ionic, kyrielle, laisse, Leonine rhyme, linked verse, long-measure, macaronic, masculine ending, masculine rhyme, metre, miurus, monometer, monorhyme, paeon, pantoum, pentameter, pentastich, Petrarchan sonnet, Pherecratean, Pindaric, poulters' measure, pyrrhic, Pythian verse, quatorzain, quatrain, reported verses, rhopalic, rhyme royal, rime riche,

rime suffisante, rondeau, rondel, rove-over, Sapphic, senarius, septenarius, sonnet, Spencerian stanza, spondee, sprung rhythm, strophe, substitution, synaphea, tetrameter, tetrapody, tetrastich, tribrach, trimeter, triolet, tripody, triseme, trochee, villanelle, virelay.

prospect n, v
▶ n **1** *the prospect of rain* chance(s), odds, probability, likelihood, likeness, possibility, hope, expectation, anticipation, outlook, future, promise **2** *a prospect of the bay* outlook, vista, view, scene, panorama, aspect, spectacle, perspective, landscape, opening
🖝 unlikelihood
▶ v explore, search, look for, seek, survey, examine, inspect, quest, fossick, *colloq.* nose

prospective *adj*
future, -to-be, would-be, intended, designate, destined, forthcoming, approaching, coming, imminent, awaited, expected, anticipated, hoped-for, likely, possible, probable, potential, aspiring

prospectus n
syllabus, manifesto, outline, synopsis, pamphlet, leaflet, brochure, catalogue, list, literature, plan, scheme, programme, *formal* conspectus

prosper v
boom, thrive, flourish, flower, bloom, succeed, be successful, get on, get on well, do well, turn out well, advance, progress, make progress, grow rich, *formal* burgeon, *colloq.* get ahead, get on in the world, go up in the world, make your pile, hit the big time, hit the jackpot, live on easy street
🖝 fail

prosperity n
boom, plenty, affluence, wealth, riches, fortune, well-being, luxury, success, good fortune, *colloq.* the good life, the life of Riley, easy street, bed of roses, land of milk and honey, clover, lap of luxury
🖝 adversity, poverty

prosperous *adj*
booming, thriving, flourishing, blooming, successful, fortunate, lucky, rich, wealthy, affluent, well-off, well-to-do, *formal* burgeoning, opulent, *colloq.* well-heeled, rolling in it, loaded, in the money, made of money, flush, on easy street
🖝 unfortunate, poor

prostitute n, v
▶ n call-girl, woman of the streets, woman of the town, woman of ill repute, loose woman, fallen woman, lady of the night, harlot, cocotte, courtesan, *fille de joie, fille des rues, lorette, colloq.* hooker, hustler, tart
▶ v cheapen, degrade, debase, demean, devalue, pervert, misapply, misuse, profane

prostitution n
vice, *colloq.* the game, the oldest profession

prostrate *adj, v*
▶ *adj* **1** FLAT, horizontal, prone, lying down, lying flat, fallen **2** OVERCOME, overwhelmed, devastated, crushed, paralysed, powerless, helpless, defenceless, laid low, brought to your knees
🖝 **1** erect **2** triumphant
▶ v lay low, flatten, level, knock down, overcome, overwhelm, crush, overthrow, bring to your knees, tire, wear out, fatigue, exhaust, sap, drain, ruin
🖝 strengthen
▷ **prostrate yourself** bow down, kneel, kowtow, submit, grovel, cringe, abase yourself

prostration n
collapse, abasement, kneeling, kowtow, submission,

depression, desolation, despair, despondency, dejection, grief, helplessness, weakness, weariness, exhaustion, paralysis, bow, *formal* slough of despond, obeisance, genuflection
🖝 elation, exaltation, happiness, triumph

protagonist n
hero, heroine, lead, principal, leader, main/chief/ leading character, title role, prime mover, champion, advocate, supporter, banker, adherent, mainstay, standard-bearer, exponent, moving spirit, *formal* proponent
🖝 critic, opponent

protean *adj*
ever-changing, changeable, versatile, inconstant, many-sided, variable, volatile, mercurial, multiform, mutable, *technical* polymorphic, polymorphous, amoebic
🖝 stable, unchanging

protect v
safeguard, defend, guard, escort, cover, screen, shield, secure, watch over, look after, care for, take care of, support, shelter, harbour, keep, keep safe, conserve, preserve, save
🖝 attack, neglect

protection n
1 *protection of the environment* care, custody, charge, guardianship, safekeeping, conservation, preservation, safety, security, safeguard, defence **2** BARRIER, buffer, bulwark, defence, guard, shield, armour, screen, cover, shelter, safeguard, refuge, security, insurance
🖝 **1** neglect, attack

protective *adj*
1 *protective clothing* waterproof, fireproof, insulating, covering, shielding, defensive **2** POSSESSIVE, defensive, motherly, maternal, fatherly, paternal, watchful, vigilant, careful, wary, overprotective, solicitous, chivalrous
🖝 **2** aggressive, threatening

protector n
1 DEFENDER, benefactor, advocate, guardian, patron, champion, counsel, bodyguard, minder, father-figure, *formal* protectress, protectrix **2** GUARD, safeguard, shield, cushion, bolster, pad, buffer
🖝 **1** attacker, threat

protégé(e) n
pupil, student, trainee, apprentice, disciple, follower, ward, charge, dependant, discovery, *colloq.* blue-eyed boy
🖝 guardian

protest v, n
▶ v **1** OBJECT, make/raise an objection to, speak out, take exception, complain, appeal, demonstrate, oppose, disapprove, disagree, argue, reject, take issue, *formal* remonstrate, demur, *colloq.* gripe, whinge, kick up a fuss **2** *protest your innocence* assert, maintain, contend, insist, profess, proclaim, announce, declare, *formal* affirm, attest, avow
🖝 **1** accept
▶ n **1** OBJECTION, disapproval, disagreement, opposition, dissent, complaint, exception, protestation, outcry, fuss, appeal, demonstration, march, boycott, riot, civil disobedience, *formal* demurral, remonstration, *colloq.* demo **2** ASSERTION, contention, declaration, proclamation, announcement, *formal* affirmation, attestation, avowal
🖝 **1** acceptance

protestation n
statement, declaration, profession, pledge, vow, assurance, oath, objection, complaint, outcry, disagreement, protest, dissent, *formal* affirmation,

asseveration, avowal, expostulation, remonstrance, remonstration

protester n
demonstrator, opposer, opponent, objector, complainer, agitator, striker, rebel, dissident, dissenter

protocol n
procedure, formalities, convention, custom, etiquette, manners, code of behaviour, civilities, good form, *formal* propriety, decorum, *colloq.* p's and q's

prototype n
original, model, mock-up, example, standard, type, pattern, precedent, *formal* archetype, exemplar, paradigm

protract v
continue, draw out, extend, keep going, lengthen, prolong, make longer, spin out, stretch out, sustain, *colloq.* drag out
🖅 shorten

protracted adj
long, lengthy, prolonged, extended, drawn-out, long-drawn-out, stretched out, spun out, overlong, endless, interminable
🖅 brief, shortened

protrude v
stick out, poke out, come through, bulge, jut out, project, extend, stand out, beetle, *formal* obtrude

protruding adj
jutting, prominent, protuberant, proud, *formal* exsertive, extrusive, extrusory, protrudent, protrusive
🖅 flat, flush

protrusion n
lump, bulge, knob, bump, outgrowth, projection, protuberance, swelling, jut, *formal* obtrusion, process

protuberance n
lump, bump, bulge, bulb, knob, outgrowth, swelling, prominence, protrusion, projection, tumour, wart, welt, tuber, tubercle, *technical* apophysis, *formal* excrescence, process

protuberant adj
swelling, swollen, jutting, prominent, popping, bulging, bulbous, protruding, proud, beetling, bunched, gibbous, *old use* astrut, *formal* protrusive, exsertive, extrusive, extrusory, protrudent
🖅 flat

proud adj
1 CONCEITED, vain, egotistical, big-headed, boastful, smug, complacent, arrogant, self-important, cocky, presumptuous, haughty, full of yourself, scornful, high-handed, imperious, pompous, overweening, puffed up, overbearing, supercilious, snobbish, *formal* hubristic, *colloq.* high and mighty, snooty, toffee-nosed, stuck-up, jumped-up, too big for your boots 2 SATISFIED, contented, gratified, pleased, delighted, happy, glad, content, thrilled, honoured 3 DIGNIFIED, noble, honourable, worthy, self-respecting 4 *a proud moment* satisfying, gratifying, pleasing, memorable, notable, splendid, marvellous, wonderful, *colloq.* red-letter 5 *a proud sight* splendid, grand, imposing, glorious, magnificent, outstanding, notable, honourable, worthy
🖅 1 humble, modest, unassuming 2 ashamed 3 deferential, ignoble

provable adj
demonstrable, establishable, confirmable, verifiable, testable, *formal* attestable, corroborable, evincible
🖅 unprovable

prove v
1 SHOW, demonstrate, verify, confirm, bear out, bear witness to, document, certify, authenticate, validate, justify, establish, determine, ascertain, try (out), test,

check, examine, analyse, *formal* attest, corroborate, substantiate 2 TURN OUT, come about, be the case, *formal* transpire, eventuate, *colloq.* pan out
🖅 1 disprove, discredit, falsify

proven adj
proved, confirmed, certified, checked, established, accepted, dependable, reliable, tested, tried, definite, authentic, trustworthy, valid, verified, undoubted, *formal* attested, corroborated
🖅 unproven

provenance n
source, origin, derivation, birthplace, *formal* provenience

provender n
food, provisions, foodstuffs, eats, supplies, rations, sustenance, groceries, edibles, comestibles, fare, feed, fodder, forage, *formal* victuals, *colloq.* eatables, *slang* grub, nosh

proverb n
saying, adage, aphorism, maxim, byword, dictum, precept, saw, gnome, *formal* apophthegm, paroemia

proverbial adj
axiomatic, accepted, conventional, traditional, customary, time-honoured, famous, famed, well-known, renowned, acknowledged, legendary, notorious, infamous, typical, archetypal

provide v
1 SUPPLY, furnish, stock, equip, outfit, kit out, prepare for, cater, serve, present, give, offer, contribute, yield, lend, add, bring, *formal* afford, impart 2 PLAN FOR, make plans for, allow, make provision, accommodate, arrange for, anticipate, take precautions, take measures/steps 3 STATE, specify, stipulate, lay down, require
🖅 1 take, remove
▷ **provide for** support, maintain, sustain, look after, take care of, keep, endow, fend for
🖅 ignore, neglect

provided conj
given, as/so long as, on condition, on the understanding, with the proviso

providence n
1 FATE, destiny, divine intervention, God's will, fortune, luck 2 PRUDENCE, far-sightedness, foresight, forethought, judgement, wisdom, caution, care, thrift, economy, *formal* sagacity, circumspection, judiciousness
🖅 2 improvidence

provident adj
prudent, far-sighted, cautious, careful, thrifty, economical, frugal, *formal* sagacious, circumspect, judicious
🖅 improvident

providential adj
fortunate, lucky, fortuitous, opportune, timely, happy, convenient, welcome, heaven-sent
🖅 untimely

provider n
supplier, supporter, benefactor, wage-earner, breadwinner, earner, giver, donor, funder, source, mainstay, *colloq.* angel

providing conj
provided, given, as long as, on condition, on the understanding, with the proviso

province n
1 REGION, area, district, zone, county, shire, department, territory, state, colony, dependency 2 RESPONSIBILITY, concern, duty, office, business, role, function, charge, field, sphere, area, department, domain, line, *colloq.* pigeon

provincial *adj, n*
▶ *adj* **1** *a provincial theatre* regional, local, rural, rustic, country **2** *provincial attitudes* PAROCHIAL, insular, inward-looking, limited, intolerant, narrow, narrow-minded, small-minded, unsophisticated, home-grown, small-town, outlying, parish-pump, *colloq.* hick
F3 1 national, metropolitan, capital, cosmopolitan, urban **2** sophisticated
▶ *n* country bumpkin, yokel, rustic, peasant, *colloq.* hillbilly, hick

provincialism *n*
parochialism, provinciality, regionalism, sectionalism, insularity, localism, narrow-mindedness
F3 sophistication

provision *n*
1 SUPPLY, giving, equipping, furnishing, preparation, service, contribution, outfitting **2** FACILITIES, amenities, services, resources **3** PLAN, arrangement, preparation, measure, step, allowance, concession, precaution **4** STIPULATION, specification, proviso, condition, term, requirement, clause, qualification, rider **5** FOOD, foodstuff, groceries, sustenance, rations, supplies, stocks, stores, *colloq.* eatables

provisional *adj*
temporary, interim, transitional, stopgap, makeshift, conditional, tentative, *colloq.* pro tem
F3 permanent, fixed, definite

provisionally *adv*
for the time being, interim, meanwhile, *colloq.* pro tem

proviso *n*
condition, term, requirement, stipulation, qualification, reservation, restriction, limitation, provision, clause, rider, *colloq.* strings

provocation *n*
1 ANNOYANCE, enraging, angering, irritation, exasperation, vexation, grievance, offence, insult, affront, injury, taunt, challenge, dare, *colloq.* aggravation **2** CAUSE, grounds, justification, reason, motive, stimulus, stimulation, motivation, incitement, inducement, inspiration, eliciting, production, generation, instigation

provocative *adj*
1 ANNOYING, irritating, infuriating, exasperating, galling, outrageous, offensive, insulting, abusive, *colloq.* aggravating **2** STIMULATING, exciting, challenging **3** EROTIC, titillating, arousing, sexy, sexually arousing, seductive, alluring, tempting, inviting, tantalizing, teasing, suggestive
F3 1 conciliatory

provoke *v*
1 ANNOY, irritate, rile, offend, insult, anger, enrage, infuriate, incense, madden, exasperate, tease, taunt, pique, vex, nettle, harass, *colloq.* aggravate, needle, hassle, wind up, make someone's blood boil, get someone's back up **2** GOAD, stir, spur, prod, prompt, stimulate, motivate, incite, rouse, inflame, instigate, *colloq.* egg on **3** CAUSE, occasion, give rise to, produce, generate, induce, elicit, evoke, call forth, engender, promote, excite, inspire, move
F3 1 please, pacify **3** result

provoking *adj*
annoying, exasperating, infuriating, irritating, offensive, maddening, obstructive, tiresome, vexatious, vexing, irking, irksome, galling, *colloq.* aggravating
F3 pleasing

prow *n*
bow(s), fore, stem, front, head, nose, forepart, cut-water
F3 stern

prowess *n*
1 ACCOMPLISHMENT, attainment, ability, capability,

aptitude, skill, skilfulness, expertise, facility, mastery, command, proficiency, talent, genius, dexterity, adeptness, adroitness **2** BRAVERY, courage, dauntlessness, fearlessness, daring, heroism, gallantry, pluck, valour, audacity, intrepidity, *colloq.* grit, nerve, guts, bottle, spunk

prowl *v*
creep, hunt, rove, roam, move stealthily, slink, sneak, stalk, lurk, skulk, steal, range, search, scavenge, cruise, patrol, nose, snook

proximity *n*
closeness, nearness, vicinity, neighbourhood, adjacency, juxtaposition, *formal* contiguity, propinquity
F3 remoteness

proxy *n*
agent, deputy, stand-in, substitute, surrogate, representative, delegate, attorney, factor

prude *n*
prig, old maid, puritan, school-marm, Mrs Grundy

prudence *n*
wisdom, judgement, good sense, common sense, care, foresight, forethought, far-sightedness, economy, heedfulness, preparedness, discretion, caution, vigilance, wariness, planning, providence, precaution, policy, canniness, frugality, saving, thrift, husbandry, *formal* circumspection, judiciousness, sagacity
F3 imprudence, rashness

prudent *adj*
wise, sensible, politic, shrewd, discerning, careful, cautious, wary, vigilant, discreet, provident, far-sighted, frugal, economical, thrifty, *formal* judicious, circumspect, sagacious
F3 imprudent, unwise, careless, rash

prudery *n*
overmodesty, primness, squeamishness, starchiness, strictness, stuffiness, priggishness, prissiness, old-maidishness, puritanism, Grundyism
F3 laxness

prudish *adj*
overmodest, overnice, proper, prim, narrow-minded, squeamish, demure, starchy, strait-laced, stuffy, puritanical, school-marmish, old-maidish, prissy, priggish, ultra-virtuous, Victorian, *colloq.* po-faced
F3 lax, *colloq.* easy-going

prune *v*
clip, trim, snip, cut, dock, lop, pare, shape, reduce, shorten

prurient *adj*
salacious, lewd, dirty, obscene, indecent, lustful, desirous, itching, erotic, pornographic, lascivious, lecherous, voyeuristic, *formal* concupiscent, cupidinous, libidinous, *colloq.* smutty, blue
F3 decent

pry *v*
meddle, interfere, intrude, peep, peer, nose, ferret, dig, delve, *colloq.* snoop, poke/stick your nose in, put your oar in
F3 mind your own business

prying *adj*
meddlesome, meddling, interfering, intrusive, nosy, curious, inquisitive, spying, peering, peery, *colloq.* snooping, snoopy
F3 uninquisitive

psalm *n*
hymn, song, poem, prayer, chant, canticle, paean, paraphrase

pseud *n*
poser, poseur, trendy, fraud, humbug, *colloq.* phoney

pseudo *adj*
false, sham, mock, pretended, imitation, fake, counterfeit, bogus, artificial, spurious, ersatz, quasi-, ungenuine, *colloq.* phoney, pseud
🆁 genuine, real, authentic

pseudonym *n*
false name, assumed name, alias, incognito, penname, nom-de-plume, stage-name, *formal* allonym

psyche *n*
spirit, soul, mind, self, deepest feelings, heart of hearts, consciousness, personality, awareness, individuality, subconscious, intellect, intelligence, understanding, *technical* anima, pneuma

psychiatrist *n*
analyst, psychoanalyst, therapist, psychotherapist, psychologist, psychoanalyser, *colloq.* headshrinker, shrink, trick cyclist, head doctor, person in a white coat

psychic *adj*
1 *psychic power* spiritual, supernatural, occult, mystic(al), clairvoyant, extrasensory, telepathic, telekinetic **2** MENTAL, psychological, intellectual, cognitive, spiritual

psychological *adj*
mental, intellectual, cognitive, emotional, subjective, subconscious, unconscious, psychosomatic, irrational, unreal, imaginary, *formal* cerebral
🆁 physical, real

psychology *n*
1 *study psychology* science of the mind, study of the mind, study of mental processes, science of human/animal behaviour **2** *the psychology of crowds* mind, mental characteristics, behavioural characteristics, mental chemistry, make-up, attitudes, habits, motives, mindset, *colloq.* what makes someone tick

psychopath *n*
lunatic, mad person, maniac, sociopath, psychotic, *colloq.* psycho

psychopathic *adj*
lunatic, mad, insane, maniacal, psychotic, deranged, unbalanced, mentally disturbed, demented

pub *n*
public house, inn, tavern, bar, saloon, taproom, lounge, lounge bar, grill, brasserie, counter, table, *colloq.* local, hostelry, watering-hole, *slang* boozer

puberty *n*
pubescence, adolescence, teens, teenage years, youth, young adulthood, growing up, maturity
🆁 childhood, immaturity, old age

public *adj, n*
▶ *adj* **1** *public buildings* state, government, national, nationalized, official, civil, community, social, civic, collective, communal, common, general, popular, universal, open, accessible, unrestricted **2** KNOWN, well-known, famous, important, influential, respected, eminent, illustrious, celebrated, popular, widespread, recognized, acknowledged, plain, overt, obvious, open, exposed, published
🆁 **1** private, privatized, personal **2** secret, exclusive
▷ **public house** bar, saloon, inn, tavern, taproom, lounge, lounge bar, grill, brasserie, counter, table, *colloq.* pub, local, hostelry, watering-hole, *slang* boozer
▶ *n* people, nation, country, population, populace, masses, citizens, society, everyone, community, voters, electorate, multitude, followers, supporters, fans, audience, spectators, patrons, clientèle, customers, buyers, consumers
▷ **in public** publicly, openly, in the open, in full view, for all to see
🆁 in secret

publican *n*
landlord, landlady, barman, barmaid, hotelier, hotelkeeper, innkeeper, taverner, mine host

publication *n*
1 *the publication of a book* publishing, production, printing, distribution, circulation, release, issue **2** BOOK, newspaper, magazine, journal, periodical, weekly, monthly, daily, quarterly, booklet, leaflet, pamphlet, brochure, handbill **3** ANNOUNCEMENT, declaration, notification, reporting, proclamation, disclosure

publicity *n*
advertising, promotion, marketing, puff, propaganda, build-up, boost, attention, limelight, splash, *colloq.* plug, hype

publicize *v*
advertise, promote, market, spotlight, broadcast, make known, announce, make public, bring to the public's attention, blaze, *formal* disseminate, promulgate, *colloq.* plug, hype, push

public-spirited *adj*
community-minded, humanitarian, philanthropic, altruistic, charitable, unselfish, generous, conscientious
🆁 selfish

publish *v*
1 *publish a book* produce, print, issue, bring out, release, distribute, circulate, spread, diffuse, *formal* disseminate, promulgate **2** ANNOUNCE, declare, communicate, report, notify, make known, make public, proclaim, import, divulge, disclose, reveal, release, publicize, advertise

pucker *v, n*
▶ *v* gather, ruffle, wrinkle, pleat, ruckle, ruck, shrivel, crinkle, crumple, crease, furrow, purse, screw up, contract, compress
▶ *n* crinkle, crumple, fold, crease, ruck, wrinkle, ruckle, shirr

puckered *adj*
creased, gathered, rucked, ruckled, wrinkled, pursy
🆁 smooth

puckish *adj*
impish, mischievous, naughty, playful, roguish, sly, waggish, whimsical, teasing, frolicsome, sportive
🆁 serious, solemn

pudding *n*
dessert, sweet, tart, pie, pastry, *colloq.* afters, pud

puddle *n*
pool, sop, plash, slop

puerile *adj*
childish, babyish, infantile, juvenile, immature, adolescent, irresponsible, silly, foolish, inane, trivial
🆁 mature

puff *n, v*
▶ *n* **1** BREATH, waft, whiff, draught, flurry, gust, blast **2** *a puff on a cigarette* pull, drag **3** ADVERTISEMENT, publicity, promotion, marketing, push, commendation, *colloq.* plug
▶ *v* **1** BREATHE, pant, gasp, gulp, wheeze, blow, waft, inflate, expand, swell **2** *puff a cigarette* smoke, pull, drag, draw, suck **3** ADVERTISE, praise, publicize, promote, market, push, commend, *colloq.* plug

puffed *adj*
out of breath, breathless, panting, winded, exhausted, gasping, *colloq.* done in
▷ **puffed up** arrogant, proud, swollen-headed, full of yourself, prideful, *colloq.* big-headed, high and mighty, too big for your boots
🆁 modest

puffy *adj*
puffed up, inflated, swollen, bloated, enlarged, *technical* oedematous, *formal* distended, dilated

pugilism *n*
boxing, fighting, prize-fighting, the noble art, the noble science, the ring, the prize-ring, *colloq.* the fancy, fistiana

pugilist *n*
boxer, fighter, prize-fighter, *colloq.* bruiser

pugnacious *adj*
hostile, aggressive, belligerent, contentious, antagonistic, argumentative, quarrelsome, bad-tempered, hot-tempered, *formal* disputatious, bellicose
Ea peaceable

puke *v*
vomit, spew, retch, regurgitate, disgorge, heave, *colloq.* throw up

pull *v, n*
▸ *v* **1** TOW, drag, haul, trail, heave, draw, tug, jerk, *colloq.* yank **2** REMOVE, take out, draw out, extract, root out, pull out, pluck, uproot, pull up, rip, tear, wrench **3** ATTRACT, draw, bring in, pull in, lure, allure, entice, tempt, magnetize **4** DISLOCATE, sprain, wrench, strain, damage, tear
Ea 1 push, press **3** repel, deter, discourage
▷ **pull apart 1** SEPARATE, part, dismember, dismantle, take to pieces, tear apart **2** CRITICIZE, take apart, attack, *colloq.* slate, slam, run down, pick holes in, pull to pieces, do a hatchet job on
Ea 1 join
▷ **pull back** draw back, withdraw, retreat, fall back, retire, disengage, back out
▷ **pull down** destroy, demolish, knock down, dismantle, bulldoze, raze to the ground
Ea build, erect, put up
▷ **pull in 1** STOP, arrive, draw in, pull up, park **2** ATTRACT, draw, bring in, lure, allure, entice **3** ARREST, capture, seize, apprehend, detain, take into custody, *colloq.* bust, nick, collar, nab, book, run in **4** EARN, receive, be paid, make, clear, take home, *colloq.* rake in
Ea 1 pull away **2** repel **3** lose
▷ **pull off 1** ACCOMPLISH, achieve, bring off, succeed, manage, carry off, carry out **2** DETACH, remove, separate, take off, tear off, rip off
Ea 1 fail **2** attach
▷ **pull out** retreat, withdraw, leave, depart, quit, move out, back out, evacuate, desert, abandon
Ea join, arrive
▷ **pull through** recover, come through, rally, recuperate, survive, weather
▷ **pull together** co-operate, work together, collaborate, team up
Ea fight
▷ **pull up 1** STOP, halt, come to a halt, park, draw up, pull in, pull over, brake **2** REPRIMAND, take to task, rebuke, scold, criticize, *colloq.* tell off, tick off, carpet
▷ **pull yourself together** control yourself, regain your self-control, get a grip on yourself
▸ *n* **1** TOW, drag, tug, haul, jerk, power, forcefulness, exertion, *colloq.* yank **2** ATTRACTION, lure, allurement, draw, drawing power, magnetism, influence, weight, *colloq.* clout, muscle

pulp *n, v*
▸ *n* flesh, marrow, paste, purée, mash, mush, pap, *formal* triturate
▸ *v* crush, squash, pulverize, mash, purée, liquidize, shred

pulpit *n*
platform, rostrum, lectern, dais, *colloq.* soapbox

pulpy *adj*
soft, sloppy, pappy, mushy, crushed, squashy, fleshy, succulent
Ea hard

pulsate *v*
pulse, beat, throb, pound, hammer, drum, thud, thump, vibrate, oscillate, quiver

pulsating *adj*
vibrating, oscillating, pulsing, palpitating, *formal* pulsatile, pulsative, pulsatory, vibrative, vibratile

pulsation *n*
vibration, oscillation, palpitation, vibratiuncle, *technical* ictus

pulse *n, v*
▸ *n* beat, stroke, rhythm, throb, pulsation, beating, throbbing, thud, thudding, thump, thumping, pounding, drumming, vibration, oscillation
▸ *v* beat, drum, pulsate, vibrate, pound, thud, throb, tick

pulverize *v*
1 CRUSH, pound, grind, mill, powder, crumble, pulp, squash, *formal* triturate **2** DEFEAT, destroy, demolish, annihilate, smash, *formal* vanquish, *colloq.* thrash, hammer, wipe the floor with

pummel *v*
hit, knock, hammer, beat, batter, pound, punch, strike, thump, bang

pump *v*
1 PUSH, drive, force, send, inject, siphon, draw, drain **2** CROSS-EXAMINE, cross-question, interrogate, quiz, *colloq.* grill, give someone the third degree
▷ **pump out** bail out, drain, draw off, empty, force out, siphon
▷ **pump up** blow up, inflate, puff up, fill

pun *n*
play on words, *double entendre*, witticism, quip, *technical* paronomasia

punch¹ *v, n*
▸ *v* hit, strike, pummel, jab, bash, knock, clout, cuff, box, slug, thump, thwack, *colloq.* sock, wallop, bop, biff
▸ *n* **1** BLOW, jab, bash, knock, hit, clout, thump, thwack, *colloq.* sock, wallop, bop, biff **2** FORCE, strength, power, impact, effectiveness, drive, vigour, forcefulness, verve, panache, *colloq.* bite, pizzazz

punch² *v*
punch a hole perforate, pierce, puncture, make a hole in, prick, bore, drill, hole, stamp, cut

punch-drunk *adj*
dazed, confused, befuddled, stupefied, unsteady, reeling, staggering, dizzy, groggy, woozy

punch-up *n*
stand-up fight, brawl, fight, row, free-for-all, argument, ruckus, *colloq.* scrap, set-to, ding-dong, dust-up, shindy

punchy *adj*
incisive, effective, forceful, aggressive, dynamic, lively, powerful, spirited, vigorous, *colloq.* zappy
Ea feeble, weak

punctilio *n*
1 SCRUPULOUSNESS, strictness, exactness, ceremony, finickiness, formality, convention, punctiliousness, precision, meticulousness, refinement, preciseness **2** FINE POINT, detail, nicety, particular, exactitude, delicacy, distinction, particularity
Ea 1 informality

punctilious *adj*
scrupulous, conscientious, meticulous, careful, painstaking, exact, precise, strict, formal, proper, particular, finicky, fussy, *colloq.* pernickety, choosy,

picky, nit-picking
F lax, informal

punctual *adj*
prompt, on time, exact, precise, well-timed, early, in good time, *colloq.* on the dot, dead on time, bang on time, on cue
F unpunctual, late

punctuality *n*
promptness, promptitude, regularity, readiness, strictness
F unpunctuality

punctually *adv*
on time, prompt, promptly, precisely, exactly, sharp, to the minute, on the dot, *colloq.* dead on, bang on, spot on
F unpunctually

punctuate *v*
interrupt, sprinkle, break, intersperse, pepper, emphasize, point, accentuate, *formal* interject

punctuation *n*

Punctuation marks include:
apostrophe, asterisk, backslash, brackets, colon, comma, dash, exclamation mark, full stop, hyphen, inverted commas, oblique stroke, parentheses, period, question mark, quotation marks, *colloq.* quotes, semicolon, solidus, speech marks, square brackets, star.

puncture *n, v*
▶ *n* **1** FLAT TYRE, blow-out, *colloq.* flat **2** LEAK, hole, holing, piercing, perforation, cut, rupture, prick, nick, slit
▶ *v* **1** PRICK, pierce, penetrate, perforate, hole, bore, spike, cut, nick, burst, rupture **2** DEFLATE, flatten, let down, humiliate, *colloq.* put down

pundit *n*
authority, expert, master, teacher, maestro, guru, sage, savant, *colloq.* buff

pungent *adj*
1 *a pungent taste/smell* strong, powerful, hot, peppery, fiery, spicy, aromatic, tangy, tart, piquant, sharp, keen, acute, sour, bitter, acid, acrid, caustic, stinging, burning, biting **2** *pungent comments* cutting, incisive, pointed, piercing, penetrating, sarcastic, scathing, caustic, stinging, burning, biting
F **1** mild, bland, tasteless **2** mild, bland

punish *v*
1 PENALIZE, discipline, correct, scold, beat, make someone pay, smack, slap, flog, whip, scourge, lash, cane, spank, knee-cap, crucify, hang, fine, imprison, *formal* chastise, castigate, *colloq.* teach someone a lesson, make an example of, bring to book, throw the book at, give someone hell **2** BEAT, defeat, trounce, batter, *colloq.* hammer, thrash, rough up **3** MISUSE, maltreat, harm, damage, abuse
F **1** reward

punishable *adj*
criminal, convictable, chargeable, unlawful, blameworthy, *formal* culpable, indictable

punishing *adj*
arduous, strenuous, crippling, crushing, burdensome, taxing, grinding, demanding, hard, harsh, severe, cruel, gruelling, fatiguing, tiring, wearying, exhausting, backbreaking
F easy

punishment *n*
discipline, correction, chastisement, penalty, sentence, deserts, retribution, revenge, *colloq.* short sharp shock
F reward

Forms of punishment include:
banishment, beating, belting, the birch, borstal, the cane, capital punishment, cashiering, chain gang, confinement, confiscation, corporal punishment, defrocking, demotion, deportation, detention, dressing-down, excommunication, execution, exile, expulsion, fine, flaying, flogging, gaol, gating, grounding, *colloq.* hiding, hitting, horsewhipping, house arrest, imprisonment, incarceration, internment, jail, jankers, keelhauling, *colloq.* larruping, lashing, leathering, lines, penal colony, prison, probation, *colloq.* being put away, the rack, rap across the knuckles, scourging, *colloq.* being sent down, being sent to Coventry, sequestration, slapping, the slipper, smacking, spanking, the stocks, suspension, *colloq.* tanning someone's hide, tarring and feathering, thrashing, torturing, transportation, unfrocking, walking the plank, walloping, whipping. *See also* EXECUTION.

punitive *adj*
1 PENAL, disciplinary, retributive, retaliatory, vindictive, *formal* chastising, castigatory **2** CRIPPLING, crushing, burdensome, demanding, hard, harsh, severe, cruel, gruelling, punishing, corrective

punter *n*
1 GAMBLER, better, backer, wagerer **2** CUSTOMER, client, consumer, person, individual, fellow, chap, *colloq.* guy, bloke

puny *adj*
weak, feeble, frail, sickly, undeveloped, underdeveloped, stunted, small, undersized, diminutive, little, tiny, insignificant, minor, inconsequential, trifling, petty, trivial, *colloq.* measly, piddling
F strong, sturdy, large, important

pupil *n*
student, scholar, schoolboy, schoolgirl, learner, apprentice, beginner, novice, disciple, protégé(e)
F teacher

puppet *n*
1 MARIONETTE, finger puppet, glove puppet, doll **2** *a mere puppet of a government* tool, instrument, dupe, cat's-paw, pawn, quisling, stooge, gull, figurehead, mouthpiece, creature

purchase *v, n*
▶ *v* buy, pay for, invest in, acquire, obtain, get, pick up, shop for, go shopping, secure, gain, earn, win, *formal* procure, *colloq.* snap up, splash out on
F sell
▶ *n* **1** ACQUISITION, gain, buy, bargain, deal, investment, asset(s), possession(s), property, goods, holdings, *formal* emption **2** GRASP, foothold, grip, hold, advantage, leverage
F **1** sale

purchaser *n*
buyer, consumer, shopper, customer, client, hirer, *formal* vendee, emptor
F seller, vendor

pure *adj*
1 *pure gold* unadulterated, unalloyed, unmixed, undiluted, 100%, flawless, perfect, neat, straight, solid, simple, natural, real, authentic, genuine, true **2** STERILE, uncontaminated, unpolluted, uninfected, germ-free, aseptic, antiseptic, disinfected, sterilized, hygienic, sanitary, clean, immaculate, spotless, clear, fresh, natural **3** SHEER, utter, complete, total, thorough, absolute, perfect, unqualified, unmitigated, downright **4** CHASTE, virgin, virginal, virtuous, unde-

filed, unsullied, moral, unblemished, upright, virtuous, honourable, honest, good, righteous, decent, noble, worthy, blameless, innocent **5** *pure mathematics* theoretical, abstract, conjectural, speculative, academic

F∃ **1** impure, adulterated **2** contaminated, polluted **4** immoral, corrupt, defiled **5** applied

pure-bred *adj*
pedigree, pedigreed, pure-blood, pure-blooded, thoroughbred, full-blooded, blooded

F∃ cross-bred, hybrid, mixed, mongrel

purely *adv*
1 UTTERLY, completely, totally, entirely, wholly, thoroughly, absolutely **2** ONLY, simply, merely, just, solely, exclusively

purgative *n, adj*
▶ *n* laxative, enema, evacuant, purge, *technical* emetic, aperient, cathartic, eccoprotic, *formal* depurative
▶ *adj* cleansing, laxative, purging, evacuant, *technical* aperient, cathartic, cathartical, eccoprotic, *formal* abstersive, depurative

purge *v, n*
▶ *v* **1** PURIFY, cleanse, clean out, scour, clear, absolve **2** OUST, remove, get rid of, rid, eject, expel, depose, root out, clear (out), dismiss, eradicate, exterminate, wipe out, kill
▶ *n* removal, ejection, expulsion, witch hunt, eradication, rooting-out, extermination, cleansing, disposal, ousting

purification *n*
1 DECONTAMINATION, refinement, cleaning, cleansing, disinfection, filtration, sanitization, fumigation, deodorization, desalination, *formal* depuration, epuration **2** SANCTIFICATION, redemption, absolution, purge, cleansing, *formal* lustration, purgation

F∃ **1** contamination, defilement, pollution

purify *v*
1 DECONTAMINATE, refine, filter, distil, clarify, clean, cleanse, sanitize, freshen, disinfect, sterilize, fumigate, deodorize, filtrate, *formal* depurate, lustrate **2** SANCTIFY, redeem, absolve, purge, cleanse, shrive, *formal* lustrate

F∃ **1** contaminate, pollute, defile

purifying *adj*
cleansing, purificatory, refining, purging, purgative, *technical* cathartic, *formal* depurative, lustral, mundificative

F∃ contaminating, defiling, polluting

purism *n*
fastidiousness, formalism, fussiness, over-precision, pedantry, restraint, strictness, orthodoxy, austerity, classicism, Atticism

F∃ liberality, open-mindedness, tolerance

purist *n, adj*
▶ *n* pedant, literalist, formalist, precisionist, dogmatist, stickler, quibbler, *colloq.* nit-picker
▶ *adj* fastidious, over-exact, over-fastidious, overmeticulous, over-particular, over-precise, pedantic, quibbling, uncompromising, strict, captious, finicky, fussy, hypercritical, puristic, *colloq.* nit-picking

F∃ liberal, open-minded, tolerant

puritan *n*
pietist, rigorist, disciplinarian, zealot, fanatic, moralist, killjoy, spoilsport, prude

F∃ hedonist, libertarian

puritanical *adj*
puritan, moralistic, disciplinarian, ascetic, abstemious, austere, severe, stern, strict, strait-laced, prim, proper, prudish, disapproving, stuffy, stiff, rigid, nar-row-minded, bigoted, fanatical, zealous

F∃ hedonistic, liberal, indulgent, broad-minded

puritanism *n*
rigorousness, self-discipline, self-denial, strictness, uncompromisingness, austerity, propriety, sternness, severity, stiffness, rigidity, zealotry, fanaticism, bigotry, narrow-mindedness, narrowness, priggishness, primness, prudishness, abstemiousness, abstinence, asceticism

F∃ broad-mindedness, hedonism, indulgence, liberality

purity *n*
1 CLEARNESS, clarity, cleanness, cleanliness, freshness, untaintedness, flawlessness, wholesomeness **2** SIMPLICITY, authenticity, genuineness, truth, perfection **3** CHASTITY, virginity, decency, morality, integrity, rectitude, uprightness, goodness, virtue, virtuousness, honour, honesty, decency, nobility, worthiness, innocence, blamelessness

F∃ **1** impurity, pollution, contamination **3** immorality

purlieus *n*
neighbourhood, surroundings, vicinity, suburbs, environs, precincts, periphery, borders, bounds, confines, limits, fringes, perimeter, outskirts

purloin *v*
steal, rob, remove, take, pilfer, *formal* appropriate, *colloq.* swipe, nick, pinch, filch, finger, lift, nobble, pocket, snaffle, snitch, thieve

purport *v, n*
▶ *v* claim, allege, profess, seem, pose as, pretend, imply, proclaim, show, mean, intend, indicate, denote, signify, suggest, express, convey, declare, assert, maintain, *formal* import, portend, betoken
▶ *n* meaning, significance, point, gist, drift, idea, spirit, substance, theme, tendency, tenor, thrust, bearing, direction, implication, *formal* import

purpose *n, v*
▶ *n* **1** INTENTION, aim, objective, end, goal, target, plan, design, vision, idea, ambition, hope, wish, desire, aspiration, point, object, reason, motive, motivation, rationale, justification, principle, result, outcome, basis **2** DETERMINATION, resolve, resolution, drive, single-mindedness, firmness, dedication, devotion, constancy, steadfastness, perseverance, persistence, doggedness, tenacity, zeal **3** USE, function, application, good, advantage, benefit, gain, effect, value, usefulness

▷ **on purpose** purposely, deliberately, intentionally, consciously, knowingly, wittingly, wilfully, by design, premeditatedly

F∃ accidentally, impulsively, spontaneously
▶ *v* intend, mean, plan, propose, resolve, decide, determine, settle, design, aspire, aim, desire, contemplate, meditate

purposeful *adj*
determined, decided, resolved, resolute, singleminded, constant, steadfast, persistent, persevering, unwavering, unfaltering, tenacious, dogged, strongwilled, positive, firm, deliberate

F∃ purposeless, aimless

purposefully *adv*
resolutely, steadfastly, single-mindedly, persistently, perseveringly, unwaveringly, unfalteringly, tenaciously

---

✍ purposefully or purposely ?

Purposefully means 'obviously, or apparently, having some purpose': *She stole purposefully towards him, clearly intent on settling things once and for all.*
Purposely means 'intentionally, on purpose': *She didn't want to go to college so she purposely failed her exams.*

purposeless *adj*
pointless, senseless, aimless, objectless, empty, goalless, thoughtless, gratuitous, unasked-for, uncalled-for, unnecessary, useless, needless, motiveless, nonsensical, vain, wanton, vacuous
F3 purposeful

purposely *adv*
on purpose, intentionally, deliberately, consciously, calculatedly, by design, specifically, wilfully, knowingly, premeditatedly, designedly, expressly, with malice aforethought
F3 unintentionally, by accident, impulsively, spontaneously

 purposely or **purposefully** ? *See panel at* PURPOSEFULLY.

purse *n, v*
▶ *n* **1** MONEY-BAG, wallet, pouch **2** MONEY, means, resources, finances, funds, coffers, treasury, exchequer **3** REWARD, award, prize, present, gift
▶ *v* pucker, wrinkle, draw together, close, tighten, contract, compress

pursuance *n*
discharge, pursuit, pursuing, performance, fulfilment, following, accomplishment, achievement, completion, *formal* effecting, effectuation, execution, prosecution

pursue *v*
1 CHASE, go after, run after, follow, track, stalk, trail, shadow, tail, dog, harass, harry, hound, hunt, seek, search for, investigate, inquire into **2** *pursue an activity* perform, engage in, practise, conduct, follow, carry on, continue, keep on, keep up, maintain, persevere in, persist in, apply yourself to, hold to **3** STRIVE FOR, aspire to, aim for, seek, search for, try for, work towards, have your goal

pursuit *n*
1 CHASE, hue and cry, tracking, pursuing, stalking, trail, tailing, shadowing, hunt **2** SEARCH, quest, aim, aspiration, goal, investigation, following, continuance, persistence, perseverance **3** ACTIVITY, interest, hobby, pastime, occupation, trade, craft, line, speciality, vocation

purvey *v*
1 SUPPLY, cater, deal in, provide, furnish, stock, sell, retail, trade in, *formal* provision, victual **2** TRANSMIT, spread, communicate, publicize, publish, put about, pass on, *formal* propagate, disseminate

purveyor *n*
1 SUPPLIER, stockist, trader, dealer, provider, provisor, retailer, *formal* victualler **2** TRANSMITTER, communicator, *formal* disseminator, propagator

push *v, n*
▶ *v* **1** PROPEL, thrust, ram, shove, jostle, hustle, manhandle, butt, jolt, elbow, prod, nudge, poke, press, depress, squeeze, plunge, squash, cram, drive, force, constrain **2** PRESS (FOR), encourage, urge, incite, impel, spur, prod, goad, force, influence, persuade, press, pressurize, coerce, bully, *colloq.* egg on, twist someone's arm, put the screws on **3** PROMOTE, advertise, market, publicize, boost, *colloq.* hype, plug
F3 **1** pull **2** discourage, dissuade
▷ **push around** bully, torment, terrorize, intimidate, victimize, pick on
▷ **push off** go away, depart, leave, move, *colloq.* push along, shove off, beat it, buzz off, clear off/out, make a move, make tracks
▶ *n* **1** KNOCK, shove, nudge, jolt, prod, poke, thrust, ram, jostle, butt **2** OFFENSIVE, assault, advance, charge, invasion, incursion, raid, foray **3** ENERGY,

vigour, vitality, drive, effort, force, forcefulness, dynamism, enterprise, initiative, ambition, determination, *colloq.* go, get-up-and-go

pushed *adj*
short of, stretched, under pressure, harassed, rushed, hard-pressed, hard-up, hurried, in difficulties, strapped, pinched, pressed, harried

pushover *n*
1 *he's a pushover* sucker, dupe, mug, stooge, gull, *colloq.* fall guy, sitting duck, sitting target, soft touch **2** *the job's a pushover, colloq.* child's play, cinch, doddle, picnic, piece of cake, walkover
F3 **2** challenge, labour

pushy *adj*
assertive, self-assertive, ambitious, forceful, aggressive, over-confident, forward, bold, brash, arrogant, presumptuous, impertinent, assuming, *colloq.* bossy
F3 unassertive, unassuming

pusillanimity *n*
cowardliness, faint-heartedness, fearfulness, feebleness, timidity, timorousness, weakness, spinelessness, cravenness, *formal* poltroonery, *colloq.* gutlessness

pusillanimous *adj*
cowardly, faint-hearted, craven, fearful, timorous, scared, weak, weak-kneed, chicken-hearted, spineless, lily-livered, feeble, timid, *colloq.* chicken, gutless, yellow, wimpish
F3 brave, courageous, strong

pussyfoot *v*
1 PREVARICATE, equivocate, hedge, *formal* tergiversate, *colloq.* mess about, beat about the bush **2** CREEP, slink, tiptoe, prowl, pad, steal

pustule *n*
boil, pimple, abscess, carbuncle, eruption, fester, ulcer, pock, whitlow, blister, papule

put *v*
1 PLACE, lay (down), deposit, set (down), fix, settle, rest, establish, stand, position, dispose, situate, locate, station, post, *colloq.* plonk, dump **2** ARRANGE, place, class, sort, classify, categorize, group, rank, grade **3** APPLY, impose, inflict, levy, assign, subject, exact, demand, require **4** *put the blame on someone* place, attribute, attach, fix, ascribe, assign, lay, pin, charge, impute **5** EXPRESS, word, phrase, formulate, frame, couch, say, speak, voice, pronounce, utter, state **6** *put a suggestion* submit, present, offer, suggest, propose, tender, set/lay before, set forth, bring forward, *formal* proffer **7** *put money/energy into a project* invest, spend, sink, devote, dedicate, give, contribute **8** TRANSLATE, transcribe, turn, render, convert **9** *put money on a horse* bet, gamble, place, lay, risk, chance
▷ **put about** tell, spread, make known, circulate, announce, *formal* disseminate
▷ **put across** put over, get across/over, communicate, convey, express, explain, clarify, make clear, make understood, spell out, bring home to, get through to
▷ **put aside** put by, set aside, lay aside/by, keep, retain, save, reserve, keep in reserve, store, stow, stockpile, hoard, salt away, put to one side, *colloq.* stash
▷ **put away 1** CONSUME, devour, eat (up), drink, swallow, down, *colloq.* wolf, tuck in, guzzle, scoff, polish off **2** IMPRISON, jail, lock up, confine, commit, certify, *colloq.* bang up, send down **3** SAVE, put aside/by, set aside, lay aside/by, keep, retain, reserve, keep in reserve, store, stow, stockpile
▷ **put back 1** DELAY, defer, postpone, reschedule, adjourn, suspend, shelve, freeze, *formal* procrastinate, *colloq.* put on ice **2** REPLACE, return, restore, reinstate, return to its place, clear away/up, tidy away/up
F3 **1** bring forward

▷ **put down 1** WRITE DOWN, note down, jot down, transcribe, enter, log, register, list, record **2** CRUSH, quash, suppress, defeat, quell, stop, stamp out, silence **3** *put down a sick dog* kill, destroy, put to sleep, put out of its misery **4** ASCRIBE, attribute, blame, charge, set down, fix, attach, lay **5** HUMILIATE, snub, slight, squash, deflate, humble, crush, shame, mortify, *formal* disparage, deprecate, *colloq.* take down a peg
▷ **put forward** advance, suggest, recommend, nominate, propose, move, table, introduce, present, submit, offer, tender, *formal* proffer
▷ **put in** insert, enter, input, submit, install, fit
▷ **put off 1** DELAY, defer, postpone, reschedule, adjourn, suspend, shelve, *formal* procrastinate, *colloq.* put on ice, put on the back burner **2** DETER, dissuade, talk out of, discourage, dishearten, demoralize, daunt, dismay, intimidate, disconcert, confuse, distract, sicken, nauseate **3** DISTRACT, divert, sidetrack, deflect, turn away/aside
🖅 **2** encourage
▷ **put on 1** *put on new clothes* get dressed in, dress in, change into, get into, slip into, wear, don, try on, *colloq.* throw on, get dolled up in **2** ATTACH, affix, apply, place, add, impose **3** PRETEND, feign, sham, fake, simulate, affect, assume **4** STAGE, mount, produce, present, do, perform
🖅 **1** take off
▷ **put out 1** PUBLISH, announce, broadcast, circulate, issue, disclose, make known, bring out **2** EXTINGUISH, quench, douse, smother, stamp out **3** INCONVENIENCE, cause inconvenience to, impose on, bother, disturb, trouble, disconcert, upset, hurt, offend, annoy, irritate, irk, anger, exasperate, provoke, infuriate, unsettle, *formal* perturb, discommode, *colloq.* faze
🖅 **2** light
▷ **put through** accomplish, achieve, complete, conclude, finalize, execute, manage, bring off
▷ **put together** assemble, join, build, construct, fit/piece together
🖅 take apart
▷ **put up 1** ERECT, build, construct, assemble, raise **2** ACCOMMODATE, house, lodge, shelter, give a room to, provide with board and lodging **3** *put up prices* raise, increase, escalate, *colloq.* jack up, hike up, bump up **4** PAY, invest, give, advance, float, provide, supply, pledge, offer **5** *put up a candidate* nominate, put forward, propose, suggest, recommend, choose
🖅 **1** take down, pull down **3** bring down
▷ **put upon** impose on, exploit, take advantage of, take for granted, take liberties, inconvenience
▷ **put up to** prompt, incite, encourage, urge, persuade, goad, *colloq.* egg on
🖅 discourage, dissuade
▷ **put up with** stand, bear, abide, stomach, endure, suffer, tolerate, allow, accept, stand for, take, brook, *colloq.* swallow, take lying down
🖅 object to, reject

putative *adj*
supposed, assumed, presumed, alleged, reported, reputed, hypothetical, theoretical, suppositional, reputative, *formal* conjectural, supposititious

put-down *n*
affront, humiliation, insult, slight, sneer, snub, rebuff, sarcasm, gibe, *formal* disparagement, *colloq.* slap in the face, dig

put-off *n*
deterrent, discouragement, disincentive, hindrance, constraint, curb, damper, obstacle, restraint
🖅 encouragement, incentive

putrefy *v*
rot, perish, go bad, decay, corrupt, mould, spoil, stink, taint, gangrene, decompose, deteriorate, fester, addle

putrescent *adj*
rotting, perishing, decaying, decomposing, putrefying, stinking, festering, *formal* mephitic

putrid *adj*
rotten, decayed, decomposed, mouldy, off, bad, rancid, addled, corrupt, contaminated, tainted, polluted, foul, rank, fetid, stinking
🖅 fresh, wholesome

put-upon *adj*
imposed on, taken advantage of, exploited, used, inconvenienced, abused, maltreated, persecuted

puzzle *v, n*
▶ *v* **1** BAFFLE, mystify, perplex, confound, confuse, stagger, bewilder, *colloq.* stump, floor, flummox, beat, nonplus **2** THINK, ponder, meditate, consider, brood, mull over, muse over, deliberate, figure, rack your brains
▷ **puzzle out** solve, work out, figure out, think out, decipher, decode, unravel, untangle, find the answer to, piece together, sort out, resolve, clear up, *colloq.* crack, get, suss (out)
▶ *n* question, poser, brain-teaser, mind-bender, crossword, rebus, anagram, acrostic, riddle, conundrum, mystery, enigma, dilemma, paradox

puzzled *adj*
baffled, mystified, perplexed, confounded, at a loss, beaten, confused, bewildered, lost, in a haze, *colloq.* stumped, nonplussed, at sea, flummoxed, floored
🖅 clear

puzzlement *n*
bafflement, perplexity, bewilderment, confusion, disorientation, astonishment, mystification, surprise, wonder, uncertainty, doubt, doubtfulness, *formal* incertitude, *colloq.* bamboozlement
🖅 certainty, clarity, lucidity

puzzling *adj*
baffling, bewildering, confusing, perplexing, unclear, queer, peculiar, strange, bizarre, mystifying, mysterious, mystical, misleading, unaccountable, unfathomable, impenetrable, inexplicable, intricate, involved, ambiguous, equivocal, mind-bending, mind-boggling, curious, enigmatic, cryptic, tortuous, knotty, Sphynx-like, *formal* abstruse, labyrinthine

pygmy *n, adj*
▶ *n* person of restricted growth, dwarf, midget, Tom Thumb, Lilliputian, manikin, thumbling, fingerling, *formal* homunculus
🖅 giant
▶ *adj* miniature, small, tiny, baby, diminutive, halfpint, undersized, minuscule, minute, pocket, elfin, stunted, dwarf, midget, dwarfish, toy, Lilliputian, *Scot.* wee, *colloq.* pint-size
🖅 gigantic

pyromaniac *n*
arsonist, incendiary, fire-raiser, *colloq.* firebug

Q

quack *n, adj*
▶ *n* charlatan, impostor, fraud, mountebank, pretender, masquerader, humbug, sham, fake, cowboy, swindler, trickster, *old use* quacksalver, *colloq.* phoney, pseud
▶ *adj* false, bogus, counterfeit, fake, pretended, fraudulent, spurious, supposed, sham, so-called, unqualified, *colloq.* phoney
✇ genuine, real

quackery *n*
charlatanism, mountebankery, mountebankism, fraud, fraudulence, sham, imposture, *colloq.* humbug, phoniness

quaff *v*
down, drink, gulp, knock back, swallow, swig, toss off, swill, carouse, drain, *formal* imbibe, *colloq.* booze, guzzle, tipple

quagmire *n*
1 BOG, marsh, quag, fen, swamp, morass, mire, slough, quicksand **2** MESS, problem, dilemma, quandary, perplexity, *colloq.* fix, hole, pickle, tight spot, hot/deep water

quail *v*
recoil, back away, shy away, shrink, flinch, pull back, draw back, cringe, cower, tremble, quake, shake, shiver, blench, shudder, falter

quaint *adj*
picturesque, charming, attractive, sweet, old-fashioned, antiquated, old-world, unusual, strange, odd, curious, droll, bizarre, fanciful, whimsical, *colloq.* twee, olde-worlde
✇ modern

quake *v*
shake, tremble, shudder, quiver, shiver, quail, vibrate, throb, pulsate, wobble, rock, sway, move, convulse, heave

qualification *n*
1 CERTIFICATE, diploma, degree, training, certification, skill, competence, proficiency, ability, capability, capacity, aptitude, suitability, fitness, accomplishment, eligibility **2** RESTRICTION, limitation, reservation, exception, allowance, exemption, condition, caveat, rider, provision, proviso, stipulation, modification, adjustment, adaptation

qualified *adj*
1 CERTIFIED, chartered, licensed, professional, trained, experienced, practised, skilled, accomplished, expert, knowledgeable, skilful, talented, proficient, competent, efficient, able, capable, adept, fit, fitted, equipped, prepared, eligible **2** *qualified praise* reserved, guarded, cautious, restricted, limited, bounded, modified, conditional, provisional, equivocal, *formal* contingent, circumscribed
✇ 1 unqualified **2** unconditional, whole-hearted

qualify *v*
1 TRAIN, prepare, make ready, teach, instruct, equip, fit, coach, ground, pass, graduate, certify, empower,

entitle, authorize, license, sanction, permit, allow, warrant **2** MODERATE, reduce, lessen, diminish, temper, soften, weaken, ease, adjust, modify, restrain, restrict, limit, delimit, make conditional, define, classify, *formal* mitigate, alleviate
✇ 1 disqualify

quality *n*
1 *of poor quality* standard, grade, class, kind, sort, type, make, variety, calibre, status, rank, level, value, worth, merit, condition **2** EXCELLENCE, superiority, eminence, pre-eminence, distinction, merit, value, worth, refinement **3** CHARACTERISTIC, property, peculiarity, attribute, aspect, feature, trait, mark, nature, character, make-up

qualm *n*
misgiving, apprehension, fear, anxiety, worry, apprehension, concern, disquiet, uneasiness, scruple, hesitation, hesitancy, disinclination, reluctance, uncertainty, doubt, *formal* compunction

quandary *n*
dilemma, predicament, impasse, perplexity, confusion, bewilderment, muddle, mess, problem, difficulty, *colloq.* fix, hole, pickle, jam, tight spot

quantity *n*
1 AMOUNT, number, sum, total, aggregate, mass, lot, share, portion, quota, allotment, measure, dose, proportion, part, content, capacity, volume, weight, bulk, size, magnitude, expanse, extent, area, length, breadth **2** *quantities of food* much, many, lots, masses, *colloq.* loads, heaps, stacks

quarantine *n*
detention, isolation, segregation, lazaret, lazaretto

quarrel *n, v*
▶ *n* row, argument, wrangle, squabble, tiff, misunderstanding, disagreement, dispute, dissension, controversy, difference, difference of opinion, conflict, clash, contention, strife, fight, brawl, fracas, feud, vendetta, schism, *formal* altercation, disputation, *colloq.* slanging match, scrap, set-to, dust-up, punch-up
✇ agreement, harmony
▶ *v* **1** ROW, argue, bicker, squabble, wrangle, be at loggerheads, fall out, disagree, dispute, dissent, differ, be at variance, clash, contend, fight, scrap, feud **2** FIND FAULT WITH, fault, criticize, dispute, censure, *colloq.* pick holes in, knock, slate, slam, pull to pieces
✇ agree

quarrelling *n, adj*
▶ *n* bickering, contention, dissension, feuding, rowing, variance, strife, wrangling, disharmony, argumentation, *formal* altercation, discord, disputation, vitilitigation, *colloq.* argy-bargying
✇ concord, harmony
▶ *adj* bickering, contending, fighting, squabbling, wrangling, warring, feuding, rowing, at odds, at variance, at loggerheads, *formal* discordant, dis-

sentient, *colloq.* scrapping
🖃 amicable, friendly

quarrelsome *adj*
argumentative, disputatious, contentious, irascible, belligerent, ill-tempered, hot-tempered, irritable, ready for a fight, *formal* bellicose, pugnacious, choleric, litigious
🖃 peaceable, placid

quarry *n*
prey, victim, object, goal, target, game, kill, prize

quarter *n, v*
▶ *n* **1** DISTRICT, sector, zone, neighbourhood, accommodation, lodgings, billet, rooms, barracks, residence, station, locality, vicinity, area, region, province, territory, division, section, part, place, spot, point, direction, side, *colloq.* digs **2** MERCY, leniency, favour, pardon, pity, compassion, grace, indulgence, forgiveness, clemency **3** *living quarters* accommodation, lodgings, billet, residence, rooms, barracks, station, post, *formal* dwelling, habitation, domicile, *colloq.* digs, pad
▶ *v* station, post, billet, accommodate, put up, lodge, board, house, shelter

quash *v*
1 ANNUL, revoke, rescind, cancel, void, invalidate, reverse, set aside, overturn, overrule, override, *formal* nullify, abrogate, countermand **2** CRUSH, squash, quell, suppress, subdue, defeat, overthrow
🖃 **1** confirm, vindicate, reinstate

quaver *v, n*
▶ *v* shake, tremble, quake, waver, shudder, quiver, vibrate, pulsate, oscillate, flutter, flicker, trill, warble
▶ *n* tremble, trembling, tremor, trill, break, quiver, shake, throb, sob, quaveriness, vibration, vibrato, warble, tremolo

quay *n*
wharf, pier, jetty, dock, harbour, berth, landing, slipway, marina, waterfront, seafront

queasy *adj*
sick, ill, unwell, queer, groggy, green, nauseated, sickened, bilious, squeamish, faint, dizzy, giddy, *colloq.* rough, under the weather, out of sorts

queen *n*
1 MONARCH, sovereign, ruler, majesty, princess, empress, consort **2** BEAUTY, belle, idol, charm, Venus

queenly *adj*
sovereign, majestic, regal, royal, imperial, imperious, noble, stately, splendid, dignified, gracious, grand, *formal* august, monarchical, sublime
🖃 undignified

queer *adj, v*
▶ *adj* **1** ODD, mysterious, strange, unusual, uncommon, weird, unnatural, extraordinary, bizarre, eccentric, outlandish, peculiar, funny, puzzling, curious, unconventional, unorthodox, abnormal, deviant, remarkable, *formal* singular **2** *I feel queer* unwell, ill, sick, queasy, light-headed, faint, giddy, dizzy, *colloq.* rough, under the weather, out of sorts **3** SUSPECT, suspicious, shifty, dubious, doubtful, irregular, peculiar, strange, *colloq.* shady, fishy, iffy
🖃 **1** ordinary, usual, common **2** well
▶ *v* spoil, harm, ruin, upset, wreck, mar, botch, thwart, impair, foil, frustrate, endanger, jeopardize, stymie

queerness *n*
oddity, peculiarity, strangeness, unusualness, uncommonness, unconventionality, unnaturalness, bizarreness, anomalousness, curiousness, abnormality, irregularity, eccentricity, unorthodoxy, *formal* singularity

quell *v*
subdue, quash, crush, squash, suppress, rout, put down, overcome, conquer, defeat, overpower, moderate, allay, soothe, calm, pacify, appease, hush, quiet, silence, stifle, extinguish, *formal* mitigate, alleviate, vanquish

quench *v*
1 *quench one's thirst* slake, satisfy, sate, cool, *formal* satiate **2** EXTINGUISH, stifle, smother, douse, put out, snuff out, stamp out

querulous *adj*
peevish, fretful, fractious, cross, irritable, complaining, grumbling, sour, testy, discontented, dissatisfied, critical, carping, captious, fault-finding, fussy, irascible, *formal* cantankerous, petulant, *colloq.* grouchy, shirty, ratty
🖃 placid, uncomplaining, contented

query *v, n*
▶ *v* ask, inquire, question, challenge, dispute, quarrel with, doubt, throw doubts on, suspect, be sceptical of, have suspicions about, distrust, mistrust, disbelieve
🖃 accept
▶ *n* question, inquiry, problem, uncertainty, doubt, suspicion, scepticism, reservation, hesitation, uneasiness, qualm(s), quibble

quest *n*
search, seeking, hunt, pursuit, investigation, inquiry, purpose, aim, goal, mission, crusade, enterprise, undertaking, venture, journey, voyage, expedition, exploration, pilgrimage, adventure

question *v, n*
▶ *v* **1** INTERROGATE, quiz, grill, pump, interview, examine, cross-examine, cross-question, debrief, ask, inquire, investigate, probe, catechize, *colloq.* give the third degree to **2** QUERY, challenge, dispute, have doubts about, have reservations/qualms about, doubt, disbelieve
▶ *n* **1** QUERY, inquiry, poser, problem, difficulty **2** ISSUE, matter, problem, subject, theme, topic, point, point at issue, proposal, proposition, motion, debate, dispute, controversy **3** DOUBT, query, debate, dispute, argument, controversy, uncertainty
▷ **out of the question** impossible, unthinkable, unbelievable, absurd, ridiculous, unacceptable, not worth considering, *colloq.* not by any stretch of the imagination
▷ **without question** without arguing, immediately, unhesitatingly, unquestionably, without a shadow of doubt

questionable *adj*
debatable, disputable, unsettled, undetermined, unproven, uncertain, arguable, controversial, vexed, doubtful, dubious, suspicious, suspect, *colloq.* shady, fishy, iffy
🖃 unquestionable, indisputable, certain

questioner *n*
interviewer, examiner, inquirer, inquisitor, interrogator, investigator, catechizer, catechist, disbeliever, doubter, sceptic, agnostic, *formal* interlocutor

questionnaire *n*
quiz, test, form, survey, opinion poll, market research

queue *n*
line, tailback, file, row, column, crocodile, procession, train, string, chain, succession, series, sequence, order, *formal* concatenation

quibble *v, n*
▶ *v* carp, cavil, split hairs, equivocate, avoid the issue, prevaricate, *colloq.* nit-pick
▶ *n* complaint, objection, criticism, query, protest, cavil, niggle, equivocation, prevarication, *colloq.* nit-picking

quibbler *n*
caviller, niggler, sophist, equivocator, casuist, *colloq.* hair-splitter, nit-picker

quibbling *adj*
niggling, critical, overnice, carping, captious, ambiguous, cavilling, evasive, casuistic, equivocating, logic-chopping, *colloq.* hair-splitting, nit-picking

quick *adj*
1 FAST, swift, rapid, speedy, nippy, express, hurried, hasty, cursory, fleeting, brief, perfunctory, prompt, ready, immediate, without delay, instant, instantaneous, sudden, brisk, nimble, sprightly, agile, *formal* expeditious **2** CLEVER, intelligent, quick-witted, smart, sharp, sharp-witted, keen, shrewd, astute, discerning, perceptive, responsive, alive, receptive
F₃ 1 slow, sluggish, lethargic **2** unintelligent, dull

quicken *v*
1 ACCELERATE, speed (up), hurry (up), hasten, dispatch, advance, *formal* precipitate, expedite **2** ANIMATE, enliven, invigorate, energize, galvanize, activate, incite, instigate, rouse, arouse, stimulate, stir (up), excite, kindle, inspire, whet, revive, refresh, reinvigorate, strengthen, revitalize, reactivate, *formal* revivify
F₃ 1 slow, retard **2** dull

quickly *adv*
rapidly, quick, fast, speedily, swiftly, express, briskly, apace, hurriedly, hastily, immediately, instantaneously, readily, soon, abruptly, instantly, promptly, unhesitatingly, cursorily, posthaste, *technical* presto, prestissimo, *formal* expeditiously, perfunctorily, *colloq.* pronto, lickety-split, at a rate of knots, at the double, before you can say Jack Robinson, by leaps and bounds, hell for leather, like a bat out of hell, like the clappers, like greased lightning
F₃ slowly, *formal* tardily

quickness *n*
1 SPEED, speediness, rapidity, swiftness, hastiness, immediacy, briskness, promptness, readiness, suddenness, instantaneousness, agility, *formal* expedition, precipitation, promptitude **2** INTELLIGENCE, shrewdness, sharpness, penetration, acuteness, astuteness, keenness, quick-wittedness, alertness
F₃ 1 slowness, *formal* tardiness **2** dullness

quick-tempered *adj*
fiery, impatient, impulsive, hot-tempered, irascible, testy, touchy, irritable, explosive, volcanic, waspish, choleric, excitable, quarrelsome, shrewish, snappy, temperamental, *formal* splenetic, petulant
F₃ cool, dispassionate

quick-witted *adj*
intelligent, clever, resourceful, keen, bright, sharp, shrewd, penetrating, acute, perceptive, smart, wide-awake, alert, astute, crafty, ingenious, witty, ready-witted, nimble-witted
F₃ dull, slow, stupid

quiescent *adj*
quiet, at rest, resting, calm, peaceful, serene, placid, tranquil, undisturbed, untroubled, still, passive, silent, motionless, inactive, inert, sleeping, asleep, latent, dormant, *formal* in abeyance, reposeful
F₃ active

quiet *adj, n*
▶ *adj* **1** SILENT, soundless, without a sound, noiseless, inaudible, hushed, soft, faint, indistinct, muffled, low, *colloq.* you could hear a pin drop **2** PEACEFUL, still, tranquil, serene, calm, mild, gentle, restrained, composed, undisturbed, untroubled, placid **3** SHY, reserved, reticent, uncommunicative, taciturn, placid, unforthcoming, undemonstrative, retiring, withdrawn, introvert, unexcitable, stoic, thoughtful, discreet, subdued, meek, *formal* imperturbable, phlegmatic, *colloq.* unflappable **4** *a quiet spot* isolated, unfrequented, lonely, secluded, undisturbed, private, sleepy, peaceful, *formal* sequestered, *colloq.* off the beaten track **5** *quiet colours* muted, subdued, soft, subtle, faint, restrained, low-key
F₃ 1 noisy, loud **2** excitable **3** extrovert **4** noisy **5** loud

Colloquial ways of telling someone to be quiet include:
belt up!, button it!, cut the cackle!, drop dead!, dry up!, enough said!, get knotted!, give it a rest!, give over!, hold your peace!, not another word!, one more word out of you!, pack it in!; pipe down!, put a sock in it!, say no more!, shut up!, shut your face!, shut your gob!, shut your mouth!, wrap up!

▶ *n* quietness, silence, hush, peace, lull, stillness, soundlessness, noiselessness, tranquillity, serenity, calm, rest, *formal* repose
F₃ noise, loudness, disturbance, bustle

quieten *v*
1 SILENCE, hush, shush, mute, soften, lower, diminish, reduce, stifle, muffle, deaden, dull, *colloq.* shut up **2** SUBDUE, pacify, quell, quiet, still, smooth, calm (down), tranquillize, soothe, compose, sober
F₃ 2 disturb, agitate

quietly *adv*
calmly, noiselessly, inaudibly, mutely, silently, softly, soundlessly, surreptitiously, placidly, tranquilly, peacefully, gently, mildly, meekly, unobtrusively, unostentatiously, undemonstratively, modestly, secretly, privately
F₃ noisily, obtrusively

quietness *n*
calm, quiet, silence, serenity, tranquillity, calmness, hush, peace, placidity, lull, still, stillness, composure, inactivity, inertia, uneventfulness, dullness, *formal* quiescence, quietude, repose
F₃ activity, bustle, commotion, disturbance, noise, racket

quietus *n*
release, end, silencing, discharge, dispatch, acquittance, death, death-blow, death-stroke, finishing stroke, *coup de grâce*, extinction, *formal* decease, demise

quilt *n*
bedcover, coverlet, bedspread, counterpane, eiderdown, duvet, continental quilt

quintessence *n*
embodiment, essence, core, distillation, marrow, pith, soul, spirit, extract, gist, heart, kernel, pattern, sum and substance, *formal* exemplar, quiddity

quintessential *adj*
essential, ideal, perfect, ultimate, complete, definitive, entire, *formal* archetypical, consummate, prototypical

quip *n, v*
▶ *n* joke, jest, crack, wisecrack, witticism, riposte, retort, gibe, epigram, pleasantry, *colloq.* gag, one-liner
▶ *v* jest, joke, retort, riposte, gibe, quirk, gag, wisecrack

quirk *n*
freak, eccentricity, curiosity, oddity, peculiarity, idiosyncrasy, mannerism, habit, trait, characteristic, feature, foible, whim, vagary, caprice, obsession, turn, twist, kink, *colloq.* thing, hang-up

quisling *n*
betrayer, traitor, turncoat, collaborator, renegade, fifth columnist, puppet, Judas, *formal* collaborationist

quit *v*
1 *quit smoking* stop, end, abandon, drop, give up, leave off, *formal* cease, discontinue, desist, abstain, *colloq.* pack in **2** LEAVE, depart, go (away), exit, decamp, desert, abandon, renounce, relinquish, surrender, give up, resign, retire, withdraw, *formal* forsake

quite *adv*
1 MODERATELY, rather, somewhat, reasonably, fairly, relatively, comparatively, to some extent/degree **2** UTTERLY, absolutely, totally, completely, entirely, wholly, fully, perfectly, exactly, precisely

quits *adj*
equal, even, level, square
▷ **call it quits** stop, break off, make peace, stop fighting, *formal* cease, discontinue, *colloq.* call it a day, bury the hatchet, lay down your arms

quitter *n*
defector, delinquent, recreant, renegade, shirker, deserter, apostate, *colloq.* rat, skiver

quiver *v, n*
▶ *v* shake, tremble, shudder, shiver, quake, quaver, vibrate, pulsate, tingle, palpitate, flutter, flicker, oscillate, wobble
▶ *n* shake, tremble, shudder, shiver, tremor, throb, vibration, palpitation, quaver, pulsation, flutter, flicker, oscillation, wobble

quixotic *adj*
unrealistic, unworldly, idealistic, impracticable, visionary, extravagant, fanciful, Utopian, fantastical, romantic, starry-eyed, impetuous, impulsive, chivalrous
◪ hard-headed, practical, realistic

quiz *n, v*
▶ *n* questionnaire, test, examination, competition, questioning, cross-examination, cross-questioning
▶ *v* question, interrogate, examine, cross-examine, cross-question, *colloq.* grill, pump, give the third degree to

quizzical *adj*
questioning, inquiring, curious, amused, humorous, teasing, mocking, satirical, sardonic, sceptical, mystified, perplexed, puzzled, baffled

quota *n*
ration, allowance, allocation, assignment, share, portion, part, slice, percentage, proportion, *colloq.* cut, whack, slice of cake

quotation *n*
1 CITATION, extract, excerpt, line, passage, selection, piece, cutting, reference, allusion, *colloq.* quote **2** ESTIMATE, tender, figure, price, cost, charge, rate, *colloq.* quote

quote *v*
cite, refer to, mention, name, reproduce, echo, repeat, recite, recall, recollect, allude to

quoted *adj*
cited, referred to, reported, reproduced, stated, above-mentioned, *formal* forementioned, instanced

quotidian *adj*
everyday, normal, ordinary, routine, workaday, regular, daily, day-to-day, repeated, common, commonplace, customary, recurrent, habitual, *formal* diurnal

R

rabbit *n, v*
- ▸ *n* bunny, cony, bunny rabbit, cottontail, daman, hyrax, dassie
- ▸ *v* ▷ **rabbit on** chatter, go on (and on), blather, blether, maunder (on), *colloq.* natter, witter (on), waffle, gab, babble

rabble *n*
1 CROWD, throng, horde, herd, mob 2 MASSES, populace, crowd, herd, mob, common people, proletariat, hoi polloi, *colloq.* riff-raff, plebs

rabble-rouser *n*
agitator, troublemaker, incendiary, firebrand, demagogue, ringleader

rabid *adj*
1 FANATICAL, ferocious, extreme, burning, ardent, raging, fervent, frantic, unreasoning, intolerant, irrational, furious, obsessive, zealous, overzealous, bigoted, narrow-minded 2 MAD, hydrophobic, maniacal, wild, berserk, frenzied, crazed, violent, hysterical

race¹ *n, v*
- ▸ *n a horse race* competition, contest, contention, rivalry, chase, pursuit, quest

> ### Types of race and famous races include:
> cycle race, cyclo-cross, road race, time trial, Milk Race, Tour de France; greyhound race, Greyhound Derby; horse race, Cheltenham Gold Cup, the Classics (Derby, Oaks, One Thousand Guineas, St. Leger, Two Thousand Guineas), Grand National, Kentucky Derby, Melbourne Cup, Prix de l'Arc de Triomphe, steeplechase, trotting race, *US* harness race; motorcycle race, motocross, scramble, speedway, Isle of Man Tourist Trophy (TT); motor-race, Grand Prix, Indianapolis 500, Le Mans, Monte Carlo rally, RAC Rally, scramble, stock car race; rowing, regatta, Boat Race; running, cross-country, *US* dash, hurdles, marathon, London Marathon, relay, sprint, steeplechase, track event; ski race, downhill, slalom; swimming race; walking race, walkathon; yacht race, Admiral's Cup, America's Cup; egg-and-spoon race, pancake race, sack race, wheelbarrow race.

- ▸ *v* run, sprint, dash, tear, fly, gallop, speed, career, dart, bolt, zoom, rush, hurry, hasten, accelerate, take part in a race, *colloq.* get a move on, go all out, get cracking, run like hell

race² *n*
a race of people nation, people, ethnic group, racial group, colour, tribe, clan, house, dynasty, family, kindred, ancestry, line, lineage, blood, ancestry, extraction, stock, parentage, strain, stirps, genus, species, breed

racecourse *n*
racetrack, course, track, circuit, lap, turf, speedway

racial *adj*
national, tribal, ethnic, folk, ethnological, genealogical, ancestral, inherited, genetic

raciness *n*
1 RIBALDRY, indecency, indelicacy, bawdiness, naughtiness, lewdness, smuttiness, suggestiveness, vulgarity, crudeness, coarseness 2 LIVELINESS, animation, zest, zestfulness, energy, exhilaration, freshness, dynamism, *formal* ebullience, *colloq.* pep

racism *n*
racialism, xenophobia, chauvinism, jingoism, discrimination, racial discrimination, prejudice, racial prejudice, apartheid, bias

racist *n, adj*
- ▸ *n* racialist, discriminator, bigot, chauvinist
- ▸ *adj* racialist, discriminatory, bigoted, intolerant

rack *n, v*
- ▸ *n* 1 HOLDER, shelf, stand, support, structure, frame, framework, trestle 2 SUFFERING, pain, misery, affliction, agony, anguish, distress, pangs, torment, torture, persecution
- ▸ *v* afflict, oppress, distress, agonize, pain, harass, convulse, shake, strain, stress, tear, stretch, wrench, wrest, wring, excruciate, harrow, lacerate, torment, torture, crucify

racket *n*
1 NOISE, din, uproar, row, fuss, outcry, clamour, shouting, yelling, tumult, commotion, disturbance, hullabaloo, pandemonium, hurly-burly, hubbub 2 SWINDLE, fraud, fiddle, deception, trick, dodge, scheme, business, *colloq.* con, game

racy *adj*
1 RIBALD, bawdy, risqué, vulgar, crude, rude, coarse, dirty, naughty, indecent, indelicate, suggestive, off-colour, smutty, *colloq.* blue 2 LIVELY, animated, spirited, vigorous, vivacious, fast-moving, energetic, dynamic, buoyant, enthusiastic, boisterous, sparkling, *formal* ebullient, *colloq.* peppy, zippy

raddled *adj*
haggard, drawn, gaunt, wasted, worn out, unkempt, dishevelled, in a mess, the worse for wear

radiance *n*
1 LIGHT, luminosity, radiation, brightness, brilliance, shine, lustre, gleam, glow, glitter, resplendence, splendour, *formal* incandescence, *formal* effulgence, refulgence 2 JOY, happiness, pleasure, delight, elation, ecstasy, bliss, rapture

radiant *adj*
1 BRIGHT, luminous, shining, illuminated, gleaming, glowing, beaming, glittering, sparkling, brilliant, splendid, glorious, *technical* incandescent, resplendent, *formal* effulgent, refulgent 2 JOYFUL, happy, delighted, elated, pleased, blissful, ecstatic, in raptures,

colloq. in seventh heaven, on top of the world, over the moon

F₃ 1 dull 2 miserable

radiate *v*
1 *radiate light/an emotion* shine, gleam, glow, beam, shed, pour, send out/forth, give off, emit, emanate, diffuse, issue 2 SPREAD (OUT), scatter, disperse, diverge, branch, *formal* disseminate, divaricate

radiation *n*
emanation, emission, rays, waves, transmission, *technical* insolation

radical *adj, n*
▶ *adj* 1 BASIC, fundamental, rudimentary, primary, elementary, elemental, essential, natural, native, innate, intrinsic, deep-seated, profound 2 *radical changes* drastic, comprehensive, thorough, sweeping, far-reaching, exhaustive, thoroughgoing, profound, complete, absolute, total, entire, utter 3 FANATICAL, militant, extreme, extremist, rebellious, revolutionary
F₃ 1 superficial 3 moderate
▶ *n* fanatic, militant, extremist, revolutionary, rebel, reformer, reformist, fundamentalist

raffish *adj*
disreputable, dissipated, dissolute, cheap, tawdry, vulgar, uncouth, trashy, bohemian, rakish, showy, sporty, jaunty, casual, careless, devil-may-care, improper, gross, flamboyant, flashy, garish, gaudy, tasteless, loud, coarse, *formal* meretricious
F₃ proper, sedate, staid, *formal* decorous

raffle *n*
draw, lottery, sweepstake, sweep, tombola

rag¹ *n*
1 *an old clothes rag* cloth, flannel, floorcloth, duster, towel 2 *dressed in rags* remnants, shreds, raggedness, tatters, tats, clouts, *colloq.* duddery, duds

rag² *v*
rag the new boy tease, badger, jeer, mock, ridicule, taunt, torment, bait, *colloq.* rib, kid, take the mickey out of

ragamuffin *n*
urchin, guttersnipe, waif, street arab, gamin

ragbag *n*
confusion, miscellany, assortment, mixture, mix, jumble, medley, pastiche, hotchpotch, salad, potpourri, *formal* assemblage, *colloq.* omnium-gatherum

rage *n, v*
▶ *n* anger, wrath, fury, frenzy, raving, madness, tumult, tantrum, temper, paroxysm
▷ **all the rage** fashionable, popular, the craze, in vogue, stylish, *colloq.* the in thing, trendy
▶ *v* fume, seethe, rant, rave, storm, thunder, explode, rampage, *colloq.* blow a fuse, blow your cool, blow your top, boil over, burst a blood vessel, do your nut, explode, flip your lid, fly off the handle, go mad, foam at the mouth, go off the deep end, go up the wall, hit the roof, lose your cool, lose your rag, raise hell, see red

ragged *adj*
1 *ragged clothes* frayed, torn, ripped, tattered, in tatters, worn-out, in holes, holey, threadbare, falling to pieces, tatty, shabby, *old use* rent 2 *ragged children* scruffy, untidy, unkempt, poor, destitute, down and out, down-at-heel, *formal* indigent 3 JAGGED, serrated, indented, notched, rugged, rough, uneven, irregular 4 *a ragged group of people* fragmented, erratic, disorganized, straggling

raging *adj*
1 VIOLENT, wild, stormy, turbulent, tumultuous 2 ANGRY, furious, enraged, infuriated, irate, fuming, incensed, raving, seething, wrathful, frenzied, mad, *formal* fulminating, furibund, ireful

raid *n, v*
▶ *n* attack, onset, assault, charge, onslaught, inroad, invasion, incursion, foray, sortie, sally, strike, blitz, swoop, robbery, break-in, hold-up, smash-and-grab raid, *slang* bust
▶ *v* loot, pillage, plunder, sack, ransack, forage, rifle, maraud, break into, attack, assail, rush, set upon, descend on, invade, storm, *slang* bust

raider *n*
attacker, invader, looter, plunderer, pillager, ransacker, marauder, robber, thief, criminal, brigand, villain, pirate, *colloq.* crook, shark

rail *v*
censure, criticize, attack, abuse, protest, decry, upbraid, vociferate, mock, jeer, revile, ridicule, scoff, *formal* arraign, castigate, denounce, fulminate, inveigh, vituperate

railing *n*
fence, fencing, paling, barrier, parapet, rail(s), balustrade

raillery *n*
mockery, teasing, jeering, jesting, banter, chaff, badinage, repartee, irony, joke, joking, ridicule, satire, sport, pleasantry, persiflage, *old use* dicacity, *formal* diatribe, invective, *colloq.* kidding, ragging, ribbing, chiacking

rain *n, v*
▶ *n* 1 RAINFALL, precipitation, raindrops, drizzle, mizzle, shower, cloudburst, downpour, deluge, torrent, storm, rainstorm, thunderstorm, squall 2 *a rain of stones* torrent, volley, shower, deluge
▶ *v* spit, drizzle, mizzle, sprinkle, shower, pour (down), tipple down, teem, pelt, deluge, *colloq.* bucket (down), rain cats and dogs, come down in buckets/sheets/stair rods/torrents, the floodgates/clouds open

rainbow *n, adj*
▶ *n* arc, arch, bow, spectrum, prism, iris
▶ *adj* rainbow-like, kaleidoscopic, prismatic, variegated, spectral, opalescent, *formal* iridescent, irisated, irised
F₃ monochrome

The colours of the rainbow are:
red, orange, yellow, green, blue, indigo, violet.

rainy *adj*
wet, damp, showery, drizzly, *formal* pluvial
F₃ dry

raise *v*
1 LIFT, lift up, elevate, hoist, uplift, heave up, jack up, put up, set up, erect, build, construct, weigh 2 INCREASE, escalate, put up, magnify, heighten, strengthen, step up, intensify, amplify, boost, enhance, upgrade, *formal* augment, *colloq.* jack up, bump up 3 *raise funds* get, obtain, collect, gather, get together, amass, accumulate, assemble, rally, muster, recruit 4 BRING UP, rear, breed, propagate, grow, cultivate, educate, produce, develop, nurture 5 *raise a subject* bring up, broach, introduce, present, put forward, moot, suggest 6 PROVOKE, cause, create, arouse, rouse, activate, evoke, excite, stir
F₃ 1 lower 2 decrease, reduce 5 suppress

raised *adj*
embossed, relief, applied, appliqué, cameo, relievo
F₃ engraved, incised, intaglio

rake¹ *v*
1 *rake the grass* scratch, hoe, scrape, graze, comb, level, smooth 2 SEARCH, scour, hunt, ransack, rifle,

rummage, comb **3** GATHER, collect, amass, accumulate

rake² *n, v*

► *n* degenerate, debauchee, playboy, roué, dissolute, libertine, hedonist, lecher, sensualist, pleasure-seeker, spendthrift, swinger, *formal* profligate, prodigal

F∃ ascetic, puritan

► *v* ▷ **rake in** earn, receive, get paid, make, *colloq.* bring in, pull in

▷ **rake up** remind, bring up, raise, mention, revive, introduce, drag up

rake-off *n*

cut, share, slice, part, portion

rakish *adj*

stylish, sporty, smart, dapper, sharp, flamboyant, flashy, jaunty, debonair, nonchalant, adventurous, casual, breezy, devil-may-care, depraved, degenerate, immoral, licentious, libertine, loose, dissipated, abandoned, debauched, dissolute, lecherous, raffish, sinful, *formal* prodigal, profligate, *colloq.* natty, snazzy

rally *n, v*

► *n* **1** GATHERING, assembly, convention, convocation, conference, meeting, mass meeting, jamboree, reunion, march, demonstration, *formal* assemblage **2** RECOVERY, recuperation, revival, comeback, improvement, resurgence, renewal

► *v* **1** GATHER, collect, come/bring together, get together, assemble, congregate, group, band together, muster, summon, round up, unite, marshal, organize, mobilize, reassemble, regroup, reorganize, reform, *formal* convene **2** RECOVER, recuperate, revive, improve, pick up, get well, get better, gain strength, pull through, *colloq.* perk up, bounce back, get back on your feet, be on the mend

ram *v*

1 HIT, strike, beat, butt, hammer, pound, drive, drum, bump, crash, smash, dash, slam **2** FORCE, drive, thrust, cram, stuff, pack, crowd, jam, squeeze, compress, wedge

ramble *v, n*

► *v* **1** WALK, hike, trek, tramp, traipse, stroll, amble, saunter, stray, straggle, wander, roam, range, jaunt, rove, diverge, meander, wind, zigzag **2** CHATTER, babble, blather, blether, digress, wander, drift, *formal* expatiate, *colloq.* rabbit (on), witter (on), waffle, go off at a tangent

► *n* walk, hike, trek, tramp, stroll, saunter, wander, roam, amble, jaunt, tour, trip, excursion

rambler *n*

hiker, walker, traveller, stroller, rover, roamer, saunterer, wanderer, drifter, wayfarer

rambling *adj*

1 SPREADING, sprawling, straggling, trailing **2** ROUND-ABOUT, digressive, wandering, wordy, long-winded, long-drawn-out, disjointed, disconnected, incoherent, *formal* verbose, circuitous, periphrastic, errant

F∃ 2 direct

ramification *n*

1 RESULT, consequence, effect, upshot, outcome, sequel **2** BRANCH, offshoot, limb, outgrowth, development, implication, complication, *formal* divarication

ramp *n*

slope, incline, gradient, rise, grade, *formal* acclivity

rampage *v, n*

► *v* run wild, run amok, run riot, go berserk, rush, rush violently/wildly, charge, tear, storm, rage, rant, rave

► *n* rage, fury, frenzy, turmoil, mayhem, storm, uproar, violence, destruction, furore

▷ **on the rampage** wild, amok, berserk, frenzied, in a frenzy, violent(ly), wild(ly), out of control

rampant *adj*

unrestrained, uncontrolled, out of control, out of hand, unbridled, unchecked, wanton, excessive, fierce, violent, raging, wild, riotous, rank, profuse, rife, widespread, prevalent, epidemic, pandemic, *colloq.* spreading like wildfire

rampart *n*

earthwork, embankment, bank, fence, barricade, bastion, bulwark, defence, stronghold, guard, wall, security, parapet, fort, fortification, breastwork, vallum

ramshackle *adj*

dilapidated, tumbledown, broken-down, run-down, crumbling, ruined, neglected, derelict, jerry-built, unsafe, rickety, shaky, flimsy, unsteady, tottering, decrepit, gone to rack and ruin

F∃ solid, stable

ranch *n*

farm, estate, plantation, station, hacienda, estancia

rancid *adj*

sour, off, bad, turned, high, overripe, unpleasant, musty, stale, rank, foul, fetid, putrid, rotten, *formal* noxious, noisome, malodorous

F∃ sweet

rancorous *adj*

resentful, bitter, acerbic, hostile, spiteful, malignant, vindictive, venomous, vengeful, implacable, virulent, *formal* acrimonious, malevolent, splenetic

rancour *n*

resentfulness, resentment, spite, hate, hatred, animosity, malice, malignity, ill-feeling, ill-will, hostility, bitterness, enmity, grudge, venom, vindictiveness, spleen, *formal* acrimony, animus, antipathy, malevolence

random *adj*

arbitrary, chance, fortuitous, casual, incidental, haphazard, irregular, sporadic, unsystematic, unarranged, unplanned, unmethodical, accidental, aimless, purposeless, indiscriminate, stray, *formal* serendipitous, *colloq.* hit-or-miss

F∃ systematic, deliberate

▷ **at random** haphazardly, incidentally, fortuitously, arbitrarily, sporadically, irregularly, unsystematically, unmethodically, aimlessly, purposelessly, indiscriminately

randy *adj*

horny, sexy, raunchy, amorous, aroused, hot, lustful, goatish, lascivious, lecherous, satyric, *formal* concupiscent, *colloq.* turned-on

range *n, v*

► *n* **1** *a range of fittings* variety, diversity, assortment, selection, array, sort, kind, type, class, order, species, genus, series, string, chain, line, row, file **2** SCOPE, compass, scale, gamut, spectrum, radius, sweep, spread, extent, distance, reach, span, confines, limits, bounds, parameters, area, field, domain, province, sphere, orbit **3** *a cooking range* stove, cooker, oven

► *v* **1** EXTEND, stretch, reach, go, run, cover, spread, vary, fluctuate **2** ALIGN, arrange, draw up, line up, order, rank, class, classify, catalogue, group, categorize, grade, pigeonhole, compartmentalize, *formal* dispose **3** ROAM, wander, stroll, stray, drift, amble, ramble

rangy *adj*

long-legged, leggy, lanky, gangling, skinny, weedy, rawboned

F∃ compact, dumpy

rank¹ *n, v*

► *n* **1** GRADE, degree, class, caste, status, standing, position, station, condition, estate, mark, echelon, level, stratum, tier, classification, sort, type, group, division, *colloq.* place in the pecking order

2 ROW, line, range, column, file, string, series, order, formation

▷ **rank and file 1** ORDINARY SOLDIERS, ordinary men, soldiers, private soldiers **2** RABBLE, masses, populace, crowd, herd, mob, common people, proletariat, hoi polloi, *colloq.* riff-raff, plebs

▶ *v* **1** GRADE, class, rate, place, position, range, sort, classify, categorize, order, arrange, organize, marshal **2** ALIGN, arrange, order, draw up, line up, *formal* dispose

rank² *adj*
1 UTTER, total, complete, absolute, unmitigated, unqualified, thorough, sheer, downright, out-and-out, arrant, gross, flagrant, glaring, blatant, outrageous **2** FOUL, repulsive, disgusting, unpleasant, offensive, disagreeable, revolting, evil-smelling, acrid, pungent, putrid, fetid, rancid, stale, *formal* malodorous, mephitic, graveolent **3** *rank disobedience* gross, coarse, shocking, outrageous, vile **4** OVERGROWN, lush, abundant, dense, profuse, vigorous, *formal* luxuriant

rankle *v*
annoy, irritate, rile, nettle, gall, irk, vex, fester, cause bitterness/resentment, embitter, anger, *colloq.* peeve, bug, get someone's blood, get someone's back up

ransack *v*
1 PLUNDER, rifle, raid, sack, strip, ravage, devastate, maraud, harry, loot, pillage, *formal* depredate **2** SEARCH, scour, comb, rummage through, go through, turn inside out, turn upside down, *formal* despoil

ransom *n, v*
▶ *n* **1** PAYMENT, price, money, pay-off **2** REDEMPTION, deliverance, rescue, freedom, setting free, liberation, restoration, release
▶ *v* buy off, buy/purchase the freedom of, redeem, deliver, rescue, liberate, free, set free, release

rant *v, n*
▶ *v* shout, cry, yell, roar, bellow, bluster, rave, harangue, rant and rave, *formal* declaim, vociferate, *colloq.* tub-thump
▶ *n* storm, shouting, crying, yelling, roaring, bluster, tirade, oration, harangue, rhetoric, bombast, *formal* declamation, diatribe, philippic, vociferation

rap *v, n*
▶ *v* **1** KNOCK, hit, strike, tap, whack, clout, clip, cuff, hammer, thump, bang, batter **2** REPROVE, reprimand, criticize, censure, punish, blame, scold, *formal* castigate, *colloq.* rail, slate, slam, knock
▶ *n* **1** KNOCK, hit, blow, tap, whack, clout, clip, cuff, hammer, thump, bang, batter **2** REBUKE, reprimand, censure, blame, punishment, *formal* castigation, *colloq.* flak, slating, slamming, knocking, stick

rapacious *adj*
uncaring, greedy, grasping, extortionate, preying, ravening, ravenous, voracious, plundering, predatory, marauding, insatiable, wolfish, wolvish, vulturish, vulturous, usurious, *formal* avaricious, esurient

rapacity *n*
greed, greediness, graspingness, avarice, insatiableness, predatoriness, rapaciousness, ravenousness, voraciousness, voracity, wolfishness, usury, *formal* avidity, esurience, esuriency, *colloq.* shark's manners

rape *v, n*
▶ *v* **1** *rape a woman* violate, ravish, assault, assault sexually, abuse, maltreat, defile **2** *rape the land* ravage, sack, ransack, strip, raid, loot, rob, pillage, plunder, devastate, violate, defile, *formal* despoil, depredate, spoliate
▶ *n* **1** *the rape of a young girl* violation, assault, sexual assault, ravishment, abuse, maltreatment, date rape, gang rape **2** *rape of the countryside* ravaging, sacking, ransacking, stripping, raid, looting, plundering, devastation, violation, defilement, *formal* rapine, despoliation, depredation, spoliation

rapid *adj*
swift, speedy, quick, fast, express, prompt, lively, brisk, hurried, hasty, headlong, *formal* precipitate, expeditious, *colloq.* like lightning
🔁 slow, leisurely, sluggish, *formal* tardy

rapidity *n*
quickness, hurry, speed, speediness, rush, haste, briskness, swiftness, velocity, fleetness, promptness, dispatch, *formal* alacrity, celerity, expedition, expeditiousness, precipitateness, promptitude
🔁 slowness

rapidly *adv*
fast, quickly, speedily, swiftly, hastily, hurriedly, briskly, promptly, *formal* expeditiously, precipitately, *colloq.* lickety-split
🔁 slowly

rapine *n*
ravaging, sacking, ransacking, rage, stripping, raid, looting, plundering, devastation, violation, defilement, *formal* despoliation, depredation, spoliation

rapport *n*
bond, link, affinity, relationship, empathy, sympathy, understanding, good understanding, harmony

rapprochement *n*
reconcilement, increased friendliness, agreement, reconciliation, reunion, détente, softening, harmonization

rapt *adj*
engrossed, absorbed, preoccupied, intent, gripped, spellbound, enthralled, bewitched, captivated, preoccupied, concentrated, fascinated, entranced, charmed, enchanted, ecstatic, delighted, thrilled, ravished, enraptured, transported

rapture *n*
delight, happiness, joy, bliss, ecstasy, elation, exhilaration, enchantment, euphoria, exaltation, transport, *formal* delectation, felicity, *colloq.* seventh heaven, cloud nine, top of the world

rapturous *adj*
joyful, joyous, overjoyed, happy, delighted, enthusiastic, blissful, ecstatic, entranced, euphoric, exalted, ravished, transported, rhapsodic, *colloq.* over the moon, on cloud nine, in seventh heaven, tickled pink, on top of the world

rare *adj*
1 UNCOMMON, unusual, exceptional, scarce, sparse, sporadic, infrequent, *colloq.* thin on the ground, few and far between, like gold dust **2** EXQUISITE, superb,

excellent, superlative, superior, outstanding, unparalleled, incomparable, matchless, exceptional, remarkable, precious, choice

F₃ 1 common, abundant, frequent, ordinary, typical

rarefied *adj*
exclusive, select, private, esoteric, refined, high, noble, sublime, special

rarely *adv*
seldom, hardly ever, scarcely ever, infrequently, occasionally, little, scarcely, hardly, intermittently, sporadically, spasmodically, *colloq.* once in a blue moon

F₃ often, frequently

raring *adj*
eager, keen, enthusiastic, ready, willing, impatient, longing, itching, desperate

rarity *n*
1 CURIOSITY, curio, gem, pearl, treasure, find, marvel, wonder, nonpareil 2 UNCOMMONNESS, unusualness, strangeness, scarcity, shortage, sparseness, infrequency

F₃ 2 commonness, frequency

rascal *n*
rogue, scoundrel, scamp, scallywag, imp, devil, villain, good-for-nothing, ne'er-do-well, mischief-maker, wastrel

rascally *adj*
dishonest, wicked, mischievous, scoundrelly, unscrupulous, villainous, good-for-nothing, evil, vicious, disreputable, base, crooked, bad, knavish, low, mean, reprobate, *colloq.* furciferous

rash¹ *adj*
a rash action impulsive, impetuous, hasty, reckless, ill-considered, foolhardy, ill-advised, madcap, harebrained, hot-headed, headstrong, headlong, unguarded, unwary, indiscreet, adventurous, audacious, imprudent, careless, premature, heedless, unthinking, *formal* precipitate, temerarious

F₃ cautious, wary, careful

rash² *n*
1 *a rash on the skin* eruption, outbreak, hives, nettlerash, heat rash, epidemic, plague, *technical* pompholyx, urticaria 2 *a rash of burglaries* spate, flood, deluge, torrent, run, rush, wave

rashness *n*
impulsiveness, incaution, hastiness, foolhardiness, carelessness, incautiousness, recklessness, thoughtlessness, adventurousness, audacity, heedlessness, brashness, indiscretion, *formal* precipitance, precipitation, precipitancy, temerity

F₃ carefulness, cautiousness, wariness

rasp *n, v*
▶ *n* grating, scrape, grinding, scratch, harshness, hoarseness, croak

▶ *v* 1 GRATE, scrape, grind, file, sand, scour, scratch, abrade, rub, *formal* excoriate 2 IRRITATE, grate, jar, *colloq.* peeve, bug, get on your nerves 3 CROAK, screech, squawk, cackle

rasping *adj*
harsh, hoarse, creaking, croaking, grating, jarring, raspy, gravelly, gruff, husky, croaky, scratchy, rough, raucous, *formal* stridulant

rate *n, v*
▶ *n* 1 SPEED, velocity, tempo, time, ratio, proportion, percentage, relation, degree, grade, rank, rating, standard, basis, measure, scale 2 CHARGE, fee, hire, toll, tariff, price, cost, value, worth, pay, payment, tax, duty, amount, figure, percentage

▷ **at any rate** in any case, anyway, in any event, nevertheless, regardless, at all

▶ *v* 1 JUDGE, regard, consider, deem, count, reckon, figure, estimate, evaluate, value, assess, weigh (up), measure, grade, rank, categorize, class, classify, *formal* appraise, esteem, adjudge 2 ADMIRE, respect, value, prize, have a high opinion of, *formal* esteem 3 DESERVE, merit, be worthy of, have a right to, warrant, justify, be entitled to

rather *adv*
1 MODERATELY, relatively, slightly, a bit, a little, somewhat, fairly, quite, to some degree/extent, pretty, noticeably, significantly, very 2 PREFERABLY, sooner, much rather, much sooner, instead, by/for preference, for/from choice

ratify *v*
approve, uphold, endorse, corroborate, sign, countersign, legalize, sanction, authorize, warrant, establish, affirm, agree to, confirm, certify, validate, authenticate

F₃ repudiate, reject

rating *n*
assessment, classification, category, score, mark, evaluation, class, rank, degree, status, standing, position, placing, order, grade, grading, *formal* appraisal, adjudging

ratio *n*
proportion, percentage, fraction, relation, relationship, correspondence, correlation, symmetry, balance

ration *n, v*
▶ *n* 1 QUOTA, allowance, allocation, allotment, share, proportion, percentage, portion, helping, part, measure, lot, amount 2 *rations in times of shortage* food, foodstuffs, provisions, supplies, stores, *formal* viands, victuals

▶ *v* allot, allocate, budget, share, deal out, distribute, hand out, divide out, measure out, dole out, dispense, supply, issue, control, restrict, limit, conserve, save, *formal* apportion

rational *adj*
logical, reasonable, sound, well-founded, realistic, sensible, clear-headed, wise, sane, normal, balanced, lucid, reasoning, thinking, intelligent, enlightened, *formal* judicious, sagacious, circumspect, prudent, cognitive, cerebral, ratiocinative

F₃ irrational, illogical, insane, crazy

rationale *n*
logic, reasoning, philosophy, thesis, principle, basis, grounds, explanation, reason(s), purpose, *raison d'être*, motive, motivation, hypothesis, theory

rationalize *v*
1 JUSTIFY, excuse, vindicate, explain, account for, make allowances for, explain away 2 REORGANIZE, streamline, trim, modernize, update, make more efficient, cut back on, cut out waste

rattle *v*
1 CLATTER, jingle, jangle, clang, clank, clink, shake, vibrate, jolt, jar, bounce, bang, rap, bump, knock 2 UNNERVE, disconcert, unsettle, disturb, confuse, upset, put off/out, shake, alarm, throw off balance, *colloq.* faze, put someone's nose out of joint

▷ **rattle off** reel off, list, list quickly, run through, recite, repeat

▷ **rattle on** chatter, gabble, jabber, prate, prattle, blether, cackle, *colloq.* gab, rabbit on, witter, yack

ratty *adj*
irritable, annoyed, angry, cross, impatient, crabbed, testy, touchy, short, snappy, short-tempered, *colloq.* peeved

F₃ calm, patient

raucous *adj*
harsh, rough, hoarse, husky, scratching, rasping, grat-

ing, jarring, screeching, piercing, ear-piercing, discordant, strident, shrill, sharp, noisy, loud

ravage v, n
▶ v destroy, devastate, lay waste, demolish, level, raze, wreck, ruin, leave in ruins, spoil, damage, loot, harry, maraud, pillage, plunder, sack, depredate, *formal* despoil
▶ n destruction, devastation, havoc, damage, ruin, ruination, looting, ransacking, desolation, wreckage, pillage, plunder, *formal* despoliation, depredation, spoliation

ravaged adj
devastated, destroyed, desolate, wrecked, ransacked, spoilt, shattered, war-worn, war-torn, battletorn, war-wasted
🖪 unspoilt

rave v, adj, n
▶ v 1 TALK WILDLY, rant and rave, shout, cry, yell, roar, bellow, babble, jabber, ramble 2 RAGE, storm, thunder, roar, rant, fume, seethe, explode, lose your temper, *colloq.* lose your cool, boil over, flip your lid, hit the roof 3 ENTHUSE, sing the praises of, wax lyrical, extol, acclaim, hail, *colloq.* be mad about
▶ adj enthusiastic, praising, rapturous, favourable, excellent, ecstatic, wonderful, *formal* laudatory
▶ n party, disco, celebration, carousal, orgy, acidhouse party, *colloq.* do, knees-up, rave-up, bash, blow-out

ravenous adj
hungry, starving, starved, famished, greedy, voracious, insatiable, wolfish

rave-up n
party, celebration, carousal, debauch, orgy, *colloq.* bash, blow-out, do, shindig, thrash

ravine n
canyon, gorge, deep narrow valley, gully, canyon, abyss, gap, pass

raving adj
mad, insane, hysterical, delirious, deranged, demented, unbalanced, wild, frenzied, furious, berserk, irrational, out of your mind, *colloq.* crazy, barmy, batty, loony, loopy, round the bend/twist
🖪 rational, sane, balanced

ravish v
1 DELIGHT, enrapture, overjoy, enchant, charm, captivate, enthral, entrance, fascinate, spellbind, bewitch 2 RAPE, violate, assault, assault sexually, abuse, maltreat, defile

ravishing adj
delightful, enchanting, bewitching, enthralling, charming, lovely, beautiful, gorgeous, stunning, radiant, dazzling, alluring, seductive

raw adj
1 *raw vegetables* uncooked, fresh 2 UNPROCESSED, unrefined, untreated, unprepared, unfinished, rough, crude, natural 3 PLAIN, bare, naked, basic, harsh, brutal, realistic, candid, blunt, outspoken, frank, forthright 4 SCRATCHED, grazed, scraped, abraded, chafed, open, bloody, sore, exposed, tender, sensitive, *formal* excoriated 5 COLD, chilly, chill, bitter, biting, nippy, piercing, freezing, bleak, wet, damp 6 *a raw recruit* inexperienced, new, green, immature, callow, ignorant, naïve, untrained, untutored, unpractised, unskilled, *colloq.* wet behind the ears
🖪 1 cooked, done 2 processed, refined, treated 5 warm 6 experienced, skilled

ray n
beam, shaft, flash, streak, stream, gleam, flicker, glimmer, twinkle, glint, spark, trace, hint, suggestion, indication

raze v
demolish, pull down, tear down, knock down, bulldoze, flatten, level, wreck, ruin, destroy, fell

re prep
about, concerning, regarding, with regard to, with reference to, on the subject of

reach v, n
▶ v 1 ARRIVE AT, get to, attain, achieve, make, make it to, amount to, come to, touch, *colloq.* hit 2 *reach for a pen* stretch (out), extend, spread, touch, contact, grasp, hold, hit, strike 3 EXTEND, stretch, spread, project, continue, come to, go as far as, go down/up to, come down/up to 4 CONTACT, get in touch with, get hold of, communicate with, get through to, write to, speak to, get onto, telephone, phone, ring, call, fax
▶ n range, scope, compass, distance, span, spread, extent, extension, stretch, ambit, latitude, grasp, command, power, influence, authority, control, jurisdiction

react v
1 RESPOND, retaliate, reciprocate, reply, answer, acknowledge, act, behave 2 *react against something* rebel, rise up, oppose, defy, resist, *formal* dissent

reaction n
response, reply, answer, acknowledgement, repercussion, counteraction, reflex, recoil, reciprocation, counterbalance, reversal, reversion, retaliation, *colloq.* feedback, backlash, kickback

reactionary adj, n
▶ adj conservative, ultraconservative, right-wing, rightist, diehard, counter-revolutionary, traditional
🖪 progressive, revolutionary
▶ n conservative, ultraconservative, right-winger, rightist, diehard, counter-revolutionary, traditionalist
🖪 progressive, revolutionary

read v, n
▶ v 1 STUDY, look at, pore over, scan, examine, scrutinize, skim, *formal* peruse, *colloq.* dip into, browse through, leaf through, thumb through, flick through 2 INTERPRET, understand, comprehend, decipher, decode, *formal* construe 3 RECITE, declaim, deliver, speak, utter 4 *the gauge read zero* indicate, show, display, register, record, measure
▷ **read into** interpret, deduce, infer, reason, misinterpret, take out of context, *formal* construe, *colloq.* read between the lines, get hold of the wrong end of the stick
▶ n study, look, perusal, scan, scanning, skimming, scrutiny, browsing

readable adj
1 LEGIBLE, decipherable, intelligible, clear, easy to read, understandable, comprehensible 2 INTERESTING, enjoyable, worth reading, entertaining, stimulating, captivating, enthralling, gripping, *colloq.* unputdownable
🖪 1 illegible 2 unreadable

readily adv
willingly, unhesitatingly, happily, gladly, eagerly, enthusiastically, promptly, quickly, swiftly, rapidly, speedily, freely, smoothly, with ease, easily, effortlessly
🖪 unwillingly, reluctantly, with difficulty

readiness n
willingness, preparedness, skill, preparation, aptitude, fitness, eagerness, keenness, inclination, quickness, rapidity, ease, promptness, facility, availability, handiness, *colloq.* gameness
▷ **in readiness** in preparation, available, prepared, on standby, standing by, on call, on full alert

reading n
1 STUDY, perusal, scrutiny, scan, browsing, examination, inspection 2 INTERPRETATION, understanding,

decoding, deciphering, rendering, version, edition, rendition, recital **3** *the reading on a meter* indication, display, register, record, measurement, figure **4** *a reading from the Bible* passage, lesson

ready *adj, v*
▶ *adj* **1** *ready to go* prepared, waiting, set, all set, fit, fitted out, equipped, rigged out, arranged, organized, completed, finished, *colloq.* geared up **2** WILLING, inclined, disposed, happy, eager, enthusiastic, keen, *formal* predisposed, *colloq.* game, psyched up **3** AVAILABLE, to hand, on hand, present, near, accessible, convenient, handy, within reach, *colloq.* at your fingertips **4** ABOUT TO, on the point of, likely to, liable to, on the verge of **5** PROMPT, immediate, quick, swift, rapid, speedy, easy, sharp, astute, perceptive, discerning, alert, resourceful
🔁 **1** unprepared **2** unwilling, reluctant, disinclined **3** unavailable, inaccessible **5** slow
▶ *v* prepare, organize, arrange, equip, order, prime, set, alert

real *adj*
1 *in the real world* actual, existing, physical, material, substantial, tangible, concrete **2** *real leather* genuine, authentic, bona fide, official, rightful, legitimate, valid, true, factual, occurring, certain, sure, positive, veritable **3** SINCERE, honest, truthful, genuine, true, from the heart, fervent, heartfelt, unfeigned, unaffected **4** *this is a real mess* right, complete, absolute, utter, thorough
🔁 **1** unreal, imaginary **2** false, imitation **3** insincere

realism *n*
1 ACTUALITY, practicality, pragmatism, sanity, saneness, sensibleness, rationality **2** LIFELIKENESS, faithfulness, truthfulness, authenticity, naturalness, genuineness

realistic *adj*
1 PRACTICAL, down-to-earth, commonsense, sensible, matter-of-fact, level-headed, clear-sighted, businesslike, hard-headed, pragmatic, matter-of-fact, rational, logical, objective, detached, unsentimental, unromantic, *colloq.* hard-boiled, hard-nosed **2** LIFELIKE, faithful, truthful, true, true-to-life, vivid, genuine, authentic, natural, close, real, real-life, graphic, representational
🔁 **1** unrealistic, impractical, irrational, idealistic **2** fake, imitation, unrealistic

reality *n*
truth, fact, certainty, realism, actuality, real world, real life, existence, materiality, tangibility, substantiality, genuineness, authenticity, validity, *formal* corporeality
🔁 fiction, fantasy

realization *n*
1 UNDERSTANDING, comprehension, grasp, recognition, discernment, perception, acceptance, appreciation, awareness, consciousness, *formal* cognizance, apprehension **2** ACHIEVEMENT, accomplishment, fulfilment, completion, implementation, performance, *formal* consummation **3** EARNING, selling, fetching, making, gain, clearing

realize *v*
1 UNDERSTAND, grasp, discover, learn, ascertain, catch on, take in, become aware/conscious of, recognize, perceive, discern, accept, appreciate, glean, *formal* comprehend, apprehend, *colloq.* cotton on, twig, tumble to **2** ACHIEVE, accomplish, fulfil, complete, implement, perform, bring about, *formal* effect, effectuate, consummate **3** SELL FOR, fetch, make, earn, gain, produce, net, clear, bring in, encash

really *adv*
1 ACTUALLY, in fact, truly, honestly, sincerely, genu-

inely, positively, surely, certainly, undoubtedly, absolutely, categorically **2** VERY, extremely, exceptionally, intensely, remarkably, highly, severely, indeed

realm *n*
1 *defence of the realm* kingdom, monarchy, principality, empire, country, state, land, territory, area, region, province, domain **2** *the realm of politics* sphere, area, region, province, domain, world, orbit, field, department

reap *v*
1 HARVEST, cut, crop, gather, mow, *formal* garner **2** GAIN, obtain, secure, acquire, get, derive, collect, realize, win

rear *n, adj, v*
▶ *n* back, stern, end, hind, tail, rump, buttocks, posterior, behind, bottom, *colloq.* backside
🔁 front
▶ *adj* back, hind, hindmost, rearmost, last, tail-end
🔁 front
▶ *v* **1** *rear a child* bring up, care for, look after, raise, breed, grow, cultivate, foster, nurse, nurture, instruct, train, educate, parent **2** RISE, rise up, loom, tower, soar, raise, elevate, lift (up), hoist

rearrange *v*
change, adjust, alter, shift, vary, reorder, reschedule, reposition, rejig

reason *n, v*
▶ *n* **1** CAUSE, motive, motivation, incentive, impetus, inducement, explanation, excuse, justification, defence, warrant, ground(s), basis, case, argument, aim, intention, purpose, object, end, goal, *formal* rationale, *raison d'être* **2** SENSE, logic, reasoning, rationality, sanity, mind, thought, wit, brain, intellect, intellectuality, intelligence, understanding, comprehension, wisdom, judgement, common sense, gumption, *formal* ratiocination, *colloq.* nous
▷ **within reason** within limits, in moderation, moderately, within bounds, with self-control
🔁 to excess
▶ *v* work out, solve, reckon, resolve, conclude, deduce, infer, think, use your brain, *formal* cerebrate, ratiocinate, cogitate, syllogize
▷ **reason with** urge, persuade, coax, move, argue with, debate with, discuss with, plead with, *formal* remonstrate with

reasonable *adj*
1 SENSIBLE, wise, well-advised, sane, intelligent, rational, logical, practical, sound, fair, reasoned, understandable, well-thought-out, plausible, credible, possible, viable, *formal* sagacious, judicious **2** *a reasonable price* acceptable, satisfactory, moderate, average, fair, just, modest, inexpensive, low **3** *a reasonable standard of work* tolerable, acceptable, satisfactory, moderate, average, fair, *colloq.* OK, not a lot to write home about, no great shakes, not to be sneezed at
🔁 **1** unreasonable, irrational **2** exorbitant, expensive **3** poor, bad

reasoned *adj*
clear, logical, methodical, organized, rational, sensible, sound, systematic, well-thought-out, *formal* judicious
🔁 illogical, unsystematic

reasoning *n*
logic, thinking, thought, analysis, interpretation, deduction, supposition, hypothesis, rationalization, argument, case, proof, *formal* rationale, ratiocination, cerebration

reassure *v*
comfort, cheer (up), encourage, hearten, brace, bolster, buoy up, nerve, rally, *formal* inspirit
🔁 alarm, unnerve

rebate n
refund, repayment, reduction, decrease, discount, deduction, allowance

rebel n, v, adj
▶ n **1** REVOLUTIONARY, agitator, insurgent, insurrectionary, guerrilla, freedom fighter, mutineer, revolter **2** DISSENTER, nonconformist, schismatic, apostate, heretic, old use recusant
▶ v revolt, mutiny, rise up, riot, run riot, dissent, disobey, oppose, defy, resist, recoil, shy away, pull back, shrink, flinch
F3 conform, obey
▶ adj revolutionary, insurgent, insurrectionary, mutinous, rebellious, defiant, disobedient, malcontent(ed), formal insubordinate

rebellion n
revolt, revolution, rising, uprising, insurrection, insurgence, mutiny, riot, military takeover, coup, coup d'état, resistance, opposition, defiance, disobedience, civil disobedience, dissent, heresy, formal insubordination

rebellious adj
rebelling, resistant, defiant, disobedient, unruly, disorderly, ungovernable, unmanageable, obstinate, revolutionary, insurrectionary, insurgent, seditious, mutinous, rioting, formal contumacious, insubordinate, intractable, recalcitrant
F3 obedient, submissive

rebirth n
restoration, revival, renewal, regeneration, renaissance, revitalization, rejuvenation, resurrection, reincarnation

rebound v, n
▶ v recoil, backfire, return, bounce (back), spring (back), ricochet, boomerang, fail, defeat itself, be self-defeating, colloq. come home to roost, score an own goal
▶ n recoil, backfiring, return, bounce, spring, ricochet, repercussion, reverberation, reflection

rebuff v, n
▶ v spurn, reject, refuse, decline, repudiate, turn down, repulse, discourage, snub, slight, cut, colloq. cold-shoulder, put down
▶ n rejection, refusal, repulse, check, discouragement, spurning, repudiation, snub, slight, colloq. brush-off, put-down, cold shoulder, slap in the face, kick in the teeth

rebuild v
restore, remake, remodel, renovate, reassemble, reconstruct, refashion, re-edify
F3 demolish, destroy

rebuke v, n
▶ v reprove, chide, scold, reprimand, upbraid, rate, censure, blame, reproach, formal castigate, admonish, remonstrate, colloq. tell off, tick off, dress down, carpet, read the riot act to, throw the book at, give an earful, tear off a strip, come down on like a ton of bricks
F3 praise, compliment
▶ n reproach, reproof, reprimand, scolding, lecture, censure, blame, formal admonition, castigation, remonstration, colloq. dressing-down, telling-off, ticking-off, carpeting
F3 praise, commendation

rebut v
refute, quash, defeat, discredit, disprove, invalidate, negate, overturn, give the lie to, formal confute, colloq. explode

rebuttal n
refutation, negation, defeat, disproof, invalidation, overthrow, formal confutation

recalcitrant adj
disobedient, defiant, uncontrollable, ungovernable, unmanageable, unruly, wayward, wilful, contrary, obstinate, stubborn, unsubmissive, unwilling, uncooperative, formal contumacious, insubordinate, intractable, refractory, renitent
F3 amenable, tractable

recall v, n
▶ v **1** REMEMBER, think of, call to mind, recollect, reminisce, think back to, cast your mind back, evoke, call up, summon up, bring back **2** ORDER BACK, summon (back), call back, order to return **3** CANCEL, revoke, withdraw, repeal, annul, formal rescind, retract, countermand, abrogate, nullify
▶ n **1** REMEMBRANCE, memory, recollection **2** CANCELLATION, annulment, repeal, withdrawal, formal abrogation, nullification, countermanding, retraction, revocation, recision

recant v
deny, disown, renounce, repudiate, rescind, apostatize, retract, revoke, withdraw, recall, unsay, formal abjure, abrogate, disavow, disclaim, forswear

recantation n
denial, renunciation, repudiation, apostasy, withdrawal, revocation, revoke, disownment, formal abjuration, disavowal, disclaimer, retractation

recapitulate v
recap, summarize, sum up, review, repeat, reiterate, restate, recount, run over, go over

recede v
1 GO BACK, return, retire, withdraw, move away, retreat **2** DIMINISH, decline, fade, dwindle, decrease, lessen, fall off, drop, shrink, slacken, subside, ebb, wane, sink, formal abate
F3 1 advance, approach **2** grow, increase

receipt n
1 VOUCHER, ticket, slip, proof of purchase, counterfoil, stub, acknowledgement **2** RECEIVING, reception, acceptance, getting, obtaining, deriving, gaining, delivery **3** MONEY RECEIVED, takings, income, earnings, proceeds, profits, gains, return(s), turnover

receive v
1 TAKE, take up, accept, get, obtain, derive, gain, acquire, come by, pick up, collect, gather, inherit **2** receive guests admit, let in, greet, welcome, entertain, take, contain, hold, accommodate **3** EXPERIENCE, undergo, go through, suffer, bear, sustain, meet with, encounter **4** REACT TO, respond to, hear, find out about, be informed of, learn about, perceive, formal apprehend
F3 1 give, donate

receiver n
1 RECIPIENT, beneficiary, donee, assignee, grantee, legatee **2** RADIO, tuner, wireless, handset
F3 1 donor

recent adj
late, latest, current, present-day, contemporary, modern, up-to-date, up-to-the-minute, new, novel, fresh, young
F3 old, out-of-date

recently adv
lately, of late, newly, freshly, in the last few days/weeks/months/years, in the past few days/weeks/months/years, not long ago, a short time ago, a little while back
F3 long ago

receptacle n
container, vessel, holder, formal repository, reservatory

reception n
1 ACCEPTANCE, admission, greeting, recognition,

welcome, entertaining, treatment, response, reaction, acknowledgement, receipt **2** PARTY, function, social, get-together, gathering, reunion, at-home, entertainment, *colloq.* do, bash, beano, shindig, rave-up

receptive *adj*
open-minded, open to reason, amenable, accommodating, suggestible, susceptible, flexible, willing, quick, sensitive, responsive, open, accessible, approachable, friendly, hospitable, welcoming, sympathetic, favourable, interested
F3 narrow-minded, resistant, unresponsive

recess *n*
1 BREAK, interval, intermission, rest, respite, time off, holiday, vacation, *colloq.* time out **2** ALCOVE, niche, nook, corner, bay, cavity, hollow, oriel, depression, indentation **3** *in the recesses of your mind* innards, heart, depths, interior, reaches, bowels, *formal* penetralia

recession *n*
slump, depression, downturn, decline, slide, trough, collapse, crash, failure
F3 boom, upturn

recherché *adj*
refined, select, choice, rare, far-fetched, exotic, *formal* esoteric, abstruse, arcane
F3 commonplace

recipe *n*
formula, prescription, ingredients, instructions, directions, method, system, way, means, procedure, guide, process, technique

recipient *n*
receiver, beneficiary, assignee, donee, grantee, legatee
F3 donor, giver

reciprocal *adj*
mutual, joint, exchanged, shared, give-and-take, returned, requited, complementary, alternating, corresponding, equivalent, interchangeable, interdependent, *formal* correlative

reciprocate *v*
respond, reply, return, give in return, exchange, swap, repay, trade, match, equal, correspond, interchange, alternate, *formal* requite, *colloq.* do the same, give as good as you get

recital *n*
1 *a music recital* performance, show, concert **2** RECITATION, reading, narration, report, telling, account, description, rendition, rendering, interpretation, repetition, *formal* declamation

recitation *n*
passage, reading, piece, party piece, poem, verse, monologue, narration, story, tale, recital, rendering, telling

recite *v*
repeat, tell, narrate, relate, recount, speak, say aloud, deliver, articulate, perform, reel off, rattle off, itemize, enumerate, *formal* declaim

reckless *adj*
heedless, thoughtless, mindless, careless, negligent, inattentive, irresponsible, imprudent, incautious, ill-advised, indiscreet, rash, hasty, foolhardy, desperate, daredevil, devil-may-care, wild, madcap, tearaway, *formal* precipitate
F3 cautious, wary, careful, prudent

recklessness *n*
carelessness, heedlessness, inattention, irresponsibility, irresponsibleness, negligence, rashness, thoughtlessness, incaution, imprudence, foolhardiness, mindlessness, madness, motorway madness
F3 carefulness, caution, prudence

reckon *v*
1 THINK, believe, imagine, fancy, suppose, assume, guess, *formal* surmise, conjecture **2** CONSIDER, regard, esteem, think of, look upon, value, rate, judge, evaluate, assess, estimate, gauge, *formal* deem, appraise **3** CALCULATE, compute, figure out, work out, add up, total, tally, count, number, enumerate
▷ **reckon on** rely on, depend on, bank on, count on, take for granted, trust in, hope for, expect, anticipate, foresee, plan for, bargain for, figure on, take into account, face
▷ **reckon with** anticipate, bargain for, consider, take into account, plan for, expect, foresee, handle, cope, deal, face, treat

reckoning *n*
1 *by my reckoning* calculation, computation, addition, working-out, total, tally, score, number, enumeration, estimate **2** BILL, account, charge, due, score, paying, payment, settlement **3** JUDGEMENT, opinion, estimation, evaluation, assessment, *formal* appraisal **4** *the day of reckoning* judgement, punishment, retribution, doom, damnation

reclaim *v*
recover, regain, get back, claim back, take back, recapture, retrieve, salvage, rescue, redeem, restore, reinstate, regenerate

recline *v*
rest, lean back, lie (down), lounge, loll, sprawl, stretch out, *formal* repose

recluse *n*
ascetic, hermit, solitary, loner, monk, eremite, stylite, solitarian, solitaire, anchorite, anchoret, anchoress

reclusive *adj*
isolated, solitary, withdrawn, secluded, retiring, recluse, cloistered, monastic, ascetic, eremitic, hermitical, anchoritic, *formal* sequestered

recognition *n*
1 IDENTIFICATION, detection, discovery, recollection, recall, remembrance, awareness, knowing, knowledge, consciousness, perception, realization, admission, confession, understanding, placing, spotting, *formal* cognizance **2** ACCEPTANCE, allowing, admittance, endorsement, grating, approval, acknowledgement, validation, sanction **3** *receive recognition for your work* appreciation, honour, reward, respect, salute, gratitude, thankfulness

recognize *v*
1 IDENTIFY, know, remember, recollect, recall, call to mind, pick out, tell, place, see, notice, spot, perceive, not miss, not mistake **2** *recognize your faults* accept, acknowledge, admit, grant, concede, allow, endorse, appreciate, discern, perceive, understand, realize, confess, own, be aware of, be conscious of, *formal* apprehend **3** *recognize a qualification* accept, allow, admit, endorse, grant, approve, acknowledge, adopt, validate, sanction **4** APPRECIATE, be thankful for, honour, respect, salute, show your gratitude/thankfulness

recoil *v, n*
▶ *v* move back, jump back, spring back, shy away, flinch, shrink, quail, rebound, react, falter, kick, backfire, boomerang, misfire
▶ *n* rebound, reaction, kick, backlash, repercussion

recollect *v*
recall, remember, call to mind, cast your mind back, reminisce

recollection *n*
memory, recall, remembrance, souvenir, reminiscence, (mental) impression

recommend *v*
commend, approve, endorse, praise, vouch for,

advocate, urge, advise, counsel, guide, suggest, propose, put forward, advance, put in a good word for, *formal* exhort, *colloq.* plug
🖃 disapprove

recommendation *n*
commendation, endorsement, approval, advice, counsel, guidance, suggestion, urging, proposal, advocacy, sanction, blessing, praise, tip, good word, special mention, reference, testimonial, *formal* exhortations, *colloq.* plug
🖃 disapproval

recompense *n, v*
▶ *n* compensation, indemnification, damages, reparation, restitution, amends, requital, satisfaction, repayment, reward, payment, remuneration, pay, wages, *formal* guerdon
▶ *v* compensate, indemnify, remunerate, pay, reward, repay, redress, reimburse, requite, satisfy, *formal* guerdon

reconcile *v*
1 *be reconciled with someone* reunite, conciliate, pacify, appease, placate, mollify, bring together, make (your) peace, put on friendly terms, *formal* propitiate, *colloq.* make up, bury the hatchet, become friends again, shake hands, forgive and forget 2 *reconcile different aims* harmonize, accommodate, adjust, resolve, settle, mend, remedy, put right, rectify, square, *formal* accord, *colloq.* patch up 3 *reconcile yourself to an unpleasant situation* resign yourself to, face up to, accept, come to accept, submit
🖃 1 estrange, alienate

reconciliation *n*
reunion, conciliation, pacification, peace, mollification, appeasement, rapprochement, détente, settlement, agreement, harmony, harmonizing, accommodation, resolution, squaring, adjustment, compromise, *formal* propitiation, accord
🖃 estrangement, separation

recondite *adj*
obscure, difficult, involved, complicated, intricate, mysterious, mystical, deep, profound, dark, concealed, hidden, secret, *formal* abstruse, arcane, esoteric
🖃 simple, straightforward

recondition *v*
renovate, repair, restore, renew, refurbish, overhaul, fix, remodel, revamp

reconnaissance *n*
exploration, reconnoitring, scouting, survey, expedition, examination, inspection, probe, observation, scrutiny, scan, investigation, search, patrol, *colloq.* recce

reconnoitre *v*
explore, survey, scan, spy out, inspect, examine, scrutinize, investigate, patrol, observe, probe, *colloq.* recce, check out, see how the land lies, see the lie of the land

reconsider *v*
think over, rethink, review, revise, re-examine, think twice, modify, reassess, think better of, have second thoughts

reconstruct *v*
remake, rebuild, reassemble, re-establish, refashion, remodel, recondition, revamp, reform, reorganize, redo, recreate, restore, renovate, regenerate

record *n, v*
▶ *n* 1 REGISTER, log, chart, report, account, minutes, memorandum, note(s), entry, document(s), file, dossier, diary, logbook, journal, chronicle, memoir, memorial, history, annals, archives, documentation, data, evidence, photography, testimony, trace 2 RECORDING,

disc, single, CD, compact disc, album, release, LP, cassette, tape, *colloq.* vinyl 3 *break the record* fastest time, best performance, furthest distance, personal best, world record 4 BACKGROUND, history, previous performance, track record, curriculum vitae, career
▷ **off the record** unofficial, unofficially, confidential, confidentially, private, privately, *formal* sub rosa
🖃 official, officially
▷ **on record** noted, documented, written down 2 *the wettest April on record* noted, documented, written down 2 *to go on record as saying* officially recorded, publicly known, documented
▶ *v* 1 NOTE, enter, inscribe, write down, transcribe, register, log, chart, put down, take down, put on record, enrol, report, list, catalogue, minute, chronicle, document, keep, preserve 2 TAPE-RECORD, make a recording of, tape, videotape, video, cut, edit 3 *the gauge records electrical activity* show, register, indicate, display, read, express

recorder *n*
1 REGISTRAR, archivist, annalist, chronicler, diarist, historian, chronologer, secretary, clerk, stenographer, scribe, scorer, score-keeper 2 TAPE RECORDER, cassette recorder, cassette-player, video recorder, videocassette recorder, *colloq.* video

recording *n*

> **Types of recording include:**
> album, audiotape, cassette, CD, compact disc, digital recording, disc, DVD (digital versatile disc), EP (extended play), 45, gramophone record, long-playing record, LP, magnetic tape, mono recording, record, 78, single, stereo recording, tape, tape-recording, tele-recording, video, videocassette, video disc, videotape, *colloq.* vinyl.

recount *v*
tell, relate, impart, communicate, report, narrate, describe, depict, portray, unfold, detail, repeat, rehearse, recite

recoup *v*
recover, retrieve, regain, get back, win back, make good, repossess, repay, refund, indemnify, reimburse, recompense, compensate

recourse *n*
appeal, resort, access, turning to, choice, option, alternative, possibility, remedy, refuge, way out

recover *v*
1 *recover from illness* get better, feel better, get well, improve, pick up, rally, mend, heal, respond to treatment, get over, recuperate, feel yourself again, revive, convalesce, gain strength, get stronger, come round, *formal* ameliorate, *colloq.* pull through, bounce back, turn the corner, get back on your feet, be on the mend 2 REGAIN, get back, win back, recoup, retrieve, retake, recapture, repossess, reclaim, recycle, restore
🖃 1 worsen 2 lose, forfeit

recovery *n*
1 RECUPERATION, convalescence, rehabilitation, mending, healing, improvement, upturn, rally, rallying, revival, restoration, *formal* amelioration 2 RETRIEVAL, salvage, reclamation, recouping, regaining, repossession, recapture, recycling
🖃 1 worsening 2 loss, forfeit

recreation *n*
fun, enjoyment, pleasure, amusement, diversion, distraction, entertainment, hobby, pastime, game, sport, play, leisure pursuit, leisure activity, leisure, relaxation, refreshment

recrimination *n*
accusation, countercharge, counter-attack, reprisal, retaliation, retort, bickering, quarrel

recruit *v, n*
▶ *v* enlist, draft, conscript, enrol, sign up, levy, engage, take on, mobilize, raise, muster, gather, assemble, put together, obtain, acquire, *formal* procure
▶ *n* beginner, newcomer, novice, new entrant, initiate, learner, trainee, apprentice, tiro, conscript, draftee, convert, *colloq.* greenhorn, rookie

rectify *v*
correct, put right, right, set right, make good, remedy, cure, repair, fix, mend, reform, improve, better, amend, adjust, *formal* emend, ameliorate, redress

rectitude *n*
integrity, uprightness, virtue, honesty, honour, goodness, justice, morality, incorruptibility, irreproachability, exactness, decency, correctness, righteousness, scrupulousness, *formal* probity

recumbent *adj*
lying down, lying flat, horizontal, resting, reclining, leaning, lounging, prostrate, prone, sprawling, *formal* supine
Ⓕ erect, upright

recuperate *v*
recover, get better, get well, get stronger, regain your strength, improve, pick up, pull through, rally, revive, mend, convalesce, *colloq.* pull through, bounce back, turn the corner, get back on your feet, be on the mend
Ⓕ worsen

recur *v*
repeat itself, happen again, persist, return, reappear

recurrent *adj*
recurring, chronic, persistent, repeated, repetitive, continual, habitual, regular, periodic, cyclical, frequent, intermittent

recycle *v*
re-use, reprocess, reclaim, recover, salvage, save

red *adj*
1 SCARLET, vermilion, cherry, ruby, crimson, rose, maroon, russet, pink, reddish, bloodshot, inflamed **2** RUDDY, florid, glowing, rosy, flushed, blushing, embarrassed, shamefaced, *technical* rufescent, *formal* rubicund **3** *red hair* ginger, carroty, auburn, chestnut, Titian **4** COMMUNIST, socialist, leftist, Bolshevik, revolutionary
▷ **in the red** overdrawn, insolvent, bankrupt, in debt, in arrears, owing money, penniless, impoverished, *colloq.* on the rocks, broke, bust, gone to the wall, on your beam-ends
Ⓕ in the black
▷ **see red** become angry, lose your temper, explode, *colloq.* blow your cool, blow your top, boil over, burst a blood vessel, fly into a rage, fly off the handle, go mad, lose your cool, lose your rag

red-blooded *adj*
virile, strong, vigorous, manly, robust, hearty, lively, lusty

redden *v*
blush, flush, colour, go red, crimson, suffuse

reddish *adj*
red, bloodshot, rosy, ruddy, russet, ginger, sandy, pink, *technical* rufescent, *formal* rubicund, rufous

redeem *v*
1 BUY BACK, repurchase, cash (in), convert, trade in, exchange, give in exchange, change, trade, ransom, reclaim, regain, get back, repossess, recoup, recover, recuperate, retrieve, salvage **2** COMPENSATE FOR, make up for, offset, outweigh **3** *Christ redeems sinners* atone for, absolve, acquit, remove guilt from, dis-charge, release, liberate, emancipate, free, set free, deliver, rescue, save, ransom, *formal* expiate

redemption *n*
1 REPURCHASE, repossession, reclamation, recovery, reparation, retrieval, exchange, reinstatement, trade-in, fulfilment, compensation **2** ATONEMENT, deliverance, expiation, emancipation, freedom, rescue, salvation, ransom, liberation, release

redolent *adj*
1 EVOCATIVE, reminiscent, suggestive, remindful **2** AROMATIC, fragrant, perfumed, scented, sweet-smelling, *formal* odorous

redoubtable *adj*
formidable, fearsome, strong, terrible, powerful, resolute, mighty, awful, dreadful, fearful

redound *v*
contribute, ensue, reflect, result, tend, *formal* conduce, effect

redress *v, n*
▶ *v* **1** RIGHT, put right, rectify, remedy, avenge, requite, recompense, make compensation for **2** ADJUST, amend, correct, balance, regulate
▶ *n* compensation, recompense, indemnification, remedy, relief, assistance, help, aid, correction, requital, restitution, satisfaction, reparation, payment, justice, atonement

reduce *v*
1 LESSEN, make less, make smaller, decrease, contract, shrink, slim, shorten, abbreviate, curtail, trim, minimize, downsize, lower, moderate, weaken, dilute, diminish, impair, deplete, take the edge off, *formal* mitigate **2** DRIVE, force, degrade, bring down, lower, downgrade, demote, humble, humiliate, impoverish, subdue, overcome, overpower, conquer, master, *formal* vanquish **3** *reduce prices* lower, decrease, cut, slash, knock down, discount, rebate, halve **4** SLIM, diet, go on a diet, lose weight, *colloq.* weight-watch
Ⓕ **1** increase, raise, boost

reduction *n*
decrease, drop, fall, decline, lessening, moderation, weakening, contraction, abbreviation, compression, shrinkage, downsizing, narrowing, shortening, curtailment, restriction, limitation, cutback, cut, discount, discounting, rebate, concession, allowance, devaluation, depreciation, deduction, subtraction, loss, *formal* diminution
Ⓕ increase, rise, enlargement

redundancy *n*
1 DISMISSAL, notice, laying-off, discharge, removal, expulsion, marching-orders, *colloq.* papers, sacking, firing, sack, push, boot, elbow **2** SUPERFLUITY, surplus, uselessness, wordiness, excess, repetition, tautology, *technical* pleonasm, *formal* prolixity, verbosity
Ⓕ **1** appointment, hiring

redundant *adj*
1 UNEMPLOYED, out of work, jobless, laid off, dismissed, *colloq.* sacked, fired **2** SUPERFLUOUS, surplus, excess, extra, unneeded, unnecessary, unwanted, inessential, *formal* supernumerary **3** WORDY, verbose, padded, repetitious, tautological, *technical* pleonastic, *formal* periphrastic
Ⓕ **2** necessary, essential, required **3** concise

reef *n*
sandbank, sandbar, ridge, cay, key

reek *v, n*
▶ *v* smell, stink, fume, *formal* exhale, *colloq.* hum, pong
▶ *n* smell, odour, stink, stench, vapour, fume(s), *formal* exhalation, effluvium, malodour, mephitis, fetor, *colloq.* pong

reel *v*
stagger, totter, wobble, rock, sway, waver, falter, stumble, fling, lurch, pitch, swim, roll, revolve, gyrate, spin, wheel, twirl, whirl, swirl

refer *v*
1 MENTION, allude, touch on, speak of, bring up, recommend, cite, quote, hint at **2** *refer to a catalogue* consult, look up, turn to, look at, resort to **3** SEND, direct, point, guide, pass on, hand on, transfer, commit, deliver, *formal* remit **4** APPLY, concern, be relevant, relate, belong, *formal* pertain

referee *n, v*
▶ *n* umpire, judge, adjudicator, arbitrator, mediator, *colloq.* ref
▶ *v* umpire, judge, adjudicate, mediate, intercede, arbitrate

reference *n*
1 MENTION, remark, allusion, hint, citation, quotation, illustration, source, authority, instance, note, footnote **2** TESTIMONIAL, recommendation, endorsement, credentials, character **3** RELATION, applicability, regard, respect, connection, bearing, *formal* pertinence

referendum *n*
poll, vote, voting, plebiscite, survey

refine *v*
1 PURIFY, process, treat, clarify, filter, sift, strain, distil, clear, cleanse **2** IMPROVE, polish, hone, perfect, elaborate, civilize, elevate, exalt

refined *adj*
1 CIVILIZED, cultured, cultivated, polished, sophisticated, stylish, urbane, genteel, gentlemanly, ladylike, well-bred, well-mannered, polite, civil, elegant, gracious, courtly, fine, delicate, subtle, precise, exact, sensitive, discriminating **2** PURIFIED, processed, treated, distilled, filtered, clear
F3 **1** coarse, vulgar, rude

refinement *n*
1 MODIFICATION, alteration, amendment, addition, improvement, *formal* amelioration **2** CULTIVATION, sophistication, culture, urbanity, gentility, breeding, style, elegance, grace, civility, good manners, polish, taste, discrimination, subtlety, finesse
F3 **1** deterioration **2** coarseness, vulgarity

reflect *v*
1 MIRROR, echo, imitate, reproduce, image, send back, throw back, bounce off **2** SHOW, portray, depict, reveal, display, exhibit, demonstrate, indicate, express, communicate, *formal* manifest, bespeak **3** THINK, ponder, consider, mull (over), dwell, brood, deliberate, contemplate, meditate, muse, *formal* ruminate, cogitate, cerebrate **4** *his behaviour reflects badly on the school* discredit, disgrace, tarnish, put in a bad light, give a bad name to

reflection *n*
1 IMAGE, likeness, echo, mirror image **2** INDICATION, impression, expression, display, demonstration, portrayal, observation, view, *formal* manifestation **3** THINKING, thought, study, consideration, deliberation, contemplation, meditation, musing, view, opinion, impression, belief, viewpoint, idea, feeling(s), *formal* rumination, cogitation, cerebration **4** DISCREDIT, slur, disgrace, shame, criticism, disrepute, blame, reproach, *formal* aspersion

reflective *adj*
thoughtful, contemplative, pondering, deliberative, meditative, pensive, reasoning, absorbed, dreamy, *formal* cogitating, ruminative

reflex *adj*
automatic, spontaneous, without thinking, unwilled, uncontrollable, involuntary, natural, *colloq.* knee-jerk

reform *v, n*
▶ *v* change, amend, improve, better, rectify, correct, mend, repair, revise, refashion, rehabilitate, rebuild, reconstruct, remodel, revamp, renovate, restore, regenerate, reconstitute, reorganize, revolutionize, purge, *formal* ameliorate, *colloq.* shake up
▶ *n* change, amendment, improvement, betterment, rectification, correction, rehabilitation, renovation, reorganization, revision, rebuilding, reconstruction, remodelling, restoration, purge, *colloq.* shake-up

reformer *n*
do-gooder, revolutionary, *colloq.* whistle-blower

refractory *adj*
stubborn, obstinate, headstrong, unmanageable, uncontrollable, naughty, unruly, wilful, unco-operative, perverse, mulish, difficult, disobedient, resistant, defiant, cantankerous, contentious, *formal* intractable, contumacious, recalcitrant, disputatious, restive
F3 co-operative, malleable, obedient

refrain[1] *v*
refrain from smoking stop, give up, do without, leave off, renounce, avoid, *formal* cease, desist, abstain, forbear, eschew, *colloq.* quit

refrain[2] *n*
sing the refrain twice chorus, response, burden, strain, melody, song, tune

refresh *v*
1 COOL, freshen, energize, stimulate, enliven, invigorate, revive, brace, restore, renew, rejuvenate, reanimate, revitalize, reinvigorate, *formal* fortify, revivify, *colloq.* breathe new life into **2** *refresh your memory* jog, stimulate, stir, prompt, prod, arouse, activate, remind
F3 **1** tire, exhaust

refreshing *adj*
1 *a refreshing bath* invigorating, energizing, stimulating, inspiring, exhilarating, reviving, cool, thirst-quenching, bracing **2** *a refreshing change from routine* different, fresh, freshening, new, novel, original, unexpected, *colloq.* not another

refreshment *n*
sustenance, food, drink(s), snack, freshening, stimulation, revival, restoration, renewal, reanimation, invigoration, reinvigoration, revitalization

refreshments *n*
aliment, drinks, food, provisions, snacks, elevenses, sustenance, titbits, *colloq.* eats, *slang* nosh, grub

refrigerate *v*
chill, cool, keep cold, freeze
F3 heat, warm

refuge *n*
sanctuary, asylum, shelter, protection, security, retreat, place of safety, hideout, hide-away, resort, harbour, haven, bolthole, island

refugee *n*
exile, émigré, displaced person, stateless person, fugitive, runaway, escapee

refulgent *adj*
brilliant, shining, beaming, bright, radiant, gleaming, glistening, glittering, *formal* irradiant, lambent, lustrous, resplendent

refund *v, n*
▶ *v* repay, pay back, reimburse, rebate, return, give back, restore
▶ *n* repayment, reimbursement, rebate, return

refurbish *v*
renovate, redecorate, re-equip, refit, remodel, revamp, repair, mend, overhaul, restore, recondition, *colloq.* do up

refusal *n*
rejection, turning-down, no, rebuff, spurning, repudiation, denial, negation, withholding
☒ acceptance, agreement

refuse¹ *v*
refuse to go; refuse permission reject, turn down, say no, spurn, repudiate, rebuff, repel, deny, withhold, *formal* decline, *colloq.* pass up, knock back, shake your head, draw the line at, dig your heels in
☒ accept, agree, allow, permit, grant

refuse² *n*
piles of refuse rubbish, waste, trash, garbage, junk, litter, debris, dregs, dross, scum, offscum, *technical* scoria, draff

refutation *n*
disproof, negation, rebuttal, overthrow, *technical* elenchus, *formal* confutation

refute *v*
disprove, rebut, give the lie to, discredit, counter, negate, overthrow, silence, deny (strongly), *formal* confute

regain *v*
recover, get back, win back, recoup, reclaim, repossess, retake, take back, recapture, retrieve, return to

regal *adj*
majestic, kingly, queenly, princely, imperial, royal, sovereign, stately, magnificent, noble, lordly

regale *v*
amuse, entertain, delight, divert, captivate, fascinate, feast, ply, gratify, serve, refresh

regard *v, n*
▶ *v* **1** CONSIDER, judge, rate, value, gauge, estimate, think, believe, suppose, imagine, contemplate, weigh up, *formal* deem, appraise **2** LOOK AT, look upon, see, view, observe, watch, gaze at, scrutinize, eye, *formal* behold, *colloq.* give the once-over **3** HEED, listen to, observe, follow, note, bear in mind, take notice of, pay attention to, take into account/consideration
▶ *n* **1** CARE, concern, consideration, attention, notice, heed, respect, deference, honour, admiration, affection, love, sympathy, approval, *formal* esteem, approbation **2** *in this regard* matter, subject, aspect, point, detail, particular **3** *send her my regards* best wishes, good wishes, greetings, respects, compliments, salutations
☒ **1** disregard, contempt
▷ **with/in regard to** as regards, concerning, with reference to, with respect to, in relation to, in connection with, re, about, as to, on the subject of, apropos

regardful *adj*
attentive, mindful, thoughtful, noticing, observant, aware, careful, considerate, watchful, respectful, dutiful, heedful, *formal* circumspect
☒ heedless, inattentive, regardless, unobservant

regarding *prep*
with regard to, in regard to, as regards, concerning, with reference to, with respect to, in relation to, in connection with, re, about, as to, on the subject of, apropos

regardless *adj, adv*
▶ *adj* disregarding, heedless, unmindful, neglectful, negligent, inattentive, unconcerned, indifferent
☒ heedful, mindful, attentive
▶ *adv* anyway, nevertheless, nonetheless, no matter what, despite everything, come what may, anyhow, *colloq.* at any price/cost

regenerate *v*
revive, reinvigorate, reawaken, rekindle, renew, restore, reconstitute, reconstruct, re-establish, renovate, refresh, uplift, change, invigorate, rejuvenate, reproduce, *formal* inspirit, revivify

regeneration *n*
renewal, renovation, restoration, re-establishment, reinvigoration, reconstruction, reconstitution, rejuvenation, reproduction, *formal* homomorphosis

regime *n*
government, rule, administration, management, leadership, command, control, direction, reign, establishment, system

regiment *n*
army, brigade, cohort, battery, band, company, platoon, squadron, group, crew, gang, body

regimented *adj*
strict, disciplined, controlled, regulated, standardized, ordered, methodical, systematic, organized, systematized
☒ free, lax, disorganized

region *n*
land, terrain, sector, neighbourhood, range, scope, expanse, sphere, world, field, ambit, orbit, division, section, part, place
▷ **in the region of** approximately, roughly, around, about, some, something like, odd, circa, more or less, loosely, round about, or thereabouts, approaching, close to, nearly, just about, not far off, in the neighbourhood/vicinity of, in round numbers, rounded up/down, *colloq.* give or take
☒ exactly

regional *adj*
district, local, localized, provincial, sectional, zonal, parochial
☒ national, international, worldwide

register *n, v*
▶ *n* roll, roster, list, listing, index, catalogue, directory, log, diary, journal, record, chronicle, annals, archives, file(s), ledger, schedule, diary, almanac
▶ *v* **1** RECORD, note, log, enter, put in writing, put down, set down, take down, inscribe, mark, list, catalogue, chronicle, enrol, enlist, sign on, check in **2** SHOW, reveal, betray, display, exhibit, indicate, demonstrate, express, say, *formal* manifest **3** *the gauge registers a measurement* read, indicate, record, show, display

registrar *n*
official, recorder, secretary, clerk, administrator, cataloguer, annalist, archivist, chronicler, protocolist

regress *v*
deteriorate, recede, relapse, retreat, return, revert, wane, backslide, degenerate, lapse, ebb, *formal* retrocede, retrogress
☒ progress

regret *v, n*
▶ *v* feel sorry, wish that you had not done, be disappointed, be distressed, rue, repent, lament, bemoan, weep, mourn, grieve, deplore
▶ *n* remorse, contrition, repentance, penitence, self-reproach, shame, sorrow, grief, disappointment, bitterness, *formal* compunction

regretful *adj*
remorseful, rueful, repentant, contrite, penitent, conscience-stricken, ashamed, sorry, apologetic, sad, sorrowful, disappointed
☒ impenitent, unashamed

📖 **regretful** or **regrettable** ?

Regretful means 'full of regret, sad, sorry'; *regrettable* means 'causing regret, to be regretted': *It is regrettable that you have behaved so foolishly, and I feel regretful that I must now ask you to leave.*

regrettable *adj*
unfortunate, unlucky, unhappy, sad, disappointing, upsetting, distressing, lamentable, deplorable, disgraceful, shameful, sorry, wrong, ill-advised, *formal* reprehensible
F₃ fortunate, happy

 regrettable or **regretful** ? *See panel at* REGRETFUL.

regular *adj*
1 ROUTINE, habitual, typical, usual, customary, time-honoured, classic, conventional, established, orthodox, correct, official, approved, proper, standard, normal, average, ordinary, common, commonplace, daily, everyday **2** PERIODIC, rhythmic, frequent, recurring, hourly, daily, weekly, monthly, yearly, steady, constant, fixed, set, unchanging, unvarying, uniform, consistent, even, level, flat, evenly spread, smooth, balanced, symmetrical, orderly, systematic, methodical, well-organized, *colloq.* regular as clockwork
F₃ 1 unusual, unconventional **2** irregular, intermittent

regulate *v*
1 CONTROL, direct, guide, govern, rule, administer, oversee, superintend, supervise, manage, handle, conduct, run, organize, order, arrange, settle, square, monitor **2** ADJUST, set, synchronize, control, tune, moderate, balance

regulation *n, adj*
▶ *n* **1** RULE, statute, law, act, ordinance, by-law, edict, decree, order, ruling, directive, command, supervision, commandment, precept, dictate, dictum, pronouncement, ordinance, requirement, procedure **2** CONTROL, direction, guidance, rule, administration, superintendence, supervision, management
▶ *adj* standard, official, statutory, obligatory, required, fixed, set, orthodox, accepted, customary, usual, normal, *formal* prescribed, mandatory

regurgitate *v*
1 VOMIT, bring up, spew, *formal* disgorge, *colloq.* puke, throw up **2** REPEAT, say/tell again, restate, recapitulate, *formal* reiterate

rehabilitate *v*
restore, renew, reinvigorate, normalize, reform, reinstate, reconstitute, re-establish, renovate, reintegrate, recondition, rebuild, convert, adjust, clear, mend, reconstruct, save, redeem

rehash *n, v*
▶ *n* reworking, rearrangement, rejig, rejigging, restatement, reshuffle, rewrite
▶ *v* rework, change, alter, rearrange, rejig, rejigger, restate, reshuffle, refashion, rewrite

rehearsal *n*
practice, drill, exercise, trial run, run-through, preparation, reading, recital, *colloq.* dry run, dummy run

rehearse *v*
1 PRACTISE, drill, train, go over, run through, prepare, try out **2** REPEAT, recite, recount, relate, narrate, go over, enumerate

reign *v, n*
▶ *v* **1** RULE, be king/queen, sit on the throne, be in power, be in charge, be in control, govern, be in government, command, be in command **2** *silence reigns* prevail, predominate, occur, hold sway, be present, exist, influence, *formal* obtain
▶ *n* rule, sway, monarchy, empire, sovereignty, supremacy, government, power, command, dominion, control, influence, *formal* ascendancy

reimburse *v*
refund, repay, pay back, give back, return, restore, recompense, compensate, indemnify, remunerate

rein *n, v*
▶ *n* check, control, curb, restraint, hold, overcheck, restriction, brake, bridle, harness
▶ *v* check, control, curb, restrain, restrict, limit, hold back, stop, hold, halt, arrest, bridle

reinforce *v*
1 STRENGTHEN, toughen, harden, stiffen, steel, brace, support, buttress, shore, prop, stay, supplement, increase, *formal* fortify, augment **2** EMPHASIZE, stress, underline, consolidate
F₃ 1 weaken, undermine

reinforcement *n*
1 STRENGTHENING, supplement, support, addition, increase, enlargement, prop, shore, stay, brace, buttress, emphasis, hardening, amplification, *formal* fortification, augmentation **2** *send reinforcements* auxiliaries, reserves, additional soldiers/police officers, supplementaries, back-up, support, help

reinstate *v*
restore, return, give back, replace, recall, reappoint, reinstall, re-establish

reinstatement *n*
restoration, return, giving back, replacement, recall, re-establishment

reiterate *v*
repeat, recapitulate, resay, restate, retell, emphasize, stress, *formal* iterate, rehearse, *colloq.* recap

reject *v, n*
▶ *v* **1** *reject a proposal* refuse, deny, decline, turn down, say no to, veto, disallow, condemn, despise, spurn, rebuff, jilt, exclude, repudiate, repel, *formal* renounce, *colloq.* have nothing to do with, not have anything to do with, take a raincheck on, wash your hands of, turn your back on, turn your nose up at, not touch with a barge pole **2** DISCARD, scrap, jettison, eliminate, cast off, throw away, set aside, *formal* forsake, *colloq.* brush off, give the cold shoulder to
F₃ 1 accept, agree **2** choose, select
▶ *n* failure, second, discard, outcast, cast-off

rejection *n*
refusal, turning-down, denial, declining, veto, dismissal, rebuff, exclusion, discarding, jettisoning, repudiation, elimination, *formal* renunciation, *colloq.* brush-off, cold shoulder, Dear John letter
F₃ acceptance, choice, selection

rejoice *v*
celebrate, revel, delight, be delighted/pleased, be joyful/happy, take pleasure, glory, exult, triumph, *old use* make merry, *colloq.* jump for joy, whoop it up

rejoicing *n*
celebration, revelry, festivity, happiness, gladness, joy, delight, pleasure, euphoria, elation, jubilation, glory, exultation, triumph, *old use* merrymaking

rejoin *v*
retort, answer, reply, respond, quip, repartee, riposte

rejoinder *n*
retort, answer, reply, response, quip, repartee, riposte

rejuvenate *v*
revitalize, reinvigorate, reanimate, revive, renew, freshen up, refresh, restore, rekindle, recharge, regenerate, *formal* revivify

relapse *v, n*
▶ *v* worsen, deteriorate, degenerate, weaken, sink, fail, lapse, revert, regress, fall away, backslide, *formal* retrogress
▶ *n* worsening, deterioration, setback, recurrence,

weakening, lapse, reversion, regression, backsliding, *formal* retrogression

relate *v*
1 LINK, connect, join, couple, ally, associate, *formal* correlate **2** REFER, apply, concern, have a bearing on, be relevant, *formal* pertain, appertain **3** *relate an anecdote* tell, recount, narrate, report, describe, recite, present, communicate, detail, *formal* delineate **4** IDENTIFY, sympathize, empathize, understand, feel for, get on (well) with, *colloq.* hit it off, speak the same language, be on the same wavelength

related *adj*
kindred, akin, affiliated, allied, associated, connected, linked, interrelated, interconnected, accompanying, joint, mutual, relevant, *formal* concomitant, correlated, cognate, consanguineous, agnate
ᴇ҉ unrelated, unconnected

relation *n*
1 LINK, linking, connection, bond, relationship, comparison, similarity, affiliation, alliance, interrelation, interconnection, interdependence, *formal* correlation **2** REGARD, reference, relevance, bearing, application, *formal* pertinence **3** RELATIVE, family, kin, kinsman, kinswoman, kinsfolk, kindred

relations *n*
1 RELATIVES, family, kin, kinsman, kinswoman, kinsfolk, kindred, *colloq.* folks **2** RELATIONSHIP, terms, rapport, liaison, interaction, affairs, dealings, connections, communications, contact(s), associations, *formal* intercourse **3** *sexual relations* intercourse, sex, intimacy, intimate relations, love-making, copulation, carnal knowledge, *formal* coition, coitus, *colloq.* sleeping with someone, going to bed with someone

relationship *n*
1 CONNECTION, bond, link, tie(s), tie-up, association, alliance, liaison, rapport, friendship, affinity, closeness, similarity, parallel, ratio, proportion, *formal* correlation, *colloq.* chemistry **2** AFFAIR, love affair, romance, intimacy, liaison, friendship, *colloq.* fling

relative *adj, n*
▸ *adj* **1** COMPARATIVE, proportional, proportionate, comparable, corresponding, respective, parallel, reciprocal, *formal* commensurate, correlative **2** APPROPRIATE, relevant, applicable, related, connected, interrelated, dependent, *formal* apposite, germane, pertinent
▸ *n* relation, family, kin, kinsman, kinswoman, kinsfolk, kindred

relatively *adv*
comparatively, in/by comparison, fairly, quite, rather, somewhat

relax *v*
1 *relax on holiday* calm (down), rest, unwind, wind down, loosen up, tranquillize, sedate, *colloq.* take it/things easy, let yourself go, make yourself at home, let your hair down, put your feet up, hang loose, cool it, chill out **2** *relax the rules* moderate, soften, ease (off), lessen, reduce, diminish, weaken, lower, slacken, loosen, *formal* abate, remit
ᴇ҉ **2** tighten

relaxation *n*
1 REST, unwinding, loosening up, refreshment, leisure, recreation, fun, amusement, entertainment, enjoyment, pleasure, *formal* repose **2** SLACKENING, loosening, weakening, lessening, reduction, softening, easing, moderation, détente, easing, *formal* abatement, *colloq.* let-up
ᴇ҉ **2** tension, intensification

relaxed *adj*
1 *feel relaxed* at ease, comfortable, uninhibited, care-

free, happy-go-lucky, cool, calm, composed, restful, collected, unhurried, leisurely **2** *a relaxed situation* INFORMAL, casual, restful, *colloq.* laid-back, easy-going
ᴇ҉ **1** tense, nervous, worried **2** formal, tense

relay *n, v*
▸ *n* **1** BROADCAST, transmission, programme, communication, message, dispatch **2** *work in relays* shift, turn, stint, time, spell, period
▸ *v* broadcast, transmit, communicate, pass on, hand on, send, circulate, spread, carry, supply

release *v, n*
▸ *v* **1** SET FREE, free, liberate, deliver, emancipate **2** LOOSEN, loose, unloose, let go, untie, undo, unlock, unfasten, unchain, unbind, unshackle, unleash **3** EXCUSE, exempt, discharge, let go, let off, acquit, absolve, *formal* exonerate **4** ISSUE, publish, make available, make known, make public, announce, disclose, reveal, circulate, distribute, present, launch, divulge, unveil
ᴇ҉ **1** imprison **3** detain
▸ *n* **1** FREEDOM, liberty, liberation, deliverance, emancipation, *formal* manumission **2** ACQUITTAL, absolution, exoneration, exemption, discharge, *colloq.* let-off **3** ISSUE, publication, publishing, disclosure, revelation, declaration, bulletin, announcement, proclamation
ᴇ҉ **1** imprisonment, detention

relegate *v*
demote, downgrade, degrade, reduce, consign, entrust, assign, refer, dispatch, delegate, transfer, banish, expatriate, deport, eject, exile, expel
ᴇ҉ promote

relent *v*
1 GIVE IN, give way, come round, yield, allow, change your mind, capitulate **2** *the storm relented* ease, let up, die down, slacken, soften, weaken, unbend, relax, *formal* abate

relentless *adj*
unrelenting, unremitting, incessant, persistent, unflagging, unceasing, ruthless, remorseless, implacable, merciless, pitiless, cold-hearted, hard-hearted, unforgiving, cruel, harsh, fierce, grim, hard, punishing, uncompromising, inflexible, unyielding, inexorable
ᴇ҉ merciful, yielding

relevant *adj*
material, significant, related, to the point, applicable, apposite, apt, appropriate, suitable, fitting, proper, admissible, *formal* pertinent, germane, congruous, apropos
ᴇ҉ irrelevant, inapplicable, inappropriate, unsuitable

reliable *adj*
unfailing, certain, sure, dependable, responsible, trusty, trustworthy, dutiful, honest, true, devoted, conscientious, faithful, constant, staunch, solid, safe, sound, well-grounded, well-founded, stable, tested, predictable, regular
ᴇ҉ unreliable, doubtful, untrustworthy

reliance *n*
dependence, trust, faith, belief, conviction, credit, confidence, assurance

relic *n*
memento, souvenir, keepsake, token, reminder, remembrance, survival, remains, artefact, heirloom, antique, remnant, scrap, fragment, vestige, trace

relief *n*
1 *relief from pain* respite, alleviation, easing, lessening, reduction, soothing, release, cure, remedy, deliverance, remission, *formal* abatement, mitigation, allaying, assuaging, palliation **2** COMFORT, reassur-

ance, happiness, relaxation, calmness, consolation **3** REST, refreshment, diversion, relaxation, respite, break, interruption, *formal* repose, *colloq.* breather, let-up **4** *famine relief* aid, help, assistance, rescue, saving, support, back-up, sustenance, *formal* succour **5** SUBSTITUTE, replacement, reserve, stand-by, stand-in, supply, locum, understudy, proxy, surrogate

relieve *v*
1 *relieve the pain* alleviate, soothe, lessen, soften, slacken, reduce, cure, heal, comfort, console, reassure, *formal* mitigate, abate, allay, assuage, palliate **2** DELIVER, set free, liberate, release, unburden, discharge **3** SUBSTITUTE, replace, stand in for, take the place of, take over from **4** HELP, aid, assist, rescue, save, support, sustain, *formal* succour **5** DISCHARGE, exempt, excuse, dismiss, expel, remove, free, release **6** *relieve the tedium* break (up), interrupt, pause, stop, bring to an end, punctuate, *formal* discontinue
Fₐ **1** aggravate, intensify

religion *n*

> **Religions include:**
> Christianity, Church of England (C of E), Baptists, Catholicism, Methodism, Protestantism, Presbyterianism, Anglicanism, Congregationalism, Calvinism, Salvation Army, evangelicalism, Jehovah's Witnesses, Mormonism, Quakerism, Amish; Bahaism, Buddhism, Confucianism, Hinduism, Islam, Jainism, Judaism, Sikhism, Taoism, Shintoism, Zen, Zoroastrianism, voodoo, druidism. *See also* SCRIPTURE; WORSHIP.

religious *adj*
1 SACRED, holy, divine, spiritual, devotional, scriptural, theological, doctrinal **2** *a religious person* believing, having a living faith, devout, godly, pious, God-fearing, church-going, practising, committed, reverent, righteous **3** CONSCIENTIOUS, scrupulous, rigorous, meticulous, strict
Fₐ **1** secular **2** irreligious, ungodly

relinquish *v*
let go, release, hand over, surrender, yield, cede, give up, resign, renounce, repudiate, waive, forgo, abandon, desert, drop, discard, *formal* forsake, cease, discontinue, desist, abstain, abdicate, *colloq.* quit
Fₐ keep, retain

relish *v, n*
▶ *v* like, enjoy, savour, appreciate, adore, love, revel in, delight in
▶ *n* **1** SEASONING, flavouring, condiment, sauce, pickle, chutney, garnish, spice, flavour, piquancy, tang **2** ENJOYMENT, pleasure, delight, appreciation, satisfaction, gusto, zest, liveliness, vivacity, vigour, charm

reluctance *n*
unwillingness, hesitancy, hesitation, dislike, distaste, loathing, aversion, backwardness, *formal* disinclination, indisposition, recalcitrance, repugnance
Fₐ eagerness, enthusiasm, willingness

reluctant *adj*
unwilling, indisposed, hesitant, slow, backward, loath, averse, unenthusiastic, grudging, *formal* disinclined
Fₐ willing, ready, eager, enthusiastic

rely *v*
depend, lean, be sure, count, bank, reckon, trust, swear by

remain *v*
stay, rest, stand, last, endure, survive, stay behind, be left over, prevail, persist, continue, linger, wait, *old*

use bide, *formal* dwell, abide, tarry
Fₐ go, leave, depart

remainder *n*
rest, balance, surplus, excess, residue, leftovers, remnant, remains, vestiges, *formal* superfluity, residuum

remaining *adj*
left, left-over, spare, unused, unspent, unfinished, residual, last, outstanding, surviving, persisting, lingering, lasting, abiding

remains *n*
1 REST, remainder, residue, dregs, leavings, leftovers, scraps, crumbs, fragments, remnants, oddments, traces, vestiges, relics, *formal* detritus, reliquiae, *colloq.* odds and ends **2** CORPSE, body, dead body, cadaver, carcase, ashes, debris

remark *v, n*
▶ *v* comment, observe, note, notice, mention, say, state, assert, pronounce, declare
▶ *n* comment, observation, opinion, reflection, mention, reference, utterance, statement, assertion, pronouncement, acknowledgement, declaration, notice

remarkable *adj*
striking, impressive, noteworthy, surprising, amazing, strange, odd, unusual, uncommon, rare, extraordinary, phenomenal, exceptional, memorable, momentous, outstanding, notable, considerable, conspicuous, prominent, important, significant, pre-eminent, signal, surpassing, distinguished, *formal* singular
Fₐ average, ordinary, commonplace, usual

remedy *n, v*
▶ *n* cure, antidote, countermeasure, corrective, restorative, medicine, medication, treatment, therapy, relief, solution, answer, panacea, *formal* medicament, physic, nostrum
▶ *v* correct, put right, redress, control, counteract, cure, heal, restore, treat, help, relieve, soothe, ease, mend, repair, sort (out), fix, solve, *formal* rectify, mitigate

remember *v*
1 RECALL, recollect, summon up, think back, think of, look back, hark back, cast your mind back, call to mind, reminisce, recognize, place **2** MEMORIZE, learn, learn by heart, commit to memory, make a mental note of, retain **3** COMMEMORATE, honour, mark, keep, recognize, celebrate, pay tribute to **4** *remember me to your parents* send good/best wishes, send greetings, send your regards/respects
Fₐ **1** forget

remembrance *n*
1 MEMORY, recollection, mind, reminder, recall, reminiscence, thought, testimonial, retrospect, nostalgia **2** COMMEMORATION, memorial, monument, souvenir, memento, token, keepsake, relic, recognition

remind *v*
prompt, nudge, hint, jog your memory, refresh your memory, bring to mind, call to mind, make you think of, call up, evoke

reminder *n*
prompt, nudge, hint, suggestion, note, memorandum, aide-mémoire, souvenir, memento, *colloq.* memo

reminisce *v*
remember, recall, recollect, think back, look back, hark back, review, retrospect

reminiscence *n*
memory, remembrance, memoir, anecdote, recollection, recall, retrospection, review, reflection

reminiscent *adj*
suggestive, evocative, nostalgic, *formal* redolent

remiss *adj*
careless, negligent, neglectful, forgetful, unmindful,

heedless, lackadaisical, inattentive, indifferent, lax, slack, slipshod, sloppy, slow, thoughtless, casual, wayward, *formal* culpable, tardy, dilatory
F₃ careful, scrupulous

remission *n*
1 LESSENING, moderation, slackening, relaxation, release, weakening, decrease, reduction, respite, reprieve, ebb, lull, *formal* abatement, alleviation, diminution, *colloq.* let-up **2** CANCELLATION, repeal, annulment, suspension, *formal* rescinding, abrogation, revocation **3** PARDON, forgiveness, acquittal, excuse, absolution, exemption, discharge, indulgence, amnesty, *formal* exoneration

 remission or **remittance** ?

Remission means 'a lessening in force or effect', as in *Remissions in that form of cancer are not unknown*, 'the shortening of a prison sentence', 'the cancelling of a debt or punishment', and, in Christian theology, 'the forgiveness (of sins)'. *Remittance* is a formal word for the sending of money in payment for something, or for the money itself: *We are grateful for your remittance of the correct sum of money.*

remit *v, n*
▶ *v* **1** SEND, transmit, dispatch, post, mail, forward, pay, settle **2** REFER, transfer, direct, pass on **3** CANCEL, set aside, hold over, suspend, repeal, *formal* rescind, abrogate, revoke
▶ *n* brief, orders, instructions, guidelines, terms of reference, scope, authorization, responsibility

remittance *n*
sending, dispatch, payment, fee, allowance, consideration

remittance or **remission** ? *See panel at* REMISSION.

remnant *n*
scrap, piece, bit, fragment, end, offcut, leftover, remainder, oddment, balance, residue, remains, shred, trace, vestige

remonstrance *n*
grievance, complaint, objection, opposition, protest, protestation, reprimand, reproof, exception, petition, *formal* expostulation

remonstrate *v*
protest, argue, challenge, oppose, take exception to, take issue with, complain, object, dispute, *formal* dissent, expostulate, *colloq.* gripe

remorse *n*
regret, ruefulness, repentance, penitence, contrition, self-reproach, shame, guilt, bad conscience, sorrow, grief, *formal* compunction

remorseful *adj*
guilty, regretful, repentant, ashamed, penitent, conscience-stricken, guilt-ridden, sorrowful, sorry, sad, apologetic, rueful, contrite, *formal* chastened, compunctious
F₃ impenitent, remorseless

remorseless *adj*
relentless, unrelenting, unremitting, unstoppable, undeviating, inexorable, implacable, pitiless, unforgiving, merciless, hard, hard-hearted, harsh, ruthless, savage, unmerciful, callous, cruel, stern, inhumane
F₃ sorry, remorseful

remote *adj*
1 DISTANT, far, faraway, far-off, outlying, out-of-the-way, inaccessible, God-forsaken, isolated, secluded, lonely, *colloq.* off the beaten track **2** DETACHED, aloof,

distant, standoffish, unapproachable, uncommunicative, unconcerned, uninvolved, reserved, withdrawn **3** *a remote possibility* slight, small, slim, poor, meagre, slender, faint, inconsiderable, negligible, doubtful, dubious, unlikely, improbable, insignificant, outside
F₃ 1 close, nearby, accessible **2** friendly, approachable **3** strong

removal *n*
1 MOVE, transferral, departure, relocation, uprooting, shift, shifting, transporting, conveyance **2** WITHDRAWAL, taking away, detachment, extraction, deletion, obliteration, abolition, purging **3** DISMISSAL, discharge, departure, riddance, ejection, ousting, eviction, expulsion, relegation, disposal, *formal* dislodgement, *colloq.* firing, sacking, sack, push, boot, elbow

remove *v*
1 MOVE, transfer, relocate, take away, shift, dislodge, transport, carry, convey **2** TAKE AWAY, withdraw, take off, detach, tear off, pull off, amputate, destroy, cut off, lop off, take out, cut out, extract, excise, pull out, get out, strip, shed, doff **3** ELIMINATE, get rid of, erase, rub out, delete, strike out, cross out, obliterate, abolish, purge, blue-pencil, *formal* expurge, efface **4** DISMISS, discharge, eject, throw out, get rid of, oust, evict, expel, dislodge, unseat, depose, cast out, cashier, relegate, *colloq.* fire, sack, boot out

remunerate *v*
pay, reimburse, recompense, compensate, reward, indemnify, redress, repay

remuneration *n*
pay, wages, salary, emolument, stipend, fee, honorarium, retainer, earnings, income, profit, reward, recompense, payment, remittance, repayment, reimbursement, compensation, indemnity

remunerative *adj*
profitable, lucrative, moneymaking, paying, rewarding, rich, (financially) worthwhile, gainful, fruitful

renaissance *n*
revival, renewal, rebirth, reawakening, awakening, resurrection, rejuvenation, regeneration, re-emergence, restoration, new birth, new dawn, reappearance, resurgence, *formal* recrudescence, renascence

renascent *adj*
revived, resurgent, renewed, re-emergent, reborn, resurrected, reawakened, reanimated, *formal* redivivus, *colloq.* born again

rend *v*
tear, split, break, burst, divide, separate, rupture, sever, rip, fracture, pierce, shatter, smash, splinter, stab, lacerate, *formal* cleave

render *v*
1 *they rendered it harmless* make, cause to be, leave, change, turn **2** GIVE, provide, supply, tender, present, contribute, furnish, submit, hand over, deliver, *formal* proffer **3** TRANSLATE, transcribe, interpret, explain, clarify, represent, perform, play, sing **4** SHOW, describe, represent, display, exhibit, depict, *formal* manifest

rendezvous *n, v*
▶ *n* **1** MEETING, appointment, engagement, assignation, date, *old use* tryst **2** MEETING-PLACE, venue, haunt, resort
▶ *v* meet, come together, gather, collect, assemble, rally, muster, converge, *formal* convene

rendition *n*
performance, presentation, version, rendering, portrayal, reading, transcription, translation, interpretation, arrangement, construction, delivery, explanation, depiction, *formal* execution

renegade n, adj
▶ n deserter, defector, traitor, turncoat, dissident, mutineer, outlaw, rebel, betrayer, apostate, backslider, runaway, *formal* tergiversator
🖪 adherent, disciple, follower
▶ adj disloyal, rebel, rebellious, recreant, traitorous, unfaithful, apostate, backsliding, dissident, mutinous, outlaw, runaway, *formal* perfidious
🖪 loyal, faithful

renege v
default, repudiate, go back on your promise, backslide, apostatize, welsh, cross the floor

renew v
1 RENOVATE, modernize, refurbish, refit, recondition, mend, repair, overhaul, remodel, re-form, transform, re-create, reconstitute, re-establish, regenerate, revive, resuscitate, refresh, rejuvenate, reinvigorate, revitalize, restore, replace, replenish, restock **2** RESUME, repeat, restate, reaffirm, extend, prolong, continue, recommence, restart, *formal* reiterate

renewal n
1 RENOVATION, reconditioning, re-creation, repair, refurbishment, reconstitution, reconstruction, reinvigoration, rejuvenation, revitalization, replenishment, resurrection, resuscitation, *formal* revivification, *colloq.* kiss of life **2** RESUMPTION, repetition, restatement, reaffirmation, continuance, recommencement, *formal* reiteration

renounce v
abandon, give up, resign, relinquish, surrender, waive, sign away, discard, reject, spurn, shun, disown, forgo, disinherit, repudiate, deny, *formal* forsake, disclaim, desist, abstain, eschew, abnegate, recant, abjure, abdicate, *colloq.* wash your hands of

renovate v
restore, renew, recondition, repair, overhaul, modernize, refurbish, refit, redecorate, remodel, re-form, rehabilitate, revamp, improve, *colloq.* do up, give a facelift

renovation n
refurbishment, improvement, modernization, repair, restoration, renewal, reconditioning, refit, *colloq.* facelift

renown n
fame, celebrity, stardom, acclaim, glory, eminence, pre-eminence, illustriousness, distinction, prestige, prominence, note, mark, reputation, repute, honour, *formal* esteem
🖪 obscurity, anonymity

renowned adj
famous, well-known, celebrated, acclaimed, famed, noted, eminent, pre-eminent, distinguished, prestigious, prominent, illustrious, notable, of repute
🖪 unknown, obscure

rent[1] n, v
▶ n *pay the rent* rental, lease, hire, payment, fee
▶ v rent out, let (out), sublet, lease, hire (out), charter

rent[2] n
a rent in the cloth tear, split, break, rip, slit, gash, chink, breach, perforation, rift, rupture, schism, slash, flaw, opening, hole, division, crack, cleavage, dissension, disunion

renunciation n
abandonment, giving up, relinquishment, surrender, waiving, discarding, rejection, spurning, shunning, disowning, disinheriting, repudiation, denial, *formal* forsaking, disclaiming, desistance, abstinence, abnegation, abdication

repair[1] v, n
▶ v *repair a faulty machine* mend, fix, patch up, sew, darn, overhaul, refit, service, maintain, put right, rectify, adjust, redress, restore, make good, heal, renovate, renew
▶ n **1** MEND, patch, darn, overhaul, service, refit, maintenance, restoration, adjustment, improvement **2** *in good/bad repair* condition, shape, state, form, (working) order, fettle, kilter, *colloq.* nick

repair[2] v
repair to a place go, move, turn, withdraw, retire, resort, remove, wend your way

reparable adj
recoverable, rectifiable, remediable, restorable, retrievable, salvageable, savable, corrigible, curable
🖪 irreparable

reparation n
amends, redress, requital, restitution, satisfaction, renewal, compensation, recompense, damages, indemnity, atonement, *technical* solatium, *formal* propitiation

repartee n
banter, badinage, jesting, wit, riposte, retort

repay v
1 REFUND, reimburse, pay back, compensate, recompense, reward, remunerate, pay, settle, settle up with, square **2** GET EVEN WITH, get back at, retaliate, reciprocate, revenge, avenge, *colloq.* get your own back on, settle the score, give as good as you get, not take it lying down

repayment n
1 REFUND, reimbursement, compensation, recompense, reward, remuneration, payment, reparation, redress, restitution, amends, requital, rebate **2** VENGEANCE, revenge, retribution, reciprocation, retaliation, *colloq.* tit for tat

repeal v, n
▶ v quash, annul, void, invalidate, cancel, set aside, recall, withdraw, reverse, abolish, *formal* revoke, rescind, abrogate, nullify, abjure, retract, countermand
🖪 enact
▶ n cancellation, invalidation, quashing, reversal, withdrawal, abolition, annulment, *formal* abrogation, nullification, rescinding, rescindment, rescission, revocation
🖪 enactment, establishment

repeat v, n
▶ v restate, say again, go over, recapitulate, echo, parrot, quote, recite, relate, retell, reproduce, duplicate, renew, rebroadcast, reshow, replay, rerun, redo, *formal* reiterate, iterate, rehearse, *colloq.* recap
▶ n repetition, restatement, recapitulation, echo, reproduction, copy, duplicate, duplication, rebroadcast, reshowing, replay, rerun, ditto

repeated adj
frequent, constant, continual, regular, recurrent, periodic, rhythmical, persistent, recurring

repeatedly adv
time after time, time and (time) again, again and again, over and over, frequently, often

repel v
1 DRIVE BACK, repulse, check, hold off, ward off, parry, resist, keep at bay, oppose, fight, force back, beat back, push back, refuse, decline, reject, spurn, rebuff **2** DISGUST, revolt, nauseate, sicken, make you sick, offend, *formal* be repugnant to, *colloq.* turn off, turn your stomach
🖪 **1** attract **2** delight

repellent adj
repulsive, revolting, disgusting, nauseating, sickening, offensive, shocking, distasteful, objectionable, off-putting, obnoxious, foul, vile, nasty, loathsome,

abominable, abhorrent, contemptible, despicable, hateful, horrid, unpleasant, disagreeable, *formal* repugnant

F3 attractive, pleasant, delightful

repent *v*
regret, rue, feel remorse, sorrow, be sorry, be ashamed, be contrite, confess, lament, deplore, turn, be converted, *formal* recant, *colloq.* go down on your knees, beat your breast, see the error of your ways, see the light, do a U-turn, wipe the slate clean

repentance *n*
penitence, confession, penance, contrition, remorse, regret, sorrow, grief, guilt, shame, conversion, *formal* compunction, recantation, *colloq.* U-turn

repentant *adj*
penitent, contrite, sorry, sorrowful, apologetic, remorseful, regretful, guilty, rueful, chastened, ashamed, conscience-stricken

F3 unrepentant

repercussion *n*
result, consequence, effect, reverberation, echo, rebound, recoil, *colloq.* backlash, ripple, shock wave

repertoire *n*
collection, list, range, repertory, reserve, reservoir, stock, store, supply, *formal* repository

repetition *n*
restatement, recapitulation, quoting, copying, echo, echoing, return, reappearance, recurrence, duplication, redundancy, superfluity, tautology, *technical* echolalia, *formal* reiteration, iterance, iteration, rehearsal, reprise

repetitious *adj*
tedious, monotonous, boring, dull, unchanging, unvaried, redundant, tautological, long-winded, verbose, wordy, windy, *technical* pleonastic(al), *formal* prolix

repetitive *adj*
recurrent, monotonous, tedious, boring, dull, mechanical, automatic, unchanging, unvaried, *colloq.* samey, soul-destroying

rephrase *v*
paraphrase, reword, put in other/different words, ask/ say differently, rewrite, recast

repine *v*
grumble, complain, murmur, fret, lament, grieve, languish, moan, brood, sulk, mope, *colloq.* beef, grouse

replace *v*
1 *replace the lid* put back, return, restore, make good, reinstate, re-establish **2** SUPERSEDE, take the place of, succeed, come after, follow, supplant, relieve, oust, deputize, substitute, stand in for, act for, fill in for

replacement *n*
substitute, stand-in, reserve, understudy, fill-in, supply, proxy, surrogate, successor

replenish *v*
refill, restock, reload, recharge, replace, restore, renew, supply, provide, furnish, stock, fill, fill up, top up, make up

replete *adj*
full, full up, filled, charged, abounding, brimful, brimming, sated, teeming, well-provided, well-stocked, glutted, gorged, jammed, stuffed, crammed, *formal* satiated, *colloq.* chock-a-block, chock-full, jam-packed

repletion *n*
fullness, overfullness, glut, completeness, superabundance, superfluity, *formal* plethora, satiation, satiety

replica *n*
model, imitation, reproduction, facsimile, copy, duplicate, clone

replicate *v*
repeat, duplicate, copy, mimic, follow, reduplicate, reproduce, recreate, clone, ape

reply *v, n*
▶ *v* answer, respond, retort, rejoin, react, acknowledge, return, come back, write back, echo, reciprocate, counter, retaliate, riposte
▶ *n* answer, response, retort, rejoinder, riposte, repartee, reaction, comeback, acknowledgement, return, echo, retaliation, *colloq.* comeback

report *n, v*
▶ *n* **1** ACCOUNT, article, piece, item, write-up, record, relation, narrative, description, story, tale, statement, communiqué, bulletin, register, chronicle, minutes, declaration, announcement, communication, information, news, word, message, note, brief, file, dossier, *formal* delineation **2** GOSSIP, hearsay, rumour, talk **3** REPUTATION, honour, character, standing, stature, opinion, credit, repute, fame, renown, celebrity, distinction, name, *formal* esteem **4** EXPLOSION, shot, bang, crack, boom, crash, reverberation, noise
▶ *v* **1** STATE, announce, declare, proclaim, air, broadcast, relay, publish, circulate, pass on, communicate, notify, tell, recount, relate, narrate, describe, detail, set forth, disclose, divulge, cover, document, chronicle, record, note, *formal* delineate **2** COMPLAIN, inform on, *colloq.* tell on, shop, squeal, rat, split, blow the whistle on, *slang* grass

reporter *n*
journalist, correspondent, columnist, newspaperman, newspaperwoman, newscaster, commentator, announcer, *colloq.* hack

repose¹ *n, v*
▶ *n* *moments of repose* rest, calm, peace, restfulness, ease, relaxation, respite, stillness, tranquillity, serenity, calmness, composure, inactivity, quietness, quiet, poise, equanimity, dignity, self-possession, sleep, *formal* aplomb, quietude, slumber

F3 activity, strain, stress
▶ *v* lie, lay, lean, rest, recline, relax, sleep, *formal* slumber, *colloq.* laze

repose² *v*
repose confidence in someone place, put, set, store, lodge, deposit, confide, entrust, invest

repository *n*
store, storehouse, depository, depot, warehouse, safe, bank, treasury, vault, archive, container, receptacle, magazine

reprehensible *adj*
disgraceful, discreditable, objectionable, shameful, unworthy, blamable, blameworthy, bad, remiss, censurable, condemnable, delinquent, erring, errant, ignoble, *formal* culpable, opprobrious

F3 creditable, good, praiseworthy

represent *v*
1 STAND FOR, symbolize, designate, denote, mean, be, amount to, constitute, correspond to, be equivalent to **2** ACT FOR, stand for, speak for, act/speak on behalf of, act as representative of, act as spokesperson for, act/speak in the name of **3** EXEMPLIFY, typify, stand for, epitomize, embody, personify, show **4** DEPICT, portray, describe, picture, display, exhibit, draw, sketch, illustrate, evoke, characterize **5** ACT AS, enact, perform, appear as

representation *n*
1 LIKENESS, image, icon, picture, portrait, illustration, sketch, model, statue, bust, depiction, portrayal, description, account, explanation, *formal* delinea-

tion **2** REPRESENTATIVE, delegate, delegation, deputy, deputation, proxy, stand-in, spokesperson, spokesman, spokeswoman, envoy, ambassador, mouthpiece, MP, member of parliament, councillor **3** PERFORMANCE, production, presentation, play, show, spectacle **4** *make representations* REQUEST, report, account, statement, allegation, protest, complaint

representative *n, adj*
▶ *n* delegate, delegation, deputy, deputation, proxy, stand-in, spokesperson, spokesman, spokeswoman, envoy, ambassador, mouthpiece, MP, member of parliament, councillor, commissioner, agent, salesman, saleswoman, traveller, *colloq.* rep
▶ *adj* **1** TYPICAL, illustrative, exemplary, characteristic, usual, normal, symbolic, indicative, *formal* archetypal **2** DELEGATED, chosen, elected, elective, nominated, appointed, commissioned, authorized, decentralized, devolved
▣ **1** unrepresentative, atypical

repress *v*
1 INHIBIT, check, control, curb, restrain, suppress, bottle up, hold back, stifle, smother, muffle, silence **2** *repress a revolt* quell, put down, crush, quash, subdue, overpower, overcome, master, dominate, domineer, oppress, *formal* subjugate, vanquish

repressed *adj*
frustrated, inhibited, withdrawn, introverted, self-restrained, *colloq.* uptight
▣ uninhibited, relaxed

repression *n*
1 OPPRESSION, suppression, quashing, quelling, crushing, suffocation, gagging, censorship, authoritarianism, dictatorship, despotism, tyranny, domination, control, constraint, coercion, *formal* subjugation **2** *repression of your feelings* suppression, inhibition, restraint, control, holding-back, stifling, smothering, muffling

repressive *adj*
oppressive, authoritarian, despotic, tyrannical, dictatorial, dominating, autocratic, totalitarian, absolute, harsh, cruel, severe, strict, tough, coercive

reprieve *v, n*
▶ *v* pardon, forgive, acquit, show mercy/pity, spare, rescue, redeem, relieve, respite, *colloq.* let off, let off the hook, forgive and forget
▶ *n* pardon, amnesty, suspension, postponement, deferment, remission, respite, relief, *formal* abeyance, abatement, *colloq.* let-up

reprimand *v, n*
▶ *v* rebuke, reprove, reproach, scold, chide, lecture, criticize, censure, blame, *formal* admonish, berate, castigate, *colloq.* tell off, tick off, slate, give someone a ticking-off, give someone a dressing-down, haul over the riot act, rap over the knuckles, give someone a rap over the knuckles, give someone a flea in their ear
▶ *n* rebuke, reproof, reproach, lecture, censure, blame, *formal* upbraiding, admonition, castigation, *colloq.* telling-off, ticking-off, talking-to, dressing-down, a flea in someone's ear, rocket, wigging, carpeting

reprisal *n*
retaliation, counter-attack, retribution, requital, revenge, vengeance, recrimination, redress, *colloq.* tit for tat, a taste of someone's own medicine

reproach *v, n*
▶ *v* rebuke, reprove, reprimand, upbraid, scold, chide, reprehend, blame, censure, condemn, criticize, find fault with, defame, *formal* disparage, admonish, *colloq.* give someone a dressing-down, give

someone a ticking-off, haul over the coals, rap over the knuckles
▶ *n* **1** REBUKE, reproof, reprimand, scolding, blame, censure, condemnation, criticism, disapproval, scorn, contempt, *formal* admonition **2** DISGRACE, shame, disrepute, disrespect, discredit, stigma, dishonour, degradation, blemish, blot, smear, stain, slur, *formal* ignominy, opprobrium, obloquy

reproachful *adj*
reproving, upbraiding, scolding, censorious, critical, fault-finding, disapproving, disappointed, scornful, *formal* castigating, disparaging, opprobrious
▣ complimentary

reprobate *adj, n*
▶ *adj* immoral, corrupt, depraved, sinful, unprincipled, vile, wicked, bad, shameless, incorrigible, dissolute, degenerate, base, abandoned, hardened, damned, *formal* profligate, reprobative, reprobatory
▣ upright, virtuous
▶ *n* degenerate, miscreant, rake, roué, wrongdoer, criminal, evildoer, sinner, rogue, rascal, scoundrel, scamp, scallywag, villain, vagabond, wretch, mischief-maker, ne'er-do-well, knave, dastard, troublemaker, *formal* profligate

reproduce *v*
1 COPY, transcribe, print, duplicate, photocopy, Xerox®, Photostat®, mirror, echo, repeat, imitate, emulate, match, follow, clone, ape, mimic, simulate, recreate, remake, redo, reconstruct, *formal* replicate **2** BREED, spawn, bear young, give birth, generate, propagate, multiply, proliferate, *formal* procreate

reproduction *n*
1 COPY, print, picture, duplicate, photocopy, Xerox®, Photostat®, facsimile, replica, clone, imitation **2** BREEDING, generation, propagation, multiplication, *formal* procreation
▣ **1** original

reproductive *adj*
generative, sexual, sex, genital, propagative, *formal* procreative, progenitive

reproof *n*
rebuke, reproach, reprimand, scolding, censure, condemnation, criticism, *formal* upbraiding, admonition, castigation, disapprobation, berating, *colloq.* dressing-down, telling-off, ticking-off, rocket, wigging, carpeting
▣ praise

reprove *v*
rebuke, reproach, reprimand, scold, chide, reprehend, censure, condemn, criticize, *formal* upbraid, admonish, berate, castigate, *colloq.* tell off, tick off, slate, give someone a dressing-down, give someone a ticking-off, haul over the coals, rap over the knuckles
▣ praise

reptile *n*

Reptiles include:
adder, puff adder, grass snake, tree snake, asp, viper, rattlesnake, sidewinder, anaconda, boa constrictor, cobra, king cobra, mamba, python; lizard, frilled lizard, chameleon, gecko, iguana, skink, slow-worm; turtle, green turtle, hawksbill turtle, terrapin, tortoise, giant tortoise; alligator, crocodile. *See also* DINOSAURS.

repudiate *v*
reject, denounce, deny, renounce, disown, discard, retract, reverse, revoke, cast off, desert, abandon, divorce, *formal* abjure, disaffirm, disavow, disclaim, disprofess, forsake, rescind, *colloq.* not touch with a

barge pole, not have anything to do with, have nothing
to do with, turn your back on
☒ admit, own

repudiation *n*
renunciation, renouncement, rejection, denial, disclaimer, disowning, *formal* abjuration, disaffirmance, disaffirmation, disavowal, recantation, retraction
☒ acceptance

repugnance *n*
reluctance, distaste, dislike, aversion, hatred, loathing, horror, repulsion, revulsion, nausea, disgust, *formal* abhorrence, odium, antipathy
☒ liking, pleasure, delight

repugnant *adj*
repellent, objectionable, obnoxious, offensive, unacceptable, antagonistic, antipathetic, hostile, averse, opposed, distasteful, inconsistent, incompatible, contradictory, adverse, disgusting, foul, vile, hateful, horrid, abominable, revolting, sickening, nauseating, loathsome, odious, *formal* abhorrent, inimical
☒ acceptable, consistent, pleasant

repulse *v, n*
▶ *v* repel, drive back, defeat, beat off, check, rebuff, reject, refuse, disregard, disdain, snub, spurn
▶ *n* check, defeat, disappointment, failure, rebuff, refusal, rejection, repudiation, reverse, snub, spurning
☒ acceptance, success

repulsion *n*
revulsion, disgust, distaste, hatred, aversion, loathing, *formal* repugnance, abhorrence, detestation, disrelish, repellence, repellency
☒ liking

repulsive *adj*
repellent, revolting, disgusting, nauseating, sickening, offensive, shocking, distasteful, objectionable, off-putting, obnoxious, foul, vile, nasty, loathsome, abominable, abhorrent, contemptible, despicable, hateful, horrid, unpleasant, disagreeable, ugly, hideous, unattractive, forbidding, *formal* repugnant, reprehensible, heinous
☒ attractive, pleasant, delightful

reputable *adj*
respectable, respected, reliable, dependable, trustworthy, upright, honourable, honest, creditable, admirable, of high/good repute, well-thought-of, worthy, good, virtuous, excellent, irreproachable, *formal* esteemed, estimable
☒ disreputable, infamous

reputation *n*
1 NAME, opinion, credit, repute, character, standing, stature, status, rank, position, infamy, notoriety, *formal* estimation **2** FAME, renown, celebrity, distinction, prestige, image, character, good name, good standing, honour, respect, respectability, *formal* esteem

repute *n*
reputation, name, standing, stature, renown, fame, good name, celebrity, distinction, *formal* esteem, estimation
☒ infamy

reputed *adj*
alleged, supposed, said, rumoured, believed, thought, considered, regarded, reckoned, estimated, held, judged, seeming, assumed, presumed, apparent, *formal* ostensible
☒ actual, true

reputedly *adv*
allegedly, apparently, seemingly, supposedly, reputatively, *formal* ostensibly
☒ actually

request *v, n*
▶ *v* ask for, demand, require, seek, desire, beg, petition, apply for, call for, appeal, *formal* solicit, entreat, requisition, supplicate, beseech, *colloq.* put in for
▶ *n* appeal, call, demand, desire, application, suit, petition, petitioning, plea, pleading, prayer, *formal* requisition, solicitation, entreaty, supplication, imploration, behest

require *v*
1 NEED, want, wish, desire, crave, lack, miss, be short of, be deficient in **2** *you are required to attend* oblige, force, compel, make, ask, request, call on, instruct, direct, command, order, demand, entail, insist on, take, involve, *formal* constrain, necessitate, enjoin

required *adj*
compulsory, essential, obligatory, recommended, demanded, necessary, stipulated, set, needed, unavoidable, vital, *formal* mandatory, prescribed, requisite
☒ optional, inessential

requirement *n*
need, necessity, essential, sine qua non, demand, lack, want, stipulation, condition, term, specification, proviso, qualification, provision, *formal* requisite, prerequisite, precondition, *colloq.* must

requisite *adj, n*
▶ *adj* required, needed, necessary, essential, obligatory, compulsory, set, vital, *formal* prescribed, prerequisite, mandatory
▶ *n* requirement, essential, due, necessity, need, condition, stipulation, specification, qualification, sine qua non, *formal* desideratum, prerequisite, precondition, desiderative, *colloq.* must
☒ inessential

requisition *v, n*
▶ *v* commandeer, take, take over, take possession of, use, confiscate, seize, occupy, request, put in for, demand, summons, *formal* appropriate
▶ *n* commandeering, confiscation, seizure, takeover, occupation, order, use, application, summons, request, call, demand, *formal* appropriation

requital *n*
amends, redress, restitution, satisfaction, recompense, compensation, indemnification, indemnity, repayment, payment, pay-off, reparation, *formal* quittance

requite *v*
repay, reciprocate, respond, retaliate, return, pay, recompense, reimburse, remunerate, reward, satisfy, redress, compensate, avenge

rescind *v*
cancel, set aside, overturn, quash, reverse, recall, repeal, annul, invalidate, void, negate, *formal* abrogate, countermand, nullify, retract, revoke
☒ enforce

rescission *n*
cancellation, negation, reversal, invalidation, annulment, recall, repeal, *formal* abrogation, nullification, rescindment, retraction, revocation, voidance
☒ enforcement

rescue *v, n*
▶ *v* save, recover, salvage, deliver, free, set free, liberate, emancipate, extricate, release, relieve, redeem, ransom
☒ capture, imprison
▶ *n* saving, recovery, salvage, deliverance, liberation, freeing, release, emancipation, relief, redemption, salvation
☒ capture

research *n, v*
▶ *n* investigation, inquiry, fact-finding, groundwork, examination, analysis, assessment, scrutiny, inspec-

tion, testing, test(s), study, review, search, probe, exploration, experiment, experimentation
▸ *v* investigate, examine, look into, analyse, scrutinize, study, inspect, search, probe, test, assess, review, explore, experiment

researcher *n*
investigator, student, analyst, inspector, inquirer, field worker, boffin

resemblance *n*
likeness, similarity, sameness, conformity, nearness, closeness, affinity, uniformity, parallel, parallelism, comparison, comparability, agreement, analogy, correspondence, image, facsimile, *formal* parity, similitude, congruity
☒ dissimilarity

resemble *v*
be like, look like, be similar to, bear resemblance to, take after, favour, mirror, echo, duplicate, parallel, approach
☒ differ from

resent *v*
grudge, begrudge, envy, feel bitter about, feel aggrieved at, be angry at, take offence at, take umbrage at, take amiss, object to, grumble at, take exception to, dislike
☒ accept, like

resentful *adj*
grudging, envious, jealous, bitter, embittered, hurt, wounded, offended, aggrieved, put out, piqued, incensed, in high dudgeon, indignant, angry, irritated, irked, vindictive, malicious, spiteful, *colloq.* miffed, peeved
☒ satisfied, contented

resentment *n*
grudge, envy, jealousy, bitterness, spite, malice, ill-will, ill-feeling, bad feelings, hard feelings, (high) dudgeon, animosity, hostility, hurt, umbrage, pique, offence, displeasure, irritation, indignation, annoyance, ire, vexation, anger, vindictiveness
☒ contentment, happiness

reservation *n*
1 DOUBT, scepticism, misgiving, qualm, scruple, hesitancy, hesitation, second thoughts, *formal* demur **2** BOOKING, engagement, appointment, arrangement, order, prearrangement **3** RESERVE, preserve, park, sanctuary, homeland, enclave, tract **4** PROVISO, stipulation, qualification, condition, limitation

reserve *v, n, adj*
▸ *v* **1** SET ASIDE, earmark, keep, retain, hold back, keep back, save, store, lay aside, set apart, stockpile, hoard, accumulate **2** *reserve a seat* book, engage, order, arrange for, secure, prearrange **3** DELAY, postpone, defer, put off, suspend, shelve, hold over, adjourn
☒ **1** use up
▸ *n* **1** STORE, stock, supply, fund, stockpile, pool, reservoir, bank, cache, hoard, accumulation, savings **2** SUBSTITUTE, replacement, stand-in, understudy, fill-in, supply, proxy, surrogate, successor **3** RESERVATION, preserve, park, area, sanctuary, tract, enclave **4** SHYNESS, reticence, unresponsiveness, secretiveness, coldness, coolness, aloofness, detachment, modesty, restraint, self-restraint, distance, remoteness, unapproachability
☒ **4** friendliness, openness, approachability
▷ **in reserve** for use when needed, available, to hand, in hand, unused, stored, spare, set aside
▸ *adj* spare, substitute, additional, auxiliary, alternative, extra, secondary

reserved *adj*
1 BOOKED, engaged, ordered, arranged, prearranged,

taken, spoken for, set aside, earmarked, meant, intended, designated, destined, saved, held, kept, retained **2** SHY, retiring, reticent, unresponsive, unforthcoming, uncommunicative, secretive, silent, taciturn, unsociable, cool, cold, aloof, standoffish, unapproachable, modest, diffident, restrained, cautious, distant, remote
☒ **1** unreserved, free, available **2** friendly, open

reservoir *n*
1 LAKE, pond, pool, *Scot.* loch **2** TANK, cistern, vat, basin, container, receptacle **3** STORE, stockpile, stock, supply, source, reserves, accumulation, fund, holder, bank, *formal* repository, reservatory

reshuffle *n, v*
▸ *n* reorganization, shake-up, upheaval, redistribution, regrouping, rearrangement, realignment, restructuring, revision, change, interchange
▸ *v* reorganize, restructure, shake up, change, interchange, shift, shuffle, revise, rearrange, regroup, realign, redistribute

reside *v*
1 LIVE, inhabit, lodge, stay, board, occupy, settle, remain, *formal* dwell, sojourn **2** BE PRESENT, exist, lie, rest, be inherent, be contained, *formal* dwell, abide

residence *n*
home, house, flat, apartment, seat, place, lodgings, quarters, hall, manor, mansion, palace, villa, country house, country seat, stay, lodging, *formal* dwelling, habitation, domicile, abode, sojourn, *colloq.* pad, digs

resident *n, adj*
▸ *n* inhabitant, citizen, local, householder, occupant, occupier, tenant, lodger, guest, patient, inmate, client, *formal* resider, dweller, sojourner
☒ non-resident
▸ *adj* live-in, living-in, dwelling, local, permanent, inhabiting, neighbourhood, settled, en poste, *old use* gremial
☒ non-resident

residential *adj*
commuter, suburban, dormitory, *formal* exurban

residual *adj*
remaining, left-over, unused, unconsumed, net, excess, surplus

residue *n*
remainder, remains, remnant, rest, surplus, excess, extra, overflow, balance, difference, lees, dregs, leftovers, *formal* residuum
☒ core

resign *v*
stand down, retire, step down, leave, abdicate, vacate, give up, hand in your notice, give in your notice, forgo, waive, surrender, yield, abandon, *formal* renounce, relinquish, forsake, *colloq.* quit
☒ join
▷ **resign yourself** reconcile yourself, accept, bow, submit, yield, come to terms, *formal* comply, acquiesce
☒ resist

resignation *n*
1 STANDING-DOWN, stepping-down, abdication, retirement, departure, notice, letter of resignation, surrender, giving-up, waiving, *formal* renunciation, relinquishment **2** ACCEPTANCE, reconciliation, submission, non-resistance, passivity, patience, stoicism, yielding, defeatism, *formal* acquiescence, compliance
☒ **2** resistance

resigned *adj*
reconciled, philosophical, stoical, patient, long-suffering, unprotesting, unresisting, passive, submis-

sive, yielding, defeatist, *formal* acquiescent
F3 resistant, protesting

resilience *n*
1 FLEXIBILITY, elasticity, springiness, spring, pliability, plasticity, suppleness, give, bounce, recoil
2 STRENGTH, toughness, hardiness, adaptability, buoyancy, irrepressibility, unshockability
F3 1 inflexibility, rigidity

resilient *adj*
1 *resilient material* flexible, pliable, supple, plastic, elastic, springy, bouncy, rubbery **2** STRONG, tough, hardy, adaptable, buoyant, irrepressible, unshockable
F3 1 rigid, brittle **2** weak

resist *v*
oppose, defy, confront, fight, struggle, contend, battle, combat, weather, withstand, stand up to, hold out against, obstruct, repel, counter, counteract, check, stop, halt, avoid, refuse, prevent, hinder, obstruct, thwart, impede, restrain, curb, stem
F3 submit, accept

resistance *n*
opposition, defiance, confrontation, fight, fighting, struggle, combat, contention, counteraction, battle, withstanding, repulsion, avoidance, refusal, prevention, thwart, hindrance, obstruction, impedance, impediment, restraint, *formal* intransigence
F3 acceptance, submission

resistant *adj*
1 OPPOSED, antagonistic, defiant, unyielding, unwilling, *formal* intransigent **2** PROOF, impervious, immune, unaffected, invulnerable, unsusceptible, tough, strong
F3 1 compliant, yielding

resolute *adj*
determined, resolved, intent, decided, dedicated, constant, serious, earnest, adamant, stalwart, set, fixed, unwavering, unyielding, unswerving, inflexible, staunch, firm, steadfast, relentless, single-minded, persevering, dogged, tenacious, stubborn, obstinate, strong-willed, undaunted, unflinching, bold, *formal* obdurate
F3 irresolute, weak-willed, half-hearted

resolution *n*
1 DECISION, judgement, finding, declaration, proposition, motion, decree, verdict, declaration **2** DETERMINATION, resolve, willpower, commitment, dedication, devotion, constancy, firmness, intentness, seriousness, earnestness, steadfastness, persistence, perseverance, doggedness, inflexibility, tenacity, zeal, courage, boldness **3** SOLVING, answer, solution, unravelling, disentangling, working out, sorting out
F3 2 half-heartedness, uncertainty, indecision

resolve *v, n*
▶ *v* **1** DECIDE, make up your mind, determine, fix, settle (on), conclude **2** SOLVE, answer, unravel, disentangle, sort out, work out **3** BREAK UP, break down, analyse, reduce, divide, separate, dissolve, disintegrate, detail, convert, anatomize, itemize
▶ *n* determination, willpower, commitment, dedication, devotion, constancy, firmness, intentness, seriousness, earnestness, steadfastness, persistence, perseverance, doggedness, inflexibility, tenacity, zeal, courage, boldness, sense of purpose
F3 indecision

resonant *adj*
deep, strong, sonorous, ringing, booming, rich, vibrant, full, plummy, resounding, reverberant, reverberating, echoing, *formal* canorous
F3 weak, faint

resort *v, n*
▶ *v* go, visit, frequent, patronize, haunt, *formal* repair
▷ **resort to** turn to, use, utilize, make use of, avail yourself of, fall back on, have recourse to, employ, exercise
▶ *n* **1** HOLIDAY CENTRE, centre, spot, health resort, spa **2** RECOURSE, refuge, course (of action), measure, step, alternative, option, chance, possibility, *formal* expedient

resound *v*
resonate, reverberate, echo, re-echo, ring, sound, boom, thunder

resounding *adj*
1 RESONANT, reverberating, echoing, ringing, loud, sonorous, booming, resonating, thunderous, full, rich, vibrant **2** *a resounding victory* decisive, conclusive, impressive, striking, outstanding, great, memorable, remarkable, notable, emphatic, thorough
F3 1 faint

resource *n*
1 *a shortage of resources* materials, supplies, reserves, holdings, funds, money, wealth, riches, capital, assets, property, means, power, wherewithal **2** SUPPLY, reserve, supply, pool, accumulation, stockpile, store, fund, source, contrivance, device, course, resort, *formal* expedient **3** RESOURCEFULNESS, initiative, enterprise, ingenuity, inventiveness, wit, imagination, talent, ability, capability

resourceful *adj*
ingenious, imaginative, creative, inventive, enterprising, innovative, original, versatile, clever, bright, sharp, quick-witted, witty, able, capable, talented, adroit

resourceless *adj*
inadequate, useless, hopeless, helpless, feeble, feckless, shiftless
F3 unimaginative

respect *v, n*
▶ *v* **1** ADMIRE, regard, have a good opinion of, think highly of, hold in high regard, set great store by, appreciate, value, praise, honour, approve of, revere, *formal* esteem, venerate **2** OBEY, observe, heed, follow, adhere to, honour, fulfil, *formal* comply with **3** CONSIDER, show consideration for, pay attention to, take into account, show regard for, *formal* take cognizance of
F3 1 despise, scorn **2** ignore, disobey
▶ *n* **1** ADMIRATION, appreciation, recognition, honour, deference, reverence, high opinion, regard, high regard, homage, *formal* esteem, veneration, approbation, obeisance **2** CONSIDERATION, attention, attentiveness, notice, regard, heed, thoughtfulness, politeness, courtesy, *formal* cognizance **3** GREETINGS, compliments, regards, salutations, best wishes, good wishes, *formal* devoirs **4** *in every respect* point, aspect, facet, feature, characteristic, particular, detail, sense, matter, way, regard, reference, bearing, relation, connection
F3 1 disrespect

respectable *adj*
1 REPUTABLE, honourable, worthy, respected, dignified, upright, honest, above-board, trustworthy, worthy, decent, good, presentable, neat, tidy, clean, clean-living, *formal* decorous **2** ACCEPTABLE, tolerable, passable, adequate, fair, reasonable, all right, appreciable, considerable, *colloq.* not bad, OK
F3 1 dishonourable, disreputable **2** inadequate, paltry

respected *adj*
admired, valued, highly regarded, highly valued, held in high regard, thought highly of, *formal* esteemed, highly esteemed

respectful *adj*
deferential, reverent, reverential, humble, polite, well-mannered, courtly, dutiful, courteous, civil, subservient
🖅 disrespectful

respecting *prep*
about, concerning, considering, in respect of, with regard to, regarding, with respect to

respective *adj*
corresponding, relevant, various, several, separate, individual, personal, own, specific, particular, special

respite *n*
1 PAUSE, rest, relief, break, adjournment, intermission, recess, relaxation, interval, interruption, halt, gap, lull, *formal* cessation, hiatus, *colloq.* breather, let-up **2** DELAY, reprieve, postponement, deferment, remission, stay, suspension, moratorium, *formal* abatement

resplendent *adj*
dazzling, shining, radiant, brilliant, bright, irradiant, luminous, beaming, gleaming, glittering, glorious, splendid, *formal* effulgent, fulgent, lustrous, refulgent, *colloq.* splendiferous
🖅 dull

respond *v*
answer, reply, acknowledge, retort, rejoin, answer back, react, return, counter, reciprocate

response *n*
answer, reply, acknowledgement, retort, rejoinder, riposte, return, reaction, feedback, *colloq.* comeback
🖅 query

responsibility *n*
1 DUTY, obligation, burden, onus, charge, care, role, task, authority, power, trust, business, affair, concern, *colloq.* baby, pidgin **2** FAULT, blame, guilt, answerability, accountability, *formal* culpability **3** DEPENDABILITY, reliability, conscientiousness, honesty, soundness, maturity, adulthood, stability

responsible *adj*
1 IN CHARGE OF, in control of, controlling, managing, leading, accountable, answerable **2** GUILTY, at fault, to blame, blameworthy, liable, answerable, accountable, *formal* culpable **3** *a responsible citizen* dependable, reliable, conscientious, trustworthy, honest, sound, steady, sober, mature, adult, stable, reasonable, sensible, rational, sane, level-headed **4** IMPORTANT, authoritative, powerful, executive, decision-making, *colloq.* high-level
🖅 **3** irresponsible, unreliable, untrustworthy

responsive *adj*
alert, aware, sensitive, awake, open, sharp, reactive, amenable, receptive, susceptible, sympathetic, perceptive, forthcoming, impressionable, alive, respondent, *formal* responsorial, *colloq.* on the ball, with it
🖅 unresponsive

rest¹ *n, v*
▶ *n* **1** LEISURE, relaxation, lie-down, sleep, snooze, nap, siesta, idleness, inactivity, ease, motionlessness, standstill, stillness, tranquillity, calm, *formal* repose, quietude, slumber **2** BREAK, pause, breathing-space, intermission, interlude, interval, recess, holiday, vacation, time off, halt, lull, respite, *formal* cessation, *colloq.* breather **3** SUPPORT, prop, stand, base, holder
🖅 **1** action, activity **2** work
▶ *v* **1** PAUSE, halt, stop, *formal* cease **2** RELAX, sit (down), recline, lounge, laze, lie down, sleep, snooze, doze, *formal* repose, *colloq.* put your feet up, take it easy, recharge your batteries **3** DEPEND, rely, hinge, hang, lie, be based **4** LEAN, prop, support, stand, steady
🖅 **1** continue **2** work

rest² *n, v*
▶ *n the rest of us stayed behind* remainder, others, balance, surplus, excess, residue, remains, leftovers, remnant(s), *formal* residuum
▶ *v* continue, remain, stay, last, endure, persist

restful *adj*
relaxing, soothing, calming, calm, tranquil, serene, peaceful, quiet, still, placid, undisturbed, relaxed, comfortable, leisurely, unhurried, *formal* languid
🖅 tiring, restless

restitution *n*
amends, reparation, requital, restoration, restoring, return, satisfaction, redress, repayment, damages, compensation, recompense, remuneration, refund, reimbursement, indemnification, indemnity

restive *adj*
1 UNRULY, impatient, wayward, wilful, turbulent, uncontrollable, undisciplined, unmanageable, *formal* recalcitrant, refractory **2** RESTLESS, agitated, fidgety, fidgeting, unsettled, nervous, uneasy, anxious, fretful, tense, edgy, *colloq.* jumpy, uptight
🖅 **2** calm, relaxed

restless *adj*
1 FIDGETY, fidgeting, unruly, turbulent, impatient, changeable, *formal* restive **2** AGITATED, nervous, anxious, worried, uneasy, fretful, edgy, troubled, unsettled, *colloq.* jittery, jumpy, uptight **3** SLEEPLESS, uncomfortable, broken, disturbed, tossing and turning
🖅 **1** still **2** calm, relaxed **3** restful, comfortable

restlessness *n*
agitation, disturbance, unsettledness, uneasiness, unrest, turbulence, turmoil, worriedness, anxiety, nervousness, fitfulness, insomnia, fretfulness, bustle, disquiet, hurry, activity, instability, movement, inconstancy, transience, *formal* inquietude, restiveness, *colloq.* edginess, jitters, jumpiness, heebie-jeebies
🖅 calmness, relaxation

restoration *n*
1 RENOVATION, repair, refurbishing, rebuilding, reconstruction, renewal, rehabilitation **2** REVIVAL, refreshment, rejuvenation, revitalization, recovery, *colloq.* kiss of life **3** RETURN, replacement, reinstallation, restitution, reinstatement, re-establishment
🖅 **1** damage **2** weakening **3** removal

restore *v*
1 *restore a building* renovate, renew, rebuild, reconstruct, redecorate, refurbish, retouch, recondition, rehabilitate, revamp, repair, mend, fix, *colloq.* do up **2** REVIVE, refresh, recover, rejuvenate, revitalize, strengthen, build up, *formal* revivify **3** REPLACE, return, give back, hand back, reinstate, re-establish, reintroduce, re-impose, re-enforce
🖅 **1** damage **2** weaken **3** remove

restrain *v*
restrain your feelings; *restrain a prisoner* hold back, keep back, suppress, subdue, repress, inhibit, check, hold in check, curb, bridle, stop, arrest, prevent, hinder, obstruct, impede, bind, tie, chain, fetter, manacle, imprison, detain, jail, confine, restrict, regulate, control, keep under control, govern, *colloq.* bottle up
🖅 encourage, liberate

restrained *adj*
1 CALM, controlled, steady, self-controlled, self-restrained, unemotional, formal, cold, aloof, uncommunicative **2** *restrained decorations* tasteful, moderate, temperate, mild, subdued, subtle, muted, quiet, soft, low-key, unobtrusive, discreet
🖅 **1** emotional, demonstrative **2** *colloq.* loud

restraint *n*
behave with restraint; *no restraints in modern life* moderation, inhibition, self-control, self-discipline,

hold, grip, check, curb, rein, bridle, suppression, bondage, captivity, confinement, imprisonment, bonds, chains, fetters, straitjacket, restriction, control, constraint, limit(s), restriction(s), duress, block, barrier, stint, limitation, tie, hindrance, prevention, *formal* judiciousness, prudence

F3 liberty

restrict *v*
limit, bound, demarcate, control, keep under control, keep within limits, regulate, confine, contain, cramp, constrain, impede, hinder, hamper, handicap, tie, restrain, curtail, *colloq.* hem in

F3 broaden, free

restricted *adj*
1 SMALL, narrow, cramped, confined, tight 2 SECRET, private, limited, exclusive, controlled, regulated

restriction *n*
limit, bound, confine, limitation, constraint, handicap, check, curb, restraint, ban, stint, embargo, control, regulation, rule, stipulation, qualification, condition, proviso

F3 freedom

result *n, v*
▶ *n* effect, consequence, sequel, repercussion, reaction, implication, outcome, upshot, end, issue, end-product, by-product, side effect, fruit(s), score, grade, mark, answer, verdict, judgement, decision, conclusion, *colloq.* pay-off, spin-off

F3 cause
▶ *v* follow, ensue, happen, occur, issue, emerge, arise, spring, derive, stem, flow, evolve, emanate, proceed, come out of, develop, end, finish, terminate, culminate, *formal* eventuate

F3 cause

resume *v*
restart, start again, begin again, recommence, reopen, reconvene, re-occupy, continue, carry on, go on, proceed, take up (again)

F3 cease

résumé *n*
summary, précis, synopsis, outline, sketch, breakdown, abstract, digest, recapitulation, review, overview, run-down, epitome

resumption *n*
restart, recommencement, reopening, renewal, re-establishment, resurgence, continuation, proceeding

F3 cessation

resurgence *n*
reappearance, re-emergence, resumption, return, rebirth, resurrection, revival, renaissance, *formal* renascence, recrudescence, revivification, risorgimento

F3 decrease

resurrect *v*
1 *Jesus Christ was resurrected* bring back to life, raise from the dead, restore, restore to life, revive 2 *resurrect an old idea* restore, revive, resuscitate, reactivate, bring back, reintroduce, re-establish, re-install, renew, revitalize

F3 1 kill, bury

resurrection *n*
1 *the resurrection of Jesus Christ* bringing back to life, raising/rising from the dead, restoration to life, return from the dead 2 *resurrection of former procedures* restoration, revival, resuscitation, renaissance, rebirth, renewal, revitalization, re-establishment, resurgence, reappearance, return, comeback

resuscitate *v*
revive, bring round, resurrect, save, rescue, reanimate, quicken, reinvigorate, breathe new life into, revitalize, restore, renew, *formal* revivify, *colloq.* give the kiss of life to

resuscitated *adj*
restored, revived, resurrected, *formal* redivivus, redintegrate(d)

retain *v*
1 KEEP, hold, keep hold of, grasp, grip, reserve, hold back, hold fast to, save, continue, maintain, preserve, *colloq.* hang on to 2 *retain information* remember, recall, recollect, memorize, bear in mind, keep in mind, call to mind 3 EMPLOY, engage, hire, pay, commission

F3 1 release 2 forget 3 dismiss

retainer *n*
1 FEE, retaining fee, deposit, advance 2 SERVANT, lackey, footman, domestic, attendant, supporter, valet, dependant, vassal, menial

retaliate *v*
reciprocate, counter-attack, get back at, pay someone back, hit back, strike back, fight back, avenge, take revenge, *colloq.* get your own back, get even with, give as good as you get, return like for like, give someone a taste of their own medicine

retaliation *n*
reprisal, counter-attack, revenge, vengeance, retribution, reciprocation, *formal* ultion, *colloq.* tit for tat, like for like, an eye for an eye and a tooth for a tooth, a taste of your own medicine

retard *v*
slow down, delay, hold up, decelerate, brake, put a/the brake on, handicap, incapacitate, obstruct, hinder, impede, check, curb, restrict

F3 speed up, accelerate

retardation *n*
slowness, slowing, incapability, mental handicap, deficiency, incapacity, impeding, hindering, hindrance, delay, lag, obstruction, dullness, *formal* retardment

F3 advancement

retch *v*
vomit, heave, reach, disgorge, regurgitate, gag, *colloq.* puke, spew, throw up

retching *n*
vomiting, nausea, reaching, gagging, *formal* vomiturition, *colloq.* puking

reticence *n*
reserve, restraint, quietness, uncommunicativeness, unforthcomingness, secretiveness, silence, taciturnity, muteness, diffidence

F3 communicativeness, forwardness, frankness

reticent *adj*
reserved, shy, restrained, uncommunicative, unforthcoming, tight-lipped, secretive, taciturn, silent, quiet, diffident

F3 communicative, forward, frank

retinue *n*
entourage, following, followers, personnel, staff, suite, train, attendants, escort, cortège, aides, servants

retire *v*
stop work, stop working, leave work, give up work, resign, leave, depart, go away, withdraw, retreat, recede, move, go, decamp, *colloq.* bow out, be put out to pasture

F3 join, enter, advance

retired *adj*
former, ex-, emeritus, past

retirement *n*
withdrawal, retreat, exit, departure, resignation, solitude, loneliness, seclusion, privacy, obscurity

retiring *adj*
shy, bashful, timid, shrinking, quiet, reticent, reserved, self-effacing, unassertive, diffident, coy, modest, unassuming, humble

F3 bold, forward, assertive

retort *v, n*
▸ *v* answer, reply, respond, rejoin, return, counter, retaliate
▸ *n* answer, reply, response, rejoinder, riposte, repartee, quip

retract *v*
take back, withdraw, recant, reverse, cancel, repeal, repudiate, disown, disclaim, deny, renounce, renege, *formal* revoke, rescind, disavow, abjure, abrogate
🔁 assert, maintain

retreat *v, n*
▸ *v* draw back, pull back, fall back, recoil, shrink, withdraw, decamp, give ground, give way, retire, leave, depart, flee, *colloq.* turn tail, quit
🔁 advance
▸ *n* **1** WITHDRAWAL, drawing back, pulling back, falling back, departure, evacuation, flight **2** SECLUSION, privacy, solitude, retirement, hide-away, hideout, den, refuge, asylum, sanctuary, shelter, harbour, haven
🔁 **1** advance, charge

retrench *v*
cut back, economize, cut, slim down, live more economically, save, reduce, lessen, limit, decrease, diminish, curtail, trim, pare, prune, husband, *colloq.* tighten your belt
🔁 increase

retrenchment *n*
cutback, cutting back, cut, economy, reduction, pruning, curtailment, cost-cutting, run-down, contraction, shrinkage, *colloq.* tightening your belt
🔁 increase

retribution *n*
punishment, reckoning, justice, satisfaction, retaliation, requital, reward, reprisal, redress, repayment, payment, compensation, recompense, revenge, vengeance, Nemesis, *colloq.* just deserts

retrieve *v*
recover, get back, fetch, bring back, regain, recapture, repossess, recoup, reclaim, put to rights, make good, salvage, save, rescue, redeem, restore, remedy, return, mend, repair
🔁 lose

retrograde *adj*
backward, reverse, retrogressive, negative, downward, worsening, declining, deteriorating
🔁 progressive

retrogress *v*
regress, retrograde, return, revert, relapse, withdraw, recede, drop, ebb, fall, sink, wane, retire, retreat, backslide, decline, deteriorate, worsen, degenerate
🔁 progress, advance

retrogression *n*
regression, regress, return, relapse, decline, worsening, deterioration, drop, ebb, fall, *formal* recidivism, retrogradation
🔁 increase, progress

retrospect *n*
hindsight, afterthought, thinking back, reflection, re-examination, review, survey, recollection, remembrance
🔁 prospect
▷ **in retrospect** retrospectively, with hindsight, looking back, thinking back, on reflection, with the wisdom of hindsight

retrospective *adj*
backward-looking, retro-active, retro-operative

return *v, n*
▸ *v* **1** COME BACK, reappear, recur, go back, get back, come home, come again, backtrack, regress, revert **2** GIVE BACK, hand back, send back, take back, deliver, put back, replace, reinstate, restore, *formal* remit **3** *return a favour* reciprocate, repay, refund, reimburse, recompense, exchange, match, equal, correspond, *formal* requite, *colloq.* do the same **4** ANSWER, reply, respond, rejoin, retort, riposte, counter **5** *return a verdict* announce, pronounce, declare, deliver, bring in
🔁 **1** leave, depart **2** take
▸ *n* **1** REAPPEARANCE, recurrence, home-coming, *colloq.* comeback **2** REPAYMENT, recompense, replacement, restoration, reinstatement, reciprocation **3** REVENUE, income, proceeds, takings, yield, gain, profit, interest, reward, advantage, benefit **4** *the return of the books* giving back, handing back, taking back, reinstatement, restoration, delivery, replacement
🔁 **1** departure, disappearance **2** removal **3** payment, expense, loss

re-use *v*
recycle, reconstitute

revamp *v*
renovate, recondition, rebuild, reconstruct, repair, restore, revise, refit, refurbish, rehabilitate, overhaul, recast, *colloq.* do up

reveal *v*
expose, bring to light, make aware, uncover, unveil, unmask, unearth, expose to view, show, display, exhibit, lay bare, manifest, disclose, divulge, give away, betray, leak, tell, let out, let slip, impart, communicate, publicize, broadcast, publish, make public, make known, announce, proclaim
🔁 hide, conceal, mask

revealing *adj*
1 *a revealing interview* indicative, significant, revelatory, give-away **2** *a revealing dress* low-cut, daring, see-through, diaphanous, sheer

revel *v, n*
▸ *v* **1** *revel in an experience* enjoy, delight, take delight, take pleasure, relish, glory, joy, indulge, thrive, wallow, savour, bask, rejoice, lap up, gloat, crow, luxuriate **2** *revelling through the night* celebrate, carouse, have a party, make merry, roist, roister, *colloq.* live it up, whoop it up, paint the town red, push the boat out, raise the roof
🔁 **1** dislike
▸ *n* celebration, party, carousal, carouse, festivity, spree, gala, merrymaking, jollification, bacchanal, debauch, saturnalia, *colloq.* rave, rave-up

revelation *n*
1 UNCOVERING, unveiling, unearthing, bringing to light, exposure, unmasking, show, display, exhibition, disclosure, divulgence, confession, admission, betrayal, broadcasting, *formal* manifestation **2** NEWS, fact, detail, information, secreted/confidential information, communication, giveaway, publication, announcement, proclamation, leak

reveller *n*
celebrator, party-goer, pleasure-seeker, merrymaker, carouser, roisterer, wassailer, bacchanal

revelry *n*
celebration, festivity, party, merrymaking, carousal, fun, jollity, jollification, debauchery
🔁 sobriety

revenge *n, v*
▸ *n* vengeance, satisfaction, reprisal, retaliation, requital, retribution, redress, vendetta, *colloq.* tit for tat, eye for an eye and a tooth for a tooth, a taste of someone's own medicine
▸ *v* avenge, repay, retaliate, settle a score/an old score, pay someone back, put someone back in their

own court, get back at, hit back, fight back, *colloq.* get your own back, get even with, give as good as you get

revengeful *adj*
bitter, resentful, implacable, vengeful, vindictive, malignant, spiteful, malicious, merciless, unmerciful, pitiless, unforgiving, *formal* malevolent
🗲 forgiving, merciful

revenue *n*
income, return, yield, interest, profit(s), gain, proceeds, receipts, rewards, takings
🗲 expenditure

reverberate *v*
echo, re-echo, resound, resonate, ring, boom, vibrate

reverberation *n*
1 ECHO, re-echoing, resounding, resonance, ringing, vibration, wave, rebound, recoil, reflection 2 *reverberations following the resignation* repercussion, effect, consequence, result, *colloq.* shock wave, ripple

revere *v*
respect, admire, honour, look up to, think highly of, pay homage to, worship, reverence, adore, exalt, *formal* esteem, venerate
🗲 despise, scorn

reverence *n, v*
▶ *n* respect, deference, honour, homage, admiration, awe, worship, exaltation, adoration, devotion, *formal* veneration, (high) esteem
🗲 contempt, scorn
▶ *v* admire, respect, honour, acknowledge, revere, adore, worship, *formal* venerate
🗲 despise, scorn

reverent *adj*
reverential, respectful, admiring, deferential, humble, dutiful, devoted, awed, solemn, pious, devout, adoring, worshipping, loving
🗲 irreverent, disrespectful

reverie *n*
daydream, daydreaming, musing, trance, abstraction, absent-mindedness, inattention, preoccupation, brown study, woolgathering

reversal *n*
1 NEGATION, cancellation, annulment, nullification, countermanding, repeal, reverse, turnabout, turnaround, volte-face, upset, *formal* revocation, rescinding, *colloq.* U-turn 2 MISFORTUNE, mishap, misadventure, adversity, affliction, hardship, trial, blow, disappointment, upset, setback, check, delay, problem, difficulty, failure, defeat
🗲 1 advancement, progress

reverse *v, n, adj*
▶ *v* 1 *reverse a car* back, move backwards, drive backwards, retreat, backtrack, withdraw, *formal* regress 2 *reverse a decision* undo, negate, set aside, cancel, annul, invalidate, overrule, repeal, quash, overthrow, *formal* countermand, revoke, rescind, retract 3 TRANSPOSE, turn round, invert, up-end, overturn, turn upside-down, put back to front, upset, change, change round, swap, alter
🗲 1 go forwards 2 advance, enforce
▶ *n* 1 UNDERSIDE, other side, back, rear, inverse, counter, converse, contrary, opposite, *formal* antithesis 2 MISFORTUNE, mishap, misadventure, adversity, affliction, hardship, trial, blow, disappointment, upset, setback, check, delay, problem, difficulty, failure, defeat, reversal, *formal* vicissitude
▶ *adj* opposite, contrary, converse, inverse, inverted, backward, back, rear, verso

revert *v*
return, go back, resume, lapse, relapse, regress

review *n, v*
▶ *n* 1 CRITICISM, critique, assessment, evaluation, appraisal, judgement, report, commentary, examination, scrutiny, analysis, study, survey, rating, recapitulation, reassessment, re-evaluation, re-examination, revision, *formal* recension, *colloq.* rethink 2 MAGAZINE, periodical, journal
▶ *v* 1 CRITICIZE, assess, evaluate, judge, weigh (up), discuss, examine, view, inspect, scrutinize, analyse, study, survey, recapitulate, *formal* appraise 2 *review the situation* reassess, re-evaluate, re-examine, reconsider, rethink, revise, take stock of, *colloq.* size up

reviewer *n*
commentator, critic, judge, observer, connoisseur, arbiter, essayist

revile *v*
despise, hate, scorn, slander, libel, defame, abuse, smear, reproach, malign, blackguard, *formal* calumniate, denigrate, traduce, vituperate, vilify
🗲 praise

revise *v*
1 *revise your opinion* change, alter, modify, amend, correct, update, edit, rewrite, reword, redraft, recast, revamp, reconsider, re-examine, review, *formal* emend 2 STUDY, learn, memorize, *colloq.* swot up, cram, bone up on, mug up

revision *n*
1 CHANGE, amendment, editing, modification, alteration, correction, recast, recasting, re-examination, reconstruction, review, rewriting, rereading, *formal* emendation 2 STUDYING, memorizing, homework, learning, updating, *colloq.* swotting

revitalize *v*
revive, renew, restore, refresh, reactivate, reanimate, rejuvenate, resurrect, *formal* revivify
🗲 dampen, suppress

revival *n*
resuscitation, revitalization, restoration, re-establishment, reintroduction, renewal, renaissance, rebirth, resurrection, reawakening, resurgence, upsurge, upturn, *colloq.* the kiss of life, comeback

revive *v*
resuscitate, bring round, reanimate, revitalize, restore, renew, refresh, animate, invigorate, quicken, rouse, awaken, recover, rally, comfort, cheer up, reawaken, breathe new life into, rekindle, reactivate, re-establish, reintroduce, *colloq.* give the kiss of life to
🗲 weary

revivify *v*
revive, revitalize, invigorate, restore, resuscitate, refresh, renew, reactivate, reanimate, *formal* inspirit
🗲 dampen, depress

reviving *adj*
refreshening, invigorating, reinvigorating, exhilarating, bracing, stimulating, tonic, reanimating, enheartening, regenerating, *formal* revivescent, revivifying, reviviscent
🗲 disheartening, exhausting

revocation *n*
revoking, repeal, repealing, quashing, reversal, withdrawal, annulment, nullification, invalidation, negation, cancellation, abolition, repudiation, *formal* countermanding, rescinding, rescission, retractation, retraction
🗲 enforcement

revoke *v*
repeal, quash, annul, nullify, invalidate, negate, cancel, abolish, reverse, withdraw, *formal* rescind, abrogate, countermand, retract
🗲 enforce

revolt *n, v*
▶ *n* revolution, rebellion, mutiny, rising, uprising, insurrection, putsch, coup (d'état), secession, defection
▶ *v* **1** REBEL, mutiny, rise, rise up, riot, resist, defect, take up arms, take to the streets, *formal* dissent **2** DISGUST, sicken, nauseate, repel, turn your stomach, offend, shock, outrage, scandalize
🔁 **1** submit **2** please, delight

revolting *adj*
disgusting, sickening, nauseating, repulsive, repellent, obnoxious, nasty, horrible, vile, hateful, foul, loathsome, abhorrent, abominable, distasteful, off-putting, offensive, shocking, appalling, *formal* repugnant, reprehensible, heinous
🔁 pleasant, delightful, attractive, palatable

revolution *n*
1 REVOLT, rebellion, mutiny, rising, uprising, insurrection, insurgence, putsch, coup (d'état) **2** CHANGE, reformation, transformation, innovation, upheaval, cataclysm, *technical* metamorphosis, *colloq.* sex change **3** ROTATION, turn, spin, wheel, whirl, cycle, circuit, round, circle, orbit, gyration

revolutionary *n, adj*
▶ *n* rebel, mutineer, insurgent, insurrectionist, anarchist, revolutionist
▶ *adj* **1** REBEL, rebellious, mutinous, insurgent, insurrectionary, subversive, seditious, extremist, anarchistic, *formal* extremist **2** *revolutionary ideas* new, innovative, progressive, experimental, avant-garde, different, drastic, radical, thoroughgoing, complete
🔁 **1** conservative

revolutionize *v*
transform, reform, restructure, cause radical changes in, reorganize, transfigure, turn upside-down

revolve *v*
1 ROTATE, turn, go, move, pivot, swivel, spin, wheel, whirl, gyrate, circle, orbit **2** *his life revolves around sport* centre on, focus on, concentrate on, be preoccupied with, turn on, hinge on, hang on

revolver *n*
gun, handgun, firearm, pistol, rifle, shotgun, airgun, six-shooter, *colloq.* shooter

revolving *adj*
rotating, turning, spinning, whirling, gyrating, gyratory
🔁 stationary

revulsion *n*
disgust, distaste, dislike, repulsion, aversion, hatred, hate, loathing, nausea, abhorrence, recoil, abomination, *formal* repugnance, detestation
🔁 delight, pleasure, approval

reward *n, v*
▶ *n* **1** *a reward for long service* present, prize, honour, medal, decoration, bounty, pay-off, bonus, premium, payment, remuneration, recompense, repayment, compensation, gain, profit, return, benefit, merit, desert **2** REQUITAL, punishment, retribution, *colloq.* just deserts
▶ *v* pay, remunerate, recompense, repay, requite, compensate, honour, decorate
🔁 punish

rewarding *adj*
profitable, remunerative, lucrative, productive, fruitful, worthwhile, valuable, advantageous, beneficial, satisfying, gratifying, pleasing, fulfilling, enriching, edifying
🔁 unrewarding

rewording *n*
rephrasing, paraphrase, revision, *technical* metaphrase, metaphrasis

rewrite *v*
revise, rework, reword, redraft, recast, correct, edit, *formal* emend

rhetoric *n*
eloquence, oratory, bombast, pomposity, hyperbole, verbosity, wordiness, long-windedness, fustian, *formal* grandiloquence, magniloquence, prolixity

rhetorical *adj*
oratorical, bombastic, pompous, high-sounding, long-winded, verbose, wordy, grand, high-flown, flowery, florid, flamboyant, showy, pretentious, artificial, insincere, *formal* grandiloquent, magniloquent, declamatory, prolix
🔁 simple

rhyme *n*
poetry, verse, poem, ode, limerick, jingle, song, ditty

rhythm *n*
beat, pulse, time, throb, tempo, metre, measure, movement, harmony, flow, lilt, swing, accent, cadence, pattern

rhythmic *adj*
rhythmical, metric, metrical, pulsating, throbbing, flowing, lilting, periodic, regular, repeated, steady

rib *n*
bone, band, bar, support, vein, moulding, ribbing, ridge, shaft, welt, wale, *formal* costa

ribald *adj*
rude, obscene, risqué, racy, off-colour, bawdy, earthy, coarse, smutty, vulgar, filthy, foul-mouthed, gross, base, scurrilous, low, mean, lewd, disrespectful, licentious, indecent, irreverent, satirical, jeering, mocking, derisive, Rabelaisian, *colloq.* blue, naughty
🔁 polite

ribaldry *n*
rudeness, obscenity, bawdiness, raciness, vulgarity, smut, smuttiness, earthiness, coarseness, filth, grossness, lowness, baseness, licentiousness, indecency, scurrility, jeering, derision, mockery, *colloq.* naughtiness

ribbon *n*
band, cord, cloth, line, sash, strip, braid, shred, tatter, jag, hair-band, headband, fillet, taenia

rich *adj*
1 WEALTHY, affluent, moneyed, prosperous, well-to-do, well-off, *colloq.* flush, well-heeled, made of money, in the money, rolling in it, with money to burn, *slang* loaded, filthy rich, stinking rich **2** EXPENSIVE, precious, valuable, priceless, costly, lavish, magnificent, sumptuous, luxurious, lush, splendid, grand, gorgeous, palatial, fine, elaborate, ornate, *formal* opulent **3** PLENTIFUL, abundant, abounding, copious, profuse, prolific, ample, full, high, packed, steeped, overflowing, well-provided, well-supplied, *formal* replete, plenteous **4** FERTILE, fruitful, productive, lush, *formal* fecund **5** *rich food* creamy, fatty, oily, full-bodied, heavy, full-flavoured, strong, spicy, savoury, tasty, delicious, luscious, juicy, sweet **6** *rich colours* deep, intense, vivid, strong, bright, brilliant, vibrant, warm **7** IRONIC, laughable, ridiculous, outrageous, preposterous **8** *a rich voice* deep, mellow, full, sonorous, resonant, *formal* mellifluous
🔁 **1** poor, impoverished **2** plain **4** barren, infertile **5** plain, bland **6** dull, soft

riches *n*
wealth, affluence, prosperity, money, gold, treasure, fortune, assets, property, substance, resources, means, *old use* (filthy) lucre, *formal* opulence
🔁 poverty

richly *adv*
1 LAVISHLY, splendidly, gorgeously, sumptuously,

elegantly, elaborately, expensively, exquisitely, luxuriously, palatially, *formal* opulently **2** FULLY, thoroughly, completely, well, strongly, suitably, appropriately, properly

F₃ 1 poorly, scantily

rickety *adj*
unsteady, wobbly, shaky, unstable, insecure, flimsy, jerry-built, decrepit, ramshackle, broken-down, dilapidated, derelict

F₃ stable, strong

rid *v*
free, deliver, relieve, unburden, clear, purge, cleanse, purify

▷ **get rid of** throw away, throw out, dispose of, discard, dump, scrap, jettison, abolish, put an end to, eliminate, do away with, *colloq.* chuck (out), ditch, junk

riddance *n*
deliverance, release, relief, removal, freedom, elimination, clearance, disposal, ejection, expulsion, extermination, purgation

F₃ burdening

riddle¹ *n*
tell me a riddle enigma, mystery, conundrum, brainteaser, puzzle, poser, problem, *technical* koan

riddle² *v*
1 PERFORATE, pierce, puncture, pepper, fill, permeate, pervade, infest **2** SIFT, sieve, strain, filter, mar, winnow

ride *v, n*
▶ *v* sit, move, go, progress, travel, journey, gallop, trot, pedal, drive, steer, control, dominate, handle, manage, *formal* bestride
▶ *n* journey, trip, outing, jaunt, spin, drive, lift

ridge *n*
band, escarpment, hill, hummock, lump, arête, drum, drumlin, esker, yardang, sastruga, hog's back, reef, ripple, saddle, knurl, wale, welt, crinkle, *formal* costa

ridicule *n, v*
▶ *n* mockery, jeering, laughter, scorn, derision, taunting, teasing, chaff, banter, badinage, satire, irony, sarcasm

F₃ praise
▶ *v* laugh at, mock, make fun of, jeer, scorn, gibe, scoff, deride, sneer, tease, humiliate, taunt, satirize, send up, caricature, lampoon, burlesque, parody, *colloq.* rib, kid, rag, pull someone's leg, pooh-pooh, take the mickey out of

F₃ praise

ridiculous *adj*
ludicrous, absurd, nonsensical, silly, foolish, stupid, contemptible, derisory, laughable, facetious, farcical, comical, funny, humorous, droll, hilarious, outrageous, shocking, preposterous, incredible, unbelievable, *formal* risible

F₃ sensible

rife *adj*
abundant, abounding, rampant, teeming, swarming, overflowing, raging, epidemic, prevalent, widespread, predominant, extensive, general, common, frequent, ubiquitous

F₃ scarce

riff-raff *n*
mob, rabble, hoi polloi, scum, dregs, undesirables, canaille, *colloq.* rent-a-mob

rifle¹ *n*
shoot with a rifle gun, airgun, firearm, shotgun, musket, carbine, firelock, flintlock, fusil, bundook

rifle² *v*
rifle through some files search, rummage, sack, pillage, plunder, ransack, rob, maraud, loot, strip, burgle, gut, *formal* despoil

rift *n*
1 SPLIT, breach, break, fracture, crack, fault, chink, cleft, fissure, slit, cavity, cranny, crevice, gap, space, opening, hole **2** DISAGREEMENT, difference, fight, split, row, feud, conflict, breach, separation, division, schism, alienation, *formal* estrangement, altercation

F₃ 2 unity

rig *n, v*
▶ *n* equipment, kit, outfit, gear, tackle, apparatus, machinery, fittings, fixtures, *formal* accoutrements
▶ *v* falsify, tamper with, doctor, fiddle, distort, twist, pervert, manipulate, massage, misrepresent, forge, fake, *colloq.* cook

▷ **rig out 1** EQUIP, kit out, outfit, fit (out), supply, provide, furnish, make ready **2** CLOTHE, dress (up), wear, put on, get into, garb, robe, trim, turn out, *formal* array, accoutre, attire, *colloq.* get up

▷ **rig up** arrange, build, assemble, construct, erect, fit up, fix up, put together, improvise, *colloq.* knock up, throw together, cobble together

F₃ dismantle

right *adj, adv, n, v*
▶ *adj* **1** *the right answer* correct, accurate, exact, precise, true, factual, actual, real, genuine, authentic, valid, *colloq.* spot on, bang on **2** PROPER, fitting, correct, accepted, approved, becoming, appropriate, suitable, fit, fitting, admissible, acceptable, satisfactory, reasonable, desirable, favourable, preferable, advantageous, convenient, opportune, *formal* propitious, auspicious, *colloq.* the done thing **3** FAIR, just, equitable, lawful, legal, honest, upright, good, virtuous, righteous, moral, ethical, proper, principled, honourable, impartial **4** RIGHT-WING, conservative, Tory, reactionary, true-blue **5** *he's a right fool* complete, absolute, utter, real, thorough

F₃ 1 wrong, incorrect, erroneous **2** improper, unsuitable **3** unfair, wrong **4** left-wing
▶ *adv* **1** CORRECTLY, accurately, exactly, precisely, factually, properly, satisfactorily, well, favourably, fairly, *colloq.* by the book **2** *right to the bottom* straight, in a straight line, directly, as the crow flies, completely, utterly, entirely, absolutely, wholly, totally, all the way, *colloq.* slap bang **3** *I'll be right back* straight, immediately, without delay

F₃ 1 wrongly, incorrectly, unfairly

▷ **right away** straight away, immediately, at once, now, instantly, directly, forthwith, without delay, promptly, *colloq.* from the word go

F₃ later, eventually
▶ *n* **1** JUSTICE, legality, lawfulness, good, goodness, virtue, righteousness, morality, ethics, honour, honesty, integrity, uprightness, truthfulness, impartiality, fairness, *formal* rectitude, propriety **2** PRIVILEGE, prerogative, due, claim, entitlement, birthright, business, authority, power, permission, warrant, freedom, opportunity, licence, charter, sanction, title deed, *technical* droit, *formal* lien

F₃ 1 wrong

▷ **by rights** rightfully, correctly, properly, rightly, justifiably, justly, lawfully, legally, legitimately, *technical* de jure

▷ **in the right** justified, right, warranted, vindicated

F₃ in the wrong, at fault

▷ **put/set to rights** rectify, correct, put in order, fix, settle, straighten (out)

▷ **within your rights** justified, entitled, permitted, allowed, reasonable, right
▶ *v* rectify, correct, put right, put in order, fix, repair, redress, vindicate, avenge, settle, straighten (out), stand up

righteous *adj*
1 *a righteous person/action* just, good, virtuous, moral, worthy, honourable, upright, fair, ethical, equitable, honest, law-abiding, blameless, irreproachable, incorrupt, guiltless, God-fearing, saintly, pure, sinless **2** *righteous anger* justifiable, defensible, excusable, warranted, reasonable, supportable, justified, lawful, legal, legitimate, acceptable, explainable, valid, well-founded, proper
F3 **1** unrighteous **2** unjustifiable

righteousness *n*
goodness, honesty, honour, virtue, uprightness, morality, integrity, justice, blamelessness, faithfulness, equity, ethicalness, purity, holiness, sanctification, *technical* dharma, *formal* probity, rectitude
F3 unrighteousness

rightful *adj*
legitimate, lawful, legal, just, bona fide, true, real, genuine, valid, authorized, correct, proper, suitable, due
F3 wrongful, unlawful

rightfully *adv*
correctly, properly, rightly, by rights, justifiably, justly, lawfully, legally, legitimately, *technical* de jure
F3 incorrectly, unjustifiably

rigid *adj*
1 STIFF, inflexible, inelastic, unbending, cast-iron, hard, firm, set, fixed, unyielding, unalterable, invariable **2** *a rigid political system* austere, harsh, severe, inflexible, unrelenting, strict, rigorous, stringent, stern, uncompromising, unyielding, Spartan, *formal* intransigent
F3 **1** flexible, elastic, bending, malleable **2** variable, weak

rigmarole *n*
process, bother, performance, fuss, palaver, nonsense, jargon, gibberish, twaddle, *colloq.* carry-on, hassle, red tape, to-do

rigorous *adj*
1 EXACT, precise, accurate, meticulous, painstaking, scrupulous, conscientious, punctilious, laborious, thorough **2** STRICT, stringent, rigid, firm, tough, harsh, hard, severe, stern, austere, exacting, uncompromising, spartan, *formal* intransigent
F3 **1** lax, superficial

rigour *n*
1 *the rigours of war* TRIAL, hardship, severity, suffering, ordeal, *formal* privation **2** THOROUGHNESS, exactness, meticulousness, accuracy, preciseness, precision, conscientiousness, punctiliousness, inflexibility **3** STRICTNESS, stringency, rigidity, firmness, toughness, harshness, hardship, hardness, severity, sternness, austerity, *formal* intransigence
F3 **3** leniency, mildness

rig-out *n*
clothing, clothes, garments, outfit, uniform, dress, costume, habit, livery, *formal* apparel, raiment, *colloq.* clobber, garb, gear, get-up, togs

rile *v*
annoy, irritate, nettle, pique, put out, upset, irk, vex, anger, exasperate, *colloq.* peeve, aggravate, bug
F3 calm, soothe

rim *n*
lip, edge, brim, brink, verge, margin, border, circumference
F3 centre, middle

rind *n*
peel, skin, husk, crust, *formal* epicarp, integument

ring¹ *n, v*
▶ *n* **1** CIRCLE, round, loop, hoop, disc, halo, band,

circlet, belt, girdle, collar, circuit, area, arena, enclosure, atoll **2** GROUP, cartel, syndicate, association, organization, league, alliance, combine, society, club, fraternity, sorority, gathering, circle, gang, crew, mob, band, cell, clique, coterie
▶ *v* surround, encircle, gird, loop, encompass, enclose, cage in, hem in, *formal* circumscribe

ring² *v, n*
▶ *v* **1** CHIME, peal, toll, knell, ding, ding-dong, tinkle, clink, jingle, clang, sound, resound, resonate, echo, reverberate, buzz **2** TELEPHONE, phone, call, ring up, *colloq.* give a buzz, give a tinkle, give a bell
▶ *n* **1** CHIME, peal, toll, knell, tinkle, clink, jingle, clang, ding-dong **2** PHONE CALL, call, *colloq.* buzz, tinkle, bell

ringleader *n*
leader, spokesman, spokeswoman, spokesperson, mouthpiece, chief, fugleman, bell-wether, *colloq.* brains

rinse *v*
swill, bathe, wash, wash clean, clean, cleanse, flush (away), wet, dip

riot *n, v*
▶ *n* **1** *a riot in the streets* insurrection, rising, uprising, revolt, rebellion, insurgence, anarchy, lawlessness, fight, brawl, fray, fracas, melee, affray, disturbance, turbulence, disorder, confusion, commotion, tumult, turmoil, uproar, row, quarrel, strife **2** REVELRY, feasting, partying, indulgence, debauchery, orgy, *old use* merrymaking, *colloq.* rave, rave-up **3** *a riot of colour* display, show, flourish, exhibition, extravaganza **4** LAUGH, *colloq.* scream, hoot
F3 **1** order, calm
▷ **run riot** rampage, run wild, run amok, go berserk, rush wildly, charge, tear, storm, rage, rant, rave
▶ *v* revolt, rebel, mutiny, rise up, run riot, run wild, run amok, go berserk, rush wildly, charge, tear, storm, rage, rant, rave, rampage, go on the rampage

riotous *adj*
1 WILD, violent, uncontrollable, unrestrained, unruly, rebellious, lawless, insurrectionary, insubordinate, disorderly, mutinous, ungovernable, wanton **2** NOISY, loud, rowdy, tumultuous, boisterous, uproarious
F3 **1** orderly, restrained

rip *v, n*
▶ *v* tear, rend, split, separate, rupture, burst, cut, shred, slit, slash, gash, lacerate, hack
▷ **rip off** overcharge, swindle, defraud, cheat, diddle, trick, dupe, exploit, *colloq.* do, fleece, con, *slang* sting
▶ *n* tear, rent, split, cleavage, rupture, cut, ladder, slit, slash, gash, hole

ripe *adj*
1 RIPENED, mature, mellow, seasoned, grown, fully-grown, developed, fully-developed, complete, finished, perfect **2** READY, suitable, fit, right, advantageous, favourable, timely, opportune, *formal* auspicious, propitious
F3 **2** untimely, inopportune, *formal* inauspicious

ripen *v*
develop, mature, bring/come to maturity, mellow, season, age

rip-off *n*
robbery, exploitation, cheat, swindle, theft, fraud, diddle, *colloq.* con, con trick, daylight robbery, *slang* sting

riposte *n, v*
▶ *n* retort, rejoinder, repartee, quip, answer, reply, response, return, sally, comeback
▶ *v* retort, rejoin, quip, reciprocate, answer, reply, respond, return

ripple *n, v*
▶ *n* **1** WAVE, disturbance, eddy, gurgle, lapping, rip-

plet, undulation, burble, babble, purl, wimple **2** RE-PERCUSSION, effect, result, consequence, reverberation, *colloq.* shock wave
▶ *v* ruffle, wrinkle, flow, undulate, purl, wimple, crease, pucker, crumple

rise *v, n*
▶ *v* **1** GO UP, move upwards, ascend, climb (up), mount, slope (up), soar, tower, loom, grow, get higher, increase, escalate, swell, intensify, rocket **2** STAND UP, get up, arise, jump up, leap up, spring up, get to your feet, get out of bed **3** ADVANCE, progress, make progress, approach, improve, prosper, be promoted **4** ORIGINATE, spring, flow, issue, emanate, emerge, appear, start, begin, *formal* commence **5** REBEL, revolt, mutiny, riot, resist, defect, take up arms, take to the streets, *formal* dissent **6** *rise to the challenge* attempt, try, do your best, respond, react to, exert yourself
F₃ **1** fall, descend **2** sit down **3** declare
▶ *n* **1** ASCENT, climb, slope, soaring, towering, incline, hill, elevation, *formal* acclivity **2** INCREASE, growth, escalation, leap, increment, upsurge, upturn, advance, progress, improvement, advancement, promotion, *US* raise, *formal* amelioration, aggrandizement
F₃ **1** descent, valley **2** fall

risible *adj*
ridiculous, ludicrous, funny, hilarious, humorous, laughable, absurd, amusing, comic, comical, droll, farcical, *colloq.* rib-tickling, side-splitting
F₃ serious, unfunny

rising *n, adj*
▶ *n* riot, revolution, revolt, uprising, insurrection
▶ *adj* ascending, growing, increasing, intensifying, mounting, soaring, swelling, advancing, emerging, approaching
F₃ decreasing

risk *n, v*
▶ *n* danger, peril, jeopardy, hazard, threat, chance, possibility, uncertainty, gamble, speculation, venture, adventure
F₃ safety, certainty
▶ *v* endanger, imperil, jeopardize, put in jeopardy, hazard, chance, take a chance, gamble, venture, dare, *colloq.* chance it, put on the line, go for broke, stick your neck out, play with fire

risky *adj*
dangerous, unsafe, perilous, hazardous, chancy, uncertain, touch-and-go, high-risk, tricky, precarious, *colloq.* dicey, dodgy, iffy
F₃ safe

risqué *adj*
indecent, improper, rude, immodest, indelicate, suggestive, coarse, crude, earthy, dirty, bawdy, racy, smutty, naughty, ribald, off-colour, *colloq.* adult, blue, near the knuckle
F₃ decent, proper

rite *n*
ceremony, custom, act, usage, office, form, formality, ceremonial, ordinance, practice, procedure, ritual, service, worship, liturgy, sacrament, observance

ritual *n, adj*
▶ *n* custom, tradition, convention, usage, practice, habit, wont, routine, procedure, ordinance, prescription, form, formality, ceremony, ceremonial, solemnity, rite, sacrament, service, liturgy, celebration, observance, act
▶ *adj* customary, traditional, conventional, habitual, routine, procedural, prescribed, set, formal, ceremonial
F₃ informal

rival *n, adj, v*
▶ *n* competitor, contestant, contender, challenger,

opponent, opposition, adversary, antagonist, vier, fellow, match, equal, peer
F₃ colleague, associate
▶ *adj* competitive, competing, in competition, in conflict, conflicting, opposed, opposing, in opposition
F₃ associate
▶ *v* compete with, contend with, vie with, oppose, compare with, measure up to, emulate, match, equal, parallel
F₃ co-operate

rivalry *n*
competitiveness, competition, contest, contention, conflict, struggle, strife, vying, opposition, antagonism
F₃ co-operation

river *n*
waterway, watercourse

Forms of river or watercourse include:
beck, billabong, bourn, broads, brook, burn, canal, channel, confluence, creek, cut, delta, estuary, firth, frith, inlet, mountain stream, mouth, rill, rillet, rivulet, runnel, source, stream, tributary, wadi, waterway.

The world's longest rivers include:
Nile (Africa), Amazon (South America), Yangtze (Asia), Mississippi-Missouri (North America), Yenisey-Angara-Selenga (Asia), Amur-Argun-Kerulen (Asia), Ob-Irtysh (Asia), Plata-Parena-Grande (South America), Yellow (Asia), Zaire (Africa).

riveting *adj*
fascinating, absorbing, interesting, exciting, gripping, arresting, captivating, engrossing, enthralling, spellbinding, magnetic, hypnotic
F₃ boring

roam *v*
wander, rove, range, travel, traverse, walk, tramp, trek, ramble, meander, stroll, amble, prowl, drift, stray, *formal* ambulate, perambulate, peregrinate
F₃ stay

roar *v, n*
▶ *v* **1** BELLOW, yell, shout, cry, scream, shriek, bawl, howl, hoot, guffaw, thunder, crash, blare, rumble **2** LAUGH, burst out laughing, shriek with laughter, guffaw, hoot, *colloq.* split your sides, fall about, break up, crease up, laugh like a drain
F₃ **1** whisper
▶ *n* bellow, yell, shout, cry, scream, shriek, bawl, howl, hoot, guffaw, thunder, crash, blare, rumble

rob *v*
steal from, hold up, raid, burgle, loot, pillage, plunder, sack, rifle, ransack, swindle, cheat, defraud, deprive, *colloq.* rip off, do, mug, *slang* sting, heist

robber *n*
thief, burglar, stealer, hijacker, bandit, swindler, embezzler, fraud, cheat, plunderer, raider, pirate, highwayman, looter, brigand, *colloq.* con man, mugger

robbery *n*
theft, stealing, larceny, break-in, housebreaking, hold-up, pilferage, raid, burglary, pillage, plunder, fraud, embezzlement, swindle, *colloq.* rip-off, mugging, *slang* stick-up, heist

robe *n, v*
▶ *n* costume, gown, vestment, habit, bathrobe, dres-

sing-gown, housecoat, peignoir, wrap, wrapper
▶ *v* clothe, dress, drape, garb, vest, *formal* apparel, attire

robot *n*
automaton, machine, android, zombie

robust *adj*
1 STRONG, sturdy, tough, hardy, energetic, vigorous, powerful, muscular, well-built, strapping, stalwart, athletic, fit, healthy, well **2** *robust opinions* strong, forceful, vigorous, straightforward, direct, *colloq.* nononsense **3** COARSE, earthy, rude, crude, ribald, risqué, raw
F₃ **1** weak, feeble, unhealthy

rock¹ *n*
rocks rolling down the hill boulder, stone, pebble, crag, outcrop

Rocks include:
basalt, breccia, chalk, coal, conglomerate, flint, gabbro, gneiss, granite, gravel, lava, limestone, marble, marl, obsidian, ore, porphyry, pumice stone, sandstone, schist, serpentine, shale, slate.

rock² *v*
1 SWAY, swing, tilt, tip, shake, wobble, roll, undulate, pitch, toss, lurch, reel, stagger, totter, oscillate, move to and fro **2** *news that rocked the nation* shock, stun, stagger, bewilder, daze, dumbfound, astound, astonish, surprise, startle, take aback

rocket *v*
soar, tower, increase quickly/suddenly, escalate, shoot up

rocky¹ *adj*
rocky moorland stony, pebbly, craggy, rugged, rough, hard, flinty
F₃ smooth, soft

rocky² *adj*
a rocky marriage unsteady, shaky, wobbly, wobbling, staggering, tottering, unstable, unreliable, uncertain, weak
F₃ steady, stable, dependable, strong

rod *n*
bar, shaft, strut, pole, stick, baton, wand, cane, switch, staff, mace, sceptre

rodent *n*

Kinds of rodent include:
agouti, bandicoot, beaver, black rat, brown rat, cane rat, capybara, cavy, chinchilla, chipmunk, cony, coypu, dormouse, ferret, fieldmouse, gerbil, gopher, grey squirrel, groundhog, guinea pig, hamster, hare, harvest mouse, hedgehog, jerboa, kangaroo rat, lemming, marmot, meerkat, mouse, muskrat, musquash, pika, porcupine, prairie dog, rabbit, rat, red squirrel, sewer-rat, squirrel, vole, water rat, water vole, woodchuck.

rogue *n*
scoundrel, rascal, scamp, villain, miscreant, deceiver, swindler, fraud, fraudster, cheat, reprobate, good-for-nothing, wastrel, ne'er-do-well, *colloq.* crook, con man, nasty piece of work

roguish *adj*
mischievous, playful, cheeky, impish, knavish, rascally, waggish, frolicsome, coquettish, swindling, villainous, deceiving, deceitful, dishonest, criminal, crooked, fraudulent, shady, unprincipled, unscrupulous
F₃ honest, serious

roister *v*
revel, rollick, celebrate, carouse, frolic, romp, strut,

swagger, brag, bluster, boast, *colloq.* paint the town red, whoop it up

roisterous *adj*
loud, noisy, wild, rowdy, uproarious, disorderly, exuberant, boisterous, clamorous, obstreperous
F₃ orderly, restrained

role *n*
part, character, representation, portrayal, impersonation, function, capacity, task, duty, job, post, position, situation, place

roll *v, n*
▶ *v* **1** ROTATE, revolve, turn (round), go round, spin, wheel, twirl, whirl, gyrate, move, go, run, pass **2** WIND, coil, furl, twist, curl, wrap, envelop, fold, enfold, bind **3** *the ship rolled* rock, sway, swing, pitch, toss, lurch, reel, billow, tumble, stagger, wallow, undulate **4** PRESS, press down, flatten, crush, smooth, level **5** RUMBLE, roar, thunder, boom, resound, reverberate
▷ **roll up** arrive, assemble, gather, congregate, convene
F₃ leave
▶ *n* **1** ROLLER, cylinder, drum, reel, spool, bobbin, scroll **2** REGISTER, roster, census, list, inventory, index, catalogue, directory, schedule, record, file, chronicle, annals **3** ROTATION, revolution, cycle, turn, spin, wheel, twirl, whirl, gyration, undulation **4** RUMBLE, roar, thunder, boom, resonance, reverberation **5** SWELL, pitching, tossing, rocking, reeling, billowing, undulation

rollicking *adj*
lively, noisy, light-hearted, hearty, romping, sprightly, exuberant, frolicsome, jovial, carefree, boisterous, joyous, merry, spirited, sportive, jaunty, cavorting, devil-may-care, roisterous, roisting, frisky, playful, rip-roaring, swashbuckling
F₃ restrained, serious

rolling *adj*
heaving, surging, waving, rippling, undulating, undulant
F₃ flat

roly-poly *adj*
fat, plump, chubby, overweight, rounded, tubby, buxom, podgy, pudgy, *formal* rotund
F₃ slim

romance *n, v*
▶ *n* **1** LOVE AFFAIR, affair, relationship, liaison, attachment, intrigue, amour, passion **2** LOVE STORY, romantic fiction, novel, story, tale, fairytale, legend, idyll, fiction, fantasy, whimsy **3** ADVENTURE, excitement, melodrama, mystery, charm, fascination, glamour, sentiment
▶ *v* **1** LIE, fantasize, exaggerate, overstate **2** GO OUT WITH, court, see, *colloq.* date, go steady with

romantic *adj, n*
▶ *adj* **1** IMAGINARY, fictitious, fanciful, fantastic, legendary, fairy-tale, idyllic, utopian, optimistic, idealistic, quixotic, visionary, starry-eyed, dreamy, unrealistic, impractical, improbable, unlikely, wild, extravagant, exciting, fascinating, mysterious **2** SENTIMENTAL, loving, amorous, passionate, tender, fond, soppy, mushy, sloppy, *colloq.* lovey-dovey
F₃ **1** real, practical **2** unromantic, unsentimental
▶ *n* sentimentalist, dreamer, visionary, idealist, utopian
F₃ realist

Romeo *n*
lover, ladies' man, Don Juan, Casanova, lady-killer, gigolo

romp *v, n*
▶ *v* gambol, frolic, skip, sport, frisk, caper, cavort,

revel, rollick, roister
► *n* caper, frolic, lark, rig, spree

rook *v*
cheat, swindle, defraud, overcharge, *colloq.* rip off, do, fleece, diddle, con, bilk, sting

room *n*
space, volume, capacity, area, headroom, legroom, elbow-room, scope, range, extent, expanse, volume, leeway, latitude, margin, allowance, chance, opportunity

roomy *adj*
spacious, large, sizeable, broad, wide, extensive, ample, generous, *formal* capacious, voluminous, commodious
🗲 cramped, small, tiny

root¹ *n, v*
► *n* **1** TUBER, rhizome, stem, radical, radicle, radix **2** ORIGIN, source, derivation, reason, cause, starting point, fount, fountainhead, seed, germ, kernel, nucleus, heart, core, nub, essence, seat, base, bottom, basis, foundation, fundamental **3** *tracing your family roots* beginning(s), origins, family, heritage, background, birthplace, home
▷ **root and branch** completely, entirely, wholly, totally, utterly, thoroughly, radically, finally
🗲 not at all, slightly
► *v* anchor, moor, fasten, fix, set, stick, implant, embed, entrench, establish, ground, base
▷ **root out** unearth, dig out, uncover, discover, uproot, eradicate, eliminate, put an end to, exterminate, destroy, abolish, clear away, remove, get rid of, *formal* extirpate

root² *v*
▷ **root around** *root around in the cupboard* rummage, ferret, poke, pry, nose, dig, delve, burrow, forage, hunt

root³ *v*
root for your team support, shout, cheer (on), encourage, applaud, hail, *US* pull

rooted *adj*
entrenched, established, felt, firm, fixed, deep, deeply, deep-seated, ingrained, confirmed, rigid, radical
🗲 superficial, temporary

rope *v*
tie, bind, lash, fasten, hitch, moor, tether
▷ **rope in** enlist, engage, involve, persuade, talk into, *formal* inveigle

ropy *adj*
poor, substandard, deficient, inadequate, inferior, unsatisfactory, rough, unwell, off-colour, *colloq.* below par
🗲 good, well

roster *n*
rota, schedule, register, roll, list, listing, index, directory

rostrum *n*
platform, stage, dais, podium

rosy *adj*
1 PINK, reddish, red, rose, rose-coloured, rose-hued, roselike, rose-pink, rose-red, rose-scented, roseate, glowing, fresh, sunny, healthy-looking, blooming, blushing, ruddy, flushed, florid, inflamed, bloodshot, *formal* rubicund **2** PROMISING, cheerful, bright, encouraging, optimistic, hopeful, reassuring, favourable, *formal* auspicious
🗲 **2** depressing, sad, unhappy

rot *v, n*
► *v* decay, decompose, fester, perish, corrode, spoil, go bad, go off, degenerate, go sour, deteriorate, crumble, disintegrate, taint, corrupt, *formal* putrefy

► *n* **1** DECAY, decomposition, deterioration, disintegration, corrosion, rust, mould, *formal* putrefaction **2** NONSENSE, rubbish, drivel, claptrap, *colloq.* poppycock, bunk, bunkum, baloney, humbug, piffle, tosh, bosh, codswallop

rotary *adj*
rotating, revolving, turning, spinning, whirling, gyrating, gyratory
🗲 fixed

rotate *v*
1 REVOLVE, turn (round), spin (round), go round, move round, reel, whirl, gyrate, pivot, swivel, roll **2** ALTERNATE, take (it) in turns, interchange, reciprocate

rotation *n*
revolution, turn, turning, spin, spinning, swivel, swivelling, whirl, whirling, gyration, orbit, cycle, alternation, sequence, succession

rotten *adj*
1 DECAYED, decomposed, putrid, addled, bad, off, sour, spoilt, tainted, mouldy, fetid, stinking, rank, foul, rotting, decaying, disintegrating, mouldering, *formal* putrescent **2** INFERIOR, bad, poor, inadequate, low-grade, lousy, mean, *colloq.* crummy, ropy **3** NASTY, evil, wicked, horrible, beastly, dirty, despicable, contemptible, dishonourable, dishonest, immoral, corrupt, unprincipled **4** ILL, sick, unwell, poorly, awful, off-colour, *colloq.* grotty, rough, ropy
🗲 **1** fresh **2, 3** good **4** well

rotter *n*
scoundrel, cad, blackguard, dastard, cur, *colloq.* bounder, blighter, stinker, swine, rat, fink, louse

rotund *adj*
1 FAT, round, stout, tubby, full, fleshy, plump, podgy, portly, chubby, roly-poly, heavy, obese, spherical, globular, spheric, spheral, spherular, bulbous, *formal* corpulent, rotundate, orbicular **2** RESONANT, rich, sonorous, full, rounded, *formal* grandiloquent, magniloquent, orotund
🗲 **1** flat, slim, gaunt

rough *adj, n, v*
► *adj* **1** UNEVEN, bumpy, lumpy, stony, rugged, craggy, jagged, irregular, gnarled, coarse, bristly, hairy, shaggy, scaly, prickly, scratchy **2** BOISTEROUS, forceful, energetic, lively, disorderly, violent, wild, noisy, rowdy, raucous **3** HARSH, severe, stern, tough, hard, difficult, insensitive, unfeeling, merciless, cruel, brutal, drastic, extreme, vulgar, impolite, coarse, brutish, brusque, curt, sharp **4** *in a rough voice* husky, throaty, gruff, harsh, hoarse, rasping, croaking, guttural, raucous, discordant, strident **5** APPROXIMATE, estimated, imprecise, inexact, hazy, vague, general, quick, cursory, hasty, sketchy, incomplete, unfinished, unpolished, unrefined, crude, basic, rudimentary **6** *rough sea* choppy, agitated, turbulent, stormy, tempestuous, violent, wild **7** ILL, sick, unhealthy, unwell, poorly, off-colour, *colloq.* below par, rotten, grotty
🗲 **1** smooth **2** gentle **3** mild **5** accurate, exact **6** calm, smooth **7** well
► *n* **1** SKETCH, mock-up, outline, draft, model **2** THUG, hooligan, bully, rowdy, ruffian, bruiser, roughneck, tough, *slang* yob, yobbo
► *v* ▷ **rough out** sketch, draft, draw in rough, outline, mock up, give a summary of
▷ **rough up** beat up, maltreat, manhandle, mistreat, *colloq.* do in, knock about, bash, mug

rough-and-ready *adj*
approximate, crude, sketchy, simple, makeshift, make-do, provisional, stop-gap, hurried, unpolished, unrefined
🗲 exact, refined

rough-and-tumble *n*
scuffle, struggle, fight, fracas, rumpus, affray, brawl, melee, *colloq.* dust-up, punch-up, scrap

roughen *v*
abrade, asperate, coarsen, granulate, graze, harshen, rough, chafe, chap, rasp, ruffle, scuff
≠ smooth

roughneck *n*
tough, thug, rough, rowdy, ruffian, hooligan, lout, bully boy, bruiser, keelie

round *adj, n, v*
▶ *adj* **1** SPHERICAL, globular, ball-shaped, circular, ring-shaped, disc-shaped, dislike, globelike, hooplike, cylindrical, rounded, curved, *formal* spheroid, discoid, discoidal, orbicular, globate **2** ROTUND, plump, stout, portly, ample, *formal* corpulent **3** APPROXIMATE, rough, imprecise, estimated
▶ *n* **1** CIRCLE, ring, band, hoop, circlet, disc, sphere, cylinder, globe, ball, orb **2** CYCLE, series, sequence, succession, period, bout, session, heat, game, level, stage **3** BEAT, circuit, route, path, lap, course, routine
▶ *v* go round, move past, circle, skirt, travel round, flank, bypass
▷ **round off** finish (off), complete, end, close, conclude, cap, crown, top off
≠ begin
▷ **round on** turn on, set upon, attack, lay into, abuse
▷ **round up** bring together, herd, marshal, assemble, gather, rally, muster, collect, group
≠ disperse, scatter

roundabout *adj*
circuitous, tortuous, twisting, winding, meandering, indirect, oblique, devious, evasive, *formal* periphrastic, circumlocutory
≠ straight, direct

roundly *adv*
completely, thoroughly, forcefully, violently, vehemently, fiercely, intensely, rigorously, severely, sharply, bluntly, openly, frankly, outspokenly
≠ mildly

round-up *n*
summary, survey, overview, précis, collation, collection, assembly, gathering, herding, marshalling, muster, rally
≠ dispersal

rouse *v*
1 WAKE (UP), awaken, arouse, call, stir, get up **2** EXCITE, move, start, disturb, agitate, anger, provoke, stimulate, instigate, incite, inflame, impel, induce, kindle, evoke, call up, galvanize, whip up
≠ **2** calm

rousing *adj*
stimulating, exciting, inspiring, lively, moving, spirited, stirring, vigorous, exhilarating, brisk, electrifying
≠ dull, boring, calming

rout *n, v*
▶ *n* defeat, conquest, overthrow, beating, trouncing, drubbing, flight, retreat, stampede, *formal* subjugation, *colloq.* thrashing
≠ win
▶ *v* defeat, conquer, overthrow, crush, beat, trounce, put to flight, chase, dispel, scatter, *formal* vanquish, subjugate, *colloq.* hammer, thrash, lick, slaughter, wipe the floor with

route *n, v*
▶ *n* course, run, path, road, avenue, way, flight path, direction, itinerary, journey, passage, circuit, round, beat
▶ *v* direct, send, forward, convey, dispatch

routine *n, adj*
▶ *n* **1** PROCEDURE, way, method, system, order, pattern, schedule, programme, formula, practice, usage, custom, wont, habit, rut **2** *comedy routine* act, piece, programme, performance, lines, *colloq.* patter, spiel, yak
▶ *adj* customary, habitual, usual, typical, ordinary, run-of-the-mill, normal, standard, common, wonted, workaday, conventional, unoriginal, predictable, familiar, everyday, banal, humdrum, dull, boring, monotonous, tedious, tiresome, hackneyed
≠ unusual, different, exciting, inspiring

rove *v*
roam, wander, ramble, range, meander, drift, cruise, stroll, stray, gallivant, traipse, *Scot.* stravaig
≠ stay

row¹ *n*
a row of seats line, tier, bank, rank, range, column, file, queue, string, chain, series, sequence, arrangement

row² *n, v*
▶ *n* **1** ARGUMENT, quarrel, disagreement, dispute, controversy, squabble, tiff, fight, conflict, fracas, brawl, *formal* altercation, *colloq.* slanging match, falling-out, set-to, scrap, dust-up **2** NOISE, racket, din, uproar, commotion, clamour, disturbance, rumpus, hubbub, tumult
≠ **2** calm
▶ *v* argue, quarrel, wrangle, bicker, squabble, fight, *colloq.* scrap

rowdy *adj, n*
▶ *adj* noisy, loud, rough, boisterous, disorderly, unruly, unrestrained, riotous, wild, obstreperous
≠ quiet, peaceful, restrained
▶ *n* rough, ruffian, tough, tearaway, hooligan, lout, brawler, apache, keelie, *colloq.* hoodlum, *slang* yahoo, yob, yobbo

royal *adj*
regal, majestic, kingly, kinglike, queenly, queenlike, princely, imperial, monarchical, sovereign, august, grand, impressive, imposing, stately, magnificent, splendid, superb

rub *v, n*
▶ *v* **1** STROKE, caress, fondle, pat, massage, scratch, knead, *formal* embrocate **2** CLEAN, smooth, polish, buff (up), burnish, shine **3** SCOUR, scratch, scrape, scrub, wipe, clean, abrade **4** PUT ON, apply, work in, spread, smear **5** CHAFE, grate, scrape, pinch
▷ **rub in** emphasize, stress, underline, highlight, make much of, insist on, harp on
▷ **rub off on** influence, affect, have an effect on, change, alter, transform
▷ **rub out 1** ERASE, obliterate, delete, cancel, *formal* efface **2** KILL, assassinate, murder, put to death, finish off, do away with, *colloq.* do in, bump off, eliminate, liquidate
▷ **rub up the wrong way** annoy, anger, irk, irritate, get, vex, niggle, get to, *colloq.* bug, get one's goat, get under one's skin, needle, peeve
≠ calm
▶ *n* **1** MASSAGE, stroke, caress, kneading **2** POLISH, shine, wipe, clean **3** DIFFICULTY, drawback, hindrance, trouble, impediment, problem, obstacle, hitch, catch, *colloq.* snag

rubbish *n*
1 REFUSE, junk, litter, scrap, waste, dross, debris, rubble, flotsam and jetsam, *US* garbage, trash, *formal* detritus **2** NONSENSE, drivel, twaddle, gibberish, gobbledegook, balderdash, *colloq.* stuff and nonsense, claptrap, poppycock, rot, cobblers, bunk, bunkum, piffle, rot, tripe, tosh, bosh, *slang* crap, bull
≠ **2** sense

rubbishy *adj*
worthless, valueless, trashy, cheap, tawdry, third-rate, grotty, paltry, petty, shoddy, throw-away, gimcrack, tatty, twopenny-halfpenny
🖛 high-quality, classy

ruction *n*
protest, quarrel, trouble, fracas, fuss, row, rout, rumpus, disturbance, dispute, commotion, racket, uproar, storm, brawl, rookery, ruffle, *formal* altercation, *colloq.* scrap, to-do
🖛 calm

ruddy *adj*
red, reddish, scarlet, crimson, blushing, flushed, rosy, glowing, healthy, blooming, florid, fresh, sunburnt, *formal* rubicund
🖛 pale, unhealthy

rude *adj*
1 IMPOLITE, discourteous, disrespectful, bad-tempered, impertinent, impudent, insolent, offensive, insulting, abusive, ill-mannered, ill-bred, unpleasant, uncouth, uncivilized, unrefined, unpolished, uneducated, untutored, uncivil, curt, brusque, abrupt, sharp, short, *colloq.* cheeky 2 *a rude joke* obscene, vulgar, coarse, improper, indecent, indelicate, dirty, filthy, risqué, ribald, lewd, bawdy, naughty, gross, *colloq.* near the bone 3 *get a rude shock* unpleasant, harsh, disagreeable, nasty, unexpected, sudden 4 SIMPLE, rough, crude, primitive, rudimentary, rough-and-ready 5 IGNORANT, illiterate, uncivilized, unrefined, uneducated, untutored, unpolished, uncouth, rough
🖛 1 polite, courteous, civil 2 clean, decent 3 pleasant 4 advanced, well-developed 5 educated

rudimentary *adj*
1 BASIC, primary, initial, introductory, elementary, fundamental 2 PRIMITIVE, undeveloped, embryonic, crude, simple, rough
🖛 1 advanced 2 developed

rudiments *n*
basics, fundamentals, essentials, principles, elements, ABC, beginnings, foundations

rue *v*
regret, be regretful, be sorry, mourn, grieve, lament, deplore, feel remorse for, bemoan, bewail, repent
🖛 rejoice

rueful *adj*
regretful, remorseful, penitent, sad, melancholy, repentant, sorrowful, sorry, mournful, dismal, apologetic, grievous, conscience-stricken, doleful, pitiable, pitiful, plaintive, self-reproachful, *formal* contrite, lugubrious, woebegone, woeful
🖛 glad, joyful

ruffian *n*
villain, scoundrel, bully, bully boy, brute, thug, lout, rowdy, rogue, cut-throat, rascal, roughneck, hooligan, bruiser, *formal* miscreant, *colloq.* hoodlum, rough, tough, yobbo, *slang* yob

ruffle *v*
1 RUMPLE, dishevel, tangle, tousle, wrinkle, crease, pucker, crumple, ripple, *formal* disarrange 2 ANNOY, upset, irritate, anger, put out, vex, irk, exasperate, fluster, rile, nettle, confuse, trouble, *formal* discompose, perturb, *colloq.* aggravate, bug, hassle, rattle
🖛 1 smooth 2 pacify

rugged *adj*
1 ROUGH, bumpy, uneven, irregular, jagged, rocky, stony, craggy, stark 2 STRONG, robust, hardy, tough, sturdy, stalwart, vigorous, burly, well-built, muscular, sinewy, weather-beaten, furrowed 3 DETERMINED, strong, robust, tough, resolute, firm, tenacious, unflinching, unwavering
🖛 1 smooth

ruin *n, v*
▶ *n* 1 DESTRUCTION, devastation, wreckage, havoc, damage, disrepair, decay, disintegration, breakdown, collapse, fall, downfall, failure, defeat, overthrow, ruination, undoing 2 *financial ruin* insolvency, bankruptcy, loss, failure, crash, disaster, *formal* indigence, penury 3 *the ruins of the castle* remains, debris, rubble, fragments, traces, vestiges, relics, remnants, chaos, devastation, havoc, shambles, *formal* detritus
🖛 1 development, reconstruction
▶ *v* 1 DAMAGE, harm, spoil, mar, botch, break, smash, shatter, injure, wreck, wreak havoc, destroy, demolish, raze, devastate, lay waste, overwhelm, overthrow, defeat, cripple, crush, *colloq.* mess up 2 IMPOVERISH, bankrupt, make bankrupt, make insolvent, cripple
🖛 1 develop, restore

ruinous *adj*
1 *ruinous costs* exorbitant, extortionate, excessive, unreasonable, immoderate, crippling 2 RUINED, in ruins, damaged, dilapidated, broken-down, ramshackle, decrepit, destroyed, devastated, wrecked, shattered, catastrophic, calamitous, devastating, cataclysmic
🖛 1 low 2 beneficial

rule *n, v*
▶ *n* 1 REGULATION, law, statute, ordinance, decree, ruling, order, command, commandment, direction, guide, corrective, restriction, precept, tenet, canon, maxim, axiom, truth, truism, principle, formula, guideline, direction, instruction, standard, criterion 2 REIGN, sovereignty, supremacy, kingship, queenship, dominion, mastery, influence, sway, power, authority, command, direction, control, influence, regime, administration, government, leadership, jurisdiction 3 CUSTOM, convention, practice, standard, routine, procedure, protocol, form, habit, wont
▷ **as a rule** usually, normally, mainly, in the main, ordinarily, generally, in general, on the whole, by and large, for the most part
▶ *v* 1 *rule a country* reign, govern, command, lead, preside over, officiate, administer, manage, direct, guide, control, be in control, administer, regulate, prevail, dominate, *colloq.* call the shots, sit in the driving seat 2 JUDGE, adjudicate, decide, find, settle, determine, resolve, establish, decree, direct, order, lay down, pronounce
▷ **rule out** exclude, eliminate, reject, dismiss, prevent, ban, prohibit, forbid, disallow, *formal* preclude, obviate

ruler *n*

ruling *n, adj*
▶ *n* judgement, adjudication, verdict, decision, finding, resolution, decree, pronouncement
▶ *adj* 1 REIGNING, sovereign, on the throne, supreme, governing, controlling, in control, in charge, commanding, leading 2 MAIN, chief, leading, principal, dominant, predominant, most influential

rum *adj*
strange, unusual, odd, peculiar, abnormal, bizarre, curious, weird, funny, freakish, queer, suspect, suspicious, *formal* singular, *colloq.* funny-peculiar

rumbustious *adj*
boisterous, loud, noisy, rowdy, disorderly, clamorous, exuberant, unmanageable, unruly, uproarious, wild, rough, wayward, wilful, robust, roisterous, roisting, *formal* obstreperous, refractory
F3 quiet, restrained, sensible

ruminate *v*
ponder, think, reflect, meditate, mull over, muse, brood, consider, contemplate, deliberate, chew over, *formal* cogitate

rummage *v, n*
▶ *v* root (around), search, turn over, poke around, hunt, explore, examine, delve, ransack, forage, rifle
▶ *n* jumble, junk, tat, bric-à-brac, odds and ends

rumour *n, v*
▶ *n* hearsay, gossip, talk, speculation, whisper, scandal, word, information, news, report, story, *formal* tidings, *colloq.* grapevine, bush telegraph, buzz
▶ *v* say, tell, hint, put about, noise abroad, report, publish, gossip, circulate, whisper, bruit

rump *n*
1 BUTTOCKS, backside, bottom, rear, seat, dock, hindquarters, haunch, nache, croup, *colloq.* bum, posterior, *US colloq.* butt **2** LEFTOVERS, remains, remainder, residue, trace, vestige

rumple *v*
wrinkle, crease, pucker, crumple, ruffle, dishevel, disorder, tousle, crinkle, crush, derange, scrunch
F3 smooth

rumpus *n*
disturbance, noise, uproar, confusion, commotion, disruption, furore, rout, row, tumult, fuss, fracas, brawl, brouhaha, ruction, *colloq.* kerfuffle
F3 calm

run *v, n*
▶ *v* **1** SPRINT, jog, race, charge, career, tear, dash, hurry, rush, speed, bolt, dart, gallop, trot, scoot, scuttle, scamper, scurry, *colloq.* step on it **2** GO, pass, move, travel, proceed, issue, flow **3** FUNCTION, work, go, operate, be in operation, perform, progress **4** *run a company* head, lead, administer, direct, operate, own, carry on, carry out, conduct, manage, superintend, supervise, organize, co-ordinate, oversee, control, be in control of, regulate, be in charge of **5** COMPETE, contend, stand, enter, take part in, put yourself forward, challenge **6** LAST, continue, go, go on, extend, reach, stretch, proceed, spread, range **7** FLOW, stream, glide, roll, course, pour, gush, issue, jet, spurt, cascade, drip, trickle **8** *run your hand over something* move, pass, spread, slide, cross **9** *run you to the station* DRIVE, take, convey, transport, give a lift **10** *run a car* own, possess, have, drive, use, keep, maintain **11** *the play ran for four years* be performed, be presented, be produced, be staged, be mounted, be played, last, go on **12** *the newspaper ran a story* publish, print, carry, feature, include, communicate, broadcast
▷ **run across** meet, encounter, come across, run into, *formal* chance upon, *colloq.* bump into
▷ **run after** chase, pursue, follow, tail
F3 flee
▷ **run away 1** ESCAPE, flee, abscond, decamp, bolt, run off, make off, *colloq.* scarper, beat it, clear off, make a run for it **2** *run away from problems* avoid, ignore, disregard, evade, neglect, overlook, take no notice of, brush aside, *colloq.* shut your eyes to, turn your back on **3** *run away with your neighbour's wife*

run off, elope, make off with, leave **4** *run away with the money* make off with, walk off with, steal, pocket, *formal* appropriate, purloin, *colloq.* pinch, nick, lift
F3 **1** stay **2** deal with
▷ **run down 1** CRITICIZE, denounce, attack, belittle, disparage, defame, *formal* denigrate *colloq.* knock, slate, slag off, rubbish **2** RUN OVER, knock down, knock over, knock to the ground, hit, strike **3** TIRE, weary, exhaust, weaken **4** *run down production* reduce, decrease, drop, cut, cut back on, trim, curtail
F3 **1** praise **4** increase
▷ **run for it** escape, flee, fly, make off, retreat, bolt, *colloq.* scarper, scram, do a bunk, skedaddle
F3 stay
▷ **run in** arrest, jail, *formal* apprehend, *colloq.* nick, pick up, nab, lift, pinch, bust, collar
▷ **run into 1** MEET, encounter, run across, *formal* chance upon, *colloq.* bump into **2** HIT, strike, collide with, bump into, crash, ram
F3 **2** miss
▷ **run off 1** RUN AWAY, escape, make off, abscond, bolt, decamp, elope, *colloq.* scarper, skedaddle **2** DUPLICATE, print, produce, xerox®, photostat®
F3 **1** stay
▷ **run off with** run away with, make off with, elope with
▷ **run on** continue, go on, carry on, last, extend, reach
▷ **run out** expire, terminate, end, close, finish, be finished, exhaust, be exhausted, dry up, give out, fail, *formal* cease
▷ **run out on** abandon, leave, strand, maroon, *formal* forsake, *colloq.* walk out on, jilt, ditch, chuck, dump, leave in the lurch
▷ **run over 1** HIT, knock down, run down, strike **2** REPEAT, go over, run through, practise, rehearse, review, overflow, survey, *formal* reiterate
▷ **run through 1** REHEARSE, go through, run over, practise, read, review, survey, examine **2** SPEND, waste, squander, exhaust, fritter away, *formal* dissipate
▷ **run to** amount to, add up to, total, come to, equal, afford, have enough of
▷ **run together** join, mix, unite, blend, combine, fuse, merge, mingle, amalgamate, coalesce, *formal* commingle
F3 separate
▶ *n* **1** JOG, gallop, race, sprint, spurt, dash, rush, hurry **2** DRIVE, ride, jaunt, excursion, outing, trip, journey, *colloq.* spin **3** SERIES, sequence, string, cycle, chain, course, round, succession, spell, stretch, period **4** COURSE, route, way, line, track, road, flight path **5** ENCLOSURE, coop, pen, pound, fold, sty, paddock, yard **6** *a run on a currency* demand, need, call, rush, clamour, pressure **7** POINT, goal, hit, mark, score **8** *different from the average run of things* sort, kind, type, class, set, variety, category **9** *a run in a stocking* ladder, rip, tear, cut, hole, split, slit, slash, snag, gash
▷ **in the long run** eventually, ultimately, at last, in the end, *colloq.* when all is said and done, at the end of the day

runaway *n, adj*
▶ *n* escaper, escapee, fugitive, absconder, truant, deserter, refugee
▶ *adj* escaped, fugitive, loose, out of control, uncontrolled, wild

run-down *n, adj*
▶ *n* **1** REDUCTION, decrease, curtailment, decline, drop, cut, cutback **2** SUMMARY, résumé, synopsis, analysis, outline, sketch, briefing, review, recap, run-through
▶ *adj* **1** WEAK, tired, weary, drained, exhausted, fa-

tigued, worn-out, unhealthy, grotty, seedy, peaky, *formal* debilitated, enervated **2** NEGLECTED, dilapidated, uncared-for, tumbledown, ramshackle, broken-down, decrepit, dingy, shabby
🔁 **1** healthy **2** well-kept

run-in *n*
fight, quarrel, argument, dispute, set-to, wrangle, skirmish, tussle, confrontation, difference of opinion, brush, contretemps, *formal* altercation, *colloq.* dust-up

runner *n*
1 JOGGER, sprinter, athlete, competitor, participant **2** COURIER, messenger, racer, dispatch rider, bearer **3** STEM, shoot, offshoot, sprout, tendril, sprig, sarmentum, stolon, *technical* flagellum

running *n, adj*
▶ *n* **1** SPRINTING, jogging, racing, rushing **2** ADMINISTRATION, direction, management, organization, coordination, superintendency, supervision, leadership, charge, control, controlling, regulation **3** FUNCTIONING, working, operation, performance, conduct **4** *out of the running* contention, contest, competition
▶ *adj* **1** UNBROKEN, uninterrupted, continuous, constant, perpetual, ceaseless, incessant, moving, flowing, *formal* unceasing **2** IN SUCCESSION, successive, consecutive, in a row, *colloq.* on the trot
🔁 **1** broken, occasional

runny *adj*
flowing, fluid, liquid, liquefied, melted, molten, watery, diluted
🔁 solid

run-of-the-mill *adj*
ordinary, common, normal, everyday, average, unexceptional, mediocre, middling, tolerable, fair, unremarkable, undistinguished, unimpressive, *colloq.* so-so, not up to much, no great shakes
🔁 exceptional, remarkable

rupture *n, v*
▶ *n* **1** SPLIT, tear, burst, puncture, break, breaking, breach, fracture, crack **2** DIVISION, separation, split, schism, rift, disagreement, quarrel, falling-out, *formal* estrangement, *colloq.* bust-up
▶ *v* split, tear, burst, puncture, break, fracture, crack, sever, separate, divide, cut off

rural *adj*
country, rustic, pastoral, agricultural, agrarian, bucolic, sylvan
🔁 urban

ruse *n*
plan, trick, deception, hoax, imposture, stratagem, tactic, manoeuvre, ploy, plot, scheme, wile, subterfuge, artifice, device, blind, sham, *colloq.* dodge

rush *v, n*
▶ *v* **1** HURRY, dash, hasten, quicken, accelerate, speed (up), press, push, dispatch, bolt, dart, shoot, fly, tear, career, race, run, sprint, scramble, gallop, stampede, charge, *colloq.* get a move on **2** ATTACK, charge, assault, storm, raid, strike
▶ *n* **1** HURRY, haste, urgency, speed, rapidity, swiftness, dash, race, scramble, stampede, charge, flow, flood, surge, stream, gush **2** BUSTLE, activity, hustle and bustle, stir, commotion, excitement, flurry, hurry, hurly-burly, *colloq.* hive of activity, comings and goings **3** ATTACK, charge, onslaught, assault, storm, raid, strike **4** DEMAND, call, need, run, clamour, pressure

rushed *adj*
busy, hurried, emergency, careless, cursory, superficial, quick, fast, rapid, swift, brisk, hasty, prompt, urgent, *formal* expeditious

rust *n, v*
▶ *n* corrosion, oxidation, verdigris, stain, decay
▶ *v* corrode, oxidize, tarnish, deteriorate, decline, decay, rot

rust-coloured *adj*
rusty, reddish-brown, brown, red, reddish, coppery, copper, auburn, chestnut, russet, ginger, gingery, sandy, tawny, Titian

rustic *adj, n*
▶ *adj* **1** PASTORAL, sylvan, bucolic, countrified, country, countryside, rural **2** PLAIN, simple, rough, crude, coarse, rude, clumsy, awkward, artless, homespun, ingenuous, unsophisticated, unrefined, uncultured, provincial, uncouth, graceless, indelicate, boorish, clodhopping, oafish, *formal* maladroit
🔁 **1** urban **2** urbane, sophisticated, cultivated, polished
▶ *n* bumpkin, countryman, countrywoman, oaf, peasant, provincial, yokel, boor, churl, clodhopper, clod, country cousin, *colloq.* hayseed, hick, hillbilly
🔁 sophisticate, dandy

rustle *v, n*
▶ *v* crackle, whoosh, swish, whisper, sigh, *formal* susurrate
▶ *n* crackle, crinkling, rustling, swish, whoosh, whisper, whispering, *formal* crepitation, crepitus, susurration, susurrus

rusty *adj*
1 CORRODED, rusted, rust-covered, oxidized, tarnished, discoloured, dull **2** RUST-COLOURED, brown, red, reddish, reddish-brown, coppery, copper, auburn, chestnut, russet, ginger, gingery, sandy, tawny, Titian **3** UNPRACTISED, out of practice, weak, poor, impaired, deficient, dated, old-fashioned, outmoded, antiquated, stale, stiff, creaking

rut *n*
1 DITCH, channel, furrow, groove, gutter, indentation, trough, track, gouge, pothole, wheelmark **2** ROUTINE, habit, pattern, system, humdrum, grind, daily grind, treadmill, same old round/place, no change of scenery

ruthless *adj*
merciless, pitiless, hard-hearted, hard, heartless, unforgiving, unmerciful, unfeeling, unsparing, callous, cruel, inhuman, grim, stern, vicious, brutal, savage, barbarous, fierce, ferocious, relentless, remorseless, unrelenting, inexorable, implacable, harsh, severe, draconian, *colloq.* cut-throat, dog-eat-dog
🔁 merciful, compassionate

S

sable *adj*
dark, black, coal-black, pitch-black, pitch-dark, pitchy, ebony, inky, jet, dusky, sombre, midnight

sabotage *v, n*
▶ *v* damage, spoil, mar, disrupt, vandalize, wreck, destroy, thwart, ruin, scupper, cripple, incapacitate, disable, undermine, impair, weaken
▶ *n* vandalism, damage, impairment, disruption, wrecking, destruction, ruin, spoiling, crippling, disabling, weakening

sac *n*
bag, pocket, pouch, pod, bladder, capsule, follicle, cyst, saccule, vesicle, *technical* bursa, theca, vesica, vesicula

saccharine *adj*
sickly, sweet, sentimental, honeyed, cloying, maudlin, mawkish, nauseating, oversweet, sugary, syrupy, sickly-sweet, *colloq.* soppy, sloppy, mushy, gushy, schmaltzy
F3 bitter, tart

sack¹ *v, n*
▶ *v* *sack 100 workers* dismiss, fire, discharge, lay off, make redundant, *colloq.* axe, send packing, boot out, fire, give someone their cards, give someone the sack/push/boot/elbow, show someone the door
▶ *n* dismissal, discharge, your cards, notice, marching orders, *colloq.* the boot, the push, the elbow, the axe, the chop, papers, sacking, firing

sack² *v, n*
▶ *v* *the army sacked the town* destroy, raid, plunder, ravage, raze, lay waste, waste, level, devastate, desecrate, demolish, maraud, pillage, rifle, rob, loot, ruin, rape, spoil, strip, *formal* depredate, despoil
▶ *n* destruction, devastation, ravage, razing, ruin, waste, levelling, looting, plunder, plundering, marauding, desecration, rape, pillage, *formal* depredation, despoliation, rapine

sacred *adj*
1 HOLY, divine, heavenly, blessed, hallowed, sanctified, consecrated, dedicated 2 RELIGIOUS, spiritual, devotional, ecclesiastical, priestly, saintly, godly 3 REVERED, venerable, respected, sacrosanct, inviolable, defended, protected, hallowed, untouchable, impregnable, secure
F3 1 profane, secular 2 temporal

sacredness *n*
holiness, divinity, godliness, sanctity, solemnity, saintliness, sacrosanctity, invulnerability, inviolability
F3 profaneness, worldliness

sacrifice *v, n*
▶ *v* 1 *sacrifice an animal in a religious ceremony* offer, offer up, slaughter, immolate 2 GIVE UP, surrender, forfeit, relinquish, let go, abandon, renounce, forego
▶ *n* 1 OFFERING, immolation, slaughter, victim, *formal* oblation 2 GIVING-UP, destruction, surrender, abandonment, renunciation, loss

sacrificial *adj*
atoning, votive, *formal* oblatory, propitiatory, expiatory, reparative, piacular

sacrilege *n*
blasphemy, profanity, heresy, desecration, profanation, violation, outrage, irreligion, impiety, irreverence, disrespect, mockery
F3 piety, reverence, respect

sacrilegious *adj*
blasphemous, profane, heretical, desecrating, disrespectful, irreverent, impious, irreligious, godless, ungodly, unholy, *formal* profanatory
F3 pious, reverent, respectful

sacrosanct *adj*
sacred, hallowed, untouchable, inviolable, impregnable, protected, secure

sad *adj*
1 UNHAPPY, sorrowful, tearful, grief-stricken, heavy-hearted, upset, distressed, miserable, low-spirited, in low spirits, downcast, glum, long-faced, crestfallen, dejected, down-hearted, despondent, melancholy, depressed, mournful, doleful, wistful, joyless, gloomy, dismal, wretched, *formal* woebegone, disconsolate, *colloq.* fed up, blue, low, down, down in the dumps, (at) rock bottom 2 *sad news* upsetting, distressing, painful, depressing, touching, poignant, heart-rending, heart-breaking, tragic, grievous, lamentable, regrettable, miserable, sorry, sorrowful, unfortunate, unhappy, serious, grave, calamitous, disastrous 3 *in a sad state* grievous, lamentable, regrettable, deplorable, disgraceful, shameful, sorry, unfortunate, wretched, pitiful, pitiable, *colloq.* pathetic
F3 1 happy, cheerful 2 fortunate, lucky 3 good

sadden *v*
upset, distress, grieve, depress, deject, dismay, discourage, dishearten, cast down, dispirit, break your heart, drive to despair, *colloq.* get someone down
F3 cheer, please, gratify, delight

saddle *v*
burden, encumber, lumber, land, impose, tax, charge, load

sadism *n*
cruelty, inhumanity, brutality, savagery, viciousness, heartlessness, ruthlessness, unnaturalness, spite, callousness, barbarity, bestiality, *formal* malevolence, *Schadenfreude*

sadistic *adj*
cruel, inhuman, brutal, savage, vicious, merciless, pitiless, barbarous, bestial, unnatural, perverted

sadness *n*
unhappiness, sorrow, sorrowfulness, grief, misery, misfortune, despondency, desolation, depression, dejection, cheerlessness, bleakness, joylessness, dolefulness, dismalness, poignancy, sombreness, mournfulness, distress, low spirits, glumness, gloominess, tearfulness, wretchedness, tragedy, pain, regret,

pathos, *formal* disconsolateness, lugubriousness, melancholy, woe, *colloq.* heartache

> **Ways of expressing sadness, sorrow or depression:**
> break your heart, be down in the dumps, feel sorry for yourself, feel low, be in mourning, have a long face, have the weight of the world on your shoulders, be in the doldrums, get the blues, weep buckets, be cut up, in the depths of despair, cry your eyes out, cry your heart out, have a good cry, have a heavy heart, down in the mouth, in low spirits, a tale of woe, my/ our deepest sympathy, it's a sad day for , parting is such sweet sorrow, weep and wail, be/feel choked, have a lump in your throat, have tears in your eyes.

F₃ happiness, cheerfulness, delight

safe *adj, n*
> ▶ *adj* **1** HARMLESS, innocuous, non-toxic, non-poisonous, uncontaminated **2** UNHARMED, undamaged, unscathed, uninjured, out of danger, unhurt, intact, secure, sound, protected, sheltered, defended, guarded, impregnable, invulnerable, unassailable, immune, *colloq.* out of harm's way, safe and sound, safe as houses, in good hands **3** DEPENDABLE, reliable, trustworthy, responsible, honest, honourable, sure, proven, tried, tested, sound, upright **4** UNADVENTUROUS, unenterprising, cautious, conservative, *formal* prudent, circumspect
> **F₃ 1** dangerous, harmful **2** vulnerable, at risk, exposed **3** risky **4** adventurous
> ▶ *n* cash box, deposit box, safety-deposit box, strongbox, chest, coffer, vault, depository, repository

safe-conduct *n*
authorization, pass, passport, permit, safeguard, warrant, licence, convoy, laissez-passer

safeguard *v, n*
> ▶ *v* protect, preserve, defend, look after, take care of, guard, shield, screen, shelter, secure
> **F₃** endanger, jeopardize
> ▶ *n* protection, defence, shield, security, surety, guarantee, assurance, insurance, cover, precaution, preventive, preventative

safekeeping *n*
protection, care, custody, keeping, charge, trust, guardianship, surveillance, supervision, ward, wardship

safety *n, adj*
> ▶ *n* **1** PROTECTION, security, safeguard, immunity, welfare, sanctuary, impregnability, safeness, harmlessness, soundness, reliability, dependability, trustworthiness **2** SANCTUARY, refuge, shelter, cover
> **F₃ 1** danger, jeopardy, risk
> ▶ *adj* precautionary, preventive, preventative, protective, fail-safe

sag *v, n*
> ▶ *v* **1** HANG LOOSELY, bend, give, bag, droop, hang **2** *prices/her spirits started to sag* fall, drop, sink, dip, decline, slump, subside, flop, fail, flag, falter, weaken, wilt
> **F₃ 1** bulge **2** rise
> ▶ *n* drop, fall, low, low point, reduction, slump, slip, slide, dip, decline, depression, downturn, dwindling
> **F₃** peak, rise

saga *n*
chronicle, epic, history, narrative, adventure, story, tale, yarn, romance, soap opera, roman fleuve, *formal* epopee, epopeia, epos

sagacious *adj*
wise, discerning, insightful, penetrating, perceptive, far-sighted, able, intelligent, knowing, acute, sharp,

astute, canny, quick, shrewd, smart, wary, wide-awake, wily, fly, *formal* prudent, judicious, percipient, perspicacious, sage, sapient
F₃ foolish, obtuse

sagacity *n*
wisdom, discernment, understanding, judgement, insight, foresight, penetration, sense, sharpness, shrewdness, acumen, knowingness, astuteness, acuteness, canniness, wariness, wiliness, *formal* prudence, judiciousness, percipience, perspicacity, sapience
F₃ folly, foolishness, obtuseness

sage *n, adj*
> ▶ *n* wise person, wise man, wise woman, teacher, master, expert, authority, pundit, savant, guru, maharishi, oracle, elder, philosopher, wiseacre, Solomon, mahatma, hakam
> **F₃** ignoramus
> ▶ *adj* wise, intelligent, discerning, knowing, learned, knowledgeable, astute, canny, politic, sensible, *formal* judicious, perspicacious, prudent, sagacious, sapient
> **F₃** foolish

sail *v, n*
> ▶ *v* **1** *sail for France* embark, set sail, leave port, weigh anchor, put to sea, put off, cruise, yacht, boat, ship, voyage **2** CAPTAIN, skipper, pilot, navigate, steer **3** GLIDE, plane, sweep, float, drift, coast, skim, scud, fly, wing, soar
> ▷ **sail into** attack, lay into, let fly, set about, tear into, turn on, assault
> ▷ **sail through** deal with successfully, succeed in/pass easily, romp through
> **F₃** scrape through

> **Types of sail include:**
> canvas, course, foreroyal, foresail, forestaysail, foretop, fore-topgallant, fore-topsail, gaff sail, gaff-topsail, genoa, headsail, jib, jigger, kite, lateen sail, lugsail, main course, mainsail, maintopsail, mizzen, moonraker, royal, skysail, spanker, spinnaker, spritsail, square sail, staysail, studdingsail, topgallant, topsail, trysail.

sailing *n*

> **Terms used in sailing include :**
> abaft, across the wind, alongside, astern, backing, bearing, beat, beating, bending on (a sail), blanketing effect, breaking out (the anchor), casting off/letting go, close-hauled, coming about, downwind, fetch, fitting out, fixing a position, going about, gybe, handing (a sail), hard on the wind, heeling (to the wind), in irons/in stays, knockdown (by the wind), laying off (a course), lay up, lee helm, lee-oh!, leeway, lift, points of sailing, port, reaching, beam reach, broad reach, close reach, ready about!, running, running goose-winged, sailing by the lee, sail trimming, sheeting in a sail, spilling wind, standing on, starboard, stepping/unstepping (the mast), tacking, port tack, starboard tack, steerage way, taking soundings, unbending (a sail), under way, upwind, veer (the anchor cable), weathering, weather helm, windward, yawing. *See also* KNOT.

> **Parts of a sailing boat include:**
> anchor, CQR anchor, Danford anchor, fisherman's anchor, fluke, ground tackle, *colloq.* hook; anti-fouling paint, batten, beam, bilge, bow, bowsprit,

bulkhead, buoyancy chamber; cleat, jamming cleat; cockpit, counter, dinghy, doghouse, draught, fender, foredeck, forepeak, guard rail, gudgeon, gymbals, hatch, heads, helm, helmsman; hull, carvel-built, catamaran, clench-built, clinker-built, glass-fibre reinforced plastic (GRP), hard-chined, single-chined, double-chined, multi-chined, mono-hull, multi-hull, moulded hull, trimaran; keel, ballast keel, bilge keels, centreboard, dagger board, fin keel, single-keel, retractable keel, triple keel; mooring, pintle, pulpit, pushpit; reefing, reef cringle, reef points, roller reefing; riding light; rigs, Bermudan rig, *US* catboat rig, cutter rig, fore-and-aft rig, gaff rig, loose-footed gaff rig, gunter rig, *US* jib-headed rig, jury rig, ketch rig, lugsail rig, *US* Marconi rig, performance rig, schooner rig, sloop rig, square rig, Una rig, spritsail rig, yawl rig; rudder, skeg rudder; self-bailer; standing rigging; running rigging; main mast, mizzen mast; boom, main boom, mizzen boom, spinnaker boom; sails, foot, tack, luff, head, leech, clew; batten, batten pocket, cringle; Genoa, *colloq.* jenny, headsail, jib, loose-footed sail, mainsail, mainsheet, mizzen sail, set (of the sails), spinnaker, storm jib, storm trysail; halyard, halyard winch, outhaul, painter, rope, sheave, sheet, sheet winch, shock cord; shroud, cap shroud, lower shroud; spring; stay, backstay, forestay; warp; block, fairlead, kicking strap; shackle; stanchion, stern, stern-post, tackle, tender, tiller, transom, trapeze, whisker pole, yard.

Types and classes of modern sailing boat include:
sloop, cutter, yawl, ketch, schooner; formula class, one-design class, restricted class; 420, 470, 5-0-5, Cadet, Conway One, Dragon, Enterprise, Finn, Fireball, Firefly, Fisher, Flying Dutchman, Flying Fifteen, Fourteen, Laser, Maxi, Minisail, Mirror, Moody, Moth, Optimist, Rival, Solo, Tasar, Topper, Tornado, Trapper, Twelve, Wayfarer, Westerley.

sailor *n*
seafarer, mariner, seaman

Types of sailor include:
AB, able seaman, bargee, bluejacket, boatman, boatswain, bosun, buccaneer, cabin boy, captain, cox, coxswain, crewman, deck hand, fisherman, galiongee, *US slang* gob, hearty, helmsman, Jack tar, lascar, leatherneck, *US colloq.* limey, marine, master, mate, *slang* matelot, navigator, oarsman, pilot, pirate, purser, rating, rower, salt, sculler, sea dog, skipper, *colloq.* tar, *Scot.* tarry-breeks, water rat, Wren, yachtsman, yachtswoman.

saintliness *n*
godliness, piety, devoutness, holiness, spirituality, blessedness, purity, spotlessness, faith, innocence, blamelessness, sinlessness, virtue, selflessness, morality, goodness, righteousness, sanctity, chastity, self-denial, self-sacrifice, asceticism, uprightness, unselfishness
🔁 godlessness, unholiness, wickedness

saintly *adj*
saintlike, godly, pious, devout, God-fearing, holy, religious, spiritual, believing, blessed, angelic, pure, spotless, innocent, blameless, sinless, virtuous, moral, ethical, good, upright, worthy, righteous

🔁 godless, unholy, wicked

sake *n*
benefit, advantage, good, welfare, wellbeing, gain, profit, behalf, interest, account, regard, respect, purpose, aim, goal, object, objective, cause, reason, consideration

salacious *adj*
prurient, bawdy, indecent, improper, obscene, scurrilous, pornographic, lecherous, lewd, carnal, coarse, erotic, horny, ribald, wanton, randy, lustful, raunchy, ruttish, *formal* concupiscent, lascivious, libidinous, lubricious, *colloq.* blue, smutty, steamy
🔁 clean, decent, proper

salaried *adj*
paid, remunerated, waged, stipendiary, *formal* emolumental, emolumentary
🔁 unpaid, voluntary, honorary

salary *n*
pay, remuneration, emolument, stipend, honorarium, wages, earnings, income, fee

sale *n*
selling, marketing, vending, bargaining, disposal, trade, market, traffic, transaction, deal
▷ **for sale** on sale, up for sale, available, obtainable, on the market, in the shops, *colloq.* up for grabs

Types of sale include:
auction, autumn sale, bargain offer, bazaar, bazumble, boot-sale, bring-and-buy, car-boot sale, charity sale, church bazaar, clearance sale, closing-down sale, cold-call, end-of-line sale, end-of-season sale, exhibition, exposition, fair, fleamarket, forced sale, garage sale, grand opening sale, introductory offer, January sale, jumble sale, mail order, market, mid-season sale, on-promotion, open market, pre-season sale, private sale, public sale, pyramid selling, remainder sale, rummage sale, sale of bankrupt stock, sale of the century, sale of work, second-hand sale, special offer, spring sale, stocktaking sale, summer sale, tabletop sale, telesales, trade show, trash and treasure sale, winter sale.

saleable *adj*
marketable, merchantable, sought-after, desirable, *formal* vendible
🔁 unmarketable, unsaleable

salesperson *n*
salesman, saleswoman, saleslady, sales assistant, clerk, salesclerk, shop assistant, shop-boy, shop-girl, salesgirl, shopkeeper, representative, *colloq.* rep

salient *adj*
important, significant, chief, main, principal, striking, arresting, conspicuous, noticeable, obvious, prominent, pronounced, outstanding, signal, remarkable

sallow *adj*
yellowish, pale, pallid, wan, waxen, pasty, sickly, jaundiced, unhealthy, anaemic, colourless
🔁 rosy, healthy

sally[1] *v, n*
▶ *v* **1** RUSH, surge, attack, sortie, charge, breeze, venture, erupt, foray, issue **2** SAUNTER, stroll, wander, promenade, *colloq.* mosey
🔁 **1** retreat
▶ *n* **1** RUSH, raid, assault, attack, foray, incursion, offensive, surge, sortie, thrust, venture, dash **2** EXCURSION, jaunt, wander, trip, drive, frolic, escapade
🔁 **1** retire, retreat

sally[2] *n*
JOKE, retort, riposte, witticism, wisecrack, jest, crack,

quip, *bon mot*, jeu d'esprit

salt *n, adj, v*
▶ *n* **1** *add a pinch of salt* seasoning, taste, flavour, savour, relish, piquancy, pungency, smack, punch, rock-salt, sea-salt **2** LIVELINESS, zest, interest, wit, vigour, zip, *formal* trenchancy **3** SAILOR, seafarer, mariner, seaman, marine, rating
▶ *adj* salted, saltish, salty, saline, brackish, briny
🖪 fresh
▶ *v* ▷ **salt away** store up, hoard, save, stash, stockpile, collect, cache, bank, accumulate, amass, hide
🖪 spend, squander

salty *adj*
1 SALT, salted, saline, briny, brackish, savoury, spicy, piquant, tangy **2** LIVELY, vigorous, witty, exciting, stimulating, animated, *formal* trenchant
🖪 fresh, sweet

salubrious *adj*
sanitary, hygienic, health-giving, healthy, healthful, wholesome, pleasant, beneficial, salutary, refreshing, invigorating

salutary *adj*
1 GOOD, beneficial, advantageous, profitable, valuable, helpful, useful, practical, timely **2** HEALTHY, sanitary, hygienic, health-giving, refreshing, invigorating

salutation *n*
greeting, address, welcome, salute, reverence, respects, homage, *formal* obeisance

salute *v, n*
▶ *v* **1** GREET, acknowledge, recognize, wave, hail, address, nod, bow, honour, present arms **2** HONOUR, acknowledge, recognize, mark, celebrate, pay tribute to
▶ *n* **1** GREETING, acknowledgement, recognition, welcome, wave, gesture, hail, address, handshake, nod, bow, reverence **2** HONOUR, celebration, recognition, acknowledgement, tribute, homage

salvage *v*
save, preserve, conserve, rescue, recover, recuperate, retrieve, get back, reclaim, redeem, repair, restore, retain
🖪 waste, abandon

salvation *n*
deliverance, liberation, rescue, saving, preservation, lifeline, redemption, reclamation, *technical* soteriology
🖪 loss, damnation

salve *n, v*
▶ *n* ointment, lotion, cream, balm, liniment, medication, preparation, application, *formal* embrocation
▶ *v* ease, lighten, relieve, calm, comfort, soothe

same *adj, n*
▶ *adj* **1** IDENTICAL, twin, indistinguishable, equal, selfsame, the very same, one and the same, very, alike, like, similar, duplicate, carbon copy, comparable, equivalent, matching, corresponding, mutual, reciprocal, interchangeable, unchanging, substitutable, synonymous, *formal* aforementioned **2** UNCHANGING, consistent, uniform, unvarying, unvariable, changeless, unchanged
🖪 **1** different **2** inconsistent, variable, changeable
▷ **all the same** nevertheless, nonetheless, still, anyway, even so, yet, however, by any means, in any case/event, by some means, anyhow, but, regardless, for all that, *formal* notwithstanding
▶ *n* the above-mentioned, the above-named, ditto, *formal* the aforementioned, the aforesaid

sameness *n*
changelessness, invariability, consistency, monotony, predictability, repetition, tedium, uniformity, standard-ization, resemblance, similarity, indistinguishability, likeness, identicalness, identity, oneness, duplication, déjà vu
🖪 variety, difference

sample *n, v, adj*
▶ *n* specimen, example, cross-section, representative, model, pattern, type, test, sampling, swatch, piece, demonstration, illustration, instance, sign, indication, foretaste
▶ *v* try, test, taste, sip, inspect, examine, experience
▶ *adj* representative, specimen, demonstrative, illustrative, typical, dummy, trial, test, pilot

sanctify *v*
1 HALLOW, consecrate, make holy, make sacred, bless, anoint, dedicate, set apart, cleanse, purify, wash, absolve, exalt, canonize **2** SANCTION, authorize, allow, permit, approve, ratify, confirm, support, back, endorse, underwrite, accredit, license, warrant, legitimize
🖪 **1** desecrate, defile **2** veto, forbid, disapprove

sanctimonious *adj*
self-righteous, holier-than-thou, pious, pietistic, moralizing, smug, superior, hypocritical, priggish, pharisaical, *formal* unctuous, *colloq.* goody-goody
🖪 humble

sanctimoniousness *n*
self-righteousness, moralizing, righteousness, hypocrisy, self-satisfaction, priggishness, pietism, preachiness, complacency, cant, smugness, humbug, pharisaism, *formal* unctuousness
🖪 humility

sanction *n, v*
▶ *n* **1** AUTHORIZATION, permission, agreement, approval, ratification, confirmation, support, backing, endorsement, licence, authority, *formal* approbation, accreditation, *colloq.* OK, go-ahead, green light, thumbs-up **2** *impose sanctions on a country* restriction, boycott, embargo, ban, prohibition, penalty, deterrent, punishment, sentence
▶ *v* authorize, allow, permit, approve, ratify, confirm, support, back, endorse, underwrite, accredit, license, warrant, legitimize, *formal* accredit, *colloq.* OK, give the go-ahead to, give the green light to, give the thumbs-up to
🖪 veto, forbid, disapprove

sanctity *n*
holiness, sacredness, inviolability, piety, godliness, saintliness, blessedness, religiousness, devotion, grace, spirituality, purity, goodness, virtue, righteousness
🖪 unholiness, secularity, worldliness, godlessness, impurity

sanctuary *n*
1 CHURCH, temple, tabernacle, shrine, altar, place of worship, holy place, holy of holies, *formal* sanctum, sanctum sanctorum **2** ASYLUM, refuge, protection, shelter, haven, retreat, hideout, hideaway **3** SAFETY, protection, security, safeguard, immunity **4** RESERVE, reservation, park, area, enclave, tract, preserve

sanctum *n*
1 HOLY PLACE, holy of holies, shrine, sanctuary, *formal* sanctum sanctorum **2** REFUGE, retreat, den, hideaway, hideout, study, cubbyhole

sand *n*
beach, shore, strand, sands, seashore, desert, wilderness, grit, rock

sandbank *n*
dune, reef, sand bar, sandhill, bar, hurst, key, yardang

sandy *adj*
gritty, ginger, rusty, tawny, reddish, reddish-yellow, yellow, yellowish, yellowy, gingerous, gingery, auburn,

coppery, red, Titian, *technical* arenaceous, psammitic

sane *adj*
normal, rational, right-minded, balanced, lucid, in your right mind, of sound mind, stable, sound, sober, level-headed, sensible, responsible, wise, reasonable, moderate, *formal* judicious, *colloq.* all there
 insane, mad, crazy, foolish

sang-froid *n*
composure, self-control, poise, self-possession, indifference, equanimity, assurance, calmness, dispassion, cool-headedness, nonchalance, coolness, imperturbability, *formal* aplomb, phlegm, *colloq.* nerve, cool, unflappability
 discomposure, excitability, hysteria, panic

sanguinary *adj*
bloody, bloodied, gory, grim, bloodthirsty, brutal, cruel, merciless, murderous, savage, pitiless, ruthless

sanguine *adj*
1 CHEERFUL, confident, hopeful, lively, expectant, optimistic, over-confident, over-optimistic, assured, animated, ardent, buoyant, spirited, unabashed, unbowed 2 RUDDY, rosy, florid, red, pink, fresh-complexioned, fresh, flushed, *formal* rubicund
 1 cynical, depressive, gloomy, melancholy, pessimistic 2 pale, sallow

sanitary *adj*
clean, pure, uncontaminated, unpolluted, aseptic, antiseptic, germ-free, disinfected, sterile, hygienic, healthy, wholesome, *formal* salubrious
 insanitary, unwholesome

sanity *n*
normality, rationality, reason, sense, common sense, good sense, balance of mind, soundness of mind, lucidity, right-mindedness, stability, soundness, level-headedness, wisdom, responsibility, *formal* judiciousness, prudence
 insanity, madness

sap *v, n*
▶ *v* bleed, drain, exhaust, weaken, wear down/away, erode, enfeeble, undermine, deplete, reduce, diminish, impair, *formal* enervate, debilitate
 strengthen, build up, increase
▶ *n* 1 *sap in a plant* lifeblood, vital fluid, juice, essence, vigour, energy 2 FOOL, idiot, imbecile, moron, *colloq.* clot, twit, nit, nitwit, *slang* jerk, prat, git, fink

sarcasm *n*
irony, satire, mockery, sneering, ridicule, scoffing, derision, scorn, contempt, gibing, cynicism, resentment, acidity, spitefulness, bitterness, *formal* acrimony, trenchancy

sarcastic *adj*
ironical, satirical, mocking, snide, taunting, sneering, derisive, derisory, scornful, sardonic, jeering, scoffing, scathing, cynical, incisive, cutting, biting, caustic, *formal* disparaging, acrimonious, acerbic, mordant, *colloq.* sarky

sardonic *adj*
mocking, jeering, sneering, derisive, scornful, contemptuous, sarcastic, dry, biting, cruel, heartless, malicious, cynical, bitter, *formal* acrimonious, acerbic, mordant

Satan *n*
the Devil, the Enemy, the Adversary, the Evil One, the Tempter, Beelzebub, Lucifer, Old Nick, Prince of Darkness, Mephistopheles, Belial, Apollyon, Abaddon

satanic *adj*
satanical, diabolical, devilish, demonic, fiendish, hellish, infernal, damned, accursed, inhuman, wicked, evil, sinful, abominable, black, dark, *formal* malevolent, iniquitous

 holy, divine, godly, saintly, benevolent

sate *v*
satisfy, overfill, saturate, surfeit, fill, glut, gorge, gratify, cloy, sicken, slake, *formal* satiate
 deprive, dissatisfy, starve

satellite *n*
1 ORBITING BODY, natural/artificial satellite, spacecraft, moon, planet, spaceship, sputnik 2 DEPENDANT, hanger-on, parasite, sycophant, subordinate, follower, attendant, aide, adherent, disciple, minion, lackey, yes-man, sidekick, retainer, vassal, *colloq.* puppet

satiate *v*
sate, overfill, overfeed, satisfy, gorge, slake, glut, cloy, engorge, stuff, surfeit, jade, nauseate
 deprive, dissatisfy, underfeed

satiety *n*
satiation, saturation, satisfaction, gratification, fullness, over-fullness, overindulgence, surfeit, *formal* repleteness, repletion

satire *n*
ridicule, irony, sarcasm, wit, burlesque, lampoon, skit, parody, caricature, travesty, *colloq.* send-up, spoof, take-off, mickey-taking

satirical *adj*
ironical, sarcastic, mocking, ridiculing, irreverent, taunting, derisive, sardonic, incisive, cutting, biting, caustic, cynical, bitter, *formal* trenchant, acerbic, mordant, acrimonious

satirist *n*
cartoonist, mocker, parodist, ridiculer, caricaturist, lampooner, lampoonist, *formal* pasquilant, pasquiler, pasquinader

satirize *v*
ridicule, mock, make fun of, poke fun at, burlesque, lampoon, parody, caricature, criticize, *formal* deride, *colloq.* send up, take off, take the mickey out of
 acclaim, honour

satisfaction *n*
1 GRATIFICATION, contentment, happiness, pleasure, enjoyment, delight, comfort, ease, well-being, fulfilment, self-satisfaction, pride, sense of achievement 2 SETTLEMENT, compensation, reimbursement, indemnification, indemnity, damages, reparation, amends, redress, recompense, requital, vindication, restitution
 1 dissatisfaction, displeasure

satisfactory *adj*
acceptable, passable, up to the mark, all right, fair, average, competent, adequate, fine, sufficient, suitable, proper, *colloq.* OK, up to scratch
 unsatisfactory, unacceptable, inadequate

satisfied *adj*
1 HAPPY, contented, pleased, self-satisfied, content, smug 2 CONVINCED, reassured, persuaded, sure, certain, positive, pacified 3 FULL, sated, satiated, *formal* replete
 1 dissatisfied, *colloq.* disgruntled 2 unconvinced 3 hungry

satisfy *v*
1 GRATIFY, indulge, content, please, delight, appease, quench, slake, sate, satiate, surfeit, *formal* assuage 2 *satisfy requirements* meet, fulfil, discharge, settle, answer, fill, be sufficient for, be adequate for, serve, qualify, *formal* comply with, suffice 3 ASSURE, reassure, convince, persuade 4 COMPENSATE FOR, indemnify, make reparation for, *formal* appease, placate, requite
 1 dissatisfy 2 fail

satisfying *adj*
pleasing, fulfilling, gratifying, cheering, pleasurable, satisfactory, convincing, persuasive, filling, cool, refreshing
🔄 dissatisfying, frustrating, unsatisfactory

saturate *v*
1 SOAK, make wet through, wet, steep, flood, souse, drench, waterlog **2** IMPREGNATE, permeate, imbue, pervade, suffuse, fill, overfill, sate, glut, surfeit

saturated *adj*
1 SOAKED, soaking, sopping, dripping, soused, steeped, drenched, flooded, wringing, waterlogged, sodden **2** IMBUED, impregnated, permeated, suffused

saturnine *adj*
morose, gloomy, unfriendly, sombre, severe, austere, dismal, dour, dull, grave, melancholy, moody, glum, stern, heavy, withdrawn, taciturn, uncommunicative, phlegmatic
🔄 cheerful, jovial

sauce *n*
1 DRESSING, relish, condiment, flavouring, dip, mayonnaise **2** CHEEKINESS, cheek, impudence, impertinence, presumption, presumptuousness, audacity, freshness, flippancy, pertness, backchat, brazenness, insolence, disrespectfulness, disrespect, irreverence, rudeness, sass, *formal* malapertness, *colloq.* brass, lip, nerve, sauciness, mouth
🔄 **2** politeness, respectfulness

saucy *adj*
impertinent, impudent, insolent, brazen, presumptuous, disrespectful, irreverent, rude, pert, forward, presumptuous, flippant, *colloq.* cheeky, fresh, lippy, *US* sassy
🔄 polite, respectful

saunter *v, n*
▶ *v* stroll, amble, wander, ramble, meander, *colloq.* mosey, mooch
▶ *n* stroll, amble, walk, constitutional, ramble, *colloq.* mosey, mooch

savage *adj, n, v*
▶ *adj* wild, untamed, undomesticated, uncivilized, primitive, barbaric, barbarous, fierce, ferocious, vicious, beastly, cruel, terrible, inhuman, grim, brutal, sadistic, bloodthirsty, bloody, murderous, pitiless, merciless, ruthless, harsh, *formal* feral, *colloq.* cutthroat, dog-eat-dog
🔄 tame, civilized, humane, mild
▶ *n* brute, boor, churl, beast, monster, barbarian, wild person, wild man, wild woman
▶ *v* **1** *savaged by a dog* attack, bite, claw, tear, tear to pieces, lacerate, maul, mangle **2** *savaged by the critics* attack, denounce, *colloq.* slate, slam, run down, tear to pieces, tear to shreds

savagery *n*
cruelty, fierceness, ferocity, viciousness, wildness, roughness, barbarity, bestiality, brutality, inhumanity, ruthlessness, mercilessness, pitilessness, murderousness, bloodthirstiness, brutishness, sadism, primitiveness, *formal* ferity
🔄 civilization, civility, humanity

savant *n*
authority, scholar, intellectual, pundit, guru, mastermind, man/woman of letters, master, philosopher, *formal* sage
🔄 amateur, ignoramus

save *v*
1 RESCUE, come to the rescue of, deliver, liberate, free, set free, release, get someone out of, redeem, salvage, recover, reclaim, *colloq.* bail out **2** *save food* conserve, preserve, keep, retain, hold, reserve, store, lay up, set aside, put by, put aside, hoard, stockpile, collect, gather, *colloq.* stash **3** ECONOMIZE, cut back, cut costs, use less, budget, buy cheaply, live on the cheap, be thrifty, scrimp and save, *colloq.* tighten your belt, cut your coat according to your cloth **4** PROTECT, guard, screen, keep, shield, safeguard, keep safe, preserve, spare, prevent, hinder, *formal* obviate
🔄 **2** waste, discard **3** spend, squander

saving *adj, n*
▶ *adj* **1** ECONOMICAL, careful, sparing, thrifty, frugal **2** *a saving grace* qualifying, compensatory, extenuating, mitigating
▶ *n* **1** ECONOMY, thrift, discount, reduction, bargain, cut, conservation, preservation **2** *put your savings in the bank* capital, investments, nest egg, fund, store, reserves, resources
🔄 **1** expense, loss, waste **2** expenditure

saviour *n*
1 RESCUER, deliverer, redeemer, liberator, emancipator, guardian, protector, defender, champion **2** *Jesus Christ, the Saviour* Redeemer, Deliverer, Lamb of God, Mediator, Emmanuel
🔄 **1** destroyer

savoir-faire *n*
capability, ability, accomplishment, confidence, assurance, discretion, expertise, finesse, poise, diplomacy, tact, urbanity, *colloq.* know-how
🔄 awkwardness, clumsiness, incompetence, inexperience

savour *n, v*
▶ *n* **1** TASTE, flavour, smack, tang, piquancy, salt, spice, relish, zest **2** SMELL, aroma, bouquet, fragrance, perfume, scent **3** TRACE, hint, suggestion, touch, smattering
▶ *v* **1** RELISH, taste to the full, enjoy, enjoy to the full, delight in, take pleasure in, revel in, like, appreciate **2** SMACK, suggest, speak, spell, seem like, have all the signs of, have the hallmarks of
🔄 **1** shrink from

savoury *adj, n*
▶ *adj* **1** TASTY, flavoursome, appetizing, delicious, mouthwatering, luscious, palatable, *colloq.* yummy, scrumptious **2** *savoury pancakes* salty, spicy, aromatic, piquant, tangy
🔄 **1** unappetizing, tasteless, insipid **2** sweet
▶ *n* appetizer, snack, hors d'oeuvre, bonne-bouche, canapé

say *v, n*
▶ *v* **1** EXPRESS, phrase, put, put into words, speak, mention, render, utter, voice, articulate, enunciate, pronounce, deliver, speak, rehearse, recite, repeat, perform, read, indicate, *formal* orate **2** ANSWER, reply, respond, rejoin, retort, exclaim, comment, remark, observe, mention, add, drawl, mutter, grunt, *formal* ejaculate **3** TELL, instruct, order, communicate, convey, intimate, report, announce, declare, state, assert, affirm, maintain, claim, allege, rumour, suggest, imply, signify, reveal, disclose, divulge **4** GUESS, estimate, reckon, judge, imagine, suppose, assume, presume, surmise
▷ **that is to say** ie, that is, in other words

croak, cry, curse, declare, demand, deny, describe, detail, disclose, dispute, divulge, echo, elaborate, elucidate, emphasize, enjoin, estimate, exclaim, expostulate, express, falter, finish, flounder, gasp, greet, groan, growl, grumble, grunt, guess, hint, howl, imagine, implore, imply, indicate, infer, inform, inquire, insinuate, insist, instruct, interrogate, interrupt, intervene, intimate, jeer, jest, joke, laugh, lecture, lie, maintain, make known, make public, mention, mimic, moan, mock, mouth, mumble, murmur, mutter, nag, observe, offer, orate, order, persist, persuade, phrase, pipe, plead, point out, predict, press, presume, proclaim, profess, proffer, prompt, pronounce, propose, protest, *colloq.* put about, query, question, quote, rage, rail, rant, read, reassure, rebuke, recite, reckon, recommend, rehearse, reiterate, rejoice, relate, remark, remonstrate, renounce, repeat, reply, report, request, resolve, respond, retaliate, retort, retract, reveal, roar, rumour, scoff, scold, scream, screech, shout, shriek, snap, snarl, speak, specify, speculate, squeak, stammer, state, storm, stutter, submit, suggest, suppose, surmise, swear, sympathize, taunt, tease, tell, testify, thunder, urge, utter, venture, voice, volunteer, vow, whine, whisper, wonder, yell.

▶ *n* **1** *have a say in something* voice, word, opinion, vote, right to express yourself, opportunity to speak, turn/chance to speak **2** *have no say in the matter* influence, power, authority, sway, weight, *colloq.* clout

saying *n*
adage, proverb, dictum, precept, axiom, aphorism, maxim, motto, slogan, phrase, catch phrase, cliché, platitude, expression, quotation, epigram, statement, remark, word/pearl of wisdom, *formal* apophthegm

say-so *n*
authorization, permission, agreement, approval, affirmation, authority, backing, assertion, assurance, word, guarantee, ratification, sanction, *formal* asseveration, consent, dictum, *colloq.* OK

scaffold *n*
1 PLATFORM, framework, scaffolding, gantry, tower **2** GALLOWS, gibbet, the rope

scald *v*
burn, sear, brand, scorch, blister, *formal* cauterize

scale¹ *n, v*
▶ *n* **1** *the Richter scale* graduation, calibration, system of measurement, measuring system, register **2** EXTENT, level, degree, measure, spread, reach, range, scope, compass, spectrum, gamut **3** *What is the scale of the map?* ratio, proportion, relative size **4** SEQUENCE, series, gamut, progression, hierarchy, ranking, order, ladder, *colloq.* pecking order
▶ *v* climb, go up, ascend, mount, clamber, scramble, shin up, conquer, surmount
▷ **scale down** decrease, make less, lessen, reduce, cut back/down, drop, contract, shrink

scale² *n*
scale in a kettle; scales on a fish encrustation, deposit, crust, layer, coat, coating, limescale, tartar, plaque, film, lamina, plate, flake, scurf, furfur, *formal* squama

scaly *adj*
flaky, scurfy, scabby, scabrous, rough, branny, *formal* lepidote, furfuraceous, furfurous, squamose, squamous, squamulose, desquamative, desquamatory

scamp *n*
rogue, rascal, scallywag, monkey, mischief-maker,

troublemaker, imp, devil, wretch, *colloq.* whippersnapper

scamper *v*
scuttle, scurry, scoot, dart, dash, run, sprint, rush, hurry, race, scramble, fly, romp, frolic, gambol, *formal* hasten

scan *v, n*
▶ *v* **1** EXAMINE, scrutinize, inspect, study, search, survey, sweep, investigate, check **2** SKIM, have a quick look at, browse through, run through, run over, go over, glance at, flick through, flip through, thumb through, leaf through, run your eye over
▶ *n* screening, examination, scrutiny, inspection, search, probe, check, study, investigation, test, survey, review

scandal *n*
1 OUTRAGE, offence, outcry, uproar, furore, discredit, dishonour, disgrace, shame, embarrassment, ignominy, *formal* obloquy, opprobrium **2** GOSSIP, rumours, libel, slander, smear, dirt, *formal* defamation, calumny, *colloq.* dirty linen/washing/laundry, skeleton in the cupboard **3** DISGRACE, shame, pity, reproach, blot, slur, smear, stain, black mark, *colloq.* crying shame

scandalize *v*
shock, horrify, appal, dismay, disgust, repel, revolt, offend, insult, affront, outrage

scandalmonger *n*
gossip, gossip-monger, tattler, tattle, talebearer, busybody, quidnunc, *formal* calumniator, defamer, traducer, *colloq.* muck-raker, nosy parker

scandalous *adj*
shocking, appalling, atrocious, abominable, monstrous, unspeakable, outrageous, blatant, flagrant, disgraceful, shameful, disreputable, dishonourable, infamous, improper, malicious, scurrilous, slanderous, libellous, untrue, *formal* unseemly, defamatory, opprobrious, *colloq.* juicy

scant *adj*
little, sparse, limited, little or no, bare, deficient, minimal, hardly any, inadequate, insufficient, *formal* exiguous, *colloq.* measly
☲ adequate, ample, sufficient

scanty *adj*
deficient, short, inadequate, insufficient, scant, little, limited, restricted, narrow, poor, meagre, insubstantial, thin, skimpy, sparse, bare
☲ adequate, sufficient, ample, plentiful, substantial

scapegoat *n*
victim, whipping-boy, sucker, *colloq.* fall guy, *US slang* patsy

scar *n, v*
▶ *n* mark, lesion, wound, injury, shock, trauma, defacement, disfigurement, discolouration, blemish, blotch, stigma
▶ *v* mark, deface, disfigure, discolour, spoil, damage, injure, shock, traumatize, brand, stigmatize

scarce *adj*
few, rare, infrequent, uncommon, unusual, sparse, scanty, scant, meagre, in short supply, too little, not enough, insufficient, inadequate, deficient, lacking, *colloq.* few and far between, like gold dust
☲ plentiful, common

scarcely *adv*
1 *I can scarcely hear you* hardly, barely, only just **2** *that is scarcely a reason to hit him* hardly, not, not at all, certainly not, definitely not

scarcity *n*
lack, shortage, dearth, deficiency, insufficiency, rareness, rarity, infrequency, uncommonness, sparse-

ness, scantness, scantiness, *formal* paucity, want, exiguity

■ glut, plenty, abundance, sufficiency, enough

scare *v, n*
► *v* frighten, startle, alarm, make afraid, make frightened, dismay, daunt, intimidate, unnerve, threaten, menace, terrorize, shock, appal, panic, terrify, petrify, *formal* perturb, *colloq.* rattle, scare out of your wits, make your blood run cold, scare the living daylights out of, make your hair stand on end, make your flesh creep, make someone jump out of their skin, put the frighteners on, put the wind up
■ reassure, calm
► *n* fright, start, shock, alarm, panic, hysteria, horror, terror, fearfulness
■ reassurance, comfort

scared *adj*
afraid, frightened, fearful, nervous, anxious, worried, startled, alarmed, cowed, shaken, panic-stricken, panicky, quivery, terrified, petrified, terrorized, terror-stricken, unnerved, jittery, nervous, *colloq.* scared out of your wits, scared to death, with your heart in your mouth, shaking like a leaf, having kittens, in a blue funk
■ confident, reassured

scaremonger *n*
alarmist, pessimist, prophet of doom, doom and gloom merchant, doomwatcher, doom-monger, jitterbug, Cassandra

scarf *n*
headscarf, headsquare, kerchief, neckerchief, muffler, necktie, shawl, stole, cravat, babushka

scarper *v*
leave, depart, go, run away, vanish, disappear, abscond, bolt, escape, flee, decamp, flit, *colloq.* clear off, beat it, bunk off, run for it, scram, skedaddle, vamoose, hightail it, do a bunk

scary *adj*
frightening, alarming, daunting, formidable, fearsome, forbidding, intimidating, disturbing, shocking, horrifying, terrifying, petrifying, hair-raising, blood-curdling, spine-chilling, chilling, creepy, eerie, *colloq.* spooky, hairy

scathing *adj*
sarcastic, scornful, critical, cutting, biting, stinging, caustic, acid, vitriolic, ferocious, fierce, severe, bitter, harsh, brutal, savage, unsparing, *formal* trenchant, mordant
■ complimentary

scatter *v*
disperse, dispel, dissipate, disband, disunite, separate, divide, break up, disintegrate, diffuse, broadcast, spread, sprinkle, sow, strew, fling, shower, *formal* disseminate
■ gather, collect

scatterbrained *adj*
forgetful, absent-minded, empty-headed, featherbrained, hare-brained, careless, inattentive, thoughtless, unreliable, impulsive, irresponsible, woolgathering, frivolous, slaphappy, carefree, *colloq.* scatty, having your head in the clouds
■ sensible, sober, efficient, careful

scattering *n*
sprinkling, few, handful, smattering, break-up
■ mass, abundance

scavenge *v*
forage, rummage, rake, search, look for, hunt, scrounge

scavenger *n*
rummager, scavager, forager, scrounger, raker

scenario *n*
1 SITUATION, scene, circumstances, state, state of affairs, sequence of events, plan, programme **2** OUTLINE, synopsis, summary, résumé, storyline, script, screenplay, plot, scheme, plan, programme, projection, sequence

scene *n*
1 PLACE, area, spot, location, locale, site, situation, position, whereabouts, locality, environment, milieu, setting, context, background, backdrop, arena, set, stage **2** LANDSCAPE, scenery, panorama, view, vista, outlook, prospect, sight, spectacle, picture, tableau, pageant **3** EPISODE, incident, proceeding, part, division, act, clip **4** *don't make a scene* fuss, commotion, outburst, furore, performance, drama, exhibition, display, show, *colloq.* to-do, kerfuffle **5** *not my scene* area of interest, area of activity, field, area, speciality

scenery *n*
landscape, terrain, panorama, view, vista, outlook, prospect, scene, background, setting, surroundings, backdrop, set, *mise-en-scène*

scenic *adj*
panoramic, picturesque, attractive, pretty, beautiful, grand, striking, impressive, spectacular, breathtaking, awe-inspiring
■ dull, dreary

scent *n, v*
► *n* **1** FRAGRANCE, aroma, perfume, bouquet, smell, odour, *formal* redolence **2** PERFUME, essence, cologne, eau-de-cologne, eau-de-toilette, toilet water **3** *follow the scent* track, trail, trace, spoor
■ **1** stink
► *v* **1** SMELL, sniff (out), nose (out), track, trail, trace **2** SENSE, become aware of, become conscious of, perceive, detect, discern, recognize

scented *adj*
perfumed, fragrant, sweet-smelling, aromatic
■ malodorous, stinking

sceptic *n*
doubter, unbeliever, disbeliever, agnostic, atheist, rationalist, questioner, scoffer, cynic, doubting Thomas
■ believer

sceptical *adj*
doubting, doubtful, unconvinced, unbelieving, disbelieving, incredulous, questioning, distrustful, mistrustful, hesitating, hesitant, dubious, suspicious, scoffing, cynical, pessimistic
■ convinced, confident, trusting

scepticism *n*
doubt, unbelief, disbelief, hesitancy, agnosticism, atheism, rationalism, distrust, doubtfulness, dubiety, suspicion, incredulity, cynicism, pessimism
■ belief, faith

schedule *n, v*
► *n* timetable, programme, agenda, diary, calendar, itinerary, plan, scheme, list, syllabus, inventory, catalogue, table, form
► *v* timetable, time, table, programme, plan, organize, arrange, appoint, assign, book, list

schematic *adj*
diagrammatic, representational, symbolic, illustrative, graphic

scheme *n, v*
► *n* **1** PROGRAMME, schedule, plan, project, strategy, tactics, system, method, procedure, course of action, idea, proposal, proposition, suggestion, draft, outline, blueprint, schema, diagram, chart, map, layout, sketch, pattern, design, shape, arrangement, *formal* configuration, disposition, delineation **2** INTRIGUE, plot, conspiracy, device, stratagem, ruse, ploy, shift, manoeuvre, tactic(s), strategy, *formal* machinations

▶ *v* plot, conspire, connive, collude, intrigue, manoeuvre, manipulate, pull strings, mastermind, plan, project, contrive, devise, frame, work out, *formal* machinate

schemer *n*
plotter, intriguer, politician, conniver, deceiver, mastermind, intrig(u)ant(e), Machiavelli, Machiavellian, éminence grise, fox, *formal* machinator, *colloq.* wangler, wheeler-dealer, wire-puller

scheming *adj*
crafty, cunning, deceitful, sly, underhand, unscrupulous, wily, devious, artful, calculating, conniving, designing, insidious, tricky, slippery, foxy, Machiavellian, *formal* duplicitous
F∃ artless, honest, open, transparent

schism *n*
1 DIVISION, split, rift, rupture, break, breach, disunion, separation, severance, discord, *formal* estrangement **2** SPLINTER, group, faction, sect, detachment

scholar *n*
1 STUDENT, pupil, learner, schoolchild, schoolboy, schoolgirl **2** ACADEMIC, intellectual, authority, expert, philosopher, mastermind, pundit, *colloq.* egghead, bookworm

scholarly *adj*
learned, erudite, lettered, academic, scholastic, school, intellectual, highbrow, bookish, studious, knowledgeable, well-read, conscientious, analytical, scientific
F∃ uneducated, illiterate

scholarship *n*
1 LEARNING, learnedness, knowledge, wisdom, education, schooling, academic achievements/attainments, *formal* erudition **2** *a scholarship to a public school* grant, award, bursary, endowment, fellowship, exhibition

scholastic *adj*
academic, scholarly, educational, pedagogic, lettered, learned, literary, bookish, analytical, pedantic, precise

school *n, v*
▶ *n* **1** *go to school* college, academy, institute, institution, university, seminary, faculty, department, division, discipline, class, group, pupils, students, yeshiva(h). *See also* EDUCATIONAL ESTABLISHMENTS. **2** *a school of artists* group, set, circle, clique, coterie, faction, association, club, society, guild, league, company
▶ *v* educate, teach, instruct, tutor, coach, train, discipline, drill, verse, prime, prepare, indoctrinate

schooling *n*
education, learning, book-learning, teaching, instruction, tuition, coaching, training, drill, preparation, grounding, guidance, indoctrination

schoolteacher *n*
teacher, instructor, educator, schoolmaster, master, schoolmistress, mistress, schoolmarm, pedagogue

science *n*
technology, discipline, specialization, knowledge, skill, proficiency, expertise, technique, dexterity, art

Sciences include:
acoustics, aerodynamics, aeronautics, agricultural science, anatomy, anthropology, archaeology, astronomy, astrophysics, behavioural science, biochemistry, biology, biophysics, botany, chemistry, chemurgy, climatology, computer science, cybernetics, diagnostics, dietetics, domestic science, dynamics, earth science, ecology, economics, electrodynamics, electronics, engineering, entomology, environmental science, food science, genetics, geochemistry, geographical science, geology, geophysics, graphology, hydraulics, information technology, inorganic chemistry, life science, linguistics, macrobiotics, materials science, mathematics, mechanical engineering, mechanics, medical science, metallurgy, meteorology, microbiology, mineralogy, morphology, natural science, nuclear physics, organic chemistry, ornithology, pathology, pharmacology, physics, physiology, political science, psychology, radiochemistry, robotics, sociology, space technology, telecommunications, thermodynamics, toxicology, ultrasonics, veterinary science, zoology.

scientific *adj*
methodical, systematic, controlled, regulated, orderly, analytical, mathematical, exact, precise, accurate, scholarly, thorough

scientific instruments

Types of scientific instrument include:
absorptiometer, barostat, cathode ray oscilloscope, centrifuge, chronograph, coherer, collimator, cryostat, decoherer, dephlegmator, dipleidoscope, electromyograph, electrosonde, eudiometer, fluoroscope, Fresnel lens, Geissler tube, heliograph, heliostat, hodoscope, humidistat, hydrophone, hydroscope, hydrostat, hygrograph, hygrostat, iconoscope, image converter, image tube, interferometer, microtome, nephograph, optical character reader, oscillograph, oscilloscope, pantograph, parametric amplifier, phonendoscope, radarscope, radiosonde, rheocord, rheostat, sliderule, spectroscope, stactometer, stauroscope, strobe, stroboscope, tachistoscope, tachograph, teinoscope, telemeter, telethermoscope, tesla coil, thermostat, thyratron, torsion-balance, transformer, transponder, tunnel diode, vernier, zymoscope. *See also* LABORATORY APPARATUS; MEDICAL EQUIPMENT.

scintillate *v*
sparkle, spark, shine, flash, gleam, glint, glisten, glitter, twinkle, blaze, wink, *formal* coruscate

scintillating *adj*
sparkling, glittering, flashing, bright, shining, brilliant, dazzling, exciting, stimulating, lively, animated, vivacious, witty, exhilarating, invigorating, *formal* ebullient
F∃ dull

scion *n*
1 CHILD, descendant, offspring, heir, successor **2** OFFSHOOT, shoot, branch, sprout, graft, twig

scoff¹ *v*
scoff at something mock, ridicule, laugh at, poke fun, taunt, tease, jeer, sneer, gibe, scorn, despise, revile, belittle, *formal* deride, disparage, *colloq.* rib, poohpooh, knock
F∃ praise, compliment, flatter

scoff² *v, n*
▶ *v* *scoff food* eat, consume, devour, finish off, gobble, guzzle, bolt, gulp, *colloq.* put away, wolf

▶ *n* food, foodstuffs, comestibles, provisions, meal, refreshments, sustenance, nourishment, nutrition, nutriment, subsistence, *colloq.* eatables, eats, tuck, *slang* grub, nosh, nosh-up, *US* chow

scoffing *adj*
mocking, taunting, sneering, derisive, scathing, cynical, sarcastic, fiendish, Mephistophelian, *formal* disparaging

scold *v*
reprimand, reprove, rebuke, chide, take to task, reproach, blame, censure, lecture, nag, *formal* admonish, upbraid, castigate, berate, lambaste, *colloq.* tell off, tick off, give someone a piece of your mind, give a dressing-down, read the riot act to, haul over the coals, rap over the knuckles
Fɜ praise, commend

scolding *n*
telling-off, reprimand, reproof, rebuke, lecture, talking-to, *formal* castigation, upbraiding, *colloq.* a piece of your mind, ticking-off, dressing-down, carpeting, wigging, earful
Fɜ praise, commendation

scoop *n, v*
▶ *n* 1 LADLE, spoon, dipper, bailer, bucket, shovel 2 EXCLUSIVE, coup, inside story, revelation, exposé, sensation, *colloq.* latest
▶ *v* gouge, scrape, hollow, empty, excavate, dig, shovel, remove, ladle, spoon, dip, bail

scoot *v*
rush, hurry, dash, dart, career, bolt, shoot, run, sprint, zip, scurry, scud, scuttle, tootle, *colloq.* vamoose, skedaddle, beat it, scarper

scope *n*
1 RANGE, compass, field, area, sphere, ambit, terms of reference, realm, confines, limits, reach, orbit, extent, span, sweep, breadth, coverage 2 *scope for improvement* room, space, capacity, elbow-room, latitude, leeway, freedom, liberty, opportunity

scorch *v*
burn, singe, char, blacken, discolour, scald, roast, sear, parch, shrivel, wither, dry up

scorching *adj*
burning, roasting, sizzling, blistering, sweltering, torrid, tropical, searing, red-hot, *colloq.* boiling, baking

score *n, v*
▶ *n* 1 RESULT, goals, runs, hits, total, sum, tally, points, marks, record, outcome 2 SCRATCH, line, groove, mark, cut, gouge, incision, nick, notch, gash, slit, scrape 3 *scores of people* crowds, lots, masses, multitudes, hundreds, thousands, millions, myriads, swarms, shoals, droves, hosts, legions 4 REASON, grounds, basis, motives, explanation, case, argument 5 *no worries on that score* matter, subject, question, issue, concern, aspect 6 *settle old scores* grievance, grudge, complaint, dispute, quarrel, argument, bone of contention
▶ *v* 1 RECORD, register, get, count, total, keep a tally, make, earn, gain, achieve, attain, win, have the advantage, have the edge, be one up, *colloq.* chalk up, notch up, hit the jackpot 2 SCRATCH, scrape, graze, mark, groove, gouge, cut, incise, engrave, indent, nick, slit, gash, slash, notch 3 *score a piece of music* set, arrange, adapt, write, orchestrate, instrument
▷ **score off** gain an advantage over, make a clever reply to, humiliate, have the edge, *colloq.* get one over on
▷ **score out** cross out, cancel, remove, strike out, erase, delete, *formal* efface, expunge, obliterate
Fɜ reinstate, restore

scorn *n, v*
▶ *n* contempt, scornfulness, disdain, sneering, derision, mockery, haughtiness, ridicule, sarcasm, disgust, *formal* disparagement, contumely
Fɜ admiration, respect
▶ *v* despise, look down on, disdain, sneer at, sniff at, scoff at, mock, laugh at, slight, rebuff, spurn, refuse, shun, reject, dismiss, *formal* deride, disparage
Fɜ admire, respect

scornful *adj*
contemptuous, disdainful, supercilious, haughty, arrogant, sneering, scoffing, derisive, mocking, jeering, sarcastic, scathing, insulting, slighting, dismissive, *formal* disparaging
Fɜ admiring, respectful

scornfully *adv*
contemptuously, disdainfully, superciliously, haughtily, arrogantly, scathingly, slightingly, sneeringly, derisively, dismissively, witheringly, *formal* disparagingly
Fɜ admiringly, respectfully

scot-free *adj*
clear, unpunished, unrebuked, unreprimanded, unreproached, unharmed, unhurt, unscathed, undamaged, safe, ininjured, without a scratch

scoundrel *n*
rogue, rascal, villain, vagabond, ruffian, ne'er-do-well, good-for-nothing, miscreant, scamp, scallywag, cheat, rotter, reprobate, *colloq.* rat, swine, *slang* louse, scab

scour[1] *v*
scour pots and pans scrub, scrape, clean, wash, cleanse, purge, flush, rub, polish, wipe, burnish, *formal* abrade

scour[2] *v*
scour the hillside search, hunt, comb, drag, ransack, rummage, turn upside-down, forage, rake

scourge *n, v*
▶ *n* 1 AFFLICTION, misfortune, torment, terror, torture, bane, evil, curse, menace, plague, trial, penalty, nuisance, punishment, thorn in your side 2 WHIP, lash, strap, flail, birch, cat-o'-nine-tails, switch, flagellum
Fɜ 1 blessing, godsend, boon
▶ *v* 1 AFFLICT, torment, torture, burden, curse, plague, devastate, punish, chastise, discipline 2 WHIP, flog, beat, lash, strap, birch, cane, flail, thrash

scout *v, n*
▶ *v* spy out, reconnoitre, explore, investigate, check out, survey, inspect, spy, snoop, search, seek, hunt, probe, look (for), watch, observe, *colloq.* recce, *slang* case
▶ *n* spy, reconnoitre, vanguard, advance guard, outrider, escort, lookout, recruiter, spotter, talent spotter

scowl *v, n*
▶ *v* frown, glower, glare, grimace, pout, lour, look daggers at
Fɜ smile, grin, beam
▶ *n* frown, glower, glare, grimace, pout, *colloq.* dirty/black look
Fɜ smile, grin, beam

scrabble *v*
clamber, scramble, scrape, scratch, claw, grope, grub, paw, dig, root

scraggy *adj*
scrawny, skinny, thin, lean, lanky, bony, raw-boned, angular, gaunt, undernourished, emaciated, wasted
Fɜ plump, sleek

scram *v*
go away, leave, depart, disappear, flee, *colloq.* take to your heels, clear out, clear off, quit, beat it, shove off, skedaddle, vamoose, do a bunk, scarper, scoot, bolt

scramble *v, n*
▸ *v* **1** CLIMB, scale, clamber, crawl, shuffle, scrabble, grope **2** RUSH, hurry, run, push, jostle, jockey, struggle, tussle, strive, vie, contend, compete, battle, *formal* hasten **3** MIX, jumble, mix up, infuse, disturb, disorganize
▸ *n* **1** CLAMBER, climb, scrabble, shuffle, scaling **2** RUSH, hurry, race, dash, hustle, bustle, scurry, commotion, confusion, muddle, struggle, tussle, vying, competition, free-for-all, melee

scrap¹ *n, v*
▸ *n* **1** *a scrap of paper* bit, piece, fragment, part, fraction, crumb, morsel, bite, mouthful, sliver, shred, snippet, tatter, atom, iota, grain, particle, mite, trace, vestige, remnant, leftover, waste, junk **2** *scraps of meat* leftovers, bits, scrapings, leavings, remains, residue, *colloq.* bits and pieces, odds and ends, *slang* odds and sods
▷ **on the scrap heap** discarded, forgotten, jettisoned, redundant, rejected, written off, *colloq.* ditched, dumped
▸ *v* discard, throw away, get rid of, jettison, shed, abandon, drop, dump, cancel, axe, demolish, break up, write off, *colloq.* chuck out, ditch, junk
☒ recover, restore

scrap² *n, v*
▸ *n* *a scrap in the school playground* fight, scuffle, brawl, quarrel, row, argument, squabble, wrangle, dispute, disagreement, tiff, fracas, *colloq.* dust-up, set-to, punch-up
☒ peace, agreement
▸ *v* fight, brawl, quarrel, argue, fall out, squabble, bicker, row, wrangle, disagree
☒ agree

scrape *v, n*
▸ *v* **1** GRATE, grind, rasp, file, scour, rub, clean, remove, erase, scrabble, claw, *formal* abrade **2** SCRATCH, graze, skin, cut, bark, scuff
▷ **scrape by** just manage to live, get by, scrimp, skimp, scarcely have enough to live on
▷ **scrape through** just pass, only just/barely win, just succeed in, *colloq.* get through by a whisker
▷ **scrape together** get together, round up, pool together, get with difficulty, collect with difficulty, obtain with difficulty, just manage to get
▸ *n* **1** GRAZE, scratch, rub, abrasion, scuff, shave **2** DIFFICULTY, dilemma, predicament, trouble, plight, distress, *colloq.* fix, mess, pickle, tight spot, pretty kettle of fish

scrappy *adj*
bitty, disjointed, piecemeal, fragmentary, incomplete, untidy, disorganized, sketchy, superficial, slapdash, slipshod
☒ complete, finished

scratch *v, n, adj*
▸ *v* claw, gouge, score, mark, cut, nick, incise, etch, engrave, scrape, rub, scuff, graze, gash, skin, tear, lacerate, *formal* abrade
▸ *n* mark, line, scrape, scuff, abrasion, graze, gash, wound, laceration
▷ **up to scratch** good enough, satisfactory, adequate, acceptable, reasonable, tolerable, competent, *colloq.* OK
☒ unsatisfactory
▸ *adj* improvised, impromptu, unrehearsed, rough-and-ready, rough, haphazard
☒ polished

scrawl *v, n*
▸ *v* scribble, write quickly, pen, jot (down), dash off, doodle
▸ *n* scribble, squiggle, writing, handwriting, bad/illegible handwriting, scratch, scrabble, *formal* cacography

scrawny *adj*
scraggy, skinny, thin, lean, lanky, angular, bony, raw-boned, underfed, undernourished, emaciated
☒ fat, plump

scream *v, n*
▸ *v* shriek, screech, cry, shout, yell, bawl, roar, howl, wail, squeal, yelp, squawk, *colloq.* holler, *US* yawp
☒ whisper
▸ *n* **1** SHRIEK, screech, cry, shout, yell, bawl, roar, howl, wail, squeal, yelp, squawk, *colloq.* holler, *US* yawp **2** *he's a scream* joker, comic, comedian, wit, *colloq.* character, hoot, laugh, riot
☒ **1** whisper **2** bore

screech *v & n*
squeal, cry, scream, shriek, howl, yell, squawk, yelp
☒ whisper

screen *n, v*
▸ *n* **1** PARTITION, divider **2** SHIELD, guard, protection, cover, mask, veil, cloak, shroud, concealment, front, façade, disguise, camouflage, shelter, shade, curtain, blind, awning, canopy, net, netting, mesh
▸ *v* **1** *screen a film* show, present, broadcast **2** SHIELD, protect, safeguard, defend, guard, cover, mask, veil, cloak, shroud, hide, conceal, disguise, camouflage, shelter, shade **3** SORT, grade, sift, sieve, riddle, filter, process, evaluate, test, check, investigate, gauge, examine, scan, vet
☒ **2** uncover, expose
▷ **screen off** partition (off), separate (off), divide (off), fence off, hide, conceal

screw *n, v*
▸ *n* fastener, pin, tack, nail, rivet, brad, bolt
▷ **put the screws on** pressurize, force, compel, constrain, dragoon, coerce, *colloq.* lean on
▸ *v* **1** FASTEN, adjust, tighten, clamp, fix, contract, compress, squeeze, turn, wind, twist, wring, distort, wrinkle **2** *screw money out of him* extract, extort, force, constrain, pressurize, *colloq.* bleed, milk
☒ **1** unscrew
▷ **screw up 1** *screw up your face* wrinkle, distort, tighten, knot, crumple, contract, pucker, contort **2** MESS UP, spoil, botch, bungle, mishandle, mismanage, *colloq.* make a hash of, *slang* louse up
☒ **2** manage

screwy *adj*
crazy, eccentric, mad, odd, weird, queer, *colloq.* daft, dotty, nutty, batty, crackers, round the twist, round the bend
☒ sane

scribble *v, n*
▸ *v* write, pen, jot (down), dash off, scrawl, doodle
▸ *n* squiggle, writing, handwriting, bad/illegible handwriting, scratch, scrabble, *formal* cacography

scrimmage *n*
brawl, fight, riot, row, struggle, scuffle, skirmish, squabble, disturbance, fray, free-for-all, affray, shindy, melee, *colloq.* bovver, dust-up, scrap, set-to

scrimp *v*
skimp, save, economize, cut back on, limit, reduce, restrict, scrape, curtail, shorten, stint, pinch, *colloq.* tighten your belt, cut your coat according to your cloth
☒ spend

script *n*
1 *a film script* text, lines, words, manuscript, dialogue, screenplay, libretto, book **2** WRITING, handwriting, hand, longhand, calligraphy, letters, manuscript, copy

scripture *n*

The sacred writings of religions include:
the word of God, the word, Holy Bible, the Gospel,

Old Testament, New Testament, Epistle, Torah, Pentateuch, Talmud, Koran, Bhagavad-Gita, Veda, Granth, Zend-Avesta.

Scrooge *n*
miser, skinflint, niggard, *colloq.* cheapskate, meanie, money-grubber, penny-pincher, tightwad
F3 spendthrift

scrounge *v*
cadge, beg, borrow, *colloq.* sponge, bum, bludge

scrounger *n*
cadger, parasite, beggar, borrower, *colloq.* sponger, bum, freeloader, bludger, moocher

scrub¹ *v*
1 *scrub the floor* rub, brush, clean, wash, cleanse, wipe, scour **2** ABOLISH, cancel, delete, abandon, give up, drop, forget, *formal* discontinue, *colloq.* axe

scrub² *n*
an area of scrub scrubland, bush, backwoods, brush

scruffy *adj*
untidy, messy, unkempt, dishevelled, bedraggled, ungroomed, run-down, tattered, shabby, down-at-heel, disreputable, slatternly, worn-out, ragged, seedy, squalid, slovenly, *colloq.* sloppy
F3 tidy, well-dressed

scrumptious *adj*
delicious, appetising, tasty, mouth-watering, succulent, luscious, delightful, exquisite, magnificent, *formal* delectable, *colloq.* morish, yummy, scrummy
F3 unappetizing, *colloq.* yucky

scrunch *v*
crunch, crumple, twist, crush, grate, grind, screw (up), mash, squash, chew, champ

scruple *n, v*
 ▸ *n* **1** RELUCTANCE, hesitation, doubt, qualm, reservation, misgiving, second thoughts, uneasiness, difficulty, perplexity, *formal* vacillation, compunction **2** *has no scruples* standards, principles, morals, ethics
 ▸ *v* hesitate, be reluctant, think twice, hold back, shrink, balk, *formal* vacillate

scrupulous *adj*
1 PAINSTAKING, meticulous, conscientious, careful, rigorous, thorough, strict, exact, precise, minute, fastidious, nice, *formal* punctilious **2** PRINCIPLED, high-principled, moral, ethical, honourable, honest, upright
F3 **1** superficial, careless, reckless **2** unscrupulous, unprincipled

scrutinize *v*
examine, inspect, study, scan, go over, go through, look over, look through, run over, run through, analyse, sift, investigate, probe, search, explore, *formal* peruse

scrutiny *n*
examination, inspection, study, analysis, investigation, inquiry, search, exploration, probe, *formal* perusal

scuff *v*
scrape, scratch, graze, rub, brush, drag, *formal* abrade

scuffle *v, n*
 ▸ *v* fight, quarrel, tussle, brawl, come to blows, grapple, struggle, contend, clash, *colloq.* scrap
 ▸ *n* fight, tussle, brawl, fray, rumpus, commotion, disturbance, affray, row, quarrel, *colloq.* scrap, set-to, dust-up

sculpt *v*
sculpture, carve, chisel, hew, cut, model, mould, cast, form, shape, fashion, represent

sculpture *n*

Types of sculpture include:
bas-relief, bronze, bust, carving, caryatid, cast, effigy, figure, figurine, group, head, herm, high-relief, maquette, marble, moulding, plaster cast, relief, statue, statuette, telamon, waxwork.

scum *n*
1 *scum floating on a liquid* froth, foam, film, layer, covering, impurities, dross, dregs **2** *they're the scum of the earth* rabble, dregs of society, undesirables, lowest of the low, rubbish, trash, *colloq.* riff-raff, plebs, the great unwashed

scupper *v*
1 *scupper a plan* foil, wreck, ruin, scuttle, disable, demolish, defeat, destroy, overthrow, overwhelm, *colloq.* put a spanner in the works **2** *scupper a ship* sink, destroy, submerge, torpedo
F3 **1** advance, promote

scurrility *n*
scurrilousness, rudeness, offensiveness, vulgarity, nastiness, obscenity, coarseness, foulness, indecency, grossness, abuse, abusiveness, *formal* invective, obloquy, vituperation
F3 politeness

scurrilous *adj*
rude, vulgar, coarse, foul, obscene, indecent, salacious, offensive, abusive, insulting, slanderous, libellous, scandalous, *formal* disparaging, defamatory, vituperative
F3 polite, courteous, complimentary

scurry *v, n*
 ▸ *v* dash, rush, hurry, bustle, scramble, scuttle, scamper, scoot, dart, run, sprint, trot, race, fly, skim, scud, *formal* hasten
 ▸ *n* rush, bustling, hurry, flurry, scampering, whirl, *colloq.* hustle and bustle
F3 calm

scurvy *adj*
contemptible, vile, dirty, shabby, worthless, dishonourable, sorry, ignoble, despicable, rotten, pitiful, mean, low, bad, base, *formal* abject, *colloq.* low-down
F3 good, honourable

scuttle *v*
scurry, hurry, rush, scutter, bustle, scamper, scramble, scud, run, *formal* hasten

sea *n, adj*
 ▸ *n* **1** OCEAN, main, deep, *colloq.* briny. *See also* OCEAN. **2** *a sea of faces* large number, multitude, abundance, profusion, host, mass, expanse
 ▸ *adj* marine, maritime, ocean, oceanic, salt, saltwater, aquatic, seafaring, afloat
F3 land, air
 ▷ **at sea** adrift, lost, confused, bewildered, baffled, puzzled, perplexed, mystified

seafaring *adj*
sea-going, ocean-going, oceanic, sailing, nautical, naval, marine, maritime

seal *v, n*
 ▸ *v* **1** *seal a jar* close (up), shut, stop (up), plug, cork, stopper, waterproof, fasten, secure, tighten, make airtight/watertight **2** SETTLE, conclude, finalize, confirm, ratify, stamp, *colloq.* clinch
F3 **1** unseal
 ▷ **seal off** block up, cordon off, close off, shut off, fence off, cut off, segregate, isolate, quarantine
F3 open up
 ▸ *n* stamp, signet, insignia, imprimatur, authentication, assurance, confirmation, ratification, *formal* attestation

sealed *adj*
closed, shut, corked, plugged, hermetic
🖅 unsealed

seam *n*
1 JOIN, joint, junction, weld, closure, line **2** *coal seam* layer, stratum, vein, lode

seaman *n*
sailor, rating, seafarer, steersman, AB, tar, deck hand, Jack tar, sea dog, *slang* matelot

seamy *adj*
disreputable, sordid, squalid, unsavoury, rough, dark, low, nasty, unpleasant, *colloq.* sleazy
🖅 respectable, wholesome, pleasant

sear *v*
burn, scorch, char, singe, brown, fry, sizzle, seal, brand, parch, shrivel, wither, wilt, dry-up, *formal* cauterize

search *v, n*
▶ *v* **1** SEEK, look, look through, go through, hunt, rummage, rifle, ransack, forage, scour, comb, sift, *colloq.* go through with a fine-tooth comb, turn upside-down/inside-out **2** EXAMINE, probe, explore, examine, scrutinize, inspect, check, investigate, inquire, pry, *colloq.* frisk
▶ *n* **1** HUNT, hunt, quest, pursuit, rummage, rifling, forage, ransacking **2** EXAMINATION, exploration, probe, scrutiny, inspection, investigation, inquiry, research, survey

searching *adj*
penetrating, piercing, alert, discerning, observant, keen, sharp, close, intent, probing, thorough, minute
🖅 vague, superficial

seaside *n*
coast, shore, seashore, beach, sands

season *n, v*
▶ *n* period, spell, phase, term, time, span, interval
▷ **in season** available, obtainable, growing plentifully, growing, on the market
▶ *v* **1** *season food* flavour, spice, salt, add flavouring, add pepper to, add herbs to, add relish/sauce to, *colloq.* pep up **2** AGE, mature, ripen, mellow, harden, toughen, train, prime, prepare, condition, treat **3** TEMPER, moderate, tone down

seasonable *adj*
timely, well-timed, welcome, opportune, providential, convenient, suitable, appropriate, fitting
🖅 unseasonable, inopportune

seasoned *adj*
mature, experienced, practised, established, well-versed, veteran, long-serving, battle-scarred, old, hardened, toughened, conditioned, acclimatized, weathered, *formal* habituated
🖅 inexperienced, novice

seasoning *n*
flavouring, spice, condiment, salt, pepper, herbs, relish, sauce, dressing

seat *n, v*
▶ *n* **1** CHAIR, bench, pew, stool, throne, stall, form, settle **2** *country seat* residence, house, mansion, stately home, *formal* abode **3** PLACE, site, situation, location, headquarters, centre, heart, hub, axis, source, cause, origin, reason, bottom, base, foundation, footing, ground
▶ *v* **1** SIT, place, put, position, deposit, set, locate, install, fit, fix, settle **2** *the theatre seats 1000* accommodate, hold, contain, take, have room for

seating *n*
seats, chairs, places, room, accommodation

secede *v*
separate, split off, withdraw, break away, break, resign, retire, leave, disaffiliate, turn your back on,

formal apostatize, *colloq.* quit
🖅 join, unite with

secession *n*
seceding, split, withdrawal, defection, break, breakaway, disaffiliation, schism, *formal* apostasy
🖅 amalgamation, unification

secluded *adj*
private, cloistered, shut away, cut off, isolated, lonely, unfrequented, solitary, remote, out-of-the-way, sheltered, hidden, concealed, *formal* sequestered
🖅 public, accessible

seclusion *n*
privacy, retirement, withdrawal, retreat, isolation, solitude, remoteness, shelter, secrecy, hiding, concealment, *formal* sequestration

second¹ *adj, n, v*
▶ *adj* **1** NEXT, following, subsequent, succeeding **2** ADDITIONAL, further, extra, supplementary, alternative, other, alternate, back-up **3** DUPLICATE, twin, double, repeated **4** SECONDARY, subordinate, lower, inferior, lesser, supporting
▶ *n* helper, assistant, backer, supporter, attendant, second-in-command, right-hand man/woman
▶ *v* approve, agree with, endorse, back, back up, support, help, assist, aid, further, advance, forward, promote, encourage

second² *n*
in ten seconds minute, moment, instant, flash, split second, twinkling, twinkling of an eye, trice, *colloq.* tick, jiffy, two shakes of a lamb's tail

second³ *v*
seconded to Australia for a year transfer, relocate, change, move, shift, assign, send

secondary *adj*
subsidiary, subordinate, lower, inferior, lesser, minor, unimportant, non-essential, ancillary, auxiliary, supporting, relief, back-up, reserve, spare, extra, second, alternative, indirect, derived, derivative, resulting
🖅 primary, main, major, essential

second-class *adj*
second-best, second-rate, mediocre, inferior, unimportant, indifferent, uninspiring, undistinguished, uninspired
🖅 valuable

second-hand *adj*
used, old, nearly-new, worn, hand-me-down, borrowed, derivative, secondary, indirect, vicarious
🖅 brand-new

second-in-command *n*
helper, assistant, backer, supporter, attendant, right-hand man/woman

second-rate *adj*
inferior, substandard, lesser, unimportant, second-class, second-best, poor, low-grade, shoddy, cheap, tawdry, mediocre, undistinguished, uninspired, uninspiring, *colloq.* tacky, lousy, tinpot, ropy
🖅 first-rate

secrecy *n*
privacy, seclusion, confidentiality, confidence, disguise, covertness, concealment, camouflage, furtiveness, surreptitiousness, stealthiness, stealth, mystery
🖅 openness

secret *adj, n*
▶ *adj* **1** PRIVATE, discreet, covert, hidden, concealed, unseen, shrouded, covered, disguised, camouflaged, undercover, furtive, surreptitious, stealthy, sly, underhand, under-the-counter, underground, backstairs, back-door, *formal* clandestine, *colloq.* cloak-and-dagger, hole-and-corner, closet **2** CLASSIFIED, re-

stricted, confidential, sensitive, unpublished, undisclosed, unrevealed, unknown, *colloq.* hush-hush, top secret, between you and me, between you, me and the gatepost **3** CRYPTIC, mysterious, occult, deep, *formal* arcane, recondite, abstruse **4** CONCEALED, private, cloistered, shut away, cut off, isolated, lonely, unfrequented, solitary, remote, close, sheltered, hidden, retired, secluded, out-of-the-way, *formal* sequestered

📷 **1** public, open **2** well-known **4** public, accessible
▶ *n* **1** CONFIDENTIAL MATTER, confidence, private matter, mystery, enigma, *colloq.* inside story **2** *the secret of eternal youth* code, key, answer, solution, formula, recipe
▷ **in secret** confidentially, in confidence, in private, under cover, privately, quietly, surreptitiously, stealthily, unobserved, covertly, furtively, on the quiet, *formal* clandestinely, in camera, privily, *colloq.* on the q.t., on the sly, behind closed doors, hugger-mugger
📷 openly

secretary *n*
personal assistant, PA, office administrator, executive assistant, typist, stenographer, clerk, person Friday, amanuensis

secrete¹ *v*
secrete a weapon hide, conceal, bury, cover, cover up, cache, screen, shroud, veil, disguise, take, appropriate, *formal* sequester, *colloq.* stash away
📷 uncover, reveal, disclose

secrete² *v*
secrete a liquid exude, discharge, release, excrete, give off, emit, send out, emanate, produce, leach, leak, ooze

secretion *n*
exudation, discharge, release, emission, emanation, leakage, oozing, *technical* osmosis

secretive *adj*
tight-lipped, close, uncommunicative, unforthcoming, reticent, taciturn, reserved, withdrawn, intent, quiet, deep, cryptic, enigmatic, *colloq.* cagey, playing your cards close to your chest
📷 open, communicative, forthcoming

secretly *adv*
confidentially, in confidence, in private, in secret, under cover, privately, quietly, surreptitiously, stealthily, unobserved, covertly, furtively, on the quiet, *formal* clandestinely, in camera, privily, *colloq.* on the q.t., on the sly, behind closed doors
📷 openly

sect *n*
denomination, cult, division, subdivision, group, splinter group, order, faction, camp, wing, party, school

sectarian *adj, n*
▶ *adj* factional, partisan, cliquish, exclusive, narrow, hidebound, limited, parochial, insular, narrow-minded, bigoted, prejudiced, fanatical, extreme, doctrinaire, dogmatic, rigid
📷 non-sectarian, broad-minded
▶ *n* bigot, fanatic, partisan, zealot, dogmatist, extremist, fractionalist

section *n*
division, subdivision, chapter, paragraph, passage, instalment, part, component, fraction, fragment, bit, piece, slice, portion, segment, sector, zone, district, area, region, department, branch, wing
📷 whole

sectional *adj*
separate, divided, exclusive, factional, separatist, regional, local, localized, partial, class, racial, sectarian
📷 general, universal

sector *n*
zone, district, quarter, area, region, branch, field, category, section, division, subdivision, part
📷 whole

secular *adj*
lay, temporal, worldly, earthly, civil, state, profane, non-religious, non-spiritual
📷 religious, spiritual

secure *adj, v*
▶ *adj* **1** SAFE, unharmed, undamaged, protected, sheltered, shielded, immune, impregnable, fast, tight, closed, sealed, fastened, locked, *formal* fortified, *colloq.* out of harm's way **2** CONFIDENT, assured, reassured, safe, comfortable, relaxed, happy, contented **3** FIXED, immovable, stable, steady, sturdy, solid, firm **4** CERTAIN, sure, well-founded, reliable, dependable, steadfast, conclusive, definite, established, settled
📷 **1** insecure, vulnerable **2** uneasy, ill at ease, embarrassed, uncomfortable
▶ *v* **1** OBTAIN, acquire, gain, get, get hold of, *formal* procure, *colloq.* come by, land **2** FASTEN, attach, fix, make fast, tie (up), moor, lash, chain, lock (up), shut, close, padlock, bolt, batten down, nail, rivet **3** PROTECT, make safe, strengthen, guard, safeguard, defend, cover, shield, screen **4** GUARANTEE, assure, ensure, establish, confirm, sponsor, underwrite, endorse
📷 **1** lose **2** unfasten

security *n*
1 SAFETY, immunity, asylum, sanctuary, refuge, cover, protection, defence, protection, invulnerability, surveillance, safe-keeping, preservation, care, custody **2** *security for a loan* collateral, surety, pledge, guarantee, warranty, assurance, insurance, precaution(s), safeguard(s), protection, defence **3** CONFIDENCE, assurance, ease, peace of mind, conviction, certainty, positiveness
📷 **1** insecurity, danger **3** anxiety, worry, embarrassment

sedate *adj, v*
▶ *adj* staid, dignified, solemn, grave, stiff, serious, earnest, sober, proper, demure, composed, unruffled, serene, tranquil, calm, quiet, unexciting, dull, cool, collected, deliberate, slow-moving, *formal* decorous, imperturbable, *colloq.* unflappable
📷 undignified, lively, agitated
▶ *v* tranquillize, calm, calm down, quieten down, soothe, relax, pacify

sedative *adj, n*
▶ *adj* calming, soothing, anodyne, lenitive, tranquillizing, relaxing, soporific, depressant
📷 rousing
▶ *n* tranquillizer, sleeping-pill, narcotic, barbiturate, opiate, calmative, depressant, *colloq.* downer

sedentary *adj*
sitting, seated, desk-bound, inactive, still, stationary, immobile, unmoving
📷 active

sediment *n*
deposit, residue, grounds, lees, dregs, silt, *formal* precipitate, residuum

sedition *n*
agitation, rabble-rousing, subversion, disloyalty, treachery, treason, mutiny, rebellion, revolt, *formal* insubordination, fomentation, incitement to riot
📷 calm, loyalty

seditious *adj*
agitating, inciting, rabble-rousing, subversive, disloyal, traitorous, mutinous, rebellious, revolutionary, *formal* insubordinate, dissident, insurrectionist, fomenting, refractory
📷 calm, loyal

seduce *v*
entice, lure, allure, attract, tempt, charm, beguile, ensnare, lead astray, mislead, deceive, corrupt, dishonour, deprave, ruin, *formal* inveigle, *colloq.* get into bed
🔁 repel

seducer *n*
charmer, philanderer, womanizer, flirt, deceiver, libertine, Don Juan, Casanova, Lothario, *colloq.* wolf, goat

seduction *n*
enticement, lure, allure, allurement, attraction, appeal, temptation, charm, beguilement, corruption, deception, misleading, ruin, *colloq.* come-on

seductive *adj*
enticing, alluring, luring, attractive, appealing, tempting, tantalizing, inviting, flirtatious, sexy, provocative, beguiling, charming, captivating, bewitching, deceiving, misleading, irresistible, sultry, *colloq.* come-hither
🔁 unattractive, repulsive

seductress *n*
femme fatale, temptress, siren, Lorelei, Circe, *colloq.* vamp

sedulous *adj*
diligent, industrious, conscientious, painstaking, persevering, persistent, laborious, busy, constant, assiduous, tireless, untiring, unflagging, unremitting, resolved, determined
🔁 half-hearted

see *v*
1 PERCEIVE, catch sight of, set eyes on, glimpse, discern, spot, make out, recognize, distinguish, identify, sight, notice, observe, watch, view, look at, get a look at, witness, mark, note **2** *I see your point* understand, comprehend, grasp, fathom, follow, know, take in, make out, realize, recognize, appreciate, regard, consider, reflect, deem, *colloq.* get, latch onto, cotton onto **3** IMAGINE, picture, visualize, envisage, forecast, foresee, predict, anticipate **4** DISCOVER, find out, ask, learn, ascertain, investigate, inquire, determine, decide **5** ACCOMPANY, usher, lead, show, take, escort **6** VISIT, consult, speak to, interview, meet, encounter, *formal* chance upon, *colloq.* bump into, run into, come across **7** GO OUT WITH, court, date, take out, keep company with
▷ **see about** arrange, attend to, deal with, take care of, look after, organize, manage, be responsible for, do, fix, repair, sort out
▷ **see through 1** *see through a trick* realize, understand, fathom, penetrate, not be deceived by, not be taken in by, *colloq.* get wise to **2** *see a task through* stick out, continue, persist, persevere, not give up, *colloq.* hang in
▷ **see to** attend to, deal with, take care of, look after, arrange, organize, manage, be responsible for, do, fix, repair, sort out, mind, ensure, make sure, make certain

seed *n*
1 *the seeds of a plant* pip, stone, kernel, nucleus, grain, germ, sperm, ovum, egg, ovule, spawn, embryo, semen, spermatozoon **2** *the seeds of rebellion* source, start, beginning, root, origin, cause, reason(s) **3** OFFSPRING, child, children, young, young one(s), family, heirs, successors, descendants
▷ **go/run to seed** deteriorate, decay, decline, degenerate, get worse, *colloq.* go downhill, got to pot, go to the dogs, go down the tubes

seedy *adj*
1 SHABBY, dirty, untidy, scruffy, tatty, mangy, squalid, run-down, dilapidated, decaying, *colloq.* grotty, crummy, sleazy **2** UNWELL, ill, sick, poorly, ailing,
off-colour, *colloq.* groggy, rough, under the weather, out of sorts
🔁 **2** well

seek *v*
look for, search for, try to find, hunt for, pursue, follow, inquire, ask, invite, request, beg, petition, want, desire, aim, try, attempt, endeavour, strive, *formal* solicit, entreat, aspire

seem *v*
appear, look, have/give the appearance of being, look like, come across as, have the look of, show signs of, give the impression of being, strike you as, feel, sound, pretend to be

seeming *adj*
apparent, outward, external, superficial, surface, supposed, pretended, quasi-, pseudo, specious, *formal* ostensible, assumed
🔁 real

seemingly *adv*
apparently, superficially, on the surface, on the face of it, as far as you can see, outwardly, allegedly, *formal* ostensibly
🔁 really

seemly *adj*
appropriate, proper, suitable, suited, befitting, fit, fitting, decent, nice, attractive, handsome, maidenly, becoming, *comme il faut*, *formal* decorous
🔁 unseemly

seep *v*
ooze, leak, exude, well, trickle, drip, dribble, percolate, drain, permeate, soak

seepage *n*
leak, leakage, dripping, oozing, exudation, percolation, *technical* osmosis

seer *n*
augur, prophet, soothsayer, sibyl, spaeman, spaewife

seesaw *v*
alternate, swing, go from one extreme to the other, fluctuate, oscillate, teeter, pitch, *colloq.* yo-yo

seethe *v*
1 BOIL, simmer, bubble, effervesce, fizz, foam, froth, ferment, rise, swell, surge, teem, swarm **2** RAGE, fume, smoulder, storm, be furious, be outraged, be livid, be incensed, *colloq.* explode, boil over, see red, foam at the mouth

see-through *adj*
transparent, translucent, sheer, filmy, gauzy, gossamer(y), flimsy
🔁 opaque

segment *n, v*
▶ *n* section, division, compartment, part, bit, piece, slice, portion, wedge
🔁 whole
▶ *v* cut up, separate, divide, split, slice, halve, anatomize

segregate *v*
separate, keep apart, set apart, cut off, isolate, dissociate, ostracize, quarantine, set apart, exclude, *formal* sequester
🔁 unite, join

segregation *n*
separation, setting apart, isolation, quarantine, dissociation, apartheid, discrimination, *formal* sequestration
🔁 unification

seize *v*
1 GRAB, snatch, grasp, clutch, grip, hold, get/take hold of, grab hold of **2** *seize property/a plane* take, confiscate, impound, usurp, appropriate, comman-

deer, hijack, annex, kidnap, abduct, *formal* sequestrate **3** *seize a criminal* catch, capture, arrest, ap-pre-
hend, *colloq.* nab, collar, nail, nobble
F₃ 1, 2 let go, release, hand back

seizure *n*
1 FIT, attack, convulsion, paroxysm, spasm **2** TAK-
ING, confiscation, commandeering, hijack, annexation, abduction, snatching, capture, arrest, apprehension, *formal* appropriation, sequestration
F₃ 2 release, liberation

seldom *adv*
rarely, infrequently, occasionally, hardly ever, scarcely
ever, *colloq.* once in a blue moon
F₃ often, usually

select *v, adj*
► *v* choose, pick, single out, decide on, settle on, appoint, elect, favour, prefer, opt for, invite
► *adj* selected, choice, top, prime, first-class, first-
rate, best, finest, supreme, high-quality, hand-picked,
élite, exclusive, limited, privileged, special, excellent,
superior, *colloq.* posh
F₃ second-rate, ordinary, general

selection *n*
1 CHOICE, pick, option, preference **2** ASSORTMENT,
variety, choice, range, line-up, miscellany, medley,
potpourri, collection, anthology

selective *adj*
particular, careful, fussy, finicky, fastidious, discerning, discriminating, *colloq.* choosy, picky, pernickety
F₃ indiscriminate

self *n*
ego, personality, identity, I, person, inner being, soul,
colloq. the real me, heart of hearts

self-assertive *adj*
forceful, pushing, aggressive, authoritarian, commanding, dictatorial, overbearing, heavy-handed,
high-handed, overweening, domineering, *formal* peremptory, *colloq.* bossy, pushy, not backward in coming forward
F₃ compliant

self-assurance *n*
confidence, overconfidence, belief in yourself, self-
confidence, assurance, self-possession, positiveness,
aplomb, cocksureness, *colloq.* cockiness
F₃ humility, unsureness

self-assured *adj*
self-confident, confident, assured, sure of oneself,
self-collected, self-possessed, overconfident, cocksure, *colloq.* cocky
F₃ humble, unsure

self-centred *adj*
selfish, self-seeking, self-serving, self-interested, ego-
tistic(al), narcissistic, self-absorbed, egocentric,
thinking only of yourself, wrapped up in yourself
F₃ altruistic

self-confident *adj*
confident, self-reliant, self-assured, assured, self-
possessed, composed, cool, bold, fearless, positive,
unabashed
F₃ unsure, self-conscious

self-conscious *adj*
uncomfortable, ill at ease, awkward, embarrassed,
blushing, shamefaced, sheepish, shy, diffident,
bashful, coy, retiring, timid, shrinking, self-effacing,
nervous, insecure, *formal* timorous
F₃ natural, unaffected, confident

self-control *n*
calmness, composure, patience, self-restraint, restraint, self-denial, temperance, self-discipline, self-
mastery, willpower, *colloq.* cool

self-denial *n*
moderation, temperance, abstemiousness, asceticism, self-sacrifice, unselfishness, selflessness, *formal* self-abnegation, self-renunciation
F₃ self-indulgence

self-esteem *n*
ego, self-respect, self-regard, self-assurance, self-
confidence, pride, self-pride, dignity, *amour-
propre*
F₃ inferiority complex

self-evident *adj*
obvious, clear, undeniable, axiomatic, unquestionable, incontrovertible, inescapable, *formal* manifest

self-glorification *n*
self-exaltation, self-aggrandizement, self-admiration,
self-advertisement, egotism, egotheism
F₃ humility

self-government *n*
autonomy, independence, home rule, democracy,
self-sovereignty, *formal* autarchy
F₃ subjection

self-importance *n*
arrogance, pompousness, conceit, conceitedness,
vanity, pomposity, big-headedness, self-opinion,
donnism, self-consequence, *colloq.* cockiness, pushiness, bumptiousness
F₃ humility

self-important *adj*
arrogant, pompous, big-headed, conceited, egoistic,
vain, proud, overbearing, swaggering, strutting, self-
consequent, swollen-headed, *colloq.* cocky, pushy,
bumptious
F₃ humble

self-indulgence *n*
extravagance, excess, self-gratification, sensualism,
dissoluteness, intemperance, high living, hedonism,
formal dissipation, profligacy
F₃ self-denial

self-indulgent *adj*
hedonistic, dissolute, extravagant, intemperate, immoderate, *formal* dissipated, profligate
F₃ abstemious

self-interest *n*
selfishness, self-love, self-regard, self-serving, self
F₃ selflessness

selfish *adj*
self-interested, self-seeking, self-serving, mean,
miserly, mercenary, greedy, covetous, self-centred, inconsiderate, egocentric, egotistic(al), *colloq.* thinking
of nobody except yourself
F₃ unselfish, selfless, generous, considerate

selfishness *n*
self-centredness, self-seeking, self-serving, self-love,
self-interest, self-regard, greed, meanness, egotism
F₃ selflessness

selfless *adj*
unselfish, altruistic, self-denying, self-sacrificing,
generous, philanthropic, *formal* magnanimous
F₃ selfish, self-centred

self-possessed *adj*
self-assured, self-collected, calm, collected, composed, confident, unruffled, poised, *colloq.* cool, unflappable, together
F₃ worried

self-possession *n*
calmness, confidence, composure, self-confidence,
coolness, self-command, poise, *formal* aplomb,
sang-froid, *colloq.* cool, unflappability

self-reliance *n*
independence, self-support, self-sufficiency, self-

sustenance, self-sustainment, *technical* autarky, *formal* self-sustentation
🖅 dependence

self-reliant *adj*
independent, self-supporting, self-sufficient, self-sustaining, *technical* autarkic(al)
🖅 dependent

self-respect *n*
pride, dignity, self-esteem, self-assurance, self-confidence, self-regard, *amour-propre*
🖅 inferiority complex

self-restraint *n*
self-discipline, self-denial, self-control, patience, forbearance, moderation, abstemiousness, self-government, temperance, self-command, willpower, *formal* encraty
🖅 licence

self-righteous *adj*
smug, complacent, superior, priggish, pious, sanctimonious, holier-than-thou, pietistic, hypocritical, pharisaical, *colloq.* goody-goody, pi
🖅 humble

self-righteousness *n*
priggishness, piousness, goodiness, sanctimoniousness, pharisaicalness, pharisaism, *colloq.* goody-goodiness
🖅 humility

self-sacrifice *n*
self-denial, selflessness, altruism, unselfishness, generosity, *formal* self-abnegation, self-renunciation
🖅 selfishness

self-satisfaction *n*
smugness, complacency, contentment, pride, self-appreciation, self-approval, *formal* self-approbation
🖅 humility

self-satisfied *adj*
smug, complacent, self-congratulatory, proud, self-righteous, *colloq.* puffed up
🖅 humble

self-seeking *adj*
mercenary, self-interested, selfish, self-loving, self-serving, self-endeared, opportunistic, acquisitive, calculating, careerist, fortune-hunting, gold-digging, *colloq.* on the make
🖅 altruistic

self-styled *adj*
self-appointed, self-titled, professed, so-called, *soi-disant*, would-be, pretended

self-supporting *adj*
self-sufficient, self-financing, self-reliant, independent, self-sustaining
🖅 dependent

self-willed *adj*
stubborn, obstinate, stiff-necked, opinionated, self-opinionative, self-opinionated, headstrong, pig-headed, ungovernable, wilful, bloody-minded, *formal* intractable, refractory, *colloq.* cussed
🖅 complaisant

sell *v*
1 *sell cars* exchange, trade, barter, auction, dispose of, vend, retail, hawk, peddle, tout, *colloq.* flog **2** STOCK, handle, deal in, carry, market, trade in, traffic in, merchandise, import, export **3** PROMOTE, advertise, market, get support/approval for, persuade, win over, *colloq.* push, hype
🖅 **1** buy
▷ **sell out 1** *sell out of fruit* run out of, have none left, be out of stock **2** BETRAY, fail, double-cross, *colloq.* rat on, sell down the river, stab in the back, *slang* fink on

seller *n*
vendor, merchant, trader, supplier, stockist
🖅 buyer, purchaser

> **Types of seller include:**
> agent, auctioneer, bagman, barrow-boy, broker, cold caller, colporteur, commercial traveller, costermonger, dealer, demonstrator, door-to-door salesman/saleswoman, estate agent, factor, hawker, huckster, jobber, knight of the road, market trader, merchandiser, milkman, milklady, pedlar, *US* peddler, *colloq.* rep, representative, retailer, sales assistant, sales clerk, sales executive, saleslady, salesman, salesperson, saleswoman, sales staff, shop assistant, shopkeeper, store clerk, storekeeper, street trader, tallyman, telephone sales-person, ticket agent, tout, tradesman, tradeswoman, traveller, wholesaler. *See also* SHOPS.

selling *n*
dealing, marketing, trading, transactions, traffic, trafficking, merchandising, salesmanship, promotion, *formal* vendition
🖅 buying

semblance *n*
appearance, air, show, pretence, guise, mask, front, façade, veneer, look, aspect, image, resemblance, likeness, similarity, *formal* apparition

seminal *adj*
influential, major, important, original, innovative, productive, creative, formative, imaginative, seminary
🖅 derivative

seminary *n*
college, institute, institution, training-college, academy, school

send *v*
1 POST, mail, get off, address, put in the post/mail, dispatch, consign, forward, redirect, convey, deliver, *formal* remit **2** TRANSMIT, broadcast, beam, relay, communicate, convey, radio, televise **3** PROPEL, drive, move, throw, cast, fling, hurl, launch, fire, shoot, discharge, project, emit, direct **4** THRILL, stimulate, excite, arouse, give pleasure to, *colloq.* turn on, give a buzz/kick
▷ **send for** summon, call for, request, order, command
🖅 dismiss
▷ **send up** satirize, mock, ridicule, parody, mimic, imitate, lampoon, *colloq.* take off, take the mickey out of

send-off *n*
goodbye, farewell, leave-taking, departure, start
🖅 arrival

send-up *n*
mockery, parody, skit, satire, imitation, *colloq.* mickey-take, spoof, take-off

senile *adj*
old, aged, doddering, decrepit, failing, confused, *formal* senescent, *colloq.* gaga

senility *n*
old age, infirmity, dotage, second childhood, senile dementia, decrepitude, anility, *formal* paracme, caducity, senescence

senior *adj*
older, elder, higher, superior, high-ranking, first, major, chief, *formal* doyen(ne), aîné(e)
🖅 junior

seniority *n*
priority, precedence, rank, standing, status, age, superiority, importance

sensation *n*
1 FEELING, sense, impression, perception, awareness, consciousness, emotion, *colloq.* vibes **2** *the report caused a sensation* commotion, stir, agitation, excitement, thrill, furore, outrage, scandal **3** SUCCESS, hit, triumph, *colloq.* winner, wow

sensational *adj*
1 EXCITING, thrilling, electrifying, breathtaking, startling, stirring, amazing, astounding, staggering, dramatic, spectacular, impressive, exceptional, excellent, wonderful, superb, marvellous, *colloq.* smashing, fantastic, terrific, fabulous **2** SCANDALOUS, shocking, horrifying, revealing, melodramatic, lurid
F3 1 ordinary, run-of-the-mill

sense *n, v*
▶ *n* **1** FEELING, sensation, impression, perception, awareness, consciousness, appreciation, faculty, *formal* sensibility **2** REASON, logic, mind, brain(s), wit(s), wisdom, common sense, intelligence, cleverness, understanding, comprehension, apprehension, discernment, judgement, appreciation, intuition, *formal* prudence, judiciousness, *colloq.* gumption, nous, savvy **3** MEANING, significance, definition, interpretation, implication, drift, tenor, nuance, point, purpose, substance, *formal* denotation, import, purport
F3 2 foolishness **3** nonsense
▷ **make sense of** understand, grasp, make out, comprehend, *colloq.* figure out, fathom, make head or tail of
▶ *v* feel, suspect, be aware of, be conscious of, discern, perceive, detect, experience, notice, observe, recognize, realize, appreciate, understand, comprehend, grasp, *formal* intuit, divine, *colloq.* pick up

senseless *adj*
1 FOOLISH, stupid, unwise, silly, idiotic, mad, crazy, moronic, ridiculous, ludicrous, absurd, meaningless, nonsensical, fatuous, irrational, illogical, unreasonable, mindless, pointless, purposeless, futile, *colloq.* daft, dotty, batty **2** UNCONSCIOUS, stunned, anaesthetized, deadened, numb, unfeeling, *formal* insensible, insensate, *colloq.* out, out cold
F3 1 sensible, meaningful, intelligent **2** conscious

sensibility *n*
1 *show sensibility* sensitiveness, sensitivity, susceptibility, discernment, perceptiveness, appreciation, awareness, responsiveness, insight, intuition, delicacy, taste **2** *offend someone's sensibilities* feelings, emotions, sentiments, susceptibilities, sensitivities
F3 1 insensibility

sensible *adj*
1 WISE, well-advised, shrewd, sharp, far-sighted, intelligent, clever, mature, level-headed, down-to-earth, commonsense, commonsensical, sober, sane, rational, logical, reasonable, realistic, practical, functional, sound, *formal* prudent, judicious, sagacious, *colloq.* with both feet on the ground, with your head screwed on (the right way) **2** SENSITIVE, responsive, aware, perceptive, discerning, susceptible, vulnerable **3** *wear sensible shoes* practical, ordinary, everyday, working, serviceable, hard-wearing, strong, tough
F3 1 senseless, foolish, unwise **2** insensitive **3** impractical, fashionable, decorative
▷ **sensible of** sensitive to, understanding, conscious of, aware of, acquainted with, mindful of, observant of, alive to, convinced of, *formal* cognizant of
F3 unaware of

sensitive *adj*
1 SUSCEPTIBLE, vulnerable, impressionable, tender, emotional, thin-skinned, temperamental, touchy, irritable, sensitized, responsive, reactive, aware, perceptive, discerning, appreciative, *formal* sentient **2** DELICATE, fine, fragile, soft, exact, precise **3** *a sensitive issue* delicate, tricky, controversial, difficult, problematic, awkward, touchy **4** *needs sensitive handling* tactful, delicate, diplomatic, careful, considerate, sympathetic, discerning, discreet, well-thought-out
F3 1 insensitive, thick-skinned **2** imprecise, approximate

sensitivity *n*
1 SUSCEPTIBILITY, vulnerability, responsiveness, awareness, perceptiveness, receptiveness, reactiveness, discernment, appreciation, sympathy **2** DELICACY, fineness, fragility, softness
F3 1 insensitivity

sensual *adj*
self-indulgent, voluptuous, sultry, worldly, physical, animal, carnal, fleshly, bodily, sexual, erotic, sexy, lustful, lecherous, lewd, licentious, *colloq.* randy
F3 ascetic

🖉 sensual or **sensuous** ?

Sensual means 'of or concerning the physical senses and the body rather than the mind', and is used especially with a connotation of sexuality or sexual arousal: *a full, sensual mouth*; *a strong desire for sensual pleasure*. *Sensuous* means 'perceived by or affecting the senses, especially in a pleasant way', as in *I find his music very sensuous*; *Her sculptures have a certain sensuous quality to them.*

---

sensuality *n*
voluptuousness, lewdness, lustfulness, salaciousness, sexiness, licentiousness, libertinism, eroticism, carnality, animalism, lasciviousness, debauchery, lecherousness, gourmandize, *formal* profligacy, prurience
F3 asceticism, Puritanism

sensuous *adj*
pleasurable, gratifying, pleasing, pleasant, voluptuous, rich, lush, luxurious, sumptuous, aesthetic
F3 ascetic, plain, simple

🖉 sensuous or **sensual** ? *See panel at* SENSUAL.

---

sentence *n, v*
▶ *n* judgement, decision, verdict, condemnation, pronouncement, ruling, decree, order, punishment
▶ *v* judge, pass judgement on, impose a sentence on, condemn, doom, punish, penalize

sententious *adj*
1 MORALIZING, moralistic, judgemental, sanctimonious, canting, pompous **2** BRIEF, concise, compact, pithy, short, terse, succinct, pointed, epigrammatic, aphoristic, laconic, axiomatic, gnomic, *colloq.* preachy
F3 1 humble **2** verbose

sentient *adj*
conscious, aware, sensitive, responsive, live, living, reactive
F3 *formal* insentient

sentiment *n*
1 THOUGHT, idea, feeling, opinion, view, point of view, judgement, belief, persuasion, attitude **2** EMOTION, sensibility, tenderness, soft-heartedness, softness, romance, romanticism, sentimentality, mawkishness

sentimental *adj*
tender, soft-hearted, emotional, loving, gushing, sugary, touching, pathetic, tear-jerking, maudlin, mawkish, nostalgic, romantic, affectionate, sloppy, soppy, *colloq.* weepy, lovey-dovey, slushy, mushy, schmaltzy, corny, sickly, gushy
F∃ unsentimental, realistic, cynical

sentimentality *n*
tenderness, sentimentalism, emotionalism, romanticism, mawkishness, nostalgia, *formal* bathos, *colloq.* corniness, gush, mush, pulp, schmaltz, sloppiness, slush

sentry *n*
sentinel, guard, picket, watchman, watch, lookout

separable *adj*
divisible, detachable, removable, distinguishable, distinct, independent, different, particular
F∃ inseparable

separate *v, adj*
▶ *v* divide, sever, take/come apart, keep apart, break off, break up, part, split (up), divorce, part company, diverge, dismantle, disconnect, uncouple, disunite, disaffiliate, disentangle, single out, segregate, isolate, cut off, partition, abstract, remove, detach, withdraw, secede, *old use* sunder, *formal* disjoin, become estranged
F∃ join, unite, combine
▶ *adj* different, distinct, unattached, unconnected, unrelated, single, individual, particular, independent, alone, solitary, segregated, isolated, apart, divorced, divided, disunited, disconnected, disjointed, detached, sundry, *formal* disparate, discrete, several, autonomous
F∃ together, attached

separated *adj*
separate, split up, divided, disconnected, parted, isolated, disunited, disassociated, apart, segregated
F∃ attached, together

separately *adv*
independently, individually, singly, apart, discriminately, discretely, alone, personally, *formal* severally
F∃ together

separating *adj*
divisive, isolating, dividing, intervening, partitioning, segregating
F∃ unifying

separation *n*
division, parting, parting of the ways, leave-taking, farewell, split-up, break-up, divorce, split, rift, schism, gap, divergence, disconnection, uncoupling, disengagement, dissociation, segregation, isolation, apartheid, detachment, *formal* severance, estrangement, disseverment
F∃ unification

septic *adj*
infected, poisoned, festering, putrefying, putrid, *formal* putrefactive, suppurating

sepulchral *adj*
gloomy, grave, melancholy, sombre, cheerless, mournful, sad, solemn, dismal, funereal, morbid, deep, hollow, *formal* lugubrious, sepulchrous, woeful
F∃ happy, cheerful

sepulchre *n*
tomb, grave, burial place, vault, mausoleum

sequel *n*
follow-up, continuation, development, result, consequence, outcome, issue, upshot, pay-off, end, conclusion

sequence *n*
succession, series, run, progression, chain, string, train, line, procession, order, arrangement, consequence, course, track, cycle, set

sequester *v*
1 ISOLATE, set apart, seclude, insulate, detach, remove, alienate, shut away, shut off 2 SEQUESTRATE, seize, confiscate, impound, take, commandeer, *formal* appropriate

sequestered *adj*
isolated, secluded, lonely, outback, out-of-the-way, private, remote, quiet, retired, unfrequented, cloistered
F∃ public, busy, frequented

sequestrate *v*
seize, confiscate, impound, take, commandeer, sequester, *formal* appropriate

seraphic *adj*
seraphical, angelic, heavenly, celestial, holy, divine, pure, saintly, innocent, blissful, *formal* beatific, sublime
F∃ demonic

serendipity *n*
chance, coincidence, happy coincidence, accident, luck, fortune, good fortune, *formal* fortuity

serene *adj*
calm, tranquil, cool, composed, placid, untroubled, undisturbed, unclouded, unruffled, still, quiet, peaceful, *formal* halcyon, imperturbable, *colloq.* unflappable
F∃ troubled, disturbed

serenity *n*
calm, calmness, stillness, tranquillity, cool, composure, placidity, peace, peacefulness, quietness, *formal* quietude, *colloq.* unflappability
F∃ anxiety, disruption

series *n*
set, cycle, succession, sequence, run, progression, row, chain, string, line, train, stream, order, arrangement, course, *formal* concatenation

serious *adj*
1 IMPORTANT, significant, weighty, momentous, crucial, critical, urgent, pressing, acute, grave, worrying, difficult, life-and-death, grim, severe, deep, far-reaching, *formal* of consequence, consequential, *colloq.* no joke, no laughing matter 2 UNSMILING, long-faced, humourless, unlaughing, grim, dour, solemn, sober, sombre, grave, grim, stern, thoughtful, quiet, pensive, preoccupied, earnest, genuine, honest, sincere, *colloq.* heavy 3 *serious injuries* severe, acute, critical, grave, bad, dangerous, precarious, life-and-death, grievous, *formal* perilous
F∃ 1 trivial 2 smiling, laughing, joking, light-hearted, facetious, frivolous 3 slight, trivial

seriously *adv*
1 SOLEMNLY, thoughtfully, earnestly, sincerely, joking apart 2 ACUTELY, gravely, badly, severely, critically, dangerously, sorely, distressingly, grievously
F∃ 1 casually 2 slightly

seriousness *n*
1 IMPORTANCE, significance, urgency, weight, gravity, *formal* moment 2 SOLEMNITY, earnestness, humourlessness, sternness, staidness, sedateness, *formal* sobriety, gravitas
F∃ 1 triviality, slightness 2 casualness

sermon *n*
address, discourse, lecture, talk, message, harangue, homily, *formal* oration, exhortation, declamation, *colloq.* talking-to

serpentine *adj*
winding, twisting, tortuous, meandering, coiling, crooked, sinuous, snakelike, snaking, snaky, *formal* serpentiform
F∃ straight

serrated *adj*
toothed, notched, indented, jagged, sawlike, saw-toothed, saw-edged, *formal* serratulate, serrulated
F₃ smooth

serried *adj*
dense, close, close-set, crowded, compact, massed
F₃ scattered

servant *n*
attendant, retainer, hireling, help, helper, assistant, ancillary
F₃ master, mistress

People whose occupation is to serve others include:
au pair, barmaid, barman, batman, *US* bell-hop, boots, butler, care assistant, carer, chambermaid, *colloq.* char, charlady, chauffeur, chauffeuse, chef, cleaner, coachman, commissionaire, cook, *colloq.* daily, *colloq.* dogsbody, domestic, domestic help, drudge, equerry, errand boy, factotum, fag, flunkey, footman, governess, groom, henchman, henchperson, henchwoman, home help, house boy, housekeeper, housemaid, kitchen-maid, lackey, lady-in-waiting, lady's maid, maid, manservant, menial, nanny, ostler, page, page-boy, parlour-maid, scullery maid, scullion, seneschal, *colloq.* skivvy, slave, steward, stewardess, *colloq.* tweeny, valet, waiter, waitress, wet nurse.

serve *v*
1 WAIT ON, attend, minister to, be employed by, work for, help, aid, assist, be of assistance to, benefit, be of benefit to, further, support, be of use to, *formal* succour, *colloq.* do a good turn to 2 *serve a purpose* fulfil, complete, answer, satisfy, perform, carry out, go through, act, function, do the work of, *formal* discharge, suffice 3 DISTRIBUTE, give out, dish up, wait, dole out, present, deliver, take care of, provide, supply

service *n, v*
▶ *n* 1 EMPLOYMENT, work, labour, business, duty, duties, job, function, performance, activity, assistance 2 USE, usefulness, utility, advantage, benefit, help, assistance, *colloq.* turn 3 SERVICING, maintenance, repair(s), overhaul, check 4 *church service* worship, observance, ceremony, rite, ritual, sacrament, ordinance 5 *armed services* forces, air force, navy, army. *See also panel at* ARMED SERVICES. 6 *railway/postal services* facilities, amenities, resources, utilities
▶ *v* maintain, overhaul, check, repair, go over, recondition, tune

serviceable *adj*
usable, useful, helpful, profitable, advantageous, beneficial, utilitarian, simple, plain, unadorned, strong, tough, durable, hard-wearing, dependable, efficient, functional, practical, sensible, convenient
F₃ unserviceable, unusable

servile *adj*
obsequious, toadying, cringing, fawning, grovelling, bootlicking, slavish, subservient, subject, submissive, humble, abject, low, lowly, mean, base, menial, *formal* sycophantic
F₃ assertive, aggressive

servility *n*
obsequiousness, toadyism, grovelling, fawning, bootlicking, self-abasement, slavishness, submissiveness, subservience, meanness, unctuousness, abjection, abjectness, baseness, *formal* sycophancy
F₃ aggressiveness, boldness

serving *n*
helping, portion, share, amount, plateful, bowlful, spoonful, ration

servitude *n*
slavery, enslavement, bondage, obedience, bonds, chains, serfdom, thrall, thraldom, vassalage, villeinage, *formal* subjugation
F₃ freedom, liberty

session *n*
1 MEETING, sitting, hearing, assembly, conference, discussion 2 PERIOD, stretch, spell, time, term, semester, year

set *v, n, adj*
▶ *v* 1 PUT, place, lay (down), locate, situate, position, station, arrange, prepare, make ready, install, lodge, insert, fix, stick, park, deposit, rest, *colloq.* plonk, dump 2 SCHEDULE, appoint, arrange, organize, designate, specify, name, prescribe, ordain, assign, allocate, impose, fix, establish, determine, stipulate, decide, conclude, confirm, settle, agree on, resolve 3 ADJUST, regulate, synchronize, co-ordinate, harmonize, put right 4 *set the table* lay, prepare, get ready, arrange, set out 5 *set something in motion* cause, start, begin, occasion, bring about, produce, prompt, set off, give rise to, lead to, result in, trigger (off) 6 *set someone a task* assign, allocate, give, grant, delegate, choose, select, consign 7 *set a record/precedent* establish, provide, inaugurate, start, begin, create, bring into being 8 *set a trap* prepare, arrange, organize, lay, set up, plan, devise 9 *set words to music* arrange, score, adapt, write, orchestrate, harmonize 10 *the sun sets* go down, go below the horizon, sink, dip, decline, subside, disappear, vanish 11 CONGEAL, thicken, gel, stiffen, become firm/hard, solidify, harden, cake, coagulate, crystallize
F₃ 10 rise
▷ **set about** begin, start, get down to, embark on, undertake, tackle, attack, *formal* commence, *colloq.* set the ball rolling
▷ **set against 1** BALANCE, compare, contrast, weigh, *formal* juxtapose 2 OPPOSE, divide, disunite, alienate, *formal* estrange
▷ **set apart** distinguish, make different, differentiate, mark off, put aside, separate
▷ **set aside 1** PUT ASIDE, lay aside, lay by, keep (back), put away, save, keep in reserve, reserve, set apart, separate, select, earmark, mothball, *colloq.* stash away 2 ANNUL, cancel, reverse, overturn, overrule, reject, ignore, discount, discard, *formal* abrogate, revoke
▷ **set back** delay, hold up, slow, thwart, check, hinder, impede, *formal* retard
▷ **set down 1** LAY DOWN, record, stipulate, assert, affirm, state, establish, formulate, prescribe 2 WRITE DOWN, note (down), record, put in writing
▷ **set forth 1** EXPLAIN, expound, describe, present, set out, clarify, *formal* delineate, elucidate, explicate 2 *set forth on a journey* depart, set out, set off, leave, start out
▷ **set in** begin, start, come, arrive, *formal* commence
▷ **set off 1** LEAVE, depart, set out, start (out), set forth, begin 2 DETONATE, blow up, light, ignite, touch off, trigger off, explode 3 ACTIVATE, trigger (off), touch off, prompt, encourage, initiate, set in motion 4 DISPLAY, show off, enhance, contrast, throw into relief, heighten, intensify
▷ **set on** set upon, attack, assault, turn on, go for, fall upon, lay into, mug, *colloq.* beat up
▷ **set out 1** LEAVE, depart, set off, start (out), begin 2 ARRANGE, lay out, display, exhibit, present, describe, explain
▷ **set up 1** BUILD, raise, elevate, erect, construct, as-

semble, compose, *formal* dispose, array **2** START, form, create, establish, institute, found, inaugurate, initiate, begin, introduce, bring into being, organize, arrange, prepare **3** FRAME, trap, incriminate, accuse falsely, *colloq.* fit up
▶ *n* **1** COLLECTION, batch, series, sequence, kit, outfit, compendium, assortment, class, category, *formal* array, assemblage **2** *a set of people* group, band, gang, crowd, circle, clique, faction **3** *the set of a film* setting, background, scene, scenery, backdrop, wings, *mise-en-scène* **4** *the set of someone's face/body* expression, turn, look, position, posture, *formal* bearing
▶ *adj* **1** FIXED, established, scheduled, appointed, arranged, prearranged, specified, decided, agreed, settled, firm, strict, rigid, inflexible, ingrained, entrenched, *formal* predetermined, prescribed, ordained **2** REGULAR, routine, usual, customary, everyday, traditional, habitual, standard, stock, stereotyped, conventional **3** READY, prepared, equipped, arranged, organized, completed, finished, all set
🔁 **1** undecided, movable **2** spontaneous **3** unprepared

setback *n*
delay, problem, hitch, hiccup, reverse, reversal, stumbling-block, impediment, hindrance, obstruction, misfortune, upset, disappointment, defeat, *colloq.* hold-up, snag, blow
🔁 boost, advance, help, advantage

setting *n*
mounting, frame, surroundings, milieu, environment, background, context, perspective, period, position, location, locale, site, scene, scenery, *mise-en-scène*

setting-up *n*
start, establishment, institution, initiation, inauguration, foundation, founding, introduction, creation, *formal* inception
🔁 abolition, termination

settle *v*
1 AGREE (ON), decide, resolve, reconcile, solve, compromise, fix, establish, determine, decide (on), settle on, choose, confirm, appoint, arrange, *colloq.* patch up, clinch **2** ARRANGE, order, put in order, organize, adjust, complete, conclude **3** SINK, subside, drop, fall, come down, descend, land, alight, light upon, *formal* repose **4** COLONIZE, occupy, populate, people, inhabit, live, make your home, put down roots, *formal* reside **5** *settle a bill* pay, clear, discharge, settle up, square (up), *colloq.* fork out, cough up, foot
▷ **settle down** calm down, make comfortable, quieten, still, soothe, compose

settlement *n*
1 RESOLUTION, agreement, arrangement, contract, decision, conclusion, reconciliation, satisfaction, *formal* termination, *colloq.* patching up **2** ARRANGEMENT, ordering, organization, completion, conclusion **3** PAYMENT, clearance, clearing, liquidation, discharge, *formal* defrayal **4** COLONY, outpost, community, kibbutz, camp, encampment, hamlet, village, plantation, establishment, colonization, occupation, population

settler *n*
colonist, colonizer, pioneer, frontiersman, frontierswoman, planter, immigrant, incomer, newcomer, squatter
🔁 native

set-to *n*
argument, quarrel, conflict, fight, row, squabble, wrangle, disagreement, exchange, fracas, brush, contest, slanging-match, *formal* altercation, *colloq.* argy-bargy, barney, dust-up, scrap, spat

set-up *n*
1 SYSTEM, structure, organization, composition, arrangement, format, framework, business, conditions, circumstances, *formal* disposition **2** FABRICATION, trap, trick, fix, trumped-up charge

sever *v*
1 CUT, split, part, separate, divide, break off, tear off, lop off, chop (off), hack, cut off, amputate, detach, disconnect, disjoin, disunite, *old use* rend, *formal* cleave **2** *sever a relationship* dissociate, alienate, break off, dissolve, end, *formal* cease, terminate, estrange
🔁 **1** join, combine, attach, unite

several *adj*
some, many, a number of, (quite) a few, various, assorted, sundry, diverse, different, distinct, separate, particular, individual, *formal* disparate

severally *adv*
separately, individually, singly, discretely, particularly, respectively, specifically, seriatim, apiece
🔁 simultaneously, together

severe *adj*
1 EXTREME, acute, intense, fierce, violent, strong, forceful, powerful, cruel, pitiless, merciless, relentless, inexorable, harsh, tough, hard, difficult, grim, forbidding, rigorous, stringent, drastic, draconian, tyrannical **2** STRICT, rigid, unbending, stern, grim, dour, cold, unsympathetic, disapproving, sober, serious, unsmiling, strait-laced **3** AUSTERE, ascetic, plain, simple, modest, start, spartan, undecorated, unembellished, unadorned, functional **4** *a severe illness* serious, grave, critical, acute, dangerous, perilous **5** HARD, difficult, demanding, rigorous, arduous, burdensome, taxing, exacting, punishing
🔁 **1** mild, kind, compassionate, sympathetic **2** lenient **3** decorated, ornate **4** minor **5** easy, simple

severely *adv*
1 EXTREMELY, acutely, intensely, badly, critically, dangerously, gravely **2** STRICTLY, rigorously, disapprovingly, sternly, hard, harshly, sharply, sorely, grimly, bitterly, coldly, unsympathetically, dourly

severity *n*
1 EXTREMITY, acuteness, severeness, intensity, strength, forcefulness, fierceness **2** HARSHNESS, hardness, toughness, sharpness, ungentleness, ruthlessness, pitilessness, mercilessness, grimness, stringency, coldness, sternness, strictness, seriousness, gravity **3** AUSTERITY, plainness, rigour, asceticism, simplicity, bareness, plainness, spartanism
🔁 **1** mildness **2** compassion, kindness, leniency

sew *v*
stitch, tack, baste, hem, darn, mend, seam, embroider

sex *n*
1 GENDER, sexuality, sex appeal, sexual desire, libido, sex attraction, sensuality, desirability, allure, seductiveness, glamour, sexiness, magnetism, voluptuousness, *formal* nubility, *colloq.* it **2** SEXUAL INTERCOURSE, intercourse, sexual relations, copulation, lovemaking, fornication, reproduction, union, intimacy, intimate relations, *formal* consummation, coitus, coition, *colloq.* sleeping with someone, going to bed with someone

sexless *adj*
asexual, unsexual, unsexed, unfeminine, unmasculine, undersexed, neuter, *technical* parthenogenetic

sexton *n*
caretaker, verger, grave-digger, grave-maker, fossor, sacristan

sexual *adj*
sex, reproductive, procreative, genital, coital, venereal, carnal, sensual, erotic

sexuality *n*

sexual instincts, sexual urge, sexual orientation, sexual desire, sexiness, sensuality, desire, carnality, eroticism, virility, lust, voluptuousness

sexy *adj*

alluring, desirable, attractive, sensual, voluptuous, nubile, seductive, inviting, flirtatious, arousing, stimulating, slinky, provoking, provocative, titillating, pornographic, erotic, salacious, suggestive, *colloq.* raunchy, beddable

F3 sexless

shabby *adj*

1 RAGGED, tattered, frayed, threadbare, worn, worn-out, mangy, moth-eaten, faded, scruffy, tatty, dowdy, disreputable **2** DILAPIDATED, run-down, broken-down, tumbledown, ramshackle, seedy, dirty, squalid, dingy, poky, in disrepair, *colloq.* tacky **3** *a shabby trick* unfair, contemptible, despicable, rotten, mean, low, cheap, shoddy, unworthy, shameful, dishonourable

F3 1, 2 smart **3** honourable, fair

shack *n*

hut, cabin, shanty, hovel, shed, hutch, lean-to, *colloq.* dump, hole

shackle *v, n*

▶ *v* **1** HAMPER, inhibit, impede, encumber, limit, restrict, restrain, secure, thwart, bind, tie, constrain, obstruct, handicap, hamstring **2** CHAIN, handcuff, bind, restrain, manacle, fetter, trammel, tether

▶ *n* bond, tether, chain, fetter, iron, handcuff, rope, manacle, trammel, *colloq.* bracelets, darbies

shade *n, v*

▶ *n* **1** SHADINESS, shadow(s), darkness, obscurity, semi-darkness, dimness, gloom, gloominess, murkiness, twilight, dusk, gloaming **2** AWNING, canopy, cover, covering, shelter, protection, screen, blind, curtain, veil, shield, visor, umbrella, parasol **3** COLOUR, hue, tint, tone, tinge **4** TRACE, dash, hint, suggestion, suspicion, touch, memory, reminder, nuance, gradation, degree, difference, amount, variety, *colloq.* tad **5** GHOST, spectre, phantom, spirit, apparition, semblance

▷ **a shade** a little, a bit, rather, slightly, a touch, a trifle

▷ **put in the shade** outshine, outclass, surpass, beat, excel, eclipse, outrank, top, dwarf

▶ *v* shield, screen, protect, cover, shroud, veil, hide, conceal, obscure, block light from, cloud, dim, darken, shadow, overshadow

shadow *n, v*

▶ *n* **1** SHADE, darkness, obscurity, inconspicuousness, semi-darkness, dimness, gloom, twilight, dusk, gloaming, cloud, cover, protection, *formal* tenebrosity **2** SILHOUETTE, shape, outline, image, representation **3** *cast a shadow over the proceedings* cloud, gloom, sadness, blight, foreboding **4** FOLLOWER, companion, inseparable companion, pal, detective, sleuth, *colloq.* sidekick **5** TRACE, hint, suggestion, suspicion, vestige, remnant

▷ **a shadow of your former self** vestige, remnant, weaker version, poor imitation

▶ *v* **1** OVERSHADOW, overhang, shade, shield, screen, obscure, darken **2** FOLLOW, tail, dog, stalk, trail, watch

shadowy *adj*

1 DARK, gloomy, murky, obscure, dim, *formal* crepuscular, tenebrous, tenebrose, tenebrious **2** VAGUE, faint, indistinct, ill-defined, indistinguishable, indeterminate, unclear, hazy, nebulous, intangible, unsubstantial, ethereal, ghostly, spectral, phantom, illusory, dreamlike, imaginary, unreal, mysterious

shady *adj*

1 SHADED, shadowy, shielded, screened, protected, covered, shrouded, veiled, dim, dark, obscure, clouded, cool, leafy, bowery, *formal* umbrageous, umbratile, umbratilous, umbriferous, umbrose, umbrous, tenebrous, tenebrose, tenebrious **2** DUBIOUS, questionable, suspect, suspicious, dishonest, crooked, unreliable, untrustworthy, disreputable, unscrupulous, unethical, underhand, *colloq.* fishy, slippery, iffy

F3 1 sunny, sunlit, bright **2** honest, trustworthy, honourable

shaft *n*

1 PASSAGE, duct, tunnel, well, flue **2** HANDLE, shank, stem, upright, pillar, pole, rod, bar, stick, arrow **3** *a shaft of light* ray, dart, pencil, beam, duct, passage, *technical* winze

shaggy *adj*

hairy, long-haired, hirsute, bushy, woolly, unshorn, dishevelled, unkempt, *formal* crinose

F3 bald, shorn, close-cropped

shake *v, n*

▶ *v* **1** *the windows are shaking in the wind* rattle, jolt, jerk, bump, roll, bounce, judder, wag, agitate, twitch, convulse, heave, throb, vibrate, oscillate **2** TREMBLE, quiver, quake, wobble, totter, sway, rock, shiver, shudder, judder, convulse **3** WAVE, swing, flourish, brandish, wield **4** *the news shook her* upset, distress, alarm, shock, shake up, frighten, unnerve, intimidate, disturb, unsettle, agitate, stir, rouse, *formal* discompose, perturb, *colloq.* rattle, faze **5** *shake someone's confidence* weaken, undermine, reduce, diminish, lower, lessen

▷ **shake a leg** hurry, get a move on, *colloq.* get cracking, step on it, look lively

▷ **shake off** get rid of, dislodge, lose, elude, escape, give the slip, leave behind, outdistance, outstrip

▷ **shake up 1** *the accident shook me up* upset, distress, alarm, shock, unnerve, unsettle, *colloq.* rattle **2** *shake up an organization* reorganize, rearrange, *colloq.* reshuffle

▶ *n* **1** JOLT, rattle, roll, bounce, rocking, jerk, judder, twitch, throbbing, vibration, oscillation **2** TREMBLING, convulsion, quiver, quake, quaking, shiver, shivering, shudder, shuddering **3** SHOCK, upset, alarm, disturbance, jolt, unsettling

shake-up *n*

reorganization, rearrangement, disturbance, upheaval, *colloq.* reshuffle

shaky *adj*

1 TREMBLING, quivering, quavery, faltering, unsteady, wobbly, tottering, tottery, staggering, doddering, tentative, uncertain, *formal* tremulous **2** UNSTABLE, unsteady, insecure, precarious, wobbly, rocky, tottery, rickety, weak **3** DUBIOUS, questionable, suspect, weak, flimsy, unreliable, unsound, unfounded, ungrounded, unsupported, untrustworthy

F3 2 firm, strong

shallow *adj*

1 *shallow water/containers* superficial, surface, skin-deep **2** *a shallow person* superficial, slight, flimsy, trivial, frivolous, foolish, idle, empty, petty, trifling, meaningless, unscholarly, ignorant, simple, insincere

F3 1 deep, profound **2** deep, profound, serious, careful

sham *n, adj, v*

▶ *n* **1** PRETENCE, fraud, counterfeit, imposture, forgery, fake, copy, imitation, simulation, feigning, hoax, *colloq.* humbug **2** IMPOSTOR, fraud, fake, charlatan, impersonator, pretender, deceiver, cheat, swindler, *colloq.* phoney, con man

▶ *adj* false, fake, counterfeit, spurious, bogus, pretended, feigned, make-believe, put-on, simulated,

artificial, mock, imitation, synthetic, *colloq.* phoney
☒ genuine, authentic, real
▶ *v* pretend, feign, put on, make believe, simulate, imitate, fake, counterfeit, *formal* affect, dissemble

shaman *n*
magician, sorcerer, witch doctor, medicine man, medicine woman, powwow, pawaw, angekok

shamble *v*
shuffle, scrape, drag, falter, limp, toddle, doddle, hobble

shambles *n*
mess, chaos, muddle, confusion, disorganization, disorder, havoc, anarchy, bedlam, wreck, *formal* disarray, *colloq.* madhouse, pigsty

shambling *adj*
awkward, clumsy, unsteady, ungainly, lumbering, lurching, shuffling, unco-ordinated, disjointed, loose
☒ agile, neat, nimble, spry

shame *n, v*
▶ *n* **1** HUMILIATION, degradation, shamefacedness, remorse, guilt, embarrassment, mortification, *formal* compunction **2** DISGRACE, dishonour, discredit, stain, stigma, disrepute, infamy, scandal, *formal* ignominy, opprobrium **3** *it's a shame* pity, disappointment, misfortune, unfortunate thing, bad luck
☒ **1** pride **2** honour, credit, distinction
▷ **put to shame** show up, humiliate, humble, embarrass, mortify, disgrace, upstage, outshine, outclass, outstrip, surpass, eclipse
▶ *v* embarrass, mortify, abash, confound, humiliate, ridicule, humble, put to shame, show up, disgrace, dishonour, discredit, debase, degrade, sully, taint, stain

shamefaced *adj*
ashamed, conscience-stricken, guilty, regretful, penitent, remorseful, contrite, apologetic, sorry, red-faced, blushing, embarrassed, mortified, abashed, humiliated, uncomfortable, *colloq.* sheepish
☒ unashamed, proud

shameful *adj*
1 *a shameful waste of money* disgraceful, outrageous, shocking, scandalous, indecent, abominable, atrocious, wicked, mean, base, low, vile, reprehensible, dishonourable, discreditable, inglorious, contemptible, unworthy, ignoble, *formal* heinous **2** EMBARRASSING, mortifying, shaming, humiliating, *formal* ignominious
☒ **1** honourable, creditable, worthy

shameless *adj*
1 UNASHAMED, unabashed, unrepentant, unregretful, impenitent, barefaced, flagrant, blatant, brazen, brash, audacious, insolent, imprudent, defiant, hardened, incorrigible **2** IMMODEST, indecent, improper, unprincipled, wanton, dissolute, corrupt, depraved, *formal* unbecoming, indecorous, unseemly
☒ **1** ashamed, shamefaced, contrite **2** modest

shanty *n*
hut, cabin, shed, shack, lean-to, hovel, bothy, hutch

shape *n, v*
▶ *n* **1** FORM, outline, outward appearance, silhouette, profile, model, mould, pattern, cut, lines, contours, figure, physique, build, structure, frame, design, format, *formal* configuration **2** APPEARANCE, guise, likeness, form, look, aspect, image, air, guise, semblance **3** *in good shape* condition, state, form, health, trim, fettle, kilter **4** PATTERN, mould, model, format, structure, character, *formal* configuration

Geometrical shapes include:
circle, semicircle, quadrant, oval, ellipse, crescent, triangle, equilateral triangle, isosceles triangle, scalene triangle, quadrilateral, square, rectangle, oblong, rhombus, diamond, kite, trapezium, parallelogram, polygon, pentagon, hexagon, heptagon, octagon, nonagon, decagon, polyhedron, cube, cuboid, prism, pyramid, tetrahedron, pentahedron, octahedron, cylinder, cone, sphere, hemisphere.

▶ *v* form, fashion, model, mould, cast, forge, sculpt, sculpture, carve, whittle, make, guide, influence, develop, produce, construct, create, design, define, devise, frame, block, plan, prepare, organize, develop, adapt, adjust, regulate, accommodate, alter, modify, remodel
▷ **shape up** develop, come on, take shape, progress, make progress, move forward, make headway, flourish

shapeless *adj*
formless, amorphous, unformed, unfashioned, undeveloped, unframed, nebulous, unstructured, irregular, misshapen, badly proportioned, ill-proportioned, deformed, dumpy

shapely *adj*
elegant, pretty, attractive, well-proportioned, well-formed, well-turned, trim, neat, graceful, gainly, curvaceous, voluptuous

shard *n*
fragment, piece, bit, part, chip, particle, splinter, shiver

share *v, n*
▶ *v* divide, split, go halves, partake, participate, have a share in, share out, distribute, dole out, give out, hand out, deal out, allot, allocate, assign, *formal* apportion, *colloq.* go fifty-fifty, go Dutch, carve up
▶ *n* portion, ration, quota, allowance, allocation, allotment, lot, part, division, proportion, percentage, dividend, due, contribution, *colloq.* cut, whack, rake-off, slice of the cake, piece/slice of the action
▷ **share out** give out, distribute, hand out, mete out, divide up, parcel out, allot, apportion, assign
☒ monopolize

shark *n*
1 *a man-eating shark*

Types of shark include:
basking, blue, dogfish, fox, ghost, goblin, great white, Greenland, grey reef, hammerhead, leopard, mackerel, mako, man-eating, nurse, porbeagle, requiem, saw, thresher, tiger, whale.

2 CROOK, extortioner, swindler, parasite, slicker, *colloq.* fleecer, sponger, wheeler-dealer

sharp *adj, adv*
▶ *adj* **1** *a sharp needle* pointed, keen, edged, knife-edged, razor-edged, razor-sharp, needle-like, cutting, serrated, jagged, barbed, spiky **2** QUICK-WITTED, quick, clever, bright, intelligent, alert, shrewd, astute, perceptive, observant, discerning, penetrating **3** HARSH, brusque, incisive, cutting, biting, cruel, hurtful, malicious, caustic, sarcastic, sardonic, scathing, vitriolic, venomous, *formal* trenchant, acrimonious **4** CLEAR, clear-cut, well-defined, distinct, crisp **5** SUDDEN, abrupt, unexpected, violent, fierce, rapid, tight, intense, extreme, severe, keen, acute, piercing, stinging, shooting, stabbing **6** PUNGENT, strong, piquant, sour, tart, vinegary, bitter, biting, acerbic, acid, acidic, burning, acrid **7** CRAFTY, clever, deceptive, dishonest, cunning, artful, wily, sly **8** *a sharp dresser* neat, tidy, smart, elegant, stylish, fashionable, *colloq.* snappy, natty
☒ **1** blunt **2** slow, stupid **3** mild **4** blurred **5** gentle **6** bland **8** shabby
▶ *adv* punctually, promptly, on the dot, exactly, pre-

cisely, abruptly, suddenly, unexpectedly
🔁 approximately, roughly

sharpen *v*
edge, whet, hone, grind, file, keen, strop, *formal* acuminate
🔁 blunt, blur

sharp-eyed *adj*
observant, perceptive, noticing, eagle-eyed, hawk-eyed, keen-sighted
🔁 short-sighted, unobservant

sharpness *n*
1 DISCERNMENT, penetration, acuteness, keenness, astuteness, shrewdness, observation, perceptiveness, incisiveness, eagerness **2** INTENSITY, fierceness, severity **3** HARSHNESS, brusqueness, cruelty, incisiveness, sarcasm, vitriol, venom **4** CLARITY, definition, precision, crispness

shatter *v*
1 BREAK, smash, splinter, shiver, crack, split, burst, explode, blast, crush, demolish, smash/blow to smithereens, *formal* pulverize **2** *shatter your hopes* destroy, devastate, dash, crush, wreck, ruin, disappoint, overturn **3** *shattered by her death* upset, devastate, crush, overwhelm, break your heart

shattered *adj*
1 OVERWHELMED, devastated, crushed, broken **2** WORN OUT, exhausted, weary, tired out, *colloq.* all in, dead beat, dog-tired, done in, knackered, zonked

shattering *adj*
devastating, damaging, crushing, overwhelming, paralysing, severe

shave *v*
cut, trim, barber, shear, crop, fleece, graze, brush, touch, pare, cut, plane, scrape

sheaf *n*
bundle, bunch, armful, truss

sheath *n*
1 SCABBARD, case, sleeve, envelope, shell, wrapping, casing, covering **2** CONDOM, protective contraceptive, *US* prophylactic

shed¹ *v*
1 DROP, cast (off), moult, discard, slough, spill **2** GET RID OF, pour, spill, scatter, diffuse, emit, shower, throw, radiate, shine

shed² *n*
a garden shed hut, outhouse, lean-to, building, outbuilding, shack

sheen *n*
lustre, gloss, shine, gleam, sparkle, shimmer, brightness, brilliance, shininess, polish, burnish, *formal* patina
🔁 dullness, tarnish

sheep *n*
ram, ewe, lamb, wether, tup, bell-wether, *Austral. colloq.* jumbuck

sheepish *adj*
ashamed, shamefaced, embarrassed, mortified, chastened, abashed, uncomfortable, self-conscious, silly, foolish
🔁 unabashed, brazen, bold

sheer¹ *adj*
1 UTTER, complete, total, absolute, thorough, mere, pure, unadulterated, downright, out-and-out, rank, veritable, thoroughgoing, unconditional, unqualified, *formal* unmitigated **2** *a sheer drop* vertical, perpendicular, precipitous, abrupt, steep, sharp **3** THIN, fine, light, delicate, flimsy, gauzy, gossamer, translucent, transparent, see-through, *formal* diaphanous
🔁 **2** gentle, gradual **3** thick, heavy

sheer² *v*
sheer away to the right swerve, turn, bend, veer, swing, shift, drift, deviate, diverge, deflect

sheet *n*
1 *cotton sheets* cover, blanket, bed-linen **2** COVERING, coating, coat, film, layer, stratum, skin, membrane, veneer, overlay, plate, piece, panel, slab, plate, pane, *formal* lamina **3** *a sheet of paper* leaf, page, folio **4** *a sheet of ice* expanse, stretch, reach, sweep, surface

shelf *n*
1 *put books on the shelf* ledge, mantelpiece, mantelshelf, sill, step, bench, bracket, counter, bar **2** *the shelf on the seabed* bank, sandbank, reef, ledge, terrace, continental shelf, sand bar, bar, step, shoal

shell *n, v*
▶ *n* **1** COVERING, hull, husk, pod, rind, crust, case, carapace, casing, body, chassis, frame, framework, structure, skeleton, *technical* integument, *US* shuck **2** EXPLOSIVE, bullet, shot, pellet, missile, grenade
▶ *v* **1** *shell nuts* hull, husk, pod, *US* shuck **2** BOMB, bombard, fire on, barrage, blitz, attack
▷ **shell out** pay out, spend, lay out, give, contribute, donate, expend, *formal* disburse, *colloq.* ante, cough up, fork out

shelter *n, v*
▶ *n* cover, roof, shade, shadow, protection, shield, screen, defence, guard, security, safety, sanctuary, asylum, haven, refuge, harbour, retreat, accommodation, lodging
🔁 exposure
▶ *v* cover, shroud, screen, shade, shadow, protect, defend, guard, safeguard, shield, harbour, hide, conceal, accommodate, put up
🔁 expose

sheltered *adj*
covered, shaded, shady, shielded, protected, screened, cosy, snug, warm, quiet, secluded, isolated, retired, withdrawn, reclusive, cloistered, unworldly
🔁 exposed

shelve *v*
postpone, defer, put off, suspend, halt, put aside, lay aside, pigeonhole, mothball, *colloq.* put on ice, put on the back burner
🔁 expedite, implement

shepherd *n, v*
▶ *n* shepherdess, herdess, shepherdling, herdsman, protector, shepherd boy, herdboy, guardian
▶ *v* guide, lead, conduct, convoy, escort, usher, steer, marshal, herd

shield *n, v*
▶ *n* buckler, defence, bulwark, rampart, support, screen, guard, cover, shelter, protection, protector, safeguard, targe, *technical* escutcheon
▶ *v* defend, guard, protect, safeguard, screen, shade, shadow, cover, shelter
🔁 expose

shift *v, n*
▶ *v* **1** CHANGE, vary, fluctuate, alter, adjust, modify, move, budge, relocate, reposition, rearrange, transfer, carry, switch, swerve, veer, *formal* transpose **2** REMOVE, dislodge, displace, get rid of
▶ *n* **1** CHANGE, variation, fluctuation, alteration, modification, move, movement, removal, switch, displacement, relocation, rearrangement, transfer, *formal* transposition, *colloq.* U-turn **2** *work shifts* period, spell, time, stretch, span, stint

shiftless *adj*
lazy, idle, unambitious, unenterprising, resourceless, aimless, directionless, goalless, incompetent, inefficient, irresponsible, inept, feckless, *formal* indolent,

ineffectual, slothful, *colloq.* good-for-nothing, lackadaisical

🔁 enterprising, ambitious, aspiring, eager

shifty *adj*
untrustworthy, dishonest, deceitful, scheming, contriving, tricky, wily, crafty, cunning, devious, evasive, furtive, underhand, dubious, *formal* duplicitous, *colloq.* shady, slippery, iffy

🔁 dependable, honest, open

shilly-shally *v*
dither, hesitate, vacillate, waver, fluctuate, falter, teeter, seesaw, *formal* prevaricate, *colloq.* dilly-dally, hem and haw, mess about

shimmer *v, n*
  ▶ *v* glisten, gleam, sparkle, glimmer, glint, glitter, scintillate, glow, flicker, twinkle
  ▶ *n* lustre, gleam, sparkle, glint, glimmer, glitter, glistening, glow, flicker, twinkle, *formal* iridescence

shimmering *adj*
glittering, glowing, glistening, gleaming, shining, shiny, lustrous, luminous, *technical* aventurine, *formal* incandescent, iridescent

🔁 dull, matt

shin *v*
climb, mount, soar, scramble, ascend, clamber, scale, shoot, swarm

shine *v, n*
  ▶ *v* **1** BEAM, radiate, glow, flash, glare, dazzle, gleam, glint, glitter, flicker, sparkle, twinkle, shimmer, glisten, glimmer, give off, emit, *formal* incandesce **2** POLISH, burnish, gloss, buff, brush, rub (up), wax **3** *shine at athletics* excel, stand out, be brilliant, be excellent, be outstanding, be pre-eminent
  ▶ *n* **1** LIGHT, radiance, glow, brightness, glare, dazzle, flash, gleam, sparkle, shimmer, glitter, glint, flicker, twinkle, *formal* effulgence, luminescence, incandescence, lambency **2** GLOSS, polish, burnish, gleam, sheen, lustre, glaze, *formal* patina

shininess *n*
brightness, gleam, glitter, shine, sheen, polish, lustre, glossiness, burnish, *formal* effulgence

🔁 dullness

shining *adj*
1 BRIGHT, radiant, glowing, beaming, flashing, gleaming, glittering, glinting, glistening, shimmering, twinkling, sparkling, flickering, luminous, brilliant, splendid, glorious, *formal* phosphorescent, resplendent, effulgent, incandescent **2** *a shining example* conspicuous, outstanding, splendid, magnificent, glorious, brilliant, leading, eminent, pre-eminent, celebrated, distinguished, illustrious

🔁 **1** dark

shiny *adj*
polished, burnished, shining, sheeny, lustrous, glossy, silky, sleek, bright, gleaming, glistening, shimmering

🔁 dull, matt

ship *n*
vessel, craft, liner, steamer, tanker, trawler, ferry, boat, yacht

---

Parts of a ship include:
anchor, berth, bilge, boiler room, bollard, bridge, brig, bulkhead, bulwarks, bunk, cabin, capstan, chain locker, chart room, cleat, companion ladder, companion way, crow's nest, davit; deck, after deck, boat deck, flight deck, gun deck, lower deck, main deck, poop deck, promenade deck, quarter deck, top deck; engine room, figurehead, forecastle (fo'c'sle), funnel, galley, gangplank, gangway, gunwale (gunnel), hammock, hatch, hatchway, hawser, head,

hold, keel, landing, mast, oar, paddle wheel, pilot house, Plimsoll line, port, porthole, prow, quarter, radio room, rigger, rowlock, rudder, sail, stabilizer, stanchion, starboard, stateroom, stern, superstructure, tiller, transom, wardroom, waterline, wheel, winch. *See also* BOAT; SAIL.

---

shipshape *adj*
tidy, neat, orderly, spruce, trim, well-organized, well-planned, businesslike, well-regulated, spick and span, trig

🔁 disorderly, untidy

shirk *v*
dodge, get out of, evade, avoid, shun, shrink from, play truant, slack, *colloq.* duck, skive

shirker *n*
dodger, slacker, idler, layabout, loafer, absentee, truant, malingerer, shirk, *colloq.* quitter, skiver

shiver¹ *v, n*
  ▶ *v shivering with cold* shudder, tremble, quiver, quake, shake, vibrate, palpitate, flutter
  ▶ *n* shudder, quiver, shake, tremor, twitch, start, vibration, flutter

shiver² *n, v*
  ▶ *n shivers of light* splinter, piece, bit, fragment, shred, sliver, shaving, chip, shard, *colloq.* smither-een(s)
  ▶ *v* shatter, break, smash, splinter, crack, split

shivery *adj*
cold, chilly, trembly, shuddery, shaking, quivery, quaking, chilled, nervous, fluttery

shoal *n*
group, mass, multitude, mob, throng, swarm, horde, flock, *formal* assemblage

shock *v, n*
  ▶ *v* disgust, revolt, repel, sicken, offend, nauseate, appal, outrage, scandalize, outrage, horrify, startle, astound, stagger, amaze, stun, daze, stupefy, numb, paralyse, traumatize, jolt, jar, shake, agitate, unsettle, upset, distress, disquiet, unnerve, bewilder, take aback, confound, dumbfound, dismay, *formal* perturb, *colloq.* bowl over

🔁 delight, please, gratify, reassure

  ▶ *n* **1** FRIGHT, start, jolt, surprise, blow, trauma, upset, distress, dismay, disgust, outrage, horror, *formal* consternation, perturbation, *colloq.* bombshell, thunderbolt, bolt from the blue, rude awakening **2** IMPACT, crash, collision, blow, shake, jolt, jarring, jerk

🔁 **1** delight, pleasure, reassurance

shocking *adj*
appalling, outrageous, scandalous, offensive, horrifying, disgraceful, deplorable, intolerable, unbearable, atrocious, abominable, monstrous, vile, foul, unspeakable, detestable, abhorrent, dreadful, loathsome, awful, terrible, frightful, ghastly, hideous, horrible, horrific, disgusting, revolting, repulsive, sickening, nauseating, unsettling, disquieting, distressing, *formal* perturbing, repugnant

🔁 acceptable, satisfactory, pleasant, delightful

shoddy *adj*
inferior, second-rate, cheap, tawdry, tatty, trashy, rubbishy, poor, poor-quality, careless, slipshod, slapdash, cheapjack, *colloq.* ropy, tacky, rubbish

🔁 superior, well-made

shoe *n*
See FOOTWEAR.

shoot *v, n*
  ▶ *v* **1** FIRE, discharge, launch, propel, kick, hit, throw, hurl, fling, lob, project, let off, aim, direct **2** HIT, kill, injure, wound, open fire, blast, bombard, gun down, shell, snipe at, pick off, *colloq.* zap **3** DART, bolt, dash,

tear, rush, race, sprint, speed, hurry, charge, fly, hurtle, streak, whisk, whiz **4** *shoot a film* film, photograph, take photographs of, video, *colloq.* snap **5** GROW, germinate, shoot up, sprout, burgeon, bolt, bud, stretch
▶ *n* sprout, bud, offshoot, branch, twig, sprig, cutting, slip, scion, graft, tendron

shop *n, v*
▶ *n* store, retail outlet, *formal* emporium

Types of shop include:
bazaar, market, indoor market, stall, mini-market, general store, corner shop, shopping precinct, shopping mall, arcade, complex, mall, plaza, galleria, chain store, department store, supermarket, superstore, hypermarket, cash-and-carry; butcher, baker, grocer, greengrocer, fishmonger, dairy, delicatessen, health-food shop, farm shop, fish and chip shop, take-away, off-licence, tobacconist, sweet shop, confectioner, tuck shop; bookshop, newsagent, stationer, chemist, pharmacy, tailor, outfitter, dress shop, boutique, milliner, shoe shop, haberdasher, draper, florist, jeweller, toy shop, hardware shop, ironmonger, saddler, radio and TV shop, video shop; launderette, hairdresser, barber, betting shop, bookmaker, *colloq.* bookie, pawnbroker, post office.

▶ *v* **1** *shop for clothes* go shopping, buy, buy things, do the shopping, stock up on, get, purchase **2** INFORM ON, betray, *colloq.* tell on, split, squeal, rat, blow the whistle on, *slang* grass

shore¹ *n*
walk along the shore seashore, beach, sand(s), shingle, strand, waterfront, front, promenade, coast, seaside, seaboard, foreshore, lakeside, bank

shore² *v*
shore up a building support, hold (up), prop (up), stay, underpin, buttress, brace, strengthen, reinforce

shorn *adj*
cut, cropped, shaved, shaven, stripped, bald, beardless, crew-cut, deprived

short *adj, adv*
▶ *adj* **1** BRIEF, cursory, fleeting, momentary, short-lived, transitory, temporary, concise, succinct, terse, crisp, pithy, to the point, compact, compressed, shortened, condensed, truncated, curtailed, abbreviated, abridged, summarized, summary, *formal* ephemeral, evanescent **2** SMALL, little, low, petite, slight, minuscule, diminutive, squat, dumpy, stubby, *Scot.* wee, *colloq.* teeny, pint-size(d) **3** INADEQUATE, insufficient, deficient, lacking, wanting, low, poor, meagre, scarce, scanty, scant, sparse, *colloq.* tight **4** BRUSQUE, curt, gruff, snappy, sharp, abrupt, terse, blunt, direct, rude, impolite, discourteous, uncivil
₣ **1** long, lasting **2** tall **3** adequate, ample **4** polite
▶ *adv* unexpectedly, suddenly, abruptly
▷ **fall short** be less than required, be lacking, be insufficient, be inadequate
▷ **in short** in brief, in a word, in a few words, in conclusion, summarizing, concisely, *colloq.* in a nutshell, to cut a long story short
▷ **short of** deficient in, lacking, missing, short on, less than, low on, other than, *formal* wanting, *colloq.* pushed for

shortage *n*
inadequacy, insufficiency, deficiency, shortfall, deficit, lack, want, need, scarcity, poverty, absence, dearth, *formal* paucity
₣ sufficiency, abundance, surplus

shortcoming *n*
defect, imperfection, fault, flaw, drawback, failing, weak point, weakness, frailty, foible

shorten *v*
cut (down), trim, prune, crop, dock, pare (down), curtail, truncate, abbreviate, abridge, condense, compress, contract, sum up, reduce, lessen, decrease, diminish, take up
₣ lengthen, enlarge, amplify

shortened *adj*
abridged, condensed, summarized, abbreviated, abstracted, *formal* abbreviatory
₣ amplified

short-lived *adj*
brief, momentary, passing, short, temporary, transient, transitory, fleeting, impermanent, *technical* caducous, *formal* ephemeral, evanescent, fugacious
₣ abiding, enduring, lasting, long-lived

shortly *adv*
1 SOON, in a little while, in a while, before long, presently, by and by **2** BRUSQUELY, curtly, gruffly, sharply, abruptly, tersely, bluntly, directly, rudely, impolitely, discourteously, uncivilly

short-sighted *adj*
1 MYOPIC, near-sighted **2** IMPROVIDENT, unwise, unthinking, impolitic, ill-advised, thoughtless, careless, rash, heedless, hasty, ill-considered, *formal* imprudent, injudicious, uncircumspect
₣ **1** long-sighted, far-sighted

short-staffed *adj*
shorthanded, understaffed, with insufficient staff, below strength

short-tempered *adj*
bad-tempered, impatient, irritable, hot-tempered, quick-tempered, fiery, irascible, choleric, crusty, *colloq.* ratty, testy, touchy
₣ calm, patient, placid

short-winded *adj*
breathless, gasping, panting, puffing

shot¹ *n*
1 GUNFIRE, discharge, blast, bang, crack, explosion **2** BULLET, ammunition, missile, projectile, ball, pellet, *colloq.* slug **3** *have a shot at goal* kick, hit, throw, fling, lob **4** PHOTOGRAPH, photo, snap, snapshot, print, picture, image **5** ATTEMPT, try, effort, endeavour, guess, turn, *colloq.* go, bash, whack, crack, stab **6** INJECTION, inoculation, immunization, vaccination, dose, *colloq.* jab, *slang* fix
▷ **call the shots** be in charge, lead, give a lead, head (up), manage, direct, supervise, command
▷ **like a shot** without delay, without hesitation, immediately, instantly, at once, eagerly, enthusiastically, willingly
▷ **shot in the arm** encouragement, stimulus, boost, fillip, lift, uplift, impetus, fresh talent
▷ **shot in the dark** guess, guesswork, wild guess, blind guess, conjecture, speculation

shot² *adj*
shot fabric variegated, mottled, watered, moiré, iridescent

shoulder *v*
1 ACCEPT, assume, take on, take upon yourself, bear, carry, sustain, support **2** PUSH, shove, jostle, thrust, press, force, elbow
▷ **rub shoulders with** meet with, associate with, socialize with, mix with, fraternize with, *colloq.* hobnob with
▷ **shoulder to shoulder** side by side, hand in hand, together, co-operatively, working together, closely, in alliance

shout *v, n*
- ▶ *v* call (out), cry (out), scream, shriek, yell, raise your voice, rant and rave, squawk, roar, bellow, bawl, howl, bay, cheer, *colloq.* holler, *US* yawp
- ▶ *n* call, cry, scream, shriek, yell, squawk, roar, bellow, bawl, howl, bay, cheer, *colloq.* holler, *US* yawp

shove *v, n*
- ▶ *v* push, thrust, drive, propel, force, barge, jolt, jostle, elbow, shoulder, press, crowd
- ▷ **shove off** leave, depart, *colloq.* beat it, clear off, push off, get lost, scram, scarper, clear out, skedaddle, vamoose, do a bunk
- ▶ *n* push, thrust, jolt, jostle, elbow, shoulder

shovel *n, v*
- ▶ *n* spade, scoop, bucket
- ▶ *v* dig, excavate, scoop, dredge, clear, move, shift, spade, heap

show *v, n*
- ▶ *v* **1** REVEAL, expose, uncover, disclose, divulge, make visible, make clear, make plain, make known, *formal* manifest **2** EXPRESS, mean, indicate, signify, register, record, portray, depict, make it clear, be evidence, bear witness to, suggest, *formal* manifest **3** TEACH, instruct, clarify, make clear, elucidate, point out, explain, demonstrate, prove, illustrate, exemplify, *formal* expound **4** DISPLAY, exhibit, demonstrate, set out, present, produce, offer **5** *show him out* lead, guide, direct, conduct, steer, take, usher, escort, accompany, attend **6** *he didn't show* appear, arrive, come, turn up
- ⊟ **1** hide, cover (up)
- ▷ **show off** parade, strut, swagger, brag, boast, flaunt, brandish, display, exhibit, demonstrate, show to advantage, advertise, set off, enhance, *colloq.* swank
- ▷ **show up 1** REVEAL, show, make visible, expose, unmask, lay bare, highlight, pinpoint **2** HUMILIATE, embarrass, mortify, shame, put to shame, disgrace, let down **3** ARRIVE, come, turn up, appear, *colloq.* materialize
- ▶ *n* **1** ENTERTAINMENT, performance, programme, production, staging, showing, spectacle, extravaganza **2** EXHIBITION, fair, parade, presentation, demonstration, display, spectacle, *formal* exposition, *colloq.* expo **3** DISPLAY, representation, demonstration, presentation, sign, indication, arrangement, *formal* manifestation, array **4** PRETENCE, semblance, façade, front, illusion, ostentation, parade, flamboyance, panache, showiness, exhibitionism, pose, *formal* affectation, *colloq.* window dressing, play-acting, pizzazz **5** APPEARANCE, air, impression, guise, display, profession **6** *Who's running the show?* affair, proceedings, organization, undertaking, operation

showdown *n*
confrontation, clash, crisis, climax, moment of truth, culmination, dénouement, face-off

shower *n, v*
- ▶ *n* rain, drizzling, stream, torrent, sprinkling, deluge, hail, volley, barrage
- ▶ *v* spray, sprinkle, rain, pour, fall, deluge, inundate, overwhelm, load, heap, lavish

showiness *n*
flamboyance, pretentiousness, glitter, glitz, ostentation, razzle-dazzle, *colloq.* flashiness, pizzazz, razzmatazz, swank
⊟ restraint

showing *n, adj*
- ▶ *n* display, evidence, impression, representation, record, presentation, performance, exhibition, show, staging, account, statement, appearance, past performance, *colloq.* track record

- ▶ *adj* explanatory, demonstrative, descriptive, illustrative, indicative, representative, significant, symbolic, *formal* explicatory, elucidative, revelatory

showing-off *n*
boasting, self-advertisement, bragging, exhibitionism, braggadocio, swagger, egotism, peacockery, *formal* vainglory, *colloq.* swank
⊟ modesty

showman *n*
performer, entertainer, impresario, publicist, ringmaster, self-advertiser, *colloq.* show-off

show-off *n*
swaggerer, braggart, boaster, exhibitionist, peacock, poser, poseur, posturer, egotist, *colloq.* swanker, know-all

showy *adj*
flashy, flamboyant, ostentatious, gaudy, garish, glittering, loud, tawdry, fancy, ornate, pretentious, pompous, *colloq.* swanky, flash
⊟ quiet, restrained

shred *n*
1 SCRAP, ribbon, tatter, rag, snippet, sliver, bit, piece, fragment, remnant, particle, modicum, speck **2** JOT, iota, atom, grain, mite, whit, trace, whisp

shred *v*
cut (up), tear (up), rip (up), chop, slice

shrew *n*
dragon, nag, scold, termagant, virago, vixen, Xanthippe, harridan, henpecker, spitfire, Fury

shrewd *adj*
astute, well-advised, calculated, far-sighted, smart, clever, intelligent, sharp, keen, acute, alert, perceptive, observant, discerning, discriminating, knowing, calculating, cunning, crafty, wily, canny, artful, sly, *formal* callid, judicious, sagacious, perspicacious
⊟ unwise, obtuse, naïve, unsophisticated

shrewdly *adv*
astutely, cleverly, far-sightedly, wisely, knowingly, perceptively, craftily, cannily, artfully, slyly, *formal* judiciously, sagaciously, perspicaciously

shrewdness *n*
discernment, intelligence, perceptiveness, sharpness, acuteness, astuteness, grasp, judgement, penetration, wisdom, acumen, canniness, *formal* perspicacity, astucity, callidity, sagacity, *colloq.* smartness
⊟ foolishness, naïvety, obtuseness

shrewish *adj*
scolding, bad-tempered, ill-tempered, ill-humoured, ill-natured, nagging, peevish, quarrelsome, complaining, discontented, fault-finding, henpecking, petulant, captious, sharp-tongued, vixenish, *formal* querulous
⊟ affectionate, peaceable, placid, supportive

shriek *v, n*
- ▶ *v* scream, screech, squawk, squeal, cry (out), shout, yell, wail, howl
- ▶ *n* scream, screech, squawk, squeal, cry, shout, yell, wail, howl

shrill *adj*
high, high-pitched, treble, sharp, acute, piercing, penetrating, screaming, screeching, ear-splitting, strident
⊟ deep, low, soft, gentle

shrine *n*
holy place, sacred place, chapel, sanctuary, church, tabernacle, temple, martyry, fane, dome, delubrum, dagoba, stupa, tope, darga, vimana

shrink *v*
1 CONTRACT, shorten, grow/become smaller, narrow, decrease, lessen, reduce, diminish, drop off, fall off,

dwindle, shrivel, wrinkle, wither, atrophy **2** RECOIL, draw back, back away, shy away, withdraw, retire, balk, quail, cower, cringe, wince, flinch, start back, shun

F3 **1** expand, stretch **2** accept, embrace

shrivel v
wrinkle, pucker (up), wither, wilt, shrink, dwindle, parch, dry (up), dehydrate, desiccate, scorch, sear, burn, frizzle, *Scot.* gizzen

shrivelled *adj*
wrinkled, puckered, shrunken, withered, emaciated, wizened, dried up, dry, desiccated, *Scot.* gizzen, *formal* sere

shroud v, n
▶ v wrap, envelop, swathe, cloak, veil, screen, cloud, hide, conceal, enshroud, blanket, cover

F3 uncover, expose

▶ n winding-sheet, cloth, graveclothes, cerecloth, cerement, pall, mantle, cloak, veil, screen, cloud, blanket, covering

shrouded *adj*
wrapped, enveloped, swathed, cloaked, enshrouded, hidden, concealed, covered, clouded, blanketed, veiled

F3 exposed, uncovered

shrub *n*

Shrubs include:
azalea, berberis, broom, buddleia, camellia, clematis, cotoneaster, daphne, dogwood, euonymus, firethorn, flowering currant, forsythia, fuchsia, heather, hebe, holly, honeysuckle, hydrangea, ivy, japonica, jasmine, laburnum, laurel, lavender, lilac, magnolia, mallow, mimosa, mock orange, peony, privet, musk rose, rhododendron, rose, spiraea, viburnum, weigela, wistaria, witch hazel. *See also* FLOWER; PLANT.

shrug v
▷ **shrug off** brush off, ignore, disregard, dismiss, neglect, take no notice of

shrunken *adj*
reduced, shrunk, shrivelled, contracted, emaciated, gaunt, *formal* cadaverous

F3 full, generous, rounded, sleek

shudder v, n
▶ v shiver, shake, tremble, quiver, quake, heave, convulse

▶ n shiver, quiver, tremble, quake, heave, tremor, spasm, convulsion

shuffle v
1 MIX (UP), intermix, jumble (up), confuse, disorder, rearrange, reorganize, move around, shift around, switch **2** *shuffle across the room* shamble, scuffle, scrape, drag, falter, limp, toddle, doddle, hobble

shun v
avoid, evade, elude, steer clear of, shy away from, keep away from, spurn, ignore, ostracize, *formal* eschew, *colloq.* give a wide berth to, cold-shoulder

F3 accept, embrace

shut v
close, slam, seal, fasten, secure, seal, put the lid on, lock, latch, bolt, bar

F3 open

▷ **shut down** close (down), stop, halt, suspend, switch off, inactivate, *formal* cease, terminate, discontinue

▷ **shut in** enclose, box in, hem in, fence in, confine, imprison, cage (in), keep in, restrain, *formal* immure

▷ **shut off** seclude, isolate, cut off, separate, segregate

▷ **shut out** **1** EXCLUDE, bar, debar, lock out, ostracize, banish, outlaw, exile **2** HIDE, conceal, cover (up), block out, mask, screen, veil

▷ **shut up** **1** SILENCE, gag, quiet, quieten, hush (up), hold your tongue, *colloq.* pipe down, clam up, keep mum **2** CONFINE, lock up, cage in, coop up, imprison, jail, intern, *formal* incarcerate, immure

shuttle v
go to and fro, travel, ply, alternate, commute, shunt, shuttlecock, seesaw

shy *adj*, v
▶ *adj* timid, bashful, reticent, reserved, demure, diffident, introverted, retiring, coy, self-conscious, embarrassed, inhibited, modest, self-effacing, shrinking, withdrawn, hesitant, cautious, chary, suspicious, nervous, *formal* timorous, *colloq.* mousy, backward in coming forward

F3 bold, assertive, confident

▷ **fight shy of** avoid, steer clear of, shun, spurn, *formal* eschew, *colloq.* give a wide berth to, keep at arm's length

▶ v ▷ **shy away** avoid, balk, shrink, recoil, wince, back away, flinch, swerve, start, quail, rear, buck

shyness n
timidity, timidness, hesitancy, diffidence, bashfulness, reticence, self-consciousness, inhibition, embarrassment, modesty, constraint, nervousness, coyness, *formal* timorousness, *colloq.* mousiness

F3 boldness, assertiveness, confidence

sibling n
brother, sister, german, twin

sick *adj*
1 ILL, unwell, laid up, poorly, ailing, sickly, weak, feeble, *formal* indisposed, *colloq.* under the weather, rough, groggy, off colour, out of sorts **2** VOMITING, retching, nauseous, queasy, bilious, travel-sick, carsick, seasick, airsick, *colloq.* throwing up, spewing up, puking **3** *sick of waiting* bored, tired, weary, disgusted, nauseated, *colloq.* fed up **4** DISGUSTED, annoyed, angry, enraged, disgruntled, *colloq.* fed up, sick and tired, cheesed off, browned off, hacked off **5** *a sick joke* cruel, black, tasteless, vulgar, gross, in bad taste

F3 **1** well, healthy

sicken v
1 NAUSEATE, revolt, disgust, repel, appal, put off, *colloq.* turn off, turn your stomach **2** BECOME ILL, catch, develop, pick up, get, go down with, come down with, become infected with, become ill with, *formal* contract, succumb to

F3 **1** delight, attract

sickening *adj*
nauseating, revolting, disgusting, offensive, appalling, shocking, distasteful, off-putting, foul, vile, loathsome, nauseous, repulsive, repellent, stomach-turning

F3 delightful, pleasing, attractive

sickly *adj*
1 UNHEALTHY, infirm, delicate, weak, feeble, frail, wan, pale, pallid, ailing, indisposed, sick, bilious, faint, languid, *colloq.* washed out **2** NAUSEATING, revolting, sweet, syrupy, cloying, mawkish, *colloq.* soppy, schmaltzy, gushy, mushy, slushy

F3 **1** healthy, robust, sturdy, strong

sickness n
1 ILLNESS, disease, ailment, complaint, ill-health, indisposition, disorder, infirmity, *formal* malady, affliction, *colloq.* bug, virus **2** VOMITING, retching, nausea, queasiness, biliousness, travel sickness, mo-

tion sickness, morning sickness, carsickness, seasickness, airsickness, *colloq.* throwing up, spewing up, puking

F3 1 health

side *n, adj, v*

▸ *n* 1 *the side of an object* face, facet, surface, end, profile 2 EDGE, margin, fringe, periphery, border, boundary, limit, end, verge, rim, brink, bank, shore, flank, hand, *technical* jamb 3 *the other side of the city* district, quarter, area, region, sector, neighbourhood, section, zone 4 ASPECT, angle, slant, facet, standpoint, view, viewpoint, point of view, profile 5 STANDPOINT, viewpoint, view, aspect, angle, slant 6 TEAM, party, faction, wing, camp, sect, splinter group, cause, interest

▷ **side by side** next to each other, close to each other, alongside each other, shoulder to shoulder

▸ *adj* 1 LATERAL, flanking, wing 2 MINOR, marginal, secondary, subsidiary, subordinate, lesser, incidental 3 OBLIQUE, wideward, wideways, sidelong

▸ *v* ▷ **side with** agree with, team up with, take someone's side, be on the side of, support, give your support, back, give your backing, join with, vote for, favour, prefer

sidelong *adj*

indirect, oblique, sideward, sideways, covert

F3 direct, overt

sidestep *v*

avoid, find a way around, dodge, evade, elude, skirt, bypass, *formal* circumvent, *colloq.* duck, shirk, give a miss

F3 tackle, deal with

sidetrack *v*

deflect, head off, lead away from, divert, distract

sideways *adv, adj*

▸ *adv* from side to side, sidewards, edgeways, edgewise, crabwise, laterally, obliquely, askance, athwart

▸ *adj* sideward, side, lateral, slanted, oblique, indirect, sidelong

sidle *v*

slink, edge, inch, creep, sneak

siege *n*

blockade, encirclement, besiegement, beleaguerment

siesta *n*

rest, sleep, relaxation, nap, doze, *formal* repose, *colloq.* catnap, forty winks, snooze

sieve *v, n*

▸ *v* sift, strain, filter, screen, riddle, separate, remove, sort, winnow

▸ *n* colander, strainer, filter, sifter, riddle, screen

sift *v*

1 SIEVE, strain, filter, riddle, screen, winnow, separate, sort 2 EXAMINE, scrutinize, investigate, analyse, study, pore over, probe, review

sigh *v*

1 BREATHE, moan, complain, lament, grieve, *formal* exhale 2 *the wind sighing through the valley* rustle, whisper, crackle, swish, *formal* susurrate

▷ **sigh for** grieve, lament, languish, long, mourn, pine, weep, yearn, cry

sight *n, v*

▸ *n* 1 VISION, eyesight, seeing, ability to see, faculty/ sense of sight, observation, perception 2 VIEW, look, glance, glimpse, range, field of vision, range of vision, visibility 3 APPEARANCE, spectacle, show, display, exhibition, scene, monstrosity, *colloq.* eyesore, fright 4 *see the sights of London* places of interest, amenities, beauties, features, curiosities, wonders, splendours, marvels

▷ **catch sight of** see, perceive, notice, note, watch,

view, look at, mark, glimpse, discern, make out, recognize, spot, identify

▷ **lose sight of** forget, omit, fail to remember, neglect, overlook, disregard, ignore, put aside, slip your mind

▷ **set your sights on** aim at, plan for, seek to, intend to, strive for, aspire towards, work towards

▸ *v* see, observe, spot, glimpse, perceive, discern, distinguish, make out

sightseer *n*

tourist, visitor, holidaymaker, tripper, excursionist, *US* rubberneck

sign *n, v*

▸ *n* 1 SYMBOL, token, character, figure, code, cipher, representation, emblem, badge, insignia, logo 2 INDICATION, mark, signal, gesture, evidence, proof, clue, pointer, token, hint, suggestion, trace, symptom, *formal* manifestation 3 GESTURE, signal, movement, motion, wave, indication, act, action, gesticulation 4 NOTICE, poster, board, placard, signpost, marker, indicator 5 PORTENT, omen, forewarning, foreboding, *formal* augury, prognostication, harbinger, presage

▸ *v* 1 *sign your name* autograph, countersign, initial, endorse, write, *formal* inscribe 2 SIGNAL, wave, gesticulate, gesture, beckon, wink, motion, nod, indicate, express, show, mark, communicate

▷ **sign over** make over, transfer, turn over, surrender, entrust, deliver, convey, consign

▷ **sign up** enlist, enrol, join (up), join the services, volunteer, register, sign on, put your name down for, recruit, take on, hire, engage, employ

signal *n, v, adj*

▸ *n* sign, indication, mark, gesture, evidence, clue, message, symptom, pointer, token, hint, light, alert, warning, tip-off, *colloq.* shot across the bows

▸ *v* wave, gesticulate, gesture, beckon, wink, motion, nod, sign, indicate, express, show, mark, communicate, *formal* signify

▸ *adj* significant, important, exceptional, notable, noteworthy, outstanding, extraordinary, impressive, memorable, momentous, remarkable, striking, eminent, distinguished, conspicuous, glorious, famous

signature *n*

autograph, name, initials, mark, endorsement, inscription, *US colloq.* John Hancock

significance *n*

importance, relevance, consequence, seriousness, solemnity, magnitude, matter, interest, consideration, weight, force, meaning, implication(s), sense, essence, gist, point, message, *formal* significance, import, purport

F3 insignificance, unimportance, pettiness

significant *adj*

1 IMPORTANT, relevant, consequential, momentous, memorable, weighty, serious, noteworthy, material, critical, vital, crucial, key, fateful, marked, considerable, appreciable 2 MEANINGFUL, symbolic, expressive, suggestive, indicative, symptomatic, eloquent, pregnant, ominous

F3 1 insignificant, unimportant, trivial 2 meaningless

significantly *adj*

1 VITALLY, crucially, considerably, appreciably, noticeably, perceptibly, critically, materially 2 MEANINGFULLY, eloquently, meaningly, knowingly, suggestively

signify *v*

1 MEAN, symbolize, be a sign of, represent, stand for, indicate, show, exhibit, signal, express, convey, transmit, communicate, declare, proclaim, intimate, imply, suggest, *formal* denote, betoken, portend 2 MATTER,

count, be of importance, be important, be relevant, have influence, carry weight, *colloq.* make waves

signpost *n*
sign, pointer, marker, indicator, placard, guidepost, finger-post, handpost, waypost, clue

silence *n, v*
▶ *n* quiet, quietness, hush, peace, peacefulness, stillness, still, calm, calmness, tranquillity, lull, noiselessness, soundlessness, muteness, dumbness, speechlessness, wordlessness, voicelessness, taciturnity, uncommunicativeness, reticence, reserve, secretiveness
🗲 noise, sound, din, uproar
▶ *v* quiet, quieten, hush, mute, strike dumb, deaden, muffle, stifle, gag, muzzle, suppress, subdue, quell, still, dumbfound, *formal* abate, *colloq.* be able to hear a pin drop

silent *adj*
inaudible, noiseless, soundless, quiet, peaceful, still, calm, hushed, muted, mute, dumb, speechless, tongue-tied, tight-lipped, taciturn, reticent, reserved, secretive, tacit, unspoken, implicit, implied, unexpressed, understood, unvoiced, voiceless, wordless, *colloq.* mum
🗲 noisy, loud, talkative

silently *adv*
noiselessly, quietly, calmly, inaudibly, soundlessly, speechlessly, wordlessly, unheard, dumbly, mutely, tacitly

silhouette *n, v*
▶ *n* outline, contour, shape, form, profile, shadow, *formal* delineation, configuration
▶ *v* outline, shadow, shape, profile, stand out, *formal* delineate, configurate, configure

silky *adj*
silken, fine, sleek, lustrous, glossy, satiny, smooth, soft, velvety, *formal* diaphanous

silly *adj, n*
▶ *adj* foolish, stupid, unintelligent, unwise, senseless, pointless, thoughtless, idiotic, ridiculous, ludicrous, preposterous, absurd, meaningless, unreasonable, irrational, illogical, frivolous, childish, puerile, inane, fatuous, immature, irresponsible, foolhardy, rash, reckless, scatterbrained, *formal* imprudent, injudicious, *colloq.* daft, soft, dotty, loopy, barmy, potty, loony, nutty
🗲 wise, sensible, sane, mature, clever, intelligent
▶ *n* fool, idiot, ignoramus, simpleton, ninny, half-wit, *colloq.* dumbo, silly-billy, clot, dope, duffer, twit, wally, goose

silt *n, v*
▶ *n* sediment, deposit, residue, sludge, mud, ooze, *formal* alluvium
▶ *v* ▷ **silt up** block, clog, dam, choke, congest

silvan *adj*
leafy, tree-covered, wooded, woodland, *formal* arboreous, forestal, forested, forestine
🗲 treeless

similar *adj*
like, alike, close, much the same, related, akin, corresponding, equivalent, comparable, uniform, *technical* homologous, *formal* analogous, homogeneous
🗲 dissimilar, different

similarity *n*
likeness, resemblance, sameness, closeness, relation, kinship, correspondence, parallelism, equivalence, comparability, compatibility, agreement, affinity, uniformity, *formal* similitude, congruence, analogy, homogeneity, concordance
🗲 dissimilarity, difference, clash

similarly *adv*
in the same way, likewise, correspondingly, uniformly, by the same token, by analogy
🗲 differently

similitude *n*
similarity, likeness, resemblance, sameness, closeness, relation, correspondence, parallelism, equivalence, comparability, compatibility, agreement, affinity, uniformity, *formal* congruence, analogy

simmer *v*
1 BOIL GENTLY, bubble, cook gently, seethe, stew **2** *simmer with anger* fume, rage, seethe, burn, smoulder
▷ **simmer down** calm down, cool down, subside, lessen, control yourself, collect yourself

simpering *adj*
self-conscious, silly, coy, giggling, missish, schoolgirlish, *formal* affected

simple *adj*
1 *a simple question*; *in simple language* easy, elementary, straightforward, uncomplicated, uninvolved, effortless, clear, lucid, plain, understandable, comprehensible, *colloq.* cushy, easy-peasy, rough and ready, a cinch, a doddle, a piece of cake, a pushover, as easy as falling off a log **2** BASIC, plain, crude, primitive, natural, undecorated, unadorned, unembellished, unsophisticated, ordinary, unpretentious, unfussy, classic, rudimentary, stark, austere, spartan, *colloq.* low-tech, no-frills **3** *the simple fact is ...* plain, basic, straightforward, bald, stark, direct, unambiguous, open, honest, sincere, candid, blunt **4** UNSOPHISTICATED, natural, innocent, artless, guileless, ingenuous, naïve, green **5** FOOLISH, stupid, silly, idiotic, half-witted, simple-minded, feeble-minded, slow, backward, retarded
🗲 **1** difficult, hard, complicated, intricate **2** elaborate, fancy, luxurious **4** sophisticated, worldly, artful **5** clever

simple-minded *adj*
unsophisticated, simple, natural, artless, stupid, foolish, idiot, idiotic, imbecile, moronic, cretinous, brainless, backward, retarded, dim-witted, feeble-minded, addle-brained, *colloq.* dopey, goofy
🗲 bright, clever

simpleton *n*
idiot, fool, moron, ninny, imbecile, dolt, dullard, dunce, dupe, jackass, flathead, *colloq.* dope, nincompoop, numskull, nitwit, stupid, twerp, clot, twit, greenhorn, soft-head, goose, blockhead, booby
🗲 brain

simplicity *n*
simpleness, ease, easiness, facility, straightforwardness, uncomplicatedness, elementariness, clarity, purity, plainness, lucidity, intelligibility, restraint, starkness, naturalness, clean lines, innocence, guilelessness, naïvety, artlessness, directness, frankness, candour, openness, sincerity, honesty, directness
🗲 difficulty, complexity, intricacy, sophistication, elaborateness

simplify *v*
disentangle, untangle, unravel, decipher, make easy/easier, make easier to understand, make (more) comprehensible, remove complexities in, explain, clarify, paraphrase, abridge, reduce, sort out, streamline
🗲 complicate, elaborate

simplistic *adj*
oversimplified, superficial, shallow, sweeping, facile, simple, naïve, pat
🗲 analytical, detailed

simply *adv*
1 MERELY, just, only, solely, purely, utterly, completely, totally, wholly, altogether, absolutely, positively, quite, really, undeniably, unquestionably, unreservedly, un-

conditionally, clearly, plainly, obviously **2** EASILY, straightforwardly, directly, intelligibly, plainly, clearly, lucidly, naturally

simulate *v*
pretend, assume, put on, act, feign, sham, fake, counterfeit, reproduce, duplicate, copy, imitate, mimic, parrot, echo, reflect, parallel, *formal* affect, *colloq.* make believe

simulated *adj*
pretended, feigned, artificial, assumed, imitation, put-on, sham, fake, mock, make-believe, bogus, spurious, substitute, synthetic, man-made, inauthentic, insincere, *colloq.* phoney, pseudo
🖅 real, genuine

simultaneous *adj*
happening at the same time, existing at the same time, done at the same time, synchronous, synchronic, co-existent, coinciding, parallel, *formal* concurrent, contemporaneous, concomitant
🖅 asynchronous

sin *n, v*
▶ *n* wrong, offence, misdeed, lapse, fault, error, crime, wrongdoing, sinfulness, wickedness, badness, evil, impiety, immorality, ungodliness, unrighteousness, irreligiousness, guilt, *formal* transgression, trespass, misdemeanour, iniquity
▶ *v* offend, commit a sin, lapse, err, misbehave, go wrong, do wrong, stray, go astray, fall, fall from grace, *formal* transgress, trespass

sincere *adj*
genuine, true, real, honest, truthful, unfeigned, bona fide, trustworthy, candid, frank, open, direct, straightforward, plain-spoken, serious, fervent, earnest, heartfelt, wholehearted, pure, unadulterated, unmixed, natural, artless, ingenuous, guileless, simple, *formal* unaffected, *colloq.* no-nonsense, above board, up front
🖅 insincere, hypocritical, affected

sincerely *adv*
genuinely, honestly, earnestly, in earnest, seriously, really, simply, truly, truthfully, wholeheartedly, unfeignedly, *formal* unaffectedly

sincerity *n*
genuineness, honour, integrity, probity, uprightness, honesty, truth, truthfulness, candour, frankness, openness, directness, straightforwardness, seriousness, earnestness, wholeheartedness, trustworthiness, artlessness, ingenuousness, guilelessness
🖅 insincerity

sinecure *n*
soft option, *colloq.* plum job, picnic, doddle, cinch, cushy job, money for jam, money for old rope, gravy train

sinewy *adj*
muscular, burly, brawny, strapping, stalwart, strong, sturdy, robust, vigorous, athletic, wiry, stringy

sinful *adj*
wrong, wrongful, criminal, evil, bad, wicked, erring, fallen, immoral, corrupt, depraved, impious, ungodly, unholy, unrighteous, irreligious, guilty, *formal* iniquitous
🖅 sinless, righteous, godly

sinfulness *n*
immorality, wickedness, sin, ungodliness, unrighteousness, impiety, corruption, guilt, *formal* iniquity, depravity, peccability, peccancy, transgression
🖅 righteousness

sing *v*
chant, intone, vocalize, burst into song, croon, serenade, yodel, trill, warble, chirp, quaver, pipe, whistle, hum

▷ **sing out** shout, yell, cry (out), call, bawl, bellow, cooee, *colloq.* holler

singe *v*
scorch, char, blacken, burn, sear

singer *n*

Singers include:
vocalist, songster, songstress, warbler, balladeer, minstrel, troubadour, opera singer, diva, prima donna, soloist, precentor, choirboy, choirgirl, chorister, chorus, folk-singer, pop star, pop singer, chanteuse, crooner, carol-singer; soprano, coloratura soprano, castrato, tenor, treble, contralto, alto, baritone, bass.

single *adj, v*
▶ *adj* **1** ONE, unique, singular, individual, particular, exclusive, sole, only, one and only, by yourself/itself, lone, solitary, isolated, separate, distinct, unshared, undivided, unbroken, simple, one-to-one, person-to-person, man-to-man, woman-to-woman **2** UNMARRIED, unwed, free, unattached, celibate, on your own, by yourself, available
🖅 **1** multiple **2** married
▶ *v* ▷ **single out** choose, select, pick, hand-pick, distinguish, identify, separate (out), set apart, decide on, isolate, highlight, pinpoint

single-handed *adj, adv*
by yourself, on your own, alone, solo, independent(ly), without help, unaided, unassisted, unaccompanied

single-minded *adj*
determined, resolute, dogged, persevering, tireless, unwavering, fixed, set, unswerving, undeviating, steadfast, dedicated, committed, devoted, obsessive, monomaniacal

singly *adv*
one by one, on their own, one at a time, individually, separately, distinctly, solely, independently

singular *adj*
1 REMARKABLE, exceptional, unusual, extraordinary, noteworthy, unique, unparalleled, pre-eminent, outstanding, eminent, conspicuous **2** PECULIAR, odd, queer, unusual, strange, uncommon, curious, eccentric, atypical
🖅 **1** usual **2** normal

singularity *n*
peculiarity, strangeness, queerness, quirk, particularity, oddness, oddity, abnormality, curiousness, eccentricity, idiosyncrasy, irregularity, extraordinariness, uniqueness, oneness, twist
🖅 normality

singularly *adv*
remarkably, exceptionally, extraordinarily, notably, outstandingly, particularly, uncommonly, unusually, especially, surprisingly, signally, conspicuously, prodigiously, bizarrely

sinister *adj*
ominous, menacing, threatening, disturbing, disquieting, terrifying, frightening, unlucky, evil, harmful, cruel, wicked, vicious, *formal* inauspicious, malevolent, portentous
🖅 harmless, innocent, *formal* auspicious

sink *v*
1 DESCEND, slip, fall, drop, go down, slump, lower, go lower, slump, plummet, plunge, stoop, succumb, lapse, droop, sag, dip, set, disappear, vanish **2** DECREASE, lessen, subside, abate, dwindle, diminish, ebb, fade, flag, weaken, fail, decline, worsen, degenerate, degrade, decay, collapse, fall (in), *formal* abate,

colloq. go downhill, go to pot **3** FOUNDER, dive, plunge, plummet, capsize, submerge, immerse, engulf, drown **4** *sink a well* bore, drill, penetrate, dig, excavate, drive, put down, embed, lay, conceal **5** *sink money into a project* invest, put in, lay out, fund, risk, plough **6** RUIN, destroy, wreck, devastate, demolish, foil, scupper, scuttle, *colloq.* put a spanner in the works
🖃 1 rise **2** increase, improve **3** float

sinless *adj*
innocent, virtuous, faultless, guiltless, immaculate, pure, unblemished, uncorrupted, undefiled, unsullied, unspotted, impeccable
🖃 sinful

sinner *n*
wrongdoer, offender, criminal, backslider, reprobate, evil-doer, *formal* malefactor, miscreant, transgressor, trespasser

sinuous *adj*
lithe, slinky, curved, curving, wavy, undulating, tortuous, twisting, winding, bending, turning, meandering, serpentine, coiling, curling, ogee
🖃 straight

sip *v, n*
▶ *v* taste, sample, drink, drink slowly, sup
▶ *n* taste, drop, drink, spoonful, mouthful

siren *n*
1 ALARM, tocsin, burglar alarm, car alarm, fire alarm, personal alarm, security alarm **2** SEDUCTRESS, *femme fatale*, temptress, vamp, charmer, Lorelei, Circe

sissy *n, adj*
▶ *n* baby, coward, weakling, softy, mummy's boy, milksop, *colloq.* wimp, namby-pamby, wet
▶ *adj* unmanly, weak, soft, cowardly, effeminate, feeble, *colloq.* wimpish, namby-pamby, wet

sister *n*
1 *brothers and sisters* sibling, blood-sister, relation, relative **2** *sisters in the struggle against injustice* comrade, friend, partner, colleague, associate, fellow, companion **3** *sisters in a convent* nun, abbess, prioress, vowess

sit *v*
1 SETTLE, sit down, take your seat, be seated, lie, hang, rest, squat (down), place, deposit, position, situate, locate, stand, perch, roost, brood, pose **2** SEAT, accommodate, hold, contain, have room/space for **3** MEET, assemble, gather, convene, consult, deliberate, be in session

site *n, v*
▶ *n* **1** LOCATION, place, spot, position, situation, locality, station, setting, scene **2** PLOT, lot, ground, area
▶ *v* locate, place, position, situate, station, put, set, install

sitting *n*
session, period, spell, meeting, assembly, hearing, consultation

situate *v*
locate, place, position, station, put, set, install

situation *n*
1 SITE, location, position, place, spot, seat, locality, locale, setting, environment, milieu, scenario **2** STATE OF AFFAIRS, case, circumstances, predicament, affairs, environment, climate, set-up, state, state of play, condition(s), status, rank, station, *colloq.* scenario, lie of the land, picture, what's going on, score **3** JOB, post, office, position, place, employment

size *n, v*
▶ *n* magnitude, measurement(s), dimensions, proportions, volume, bulk, mass, expanse, height, length, area, extent, range, scale, amount, greatness, largeness, bigness, vastness, immensity

▶ *v* ▷ **size up** gauge, assess, evaluate, judge, weigh up, estimate, rate, measure, *formal* appraise, *colloq.* suss out

sizeable *adj*
substantial, fairly large, considerable, respectable, goodly, largish, biggish, decent, generous
🖃 small, tiny

sizzle *v*
hiss, crackle, spit, sputter, fry, frizzle

skeletal *adj*
skin-and-bone, wasted, drawn, emaciated, gaunt, haggard, hollow-cheeked, shrunken, fleshless, *formal* cadaverous

skeleton *n, adj*
▶ *n* bones, frame, structure, framework, support, bare bones, outline, blueprint, plan, draft, sketch
▶ *adj* smallest, lowest, minimum, reduced, basic

sketch *v, n*
▶ *v* draw, depict, portray, represent, pencil, paint, outline, delineate, draft, rough out, block out
▶ *n* drawing, vignette, design, plan, diagram, outline, skeleton, plan, abstract, draft, representation, description, *formal* delineation, *croquis*, *ébauche*, *esquisse*

sketchily *adv*
roughly, vaguely, incompletely, inadequately, imperfectly, patchily, cursorily, perfunctorily, hastily
🖃 fully

sketchy *adj*
rough, vague, incomplete, unpolished, unfinished, scrappy, crude, provisional, patchy, bitty, imperfect, inadequate, insufficient, defective, deficient, slight, superficial, cursory, meagre, perfunctory, hasty
🖃 full, complete

skilful *adj*
able, capable, adept, competent, proficient, efficient, good, dexterous, deft, adroit, handy, expert, (well-) versed, masterly, clever, smart, accomplished, skilled, gifted, talented, practised, experienced, trained, professional, tactical, cunning
🖃 inept, clumsy, awkward

skill *n*
skilfulness, ability, aptitude, facility, handiness, adeptness, deftness, adroitness, talent, knack, art, technique, training, experience, expertise, expertness, professionalism, finesse, mastery, proficiency, competence, efficiency, accomplishment, cleverness, smartness, intelligence

skilled *adj*
trained, schooled, qualified, professional, experienced, practised, accomplished, gifted, talented, expert, masterly, proficient, competent, efficient, able, capable, good, adept, skilful
🖃 unskilled, inexperienced

skim *v*
1 BRUSH, touch, skate, plane, float, sail, glide, graze, fly, skip, bounce **2** SCAN, look through, glance at, skip, read (through) quickly, run through/over, have a quick look at, browse through, flick through, flip through, thumb through, leaf through **3** CREAM, separate, *formal* despumate

skimp *v*
economize, be economical, cut back on, scrimp, pinch, stint, withhold, *colloq.* cut corners, tighten your belt, cut your coat according to your cloth
🖃 squander, waste

skimpy *adj*
small, scanty, short, sparse, thin, tight, sketchy, meagre, miserly, niggardly, inadequate, insufficient, insubstantial, beggarly, *formal* exiguous, *colloq.* measly
🖃 generous

skin *n, v*
- ▸ *n* hide, fleece, fell, pelt, membrane, film, coating, layer, surface, covering, cover, outside, peel, rind, husk, hull, pod, casing, crust, *technical* corium, derma, dermis, cutis, integument, tegument, epidermis, *formal* cuticle
- ▸ *v* flay, fleece, strip, peel, scrape, graze

skin-deep *adj*
  shallow, superficial, surface, external, outward, artificial, empty, meaningless

skinflint *n*
  miser, niggard, cheeseparer, Scrooge, *colloq.* meanie, penny-pincher
  🖪 spendthrift

skinny *adj*
  thin, lean, scrawny, scraggy, skeletal, emaciated, underfed, undernourished, *colloq.* (all) skin-and-bone
  🖪 fat, plump

skip *v*
  1 HOP, jump, leap, dance, spring, bounce, bob, bound, cavort, gambol, frisk, caper, prance **2** *skip a page* miss (out), omit, leave out, *colloq.* dodge, cut **3** *skip from one thing to another* move quickly, jump, rush, pass, dart, tear, race

skirmish *n, v*
- ▸ *n* fight, combat, battle, engagement, encounter, confrontation, conflict, clash, brush, affray, fracas, melee, tussle, argument, dispute, difference of opinion, *formal* altercation, *colloq.* scrap, set-to, dust-up, punch-up
- ▸ *v* clash, fight, tussle, brawl, scuffle, combat, battle, contend, argue, quarrel, wrangle, *colloq.* scrap, fall out, be at each other's throats

skirt *v*
  1 CIRCLE, move/go round, border, edge, flank, *formal* circumnavigate **2** AVOID, evade, bypass, find a way round, *formal* circumvent

skit *n*
  satire, parody, caricature, burlesque, sketch, *colloq.* spoof, take-off, send-up, mickey-taking

skittish *adj*
  nervous, excitable, fidgety, lively, high-spirited, playful, jumpy, highly-strung, frivolous, fickle, *formal* restive

skive *v*
  dodge, laze, idle, shirk, malinger, skulk, slack, *colloq.* swing the lead

skiver *n*
  dodger, idler, do-nothing, shirker, slacker, loafer, malingerer

skulduggery *n*
  trickery, swindling, fraudulence, double-dealing, underhandedness, unscrupulousness, chicanery, *formal* duplicity, machinations, *colloq.* jiggery-pokery, shenanigans, hanky-panky

skulk *v*
  lurk, hide, prowl, sneak, creep, slink, lie in wait, steal, slide, pad, pussyfoot, loiter

sky *n*
  space, atmosphere, air, heavens, the blue, firmament, *formal* vault of heaven, empyrean, welkin

slab *n*
  piece, block, lump, chunk, hunk, brick, briquette, wedge, slice, portion, *colloq.* wodge

slack *adj, n, v*
- ▸ *adj* **1** LOOSE, relaxed, flexible, limp, hanging, sagging, flapping, flabby, baggy, *formal* flaccid **2** *a slack period* sluggish, slow, quiet, idle, lazy, inactive **3** NEGLECTFUL, negligent, careless, inattentive, permissive, lax, relaxed, *formal* remiss, tardy, *colloq.* easy-going, sloppy
- 🖪 **1** tight, taut, stiff, rigid **2** busy **3** diligent
- ▸ *n* looseness, give, play, room, leeway, excess, spare capacity
- ▸ *v* idle, shirk, dodge, malinger, neglect, *colloq.* skive

slacken *v*
  ▷ **slacken off** loosen, release, relax, ease, moderate, reduce, lessen, get less, decrease, diminish, slow (down), become slower, become less intense/active, *formal* abate, *colloq.* take it easy
  🖪 tighten, increase, intensify, quicken

slacker *n*
  idler, shirker, dawdler, loafer, malingerer, clock-watcher, good-for-nothing, layabout, *colloq.* skiver

slag *v*
  ▷ **slag off** criticize, abuse, mock, malign, insult, *formal* berate, deride, lambaste, *colloq.* slam, slate

slake *v*
  satisfy, satiate, quench, moisten, sate, gratify, allay, reduce, extinguish, moderate, *formal* abate, assuage, mitigate

slam *v*
  1 BANG, crash, dash, smash, thump, slap, throw, hurl, fling **2** CRITICIZE, attack, denounce, find fault with, *colloq.* slate, pan, rubbish, run down, pull/tear to pieces, tear to shreds, do a hatchet job on

slander *n, v*
- ▸ *n* defamation, misrepresentation, libel, scandal, smear, smear campaign, slur, denigration, backbiting, *formal* aspersion, disparagement, calumny, vilification, traducement, obloquy, *colloq.* muck-raking, mudslinging
- ▸ *v* defame, malign, disparage, libel, smear, blacken the name of, slur, backbite, *formal* vilify, cast aspersions on, denigrate, vilipend, calumniate, traduce, *colloq.* sling/throw mud at, drag someone's name through the mud, *US* badmouth
- 🖪 praise, compliment

 slander or **libel** ? *See panel at* LIBEL.

slanderous *adj*
  defamatory, false, untrue, libellous, damaging, malicious, abusive, insulting, backbiting, *formal* aspersory, aspersive, calumniatory, calumnious

slang *n*
  cant, jargon, argot, patois, patter, cockney, cockney rhyming slang, vulgarism, doublespeak, gobbledygook, colloquialism, informal expressions, *colloq.* lingo, mumbo-jumbo

slanging match
  argument, row, quarrel, dispute, shouting match, *formal* altercation, *colloq.* argy-bargy, barney, set-to, spat

slant *v, n*
- ▸ *v* **1** TILT, slope, incline, lean, list, dip, skew, be askew, angle, shelve **2** DISTORT, twist, warp, bend, weight, bias, skew, colour
- ▸ *n* **1** SLOPE, incline, inclination, leaning, gradient, ramp, camber, pitch, tilt, dip, angle, diagonal **2** BIAS, prejudice, distortion, twist, one-sidedness, emphasis, attitude, angle, opinion, view, viewpoint, point of view

slanting *adj*
  sloping, tilting, tilted, inclining, leaning, listing, dipping, on an incline, at a slant, askew, oblique, diagonal

slap *n, v, adv*
- ▸ *n* smack, spank, cuff, blow, hit, bang, clap, thump, whack, punch, *colloq.* wallop, clout, biff, sock, clobber

▷ **slap in the face** insult, humiliation, blow, affront, rejection, repulse, snub, rebuke, rebuff, indignity, *colloq.* put-down

▶ *v* **1** SMACK, spank, hit, strike, thump, whack, punch, cuff, bang, clap, *colloq.* clout, wallop, biff, sock, clobber **2** PUT DOWN, set (down), plump, plonk, slam, stick **3** DAUB, plaster, spread, apply

▶ *adv* right, directly, straight, exactly, precisely, dead, plumb, *colloq.* bang, slap-bang, smack

slapdash *adj*
careless, thoughtless, haphazard, slovenly, disorderly, clumsy, offhand, negligent, messy, slipshod, thrown-together, untidy, hurried, last-minute, hasty, rash, perfunctory, *formal* sloppy
F3 careful, orderly

slap-happy *adj*
casual, irresponsible, boisterous, haphazard, reeling, happy-go-lucky, nonchalant, reckless, slapdash, hit-or-miss, dazed, giddy, punch-drunk, woozy

slapstick *n*
comedy, farce, buffoonery, tomfoolery, knockabout, horseplay

slap-up *adj*
excellent, splendid, lavish, elaborate, first-class, first-rate, magnificent, superb, sumptuous, luxurious, princely, superlative

slash *v, n*
▶ *v* **1** *slash your wrists* cut, slit, gash, lacerate, knife, rip, tear, hack, score, rend **2** *slash costs* cut, reduce, decrease, curb, curtail, prune, *colloq.* axe
▶ *n* cut, incision, slit, gash, laceration, score, rip, tear, rent

slate *v*
scold, rebuke, reprimand, berate, censure, blame, criticize, *colloq.* slam, pan, rubbish, run down, pull/tear to pieces, tear to shreds, do a hatchet job on
F3 praise

slatternly *adj*
slovenly, sloppy, dirty, slipshod, untidy, unkempt, unclean, dowdy, bedraggled, dishevelled, frowzy, frumpish, frumpy

slaughter *v, n*
▶ *v* kill, put to death, slay, butcher, murder, massacre, exterminate, liquidate, annihilate
▶ *n* killing, putting to death, murder, massacre, extermination, liquidation, annihilation, butchery, carnage, blood-bath, bloodshed

slave *n, v*
▶ *n* servant, drudge, menial, lackey, vassal, serf, villein, captive, thrall, bondservant, bond-slave, bond(s)man, bond(s)woman, *colloq.* skivvy
▶ *v* toil, labour, drudge, sweat, grind, slog, work your fingers to the bone, work your guts out

slaver *v*
dribble, drivel, slobber, drool, *formal* salivate

slavery *n*
servitude, bondage, yoke, captivity, enslavement, serfdom, vassalage, thrall, thraldom, *formal* subjugation
F3 freedom, liberty

slavish *adj*
1 UNORIGINAL, imitative, unimaginative, uninspired, literal, strict **2** SERVILE, abject, submissive, sycophantic, obsequious, deferential, grovelling, cringing, fawning, menial, low, mean
F3 **1** original, imaginative **2** independent, assertive

slay *v*
kill, butcher, massacre, murder, dispatch, destroy, eliminate, execute, slaughter, annihilate, assassinate, exterminate, *colloq.* rub out

slaying *n*
murder, killing, butchery, slaughter, assassination, massacre, destruction, dispatch, elimination, annihilation, extermination, *formal* mactation

sleazy *adj*
disreputable, low, seedy, sordid, squalid, crummy, run-down, *colloq.* tacky

sleek *adj*
shiny, glossy, lustrous, smooth, silky, silken, soft, well-groomed, stylish, thriving, prosperous
F3 rough, unkempt

sleep *v, n*
▶ *v* be asleep, get some sleep, fall asleep, doze, hibernate, drop off, go off, drift off, nod off, nap, rest, *formal* slumber, repose, *colloq.* snooze, have a snooze, have forty winks, be in the land of Nod, sleep like a log, flake out, crash out, go out like a light, *slang* kip, doss (down)
▶ *n* doze, nap, catnap, hibernation, rest, siesta, *formal* slumber, repose, *colloq.* snooze, forty winks, shut-eye, *slang* kip

sleepiness *n*
drowsiness, doziness, heaviness, lethargy, torpor, *formal* languor, oscitancy, oscitation, somnolence
F3 alertness, wakefulness

sleeping *adj*
asleep, daydreaming, idle, inactive, unaware, becalmed, passive, off guard, inattentive, dormant, hibernating, *formal* slumbering
F3 alert, awake

sleepless *adj*
unsleeping, awake, wide-awake, alert, vigilant, watchful, wakeful, restless, disturbed, insomniac

sleeplessness *n*
insomnia, wakefulness, *formal* insomnolence

sleepwalker *n*
somnambulist, noctambulist

sleepwalking *n*
somnambulism, somnambulation, noctambulism, noctambulation

sleepy *adj*
1 DROWSY, tired, weary, heavy, slow, sluggish, torpid, lethargic, inactive, quiet, dull, soporific, hypnotic, *technical* comatose, *formal* somnolent, languid, languorous **2** *a sleepy little village* quiet, dull, peaceful, still, isolated, lonely, unfrequented, undisturbed, *formal* sequestered, *colloq.* off the beaten track
F3 **1** awake, alert, wakeful, restless

sleight of hand
trickery, skill, artifice, dexterity, legerdemain, deception, magic, adroitness, manipulation, *formal* prestidigitation

slender *adj*
1 SLIM, thin, lean, slight, svelte, graceful, trim, sylphlike, willowy, willowish **2** *a slender chance* faint, remote, small, little, slim, slight, inconsiderable, tenuous, flimsy, feeble, deficient, inadequate, insufficient, meagre, scant, scanty
F3 **1** fat **2** appreciable, considerable, ample

sleuth *n*
detective, private investigator, shadow, tail, tracker, *colloq.* private eye, bloodhound, dick, gumshoe

slice *n, v*
▶ *n* piece, sliver, wafer, rasher, tranche, slab, wedge, segment, section, hunk, chunk, part, share, portion, allocation, allotment, helping, *colloq.* cut, whack, slice of the cake
▶ *v* carve, cut (up), chop, sever, divide, separate, segment

slick *adj*

1 GLIB, plausible, easy, simplistic, deft, adroit, sharp, dexterous, skilful, smooth, professional, efficient, masterly **2** SMOOTH, sleek, glossy, shiny, polished, quick, streamlined, well-oiled, well-organized **3** INSINCERE, glib, smarmy, smooth-speaking, smooth-talking, persuasive, polished, sophisticated, suave, unctuous

slide *v*

1 MOVE SMOOTHLY, go smoothly, slip, slither, skid, skate, ski, toboggan, glide, plane, coast, skim **2** DETERIORATE, lessen, decrease, decline, fall, drop, plummet, plunge, lapse, worsen, get worse, depreciate

slight *adj, v, n*

▶ *adj* **1** MINOR, unimportant, insignificant, inconsequential, negligible, inappreciable, imperceptible, trivial, petty, scant, paltry, subtle, modest, small, little, minute, inconsiderable, insubstantial **2** SLENDER, slim, small, dainty, diminutive, petite, frail, fragile, delicate, elfin

🔁 **1** major, significant, noticeable, considerable **2** large, muscular

▶ *v* scorn, despise, disdain, insult, affront, offend, snub, spurn, slur, cut, ignore, disregard, neglect, *formal* disparage, *colloq.* giving the cold shoulder to, cold-shoulder

🔁 respect, praise, compliment, flatter

▶ *n* insult, affront, scorn, slur, snub, rebuff, rudeness, discourtesy, disrespect, contempt, disdain, indifference, disregard, neglect, *colloq.* cold shoulder, slap in the face, kick in the teeth

slighting *adj*

disdainful, disrespectful, belittling, insulting, scornful, offensive, defamatory, derogatory, slanderous, abusive, supercilious, uncomplimentary, *formal* disparaging

🔁 complimentary

slightly *adj*

rather, quite, a little, a bit, to some degree, to some extent

slim *adj, v*

▶ *adj* **1** SLENDER, thin, slight, lean, svelte, trim, graceful, sylphlike, willowy, willowish **2** SLIGHT, remote, faint, poor, small, little, scant, scanty, meagre, inconsiderable, tenuous, flimsy, insufficient, inadequate

🔁 **1** fat, chubby **2** strong, considerable

▶ *v* lose weight, diet, go on a diet, reduce

slime *n*

mud, ooze, muck, mess, *colloq.* goo, gunk, yuck

slimy *adj*

1 MUDDY, miry, sludgy, oozy, sticky, mucous, viscous, oily, greasy, slippery **2** SERVILE, obsequious, sycophantic, toadying, ingratiating, grovelling, creeping, oily, unctuous, *colloq.* smarmy

sling *v, n*

▶ *v* **1** THROW, hurl, fling, catapult, heave, pitch, lob, toss, shy, *colloq.* chuck **2** HANG, suspend, dangle, swing

▶ *n* bandage, loop, strap, support, band, catapult

slink *v*

sneak, steal, creep, sidle, slip, lurk, prowl, skulk

slinky *adj*

close-fitting, figure-hugging, clinging, skin-tight, sleek, sinuous

slip¹ *v, n*

▶ *v* **1** SLIDE, glide, skate, skid, stumble, lose your balance, trip, lose your footing, fall, slither, slink, sneak, steal, creep **2** *slip into/out of clothes* put on, get dressed in, change into, get into, take off, change out of, pull on, wear, don **3** *standards are slipping* fall, drop, sink, decrease, decline, plummet, plunge, slump, deteriorate, worsen, lapse, get worse, *colloq.*

go to the dogs, go to pot, go down the tube

▷ **let slip** let out, reveal, divulge, give away, betray, leak, tell

▷ **slip up** make a mistake, go wrong, get wrong, miscalculate, bungle, blunder, err, stumble, *colloq.* boob, botch, goof, fluff, *slang* screw up

▶ *n* mistake, error, blunder, fault, indiscretion, omission, oversight, failure, *colloq.* slip-up, bloomer, boob, booboo, howler, clanger

▷ **give someone the slip** escape from, run away from, get away from, flee from, break loose from, shake off, *colloq.* slip through someone's fingers, dodge, duck

slip² *n*

a slip of paper piece, strip, paper, note, voucher, chit, coupon, certificate

▷ **a slip of a** small, thin, slender, slim, slight, delicate, fragile, young

slipper *n*

houseshoe, moccasin, mule, flip-flop, sandal, pump, loafer, pabouche, pantof(f)le, pantoufle, pantable, *Scot.* panton

slippery *adj*

1 SLIPPY, icy, wet, greasy, oily, slimy, glassy, smooth, dangerous, treacherous, perilous, *colloq.* skiddy **2** *a slippery character* dishonest, untrustworthy, unreliable, false, two-faced, crafty, cunning, devious, clever, shifty, deceitful, foxy, evasive, smooth, smarmy, *formal* duplicitous, perfidious

🔁 **1** rough **2** trustworthy, reliable

slipshod *adj*

careless, slapdash, sloppy, slovenly, untidy, disorganized, negligent, lax, casual

🔁 careful, fastidious, neat, tidy, methodical, organized

slip-up *n*

slip, mistake, error, blunder, fault, indiscretion, omission, oversight, failure, *colloq.* bloomer, boob, booboo, howler, clanger

slit *v, n*

▶ *v* cut, gash, slash, slice, split, pierce, lance, knife, rip, tear, *formal* rend

▶ *n* opening, aperture, fissure, vent, cut, incision, gash, slash, split, rip, tear, *formal* rent

slither *v*

slide, skid, slip, glide, slink, creep, snake, worm, undulate

sliver *n*

flake, shaving, paring, slice, wafer, shred, fragment, piece, bit, scrap, chip, splinter, shiver, shard

slob *n*

lout, oaf, sloven, churl, boor, philistine, *colloq.* yob

slobber *v*

drool, dribble, drivel, slaver, foam at the mouth, *formal* salivate

slog *v, n*

▶ *v* **1** HIT, strike, thump, belt, *formal* smite, *colloq.* bash, slosh, slug, sock, wallop **2** PERSEVERE, labour, slave, work, plough through, toil, plod, trudge, trek, tramp

▶ *n* struggle, effort, exertion, grind, labour, hike, trek, trudge, tramp

slogan *n*

jingle, motto, catch phrase, catchword, watchword, battle-cry, rallying cry, war cry, logo

slop *v*

spill, overflow, slosh, splash, splatter, spatter

slope *v*

slant, lean, tilt, tip, dip, pitch, incline, rise, fall (away), drop

▷ **slope off** slip away, sneak off, steal away, leave quietly

sloping *adj*
inclined, inclining, slanting, leaning, oblique, tilting, askew, angled, canting, bevelled, *formal* acclivitous, acclivous, declivitous, declivous
𝔼 level

sloppy *adj*
1 WATERY, wet, liquid, runny, soggy, splashy, mushy, slushy **2** *sloppy work* careless, hit-or-miss, slapdash, slipshod, hurried, hasty, slovenly, untidy, disorganized, messy, clumsy, amateurish **3** SENTIMENTAL, gushy, gushing, mawkish, maudlin, *colloq.* mushy, soppy, schmaltzy, slushy, sickly, corny
𝔼 **1** solid **2** careful, exact, precise, organized, methodical

slosh *v*
1 SPLASH, wade, slop, slog, pour, shower, flounder, spray, swash **2** HIT, strike, thump, thwack, slap, swipe, punch, *colloq.* bash, biff, slug, sock, wallop

slot *n, v*
▶ *n* **1** HOLE, opening, aperture, crack, slit, vent, notch, groove, channel **2** *a slot in your schedule* gap, space, time, vacancy, place, opening, spot, position, niche, *colloq.* window
▶ *v* insert, fit, put, install, place, position, assign, pigeonhole

sloth *n*
laziness, idleness, inactivity, slackness, listlessness, slothfulness, sluggishness, torpor, inertia, *formal* indolence, acedia, accidie, fainéance
𝔼 diligence, industriousness, *formal* sedulity

slothful *adj*
lazy, idle, inactive, inert, slack, listless, sluggish, workshy, torpid, do-nothing, *formal* indolent, fainéant, *colloq.* skiving
𝔼 diligent, industrious, *formal* sedulous

slouch *v*
stoop, hunch, bend, droop, slump, lounge, loll, shuffle, shamble

slovenly *adj*
sloppy, careless, slipshod, untidy, messy, disorganized, scruffy, unclean, dirty, unkempt, slatternly
𝔼 careful, tidy, neat, smart

slow *adj, v*
▶ *adj* **1** LEISURELY, unhurried, lingering, loitering, lagging, dawdling, lazy, sluggish, slow-moving, slow-motion, ponderous, creeping, gradual, deliberate, measured, plodding, at a snail's pace, delayed, late, *formal* tardy, dilatory **2** STUPID, unintelligent, slow-witted, dim, dull, dull-witted, dense, retarded, daft, *colloq.* thick, dumb, dopey **3** PROLONGED, time-consuming, protracted, long-drawn-out, tedious, boring, dull, tiresome, wearisome, uninteresting, uneventful **4** QUIET, sleepy, dull, slack, sluggish, stagnant, dead **5** *slow to anger* unwilling, reluctant, hesitant, averse, disinclined, loath, indisposed
𝔼 **1** fast, quick, swift, rapid, speedy **2** bright, clever, intelligent **3** brief, exciting **4** brisk, lively, exciting
▶ *v* brake, decelerate, ease up, reduce speed, put the brakes on, delay, hold up, handicap, check, curb, detain, keep/hold back, restrict, *formal* retard
𝔼 speed, accelerate

slowly *adv*
leisurely, at a leisurely pace, slowly but surely, unhurriedly, gradually, little by little, by degrees, steadily, lazily, ploddingly, ponderously, sluggishly, at a snail's pace, *technical* lento, adagio, largo, larghetto
𝔼 fast, quickly

sludge *n*
mud, ooze, mire, muck, residue, sediment, silt, slime,

slush, swill, slop, slag, dregs, *colloq.* gunge, gunk

sluggard *n*
idler, loafer, dawdler, slacker, lounger, shirker, good-for-nothing, laggard, waster, wastrel, layabout, do-nothing, *formal* sloth, *colloq.* lazybones

sluggish *adj*
lethargic, listless, torpid, heavy, dull, slow, slow-moving, slothful, languid, lazy, idle, inactive, apathetic, lifeless, unresponsive, phlegmatic, *formal* languorous, indolent, somnolent
𝔼 brisk, vigorous, lively, dynamic

sluggishness *n*
lethargy, listlessness, torpor, phlegm, heaviness, inertia, dullness, slowness, slothfulness, apathy, drowsiness, stagnation, lassitude, *formal* indolence, languor, somnolence, fainéance
𝔼 dynamism, eagerness, quickness

sluice *v*
wash, cleanse, drain, flush, swill, drench, irrigate, slosh

slumber *n, v*
▶ *n* sleep, rest, doze, nap, *formal* repose, *colloq.* snooze, forty winks, shut-eye, *slang* kip
▶ *v* doze, drowse, nap, rest, sleep, *formal* repose, *colloq.* snooze

slummy *adj*
run-down, squalid, dirty, decayed, seedy, sleazy, sordid, ramshackle, overcrowded, wretched

slump *v, n*
▶ *v* **1** COLLAPSE, fall, go down, decrease, drop, plunge, plummet, sink, subside, nosedive, decline, deteriorate, worsen, crash, fail, *colloq.* go down hill **2** DROOP, sag, bend, stoop, slouch, loll, lounge, flop
▶ *n* recession, depression, stagnation, devaluation, downturn, slide, low, lowering, trough, downswing, decline, deterioration, worsening, fall, drop, decrease, plunge, collapse, crash, failure
𝔼 boom, upturn

slur *n, v*
▶ *n* smear, slight, insult, disgrace, discredit, reproach, slander, libel, affront, stain, blot, innuendo, insinuation, stigma, *formal* aspersion, calumny
▶ *v* mumble, speak unclearly, splutter, stumble

slush *n*
1 SNOW, melting snow, wet snow **2** SENTIMENTALITY, emotionalism, romanticism, mawkishness, *colloq.* mush, gush, pulp, schmaltz, soppiness, sloppiness

sly *adj*
wily, foxy, crafty, cunning, artful, guileful, clever, canny, shrewd, smart, astute, knowing, subtle, devious, shifty, tricky, furtive, stealthy, surreptitious, insidious, underhand, covert, secret, secretive, scheming, conniving, mischievous, impish, roguish, *formal* clandestine, *colloq.* sneaky
𝔼 honest, frank, candid, open
▷ **on the sly** in secret, secretly, in private, under cover, privately, stealthily, surreptitiously, underhandedly, furtively, covertly, *formal* clandestinely, *colloq.* on the q.t.
𝔼 openly

smack¹ *v, n, adv*
▶ *v* *Do you ever smack your children?* hit, strike, slap, spank, clap, box, thump, punch, bang, crash, thud, cuff, pat, tap, *colloq.* whack, thwack, belt, clout, wallop, biff, sock, clobber, put over your knee, give a hiding to
▶ *n* blow, slap, spank, box, thump, punch, bang, crash, thud, cuff, pat, tap, *colloq.* whack, thwack, belt, clout, wallop, biff, sock, clobber
▶ *adv* bang, slap-bang, right, plumb, straight, directly, exactly, precisely
▷ **smack your lips** enjoy, relish, savour, drool over,

delight in, anticipate, take pleasure in

smack² *v, n*
- ▶ *v his attitude smacks of hypocrisy* suggest, savour of, hint at, give the impression of, intimate, evoke, bring to mind, remind you of
- ▶ *n* **1** TASTE, flavour, savour, tang, relish, piquancy, zest **2** SUGGESTION, hint, trace, impression, intimation, tinge, touch, dash, speck, whiff, nuance

small *adj*
1 LITTLE, tiny, minute, minuscule, short, slight, puny, petite, diminutive, compact, pocket, cramped, poky, miniature, microscopic, infinitesimal, teeny, mini, pocket, pocket-sized, young, *Scot.* wee, *colloq.* pint-size(d), knee-high to a grasshopper **2** PETTY, trifling, trivial, unimportant, insignificant, minor, inconsiderable, inappreciable, negligible **3** INADEQUATE, insufficient, scanty, meagre, paltry, mean, limited **4** *make you feel small* humiliated, ashamed, embarrassed, crushed, broken, deflated, degraded, disgraced, stupid, unimportant, insignificant
F3 1 big, large, tall, huge **2** great, major, considerable **3** ample

small-minded *adj*
petty, mean, ungenerous, illiberal, intolerant, bigoted, narrow-minded, prejudiced, biased, parochial, insular, rigid, hidebound
F3 liberal, generous, tolerant, broad-minded, open-minded

small-time *adj*
unimportant, minor, insignificant, petty, piddling, inconsequential, no-account
F3 important, major, big-time

smarminess *n*
obsequiousness, unctuousness, oiliness, servility, sycophancy, toadying, suavity, *formal* unctuosity

smarmy *adj*
smooth, oily, unctuous, servile, obsequious, sycophantic, bootlicking, suave, toadying, ingratiating, crawling, fawning

smart *adj, v*
- ▶ *adj* **1** *smart clothes* elegant, stylish, chic, fashionable, modish, neat, tidy, spruce, trim, presentable, dapper, well-dressed, well-groomed, well-turned-out, *colloq.* natty, cool, snazzy **2** CLEVER, intelligent, bright, sharp, acute, shrewd, astute **3** *a smart hotel* fashionable, elegant, expensive, stylish, chic, modish, *colloq.* posh, glitzy, ritzy
F3 1 dowdy, unfashionable, untidy, scruffy **2** stupid, slow **3** cheap
- ▶ *v* sting, hurt, prick, burn, nip, ache, tingle, twinge, throb

smarten *v*
neaten, make neat, tidy (up), make tidy, spruce up, groom, clean, polish, beautify

smash *v, n*
- ▶ *v* **1** *smash a window* break, shatter, crack, splinter, disintegrate, shiver, ruin, wreck, demolish, destroy, dash, defeat, crush, *formal* pulverize **2** CRASH, collide, wreck, strike, bang, bump, drive, go, run, knock, hit, plough, bash, thump
- ▶ *n* accident, crash, collision, pile-up, bump, wreck, *colloq.* smash-up, prang

smashing *adj*
excellent, wonderful, marvellous, superb, terrific, tremendous, great, fantastic, magnificent, sensational, superlative, stupendous, super, exhilarating, first-class, first-rate, fabulous

smattering *n*
bit, modicum, dash, sprinkling, basics, rudiments, elements

smear *v, n*
- ▶ *v* **1** DAUB, plaster, spread, cover, slap, coat, rub, smudge, streak **2** SULLY, blacken, stain, tarnish, slur, taint, *formal* defame, malign, vilify, calumniate, *colloq.* drag someone's name through the mud, *US* badmouth
- ▶ *n* **1** STREAK, smudge, blot, spot, patch, blotch, splodge, splotch, daub **2** *a smear campaign against a politician* taint, slur, stain, slander, libel, *formal* defamation, aspersion, vilification, obloquy, *colloq.* mudslinging, muck-raking

smell *n*

> **Words used for types of smell include:**
> *pleasant:* aroma, bouquet, fragrance, incense, nose, odour, pot pourri, perfume, redolence, scent;
> *unpleasant:* b.o. (body odour), fetor, *US* funk, hum, malodour, mephitis, miasma, *slang* niff,
> *colloq.* pong, pungency, reek, sniff, stench, stink, whiff.

smelly *adj*
stinking, reeking, foul, bad, off, putrid, high, strong-smelling, *formal* malodorous, fetid, mephitic, noisome, *colloq.* pongy, humming

smile *n*
grin, beam, simper, smirk, leer, sneer, laugh, chuckle, giggle, snigger, titter, *colloq.* someone's face lights up, be all smiles

smirk *n*
grin, sneer, snigger, leer, simper

smitten *adj*
obsessed, bewitched, beguiled, charmed, attracted, enthusiastic, captivated, infatuated, enamoured, afflicted, plagued, struck, troubled, burdened, beset, *colloq.* bowled over

smog *n*
fog, pea-souper, smoke, pollution, exhaust, fumes, haze, mist, vapour

smoke *n, v*
- ▶ *n* fumes, exhaust, gas, vapour, mist, fog, smog
- ▶ *v* fume, draw (on), puff (on), light up, smoulder, preserve, cure, dry

smoky *adj*
sooty, black, grey, dark, grimy, murky, cloudy, hazy, foggy, smoggy

smooth *adj, v*
- ▶ *adj* **1** LEVEL, plane, even, flat, horizontal, flush **2** STEADY, even, unbroken, uninterrupted, continuous, flowing, regular, uniform, rhythmic, easy, simple, effortless, problem-free, trouble-free, *colloq.* plain sailing **3** SHINY, polished, burnished, glossy, silky, silken, velvety, sleek, like a mirror, glassy **4** CALM, still, undisturbed, serene, tranquil, peaceful **5** SUAVE, agreeable, smooth-talking, urbane, sophisticated, over-confident, glib, plausible, persuasive, slick, unctuous, ingratiating, crawling, fawning, *colloq.* smarmy
F3 1 rough, coarse, lumpy **2** troublesome, irregular, erratic, unsteady **4** bumpy, rough, choppy
- ▶ *v* **1** IRON, press (down), roll, flatten, plaster (down), slick, rub down, level, plane, even (out), file, sand, grind, polish **2** EASE, alleviate, pacify, soothe, allay, calm (down), palliate, mollify, *formal* assuage, mitigate, appease **3** *smooth the way* make easier, facilitate, ease, help, assist, aid, encourage, clear the way for
F3 1 roughen, wrinkle, crease

smoothly *adv*
evenly, calmly, steadily, soothingly, peacefully, tranquilly, serenely, pleasantly, mildly, easily, effortlessly, equably, fluently

smoothness *n*
1 LEVELNESS, evenness, flatness **2** STEADINESS, evenness, flow, regularity, rhythm, unbrokenness, ease, efficiency, effortlessness, facility, fluency, finish **3** SHINE, polish, silkiness, velvetiness, sleekness, glassiness, serenity, calmness, stillness, softness
F₃ **1** roughness, coarseness

smooth-talking *adj*
persuasive, plausible, slick, suave, silver-tongued, facile, glib, bland, *colloq.* smooth

smother *v*
suffocate, asphyxiate, strangle, throttle, choke, stifle, put out, extinguish, snuff, damp (down), dampen, muffle, inundate, overwhelm, suppress, repress, keep back, hide, conceal, cover, shroud, cocoon, envelop, surround, wrap

smoulder *v*
burn, smoke, fume, rage, foam, boil, seethe, fester, simmer

smudge *n, v*
▶ *n* (dirty) mark, blot, blotch, stain, spot, blemish, blur, smear, streak, smutch
▶ *v* blur, smear, streak, daub, mark, spot, stain, dirty, make dirty, soil, blacken, besmirch

smug *adj*
complacent, self-satisfied, superior, holier-than-thou, self-righteous, pleased with yourself, priggish, conceited
F₃ humble, modest

smuggler *n*
runner, contrabandist, moonshiner, courier, *colloq.* bootlegger, mule

smutty *adj*
dirty, crude, coarse, filthy, indecent, improper, indelicate, obscene, pornographic, risqué, racy, bawdy, suggestive, vulgar, gross, lewd, salacious, ribald, *formal* prurient, *colloq.* blue, off colour, raunchy, sleazy
F₃ clean, decent

snack *n*
refreshment(s), light meal, sandwich, bite, nibble(s), titbit, buffet, *colloq.* elevenses, bite to eat, pick-me-up

snag *n, v*
▶ *n* disadvantage, inconvenience, drawback, catch, problem, difficulty, complication, setback, hitch, obstacle, stumbling-block
▶ *v* catch, rip, tear, hole, ladder

snap *v, n, adj*
▶ *v* **1** *the twig snapped* break, crack, split, splinter, fracture, separate, crackle **2** BITE, nip, bark, growl, snarl, retort, crackle **3** SNATCH, seize, catch, grasp, grip **4** *speak angrily to* growl at, snarl at, lash out at, bark at, speak sharply/brusquely to **5** PHOTOGRAPH, take, film, shoot, record
▷ **snap up** grab, grasp, seize, snatch, pounce on, pick up, pluck, *colloq.* nab
▶ *n* **1** BREAK, crack, bite, nip, flick, fillip, crackle **2** *a cold snap* spell, period, time, stretch, span, stint **3** PHOTOGRAPH, photo, snapshot, print, shot, still, picture
▶ *adj* sudden, immediate, instant, on-the-spot, abrupt

snappy *adj*
1 SMART, stylish, chic, elegant, fashionable, up-to-date, up-to-the-minute, modish, *colloq.* trendy, snazzy, natty **2** QUICK, hasty, brisk, lively, energetic **3** CROSS, irritable, edgy, touchy, brusque, bad-tempered, quick-tempered, ill-tempered, ill-natured, irascible, crabbed, testy, crotchety
F₃ **1** dowdy **2** slow

snare *v, n*
▶ *v* trap, ensnare, entrap, catch, capture, seize, net
▶ *n* trap, wire, net, noose, gin, springe, catch, pitfall

snarl[1] *v*
the dog snarled growl, show your teeth, snap, bark, howl, yelp, lash out at, grumble, complain

snarl[2] *v*
TANGLE, knot, ravel, twist, entangle, enmesh, entwine, embroil, confuse, muddle, jumble, complicate

snarl-up *n*
muddle, tangle, mess, mix-up, jumble, confusion, entanglement, traffic jam, gridlock

snatch *v, n*
▶ *v* grab, seize, steal, kidnap, abduct, take as hostage, make off with, take, take/get hold of, pluck, pull, wrench, wrest, gain, win, clutch, pounce on, grasp, grip, secure, *colloq.* nab, swipe, bag, collar, nail
▶ *n* part, piece, bit, section, segment, fraction, fragment, smattering, snippet, spell

snazzy *adj*
stylish, showy, fashionable, smart, attractive, flamboyant, raffish, sporty, dashing, sophisticated, *colloq.* flashy, jazzy, ritzy, snappy, swinging, with it
F₃ drab, unfashionable

sneak *v, n, adj*
▶ *v* **1** CREEP, steal, slip, slink, sidle, slide, skulk, pad, lurk, prowl, smuggle, spirit **2** TELL TALES, inform on, *colloq.* split, squeal, snitch, blow the whistle on, shop, rat, *slang* grass on
▶ *n* tell-tale, informer, *colloq.* squealer, mole, rat, whistle-blower, *slang* grass
▶ *adj* secret, surprise, quick, covert, furtive, stealthy, surreptitious, *formal* clandestine

sneaking *adj*
private, secret, furtive, surreptitious, hidden, lurking, suppressed, unvoiced, unexpressed, grudging, nagging, niggling, persistent, worrying, uncomfortable, intuitive

sneaky *adj*
shady, shifty, furtive, dishonest, devious, guileful, deceitful, unethical, unreliable, unscrupulous, untrustworthy, sly, snide, double-dealing, base, contemptible, cowardly, nasty, mean, low, low-down, malicious, *formal* disingenuous, *colloq.* slippery
F₃ honest, open, *colloq.* up front

sneer *v, n*
▶ *v* scorn, disdain, look down on, scoff, jeer, mock, ridicule, insult, taunt, slight, gibe, laugh, snigger, snicker, smirk, *formal* deride
▶ *n* scorn, disdain, derision, jeer, mockery, ridicule, insult, taunt, slight, gibe, snigger, snicker, smirk

snicker *v & n*
snigger, laugh, giggle, titter, chuckle, chortle, sneer

snide *adj*
derogatory, sarcastic, cynical, scornful, sneering, hurtful, mocking, taunting, jeering, scoffing, derisive, scathing, biting, caustic, unkind, nasty, mean, spiteful, malicious, ill-natured, *formal* disparaging
F₃ complimentary

sniff *v, n*
▶ *v* **1** BREATHE, inhale, snuff, snuffle **2** SMELL, nose, scent, whiff, get a whiff of
▷ **sniff at** look down on, disdain, sneer at, scoff at, mock, laugh at, slight, spurn, shun, reject, dismiss, disregard, overlook, *formal* deride, disparage
F₃ admire, respect
▶ *n* **1** SMELL, scent, whiff, aroma **2** HINT, whiff, suggestion, trace, impression, intimation

sniffy *adj*
snobbish, snobby, contemptuous, scoffing, sneering,

scornful, condescending, superior, supercilious, disdainful, haughty

snigger *v, n*
snicker, laugh, giggle, titter, chuckle, chortle, sneer, smirk

snip *v, n*
▶ *v* cut, clip, trim, crop, dock, prune, slit, nick, snick, notch, incise
▶ *n* **1** CUT, clip, trim, crop, prune, slit, clipping **2** BIT, fragment, piece, scrap, shred, snippet **3** BARGAIN, giveaway, special offer, good buy, discount, reduction, value for money, *colloq.* steal

snippet *n*
piece, scrap, bit, cutting, clipping, fragment, particle, shred, snatch, part, portion, segment, section

snivel *v*
cry, weep, bawl, sniff, sniffle, snuffle, sob, blub, blubber, whimper, grizzle, moan, whinge, whine

snivelling *adj*
crying, weeping, sniffling, snuffling, blubbering, whimpering, grizzling, moaning, whingeing, whining

snobbery *n*
snobbishness, superciliousness, airs, loftiness, arrogance, haughtiness, pride, pretension, condescension, superiority, disdain, airs and graces, *colloq.* snootiness, uppishness, side

snobbish *adj*
supercilious, disdainful, proud, haughty, snobby, superior, lofty, high and mighty, arrogant, pretentious, affected, condescending, patronizing, *colloq.* snooty, stuck-up, toffee-nosed, uppity, jumped-up, hoity-toity, too big for your boots

snoop *v, n*
▶ *v* spy, sneak, pry, nose, interfere, meddle, *colloq.* poke/stick your nose in, stick/put your oar in
▶ *n* **1** *have a snoop around* sneak, pry, nose, interference, meddling **2** SNOOPER, spy, busybody, pry, meddler, *colloq.* nosy parker, Paul Pry

snooze *v, n*
▶ *v* nap, drop off, nod off, catnap, doze, sleep, *formal* slumber, *colloq.* have forty winks, *slang* kip
▶ *n* nap, catnap, doze, siesta, sleep, *formal* slumber, repose, *colloq.* forty winks, shut-eye, *slang* kip

snout *n*
nose, muzzle, neb, trunk, *formal* proboscis, *colloq.* schnozzle, snitch

snow *n*
snowfall, snowstorm, snowflakes, snowdrift, blizzard, snow flurries, sleet, slush, ice

snub *v, n*
▶ *v* rebuff, shun, spurn, insult, disregard, ignore, brush off, cut, slight, rebuke, put down, squash, humble, shame, humiliate, mortify, *formal* affront, *colloq.* cold-shoulder, give the cold-shoulder to, slap in the face, kick in the teeth
▶ *n* rebuff, brush-off, slight, affront, insult, rebuke, put-down, humiliation, *colloq.* slap in the face, kick in the teeth

snug *adj*
cosy, warm, comfortable, homely, friendly, intimate, sheltered, secure, tight, skintight, figure-hugging, close-fitting, *colloq.* comfy, snug as a bug in a rug

snuggle *v*
nestle, nuzzle, curl up, cuddle, embrace, hug

soak *v*
wet, drench, saturate, penetrate, permeate, infuse, bathe, marinate, souse, steep, submerge, immerse, imbue, ret

soaking *adj*
soaked, soaked to the skin, wet through, drenched,

sodden, waterlogged, saturated, sopping, sopping wet, wringing, dripping, streaming
🔁 dry

soar *v*
fly, wing, glide, plane, tower, rise, take off, ascend, climb, mount, escalate, spiral, rocket, skyrocket
🔁 fall, plummet

sob *v*
cry, weep, shed tears, bawl, howl, blubber, snivel, *colloq.* boohoo

sober *adj*
1 TEETOTAL, temperate, moderate, abstinent, abstemious, clear-headed, *colloq.* sober as a judge, dry, drying out, stone-cold sober, on the wagon, off the bottle, having signed the pledge **2** SOLEMN, dignified, serious, earnest, grave, thoughtful, staid, steady, sedate, quiet, serene, calm, composed, unruffled, unexcited, cool, dispassionate, level-headed, practical, realistic, reasonable, rational, clear-headed, self-controlled **3** *sober dress* sombre, staid, drab, dull, dark, plain, severe, austere, subdued, restrained
🔁 **1** drunk, intemperate **2** frivolous, excited, unrealistic, irrational **3** flashy, garish

sobriety *n*
1 ABSTEMIOUSNESS, soberness, abstinence, moderation, temperance, teetotalism **2** SOLEMNITY, seriousness, staidness, steadiness, calmness, composure, level-headedness, coolness, sedateness, restraint, self-restraint, gravity
🔁 **1** drunkenness **2** excitement, frivolity

so-called *adj*
alleged, supposed, ostensible, nominal, self-styled, professed, would-be, pretended, *soi-disant*, *formal* purported

sociability *n*
friendliness, companionability, congeniality, conviviality, cordiality, affability, neighbourliness, gregariousness, *colloq.* chumminess

sociable *adj*
friendly, outgoing, gregarious, affable, companionable, genial, convivial, cordial, warm, hospitable, neighbourly, approachable, accessible, familiar, *colloq.* chummy
🔁 unsociable, withdrawn, unfriendly, hostile

> 📝 **sociable** or **social** ?
>
> *Sociable* is usually applied to people and means 'friendly, fond of the company of others': *Our new neighbours aren't very sociable*; *He's a cheerful, sociable sort of bloke. Social* means 'of or concerning society': *Problems such as this are social rather than medical in origin*; *social class. Social* also means 'concerning the gathering together or meeting of people for recreation and amusement': *a social club*; *His reasons for calling round were purely social.*

---

social *adj, n*
▶ *adj* **1** *social policies* communal, public, community, civic, common, general, collective, group, organized **2** *social activities* leisure, entertainment, amusement
▶ *n* party, get-together, gathering, dance, *colloq.* do

> 📝 **social** or **sociable** ? *See panel at* SOCIABLE.

---

socialism *n*
leftism, communism, welfarism, Leninism, Marxism, Stalinism, Trotskyism

socialist *adj, n*
▶ *adj* left-wing, leftist, communist, Trotskyist, Trotskyite, *colloq.* commie, leftie, red, Trot

▶ *n* left-winger, leftist, communist, welfarist, Trotskyist, Trotskyite, *colloq.* commie, leftie, red, Trot

socialize *v*
mix, mingle, be sociable, meet people, meet socially, fraternize, get together, go out, entertain, *colloq.* hobnob

society *n*
1 COMMUNITY, population, culture, civilization, nation, public, people, mankind, humanity, human race, humankind **2** CLUB, circle, group, band, body, association, organization, company, corporation, federation, alliance, league, union, guild, fellowship, fraternity, brotherhood, sisterhood, sorority **3** FRIENDSHIP, companionship, camaraderie, fellowship, company **4** UPPER CLASSES, high society, aristocracy, gentry, nobility, elite, *colloq.* nobs, toffs, swells, top drawer, the smart set, the upper crust, Sloane Rangers

sodden *adj*
wet, soaking, soaked, wet, drenched, saturated, sopping, waterlogged, soggy, marshy, boggy, miry, *Scot.* drookit
Fꜱ dry

soft *adj*
1 YIELDING, pliable, flexible, pliant, elastic, springy, plastic, supple, malleable, tender, spongy, squashy, mushy, squelchy, pulpy, *formal* ductile, *colloq.* squishy **2** *soft colours*; *speak in a soft voice* pale, light, pastel, delicate, subdued, shaded, muted, restrained, quiet, low, low-key, whispered, hushed, dim, faint, diffuse, mild, bland, gentle, flowing, soothing, sweet, mellow, melodious, dulcet, pleasant, *formal* mellifluous **3** FURRY, downy, fleecy, velvety, silky, silken, smooth **4** LENIENT, lax, liberal, permissive, indulgent, tolerant, forgiving, forbearing, weak, *colloq.* easy-going, spineless **5** TENDER, kind, generous, sympathetic, affectionate, gentle, merciful, softhearted, sensitive **6** *a soft life* easy, comfortable, luxurious, successful, prosperous, *colloq.* cushy, easy-going, a bed of roses, all beer and skittles
Fꜱ 1 hard, firm **2** harsh, hard, sharp, bright, loud **3** rough **4** hard, strict, severe **5** unsympathetic, cruel **6** hard
▷ **soft spot** fondness, liking, partiality, weakness, *formal* penchant

soften *v*
1 MODERATE, temper, lessen, diminish, alleviate, ease, cushion, soothe, palliate, quell, subdue, mollify, appease, calm (down), still, relax, *formal* mitigate, abate, assuage **2** MELT, liquefy, dissolve, reduce **3** CUSHION, pad, muffle, quicken, lower, lighten
▷ **soften up** persuade, conciliate, disarm, win over, weaken, melt, *colloq.* butter up, soft-soap

soft-hearted *adj*
sympathetic, compassionate, gentle, kind, benevolent, charitable, generous, warm-hearted, tender, affectionate, sentimental
Fꜱ hard-hearted, callous

soft-pedal *v*
moderate, go easy, play down, subdue, tone down
Fꜱ highlight, emphasize

soggy *adj*
wet, damp, moist, soaked, soaking, drenched, sodden, waterlogged, saturated, sopping, sopping wet, dripping, heavy, boggy, spongy, pulpy

soil¹ *n*
1 EARTH, clay, loam, humus, dirt, dust, ground **2** LAND, region, country, territory, *formal* terra firma

soil² *v*
1 DIRTY, begrime, stain, spot, smudge, smear, foul, muddy, pollute, defile **2** *soil your reputation* besmirch, stain, smear, sully, tarnish, defile

soiled *adj*
dirty, grimy, stained, spotted, sullied, polluted, tarnished, *formal* maculate, *colloq.* manky
Fꜱ clean, immaculate

sojourn *n*, *v*
▶ *n* stay, rest, visit, stop, stopover, *formal* peregrination
▶ *v* lodge, rest, stay, stop, *formal* dwell, reside, abide, tarry, tabernacle

solace *n*, *v*
▶ *n* comfort, consolation, relief, alleviation, support, condolence, cheer, *formal* succour
▶ *v* comfort, console, support, allay, alleviate, soften, soothe, *formal* mitigate, succour

soldier *n*, *v*

Types of soldier include:
cadet, private, sapper, NCO, orderly, officer, gunner, infantryman, trooper, fusilier, rifleman, paratrooper, sentry, guardsman, marine, commando, tommy, dragoon, cavalryman, lancer, hussar, conscript, recruit, regular, private, Territorial, *US* GI, warrior, mercenary, legionnaire, guerrilla, partisan, centurion; fighter, serviceman, troops. *See also* RANK¹.

v ▷ **soldier on** continue, persevere, keep on, keep going, remain, hold on, hang on, *colloq.* keep at it, stick at it, plug away

sole *adj*
only, unique, exclusive, individual, single, singular, one, lone, solitary, alone
Fꜱ shared, multiple

solecism *n*
error, mistake, blunder, lapse, gaucherie, impropriety, absurdity, cacology, *faux pas*, *technical* anacoluthon, *formal* incongruity, indecorum, *colloq.* boob, booboo, howler, gaffe

solely *adv*
exclusively, only, singly, uniquely, merely, completely, entirely, alone, single-handedly

solemn *adj*
1 *a solemn expression* serious, grave, sober, sedate, sombre, glum, thoughtful, earnest, formal, awed, reverential **2** GRAND, stately, majestic, ceremonial, ritual, formal, ceremonious, pompous, dignified, august, venerable, awe-inspiring, impressive, imposing, momentous **3** *a solemn promise* sincere, formal, earnest, genuine, wholehearted, committed, grave
Fꜱ 1 light-hearted **2** frivolous

solemnity *n*
1 SERIOUSNESS, earnestness, gravity, sacredness, sanctity, momentousness, dignity, impressiveness, grandeur, stateliness, *formal* portentousness **2** CEREMONY, celebration, observance, rite, ritual, ceremonial, proceedings, formalities
Fꜱ 1 frivolity

solemnize *v*
keep, honour, observe, commemorate, celebrate, dignify

solicit *v*
ask (for), request, crave, beg, implore, plead, pray, apply (for), petition, canvass, *formal* seek, beseech, entreat, supplicate, sue, importune, *colloq.* tout, hustle

solicitor *n*
lawyer, advocate, attorney, barrister, QC

solicitous *adj*
caring, attentive, considerate, concerned, anxious, worried, apprehensive, uneasy, troubled, eager, earnest, zealous

solicitude *n*
care, concern, attentiveness, considerateness, consideration, regard, worry, anxiety, uneasiness, disquiet, trouble

solid *adj*
1 HARD, firm, dense, thick, compact, compressed, strong, concrete, sturdy, substantial, stable, sound, well-built, durable, long-lasting, unshakable **2** RELIABLE, dependable, trusty, trustworthy, worthy, decent, upstanding, upright, sensible, level-headed, steadfast, stable, serious, sober, respectable **3** *solid evidence* reliable, sound, valid, strong, firm, authoritative, weighty, well-grounded, well-founded, *formal* cogent **4** REAL, genuine, pure, concrete, tangible, unadulterated, unmixed, unalloyed **5** *a solid white line* unbroken, continuous, undivided, uninterrupted
◨ **1** liquid, gaseous, hollow **2** unreliable, unstable **3** unsound, unreliable **4** unreal **5** broken, dotted

solidarity *n*
unity, agreement, accord, unanimity, consensus, harmony, concord, cohesion, like-mindedness, singlemindedness, camaraderie, team spirit, *esprit de corps*, soundness, stability
◨ discord, division, schism

solidify *v*
harden, go/become hard, set, gel, jell, congeal, coagulate, clot, cake, crystallize
◨ soften, liquefy, dissolve

solitary *adj, n*
▶ *adj* **1** LONELY, sole, single, lone, alone, lonesome, by yourself, friendless, companionless, unsociable, introverted, reclusive, hermitical, withdrawn, retired **2** REMOTE, lonely, separate, isolated, desolate, out-of-the-way, inaccessible, cloistered, secluded, unfrequented, unvisited, untrodden, *formal* sequestered
◨ **1** accompanied, gregarious, busy **2** accessible
▶ *n* loner, individualist, hermit, recluse, ascetic, monk, anchorite, anchoress, ancress, eremite, stylite, *colloq.* lone wolf

solitude *n*
aloneness, loneliness, singleness, friendlessness, lonesomeness, introversion, unsociability, reclusiveness, retirement, privacy, seclusion, isolation, remoteness, desolation
◨ companionship

solution *n*
1 ANSWER, result, explanation, resolution, key, remedy, way out, panacea, cure-all, clarification, decipherment, disentanglement, unfolding, unravelling, *formal* elucidation, *colloq.* (quick) fix **2** MIXTURE, blend, mix, compound, suspension, emulsion, liquid, solvent

solve *v*
work out, figure out, puzzle out, decipher, crack, disentangle, unravel, unfold, answer, resolve, put right, remedy, settle, clear up, clarify, explain, interpret, get to the bottom of, *formal* rectify, expound, *colloq.* fathom, crack

solvent *adj*
sound, financially sound, able to pay, creditworthy, out of debt, unindebted, *colloq.* in the black
◨ insolvent

sombre *adj*
dark, funereal, drab, dull, dim, obscure, shady, shadowy, gloomy, dismal, dingy, melancholy, mournful, sad, depressed, doleful, morose, joyless, sober, serious, grave, solemn, *formal* funereal, lugubrious
◨ bright, cheerful, happy

somebody *n*
someone, celebrity, dignitary, name, personage, star, superstar, VIP, notable, luminary, magnate, mogul, heavyweight, nabob, panjandrum, *colloq.* household name, bigwig, big noise, big shot, big wheel
◨ nobody

someday *adv*
sometime, at some time in the future, one day, one of these (fine) days, sooner or later, later, later on, in due course, by and by, eventually, ultimately
◨ never

somehow *adv*
by some means, one way or another, come what may, *colloq.* by fair means or foul, by hook or by crook, come hell or high water

sometime *adv, adj*
▶ *adv* someday, one day, at some time in the future, at some time in the past, another time, in the past, then, previously, earlier
▶ *adj* former, previous, one-time, late, retired, emeritus, *formal* erstwhile, quondam, *colloq.* ex

sometimes *adv*
occasionally, on occasion(s), now and again, now and then, on and off, off and on, every so often, once in a while, at times, from time to time
◨ always, never

somnolent *adj*
sleepy, drowsy, dozy, half-awake, heavy-eyed, soporific, torpid, *technical* comatose, *formal* oscitant

son *n*
boy, child, lad(die), offspring, descendant, inhabitant, native, disciple

song *n*

Types of song include:
air, anthem, aria, ballad, barcarole, bird call, bird song, blues, calypso, cantata, canticle, cantilena, canzone, canzonet, carol, chanson, chansonette, chant, chorus, descant, dirge, dithyramb, ditty, elegy, epinikion, epithalamium, folk-song, gospel song, hymn, jingle, lay, love-song, lied, lilt, lullaby, lyric(s), madrigal, melody, number, nursery rhyme, ode, plainchant, plainsong, pop song, psalm, recitative, refrain, requiem, rock and roll, roundelay, serenade, shanty, spiritual, Negro spiritual, threnody, tune, war song, wassail, yodel. *See also* POEM.

songster *n*
singer, vocalist, chorister, balladeer, chanteuse, minstrel, troubadour, crooner, warbler

sonorous *adj*
resonant, resounding, ringing, rich, rounded, orotund, ororotund, full, full-mouthed, full-voiced, full-throated, loud, sounding, high-flown, high-sounding, *formal* grandiloquent, plangent

soon *adv*
shortly, presently, in a little while, in no time (at all), in a short time, in a minute, in a moment (or two), any minute (now), before long, in the near future, *colloq.* pronto, in a jiffy, in a tick, in two shakes of a lamb's tail, before you can say Jack Robinson

soothe *v*
alleviate, relieve, ease, salve, comfort, allay, calm (down), compose, tranquillize, settle (down), still, quiet, quieten (down), hush, lull, pacify, mollify, soften, palliate, temper, *formal* appease, assuage, mitigate
◨ aggravate, irritate, annoy, vex

soothing *adj*
relaxing, restful, calming, easeful, emollient, lenitive, balmy, palliative, balsamic, *technical* anetic, *formal* assuasive, demulcent

⊞ annoying, irritating, vexing

soothsayer *n*
prophet, diviner, foreteller, seer, sibyl, augur, Chaldee, *formal* haruspex

sophisticated *adj*
1 URBANE, cosmopolitan, worldly, worldly-wise, experienced, seasoned, cultured, cultivated, stylish, elegant, refined, polished, suave **2** *sophisticated technology* advanced, highly-developed, complicated, complex, intricate, elaborate, delicate, subtle
⊞ **1** unsophisticated, naïve **2** primitive, simple

sophistication *n*
urbanity, worldliness, culture, experience, elegance, finesse, poise, *savoir-faire*, *savoir-vivre*
⊞ naïvety, simplicity

sophistry *n*
casuistry, sophism, quibble, fallacy, *technical* paralogism, elenchus

soporific *adj, n*
▶ *adj* sleep-inducing, hypnotic, sedative, opiate, narcotic, tranquillizing, sleepy, *formal* somnolent
⊞ stimulating, invigorating
▶ *n* tranquillizer, sleeping pill, sleeping tablet, sedative, opiate, narcotic, hypnotic, anaesthetic, hypnic
⊞ stimulant

soppy *adj*
sentimental, overemotional, mawkish, maudlin, cloying, soft, crazy, wild, silly, *colloq.* slushy, mushy, sloppy, lovey-dovey, weepy, schmaltzy, corny, wet, wimpish, daft

sorcerer *n*
sorceress, wizard, warlock, witch, magician, enchanter, magus, mage, magian, reim-kennar, necromancer, voodoo, angek(k)ok, *formal* thaumaturgist

sorcery *n*
magic, black magic, witchcraft, wizardry, necromancy, voodoo, spell, incantation, charm, enchantment, pishogue, *formal* thaumaturgy

sordid *adj*
1 DIRTY, filthy, unclean, foul, vile, squalid, grimy, stained, soiled, sleazy, mucky, seamy, seedy, disreputable, shabby, tawdry **2** CORRUPT, degraded, degenerate, immoral, debased, dishonest, dishonourable, disreputable, debauched, low, base, vile, foul, despicable, shameful, wretched, mean, miserly, niggardly, grasping, mercenary, self-seeking, *formal* abhorrent, ignominious
⊞ **1** clean, pure **2** honourable, upright

sore *adj, n*
▶ *adj* **1** PAINFUL, hurting, aching, smarting, stinging, burning, chafed, tender, sensitive, inflamed, red, reddened, bruised, injured, raw, wounded **2** ANNOYED, irritated, vexed, angry, upset, hurt, wounded, afflicted, aggrieved, offended, bitter, resentful, distressed
⊞ **2** pleased, happy
▶ *n* wound, cut, graze, laceration, lesion, scrape, abrasion, chafe, swelling, inflammation, boil, abscess, ulcer

sorrow *n, v*
▶ *n* **1** SADNESS, unhappiness, grief, mourning, misery, woe, distress, suffering, pain, dejection, anguish, heartache, heartbreak, misfortune, wretchedness, *formal* affliction, disconsolateness, dolour **2** TROUBLE, misfortune, hardship, worry, trial, regret, remorse, *formal* tribulation, affliction
⊞ **1** happiness, joy **2** joy
▶ *v* grieve, lament, bewail, bemoan, be/feel sad, be/feel miserable, weep, agonize, moan, mourn, pine
⊞ rejoice

sorrowful *adj*
miserable, mournful, sad, unhappy, tearful, sorry, distressing, depressed, dejected, wretched, painful, lamentable, woeful, melancholy, grievous, doleful, heartbroken, heart-rending, heavy-hearted, piteous, rueful, *Scot.* wae, *formal* afflicted, disconsolate, lugubrious, woebegone
⊞ happy, joyful

sorry *adj*
1 APOLOGETIC, regretful, ashamed, remorseful, contrite, penitent, repentant, conscience-stricken, guilt-ridden, shamefaced **2** *sorry to hear the news* sad, unhappy, upset, distressed, *colloq.* down **3** SYMPATHETIC, compassionate, understanding, pitying, concerned, moved **4** *in a sorry state* pathetic, pitiful, poor, wretched, miserable, sad, unhappy, dismal, grievous, heart-rending, shameful
⊞ **1** impenitent, unashamed **2** happy, pleased **3** uncaring **4** happy, cheerful

sort *n, v*
▶ *n* kind, type, ilk, family, race, breed, species, variety, order, class, set, category, group, denomination, style, make, brand, stamp, quality, nature, character, description, *technical* genus, *formal* genre
▷ **out of sorts 1** UNWELL, ill, sick, poorly, laid up, ailing, off-colour, seedy, queasy, diseased, unhealthy, infirm, frail, weak, feeble, bedridden, *colloq.* in a bad way, dicky, below par, down in the dumps, down in the mouth, under the weather, run down, rough, groggy **2** BAD-TEMPERED, irritable, cross, snappy, quick-tempered, grumpy, fractious, in a (bad) mood, narky, impatient, choleric, *colloq.* crotchety, crabbed, crabby, grouchy, stroppy, shirty, ratty, in a huff, in a sulk
▶ *v* class, group, categorize, distribute, divide, separate, segregate, sift, screen, grade, rank, order, classify, catalogue, arrange, put in order, organize, systematize
▷ **sort out 1** ARRANGE, order, put in order, organize, work out **2** CLASSIFY, class, group, categorize, rank, order, grade, separate, divide, segregate, choose, select **3** RESOLVE, clear up, work out, put right, solve

sortie *n*
foray, raid, offensive, attack, charge, assault, sally, swoop, invasion, rush

so-so *adj*
average, middling, moderate, indifferent, fair, adequate, ordinary, respectable, neutral, tolerable, unexceptional, undistinguished, passable, *colloq.* fair to middling, not bad, OK, run-of-the-mill

soul *n*
1 SPIRIT, psyche, mind, reason, intellect, character, inner being, inner self, essence, life, life-giving principle, vital force, *colloq.* heart of hearts **2** INDIVIDUAL, person, human being, man, woman, creature, *colloq.* character **3** *a singer with no soul* sensitivity, sympathy, compassion, feeling, humanity, understanding, appreciation, tenderness, inspiration **4** *he's the soul of discretion* epitome, personification, embodiment, essence, model, example
⊞ **1** body

soulful *adj*
sensitive, emotional, expressive, heartfelt, moving, profound, mournful, meaningful, eloquent
⊞ soulless

soulless *adj*
unfeeling, spiritless, unsympathetic, inhuman, lifeless, cold, callous, cruel, unkind, dead, uninteresting, ignoble, mean, mean-spirited, soul-destroying, mechanical
⊞ soulful

sound¹ *n, v*

▸ *n hear a tapping sound* noise, din, report, resonance, reverberation, tone, timbre, tenor, description

▸ *v* **1** RING, toll, chime, peal, resound, resonate, reverberate, echo, go off **2** ARTICULATE, enunciate, pronounce, voice, express, utter, say, declare, announce

Sounds include:
bang, beep, blare, blast, bleep, boom, bubble, buzz, chime, chink, chug, clack, clang, clank, clap, clash, clatter, click, clink, crack, crackle, crash, creak, crunch, cry, drone, echo, explode, fizz, grate, grizzle, groan, gurgle, hiccup, hiss, honk, hoot, hum, jangle, jingle, knock, moan, murmur, patter, peal, ping, pip, plop, pop, rattle, report, reverberate, ring, roar, rumble, rustle, scrape, scream, screech, sigh, sizzle, skirl, slam, slurp, smack, snap, sniff, snore, snort, sob, splash, splutter, squeak, squeal, squelch, swish, tap, throb, thud, thump, thunder, tick, ting, tinkle, toot, twang, wail, whimper, whine, whirr, whistle, whoop, yell.

Animals sounds include:
bark, bay, bellow, bleat, bray, cackle, caw, chirp, chirrup, cluck, coo, croak, crow, gobble, growl, grunt, hiss, hoot, howl, low, mew, miaow, moo, neigh, purr, quack, roar, screech, snarl, squawk, squeak, tweet, twitter, warble, whinny, woof, yap, yelp, yowl.

sound² *adj*

1 FIT, well, healthy, in good health, in good condition/shape, vigorous, robust, sturdy, firm, solid, whole, sane, complete, intact, perfect, disease-free, unbroken, undamaged, unimpaired, unhurt, uninjured, *colloq.* in fine fettle, sound as a bell **2** VALID, well-founded, well-grounded, reasonable, rational, logical, orthodox, authoritative, weighty, right, true, proven, reliable, dependable, trustworthy, secure, substantial, solid, sturdy, thorough, good, complete, *formal* judicious, cogent

🗷 **1** unfit, ill, shaky **2** unsound, unreliable, poor

sound³ *v*

to sound the depths measure, plumb, fathom, probe, examine, test, inspect, investigate

▷ **sound out** ask, canvass, examine, investigate, research, survey, probe, pump, question, *colloq.* suss out

sound *n*

the Sound of Jura channel, estuary, inlet, passage, strait, firth, fjord, voe

soup *n*

broth, potage, consommé, stock, chowder, bisque, cockieleekie, borsch, gazpacho, mulligatawny, julienne

sour *adj, v*

▸ *adj* **1** TART, sharp, acid, tangy, acidy, aciduous, acetic, pungent, vinegary, bitter, rancid, curdled, turned, *colloq.* off, bad **2** EMBITTERED, bad-tempered, surly, churlish, ill-tempered, peevish, crusty, resentful, unpleasant, nasty, disagreeable, *formal* acrimonious, *colloq.* crabbed, grouchy, shirty, ratty

🗷 **1** sweet, sugary **2** good-natured, generous

▸ *v* disenchant, embitter, make better, exacerbate, exasperate, alienate, spoil, envenom

source *n*

origin, derivation, beginning, start, cause, root, rise, spring, wellspring, fountainhead, wellhead, supply, mine, originator, author, authority, informant, *tech-*

nical ylem, *formal* commencement, provenance, primordium, *fons et origo*

sourpuss *n*

misery, grumbler, killjoy, shrew, whiner, kvetch, *colloq.* crosspatch, grouse, grump, whinger

souse *v*

douse, drench, dunk, sink, immerse, marinate, marinade, pickle, plunge, soak, saturate, steep, dip, submerge

souvenir *n*

memento, reminder, remembrance, keepsake, relic, token, trophy

sovereign *n, adj*

▸ *n* ruler, monarch, king, queen, emperor, empress, tsar, chief, *formal* potentate

▸ *adj* **1** RULING, royal, kingly, queenly, princely, imperial, majestic, absolute, unlimited, supreme, paramount, predominant, principal, chief, dominant, independent, autonomous, self-governing, self-ruling **2** UNRIVALLED, outstanding, utmost, extreme, unequalled

sovereignty *n*

autonomy, independence, supremacy, domination, sway, dominion, kingship, queenship, regality, primacy, raj, *formal* ascendancy, imperium, suzerainty

sow *v*

plant, seed, scatter, strew, bestrew, spread, distribute, disperse, broadcast, lodge, implant, *formal* disseminate

space *n, v*

▸ *n* **1** ROOM, place, seat, accommodation, capacity, area, volume, extent, expanse, sweep, stretch, expansion, latitude, scope, range, play, clearance, elbow-room, leeway, margin, *formal* amplitude **2** BLANK, omission, gap, break, empty space, opening, interval, intermission, chasm, *formal* lacuna, interstice **3** *in a short space of time* period, stretch, span, spell, time, shift, stint **4** OUTER SPACE, the milky way, galaxy, universe, cosmos, solar system, deep space

▸ *v* arrange, order, put in order, range, be apart, set apart, space out, stretch out, string out, place at intervals, *formal* array, dispose

spacious *adj*

roomy, ample, big, large, sizable, broad, wide, huge, vast, immense, extensive, expansive, open, uncrowded, *formal* capacious, commodious

🗷 small, narrow, cramped, confined, *colloq.* poky

spadework *n*

foundation, groundwork, homework, preparation, labour, drudgery, *colloq.* donkey-work

span *n, v*

▸ *n* spread, stretch, reach, range, scope, compass, extent, length, distance, duration, time, interval, term, period, spell

▸ *v* arch, vault, bridge, link, cross, traverse, range, extend, stretch, last, cover, include, *formal* bestride

spank *v*

smack, slap, thrash, slipper, cane, *colloq.* wallop, whack, thwack, tan, put over your knee

spanking *adj, adv*

▸ *adj* brisk, fast, quick, lively, smart, speedy, swift, vigorous, energetic, snappy, invigorating, fine, gleaming

🗷 slow

▸ *adv* absolutely, completely, utterly, totally, exactly, strikingly, positively, brand

spar *v*

argue, dispute, contest, fall out, contend, wrangle, squabble, bicker, wrestle, box, skirmish, *colloq.* scrap, spat, tiff

spare *adj, v*

▶ *adj* **1** RESERVE, emergency, extra, additional, supplementary, leftover, remaining, unused, over, surplus, surplus to requirements, superfluous, supernumerary, auxiliary, unwanted **2** *spare time* free, unoccupied, leisure **3** LEAN, thin, skinny, bony, gaunt, lank, slim, slender, scraggy, scrawny, *colloq.* all skin and bones **4** FRUGAL, scanty, scant, meagre, modest, sparing

🖬 **1** necessary, vital, used **3** fat

▷ **to spare** left over, remaining, extra, in reserve, unused, surplus

▶ *v* **1** PARDON, let off, reprieve, show mercy to, forgive, release, free **2** GRANT, allow, provide, give, afford, part with, do without, manage without, *formal* dispense with **3** NOT HARM, protect, save, guard, safeguard, secure, take care of, defend

sparing *adj*
economical, thrifty, careful, frugal, meagre, miserly, tight-fisted, close-fisted, *formal* prudent, penurious, *colloq.* stingy, mingy

🖬 unsparing, liberal, lavish

spark *n, v*

▶ *n* **1** FLASH, flare, gleam, glint, glimmer, flicker **2** *not a spark of intelligence* flicker, hint, trace, vestige, scrap, bit, touch, suggestion, iota, atom, jot

▶ *v* ▷ **spark off** kindle, set off, trigger (off), start (off), cause, touch off, occasion, prompt, provoke, stimulate, stir, incite, excite, inspire, *formal* precipitate

sparkle *v, n*

▶ *v* **1** TWINKLE, glitter, scintillate, flash, flicker, gleam, glint, glisten, glow, glimmer, shimmer, shine, beam, *formal* coruscate **2** EFFERVESCE, fizz, bubble **3** BE LIVELY, be animated, be spirited, be enthusiastic, be witty, be vivacious, be effervescent, *formal* be ebullient, *colloq.* be bubbly

▶ *n* **1** TWINKLE, glitter, flash, shimmer, gleam, glow, shine, glint, flicker, spark, radiance, brilliance, dazzle, *formal* coruscation **2** SPIRIT, vitality, life, animation, vivacity, liveliness, energy, dash, enthusiasm, *formal* ebullience, *colloq.* get-up-and-go, vim, pizzazz

sparkling *adj*
1 EFFERVESCENT, fizzy, carbonated, bubbly **2** TWINKLING, flashing, glittering, glistening, gleaming, *formal* coruscating **3** LIVELY, animated, scintillating, witty

🖬 **1** flat **3** dull

sparse *adj*
scarce, scanty, meagre, slight, scattered, infrequent, sporadic

🖬 plentiful, thick, dense

spartan *adj*
austere, harsh, severe, rigorous, strict, disciplined, self-denying, ascetic, abstemious, stringent, temperate, frugal, plain, simple, bleak, joyless

🖬 luxurious, self-indulgent

spasm *n*
burst, eruption, outburst, frenzy, fit, bout, convulsion, seizure, attack, paroxysm, contraction, cramp, jerk, twitch, tic, *formal* access

spasmodic *adj*
sporadic, occasional, intermittent, erratic, periodic, irregular, fitful, jerky

🖬 continuous, uninterrupted

spate *n*
flood, deluge, torrent, rush, outpouring, flow

spatter *v*
splatter, splash, splodge, spray, sprinkle, shower, speckle, scatter, daub, bedaub, bestrew, besprinkle, bespatter, dirty, soil

spay *n*
neuter, sterilize, castrate, emasculate, doctor, geld

speak *v*
talk, say, state, declare, express, utter, voice, articulate, enunciate, pronounce, tell, chat, communicate, address, lecture, harangue, hold forth, argue, discuss, *formal* converse, declaim, *colloq.* have a word with, chatter, gab, witter, yak

▷ **speak for** speak on behalf of, represent, act for, stand for, act as spokesperson for

▷ **speak of** refer to, make reference to, mention, make mention of, discuss

▷ **speak out/up** say publicly, speak openly, defend, support, protest, *colloq.* stand up and be counted

▷ **speak to** rebuke, reprimand, scold, warn, lecture, accost, address, *formal* admonish, upbraid, *colloq.* bring to book, dress down, tell off, tick off

▷ **speak up** talk (more) loudly, raise your voice, make yourself heard

speaker *n*
talker, lecturer, orator, spokesperson, spokesman, spokeswoman, mouthpiece, *formal* prolocutor

spearhead *v, n*

▶ *v* lead, head, initiate, launch, front, pioneer

▶ *n* vanguard, front line, leading position, pioneer, trailblazer, leader, guide, overseer, *colloq.* van, cutting edge

special *adj*
1 *a special occasion* important, significant, momentous, major, noteworthy, notable, distinguished, distinctive, memorable, remarkable, extraordinary, outstanding, exceptional, unusual, *colloq.* out of the ordinary, red-letter **2** DIFFERENT, distinctive, characteristic, peculiar, individual, unique, exclusive, select, choice, particular, exact, specific, precise, detailed, *formal* singular

🖬 **1** normal, ordinary, usual, *colloq.* run of the mill **2** general, common

specialist *n*
consultant, authority, expert, master, professional, connoisseur, *colloq.* brains

speciality *n*
strength, feature, forte, talent, gift, field/area of study, field, *pièce de résistance*, *US* specialty

specially *adv*
for a special purpose, for a particular purpose, particularly, exclusively, uniquely, in particular, specifically, explicitly, distinctly, expressly

species *n*
class, kind, breed, sort, type, category, variety, genus, group, collection, description

specific *adj*
precise, exact, fixed, set, limited, determined, particular, special, definite, well-defined, unequivocal, clear-cut, detailed, explicit, express, unambiguous

🖬 vague, approximate, unspecific

specification *n*
requirement, condition, qualification, stipulation, instruction, description, listing, naming, statement, designation, item, particular, detail, *formal* delineation

specify *v*
stipulate, spell out, set out, define, particularize, detail, itemize, particularize, enumerate, list, mention, state, cite, name, designate, indicate, describe, *formal* delineate

specimen *n*
sample, example, instance, illustration, model, pattern, type, representative, copy, exhibit, *formal* paradigm, exemplar

specious *adj*
false, misleading, unsound, untrue, deceptive, plausible, *formal* fallacious, casuistic, sophistic, sophistical
F₃ valid, true

speck *n*
mark, fleck, dot, speckle, shred, grain, particle, bit, blot, defect, blemish, fault, flaw, stain, spot, atom, mite, iota, jot, trace, whit, tittle

speckled *adj*
spotted, spotty, flecked, dotted, dappled, mottled, sprinkled, stippled, brinded, brindle(d), fleckered, freckled, *technical* lentiginous

spectacle *n*
show, performance, display, exhibition, parade, pageant, extravaganza, scene, sight, picture, curiosity, wonder, marvel, phenomenon

spectacles *n*

Types of spectacles include:
bifocals, diving mask, eyeglass, goggles, half-glasses, lorgnette, monocle, pince-nez, Polaroid® glasses, quizzing glass, reading glasses, safety glasses, shooting glasses, sports spex, sunglasses, trifocals, varifocals.

spectacular *adj, n*
▶ *adj* grand, splendid, magnificent, sensational, impressive, glorious, striking, stunning, staggering, amazing, astonishing, extraordinary, outstanding, remarkable, dramatic, daring, breathtaking, dazzling, eye-catching, colourful, ostentatious, flamboyant, *formal* resplendent, opulent
F₃ unimpressive, ordinary
▶ *n* extravaganza, show, display, exhibition, pageant, spectacle

spectator *n*
watcher, viewer, onlooker, looker-on, bystander, passer-by, witness, eye-witness, observer, *formal* beholder, *US slang* rubberneck
F₃ player, participant

spectral *adj*
ghostly, incorporeal, insubstantial, disembodied, supernatural, unearthly, weird, uncanny, phantom, shadowy, eerie, *colloq.* spooky

spectre *n*
1 GHOST, phantom, spirit, wraith, apparition, vision, presence, shade, shadow, revenant, visitant, *colloq.* spook 2 THREAT, menace, fear, dread

spectrum *n*
See RAINBOW.

speculate *v*
1 GUESS, wonder, contemplate, meditate, muse, reflect, consider, deliberate, theorize, suppose, *formal* conjecture, surmise, hypothesize, cogitate 2 GAMBLE, risk, hazard, venture

speculation *n*
1 GUESS, guesswork, consideration, supposition, theory, hypothesis, contemplation, deliberation, flight of fancy, *formal* conjecture, surmise 2 GAMBLE, gambling, hazard, risk

speculative *adj*
conjectural, hypothetical, theoretical, notional, indefinite, vague, abstract, academic, tentative, risky, hazardous, uncertain, unpredictable, unproven, *formal* suppositional, *colloq.* iffy, chancy, dicey

speech *n*
1 COMMUNICATION, spoken communication, language, dialogue, conversation, talk, articulation, pronunciation, diction, enunciation, elocution, accent,

delivery, utterance, voice, tongue, parlance, dialect, jargon, *colloq.* lingo 2 *make a speech* oration, address, discourse, talk, lecture, harangue, patter, conversation, dialogue, monologue, soliloquy, tirade, *formal* diatribe, philippic, *colloq.* spiel

speechless *adj*
dumbfounded, dumbstruck, thunderstruck, amazed, astounded, shocked, aghast, tongue-tied, inarticulate, mute, dumb, silent, mum, *formal* obmutescent
F₃ talkative

speed *n, v*
▶ *n* velocity, rate, pace, tempo, momentum, quickness, swiftness, promptness, rapidity, alacrity, haste, hurry, dispatch, rush, acceleration, *formal* celerity, expeditiousness
F₃ slowness, delay
▶ *v* race, tear, zoom, career, bowl along, sprint, gallop, hurry, rush, dash, accelerate, quicken, *formal* hasten, *colloq.* belt, hurtle, pelt, put your foot down, step on it/the gas/the juice
F₃ slow, delay
▷ **speed up 1** ACCELERATE, quicken, speed, drive faster, go faster, pick up/gather speed, gain momentum, *colloq.* open up, put your foot down, step on it/the gas/the juice, put on a spurt **2** *speed up a process* hurry, step up, stimulate, facilitate, advance, further, promote, spur on, forward, *formal* hasten, expedite, precipitate

speedily *adv*
fast, quickly, rapidly, swiftly, hastily, hurriedly, promptly, posthaste
F₃ slowly

speedy *adj*
fast, quick, swift, rapid, nimble, express, prompt, immediate, hurried, hasty, cursory, summary, *formal* precipitate, expeditious, *colloq.* nippy, zippy
F₃ slow, leisurely

spell¹ *v*
his expression spelt trouble signal, suggest, mean, indicate, imply, promise, signify, herald, *formal* augur, portend, presage
▷ **spell out** explain, clarify, make clear, elucidate, emphasize, detail, stipulate, specify

spell² *n*
a spell of sunny weather period, time, bout, session, term, season, interval, extent, course, stretch, span, patch, turn, shift, stint

spell³ *n*
1 CHARM, incantation, abracadabra, magic, sorcery, witchery, bewitchment, enchantment, trance 2 FASCINATION, charm, glamour, pull, attraction, drawing power, allure, magnetism

spellbinding *adj*
gripping, fascinating, riveting, enthralling, captivating, enchanting, bewitching, entrancing, mesmerizing

spellbound *adj*
transfixed, hypnotized, mesmerized, fascinated, enthralled, gripped, entranced, riveted, captivated, bewitched, transported, enraptured, enchanted, charmed, rapt

spend *v*
1 *spend money* pay out, invest, lay out, waste, squander, fritter, expend, consume, use up, exhaust, finish, *formal* disburse, *colloq.* fork out, shell out, splash out, blow, spend like water, dip/dig into your pocket **2** *spend time* pass, fill, occupy, use (up), take up, while away, put in, employ, apply, devote, *colloq.* do, kill
F₃ **1** save, hoard

spendthrift *n, adj*
▶ *n* squanderer, prodigal, wastrel, *formal* profligate

🖬 miser, hoarder, saver
▶ *adj* improvident, extravagant, prodigal, wasteful, squandering, *formal* profligate

spent *adj*
1 USED (UP), finished, expended, exhausted, consumed, gone **2** TIRED OUT, exhausted, weary, wearied, drained, weakened, *formal* debilitated, effete, *colloq.* worn out, fagged (out), burnt out, all in, bushed, dead beat, dog-tired, done in, jiggered, knackered, shattered, whacked, zonked

spew *v*
vomit, spit out, spurt, gush, issue, retch, regurgitate, disgorge, belch, *colloq.* puke, throw up

sphere *n*
1 BALL, globe, orb, round, globule **2** DOMAIN, realm, province, department, territory, discipline, speciality, field, area, range, scope, compass, extent, rank, function, capacity **3** *a sphere of people* circle, class, group, set, band, crowd, clique

spherical *adj*
round, ball-shaped, globe-shaped, globular, *formal* rotund, globoid, globate, globose, orbicular

spice *n, v*
▶ *n* **1** FLAVOURING, seasoning, piquancy, relish, savour, tang. *See also* HERBS. **2** EXCITEMENT, life, colour, zest, gusto, *colloq.* kick, pep, zap, zip
▶ *v* liven (up), enliven, vitalize, put life into, rouse, invigorate, animate, energize, brighten, stir (up), *colloq.* buck up, pep up, perk up, hot up

spicy *adj*
1 PIQUANT, hot, peppery, pungent, sharp, tangy, tart, seasoned, well-seasoned, flavoured, strongly flavoured, flavoursome, aromatic, fragrant **2** RACY, risqué, ribald, suggestive, indelicate, indecent, improper, scandalous, sensational, *formal* indecorous, unseemly, *colloq.* raunchy, juicy, blue, adult, near the bone/knuckle
🖬 **1** bland, insipid **2** decent

spiel *n*
patter, pitch, sales patter, speech, recital, *formal* oration

spike *n, v*
▶ *n* point, prong, projection, tine, spine, barb, nail, stake, rowel
▶ *v* **1** IMPALE, stick, prick, spear, skewer, spit **2** *spike a drink* lace, drug, add, mix in, contaminate

spill *v, n*
▶ *v* overturn, upset, slop, flow, overflow, disgorge, run (out/over), pour, tip, discharge, well, shed, scatter
▶ *n* fall, accident, tumble, overturn, upset, *colloq.* cropper

spin *v, n*
▶ *v* **1** TURN (ROUND), go round, revolve, rotate, circle, twist, gyrate, twirl, swivel, pirouette, wheel, whirl, whirr, swirl, reel **2** *spin a story/yarn* tell, narrate, relate, make up, invent, fabricate, dream up
▷ **spin out** prolong, extend, lengthen, amplify, pad out, *formal* protract
▶ *n* **1** TURN, revolution, rotation, circle, twist, gyration, twirl, swivel, pirouette, wheel, whirl, swirl, reel **2** COMMOTION, agitation, panic, *colloq.* flap, state, dither, fluster, tizzy, tizz **3** DRIVE, ride, run, trip, journey, outing, jaunt

spindle *n*
axis, pivot, pin, rod, axle, *technical* arbor, fusee

spindly *adj*
long, thin, lanky, gangly, gangling, skinny, spidery, skeletal, spindle-shanked, *formal* attenuate(d), *colloq.* weedy
🖬 stocky, thickset

spine *n*
1 BACKBONE, spinal column, vertebral column, vertebrae, dorsum, rachis **2** THORN, barb, prickle, bristle, spike, needle, quill, rachis **3** STRENGTH OF CHARACTER, courage, bravery, determination, spirit, resolution, mettle, pluck, *formal* fortitude, *colloq.* guts, bottle, grit, spunk

spine-chilling *adj*
frightening, hair-raising, horrifying, scary, terrifying, bloodcurdling, eerie, *colloq.* spooky

spineless *adj*
weak, feeble, irresolute, indecisive, ineffective, cowardly, faint-hearted, spiritless, lily-livered, soft, submissive, weak-kneed, timid, *formal* timorous, *colloq.* chicken, yellow, wet, wimpish
🖬 strong, brave, courageous

spiny *adj*
thorny, thistly, prickly, briery, *formal* spinose, spinous, acanthaceous, acanthous, spinigerous, spiniferous, spicular, spiculate

spiral *adj, n, v*
▶ *adj* winding, twisting, coiled, corkscrew, helical, whorled, scrolled, circular, *technical* cochlear, *formal* cochleate(d)
▶ *n* coil, helix, corkscrew, screw, twist, whorl, convolution, wreath, curlicue, *technical* cochlea, *formal* gyre, volute, volution, volute(d)
▶ *v* **1** WIND, twist, coil, circle, screw, whorl, wreathe, gyrate, gyre **2** *costs spiralling* rise, increase, go up, soar, climb, escalate, rocket, skyrocket

spire *n*
steeple, belfry, tower, turret, pinnacle, peak, summit, crest, top, tip, point, spike

spirit *n, v*
▶ *n* **1** SOUL, psyche, inner being, inner self, mind, breath, life, life-giving principle, vital force, *élan vital* **2** GHOST, spectre, phantom, apparition, supernatural being, presence, wraith, shade, shadow, revenant, visitant, angel, demon, fiend, devil, fairy, sprite, *colloq.* spook **3** MOOD, atmosphere, air, humour, temper, disposition, temperament, character, complexion, feeling(s), morale, make-up, quality, state/frame of mind, attitude, outlook **4** DETERMINATION, strength of character, resolution, willpower, courage, bravery, backbone, mettle, pluck, dauntlessness, stouteartedness, *colloq.* guts, bottle, grit, spunk **5** TENDENCY, characteristic, principle, essence, essential quality, force **6** LIVELINESS, vivacity, animation, sparkle, vigour, energy, zest, fire, ardour, motivation, enthusiasm, zeal, enterprise, *colloq.* pizzazz, zip, kick **7** *the spirit of the law* meaning, sense, substance, essence, drift, gist, tenor, implication, character, quality, *formal* purport
▶ *v* ▷ **spirit away** remove, capture, carry, convey, abstract, seize, kidnap, steal, whisk, *formal* purloin, *colloq.* abduct, snaffle

spirited *adj*
lively, vivacious, animated, sparkling, high-spirited, vigorous, energetic, fiery, passionate, active, ardent, zealous, bold, determined, resolute, courageous, valiant, mettlesome, plucky, confident, *formal* valorous, *colloq.* feisty
🖬 spiritless, lethargic, cowardly

spiritless *adj*
apathetic, weak, lifeless, listless, dull, unenthusiastic, unmoved, lacklustre, anaemic, despondent, depressed, dejected, dispirited, low, melancholy, torpid, droopy, *formal* languid, *colloq.* wishy-washy
🖬 spirited

spirits *n*
1 LIQUOR, alcohol, strong drink, strong liquor, moon-

shine, *colloq.* fire-water, hooch, the hard stuff **2** FEEL-INGS, emotions, mood, temperament, temper, attitude, humour

spiritual *adj*
1 UNWORLDLY, incorporeal, immaterial, ethereal, otherworldly, intangible **2** RELIGIOUS, devotional, heavenly, divine, holy, sacred, ecclesiastical
🖅 **1** physical, material, temporal **2** secular

spit *v, n*
▶ *v* eject, discharge, issue, rasp, hawk, splutter, hiss, *formal* expectorate
▷ **spitting image** likeness, exact likeness, double, lookalike, picture, replica, spit, twin, clone, *colloq.* dead spit, dead ringer, ringer
▶ *n* spittle, saliva, slaver, drool, dribble, sputum, phlegm, *formal* expectoration

spite *n, v*
▶ *n* spitefulness, malice, maliciousness, venom, gall, bitterness, resentment, rancour, animosity, ill-feeling, ill-will, grudge, vengeance, vindictiveness, ill nature, hostility, evil, hate, hatred, *formal* malevolence, malignity, *colloq.* hard feelings
🖅 goodwill, compassion, affection
▷ **in spite of** despite, regardless of, undeterred by, against, defying, in the face of, *formal* notwithstanding
▶ *v* annoy, irritate, irk, vex, provoke, gall, hurt, upset, injure, wound, offend, put out

spiteful *adj*
malicious, venomous, snide, barbed, resentful, bitter, cruel, hostile, rancorous, vindictive, vengeful, ill-natured, ill-disposed, nasty, *formal* malevolent, malignant, *colloq.* catty, bitchy
🖅 charitable, affectionate

splash *v, n*
▶ *v* **1** BATHE, wallow, paddle, wade, dabble, plunge, wet, wash, shower, spray, squirt, sprinkle, spatter, splatter, splodge, splotch, scatter, spread, daub, plaster, slop, slosh, plop, surge, break, dash, beat, strike, batter, buffet, smack **2** PUBLICIZE, show, display, exhibit, flaunt, blazon, trumpet, plaster
▷ **splash out** invest in, lash out, spend, splurge, be extravagant, *colloq.* push the boat out
▶ *n* **1** SPOT, patch, splatter, splodge, splotch, splurge, stain, burst, touch, streak, dash, beating **2** PUBLICITY, display, ostentation, effect, impression, impact, stir, excitement, sensation, *colloq.* splurge

spleen *n*
anger, bad temper, bitterness, resentment, hatred, hostility, ill-will, ill-humour, spite, spitefulness, vindictiveness, peevishness, venom, malignity, wrath, pique, rancour, bile, biliousness, gall, animosity, *formal* acrimony, animus, malevolence, malice, petulance

splendid *adj*
brilliant, dazzling, glittering, lustrous, bright, radiant, glowing, glorious, magnificent, gorgeous, sumptuous, luxurious, lavish, rich, fine, grand, stately, imposing, impressive, great, distinguished, illustrious, renowned, celebrated, outstanding, remarkable, exceptional, sublime, supreme, superb, excellent, first-class, wonderful, marvellous, admirable, *formal* resplendent, opulent, refulgent, *colloq.* fabulous, terrific, super
🖅 drab, ordinary, run-of-the-mill

splendour *n*
brightness, radiance, brilliance, dazzle, glow, gleam, lustre, glory, luxury, sumptuousness, magnificence, richness, grandeur, majesty, illustriousness, solemnity, pomp, ceremony, display, show, spectacle, *formal* resplendence, opulence
🖅 drabness, squalor

splenetic *adj*
angry, cross, bad-tempered, irritable, irascible, sullen, spiteful, choleric, morose, peevish, churlish, fretful, bilious, envenomed, acid, crabby, sour, testy, touchy, *formal* petulant, rancorous, *colloq.* bitchy, crabbed, ratty

splice *v*
join, fasten, connect, marry, bind, tie, plait, braid, interweave, interlace, intertwine, entwine, mesh, knit, graft
▷ **get spliced** get married, wed, become husband and wife, *colloq.* get hitched, tie the knot, take the plunge

splinter *n, v*
▶ *n* sliver, shiver, chip, shard, fragment, bit, piece, shred, flake, shaving, paring, *colloq.* smithereens
▶ *v* split, break, break into pieces, fracture, smash, shatter, shiver, crumble, fragment, disintegrate, *formal* cleave

split *v, n, adj*
▶ *v* **1** *split the logs; the cloth split* break, cut, splinter, shiver, crack, burst, rupture, tear, rip, chop, slit, slash, open, *old use* rend, *formal* cleave **2** *split in two* divide, separate, partition, halve, bisect, share **3** *split the profits* share, separate, divide, halve, allocate, allot, apportion, distribute, hand out, dole out, parcel out, *colloq.* carve up **4** PART COMPANY, part, disunite, disband, break up, set apart, dissociate from, divide, separate, divorce, become estranged, become alienated **5** INFORM ON, betray, incriminate, *colloq.* tell on, shop, squeal, rat, blow the whistle on, *slang* grass
▷ **split hairs** find fault, quibble, pettifog, over-refine, cavil, *colloq.* nit-pick
▷ **split up** part, part company, disband, break up, separate, divorce, get divorced
▶ *n* **1** DIVISION, separation, partition, break, cut, breach, gap, cleft, crevice, crack, fissure, rupture, tear, rip, rift, slit, slash **2** SCHISM, disunion, dissension, discord, difference, division, separation, rupture, estrangement, alienation, divergence, break-up
▶ *adj* divided, cleft, bisected, dual, twofold, broken, fractured, cracked, ruptured, *formal* cloven

split-up *n*
break-up, separation, divorce, estrangement, alienation, parting, parting of the ways

spoil *v*
1 MAR, upset, wreck, ruin, destroy, damage, bodge, impair, harm, hurt, injure, deface, disfigure, blemish, taint, contaminate, pollute, foul, tarnish, deform, obliterate, poison, *colloq.* mess up, throw a spanner in the works, pour cold water on, put a damper on, cast a shadow over, *slang* louse up, screw up **2** *spoil a child* indulge, overindulge, pamper, cosset, coddle, mollycoddle, baby, spoon-feed, *colloq.* wait on hand and foot **3** DETERIORATE, go bad, go off, go sour, sour, turn, curdle, decay, decompose, rot, go/become rotten
▷ **spoil for** be eager for, be keen on, be intent on, long for, yearn for

spoils *n*
plunder, loot, booty, haul, gain, benefit, profit, acquisitions, prizes, winnings, *formal* spoliation, *colloq.* pickings, *slang* swag

spoilsport *n*
misery, killjoy, party-pooper, meddler, damper, *colloq.* dog in the manger, wet blanket, wowser

spoken *adj*
verbal, oral, voiced, said, stated, told, uttered, phonetic, expressed, declared, unwritten, viva voce

☱ unspoken, unexpressed, written

spokesman, spokeswoman *n*
spokesperson, representative, delegate, agent, voice, negotiator, arbitrator, intermediary, mediator, go-between, broker, mouthpiece, propagandist

sponge *v*
1 WIPE, mop, clean, wash, swab 2 *sponge off/on other people* cadge, beg, borrow, scrounge, *colloq.* bum, bludge, freeload

sponger *n*
cadger, scrounger, parasite, hanger-on, beggar, borrower, *colloq.* freeloader, bum, moocher, bludger

spongy *adj*
soft, cushioned, cushiony, yielding, elastic, resilient, springy, squashy, porous, absorbent, light

sponsor *n, v*
▶ *n* patron, supporter, backer, friend, promoter, subsidizer, underwriter, guarantor, surety, *colloq.* angel
▶ *v* finance, fund, bankroll, subsidize, patronize, be a patron of, back, support, promote, underwrite, guarantee, put up the money for

spontaneous *adj*
1 UNPLANNED, voluntary, unprompted, uncompelled, impromptu, extempore, unrehearsed, unpremeditated, free, willing, unhesitating, *colloq.* spur of the moment, knee-jerk 2 NATURAL, unforced, untaught, instinctive, impulsive
☱ 1 planned, deliberate 2 forced, studied

spontaneously *adv*
voluntarily, willingly, freely, impromptu, extempore, impulsively, on impulse, unplanned, unprompted, instinctively, of your own accord, on the spur of the moment, *colloq.* off the cuff, off the top of your head

spoof *n*
joke, hoax, game, travesty, trick, prank, fake, deception, caricature, bluff, burlesque, parody, mockery, satire, lampoon, *colloq.* send-up, take-off, con, leg-pull

spooky *adj*
creepy, chilling, frightening, hair-raising, ghostly, scary, mysterious, spine-chilling, supernatural, weird, unearthly, uncanny, eerie

spoon-feed *v*
indulge, overindulge, cosset, pamper, spoil, mollycoddle, baby, featherbed, *colloq.* wait on hand and foot

sporadic *adj*
occasional, intermittent, infrequent, isolated, spasmodic, erratic, irregular, uneven, random, scattered
☱ frequent, regular

sport *n, v*
▶ *n* 1 GAME, exercise, activity, physical activity, pastime, amusement, entertainment, diversion, recreation, pleasure, fun, play 2 FUN, mirth, humour, joking, jesting, banter, teasing, mockery, ridicule, sneering, *colloq.* kidding

Sports include:
badminton, fives, lacrosse, squash, table-tennis, *colloq.* ping-pong, tennis; American football, baseball, basketball, billiards, boules, bowls, cricket, croquet, football, golf, handball, hockey, netball, pétanque, pitch and putt, polo, pool, putting, rounders, Rugby, snooker, soccer, tenpin bowling, volleyball; athletics, cross-country, decathlon, discus, high-jump, hurdling, javelin, long-jump, marathon, pentathlon, pole vault, running, shot put, triple-jump; angling, canoeing, diving, fishing, rowing, sailing, skin-diving, surfing,

swimming, synchronized swimming, water polo, water-skiing, windsurfing, yachting; bobsleigh, curling, ice-hockey, ice-skating, skiing, speed skating, tobogganing (luging); aerobics, fencing, gymnastics, jogging, keep-fit, roller-skating, trampolining; archery, darts, quoits; boxing, judo, jujitsu, karate, kung fu, tae kwon do, weightlifting, wrestling; climbing, mountaineering, rock-climbing, walking, orienteering, pot-holing; cycle racing, drag-racing, go-karting, motor racing, speedway racing, stock-car racing, greyhound-racing, horse-racing, show-jumping, trotting, hunting, shooting, clay-pigeon shooting; gliding, sky-diving.

▶ *v* wear, display, exhibit, show off

sporting *adj*
sportsmanlike, decent, modest, considerate, fair, reasonable, respectable, just, honourable, gentlemanly, ladylike
☱ unsporting, ungentlemanly, unfair

sportive *adj*
playful, lively, frisky, frolicsome, gamesome, gay, jaunty, merry, skittish, sprightly, prankish, rollicking, coltish, kittenish

sports equipment

Kinds of sports equipment:
ball, basketball, boule, bowl, jack, wood, football, netball, rugby ball, tenpin bowling ball, volleyball; fishing-rod, fly rod, spinning rod, fishing-line, paternoster, reel, fly reel, hook, gaff, gang-hook, jig, trace, lure, bait, fly, float, net, keep-net, priest, disgorger; bow, arrow, crossbow, bolt; badminton racket, shuttlecock, net; baseball bat, baseball, mitt, catcher's glove; boxing glove, gum shield, punch-bag, punch-ball; cricket bat, cricket ball, wicket, stump, bail, nets; épée, foil, sabre, face-guard, mask; discus, hammer, javelin, shot; golf club, golfball, tee, golfing glove; asymmetrical bars, horizontal bar, isometric bar, parallel-bars, beam, balance-beam, mat, pommel horse, vaulting horse, rings, rope, springboard, trampoline; hockey stick, hockey ball, ice-hockey stick, puck, hockey skate; curling stone; ice-skate, roller-skate, rollerblade, roller boot, speed skate, skateboard; ski, ski stick, snow board, toboggan; snooker ball, billiard ball, cue ball, table, cue, rest, bridge, rack, chalk; squash racket, squash ball; table-tennis bat, table-tennis ball, net; tennis racket, tennis ball, net, racket press; oar, aqualung, snorkel, water-ski, sailboard, surfboard. *See also* GOLF CLUB.

sporty *adj*
1 ATHLETIC, fit, energetic, outdoor 2 STYLISH, jaunty, showy, loud, flashy, casual, informal, *colloq.* trendy, natty, snazzy

spot *n, v*
▶ *n* 1 DOT, speckle, fleck, mark, speck, blotch, blot, splodge, splotch, smudge, daub, splash, stain, discoloration, blemish, flaw 2 PIMPLE, blackhead, boil, pock, papula, papule, pustule 3 PLACE, point, position, situation, location, site, scene, setting, locality, local, area 4 *have a spot of lunch* bit, little, some, small amount, bite, morsel 5 *have a spot on television* slot, niche, opening, position, place, time, airtime, show, programme 6 PLIGHT, predicament, quandary, difficulty, trouble, mess, *colloq.* fix, hole, jam, scrape, pickle

▶ *v* **1** NOTICE, see, observe, detect, discern, identify, recognize, make out, catch sight of, *formal* descry, espy **2** MARK, dot, speckle, fleck, soil, blemish, taint, stain

spotless *adj*
immaculate, clean, white, gleaming, shining, spick and span, unmarked, unstained, unblemished, unsullied, untainted, pure, chaste, virgin, virginal, untouched, innocent, blameless, faultless, irreproachable
☒ dirty, impure

spotlight *v, n*
▶ *v* emphasize, stress, accentuate, focus on, highlight, underline, illuminate, feature, point up, draw attention to, give prominence to, throw into relief
☒ tone down, play down
▶ *n* attention, public attention, public eye, fame, emphasis, notoriety, interest, *colloq.* limelight

spotted *adj*
dotted, speckled, flecked, mottled, dappled, pied, piebald, brindled, polka-dot, spotty, *formal* macular, guttate(d)

spotty *adj*
1 PIMPLY, pimpled, blotchy, spotted, speckled, dotted, flecked, mottled, dappled, pied, piebald **2** PATCHY, uneven, inconsistent, varying, erratic, bitty

spouse *n*
husband, wife, partner, companion, consort, mate, *colloq.* better half, other half, hubby, missus

spout *v, n*
▶ *v* **1** SPURT, jet, squirt, spray, shoot, gush, flow, stream, pour, surge, erupt, emit, discharge, disgorge, spew **2** *spouting poetry* pontificate, go on, rant, hold forth, spout off/forth, *formal* expatiate, sermonize, orate, *colloq.* spiel, rabbit on, waffle, witter (on)
▶ *n* stream, jet, fountain, geyser, gargoyle, outlet, nozzle, rose, spray

sprawl *v*
1 *sprawl on the couch* flop, slump, stretch, slouch, recline, *formal* repose, *colloq.* loll, lounge **2** STRAGGLE, spread, stretch, trail, ramble

spray[1] *n, v*
▶ *n* **1** MOISTURE, drizzle, mist, foam, froth, spume, shower, jet, spindrift **2** AEROSOL, atomizer, sprinkler, vaporizer
▶ *v* shower, spatter, spout, sprinkle, scatter, diffuse, disperse, gush, jet, wet, drench, *formal* disseminate

spray[2] *n*
a spray of flowers/leaves sprig, branch, corsage, posy, nosegay, bouquet, garland, wreath

spread *v, n*
▶ *v* **1** STRETCH, extend, sprawl, broaden, widen, dilate, enlarge, develop, grow, increase, advance, expand, grow/become bigger, swell, mushroom, proliferate, escalate, spill over, open (out), unroll, unfurl, unfold, fan out, cover, lay (out), order, set, arrange **2** SCATTER, strew, diffuse, radiate, fan out, broadcast, transmit, communicate, propagate, make public, make known, publicize, advertise, publish, circulate, go/get round, distribute, *formal* disseminate, promulgate **3** COAT, cover, put on, apply, smear, layer
☒ **1** close, fold **2** suppress
▶ *n* **1** STRETCH, reach, span, extent, expanse, sweep, compass **2** *the spread of disease* advance, development, expansion, increase, proliferation, escalation, swelling, mushrooming, diffusion, dispersion, distribution, transmission, broadcasting, communication, propagation, *formal* dissemination **3** LARGE MEAL, banquet, feast, party, dinner, dinner party, treat, *formal* repast, *colloq.* blow-out

spree *n*
bout, fling, orgy, revel, carouse, debauch, *colloq.* binge, splurge, razzle, razzle-dazzle, bender

sprig *n*
twig, stem, spray, shoot, branch, bough

sprightly *adj*
agile, nimble, spry, active, energetic, lively, animated, spirited, vivacious, hearty, brisk, jaunty, playful, frolicsome, cheerful, light-hearted, blithe, airy, *colloq.* perky
☒ doddering, inactive, lifeless

spring *v, n*
▶ *v* **1** JUMP, leap, vault, bound, hop, bounce, rebound, recoil **2** ORIGINATE, derive, come, stem, arise, start, proceed, issue, descend, emerge, emanate, appear, sprout, grow, develop **3** *spring the news on someone* tell unexpectedly, reveal suddenly, present without warning
▷ **spring up** appear suddenly, come into existence, come into being, develop, grow, shoot up, sprout up, proliferate, mushroom
▶ *n* **1** JUMP, leap, vault, bound, hop, bounce, rebound, recoil **2** SPRINGINESS, resilience, give, flexibility, elasticity, bounciness, buoyancy **3** LIVELINESS, energy, spirit, briskness, cheerfulness, light-heartedness, animation **4** SOURCE, origin, beginning, basis, cause, root, fountainhead, wellhead, wellspring, well, geyser, spa

springy *adj*
bouncy, resilient, flexible, elastic, stretchy, rubbery, spongy, buoyant, tensible, tensile
☒ hard, stiff, rigid

sprinkle *v*
shower, spray, spatter, splash, trickle, scatter, strew, dot, pepper, dust, powder

sprinkling *n*
few, handful, dash, scattering, scatter, smattering, sprinkle, trickle, touch, trace, dusting, *formal* admixture

sprint *v*
run, race, dash, tear, fly, dart, career, shoot, *colloq.* belt, scoot, zip

sprite *n*
spirit, elf, fairy, goblin, imp, kelpie, nymph, naiad, puck, pouke, pixie, sylph, brownie, leprechaun, dryad, apparition

sprout *v*
shoot, bud, germinate, grow, develop, come up, put forth, spring up

spruce *adj, v*
▶ *adj* smart, elegant, neat, trim, dapper, well-dressed, chic, well-turned-out, well-groomed, sleek, *colloq.* natty, cool, snazzy
☒ scruffy, untidy
▶ *v* ▷ **spruce up** neaten, tidy (up), smarten up, groom, preen, primp, titivate

spry *adj*
sprightly, quick, alert, agile, energetic, brisk, ready, nimble, active, supple, *colloq.* nippy, peppy
☒ doddering, inactive, lethargic

spume *n*
foam, froth, lather, suds, head, bubbles, fizz, effervescence

spunk *n*
courage, nerve, spirit, pluck, resolution, toughness, gameness, heart, mettle, chutzpah, *colloq.* guts, grit, bottle, backbone
☒ *colloq.* funk

spur *v, n*
▶ *v* stimulate, prompt, incite, drive, propel, impel, urge,

induce, encourage, motivate, goad, prod, poke, prick
F3 curb, discourage
▶ *n* incentive, encouragement, inducement, motive, motivation, stimulus, stimulant, urge, incitement, impetus, prompt, fillip
F3 curb, disincentive, discouragement
▷ **on the spur of the moment** on impulse, impulsively, impetuously, spontaneously, impromptu, unexpectedly, suddenly, thoughtlessly, unpremeditatedly, without planning, *colloq.* on the spot

spurious *adj*
false, fake, counterfeit, forged, fraudulent, deceitful, contrived, bogus, mock, sham, feigned, pretended, simulated, imitation, artificial, *colloq.* make-believe, pseudo, phoney, trumped-up
F3 genuine, authentic, real

spurn *v*
reject, turn down, turn away, say no to, scorn, condemn, despise, disdain, rebuff, repulse, repudiate, slight, snub, ignore, disregard, *colloq.* cold-shoulder, look down on
F3 accept, embrace

spurt *v, n*
▶ *v* gush, spray, squirt, jet, shoot, pour, stream, well, burst, erupt, issue, surge
▶ *n* **1** JET, gush, stream, spray, squirt, outpouring, welling, eruption **2** *a spurt of activity* burst, rush, surge, rush, increase, spate, fit, access

spy *n, v*
▶ *n* secret agent, undercover agent, foreign agent, enemy agent, double agent, fifth columnist, scout, snooper, *colloq.* mole
▶ *v* spot, glimpse, notice, see, observe, discern, discover, make out, catch sight of, *formal* espy, descry
▷ **spy on** watch, observe (closely), keep an eye on, keep tabs on, keep under surveillance

squabble *v, n*
▶ *v* bicker, wrangle, fight, quarrel, row, argue, dispute, have words, clash, brawl, *colloq.* scrap, set to
▶ *n* row, clash, dispute, fight, argument, disagreement, spat, *colloq.* barney, scrap, set-to, tiff

squad *n*
crew, team, gang, band, group, company, unit, brigade, platoon, troop, force, outfit

squalid *adj*
1 DIRTY, filthy, unclean, grimy, grubby, mucky, foul, disgusting, repulsive, sordid, seedy, dingy, untidy, slovenly, unkempt, broken-down, run-down, ramshackle, dilapidated, neglected, uncared-for, *colloq.* sleazy, grotty **2** REPULSIVE, low, mean, nasty, sordid, unpleasant, wretched, vile, shameful, obscene, offensive, disgraceful
F3 **1** clean, attractive **2** pleasant

squall *n, v*
▶ *n* wind, storm, gale, gust, hurricane, blow, tempest, windstorm
▶ *v* wail, yell, cry, howl, yowl, moan, groan

squally *adj*
windy, stormy, rough, wild, gusty, blowy, blustery, tempestuous, turbulent

squalor *n*
squalidness, dirtiness, dirt, filthiness, filth, foulness, uncleanness, grime, griminess, grubbiness, muckiness, dinginess, decay, neglect, meanness, wretchedness, *colloq.* sleaziness

squander *v*
waste, misspend, misuse, lavish, fritter away, throw away, dissipate, scatter, spend, expend, consume, *colloq.* splash out on, splurge, throw/pour down the drain, spend money like water, spend money as if it grows on trees, spend money as if it's going out of

style/fashion, spend money like there's no tomorrow, *slang* blow

square *n, v, adj*
▶ *n* **1** QUADRANGLE, market square, town square, plaza, *colloq.* quad **2** TRADITIONALIST, conservative, conventionalist, conformer, conformist, diehard, *colloq.* fuddy-duddy, (old) fogey, stick-in-the-mud
▶ *v* settle (up), reconcile, tally, agree, harmonize, conform, correspond, match, be compatible with, balance, straighten, level, align, even, make equal, adjust, regulate, set/put right, adapt, tailor, fit, suit, *formal* accord, be congruous with
▶ *adj* **1** QUADRILATERAL, rectangular, right-angled, perpendicular, straight, true, even, level **2** FAIR, equitable, just, ethical, upright, straight, honourable, honest, genuine, above-board, *colloq.* on the level **3** TRADITIONALIST, conservative, conventionalist, conformist, diehard, old-fashioned, strait-laced, *colloq.* fuddy-duddy

squash *v*
1 CRUSH, flatten, press, squeeze, compress, crowd, pack, jam, trample, stamp, pound, grind, pulp, mash, smash, distort, *formal* macerate, pulverize **2** SUPPRESS, silence, quell, quash, annihilate, put down, squelch, snub, humiliate
F3 **1** stretch, expand

squashy *adj*
soft, spongy, squelchy, mushy, pappy, pulpy, squishy, yielding
F3 firm

squat *v, adj*
▶ *v* crouch, stoop, bend, kneel, hunch, sit on your haunches, sit
▶ *adj* short, stocky, thickset, dumpy, chunky, stubby
F3 slim, lanky, slender

squawk *v, n*
screech, shriek, cry, scream, yelp, croak, cackle, crow, hoot

squeak *v, n*
squeal, whine, creak, peep, cheep, pipe

squeal *v, n*
▶ *v* **1** CRY, shout, yell, howl, yelp, wail, scream, screech, shriek, squawk **2** INFORM, tell tales, sneak, betray, *colloq.* tell, shop, snitch, split, rat, *slang* grass
▶ *n* cry, shout, yell, howl, yelp, wail, scream, screech, shriek, squawk

squeamish *adj*
queasy, nauseated, nauseous, sick, delicate, fastidious, finicky, particular, punctilious, prudish, strait-laced, scrupulous

squeeze *v, n*
▶ *v* **1** PRESS, squash, crush, pulp, mash, pinch, nip, tighten, compress, twist, wring, extract, grip, clasp, clutch, pinch, hold tight, hug, embrace, enfold, cuddle **2** *squeeze into a corner* cram, stuff, pack, crowd, crush, squash, wedge, jam, force, ram, push, thrust, shove, jostle **3** WRING, wrest, extort, milk, force, pressurize, pressure, *colloq.* bleed, lean on, put the screws on
▶ *n* **1** PRESS, squash, crush, crowd, congestion, jam **2** HUG, embrace, cuddle, hold, grasp, grip, clutch, clasp

squint *adj*
crooked, indirect, oblique, off-centre, aslant, askew, awry, cock-eyed, *technical* strabismic, *colloq.* skew-whiff
F3 straight

squirm *v*
wriggle, twist, writhe, squiggle, move, shift, wiggle, fidget, agonize, flounder

squirt v, n
▶ v spray, spurt, jet, shoot, spout, gush, stream, spew (out), ejaculate, discharge, issue, pour, well, surge, emit, eject, expel
▶ n spray, spurt, jet, stream, gush, surge

stab v, n
▶ v pierce, puncture, cut, wound, injure, gore, knife, spear, skewer, slash, bayonet, transfix, stick, push, jab, thrust
▷ **stab in the back** betray, deceive, let down, slander, double-cross, inform on, sell out, *colloq.* sell down the river
▶ n **1** ACHE, pang, pain, spasm, throb, twinge, prick **2** CUT, puncture, incision, slash, gash, injury, wound, jab **3** TRY, attempt, go, endeavour, venture, *formal* essay, *colloq.* bash, crack, shot, whirl

stabbing adj
shooting, stinging, piercing, throbbing, painful, acute

stability n
steadiness, firmness, secureness, soundness, sturdiness, solidity, reliability, durability, uniformity, constancy, regularity, unchangeability
🔳 instability, unsteadiness, insecurity, weakness

stable adj
1 *a stable structure* balanced, fixed, static, steady, firm, secure, fast, sound, strong, sturdy, solid, sure, reliable **2** *a stable government/relationship* established, well-founded, deep-rooted, lasting, long-lasting, durable, enduring, abiding, permanent, dependable, reliable, unchangeable, invariable, unwavering, unswerving **3** *the patient's condition is stable* regular, uniform, steady, constant, unchanging
🔳 **1** wobbly, shaky, weak, unstable **2** unstable **3** irregular, erratic, unstable

stack n, v
▶ n **1** HEAP, pile, mound, mass, load, collection, accumulation, store, hoard, stock, stockpile **2** *stacks of money* a large amount, lot, great numbers, many, a good/great deal, *colloq.* oodles, tons, loads, masses, heaps, piles
▶ v heap, pile, load, amass, accumulate, assemble, gather, save, hoard, stockpile

stadium n
sports ground, sports field, field, arena, bowl, ring, track, pitch

staff n, v
▶ n **1** *member of staff* personnel, workforce, workers, employees, crew, team, teachers, officers **2** STICK, pole, cane, crook, rod, baton, crutch, wand, truncheon, prop, crosier
▶ v man, work, operate, occupy, provide, supply, equip

stage n, v
▶ n **1** PHASE, point, juncture, step, time, period, division, lap, leg, length, level, floor **2** PLATFORM, podium, dais, rostrum, stand, apron, *colloq.* soapbox **3** ARENA, setting, scene, sphere, field, realm, background, backdrop
▷ **the stage** theatre, drama, the play, dramatics, theatrics, show business, *formal* Thespian art, *colloq.* the boards, the footlights, rep
▶ v mount, put on, lay on, put together, present, produce, give, do, perform, direct, arrange, organize, stage-manage, orchestrate, engineer

stagger v
1 LURCH, totter, teeter, wobble, sway, rock, roll, pitch, reel, falter, hesitate, waver **2** SURPRISE, amaze, astound, astonish, stun, stupefy, dumbfound, shake, shock, confound, overwhelm, *colloq.* flabbergast, nonplus, bowl over

staggering adj
amazing, astounding, astonishing, surprising, dra-

matic, shocking, stunning, stupefying, unexpected, unforeseen, *colloq.* mind-boggling

stagnant adj
1 *stagnant water* still, motionless, unflowing, standing, brackish, stale, foul, dirty, filthy, smelly, unhealthy **2** *a stagnant economy* inactive, slow, quiet, dull, sluggish, torpid, lethargic
🔳 **1** fresh, moving **2** busy

stagnate v
vegetate, become stagnant, idle, languish, do nothing, decline, deteriorate, degenerate, decay, rot, putrefy, fester, rust

staid adj
sedate, calm, composed, sober, demure, solemn, serious-minded, serious, proper, formal, grave, sombre, quiet, steady, stiff, starchy, prim, *formal* decorous
🔳 jaunty, debonair, frivolous, adventurous

stain v, n
▶ v **1** MARK, spot, blemish, blot, blotch, smear, smudge, discolour, dirty, soil, taint, contaminate, corrupt, sully, tarnish, blacken, disgrace, damage, injure, *formal* besmirch **2** DYE, tint, tinge, colour, paint, varnish
▶ n mark, spot, blemish, blot, blotch, smear, splodge, smudge, discoloration, smear, slur, taint, disgrace, shame, dishonour, damage, injury

stake¹ n, v
▶ n *a stake supporting a young tree* post, pole, standard, picket, pale, paling, spike, stick, rod
▶ v **1** SUPPORT, fasten, brace, tie, tie up, prop (up), secure, hold (up), tether, pierce **2** *stake a claim* establish, lay claim to, state, declare, demand, put in, *formal* requisition
▷ **stake out** demarcate, define, delimit, stake off, mark out, outline, reserve, survey, watch, keep an eye on

stake² n, v
▶ n **1** INVESTMENT, share, claim, involvement, concern, (financial) interest, bet, wager, pledge, *colloq.* ante **2** *the leadership stakes* contest, competition, race, prize, winnings
▶ v risk, gamble, bet, wager, pledge, chance, hazard, venture, *colloq.* ante

stale adj
1 *stale bread* dry, hard, hardened, old, musty, mouldy, fusty, flat, insipid, tasteless, sour, *colloq.* (gone) off **2** OVERUSED, hackneyed, corny, clichéd, clichéridden, stock, stereotyped, tired, jaded, worn-out, unoriginal, uninspired, flat, trite, insipid, banal, commonplace, *formal* platitudinous, *colloq.* run of the mill
🔳 **1** crisp, fresh **2** new, original, imaginative

stalemate n
draw, tie, deadlock, impasse, standstill, halt, blockade, stand-off, *zugzwang*
🔳 progress

stalk¹ n
the stalk of a flower stem, shoot, twig, branch, trunk, *technical* peduncle, petiole

stalk² v
stalk a person/an animal **1** TRAIL, track, hunt, chase, give chase, follow, pursue, shadow, track down, tail, haunt **2** STRIDE, walk, step, pace, march

stall¹ v
stall them to give you more time temporize, play for time, delay, hold up, put off, defer, postpone, hedge, equivocate, obstruct, stonewall, *colloq.* beat about the bush, drag your feet, put on ice, put on the back burner

stall² *n*

1 STAND, table, booth, kiosk, counter, surface, place, platform **2** CUBICLE, compartment, enclosure, coop, pen

stalwart *adj*

1 STAUNCH, loyal, faithful, devoted, committed, steadfast, steady, trusty, reliable, dependable, vigorous, valiant, daring, intrepid, indomitable, determined, resolute **2** STRONG, sturdy, robust, rugged, stout, hardy, strapping, muscular, athletic, brawny, burly
🖬 **1** disloyal, unfaithful **2** weak, feeble, timid

stamina *n*

energy, vigour, strength, power, force, grit, resilience, resistance, endurance, indefatigability, staying power, *formal* fortitude, *colloq.* grit
🖬 weakness

stammer *v, n*

▶ *v* stutter, stumble, falter, hesitate, splutter, lisp, mumble, gibber, babble
▶ *n* stutter, speech impediment, speech defect

stamp *v, n*

▶ *v* **1** TRAMPLE, tread, crush, beat, pound, pulp, mash, squash **2** IMPRINT, impress, print, inscribe, engrave, emboss, mark, brand, fix, label, categorize, designate, identify, characterize
▷ **stamp out** eradicate, suppress, crush, quell, quash, put down, scotch, destroy, eliminate, end, extinguish, quench, kill, *formal* extirpate
▶ *n* print, imprint, impression, seal, signature, authorization, mark, hallmark, tag, label, brand, cast, mould, cut, form, fashion, sort, kind, type, quality, variety, breed, character, description, *formal* attestation

stampede *n, v*

▶ *n* charge, rush, onrush, dash, sprint, flight, rout, scattering
▶ *v* charge, rush, dash, tear, run, race, sprint, gallop, shoot, fly, flee, scatter

stance *n*

position, posture, deportment, carriage, bearing, stand, standpoint, viewpoint, policy, angle, slant, line, point of view, opinion, attitude

stanch *v*

stem, stop, check, block, arrest, stay, halt, plug, dam
🖬 increase, promote

📖 **stanch** or **staunch** ?

In the sense of 'to stop the flow of', either form is correct, but *staunch* is the commoner: *staunched the flow of blood from the wound*; *staunch the decline of royal authority*; *This helped to staunch the Danish invasion*. As an adjective, the form to use is *staunch*, meaning 'loyal, trusty, steadfast': *a staunch ally/ Catholic/opponent*.

---

stand *v, n*

▶ *v* **1** RISE, rise to your feet, get on/to your feet, get up, stand up, be on your feet, straighten up, be erect, be upright **2** PUT, place, set, erect, up-end, place, position, station, locate **3** *I can't stand it* bear, tolerate, put up with, cope with, endure, allow, brook, suffer, experience, live with, undergo, withstand, weather, *formal* abide, *colloq.* stomach **4** *the offer still stands* exist, be, remain, hold, be valid, be in effect, be in force, *formal* prevail, obtain
▷ **stand by** support, back, champion, defend, stand up for, stick up for, uphold, side with, adhere to, hold to, stick by
🖬 let down

▷ **stand down** step down, resign, abdicate, quit, give up, retire, withdraw
🖬 join
▷ **stand for 1** REPRESENT, symbolize, mean, signify, denote, indicate, *formal* betoken **2** *not stand for such nonsense* put up with, tolerate, bear, endure, allow, brook, *colloq.* stomach
▷ **stand in for** deputize for, cover for, understudy, replace, take the place of, substitute for, *colloq.* hold the fort for
▷ **stand out** show, be noticeable, be obvious, be conspicuous, stick out, jut out, extend, project, poke out, *colloq.* catch the eye, stick out a mile
▷ **stand up 1** RISE, rise to your feet, get up, get to your feet, straighten up, stand **2** COHERE, hold up, hold water, stand, *colloq.* wash
▷ **stand up for** defend, stick up for, side with, fight for, stand by, support, protect, champion, uphold, adhere
🖬 attack
▷ **stand up to** defy, oppose, resist, withstand, challenge, endure, face, face up to, confront, brave
🖬 give in to
▶ *n* **1** BASE, pedestal, support, shelf, case, frame, rack **2** STALL, booth, counter, table, stage, dais, platform, place **3** STANCE, position, standpoint, viewpoint, policy, angle, slant, line, point of view, opinion, attitude

standard *n, adj*

▶ *n* **1** NORM, average, type, model, pattern, example, sample, guide, guideline, benchmark, touchstone, yardstick, principle, rule, measure, gauge, criterion, requirement, specification, grade, level, quality, *formal* archetype, paradigm, exemplar **2** PRINCIPLE, scruple, ethic, moral, code, ideal **3** FLAG, ensign, pennant, pennon, streamer, colours, banner, gonfalon, *technical* vexillum
▶ *adj* normal, average, typical, stock, classic, basic, staple, usual, ordinary, customary, habitual, popular, prevailing, regular, approved, accepted, recognized, official, authoritative, orthodox, conventional, set, fixed, established, definitive
🖬 abnormal, unusual, irregular

standardize *v*

normalize, equalize, systematize, regiment, regularize, homogenize, stereotype, mass-produce
🖬 differentiate

stand-in *n*

deputy, representative, delegate, proxy, substitute, surrogate, second, second-in-command, understudy, locum

standing *n, adj*

▶ *n* **1** REPUTATION, status, rank, position, seniority, eminence, station, repute, experience, footing **2** DURATION, existence, continuance
▶ *adj* **1** UPRIGHT, erect, perpendicular, vertical, upended, on your feet **2** PERMANENT, perpetual, lasting, fixed, regular, repeated
🖬 **1** horizontal, lying **2** temporary

stand-off *n*

deadlock, impasse, standstill, halt, blockade

standoffish *adj*

aloof, remote, distant, unapproachable, unsociable, unfriendly, uncommunicative, withdrawn, detached, reserved, cold, cool
🖬 friendly, approachable

standpoint *n*

viewpoint, angle, slant, point of view, perspective, position, station, vantage point, stance

standstill *n*

stop, halt, pause, lull, rest, stoppage, jam, log-jam, hold-up, dead stop, impasse, deadlock, stalemate,

staple *v*

formal cessation

⧇ advance, progress

staple *adj*

basic, fundamental, primary, key, main, chief, major, important, foremost, principal, essential, indispensable, vital, necessary, standard

⧇ minor, dispensable

star *n, adj*

▶ *n* **1** *the stars in the sky* asteroid, planet, sun, moon, heavenly/celestial body, sphere, orb, satellite

Types of star include:
nova, supernova, pulsar, quasar, falling-star, shooting-star, meteor, comet, Halley's comet, red giant, supergiant, white dwarf, red dwarf, brown dwarf, neutron star, Pole Star, Polaris, North Star. *See also* CONSTELLATION.

2 CELEBRITY, personage, luminary, idol, lead, leading man, leading lady, superstar, principal, *colloq.* household name, big name, bigwig, big shot, leading light

▶ *adj* brilliant, well-known, famous, leading, illustrious, celebrated, prominent, talented, principal, major, pre-eminent, paramount

⧇ minor

starchy *adj*

formal, stiff, prim, punctilious, ceremonious, conventional, stuffy, strait-laced

⧇ informal

stare *v, n*

▶ *v* gaze, look, watch, gape, gawp, gawk, goggle, glare

▶ *n* gaze, look, glare, gawp

▷ **be staring you in the face** be very obvious, be glaringly obvious, be blatant, be conspicuous, *colloq.* stick out a mile

stark *adj, adv*

▶ *adj* **1** *faced with the stark reality* bald, bare, plain, simple, blunt, harsh, grim, severe, undecorated, unembellished, unadorned **2** *a stark landscape* bare, barren, desolate, bleak, austere, forsaken, empty, harsh, severe, grim, dreary, gloomy, depressing **3** UTTER, complete, unmitigated, unqualified, total, absolute, sheer, pure, downright, thorough, out-and-out, flagrant, arrant, *formal* consummate

▶ *adv* completely, entirely, wholly, totally, absolutely, altogether, quite, utterly, clean

⧇ mildly, slightly

stark-naked *adj*

naked, nude, in the nude, stripped, undressed, *formal* unclad, *colloq.* in the altogether, in the buff, in your birthday suit, in the raw, starkers

⧇ clothed, dressed

start *v, n*

▶ *v* **1** BEGIN, originate, initiate, introduce, pioneer, create, embark on/upon, bring/come into being, bring/come into existence, get under way, found, establish, set up, institute, inaugurate, launch, open, instigate, activate, turn on, trigger (off), set off, get going, get out, leave, depart, appear, arise, issue, *formal* commence, *colloq.* kick off, set the ball rolling, get things moving, get cracking, fire away **2** JUMP, jerk, leap, twitch, flinch, shrink, wince, recoil

⧇ **1** stop, finish, end

▶ *n* **1** BEGINNING, outset, dawn, birth, break, outburst, onset, origin, origination, initiation, introduction, foundation, institution, inauguration, launch, opening, emergence, *formal* commencement, inception, *colloq.* kick-off **2** JUMP, jerk, leap, twitch, flinch, wince, spasm, convulsion, fit

⧇ **1** stop, finish, end

startle *v*

surprise, amaze, astonish, astound, shock, make you jump, scare, frighten, alarm, agitate, upset, unsettle, disturb, *formal* perturb

⧇ calm

startling *adj*

surprising, astonishing, astounding, extraordinary, shocking, staggering, unexpected, sudden, dramatic, alarming, unforeseen, electrifying

⧇ boring, calming, ordinary

starvation *n*

hunger, extreme hunger, undernourishment, malnutrition, famine, fasting, death

⧇ plenty, excess

starve *v*

hunger, fast, diet, deprive, deny, die, perish, faint

⧇ feed, gorge

starving *adj*

(very) hungry, underfed, undernourished, ravenous, famished, faint, dying

stash *v, n*

▶ *v* store, hide, conceal, hoard, closet, lay up, save up, stockpile, stow, cache, *formal* secrete, *colloq.* salt away

⧇ bring out, uncover

▶ *n* hoard, store, collection, accumulation, mass, heap, pile, fund, reservoir, reserve, stockpile, cache

state *n, v, adj*

▶ *n* **1** CONDITION, shape, situation, position, circumstances, case, predicament **2** NATION, country, land, territory, kingdom, republic, realm, government, federation **3** PANIC, bother, plight, predicament, *colloq.* fluster, flap, tizzy **4** GOVERNMENT, administration, authorities, parliament, council, establishment **5** POMP, ceremony, dignity, majesty, grandeur, glory, splendour, display

▷ **in a state** agitated, anxious, worried, distressed, troubled, upset, worked up, panic-stricken, ruffled, *colloq.* flustered, hassled, het up, in a stew, in a tizzy

⧇ calm

▷ **state of affairs** case, situation, position, circumstances, condition, plight, predicament, crisis, juncture, *colloq.* kettle of fish, lie of the land

▶ *v* say, declare, tell, announce, report, communicate, assert, affirm, specify, present, express, put, set out, make known, proclaim, formulate, articulate, voice, utter, reveal, divulge, disclose, *formal* aver, promulgate

▶ *adj* national, governmental, parliamentary, public, official, formal, ceremonial, pompous, stately

⧇ private, commercial

stately *adj*

grand, imposing, impressive, splendid, glorious, magnificent, elegant, majestic, regal, royal, imperial, noble, lofty, pompous, dignified, measured, deliberate, solemn, ceremonial, ceremonious, graceful, *formal* august

⧇ informal, unimpressive

statement *n*

account, report, bulletin, communiqué, announcement, declaration, assertion, proclamation, communication, presentation, utterance, revelation, divulgence, disclosure, testimony, *formal* affirmation, averment, promulgation

statesman, stateswoman *n*

politician, leader, elder statesman, diplomat, GOM, *colloq.* grand old man

static *adj*

stationary, motionless, immobile, unmoving, still, at a standstill, inert, resting, fixed, constant, steady, change-

less, unchanging, undeviating, unvarying, stable
☒ dynamic, mobile, varying

station *n, v*
▶ *n* **1** *a bus/railway station* stop, stopping-place, halt, fare-stage, terminus, exchange, park-and-ride **2** OFFICE, base, depot, headquarters **3** *your station in life* status, standing, position, rank, level, grade, class **4** PLACE OF DUTY, post, place, site, location, position
▶ *v* locate, set, establish, install, garrison, post, send, appoint, assign

stationary *adj*
motionless, immobile, unmoving, still, at a standstill, static, constant, inert, standing, resting, parked, moored, fixed
☒ mobile, moving, active

stationery *n*

Items of stationery include:
account book, address book, adhesive tape, blotter, bulldog clip, calendar, carbon paper, card index, cartridge ribbon, cash book, clipboard, computer disk, copying paper, correcting paper, correction fluid, correction ribbon, desk-diary, diary, divider, document folder, document wallet, drawing pin, dry-transfer lettering, elastic band, envelope, brown manila envelope, reply-paid envelope, self-seal envelope, window envelope, eraser, expanding file, file, file tab, filing tray, Filofax®, flip chart, floppy disk, folder, graph paper, headed notepaper, index card, ink, Jiffy bag®, label, lever arch file, marker, memo pad, notepaper, paper clip, paper fastener, paper knife, pen, pencil, pencil-sharpener, personal organizer, pin, pocket calculator, pocket folder, Post-it note®, printer label, printer paper, printer ribbon, reinforcement ring, ring binder, rubber, rubber band, rubber stamp, ruler, scissors, Sellotape®, shorthand notebook, spiral notebook, stamp pad, staple, suspension file, tape dispenser, Tipp-Ex®, toner, treasury tag, typewriter ribbon, wall chart, writing paper. *See also* PAPER.

statue *n*
figure, head, bust, effigy, image, idol, statuette, figurine, carving, sculpture, bronze, representation

statuesque *adj*
dignified, imposing, impressive, majestic, stately, regal, handsome
☒ small

stature *n*
1 HEIGHT, tallness, elevation, attitude, loftiness, size **2** IMPORTANCE, reputation, standing, prominence, prestige, fame, renown, eminence, rank, consequence, weight
☒ **2** unimportance

status *n*
1 POSITION, rank, grade, degree, level, class, station, standing, state, condition **2** IMPORTANCE, prestige, eminence, distinction, reputation, consequence, weight
☒ **2** unimportance, insignificance

statute *n*
law, rule, regulation, act, decree, ordinance, edict, enactment, ukase, *formal* interlocution

staunch[1] *adj*
a staunch supporter loyal, faithful, devoted, hearty, strong, stout, firm, resolute, sound, sure, constant, true, trusty, trustworthy, committed, reliable, dependable, steadfast
☒ unfaithful, weak, unreliable

 staunch or **stanch** ? *See panel at* STANCH.

staunch[2] *v*
staunch the flow of blood stem, stop, check, block, arrest, stay, halt, plug
☒ increase, promote

 staunch or **stanch** ? *See panel at* STANCH.

stave *v*
▷ **stave off** fend off, ward off, avoid, avert, deflect, repel, repulse, turn aside, parry, foil, keep back, keep at bay
☒ cause, encourage

stay[1] *v, n*
▶ *v* **1** REMAIN, last, continue, endure, linger, persist, keep, stay put, *formal* abide, tarry **2** *stay in a hotel* live, settle, stop, board, lodge, put up, rest, halt, pause, wait, visit, be accommodated at, take a room at, *formal* reside, dwell, sojourn **3** *stay judgement* suspend, halt, postpone, put off, delay, defer, adjourn, reprieve, *formal* prorogue **4** *stay your anger* control, restrain, arrest, check, curb, stop, halt, prevent, hinder, block, obstruct
▶ *n* **1** VISIT, holiday, vacation, stopover, *formal* sojourn **2** *a stay of execution* suspension, postponement, deferment, delay, reprieve, *formal* remission

stay[2] *n*
a stay supporting a mast prop, brace, buttress, reinforcement, stanchion, support, shoring

staying power
stamina, energy, vigour, strength, power, force, grit, resilience, resistance, endurance, indefatigability, fibre, *formal* fortitude, *colloq.* grit

steadfast *adj*
firm, fixed, resolute, stable, steady, intent, single-minded, loyal, faithful, stout-hearted, sturdy, dedicated, constant, dependable, staunch, reliable, established, persevering, unswerving, unwavering, unfaltering, implacable, unflinching
☒ unreliable, wavering, weak

steady *adj, v*
▶ *adj* **1** *hold the camera steady* stable, balanced, well-balanced, poised, fixed, secure, immovable, unmoving, motionless, firm **2** *make steady progress* regular, even, uniform, consistent, unvarying, unvariable, unchanging, ceaseless, perpetual, constant, persistent, uninterrupted, unbroken, unfaltering, unwavering, *formal* incessant, unremitting **3** CALM, stable, settled, controlled, self-controlled, well-balanced, still, imperturbable, unexcitable, unexcited, *colloq.* unflappable **4** RELIABLE, dependable, balanced, well-balanced, serious, sober, sensible, steadfast **5** *a steady boyfriend* regular, constant, usual, customary, established, habitual
☒ **1** unsteady, shaky, wobbly **2** uneven, irregular, variable, wavering **3** excitable, worried **4** unreliable
▶ *v* **1** STABILIZE, balance, fix, secure, brace, support **2** COMPOSE, control, soothe, relax, tranquillize, still, subdue, check, restrain

steal *v, n*
▶ *v* **1** *steal a car* thieve, pilfer, filch, take, misappropriate, snatch, break in, swipe, pocket, shoplift, poach, embezzle, kidnap, abduct, plagiarize, *formal* appropriate, purloin, peculate, *colloq.* pinch, nick, lift, snaffle, knock up, nobble, rip off, knock off, help yourself to, make off/away with, run off with, go/walk off with, have your fingers in the till, *slang* heist **2** CREEP, tiptoe, slip, slink, slide, slither, sneak
☒ **1** return, give back

▶ *n* bargain, giveaway, special offer, good buy, value for money, discount, reduction, *colloq.* snip

stealing *n*
theft, robbery, thieving, shoplifting, pilfering, pilferage, burglary, break-in, embezzlement, larceny, misappropriation, plagiarism, poaching, piracy, thievery, *formal* peculation, appropriation, purloining, *colloq.* rip-off, filching, pinching, nicking, stick-up job

stealth *n*
stealthiness, furtiveness, surreptitiousness, covertness, secrecy, slyness, sneakiness, unobtrusiveness

stealthy *adj*
surreptitious, covert, secret, unobtrusive, secretive, quiet, furtive, sly, cunning, sneaky, underhand, *formal* clandestine

steam *n, v*
▶ *n* 1 VAPOUR, mist, haze, exhalation, condensation, moisture, dampness 2 *run out of steam* energy, activity, enthusiasm, eagerness, liveliness, vigour, stamina
▷ **under your own steam** by your own efforts, independently, by yourself, alone, without (other's) help
▶ *v* ▷ **get steamed up** get annoyed, get angry, get flustered, get excited, *colloq.* get het up, boil over, fly into a rage
▷ **steam up** mist up, fog up, become covered with steam, become covered with mist

steamy *adj*
1 HUMID, hot, steaming, sweltering, hazy, muggy, sticky, misty, sweaty, close, damp, sultry, stewy, vaporous, vapourish, vapoury, gaseous, *formal* vaporiform 2 EROTIC, passionate, sensual, lustful, amorous, seductive, *colloq.* sexy, raunchy, blue

steel *v*
brace, harden, toughen, nerve, prepare, *formal* fortify
⊟ weaken

steely *adj*
1 GREY, steel-coloured, steel-blue, blue-grey 2 DETERMINED, firm, resolute, strong, hard, harsh, inflexible, pitiless, merciless, unyielding

steep[1] *adj*
1 *a steep slope* sheer, precipitous, headlong, abrupt, sudden, sharp, vertical, perpendicular, *formal* acclivitous, declivitous 2 EXCESSIVE, extreme, stiff, unreasonable, uncalled-for, high, exorbitant, extortionate, inordinate, expensive, costly, dear, overpriced, *colloq.* over the top
⊟ 1 gentle, gradual 2 moderate, low

steep[2] *v*
steep something in liquid saturate, seethe, soak, damp, moisten, souse, submerge, suffuse, drench, fill, imbrue, imbue, immerse, infuse, permeate, pervade, marinate, pickle, brine, macerate

steeple *n*
spire, beltry, tower, turret

steer *v*
pilot, guide, direct, control, drive, govern, conduct, navigate, cox, lead, usher
▷ **steer clear of** avoid, shun, evade, bypass, escape, skirt, *formal* circumvent, eschew, *colloq.* dodge, give a wide berth to
⊟ seek

stem[1] *n, v*
▶ *n the stem of a plant* stalk, shoot, stock, branch, trunk, *technical* peduncle
▶ *v* come, develop, flow, originate, derive, emanate, spring, issue, arise
⊟ give rise to, cause

stem[2] *v*
stem the flow of blood stop, halt, arrest, stanch,

staunch, block, dam, check, curb, restrain, contain, resist, oppose
⊟ encourage

stench *n*
stink, reek, smell, odour, whiff, *formal* mephitis, miasma, *colloq.* pong, *slang* niff

stentorian *adj*
loud, strong, booming, thunderous, thundering, resonant, sonorous, ringing, full, vibrant, reverberating, strident

step *n, v*
▶ *n* 1 PACE, stride, footstep, walk, gait, tread, tramp, footprint, print, impression, trace, track 2 MOVE, act, action, course of action, deed, measure, procedure, process, proceeding, progression, advance, development, movement, manoeuvre, expedient, effort, stage, rank, grade, level, phase, degree 3 RUNG, stair, level, rank, point
▷ **in step** together, in agreement, in harmony, in unison
▷ **out of step** in disagreement, not in step, having different opinions, at odds, at loggerheads
▷ **step by step** gradually, slowly, progressively, bit by bit, gradatim
▷ **watch your step** be careful, look out, watch out, take care, be attentive, *colloq.* mind how you go
▶ *v* pace, stride, tread, stamp, walk, move, advance, progress
▷ **step down** stand down, resign, abdicate, quit, leave, retire, withdraw, give up your post
▷ **step in** intervene, mediate, arbitrate, intercede, interfere, interrupt, intrude, involve yourself in
▷ **step up** increase, raise, boost, build up, intensify, escalate, accelerate, speed up, *formal* augment
⊟ decrease

stereotype *n, v*
▶ *n* formula, convention, mould, pattern, model, cliché, hackneyed expression, conventional/standardized image, fixed set of ideas
▶ *v* typecast, pigeonhole, standardize, formalize, tag, label, conventionalize, mass-produce, categorize
⊟ differentiate

stereotyped *adj*
conventional, stereotypical, standardized, standard, unoriginal, stock, overused, mass-produced, hackneyed, clichéd, cliché-ridden, banal, stale, trite, tired, threadbare, corny, *formal* platitudinous
⊟ different, unconventional

sterile *adj*
1 GERM-FREE, germless, clean, pure, aseptic, sterilized, disinfected, antiseptic, uncontaminated, uninfected 2 INFERTILE, barren, arid, bare, unproductive, unprofitable, fruitless, unfruitful, pointless, futile, vain, useless, unyielding, abortive, *formal* infecund, ineffectual
⊟ 1 septic 2 fertile, fruitful

sterility *n*
1 CLEANNESS, purity, disinfection, *technical* asepsis 2 INFERTILITY, barrenness, unfruitfulness, unproductiveness, impotence, fruitlessness, futility, pointlessness, uselessness, ineffectiveness, *technical* atocia, *formal* inefficacy, unfecundity
⊟ 1 infection, contamination 2 fertility, fruitfulness

sterilize *v*
1 DISINFECT, fumigate, purify, clean, cleanse 2 MAKE INFERTILE, castrate, neuter, doctor, geld, spay
⊟ 1 contaminate, infect

sterling *adj*
excellent, great, superlative, first-class, genuine, real, sound, standard, authentic, true, pure, worthy
⊟ false, poor

stern¹ *adj*
  a stern look/person strict, severe, authoritarian, rigid, inflexible, unyielding, hard, tough, rigorous, demanding, exacting, stringent, harsh, cruel, tyrannical, draconian, unsparing, relentless, unrelenting, grim, sombre, forbidding, stark, austere
  F₃ kind, gentle, mild, lenient

stern² *n*
  the stern of the ship rear, back, tail, tail end, poop
  F₃ bow

stew *v, n*
  ▶ *v* **1** stew the meat boil, simmer, braise, cook, casserole **2** let him stew in his own juice worry, sweat, fret, fuss, agonize
  ▶ *n* **1** beef stew casserole, goulash, pot-au-feu, daube, ragout, hash, chowder, lobscouse, bouillabaisse **2** FLUSTER, worry, fuss, bother, agitation, pother, fret, *colloq.* tizzy

steward *n*
  attendant, flight attendant, air hostess, waiter, waitress, official, butler, supervisor, overseer, custodian, caretaker, marshal, factor, chamberlain, manciple, *major-domo, homme d'affaires, maître d'hôtel*

stick¹ *v*
  1 THRUST, poke, stab, jab, push, pierce, prick, penetrate, insert, puncture, spear, impale, transfix **2** GLUE, gum, paste, cement, bond, fuse, weld, solder, tape, adhere, grip, cling, hold, attach, affix, fasten, secure, fix, pin, tack, join, bind **3** PUT, place, lay, position, site, locate, set (down), install, deposit, drop **4** the car got stuck in the mud fix, jam, clog (up), get bogged down, trap, stop, come to a halt, come to a standstill **5** REMAIN, stay, linger, persist, continue, carry on, rest, last, endure, *formal* dwell, abide **6** TOLERATE, bear, stand, endure, put up with, *formal* abide, *colloq.* stomach
  ▷ **stick at 1** PERSEVERE, persist, continue, keep at, *colloq.* plug away **2** HESITATE, recoil, shrink from, stop at, doubt, pause, balk, scruple, *formal* demur, *colloq.* draw the line at
  F₃ 1 give up
  ▷ **stick by** stand by, support, back, champion, defend, stand up for, stick up for, uphold, side with, adhere to, hold to
  F₃ let down
  ▷ **stick it out** persevere, persist, continue, *colloq.* plug away, see things through to the end, keep at it, hang in there
  ▷ **stick out** protrude, jut out, poke out, bulge, project, extend, be noticeable, be obvious, be conspicuous
  ▷ **stick up for** stand up for, speak up for, fight for, stand by, defend, protect, champion, support, uphold, take the side/part of
  F₃ attack

stick² *n*
  gather dry sticks **1** BRANCH, branch, twig, switch **2** CRITICISM, hostility, punishment, reproof, blame, abuse, *colloq.* flak
  F₃ praise
  ▷ **the sticks** remote areas, backwoods, bush, outback, *colloq.* middle of nowhere, end of the earth, hickdom, yokeldom, *US* boondocks, boonies

stickiness *n*
  adhesiveness, gumminess, glueyness, tackiness, syrupiness, *formal* glutinousness, viscidity, *colloq.* goo, gooeyness

stick-in-the-mud *adj, n*
  ▶ *adj* fuddy-duddy, unadventurous, conservative, fossilized, fogeyish, outmoded, antiquated, antediluvian, Victorian, *colloq.* square

F₃ adventurous, modern
  ▶ *n* fuddy-duddy, conservative, *colloq.* (old) fogey, back number, fossil

stickler *n*
  fanatic, maniac, perfectionist, pedant, purist, precisionist, fusspot, *colloq.* nut

sticky *adj*
  1 ADHESIVE, gummed, tacky, gluey, gummy, viscous, *formal* glutinous, viscoid, *colloq.* gooey **2** a sticky situation difficult, tricky, thorny, unpleasant, awkward, embarrassing, delicate, sensitive, ticklish **3** HUMID, clammy, muggy, close, oppressive, sweltering, sultry
  F₃ 1 dry **2** easy **3** fresh, cool

stiff *adj*
  1 RIGID, unbending, unyielding, inflexible, hard, solid, hardened, solidified, firm, tight, taut, inelastic, tense **2** stiff muscles/joints aching, arthritic, rheumatic, tight, tense, rheumaticky **3** DIFFICULT, hard, tough, tiring, harsh, arduous, laborious, awkward, demanding, exacting, challenging, rigorous **4** FORMAL, ceremonial, ceremonious, reserved, pompous, standoffish, cold, chilly, awkward, prim, priggish, *formal* decorous **5** SEVERE, extreme, rigorous, hard, harsh, tough, demanding, austere, strict, drastic, stringent, draconian **6** a stiff breeze strong, fresh, brisk, windy, forceful, vigorous **7** a stiff drink large, alcoholic, strong, intoxicating
  F₃ 1 flexible, supple **3** easy **4** informal, relaxed, friendly **6** light

stiffen *v*
  1 HARDEN, solidify, tighten, tense (up), starch, congeal, coagulate, thicken, jell, set **2** STRENGTHEN, steel, brace, harden, reinforce, *formal* fortify

stiff-necked *adj*
  proud, stubborn, obstinate, arrogant, haughty, uncompromising, opinionated, *formal* contumacious
  F₃ humble, flexible

stifle *v*
  1 stifle opposition repress, silence, hush, suppress, quell, quash, check, curb, restrain, keep in, hold back, smother, crush, subdue, extinguish, muffle, dampen, deaden **2** SMOTHER, suffocate, asphyxiate, strangle, choke
  F₃ 1 encourage

stigma *n*
  brand, mark, stain, blot, spot, blemish, slur, taint, disgrace, shame, dishonour
  F₃ credit, honour

stigmatize *v*
  stain, mark, blemish, disgrace, shame, condemn, denounce, discredit, brand, label, mark, *formal* vilify, vilipend
  F₃ praise

still *adj, v, adv, n*
  ▶ *adj* **1** STATIONARY, motionless, immobile, unmoving, unstirring, static, stock-still, lifeless, stagnant, inert, inactive, sedentary **2** QUIET, undisturbed, unruffled, calm, smooth, tranquil, serene, mild, restful, peaceful, hushed, silent, noiseless
  F₃ 1 moving, active **2** disturbed, agitated, noisy
  ▶ *v* calm, soothe, allay, tranquillize, subdue, restrain, hush, quieten, silence, pacify, settle, moderate, smooth, *formal* assuage, appease, abate
  F₃ agitate, stir up
  ▶ *adv* **1** UNTIL NOW, up to the present time, up to this time, yet **2** YET, but, even so, though, although, nevertheless, nonetheless, however, in spite of this/that, for all that, *formal* notwithstanding
  ▶ *n* stillness, quiet, quietness, hush, peace, peacefulness, silence, noiselessness, serenity, tranquillity

🔄 agitation, disturbance, noise

stilted *adj*
artificial, unnatural, laboured, stiff, wooden, forced, constrained
🔄 natural, relaxed, fluent, flowing

stimulant *n*
tonic, restorative, reviver, *technical* analeptic, *colloq.* pick-me-up, pep pill

stimulate *v*
rouse, arouse, animate, quicken, kindle, fan, fire, inflame, excite, inspire, motivate, encourage, induce, fillip, urge, impel, spur, prompt, goad, provoke, incite, instigate, trigger (off), *colloq.* whip up
🔄 discourage, hinder, prevent

stimulating *adj*
inspiring, rousing, stirring, interesting, exciting, exhilarating, intriguing, provoking, provocative, thought-provoking, galvanic
🔄 uninspiring, boring, depressing

stimulus *n*
incentive, encouragement, impetus, inducement, spur, goad, prod, provocation, incitement, fillip, push, drive, jolt, jog, *colloq.* shot in the arm
🔄 discouragement

sting *v, n*
▶ *v* **1** *bees sting* bite, prick, hurt, injure, wound **2** SMART, tingle, burn, pain, irritate **3** HURT, distress, wound, upset, offend, annoy, grieve, torment, provoke, exasperate, incense, needle, nettle **4** CHEAT, swindle, defraud, deceive, trick, fiddle, *colloq.* do, fleece, rip off, con, take for a ride, take to the cleaners
▶ *n* **1** PRICK, bite, nip, wound, injury, hurt, pain, smart, tingle, irritate **2** *the memory lost its sting* sharpness, viciousness, spite, malice, pungency, incisiveness, sarcasm, causticness, causticity, edge, bite

stinging *adj*
burning, smarting, tingling, irritating, hurtful, injurious, wounding, offensive, distressing, *formal* urent, urticant, aculeate(d)
🔄 mild, soothing, comforting

stingy *adj*
mean, miserly, niggardly, cheeseparing, *formal* parsimonious, penurious, *colloq.* tight-fisted, mingy, penny-pinching
🔄 generous, liberal

stink *v, n*
▶ *v* **1** SMELL, reek, *colloq.* pong, hum **2** *the whole set-up stinks* be bad, be awful, be nasty, be unpleasant, be despicable
▶ *n* **1** SMELL, bad/foul smell, odour, stench, *formal* malodour, *colloq.* pong, *slang* niff **2** FUSS, trouble, bother, furore, row, commotion, stir, fluster, *colloq.* hassle, hoo-ha, flap, song and dance

stinker *n*
1 PROBLEM, difficulty, predicament, plight, impediment, horror, shocker **2** SCOUNDREL, creep, cur, rotter, *slang* rat, swine

stinking *adj*
bad, unpleasant, vile, awful, nasty, contemptible, disgusting, foul, rotten
🔄 good, pleasant

stint *n, v*
▶ *n* spell, stretch, period, time, shift, turn, bit, share, quota
▶ *v* economize, save, withhold, pinch, begrudge, scrimp, *colloq.* skimp on

stipulate *v*
specify, lay down, set down, require, demand, insist on

stipulation *n*
specification, requirement, point, demand, condition, proviso, *formal* precondition, prerequisite

stir *v, n*
▶ *v* **1** MOVE, budge, shift, rouse, disturb, agitate, shake, tremble, twitch, quiver, flutter, rustle **2** MIX, blend, whip, beat **3** AFFECT, touch, inspire, excite, thrill
▷ **stir up** encourage, rouse, arouse, awaken, waken, inspire, animate, quicken, kindle, fire, inflame, excite, stimulate, spur, motivate, drive, impel, prompt, provoke, incite, instigate, agitate, electrify, galvanize
🔄 calm, discourage
▶ *n* activity, movement, bustle, flurry, commotion, ado, fuss, uproar, tumult, disturbance, disorder, agitation, excitement, ferment, *colloq.* to-do, hoo-ha, flap, kerfuffle, tizzy, song and dance
🔄 calm

stirring *adj*
rousing, exciting, spirited, inspiring, stimulating, moving, animating, thrilling, exhilarating, heady, emotive, dramatic, lively, impassioned, intoxicating
🔄 calming, uninspiring

stitch *v*
sew, stitch, tack, darn, mend, repair, seam, embroider, hem. *See panel at* EMBROIDERY.

stock *n, adj, v*
▶ *n* **1** GOODS, merchandise, wares, commodities, inventory, repertoire, quantity, collection, range, selection, variety, assortment, source, supply, quantity, fund, reservoir, store, reserve, cache, stockpile, hoard, heap, pile, amassment, accumulation **2** *stocks and shares* investment, holding, shares, bonds, securities, equities, portfolio, money, capital, funds, assets **3** PARENTAGE, ancestry, genealogy, background, descent, extraction, family, relatives, line, lineage, pedigree, race, breed, strain, species, blood **4** LIVESTOCK, animals, farm animals, cattle, cows, pigs, horses, sheep, herds, flocks
▷ **in stock** available, for sale, on sale, on the market, on the shelves
▷ **take stock** assess, reassess, estimate, review, survey, evaluate, re-evaluate, re-examine, size up, weigh up, *formal* appraise
▶ *adj* standard, basic, regular, routine, ordinary, average, run-of-the-mill, usual, common, customary, essential, basic, traditional, conventional, set, stereotyped, tired, worn-out, hackneyed, clichéd, overused, banal, trite
🔄 original, unusual
▶ *v* keep, carry, sell, market, trade in, traffic in, merchandise, deal in, handle, carry, supply, provide, furnish, equip, *formal* accoutre, *colloq.* kit out
▷ **stock up** gather, accumulate, amass, lay in, fill (up), load, store (up), buy (up), put aside, put away, save, hoard, stockpile, stack up, pile up, heap (up), *formal* provision, replenish, *colloq.* salt away, stash away

stockpile *v, n*
▶ *v* hoard, store (up), save, gather, accumulate, amass, pile up, heap (up), keep, put aside, put away
▶ *n* store, hoard, fund, reservoir, reserve, cache, pile, heap, amassment, accumulation

stock-still *adj*
motionless, unmoving, unstirring, static, still, immobile, inactive, inert, stationary

stocky *adj*
sturdy, solid, thickset, chunky, broad, short, squat, dumpy, stubby, stumpy, *formal* mesomorphic
🔄 tall, skinny

stodgy *adj*
 1 *stodgy food* solid, heavy, indigestible, filling, starchy, substantial **2** STUFFY, unimaginative, uninspired, unexciting, unenterprising, solemn, heavy, boring, dull, tedious, staid, formal, leaden, laboured, turgid, spiritless, *colloq.* fuddy-duddy
 Fᴈ exciting, informal, light

stoical *adj*
 patient, long-suffering, uncomplaining, accepting, resigned, philosophical, indifferent, impassive, unexcitable, unemotional, dispassionate, self-disciplined, self-controlled, forbearing, cool, calm, imperturbable, *formal* phlegmatic
 Fᴈ excitable, anxious

stoicism *n*
 patience, long-suffering, resignation, indifference, dispassion, unexcitability, impassivity, calmness, acceptance, forbearance, imperturbability, stolidity, fatalism, *formal* fortitude, ataraxia, ataraxy
 Fᴈ anxiety, depression, fury

stolid *adj*
 slow, heavy, dull, bovine, wooden, blockish, lumpish, impassive, unemotional, uninspiring, unimaginative, solemn, indifferent, apathetic, *formal* phlegmatic
 Fᴈ lively, interested

stomach *n, v*
 ▸ *n* **1** GUT, inside(s), belly, abdomen, paunch, potbelly, *colloq.* tummy, corporation, *slang* bread basket **2** *have the stomach for food* desire, relish, hunger, appetite, taste, zest **3** *not have the stomach for a fight* courage, determination, desire, inclination, liking, passion, appetite, *colloq.* guts
 ▸ *v* tolerate, bear, stand, endure, suffer, approve of, submit to, take, brook, put up with, *formal* abide

stone *n*
 1 ROCK, boulder, cobble, pebble, *formal* concretion **2** *precious stones* jewel, gemstone, gem, lapis **3** GRAVESTONE, tombstone, headstone, slab, flagstone, set(t) **4** PIP, kernel, pit, seed, *technical* endocarp

stony *adj*
 1 *stony beach* pebbly, shingly, rocky, gravelly, gritty **2** BLANK, expressionless, deadpan, poker-faced, hard, cold, frigid, icy, frosty, chilly, indifferent, unfeeling, heartless, adamant, steely, unresponsive, callous, merciless, pitiless, severe, stern, unforgiving, inexorable, hostile
 Fᴈ **2** warm, soft-hearted, friendly

stooge *n*
 puppet, pawn, lackey, henchman, dupe, foil, butt, *colloq.* cat's paw, fall guy

stoop *v, n*
 ▸ *v* **1** HUNCH, bow, bend, lower, incline, lean, duck, squat, crouch, kneel **2** *stoop to blackmail* descend, sink, lower yourself, resort, go so far as, condescend, go so low as, deign, *formal* vouchsafe
 ▸ *n* droop, hunching, round-shoulderedness, sag, slouch, slump, bending, inclination, lowering, ducking

stop *v, n*
 ▸ *v* **1** HALT, end, finish, conclude, discontinue, abandon, bring/come to an end, suspend, interrupt, pause, quit, *formal* cease, terminate, arrest, refrain, desist, *colloq.* quit, wind up, pack in, kick, knock off, leave off, give over **2** PREVENT, bar, frustrate, thwart, intercept, hinder, impede, obstruct, block, check, restrain, stall **3** SEAL, close, plug, block, bung, stop up, cover, obstruct, arrest, stem, stanch, staunch **4** STAY, live, settle, lodge, board, visit, put up, rest, pause, break your journey, *formal* reside, dwell, sojourn
 Fᴈ **1** begin, start, continue
 ▸ *n* **1** HALT, standstill, stoppage, end, finish, close,

conclusion, *formal* cessation, termination, discontinuance, discontinuation **2** STATION, halt, bus stop, fare stage, stopping-place, terminus, destination **3** REST, break, stay, pause, stage, stopover, visit, *formal* sojourn
 Fᴈ **1** start, beginning, continuation

stopgap *n, adj*
 ▸ *n* improvisation, makeshift, substitute, temporary substitute, expedient, resort, shift
 ▸ *adj* improvised, makeshift, provisional, temporary, emergency, impromptu, *formal* expediential, *colloq.* rough-and-ready
 Fᴈ finished, permanent

stopover *n*
 stop-off, stop, visit, rest, break, overnight stay, *formal* sojourn

stoppage *n*
 1 STOP, halt, standstill, arrest, blockage, obstacle, obstruction, check, hindrance, interruption, *formal* cessation, termination, discontinuance, discontinuation, occlusion **2** STRIKE, shutdown, closure, walk-out, sit-in, industrial action **3** DEDUCTION, subtraction, reduction, decrease, taking away/off, withdrawal, removal, discount, allowance
 Fᴈ **1** start, continuation

store *v, n*
 ▸ *v* save, keep, put aside, lay by, reserve, stock, stock up with, lay in, deposit, put down, lay down, lay up, bank, gather, collect, accumulate, hoard, stockpile, *colloq.* salt away, stash, save for a rainy day
 Fᴈ use
 ▸ *n* **1** STOCK, supply, provision, fund, reserve, mine, reservoir, hoard, cache, stockpile, heap, load, accumulation, amassment, deposit, quantity, abundance, plenty, lot **2** SHOP, retail outlet, supermarket, hypermarket, chain store, department store, corner shop. *See panel at* SHOP. **3** STOREROOM, storehouse, warehouse, repository, depository, larder, buttery
 Fᴈ **1** scarcity
 ▷ **set/lay store by** value, think highly of, consider highly, admire, hold in high regard, *formal* esteem

storehouse *n*
 repository, warehouse, treasury, wealth, vault, depository, depot, garner, granary, hold, cellar, armoury, arsenal, fund, entrepot, repertory, barn, buttery, larder, pantry, silo

storey *n*
 floor, level, stage, tier, flight, deck, *formal* stratum

storm *n, v*
 ▸ *n* outburst, uproar, furore, outcry, row, rumpus, commotion, disturbance, clamour, tumult, brouhaha, turmoil, stir, agitation, rage, roar, outbreak, offensive, attack, assault, onslaught, *colloq.* to-do, kerfuffle
 Fᴈ calm

Kinds of storm include:
blizzard, buran, cloudburst, cyclone, downpour, dust-devil, dust-storm, electrical storm, gale, haboob, hailstorm, hurricane, monsoon, rainstorm, sand storm, snow storm, squall, tempest, thunderstorm, tornado, typhoon, whirlwind. *See also* WIND.

 ▸ *v* **1** *storm a citadel* CHARGE, rush, attack, assault, assail **2** RAGE, roar, rant, rave, shout, fume, thunder, explode, seethe, *colloq.* hit the roof, lose your cool, foam at the mouth **3** *storm out of the room* charge, rush, stamp, tear, flounce

stormy *adj*
 tempestuous, squally, rough, choppy, turbulent, rainy,

wild, raging, windy, gusty, blustery, foul
☒ calm, peaceful

story *n*
1 TALE, fiction, anecdote, episode, plot, storyline, narrative, history, chronicle, record, account, relation, recital, report, item, article, feature

Types of story include:
adventure story, anecdote, bedtime story, *colloq.* blockbuster, children's story, comedy, black comedy, crime story, detective story, fable, fairy story, fairy tale, fantasy, folk tale, ghost story, historical novel, horror story, legend, love story, Mills & Boon®, mystery, myth, novel, novella, parable, romance, saga, science fiction, *colloq.* sci-fi, short story, spiel, spine-chiller, spy story, supernatural tale, tall story, thriller, western, *colloq.* whodunit, *colloq.* yarn.

2 LIE, falsehood, untruth, *colloq.* rib, untruth

storyteller *n*
narrator, writer, author, novelist, raconteur, raconteuse, anecdotist, chronicler, bard, romancer, tell-tale

stout *adj*
1 FAT, stocky, plump, fleshy, portly, obese, overweight, heavy, tubby, bulky, big, brawny, beefy, hulking, thick-set, burly, muscular, athletic, *formal* corpulent **2** *stout packaging* strong, tough, durable, thick, solid, heavy, sturdy, substantial, robust, hardy, vigorous **3** BRAVE, courageous, valiant, plucky, tough, fearless, bold, gallant, heroic, intrepid, dauntless, resolute, stalwart, determined, strong, forceful, fierce, *formal* valorous, *colloq.* gutsy, spunky, gritty
☒ **1** thin, lean, slim **2** weak **3** cowardly, timid, afraid

stow *v*
put away, store, place, deposit, load, pack, cram, bundle, stuff, *colloq.* stash
☒ unload

straggle *v*
stray, wander, drift, lag, amble, loiter, ramble, roam, rove, trail, range, scatter, spread, string out, *colloq.* dilly-dally

straggly *adj*
untidy, rambling, drifting, straying, straggling, aimless, disorganized, irregular, random, spreading, loose, strung out
☒ tidy, organized, grouped

straight *adj, adv*
▸ *adj* **1** *a straight line* DIRECT, undeviating, unswerving, unbending, unbent, uncurving **2** LEVEL, even, flat, horizontal, upright, vertical, aligned, true, right **3** FRANK, honest, candid, blunt, forthright, direct, outspoken, straightforward **4** CONSECUTIVE, successive, continuous, unbroken, uninterrupted, one after the other **5** TIDY, neat, in order, orderly, shipshape, arranged, organized **6** HONOURABLE, honest, law-abiding, respectable, upright, trustworthy, reliable, upstanding, decent, straightforward, fair, just, faithful, sincere, conventional **7** *straight whisky* undiluted, neat, pure, unadulterated, unmixed
☒ **1** bent, crooked, curved, wavy, curly **2** sloping **3** evasive **5** untidy **6** dishonest **7** diluted
▸ *adv* **1** DIRECTLY, with no changes of direction, without deviating, as the crow flies **2** IMMEDIATELY, directly, instantly, promptly, right away, without delay, at once, as soon as possible, *colloq.* pronto **3** *tell someone straight* frankly, honestly, candidly, bluntly, directly, plainly, clearly, forthrightly, straightforwardly, point-blank, *colloq.* not pulling any punches, straight from the shoulder **4** CONSECUTIVELY, successively,

continuously, uninterruptedly, one after the other, *colloq.* on the trot
▷ **straight away** at once, immediately, instantly, right away, directly, without delay, now, there and then, *colloq.* pronto
☒ later, eventually

straighten *v*
unbend, align, tidy (up), neaten, order, arrange, adjust, put in order, put right
☒ bend, twist
▷ **straighten out** clear up, sort out, settle, resolve, correct, realign, disentangle, regularize, tidy up, put in order, put right, *formal* rectify
☒ confuse, muddle
▷ **straighten up** stand up, stand, stand erect, stand upright, straighten your back/body

straightforward *adj*
1 EASY, simple, uncomplicated, clear, elementary, unexacting, undemanding, *colloq.* child's play, a piece of cake, like falling off a log **2** HONEST, truthful, sincere, genuine, open, frank, candid, direct, forthright, outspoken, plain-speaking
☒ **1** difficult, complicated, tricky **2** evasive, devious

strain¹ *v, n*
▸ *v* **1** PULL, heave, tug, wrench, twist, sprain, hurt, injure, wrick, tear, stretch, extend, elongate, tighten, tauten, *formal* distend **2** SIEVE, sift, screen, separate, filter, percolate, riddle, purify, drain, wring, squeeze, compress, express **3** WEAKEN, tire, fatigue, tax, overtax, overwork, pressure, labour, try, endeavour, struggle, strive, exert, force, drive, push to/beyond the limit, make every effort, do your utmost, *colloq.* go all out, put your heart and soul into, pull out all the stops
▸ *n* **1** SPRAIN, pull, wrench, twist, injury, wrick **2** PRESSURE, tension, stress, anxiety, worry, duress, effort, struggle, exertion, pressure, force, burden, demand, tiredness, weariness, fatigue, exhaustion, overwork
☒ **2** relaxation

strain² *n*
1 STOCK, ancestry, descent, extraction, breed, family, lineage, pedigree, blood, variety, type, sort, kind **2** TRAIT, streak, quality, characteristic, vein, tendency, way, trace, element, suggestion, suspicion, *formal* disposition, proclivity **3** *the strains of music* theme, tune, melody, song, air

strained *adj*
forced, constrained, laboured, false, artificial, unnatural, stiff, wooden, tense, unrelaxed, uneasy, uncomfortable, awkward, embarrassed, self-conscious
☒ natural, relaxed

strainer *n*
sieve, colander, sifter, filter, screen, riddle

strait *n*
1 *the Straits of Gibraltar* sound, narrows, inlet, channel, kyle **2** *in desperate straits* crisis, difficulty, emergency, hardship, predicament, plight, perplexity, distress, dilemma, embarrassment, extremity, poverty, *colloq.* hole, mess, fix, pickle

straitened *adj*
poor, reduced, difficult, distressed, restricted, limited, impoverished, embarrassed
☒ easy, well-off

strait-laced *adj*
prudish, stuffy, starchy, prim, priggish, proper, strict, narrow, narrow-minded, puritanical, moralistic
☒ broad-minded

strand¹ *n*
1 FIBRE, filament, wire, thread, string, piece, length

2 *the strands of a theory* element, feature, component, factor, ingredient

strand² *n*
walk along the strand shore, beach, seashore, foreshore, sand(s), waterfront, front

stranded *adj*
marooned, high and dry, abandoned, helpless, penniless, aground, grounded, beached, shipwrecked, wrecked, *formal* forsaken, *colloq.* (left) in the lurch

strange *adj*
1 ODD, peculiar, curious, queer, weird, bizarre, eccentric, abnormal, irregular, uncommon, unusual, unexpected, exceptional, remarkable, fantastic, extraordinary, unreal, surreal, mystifying, perplexing, unexplained, inexplicable, uncanny, *formal* singular, *colloq.* funny, freaky, wacky, oddball, offbeat, kinky **2** NEW, novel, untried, unknown, unheard-of, unfamiliar, unaccustomed, unacquainted, foreign, alien, exotic
Fa 1 ordinary, common **2** well-known, familiar

strangeness *n*
oddity, oddness, peculiarity, bizarreness, extraordinariness, irregularity, abnormality, queerness, eccentricity, uncanniness, eeriness, exoticness, *formal* singularity
Fa ordinariness

stranger *n*
newcomer, new arrival, visitor, guest, non-member, outsider, incomer, foreigner, alien
Fa local, native
▷ **a stranger to** unfamiliar with, inexperienced in, unversed in, unacquainted with, unaccustomed to

strangle *v*
1 THROTTLE, choke, asphyxiate, suffocate, stifle, smother **2** SUPPRESS, gag, repress, inhibit, restrain, check, keep in, hold back, stifle, smother

strap *n, v*
▶ *n* thong, tie, band, belt, cord, leash
▶ *v* **1** BEAT, lash, whip, flog, belt, scourge **2** FASTEN, secure, tie, bind, truss, lash, bandage

strapping *adj*
brawny, strong, sturdy, well-built, beefy, big, burly, hefty, robust, hulking, husky, *colloq.* hunky
Fa puny

stratagem *n*
plan, scheme, plot, intrigue, ruse, ploy, trick, deception, dodge, manoeuvre, device, tactic, artifice, wile, subterfuge, *formal* machination

---

✎ stratagem or strategy ?

A *stratagem* is a plan or trick, intended to deceive someone or gain an advantage over them: *He was a master of the cunning stratagem and the bare-faced lie.* *Strategy* is used to describe tactics, especially in a long-term plan of campaign: *adopt a strategy of civil disobedience; guerrilla tactics were replaced by a strategy of conventional warfare.*

---

strategic *adj*
important, key, critical, decisive, crucial, vital, essential, tactical, planned, calculated, deliberate, politic, diplomatic
Fa unimportant

strategy *n*
tactics, planning, policy, approach, procedure, plan, plan of action, programme, schedule, design, scheme, *colloq.* blueprint, game, plan

---

✎ strategy or stratagem ? *See panel at* STRATAGEM.

---

stratum *n*
1 LEVEL, grade, class, rank, table, tier, category, bracket, caste, station, group, region **2** LAYER, seam, vein, lode, bed, stratification

stray *v, adj*
▶ *v* wander (off), get lost, err, go astray, ramble, saunter, amble, roam, rove, range, meander, straggle, drift, diverge, deviate, digress, go off the subject, *colloq.* go off at a tangent
▶ *adj* **1** LOST, abandoned, homeless, wandering, roaming, drifting **2** RANDOM, chance, occasional, accidental, freak, odd, erratic, scattered, isolated

streak *n, v*
▶ *n* **1** LINE, stroke, smear, band, stripe, strip, layer, vein **2** TRACE, dash, touch, element, strain **3** *on a lucky streak* spell, time, period, stint, stretch
▶ *v* **1** BAND, stripe, mark, fleck, smear, smudge, daub, *formal* striate **2** SPEED, tear, rush, hurtle, sprint, race, gallop, fly, dart, dash, flash, whistle, zoom, whizz, sweep, scurry

streaked *adj*
flecked, fleckered, streaky, lined, banded, barred, brinded, brindle(d), *formal* striate

stream *n, v*
▶ *n* **1** RIVER, creek, brook, beck, burn, rill, rillet, rivulet, tributary **2** *a stream of traffic* course, drift, flow, surge, current, outpouring, jet, run, gush, rush, tide, flood, deluge, cascade, torrent, volley, burst, *formal* efflux
▶ *v* **1** ISSUE, well, surge, run, flow, course, pour, spout, gush, flood, cascade, crowd, spill, shed **2** *streaming in the wind* float, trail, flap, fly, flutter

streamlined *adj*
1 AERODYNAMIC, smooth, sleek, graceful **2** EFFICIENT, well-run, smooth-running, rationalized, time-saving, organized, modernized, slick, *colloq.* up-to-the-minute
Fa 2 clumsy, inefficient

street *n*
road, thoroughfare, lane, avenue, boulevard

strength *n*
1 POWER, force, energy, vigour, brawn, muscle, sinew, stoutness, toughness, stamina, fitness, health, vigour, *colloq.* clout **2** TOUGHNESS, resilience, robustness, sturdiness, impregnability, durability, solidity, solidness, resistance, firmness, soundness, hardiness **3** DETERMINATION, resolution, forcefulness, firmness, assertiveness, persistence, spirit, bravery, courage, *formal* fortitude, *colloq.* guts **4** INTENSITY, depth, vividness, graphicness, sharpness, keenness, pungency, passion, fervency, ardour, vehemence **5** FORCEFULNESS, effectiveness, power, force, potency, persuasiveness, weight, validity, soundness, urgency, *formal* cogency **6** STRONG POINT, talent, gift, aptitude, advantage, asset, bent, forte, specialty, speciality, métier, *colloq.* thing
Fa 1 weakness, frailty **2** weakness **3** weakness, feebleness **4** mildness, blandness, faintness **5** weakness, ineffectiveness **6** weakness
▷ **on the strength of** because of, because of the influence of, on account of, based on, on the basis of, *formal* by virtue of

strengthen *v*
reinforce, brace, steel, buttress, build up, prop up, shore up, bolster, support, back up, toughen, harden, stiffen, consolidate, substantiate, corroborate, confirm, encourage, hearten, refresh, restore, rally, invigorate, nourish, increase, heighten, intensify, *formal* fortify, *colloq.* beef up
Fa weaken, undermine

strenuous *adj*

1 *strenuous work* hard, tough, demanding, gruelling, taxing, difficult, laborious, heavy, uphill, arduous, tiring, exhausting, weighty **2** ACTIVE, energetic, vigorous, eager, keen, earnest, tenacious, determined, forceful, resolute, spirited, bold, tireless, indefatigable

Fa 1 easy, effortless

stress *n, v*

▶ *n* **1** PRESSURE, strain, tension, worry, uneasiness, apprehension, anxiety, distress, difficulty, trouble, weight, burden, trauma, *colloq.* hassle **2** EMPHASIS, accent, accentuation, beat, force, weight, value, priority, importance, significance, *technical* ictus

Fa 1 relaxation

▶ *v* emphasize, accentuate, highlight, underline, underscore, point up, spotlight, repeat, exaggerate

Fa understate, play down, moderate, downplay, tone down

stretch *v, n*

▶ *v* **1** LENGTHEN, extend, make/become longer, broaden, widen, make/become wider, expand, spread, elongate, prolong, draw out, *formal* protract **2** *stretch from one point to another* reach, extend, spread, unfold, unroll, continue, project, go as far as, go/come down/up to, last, range **3** TIGHTEN, pull, tauten, strain **4** REACH OUT, straighten, extend, hold out, present, offer, *formal* proffer **5** *the job will stretch you* challenge, extend, push, test, tax, try

Fa 1 shorten, condense, compress

▷ **stretch your legs** exercise, go for a walk, move about, stroll, take a walk, take the air, *formal* promenade, *colloq.* take a breather

▷ **stretch out** extend, relax, hold out, put out, lie down, sprawl, reach, *formal* recline

Fa draw back

▶ *n* **1** EXPANSE, spread, sweep, reach, extent, distance, space, area, tract **2** PERIOD, time, term, spell, stint, run

strew *v*

scatter, spread, disperse, bestrew, litter, sprinkle, toss

Fa gather

stricken *adj*

affected, afflicted, hit, struck, injured, wounded, smitten

Fa unaffected

strict *adj*

1 *a strict teacher* stern, authoritarian, no-nonsense, hard, firm, rigid, inflexible, uncompromising, stringent, rigorous, disciplinarian, harsh, tough, severe, austere, narrow **2** EXACT, precise, accurate, clear, clear-cut, literal, faithful, close, true, absolute, utter, total, complete, thoroughgoing, meticulous, scrupulous, conscientious, particular, orthodox, religious

Fa 1 liberal, soft, flexible, *colloq.* easy-going **2** loose

strictness *n*

1 STERNNESS, authoritarianism, firmness, harshness, rigidity, rigidness, severity, stringency, stringentness, austerity **2** EXACTNESS, precision, accuracy, meticulousness, rigorousness, rigour, scrupulousness

Fa 1 flexibility, mildness

stricture *n*

1 CRITICISM, rebuke, reproof, blame, censure, *formal* animadversion, *colloq.* flak **2** RESTRICTION, limit, bound, confine, constraint, restraint, control, tightness

Fa 1 praise

stride *v, n*

▶ *v* walk, step, pace, tread, advance, progress

▶ *n* step, pace, walk, tread, movement, advance, progression

strident *adj*

loud, thundering, roaring, booming, clamorous, vociferous, harsh, rough, raucous, grating, rasping, shrill, screeching, unmusical, discordant, clashing, jarring, jangling, *formal* stentorian, stridulant, stridulous

Fa quiet, soft

strife *n*

conflict, disagreement, discord, dissension, controversy, animosity, hostility, friction, rivalry, contention, ill-feeling, ill-will, quarrel, quarrelling, row, argument, dispute, bickering, wrangling, struggle, fighting, combat, battle, warfare

Fa peace

strike *n, v*

▶ *n* **1** INDUSTRIAL ACTION, work-to-rule, go-slow, stoppage, sit-in, walk-out, mutiny, revolt **2** HIT, blow, stroke, slap, smack, thump, thwack, *colloq.* wallop, clobber, whack, belt, biff **3** ATTACK, charge, aid, storming, assault, rush, ambush, trap

▶ *v* **1** STOP WORK, down tools, take industrial action, work to rule, walk out, protest, mutiny, revolt **2** HIT, knock, collide with, slap, smack, cuff, thump, thwack, thrash, rap, beat, bang, pound, punch, box, hammer, buffet, batter, *colloq.* clout, wallop, sock, clobber, swipe, whack, belt, biff **3** ATTACK, charge, storm, assail, assault, raid, rush, set about, pounce on, ambush, trap **4** FIND, discover, come upon, unearth, uncover, encounter, reach, *formal* chance upon, happen upon **5** *the idea suddenly struck me* occur to, hit, come to, come to mind, dawn on, register **6** *it strikes me as odd* seem, appear, look, look like, feel, sound, give the impression, impress, affect, touch, have the look of **7** *strike a particular pose* adopt, take on, assume, embrace, affect **8** *strike a bargain* reach, come to, agree on, come to an agreement on, settle on, arrive at, achieve, *colloq.* clinch

▷ **strike back** retaliate, hit back, fight back, reciprocate, get back at, pay someone back, *colloq.* get your own back, get even with

▷ **strike down** afflict, ruin, destroy, kill, murder, assassinate, *formal* slay, smite

▷ **strike out** cross out, delete, rub out, erase, strike through, cancel, strike off, remove, obliterate

Fa add

▷ **strike up** begin, start, initiate, instigate, introduce, establish, *formal* commence, *colloq.* kick off

striking *adj*

1 NOTICEABLE, conspicuous, obvious, evident, salient, outstanding, remarkable, extraordinary, memorable, distinct, visible, impressive, dazzling, arresting, astonishing, stunning **2** ATTRACTIVE, stunning, beautiful, good-looking, gorgeous, pretty, glamorous

Fa 1 unimpressive **2** ugly

string *n, v*

▶ *n* **1** *a piece of string* twine, cord, rope, yarn, cable, line, strand, fibre **2** SERIES, succession, sequence, chain, line, row, column, file, queue, procession, stream, train **3** *with no strings attached* qualifications, conditions, limitations, restrictions, stipulations, provisos, obligations, requirements, catches, *formal* prerequisites

▶ *v* thread, link, connect, fasten, tie up, sling, hang, suspend, festoon, loop

▷ **string along** deceive, fool, bluff, dupe, play (someone) false, hoax, humbug, *colloq.* play fast and loose with, put one over on, take for a ride

▷ **string out** space out, spread out, stretch out, straggle, fan out, disperse, extend, lengthen, wander, *formal* protract

Fa gather, shorten

▷ **string up** hang, kill, lynch, send to the gallows/

scaffold/gibbet, *colloq.* top

stringent *adj*
binding, strict, severe, rigorous, tough, firm, rigid, inflexible, uncompromising, exacting, demanding, tight, hard, harsh
☒ lax, flexible

stringy *adj*
tough, gristly, chewy, fibrous, sinewy, leathery, wiry, ropy
☒ tender

strip *v, n*
▶ *v* **1** UNDRESS, take your clothes off, unclothe, remove your clothes, uncover, expose, lay bare, *formal* disrobe, denude **2** CLEAN OUT, clear, empty, divest, deprive, dispossess, gut, ransack, pillage, plunder, loot **3** PEEL, skin, flay, flake off, *formal* excoriate **4** DISMANTLE, take apart, disassemble, separate, pull apart, take to pieces
☒ **1** clothe, dress, get dressed **2** cover, fill **4** put together, assemble
▶ *n* ribbon, thong, strap, belt, sash, band, bar, stripe, swathe, lath, slat, piece, bit, slip, shred

stripe *n*
band, line, bar, chevron, flash, streak, fleck, strip, belt

striped *adj*
banded, barred, streaky, stripy, variegated, striated, vittate

stripling *n*
boy, fledgling, lad, teenager, adolescent, youth, youngster, *colloq.* young'un

strive *v*
1 TRY, attempt, endeavour, struggle, strain, work, toil, labour, try hard, campaign, exert yourself, give your all, do your best, do your utmost **2** FIGHT, battle, contend, engage, contest, combat, do battle, vie, compete

stroke *n, v*
▶ *n* **1** CARESS, pat, rub **2** BLOW, hit, knock, swipe, slap, thwack, thump, smack, *colloq.* wallop, clobber, whack, belt, biff **3** SWEEP, flourish, movement, action, move, motion, line **4** ACCOMPLISHMENT, achievement, coup **5** COLLAPSE, shock, spasm, attack, seizure, thrombosis, cerebral haemorrhage
▶ *v* caress, fondle, pet, touch, pat, rub, massage

stroll *v, n*
▶ *v* saunter, amble, dawdle, ramble, wander, meander, go for a walk, *colloq.* stretch your legs
▶ *n* walk, saunter, amble, constitutional, turn, ramble

stroller *n*
saunterer, rambler, walker, wanderer, dawdler

strong *adj*
1 POWERFUL, mighty, potent, lusty, strapping, sturdy, stout, burly, well-built, beefy, brawny, muscular, sinewy, athletic, fit, well, healthy **2** TOUGH, resilient, durable, hard-wearing, heavy-duty, solid, long-lasting, well-built, well-protected, reinforced, robust, hardy, sturdy, vigorous, stalwart, rugged **3** DETERMINED, forceful, firm, confident, resolute, assertive, aggressive, formidable, strong-willed, strong-minded, single-minded, persistent, brave, courageous, *colloq.* gutsy **4** *a strong colour/point* INTENSE, deep, vivid, graphic, fierce, violent, powerful, sharp, heady, keen, pungent, piquant, biting, highly-flavoured, highly-seasoned, hot, spicy **5** *a strong impression* marked, clear, clear-cut, obvious, evident, remarkable, pronounced **6** *take strong action* decisive, firm, positive, active, severe, resolute, forceful **7** *a strong interest in railways* keen, enthusiastic, eager, devoted, committed, passionate **8** *a strong case/argument* convincing, persuasive, powerful, potent, plausible, valid, sound, effective, telling, forceful, weighty, compelling, urgent, *formal*

efficacious **9** *strong feelings* intense, passionate, fervent, great, powerful, deep, profound, ardent, vehement **10** UNDILUTED, concentrated, potent
☒ **1** weak, frail, sickly, unhealthy **2** weak, insubstantial **3** feeble, weak **4** weak, faint, mild, bland **6** weak, indecisive **8** weak, unconvincing **9** weak, feeble **10** diluted
▷ **strong point** strength, talent, gift, aptitude, advantage, asset, bent, forte, speciality, specialty, métier, *colloq.* thing

strongarm *adj*
forceful, physical, violent, oppressive, terror, aggressive, bullying, coercive, threatening, intimidatory, thuggish
☒ gentle

stronghold *n*
citadel, bastion, fort, fortress, castle, tower, keep, refuge

strong-minded *adj*
resolute, steadfast, strong-willed, tenacious, firm, determined, independent, iron-willed, uncompromising, unbending, unwavering
☒ weak-willed

strong-willed *adj*
stubborn, obstinate, intractable, wayward, inflexible, wilful, self-willed, *formal* obdurate, refractory, recalcitrant, intransigent

stroppy *adj*
bad-tempered, difficult, unhelpful, unco-operative, perverse, awkward, bloody-minded, quarrelsome, rowdy, cantankerous, obstreperous, *formal* refractory
☒ co-operative, sweet-tempered

structural *adj*
design, constructional, organizational, *technical* tectonic, *formal* configurational, formational

structure *n, v*
▶ *n* **1** *the structure of society* framework, frame, construction, fabric, form, shape, design, make-up, formation, arrangement, organization, composition, constitution, system, set-up, *formal* configuration, conformation **2** BUILDING, construction, edifice, erection
▶ *v* construct, assemble, build, form, shape, design, arrange, organize

struggle *v, n*
▶ *v* **1** STRIVE, work, toil, labour, strain, try hard, exert yourself, give your all, do your best, do your utmost, agonize **2** FIGHT, battle, wrestle, grapple, engage, contest, combat, contend, compete, vie
☒ **2** yield, give in
▶ *n* difficulty, problem, effort, exertion, trouble, pains, agony, work, labour, toil, clash, conflict, strife, fight, battle, skirmish, encounter, combat, scuffle, brawl, hostilities, contest, competition
☒ ease, submission, co-operation

strut *v*
parade, prance, stalk, swagger, peacock, *colloq.* swank

stub *n*
end, stump, remnant, butt, counterfoil, *colloq.* fag end, dog-end

stubborn *adj*
obstinate, stiff-necked, mulish, pig-headed, rigid, uncompromising, inflexible, unbending, unyielding, dogged, persistent, tenacious, headstrong, self-willed, strong-willed, adamant, hidebound, wilful, difficult, unmanageable, stubborn as a mule, not listening/open to reason, *formal* obdurate, intransigent, refractory, intractable, recalcitrant
☒ compliant, flexible, yielding

stubby *adj*
stumpy, dumpy, chunky, short, squat, thickset
🖪 long, tall, thin

stuck *adj*
1 FAST, jammed, firm, fixed, embedded, rooted, fastened, unmovable, immobile, joined, glued, cemented, *colloq.* bogged down **2** BEATEN, baffled, *colloq.* stumped, perplexed, at a loss, at your wits' end, nonplussed
🖪 **1** loose
▷ **get stuck into** set about, tackle, get down to, start, begin, embark on
▷ **stuck on** fond of, enthusiastic about, keen on, obsessed with, infatuated with, wild about, crazy about, *colloq.* dotty about, mad on, nuts on
🖪 indifferent to

stuck-up *adj*
snobbish, supercilious, haughty, patronizing, condescending, proud, arrogant, conceited, *colloq.* snooty, bigheaded, toffee-nosed, high and mighty, hoity-toity, uppish
🖪 humble, modest

studded *adj*
dotted, flecked, set, spotted, speckled, sprinkled, ornamented, spangled, scattered

student *n*
undergraduate, postgraduate, scholar, schoolboy, schoolgirl, pupil, disciple, learner, probationer, apprentice, trainee

studied *adj*
deliberate, conscious, wilful, intentional, premeditated, planned, purposeful, calculated, contrived, forced, affected, unnatural, artificial, over-elaborate
🖪 unplanned, impulsive, natural

studio *n*
workshop, workroom, school, atelier

studious *adj*
scholarly, academic, intellectual, bookish, serious, thoughtful, reflective, diligent, hard-working, industrious, meticulous, thorough, assiduous, careful, attentive, earnest, eager, *formal* sedulous
🖪 lazy, idle, negligent

study *v, n*
▶ *v* read, learn, train, revise, cram, read up, research, major in, investigate, analyse, survey, scan, examine, scrutinize, peruse, pore over, contemplate, meditate, ponder, consider, deliberate, *colloq.* swot, mug up, bone up
▶ *n* **1** READING, homework, preparation, learning, scholarship, revision, cramming, research, investigation, inquiry, analysis, examination, scrutiny, inspection, contemplation, thought, consideration, attention, *colloq.* swotting

Subjects of study include:
accountancy, agriculture, anatomy, anthropology, archaeology, architecture, art, astrology, astronomy, biology, botany, building studies, business studies, calligraphy, chemistry, CDT (craft, design and technology), civil engineering, the Classics, commerce, computer studies, cosmology, craft, dance, design, domestic science, drama, dressmaking, driving, ecology, economics, education, electronics, engineering, environmental studies, ethnology, eugenics, fashion, fitness, food technology, forensics, genetics, geography, geology, heraldry, history, home economics, horticulture, information technology (IT), journalism, languages, law, leisure studies, lexicography, linguistics, literature,

logistics, management studies, marketing, mathematics, mechanics, media studies, medicine, metallurgy, metaphysics, meteorology, music, mythology, natural history, oceanography, ornithology, pathology, penology, personal and social education (PSE), personal, health and social education (PHSE), pharmacology, philosophy, photography, physics, physiology, politics, pottery, psychology, religious studies, science, shorthand, social sciences, sociology, sport, statistics, surveying, technology, theology, typewriting, visual arts, word processing, writing, zoology.

2 REPORT, essay, thesis, paper, monograph, work, survey, review, critique **3** OFFICE, studio, library, workroom, *colloq.* den

stuff *v, n*
▶ *v* **1** PACK, stow, load, fill, pad, press, cram, crowd, force, push, ram, thrust, wedge, jam, squeeze, stow, compress, block, obstruct, bung up, *colloq.* shove **2** GORGE, gormandize, overindulge, guzzle, gobble, sate, satiate, *colloq.* pig out, gross out, make a pig of yourself
🖪 **1** unload, empty **2** nibble
▶ *n* **1** MATERIAL, fabric, matter, substance, essence **2** BELONGINGS, possessions, things, objects, articles, items, goods, luggage, paraphernalia, kit, tackle, equipment, materials, *colloq.* gear, clobber

stuffing *n*
padding, wadding, quilting, packing, kapok, filling, forcemeat, farce

stuffy *adj*
1 *a stuffy room* musty, stale, airless, unventilated, suffocating, stifling, oppressive, heavy, close, muggy, sultry, fuggy **2** STAID, strait-laced, prim, conventional, old-fashioned, pompous, dull, dreary, uninteresting, stodgy, stiff, starchy, *colloq.* fuddy-duddy
🖪 **1** airy, well-ventilated **2** informal, modern, lively

stultify *v*
blunt, dull, stupefy, numb, smother, stifle, suppress, thwart, invalidate, negate, nullify, *formal* hebetate
🖪 prove, sharpen, electrify

stumble *v*
1 TRIP, slip, fall, lurch, reel, stagger, flounder, blunder, lose your balance **2** STAMMER, stutter, hesitate, falter
▷ **stumble on** come across, find, discover, encounter, *formal* chance upon, happen upon

stumbling-block *n*
obstacle, hurdle, barrier, bar, obstruction, hindrance, impediment, difficulty, snag

stump *n, v*
▶ *n* end, remnant, trunk, stub, butt, remains, *colloq.* fag end, dog-end
▶ *v* defeat, outwit, confound, perplex, puzzle, baffle, mystify, confuse, bewilder, dumbfound, foil, *colloq.* flummox, bamboozle, nonplus
🖪 assist
▷ **stump up** pay, pay out/up, hand over, donate, contribute, *colloq.* fork out, shell out, chip in, cough up
🖪 receive

stumped *adj*
perplexed, stuck, baffled, *colloq.* floored, bamboozled, flummoxed, nonplussed, stymied

stumpy *adj*
chunky, heavy, short, squat, stocky, stubby, thickset, thick, dumpy
🖪 long, tall, thin

stun *v*
amaze, astonish, astound, stagger, shock, daze, stupefy, dumbfound, overcome, overpower, confound,

confuse, bewilder, *colloq.* flabbergast, knock out, knock for six, bowl over, take your breath away

stunned *adj*
amazed, astounded, devastated, dumbfounded, dazed, numb, shocked, staggered, stupefied, *colloq.* flabbergasted, floored, gobsmacked
☒ indifferent

stunner *n*
beauty, charmer, good-looker, sensation, dazzler, heart-throb, looker, *femme fatale*, lovely, siren, *colloq.* smasher, knock-out, peach, wow, eye-catcher

stunning *adj*
beautiful, lovely, gorgeous, ravishing, dazzling, brilliant, striking, impressive, spectacular, remarkable, extraordinary, amazing, wonderful, marvellous, great, sensational, incredible, staggering, *colloq.* smashing, fabulous
☒ ugly, awful

stunt¹ *n*
a publicity stunt feat, exploit, act, deed, action, enterprise, trick, turn, performance, *colloq.* wheeze

stunt² *v*
stunt someone's growth stop, arrest, check, restrict, curb, slow, hinder, hamper, impede, dwarf, *formal* retard
☒ promote, encourage

stunted *adj*
small, little, tiny, undersized, diminutive, dwarfed, dwarfish
☒ large, sturdy

stupefaction *n*
daze, numbness, state of shock, blackout, senselessness, bewilderment, wonder, bafflement, amazement, astonishment

stupefy *v*
daze, stun, numb, dumbfound, shock, devastate, stagger, dull, amaze, astound, *colloq.* knock out, knock for six, bowl over

stupendous *adj*
huge, enormous, immense, gigantic, colossal, vast, phenomenal, tremendous, breathtaking, wonderful, extraordinary, overwhelming, staggering, stunning, amazing, astounding, fabulous, superb, marvellous, *formal* prodigious, *colloq.* fantastic
☒ ordinary, unimpressive

stupid *adj*
1 SILLY, foolish, irresponsible, ill-advised, indiscreet, foolhardy, rash, senseless, mad, lunatic, brainless, mindless, half-witted, idiotic, imbecilic, moronic, feeble-minded, simple-minded, slow, dim, dull, dull-witted, dense, crass, inane, fatuous, puerile, futile, pointless, meaningless, nonsensical, absurd, ludicrous, laughable, *formal* injudicious, *colloq.* gormless, thick, dumb, dopey, not all there, slow on the uptake, thick as a plank/two short planks 2 DAZED, groggy, stupefied, stunned, sluggish, semiconscious, unconscious
☒ 1 sensible, wise, clever, intelligent 2 alert

stupidity *n*
silliness, folly, foolishness, foolhardiness, irresponsibility, indiscretion, rashness, senselessness, madness, lunacy, denseness, crassness, absurdity, dimness, asininity, feeble-mindedness, dullness, puerility, fatuousness, fatuity, futility, impracticality, brainlessness, idiocy, imbecility, inanity, ineptitude, naïvety, obtuseness, pointlessness, ludicrousness, slowness, *colloq.* dopiness, doziness, dumbness, thickness
☒ intelligence, alertness, cleverness

stupor *n*
daze, state of shock, stupefaction, lethargy, inertia, trance, blackout, coma, numbness, oblivion, insens-

ibility, unconsciousness, *formal* torpor
☒ alertness, consciousness

sturdy *adj*
strong, robust, durable, well-made, stout, substantial, solid, well-built, powerful, muscular, athletic, hardy, vigorous, flourishing, hearty, staunch, stalwart, steadfast, firm, resolute, determined, tenacious, *formal* mighty
☒ weak, flimsy, puny

stutter *v*
stammer, hesitate, splutter, falter, stumble, mumble

style *n, v*
▶ *n* 1 APPEARANCE, cut, design, pattern, shape, form, sort, type, kind, variety, category, *formal* genre 2 ELEGANCE, smartness, chic, flair, panache, stylishness, dash, taste, polish, refinement, sophistication, urbanity, suaveness, fashion, vogue, trend, mode, dressiness, flamboyance, wealth, affluence, comfort, luxury, grandeur 3 *style of working* technique, approach, method, methodology, manner, fashion, way, custom, *formal* mode 4 WORDING, phrasing, expression, language, tone, tenor
☒ 2 inelegance, tastelessness
▶ *v* 1 DESIGN, cut, tailor, fashion, make, shape, produce, adapt 2 DESIGNATE, term, name, call, address, title, dub, tag, label, *formal* denominate

stylish *adj*
chic, fashionable, *à la mode*, modish, in vogue, voguish, snappy, dressy, smart, elegant, polished, refined, sophisticated, urbane, *colloq.* trendy, natty, snazzy, classy, ritzy
☒ old-fashioned, shabby

stylus *n*
needle, pointer, pen, index, hand, style, probe, *formal* graphium

stymie *v*
foil, frustrate, hinder, stump, thwart, defeat, confound, baffle, balk, mystify, puzzle, *colloq.* flummox, bamboozle, nonplus, snooker
☒ help, assist

suave *adj*
debonair, refined, polite, courteous, charming, civil, civilized, agreeable, affable, soft-spoken, smooth, polished, bland, unctuous, glib, sophisticated, urbane, worldly
☒ rude, unsophisticated

suavity *n*
refinement, politeness, courtesy, sophistication, urbanity, charm, civility, agreeability, blandness, smoothness, unctuousness, worldliness
☒ coarseness

subaquatic *adj*
underwater, undersea, submersed, submarine, *formal* subaqua, subaqueous, demersal

subconscious *adj, n*
▶ *adj* subliminal, unconscious, intuitive, instinctive, inner, innermost, deep, hidden, latent, underlying, repressed, suppressed
☒ conscious
▶ *n* psyche, unconscious, unconscious self, ego, super-ego, id

subdue *v*
overcome, quell, suppress, repress, overpower, crush, quash, defeat, conquer, overrun, subject, gain mastery over, get the better of, humble, break, tame, master, discipline, control, check, stifle, restrain, moderate, reduce, soften, quieten, damp, mellow, *formal* vanquish, subjugate
☒ arouse, awaken

subdued *adj*
1 SAD, downcast, dejected, crestfallen, depressed,

quiet, unexcited, lifeless, serious, grave, solemn, *colloq.* down in the dumps **2** QUIET, muted, hushed, silent, noiseless, still, soft, softened, pastel, dim, shaded, sombre, sober, restrained, delicate, unobtrusive, low-key, subtle, toned down
🖅 1 cheerful, lively, excited **2** bright, loud, striking, obtrusive

subject *n, adj, v*
▶ *n* **1** TOPIC, theme, matter, issue, question, aspect, point, substance, case, affair, business, discipline, area of study, field, field of study, motif **2** NATIONAL, citizen, participant, client, patient, victim **3** SUBORDINATE, vassal, liegeman, inferior, dependant, captive, *colloq.* underling
🖅 3 monarch, ruler, master
▶ *adj* **1** LIABLE, disposed, prone, susceptible, vulnerable, likely, apt, open, exposed **2** *subject to a law* captive, bound, constrained, obedient, answerable, accountable, subordinate, inferior, subservient, submissive, *formal* subjugated **3** DEPENDENT, conditional, *formal* contingent
🖅 1 invulnerable **2** free, superior **3** unconditional
▶ *v* expose, lay open, submit, subdue, submit, *formal* subjugate

subjection *n*
captivity, bondage, slavery, oppression, domination, mastery, defeat, enslavement, chains, shackles, *formal* subjugation

subjective *adj*
biased, prejudiced, bigoted, personal, individual, idiosyncratic, emotional, intuitive, instinctive
🖅 objective, unbiased, impartial

subjugate *v*
conquer, overpower, overcome, master, overthrow, gain mastery over, get the better of, crush, defeat, subdue, suppress, oppress, quell, reduce, enslave, tame, thrall, *formal* vanquish
🖅 free, liberate

sublimate *v*
channel, divert, transfer, redirect, turn, exalt, elevate, heighten, purify, refine, *formal* transmute
🖅 let out

sublime *adj*
1 GLORIOUS, exalted, elevated, high, lofty, noble, majestic, great, grand, imposing, magnificent, transcendent, spiritual **2** SUPREME, great, intense, extreme, complete, utter
🖅 1 lowly, base

submerge *v*
submerse, immerse, plunge, plummet, duck, dip, dunk, sink, go down, go/put under water, drown, engulf, overwhelm, swamp, overflow, flood, inundate, deluge, bury
🖅 surface

submerged *adj*
submersed, immersed, underwater, sunk, sunken, drowned, swamped, inundated, hidden, concealed, cloaked, veiled, unseen

submission *n*
1 SURRENDER, giving in, capitulation, resignation, agreement, acquiescence, compliance, obedience, deference, submissiveness, meekness, passivity, *formal* assent **2** PRESENTATION, offering, contribution, entry, introduction, tendering, tabling, tender, suggestion, proposal, statement, assertion, *formal* averment
🖅 1 resistance, opposition, intransigence, intractability **2** withdrawal

submissive *adj*
yielding, unresisting, resigned, patient, uncomplaining, accommodating, malleable, biddable, compliant,

acquiescent, obedient, deferential, ingratiating, subservient, resisting, servile, humble, meek, self-effacing, docile, weak, weak-willed, downtrodden, subdued, passive, *formal* supine
🖅 intractable, assertive, *formal* intransigent

submit *v*
1 YIELD, give in, give way, surrender, lay down your arms, capitulate, knuckle under, bow, bend, stoop, succumb, agree, comply, defer, acquiesce, *formal* accede **2** PRESENT, tender, offer, put forward, suggest, propose, introduce, table, move, state, claim, assert, argue, *formal* proffer, propound, aver
🖅 1 resist, oppose **2** withdraw

subnormal *adj*
below normal, below average, low, backward, inferior, slow, retarded, feeble-minded
🖅 gifted

subordinate *adj, n*
▶ *adj* secondary, auxiliary, ancillary, subsidiary, dependent, inferior, lower, lower in rank, lower-ranking, junior, minor, lesser, subservient, lowly
🖅 superior, senior
▶ *n* inferior, junior, assistant, attendant, second, deputy, aide, dependant, menial, vassal, *colloq.* underling, sidekick, skivvy, dogsbody,
second fiddle
🖅 superior, boss

subordination *n*
inferiority, subjection, submission, dependence, servitude, subservience
🖅 superiority

subscribe *v*
1 *subscribe to a magazine* pay for regularly, buy regularly, receive/take regularly **2** DONATE, give, contribute, pledge, *colloq.* shell out, fork **3** *subscribe to a theory* support, endorse, back, approve, agree, underwrite, *formal* advocate, consent, accede

subscription *n*
membership fee, dues, payment, donation, contribution, offering, gift

subsequent *adj*
following, later, future, next, succeeding, resulting, consequent, ensuing
🖅 previous, earlier, prior

subsequently *adv*
later, after, afterwards, consequently
🖅 previously

subservient *adj*
1 SERVILE, deferential, submissive, fawning, ingratiating, unctuous, obsequious, toadying, *formal* sycophantic, *colloq.* bootlicking **2** SUBORDINATE, less important, secondary, ancillary, auxiliary, subsidiary, dependent, inferior, lower, junior, minor, lesser, conducive, useful, instrumental
🖅 1 domineering, rebellious **2** superior, senior, more important, unhelpful

subside *v*
1 DECREASE, lower, get lower, lessen, diminish, decline, dwindle, wane, ebb, recede, moderate, die down, quieten, let up, fall, slacken, ease, *formal* abate, *colloq.* peter out **2** SINK, collapse, cave in, settle, descend, lower, fall, drop
🖅 1 rise, increase

subsidence *n*
decline, decrease, descent, settlement, sinking, slackening, lessening, ebb, de-escalation, settling, *formal* abatement, detumescence, diminution
🖅 increase

subsidiary *adj, n*
▶ *adj* auxiliary, supplementary, additional, supple-

mentary, ancillary, assistant, supporting, contributory, secondary, subordinate, subservient, lesser, minor

Ⓕ primary, chief, major

▸ *n* branch, offshoot, division, section, part, wing

subsidize *v*
support, back, endorse, underwrite, sponsor, finance, fund, invest in, give a subsidy to, pay part of the cost of, contribute to, aid, promote

subsidy *n*
grant, allowance, assistance, help, aid, contribution, sponsorship, finance, funding, investment, support, backing, endorsement, underwriting, *formal* subvention

subsist *v*
exist, continue, endure, hold out, live, survive, remain, last, eke out an existence

subsistence *n*
living, survival, existence, continuance, livelihood, maintenance, support, keep, sustenance, nourishment, food, provisions, rations, aliment

substance *n*
1 MATTER, material, stuff, fabric, essence, mass, medium, entity, body, solidity, materiality, tangibility, concreteness, reality, actuality, ground, foundation, *formal* corporeality **2** SUBJECT, subject matter, matter, topic, theme, text, burden, pith, gist, meaning, meaningfulness, significance, validity, truth, foundation, ground, basis, force, power, weight, *formal* import **3** *a person of substance* wealth, money, prosperity, riches, assets, means, resources, affluence, power, influence

substandard *adj*
second-rate, inferior, imperfect, damaged, shoddy, poor, inadequate, unacceptable, *colloq.* below par, not up to scratch

Ⓕ first-rate, superior, perfect

substantial *adj*
1 LARGE, big, sizable, ample, generous, great, considerable, significant, important, meaningful, notable, remarkable, weighty, worthwhile, valuable, *colloq.* tidy **2** WELL-BUILT, solid, stout, sturdy, strong, tough, durable, sound **3** TANGIBLE, material, existing, concrete, real, actual, true, *formal* corporeal **4** BASIC, essential, central, primary, main, principal, fundamental, inherent, intrinsic **5** WEALTHY, prosperous, rich, successful, affluent, powerful, influential

Ⓕ **1** small, insignificant **2** flimsy **3** insubstantial, imaginary **5** poor

substantially *adv*
1 SIGNIFICANTLY, largely, considerably, to a great extent **2** ESSENTIALLY, fundamentally, mainly, in the main, materially, to all intents and purposes

Ⓕ **1** slightly

substantiate *v*
prove, verify, confirm, uphold, support, back up, bear out, authenticate, validate, *formal* corroborate

Ⓕ disprove, refute

substitute *v, n, adj*
▸ *v* **1** CHANGE, exchange, swap, switch, interchange, replace, use instead **2** STAND IN, cover, deputize, understudy, relieve, take over, take the place of, double, act instead of, *colloq.* fill in, sub

▸ *n* reserve, stand-by, supply, locum, understudy, stand-in, replacement, relief, surrogate, proxy, agent, deputy, makeshift, stopgap, *formal locum tenens, colloq.* temp, fill in

▸ *adj* reserve, temporary, relief, acting, deputy, surrogate, proxy, replacement, alternative, stand-by, stand-in

substitution *n*
change, exchange, replacement, interchange, swap,

swapping, switch, switching

subterfuge *n*
trick, stratagem, scheme, ploy, ruse, wile, intrigue, expedient, manoeuvre, deviousness, evasion, deception, artifice, pretence, excuse, pretext, *formal* machination, duplicity, *colloq.* dodge

Ⓕ openness, honesty

subtle *adj*
1 DELICATE, understated, implied, indirect, low-key, slight, minute, tenuous, elusive, faint, indistinct, indefinite, mild, toned down, fine, nice, refined, sophisticated, deep, profound **2** ARTFUL, cunning, crafty, sly, devious, wily, indirect, shrewd, astute, discreet, discriminating, tactful, clever, strategic, intricate, complex

Ⓕ **1** blatant, obvious **2** artless, open, indiscreet, tactless

subtlety *n*
1 DELICACY, nicety, nuance, refinement, finesse, faintness, indistinctness, indefiniteness, mutedness, sophistication **2** ARTFULNESS, cunning, wiliness, guile, deviousness, craftiness, cleverness, discernment, astuteness, skill, discrimination, intricacy, slyness, acuteness, acumen, *formal* sagacity

subtract *v*
deduct, take away, remove, dock, withdraw, debit, detract, diminish

Ⓕ add

suburb *n*
suburbia, outskirts, commuter belt, residential area, dormitory town, *formal* purlieus

Ⓕ centre, heart

suburban *adj*
1 *a suburban railway* commuter, residential **2** *suburban attitudes* conventional, dull, unimaginative, narrow, narrow-minded, parochial, provincial, insular, bourgeois, middle-class

subversive *adj, n*
▸ *adj* seditious, treasonous, treacherous, traitorous, revolutionary, inflammatory, incendiary, disruptive, troublemaking, riotous, weakening, undermining, discrediting, destructive

Ⓕ loyal

▸ *n* seditionist, terrorist, dissident, traitor, quisling, *colloq.* freedom fighter, fifth columnist

subvert *v*
undermine, destroy, ruin, pervert, corrupt, confound, deprave, demoralize, contaminate, poison, overturn, upset, disrupt, invalidate, wreck, demolish, debase, raze, sabotage, *formal* vitiate

Ⓕ boost, uphold

subway *n*
1 UNDERGROUND RAILWAY, underground, metro, *colloq.* tube **2** UNDERPASS, tunnel, pedestrian tunnel, underground passage

succeed *v*
1 TRIUMPH, do well, be successful, thrive, flourish, prosper, make good, manage, carry out, complete, achieve, accomplish, reach, realize, attain, fulfil, prevail, work, work out, get results, *colloq.* make it, get on, bring off, pull off, turn up trumps, take over, steal the show, go places, win the day, land/fall on your feet, bring home the bacon, strike gold, hit the jackpot **2** *winter succeeds autumn* follow, come after, replace, take the place of, result, ensue

Ⓕ **1** fail, *colloq.* flop **2** precede

▷ **succeed to** come into, enter upon, inherit, replace, take over, supersede, *formal* accede, assume

Ⓕ abdicate, precede

ᐧ**succeeding** *adj*
following, next, subsequent, ensuing, coming, to

come, later, successive
🔁 previous, earlier, prior

success n
1 TRIUMPH, victory, positive result, luck, fortune, prosperity, happiness, fame, eminence, completion, achievement, accomplishment, realization, attainment, fulfilment **2** CELEBRITY, star, winner, bestseller, hit, sensation, *colloq.* somebody, VIP, big name, bigwig, big shot, wow, sell-out, box-office hit
🔁 **1** failure, disaster **2** failure, loser, *colloq.* write-off, flop, dead loss

successful adj
1 VICTORIOUS, triumphant, winning, lucky, fortunate, prosperous, wealthy, affluent, thriving, flourishing, booming, moneymaking, lucrative, profitable, rewarding, satisfying, fruitful, productive **2** *a successful writer* famous, well-known, popular, leading, bestselling, top, unbeaten
🔁 **1** unsuccessful, unprofitable, fruitless **2** unknown

successfully adv
great, fine, well, victoriously, beautifully, famously, *colloq.* swimmingly
🔁 unsuccessfully

succession n
1 SERIES, sequence, order, progression, run, chain, string, cycle, continuation, flow, course, line, train, procession **2** *the succession to the throne* accession, attaining, elevation, inheritance, *formal* assumption
▷ **in succession** successively, consecutively, sequentially, uninterruptedly, running, one after the other, *colloq.* on the trot

successive adj
consecutive, sequential, following, succeeding, running, serial

successively adv
consecutively, in succession, sequentially, uninterruptedly, running, one after the other, *colloq.* on the trot

successor n
replacement, substitute, relief, descendant, beneficiary, heir, co-heir, inheritor, next in line

succinct adj
concise, short, brief, terse, crisp, pithy, compact, condensed, summary, to the point, in a word
🔁 long, lengthy, wordy, verbose

succour n, v
▶ n help, aid, assistance, support, comfort, relief, *formal* ministrations, *colloq.* helping hand
▶ v help, help out, aid, assist, comfort, encourage, support, relieve, foster, minister to, nurse, befriend
🔁 undermine

succulent adj
fleshy, juicy, moist, luscious, mouthwatering, lush, rich, mellow
🔁 dry

succumb v
1 GIVE IN, give way, yield, submit, knuckle under, surrender, capitulate, collapse, fall **2** *succumb to an illness* catch, go down with, pick up, die of, *formal* contract
🔁 **1** overcome, overwhelm, master

suck v
draw (in), imbibe, absorb, blot up, soak up, extract, drain
▷ **suck up to** fawn, flatter, ingratiate, toady, curry favour, truckle, *colloq.* lick someone's boots

sucker n
fool, victim, dupe, stooge, sap, leech, *colloq.* pushover, mug, butt, cat's-paw

suckle v
breastfeed, feed, nurse

sudden adj
unexpected, unforeseen, unanticipated, surprising, startling, dramatic, abrupt, sharp, quick, fast, swift, rapid, speedy, meteoric, immediate, instantaneous, prompt, hurried, hasty, rash, impetuous, impulsive, *colloq.* snap, spur-of-the-moment
🔁 expected, predictable, gradual, slow

suddenly adv
unexpectedly, all of a sudden, quickly, sharply, abruptly, immediately, instantaneously, without warning, *colloq.* out of the blue, from out of nowhere

suddenness n
unexpectedness, abruptness, hurriedness, haste, hastiness, impulsiveness
🔁 slowness

sue v
1 PROSECUTE, charge, bring charges against, take (legal) action against, indict, take to court, bring to trial **2** SUMMON, solicit, appeal, beg, petition, plead, *formal* beseech

suffer v
1 HURT, ache, be in pain, be afflicted, agonize, grieve, sorrow, *colloq.* go through the mill **2** UNDERGO, experience, go through, feel, meet with, endure, sustain **3** BEAR, support, stand, put up with, tolerate, endure, *formal* abide

suffering n
pain, discomfort, hurt, hurting, agony, anguish, affliction, distress, misery, hardship, wretchedness, plight, adversity, ordeal, torment, torture
🔁 ease, comfort

suffice v
do, satisfy, be sufficient, be adequate, answer, measure up, serve, content, *colloq.* fit/fill the bill

sufficiency n
adequateness, adequacy, enough, plenty, satiety, competence, *formal* sufficience
🔁 insufficiency, inadequacy

sufficient adj
enough, adequate, ample, plenty, satisfactory, effective, *colloq.* decent
🔁 insufficient, inadequate

suffocate v
asphyxiate, smother, stifle, choke, strangle, throttle, be/make breathless

suffrage n
franchise, right to vote, right of representation, *formal* enfranchisement

suffuse v
spread, imbue, infuse, permeate, pervade, steep, transfuse, cover, flood, mantle, bathe, colour, redden

sugar n

Kinds of sugar include:
beet sugar, brown sugar, cane sugar, caster sugar, crystallized sugar, demerara, dextrose, fructose, glucose, golden syrup, granulated sugar, icing sugar, invert sugar, jaggery, lactose, maltose, maple syrup, molasses, powdered sugar, refined sugar, sucrose, sugar loaf, sugar lump, sweets, *US* candy, *US* sugar candy, syrup, treacle, unrefined sugar.

Artificial sweeteners include:
acesulfame K, aspartame, Canderel®, cyclamate, Hermesetas®, NutraSweet®, saccharin, sorbitol, Sweetex®. *See also* SWEETS.

sugary adj
sentimental, emotional, gushing, touching, maudlin,

mawkish, sloppy, soppy, *colloq.* lovey-dovey, slushy, mushy, schmaltzy, corny, sickly, gushy

suggest *v*
1 PROPOSE, put forward, advocate, recommend, submit, advise, counsel, move, table, nominate, *colloq.* float **2** IMPLY, insinuate, hint, intimate, evoke, bring to mind, indicate, give the impression

suggestion *n*
1 PROPOSAL, proposition, motion, recommendation, submission, idea, plan, hint, piece of advice, pointer **2** IMPLICATION, insinuation, intimation, innuendo **3** HINT, intimation, suspicion, trace, touch, indication

suggestive *adj*
1 EVOCATIVE, reminiscent, expressive, meaning, indicative, *formal* redolent **2** *a suggestive remark* indecent, immodest, improper, indelicate, titillating, off-colour, sexual, risqué, bawdy, dirty, smutty, ribald, lewd, provocative, *colloq.* blue
F3 1 inexpressive **2** decent, clean

suicide *n*
killing yourself, self-destruction, self-murder, taking of your (own) life, self-slaughter, hara-kiri, suttee, *formal* felo de se, self-immolation, *colloq.* topping yourself, ending it all

suit *n, v*
▸ *n* **1** *wear a suit* outfit, costume, dress, clothing, set of clothes, ensemble **2** LAWSUIT, action, case, cause, dispute, argument, contest, prosecution, litigation, proceedings, process, trial
▸ *v* **1** GO WELL WITH, complement, match, tally with, agree with, harmonize with, fit, befit, become, look good/attractive on, flatter **2** PLEASE, satisfy, answer, gratify **3** BE CONVENIENT FOR, be suitable for, be appropriate, be applicable, be acceptable, be satisfactory, qualify, *formal* suffice, *colloq.* fit/fill the bill
F3 1 clash **2** displease **3** be unsuitable for, be inconvenient for

suitability *n*
appropriateness, aptness, fitness, fittingness, opportuneness, timeliness, convenience, rightness, *formal* appositeness
F3 unsuitability, inappropriateness

suitable *adj*
appropriate, fitting, convenient, opportune, suited, in keeping, right, compatible, well-suited, well-matched, due, apt, relevant, applicable, fit, adequate, satisfactory, acceptable, befitting, becoming, proper, right, *formal* apposite, pertinent, *colloq.* (right/just) up someone's street
F3 unsuitable, inappropriate

suitably *adv*
appropriately, fittingly, properly, fitly, acceptably, accordingly, quite
F3 unsuitably

suitcase *n*
case, vanity-case, bag, holdall, portmanteau, valise, overnight-bag, flight bag, hand-luggage, travel bag, attaché case, portfolio, trunk

suite *n*
1 APARTMENT, rooms, set of rooms, household **2** SET, series, collection, sequence, train, furniture **3** ATTENDANTS, retinue, entourage, escort, followers, retainers, servants

suitor *n*
admirer, boyfriend, lover, young man, wooer, beau, follower, pretendant

sulk *v, n*
▸ *v* mope, brood, pout, grouse, grump, *colloq.* be

miffed, be in a huff
▸ *n* mood, temper, bad mood, bad temper, pique, *colloq.* huff, miff

sulky *adj*
brooding, moody, morose, resentful, grudging, disgruntled, put out, cross, moping, grumpy, out of sorts, bad-tempered, sullen, aloof, unsociable, *colloq.* miffed, ratty, huffy
F3 cheerful, good-tempered, sociable

sullen *adj*
1 SULKY, moody, morose, glum, gloomy, silent, uncommunicative, surly, sour, cross, churlish, perverse, obstinate, stubborn, resentful **2** DARK, gloomy, dismal, sombre, cheerless, dull, leaden, heavy
F3 1 cheerful, happy **2** fine, clear

sullenness *n*
moroseness, sulkiness, surliness, moodiness, brooding, glowering, sourness, glumness, heaviness
F3 cheerfulness

sully *v*
dirty, soil, defile, pollute, contaminate, taint, spoil, mar, spot, blemish, besmirch, stain, tarnish, damage, disgrace, dishonour
F3 cleanse, honour

sultry *adj*
1 *sultry weather* hot, sweltering, stifling, stuffy, oppressive, suffocating, close, airless, humid, muggy, sticky **2** SENSUAL, voluptuous, passionate, attractive, sexy, provocative, seductive, tempting, alluring
F3 1 cool, cold

sum *n, v*
▸ *n* total, sum total, aggregate, whole, entirety, number, quantity, amount, tally, reckoning, score, result, answer, summary, culmination
▸ *v* ▷ **sum up 1** SUMMARIZE, review, recapitulate, conclude, close, *colloq.* put in a nutshell **2** EPITOMIZE, embody, encapsulate, exemplify

summarily *adv*
immediately, promptly, speedily, swiftly, without delay, hastily, abruptly, arbitrarily, *formal* expeditiously, peremptorily, forthwith

summarize *v*
outline, précis, condense, abridge, shorten, abbreviate, sum up, epitomize, encapsulate, review, sketch, outline, *colloq.* recap
F3 expand (on)

summary *n, adj*
▸ *n* synopsis, résumé, outline, main points, abstract, précis, condensation, digest, compendium, abridgement, summing-up, review, recapitulation, overview, plan, *colloq.* rundown
▸ *adj* short, succinct, brief, cursory, swift, speedy, hasty, prompt, without delay, immediate, instant, instantaneous, direct, unceremonious, without formality, arbitrary, *formal* peremptory
F3 lengthy, careful

summerhouse *n*
belvedere, gazebo, pavilion

summit *n*
top, peak, pinnacle, point, crest, crown, head, vertex, acme, climax, culmination, height, *formal* apex, zenith, apogee
F3 bottom, foot, nadir

summon *v*
call, send for, order, demand, invite, bid, beckon, gather, assemble, convene, rally, muster, mobilize, rouse, arouse, *formal* convoke
F3 dismiss
▷ **summon up** gather, assemble, convene, rally, muster, mobilize, rouse, arouse, evoke, revive, call to mind

summons *n*
writ, subpoena, citation, order, call, injunction

sumptuous *adj*
luxurious, plush, lavish, extravagant, rich, costly, expensive, dear, splendid, magnificent, gorgeous, superb, grand, de luxe, *formal* opulent
🔁 plain, poor

sun *n, v*
▶ *n* star, daystar, sunlight, light, daylight, sunshine
▶ *v* sunbathe, tan, brown, bake, bask, *formal* insolate

sunbathe *v*
sun, bask, tan, brown, bake, sunbake, *formal* insolate

sunburnt *adj*
brown, tanned, sun-tanned, bronzed, weather-beaten, burnt, red, blistered, blistering, peeling, inflamed
🔁 pale

sunder *v*
split, separate, divide, part, cut, chop, sever, *formal* cleave, dissever, dissunder
🔁 join

sundry *adj*
various, diverse, miscellaneous, assorted, varied, different, several, some, a few

sunk *adj*
failed, lost, ruined, finished, doomed, *colloq.* done for, up the creek, up the spout, in a fix/jam

sunken *adj*
1 SUBMERGED, buried, recessed, lower, lowered, below ground level **2** *sunken eyes* depressed, concave, hollow, haggard, drawn

sunless *adj*
bleak, overcast, dark, cloudy, grey, hazy, gloomy, depressing, dismal, dreary, sombre, cheerless
🔁 sunny, bright

sunny *adj*
1 FINE, cloudless, unclouded, clear, summery, sunshiny, sunlit, bright, brilliant **2** CHEERFUL, happy, joyful, smiling, cheery, glad, bright, merry, beaming, radiant, light-hearted, bubbly, bouncy, buoyant, optimistic, hopeful, pleasant, *formal* blithe
🔁 **1** sunless, cloudy, dull **2** gloomy

sunrise *n*
dawn, crack of dawn, break of day, daybreak, daylight, first light, sun-up, cock-crow, aurora

sunset *n*
sundown, dusk, twilight, gloaming, evening, close of day, nightfall

super *adj*
great, excellent, superb, wonderful, outstanding, marvellous, magnificent, glorious, incomparable, peerless, matchless, sensational, *colloq.* smashing, terrific, top-notch, neat, ace, brill, *slang* mega, cool, wicked
🔁 poor, *colloq.* lousy

superannuated *adj*
antiquated, old, elderly, pensioned off, obsolete, senile, retired, aged, decrepit, *formal* moribund, *colloq.* past it, put out to grass
🔁 young

superb *adj*
excellent, first-rate, first-class, superior, superlative, choice, fine, exquisite, brilliant, gorgeous, magnificent, splendid, lavish, grand, wonderful, great, outstanding, remarkable, unrivalled, unsurpassed, marvellous, admirable, impressive, breathtaking, dazzling, *colloq.* fabulous, smashing, terrific, neat, ace, brill
🔁 bad, poor, inferior

supercilious *adj*
arrogant, condescending, patronizing, overbearing, scornful, lofty, lordly, imperious, insolent, proud, disdainful, haughty, contemptuous, *formal* vainglorious, *colloq.* snooty, snotty, stuck-up, toffee-nosed, uppish, uppity, hoity-toity, jumped up, too big for your boots
🔁 humble, self-effacing

superficial *adj*
surface, external, exterior, peripheral, outer, outward, apparent, alleged, seeming, cosmetic, skin-deep, shallow, slight, trivial, facile, lightweight, insignificant, frivolous, casual, cursory, sketchy, careless, slapdash, perfunctory, hasty, hurried, passing, *formal* ostensible
🔁 internal, deep, thorough

superficially *adv*
externally, on the surface, apparently, seemingly, casually, carelessly, hurriedly, *formal* ostensibly
🔁 in depth

superfluity *n*
redundancy, excess, surfeit, surplus, extra, exuberance, glut, superabundance, excessiveness, *technical* pleonasm, *formal* plethora
🔁 lack

superfluous *adj*
extra, spare, excess, surplus, remaining, redundant, to spare, unnecessary, unneeded, needless, gratuitous, unwanted, unwarranted, uncalled-for, excessive, *formal* supernumerary
🔁 necessary, needed, required, wanted, essential

superhuman *adj*
great, immense, supernatural, herculean, heroic, stupendous, divine, paranormal, phenomenal, *formal* preternatural, prodigious
🔁 average, ordinary

superintend *v*
supervise, oversee, overlook, inspect, run, manage, administer, direct, be in charge of, be responsible for, control, be in control of, handle, steer

superintendence *n*
supervision, oversight, inspection, direction, control, government, charge, care, management, administration, running, guidance, surveillance

superintendent *n*
supervisor, overseer, director, governor, controller, conductor, administrator, manager, inspector, chief, curator, *colloq.* gaffer, boss

superior *adj, n*
▶ *adj* **1** EXCELLENT, first-class, first-rate, high-class, high-quality, exclusive, prime, quality, prize, choice, select, fine, de luxe, admirable, distinguished, exceptional, unrivalled, par excellence, *colloq.* top-notch, top-flight **2** BETTER, preferred, greater, higher, higher in rank, senior **3** HAUGHTY, lordly, lofty, pretentious, snobbish, supercilious, disdainful, condescending, patronizing, *colloq.* snooty, stuck-up, toffee-nosed, uppish, uppity, jumped up, too big for your boots
🔁 **1** inferior, average **2** inferior, worse, lower **3** self-effacing, humble
▶ *n* senior, elder, better, boss, chief, principal, director, manager, foreman, supervisor, chief
🔁 subordinate, inferior, junior, assistant

superiority *n*
advantage, lead, edge, supremacy, pre-eminence, eminence, dominance, predominance, *formal* ascendancy
🔁 inferiority

superlative *adj*
best, greatest, highest, first-class, first-rate, supreme, unbeatable, unrivalled, unparalleled, matchless, peerless, unsurpassed, unbeaten, excellent, brilliant,

magnificent, outstanding, *formal* transcendent, consummate, *colloq.* ace, brill
F3 poor, average, mediocre

supernatural *adj*
paranormal, unnatural, abnormal, otherworldly, metaphysical, spiritual, psychic, mystic, mystical, occult, hidden, mysterious, miraculous, magical, magic, phantom, ghostly, eerie, weird, *formal* preternatural
F3 natural, normal

supernumerary *adj*
superfluous, surplus, redundant, spare, excess, excessive, extra, extraordinary
F3 necessary

supersede *v*
succeed, replace, supplant, usurp, oust, displace, take the place of, take over from, remove

superstition *n*
myth, old wives' tale, fallacy, delusion, illusion, magic

superstitious *adj*
mythical, false, fallacious, irrational, groundless, delusive, illusory
F3 rational, logical, factual

supervise *v*
oversee, watch (over), look after, keep an eye on, inspect, superintend, run, manage, administer, direct, guide, conduct, preside over, be in charge of, be responsible for, be in control of, control, handle

supervision *n*
surveillance, care, charge, superintendence, oversight, running, management, administration, direction, control, guidance, inspection, instruction

supervisor *n*
overseer, inspector, superintendent, boss, chief, director, administrator, manager, steward, foreman, forewoman

supervisory *adj*
administrative, managerial, executive, overseeing, superintendent, *formal* directorial

supine *adj*
1 PROSTRATE, flat, horizontal, *formal* recumbent **2** LAZY, idle, inactive, lethargic, careless, heedless, resigned, bored, uninterested, apathetic, indifferent, sluggish, slothful, inert, languid, negligent, passive, listless, spiritless, unresisting, *formal* indolent, torpid, *colloq.* spineless
F3 **1** upright **2** alert

supper *n*
dinner, evening meal, tea, snack

supplant *v*
replace, supersede, usurp, oust, displace, take the place of, take over from, remove, overthrow, topple, unseat

supple *adj*
flexible, bending, stretching, elastic, pliant, pliable, plastic, lithe, supple, limber, graceful, loose-limbed, double-jointed
F3 stiff, rigid, inflexible

supplement *n, v*
▶ *n* addition, additive, extra, insert, pull-out, add-on, addendum, appendix, rider, postscript, sequel, *technical* codicil
▶ *v* add to, boost, reinforce, increase, fill up, top up, complement, extend, eke out, *formal* augment
F3 deplete, use up

> 📖 **supplement**, **complement** or **compliment** ? *See panel at* COMPLEMENT.

supplementary *adj*
additional, extra, added, auxiliary, secondary, attached, complementary, accompanying

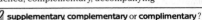

> 📖 **supplementary**, **complementary** or **complimentary** ? *See panel at* COMPLEMENTARY.

suppliant *adj*
begging, entreating, imploring, supplicating, craving, *formal* beseeching, importunate

supplicant *n*
petitioner, pleader, suitor, applicant, suppliant, *formal* postulant

supplicate *v*
request, entreat, appeal, petition, plead, pray, solicit, *formal* invoke, beseech

supplication *n*
request, appeal, entreaty, petition, plea, pleading, prayer, orison, suit, *formal* invocation, imploration, solicitation, rogation

supplicatory *adj*
begging, petitioning, supplicating, imploring, *formal* beseeching, imprecatory, precative, precatory

supplier *n*
dealer, seller, vendor, wholesaler, retailer, outfitter, provider, contributor, donor

supply *v, n*
▶ *v* provide, furnish, equip, outfit, fit out, stock, fill, replenish, give, donate, grant, endow, contribute, yield, produce, sell, *formal* endue, proffer
F3 take, receive
▶ *n* **1** STOCK, source, amount, quantity, fund, reservoir, store, reserve, heap, mass, pile, stockpile, hoard, cache **2** PROVISIONS, stores, food, rations, equipment, materials, necessities

support *v, n*
▶ *v* **1** BACK, second, defend, champion, advocate, further, be in favour of, be in sympathy with, be behind/with, promote, foster, help, aid, assist, rally round, *formal* espouse, *colloq.* run with, throw your weight behind **2** HELP, encourage, comfort, motivate, befriend, care for, sympathize with, be kind to, give strength to, give moral support to, be supportive to **3** HOLD UP, bear, carry, take the weight of, sustain, brace, reinforce, strengthen, prop (up), shore up, buttress, underpin, bolster (up) **4** MAINTAIN, keep, look after, take care of, provide for, sustain, feed, nourish **5** *support a statement* endorse, confirm, back up, bear out, verify, authenticate, substantiate, validate, ratify, document, *formal* corroborate **6** FINANCE, fund, subsidize, underwrite, back, sponsor, contribute to, give a donation to
F3 **1** oppose **4** live off **5** contradict
▶ *n* **1** BACKING, allegiance, loyalty, defence, protection, patronage, approval, encouragement, comfort, relief, help, aid, assistance, *formal* espousal **2** PROP, stay, post, pillar, brace, buttress, bolster, trestle, crutch, foundation(s), underpinning, substructure, skeleton, base **3** HELP, encouragement, comfort, care, sympathy, motivation, strength, friendship, moral support, *colloq.* tower of strength **4** MAINTENANCE, keep, provision, sustenance, food, subsistence **5** FINANCE, funding, sponsorship, grant, donation, subsidy, contribution, patronage **6** EVIDENCE, confirmation, backing, verification, authentication, substantiation, validation, ratification
F3 **1** opposition, hostility

supporter *n*
fan, follower, adherent, advocate, champion, defender, promoter, sympathizer, seconder, patron, sponsor, donor, contributor, partner, co-worker,

helper, ally, friend, voter, well-wisher, apologist
☒ opponent

supportive *adj*
helpful, caring, attentive, sympathetic, understanding, comforting, reassuring, encouraging
☒ discouraging

suppose *v*
1 THINK, guess, believe, consider, imagine, reckon, fancy, judge, expect, infer, conclude, take for granted, *formal* conjecture, surmise **2** ASSUME, presume, imply, require, *formal* postulate, hypothesize, posit, presuppose

supposed *adj*
alleged, reported, rumoured, assumed, presumed, reputed, so-called, believed, imagined, hypothetical, *formal* putative
▷ **supposed to** meant to, intended to, expected to, required to, obliged to

supposition *n*
assumption, presumption, guess, speculation, theory, idea, notion, *formal* conjecture, surmise, postulation, hypothesis, presupposition
☒ knowledge

suppress *v*
crush, stamp out, put an end to, quash, squash, quell, subdue, stop, silence, censor, stifle, smother, strangle, conceal, withhold, hold back, control, keep under control, contain, restrain, check, keep in check, repress, inhibit, *formal* vanquish, *colloq.* crack/clamp down on
☒ encourage, incite

suppression *n*
crushing, quashing, quelling, elimination, prohibition, censorship, check, inhibition, dissolution, coverup, smothering, termination, extinction, *colloq.* clampdown, crackdown
☒ encouragement, incitement

suppurate *v*
gather, discharge, fester, ooze, weep, *technical* maturate

suppuration *n*
festering, pus, mattering, *technical* diapyesis

supremacy *n*
dominance, domination, dominion, mastery, lordship, rule, power, control, predominance, primacy, sovereignty, sway, pre-eminence, *formal* ascendancy, hegemony, paramountcy

supreme *adj*
1 GREATEST, best, highest, excellent, top, crowning, culminating, first, first-rate, first-class, leading, foremost, chief, principal, head, sovereign, pre-eminent, predominant, prevailing, world-beating, second-to-none, unsurpassed, incomparable, peerless, matchless, consummate, transcendent, superlative, prime **2** *the supreme sacrifice* utmost, extreme, ultimate, final, last, greatest, highest
☒ **1** lowly, poor

sure *adj*
1 CERTAIN, convinced, assured, confident, decided, positive, definite, unmistakable, unfaltering, unwavering, clear, accurate, precise, unquestionable, indisputable, undoubted, undeniable, irrevocable, inevitable, guaranteed, bound, *colloq.* as sure as eggs is eggs **2** SAFE, secure, fast, solid, firm, steady, stable, guaranteed, reliable, dependable, tested, loyal, faithful, trustworthy, steadfast, unwavering, unerring, unfailing, never-failing, infallible, effective, foolproof, *formal* efficacious, *colloq.* home and dry, sure-fire, sure-footed, safe as houses
☒ **1** unsure, uncertain, hesitating, doubtful **2** unsafe, insecure

surely *adv*
certainly, without doubt, doubtlessly, undoubtedly, unquestionably, indubitably, definitely, assuredly, firmly, confidently, inevitably, inexorably

surety *n*
guarantee, indemnity, pledge, security, safety, warrant, warranty, certainty, bail, insurance, mortgagor, sponsor, bond, deposit, guarantor, hostage, bondsman

surface *n, v, adj*
▸ *n* outside, outward appearance, exterior, façade, veneer, covering, skin, top, side, face, plane
☒ inside, interior
▷ **on the surface** superficially, externally, outwardly, apparently, at first glance, seemingly, to all appearances, *formal* ostensibly
▸ *v* rise, arise, come up, come to the surface, emerge, appear, reappear, materialize, come to light
☒ sink, disappear, vanish
▸ *adj* superficial, outer, outside, outward, exterior, external, apparent
☒ interior

surfeit *n, v*
▸ *n* surplus, superfluity, excess, glut, satiety, superabundance, overindulgence, *formal* plethora, *colloq.* bellyful
☒ lack
▸ *v* fill, overfill, overfeed, stuff, cram, glut, gorge, satiate

surge *n, v*
▸ *n* **1** RUSH, gush, stream, sweep, pouring, flow, wave(s), billow, breaker, roller, swell, eddy, *formal* efflux **2** INCREASE, upswing, upsurge, rise, escalation, intensification
▸ *v* **1** RUSH, gush, stream, sweep, pour, flow, break, swell, swirl, eddy, heave, roll, seethe **2** INCREASE, rise, escalate

surly *adj*
gruff, brusque, churlish, ungracious, uncivil, ill-natured, bad-tempered, cross, grouchy, crusty, grumpy, testy, cantankerous, irascible, sullen, sulky, morose, *colloq.* crabbed, crotchety
☒ friendly, polite

surmise *v, n*
▸ *v* infer, suppose, presume, assume, conclude, deduce, imagine, fancy, guess, consider, speculate, suspect, *formal* conjecture, opine
☒ know
▸ *n* inference, conclusion, deduction, assumption, presumption, speculation, guess, idea, suspicion, thought, opinion, notion, possibility, *formal* conjecture, hypothesis, supposition
☒ certainty

surmount *v*
overcome, get over, conquer, master, triumph over, prevail over, surpass, exceed, *formal* vanquish

surpass *v*
beat, outdo, exceed, outstrip, outclass, better, excel, transcend, tower above, outshine, overshadow, eclipse

surpassing *adj*
exceptional, incomparable, outstanding, matchless, unrivalled, unsurpassed, rare, inimitable, extraordinary, supreme, phenomenal, transcendent
☒ poor

surplus *n, adj*
▸ *n* excess, residue, remainder, balance, superfluity, glut, surfeit, leftovers
☒ lack, shortage
▸ *adj* excess, superfluous, redundant, extra, spare, remaining, unused, left over

surprise v, n

▶ v **1** AMAZE, startle, astonish, astound, stagger, take aback, stun, bewilder, confuse, disconcert, dismay, *colloq.* flabbergast, nonplus, bowl over, wow, knock for six, knock someone down with a feather, take someone's breath away **2** CATCH RED-HANDED, catch in the act, catch unawares, expose, unmask, startle, burst in on, find (out), *colloq.* catch someone with their pants/trousers down

▶ n amazement, astonishment, incredulity, wonder, bewilderment, dismay, shock, start, revelation, *colloq.* bombshell, thunderbolt, bolt from the blue

🔁 composure

Expressions of surprise include:

bless my soul!, blow me down!, by Jove!, come off it!, did you ever!, fancy that!, for goodness sake!, for heaven's sake!, good heavens!, Gordon Bennett!, great Scott!, heavens above!, holy smoke!, how about that, then!, I ask you!, I don't know!, I'll be blessed!, I'll be damned!, imagine that!, in heaven's name!, just a moment!, my eye!, my foot!, my goodness!, my word!, no kidding!, of all the ...!, oh mother!, oh my!, stone me!, that'll be the day!, that's news to me!, the (very) idea!, to think!, well, did you ever!, well, I'll be blowed!, well I never!, wonders will never cease!, would you believe it!, you don't say!, you're joking!, you're kidding!

---

surprised adj

startled, amazed, astonished, astounded, staggered, thunderstruck, dumbfounded, speechless, lost for words, open-mouthed, shocked, stunned, *colloq.* flabbergasted, nonplussed, gobsmacked

🔁 unsurprised, composed

surprising adj

amazing, astonishing, astounding, staggering, stunning, incredible, extraordinary, remarkable, wonderful, startling, unexpected, unforeseen, unlooked-for

🔁 unsurprising, expected

surrender v, n

▶ v capitulate, submit, resign, concede, yield, give in, cede, give up, leave behind, let go of, relinquish, abandon, renounce, abdicate, forego, waive, *formal* succumb, *colloq.* quit, throw in the towel/sponge

▶ n capitulation, resignation, submission, yielding, relinquishing, renunciation, abandonment, abdication, waiving, *formal* cession

surreptitious adj

furtive, stealthy, sly, covert, veiled, hidden, secret, underhand, unauthorized, *formal* clandestine, *colloq.* sneaky

🔁 open, obvious

surrogate n

substitute, replacement, representative, stand-in, deputy, proxy

surround v

encircle, ring, go round, gird, girdle, encompass, confine, envelop, encase, enclose, fence in, hem in, besiege, beset, *formal* environ

surrounding adj

encircling, bordering, adjacent, adjoining, neighbouring, nearby

surroundings n

neighbourhood, vicinity, locality, scene, setting, environment, habitat, environs, background, milieu, element, ambience

surveillance n

watch, observation, inspection, superintendence, supervision, vigilance, stewardship, guardianship,

monitoring, scrutiny, check, care, charge, control, direction, regulation

survey v, n

▶ v **1** VIEW, contemplate, observe, look at, look over, supervise, scan, scrutinize, examine, inspect, study, research, poll, review, consider **2** ASSESS, estimate, evaluate, measure, plot, plan, map, chart, reconnoitre, *formal* appraise, *colloq.* size up, recce

▶ n **1** REVIEW, overview, scrutiny, examination, inspection, consideration, study, poll, appraisal, assessment, measurement, valuation **2** QUESTIONNAIRE, quiz, test, form, study, probe, opinion poll, market research

surveyor n

inspector, examiner, assessor, *technical* geodesist

survive v

outlive, outlast, endure, last, continue, persist, stay, remain, live (on), exist, withstand, hold out, cope, manage, weather, recover, rally, *formal* be extant, *colloq.* pull through, make it, keep your head above water

🔁 succumb, die

susceptibility n

liability, openness, vulnerability, defencelessness, weakness, proneness, responsiveness, sensitivity, suggestibility, gullibility, tendency, *formal* predisposition, proclivity, propensity

🔁 impregnability, resistance

susceptible adj

liable, prone, inclined, disposed, given, subject, receptive, responsive, impressionable, easily led, credulous, gullible, suggestible, weak, vulnerable, defenceless, open, sensitive, tender

🔁 resistant, immune

suspect v, adj

▶ v **1** DOUBT, have doubts about, distrust, mistrust, be wary of, have misgivings/qualms about, be uneasy about, call into question, *colloq.* smell a rat **2** *I suspect you're right* believe, fancy, feel, guess, suppose, speculate, consider, conclude, infer, *formal* conjecture, surmise, *colloq.* have a hunch, get it into your head

▶ adj suspicious, doubtful, dubious, questionable, debatable, unreliable, *colloq.* iffy, dodgy, fishy

🔁 acceptable, reliable

suspend v

1 HANG, dangle, swing **2** ADJOURN, interrupt, delay, defer, postpone, put off, arrest, shelve, pigeonhole, *formal* discontinue, cease, put in abeyance, prorogue, *colloq.* put on ice, put on the back burner, take a raincheck on **3** EXPEL, dismiss, exclude, remove, debar, keep out, shut out, unfrock

🔁 **2** continue, carry on **3** restore, reinstate

suspended adj

1 HANGING, dangling, *formal* pendent, pensile **2** POSTPONED, delayed, deferred, put off, shelved, pending, *colloq.* put on ice

suspense n

uncertainty, insecurity, doubt, doubtfulness, anxiety, tension, nervousness, apprehension, anticipation, expectation, expectancy, excitement

🔁 certainty, knowledge

suspension n

1 ADJOURNMENT, interruption, break, intermission, respite, remission, stay, moratorium, delay, deferral, deferment, postponement, *formal* cessation, abeyance **2** EXPULSION, dismissal, exclusion, removal, debarment, unfrocking

🔁 **1** continuation

suspicion n

1 DOUBT, scepticism, distrust, mistrust, chariness, wariness, qualm(s), caution, misgiving(s), apprehen-

sion **2** TRACE, hint, suggestion, soupçon, touch, tinge, shade, glimmer, shadow, scintilla **3** IDEA, notion, feeling, belief, opinion, *colloq.* hunch, sixth sense, funny feeling
F3 1 trust

suspicious *adj*
1 DOUBTFUL, sceptical, unbelieving, disbelieving, suspecting, unsure, distrustful, mistrustful, wary, chary, apprehensive, uneasy **2** DUBIOUS, questionable, suspect, irregular, strange, odd, funny, peculiar, dishonest, guilty, shifty, *colloq.* shady, dodgy, fishy, iffy
F3 1 trustful, confident **2** trustworthy, innocent

sustain *v*
1 NOURISH, feed, provide for, nurture, foster, help, aid, assist, comfort, encourage, relieve, support, uphold, give strength to, endorse, bear, carry **2** MAINTAIN, keep going, keep up, carry on, continue, prolong, hold, *formal* protract **3** SUFFER, go through, experience, undergo, endure, receive, happen to

sustained *adj*
prolonged, long-drawn-out, steady, continuous, continuing, constant, perpetual, *formal* protracted, unremitting
F3 broken, interrupted, intermittent, spasmodic

sustenance *n*
nourishment, food, provisions, fare, maintenance, subsistence, support, livelihood, *formal* refection, aliment, comestibles, provender, viands, victuals, *colloq.* grub, nosh, scoff

svelte *adj*
slender, slim, lithe, elegant, graceful, lissom, willowy, sylphlike, shapely, sophisticated, urbane, polished
F3 bulky, ungainly

swagger *v, n*
▶ *v* bluster, boast, crow, brag, prance, parade, strut, *colloq.* swank, show off, play to the gallery, make an exhibition of yourself, go over the top
▶ *n* bluster, show, ostentation, arrogance, prancing, parading

swallow *v*
1 CONSUME, devour, eat, gobble up, drink, quaff, gulp, *formal* ingest, *colloq.* guzzle, knock back, down, scoff, swig, polish off **2** ACCEPT, believe, trust, be certain of, *colloq.* buy, fall for, swallow hook line and sinker **3** STIFLE, smother, repress, hold back, contain, suppress **4** TOLERATE, put up with, accept, endure, stand, take, abide, bear, *colloq.* stomach
▷ **swallow up** overwhelm, overrun, engulf, enfold, envelop, absorb, assimilate

swamp *n, v*
▶ *n* bog, marsh, fen, slough, quagmire, quag, quicksand, mire, morass, mud
▶ *v* flood, inundate, deluge, engulf, submerge, sink, drench, saturate, waterlog, wash out, weigh down, overload, overwhelm, besiege, beset

swampy *adj*
boggy, marshy, wet, miry, fenny, soggy, quaggy, squelchy, waterlogged, *formal* paludal, uliginous
F3 arid, dehydrated, dry

swank *v, n*
▶ *v* brag, boast, show off, strut, swagger, parade, posture, preen yourself, attitudinize
▶ *n* bragging, boastfulness, pretentiousness, show, display, showing-off, ostentation, conceit, conceitedness, swagger, self-advertisement, *formal* vainglory
F3 modesty, restraint

swanky *adj*
glamorous, ostentatious, fashionable, expensive, luxurious, rich, lavish, smart, grand, stylish, showy, exclusive, de luxe, sumptuous, fancy, pretentious, *colloq.* flash, flashy, plush, plushy, posh, ritzy, swish

F3 discreet, unobtrusive

swap, swop *v*
exchange, transpose, switch, interchange, substitute, barter, trade, bandy, traffic

swarm *n, v*
▶ *n* crowd, throng, mob, mass, stream, body, multitude, myriad, host, army, horde, pack, herd, flock, drove, shoal
▶ *v* flock, flood, surge, stream, mass, congregate, crowd, throng
▷ **be swarming with** be crowded with, be teeming with, be overrun with, be crawling with, be bristling with, be thronged with, abound in

swarthy *adj*
dark, dark-complexioned, dark-skinned, tanned, brown, dusky, black
F3 fair, pale

swashbuckling *adj*
daring, courageous, adventurous, bold, spirited, swaggering, exciting, gallant, flamboyant, dare-devil, dashing, robust
F3 tame, unadventurous, unexciting

swathe *v*
wrap, bandage, bind, wind, cloak, envelop, drape, enshroud, enwrap, fold, shroud, swaddle, lap, sheathe, furl
F3 unwind, unwrap

sway *v, n*
▶ *v* **1** ROCK, roll, reel, lurch, stagger, swing, wave, shake, wobble, oscillate, fluctuate, bend, incline, lean, divert, veer, swerve **2** INFLUENCE, affect, persuade, win over, bring round, induce, convince, convert, overrule, rule, direct, dominate, govern, *formal* prevail upon
▶ *n* control, command, authority, power, influence, leadership, government, rule, sovereignty, dominion, predominance, jurisdiction, *technical* hegemony, *formal* ascendancy, preponderance, *colloq.* clout

swear *v*
1 VOW, promise, promise solemnly, pledge, pledge yourself, take an oath, be on/under oath, take the oath, testify, affirm, assert, declare, insist, *formal* avow, attest, asseverate, aver, abjure **2** CURSE, blaspheme, utter profanities, use bad language, blind, take the lord's name in vain, turn the air blue, *formal* imprecate, maledict, *colloq.* cuss, eff and blind
▷ **swear by** believe in, trust in, depend on, rely on, have confidence in, have faith in

swearing *n*
bad language, foul language, cursing, profanity, expletives, blasphemy, *technical* coprolalia, *formal* imprecations, maledictions, *colloq.* cussing, effing and blinding

swear-word *n*
expletive, four-letter word, curse, oath, obscenity, profanity, blasphemy, swearing, bad language, foul language, *formal* imprecation

sweat *n, v*
▶ *n* **1** PERSPIRATION, moisture, stickiness, *technical* sudor, diaphoresis, hidrosis **2** ANXIETY, worry, agitation, panic, fuss, dither, *colloq.* fluster, flap, tizzy **3** TOIL, labour, drudgery, chore, effort
▶ *v* perspire, secrete, swelter, drip, break out in a sweat, *technical* sudate, *formal* exude, *colloq.* sweat like a pig, sweat buckets

sweaty *adj*
damp, moist, clammy, sticky, sweating, perspiring
F3 dry, cool

sweep *v, n*
▶ *v* **1** *sweep the floor* brush, dust, clean (up), clear

(up), remove, vacuum **2** PUSH, thrust, drive, move quickly, spread quickly, force, shove, drag, jostle, elbow, poke **3** PASS, sail, fly, glide, scud, skim, glance, whisk, race, whip, tear, hurtle
▶ *n* **1** ARC, curve, bend, swing, stroke, move, movement, action, gesture, stroke, *formal* curvature **2** SCOPE, compass, range, extent, span, stretch, vastness, immensity, expanse, vista

sweeping *adj*
general, global, all-inclusive, all-embracing, broad, wide, wide-ranging, extensive, far-reaching, comprehensive, thorough, thoroughgoing, radical, wholesale, indiscriminate, oversimplified, simplistic, *colloq.* blanket, across-the-board
🖅 specific, narrow

sweepstake *n*
draw, lottery, gambling, sweep, sweepstakes

sweet *adj, n*
▶ *adj* **1** SUGARY, syrupy, sickly, sweetened, sickly sweet, honeyed, candied, glacé, saccharine, luscious, delicious, ripe **2** AROMATIC, fragrant, perfumed, balmy, sweet-scented, *formal* ambrosial, odoriferous, odorous, redolent **3** *sweet music* melodious, tuneful, harmonious, sweet-sounding, euphonious, musical, dulcet, soft, mellow, *formal* mellifluous **4** PLEASANT, delightful, pleasing, lovely, attractive, beautiful, pretty, winsome, winning, cute, engaging, appealing, likeable, lovable, adorable, charming, agreeable, amiable, affectionate, tender, kind, kindly, treasured, precious, cherished, dear, darling **5** FRESH, clean, wholesome, pure, clear
🖅 **1** savoury, salty, sour, bitter **2** foul **3** discordant **4** unpleasant, nasty, ugly **5** foul
▷ **sweet on** fond of, liking, keen on, having a soft spot for, infatuated with, ravished with, *colloq.* crazy about, mad about, far gone on
▶ *n* **1** DESSERT, pudding, *colloq.* afters **2** BONBON, candy, sweetmeat, confectionery, *formal* confection, *colloq.* sweetie

Sweets include:
barley sugar, bull's eye, butterscotch, caramel, chewing-gum, chocolate, fondant, fruit pastille, fudge, gobstopper, gumdrop, humbug, jelly, jelly bean, Kit-Kat®, liquorice, liquorice allsort, lollipop, Mars®, marshmallow, marzipan, nougat, peppermint, praline, rock, Edinburgh rock, toffee, toffee apple, truffle, Turkish delight.

sweeten *v*
1 SUGAR, add sugar to, honey **2** MELLOW, soften, soothe, mollify, appease **3** TEMPER, cushion, alleviate, ease, relieve, *formal* mitigate
🖅 **2** sour, embitter

sweetheart *n*
darling, dear, boyfriend, girlfriend, love, lover, truelove, suitor, valentine, admirer, beloved, betrothed, follower, inamorata, inamorato, Romeo, *colloq.* flame, steady, sweetie

sweetness *n*
1 SUGARINESS, syrup, succulence, lusciousness, mellowness, freshness **2** FRAGRANCE, balminess, aroma **3** KINDNESS, amiability, winsomeness, tenderness, sweet temper, love, loveliness, charm **4** HARMONY, euphony, *formal* dulcitude
🖅 **1** saltness, sourness, bitterness, acidity **2** foulness **3** nastiness **4** cacophony

sweet-smelling *adj*
aromatic, fragrant, perfumed, balmy, sweet-scented, *formal* ambrosial, odoriferous, odorous, redolent

🖅 fetid, malodorous

swell *v, n, adj*
▶ *v* **1** EXPAND, inflate, blow up, puff up, bloat, fatten, bulge, balloon, billow, *formal* dilate, distend **2** RISE, surge, mount, increase, enlarge, grow larger, escalate, extend, grow, step up, accelerate, mushroom, proliferate, snowball, skyrocket, heighten, intensify, *formal* augment
🖅 **1** shrink, contract **2** decrease, dwindle
▶ *n* **1** BILLOW, wave, undulation, surge, rise, increase, enlargement **2** DANDY, fop, beau, dude, cockscomb, *colloq.* bigwig
🖅 **2** down-and-out, scarecrow, tramp
▶ *adj* great, grand, smart, stylish, exclusive, fashionable, de luxe, *colloq.* flashy, posh, ritzy, swanky
🖅 seedy, shabby

swelling *n*
lump, tumour, bump, bruise, blister, boil, inflammation, bulge, protuberance, puffiness, enlargement, *formal* distension, tumescence

sweltering *adj*
hot, tropical, baking, boiling, roasting, scorching, torrid, stifling, suffocating, airless, oppressive, sultry, clammy, muggy, steamy, sticky, humid, *colloq.* baking, roasting, sizzling
🖅 cold, cool, fresh, breezy, airy

swerve *v*
change direction suddenly, turn, bend, incline, veer, swing, twist, shift, deviate, stray, wander, diverge, deflect, skew, sheer

swift *adj*
fast, quick, rapid, brisk, speedy, express, flying, hurried, hasty, short, brief, sudden, abrupt, immediate, prompt, ready, agile, lively, nimble, *formal* expeditious, *colloq.* nippy
🖅 slow, sluggish, unhurried

swiftly *adv*
quickly, posthaste, fast, rapidly, speedily, express, hurriedly, instantly, promptly, at full tilt, *formal* expeditiously, *colloq.* double-quick, hotfoot
🖅 slowly, *formal* tardily

swiftness *n*
quickness, rapidity, speed, speediness, suddenness, velocity, immediacy, immediateness, instantaneity, readiness, promptness, dispatch, *formal* alacrity, celerity, expedition
🖅 delay, slowness, *formal* tardiness

swill *v, n*
▶ *v* drink, swallow, swig, quaff, gulp, guzzle, drain, consume, *formal* imbibe, *colloq.* knock back, toss off
▷ **swill out** wash out, wash down, rinse, clean, cleanse, drench, flush, sluice
▶ *n* **1** DRINK, gulp, swallow, swig **2** WASTE, slops, hogwash, pigswill, scourings, refuse

swim *v*
bathe, take a dip, tread water, float, bob, snorkel

The main swimming strokes include:
backstroke, breaststroke, butterfly, crawl, doggy-paddle, sidestroke

swimming-pool *n*
swimming-bath, leisure pool, lido, swimming-pond

swimsuit *n*
swimming costume, bathing costume, bathing suit, bikini, trunks

swindle *v, n*
▶ *v* cheat, defraud, diddle, overcharge, exploit, fleece, trick, deceive, dupe, *colloq.* do, rip off, con, bamboozle, sting, rook, put one over on, take for a

ride, take to the cleaners, pull the wool over someone's eyes
▸ *n* fraud, fiddle, diddle, racket, trickery, deception, sharp practice, double-dealing, *colloq.* con, rip-off, scam

swindler *n*
cheat, fraud, fiddler, impostor, trickster, rogue, rascal, charlatan, mountebank, *colloq.* con man, shark, rook, hustler, hood, hoodlum

swine *n*
1 PIG, beast, boar, hog **2** SCOUNDREL, rogue, rascal, good-for-nothing, brute, boor

swing *v, n*
▸ *v* **1** HANG, dangle, wave, spin, rotate, pivot, sway, rock **2** SWERVE, veer, turn, twist, wind, curve, bend, incline, lean, oscillate, fluctuate, change, vary, *formal* pendulate **3** ARRANGE, achieve, get, set up, make, organize, *colloq.* fix (up)
▸ *n* sway, rock, oscillation, waving, vibration, fluctuation, variation, change, shift, move, movement, motion, stroke, rhythm

swingeing *adj*
harsh, severe, stringent, drastic, serious, punishing, devastating, excessive, extortionate, exorbitant, oppressive, heavy, draconian, *colloq.* thumping
≠ mild

swinging *adj*
lively, exciting, dynamic, fashionable, contemporary, modern, up-to-date, up-to-the-minute, stylish, *colloq.* jet-setting, trendy, with it, *slang* hip
≠ old-fashioned, fuddy-duddy

swipe *v, n*
▸ *v* **1** HIT, strike, lunge, lash out, slap, *colloq.* whack, wallop, sock, biff, clout **2** STEAL, pilfer, lift, *colloq.* pinch, whip, nick, filch
▸ *n* stroke, blow, slap, smack, *colloq.* clout, whack, wallop, biff

swirl *v*
churn, agitate, spin, revolve, circulate, twirl, whirl, wheel, eddy, twist, curl

swish[1] *v*
the horses swished their tails flourish, whisk, swing, swirl, thrash, flog, lash, birch, whip, rustle, twirl, whizz, swoosh, wave, brandish, whirl, whistle, whoosh

swish[2] *adj*
a swish hotel smart, grand, fashionable, exclusive, plush, stylish, elegant, sumptuous, de luxe, *colloq.* flash, posh, ritzy, swanky, swell
≠ seedy, shabby

switch *v, n*
▸ *v* change, exchange, swap, trade, barter, interchange, substitute, replace, shift, rearrange, turn, put, veer, deviate, divert, deflect, *formal* transpose, *colloq.* chop and change
▸ *n* **1** CHANGE, alteration, shift, exchange, swap, interchange, substitution, replacement, reversal, about-turn **2** TWIG, shoot, branch, cane, rod, birch, lash, twitch, whisk, whip, thong

swivel *v*
pivot, spin, rotate, revolve, turn, twirl, pirouette, gyrate, wheel

swollen *adj*
bloated, inflated, tumid, puffed up, puffy, inflamed, enlarged, expanded, bulbous, bulging, *formal* distended, dilated, tumescent
≠ shrunken, shrivelled

swoop *v, n*
▸ *v* dive, plunge, drop, fall, descend, stoop, pounce, lunge, rush
▸ *n* dive, plunge, drop, descent, pounce, lunge, rush, attack, onslaught

swop *see* SWAP.

sword *n*
blade, foil, rapier, sabre, scimitar, steel, épée, katana
▷ **cross swords** disagree, argue, quarrel, fight, contend, dispute, contest, wrangle, bicker, be at odds, be at loggerheads

sworn *adj*
devoted, confirmed, eternal, implacable, inveterate, relentless, *formal* attested

swot *v*
study, work, learn, memorize, revise, cram, apply oneself, read up, *colloq.* mug up, bone up, burn the midnight oil

sybarite *n*
parasite, pleasurer, pleasure-seeker, sensualist, bon vivant, epicure, epicurean, hedonist, playboy, voluptuary, one of the idle rich
≠ ascetic, toiler

sybaritic *adj*
easy, pleasure-loving, pleasure-seeking, self-indulgent, sensual, voluptuous, hedonistic, epicurean, luxurious, parasitic
≠ ascetic

sycophancy *n*
cringing, fawning, flattery, toadyism, grovelling, servility, slavishness, kowtowing, backscratching, adulation, truckling, *formal* obsequiousness, *colloq.* bootlicking

sycophant *n*
cringer, fawner, flatterer, groveller, backscratcher, slave, parasite, hanger-on, toady, toad-eater, truckler, *colloq.* bootlicker, sponger, yes-man

sycophantic *adj*
cringing, fawning, flattering, grovelling, servile, slavish, ingratiating, parasitical, backscratching, slimy, toad-eating, toadying, time-serving, unctuous, truckling, *formal* obsequious, *colloq.* bootlicking, smarmy

syllabus *n*
curriculum, course, programme, schedule, plan, outline

syllogism *n*
deduction, argument, proposition, *technical* epicheirema

sylph-like *adj*
slim, slight, slender, elegant, graceful, lithe, willowy, streamlined, svelte
≠ bulky, plump

symbiotic *adj*
co-operative, interactive, interdependent, *technical* endophytic, epizoan, epizoic, epizootic, *formal* commensal, synergetic

symbol *n*
sign, token, representation, mark, emblem, badge, logo, character, ideograph, figure, image, *formal* type

symbolic *adj*
symbolical, representative, typical, illustrative, emblematic, token, figurative, metaphorical, allegorical, meaningful, significant

symbolize *v*
represent, stand for, denote, mean, signify, typify, exemplify, epitomize, personify, *formal* betoken

symmetrical *adj*
balanced, even, regular, well-proportioned, parallel, uniform, consistent, harmonious, corresponding, proportional
≠ asymmetrical, irregular

symmetry *n*
balance, evenness, regularity, parallelism, correspondence, proportion(s), harmony, uniformity, con-

sistency, agreement, *formal* congruity
🔁 asymmetry, irregularity

sympathetic *adj*
understanding, appreciative, supportive, comforting, encouraging, consoling, commiserating, pitying, interested, concerned, caring, compassionate, tolerant, tender, kind, kindly, warm, warm-hearted, kindhearted, well-disposed, affectionate, agreeable, favourable, considerate, solicitous, friendly, pleasant, likeable, companionable, congenial, sociable, neighbourly, like-minded, compatible, *formal* solicitous
🔁 unsympathetic, indifferent, callous, antipathetic

sympathetically *adv*
appreciatively, supportively, understandingly, compassionately, comfortingly, consolingly, responsively, sensitively, warmly, warm-heartedly, feelingly, kindly, pityingly

sympathize *v*
understand, comfort, console, encourage, be supportive, appreciate, show concern/interest, care for, offer condolences, commiserate, pity, feel sorry for, feel for, your heart goes out, empathize, identify with, respond to
🔁 ignore, disregard

sympathizer *n*
supporter, friend in need, condoler, admirer, backer, adherent, well-wisher, fan, fellow-traveller, partisan
🔁 enemy, opponent, adversary

sympathy *n*
1 UNDERSTANDING, comfort, encouragement, support, appreciation, consolation, condolences, commiseration, pity, compassion, tenderness, kindness, warmth, warm-heartedness, thoughtfulness, empathy, fellow-feeling, closeness, consideration, affinity, rapport, *formal* solace 2 AGREEMENT, approval, correspondence, harmony, *formal* accord, approbation
🔁 1 indifference, insensitivity, callousness 2 disagreement

symptom *n*
sign, indication, signal, evidence, expression, display, demonstration, note, feature, characteristic, mark, token, warning, *technical* prodrome, prodromus, *formal* manifestation

symptomatic *adj*
indicative, typical, characteristic, associated, suggesting, suggestive

syndicate *n*
association, alliance, combination, group, bloc, cartel, ring, combine

synonymous *adj*
interchangeable, substitutable, the same, identical, similar, comparable, tantamount, equivalent, corresponding
🔁 antonymous, opposite

synopsis *n*
outline, abstract, summary, sketch, résumé, précis, condensation, digest, abridgement, review, recapitulation, compendium, *formal* summation, conspectus, *colloq.* run-down

synthesis *n*
amalgamation, combination, compound, fusion, integration, union, welding, blend, alloy, amalgam, coalescence, composite, pastiche, *formal* unification

synthesize *v*
unite, combine, amalgamate, integrate, merge, blend, compound, alloy, fuse, weld, coalesce, unify
🔁 separate, analyse, resolve

synthetic *adj*
manufactured, man-made, simulated, artificial, ersatz, imitation, fake, bogus, mock, sham, pseudo
🔁 genuine, real, natural

syrupy *adj*
1 SWEET, sugary, sickly sweet, sweetened, honeyed, saccharine 2 SENTIMENTAL, emotional, loving, gushing, sugary, pathetic, tear-jerking, maudlin, mawkish, romantic, affectionate, sloppy, soppy, *colloq.* weepy, lovey-dovey, slushy, mushy, schmaltzy, corny, sickly, gushy

system *n*
1 METHOD, technique, procedure, process, routine, practice, approach, way, means, usage, rule, *modus operandi*, *formal* mode 2 ORGANIZATION, structure, set-up, systematization, co-ordination, orderliness, methodology, logic, classification, arrangement, network, framework, order, plan, scheme, apparatus, mechanism

systematic *adj*
methodical, logical, ordered, well-ordered, planned, well-planned, organized, well-organized, structured, systematized, standardized, scientific, orderly, businesslike, efficient
🔁 unsystematic, arbitrary, disorderly, inefficient

systematize *v*
arrange, order, structure, plan, organize, rationalize, methodize, standardize, schematize, regulate, regiment, classify, tabulate, make uniform, *formal* dispose

tab *n*
flap, tag, marker, label, sticker, ticket
▷ **keep tabs on** watch closely, keep an eye on, observe, keep a close watch on, keep a close check on

tabby *adj*
stripy, striped, streaked, wavy, mottled, variegated, banded, brindled

table *n, v*
► *n* **1** BOARD, slab, counter, bar, worktop, desk, bench, stand **2** DIAGRAM, chart, figure, graph, timetable, schedule, programme, plan, list, inventory, catalogue, tabulation, index, register, record **3** FOOD, board, diet, fare, dish, speciality, menu, *colloq.* tuck, *slang* grub, nosh, *US* chow
► *v* propose, suggest, submit, put forward, move

tableau *n*
representation, picture, portrayal, scene, spectacle, vignette, diorama, *tableau vivant*

tablet *n*
pill, capsule, lozenge, pellet, ball, bolus

taboo *adj, n*
► *adj* forbidden, prohibited, banned, ruled out, vetoed, sacrosanct, unacceptable, unmentionable, unthinkable, *formal* proscribed
▣ permitted, acceptable
► *n* ban, prohibition, veto, restriction, anathema, curse, *formal* interdiction, proscription
▣ permission, acceptance

tabulate *v*
order, arrange, arrange in columns, chart, classify, list, sort, systematize, table, catalogue, categorize, range, index, codify, tabularize

tacit *adj*
unspoken, unexpressed, unstated, unvoiced, silent, wordless, understood, implicit, implied, inferred
▣ express, explicit

taciturn *adj*
silent, quiet, uncommunicative, unforthcoming, close-mouthed, tight-lipped, reticent, reserved, withdrawn, aloof, detached, distant, cold, dumb, mute
▣ talkative, communicative, forthcoming

tack *n, v*
► *n* **1** NAIL, pin, drawing-pin, staple, *US* thumbtack **2** COURSE, path, bearing, heading, direction, line, line of action, course of action, approach, method, way, technique, procedure, process, policy, strategy, plan, tactic, attack
► *v* **1** ADD, append, attach, annex **2** FIX, fasten, affix, nail, pin, staple, stitch, sew, baste

tackle *n, v*
► *n* **1** *a rugby tackle* attack, challenge, interception, intervention, block **2** EQUIPMENT, tools, implements, apparatus, rig, outfit, gear, things, trappings, paraphernalia, harness, *formal* accoutrements, *colloq.* stuff

► *v* **1** BEGIN, embark on, set about, go about, try, attempt, undertake, take on, challenge, confront, encounter, face up to, grapple with, get to grips with, apply yourself to, address, deal with, attend to, handle, grab, seize, grasp, take hold of **2** INTERCEPT, block, take, halt, stop, deflect, catch, grapple with, obstruct
▣ **1** avoid, sidestep

tacky¹ *adj*
tacky paint sticky, adhesive, gluey, gummy, *colloq.* gooey

tacky² *adj*
1 SHABBY, scruffy, tatty, threadbare, shoddy, dingy, tattered, ragged, untidy, messy, sloppy, *colloq.* grotty **2** TASTELESS, vulgar, tawdry, flashy, gaudy, kitschy, *colloq.* naff

tact *n*
tactfulness, diplomacy, discretion, prudence, delicacy, subtlety, sensitivity, perception, discernment, judgement, understanding, thoughtfulness, consideration, skill, dexterity, adroitness, finesse, *savoir-faire*, *formal* judiciousness
▣ tactlessness, indiscretion

tactful *adj*
diplomatic, discreet, politic, prudent, careful, delicate, subtle, sensitive, perceptive, discerning, understanding, thoughtful, considerate, polite, skilful, adroit, *formal* judicious
▣ tactless, indiscreet, thoughtless, rude

tactic *n*
1 APPROACH, course, course of action, way, means, method, procedure, plan, stratagem, scheme, ruse, ploy, subterfuge, trick, device, shift, expedient, move, manoeuvre **2** *military tactics* strategy, campaign, plan, policy, approach, line of attack, moves, manoeuvres

tactical *adj*
strategic, planned, calculated, artful, cunning, shrewd, adroit, skilful, clever, smart, prudent, politic, *formal* judicious

tactician *n*
strategist, orchestrator, planner, politician, diplomat, director, campaigner, co-ordinator, mastermind, *colloq.* brain

tactless *adj*
undiplomatic, indiscreet, indelicate, unsubtle, inappropriate, impolitic, imprudent, careless, clumsy, awkward, blundering, gauche, insensitive, unfeeling, hurtful, unkind, thoughtless, inconsiderate, rude, rough, impolite, discourteous, *formal* injudicious, maladroit
▣ tactful, diplomatic, discreet

tactlessness *n*
insensitivity, impoliteness, indelicacy, indiscretion, thoughtlessness, discourtesy, rudeness, ineptitude, bad timing, clumsiness, gaucherie, boorishness,

formal maladroitness
🖪 tact, tactfulness, diplomacy

tag *n, v*
▶ *n* **1** LABEL, sticker, tab, ticket, mark, identification, note, slip, docket **2** IDENTIFICATION, label, description, name, title, nickname, epithet, badge **3** QUOTATION, saying, expression, phrase, maxim, moral, motto, proverb, dictum, epithet, allusion, stock phrase, *colloq.* quote
▶ *v* **1** LABEL, mark, identify, designate, term, title, entitle, call, name, christen, nickname, style, dub **2** ADD, attach, append, annex, adjoin, affix, fasten, tack
▷ **tag along** follow, shadow, tail, trail, accompany

tail *n, v*
▶ *n* **1** END, extremity, rear, rear end, bottom, back, rump, appendage, conclusion, *formal* termination, *colloq.* behind, posterior, backside **2** DETECTIVE, (private) investigator, *colloq.* private eye, sleuth, gumshoe, shamus
▷ **turn tail** run away, escape, flee, abscond, decamp, bolt, *colloq.* skedaddle, scarper, beat it
▶ *v* follow, pursue, shadow, dog, stalk, track, trail, dog
▷ **tail off** decrease, decline, drop (off), fall away, fade, wane, dwindle, taper off, peter out, die (out)
🖪 increase, grow

tailor *n, v*
▶ *n* outfitter, dressmaker, costumer, costumier, couturier, seamster, seamstress, modiste, clothier
▶ *v* fit, suit, cut, trim, style, fashion, shape, mould, alter, modify, convert, adapt, adjust, accommodate

tailor-made *adj*
made-to-measure, custom-built, bespoke, ideal, perfect, right, suited, fitted
🖪 off the peg, ready-made

taint *v, n*
▶ *v* contaminate, infect, pollute, adulterate, corrupt, deprave, stain, blemish, blot, smear, tarnish, blacken, dirty, soil, muddy, defile, sully, harm, damage, injure, blight, spoil, ruin, shame, disgrace, dishonour, *formal* befoul
▶ *n* contamination, infection, contagion, adulteration, pollution, corruption, stain, blemish, fault, flaw, defect, spot, blot, smear, stain, stigma, shame, disgrace, dishonour

take *v, n*
▶ *v* **1** SEIZE, grab, snatch, clutch, grasp, hold, get hold of, grip, catch, capture, get, obtain, acquire, secure, gain, receive, win, derive, adopt, assume, pick, choose, select, decide on, settle on, accept, receive, *formal* procure **2** REMOVE, eliminate, take away, subtract, deduct, steal, seize, kidnap, abduct, carry off, confiscate, *formal* purloin, appropriate, *colloq.* filch, nick, pinch, lift, have your fingers in the till **3** *take me home* convey, carry, bring, fetch, deliver, drive, transport, ferry, accompany, escort, show, lead, guide, conduct, usher, shepherd, *formal* bear, *colloq.* whisk **4** BEAR, tolerate, put up with, stand, stomach, abide, endure, suffer, undergo, experience, withstand **5** *the journey takes 6 hours* NEED, necessitate, require, demand, call for, use (up), last **6** CAPTURE, win, seize, conquer, occupy, *formal* vanquish **7** *take pleasure in something* derive, obtain, draw, gain, receive, attain, secure, achieve, be given, come by, get, *formal* procure **8** *take the blame/responsibility* accept, bear, be responsible for, admit, acknowledge, undertake **9** CONSIDER, believe, assume, presume, suppose, note, remember, examine, bear in mind **10** UNDERSTAND, comprehend, grasp, gather, apprehend, follow, fathom (out), *colloq.* cotton on, twig **11** *take the news badly* react to, accept, respond to, cope with, deal with, handle **12** *take him for a fool* believe, think,

consider, regard, look upon, view, reckon, suppose, hold, *formal* deem **13** *the hall takes 400 people* hold, contain, accommodate, seat, have a capacity of, have room for, have space for **14** *take a measurement* find out, discover, measure, establish, determine, ascertain **15** BUY, purchase, rent, hire, lease, pay for, book, receive **16** *take a subject at university* study, learn, pursue, be taught, research, read, major in **17** *take the new road* use, travel along, drive along, go along, follow **18** *take food/drink* consume, swallow, eat, drink, devour, *formal* imbibe, *colloq.* tuck in, guzzle, scoff **19** *Will the drug take?* succeed, work, produce results, be effective, *formal* be efficacious
🖪 **1** leave, refuse **2** replace, put back **6** lose **15** sell **19** fail
▷ **take aback** surprise, astonish, astound, stagger, stun, shock, startle, disconcert, bewilder, dismay, upset
▷ **take after** resemble, look like, be like, be similar to, favour, mirror, echo
▷ **take against** dislike, object to, disapprove of, despise, regard with distaste
🖪 take to
▷ **take apart** take to pieces, separate, dismantle, analyse, *formal* disassemble
▷ **take back 1** WITHDRAW, retract, recant, repudiate, renounce, disclaim, deny, *colloq.* eat one's words **2** REPOSSESS, reclaim, regain, get back **3** RETURN, replace, restore, give back, hand back, send back
▷ **take down 1** DISMANTLE, disassemble, demolish, raze, level, lower **2** NOTE, make a note of, record, write down, put down, set down, get down, transcribe, put on paper
🖪 put up
▷ **take in 1** ABSORB, assimilate, digest, realize, appreciate, understand, comprehend, grasp **2** ACCOMMODATE, admit, receive, shelter, welcome **3** INCLUDE, contain, comprise, incorporate, embrace, encompass, cover **4** DECEIVE, fool, dupe, mislead, trick, hoodwink, cheat, swindle, *colloq.* con, bamboozle, lead up the garden path
▷ **take off 1** *watch the plane take off* depart, fly, lift off, ascend, climb, rise, soar, mount, become airborne **2** REMOVE, undress, get undressed, strip, divest, shed, discard, detach, pull off, throw off, tear off, drop, doff **3** SUBTRACT, take away, remove, deduct, discount **4** LEAVE, depart, go, run away, decamp, disappear, flee, abscond, *colloq.* skedaddle, scarper, bunk off, do a runner **5** IMITATE, mimic, parody, caricature, satirize, mock, *colloq.* send up **6** *the project has really taken off* succeed, work, do well, become fashionable, become popular, catch on, prosper, flourish, *colloq.* make it, become all the rage, go places, hit the jackpot, strike gold
▷ **take on 1** ACCEPT, assume, acquire, undertake, tackle, face **2** COMPETE WITH, contend with, fight, oppose, vie with, tackle **3** *take on staff* employ, hire, enlist, recruit, engage, enrol, retain
▷ **take out 1** REMOVE, extract, get out, detach, excise, cut out, pull out **2** *take someone out to a restaurant* go with, go out with, accompany, escort, see **3** *take out a loan* arrange, organize, set up, settle on, work out, *colloq.* fix **4** *take out a book from the library* borrow, use temporarily, have a loan, be lent
▷ **take over** gain control of, take charge of, become responsible for, assume responsibility for, buy out
▷ **take to 1** LIKE, find pleasant, find attractive, become friendly with, become keen on, appreciate **2** BEGIN, start, launch into, undertake, set about, *formal* commence
▷ **take up 1** OCCUPY, fill, engage, engross, absorb, become interested in, monopolize, use (up), consume **2** RAISE, lift, pick up **3** *take up a hobby* start, begin, embark on, pursue, *formal* commence **4**

RESUME, carry on, continue, pick up, *colloq.* pick up the threads **5** ACCEPT, adopt, assume, agree to
F3 5 refuse
▶ *n* **1** CATCH, gate, haul, bag, yield **2** INCOME, revenue, takings, proceeds, profit(s), receipts, return(s), yield, gate, gate-money

take-off *n*
1 DEPARTURE, flight, flying, lift-off, ascent, climbing **2** IMITATION, mimicry, impersonation, parody, caricature, travesty, *colloq.* spoof, send-up

takeover *n*
gaining of control, merger, amalgamation, combination, incorporation, buyout, coalition, coup

taking *adj, n*
▶ *adj* catching, attractive, charming, pleasing, delightful, winning, winsome, appealing, fascinating, fetching, engaging, enchanting, compelling, alluring, beguiling, captivating, intriguing, prepossessing
F3 repellent, repulsive, unattractive
▶ *n* receipts, proceeds, profits, gain, returns, income, revenue, yield, income, earnings, winnings, pickings, gate, gate money

tale *n*
1 STORY, yarn, anecdote, narrative, account, report, rumour, tall story, old wives' tale, superstition, fable, myth, legend, epic, saga, parable, allegory, *colloq.* spiel **2** LIE, falsehood, untruth, fabrication, *colloq.* fib, whopper, porky, tall story, cock-and-bull story

talent *n*
gift, endowment, genius, flair, feel, knack, bent, aptitude, faculty, facility, skill, ability, capacity, aptness, power, strength, strong point, forte
F3 inability, weakness

talented *adj*
gifted, brilliant, well-endowed, versatile, able, capable, accomplished, proficient, adept, adroit, deft, artistic, clever, skilful
F3 inept

talisman *n*
amulet, charm, fetish, mascot, totem, symbol, idol, juju, phylactery, periapt, abraxas

talk *v, n*
▶ *v* **1** SPEAK, say, utter, articulate, voice, communicate, express, have a conversation/discussion, *formal* converse, confer, orate, *colloq.* natter, jabber, babble, prattle, chinwag, jaw **2** NEGOTIATE, discuss, bargain, haggle, work out an agreement **3** GOSSIP, spread rumours, chat, chatter, natter **4** *talk to the police* tell, confess, give (secret) information to, inform on, *colloq.* tell tales, squeal, blab, spill the beans, let the cat out of the bag, give the game away, *slang* grass
▷ **talk back** answer back, answer rudely, be cheeky to, retort, riposte, retaliate
▷ **talk big** bluster, boast, brag, show off, crow, exaggerate, swank, vaunt
▷ **talk down to** patronize, speak condescendingly towards, look down on, despise
▷ **talk into** encourage, coax, sway, persuade, convince, bring round, win over
F3 dissuade, talk out of
▷ **talk out of** discourage, deter, put off, prevent, stop, dissuade
F3 persuade, convince, talk into
▶ *n* **1** CONVERSATION, dialogue, discussion, chat, chatter, tête-à-tête, *colloq.* natter, confab, jaw, chinwag **2** *give a talk* lecture, seminar, symposium, speech, address, discourse, sermon, *formal* disquisition, oration, *colloq.* spiel **3** GOSSIP, hearsay, rumour, tittle-tattle **4** *the two sides are holding talks* NEGOTIATION, discussion, interview, meeting, consultation, debate, conference, summit conference, dialogue,

seminar, symposium, bargaining, haggling, *formal* conclave **5** LANGUAGE, dialect, slang, cant, jargon, speech, utterance, words, *technical* idiolect, *colloq.* lingo

talkative *adj*
garrulous, vocal, communicative, forthcoming, unreserved, expansive, chatty, gossipy, verbose, wordy, longwinded, *formal* voluble, loquacious, *colloq.* gabby, gassy, mouthy, can talk the hind legs of a donkey
F3 taciturn, quiet, reserved

talker *n*
speaker, conversationalist, communicator, lecturer, speech-maker, *formal* orator, *colloq.* chatterbox

talking-to *n*
lecture, scolding, reprimand, rebuke, reproof, reproach, criticism, *colloq.* dressing-down, telling-off, carpeting, ticking-off
F3 praise, commendation

tall *adj*
1 HIGH, lofty, elevated, soaring, towering, sky-high, lanky, big, great, giant, gigantic **2** *a tall story* unlikely, unbelievable, incredible, improbable, remarkable, implausible, absurd, far-fetched, exaggerated, dubious, preposterous, overblown **3** *a tall order* difficult, demanding, exacting, taxing, hard, challenging, trying
F3 1 short, low, small **2** reasonable **3** easy

tallness *n*
altitude, height, loftiness, stature

tally *n, v*
▶ *n* **1** RECORD, count, total, sum, score, enumeration, reckoning, account, register, list, roll **2** COUNTERFOIL, counterpart, duplicate, ticket, tag, tab, stub
▶ *v* **1** AGREE, tie in, square, accord, harmonize, coincide, correspond, match, conform, suit, fit, *formal* concur **2** ADD (UP), total, count, reckon, figure
F3 1 disagree, differ

tame *adj, v*
▶ *adj* **1** *a tame rabbit* domesticated, broken in, trained, disciplined, manageable, tractable, amenable, gentle, docile, meek, subdued, submissive, unresisting, obedient, biddable **2** DULL, boring, tedious, uninteresting, unexciting, humdrum, flat, bland, insipid, weak, feeble, uninspired, unadventurous, unenterprising, wearisome, lifeless, spiritless, vapid
F3 1 wild, unmanageable, rebellious **2** exciting, adventurous
▶ *v* domesticate, house-train, break in, train, discipline, master, overcome, conquer, bring to heel, bridle, curb, repress, suppress, quell, subdue, temper, soften, mellow, calm, pacify, humble, *formal* subjugate

tamper *v*
interfere, meddle, tinker, fiddle, manipulate, juggle, alter, damage, *colloq.* mess about, muck about, monkey, fix, rig, poke/stick your nose in, stick/put your oar in

tan *adj, v*
▶ *adj* brown, light brown, yellowish brown
▶ *v* **1** BROWN, go/turn brown, make/become darker, bronze, sunburn **2** BEAT, flog, lash, thrash, whip, flay, cane, birch, strap, spank, *colloq.* wallop, whack, belt, clout

tang *n*
1 SHARPNESS, piquancy, spice, pungency, taste, flavour, savour, smack, smell, aroma, scent, whiff, *colloq.* bite, edge, kick, pep, punch **2** TINGE, touch, trace, hint, suggestion, overtone

tangible *adj*
touchable, palpable, solid, concrete, material, sub-

stantial, physical, real, actual, hard, perceptible, discernible, visible, evident, definite, well-defined, unmistakable, positive, *formal* tactile, manifest

🔁 intangible, abstract, unreal

tangle *n, v*

▶ *n* **1** KNOT, snarl-up, twist, coil, mesh, mat, web, maze, labyrinth, *formal* convolution **2** MESS, muddle, jumble, mix-up, confusion, entanglement, embroilment, complication, imbroglio

▶ *v* **1** ENTANGLE, knot, snarl, ravel, twist, coil, interweave, interlace, intertwine, intertwist, catch, ensnare, entrap, enmesh, *formal* convolve **2** INVOLVE, embroil, ensnare, entrap, enmesh, implicate, muddle, confuse

🔁 **1, 2** disentangle

tangled *adj*

1 *tangled hair* knotty, knotted, twisted, snarled, matted, tousled, dishevelled, messy, entangled **2** CONFUSED, muddled, jumbled, twisted, tortuous, involved, mixed up, complicated, complex, intricate, *formal* convoluted

tangy *adj*

sharp, biting, acid, tart, spicy, piquant, pungent, strong, fresh

🔁 tasteless, insipid

tank *n*

1 *a hot-water tank* container, reservoir, receptacle, cistern, aquarium, vat, basin **2** *anti-tank missiles* armoured car, armoured vehicle, panzer

tankard *n*

mug, cup, beaker, goblet, chalice

tantalize *v*

tease, taunt, torment, torture, provoke, lead on, titillate, tempt, allure, entice, beguile, bait, balk, frustrate, thwart, disappoint

🔁 gratify, satisfy, fulfil

tantamount *adj*

as good as, equivalent, equal, synonymous, the same as, *formal* commensurate

tantrum *n*

temper, rage, fury, storm, outburst, fit, fit of temper, flare-up, pet, scene, paroxysm, *colloq.* paddy

tap¹ *v, n*

▶ *v* *tap someone on the shoulder* hit, strike, knock, rap, beat, drum, pat, touch

▶ *n* knock, rap, beat, pat, touch, light blow

tap² *n, v*

▶ *n* **1** STOPCOCK, valve, faucet, spigot, spout **2** STOPPER, plug, bung **3** BUG, listening device, hidden microphone, receiver

▷ **on tap** available, ready, on/at hand, handy, accessible

▶ *v* use, utilize, exploit, mine, quarry, siphon, bleed, milk, drain

tape *n, v*

▶ *n* **1** BAND, strip, string, binding, ribbon **2** VIDEO, videotape, cassette, videocassette, recording, taperecording, video recording, audiotape, magnetic tape **3** *with tape over their mouths* adhesive tape, Sellotape®, masking tape, sticky tape

▶ *v* **1** BIND, secure, tie, fasten, stick, seal **2** RECORD, tape-record, video, video-record

taper *v, n*

▶ *v* narrow, make/become narrow, thin, thin out, make/become thin, slim, decrease, reduce, lessen, diminish, dwindle, fade, wane, peter out, tail off, die away/off, *formal* attenuate

🔁 widen, flare, swell, increase

▶ *n* spill, candle, wick

tardily *adv*

late, slowly, unpunctually, sluggishly, late in the day,

at the last minute, *formal* belatedly, *colloq.* at the eleventh hour

🔁 promptly, punctually

tardiness *n*

lateness, delay, slowness, unpunctuality, sluggishness, dawdling, *formal* procrastination, dilatoriness, belatedness

🔁 promptness, punctuality

tardy *adj*

slow, slack, sluggish, late, unpunctual, overdue, delayed, dawdling, loitering, behindhand, backward, last-minute, eleventh-hour, *formal* belated, dilatory, procrastinating, retarded

🔁 prompt, punctual

target *n*

1 MARK, aim, goal, bull's eye, victim, butt, game, prey, quarry **2** AIM, object, objective, end, purpose, intention, ambition, goal, destination

tariff *n*

1 TOLL, tax, levy, customs, excise, duty **2** PRICE LIST, schedule, (list of) charges, menu, bill of fare, rate

tarnish *v, n*

▶ *v* discolour, corrode, rust, darken, blacken, dull, dim, sully, taint, stain, blemish, spot, blot, mar, spoil, *formal* befoul, besmirch

🔁 polish, brighten

▶ *n* blemish, spot, stain, taint, blot, discoloration, blackening, film, rust, patina

🔁 brightness, polish

tarry *v*

linger, remain, stay, stop, rest, wait, pause, delay, lag, dally, dawdle, loiter, *formal* abide, bide, sojourn, *colloq.* hang around/about

🔁 hurry, rush

tart¹ *n, v*

▶ *n* pie, flan, pastry, tartlet, patty, quiche, strudel

▶ *v* ▷ **tart up** smarten (up), renovate, decorate, redecorate, embellish, *colloq.* doll up

tart² *adj*

1 *the food tastes tart* sharp, acid, sour, bitter, vinegary, tangy, piquant, pungent, *formal* acidulous **2** *tart remarks* biting, sharp, cutting, sarcastic, incisive, caustic, acid, acerbic, scathing, sardonic, *formal* trenchant, astringent

🔁 **1** bland, sweet **2** kind

task *n*

job, chore, duty, charge, imposition, assignment, commission, exercise, mission, engagement, errand, undertaking, enterprise, business, occupation, activity, employment, work, piece of work, labour, toil, burden

▷ **take to task** reprimand, rebuke, criticize, blame, scold, reproach, reprove, censure, lecture, *formal* upbraid, *colloq.* tell off, tick off

🔁 commend, praise

taste *n, v*

▶ *n* **1** FLAVOUR, savour, relish, smack, tang

Ways of describing taste include:

acid, acrid, appetizing, bitter, bittersweet, citrus, creamy, delicious, flavoursome, fruity, hot, meaty, moreish, *colloq.* mouth-watering, peppery, piquant, pungent, salty, sapid, savoury, *colloq.* scrumptious, sharp, sour, spicy, sugary, sweet, tangy, tart, tasty, vinegary, *colloq.* yummy.

---

2 SAMPLE, bit, piece, morsel, titbit, bite, nibble, mouthful, sip, drop, dash, soupçon **3** *a taste for adventure* liking, fondness, partiality, preference, inclination, bent, leaning, hankering, desire, hunger, thirst,

appetite, *formal* penchant, predilection **4** DISCRIM-
INATION, discernment, judgement, perception, appreciation, sensitivity, refinement, polish, culture,
cultivation, breeding, decorum, stylishness, etiquette,
finesse, style, grace, elegance, tastefulness, propriety
F3 **1** blandness **3** distaste **4** tastelessness
▶ *v* **1** SAMPLE, nibble, sip, try, test **2** SAVOUR, smack,
relish **3** EXPERIENCE, undergo, feel, encounter, meet,
know **4** DIFFERENTIATE, distinguish, discern, make
out, perceive

tasteful *adj*
refined, polished, cultured, cultivated, elegant, pleasing, charming, smart, stylish, aesthetic, artistic, harmonious, beautiful, pretty, exquisite, delicate,
graceful, restrained, well-judged, correct, fastidious,
discriminating, *formal* judicious
F3 tasteless, garish, tawdry

tasteless *adj*
1 FLAVOURLESS, insipid, bland, mild, weak, thin,
watery, watered-down, flat, plain, stale, dull, boring,
uninteresting, vapid **2** INELEGANT, graceless, unseemly, improper, unfitting, indiscreet, crass, rude,
tactless, crude, vulgar, kitsch, cheap, tawdry, flashy,
showy, gaudy, garish, loud, uncouth, *colloq.* tacky,
slang naff
F3 **1** tasty **2** tasteful, elegant

tasting *n*
testing, sampling, trial, assay, assessment, *formal*
gustation

tasty *adj*
luscious, palatable, appetizing, mouth-watering, delicious, flavoursome, succulent, tangy, spicy, piquant,
savoury, sweet, delectable, *formal* flavorous, *colloq.*
scrumptious, *slang* yummy
F3 tasteless, insipid

tatter *n*
▷ **in tatters 1** IN RAGS, in shreds, in ribbons, in bits,
in pieces **2** DESTROYED, ruined, wrecked, broken,
shattered, devastated

tattered *adj*
ragged, frayed, threadbare, ripped, torn, tatty, shabby,
scruffy
F3 smart, neat

tattler *n*
gossip, busybody, tell-tale, scandalmonger, tale-
teller, newsmonger, rumour-monger, talebearer

taunt *v, n*
▶ *v* tease, torment, provoke, bait, goad, jeer, mock,
ridicule, make fun of, poke fun at, gibe, deride, sneer,
insult, revile, reproach, *colloq.* rib
▶ *n* jeer, catcall, gibe, dig, barb, sneer, insult, reproach, taunting, teasing, provocation, mockery, ridicule, sarcasm, derision, censure, *colloq.* brickbat

taut *adj*
tight, stretched, tightened, contracted, strained,
tense, tensed, unrelaxed, stiff, rigid
F3 slack, loose, relaxed

tautological *adj*
repetitive, superfluous, redundant, wordy, *technical*
pleonastic, *formal* verbose
F3 succinct, economical

tautology *n*
repetition, repetitiveness, duplication, superfluity, redundancy, *technical* pleonasm, perissology, *formal*
iteration, verbosity

tavern *n*
public house, local, inn, bar, alehouse, tap-house, road-
house, *colloq.* dive, hostelry, joint, pub, *slang* boozer

tawdry *adj*
cheap, vulgar, tasteless, fancy, showy, flashy, gaudy,

garish, tinselly, glittering, *colloq.* tacky
F3 fine, tasteful

tawny *adj*
golden, golden brown, khaki, sandy, yellow, tan, fawn,
formal fulvous, fulvid, xanthous

tax *n, v*
▶ *n* **1** LEVY, charge, rate, duty, tariff, customs, contribution, *formal* imposte

Taxes include:
airport tax, capital gains tax, capital transfer tax,
capitation, community charge, corporation tax,
council tax, customs, death duty, estate duty,
excise, income tax, inheritance tax, insurance tax,
PAYE, poll tax, property tax, rates, surtax, tithe, toll,
value added tax (VAT).

2 BURDEN, load, strain, stress, pressure, imposition,
weight
▶ *v* **1** LEVY, charge, demand, exact, assess, impose
2 BURDEN, weigh (down), load, overload, strain,
stretch, encumber, impose, exact, try, test, tire, wear
out, weary, exhaust, drain, sap, weaken, make demands on, *formal* enervate

taxi *n*
cab, minicab, taxicab, hansom-cab, hackney coach,
fiacre

taxing *adj*
burdensome, exacting, demanding, exhausting, punishing, stressful, heavy, tough, hard, tiring, trying, onerous, draining, wearing, wearying, wearisome, *formal* enervating
F3 easy, gentle, mild

teach *v*
instruct, train, coach, tutor, lecture, drill, give lessons,
ground, verse, discipline, school, educate, enlighten,
edify, inform, impart, indoctrinate, condition, brainwash, advise, counsel, guide, direct, show, demonstrate, *formal* inculcate
F3 learn

teacher *n*
schoolteacher, educator, guide
F3 pupil

Kinds of teacher include:
adviser, coach, college lecturer, counsellor,
crammer, dean, demonstrator, deputy head,
doctor, don, duenna, fellow, form teacher,
governess, guru, head of department, head of year,
headmaster, headmistress, headteacher,
housemaster, housemistress, instructor, lecturer,
maharishi, master, mentor, middle school teacher,
mistress, nursery school teacher, pastoral head,
pedagogue, pedant, preceptor, preceptress,
primary school teacher, principal, private tutor,
professor, pundit, reception teacher, school-
ma'am, schoolmaster, schoolmistress,
schoolteacher, secondary school teacher, senior
lecturer, student teacher, subject co-ordinator,
supply teacher, trainer, tutor, university lecturer,
upper school teacher.

teaching *n*
1 INSTRUCTION, tuition, education, pedagogy

Methods of teaching include:
apprenticeship, briefing, coaching, computer-
aided learning, correspondence course,
counselling, demonstration, distance learning,
drilling, familiarization, grounding, guidance,

hands-on training, home-learning, indoctrination, induction training, in-service training, instruction, job training, lecturing, lesson, master-class, on-the-job training, practical, preaching, private tuition, role play, rote learning, schooling, seminar, shadowing, special tuition, theory, training, tuition, tutelage, tutorial, vocational training, work experience.

2 DOGMA, doctrine, tenet, precept, principle

team *n, v*
▶ *n* side, line-up, squad, shift, crew, gang, band, group, set, troupe, bunch, company, stable
▶ *v* ▷ **team up** join, unite, couple, combine, band together, co-operate, collaborate, work together, match, yoke

teamwork *n*
collaboration, co-operation, co-ordination, joint effort, team spirit, fellowship, *esprit de corps*
Ⓕ disharmony, disunity

tear¹ *v, n*
▶ *v* **1** RIP, rend, divide, pull apart, break apart, split, ladder, rupture, sever, shred, scratch, claw, gash, wound, injure, lacerate, slash, mutilate, mangle **2** PULL, snatch, grab, seize, pluck, wrest, *colloq.* yank **3** *tear down the street* dash, rush, hurry, speed, race, run, sprint, fly, shoot, dart, bolt, career, gallop, charge, *colloq.* belt, nip, rip, whizz, vroom, zap, zing, zip, zoom, step on it
▶ *n* rip, rent, slit, hole, split, run, rupture, scratch, gash, wound, injury, laceration, slash, mutilation

tear² *n*
▷ **in tears** crying, weeping, sobbing, wailing, whimpering, blubbering, sad, sorrowful, upset, distressed, emotional, *colloq.* weepy

tearaway *n*
rough, tough, rowdy, ruffian, rascal, daredevil, delinquent, hooligan, hoodlum, hothead, madcap, roughneck, *colloq.* good-for-nothing

tearful *adj*
crying, weeping, sobbing, whimpering, blubbering, sad, sorrowful, upset, distressed, emotional, upsetting, distressing, mournful, doleful, *formal* lachrymose, *colloq.* weepy
Ⓕ happy, smiling, laughing

tease *v*
taunt, provoke, bait, goad, annoy, vex, irritate, badger, worry, pester, plague, torment, tantalize, mock, ridicule, gibe, banter, *colloq.* aggravate, needle, rag, kid, rib

technical *adj*
mechanical, scientific, technological, electronic, computerized, specialist, specialized, practical, applied, expert, professional

technique *n*
1 METHOD, system, procedure, manner, fashion, style, way, means, approach, course, performance, execution, *modus operandi, formal* mode **2** SKILL, skilfulness, ability, capability, delivery, artistry, mastery, craftsmanship, dexterity, skill, facility, proficiency, expertise, art, craft, knack, touch, *colloq.* know-how

tedious *adj*
boring, monotonous, uninteresting, unexciting, dull, dreary, uninspired, unvaried, lifeless, flat, drab, humdrum, banal, routine, tiresome, wearisome, wearying, tiring, laborious, long-winded, long-drawn-out, *formal* prosaic, *colloq.* run-of-the-mill, samey
Ⓕ lively, interesting, exciting

tedium *n*
boredom, tediousness, monotony, dullness, dreari-

ness, lifelessness, drabness, banality, sameness, routine, prosiness, ennui, vapidity
Ⓕ excitement, interest

teem *v*
swarm, bristle, crawl, burst, proliferate, abound, increase, multiply, overflow, produce, bear, brim, *formal* pullulate
Ⓕ lack, want

teeming *adj*
swarming, crawling, alive, bristling, seething, full, packed, brimming, overflowing, bursting, numerous, abundant, fruitful, thick, *formal* replete, pullulating, *colloq.* chock-a-block, chock-full
Ⓕ lacking, sparse, rare

teenage *adj*
teenaged, adolescent, young, youthful, juvenile, immature

teenager *n*
young person, young adult, adolescent, youth, boy, girl, minor, juvenile

teeny *adj*
tiny, minute, minuscule, miniature, diminutive, microscopic, *Scot.* wee, *colloq.* titchy, teeny-weeny, teensy-weensy

teeter *v*
sway, rock, roll, reel, stagger, totter, shake, tremble, waver, wobble, balance, lurch, pitch, pivot, seesaw

teetotal *adj*
temperate, abstinent, abstemious, sober, *colloq.* on the wagon

teetotaller *n*
non-drinker, abstainer, nephalist, Rechabite, water-drinker

telegram *n*
Telemessage®, cable, telex, fax, telegraph, *colloq.* wire

telegraph *n, v*
▶ *n* cable, teleprinter, telex, telegram, radiotelegraph, *colloq.* wire
▶ *v* send, transmit, signal, cable, telex, *colloq.* wire

telepathy *n*
mind-reading, thought transference, sixth sense, ESP, extrasensory perception, clairvoyance

telephone *n, v*
▶ *n* phone, handset, receiver, *colloq.* blower, hot line

Types of telephone include:
Ansaphone®, answering machine, caller display phone, cardphone, carphone, cashphone, cellphone, cellular phone, corded phone, cordless phone, fax, fax-phone, hazardous area phone, Minicom®, mobile phone, pager, payphone, push-button telephone, system phone, textphone, tone-dialling phone, Touchtone®, Uniphone®, videophone, weather-resistant phone.

▶ *v* phone, ring (up), call (up), dial, contact, get in touch, *colloq.* buzz, give a buzz, give a tinkle, give a bell

telescope *v*
contract, shrink, compress, condense, abridge, squash, squeeze, crush, shorten, compact, curtail, truncate, abbreviate, reduce, cut, trim, concertina

televise *v*
broadcast, screen, show, put on, transmit, air, beam, relay, cable

television *n*
TV, receiver, set, small screen, *colloq.* telly, the box, goggle-box, idiot box, the tube, *US* boob tube

Parts of a television set include:
aerial, aerial socket, amplifier, cathode-ray tube, chrominance signal extractor, colour decoder module, deflector coil, electron gun, horizontal synchronizing module, intermediate frequency amplifier module, loudspeaker, luminance signal amplifier, phospher dots, picture tube, remote control, scanning current generator, screen, set-top-box, shadow mask, sound demodulator, stand-by switch, synchronizing pulse separator, tuner.

tell *v*
1 INFORM, notify, let know, brief, mention, acquaint, impart, communicate, make known, report, speak, utter, say, state, confess, divulge, show, disclose, reveal, announce, broadcast, declare, proclaim, *formal* apprise, *colloq.* give the low-down **2** *tell a story* narrate, recount, relate, recite, report, announce, describe, sketch, portray, mention, *formal* delineate **3** ORDER, command, direct, instruct, require, charge, bid, dictate, advise, authorize, decree **4** DIFFERENTI-ATE, distinguish, discriminate, tell apart, discern, recognize, identify, discover, see, perceive, make out, understand, comprehend **5** AFFECT, have an effect on, take its toll of, exhaust, drain, change, transform, alter **6** INFORM ON, talk, betray, denounce, *colloq.* rat, squeal, tell tales, blab, blow the whistle on, spill the beans, let the cat out of the bag, give the game away, *slang* grass, shop
▷ **tell off** scold, chide, reprimand, rebuke, reprove, lecture, reproach, censure, *formal* upbraid, berate, *colloq.* tick off, dress down, give a talking-to

telling *adj*
revealing, significant, impressive, marked, effective, powerful, convincing, persuasive, impressive, *formal* cogent

telling-off *n*
scolding, chiding, rebuke, reprimand, reproach, reproof, lecture, row, *formal* castigation, upbraiding, *colloq.* dressing-down, ticking-off, bawling-out

tell-tale *adj, n*
▶ *adj* revealing, meaningful, revelatory, noticeable, perceptible, unmistakable, *colloq.* give-away
▶ *n* informer, secret agent, sneak, spy, *Scot.* clype, *colloq.* squealer, snake in the grass, snitch, snitcher, *slang* grass

temerity *n*
presumption, impudence, impertinence, effrontery, gall, audacity, boldness, daring, rashness, recklessness, impulsiveness, *colloq.* cheek, nerve
☒ caution, prudence

temper *n, v*
▶ *n* **1** MOOD, humour, nature, temperament, character, attitude, disposition, constitution, frame/state of mind **2** ANGER, bad mood, rage, fury, passion, tantrum, fit of temper, scene, storm, annoyance, resentment, irritability, petulance, ill-humour, *colloq.* paddy, wax, flare-up **3** CALM, calmness, composure, self-control, tranquillity, *slang* cool
☒ **2** calmness, self-control **3** anger, rage
▷ **lose your temper** get angry, boil over, get all steamed up, foam at the mouth, fly off the handle, go mad, see red, get up in arms, get aggravated, blow a fuse, blow a gasket, blow your cool, blow your top, burst a blood vessel, do your nut, explode, flip your lid, fly into a rage, go off the deep end, go up the wall, hit the ceiling, hit the roof, lose your cool, lose your rag, lose your patience, raise hell, throw a tantrum, throw a wobbly
▶ *v* **1** MODERATE, lessen, weaken, reduce, calm,

soothe, allay, alleviate, palliate, modify, soften, *formal* mitigate, assuage, *colloq.* tone down **2** HARDEN, roughen, toughen, strengthen, *technical* anneal, *formal* fortify

temperament *n*
1 CHARACTER, nature, personality, disposition, tendency, bent, constitution, make-up, complexion, soul, spirit, mood, humour, temper, frame/state of mind, attitude, outlook **2** MOODINESS, excitability, sensitivity, touchiness, irritability, impatience, fieriness, explosiveness, hot-headedness, volatility

temperamental *adj*
1 MOODY, emotional, over-emotional, neurotic, highly-strung, sensitive, hypersensitive, touchy, irritable, impatient, passionate, fiery, excitable, explosive, hot-blooded, hot-headed, petulant, volatile, mercurial, capricious, unpredictable, unreliable **2** NAT-URAL, inborn, innate, inherent, constitutional, ingrained, congenital
☒ **1** calm, level-headed, steady

temperance *n*
teetotalism, prohibition, abstinence, abstemiousness, sobriety, continence, moderation, restraint, self-restraint, self-control, self-discipline, self-denial, austerity
☒ intemperance, excess

temperate *adj*
1 *temperate climate* mild, clement, balmy, fair, equable, balanced, stable, moderate, gentle, pleasant, agreeable **2** TEETOTAL, abstinent, abstemious, self-denying, sober, continent, moderate, restrained, self-restrained, controlled, self-controlled, even-tempered, calm, composed, reasonable, sensible
☒ **2** intemperate, extreme, excessive

tempest *n*
1 STORM, gale, squall, tornado, typhoon, hurricane, cyclone **2** FURORE, upheaval, uproar, ferment, disturbance, commotion, tumult

tempestuous *adj*
stormy, windy, gusty, blustery, squally, turbulent, tumultuous, rough, wild, uncontrolled, violent, furious, raging, heated, boisterous, impassioned, fierce, feverish, passionate, intense
☒ calm, peaceful, quiet

temple *n*
place of worship, shrine, sanctuary, church, tabernacle, mosque, pagoda. *See also* WORSHIP.

tempo *n*
time, rhythm, metre, measure, beat, cadence, pulse, throb, speed, velocity, rate, pace

temporal *adj*
secular, profane, worldly, earthly, terrestrial, material, carnal, fleshly, mortal
☒ spiritual

temporarily *adv*
for the time being, momentarily, in the interim, pro tem, transiently, transitorily, briefly, fleetingly
☒ permanently

temporary *adj*
impermanent, provisional, interim, short-term, fill-in, makeshift, stopgap, pro tem, temporal, transient, transitory, passing, fleeting, brief, short-lived, momentary, *formal* ephemeral, evanescent, fugacious
☒ permanent, everlasting

temporize *v*
delay, hang back, pause, stall, equivocate, play for time, *formal* procrastinate, tergiversate, *colloq.* hum and haw

tempt *v*
1 ENTICE, coax, cajole, persuade, woo, bait, lure,

educe, provoke, incite, egg on, *formal* inveigle **2** AL-
LURE, attract, draw, invite, tantalize, *colloq.* make
someone's mouth water

☒ 1 discourage, dissuade **2** repel

temptation *n*

enticement, inducement, incitement, coaxing, cajolery, persuasion, urging, bait, lure, allure, appeal,
attraction, influence, draw, pull, seduction, invitation

tempting *adj*

attractive, inviting, alluring, tantalizing, enticing, appetizing, mouthwatering, seductive

☒ unattractive, uninviting

temptress *n*

enchantress, seductress, siren, vamp, flirt, sorceress,
femme fatale, coquette, Delilah

tenable *adj*

credible, defensible, justifiable, reasonable, rational,
sound, arguable, believable, defendable, plausible,
maintainable, supportable, viable, feasible

☒ untenable, indefensible, unjustifiable

tenacious *adj*

1 DETERMINED, persistent, dogged, firm, single-
minded, adamant, resolute, purposeful, steadfast,
relentless, unyielding, unshakeable, unswerving,
obstinate, stubborn, *formal* intransigent, obdurate
2 ADHESIVE, cohesive, sticky, clinging, secure, firm,
tight, fast

☒ 1 loose, slack, weak

tenacity *n*

determination, persistence, single-mindedness, firmness, fastness, perseverance, doggedness, resoluteness, resolution, resolve, steadfastness, staunchness, toughness, diligence, power, solidity, solidness,
strength, force, forcefulness, inflexibility, indomitability, application, stubbornness, obstinacy, *formal* intransigence, obduracy, pertinacity

☒ looseness, slackness, weakness

tenancy *n*

occupancy, possession, renting, residence, tenure,
holding, lease, leasehold, occupation, incumbency

tenant *n*

renter, lessee, leaseholder, occupier, occupant, resident, inhabitant, landholder, incumbent

tend¹ *v*

tends to arrive late incline, lean, show a tendency,
bend, bear, head, aim, point, lead, go, move, gravitate

tend² *v*

tend someone who is ill look after, take care of, care
for, cultivate, keep, maintain, see to, manage, handle,
guard, protect, watch (over), keep an eye on, mind,
nurture, nurse, minister to, serve, attend (to), wait on

☒ neglect, ignore

tendency *n*

trend, drift, movement, course, direction, trend, bearing, heading, bias, partiality, readiness, liability, susceptibility, proneness, inclination, leaning, bent,
aptness, disposition, *formal* predisposition, propensity, proclivity, conatus

tender¹ *adj*

1 KIND, gentle, caring, humane, generous, benevolent, considerate, compassionate, sympathetic,
warm, kindly, fond, affectionate, loving, amorous, romantic, sentimental, emotional, evocative, sensitive,
vulnerable, tender-hearted, soft-hearted **2** YOUNG,
youthful, immature, green, raw, new, early, callow, inexperienced, impressionable, vulnerable **3** SOFT,
succulent, fleshy, juicy, dainty, delicate, fragile, frail,
sensitive, weak, feeble **4** SORE, painful, aching,
smarting, bruised, throbbing, inflamed, red, raw, sensitive

☒ 1 hard-hearted, callous **2** mature **3** tough, hard

tender² *v, n*

▸ *v tender an apology* offer, extend, give, present,
submit, propose, suggest, advance, volunteer, bid,
proffer

▸ *n* **1** *legal tender* currency, money **2** OFFER, bid, estimate, quotation, price, proposal, proposition, suggestion, submission

tender-hearted *adj*

caring, gentle, kind, kind-hearted, kindly, mild, warm,
warm-hearted, sympathetic, soft-hearted, feeling,
considerate, compassionate, benevolent, loving,
fond, affectionate, responsive, sensitive, humane,
merciful, pitying, sentimental, benign

☒ callous, cruel, hard-hearted, unfeeling

tenderness *n*

1 KINDNESS, gentleness, warmth, warm-heartedness,
tender-heartedness, sympathy, sweetness, sensitivity,
loving-kindness, humaneness, benevolence,
attachment, devotion, affection, fondness, amorousness, love, liking, mercy, pity, care, compassion,
consideration, humanity, sentimentality, vulnerability, soft-heartedness **2** YOUTH, youthfulness, immaturity, callowness, greenness, inexperience **3** SOFT-
NESS, weakness, delicateness, frailness, fragility,
feebleness **4** SORENESS, rawness, bruising, sensitiveness, ache, aching, inflammation, irritation, pain,
painfulness

☒ 1 cruelty, hardness, harshness **2** maturity **3** toughness, hardness

tenet *n*

principle, belief, precept, presumption, conviction,
opinion, teaching, rule, thesis, view, doctrine, dogma,
maxim, creed, credo, canon, article of faith

tenor *n*

meaning, tendency, theme, trend, essence, substance, gist, aim, point, direction, drift, purpose,
sense, spirit, intent, course, path, way, burden, *formal*
purport

tense *adj, v*

▸ *adj* **1** TIGHT, taut, stretched, strained, stiff, rigid
2 NERVOUS, anxious, worried, strained, distraught,
under pressure, jittery, uneasy, apprehensive, edgy,
fidgety, restless, jumpy, overwrought, keyed up,
colloq. edgy, uptight, stressed out, *slang* screwed up
3 STRESSFUL, exciting, worrying, uneasy, strained,
charged, fraught, nerve-racking, nail-biting

☒ 1 loose, slack **2** calm, relaxed

▸ *v* tighten, contract, brace, stretch, strain, stiffen,
work

☒ loosen, relax

tension *n*

1 TIGHTNESS, tautness, stiffness, rigidity, strain,
straining, stretching, stress, pressure **2** NERVOUS-
NESS, anxiety, worry, strain, stress, pressure, uneasiness, apprehension, edginess, restlessness, agitation, disquiet, distress, suspense, *colloq.* nerves **3**
CONFLICT, disagreement, friction, quarrel, dissension, dispute, opposition, antagonism, hostility, strife,
unrest, confrontation, feud, discord, contention, ill-
will, difference of opinion, variance, clash, *formal* antipathy

☒ 1 looseness **2** calm(ness), relaxation **3** harmony

tentative *adj*

1 PROVISIONAL, experimental, exploratory, speculative, test, trial, pilot, indefinite, unconfirmed, unproven, *formal* conjectural **2** HESITANT, wavering,
faltering, cautious, unsure, uncertain, timid, doubtful, undecided

☒ 1 definite, conclusive, final, firm **2** decisive, confident

tenterhooks *n*
▷ **on tenterhooks** anxious, in suspense, impatient, nervous, excited, waiting, watchful, eager, with bated breath

tenuous *adj*
thin, slim, slender, fine, slight, insubstantial, flimsy, fragile, delicate, weak, vague, hazy, shaky, indefinite, doubtful, dubious, questionable
▰ strong, substantial

tenure *n*
possession, proprietorship, residence, tenancy, term, time, holding, occupancy, occupation, incumbency, *formal* habitation

tepid *adj*
lukewarm, cool, warmish, half-hearted, indifferent, unenthusiastic, apathetic
▰ cold, hot, passionate

term *n, v*
▶ *n* **1** WORD, name, title, epithet, phrase, expression, *formal* designation, denomination, appellation, locution **2** TIME, period, course, duration, spell, span, stretch, interval, space, semester, session, season **3** *on good terms* relations, relationship, footing, standing, position **4** *the terms of the contract* conditions, points, details, specifications, stipulations, clauses, provisos, provisions, qualifications, particulars **5** CHARGES, rates, fees, prices, costs, tariff **6** END, interval, conclusion, limit, finish, duration, period, culmination, close, bound, boundary, fruition, terminus
▷ **come to terms** become reconciled, reconcile yourself, resign yourself, accept, come to accept, submit
▷ **in terms of** in relation to, as regards, with/in regard to, with respect to
▶ *v* call, name, dub, style, designate, label, tag, title, entitle, *formal* denominate

terminal *adj, n*
▶ *adj* **1** LAST, final, concluding, ultimate, extreme, utmost, ending, confining, limiting **2** *terminal illness* fatal, deadly, lethal, mortal, incurable, dying, killing
▰ **1** initial, first
▶ *n* **1** END, extremity, limit, termination, boundary, depot, terminus **2** *a computer terminal* VDU, computer workstation, input-output device, keyboard, console, monitor

terminate *v*
finish, bring/come to an end, complete, conclude, end, stop, close, cut off, result, put an end to, abort, lapse, run out, expire, *formal* cease, discontinue, *colloq.* wind up
▰ begin, start, initiate

termination *n*
end, ending, finish, conclusion, close, abortion, completion, issue, result, consequence, effect, dénouement, expiry, finale, finis, *formal* demise, cessation, discontinuation
▰ beginning, initiation, start

terminology *n*
language, jargon, phraseology, vocabulary, words, expressions, terms, nomenclature

terminus *n*
end, close, termination, extremity, limit, boundary, destination, goal, target, depot, station, garage, terminal

terrain *n*
land, ground, territory, country, countryside, landscape, topography

terrestrial *adj*
earthly, worldly, global, mundane
▰ cosmic, heavenly

terrible *adj*
1 BAD, awful, frightful, dreadful, shocking, appalling, outrageous, disgusting, revolting, repulsive, nasty, offensive, abhorrent, hateful, horrid, horrible, unpleasant, obnoxious, foul, vile, hideous, gruesome, horrific, harrowing, grim, distressing, unspeakable, harsh, grave, desperate, incompetent, poor, incorrigible **2** EXTREME, serious, severe, great, intense, exceptional, big, large, *colloq.* frightful, awful
▰ **1** excellent, wonderful, superb

terribly *adv*
very, much, greatly, extremely, exceedingly, thoroughly, desperately, decidedly, seriously, *colloq.* frightfully, awfully

terrific *adj*
1 EXCELLENT, wonderful, great, marvellous, super, remarkable, outstanding, brilliant, magnificent, superb, sensational, amazing, stupendous, breathtaking, *colloq.* smashing, fabulous, fantastic, smashing, neat, ace, brill, crack, out of this world, *slang* mega, cool, wicked, awesome, crucial **2** HUGE, enormous, gigantic, tremendous, great, intense, extreme, excessive, extraordinary
▰ **1** awful, terrible, appalling

terrified *adj*
frightened, petrified, scared, scared stiff, panic-stricken, intimidated, horrified, horror-struck, dismayed, appalled, alarmed, awed, *colloq.* scared out of your wits, scared to death, having kittens, in a blue funk

terrify *v*
petrify, horrify, appal, shock, terrorize, intimidate, frighten, scare, scare stiff, panic, alarm, dismay, paralyse, numb, *colloq.* rattle, scare out of your wits, make your blood run cold, scare the living daylights out of, make your hair stand on end, make someone jump out of their skin, put the frighteners on, put the wind up

territorial *adj*
geographical, area, district, zonal, regional, sectional, topographic, localized, *formal* domainal

territory *n*
country, land, state, dependency, province, domain, preserve, jurisdiction, sector, region, area, district, county, zone, tract, terrain, field

terror *n*
1 FEAR, panic, dread, trepidation, horror, shock, fright, alarm, dismay, terrorism, intimidation, *formal* consternation, *colloq.* blue funk **2** *that child's a terror* rascal, rogue, horror, tearaway **3** FIEND, monster, devil, demon

terrorize *v*
threaten, menace, intimidate, oppress, coerce, bully, browbeat, frighten, scare, alarm, terrify, petrify, horrify, shock, *colloq.* strongarm, put the frighteners on, put the wind up

terse *adj*
short, brief, succinct, concise, to the point, compact, crisp, elliptical, condensed, pithy, incisive, snappy, curt, blunt, brusque, abrupt, laconic, *formal* epigrammatic, elliptical, gnomic
▰ long-winded, verbose

test *v, n*
▶ *v* **1** *test them on spelling* try (out), experiment, examine, assess, evaluate, check, scrutinize, inspect, investigate, study, analyse, screen, sample, prove, verify, *formal* appraise, assay, *colloq.* probe **2** *test someone's patience* strain, burden, load, overload, stretch, encumber, impose, exact, try, test, tire, wear out, weary, exhaust, drain, sap, weaken, make demands on, *formal* enervate
▶ *n* trial, try-out, experiment, examination, audition,

pilot study, assessment, evaluation, questions, questionnaire, quiz, check, check-up, scrutinization, investigation, inspection, analysis, exploration, proof, probation, ordeal

testament *n*
testimony, witness, demonstration, proof, evidence, exemplification, tribute, will, earnest, *formal* attestation

testify *v*
give evidence, state, declare, assert, swear, vouch, certify, confirm, verify, establish, demonstrate, substantiate, show, bear witness, back up, support, endorse, *formal* depose, avow, attest, corroborate, affirm

testimonial *n*
reference, character, credential, certificate, (letter of) recommendation, endorsement, commendation, tribute

---

 testimonial or **testimony** ?

A *testimonial* is a letter describing a person's character and abilities. A *testimony* is a statement of evidence, for example that of a witness at a trial: *He was convicted mainly by the testimony of his former partner; Her book is a remarkable testimony to her vision for the future of her country.*

---

testimony *n*
evidence, statement, submission, declaration, profession, assertion, support, proof, verification, confirmation, witness, demonstration, indication, *technical* affidavit, deposition, *formal* attestation, affirmation, corroboration, manifestation

---

testimony or **testimonial** ? *See panel at* TESTIMONIAL.

---

testy *adj*
bad-tempered, cross, quarrelsome, crusty, quick-tempered, short-tempered, irritable, impatient, grumpy, irascible, snappish, snappy, waspish, sullen, fretful, peevish, splenetic, petulant, captious, *formal* cantankerous, *colloq.* crabbed, tetchy, touchy, crotchety, stroppy, shirty, ratty
🔁 even-tempered, good-humoured

tetchy *adj*
irritable, irascible, peevish, bad-tempered, crusty, grumpy, short-tempered, snappish, *colloq.* touchy, crotchety, shirty, ratty

tête-à-tête *n*
conversation, chat, talk, heart-to-heart, dialogue, *colloq.* confab, natter

tether *n, v*
▶ *n* chain, rope, cord, line, lead, leash, bond, fetter, shackle, restraint, fastening
▶ *v* tie, fasten, secure, restrain, chain, rope, leash, bind, lash, fetter, shackle, manacle

text *n*
1 WORDS, wording, content, matter, main matter, body **2** SUBJECT, subject matter, topic, theme, issue, point **3** READING, passage, verse, chapter, paragraph, sentence **4** BOOK, set book, textbook, source

textile *n*
cloth, fabric, material

texture *n*
consistency, feel, touch, surface, finish, grain, appearance, weave, tissue, fabric, structure, composition, constitution, character, quality

thank *v*
say thank you, be grateful, show/express your gratitude, express your thanks, appreciate, show your appreciation, acknowledge, recognize, credit

thankful *adj*
grateful, appreciative, obliged, indebted, pleased, contented, relieved, *formal* beholden
🔁 ungrateful, unappreciative

thankless *adj*
unrecognized, unappreciated, unacknowledged, unrequited, unrewarded, unrewarding, unprofitable, useless, fruitless
🔁 rewarding, worthwhile

thanks *n, interj*
▶ *n* gratitude, gratefulness, appreciation, acknowledgement, recognition, credit, thanksgiving, thank-offering
▶ *interj*

Expressions used when thanking someone include:

how can I ever thank you?, how kind of you!, I can't thank you enough, I'm so/very grateful, many thanks, bless you, much obliged, please accept my grateful/sincere thanks, cheers, ta, thanks a lot, thanks be (to), thanks for that, that's very good of you, that's very kind of you, you're too kind, you shouldn't have.

▷ **thanks to** because of, owing to, due to, on account of, as a result of, through

thaw *v*
1 MELT, defrost, defreeze, de-ice, soften, liquefy, dissolve, warm, heat up **2** BECOME FRIENDLIER, become more relaxed, relax, loosen up
🔁 **1** freeze

theatre *n*
1 *go to the theatre* auditorium, hall, playhouse, amphitheatre, lyceum, odeon, opera house **2** DRAMA, the stage, dramatics, theatrics, show business, *formal* Thespian art, *colloq.* the boards, the footlights, rep

---

Parts of a theatre include:

apron, auditorium, backstage, balcony, border, box, bridge, catwalk, circle, coulisse, cut drop, cyclorama, decor, downstage, flat, flies, forestage, fourth wall, gallery, *colloq.* the gods, green room, grid, leg drop, lights, floats, floods, footlights, spots, loge, loggia, logum, mezzanine, open stage, opposite prompt, orchestra pit, picture-frame stage, pit, prompt side, proscenium, proscenium arch, revolving stage, rostrum, safety curtain, scruto, set, stage, stalls, tormentor, trapdoor, upper circle, upstage, wings.

---

theatrical *adj*
1 DRAMATIC, thespian

Theatrical forms include:
ballet, burlesque, cabaret, circus, comedy, black comedy, comedy of humours, comedy of manners, comedy of menace, commedia dell' arte, duologue, farce, fringe theatre, Grand Guignol, kabuki, Kitchen-Sink, legitimate drama, masque, melodrama, mime, miracle play, monologue, morality play, mummery, music hall, musical, musical comedy, mystery play, Noh, opera, operetta, pageant, pantomime, play, Punch and Judy, puppet theatre, revue, street theatre, tableau,

theatre-in-the-round, Theatre of the Absurd, Theatre of Cruelty, tragedy.

2 MELODRAMATIC, histrionic, dramatic, mannered, affected, unreal, artificial, forced, pompous, ostentatious, showy, extravagant, emotional, exaggerated, overdone

theft *n*
robbery, thieving, burglary, stealing, pilfering, larceny, shoplifting, kleptomania, fraud, swindling, embezzlement, *formal* purloining, *colloq.* pinching, nicking, swiping, lifting, nobbling

thematic *adj*
conceptual, notional, classificatory, *formal* taxonomic

theme *n*
1 SUBJECT, topic, subject matter, thread, motif, keynote, idea, gist, essence, burden, argument, *formal* leitmotif **2** THESIS, paper, dissertation, composition, essay, text, matter **3** MELODY, tune, motif

then *adv*
1 AT THAT TIME, at that point, at that moment, in those days, by that time, *formal* whereupon **2** AFTERWARDS, after, next, soon, subsequently, at a later date **3** IN ADDITION, additionally, also, as well, moreover, besides, too, further, furthermore **4** THEREFORE, so and so, accordingly, consequently, as a result, *formal* thus

theological *adj*
religious, divine, doctrinal, ecclesiastical, scriptural, *technical* hierological

theorem *n*
formula, principle, rule, statement, deduction, proposition, hypothesis, *formal* dictum, postulate

theoretical *adj*
hypothetical, speculative, abstract, conceptual, notional, academic, doctrinaire, pure, ideal, *formal* conjectural, suppositional, *colloq.* on paper
◪ practical, applied, concrete

theorize *v*
suppose, guess, speculate, formulate, *formal* hypothesize, conjecture, postulate, propound

theory *n*
hypothesis, supposition, assumption, presumption, surmise, guess, speculation, idea, view, opinion, notion, abstraction, philosophy, thesis, plan, proposal, scheme, system, *formal* conjecture, postulation
◪ certainty, practice

therapeutic *adj*
remedial, curative, healing, curing, restorative, tonic, medicinal, corrective, good, advantageous, beneficial, salutary, health-giving, *formal* ameliorative, sanative
◪ harmful, detrimental

therapy *n*
treatment, remedy, cure, healing, tonic

Types of therapy include:
acupressure, acupuncture, Alexander technique, aromatherapy, art therapy, aversion therapy, beauty therapy, behaviour therapy, biofeedback, chemotherapy, chiropractic, cognitive therapy, confrontation therapy, drama therapy, electroconvulsive therapy, electrotherapy, faith healing, family therapy, Gestalt therapy, group therapy, heat treatment, herbalism, homeopathy, hormone-replacement therapy, horticulture therapy, hydrotherapy, hypnotherapy, irradiation, moxibustion, music therapy, naturopathy, occupational therapy, osteopathy, phototherapy, physiotherapy, play therapy, primal therapy, psychotherapy, radiotherapy, reflexology,

regression therapy, reminiscence therapy, Rolfing, sex therapy, shiatsu, speech therapy, ultrasound, zone therapy.

thereabouts *adv*
about, approximately, roughly, near that number, near that date

thereafter *adv*
subsequently, afterwards, after that, after that time, next

therefore *adv*
so, and so, then, accordingly, consequently, as a result, *formal* thus, ergo

thesaurus *n*
dictionary, lexicon, wordbook, vocabulary, synonymy, encyclopedia, storehouse, repository, treasury

thesis *n*
1 *doctoral thesis* dissertation, essay, composition, treatise, paper, monograph, *formal* disquisition **2** SUBJECT, topic, theme, idea, opinion, view, theory, hypothesis, proposal, proposition, premise, statement, argument, contention

thick *adj, n*
▶ *adj* **1** WIDE, broad, fat, stout, chunky, heavy, bulky, deep, big, substantial, stiff, solid, dense, impenetrable, close, compact, concentrated, condensed, viscous, coagulated, creamy, lumpy, clotted **2** FULL, packed, crowded, filled, overflowing, swarming, teeming, bristling, brimming, crawling, bursting, numerous, abounding, abundant, *colloq.* chock-a-block **3** *thick fog* impenetrable, dense, heavy, murky, smoggy, soupy, opaque, concentrated **4** *a thick voice* husky, rough, unclear, indistinct, throaty, guttural, croaky, croaking, gruff, gravelly, rasping **5** *a thick accent* strong, pronounced, broad, marked, definite, obvious, noticeable, striking **6** STUPID, foolish, slow, dense, dull, dim-witted, brainless, simple, *colloq.* dumb, gormless, dopey, thick as a plank/two short planks
◪ **1** thin, slim, slender, slight **2** sparse **4** clear **5** faint, vague **6** clever, intelligent, *colloq.* brainy
▶ *n* middle, centre, focus, midst, hub, heart

thicken *v*
1 *thicken a soup* make/become more solid, solidify, stiffen, condense, congeal, coagulate, clot, cake, gel, jell, set **2** *the plot thickens* become more mysterious, become more complicated, become more involved, become more intricate
◪ **1** thin

thickhead *n*
fool, idiot, dunce, *colloq.* nitwit, twit, numskull, fathead, blockhead, dimwit, dope, clot, dummy, pinhead, chump, imbecile, moron

thick-headed *adj*
stupid, foolish, dense, slow, brainless, obtuse, dim-witted, dull-witted, idiotic, imbecilic, moronic, asinine, doltish, slow-witted, *colloq.* blockheaded, dopey, thick, gormless
◪ clever, intelligent, sharp, *colloq.* brainy

thickness *n*
1 WIDTH, breadth, diameter, extent, density, viscosity, consistency, bulk, bulkiness, body, solidness, closeness **2** LAYER, stratum, seam, vein, band, deposit, bed, ply, sheet, coat, film, lamina
◪ **1** thinness

thickset *adj*
stocky, heavy, heavily built, well-built, sturdy, powerful, strong, muscular, burly, solid, bulky, squabby, squat, dense, *colloq.* beefy, brawny,
◪ lanky

thick-skinned *adj*
insensitive, unfeeling, callous, tough, invulnerable, hardened, case-hardened, inured, *colloq.* hard-boiled, hard-nosed, tough as old boots
🖪 thin-skinned, sensitive, vulnerable

thief *n*
robber, bandit, pickpocket, shoplifter, burglar, housebreaker, plunderer, poacher, stealer, pilferer, kleptomaniac, fraud, fraudster, swindler, embezzler, brigand, *colloq.* mugger, filcher, nicker, nobbler

thieve *v*
steal, rob, pinch, cheat, swindle, misappropriate, embezzle, pilfer, plunder, poach, abstract, *formal* peculate, purloin, *colloq.* make/run off with, nobble, snaffle, filch, knock off, lift, nick, rip off, swipe, *slang* heist

thieving *n*
stealing, theft, robbery, burglary, pilferage, pilfering, shoplifting, plundering, embezzlement, larceny, thievery, banditry, crookedness, piracy, *formal* peculation, *colloq.* mugging, knocking off, ripping off, lifting, nicking, filching

thin *adj, v*
▶ *adj* **1** LEAN, slim, slender, fine, light, svelte, narrow, paper-thin, wafer-thin, attenuated, slight, skinny, bony, skeletal, scraggy, scrawny, spindly, lanky, gaunt, spare, anorexic, wasted, shrunken, underweight, undernourished, emaciated, *colloq.* thin as a rake **2** *thin fabric* fine, delicate, light, flimsy, filmy, gauzy, gossamer, sheer, see-through, transparent, translucent, *formal* diaphanous **3** SPARSE, scarce, scattered, scant, paltry, meagre, poor, inadequate, deficient, scanty, skimpy, straggly, wispy **4** WEAK, feeble, runny, watery, diluted, dilute, *colloq.* wishy-washy **5** *the evidence is thin* weak, flimsy, unconvincing, implausible, feeble, lame, inadequate, inconclusive, untenable, defective, deficient **6** *a thin voice/sound* high-pitched, soft, quiet, weak, faint
🖪 **1** fat, broad **2** substantial, thick, dense, solid **3** thick, plentiful, abundant **4** strong, thick **5** strong, substantial
▷ **on thin ice** precarious, unsafe, at risk, vulnerable, insecure, in jeopardy, open to attack
▶ *v* **1** DIMINISH, reduce, dwindle, decrease, lessen, make/become less in number, trim, narrow, weed out, *formal* attenuate **2** WEAKEN, dilute, make more watery, water down, rarefy, refine

thing *n*
1 ARTICLE, item, object, entity, creature, body, substance **2** DEVICE, contrivance, gadget, tool, implement, instrument, apparatus, machine, mechanism, *colloq.* gismo, doodah, thingy, thingummy, thingamy, thingummyjig, thingummybob, what-d'you-call-it, whatsit, what's-its-name **3** *take your things with you* clothes, clothing, garments, belongings, possessions, paraphernalia, goods, luggage, baggage, equipment, tools, apparatus, tackle, oddments, odds and ends, bits and pieces, *formal* apparel, attire, effects, *colloq.* stuff, gear, togs, bits and bobs, clobber **4** ASPECT, detail, particular, characteristic, trait, feature, quality, property, factor, element, attribute, point, fact, concept, notion, thought, idea **5** ACT, deed, feat, exploit, action, undertaking, job, chore, task, responsibility, problem **6** CIRCUMSTANCE, situation, eventuality, happening, occurrence, event, episode, matter, incident, phenomenon, affair, proceeding, arrangement, condition **7** OBSESSION, preoccupation, fixation, *idée fixe*, fetish, phobia, dislike, fear, horror, aversion, *colloq.* hang-up, one-track mind **8** LIKING, fondness, love, affection, preference, partiality, affinity, taste, attraction, appreciation, proneness, inclination, tendency, bias, leaning, bent, desire, weakness, fancy, *formal* predilection, penchant, propensity, proclivity, *colloq.* soft spot

think *v, n*
▶ *v* **1** BELIEVE, hold, consider, regard, judge, estimate, reckon, calculate, determine, conclude, reason, *formal* esteem, deem, opine, *colloq.* figure, reckon **2** CONCEIVE, imagine, suppose, guess, presume, expect, foresee, envisage, visualize, anticipate, *formal* surmise, conjecture **3** *think it over* ponder, mull over, chew over, brood, ruminate, meditate, contemplate, muse, reflect, concentrate, deliberate, weigh up, recall, review, take stock, recollect, remember, *formal* cogitate, cerebrate, *colloq.* sleep on it
▷ **think better of** change your mind about, think again, think twice, reconsider, rethink, revise, have second thoughts about, decide not to do, *colloq.* get cold feet
▷ **think much of** think highly of, admire, prize, respect, value, set store by, rate, *formal* esteem
🖪 abominate
▷ **think nothing of** consider normal, consider usual
▷ **think over** reflect upon, consider, weigh up, contemplate, meditate, ponder, chew over, ruminate, mull over
▷ **think up** devise, contrive, dream up, imagine, conceive, visualize, invent, design, create, concoct
▶ *n* consideration, contemplation, deliberation, reflection, meditation, assessment, evaluation, *formal* cogitation

thinkable *adj*
likely, imaginable, possible, feasible, reasonable, supposable, conceivable, *formal* cogitable
🖪 unthinkable

thinker *n*
philosopher, scholar, theorist, ideologist, intellect, sage, mastermind, *colloq.* brain

thinking *n, adj*
▶ *n* reasoning, philosophy, thought(s), conclusion(s), theory, idea, opinion, view, outlook, position, judgement, assessment, evaluation, appraisal
▶ *adj* reasoning, rational, sensible, intellectual, intelligent, cultured, sophisticated, philosophical, analytical, logical, reflective, contemplative, meditative, thoughtful

thin-skinned *adj*
sensitive, easily upset, snappish, soft, susceptible, tender, vulnerable, hypersensitive, irritable, *colloq.* touchy
🖪 thick-skinned, unfeeling, callous

third-rate *adj*
low-grade, low-quality, poor, bad, awful, inferior, unsatisfactory, mediocre, indifferent, slipshod, shoddy, cheap and nasty, *colloq.* ropy, *slang* naff
🖪 first-rate

thirst *n, v*
▶ *n* **1** THIRSTINESS, dryness, drought, parchedness, aridity, drouth, drouthiness **2** DESIRE, longing, yearning, hankering, craving, hunger, appetite, lust, passion, eagerness, keenness, *colloq.* yen
▶ *v* hunger, desire, long, yearn, hanker, crave, lust

thirsty *adj*
1 DRY, dehydrated, arid, *colloq.* parched, gasping **2** *thirsty for knowledge* desirous, longing, yearning, hankering, craving, hungry, thirsting, burning, itching, dying, eager, keen, avid, greedy

thorn *n*
spike, point, barb, prickle, spine, bristle, needle

thorny *adj*
1 SPIKY, pointed, sharp, barbed, prickly, spiny, bristly, *formal* acanthous, spinous, spinose **2** *a thorny problem* difficult, troublesome, irksome, vexed, worrying, trying, upsetting, problematic, knotty, complex, intricate, tough, awkward, delicate, tricky, ticklish, *formal* convoluted

thorough *adj*
1 *a thorough person* painstaking, scrupulous, meticulous, careful, conscientious, efficient, methodical 2 *thorough research* sweeping, all-embracing, comprehensive, all-inclusive, exhaustive, scrupulous, meticulous, extensive, deep, thoroughgoing, intensive, widespread, in-depth 3 *a thorough waste of time* full, complete, total, entire, utter, absolute, perfect, pure, sheer, unqualified, unmitigated, out-and-out, downright
⊞ 1, 2 partial, superficial, careless

thoroughbred *adj*
pedigree, pedigreed, pure-blood, pure-blooded, full-blooded, blooded
⊞ cross-bred, hybrid, mixed, mongrel

thoroughfare *n*
road, street, roadway, way, highway, avenue, motorway, passage, passageway, access, turnpike, boulevard, concourse

thoroughly *adv*
1 CAREFULLY, painstakingly, meticulously, scrupulously, intensively, conscientiously, assiduously, efficiently, comprehensively, sweepingly, exhaustively, root and branch, inside out 2 FULLY, perfectly, completely, absolutely, downright, entirely, quite, totally, utterly, *colloq.* every inch, with a fine-tooth comb
⊞ 1 carelessly, haphazardly **2** partially

though *conj, adv*
▶ *conj* although, even if, while, allowing, granted, *formal* notwithstanding
▶ *adv* however, but, nevertheless, nonetheless, yet, still, even so, for all that, *colloq.* all the same

thought *n*
1 THINKING, attention, care, heed, regard, consideration, reasoning, study, scrutiny, introspection, meditation, pondering, contemplation, musing, rumination, reflection, deliberation, *formal* cogitation, cerebration 2 IDEA, notion, concept, conception, belief, conviction, opinion, view, point of view, feeling, judgement, theory, assessment, estimation, appraisal, conclusion, plan, design, intention, purpose, reason, aim, hope, dream, prospect, expectation, anticipation, aspiration 3 THOUGHTFULNESS, consideration, kindness, care, concern, regard, compassion, sympathy, tenderness, gesture, touch, *formal* solicitude

thoughtful *adj*
1 PENSIVE, wistful, dreamy, abstracted, reflective, contemplative, introspective, thinking, absorbed, studious, serious, solemn, quiet, lost in thought, deep, profound, *formal* cogitative, *colloq.* in a brown study 2 CONSIDERATE, kind, unselfish, helpful, caring, compassionate, sympathetic, tender, attentive, mindful, careful, prudent, cautious, wary, *formal* heedful, solicitous
⊞ 2 thoughtless, insensitive, selfish

thoughtless *adj*
1 INCONSIDERATE, unthinking, insensitive, unfeeling, tactless, undiplomatic, indiscreet, unkind, rude, impolite, selfish, uncaring 2 ABSENT-MINDED, inattentive, heedless, mindless, foolish, stupid, silly, rash, hasty, reckless, ill-considered, ill-advised, unwise, imprudent, careless, negligent, remiss, *formal* precipitate
⊞ 1 thoughtful, considerate **2** careful

thrall *n*
thraldom, power, bondage, enslavement, servitude, slavery, subjection, serfdom, vassalage, *formal* subjugation
⊞ freedom

thrash *v*
1 PUNISH, beat, whip, lash, flog, scourge, cane,

spank, clobber, lay into, *colloq.* wallop, tan, whack, belt 2 DEFEAT, beat, trounce, drub, be more than a match for, have the edge on, crush, overwhelm, rout, *formal* vanquish, *colloq.* hammer, slaughter, clobber, lick, wipe the floor with 3 THRESH, flail, hit, flog, toss, jerk, swish, writhe
▷ **thrash out** discuss, debate, negotiate, hammer out, settle, resolve, clear the air

thrashing *n*
1 PUNISHMENT, flogging, lashing, caning, hiding, beating, tanning, whipping, leathering, pasting, *formal* chastisement, *colloq.* belting 2 DEFEAT, drubbing, beating, rout, crushing, trouncing, lamming, *colloq.* hammering, clobbering, licking

thread *n, v*
▶ *n* 1 YARN, strand, fibre, filament, string, line, strip, streak 2 COURSE, direction, drift, tenor, theme, subject, motif, plot, storyline, train of thought
▶ *v* pass, ease, move, push, inch, meander, wind, string, weave

threadbare *adj*
1 *threadbare clothes* worn, frayed, ragged, moth-eaten, scruffy, tatty, tattered, shabby 2 HACKNEYED, overused, old, stale, tired, trite, worn-out, well-worn, clichéridden, commonplace, stock, stereotyped, *colloq.* corny
⊞ 1 new **2** fresh

threat *n*
menace, warning, ultimatum, omen, foreboding, danger, risk, hazard, peril, *formal* portent, presage, commination

threaten *v*
1 MENACE, intimidate, browbeat, cow, pressurize, bully, extort, blackmail, terrorize, warn, warn (off), endanger, jeopardize, imperil, *colloq.* push around, lean on, put the frighteners on, put the screws on 2 BE IMMINENT, be in the offing, approach, loom (up), forebode, foreshadow, *formal* portend, presage, augur, comminate

threatening *adj*
menacing, intimidatory, warning, cautionary, ominous, foreboding, sinister, grim, looming, *formal* inauspicious, impending, minacious, minatory

threesome *n*
trio, trilogy, triple, triplet, triumvirate, triad, triune, troika, trinity, triptych

threshold *n*
doorstep, sill, doorway, door, entrance, entry, brink, verge, starting-point, dawn, beginning, start, commencement, outset, opening, *formal* inception

thrift *n*
economy, husbandry, saving, conservation, frugality, carefulness, *formal* prudence, parsimony, *colloq.* scrimping and saving
⊞ extravagance, waste

thriftless *adj*
extravagant, lavish, spendthrift, unthrifty, wasteful, prodigal, *formal* imprudent, improvident, dissipative, profligate
⊞ thrifty

thrifty *adj*
economical, saving, frugal, sparing, careful, conserving, *formal* prudent, parsimonious
⊞ extravagant, profligate, prodigal, wasteful

thrill *n, v*
▶ *n* excitement, adventure, pleasure, delight, joy, stimulation, charge, sensation, feeling, glow, tingle, throb, frisson, shudder, flutter, vibration, quiver, tremor, *colloq.* kick, buzz
▶ *v* excite, exhilarate, rouse, arouse, move, stir, stimulate, electrify, galvanize, flush, glow, tingle, throb,

shudder, flutter, vibrate, tremble, shiver, quiver, shake, *colloq.* give a buzz/kick to
🗲 bore

thrilling *adj*
exciting, stimulating, stirring, rousing, riveting, sensational, exhilarating, gripping, electrifying, riproaring, heart-stirring, soul-stirring, shaking, shuddering, shivering, trembling, vibrating, quaking, *colloq.* hair-raising

thrive *v*
flourish, prosper, boom, grow, increase, advance, develop, bloom, blossom, gain, profit, succeed, do well, make progress, make headway, *formal* burgeon
🗲 languish, stagnate, fail, die

thriving *adj*
prosperous, successful, blossoming, booming, developing, flourishing, growing, healthy, wealthy, affluent, well, comfortable, blooming, *formal* burgeoning
🗲 ailing, failing, languishing, stagnating, dying

throat *n*
throttle, windpipe, gullet, gorge, oesophagus, craw, thropple, fauces, halse, *Scot.* thrapple, *colloq.* the Red Lane

throaty *adj*
guttural, hoarse, rasping, raucous, low, husky, deep, gruff, thick

throb *v, n*
▶ *v* pulse, pulsate, beat, palpitate, vibrate, pound, thump, drum
▶ *n* pulse, pulsation, beat, palpitation, vibration, pounding, thumping, drumming

throe *n*
convulsion, fit, pain, pang, paroxysm, seizure, spasm, stab, suffering, distress, agony, anguish, torture, *formal* travail

throng *n, v*
▶ *n* crowd, mass, mob, multitude, pack, press, crush, jam, swarm, flock, congregation, herd, bevy, horde, host, *formal* assemblage
▶ *v* flock, fill, crowd, cram, converge, herd, press, swarm, pack, bunch, congregate, jam, *colloq.* mill around

throttle *v*
1 STRANGLE, strangulate, choke, asphyxiate, suffocate, smother, stifle 2 SUPPRESS, gag, silence, inhibit, restrain, check, keep in, hold back, strangle, stifle, smother

through *prep, adj*
▶ *prep* 1 ACROSS, all the way across, from one side of to the other, from one end of to the other 2 BETWEEN, by, with the help of, via, by way of, by means of, using, through the agency of, *formal* through the good offices of, by virtue of 3 *all through the night* throughout, during, in, to/until the end of, from the beginning to the end of, without a break/interruption in 4 BECAUSE OF, as a result of, owing to, due to, thanks to, on account of, by virtue of
▷ **through and through** completely, totally, thoroughly, utterly, wholly, entirely, fully, unreservedly, altogether, to the core, from top to bottom
▶ *adj* 1 FINISHED, ended, completed, done, no longer having anything to do with, no longer involved with, *formal* terminated 2 *through train* direct, express, non-stop

throughout *adv, prep*
▶ *adv* everywhere, in every part, extensively, widely, completely, from beginning to end, *formal* ubiquitously
▶ *prep* 1 DURING, during/in the whole of, all through, in the course of, for the duration of 2 IN ALL PARTS, in every part of, all over, all round, everywhere

throw *v, n*
▶ *v* 1 HURL, heave, lob, pitch, sling, cast, fling, toss, shy, launch, project, propel, catapult, send, *colloq.* chuck 2 MOVE QUICKLY, fling, turn, force, put, cast 3 *throw light* shed, cast, project, send, direct, cause to fall, emit, radiate, give off 4 BRING DOWN, floor, fell, prostrate, upset, overturn, dislodge, unseat, unsaddle, unhorse 5 *throw a switch* put on, switch on, operate, work 6 PERPLEX, baffle, confound, disturb, put out, confuse, disconcert, surprise, astonish, dumbfound, *formal* discomfit, *colloq.* floor 7 *throw a party* arrange, organize, give, put on, lay on
▷ **throw away** 1 DISCARD, jettison, get rid of, reject, scrap, dispose of, throw out, *formal* dispense with, *colloq.* dump, ditch, chuck away/out 2 WASTE, lose, squander, fritter away, *slang* blow
🗲 1 keep, preserve, salvage, rescue 2 exploit, make use of, capitalize on
▷ **throw off** shed, cast off, drop, abandon, shake off, free yourself from, get rid of, discard, jettison, elude, escape from
▷ **throw out** 1 EVICT, turn out, expel, eject, *colloq.* turf out 2 REJECT, discard, dismiss, turn down, jettison, throw away, scrap, *formal* dispense with, *colloq.* dump, ditch 3 EMIT, emit, radiate, give off, emanate, exude, send out, diffuse, produce 4 MENTION, speak about, refer to, bring up, point out, introduce
▷ **throw over** abandon, desert, discard, drop, finish with, jilt, leave, reject, *formal* forsake, *colloq.* chuck, quit
▷ **throw up** 1 VOMIT, spew, regurgitate, disgorge, retch, heave, gag, *colloq.* puke 2 ABANDON, renounce, resign, quit, leave, *formal* relinquish, *colloq.* chuck in, pack in, jack in
▶ *n* heave, lob, pitch, sling, fling, toss, cast, *colloq.* chuck

throwaway *adj*
1 *throwaway comments* careless, casual, offhand, passing, unemphatic, undramatic 2 *a throwaway product* disposable, cheap, expendable, non-returnable, biodegradable

thrust *v, n*
▶ *v* 1 PUSH, shove, butt, ram, jam, wedge, stick, poke, prod, jab, lunge, pierce, stab, plunge, drive, press, force, impel, drive, propel 2 IMPOSE, press, urge, force, inflict, burden, saddle, encumber, foist
▶ *n* 1 PUSH, shove, poke, prod, lunge, jab, ram, prod, stab 2 DRIVE, motive, power, force, pressure, impetus, momentum 3 *the thrust of an argument* gist, essence, drift, tenor, theme, message, point, substance

thud *n, v*
thump, clump, knock, clunk, clonk, smack, bash, crash, bang, thunder, *colloq.* wallop, wham

thug *n*
ruffian, tough, rough, roughneck, robber, bandit, killer, murderer, cut-throat, assassin, hoodlum, gangster, hooligan, villain, *colloq.* mugger

thumb *v*
▷ **thumb through** glance at, scan, skim, peruse, browse through, flick through, flip through, leaf through

thumbnail *adj*
short, brief, concise, pithy, quick, small, compact, succinct, miniature

thumbs-down
refusal, rejection, disapproval, negation, rebuff, no, turn-down
🗲 thumbs-up

thumbs-up
approval, encouragement, acceptance, yes, sanc-

tion, *formal* affirmation, *colloq.* go-ahead, green light, OK

🔁 thumbs-down

thump *v, n*
▶ *v* **1** HIT, strike, knock, punch, box, cuff, smack, thrash, slap, rap, thwack, crash, bang, thud, batter, *colloq.* clout, whack, wallop **2** THROB, pound, hammer, beat, pulsate, palpitate
▶ *n* knock, blow, punch, box, cuff, smack, rap, thwack, crash, bang, thud, beat, throb, *colloq.* clout, whack, wallop

thumping *adj, adv*
▶ *adj* big, enormous, great, intense, extreme, severe, immense, massive, huge, colossal, monumental, terrific, thundering, tremendous, impressive, mammoth, excessive, exorbitant, gigantic, towering, gargantuan, titanic, *colloq.* whopping
🔁 insignificant, petty, trivial, *colloq.* piddling
▶ *adv* extremely, very, intensely, really, greatly, severely, unusually

thunder *n, v*
▶ *n* boom, reverberation, crash, crashing, bang, crack, clap, peal, rumble, roll, roar, outburst, blast, explosion
▶ *v* boom, resound, reverberate, crash, bang, crack, clap, peal, rumble, roll, roar, bellow, blast

thundering *adj, adv*
▶ *adj* great, enormous, excessive, remarkable, monumental, tremendous, unmitigated
▶ *adv* extremely, very, intensely, really, greatly, severely, unusually

thunderous *adj*
booming, resounding, reverberating, roaring, rumbling, loud, noisy, deafening, tumultuous, ear-splitting

thunderstruck *adj*
stunned, shocked, staggered, amazed, astonished, astounded, dazed, dumbfounded, open-mouthed, paralysed, aghast, agape, petrified, *colloq.* flabbergasted, floored, flummoxed, nonplussed, bowled over, knocked for six

thus *adv*
1 THEREFORE, so, consequently, then, accordingly, *formal* hence, ergo **2** LIKE THIS, in this way, so, as follows

thwack *v, n*
▶ *v* beat, bash, hit, flog, smack, thump, slap, buffet, cuff, *colloq.* clout, wallop, whack
▶ *n* blow, bash, slap, thump, smack, cuff, buffet, *colloq.* wallop, whack

thwart *v*
frustrate, foil, defeat, hinder, hamper, impede, obstruct, block, balk, check, baffle, stop, prevent, oppose, cross, nobble, *colloq.* stymie
🔁 help, assist, aid

tic *n*
jerk, spasm, twitch, tic douloureux

tick *n, v*
▶ *n* **1** CLICK, tap, stroke, beat, tick-tock **2** *wait a tick* moment, instant, flash, second, minute, twinkling, *colloq.* jiffy, sec, trice **3** MARK, line, stroke, *US* check
▶ *v* **1** MARK, indicate, choose, select, *US* check **2** CLICK, tap, beat
▷ **tick off 1** *tick off items on a list* put a tick against, mark, indicate, *US* check (off) **2** SCOLD, chide, reprimand, rebuke, reproach, reprove, *formal* upbraid, *colloq.* tell off, give someone a dressing-down, haul over the coals, tear off a strip
🔁 **2** praise, compliment

ticket *n*
pass, card, certificate, token, voucher, coupon, stub,

docket, counterfoil, slip, label, tag, sticker

tickle *v*
touch, stroke, excite, thrill, delight, please, gratify, amuse, entertain, divert, interest, stimulate

ticklish *adj*
sensitive, touchy, delicate, thorny, awkward, problematic, difficult, tricky, knotty, critical, risky, hazardous, precarious, *colloq.* dodgy
🔁 easy, simple, straightforward

tide *n, v*
▶ *n* **1** CURRENT, ebb, flow, stream, flux, movement **2** COURSE, movement, run, direction, drift, trend, tendency, tenor
▶ *v* ▷ **tide over** help (through), help out, assist, aid, see through, keep going

tidings *n*
news, communication, report, bulletin, message, advice, word, information, intelligence, greetings, *colloq.* dope, gen

tidy *adj, v*
▶ *adj* **1** NEAT, orderly, methodical, efficient, businesslike, systematic, organized, in order, well-ordered, ordered, uncluttered, clean, spick-and-span, immaculate, shipshape, smart, spruce, trim, well-groomed, well-kept **2** *a tidy sum* large, substantial, sizeable, considerable, fair, respectable, good, generous, ample
🔁 **1** untidy, messy, disorganized **2** small, insignificant
▶ *v* neaten, straighten (out), straighten up, order, arrange, clean (up), clear up, smarten, spruce up, groom

tie *v, n*
▶ *v* **1** FASTEN, knot, fix, secure, moor, tether, attach, join, connect, link, couple, unite, rope, lash, strap, chain, bind **2** RESTRAIN, restrict, confine, limit, curb, constrain, hamper, impede, hinder, cramp, shackle **3** DRAW, be equal, be even, *colloq.* be all square
▷ **tie down** restrain, constrain, restrict, confine, limit, hamper, hinder
▷ **tie up 1** MOOR, tether, attach, fasten, secure, rope, lash, chain, bind, connect, truss, wrap up, restrain, *colloq.* do up **2** CONCLUDE, settle, finalize, *formal* terminate, *colloq.* wind up, wrap up **3** OCCUPY, engage, engross, keep busy
▶ *n* **1** KNOT, fastening, link, band, bond, ribbon, tape, clip **2** CONNECTION, link, liaison, relationship, bond, friendship, affiliation, allegiance, kinship **3** OBLIGATION, commitment, duty, restraint, constraint, restriction, limit, limitation, hindrance **4** DRAW, dead heat, stalemate, deadlock

tie-in *n*
connection, relationship, link, relation, co-ordination, association, liaison, tie-up, affiliation, *colloq.* hook-up

tier *n*
floor, storey, level, stage, layer, stratum, belt, zone, band, echelon, rank, row, line, bank

tiff *n*
disagreement, squabble, row, difference, difference of opinion, quarrel, words, dispute, temper, ill-humour, sulk, tantrum, *colloq.* falling-out, huff, scrap, set-to, pet, barney, spat

tight *adj*
1 TAUT, stretched, tense, strained, strained, rigid, stiff, firm, fixed, fast, secure, close, cramped, clenched, constricted, compressed, limited, restricted, compact, snug, close-fitting, skin-tight, figure-hugging **2** SEALED, hermetic, sound-proof, impervious, impenetrable, airtight, watertight **3** *tight security* strict, tough, firm, severe, stringent, rigorous, hard, harsh, rigid, inflexible **4** *money is tight* scarce, limited, insufficient, inadequate, too little, not enough,

in short supply **5** *a tight contest* close, evenly matched, well-matched, hard-fought, *colloq.* neck and neck **6** *in a tight corner/spot* difficult, awkward, problematic, tricky, delicate, *colloq.* dodgy **7** MEAN, stingy, miserly, niggardly, penny-pinching, *formal* parsimonious, *colloq.* tight-fisted **8** DRUNK, intoxicated, tipsy, *colloq.* under the influence, sloshed, sozzled, plastered, tiddly, merry, well-oiled, legless, *slang* stoned, tanked up, smashed
◪ **1** loose, slack **2** open **3** lax **4** plentiful **6** easy **7** generous **8** sober

tighten *v*
tauten, stretch, pull tight, tense, stiffen, fix, fasten, make fast, secure, narrow, close, cramp, constrict, crush, squeeze, *formal* rigidify, constringe
◪ loosen, relax

tight-fisted *adj*
mean, stingy, miserly, niggardly, penny-pinching, sparing, grasping, *formal* parsimonious, *colloq.* mingy, tight
◪ generous, charitable

tight-lipped *adj*
silent, uncommunicative, unforthcoming, close-lipped, close-mouthed, quiet, reticent, taciturn, reserved, secretive, mum, mute
◪ talkative, forthcoming, garrulous

till ¹ *prep*
till the end of June until, up to, to, up to the time of, all through, *US* through

till ² *v*
till the land cultivate, work, plough, dig, farm

tilt *v*, *n*
▶ *v* **1** SLOPE, incline, slant, pitch, list, tip, lean, cant **2** ATTACK, charge, rush, fight, contend, encounter, clash, duel, spar, joust
▶ *n* **1** SLOPE, incline, angle, inclination, slant, pitch, list **2** ATTACK, charge, fight, contest, encounter, combat, clash, duel, spar, joust, tournament
▷ **at full tilt** very quickly, very fast, at full speed, at top speed, at full blast, at full pelt, with full force, *colloq.* all out, flat out

timber *n*
1 WOOD, trees, forest, *US* lumber **2** BEAM, lath, plank, pole, spar, board, log

timbre *n*
quality, voice quality, tone, tonality, resonance, ring, colour, *technical* klang

time *n*, *v*
▶ *n* **1** SPELL, stretch, period, term, season, session, span, duration, interval, space, while **2** TEMPO, beat, rhythm, metre, measure **3** MOMENT, point, juncture, stage, instance, instant, occasion, date **4** AGE, era, epoch, life, lifetime, lifespan, generation, heyday, peak

Periods of time include:
eternity, eon, era, age, generation, period, epoch, millennium, chiliad, century, lifetime, decade, decennium, quinquennium, year, light-year, yesteryear, quarter, month, fortnight, week, midweek, weekend, long weekend, day, today, tonight, yesterday, tomorrow, morrow, weekday, hour, minute, second, moment, instant, millisecond, microsecond, nanosecond; dawn, sunrise, sun-up, the early hours, *colloq.* wee small hours, morning, morn, a.m., daytime, midday, noon, high noon, p.m., afternoon, tea-time, evening, twilight, dusk, sunset, nightfall, bedtime, night, night-time; season, spring, summer, midsummer, autumn, *US* fall, winter.

▷ **all the time** continually, constantly, perpetually, incessantly, interminably, always, forever
◪ never
▷ **at one time** once, formerly, previously, at one point, long ago, in times past
▷ **at the same time 1** SIMULTANEOUSLY, all together, in parallel, *formal* concurrently **2** NEVERTHELESS, nonetheless, still, but, however, anyway, even so, for all that
▷ **at times** sometimes, on occasions, from time to time, now and again, now and then, off and on, every so often
▷ **behind time** late, overdue, unpunctual, delayed, behind, behind schedule, *formal* tardy
◪ early
▷ **behind the times** old-fashioned, out of date, dated, old, unfashionable, out of fashion, obsolete, past, *colloq.* fuddy-duddy, old hat, past its sell-by date
◪ up to date
▷ **for the time being** at present, for now, right now, just now, at the moment, for the moment, for the present, at the present time, temporarily, (in the) meantime, meanwhile, pro tem
▷ **from time to time** now and again, now and then, at times, sometimes, occasionally, on occasion, once in a while, periodically, intermittently, spasmodically, sporadically, every now and then, every so often
◪ constantly, always
▷ **in good time** early, with time to spare, ahead of time, ahead of schedule, punctually, on time
◪ late
▷ **in time** not too late, early enough, punctually, on time
▷ **on time** punctually, promptly, exactly, precisely, sharp, on the dot, *colloq.* dead on, bang on, spot on
◪ late
▷ **play for time** delay, hesitate, stall, temporize, stonewall, hang fire, filibuster, *formal* procrastinate, *colloq.* drag your feet
▷ **time after time** repeatedly, frequently, often, recurrently, many times, on many occasions, time and (time) again, again and again, over and over again
▶ *v* **1** ARRANGE, set, schedule, programme, timetable, fix **2** MEASURE, clock, calculate, count, meter, regulate, control, adjust

time-honoured *adj*
age-old, traditional, long-established, usual, accustomed, conventional, customary, established, fixed, old, ancient, historic, venerable

timeless *adj*
ageless, immortal, deathless, everlasting, eternal, endless, permanent, lasting, enduring, changeless, unchanging, unending, indestructible, imperishable, *formal* immutable, abiding

timely *adj*
well-timed, at the right time, seasonable, suitable, appropriate, convenient, opportune, prompt, punctual, *formal* propitious, felicitous
◪ ill-timed, unsuitable, inappropriate

timetable *n*, *v*
▶ *n* schedule, programme, agenda, calendar, diary, rota, roster, list, listing, curriculum
▶ *v* schedule, programme, diarize, set, fix, arrange, list

time-worn *adj*
worn, old, aged, dog-eared, out of date, *passé*, outworn, ruined, well-worn, tired, trite, stock, stale, threadbare, bromidic, clichéed, hackneyed, dated, weathered, decrepit, ancient, broken-down, rundown, shabby, ragged, hoary, wrinkled, lined
◪ fresh, new

timid *adj*
shy, bashful, modest, shrinking, retiring, nervous, apprehensive, afraid, scared, frightened, fearful, cowardly, faint-hearted, spineless, irresolute, *formal* timorous, pusillanimous, *colloq.* chicken, yellow, gutless, wimpish, lily-livered
🔁 brave, bold, confident

timorous *adj*
shy, timid, bashful, afraid, fearful, scared, frightened, apprehensive, shrinking, retiring, faint-hearted, nervous, diffident, coy, tentative, irresolute, modest, unadventurous, cowardly, trembling, *formal* pusillanimous, *colloq.* mousy
🔁 assertive, assured, bold

tincture *n, v*
  ▶ *n* trace, flavour, touch, tinge, tint, colour, hint, hue, dash, suggestion, shade, stain, seasoning, smack, aroma
  ▶ *v* flavour, scent, season, stain, tinge, tint, colour, dye, infuse, permeate, imbue, suffuse

tinge *n, v*
  ▶ *n* **1** TRACE, touch, suggestion, hint, smack, flavour, pinch, drop, dash, bit, sprinkling, smattering **2** TINT, dye, colour, shade, wash, tincture
  ▶ *v* tint, dye, stain, colour, flavour, shade, suffuse, imbue

tingle *v, n*
  ▶ *v* sting, prickle, tickle, itch, prick, thrill, throb, tremble, quiver, vibrate
  ▶ *n* stinging, prickling, tickle, tickling, itch, itching, thrill, tremor, throb, quiver, shiver, gooseflesh, goose-pimples, *colloq.* pins and needles

tinker *v, n*
  ▶ *v* fiddle, play, toy, trifle, potter, dabble, meddle, fool about/around, tamper, *colloq.* mess about/around
  ▶ *n* itinerant, Gypsy, fixer, mender, botcher, bungler

tinkle *v, n*
  ▶ *v* ring, ding, jingle, jangle, clink, chink, peal, chime
  ▶ *n* **1** *the tinkle of the bell* ring, ding, jingle, jangle, clink, chink, peal, chime **2** *give you a tinkle* ring, phone call, call, *colloq.* buzz, bell

tinsel *adj, n*
  ▶ *adj* showy, ostentatious, cheap, gaudy, tawdry, trashy, superficial, specious, gimcrack, sham, *formal* meretricious, *colloq.* flashy
  ▶ *n* glitter, spangle, frippery, show, triviality, display, ostentation, flamboyance, garishness, gaudiness, sham, worthlessness, artificiality, meaninglessness, insignificance, pretension

tint *n, v*
  ▶ *n* dye, stain, rinse, wash, colour, hue, shade, tincture, tinge, tone, cast, streak, trace, touch
  ▶ *v* dye, colour, tinge, streak, stain, taint, affect

tiny *adj*
minute, microscopic, infinitesimal, minuscule, small, little, slight, trifling, negligible, insignificant, diminutive, petite, dwarfish, midget, pocket, miniature, Lilliputian, *Scot.* wee, *colloq.* pint-sized, mini, teeny, teeny-weeny, itsy-bitsy
🔁 huge, enormous, immense

tip¹ *n, v*
  ▶ *n* *the tip of a finger* end, extremity, point, nib, apex, peak, pinnacle, summit, acme, top, cap, crown, head
  ▶ *v* cap, crown, top, surmount

tip² *v, n*
  ▶ *v* *tip your head* lean, incline, slant, list, tilt, cant, topple (over), capsize, upset, overturn, spill, pour (out), empty, unload, dump
  ▶ *n* dump, rubbish-heap, refuse-heap, slag heap, midden

tip³ *n, v*
  ▶ *n* **1** HINT, pointer, clue, suggestion, advice, recom-

mendation, warning, tip-off, information, inside information, forecast **2** GRATUITY, gift, bonus, reward, gift, present, baksheesh, *pourboire*, *formal* perquisite, *colloq.* perk
  ▶ *v* **1** ADVISE, suggest, warn, caution, forewarn, tip off, inform, tell **2** *tip the driver* reward, remunerate

tip-off *n*
hint, pointer, clue, suggestion, warning, information, inside information

tipple *v, n*
  ▶ *v* drink, imbibe, indulge, quaff, bib, *colloq.* swig, booze
  ▶ *n* drink, regular drink, favourite drink, alcohol, liquor, *colloq.* booze, poison, usual

tippler *n*
drinker, hard drinker, drunk, drunkard, dipso(maniac), bibber, inebriate, wine-bag, *colloq.* boozer, sponge, *slang* lush, soak, sot, toper, wino

tipsy *adj*
drunk, under the influence, *colloq.* merry, happy, mellow, squiff(y), tiddly, tight
🔁 sober

tirade *n*
harangue, diatribe, denunciation, abuse, lecture, outburst, rant, *formal* fulmination, invective, philippic

tire *v*
weary, fatigue, wear out, tire out, exhaust, tax, strain, drain, drop, flag, bore, *formal* enervate
🔁 enliven, invigorate, refresh

tired *adj*
1 WEARY, drowsy, sleepy, flagging, fatigued, wearied, worn out, exhausted, dog-tired, drained, jaded, *formal* enervated, *colloq.* fagged out, bushed, whacked, shattered, beat, dead-beat, all in, knackered, ready to drop, washed-out, hardly able to keep your eyes open **2** *tired of waiting* bored, sick, *colloq.* fed up, sick and tired **3** HACKNEYED, old, stale, worn-out, trite, clichéd, *colloq.* corny, past its sell-by date
🔁 **1** lively, energetic, rested, refreshed **3** new

tireless *adj*
untiring, unwearied, unflagging, indefatigable, energetic, vigorous, diligent, industrious, resolute, determined
🔁 tired, lazy, unenthusiastic

tiresome *adj*
troublesome, trying, annoying, irritating, exasperating, irksome, vexatious, wearisome, dull, boring, routine, humdrum, tedious, monotonous, uninteresting, unexciting, tiring, fatiguing, laborious
🔁 interesting, stimulating, easy

tiring *adj*
wearying, wearisome, fatiguing, exhausting, draining, demanding, hard, tough, difficult, exacting, taxing, arduous, strenuous, laborious, *formal* enervating

tiro, tyro *n*
beginner, novice, apprentice, freshman, learner, pupil, starter, student, trainee, tenderfoot, greenhorn, initiate, neophyte, novitiate, catechumen
🔁 veteran, *colloq.* old hand

tissue *n*
1 MATTER, substance, material **2** *a box of tissues* paper handkerchief, disposable handkerchief, Kleenex®, facial tissue, toilet paper, toilet tissue **3** *tissue paper* fabric, stuff, gauze, gossamer **4** *a tissue of lies* web, mesh, network, structure, texture

titanic *adj*
colossal, huge, enormous, massive, vast, immense, giant, gigantic, jumbo, mammoth, monumental, pro-

digious, stupendous, towering, mountainous, monstrous, herculean, cyclopean, *formal* mighty *colloq.* - ginormous

F3 insignificant, small

titbit *n*
morsel, scrap, appetizer, snack, delicacy, dainty, treat, bonne-bouche

tithe *n, v*
▶ *n* tenth, tax, levy, duty, tariff, toll, tribute, rent, assessment, impost
▶ *v* give, hand over, pay, take in, tax, assess, charge, levy, rate

titillate *v*
stimulate, arouse, excite, thrill, tickle, provoke, tease, tantalize, intrigue, interest, *colloq.* turn on

titillating *adj*
stimulating, arousing, exciting, sexy, erotic, seductive, lewd, lurid, thrilling, provocative, sensational, suggestive, intriguing, interesting, teasing, captivating

titivate *v*
smarten up, touch up, refurbish, preen, make up, primp, prink, *colloq.* doll up, tart up

title *n, v*
▶ *n* **1** NAME, term, designation, form of address, label, epithet, nickname, sobriquet, pseudonym, *nom-de-plume*, rank, status, office, position, *formal* appellation, denomination, *colloq.* handle, moniker **2** HEADING, headline, caption, legend, inscription, credit(s) **3** RIGHT, prerogative, privilege, claim, entitlement, ownership, proprietorship, deeds **4** CHAMPIONSHIP, match, contest, competition, game, prize, trophy, stakes, laurels, crown
▶ *v* entitle, name, call, dub, style, term, designate, tag, label

titter *v & n*
giggle, snigger, snicker, chuckle, cackle, laugh, chortle

tittle-tattle *n, v*
▶ *n* gossip, rumour, hearsay, chatter, cackle, prattle, *colloq.* chitchat, babble, blather, blether, jaw, natter, twaddle, ya(c)k, yackety-yak
▶ *v* gossip, chat, chatter, cackle, prattle, *colloq.* chitchat, tell tales, witter, babble, blather, blether, jaw, natter, ya(c)k, yackety-yak

titular *adj*
nominal, token, so-called, self-styled, honorary, formal, official, *formal* putative, *colloq.* puppet

toady *n, v*
▶ *n* fawner, flatterer, sycophant, groveller, lackey, minion, parasite, flunkey, jackal, *colloq.* yes-man, sucker, bootlicker, crawler, creep, hanger-on, truckler
▶ *v* curry favour, crawl, flatter, grovel, fawn, creep, cringe, kowtow, *colloq.* bootlick, bow and scrape, butter up, kiss the feet, suck up, truckle

toast *v, n*
▶ *v* **1** *toast bread* grill, brown, roast, crisp, bake, heat (up), warm (up), barbecue **2** *toast the bride and groom* drink to, drink the health of, honour, salute, pledge
▶ *n* drink, pledge, tribute, salute, salutation, compliment(s), best wishes, health

---

Toasts include:
all the best!, *auf Ihre Gesundheit*, *à votre santé*, bottoms up!, cheers!, down the hatch!, good health!, good luck!, happy landings!, here's how!, here's looking at you!, here's mud in your eye!, here's to ...!, here's to you!, *prosit!*, skoal!, *slàinte!*, to absent friends!, your health!

---

tobacco *n*

Forms of tobacco include:
colloq. baccy, cheroot, chewing tobacco; cigar, Havana cigar; cigarette, cork-tipped cigarette, filter-tip cigarette, king-size cigarette, menthol cigarette, Russian cigarette; *colloq.* ciggie, *slang* coffin nail, *colloq.* fag; cigarette end, cigarette butt, *slang* dog-end, *slang* fag end; cigarillo, corona, high-tar, low-tar, panatella, plug, snuff, flake tobacco, pipe tobacco, shag tobacco, Turkish tobacco, Virginia tobacco, *colloq.* the weed.

Tobacco accessories include:
ashtray, cigar box, cigar case, cigar cutter, cigar-holder, cigarette box, cigarette case, cigarette-holder, cigarette lighter, gas lighter, petrol lighter, cigarette machine, cigarette paper, cigarette roller, humidor, match, matchbook, box of matches, match striker, pipe, chibouk, church-warden, clay pipe, hookah, meerschaum, narghile, peace pipe (pipe of peace), tobacco pipe, pipe-cleaner, pipe-rack, pipe-rest, smoker's companion, snuffbox, tobacco-pouch, vesta.

---

today *n, adv*
1 THIS DAY, the present day, this very day, the present time, this morning, this afternoon, this evening **2** AT THIS MOMENT, at this moment in time, now, right now, just now, at the present time, these days, nowadays

toddle *v*
walk/move unsteadily, totter, wobble, waddle, stagger, reel, lurch, stumble, falter, waver, teeter, sway, rock, shake

to-do *n*
commotion, fuss, furore, bother, disturbance, flurry, stir, tumult, turmoil, uproar, unrest, excitement, bustle, agitation, rumpus, ruction, quarrel, *colloq.* performance, brouhaha, flap, hoo-ha, stew

together *adv, adj*
▶ *adv* **1** UNITED, collectively, jointly, mutually, in concert, in unison, working together, in collaboration, in conjunction, as one, as a partnership, as a team **2** *travel together* side by side, shoulder to shoulder, hand in hand, in a row **3** SIMULTANEOUSLY, at the same time, at one time, all at once, *formal* concurrently **4** CONTINUOUSLY, consecutively, successively, in succession, without a break, without interruption, on end, *colloq.* on the trot, back to back
F3 **1** separately, individually **2** alone
▶ *adj* well-balanced, well-adjusted, stable, organized, well-organized, level-headed, sensible, down-to-earth, composed, calm, commonsensical, *colloq.* cool

toil *n, v*
▶ *n* labour, hard work, slog, drudgery, sweat, slaving, industry, application, effort, exertion, *colloq.* donkey-work, graft, elbow grease
▶ *v* labour, work, slave, drudge, sweat, grind, push yourself, slog, persevere, strive, struggle, *colloq.* graft, plug away, work like a Trojan, work your fingers to the bone

toiler *n*
worker, workaholic, drudge, grafter, slogger, struggler, slave, workhorse, labourer, menial, navvy
F3 idler, loafer, shirker

toilet *n*
lavatory, WC, bathroom, cloakroom, washroom, pub-

lic convenience, urinal, latrine, convenience, powder room, *US* rest room, *colloq.* loo, bog, the ladies, the gents, *slang* kazi, *US slang* john

toilsome *adj*
difficult, hard, laborious, arduous, burdensome, backbreaking, fatiguing, painful, tough, wearisome, severe, strenuous, taxing, tedious, tiresome, uphill, herculean

token *n, adj*
► *n* 1 SYMBOL, emblem, representation, mark, sign, indication, demonstration, expression, evidence, proof, recognition, clue, warning, signal, index, reminder, remembrance, memorial, memento, souvenir, keepsake, *formal* manifestation 2 *gift token* voucher, coupon, counter, disc
► *adj* symbolic, emblematic, nominal, slight, minimal, perfunctory, superficial, cosmetic, hollow, insincere

tolerable *adj*
1 BEARABLE, endurable, sufferable 2 ACCEPTABLE, satisfactory, passable, adequate, reasonable, fair, fairly good, average, all right, mediocre, indifferent, unexceptional, ordinary, middling, *colloq.* OK, so-so, run-of-the-mill, not bad, nothing (much) to write home about, no great shakes, not much cop
🖪 intolerable, unbearable, insufferable

tolerance *n*
1 TOLERATION, patience, forbearance, liberalism, open-mindedness, broad-mindedness, sympathy, understanding, leniency, lenity, laxness, indulgence, permissiveness, *formal* magnanimity 2 VARIATION, fluctuation, allowance, clearance, *colloq.* play, give, swing 3 RESISTANCE, resilience, toughness, endurance, stamina, *formal* fortitude
🖪 1 intolerance, prejudice, bias, bigotry, narrow-mindedness

tolerant *adj*
patient, forbearing, long-suffering, open-minded, fair, unprejudiced, broad-minded, catholic, liberal, charitable, kind-hearted, sympathetic, understanding, forgiving, lenient, compliant, indulgent, permissive, lax, soft, *formal* magnanimous, *colloq.* easygoing
🖪 intolerant, biased, prejudiced, bigoted, unsympathetic

tolerate *v*
endure, suffer, put up with, bear, stand, swallow, take, receive, accept, admit, allow, permit, warrant, sanction, condone, indulge, *formal* abide, countenance, *colloq.* stomach

toleration *n*
1 PATIENCE, forbearance, open-mindedness, broad-mindedness, liberalism, sympathy, understanding, leniency, lenity, laxness, indulgence, permissiveness, *formal* magnanimity 2 RESISTANCE, resilience, toughness, endurance, stamina, *formal* fortitude 3 ACCEPTANCE, allowance, endurance, sufferance, sanction, indulgence

toll¹ *v*
the bell tolls ring, peal, chime, knell, sound, strike, clang, announce, call, signal, warn, herald

toll² *n*
1 *motorway tolls* charge, fee, payment, levy, tax, duty, tariff, rate, cost, penalty, demand 2 *the casualty toll* cost, loss, damage, injury, death

tomb *n*
grave, burial-place, vault, crypt, sepulchre, catacomb, mausoleum, cenotaph

tombstone *n*
gravestone, headstone, stone, memorial, monument

tome *n*
book, volume, work, opus

tomfoolery *n*
mischief, horseplay, silliness, stupidity, messing about, messing on, foolishness, childishness, idiocy, inanity, skylarking, clowning, buffoonery, hooey, *colloq.* larking about, larks, shenanigans

tone *n, v*
► *n* 1 *tone of voice* note, timbre, pitch, sound, quality, volume, expression, intonation, modulation, inflection, accent, accentuation, stress, emphasis, force, strength 2 TINT, tinge, colour, hue, shade, cast, tonality, tincture 3 AIR, manner, attitude, mood, spirit, humour, temper, character, quality, feel, style, effect, vein, tenor, drift
► *v* match, co-ordinate, suit, blend, harmonize, go (well) with
▷ **tone down** moderate, temper, subdue, restrain, soften, lighten, dim, dampen, play down, reduce, alleviate, *formal* assuage, mitigate, *colloq.* soft-pedal
▷ **tone up** shape up, touch up, trim, tune up, sharpen up, limber up, freshen, invigorate, brighten

tongue *n*
language, speech, discourse, talk, utterance, articulation, vernacular, idiom, dialect, patois, jargon, slang, argot, cant, *formal* parlance, *colloq.* lingo

tongue-tied *adj*
speechless, dumbstruck, inarticulate, silent, mute, dumb, wordless, voiceless, lost for words
🖪 talkative, garrulous, voluble

tonic *n*
cordial, pick-me-up, restorative, refresher, bracer, stimulant, analeptic, boost, fillip, *colloq.* shot in the arm

too *adv*
1 ALSO, as well, in addition, furthermore, besides, moreover, likewise 2 EXCESSIVELY, inordinately, unduly, overly, unreasonably, ridiculously, extremely, very

tool *n, v*
► *n* 1 IMPLEMENT, instrument, utensil, gadget, device, contraption, contrivance, apparatus, artefact, appliance, machine, means, vehicle, medium, agency, agent, intermediary, *colloq.* gismo 2 PUPPET, pawn, dupe, stooge, flunkey, minion, hireling, cat's paw

Types of tool include:
axe, bolster, caulking-iron, crowbar, hod, jackhammer, jointer, mattock, pick, pick-axe, plumb-line, sledgehammer; chaser, clamp, dividers, dolly, drill, hacksaw, jack, pincers, pliers, protractor, punch, rule, sander, scriber, snips, socket-wrench, soldering-iron, spraygun, tommy bar, vice, wrench; auger, awl, bevel, brace and bit, bradawl, chisel, file, fretsaw, hammer, handsaw, jack-plane, jig-saw, level, mallet, plane, rasp, saw, screwdriver, set-square, spirit level, tenon-saw, T-square; billhook, chainsaw, chopper, dibber, fork, grass-rake, hay fork, hoe, pitchfork, plough, pruning-knife, pruning-shears, rake, scythe, secateurs, shears, shovel, sickle, spade, thresher, trowel; needle, scissors, pinking-shears, bodkin, crochet hook, forceps, scalpel, tweezers, tongs, cleaver, steel, gimlet, mace, mortar, pestle, paper-cutter, paper-knife, stapler, pocket-knife, penknife

► *v* work, machine, cut, shape, decorate, fashion, ornament, chase

tooth *n*
cog, denticle, denticulation, dentil, fang, incisor, jag, masticator, molar, prong, tush, tusk

Types of tooth include:
baby tooth, back tooth, bicuspid, bucktooth, canine, carnassial, dog-tooth, eye tooth, fang, first tooth, gold tooth, grinder, incisor, central incisor, lateral incisor, milk tooth, molar, first molar, second molar, third molar, premolar, first premolar, second premolar, snaggletooth, tush, tusk, wisdom tooth; false tooth, false teeth, bridge, cap, crown, denture, dentures, plate.

toothsome *adj*
appetizing, delicious, tasty, tempting, mouth-watering, palatable, nice, agreeable, flavoursome, sweet, luscious, savoury, dainty, delectable, *colloq.* scrumptious, yummy
◼ disagreeable, unpleasant

top *n, adj, v*
▶ *n* **1** HEAD, tip, highest point, apex, crest, crown, peak, pinnacle, summit, climax, culmination, height, *technical* vertex, acme, zenith, apogee **2** LID, cap, cover, cork, stopper **3** *a sleeveless top* blouse, shirt, sweatshirt, T-shirt, tee shirt, jumper, jersey, sweater, pullover, tank top, smock
◼ **1** bottom, base, nadir **3** bottoms
▷ **on top of the world** thrilled, happy, overjoyed, ecstatic, elated, exhilarated, exultant, *colloq.* on cloud nine, over the moon
▷ **over the top** excessive, immoderate, inordinate, extreme, too much, undue, uncalled-for, disproportionate, unreasonable, lavish, exorbitant, extravagant, *colloq.* a bit much
▶ *adj* highest, topmost, upmost, uppermost, upper, superior, head, chief, leading, main, first, foremost, principal, sovereign, ruling, pre-eminent, dominant, prime, paramount, utmost, greatest, maximum, best, finest, supreme, crowning, culminating
◼ bottom, lowest, inferior
▶ *v* **1** TIP, cap, crown, cover, finish (off), decorate, garnish **2** BEAT, exceed, outstrip, better, excel, best, surpass, eclipse, outshine, outdo, surmount, transcend **3** HEAD, lead, be first in, rule, command
▷ **top up** refill, recharge, reload, add to, supplement, increase, boost, *formal* replenish, augment

topic *n*
subject, subject matter, theme, issue, question, argument, matter, point, talking point, thesis, text

topical *adj*
current, contemporary, up-to-date, up-to-the-minute, recent, newsworthy, relevant, popular, familiar

topmost *adj*
uppermost, highest, loftiest, top, upper, supreme, first, leading, foremost, principal, maximum, paramount, dominant, *technical* apical
◼ bottom, bottommost, lowest

top-notch *adj*
first rate, first-class, second-to-none, matchless, peerless, top, top-flight, leading, supreme, superior, prime, excellent, outstanding, superlative, premier, exceptional, splendid, superb, fine, admirable, *colloq.* super, A1, ace, crack, out of this world

topple *v*
1 OVERBALANCE, totter, tumble, fall (over), collapse, upset, tip over, knock over/down, keel over, overturn, capsize **2** OVERTHROW, oust, bring down, unseat, displace, dethrone

topsy-turvy *adj*
confused, in confusion, jumbled, chaotic, inside out, upside down, disorganized, disarranged, disorderly, in disorder, untidy, mixed-up, messy
◼ ordered, tidy

torch *n*
light, firebrand, brand, flambeau, *US* flashlight

torment *n, v*
▶ *n* **1** ANGUISH, distress, misery, affliction, suffering, pain, agony, ordeal, worry, torture, persecution **2** ANNOYANCE, provocation, irritation, vexation, bane, scourge, curse, pest, trouble, bother, nuisance, harassment, worry, *colloq.* thorn in the flesh, pain in the neck
▶ *v* **1** AFFLICT, plague, distress, trouble, distress, harrow, pain, torture, persecute **2** ANNOY, tease, provoke, irritate, vex, trouble, worry, harass, hound, pester, bother, plague, badger, bedevil

torn *adj*
1 CUT, ragged, ripped, slit, split, rent, lacerated **2** DIVIDED, uncertain, undecided, unsure, irresolute, vacillating, wavering, dithering

tornado *n*
storm, cyclone, gale, hurricane, whirlwind, typhoon, monsoon, tempest, squall, *colloq.* twister

torpid *adj*
sluggish, lethargic, slow, dull, lifeless, inert, inactive, apathetic, lazy, passive, listless, drowsy, sleepy, dead, deadened, numb, nerveless, insensible, *formal* languorous, somnolent, supine, indolent
◼ active, lively, vigorous

torpor *n*
torpidity, sluggishness, lethargy, listlessness, slowness, dullness, lifelessness, inactivity, inertia, inertness, drowsiness, sleepiness, numbness, apathy, laziness, passivity, sloth, *formal* indolence, languor, somnolence, hebetude
◼ activity, vigour, enthusiasm

torrent *n*
1 *torrent of water* stream, gush, rush, flood, storm, outburst, volley, barrage, inundation, spate, deluge, cascade, downpour **2** *a torrent of abuse* outburst, volley, barrage, stream, gush, rush, flood, storm, inundation, spate, deluge
◼ **1, 2** trickle

torrid *adj*
1 HOT, blazing, sweltering, blistering, boiling, sizzling, scorching, tropical, stifling, arid, parched, scorched, waterless, desert **2** PASSIONATE, erotic, red-hot, sexy, amorous, *colloq.* steamy

tortuous *adj*
1 *a tortuous road* twisting, winding, meandering, curving, serpentine, zigzag, circuitous, roundabout, indirect, *formal* sinuous **2** COMPLICATED, involved, serpentine, zigzag, circuitous, roundabout, indirect, *formal* convoluted
◼ **1** straight **2** straightforward

torture *v, n*
▶ *v* pain, agonize, excruciate, crucify, rack, martyr, persecute, abuse, ill-treat, mistreat, torment, harrow, plague, punish, afflict, worry, distress, trouble
▶ *n* pain, agony, suffering, affliction, distress, punishment, misery, anguish, torment, abuse, ill-treatment, mistreatment, martyrdom, persecution

toss *v, n*
▶ *v* **1** FLIP, cast, fling, throw, pitch, heave, sling, hurl, lob, shy, *colloq.* chuck **2** ROLL, heave, sway, pitch, lurch, jolt, shake, jerk, agitate, rock, thrash, squirm, writhe, wriggle
▶ *n* flip, cast, fling, throw, pitch, *colloq.* chuck

tot¹ *n*
1 TODDLER, child, infant, mite, baby, *Scot.* bairn **2** *a tot of whisky* DRAM, measure, nip, shot, slug, finger

tot² *v*
▷ **tot up** add (up), calculate, compute, count (up),

reckon, mount (up), sum, tally, total

total *n, adj, v*
▶ *n* sum, whole, entirety, grand total, subtotal, totality, all, lot, mass, amount, *formal* aggregate
▶ *adj* full, complete, entire, whole, comprehensive, integral, all-out, utter, absolute, unconditional, unqualified, outright, undisputed, perfect, thoroughgoing, rank, sheer, downright, thorough, *formal* consummate, unmitigated
🠶 partial, limited, restricted
▶ *v* add (up), sum (up), tot (up), count (up), reckon, amount to, come to, reach, make

totalitarian *adj*
authoritarian, one-party, despotic, dictatorial, oppressive, tyrannous, monolithic, undemocratic, *formal* omnipotent, monocratic
🠶 democratic

totality *n*
total, sum, whole, wholeness, entirety, entireness, everything, fullness, completeness, all, cosmos, universe, *formal* aggregate, pleroma

totally *adv*
completely, fully, wholly, entirely, perfectly, utterly, quite, thoroughly, wholeheartedly, absolutely, unconditionally, comprehensively, undividedly, undisputedly, *formal* consummately, unmitigatedly
🠶 partially

totter *v*
1 STAGGER, waddle, move unsteadily, reel, lurch, stumble, falter, waver, teeter, sway, roll, rock, shake, wobble, quiver, tremble 2 *the economy is tottering* be unstable, be unsteady, be insecure, be shaky, be precarious, be about to collapse, *colloq.* wobble

touch *v, n*
▶ *v* 1 FEEL, handle, hold, finger, run your finger over, brush, skim, graze, stroke, caress, fondle, pet, tickle, pat, tap, hit, strike, contact 2 ADJOIN, bring/come into contact, meet, abut, border, impinge, *formal* be contiguous to 3 MOVE, stir, upset, sadden, disturb, impress, inspire, influence, affect, have an effect on, have an influence/impact on, involve, concern, regard 4 EQUAL, match, rival, better, come near, approach, *colloq.* hold a candle to 5 REACH, attain, make, come to, *colloq.* hit 6 *not touch alcohol* consume, use, eat, drink, take, devour 7 MENTION, broach, speak of, remark on, refer to, allude to, cover, deal with
▷ **touch off** spark off, trigger (off), begin, cause, set off, initiate, provoke, foment, fire, ignite, inflame, light, arouse, *formal* actuate
▷ **touch up** renovate, improve, brush up, retouch, revamp, enhance, finish off, round off, patch up, perfect, polish up
▶ *n* 1 FEEL, brush, stroke, caress, pat, tap, blow, hit, contact, tactility 2 TEXTURE, feel, surface, finish, grain, weave 3 SKILL, art, knack, flair, craftsmanship, dexterity, style, method, manner, technique, approach, direction 4 *finishing touches* DETAIL, feature, point, addition, aspect, nicety, minutiae 5 *keep/lose touch* contact, communication, correspondence, connection, association 6 *a touch of garlic* trace, spot, dash, pinch, taste, soupçon, suspicion, hint, suggestion, bit, speck, jot, tinge, smack, *colloq.* whiff

touch-and-go *adj*
close, critical, dangerous, uncertain, hazardous, near, nerve-racking, offhand, perilous, dire, precarious, risky, sticky, tricky, *formal* parlous, *colloq.* dodgy, hairy

touched *adj*
1 MOVED, stirred, inspired, influenced, affected, impressed, disturbed, upset 2 MAD, crazy, insane, de-

ranged, disturbed, eccentric, unbalanced, *colloq.* dotty, daft, barmy, nutty, bonkers, batty, loopy

touchiness *n*
bad temper, irritability, grouchiness, grumpiness, irascibility, peevishness, pettishness, surliness, testiness, tetchiness, petulance, crabbedness, captiousness

touching *adj*
moving, stirring, impressive, affecting, upsetting, disturbing, poignant, pitiable, pitiful, heart-breaking, heart-rending, pathetic, sad, emotional, tender, *formal* piteous

touchstone *n*
criterion, standard, test, norm, proof, measure, gauge, guide, model, pattern, template, benchmark, yardstick

touchy *adj*
irritable, bad-tempered, quick-tempered, grumpy, cross, over-sensitive, thin-skinned, peevish, grouchy, crabbed, captious, irascible, *colloq.* edgy, prickly
🠶 calm, imperturbable

tough *adj, n*
▶ *adj* 1 STRONG, durable, resilient, resistant, firm, hardy, sturdy, solid, rigid, stiff, inflexible, hard, leathery 2 *tough criminal* rough, violent, disorderly, rowdy, vicious, callous, hardened, obstinate 3 HARSH, severe, strict, stern, firm, resolute, adamant, determined, tenacious, unyielding, uncompromising 4 ARDUOUS, strenuous, laborious, exacting, hard, taxing, grim, difficult, puzzling, perplexing, baffling, knotty, thorny, troublesome, *colloq.* uphill 5 FIT, muscular, hardy, burly, well-built, robust, sturdy, rugged, vigorous, stalwart 6 *the meat is tough* rubbery, chewy, fibrous, gristly, *colloq.* tough as leather 7 *tough luck* hard, unpleasant, unfortunate, unlucky, uncomfortable, distressing
🠶 1 fragile, delicate, weak, tender 2 gentle, soft 3 gentle 4 easy, simple 5 weak 6 tender 7 good
▶ *n* brute, thug, bully, ruffian, hooligan, lout, bully, rowdy, roughneck, *slang* yob

toughen *v*
strengthen, harden, reinforce, brace, stiffen, consolidate, substantiate, make stricter, *formal* fortify

toughness *n*
strength, resilience, resistance, firmness, hardiness, sturdiness, tenacity, determination, inflexibility, ruggedness, obduracy, *colloq.* grit
🠶 weakness, vulnerability, softness, liberality

tour *n, v*
▶ *n* circuit, round, visit, expedition, journey, trip, outing, excursion, inspection, drive, ride, jaunt, course, *formal* peregrination, *colloq.* walkabout
▶ *v* visit, go round, sightsee, explore, travel round, journey through, drive through, ride

tourist *n*
holidaymaker, visitor, sightseer, tripper, day-tripper, excursionist, traveller, voyager, globetrotter, *formal* sojourner, *US slang* rubberneck

tournament *n*
championship, series, competition, contest, match, event, meeting, meet, joust

tousled *adj*
dishevelled, ruffled, messed up, disordered, disarranged, tangled, rumpled, tumbled

tout *v*
1 SELL, hawk, peddle, trade 2 ADVERTISE, promote, market, solicit, petition, ask, appeal, seek, *colloq.* plug, hype, push

tow *v, n*
▶ *v* pull, tug, draw, trail, drag, lug, haul, transport
▶ *n* pull, tug, haul, trail, lug

▷ **in tow** following closely, accompanying, by your side, in convoy

towards *prep*
1 TO, in the direction of, on the way to, approaching, nearing, close to, nearly, almost, -wards 2 *his feelings towards her* regarding, with regard to, with respect to, concerning, about, for

tower *v*
rise, rear, ascend, mount, soar, loom, overlook, dominate, surpass, transcend, overshadow, eclipse, exceed, excel, top, cap

towering *adj*
1 HIGH, soaring, tall, lofty, elevated, monumental, colossal, gigantic, great 2 MAGNIFICENT, imposing, impressive, outstanding, sublime, supreme, incomparable, unrivalled, surpassing, overpowering, extraordinary, extreme, inordinate
🔁 1 low, small, tiny 2 minor, trivial

town *n*
borough, village, municipality, burgh, market town, county town, new town, city, suburbs, outskirts, conurbation, metropolis, urban district, settlement, township, pueblo
🔁 country

town-dweller *n*
citizen, townsman, townswoman, burgher, urbanite, *formal* oppidan, *colloq.* towny
🔁 country-dweller, rustic

toxic *adj*
poisonous, harmful, noxious, unhealthy, dangerous, deadly, lethal, baneful
🔁 harmless, safe

toy *n, v*
▶ *n* plaything, knick-knack, trinket, trifle, bauble

Kinds of toy include:
Action Man®, activity centre, aeroplane, baby-bouncer, baby-walker, ball, balloon; bicycle, *colloq.* bike, mountain bike; blackboard and easel, boxing-gloves, building-block, building-brick, catapult, climbing-frame, computer game, crayon; doll, Barbie doll®, kewpie doll, rag-doll, Sindy doll®, Tiny-Tears doll®, doll's buggy, doll's cot, doll's house, doll's pram; drum set, electronic game, executive toy, farm, fivestones, football, fort, Frisbee®, game, garage, glove puppet, go-kart, guitar, gun, cap-gun, pop-gun, gyroscope, hobby-horse, hula-hoop, jack-in-the-box, jigsaw puzzle, kaleidoscope, kite, box-kite, Lego®, marble, Matchbox®, Meccano®, model car, model kit, model railway, modelling clay, musical box, ocarina, paddling-pool, paints, pantograph, pedal-car, peashooter, Plasticene®, Play-Doh®, playhouse, pogo stick, Pokémon®, Power Rangers®, puzzle, rattle, rocker, rocking-horse, Rubik's Cube®, sandpit, Scalextric®, scooter, seesaw, sewing machine, shape-sorter, skateboard, skipping-rope, slide, soft-toy, spacehopper, Space Invaders®, spinning top, Subbuteo®, swing, swingball, teaset, teddy-bear, toy soldier, train set, trampoline, tricycle, *colloq.* trike, Turtles®, typewriter; video game, Game Boy®, Dreamcast®, Nintendo®, Sega®, Super Mario®; *colloq.* walkie-talkie, water pistol, Wendy house, yo-yo. *See also* GAME.

▶ *v* play, tinker, fiddle, sport, trifle, dally, flirt, *colloq.* mess about/around

trace *n, v*
▶ *n* 1 *leave traces of blood* hint, suggestion, suspicion, soupçon, dash, pinch, drop, spot, bit, jot, touch, tinge, shadow, smack 2 MARK, token, sign, indication, evidence, record, relic, remains, remnant, vestige, trail, track, spoor, footprint, footmark, scent
▶ *v* 1 FIND, discover, detect, unearth, track (down), uncover, dig up, trail, track, stalk, hunt, seek, follow, pursue, dog, shadow, *colloq.* run down 2 COPY, draw, draft, sketch, outline, show, depict, mark (out), record, map, chart, *formal* delineate

track *n, v*
▶ *n* 1 WAY, rail, path, way, route, orbit, line, trail, trajectory, slot, groove, course, drift, sequence, argument 2 FOOTPRINT, footstep, footmark, scent, spoor, trail, wake, mark, trace
▷ **keep track of** monitor, check, watch, follow, observe, record, keep an eye on
🔁 lose track of
▷ **make tracks** leave, go, depart, make off, dash (off), disappear, *colloq.* scram, beat it, hit the road
▶ *v* stalk, trail, hunt, trace, follow, pursue, chase, dog, tail, shadow
▷ **track down** find, discover, trace, hunt down, run to earth, nose out, sniff out, ferret out, turn up, dig up, uncover, unearth, expose, catch, capture, *colloq.* run down

tract *n*
1 *a tract of land* stretch, extent, expanse, plot, lot, territory, area, region, zone, district, quarter 2 *a religious tract* booklet, leaflet, brochure, pamphlet, treatise, sermon, essay, dissertation, homily, discourse, monograph, *formal* disquisition

tractable *adj*
pliant, pliable, manageable, obedient, persuadable, willing, submissive, docile, controllable, amenable, biddable, governable, malleable, compliant, yielding, workable, tame, tractile, *formal* complaisant
🔁 headstrong, intractable, obstinate, refractory, stubborn, unruly, wilful

traction *n*
drawing, pull, pulling, haulage, propulsion, drag, draught, grip, friction, adhesion

trade *n, v*
▶ *n* 1 COMMERCE, traffic, trafficking, business, dealing, buying, selling, marketing, shopkeeping, barter, exchange, switch, swap, transactions, custom 2 OCCUPATION, employment, job, work, business, line (of work), profession, career, calling, vocation, métier, craft, skill
▶ *v* do business, deal, transact, buy, sell, run, traffic, peddle, market, merchandise, barter, exchange, swap, switch, bargain

trademark *n*
1 *a registered trademark* brand, brand name, trade-name, proprietary name, proprietary brand, label, name, sign, symbol, logo, insignia, crest, emblem, badge 2 HALLMARK, stamp, mark, speciality, typical quality, (distinctive) feature, attribute, characteristic, idiosyncrasy, peculiarity, quirk

trader *n*
merchant, tradesman, tradeswoman, broker, dealer, buyer, seller, marketeer, marketer, vendor, supplier, wholesaler, retailer, shopkeeper, trafficker, peddler

tradesman, tradeswoman *n*
1 SHOPKEEPER, retailer, buyer, seller, merchant, dealer, vendor 2 ARTISAN, craftsman, craftswoman, worker, mechanic, journeyman

tradition *n*
convention, custom, belief, ceremony, usage, way, habit, routine, practice, observance, ritual, rite, insti-

tution, folklore, *formal* praxis

traditional *adj*
conventional, customary, habitual, usual, routine, accustomed, ceremonial, established, fixed, set, long-established, time-honoured, old, age-old, historic, folk, oral, unwritten
F3 unconventional, innovative, new, modern, contemporary

traduce *v*
misrepresent, slander, revile, deprecate, decry, defame, blacken, abuse, insult, malign, smear, *formal* disparage, detract, asperse, denigrate, depreciate, calumniate, vilify, *colloq.* knock, run down, slag

traducer *n*
defamer, slanderer, disparager, abuser, smearer, *formal* asperser, calumniator, denigrator, deprecator, detractor, vilifier, *colloq.* knocker, mud-slinger

traffic *n, v*
▶ *n* **1** VEHICLES, cars, shipping, transport, transportation, freight, passengers **2** TRADE, commerce, business, dealing, trading, trafficking, buying and selling, peddling, barter, exchange **3** COMMUNICATION, dealings, relations, contact, *formal* intercourse
▶ *v* peddle, buy, sell, trade, do business, deal, peddle, bargain, barter, exchange

trafficker *n*
dealer, merchant, trader, broker, peddler, monger

tragedy *n*
adversity, misfortune, unhappiness, affliction, blow, calamity, disaster, catastrophe
F3 success, triumph

tragic *adj*
calamitous, disastrous, catastrophic, deadly, fatal, sad, sorrowful, miserable, terrible, unhappy, unfortunate, wretched, unlucky, ill-fated, pitiable, pathetic, heartbreaking, shocking, appalling, dreadful, awful, deplorable, dire
F3 happy, comic, successful

trail *n, v*
▶ *n* track, path, footpath, road, route, way, wake, footprints, footmarks, scent, spoor, sign, trace
▶ *v* **1** DRAG, pull, tow, haul, draw, droop, dangle, hang, extend, reach, stream, sweep, straggle, dawdle, lag, loiter, linger **2** TRACK, stalk, hunt, follow, pursue, chase, dog, shadow, tail
▷ **trail away** decrease, die away, diminish, disappear, dwindle, fade (away), fall away, melt away, lessen, peter out, shrink, sink, subside, tail off, taper off, trail off, weaken

train *n, v*
▶ *n* **1** *a train of events* sequence, succession, series, progression, order, set, suite, string, chain, trail, line, path, track, stream, file, procession, column, convoy, cortège, caravan, *formal* concatenation **2** RETINUE, entourage, attendants, court, household, staff, followers, following, cortège
▶ *v* **1** TEACH, instruct, coach, tutor, educate, improve, school, indoctrinate, discipline, prepare, drill, ground, exercise, work out, practise, rehearse, groom, *formal* inculcate **2** LEARN, study, be trained, be taught, be prepared **3** POINT, direct, aim, focus, level

trainer *n*
teacher, instructor, coach, tutor, handler, educator

training *n*
teaching, instruction, coaching, tuition, tutoring, education, schooling, learning, lessons, discipline, preparation, grounding, drill, exercise, workout, working-out, practice, learning, apprenticeship

traipse *v, n*
▶ *v* trudge, tramp, plod, slouch, trail

▶ *n* trudge, trek, slog, plod, tramp

trait *n*
feature, attribute, quality, property, characteristic, idiosyncrasy, peculiarity, quirk

traitor *n*
betrayer, informer, deceiver, double-crosser, double-dealer, turncoat, renegade, deserter, defector, quisling, collaborator, fifth columnist, Judas, *colloq.* backstabber, two-timer
F3 loyalist, supporter, defender

traitorous *adj*
disloyal, unfaithful, faithless, false, untrue, treasonable, dishonourable, double-crossing, renegade, double-dealing, treacherous, apostate, *formal* perfidious, seditious
F3 faithful, loyal, patriotic

trajectory *n*
line, orbit, path, route, flight, flight path, course, track, trail

trammel *n, v*
▶ *n* bar, block, bond, fetter, rein, shackle, check, clog, chain, hamper, curb, handicap, hindrance, impediment, obstacle, stumbling-block
▶ *v* bar, block, clog, restrict, restrain, fetter, catch, check, tie, enmesh, ensnare, entrap, shackle, inhibit, impede, hinder, handicap, hamper, curb, capture, net

tramp *n, v*
▶ *n* **1** VAGRANT, vagabond, hobo, down-and-out, derelict, *slang* dosser, bum **2** TRUDGE, march, tread, walk, trek, hike, ramble
▶ *v* walk, march, tread, stamp, stomp, stump, plod, trudge, traipse, trail, trek, hike, ramble, roam, rove

trample *v*
tread, stamp, crush, squash, flatten, compress, pound, mangle, pulp, pulverize

trance *n*
dream, reverie, daze, stupor, unconsciousness, catalepsy, spell, ecstasy, rapture

tranquil *adj*
calm, peaceful, quiet, serene, composed, cool, imperturbable, unexcited, even-tempered, placid, sedate, relaxed, restful, still, undisturbed, untroubled, silent, hushed, *formal* reposeful, *colloq.* laid-back, unflappable
F3 agitated, disturbed, troubled, noisy

tranquillity *n*
calm, peace, peacefulness, serenity, calmness, composure, quiet, quietness, rest, restfulness, stillness, hush, silence, imperturbability, coolness, equanimity, sedateness, placidity, *technical* ataraxia, ataraxy, *formal* quietude, repose
F3 disturbance, agitation, noise

tranquillize *v*
calm, quiet, pacify, relax, sedate, soothe, quell, lull, compose, *technical* narcotize, opiate
F3 disturb, agitate, upset

tranquillizer *n*
sedative, calmative, sleeping pill, opiate, narcotic, barbiturate, *colloq.* downer

transact *v*
carry out, conduct, do, perform, settle, handle, manage, carry on, accomplish, negotiate, conclude, dispatch, discharge, enact, execute, *formal* prosecute

transaction *n*
1 *bank transactions* deal, bargain, agreement, arrangement, negotiation, business, affair, matter, proceeding, enterprise, undertaking, deed, action, handling, settlement, enactment, execution, discharge **2** *the transactions of a learned society* reports, proceedings, record, minutes, concerns, annals, affairs,

doings, *colloq.* goings-on

transcend *v*
surpass, excel, outshine, eclipse, outdo, outstrip, leave behind, beat, surmount, exceed, go beyond, rise above, overstep

transcendence *n*
transcendency, superiority, supremacy, predominance, pre-eminence, incomparability, matchlessness, paramoun(t)cy, excellence, greatness, *formal* ascendancy, sublimity

transcendent *adj*
1 SURPASSING, supreme, sublime, superlative, excelling, excellent, magnificent, incomparable, matchless, peerless, unparalleled, unsurpassable **2** SUPERHUMAN, supernatural, spiritual, *formal* ineffable, numinous

transcendental *adj*
supernatural, spiritual, otherworldly, metaphysical, mystical, mysterious, *formal* preternatural

transcribe *v*
write out, write up, copy out, copy up, reproduce, rewrite, transliterate, translate, render, take down, note, record

transcript *n*
transcription, copy, reproduction, duplicate, transliteration, translation, version, note, record, manuscript

transfer *v, n*
▶ *v* **1** CHANGE, transpose, move, shift, remove, relocate, transplant, transport, carry, take, convey **2** *transfer land* assign, convey, transmit, consign, grant, hand over
▶ *n* change, changeover, transposition, move, shift, removal, relocation, displacement, transmission, handover, assignment, transference, *technical* conveyance

transfigure *v*
transform, change, alter, convert, exalt, glorify, idealize, *formal* transmute, translate, metamorphose, apotheosize

transfix *v*
1 FASCINATE, spellbind, mesmerize, hypnotize, paralyse, stun, hold, engross, rivet, petrify **2** IMPALE, pierce, run through, spear, skewer, spike, stick

transform *v*
change, alter, adapt, convert, remodel, rebuilt, reconstruct, renew, transfigure, revolutionize, *formal* transmute, metamorphose, *colloq.* transmogrify
☲ preserve, maintain

transformation *n*
change, alteration, conversion, transfiguration, revolution, *technical* metastasis, *formal* mutation, transmutation, metamorphosis, *colloq.* sea change, transmogrification
☲ preservation, conservation

transfuse *v*
transfer, imbue, pervade, instil, permeate, suffuse

transgress *v*
break, offend, sin, contravene, disobey, misbehave, overstep, exceed, violate, breach, defy, infringe, encroach, lapse, err, *formal* trespass
☲ keep, obey

transgression *n*
wrong, wrongdoing, offence, infringement, lapse, crime, sin, violation, fault, error, iniquity, misdeed, peccadillo, misbehaviour, misdemeanour, breach, contravention, encroachment, debt, *formal* infraction, trespass

transgressor *n*
lawbreaker, offender, wrongdoer, evil-doer, criminal, culprit, delinquent, debtor, miscreant, felon, sinner, villain, *formal* trespasser, malefactor

transience *n*
transitoriness, shortness, briefness, brevity, impermanence, deciduousness, *technical* caducity, *formal* ephemerality, evanescence, fugacity, fugitiveness, *colloq.* fleetingness
☲ permanence

transient *adj*
transitory, passing, flying, fleeting, brief, short, momentary, short-lived, temporary, short-term, impermanent, *formal* ephemeral, evanescent, fugacious
☲ lasting, permanent

transit *n*
passage, journey, journeying, travel, crossing, route, movement, transfer, transportation, conveyance, carriage, haulage, shipment
▷ **in transit** en route, on the way, travelling, by road, by rail, by air, by sea

transition *n*
passage, passing, progress, progression, development, evolution, move, movement, flux, change, change-over, alteration, conversion, transformation, shift, switch, *formal* metamorphosis, transmutation

transitional *adj*
provisional, temporary, passing, intermediate, developmental, evolutionary, changing, fluid, unsettled
☲ initial, final

transitory *adj*
transient, passing, flying, fleeting, brief, short, momentary, short-lived, temporary, short-term, impermanent, *formal* ephemeral, evanescent, fugacious
☲ lasting, permanent

translate *v*
1 *translate into German* put, render, paraphrase, reword, explain, interpret, simplify, decode, decipher, transliterate, transcribe, *formal* construe **2** CHANGE, alter, convert, transform, improve, move, transfer, relocate, shift, *formal* transmute, *colloq.* transmogrify

translation *n*
1 *a translation from Spanish* rendering, version, rendition, explanation, interpretation, gloss, crib, rewording, rephrasing, paraphrase, simplification, transliteration, transcription, *formal* metaphrasis **2** CHANGE, alteration, conversion, transformation, move, transfer, shift, *formal* transmutation, metamorphosis, *colloq.* transmogrification

translator *n*
linguist, polyglot, paraphraser, interpreter, glosser, dragoman, *formal* exegete, exegetist, glossarist, glossator, metaphrast, paraphrast

translucent *adj*
transparent, clear, see-through, pellucid, translucid, limpid, *formal* diaphanous
☲ opaque

transmigration *n*
transformation, rebirth, reincarnation, *formal* metempsychosis, Pythagoreanism

transmission *n*
1 BROADCASTING, diffusion, spread, communication, conveyance, carriage, transport, shipment, sending, dispatch, relaying, transfer, transference, imparting, *formal* dissemination **2** *a live transmission* broadcast, programme, show, performance, production, presentation, episode, simulcast, signal
☲ **1** reception

transmit *v*
communicate, impart, convey, carry, bear, impart, transport, send, pass on, dispatch, forward, relay, transfer, broadcast, radio, network, diffuse, spread, *formal* disseminate, remit
☲ receive

transmute *v*
transform, alter, change, convert, remake, transfigure, transverse, *formal* metamorphose, translate, *colloq.* transmogrify
▪ retain

transparency *n*
1 CLEARNESS, clarity, translucence, translucency, sheerness, gauziness, filminess, pellucidity, pellucidness, perspicuousness, limpidity, limpidness, translucidity, water, *formal* diaphanousness **2** PLAINNESS, clearness, clarity, obviousness, apparentness, distinctness, unambiguousness, straightforwardness, directness, openness, patentness, frankness, forthrightness, explicitness, candidness **3** *holiday transparencies* slide, photograph, photo, picture
▪ **1** opacity **2** ambiguity, unclearness

transparent *adj*
1 *transparent plastic* clear, see-through, translucent, sheer, pellucid, diaphanous, gauzy, filmy **2** PLAIN, distinct, clear, lucid, explicit, unambiguous, unequivocal, unmistakable, apparent, visible, obvious, noticeable, discernible, perceptible, evident, patent, undisguised, open, direct, forthright, candid, straightforward, *formal* manifest
▪ **1** opaque **2** unclear, ambiguous

transpire *v*
1 BECOME KNOWN, turn out, come to light, come out, be disclosed, become apparent, appear, prove **2** HAPPEN, occur, take place, ensue, arise, come about, come to pass, *formal* befall

transplant *v*
move, shift, displace, remove, uproot, graft, transfer, relocate, resettle, repot, replant
▪ leave

transport *v, n*
▸ *v* **1** CONVEY, carry, bear, take, fetch, bring, move, run, shift, transfer, ship, haul, remove, deport, exile **2** DELIGHT, enrapture, entrance, captivate, electrify, spellbind, *colloq.* carry away
▸ *n* **1** CONVEYANCE, transit, vehicle, carriage, transfer, transportation, shipment, shipping, haulage, freight, removal **2** *transports of delight* rapture, ecstasy, bliss, euphoria, elation, exhilaration, frenzy, fit, *colloq.* seventh heaven

transportation *n*
conveyance, transit, carriage, transfer, shipment, shipping, haulage, freight

transpose *v*
swap, exchange, switch, interchange, transfer, shift, invert, rearrange, reorder, change, convert, alter, move, substitute

transverse *adj*
cross, crossways, crosswise, transversal, diagonal, oblique

trap *n*
▸ *n* snare, net, mesh, noose, springe, gin, boobytrap, pitfall, danger, hazard, ambush, trick, wile, ruse, stratagem, device, trickery, ploy, artifice, subterfuge, deception
▸ *v* snare, net, entrap, ensnare, enmesh, confine, catch, take, ambush, lure, beguile, corner, trick, deceive, dupe, *formal* inveigle

trapped *adj*
caught, beguiled, cornered, ensnared, ambushed, snared, stuck, netted, surrounded, tricked, deceived, duped, *formal* inveigled
▪ free

trappings *n*
ornaments, accompaniments, clothes, adornments, dress, decorations, fripperies, equipment, paraphernalia, fixtures, fittings, furnishings, housings, finery,
livery, gear, trimmings, *formal* accoutrements, panoply, raiment, *colloq.* things

trash *n*
1 RUBBISH, garbage, refuse, junk, waste, litter, sweepings, offscourings, scum, dregs **2** NONSENSE, rubbish, garbage, junk, drivel, balderdash, gibberish, gobbledygook, *colloq.* bunk, rot, tripe, bull **3** UNDESIRABLES, riff-raff, rabble, scum, dregs, *canaille*

trashy *adj*
rubbishy, worthless, shabby, tawdry, tinsel, flimsy, third-rate, cheap, cheap-jack, kitschy, shoddy, inferior, *formal* meretricious, *colloq.* grotty, naff
▪ first-rate

trauma *n*
injury, wound, hurt, lesion, damage, pain, suffering, anguish, agony, torture, distress, ordeal, shock, disorder, jolt, upset, disturbance, upheaval, strain, stress
▪ healing

traumatic *adj*
painful, harmful, hurtful, injurious, wounding, shocking, agonizing, upsetting, distressing, disturbing, unpleasant, frightening, stressful
▪ healing, relaxing

travail *n*
1 TOIL, hardship, exertion, effort, drudgery, slog, strain, stress, suffering, distress, grind, tears, sweat, *formal* tribulation **2** LABOUR PAINS, childbirth, birthpangs, labour, throes
▪ rest

travel *v, n*
▸ *v* journey, voyage, tour, make a trip, explore, go, go abroad/overseas, wend, make your way, move, advance, proceed, progress, wander, ramble, roam, rove, tour, cover, cross, traverse, *colloq.* see the world
▪ stay, remain

Methods of travel include:
fly, aviate, pilot, shuttle, sail, cruise, punt, paddle, row, steam, ride, cycle, *colloq.* bike, freewheel, drive, motor, bus, tour, walk, hike, march, ramble, trek, orienteer, hitch-hike, commute.

Forms of travel include:
flight, cruise, sail, voyage, ride, drive, march, walk, hike, ramble, excursion, holiday, jaunt, outing, tour, trip, visit, expedition, safari, trek, circumnavigation, exploration, journey, migration, mission, pilgrimage.

▸ *n* **1** TRAVELLING, touring, journeying, tourism, *colloq.* globetrotting **2** *travels abroad* voyage, expedition, passage, journey, trip, excursion, sightseeing, tour, wanderings, *colloq.* globetrotting

traveller *n*
1 TOURIST, explorer, voyager, globetrotter, sightseer, holidaymaker, tourer, excursionist, passenger, commuter, wanderer, rambler, hiker, *colloq.* tripper **2** WANDERER, wayfarer, migrant, nomad, gypsy, itinerant, tinker, vagrant, tramp, drifter **3** SALES REPRESENTATIVE, salesman, saleswoman, representative, commercial traveller, agent, *colloq.* rep

travelling *adj*
touring, wandering, roaming, roving, wayfaring, migrating, migrant, migratory, nomadic, itinerant, mobile, moving, vagrant, homeless, unsettled, *formal* peripatetic
▪ fixed, settled

travel-worn *adj*
weary, tired, jet-lagged, saddle-sore, travel-weary, footsore, waygone, wayworn
▪ fresh

traverse v
cross, pass over/through, go across/through, travel across/through, negotiate, bridge, span, ford, ply, range, roam, wander, *formal* peregrinate

travesty n
mockery, parody, burlesque, farce, caricature, perversion, corruption, distortion, misrepresentation, sham, apology, *colloq.* take-off, send-up, wind-up, spoof, tall story

treacherous adj
1 TRAITOROUS, disloyal, unfaithful, faithless, unreliable, untrustworthy, false, untrue, deceitful, *formal* duplicitous, perfidious, *colloq.* double-crossing, back-stabbing, two-timing 2 *treacherous roads* dangerous, hazardous, risky, perilous, precarious, unsafe, icy, slippery
🔁 1 loyal, faithful, dependable 2 safe, stable

treacherously adv
deceitfully, falsely, disloyally, faithlessly, *formal* perfidiously
🔁 loyally

treachery n
treason, betrayal, sabotage, unfaithfulness, faithlessness, disloyalty, infidelity, falseness, deceitfulness, *formal* duplicity, perfidity, *colloq.* double-dealing, double-crossing, back-stabbing, two-timing
🔁 loyalty, dependability

tread v, n
▶ v walk, step, pace, stride, march, go, hike, trek, tramp, trudge, plod, stamp, trample, walk on, press (down), crush, squash, flatten
▷ **tread on someone's toes** offend, hurt, upset, vex, irk, annoy, infringe, injure, affront, bruise, inconvenience, *formal* discommode, *colloq.* disgruntle
🔁 soothe
▶ n walk, footstep, step, pace, stride, tramp, gait, footprint, footmark, footfall

treason n
treachery, disloyalty, subversion, mutiny, rebellion, disaffection, lese-majesty, *formal* perfidy, duplicity, sedition
🔁 loyalty

treasonable adj
traitorous, disloyal, false, unfaithful, faithless, subversive, seditious, mutinous, rebellious, *formal* perfidious
🔁 loyal

treasure n, v
▶ n 1 FORTUNE, wealth, valuables, riches, money, cash, gold, jewels, gems, hoard, cache 2 *she's a real treasure* gem, prize, masterpiece, pride and joy, darling, *pièce de résistance*, crème de la crème
▶ v prize, value, hold dear, revere, worship, love, adore, idolize, dote on, cherish, think highly of, preserve, guard, *formal* esteem
🔁 disparage, belittle

treasurer n
bursar, cashier, purser

treasury n
bank, exchequer, repository, resources, revenues, finances, capital, money, funds, assets, coffers, cache, hoard, vault, store, storehouse, thesaurus, corpus

treat n, v
▶ n indulgence, gratification, pleasure, delight, enjoyment, fun, entertainment, amusement, excursion, outing, party, celebration, feast, banquet, gift, present, surprise, thrill
▶ v 1 DEAL WITH, manage, handle, use, attend to, behave towards, view, regard, consider, study, discuss, cover, review 2 TEND, nurse, minister to, attend to,

care for, look after, heal, cure, medicate 3 PAY FOR, buy, stand, give, pay/foot the bill, provide, take out, entertain, amuse, delight, regale, feast 4 *wood treated with creosote* put on, apply, spread on, lay on, cover with, paint, smear, rub

treatise n
essay, dissertation, thesis, monograph, paper, pamphlet, tract, study, discourse, *formal* exposition, disquisition, prodrome

treatment n
1 HEALING, cure, remedy, medication, medicament, therapy, surgery, care, nursing, manipulation, therapeutics 2 MANAGEMENT, handling, dealing(s), use, usage, conduct, behaviour, action, discussion, coverage

treaty n
pact, convention, agreement, covenant, compact, negotiation, bargain, contract, deal, pledge, bond, alliance, *formal* concordat

treble adj
1 HIGH, high-pitched, shrill, sharp, piping 2 TRIPLE, threefold
🔁 1 deep

tree n
bush, shrub, evergreen, conifer

Trees include: acacia, acer, alder, almond, apple, ash, aspen, balsa, bay, beech, birch, blackthorn, blue gum, box, cedar, cherry, chestnut, coconut palm, cottonwood, cypress, date palm, dogwood, Dutch elm, ebony, elder, elm, eucalyptus, fig, fir, gum, hawthorn, hazel, hickory, hornbeam, horse chestnut, jacaranda, Japanese maple, larch, laurel, lime, linden, mahogany, maple, monkey puzzle, mountain ash, oak, palm, pear, pine, plane, plum, poplar, prunus, pussy willow, redwood, rowan, rubber tree, sandalwood, sapele, sequoia, silver birch, silver maple, spruce, sycamore, tamarisk, teak, walnut, weeping willow, whitebeam, willow, witch hazel, yew, yucca; bonsai, conifer, deciduous, evergreen, fruit, hardwood, ornamental, palm, softwood.

trek v, n
▶ v hike, journey, walk, march, tramp, traipse, trudge, plod, slog, journey, ramble, rove, roam
▶ n hike, walk, march, tramp, ramble, journey, trip, expedition, safari, odyssey

trellis n
framework, mesh, grid, net, network, lattice, grate, grating, grille, *formal* reticulation

tremble v, n
▶ v shake, vibrate, quake, shiver, shudder, judder, wobble, rock
▶ n shake, vibration, quake, shiver, shudder, judder, quiver, tremor, wobble
🔁 steadiness

trembling n
shaking, vibration, quaking, quavering, quivering, shuddering, juddering, shivering, heart-quake, oscillation, rocking, *colloq.* shakes
🔁 steadiness

tremendous adj
1 WONDERFUL, marvellous, stupendous, remarkable, sensational, spectacular, exceptional, extraordinary, great, amazing, incredible, impressive, *colloq.* terrific, smashing, out of this world, *slang* wicked 2 HUGE, immense, vast, great, enormous, massive, colossal, gigantic, towering, formidable
🔁 1 ordinary, unimpressive

tremor n
shake, quiver, tremble, trembling, shiver, quake, quaver, wobble, vibration, agitation, thrill, shock, earthquake
🖃 steadiness

tremulous adj
unsteady, shaking, wavering, vibrating, trembling, shivering, jumpy, jittery, quavering, quivering, quivery, agitated, trembly, afraid, scared, frightened, fearful, nervous, anxious, excited, timid
🖃 steady, firm, calm

trench n
ditch, channel, excavation, trough, waterway, earthwork, furrow, gutter, pit, cut, drain, rill, sap, entrenchment, fosse

trenchant adj
1 INCISIVE, pungent, caustic, biting, scathing, acerbic, penetrating, acute, astute, sharp, clear, perceptive, effective, clear-cut, formal mordant, perspicacious **2** FORTHRIGHT, vigorous, forceful, emphatic, blunt, terse, unequivocal, colloq. no-nonsense
🖃 woolly

trend n
1 TENDENCY, course, flow, current, drift, direction, bearing, inclination, leaning **2** FASHION, craze, mode, vogue, style, look, colloq. rage, fad, latest

trendy adj
fashionable, latest, modish, stylish, up to the minute, voguish, colloq. all the rage, natty, hip, cool, funky, in, groovy, with it
🖃 unfashionable

trepidation n
fear, apprehension, alarm, dread, anxiety, worry, unease, qualms, disquiet, misgivings, dismay, uneasiness, excitement, emotion, trembling, nervousness, shaking, agitation, quivering, tremor, palpitation, fright, formal consternation, perturbation, colloq. butterflies, cold sweat, jitters, nerves
🖃 calm

trespass v, n
▶ v invade, intrude, encroach, impinge, poach, infringe, violate, offend, sin, wrong, formal obdurate, transgress
🖃 obey, keep to
▶ n invasion, intrusion, encroachment, poaching, infringement, violation, wrongdoing, contravention, offence, sin, misdemeanour, formal transgression

trespasser n
intruder, encroacher, poacher, offender, criminal, delinquent, evil-doer, sinner, formal transgressor

tress n
hair, curl, lock, braid, bunch, plait, pigtail, ringlet, tail

trial n, adj
▶ n **1** LITIGATION, case, lawsuit, hearing, inquiry, examination, tribunal, appeal, retrial **2** EXPERIMENT, test, examination, check, dummy run, try-out, practice, rehearsal, audition, contest, competition, selection, probation, formal assay, colloq. dry run **3** SUFFERING, grief, misery, distress, adversity, hardship, ordeal, trouble, nuisance, annoyance, burden, vexation, bother, bane, cross, cross to bear, formal affliction, tribulation, colloq. hassle, pest, pain in the neck, thorn in the flesh
🖃 **3** relief, happiness
▶ adj experimental, test, testing, pilot, exploratory, provisional, probationary, dummy, colloq. dry

triangle n

Types of triangle include:
acute-angled, congruent, equilateral, isosceles, obtuse-angled, right-angled, scalene, similar.

triangular adj
triangle-shaped, three-sided, three-cornered, trilateral, technical trigonous, formal trigonal, trigonic

tribal adj
ethnic, family, native, indigenous, class, group, sectional

tribe n
race, nation, people, clan, sept, family, house, dynasty, blood, stock, group, ethnic group, caste, class, division, branch

tribulation n
suffering, grief, pain, sorrow, vexation, ordeal, misery, unhappiness, misfortune, wretchedness, worry, care, woe, burden, blow, distress, heartache, trial, reverse, adversity, hardship, trouble, curse, formal affliction, travail
🖃 happiness, rest

tribunal n
court, committee, hearing, examination, inquisition, trial, bar, bench

tribute n
1 PRAISE, commendation, compliment, high/good opinion, good word, accolade, present, gift, homage, respect, honour, applause, testimonial, credit, acknowledgement, evidence, proof, recognition, gratitude, formal eulogy, paean, panegyric, enconium **2** PAYMENT, levy, charge, tax, tariff, duty, gift, offering, contribution

trice n
moment, minute, second, instant, flash, twinkling, colloq. jiffy, sec, shake, tick

trick n, adj, v
▶ n **1** FRAUD, swindle, deception, deceit, artifice, ploy, ruse, dodge, subterfuge, trap, device, manoeuvre, colloq. con, rip-off, scam, diddle **2** HOAX, practical joke, joke, prank, antic, caper, frolic, gag, jape, feat, stunt, colloq. leg-pull, frame-up, fast one, scam **3** ILLUSION, apparition, mirage, fantasy, trick of light, legerdemain **4** KNACK, gift, talent, technique, skill, art, flair, ability, capability, faculty, facility, capacity, secret, genius, colloq. know-how, hang
▶ adj false, mock, artificial, imitation, ersatz, fake, forged, counterfeit, feigned, sham, bogus
🖃 real, genuine
▶ v deceive, delude, dupe, fool, hoodwink, beguile, mislead, take in, bluff, hoax, cheat, swindle, diddle, defraud, trap, outwit, colloq. con, pull someone's leg, kid, have on, do, take for a ride, pull a fast one on, pull one over, lead up the garden path, pull the wool over someone's eyes

trickery n
deception, deceit, cunning, illusion, sleight of hand, pretence, artifice, guile, wiliness, subterfuge, deceit, dishonesty, cheating, swindling, fraud, imposture, double-dealing, monkey business, chicanery, skulduggery, formal duplicity, colloq. funny business, hankypanky, jiggery-pokery, hocus-pocus, shenanigans
🖃 straightforwardness, honesty

trickle v, n
▶ v dribble, run, leak, seep, ooze, flow slowly, exude, drip, drop, filter, percolate
🖃 stream, gush
▶ n dribble, drip, drop, leak, seepage
🖃 stream, gush

trickster n
cheat, swindler, deceiver, fraud, hoaxer, impostor, joker, pretender, tricker, cozener, formal dissembler, colloq. con man, diddler

tricky adj
1 a tricky problem difficult, awkward, problematic, complicated, knotty, thorny, sensitive, delicate, tick-

lish, *colloq.* dodgy **2** CRAFTY, artful, cunning, sly, wily, foxy, subtle, devious, slippery, scheming, deceitful, *colloq.* dodgy

F∃ **1** easy, simple **2** honest

tried *adj*
tested, proved, reliable, dependable, trusted, trustworthy, established

trifle *n, v*
▶ *n* **1** LITTLE, bit, small amount, spot, drop, dash, touch, trace **2** TOY, plaything, trinket, bauble, knick-knack, triviality, nothing, trivia, inessential, minor consideration
▶ *v* toy, play, sport, flirt, treat frivolously, dally, dabble, fiddle, meddle, fool, potter, *colloq.* mess about/around

trifling *adj*
small, paltry, slight, negligible, inconsiderable, unimportant, insignificant, minor, trivial, superficial, petty, silly, foolish, frivolous, idle, empty, shallow, worthless, *formal* inconsequential

F∃ important, significant, serious

trigger *v, n*
▶ *v* cause, start, initiate, activate, bring about, set off, spark off, provoke, prompt, elicit, generate, produce, set in motion, *colloq.* set/start the ball rolling
▶ *n* lever, catch, switch, spur, stimulus

trim *adj, v, n*
▶ *adj* **1** NEAT, tidy, orderly, shipshape, in good order, spick-and-span, spruce, smart, well-turned-out, well-groomed, well-dressed, presentable, dapper, *colloq.* natty, cool, snazzy **2** SLIM, slender, svelte, streamlined, fit, compact

F∃ **1** untidy, scruffy

▶ *v* **1** CUT, clip, crop, dock, snip, prune, pare, shave, shear, chop **2** DECREASE, reduce, cut (down), cut back on, diminish, curtail, contract, scale down **3** DECORATE, ornament, embellish, garnish, adorn, festoon, dress, fringe, edge, adjust, arrange, order, neaten, tidy (up), *formal* array
▶ *n* **1** CONDITION, state, order, form, shape, fitness, health, fettle **2** TRIMMING, braid, border, edging, fringe, frill

trimming *n*
1 ADORNMENT, decoration, braid, border, edging, fringe, frill, embellishment, garnish, ornamentation, trim, extra, accessory, piping, falbala, frou-frou, passement, passementerie, *technical* fimbriation **2** CUTTING, clipping, paring, end

trinket *n*
bauble, jewel, ornament, knick-knack, trifle, gimcrack, gewgaw, bagatelle, whim-wham

trio *n*
threesome, triad, trinity, triune, triunity, triplet, triplicity, trilogy, *formal* triumvirate, troika

trip *n, v*
▶ *n* **1** OUTING, excursion, tour, jaunt, ride, drive, spin, run, journey, voyage, expedition, foray **2** FALL, slip, stumble, tumble, false step **3** ERROR, blunder, mistake, inaccuracy, slip, gaffe, *faux pas*, *colloq.* howler, bloomer, clanger, booboo **4** HALLUCINATION, illusion, vision, apparition, fantasy, dream, experience, *slang* freak-out, buzz
▶ *v* **1** STUMBLE, slip, slide, fall, tumble, stagger, totter, lose your footing **2** DANCE, skip, gambol, hop, spring, caper, tiptoe
▷ **trip up** catch (out), trap, snare, ensnare, ambush, waylay, outsmart, outwit, surprise, trick

tripe *n*
rubbish, nonsense, bunkum, drivel, garbage, inanity, claptrap, trash, guff, *colloq.* balderdash, hogwash, twaddle, tosh, rot, poppycock, blah, bosh, cobblers, *slang* crap

F∃ sense

triple *adj, v, n*
▶ *adj* treble, three times, triplicate, threefold, three-ply, three-way, tripartite
▶ *v* treble, triplicate
▶ *n* trio, threesome, triad, trinity, triune, triunity, triplet, triplicity, trilogy, *formal* triumvirate, troika

tripper *n*
tourist, sightseer, traveller, voyager, holidaymaker, excursionist, *colloq.* grockle

trite *adj*
banal, commonplace, common, ordinary, run-of-the-mill, stale, tired, worn, worn-out, threadbare, unoriginal, uninspired, dull, routine, hackneyed, overdone, overused, stock, stereotyped, clichéd, *formal* platitudinous, *colloq.* corny

F∃ original, new, fresh, imaginative, inspired

triumph *n, v*
▶ *n* **1** WIN, victory, conquest, walk-over, success, mastery, achievement, accomplishment, attainment, feat, coup, masterstroke, hit, sensation, *colloq.* walkover **2** EXULTATION, jubilation, rejoicing, celebration, elation, joy, happiness

F∃ **1** failure

▶ *v* **1** WIN, succeed, prosper, conquer, defeat, beat, overcome, overwhelm, gain mastery, dominate, *formal* vanquish, prevail, *colloq.* win the day **2** CELEBRATE, rejoice, glory, gloat, exult, revel, swagger, crow, *formal* jubilate

F∃ **1** lose, fail

triumphant *adj*
winning, victorious, conquering, successful, prize-winning, exultant, jubilant, rejoicing, celebratory, glorious, elated, joyful, proud, boastful, gloating, swaggering, *colloq.* cock-a-hoop

F∃ defeated, humble

trivia *n*
details, trifles, trivialities, irrelevancies, minutiae, *colloq.* pap

F∃ essentials

trivial *adj*
unimportant, insignificant, incidental, minor, petty, paltry, trifling, flimsy, small, little, inconsiderable, negligible, worthless, meaningless, frivolous, banal, trite, commonplace, everyday, *formal* inconsequential, *colloq.* measly, piddling, no great shakes, cutting no ice

F∃ important, significant, profound, substantial

triviality *n*
unimportance, insignificance, pettiness, smallness, worthlessness, meaninglessness, foolishness, frivolity, trifle, detail, technicality

F∃ importance, essential

trivialize *v*
minimize, play down, underestimate, underplay, undervalue, devalue, belittle, depreciate, scoff at

F∃ exalt

troop *n, v*
▶ *n* **1** *send in troops* army, military, soldiers, armed forces, servicemen, servicewomen **2** *a troop of soldiers/children* contingent, squadron, unit, division, company, squad, team, crew, gang, band, bunch, group, body, pack, squad, herd, flock, horde, crowd, throng, mob, gathering, multitude, *formal* assemblage
▶ *v* go, march, parade, stream, flock, swarm, throng, traipse, trudge

trophy *n*
cup, prize, laurels, award, spoils, souvenir, memento

tropical *adj*
hot, torrid, sultry, boiling, sweltering, stifling, steamy, humid

🔁 arctic, cold, cool, temperate

trot v, n
- ▶ v jog, canter, run, pace, scamper, scuttle, bustle, scurry
- ▷ **trot out** bring out, bring up, drag up, relate, repeat, bring forward, exhibit, reiterate, *formal* adduce, recite, rehearse
- ▶ n jog, canter, run

trouble n, v
- ▶ n 1 PROBLEM, difficulty, struggle, annoyance, irritation, vexation, bother, nuisance, inconvenience, hardship, misfortune, adversity, trial, torment, burden, pain, suffering, distress, grief, woe, heartache, concern, unease, uneasiness, worry, anxiety, agitation, *formal* tribulation, affliction, disquiet, *colloq.* hassle, headache, hot water, mess, corner, fix, scrape, jam, pickle, tight spot 2 UNREST, strife, fighting, tumult, commotion, disturbance, disorder, upheaval 3 *back trouble* disorder, complaint, ailment, illness, disease, disability, defect 4 *engine trouble* problem(s), failure, breakdown, cutting-out, shutdown, stopping, stalling, *formal* malfunction, *colloq.* packing-up, *slang* conking-out 5 EFFORT, exertion, pains, care, attention, thought, thoughtfulness, bother, fuss, ado, inconvenience, *colloq.* hassle
- 🔁 1 relief, calm 2 order 3 health
- ▶ v annoy, vex, harass, torment, bother, make the effort, inconvenience, disturb, upset, distress, sadden, pain, afflict, weigh (down), burden, worry, agitate, irritate, disconcert, perplex, *formal* discommode, perturb, *colloq.* put out, hassle
- 🔁 reassure, help

troublemaker n
agitator, rabble-rouser, incendiary, instigator, inciter, ringleader, stirrer, *agent provocateur*, mischiefmaker
- 🔁 peacemaker

troublesome adj
1 ANNOYING, irritating, vexatious, irksome, bothersome, worrisome, disturbing, inconvenient, difficult, hard, awkward, tricky, thorny, taxing, demanding, exacting, laborious, tiresome, wearisome, *formal* perturbing 2 UNRULY, mischievous, rowdy, turbulent, trying, unco-operative, insubordinate, rebellious
- 🔁 1 easy, simple 2 helpful

trough n
1 MANGER, feeding trough, feeder, crib 2 GUTTER, conduit, drain, trench, ditch, gully, channel, duct, groove, furrow, flame, hollow, depression

trounce v
defeat, rout, beat, thrash, overwhelm, paste, punish, best, crush, *colloq.* wallop, wipe the floor with, slaughter, hammer, clobber, lick, drub

troupe n
company, group, set, band, cast, troop

trouper n
actor, performer, player, theatrical, artiste, entertainer, veteran, *formal* thespian, *colloq.* old hand

trousers n
slacks, jeans, denims, Levis®, flannels, dungarees, breeches, shorts, *US* pants

truancy n
absence, absenteeism, shirking, malingering, French leave, *colloq.* skiving
- 🔁 attendance

truant n, adj, v
- ▶ n absentee, deserter, runaway, idler, shirker, dodger, malingerer, *colloq.* skiver
- ▶ adj absent, missing, runaway
- ▶ v play truant, desert, dodge, shirk, malinger, *colloq.* skive, skive off, play hooky

truce n
cease-fire, peace, armistice, cessation, moratorium, suspension, stay, respite, lull, rest, break, interval, intermission, *colloq.* let-up
- 🔁 war, hostilities

truck¹ n
heavy trucks on the road lorry, heavy goods vehicle (HGV), van, wagon, float

truck² n
have no truck with someone contact, communication, connection, relations, dealings, business, trade, commerce, traffic, exchange, *formal* intercourse

truculent adj
aggressive, belligerent, defiant, disobedient, quarrelsome, antagonistic, contentious, hostile, violent, savage, combative, fierce, argumentative, rude, bad-tempered, ill-tempered, sullen, cross, obstreperous, discourteous, disrespectful, *formal* bellicose, pugnacious
- 🔁 co-operative, good-natured

trudge v, n
- ▶ v tramp, plod, clump, stump, lumber, traipse, slog, toil, labour, trek, hike, walk, march, shuffle
- ▶ n tramp, traipse, slog, haul, trek, hike, walk, march

true adj, adv
- ▶ adj 1 REAL, genuine, authentic, actual, veritable, exact, precise, accurate, close, correct, right, factual, truthful, veracious, sincere, honest, legitimate, faithful, unerring, valid, rightful, proper, *formal* veracious 2 FAITHFUL, loyal, constant, steadfast, fast, staunch, firm, dependable, reliable, trustworthy, trusty, honourable, sincere, dedicated, devoted
- 🔁 1 false, wrong, untrue, incorrect, inaccurate 2 unfaithful, faithless
- ▶ adv accurately, exactly, correctly, faithfully, honestly, precisely, rightly, truly, truthfully, unerringly, properly, perfectly, veritably, *formal* veraciously
- 🔁 falsely, inaccurately

true-blue adj
card-carrying, committed, confirmed, constant, dedicated, devoted, dyed-in-the-wool, faithful, loyal, orthodox, staunch, true, trusty, uncompromising, unwavering
- 🔁 superficial, wavering

truism n
platitude, self-evident truth, truth, commonplace, cliché, bromide, axiom

truly adv
very, greatly, extremely, exceptionally, really, genuinely, sincerely, honestly, constantly, steadfastly, truthfully, surely, definitely, certainly, undoubtedly, undeniably, indeed, in fact, in reality, actually, exactly, precisely, correctly, rightly, properly, *formal* indubitably
- 🔁 slightly, falsely, incorrectly

trump v
- ▷ **trump up** invent, fake, fabricate, create, devise, make up, concoct, contrive, *colloq.* cook up

trumped-up adj
false, fabricated, fake, faked, falsified, invented, made-up, untrue, cooked-up, concocted, contrived, spurious, *colloq.* phoney
- 🔁 genuine, real, true, veritable, authentic, actual, bona fide, sound

trumpery adj
worthless, useless, valueless, shabby, trifling, showy, cheap, flashy, nasty, rubbishy, shoddy, tawdry, trashy, *formal* meretricious, *colloq.* grotty
- 🔁 first-rate

trumpet n, v
- ▶ n bugle, horn, clarion, blare, blast, roar, bellow, cry, call
- ▶ v blare, blast, roar, bellow, bay, shout, proclaim,

announce, herald, broadcast, advertise

truncate *v*
shorten, abbreviate, curtail, reduce, diminish, cut, lop, dock, prune, pare, clip, trim, crop
🔁 lengthen, extend

truncheon *n*
baton, club, cudgel, cosh, stick, staff, shillelagh, knobkerrie

trunk *n*
1 STEM, shaft, stock, stalk **2** CASE, suitcase, chest, coffer, box, crate, portmanteau **3** SNOUT, nose, *technical* proboscis **4** TORSO, body, frame

truss *v, n*
▶ *v* tie, strap, bind, pinion, fasten, tether, secure, bundle, wrap, pack
🔁 untie, loosen
▶ *n* binding, bandage, pad, support, brace, prop, stay, shore, buttress, strut, joist

trust *n, v*
▶ *n* **1** FAITH, belief, credence, credit, hope, expectation, reliance, confidence, assurance, conviction, certainty **2** CARE, charge, custody, safekeeping, guardianship, trusteeship, protection, obligation, responsibility, duty, commitment
🔁 **1** distrust, mistrust, scepticism, doubt
▶ *v* **1** RELY ON, depend on, put your confidence in, have confidence in, be sure of, count on, bank on, swear by **2** BELIEVE, imagine, assume, presume, suppose, hope, expect, *formal* surmise **3** ENTRUST, commit, consign, confide, give, assign, turn over, delegate
🔁 **2** distrust, mistrust, doubt, disbelieve

trustee *n*
keeper, administrator, agent, custodian, guardian, executor, executrix, fiduciary, depositary

trusting *adj*
trustful, credulous, gullible, naïve, innocent, ingenuous, unquestioning, unsuspecting, unguarded, unwary
🔁 distrustful, suspicious, cautious

trustworthy *adj*
honest, upright, honourable, principled, ethical, dependable, reliable, steadfast, stable, staunch, true, committed, devoted, faithful, loyal, responsible, sensible, level headed, *colloq.* (as) good as your word
🔁 untrustworthy, dishonest, unreliable, irresponsible

trusty *adj*
faithful, dependable, reliable, responsible, strong, supportive, firm, honest, loyal, staunch, trustworthy, true, solid, straightforward, steady, upright
🔁 unreliable

truth *n*
1 TRUTHFULNESS, candour, frankness, honesty, sincerity, genuineness, authenticity, realism, exactness, precision, correctness, accuracy, validity, legitimacy, rightness, honour, honourableness, integrity, uprightness, faithfulness, loyalty, constancy, *formal* veracity, fidelity **2** *tell the truth* facts, reality, actuality, fact, the gospel truth, axiom, maxim, principle, truism, *colloq.* home truth
🔁 **1** deceit, dishonesty, falseness **2** lie, falsehood

truthful *adj*
frank, candid, straight, honest, open, forthright, true, sincere, veritable, exact, precise, right, factual, accurate, correct, valid, realistic, faithful, trustworthy, reliable, *formal* veracious
🔁 untruthful, deceitful, false, untrue

truthfulness *n*
frankness, candour, honesty, openness, sincerity, straightness, uprightness, righteousness, *formal* veracity
🔁 untruthfulness

try *v, n*
▶ *v* **1** ATTEMPT, endeavour, venture, undertake, seek, strive, aim, *formal* assay, *colloq.* have a go, have a bash/crack/shot/stab, give something your best shot, give something a whirl **2** HEAR, judge **3** EXPERIMENT, test, try out, sample, taste, inspect, examine, investigate, evaluate, *formal* appraise **4** *try someone's patience* tax, make demands on, strain, stress, tire, wear out, weary, exhaust, drain, sap, weaken, stretch
▷ **try out** test, evaluate, try on, check out, inspect, sample, taste, *formal* appraise
▶ *n* **1** ATTEMPT, endeavour, effort, *colloq.* go, bash, crack, shot, stab, whirl **2** EXPERIMENT, test, trial, evaluation, sample, taste, *formal* appraisal

trying *adj*
annoying, irritating, vexatious, exasperating, troublesome, tiresome, wearisome, bothersome, difficult, hard, tough, arduous, taxing, demanding, testing, *colloq.* aggravating
🔁 easy

tub *n*
bath, bathtub, basin, vat, tun, butt, cask, barrel, keg

tubby *adj*
chubby, plump, portly, podgy, paunchy, stout, pudgy, roly-poly, fat, overweight, obese, buxom, well-upholstered, *formal* corpulent, rotund
🔁 slim

tube *n*
hose, pipe, cylinder, duct, conduit, spout, channel, shaft, inlet, outlet

tubular *adj*
tubelike, pipelike, pipy, *formal* tubulous, tubulate, tubiform, tubate, vasiform

tuck *v, n*
▶ *v* **1** INSERT, push, ease, thrust, stuff, cram **2** FOLD, pleat, gather, crease, ruffle
▷ **tuck away** stash away, save (up), store, hide, conceal, hoard
▷ **tuck in/into** eat, eat up, gorge, devour, dine, feast, *colloq.* gobble, scoff, wolf down
▷ **tuck in/up** put to bed, make comfortable, make snug, cover up, wrap up, fold in/under
▶ *n* **1** FOLD, pleat, gather, pucker, crease **2** FOOD, comestibles, meals, snack(s), *colloq.* eats, *slang* grub, nosh, scoff

tuft *n*
crest, beard, tassel, truss, knot, clump, cluster, bunch, wisp, *formal* flocculus

tug *v, n*
▶ *v* pull, draw, tow, haul, drag, lug, heave, wrench, jerk, pluck, *colloq.* yank
▶ *n* pull, tow, haul, heave, wrench, jerk, pluck, *colloq.* yank

tuition *n*
teaching, instruction, coaching, training, guidance, lessons, schooling, education

tumble *v, n*
▶ *v* **1** FALL, trip (up), topple, stumble, drop, flop, knock down, unseat, overthrow **2** PITCH, roll, toss, lurch, sway, reel, heave **3** *prices are tumbling* decrease, fall, decline, collapse, slide, plummet, dive, nosedive, plunge, fall headlong
▷ **tumble to** understand, realize, grasp, perceive, become aware of, *colloq.* cotton on to, twig
▶ *n* **1** FALL, stumble, trip, drop, roll, toss **2** DECREASE, fall, decline, collapse, slide, dive, nosedive

tumbledown *adj*
broken-down, ramshackle, rickety, dilapidated, unstable, unsteady, shaky, unsafe, ruinous, ruined, crumbling, crumbly, disintegrating, decrepit, tottering
🔁 well-kept

tumbler *n*
1 ACROBAT, gymnast, contortionist 2 DRINKING-GLASS, glass, beaker, cup, drinking-glass, goblet, mug

tumid *adj*
1 SWOLLEN, enlarged, bulging, protuberant, bloated, puffed up, bulbous, *formal* distended, tumescent 2 BOMBASTIC, pompous, affected, overblown, grandiose, high-flown, inflated, pretentious, fulsome, flowery, stilted, turgid, *formal* euphuistic, grandiloquent, magniloquent
🖃 1 flat 2 simple

tumour *n*
cancer, growth, lump, swelling, *technical* carcinoma, melanoma, lymphoma, myeloma, sarcoma, neoplasm

tumult *n*
commotion, turmoil, disturbance, upheaval, stir, agitation, unrest, disorder, confusion, chaos, pandemonium, bedlam, babel, noise, clamour, shouting, din, racket, hubbub, hullabaloo, row, rumpus, uproar, riot, fracas, brawl, affray, strife, *formal* disarray
🖃 peace, calm, composure

tumultuous *adj*
turbulent, stormy, raging, frenzied, fierce, violent, wild, vehement, fervent, hectic, boisterous, rowdy, noisy, loud, deafening, clamorous, disorderly, unruly, riotous, uncontrolled, restless, agitated, troubled, disturbed, excited
🖃 calm, peaceful, quiet

tune *n, v*
▶ *n* melody, theme, motif, song, air, strain
▷ **change your tune** change your mind, change your attitude/opinions, change your approach
▷ **in tune with** in agreement with, in sympathy with, agreeing with, in harmony with, *formal* in accord with
▶ *v* pitch, harmonize, set, regulate, adjust, adapt, temper, synchronize, *formal* attune

tuneful *adj*
melodious, melodic, catchy, musical, euphonious, harmonious, pleasant, agreeable, mellow, sonorous, *formal* mellifluous
🖃 tuneless, discordant

tuneless *adj*
unmelodic, unmelodious, unmusical, unpleasant, disagreeable, harsh, clashing, discordant, cacophonous, dissonant, *formal* atonal, horrisonant
🖃 tuneful

tunnel *n, v*
▶ *n* passage, underground passage, passageway, gallery, subway, underpass, burrow, hole, mine, shaft, chimney
▶ *v* burrow, dig, excavate, mine, bore, penetrate, undermine, sap

turbid *adj*
cloudy, clouded, hazy, dense, dim, foggy, fuzzy, muddy, murky, unclear, thick, muddled, opaque, confused, disordered, turbulent, unsettled, impure, incoherent, foul, *formal* feculent
🖃 clear

turbulence *n*
roughness, storm, unrest, boiling, upheaval, agitation, turmoil, tumult, confusion, commotion, chaos, disorder, disruption, instability, pandemonium
🖃 calm

turbulent *adj*
rough, choppy, foaming, stormy, blustery, tempestuous, raging, furious, violent, wild, tumultuous, unbridled, boisterous, rowdy, disorderly, unruly, undisciplined, obstreperous, rebellious, mutinous, riotous, agitated, in turmoil, unsettled, unstable, confused, disordered

🖃 calm, composed

turf *n, v*
▶ *n* grass, clod, sod, divot, sward, green, lawn, glebe
▶ *v* ▷ **turf out** discharge, dismiss, eject, turn out, throw out, evict, banish, fling out, expel, oust, *formal* dispossess, *colloq.* kick out, chuck out, elbow, fire, sack, give the elbow to

turgid *adj*
pompous, bombastic, flowery, fulsome, grandiose, high-flown, inflated, ostentatious, extravagant, overblown, pretentious, stilted, affected, *formal* grandiloquent, magniloquent
🖃 simple

turmoil *n*
confusion, disorder, tumult, commotion, disturbance, trouble, disquiet, agitation, turbulence, stir, ferment, flurry, bustle, chaos, pandemonium, bedlam, noise, din, hubbub, row, uproar, upheaval, *formal* disarray
🖃 calm, peace, quiet

turn *v, n*
▶ *v* 1 REVOLVE, circle, spin, go round, go round and round, go round in circles, twirl, whirl, spiral, wind, reel, twist, gyrate, pivot, hinge, swivel, rotate, roll, move, shift, invert, reverse, bend, veer, swing, swerve, pass, point, direct, aim, divert 2 MAKE, transform, change, alter, modify, convert, adapt, adjust, fit, mould, shape, cast, form, fashion, remodel, *formal* mutate, transmute, metamorphose 3 *turn cold* go, become, grow, come to be 4 RESORT, have recourse, apply, appeal 5 SOUR, curdle, spoil, go off, go bad, make, become rancid
▷ **turn against** dislike, disapprove of, distrust, make/become hostile to
🖃 like, trust, support
▷ **turn aside** deviate, depart, diverge, deflect, ward off, fend off, parry, avert
▷ **turn away** reject, avert, deflect, deviate, depart, move away, *colloq.* cold shoulder
🖃 accept, help, receive
▷ **turn down** 1 *turn down an offer* reject, decline, refuse, spurn, rebuff, repudiate, veto 2 LOWER, decrease, reduce, lessen, make quieter, quieten, soften, mute, muffle
🖃 1 accept 2 turn up
▷ **turn in** 1 GO TO BED, retire, *colloq.* hit the hay, hit the sack 2 HAND IN, give in, tender, submit, return, give back, hand over, give up, surrender, deliver
🖃 1 get up 2 keep
▷ **turn off** 1 BRANCH OFF, leave, depart from, deviate, divert, go along a different road, *colloq.* quit 2 SWITCH OFF, turn out, stop, shut down, unplug, disconnect, pull off 3 REPEL, sicken, nauseate, disgust, offend, displease, disenchant, alienate, bore, discourage, put off, turn against
🖃 1 join 2 turn on 3 *colloq.* turn on
▷ **turn on** 1 SWITCH ON, start (up), activate, plug (in), connect 2 AROUSE, stimulate, excite, thrill, please, attract 3 HINGE ON, depend on, rest on, hang on, *formal* be contingent on 4 ATTACK, round on, fall on, set upon, lay into
🖃 1 turn off 2 *colloq.* turn off
▷ **turn out** 1 HAPPEN, come about, ensue, result, end up, become, develop, emerge, *formal* transpire, *colloq.* pan out 2 SWITCH OFF, turn off, unplug, disconnect 3 APPEAR, present, dress, clothe 4 ATTEND, turn up, come, go, arrive, appear, be present, *colloq.* show up 5 PRODUCE, make, manufacture, fabricate, assemble, *colloq.* churn out 6 EVICT, throw out, expel, deport, banish, dismiss, discharge, drum out, *colloq.* chuck out, kick out, turf out, sack, fire 7 *turn out the attic* empty, clear (out), clean out
🖃 2 turn on 6 admit, receive 7 fill

▷ **turn over 1** THINK OVER, think about, mull over, ponder, deliberate, reflect on, contemplate, consider, examine, *formal* ruminate **2** HAND OVER, surrender, deliver, transfer, assign, consign **3** OVERTURN, upset, upend, turn turtle, invert, reverse, capsize, keel over
▷ **turn over a new leaf** change, change your ways, improve, mend your ways, amend, reform, begin again, *colloq.* pull one's socks up
▷ **turn up 1** ATTEND, turn out, come, arrive, appear, be present, *colloq.* show up **2** AMPLIFY, make louder, intensify, raise, increase **3** DISCOVER, find, uncover, unearth, dig up, expose, disclose, reveal, show, bring to light
Ⅎ 1 stay away **2** turn down
▶ *n* **1** REVOLUTION, cycle, round, circle, rotation, spin, twirl, whirl, twist, swivel, gyration, bend, curve, corner, loop, reversal **2** CHANGE, alteration, shift, variation, difference, deviation, divergence **3** *it's your turn* go, chance, opportunity, occasion, time, stint, period, spell, *colloq.* crack, stab, bash **4** ACT, appearance, routine, performance, performer **5** TREND, tendency, inclination, direction, bias, leaning, drift, *formal* propensity **6** *gave her quite a turn* illness, nervousness, faintness, shock, fright, scare
▷ **to a turn** perfectly, exactly, correctly, precisely, to perfection
▷ **turn of events** incident, happening, occurrence, result, affair, outcome, phenomenon
▷ **turn of phrase** expression, idiom, saying, style, diction, metaphor, phraseology, *formal* locution

turning *n*
turn-off, junction, crossroads, fork, bend, curve, turn

turning-point *n*
crossroads, watershed, crux, crisis, critical/decisive moment, moment of truth

turnout *n*
1 ATTENDANCE, audience, gate, crowd, gathering, assembly, congregation, number, *formal* assemblage **2** APPEARANCE, outfit, dress, clothes, *formal* attire, array, *colloq.* gear, clobber, togs, get-up

turnover *n*
income, profits, productivity, business, production, output, yield, volume, outturn, change, movement, flow, replacement

turpitude *n*
baseness, corruption, badness, corruptness, evil, criminality, immorality, vileness, wickedness, viciousness, depravity, degeneracy, foulness, sinfulness, villainy, *formal* flagitiousness, nefariousness, iniquity
Ⅎ honour

tussle *v, n*
▶ *v* struggle, battle, wrestle, compete, vie, fight, contend, grapple, scrap, brawl, scuffle, scramble
▶ *n* struggle, battle, conflict, contest, scramble, fight, brawl, bout, fracas, fray, melee, punch-up, scrap, scuffle, scrum, set-to, competition, contention, scrimmage, *colloq.* dust-up

tutelage *n*
guidance, charge, custody, care, protection, guardianship, wardship, patronage, vigilance, eye, teaching, instruction, education, schooling, tuition, preparation, *formal* aegis

tutor *n, v*
▶ *n* teacher, instructor, coach, educator, lecturer, supervisor, guide, mentor, guru, guardian
▶ *v* teach, instruct, train, drill, coach, educate, school, lecture, supervise, direct, guide

tutorial *n, adj*
▶ *n* class, lesson, seminar, teach-in
▶ *adj* coaching, didactic, educative, educatory, guiding, instructional, teaching

TV *n*
television, receiver, set, small screen, *colloq.* telly, the box, goggle-box, idiot box, the tube, *US* boob tube

twaddle *n*
drivel, rubbish, nonsense, trash, garbage, gabble, waffle, blather, blether, guff, gossip, tattle, balderdash, bunk, bunkum, claptrap, inanity, gobbledygook, poppycock, stuff, *colloq.* hogwash, hot air, piffle, rot, tosh
Ⅎ sense

tweak *v, n*
twist, pinch, squeeze, nip, pull, tug, jerk, twitch

twee *adj*
sweet, cute, pretty, dainty, quaint, sentimental, affected, precious

twiddle *v*
turn, twirl, swivel, twist, wiggle, adjust, fiddle, finger, play with

twig¹ *n*
dried twigs branch, spring, spray, shoot, offshoot, stick, wattle, whip, withe, withy, *formal* ramulus

twig² *v*
then I twigged understand, see, get, comprehend, grasp, fathom, rumble, *colloq.* catch on, cotton on, tumble to

twilight *n, adj*
▶ *n* dusk, half-light, gloaming, gloom, dimness, sunset, evening, decline, ebb, *formal* crepuscule
▶ *adj* darkening, dim, declining, evening, shadowy, final, last, ebbing, dying, *formal* crepuscular

twin *n, adj, v*
▶ *n* double, look-alike, likeness, duplicate, clone, match, counterpart, equivalent, complement, fellow, mate, *formal* corollary, *colloq.* (dead) ringer
▶ *adj* identical, matching, corresponding, symmetrical, parallel, matched, paired, double, dual, duplicate, twofold
▶ *v* match, pair, couple, link, join, yoke

twine *n, v*
▶ *n* string, cord, thread, yarn
▶ *v* wind, coil, spiral, loop, curl, bend, twist, tangle, wreathe, wrap, surround, encircle, entwine, plait, braid, knit, weave

twinge *n*
pain, pang, throb, spasm, ache, throe, stab, stitch, cramp, pinch, prick

twinkle *v, n*
▶ *v* sparkle, glitter, shimmer, glisten, glimmer, flicker, wink, flash, glint, gleam, shine, scintillate, *formal* coruscate
▶ *n* sparkle, scintillation, glitter, shimmer, glisten, glimmer, flicker, wink, flash, glint, shining, gleam, light, *formal* coruscation

twinkling *adj, n*
▶ *adj* bright, sparkling, glittering, shimmering, glistening, glimmering, flickering, gleaming, flashing, blinking, scintillating, shining, winking, polished, *formal* coruscating, nitid
▶ *n* moment, flash, instant, second, *colloq.* sec, tick, jiff, jiffy, mo, trice, shake, no time, two shakes of a lamb's tail

twirl *v, n*
▶ *v* spin, whirl, pirouette, wheel, rotate, revolve, swivel, pivot, turn, curl, twist, gyrate, wind, coil
▶ *n* spin, whirl, pirouette, rotation, revolution, turn, curl, twist, gyration, convolution, spiral, coil

twirling *adj*
spinning, whirling, pirouetting, rotating, revolving, pivoting, pivotal, gyratory, swivelling, *formal* gyral, rotatory

twist v, n

▶ v **1** TURN, screw, wring, spin, rotate, revolve, swivel, wind, zigzag, bend, coil, spiral, curl, wreathe, twirl, twine, entwine, intertwine, weave, braid, plait, entangle, wriggle, squirm, writhe, skew **2** *twist your ankle* wrench, rick, sprain, strain **3** CHANGE, alter, garble, falsify, misquote, misrepresent, misreport, distort, contort, warp, bend, misshape, deform, pervert

▷ **twist someone's arm** persuade, force, intimidate, pressurize, bulldoze, bully, coerce, dragoon, *colloq.* lean on, put the screws on

▶ n **1** TURN, screw, spin, roll, bend, curve, arc, kink, curl, loop, zigzag, coil, spiral, convolution, squiggle, tangle **2** WRENCH, rick, sprain, strain **3** CHANGE, variation, break, turn, surprise, turnabout **4** PERVERSION, distortion, contortion, imperfection, defect, flaw, *formal* aberration **5** QUIRK, oddity, peculiarity, idiosyncrasy, foible, freak, whim

twisted *adj*
winding, wavy, squiggly, warped, perverted, deviant, unnatural, strange, peculiar, odd, *formal* sinuous
🔁 straight

twister n
swindler, cheat, crook, fraud, rogue, deceiver, trickster, scoundrel, blackguard, *colloq.* con man, phoney

twit n
idiot, fool, simpleton, blockhead, clown, *colloq.* ass, ninny, halfwit, dope, twerp, nitwit, clot, nincompoop, chump

twitch v, n

▶ v jerk, jump, start, blink, tremble, quiver, flutter, shake, pull, tug, tweak, snatch, pluck

▶ n spasm, convulsion, tic, tremor, shiver, quiver, flutter, jerk, jump, start

twitter v, n

▶ v **1** CHIRP, chirrup, tweet, cheep, sing, warble, whistle, chatter **2** PRATTLE, witter, gabble, gossip, twaddle, blather, blether

▶ n chirping, chirruping, tweeting, song, cry, warble, chatter

two-faced *adj*
hypocritical, insincere, false, lying, deceitful, double-dealing, treacherous, devious, untrustworthy, Janus-faced, *formal* perfidious, dissembling, duplicitous
🔁 honest, candid, frank

tycoon n
industrialist, entrepreneur, captain of industry, magnate, mogul, baron, supremo, capitalist, financier, *colloq.* fat cat, big noise, big cheese, moneybags, moneyspinner

type n
1 SORT, kind, form, set, style, variety, strain, species, breed, group, class, category, subdivision, classification, description, designation, stamp, mark, order, brand, model, make, standard, *technical* genus, *formal* genre **2** EMBODIMENT, prototype, original, model, pattern, specimen, example, *formal* archetype, exemplar, quintessence **3** PRINT, printing, character(s), letter(s), number(s), symbol(s), lettering, face, fount, font

typhoon n
whirlwind, cyclone, tornado, hurricane, tempest, storm, squall, *colloq.* twister

typical *adj*
standard, normal, usual, average, ordinary, conventional, orthodox, classic, true, stereotype, stock, model, representative, illustrative, indicative, characteristic, distinctive, *formal* archetypal, quintessential, *colloq.* run-of-the-mill
🔁 atypical, unusual

typically *adv*
usually, normally, ordinarily, characteristically, customarily, routinely, habitually, as a rule, *formal* quintessentially

typify v
embody, epitomize, encapsulate, personify, characterize, exemplify, symbolize, indicate, represent, illustrate

tyrannical *adj*
dictatorial, despotic, autocratic, absolute, totalitarian, arbitrary, authoritarian, domineering, overbearing, high-handed, imperious, magisterial, ruthless, harsh, severe, strict, cruel, oppressive, repressive, overpowering, unjust, unreasonable, Neronian, *formal* peremptory
🔁 liberal, tolerant

tyrannize v
oppress, crush, intimidate, terrorize, coerce, repress, suppress, dictate, domineer, enslave, browbeat, bully, lord it over, *formal* subjugate

tyranny n
dictatorship, despotism, autocracy, absolutism, authoritarianism, imperiousness, high-handedness, ruthlessness, harshness, severity, strictness, cruelty, oppression, injustice
🔁 democracy, freedom

tyrant n
dictator, despot, autocrat, absolutist, authoritarian, bully, oppressor, slave-driver, taskmaster, martinet

tyro *see* TIRO.

ubiquitous *adj*
ever-present, everywhere, universal, global, pervasive, common, frequent, *formal* omnipresent
F3 rare, scarce

ugly *adj*
1 UNATTRACTIVE, unsightly, plain, unlovely, unprepossessing, ill-favoured, hideous, revolting, repulsive, grotesque, monstrous, misshapen, deformed, *US* homely, *colloq.* ugly as sin **2** UNPLEASANT, disagreeable, nasty, horrid, hideous, objectionable, offensive, shocking, disgusting, loathsome, revolting, foul, repulsive, vile, frightful, obnoxious, terrible **3** DANGEROUS, threatening, alarming, sinister, grave, nasty, hostile, evil
F3 **1** attractive, good-looking, beautiful, handsome, pretty **2** pleasant

ulcer *n*
sore, open sore, fester, abscess, boil, canker, ulceration, noma

ulterior *adj*
secondary, hidden, concealed, undisclosed, unexpressed, unrevealed, covert, secret, private, personal, selfish
F3 overt, declared

ultimate *adj, n*
▶ *adj* **1** FINAL, last, closing, concluding, eventual, terminal, furthest, end, remotest, extreme **2** RADICAL, basic, fundamental, primary, *formal* elemental **3** BEST, utmost, greatest, topmost, highest, supreme, superlative, maximum, perfect
▶ *n* best, greatest, peak, perfection, summit, culmination, greatest achievement, masterpiece, *chef d'oeuvre*, height, extreme, *formal* consummation, epitome, *colloq.* daddy of them all, last word

ultimately *adv*
1 FINALLY, eventually, at last, in the end, after all, sooner or later **2** BASICALLY, fundamentally, primarily

ultra- *prefix*
extremely, excessively, especially, exceptionally, unusually, extraordinarily, remarkably, extra

ululate *v*
howl, wail, screech, moan, lament, keen, mourn, cry, scream, weep, sob, holler, hoot

umbrage *n*
▷ **take umbrage** take offence, resent, be angry, be annoyed, be exasperated, be hurt, be offended, be insulted, be upset, be/feel put out, take exception, take personally, *colloq.* be miffed, get huffy, get your nose out of joint

umbrella *n*
1 *put up your umbrella* parasol, sunshade, *colloq.* brolly, gamp **2** PROTECTION, cover, agency, patronage, *formal* aegis

umpire *n, v*
▶ *n* referee, linesman, judge, adjudicator, arbiter, arbitrator, mediator, moderator, *colloq.* ref
▶ *v* referee, judge, adjudicate, arbitrate, mediate, moderate, control

umpteen *adj*
numerous, very many, plenty, thousands, millions, countless, innumerable, *colloq.* a good many
F3 few

unabashed *adj*
unashamed, unembarrassed, brazen, blatant, bold, confident, undaunted, unconcerned, undismayed
F3 abashed, sheepish

unable *adj*
incapable, powerless, impotent, unequipped, unqualified, unfit, incompetent, inadequate, *formal* ineffectual
F3 able, capable, *colloq.* up to

unabridged *adj*
complete, entire, full-length, full, whole, uncondensed, unshortened, uncut, unexpurgated
F3 abridged, shortened

unacceptable *adj*
intolerable, inadmissible, unsatisfactory, unsuitable, disappointing, undesirable, unwelcome, objectionable, disagreeable, offensive, unpleasant, obnoxious
F3 acceptable, satisfactory

unaccommodating *adj*
inflexible, uncompromising, unco-operative, unbending, unyielding, obstinate, stubborn, perverse, rigid, disobliging, *formal* intransigent, uncomplaisant
F3 flexible, obliging

unaccompanied *adj*
alone, unescorted, unattended, by yourself, on your own, lone, solo, single, single-handed
F3 accompanied

unaccountable *adj*
1 INEXPLICABLE, unexplainable, unfathomable, impenetrable, insoluble, incomprehensible, baffling, puzzling, mysterious, astonishing, extraordinary, strange, odd, peculiar, singular, curious, bizarre, queer, unusual, uncommon, unheard-of **2** *unaccountable to the public* not responsible, not answerable, free, immune
F3 **1** explicable, explainable **2** accountable, bound

unaccustomed *adj*
1 *unaccustomed to such luxury* unused, unacquainted, unfamiliar, unpractised, inexperienced, *formal* unwonted **2** STRANGE, unusual, uncommon, different, new, unexpected, surprising, extraordinary, remarkable, unfamiliar, uncharacteristic, unprecedented
F3 **1** accustomed, familiar **2** customary

unacquainted *adj*
unfamiliar, unaccustomed, unused, inexperienced, strange, ignorant

unadorned *adj*
plain, simple, straightforward, undecorated, unorna-

mented, unembellished, unvarnished, severe, stark, restrained
F₃ decorated, embellished, ornate

unaffected *adj*
1 UNMOVED, unconcerned, indifferent, impervious, untouched, unchanged, unaltered **2** UNSOPHIST-ICATED, artless, naïve, ingenuous, guileless, unspoilt, plain, simple, straightforward, natural, unpretentious, unassuming, candid, true, sincere, honest, genuine
F₃ 1 moved, impressed, influenced **2** affected, pretentious, insincere

unafraid *adj*
fearless, confident, daring, dauntless, brave, courageous, imperturbable, intrepid, unshakable
F₃ afraid, fearful, nervous

unalterable *adj*
unchangeable, invariable, unchanging, immutable, final, inflexible, unyielding, rigid, fixed, permanent
F₃ alterable, flexible

unanimity *n*
consensus, unity, agreement, concurrence, like-mindedness, consistency, harmony, unison, concert, *formal* accord, concord, congruence
F₃ disagreement, disunity

unanimous *adj*
united, concerted, joint, common, as one, in agreement, like-minded, consistent, harmonious, *formal* in accord, concordant
F₃ disunited, divided

unanimously *adv*
unopposed, without opposition, without exception, as one, of one mind, with one voice, by common consent, in concert, *nem con*, *formal* conjointly

unanswerable *adj*
incontestable, incontrovertible, indisputable, unarguable, undeniable, absolute, final, conclusive, *formal* irrefragable, irrefutable
F₃ answerable, refutable

unappetizing *adj*
unpleasant, tasteless, unpalatable, off-putting, distasteful, disagreeable, uninviting, unsavoury, insipid, unappealing, unattractive, unexciting, uninteresting
F₃ appetising

unapproachable *adj*
inaccessible, remote, distant, aloof, remote, standoffish, withdrawn, reserved, unsociable, unfriendly, unresponsive, uncommunicative, forbidding, cold, cool
F₃ approachable, friendly

unapt *adj*
unsuitable, unfit, unfitted, unsuited, inappropriate, inapplicable, untimely, unseasonable, inapt, *formal* inapposite, malapropos
F₃ apt

unarmed *adj*
defenceless, unprotected, exposed, open, vulnerable, weak, helpless
F₃ armed, protected

unashamed *adj*
shameless, unabashed, impenitent, unrepentant, unconcealed, undisguised, open, honest, blatant
F₃ ashamed, abashed

unasked *adj*
uninvited, unbidden, unrequested, unsought, unsolicited, unwanted, voluntary, spontaneous, unannounced
F₃ invited, wanted

unassailable *adj*
invulnerable, incontestable, impregnable, incontrovertible, indisputable, secure, sound, positive, proven, absolute, conclusive, invincible, inviolable, undeniable, well-armed, *formal* well-fortified, irrefutable
F₃ assailable

unassertive *adj*
self-effacing, unassuming, backward, bashful, quiet, retiring, shy, timid, meek, mousy, diffident, timorous
F₃ assertive

unassuming *adj*
unassertive, self-effacing, retiring, modest, shy, demure, humble, meek, quiet, reticent, unobtrusive, unpretentious, simple, natural, restrained
F₃ presumptuous, assertive, pretentious

unattached *adj*
unmarried, unengaged, uncommitted, single, on your own, by yourself, free, available, footloose, fancy-free, independent, unaffiliated
F₃ engaged, committed

unattended *adj*
ignored, disregarded, abandoned, neglected, forgotten, unguarded, unwatched, unsupervised, unaccompanied, unescorted, alone, *formal* forsaken
F₃ attended, escorted, looked after

unauthorized *adj*
unofficial, unlicensed, unlawful, forbidden, prohibited, illegal, illicit, illegitimate, irregular, unapproved, unsanctioned, unwarranted
F₃ authorized, legal, *formal* accredited

unavailing *adj*
unsuccessful, failed, abortive, vain, futile, useless, ineffective, fruitless, unproductive, unprofitable, sterile, luckless, unlucky, unfortunate, losing, beaten, defeated, frustrated, thwarted
F₃ successful, effective

unavoidable *adj*
inevitable, inescapable, inexorable, certain, sure, fated, destined, predestined, obligatory, required, compulsory, necessary, *formal* mandatory, ineluctable
F₃ avoidable

unaware *adj*
oblivious, unconscious, ignorant, uninformed, unenlightened, in the dark, unknowing, unsuspecting, unmindful, heedless, blind, deaf, *formal* insentient
F₃ aware, conscious

unawares *adv*
off guard, by surprise, accidentally, inadvertently, mistakenly, suddenly, unexpectedly, aback, abruptly, unintentionally, unconsciously, unknowingly, unprepared, unthinkingly, unwittingly, insidiously, *colloq.* on the hop

unbalanced *adj*
1 INSANE, mad, lunatic, deranged, disturbed, demented, irrational, unsound, unstable, mentally ill, *colloq.* crazy, barmy, crackers, round the bend/twist, needing your head examining **2** *an unbalanced report* biased, prejudiced, one-sided, partisan, unfair, unjust, unequal, uneven, asymmetrical, lopsided, unsteady, unstable, *formal* inequitable
F₃ 1 sane, sound **2** unbiased

unbearable *adj*
intolerable, unacceptable, insupportable, insufferable, unendurable, excruciating, *colloq.* too much, too bad, the limit, the last straw, the straw that broke the camel's back
F₃ bearable, acceptable

unbeatable *adj*
invincible, unconquerable, unstoppable, unsurpassable, matchless, supreme, best, excellent, *formal* indomitable

unbeaten *adj*
undefeated, unconquered, victorious, winning, supreme, triumphant, unsubdued, unsurpassed, unbowed, *formal* unvanquished
🗲 defeated, *formal* vanquished

unbecoming *adj*
unseemly, improper, unsuitable, inappropriate, unbefitting, indelicate, ungentlemanly, unladylike, unattractive, unsightly, *formal* indecorous, unseemly
🗲 suitable, attractive

unbelief *n*
atheism, agnosticism, scepticism, doubt, incredulity, disbelief
🗲 belief, faith

unbelievable *adj*
incredible, inconceivable, unthinkable, unimaginable, amazing, astonishing, staggering, extraordinary, impossible, improbable, unlikely, implausible, unconvincing, far-fetched, preposterous, outlandish
🗲 believable, credible

unbeliever *n*
disbeliever, agnostic, atheist, doubter, sceptic, doubting Thomas, infidel, *formal* nullifidian
🗲 believer, supporter

unbelieving *adj*
sceptical, suspicious, disbelieving, distrustful, doubtful, doubting, dubious, unconvinced, unpersuaded, incredulous, *formal* nullifidian
🗲 credulous, trustful

unbend *v*
loosen up, relax, become less formal/strict, thaw, unfreeze, unbutton, uncoil, uncurl, straighten
🗲 stiffen, withdraw

unbending *adj*
rigid, inflexible, strict, tough, uncompromising, unyielding, resolute, firm, formal, formidable, stubborn, severe, stiff, stern, hard-line, forbidding, aloof, distant, reserved, *formal* intransigent
🗲 approachable, friendly, relaxed

unbiased *adj*
impartial, unprejudiced, objective, just, fair, fair-minded, open-minded, independent, equitable, even-handed, disinterested, dispassionate, neutral, uninfluenced, uncoloured
🗲 biased

unbidden *adj*
spontaneous, unforced, free, voluntary, unsolicited, unprompted, uninvited, willing, unasked, unwanted, unwelcome
🗲 invited, solicited

unbind *v*
untie, unfasten, unloose, unloosen, unchain, undo, unshackle, free, liberate, loose, loosen, release, unyoke, unfetter
🗲 bind, restrain

unblemished *adj*
untarnished, unspotted, unstained, unsullied, unimpeachable, unflawed, pure, clear, perfect, spotless, immaculate, irreproachable, flawless
🗲 blemished, flawed, imperfect

unblinking *adj*
steady, unfaltering, unflinching, unshrinking, unwavering, imperturbable, emotionless, unemotional, fearless, unafraid, assured, calm, impassive, cool, composed
🗲 fearful, cowed

unblushing *adj*
shameless, brazen, blatant, bold, immodest, unabashed, unashamed, unembarrassed, conscience-proof, amoral
🗲 abashed, ashamed

unborn *adj*
embryonic, *in utero*, expected, awaited, coming, to-come, future, subsequent, succeeding

unbosom *v*
unburden, confess, admit, reveal, tell, lay bare, divulge, disclose, confide, uncover, let out, pour out, bare, *colloq.* tell all
🗲 hide, conceal, suppress

unbounded *adj*
boundless, limitless, unlimited, unrestricted, unrestrained, uncontrolled, unchecked, unbridled, infinite, endless, immeasurable, vast
🗲 limited, restrained

unbreakable *adj*
indestructible, shatterproof, toughened, resistant, shatterproof, durable, strong, tough, rugged, solid, *formal* infrangible
🗲 breakable, fragile

unbridled *adj*
immoderate, excessive, rampant, riotous, wild, uncontrolled, unrestrained, unconstrained, ungoverned, uncurbed, unchecked, intemperate, licentious, profligate

unbroken *adj*
1 INTACT, whole, entire, complete, solid, undivided **2** UNINTERRUPTED, continuous, endless, non-stop, ceaseless, incessant, unceasing, constant, perpetual, progressive, successive, *formal* unremitting **3** *unbroken record* unbeaten, unsurpassed, unrivalled, unequalled, unmatched
🗲 **1** broken, damaged **2** intermittent, fitful

unburden *v*
confess, admit, reveal, tell, lay bare, divulge, offload, disclose, confide, uncover, let out, pour out, bare, *colloq.* tell all
🗲 hide, conceal, suppress

uncalled-for *adj*
unwarranted, gratuitous, unprovoked, unjustified, unasked, unsought, unsolicited, unprompted, undeserved, unwelcome, unnecessary, needless
🗲 timely

uncanny *adj*
weird, strange, queer, odd, bizarre, mysterious, unaccountable, incredible, remarkable, exceptional, extraordinary, fantastic, unnatural, unearthly, supernatural, eerie, creepy, *Scot.* eldritch, *formal* preternatural, *colloq.* spooky

uncaring *adj*
unconcerned, unmoved, unsympathetic, inconsiderate, unfeeling, cold, callous, indifferent, uninterested
🗲 caring, concerned

unceasing *adj*
ceaseless, incessant, unending, endless, never-ending, non-stop, continuous, unbroken, constant, perpetual, continual, persistent, relentless, unrelenting, unremitting
🗲 intermittent, spasmodic

uncertain *adj*
1 UNSURE, unconvinced, doubtful, dubious, undecided, unresolved, open, equivocating, ambivalent, hesitant, wavering, vacillating, *colloq.* in two minds **2** INCONSTANT, changeable, variable, erratic, irregular, shaky, fitful, unsteady, unreliable **3** UNPREDICTABLE, unforeseeable, undetermined, unsettled, unresolved, unconfirmed, unknown, unclear, speculative, indefinite, vague, insecure, risky, *colloq.* iffy, up in the air, touch and go, (hanging) in the balance, in the lap of the gods
🗲 **1** certain, sure **2** steady **3** predictable

uncertainty *n*
doubt, scepticism, irresolution, dilemma, ambiguity, ambivalence, hesitation, misgiving, qualm(s), uneasiness, confusion, vagueness, bewilderment, perplexity, puzzlement, unreliability, unpredictability, riskiness, insecurity
F≥ certainty

unchangeable *adj*
changeless, unchanging, invariable, irreversible, permanent, final, eternal, *formal* immutable, intransmutable
F≥ changeable

unchanging *adj*
unvarying, changeless, same, invariable, steady, steadfast, constant, perpetual, lasting, enduring, abiding, eternal, permanent
F≥ changing, changeable

uncharitable *adj*
unkind, cruel, hard-hearted, callous, hard, harsh, stern, severe, unfeeling, insensitive, unsympathetic, uncompassionate, unfriendly, mean, ungenerous, unforgiving
F≥ kind, sensitive, charitable, generous

uncharted *adj*
unexplored, unsurveyed, undiscovered, unplumbed, foreign, alien, strange, unknown, unfamiliar, new, virgin
F≥ familiar

unchaste *adj*
immoral, depraved, defiled, dissolute, dishonest, impure, immodest, promiscuous, fallen, loose, licentious, wanton, lewd
F≥ chaste

uncivil *adj*
rude, impolite, discourteous, disrespectful, bad-mannered, ill-mannered, ill-bred, uncouth, unmannerly, ungracious, churlish, brusque, abrupt, gruff, curt, boorish, bearish, surly
F≥ civil, polite

uncivilized *adj*
primitive, barbaric, barbarian, savage, wild, rough, boorish, brutish, untamed, uncultured, unrefined, unsophisticated, unenlightened, uneducated, illiterate, uncouth, antisocial
F≥ civilized, cultured

unclassifiable *adj*
doubtful, indistinct, uncertain, undefinable, indescribable, unidentifiable, vague, elusive, ill-defined, indefinable, indefinite, indeterminate
F≥ conformable, definable, identifiable

unclean *adj*
dirty, soiled, filthy, grimy, grubby, foul, polluted, contaminated, tainted, impure, unhygienic, unwholesome, corrupt, adulterated, defiled, sullied, bad, evil, wicked
F≥ clean, hygienic

unclear *adj*
indistinct, hazy, foggy, dim, obscure, vague, indefinite, ambiguous, equivocal, uncertain, undetermined, unsettled, unsure, doubtful, dubious, *colloq.* iffy
F≥ clear, evident

unclothed *adj*
naked, nude, stripped, undressed, bare, *formal* disrobed, unclad, *colloq.* stark naked, in your birthday suit, in the altogether, in the buff, starkers,
F≥ clothed, dressed

uncomfortable *adj*
1 CRAMPED, hard, cold, ill-fitting, irritating, painful, disagreeable **2** AWKWARD, embarrassed, self-conscious, nervous, uneasy, tense, troubled, worried, anxious, disturbed, distressed, disquieted, conscience-stricken, *formal* discomfited, *colloq.* on edge
F≥ **1** comfortable **2** relaxed

uncommitted *adj*
unattached, uninvolved, undecided, available, free, fancy-free, floating, non-aligned, non-partisan, neutral
F≥ committed

uncommon *adj*
rare, scarce, infrequent, unusual, abnormal, atypical, unfamiliar, strange, odd, peculiar, queer, singular, curious, bizarre, extraordinary, remarkable, notable, outstanding, striking, exceptional, distinctive, special, *colloq.* thin on the ground, few and far between, like gold dust
F≥ common, usual, normal

uncommonly *adv*
exceptionally, abnormally, peculiarly, remarkably, strangely, unusually, occasionally, singularly, rarely, seldom, infrequently, extremely, outstandingly, particularly, very
F≥ commonly, frequently

uncommunicative *adj*
silent, taciturn, tight-lipped, close, secretive, unforthcoming, unresponsive, curt, brief, reticent, quiet, reserved, shy, retiring, diffident, withdrawn, aloof, unsociable
F≥ communicative, forthcoming, talkative, conversational

uncomplicated *adj*
simple, easy, straightforward, direct, uninvolved, clear, undemanding
F≥ complicated, complex, involved

uncompromising *adj*
unyielding, unbending, inflexible, unaccommodating, rigid, firm, stiff, strict, tough, hard-line, immovable, inexorable, stubborn, obstinate, die-hard, *formal* obdurate, intransigent
F≥ flexible, yielding

unconcealed *adj*
open, obvious, patent, evident, conspicuous, overt, undistinguished, admitted, visible, blatant, frank, apparent, noticeable, unashamed, ill-concealed, self-confessed, *formal* manifest
F≥ hidden, secret

unconcern *n*
aloofness, detachment, remoteness, apathy, nonchalance, indifference, uninterestedness, negligence, callousness, *formal* insouciance, pococurantism
F≥ concern

unconcerned *adj*
indifferent, apathetic, uninterested, nonchalant, carefree, relaxed, casual, complacent, cool, composed, untroubled, unworried, unruffled, unmoved, uncaring, unsympathetic, callous, aloof, remote, distant, detached, dispassionate, uninvolved, oblivious, *formal* unperturbed, insouciant, pococurante
F≥ concerned, worried, interested

unconditional *adj*
unqualified, unreserved, unrestricted, unlimited, absolute, utter, full, plenary, total, complete, entire, whole-hearted, thoroughgoing, downright, outright, out-and-out, positive, define, conclusive, categorical, unequivocal
F≥ conditional, qualified, limited

unconfirmed *adj*
unproven, unproved, unratified, unverified, unauthenticated, unsubstantiated, *formal* uncorroborated
F≥ confirmed

unconformity *n*
discontinuity, irregularity, unconformability, *formal* disconformity
F3 conformability

uncongenial *adj*
unfriendly, uninviting, unappealing, unattractive, unpleasant, displeasing, disagreeable, antagonistic, unsympathetic, incompatible, unsuited, unsavoury, discordant, distasteful, *formal* antipathetic
F3 congenial

unconnected *adj*
1 IRRELEVANT, unrelated, beside/off the point, inappropriate, unattached, detached, separate, independent, *colloq.* neither here nor there **2** DISCONNECTED, incoherent, irrational, illogical, confused, unco-ordinated, disjointed
F3 1 connected, relevant

unconquerable *adj*
irrepressible, enduring, ingrained, inveterate, undefeatable, unbeatable, invincible, unyielding, insuperable, insurmountable, irresistible, overpowering, *formal* indomitable
F3 weak, yielding

unconscionable *adj*
unprincipled, amoral, outrageous, unethical, unjustifiable, unscrupulous, unreasonable, unwarrantable, unpardonable, preposterous, criminal, exorbitant, extreme, extravagant, excessive, immoderate, inordinate

unconscious *adj*
1 STUNNED, knocked out, dazed, out, fainted, collapsed, drugged, in a coma, concussed, blacked out, senseless, asleep, *technical* comatose, *formal* insensible, *colloq.* out cold, out for the count, zonked, dead to the world **2** UNAWARE, oblivious, blind, deaf, heedless, unmindful, ignorant, *formal* insensible, incognizant **3** *an unconscious reaction* involuntary, automatic, reflex, instinctive, impulsive, innate, subconscious, subliminal, repressed, suppressed, latent, unthinking, unwitting, inadvertent, accidental, unintentional
F3 1 conscious 2 aware 3 intentional

unconstraint *n*
unreserve, unrestraint, openness, freedom, liberality, relaxation, abandon, laissez-faire

uncontrollable *adj*
ungovernable, unmanageable, unruly, out of control, disorderly, wild, mad, furious, violent, strong, irrepressible, *formal* intractable
F3 controllable, manageable

uncontrolled *adj*
unrestrained, unbridled, unchecked, rampant, violent, wild, boisterous, riotous, unruly, uncurbed, undisciplined, unhindered
F3 controlled, restrained

unconventional *adj*
unorthodox, alternative, different, offbeat, eccentric, bohemian, idiosyncratic, individual, original, odd, unusual, uncommon, rare, uncustomary, irregular, abnormal, bizarre, *colloq.* fringe, out of the ordinary, freaky, wacky, oddball, zany, *slang* way-out, far-out
F3 conventional, orthodox

unconvincing *adj*
implausible, unlikely, improbable, questionable, doubtful, dubious, suspect, weak, feeble, flimsy, lame, *colloq.* fishy
F3 convincing, plausible

unco-ordinated *adj*
clumsy, awkward, ungainly, ungraceful, bungling, bumbling, clodhopping, inept, disjointed, *formal* maladroit
F3 graceful

uncouth *adj*
coarse, crude, vulgar, rude, bad-mannered, ill-mannered, impolite, improper, clumsy, awkward, boorish, loutish, gauche, graceless, unrefined, uncultivated, unsophisticated, uncultured, uncivilized, rough, *formal* unseemly
F3 polite, refined, urbane

uncover *v*
unveil, unmask, unwrap, strip, bare, lay bare, open, peel, expose, reveal, bring to light, show, disclose, divulge, make known, leak, unearth, dig up, exhume, discover, detect
F3 cover, conceal, suppress

uncritical *adj*
undiscerning, undiscriminating, unselective, unquestioning, credulous, accepting, trusting, gullible, naïve, non-judgemental, unfussy, superficial
F3 discerning, discriminating, sceptical

unctuous *adj*
1 INSINCERE, fawning, ingratiating, smooth, suave, sycophantic, gushing, slick, plausible, glib, sanctimonious, obsequious, servile, pietistic, *colloq.* smarmy **2** GREASY, oily, creamy

uncultivated *adj*
fallow, wild, rough, natural
F3 cultivated

uncultured *adj*
unsophisticated, unrefined, uncultivated, uncivilized, unintellectual, rough, uncouth, boorish, rustic, hick, coarse, crude, ill-bred
F3 cultured, sophisticated

undaunted *adj*
undeterred, undiscouraged, undismayed, unbowed, unflagging, resolute, steadfast, brave, courageous, fearless, bold, brave, unalarmed, intrepid, dauntless, indomitable
F3 discouraged, timorous

undecided *adj*
uncertain, unsure, unknown, ambivalent, doubtful, hesitant, dithering, equivocating, wavering, irresolute, uncommitted, unestablished, indefinite, vague, dubious, debatable, moot, unresolved, unsettled, open, *colloq.* in two minds, the jury is still out on, up in the air
F3 decided, certain, definite

undefeated *adj*
unbeaten, unconquered, victorious, winning, supreme, triumphant, unsubdued, unsurpassed, unbowed, *formal* unvanquished
F3 defeated, *formal* vanquished

undefended *adj*
defenceless, exposed, vulnerable, unprotected, unguarded, open, unarmed, naked, pregnable, *formal* unfortified
F3 armed, defended, *formal* fortified

undefiled *adj*
pure, spotless, unblemished, unsoiled, unspotted, immaculate, flawless, sinless, chaste, clean, clear, unstained, unsullied, intact, virginal, *formal* inviolate

undefined *adj*
vague, hazy, ill-defined, indefinite, unclear, unexplained, unspecified, indistinct, inexact, imprecise, woolly, nebulous, formless, shadowy, tenuous, *formal* indeterminate
F3 definite, precise

undemonstrative *adj*
aloof, distant, remote, withdrawn, reserved, reticent, uncommunicative, unresponsive, stiff, formal, cool, cold, unemotional, restrained, impassive, phlegmatic
F3 demonstrative, communicative

undeniable *adj*
indisputable, incontrovertible, unquestionable, sure, certain, undoubted, indubitable, beyond doubt, beyond question, definite, positive, proven, clear, obvious, patent, evident, unmistakable, *formal* irrefutable, manifest
Fx questionable

undependable *adj*
unreliable, inconsistent, changeable, erratic, uncertain, fickle, capricious, irresponsible, inconstant, unpredictable, unstable, untrustworthy, variable, mercurial, treacherous, fair-weather
Fx dependable, reliable

under *prep, adv*
▶ *prep* **1** BELOW, underneath, beneath, lower than, less than **2** INFERIOR TO, secondary to, junior to, subordinate to, subservient to
Fx **1** over, above
▶ *adv* below, underneath, beneath, down, downward, less, lower

underclothes *n*
underwear, underclothing, undergarments, underlinen, frillies, lingerie, *colloq.* smalls, undies, unmentionables

undercover *adj*
secret, private, confidential, sly, intelligence, underground, surreptitious, stealthy, furtive, covert, hidden, concealed, *formal* clandestine, *colloq.* hush-hush
Fx open, unconcealed

undercurrent *n*
1 *an undercurrent in the sea* undertow, underflow **2** FEELING, undertone, overtone, hint, suggestion, tinge, flavour, aura, atmosphere, sense, movement, tendency, trend, drift, undertow

undercut *v*
1 UNDERPRICE, undersell, undercharge, underbid, undermine **2** EXCAVATE, hollow out, mine, gouge out, scoop out

underestimate *v*
underrate, undervalue, misjudge, miscalculate, fail to appreciate, minimize, belittle, dismiss, look down on, sell short, trivialize, *formal* disparage, *colloq.* play down
Fx overestimate, exaggerate

undergo *v*
experience, suffer, sustain, submit to, go through, put up with, tolerate, bear, stand, endure, weather, withstand

underground *adj, n, adv*
▶ *adj* **1** *an underground passage* subterranean, buried, sunken, covered, hidden, concealed **2** SECRET, covert, furtive, surreptitious, undercover, revolutionary, subversive, radical, experimental, avant-garde, alternative, unorthodox, unofficial, illegal, *formal* clandestine
▶ *n* subway, metro, *colloq.* tube
▶ *adv* below the surface, below ground level, below ground

undergrowth *n*
brush, brushwood, scrub, vegetation, ground cover, bracken, thicket, bushes, brambles, briars

underhand *adj*
unscrupulous, unethical, immoral, improper, sly, crafty, sneaky, stealthy, secret, surreptitious, furtive, devious, dishonest, deceitful, deceptive, fraudulent, scheming, *formal* clandestine, *colloq.* crooked, shady
Fx honest, open, *colloq.* above board

underline *v*
mark, underscore, stress, emphasize, draw attention to, accentuate, italicize, highlight, point up
Fx play down, soft-pedal

underling *n*
minion, subordinate, inferior, lackey, menial, nonentity, flunkey, hireling, servant, slave, nobody
Fx boss, leader, master

underlying *adj*
basic, fundamental, essential, primary, elementary, root, intrinsic, latent, hidden, concealed, lurking, veiled, *formal* basal

undermine *v*
1 WEAKEN, make less secure, destroy, erode, wear away, sap, damage, sabotage, subvert, injure, mar, impair, *formal* vitiate **2** MINE, tunnel, dig, excavate
Fx **1** strengthen, fortify

underprivileged *adj*
disadvantaged, deprived, poor, needy, in need, in distress, in want, impoverished, destitute, oppressed, *formal* impecunious
Fx privileged, fortunate, affluent

underrate *v*
underestimate, undervalue, fail to appreciate, belittle, depreciate, dismiss, look down on, sell short, *formal* disparage
Fx overrate, exaggerate

undersell *v*
undercharge, undercut, cut, mark down, reduce, slash, sell short, depreciate, play down, understate, *formal* disparage

undersized *adj*
little, small, tiny, minute, miniature, pygmy, dwarf, stunted, underdeveloped, underweight, puny, runtish, atrophied, *technical* achondroplastic, *colloq.* pint-(sized)
Fx oversized, big, overweight

understand *v*
1 *I don't understand* grasp, take in, follow, fathom, penetrate, make out, figure out, discern, perceive, see, realize, recognize, appreciate, accept, *formal* comprehend, apprehend, *colloq.* get, cotton on, click, twig, tumble to, latch onto, get the hang of, rumble, suss out, get the message, get the picture, get wise, get your head/mind round, *slang* savvy **2** SYMPATHIZE, empathize, commiserate, comfort, feel sorry for, feel for, identify with, support **3** BELIEVE, think, know, hear, learn, gather, assume, presume, suppose, conclude
Fx **1** misunderstand

understanding *n, adj*
▶ *n* **1** GRASP, knowledge, wisdom, intelligence, intellect, sense, judgement, discernment, insight, appreciation, awareness, impression, feeling, perception, view, belief, idea, notion, opinion, interpretation, *formal* comprehension, apprehension **2** AGREEMENT, arrangement, pact, bargain, harmony, *formal* accord, compact, entente **3** SYMPATHY, empathy, compassion, comfort, support, consolation, commiseration, trust
▶ *adj* sympathetic, compassionate, kind, considerate, supportive, sensitive, thoughtful, tender, loving, patient, lenient, tolerant, forbearing, forgiving
Fx unsympathetic, insensitive, impatient, intolerant

understate *v*
underplay, play down, minimize, make light of, belittle, dismiss, *colloq.* soft-pedal
Fx exaggerate, emphasize

understood *adj*
accepted, assumed, presumed, implied, implicit, inferred, tacit, unstated, unspoken, unwritten

understudy *n*
stand-in, double, substitute, replacement, reserve, deputy, relief, locum, *colloq.* fill in

undertake v

1 PLEDGE, promise, guarantee, agree, contract, covenant **2** BEGIN, embark on, tackle, set about, try, attempt, endeavour, take on, accept, assume, *formal* commence

undertaker n

funeral director, funeral furnisher, *US* mortician

undertaking n

1 ENTERPRISE, venture, business, affair, task, project, operation, attempt, endeavour, effort, job, plan, campaign, scheme **2** PLEDGE, commitment, promise, vow, word, assurance, guarantee, warrant

undertone n

hint, suggestion, whisper, murmur, intimation, trace, tinge, touch, flavour, feeling, aura, atmosphere, undercurrent

undervalue v

underrate, underestimate, misjudge, minimize, depreciate, dismiss, look down on, sell short, *formal* disparage

☒ overrate, exaggerate

underwater adj

subaquatic, undersea, submarine, immersed, submerged, sunken, *formal* subaqueous

underwear n

underclothes, undergarments, lingerie, frillies, *colloq.* undies, smalls, unmentionables

underweight adj

thin, undersized, underfed, undernourished, half-starved

☒ overweight

underworld n

1 CRIMINAL WORLD, organized crime, gangland, *slang* the mob **2** NETHER WORLD, infernal regions, hades, hell, the inferno

underwrite v

endorse, authorize, sanction, approve, confirm, back, guarantee, insure, sponsor, support, fund, finance, subsidize, subscribe, sign, initial, countersign

undesirable adj

unwanted, unwelcome, unacceptable, unwished-for, disliked, unsuitable, unpleasant, disagreeable, distasteful, offensive, objectionable, foul, nasty, obnoxious, *formal* repugnant

☒ desirable, pleasant

undeveloped adj

1 *undeveloped nations* developing, underdeveloped, less advanced, Third World **2** UNFORMED, embryonic, potential, latent, immature, stunted, dwarfed, *formal* inchoate, primordial

☒ **1** advanced, industrialized **2** developed, mature

undignified adj

inelegant, ungainly, clumsy, foolish, improper, unsuitable, inappropriate, unbecoming, *formal* unseemly, indecorous

☒ dignified, elegant

undisciplined adj

wild, unrestrained, unruly, uncontrolled, wayward, disobedient, obstreperous, wilful, unpredictable, unreliable, unschooled, unsteady, untrained, disorganized, unsystematic

☒ disciplined, self-controlled

undisguised adj

unconcealed, open, overt, explicit, frank, genuine, apparent, patent, obvious, evident, transparent, blatant, naked, unadorned, stark, utter, outright, thoroughgoing, *formal* manifest

☒ secret, concealed, hidden

undisputed adj

uncontested, unchallenged, unquestioned, undoubted, indisputable, incontrovertible, undeniable, accepted, acknowledged, recognized, sure, certain, conclusive, *formal* irrefutable

☒ debatable, uncertain

undistinguished adj

unexceptional, unremarkable, unimpressive, ordinary, everyday, common, pedestrian, banal, indifferent, mediocre, inferior, *colloq.* run-of-the-mill, so-so, not up to much, not all that it is cracked up to be, nothing much to write about, no great shakes, not much cop

☒ distinguished, exceptional, remarkable

undisturbed adj

untouched, calm, composed, equable, collected, even, quiet, placid, serene, tranquil, untroubled, motionless, unconcerned, unaffected, uninterrupted, unruffled, *formal* unperturbed

☒ disturbed, interrupted

undivided adj

solid, unbroken, intact, whole, total, entire, full, complete, combined, united, unanimous, unqualified, unreserved, concentrated, exclusive, wholehearted, serious, dedicated, sincere

undo v

1 UNFASTEN, untie, unbuckle, unbutton, unhook, unzip, unlock, unwrap, unwind, open, free, release, loose, loosen, separate, disentangle **2** ANNUL, invalidate, cancel, offset, neutralize, reverse, overturn, repeal, revoke, set aside, upset, quash, defeat, undermine, subvert, mar, spoil, ruin, wreck, crush, shatter, destroy, obliterate, *formal* nullify

☒ **1** fasten, do up

undoing n

downfall, ruin, ruination, collapse, destruction, defeat, overthrow, reversal, weakness, shame, disgrace

undone adj

1 UNACCOMPLISHED, unfulfilled, unfinished, uncompleted, incomplete, outstanding, left, omitted, neglected, ignored, forgotten, passed over **2** UNFASTENED, untied, unlaced, unbuttoned, unlocked, open, loose **3** RUINED, lost, destroyed, betrayed

☒ **1** done, accomplished, complete **2** fastened

undoubted adj

unchallenged, undisputed, acknowledged, uncontested, unquestionable, indisputable, incontrovertible, undesirable, sure, certain, definite, obvious, patent, *formal* indubitable, irrefutable

undoubtedly adv

certainly, definitely, doubtless, without doubt, no doubt, beyond doubt, surely, of course, undeniably, unquestionably, unmistakably, assuredly, *formal* indubitably

undreamed-of adj

undreamt, inconceivable, unheard-of, unhoped-for, unimagined, unexpected, incredible, unforeseen, unsuspected, amazing, astonishing, miraculous

undress v, n

▶ v strip, disrobe, take off, remove, shed, unclothe, *formal* divest, *colloq.* peel off

▶ n nakedness, nudity, dishabille, déshabillé, *formal* disarray

undressed adj

unclothed, disrobed, stripped, naked, stark naked, nude

☒ clothed

undue adj

unnecessary, needless, uncalled-for, unwarranted, undeserved, unjustified, unreasonable, disproportionate, excessive, immoderate, inordinate, extreme, superfluous, extravagant, improper, inappropriate

☒ reasonable, moderate, proper

undulate *v*
rise and fall, swell, roll, surge, wave, ripple, billow, heave

undulating *adj*
rolling, wavy, rippling, billowing, sinuous, *formal* flexuose, flexuous, undate, undulant
F∃ flat

unduly *adv*
too, over, excessively, immoderately, inordinately, disproportionately, out of all proportions, unreasonably, unjustifiably, unnecessarily
F∃ moderately, reasonably

undying *adj*
eternal, deathless, lasting, perpetual, everlasting, immortal, infinite, continuing, constant, perennial, permanent, unending, unfading, indestructible, inextinguishable, imperishable, undiminished, *formal* abiding, sempiternal
F∃ impermanent, inconstant

unearth *v*
dig up, exhume, disinter, excavate, uncover, expose, reveal, bring to light, find, discover, detect
F∃ bury

unearthly *adj*
1 SUPERNATURAL, ghostly, phantom, eerie, uncanny, weird, strange, spine-chilling, other-worldly, *Scot.* eldritch, *formal* preternatural, *colloq.* creepy **2** *at this unearthly hour* unreasonable, preposterous, appalling, outrageous, ungodly, *colloq.* horrendous
F∃ 2 reasonable

uneasiness *n*
anxiety, alarm, apprehension, apprehensiveness, worry, doubt, qualms, unease, misgiving, nervousness, suspicion, disquiet, dis-ease, agitation, *formal* inquietude, perturbation
F∃ calm, composure

uneasy *adj*
1 UNCOMFORTABLE, anxious, worried, alarmed, apprehensive, tense, strained, nervous, agitated, shaky, edgy, upset, troubled, disturbed, unsettled, restless, impatient, unsure, insecure, *formal* perturbed, *colloq.* on edge, nervy, twitchy, keyed up, wound up, jittery **2** WORRYING, troubling, disturbing, unsettling, unnerving, disconcerting, *formal* perturbing
F∃ 1 calm, composed

uneconomic *adj*
unprofitable, uncommercial, loss-making, non-profit-making
F∃ economic, profitable, profit-making, remuneration

uneducated *adj*
unschooled, untaught, unread, ignorant, illiterate, uncultivated, uncultured, philistine, benighted
F∃ educated

unemotional *adj*
cool, cold, unfeeling, impassive, reserved, indifferent, apathetic, passionless, unresponsive, undemonstrative, unexcitable, phlegmatic, detached, objective, dispassionate
F∃ emotional, excitable

unemphatic *adj*
understated, unobtrusive, unostentatious, underplayed, played-down, *colloq.* down-beat, soft-pedalled

unemployed *adj*
jobless, out of work, laid off, redundant, unwaged, idle, unoccupied, *colloq.* on the dole
F∃ employed, occupied

unending *adj*
endless, never-ending, unceasing, ceaseless, incessant, interminable, continuous, uninterrupted, constant, continual, perpetual, everlasting, eternal, undying, *formal* unremitting
F∃ transient, intermittent

unendurable *adj*
intolerable, unbearable, overwhelming, shattering, insufferable, insupportable
F∃ bearable, endurable

unenthusiastic *adj*
uninterested, unimpressed, cool, half-hearted, apathetic, bored, neutral, nonchalant, indifferent, unmoved, unresponsive, blasé, lukewarm, Laodicean
F∃ enthusiastic

unenviable *adj*
undesirable, unpleasant, disagreeable, uncongenial, uncomfortable, thankless, difficult, dangerous
F∃ enviable, desirable

unequal *adj*
1 DIFFERENT, varying, dissimilar, unlike, unfair, unjust, biased, inequitable, discriminatory **2** UNMATCHED, uneven, unbalanced, lopsided, disproportionate, asymmetrical, irregular **3** *unequal to a task* incapable, unqualified, inadequate, unsuited, unfitted, incompetent, *colloq.* not up to, not cut out for
F∃ 1, 2, 3 equal

unequalled *adj*
unmatched, unsurpassed, unrivalled, peerless, unique, paramount, matchless, incomparable, unparalleled, pre-eminent, surpassing, transcendent, supreme, exceptional, inimitable, *formal* nonpareil

unequivocal *adj*
unambiguous, explicit, clear, plain, evident, distinct, unmistakable, express, direct, straight, straightforward, definite, positive, categorical, incontrovertible, absolute, outright, unqualified, unreserved
F∃ ambiguous, vague, qualified

unerring *adj*
unfailing, perfect, impeccable, infallible, faultless, exact, certain, sure, accurate, uncanny, *colloq.* dead
F∃ fallible

unethical *adj*
unprofessional, immoral, improper, wrong, wicked, evil, unscrupulous, unprincipled, dishonourable, disreputable, illegal, illicit, dishonest, underhand, *colloq.* shady
F∃ ethical

uneven *adj*
1 *uneven ground* rough, bumpy, lumpy, stony, rugged, craggy, jagged, irregular, coarse **2** ODD, unequal, inequitable, unfair, unbalanced, one-sided, ill-matched, asymmetrical, lopsided, crooked **3** IRREGULAR, intermittent, spasmodic, fitful, jerky, unsteady, variable, changeable, fluctuating, erratic, inconsistent, patchy
F∃ 1 even, flat, level **2** even, equal **3** regular, consistent

uneventful *adj*
uninteresting, unexciting, quiet, unvaried, boring, monotonous, tedious, dull, routine, humdrum, ordinary, everyday, commonplace, unremarkable, unexceptional, unmemorable, *colloq.* run-of-the-mill
F∃ eventful, memorable, remarkable

unexampled *adj*
unprecedented, never before seen, incomparable, unequalled, unparalleled, unheard-of, unmatched, unique, novel

unexceptional *adj*
unremarkable, unmemorable, typical, average, normal, usual, ordinary, common, everyday, indifferent, mediocre, unimpressive, undistinguished, *colloq.* run-of-the-mill, so-so, not up to much, not all that it is

cracked up to be, nothing much to write about, no great shakes, not much cop

F3 exceptional, impressive

unexpected *adj*

unforeseen, unanticipated, unpredictable, unlooked-for, chance, accidental, fortuitous, sudden, abrupt, surprising, startling, amazing, astonishing, unusual

F3 expected, predictable

unexpectedly *adv*

suddenly, surprisingly, unpredictably, without warning, abruptly, by chance, fortuitously, *colloq.* out of the blue

unexpressive *adj*

expressionless, emotionless, impassive, inexpressive, inscrutable, vacant, blank, dead-pan, immobile

F3 expressive, mobile

unfading *adj*

lasting, imperishable, durable, enduring, undying, unfailing, fadeless, fast, evergreen, *formal* abiding, immarcescible

F3 changeable, transient

unfailing *adj*

constant, certain, dependable, reliable, sure, steady, true, steadfast, faithful, loyal, staunch, undying, unfading, inexhaustible, infallible

F3 fickle, impermanent, transient

unfair *adj*

1 UNJUST, partial, biased, prejudiced, bigoted, discriminatory, unbalanced, weighted, one-sided, slanted, partisan, arbitrary, undeserved, unmerited, unwarranted, unreasonable, uncalled-for, *formal* inequitable **2** UNETHICAL, unscrupulous, unprincipled, wrongful, deceitful, dishonest, *colloq.* crooked, bent, shady, below the belt

F3 **1** fair, just, unbiased, deserved **2** honest, ethical

unfairness *n*

injustice, inequity, one-sidedness, partiality, partisanship, prejudice, bigotry, bias, discrimination

F3 fairness, equity

unfaithful *adj*

disloyal, treacherous, false, untrue, insincere, deceitful, dishonest, untrustworthy, unreliable, fickle, inconstant, adulterous, cheating, double-dealing, faithless, unbelieving, godless, *formal* duplicitous, perfidious, *colloq.* two-timing

F3 faithful, loyal, reliable

unfaltering *adj*

unfailing, unwavering, unyielding, unswerving, untiring, tireless, unflagging, unflinching, constant, firm, indefatigable, steady, steadfast, resolute, fixed, *formal* pertinacious

F3 faltering, uncertain, wavering

unfamiliar *adj*

1 STRANGE, unusual, uncommon, curious, alien, foreign, uncharted, unexplored, unknown, different, new, novel **2** UNACCUSTOMED, unacquainted, uninformed, inexperienced, unpractised, unskilled, unversed, unconversant

F3 **1** familiar, customary **2** conversant

unfashionable *adj*

outmoded, dated, out of date, out, *passé*, *démodé*, old-fashioned, antiquated, obsolete, unpopular, *colloq.* old hat, square

F3 fashionable

unfasten *v*

undo, untie, loosen, unwrap, unclasp, unlock, open, uncouple, disconnect, separate, detach

F3 fasten, do up, bolt, lock

unfathomable *adj*

inexplicable, incomprehensible, impenetrable, baffling, fathomless, immeasurable, unknowable, mysterious, deep, profound, hidden, bottomless, unplumbed, unsounded, inscrutable, indecipherable, *formal* abstruse, esoteric

F3 comprehensible, explicable, penetrable

unfavourable *adj*

1 UNPROMISING, ominous, threatening, discouraging, inopportune, untimely, unseasonable, ill-suited, unfortunate, unlucky, disadvantageous, bad, poor, adverse, contrary, negative, *formal* inauspicious **2** HOSTILE, critical, adverse, negative, bad, poor, unfriendly, uncomplimentary, *formal* inimical

F3 **1** favourable, promising, *formal* auspicious **2** good, friendly, complimentary

unfeeling *adj*

insensitive, cold, hard, stony, callous, heartless, hard-hearted, harsh, cruel, inhuman, pitiless, uncaring, unsympathetic, apathetic

F3 sensitive, sympathetic

unfeigned *adj*

genuine, natural, pure, real, sincere, unaffected, frank, spontaneous, wholehearted, unforced, heartfelt

F3 insincere, pretended, feigned

unfettered *adj*

unconstrained, free, unhampered, unrestrained, unhindered, unconfined, unchecked, unbridled, uninhibited, unshackled, untrammelled

F3 constrained, fettered

unfinished *adj*

incomplete, uncompleted, half-done, sketchy, rough, crude, imperfect, lacking, wanting, deficient, undone, unaccomplished, unfulfilled

F3 finished, perfect

unfit *adj*

1 UNSUITABLE, inappropriate, unsuited, inapt, ill-equipped, unqualified, ineligible, untrained, unprepared, unequal, incapable, unable, incompetent, inadequate, ineffective, useless **2** UNHEALTHY, out of condition, flabby, feeble, weak, decrepit, *formal* debilitated

F3 **1** fit, suitable, competent **2** healthy, fit

unflagging *adj*

unfaltering, unfailing, untiring, tireless, unswerving, unceasing, undeviating, persevering, persistent, never-failing, indefatigable, constant, steady, fixed, single-minded, staunch, *formal* unremitting

F3 faltering, inconstant

unflappable *adj*

calm, collected, composed, level-headed, unworried, unexcitable, unruffled, equable, cool, impassive, self-possessed, phlegmatic, *formal* imperturbable

F3 excitable, nervous, temperamental, *colloq.* panicky

unflattering *adj*

unbecoming, uncomplimentary, unfavourable, unprepossessing, critical, honest, blunt, candid, outspoken

F3 complimentary, flattering

unflinching *adj*

steady, unfaltering, unwavering, unshaken, unshrinking, unswerving, firm, fixed, determined, constant, staunch, steadfast, sure, bold, resolute, stalwart, unblinking

F3 unsteady, scared

unfold *v*

1 DEVELOP, evolve, grow, work out, come about, result, emerge **2** REVEAL, disclose, show, present, tell, relate, make known, describe, explain, clarify, elaborate, narrate **3** *unfold a map* open (out), spread (out), flatten, straighten (out), stretch out, undo, unfurl,

unroll, uncoil, unravel, unwrap, uncover
F∃ 2 withhold, suppress **3** fold, wrap

unforeseen *adj*
unpredicted, unpredictable, unexpected, unanticipated, unlooked-for, surprising, amazing, astonishing, startling, sudden, unavoidable, unusual
F∃ expected, predictable

unforgettable *adj*
memorable, momentous, historic, noteworthy, notable, impressive, remarkable, significant, exceptional, extraordinary, striking, important, special, distinctive
F∃ unmemorable, unexceptional

unforgivable *adj*
unpardonable, inexcusable, unjustifiable, indefensible, intolerable, shameful, outrageous, disgraceful, deplorable, contemptible, *formal* reprehensible
F∃ forgivable, venial

unforgiven *adj*
unredeemed, unabsolved, unregenerate, unrepentant
F∃ absolved, forgiven

unfortunate *adj*
1 UNLUCKY, luckless, unsuccessful, poor, wretched, unhappy, doomed, ill-fated, hopeless, calamitous, disastrous, ruinous, adverse, unpleasant, disadvantageous, untoward, *formal* hapless **2** REGRETTABLE, lamentable, deplorable, adverse, unfavourable, unsuitable, inappropriate, inopportune, untimely, ill-timed, ill-advised, *formal* injudicious
F∃ 1 fortunate, happy **2** favourable, appropriate

unfortunately *adv*
regrettably, unhappily, unluckily, sadly, alas, sad to say, sad to relate, *colloq.* worse luck
F∃ fortunately

unfounded *adj*
baseless, groundless, unsupported, unsubstantiated, unproven, unjustified, idle, false, spurious, trumped-up, fabricated, without foundation, *formal* uncorroborated, conjectural
F∃ substantiated, justified

unfrequented *adj*
lonely, remote, secluded, uninhabited, unvisited, isolated, deserted, desolate, solitary, lone, God-forsaken, *formal* sequestered
F∃ busy, crowded, populous

unfriendly *adj*
unsociable, standoffish, aloof, distant, unapproachable, inhospitable, uncongenial, unneighbourly, unwelcoming, unkind, cold, chilly, cool, frosty, hostile, strained, aggressive, quarrelsome, antagonistic, ill-disposed, unpleasant, disagreeable, surly, sour, *formal* inimical, inauspicious
F∃ friendly, amiable, agreeable

unfruitful *adj*
unproductive, fruitless, barren, exhausted, impoverished, infertile, sterile, arid, unprofitable, unprolific, unrewarding, *formal* infecund, infructuous
F∃ fruitful, productive

ungainly *adj*
clumsy, awkward, gauche, inelegant, ungraceful, gawky, unco-ordinated, lumbering, gangling, unwieldy, uncouth, loutish, *formal* maladroit
F∃ graceful, elegant

ungodly *adj*
1 UNREASONABLE, outrageous, preposterous, intolerable, unearthly, unsocial, *colloq.* horrendous **2** IMPIOUS, irreligious, godless, blasphemous, profane, immoral, corrupt, depraved, sinful, wicked, *formal* iniquitous

ungovernable *adj*
uncontrollable, wild, disorderly, unmanageable, unrestrainable, unruly, ungoverned, rebellious, masterless, *formal* refractory

ungracious *adj*
discourteous, uncivil, impolite, rude, disrespectful, graceless, bad-mannered, ill-bred, unmannerly, offhand, boorish, churlish
F∃ gracious, polite

ungrateful *adj*
unthankful, unappreciative, rude, impolite, uncivil, ill-mannered, ungracious, selfish, thankless, heedless
F∃ grateful, thankful

unguarded *adj*
1 *in an unguarded moment* unwary, careless, inattentive, off guard, incautious, indiscreet, undiplomatic, thoughtless, unthinking, heedless, foolish, foolhardy, rash, ill-considered, *formal* imprudent, impolitic, uncircumspect **2** UNDEFENDED, unprotected, exposed, vulnerable, defenceless, unpatrolled
F∃ 1 guarded, cautious **2** defended, protected

unhappily *adv*
unfortunately, regrettably, unluckily, sadly, alas, sad to say, sad to relate, *colloq.* worse luck
F∃ fortunately

unhappy *adj*
1 SAD, sorrowful, miserable, melancholy, depressed, dispirited, glum, despondent, dejected, downcast, crestfallen, long-faced, gloomy, mournful, *formal* woebegone, disconsolate, *colloq.* down, blue, fed up, low, down in the dumps **2** UNFORTUNATE, unlucky, ill-fated, ill-starred, unsuitable, inappropriate, inapt, ill-chosen, ill-advised, tactless, awkward, clumsy, *formal* hapless, injudicious
F∃ 1 happy **2** fortunate, suitable

unharmed *adj*
undamaged, unhurt, uninjured, unscathed, untouched, whole, intact, safe, sound
F∃ harmed, injured, hurt

unhealthy *adj*
1 UNWELL, sick, ill, poorly, ailing, sickly, infirm, invalid, weak, feeble, frail, unsound, *formal* indisposed, debilitated **2** UNWHOLESOME, insanitary, unhygienic, harmful, injurious, insalutary, detrimental, noxious, morbid, unnatural, *formal* insalubrious
F∃ 1 healthy, fit **2** wholesome, hygienic, natural

unheard-of *adj*
1 UNTHINKABLE, inconceivable, unbelievable, unimaginable, undreamed-of, unprecedented, extraordinary, exceptional, unacceptable, offensive, shocking, outrageous, preposterous **2** UNKNOWN, unfamiliar, new, unusual, obscure, unsung, unheralded, undiscovered
F∃ 1 normal, acceptable **2** famous

unheeded *adj*
ignored, disregarded, disobeyed, unnoticed, unnoted, unobserved, unremarked, overlooked, neglected, forgotten
F∃ noted, observed

unheralded *adj*
unsung, unrecognized, unproclaimed, unpublicized, unnoticed, surprise, unadvertised, unannounced, unexpected, unforeseen
F∃ advertised, publicized, trumpeted, acclaimed

unhesitating *adj*
immediate, instant, instantaneous, prompt, ready, automatic, spontaneous, unquestioning, unwavering, unfaltering, wholehearted, confident, implicit
F∃ hesitant, tentative

unhinge *v*
unbalance, unnerve, unsettle, upset, confuse, distract, disorder, drive mad, madden, craze, derange

unholy *adj*
1 IMPIOUS, irreligious, godless, ungodly, blasphemous, sinful, immoral, corrupt, depraved, wicked, evil, *formal* iniquitous **2** *an unholy mess* unreasonable, shocking, outrageous, ungodly, unearthly, *colloq.* horrendous
F3 1 holy, pious, godly 2 reasonable

unhoped-for *adj*
unexpected, unforeseen, unanticipated, unimaginable, unlooked-for, unbelievable, undreamed-of, incredible, surprising

unhurried *adj*
slow, leisurely, deliberate, easy, relaxed, calm, sedate, *colloq.* easy-going, laid-back
F3 hurried, hasty, rushed

unhurt *adj*
unharmed, uninjured, unscathed, untouched, whole, intact, safe, sound
F3 hurt, injured

unidentified *adj*
unknown, unrecognized, unmarked, unnamed, nameless, anonymous, incognito, unfamiliar, strange, mysterious, obscure, unclassified
F3 identified, known, named

unification *n*
union, uniting, merger, alliance, amalgamation, combination, federation, fusion, incorporation, coalescence, coalition, confederation, *formal* enosis
F3 separation, split, division

uniform *n, adj*
▶ *n* outfit, costume, livery, insignia, regalia, robes, dress, suit, regimentals, *colloq.* garb, rig
▶ *adj* same, identical, like, alike, similar, homogeneous, consistent, regular, equal, smooth, even, flat, monotonous, unvarying, unchanging, constant, unbroken, stable, invariable, undeviating
F3 different, varied, changing

uniformity *n*
sameness, constancy, invariability, regularity, similarity, evenness, flatness, monotony, drabness, dullness, tedium, *formal* homogeneity, homomorphism, similitude
F3 difference, dissimilarity, variation

unify *v*
unite, bring/come together, join, bind, combine, integrate, mix, blend, merge, amalgamate, consolidate, coalesce, fuse, weld
F3 separate, divide, split

unimaginable *adj*
inconceivable, unbelievable, incredible, amazing, astonishing, staggering, extraordinary, preposterous, impossible, fantastic, undreamed-of, unthinkable, unheard-of, implausible, unlikely, unconvincing, far-fetched, outlandish, *colloq.* mind-boggling

unimaginative *adj*
uninspired, unoriginal, predictable, hackneyed, banal, mundane, pedestrian, ordinary, dull, boring, routine, usual, dry, barren, lifeless, stale, unexciting, tame, *colloq.* matter-of-fact, samey
F3 imaginative, creative, original

unimpeachable *adj*
blameless, perfect, unblemished, spotless, faultless, immaculate, impeccable, irreproachable, unchallengeable, unquestionable, unassailable, reliable, dependable
F3 blameworthy, faulty

unimpeded *adj*
unrestrained, unconstrained, free, open, clear, unhindered, unblocked, unchecked, unhampered, uninhibited, untrammelled, *colloq.* all-round
F3 hampered, impeded

unimportant *adj*
insignificant, inconsequential, irrelevant, immaterial, insubstantial, minor, secondary, incidental, marginal, peripheral, trivial, trifling, petty, slight, negligible, worthless, *formal* nugatory, *colloq.* no great shakes, no big deal, not worth mentioning
F3 important, significant, relevant, vital

uninhabited *adj*
unoccupied, vacant, empty, deserted, abandoned, desolate, unpeopled, unpopulated, unsettled

uninhibited *adj*
unconstrained, unreserved, unselfconscious, liberated, free, unrestricted, uncontrolled, unrestrained, abandoned, natural, spontaneous, frank, outspoken, candid, open, relaxed, informal
F3 inhibited, repressed, constrained, restrained

uninspired *adj*
ordinary, boring, commonplace, dull, indifferent, stale, trite, stock, unexciting, unimaginative, uninspiring, uninteresting, undistinguished, unoriginal, pedestrian, prosaic, humdrum
F3 original, inspired, exciting

unintelligent *adj*
stupid, foolish, silly, slow, half-witted, empty-headed, fatuous, unreasoning, unthinking, dense, dull, obtuse, brainless, *colloq.* thick, dumb, gormless
F3 intelligent

unintelligible *adj*
incomprehensible, incoherent, inarticulate, garbled, scrambled, jumbled, muddled, indecipherable, unreadable, illegible, impenetrable, unfathomable, puzzling, mysterious, obscure, complicated, complex, involved, *colloq.* double Dutch
F3 intelligible, comprehensible, clear

unintentional *adj*
unintended, accidental, inadvertent, unplanned, unpremeditated, uncalculated, involuntary, unconscious, unwitting, careless, *formal* fortuitous
F3 intentional, deliberate

uninterested *adj*
indifferent, unconcerned, uninvolved, bored, listless, apathetic, unenthusiastic, blasé, impassive, distant, unresponsive
F3 interested, concerned, enthusiastic, responsive, curious

> *uninterested* or *disinterested* ? *See panel at* DIS-INTERESTED.

uninteresting *adj*
boring, tedious, monotonous, humdrum, dull, drab, dreary, dry, flat, tame, stale, prosaic, pedestrian, uneventful, unexciting, uninspiring, unimpressive, tiresome, wearisome
F3 interesting, exciting, entertaining

uninterrupted *adj*
unbroken, continuous, non-stop, unending, unceasing, ceaseless, endless, constant, continual, steady, sustained, undisturbed, peaceful, *formal* unremitting
F3 broken, intermittent

uninvited *adj*
unasked, unsought, unsolicited, unwanted, unwelcome
F3 invited

uninviting *adj*
unappealing, unattractive, undesirable, unpleasant, unwelcoming, repellent, repulsive, offensive, off-

putting, unsavoury, disagreeable, distasteful, unappetizing

🖃 inviting, welcome

union *n*

1 FUSION, unification, unity, alliance, coalition, association, league, confederation, amalgamation, merger, combination, joining, juncture, consolidation, mixture, synthesis, blend **2** ASSOCIATION, trade union, alliance, coalition, league, club, federation, confederacy, consortium, confederacy **3** AGREEMENT, harmony, unity, unanimity, *formal* accord, concurrence **4** MARRIAGE, wedding, *formal* matrimony, nuptials

🖃 **1** separation, alienation, *formal* estrangement **4** divorce

unique *adj*

single, one-off, sole, only, one and only, one of a kind, lone, solitary, unmatched, matchless, peerless, unequalled, unparalleled, unrivalled, incomparable, unprecedented, inimitable, *formal* nonpareil, *sui generis*

🖃 common

unison *n*

concert, co-operation, unanimity, unity, *formal* accord, concord

unit *n*

item, part, element, constituent, piece, component, module, section, segment, portion, entity, whole, one, system, assembly

unite *v*

join, connect, link, couple, marry, ally, co-operate, band, associate, federate, confederate, combine, join forces, pool, amalgamate, merge, blend, unify, consolidate, coalesce, weld, fuse, *colloq.* pull together

🖃 separate, sever

united *adj*

allied, affiliated, corporate, unified, combined, amalgamated, pooled, collective, concerted, one, unanimous, agreed, in agreement, like-minded, co-operative, *formal* in accord

🖃 disunited

unity *n*

1 AGREEMENT, harmony, peace, consensus, unanimity, solidarity, *formal* accord, concord, concert, *colloq.* togetherness **2** UNION, integrity, oneness, wholeness, amalgamation, unification

🖃 **1** disunity, disagreement, discord, strife

universal *adj*

worldwide, global, cosmic, all-embracing, all-inclusive, general, comprehensive, common, across-the-board, total, whole, entire, all-round, unlimited, *formal* ubiquitous, omnipresent

universality *n*

commonness, comprehensiveness, all-inclusiveness, entirety, totality, completeness, generalization, generality, predominance, prevalence, *formal* ubiquity

universally *adv*

always, everywhere, uniformly, invariably, *formal* ubiquitously

universe *n*

cosmos, world, nature, creation, firmament, heavens, *formal* macrocosm

university *n*

college, institute, varsity, academy, *formal* academia

unjust *adj*

unfair, wrong, partial, biased, prejudiced, one-sided, partisan, unreasonable, unjustified, undeserved, *formal* inequitable

🖃 just, fair, reasonable

unjustifiable *adj*

indefensible, inexcusable, unforgivable, unpardon-

able, unreasonable, uncalled-for, unwarranted, immoderate, excessive, unacceptable, outrageous

🖃 justifiable, acceptable

unkempt *adj*

dishevelled, tousled, rumpled, uncombed, ungroomed, untidy, disordered, messy, scruffy, shabby, slovenly, *colloq.* sloppy, shambolic, slobbish

🖃 well-groomed, tidy

unkind *adj*

cruel, harsh, inhuman, inhumane, callous, hard-hearted, cold-hearted, heartless, unfeeling, insensitive, thoughtless, inconsiderate, uncharitable, pitiless, ruthless, nasty, malicious, vicious, snide, spiteful, mean, unfriendly, uncaring, unsympathetic, *formal* malevolent, *colloq.* shabby, bitchy

🖃 kind, kindly, considerate, generous, sympathetic

unkindness *n*

cruelty, harshness, uncharitableness, unfriendliness, inhumanity, callousness, hard-heartedness, insensitivity, maliciousness, meanness, spite

🖃 kindness, friendship

unknown *adj*

unfamiliar, unheard-of, strange, alien, foreign, mysterious, dark, obscure, hidden, concealed, undisclosed, secret, undivulged, untold, new, uncharted, unexplored, undiscovered, unrevealed, unidentified, unnamed, nameless, anonymous, unheard-of, incognito

🖃 known, familiar

unlawful *adj*

illegal, criminal, illicit, illegitimate, against the law, unconstitutional, outlawed, banned, prohibited, forbidden, unauthorized, unlicensed, unsanctioned

🖃 lawful, legal, allowed, permitted

unleash *v*

loose, let loose, free, release, unloose, untie, untether

🖃 restrain

unlettered *adj*

illiterate, ignorant, uneducated, unlearned, unschooled, untaught, untutored, unlessoned

🖃 educated

unlike *adj, prep*

▶ *adj* dissimilar, different, distinct, opposite, opposed, incompatible, contrasted, ill-matched, unrelated, unequal, divergent, diverse, *formal* disparate

🖃 similar, related

▶ *prep* dissimilar to, different from, in contrast to, as opposed to, as against

🖃 like

unlikely *adj*

1 IMPROBABLE, implausible, far-fetched, unconvincing, unbelievable, incredible, inconceivable, unimaginable, unexpected, doubtful, dubious, questionable, suspect, suspicious **2** SLIGHT, faint, remote, distant, slim, small, inconsiderable

🖃 **1** likely, plausible

unlimited *adj*

limitless, unrestricted, unbounded, boundless, illimitable, infinite, endless, countless, incalculable, immeasurable, untold, vast, immense, extensive, great, indefinite, absolute, total, unconditional, unqualified, all-encompassing, total, complete, full, unconstrained, unhampered, unimpeded, uncontrolled, unchecked

🖃 limited

unload *v*

unpack, empty, discharge, dump, offload, unburden, relieve

🖃 load

unlock *v*
unbolt, unlatch, unfasten, undo, unbar, open, free, release
F3 lock, fasten

unlooked-for *adj*
unexpected, unforeseen, unanticipated, unpredicted, unhoped-for, unthought-of, undreamed-of, surprising, surprise, fortunate, chance, lucky, *formal* fortuitous
F3 expected, predictable

unloved *adj*
unpopular, disliked, hated, detested, unwanted, rejected, spurned, loveless, uncared-for, neglected, *formal* forsaken, *colloq.* dumped
F3 loved

unlucky *adj*
1 UNFORTUNATE, luckless, unsuccessful, poor, wretched, unhappy, miserable, ill-fated, ill-starred, star-crossed, jinxed, doomed, cursed, *formal* hapless, *colloq.* down on your luck **2** UNFAVOURABLE, adverse, unfortunate, unpleasant, unpromising, doomed, ill-fated, ominous, disadvantageous, untoward, calamitous, disastrous, catastrophic, *formal* inauspicious, unpropitious
F3 **1** fortunate, lucky **2** favourable, lucky

unmanageable *adj*
1 UNWIELDY, bulky, cumbersome, awkward, inconvenient, unhandy, *formal* incommodious **2** UNCONTROLLABLE, wild, unruly, disorderly, ungovernable, obstreperous, difficult, *formal* recalcitrant, refractory
F3 **1** manageable **2** controllable

unmanly *adj*
effeminate, dishonourable, feeble, weak, weak-kneed, soft, weedy, cowardly, chicken-hearted, craven, namby-pamby, *colloq.* sissy, wet, yellow, wimpish
F3 manly

unmannerly *adj*
impolite, rude, uncivil, uncouth, discourteous, ill-mannered, badly-behaved, bad-mannered, disrespectful, graceless, ungracious, ill-bred, boorish, low-bred
F3 polite

unmarried *adj*
single, unwed, divorced, celibate, unattached, available, lone, on your own
F3 married

unmask *v*
unveil, uncloak, uncover, bare, expose, reveal, show, disclose, discover, detect
F3 mask, conceal

unmatched *adj*
unrivalled, unique, unparalleled, unequalled, unsurpassed, incomparable, beyond compare, matchless, supreme, peerless, paramount, unexampled, *formal* consummate, nonpareil

unmentionable *adj*
unspeakable, unutterable, taboo, immodest, indecent, embarrassing, unpleasant, shocking, scandalous, shameful, disgraceful, abominable

unmerciful *adj*
merciless, pitiless, ruthless, cruel, brutal, hard, callous, sadistic, heartless, implacable, relentless, remorseless, unrelenting, unsparing, uncaring, unfeeling
F3 merciful

unmethodical *adj*
unorganized, confused, muddled, disorderly, haphazard, illogical, irregular, unsystematic, uncoordinated, random, *formal* desultory
F3 methodical

unmindful *adj*
heedless, careless, negligent, remiss, unheeding, neglectful, lax, slack, indifferent, inattentive, unaware, unconscious, oblivious, forgetful, blind, deaf, regardless
F3 mindful, aware, heedful

unmistakable *adj*
clear, plain, distinct, pronounced, obvious, evident, patent, glaring, blatant, striking, explicit, conspicuous, clear-cut, well-defined, unambiguous, unequivocal, positive, definite, sure, certain, unquestionable, beyond question, indisputable, undeniable, *formal* manifest, indubitable
F3 unclear, ambiguous

unmitigated *adj*
utter, absolute, complete, pure, rank, perfect, outright, downright, out-and-out, thorough, thoroughgoing, sheer, relentless, persistent, intense, unqualified, unalleviated, unrelieved, unbroken, unrelenting, unredeemed, unmodified, undiminished, harsh, grim, *formal* arrant, consummate, unabated, unremitting

unmoved *adj*
unaffected, untouched, unshaken, unstirred, dry-eyed, unfeeling, cold, dispassionate, indifferent, impassive, unresponsive, unconcerned, unimpressed, firm, adamant, inflexible, unbending, undeviating, unwavering, steady, unchanged, resolute, resolved, determined
F3 moved, affected, shaken

unnatural *adj*
1 ABNORMAL, anomalous, freakish, irregular, unusual, strange, odd, peculiar, queer, bizarre, extraordinary, uncommon, uncanny, supernatural, inhuman, perverted **2** AFFECTED, feigned, artificial, false, insincere, unspontaneous, contrived, laboured, stilted, forced, strained, staged, self-conscious, stiff
F3 **1** natural, normal **2** sincere, fluent

unnecessary *adj*
unneeded, needless, uncalled-for, unrequired, wasted, unwanted, gratuitous, non-essential, inessential, dispensable, expendable, superfluous, redundant, tautological
F3 necessary, essential, indispensable

unnerve *v*
daunt, intimidate, frighten, scare, alarm, discourage, deject, demoralize, dishearten, dismay, disconcert, put out, disquiet, unsettle, upset, worry, shake, confound, fluster, unman, *formal* perturb, *colloq.* rattle
F3 nerve, brace, steel

unnoticed *adj*
unobserved, unremarked, unseen, unrecognized, undiscovered, overlooked, ignored, disregarded, neglected, unheeded
F3 noticed, noted

unobtrusive *adj*
inconspicuous, unnoticeable, unassertive, self-effacing, humble, modest, unassuming, unaggressive, unostentatious, unpretentious, restrained, low-key, subdued, quiet, retiring
F3 prominent, obtrusive, ostentatious

unobtrusively *adv*
inconspicuously, quietly, modestly, on the quiet, unostentatiously, surreptitiously, humbly, unpretentiously
F3 obtrusively, ostentatiously, showily, aggressively

unoccupied *adj*
1 UNINHABITED, vacant, empty, deserted, *formal* forsaken **2** JOBLESS, free, idle, inactive, workless, unemployed
F3 **1** occupied **2** busy

unofficial *adj*
unauthorized, illegal, informal, off-the-record, personal, private, confidential, undeclared, unconfirmed, unratified
☒ official, ratified, *formal* accredited, substantiated, corroborated

unoriginal *adj*
unimaginative, uninspired, hackneyed, stale, trite, copied, cliché-ridden, derivative, cribbed, secondhand, derived
☒ original, imaginative, creative, innovative, fresh

unorthodox *adj*
unconventional, nonconformist, heterodox, alternative, fringe, irregular, abnormal, unusual, eccentric, creative, innovative, new, novel, fresh
☒ orthodox, conventional

unpaid *adj*
1 *unpaid bills* outstanding, overdue, unsettled, owing, due, payable, pending, uncollected, remaining 2 *unpaid work* voluntary, honorary, unsalaried, unwaged, unremunerative, free
☒ 1 paid

unpalatable *adj*
1 UNAPPETIZING, distasteful, insipid, bitter, uneatable, inedible, unsavoury, disgusting 2 UNPLEASANT, disagreeable, unattractive, distasteful, unsavoury, offensive, nasty, repellent, *formal* repugnant
☒ 1 palatable 2 pleasant

unparalleled *adj*
unequalled, without equal, unmatched, matchless, peerless, beyond compare, incomparable, unrivalled, unsurpassed, supreme, superlative, rare, unique, exceptional, unprecedented

unpardonable *adj*
unforgivable, inexcusable, unjustifiable, indefensible, outrageous, deplorable, disgraceful, shocking, shameful, scandalous, *formal* irremissible, reprehensible, unconscionable
☒ forgivable, understandable

unperturbed *adj*
calm, unexcited, unflustered, untroubled, unworried, undisturbed, unruffled, unflinching, self-possessed, composed, collected, tranquil, serene, placid, poised, cool, impassive
☒ anxious, perturbed

unpleasant *adj*
1 *an unpleasant smell* disagreeable, nasty, objectionable, offensive, distasteful, unpalatable, unappetizing, unattractive, repulsive, bad, foul, troublesome, disgusting, undesirable, *formal* repugnant, noisome 2 *an unpleasant person* unfriendly, unkind, disagreeable, rude, impolite, discourteous, bad-tempered, ill-natured, nasty, objectionable, hostile, aggressive, quarrelsome, surly, sour, mean
☒ 1, 2 pleasant, agreeable, nice

unpleasantness *n*
annoyance, nastiness, trouble, upset, bother, embarrassment, fuss, furore, ill-feeling, scandal

unpolished *adj*
unfinished, unworked, rough and ready, sketchy, unrefined, unfashioned, unsophisticated, uncultivated, uncultured, uncivilized, coarse, crude, rough, homebred, rude, uncouth, vulgar
☒ finished, polished, refined

unpopular *adj*
disliked, hated, detested, unloved, friendless, undesirable, unattractive, unsought-after, unfashionable, undesirable, unwelcome, unwanted, rejected, ignored, neglected, shunned, avoided,
☒ popular, fashionable

unprecedented *adj*
new, original, revolutionary, unknown, unheard-of, exceptional, remarkable, extraordinary, abnormal, unusual, uncommon, freakish, unparalleled, unrivalled, unequalled
☒ usual

unpredictable *adj*
unforeseeable, unexpected, changeable, variable, inconstant, unreliable, fickle, unstable, volatile, erratic, random, chance, *formal* mercurial, capricious
☒ predictable, foreseeable, constant, reliable

unprejudiced *adj*
unbiased, fair, fair-minded, impartial, just, objective, non-partisan, open-minded, even-handed, balanced, detached, uncoloured, dispassionate, enlightened
☒ prejudiced, narrow-minded

unpremeditated *adj*
spontaneous, unintentional, unplanned, unprepared, unrehearsed, offhand, impulsive, impromptu, extempore, *formal* fortuitous, *colloq.* off-the-cuff, spur-of-the-moment
☒ premeditated

unprepared *adj*
unready, surprised, unsuspecting, ill-equipped, unwilling, unfinished, incomplete, half-baked, unplanned, unrehearsed, spontaneous, improvised, ad-lib, *colloq.* off-the-cuff
☒ prepared, ready

unpretentious *adj*
unaffected, natural, plain, simple, ordinary, unobtrusive, honest, straightforward, humble, modest, unassuming, unostentatious
☒ pretentious, show, ostentatious

unprincipled *adj*
unscrupulous, unprofessional, unethical, dishonest, dishonourable, immoral, underhand, deceitful, devious, corrupt, discreditable, *colloq.* crooked
☒ ethical, principled

unproductive *adj*
infertile, sterile, barren, dry, arid, unfruitful, fruitless, futile, vain, idle, worthless, useless, ineffective, unprofitable, unremunerative, unrewarding, *formal* inefficacious, otiose
☒ productive, fertile

unprofessional *adj*
amateurish, inexpert, unskilled, incompetent, inexperienced, untrained, inefficient, casual, negligent, lax, unethical, unprincipled, unscrupulous, improper, unacceptable, inadmissible, *formal* unseemly, indecorous, *colloq.* sloppy
☒ professional, skilful

unpromising *adj*
unfavourable, adverse, discouraging, gloomy, depressing, doubtful, dispiriting, inauspicious, ominous, *formal* unpropitious
☒ promising, favourable, auspicious

unprotected *adj*
defenceless, unguarded, unattended, undefended, unfortified, unarmed, unshielded, unsheltered, uncovered, exposed, open, naked, vulnerable, liable, helpless
☒ protected, safe, immune

unqualified *adj*
1 UNTRAINED, inexperienced, amateur, ineligible, unlicensed, unfit, incompetent, incapable, unprepared, ill-equipped 2 ABSOLUTE, categorical, utter, total, complete, perfect, positive, thorough, downright, unmitigated, unreserved, wholehearted, outright, out and out, unconditional, unequivocal, unrestricted, *formal* consummate
☒ 1 qualified, professional 2 conditional, tentative

unquestionable *adj*
unequivocal, beyond question, incontestable, faultless, flawless, indisputable, obvious, patent, clear, conclusive, definite, absolute, sure, certain, self-evident, unchallenged, undeniable, unmistakable, *formal* incontrovertible, indubitable, irrefutable, manifest
🖅 dubious, questionable

unquestioning *adj*
implicit, unhesitating, questionless, unconditional, unqualified, wholehearted
🖅 doubtful

unravel *v*
unwind, undo, untangle, disentangle, free, extricate, separate, unknot, straighten out, resolve, sort out, clear up, solve, work out, figure out, puzzle out, penetrate, interpret, explain
🖅 tangle, complicate

unreadable *adj*
unintelligible, too difficult to read, incomprehensible, incoherent, inarticulate, garbled, scrambled, muddled, jumbled, indecipherable, unreadable, illegible, impenetrable, unfathomable, puzzling, mysterious, obscure, complicated, complex, involved, *colloq.* double Dutch
🖅 intelligible, comprehensible, clear

unreal *adj*
false, artificial, synthetic, mock, fake, sham, imaginary, visionary, fanciful, make-believe, fictitious, made-up, fairy-tale, legendary, mythical, fantastic, bizarre, illusory, immaterial, insubstantial, nebulous, hypothetical, non-existent, *formal* chimerical, phantasmagorical, *colloq.* pretend
🖅 real, genuine, authentic

unrealistic *adj*
impractical, idealistic, theoretical, romantic, quixotic, impracticable, unworkable, unreasonable, impossible, over-optimistic
🖅 realistic, pragmatic

unreasonable *adj*
1 UNFAIR, unjust, biased, unjustifiable, unjustified, unwarranted, unacceptable, undue, uncalled-for **2** IRRATIONAL, illogical, inconsistent, arbitrary, absurd, nonsensical, ludicrous, far-fetched, outrageous, preposterous, mad, senseless, silly, foolish, stupid, headstrong, opinionated, perverse **3** *unreasonable prices* excessive, immoderate, extravagant, outrageous, expensive, exorbitant, extortionate, undue, *colloq.* steep
🖅 **1** reasonable, fair **2** rational, sensible **3** moderate

unrecognizable *adj*
unidentifiable, disguised, incognito, changed, altered, unknowable, *formal* incognizable

unrecognized *adj*
unnoticed, unobserved, unremarked, unseen, undiscovered, overlooked, ignored, disregarded, neglected, unheeded
🖅 recognized, noticed, noted

unrefined *adj*
raw, untreated, unprocessed, unpurified, unfinished, unpolished, crude, coarse, vulgar, unsophisticated, uncultivated, uncultured
🖅 refined, finished

unregenerate *adj*
unconverted, hardened, impenitent, stubborn, obstinate, unreformed, unrepentant, persistent, abandoned, shameless, wicked, sinful, *formal* intractable, obdurate, incorrigible, recalcitrant, refractory
🖅 reformed, repentant

unrelated *adj*
unconnected, unassociated, irrelevant, beside/off

the point, extraneous, different, dissimilar, unlike, distinct, foreign, separate, independent, *formal* disparate, *colloq.* neither here nor there
🖅 related, similar

unrelenting *adj*
relentless, uncompromising, inexorable, unceasing, ceaseless, endless, unbroken, continuous, constant, continual, perpetual, steady, remorseless, ruthless, cruel, unmerciful, merciless, pitiless, unforgiving, unsparing, *formal* unremitting, incessant, unabated, intransigent
🖅 spasmodic, intermittent

unreliable *adj*
unsound, fallible, deceptive, false, mistaken, erroneous, inaccurate, doubtful, unconvincing, implausible, uncertain, undependable, untrustworthy, unstable, fickle, irresponsible, *colloq.* iffy, slippery
🖅 reliable, dependable, trustworthy, sound

unremitting *adj*
unrelenting, unceasing, ceaseless, remorseless, relentless, tireless, constant, continual, continuous, perpetual, unbroken, *formal* incessant, unabated
🖅 spasmodic, intermittent

unrepentant *adj*
impenitent, unapologetic, unabashed, unashamed, shameless, confirmed, hardened, callous, *formal* incorrigible, obdurate
🖅 repentant, penitent, ashamed

unreserved *adj*
unqualified, unrestrained, unconditional, unhesitating, uninhibited, unlimited, complete, full, absolute, free, total, open, wholehearted, entire, frank, forthright, direct, candid, demonstrative, extrovert, outgoing, outspoken
🖅 inhibited, tentative, hesitant

unreservedly *adv*
completely, entirely, utterly, wholeheartedly, outright, unhesitatingly

unresolved *adj*
undecided, unanswered, undetermined, unsettled, unsolved, vexed, vague, indefinite, doubtful, problematical, pending, moot, *colloq.* up in the air
🖅 definite, determined

unresponsive *adj*
unaffected, unmoved, unsympathetic, uninterested, indifferent, aloof, apathetic, cool
🖅 responsive, sympathetic

unrest *n*
protest, rebellion, turmoil, agitation, disorder, restlessness, dissatisfaction, dissension, worry, turmoil, disquiet, discontent, unease, uneasiness, *formal* disaffection, discord, perturbation
🖅 peace, calm

unrestrained *adj*
unbridled, uncontrolled, unhindered, uninhibited, unrepressed, unreserved, unchecked, unconstrained, unbounded, irrepressible, inordinate, immoderate, intemperate, free, natural, rampant, abandoned, boisterous
🖅 restrained, inhibited

unrestricted *adj*
unlimited, unbounded, unopposed, unhindered, unimpeded, unobstructed, clear, free, open, public, unconditional, absolute, *colloq.* free-for-all
🖅 restricted, limited

unrivalled *adj*
unequalled, unparalleled, unmatched, matchless, peerless, incomparable, unsurpassed, without equal, beyond compare, supreme, superlative, *formal* inimitable, nonpareil ▭

unruffled *adj*
undisturbed, untroubled, imperturbable, collected, composed, cool, calm, tranquil, serene, peaceful, smooth, level, even, *formal* unperturbed
F3 troubled, anxious

unruly *adj*
uncontrollable, unmanageable, ungovernable, disorderly, wild, rowdy, riotous, rebellious, mutinous, lawless, insubordinate, disobedient, wayward, wilful, headstrong, obstreperous, *formal* recalcitrant, refractory, intractable
F3 manageable, orderly

unsafe *adj*
dangerous, perilous, risky, high-risk, hazardous, treacherous, chancy, unreliable, uncertain, unsound, unstable, precarious, insecure, vulnerable, exposed, defenceless, *colloq.* dicey, hairy
F3 safe, secure

unsaid *adj*
unspoken, unstated, unexpressed, unvoiced, unmentioned, undeclared, unuttered, unpronounced
F3 spoken

unsatisfactory *adj*
unacceptable, imperfect, defective, faulty, inferior, poor, mediocre, weak, inadequate, insufficient, deficient, unsuitable, displeasing, dissatisfying, unsatisfying, frustrating, disappointing, *colloq.* leaving a lot to be desired
F3 satisfactory, adequate, pleasing

unsavoury *adj*
distasteful, disagreeable, unpleasant, disgusting, nauseating, revolting, sickening, nasty, undesirable, repulsive, objectionable, obnoxious, offensive, repellent, unattractive, sordid, squalid, unpalatable, unappetizing, *formal* repugnant
F3 palatable, pleasant

unscathed *adj*
unhurt, uninjured, unharmed, undamaged, untouched, whole, intact, safe, sound
F3 hurt, injured, harmed

unscrupulous *adj*
unprincipled, ruthless, shameless, dishonourable, dishonest, corrupt, immoral, unethical, improper, *colloq.* crooked
F3 scrupulous, ethical, proper

unseasonable *adj*
inappropriate, ill-timed, unsuitable, un-timely, mistimed, *formal* inopportune, inexpedient, intempestive, malapropos
F3 seasonable, timely

unseat *v*
remove, depose, dethrone, dismount, displace, dismiss, discharge, oust, throw, overthrow, topple, unhorse, unsaddle, dishorse

unseemly *adj*
improper, indelicate, unbecoming, undignified, unrefined, disreputable, discreditable, undue, inappropriate, unsuitable, unbefitting, in poor taste, *formal* indecorous
F3 seemly, decorous

unseen *adj*
unnoticed, unobserved, undetected, unobtrusive, invisible, hidden, concealed, veiled, obscure, lurking
F3 visible

unselfish *adj*
selfless, altruistic, self-denying, self-sacrificing, self-forgetting, disinterested, noble, kind, generous, open-handed, liberal, charitable, philanthropic, public-spirited, humanitarian, *formal* magnanimous
F3 selfish

unsettle *v*
disturb, upset, trouble, bother, discompose, ruffle, fluster, unbalance, destabilize, shake, agitate, disconcert, confuse, *formal* perturb, discomfit, *colloq.* rattle, throw

unsettled *adj*
1 DISTURBED, upset, troubled, agitated, anxious, uneasy, tense, edgy, fidgety, flustered, shaken, unnerved, disoriented, confused, *colloq.* on edge **2** UNRESOLVED, undetermined, undecided, to be decided, open, uncertain, doubtful, *colloq.* up in the air, in the balance **3** *unsettled weather* changeable, variable, unpredictable, inconstant, unstable, uncertain, insecure, unsteady, shaky **4** UNPAID, outstanding, owing, in arrears, payable, overdue **5** UNINHABITED, unoccupied, deserted, abandoned, desolate, unpeopled, unpopulated
F3 1 composed 2 decided, certain 3 settled 4 paid 5 settled, peopled

unshakable *adj*
firm, well-founded, fixed, stable, immovable, unassailable, unswerving, unwavering, constant, steadfast, staunch, sure, resolute, determined
F3 insecure

unsightly *adj*
ugly, unattractive, unprepossessing, hideous, revolting, repulsive, repugnant, off-putting, unpleasant, disagreeable
F3 attractive

unskilful *adj*
unskilled, amateurish, inexperienced, unprofessional, unqualified, untaught, untrained, uneducated, untalented, unpractised, incompetent, awkward, clumsy, fumbling, bungling, inept, inexpert, gauche, *formal* maladroit
F3 skilful, skilled

unskilled *adj*
untrained, unqualified, inexperienced, unpractised, inexpert, unprofessional, amateurish, incompetent
F3 skilled, professional

unsociable *adj*
unfriendly, aloof, distant, standoffish, withdrawn, introverted, reclusive, solitary, retiring, reserved, taciturn, unforthcoming, uncommunicative, cold, chilly, cool, uncongenial, unneighbourly, inhospitable, hostile
F3 sociable, friendly, congenial

unsolicited *adj*
unrequested, unsought, uninvited, unasked, unwanted, unwelcome, uncalled-for, unasked-for, gratuitous, voluntary, spontaneous
F3 requested, invited

unsophisticated *adj*
1 *an unsophisticated person* artless, guileless, innocent, ingenuous, naïve, inexperienced, simple, unworldly, childlike, natural, unaffected, unpretentious **2** CRUDE, unrefined, plain, simple, basic, straightforward, rudimentary, undeveloped, uncomplicated, uninvolved
F3 1 sophisticated, worldly 2 complex

unsound *adj*
1 *unsound reasoning* faulty, flawed, defective, ill-founded, unfounded, false, weak, erroneous, invalid, illogical, shaky, *formal* fallacious **2** UNHEALTHY, unwell, ill, diseased, weak, ailing, delicate, frail, unbalanced, deranged, unhinged **3** UNSTABLE, unsteady, rickety, wobbly, shaky, insecure, broken, dangerous, unsafe, unreliable
F3 1 sound 2 well 3 stable

unsparing *adj*
1 GENEROUS, lavish, liberal, open-handed, unstinting,

ungrudging, plenteous, abundant, bountiful, profuse, *formal* munificent **2** HARSH, hard, merciless, unmerciful, ruthless, severe, stern, relentless, implacable, uncompromising, unforgiving
F3 forgiving, mean, sparing

unspeakable *adj*
unutterable, inexpressible, indescribable, awful, dreadful, frightful, terrible, horrible, shocking, appalling, monstrous, inconceivable, unimaginable, unthinkable, unbelievable, *formal* execrable

unspoilt *adj*
preserved, unchanged, untouched, natural, unaffected, unsophisticated, unharmed, undamaged, unimpaired, unblemished, perfect
F3 spoilt, affected

unspoken *adj*
unstated, undeclared, unuttered, unexpressed, unsaid, voiceless, wordless, silent, tacit, implicit, implied, inferred, understood, assumed
F3 stated, explicit

unstable *adj*
1 CHANGEABLE, variable, fluctuating, vacillating, wavering, fitful, erratic, moody, inconsistent, volatile, inconstant, unpredictable, unreliable, untrustworthy, *formal* capricious, mercurial **2** UNSTEADY, wobbly, shaky, rickety, insecure, unsafe, risky, precarious, tottering, unbalanced **3** *emotionally/mentally unstable* deranged, insane, mad, disturbed, unsound, unhinged, *colloq.* crazy, barmy, crackers
F3 1 stable **2** steady **3** stable, sane

unsteady *adj*
unstable, wobbly, shaky, rickety, doddery, insecure, unsafe, treacherous, precarious, tottering, unreliable, inconstant, irregular, flickering
F3 steady, firm, stable

unstinting *adj*
abounding, abundant, ample, bountiful, full, generous, large, lavish, liberal, plentiful, profuse, unsparing, ungrudging, *formal* munificent, prodigal
F3 grudging, mean

unsubstantiated *adj*
unconfirmed, debatable, dubious, questionable, disputable, unestablished, unproved, unproven, unsupported, unverified, *formal* unattested, uncorroborated
F3 proved, proven

unsuccessful *adj*
failed, abortive, vain, futile, useless, ineffective, unavailing, fruitless, unproductive, unprofitable, sterile, luckless, unlucky, unfortunate, losing, beaten, defeated, frustrated, thwarted, *formal* ineffectual
F3 successful, effective, fortunate, winning

unsuitable *adj*
inappropriate, inapt, unsuited, unfit, unacceptable, out of place, improper, incompatible, *formal* unseemly, unbecoming, incongruous, inapposite, infelicitous, malapropos
F3 suitable, appropriate

unsullied *adj*
untainted, unspotted, spotless, unstained, stainless, untarnished, unblemished, uncorrupted, undefiled, unspoiled, unsoiled, untouched, perfect, clean, pure, immaculate, intact, unblackened, *formal* pristine
F3 dirty, stained

unsung *adj*
unhonoured, unpraised, unacknowledged, uncelebrated, unhailed, unacclaimed, unknown, unrecognized, overlooked, disregarded, neglected, forgotten, unknown, anonymous, obscure
F3 honoured, famous, renowned

unsure *adj*
1 *unsure of yourself* uncertain, hesitant, insecure, lacking self-confidence, tentative, doubtful, dubious, suspicious, sceptical, unconvinced, unpersuaded, undecided **2** *unsure about what to do* undecided, uncertain, unknown, ambivalent, doubtful, hesitant, dithering, equivocating, wavering, irresolute, uncommitted, indefinite, vague, *colloq.* in two minds
F3 1 confident, sure, certain **2** sure, certain, decided

unsurpassed *adj*
surpassing, supreme, transcendent, unbeaten, unexcelled, unequalled, unparalleled, unrivalled, incomparable, matchless, superlative, exceptional
F3 surpassed

unsuspecting *adj*
unwary, unaware, off guard, unconscious, trusting, trustful, unsuspicious, credulous, gullible, ingenuous, naïve, innocent
F3 suspicious, knowing

unswerving *adj*
unflagging, unwavering, unfaltering, untiring, undeviating, staunch, steadfast, dedicated, devoted, steady, sure, true, firm, constant, fixed, immovable, resolute, single-minded, direct
F3 irresolute, tentative

unsympathetic *adj*
unpitying, unconcerned, uncaring, unmoved, unresponsive, indifferent, insensitive, unfeeling, cold, heartless, pitiless, soulless, hard-hearted, harsh, callous, cruel, inhuman, unkind, hard, stony, hostile, antagonistic
F3 sympathetic, compassionate

unsystematic *adj*
unmethodical, unco-ordinated, irregular, disorganized, unorganized, unplanned, disorderly, untidy, haphazard, illogical, confused, muddled, jumbled, chaotic, indiscriminate, random, slapdash, shambolic, *colloq.* sloppy
F3 logical, systematic

untamed *adj*
wild, fierce, savage, undomesticated, unmellowed, untameable, barbarous, *formal* feral
F3 domesticated, tame

untangle *v*
disentangle, extricate, unravel, undo, resolve, solve, work out, straighten out
F3 tangle, complicate

untarnished *adj*
unblemished, unstained, stainless, unspotted, spotless, unsullied, unsoiled, unspoilt, clean, immaculate, impeccable, intact, bright, pure, burnished, shining, glowing, polished, unimpeachable, *formal* pristine
F3 tarnished, blemished

untenable *adj*
indefensible, unreasonable, unmaintainable, unsound, unjustifiable, inexcusable, insupportable, unsustainable, flawed, illogical, fallacious, rocky, shaky
F3 tenable, sound

unthinkable *adj*
inconceivable, unimaginable, unheard-of, unbelievable, incredible, impossible, improbable, unlikely, implausible, unreasonable, illogical, absurd, preposterous, outrageous, shocking, staggering

unthinking *adj*
thoughtless, inconsiderate, insensitive, tactless, indiscreet, undiplomatic, unkind, rude, impolite, heedless, careless, negligent, rash, impulsive, instinctive, involuntary, unconscious, automatic, mechanical
F3 considerate, conscious

untidy *adj*
messy, cluttered, disorderly, muddled, jumbled, unsystematic, chaotic, haywire, disorganized, shambolic, topsy-turvy, scruffy, bedraggled, rumpled, dishevelled, unkempt, slovenly, slipshod, *colloq.* sloppy, higgledy-piggledy
F3 tidy, neat

untie *v*
undo, unfasten, unhitch, unknot, unbind, unwrap, free, release, loose, loosen
F3 tie, fasten

untimely *adj*
early, premature, unseasonable, ill-timed, inopportune, inconvenient, awkward, unsuitable, inappropriate, unfortunate, *formal* inauspicious, infelicitous, malapropos
F3 timely, opportune

untiring *adj*
unflagging, unfaltering, tireless, indefatigable, dogged, persevering, persistent, tenacious, determined, resolute, devoted, dedicated, constant, incessant, unceasing, steady, staunch, unfailing, *formal* unremitting
F3 inconstant, wavering

untold *adj*
1 *cause untold damage* indescribable, unimaginable, inconceivable, inexpressible, unutterable **2** COUNTLESS, uncounted, unnumbered, unreckoned, incalculable, innumerable, uncountable, infinite, measureless, immeasurable, boundless, inexhaustible, undreamed-of, unimaginable

untouched *adj*
unharmed, undamaged, unimpaired, unhurt, uninjured, unscathed, safe, intact, unchanged, unaltered, unaffected, unimpressed, unstirred
F3 damaged, affected

untoward *adj*
unfortunate, troublesome, inconvenient, annoying, adverse, unfavourable, unexpected, unsuitable, unfitting, untimely, vexatious, irritating, worrying, awkward, disastrous, improper, contrary, unlucky, inappropriate, inauspicious, ominous, ill-timed, *formal* indecorous, inopportune, unbecoming, unpropitious, unseemly
F3 suitable, auspicious

untrained *adj*
unskilled, untaught, unschooled, uneducated, inexperienced, unpractised, unqualified, amateur, unprofessional, inexpert, incompetent
F3 trained, expert

untried *adj*
untested, unproved, unestablished, experimental, exploratory, new, novel, innovative, innovatory
F3 tried, tested, proven

untroubled *adj*
unworried, unconcerned, undisturbed, unexcited, unstirred, unflustered, unruffled, steady, calm, composed, peaceful, impassive, cool, placid, serene, tranquil, *formal* unperturbed, *colloq.* unflappable
F3 anxious, troubled

untrue *adj*
1 FALSE, fallacious, deceptive, misleading, wrong, incorrect, inaccurate, inexact, mistaken, erroneous, fabricated, *colloq.* made-up, trumped-up **2** UNFAITHFUL, disloyal, untrustworthy, dishonest, deceitful, fraudulent, untruthful, *formal* perfidious, *colloq.* two-faced
F3 **1** true, correct **2** faithful, honest

untrustworthy *adj*
dishonest, deceitful, untruthful, disloyal, unfaithful, faithless, treacherous, false, untrue, dishonourable,

capricious, fickle, fly-by-night, unreliable, untrusty, *formal* duplicitous, *colloq.* two-faced
F3 trustworthy, reliable

untruth *n*
lie, story, tale, fiction, invention, fabrication, falsehood, lying, untruthfulness, deceit, perjury, *colloq.* fib, whopper, porky, tall story, made-up story, cock-and-bull story
F3 truth

untruthful *adj*
lying, deceitful, dishonest, hypocritical, insincere, false, untrue, fictional, fabricated, invented, erroneous, fallacious, *formal* mendacious, unveracious, *colloq.* crooked, two-faced
F3 truthful, honest

untutored *adj*
untrained, unschooled, unpractised, uneducated, unlearned, unversed, inexperienced, inexpert, illiterate, ignorant, unrefined, unsophisticated, simple, artless, unlessoned
F3 educated, trained

unused *adj*
1 LEFTOVER, remaining, surplus, extra, spare, available, new, fresh, blank, clean, untouched, unexploited, untapped, unemployed, idle **2** UNACCUSTOMED, unacquainted, unfamiliar, unpractised, inexperienced, *formal* unwonted
F3 **1, 2** used

unusual *adj*
uncommon, rare, unfamiliar, strange, odd, curious, queer, bizarre, weird, unconventional, unorthodox, irregular, abnormal, atypical, phenomenal, extraordinary, out of the ordinary, remarkable, special, exceptional, different, anomalous, surprising, unexpected, unprecedented, *formal* singular, *colloq.* offbeat
F3 usual, normal, ordinary

unutterable *adj*
unspeakable, indescribable, unimaginable, extreme, overwhelming, ineffable, *formal* egregious, nefandous

unvarnished *adj*
unembellished, unadorned, straightforward, undisguised, simple, sincere, plain, candid, frank, bare, naked, honest, pure, sheer, stark
F3 disguised, embellished, exaggerated

unveil *v*
uncover, expose, lay open, bare, lay bare, unmask, betray, reveal, disclose, divulge, bring to light, bring out into the open, make known, discover, *colloq.* take the lid off
F3 cover, hide

unwanted *adj*
undesired, uninvited, unwelcome, outcast, rejected, unrequired, unneeded, unnecessary, surplus, extra, superfluous, redundant, useless, *technical* otiose, *formal* unsolicited
F3 wanted, needed, necessary

unwarranted *adj*
unjustified, undeserved, unprovoked, uncalled-for, gratuitous, unnecessary, groundless, unreasonable, unjust, wrong, inexcusable, unjustifiable, indefensible
F3 warranted, justifiable, deserved

unwary *adj*
unguarded, off guard, incautious, careless, indiscreet, thoughtless, unthinking, heedless, reckless, rash, hasty, *formal* imprudent
F3 wary, cautious

unwavering *adj*
unswerving, unshakable, unfaltering, undeviating, unshaken, untiring, unflagging, unquestioning,

staunch, steadfast, steady, sturdy, dedicated, consistent, determined, resolute, single-minded, tenacious
F3 wavering, fickle

unwelcome *adj*
1 UNWANTED, undesirable, unpopular, uninvited, excluded, rejected 2 *unwelcome news* unpleasant, disagreeable, upsetting, worrying, distasteful, unpalatable, unacceptable
F3 1 welcome, desirable 2 pleasant

unwell *adj*
ill, sick, poorly, off-colour, ailing, sickly, unhealthy, unfit, *formal* indisposed, debilitated, *colloq.* in a bad way, dicky, out of sorts, under the weather, run down, rough, groggy, like death warmed up
F3 well, healthy

unwholesome *adj*
unhealthy, bad, harmful, demoralizing, evil, wicked, immoral, degrading, depraving, corrupting, perverting, sickly, tainted, unhygienic, poisonous, insanitary, innutritious, pasty, noxious, wan, pale, pallid, anaemic, *formal* insalubrious, insalutary, *colloq.* junk
F3 salubrious, wholesome

unwieldy *adj*
unmanageable, inconvenient, awkward, clumsy, ungainly, bulky, massive, hefty, hulking, weighty, ponderous, cumbersome, *formal* incommodious
F3 handy, dainty

unwilling *adj*
reluctant, disinclined, hesitant, resistant, opposed, averse, loath, slow, unenthusiastic, grudging, *formal* indisposed, loathful
F3 willing, enthusiastic

unwind *v*
1 UNROLL, unreel, unwrap, undo, uncoil, untwist, unravel, disentangle 2 RELAX, wind down, calm down, *colloq.* take it/things easy, let yourself go, make yourself at home, let your hair down, put your feet up, hang loose, cool it, chill out
F3 1 wind, roll

unwise *adj*
ill-advised, inadvisable, inexpedient, short-sighted, improvident, ill-considered, ill-judged, foolish, stupid, silly, senseless, thoughtless, indiscreet, foolhardy, irresponsible, rash, reckless, *formal* impolitic, imprudent, injudicious
F3 wise, sensible, *formal* prudent

unwitting *adj*
1 UNAWARE, unknowing, unsuspecting, unthinking, unconscious, involuntary 2 INADVERTENT, accidental, chance, unintentional, unintended, unplanned
F3 1 knowing 2 conscious, deliberate

unwonted *adj*
unusual, uncommon, unfamiliar, unexpected, unheard-of, strange, rare, peculiar, infrequent, exceptional, extraordinary, unaccustomed, uncustomary, atypical, *formal* singular
F3 wonted, usual

unworldly *adj*
1 NAÏVE, visionary, idealistic, impractical, unsophisticated, inexperienced, innocent, gullible, ingenuous, *colloq.* green 2 SPIRITUAL, transcendental, metaphysical, otherworldly, extra-terrestrial
F3 1 sophisticated, worldly 2 worldly, materialistic

unworthy *adj*
undeserving, inferior, ineligible, unsuitable, inappropriate, unfitting, improper, unprofessional, shameful, disgraceful, dishonourable, disreputable, discreditable, ignoble, base, contemptible, despicable, *formal* unbecoming, unseemly, unbefitting, incongruous
F3 worthy, commendable

unwritten *adj*
verbal, oral, word-of-mouth, unrecorded, tacit, implicit, understood, accepted, recognized, traditional, customary, conventional
F3 written, recorded

unyielding *adj*
unrelenting, uncompromising, relentless, unwavering, unbending, immovable, inflexible, hard-line, adamant, steadfast, stubborn, obstinate, tough, firm, determined, resolute, staunch, rigid, solid, *formal* implacable, inexorable, intractable, intransigent, obdurate
F3 yielding, flexible

up-and-coming *adj*
promising, ambitious, eager, assertive, enterprising, *colloq.* go-getting, pushing

upbeat *adj*
positive, buoyant, hopeful, optimistic, encouraging, favourable, promising, forward-looking, bright, cheerful, heartening, cheery, rosy, *colloq.* bullish
F3 downbeat, gloomy

upbraid *v*
reprimand, admonish, rebuke, reprove, reproach, scold, chide, criticize, censure, *formal* castigate, berate
F3 praise, commend

upbringing *n*
bringing-up, raising, rearing, breeding, parenting, care, nurture, cultivation, tending, education, training, instruction, teaching

update *v*
modernize, revise, amend, correct, renew, renovate, revamp, upgrade

upgrade *v*
improve, make better, better, modernize, enhance, promote, advance, elevate, raise, *formal* ameliorate
F3 downgrade, demote

upheaval *n*
disruption, disturbance, upset, chaos, confusion, disorder, turmoil, revolution, overthrow, *colloq.* shake-up

uphill *adj*
hard, difficult, arduous, tough, taxing, strenuous, laborious, tiring, wearisome, exhausting, gruelling, punishing, burdensome, onerous
F3 easy, downhill

uphold *v*
support, maintain, confirm, keep, hold to, stand by, defend, champion, advocate, promote, back, endorse, sustain, strengthen, justify, vindicate, *formal* fortify
F3 abandon, reject

upkeep *n*
1 MAINTENANCE, preservation, conservation, care, running, repair, support, sustenance, subsistence, keep 2 RUNNING COSTS, expenditure, outlay, overheads, operating costs, oncosts, expenses
F3 1 neglect

uplift *v, n*
▶ *v* improve, better, boost, upgrade, advance, enlighten, exalt, inspire, elate, lift, elevate, raise, hoist, heave, refine, cultivate, edify, civilize, *formal* ameliorate
▶ *n* improvement, lift, enlightenment, enrichment, advancement, enhancement, refinement, edification, boost, cultivation, *formal* betterment

upper *adj*
higher, loftier, superior, greater, senior, top, topmost, uppermost, high, elevated, exalted, eminent, important
F3 lower, inferior, junior

▷ **upper hand** advantage, dominance, control, sway, supremacy, superiority, mastery, domination, dominion, *formal* ascendancy, *colloq.* edge

upper-class *adj*
aristocratic, noble, well-bred, well-born, high-born, high-class, patrician, blue-blooded, exclusive, elite, *colloq.* swanky, top-drawer
🔁 humble, working-class

uppermost *adj*
highest, loftiest, top, topmost, greatest, supreme, first, primary, foremost, leading, principal, main, major, chief, dominant, predominant, paramount, pre-eminent
🔁 lowest

uppity *adj*
arrogant, self-important, conceited, presumptuous, snobbish, supercilious, impertinent, affected, assuming, big-headed, overweening, bumptious, cocky, *colloq.* hoity-toity, stuck-up, swanky, toffee-nosed
🔁 unassertive, diffident

upright *adj*
1 VERTICAL, perpendicular, erect, straight, at right angles, sheer, steep **2** RIGHTEOUS, good, virtuous, upstanding, noble, worthy, decent, respectable, reputable, honourable, moral, ethical, principled, high-minded, incorruptible, honest, trustworthy
🔁 **1** horizontal, flat **2** dishonest

uprising *n*
rebellion, revolt, mutiny, rising, overthrow, insurgence, insurrection, revolution, *coup d'état*, putsch

uproar *n*
noise, din, racket, hubbub, hullabaloo, brouhaha, pandemonium, tumult, turmoil, turbulence, commotion, confusion, disorder, mayhem, bedlam, clamour, outcry, furore, riot, rumpus, fracas, ruction

uproarious *adj*
hilarious, riotous, rip-roaring, side-splitting, hysterical, boisterous, noisy, loud, rollicking, rowdy, confused, clamorous, deafening, wild, unrestrained, *colloq.* killing, rib-tickling
🔁 quiet

uproot *v*
pull up, rip up, root out, weed out, remove, displace, eradicate, destroy, wipe out

upset *v, n, adj*
▸ *v* **1** DISTRESS, grieve, dismay, trouble, worry, agitate, disturb, hurt, bother, fluster, ruffle, sadden, discompose, shake (up), unnerve, disconcert, put out, confuse, disorganize, *formal* perturb **2** TIP, spill, overturn, capsize, topple, knock over, overthrow, destabilize, unsteady
▸ *n* **1** TROUBLE, worry, agitation, distress, disturbance, bother, disruption, upheaval, reverse, surprise, shock, *formal* perturbation, *colloq.* shake-up **2** stomach upset disorder, complaint, illness, sickness, ailment, *formal* malady, *colloq.* bug
▸ *adj* distressed, grieved, hurt, annoyed, dismayed, troubled, worried, agitated, disturbed, unsettled, discomposed, put out, flustered, bothered, shaken, disconcerted, confused, *formal* perturbed, *colloq.* in a state, het up, uptight, worked up

upshot *n*
result, consequence, outcome, issue, end, conclusion, finish, culmination, dénouement, *colloq.* pay-off

upside down
inverted, upturned, up-ended, wrong way up, wrong side up, upset, overturned, disordered, muddled, jumbled, confused, topsy-turvy, chaotic, *colloq.* messed up

upstanding *adj*
upright, honest, honourable, strong, true, trust-

worthy, ethical, moral, principled, incorruptible, erect, good, virtuous, firm, four-square
🔁 untrustworthy

upstart *n*
social climber, arriviste, parvenu, parvenue, *nouveau riche*, nobody

uptight *adj*
edgy, tense, uneasy, anxious, hung-up, irritated, nervy, *colloq.* prickly, on edge
🔁 calm, cool, relaxed

up-to-date *adj*
current, contemporary, modern, present-day, fashionable, in fashion, prevalent, latest, recent, new, *colloq.* trendy, in, all the rage, cool, state-of-the-art
🔁 out-of-date, old-fashioned

upturn *n*
revival, recovery, upsurge, upswing, rise, increase, boost, improvement, betterment, *formal* amelioration
🔁 downturn, drop

urban *adj*
town, city, inner-city, metropolitan, municipal, civic, built-up, *formal* oppidan
🔁 country, rural

📝 **urban** or **urbane**?
Urban means 'of a town': *urban development*; *urban life*; *urban violence*. *Urbane* means 'cultured, elegant, refined': *urbane wit*.
---

urbane *adj*
cultivated, suave, sophisticated, refined, polished, mannerly, civilized, courteous, cultured, debonair, well-bred, well-mannered, civil, elegant, smooth
🔁 gauche, uncouth

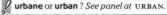
📝 **urbane** or **urban**? *See panel at* URBAN.

urbanity *n*
refinement, cultivation, sophistication, suavity, mannerliness, polish, ease, smoothness, grace, elegance, culture, civility, courtesy, charm, worldliness
🔁 awkwardness, gaucheness

urchin *n*
brat, guttersnipe, ragamuffin, waif, gamin, street Arab, kid

urge *v, n*
▸ *v* **1** PERSUADE, encourage, press, push, incite, drive, impel, prod, goad, spur, constrain, compel, force, hasten, induce, instigate, stimulate, *colloq.* egg on **2** BEG, entreat, appeal, implore, plead, *formal* beseech **3** ADVISE, counsel, recommend, advocate, encourage, *formal* exhort
🔁 **1** discourage, dissuade, deter, hinder
▸ *n* desire, wish, inclination, fancy, longing, yearning, impulse, compulsion, need, impetus, drive, eagerness, *colloq.* itch, yen
🔁 disinclination

urgency *n*
hurry, haste, pressure, stress, priority, importance, seriousness, extremity, gravity, imperativeness, need, necessity, *formal* exigency, importunity

urgent *adj*
1 PRESSING, immediate, instant, top-priority, important, critical, necessary, vital, essential, crucial, imperative, *formal* exigent **2** COMPELLING, persuasive, earnest, serious, grave, eager, insistent, persistent
🔁 **1** unimportant

urinate *v*
pass water, relieve yourself, *formal* micturate, *colloq.*

leak, pee, piddle, spend a penny, tinkle, wee

usable *adj*
working, operational, serviceable, functional, fit to use, practical, exploitable, available, current, valid
🖪 unusable, useless

usage *n*
1 TREATMENT, handling, management, control, running, operation, employment, application, use 2 TRADITION, custom, practice, habit, convention, etiquette, rule, regulation, form, routine, procedure, way, method, *formal* mode

use *v, n*
▶ *v* 1 UTILIZE, employ, make use of, exercise, service, practise, operate, work, apply, ply, wield, handle, deal with, treat, manoeuvre, enjoy, resort to, draw on, take advantage of, bring into play, put to use 2 EXPLOIT, manipulate, take advantage of, impose on, misuse, abuse, take liberties with, *colloq.* cash in on, bleed, milk, wrap/twist someone round your little finger 3 CONSUME, exhaust, get through, go through, expend, spend, waste
▷ **use up** finish, exhaust, drain, sap, deplete, consume, devour, absorb, waste, squander, fritter
▷ **used to** accustomed to, adjusted to, in the habit of, familiar with, acclimatized to, given to, prone to, *formal* habituated to, inured to, wont to, *colloq.* at home with, no stranger to
▶ *n* 1 USAGE, application, employment, operation, exercise, utilization, manipulation, exploitation 2 USEFULNESS, value, worth, profit, service, advantage, benefit, good, avail, help, point, object, end, purpose 3 *have the use of the car* right, permission, privilege, ability 4 EXPLOITATION, manipulation, imposition, misuse, abuse 5 NEED, cause, occasion, necessity, demand, call

used *adj*
second-hand, cast-off, hand-me-down, nearly new, worn, dog-eared, soiled
🖪 unused, new, fresh

useful *adj*
1 CONVENIENT, handy, all-purpose, practical, effective, productive, fruitful, profitable, valuable, worthwhile, rewarding, advantageous, beneficial, helpful, functional, general-purpose, *colloq.* nifty 2 SKILLED, proficient, practised, experienced, expert, able, skilful, handy
🖪 1 useless, ineffective, worthless

useless *adj*
1 FUTILE, fruitless, unproductive, vain, idle, unavailing, to no avail, hopeless, unhelpful, pointless, worthless, unusable, unprofitable, broken-down, unworkable, impractical, *formal* ineffectual, inefficacious, *colloq.* clapped-out 2 INCOMPETENT, ineffective, incapable, inefficient, bad, weak, *colloq.* hopeless
🖪 1 useful, helpful, effective 2 good

usher *n, v*
▶ *n* usherette, doorkeeper, attendant, escort, guide
▶ *v* escort, accompany, conduct, lead, direct, guide, show, pilot, steer
▷ **usher in** herald, inaugurate, initiate, introduce, launch, precede, announce, signal, ring in, pave the way for

usual *adj*
normal, typical, stock, standard, regular, routine, habitual, customary, conventional, traditional, orthodox, accepted, recognized, accustomed, established, familiar, common, everyday, general, ordinary, average, unexceptional, expected, predictable, *formal* wonted

🖪 unusual, strange, rare

usually *adv*
normally, generally, as a rule, ordinarily, typically, traditionally, regularly, routinely, commonly, by and large, on the whole, mainly, chiefly, mostly, for the most part, on average, in the main, *colloq.* nine times out of ten
🖪 exceptionally

usurer *n*
extortionist, money-lender, Shylock, *colloq.* loan-shark

usurp *v*
take over, assume, arrogate, seize, take, take possession of, annex, appropriate, commandeer, steal

usury *n*
money-lending, extortion, interest

utensil *n*
tool, implement, instrument, device, contrivance, gadget, apparatus, appliance

utilitarian *adj*
functional, practical, convenient, serviceable, sensible, useful, unpretentious, effective, efficient, pragmatic, down-to-earth, lowly
🖪 decorative, impractical

utility *n*
usefulness, use, value, worth, profit, advantage, benefit, good, help, avail, service, convenience, practicality, efficiency, fitness, serviceableness, *formal* efficacy

utilize *v*
use, employ, make use of, put to use, resort to, take advantage of, turn to account, exploit, adapt

utmost *adj, n*
▶ *adj* 1 *with the utmost care* extreme, maximum, most, greatest, highest, supreme, paramount 2 FARTHEST, furthest, furthermost, remotest, outermost, ultimate, final, last
▶ *n* best, hardest, most, maximum, top, peak

Utopia *n*
paradise, Eden, Garden of Eden, bliss, Elysium, heaven, heaven on earth, Shangri-la, *colloq.* seventh heaven

Utopian *adj*
ideal, idealistic, illusory, imaginary, perfect, visionary, wishful, fanciful, fantastic, airy, dream, romantic, unworkable, impractical, Elysian, *formal* chimerical

utter[1] *v*
not utter a word speak, say, voice, vocalize, verbalize, put into words, express, articulate, enunciate, sound, pronounce, deliver, state, declare, announce, proclaim, tell, reveal, divulge

utter[2]
to my utter amazement absolute, complete, total, entire, thoroughgoing, thorough, out-and-out, downright, sheer, stark, arrant, unmitigated, unqualified, positive, categorical, perfect, consummate

utterance *n*
statement, remark, comment, opinion, expression, word, articulation, delivery, speech, declaration, announcement, proclamation, pronouncement, enunciation

utterly *adv*
absolutely, completely, totally, fully, entirely, wholly, thoroughly, downright, perfectly, categorically

U-turn *n*
about-turn, volte-face, reversal, backtrack

V

vacancy *n*
opportunity, opening, position, post, job, place, room, situation

vacant *adj*
1 EMPTY, unoccupied, unfilled, free, available, void, not in use, unused, deserted, abandoned, uninhabited 2 BLANK, expressionless, vacuous, inane, poker-faced, straight-faced, deadpan, impassive, inattentive, absent, absent-minded, unthinking, dreamy, dreaming
🔁 1 occupied, engaged, in use, busy

vacate *v*
leave, depart, evacuate, abandon, withdraw, *colloq.* quit

vacation *n*
holiday, trip, leave, leave of absence, time off, break, rest, recess, furlough

vacillate *v*
waver, hesitate, fluctuate, shilly-shally, sway, oscillate, keep changing your mind, haver, temporize, *formal* tergiversate

vacillating *adj*
wavering, hesitant, irresolute, uncertain, unresolved, shilly-shallying, shuffling, oscillating
🔁 resolute, unhesitating

vacillation *n*
wavering, inconstancy, hesitancy, hesitation, fluctuation, irresolution, shilly-shallying, indecision, indecisiveness, unsteadiness, temporization, *formal* tergiversation

vacuity *n*
emptiness, space, nothingness, blankness, vacuousness, vacuum, void, apathy, inanity, incomprehension, incuriosity, *formal* incognizance

vacuous *adj*
empty, blank, vacant, void, unfilled, inane, unintelligent, stupid, uncomprehending, incurious, apathetic, idle

vacuum *n*
emptiness, void, nothingness, hollowness, vacuity, space, chasm, gap, *formal* lacuna

vagabond *n*
vagrant, tramp, wanderer, wayfarer, down-and-out, hobo, rascal, beggar, rover, runabout, itinerant, migrant, outcast, nomad, *slang* bum

vagary *n*
fancy, notion, prank, quirk, whim, whimsy, humour, crotchet, *Scot.* megrim, *formal* caprice

vagrant *n, adj*
▶ *n* tramp, wanderer, drifter, itinerant, stroller, hobo, beggar, *Scot.* gangrel, *colloq.* rolling stone, *slang* bum
▶ *adj* wandering, vagabond, travelling, shiftless, rootless, unsettled, roaming, roving, nomadic, itinerant, homeless

vague *adj*
1 ILL-DEFINED, blurred, unfocused, out of focus, in-

distinct, hazy, dim, faint, shadowy, foggy, misty, fuzzy, nebulous, obscure, *formal* amorphous 2 INDEFINITE, imprecise, unclear, unsure, uncertain, undefined, undetermined, unspecific, unspecified, rough, approximate, generalized, inexact, ambiguous, evasive, loose, lax, woolly, *formal* indeterminate
🔁 1 clear 2 definite, precise, specific

vaguely *adv*
slightly, imprecisely, faintly, dimly, inexactly, obscurely, vacantly, absent-mindedly

vagueness *n*
unclearness, fuzziness, haziness, uncertainty, dimness, faintness, obscurity, imprecision, looseness, ambiguity, inexactitude, woolliness, *formal* amorphousness
🔁 clarity, precision

vain *adj*
1 *a vain attempt* useless, worthless, futile, fruitless, pointless, unproductive, unprofitable, unavailing, hollow, groundless, empty, idle, trivial, insubstantial, unimportant, insignificant, *formal* abortive, nugatory 2 CONCEITED, proud, haughty, self-satisfied, arrogant, self-important, self-conceited, self-glorious, egotistical, affected, pretentious, ostentatious, swaggering, narcissistic, peacockish, *colloq.* big-headed, swollen-headed, stuck-up, snooty, high and mighty
🔁 1 fruitful, successful 2 modest, self-effacing
▷ **in vain** to no avail, unsuccessfully, uselessly, fruitlessly, vainly, *formal* ineffectually
🔁 successfully

valediction *n*
goodbye, farewell, leave-taking, adieu, *colloq.* send-off
🔁 welcome, greeting

valedictory *adj*
farewell, parting, departing, final, last

valetudinarian *adj*
sickly, invalid, infirm, weakly, feeble, frail, delicate, hypochondriac, neurotic

valiant *adj*
brave, courageous, gallant, fearless, intrepid, bold, dauntless, audacious, heroic, plucky, staunch, stout-hearted, lion-hearted, *formal* indomitable, valorous
🔁 cowardly, fearful, dismayed

valid *adj*
1 LOGICAL, well-founded, well-grounded, reasonable, justifiable, sound, good, convincing, telling, conclusive, credible, reliable, substantial, forceful, weighty, powerful, just, *formal* cogent 2 OFFICIAL, legal, lawful, legitimate, authentic, effective, bona fide, genuine, binding, contractual, proper
🔁 1 false, weak 2 unofficial, invalid

validate *v*
confirm, authenticate, endorse, legalize, authorize, substantiate, underwrite, ratify, certify, *formal* attest, corroborate

validity *n*
soundness, legality, lawfulness, legitimacy, foundation, grounds, justifiability, strength, power, force, weight, substance, logic, point, authority, *formal* cogency
F3 invalidity

valley *n*
dale, vale, dell, glen, hollow, cwm, depression, slade, gulch, *Scot.* strath

valorous *adj*
brave, bold, heroic, courageous, fearless, plucky, lion-hearted, stout-hearted, valiant, intrepid, gallant, hardy, mettlesome, dauntless, doughty, stalwart
F3 cowardly, weak

valour *n*
boldness, courage, bravery, heroism, intrepidity, lion-heartedness, fearlessness, mettle, spirit, gallantry, hardiness, doughtiness, *formal* fortitude
F3 cowardice, weakness

valuable *adj*
1 *valuable necklace* precious, prized, valued, costly, expensive, dear, high-priced, treasured, cherished, priceless, estimable, *colloq.* worth a pretty penny, worth its weight in gold **2** *valuable suggestions* helpful, worthwhile, useful, beneficial, invaluable, constructive, fruitful, profitable, advantageous, important, serviceable, worthy, handy
F3 1 worthless **2** useless

valuation *n*
evaluation, assessment, estimate, computation, survey, *formal* appraisement

value *n, v*
▶ *n* **1** COST, price, rate, worth **2** WORTH, use, usefulness, utility, merit, importance, desirability, benefit, advantage, significance, good, profit, gain, avail **3** *moral values* morals, principles, moral, principles, standards, ethics
▶ *v* **1** PRIZE, appreciate, treasure, hold dear, admire, respect, cherish, set great store by, *formal* esteem **2** EVALUATE, assess, estimate, price, put a price on, survey, rate, *formal* appraise
F3 1 disregard, neglect **2** undervalue

valued *adj*
highly regarded, cherished, treasured, prized, respected, dear, loved, beloved, *formal* esteemed

vanguard *n*
forefront, most advanced part, front, front line, firing line, spearhead, lead, fore, leading/foremost position

vanish *v*
disappear, fade, fade away/out, dissolve, evaporate, disperse, melt (away), die out, leave, depart, exit, fizzle out, peter out, *formal* evanesce
F3 appear, materialize

vanity *n*
1 CONCEIT, conceitedness, pride, arrogance, haughtiness, self-conceit, self-love, self-satisfaction, self-glorification, narcissism, egotism, pretension, ostentation, affectation, airs, *colloq.* big-headedness, swollen-headedness, snootiness **2** WORTHLESSNESS, uselessness, emptiness, futility, pointlessness, unreality, unproductiveness, unprofitableness, hollowness, fruitlessness, triviality, idleness, unimportance, insignificance
F3 1 modesty, worth

vanquish *v*
defeat, conquer, beat, triumph over, overcome, overpower, overwhelm, subdue, humble, master, repress, quell, confound, crush, rout, *formal* subjugate, *colloq.* hammer, slaughter, clobber, wipe the floor with

vapid *adj*
vacuous, uninteresting, lifeless, dead, banal, bland, boring, dull, tedious, flat, insipid, limp, stale, tame, flavourless, tasteless, watery, wishy-washy, colourless, tiresome, trite, weak, uninspiring
F3 interesting, vigorous

vapour *n*
steam, mist, fog, smoke, breath, fumes, haze, damp, dampness, exhalation

variable *adj, n*
▶ *adj* changeable, inconstant, varying, shifting, mutable, unpredictable, fluctuating, fitful, unstable, unsteady, uneven, wavering, vacillating, temperamental, fickle, flexible, *formal* chameleonic, protean
F3 fixed, invariable, stable
▶ *n* factor, parameter

variance *n*
1 VARIATION, difference, discrepancy, divergence, inconsistency, disagreement **2** DISAGREEMENT, disharmony, conflict, discord, division, dissent, dissension, quarrelling, opposition, strife, odds
F3 1 agreement **2** agreement, harmony

variant *n, adj*
▶ *n* alternative, variation, modification, development, deviant, rogue
▶ *adj* alternative, different, divergent, modified, derived, deviant, exceptional
F3 normal, standard, usual

variation *n*
diversity, variety, deviation, discrepancy, diversification, alteration, change, difference, vacillation, fluctuation, departure, modification, modulation, inflection, novelty, innovation
F3 monotony, uniformity

varied *adj*
assorted, diverse, miscellaneous, mixed, various, sundry, motley, different, wide-ranging, *formal* heterogeneous, multifarious
F3 standardized, uniform

variegated *adj*
multicoloured, many-coloured, parti-coloured, varicoloured, speckled, mottled, dappled, pied, streaked, marbled, jaspe, motley, *technical* poikilitic
F3 monochrome, plain

variety *n*
1 ASSORTMENT, miscellany, mixture, collection, medley, pot-pourri, range **2** DIVERSITY, difference, dissimilarity, discrepancy, variation, *formal* multiplicity, multifariousness **3** SORT, kind, class, category, species, type, breed, brand, make, strain, classification
F3 2 uniformity, *formal* similitude

various *adj*
different, differing, dissimilar, unlike, diverse, varied, varying, assorted, miscellaneous, distinct, diversified, mixed, many, several, motley, *formal* heterogeneous, disparate, variegated

varnish *n, v*
▶ *n* lacquer, lac, glaze, enamel, shellac, resin, polish, gloss, coating, veneer, japan
▶ *v* lacquer, glaze, enamel, shellac, polish, gloss, coat, veneer, japan

vary *v*
1 CHANGE, alter, modify, modulate, diversify, reorder, transform, alternate, inflect, permutate, *formal* metamorphose **2** DIFFER, diverge, disagree, depart, fluctuate, be dissimilar, clash, be in conflict, be at odds

vase *n*
container, jar, jug, pitcher, urn, vessel, ewer, amphora, hydria

vassal *n*
serf, slave, subject, thrall, bondman, bondsman, bondservant, retainer, villein, liege, liegeman

vassalage *n*
dependence, bondage, servitude, slavery, subjection, serfdom, thraldom, villeinage, *formal* subjugation

vast *adj*
huge, immense, massive, gigantic, enormous, great, colossal, bulky, extensive, tremendous, sweeping, extensive, unlimited, fathomless, limitless, boundless, immeasurable, never-ending, monumental, monstrous, far-flung, *formal* prodigious

vault¹ *v*
vault over the wall leap, spring, bound, clear, jump, hurdle, leap-frog

vault² *n*
1 CELLAR, crypt, strongroom, repository, cavern, depository, wine-cellar, underground chamber, basement, tomb, mausoleum 2 ARCH, roof, span, concave

vaunt *v*
boast, brag, exult in, flaunt, parade, trumpet, crow, *colloq.* show off, swank, blow your own trumpet, *US* blow your own horn
🗲 belittle, minimize

veer *v*
swerve, swing, change, shift, diverge, deviate, wheel, turn, sheer, tack

vegetable *n*

Vegetables include:
artichoke, asparagus, aubergine, bean, beetroot, broad bean, broccoli, Brussels sprout, butter bean, cabbage, calabrese, capsicum, carrot, cauliflower, celeriac, celery, chicory, courgette, cress, cucumber, *US* eggplant, endive, fennel, French bean, garlic, kale, leek, lentil, lettuce, mange tout, marrow, mushroom, okra, onion, parsnip, pea, pepper, petit pois, potato, *colloq.* spud, pumpkin, radish, runner bean, shallot, soya bean, spinach, spring onion, swede, sweetcorn, sweet-potato, turnip, watercress, yam, *US* zucchini.

Vegetable dishes include:
aubergine roll, baba ganoush, bhaji, onion bhaji, bubble and squeak, cauliflower cheese, champ, chillada, colcannon, coleslaw, couscous, crudités, dal, dolma, duchesse potatoes, fasolia, felafel, fondue, gado-gado, gnocchi, guacamole, gumbo, hummus, imam bayildi, latke, macaroni cheese, macedoine, mushy peas, nut cutlet, paella, pakora, pease pudding, peperonata, pilau, pissaladière, polenta, ratatouille, raita, risotto, rösti, salad, caesar salad, green salad, hot salad, mixed salad, salad nicoise, Waldorf salad, winter salad; sauerkraut, stovies, stuffed marrow, stuffed mushroom, succotash, tabbouleh, tahina, tsatsiki, vegetable chilli, vegetable curry, vegetable soup, vegetarian goulash, vichyssoise.

vegetate *v*
stagnate, degenerate, deteriorate, rusticate, go to seed, idle, rust, languish, moulder, do nothing

vegetation *n*
plants, trees, flowers, flora, green plants, greenery, *formal* herbage, verdure

vehemence *n*
passion, energy, enthusiasm, keenness, fervency, eagerness, earnestness, emphasis, strength, power, animation, intensity, zeal, verve, vigour, ardour, fervour, force, forcefulness, urgency, impetuosity, violence, warmth, heat, fire

🗲 indifference

vehement *adj*
impassioned, passionate, ardent, fervent, intense, forceful, emphatic, heated, strong, powerful, spirited, vigorous, urgent, enthusiastic, animated, eager, keen, earnest, forcible, fierce, violent, zealous, *formal* fervid
🗲 apathetic, indifferent

vehicle *n*
1 CONVEYANCE, transport

Vehicles include:
plane, boat, ship, car, taxi, hackney-carriage, bicycle, *colloq.* bike, cycle, tandem, tricycle, *colloq.* boneshaker, penny-farthing, motor-cycle, motor-bike, scooter; bus, omnibus, minibus, *colloq.* double-decker, coach, charabanc, caravan, caravanette, camper; train, Pullman, sleeper, wagon-lit, tube, tram, monorail, maglev, trolleybus; van, Transit®, lorry, truck, juggernaut, pantechnicon, trailer, tractor, fork-lift truck, steam-roller, tank, wagon; bobsleigh, sled, sledge, sleigh, toboggan, troika; barouche, brougham, dog-cart, dray, four-in-hand, gig, hansom, landau, phaeton, post-chaise, stagecoach, sulky, surrey, trap; rickshaw, sedan-chair, litter. *See also* AIRCRAFT; BOATS AND SHIPS; CAR.

2 MEANS, agency, channel, medium, mechanism, instrument, organ

veil *v, n*
▶ *v* screen, cloak, cover (up), mask, mantle, blanket, shadow, shield, obscure, conceal, hide, shroud, disguise, shade, camouflage
🗲 expose, uncover
▶ *n* cover, covering, cloak, curtain, mask, mantle, blanket, screen, disguise, film, blind, shade, canopy, shroud, purdah

vein *n*
1 STREAK, stripe, stratum, seam, lode, blood vessel
2 MOOD, tendency, bent, strain, streak, temper, tenor, tone, frame of mind, humour, mode, style, disposition, temperament, attitude, inclination

velocity *n*
speed, rate, quickness, rapidity, pace, impetus, swiftness, *formal* celerity

venal *adj*
corrupt, corruptible, bribable, mercenary, grafting, simoniacal, *colloq.* bent, buyable
🗲 incorruptible

vendetta *n*
feud, blood-feud, enmity, rivalry, quarrel, bad blood, bitterness

vendor *n*
seller, trader, salesperson, merchant, supplier, stockist. *See panel at* SELLER.

veneer *n*
1 FAÇADE, front, appearance, display, show, mask, gloss, camouflage, pretence, guise 2 LAYER, coating, surface, finish, gloss, covering

venerable *adj*
respected, revered, honoured, venerated, dignified, grave, wise, august, aged, worshipped, *formal* esteemed, hallowed

venerate *v*
revere, respect, honour, worship, adore, *formal* esteem, hallow
🗲 despise, anathematize

veneration *n*
respect, reverence, deference, adoration, awe, worship, devotion, *formal* esteem

vengeance n
retribution, revenge, retaliation, reprisal, requital, *colloq.* tit for tat, an eye for an eye and a tooth for a tooth
F3 forgiveness, mercy, pardon, remission, forbearance, exoneration, acquittal, absolution
▷ **with a vengeance 1** FORCEFULLY, violently, vigorously, powerfully, energetically, furiously, *colloq.* flat out, like crazy **2** TO A GREAT DEGREE, greatly, to a great extent, fully, to the full, to the utmost, *colloq.* with no holds barred

vengeful adj
spiteful, unforgiving, vindictive, avenging, revengeful, retaliatory, relentless, retributive, punitive, implacable, *formal* rancorous
F3 forgiving

venial adj
forgivable, excusable, pardonable, slight, minor, insignificant, trivial, trifling, negligible
F3 mortal, unforgivable, unpardonable

venom n
1 POISON, toxin **2** RANCOUR, ill-will, malice, vindictiveness, spite, bitterness, resentment, hate, enmity, hostility, animosity, virulence, *formal* malevolence, acrimony

venomous adj
1 POISONOUS, toxic, lethal, deadly, fatal, virulent, harmful, *formal* noxious **2** MALICIOUS, spiteful, vicious, vindictive, bitter, resentful, baleful, hostile, malignant, baneful, *formal* rancorous, malevolent
F3 1 harmless

vent n, v
▶ n opening, hole, aperture, outlet, gap, passage, orifice, duct
▶ v air, express, voice, utter, release, discharge, emit, let out, pour out

ventilate v
1 *ventilate a room* air, aerate, freshen, cool **2** *ventilate your feelings* express, air, broadcast, debate, discuss, bring out into the open

venture v, n
▶ v **1** DARE, advance, go, make bold, put forward, presume, suggest, volunteer **2** RISK, hazard, chance, endanger, imperil, jeopardize, put in jeopardy, speculate, gamble, wager, stake
▶ n risk, chance, hazard, speculation, gamble, undertaking, project, adventure, exploit, endeavour, enterprise, operation, fling

venturesome adj
adventurous, enterprising, courageous, bold, brave, daring, fearless, intrepid, spirited, plucky, audacious, dauntless, doughty, *colloq.* daredevil
F3 unenterprising, cowardly

veracious adj
truthful, true, trustworthy, genuine, frank, honest, reliable, credible, dependable, straightforward, exact, factual, faithful, accurate
F3 untruthful

veracity n
truthfulness, truth, trustworthiness, integrity, honesty, frankness, precision, accuracy, candour, credibility, exactitude, *formal* probity, rectitude
F3 untruthfulness

verbal adj
spoken, oral, said, uttered, vocal, linguistic, verbatim, unwritten, word-of-mouth
F3 written

verbatim adv
word for word, exactly, literally, to the letter, precisely, closely

verbiage n
repetition, verbosity, waffle, *formal* circumlocution, pleonasm, periphrasis, prolixity
F3 succinctness, briefness

verbose adj
long-winded, wordy, windy, garrulous, diffuse, *formal* prolix, loquacious, circumlocutory, periphrastic, pleonastic
F3 succinct, brief

verbosity n
verboseness, windiness, wordiness, long-windedness, garrulity, logorrhoea, verbiage, *formal* loquaciousness, loquacity, multiloquy, prolixity
F3 economy, succinctness

verdant adj
lush, green, grassy, fresh, leafy, *formal* viridescent, virid, graminaceous, gramineous

verdict n
decision, judgement, conclusion, finding, adjudication, assessment, opinion, ruling, sentence

verge n, v
▶ n border, edge, margin, limit, rim, brim, brink, boundary, threshold, brink, extreme, extremity, edging
▶ v ▷ **verge on** approach, border on, come close to, near, tend towards

verification n
confirmation, checking, proof, substantiation, validation, authentication, *formal* attestation, corroboration

verify v
confirm, substantiate, authenticate, bear out, prove, support, endorse, validate, testify, *formal* corroborate, attest, accredit
F3 invalidate, discredit

verisimilitude n
authenticity, credibility, resemblance, realism, likeliness, plausibility, semblance, colour, *colloq.* ring of truth
F3 implausibility

verity n
truth, truthfulness, validity, factuality, actuality, authenticity, soundness, *formal* veracity
F3 untruth

vernacular adj, n
▶ adj indigenous, local, native, popular, vulgar, informal, colloquial, common
▶ n language, speech, tongue, parlance, dialect, idiom, cant, jargon, *colloq.* lingo

versatile adj
adaptable, flexible, all-round, all-purpose, multipurpose, multifaceted, adjustable, many-sided, general-purpose, functional, resourceful, handy, variable
F3 inflexible

versed adj
skilled, proficient, practised, experienced, familiar, acquainted, learned, read, knowledgeable, conversant, seasoned, qualified, competent, accomplished

version n
1 RENDERING, reading, interpretation, understanding, account, report, translation, paraphrase, adaptation, portrayal **2** TYPE, kind, variant, form, model, style, design, reproduction

vertex n
peak, top, apex, summit, height, highest point, pinnacle, culmination, crown, extremity, *technical* acme, apogee, zenith
F3 nadir

vertical adj
upright, perpendicular, straight up, upstanding, sheer, erect, on end
F3 horizontal

vertigo n
dizziness, giddiness, light-headedness, sickness

verve n
vitality, vivacity, animation, energy, dash, élan, liveliness, sparkle, vigour, passion, fervour, enthusiasm, gusto, life, relish, spirit, force, brio, *colloq.* pizzazz, zip
F∃ apathy, lethargy

very adv, adj
▶ *adv* extremely, greatly, highly, deeply, truly, remarkably, excessively, exceeding(ly), exceptionally, acutely, particularly, really, quite, absolutely, noticeably, unbelievably, incredibly, unusually, uncommonly, *colloq.* pretty, terribly, dreadfully, awfully
F∃ slightly, scarcely
▶ *adj* actual, real, same, selfsame, identical, true, genuine, simple, utter, sheer, pure, perfect, ideal, plain, mere, bare, exact, suitable, appropriate, fitting

vessel n
1 SHIP, boat, craft, barque 2 CONTAINER, bowl, receptacle, holder, jar, pot, pitcher, jug

vest v
give, endow, supply, grant, empower, authorize, sanction, *formal* bestow, confer

vestibule n
foyer, hall, entrance, entrance hall, entranceway, lobby, porch, anteroom, portico

vestige n
trace, suspicion, touch, indication, sign, mark, track, impression, print, hint, evidence, inkling, glimmer, token, scrap, remains, remainder, remnant, residue, relics, *colloq.* whiff

vestigial adj
remaining, surviving, rudimentary, undeveloped, imperfect, incomplete, reduced, functionless

vet v
investigate, examine, check (out), scrutinize, scan, inspect, survey, review, audit, *formal* appraise

veteran n, adj
▶ *v* master, pastmaster, old hand, old stager, old-timer, warhorse, *colloq.* pro
F∃ novice, recruit
▶ *adj* experienced, practised, seasoned, proficient, expert, adept, long-serving, old, battle-scarred
F∃ inexperienced

veto v, n
▶ *v* reject, turn down, forbid, ban, prohibit, rule out, block, *formal* disallow, proscribe, interdict, *colloq.* give the thumbs-down to
F∃ approve, sanction
▶ *n* rejection, ban, embargo, prohibition, *formal* proscription, *colloq.* thumbs-down
F∃ approval, assent

vex v
irritate, annoy, provoke, pester, trouble, upset, worry, bother, harass, disturb, distress, agitate, enrage, exasperate, torment, fret, *formal* perturb, *colloq.* put out, hassle, aggravate, needle, bug, get someone's blood up, get someone's back up
F∃ calm, soothe

vexation n
annoyance, exasperation, displeasure, chagrin, anger, fury, pique, dissatisfaction, frustration, nuisance, misfortune, irritant, problem, trouble, upset, worry, bother, difficulty, bore, *colloq.* headache, pain, bind, thorn in the flesh, aggravation, *slang* pain in the backside, *US* pain in the butt

vexatious adj
annoying, irritating, troublesome, upsetting, worrying, irksome, nagging, exasperating, infuriating, distressing, disappointing, bothersome, burdensome, disagreeable, unpleasant, trying, worrisome, provoking, teasing, tormenting, afflicting, *formal* pestiferous, *colloq.* aggravating, pesky
F∃ pleasant, soothing

vexed adj
1 IRRITATED, annoyed, provoked, upset, troubled, worried, irate, incensed, infuriated, put out, exasperated, bothered, confused, perplexed, harassed, ruffled, riled, disturbed, flustered, distressed, displeased, agitated, *colloq.* nettled, aggravated, hassled, peeved, miffed, narked 2 *a vexed question* difficult, controversial, contested, disputed, in dispute, debated, *formal* moot

viable adj
feasible, practicable, possible, workable, usable, operable, achievable, sustainable, sound
F∃ impossible, unworkable

vibes n
atmosphere, aura, ambience, feel, feelings, emotions, vibrations, reaction, response, emanation

vibrant adj
1 ANIMATED, vivacious, lively, energetic, vigorous, responsive, sparkling, spirited, sensitive, thrilling, dynamic, electrifying, electric 2 *vibrant colours* vivid, bright, brilliant, colourful, striking

vibrate v
quiver, pulsate, shudder, shiver, resonate, reverberate, resound, throb, oscillate, tremble, undulate, sway, swing, shake

vibration n
quiver, pulsation, pulse, shudder, judder, juddering, resonance, reverberation, resounding, throb, throbbing, oscillation, trembling, tremor, shaking, frisson

vicarious adj
indirect, second-hand, substituted, surrogate, delegated, deputed, acting, commissioned, *formal* empathetic

vice n
1 EVIL, evil-doing, wrongdoing, immorality, depravity, immorality, wickedness, sin, corruption, degeneracy, *formal* iniquity, profligacy, transgression 2 FAULT, failing, defect, shortcoming, weakness, imperfection, foible, flaw, blemish, bad habit, besetting sin
F∃ 1 virtue, morality

vice versa
reciprocally, oppositely, contrariwise, the other way round, inversely

vicinity n
neighbourhood, surroundings, area, locality, district, precincts, environs, proximity, *formal* propinquity

vicious adj
1 SAVAGE, wild, violent, fierce, barbarous, brutal, cruel, ferocious, dangerous 2 MALICIOUS, spiteful, vindictive, virulent, cruel, mean, nasty, slanderous, venomous, caustic, defamatory, *formal* malevolent, *colloq.* bitchy, catty 3 WICKED, bad, wrong, immoral, depraved, unprincipled, degenerate, diabolical, corrupt, debased, perverted, vile, heinous, *formal* profligate
F∃ 1 gentle 2 kind 3 virtuous

viciousness n
savagery, brutality, cruelty, ferocity, virulence, spite, spitefulness, venom, malice, wickedness, badness, immorality, corruption, sinfulness, depravity, *formal* profligacy, rancour, *colloq.* bitchiness
F∃ goodness, gentleness, virtue

vicissitude n
change, variation, alteration, alternation, shift, turn,

revolution, deviation, divergence, fluctuation, twist, *formal* mutation

victim *n*
sufferer, casualty, prey, quarry, scapegoat, martyr, sacrifice, fatality, *colloq.* dupe, sucker, fall guy, sitting target, sucker
🖬 offender, attacker

victimize *v*
1 OPPRESS, persecute, discriminate against, pick on, prey on, bully, exploit, take (unfair) advantage of **2** CHEAT, deceive, trick, defraud, dupe, hoodwink, fool, *colloq.* swindle

victor *n*
winner, conqueror, champion, first, prize-winner, *formal* subjugator, vanquisher, victor ludorum, *colloq.* champ, top dog
🖬 loser, *formal* vanquished

victorious *adj*
conquering, champion, triumphant, winning, unbeaten, successful, prize-winning, top, first, *formal* vanquishing
🖬 defeated, unsuccessful

victory *n*
conquest, win, triumph, success, superiority, mastery, vanquishment, subjugation, overcoming
🖬 defeat, loss, failure

victuals *n*
food, provisions, supplies, stores, edibles, bread, rations, sustenance, comestibles, *formal* aliment, viands, *colloq.* eatables, eats, tuck, *slang* grub, nosh

vie *v*
strive, compete, contend, struggle, contest, fight, rival

view *n*, *v*
▶ *n* **1** OPINION, attitude, belief, judgement, point of view, viewpoint, angle, thought, conviction, estimation, feeling, sentiment, impression, idea, notion **2** SIGHT, scene, vision, range of vision, vista, spectacle, outlook, prospect, perspective, panorama, landscape, composition **3** SURVEY, inspection, examination, observation, study, contemplation, scrutiny, scan, assessment, review
▶ *v* **1** OBSERVE, watch, see, look at, examine, inspect, look at, gaze at, scrutinize, scan, survey, witness, perceive **2** CONSIDER, regard, contemplate, judge, reflect on, think about, speculate

viewer *n*
spectator, watcher, observer, onlooker

viewpoint *n*
attitude, position, perspective, slant, standpoint, stance, opinion, angle, feeling

vigil *n*
watch, wakefulness, wake, lookout, sleeplessness, stake-out, *formal* pernoctation

vigilance *n*
watchfulness, alertness, attentiveness, observation, carefulness, caution, guardedness, wakefulness, *formal* circumspection

vigilant *adj*
watchful, alert, attentive, observant, on your guard, on the lookout, cautious, aware, careful, wide-awake, sleepless, unsleeping, *formal* circumspect
🖬 careless

vigorous *adj*
1 HEALTHY, energetic, active, lively, strong, strenuous, tough, athletic, robust, lusty, sound, vital **2** DYNAMIC, forceful, forcible, powerful, stout, spirited, full-blooded, effective, efficient, brisk, enterprising, flourishing, lively, animated, sparkling, intense
🖬 **1, 2** weak, feeble

vigorously *adv*
briskly, hard, forcefully, energetically, eagerly, heartily, powerfully, strongly, strenuously, lustily
🖬 feebly, weakly

vigour *n*
energy, vitality, liveliness, health, robustness, stamina, strength, resilience, sturdiness, toughness, soundness, spirit, verve, gusto, activity, animation, power, potency, force, forcefulness, might, dash, dynamism, *formal* vivacity, *colloq.* zip, oomph, pep, brio
🖬 weakness

vile *adj*
1 *vile weather; a vile meal* disgusting, foul, nasty, unpleasant, disagreeable, horrible, horrid, nauseating, sickening, repulsive, repugnant, revolting, obnoxious, offensive, distasteful, loathsome, *formal* noxious **2** EVIL, base, contemptible, debased, low, depraved, degenerate, bad, wicked, wretched, worthless, sinful, miserable, mean, impure, corrupt, despicable, disgraceful, degrading, vicious, appalling, *formal* iniquitous
🖬 **1** pleasant, lovely **2** pure, worthy

vilification *n*
criticism, defamation, abuse, denigration, scurrility, *formal* aspersion, calumniation, calumny, contumely, disparagement, invective, revilement, vituperation, *colloq.* mud-slinging

vilify *v*
criticize, revile, denigrate, denounce, slander, defame, stigmatize, abuse, smear, debase, *formal* malign, disparage, asperse, berate, calumniate, decry, traduce, vilipend, vituperate, *colloq.* badmouth, slate, slam
🖬 praise, compliment, adore, eulogize, glorify

village *n*
hamlet, community, settlement, town, *colloq.* one-horse town

villain *n*
evildoer, wrongdoer, scoundrel, rogue, criminal, reprobate, knave, rascal, wretch, devil, *formal* miscreant, malefactor, *colloq.* baddy
🖬 hero, heroine, *colloq.* goody

villainous *adj*
wicked, bad, criminal, evil, sinful, vicious, notorious, cruel, inhuman, vile, depraved, debased, degenerate, disgraceful, terrible, fiendish, *formal* heinous, nefarious, iniquitous, opprobrious
🖬 good

villainy *n*
wickedness, viciousness, badness, crime, criminality, delinquency, atrocity, depravity, baseness, vice, sin, rascality, roguery, knavery, *formal* iniquity, turpitude

vindicate *v*
1 CLEAR, acquit, excuse, absolve, rehabilitate, *formal* exonerate, exculpate **2** JUSTIFY, uphold, support, back, maintain, sustain, champion, defend, establish, advocate, assert, verify, confirm, warrant, *formal* corroborate

vindication *n*
justification, defence, plea, excuse, assertion, apology, support, maintenance, substantiation, verification, rehabilitation, extenuation, *formal* exculpation, exoneration
🖬 accusation, conviction

vindictive *adj*
spiteful, unforgiving, implacable, vengeful, relentless, unrelenting, revengeful, resentful, punitive, venomous, malicious, *formal* malevolent, rancorous
🖬 forgiving

vintage *n*, *adj*
▶ *n* year, period, era, epoch, generation, time, origin,

harvest, gathering, crop
► *adj* choice, best, fine, prime, quality, high-quality, select, superior, supreme, rare, mature, old, ripe, enduring, classic, venerable, veteran

violate *v*
1 CONTRAVENE, disobey, disregard, break, flout, infringe, breach, *formal* transgress, infract 2 OUTRAGE, debauch, defile, rape, ravish, molest, dishonour, desecrate, profane, invade, disturb, interfere with, disrupt, invade, wreck
Ⓕ 1 observe

violation *n*
breach, contravention, offence, outrage, infringement, trespass, abuse, disruption, encroachment, profanation, sacrilege, defilement, desecration, *formal* infraction, spoliation, transgression
Ⓕ obedience, observance

violence *n*
1 FORCE, strength, power, forcefulness, vehemence, intensity, passion, ferocity, fierceness, severity, tumult, turbulence, wildness, *formal* might 2 BRUTALITY, aggression, roughness, destructiveness, cruelty, bloodshed, murderousness, savagery, passion, wildness, fighting, frenzy, fury, hostilities

violent *adj*
1 INTENSE, strong, severe, sharp, acute, extreme, great, dramatic, harmful, destructive, devastating, injurious, powerful, painful, agonizing, excruciating, forceful, forcible, harsh, ruinous, rough, vehement, passionate, tumultuous, turbulent 2 CRUEL, brutal, aggressive, fierce, ferocious, bloodthirsty, impetuous, hot-headed, headstrong, murderous, savage, wild, vicious, unrestrained, uncontrollable, ungovernable, passionate, furious, intemperate, maddened, outrageous, riotous, fiery, destructive
Ⓕ 1 calm, moderate 2 peaceful, gentle

VIP *n*
celebrity, luminary, magnate, somebody, notable, personage, dignitary, star, headliner, lion, *colloq.* bigwig, big name, big noise, big shot, big cheese, heavyweight
Ⓕ nobody, nonentity

virago *n*
shrew, termagant, vixen, tartar, scold, harridan, dragon, fury, gorgon, Xanthippe, *colloq.* battle-axe

virgin *n, adj*
► *n* girl, maiden, celibate, vestal
► *adj* virginal, chaste, intact, immaculate, maidenly, pure, modest, new, fresh, spotless, stainless, undefiled, unblemished, untainted, untouched, unspoilt, unsullied

virginal *adj*
pure, spotless, virgin, untouched, undefiled, uncorrupted, undisturbed, stainless, white, snowy, vestal, immaculate, chaste, fresh, celibate, maidenly, *formal* pristine

virginity *n*
purity, chastity, chasteness, maidenhood, virtue

virile *adj*
man-like, masculine, male, manly, robust, muscular, strapping, vigorous, potent, lusty, red-blooded, forceful, strong, rugged, *colloq.* macho
Ⓕ effeminate, impotent

virility *n*
manhood, manliness, masculinity, ruggedness, vigour, huskiness, potency, machismo
Ⓕ effeminacy, impotence, weakness

virtual *adj*
effective, in effect, essential, practical, for all practical purposes, in all but name, implied, implicit, potential, prospective

virtually *adv*
practically, effectively, in effect, almost, nearly, as good as, more or less, for all practical purposes, in all but name, in essence, conceivably

virtue *n*
1 GOODNESS, morality, uprightness, worthiness, righteousness, integrity, honesty, honour, incorruptibility, justice, high-mindedness, excellence, *formal* rectitude, probity 2 QUALITY, worth, merit, advantage, benefit, asset, credit, strength, *colloq.* plus
Ⓕ 1 vice
▷ **by virtue of** because of, on account of, by means of, owing to, with the help of, thanks to, by way of, *formal* by dint of

virtuosity *n*
skill, mastery, expertise, artistry, brilliance, polish, finesse, flair, panache, éclat, finish, wizardry, bravura

virtuoso *n, adj*
► *n* expert, master, maestro, prodigy, genius
► *adj* skilful, masterly, expert, brilliant, excellent, dazzling,

virtuous *adj*
good, moral, righteous, upright, upstanding, worthy, honourable, honest, irreproachable, incorruptible, exemplary, unimpeachable, ethical, high-principled, blameless, respectable, decent, clean-living, excellent, innocent, angelic
Ⓕ immoral, vicious

virulence *n*
1 POISON, venom, toxicity, deadliness 2 HOSTILITY, bitterness, resentment, hurtfulness, harmfulness, spite, vindictiveness, viciousness, acrimony, antagonism, malevolence, malice, malignancy, spleen, vitriol, hatred, *formal* rancour

virulent *adj*
1 POISONOUS, toxic, venomous, deadly, fatal, lethal, malignant, injurious, pernicious, severe, intense, extreme 2 HOSTILE, resentful, spiteful, acrimonious, bitter, vicious, vindictive, malicious, vitriolic, *formal* malevolent, rancorous
Ⓕ 1 harmless

viscous *adj*
sticky, adhesive, gluey, thick, clammy, mucous, tacky, syrupy, treacly, gummy, tenacious, viscid, *formal* gelatinous, glutinous, mucilaginous, *colloq.* gooey
Ⓕ runny, thin, watery

visible *adj*
perceptible, discernible, detectable, apparent, noticeable, observable, perceivable, recognizable, distinguishable, discoverable, evident, unconcealed, undisguised, unmistakable, conspicuous, showing, clear, exposed, obvious, open, overt, palpable, plain, patent, *formal* manifest
Ⓕ invisible, indiscernible, hidden

vision *n*
1 SIGHT, seeing, eyesight, perception, discernment, far-sightedness, foresight, penetration 2 IDEA, ideal, conception, insight, perception, intuition, view, picture, image, mental image, mental picture, imagination, fantasy, dream, daydream 3 APPARITION, hallucination, dream, illusion, optical illusion, delusion, mirage, phantom, ghost, chimera, spectre, wraith

visionary *adj, n*
► *adj* idealistic, impractical, romantic, dreamy, unrealistic, utopian, quixotic, unreal, fanciful, prophetic, perceptive, discerning, far-sighted, speculative, unworkable, illusory, imaginary, *colloq.* moonshiny, ivory-tower
► *n* idealist, romantic, dreamer, daydreamer, fantasist, prophet, mystic, seer, utopian, Don Quixote, rainbow-chaser, theorist

⊟ pragmatist

visit *v, n*
▸ *v* **1** *visit her brother* call on, call in, go and see, go round/over to, stay with, stay at, look in, look up, see, spend time with, *colloq.* drop in on, drop by, stop by, pop in, blow in **2** INFLICT, punish, trouble, afflict, curse, plague
▸ *n* call, stay, stop, excursion, *formal* sojourn

visitation *n*
1 VISIT, inspection, examination **2** INFLICTION, punishment, retribution, catastrophe, disaster, calamity, bane, blight, scourge, ordeal, trial, cataclysm **3** APPEARANCE, manifestation

visitor *n*
caller, guest, company, tourist, traveller, holiday-maker

vista *n*
view, prospect, panorama, perspective, outlook, scene, vision

visual *adj*
visible, observable, discernible, perceptible, optical, *formal* ocular, optic, specular

visualize *v*
picture, envisage, imagine, conceive, see, conceive of, contemplate

vital *adj*
1 CRITICAL, crucial, important, imperative, key, significant, basic, fundamental, essential, necessary, indispensable, urgent, life-and-death, decisive, forceful, *formal* requisite **2** LIVELY, alive, living, life-giving, invigorating, spirited, vivacious, vibrant, vigorous, forceful, dynamic, animated, energetic, *formal* quickening
⊟ 1 inessential, peripheral **2** dead

vitality *n*
life, liveliness, animation, vigour, energy, vivacity, spirit, sparkle, exuberance, zest, strength, stamina, *colloq.* go, get-up-and-go, oomph, pizzazz

vitamin *n*

Vitamins include:
retinol, aneurin (thiamine), riboflavin, pantothenic acid, nicotinic acid (niacin), pyridoxine (adermin), cyanocobalamin, folic acid, pteroic acid, ascorbic acid, calciferol, cholecalciferol, ergocalciferol, tocopherol, linoleic acid, linolenic acid, biotin, phylloquinone, menadione, bioflavonoid/citrin.

vitiate *v*
spoil, mar, weaken, undermine, deteriorate, harm, injure, blemish, ruin, sully, taint, corrupt, pervert, pollute, debase, contaminate, blight, defile, invalidate, nullify, devalue, deprave, impair

vitriolic *adj*
bitter, abusive, virulent, vicious, venomous, malicious, caustic, biting, sardonic, scathing, destructive, *formal* acrimonious, acerbic, mordant, trenchant, vituperative

vituperate *v*
blame, revile, reproach, censure, denounce, abuse, *formal* berate, castigate, upbraid, vilify, *colloq.* slam, slate, slag off
⊟ praise, applaud, extol

vituperation *n*
censure, rebuke, reprimand, reproach, blame, abuse, fault-finding, scurrility, *formal* castigation, invective, obloquy, revilement, contumely, diatribe, philippic, vilification, objurgation, *colloq.* flak, stick
⊟ acclaim, praise

vituperative *adj*
censorious, harsh, insulting, abusive, scornful, derogatory, defamatory, scurrilous, withering, belittling, sardonic, *formal* calumniatory, denunciatory, fulminatory, opprobrious
⊟ laudatory

vivacious *adj*
lively, animated, spirited, high-spirited, effervescent, cheerful, jolly, merry, sparkling, light-hearted, *formal* ebullient, *colloq.* bubbly

vivacity *n*
liveliness, spirit, animation, energy, quickness, vitality, dynamism, activity, élan, effervescence, light-heartedness, merriness, *formal* ebullience, *colloq.* brio

vivid *adj*
1 BRIGHT, colourful, intense, strong, rich, vibrant, brilliant, glowing, dazzling, glaring, lurid, vigorous, expressive, dramatic, flamboyant, animated, dynamic, lively, lifelike, spirited **2** MEMORABLE, powerful, graphic, clear, distinct, striking, dramatic, lively, sharp, realistic
⊟ 1 colourless, dull **2** vague

vividness *n*
intensity, strength, glow, brilliancy, brightness, lucidity, radiance, realism, clarity, sharpness, immediacy, life, liveliness, distinctness, *formal* refulgence, resplendence
⊟ dullness, lifelessness

vocabulary *n*
language, words, glossary, lexicon, dictionary, wordbook, thesaurus, idiom, *technical* lexis

vocal *adj*
1 SPOKEN, said, oral, uttered, expressed, voiced **2** ARTICULATE, eloquent, expressive, noisy, clamorous, shrill, strident, outspoken, frank, blunt, forthright, plain-spoken, vociferous
⊟ 1 unspoken **2** inarticulate

vocation *n*
calling, pursuit, career, métier, mission, profession, occupation, trade, employment, work, craft, role, line, post, job, business, office

vociferous *adj*
noisy, vocal, clamorous, loud, obstreperous, strident, vehement, thundering, shouting, outspoken, frank, blunt, forthright
⊟ quiet

vogue *n*
fashion, style, taste, craze, popularity, trend, prevalence, acceptance, custom, *formal* mode, *colloq.* fad, the latest, the rage, the thing
▷ **in vogue** fashionable, modish, popular, stylish, trendy, up-to-the-minute, voguish, current, prevalent, *colloq.* in, with it

voice *n, v*
▸ *n* **1** SPEECH, utterance, articulation, language, words, sound, tone, intonation, inflection, expression, mouthpiece, agency, vehicle, medium, instrument, organ **2** SAY, vote, opinion, view, decision, option, will, desire, wish, airing
▸ *v* express, say, utter, air, articulate, speak of, talk of, mention, verbalize, assert, convey, disclose, divulge, declare, enunciate

void *adj, n, v*
▸ *adj* **1** EMPTY, emptied, free, unfilled, unoccupied, vacant, clear, bare, blank, drained, lacking, devoid **2** ANNULLED, inoperative, invalid, cancelled, nullified, ineffective, futile, useless, vain, worthless, nugatory
⊟ 1 full **2** valid, binding
▸ *n* emptiness, vacuity, vacuum, abyss, chasm, blank, blankness, space, lack, want, cavity, gap, hol-

low, opening, *formal* lacuna
▶ *v* **1** NULLIFY, cancel, annul, invalidate, rescind, *formal* abnegate **2** DISCHARGE, eject, defecate, emit, empty, drain, evacuate
F∃ **1** validate **2** fill

volatile *adj*
changeable, inconstant, unstable, variable, erratic, irregular, temperamental, unsteady, unsettled, fickle, whimsical, unpredictable, fitful, restless, giddy, flighty, lively, volcanic, explosive, *formal* mercurial, capricious, *colloq.* up and down
F∃ constant, steady

volcano *n*

> The world's active volcanoes include:
> Mayon (Philippines); Hudson (Chile); Kilauea (Hawaii); Pinatubo, Mt (Philippines); Vulcano (Italy), St Helens, Mt (USA); Etna (Italy); Ruapehu (New Zealand); Stromboli (Italy); Klyuchevskoy (Russia); Mauna Loa (Hawaii); Nyamuragira (Zaire); Hekla (Iceland); Krakatoa (Sumatra); Taal (Philippines); Vesuvius (Italy).

volition *n*
will, free will, choice, choosing, determination, option, election, preference, discretion, purpose, resolution

volley *n*
barrage, salvo, bombardment, cannonade, fusillade, hail, shower, burst, blast, discharge, explosion

voluble *adj*
fluent, glib, articulate, talkative, forthcoming, garrulous, *formal* loquacious, *colloq.* chatty

volume *n*
1 BULK, size, capacity, space, dimensions, amount, mass, quantity, aggregate, amplitude, sound, loudness, body **2** BOOK, tome, publication, *formal* omnibus

voluminous *adj*
roomy, big, ample, spacious, billowing, vast, full, bulky, huge, large, *formal* capacious

voluntarily *adv*
willingly, freely, intentionally, consciously, deliberately, purposely, spontaneously, of your own free will, by choice, on your own initiative, of your own accord
F∃ involuntarily, unwillingly

voluntary *adj*
1 FREE, gratuitous, optional, spontaneous, unforced, willing, volunteer, unpaid, honorary **2** CONSCIOUS, deliberate, purposeful, intended, intentional, wilful, optional, of your own free will, *formal* of your own volition
F∃ **1** compulsory, obligatory **2** involuntary

volunteer *v*
offer, propose, put forward, present, suggest, step forward, advance, tender, *formal* proffer

voluptuary *n*
hedonist, sensualist, epicurean, pleasure-seeker, libertine, sybarite, debauchee, *bon vivant*, *formal* profligate, *colloq.* playboy
F∃ ascetic

voluptuous *adj*
1 SENSUAL, licentious, luxurious, self-indulgent, hedonistic, sensuous, opulent **2** EROTIC, shapely, buxom, full-figured, seductive, provocative, enticing, *colloq.* sexy

vomit *v*
be sick, bring up, heave, retch, regurgitate, *colloq.* throw up, puke, spew, heave, fetch, *US slang* barf

voracious *adj*
insatiable, greedy, hungry, gluttonous, acquisitive, avid, devouring, ravenous, ravening, uncontrolled, unquenchable, *formal* edacious, omnivorous, prodigious, rapacious

voracity *n*
greed, hunger, ravenousness, eagerness, acquisitiveness, avidity, *formal* edacity, rapacity

vortex *n*
whirlpool, maelstrom, eddy, whirlwind, whirl

votary *n*
believer, follower, disciple, devotee, addict, adherent

vote *n, v*
▶ *n* **1** *to cast your vote* ballot, poll, election, franchise, referendum, plebiscite **2** *give everyone the vote* franchise, suffrage, enfranchisement
F∃ disenfranchisement
▶ *v* elect, ballot, go to the polls, re-elect, choose, opt, plump for, suggest, put in, declare, return

vouch *v*
▷ **vouch for** guarantee, assure, warrant, support, back, endorse, confirm, answer for, certify, affirm, verify, assert, speak for, swear to, uphold, *formal* attest to, asseverate

voucher *n*
coupon, token, ticket, document, paper

vouchsafe *v*
give, grant, impart, deign, yield, cede, *formal* bestow, confer, accord

vow *v, n*
▶ *v* promise, pledge, swear, give your word, undertake, dedicate, devote, profess, consecrate, affirm
▶ *n* promise, oath, pledge

voyage *n, v*
▶ *n* journey, travel(s), trip, passage, expedition, crossing, cruise, sail, tour, safari, *formal* odyssey
▶ *v* journey, travel, go, cruise, sail, tour

vulgar *adj*
1 INDECENT, obscene, coarse, improper, dirty, filthy, crude, suggestive, risqué, rude, indelicate, distasteful, offensive, off-colour, ribald, lewd, bawdy, *colloq.* near the bone **2** UNREFINED, uncouth, coarse, rude, rough, common, crude, ill-bred, impolite, boorish, *formal* indecorous **3** TASTELESS, flashy, showy, ostentatious, kitsch, garish, loud, gaudy, tawdry, *colloq.* cheap and nasty, tacky, glitzy **4** ORDINARY, general, popular, vernacular, common, low, unsophisticated, uncultured
F∃ **1** decent **2** correct **3** tasteful, refined **4** sophisticated

vulgarity *n*
1 CRUDENESS, indecency, crudity, dirtiness, rudeness, suggestiveness, ribaldry, coarseness **2** TASTELESSNESS, tawdriness, gaudiness, showiness, ostentation, garishness
F∃ **1** decency, politeness **2** tastefulness

vulnerable *adj*
unprotected, exposed, unguarded, insecure, defenceless, susceptible, weak, powerless, helpless, sensitive, open, open to attack, wide open
F∃ protected, strong, safe

wacky *adj*
crazy, silly, wild, eccentric, irrational, odd, unpredictable, zany, erratic, daft, *colloq.* goofy, loony, loopy, nutty, screwy, off beat
 sensible

wad *n*
chunk, plug, roll, bundle, ball, lump, hunk, mass, block, *colloq.* wodge

wadding *n*
packing, padding, stuffing, filling, filler, lining, cotton-wool

waddle *v*
toddle, totter, wobble, sway, rock, shuffle

wade *v*
cross, ford, loll, lie, wallow, roll, welter, lurch, flounder, splash, *formal* traverse
▷ **wade in** pitch in, launch in, tear in, set to, get stuck in, wade through, trawl through, plough through

waffle *v, n*
▶ *v* jabber, prattle, blather, babble, *colloq.* rabbit on, witter on
▶ *n* blather, prattle, wordiness, padding, nonsense, *formal* verbosity, *colloq.* gobbledygook, hot air, guff

waft *v, n*
▶ *v* drift, float, glide, blow, transport, carry, transmit
▶ *n* breath, puff, draught, current, breeze, scent, whiff

wag *v, n*
▶ *v* shake, waggle, wave, sway, swing, bob, nod, wiggle, oscillate, wobble, flutter, vibrate, quiver, rock
▶ *n* wit, joker, humorist, jester, comic, comedian, clown, fool, droll, banterer

wage *n, v*
▶ *n* pay, fee, earnings, salary, wage-packet, payment, stipend, remuneration, allowance, reward, hire, compensation, returns, recompense, *formal* emolument
▶ *v* carry on, conduct, engage in, undertake, execute, practise, pursue

wager *v, n*
▶ *v* bet, gamble, chance, risk, speculate, venture, stake, pledge, lay odds, hazard, punt
▶ *n* bet, gamble, speculation, stake, venture, hazard, pledge, punt, flutter

waggish *adj*
amusing, mischievous, playful, sportive, funny, humorous, comical, droll, facetious, witty, impish, roguish, jesting, frolicsome, puckish, merry, jocular, jocose, bantering, *formal* risible
 grave, serious, staid

waggle *v*
wiggle, wobble, shake, jiggle, wave, oscillate, wag, bobble, flutter

waif *n*
orphan, stray, foundling

wail *v, n*
▶ *v* moan, cry, howl, lament, weep, sob, complain, groan, keen, *formal* ululate, *colloq.* yowl
▶ *n* moan, cry, howl, lament, complaint, groan, weeping, sob, *formal* ululation

wait *v, n*
▶ *v* delay, linger, hold back, hesitate, pause, remain, rest, stand by, sit out, stay, await, *formal* abide, tarry, bide your time, *colloq.* hang around, hang on, hang fire
 proceed, go ahead

> **Colloquial ways of telling someone to wait include:**
> all in good time, bear with me, half a mo, half a moment, half a tick, hang on, hold on, hold your horses, I'll be right with you, just a jiffy, just a minute, just a moment, just a second, just a tick, wait a minute, wait a moment.

▷ **wait on** serve, attend to, minister to, look after, take care of, tend, work for
▶ *n* hold-up, hesitation, delay, interval, pause, halt

waiter, waitress *n*
server, attendant, steward, stewardess, host, hostess, butler

waive *v*
give up, do without, abandon, set aside, resign, surrender, yield, cede, postpone, defer, *formal* renounce, relinquish, forego
 enforce, claim, maintain

waiver *n*
disclaimer, postponement, resignation, surrender, abandonment, *formal* abdication, deferral, relinquishment, remission, renunciation

wake[1] *v, n*
▶ *v* **1** RISE, get up, arise, waken, awake, awaken, rouse, stir, came to, bring round **2** STIMULATE, stir, activate, arouse, animate, excite, fire, galvanize, prod, goad, whet, *colloq.* egg on **3** ALERT, notify, warn, signal, make/become aware of, make/become conscious of
 1 sleep
▶ *n* funeral, death-watch, vigil, watch, funeral

wake[2] *n*
in the wake of the ship trail, track, path, aftermath, backwash, wash, rear, train, waves

wakeful *adj*
sleepless, restless, insomniac, unsleeping, watchful, vigilant, observant, heedful, attentive, alert, wary
 inattentive, sleepy, unwary

waken *v*
wake, rise, get up, awake, awaken, arouse, rouse, stimulate, stir, whet, quicken, animate, activate, enliven, kindle, fire, ignite, galvanize

walk v, n
▶ v **1** *walk along the street*

Ways of walking include:
amble, clump, crawl, creep, dodder, *colloq.* go by shanks's pony, hike, hobble, *colloq.* hoof it, limp, lope, lurch, march, mince, *colloq.* mooch, pace, pad, paddle, parade, patter, *formal* perambulate, plod, potter, promenade, prowl, ramble, roam, saunter, scuttle, shamble, shuffle, slink, sneak, stagger, stalk, steal, step, stomp, *colloq.* stretch your legs, stride, stroll, strut, stumble, swagger, tiptoe, *colloq.* toddle, totter, traipse, tramp, trample, tread, trek, trip, troop, trot, trudge, trundle, waddle, wade, wander, *colloq.* yomp.

2 ACCOMPANY, escort, guide, lead, conduct, usher, shepherd
▷ **walk off/away with** go off with, walk away with, make off with, run off with, steal, pocket, *colloq.* pinch, nick, lift
▷ **walk out** go on strike, strike, stop work, down tools, protest, mutiny, revolt, take industrial action
▷ **walk out on** abandon, desert, *formal* forsake, *colloq.* run out on, jilt, dump, leave in the lurch, leave high and dry
▶ n **1** *he has an odd walk* carriage, gait, step, pace, stride **2** *go for a walk* stroll, amble, ramble, saunter, march, hike, tramp, promenade, trek, traipse, trudge, trail **3** *a tree-lined walk* footpath, path, walkway, avenue, pathway, promenade, alley, esplanade, lane, drive, track, pavement, sidewalk **4** BEAT, round, rounds, circuit, way, path, route, trail

walker n
pedestrian, rambler, hiker

walk-out n
strike, stoppage, industrial action, protest, rebellion, revolt

walk-over n
colloq. pushover, doddle, child's play, piece of cake, cinch

wall n

Types of wall and famous walls include:
abutment, bailey, barricade, barrier, block, breeze-block wall, brick wall, bulkhead, bulwark, buttress, cavity wall, curtain wall, dam, dike, divider, embankment, enclosure wall, fence, flying buttress, fortification, garden wall, Great Wall of China, Hadrian's Wall, hedge, inner wall, load-bearing wall, mural, obstacle, outer bailey, paling, palisade, parapet, partition, party wall, rampart, retaining wall, screen, sea-wall, shield wall, stockade, stud partition, wall of death.

wallet n
pouch, purse, folder, holder, case, notecase, pochette, *US* bill-fold

wallop v, n
▶ v beat, hit, smack, punch, pummel, buffet, swat, swipe, bash, strike, thrash, thump, pound, clobber, batter, thwack, defeat, crush, trounce, rout, drub, hammer, *formal* vanquish, *colloq.* clout, belt, lick, paste, whack
▶ n blow, hit, kick, thump, thwack, whack, swat, swipe, smack, punch, bash

wallow v
1 *wallow in mud* loll, lie, roll, wade, welter, lurch, flounder, splash **2** *wallow in nostalgia* indulge, relish, revel, bask, enjoy, glory, delight, *formal* luxuriate

wan adj
pale, washed out, ashen, white, weak, discoloured, faint, colourless, anaemic, ghastly, feeble, whey-faced, waxen, pallid, pasty, sickly, bleak, mournful, weary

wand n
rod, baton, staff, stick, sprig, mace, sceptre, twig, withe, withy

wander v, n
▶ v **1** ROAM, rove, ramble, meander, saunter, stroll, prowl, drift, range, traipse, stray, straggle, *formal* peregrinate **2** DIGRESS, diverge, deviate, depart, go astray, stray, swerve, veer, err, lose your way **3** RAMBLE, rave, babble, gibber, talk nonsense
▶ n excursion, ramble, amble, stroll, saunter, meander, prowl, cruise

wanderer n
itinerant, traveller, voyager, drifter, rover, rambler, stroller, stray, straggler, ranger, wayfarer, nomad, Gypsy, vagrant, vagabond, *colloq.* rolling stone

wandering adj, n
▶ adj itinerant, travelling, rambling, wayfaring, roving, strolling, voyaging, rootless, homeless, unsettled, drifting, migratory, nomadic, vagabond, vagrant, *formal* peripatetic
▶ n travels, drift(ing), journey(ing), meander(ing), walkabout, *formal* odyssey, peregrination

wane v, n
▶ v diminish, decrease, decline, weaken, subside, fade (away), dwindle, ebb, lessen, abate, sink, drop, taper off, peter out, dim, droop, contract, shrink, fail, wither, vanish, *formal* abate
☲ increase, wax
▶ n fading, dwindling, decline, decrease, lessening, sinking, ebb, contraction, subsidence, weakening, decay, degeneration, failure, fall, drop, tapering off, atrophy, *formal* abatement, diminution
☲ increase
▷ **on the wane** deteriorating, declining, degenerating, weakening, withering, fading, subsiding, dwindling, lessening, ebbing, tapering off, dropping, on the decline, obsolescent, *formal* moribund, *colloq.* on its last legs, on the way out

wangle v
manipulate, arrange, contrive, engineer, fix, scheme, manoeuvre, work, pull off, manage, *colloq.* fiddle, wheel and deal

want v, n
▶ v **1** DESIRE, wish, like, feel like, crave, covet, fancy, hope for, long for, pine for, yearn for, hunger for, thirst for **2** NEED, require, demand, lack, miss, be without, be deficient in, call for
▶ n **1** DESIRE, demand, longing, pining, yearning, craving, coveting, hunger, thirst, requirement, wish, need, lust, appetite **2** LACK, dearth, insufficiency, absence, deficiency, shortage, inadequacy, scarcity, scantiness, *formal* paucity **3** POVERTY, destitution, *formal* privation, indigence, penury

wanting adj
1 ABSENT, missing, lacking, short, insufficient **2** INADEQUATE, imperfect, faulty, defective, substandard, poor, deficient, unsatisfactory, unacceptable, disappointing, *colloq.* not up to scratch
☲ **1** sufficient **2** adequate

wanton adj, n
▶ adj **1** *a wanton action* malicious, arbitrary, unprovoked, unjustifiable, groundless, gratuitous, pointless, unrestrained, rash, reckless, wild, extravagant, *formal* malevolent **2** *a wanton woman* immoral, promiscuous, shameless, immodest, impure, abandoned, dissipated, dissolute, lewd, lecherous

▶ *n* voluptuary, debauchee, lecher, libertine, rake, roué, Don Juan, Casanova

war *n, v*
▶ *n* warfare, hostilities, fighting, fight, battle, combat, conflict, clash, skirmish, strife, struggle, bloodshed, contest, confrontation, campaign, contention, enmity, antagonism, ill-will
⊟ peace, cease-fire

Types of war include:
ambush, armed conflict, assault, attack, battle, biological warfare, blitz, blitzkrieg, bombardment, chemical warfare, civil war, cold war, counter-attack, engagement, germ warfare, guerrilla warfare, holy war, hot war, invasion, jihad, jungle warfare, limited war, manoeuvres, nuclear war, private war, resistance, skirmish, state of siege, struggle, total war, trade war, war of attrition, war of nerves, world war.

Famous wars include:
American Civil War (Second American Revolution), American Revolution (War of Independence), Boer War, Cod wars, Crimean War, Crusades, English Civil War, Falklands War, Franco-Prussian War, Gulf War, Hundred Years War, Indian Wars, Iran-Iraq War, Korean War, Mexican War, Napoleonic War, Opium Wars, Peasants' War, Russo-Finnish War (Winter War), Russo-Japanese War, Russo-Turkish Wars, Seven Years War, Six-Day War, Spanish-American War, Spanish-American Wars of Independence, Spanish Civil War, Suez Crisis, Thirty Years War, Vietnam War, War of 1812, War of the Pacific, Wars of the Roses, World War I (the Great War), World War II.

▷ **war cry** rallying-cry, battle cry, war-song, slogan, watchword
▶ *v* wage war, fight, take up arms, cross swords, make war, battle, clash, combat, strive, skirmish, struggle, contest, contend

warble *v, n*
▶ *v* sing, chirrup, chirp, twitter, quaver, yodel, trill
▶ *n* song, cry, call, chirp, chirrup, quaver, trill, twitter

ward *n, v*
▶ *n* **1** ROOM, apartment, compartment, cubicle, unit **2** DIVISION, area, district, quarter, precinct, zone **3** CHARGE, dependant, protégé(e), pupil, minor
▶ *v* ▷ **ward off** avert, fend off, deflect, parry, repel, drive back, stave off, thwart, beat off, forestall, evade, turn aside, turn away, block, avoid, *colloq.* dodge

warden *n*
keeper, custodian, guardian, protector, warder, caretaker, curator, ranger, steward, watchman, superintendent, supervisor, overseer, administrator, janitor

warder *n*
jailer, keeper, prison officer, guard, wardress, custodian, warden, *slang* screw

wardrobe *n*
1 CUPBOARD, closet **2** CLOTHES, outfit, *formal* attire, apparel

warehouse *n*
store, storehouse, depot, depository, repository, stockroom, entrepot

wares *n*
goods, merchandise, commodities, stock, products, produce, stuff

warfare *n*
war, fighting, hostilities, battle, arms, combat, strife,

struggle, passage of arms, contest, confrontation, campaign, conflict, contention, discord, blows
⊟ peace

warily *adv*
cautiously, carefully, guardedly, watchfully, vigilantly, hesitantly, apprehensively, gingerly, cagily, charily, suspiciously, uneasily, distrustfully, *formal* circumspectly
⊟ heedlessly, recklessly, thoughtlessly, unwarily

wariness *n*
caution, carefulness, attention, mindfulness, alertness, care, heedfulness, watchfulness, vigilance, foresight, discretion, caginess, apprehension, hesitancy, suspicion, distrust, unease, *formal* circumspection, prudence
⊟ heedlessness, recklessness, thoughtlessness

warlike *adj*
martial, belligerent, aggressive, combative, bloodthirsty, war-mongering, militaristic, militant, hostile, antagonistic, hawkish, unfriendly, *formal* bellicose, pugnacious
⊟ friendly, peaceable

warlock *n*
witch, wizard, sorcerer, enchanter, conjurer, magician, demon, *formal* necromancer

warm *adj, v*
▶ *adj* **1** HEATED, tepid, lukewarm **2** ARDENT, passionate, fervent, vehement, intense, earnest, eager, enthusiastic, heart-felt, sincere, zealous **3** *warm colours* rich, intense, mellow, cheerful, relaxing **4** FRIENDLY, amiable, cordial, affable, kind, kindly, genial, hearty, hospitable, caring, sympathetic, loving, affectionate, tender **5** FINE, sunny, balmy, temperate, close
⊟ **1** cool **2** indifferent **3** cold, cool **4** unfriendly **5** cool
▶ *v* **1** HEAT (UP), make warm, reheat, melt, thaw **2** ANIMATE, interest, please, delight, stimulate, liven up, enliven, put some life into, stir, rouse, excite, cheer up
⊟ **1** cool

warm-blooded *adj*
passionate, enthusiastic, excitable, fervent, hot-blooded, emotional, ardent, earnest, lively, spirited, vivacious, impetuous, rash

warm-hearted *adj*
kind, kind-hearted, kindly, affectionate, loving, sympathetic, tender, tender-hearted, compassionate, generous, cordial, ardent, genial
⊟ cold, unsympathetic

warmth *n*
1 WARMNESS, heat, hotness, fire **2** FRIENDLINESS, affection, cordiality, tenderness, kindness, kindliness, care, love, compassion, sympathy, hospitality **3** ARDOUR, enthusiasm, passion, fervour, zeal, vehemence, intensity, eagerness, sincerity
⊟ **1** coldness **2** unfriendliness **3** indifference

warn *v*
1 INFORM, notify, tell, let know, advise, alert, give (advance) notice, put on your guard, sound the alarm, *formal* forewarn, *colloq.* tip off **2** ADVISE, counsel, urge, caution, exhort **3** REBUKE, caution, reprimand, reprove, *formal* admonish

warning *n, adj*
▶ *n* **1** CAUTION, alert, advice, notification, information, notice, advance notice, counsel, hint, lesson, alarm, threat, *formal* admonition, *colloq.* tip-off, shot across the bows **2** OMEN, threat, sign, signal, *formal* augury, premonition, presage, portent
▶ *adj* ominous, threatening, cautionary, *formal* admonitory, premonitory, monitory

warp *v, n*
▶ *v* twist, bend, contort, deform, distort, kink, misshape, pervert, corrupt, deviate
⊟ straighten

▶ *n* twist, bend, contortion, deformation, distortion, bias, kink, irregularity, turn, bent, defect, deviation, quirk, perversion

warrant *n, v*
▶ *n* authorization, authority, sanction, validation, permit, permission, licence, guarantee, warranty, security, pledge, commission, voucher, *formal* consent
▶ *v* **1** GUARANTEE, pledge, swear, certify, assure, declare, affirm, vouch for, answer for, underwrite, uphold, support, back, endorse, *formal* avouch **2** AUTHORIZE, entitle, empower, sanction, permit, allow, license, justify, excuse, approve, support, call for, commission, require, *formal* necessitate, consent to

warrantable *adj*
permissible, allowable, defensible, excusable, justifiable, right, reasonable, proper, legal, lawful, accountable, necessary
▣ indefensible, unjustifiable, unwarrantable

warranty *n*
guarantee, contract, certificate, bond, authorization, assurance, pledge, justification, *formal* covenant

warring *adj*
fighting, hostile, opposing, opposed, conflicting, contending, combatant, embattled, belligerent, at war, at daggers drawn

warrior *n*
fighter, soldier, fighting man, combatant, champion, warhorse, wardog

wary *adj*
cautious, guarded, careful, chary, on your guard, on the lookout, distrustful, suspicious, heedful, attentive, alert, on the alert, watchful, vigilant, wide-awake, cagey, *formal* prudent, circumspect
▣ unwary, careless, heedless

wash *v, n*
▶ *v* **1** CLEAN, cleanse, launder, shampoo, scrub, mop, swab down, sponge, wipe, rinse, soak, swill **2** BATHE, bath, freshen up, get cleaned up, have a wash, have a bath, shower, have a shower, douche, shampoo **3** FLOW, sweep, wave, swell, stream, beat, splash, dash **4** *that excuse won't wash* be unbelievable, be implausible, not be accepted, hold, stand up, bear examination, bear scrutiny, carry weight, pass muster, *colloq.* stick
▷ **wash your hands** abandon, give up on, have nothing to do with, leave to your own devices, abdicate responsibility
▶ *n* **1** CLEANING, cleansing, bath, bathe, laundry, laundering, scrub, shower, shampoo, washing, rinse **2** FLOW, roll, sweep, wave, swell, surge **3** LAYER, coat, coating, rinse, stain

washed-out *adj*
pale, pallid, blanched, bleached, faded, wan, colourless, drained, drawn, exhausted, tired-out, fatigued, worn-out, weary, spent, flat, lacklustre, haggard, *colloq.* all in, dead on your feet, dog-tired, knackered

washout *n*
failure, disaster, disappointment, fiasco, debacle, messy, *colloq.* flop, lead balloon
▣ success, triumph

waspish *adj*
critical, irritable, bad-tempered, cross, ill-tempered, captious, irascible, peevish, snappish, testy, grumpy, *formal* cantankerous, petulant, *colloq.* bitchy, crabbed, crabby, crotchety, grouchy, prickly, touchy

waste *v, n, adj*
▶ *v* **1** SQUANDER, misspend, misuse, fritter away, lavish, spend, throw away, get through, go through, *formal* dissipate, *colloq.* blow, splurge **2** CONSUME, erode, exhaust, drain, destroy, spoil, devastate **3** WITHER, shrivel, shrink, become emaciated, *formal*

atrophy, debilitate **4** LAY WASTE, desolate, ravage, destroy, devastate, raze, ruin, sack, spoil, pillage, rape, *formal* depredate, despoil
▣ **1** economize **2** preserve
▶ *n* **1** SQUANDERING, wastefulness, extravagance, loss, *formal* dissipation, prodigality **2** MISAPPLICATION, misuse, abuse, neglect **3** RUBBISH, refuse, leftovers, debris, dregs, effluent, litter, scrap, slops, offscouring(s), dross, *US* trash, garbage
▣ **1** thriftiness
▶ *adj* **1** USELESS, worthless, unwanted, unused, leftover, superfluous, extra, *formal* supernumerary **2** BARREN, desolate, empty, uninhabited, bare, devastated, uncultivated, unprofitable, unproductive, wild, dismal, bleak, dreary

wasteful *adj*
extravagant, spendthrift, prodigal, uneconomical, thriftless, unthrifty, ruinous, lavish, improvident, *formal* profligate
▣ economical, thrifty

wasteland *n*
wilderness, desert, barrenness, waste, wild(s), void, emptiness, barrenness

wastrel *n*
good-for-nothing, idler, layabout, loafer, ne'er-do-well, malingerer, spendthrift, *formal* profligate, *colloq.* lounger, shirker, skiver

watch *v, n*
▶ *v* **1** OBSERVE, see, look at, look on, regard, note, notice, mark, stare at, peer at, gape at, contemplate, scan, survey, gaze at, view **2** GUARD, look after, keep an eye on, mind, protect, superintend, inspect, take care of, keep, *colloq.* keep tabs on, not take your eyes off **3** PAY ATTENTION, be careful, take care, take heed, look out
▷ **watch out** notice, be vigilant, look out, keep a lookout, keep your eyes open, *colloq.* keep your eyes peeled, keep your eyes skinned
▷ **watch over** guard, protect, stand guard over, keep an eye on, look after, take care of, mind, shield, defend, shelter
▶ *n* **1** TIMEPIECE, wristwatch, clock, *formal* chronometer **2** VIGILANCE, watchfulness, vigil, guard, observation, surveillance, notice, lookout, attention, heed, alertness, inspection, supervision

watchdog *n*
1 GUARD DOG, house-dog **2** MONITOR, inspector, scrutineer, vigilante, ombudsman, guardian, custodian, protector

watcher *n*
spectator, observer, onlooker, looker-on, viewer, (member of the) audience, lookout, spy, witness

watchful *adj*
vigilant, attentive, heedful, observant, alert, guarded, on your guard, wide awake, keep your eyes open/peeled/skinned, on the lookout, suspicious, wary, chary, cautious, *formal* circumspect, on the qui vive
▣ unobservant, inattentive

watchfulness *n*
vigilance, alertness, attention, attentiveness, heedfulness, caution, cautiousness, circumspection, suspicion, suspiciousness, wariness
▣ inattention

watchman *n*
guard, security guard, caretaker, custodian, caretaker

watchword *n*
catch phrase, slogan, catchword, maxim, password, motto, rallying-cry, battle-cry, signal, byword, buzz word, magic word, shibboleth

water *n, v*
▶ *n* rain, sea, ocean, lake, river, current, stream,

moisture, flooding, torrent
▶ *v* wet, moisten, dampen, soak, spray, sprinkle, irrigate, saturate, drench, flood, hose, douse
▣ dry out, parch
▷ **water down** dilute, thin, water, weaken, adulterate, mix, tone down, play down, soften, qualify, *formal* mitigate, *colloq.* soft-pedal

waterfall *n*
fall, falls, cascade, chute, cataract, torrent

waterproof *adj*
impervious, water-resistant, damp-proof, rubberized, impermeable, water-repellent, coated, proofed
▣ leaky

watertight *adj*
1 WATERPROOF, sound, hermetic **2** IMPREGNABLE, unassailable, incontrovertible, indisputable, airtight, flawless, foolproof, firm, sound
▣ **1** leaky

watery *adj*
1 LIQUID, fluid, moist, wet, damp, *technical* hydrous, *formal* aqueous **2** WEAK, watered-down, diluted, adulterated, insipid, tasteless, thin, runny, soggy, squelchy, flavourless, washy, *colloq.* wishy-washy
▣ **1** dry

wave *v, n*
▶ *v* **1** BECKON, gesture, gesticulate, indicate, sign, signal, direct **2** BRANDISH, flourish, flap, flutter, stir, shake, sway, swing, waft, quiver, ripple, surge, move from side to side, *formal* undulate
▷ **wave aside** dismiss, brush aside, disregard, reject, set aside, shelve, spurn, *colloq.* pour cold water on
▶ *n* **1** BREAKER, roller, billow, ripple, comber, foam, froth, swell, surf, tidal wave, wavelet, undulation, *colloq.* white horse **2** SURGE, sweep, swell, flow, upsurge, ground swell, current, drift, movement, rush, tendency, trend, stream, flood, outbreak, rash

waver *v*
1 VACILLATE, falter, hesitate, dither, fluctuate, vary, seesaw, equivocate, *colloq.* shilly-shally, hum and haw **2** TREMBLE, oscillate, shake, sway, wobble, stagger, teeter, totter, rock
▣ **1** decide

wavy *adj*
undulating, rippled, curly, curling, curvy, curving, ridged, sinuous, winding, zigzag

wax *v*
grow, increase, get bigger, rise, swell, develop, enlarge, expand, extend, spread, magnify, broaden, widen, mount, fill out, become
▣ decrease, wane

waxen *adj*
pale, colourless, ashen, wan, white, whitish, pallid, ghastly, anaemic, bloodless, livid
▣ ruddy

waxy *adj*
soft, pallid, pasty, waxen, impressible, impressionable, *formal* ceraceous, cereous

way *n*
1 METHOD, approach, manner, technique, process, plan, course of action, strategy, procedure, means, instrument, tool, system, style, fashion, lines, *formal* mode, instrumentality **2** CUSTOM, practice, behaviour, manner, habit, usage, characteristic, idiosyncrasy, peculiarity, mannerism, personality, temper, temperament, disposition, trait, style, conduct, nature, *formal* wont **3** DIRECTION, course, route, path, pathway, road, channel, access, avenue, track, passage, highway, roadway, street, thoroughfare, lane
▷ **by the way** incidentally, in passing, secondarily, parenthetically, *en passant*
▷ **give way 1** COLLAPSE, break, fall in, sink, disin-

tegrate, subside, cave in **2** GIVE IN, yield, surrender, capitulate, submit, concede
▷ **under way** in progress, moving, in motion, going, begun, started, in operation, afoot
▷ **way of life** lifestyle, life, living conditions, position, situation, world
▷ **ways and means** methods, procedure, way, resources, wherewithal, capability, capacity, tools, cash, funds, reserves, capital

wayfarer *n*
traveller, walker, wanderer, journeyer, globetrotter, rover, trekker, voyager, itinerant, nomad, Gypsy
▣ resident, stay-at-home

wayfaring *adj*
journeying, walking, travelling, wandering, rambling, roving, drifting, itinerant, voyaging, nomadic, *formal* peripatetic
▣ resident, stay-at-home

waylay *v*
lie in wait for, ambush, attack, accost, set upon, surprise, catch, hold up, intercept, seize, buttonhole

way-out *adj*
weird, crazy, bizarre, outlandish, unusual, unorthodox, unconventional, fantastic, eccentric, wild, experimental, avant-garde, progressive, *colloq.* far-out, freaky, off-beat
▣ ordinary

wayward *adj*
wilful, perverse, contrary, changeable, fickle, unpredictable, stubborn, self-willed, unmanageable, ungovernable, headstrong, obstinate, disobedient, rebellious, insubordinate, unruly, incorrigible, *formal* intractable, obdurate, contumacious, refractory, capricious
▣ tractable, good-natured

weak *adj*
1 FEEBLE, frail, infirm, shaky, unhealthy, sickly, puny, delicate, exhausted, worn out, fatigued, fragile, flimsy, *formal* debilitated, indisposed, enervated, *colloq.* weedy **2** VULNERABLE, unprotected, unguarded, defenceless, exposed **3** POWERLESS, impotent, spineless, cowardly, indecisive, irresolute, poor, flimsy, feeble, lacking, lame, inadequate, faulty, imperfect, useless, defective, deficient, inconclusive, unconvincing, unsound, untenable, *formal* ineffectual **4** FAINT, slight, dim, low, soft, muffled, stifled, dull, imperceptible **5** INSIPID, tasteless, watery, thin, diluted, runny, adulterated
▣ **1** strong **2** secure **3** powerful, determined **4** strong **5** strong

weaken *v*
1 ENFEEBLE, tire, exhaust, sap, undermine, incapacitate, disable, paralyse, cripple, incapacitate, dilute, diminish, lower, lessen, reduce, moderate, mitigate, temper, soften (up), thin, water down, *formal* debilitate, enervate **2** TIRE, flag, fail, give way, droop, fade, ease up, dwindle, *formal* abate
▣ **1** strengthen

weakling *n*
coward, underling, underdog, mouse, *colloq.* wimp, wet, wally, weed, drip, doormat, sissy
▣ hero, stalwart

weak-minded *adj*
pliable, faint-hearted, irresolute, persuasible, submissive, compliant, weak-kneed, persuadable, *formal* complaisant, pusillanimous, *colloq.* spineless
▣ strong-willed

weakness *n*
1 FEEBLENESS, infirmity, impotence, incapacity, delicateness, frailty, powerlessness, vulnerability, *formal* debility, enervation **2** FAULT, failing, flaw, im-

perfection, shortcoming, blemish, defect, deficiency, foible, weak point, achilles' heel **3** LIKING, inclination, fondness, passion, *formal* penchant, predilection, proclivity, predisposition, *colloq.* soft spot
F₃ 1 strength **2** strength **3** dislike

weal *n*
welt, stripe, streak, scar, ridge, mark, wound, contusion, cicatrice, cicatrix

wealth *n*
1 MONEY, cash, riches, assets, affluence, prosperity, funds, mammon, fortune, treasure, capital, finance, means, substance, resources, goods, possessions, property, estate, *formal* opulence **2** ABUNDANCE, plenty, mass, bounty, fullness, store, copiousness, *formal* cornucopia, profusion, plenitude
F₃ 1 poverty

wealthy *adj*
rich, prosperous, affluent, well-off, moneyed, comfortable, well-heeled, well-to-do, *formal* opulent
F₃ poor, impoverished, *colloq.* flush, rolling in it, made of money, *slang* loaded, filthy rich, stinking rich

weapon *n*

Weapons include:
gun, airgun, pistol, revolver, automatic, Colt®, Luger®, magnum, Mauser, six-gun, six-shooter, rifle, air rifle, Winchester® rifle, carbine, shotgun, blunderbuss, musket, elephant gun, machine-gun, kalashnikov, submachine-gun, tommy-gun, sten gun, Bren gun, cannon, field gun, gatling-gun, howitzer, mortar, turret-gun; knife, bowie knife, flick-knife, stiletto, dagger, dirk, poniard, sword, épée, foil, rapier, sabre, scimitar, bayonet, broadsword, claymore, lance, spear, pike, machete; bomb, atom bomb, H-bomb, cluster-bomb, depth-charge, incendiary bomb, Mills bomb, mine, land-mine, napalm bomb, time-bomb; bow and arrow, longbow, crossbow, blowpipe, catapult, boomerang, sling, harpoon, bolas, rocket, bazooka, ballistic missile, Cruise missile, Exocet®, *colloq.* Scud, torpedo, hand grenade, flame-thrower; battleaxe, pole-axe, halberd, tomahawk, cosh, cudgel, knuckleduster, shillelagh, truncheon; gas, Agent Orange, CS gas, *US* Mace®, mustard gas, tear-gas.

wear *v, n*
▶ *v* **1** DRESS IN, be dressed in, have on, put on, be clothed in, don, sport, carry, bear, have, display, show, exhibit, assume **2** DETERIORATE, erode, corrode, consume, fray, become thinner, become weaker, become threadbare, rub, abrade, waste, grind
▷ **wear down** reduce, rub away, corrode, abrade, erode, grind down, chip away at, consume, undermine, diminish, lessen, overcome, *formal* macerate
▷ **wear off** decrease, dwindle, diminish, subside, wane, weaken, fade, lessen, ebb, peter out, disappear, *formal* abate
F₃ increase
▷ **wear on** go on, go by, pass, elapse
▷ **wear out 1** EXHAUST, fatigue, tire (out), strain, stress, drain, sap, *formal* enervate **2** DETERIORATE, wear through, erode, impair, consume, fray
▶ *n* **1** CLOTHES, clothing, dress, garments, outfit, costume, *formal* attire **2** DETERIORATION, erosion, corrosion, damage, wear and tear, friction, abrasion **3** USE, service, employment, usefulness, utility, durability

weariness *n*
fatigue, tiredness, exhaustion, lassitude, lethargy, ennui, drowsiness, sleepiness, listlessness, prostration,

formal enervation, languor
F₃ freshness

wearing *adj*
exhausting, fatiguing, tiring, tiresome, wearisome, trying, taxing, oppressive, irksome, exasperating, erosive
F₃ refreshing

wearisome *adj*
tiresome, troublesome, wearing, fatiguing, exhausting, dreary, burdensome, bothersome, boring, monotonous, humdrum, tedious, annoying, trying, exasperating, irksome, vexatious, dull
F₃ refreshing

weary *adj, v*
▶ *adj* **1** TIRED, exhausted, fatigued, sleepy, worn out, drained, drowsy, jaded, *colloq.* all in, done in, fagged out, knackered, bushed, pooped, dead beat, whacked, dog-tired **2** *weary of trying to please him* bored, unenthusiastic, tired, uninterested, unexcited, *colloq.* sick and tired, bored to tears, browned off, brassed off, cheesed off
F₃ 1 refreshed **2** excited, interested
▶ *v* tire, tire out, wear out, fatigue, bore, fail, jade, sap, sicken, drain, burden, fade, annoy, irritate, exasperate, irk, tax, *formal* debilitate, enervate, *colloq.* bug, fag

weather *n, v*
▶ *n* climate, conditions, temperature, humidity, dryness, windiness, sunniness, cloudiness, meteorological reports, atmospheric conditions, forecast, outlook
▷ **under the weather** ill, sick, poorly, queer, ailing, off-colour, the worse for wear, seedy, groggy, below par, squeamish, nauseous, hung over, out of sorts, *formal* indisposed
▶ *v* **1** ENDURE, survive, live through, come through, get through, ride out, rise above, stick out, withstand, surmount, stand, brave, overcome, resist, pull through, suffer **2** EXPOSE, toughen, season, harden, dry
F₃ 1 succumb

weave *v*
1 INTERLACE, lace, plait, braid, intertwine, spin, knit, entwine, intercross, interwork, fuse, merge, unite **2** CREATE, compose, construct, contrive, make up, put together, fabricate **3** WIND, twist, zigzag, crisscross

web *n*
network, net, netting, lattice, lacework, mesh, complex, webbing, interlacing, weft, snare, knot, tangle, trap

wed *v*
1 MARRY, get married, yoke, *formal* espouse, *colloq.* get hitched, splice, tie the knot, **2** JOIN, unite, unify, coalesce, blend, ally, combine, link, interweave, fuse, merge, *formal* commingle
F₃ 1 divorce

wedded *adj*
married, marital, joined, husbandly, wifely, *formal* conjugal, connubial, matrimonial, nuptial, spousal

wedding *n, adj*
▶ *n* marriage, union, marriage service, marriage ceremony, celebration of marriage, *formal* matrimony, nuptials
F₃ divorce
▶ *adj* marriage, *formal* bridal, matrimonial, nuptial, hymeneal, hymenean, epithalamic

wedge *n, v*
▶ *n* lump, block, piece, chunk, wodge, chock, triangle
▶ *v* jam, cram, pack, ram, squeeze, stuff, push, lodge, fit, block, thrust, crowd, force

wedlock *n*
marriage, union, *formal* holy matrimony, matrimony

wee *adj*
small, little, tiny, miniature, minute, negligible, insignificant, diminutive, minuscule, microscopic, midget, Lilliputian, *colloq.* itsy-bitsy, teeny, teeny-weeny, weeny
F3 big, large

weed *v*
▷ **weed out** get rid of, remove, root out, eradicate, eliminate, purge, *formal* extirpate
F3 add, fix, infiltrate

weedy *adj*
thin, skinny, puny, scrawny, undersized, gangling, weak, feeble, frail, weak-kneed, insipid, *colloq.* wet, wimpish
F3 strong

weekly *adv, adj*
▶ *adv* every week, by the week, once a week, *formal* hebdomadally
▶ *adj formal* hebdomadal, hebdomadary

weep *v, n*
▶ *v* cry, sob, be in tears, shed tears, moan, lament, wail, mourn, grieve, bawl, blubber, snivel, whine, whimper, *colloq.* blub
F3 rejoice
▶ *n* cry, sob, moan, snivel, blub, lament

weepy *adj, n*
▶ *adj* crying, tearful, sobbing, blubbering, weeping, teary, *formal* labile, lachrymose
▶ *n* melodrama, sob-stuff, tear-jerker

weigh *v*
1 *weigh the apples* measure the weight of, see/measure how heavy something is **2** BEAR DOWN, oppress, burden, depress, afflict, trouble, worry, *colloq.* get down **3** CONSIDER, contemplate, evaluate, meditate on, mull over, ponder, think over, examine, reflect on, deliberate
▷ **weigh down** oppress, overload, load, burden, bear down, weigh upon, press down, depress, afflict, trouble, worry, *colloq.* get down
F3 lighten, hearten
▷ **weigh up** assess, examine, size up, evaluate, balance, compare, consider, contemplate, deliberate, mull over, ponder, think over, discuss, *colloq.* chew over

weight *n, v*
▶ *n* **1** HEAVINESS, gravity, burden, load, pressure, mass, quantity, force, ballast, tonnage, poundage, *formal* avoirdupois **2** IMPORTANCE, significance, substance, consequence, impact, moment, influence, force, value, authority, power, consideration, *formal* preponderance, *colloq.* clout **3** BURDEN, load, onus, responsibility, duty, worry, trouble, strain, encumbrance
F3 **1** lightness
▶ *v* **1** LOAD, weigh down, burden, oppress, handicap **2** BIAS, unbalance, slant, prejudice, angle, load, twist, sway

weightless *adj*
light, insubstantial, airy, *formal* imponderous
F3 heavy

weighty *adj*
1 HEAVY, substantial, massive, bulky, hefty **2** IMPORTANT, significant, consequential, crucial, critical, momentous, vital, serious, influential, authoritative, grave, solemn **3** DEMANDING, burdensome, onerous, difficult, exacting, taxing
F3 **1** light **2** unimportant, significant

weird *adj*
strange, uncanny, bizarre, eerie, creepy, supernatural, unnatural, ghostly, freakish, mysterious, queer, grotesque, *formal* preternatural, *colloq.*
spooky, far-out, way-out
F3 normal, usual

weirdo *n*
eccentric, freak, crank, cure, *colloq.* crackpot, oddball, nutcase, loony, fruitcake, nut, nutter, queer fish

welcome *adj, n, v*
▶ *adj* acceptable, desirable, popular, pleasing, pleasant, agreeable, gratifying, appreciated, delightful, refreshing
F3 unwelcome
▶ *n* reception, greeting, acceptance, hospitality, *colloq.* salutation, red carpet
▶ *v* greet, hail, receive, salute, meet, accept, approve of, be pleased with, be satisfied with, embrace, *colloq.* roll out the red carpet for
F3 reject, snub

weld *v, n*
▶ *v* fuse, unite, bond, join, solder, bind, connect, seal, link, cement
F3 separate
▶ *n* joint, bond, seal, seam

welfare *n*
1 WELL-BEING, health, prosperity, happiness, comfort, soundness, security, benefit, good, fortune, advantage, interest, profit, success **2** *live off welfare* benefit, income, allowance, pension, sick pay, payment

well ¹ *adv, adj*
▶ *adv* **1** *speak Czech well* competently, skilfully, properly, ably, expertly, proficiently, effectively, adeptly, excellently, rightly, correctly, successfully **2** *everything turned out well* satisfactorily, adequately, suitably, fittingly, sufficiently **3** *treat someone well* kindly, genially, generously, hospitably, agreeably, pleasantly, happily **4** *Did you know her well?* thoroughly, properly, carefully, industriously, fully, deeply, profoundly, closely, completely, greatly, considerably **5** *live well* successfully, prosperously, comfortably, splendidly, luckily, fortunately **6** *think/speak well of someone* highly, approvingly, favourably, glowingly, warmly **7** *well over a thousand people* substantially, considerably, very much, to a great extent, far **8** *you may well be right* conceivably, quite possibly, very likely, probably, certainly
F3 **1** badly, inadequately, incompetently, wrongly **2, 3** badly **5** poorly **6** unfavourably
▷ **as well** too, also, in addition, furthermore, besides, moreover, *colloq.* into the bargain
▷ **as well as** in addition to, together with, along with, including, over and above, not to mention, to say nothing of
▷ **well done** bravo, congratulations, hurrah, encore
▶ *adj* **1** HEALTHY, in good health, fit, able-bodied, sound, robust, strong, thriving, flourishing, hale and hearty **2** SATISFACTORY, right, all right, good, pleasing, proper, agreeable, fine, lucky, fortunate, *colloq.* OK
F3 **1** ill **2** bad

well ² *n, v*
▶ *n* *dig a well* spring, well-spring, fountain, fount, source, reservoir, pool, well-head

Types of well include:
artesian well, borehole, draw-well, gas well, geyser, gusher, hot spring, inkwell, lift-shaft, mineral spring, oil-well, pump-well, stairwell, thermal spring, waterhole, wishing-well.

▶ *v* flow, spring, surge, gush, stream, brim over, jet, spout, spurt, swell, issue, rush, pour, flood, ooze, run, trickle, rise, seep

well-balanced *adj*
 1 RATIONAL, reasonable, level-headed, well-adjusted, stable, sensible, sane, sound, sober, *colloq.* together 2 SYMMETRICAL, even, harmonious, balanced, well-proportioned, well-ordered
 ☒ 1 unbalanced, maladjusted 2 asymmetrical, disordered

well-behaved *adj*
 well-mannered, good, polite, respectful, under control, obedient, considerate, co-operative, *formal* compliant, *colloq.* good as gold
 ☒ disobedient, naughty

well-being *n*
 welfare, happiness, comfort, health, good health, good

well-bred *adj*
 well-mannered, polite, well-brought-up, mannerly, courteous, civil, refined, cultivated, cultured, genteel, gentlemanly, ladylike, aristocratic, blue-blooded, upper-crust, gallant, urbane
 ☒ ill-bred

well-built *adj*
 strong, muscular, brawny, strapping, burly, beefy, stout

well-disposed *adj*
 favourable, friendly, well-placed, sympathetic, agreeable, amicable, well-arranged, well-minded, well-aimed
 ☒ ill-disposed

well-dressed *adj*
 smart, well-groomed, elegant, fashionable, chic, stylish, neat, trim, dapper, spruce, tidy, *colloq.* natty
 ☒ badly dressed, scruffy

well-founded *adj*
 justifiable, reasonable, acceptance, reasonable, warranted, sustainable, right, sensible, sound, proper, fit, valid, plausible

well-groomed *adj*
 neat, tidy, smart, trim, spruce, dapper, well-turned-out, well-dressed

well-known *adj*
 famous, renowned, celebrated, famed, eminent, notable, noted, illustrious, familiar, widely-known, usual, common
 ☒ unknown

well-nigh *adv*
 almost, nearly, practically, virtually, all but, just about, to all intents and purposes

well-off *adj*
 1 RICH, wealthy, affluent, prosperous, well-to-do, moneyed, thriving, successful, comfortable, *colloq.* well-heeled, flush, rolling in it, *slang* loaded, filthy rich, stinking rich 2 FORTUNATE, lucky, prosperous, thriving, successful, comfortable
 ☒ 1 poor, badly-off 2 unfortunate, unlucky

well-spoken *adj*
 articulate, fluent, eloquent, clear, coherent, well-expressed

well-thought-of *adj*
 respected, highly regarded, admired, looked up to, honoured, revered, *formal* esteemed, venerated
 ☒ despised, looked down on

well-to-do *adj*
 rich, wealthy, affluent, moneyed, prosperous, well-off, comfortable, *colloq.* flush, well-heeled, rolling in it, *slang* loaded
 ☒ poor

well-worn *adj*
 1 *a well-worn phrase* timeworn, stale, tired, trite, over-used, unoriginal, hackneyed, commonplace, stereo-typed, threadbare, *colloq.* corny 2 *well-worn clothing* threadbare, worn, worn out, frayed, ragged, scruffy, shabby
 ☒ 1 original 2 new

welsh *v*
 cheat, defraud, swindle, *colloq.* diddle, do

welter *v, n*
 ▶ *v* roll, flounder, pitch, toss, wallow, splash, wade, lurch, heave
 ▶ *n* mess, confusion, jumble, muddle, tangle, web, hotchpotch, *colloq.* mish-mash

wend *v*
 ▷ **wend your way** go, move, make your way, proceed, progress, travel, walk, hike, wander, trudge, plod, meander
 ☒ stay

wet *adj, n, v*
 ▶ *adj* 1 DAMP, moist, soaked, soaking, sodden, saturated, soggy, sopping, sopping wet, watery, waterlogged, drenched, dripping, spongy, dank, clammy 2 RAINING, rainy, showery, teeming, pouring, drizzling, dank, damp, humid 3 WEAK, feeble, weedy, spineless, soft, namby-pamby, irresolute, *formal* ineffectual, timorous, effete, *colloq.* pathetic, wimpish
 ☒ 1 dry 2 dry 3 strong
 ▷ **wet behind the ears** new, untrained, inexperienced, immature, raw, innocent, naïve, callow, *colloq.* green
 ☒ experienced
 ▶ *n* 1 WETNESS, moisture, moistness, damp, dampness, liquid, water, clamminess, condensation, humidity, rain, drizzle 2 *don't be such a wet* fool, idiot, softy, weakling, milksop, *colloq.* wimp, wally, drip, *slang* jerk, nerd
 ☒ 1 dryness
 ▶ *v* moisten, damp, dampen, soak, saturate, drench, steep, flood, swamp, water, irrigate, spray, splash, sprinkle, imbue, douse, dip
 ☒ dry

wetness *n*
 damp, dampness, moisture, wet, water, liquid, soddenness, sogginess, condensation, dankness, clamminess, humidity
 ☒ dryness

whack *v, n*
 ▶ *v* hit, strike, smack, thrash, slap, beat, bang, cuff, thump, box, buffet, rap, *colloq.* bash, wallop, belt, clobber, clout, sock
 ▶ *n* 1 SMACK, slap, blow, hit, rap, stroke, thump, cuff, box, bang, *colloq.* clout, bash, wallop 2 SHARE, portion, quota, allowance, allocation, lot, part, division, stint, proportion, percentage, *colloq.* cut, rake-off, slice of the cake

wharf *n*
 dock, quay, quayside, jetty, landing-stage, dockyard, marina, pier

what's-its-name *n*
 thingummy, thingummyjig, thingummybob, what-d'you-call-it, *colloq.* whatsit, doodah, whatnot

wheedle *v*
 cajole, coax, persuade, talk into, win over, charm, flatter, beguile, entice, induce, court, draw, *formal* inveigle
 ☒ force

wheel *n, v*
 ▶ *n* turn, revolution, circle, rotation, gyration, pivot, roll, spin, twirl, whirl

Types of wheel include:
 balance-wheel, big wheel, buff-wheel, cartwheel, castor, Catherine wheel, charka, cogwheel, crown-

wheel, drive-wheel, escape wheel, Ferris wheel, flywheel, gearwheel, idle wheel, mill wheel, paddle wheel, potter's wheel, prayer wheel, ratchet-wheel, roulette wheel, spinning-jenny, spinning-wheel, sprocket, spur gear, steering-wheel, wagon wheel, water-wheel, wheel of fortune, worm wheel.

▷ **at the wheel 1** DRIVING, steering, behind the wheel, in the driver's seat, turning **2** IN CHARGE, at the helm, in control, in command, responsible, directing, *colloq.* heading up
▶ *v* turn, rotate, circle, gyrate, orbit, spin, go round, pivot, twirl, whirl, swing, roll, revolve, swivel

wheeze *v, n*
▶ *v* pant, gasp, cough, hiss, rasp, whistle
▶ *n* **1** RASP, gasp, cough, hiss, whistle **2** TRICK, joke, gag, crack, prank, ruse, practical joke, ploy, scheme, plan, stunt, idea, story, anecdote, catch phrase, *colloq.* chestnut, one-liner, wrinkle

whereabouts *n*
location, position, place, situation, site, vicinity

wherewithal *n*
means, resources, supplies, money, cash, funds, capital, necessary, *colloq.* readies

whet *v*
1 SHARPEN, hone, file, grind, edge **2** STIMULATE, stir, rouse, arouse, excite, provoke, kindle, quicken, incite, awaken, titillate, increase
F **1** blunt **2** dampen

whiff *n*
1 *a whiff of fresh air* breath, puff, hint, trace, blast, gust, draught, odour, smell, aroma, sniff, scent, reek, stink, stench **2** *a whiff of scandal/danger* trace, hint, suspicion, suggestion, touch

while *n, v*
▶ *n* time, period, spell, stretch, season, span, interval
▶ *v* ▷ **while away** spend, pass, occupy, use (up), devote

whim *n*
fancy, caprice, notion, idea, quirk, freak, humour, conceit, fad, craze, passion, vagary, urge, impulse

whimper *v, n*
▶ *v* cry, sob, weep, snivel, sniffle, whine, grizzle, mewl, moan, groan, *colloq.* whinge
▶ *n* sob, cry, snivel, whine, moan, groan

whimsical *adj*
fanciful, quirky, playful, mischievous, impulsive, unpredictable, eccentric, funny, droll, curious, queer, unusual, weird, odd, peculiar, quaint, *formal* capricious, *colloq.* dotty

whine *v, n*
▶ *v* **1** CRY, sob, whimper, grizzle, moan, wail **2** COMPLAIN, carp, grumble, moan, groan, grouse, *colloq.* gripe, whinge, grouch, beef, belly-ache
▶ *n* **1** CRY, sob, whimper, moan, wail **2** COMPLAINT, moan, grumble, groan, grouse, *colloq.* gripe, grouch, beef, belly-ache

whinge *v, n*
▶ *v* complain, grumble, moan, carp, *colloq.* gripe, grouse, beef, belly-ache
▶ *n* complaint, grumble, moan, groan, grouse, *colloq.* gripe, beef, belly-ache

whip *v, n*
▶ *v* **1** BEAT, flog, lash, scourge, birch, cane, strap, thrash, punish, discipline, *formal* flagellate, chastise, castigate, *colloq.* tan, belt, whack, clout, wallop, give someone a good hiding **2** PULL, jerk, snatch, whisk, flash, *colloq.* yank **3** DASH, dart, rush, tear, flit, fly **4** *whip the cream* stir, mix, whisk, beat **5** GOAD, drive, spur, prod, push, urge, stir, rouse, agitate, incite,

provoke, prompt, instigate
▷ **whip up** stir up, work up, agitate, excite, arouse, incite, inflame, kindle, instigate, provoke, foment, *colloq.* psych up
F dampen, deter
▶ *n* lash, scourge, switch, birch, cane, horsewhip, crop, riding-crop, cat-o'-nine-tails

whipping *n*
beating, punishment, spanking, flogging, lashing, thrashing, birching, caning, *formal* castigation, flagellation, *colloq.* belting, hiding, tanning, walloping

whirl *v, n*
▶ *v* spin, swirl, turn, twist, twirl, pivot, pirouette, swivel, wheel, rotate, revolve, turn round, reel, roll, gyrate, circle
▶ *n* **1** SPIN, twirl, twist, gyration, revolution, pirouette, swirl, turn, wheel, rotation, circle, reel, roll, pivot, roll **2** BUSTLE, flurry, round, series, succession, merry-go-round, commotion, agitation, hubbub, hurly-burly, confusion, daze, muddle, jumble, giddiness, tumult, uproar
▷ **give something a whirl** try, attempt, strive, endeavour, venture, *colloq.* have a go, have a bash/crack/shot/stab

whirlpool *n*
maelstrom, vortex, *Scot.* weel

whirlwind *n, adj*
▶ *n* tornado, cyclone, vortex
▶ *adj* hasty, impulsive, quick, rapid, speedy, swift, lightning, headlong, impetuous, rash
F deliberate, slow

whisk *v, n*
▶ *v* **1** WHIP, beat, stir, mix **2** DART, dash, rush, hurry, speed, fly, tears, bolt, hasten, race, shoot, dive, whip **3** BRUSH, sweep, flick, wipe, twitch
▶ *n* beater, brush, swizzle-stick

whisky *n*
whiskey, Scotch, bourbon, rye, usquebaugh, moonshine, malt

whisper *v, n*
▶ *v* **1** MURMUR, mutter, mumble, say/speak quietly, breathe, hiss, rustle, sigh, sough, *formal* susurrate **2** HINT, intimate, insinuate, gossip, divulge
F **1** shout
▶ *n* **1** MURMUR, soft/quiet/low voice, undertone, sigh, hiss, rustle, sough **2** HINT, suggestion, suspicion, breath, whiff, rumour, report, innuendo, insinuation, trace, tinge, soupçon, buzz

whistle *v, n*
▶ *v* pipe, sing, call, cheep, chirp, warble
▶ *n* song, call, cheep, warble, chirp, siren, hooter

whit *n*
atom, little, drop, bit, scrap, shred, piece, fragment, particle, crumb, pinch, speck, trace, iota, jot, grain, mite, modicum, dash, hoot
F lot

white *adj*
1 PALE, light-skinned, pallid, wan, ashen, colourless, anaemic, pasty, waxen **2** LIGHT, snowy, milky, creamy, ivory, hoary, silver, grey **3** PURE, immaculate, spotless, stainless, undefiled
F **1** black, dark, ruddy **2** dark **3** defiled

white-collar *adj*
executive, office, professional, salaried, clerical, nonmanual
F blue-collar, manual

whiten *v*
bleach, blanch, whitewash, pale, fade, whitewash, *formal* etiolate
F blacken, darken

whitewash *n, v*
▶ *n* cover-up, concealment, deception, camouflage, pretext
F﹢ exposure
▶ *v* **1** COVER UP, conceal, hide, make light of, suppress, gloss over, camouflage **2** THRASH, beat, crush, drub, best, *colloq.* clobber, hammer, lick, paste, trounce
F﹢ **1** expose

whittle *v*
1 CARVE, cut, scrape, shave, trim, pare, hew, shape **2** ERODE, eat away, wear away, diminish, consume, use (up), reduce, undermine

whole *adj, n*
▶ *adj* **1** COMPLETE, entire, integral, full, total, unabridged, uncut, undivided, unedited **2** INTACT, unharmed, undamaged, unbroken, perfect, sound, in one piece, mint, uninjured, unhurt, *formal* inviolate **3** WELL, healthy, fit, sound, strong
F﹢ **1** damaged **3** ill
▶ *n* total, aggregate, sum total, entirety, all, fullness, totality, ensemble, entity, unit, lot, piece, everything
F﹢ part
▷ **on the whole** generally, mostly, in general, generally speaking, in the main, as a rule, for the most part, all in all, all things considered, by and large, predominantly

wholehearted *adj*
enthusiastic, earnest, committed, dedicated, devoted, hearty, passionate, heartfelt, emphatic, warm, sincere, unfeigned, genuine, unreserved, unstinting, unqualified, complete, true, real, zealous
F﹢ half-hearted

wholesale *adj, adv*
▶ *adj* comprehensive, far-reaching, extensive, sweeping, wide-ranging, mass, broad, all-inclusive, outright, total, massive, indiscriminate
F﹢ partial
▶ *adv* indiscriminately, totally, extensively, comprehensively, massively, en bloc
F﹢ partially

wholesome *adj*
1 *wholesome food*; *a wholesome climate* good, healthy, healthful, hygienic, sanitary, nutritious, nourishing, beneficial, salutary, refreshing, invigorating, bracing, *formal* salubrious **2** *wholesome entertainment* moral, decent, clean, proper, improving, edifying, uplifting, pure, virtuous, righteous, beneficial, helpful, ethical, honourable, respectable
F﹢ **1** unhealthy **2** unwholesome, immoral

wholly *adv*
completely, entirely, fully, purely, absolutely, totally, utterly, comprehensively, altogether, perfectly, thoroughly, all, exclusively, only, in every respect, *colloq.* one hundred per cent
F﹢ partly

whoop *v, n*
shout, cry, yell, cheer, scream, shriek, roar, hoop, hoot, hurrah, *colloq.* holler

whopper *n*
lie, falsehood, fabrication, deception, falsification, invention, fiction, deceit, falsity, untruth, fable, *colloq.* cracker, fairy story, tall story, porky, fib, cock-and-bull story

whopping *adj*
large, big, huge, massive, extraordinary, immense, vast, great, mammoth, tremendous, staggering, monumental, enormous, giant, gigantic, whacking, *formal* prodigious
F﹢ tiny

whorl *n*
spiral, twist, turn, coil, helix, vortex, corkscrew, *formal* convolution

wicked *adj*
1 EVIL, sinful, immoral, bad, depraved, corrupt, vicious, unprincipled, debased, abominable, ungodly, devilish, unrighteous, shameful, black-hearted, villainous, *formal* iniquitous, heinous, dissolute, egregious, nefarious **2** BAD, unpleasant, harmful, offensive, scandalous, vile, worthless, difficult, terrible, dreadful, distressing, awful, atrocious, severe, intense, nasty, injurious, troublesome, terrible, foul, fierce **3** NAUGHTY, mischievous, roguish, impish, rascally **4** EXCELLENT, admirable, *colloq.* cool
F﹢ **1** good, upright **2** harmless

wickedness *n*
evil, depravity, vileness, atrocity, abomination, corruption, corruptness, foulness, fiendishness, immorality, shamefulness, sin, sinfulness, impiety, unrighteousness, devilishness, enormity, amorality, *formal* dissoluteness, heinousness, iniquity, reprobacy
F﹢ uprightness

wide *adj, adv*
▶ *adj* **1** BROAD, roomy, spacious, extensive, vast, immense, ample **2** DILATED, expanded, full **3** EXTENSIVE, wide-ranging, comprehensive, great, broad, vast, immense, far-reaching, general **4** LOOSE, baggy, full, roomy, *formal* capacious **5** OFF-TARGET, off-course, off the mark, distant, remote
F﹢ **1** narrow **3** restricted **5** near
▶ *adv* **1** ASTRAY, off course, off target, off the mark **2** FULLY, completely, to the full extent, all the way
F﹢ **1** on target

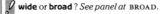
wide or **broad** ? *See panel at* BROAD.

wide-awake *adj*
conscious, aware, fully awake, wakened, observant, watchful, vigilant, wary, sharp, alert, astute, roused, heedful, keen, quick-witted, on your toes, on the alert, on the qui vive, *colloq.* on the ball
F﹢ asleep

wide-eyed *adj*
credulous, naïve, gullible, trusting, overtrusting, dupable, unsuspecting, uncritical, unseasoned, fresh, unsophisticated, innocent, *colloq.* green, wet behind the ears, out of your depth
F﹢ knowing, suspicious, sophisticated

widely *adv*
broadly, extensively, generally, comprehensively

widen *v*
broaden, expand, extend, spread, increase, stretch, enlarge, *formal* distend, dilate
F﹢ narrow

wide-open *adj*
open, gaping, wide, outspread, outstretched, spread, unprotected, vulnerable, defenceless, exposed, susceptible, *formal* unfortified
F﹢ closed, narrow

wide-ranging *adj*
far-reaching, broad, extensive, widespread, comprehensive, thorough, important, significant, momentous, sweeping

widespread *adj*
extensive, prevalent, rife, general, sweeping, universal, wholesale, far-reaching, unlimited, broad, common, pervasive, far-flung
F﹢ limited

width *n*
breadth, broadness, diameter, wideness, compass,

wield

thickness, largeness, span, scope, range, measure, girth, beam, amplitude, extent, extensiveness, reach

wield *v*
1 *wield a weapon* brandish, flourish, swing, wave, handle, ply, shake, manage, manipulate **2** *wield power* have, hold, possess, employ, exert, exercise, use, utilize, control, maintain, command

wife *n*
partner, spouse, companion, mate, bride, *colloq.* better half, other half, missus

wiggle *v & n*
jiggle, shake, jerk, wriggle, wag, waggle, twist, squirm, twitch, writhe

wild *adj*
1 UNTAMED, undomesticated, savage, barbarous, primitive, uncivilized, natural, unbroken, ferocious, fierce, brutish, *formal* feral **2** UNCULTIVATED, natural, desolate, waste, barren, forsaken, unpopulated, uninhabited, unsettled, rugged, inhospitable **3** UNRESTRAINED, unruly, undisciplined, unmanageable, violent, turbulent, rowdy, lawless, out of control, uncontrollable, ungovernable, rampant, disorderly, riotous, boisterous **4** STORMY, tempestuous, raging, rough, furious, violent, blustery, choppy, turbulent **5** UNTIDY, unkempt, messy, dishevelled, tousled, uncombed **6** RECKLESS, rash, impulsive, foolish, foolhardy, impracticable, irrational, outrageous, preposterous, wayward, extravagant, fantastic, unwise, *formal* imprudent **7** MAD, frenzied, distraught, demented, berserk, frantic, beside yourself, *colloq.* crazy, nuts, nutty, bonkers, bananas **8** ANGRY, furious, raging, enraged, infuriated, incensed, blazing, fuming, *colloq.* crazy, mad, hopping mad, foaming at the mouth **9** ENTHUSIASTIC, keen, fervent, vehement, passionate, excited, fanatical, *colloq.* crazy, mad, nuts, daft, potty
 1 tame, civilized **2** cultivated **3** restrained **4** calm **5** tidy **6** sensible **7** sane

wilderness *n*
desert, wasteland, waste, wilds, jungle

wild flower

Wild flowers include:
Aaron's rod, ale hoof, bird's foot trefoil, birth-wort, bistort, black-eyed susan, bladder campion, bluebell, broomrape, butter-and-eggs, buttercup, campion, celandine, clary, clustered bellflower, clover, columbine, comfrey, common evening-primrose, common mallow, common toadflax, cowslip, crane's bill, crowfoot, cuckoo flower, daisy, edelweiss, field cow-wheat, foxglove, goatsbeard, goldcup, goldenrod, great mullein, harebell, heartsease, heather, horsetail, lady's slipper, lady's smock, lungwort, marguerite, masterwort, moneywort, multiflora rose, New England aster, oxeye daisy, oxslip, pennyroyal, poppy, primrose, ragged robin, rock rose, rough-fruited cinquefoil, self-heal, shepherd's club, solomon's seal, stiff-haired sunflower, stonecrop, teasel, toadflax, violet, water lily, white campion, wild chicory, wild endive, wild gladiolus, wild iris, wild orchid, wild pansy, wood anemone, yarrow, yellow rocket.

wildlife *n*
animals, fauna

wilds *n*
outback, remote areas, wasteland, wilderness, desert, *colloq.* the back of beyond, the sticks, the middle of nowhere, the boondocks

wiles *n*
trick, stratagem, ruse, ploy, device, contrivance, guile, manoeuvre, subterfuge, cunning, deceit, deception, cheating, trickery, fraud, craftiness, artfulness, chicanery, *colloq.* dodge
 guilelessness

wilful *adj*
1 DELIBERATE, conscious, intentional, voluntary, calculated, planned, premeditated **2** SELF-WILLED, headstrong, obstinate, stubborn, pig-headed, mulish, inflexible, unyielding, uncompromising, perverse, wayward, contrary, determined, dogged, *formal* obdurate, refractory, intransigent, intractable
 1 unintentional, spontaneous **2** good-natured

will *n, v*
▶ *n* **1** VOLITION, choice, option, preference, decision, discretion **2** WISH, desire, inclination, feeling, fancy, disposition, mind **3** PURPOSE, resolve, resolution, determination, purposefulness, willpower, single-mindedness, aim, intention, command
▶ *v* **1** WANT, desire, wish, intend, choose, compel, direct, command, decree, order, ordain **2** BEQUEATH, leave, hand down, pass on, pass down, dispose of, *formal* transfer, confer

willing *adj*
disposed, inclined, agreeable, ready, prepared, consenting, content, amenable, biddable, co-operative, pleased, well-disposed, so-minded, favourable, happy, glad, eager, enthusiastic, keen, *formal* compliant, *colloq.* game
 unwilling, disinclined, reluctant

willingly *adv*
readily, unhesitatingly, eagerly, freely, happily, cheerfully, by choice, voluntarily, gladly, nothing loth
 unwillingly

willingness *n*
readiness, inclination, will, wish, consent, desire, favour, enthusiasm, agreeableness, agreement, disposition, volition, *formal* complaisance, compliance
 unwillingness

willowy *adj*
slender, slim, graceful, svelte, sylph-like, limber, lissom, lithe, lithesome, supple
 buxom

willpower *n*
determination, resolution, resolve, single-mindedness, commitment, will, self-control, self-discipline, self-mastery, self-command, persistence, doggedness, drive, *colloq.* grit

willy-nilly *adv*
necessarily, compulsorily, of necessity, *formal* perforce

wilt *v*
droop, sag, wither, shrivel, flop, flag, dwindle, weaken, faint, diminish, lessen, grow less, fail, fade, languish, ebb, sink, wane
 perk up

wily *adj*
shrewd, cunning, scheming, artful, sharp, crafty, foxy, intriguing, tricky, underhand, shifty, deceitful, cheating, deceptive, astute, sly, guileful, designing, crooked, *colloq.* fly
 guileless

wimp *n*
fool, softy, clown, milksop, *colloq.* clot, drip, wally, wet, *slang* jerk, nerd

win *v, n*
▶ *v* **1** BE VICTORIOUS, triumph, succeed, achieve, success, prevail, overcome, conquer, come (in) first, carry off, finish first, *colloq.* win the day, win hands down, come out on top, turn up trumps, strike gold,

hit the jackpot **2** GAIN, acquire, achieve, attain, accomplish, receive, secure, obtain, get, earn, collect, catch, net, *formal* procure
F₃ 1 fail, lose
▷ **win over** persuade, convince, influence, convert, sway, talk round, bring round, charm, allure, attract, *formal* prevail upon
▶ *n* victory, triumph, conquest, success, mastery
F₃ defeat

wince *v, n*
▶ *v* start, jump, draw back, recoil, flinch, jerk, shrink, cringe, blench, cower, quail
▶ *n* start, cringe, flinch, jerk

wind¹ *n*
blowing in the wind air, breeze, draught, gust, puff, breath, air-current, blast, current, bluster, gale, hurricane, tornado

Types of wind include:
anticyclone, austral wind, berg wind, bise, bora, Cape doctor, chinook, cyclone, doctor, east wind, El Niño, etesian, Favonian wind, föhn, gregale, harmattan, helm wind, khamsin, levant, libeccio, meltemi, mistral, monsoon, north wind, nor'wester, pampero, prevailing wind, samiel, simoom, sirocco, snow eater, southerly, southerly buster, trade wind, tramontana, westerly, wet chinook, williwaw, willy-willy, zephyr, zonda.

▷ **in the wind** likely, probable, expected, about to happen, *colloq.* on the cards
▷ **put the wind up** scare, frighten, discourage, alarm, unnerve, startle, panic, agitate, daunt, sound the alarm, *formal* perturb

wind² *v, n*
▶ **1** CURVE, bend, loop, spiral, zigzag, twine, snake, deviate, meander, ramble **2** COIL, wrap, twist, turn, curl, twine, encircle, furl, wreathe, roll, reel
▷ **wind down 1** SLOW (DOWN), slacken off, lessen, reduce, subside, diminish, dwindle, decline, stop, bring/come to an end **2** RELAX, unwind, quieten down, ease up, calm down
F₃ 1 increase
▷ **wind up 1** CLOSE (DOWN), end, finalize, finish, stop, bring to a close, bring to an end, liquidate, *formal* conclude, terminate **2** END UP, finish up, find yourself, settle **3** ANNOY, irritate, disconcert, fool, trick, make fun of, *colloq.* kid, pull someone's leg, rub someone up the wrong way
F₃ 1 begin
▶ *n* bend, curve, turn, twist, zigzag, meander

windbag *n*
boaster, gossip, bore, braggart, blether, *colloq.* gasbag, big-mouth

winded *adj*
puffed out, breathless, out of breath, panting, puffed, out of puff
F₃ fresh

windfall *n*
stroke of luck, bonanza, godsend, jackpot, treasure-trove, stroke of luck, find, manna, pennies from heaven

winding *adj*
curving, turning, twisting, bending, crooked, tortuous, indirect, roundabout, spiral, circuitous, meandering, serpentine, *formal* sinuous, sinuate(d), flexuose, flexuous, anfractuous, convoluted
F₃ straight

windy *adj*
1 *windy weather* breezy, blowy, blustery, squally, windswept, stormy, wild, tempestuous, gusty **2** *windy*

speech long-winded, wordy, verbose, garrulous, rambling, turgid, pompous, bombastic, *formal* prolix **3** NERVOUS, uneasy, afraid, frightened, scared, timid, *colloq.* chicken, nervy, on edge
F₃ 1 calm, windless **3** fearless

wine *n*

Types of wine include:
alcohol-free, dry, brut, sec, demi-sec, sweet, sparkling, table wine, house wine, red wine, *colloq.* house red, white wine, *colloq.* house white, rosé, blush wine, fortified wine, mulled wine, tonic wine, vintage wine, *colloq.* plonk; sherry, dry sherry, fino, medium sherry, amontillado, sweet sherry, oloroso; port, ruby, tawny, white port, vintage port.

Varieties of wine include:
Alsace, Asti, Auslese, Beaujolais, Beaujolais Nouveau, Beaune, Bordeaux, Burgundy, cabernet sauvignon, Chablis, Chambertin, champagne, Chardonnay, Chianti, claret, Côtes du Rhône, Dao, Douro, Frascati, Graves, hock, Lambrusco, Liebfraumilch, Mâcon, Madeira, Malaga, Marsala, Mateus Rosé, Médoc, Merlot, moselle, Muscadet, muscatel, Niersteiner, retsina, Riesling, Rioja, Sauterne, Sekt, Soave, Spätlese, Tarragona, Valpolicella, vinho verde.

wine-bottle sizes

Sizes of wine-bottles include:
magnum, flagon, jeroboam, methuselah, rehoboam, salmanazar, balthazar, nebuchadnezzar.

wing *n, v*
▶ *n* **1** SECTION, branch, arm, faction, group, grouping, flank, circle, coterie, set, segment, side **2** ANNEXE, adjunct, extension, attachment, side
▶ *v* fly, glide, flit, hurry, move, travel, pass, speed, race, soar, zoom, *formal* hasten

wink *v, n*
▶ *v* blink, flutter, glimmer, glint, glitter, twinkle, gleam, sparkle, flicker, flash, *formal* nictate, nictitate
▷ **wink at** ignore, disregard, overlook, neglect, pass over, condone, take no notice of, *colloq.* turn a blind eye to
▶ *n* **1** BLINK, flutter, sparkle, twinkle, glimmering, gleam, glitter, glint, flash, *formal* nictation, nictitation **2** INSTANT, moment, second, split second, flash

winkle *v*
extract, extricate, draw out, worm, force, prise, flush

winner *n*
champion, victor, prizewinner, medallist, title-holder, world-beater, conqueror, *formal* vanquisher, *colloq.* champ
F₃ loser

winning *adj*
1 CONQUERING, triumphant, unbeaten, undefeated, victorious, successful, *formal* vanquishing **2** WINSOME, charming, attractive, captivating, engaging, beguiling, bewitching, fetching, enchanting, endearing, delightful, amiable, alluring, lovely, pleasing, sweet
F₃ 1 losing **2** unappealing

winnings *n*
jackpot, gains, proceeds, profits, takings, prize(s), booty, spoils
F₃ losses

winnow v
sift, separate, screen, divide, cull, select, sort, part, comb, fan

winsome adj
charming, attractive, captivating, engaging, beguiling, bewitching, fetching, enchanting, endearing, delightful, amiable, alluring, lovely, pleasing, pretty, prepossessing, sweet, formal delectable
Ӻ unattractive

wintry adj
1 wintry weather cold, chilly, bleak, cheerless, biting, piercing, raw, desolate, dismal, harsh, snowy, arctic, frosty, freezing, frozen, icy, glacial, formal hibernal, hiemal 2 UNFRIENDLY, hostile, bleak, cheerless, desolate, dismal, cold, frosty, icy, cool, harsh

wipe v, n
► v 1 RUB, clean, dry, dust, brush, mop, swab, sponge, clear 2 REMOVE, erase, take away, take off, get rid of
▷ **wipe out** eradicate, obliterate, destroy, massacre, exterminate, annihilate, erase, expunge, raze, abolish, blot out, demolish, formal efface, extirpate
► n rub, clean, dry, dust, brush, mop, sponge, swab

wiry adj
1 SINEWY, muscular, lean, tough, strong 2 wiry hair coarse, wavy, rough
Ӻ 1 puny, flabby 2 soft

wisdom n
discernment, penetration, reason, sense, astuteness, comprehension, enlightenment, judgement, insight, common sense, understanding, knowledge, learning, intelligence, foresight, formal sagacity, judiciousness, erudition, prudence, circumspection, sapience
Ӻ folly, stupidity

wise adj
1 DISCERNING, perceptive, rational, informed, well-informed, understanding, enlightened, knowing, educated, knowledgeable, intelligent, clever, aware, experienced, formal sagacious, erudite, sapient 2 WELL-ADVISED, reasonable, sensible, sound, far-sighted, long-sighted, shrewd, politic, formal prudent, judicious, sagacious, circumspect
Ӻ 1 foolish, stupid 2 ill-advised
▷ **put wise** inform, notify, tip off, warn, tell, alert, fill in, intimate to, put in the picture, clue in, formal apprise, colloq. wise up

wisecrack n
quip, joke, jest, funny, witticism, gag, barb, gibe, pun, in-joke, colloq. one-liner

wish v, n
► v 1 DESIRE, want, yearn, long, hanker, pine, covet, crave, aspire, hope, fancy, hunger, thirst, prefer, need, lust, colloq. yen 2 ASK, bid, require, order, instruct, direct, command
► n 1 DESIRE, want, hankering, aspiration, inclination, longing, craving, hunger, thirst, liking, fondness, preference, yearning, urge, whim, hope, fancy, colloq. yen 2 REQUEST, desire, bidding, order, instruction, command, will

wishy-washy adj
feeble, weak, insipid, thin, watered-down, watery, flat, bland, ineffective, vapid, tasteless, formal ineffectual, colloq. namby-pamby
Ӻ strong, firm

wisp n
shred, strand, thread, twist, piece, lock

wispy adj
thin, straggly, frail, fine, insubstantial, light, flimsy, fragile, delicate, ethereal, gossamer, faint, formal attenuated
Ӻ substantial

wistful adj
1 THOUGHTFUL, pensive, musing, reflective, wishful, contemplative, dreamy, dreaming, meditative 2 MELANCHOLY, sad, forlorn, longing, yearning, mournful, formal disconsolate

wit n
1 HUMOUR, funniness, repartee, facetiousness, drollery, banter, badinage, jocularity, levity, waggishness 2 INTELLIGENCE, cleverness, sense, reason, common sense, wisdom, understanding, judgement, insight, shrewdness, astuteness, faculties, intellect, formal sagacity, colloq. brains, gumption, nous, marbles 3 HUMORIST, comedian, comic, satirist, joker, wag
Ӻ 1 seriousness 2 stupidity

witch n
sorceress, enchantress, occultist, magician, hex, hag, formal necromancer

witchcraft n
sorcery, magic, wizardry, occultism, the occult, the black art, black magic, enchantment, voodoo, spell, incantation, divination, formal necromancy, conjuration

withdraw v
1 REMOVE, take away, pull back, draw back, draw out, pull out, extract 2 DEPART, go (away), absent yourself, retire, remove, leave, back out, draw back, fall back, recede, drop out, retreat, secede, scratch 3 RECANT, disclaim, take back, revoke, retract, cancel, recall, take away, formal rescind, abjure, nullify, annul 4 RECOIL, shrink back, draw back, pull back

withdrawal n
1 REMOVAL, taking away, pulling back, drawing back/out, extraction 2 DEPARTURE, exit, exodus, falling back, retirement, retreat, evacuation, disengagement 3 REPUDIATION, recantation, disclaimer, revocation, recall, secession, formal disavowal, abjuration

withdrawn adj
1 RESERVED, unsociable, shy, introvert, introverted, quiet, retiring, aloof, detached, shrinking, private, uncommunicative, unforthcoming, taciturn, silent 2 REMOTE, isolated, distant, secluded, out-of-the-way, private, hidden, solitary
Ӻ 1 extrovert, outgoing, forthcoming

wither v
shrink, shrivel, dry (up), wilt, droop, weaken, decay, disintegrate, dwindle, wane, perish, die (off), disappear, fade (away), languish, decline, waste
Ӻ flourish, thrive

withering adj
scornful, contemptuous, scathing, snubbing, humiliating, mortifying, wounding, destructive, deadly, death-dealing, devastating
Ӻ encouraging, supportive

withhold v
keep back, retain, hold back, suppress, restrain, repress, control, curb, check, keep in check, reserve, deduct, refuse, hide, conceal, formal decline
Ӻ give, accord

withstand v
resist, oppose, stand fast, stand your ground, stand, stand up to, stand firm/fast, fight, confront, brave, face, cope with, take on, thwart, defy, hold your ground, hold out, last out, hold off, endure, bear, tolerate, put up with, survive, weather
Ӻ give in, yield

witless adj
stupid, mindless, foolish, silly, senseless, inane, crazy, imbecilic, idiotic, moronic, daft, gormless, dull, empty-headed, half-witted, cretinous
Ӻ intelligent

witness *n, v*

▶ *n* **1** *witness in a court* testifier, *formal* attestant, deponent **2** ONLOOKER, eye-witness, looker-on, observer, spectator, viewer, watcher, bystander
▶ *v* **1** SEE, observe, notice, note, view, watch, look on, mark, perceive **2** TESTIFY, bear witness, give evidence, confirm, prove, verify, support, endorse, be evidence of, bear out, *formal* attest, depose, corroborate, affirm **3** ENDORSE, sign, countersign

witticism *n*

quip, riposte, pun, repartee, pleasantry, *bon mot*, wisecrack, epigram, *colloq.* one-liner

witty *adj*

humorous, amusing, comic, sharp-witted, droll, whimsical, original, brilliant, clever, ingenious, lively, sparkling, funny, facetious, waggish, fanciful, jocular
F₃ dull, unamusing

wizard *n, adj*

▶ *n* **1** SORCERER, magician, warlock, enchanter, occultist, witch, conjurer, *formal* necromancer, thaumaturge **2** EXPERT, adept, virtuoso, ace, master, maestro, prodigy, genius, *colloq.* star, whiz, hotshot
▶ *adj* fantastic, wonderful, great, good, marvellous, brilliant, enjoyable, tremendous, super, superb, smashing, sensational, *colloq.* fab, terrific, smashing

wizened *adj*

shrivelled, shrunken, dried up, withered, wrinkled, gnarled, thin, worn, lined

wobble *v, n*

▶ *v* shake, oscillate, tremble, quake, sway, stagger, teeter, totter, rock, seesaw, vibrate, waver, quiver, dodder, fluctuate, hesitate, dither, vacillate, *colloq.* shilly-shally
▶ *n* shake, unsteadiness, tremor, quaking, rock, tremble, vibration, oscillation

wobbly *adj*

unstable, shaky, rickety, unsteady, quavering, trembling, teetering, tottering, doddering, doddery, uneven, unbalanced, unsafe, *colloq.* wonky
F₃ stable, steady

woe *n*

misery, adversity, distress, sadness, sorrow, unhappiness, wretchedness, grief, melancholy, misfortune, suffering, hardship, trouble, pain, agony, anguish, gloom, curse, trial, depression, dejection, burden, disaster, calamity, heartache, heartbreak, tears, *formal* affliction, tribulation
F₃ joy

woebegone *adj*

miserable, wretched, sad, sorrowful, troubled, downcast, downhearted, gloomy, forlorn, grief-stricken, long-faced, dejected, crestfallen, mournful, doleful, dispirited, tearful, tear-stained, *formal* disconsolate, lugubrious, *colloq.* blue, down in the mouth
F₃ joyful

woeful *adj*

1 SAD, miserable, wretched, mournful, sorry, unhappy, gloomy, grieving, grievous, heartbreaking, heartrending, *formal* disconsolate, doleful **2** DISTRESSING, disappointing, lamentable, pitiable, disgraceful, deplorable, shocking, sorrowful, tragic, cruel, hopeless, inadequate, mean, paltry, feeble, dreadful, appalling, awful, bad, terrible, poor, rotten, calamitous, catastrophic, disastrous, *colloq.* lousy, pathetic
F₃ joyful

wolf *n, v*

▶ *n* womanizer, seducer, ladies' man, lady-killer, lecher, philanderer, Casanova, Don Juan, Romeo
▶ *v* ▷ **wolf down** put away, pack away, gobble, gulp, devour, cram, bolt, stuff, gorge, scoff
F₃ nibble

woman *n*

female, lady, girl, maiden, maid

womanhood *n*

1 ADULTHOOD, maturity, *formal* muliebrity **2** WOMANKIND, woman, womenkind, womenfolk(s)

womanizer *n*

philanderer, seducer, wolf, lady-killer, ladies' man, lecher, Casanova, Don Juan, Romeo

womanly *adj*

feminine, female, ladylike, womanish, motherly, kind, warm, tender, effeminate

wonder *n, v*

▶ *n* **1** AWE, amazement, astonishment, admiration, wonderment, fascination, surprise, pleasure, bewilderment **2** MARVEL, phenomenon, miracle, prodigy, sight, spectacle, rarity, curiosity, *formal* nonpareil

The seven wonders of the world are:
Pyramids of Egypt, Hanging Gardens of Babylon, Statue of Zeus at Olympia, Temple of Artemis at Ephesus, Mausoleum of Halicarnassus, Colossus of Rhodes, Pharos of Alexandria.

▶ *v* **1** ASK YOURSELF, meditate, speculate, ponder, question, puzzle, inquire, query, doubt, think, reflect, *formal* conjecture **2** MARVEL, gape, be amazed, be surprised, be astonished, be astounded, stand in awe, be dumbfounded, be lost for words

wonderful *adj*

1 MARVELLOUS, magnificent, outstanding, excellent, superb, admirable, delightful, phenomenal, sensational, stupendous, tremendous, *colloq.* super, terrific, brilliant, great, fabulous, fantastic, smashing, ace, out of this world, *slang* cool, wicked **2** AMAZING, astonishing, astounding, startling, surprising, extraordinary, incredible, remarkable, staggering, awesome, strange
F₃ **1** appalling, awful, dreadful **2** ordinary

wonky *adj*

shaky, wobbly, weak, wrong, unsound, unsteady, askew, skew-whiff, amiss
F₃ stable, straight, balanced

wont *adj, n*

▶ *adj* inclined, used, accustomed, given, *formal* habituated
▶ *n* habit, custom, routine, practice, rule, use, way

wonted *adj*

usual, customary, familiar, normal, regular, common, daily, frequent, accustomed, conventional, *formal* habitual
F₃ unwonted

woo *v*

1 *woo a lover* court, pay court to, chase, pursue, seek the hand of **2** *woo custom* encourage, cultivate, attract, look for, seek, pursue

wood *n*

1 TIMBER, lumber, planks

Types of wood include:
timber, *US* lumber, hardwood, softwood, heartwood, sapwood, seasoned wood, green wood, bitterwood, brushwood, cordwood, firewood, kindling, matchwood, plywood, pulpwood, whitewood, chipboard, hardboard, wood veneer; afrormosia, ash, balsa, beech, cedar, cherry, chestnut, cottonwood, deal, ebony, elm, mahogany, African mahogany, maple, oak, pine, redwood, rosewood, sandalwood, sapele, satinwood, teak, walnut, willow. *See also* TREE.

2 FOREST, woods, woodland, trees, plantation, thicket, grove, coppice, copse, spinney
▷ **out of the wood(s)** out of danger, safe, safe and sound, secure, in the clear, out of difficulty, home and dry

wooded *adj*
forested, timbered, woody, tree-covered, *formal* sylvan
🔁 open

wooden *adj*
1 TIMBER, woody **2** EMOTIONLESS, expressionless, awkward, clumsy, stilted, stodgy, lifeless, spiritless, graceless, impassive, unemotional, unresponsive, stiff, rigid, leaden, deadpan, blank, empty, vacant, vacuous, slow
🔁 **2** lively

wool *n*
fleece, down, hair, floccus, yarn
▷ **pull the wool over someone's eyes** deceive, fool, trick, hoodwink, take in, bamboozle, delude, dupe, *colloq.* con, lead up the garden path, pull a fast one on, put one over on

wool-gathering *n*
absent-mindedness, day-dreaming, forgetfulness, distraction, inattention, preoccupation

woolly *adj, n*
▶ *adj* **1** WOOLLEN, fleecy, woolly-haired, hairy, downy, fluffy, shaggy, fuzzy, frizzy, *formal* flocculent **2** UNCLEAR, indistinct, ill-defined, hazy, fuzzy, blurred, foggy, cloudy, confused, muddled, vague, indefinite, nebulous
🔁 **2** clear, distinct
▶ *n* jumper, sweater, jersey, pullover, cardigan

woozy *adj*
dazed, dizzy, nauseated, fuddled, confused, blurred, wobbly, unsteady, rocky, befuddled, bemused, tipsy
🔁 alert

word *n, v*
▶ *n* **1** NAME, term, expression, designation, utterance, *formal* vocable **2** CONVERSATION, chat, talk, discussion, consultation, tête-à-tête **3** INFORMATION, news, report, communication, notice, message, bulletin, communiqué, intelligence, statement, utterance, dispatch, declaration, comment, assertion, account, remark, advice, warning, *formal* tidings, *colloq.* gen, info, low-down, dope **4** PROMISE, pledge, oath, assurance, honour, vow, guarantee, undertaking **5** COMMAND, signal, order, decree, will, commandment, mandate, *colloq.* go-ahead, green light, thumbs-up **6** RUMOUR, hearsay, gossip, talk, speculation, scandal, whisper **7** *the words of a song* lyrics, libretto, script, text, book
▷ **have words** argue, dispute, quarrel, disagree, row, squabble, bicker
▷ **in a word** briefly, in short, in brief, to be brief, to put it briefly, concisely, succinctly, summarizing, to sum up, *colloq.* in a nutshell, to cut a long story short
▶ *v* phrase, express, couch, put, say, state, explain, write

wording *n*
words, choice of words, language, phrasing, expression, phraseology, terminology, style, diction, wordage, verbiage

word-perfect *adj*
accurate, faithful, exact, spot-on, letter-perfect
🔁 inaccurate

wordplay *n*
puns, punning, wit, witticisms, repartee, *technical* paronomasia

wordy *adj*
verbose, long-winded, garrulous, rambling, diffuse,

discursive, *formal* loquacious, prolix
🔁 concise

work *n, v*
▶ *n* **1** OCCUPATION, job, employment, profession, trade, business, career, calling, vocation, pursuit, field, line, line of business, métier, livelihood, craft, skill, art, workmanship **2** TASK, assignment, undertaking, job, chore, responsibility, duty, charge, mission, commission **3** TOIL, labour, drudgery, trouble, effort, exertion, industry, *formal* travail, *colloq.* slog, graft, elbow grease **4** CREATION, production, achievement, accomplishment, composition, piece, poem, painting, book, play, writing, œuvre, opus **5** *steel works* factory, plant, workshop, mill, foundry, shop **6** *good works* actions, acts, doings, deed **7** *the works of a clock* machinery, mechanism, workings, action, movement, parts, working parts, installations, *colloq.* innards, guts
🔁 **1** play, rest, hobby
▶ *v* **1** BE EMPLOYED, have a job, earn your living **2** LABOUR, toil, exert yourself, drudge, slave, *colloq.* slog, peg away, plug away, work your fingers to the bone, slog your guts out **3** FUNCTION, go, operate, perform, run, handle **4** OPERATE, run, handle, manage, use, drive, control **5** BRING ABOUT, accomplish, perform, execute, achieve, create, do, cause, *formal* effect, *colloq.* pull off **6** BE SUCCESSFUL, succeed, be effective, be satisfactory, have the desired effect, go well, prosper **7** MANIPULATE, manoeuvre, engineer, arrange, contrive, *colloq.* fix, fiddle, wangle **8** *work your way forward* shift, guide, edge, move, make, penetrate, manoeuvre **9** CULTIVATE, farm, dig, till **10** MOULD, manipulate, knead, shape, form, fashion, model, make, process
🔁 **1** be unemployed **2** play, rest **3** fail
▷ **work out 1** SOLVE, resolve, calculate, figure out, puzzle out, sort out, understand, clear up **2** DEVELOP, evolve, go well, succeed, be effective, prosper, turn out, *colloq.* pan out **3** PLAN, devise, organize, arrange, contrive, invent, construct, formulate, develop, put together **4** ADD UP TO, amount to, total, come out, come to **5** EXERCISE, train, drill, practise, keep fit, warm up
▷ **work up 1** *work up a crowd* excite, agitate, incite, arouse, stir up, move **2** *work something up* incite, stir up, rouse, arouse, animate, move, stimulate, build up, inflame, spur, instigate, kindle, agitate, generate, whet

workable *adj*
practicable, feasible, possible, practical, realistic, viable, doable
🔁 unworkable

workaday *adj*
everyday, ordinary, routine, work-day, working, practical, mundane, humdrum, dull, common, commonplace, familiar, labouring, toiling, *colloq.* run-of-the-mill
🔁 exciting

worker *n*
employee, labourer, working man, working woman, member of staff, artisan, workman, workwoman, craftsman, craftswoman, tradesman, hand, operative, wage-earner, breadwinner, proletarian, *colloq.* workhorse, workaholic

workforce *n*
workers, employees, personnel, labour force, staff, labour, manpower, work-people, shop floor

working *n, adj*
▶ *n* **1** FUNCTIONING, operation, running, routine, manner, process, system, method, action **2** *mine workings* mine, quarry, pit, shaft, diggings, excavations **3** *the workings of a clock* works, machinery, me-

chanism, action, movement, parts, working parts, installations, *colloq.* innards, guts
► *adj* **1** FUNCTIONING, operational, running, operating, operative, going, in working order, *colloq.* up and running **2** EMPLOYED, active
🔁 **1** inoperative **2** idle

workman, workwoman *n*
worker, employee, labourer, hand, artisan, craftsman, craftswoman, operative, tradesperson, mechanic, journeyman, navvy, artificer

workmanlike *adj*
efficient, proficient, satisfactory, careful, adept, skilful, skilled, thorough, painstaking, expert, professional, masterly
🔁 amateurish

workmanship *n*
skill, craft, craftsmanship, expertise, art, artistry, handicraft, handiwork, technique, execution, manufacture, work, finish

workmate *n*
colleague, associate, co-worker, fellow-worker, workfellow, yoke-fellow

workout *n*
exercise, training, drill, practice, warm-up, aerobic, gymnastics, isometrics, eurhythmics, callisthenics

workshop *n*
1 WORKS, workroom, atelier, studio, garage, factory, plant, mill, shop **2** STUDY GROUP, seminar, symposium, discussion group, class

world *n*
1 EARTH, globe, sphere, planet, star, heavenly body, universe, cosmos, creation, nature **2** EVERYBODY, everyone, people, human race, humankind, humanity, mankind, man **3** SPHERE, realm, field, area, domain, department, division, section, group, system, society, province, kingdom **4** TIMES, epoch, era, period, age, days, life **5** WAY OF LIFE, life, reality, existence, experience, situation
▷ **out of this world** wonderful, excellent, incredible, marvellous, remarkable, great, fantastic, superb, unbelievable, phenomenal, indescribable, *colloq.* fabulous

worldly *adj*
1 TEMPORAL, earthly, material, mundane, terrestrial, physical, secular, unspiritual, profane, carnal, *formal* corporeal **2** WORLDLY-WISE, sophisticated, urbane, cosmopolitan, experienced, knowing, *colloq.* streetwise **3** MATERIALISTIC, selfish, ambitious, grasping, greedy, covetous, avaricious
🔁 **1** spiritual, eternal **2** unsophisticated

worldwide *adj*
international, global, general, universal, catholic, *formal* mondial, ubiquitous
🔁 local

worn *adj*
1 SHABBY, threadbare, worn-out, tatty, tattered, in tatters, frayed, ragged **2** EXHAUSTED, tired, weary, spent, fatigued, careworn, drawn, strained, haggard, jaded, *colloq.* done in, all in, dog-tired, bushed, knackered
🔁 **1** new, unused **2** fresh
▷ **worn out 1** SHABBY, threadbare, useless, used, tatty, tattered, on its last legs, ragged, moth-eaten, frayed, decrepit **2** TIRED OUT, exhausted, weary, *colloq.* done in, all in, dog-tired, bushed, knackered
🔁 **1** new, unused **2** fresh

worried *adj*
anxious, troubled, uneasy, ill at ease, apprehensive, concerned, bothered, upset, fearful, afraid, frightened, overwrought, tense, strained, nervous, disturbed, distraught, distracted, disquieted, dismayed, fretful, distressed, agonized, *formal* perturbed, *colloq.* on edge, uptight, (all) hot and bothered, *slang* wired

🔁 calm, unworried, unconcerned

worrisome *adj*
worrying, upsetting, anxious, troublesome, frightening, bothersome, agonizing, distressing, uneasy, disturbing, insecure, fretful, apprehensive, vexing, irksome, disquieting, jittery, *formal* perturbing, *colloq.* nail-biting
🔁 calm, reassuring

worry *v, n*
► *v* **1** BE ANXIOUS, be troubled, be distressed, agonize, fret **2** IRRITATE, plague, pester, torment, upset, unsettle, agitate, annoy, bother, disturb, trouble, concern, vex, tease, nag, harass, harry, *formal* perturb, *colloq.* aggravate, bug, hassle **3** ATTACK, go for, tear at, bite, savage
🔁 **1** be unconcerned **2** comfort
► *n* **1** PROBLEM, trouble, responsibility, burden, concern, care, trial, annoyance, nuisance, pest, plague, irritation, vexation **2** ANXIETY, apprehension, trouble, distress, disquiet, concern, unease, misgiving, fear, fearfulness, tension, stress, strain, disturbance, agitation, torment, anguish, misery, perplexity, *formal* perturbation, *colloq.* hang-up, tizzy, tiz, stew
🔁 **2** comfort, reassurance

worrying *adj*
anxious, troublesome, trying, unsettling, upsetting, niggling, disturbing, distressing, harassing, disquieting, worrisome, uneasy, *formal* perturbing, *colloq.* nail-biting
🔁 calm, reassuring

worsen *v*
1 AGGRAVATE, exacerbate, intensify, increase, heighten **2** GET WORSE, weaken, deteriorate, degenerate, decline, slip, sink, *colloq.* go from bad to worse, go down the tube(s), go to pot, go downhill
🔁 improve

worship *v, n*
► *v* revere, reverence, adore, exalt, glorify, honour, praise, idolize, adulate, admire, love, extol, respect, pray to, deify, *formal* venerate, laud
🔁 despise, hate
► *n* reverence, adoration, devotion(s), homage, honour, glory, glorification, exaltation, praise, prayer(s), respect, regard, love, adulation, deification, idolatry, *formal* veneration, laudation

Places of worship include:
abbey, bethel, cathedral, chantry, church, fane, kirk, masjid, meeting-house, minster, mosque, pagoda, shrine, shul, synagogue, tabernacle, temple, wat. *See also* RELIGIONS.

worst *v*
beat, defeat, get the better of, overcome, overpower, overthrow, conquer, crush, master, subdue, drub, whitewash, best, *formal* subjugate, vanquish

worth *n*
worthiness, merit, value, benefit, profit, gain, advantage, importance, significance, eminence, use, usefulness, utility, service, quality, good, virtue, excellence, credit, desert(s), cost, rate, price, help, assistance, avail
🔁 worthlessness

worthless *adj*
1 VALUELESS, useless, pointless, meaningless, futile, unavailing, unimportant, insignificant, trivial, unusable, cheap, poor, rubbishy, trashy, trifling, paltry, *formal* ineffectual, nugatory, *slang* naff **2** CONTEMPTIBLE, despicable, good-for-nothing, corrupt, vile, low, useless
🔁 **1** valuable **2** worthy

worthwhile *adj*
profitable, useful, valuable, worthy, good, helpful, advantageous, beneficial, constructive, gainful, justifiable, productive
F3 worthless

worthy *adj, n*
▶ *adj* praiseworthy, creditable, commendable, valuable, worthwhile, admirable, reliable, fit, deserving, appropriate, respectable, trustworthy, reputable, good, moral, honest, honourable, excellent, decent, upright, righteous, virtuous, *formal* laudable, meritorious
F3 unworthy, disreputable
▶ *n* dignitary, personage, name, luminary, notable, *colloq.* bigwig, big cheese, big noise, big shot

would-be *adj*
aspiring, budding, striving, endeavouring, ambitious, enterprising, keen, eager, hopeful, optimistic, wishful, longing

wound *n, v*
▶ *n* **1** INJURY, trauma, hurt, cut, gash, graze, scratch, lesion, laceration, scar **2** HURT, distress, trauma, torment, heartbreak, blow, harm, damage, pain, ache, anguish, grief, shock
▶ *v* **1** DAMAGE, harm, hurt, injure, hit, cut, gash, tear, graze, scratch, lacerate, slash, stab, puncture, pierce **2** DISTRESS, hurt, offend, shock, insult, pain, traumatize, mortify, upset, slight, grieve

wraith *n*
ghost, spirit, phantom, apparition, spectre, revenant, shade, *colloq.* spook

wrangle *n, v*
▶ *n* argument, quarrel, dispute, controversy, squabble, tussle, tiff, bickering, disagreement, clash, contest, *formal* altercation, *colloq.* row, slanging match, set-to, barney, argy-bargy
F3 agreement
▶ *v* argue, quarrel, disagree, dispute, bicker, contend, have words, clash, row, squabble, scrap, fight, spar, *formal* altercate, *colloq.* fall out
F3 agree

wrap *v, n*
▶ *v* envelop, fold, enfold, enclose, cover, pack, shroud, wind, surround, package, parcel (up), muffle, cocoon, encase, cloak, roll up, bind, bundle up, swathe, immerse
F3 unwrap
▷ **wrap up 1** WRAP, pack up, package, parcel (up) **2** CONCLUDE, finish off, end, bring to a close, terminate, wind up, complete, round off **3** SHUT UP, *colloq.* dry up, belt up, pipe down, give it a rest, hold your tongue, put a sock in it, shut your mouth
▶ *n* shawl, stole, cape, robe, cloak, mantle

wrapper *n*
wrapping, packaging, envelope, Jiffy bag®, cover, covering, jacket, dust jacket, sheath, casing, case, sleeve, paper

wrath *n*
anger, bitterness, rage, fury, exasperation, indignation, irritation, annoyance, temper, resentment, passion, displeasure, spleen, choler, *formal* ire
F3 calm, pleasure

wrathful *adj*
angry, furious, incensed, enraged, infuriated, raging, indignant, bitter, displeased, irate, ireful, *formal* furibund, *colloq.* in a paddy, on the warpath
F3 calm, pleased

wreak *v*
inflict, exercise, create, cause, bring about, perpetrate, vent, unleash, express, execute, carry out, *formal* bestow

wreath *n*
garland, coronet, chaplet, festoon, crown, band, loop, ring, circle, circlet

wreathe *v*
encircle, surround, enfold, entwine, twine, twist, wind, coil, wrap, envelop, crown, adorn, shroud, enwrap, festoon, intertwine, interweave

wreck *v, n*
▶ *v* destroy, ruin, demolish, devastate, shatter, smash, break, sink, spoil, mar, play havoc with, torpedo, ravage, write off
F3 conserve, repair
▶ *n* ruin, destruction, devastation, shattering, smashing, breaking, mess, demolition, ruination, write-off, disaster, loss, undoing, disruption, shipwreck, derelict, debris, remains, rubble, ruin, fragments, flotsam, pieces

wreckage *n*
debris, remains, rubble, ruin, fragments, flotsam, pieces, *formal* detritus

wrench *v, n*
▶ *v* yank, wrest, jerk, pull, tug, force, sprain, strain, rick, tear, twist, wring, rip, distort
▶ *n* **1** PULL, jerk, tear, twist, tug, sprain, pain, ache, pang **2** UPROOTING, upheaval, shock, sorrow, sadness, blow

wrest *v*
seize, force, extract, pull, take, win, wring, wrench, twist, strain

wrestle *v*
struggle, strive, fight, scuffle, grapple, tussle, combat, contend, contest, vie, battle

wretch *n*
scoundrel, rogue, villain, good-for-nothing, ruffian, rascal, vagabond, miscreant, outcast, devil, *colloq.* rat, swine, worm

wretched *adj*
1 MISERABLE, sad, unhappy, sorry, melancholy, depressed, dejected, disconsolate, downcast, forlorn, gloomy, doleful, distressed, broken-hearted, crestfallen **2** PATHETIC, pitiable, pitiful, sad, unhappy, miserable, piteous, unfortunate, unlucky, sorry, hopeless, poor, *formal* hapless **3** CONTEMPTIBLE, despicable, vile, worthless, shameful, inferior, bad, low, base, mean, vile, paltry **4** ATROCIOUS, awful, deplorable, appalling, shocking, outrageous, dreadful, terrible, horrible
F3 **1** happy **2** enviable **3** worthy **4** excellent

wriggle *v, n*
▶ *v* squirm, writhe, wiggle, worm, twist, snake, slink, crawl, edge, sidle, manoeuvre, squiggle, dodge, extricate, zigzag, waggle, turn
▶ *n* wiggle, twist, squirm, writhe, jiggle, jerk, turn, twitch

wring *v*
1 SQUEEZE, twist, wrench, wrest, extract, mangle, screw **2** EXACT, extort, coerce, force **3** DISTRESS, pain, hurt, rack, tear, rend, pierce, torture, wound, lacerate, stab, tear

wrinkle *n, v*
▶ *n* furrow, crease, corrugation, line, ridge, fold, gather, pucker, crumple, rumple, wimple, frounce
▶ *v* crease, corrugate, furrow, line, fold, crinkle, crumple, rumple, shrivel, gather, pucker

wrinkled *adj*
crumpled, wrinkly, crinkled, creased, furrowed, ridged, puckered, rivelled, rumpled, crinkly, *formal* rugose, rugate, rugous
F3 smooth

writ *n*
court order, summons, decree, subpoena

write *v*
pen, inscribe, record, register, jot down, note (down), set down, put down, take down, make a note of, transcribe, print, scribble, scrawl, correspond, communicate, draft, draw up, copy, compose, create, *colloq.* dash off, put down in black and white
▷ **write off 1** DELETE, cancel, cross out, wipe out, disregard, *formal* annul, nullify **2** WRECK, destroy, crash, demolish, smash (up)

writer *n*

Writers include:
annalist, author, autobiographer, bard, biographer, calligraphist, chronicler, clerk, columnist, composer, contributor, copyist, copywriter, correspondent, court reporter, diarist, dramatist, editor, essayist, fabler, fiction writer, ghost writer, hack, historian, journalist, leaderwriter, lexicographer, librettist, lyricist, novelist, pen-friend, penman, pen-pal, *colloq.* penpusher, penwoman, playwright, poet, poet laureate, reporter, rhymer, satirist, scribbler, scribe, scriptwriter, short-story writer, sonneteer, stenographer, *colloq.* storyteller.

writhe *v*
squirm, wriggle, thresh, thrash, twist, wiggle, jerk, toss, coil, contort, struggle, *colloq.* twist and turn

writing *n*
1 HANDWRITING, calligraphy, script, penmanship, scrawl, scribble, hand, text, words, print **2** DOCUMENT, composition, work, opus, volume, publication

writing instrument

Types of writing instruments include:
pen, ballpoint, Biro®, calligraphy pen, cartridge pen, dip pen, eraser pen, felt-tip pen, fountain pen; marker pen, rollerball pen; writing brush, pencil, chinagraph pencil, coloured pencil, crayon, ink pencil, lead-pencil, propelling pencil, board marker, laundry marker, permanent marker, highlighter; cane pen, quill, reed, Roman metal pen, steel pen, stylus; brailler, typewriter, word-processor.

written *adj*
set down, recorded, drawn up, transcribed, documented, documentary, *formal* documental
Fa unwritten, verbal

wrong *adj, adv, n, v*
▶ *adj* **1** INACCURATE, incorrect, mistaken, erroneous, false, in error, imprecise, *formal* fallacious, *colloq.* wide of the mark, off beam, off target **2** INAPPROPRIATE, unsuitable, improper, unconventional, unfitting, inapt, *formal* unseemly, indecorous, incongruous, infelicit-

ous, inapposite, malapropos, *colloq.* hardly the place/ time **3** UNJUST, unethical, unfair, unlawful, immoral, illegal, illicit, dishonourable, unjustified, dishonest, criminal, blameworthy, guilty, to blame, bad, wicked, sinful, evil, *formal* reprehensible, iniquitous, felonious, *colloq.* crooked **4** DEFECTIVE, faulty, out of order, amiss, awry, *colloq.* up the spout **5** REVERSE, opposite, inside, inverse, inverted, back, contrary
Fa **1** correct, right **2** suitable, right **3** good, moral **4** in order **5** right, front
▶ *adv* amiss, astray, awry, inaccurately, incorrectly, inexactly, imprecisely, wrongly, mistakenly, faultily, badly, erroneously, improperly
Fa right
▷ **go wrong 1** BREAK DOWN, stop working, fail, *formal* malfunction, *colloq.* pack up, conk out, seize up **2** FAIL, be unsuccessful, collapse, come to grief, come to nothing, stray, go astray, *colloq.* not make it, come a cropper, become unstuck
▶ *n* sin, misdeed, offence, crime, immorality, sinfulness, wickedness, unlawfulness, wrongdoing, grievance, abuse, injustice, iniquity, inequity, infringement, unfairness, error, *formal* transgression, trespass, injury
Fa right
▷ **in the wrong** at fault, guilty, in error, mistaken, to blame, blameworthy
Fa in the right
▶ *v* abuse, ill-treat, mistreat, maltreat, injure, ill-use, hurt, harm, discredit, dishonour, misrepresent, malign, oppress, cheat

wrongdoer *n*
offender, law-breaker, criminal, delinquent, felon, miscreant, evil-doer, sinner, trespasser, culprit, *formal* transgressor, malefactor

wrongdoing *n*
crime, offence, error, evil, misdeed, fault, felony, immorality, delinquency, sin, sinfulness, wickedness, mischief, *formal* iniquity, maleficence, transgression

wrongful *adj*
immoral, improper, unfair, unethical, unjust, unlawful, illegal, illegitimate, illicit, dishonest, criminal, blameworthy, dishonourable, wrong, unjustified, unwarranted, reprehensible, wicked, evil
Fa rightful

wrongly *adv*
incorrectly, mistakenly, badly, by mistake, in error, inaccurately, erroneously
Fa rightly

wrought *adj*
shaped, fashioned, hammered, beaten, made, manufactured, ornamental, ornate, decorative, ornamented

wry *adj*
1 *wry humour* ironic, sardonic, dry, witty, sarcastic, mocking, droll **2** TWISTED, distorted, deformed, contorted, warped, uneven, askew, crooked
Fa **2** straight

X,Y,Z

xenophobia *n*
racism, ethnocentrism, racialism, xenophoby
⊞ xenomania

xenophobic *adj*
racist, racialist, parochial, ethnocentrist

xerox *v*
photocopy, copy, duplicate, Photostat®, reproduce, print, run off

Xerox® *n*
photocopy, duplicate, facsimile, Photostat®

yack *v, n*
▶ *v* chatter, gossip, prattle, tattle, twattle, jabber, witter on, blather, *colloq.* jaw, gab, yap
▶ *n* chat, gossip, prattle, rant, harp on, twattle, jaw, blather, *colloq.* blah, chinwag, yackety-yack, confab, hot air

yank *v & n*
jerk, tug, pull, wrench, snatch, haul, heave

yap *v*
1 BARK, yelp 2 CHATTER, jabber, babble, prattle, yatter, *colloq.* jaw, gab

yard *n*
courtyard, court, garden, quadrangle, *colloq.* quad

yardstick *n*
measure, gauge, criterion, standard, scale, guideline, benchmark, touchstone, comparison

yarn *n*
1 THREAD, fibre, strand 2 STORY, tale, anecdote, fable, fabrication, *colloq.* tall story, cock-and-bull story

yawning *adj*
gaping, wide, wide-open, huge, vast, cavernous

yearly *adj, adv*
▶ *adj* annual, per year, per annum, perennial
▶ *adv* annually, every year, once a year, perennially

yearn *v*
long, pine, desire, want, wish, crave, covet, hunger, thirst, hanker, ache, fancy, languish, itch, *colloq.* yen

yearning *n*
longing, pining, desire, wish, craving, hunger, thirst, hankering, fancy, *colloq.* yen

yell *v, n*
▶ *v* shout, scream, cry (out), bellow, roar, bawl, shriek, squeal, howl, screech, squall, yelp, yowl, whoop, *colloq.* holler
⊞ whisper
▶ *n* shout, scream, cry, roar, bellow, shriek, howl, screech, squall, whoop, *colloq.* holler
⊞ whisper

yellow *adj*
lemon, gold, golden, buff, tawny, canary, primrose, saffron, flaxen, *technical* xanthous, xanthic, xanthochroic,
vitellary, vitelline, *formal* flavescent, fulvous, fulvid

yelp *v, n*
▶ *v* yap, bark, squeal, cry, yell, yowl, bay
▶ *n* yap, bark, yip, squeal, cry, yell, yowl

yen *n*
longing, yearning, hunger, desire, craving, hankering, itch, passion, lust, *colloq.* thing
⊞ dislike

yes *adv*
right, quite, absolutely, certainly, agreed, of course, affirmative, *colloq.* yeah, yep
⊞ no

yes-man *n*
sycophant, crawler, toady, lackey, minion, bootlicker, backscratcher

yet *adv, conj*
▶ *adv* 1 UP TILL NOW, until now, up to this time, up till then, by now, by then, now, already, as yet, *formal* thus far, hitherto, heretofore 2 IN ADDITION, still, even, too, also, furthermore, besides, moreover, *colloq.* into the bargain
▶ *conj* but, however, nevertheless, nonetheless, anyway, even so, all/just the same, for all that, *formal* notwithstanding

yield *v, n*
▶ *v* 1 SURRENDER, give up, abandon, abdicate, cede, part with, *formal* relinquish, forego, renounce 2 GIVE WAY, capitulate, surrender, concede, submit, succumb, give in, admit defeat, bow, cave in, knuckle under, resign yourself, go along with, permit, allow, accede, agree, comply, consent, *formal* acquiesce, *colloq.* throw in the towel/sponge 3 PRODUCE, bear, supply, provide, give, generate, bring in, bring forth, furnish, return, earn, fetch, pay, net, gross, *formal* fructify, fructuate
⊞ 1 hold 2 resist, withstand
▶ *n* return, product, earnings, harvest, crop, produce, output, profit, revenue, takings, proceeds, income, haul

yielding *adj*
1 FLEXIBLE, pliable, pliant, resilient, elastic, springy, soft, supple, spongy, quaggy 2 SUBMISSIVE, obedient, amenable, biddable, obliging, unresisting, accommodating, easy, *formal* acquiescent, complaisant, compliant, tractable
⊞ 1 solid 2 obstinate

yoke *n, v*
▶ *n* 1 HARNESS, bond, link, tie, coupling 2 BURDEN, bondage, enslavement, slavery, tyranny, oppression, servility, *formal* servitude, subjugation
▶ *v* couple, link, join, tie, bond, harness, hitch, connect, bracket, unite

yokel *n*
country bumpkin, clodhopper, country cousin, hick, peasant, rustic, boor, bucolic, *colloq.* hillbilly
⊞ sophisticate, towny

young *adj, n*
▶ *adj* **1** YOUTHFUL, juvenile, childlike, baby, infant, junior, small, little, teenage, adolescent, *colloq.* kid **2** IMMATURE, childish, early, new, recent, green, growing, fledgling, unfledged, inexperienced, undeveloped
⊟ 1 adult, old **2** mature, old
▶ *n* offspring, babies, little ones, issue, litter, brood, children, family, *formal* progeny

youngster *n*
child, boy, lad, girl, lass, toddler, young person, young adult, young man, youth, young woman, teenager, adolescent, *colloq.* kid, shaver

youth *n*
1 ADOLESCENT, teenager, youngster, juvenile, boy, lad, young man, *colloq.* kid **2** YOUNG PEOPLE, the young, younger generation **3** ADOLESCENCE, teenage years, teens, childhood, immaturity, inexperience, boyhood, girlhood
⊟ 3 adulthood, maturity

youthful *adj*
young, boyish, girlish, childish, immature, juvenile, inexperienced, fresh, active, vigorous, lively, spry, sprightly, well-preserved
⊟ aged

youthfulness *n*
liveliness, vigour, spryness, sprightliness, vivaciousness, freshness, juvenileness, juvenility, *formal* vivacity
⊟ agedness, languor

yowl *v, n*
▶ *v* wail, yell, yelp, cry, howl, screech, squall, bay, caterwaul, *formal* ululate
▶ *n* wail, cry, howl, screech, yell, yelp

yucky *adj*
disgusting, revolting, horrible, unpleasant, messy, mucky, filthy, dirty, foul, sickly, sentimental, saccharine, *colloq.* grotty
⊟ nice

zany *adj* comical, funny, amusing, eccentric, odd, absurd, ridiculous, droll, clownish, *colloq.* crazy, daft, loony, wacky, *US* kooky
⊟ serious

zap *v*
kill, destroy, hit, shoot, finish off, *colloq.* do in, bump off, rub out, wipe out

zeal *n*
enthusiasm, ardour, fervour, passion, warmth, fire, devotion, spirit, energy, vigour, keenness, zest, eagerness, earnestness, dedication, commitment, vehemence, intensity, fanaticism, gusto, verve
⊟ apathy, indifference

zealot *n*
fanatic, radical, extremist, bigot, militant, partisan

zealous *adj*
ardent, fervent, impassioned, passionate, devoted, burning, fiery, enthusiastic, intense, warm, fanatical,

militant, keen, committed, dedicated, eager, earnest, spirited, *formal* fervid
⊟ apathetic, indifferent

zenith *n*
summit, peak, height, pinnacle, apex, high point, highest point, top, optimum, climax, culmination, meridian, *technical* acme, vertex, apogee
⊟ nadir

zero *n, v*
▶ *n* nothing, nought, naught, nil, nadir, bottom, cipher, duck, love, *colloq.* zilch
▶ *v* ▷ **zero in on** aim for, concentrate on, converge on, home in on, direct at, level at, pinpoint, fix on, focus on, train on, head for

zest *n*
1 GUSTO, appetite, enthusiasm, enjoyment, relish, keenness, zeal, eagerness, liveliness, vigour, exuberance, interest, *joie de vivre*, *colloq.* zing **2** FLAVOUR, taste, relish, savour, spice, tang, piquancy
⊟ 1 apathy

zigzag *v, adj*
▶ *v* meander, snake, wind, twist, curve
▶ *adj* meandering, crooked, serpentine, sinuous, twisting, winding
⊟ straight

zing *n*
liveliness, life, energy, vitality, vigour, spirit, animation, zest, sparkle, élan, joie de vivre, *colloq.* go, oomph, pizzazz, zip, dash, brio
⊟ listlessness

zip *n, v*
▶ *n* energy, verve, vitality, life, liveliness, enthusiasm, drive, sparkle, spirit, vigour, zest, gusto, élan, *colloq.* go, get-up-and-go, oomph, pizzazz, pep, punch, zing
⊟ listlessness
▶ *v* fly, dash, tear, rush, race, hurry, speed, shoot, flash, scoot, zoom, *colloq.* whiz, whoosh

zodiac *n*

The signs of the zodiac (with their symbols) are: Aries (Ram), Taurus (Bull), Gemini (Twins), Cancer (Crab), Leo (Lion), Virgo (Virgin), Libra (Balance), Scorpio (Scorpion), Sagittarius (Archer), Capricorn (Goat), Aquarius (Waterbearer), Pisces (Fishes).

zone *n*
region, area, district, territory, province, section, sector, belt, sphere, tract, stratum

zoo *n*
zoological gardens, safari park, animal park, aquarium, aviary, menagerie

zoom *v*
race, rush, tear, dash, speed, fly, hurtle, streak, flash, shoot, whirl, dive, buzz, zip, *colloq.* go all out, vroom, whiz, zap

STUDY SUPPLEMENT

PART ONE

USING WORDS APPROPRIATELY

An effective use of language helps us to get what we want. Whether that is good exam results, a higher essay grade, a new job or to get out of a tight spot, it is crucial to express ourselves creatively, accurately and in an interesting way that makes people listen to what we have to say.

CHOOSING THE RIGHT WORD

'The difference between the almost right word and the right word is really a large matter – it's the difference between the lightning bug* and the lightning.'

MarkTwain

Our choice of word in any situation is subconsciously influenced by several factors:

○ *Context* – where we are, and in what kind of situation

○ *Audience* – who we are communicating with, and their relationship to us

○ *Aim* – what effect we wish to have on our audience, and the desired end result

and many others. All these are taken into account before we even open our mouths, or put pen to paper.

When we use a thesaurus, this process of selecting the appropriate word becomes a conscious one. This is especially true as we may be using words with which we are unfamiliar.

Context

The most important factor to remember when choosing a word from the *Study Thesaurus* is the context in which you will use it. No matter how apt a word may appear, if you use it out of context it will be inappropriate, and may even have the opposite effect to the one that you hoped for. Using a slang expression in a job interview is unlikely to help you get the job, but using a very formal term amongst friends will make them laugh.

Examples of the right and wrong context are given throughout this section to help you choose the right word for the situation.

Audience

'A politician's words reveal less about what he thinks about his subject than what he thinks about his audience.'

George F. Will

Your audience is not necessarily a group of people sitting in front of you. The audience is the person or people who will be hearing or reading your words: your teacher, your friends and classmates, the manager of a business for which you want to work, your bank manager, or anyone else that you wish to communicate with. Ask yourself:

---

* The American term for a firefly.

○ What is the audience's prior knowledge and level of understanding of the subject?

○ Will they understand and appreciate simple or more complicated vocabulary?

○ What is their relationship to you – are they in authority, or is it an informal relationship?

Think about who your audience is, and then tailor your choice of words to them.

Aim

Your aim in speaking or writing might seem obvious. You want to convey the right information so you get a good mark in an essay, or you want to receive a pay rise, or you want to make people laugh, or you want to persuade people that your point of view is the right one. Consider your aim when choosing words so that you have the best chance of achieving it.

✗ 'I *deserve* a good grade on this essay because I *worked* hard.'

✓ 'I have *earned* a good grade on this essay because I *researched* it, *studied* the issues closely, and have *presented* them clearly.'

The first example says what you think. The second example has more chance of persuading someone, because the words emphasize *why* you think this – and so you have a better chance of achieving your aim.

Appropriateness

Bearing in mind the context, your audience, and your aim will help you to choose the right word. But it is also important to check the meaning of any word that you are unsure about in an English dictionary, such as *Chambers Study Dictionary*, before using it. Not all synonyms listed are interchangeable, and so not all can be used in the same situation.

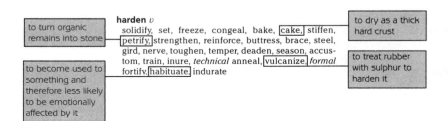

Although in their own way each of these words means *harden*, each only applies to a specific form of hardening, and if you use them inappropriately your sentence can become gobble-degook:

✗ She was *vulcanized* to his whining by now, so ignored him as they drove to see the *caked* forest, the mud from the rough track becoming *habituated* on the *petrified* tyres.

✓ She was *habituated* to his whining by now, so ignored him as they drove to see the *petrified* forest, the mud from the rough track becoming *caked* on the *vulcanized* tyres.

USING THE LABELS

The italic labels used in the *Study Thesaurus* indicate, for example, the register of a term (*formal*, *slang*) or the geographical location where it is most used (*US*, *Scot*). Because language is fluid, there is frequently some overlap between different language types. There is often similarity between *old-fashioned* and *formal* language, and between *formal* and *technical* language, for example, and the distinction between *colloquial* language and *slang* can be a subtle one. Also, a word may have more than one element in its label, for example *US slang*.

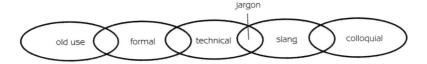

So the labels are there as a *guide* to help you in your choice of words. Use them to help you choose the most appropriate word for any situation.

REGISTER

What is register?

Register is the style of language suitable for certain situations or subjects. People use different words in a formal situation, for example at work or in an exam, from those that they use when chatting with friends. Most of the time this choice of language is made instinctively. But when using a thesaurus to choose words that might be unfamiliar to you, it is important to be careful. If a word is used in the wrong context, the result may be incongruous or inappropriate, or even cause trouble – the opposite of the effect that you are trying to create.

Register labels

Most of the words in the *Study Thesaurus* are Standard English. However, some words are marked by register labels, which indicate in which context the word might be used. They should help you to choose the right word for the right occasion.

- ○ *formal* – words which would be used in a more formal context
- ○ *colloq.* – words which would be suitable in an informal context
- ○ *slang* – words which should only be used in a very informal context
- ○ *old use* – words which are now considered to be old-fashioned

The synonyms given for a word in the *Study Thesaurus* may include words from several different registers:

> **kiss** *v, n*
> ▶ *v* **1** CARESS, *formal* osculate, *colloq.* peck, give someone a peck, smooch, neck, canoodle, bill and coo, *slang* snog

Standard   ✓ Linzi fondly **kissed** her brothers goodbye as she waved them off at the station.

formal   ✓ 'Male kissing gouramis, *Helostoma temmincki*, press lips and appear to *osculate*, but this is actually attempting to establish territorial dominance,' explained the tropical fish expert.

colloq. ✓ 'You'll never guess who I saw Ben *smooching* with at the cinema last night!' gossiped Fozia.

slang ✓ 'Ooh, I love Robbie,' squealed Alix, 'I'd *snog* him any time!'

These different registers are discussed in detail below.

Standard English

Standard English is the form of English generally used throughout the English-speaking world in education, business, official bodies, the media, and in all other everyday conventional speech and writing. It is understood by all speakers of English, and exists with very little variation from one English-speaking country to another. It can be seen as the 'common core' of English, what would remain if all the other variations were removed.

Standard English terms are not labelled in the *Study Thesaurus*.

Formal language

Formal language is frequently used in official or business situations. Like Standard English, it is strictly correct with regard to grammar, style and choice of words. However, formal language varies both in terms of the words used, and the way the language is structured. Standard English words that are not markedly formal can still be used in a formal context, but informal or slang words should not be used.

◻ Structure

Formal language is more restrictive in its structure than conversational language. Contractions and abbreviations are little used. Passive and impersonal constructions are used more. Both the words and sentences may be longer:

✗ We hope that he'll phone in, as we don't have much time to put this right.

✓ It is to be hoped that he will telephone the office, given the time constraints within which the situation must be rectified.

◻ Vocabulary

Formal words are not frequently used in everyday conversation. However, they may come in useful when addressing authority, or for adding weight to your words.

These words are labelled *formal* in the *Study Thesaurus*.

> **drunk** *adj, n*
> ▶ *adj* under the influence, drunken, *formal* inebriated, intoxicated, crapulent, *colloq.* merry, tight, tipsy, tiddly, well-oiled, blotto, drunk as a lord/newt, blind drunk, roaring drunk, the worse for drink, soused, squiffy, happy, legless, plastered, sozzled, pickled, bibulous, woozy, one over the eight, under the table, bevvied, having had a few

✗ 'Your Honour, I solemnly swear that on the night in question I was neither *squiffy* nor *plastered*.'

✓ 'Your Honour, I solemnly swear that on the night in question I was not *inebriated*.'

◻ Potential pitfalls

It is important not to overuse formal words, as there is a risk of sounding pompous or pretentious, or losing sight of the meaning of the sentence:

✗ His *propensity* for *prolixity* and *magniloquence obfuscated* his *elucidation* of the *eventuality*.

✓ His *explanation* of what *happened* was *unclear* because of his *pomposity* and *long-windedness*.

❑ **Context**

The context of formal words is also very important. They are unlikely, for example, to be used by children, or to be dropped casually into conversation:

> **yellow** *adj*
> lemon, gold, golden, buff, tawny, canary, primrose, saffron, flaxen, *technical* xanthous, xanthic, xantho-chroic, vitellary, vitelline, *formal* flavescent, fulvous, fulvid

✗ 'Look at the *flavescent* flower!' laughed four-year-old Debbie.

✓ 'The wings of the Blue Dasher dragonfly, *Pachydiplax longipennis*, are usually clear but may sometimes be *flavescent*...' droned Professor Pocklington, as his students nodded off.

Informal language

Informal language, which is also sometimes called colloquial language, is used when you are familiar with your audience, in a more relaxed or everyday situation. It uses vocabulary, idioms and structures characteristic of conversational speech. It is characterized by a lack of formality and tends to be more flexible in its construction and more expressive than formal language. It should not be used in a formal context.

These words are labelled *colloq.* in the *Study Thesaurus*.

> **depart** *v*
> **1** GO, leave, withdraw, exit, make off, decamp, take your leave, absent yourself, set off, set out, start out, pull out, get going, remove, retreat, migrate, escape, disappear, retire, vanish, *colloq.* push along/off, make tracks, quit, scat, scoot, scram, take off, take to your heels, make yourself scarce, shove off, bunk off, clear off, split, scarper, skedaddle, vamoose, skive, do a runner, do a bunk, do a moonlight flit, hit the road/ trail, make a bolt/break for it, up sticks, hightail it, sling your hook

✗ 'Prince Charles Edward Stuart *hightailed* it to Skye', she wrote in her history examination.

✓ The red wine stain wouldn't come out of the carpet, so Kieran *hightailed* it out of the house.

Remember that not only should informal words only be used in an informal context, but that not all the words listed mean exactly the same thing:

✗ 'The train will *skedaddle* at 16.20 – so we'd better run!' he shouted.

✓ They grabbed the box of chocolates and *skedaddled* as fast as their legs could carry them.

❑ **Idioms**

Informal language often contains idioms. An idiom is an expression with a meaning that cannot be understood from the usual meanings of the words which form it. Idioms add colour to your speech and writing, making it more lively and interesting for your audience. Many colloquial phrases are idiomatic. As with all informal language, such idioms are often inappropriate in more formal situations.

> **Colloquial ways of expressing becoming angry and losing your temper include:**
> blow up, blow a fuse, blow a gasket, blow your cool, blow your stack, blow your top, boil over, burst a blood vessel, do your nut, explode, flip your lid, fly into a rage, fly off the handle, go mad, go off the deep end, go up the wall, hit the ceiling, hit the roof, lose your cool, lose your patience, lose your rag, raise Cain, raise hell, see red, throw a tantrum, throw a wobbly, foam at the mouth, get all steamed up

✗ The Chief Executive shocked the Board of Directors when she *threw a wobbly* about the sales figures.

✓ Caitlin *threw a wobbly* when Helen sneakily finished off the last of the chocolate fudge cake.

Be careful not to overuse idioms, or the effectiveness will be lost and the meaning will be unclear:

✗ He had *cold feet* about *pulling the wool over their eyes*, but he was at the *end of his tether* about the *top dog throwing his weight about* and this was the *final straw*.

Slang

'Slang is a language that rolls up its sleeves, spits on its hands, and goes to work.'

Carl Sandburg

The most informal of all language is slang. Slang has been around for hundreds of years, but the words that are considered to be slang are constantly changing, and many terms that were once slang are now thought to be Standard English. *Donkey*, for example, was a slang term in the 1800s! As a general rule, slang should not be used in a formal context, and should always be used with caution. It can also be very specific to one region or group of people.

These words are labelled *slang* in the *Study Thesaurus*.

> **money** *n*
> currency, cash, legal tender, banknotes, coin, funds, finances, assets, means, savings, resources, capital, riches, wealth, prosperity, affluence, *colloq.* the necessary, readies, *slang* megabucks, dough, dosh, bread, lolly, spondulicks, brass, loot, gravy

✗ 'I should invest your *spondulicks* in a high-interest, fixed-rate savings account,' said the financial adviser.

✓ 'Swindle the store, hit the highway, and we'll visit Vegas to spend the *spondulicks*,' growled the infamous gangster 'Red' Rogers.

Old-fashioned language

Language is constantly evolving, as new words are coined and old ones become disused. Some old words become obsolete and disappear entirely except from the pages of dictionaries. More, however, remain on the fringes of everyday language, infrequently used but still occasionally encountered – in novels, historical texts or scientific works written in previous centuries. They may sound archaic, but are useful if you are writing in a historical or old-fashioned style.

These words are labelled *old use* in the *Study Thesaurus*.

> **rendezvous** *n, v*
> ▶ *n* **1** MEETING, appointment, engagement, assignation, date, *old use* tryst

✗ Graham waited nervously for his *tryst* at the nightclub that night with Hannah.

✓ Sir Lancelot waited silently in the forest for a secret *tryst* with Guinevere.

GEOGRAPHICAL VARIATIONS

Dialect

A dialect is a particular form of a language used by a particular group of people in a region or social class, and is distinguished by its vocabulary and grammar. Within any geographical region there will be some variation from Standard English. Some, such as Scots English, have many words not found in Standard English.

For example, in the *Study Thesaurus* words which are primarily Scottish are labelled *Scot.*

> **baby** *n, adj*
> ▶ *n* babe, infant, newborn baby, suckling, child, toddler, tiny tot, *Scot.* bairn, *technical* neonate, *slang* sprog

✗ Princess Agnetha proudly showed off her newborn *bairn* to her adoring family.

✓ 'Our Willie was a bonnie wee *bairn*,' said Betty McIntosh wistfully to her neighbour.

Be careful when using dialect words, as they might not be understood by an English speaker from another region or country.

English worldwide

'We have really everything in common with America nowadays, except, of course, language.'

Oscar Wilde

English is spoken by millions of people around the globe, but varies slightly from country to country, as it is influenced by the other languages spoken there and the particular culture of each country. For example, there are differences between the English spoken in the United Kingdom and the English spoken in the United States of America. Terms that are used primarily in the United States are labelled *US* in the *Study Thesaurus*.

There are many differences of meaning, pronunciation, spelling and syntax between British and US English. This means that the context in which a word is used is very important. In the example below, 'pants' is an American term meaning trousers, and it is acceptable to use the word in this way if writing in an American context or style. However, if you were writing outside the US it has a different meaning, and should not be used in this sense:

> **trousers** *n*
> slacks, jeans, denims, Levis®, flannels, dungarees, breeches, shorts, *US* pants

✗ An English gentleman must always carry an umbrella and wear a bowler hat, and his shirt and *pants* should be immaculate.

✓ Movie star Brock Beagle looked gorgeous as he cruised through New York City in casual T-shirt and *pants*.

TECHNICAL LANGUAGE

In the field of science and technology there is a tendency for objects and concepts to have a technical or scientific name, as well as a common name. These technical terms are labelled *technical* in the *Study Thesaurus*. It is important to be careful when using these kind of words. Not only may they be more specific than the standard term, they are also unlikely to be readily interchangeable with other terms listed:

> **accelerate** *v*
> **2** *accelerate a process* speed up, hurry, step up, stimulate, facilitate, advance, further, promote, spur on, forward, *technical* festinate

✗ The racing car *festinated* down the straight into the final lap.

✓ Dr Martin explained that the patient may take tiny steps, *festinate* or fall when walking.

There is also a risk of confusing your audience if you use too many technical terms on a topic with which they are unfamiliar. However, if they already know something about the subject, then it is appropriate to use the technical term.

> **baby** *n, adj*
> ▶ *n* babe, infant, newborn baby, suckling, child, toddler, tiny tot, *Scot.* bairn, *technical* neonate, *slang* sprog

✗ 'You were a *neonate* once', explained Rajiv to three-year old Tim, who wailed and burst into tears.

✓ The second-year nursing students made notes as the lecturer explained how to care for the needs of the *neonate*.

Beware! The majority of the terms labelled as technical have very specific meanings. It may be that a word only applies in a certain context, or refers only to a specific type of the headword:

> **fossil** *n*
> remains, remnant, petrified remains/impression, ammonite, relic, reliquiae, *technical* graptolite, coprolite, trilobite

✗ Prehistoric plants which grew over forty million years ago can now be found as *trilobites*.

✓ The renowned palaeontologist Dr Celia Kanth explained the differences between *ammonites*, *graptolites* and *trilobites*.

Technical terms may also be found in the panels that list language specific to a certain subject or item. In these panels they are not labelled because all the words listed are relatively specialist terms.

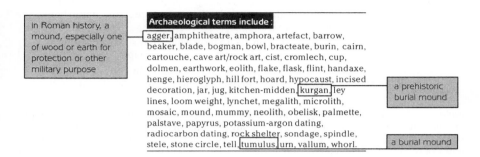

In Roman history, a mound, especially one of wood or earth for protection or other military purpose

Archaeological terms include :
agger, amphitheatre, amphora, artefact, barrow, beaker, blade, bogman, bowl, bracteate, burin, cairn, cartouche, cave art/rock art, cist, cromlech, cup, dolmen, earthwork, eolith, flake, flask, flint, handaxe, henge, hieroglyph, hill fort, hoard, hypocaust, incised decoration, jar, jug, kitchen-midden, kurgan, ley lines, loom weight, lynchet, megalith, microlith, mosaic, mound, mummy, neolith, obelisk, palmette, palstave, papyrus, potassium-argon dating, radiocarbon dating, rock shelter, sondage, spindle, stele, stone circle, tell, tumulus, urn, vallum, whorl.

a prehistoric burial mound

a burial mound

It is always important to look up technical words in an English dictionary before you use them. For example, although *agger*, *kurgan* and *tumulus* are all kinds of mound, they could not be substituted for each other without changing the meaning of the sentence.

Technical language is sometimes called jargon. Jargon is the specialized vocabulary of a particular trade, activity, group or profession. Be careful if you use jargon; even if you are sure what it means, your audience might not be. You risk confusing them, and so failing to communicate clearly. It is also important not to use jargon in a pretentious or meaningless way just because it may *sound* impressive.

SENSITIVE LANGUAGE

'There is a wonderful cliché – sticks and stones may break my bones but words can never hurt me. That is nonsense. Words can and do hurt people every day of their lives....Words are all important....Words have influence. Words have power.'

Gurbux Singh, Chair of the Commission for Racial Equality

Sometimes language can be a minefield. Even seemingly innocent language can have unwanted effects if it is used without sensitivity. Language can reinforce unhelpful stereotypes, promote negative opinions and patronize people. On the other hand, sensitive use of language can have the opposite effect. It is useful to be aware that there are occasions when you risk causing offence if you do not use language with care.

Sensitive use of language is a complicated and emotive area. There are no fixed rules about what is acceptable and what is inappropriate, and people often disagree. However, the following general principles may be helpful.

  o Some traditional ways of referring to people may reinforce stereotypical (and often incorrect) notions, for example that men naturally hold positions of authority in society, or that members of minority groups are inferior or abnormal.

  o People usually prefer to be treated as individuals rather than merely as members of a group.

  o It is often not relevant to refer to people's race, gender or disabilities if you wish to talk about them. Consider whether such information is really appropriate.

○ Try to be aware of terms people use to describe themselves and respect the right of people to choose how they are called.

○ Terms which are regarded as appropriate in one country or region may sometimes be regarded as offensive in another.

○ Terms which were formerly regarded as acceptable may now be regarded as derogatory, and it is possible that terms which are now acceptable may in time come to be regarded as offensive.

○ Sometimes a group may use within itself a term which may still be regarded as offensive when used by people who are not part of the group.

○ Although it is often used out of the best of motives, politically correct language can impair clarity of expression or appear ridiculous when taken to extremes.

Following these general principles may help you to use language carefully. These principles are reinforced below by some more specific suggestions on how to use language sensitively with reference to gender, race and religion, disability, and sexuality. However, these are only a few of the areas which call for sensitivity. You should also be careful when speaking, for example, about age, marital or family status, nationality, and political beliefs.

Gender

You risk offending many of your readers if you use language in a way that implies that there is only one gender, or that one gender is superior to the other. This can sometimes be difficult to achieve, however, as many traditional uses of language treat the masculine gender as a privileged form.

○ Some people disapprove of the words *he, his* and *him* being used to refer to someone who could be of either sex.

✗ *Every applicant for the job* should include *his* curriculum vitae.

Some people prefer to use the plural words *they, their* and *them* (which imply no specific gender) in such situations. This usage is becoming widely acceptable, although some people still regard it as ungrammatical.

Every applicant for the job should include *their* curriculum vitae.

Other people prefer to use *he* or *she, his* or *hers*, and *him* or *her*, but this can be clumsy, especially when these phrases have to be repeated frequently.

Every applicant for the job should include *his* or *her* curriculum vitae.

The best solution in many cases is to rewrite the sentence in such a way that the problem is avoided altogether. This can often be done by making the subject into a plural:

✓ *Every applicant for the job* should include *a* curriculum vitae.

✓ *All applicants for the job* should include *their* curriculum vitae.

○ Some people object to words such as *man, men* or *mankind* as terms to denote both men and women. There are plenty of alternative terms, such as *people, humanity,* or *human beings* which can avoid this usage.

○ Be careful about using words which reinforce stereotypical images of the sexes, such as saying that men *converse* while women *gossip,* or that a woman is *hysterical* whilst a man is *angry.*

○ If you are talking about two people, you should, other things being equal, use equivalent terms to refer to each of them. Beware of defining women by appearance, age and the number of children they have, and men by career or achievement:

> ✗ Famous actor Brock Beagle was accompanied by his sister, a stunningly attractive blonde mother-of-two.

> ✓ Famous actor Brock Beagle was accompanied by his sister Brenda Beagle, the award-winning photographer.

○ Many occupations have traditional titles which imply that they are done only by one sex. There is usually a non-gender-specific term which can be used instead: for example, *flight attendant* in place of *air stewardess*, and *fire fighter* in place of *fireman*. These titles should be used consistently − if you use the title *police officer* when talking about men, you should use the same term when talking about women who do the same job, and vice versa.

○ Do not make assumptions about people's gender from their occupations. The job titles *nurse*, *doctor* and *secretary*, for example, can refer to people of both sexes. There is no need to use *male nurse*, *female doctor*, or *male secretary*.

Race and Religion

Sensitive use of language with reference to race and religion does not refer solely to avoiding deliberately offensive terms for racial and religious groups. You can show sensitivity by respecting the wishes of people to use their own preferred names and by using language in a way that does not perpetuate negative or stereotypical images.

○ It is advisable to avoid language which suggests that one group of people are normal and that all others are abnormal. Beware of defining minority groups solely in terms of their differences from the majority group.

○ People generally prefer to be identified positively rather than be defined by what they are not. Terms such as *non-white* are best used only when the context makes them relevant.

> ✗ *Non-whites* took to the streets today to protest against racism.

> ✓ An investigation into equal opportunities at the company found that *non-white* employees were paid less than their *white* colleagues.

○ People are likely to be offended by over-generalizations, such as using *black* as a generic word for absolutely everyone who is not white.

○ You risk causing offence if you use words inaccurately. For example, *immigrants* are people who have come to a foreign country with the intention of settling in it. The term is not appropriate to describe people of a different racial group who were born in the country.

○ Try to avoid describing people by using stereotypical images of the race or religion to which they belong. For example, people of Chinese origin are likely to be offended if they are associated with adjectives such as *inscrutable*, especially if such words would not be used of other people in the same situation. Even associations that might be intended to be positive, such as regarding people of Indian origin as *industrious* or Germans as *efficient*, can cause offence because they treat people as stereotypes rather than individuals.

✗ Bruce looks after the company's finances with *typical Scottish thrift.*

✓ Bruce keeps tight control over the company's finances.

○ Be aware of the names by which different racial groups prefer to be called. In Britain, terms such as *Afro/Caribbean* or *Afro-Caribbean* are preferable to *West Indian*, whilst *British Asian* is preferred for British citizens whose families originate from the Indian subcontinent. In the United States, words like *African American* or *Chinese American* are preferred, as these indicate a person's ethnic group whilst still denoting that someone is an American. In Australia, it is normal to use *Aboriginal people* or the individual group name (for example *Pitjantjatjara*) in preference to *Aborigine*.

It is increasingly common to respect peoples' own preferred names for themselves and for local places rather than using names imposed by colonizers – for example, *Inuit* is now preferred to *Eskimo*, *Ayers Rock* is now known by its Aboriginal name *Uluru*, and *Mount McKinley* is known as *Denali*, the name given to it by the Athabascan native people of Alaska. Similarly, the spelling and pronunciation of place names increasingly reflects the usage of indigenous peoples – for example *Makkah* being preferred to *Mecca*, when referring to the holy city of Islam.

Disability

'The language we use reflects the way we think. It also shapes the way we think. The language we use about disability is an important way of influencing our own and society's attitudes.'

Scope (British cerebral palsy charity)

Some of the language traditionally used when referring to people with disabilities frequently has associations of passivity, pity and limitation. It often stresses the disability at the expense of the person. Sensitive use of language recognizes the abilities as well as the disabilities of a person, and avoids making judgements that may be at odds with the facts.

○ Beware of describing someone solely in terms of the disability they have, as though that defined their personality. It is preferable to talk of *a person with a disability* or *a disabled person* rather than *a cripple* or *an invalid*. Similarly, it is preferable to talk of *people with epilepsy* or *deaf people* rather than *epileptics* or *the deaf.*

○ Many *disabled people* dislike being referred to as *handicapped* on the grounds that a handicap is created by external surroundings or by other people's attitudes (for example a building without a lift for a wheelchair user, or discrimination in the workplace) and not by the disability itself.

○ You may cause offence if you use terms which imply some judgement, such as *sufferer* or *victim*. It is preferable to say that someone *has* a certain disability, rather than making the judgement that they are *afflicted* by it or *suffer* as a result. Similarly, it is preferable to refer to a *wheelchair user* or someone who *uses a wheelchair*, rather than saying that they are *confined to a wheelchair* or *wheelchair bound*, which implies restriction and passivity.

✗ Sam is afflicted by cerebral palsy. How the poor girl must suffer!

✓ Paul uses a wheelchair to go out with his friends.

○ Beware of using inaccurate or outdated terms. Where a recognized scientific term exists, such as *cerebral palsy* or *Down's syndrome*, it is advisable to use this.

○ It is usually best to use precise terms to describe disabilities rather than vague and evasive constructions such as *differently abled, physically challenged* and *special.*

○ You may cause offence if you refer to people who do not have a particular disability as *normal,* when in fact they are just people without that disability.

○ Remember that people may have individual preferences. Some people who are deaf dislike being called *hearing impaired.* Some people dislike the terms *blind* or *partially sighted,* and prefer *people with impaired vision* or *people with a visual disability.* Respect a person's wish if they express a preference for a certain term.

Sexuality

As is the case with language relating to race and religion, using sensitive language with regard to sexuality goes beyond simply avoiding terms of abuse. It takes account of differences and avoids crude categorizations.

○ Many people prefer to use the term *partner,* as this is regarded as inclusive, whereas terms like *husband, wife, boyfriend, girlfriend* or *spouse* make assumptions about people's sexuality.

○ Try to avoid language which stereotypes people, or which makes assumptions based on prejudice or misinformation about their character or lifestyle.

PART TWO

USING WORDS CREATIVELY

'Words set things in motion. I've seen them doing it. Words set up atmospheres, electrical fields, charges. I've felt them doing it. Words conjure.'

Toni Cade Bambara

LIVELY LANGUAGE

The more creative your choice of words, the more interesting your speech or writing will be, and the more influence it will have on your audience. Lively language elicits a response from the audience: it arouses their emotions, changes their point of view, or creates a strong impression. Choose the right word to add interest, impact and a deeper meaning to your speech or writing.

□ Colourful descriptions

The most memorable communication creates a vivid mental image for the audience. It is tempting to rely on overused words because they can often be used in a variety of contexts – *big*, for example, can mean *sizable, elder, significant, famous* or *generous*. Use the *Study Thesaurus* to exchange uninspiring and overused words for ones with impact and interest.

> **nice** *adj*
> **1** *have a nice time* pleasant, agreeable, enjoyable, lovely, good, delightful, satisfying, acceptable, pleasurable, fine, appealing, amusing, entertaining, welcome, *formal* delectable **2** *he seems a nice man* pleasant, agreeable, delightful, charming, likeable, attractive, good, good-natured, good-humoured, kind, kindly, friendly, genial, sweet, amiable, sympathetic, understanding, endearing, well-mannered, polite, respectable, civil, courteous

✗ 'He's a *nice* guy,' said Kathryn, 'I quite like him.'

✓ 'He's *attractive, polite, good-humoured, sympathetic, understanding* and *kind*,' said Kathryn, 'I adore him!'

You should also be careful not to pepper your work with intensifiers such as *really* or *very* because these will actually reduce the impact of what you want to say. Mark Twain had the following advice:

> 'Substitute *damn* every time you're inclined to write *very*; your editor will delete it and the writing will be just as it should be.'

Although this is not advisable for writing at school or college, the principle holds true!

> **very** *adv, adj*
> ▶ *adv* extremely, greatly, highly, deeply, truly, remarkably, excessively, exceeding(ly), exceptionally, acutely, particularly, really, quite, absolutely, noticeably, unbelievably, incredibly, exceptionally, unusually, uncommonly, *colloq.* pretty, terribly, dreadfully, awfully

✗ 'It was a *very* dangerous expedition,' declared 'Fearless' Floyd, ' *Very* difficult terrain and the temperatures in the jungle were *very* high, not to mention the insects which were *very* persistent and bit us *very* often. We were all *very* ill from fevers and suffered *very* much. We are *very* relieved to be home.'

✓ 'It was an *exceptionally* dangerous expedition,' declared 'Fearless' Floyd, '*Remarkably* difficult terrain and the temperatures in the jungle were *uncommonly* high, not to mention the insects which were *incredibly* persistent and bit us *excessively.* We were all *acutely* ill from fevers and suffered *dreadfully.* We are *extremely* relieved to be home.'

Your language will become more evocative if you substitute colourful words for dull ones.

✗ The *big, dry* desert was *hot* and the *lost* explorers were *very thirsty.*

✓ The *vast, arid* desert was *sweltering* and the *disorientated* explorers were *extremely dehydrated.*

❑ Vigorous verbs

Many commonly overused verbs, such as *say, do* and *like*, offer a simple way of expressing an idea, but they can also be rather bland. To add interest you can employ an adverb to describe the tone of voice or way in which the action is performed. However, this can still lack impact. Try using a more forceful verb in place of the overused word:

✗ 'You told her my secret!' he *said accusingly.*

✓ 'You told her my secret!' he *accused.*

The second example is stylistically better, makes a stronger impression, and is more likely to grab the reader's attention. Throughout the *Study Thesaurus* you will find panels which list these useful verbs. Use them to enliven your writing:

> **Ways of walking include:**
> amble, clump, crawl, creep, dodder, *colloq.* go by shanks's pony, hike, hobble, *colloq.* hoof it, limp, lope, lurch, march, mince, *colloq.* mooch, pace, pad, paddle, parade, patter, *formal* perambulate, plod, potter, promenade, prowl, ramble, roam, saunter, scuttle, shamble, shuffle, slink, sneak, stagger, stalk, steal, step, stomp, *colloq.* stretch your legs, stride, stroll, strut, stumble, swagger, tiptoe, *colloq.* toddle, totter, traipse, tramp, trample, tread, trek, trip, troop, trot, trudge, trundle, waddle, wade, wander, *colloq.* yomp.

✗ Russell *walked* out of Tipsy Tallulah's Tavern.

✓ Russell *lurched* out of Tipsy Tallulah's Tavern.

✓ Russell *sneaked* out of Tipsy Tallulah's Tavern.

✓ Russell *marched* out of Tipsy Tallulah's Tavern.

The first example lacks interest because it provides little information or colour, but the following sentences capture the reader's attention. He lurches (is he drunk?), he sneaks (is someone searching for him?) and he marches (is he disgusted with the goings-on inside?). The carefully chosen word adds meaning to the sentence beyond the literal fact of his leaving the bar. This is an economic way of revealing information whilst developing a concise, colourful and interesting style. Tone, atmosphere and character can all be conveyed in this way:

> **Other words for say include:**
> correct, counter, croak, cry, curse, declare,
> demand, deny, describe, detail, disclose, dispute,
> divulge, echo, elaborate, elucidate, emphasize,
> enjoin, estimate, exclaim, expostulate, express,
> falter, finish, flounder, gasp, greet, groan, growl,
> grumble, grunt, guess, hint, howl, imagine,
> implore, imply, indicate, infer, inform, inquire,
> insinuate, insist, instruct, interrogate, interrupt,
> intervene, intimate, jeer, jest, joke, laugh, lecture,
> lie, maintain, make known, make public, mention,
> mimic, moan, mock, mouth, mumble, murmur,
> mutter, nag, observe, offer, orate, order...

✗ 'I'm not afraid of you!' he *said*.
✓ 'I'm not afraid of you!' he *croaked*.
✓ 'I'm not afraid of you!' he *exclaimed*.
✓ 'I'm not afraid of you!' he *growled*.
✓ 'I'm not afraid of you!' he *jeered*.
✓ 'I'm not afraid of you!' he *mumbled*.

By varying the verb, the entire situation changes. Is the speaker brave, terrified, or subdued? The verb can even undermine the spoken words: if the speaker is not afraid, as he says, why does he mumble?

Making your audience think about your meaning rather than simply stating the information blandly involves them in what you are writing and keeps their attention. Your words will have more power if you let them draw conclusions for themselves.

❏ Manipulating meaning

Remember that your choice of word affects both the explicit and the implied meaning of what you are trying to communicate.

✓ 'I've not seen his wife for days, and now he's digging the garden at midnight!' *whispered* Mrs Meddle, *peeking furtively* through her net curtains at her neighbour's *shadowy* activities in the back yard.

Her suspicion that her neighbour is doing something more sinister than just planting dahlias is clearly suggested and reinforced by the choice of the words *whispered, peeking, furtively* and *shadowy*. Consider too how to convey *tone* through your words:

✓ '*Of course* your bottom doesn't look big in that dress!' *smirked* the *supercilious* sales assistant.

Associations and connotations

Just as some synonyms in a list can apply to only one sense of a headword or have a very specific meaning, so some words can carry certain connotations or associations.

- ○ A *connotation* is an idea or feeling suggested in addition to the literal meaning of a word.
- ○ An *association* is a connection in the mind between a word and emotions or sensations.

The connotations or associations of a word often vary from person to person, and words which are positive for one person can seem negative to another. This is because our own personal experiences provide different impressions. However, many words have widely re-cognised associations shared by most people. This means that many words have both a literal meaning and inherent connotations.

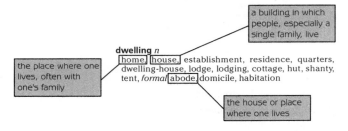

a building in which people, especially a single family, live

dwelling *n*
home, house, establishment, residence, quarters, dwelling-house, lodge, lodging, cottage, hut, shanty, tent, *formal* abode, domicile, habitation

the place where one lives, often with one's family

the house or place where one lives

The definitions of these words are more or less interchangeable but their connotations vary. A *home* suggests security and happiness, and perhaps a place of refuge and relaxation. A *house*, on the other hand, is associated more with the physical structure of the building than any feelings towards it, whilst an *abode* is a formal term which elicits little emotional re-sponse. This difference in connotations is often exploited by, for example, construction com-panies who style themselves as *creators of homes* rather than *builders of houses*.

✓ Hannah bought candles, bright curtains, colourful rugs and comfy cushions to turn her drab new *house* into a *home*.

Use these connotations and associations to add extra meaning and depth to your words, or to help you create a certain effect.

Language traps to avoid

◻ Clichés and collocations

- ○ A *cliché* is a once striking and effective phrase or combination of words which has become stale and hackneyed through overuse. Clichés are often over-used idioms, metaphors or similes.
- ○ A *collocation* is a number of words which frequently occur alongside one another. Many collocations are used so often that they have become clichéd.

Whilst a cliché may seem apt and easy to use, you are more likely to express yourself exactly and with interest if you choose your own words, and think more carefully about what it is that you want to communicate.

✗ *'Plenty more fish in the sea,'* observed Stewart's father cheerily, 'She wasn't worth
  it anyway, and *if you ask me* you're better off alone, son. *Things could be worse.*
  Just remember that *it's better to have loved and lost, than never to have loved at
  all.* And *at the end of the day, all's fair in love and war.'*

Common collocations are also easy to use without thinking. We are so used to following one
word with another almost automatically that we often forget to ask ourselves whether they
actually mean anything. The next time that you are tempted use terms like *vast majority* or
tragic accident, pause and consider if this really is what you intend to say, or if you are just
pairing the words because they are so commonly found together.

✗ 'The *burning question* is whether we can live in *blissful ignorance* when there's
  such a *gaping hole* in our knowledge. Having given *active consideration* to the
  graphic details of this case, we must issue a *categorical denial.'*

Some of the well-known idioms listed in the *Study Thesaurus* might be considered clichéd by
some people, so exercise caution when using them.

> **Colloquial expressions showing determination
> include:**
> mean business, stick to your guns, go to great
> lengths, go all out, go to extremes, go the whole
> hog, go for it, move heaven and earth, stop at
> nothing, do your utmost, give your all, leave no
> stone unturned, pull out all the stops, put your heart
> and soul into, strain every nerve, be hell-bent, get
> stuck into.

✗ I can assure you that the private investigator will *leave no stone unturned.*

✓ I can assure you that the private investigator is *persistent*, and is *determined* to
  scrutinize every possibility.

❏ Verbosity
Verbosity means using too many words, and so becoming boringly or irritatingly long-
winded. Stop and think whenever you are tempted to use five words where one might do.
Try to avoid needless repetition. For example, there is no need to write *by virtue of the fact that*
when you could just use *because*, and *now* is just as good as *at this moment in time.*

❏ Tautology
Tautology means saying the same thing twice. For example:

✗ Let's *continue on* to the next village and find a guesthouse, as I don't want to
  camp here in the rain.

✗ *Finally*, I would like to say *in conclusion* that you should always look on the
  bright side of life.

✗ *Everyone* was *unanimous* in their hatred of Monday mornings.

Such structures are clumsy and unnecessary. It is especially important to be aware of them if
you are writing an essay or other document with a strict word limit.

❏ Redundancy
A redundant word or phrase can be omitted without affecting the overall meaning of what
you are saying. For example, *in the present crisis situation* could be rewritten as *in the present
crisis* without changing its meaning, and instead of *on a daily basis* you could just write *daily.*

✗ They had a *confrontation of a most distressing nature* in the supermarket, and
  ended up fighting at the fish counter.

✓ They had a *most distressing confrontation* in the supermarket, and ended up fighting at the fish counter.

Presenting facts and opinions

Many newspaper articles, television programmes, websites and communications between friends or colleagues are made up of a mixture of facts and opinions.

○ A *fact* is a thing which is known to be true, exist, or have happened.

○ An *opinion* is a belief or judgement which seems likely to be true, but which is not based on proof. It is what someone thinks about somebody or something.

Often an author will intermingle facts and opinions, and will use language skilfully to blur the distinctions between the two.

✓ The Hungry Moose Steakhouse on the High Street serves a varied and interesting menu at reasonable prices. The succulent steak was deliciously tender, drowned in a sumptuous brandy and peppercorn sauce and accompanied by a mound of golden fries, whilst my companion's beefburger came loaded with crispy lettuce, smooth mayonnaise and dripping with melted cheese.

In this review, the restaurant critic has mixed facts (for example that the restaurant is on the High Street, that the steak was served with chips, and that his or her companion had a burger) and opinions (for example that the prices are reasonable, there was a lot of sauce with the steak, and that the lettuce was crispy). Keep an eye out for words such as *varied, interesting* or *delicious* as these words are value judgements: an assessment of worth or merit based on personal opinion rather than objective fact.

Whilst the restaurant critic did not point out which words were facts and which were opinions, there are words you can use as pointers in your own writing to identify which statements are which. This might be useful if writing an essay, as you must be careful not to state an idea as a fact just because you believe it to be right.

You can look under these key headwords in the *Study Thesaurus* for:

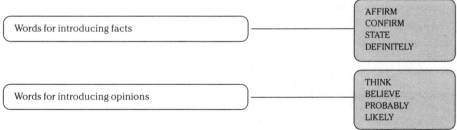

| Words for introducing facts | AFFIRM
CONFIRM
STATE
DEFINITELY |

| Words for introducing opinions | THINK
BELIEVE
PROBABLY
LIKELY |

✓ The teacher *confirmed* that there would *definitely* be a question about French cinema in the exam.

✓ Jia-Ling *believed* that there would *probably* be a question about French cinema in the exam.

Besides being important at school or college, it is also important to distinguish between facts and opinions in the wider world. Most countries have laws which regulate what can and cannot be presented as a fact about someone or something. Words such as *claim, suggest* and *allege* are sometimes used to suggest a certain meaning without having to provide evidence to substantiate it.

> **say** *v*
> **3** TELL, instruct, order, communicate, convey, inti-
> mate, report, announce, declare, state, assert, affirm,
> maintain, claim, allege, rumour, suggest, imply, sig-
> nify, reveal, disclose, divulge

fact   ✓ It has been *announced* that singing sensation Felicity Fizgig is engaged to movie star Brock Beagle.

opinion ✓ It has been *reported* that singing sensation Felicity Fizgig is engaged to movie star Brock Beagle.

opinion ✓ It has been *rumoured* that singing sensation Felicity Fizgig is engaged to movie star Brock Beagle.

The use of such words in speech or writing should alert you to the fact that there may be a mixture of facts and opinions. You should also be careful if, for example, a report is written in the conditional tense or contains words like *likely*:

> ✓ It is *believed* that Brock Beagle and Felicity Fizgig *could* be engaged. Sources say it is *likely* that they *would* wed in Fizgig's hometown of Vancouver, although Beagle's *reported* love of Scotland *may point to* a romantic Highland wedding.

◻ Vagueness and ambiguity

- ○ An *ambiguous* word or statement can be interpreted in more than one way.
- ○ *Vagueness* is expression without clarity, and imprecise use of language.

Be careful when using words from the *Study Thesaurus* to make sure that your meaning is clear. However, you should also be aware that vagueness and ambiguity are sometimes em- ployed deliberately, especially in areas such as politics or advertising. Words such as *fresh, pure, natural* or *traditional* might be interpreted by different people in different ways, and can be used in an ambiguous way to influence people's view of a product.

> ✗ Our foods are *naturally fresh*: the *healthy* choice for you and your family.

Fresh may mean different things to different people. Has a fresh item been processed, pre- served, salted, frozen or tinned? How much time may have elapsed between it being pro- duced and when it reaches the customer? Your ideas on what constitutes *fresh* food may vary from those of people around you. So be cautious when encountering such words and remember that they may be used in a deliberately ambiguous way.

Bias and objectivity

- ○ *Objective* language is detached; it does not incite the audience to become emotionally involved, and presents facts without prejudice.
- ○ *Subjective* language is emotive, biased and calculated to arouse emotion to influence the audience.

It is useful to develop a discriminating eye when reading reports and articles. You can then use the same techniques to persuade and influence in your own work.

Imagine that a construction company has applied for planning permission to build a new housing development on a greenfield, or previously undeveloped, site. The local newspaper could report this as:

against A development scheme which *threatens* to *devastate* a wildlife reserve was revealed today.

for   A development scheme which *promises* to *create* homes and jobs was revealed today.

Not only does the focus of the article change from the effect on the environment to the effect on the community, but changing the blue text from words with negative associations to words with positive associations changes the tone of the piece.

Many entries in the *Study Thesaurus* give *antonyms*, words which mean the opposite of the headword. Antonyms are useful if you want to change the bias of a report. For example:

selfish *adj*
  self-interested, self-seeking, self-serving, mean, miserly, mercenary, greedy, covetous, self-centred, inconsiderate, egocentric, egotistic(al), *colloq.* thinking of nobody except yourself
  ⊠ unselfish, selfless, **generous**, considerate
	generous *adj*
	  2 MAGNANIMOUS, charitable, philanthropic, publicspirited, unselfish, selfless, altruistic, kind, bighearted, benevolent, good, high-minded, noble, lofty, *formal* beneficent, munificent, *colloq.* big
	  ⊠ **2 selfish**

against   The *selfish* schemes of *greedy* developers will mean destruction for the environment.

for   The *public-spirited* schemes of *generous* developers will provide jobs and homes.

Remember the points about connotations and associations, about fact and opinions, and also about adding colour to your work. Using these techniques together can create a forceful report on one side of the argument.

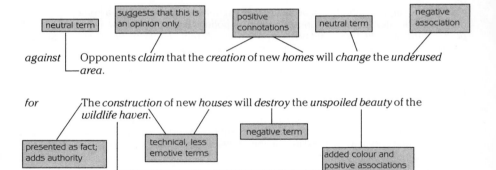

Biased and emotive language is often used to persuade an audience. Consider the response which you want to create in your audience, then use words skilfully to elicit this response from them.

LANGUAGE FOR SCHOOL AND COLLEGE

'There are no dull subjects. There are only dull writers.'

HL Mencken

The *Study Thesaurus* can help you to express yourself effectively at school or college. It can help you to use clear and interesting language to convey your thoughts, and so create a positive impression, whether in a speech, essay or an exam. Remember that no matter how careful your research, how novel your ideas, how well organised your work, if the words you use are dull then your grade will suffer as a result.

◻ Getting help with essays and coursework

Your teachers and lecturers can advise you on essay writing and exam techniques. In addition, many websites provide useful information on topics such as research, structure, references and common writing errors. *Chambers Study Dictionary* has a comprehensive supplement on all aspects of essay writing. It may also be useful to look at sample answers or previous students' essays, to see how others have approached the subject and how they have presented their ideas.

Use the *Study Thesaurus* to improve your word choice and vocabulary. This means using lively, interesting language, *and* avoiding overused words. The examples which follow show words being overused within paragraphs. However, it is possible to overuse a word throughout an entire essay, so review your work as a whole.

Key question words

In the wording of questions you may be asked to do one of several things:

analyse	contrast	examine	outline
appraise	define	explain	review
argue	describe	explore	state
assess	discuss	illustrate	summarize
compare	evaluate	justify	trace

These key words indicate the response which your teacher or the examiner is looking for. It is always helpful to look these key words up in the *Study Thesaurus* as this can help you understand what the question is asking, as well as give you vocabulary that might be useful in your answer.

For example, a question might ask you to *contrast* different views on a subject. Looking at the entry for *contrast* you can see that you are being asked to *differentiate* between opinions, to discuss how people may *disagree*. Looking at the synonyms for the key question word can encourage you to think around the subject, and help you to a clearer understanding of the question.

> **contrast** *n, v*
> ▶ *v* **1** *contrast two people* compare, differentiate, distinguish, discriminate **2** *her expression contrasted sharply with her dress* disagree, contradict, clash, conflict, differ, oppose, go against, be at variance, be at odds, be in conflict, be inconsistent with

✓ In his autobiography, Sir Richard *opposes* the widely-held belief that he *clashed* on many occasions with other members of the government. He argues that although his views did *conflict* with those of some senior politicians, he never *contradicted* official statements and remained loyal throughout his career.

Enlivening your answer

Your tone or language need not be sombre and dull just because you are writing an essay or exam paper. Whilst your subject matter may be serious, you can still make it engaging through a careful choice of words. Your teacher or the examiner may have to mark hundreds of papers. An interesting essay will be easier to read and will create a stronger, more positive impression.

✗ The two sides tried to take charge for a long while but then the Duke lost an important fight and was quickly killed.

✓ The rival factions struggled for supremacy for nine years before the Duke was defeated in a decisive battle and swiftly beheaded.

The second example is not only more striking and holds the attention, but also shows a better grasp of the issues (*rival factions, nine years*) and precise detail (*beheaded* rather than the vague *killed*). Remember that the marker will be looking for freshness and originality of approach, with varied sentences and paragraphs. Hold their attention and you will increase your chance of an improved grade.

Overused words for causes and effects

In a longer piece it is easy to repeat words excessively, or to struggle to find fresh ways of explaining something. As statements must always be backed up with evidence, you may find that words which describe a causal link are easy to overuse. If you feel that a word is becoming overworked, look it up in the *Study Thesaurus* and vary your word choices accordingly.

> **because** *conj*
> as, for, since, owing to, due to, on account of, as a result of, the reason is ..., through, thanks to, in view of the fact that, *formal* by reason of, by virtue of, forasmuch, *colloq.* seeing as

✗ The Venus Fly Trap cannot absorb much nitrogen *because* it grows in poor soil with few nutrients. *Because* of this it has developed traps to catch flies, *because* it can digest the caught insects and so absorb their nutrients. It is known as a 'carnivorous plant' *because* of this.

✓ The Venus Fly Trap cannot absorb much nitrogen *since* it grows in poor soil with few nutrients. *On account* of this it has developed traps to catch flies, *as* it can digest the caught insects and so absorb their nutrients. It is known as a 'carnivorous plant' *as a result*.

However, remember what has been said about verbosity – in some instances it might be better to repeat *because* than to use longer terms such as *by virtue of*. It may also be better to restructure your sentences to avoid the repetition:

✓ 'Carnivorous plants' such as the Venus Fly Trap cannot absorb much nitrogen from the nutrient-poor soil in which they grow. They have therefore developed traps which catch and digest flies, thus absorbing the insects' nutrients.

Words listed under these headwords may also be useful:

| Key words for relationships between two factors | BECAUSE THEREFORE RESULT CONSEQUENTLY |

Overused verbs

Verbs such as *show* or *demonstrate* are also easy to overuse, as you will often need to cite evidence and discuss its significance.

> **show** *v, n*
> ▶ *v* **1** REVEAL, expose, uncover, disclose, divulge, make visible, make clear, make plain, make known, *formal* manifest **2** EXPRESS, mean, indicate, signify, register, record, portray, depict, make it clear, be evidence, bear witness to, suggest, *formal* manifest **3** TEACH, instruct, clarify, make clear, elucidate, point out, explain, demonstrate, prove, illustrate, exemplify, *formal* expound

✗ The hero's actions here *show* his character. He is *shown* to be stubborn and short-sighted, and his comparison with a mule *shows* that he is obstinate. This passage *shows* an example of his destructive behaviour.

✓ The hero's actions here *expose* his character. He is *depicted* as being stubborn and short-sighted, and his comparison with a mule *suggests* that he is obstinate. This passage *exemplifies* his destructive behaviour.

It is important to distinguish between your thoughts and ideas and those of critics or experts whom you wish to quote in order to add weight to your argument, or to comment upon their views.

> **remark** *v, n*
> ▶ *v* comment, observe, note, notice, mention, say, state, assert, pronounce, declare

✗ *Remarking* upon the absence of written records, Professor Jones *remarks* that research into the period is vitally important. She *remarks* that archaeological digs have increased our knowledge but *remarks* that funding for such research is badly needed.

✓ *Commenting* upon the absence of written records, Professor Jones *notes* that research into the period is vitally important. She *observes* that archaeological digs have increased our knowledge but *states* that funding for such research is badly needed.

Words listed under these headwords may also be useful:

| Key words for explaining facts and ideas | DEMONSTRATE MEAN^1 INDICATE PORTRAY |

Choosing language for school and college

Consider not only the points in this section but elsewhere in the supplement about audience, appropriateness, aim, bias and objectivity, facts and opinions, avoiding clichés and repetition, and adding colour and interest. In particular:

○ *Use Standard English.* Of course in some situations you may be writing creatively and so wish to use dialect or slang. However, ensure that the context is appropriate. Do not use contractions such as *don't* or *he'd.*

○ *A serious subject does not need excessively formal language.* Your writing or speech should be clear, easy and interesting to read, so be careful not to inflate it with pretentious words or formal language.

✗ He is perambulating in the direction of the emporium to procure a quantity of delectable comestibles from the victualler.

✓ He is walking to the shop to buy some tasty food from the grocer.

○ *Double-check that your spelling, grammar and punctuation are accurate.* Make sure that the words you have used mean what you intend them to mean, and that you have not confused similar-sounding words.

✗ A priest was brought in to *exercise* the ghost.

✓ A priest was brought in to *exorcize* the ghost.

○ *Use precise, accurate terminology* which indicates your understanding of the subject. Give appropriate detail, and choose dynamic words which convey your ideas clearly and retain the reader's attention. You will probably have a strict word or time limit, so avoid words which add little to your work.

LANGUAGE FOR FINDING WORK

A confident and creative use of language will not just help you to achieve better marks in your essays or exams. A good vocabulary can also help you to succeed in the wider world beyond school, in practical situations such as applying for jobs or for a place at college or university. This section focuses on using words effectively to find work, but it will also be relevant when applying for a place in higher education and to other types of application.

What is a CV and what is a covering letter?

- A *CV*, or *résumé* as it is called in North America, is a concise list of your skills, experience, qualifications and perhaps a little additional information.
- A brief *covering letter* should always accompany your CV. It is an opportunity to communicate something of your personality, your interest in the company, and why you think that you are the right person for the job.

Both your covering letter and your CV should be short and to the point – normally no longer than two A4 pages. Because you do not have much space, it is vitally important that the words you choose are the right ones – accurate, interesting, informative and dynamic.

Getting help with CVs and covering letters

In addition to the large range of books and written information on this subject, there are many careers websites which will give you helpful tips (see the box below). Your school or local public library should have a careers section with useful information, and many schools also have a Careers Adviser. These resources will help you to choose which of your skills, achievements and experience to include on your CV, and how to present this information.

SOME CAREERS WEBSITES

www.activatecareers.co.uk
www.all4resumes.com
www.bbc.co.uk/education/work
www.careersign.com
www.careerworld.net
www.cvservices.net

Writing CVs and covering letters

The *way* in which you express yourself can be just as important as *what* you say. The *Study Thesaurus* can help you select the right words to present your experience in the most favourable light. There may be hundreds of applications for one job and choosing the right words with which to express yourself in your CV could make all the difference.

Overused words

Many of the words which are commonly overused in everyday situations are the same ones which crop up again and again in CVs and covering letters. They reduce the impact of what you have to say and increase the likelihood of your CV being discarded rather than put in the 'interview' pile. Some typically overused words are:

do	like	enjoy	really
very	well	lots	good
success	want	show	go

This is not to say that these words should never be used. However, consider whether there is a better word that you could use to make a greater impact.

> ✗ I *like doing well* at work, and can *give lots* of examples to *show* how I *really* am *good* at it.

> ✓ I am *motivated* to work hard to *achieve* the best *results*. I have *demonstrated* my *ability* to *succeed*.

Key words to describe your skills and experience

Look under these key headwords in the *Study Thesaurus* for forceful verbs.

What do you want to describe?	**Helpful headwords**
What you have done, and to what purpose	DO CARRY OUT CONSTRUCT CHANGE MODERNIZE
Results or the effect of your actions	INCREASE ACCELERATE CONSOLIDATE MINIMIZE
Situations in which you have succeeded or done something well	ACHIEVE
Setting up something new, or starting something	INITIATE DESIGN SET UP
Instances of team work, where you have supported or helped other people	PARTICIPATE LIAISE
Interpersonal skills, how you interact with others	NEGOTIATE COMMUNICATE
Positions of responsibility or leadership	GUIDE CO-ORDINATE
Investigative skills, your ability to evaluate	ANALYZE MONITOR

These headwords are just a starting point. Consult the *Study Thesaurus* to check any word which you think is overused or which sounds trite, and the words listed should suggest some more effective ways of expressing yourself. Even a simple change of word can have a considerable effect.

> **achieve** *v*
> accomplish, do, attain, reach, get, obtain, acquire, gain, earn, win, succeed, manage, do, perform, carry out, execute, fulfil, finish, complete, bring about, realize, produce, *formal* procure, consummate, effect, effectuate
> ▰ miss, fail

✗ I *got* three Bs in my exams and *got to go* to college.

✓ I *achieved* three Bs in my exams and *earned my place* at college.

Key words to describe yourself

One of the most difficult aspects of writing a CV or covering letter is how to express your personality. Here are some hints on where to find positive adjectives in the *Study Thesaurus* so you can present yourself in the best possible light.

What do you think about yourself ?	Helpful headwords
I can be trusted to do a job well. / I try to do things quickly – but without cutting corners. / I care about my work and always try to get things right.	RESPONSIBLE / EFFICIENT / CAREFUL
I am full of ideas. / I like challenges. / I can think through a problem and come up with an answer.	CREATIVE / ENTERPRISING / LOGICAL
I work hard – if it's worth doing it's worth doing well. / I've done this before and know what I'm doing.	HARDWORKING / EXPERIENCED
I am enthusiastic and want to do well. / If I start something, I want to stick with it and finish it.	KEEN / DETERMINED
People can count on me to do what I say I will. / I don't give up easily. / I am loyal to my friends and colleagues.	RELIABLE / DEDICATED
I know when to be discreet. / I never break someone's confidence. / I try to bear in mind people's feelings.	TACTFUL / HONEST / TRUSTWORTHY
I am friendly and get on well with people. / I like meeting new people. / I have a lot of energy.	ACTIVE / POSITIVE / PERSONABLE

It is unlikely that all of the above characteristics will apply to you, and no doubt you will have other qualities that are not covered here. Think carefully about your own character: what you enjoy, what you do well, and where your strengths lie. Then choose positive words to express this in your CV or covering letter.

> **enterprise** *n*
> **1** UNDERTAKING, venture, project, plan, effort, opera-
> tion, campaign, programme, endeavour, task,
> scheme **2** INITIATIVE, resourcefulness, drive, adven-
> turousness, courage, boldness, ambition, energy,
> enthusiasm, strong feeling, spirit, vitality, *colloq.* get-
> up-and-go, push, oomph **3** BUSINESS, company, firm,
> establishment, operation, concern, industry

✗ I am always thinking up get-rich-quick schemes. They never work, and I end up broke and in trouble with someone or other. But by then I am already concocting the next money-making plan.

✓ I have a *resourceful* character with *entrepreneurial* flair. I am *enthusiastic* and *ambitious*, display great *determination* and have an *adventurous* nature.

Using words for CV success

Here are a few tips to bear in mind when choosing synonyms from the *Study Thesaurus*:

○ *Make sure that the CV or covering letter is written in your voice.* The dynamic words should let you put your personality, skills and experience across more clearly. The text should not sound as if someone else has written it for you.

○ *Do not lie or exaggerate.* The interviewer will soon realize if you have bent the truth, and you will not get the job. Do use positive words to minimize your weak points and play up your strengths, but do not be bigheaded.

○ *Try not to pepper your CV with powerful words used at random.* Use them for a purpose and know exactly what each one means. You may have to support what you have said with examples in an interview, so if you say that you are trustworthy, be prepared to talk about a situation where you demonstrated this quality.

○ *Try not to overload your CV with lively adjectives and forceful verbs.* Use them carefully for maximum effect, and make sure your meaning is clear. If you cram in too many powerful words, your CV may sound pretentious, look ridiculous, and will not make sense.

○ *Make sure that the words you select are appropriate for this kind of writing.* Do not use slang or informal words, but at the same time do not be overly formal or technical. Keep the tone businesslike. (Bear in mind the points in Part One about register and context.)

○ *Ensure that every word is spelt correctly and that your grammar and punctuation are accurate.* Try to write in an impersonal way in the CV – it is better to use a list, which avoids using 'I' altogether. In the covering letter, however, writing in the first person is acceptable.